Every Day
with Jesus

ONE YEAR
BIBLE

CWR

NIV✝™

Contents

Every Day with Jesus: 5
A history

NIV 2011 Introduction   7

January   13

February   139

March   252

April   376

May   506

June   635

July   771

August   909

September   1051

October   1186

November   1337

December   1474

Every Day with Jesus: A history

A note from Selwyn Hughes, 1928-2006
(author of *Every Day with Jesus* for over forty years):
a vision for spending every day with Jesus

I have talked in my time to many Christians who say that though they regard the Bible as God's Word they do not read or study it on a regular basis. When I have enquired why this is so the problems appear to be threefold: one, they find the Bible dull and uninteresting. Two, they don't know how to approach it – where to read, what to read, how to read. And three, they lack time. Part of the purpose of these devotional notes is to address these problems head on and consider ways by which they can be overcome.

Christians, it must be remembered, are people of God's Word, called to take it to heart, apply it in their daily living, and to be formed as persons by the sound of His voice. Amid the din of voices that ring in our ears, God is trying to say something too. How can we heed what He says unless we give time to listening to His voice speaking to us through His Word and in private prayer?

'Man does not live on bread alone ...' said Jesus, '... but on every word that comes from the mouth of God' (Matt. 4:4). To live, that is really live, we need much more than physical nourishment; we need spiritual nourishment also. The kind that comes only from the Word of God.

My prayer is that you will catch the spirit of the Bereans referred to in the text below and call no day complete unless it has included some time spent in the Bible.

'Now the Bereans were of more noble character ... for they received the message with great eagerness and examined the Scriptures every day to see if what Paul said was true.' (Acts 17:11)

A note from the publishers: how *Every Day with Jesus* is changing lives

Since its inception in 1965 *Every Day with Jesus* has engaged with millions of readers worldwide. Not only does the English language edition get shipped in its thousands to Algeria, New Zealand, Singapore, South Africa, Ghana, Hong Kong and many other places, but locally printed versions are also available in India, Kenya and Nigeria. Concurrent translated editions are available in Sri Lanka in Tamil and Sinhala, and regular Serbian translations are available in print and on radio. Add to these the many translated editions (including French, Mandarin, Czech, German and Slovak) and the numerous compilations editions in, amongst other languages English, Malayalam and Persian, and the amazing reach and impact of this publication begins to be seen.

Selected meditations are made available on CD; Braille editions are being painstakingly created, and we have also entered the digital arena with eSubscriptions and eBooks.

This one publication, commenced over 40 years ago on the back of a postcard, continues to change lives on every continent.

About the NIV

The goal of the New International Version (NIV) is to enable English-speaking people from around the world to read and hear God's eternal Word in their own language. Our work as translators is motivated by our conviction that the Bible is God's Word in written form. We believe that the Bible contains the divine answer to the deepest needs of humanity, sheds unique light on our path in a dark world and sets forth the way to our eternal well-being. Out of these deep convictions, we have sought to recreate as far as possible the experience of the original audience – blending transparency to the original text with accessibility for the millions of English speakers around the world. We have prioritised accuracy, clarity and literary quality with the goal of creating a translation suitable for public and private reading, evangelism, teaching, preaching, memorising and liturgical use. We have also sought to preserve a measure of continuity with the long tradition of translating the Scriptures into English.

The complete NIV Bible was first published in 1978. It was a completely new translation made by over a hundred scholars working directly from the best available Hebrew, Aramaic and Greek texts. The translators came from the United States, Great Britain, Canada, Australia and New Zealand, giving the translation an international scope. They were from many denominations and churches – including Anglican, Assemblies of God, Baptist, Brethren, Christian Reformed, Church of Christ, Evangelical Covenant, Evangelical Free, Lutheran, Mennonite, Methodist, Nazarene, Presbyterian, Wesleyan and others. This breadth of denominational and theological perspective helped to safeguard the translation from sectarian bias. For these reasons, and by the grace of God, the NIV has gained a wide readership in all parts of the English-speaking world.

The work of translating the Bible is never finished. As good as they are, English translations must be regularly updated so that they will continue to communicate accurately the meaning of God's Word. Updates are needed in order to reflect the latest developments in our understanding of the biblical world and its languages and to keep pace with changes in English usage. Recognising, then, that the NIV would retain its ability to communicate God's Word accurately only if it were regularly updated, the original translators established The Committee on Bible Translation (CBT). The committee is a self-perpetuating group of biblical scholars charged with keeping abreast of advances in biblical scholarship and changes in English and issuing periodic updates to the NIV. CBT is an independent, self-governing body and has sole responsibility for the NIV text. The committee mirrors the original group of translators in its diverse international and denominational makeup and in its unifying commitment to the Bible as God's inspired Word.

In obedience to its mandate, the committee has issued periodic updates to the NIV. An initial revision was released in 1984. A more thorough revision process was completed in 2005, resulting in the separately published Today's New International Version (TNIV). The updated NIV you now have in your hands builds on both the original NIV and the TNIV and represents the latest effort of the committee to articulate God's unchanging Word in the way the original authors might have said it had they been speaking in English to the global English speaking audience today.

The first concern of the translators has continued to be the accuracy of the translation and its faithfulness to the intended meaning of the biblical writers. This has moved the translators to go beyond a formal word-for-word rendering of the original texts. Because thought patterns and syntax differ from language to language, accurate communication of the meaning of the biblical authors demands constant regard for varied contextual uses of words and idioms and for frequent modifications in sentence structures.

For the Old Testament the standard Hebrew text, the Masoretic Text as published in the latest edition of Biblia Hebraica, has been used throughout. The Masoretic Text tradition contains marginal notations that offer variant readings. These have sometimes been followed instead of the text itself. Because such instances involve variants within the Masoretic tradition, they have not been indicated in the textual notes. In a few cases, words in the basic consonantal text have been divided differently than in the Masoretic Text. The Dead Sea Scrolls contain biblical texts that represent an earlier stage of the transmission of the Hebrew text. They have been consulted, as have been the Samaritan Pentateuch and the ancient scribal traditions concerning deliberate textual changes. The translators also consulted the more important early versions - the Greek Septuagint, Aquila, Symmachus and Theodotion, the Latin Vulgate, the Syriac Peshitta, the Aramaic Targums and, for the Psalms, the Juxta Hebraica of Jerome. Readings from these versions, the Dead Sea Scrolls and the scribal traditions were occasionally followed where the Masoretic Text seemed doubtful and where accepted principles of textual criticism showed that one or more of these textual witnesses appeared to provide the correct reading. In rare cases, the committee has emended the Hebrew text where it appears to have become corrupted at an even earlier stage of its transmission. Sometimes the vowel indicators (which are later additions to the basic consonantal text) found in the Masoretic Text did not, in the judgment of the committee, represent the correct vowels for the original text. Accordingly, some words have been read with a different set of vowels.

The Greek text used in translating the New Testament is an eclectic one, based on the latest editions of the Nestle-Aland/United Bible Societies' Greek New Testament. The committee has made its choices among the variant readings in accordance with widely accepted principles of New Testament textual criticism.

The New Testament authors, writing in Greek, often quote the Old Testament from its ancient Greek version, the Septuagint. This is one reason why some of the Old Testament quotations in the NIV New Testament are not identical to the corresponding passages in the NIV Old Testament.

It should be noted that references to diseases, minerals, flora and fauna, architectural details, clothing, jewellery, musical instruments and other articles cannot always be identified with precision. Also, linear measurements and measures of capacity can only be approximated (see the Appendix). Although Selah, used mainly in the Psalms, is probably a musical term, its meaning is uncertain. Since it may interrupt reading and distract the reader, this word has not been kept in the English text.

One of the main reasons the task of Bible translation is never finished is the change in our own language, English. Although a basic core of the language remains relatively stable, many diverse and complex linguistic factors continue to bring about subtle shifts in the meanings and/or connotations of even old, well established words and phrases. One of the shifts that creates particular challenges to writers and translators alike is the manner in which gender is presented. The original NIV (1978) was published in a time when 'a man' would naturally be understood, in many contexts, to be referring to a person, whether male or female. But most English speakers today tend to hear a distinctly male connotation in this word. In recognition of this change in English, this edition of the NIV, along with almost all other recent English translations, substitutes other expressions when the original text intends to refer generically to men and women equally. Thus, for instance, the NIV (1984) rendering of 1 Corinthians 8:3, 'But the man who loves God is known by God' becomes in this edition 'But whoever loves God is known by God.' On the other hand, 'man' and 'mankind', as ways of denoting the human race, are still widely used. This edition of the NIV therefore continues to use these words, along with other expressions, in this way.

A related shift in English creates a greater challenge for modern translations: the move away from using the third-person masculine singular pronouns – 'he/him/his' – to refer to men and women equally. This usage does persist at a low level in some forms of English, and this revision therefore occasionally uses these pronouns in a generic sense. But the tendency, recognised in day-to-day usage and confirmed by extensive research, is away from the generic use of 'he,' 'him', and 'his.' In recognition of this shift in language and in an effort to translate into the 'common' English that people are actually using, this revision of the NIV generally uses other constructions when the biblical text is plainly addressed to men and women equally. The reader will frequently encounter a 'they', 'them' or 'their' to express a generic singular idea. Thus, for instance, Mark 8:36 reads:

'What good is it for someone to gain the whole world, yet forfeit their soul?' This generic use of the indefinite or 'singular' 'they/them/their' has a venerable place in English idiom and has quickly become established as standard English, spoken and written, all over the world. Where an individual emphasis is deemed to be present, 'anyone' or 'everyone' or some other equivalent is generally used as the antecedent of such pronouns.

Sometimes the chapter and/or verse numbering in English translations of the Old Testament differs from that found in published Hebrew texts. This is particularly the case in the Psalms, where the traditional titles are often included in the Hebrew verse numbering. Such differences are indicated in the footnotes at the bottom of the page. In the New Testament, verse numbers that marked off portions of the traditional English text not supported by the best Greek manuscripts now appear in brackets, with a footnote indicating the text that has been omitted (see, for example, Matthew 17:[21]).

Mark 16:9 - 20 and John 7:53 - 8:11, although long accorded virtually equal status with the rest of the Gospels in which they stand, have a very questionable - and confused - standing in the textual history of the New Testament, as noted in the bracketed annotations with which they are set off. A smaller typeface has been chosen for these passages to indicate even more clearly their uncertain status.

Basic formatting of the text, such as lining the poetry, paragraphing (both prose and poetry), setting up of (administrative-like) lists and indenting letters and lengthy prayers within narratives, has been the work of the committee. However, the choice between single-column and double-column formats has been left to the publishers.

The committee has again been reminded that every human effort is flawed - including this revision of the NIV. We trust, however, that many will find in it an improved representation of the Word of God, through which they hear His call to faith in our Lord Jesus Christ and to service in His kingdom. We offer this version of the Bible to Him in whose name and for whose glory it has been made.

The Committee on Bible Translation
September 2010

Royalties from all sales of the NIV® Bible help Biblica in their work of translating and distributing Bibles around the world.

Biblica provides God's Word to people through translation, publishing and Bible engagement in Africa, Asia Pacific, Europe, Latin America, Middle East and North America. Through its worldwide reach, Biblica engages people with God's Word so that their lives are transformed through a relationship with Jesus Christ.

January I

■ GENESIS 1:1–2:25

1 In the beginning God created the heavens and the earth. ²Now the earth was formless and empty, darkness was over the surface of the deep, and the Spirit of God was hovering over the waters.

³And God said, 'Let there be light,' and there was light. ⁴God saw that the light was good, and he separated the light from the darkness. ⁵God called the light 'day', and the darkness he called 'night'. And there was evening, and there was morning – the first day.

⁶And God said, 'Let there be a vault between the waters to separate water from water.' ⁷So God made the vault and separated the water under the vault from the water above it. And it was so. ⁸God called the vault 'sky'. And there was evening, and there was morning – the second day.

⁹And God said, 'Let the water under the sky be gathered to one place, and let dry ground appear.' And it was so. ¹⁰God called the dry ground 'land', and the gathered waters he called 'seas'. And God saw that it was good.

¹¹Then God said, 'Let the land produce vegetation: seed-bearing plants and trees on the land that bear fruit with seed in it, according to their various kinds.' And it was so. ¹²The land produced vegetation: plants bearing seed according to their kinds and trees bearing fruit with seed in it according to their kinds. And God saw that it was good. ¹³And there was evening, and there was morning – the third day.

¹⁴And God said, 'Let there be lights in the vault of the sky to separate the day from the night, and let them serve as signs to mark sacred times, and days and years, ¹⁵and let them be lights in the vault of the sky to give light on the earth.' And it was so. ¹⁶God made two great lights – the greater light to govern the day and the lesser light to govern the night. He also made the stars. ¹⁷God set them in the vault of the sky to give light on the earth, ¹⁸to govern the day and the night, and to separate light from darkness. And God saw that it was good. ¹⁹And there was evening, and there was morning – the fourth day.

²⁰And God said, 'Let the water teem with living creatures, and let birds fly above the earth across the vault of the sky.' ²¹So God created the great creatures of the sea and every living thing with which the water teems and that moves about in it, according to their kinds, and every winged bird according to its kind. And God saw that it was good. ²²God blessed them and said, 'Be fruitful and increase in number and fill the water in the seas, and let the birds increase on the earth.' ²³And there was evening, and there was morning – the fifth day.

²⁴And God said, 'Let the land produce living creatures according to their kinds: the livestock, the creatures that move along the ground, and the wild animals, each according to its kind.' And it was so. ²⁵God made the wild animals according to their kinds, the livestock according to their kinds, and all the creatures that move along the ground according to

their kinds. And God saw that it was good.

²⁶Then God said, 'Let us make mankind in our image, in our likeness, so that they may rule over the fish in the sea and the birds in the sky, over the livestock and all the wild animals, and over all the creatures that move along the ground.'

²⁷So God created mankind in his own image, in the image of God he created them; male and female he created them.

²⁸God blessed them and said to them, 'Be fruitful and increase in number; fill the earth and subdue it. Rule over the fish in the sea and the birds in the sky and over every living creature that moves on the ground.'

²⁹Then God said, 'I give you every seed-bearing plant on the face of the whole earth and every tree that has fruit with seed in it. They will be yours for food. ³⁰And to all the beasts of the earth and all the birds in the sky and all the creatures that move along the ground – everything that has the breath of life in it – I give every green plant for food.' And it was so.

³¹God saw all that he had made, and it was very good. And there was evening, and there was morning – the sixth day.

2 Thus the heavens and the earth were completed in all their vast array.

²By the seventh day God had finished the work he had been doing; so on the seventh day he rested from all his work. ³Then God blessed the seventh day and made it holy, because on it he rested from all the work of creating that he had done.

⁴This is the account of the heavens and the

earth when they were created, when the LORD God made the earth and the heavens.

⁵Now no shrub had yet appeared on the earth and no plant had yet sprung up, for the LORD God had not sent rain on the earth and there was no one to work the ground, ⁶but streams came up from the earth and watered the whole surface of the ground. ⁷Then the LORD God formed a man from the dust of the ground and breathed into his nostrils the breath of life, and the man became a living being.

⁸Now the LORD God had planted a garden in the east, in Eden; and there he put the man he had formed. ⁹The LORD God made all kinds of trees grow out of the ground – trees that were pleasing to the eye and good for food. In the middle of the garden were the tree of life and the tree of the knowledge of good and evil.

¹⁰A river watering the garden flowed from Eden; from there it was separated into four headwaters. ¹¹The name of the first is the Pishon; it winds through the entire land of Havilah, where there is gold. ¹²(The gold of that land is good; aromatic resin and onyx are also there.) ¹³The name of the second river is the Gihon; it winds through the entire land of Cush. ¹⁴The name of the third river is the Tigris; it runs along the east side of Ashur. And the fourth river is the Euphrates.

¹⁵The LORD God took the man and put him in the Garden of Eden to work it and take care of it. ¹⁶And the LORD God commanded the man, 'You are free to eat from any tree in the garden; ¹⁷but you must not eat from the tree of the knowledge of good and evil, for when you eat from it you will certainly die.'

¹⁸The LORD God said, 'It is not good for the man to be alone. I will make a helper suitable for him.'

¹⁹Now the LORD God had formed out of the ground all the wild animals and all the

birds in the sky. He brought them to the man to see what he would name them; and whatever the man called each living creature, that was its name. [20] So the man gave names to all the livestock, the birds in the sky and all the wild animals.

But for Adam no suitable helper was found. [21] So the LORD God caused the man to fall into a deep sleep; and while he was sleeping, he took one of the man's ribs and then closed up the place with flesh. [22] Then the LORD God made a woman from the rib he had taken out of the man, and he brought her to the man.

[23] The man said,

'This is now bone of my bones
    and flesh of my flesh;
she shall be called "woman",
    for she was taken out of man.'

[24] That is why a man leaves his father and mother and is united to his wife, and they become one flesh.

[25] Adam and his wife were both naked, and they felt no shame.

■ PSALM 1:1-6

1 [1] Blessed is the one
    who does not walk in step with the
        wicked
    or stand in the way that sinners take
    or sit in the company of mockers,
[2] but whose delight is in the law of the LORD,
    and who meditates on his law day
        and night.
[3] That person is like a tree planted by
        streams of water,
    which yields its fruit in season
    and whose leaf does not wither –
        whatever they do prospers.

[4] Not so the wicked!
    They are like chaff

that the wind blows away.
[5] Therefore the wicked will not stand in
        the judgment,
    nor sinners in the assembly of the
        righteous.

[6] For the LORD watches over the way of the
        righteous,
    but the way of the wicked leads to
        destruction.

■ PROVERBS 1:1-4

1 The proverbs of Solomon son of David,
  king of Israel:

[2] for gaining wisdom and instruction;
    for understanding words of insight;
[3] for receiving instruction in prudent
        behaviour,
    doing what is right and just and fair;
[4] for giving prudence to those who are
        simple,
    knowledge and discretion to the young –

■ MATTHEW 1:1-25

1 This is the genealogy of Jesus the Messiah the son of David, the son of Abraham:

[2] Abraham was the father of Isaac,
    Isaac the father of Jacob,
    Jacob the father of Judah and his
        brothers,
[3] Judah the father of Perez and Zerah,
        whose mother was Tamar,
    Perez the father of Hezron,
    Hezron the father of Ram,
[4] Ram the father of Amminadab,
    Amminadab the father of Nahshon,
    Nahshon the father of Salmon,
[5] Salmon the father of Boaz, whose
        mother was Rahab,
    Boaz the father of Obed, whose

mother was Ruth,
Obed the father of Jesse,
[6] and Jesse the father of King David.

David was the father of Solomon, whose
mother had been Uriah's wife,
[7] Solomon the father of Rehoboam,
Rehoboam the father of Abijah,
Abijah the father of Asa,
[8] Asa the father of Jehoshaphat,
Jehoshaphat the father of Jehoram,
Jehoram the father of Uzziah,
[9] Uzziah the father of Jotham,
Jotham the father of Ahaz,
Ahaz the father of Hezekiah,
[10] Hezekiah the father of Manasseh,
Manasseh the father of Amon,
Amon the father of Josiah,
[11] and Josiah the father of Jeconiah
and his brothers at the time of the
exile to Babylon.

[12] After the exile to Babylon:
Jeconiah was the father of Shealtiel,
Shealtiel the father of Zerubbabel,
[13] Zerubbabel the father of Abihud,
Abihud the father of Eliakim,
Eliakim the father of Azor,
[14] Azor the father of Zadok,
Zadok the father of Akim,
Akim the father of Elihud,
[15] Elihud the father of Eleazar,
Eleazar the father of Matthan,
Matthan the father of Jacob,
[16] and Jacob the father of Joseph, the
husband of Mary, and Mary was

the mother of Jesus who is called
the Messiah.

[17] Thus there were fourteen generations in
all from Abraham to David, fourteen from
David to the exile to Babylon, and fourteen
from the exile to the Messiah.

[18] This is how the birth of Jesus the Messiah came about: his mother Mary was
pledged to be married to Joseph, but before they came together, she was found to
be pregnant through the Holy Spirit. [19] Because Joseph her husband was faithful
to the law, and yet did not want to expose
her to public disgrace, he had in mind to
divorce her quietly.

[20] But after he had considered this, an angel of the Lord appeared to him in a dream
and said, 'Joseph son of David, do not be
afraid to take Mary home as your wife, because what is conceived in her is from the
Holy Spirit. [21] She will give birth to a son, and
you are to give him the name Jesus, because
he will save his people from their sins.'

[22] All this took place to fulfil what the
Lord had said through the prophet: [23] 'The
virgin will conceive and give birth to a son,
and they will call him Immanuel' (which
means 'God with us').

[24] When Joseph woke up, he did what the
angel of the Lord had commanded him and
took Mary home as his wife. [25] But he did
not consummate their marriage until she
gave birth to a son. And he gave him the
name Jesus.

The Primary Focus

'In the beginning God ...' **Genesis 1:1**

We focus on what is without doubt the most noble and loftiest of
themes: the nature and character of God. I have noticed that
Christians, generally speaking, seem to be preoccupied with knowing
more about themselves rather than knowing more about God. Ask any

Christian bookshop manager: 'What are the best-selling books?' Not those that unfold for us the nature of God, but those that direct us toward such things as how to get a better self-image, how to manage money, how to find inner healing, how to get more excitement out of life, and so on. Not that these subjects are unimportant, but they are explored in a self-absorbed way that gives the idea that the most important thing in life is knowing ourselves better. It isn't. The most important thing in life is knowing God better.

John Lancaster, a minister in Cardiff, South Wales, in an article entitled 'Where on Earth Is God?' asks the question: 'Given a choice between attending a seminar, say, on the "Glory of God in Isaiah" and one on "The Christian and Sex," to which would you go?' He makes the point also that although the Church often answers the questions that people are asking, the real problem may be that people are not asking the right questions. In today's Church we are far too man-centred and not God-centred.

It is not by accident, I believe, that the Bible opens with the thunderous acclaim: 'In the beginning God.' I tell you with all the conviction of which I am capable: if God is not our primary focus, then everything else will soon get out of focus.

(handwritten margin note: Jesus should be at the centre of everything we do, the main focus.)

PRAYER

O Father, from this day help me determine to make You my primary focus. And give me the grace and strength to maintain it, through all the changes and uncertainties of the days ahead. In Jesus' name I pray. Amen.

FURTHER STUDY

John 1:1-5; Col. 1:15-20; Heb. 12:2; Rev. 1:8
- What did the Lord declare to John?
- What did the apostle John declare?

January 2

■ GENESIS 3:1–4:26

3 Now the snake was more crafty than any of the wild animals the LORD God had made. He said to the woman, 'Did God really say, "You must not eat from any tree in the garden"?'

² The woman said to the snake, 'We may eat fruit from the trees in the garden, ³ but God did say, "You must not eat fruit from the tree that is in the middle of the garden, and you must not touch it, or you will die."'

⁴ 'You will not certainly die,' the snake said to the woman. ⁵ 'For God knows that when you eat from it your eyes will be opened, and you will be like God, knowing good and evil.'

⁶ When the woman saw that the fruit of the tree was good for food and pleasing to the eye, and also desirable for gaining wisdom, she took some and ate it. She also gave some to her husband, who was with her, and he ate it. ⁷ Then the eyes of both of them were opened, and they realised that they

were naked; so they sewed fig leaves together and made coverings for themselves.

⁸ Then the man and his wife heard the sound of the Lord God as he was walking in the garden in the cool of the day, and they hid from the Lord God among the trees of the garden. ⁹ But the Lord God called to the man, 'Where are you?'

¹⁰ He answered, 'I heard you in the garden, and I was afraid because I was naked; so I hid.'

¹¹ And he said, 'Who told you that you were naked? Have you eaten from the tree from which I commanded you not to eat?'

¹² The man said, 'The woman you put here with me – she gave me some fruit from the tree, and I ate it.'

¹³ Then the Lord God said to the woman, 'What is this you have done?'

The woman said, 'The snake deceived me, and I ate.'

¹⁴ So the Lord God said to the snake, 'Because you have done this,

'Cursed are you above all livestock
and all wild animals!
You will crawl on your belly
and you will eat dust
all the days of your life.
¹⁵ And I will put enmity
between you and the woman,
and between your offspring and hers;
he will crush your head,
and you will strike his heel.'

¹⁶ To the woman he said,

'I will make your pains in childbearing
very severe;
with painful labour you will give birth
to children.
Your desire will be for your husband,
and he will rule over you.'

¹⁷ To Adam he said, 'Because you listened to your wife and ate fruit from the tree about which I commanded you, "You must not eat from it,"

'Cursed is the ground because of you;
through painful toil you will eat food
from it
all the days of your life.
¹⁸ It will produce thorns and thistles for
you,
and you will eat the plants of the field.
¹⁹ By the sweat of your brow
you will eat your food
until you return to the ground,
since from it you were taken;
for dust you are
and to dust you will return.'

²⁰ Adam named his wife Eve, because she would become the mother of all the living.

²¹ The Lord God made garments of skin for Adam and his wife and clothed them. ²² And the Lord God said, 'The man has now become like one of us, knowing good and evil. He must not be allowed to reach out his hand and take also from the tree of life and eat, and live for ever.' ²³ So the Lord God banished him from the Garden of Eden to work the ground from which he had been taken. ²⁴ After he drove the man out, he placed on the east side of the Garden of Eden cherubim and a flaming sword flashing back and forth to guard the way to the tree of life.

4 Adam made love to his wife Eve, and she became pregnant and gave birth to Cain. She said, 'With the help of the Lord I have brought forth a man.' ² Later she gave birth to his brother Abel.

Now Abel kept flocks, and Cain worked the soil. ³ In the course of time Cain brought some of the fruits of the soil as an offering to the Lord. ⁴ But Abel also brought an offering – fat portions from some of the firstborn of his flock. The Lord looked with favour on Abel and his offering, ⁵ but on Cain and his offering he did not look with favour. So Cain was very angry, and his face was downcast.

[6] Then the LORD said to Cain, 'Why are you angry? Why is your face downcast? [7] If you do what is right, will you not be accepted? But if you do not do what is right, sin is crouching at your door; it desires to have you, but you must rule over it.'

[8] Now Cain said to his brother Abel, 'Let's go out to the field.' While they were in the field, Cain attacked his brother Abel and killed him.

[9] Then the LORD said to Cain, 'Where is your brother Abel?'

'I don't know,' he replied. 'Am I my brother's keeper?'

[10] The LORD said, 'What have you done? Listen! Your brother's blood cries out to me from the ground. [11] Now you are under a curse and driven from the ground, which opened its mouth to receive your brother's blood from your hand. [12] When you work the ground, it will no longer yield its crops for you. You will be a restless wanderer on the earth.'

[13] Cain said to the LORD, 'My punishment is more than I can bear. [14] Today you are driving me from the land, and I will be hidden from your presence; I will be a restless wanderer on the earth, and whoever finds me will kill me.'

[15] But the LORD said to him, 'Not so; anyone who kills Cain will suffer vengeance seven times over.' Then the LORD put a mark on Cain so that no one who found him would kill him. [16] So Cain went out from the LORD's presence and lived in the land of Nod, east of Eden.

[17] Cain made love to his wife, and she became pregnant and gave birth to Enoch. Cain was then building a city, and he named it after his son Enoch. [18] To Enoch was born Irad, and Irad was the father of Mehujael, and Mehujael was the father of Methushael, and Methushael was the father of Lamech. [19] Lamech married two women, one named Adah and the other Zillah. [20] Adah gave birth to Jabal; he was the father of those who live in tents and raise livestock. [21] His brother's name was Jubal; he was the father of all who play stringed instruments and pipes. [22] Zillah also had a son, Tubal-Cain, who forged all kinds of tools out of bronze and iron. Tubal-Cain's sister was Naamah.

[23] Lamech said to his wives,

'Adah and Zillah, listen to me;
    wives of Lamech, hear my words.
I have killed a man for wounding me,
    a young man for injuring me.
[24] If Cain is avenged seven times,
    then Lamech seventy-seven times.'

[25] Adam made love to his wife again, and she gave birth to a son and named him Seth, saying, 'God has granted me another child in place of Abel, since Cain killed him.' [26] Seth also had a son, and he named him Enosh.

At that time people began to call on the name of the LORD.

▬ PSALM 2:1-6

[1] Why do the nations conspire
    and the peoples plot in vain?
[2] The kings of the earth rise up
    and the rulers band together
    against the LORD and against his
        anointed, saying,
[3] 'Let us break their chains
    and throw off their shackles.'

[4] The One enthroned in heaven laughs;
    the Lord scoffs at them.
[5] He rebukes them in his anger
    and terrifies them in his wrath,
        saying,
[6] 'I have installed my king
    on Zion, my holy mountain.'

▬ PROVERBS 1:5-6

⁵ let the wise listen and add to their
    learning,
    and let the discerning get guidance –
⁶ for understanding proverbs and
    parables,
    the sayings and riddles of the wise.

▬ MATTHEW 2:1-23

2 After Jesus was born in Bethlehem in
Judea, during the time of King Herod,
Magi from the east came to Jerusalem ² and
asked, 'Where is the one who has been born
king of the Jews? We saw his star when it
rose and have come to worship him.'

³ When King Herod heard this he was disturbed, and all Jerusalem with him. ⁴ When
he had called together all the people's chief
priests and teachers of the law, he asked them
where the Messiah was to be born. ⁵ 'In Bethlehem in Judea,' they replied, 'for this is what
the prophet has written:

⁶ ' "But you, Bethlehem, in the land of
        Judah,
    are by no means least among the
        rulers of Judah;
    for out of you will come a ruler
        who will shepherd my people Israel." '

⁷ Then Herod called the Magi secretly
and found out from them the exact time
the star had appeared. ⁸ He sent them to
Bethlehem and said, 'Go and search carefully for the child. As soon as you find
him, report to me, so that I too may go and
worship him.'

⁹ After they had heard the king, they
went on their way, and the star they had
seen when it rose went ahead of them
until it stopped over the place where the
child was. ¹⁰ When they saw the star, they
were overjoyed. ¹¹ On coming to the house,

they saw the child with his mother Mary,
and they bowed down and worshipped
him. Then they opened their treasures
and presented him with gifts of gold,
frankincense and myrrh. ¹² And having
been warned in a dream not to go back to
Herod, they returned to their country by
another route.

¹³ When they had gone, an angel of the
Lord appeared to Joseph in a dream. 'Get
up,' he said, 'take the child and his mother
and escape to Egypt. Stay there until I tell
you, for Herod is going to search for the
child to kill him.'

¹⁴ So he got up, took the child and his
mother during the night and left for Egypt,
¹⁵ where he stayed until the death of Herod.
And so was fulfilled what the Lord had said
through the prophet: 'Out of Egypt I called
my son.'

¹⁶ When Herod realised that he had been
outwitted by the Magi, he was furious, and
he gave orders to kill all the boys in Bethlehem and its vicinity who were two years
old and under, in accordance with the time
he had learned from the Magi. ¹⁷ Then what
was said through the prophet Jeremiah was
fulfilled:

¹⁸ 'A voice is heard in Ramah,
    weeping and great mourning,
    Rachel weeping for her children
    and refusing to be comforted,
    because they are no more.'

¹⁹ After Herod died, an angel of the Lord
appeared in a dream to Joseph in Egypt
²⁰ and said, 'Get up, take the child and his
mother and go to the land of Israel, for
those who were trying to take the child's life
are dead.'

²¹ So he got up, took the child and his
mother and went to the land of Israel. ²² But
when he heard that Archelaus was reigning in Judea in place of his father Herod, he
was afraid to go there. Having been warned

in a dream, he withdrew to the district of Galilee, ²³and he went and lived in a town called Nazareth. So was fulfilled what was said through the prophets, that he would be called a Nazarene.

God's Great Intolerance

'He rebukes them in his anger and terrifies them in his wrath ...' **Psalm 2:5**

Wrath is not a defect in the divine character; rather, it would be a defect if wrath were absent *from* Him. Those who see God's wrath as petulance or retaliation, inflicting punishment just for the sake of it or in return for some injury received, do not really understand it. Divine wrath is not vindictiveness; it is divine perfection, issuing forth from God because it is right.

Human beings tend to make God in their own image. He made us in His image, but we want to return the compliment, and it is there that so often we go wrong. Instead of reasoning from the divine down to the human, recognising that sin has marred the divine image within us, we reason from our fallen condition and project our own feelings and ideas onto God.

Thus, when thinking of the wrath of God, we tend to look at what happens in our own hearts when we get angry, and we imagine God to be the same. But divine anger must never be confused with human anger. Most of what goes on in our hearts whenever we are angry is a mixture of unpredictable petulance, retaliation, hostility and self-concern. God's anger is always predictable, always steadfast and always set against sin. We must never forget that God's nature is uncompromisingly set against sin. We may tolerate it; He never.

Sin has been defined as 'God's one great intolerance,' and for that we ought to be eternally grateful. As His children we ought to rejoice that He will not tolerate anything that is harmful to us.

PRAYER

O Father, what a change comes over me when I realise that Your wrath is not so much directed at persons as at the sin that demeans and destroys them. You are not against me for my sin, but for me against my sin. I am deeply, deeply grateful. Amen.

FURTHER STUDY

Psa. 5:1-6; 11:5; Hab. 1:12-13; Zech. 8:16-17
• How did the psalmist express God's great intolerance?
• What does the Lord hate?

January 3

■ **GENESIS 5:1–6:22**

5 This is the written account of Adam's family line.

When God created mankind, he made them in the likeness of God. ²He created them male and female and blessed them. And he named them 'Mankind' when they were created.

³When Adam had lived 130 years, he had a son in his own likeness, in his own image; and he named him Seth. ⁴After Seth was born, Adam lived 800 years and had other sons and daughters. ⁵Altogether, Adam lived a total of 930 years, and then he died.

⁶When Seth had lived 105 years, he became the father of Enosh. ⁷After he became the father of Enosh, Seth lived 807 years and had other sons and daughters. ⁸Altogether, Seth lived a total of 912 years, and then he died.

⁹When Enosh had lived 90 years, he became the father of Kenan. ¹⁰After he became the father of Kenan, Enosh lived 815 years and had other sons and daughters. ¹¹Altogether, Enosh lived a total of 905 years, and then he died.

¹²When Kenan had lived 70 years, he became the father of Mahalalel. ¹³After he became the father of Mahalalel, Kenan lived 840 years and had other sons and daughters. ¹⁴Altogether, Kenan lived a total of 910 years, and then he died.

¹⁵When Mahalalel had lived 65 years, he became the father of Jared. ¹⁶After he became the father of Jared, Mahalalel lived 830 years and had other sons and daughters. ¹⁷Altogether, Mahalalel lived a total of 895 years, and then he died.

¹⁸When Jared had lived 162 years, he became the father of Enoch. ¹⁹After he became the father of Enoch, Jared lived 800 years and had other sons and daughters. ²⁰Altogether, Jared lived a total of 962 years, and then he died.

²¹When Enoch had lived 65 years, he became the father of Methuselah. ²²After he became the father of Methuselah, Enoch walked faithfully with God 300 years and had other sons and daughters. ²³Altogether, Enoch lived a total of 365 years. ²⁴Enoch walked faithfully with God; then he was no more, because God took him away.

²⁵When Methuselah had lived 187 years, he became the father of Lamech. ²⁶After he became the father of Lamech, Methuselah lived 782 years and had other sons and daughters. ²⁷Altogether, Methuselah lived a total of 969 years, and then he died.

²⁸When Lamech had lived 182 years, he had a son. ²⁹He named him Noah and said, 'He will comfort us in the labour and painful toil of our hands caused by the ground the LORD has cursed.' ³⁰After Noah was born, Lamech lived 595 years and had other sons and daughters. ³¹Altogether, Lamech lived a total of 777 years, and then he died.

³²After Noah was 500 years old, he became the father of Shem, Ham and Japheth.

6 When human beings began to increase in number on the earth and daughters were born to them, ²the sons of God saw that the daughters of humans were beautiful, and they married any of them they chose. ³Then the LORD said, 'My Spirit will not contend with humans for ever, for they are mortal; their days will be a hundred and twenty years.'

⁴The Nephilim were on the earth in those

days – and also afterwards – when the sons of God went to the daughters of humans and had children by them. They were the heroes of old, men of renown.

⁵ The LORD saw how great the wickedness of the human race had become on the earth, and that every inclination of the thoughts of the human heart was only evil all the time. ⁶ The LORD regretted that he had made human beings on the earth, and his heart was deeply troubled. ⁷ So the LORD said, 'I will wipe from the face of the earth the human race I have created – and with them the animals, the birds and the creatures that move along the ground – for I regret that I have made them.' ⁸ But Noah found favour in the eyes of the LORD.

⁹ This is the account of Noah and his family.

Noah was a righteous man, blameless among the people of his time, and he walked faithfully with God. ¹⁰ Noah had three sons: Shem, Ham and Japheth.

¹¹ Now the earth was corrupt in God's sight and was full of violence. ¹² God saw how corrupt the earth had become, for all the people on earth had corrupted their ways. ¹³ So God said to Noah, 'I am going to put an end to all people, for the earth is filled with violence because of them. I am surely going to destroy both them and the earth. ¹⁴ So make yourself an ark of cypress wood; make rooms in it and coat it with pitch inside and out. ¹⁵ This is how you are to build it: The ark is to be three hundred cubits long, fifty cubits wide and thirty cubits high. ¹⁶ Make a roof for it, leaving below the roof an opening one cubit high all around. Put a door in the side of the ark and make lower, middle and upper decks. ¹⁷ I am going to bring floodwaters on the earth to destroy all life under the heavens, every creature that has the breath of life in it. Everything on earth will perish. ¹⁸ But I will establish my covenant with you, and

you will enter the ark – you and your sons and your wife and your sons' wives with you. ¹⁹ You are to bring into the ark two of all living creatures, male and female, to keep them alive with you. ²⁰ Two of every kind of bird, of every kind of animal and of every kind of creature that moves along the ground will come to you to be kept alive. ²¹ You are to take every kind of food that is to be eaten and store it away as food for you and for them.'

²² Noah did everything just as God commanded him.

··

■ PSALM 2:7-12

⁷ I will proclaim the LORD's decree:

He said to me, 'You are my son;
    today I have become your father.
⁸ Ask me,
    and I will make the nations your
        inheritance,
    the ends of the earth your possession.
⁹ You will break them with a rod of iron;
    you will dash them to pieces like
        pottery.'

¹⁰ Therefore, you kings, be wise;
    be warned, you rulers of the earth.
¹¹ Serve the LORD with fear
    and celebrate his rule with trembling.
¹² Kiss his son, or he will be angry
    and your way will lead to your
        destruction,
for his wrath can flare up in a moment.
    Blessed are all who take refuge in him.

··

■ PROVERBS 1:7

⁷ The fear of the LORD is the beginning of
        knowledge,
    but fools despise wisdom and
        instruction.

■ MATTHEW 3:1-17

3 In those days John the Baptist came, preaching in the wilderness of Judea ²and saying, 'Repent, for the kingdom of heaven has come near.' ³This is he who was spoken of through the prophet Isaiah:

'A voice of one calling in the wilderness,
"Prepare the way for the Lord,
    make straight paths for him."'

⁴John's clothes were made of camel's hair, and he had a leather belt round his waist. His food was locusts and wild honey. ⁵People went out to him from Jerusalem and all Judea and the whole region of the Jordan. ⁶Confessing their sins, they were baptised by him in the River Jordan.

⁷But when he saw many of the Pharisees and Sadducees coming to where he was baptising, he said to them: 'You brood of vipers! Who warned you to flee from the coming wrath? ⁸Produce fruit in keeping with repentance. ⁹And do not think you can say to yourselves, "We have Abraham as our father." I tell you that out of these stones God can raise up children for Abraham. ¹⁰The axe has been laid to the root of the trees, and every tree that does not produce good fruit will be cut down and thrown into the fire.

¹¹'I baptise you with water for repentance. But after me comes one who is more powerful than I, whose sandals I am not worthy to carry. He will baptise you with the Holy Spirit and fire. ¹²His winnowing fork is in his hand, and he will clear his threshing-floor, gathering his wheat into the barn and burning up the chaff with unquenchable fire.'

¹³Then Jesus came from Galilee to the Jordan to be baptised by John. ¹⁴But John tried to deter him, saying, 'I need to be baptised by you, and do you come to me?'

¹⁵Jesus replied, 'Let it be so now; it is proper for us to do this to fulfil all righteousness.' Then John consented.

¹⁶As soon as Jesus was baptised, he went up out of the water. At that moment heaven was opened, and he saw the Spirit of God descending like a dove and alighting on him. ¹⁷And a voice from heaven said, 'This is my Son, whom I love; with him I am well pleased.'

On This Truth We Stand

'[Jesus] saw the Spirit of God descending ... And a voice from heaven said, "This is my Son, whom I love ..."'
Matthew 3:16-17

Those who accept Scripture's teaching concerning God must be prepared to say that He is not only personal, but that He is a plurality of Persons - a Trinity. The doctrine of the Trinity, that God is one yet three separate Persons, is not easy to understand, but it is clear in Scripture. The term 'Trinity' nowhere appears in the Bible (it was first used by Tertullian around AD 210), but its roots are deeply embedded in the Word of God. It is mainly a revelation of the New Testament, but there are glimpses of the truth to be seen in the Old Testament also.

'Let us make mankind in our image' (Gen. 1:26). To whom was God speaking? Some say the angels, but nowhere in Scripture are angels seen as being involved in the act of creation or as being on the same level as God. Read Colossians 1:16 and it will become clear to whom God was speaking.

Other examples of the Trinity being mentioned in the Old Testament include these: 'The man has now become like one of us' (Gen. 3:22) and in Isaiah 6:8 God says: 'Whom shall I send? And who will go for us?'

'Go to the Jordan,' wrote Augustine, 'and you find the Trinity. There at the baptism of Jesus, the three Persons in the Godhead are simultaneously in evidence. The Father is heard speaking directly from heaven, the Son is seen being immersed in the river, and John the Baptist beholds the Spirit descending upon the Christ.' Three in One and One in Three. On this truth we must stand, though we may not fully understand.

PRAYER

Blessed Trinity, Three in One and One in Three, my spirit joins with Your Spirit this day to worship You in spirit and in truth. Though sometimes darkness to my intellect, Your truth is nevertheless sunshine to my heart. Amen.

FURTHER STUDY

Matt. 28:16-20;
John 14:26-27; 15:26-27
• How were the disciples to baptise new converts?
• How did Jesus confirm the truth of the Trinity?

January 4

■ GENESIS 7:1–9:7

7 The LORD then said to Noah, 'Go into the ark, you and your whole family, because I have found you righteous in this generation. ²Take with you seven pairs of every kind of clean animal, a male and its mate, and one pair of every kind of unclean animal, a male and its mate, ³and also seven pairs of every kind of bird, male and female, to keep their various kinds alive throughout the earth. ⁴Seven days from now I will send rain on the earth for forty days and forty nights, and I will wipe from the face of the earth every living creature I have made.'

⁵And Noah did all that the LORD commanded him.

⁶Noah was six hundred years old when the floodwaters came on the earth. ⁷And Noah and his sons and his wife and his sons'

wives entered the ark to escape the waters of the flood. ⁸Pairs of clean and unclean animals, of birds and of all creatures that move along the ground, ⁹male and female, came to Noah and entered the ark, as God had commanded Noah. ¹⁰And after the seven days the floodwaters came on the earth.

¹¹In the six hundredth year of Noah's life, on the seventeenth day of the second month – on that day all the springs of the great deep burst forth, and the floodgates of the heavens were opened. ¹²And rain fell on the earth for forty days and forty nights.

¹³On that very day Noah and his sons, Shem, Ham and Japheth, together with his wife and the wives of his three sons, entered the ark. ¹⁴They had with them every wild animal according to its kind, all livestock according to their kinds, every creature that moves along the ground according

to its kind and every bird according to its kind, everything with wings. ¹⁵ Pairs of all creatures that have the breath of life in them came to Noah and entered the ark. ¹⁶ The animals going in were male and female of every living thing, as God had commanded Noah. Then the LORD shut him in.

¹⁷ For forty days the flood kept coming on the earth, and as the waters increased they lifted the ark high above the earth. ¹⁸ The waters rose and increased greatly on the earth, and the ark floated on the surface of the water. ¹⁹ They rose greatly on the earth, and all the high mountains under the entire heavens were covered. ²⁰ The waters rose and covered the mountains to a depth of more than fifteen cubits. ²¹ Every living thing that moved on land perished – birds, livestock, wild animals, all the creatures that swarm over the earth, and all mankind. ²² Everything on dry land that had the breath of life in its nostrils died. ²³ Every living thing on the face of the earth was wiped out; people and animals and the creatures that move along the ground and the birds were wiped from the earth. Only Noah was left, and those with him in the ark.

²⁴ The waters flooded the earth for a hundred and fifty days.

8 But God remembered Noah and all the wild animals and the livestock that were with him in the ark, and he sent a wind over the earth, and the waters receded. ² Now the springs of the deep and the floodgates of the heavens had been closed, and the rain had stopped falling from the sky. ³ The water receded steadily from the earth. At the end of the hundred and fifty days the water had gone down, ⁴ and on the seventeenth day of the seventh month the ark came to rest on the mountains of Ararat. ⁵ The waters continued to recede until the tenth month, and on the first day of the tenth month the tops of the mountains became visible.

⁶ After forty days Noah opened a window he had made in the ark ⁷ and sent out a raven, and it kept flying back and forth until the water had dried up from the earth. ⁸ Then he sent out a dove to see if the water had receded from the surface of the ground. ⁹ But the dove could find nowhere to perch because there was water over all the surface of the earth; so it returned to Noah in the ark. He reached out his hand and took the dove and brought it back to himself in the ark. ¹⁰ He waited seven more days and again sent out the dove from the ark. ¹¹ When the dove returned to him in the evening, there in its beak was a freshly plucked olive leaf! Then Noah knew that the water had receded from the earth. ¹² He waited seven more days and sent the dove out again, but this time it did not return to him.

¹³ By the first day of the first month of Noah's six hundred and first year, the water had dried up from the earth. Noah then removed the covering from the ark and saw that the surface of the ground was dry. ¹⁴ By the twenty-seventh day of the second month the earth was completely dry.

¹⁵ Then God said to Noah, ¹⁶ 'Come out of the ark, you and your wife and your sons and their wives. ¹⁷ Bring out every kind of living creature that is with you – the birds, the animals, and all the creatures that move along the ground – so they can multiply on the earth and be fruitful and increase in number on it.'

¹⁸ So Noah came out, together with his sons and his wife and his sons' wives. ¹⁹ All the animals and all the creatures that move along the ground and all the birds – everything that moves on land – came out of the ark, one kind after another.

²⁰ Then Noah built an altar to the LORD and, taking some of all the clean animals and clean birds, he sacrificed burnt offerings on it. ²¹ The LORD smelled the pleasing aroma and said in his heart: 'Never again will I curse the ground because of humans, even though every inclination of the human heart is evil from childhood. And never

again will I destroy all living creatures, as I have done.

22 'As long as the earth endures,
    seedtime and harvest,
    cold and heat,
    summer and winter,
    day and night
    will never cease.'

9 Then God blessed Noah and his sons, saying to them, 'Be fruitful and increase in number and fill the earth. ²The fear and dread of you will fall on all the beasts of the earth, and on all the birds in the sky, on every creature that moves along the ground, and on all the fish in the sea; they are given into your hands. ³Everything that lives and moves about will be food for you. Just as I gave you the green plants, I now give you everything.

⁴'But you must not eat meat that has its lifeblood still in it. ⁵And for your lifeblood I will surely demand an accounting. I will demand an accounting from every animal. And from each human being, too, I will demand an accounting for the life of another human being.

⁶'Whoever sheds human blood,
    by humans shall their blood be shed;
for in the image of God
    has God made mankind.

⁷As for you, be fruitful and increase in number; multiply on the earth and increase upon it.'

. . . .

■ PSALM 3:1–8

¹ LORD, how many are my foes!
    How many rise up against me!
² Many are saying of me,
    'God will not deliver him.'

³ But you, LORD, are a shield around me,

my glory, the One who lifts my head high.
⁴ I call out to the LORD,
    and he answers me from his holy mountain.

⁵ I lie down and sleep;
    I wake again, because the LORD sustains me.
⁶ I will not fear though tens of thousands assail me on every side.

⁷ Arise, LORD!
    Deliver me, my God!
Strike all my enemies on the jaw;
    break the teeth of the wicked.

⁸ From the LORD comes deliverance.
    May your blessing be on your people.

. . . .

■ PROVERBS 1:8–9

⁸ Listen, my son, to your father's
    instruction
    and do not forsake your mother's
    teaching.
⁹ They are a garland to grace your head
    and a chain to adorn your neck.

. . . .

■ MATTHEW 4:1–20

4 Then Jesus was led by the Spirit into the wilderness to be tempted by the devil. ²After fasting for forty days and forty nights, he was hungry. ³The tempter came to him and said, 'If you are the Son of God, tell these stones to become bread.'

⁴Jesus answered, 'It is written: "Man shall not live on bread alone, but on every word that comes from the mouth of God."'

⁵Then the devil took him to the holy city and set him on the highest point of the temple. ⁶'If you are the Son of God,' he said, 'throw yourself down. For it is written:

He will protect me →

" He will command his angels
concerning you,
and they will lift you up in their hands,
so that you will not strike your foot
against a stone."'

⁷Jesus answered him, 'It is also written:
"Do not put the Lord your God to the test."'

⁸Again, the devil took him to a very high
mountain and showed him all the kingdoms of the world and their splendour. ⁹'All
this I will give you,' he said, 'if you will bow
down and worship me.'

¹⁰Jesus said to him, 'Away from me,
Satan! For it is written: "Worship the Lord
your God, and serve him only."'

¹¹Then the devil left him, and angels
came and attended him.

¹²When Jesus heard that John had been
put in prison, he withdrew to Galilee.
¹³Leaving Nazareth, he went and lived in
Capernaum, which was by the lake in the
area of Zebulun and Naphtali – ¹⁴to fulfil
what was said through the prophet Isaiah:

¹⁵'Land of Zebulun and land of Naphtali,
the Way of the Sea, beyond the Jordan,
Galilee of the Gentiles –
¹⁶the people living in darkness
have seen a great light;
on those living in the land of the shadow
of death
a light has dawned.'

¹⁷From that time on Jesus began to
preach, 'Repent, for the kingdom of heaven
has come near.'

¹⁸As Jesus was walking beside the Sea of
Galilee, he saw two brothers, Simon called
Peter and his brother Andrew. They were
casting a net into the lake, for they were fishermen. ¹⁹'Come, follow me,' Jesus said, 'and
I will send you out to fish for people.' ²⁰At
once they left their nets and followed him.

Influence or Intelligence?

'Jesus said to him, "Away from me, Satan! For it is
written ..."' **Matthew 4:10**

Some of the names given to the devil in Scripture show him to be a
real personality. In the passage that is before us today, Jesus is
seen in direct confrontation with the devil, even engaging in conversation
with him. Some liberal theologians explain this in these terms: Christ
was having a conversation with the dark thoughts that arose within His
nature, so any 'devil' that was present was subjective, not objective.

If we allow the notion that Christ had dark thoughts within His nature,
then the whole scheme of redemption tumbles like a pack of cards, for
a Saviour who is not perfect could never fully atone for our sins. As Dr
Handley Moule puts it: 'A Saviour who is not perfect is like a bridge
broken at one end and is not a reliable passage of access.' Once we try
to get around Scripture, we create endless difficulties for ourselves and
finish up looking foolish. Far better to accept the Bible as it stands and
believe its testimony on everything.

It is actually to Satan's advantage to get us to believe that he is not a
personal being, for if there is no personal devil, there can be no personal
resistance. Don't allow yourself to be deceived into thinking that the term

devil is a synonym for the evil influence that is in the world. The devil is more than an evil influence; he is an evil intelligence. Only when we recognise this fact will we be motivated to take effective steps to resist him.

PRAYER

Father, help me see that the first step in spiritual warfare is to 'know the enemy.' For until I know and understand my enemy, I will not be able to defeat him. Deepen my knowledge of these important truths, I pray. In Jesus' name. Amen.

FURTHER STUDY

1 John 3:1-8; Heb. 2:14;
John 12:30-31
• Why did the Son of God
  appear?
• What did He declare?

January 5

▬ GENESIS 9:8–10:32

⁸ Then God said to Noah and to his sons with him: ⁹ 'I now establish my covenant with you and with your descendants after you ¹⁰ and with every living creature that was with you – the birds, the livestock and all the wild animals, all those that came out of the ark with you – every living creature on earth. ¹¹ I establish my covenant with you: Never again will all life be destroyed by the waters of a flood; never again will there be a flood to destroy the earth.'

¹² And God said, 'This is the sign of the covenant I am making between me and you and every living creature with you, a covenant for all generations to come: ¹³ I have set my rainbow in the clouds, and it will be the sign of the covenant between me and the earth. ¹⁴ Whenever I bring clouds over the earth and the rainbow appears in the clouds, ¹⁵ I will remember my covenant between me and you and all living creatures of every kind. Never again will the waters become a flood to destroy all life. ¹⁶ Whenever the rainbow appears in the clouds, I will see it and remember the everlasting covenant between God and all living creatures of every kind on the earth.'

¹⁷ So God said to Noah, 'This is the sign of the covenant I have established between me and all life on the earth.'

¹⁸ The sons of Noah who came out of the ark were Shem, Ham and Japheth. (Ham was the father of Canaan.) ¹⁹ These were the three sons of Noah, and from them came the people who were scattered over the whole earth.

²⁰ Noah, a man of the soil, proceeded to plant a vineyard. ²¹ When he drank some of its wine, he became drunk and lay uncovered inside his tent. ²² Ham, the father of Canaan, saw his father naked and told his two brothers outside. ²³ But Shem and Japheth took a garment and laid it across their shoulders; then they walked in backwards and covered their father's naked body. Their faces were turned the other way so that they would not see their father naked.

²⁴ When Noah awoke from his wine and found out what his youngest son had done to him, ²⁵ he said,

'Cursed be Canaan!
    The lowest of slaves
      will he be to his brothers.'

[26] He also said,

'Praise be to the LORD, the God of Shem!
   May Canaan be the slave of Shem.
[27] May God extend Japheth's territory;
   may Japheth live in the tents of Shem,
   and may Canaan be the slave of
      Japheth.'

[28] After the flood Noah lived 350 years. [29] Noah lived a total of 950 years, and then he died.

10 This is the account of Shem, Ham and Japheth, Noah's sons, who themselves had sons after the flood.

[2] The sons of Japheth:
   Gomer, Magog, Madai, Javan, Tubal,
   Meshek and Tiras.
[3] The sons of Gomer:
   Ashkenaz, Riphath and Togarmah.
[4] The sons of Javan:
   Elishah, Tarshish, the Kittites and
   the Rodanites. [5] (From these the
   maritime peoples spread out into
   their territories by their clans within their nations, each with its own
   language.)
[6] The sons of Ham:
   Cush, Egypt, Put and Canaan.
[7] The sons of Cush:
   Seba, Havilah, Sabtah, Raamah and
   Sabteka.
   The sons of Raamah:
   Sheba and Dedan.

[8] Cush was the father of Nimrod, who became a mighty warrior on the earth. [9] He was a mighty hunter before the LORD; that is why it is said, 'Like Nimrod, a mighty hunter before the LORD.' [10] The first centres of his kingdom were Babylon, Uruk, Akkad and Kalneh, in Shinar. [11] From that land he went to Assyria, where he built Nineveh, Rehoboth Ir, Calah [12] and Resen, which is between Nineveh and Calah – which is the great city.

[13] Egypt was the father of
   the Ludites, Anamites, Lehabites,
   Naphtuhites, [14] Pathrusites, Kaslu-
   hites (from whom the Philistines
   came) and Caphtorites.
[15] Canaan was the father of
   Sidon his firstborn, and of the
   Hittites, [16] Jebusites, Amorites,
   Girgashites, [17] Hivites, Arkites,
   Sinites, [18] Arvadites, Zemarites and
   Hamathites.

Later the Canaanite clans scattered [19] and the borders of Canaan reached from Sidon towards Gerar as far as Gaza, and then towards Sodom, Gomorrah, Admah and Zeboyim, as far as Lasha.

[20] These are the sons of Ham by their clans and languages, in their territories and nations.

[21] Sons were also born to Shem, whose elder brother was Japheth; Shem was the ancestor of all the sons of Eber.

[22] The sons of Shem:
   Elam, Ashur, Arphaxad, Lud and
   Aram.
[23] The sons of Aram:
   Uz, Hul, Gether and Meshek.
[24] Arphaxad was the father of Shelah,
   and Shelah the father of Eber.
[25] Two sons were born to Eber:
   One was named Peleg, because in
   his time the earth was divided; his
   brother was named Joktan.
[26] Joktan was the father of
   Almodad, Sheleph, Hazarmaveth,
   Jerah, [27] Hadoram, Uzal, Diklah,
   [28] Obal, Abimael, Sheba, [29] Ophir,
   Havilah and Jobab. All these were
   sons of Joktan.

[30] The region where they lived stretched from Mesha towards Sephar, in the eastern hill country. [31] These are the sons of Shem by their

clans and languages, in their territories and nations.

³²These are the clans of Noah's sons, according to their lines of descent, within their nations. From these the nations spread out over the earth after the flood.

....

■ PSALM 4:1-8

¹Answer me when I call to you,
    my righteous God.
  Give me relief from my distress;
    have mercy on me and hear my prayer.

²How long will you people turn my glory
      into shame?
  How long will you love delusions and
      seek false gods?
³Know that the LORD has set apart his
      faithful servant for himself;
  the LORD hears when I call to him.

⁴Tremble and do not sin;
    when you are on your beds,
    search your hearts and be silent.
⁵Offer the sacrifices of the righteous
    and trust in the LORD.

⁶Many, LORD, are asking, 'Who will bring
      us prosperity?'
  Let the light of your face shine on us.
⁷Fill my heart with joy
    when their grain and new wine abound.

⁸In peace I will lie down and sleep,
    for you alone, LORD,
    make me dwell in safety.

....

■ PROVERBS 1:10-14

¹⁰My son, if sinful men entice you,
    do not give in to them.
¹¹If they say, 'Come along with us;

let's lie in wait for innocent blood,
    let's ambush some harmless soul;
¹²let's swallow them alive, like the grave,
    and whole, like those who go down to
      the pit;
¹³we will get all sorts of valuable things
    and fill our houses with plunder;
¹⁴cast lots with us;
    we will all share the loot' –

....

■ MATTHEW 4:21–5:12

²¹Going on from there, he saw two other brothers, James son of Zebedee and his brother John. They were in a boat with their father Zebedee, preparing their nets. Jesus called them, ²²and immediately they left the boat and their father and followed him.

²³Jesus went throughout Galilee, teaching in their synagogues, proclaiming the good news of the kingdom, and healing every disease and illness among the people. ²⁴News about him spread all over Syria, and people brought to him all who were ill with various diseases, those suffering severe pain, the demon-possessed, those having seizures, and the paralysed; and he healed them. ²⁵Large crowds from Galilee, the Decapolis, Jerusalem, Judea and the region across the Jordan followed him.

5 Now when Jesus saw the crowds, he went up on a mountainside and sat down. His disciples came to him, ²and he began to teach them.
He said:

³'Blessed are the poor in spirit,
    for theirs is the kingdom of heaven.
⁴Blessed are those who mourn,
    for they will be comforted.
⁵Blessed are the meek,
    for they will inherit the earth.
⁶Blessed are those who hunger and thirst
      for righteousness,
    for they will be filled.

7 Blessed are the merciful,
 for they will be shown mercy.
8 Blessed are the pure in heart,
 for they will see God.
9 Blessed are the peacemakers,
 for they will be called children of God.
10 Blessed are those who are persecuted
 because of righteousness,
 for theirs is the kingdom of heaven.

11 'Blessed are you when people insult you, persecute you and falsely say all kinds of evil against you because of me. 12 Rejoice and be glad, because great is your reward in heaven, for in the same way they persecuted the prophets who were before you.

False Accusation

'Blessed are you when people ... falsely say all kinds of evil against you because of me.' **Matthew 5:11**

Today we examine a hurt that often arises within the human heart - false accusation. Has someone accused you of a wrong for which you were not responsible, and though you try to explain or defend yourself, no one seems to believe you? It hurts, doesn't it? I have known many Christians who, when faced with the hurt of false accusation, turned away from the Christian life altogether. How sad! I have a friend who was falsely accused by fellow Christians in a church, and although I and many others knew the accusation was not true and passionately defended him, he broke down and was placed in a mental institution.

People (even Christians) have their own ways of trying to cope with the feelings that arise when they are falsely accused. Some turn to alcohol. They want to dull the pain inside them, and so they take what seems to them to be an easy way to that end. But it doesn't work, for there is always the morning after.

Some turn to books. That was the advice Edmund Gosse gave to his friend Robert Ross when he became involved in the Oscar Wilde scandal at the end of the nineteenth century. 'Turn for consolation to books,' he said. But it didn't work. Others might turn to nature, to art, or to music.

There is, however, a better way. If you are a Christian, and your heart is heavy because of a false accusation, then I assure you that the blessed Comforter is alongside you even now. Offer the hurt to Him. He delights to heal.

PRAYER

Blessed Lord Jesus, You who knew the hurt of being falsely accused, draw near in the power of Your Spirit and heal me now. I take - and You undertake. Thank You, Saviour. Amen.

FURTHER STUDY

James 3; 1 Pet. 3:16; 2:1;
Luke 6:7
• What is the hardest thing to tame?
• For what should we use our tongues?

January 6

■ **GENESIS 11:1–12:20**

11 Now the whole world had one language and a common speech. ²As people moved eastward, they found a plain in Shinar and settled there.

³They said to each other, 'Come, let's make bricks and bake them thoroughly.' They used brick instead of stone, and bitumen for mortar. ⁴Then they said, 'Come, let us build ourselves a city, with a tower that reaches to the heavens, so that we may make a name for ourselves; otherwise we will be scattered over the face of the whole earth.'

⁵But the LORD came down to see the city and the tower the people were building. ⁶The LORD said, 'If as one people speaking the same language they have begun to do this, then nothing they plan to do will be impossible for them. ⁷Come, let us go down and confuse their language so they will not understand each other.'

⁸So the LORD scattered them from there over all the earth, and they stopped building the city. ⁹That is why it was called Babel – because there the LORD confused the language of the whole world. From there the LORD scattered them over the face of the whole earth.

¹⁰This is the account of Shem's family line.

Two years after the flood, when Shem was 100 years old, he became the father of Arphaxad. ¹¹And after he became the father of Arphaxad, Shem lived 500 years and had other sons and daughters.

¹²When Arphaxad had lived 35 years, he became the father of Shelah. ¹³And after he became the father of Shelah, Arphaxad lived 403 years and had other sons and daughters.

¹⁴When Shelah had lived 30 years, he became the father of Eber. ¹⁵And after he became the father of Eber, Shelah lived 403 years and had other sons and daughters.

¹⁶When Eber had lived 34 years, he became the father of Peleg. ¹⁷And after he became the father of Peleg, Eber lived 430 years and had other sons and daughters.

¹⁸When Peleg had lived 30 years, he became the father of Reu. ¹⁹And after he became the father of Reu, Peleg lived 209 years and had other sons and daughters.

²⁰When Reu had lived 32 years, he became the father of Serug. ²¹And after he became the father of Serug, Reu lived 207 years and had other sons and daughters.

²²When Serug had lived 30 years, he became the father of Nahor. ²³And after he became the father of Nahor, Serug lived 200 years and had other sons and daughters.

²⁴When Nahor had lived 29 years, he became the father of Terah. ²⁵And after he became the father of Terah, Nahor lived 119 years and had other sons and daughters.

²⁶After Terah had lived 70 years, he became the father of Abram, Nahor and Haran.

²⁷This is the account of Terah's family line.

Terah became the father of Abram, Nahor and Haran. And Haran became the father of Lot. ²⁸While his father Terah was still alive, Haran died in Ur of the Chaldeans, in the land of his birth. ²⁹Abram and Nahor both married. The name of Abram's wife was Sarai, and the name of Nahor's wife was Milkah; she was the daughter of Haran, the father of both Milkah and Iskah.

30 Now Sarai was childless because she was not able to conceive.

31 Terah took his son Abram, his grandson Lot son of Haran, and his daughter-in-law Sarai, the wife of his son Abram, and together they set out from Ur of the Chaldeans to go to Canaan. But when they came to Harran, they settled there.

32 Terah lived 205 years, and he died in Harran.

12 The LORD had said to Abram, 'Go from your country, your people and your father's household to the land I will show you.

2 'I will make you into a great nation,
    and I will bless you;
I will make your name great,
    and you will be a blessing.
3 I will bless those who bless you,
    and whoever curses you I will curse;
and all peoples on earth
    will be blessed through you.'

4 So Abram went, as the LORD had told him; and Lot went with him. Abram was seventy-five years old when he set out from Harran. 5 He took his wife Sarai, his nephew Lot, all the possessions they had accumulated and the people they had acquired in Harran, and they set out for the land of Canaan, and they arrived there.

6 Abram travelled through the land as far as the site of the great tree of Moreh at Shechem. At that time the Canaanites were in the land. 7 The LORD appeared to Abram and said, 'To your offspring I will give this land.' So he built an altar there to the LORD, who had appeared to him.

8 From there he went on towards the hills east of Bethel and pitched his tent, with Bethel on the west and Ai on the east. There he built an altar to the LORD and called on the name of the LORD.

9 Then Abram set out and continued towards the Negev.

10 Now there was a famine in the land, and Abram went down to Egypt to live there for a while because the famine was severe. 11 As he was about to enter Egypt, he said to his wife Sarai, 'I know what a beautiful woman you are. 12 When the Egyptians see you, they will say, "This is his wife." Then they will kill me but will let you live. 13 Say you are my sister, so that I will be treated well for your sake and my life will be spared because of you.'

14 When Abram came to Egypt, the Egyptians saw that Sarai was a very beautiful woman. 15 And when Pharaoh's officials saw her, they praised her to Pharaoh, and she was taken into his palace. 16 He treated Abram well for her sake, and Abram acquired sheep and cattle, male and female donkeys, male and female servants, and camels.

17 But the LORD inflicted serious diseases on Pharaoh and his household because of Abram's wife Sarai. 18 So Pharaoh summoned Abram. 'What have you done to me?' he said. 'Why didn't you tell me she was your wife? 19 Why did you say, "She is my sister," so that I took her to be my wife? Now then, here is your wife. Take her and go!' 20 Then Pharaoh gave orders about Abram to his men, and they sent him on his way, with his wife and everything he had.

■ PSALM 5:1-6

1 Listen to my words, LORD,
    consider my lament.
2 Hear my cry for help,
    my King and my God,
    for to you I pray.

3 In the morning, LORD, you hear my voice;
    in the morning I lay my requests
        before you
    and wait expectantly.
4 For you are not a God who is pleased
    with wickedness;

with you, evil people are not welcome.
⁵ The arrogant cannot stand
     in your presence.
You hate all who do wrong;
⁶   you destroy those who tell lies.
The bloodthirsty and deceitful
     you, Lord, detest.

▬ PROVERBS 1:15-16

¹⁵ my son, do not go along with them,
     do not set foot on their paths;
¹⁶ for their feet rush into evil,
     they are swift to shed blood.

▬ MATTHEW 5:13-32

¹³ 'You are the salt of the earth. But if the salt loses its saltiness, how can it be made salty again? It is no longer good for anything, except to be thrown out and trampled underfoot. ¹⁴ 'You are the light of the world. A town built on a hill cannot be hidden. ¹⁵ Neither do people light a lamp and put it under a bowl. Instead they put it on its stand, and it gives light to everyone in the house. ¹⁶ In the same way, let your light shine before others, that they may see your good deeds and glorify your Father in heaven.

¹⁷ 'Do not think that I have come to abolish the Law or the Prophets; I have not come to abolish them but to fulfil them. ¹⁸ For truly I tell you, until heaven and earth disappear, not the smallest letter, not the least stroke of a pen, will by any means disappear from the Law until everything is accomplished. ¹⁹ Therefore anyone who sets aside one of the least of these commands and teaches others accordingly will be called least in the kingdom of heaven, but whoever practises and teaches these commands will be called great in the kingdom of heaven. ²⁰ For I tell you that unless your righteousness surpasses that of the Pharisees and the teachers of the law, you will certainly not enter the kingdom of heaven.

²¹ 'You have heard that it was said to the people long ago, "You shall not murder, and anyone who murders will be subject to judgment." ²² But I tell you that anyone who is angry with a brother or sister will be subject to judgment. Again, anyone who says to a brother or sister, "Raca," is answerable to the court. And anyone who says, "You fool!" will be in danger of the fire of hell.

²³ 'Therefore, if you are offering your gift at the altar and there remember that your brother or sister has something against you, ²⁴ leave your gift there in front of the altar. First go and be reconciled to them; then come and offer your gift.

²⁵ 'Settle matters quickly with your adversary who is taking you to court. Do it while you are still together on the way, or your adversary may hand you over to the judge, and the judge may hand you over to the officer, and you may be thrown into prison. ²⁶ Truly I tell you, you will not get out until you have paid the last penny.

²⁷ 'You have heard that it was said, "You shall not commit adultery." ²⁸ But I tell you that anyone who looks at a woman lustfully has already committed adultery with her in his heart. ²⁹ If your right eye causes you to stumble, gouge it out and throw it away. It is better for you to lose one part of your body than for your whole body to be thrown into hell. ³⁰ And if your right hand causes you to stumble, cut it off and throw it away. It is better for you to lose one part of your body than for your whole body to go into hell.

³¹ 'It has been said, "Anyone who divorces his wife must give her a certificate of divorce." ³² But I tell you that anyone who divorces his wife, except for sexual immorality, makes her the victim of adultery, and anyone who marries a divorced woman commits adultery.

The Unyielding Judge

'Settle matters quickly with your adversary ... or [he] may hand you over to the judge ...' **Matthew 5:25**

'God's wrath,' said George MacDonald, 'is always judicial. It is always the wrath of the Judge administering justice. Cruelty is always immoral, but true justice – never.' This may sound hard, but it is true.

There is great wisdom in the words of our Lord in the passage before us today. Settle matters with an adversary, He says, before he drags you to court. Do at once what you must one day do anyway. There may be no escape from payment, but why not escape at least from the prison sentence that will enforce it?

The point our Lord is making is that we ought not to drive justice to extremities. God requires righteousness of us, does He not? It is utterly useless to think, then, that we can escape the eternal law. So yield yourself rather than be compelled.

To those whose hearts are true, the idea of judgment is right; to those whose hearts are untrue, the idea of judgment is wrong. Many people live under the illusion that perhaps it might be possible to find a way of escaping all that is required of us in this world. But there is no escape. A way to avoid the demands of righteousness, apart from the righteousness which God accounts to us at the cross, would not be moral. When a man or woman accepts the payment God has made for them in Christ, the whole wealth of heaven is theirs; their debt is cleared. Those who deny that debt or who, acknowledging it, do nothing to avail themselves of the payment made for them on Calvary, face an unyielding Judge and an everlasting prison.

PRAYER

O Father, how serious and solemn is all this, but yet how true. Sin must ultimately be punished. I am so grateful that in Christ my debt has been paid, and availing myself of Your offer I am eternally free. Blessed be Your name forever. Amen.

FURTHER STUDY

Zeph. 3:1-5; Psa. 103:6; John 5:30; Rom. 2:2
• What does God do morning by morning?
• What is God's judgment based on?

January 7

■ GENESIS 13:1–15:6

13 So Abram went up from Egypt to the Negev, with his wife and everything he had, and Lot went with him. ² Abram had become very wealthy in livestock and in silver and gold.

³ From the Negev he went from place to place until he came to Bethel, to the place between Bethel and Ai where his tent had been earlier ⁴ and where he had first built an altar. There Abram called on the name of the LORD.

⁵ Now Lot, who was moving about with Abram, also had flocks and herds and tents. ⁶ But the land could not support them while they stayed together, for their possessions were so great that they were not able to stay together. ⁷ And quarrelling arose between Abram's herdsmen and Lot's. The Canaanites and Perizzites were also living in the land at that time.

⁸ So Abram said to Lot, 'Let's not have any quarrelling between you and me, or between your herdsmen and mine, for we are close relatives. ⁹ Is not the whole land before you? Let's part company. If you go to the left, I'll go to the right; if you go to the right, I'll go to the left.'

¹⁰ Lot looked around and saw that the whole plain of the Jordan towards Zoar was well watered, like the garden of the LORD, like the land of Egypt. (This was before the LORD destroyed Sodom and Gomorrah.) ¹¹ So Lot chose for himself the whole plain of the Jordan and set out towards the east. The two men parted company: ¹² Abram lived in the land of Canaan, while Lot lived among the cities of the plain and pitched his tents near Sodom. ¹³ Now the people of Sodom were wicked and were sinning greatly

against the LORD.

¹⁴ The LORD said to Abram after Lot had parted from him, 'Look around from where you are, to the north and south, to the east and west. ¹⁵ All the land that you see I will give to you and your offspring for ever. ¹⁶ I will make your offspring like the dust of the earth, so that if anyone could count the dust, then your offspring could be counted. ¹⁷ Go, walk through the length and breadth of the land, for I am giving it to you.'

¹⁸ So Abram went to live near the great trees of Mamre at Hebron, where he pitched his tents. There he built an altar to the LORD.

14 At the time when Amraphel was king of Shinar, Arioch king of Ellasar, Kedorlaomer king of Elam and Tidal king of Goyim, ² these kings went to war against Bera king of Sodom, Birsha king of Gomorrah, Shinab king of Admah, Shemeber king of Zeboyim, and the king of Bela (that is, Zoar). ³ All these latter kings joined forces in the Valley of Siddim (that is, the Dead Sea Valley). ⁴ For twelve years they had been subject to Kedorlaomer, but in the thirteenth year they rebelled.

⁵ In the fourteenth year, Kedorlaomer and the kings allied with him went out and defeated the Rephaites in Ashteroth Karnaim, the Zuzites in Ham, the Emites in Shaveh Kiriathaim ⁶ and the Horites in the hill country of Seir, as far as El Paran near the desert. ⁷ Then they turned back and went to En Mishpat (that is, Kadesh), and they conquered the whole territory of the Amalekites, as well as the Amorites who were living in Hazezon Tamar.

⁸ Then the king of Sodom, the king of Gomorrah, the king of Admah, the king of Zeboyim and the king of Bela (that is, Zoar) marched out and drew up their battle lines

in the Valley of Siddim ⁹against Kedorlaomer king of Elam, Tidal king of Goyim, Amraphel king of Shinar and Arioch king of Ellasar – four kings against five. ¹⁰Now the Valley of Siddim was full of tar pits, and when the kings of Sodom and Gomorrah fled, some of the men fell into them and the rest fled to the hills. ¹¹The four kings seized all the goods of Sodom and Gomorrah and all their food; then they went away. ¹²They also carried off Abram's nephew Lot and his possessions, since he was living in Sodom.

¹³A man who had escaped came and reported this to Abram the Hebrew. Now Abram was living near the great trees of Mamre the Amorite, a brother of Eshkol and Aner, all of whom were allied with Abram. ¹⁴When Abram heard that his relative had been taken captive, he called out the 318 trained men born in his household and went in pursuit as far as Dan. ¹⁵During the night Abram divided his men to attack them and he routed them, pursuing them as far as Hobah, north of Damascus. ¹⁶He recovered all the goods and brought back his relative Lot and his possessions, together with the women and the other people.

¹⁷After Abram returned from defeating Kedorlaomer and the kings allied with him, the king of Sodom came out to meet him in the Valley of Shaveh (that is, the King's Valley).

¹⁸Then Melchizedek king of Salem brought out bread and wine. He was priest of God Most High, ¹⁹and he blessed Abram, saying,

'Blessed be Abram by God Most High,
    Creator of heaven and earth.
²⁰And praise be to God Most High,
    who delivered your enemies into your
        hand.'

Then Abram gave him a tenth of everything.

²¹The king of Sodom said to Abram, 'Give me the people and keep the goods for yourself.'

²²But Abram said to the king of Sodom, 'With raised hand I have sworn an oath to the LORD, God Most High, Creator of heaven and earth, ²³that I will accept nothing belonging to you, not even a thread or the strap of a sandal, so that you will never be able to say, "I made Abram rich." ²⁴I will accept nothing but what my men have eaten and the share that belongs to the men who went with me – to Aner, Eshkol and Mamre. Let them have their share.'

15 After this, the word of the LORD came to Abram in a vision:

'Do not be afraid, Abram.
    I am your shield,
    your very great reward.'

²But Abram said, 'Sovereign LORD, what can you give me since I remain childless and the one who will inherit my estate is Eliezer of Damascus?' ³And Abram said, 'You have given me no children; so a servant in my household will be my heir.'

⁴Then the word of the LORD came to him: 'This man will not be your heir, but a son who is your own flesh and blood will be your heir.' ⁵He took him outside and said, 'Look up at the sky and count the stars – if indeed you can count them.' Then he said to him, 'So shall your offspring be.'

⁶Abram believed the LORD, and he credited it to him as righteousness.

▬ PSALM 5:7-12

⁷But I, by your great love,
    can come into your house;
in reverence I bow down
    towards your holy temple.

⁸Lead me, LORD, in your righteousness
    because of my enemies –
    make your way straight before me.

⁹ Not a word from their mouth can be
 trusted;
 their heart is filled with malice.
 Their throat is an open grave;
 with their tongues they tell lies.
¹⁰ Declare them guilty, O God!
 Let their intrigues be their downfall.
 Banish them for their many sins,
 for they have rebelled against you.
¹¹ But let all who take refuge in you be glad;
 let them ever sing for joy.
 Spread your protection over them,
 that those who love your name may
 rejoice in you.

¹² Surely, LORD, you bless the righteous;
 you surround them with your favour
 as with a shield.

▬ PROVERBS 1:17-19

¹⁷ How useless to spread a net
 where every bird can see it!
¹⁸ These men lie in wait for their own
 blood;
 they ambush only themselves!
¹⁹ Such are the paths of all who go after
 ill-gotten gain;
 it takes away the life of those who
 get it.

▬ MATTHEW 5:33–6:4

³³ 'Again, you have heard that it was said
to the people long ago, "Do not break your
oath, but fulfil to the Lord the oaths you
have made." ³⁴ But I tell you, do not swear
an oath at all: either by heaven, for it is
God's throne; ³⁵ or by the earth, for it is his
footstool; or by Jerusalem, for it is the city
of the Great King. ³⁶ And do not swear by
your head, for you cannot make even one
hair white or black. ³⁷ All you need to say is
simply "Yes," or "No"; anything beyond this
comes from the evil one.

³⁸ 'You have heard that it was said, "Eye
for eye, and tooth for tooth." ³⁹ But I tell you,
do not resist an evil person. If anyone slaps
you on the right cheek, turn to them the
other cheek also. ⁴⁰ And if anyone wants to
sue you and take your shirt, hand over your
coat as well. ⁴¹ If anyone forces you to go one
mile, go with them two miles. ⁴² Give to the
one who asks you, and do not turn away
from the one who wants to borrow from
you.

⁴³ 'You have heard that it was said, "Love
your neighbour and hate your enemy."
⁴⁴ But I tell you, love your enemies and pray
for those who persecute you, ⁴⁵ that you
may be children of your Father in heaven.
He causes his sun to rise on the evil and the
good, and sends rain on the righteous and
the unrighteous. ⁴⁶ If you love those who
love you, what reward will you get? Are not
even the tax collectors doing that? ⁴⁷ And if
you greet only your own people, what are
you doing more than others? Do not even
pagans do that? ⁴⁸ Be perfect, therefore, as
your heavenly Father is perfect.

6 'Be careful not to practise your righteousness in front of others to be seen
by them. If you do, you will have no reward
from your Father in heaven.

² 'So when you give to the needy, do not
announce it with trumpets, as the hypocrites do in the synagogues and on the
streets, to be honoured by others. Truly I
tell you, they have received their reward in
full. ³ But when you give to the needy, do
not let your left hand know what your right
hand is doing, ⁴ so that your giving may be
in secret. Then your Father, who sees what
is done in secret, will reward you.

'I Am Your Shield'

'Abram believed the LORD, and he credited it to him as righteousness.' **Genesis 15:6**

It is no good saying you believe God is stronger than the devil if you do not act on that belief. Faith not only believes this but acts on it by quickly standing up to the devil and saying something similar to what David said when he stood before Goliath: 'You come against me with sword and spear and javelin, but I come against you in the name of the LORD Almighty ...' (1 Sam. 17:45). You must never forget that God is much more powerful than the devil. Hold on to that and quickly raise your shield whenever you experience an attack of Satan's 'fiery darts.'

The passage that introduces this devotion focuses on an incident in Abraham's life that took place when he was exhausted after making a great stand. Doubtless, Satan would have attacked him with thoughts like: 'What is the point of all this action of God on your behalf and all these promises when you do not have an heir to carry on your line? God doesn't seem to have as much power as it would appear.'

Abraham was fearful at this point until the Lord came to him and gave him these glorious words: 'Do not be afraid, Abram. I am your shield your very great reward' (Gen. 15:1).

'I am your shield.' Hold on to that great truth, my friend, and when under attack, quickly lift it up and remind the devil that you belong to One whose power is endless and eternal. His promises are ever sure. That is what it means to hold up the shield of faith.

PRAYER

O God, how grateful I am for the sureness and certainty of Your Word. Once again I feel it entering into the core of my being. Help me to put these truths into practice the very moment I come under satanic attack. In Jesus' name I pray. Amen.

FURTHER STUDY

Prov. 30:1-5; Deut. 33:29; Psa. 33:20; 59:11; 84:9
• Why was Israel blessed?
• What was the psalmist's continual testimony?

January 8

■ **GENESIS 15:7–17:27**

7 He also said to him, 'I am the LORD, who brought you out of Ur of the Chaldeans to give you this land to take possession of it.'

8 But Abram said, 'Sovereign LORD, how can I know that I shall gain possession of it?'

⁹So the LORD said to him, 'Bring me a heifer, a goat and a ram, each three years old, along with a dove and a young pigeon.'

¹⁰Abram brought all these to him, cut them in two and arranged the halves opposite each other; the birds, however, he did not cut in half. ¹¹Then birds of prey came down on the carcasses, but Abram drove them away.

¹²As the sun was setting, Abram fell into a deep sleep, and a thick and dreadful darkness came over him. ¹³Then the LORD said to him, 'Know for certain that for four hundred years your descendants will be strangers in a country not their own and that they will be enslaved and ill-treated there. ¹⁴But I will punish the nation they serve as slaves, and afterwards they will come out with great possessions. ¹⁵You, however, will go to your ancestors in peace and be buried at a good old age. ¹⁶In the fourth generation your descendants will come back here, for the sin of the Amorites has not yet reached its full measure.'

¹⁷When the sun had set and darkness had fallen, a smoking brazier with a blazing torch appeared and passed between the pieces. ¹⁸On that day the LORD made a covenant with Abram and said, 'To your descendants I give this land, from the Wadi of Egypt to the great river, the Euphrates – ¹⁹the land of the Kenites, Kenizzites, Kadmonites, ²⁰Hittites, Perizzites, Rephaites, ²¹Amorites, Canaanites, Girgashites and Jebusites.'

16 Now Sarai, Abram's wife, had borne him no children. But she had an Egyptian slave named Hagar; ²so she said to Abram, 'The LORD has kept me from having children. Go, sleep with my slave; perhaps I can build a family through her.'

Abram agreed to what Sarai said. ³So after Abram had been living in Canaan ten years, Sarai his wife took her Egyptian slave Hagar and gave her to her husband to be his wife. ⁴He slept with Hagar, and she conceived.

When she knew she was pregnant, she began to despise her mistress. ⁵Then Sarai said to Abram, 'You are responsible for the wrong I am suffering. I put my slave in your arms, and now that she knows she is pregnant, she despises me. May the LORD judge between you and me.'

⁶'Your slave is in your hands,' Abram said. 'Do with her whatever you think best.' Then Sarai ill-treated Hagar; so she fled from her.

⁷The angel of the LORD found Hagar near a spring in the desert; it was the spring that is beside the road to Shur. ⁸And he said, 'Hagar, slave of Sarai, where have you come from, and where are you going?'

'I'm running away from my mistress Sarai,' she answered.

⁹Then the angel of the LORD told her, 'Go back to your mistress and submit to her.' ¹⁰The angel added, 'I will increase your descendants so much that they will be too numerous to count.'

¹¹The angel of the LORD also said to her:

'You are now pregnant
   and you will give birth to a son.
You shall name him Ishmael,
   for the LORD has heard of your misery.
¹²He will be a wild donkey of a man;
   his hand will be against everyone
   and everyone's hand against him,
and he will live in hostility
   towards all his brothers.'

¹³She gave this name to the LORD who spoke to her: 'You are the God who sees me,' for she said, 'I have now seen the One who sees me.' ¹⁴That is why the well was called Beer Lahai Roi; it is still there, between Kadesh and Bered.

¹⁵So Hagar bore Abram a son, and Abram gave the name Ishmael to the son she had borne. ¹⁶Abram was eighty-six years old when Hagar bore him Ishmael.

17 When Abram was ninety-nine years old, the LORD appeared to him and said, 'I am God Almighty; walk before me faithfully and be blameless. ²Then I will make my covenant between me and you and will greatly increase your numbers.'

³Abram fell face down, and God said to him, ⁴'As for me, this is my covenant with you: you will be the father of many nations. ⁵No longer will you be called Abram; your name will be Abraham, for I have made you a father of many nations. ⁶I will make you very fruitful; I will make nations of you, and kings will come from you. ⁷I will establish my covenant as an everlasting covenant between me and you and your descendants after you for the generations to come, to be your God and the God of your descendants after you. ⁸The whole land of Canaan, where you now reside as a foreigner, I will give as an everlasting possession to you and your descendants after you; and I will be their God.'

⁹Then God said to Abraham, 'As for you, you must keep my covenant, you and your descendants after you for the generations to come. ¹⁰This is my covenant with you and your descendants after you, the covenant you are to keep: every male among you shall be circumcised. ¹¹You are to undergo circumcision, and it will be the sign of the covenant between me and you. ¹²For the generations to come every male among you who is eight days old must be circumcised, including those born in your household or bought with money from a foreigner – those who are not your offspring. ¹³Whether born in your household or bought with your money, they must be circumcised. My covenant in your flesh is to be an everlasting covenant. ¹⁴Any uncircumcised male, who has not been circumcised in the flesh, will be cut off from his people; he has broken my covenant.'

¹⁵God also said to Abraham, 'As for Sarai your wife, you are no longer to call her Sarai; her name will be Sarah. ¹⁶I will bless her and will surely give you a son by her. I will bless her so that she will be the mother of nations; kings of peoples will come from her.'

¹⁷Abraham fell face down; he laughed and said to himself, 'Will a son be born to a man a hundred years old? Will Sarah bear a child at the age of ninety?' ¹⁸And Abraham said to God, 'If only Ishmael might live under your blessing!'

¹⁹Then God said, 'Yes, but your wife Sarah will bear you a son, and you will call him Isaac. I will establish my covenant with him as an everlasting covenant for his descendants after him. ²⁰And as for Ishmael, I have heard you: I will surely bless him; I will make him fruitful and will greatly increase his numbers. He will be the father of twelve rulers, and I will make him into a great nation. ²¹But my covenant I will establish with Isaac, whom Sarah will bear to you by this time next year.' ²²When he had finished speaking with Abraham, God went up from him.

²³On that very day Abraham took his son Ishmael and all those born in his household or bought with his money, every male in his household, and circumcised them, as God told him. ²⁴Abraham was ninety-nine years old when he was circumcised, ²⁵and his son Ishmael was thirteen; ²⁶Abraham and his son Ishmael were both circumcised on that very day. ²⁷And every male in Abraham's household, including those born in his household or bought from a foreigner, was circumcised with him.

....

■ PSALM 6:1-5

¹LORD, do not rebuke me in your anger
    or discipline me in your wrath.
²Have mercy on me, LORD, for I am faint;
    heal me, LORD, for my bones are in
    agony.

³ My soul is in deep anguish.
How long, LORD, how long?

⁴ Turn, LORD, and deliver me;
save me because of your unfailing
love.
⁵ Among the dead no one proclaims your
name.
Who praises you from his grave?

▬ PROVERBS 1:20-23

²⁰ Out in the open wisdom calls aloud,
she raises her voice in the public square;
²¹ on top of the wall she cries out,
at the city gate she makes her speech:

²² 'How long will you who are simple love
your simple ways?
How long will mockers delight in
mockery
and fools hate knowledge?
²³ Repent at my rebuke!
Then I will pour out my thoughts to
you,
I will make known to you my
teachings.

▬ MATTHEW 6:5-24

⁵ 'And when you pray, do not be like the
hypocrites, for they love to pray standing in
the synagogues and on the street corners to
be seen by others. Truly I tell you, they have
received their reward in full. ⁶ But when you
pray, go into your room, close the door and
pray to your Father, who is unseen. Then
your Father, who sees what is done in secret,
will reward you. ⁷ And when you pray, do not
keep on babbling like pagans, for they think
they will be heard because of their many
words. ⁸ Do not be like them, for your Father
knows what you need before you ask him.

⁹ 'This, then, is how you should pray:

' "Our Father in heaven,
hallowed be your name,
¹⁰ your kingdom come,
your will be done,
on earth as it is in heaven.
¹¹ Give us today our daily bread.
¹² And forgive us our debts,
as we also have forgiven our debtors.
¹³ And lead us not into temptation,
but deliver us from the evil one." '

¹⁴ For if you forgive other people when they
sin against you, your heavenly Father will
also forgive you. ¹⁵ But if you do not forgive others their sins, your Father will not
forgive your sins.

¹⁶ 'When you fast, do not look sombre as
the hypocrites do, for they disfigure their
faces to show others they are fasting. Truly I tell you, they have received their reward
in full. ¹⁷ But when you fast, put oil on your
head and wash your face, ¹⁸ so that it will not
be obvious to others that you are fasting,
but only to your Father, who is unseen; and
your Father, who sees what is done in secret,
will reward you.

¹⁹ 'Do not store up for yourselves treasures on earth, where moths and vermin destroy, and where thieves break in and steal.
²⁰ But store up for yourselves treasures in
heaven, where moths and vermin do not destroy, and where thieves do not break in and
steal. ²¹ For where your treasure is, there
your heart will be also.

²² 'The eye is the lamp of the body. If your
eyes are healthy, your whole body will be
full of light. ²³ But if your eyes are unhealthy,
your whole body will be full of darkness. If
then the light within you is darkness, how
great is that darkness!

²⁴ 'No one can serve two masters. Either
you will hate the one and love the other, or
you will be devoted to the one and despise
the other. You cannot serve both God and
Money.

Jesus' Pattern of Prayer

'This, then, is how you should pray: "Our Father in heaven, hallowed be your name ..."' **Matthew 6:9**

One of the most precious passages in the whole of the New Testament is the Lord's Prayer. These words of Jesus, so seemingly simple, encompass every conceivable element in prayer and reduce it to a clearly understood pattern.

The Lord's Prayer (or, more correctly, The Disciples' Prayer) is, among other things, a miracle of condensation. In the short compass of sixty-six words, the Master presents a model of praying that touches on every major aspect of prayer. One writer says of it: 'The Lord's Prayer sets the standard for all praying. Everything every man ever needed to understand about prayer is latent in the choice disclosure of these words.' That might sound like an astonishing claim, but it is true. No set of theological volumes, no sermon, no series of writings could ever capture the fullness of everything prayer is, as does this simple yet profound model.

The more we understand this model, and the more we pray in line with it, the more powerful and productive our prayer life will become. Because this communication is so important, the enemy seeks to disrupt it. This is why we face the necessity to constantly refocus our thinking on the subject, and seek to deepen and enhance our prowess in the art of prayer. If the Lord's Prayer sets the standard for all praying, then we must lay our praying alongside His pattern in order that our prayers might become more and more like His.

PRAYER

O God, as I begin this quest for a deeper and more effective prayer life, my heart cries out: 'Lord, teach me to pray.' For I know that when I learn to pray, I learn to live – vitally and victoriously. Amen.

FURTHER STUDY

1 Tim. 2:1-8; 1 Chron. 16:11; Luke 18:1; 1 Thess. 5:17
• What was Christ's injunction?
• What is Paul's desire?

January 9

■ GENESIS 18:1–19:22

18 The LORD appeared to Abraham near the great trees of Mamre while he was sitting at the entrance to his tent in the heat of the day. ²Abraham looked up and saw three men standing nearby. When he saw them, he hurried from the entrance of his tent to meet them and bowed low to the ground.

³ He said, 'If I have found favour in your eyes, my lord, do not pass your servant by. ⁴ Let a little water be brought, and then you may all wash your feet and rest under this tree. ⁵ Let me get you something to eat, so you can be refreshed and then go on your way – now that you have come to your servant.'

'Very well,' they answered, 'do as you say.'

⁶ So Abraham hurried into the tent to Sarah. 'Quick,' he said, 'get three seahs of the finest flour and knead it and bake some bread.'

⁷ Then he ran to the herd and selected a choice, tender calf and gave it to a servant, who hurried to prepare it. ⁸ He then brought some curds and milk and the calf that had been prepared, and set these before them. While they ate, he stood near them under a tree.

⁹ 'Where is your wife Sarah?' they asked him.

'There, in the tent,' he said.

¹⁰ Then one of them said, 'I will surely return to you about this time next year, and Sarah your wife will have a son.'

Now Sarah was listening at the entrance to the tent, which was behind him. ¹¹ Abraham and Sarah were already very old, and Sarah was past the age of childbearing. ¹² So Sarah laughed to herself as she thought, 'After I am worn out and my lord is old, will I now have this pleasure?'

¹³ Then the LORD said to Abraham, 'Why did Sarah laugh and say, "Will I really have a child, now that I am old?" ¹⁴ Is anything too hard for the LORD? I will return to you at the appointed time next year, and Sarah will have a son.'

¹⁵ Sarah was afraid, so she lied and said, 'I did not laugh.'

But he said, 'Yes, you did laugh.'

¹⁶ When the men got up to leave, they looked down towards Sodom, and Abraham walked along with them to see them on their way. ¹⁷ Then the LORD said,

'Shall I hide from Abraham what I am about to do? ¹⁸ Abraham will surely become a great and powerful nation, and all nations on earth will be blessed through him. ¹⁹ For I have chosen him, so that he will direct his children and his household after him to keep the way of the LORD by doing what is right and just, so that the LORD will bring about for Abraham what he has promised him.'

²⁰ Then the LORD said, 'The outcry against Sodom and Gomorrah is so great and their sin so grievous ²¹ that I will go down and see if what they have done is as bad as the outcry that has reached me. If not, I will know.'

²² The men turned away and went towards Sodom, but Abraham remained standing before the LORD. ²³ Then Abraham approached him and said: 'Will you sweep away the righteous with the wicked? ²⁴ What if there are fifty righteous people in the city? Will you really sweep it away and not spare the place for the sake of the fifty righteous people in it? ²⁵ Far be it from you to do such a thing – to kill the righteous with the wicked, treating the righteous and the wicked alike. Far be it from you! Will not the Judge of all the earth do right?'

²⁶ The LORD said, 'If I find fifty righteous people in the city of Sodom, I will spare the whole place for their sake.'

²⁷ Then Abraham spoke up again: 'Now that I have been so bold as to speak to the Lord, though I am nothing but dust and ashes, ²⁸ what if the number of the righteous is five less than fifty? Will you destroy the whole city for lack of five people?'

'If I find forty-five there,' he said, 'I will not destroy it.'

²⁹ Once again he spoke to him, 'What if only forty are found there?'

He said, 'For the sake of forty, I will not do it.'

³⁰ Then he said, 'May the Lord not be angry, but let me speak. What if only thirty can be found there?'

He answered, 'I will not do it if I find

thirty there.'

³¹Abraham said, 'Now that I have been so bold as to speak to the Lord, what if only twenty can be found there?'

He said, 'For the sake of twenty, I will not destroy it.'

³²Then he said, 'May the Lord not be angry, but let me speak just once more. What if only ten can be found there?'

He answered, 'For the sake of ten, I will not destroy it.'

³³When the LORD had finished speaking with Abraham, he left, and Abraham returned home.

19 The two angels arrived at Sodom in the evening, and Lot was sitting in the gateway of the city. When he saw them, he got up to meet them and bowed down with his face to the ground. ²'My lords,' he said, 'please turn aside to your servant's house. You can wash your feet and spend the night and then go on your way early in the morning.'

'No,' they answered, 'we will spend the night in the square.'

³But he insisted so strongly that they did go with him and entered his house. He prepared a meal for them, baking bread without yeast, and they ate. ⁴Before they had gone to bed, all the men from every part of the city of Sodom – both young and old – surrounded the house. ⁵They called to Lot, 'Where are the men who came to you tonight? Bring them out to us so that we can have sex with them.'

⁶Lot went outside to meet them and shut the door behind him ⁷and said, 'No, my friends. Don't do this wicked thing. ⁸Look, I have two daughters who have never slept with a man. Let me bring them out to you, and you can do what you like with them. But don't do anything to these men, for they have come under the protection of my roof.'

⁹'Get out of our way,' they replied. 'This fellow came here as a foreigner, and now he wants to play the judge! We'll treat you

worse than them.' They kept bringing pressure on Lot and moved forward to break down the door.

¹⁰But the men inside reached out and pulled Lot back into the house and shut the door. ¹¹Then they struck the men who were at the door of the house, young and old, with blindness so that they could not find the door.

¹²The two men said to Lot, 'Do you have anyone else here – sons-in-law, sons or daughters, or anyone else in the city who belongs to you? Get them out of here, ¹³because we are going to destroy this place. The outcry to the LORD against its people is so great that he has sent us to destroy it.'

¹⁴So Lot went out and spoke to his sons-in-law, who were pledged to marry his daughters. He said, 'Hurry and get out of this place, because the LORD is about to destroy the city!' But his sons-in-law thought he was joking.

¹⁵With the coming of dawn, the angels urged Lot, saying, 'Hurry! Take your wife and your two daughters who are here, or you will be swept away when the city is punished.'

¹⁶When he hesitated, the men grasped his hand and the hands of his wife and of his two daughters and led them safely out of the city, for the LORD was merciful to them. ¹⁷As soon as they had brought them out, one of them said, 'Flee for your lives! Don't look back, and don't stop anywhere in the plain! Flee to the mountains or you will be swept away!'

¹⁸But Lot said to them, 'No, my lords, please! ¹⁹Your servant has found favour in your eyes, and you have shown great kindness to me in sparing my life. But I can't flee to the mountains; this disaster will overtake me, and I'll die. ²⁰Look, here is a town near enough to run to, and it is small. Let me flee to it – it is very small, isn't it? Then my life will be spared.'

²¹He said to him, 'Very well, I will grant this request too; I will not overthrow the town you speak of. ²²But flee there quickly,

because I cannot do anything until you reach it.' (That is why the town was called Zoar.)

....

▬ PSALM 6:6-10

⁶ I am worn out from my groaning.

All night long I flood my bed with weeping
and drench my couch with tears.
⁷ My eyes grow weak with sorrow;
they fail because of all my foes.

⁸ Away from me, all you who do evil,
for the LORD has heard my weeping.
⁹ The LORD has heard my cry for mercy;
the LORD accepts my prayer.
¹⁰ All my enemies will be overwhelmed
with shame and anguish;
they will turn back and suddenly be
put to shame.

....

▬ PROVERBS 1:24-27

²⁴ But since you refuse to listen when I call
and no one pays attention when I
stretch out my hand,
²⁵ since you disregard all my advice
and do not accept my rebuke,
²⁶ I in turn will laugh when disaster strikes
you;
I will mock when calamity overtakes
you –
²⁷ when calamity overtakes you like a
storm,
when disaster sweeps over you like a
whirlwind,
when distress and trouble overwhelm
you.

....

▬ MATTHEW 6:25–7:12

²⁵ 'Therefore I tell you, do not worry
about your life, what you will eat or drink;
or about your body, what you will wear. Is
not life more than food, and the body more
than clothes? ²⁶ Look at the birds of the air;
they do not sow or reap or store away in
barns, and yet your heavenly Father feeds
them. Are you not much more valuable than
they? ²⁷ Can any one of you by worrying add
a single hour to your life?

²⁸ 'And why do you worry about clothes?
See how the flowers of the field grow. They
do not labour or spin. ²⁹ Yet I tell you that
not even Solomon in all his splendour was
dressed like one of these. ³⁰ If that is how
God clothes the grass of the field, which is
here today and tomorrow is thrown into the
fire, will he not much more clothe you – you
of little faith? ³¹ So do not worry, saying,
"What shall we eat?" or "What shall we
drink?" or "What shall we wear?" ³² For the
pagans run after all these things, and your
heavenly Father knows that you need them.
³³ But seek first his kingdom and his righteousness, and all these things will be giv-
en to you as well. ³⁴ Therefore do not worry
about tomorrow, for tomorrow will worry
about itself. Each day has enough trouble of
its own.

7 'Do not judge, or you too will be judged.
² For in the same way as you judge others, you will be judged, and with the measure you use, it will be measured to you.

³ 'Why do you look at the speck of sawdust
in your brother's eye and pay no attention
to the plank in your own eye? ⁴ How can you
say to your brother, "Let me take the speck
out of your eye," when all the time there is
a plank in your own eye? ⁵ You hypocrite,
first take the plank out of your own eye, and
then you will see clearly to remove the speck
from your brother's eye.

⁶ 'Do not give dogs what is sacred; do not
throw your pearls to pigs. If you do, they
may trample them under their feet, and
turn and tear you to pieces.

⁷ 'Ask and it will be given to you; seek and

you will find; knock and the door will be opened to you. [8] For everyone who asks receives; the one who seeks finds; and to the one who knocks, the door will be opened.

[9] 'Which of you, if your son asks for bread, will give him a stone? [10] Or if he asks for a fish, will give him a snake? [11] If you,

then, though you are evil, know how to give good gifts to your children, how much more will your Father in heaven give good gifts to those who ask him! [12] So in everything, do to others what you would have them do to you, for this sums up the Law and the Prophets.

'Your Kingdom Come'

'But seek first his kingdom and his righteousness, and all these things will be given to you as well.'
Matthew 6:33

Let us examine the fourth phrase in the Lord's Prayer: 'Your kingdom come.' Jesus, after making clear that the first consideration in prayer is to focus on God's character, puts as the next issue the establishing of God's kingdom. Any pattern of praying that does not make the kingdom a priority is not Christian praying. Our text today tells us: 'Seek first his kingdom and his righteousness, and all these things will be given to you as well.' If you seek something else first, then your life will be off balance.

A newspaper report tells of a small town in Alaska where all the electric clocks were showing the wrong time. The fault, it appears, was in the local power plant. It failed to run with systematic regularity and thus all the electric clocks were 'out.' When your primary concern is for something other than the kingdom of God, then everything in your life will be 'out,' too. One of the sad things about church history is that the Church has never really been gripped by the vision of the kingdom of God. There are notable exceptions, of course, but by and large the Church has missed its way in this matter. One theologian points out that when the Church drew up its creeds – the Apostle's, the Athanasian, the Nicene – it mentioned the kingdom once in all three of them, and then only marginally. The Church will never move into the dimension God has planned for it until it puts the kingdom where Jesus put it in this prayer – in a place of primary consideration and primary allegiance.

PRAYER

Gracious Father, I begin to see that there is something here that demands my thought and attention, and I don't want to miss it. Prepare me in mind and spirit for what You want to teach me in the days ahead. In Jesus' name. Amen.

FURTHER STUDY

Luke 9:51-62; Matt. 5:3; John 3:3; James 2:5
• What did Jesus teach about the kingdom?
• What did Jesus say to His would-be followers?

January 10

▬ GENESIS 19:23–21:21

²³ By the time Lot reached Zoar, the sun had risen over the land. ²⁴ Then the LORD rained down burning sulphur on Sodom and Gomorrah – from the LORD out of the heavens. ²⁵ Thus he overthrew those cities and the entire plain, destroying all those living in the cities – and also the vegetation in the land. ²⁶ But Lot's wife looked back, and she became a pillar of salt.

²⁷ Early the next morning Abraham got up and returned to the place where he had stood before the LORD. ²⁸ He looked down towards Sodom and Gomorrah, towards all the land of the plain, and he saw dense smoke rising from the land, like smoke from a furnace.

²⁹ So when God destroyed the cities of the plain, he remembered Abraham, and he brought Lot out of the catastrophe that overthrew the cities where Lot had lived.

³⁰ Lot and his two daughters left Zoar and settled in the mountains, for he was afraid to stay in Zoar. He and his two daughters lived in a cave. ³¹ One day the elder daughter said to the younger, 'Our father is old, and there is no man round here to give us children – as is the custom all over the earth. ³² Let's get our father to drink wine and then sleep with him and preserve our family line through our father.'

³³ That night they got their father to drink wine, and the elder daughter went in and slept with him. He was not aware of it when she lay down or when she got up.

³⁴ The next day the elder daughter said to the younger, 'Last night I slept with my father. Let's get him to drink wine again tonight, and you go in and sleep with him so we can preserve our family line through

our father.' ³⁵ So they got their father to drink wine that night also, and the younger daughter went in and slept with him. Again he was not aware of it when she lay down or when she got up.

³⁶ So both of Lot's daughters became pregnant by their father. ³⁷ The elder daughter had a son, and she named him Moab; he is the father of the Moabites of today. ³⁸ The younger daughter also had a son, and she named him Ben-Ammi; he is the father of the Ammonites of today.

20 Now Abraham moved on from there into the region of the Negev and lived between Kadesh and Shur. For a while he stayed in Gerar, ² and there Abraham said of his wife Sarah, 'She is my sister.' Then Abimelek king of Gerar sent for Sarah and took her.

³ But God came to Abimelek in a dream one night and said to him, 'You are as good as dead because of the woman you have taken; she is a married woman.'

⁴ Now Abimelek had not gone near her, so he said, 'Lord, will you destroy an innocent nation? ⁵ Did he not say to me, "She is my sister," and didn't she also say, "He is my brother"? I have done this with a clear conscience and clean hands.'

⁶ Then God said to him in the dream, 'Yes, I know you did this with a clear conscience, and so I have kept you from sinning against me. That is why I did not let you touch her. ⁷ Now return the man's wife, for he is a prophet, and he will pray for you and you will live. But if you do not return her, you may be sure that you and all who belong to you will die.'

⁸ Early the next morning Abimelek summoned all his officials, and when he told them all that had happened, they were very

much afraid. ⁹Then Abimelek called Abraham in and said, 'What have you done to us? How have I wronged you that you have brought such great guilt upon me and my kingdom? You have done things to me that should never be done.' ¹⁰And Abimelek asked Abraham, 'What was your reason for doing this?'

¹¹Abraham replied, 'I said to myself, "There is surely no fear of God in this place, and they will kill me because of my wife." ¹²Besides, she really is my sister, the daughter of my father though not of my mother; and she became my wife. ¹³And when God caused me to wander from my father's household, I said to her, "This is how you can show your love to me: Everywhere we go, say of me, 'He is my brother.'"'

¹⁴Then Abimelek brought sheep and cattle and male and female slaves and gave them to Abraham, and he returned Sarah his wife to him. ¹⁵And Abimelek said, 'My land is before you; live wherever you like.'

¹⁶To Sarah he said, 'I am giving your brother a thousand shekels of silver. This is to cover the offence against you before all who are with you; you are completely vindicated.'

¹⁷Then Abraham prayed to God, and God healed Abimelek, his wife and his female slaves so they could have children again, ¹⁸for the LORD had kept all the women in Abimelek's household from conceiving because of Abraham's wife Sarah.

21 Now the LORD was gracious to Sarah as he had said, and the LORD did for Sarah what he had promised. ²Sarah became pregnant and bore a son to Abraham in his old age, at the very time God had promised him. ³Abraham gave the name Isaac to the son Sarah bore him. ⁴When his son Isaac was eight days old, Abraham circumcised him, as God commanded him. ⁵Abraham was a hundred years old when his son Isaac was born to him.

⁶Sarah said, 'God has brought me laughter, and everyone who hears about this will laugh with me.' ⁷And she added, 'Who would have said to Abraham that Sarah would nurse children? Yet I have borne him a son in his old age.'

⁸The child grew and was weaned, and on the day Isaac was weaned Abraham held a great feast. ⁹But Sarah saw that the son whom Hagar the Egyptian had borne to Abraham was mocking, ¹⁰and she said to Abraham, 'Get rid of that slave woman and her son, for that woman's son will never share in the inheritance with my son Isaac.'

¹¹The matter distressed Abraham greatly because it concerned his son. ¹²But God said to him, 'Do not be so distressed about the boy and your slave woman. Listen to whatever Sarah tells you, because it is through Isaac that your offspring will be reckoned. ¹³I will make the son of the slave into a nation also, because he is your offspring.'

¹⁴Early the next morning Abraham took some food and a skin of water and gave them to Hagar. He set them on her shoulders and then sent her off with the boy. She went on her way and wandered in the Desert of Beersheba.

¹⁵When the water in the skin was gone, she put the boy under one of the bushes. ¹⁶Then she went off and sat down about a bow-shot away, for she thought, 'I cannot watch the boy die.' And as she sat there, she began to sob.

¹⁷God heard the boy crying, and the angel of God called to Hagar from heaven and said to her, 'What is the matter, Hagar? Do not be afraid; God has heard the boy crying as he lies there. ¹⁸Lift the boy up and take him by the hand, for I will make him into a great nation.'

¹⁹Then God opened her eyes and she saw a well of water. So she went and filled the skin with water and gave the boy a drink.

²⁰God was with the boy as he grew up. He lived in the desert and became an archer. ²¹While he was living in the Desert of Paran,

his mother got a wife for him from Egypt.

▬ PSALM 7:1-8

¹ LORD my God, I take refuge in you;
>   save and deliver me from all who
>   pursue me,
² or they will tear me apart like a lion
>   and rip me to pieces with no one to
>   rescue me.

³ LORD my God, if I have done this
>   and there is guilt on my hands –
⁴ if I have repaid my ally with evil
>   or without cause have robbed my foe –
⁵ then let my enemy pursue and overtake
>   me;
>   let him trample my life to the ground
>   and make me sleep in the dust.

⁶ Arise, LORD, in your anger;
>   rise up against the rage of my enemies.
>   Awake, my God; decree justice.
⁷ Let the assembled peoples gather round
>   you,
>   while you sit enthroned over them on
>   high.
⁸   Let the LORD judge the peoples.
> Vindicate me, LORD, according to my
>   righteousness,
>   according to my integrity, O Most High.

▬ PROVERBS 1:28-31

²⁸ 'Then they will call to me but I will not
>   answer;
>   they will look for me but will not
>   find me,
²⁹ since they hated knowledge
>   and did not choose to fear the LORD.
³⁰ Since they would not accept my advice
>   and spurned my rebuke,
³¹ they will eat the fruit of their ways

and be filled with the fruit of their
>   schemes.

▬ MATTHEW 7:13-8:4

¹³ 'Enter through the narrow gate. For wide is the gate and broad is the road that leads to destruction, and many enter through it. ¹⁴ But small is the gate and narrow the road that leads to life, and only a few find it.

¹⁵ 'Watch out for false prophets. They come to you in sheep's clothing, but inwardly they are ferocious wolves. ¹⁶ By their fruit you will recognise them. Do people pick grapes from thorn-bushes, or figs from thistles? ¹⁷ Likewise, every good tree bears good fruit, but a bad tree bears bad fruit. ¹⁸ A good tree cannot bear bad fruit, and a bad tree cannot bear good fruit. ¹⁹ Every tree that does not bear good fruit is cut down and thrown into the fire. ²⁰ Thus, by their fruit you will recognise them.

²¹ 'Not everyone who says to me, "Lord, Lord," will enter the kingdom of heaven, but only the one who does the will of my Father who is in heaven. ²² Many will say to me on that day, "Lord, Lord, did we not prophesy in your name and in your name drive out demons and in your name perform many miracles?" ²³ Then I will tell them plainly, "I never knew you. Away from me, you evildoers!"

²⁴ 'Therefore everyone who hears these words of mine and puts them into practice is like a wise man who built his house on the rock. ²⁵ The rain came down, the streams rose, and the winds blew and beat against that house; yet it did not fall, because it had its foundation on the rock. ²⁶ But everyone who hears these words of mine and does not put them into practice is like a foolish man who built his house on sand. ²⁷ The rain came down, the streams rose, and the winds blew and beat against that house, and it fell with a great crash.'

²⁸When Jesus had finished saying these things, the crowds were amazed at his teaching, ²⁹because he taught as one who had authority, and not as their teachers of the law.

8 When Jesus came down from the mountainside, large crowds followed him. ²A man with leprosy came and knelt before him and said, 'Lord, if you are willing, you can make me clean.'

³Jesus reached out his hand and touched the man. 'I am willing,' he said. 'Be clean!' Immediately he was cleansed of his leprosy. ⁴Then Jesus said to him, 'See that you don't tell anyone. But go, show yourself to the priest and offer the gift Moses commanded, as a testimony to them.'

Sudden Conversions

'By their fruit you will recognise them.' **Matthew 7:16**

Every day the Holy Spirit comes to people who have no idea that before the day ends they will enter into a personal relationship with Jesus Christ. Lacordaire, the French pastor who once occupied the pulpit of the Cathedral of Notre Dame in Paris, said: 'I was unbelieving in the evening, on the morrow a Christian, certain with an invincible certainty.'

The biographer of John Duncan, a Scottish divine, wrote: 'He was the most sceptical of men who was transformed in a moment into the most believing of men. We have a picture of a strong man suddenly arrested, struck down in mid career of linguistic study and speculative daring by the realities of the unseen world; his was one of those swift upheavals of experience which attest the agency of a Higher Power working in the spirit of man.' Sudden conversions do occur; they can only be explained vertically.

Think back now to your own conversion. Reflect on how it happened. Did it take place in a crisis? Or was it a slow dawning of the fact that though you were lost, you were now found. Some conversions are gradual and some are sudden. Some unfold like the flower to the sun - little by little. Others are a sudden leap to the breast of God.

Which of these two types of experience is the most valid? Both are. It is not the phenomena that surround conversion which make it valid; it is that 'by their fruit you will recognise them.'

PRAYER

My Father and my God, help me to lay hold of the fact that Your offer is not simply to help me realise what sin is, but to release me from it. May I enter more and more into that glorious deliverance day by day. Amen.

FURTHER STUDY

Rom. 7 & 8; 6:11; John 8:34
• What set Paul free?
• What is the obligation we have?

January II

²²At that time Abimelek and Phicol the commander of his forces said to Abraham, 'God is with you in everything you do. ²³Now swear to me here before God that you will not deal falsely with me or my children or my descendants. Show to me and the country where you now reside as a foreigner the same kindness that I have shown to you.'

²⁴Abraham said, 'I swear it.'

²⁵Then Abraham complained to Abimelek about a well of water that Abimelek's servants had seized. ²⁶But Abimelek said, 'I don't know who has done this. You did not tell me, and I heard about it only today.'

²⁷So Abraham brought sheep and cattle and gave them to Abimelek, and the two men made a treaty. ²⁸Abraham set apart seven ewe lambs from the flock, ²⁹and Abimelek asked Abraham, 'What is the meaning of these seven ewe lambs you have set apart by themselves?'

³⁰He replied, 'Accept these seven lambs from my hand as a witness that I dug this well.'

³¹So that place was called Beersheba, because the two men swore an oath there.

³²After the treaty had been made at Beersheba, Abimelek and Phicol the commander of his forces returned to the land of the Philistines. ³³Abraham planted a tamarisk tree in Beersheba, and there he called on the name of the LORD, the Eternal God. ³⁴And Abraham stayed in the land of the Philistines for a long time.

22 Some time later God tested Abraham. He said to him, 'Abraham!'

'Here I am,' he replied.

²Then God said, 'Take your son, your only son, whom you love – Isaac – and go to the region of Moriah. Sacrifice him there as a burnt offering on a mountain that I will show you.'

³Early the next morning Abraham got up and loaded his donkey. He took with him two of his servants and his son Isaac. When he had cut enough wood for the burnt offering, he set out for the place God had told him about. ⁴On the third day Abraham looked up and saw the place in the distance. ⁵He said to his servants, 'Stay here with the donkey while I and the boy go over there. We will worship and then we will come back to you.'

⁶Abraham took the wood for the burnt offering and placed it on his son Isaac, and he himself carried the fire and the knife. As the two of them went on together, ⁷Isaac spoke up and said to his father Abraham, 'Father?'

'Yes, my son?' Abraham replied.

'The fire and wood are here,' Isaac said, 'but where is the lamb for the burnt offering?'

⁸Abraham answered, 'God himself will provide the lamb for the burnt offering, my son.' And the two of them went on together.

⁹When they reached the place God had told him about, Abraham built an altar there and arranged the wood on it. He bound his son Isaac and laid him on the altar, on top of the wood. ¹⁰Then he reached out his hand and took the knife to slay his son. ¹¹But the angel of the LORD called out to him from heaven, 'Abraham! Abraham!'

'Here I am,' he replied.

¹²'Do not lay a hand on the boy,' he said. 'Do not do anything to him. Now I know that you fear God, because you have not withheld from me your son, your only son.'

¹³Abraham looked up and there in a

thicket he saw a ram caught by its horns. He went over and took the ram and sacrificed it as a burnt offering instead of his son. [14] So Abraham called that place The LORD Will Provide. And to this day it is said, 'On the mountain of the LORD it will be provided.'

[15] The angel of the LORD called to Abraham from heaven a second time [16] and said, 'I swear by myself, declares the LORD, that because you have done this and have not withheld your son, your only son, [17] I will surely bless you and make your descendants as numerous as the stars in the sky and as the sand on the seashore. Your descendants will take possession of the cities of their enemies, [18] and through your offspring all nations on earth will be blessed, because you have obeyed me.'

[19] Then Abraham returned to his servants, and they set off together for Beersheba. And Abraham stayed in Beersheba.

[20] Some time later Abraham was told, 'Milkah is also a mother; she has borne sons to your brother Nahor: [21] Uz the firstborn, Buz his brother, Kemuel (the father of Aram), [22] Kesed, Hazo, Pildash, Jidlaph and Bethuel.' [23] Bethuel became the father of Rebekah. Milkah bore these eight sons to Abraham's brother Nahor. [24] His concubine, whose name was Reumah, also had sons: Tebah, Gaham, Tahash and Maakah.

23 Sarah lived to be a hundred and twenty-seven years old. [2] She died at Kiriath Arba (that is, Hebron) in the land of Canaan, and Abraham went to mourn for Sarah and to weep over her.

[3] Then Abraham rose from beside his dead wife and spoke to the Hittites. He said, [4] 'I am a foreigner and stranger among you. Sell me some property for a burial site here so that I can bury my dead.'

[5] The Hittites replied to Abraham, [6] 'Sir, listen to us. You are a mighty prince among us. Bury your dead in the choicest of our tombs. None of us will refuse you his tomb

for burying your dead.'

[7] Then Abraham rose and bowed down before the people of the land, the Hittites. [8] He said to them, 'If you are willing to let me bury my dead, then listen to me and intercede with Ephron son of Zohar on my behalf [9] so that he will sell me the cave of Machpelah, which belongs to him and is at the end of his field. Ask him to sell it to me for the full price as a burial site among you.'

[10] Ephron the Hittite was sitting among his people and he replied to Abraham in the hearing of all the Hittites who had come to the gate of his city. [11] 'No, my lord,' he said. 'Listen to me; I give you the field, and I give you the cave that is in it. I give it to you in the presence of my people. Bury your dead.'

[12] Again Abraham bowed down before the people of the land [13] and he said to Ephron in their hearing, 'Listen to me, if you will. I will pay the price of the field. Accept it from me so that I can bury my dead there.'

[14] Ephron answered Abraham, [15] 'Listen to me, my lord; the land is worth four hundred shekels of silver, but what is that between you and me? Bury your dead.'

[16] Abraham agreed to Ephron's terms and weighed out for him the price he had named in the hearing of the Hittites: four hundred shekels of silver, according to the weight current among the merchants.

[17] So Ephron's field in Machpelah near Mamre – both the field and the cave in it, and all the trees within the borders of the field – was legally made over [18] to Abraham as his property in the presence of all the Hittites who had come to the gate of the city. [19] Afterwards Abraham buried his wife Sarah in the cave in the field of Machpelah near Mamre (which is at Hebron) in the land of Canaan. [20] So the field and the cave in it were legally made over to Abraham by the Hittites as a burial site.

▬ PSALM 7:9-17

9 Bring to an end the violence of the wicked
    and make the righteous secure –
  you, the righteous God
    who probes minds and hearts.

10 My shield is God Most High,
    who saves the upright in heart.
11 God is a righteous judge,
    a God who displays his wrath every day.
12 If he does not relent,
    he will sharpen his sword;
    he will bend and string his bow.
13 He has prepared his deadly weapons;
    he makes ready his flaming arrows.

14 Whoever is pregnant with evil
    conceives trouble and gives birth to
        disillusionment.
15 Whoever digs a hole and scoops it out
    falls into the pit they have made.
16 The trouble they cause recoils on them;
    their violence comes down on their
        own heads.

17 I will give thanks to the LORD because of
        his righteousness;
    I will sing the praises of the name of
        the LORD Most High.

▬ PROVERBS 1:32-33

32 For the waywardness of the simple will
        kill them,
    and the complacency of fools will
        destroy them;
33 but whoever listens to me will live in
        safety
    and be at ease, without fear of harm.'

▬ MATTHEW 8:5-27

5 When Jesus had entered Capernaum,
a centurion came to him, asking for help.
6 'Lord,' he said, 'my servant lies at home
paralysed, suffering terribly.'

7 Jesus said to him, 'Shall I come and heal
him?'

8 The centurion replied, 'Lord, I do not
deserve to have you come under my roof.
But just say the word, and my servant will
be healed. 9 For I myself am a man under
authority, with soldiers under me. I tell
this one, "Go," and he goes; and that one,
"Come," and he comes. I say to my servant,
"Do this," and he does it.'

10 When Jesus heard this, he was amazed
and said to those following him, 'Truly I tell
you, I have not found anyone in Israel with
such great faith. 11 I say to you that many will
come from the east and the west, and will
take their places at the feast with Abraham,
Isaac and Jacob in the kingdom of heaven.
12 But the subjects of the kingdom will be
thrown outside, into the darkness, where
there will be weeping and gnashing of teeth.'

13 Then Jesus said to the centurion, 'Go!
Let it be done just as you believed it would.'
And his servant was healed at that moment.

14 When Jesus came into Peter's house, he
saw Peter's mother-in-law lying in bed with a
fever. 15 He touched her hand and the fever left
her, and she got up and began to wait on him.

16 When evening came, many who were
demon-possessed were brought to him,
and he drove out the spirits with a word
and healed all who were ill. 17 This was to
fulfil what was spoken through the prophet
Isaiah:

'He took up our infirmities
    and bore our diseases.'

18 When Jesus saw the crowd around him,
he gave orders to cross to the other side of
the lake. 19 Then a teacher of the law came
to him and said, 'Teacher, I will follow you
wherever you go.'

20 Jesus replied, 'Foxes have dens and
birds have nests, but the Son of Man has

nowhere to lay his head.'

²¹Another disciple said to him, 'Lord, first let me go and bury my father.'

²²But Jesus told him, 'Follow me, and let the dead bury their own dead.'

²³Then he got into the boat and his disciples followed him. ²⁴Suddenly a furious storm came up on the lake, so that the waves swept over the boat. But Jesus was sleeping.

²⁵The disciples went and woke him, saying, 'Lord, save us! We're going to drown!'

²⁶He replied, 'You of little faith, why are you so afraid?' Then he got up and rebuked the winds and the waves, and it was completely calm.

²⁷The men were amazed and asked, 'What kind of man is this? Even the winds and the waves obey him!'

A Little-Known Sin

'... the righteous God who probes minds and hearts ...'
Psalm 7:9

Focusing only on correcting obvious sin (sins of behaviour) without understanding what it means to deal with the issues of the heart will bring about a condition akin to that of the Pharisees – more smug than spiritual.

One of the things I have noticed about myself is that whenever I feel I am not pursuing God in the way I should, I tend to focus on the surface issues of my life – my above-the-waterline problems – and work at them all I can. But sin involves far more than what goes on above the surface; there is also something going on in the deep recesses of my heart.

As there is little need for me to discuss the sins that are obvious, I want to focus now on those that are not. I imagine that those of you who have been Christians for some time will expect me at this stage to identify the hidden sins of the heart under such categories as resentment, lukewarmness, impatience, jealousy, and so on. My concern, however, is with a category of sin that is not easily recognised and not very well known. This sin is probably more deeply buried in our hearts than any other, and it acts, in my opinion, as a trigger to them.

The sin I refer to is – demandingness. You won't find the word in the Bible, but you will certainly see it illustrated there. Demandingness is insisting that our interests be served irrespective of others.

Clearly, if Christ is to live in us, then this has to die in us.

PRAYER

Father, I see that again You are about to face me with a strong and serious challenge. Forgive me if I draw back when Your lance plunges deep. I have lived with demandingness for so long that I might not even be able to recognise it. Help me, Lord. Amen.

FURTHER STUDY

Gal. 2:11-21; Isa. 29:15; 30:1-2; 1 Cor. 10:24
• How did Paul describe 'demandingness'?
• What were the children of Israel doing?

January 12

▬ GENESIS 24:1-54

24 Abraham was now very old, and the LORD had blessed him in every way. ²He said to the senior servant in his household, the one in charge of all that he had, 'Put your hand under my thigh. ³I want you to swear by the LORD, the God of heaven and the God of earth, that you will not get a wife for my son from the daughters of the Canaanites, among whom I am living, ⁴but will go to my country and my own relatives and get a wife for my son Isaac.'

⁵The servant asked him, 'What if the woman is unwilling to come back with me to this land? Shall I then take your son back to the country you came from?'

⁶'Make sure that you do not take my son back there,' Abraham said. ⁷'The LORD, the God of heaven, who brought me out of my father's household and my native land and who spoke to me and promised me on oath, saying, "To your offspring I will give this land" – he will send his angel before you so that you can get a wife for my son from there. ⁸If the woman is unwilling to come back with you, then you will be released from this oath of mine. Only do not take my son back there.' ⁹So the servant put his hand under the thigh of his master Abraham and swore an oath to him concerning this matter.

¹⁰Then the servant left, taking with him ten of his master's camels loaded with all kinds of good things from his master. He set out for Aram Naharaim and made his way to the town of Nahor. ¹¹He made the camels kneel down near the well outside the town; it was towards evening, the time the women go out to draw water.

¹²Then he prayed, 'LORD, God of my master Abraham, make me successful today, and show kindness to my master Abraham. ¹³See, I am standing beside this spring, and the daughters of the townspeople are coming out to draw water. ¹⁴May it be that when I say to a young woman, "Please let down your jar that I may have a drink," and she says, "Drink, and I'll water your camels too" – let her be the one you have chosen for your servant Isaac. By this I will know that you have shown kindness to my master.'

¹⁵Before he had finished praying, Rebekah came out with her jar on her shoulder. She was the daughter of Bethuel son of Milkah, who was the wife of Abraham's brother Nahor. ¹⁶The woman was very beautiful, a virgin; no man had ever slept with her. She went down to the spring, filled her jar and came up again.

¹⁷The servant hurried to meet her and said, 'Please give me a little water from your jar.'

¹⁸'Drink, my lord,' she said, and quickly lowered the jar to her hands and gave him a drink.

¹⁹After she had given him a drink, she said, 'I'll draw water for your camels too, until they have had enough to drink.' ²⁰So she quickly emptied her jar into the trough, ran back to the well to draw more water, and drew enough for all his camels. ²¹Without saying a word, the man watched her closely to learn whether or not the LORD had made his journey successful.

²²When the camels had finished drinking, the man took out a gold nose ring weighing a beka and two gold bracelets weighing ten shekels. ²³Then he asked, 'Whose daughter are you? Please tell me, is there room in your father's house for us to spend the night?'

²⁴She answered him, 'I am the daughter

of Bethuel, the son that Milkah bore to Nahor.' ²⁵And she added, 'We have plenty of straw and fodder, as well as room for you to spend the night.'

²⁶Then the man bowed down and worshipped the LORD, ²⁷saying, 'Praise be to the LORD, the God of my master Abraham, who has not abandoned his kindness and faithfulness to my master. As for me, the LORD has led me on the journey to the house of my master's relatives.'

²⁸The young woman ran and told her mother's household about these things. ²⁹Now Rebekah had a brother named Laban, and he hurried out to the man at the spring. ³⁰As soon as he had seen the nose ring, and the bracelets on his sister's arms, and had heard Rebekah tell what the man said to her, he went out to the man and found him standing by the camels near the spring. ³¹'Come, you who are blessed by the LORD,' he said. 'Why are you standing out here? I have prepared the house and a place for the camels.'

³²So the man went to the house, and the camels were unloaded. Straw and fodder were brought for the camels, and water for him and his men to wash their feet. ³³Then food was set before him, but he said, 'I will not eat until I have told you what I have to say.'

'Then tell us,' Laban said.

³⁴So he said, 'I am Abraham's servant. ³⁵The LORD has blessed my master abundantly, and he has become wealthy. He has given him sheep and cattle, silver and gold, male and female servants, and camels and donkeys. ³⁶My master's wife Sarah has borne him a son in her old age, and he has given him everything he owns. ³⁷And my master made me swear an oath, and said, "You must not get a wife for my son from the daughters of the Canaanites, in whose land I live, ³⁸but go to my father's family and to my own clan, and get a wife for my son."

³⁹'Then I asked my master, "What if the woman will not come back with me?"

⁴⁰'He replied, "The LORD, before whom I have walked faithfully, will send his angel with you and make your journey a success, so that you can get a wife for my son from my own clan and from my father's family. ⁴¹You will be released from my oath if, when you go to my clan, they refuse to give her to you – then you will be released from my oath.'

⁴²'When I came to the spring today, I said, "LORD, God of my master Abraham, if you will, please grant success to the journey on which I have come. ⁴³See, I am standing beside this spring. If a young woman comes out to draw water and I say to her, 'Please let me drink a little water from your jar,' ⁴⁴and if she says to me, 'Drink, and I'll draw water for your camels too,' let her be the one the LORD has chosen for my master's son."

⁴⁵'Before I finished praying in my heart, Rebekah came out, with her jar on her shoulder. She went down to the spring and drew water, and I said to her, "Please give me a drink."

⁴⁶'She quickly lowered her jar from her shoulder and said, "Drink, and I'll water your camels too." So I drank, and she watered the camels also.

⁴⁷'I asked her, "Whose daughter are you?"

'She said, "The daughter of Bethuel son of Nahor, whom Milkah bore to him."

'Then I put the ring in her nose and the bracelets on her arms, ⁴⁸and I bowed down and worshipped the LORD. I praised the LORD, the God of my master Abraham, who had led me on the right road to get the granddaughter of my master's brother for his son. ⁴⁹Now if you will show kindness and faithfulness to my master, tell me; and if not, tell me, so I may know which way to turn.'

⁵⁰Laban and Bethuel answered, 'This is from the LORD; we can say nothing to you one way or the other. ⁵¹Here is Rebekah; take her and go, and let her become the wife of your master's son, as the LORD has directed.'

[52] When Abraham's servant heard what they said, he bowed down to the ground before the LORD. [53] Then the servant brought out gold and silver jewellery and articles of clothing and gave them to Rebekah; he also gave costly gifts to her brother and to her mother. [54] Then he and the men who were with him ate and drank and spent the night there.

When they got up the next morning, he said, 'Send me on my way to my master.'

■ PSALM 8:1–9

[1] LORD, our Lord,
  how majestic is your name in all the
    earth!

You have set your glory
  in the heavens.
[2] Through the praise of children and
    infants
  you have established a stronghold
    against your enemies,
  to silence the foe and the avenger.
[3] When I consider your heavens,
  the work of your fingers,
  the moon and the stars,
  which you have set in place,
[4] what is mankind that you are mindful of
    them,
  human beings that you care for them?

[5] You have made them a little lower than
    the angels
  and crowned them with glory and
    honour.
[6] You made them rulers over the works of
    your hands;
  you put everything under their feet:
[7] all flocks and herds,
  and the animals of the wild,
[8] the birds in the sky,
  and the fish in the sea,
  all that swim the paths of the seas.

[9] LORD, our Lord,
  how majestic is your name in all the
    earth!

■ PROVERBS 2:1–5

2 My son, if you accept my words
  and store up my commands within you,
[2] turning your ear to wisdom
  and applying your heart to
    understanding –
[3] indeed, if you call out for insight
  and cry aloud for understanding,
[4] and if you look for it as for silver
  and search for it as for hidden
    treasure,
[5] then you will understand the fear of the
  LORD
  and find the knowledge of God.

■ MATTHEW 8:28–9:17

[28] When he arrived at the other side in the region of the Gadarenes, two demon-possessed men coming from the tombs met him. They were so violent that no one could pass that way. [29] 'What do you want with us, Son of God?' they shouted. 'Have you come here to torture us before the appointed time?'

[30] Some distance from them a large herd of pigs was feeding. [31] The demons begged Jesus, 'If you drive us out, send us into the herd of pigs.'

[32] He said to them, 'Go!' So they came out and went into the pigs, and the whole herd rushed down the steep bank into the lake and died in the water. [33] Those tending the pigs ran off, went into the town and reported all this, including what had happened to the demon-possessed men. [34] Then the whole town went out to meet Jesus. And when they saw him, they pleaded with him to leave their region.

9 Jesus stepped into a boat, crossed over and came to his own town. ²Some men brought to him a paralysed man, lying on a mat. When Jesus saw their faith, he said to the man, 'Take heart, son; your sins are forgiven.'

³At this, some of the teachers of the law said to themselves, 'This fellow is blaspheming!'

⁴Knowing their thoughts, Jesus said, 'Why do you entertain evil thoughts in your hearts? ⁵Which is easier: to say, "Your sins are forgiven," or to say, "Get up and walk"? ⁶But I want you to know that the Son of Man has authority on earth to forgive sins.' So he said to the paralysed man, 'Get up, take your mat and go home.' ⁷Then the man got up and went home. ⁸When the crowd saw this, they were filled with awe; and they praised God, who had given such authority to man.

⁹As Jesus went on from there, he saw a man named Matthew sitting at the tax collector's booth. 'Follow me,' he told him, and Matthew got up and followed him.

¹⁰While Jesus was having dinner at Matthew's house, many tax collectors and sinners came and ate with him and his disciples. ¹¹When the Pharisees saw this, they asked his disciples, 'Why does your teacher eat with tax collectors and sinners?'

¹²On hearing this, Jesus said, 'It is not the healthy who need a doctor, but those who are ill. ¹³But go and learn what this means: "I desire mercy, not sacrifice." For I have not come to call the righteous, but sinners.'

¹⁴Then John's disciples came and asked him, 'How is it that we and the Pharisees fast often, but your disciples do not fast?'

¹⁵Jesus answered, 'How can the guests of the bridegroom mourn while he is with them? The time will come when the bridegroom will be taken from them; then they will fast.

¹⁶'No one sews a patch of unshrunk cloth on an old garment, for the patch will pull away from the garment, making the tear worse. ¹⁷Neither do people pour new wine into old wineskins. If they do, the skins will burst; the wine will run out, and the wineskins will be ruined. No, they pour new wine into new wineskins, and both are preserved.'

Who Can Forgive?

'... the Son of Man has authority on earth to forgive sins ...' **Matthew 9:6**

Perhaps one of the most significant ways in which Jesus is unlike anyone else who has ever lived is that He has the ability to forgive sins. I am sure you will know the words of Charles Wesley's famous hymn that refers to the forgiveness offered by Christ:

He breaks the power of cancelled sin,
He sets the prisoner free.

I know of no one else who can do that. Some psychoanalysts try to rid the soul of guilt, but though they may be successful with pseudo-guilt (guilt that is imagined rather than real), they are powerless to deal with the stain of sin that is deeply ingrained in every human soul. The secular therapist will examine the stuff of your dreams, invite you to answer a series of questions and perhaps find the source of all your trouble –

some past transgression or sin. But even the most highly trained team of psychoanalysts cannot forgive. They may expose an old wound, but they cannot heal it. They may show you that your trouble is an ancient sin, but they cannot cleanse it from the system. And that is what our sick souls need most of all – forgiveness.

A man I talked to once said he went to a professional counsellor, a non-Christian, who found the root of his trouble – an old sin. 'Now,' said the man, 'tell me the cure.' 'Just forgive yourself,' said the analyst. Forgive yourself? It's a lot easier to do that when you know that you yourself have been forgiven.

PRAYER

Lord Jesus, not only have You forgiven me, but You keep on forgiving me. Help me realise, however, that though Your forgiveness is free, it is not cheap. For You had to die in order to bring me forgiveness. Help me never forget that. Amen.

FURTHER STUDY

Matt. 26:17-30; Acts 2:38; 13:38; Heb. 9:22
• Why is forgiveness available?
• Seek forgiveness for your sin today.

January 13

■ GENESIS 24:55–26:11

⁵⁵ But her brother and her mother replied, 'Let the young woman remain with us ten days or so; then you may go.'
⁵⁶ But he said to them, 'Do not detain me, now that the LORD has granted success to my journey. Send me on my way so I may go to my master.'
⁵⁷ Then they said, 'Let's call the young woman and ask her about it.' ⁵⁸ So they called Rebekah and asked her, 'Will you go with this man?'

'I will go,' she said.
⁵⁹ So they sent their sister Rebekah on her way, along with her nurse and Abraham's servant and his men. ⁶⁰ And they blessed Rebekah and said to her,

'Our sister, may you increase

to thousands upon thousands;
may your offspring possess
the cities of their enemies.'

⁶¹ Then Rebekah and her attendants got ready and mounted the camels and went back with the man. So the servant took Rebekah and left.
⁶² Now Isaac had come from Beer Lahai Roi, for he was living in the Negev. ⁶³ He went out to the field one evening to meditate, and as he looked up, he saw camels approaching. ⁶⁴ Rebekah also looked up and saw Isaac. She got down from her camel ⁶⁵ and asked the servant, 'Who is that man in the field coming to meet us?'

'He is my master,' the servant answered. So she took her veil and covered herself.
⁶⁶ Then the servant told Isaac all he had done. ⁶⁷ Isaac brought her into the tent of

his mother Sarah, and he married Rebekah. So she became his wife, and he loved her; and Isaac was comforted after his mother's death.

25 Abraham had taken another wife, whose name was Keturah. ²She bore him Zimran, Jokshan, Medan, Midian, Ishbak and Shuah. ³Jokshan was the father of Sheba and Dedan; the descendants of Dedan were the Ashurites, the Letushites and the Leummites. ⁴The sons of Midian were Ephah, Epher, Hanok, Abida and Eldaah. All these were descendants of Keturah.

⁵Abraham left everything he owned to Isaac. ⁶But while he was still living, he gave gifts to the sons of his concubines and sent them away from his son Isaac to the land of the east.

⁷Abraham lived a hundred and seventy-five years. ⁸Then Abraham breathed his last and died at a good old age, an old man and full of years; and he was gathered to his people. ⁹His sons Isaac and Ishmael buried him in the cave of Machpelah near Mamre, in the field of Ephron son of Zohar the Hittite, ¹⁰the field Abraham had bought from the Hittites. There Abraham was buried with his wife Sarah. ¹¹After Abraham's death, God blessed his son Isaac, who then lived near Beer Lahai Roi.

¹²This is the account of the family line of Abraham's son Ishmael, whom Sarah's slave, Hagar the Egyptian, bore to Abraham.

¹³These are the names of the sons of Ishmael, listed in the order of their birth: Nebaioth the firstborn of Ishmael, Kedar, Adbeel, Mibsam, ¹⁴Mishma, Dumah, Massa, ¹⁵Hadad, Tema, Jetur, Naphish and Kedemah. ¹⁶These were the sons of Ishmael, and these are the names of the twelve tribal rulers according to their settlements and camps. ¹⁷Ishmael lived a hundred and thirty-seven years. He breathed his last and died, and he was gathered to his people.

¹⁸His descendants settled in the area from Havilah to Shur, near the eastern border of Egypt, as you go towards Ashur. And they lived in hostility towards all the tribes related to them.

¹⁹This is the account of the family line of Abraham's son Isaac.

Abraham became the father of Isaac, ²⁰and Isaac was forty years old when he married Rebekah daughter of Bethuel the Aramean from Paddan Aram and sister of Laban the Aramean.

²¹Isaac prayed to the LORD on behalf of his wife, because she was childless. The LORD answered his prayer, and his wife Rebekah became pregnant. ²²The babies jostled each other within her, and she said, 'Why is this happening to me?' So she went to enquire of the LORD.

²³The LORD said to her,

'Two nations are in your womb,
    and two peoples from within you will
        be separated;
    one people will be stronger than the other,
        and the elder will serve the younger.'

²⁴When the time came for her to give birth, there were twin boys in her womb. ²⁵The first to come out was red, and his whole body was like a hairy garment; so they named him Esau. ²⁶After this, his brother came out, with his hand grasping Esau's heel; so he was named Jacob. Isaac was sixty years old when Rebekah gave birth to them.

²⁷The boys grew up, and Esau became a skilful hunter, a man of the open country, while Jacob was content to stay at home among the tents. ²⁸Isaac, who had a taste for wild game, loved Esau, but Rebekah loved Jacob.

²⁹Once when Jacob was cooking some stew, Esau came in from the open country, famished. ³⁰He said to Jacob, 'Quick, let me

have some of that red stew! I'm famished!' (That is why he was also called Edom.)

³¹Jacob replied, 'First sell me your birthright.'

³²'Look, I am about to die,' Esau said. 'What good is the birthright to me?'

³³But Jacob said, 'Swear to me first.' So he swore an oath to him, selling his birthright to Jacob.

³⁴Then Jacob gave Esau some bread and some lentil stew. He ate and drank, and then got up and left.

So Esau despised his birthright.

26 Now there was a famine in the land – besides the previous famine in Abraham's time – and Isaac went to Abimelek king of the Philistines in Gerar. ²The LORD appeared to Isaac and said, 'Do not go down to Egypt; live in the land where I tell you to live. ³Stay in this land for a while, and I will be with you and will bless you. For to you and your descendants I will give all these lands and will confirm the oath I swore to your father Abraham. ⁴I will make your descendants as numerous as the stars in the sky and will give them all these lands, and through your offspring all nations on earth will be blessed, ⁵because Abraham obeyed me and did everything I required of him, keeping my commands, my decrees and my instructions.' ⁶So Isaac stayed in Gerar.

⁷When the men of that place asked him about his wife, he said, 'She is my sister,' because he was afraid to say, 'She is my wife.' He thought, 'The men of this place might kill me on account of Rebekah, because she is beautiful.'

⁸When Isaac had been there a long time, Abimelek king of the Philistines looked down from a window and saw Isaac caressing his wife Rebekah. ⁹So Abimelek summoned Isaac and said, 'She is really your wife! Why did you say, "She is my sister"?'

Isaac answered him, 'Because I thought I might lose my life on account of her.'

¹⁰Then Abimelek said, 'What is this you have done to us? One of the men might well have slept with your wife, and you would have brought guilt upon us.'

¹¹So Abimelek gave orders to all the people: 'Anyone who harms this man or his wife shall surely be put to death.'

▪ PSALM 9:1-6

¹I will give thanks to you, LORD, with all
    my heart;
    I will tell of all your wonderful deeds.
²I will be glad and rejoice in you;
    I will sing the praises of your name,
        O Most High.

³My enemies turn back;
    they stumble and perish before you.
⁴For you have upheld my right and my
    cause,
        sitting enthroned as the righteous
            judge.
⁵You have rebuked the nations and
        destroyed the wicked;
    you have blotted out their name for
        ever and ever.
⁶Endless ruin has overtaken my enemies,
    you have uprooted their cities;
    even the memory of them has
        perished.

▪ PROVERBS 2:6-8

⁶For the LORD gives wisdom;
    from his mouth come knowledge and
        understanding.
⁷He holds success in store for the upright,
    he is a shield to those whose way of life
        is blameless,
⁸for he guards the course of the just
    and protects the way of his faithful ones.

▬ MATTHEW 9:18-38

[18] While he was saying this, a synagogue leader came and knelt before him and said, 'My daughter has just died. But come and put your hand on her, and she will live.' [19] Jesus got up and went with him, and so did his disciples.

[20] Just then a woman who had been subject to bleeding for twelve years came up behind him and touched the edge of his cloak. [21] She said to herself, 'If I only touch his cloak, I will be healed.'

[22] Jesus turned and saw her. 'Take heart, daughter,' he said, 'your faith has healed you.' And the woman was healed at that moment.

[23] When Jesus entered the synagogue leader's house and saw the noisy crowd and the people playing pipes, [24] he said, 'Go away. The girl is not dead but asleep.' But they laughed at him. [25] After the crowd had been put outside, he went in and took the girl by the hand, and she got up. [26] News of this spread through all that region.

[27] As Jesus went on from there, two blind men followed him, calling out, 'Have mercy on us, Son of David!'

[28] When he had gone indoors, the blind men came to him, and he asked them, 'Do you believe that I am able to do this?'

'Yes, Lord,' they replied.

[29] Then he touched their eyes and said, 'According to your faith let it be done to you'; [30] and their sight was restored. Jesus warned them sternly, 'See that no one knows about this.' [31] But they went out and spread the news about him all over that region.

[32] While they were going out, a man who was demon-possessed and could not talk was brought to Jesus. [33] And when the demon was driven out, the man who had been mute spoke. The crowd was amazed and said, 'Nothing like this has ever been seen in Israel.'

[34] But the Pharisees said, 'It is by the prince of demons that he drives out demons.'

[35] Jesus went through all the towns and villages, teaching in their synagogues, proclaiming the good news of the kingdom and healing every disease and illness. [36] When he saw the crowds, he had compassion on them, because they were harassed and helpless, like sheep without a shepherd. [37] Then he said to his disciples, 'The harvest is plentiful but the workers are few. [38] Ask the Lord of the harvest, therefore, to send out workers into his harvest field.'

Another Kingdom

'Jesus went through all the towns and villages, teaching in their synagogues, proclaiming the good news of the kingdom and healing every disease and illness.' **Matthew 9:35**

While we focus our thoughts on the kingdom of God, we must not forget that there exists in the universe another kingdom - the kingdom of Satan. The Bible shows us that in ages past there was just one kingdom, the kingdom of God. But, through the rebellion of an angel named Lucifer (now known as Satan), another kingdom was established over which the Prince of Darkness rules.

Every person since Adam (with the single exception of Jesus Christ) comes under the dominion of Satan and is, in fact, classified as a citizen of the devil's kingdom (Eph. 2:1-2). When, through conversion, we become followers of the Lord Jesus Christ, we become citizens of the kingdom of God (Col. 1:13). Once we receive this new citizenship, whether we realise it or not, we are thrust into the front line of the age-long conflict which has existed between God and Satan, and we become participators in the Almighty's plan to bring about Satan's defeat and to bring the universe once again under the control of God and His kingdom.

Standing as we do on the cutting edge between the kingdom of God and the kingdom of Satan, the Almighty has given us the most powerful weapon in all the armouries of heaven. That weapon is prayer. Our citizenship in God's kingdom entitles and enables us to pray, 'Thy kingdom come.' And when said with sincerity and trust, those words spell out every time they are spoken the ultimate triumph of the kingdom of God.

PRAYER

Father, I am utterly amazed when I realise You have not only taken me out of Satan's kingdom, but You are using my prayer, when it is in line with Your pattern, to demolish his kingdom and re-establish Yours. Help me participate with all my might. Amen.

FURTHER STUDY

Eph. 1:17-2:7; 6:1;
2 Cor. 4:4; 11:3
• What is Christ's position?
• What is our position?

January 14

■ GENESIS 26:12–27:29

[12] Isaac planted crops in that land and the same year reaped a hundredfold, because the LORD blessed him. [13] The man became rich, and his wealth continued to grow until he became very wealthy. [14] He had so many flocks and herds and servants that the Philistines envied him. [15] So all the wells that his father's servants had dug in the time of his father Abraham, the Philistines stopped up, filling them with earth.

[16] Then Abimelek said to Isaac, 'Move away from us; you have become too powerful for us.'

[17] So Isaac moved away from there and camped in the Valley of Gerar, where he settled. [18] Isaac reopened the wells that had been dug in the time of his father Abraham, which the Philistines had stopped up after Abraham died, and he gave them the same names his father had given them.

[19] Isaac's servants dug in the valley and discovered a well of fresh water there. [20] But the herdsmen of Gerar quarrelled with those of Isaac and said, 'The water is ours!' So he named the well Esek, because they disputed with him. [21] Then they dug another well, but they quarrelled over that one also; so he named it Sitnah. [22] He moved on from there and dug another well, and no one quarrelled over it. He named it Rehoboth,

saying, 'Now the LORD has given us room and we will flourish in the land.'

²³ From there he went up to Beersheba. ²⁴ That night the LORD appeared to him and said, 'I am the God of your father Abraham. Do not be afraid, for I am with you; I will bless you and will increase the number of your descendants for the sake of my servant Abraham.'

²⁵ Isaac built an altar there and called on the name of the LORD. There he pitched his tent, and there his servants dug a well.

²⁶ Meanwhile, Abimelek had come to him from Gerar, with Ahuzzath his personal advisor and Phicol the commander of his forces. ²⁷ Isaac asked them, 'Why have you come to me, since you were hostile to me and sent me away?'

²⁸ They answered, 'We saw clearly that the LORD was with you; so we said, "There ought to be a sworn agreement between us" – between us and you. Let us make a treaty with you ²⁹ that you will do us no harm, just as we did not harm you but always treated you well and sent you away peacefully. And now you are blessed by the LORD.'

³⁰ Isaac then made a feast for them, and they ate and drank. ³¹ Early the next morning the men swore an oath to each other. Then Isaac sent them on their way, and they went away peacefully.

³² That day Isaac's servants came and told him about the well they had dug. They said, 'We've found water!' ³³ He called it Shibah, and to this day the name of the town has been Beersheba.

³⁴ When Esau was forty years old, he married Judith daughter of Beeri the Hittite, and also Basemath daughter of Elon the Hittite. ³⁵ They were a source of grief to Isaac and Rebekah.

27 When Isaac was old and his eyes were so weak that he could no longer see, he called for his elder son Esau and said to him, 'My son.'

'Here I am,' he answered.

² Isaac said, 'I am now an old man and don't know the day of my death. ³ Now then, get your equipment – your quiver and bow – and go out to the open country to hunt some wild game for me. ⁴ Prepare me the kind of tasty food I like and bring it to me to eat, so that I may give you my blessing before I die.'

⁵ Now Rebekah was listening as Isaac spoke to his son Esau. When Esau left for the open country to hunt game and bring it back, ⁶ Rebekah said to her son Jacob, 'Look, I overheard your father say to your brother Esau, ⁷ "Bring me some game and prepare me some tasty food to eat, so that I may give you my blessing in the presence of the LORD before I die." ⁸ Now, my son, listen carefully and do what I tell you: ⁹ go out to the flock and bring me two choice young goats, so that I can prepare some tasty food for your father, just the way he likes it. ¹⁰ Then take it to your father to eat, so that he may give you his blessing before he dies.'

¹¹ Jacob said to Rebekah his mother, 'But my brother Esau is a hairy man while I have smooth skin. ¹² What if my father touches me? I would appear to be tricking him and would bring down a curse on myself rather than a blessing.'

¹³ His mother said to him, 'My son, let the curse fall on me. Just do what I say; go and get them for me.'

¹⁴ So he went and got them and brought them to his mother, and she prepared some tasty food, just the way his father liked it. ¹⁵ Then Rebekah took the best clothes of her elder son Esau, which she had in the house, and put them on her younger son Jacob. ¹⁶ She also covered his hands and the smooth part of his neck with the goatskins. ¹⁷ Then she handed to her son Jacob the tasty food and the bread she had made.

¹⁸ He went to his father and said, 'My father.'

'Yes, my son,' he answered. 'Who is it?'

¹⁹ Jacob said to his father, 'I am Esau your firstborn. I have done as you told me. Please

sit up and eat some of my game, so that you may give me your blessing.'

²⁰ Isaac asked his son, 'How did you find it so quickly, my son?'

'The LORD your God gave me success,' he replied.

²¹ Then Isaac said to Jacob, 'Come near so I can touch you, my son, to know whether you really are my son Esau or not.'

²² Jacob went close to his father Isaac, who touched him and said, 'The voice is the voice of Jacob, but the hands are the hands of Esau.' ²³ He did not recognise him, for his hands were hairy like those of his brother Esau; so he proceeded to bless him. ²⁴ 'Are you really my son Esau?' he asked.

'I am,' he replied.

²⁵ Then he said, 'My son, bring me some of your game to eat, so that I may give you my blessing.'

Jacob brought it to him and he ate; and he brought some wine and he drank. ²⁶ Then his father Isaac said to him, 'Come here, my son, and kiss me.'

²⁷ So he went to him and kissed him. When Isaac caught the smell of his clothes, he blessed him and said,

'Ah, the smell of my son
    is like the smell of a field
    that the LORD has blessed.
²⁸ May God give you heaven's dew
    and earth's richness –
    an abundance of grain and new wine.
²⁹ May nations serve you
    and peoples bow down to you.
Be lord over your brothers,
    and may the sons of your mother bow
       down to you.
May those who curse you be cursed
    and those who bless you be blessed.'

■ PSALM 9:7-12

⁷ The LORD reigns for ever;

he has established his throne for
    judgment.
⁸ He rules the world in righteousness
    and judges the peoples with equity.
⁹ The LORD is a refuge for the oppressed,
    a stronghold in times of trouble.
¹⁰ Those who know your name trust in you,
    for you, LORD, have never forsaken
       those who seek you.

¹¹ Sing the praises of the LORD, enthroned
    in Zion;
    proclaim among the nations what he
       has done.
¹² For he who avenges blood remembers;
    he does not ignore the cries of the
       afflicted.

■ PROVERBS 2:9-10

⁹ Then you will understand what is right
    and just
    and fair – every good path.
¹⁰ For wisdom will enter your heart,
    and knowledge will be pleasant to
       your soul.

■ MATTHEW 10:1-20

10 Jesus called his twelve disciples to him and gave them authority to drive out impure spirits and to heal every disease and illness.

² These are the names of the twelve apostles: first, Simon (who is called Peter) and his brother Andrew; James son of Zebedee, and his brother John; ³ Philip and Bartholomew; Thomas and Matthew the tax collector; James son of Alphaeus, and Thaddaeus; ⁴ Simon the Zealot and Judas Iscariot, who betrayed him.

⁵ These twelve Jesus sent out with the following instructions: 'Do not go among the Gentiles or enter any town of the

Samaritans. ⁶Go rather to the lost sheep of Israel. ⁷As you go, proclaim this message: "The kingdom of heaven has come near." ⁸Heal those who are ill, raise the dead, cleanse those who have leprosy, drive out demons. Freely you have received; freely give.

⁹'Do not get any gold or silver or copper to take with you in your belts – ¹⁰no bag for the journey or extra shirt or sandals or a staff, for the worker is worth his keep. ¹¹Whatever town or village you enter, search there for some worthy person and stay at their house until you leave. ¹²As you enter the home, give it your greeting. ¹³If the home is deserving, let your peace rest on it; if it is not, let your peace return to you. ¹⁴If anyone will not welcome you or listen to your words, leave that home or town and shake the dust off your feet. ¹⁵Truly I tell you, it will be more bearable for Sodom and Gomorrah on the day of judgment than for that town.

¹⁶'I am sending you out like sheep among wolves. Therefore be as shrewd as snakes and as innocent as doves. ¹⁷Be on your guard; you will be handed over to the local councils and be flogged in the synagogues. ¹⁸On my account you will be brought before governors and kings as witnesses to them and to the Gentiles. ¹⁹But when they arrest you, do not worry about what to say or how to say it. At that time you will be given what to say, ²⁰for it will not be you speaking, but the Spirit of your Father speaking through you.

A World-view for Reading and Meditation

'The LORD is a refuge for the oppressed, a stronghold in times of trouble.' **Psalm 9:9**

Philosophers have said that if we are to live effectively and securely in this world, then we must have a world-view of things – a cosmic framework in which to live, think and work. The Germans call it *weltanschauung* – the big picture. When we have a cosmic framework, it gives a sense of validity and meaning to all we do. It makes us feel we are a part of a universal purpose. Many modern thinkers believe that the reason there is so much insecurity in the hearts of men and women is that there is a breakdown of this world frame of reference. One writer says: 'Modern man is homesick. He is going on a hand-to-mouth existence day by day, and what he does and thinks does not seem to be related to the Whole. This has made life empty and jittery because it is insecure.'

The Chinese have a saying: 'In a broken nest there are no whole eggs.' The nest, the world in which we live and think and work, has been broken up by sin, and therefore our central unity has gone. This can sometimes be seen on a small scale when the home is 'broken'. The framework in which the family operates has broken down and it can leave members inwardly disrupted and confused.

Can you see now why Jesus taught us to have a world-view of things?

With our eyes focused on the kingdom, we know that at the heart of things there is utter security.

PRAYER

O God, I am so grateful that I am not an orphan in this universe. I have a homeland, the kingdom of God. And because nothing can hinder the establishing of that kingdom, I have a peace that nothing can disturb. I am so grateful. Amen.

FURTHER STUDY

Psa. 24:1-10; 2 Chron. 20:6; 1 Tim. 1:17; Rev. 19:6
• What picture does the psalmist give us?
• What is his exhortation?

January 15

■ GENESIS 27:30–29:12

30 After Isaac finished blessing him, and Jacob had scarcely left his father's presence, his brother Esau came in from hunting. 31 He too prepared some tasty food and brought it to his father. Then he said to him, 'My father, please sit up and eat some of my game, so that you may give me your blessing.'

32 His father Isaac asked him, 'Who are you?'

'I am your son,' he answered, 'your first-born, Esau.'

33 Isaac trembled violently and said, 'Who was it, then, that hunted game and brought it to me? I ate it just before you came and I blessed him – and indeed he will be blessed!'

34 When Esau heard his father's words, he burst out with a loud and bitter cry and said to his father, 'Bless me – me too, my father!'

35 But he said, 'Your brother came deceitfully and took your blessing.'

36 Esau said, 'Isn't he rightly named Jacob? This is the second time he has taken advantage of me: he took my birthright, and now he's taken my blessing!' Then he asked, 'Haven't you reserved any blessing for me?'

37 Isaac answered Esau, 'I have made him lord over you and have made all his relatives his servants, and I have sustained him with grain and new wine. So what can I possibly do for you, my son?'

38 Esau said to his father, 'Do you have only one blessing, my father? Bless me too, my father!' Then Esau wept aloud.

39 His father Isaac answered him,

'Your dwelling will be
    away from the earth's richness,
    away from the dew of heaven
        above.
40 You will live by the sword
    and you will serve your brother.
But when you grow restless,
    you will throw his yoke
    from off your neck.'

41 Esau held a grudge against Jacob because of the blessing his father had given him. He said to himself, 'The days of mourning for my father are near; then I will kill my brother Jacob.'

42 When Rebekah was told what her elder son Esau had said, she sent for her younger son Jacob and said to him, 'Your brother

Esau is planning to avenge himself by killing you. ⁴³Now then, my son, do what I say: flee at once to my brother Laban in Harran. ⁴⁴Stay with him for a while until your brother's fury subsides. ⁴⁵When your brother is no longer angry with you and forgets what you did to him, I'll send word for you to come back from there. Why should I lose both of you in one day?'

⁴⁶Then Rebekah said to Isaac, 'I'm disgusted with living because of these Hittite women. If Jacob takes a wife from among the women of this land, from Hittite women like these, my life will not be worth living.'

28 So Isaac called for Jacob and blessed him. Then he commanded him: 'Do not marry a Canaanite woman. ²Go at once to Paddan Aram, to the house of your mother's father Bethuel. Take a wife for yourself there, from among the daughters of Laban, your mother's brother. ³May God Almighty bless you and make you fruitful and increase your numbers until you become a community of peoples. ⁴May he give you and your descendants the blessing given to Abraham, so that you may take possession of the land where you now reside as a foreigner, the land God gave to Abraham.' ⁵Then Isaac sent Jacob on his way, and he went to Paddan Aram, to Laban son of Bethuel the Aramean, the brother of Rebekah, who was the mother of Jacob and Esau.

⁶Now Esau learned that Isaac had blessed Jacob and had sent him to Paddan Aram to take a wife from there, and that when he blessed him he commanded him, 'Do not marry a Canaanite woman,' ⁷and that Jacob had obeyed his father and mother and had gone to Paddan Aram. ⁸Esau then realised how displeasing the Canaanite women were to his father Isaac; ⁹so he went to Ishmael and married Mahalath, the sister of Nebaioth and daughter of Ishmael son of Abraham, in addition to the wives he already had.

¹⁰Jacob left Beersheba and set out for Harran. ¹¹When he reached a certain place, he stopped for the night because the sun had set. Taking one of the stones there, he put it under his head and lay down to sleep. ¹²He had a dream in which he saw a stairway resting on the earth, with its top reaching to heaven, and the angels of God were ascending and descending on it. ¹³There above it stood the LORD, and he said: 'I am the LORD, the God of your father Abraham and the God of Isaac. I will give you and your descendants the land on which you are lying. ¹⁴Your descendants will be like the dust of the earth, and you will spread out to the west and to the east, to the north and to the south. All peoples on earth will be blessed through you and your offspring. ¹⁵I am with you and will watch over you wherever you go, and I will bring you back to this land. I will not leave you until I have done what I have promised you.'

¹⁶When Jacob awoke from his sleep, he thought, 'Surely the LORD is in this place, and I was not aware of it.' ¹⁷He was afraid and said, 'How awesome is this place! This is none other than the house of God; this is the gate of heaven.'

¹⁸Early the next morning Jacob took the stone he had placed under his head and set it up as a pillar and poured oil on top of it. ¹⁹He called that place Bethel, though the city used to be called Luz.

²⁰Then Jacob made a vow, saying, 'If God will be with me and will watch over me on this journey I am taking and will give me food to eat and clothes to wear ²¹so that I return safely to my father's household, then the LORD will be my God ²²and this stone that I have set up as a pillar will be God's house, and of all that you give me I will give you a tenth.'

29 Then Jacob continued on his journey and came to the land of the eastern peoples. ²There he saw a well in the open country, with three flocks of sheep lying near it because the flocks were watered from that well. The stone over the mouth of the well was large. ³When all the flocks were gathered there, the shepherds would roll the stone away from the well's mouth and water the sheep. Then they would return the stone to its place over the mouth of the well.

⁴Jacob asked the shepherds, 'My brothers, where are you from?'

'We're from Harran,' they replied.

⁵He said to them, 'Do you know Laban, Nahor's grandson?'

'Yes, we know him,' they answered.

⁶Then Jacob asked them, 'Is he well?'

'Yes, he is,' they said, 'and here comes his daughter Rachel with the sheep.'

⁷'Look,' he said, 'the sun is still high; it is not time for the flocks to be gathered. Water the sheep and take them back to pasture.'

⁸'We can't,' they replied, 'until all the flocks are gathered and the stone has been rolled away from the mouth of the well. Then we will water the sheep.'

⁹While he was still talking with them, Rachel came with her father's sheep, for she was a shepherd. ¹⁰When Jacob saw Rachel daughter of his uncle Laban, and Laban's sheep, he went over and rolled the stone away from the mouth of the well and watered his uncle's sheep. ¹¹Then Jacob kissed Rachel and began to weep aloud. ¹²He had told Rachel that he was a relative of her father and a son of Rebekah. So she ran and told her father.

▬ PSALM 9:13-20

¹³LORD, see how my enemies persecute me!
    Have mercy and lift me up from the
        gates of death,
¹⁴that I may declare your praises
    in the gates of Daughter Zion,
        and there rejoice in your salvation.

¹⁵The nations have fallen into the pit they
    have dug;

their feet are caught in the net they
    have hidden.
¹⁶The LORD is known by his acts of justice;
    the wicked are ensnared by the work
        of their hands.
¹⁷The wicked go down to the realm of the
        dead,
    all the nations that forget God.
¹⁸But God will never forget the needy;
    the hope of the afflicted will never
        perish.

¹⁹Arise, LORD, do not let mortals triumph;
    let the nations be judged in your
        presence.
²⁰Strike them with terror, LORD;
    let the nations know they are only
        mortal.

▬ PROVERBS 2:11-15

¹¹Discretion will protect you,
    and understanding will guard you.

¹²Wisdom will save you from the ways of
        wicked men,
    from men whose words are perverse,
¹³who have left the straight paths
    to walk in dark ways,
¹⁴who delight in doing wrong
    and rejoice in the perverseness of evil,
¹⁵whose paths are crooked
    and who are devious in their ways.

▬ MATTHEW 10:21-42

²¹'Brother will betray brother to death, and a father his child; children will rebel against their parents and have them put to death. ²²You will be hated by everyone because of me, but the one who stands firm to the end will be saved. ²³When you are persecuted in one place, flee to another. Truly I tell you, you will not finish going

through the towns of Israel before the Son of Man comes.

24'The student is not above the teacher, nor a servant above his master. 25It is enough for students to be like their teachers, and servants like their masters. If the head of the house has been called Beelzebul, how much more the members of his household!

26'So do not be afraid of them, for there is nothing concealed that will not be disclosed, or hidden that will not be made known. 27What I tell you in the dark, speak in the daylight; what is whispered in your ear, proclaim from the roofs. 28Do not be afraid of those who kill the body but cannot kill the soul. Rather, be afraid of the One who can destroy both soul and body in hell. 29Are not two sparrows sold for a penny? Yet not one of them will fall to the ground outside your Father's care. 30And even the very hairs of your head are all numbered. 31So don't be afraid; you are worth more than many sparrows.

32'Whoever acknowledges me before others, I will also acknowledge before my Father in heaven. 33But whoever disowns me before others, I will disown before my Father in heaven.

34'Do not suppose that I have come to bring peace to the earth. I did not come to bring peace, but a sword. 35For I have come to turn

' "a man against his father,
    a daughter against her mother,
  a daughter-in-law against her
      mother-in-law –
36   a man's enemies will be the members
      of his own household."

37'Anyone who loves their father or mother more than me is not worthy of me; anyone who loves their son or daughter more than me is not worthy of me. 38Whoever does not take up their cross and follow me is not worthy of me. 39Whoever finds their life will lose it, and whoever loses their life for my sake will find it.

40'Anyone who welcomes you welcomes me, and anyone who welcomes me welcomes the one who sent me. 41Whoever welcomes a prophet as a prophet will receive a prophet's reward, and whoever welcomes a righteous person as a righteous person will receive a righteous person's reward. 42And if anyone gives even a cup of cold water to one of these little ones who is my disciple, truly I tell you, that person will certainly not lose their reward.'

The Example of Jacob

'... "if God will be with me and will watch over me ... so that I return safely ... then the LORD will be my God ..."'
Genesis 28:20-21

One of the things we discover about ourselves when we look deep into our hearts is a spirit of demandingness. We demand that people treat us in the way we believe they should. We demand that life should go well for us. We demand that people respond to our every need. Wedged tightly in the recesses of our heart is this ugly splinter that, if not removed, will produce a poison that will infect every part of our lives.

Let there be no mistaking this issue – if we are to pursue God wholeheartedly, then the spirit of demandingness that resides in every human heart must be identified and removed.

Jacob is probably one of the clearest biblical illustrations of a demanding spirit. He insisted on having his father's blessing for himself and took advantage of his brother's hunger, buying his birthright for a plate of stew. Later, Jacob went through a kind of half conversion, making God his God and giving Him a tenth and so on, but deep in his heart there was still residing this spirit of demandingness.

It shows itself again at Paddan-aram where, after marrying Rachel, he worked out a scheme to make himself rich at his father-in-law's expense (Gen. 30:41-43). He was still Jacob – the man who demanded to have his own way. He had talked about himself in terms of honesty – 'my honesty will testify for me' (Gen. 30:33) – but it was nothing more than above-the-waterline honesty. His mind was changed, but not his heart.

PRAYER

O Father, I am so grateful that You have recorded in Scripture so many illustrations of the truths You want me to know. I see so much of myself in Jacob. Help me from this day forward to be less and less like him in this. In Jesus' name I pray. Amen.

FURTHER STUDY

Luke 15:11-32; Matt. 20:1-16
• How did the prodigal's brother display demandingness?
• How did Jesus illustrate it?

January 16

■ GENESIS 29:13–30:43

¹³ As soon as Laban heard the news about Jacob, his sister's son, he hurried to meet him. He embraced him and kissed him and brought him to his home, and there Jacob told him all these things. ¹⁴ Then Laban said to him, 'You are my own flesh and blood.'

After Jacob had stayed with him for a whole month, ¹⁵ Laban said to him, 'Just because you are a relative of mine, should you work for me for nothing? Tell me what your wages should be.'

¹⁶ Now Laban had two daughters; the name of the elder one was Leah, and the name of the younger was Rachel. ¹⁷ Leah had weak eyes, but Rachel had a lovely figure and was beautiful. ¹⁸ Jacob was in love with

Rachel and said, 'I'll work for you seven years in return for your younger daughter Rachel.'

¹⁹ Laban said, 'It's better that I give her to you than to some other man. Stay here with me.' ²⁰ So Jacob served seven years to get Rachel, but they seemed like only a few days to him because of his love for her.

²¹ Then Jacob said to Laban, 'Give me my wife. My time is completed, and I want to make love to her.'

²² So Laban brought together all the people of the place and gave a feast. ²³ But when evening came, he took his daughter Leah and brought her to Jacob, and Jacob made love to her. ²⁴ And Laban gave his servant Zilpah to his daughter as her attendant.

²⁵ When morning came, there was Leah!

So Jacob said to Laban, 'What is this you have done to me? I served you for Rachel, didn't I? Why have you deceived me?'

²⁶Laban replied, 'It is not our custom here to give the younger daughter in marriage before the elder one. ²⁷Finish this daughter's bridal week; then we will give you the younger one also, in return for another seven years of work.'

²⁸And Jacob did so. He finished the week with Leah, and then Laban gave him his daughter Rachel to be his wife. ²⁹Laban gave his servant Bilhah to his daughter Rachel as her attendant. ³⁰Jacob made love to Rachel also, and his love for Rachel was greater than his love for Leah. And he worked for Laban another seven years.

³¹When the LORD saw that Leah was not loved, he enabled her to conceive, but Rachel remained childless. ³²Leah became pregnant and gave birth to a son. She named him Reuben, for she said, 'It is because the LORD has seen my misery. Surely my husband will love me now.'

³³She conceived again, and when she gave birth to a son she said, 'Because the LORD heard that I am not loved, he gave me this one too.' So she named him Simeon.

³⁴Again she conceived, and when she gave birth to a son she said, 'Now at last my husband will become attached to me, because I have borne him three sons.' So he was named Levi.

³⁵She conceived again, and when she gave birth to a son she said, 'This time I will praise the LORD.' So she named him Judah. Then she stopped having children.

30 When Rachel saw that she was not bearing Jacob any children, she became jealous of her sister. So she said to Jacob, 'Give me children, or I'll die!'

²Jacob became angry with her and said, 'Am I in the place of God, who has kept you from having children?'

³Then she said, 'Here is Bilhah, my servant. Sleep with her so that she can bear children for me and I too can build a family through her.'

⁴So she gave him her servant Bilhah as a wife. Jacob slept with her, ⁵and she became pregnant and bore him a son. ⁶Then Rachel said, 'God has vindicated me; he has listened to my plea and given me a son.' Because of this she named him Dan.

⁷Rachel's servant Bilhah conceived again and bore Jacob a second son. ⁸Then Rachel said, 'I have had a great struggle with my sister, and I have won.' So she named him Naphtali.

⁹When Leah saw that she had stopped having children, she took her servant Zilpah and gave her to Jacob as a wife. ¹⁰Leah's servant Zilpah bore Jacob a son. ¹¹Then Leah said, 'What good fortune!' So she named him Gad.

¹²Leah's servant Zilpah bore Jacob a second son. ¹³Then Leah said, 'How happy I am! The women will call me happy.' So she named him Asher.

¹⁴During wheat harvest, Reuben went out into the fields and found some mandrake plants, which he brought to his mother Leah. Rachel said to Leah, 'Please give me some of your son's mandrakes.'

¹⁵But she said to her, 'Wasn't it enough that you took away my husband? Will you take my son's mandrakes too?'

'Very well,' Rachel said, 'he can sleep with you tonight in return for your son's mandrakes.'

¹⁶So when Jacob came in from the fields that evening, Leah went out to meet him. 'You must sleep with me,' she said. 'I have hired you with my son's mandrakes.' So he slept with her that night.

¹⁷God listened to Leah, and she became pregnant and bore Jacob a fifth son. ¹⁸Then Leah said, 'God has rewarded me for giving my servant to my husband.' So she named him Issachar.

¹⁹Leah conceived again and bore Jacob a sixth son. ²⁰Then Leah said, 'God has

presented me with a precious gift. This time my husband will treat me with honour, because I have borne him six sons.' So she named him Zebulun.

²¹ Some time later she gave birth to a daughter and named her Dinah.

²² Then God remembered Rachel; he listened to her and enabled her to conceive. ²³ She became pregnant and gave birth to a son and said, 'God has taken away my disgrace.' ²⁴ She named him Joseph, and said, 'May the LORD add to me another son.'

²⁵ After Rachel gave birth to Joseph, Jacob said to Laban, 'Send me on my way so that I can go back to my own homeland. ²⁶ Give me my wives and children, for whom I have served you, and I will be on my way. You know how much work I've done for you.'

²⁷ But Laban said to him, 'If I have found favour in your eyes, please stay. I have learned by divination that the LORD has blessed me because of you.' ²⁸ He added, 'Name your wages, and I will pay them.'

²⁹ Jacob said to him, 'You know how I have worked for you and how your livestock has fared under my care. ³⁰ The little you had before I came has increased greatly, and the LORD has blessed you wherever I have been. But now, when may I do something for my own household?'

³¹ 'What shall I give you?' he asked.

'Don't give me anything,' Jacob replied. 'But if you will do this one thing for me, I will go on tending your flocks and watching over them: ³² let me go through all your flocks today and remove from them every speckled or spotted sheep, every dark-coloured lamb and every spotted or speckled goat. They will be my wages. ³³ And my honesty will testify for me in the future, whenever you check on the wages you have paid me. Any goat in my possession that is not speckled or spotted, or any lamb that is not dark-coloured, will be considered stolen.'

³⁴ 'Agreed,' said Laban. 'Let it be as you have said.' ³⁵ That same day he removed all the male goats that were streaked or spotted, and all the speckled or spotted female goats (all that had white on them) and all the dark-coloured lambs, and he placed them in the care of his sons. ³⁶ Then he put a three-day journey between himself and Jacob, while Jacob continued to tend the rest of Laban's flocks.

³⁷ Jacob, however, took fresh-cut branches from poplar, almond and plane trees and made white stripes on them by peeling the bark and exposing the white inner wood of the branches. ³⁸ Then he placed the peeled branches in all the watering troughs, so that they would be directly in front of the flocks when they came to drink. When the flocks were in heat and came to drink, ³⁹ they mated in front of the branches. And they bore young that were streaked or speckled or spotted. ⁴⁰ Jacob set apart the young of the flock by themselves, but made the rest face the streaked and dark-coloured animals that belonged to Laban. Thus he made separate flocks for himself and did not put them with Laban's animals. ⁴¹ Whenever the stronger females were in heat, Jacob would place the branches in the troughs in front of the animals so that they would mate near the branches, ⁴² but if the animals were weak, he would not place them there. So the weak animals went to Laban and the strong ones to Jacob. ⁴³ In this way the man grew exceedingly prosperous and came to own large flocks, and female and male servants, and camels and donkeys.

▬ PSALM 10:1-6

¹ Why, LORD, do you stand far off?
    Why do you hide yourself in times of
       trouble?

² In his arrogance the wicked man hunts
       down the weak,

who are caught in the schemes he
devises.
[3] He boasts about the cravings of his heart;
he blesses the greedy and reviles the
LORD.
[4] In his pride the wicked man does not
seek him;
in all his thoughts there is no room for
God.
[5] His ways are always prosperous;
your laws are rejected by him;
he sneers at all his enemies.
[6] He says to himself, 'Nothing will ever
shake me.'
He swears, 'No one will ever do me
harm.'

PROVERBS 2:16-19

[16] Wisdom will save you also from the
adulterous woman,
from the wayward woman with her
seductive words,
[17] who has left the partner of her youth
and ignored the covenant she made
before God.
[18] Surely her house leads down to death
and her paths to the spirits of the
dead.
[19] None who go to her return
or attain the paths of life.

MATTHEW 11:1-19

11 After Jesus had finished instructing
his twelve disciples, he went on from
there to teach and preach in the towns of
Galilee.
[2] When John, who was in prison, heard
about the deeds of the Messiah, he sent his
disciples [3] to ask him, 'Are you the one who is
to come, or should we expect someone else?'
[4] Jesus replied, 'Go back and report to
John what you hear and see: [5] the blind

receive sight, the lame walk, those who have
leprosy are cleansed, the deaf hear, the dead
are raised, and the good news is proclaimed
to the poor. [6] Blessed is anyone who does not
stumble on account of me.'
[7] As John's disciples were leaving, Jesus
began to speak to the crowd about John:
'What did you go out into the wilderness
to see? A reed swayed by the wind? [8] If not,
what did you go out to see? A man dressed
in fine clothes? No, those who wear fine
clothes are in kings' palaces. [9] Then what
did you go out to see? A prophet? Yes, I tell
you, and more than a prophet. [10] This is the
one about whom it is written:

'"I will send my messenger ahead of you,
who will prepare your way before you."

[11] Truly I tell you, among those born of wom-
en there has not risen anyone greater than
John the Baptist; yet whoever is least in
the kingdom of heaven is greater than he.
[12] From the days of John the Baptist until
now, the kingdom of heaven has been subjected to violence, and violent people have
been raiding it. [13] For all the Prophets and
the Law prophesied until John. [14] And if you
are willing to accept it, he is the Elijah who
was to come. [15] Whoever has ears, let them
hear.
[16] 'To what can I compare this generation?
They are like children sitting in the market-
places and calling out to others:

[17] '"We played the pipe for you,
and you did not dance;
we sang a dirge,
and you did not mourn."

[18] For John came neither eating nor drinking, and they say, "He has a demon." [19] The
Son of Man came eating and drinking, and
they say, "Here is a glutton and a drunkard, a friend of tax collectors and sinners."
But wisdom is proved right by her deeds.'

Stop Arguing!

'He says to himself, "Nothing will shake me." He swears, "No one will ever do me harm."' **Psalm 10:6**

'At life's core,' says Dr Larry Crabb, 'the real issues are theological issues.' When life is brought down to its irreducible minimum, the issue always is – God. What do we make of Him? How does He fit into our lives?

Have you not found that whenever you make sure God is in His place, everything around you falls into place too? You see things from a different perspective. God is sovereign, Solomon says in Ecclesiastes 6:10. '... no one can contend with someone who is stronger,' and the sooner we recognise that the better. A purpose was written into the universe long before we arrived, and though at times it may look as if God is not in control, this is not so. And, he adds, because God is bigger than we are, it is useless to put ourselves in conflict with Him. C. S. Lewis put it well when he said in *The Problem of Pain*: 'To argue with God is to argue with the very power that makes it possible to argue at all.'

How different life would be for us if we would get hold of the fact that God is sovereign and that we are His subjects. God is the Potter; we are the clay. God is omnipotent; we are impotent – relatively speaking, anyway. God is consistent; we are inconsistent. God has a crystal-clear perspective on everything; we more often than not are confused. What is all this saying to us? Arguing against the divine purpose is a waste of time. Better to trust the Almighty; He always knows what He is doing.

PRAYER

My Father and my God, I have gathered some wisdom on my journey through life, but now I pray for the kind of wisdom that is greater and sharper than all earthly wisdom – Your wisdom. Make me a wise person, my Father. In Jesus' name. Amen.

FURTHER STUDY

Prov. 2:1-3:35
- What are we not to let out of our sight?
- What do the wise inherit?

January 17

■ GENESIS 31:1-55

31 Jacob heard that Laban's sons were saying, 'Jacob has taken everything our father owned and has gained all this wealth from what belonged to our father.' [2] And Jacob noticed that Laban's attitude towards him was not what it had been.

³Then the LORD said to Jacob, 'Go back to the land of your fathers and to your relatives, and I will be with you.'

⁴So Jacob sent word to Rachel and Leah to come out to the fields where his flocks were. ⁵He said to them, 'I see that your father's attitude towards me is not what it was before, but the God of my father has been with me. ⁶You know that I've worked for your father with all my strength, ⁷yet your father has cheated me by changing my wages ten times. However, God has not allowed him to harm me. ⁸If he said, "The speckled ones will be your wages," then all the flocks gave birth to speckled young; and if he said, "The streaked ones will be your wages," then all the flocks bore streaked young. ⁹So God has taken away your father's livestock and has given them to me.

¹⁰'In the breeding season I once had a dream in which I looked up and saw that the male goats mating with the flock were streaked, speckled or spotted. ¹¹The angel of God said to me in the dream, "Jacob." I answered, "Here I am." ¹²And he said, "Look up and see that all the male goats mating with the flock are streaked, speckled or spotted, for I have seen all that Laban has been doing to you. ¹³I am the God of Bethel, where you anointed a pillar and where you made a vow to me. Now leave this land at once and go back to your native land."'

¹⁴Then Rachel and Leah replied, 'Do we still have any share in the inheritance of our father's estate? ¹⁵Does he not regard us as foreigners? Not only has he sold us, but he has used up what was paid for us. ¹⁶Surely all the wealth that God took away from our father belongs to us and our children. So do whatever God has told you.'

¹⁷Then Jacob put his children and his wives on camels, ¹⁸and he drove all his livestock ahead of him, along with all the goods he had accumulated in Paddan Aram, to go to his father Isaac in the land of Canaan.

¹⁹When Laban had gone to shear his sheep, Rachel stole her father's household gods. ²⁰Moreover, Jacob deceived Laban the Aramean by not telling him he was running away. ²¹So he fled with all he had, crossed the River Euphrates, and headed for the hill country of Gilead.

²²On the third day Laban was told that Jacob had fled. ²³Taking his relatives with him, he pursued Jacob for seven days and caught up with him in the hill country of Gilead. ²⁴Then God came to Laban the Aramean in a dream at night and said to him, 'Be careful not to say anything to Jacob, either good or bad.'

²⁵Jacob had pitched his tent in the hill country of Gilead when Laban overtook him, and Laban and his relatives camped there too. ²⁶Then Laban said to Jacob, 'What have you done? You've deceived me, and you've carried off my daughters like captives in war. ²⁷Why did you run off secretly and deceive me? Why didn't you tell me, so that I could send you away with joy and singing to the music of tambourines and harps? ²⁸You didn't even let me kiss my grandchildren and my daughters goodbye. You have done a foolish thing. ²⁹I have the power to harm you; but last night the God of your father said to me, "Be careful not to say anything to Jacob, either good or bad." ³⁰Now you have gone off because you longed to return to your father's household. But why did you steal my gods?'

³¹Jacob answered Laban, 'I was afraid, because I thought you would take your daughters away from me by force. ³²But if you find anyone who has your gods, that person shall not live. In the presence of our relatives, see for yourself whether there is anything of yours here with me; and if so, take it.' Now Jacob did not know that Rachel had stolen the gods.

³³So Laban went into Jacob's tent and into Leah's tent and into the tent of the two

female servants, but he found nothing. After he came out of Leah's tent, he entered Rachel's tent. ³⁴Now Rachel had taken the household gods and put them inside her camel's saddle and was sitting on them. Laban searched through everything in the tent but found nothing.

³⁵Rachel said to her father, 'Don't be angry, my lord, that I cannot stand up in your presence; I'm having my period.' So he searched but could not find the household gods.

³⁶Jacob was angry and took Laban to task. 'What is my crime?' he asked Laban. 'How have I wronged you that you hunt me down? ³⁷Now that you have searched through all my goods, what have you found that belongs to your household? Put it here in front of your relatives and mine, and let them judge between the two of us.

³⁸'I have been with you for twenty years now. Your sheep and goats have not miscarried, nor have I eaten rams from your flocks. ³⁹I did not bring you animals torn by wild beasts; I bore the loss myself. And you demanded payment from me for whatever was stolen by day or night. ⁴⁰This was my situation: The heat consumed me in the daytime and the cold at night, and sleep fled from my eyes. ⁴¹It was like this for the twenty years I was in your household. I worked for you fourteen years for your two daughters and six years for your flocks, and you changed my wages ten times. ⁴²If the God of my father, the God of Abraham and the Fear of Isaac, had not been with me, you would surely have sent me away empty-handed. But God has seen my hardship and the toil of my hands, and last night he rebuked you.'

⁴³Laban answered Jacob, 'The women are my daughters, the children are my children, and the flocks are my flocks. All you see is mine. Yet what can I do today about these daughters of mine, or about the children they have borne? ⁴⁴Come now, let's make a covenant, you and I, and let it serve as a witness between us.'

⁴⁵So Jacob took a stone and set it up as a pillar. ⁴⁶He said to his relatives, 'Gather some stones.' So they took stones and piled them in a heap, and they ate there by the heap. ⁴⁷Laban called it Jegar Sahadutha, and Jacob called it Galeed.

⁴⁸Laban said, 'This heap is a witness between you and me today.' That is why it was called Galeed. ⁴⁹It was also called Mizpah, because he said, 'May the LORD keep watch between you and me when we are away from each other. ⁵⁰If you ill-treat my daughters or if you take any wives besides my daughters, even though no one is with us, remember that God is a witness between you and me.'

⁵¹Laban also said to Jacob, 'Here is this heap, and here is this pillar I have set up between you and me. ⁵²This heap is a witness, and this pillar is a witness, that I will not go past this heap to your side to harm you and that you will not go past this heap and pillar to my side to harm me. ⁵³May the God of Abraham and the God of Nahor, the God of their father, judge between us.'

So Jacob took an oath in the name of the Fear of his father Isaac. ⁵⁴He offered a sacrifice there in the hill country and invited his relatives to a meal. After they had eaten, they spent the night there.

⁵⁵Early the next morning Laban kissed his grandchildren and his daughters and blessed them. Then he left and returned home.

▬ PSALM 10:7-12

⁷His mouth is full of lies and threats;
  trouble and evil are under his tongue.
⁸He lies in wait near the villages;
  from ambush he murders the
    innocent.
His eyes watch in secret for his victims;

⁹   like a lion in cover he lies in wait.
   He lies in wait to catch the helpless;
      he catches the helpless and drags them
         off in his net.
¹⁰ His victims are crushed, they collapse;
      they fall under his strength.
¹¹ He says to himself, 'God will never
         notice;
      he covers his face and never sees.'

¹² Arise, LORD! Lift up your hand, O God.
   Do not forget the helpless.

▬ PROVERBS 2:20-22

²⁰ Thus you will walk in the ways of the
         good
      and keep to the paths of the righteous.
²¹ For the upright will live in the land,
      and the blameless will remain in it;
²² but the wicked will be cut off from the
         land,
      and the unfaithful will be torn from it.

▬ MATTHEW 11:20–12:8

²⁰ Then Jesus began to denounce the towns in which most of his miracles had been performed, because they did not repent. ²¹ 'Woe to you, Chorazin! Woe to you, Bethsaida! For if the miracles that were performed in you had been performed in Tyre and Sidon, they would have repented long ago in sackcloth and ashes. ²² But I tell you, it will be more bearable for Tyre and Sidon on the day of judgment than for you. ²³ And you, Capernaum, will you be lifted to the heavens? No, you will go down to Hades. For if the miracles that were performed in you had been performed in Sodom, it would

have remained to this day. ²⁴ But I tell you that it will be more bearable for Sodom on the day of judgment than for you.'

²⁵ At that time Jesus said, 'I praise you, Father, Lord of heaven and earth, because you have hidden these things from the wise and learned, and revealed them to little children. ²⁶ Yes, Father, for this is what you were pleased to do.

²⁷ 'All things have been committed to me by my Father. No one knows the Son except the Father, and no one knows the Father except the Son and those to whom the Son chooses to reveal him.

²⁸ 'Come to me, all you who are weary and burdened, and I will give you rest. ²⁹ Take my yoke upon you and learn from me, for I am gentle and humble in heart, and you will find rest for your souls. ³⁰ For my yoke is easy and my burden is light.'

12 At that time Jesus went through the cornfields on the Sabbath. His disciples were hungry and began to pick some ears of corn and eat them. ² When the Pharisees saw this, they said to him, 'Look! Your disciples are doing what is unlawful on the Sabbath.'

³ He answered, 'Haven't you read what David did when he and his companions were hungry? ⁴ He entered the house of God, and he and his companions ate the consecrated bread – which was not lawful for them to do, but only for the priests. ⁵ Or haven't you read in the Law that the priests on Sabbath duty in the temple desecrate the Sabbath and yet are innocent? ⁶ I tell you that something greater than the temple is here. ⁷ If you had known what these words mean, "I desire mercy, not sacrifice," you would not have condemned the innocent. ⁸ For the Son of Man is Lord of the Sabbath.'

An Island Within

'I rise before dawn and cry for help; I have put my hope in your word.' **Psalm 119:147**

Some Bible teachers say: 'If you are filled with the Spirit, then you can draw from God's resources, not just at the beginning of the day, but every hour of the day. Better a fountain in the heart than a fountain by the way.' This confuses two quite separate issues. It is perfectly true that by reason of the Spirit's indwelling, we can draw upon His resources moment by moment, but that does not do away with the need for a daily quiet time. Dr E Stanley Jones puts it like this: 'Those who say they can live in a state of prayer without stated times for prayer will probably find themselves without both. It is as futile as thinking that you can live in a state of physical nourishment without stated times for nourishment.' I believe with all my heart that the divine Shepherd seeks daily to lead His sheep to the 'still waters' of His Word, and how sad it is that so many Christians prefer to drink from the polluted pools of the world.

God has given us infinite resources through prayer and the reading of the Scriptures. They are ours for the asking and the taking. The quiet time creates an island of quiet within us, and that becomes the atmosphere of the day.

PRAYER

O Father, help me come to the quiet time with quiet expectancy – expectancy that here my weakness shall become strength, my doubt become faith, my fears become courage, and my sin become redemption. I ask this for Your own dear name's sake. Amen.

FURTHER STUDY

Jer. 15:1-16; Deut. 8:3; Job 23:12; Psa. 119:103
- What was Jeremiah's experience?
- What did the children of Israel have to learn?

January 18

▬ GENESIS 32:1–33:20

32 Jacob also went on his way, and the angels of God met him. ²When Jacob saw them, he said, 'This is the camp of God!' So he named that place Mahanaim.

³Jacob sent messengers ahead of him to his brother Esau in the land of Seir, the country of Edom. ⁴He instructed them: 'This is what you are to say to my lord Esau: "Your servant Jacob says, I have been staying with Laban and have remained there till now. ⁵I have cattle and donkeys, sheep and goats, male and female servants. Now I am

sending this message to my lord, that I may find favour in your eyes."'

⁶When the messengers returned to Jacob, they said, 'We went to your brother Esau, and now he is coming to meet you, and four hundred men are with him.'

⁷In great fear and distress Jacob divided the people who were with him into two groups, and the flocks and herds and camels as well. ⁸He thought, 'If Esau comes and attacks one group, the group that is left may escape.'

⁹Then Jacob prayed, 'O God of my father Abraham, God of my father Isaac, LORD, you who said to me, "Go back to your country and your relatives, and I will make you prosper," ¹⁰I am unworthy of all the kindness and faithfulness you have shown your servant. I had only my staff when I crossed this Jordan, but now I have become two camps. ¹¹Save me, I pray, from the hand of my brother Esau, for I am afraid he will come and attack me, and also the mothers with their children. ¹²But you have said, "I will surely make you prosper and will make your descendants like the sand of the sea, which cannot be counted."'

¹³He spent the night there, and from what he had with him he selected a gift for his brother Esau: ¹⁴two hundred female goats and twenty male goats, two hundred ewes and twenty rams, ¹⁵thirty female camels with their young, forty cows and ten bulls, and twenty female donkeys and ten male donkeys. ¹⁶He put them in the care of his servants, each herd by itself, and said to his servants, 'Go ahead of me, and keep some space between the herds.'

¹⁷He instructed the one in the lead: 'When my brother Esau meets you and asks, "Who do you belong to, and where are you going, and who owns all these animals in front of you?" ¹⁸then you are to say, "They belong to your servant Jacob. They are a gift sent to my lord Esau, and he is

coming behind us."'

¹⁹He also instructed the second, the third and all the others who followed the herds: 'You are to say the same thing to Esau when you meet him. ²⁰And be sure to say, "Your servant Jacob is coming behind us."' For he thought, 'I will pacify him with these gifts I am sending on ahead; later, when I see him, perhaps he will receive me.' ²¹So Jacob's gifts went on ahead of him, but he himself spent the night in the camp.

²²That night Jacob got up and took his two wives, his two female servants and his eleven sons and crossed the ford of the Jabbok. ²³After he had sent them across the stream, he sent over all his possessions. ²⁴So Jacob was left alone, and a man wrestled with him till daybreak. ²⁵When the man saw that he could not overpower him, he touched the socket of Jacob's hip so that his hip was wrenched as he wrestled with the man. ²⁶Then the man said, 'Let me go, for it is daybreak.'

But Jacob replied, 'I will not let you go unless you bless me.'

²⁷The man asked him, 'What is your name?'

'Jacob,' he answered.

²⁸Then the man said, 'Your name will no longer be Jacob, but Israel, because you have struggled with God and with humans and have overcome.'

²⁹Jacob said, 'Please tell me your name.'

But he replied, 'Why do you ask my name?' Then he blessed him there.

³⁰So Jacob called the place Peniel, saying, 'It is because I saw God face to face, and yet my life was spared.'

³¹The sun rose above him as he passed Peniel, and he was limping because of his hip. ³²Therefore to this day the Israelites do not eat the tendon attached to the socket of the hip, because the socket of Jacob's hip was touched near the tendon.

33 Jacob looked up and there was Esau, coming with his four hundred men; so he divided the children among Leah, Rachel and the two female servants. ²He put the female servants and their children in front, Leah and her children next, and Rachel and Joseph in the rear. ³He himself went on ahead and bowed down to the ground seven times as he approached his brother.

⁴But Esau ran to meet Jacob and embraced him; he threw his arms around his neck and kissed him. And they wept. ⁵Then Esau looked up and saw the women and children. 'Who are these with you?' he asked.

Jacob answered, 'They are the children God has graciously given your servant.'

⁶Then the female servants and their children approached and bowed down. ⁷Next, Leah and her children came and bowed down. Last of all came Joseph and Rachel, and they too bowed down.

⁸Esau asked, 'What's the meaning of all these flocks and herds I met?'

'To find favour in your eyes, my lord,' he said.

⁹But Esau said, 'I already have plenty, my brother. Keep what you have for yourself.'

¹⁰'No, please!' said Jacob. 'If I have found favour in your eyes, accept this gift from me. For to see your face is like seeing the face of God, now that you have received me favourably. ¹¹Please accept the present that was brought to you, for God has been gracious to me and I have all I need.' And because Jacob insisted, Esau accepted it.

¹²Then Esau said, 'Let us be on our way; I'll accompany you.'

¹³But Jacob said to him, 'My lord knows that the children are tender and that I must care for the ewes and cows that are nursing their young. If they are driven hard just one day, all the animals will die. ¹⁴So let my lord go on ahead of his servant, while I move along slowly at the pace of the flocks and herds before me and the pace of the children, until I come to my lord in Seir.'

¹⁵Esau said, 'Then let me leave some of my men with you.'

'But why do that?' Jacob asked. 'Just let me find favour in the eyes of my lord.'

¹⁶So that day Esau started on his way back to Seir. ¹⁷Jacob, however, went to Sukkoth, where he built a place for himself and made shelters for his livestock. That is why the place is called Sukkoth.

¹⁸After Jacob came from Paddan Aram, he arrived safely at the city of Shechem in Canaan and camped within sight of the city. ¹⁹For a hundred pieces of silver, he bought from the sons of Hamor, the father of Shechem, the plot of ground where he pitched his tent. ²⁰There he set up an altar and called it El Elohe Israel.

▬ PSALM 10:13-18

¹³Why does the wicked man revile God?
  Why does he say to himself,
    'He won't call me to account'?
¹⁴But you, God, see the trouble of the
    afflicted;
  you consider their grief and take it in
    hand.
The victims commit themselves to you;
  you are the helper of the fatherless.
¹⁵Break the arm of the wicked man;
  call the evildoer to account for his
    wickedness
  that would not otherwise be found out.

¹⁶The LORD is King for ever and ever;
  the nations will perish from his land.
¹⁷You, LORD, hear the desire of the afflicted;
  you encourage them, and you listen to
    their cry,
¹⁸defending the fatherless and the
    oppressed,
  so that mere earthly mortals
  will never again strike terror.

▬ PROVERBS 3:1-2

3 My son, do not forget my teaching,
but keep my commands in your heart,
² for they will prolong your life many years
and bring you peace and prosperity.

▬ MATTHEW 12:9-37

⁹ Going on from that place, he went into their synagogue, ¹⁰ and a man with a shrivelled hand was there. Looking for a reason to bring charges against Jesus, they asked him, 'Is it lawful to heal on the Sabbath?'

¹¹ He said to them, 'If any of you has a sheep and it falls into a pit on the Sabbath, will you not take hold of it and lift it out? ¹² How much more valuable is a person than a sheep! Therefore it is lawful to do good on the Sabbath.'

¹³ Then he said to the man, 'Stretch out your hand.' So he stretched it out and it was completely restored, just as sound as the other. ¹⁴ But the Pharisees went out and plotted how they might kill Jesus.

¹⁵ Aware of this, Jesus withdrew from that place. A large crowd followed him, and he healed all who were ill. ¹⁶ He warned them not to tell others about him. ¹⁷ This was to fulfil what was spoken through the prophet Isaiah:

¹⁸ 'Here is my servant whom I have chosen,
the one I love, in whom I delight;
I will put my Spirit on him,
and he will proclaim justice to the
nations.
¹⁹ He will not quarrel or cry out;
no one will hear his voice in the streets.
²⁰ A bruised reed he will not break,
and a smouldering wick he will not
snuff out,
till he has brought justice through to
victory.

²¹ In his name the nations will put their
hope.'

²² Then they brought him a demon-possessed man who was blind and mute, and Jesus healed him, so that he could both talk and see. ²³ All the people were astonished and said, 'Could this be the Son of David?'

²⁴ But when the Pharisees heard this, they said, 'It is only by Beelzebul, the prince of demons, that this fellow drives out demons.'

²⁵ Jesus knew their thoughts and said to them, 'Every kingdom divided against itself will be ruined, and every city or household divided against itself will not stand. ²⁶ If Satan drives out Satan, he is divided against himself. How then can his kingdom stand? ²⁷ And if I drive out demons by Beelzebul, by whom do your people drive them out? So then, they will be your judges. ²⁸ But if it is by the Spirit of God that I drive out demons, then the kingdom of God has come upon you.

²⁹ 'Or again, how can anyone enter a strong man's house and carry off his possessions unless he first ties up the strong man? Then he can plunder his house.

³⁰ 'Whoever is not with me is against me, and whoever does not gather with me scatters. ³¹ And so I tell you, every kind of sin and slander can be forgiven, but blasphemy against the Spirit will not be forgiven. ³² Anyone who speaks a word against the Son of Man will be forgiven, but anyone who speaks against the Holy Spirit will not be forgiven, either in this age or in the age to come.

³³ 'Make a tree good and its fruit will be good, or make a tree bad and its fruit will be bad, for a tree is recognised by its fruit. ³⁴ You brood of vipers, how can you who are evil say anything good? For the mouth speaks what the heart is full of. ³⁵ A good man brings good things out of the good stored up in him, and an evil man brings

evil things out of the evil stored up in him. ³⁶But I tell you that everyone will have to give account on the day of judgment for every empty word they have spoken. ³⁷For by your words you will be acquitted, and by your words you will be condemned.'

'What Is Your Name?'

'Jacob was left alone, and a man wrestled with him till daybreak.' **Genesis 32:24**

The way in which God helped Jacob to be rid of his spirit of demand-ingness is revealing – 'a man wrestled with him till daybreak.' Like the Hound of Heaven, the love of God pursued him down the years, awaiting the hour when he would be ready to admit that he was beaten.

This man (probably an angelic representative) wrestled with him until Jacob's strength was diminished, at which point he asked him, 'What is your name?' To us it seems a simple question, but in those days one's name was the expression of one's character; if the character changed, the name was changed. So Jacob, after a tremendous struggle, made the crucial confession, 'Jacob,' – which means 'the supplanter'. The depths were uncovered. Jacob's heart was naked before God. The real problem was identified.

If you have not reached this place in your spiritual experience, I suggest you stop everything and tell God your name. You might have to confess, 'My name is Demandingness; I insist on having my own way in everything.' This may be hard to say, but get it out no matter what the cost, for there will be no new name until you say the old name.

The saying of the old name is a confession, a catharsis. When Jacob said his name, the angel said, 'Your name will no longer be Jacob, but Israel' (v. 28) – a striver with God. The new nation of Israel would be named for this crooked man made straight. Jacob was buried; Israel was alive for evermore.

PRAYER

God, help me to tell You my name – my real name. Help me to dodge no longer; the game is up. Take out of me the spirit of demandingness. Change my name and change my character. Save me from myself. In Jesus' name I pray. Amen.

FURTHER STUDY

1 John 1:1-9; Ezra 10:11;
2 Sam. 12:13
• What are we to do with our sin?
• How did Nathan respond to David?

January 19

■ GENESIS 34:1–35:29

34 Now Dinah, the daughter Leah had borne to Jacob, went out to visit the women of the land. ² When Shechem son of Hamor the Hivite, the ruler of that area, saw her, he took her and raped her. ³ His heart was drawn to Dinah daughter of Jacob; he loved the young woman and spoke tenderly to her. ⁴ And Shechem said to his father Hamor, 'Get me this girl as my wife.'

⁵ When Jacob heard that his daughter Dinah had been defiled, his sons were in the fields with his livestock; so he did nothing about it until they came home.

⁶ Then Shechem's father Hamor went out to talk with Jacob. ⁷ Meanwhile, Jacob's sons had come in from the fields as soon as they heard what had happened. They were shocked and furious, because Shechem had done an outrageous thing in Israel by sleeping with Jacob's daughter – a thing that should not be done.

⁸ But Hamor said to them, 'My son Shechem has his heart set on your daughter. Please give her to him as his wife. ⁹ Intermarry with us; give us your daughters and take our daughters for yourselves. ¹⁰ You can settle among us; the land is open to you. Live in it, trade in it, and acquire property in it.'

¹¹ Then Shechem said to Dinah's father and brothers, 'Let me find favour in your eyes, and I will give you whatever you ask. ¹² Make the price for the bride and the gift I am to bring as great as you like, and I'll pay whatever you ask me. Only give me the young woman as my wife.'

¹³ Because their sister Dinah had been defiled, Jacob's sons replied deceitfully as they spoke to Shechem and his father

Hamor. ¹⁴ They said to them, 'We can't do such a thing; we can't give our sister to a man who is not circumcised. That would be a disgrace to us. ¹⁵ We will enter into an agreement with you on one condition only: that you become like us by circumcising all your males. ¹⁶ Then we will give you our daughters and take your daughters for ourselves. We'll settle among you and become one people with you. ¹⁷ But if you will not agree to be circumcised, we'll take our sister and go.'

¹⁸ Their proposal seemed good to Hamor and his son Shechem. ¹⁹ The young man, who was the most honoured of all his father's family, lost no time in doing what they said, because he was delighted with Jacob's daughter. ²⁰ So Hamor and his son Shechem went to the gate of their city to speak to the men of their city. ²¹ 'These men are friendly towards us,' they said. 'Let them live in our land and trade in it; the land has plenty of room for them. We can marry their daughters and they can marry ours. ²² But the men will agree to live with us as one people only on the condition that our males be circumcised, as they themselves are. ²³ Won't their livestock, their property and all their other animals become ours? So let us agree to their terms, and they will settle among us.'

²⁴ All the men who went out of the city gate agreed with Hamor and his son Shechem, and every male in the city was circumcised.

²⁵ Three days later, while all of them were still in pain, two of Jacob's sons, Simeon and Levi, Dinah's brothers, took their swords and attacked the unsuspecting city, killing every male. ²⁶ They put Hamor and his son Shechem to the sword and took Dinah from

Shechem's house and left. ²⁷ The sons of Jacob came upon the dead bodies and looted the city where their sister had been defiled. ²⁸ They seized their flocks and herds and donkeys and everything else of theirs in the city and out in the fields. ²⁹ They carried off all their wealth and all their women and children, taking as plunder everything in the houses.

³⁰ Then Jacob said to Simeon and Levi, 'You have brought trouble on me by making me obnoxious to the Canaanites and Perizzites, the people living in this land. We are few in number, and if they join forces against me and attack me, I and my household will be destroyed.'

³¹ But they replied, 'Should he have treated our sister like a prostitute?'

35 Then God said to Jacob, 'Go up to Bethel and settle there, and build an altar there to God, who appeared to you when you were fleeing from your brother Esau.'

² So Jacob said to his household and to all who were with him, 'Get rid of the foreign gods you have with you, and purify yourselves and change your clothes. ³ Then come, let us go up to Bethel, where I will build an altar to God, who answered me in the day of my distress and who has been with me wherever I have gone.' ⁴ So they gave Jacob all the foreign gods they had and the rings in their ears, and Jacob buried them under the oak at Shechem. ⁵ Then they set out, and the terror of God fell on the towns all around them so that no one pursued them.

⁶ Jacob and all the people with him came to Luz (that is, Bethel) in the land of Canaan. ⁷ There he built an altar, and he called the place El Bethel, because it was there that God revealed himself to him when he was fleeing from his brother.

⁸ Now Deborah, Rebekah's nurse, died and was buried under the oak outside Bethel. So it was named Allon Bakuth.

⁹ After Jacob returned from Paddan Aram, God appeared to him again and blessed him. ¹⁰ God said to him, 'Your name is Jacob, but you will no longer be called Jacob; your name will be Israel.' So he named him Israel.

¹¹ And God said to him, 'I am God Almighty; be fruitful and increase in number. A nation and a community of nations will come from you, and kings will be among your descendants. ¹² The land I gave to Abraham and Isaac I also give to you, and I will give this land to your descendants after you.' ¹³ Then God went up from him at the place where he had talked with him.

¹⁴ Jacob set up a stone pillar at the place where God had talked with him, and he poured out a drink offering on it; he also poured oil on it. ¹⁵ Jacob called the place where God had talked with him Bethel.

¹⁶ Then they moved on from Bethel. While they were still some distance from Ephrath, Rachel began to give birth and had great difficulty. ¹⁷ And as she was having great difficulty in childbirth, the midwife said to her, 'Don't despair, for you have another son.' ¹⁸ As she breathed her last – for she was dying – she named her son Ben-Oni. But his father named him Benjamin.

¹⁹ So Rachel died and was buried on the way to Ephrath (that is, Bethlehem). ²⁰ Over her tomb Jacob set up a pillar, and to this day that pillar marks Rachel's tomb.

²¹ Israel moved on again and pitched his tent beyond Migdal Eder. ²² While Israel was living in that region, Reuben went in and slept with his father's concubine Bilhah, and Israel heard of it.

Jacob had twelve sons:
²³ The sons of Leah:
    Reuben the firstborn of Jacob,
    Simeon, Levi, Judah, Issachar and
    Zebulun.
²⁴ The sons of Rachel:

Joseph and Benjamin.

25 The sons of Rachel's servant Bilhah: Dan and Naphtali.

26 The sons of Leah's servant Zilpah: Gad and Asher.

These were the sons of Jacob, who were born to him in Paddan Aram.

27 Jacob came home to his father Isaac in Mamre, near Kiriath Arba (that is, Hebron), where Abraham and Isaac had stayed. 28 Isaac lived a hundred and eighty years. 29 Then he breathed his last and died and was gathered to his people, old and full of years. And his sons Esau and Jacob buried him.

▬ PSALM 11:1-3

1 In the LORD I take refuge.
    How then can you say to me:
    'Flee like a bird to your mountain.
2 For look, the wicked bend their bows;
    they set their arrows against the
        strings
    to shoot from the shadows
        at the upright in heart.
3 When the foundations are being
        destroyed,
    what can the righteous do?'

▬ PROVERBS 3:3-4

3 Let love and faithfulness never leave you;
    bind them round your neck,
    write them on the tablet of your heart.
4 Then you will win favour and a good name
    in the sight of God and man.

▬ MATTHEW 12:38-13:9

38 Then some of the Pharisees and teachers of the law said to him, 'Teacher, we want to see a sign from you.'

39 He answered, 'A wicked and adulterous generation asks for a sign! But none will be given it except the sign of the prophet Jonah. 40 For as Jonah was three days and three nights in the belly of a huge fish, so the Son of Man will be three days and three nights in the heart of the earth. 41 The men of Nineveh will stand up at the judgment with this generation and condemn it; for they repented at the preaching of Jonah, and now something greater than Jonah is here. 42 The Queen of the South will rise at the judgment with this generation and condemn it; for she came from the ends of the earth to listen to Solomon's wisdom, and now something greater than Solomon is here.

43 'When an impure spirit comes out of a person, it goes through arid places seeking rest and does not find it. 44 Then it says, "I will return to the house I left." When it arrives, it finds the house unoccupied, swept clean and put in order. 45 Then it goes and takes with it seven other spirits more wicked than itself, and they go in and live there. And the final condition of that person is worse than the first. That is how it will be with this wicked generation.'

46 While Jesus was still talking to the crowd, his mother and brothers stood outside, wanting to speak to him. 47 Someone told him, 'Your mother and brothers are standing outside, wanting to speak to you.'

48 He replied to him, 'Who is my mother, and who are my brothers?' 49 Pointing to his disciples, he said, 'Here are my mother and my brothers. 50 For whoever does the will of my Father in heaven is my brother and sister and mother.'

13 That same day Jesus went out of the house and sat by the lake. 2 Such large crowds gathered round him that he got into a boat and sat in it, while all the people stood on the shore. 3 Then he told them many things in parables, saying: 'A

farmer went out to sow his seed. ⁴As he was scattering the seed, some fell along the path, and the birds came and ate it up. ⁵Some fell on rocky places, where it did not have much soil. It sprang up quickly, because the soil was shallow. ⁶But when the sun came up, the plants were scorched, and they withered because they had no root. ⁷Other seed fell among thorns, which grew up and choked the plants. ⁸Still other seed fell on good soil, where it produced a crop – a hundred, sixty or thirty times what was sown. ⁹Whoever has ears, let them hear.'

The Mystery Rolled Back

'Where, O death, is your victory? Where, O death, is your sting?' **1 Corinthians 15:55**

Mark's observation 'that the stone, which was very large, had been rolled away' (Mark 16:4) seems a simple statement, but behind it lies a truth that is positively staggering in its implications. One is that no longer can death be an intimidator. 'Death,' said Diana Wallis, 'is the great enigma of life. Humanly speaking ... it is the one secret of the universe which is kept, the silence that is never broken.' To the weary and despairing, death may come as a friend; the cynical and disillusioned may meet it with indifference; to the healthy and the happy it may appear as a foe; but it comes to all. Death is like a great stone that blocks the path of human aspiration. How certain can we be of the continuity of life beyond death? What modest person would find in himself anything worthy to endure for all eternity? Such questions have been asked down the centuries. Death is a mystery – 'the undiscovered country from which no traveller returns.' Then came the first Easter Day, and the stone was rolled away. One Traveller did return. Death is an abysmal cavern no longer but a tunnel with light at the farther end. If people have seen it as a blind alley, then they need think no longer in those terms. It is now a thoroughfare, a highway. "'Tis death is dead, not He," said the hymnist. The mystery is a mystery no more. The stone that was rolled away the first Easter morn was not just the rock that sealed the tomb. Our Lord rolled back for us the mystery of death also.

PRAYER

O Father, how can I ever sufficiently thank You that the work of salvation is complete? Nothing more needs to be done than has been done. Your Coronation spells it out in the clearest of terms. I am so deeply, deeply grateful. Amen.

FURTHER STUDY

Heb. 1:1-9; Luke 22:69; Col. 1:18
• What did God the Father say about the Son?
• What did God the Father say to the Son?

January 20

■ GENESIS 36:1-43

36 This is the account of the family line of Esau (that is, Edom).

2 Esau took his wives from the women of Canaan: Adah daughter of Elon the Hittite, and Oholibamah daughter of Anah and granddaughter of Zibeon the Hivite – 3 also Basemath daughter of Ishmael and sister of Nebaioth.

4 Adah bore Eliphaz to Esau, Basemath bore Reuel, 5 and Oholibamah bore Jeush, Jalam and Korah. These were the sons of Esau, who were born to him in Canaan.

6 Esau took his wives and sons and daughters and all the members of his household, as well as his livestock and all his other animals and all the goods he had acquired in Canaan, and moved to a land some distance from his brother Jacob. 7 Their possessions were too great for them to remain together; the land where they were staying could not support them both because of their livestock. 8 So Esau (that is, Edom) settled in the hill country of Seir.

9 This is the account of the family line of Esau the father of the Edomites in the hill country of Seir.

10 These are the names of Esau's sons:
Eliphaz, the son of Esau's wife Adah, and Reuel, the son of Esau's wife Basemath.
11 The sons of Eliphaz:
Teman, Omar, Zepho, Gatam and Kenaz.
12 Esau's son Eliphaz also had a concubine named Timna, who bore him Amalek. These were grandsons of Esau's wife Adah.
13 The sons of Reuel:
Nahath, Zerah, Shammah and Mizzah. These were grandsons of Esau's wife Basemath.
14 The sons of Esau's wife Oholibamah daughter of Anah and granddaughter of Zibeon, whom she bore to Esau:
Jeush, Jalam and Korah.

15 These were the chiefs among Esau's descendants:
The sons of Eliphaz the firstborn of Esau:
Chiefs Teman, Omar, Zepho, Kenaz, 16 Korah, Gatam and Amalek. These were the chiefs descended from Eliphaz in Edom; they were grandsons of Adah.
17 The sons of Esau's son Reuel:
Chiefs Nahath, Zerah, Shammah and Mizzah. These were the chiefs descended from Reuel in Edom; they were grandsons of Esau's wife Basemath.
18 The sons of Esau's wife Oholibamah:
Chiefs Jeush, Jalam and Korah. These were the chiefs descended from Esau's wife Oholibamah daughter of Anah.
19 These were the sons of Esau (that is, Edom), and these were their chiefs.

20 These were the sons of Seir the Horite, who were living in the region:
Lotan, Shobal, Zibeon, Anah, 21 Dishon, Ezer and Dishan. These sons of Seir in Edom were Horite chiefs.
22 The sons of Lotan:

Hori and Homam. Timna was Lotan's sister.

²³ The sons of Shobal:

Alvan, Manahath, Ebal, Shepho and Onam.

²⁴ The sons of Zibeon:

Aiah and Anah. This is the Anah who discovered the hot springs in the desert while he was grazing the donkeys of his father Zibeon.

²⁵ The children of Anah:

Dishon and Oholibamah daughter of Anah.

²⁶ The sons of Dishon;

Hemdan, Eshban, Ithran and Keran.

²⁷ The sons of Ezer:

Bilhan, Zaavan and Akan.

²⁸ The sons of Dishan:

Uz and Aran.

²⁹ These were the Horite chiefs:

Lotan, Shobal, Zibeon, Anah, ³⁰ Dishon, Ezer and Dishan. These were the Horite chiefs, according to their divisions, in the land of Seir.

³¹ These were the kings who reigned in Edom before any Israelite king reigned:

³² Bela son of Beor became king of Edom. His city was named Dinhabah.

³³ When Bela died, Jobab son of Zerah from Bozrah succeeded him as king.

³⁴ When Jobab died, Husham from the land of the Temanites succeeded him as king.

³⁵ When Husham died, Hadad son of Bedad, who defeated Midian in the country of Moab, succeeded him as king. His city was named Avith.

³⁶ When Hadad died, Samlah from Masrekah succeeded him as king.

³⁷ When Samlah died, Shaul from Rehoboth on the river succeeded him as king.

³⁸ When Shaul died, Baal-Hanan son of Akbor succeeded him as king.

³⁹ When Baal-Hanan son of Akbor died, Hadad succeeded him as king.

His city was named Pau, and his wife's name was Mehetabel daughter of Matred, the daughter of Me-Zahab.

⁴⁰ These were the chiefs descended from Esau, by name, according to their clans and regions:

Timna, Alvah, Jetheth, ⁴¹ Oholibamah, Elah, Pinon, ⁴² Kenaz, Teman, Mibzar, ⁴³ Magdiel and Iram. These were the chiefs of Edom, according to their settlements in the land they occupied.

This is the family line of Esau, the father of the Edomites.

PSALM 11:4-7

⁴ The LORD is in his holy temple;
    the LORD is on his heavenly throne.
He observes everyone on earth;
    his eyes examine them.
⁵ The LORD examines the righteous,
    but the wicked, those who love
        violence,
    he hates with a passion.
⁶ On the wicked he will rain
    fiery coals and burning sulphur;
    a scorching wind will be their lot.

⁷ For the LORD is righteous,
    he loves justice;
    the upright will see his face.

PROVERBS 3:5-6

⁵ Trust in the LORD with all your heart
    and lean not on your own
        understanding;
⁶ in all your ways submit to him,
    and he will make your paths straight.

▬ MATTHEW 13:10-35

¹⁰The disciples came to him and asked, 'Why do you speak to the people in parables?'

¹¹He replied, 'Because the knowledge of the secrets of the kingdom of heaven has been given to you, but not to them. ¹²Whoever has will be given more, and they will have an abundance. Whoever does not have, even what they have will be taken from them. ¹³This is why I speak to them in parables:

'Though seeing, they do not see;
    though hearing, they do not hear or
        understand.

¹⁴In them is fulfilled the prophecy of Isaiah:

' "You will be ever hearing but never
        understanding;
    you will be ever seeing but never
        perceiving.
¹⁵For this people's heart has become
        calloused;
    they hardly hear with their ears,
    and they have closed their eyes.
Otherwise they might see with their eyes,
    hear with their ears,
    understand with their hearts
and turn, and I would heal them." '

¹⁶But blessed are your eyes because they see, and your ears because they hear. ¹⁷For truly I tell you, many prophets and righteous people longed to see what you see but did not see it, and to hear what you hear but did not hear it.

¹⁸'Listen then to what the parable of the sower means: ¹⁹when anyone hears the message about the kingdom and does not understand it, the evil one comes and snatches away what was sown in their heart. This is the seed sown along the path. ²⁰The seed falling on rocky ground refers to someone who hears the word and at once receives it with joy. ²¹But since they have no root, they last only a short time. When trouble or persecution comes because of the word, they quickly fall away. ²²The seed falling among the thorns refers to someone who hears the word, but the worries of this life and the deceitfulness of wealth choke the word, making it unfruitful. ²³But the seed falling on good soil refers to someone who hears the word and understands it. This is the one who produces a crop, yielding a hundred, sixty or thirty times what was sown.'

²⁴Jesus told them another parable: 'The kingdom of heaven is like a man who sowed good seed in his field. ²⁵But while everyone was sleeping, his enemy came and sowed weeds among the wheat, and went away. ²⁶When the wheat sprouted and formed ears, then the weeds also appeared.

²⁷'The owner's servants came to him and said, "Sir, didn't you sow good seed in your field? Where then did the weeds come from?"

²⁸' "An enemy did this," he replied.

'The servants asked him, "Do you want us to go and pull them up?"

²⁹' "No," he answered, "because while you are pulling up the weeds, you may uproot the wheat with them. ³⁰Let both grow together until the harvest. At that time I will tell the harvesters: first collect the weeds and tie them in bundles to be burned; then gather the wheat and bring it into my barn." '

³¹He told them another parable: 'The kingdom of heaven is like a mustard seed, which a man took and planted in his field. ³²Though it is the smallest of all seeds, yet when it grows, it is the largest of garden plants and becomes a tree, so that the birds come and perch in its branches.'

³³He told them still another parable: 'The kingdom of heaven is like yeast that a woman took and mixed into about thirty kilograms of flour until it worked all through

the dough.'

³⁴Jesus spoke all these things to the crowd in parables; he did not say anything to them without using a parable. ³⁵So was fulfilled what was spoken through the prophet:

'I will open my mouth in parables,
   I will utter things hidden since the
      creation of the world.'

Heart of the Matter

'Trust in the LORD with all your heart and lean not on your own understanding.' **Proverbs 3:5**

What is the essential difference between the heart and mind? Many believe there is no difference and that they are really the same thing. But I see a clear difference between the heart and the mind: the mind is the part of us that thinks and reasons; the heart is the part of us that contains our deep longings and desires. Although the mind is important, the heart is even more important because it is the engine room of our personality – the part from which come our drive and motivation. That is why our Lord says, 'for the mouth speaks what the heart is full of' (Matt. 12:34).

Christ said that the words He spoke were the words given to Him by His Father (John 14:24). Does this mean the Father wrote out the words which He wanted Christ to say, and then Jesus had to learn them by heart? No – the heart of Jesus Christ was the very heart of God the Father; consequently, the words Christ spoke were the exact expression of God's thought. Jesus' tongue was always in its rightful place. He spoke not just from His head but from His heart; His heart and His mind were one.

Oswald Chambers put it like this: 'The heart is the central altar and the mind the outer court. What we offer on the central altar will show itself in due course through the outer extremities of personality.' In the search for unity of purpose and integration, there is no doubt that the heart of the matter is the matter of the heart.

PRAYER

O God, help me to be like Jesus, to pass on to others not just the things that come into my head, but the things that flow out of my heart. Bring my heart in closer contact with Your heart, dear Father. In Jesus' name I pray. Amen.

FURTHER STUDY

Mark 7:14-23; Prov. 4:23; Rom. 10:10
• What comes from the heart?
• What was Jesus' teaching?

January 21

■ GENESIS 37:1–38:30

37 Jacob lived in the land where his father had stayed, the land of Canaan.

² This is the account of Jacob's family line.

Joseph, a young man of seventeen, was tending the flocks with his brothers, the sons of Bilhah and the sons of Zilpah, his father's wives, and he brought their father a bad report about them. ³ Now Israel loved Joseph more than any of his other sons, because he had been born to him in his old age; and he made an ornate robe for him. ⁴ When his brothers saw that their father loved him more than any of them, they hated him and could not speak a kind word to him.

⁵ Joseph had a dream, and when he told it to his brothers, they hated him all the more. ⁶ He said to them, 'Listen to this dream I had: ⁷ We were binding sheaves of corn out in the field when suddenly my sheaf rose and stood upright, while your sheaves gathered round mine and bowed down to it.'

⁸ His brothers said to him, 'Do you intend to reign over us? Will you actually rule us?' And they hated him all the more because of his dream and what he had said.

⁹ Then he had another dream, and he told it to his brothers. 'Listen,' he said, 'I had another dream, and this time the sun and moon and eleven stars were bowing down to me.'

¹⁰ When he told his father as well as his brothers, his father rebuked him and said, 'What is this dream you had? Will your mother and I and your brothers actually come and bow down to the ground before you?' ¹¹ His brothers were jealous of him, but his father kept the matter in mind.

¹² Now his brothers had gone to graze their father's flocks near Shechem, ¹³ and Israel said to Joseph, 'As you know, your brothers are grazing the flocks near Shechem. Come, I am going to send you to them.'

'Very well,' he replied.

¹⁴ So he said to him, 'Go and see if all is well with your brothers and with the flocks, and bring word back to me.' Then he sent him off from the Valley of Hebron.

When Joseph arrived at Shechem, ¹⁵ a man found him wandering around in the fields and asked him, 'What are you looking for?'

¹⁶ He replied, 'I'm looking for my brothers. Can you tell me where they are grazing their flocks?'

¹⁷ 'They have moved on from here,' the man answered. 'I heard them say, "Let's go to Dothan."'

So Joseph went after his brothers and found them near Dothan. ¹⁸ But they saw him in the distance, and before he reached them, they plotted to kill him.

¹⁹ 'Here comes that dreamer!' they said to each other. ²⁰ 'Come now, let's kill him and throw him into one of these cisterns and say that a ferocious animal devoured him. Then we'll see what comes of his dreams.'

²¹ When Reuben heard this, he tried to rescue him from their hands. 'Let's not take his life,' he said. ²² 'Don't shed any blood. Throw him into this cistern here in the wilderness, but don't lay a hand on him.' Reuben said this to rescue him from them and take him back to his father.

²³ So when Joseph came to his brothers, they stripped him of his robe – the ornate robe he was wearing – ²⁴ and they took him and threw him into the cistern. The cistern was empty; there was no water in it.

²⁵As they sat down to eat their meal, they looked up and saw a caravan of Ishmaelites coming from Gilead. Their camels were loaded with spices, balm and myrrh, and they were on their way to take them down to Egypt.

²⁶Judah said to his brothers, 'What will we gain if we kill our brother and cover up his blood? ²⁷Come, let's sell him to the Ishmaelites and not lay our hands on him; after all, he is our brother, our own flesh and blood.' His brothers agreed.

²⁸So when the Midianite merchants came by, his brothers pulled Joseph up out of the cistern and sold him for twenty shekels of silver to the Ishmaelites, who took him to Egypt.

²⁹When Reuben returned to the cistern and saw that Joseph was not there, he tore his clothes. ³⁰He went back to his brothers and said, 'The boy isn't there! Where can I turn now?'

³¹Then they got Joseph's robe, slaughtered a goat and dipped the robe in the blood. ³²They took the ornate robe back to their father and said, 'We found this. Examine it to see whether it is your son's robe.'

³³He recognised it and said, 'It is my son's robe! Some ferocious animal has devoured him. Joseph has surely been torn to pieces.'

³⁴Then Jacob tore his clothes, put on sackcloth and mourned for his son many days. ³⁵All his sons and daughters came to comfort him, but he refused to be comforted. 'No,' he said, 'I will continue to mourn until I join my son in the grave.' So his father wept for him.

³⁶Meanwhile, the Midianites sold Joseph in Egypt to Potiphar, one of Pharaoh's officials, the captain of the guard.

38 At that time, Judah left his brothers and went down to stay with a man of Adullam named Hirah. ²There Judah met the daughter of a Canaanite man named Shua. He married her and made love to her; ³she became pregnant and gave birth to a son, who was named Er. ⁴She conceived again and gave birth to a son and named him Onan. ⁵She gave birth to still another son and named him Shelah. It was at Kezib that she gave birth to him.

⁶Judah got a wife for Er, his firstborn, and her name was Tamar. ⁷But Er, Judah's firstborn, was wicked in the Lord's sight; so the Lord put him to death.

⁸Then Judah said to Onan, 'Sleep with your brother's wife and fulfil your duty to her as a brother-in-law to raise up offspring for your brother.' ⁹But Onan knew that the child would not be his; so whenever he slept with his brother's wife, he spilled his semen on the ground to avoid providing offspring for his brother. ¹⁰What he did was wicked in the Lord's sight; so the Lord put him to death also.

¹¹Judah then said to his daughter-in-law Tamar, 'Live as a widow in your father's household until my son Shelah grows up.' For he thought, 'He may die too, just like his brothers.' So Tamar went to live in her father's household.

¹²After a long time Judah's wife, the daughter of Shua, died. When Judah had recovered from his grief, he went up to Timnah, to the men who were shearing his sheep, and his friend Hirah the Adullamite went with him.

¹³When Tamar was told, 'Your father-in-law is on his way to Timnah to shear his sheep,' ¹⁴she took off her widow's clothes, covered herself with a veil to disguise herself, and then sat down at the entrance to Enaim, which is on the road to Timnah. For she saw that, though Shelah had now grown up, she had not been given to him as his wife.

¹⁵When Judah saw her, he thought she was a prostitute, for she had covered her face. ¹⁶Not realising that she was his daughter-in-law, he went over to her by the roadside and said, 'Come now, let me sleep with you.'

'And what will you give me to sleep with you?' she asked.

¹⁷ 'I'll send you a young goat from my flock,' he said.

'Will you give me something as a pledge until you send it?' she asked.

¹⁸ He said, 'What pledge should I give you?'

'Your seal and its cord, and the staff in your hand,' she answered. So he gave them to her and slept with her, and she became pregnant by him. ¹⁹ After she left, she took off her veil and put on her widow's clothes again.

²⁰ Meanwhile Judah sent the young goat by his friend the Adullamite in order to get his pledge back from the woman, but he did not find her. ²¹ He asked the men who lived there, 'Where is the shrine-prostitute who was beside the road at Enaim?'

'There hasn't been any shrine-prostitute here,' they said.

²² So he went back to Judah and said, 'I didn't find her. Besides, the men who lived there said, "There hasn't been any shrine-prostitute here."'

²³ Then Judah said, 'Let her keep what she has, or we will become a laughing-stock. After all, I did send her this young goat, but you didn't find her.'

²⁴ About three months later Judah was told, 'Your daughter-in-law Tamar is guilty of prostitution, and as a result she is now pregnant.'

Judah said, 'Bring her out and let her be burned to death!'

²⁵ As she was being brought out, she sent a message to her father-in-law. 'I am pregnant by the man who owns these,' she said. And she added, 'See if you recognise whose seal and cord and staff these are.'

²⁶ Judah recognised them and said, 'She is more righteous than I, since I wouldn't give her to my son Shelah.' And he did not sleep with her again.

²⁷ When the time came for her to give birth, there were twin boys in her womb. ²⁸ As she was giving birth, one of them put out his hand; so the midwife took a scarlet thread and tied it on his wrist and said,

'This one came out first.' ²⁹ But when he drew back his hand, his brother came out, and she said, 'So this is how you have broken out!' And he was named Perez. ³⁰ Then his brother, who had the scarlet thread on his wrist, came out. And he was named Zerah.

■ PSALM 12:1-5

¹ Help, LORD, for no one is faithful any more;
  those who are loyal have vanished
    from the human race.
² Everyone lies to their neighbour;
  they flatter with their lips
    but harbour deception in their hearts.
³ May the LORD silence all flattering lips
  and every boastful tongue –
⁴ those who say,
  'By our tongues we will prevail;
  our own lips will defend us – who is
    lord over us?'
⁵ 'Because the poor are plundered and the needy groan,
  I will now arise,' says the LORD.
  'I will protect them from those who
    malign them.'

■ PROVERBS 3:7-8

⁷ Do not be wise in your own eyes;
  fear the LORD and shun evil.
⁸ This will bring health to your body
  and nourishment to your bones.

■ MATTHEW 13:36-58

³⁶ Then he left the crowd and went into the house. His disciples came to him and said, 'Explain to us the parable of the weeds in the field.'

³⁷He answered, 'The one who sowed the good seed is the Son of Man. ³⁸The field is the world, and the good seed stands for the people of the kingdom. The weeds are the people of the evil one, ³⁹and the enemy who sows them is the devil. The harvest is the end of the age, and the harvesters are angels.

⁴⁰'As the weeds are pulled up and burned in the fire, so it will be at the end of the age. ⁴¹The Son of Man will send out his angels, and they will weed out of his kingdom everything that causes sin and all who do evil. ⁴²They will throw them into the blazing furnace, where there will be weeping and gnashing of teeth. ⁴³Then the righteous will shine like the sun in the kingdom of their Father. Whoever has ears, let them hear.

⁴⁴'The kingdom of heaven is like treasure hidden in a field. When a man found it, he hid it again, and then in his joy went and sold all he had and bought that field.

⁴⁵'Again, the kingdom of heaven is like a merchant looking for fine pearls. ⁴⁶When he found one of great value, he went away and sold everything he had and bought it.

⁴⁷'Once again, the kingdom of heaven is like a net that was let down into the lake and caught all kinds of fish. ⁴⁸When it was full, the fishermen pulled it up on the shore. Then they sat down and collected the good fish in baskets, but threw the bad away. ⁴⁹This is how it will be at the end of the age. The angels will come and separate the wicked from the righteous ⁵⁰and throw them into the blazing furnace, where there will be weeping and gnashing of teeth.

⁵¹'Have you understood all these things?' Jesus asked.

'Yes,' they replied.

⁵²He said to them, 'Therefore every teacher of the law who has become a disciple in the kingdom of heaven is like the owner of a house who brings out of his storeroom new treasures as well as old.'

⁵³When Jesus had finished these parables, he moved on from there. ⁵⁴Coming to his home town, he began teaching the people in their synagogue, and they were amazed. 'Where did this man get this wisdom and these miraculous powers?' they asked. ⁵⁵'Isn't this the carpenter's son? Isn't his mother's name Mary, and aren't his brothers James, Joseph, Simon and Judas? ⁵⁶Aren't all his sisters with us? Where then did this man get all these things?' ⁵⁷And they took offence at him.

But Jesus said to them, 'A prophet is not without honour except in his own town and in his own home.'

⁵⁸And he did not do many miracles there because of their lack of faith.

Prevenient Grace

'... his brothers pulled Joseph up out of the cistern and sold him for twenty shekels of silver to the Ishmaelites who took him to Egypt.' **Genesis 37:28**

'So then, it was not you who sent me here, but God.' **Genesis 45:8**

Sometimes God – the Divine Eagle – disturbs the nest to further His purposes. An illustration of this concerns that remarkable Old Testament character, Joseph. When Joseph's anxious and unenlightened brothers are ushered into his presence, they fall before him on their faces. What a moment! Joseph must have seen in a flash the panorama of his strange and eventful life: his boyhood in Canaan; the dreams by which he had been haunted; the growing hostility of his brothers; the awful day when they fell upon him, cast him into a pit, and sold him to the Ishmaelites; the journey down into Egypt, and his life as a slave. He must have remembered, too, the extraordinary events that led to his becoming the Keeper of the Royal Seal with an authority second only to the throne.

But it is not the events, significant as they are, that interest me most, but the conclusions to which he comes as he ponders the past. 'Don't be worried or angry with yourselves,' he says, 'for selling me here, because God sent me ... ' Three times he says it: 'God sent me ahead of you ...' and 'It was not you who sent me here, but God ... '. The astonishing thing is that there was no anger or bitterness in his heart. And why? Because he recognised the work of the Divine Eagle who had pushed him out of the nest in Canaan in order that he might be the provider for his family in time of famine. God moved him into a position of greater usefulness. 'You sold me,' he said, 'but God sent me.'

PRAYER

O Father, as I look back, the whole meaning of my life is made plain. Many times I have rebelled against the stirring of my own nest, but now I see it was for Your glory and my eternal good. I am so thankful. Amen.

FURTHER STUDY

Gen. 37; 47:11-12, 27; 50:15-21
• How was Joseph used as an instrument in God's hand?
• What was his final response to his brothers?

January 22

▬ GENESIS 39:1-41:7

39 Now Joseph had been taken down to Egypt. Potiphar, an Egyptian who was one of Pharaoh's officials, the captain of the guard, bought him from the Ishmaelites who had taken him there.

[2] The LORD was with Joseph so that he prospered, and he lived in the house of his Egyptian master. [3] When his master saw that the LORD was with him and that the LORD gave him success in everything he did, [4] Joseph found favour in his eyes and became his attendant. Potiphar put him in charge of his household, and he entrusted to his care everything he owned. [5] From the time he put him in charge of his household and of all that he owned, the LORD blessed the household of the Egyptian because of Joseph. The blessing of the LORD was on everything Potiphar had, both in the house and in the field. [6] So Potiphar left everything he had in Joseph's care; with Joseph in charge, he did not concern himself with anything except the food he ate.

Now Joseph was well-built and handsome, [7] and after a while his master's wife took notice of Joseph and said, 'Come to bed with me!'

[8] But he refused. 'With me in charge,' he

told her, 'my master does not concern himself with anything in the house; everything he owns he has entrusted to my care. ⁹No one is greater in this house than I am. My master has withheld nothing from me except you, because you are his wife. How then could I do such a wicked thing and sin against God?' ¹⁰And though she spoke to Joseph day after day, he refused to go to bed with her or even to be with her.

¹¹One day he went into the house to attend to his duties, and none of the household servants was inside. ¹²She caught him by his cloak and said, 'Come to bed with me!' But he left his cloak in her hand and ran out of the house.

¹³When she saw that he had left his cloak in her hand and had run out of the house, ¹⁴she called her household servants. 'Look,' she said to them, 'this Hebrew has been brought to us to make sport of us! He came in here to sleep with me, but I screamed. ¹⁵When he heard me scream for help, he left his cloak beside me and ran out of the house.'

¹⁶She kept his cloak beside her until his master came home. ¹⁷Then she told him this story: 'That Hebrew slave you brought us came to me to make sport of me. ¹⁸But as soon as I screamed for help, he left his cloak beside me and ran out of the house.'

¹⁹When his master heard the story his wife told him, saying, 'This is how your slave treated me,' he burned with anger. ²⁰Joseph's master took him and put him in prison, the place where the king's prisoners were confined.

But while Joseph was there in the prison, ²¹the LORD was with him; he showed him kindness and granted him favour in the eyes of the prison warder. ²²So the warder put Joseph in charge of all those held in the prison, and he was made responsible for all that was done there. ²³The warder paid no attention to anything under Joseph's care, because the LORD was with Joseph and gave him success in whatever he did.

40 Some time later, the cupbearer and the baker of the king of Egypt offended their master, the king of Egypt. ²Pharaoh was angry with his two officials, the chief cupbearer and the chief baker, ³and put them in custody in the house of the captain of the guard, in the same prison where Joseph was confined. ⁴The captain of the guard assigned them to Joseph, and he attended them.

After they had been in custody for some time, ⁵each of the two men – the cupbearer and the baker of the king of Egypt, who were being held in prison – had a dream the same night, and each dream had a meaning of its own.

⁶When Joseph came to them the next morning, he saw that they were dejected. ⁷So he asked Pharaoh's officials who were in custody with him in his master's house, 'Why do you look so sad today?'

⁸'We both had dreams,' they answered, 'but there is no one to interpret them.'

Then Joseph said to them, 'Do not interpretations belong to God? Tell me your dreams.'

⁹So the chief cupbearer told Joseph his dream. He said to him, 'In my dream I saw a vine in front of me, ¹⁰and on the vine were three branches. As soon as it budded, it blossomed, and its clusters ripened into grapes. ¹¹Pharaoh's cup was in my hand, and I took the grapes, squeezed them into Pharaoh's cup and put the cup in his hand.'

¹²'This is what it means,' Joseph said to him. 'The three branches are three days. ¹³Within three days Pharaoh will lift up your head and restore you to your position, and you will put Pharaoh's cup in his hand, just as you used to do when you were his cupbearer. ¹⁴But when all goes well with you, remember me and show me kindness; mention me to Pharaoh and get me out of this prison. ¹⁵I was forcibly carried off from the land of the Hebrews, and even here I have done nothing to deserve being put in a dungeon.'

¹⁶ When the chief baker saw that Joseph had given a favourable interpretation, he said to Joseph, 'I too had a dream: on my head were three baskets of bread. ¹⁷ In the top basket were all kinds of baked goods for Pharaoh, but the birds were eating them out of the basket on my head.'

¹⁸ 'This is what it means,' Joseph said. 'The three baskets are three days. ¹⁹ Within three days Pharaoh will lift off your head and impale your body on a pole. And the birds will eat away your flesh.'

²⁰ Now the third day was Pharaoh's birthday, and he gave a feast for all his officials. He lifted up the heads of the chief cupbearer and the chief baker in the presence of his officials: ²¹ He restored the chief cupbearer to his position, so that he once again put the cup into Pharaoh's hand – ²² but he impaled the chief baker, just as Joseph had said to them in his interpretation.

²³ The chief cupbearer, however, did not remember Joseph; he forgot him.

41 When two full years had passed, Pharaoh had a dream: He was standing by the Nile, ² when out of the river there came up seven cows, sleek and fat, and they grazed among the reeds. ³ After them, seven other cows, ugly and gaunt, came up out of the Nile and stood beside those on the river-bank. ⁴ And the cows that were ugly and gaunt ate up the seven sleek, fat cows. Then Pharaoh woke up.

⁵ He fell asleep again and had a second dream: seven ears of corn, healthy and good, were growing on a single stalk. ⁶ After them, seven other ears of corn sprouted – thin and scorched by the east wind. ⁷ The thin ears of corn swallowed up the seven healthy, full ears. Then Pharaoh woke up; it had been a dream.

PSALM 12:6-8

⁶ And the words of the LORD are flawless,

like silver purified in a crucible,
like gold refined seven times.

⁷ You, LORD, will keep the needy safe
  and will protect us for ever from the wicked,
⁸ who freely strut about
  when what is vile is honoured by the human race.

PROVERBS 3:9-10

⁹ Honour the LORD with your wealth,
  with the firstfruits of all your crops;
¹⁰ then your barns will be filled to overflowing,
  and your vats will brim over with new wine.

MATTHEW 14:1-21

14 At that time Herod the tetrarch heard the reports about Jesus, ² and he said to his attendants, 'This is John the Baptist; he has risen from the dead! That is why miraculous powers are at work in him.'

³ Now Herod had arrested John and bound him and put him in prison because of Herodias, his brother Philip's wife, ⁴ for John had been saying to him: 'It is not lawful for you to have her.' ⁵ Herod wanted to kill John, but he was afraid of the people, because they considered John a prophet.

⁶ On Herod's birthday the daughter of Herodias danced for the guests and pleased Herod so much ⁷ that he promised with an oath to give her whatever she asked. ⁸ Prompted by her mother, she said, 'Give me here on a dish the head of John the Baptist.' ⁹ The king was distressed, but because of his oaths and his dinner guests, he ordered that her request be granted ¹⁰ and had John beheaded in the

prison. [11] His head was brought in on a dish and given to the girl, who carried it to her mother. [12] John's disciples came and took his body and buried it. Then they went and told Jesus.

[13] When Jesus heard what had happened, he withdrew by boat privately to a solitary place. Hearing of this, the crowds followed him on foot from the towns. [14] When Jesus landed and saw a large crowd, he had compassion on them and healed those who were ill.

[15] As evening approached, the disciples came to him and said, 'This is a remote place, and it's already getting late. Send the crowds away, so that they can go to the villages and buy themselves some food.'

[16] Jesus replied, 'They do not need to go away. You give them something to eat.'

[17] 'We have here only five loaves of bread and two fish,' they answered.

[18] 'Bring them here to me,' he said. [19] And he told the people to sit down on the grass. Taking the five loaves and the two fish and looking up to heaven, he gave thanks and broke the loaves. Then he gave them to the disciples, and the disciples gave them to the people. [20] They all ate and were satisfied, and the disciples picked up twelve basketfuls of broken pieces that were left over. [21] The number of those who ate was about five thousand men, besides women and children.

Not the End - Beginning

'... stay in the city until you have been clothed with power from on high.' **Luke 24:49**

Writing on the subject of the Holy Spirit has whetted my appetite for more of His fullness and His power. I can never be the same again. I hope something similar happens to you.

The Holy Spirit coordinates and unifies the conscious and the subconscious, He comforts and contributes, He clothes and convinces. There is much more that could be said, of course, about His ministry in our lives, but let me draw your attention to something else - God is willing to give you as much of His Spirit as you are willing to receive.

If you believe that you received all of the Spirit at conversion, then the question for you is this: How much is He ruling and reigning in your life at this present moment? If you believe that the Holy Spirit is given subsequent to conversion, then permit me to ask you this: What steps have you taken to open your entire being to Him in order that you might be filled with all His fullness? Don't, I beg you, remain stagnant because of some doctrinal position you might hold. Seek Him afresh today, that He might flow through your life in the fullness of His power.

And don't just focus on being filled for the blessing you might enjoy. Remember, the Holy Spirit is like electricity - He won't come in unless He can get out. Tell Him you want to be a channel, not just a consumer, and today will be not an end, but a beginning.

PRAYER

O God, now as I take all barriers down, come in by Your Holy Spirit's power and flood my life with Your divine glory. May the receiving flow out in giving. This I ask for Your own dear name's sake. Amen.

FURTHER STUDY

John 7:32-44; Matt. 5:6;
Isa. 55:1; Rev. 22:17
• What was the promise of Jesus?
• How thirsty and hungry are you today?

January 23

■ GENESIS 41:8–42:4

⁸In the morning his mind was troubled, so he sent for all the magicians and wise men of Egypt. Pharaoh told them his dreams, but no one could interpret them for him.

⁹Then the chief cupbearer said to Pharaoh, 'Today I am reminded of my shortcomings. ¹⁰Pharaoh was once angry with his servants, and he imprisoned me and the chief baker in the house of the captain of the guard. ¹¹Each of us had a dream the same night, and each dream had a meaning of its own. ¹²Now a young Hebrew was there with us, a servant of the captain of the guard. We told him our dreams, and he interpreted them for us, giving each man the interpretation of his dream. ¹³And things turned out exactly as he interpreted them to us: I was restored to my position, and the other man was impaled.'

¹⁴So Pharaoh sent for Joseph, and he was quickly brought from the dungeon. When he had shaved and changed his clothes, he came before Pharaoh.

¹⁵Pharaoh said to Joseph, 'I had a dream, and no one can interpret it. But I have heard it said of you that when you hear a dream you can interpret it.'

¹⁶'I cannot do it,' Joseph replied to Pharaoh, 'but God will give Pharaoh the answer he desires.'

¹⁷Then Pharaoh said to Joseph, 'In my dream I was standing on the bank of the Nile, ¹⁸when out of the river there came up seven cows, fat and sleek, and they grazed among the reeds. ¹⁹After them, seven other cows came up – scrawny and very ugly and lean. I had never seen such ugly cows in all the land of Egypt. ²⁰The lean, ugly cows ate up the seven fat cows that came up first. ²¹But even after they ate them, no one could tell that they had done so; they looked just as ugly as before. Then I woke up.

²²'In my dream I saw seven ears of corn, full and good, growing on a single stalk. ²³After them, seven other ears sprouted – withered and thin and scorched by the east wind. ²⁴The thin ears of corn swallowed up the seven good ears. I told this to the magicians, but none of them could explain it to me.'

²⁵Then Joseph said to Pharaoh, 'The dreams of Pharaoh are one and the same. God has revealed to Pharaoh what he is about to do. ²⁶The seven good cows are seven years, and the seven good ears of corn are seven years; it is one and the same dream. ²⁷The seven lean, ugly cows that came up afterwards are seven years, and so are the seven worthless ears of corn scorched by the east wind: they are seven years of famine.

²⁸'It is just as I said to Pharaoh: God has shown Pharaoh what he is about to do.

²⁹Seven years of great abundance are coming throughout the land of Egypt, ³⁰but seven years of famine will follow them. Then all the abundance in Egypt will be forgotten, and the famine will ravage the land. ³¹The abundance in the land will not be remembered, because the famine that follows it will be so severe. ³²The reason the dream was given to Pharaoh in two forms is that the matter has been firmly decided by God, and God will do it soon.

³³'And now let Pharaoh look for a discerning and wise man and put him in charge of the land of Egypt. ³⁴Let Pharaoh appoint commissioners over the land to take a fifth of the harvest of Egypt during the seven years of abundance. ³⁵They should collect all the food of these good years that are coming and store up the grain under the authority of Pharaoh, to be kept in the cities for food. ³⁶This food should be held in reserve for the country, to be used during the seven years of famine that will come upon Egypt, so that the country may not be ruined by the famine.'

³⁷The plan seemed good to Pharaoh and to all his officials. ³⁸So Pharaoh asked them, 'Can we find anyone like this man, one in whom is the spirit of God?'

³⁹Then Pharaoh said to Joseph, 'Since God has made all this known to you, there is no one so discerning and wise as you. ⁴⁰You shall be in charge of my palace, and all my people are to submit to your orders. Only with respect to the throne will I be greater than you.'

⁴¹So Pharaoh said to Joseph, 'I hereby put you in charge of the whole land of Egypt.' ⁴²Then Pharaoh took his signet ring from his finger and put it on Joseph's finger. He dressed him in robes of fine linen and put a gold chain round his neck. ⁴³He made him ride in a chariot as his second-in-command, and people shouted before him, 'Make way!' Thus he put him in charge of the whole land of Egypt.

⁴⁴Then Pharaoh said to Joseph, 'I am Pharaoh, but without your word no one will lift hand or foot in all Egypt.' ⁴⁵Pharaoh gave Joseph the name Zaphenath-Paneah and gave him Asenath daughter of Potiphera, priest of On, to be his wife. And Joseph went throughout the land of Egypt.

⁴⁶Joseph was thirty years old when he entered the service of Pharaoh king of Egypt. And Joseph went out from Pharaoh's presence and travelled throughout Egypt. ⁴⁷During the seven years of abundance the land produced plentifully. ⁴⁸Joseph collected all the food produced in those seven years of abundance in Egypt and stored it in the cities. In each city he put the food grown in the fields surrounding it. ⁴⁹Joseph stored up huge quantities of grain, like the sand of the sea; it was so much that he stopped keeping records because it was beyond measure.

⁵⁰Before the years of famine came, two sons were born to Joseph by Asenath daughter of Potiphera, priest of On. ⁵¹Joseph named his firstborn Manasseh and said, 'It is because God has made me forget all my trouble and all my father's household.' ⁵²The second son he named Ephraim and said, 'It is because God has made me fruitful in the land of my suffering.'

⁵³The seven years of abundance in Egypt came to an end, ⁵⁴and the seven years of famine began, just as Joseph had said. There was famine in all the other lands, but in the whole land of Egypt there was food. ⁵⁵When all Egypt began to feel the famine, the people cried to Pharaoh for food. Then Pharaoh told all the Egyptians, 'Go to Joseph and do what he tells you.'

⁵⁶When the famine had spread over the whole country, Joseph opened all the storehouses and sold grain to the Egyptians, for the famine was severe throughout Egypt. ⁵⁷And all the world came to Egypt to buy grain from Joseph, because the famine was severe everywhere.

42 When Jacob learned that there was grain in Egypt, he said to his sons, 'Why do you just keep looking at each other?' ²He continued, 'I have heard that there is grain in Egypt. Go down there and buy some for us, so that we may live and not die.'

³Then ten of Joseph's brothers went down to buy grain from Egypt. ⁴But Jacob did not send Benjamin, Joseph's brother, with the others, because he was afraid that harm might come to him.

▬ PSALM 13:1-6

¹How long, LORD? Will you forget me for ever?
How long will you hide your face from me?
²How long must I wrestle with my thoughts and day after day have sorrow in my heart?
How long will my enemy triumph over me?

³Look on me and answer, LORD my God.
Give light to my eyes, or I will sleep in death,
⁴and my enemy will say, 'I have overcome him,'
and my foes will rejoice when I fall.

⁵But I trust in your unfailing love;
my heart rejoices in your salvation.
⁶I will sing the LORD's praise,
for he has been good to me.

▬ PROVERBS 3:11-12

¹¹My son, do not despise the LORD's discipline,
and do not resent his rebuke,
¹²because the LORD disciplines those he loves,
as a father the son he delights in.

▬ MATTHEW 14:22–15:9

²²Immediately Jesus made the disciples get into the boat and go on ahead of him to the other side, while he dismissed the crowd. ²³After he had dismissed them, he went up on a mountainside by himself to pray. Later that night, he was there alone, ²⁴and the boat was already a considerable distance from land, buffeted by the waves because the wind was against it.

²⁵Shortly before dawn Jesus went out to them, walking on the lake. ²⁶When the disciples saw him walking on the lake, they were terrified. 'It's a ghost,' they said, and cried out in fear.

²⁷But Jesus immediately said to them: 'Take courage! It is I. Don't be afraid.'

²⁸'Lord, if it's you,' Peter replied, 'tell me to come to you on the water.'

²⁹'Come,' he said.

Then Peter got down out of the boat, walked on the water and came towards Jesus. ³⁰But when he saw the wind, he was afraid and, beginning to sink, cried out, 'Lord, save me!'

³¹Immediately Jesus reached out his hand and caught him. 'You of little faith,' he said, 'why did you doubt?'

³²And when they climbed into the boat, the wind died down. ³³Then those who were in the boat worshipped him, saying, 'Truly you are the Son of God.'

³⁴When they had crossed over, they landed at Gennesaret. ³⁵And when the men of that place recognised Jesus, they sent word to all the surrounding country. People brought all who were ill to him ³⁶and begged him to let those who were ill just touch the edge of his cloak, and all who touched it were healed.

15 Then some Pharisees and teachers of the law came to Jesus from Jerusalem and asked, ²'Why do your disciples break the tradition of the elders? They don't wash their hands before they eat!'

³Jesus replied, 'And why do you break

the command of God for the sake of your tradition? [4]For God said, "Honour your father and mother" and "Anyone who curses their father or mother is to be put to death." [5]But you say that if anyone declares that what might have been used to help their father or mother is "devoted to God," [6]they are not to "honour their father or mother" with it. Thus you nullify the word of God

for the sake of your tradition. [7]You hypocrites! Isaiah was right when he prophesied about you:

[8]"'These people honour me with their lips, but their hearts are far from me. [9]They worship me in vain; their teachings are merely human rules.'"

Correcting Your Doubt

'Immediately, Jesus reached out his hand and caught him. "You of little faith," he said, 'why did you doubt?'"
Matthew 14:31

While it is possible for us to distinguish between doubt and unbelief in theory, it is not so easy in practice. Doubt can move in the direction of unbelief and cross the borderline, but when it does, it ceases to be doubt. The idea of 'total' or 'complete' doubt is a contradiction in terms, for doubt that is total can no longer be classified as doubt; it is unbelief.

Os Guinness points out that when we attempt to undertake a biblical analysis of doubt, we can come out with either a 'hard' or 'soft' view of the subject. Those who take a 'soft' view of doubt point to how vastly different doubt is from unbelief, and those who take a 'hard' view of doubt point out its similarities.

Both views can be drawn out of the Scriptures. Error is usually truth out of balance, and it is important, therefore, that we get a balanced view of what the Bible has to say about doubt. In my view it can be summarised like this – doubt is not the same as unbelief, but unless corrected, doubt can naturally lead to unbelief.

This view has helped me avoid what I consider to be the extremes of being too hard or too soft on doubt. It is a condition which must be regarded as serious, but it need not be fatal. Don't allow your doubts to bring you into condemnation, for when faced and brought into clear perspective, they can be the catalyst to a deeper pursuit of God.

PRAYER

Father, when will I learn that in You all things serve – even doubt? Show me how to turn my doubts into stepping stones and use them to come into an even closer relationship with You. Amen.

FURTHER STUDY

Matt. 8:1-26; 6:30; 16:8
• What phrase did Jesus often use?
• What did He say of the centurion?

January 24

■ GENESIS 42:5–43:14

⁵ So Israel's sons were among those who went to buy grain, for there was famine in the land of Canaan also.

⁶ Now Joseph was the governor of the land, the person who sold grain to all its people. So when Joseph's brothers arrived, they bowed down to him with their faces to the ground. ⁷ As soon as Joseph saw his brothers, he recognised them, but he pretended to be a stranger and spoke harshly to them. 'Where do you come from?' he asked.

'From the land of Canaan,' they replied, 'to buy food.'

⁸ Although Joseph recognised his brothers, they did not recognise him. ⁹ Then he remembered his dreams about them and said to them, 'You are spies! You have come to see where our land is unprotected.'

¹⁰ 'No, my lord,' they answered. 'Your servants have come to buy food. ¹¹ We are all the sons of one man. Your servants are honest men, not spies.'

¹² 'No!' he said to them. 'You have come to see where our land is unprotected.'

¹³ But they replied, 'Your servants were twelve brothers, the sons of one man, who lives in the land of Canaan. The youngest is now with our father, and one is no more.'

¹⁴ Joseph said to them, 'It is just as I told you: you are spies! ¹⁵ And this is how you will be tested: as surely as Pharaoh lives, you will not leave this place unless your youngest brother comes here. ¹⁶ Send one of your number to get your brother; the rest of you will be kept in prison, so that your words may be tested to see if you are telling the truth. If you are not, then as surely as Pharaoh lives, you are spies!' ¹⁷ And he put them all in custody for three days.

¹⁸ On the third day, Joseph said to them, 'Do this and you will live, for I fear God: ¹⁹ if you are honest men, let one of your brothers stay here in prison, while the rest of you go and take grain back for your starving households. ²⁰ But you must bring your youngest brother to me, so that your words may be verified and that you may not die.' This they proceeded to do.

²¹ They said to one another, 'Surely we are being punished because of our brother. We saw how distressed he was when he pleaded with us for his life, but we would not listen; that's why this distress has come on us.'

²² Reuben replied, 'Didn't I tell you not to sin against the boy? But you wouldn't listen! Now we must give an accounting for his blood.' ²³ They did not realise that Joseph could understand them, since he was using an interpreter.

²⁴ He turned away from them and began to weep, but then came back and spoke to them again. He had Simeon taken from them and bound before their eyes.

²⁵ Joseph gave orders to fill their bags with grain, to put each man's silver back in his sack, and to give them provisions for their journey. After this was done for them, ²⁶ they loaded their grain on their donkeys and left.

²⁷ At the place where they stopped for the night one of them opened his sack to get feed for his donkey, and he saw his silver in the mouth of his sack. ²⁸ 'My silver has been returned,' he said to his brothers. 'Here it is in my sack.'

Their hearts sank and they turned to each other trembling and said, 'What is this that God has done to us?'

²⁹ When they came to their father Jacob in the land of Canaan, they told him all that had happened to them. They said, ³⁰ 'The

man who is lord over the land spoke harshly to us and treated us as though we were spying on the land. [31] But we said to him, "We are honest men; we are not spies. [32] We were twelve brothers, sons of one father. One is no more, and the youngest is now with our father in Canaan."

[33] 'Then the man who is lord over the land said to us, "This is how I will know whether you are honest men: leave one of your brothers here with me, and take food for your starving households and go. [34] But bring your youngest brother to me so I will know that you are not spies but honest men. Then I will give your brother back to you, and you can trade in the land."'

[35] As they were emptying their sacks, there in each man's sack was his pouch of silver! When they and their father saw the money pouches, they were frightened. [36] Their father Jacob said to them, 'You have deprived me of my children. Joseph is no more and Simeon is no more, and now you want to take Benjamin. Everything is against me!'

[37] Then Reuben said to his father, 'You may put both of my sons to death if I do not bring him back to you. Entrust him to my care, and I will bring him back.'

[38] But Jacob said, 'My son will not go down there with you; his brother is dead and he is the only one left. If harm comes to him on the journey you are taking, you will bring my grey head down to the grave in sorrow.'

43 Now the famine was still severe in the land. [2] So when they had eaten all the grain they had brought from Egypt, their father said to them, 'Go back and buy us a little more food.'

[3] But Judah said to him, 'The man warned us solemnly, "You will not see my face again unless your brother is with you." [4] If you will send our brother along with us, we will go down and buy food for you. [5] But if you will not send him, we will not go down, because the man said to us, "You will not see my face again unless your brother is with you."'

[6] Israel asked, 'Why did you bring this trouble on me by telling the man you had another brother?'

[7] They replied, 'The man questioned us closely about ourselves and our family. "Is your father still living?" he asked us. "Do you have another brother?" We simply answered his questions. How were we to know he would say, "Bring your brother down here"?'

[8] Then Judah said to Israel his father, 'Send the boy along with me and we will go at once, so that we and you and our children may live and not die. [9] I myself will guarantee his safety; you can hold me personally responsible for him. If I do not bring him back to you and set him here before you, I will bear the blame before you all my life. [10] As it is, if we had not delayed, we could have gone and returned twice.'

[11] Then their father Israel said to them, 'If it must be, then do this: put some of the best products of the land in your bags and take them down to the man as a gift – a little balm and a little honey, some spices and myrrh, some pistachio nuts and almonds. [12] Take double the amount of silver with you, for you must return the silver that was put back into the mouths of your sacks. Perhaps it was a mistake. [13] Take your brother also and go back to the man at once. [14] And may God Almighty grant you mercy before the man so that he will let your other brother and Benjamin come back with you. As for me, if I am bereaved, I am bereaved.'

PSALM 14:1-7

[1] The fool says in his heart,
    'There is no God.'
They are corrupt, their deeds are vile;
    there is no one who does good.

[2] The LORD looks down from heaven
    on all mankind
to see if there are any who understand,

any who seek God.
³ All have turned away, all have become
    corrupt;
  there is no one who does good,
    not even one.

⁴ Do all these evildoers know nothing?

  They devour my people as though eating
    bread;
  they never call on the LORD.
⁵ But there they are, overwhelmed with
    dread,
  for God is present in the company of
    the righteous.
⁶ You evildoers frustrate the plans of the
    poor,
  but the LORD is their refuge.

⁷ Oh, that salvation for Israel would come
    out of Zion!
  When the LORD restores his people,
    let Jacob rejoice and Israel be glad!

▬ PROVERBS 3:13-14

¹³ Blessed are those who find wisdom,
    those who gain understanding,
¹⁴ for she is more profitable than silver
    and yields better returns than gold.

▬ MATTHEW 15:10-39

¹⁰ Jesus called the crowd to him and said,
'Listen and understand. ¹¹What goes into
someone's mouth does not defile them, but
what comes out of their mouth, that is what
defiles them.'
¹² Then the disciples came to him and
asked, 'Do you know that the Pharisees
were offended when they heard this?'
¹³ He replied, 'Every plant that my heavenly Father has not planted will be pulled
up by the roots. ¹⁴Leave them; they are blind

guides. If the blind lead the blind, both will
fall into a pit.'
¹⁵ Peter said, 'Explain the parable to us.'
¹⁶ 'Are you still so dull?' Jesus asked them.
¹⁷ 'Don't you see that whatever enters the
mouth goes into the stomach and then out
of the body? ¹⁸But the things that come out
of a person's mouth come from the heart,
and these defile them. ¹⁹For out of the heart
come evil thoughts – murder, adultery,
sexual immorality, theft, false testimony,
slander. ²⁰These are what defile a person;
but eating with unwashed hands does not
defile them.'
²¹ Leaving that place, Jesus withdrew to
the region of Tyre and Sidon. ²²A Canaanite
woman from that vicinity came to him, crying out, 'Lord, Son of David, have mercy on
me! My daughter is demon-possessed and
suffering terribly.'
²³ Jesus did not answer a word. So his disciples came to him and urged him, 'Send
her away, for she keeps crying out after us.'
²⁴ He answered, 'I was sent only to the lost
sheep of Israel.'
²⁵ The woman came and knelt before
him. 'Lord, help me!' she said.
²⁶ He replied, 'It is not right to take the
children's bread and toss it to the dogs.'
²⁷ 'Yes it is, Lord,' she said. 'Even the dogs
eat the crumbs that fall from their master's
table.'
²⁸ Then Jesus said to her, 'Woman, you
have great faith! Your request is granted.' And her daughter was healed at that
moment.
²⁹ Jesus left there and went along the Sea
of Galilee. Then he went up on a mountainside and sat down. ³⁰Great crowds came
to him, bringing the lame, the blind, the
crippled, the mute and many others, and
laid them at his feet; and he healed them.
³¹ The people were amazed when they saw
the mute speaking, the crippled made well,
the lame walking and the blind seeing. And
they praised the God of Israel.

³²Jesus called his disciples to him and said, 'I have compassion for these people; they have already been with me three days and have nothing to eat. I do not want to send them away hungry, or they may collapse on the way.'

³³His disciples answered, 'Where could we get enough bread in this remote place to feed such a crowd?'

³⁴'How many loaves do you have?' Jesus asked.

'Seven,' they replied, 'and a few small fish.'

³⁵He told the crowd to sit down on the ground. ³⁶Then he took the seven loaves and the fish, and when he had given thanks, he broke them and gave them to the disciples, and they in turn to the people. ³⁷They all ate and were satisfied. Afterwards the disciples picked up seven basketfuls of broken pieces that were left over. ³⁸The number of those who ate was four thousand men, besides women and children. ³⁹After Jesus had sent the crowd away, he got into the boat and went to the vicinity of Magadan.

The God Who Is There

'The fool says in his heart, "There is no God."'
Psalm 14:1

The idea of a living, personal God gives men and women the jitters. They sense deep within that they are accountable to Him, but they don't know just what to do about it.

C. S. Lewis put it like this: 'The Pantheist's God does nothing, demands nothing. He is there if you wish for Him, like a book on a shelf. He will not pursue you. There is no danger that at any time heaven and earth should feel awe at His glance. But Christ the Creator King is there. And His intervening presence is terribly startling to discover.' Lewis goes on to compare the shock of discovering that there is a living, personal God in the universe to sitting alone in the dark and sensing someone breathing beside you. 'It is always shocking,' he says, 'to meet life where we thought we were alone.'

Listen to this paragraph by Lewis which I quote in full, as it puts the truth in a way that cannot be equalled: 'There comes a moment when the children who have been playing at burglars hush suddenly; was that a real footstep in the hall? There comes a moment when people who have been dabbling in religion suddenly draw back. Supposing we really found Him! We never meant it to come to that! Worse still, supposing He has found us? So it is a sort of Rubicon. One goes across, or not. But if one does, there is no manner of security against miracles. One may be in for anything.'

No one need worry about getting any shocks when they steadfastly resist believing in a personal God. No shocks, but no salvation either.

JANUARY 25

PRAYER

Gracious God, how can I ever sufficiently thank You for bringing me to Yourself? The thought of a God who is alive, taking a personal interest in me, is more than I can comprehend. Yet I believe it. With all my heart. Thank You, dear Father. Amen.

FURTHER STUDY

Psa. 10:1-4; 36:1-4; 1 John 2:22
- What is at the heart of the atheist?
- How does John describe those who deny Christ?

January 25

■ GENESIS 43:15–44:34

¹⁵ So the men took the gifts and double the amount of silver, and Benjamin also. They hurried down to Egypt and presented themselves to Joseph. ¹⁶ When Joseph saw Benjamin with them, he said to the steward of his house, 'Take these men to my house, slaughter an animal and prepare a meal; they are to eat with me at noon.'

¹⁷ The man did as Joseph told him and took the men to Joseph's house. ¹⁸ Now the men were frightened when they were taken to Joseph's house. They thought, 'We were brought here because of the silver that was put back into our sacks the first time. He wants to attack us and overpower us and seize us as slaves and take our donkeys.'

¹⁹ So they went up to Joseph's steward and spoke to him at the entrance to the house. ²⁰ 'We beg your pardon, our lord,' they said, 'we came down here the first time to buy food. ²¹ But at the place where we stopped for the night we opened our sacks and each of us found his silver – the exact weight – in the mouth of his sack. So we have brought it back with us. ²² We have also brought additional silver with us to buy food. We don't know who put our silver in our sacks.'

²³ 'It's all right,' he said. 'Don't be afraid. Your God, the God of your father, has given you treasure in your sacks; I received your silver.' Then he brought Simeon out to them.

²⁴ The steward took the men into Joseph's house, gave them water to wash their feet and provided fodder for their donkeys. ²⁵ They prepared their gifts for Joseph's arrival at noon, because they had heard that they were to eat there.

²⁶ When Joseph came home, they presented to him the gifts they had brought into the house, and they bowed down before him to the ground. ²⁷ He asked them how they were, and then he said, 'How is your aged father you told me about? Is he still living?'

²⁸ They replied, 'Your servant our father is still alive and well.' And they bowed down, prostrating themselves before him.

²⁹ As he looked about and saw his brother Benjamin, his own mother's son, he asked, 'Is this your youngest brother, the one you told me about?' And he said, 'God be gracious to you, my son.' ³⁰ Deeply moved at the sight of his brother, Joseph hurried out and looked for a place to weep. He went into his private room and wept there.

³¹ After he had washed his face, he came out and, controlling himself, said, 'Serve the food.'

³²They served him by himself, the brothers by themselves, and the Egyptians who ate with him by themselves, because Egyptians could not eat with Hebrews, for that is detestable to Egyptians. ³³The men had been seated before him in the order of their ages, from the firstborn to the youngest; and they looked at each other in astonishment. ³⁴When portions were served to them from Joseph's table, Benjamin's portion was five times as much as anyone else's. So they feasted and drank freely with him.

44 Now Joseph gave these instructions to the steward of his house: 'Fill the men's sacks with as much food as they can carry, and put each man's silver in the mouth of his sack. ²Then put my cup, the silver one, in the mouth of the youngest one's sack, along with the silver for his grain.' And he did as Joseph said.

³As morning dawned, the men were sent on their way with their donkeys. ⁴They had not gone far from the city when Joseph said to his steward, 'Go after those men at once, and when you catch up with them, say to them, "Why have you repaid good with evil? ⁵Isn't this the cup my master drinks from and also uses for divination? This is a wicked thing you have done."'

⁶When he caught up with them, he repeated these words to them. ⁷But they said to him, 'Why does my lord say such things? Far be it from your servants to do anything like that! ⁸We even brought back to you from the land of Canaan the silver we found inside the mouths of our sacks. So why would we steal silver or gold from your master's house? ⁹If any of your servants is found to have it, he will die; and the rest of us will become my lord's slaves.'

¹⁰'Very well, then,' he said, 'let it be as you say. Whoever is found to have it will become my slave; the rest of you will be free from blame.'

¹¹Each of them quickly lowered his sack to the ground and opened it. ¹²Then the steward proceeded to search, beginning with the eldest and ending with the youngest. And the cup was found in Benjamin's sack. ¹³At this, they tore their clothes. Then they all loaded their donkeys and returned to the city.

¹⁴Joseph was still in the house when Judah and his brothers came in, and they threw themselves to the ground before him. ¹⁵Joseph said to them, 'What is this you have done? Don't you know that a man like me can find things out by divination?'

¹⁶'What can we say to my lord?' Judah replied. 'What can we say? How can we prove our innocence? God has uncovered your servants' guilt. We are now my lord's slaves – we ourselves and the one who was found to have the cup.'

¹⁷But Joseph said, 'Far be it from me to do such a thing! Only the man who was found to have the cup will become my slave. The rest of you, go back to your father in peace.'

¹⁸Then Judah went up to him and said: 'Pardon your servant, my lord, let me speak a word to my lord. Do not be angry with your servant, though you are equal to Pharaoh himself. ¹⁹My lord asked his servants, "Do you have a father or a brother?" ²⁰And we answered, "We have an aged father, and there is a young son born to him in his old age. His brother is dead, and he is the only one of his mother's sons left, and his father loves him."

²¹'Then you said to your servants, "Bring him down to me so I can see him for myself." ²²And we said to my lord, "The boy cannot leave his father; if he leaves him, his father will die." ²³But you told your servants, "Unless your youngest brother comes down with you, you will not see my face again." ²⁴When we went back to your servant my father, we told him what my lord had said.

²⁵'Then our father said, "Go back and buy a little more food." ²⁶But we said, "We cannot go down. Only if our youngest brother is with us will we go. We cannot see

the man's face unless our youngest brother is with us."

²⁷ 'Your servant my father said to us, "You know that my wife bore me two sons. ²⁸ One of them went away from me, and I said, 'He has surely been torn to pieces.' And I have not seen him since. ²⁹ If you take this one from me too and harm comes to him, you will bring my grey head down to the grave in misery."

³⁰ 'So now, if the boy is not with us when I go back to your servant my father, and if my father, whose life is closely bound up with the boy's life, ³¹ sees that the boy isn't there, he will die. Your servants will bring the grey head of our father down to the grave in sorrow. ³² Your servant guaranteed the boy's safety to my father. I said, "If I do not bring him back to you, I will bear the blame before you, my father, all my life!"

³³ 'Now then, please let your servant remain here as my lord's slave in place of the boy, and let the boy return with his brothers. ³⁴ How can I go back to my father if the boy is not with me? No! Do not let me see the misery that would come on my father.'

■ PSALM 15:1-5

¹ LORD, who may dwell in your sacred tent?
   Who may live on your holy mountain?

² The one whose way of life is blameless,
   who does what is righteous,
   who speaks the truth from their heart;
³ whose tongue utters no slander,
   who does no wrong to a neighbour,
   and casts no slur on others;
⁴ who despises a vile person
   but honours those who fear the LORD;
   who keeps an oath even when it hurts,
   and does not change their mind;
⁵ who lends money to the poor without
   interest;

who does not accept a bribe against
   the innocent.

Whoever does these things
   will never be shaken.

■ PROVERBS 3:15-16

¹⁵ She is more precious than rubies;
   nothing you desire can compare with
      her.
¹⁶ Long life is in her right hand;
   in her left hand are riches and honour.

■ MATTHEW 16:1-20

16 The Pharisees and Sadducees came to Jesus and tested him by asking him to show them a sign from heaven.

² He replied, 'When evening comes, you say, "It will be fair weather, for the sky is red," ³ and in the morning, "Today it will be stormy, for the sky is red and overcast." You know how to interpret the appearance of the sky, but you cannot interpret the signs of the times. ⁴ A wicked and adulterous generation looks for a sign, but none will be given it except the sign of Jonah.' Jesus then left them and went away.

⁵ When they went across the lake, the disciples forgot to take bread. ⁶ 'Be careful,' Jesus said to them. 'Be on your guard against the yeast of the Pharisees and Sadducees.'

⁷ They discussed this among themselves and said, 'It is because we didn't bring any bread.'

⁸ Aware of their discussion, Jesus asked, 'You of little faith, why are you talking among yourselves about having no bread? ⁹ Do you still not understand? Don't you remember the five loaves for the five thousand, and how many basketfuls you gathered? ¹⁰ Or the seven loaves for the four thousand, and

how many basketfuls you gathered? [11] How is it you don't understand that I was not talking to you about bread? But be on your guard against the yeast of the Pharisees and Sadducees.' [12] Then they understood that he was not telling them to guard against the yeast used in bread, but against the teaching of the Pharisees and Sadducees.

[13] When Jesus came to the region of Caesarea Philippi, he asked his disciples, 'Who do people say the Son of Man is?'

[14] They replied, 'Some say John the Baptist; others say Elijah; and still others, Jeremiah or one of the prophets.'

[15] 'But what about you?' he asked. 'Who do you say I am?'

[16] Simon Peter answered, 'You are the Messiah, the Son of the living God.'

[17] Jesus replied, 'Blessed are you, Simon son of Jonah, for this was not revealed to you by flesh and blood, but by my Father in heaven. [18] And I tell you that you are Peter, and on this rock I will build my church, and the gates of Hades will not overcome it. [19] I will give you the keys of the kingdom of heaven; whatever you bind on earth will be bound in heaven, and whatever you loose on earth will be loosed in heaven.' [20] Then he ordered his disciples not to tell anyone that he was the Messiah.

A Test of Honesty

'The one whose way of life is blameless, who does what is righteous, who speaks the truth from their heart ...' **Psalm 15:2**

One of the steps toward producing a perfect coordination between our head and our heart involves facing this question: when I pray or seek the Lord, is my heart fully and enthusiastically behind what I am asking for with my lips? If not, we will fail to surmount the heights of God 'with all four feet'.

One of the things that used to puzzle me greatly in the early days of my pastoral ministry was to sit down with people who were not getting what they longed for spiritually and, after hours of counselling, sometimes to discover that although they were asking God for something with their lips, they were not really desiring it deep down in their hearts.

I am thinking specifically of a woman I knew who prayed earnestly (and loudly) in church for the conversion of her non-Christian husband. One day, however, in a moment of great openness and honesty (such as often occurs in counselling) she admitted that deep down in her heart she didn't really want her husband to be converted because she was afraid that if he was, the attention and sympathy she was getting from people in the church would no longer be there. Once she realised what was going on inside her, however, she was able to deal with it and became one of the most spiritually released women I have ever known. Her whole life (not just her prayer life) became one of deep, quiet conviction, and eventually - many years later - she had the joy of seeing her husband surrender to Christ.

PRAYER

My Father, one thing is clear – such are the subterfuges of the human heart that without Your light and guidance, I can be self-deceived. Help me to apply the test of honesty and openness to my own spiritual life. In Jesus' name. Amen.

FURTHER STUDY

Jer. 17:1-10; 23:24; 1 Cor. 3:20
• How does Jeremiah describe the heart?
• How does the Lord view the thoughts of the worldly wise?

January 26

■ GENESIS 45:1–46:27

45 Then Joseph could no longer control himself before all his attendants, and he cried out, 'Make everyone leave my presence!' So there was no one with Joseph when he made himself known to his brothers. ²And he wept so loudly that the Egyptians heard him, and Pharaoh's household heard about it.

³Joseph said to his brothers, 'I am Joseph! Is my father still living?' But his brothers were not able to answer him, because they were terrified at his presence.

⁴Then Joseph said to his brothers, 'Come close to me.' When they had done so, he said, 'I am your brother Joseph, the one you sold into Egypt! ⁵And now, do not be distressed and do not be angry with yourselves for selling me here, because it was to save lives that God sent me ahead of you. ⁶For two years now there has been famine in the land, and for the next five years there will be no ploughing and reaping. ⁷But God sent me ahead of you to preserve for you a remnant on earth and to save your lives by a great deliverance.

⁸'So then, it was not you who sent me here, but God. He made me father to Pharaoh, lord of his entire household and ruler of all Egypt. ⁹Now hurry back to my father and say to him, "This is what your son Joseph says: God has made me lord of all Egypt. Come down to me; don't delay. ¹⁰You shall live in the region of Goshen and be near me – you, your children and grandchildren, your flocks and herds, and all you have. ¹¹I will provide for you there, because five years of famine are still to come. Otherwise you and your household and all who belong to you will become destitute."

¹²'You can see for yourselves, and so can my brother Benjamin, that it is really I who am speaking to you. ¹³Tell my father about all the honour accorded me in Egypt and about everything you have seen. And bring my father down here quickly.'

¹⁴Then he threw his arms around his brother Benjamin and wept, and Benjamin embraced him, weeping. ¹⁵And he kissed all his brothers and wept over them. Afterwards his brothers talked with him.

¹⁶When the news reached Pharaoh's palace that Joseph's brothers had come, Pharaoh and all his officials were pleased. ¹⁷Pharaoh said to Joseph, 'Tell your brothers, "Do this: load your animals and return to the land of Canaan, ¹⁸and bring your father and your families back to me. I will give you the best of the land of Egypt and you can enjoy the fat of the land."

¹⁹'You are also instructed to tell them,

"Do this: take some carts from Egypt for your children and your wives, and get your father and come. ²⁰Never mind about your belongings, because the best of all Egypt will be yours."'

²¹So the sons of Israel did this. Joseph gave them carts, as Pharaoh had commanded, and he also gave them provisions for their journey. ²²To each of them he gave new clothing, but to Benjamin he gave three hundred shekels of silver and five sets of clothes. ²³And this is what he sent to his father: ten donkeys loaded with the best things of Egypt, and ten female donkeys loaded with grain and bread and other provisions for his journey. ²⁴Then he sent his brothers away, and as they were leaving he said to them, 'Don't quarrel on the way!'

²⁵So they went up out of Egypt and came to their father Jacob in the land of Canaan. ²⁶They told him, 'Joseph is still alive! In fact, he is ruler of all Egypt.' Jacob was stunned; he did not believe them. ²⁷But when they told him everything Joseph had said to them, and when he saw the carts Joseph had sent to carry him back, the spirit of their father Jacob revived. ²⁸And Israel said, 'I'm convinced! My son Joseph is still alive. I will go and see him before I die.'

46 So Israel set out with all that was his, and when he reached Beersheba, he offered sacrifices to the God of his father Isaac.

²And God spoke to Israel in a vision at night and said, 'Jacob! Jacob!'

'Here I am,' he replied.

³'I am God, the God of your father,' he said. 'Do not be afraid to go down to Egypt, for I will make you into a great nation there. ⁴I will go down to Egypt with you, and I will surely bring you back again. And Joseph's own hand will close your eyes.'

⁵Then Jacob left Beersheba, and Israel's sons took their father Jacob and their children and their wives in the carts that Pharaoh had sent to transport him. ⁶So Jacob and all his offspring went to Egypt, taking with them their livestock and the possessions they had acquired in Canaan. ⁷Jacob brought with him to Egypt his sons and grandsons and his daughters and granddaughters – all his offspring.

⁸These are the names of the sons of Israel (Jacob and his descendants) who went to Egypt:

Reuben the firstborn of Jacob.
⁹The sons of Reuben:
Hanok, Pallu, Hezron and Karmi.
¹⁰The sons of Simeon:
Jemuel, Jamin, Ohad, Jakin, Zohar and Shaul the son of a Canaanite woman.
¹¹The sons of Levi:
Gershon, Kohath and Merari.
¹²The sons of Judah:
Er, Onan, Shelah, Perez and Zerah (but Er and Onan had died in the land of Canaan).
The sons of Perez:
Hezron and Hamul.
¹³The sons of Issachar:
Tola, Puah, Jashub and Shimron.
¹⁴The sons of Zebulun:
Sered, Elon and Jahleel.
¹⁵These were the sons Leah bore to Jacob in Paddan Aram, besides his daughter Dinah. These sons and daughters of his were thirty-three in all.

¹⁶The sons of Gad:
Zephon, Haggi, Shuni, Ezbon, Eri, Arodi and Areli.
¹⁷The sons of Asher:
Imnah, Ishvah, Ishvi and Beriah.
Their sister was Serah.
The sons of Beriah:
Heber and Malkiel.
¹⁸These were the children born to Jacob by Zilpah, whom Laban had given to his daughter Leah – sixteen in all.

¹⁹ The sons of Jacob's wife Rachel:
Joseph and Benjamin. ²⁰ In Egypt,
Manasseh and Ephraim were born
to Joseph by Asenath daughter of
Potiphera, priest of On.
²¹ The sons of Benjamin:
Bela, Beker, Ashbel, Gera, Naaman,
Ehi, Rosh, Muppim, Huppim and
Ard.
²² These were the sons of Rachel who were
born to Jacob – fourteen in all.

²³ The son of Dan:
Hushim.
²⁴ The sons of Naphtali:
Jahziel, Guni, Jezer and Shillem.
²⁵ These were the sons born to Jacob
by Bilhah, whom Laban had given to his
daughter Rachel – seven in all.

²⁶ All those who went to Egypt with
Jacob – those who were his direct descendants, not counting his sons' wives – numbered sixty-six persons. ²⁷ With the two
sons who had been born to Joseph in Egypt,
the members of Jacob's family, which went
to Egypt, were seventy in all.

■ PSALM 16:1-6

¹ Keep me safe, my God,
for in you I take refuge.

² I say to the LORD, 'You are my Lord;
apart from you I have no good thing.'
³ I say of the holy people who are in the land,
'They are the noble ones in whom is all
my delight.'
⁴ Those who run after other gods will
suffer more and more.
I will not pour out libations of blood to
such gods
or take up their names on my lips.

⁵ LORD, you alone are my portion and my
cup;
you make my lot secure.
⁶ The boundary lines have fallen for me in
pleasant places;
surely I have a delightful inheritance.

■ PROVERBS 3:17-18

¹⁷ Her ways are pleasant ways,
and all her paths are peace.
¹⁸ She is a tree of life to those who take hold
of her;
those who hold her fast will be blessed.

■ MATTHEW 16:21–17:13

²¹ From that time on Jesus began to explain to his disciples that he must go to
Jerusalem and suffer many things at the
hands of the elders, the chief priests and
the teachers of the law, and that he must be
killed and on the third day be raised to life.
²² Peter took him aside and began to rebuke him. 'Never, Lord!' he said. 'This shall
never happen to you!'
²³ Jesus turned and said to Peter, 'Get behind me, Satan! You are a stumbling-block
to me; you do not have in mind the concerns
of God, but merely human concerns.'
²⁴ Then Jesus said to his disciples, 'Whoever wants to be my disciple must deny
themselves and take up their cross and follow me. ²⁵ For whoever wants to save their
life will lose it, but whoever loses their life
for me will find it. ²⁶ What good will it be for
someone to gain the whole world, yet forfeit
their soul? Or what can anyone give in exchange for their soul? ²⁷ For the Son of Man
is going to come in his Father's glory with
his angels, and then he will reward each
person according to what they have done.
²⁸ 'Truly I tell you, some who are standing here will not taste death before they see

the Son of Man coming in his kingdom.'

17 After six days Jesus took with him Peter, James and John the brother of James, and led them up a high mountain by themselves. ²There he was transfigured before them. His face shone like the sun, and his clothes became as white as the light. ³Just then there appeared before them Moses and Elijah, talking with Jesus.

⁴Peter said to Jesus, 'Lord, it is good for us to be here. If you wish, I will put up three shelters – one for you, one for Moses and one for Elijah.'

⁵While he was still speaking, a bright cloud covered them, and a voice from the cloud said, 'This is my Son, whom I love; with him I am well pleased. Listen to him!'

⁶When the disciples heard this, they fell face down to the ground, terrified. ⁷But Jesus came and touched them. 'Get up,' he said. 'Don't be afraid.' ⁸When they looked up, they saw no one except Jesus.

⁹As they were coming down the mountain, Jesus instructed them, 'Don't tell anyone what you have seen, until the Son of Man has been raised from the dead.'

¹⁰The disciples asked him, 'Why then do the teachers of the law say that Elijah must come first?'

¹¹Jesus replied, 'To be sure, Elijah comes and will restore all things. ¹²But I tell you, Elijah has already come, and they did not recognise him, but have done to him everything they wished. In the same way the Son of Man is going to suffer at their hands.' ¹³Then the disciples understood that he was talking to them about John the Baptist.

'To Look at You'

'... they saw no-one except Jesus.' **Matthew 17:8**

When we gaze at Christ's face and make Him the centre of our attention and love, then we are gradually and continuously changed into the likeness of Christ. Thus we are transformed from one degree of glory to another, the Spirit within us being the silent Artist who makes us into His image. We become like Him in character and in countenance.

A young man was so much like his father in appearance that it prompted everyone who knew him to comment on the fact. The mother said: 'It's strange, because when Andrew was a small child, he looked so much like me. Then, when he was about five, he became intrigued with being with his father. He used to go into his father's study and sit there until his father would say, "Is there anything you want?" Andrew would reply, "No, I don't want anything; I just want to look at you." He would sit there and lovingly gaze into his father's face for such a long time that I honestly believe this is how he has come to look so much like him.'

Just as there is a law in photography that says: 'The angle of incidence equals the angle of reflection' - in other words, if you want a full-face reproduction, you must look full-face into the camera - so there is a law in life that causes us to become like that on which we gaze. If we look sideways on Christ, we get only a partial reflection. If we look fully at Him, we get a full reflection. We become like that on which we gaze.

January 27

■ GENESIS 46:28–48:22

28 Now Jacob sent Judah ahead of him to Joseph to get directions to Goshen. When they arrived in the region of Goshen, 29 Joseph had his chariot made ready and went to Goshen to meet his father Israel. As soon as Joseph appeared before him, he threw his arms around his father and wept for a long time.

30 Israel said to Joseph, 'Now I am ready to die, since I have seen for myself that you are still alive.'

31 Then Joseph said to his brothers and to his father's household, 'I will go up and speak to Pharaoh and will say to him, "My brothers and my father's household, who were living in the land of Canaan, have come to me. 32 The men are shepherds; they tend livestock, and they have brought along their flocks and herds and everything they own." 33 When Pharaoh calls you in and asks, "What is your occupation?" 34 you should answer, "Your servants have tended livestock from our boyhood on, just as our fathers did." Then you will be allowed to settle in the region of Goshen, for all shepherds are detestable to the Egyptians.'

47 Joseph went and told Pharaoh, 'My father and brothers, with their flocks and herds and everything they own,

have come from the land of Canaan and are now in Goshen.' 2 He chose five of his brothers and presented them before Pharaoh.

3 Pharaoh asked the brothers, 'What is your occupation?'

'Your servants are shepherds,' they replied to Pharaoh, 'just as our fathers were.' 4 They also said to him, 'We have come to live here for a while, because the famine is severe in Canaan and your servants' flocks have no pasture. So now, please let your servants settle in Goshen.'

5 Pharaoh said to Joseph, 'Your father and your brothers have come to you, 6 and the land of Egypt is before you; settle your father and your brothers in the best part of the land. Let them live in Goshen. And if you know of any among them with special ability, put them in charge of my own livestock.'

7 Then Joseph brought his father Jacob in and presented him before Pharaoh. After Jacob blessed Pharaoh, 8 Pharaoh asked him, 'How old are you?'

9 And Jacob said to Pharaoh, 'The years of my pilgrimage are a hundred and thirty. My years have been few and difficult, and they do not equal the years of the pilgrimage of my fathers.' 10 Then Jacob blessed Pharaoh and went out from his presence.

11 So Joseph settled his father and his

brothers in Egypt and gave them property in the best part of the land, the district of Rameses, as Pharaoh directed. ¹²Joseph also provided his father and his brothers and all his father's household with food, according to the number of their children.

¹³There was no food, however, in the whole region because the famine was severe; both Egypt and Canaan wasted away because of the famine. ¹⁴Joseph collected all the money that was to be found in Egypt and Canaan in payment for the grain they were buying, and he brought it to Pharaoh's palace. ¹⁵When the money of the people of Egypt and Canaan was gone, all Egypt came to Joseph and said, 'Give us food. Why should we die before your eyes? Our money is all gone.'

¹⁶'Then bring your livestock,' said Joseph. 'I will sell you food in exchange for your livestock, since your money is gone.' ¹⁷So they brought their livestock to Joseph, and he gave them food in exchange for their horses, their sheep and goats, their cattle and donkeys. And he brought them through that year with food in exchange for all their livestock.

¹⁸When that year was over, they came to him the following year and said, 'We cannot hide from our lord the fact that since our money is gone and our livestock belongs to you, there is nothing left for our lord except our bodies and our land. ¹⁹Why should we perish before your eyes – we and our land as well? Buy us and our land in exchange for food, and we with our land will be in bondage to Pharaoh. Give us seed so that we may live and not die, and that the land may not become desolate.'

²⁰So Joseph bought all the land in Egypt for Pharaoh. The Egyptians, one and all, sold their fields, because the famine was too severe for them. The land became Pharaoh's, ²¹and Joseph reduced the people to servitude, from one end of Egypt to the other. ²²However, he did not buy the land of the priests, because they received a fixed allowance from Pharaoh and had food enough from the allowance Pharaoh gave them. That is why they did not sell their land.

²³Joseph said to the people, 'Now that I have bought you and your land today for Pharaoh, here is seed for you so you can plant the ground. ²⁴But when the crop comes in, give a fifth of it to Pharaoh. The other four-fifths you may keep as seed for the fields and as food for yourselves and your households and your children.'

²⁵'You have saved our lives,' they said. 'May we find favour in the eyes of our lord; we will be in bondage to Pharaoh.'

²⁶So Joseph established it as a law concerning land in Egypt – still in force today – that a fifth of the produce belongs to Pharaoh. It was only the land of the priests that did not become Pharaoh's.

²⁷Now the Israelites settled in Egypt in the region of Goshen. They acquired property there and were fruitful and increased greatly in number.

²⁸Jacob lived in Egypt seventeen years, and the years of his life were a hundred and forty-seven. ²⁹When the time drew near for Israel to die, he called for his son Joseph and said to him, 'If I have found favour in your eyes, put your hand under my thigh and promise that you will show me kindness and faithfulness. Do not bury me in Egypt, ³⁰but when I rest with my fathers, carry me out of Egypt and bury me where they are buried.'

'I will do as you say,' he said.

³¹'Swear to me,' he said. Then Joseph swore to him, and Israel worshipped as he leaned on the top of his staff.

48 Some time later Joseph was told, 'Your father is ill.' So he took his two sons Manasseh and Ephraim along with him. ²When Jacob was told, 'Your son Joseph has come to you,' Israel rallied his strength and sat up on the bed.

³Jacob said to Joseph, 'God Almighty appeared to me at Luz in the land of Canaan,

and there he blessed me [4] and said to me, "I am going to make you fruitful and increase your numbers. I will make you a community of peoples, and I will give this land as an everlasting possession to your descendants after you."

[5] 'Now then, your two sons born to you in Egypt before I came to you here will be reckoned as mine; Ephraim and Manasseh will be mine, just as Reuben and Simeon are mine. [6] Any children born to you after them will be yours; in the territory they inherit they will be reckoned under the names of their brothers. [7] As I was returning from Paddan, to my sorrow Rachel died in the land of Canaan while we were still on the way, a little distance from Ephrath. So I buried her there beside the road to Ephrath' (that is, Bethlehem).

[8] When Israel saw the sons of Joseph, he asked, 'Who are these?'

[9] 'They are the sons God has given me here,' Joseph said to his father.

Then Israel said, 'Bring them to me so that I may bless them.'

[10] Now Israel's eyes were failing because of old age, and he could hardly see. So Joseph brought his sons close to him, and his father kissed them and embraced them.

[11] Israel said to Joseph, 'I never expected to see your face again, and now God has allowed me to see your children too.'

[12] Then Joseph removed them from Israel's knees and bowed down with his face to the ground. [13] And Joseph took both of them, Ephraim on his right towards Israel's left hand and Manasseh on his left towards Israel's right hand, and brought them close to him. [14] But Israel reached out his right hand and put it on Ephraim's head, though he was the younger, and crossing his arms, he put his left hand on Manasseh's head, even though Manasseh was the firstborn. [15] Then he blessed Joseph and said,

'May the God before whom my fathers

Abraham and Isaac walked faithfully,
the God who has been my shepherd
  all my life to this day,
[16] the Angel who has delivered me from all
  harm
  – may he bless these boys.
May they be called by my name
  and the names of my fathers Abraham
    and Isaac,
and may they increase greatly
  on the earth.'

[17] When Joseph saw his father placing his right hand on Ephraim's head he was displeased; so he took hold of his father's hand to move it from Ephraim's head to Manasseh's head. [18] Joseph said to him, 'No, my father, this one is the firstborn; put your right hand on his head.'

[19] But his father refused and said, 'I know, my son, I know. He too will become a people, and he too will become great. Nevertheless, his younger brother will be greater than he, and his descendants will become a group of nations.' [20] He blessed them that day and said,

'In your name will Israel pronounce this
    blessing:
  "May God make you like Ephraim and
    Manasseh."'

So he put Ephraim ahead of Manasseh.

[21] Then Israel said to Joseph, 'I am about to die, but God will be with you and take you back to the land of your fathers. [22] And to you I give one more ridge of land than to your brothers, the ridge I took from the Amorites with my sword and my bow.'

▬ PSALM 16:7-11

[7] I will praise the LORD, who counsels me;
  even at night my heart instructs me.
[8] I keep my eyes always on the LORD.

With him at my right hand, I shall not
be shaken.

9 Therefore my heart is glad and my
tongue rejoices;
my body also will rest secure,
10 because you will not abandon me to the
realm of the dead,
nor will you let your faithful one see
decay.
11 You make known to me the path of life;
you will fill me with joy in your
presence,
with eternal pleasures at your right
hand.

■ PROVERBS 3:19-20

19 By wisdom the LORD laid the earth's
foundations,
by understanding he set the heavens
in place;
20 by his knowledge the watery depths were
divided,
and the clouds let drop the dew.

■ MATTHEW 17:14-18:9

14 When they came to the crowd, a man
approached Jesus and knelt before him.
15 'Lord, have mercy on my son,' he said.
'He has seizures and is suffering greatly.
He often falls into the fire or into the water.
16 I brought him to your disciples, but they
could not heal him.'
17 'You unbelieving and perverse generation,' Jesus replied, 'how long shall I stay
with you? How long shall I put up with you?
Bring the boy here to me.' 18 Jesus rebuked
the demon, and it came out of the boy, and
he was healed at that moment.
19 Then the disciples came to Jesus in
private and asked, 'Why couldn't we drive
it out?'

20 He replied, 'Because you have so little
faith. Truly I tell you, if you have faith as
small as a mustard seed, you can say to this
mountain, "Move from here to there," and
it will move. Nothing will be impossible for
you.' [21] a
22 When they came together in Galilee,
he said to them, 'The Son of Man is going to
be delivered into the hands of men. 23 They
will kill him, and on the third day he will be
raised to life.' And the disciples were filled
with grief.
24 After Jesus and his disciples arrived
in Capernaum, the collectors of the two-
drachma temple tax came to Peter and
asked, 'Doesn't your teacher pay the temple
tax?'
25 'Yes, he does,' he replied.
When Peter came into the house, Jesus
was the first to speak. 'What do you think,
Simon?' he asked. 'From whom do the kings
of the earth collect duty and taxes – from
their own children or from others?'
26 'From others,' Peter answered.
'Then the children are exempt,' Jesus
said to him. 27 'But so that we may not cause
offence, go to the lake and throw out your
line. Take the first fish you catch; open its
mouth and you will find a four-drachma
coin. Take it and give it to them for my tax
and yours.'

18 At that time the disciples came to
Jesus and asked, 'Who, then, is the
greatest in the kingdom of heaven?'
2 He called a little child to him, and placed
the child among them. 3 And he said: 'Truly I tell you, unless you change and become
like little children, you will never enter the
kingdom of heaven. 4 Therefore, whoever
takes the lowly position of this child is the
greatest in the kingdom of heaven. 5 And
whoever welcomes one such child in my
name welcomes me.
6 'If anyone causes one of these little

a Some manuscripts include here words similar to Mark 9:29

ones – those who believe in me – to stumble, it would be better for them to have a large millstone hung round their neck and to be drowned in the depths of the sea. [7] Woe to the world because of the things that cause people to stumble! Such things must come, but woe to the person through whom they come! [8] If your hand or your foot causes you to stumble, cut it off and throw it away. It is better for you to enter life maimed or crippled than to have two hands or two feet and be thrown into eternal fire. [9] And if your eye causes you to stumble, gouge it out and throw it away. It is better for you to enter life with one eye than to have two eyes and be thrown into the fire of hell.

Stirred, But Not Shaken

'With him at my right hand, I shall not be shaken.'
Psalm 16:8

Whenever I have the opportunity to address Christian counsellors, I try to encourage them to put first the work of God in an individual's life. A good deal of Christian counselling today follows the client-centred approach, where the person is all-important. There is a danger that an unbalanced attention and focus is given to the person and how they have been hurt by others, missing the vital elements of God dependency and thus allowing a victim mentality to develop. This is, however, a delicate and sensitive issue and is explored when other issues have been understood. But ultimately, however, this is the issue we must all face, whether we are in counselling or not.

Ask yourself this question now: do I allow myself to be more overwhelmed by the wrong which people have done to me than the wrong I might have done (and may still be doing) to God by my unwillingness to trust Him? Putting the glory of God before our well-being does not go down well with some modern-day Christians brought up in the 'me' generation. It means that we have to break away from the idea that life revolves around our desires, our ambitions, our self-image, our personal comfort, our hurts, and our problems, and embrace the fact that it revolves instead around the glory and the will of God. When we learn to apply the great text before us today to our lives, we will find, as did the psalmist, that when we set the Lord always before us, then no matter what happens, we will be stirred but not shaken.

PRAYER

Father, thank You for reminding me that I cannot avoid my soul being 'stirred' by life's problems, but when I have set You ever before me, then I can avoid being 'shaken'. Drive this truth deep into my being this very day. In Jesus' name. Amen.

FURTHER STUDY

1 Sam. 4:1-22; Exod. 33:12-18; Psa. 29:1-2
• Is there a parallel between this account and today's church?
• What was Moses' request?

January 28

▬ GENESIS 49:1–50:26

49 Then Jacob called for his sons and said: 'Gather round so that I can tell you what will happen to you in days to come.

2 'Assemble and listen, sons of Jacob;
    listen to your father Israel.

3 'Reuben, you are my firstborn,
    my might, the first sign of my strength,
    excelling in honour, excelling in power.
4 Turbulent as the waters, you will no
        longer excel,
    for you went up onto your father's bed,
    onto my couch and defiled it.

5 'Simeon and Levi are brothers –
    their swords are weapons of violence.
6 Let me not enter their council,
    let me not join their assembly,
    for they have killed men in their anger
    and hamstrung oxen as they pleased.
7 Cursed be their anger, so fierce,
    and their fury, so cruel!
I will scatter them in Jacob
    and disperse them in Israel.

8 'Judah, your brothers will praise you;
    your hand will be on the neck of your
        enemies;
    your father's sons will bow down to
        you.
9 You are a lion's cub, Judah;
    you return from the prey, my son.
Like a lion he crouches and lies down,
    like a lioness – who dares to rouse him?
10 The sceptre will not depart from Judah,
    nor the ruler's staff from between his
        feet,
    until he to whom it belongs shall come

and the obedience of the nations shall
    be his.
11 He will tether his donkey to a vine,
    his colt to the choicest branch;
    he will wash his garments in wine,
    his robes in the blood of grapes.
12 His eyes will be darker than wine,
    his teeth whiter than milk.

13 'Zebulun will live by the seashore
    and become a haven for ships;
    his border will extend towards Sidon.

14 'Issachar is a scrawny donkey
    lying down among the sheepfolds.
15 When he sees how good is his resting
        place
    and how pleasant is his land,
    he will bend his shoulder to the burden
    and submit to forced labour.

16 'Dan will provide justice for his people
    as one of the tribes of Israel.
17 Dan will be a snake by the roadside,
    a viper along the path,
    that bites the horse's heels
    so that its rider tumbles backwards.

18 'I look for your deliverance, LORD.

19 'Gad will be attacked by a band of raiders,
    but he will attack them at their heels.

20 'Asher's food will be rich;
    he will provide delicacies fit for a king.

21 'Naphtali is a doe set free
    that bears beautiful fawns.

22 'Joseph is a fruitful vine,
    a fruitful vine near a spring,

whose branches climb over a wall.
23 With bitterness archers attacked him;
    they shot at him with hostility.
24 But his bow remained steady,
    his strong arms stayed supple,
  because of the hand of the Mighty One of
    Jacob,
  because of the Shepherd, the Rock of
    Israel,
25 because of your father's God, who helps
    you,
  because of the Almighty, who blesses
    you
  with blessings of the skies above,
    blessings of the deep springs below,
    blessings of the breast and womb.
26 Your father's blessings are greater
    than the blessings of the ancient
    mountains,
    than the bounty of the age-old hills.
  Let all these rest on the head of Joseph,
    on the brow of the prince among his
    brothers.

27 'Benjamin is a ravenous wolf;
    in the morning he devours the prey,
    in the evening he divides the plunder.'

28 All these are the twelve tribes of Isra-el, and this is what their father said to them when he blessed them, giving each the blessing appropriate to him.

29 Then he gave them these instructions: 'I am about to be gathered to my people. Bury me with my fathers in the cave in the field of Ephron the Hittite, 30 the cave in the field of Machpelah, near Mamre in Canaan, which Abraham bought along with the field as a burial place from Ephron the Hittite. 31 There Abraham and his wife Sarah were buried, there Isaac and his wife Rebekah were buried, and there I buried Leah. 32 The field and the cave in it were bought from the Hittites.'

33 When Jacob had finished giving in-structions to his sons, he drew his feet up into the bed, breathed his last and was gatherered to his people.

50 Joseph threw himself on his fa-ther and wept over him and kissed him. 2 Then Joseph directed the physicians in his service to embalm his father Israel. So the physicians embalmed him, 3 taking a full forty days, for that was the time re-quired for embalming. And the Egyptians mourned for him seventy days.

4 When the days of mourning had passed, Joseph said to Pharaoh's court, 'If I have found favour in your eyes, speak to Phar-aoh for me. Tell him, 5 "My father made me swear an oath and said, 'I am about to die; bury me in the tomb I dug for myself in the land of Canaan.' Now let me go up and bury my father; then I will return."'

6 Pharaoh said, 'Go up and bury your fa-ther, as he made you swear to do.'

7 So Joseph went up to bury his father. All Pharaoh's officials accompanied him – the dignitaries of his court and all the digni-taries of Egypt – 8 besides all the members of Joseph's household and his brothers and those belonging to his father's household. Only their children and their flocks and herds were left in Goshen. 9 Chariots and horsemen also went up with him. It was a very large company.

10 When they reached the threshing-floor of Atad, near the Jordan, they lamented loudly and bitterly; and there Joseph ob-served a seven-day period of mourning for his father. 11 When the Canaanites who lived there saw the mourning at the threshing-floor of Atad, they said, 'The Egyptians are holding a solemn ceremony of mourning.' That is why that place near the Jordan is called Abel Mizraim.

12 So Jacob's sons did as he had command-ed them: 13 they carried him to the land of Canaan and buried him in the cave in the field of Machpelah, near Mamre, which Abraham had bought along with the field as a burial place from Ephron the Hittite.

¹⁴ After burying his father, Joseph returned to Egypt, together with his brothers and all the others who had gone with him to bury his father.

¹⁵ When Joseph's brothers saw that their father was dead, they said, 'What if Joseph holds a grudge against us and pays us back for all the wrongs we did to him?' ¹⁶ So they sent word to Joseph, saying, 'Your father left these instructions before he died: ¹⁷ "This is what you are to say to Joseph: I ask you to forgive your brothers the sins and the wrongs they committed in treating you so badly." Now please forgive the sins of the servants of the God of your father.' When their message came to him, Joseph wept.

¹⁸ His brothers then came and threw themselves down before him. 'We are your slaves,' they said.

¹⁹ But Joseph said to them, 'Don't be afraid. Am I in the place of God? ²⁰ You intended to harm me, but God intended it for good to accomplish what is now being done, the saving of many lives. ²¹ So then, don't be afraid. I will provide for you and your children.' And he reassured them and spoke kindly to them.

²² Joseph stayed in Egypt, along with all his father's family. He lived a hundred and ten years ²³ and saw the third generation of Ephraim's children. Also the children of Makir son of Manasseh were placed at birth on Joseph's knees.

²⁴ Then Joseph said to his brothers, 'I am about to die. But God will surely come to your aid and take you up out of this land to the land he promised on oath to Abraham, Isaac and Jacob.' ²⁵ And Joseph made the Israelites swear an oath and said, 'God will surely come to your aid, and then you must carry my bones up from this place.'

²⁶ So Joseph died at the age of a hundred and ten. And after they embalmed him, he was placed in a coffin in Egypt.

▬ PSALM 17:1-5

¹ Hear me, LORD, my plea is just;
    listen to my cry.
Hear my prayer –
    it does not rise from deceitful lips.
² Let my vindication come from you;
    may your eyes see what is right.

³ Though you probe my heart,
    though you examine me at night and
        test me,
you will find that I have planned no evil;
    my mouth has not transgressed.
⁴ Though people tried to bribe me,
    I have kept myself from the ways of the
        violent
through what your lips have
        commanded.
⁵ My steps have held to your paths;
    my feet have not stumbled.

▬ PROVERBS 3:21-24

²¹ My son, do not let wisdom and
        understanding out of your sight,
    preserve sound judgment and
        discretion;
²² they will be life for you,
    an ornament to grace your neck.
²³ Then you will go on your way in safety,
    and your foot will not stumble.
²⁴ When you lie down, you will not be afraid;
    when you lie down, your sleep will be
        sweet.

▬ MATTHEW 18:10-35

¹⁰ 'See that you do not despise one of these little ones. For I tell you that their angels in heaven always see the face of my Father in heaven. [11] a

---

a Some manuscripts include here the words of Luke 19:10

12 'What do you think? If a man owns a hundred sheep, and one of them wanders away, will he not leave the ninety-nine on the hills and go to look for the one that wandered off? 13 And if he finds it, truly I tell you, he is happier about that one sheep than about the ninety-nine that did not wander off. 14 In the same way your Father in heaven is not willing that any of these little ones should perish.

15 'If your brother or sister sins, go and point out their fault, just between the two of you. If they listen to you, you have won them over. 16 But if they will not listen, take one or two others along, so that "every matter may be established by the testimony of two or three witnesses." 17 If they still refuse to listen, tell it to the church; and if they refuse to listen even to the church, treat them as you would a pagan or a tax collector.

18 'Truly I tell you, whatever you bind on earth will be bound in heaven, and whatever you loose on earth will be loosed in heaven.

19 'Again, truly I tell you that if two of you on earth agree about anything they ask for, it will be done for them by my Father in heaven. 20 For where two or three gather in my name, there am I with them.'

21 Then Peter came to Jesus and asked, 'Lord, how many times shall I forgive my brother or sister who sins against me? Up to seven times?'

22 Jesus answered, 'I tell you, not seven times, but seventy-seven times.

23 'Therefore, the kingdom of heaven is like a king who wanted to settle accounts with his servants. 24 As he began the settlement, a man who owed him ten thousand bags of gold was brought to him. 25 Since he was not able to pay, the master ordered that he and his wife and his children and all that he had be sold to repay the debt.

26 'At this the servant fell on his knees before him. "Be patient with me," he begged, "and I will pay back everything." 27 The servant's master took pity on him, cancelled the debt and let him go.

28 'But when that servant went out, he found one of his fellow servants who owed him a hundred silver coins. He grabbed him and began to choke him. "Pay back what you owe me!" he demanded.

29 'His fellow servant fell to his knees and begged him, "Be patient with me, and I will pay it back."

30 'But he refused. Instead, he went off and had the man thrown into prison until he could pay the debt. 31 When the other servants saw what had happened, they were outraged and went and told their master everything that had happened.

32 'Then the master called the servant in. "You wicked servant," he said, "I cancelled all that debt of yours because you begged me to. 33 Shouldn't you have had mercy on your fellow servant just as I had on you?" 34 In anger his master handed him over to the jailers to be tortured, until he should pay back all he owed.

35 'This is how my heavenly Father will treat each of you unless you forgive your brother or sister from your heart.'

Sand in the Machinery

'"I cancelled all that debt of yours because you begged me to. Shouldn't you have had mercy on your fellow-servant just as I had on you?"' **Matthew 18:32-33**

I f we are to maintain spiritual freshness, we must determine to forgive everyone who hurts us and refuse to nurse a grudge. Grudges become glooms.

A few years after World War II, a Christian Japanese boy at a public speaking contest announced that his subject would be 'The Sacredness of Work.' Some people smiled at his choice, but when they heard his story, their smiles turned to tears. His parents and home were burned to ashes in the atomic bomb explosion at Nagasaki. He was the eldest of three surviving children, and together they knelt in the ashes of their home and prayed to know what to do. One of them said, 'I know - we can work.' So they set to work, gathering bits of tin and boards, and soon they had built a little hut in which to live. They could have nursed their grudge and become gloomy; instead they forgave, forgot, and went to work.

No one who wants to maintain spiritual freshness can afford to nurse a grudge. It will poison both spirit and body. As one doctor put it, 'Grudges put the whole physical and mental system on a war basis instead of on a peace basis.'

Walter Alvarez, who is both a medical doctor and counsellor, says, 'I often tell patients they cannot afford to carry grudges or maintain hates. Such things can make them ill and tire them out. I once saw a man kill himself inch by inch, simply by thinking of nothing but hatred for a relative who had sued him. Within a year or two he was dead.' A grudge or a resentment is sand in the machinery of living.

PRAYER

O Father, teach me how to get the splinters of resentment out of my soul and also out of my body. Help me to decide that it is the oil of love, not the sand of resentments, that shall go into the machinery of my life day by day. Amen.

FURTHER STUDY

Eph.4:21-32; Rom. 3:14; Heb. 12:15
• What should not come out of our mouths?
• What are we to do?

January 29

EXODUS 1:1–2:25

1 These are the names of the sons of Israel who went to Egypt with Jacob, each with his family: ² Reuben, Simeon, Levi and Judah; ³ Issachar, Zebulun and Benjamin; ⁴ Dan and Naphtali; Gad and Asher. ⁵ The descendants of Jacob numbered seventy in all; Joseph was already in Egypt.

⁶ Now Joseph and all his brothers and all that generation died, ⁷ but the Israelites were exceedingly fruitful; they multiplied greatly, increased in numbers and became so numerous that the land was filled with them.

⁸ Then a new king, to whom Joseph meant

nothing, came to power in Egypt. ⁹'Look,' he said to his people, 'the Israelites have become far too numerous for us. ¹⁰Come, we must deal shrewdly with them or they will become even more numerous and, if war breaks out, will join our enemies, fight against us and leave the country.'

¹¹So they put slave masters over them to oppress them with forced labour, and they built Pithom and Rameses as store cities for Pharaoh. ¹²But the more they were oppressed, the more they multiplied and spread; so the Egyptians came to dread the Israelites ¹³and worked them ruthlessly. ¹⁴They made their lives bitter with harsh labour in brick and mortar and with all kinds of work in the fields; in all their harsh labour, the Egyptians worked them ruthlessly.

¹⁵The king of Egypt said to the Hebrew midwives, whose names were Shiphrah and Puah, ¹⁶'When you are helping the Hebrew women during childbirth on the delivery stool, if you see that the baby is a boy, kill him; but if it is a girl, let her live.' ¹⁷The midwives, however, feared God and did not do what the king of Egypt had told them to do; they let the boys live. ¹⁸Then the king of Egypt summoned the midwives and asked them, 'Why have you done this? Why have you let the boys live?'

¹⁹The midwives answered Pharaoh, 'Hebrew women are not like Egyptian women; they are vigorous and give birth before the midwives arrive.'

²⁰So God was kind to the midwives and the people increased and became even more numerous. ²¹And because the midwives feared God, he gave them families of their own.

²²Then Pharaoh gave this order to all his people: 'Every Hebrew boy that is born you must throw into the Nile, but let every girl live.'

2 Now a man of the tribe of Levi married a Levite woman, ²and she became pregnant and gave birth to a son. When she saw that he was a fine child, she hid him for three months. ³But when she could hide him no longer, she got a papyrus basket for him and coated it with tar and pitch. Then she placed the child in it and put it among the reeds along the bank of the Nile. ⁴His sister stood at a distance to see what would happen to him.

⁵Then Pharaoh's daughter went down to the Nile to bathe, and her attendants were walking along the river-bank. She saw the basket among the reeds and sent her female slave to get it. ⁶She opened it and saw the baby. He was crying, and she felt sorry for him. 'This is one of the Hebrew babies,' she said.

⁷Then his sister asked Pharaoh's daughter, 'Shall I go and get one of the Hebrew women to nurse the baby for you?'

⁸'Yes, go,' she answered. So the girl went and got the baby's mother. ⁹Pharaoh's daughter said to her, 'Take this baby and nurse him for me, and I will pay you.' So the woman took the baby and nursed him. ¹⁰When the child grew older, she took him to Pharaoh's daughter and he became her son. She named him Moses, saying, 'I drew him out of the water.'

¹¹One day, after Moses had grown up, he went out to where his own people were and watched them at their hard labour. He saw an Egyptian beating a Hebrew, one of his own people. ¹²Looking this way and that and seeing no one, he killed the Egyptian and hid him in the sand. ¹³The next day he went out and saw two Hebrews fighting. He asked the one in the wrong, 'Why are you hitting your fellow Hebrew?'

¹⁴The man said, 'Who made you ruler and judge over us? Are you thinking of killing me as you killed the Egyptian?' Then Moses was afraid and thought, 'What I did must have become known.'

¹⁵When Pharaoh heard of this, he tried to kill Moses, but Moses fled from Pharaoh and went to live in Midian, where he

sat down by a well. [16] Now a priest of Midian had seven daughters, and they came to draw water and fill the troughs to water their father's flock. [17] Some shepherds came along and drove them away, but Moses got up and came to their rescue and watered their flock.

[18] When the girls returned to Reuel their father, he asked them, 'Why have you returned so early today?'

[19] They answered, 'An Egyptian rescued us from the shepherds. He even drew water for us and watered the flock.'

[20] 'And where is he?' Reuel asked his daughters. 'Why did you leave him? Invite him to have something to eat.'

[21] Moses agreed to stay with the man, who gave his daughter Zipporah to Moses in marriage. [22] Zipporah gave birth to a son, and Moses named him Gershom, saying, 'I have become a foreigner in a foreign land.'

[23] During that long period, the king of Egypt died. The Israelites groaned in their slavery and cried out, and their cry for help because of their slavery went up to God. [24] God heard their groaning and he remembered his covenant with Abraham, with Isaac and with Jacob. [25] So God looked on the Israelites and was concerned about them.

▬ PSALM 17:6-12

[6] I call on you, my God, for you will answer
        me;
    turn your ear to me and hear my prayer.
[7] Show me the wonders of your great love,
    you who save by your right hand
    those who take refuge in you from
        their foes.
[8] Keep me as the apple of your eye;
    hide me in the shadow of your wings
[9] from the wicked who are out to destroy
        me,

from my mortal enemies who
    surround me.
[10] They close up their callous hearts,
    and their mouths speak with
        arrogance.
[11] They have tracked me down, they now
        surround me,
    with eyes alert, to throw me to the
        ground.
[12] They are like a lion hungry for prey,
    like a fierce lion crouching in cover.

▬ PROVERBS 3:25-26

[25] Have no fear of sudden disaster
    or of the ruin that overtakes the
        wicked,
[26] for the LORD will be at your side
    and will keep your foot from being
        snared.

▬ MATTHEW 19:1-22

19 When Jesus had finished saying these things, he left Galilee and went into the region of Judea to the other side of the Jordan. [2] Large crowds followed him, and he healed them there.

[3] Some Pharisees came to him to test him. They asked, 'Is it lawful for a man to divorce his wife for any and every reason?'

[4] 'Haven't you read,' he replied, 'that at the beginning the Creator "made them male and female," [5] and said, "For this reason a man will leave his father and mother and be united to his wife, and the two will become one flesh"? [6] So they are no longer two, but one flesh. Therefore what God has joined together, let no one separate.'

[7] 'Why then,' they asked, 'did Moses command that a man give his wife a certificate of divorce and send her away?'

[8] Jesus replied, 'Moses permitted you

to divorce your wives because your hearts were hard. But it was not this way from the beginning. ⁹ I tell you that anyone who divorces his wife, except for sexual immorality, and marries another woman commits adultery.'

¹⁰ The disciples said to him, 'If this is the situation between a husband and wife, it is better not to marry.'

¹¹ Jesus replied, 'Not everyone can accept this word, but only those to whom it has been given. ¹² For there are eunuchs who were born that way, and there are eunuchs who have been made eunuchs by others – and there are those who choose to live like eunuchs for the sake of the kingdom of heaven. The one who can accept this should accept it.'

¹³ Then people brought little children to Jesus for him to place his hands on them and pray for them. But the disciples rebuked them.

¹⁴ Jesus said, 'Let the little children come to me, and do not hinder them, for the kingdom of heaven belongs to such as these.' ¹⁵ When he had placed his hands on them, he went on from there.

¹⁶ Just then a man came up to Jesus and asked, 'Teacher, what good thing must I do to get eternal life?'

¹⁷ 'Why do you ask me about what is good?' Jesus replied. 'There is only One who is good. If you want to enter life, keep the commandments.'

¹⁸ 'Which ones?' he enquired.

Jesus replied, ' "You shall not murder, you shall not commit adultery, you shall not steal, you shall not give false testimony, ¹⁹ honour your father and mother," and "love your neighbour as yourself." '

²⁰ 'All these I have kept,' the young man said. 'What do I still lack?'

²¹ Jesus answered, 'If you want to be perfect, go, sell your possessions and give to the poor, and you will have treasure in heaven. Then come, follow me.'

²² When the young man heard this, he went away sad, because he had great wealth.

Divine Re-parenting

'I call on you, my God, for you will answer me.' **Psalm 17:6**

Using the Scriptures, we can build up a picture of God. So set up a canvas in your soul and allow the Holy Spirit to paint a picture for you of the Father using the palette of God's Word. As you read, let God re-parent you, and a fresh, clear and accurate picture of the Father will be drawn.

The first thing you need to know about your heavenly Father is: He is never too busy for you. Were your parents ever too busy for you? Were there occasions when you cried out for them and they were not there? Well, be assured that your heavenly Father is not like that. Even though He has a million and one things calling for His attention and a gigantic universe to run, He pays as much attention to you as if you were the only person on the face of the earth. Such is His relationship with you that it is as if there were not another soul in the universe. You don't have to share His attention with anyone - except, of course, when you are in prayer or fellowship with others. And even then He relates to you as if you were the only being in existence.

You may be too busy for your heavenly Father, but, take it from me, your heavenly Father is never too busy for you. Look once again at the opening text. It is written specially for you.

PRAYER

O Father, burn this thought deep into my soul – I am Your special child. You relate to me as if I were the only one on the face of the earth. How wonderful. How truly wonderful. Thank You, Father. Amen.

FURTHER STUDY

2 Sam. 22:7; Psa. 139:11-18; Matt. 6:6-8; 1 John 3:21-22
• Why can we pray with confidence?
• Now pray confidently!

January 30

■ EXODUS 3:1–4:31

3 Now Moses was tending the flock of Jethro his father-in-law, the priest of Midian, and he led the flock to the far side of the wilderness and came to Horeb, the mountain of God. ²There the angel of the LORD appeared to him in flames of fire from within a bush. Moses saw that though the bush was on fire it did not burn up. ³So Moses thought, 'I will go over and see this strange sight – why the bush does not burn up.'

⁴When the LORD saw that he had gone over to look, God called to him from within the bush, 'Moses! Moses!'

And Moses said, 'Here I am.'

⁵'Do not come any closer,' God said. 'Take off your sandals, for the place where you are standing is holy ground.' ⁶Then he said, 'I am the God of your father, the God of Abraham, the God of Isaac and the God of Jacob.' At this, Moses hid his face, because he was afraid to look at God.

⁷The LORD said, 'I have indeed seen the misery of my people in Egypt. I have heard them crying out because of their slave drivers, and I am concerned about their suffering. ⁸So I have come down to rescue them from the hand of the Egyptians and to bring them up out of that land into a good and spacious land, a land flowing with milk and honey – the home of the Canaanites, Hittites, Amorites, Perizzites, Hivites and Jebusites. ⁹And now the cry of the Israelites has reached me, and I have seen the way the Egyptians are oppressing them. ¹⁰So now, go. I am sending you to Pharaoh to bring my people the Israelites out of Egypt.'

¹¹But Moses said to God, 'Who am I that I should go to Pharaoh and bring the Israelites out of Egypt?'

¹²And God said, 'I will be with you. And this will be the sign to you that it is I who have sent you: when you have brought the people out of Egypt, you will worship God on this mountain.'

¹³Moses said to God, 'Suppose I go to the Israelites and say to them, "The God of your fathers has sent me to you," and they ask me, "What is his name?" Then what shall I tell them?'

¹⁴God said to Moses, 'I AM WHO I AM. This is what you are to say to the Israelites: "I AM has sent me to you."'

¹⁵God also said to Moses, 'Say to the Israelites, "The LORD, the God of your fathers – the God of Abraham, the God of Isaac and the God of Jacob – has sent me to you."

'This is my name for ever,
the name you shall call me
from generation to generation.

¹⁶ 'Go, assemble the elders of Israel and say to them, "The LORD, the God of your fathers – the God of Abraham, Isaac and Jacob – appeared to me and said: I have watched over you and have seen what has been done to you in Egypt. ¹⁷ And I have promised to bring you up out of your misery in Egypt into the land of the Canaanites, Hittites, Amorites, Perizzites, Hivites and Jebusites – a land flowing with milk and honey."

¹⁸ 'The elders of Israel will listen to you. Then you and the elders are to go to the king of Egypt and say to him, "The LORD, the God of the Hebrews, has met with us. Let us take a three-day journey into the wilderness to offer sacrifices to the LORD our God." ¹⁹ But I know that the king of Egypt will not let you go unless a mighty hand compels him. ²⁰ So I will stretch out my hand and strike the Egyptians with all the wonders that I will perform among them. After that, he will let you go.

²¹ 'And I will make the Egyptians favourably disposed towards this people, so that when you leave you will not go empty-handed. ²² Every woman is to ask her neighbour and any woman living in her house for articles of silver and gold and for clothing, which you will put on your sons and daughters. And so you will plunder the Egyptians.'

4 Moses answered, 'What if they do not believe me or listen to me and say, "The LORD did not appear to you"?'

² Then the LORD said to him, 'What is that in your hand?'

'A staff,' he replied.

³ The LORD said, 'Throw it on the ground.' Moses threw it on the ground and it became a snake, and he ran from it. ⁴ Then the LORD said to him, 'Reach out your hand and take it by the tail.' So Moses reached out and took hold of the snake and it turned back into a staff in his hand. ⁵ 'This,' said the LORD, 'is so that they may believe that the LORD, the God of their fathers – the God of Abraham, the God of Isaac and the God of Jacob – has appeared to you.'

⁶ Then the LORD said, 'Put your hand inside your cloak.' So Moses put his hand into his cloak, and when he took it out, the skin was leprous – it had become as white as snow.

⁷ 'Now put it back into your cloak,' he said. So Moses put his hand back into his cloak, and when he took it out, it was restored, like the rest of his flesh.

⁸ Then the LORD said, 'If they do not believe you or pay attention to the first sign, they may believe the second. ⁹ But if they do not believe these two signs or listen to you, take some water from the Nile and pour it on the dry ground. The water you take from the river will become blood on the ground.'

¹⁰ Moses said to the LORD, 'Pardon your servant, Lord. I have never been eloquent, neither in the past nor since you have spoken to your servant. I am slow of speech and tongue.'

¹¹ The LORD said to him, 'Who gave human beings their mouths? Who makes them deaf or mute? Who gives them sight or makes them blind? Is it not I, the LORD? ¹² Now go; I will help you speak and will teach you what to say.'

¹³ But Moses said, 'Pardon your servant, Lord. Please send someone else.'

¹⁴ Then the LORD's anger burned against Moses and he said, 'What about your brother, Aaron the Levite? I know he can speak well. He is already on his way to meet you, and he will be glad to see you. ¹⁵ You shall speak to him and put words in his mouth; I will help both of you speak and will teach you what to do. ¹⁶ He will speak to the people for you, and it will be as if he were your mouth and as if you were God to him. ¹⁷ But

take this staff in your hand so that you can perform the signs with it.'

¹⁸ Then Moses went back to Jethro his father-in-law and said to him, 'Let me return to my own people in Egypt to see if any of them are still alive.'

Jethro said, 'Go, and I wish you well.'

¹⁹ Now the LORD had said to Moses in Midian, 'Go back to Egypt, for all those who wanted to kill you are dead.' ²⁰ So Moses took his wife and sons, put them on a donkey and started back to Egypt. And he took the staff of God in his hand.

²¹ The LORD said to Moses, 'When you return to Egypt, see that you perform before Pharaoh all the wonders I have given you the power to do. But I will harden his heart so that he will not let the people go. ²² Then say to Pharaoh, "This is what the LORD says: Israel is my firstborn son, ²³ and I told you, 'Let my son go, so that he may worship me.' But you refused to let him go; so I will kill your firstborn son."'

²⁴ At a lodging place on the way, the LORD met Moses and was about to kill him. ²⁵ But Zipporah took a flint knife, cut off her son's foreskin and touched Moses' feet with it. 'Surely you are a bridegroom of blood to me,' she said. ²⁶ So the LORD let him alone. (At that time she said 'bridegroom of blood', referring to circumcision.)

²⁷ The LORD said to Aaron, 'Go into the wilderness to meet Moses.' So he met Moses at the mountain of God and kissed him. ²⁸ Then Moses told Aaron everything the LORD had sent him to say, and also about all the signs he had commanded him to perform.

²⁹ Moses and Aaron brought together all the elders of the Israelites, ³⁰ and Aaron told them everything the LORD had said to Moses. He also performed the signs before the people, ³¹ and they believed. And when they heard that the LORD was concerned about them and had seen their misery, they bowed down and worshipped.

▬ PSALM 17:13–15

¹³ Rise up, LORD, confront them, bring them down;
  with your sword rescue me from the wicked.
¹⁴ By your hand save me from such people, LORD,
  from those of this world whose reward is in this life.
May what you have stored up for the wicked fill their bellies;
  may their children gorge themselves on it,
  and may there be leftovers for their little ones.

¹⁵ As for me, I shall be vindicated and shall see your face;
  when I awake, I shall be satisfied with seeing your likeness.

▬ PROVERBS 3:27–28

²⁷ Do not withhold good from those to whom it is due,
  when it is in your power to act.
²⁸ Do not say to your neighbour,
  'Come back tomorrow and I'll give it to you' –
  when you already have it with you.

▬ MATTHEW 19:23–20:19

²³ Then Jesus said to his disciples, 'Truly I tell you, it is hard for someone who is rich to enter the kingdom of heaven. ²⁴ Again I tell you, it is easier for a camel to go through the eye of a needle than for someone who is rich to enter the kingdom of God.'

²⁵ When the disciples heard this, they were greatly astonished and asked, 'Who then can be saved?'

²⁶ Jesus looked at them and said, 'With

man this is impossible, but with God all things are possible.'

²⁷ Peter answered him, 'We have left everything to follow you! What then will there be for us?'

²⁸ Jesus said to them, 'Truly I tell you, at the renewal of all things, when the Son of Man sits on his glorious throne, you who have followed me will also sit on twelve thrones, judging the twelve tribes of Israel. ²⁹ And everyone who has left houses or brothers or sisters or father or mother or wife or children or fields for my sake will receive a hundred times as much and will inherit eternal life. ³⁰ But many who are first will be last, and many who are last will be first.

20 'For the kingdom of heaven is like a landowner who went out early in the morning to hire workers for his vineyard. ² He agreed to pay them a denarius for the day and sent them into his vineyard.

³ 'About nine in the morning he went out and saw others standing in the market-place doing nothing. ⁴ He told them, "You also go and work in my vineyard, and I will pay you whatever is right." ⁵ So they went.

'He went out again about noon and about three in the afternoon and did the same thing. ⁶ About five in the afternoon he went out and found still others standing around. He asked them, "Why have you been standing here all day long doing nothing?"

⁷ '"Because no one has hired us," they answered.

'He said to them, "You also go and work in my vineyard."

⁸ 'When evening came, the owner of the vineyard said to his foreman, "Call the workers and pay them their wages, beginning with the last ones hired and going on to the first."

⁹ 'The workers who were hired about five in the afternoon came and each received a denarius. ¹⁰ So when those came who were hired first, they expected to receive more. But each one of them also received a denarius. ¹¹ When they received it, they began to grumble against the landowner. ¹² "These who were hired last worked only one hour," they said, "and you have made them equal to us who have borne the burden of the work and the heat of the day."

¹³ 'But he answered one of them, "I am not being unfair to you, friend. Didn't you agree to work for a denarius? ¹⁴ Take your pay and go. I want to give the one who was hired last the same as I gave you. ¹⁵ Don't I have the right to do what I want with my own money? Or are you envious because I am generous?"

¹⁶ 'So the last will be first, and the first will be last.'

¹⁷ Now Jesus was going up to Jerusalem. On the way, he took the Twelve aside and said to them, ¹⁸ 'We are going up to Jerusalem, and the Son of Man will be delivered over to the chief priests and the teachers of the law. They will condemn him to death ¹⁹ and will hand him over to the Gentiles to be mocked and flogged and crucified. On the third day he will be raised to life!'

'Jehovah' - No Such Word

'God said to Moses, "I AM WHO I AM."' **Exodus 3:14**

Honouring the name of God is not just esteeming the letters in His name, nor speaking His name in hushed or quiet tones. The ancient Israelites attached such a sacredness to the name of God that they would not say it aloud. They thought that hallowing God's name meant hallowing the name itself. They paid honour to the actual letters of God's name, yet, on occasion, thought nothing about disobeying His Word and denying His truth.

One great Hebrew scholar points out that there is no such word as 'Jehovah' in the Hebrew language, although it appears in English translations of the Old Testament. The name of God in Exodus 3:14, where the Almighty gave His name to Moses – 'I AM WHO I AM' – is Yahweh, the English equivalent of which is 'Jehovah'. The Israelites would not say the word 'Yahweh', and eventually the vowels were taken out and mixed with the consonants of another Hebrew word to form the word 'Adonai'. This was done as a device to avoid having to say the real word 'Yahweh'.

Let us be quite clear, then, about what Jesus meant when He taught us to pray, 'hallowed be your name'. God's name stands for who He is – His mercy, His compassion, His love, His power, His eternity and so on. When, as God's children, we come to Him to honour His name, we do more than enter into a religious routine. We contemplate all that His name stands for and reverence Him for who He is.

PRAYER

Father, I see that prayer, true prayer, is not just a technique; it is an art. Help me to learn this art and to implement what You are teaching me in my prayer life day by day. For Jesus' sake. Amen.

FURTHER STUDY

Gen. 15; 22:14; Exod. 15:26; 17:15; Judg. 6:24; Psa. 23:1; Jer. 23:6; Ezek. 48:35
• List some of the names of God.
• What do they mean?

January 31

■ EXODUS 5:1–6:30

5 Afterwards Moses and Aaron went to Pharaoh and said, 'This is what the LORD, the God of Israel, says: "Let my people go, so that they may hold a festival to me in the wilderness."'

² Pharaoh said, 'Who is the LORD, that I should obey him and let Israel go? I do not know the LORD and I will not let Israel go.'

³ Then they said, 'The God of the Hebrews has met with us. Now let us take a three-day journey into the wilderness to offer sacrifices to the LORD our God, or he may strike us

with plagues or with the sword.'

⁴ But the king of Egypt said, 'Moses and Aaron, why are you taking the people away from their labour? Get back to your work!' ⁵ Then Pharaoh said, 'Look, the people of the land are now numerous, and you are stopping them from working.'

⁶ That same day Pharaoh gave this order to the slave drivers and overseers in charge of the people: ⁷ 'You are no longer to supply the people with straw for making bricks; let them go and gather their own straw. ⁸ But require them to make the same number of bricks as before; don't reduce the quota.

They are lazy; that is why they are crying out, "Let us go and sacrifice to our God." ⁹ Make the work harder for the people so that they keep working and pay no attention to lies.'

¹⁰ Then the slave drivers and the overseers went out and said to the people, 'This is what Pharaoh says: "I will not give you any more straw. ¹¹ Go and get your own straw wherever you can find it, but your work will not be reduced at all." ' ¹² So the people scattered all over Egypt to gather stubble to use for straw. ¹³ The slave drivers kept pressing them, saying, 'Complete the work required of you for each day, just as when you had straw.' ¹⁴ And Pharaoh's slave drivers beat the Israelite overseers they had appointed, demanding, 'Why haven't you met your quota of bricks yesterday or today, as before?'

¹⁵ Then the Israelite overseers went and appealed to Pharaoh: 'Why have you treated your servants this way? ¹⁶ Your servants are given no straw, yet we are told, "Make bricks!" Your servants are being beaten, but the fault is with your own people.'

¹⁷ Pharaoh said, 'Lazy, that's what you are – lazy! That is why you keep saying, "Let us go and sacrifice to the LORD." ¹⁸ Now get to work. You will not be given any straw, yet you must produce your full quota of bricks.'

¹⁹ The Israelite overseers realised they were in trouble when they were told, 'You are not to reduce the number of bricks required of you for each day.' ²⁰ When they left Pharaoh, they found Moses and Aaron waiting to meet them, ²¹ and they said, 'May the LORD look on you and judge you! You have made us obnoxious to Pharaoh and his officials and have put a sword in their hand to kill us.'

²² Moses returned to the LORD and said, 'Why, Lord, why have you brought trouble on this people? Is this why you sent me? ²³ Ever since I went to Pharaoh to speak in your name, he has brought trouble on this people, and you have not rescued your people at all.'

6 Then the LORD said to Moses, 'Now you will see what I will do to Pharaoh: because of my mighty hand he will let them go; because of my mighty hand he will drive them out of his country.'

² God also said to Moses, 'I am the LORD. ³ I appeared to Abraham, to Isaac and to Jacob as God Almighty, but by my name the LORD I did not make myself known to them. ⁴ I also established my covenant with them to give them the land of Canaan, where they resided as foreigners. ⁵ Moreover, I have heard the groaning of the Israelites, whom the Egyptians are enslaving, and I have remembered my covenant.

⁶ 'Therefore, say to the Israelites: "I am the LORD, and I will bring you out from under the yoke of the Egyptians. I will free you from being slaves to them, and I will redeem you with an outstretched arm and with mighty acts of judgment. ⁷ I will take you as my own people, and I will be your God. Then you will know that I am the LORD your God, who brought you out from under the yoke of the Egyptians. ⁸ And I will bring you to the land I swore with uplifted hand to give to Abraham, to Isaac and to Jacob. I will give it to you as a possession. I am the LORD." '

⁹ Moses reported this to the Israelites, but they did not listen to him because of their discouragement and harsh labour.

¹⁰ Then the LORD said to Moses, ¹¹ 'Go, tell Pharaoh king of Egypt to let the Israelites go out of his country.'

¹² But Moses said to the LORD, 'If the Israelites will not listen to me, why would Pharaoh listen to me, since I speak with faltering lips?'

¹³ Now the LORD spoke to Moses and Aaron about the Israelites and Pharaoh king of Egypt, and he commanded them to bring the Israelites out of Egypt.

¹⁴ These were the heads of their families:

The sons of Reuben the firstborn

son of Israel were Hanok and Pallu, Hezron and Karmi. These were the clans of Reuben.

¹⁵The sons of Simeon were Jemuel, Jamin, Ohad, Jakin, Zohar and Shaul the son of a Canaanite woman. These were the clans of Simeon.

¹⁶These were the names of the sons of Levi according to their records: Gershon, Kohath and Merari. Levi lived 137 years.

¹⁷The sons of Gershon, by clans, were Libni and Shimei.

¹⁸The sons of Kohath were Amram, Izhar, Hebron and Uzziel. Kohath lived 133 years.

¹⁹The sons of Merari were Mahli and Mushi.

These were the clans of Levi according to their records.

²⁰Amram married his father's sister Jochebed, who bore him Aaron and Moses. Amram lived 137 years.

²¹The sons of Izhar were Korah, Nepheg and Zikri.

²²The sons of Uzziel were Mishael, Elzaphan and Sithri.

²³Aaron married Elisheba, daughter of Amminadab and sister of Nahshon, and she bore him Nadab and Abihu, Eleazar and Ithamar.

²⁴The sons of Korah were Assir, Elkanah and Abiasaph. These were the Korahite clans.

²⁵Eleazar son of Aaron married one of the daughters of Putiel, and she bore him Phinehas.

These were the heads of the Levite families, clan by clan.

²⁶It was this Aaron and Moses to whom the LORD said, 'Bring the Israelites out of Egypt by their divisions.' ²⁷They were the ones who spoke to Pharaoh king of Egypt about bringing the Israelites out of

Egypt – this same Moses and Aaron.

²⁸Now when the LORD spoke to Moses in Egypt, ²⁹he said to him, 'I am the LORD. Tell Pharaoh king of Egypt everything I tell you.'

³⁰But Moses said to the LORD, 'Since I speak with faltering lips, why would Pharaoh listen to me?'

■ PSALM 18:1-6

¹I love you, LORD, my strength.

²The LORD is my rock, my fortress and my
   deliverer;
   my God is my rock, in whom I take
      refuge,
   my shield and the horn of my
      salvation, my stronghold.

³I called to the LORD, who is worthy of
      praise,
   and I have been saved from my
      enemies.

⁴The cords of death entangled me;
   the torrents of destruction
      overwhelmed me.

⁵The cords of the grave coiled around me;
   the snares of death confronted me.

⁶In my distress I called to the LORD;
   I cried to my God for help.
From his temple he heard my voice;
   my cry came before him, into his ears.

■ PROVERBS 3:29-32

²⁹Do not plot harm against your
      neighbour,
   who lives trustfully near you.

³⁰Do not accuse anyone for no reason –
   when they have done you no harm.

³¹Do not envy the violent
   or choose any of their ways.

³² For the LORD detests the perverse
but takes the upright into his
confidence.

···

■ MATTHEW 20:20–21:11

²⁰ Then the mother of Zebedee's sons
came to Jesus with her sons and, kneeling
down, asked a favour of him.

²¹ 'What is it you want?' he asked.

She said, 'Grant that one of these two
sons of mine may sit at your right and the
other at your left in your kingdom.'

²² 'You don't know what you are asking,'
Jesus said to them. 'Can you drink the cup I
am going to drink?'

'We can,' they answered.

²³ Jesus said to them, 'You will indeed
drink from my cup, but to sit at my right or
left is not for me to grant. These places belong to those for whom they have been prepared by my Father.'

²⁴ When the ten heard about this, they
were indignant with the two brothers.
²⁵ Jesus called them together and said, 'You
know that the rulers of the Gentiles lord it
over them, and their high officials exercise
authority over them. ²⁶ Not so with you.
Instead, whoever wants to become great
among you must be your servant, ²⁷ and
whoever wants to be first must be your
slave – ²⁸ just as the Son of Man did not
come to be served, but to serve, and to give
his life as a ransom for many.'

²⁹ As Jesus and his disciples were leaving
Jericho, a large crowd followed him. ³⁰ Two
blind men were sitting by the roadside, and
when they heard that Jesus was passing
by, they shouted, 'Lord, Son of David, have
mercy on us!'

³¹ The crowd rebuked them and told them
to be quiet, but they shouted all the louder,
'Lord, Son of David, have mercy on us!'

³² Jesus stopped and called them. 'What
do you want me to do for you?' he asked.

³³ 'Lord,' they answered, 'we want our
sight.'

³⁴ Jesus had compassion on them and
touched their eyes. Immediately they
received their sight and followed him.

21 As they approached Jerusalem and
came to Bethphage on the Mount of
Olives, Jesus sent two disciples, ² saying to
them, 'Go to the village ahead of you, and at
once you will find a donkey tied there, with
her colt by her. Untie them and bring them
to me. ³ If anyone says anything to you, say
that the Lord needs them, and he will send
them right away.'

⁴ This took place to fulfil what was spo-
ken through the prophet:

⁵ 'Say to Daughter Zion,
    "See, your king comes to you,
gentle and riding on a donkey,
    and on a colt, the foal of a donkey." '

⁶ The disciples went and did as Jesus had
instructed them. ⁷ They brought the donkey and the colt and placed their cloaks on
them for Jesus to sit on. ⁸ A very large crowd
spread their cloaks on the road, while others
cut branches from the trees and spread them
on the road. ⁹ The crowds that went ahead of
him and those that followed shouted,

'Hosanna to the Son of David!'

'Blessed is he who comes in the name of
    the Lord!'

'Hosanna in the highest heaven!'

¹⁰ When Jesus entered Jerusalem, the whole
city was stirred and asked, 'Who is this?'

¹¹ The crowds answered, 'This is Jesus, the
prophet from Nazareth in Galilee.'

Ulterior Motives

'You don't know what you are asking.' Matthew 20:22

There are many people in the Scriptures who appear to be spiritually minded but whose hearts harbour deeply unspiritual motives. Take the mother of the sons of Zebedee, for example, who according to Matthew 27:55 was one of the women who followed Jesus from Galilee in order to minister to Him.

Most commentators believe this small band of women to have been devotees of Christ, assisting Him and the disciples by preparing meals, washing and repairing clothes, and so on. Onlookers would have classified them as deeply spiritual, willing to give up their time to minister to Jesus – and of course, in the main, they were. In one place, however, the Scripture draws aside the veil from the heart of one of them, the mother of James and John, and shows her approaching Jesus with the request: 'Grant that one of these two sons of mine may sit at your right and the other at your left in your kingdom.' 'You don't know what you are asking,' Jesus said (Matt. 20:21-22).

Yes, she served Jesus. Of that there can be no doubt. But she had a secret and selfish motive in her heart: a privileged position for her sons. It is easy to excuse her action, as many have done, on the grounds that she was doing only what any other concerned mother would have done – attempting to get the best for her children. But Jesus saw right into her heart and said: 'You don't know what you're asking.' How sad that her beautiful ministry to Jesus was spoiled by ulterior motives.

PRAYER

My Father, help me to see that I cannot be a fully integrated person when I harbour within me two mutually exclusive loves. I cannot love You fully when I love my own interests fully. Set me free, dear Lord, to live only for You. Amen.

FURTHER STUDY

James 2; Eph. 2:3;
1 John 2:15-16
• What motive was James exposing?
• What did he say about the law?

February 1

▬ EXODUS 7:1–8:32

7 Then the LORD said to Moses, 'See, I have made you like God to Pharaoh, and your brother Aaron will be your prophet. ²You are to say everything I command you, and your brother Aaron is to tell Pharaoh to let the Israelites go out of his country.

³But I will harden Pharaoh's heart, and though I multiply my signs and wonders in Egypt, ⁴he will not listen to you. Then I will lay my hand on Egypt and with mighty acts of judgment I will bring out my divisions, my people the Israelites. ⁵And the Egyptians will know that I am the LORD when I stretch out my hand against Egypt and bring the Israelites out of it.'

⁶Moses and Aaron did just as the LORD commanded them. ⁷Moses was eighty years old and Aaron eighty-three when they spoke to Pharaoh.

⁸The LORD said to Moses and Aaron, ⁹'When Pharaoh says to you, "Perform a miracle," then say to Aaron, "Take your staff and throw it down before Pharaoh," and it will become a snake.'

¹⁰So Moses and Aaron went to Pharaoh and did just as the LORD commanded. Aaron threw his staff down in front of Pharaoh and his officials, and it became a snake. ¹¹Pharaoh then summoned the wise men and sorcerers, and the Egyptian magicians also did the same things by their secret arts: ¹²each one threw down his staff and it became a snake. But Aaron's staff swallowed up their staffs. ¹³Yet Pharaoh's heart became hard and he would not listen to them, just as the LORD had said.

¹⁴Then the LORD said to Moses, 'Pharaoh's heart is unyielding; he refuses to let the people go. ¹⁵Go to Pharaoh in the morning as he goes out to the river. Confront him on the bank of the Nile, and take in your hand the staff that was changed into a snake. ¹⁶Then say to him, "The LORD, the God of the Hebrews, has sent me to say to you: Let my people go, so that they may worship me in the wilderness. But until now you have not listened. ¹⁷This is what the LORD says: by this you will know that I am the LORD: with the staff that is in my hand I will strike the water of the Nile, and it will be changed into blood. ¹⁸The fish in the Nile will die, and the river will stink;

the Egyptians will not be able to drink its water."'

¹⁹The LORD said to Moses, 'Tell Aaron, "Take your staff and stretch out your hand over the waters of Egypt – over the streams and canals, over the ponds and all the reservoirs – and they will turn to blood." Blood will be everywhere in Egypt, even in vessels of wood and stone.'

²⁰Moses and Aaron did just as the LORD had commanded. He raised his staff in the presence of Pharaoh and his officials and struck the water of the Nile, and all the water was changed into blood. ²¹The fish in the Nile died, and the river smelled so bad that the Egyptians could not drink its water. Blood was everywhere in Egypt.

²²But the Egyptian magicians did the same things by their secret arts, and Pharaoh's heart became hard; he would not listen to Moses and Aaron, just as the LORD had said. ²³Instead, he turned and went into his palace, and did not take even this to heart. ²⁴And all the Egyptians dug along the Nile to get drinking water, because they could not drink the water of the river.

²⁵Seven days passed after the LORD struck the Nile. **8** ¹Then the LORD said to Moses, 'Go to Pharaoh and say to him, "This is what the LORD says: let my people go, so that they may worship me. ²If you refuse to let them go, I will send a plague of frogs on your whole country. ³The Nile will teem with frogs. They will come up into your palace and your bedroom and onto your bed, into the houses of your officials and on your people, and into your ovens and kneading troughs. ⁴The frogs will come up on you and your people and all your officials."'

⁵Then the LORD said to Moses, 'Tell Aaron, "Stretch out your hand with your staff over the streams and canals and ponds, and make frogs come up on the land of Egypt."'

⁶So Aaron stretched out his hand over

the waters of Egypt, and the frogs came up and covered the land. [7] But the magicians did the same things by their secret arts; they also made frogs come up on the land of Egypt.

[8] Pharaoh summoned Moses and Aaron and said, 'Pray to the LORD to take the frogs away from me and my people, and I will let your people go to offer sacrifices to the LORD.'

[9] Moses said to Pharaoh, 'I leave to you the honour of setting the time for me to pray for you and your officials and your people that you and your houses may be rid of the frogs, except for those that remain in the Nile.'

[10] 'Tomorrow,' Pharaoh said.

Moses replied, 'It will be as you say, so that you may know there is no one like the LORD our God. [11] The frogs will leave you and your houses, your officials and your people; they will remain only in the Nile.'

[12] After Moses and Aaron left Pharaoh, Moses cried out to the LORD about the frogs he had brought on Pharaoh. [13] And the LORD did what Moses asked. The frogs died in the houses, in the courtyards and in the fields. [14] They were piled into heaps, and the land reeked of them. [15] But when Pharaoh saw that there was relief, he hardened his heart and would not listen to Moses and Aaron, just as the LORD had said.

[16] Then the LORD said to Moses, 'Tell Aaron, "Stretch out your staff and strike the dust of the ground," and throughout the land of Egypt the dust will become gnats.' [17] They did this, and when Aaron stretched out his hand with the staff and struck the dust of the ground, gnats came on people and animals. All the dust throughout the land of Egypt became gnats. [18] But when the magicians tried to produce gnats by their secret arts, they could not.

Since the gnats were on people and animals everywhere, [19] the magicians said to Pharaoh, 'This is the finger of God.' But Pharaoh's heart was hard and he would not listen, just as the LORD had said.

[20] Then the LORD said to Moses, 'Get up early in the morning and confront Pharaoh as he goes to the river and say to him, "This is what the LORD says: let my people go, so that they may worship me. [21] If you do not let my people go, I will send swarms of flies on you and your officials, on your people and into your houses. The houses of the Egyptians will be full of flies; even the ground will be covered with them.

[22] "'But on that day I will deal differently with the land of Goshen, where my people live; no swarms of flies will be there, so that you will know that I, the LORD, am in this land. [23] I will make a distinction between my people and your people. This sign will occur tomorrow.'"

[24] And the LORD did this. Dense swarms of flies poured into Pharaoh's palace and into the houses of his officials; throughout Egypt the land was ruined by the flies.

[25] Then Pharaoh summoned Moses and Aaron and said, 'Go, sacrifice to your God here in the land.'

[26] But Moses said, 'That would not be right. The sacrifices we offer the LORD our God would be detestable to the Egyptians. And if we offer sacrifices that are detestable in their eyes, will they not stone us? [27] We must take a three-day journey into the wilderness to offer sacrifices to the LORD our God, as he commands us.'

[28] Pharaoh said, 'I will let you go to offer sacrifices to the LORD your God in the wilderness, but you must not go very far. Now pray for me.'

[29] Moses answered, 'As soon as I leave you, I will pray to the LORD, and tomorrow the flies will leave Pharaoh and his officials and his people. Only let Pharaoh be sure that he does not act deceitfully again by not letting the people go to offer sacrifices to the LORD.'

[30] Then Moses left Pharaoh and prayed

to the LORD, ³¹and the LORD did what Moses asked. The flies left Pharaoh and his officials and his people; not a fly remained. ³²But this time also Pharaoh hardened his heart and would not let the people go.

■ PSALM 18:7-12

⁷The earth trembled and quaked,
 and the foundations of the mountains
  shook;
 they trembled because he was angry.
⁸Smoke rose from his nostrils;
 consuming fire came from his mouth,
 burning coals blazed out of it.
⁹He parted the heavens and came down;
 dark clouds were under his feet.
¹⁰He mounted the cherubim and flew;
 he soared on the wings of the wind.
¹¹He made darkness his covering, his
  canopy around him –
 the dark rain clouds of the sky.
¹²Out of the brightness of his presence
  clouds advanced,
 with hailstones and bolts of lightning.

■ PROVERBS 3:33-35

³³The LORD's curse is on the house of the
  wicked,
 but he blesses the home of the righteous.
³⁴He mocks proud mockers
 but shows favour to the humble and
  oppressed.
³⁵The wise inherit honour,
 but fools get only shame.

■ MATTHEW 21:12-27

¹²Jesus entered the temple courts and drove out all who were buying and selling there. He overturned the tables of the money-changers and the benches of those selling doves. ¹³'It is written,' he said to them, '"My house will be called a house of prayer," but you are making it "a den of robbers."'

¹⁴The blind and the lame came to him at the temple, and he healed them. ¹⁵But when the chief priests and the teachers of the law saw the wonderful things he did and the children shouting in the temple courts, 'Hosanna to the Son of David,' they were indignant.

¹⁶'Do you hear what these children are saying?' they asked him.

'Yes,' replied Jesus, 'have you never read,

'"From the lips of children and infants
 you, Lord, have called forth your
  praise"?'

¹⁷And he left them and went out of the city to Bethany, where he spent the night.

¹⁸Early in the morning, as Jesus was on his way back to the city, he was hungry. ¹⁹Seeing a fig-tree by the road, he went up to it but found nothing on it except leaves. Then he said to it, 'May you never bear fruit again!' Immediately the tree withered.

²⁰When the disciples saw this, they were amazed. 'How did the fig-tree wither so quickly?' they asked.

²¹Jesus replied, 'Truly I tell you, if you have faith and do not doubt, not only can you do what was done to the fig-tree, but also you can say to this mountain, "Go, throw yourself into the sea," and it will be done. ²²If you believe, you will receive whatever you ask for in prayer.'

²³Jesus entered the temple courts, and, while he was teaching, the chief priests and the elders of the people came to him. 'By what authority are you doing these things?' they asked. 'And who gave you this authority?'

²⁴Jesus replied, 'I will also ask you one question. If you answer me, I will tell you by what authority I am doing these things.

²⁵ John's baptism – where did it come from? Was it from heaven, or of human origin?'

They discussed it among themselves and said, 'If we say, "From heaven", he will ask, "Then why didn't you believe him?" ²⁶ But if we say, "Of human origin" – we are afraid of the people, for they all hold that John was a prophet.'

²⁷ So they answered Jesus, 'We don't know.'

Then he said, 'Neither will I tell you by what authority I am doing these things.

'Faith in Two Minds'

'... if you have faith ... you can say to this mountain, "Go, throw yourself into the sea," and it will be done.'
Matthew 21:21

If we are to have feet like 'hinds' feet,' we must learn how to face and handle any doubts that may arise in our hearts.

Most of us have to face the problem of doubt at some time or another, and unless we have a clear understanding of what is involved when we doubt and how to deal with it, our pursuit of God can be greatly hindered. The English word doubt comes from the Latin *dubitare*, which is rooted in an Aryan word meaning 'two'. To doubt means to take two positions on something or to have a divided heart.

A major misconception concerning doubt – and one that has brought great anxiety to many a Christian's heart – is to view doubt as the opposite of faith, which it is not. Unbelief is the opposite of faith.

Os Guinness puts it like this: 'To believe is to be "in one mind" about accepting something as true; to disbelieve is to be "in one mind" about rejecting it. To doubt is to waver between the two, to believe and disbelieve all at once, and so to be "in two minds."'

Donald Bridge, in his book *When Christians Doubt*, refers to doubt as 'faith asking questions.' Some might think this definition elevates doubt to a position it does not deserve and masks its true nature – but not so. It is only when we understand what doubt really is that we can deal with it in the way we should. Doubt is, as Guinness puts it, 'faith in two minds.'

PRAYER

My God and Father, I would be at my best – at Your best. But Your best cannot get across to me if doubt remains in my heart. Show me the steps I must take to overcome doubt. Amen.

FURTHER STUDY

Matt. 14:22-33;
Luke 24:13-35
• How does Peter illustrate being 'in two minds'?
• What did Jesus mean by slow to believe in your hearts?

February 2

■ EXODUS 9:1–10:20

9 Then the LORD said to Moses, 'Go to Pharaoh and say to him, "This is what the LORD, the God of the Hebrews, says: 'Let my people go, so that they may worship me.' ²If you refuse to let them go and continue to hold them back, ³the hand of the LORD will bring a terrible plague on your livestock in the field – on your horses, donkeys and camels and on your cattle, sheep and goats. ⁴But the LORD will make a distinction between the livestock of Israel and that of Egypt, so that no animal belonging to the Israelites will die."'

⁵The LORD set a time and said, 'Tomorrow the LORD will do this in the land.' ⁶And the next day the LORD did it: all the livestock of the Egyptians died, but not one animal belonging to the Israelites died. ⁷Pharaoh investigated and found that not even one of the animals of the Israelites had died. Yet his heart was unyielding and he would not let the people go.

⁸Then the LORD said to Moses and Aaron, 'Take handfuls of soot from a furnace and let Moses toss it into the air in the presence of Pharaoh. ⁹It will become fine dust over the whole land of Egypt, and festering boils will break out on people and animals throughout the land.'

¹⁰So they took soot from a furnace and stood before Pharaoh. Moses tossed it into the air, and festering boils broke out on people and animals. ¹¹The magicians could not stand before Moses because of the boils that were on them and on all the Egyptians. ¹²But the LORD hardened Pharaoh's heart and he would not listen to Moses and Aaron, just as the LORD had said to Moses.

¹³Then the LORD said to Moses, 'Get up early in the morning, confront Pharaoh and say to him, "This is what the LORD, the God of the Hebrews, says: let my people go, so that they may worship me, ¹⁴or this time I will send the full force of my plagues against you and against your officials and your people, so you may know that there is no one like me in all the earth. ¹⁵For by now I could have stretched out my hand and struck you and your people with a plague that would have wiped you off the earth. ¹⁶But I have raised you up for this very purpose, that I might show you my power and that my name might be proclaimed in all the earth. ¹⁷You still set yourself against my people and will not let them go. ¹⁸Therefore, at this time tomorrow I will send the worst hailstorm that has ever fallen on Egypt, from the day it was founded till now. ¹⁹Give an order now to bring your livestock and everything you have in the field to a place of shelter, because the hail will fall on every person and animal that has not been brought in and is still out in the field, and they will die."'

²⁰Those officials of Pharaoh who feared the word of the LORD hurried to bring their slaves and their livestock inside. ²¹But those who ignored the word of the LORD left their slaves and livestock in the field.

²²Then the LORD said to Moses, 'Stretch out your hand towards the sky so that hail will fall all over Egypt – on people and animals and on everything growing in the fields of Egypt.' ²³When Moses stretched out his staff towards the sky, the LORD sent thunder and hail, and lightning flashed down to the ground. So the LORD rained hail on the land of Egypt; ²⁴hail fell and lightning flashed back and forth. It was the worst storm in all the land of Egypt since it had become a nation. ²⁵Throughout Egypt hail

struck everything in the fields – both people and animals; it beat down everything growing in the fields and stripped every tree. ²⁶ The only place it did not hail was the land of Goshen, where the Israelites were.

²⁷ Then Pharaoh summoned Moses and Aaron. 'This time I have sinned,' he said to them. 'The LORD is in the right, and I and my people are in the wrong. ²⁸ Pray to the LORD, for we have had enough thunder and hail. I will let you go; you don't have to stay any longer.'

²⁹ Moses replied, 'When I have gone out of the city, I will spread out my hands in prayer to the LORD. The thunder will stop and there will be no more hail, so you may know that the earth is the LORD's. ³⁰ But I know that you and your officials still do not fear the LORD God.'

³¹ (The flax and barley were destroyed, since the barley was in the ear and the flax was in bloom. ³² The wheat and spelt, however, were not destroyed, because they ripen later.)

³³ Then Moses left Pharaoh and went out of the city. He spread out his hands towards the LORD; the thunder and hail stopped, and the rain no longer poured down on the land. ³⁴ When Pharaoh saw that the rain and hail and thunder had stopped, he sinned again: he and his officials hardened their hearts. ³⁵ So Pharaoh's heart was hard and he would not let the Israelites go, just as the LORD had said through Moses.

10 Then the LORD said to Moses, 'Go to Pharaoh, for I have hardened his heart and the hearts of his officials so that I may perform these signs of mine among them ² that you may tell your children and grandchildren how I dealt harshly with the Egyptians and how I performed my signs among them, and that you may know that I am the LORD.'

³ So Moses and Aaron went to Pharaoh and said to him, 'This is what the LORD, the God of the Hebrews, says: "How long will

you refuse to humble yourself before me? Let my people go, so that they may worship me. ⁴ If you refuse to let them go, I will bring locusts into your country tomorrow. ⁵ They will cover the face of the ground so that it cannot be seen. They will devour what little you have left after the hail, including every tree that is growing in your fields. ⁶ They will fill your houses and those of all your officials and all the Egyptians – something neither your parents nor your ancestors have ever seen from the day they settled in this land till now."' Then Moses turned and left Pharaoh.

⁷ Pharaoh's officials said to him, 'How long will this man be a snare to us? Let the people go, so that they may worship the LORD their God. Do you not yet realise that Egypt is ruined?'

⁸ Then Moses and Aaron were brought back to Pharaoh. 'Go, worship the LORD your God,' he said. 'But tell me who will be going.'

⁹ Moses answered, 'We will go with our young and our old, with our sons and our daughters, and with our flocks and herds, because we are to celebrate a festival to the LORD.'

¹⁰ Pharaoh said, 'The LORD be with you – if I let you go, along with your women and children! Clearly you are bent on evil. ¹¹ No! Let only the men go and worship the LORD, since that's what you have been asking for.' Then Moses and Aaron were driven out of Pharaoh's presence.

¹² And the LORD said to Moses, 'Stretch out your hand over Egypt so that locusts swarm over the land and devour everything growing in the fields, everything left by the hail.'

¹³ So Moses stretched out his staff over Egypt, and the LORD made an east wind blow across the land all that day and all that night. By morning the wind had brought the locusts; ¹⁴ they invaded all Egypt and settled down in every area of the country in

great numbers. Never before had there been such a plague of locusts, nor will there ever be again. ¹⁵They covered all the ground until it was black. They devoured all that was left after the hail – everything growing in the fields and the fruit on the trees. Nothing green remained on tree or plant in all the land of Egypt.

¹⁶Pharaoh quickly summoned Moses and Aaron and said, 'I have sinned against the LORD your God and against you. ¹⁷Now forgive my sin once more and pray to the LORD your God to take this deadly plague away from me.'

¹⁸Moses then left Pharaoh and prayed to the LORD. ¹⁹And the LORD changed the wind to a very strong west wind, which caught up the locusts and carried them into the Red Sea. Not a locust was left anywhere in Egypt. ²⁰But the LORD hardened Pharaoh's heart, and he would not let the Israelites go.

■ PSALM 18:13-19

¹³The LORD thundered from heaven;
    the voice of the Most High resounded.
¹⁴He shot his arrows and scattered the
        enemy,
    with great bolts of lightning he routed
        them.
¹⁵The valleys of the sea were exposed
    and the foundations of the earth laid
        bare
    at your rebuke, LORD,
        at the blast of breath from your nostrils.

¹⁶He reached down from on high and took
        hold of me;
    he drew me out of deep waters.
¹⁷He rescued me from my powerful enemy,
    from my foes, who were too strong for
        me.
¹⁸They confronted me in the day of my
        disaster,
    but the LORD was my support.

¹⁹He brought me out into a spacious place;
    he rescued me because he delighted
        in me.

■ PROVERBS 4:1-2

4 Listen, my sons, to a father's instruction;
    pay attention and gain
        understanding.
²I give you sound learning,
    so do not forsake my teaching.

■ MATTHEW 21:28-46

²⁸'What do you think? There was a man who had two sons. He went to the first and said, "Son, go and work today in the vineyard."

²⁹'"I will not," he answered, but later he changed his mind and went.

³⁰'Then the father went to the other son and said the same thing. He answered, "I will, sir," but he did not go.

³¹'Which of the two did what his father wanted?'

'The first,' they answered.

Jesus said to them, 'Truly I tell you, the tax collectors and the prostitutes are entering the kingdom of God ahead of you. ³²For John came to you to show you the way of righteousness, and you did not believe him, but the tax collectors and the prostitutes did. And even after you saw this, you did not repent and believe him.

³³'Listen to another parable: there was a landowner who planted a vineyard. He put a wall round it, dug a winepress in it and built a watchtower. Then he rented the vineyard to some farmers and moved to another place. ³⁴When the harvest time approached, he sent his servants to the tenants to collect his fruit.

³⁵'The tenants seized his servants; they beat one, killed another, and stoned a third.

36 Then he sent other servants to them, more than the first time, and the tenants treated them in the same way. 37 Last of all, he sent his son to them. "They will respect my son," he said.

38 'But when the tenants saw the son, they said to each other, "This is the heir. Come, let's kill him and take his inheritance." 39 So they took him and threw him out of the vineyard and killed him.

40 'Therefore, when the owner of the vineyard comes, what will he do to those tenants?'

41 'He will bring those wretches to a wretched end,' they replied, 'and he will rent the vineyard to other tenants, who will give him his share of the crop at harvest time.'

42 Jesus said to them, 'Have you never read in the Scriptures:

' "The stone the builders rejected
    has become the cornerstone;
the Lord has done this,
    and it is marvellous in our eyes"?

43 'Therefore I tell you that the kingdom of God will be taken away from you and given to a people who will produce its fruit. 44 Anyone who falls on this stone will be broken to pieces; anyone on whom it falls will be crushed.'

45 When the chief priests and the Pharisees heard Jesus' parables, they knew he was talking about them. 46 They looked for a way to arrest him, but they were afraid of the crowd because the people held that he was a prophet.

The Final Word

'... he drew me out of deep waters. He rescued me from my powerful enemy ...' **Psalm 18:16-17**

Once we become Christians, we are involved in a fight against Satan and his forces. God, however, has given us a defence against Satan and his tactics, which consists of six separate pieces of spiritual equipment outlined in Ephesians 6.

First, He has given us the belt of truth - a willingness to let God's truth govern every part of our lives. Second, the breastplate of righteousness - seeing clearly that we are not saved by our own righteousness but Christ's. Third, we must have our feet sandalled with the readiness that comes from the gospel of peace - our determination to stand firmly in the faith. Fourth, we must raise the shield of faith - the quick action by which we act upon God's truth and refuse Satan's lies. Fifth, we must put on the helmet of salvation - the glorious hope that, one day, the Lord will right all wrongs and establish His eternal kingdom. And sixth, we must take up the sword of the Spirit, the Word of God, and wield the written Scriptures in the same way our Lord did in His wilderness temptations.

Having done all this, it is still possible to be defeated by the devil unless we know how to pray in the power of the Spirit. We must pray not only when things are going wrong but continuously, fervently, powerfully, and perseveringly. Our prayers must catch alight and burst into flame. Against such praying, the principalities and powers are helpless.

PRAYER

My Father, now that I have seen the resources that are available to me in Christ, I realise that my responsibility to avail myself of these resources is greater than ever. Help me to put everything I have learned into action. For Your own dear name's sake. Amen.

FURTHER STUDY

Psa. 18; 65:6; Hab. 3:19; Isa. 41:10

- With what was David armed?
- Have you put on your armour today?

February 3

■ EXODUS 10:21–12:36

²¹ Then the LORD said to Moses, 'Stretch out your hand towards the sky so that darkness spreads over Egypt – darkness that can be felt.' ²² So Moses stretched out his hand towards the sky, and total darkness covered all Egypt for three days. ²³ No one could see anyone else or move about for three days. Yet all the Israelites had light in the places where they lived.

²⁴ Then Pharaoh summoned Moses and said, 'Go, worship the LORD. Even your women and children may go with you; only leave your flocks and herds behind.'

²⁵ But Moses said, 'You must allow us to have sacrifices and burnt offerings to present to the LORD our God. ²⁶ Our livestock too must go with us; not a hoof is to be left behind. We have to use some of them in worshipping the LORD our God, and until we get there we will not know what we are to use to worship the LORD.'

²⁷ But the LORD hardened Pharaoh's heart, and he was not willing to let them go. ²⁸ Pharaoh said to Moses, 'Get out of my sight! Make sure you do not appear before me again! The day you see my face you will die.'

²⁹ 'Just as you say,' Moses replied. 'I will never appear before you again.'

11 Now the LORD said to Moses, 'I will bring one more plague on Pharaoh and on Egypt. After that, he will let you go from here, and when he does, he will drive you out completely. ² Tell the people that men and women alike are to ask their neighbours for articles of silver and gold.' ³ (The LORD made the Egyptians favourably disposed towards the people, and Moses himself was highly regarded in Egypt by Pharaoh's officials and by the people.)

⁴ So Moses said, 'This is what the LORD says: "About midnight I will go throughout Egypt. ⁵ Every firstborn son in Egypt will die, from the firstborn son of Pharaoh, who sits on the throne, to the firstborn son of the female slave, who is at her hand mill, and all the firstborn of the cattle as well. ⁶ There will be loud wailing throughout Egypt – worse than there has ever been or ever will be again. ⁷ But among the Israelites not a dog will bark at any person or animal." Then you will know that the LORD makes a distinction between Egypt and Israel. ⁸ All these officials of yours will come to me, bowing down before me and saying, "Go, you and all the people who follow you!" After that I will leave.' Then Moses, hot with anger, left Pharaoh.

⁹ The LORD had said to Moses, 'Pharaoh

will refuse to listen to you – so that my wonders may be multiplied in Egypt.' ¹⁰ Moses and Aaron performed all these wonders before Pharaoh, but the LORD hardened Pharaoh's heart, and he would not let the Israelites go out of his country.

12 The LORD said to Moses and Aaron in Egypt, ²'This month is to be for you the first month, the first month of your year. ³ Tell the whole community of Israel that on the tenth day of this month each man is to take a lamb for his family, one for each household. ⁴ If any household is too small for a whole lamb, they must share one with their nearest neighbour, having taken into account the number of people there are. You are to determine the amount of lamb needed in accordance with what each person will eat. ⁵ The animals you choose must be year-old males without defect, and you may take them from the sheep or the goats. ⁶ Take care of them until the fourteenth day of the month, when all the members of the community of Israel must slaughter them at twilight. ⁷ Then they are to take some of the blood and put it on the sides and tops of the door-frames of the houses where they eat the lambs. ⁸ That same night they are to eat the meat roasted over the fire, along with bitter herbs, and bread made without yeast. ⁹ Do not eat the meat raw or boiled in water, but roast it over a fire – with the head, legs and internal organs. ¹⁰ Do not leave any of it till morning; if some is left till morning, you must burn it. ¹¹ This is how you are to eat it: with your cloak tucked into your belt, your sandals on your feet and your staff in your hand. Eat it in haste; it is the LORD's Passover.

¹²'On that same night I will pass through Egypt and strike down every firstborn of both people and animals, and I will bring judgment on all the gods of Egypt. I am the LORD. ¹³ The blood will be a sign for you on the houses where you are, and when I see the blood, I will pass over you. No destructive plague will touch you when I strike Egypt.

¹⁴'This is a day you are to commemorate; for the generations to come you shall celebrate it as a festival to the LORD – a lasting ordinance. ¹⁵ For seven days you are to eat bread made without yeast. On the first day remove the yeast from your houses, for whoever eats anything with yeast in it from the first day until the seventh must be cut off from Israel. ¹⁶ On the first day hold a sacred assembly, and another one on the seventh day. Do no work at all on these days, except to prepare food for everyone to eat; that is all you may do.

¹⁷'Celebrate the Festival of Unleavened Bread, because it was on this very day that I brought your divisions out of Egypt. Celebrate this day as a lasting ordinance for the generations to come. ¹⁸ In the first month you are to eat bread made without yeast, from the evening of the fourteenth day until the evening of the twenty-first day. ¹⁹ For seven days no yeast is to be found in your houses. And anyone, whether foreigner or native-born, who eats anything with yeast in it must be cut off from the community of Israel. ²⁰ Eat nothing made with yeast. Wherever you live, you must eat unleavened bread.'

²¹ Then Moses summoned all the elders of Israel and said to them, 'Go at once and select the animals for your families and slaughter the Passover lamb. ²² Take a bunch of hyssop, dip it into the blood in the basin and put some of the blood on the top and on both sides of the door-frame. None of you shall go out of the door of your house until morning. ²³ When the LORD goes through the land to strike down the Egyptians, he will see the blood on the top and sides of the door-frame and will pass over that doorway, and he will not permit the destroyer to enter your houses and strike you down.

²⁴'Obey these instructions as a lasting ordinance for you and your descendants. ²⁵ When you enter the land that the LORD will give you as he promised, observe this ceremony. ²⁶ And when your children ask

you, "What does this ceremony mean to you?" ²⁷then tell them, "It is the Passover sacrifice to the LORD, who passed over the houses of the Israelites in Egypt and spared our homes when he struck down the Egyptians."' Then the people bowed down and worshipped. ²⁸The Israelites did just what the LORD commanded Moses and Aaron.

²⁹At midnight the LORD struck down all the firstborn in Egypt, from the firstborn of Pharaoh, who sat on the throne, to the firstborn of the prisoner, who was in the dungeon, and the firstborn of all the livestock as well. ³⁰Pharaoh and all his officials and all the Egyptians got up during the night, and there was loud wailing in Egypt, for there was not a house without someone dead.

³¹During the night Pharaoh summoned Moses and Aaron and said, 'Up! Leave my people, you and the Israelites! Go, worship the LORD as you have requested. ³²Take your flocks and herds, as you have said, and go. And also bless me.'

³³The Egyptians urged the people to hurry and leave the country. 'For otherwise,' they said, 'we will all die!' ³⁴So the people took their dough before the yeast was added, and carried it on their shoulders in kneading troughs wrapped in clothing. ³⁵The Israelites did as Moses instructed and asked the Egyptians for articles of silver and gold and for clothing. ³⁶The LORD had made the Egyptians favourably disposed towards the people, and they gave them what they asked for; so they plundered the Egyptians.

▬ PSALM 18:20-24

²⁰The LORD has dealt with me according to
    my righteousness;
  according to the cleanness of my
    hands he has rewarded me.
²¹For I have kept the ways of the LORD;

I am not guilty of turning from my
    God.
²²All his laws are before me;
  I have not turned away from his
    decrees.
²³I have been blameless before him
  and have kept myself from sin.
²⁴The LORD has rewarded me according to
    my righteousness,
  according to the cleanness of my
    hands in his sight.

▬ PROVERBS 4:3-4

³For I too was a son to my father,
  still tender, and cherished by my
    mother.
⁴Then he taught me, and he said to me,
  'Take hold of my words with all your
    heart;
  keep my commands, and you will live.

▬ MATTHEW 22:1-22

22 Jesus spoke to them again in parables, saying: ²'The kingdom of heaven is like a king who prepared a wedding banquet for his son. ³He sent his servants to those who had been invited to the banquet to tell them to come, but they refused to come.

⁴'Then he sent some more servants and said, "Tell those who have been invited that I have prepared my dinner: my oxen and fattened cattle have been slaughtered, and everything is ready. Come to the wedding banquet."

⁵'But they paid no attention and went off – one to his field, another to his business. ⁶The rest seized his servants, ill-treated them and killed them. ⁷The king was enraged. He sent his army and destroyed those murderers and burned their city.

⁸'Then he said to his servants, "The

wedding banquet is ready, but those I invited did not deserve to come. ⁹So go to the street corners and invite to the banquet anyone you find." ¹⁰So the servants went out into the streets and gathered all the people they could find, the bad as well as the good, and the wedding hall was filled with guests.

¹¹'But when the king came in to see the guests, he noticed a man there who was not wearing wedding clothes. ¹²He asked, "How did you get in here without wedding clothes, friend?" The man was speechless.

¹³'Then the king told the attendants, "Tie him hand and foot, and throw him outside, into the darkness, where there will be weeping and gnashing of teeth."

¹⁴'For many are invited, but few are chosen.'

¹⁵Then the Pharisees went out and laid plans to trap him in his words. ¹⁶They sent their disciples to him along with the Herodians. 'Teacher,' they said, 'we know that you are a man of integrity and that you teach the way of God in accordance with the truth. You aren't swayed by others, because you pay no attention to who they are. ¹⁷Tell us then, what is your opinion? Is it right to pay the poll-tax to Caesar or not?'

¹⁸But Jesus, knowing their evil intent, said, 'You hypocrites, why are you trying to trap me? ¹⁹Show me the coin used for paying the tax.' They brought him a denarius, ²⁰and he asked them, 'Whose image is this? And whose inscription?'

²¹'Caesar's,' they replied.

Then he said to them, 'So give back to Caesar what is Caesar's, and to God what is God's.'

²²When they heard this, they were amazed. So they left him and went away.

The Coal Miner

'For I too was a son to my father ... he taught me, and he said to me, "Take hold of my words with all your heart ..."' **Proverbs 4:3-4**

Some of you reading these lines may not have had the benefits of a good or extensive education. But here is the encouraging thing – this is not important when it comes to the matter of defeating Satan.

I remember being present some years ago in a church in South Wales when a debate was held between a university professor and an ordinary coal miner. The subject was: 'Is the Bible true?' The university professor presented his arguments in a clear fashion, and I remember feeling quite sorry for the miner as I envisaged some of the difficulties he might face when making his reply. After the professor had finished, the miner stood to his feet. And for over an hour, I witnessed one of the most amazing demonstrations of the Holy Spirit at work that I have ever seen in my life.

The miner began by asking everyone to bow their heads as he prayed a prayer which went something like this, 'Lord, I have not had much education, but You know that I love Your Word and have spent my life searching its pages. Help me now to say something that will convince my friends here that Your Word is true.' He then proceeded to demolish the arguments of the professor simply by quoting appropriate Scriptures without making even a simple comment.

When he finished, there was thunderous applause. The professor's well-articulated, highly intellectual arguments had been torn to pieces by the sharp edges of the sword of the Spirit - by that and by that alone.

PRAYER

O Father, the more I hear, the more I want to hear. For I was created by Your Word, designed according to Your Word, and I can never remain content until I am indwelt *with* Your Word. Teach me even more. In Jesus' name. Amen.

FURTHER STUDY

Jer. 5:1-14; 23:29;
Psa. 119:105, 130; Heb. 4:12
• What was God's Word in Jeremiah's mouth?
• What was it to the psalmist?

February 4

■ EXODUS 12:37–14:20

37 The Israelites journeyed from Rameses to Sukkoth. There were about six hundred thousand men on foot, besides women and children. 38 Many other people went up with them, and also large droves of livestock, both flocks and herds. 39 With the dough the Israelites had brought from Egypt, they baked loaves of unleavened bread. The dough was without yeast because they had been driven out of Egypt and did not have time to prepare food for themselves.

40 Now the length of time the Israelite people lived in Egypt was 430 years. 41 At the end of the 430 years, to the very day, all the LORD's divisions left Egypt. 42 Because the LORD kept vigil that night to bring them out of Egypt, on this night all the Israelites are to keep vigil to honour the LORD for the generations to come.

43 The LORD said to Moses and Aaron, 'These are the regulations for the Passover meal:

'No foreigner may eat it. 44 Any slave you have bought may eat it after you have circumcised him, 45 but a temporary resident or a hired worker may not eat it.

46 'It must be eaten inside the house; take none of the meat outside the house. Do not break any of the bones. 47 The whole community of Israel must celebrate it.

48 'A foreigner residing among you who wants to celebrate the LORD's Passover must have all the males in his household circumcised; then he may take part like one born in the land. No uncircumcised male may eat it. 49 The same law applies both to the native-born and to the foreigner residing among you.'

50 All the Israelites did just what the LORD had commanded Moses and Aaron. 51 And on that very day the LORD brought the Israelites out of Egypt by their divisions.

13 The LORD said to Moses, 2 'Consecrate to me every firstborn male. The first offspring of every womb among the Israelites belongs to me, whetsher human or animal.'

3 Then Moses said to the people, 'Commemorate this day, the day you came out of Egypt, out of the land of slavery, because the LORD brought you out of it with a mighty hand. Eat nothing containing yeast. 4 Today, in the month of Aviv, you are leaving.

⁵When the LORD brings you into the land of the Canaanites, Hittites, Amorites, Hivites and Jebusites – the land he swore to your ancestors to give you, a land flowing with milk and honey – you are to observe this ceremony in this month: ⁶for seven days eat bread made without yeast and on the seventh day hold a festival to the LORD. ⁷Eat unleavened bread during those seven days; nothing with yeast in it is to be seen among you, nor shall any yeast be seen anywhere within your borders. ⁸On that day tell your son, "I do this because of what the LORD did for me when I came out of Egypt." ⁹This observance will be for you like a sign on your hand and a reminder on your forehead that this law of the LORD is to be on your lips. For the LORD brought you out of Egypt with his mighty hand. ¹⁰You must keep this ordinance at the appointed time year after year.

¹¹'After the LORD brings you into the land of the Canaanites and gives it to you, as he promised on oath to you and your ancestors, ¹²you are to give over to the LORD the first offspring of every womb. All the firstborn males of your livestock belong to the LORD. ¹³Redeem with a lamb every firstborn donkey, but if you do not redeem it, break its neck. Redeem every firstborn among your sons.

¹⁴'In days to come when your son asks you, "What does this mean?" say to him, "With a mighty hand the LORD brought us out of Egypt, out of the land of slavery. ¹⁵When Pharaoh stubbornly refused to let us go, the LORD killed the firstborn of both people and animals in Egypt. This is why I sacrifice to the LORD the first male offspring of every womb and redeem each of my firstborn sons." ¹⁶And it will be like a sign on your hand and a symbol on your forehead that the LORD brought us out of Egypt with his mighty hand.'

¹⁷When Pharaoh let the people go, God did not lead them on the road through the Philistine country, though that was shorter. For God said, 'If they face war, they might change their minds and return to Egypt.' ¹⁸So God led the people around by the desert road towards the Red Sea. The Israelites went up out of Egypt ready for battle.

¹⁹Moses took the bones of Joseph with him because Joseph had made the Israelites swear an oath. He had said, 'God will surely come to your aid, and then you must carry my bones up with you from this place.'

²⁰After leaving Sukkoth they camped at Etham on the edge of the desert. ²¹By day the LORD went ahead of them in a pillar of cloud to guide them on their way and by night in a pillar of fire to give them light, so that they could travel by day or night. ²²Neither the pillar of cloud by day nor the pillar of fire by night left its place in front of the people.

14 Then the LORD said to Moses, ²'Tell the Israelites to turn back and camp near Pi Hahiroth, between Migdol and the sea. They are to camp by the sea, directly opposite Baal Zephon. ³Pharaoh will think, "The Israelites are wandering around the land in confusion, hemmed in by the desert." ⁴And I will harden Pharaoh's heart, and he will pursue them. But I will gain glory for myself through Pharaoh and all his army, and the Egyptians will know that I am the LORD.' So the Israelites did this.

⁵When the king of Egypt was told that the people had fled, Pharaoh and his officials changed their minds about them and said, 'What have we done? We have let the Israelites go and have lost their services!' ⁶So he had his chariot made ready and took his army with him. ⁷He took six hundred of the best chariots, along with all the other chariots of Egypt, with officers over all of them. ⁸The LORD hardened the heart of Pharaoh king of Egypt, so that he pursued the Israelites, who were marching out boldly. ⁹The Egyptians – all Pharaoh's horses and chariots, horsemen and troops – pursued the Israelites and overtook them as they camped by the sea near Pi Hahiroth, opposite Baal Zephon.

¹⁰As Pharaoh approached, the Israelites looked up, and there were the Egyptians, marching after them. They were terrified and cried out to the LORD. ¹¹They said to Moses, 'Was it because there were no graves in Egypt that you brought us to the desert to die? What have you done to us by bringing us out of Egypt? ¹²Didn't we say to you in Egypt, "Leave us alone; let us serve the Egyptians"? It would have been better for us to serve the Egyptians than to die in the desert!'

¹³Moses answered the people, 'Do not be afraid. Stand firm and you will see the deliverance the LORD will bring you today. The Egyptians you see today you will never see again. ¹⁴The LORD will fight for you; you need only to be still.'

¹⁵Then the LORD said to Moses, 'Why are you crying out to me? Tell the Israelites to move on. ¹⁶Raise your staff and stretch out your hand over the sea to divide the water so that the Israelites can go through the sea on dry ground. ¹⁷I will harden the hearts of the Egyptians so that they will go in after them. And I will gain glory through Pharaoh and all his army, through his chariots and his horsemen. ¹⁸The Egyptians will know that I am the LORD when I gain glory through Pharaoh, his chariots and his horsemen.'

¹⁹Then the angel of God, who had been travelling in front of Israel's army, withdrew and went behind them. The pillar of cloud also moved from in front and stood behind them, ²⁰coming between the armies of Egypt and Israel. Throughout the night the cloud brought darkness to the one side and light to the other; so neither went near the other all night long.

▬ PSALM 18:25-29

²⁵To the faithful you show yourself faithful,
 to the blameless you show yourself blameless,

²⁶to the pure you show yourself pure,
 but to the devious you show yourself shrewd.

²⁷You save the humble
 but bring low those whose eyes are haughty.

²⁸You, LORD, keep my lamp burning;
 my God turns my darkness into light.

²⁹With your help I can advance against a troop;
 with my God I can scale a wall.

▬ PROVERBS 4:5-6

⁵Get wisdom, get understanding;
 do not forget my words or turn away from them.

⁶Do not forsake wisdom, and she will protect you;
 love her, and she will watch over you.

▬ MATTHEW 22:23-46

²³That same day the Sadducees, who say there is no resurrection, came to him with a question. ²⁴'Teacher,' they said, 'Moses told us that if a man dies without having children, his brother must marry the widow and raise up offspring for him. ²⁵Now there were seven brothers among us. The first one married and died, and since he had no children, he left his wife to his brother. ²⁶The same thing happened to the second and third brother, right on down to the seventh. ²⁷Finally, the woman died. ²⁸Now then, at the resurrection, whose wife will she be of the seven, since all of them were married to her?'

²⁹Jesus replied, 'You are in error because you do not know the Scriptures or the power of God. ³⁰At the resurrection people will neither marry nor be given in marriage; they will be like the angels in heaven. ³¹But about the resurrection of the dead – have

you not read what God said to you, [32]"I am the God of Abraham, the God of Isaac, and the God of Jacob"? He is not the God of the dead but of the living.'

[33] When the crowds heard this, they were astonished at his teaching.

[34] Hearing that Jesus had silenced the Sadducees, the Pharisees got together. [35] One of them, an expert in the law, tested him with this question: [36] 'Teacher, which is the greatest commandment in the Law?'

[37] Jesus replied: ' "Love the Lord your God with all your heart and with all your soul and with all your mind." [38] This is the first and greatest commandment. [39] And the second is like it: "Love your neighbour as yourself." [40] All the Law and the Prophets hang on these two commandments.'

[41] While the Pharisees were gathered together, Jesus asked them, [42] 'What do you think about the Messiah? Whose son is he?'

'The son of David,' they replied.

[43] He said to them, 'How is it then that David, speaking by the Spirit, calls him "Lord"? For he says,

[44] ' "The Lord said to my Lord:
    'Sit at my right hand
    until I put your enemies
      under your feet.' "

[45] If then David calls him "Lord", how can he be his son?' [46] No one could say a word in reply, and from that day on no one dared to ask him any more questions.

The Need to Know

'At the end of the 430 years, to the very day, all the LORD's divisions left Egypt.' **Exodus 12:41**

The Bible is a veritable mine of information on the fact of God's faithfulness. More than 4,000 years ago He said, 'As long as the earth endures, seedtime and harvest, cold and heat, summer and winter, day and night will never cease' (Gen. 8:22). Every year furnishes us with fresh evidence that He has not gone back on His Word.

In Genesis 15:13-14, God declared to Abram, 'Know for certain that for four hundred years your descendants will be strangers in a country not their own and that they will be enslaved and ill-treated there.' However, '... afterwards they will come out with great possessions.' Did that happen? Exodus 12:41 says: 'At the end of the 430 years, to the very day, all the LORD's divisions left Egypt.'

The prophet Isaiah predicted that a virgin would conceive and bear a son whose name would be Immanuel (Isa. 7:14). Centuries later the prediction came to pass. In Galatians 4:4 we read: 'But when the set time had fully come, God sent his Son, born of a woman ... .'

I wish I had the space to take you through the pages of Scripture and show you how faithful God has been to His Word. But you have a Bible for yourself; study it. Read it to know God. This is the basis of our confidence in Him. And this is why the Bible fairly bulges with this great and gripping truth. The more of God's truth we pack into our souls, the better equipped we are for the road that lies ahead.

PRAYER

Gracious and loving Father, the more I learn about Your nature and character, the more I want to know. Just these glimpses I am getting set my soul on fire to know You more intimately. Take me deeper, dear Lord. In Jesus' name. Amen.

FURTHER STUDY

Mal. 3:7; Psa. 103:17; 102:27; James 1:1-17
• What did the Lord declare to Israel?
• How did James put it?

February 5

■ EXODUS 14:21–16:20

²¹ Then Moses stretched out his hand over the sea, and all that night the LORD drove the sea back with a strong east wind and turned it into dry land. The waters were divided, ²² and the Israelites went through the sea on dry ground, with a wall of water on their right and on their left.

²³ The Egyptians pursued them, and all Pharaoh's horses and chariots and horsemen followed them into the sea. ²⁴ During the last watch of the night the LORD looked down from the pillar of fire and cloud at the Egyptian army and threw it into confusion. ²⁵ He jammed the wheels of their chariots so that they had difficulty driving. And the Egyptians said, 'Let's get away from the Israelites! The LORD is fighting for them against Egypt.'

²⁶ Then the LORD said to Moses, 'Stretch out your hand over the sea so that the waters may flow back over the Egyptians and their chariots and horsemen.' ²⁷ Moses stretched out his hand over the sea, and at daybreak the sea went back to its place. The Egyptians were fleeing towards it, and the LORD swept them into the sea. ²⁸ The water flowed back and covered the chariots and horsemen – the entire army of Pharaoh that had followed the Israelites into the sea. Not one

of them survived.

²⁹ But the Israelites went through the sea on dry ground, with a wall of water on their right and on their left. ³⁰ That day the LORD saved Israel from the hands of the Egyptians, and Israel saw the Egyptians lying dead on the shore. ³¹ And when the Israelites saw the mighty hand of the LORD displayed against the Egyptians, the people feared the LORD and put their trust in him and in Moses his servant.

15 Then Moses and the Israelites sang this song to the LORD:

'I will sing to the LORD,
  for he is highly exalted.
Both horse and driver
  he has hurled into the sea.
² 'The LORD is my strength and my
    defence;
  he has become my salvation.
He is my God, and I will praise him,
  my father's God, and I will exalt
    him.
³ The LORD is a warrior;
  the LORD is his name.
⁴ Pharaoh's chariots and his army
  he has hurled into the sea.
The best of Pharaoh's officers
  are drowned in the Red Sea.

⁵ The deep waters have covered them;
   they sank to the depths like a stone.
⁶ Your right hand, LORD,
   was majestic in power.
Your right hand, LORD,
   shattered the enemy.

⁷ 'In the greatness of your majesty
   you threw down those who opposed
   you.
You unleashed your burning anger;
   it consumed them like stubble.
⁸ By the blast of your nostrils
   the waters piled up.
The surging waters stood up like a
   wall;
   the deep waters congealed in the
   heart of the sea.
⁹ The enemy boasted,
   "I will pursue, I will overtake them.
I will divide the spoils;
   I will gorge myself on them.
I will draw my sword
   and my hand will destroy them."
¹⁰ But you blew with your breath,
   and the sea covered them.
They sank like lead
   in the mighty waters.
¹¹ Who among the gods
   is like you, LORD?
Who is like you –
   majestic in holiness,
awesome in glory,
   working wonders?

¹² 'You stretch out your right hand,
   and the earth swallows your
   enemies.
¹³ In your unfailing love you will lead
   the people you have redeemed.
In your strength you will guide them
   to your holy dwelling.
¹⁴ The nations will hear and tremble;
   anguish will grip the people of
   Philistia.
¹⁵ The chiefs of Edom will be terrified,

the leaders of Moab will be seized
   with trembling,
the people of Canaan will melt away;
¹⁶   terror and dread will fall on them.
By the power of your arm
   they will be as still as a stone –
until your people pass by, LORD,
   until the people you bought pass by.
¹⁷ You will bring them in and plant them
   on the mountain of your
   inheritance –
the place, LORD, you made for your
   dwelling,
   the sanctuary, Lord, your hands
   established.

¹⁸ 'The LORD reigns
   for ever and ever.'

¹⁹ When Pharaoh's horses, chariots and horsemen went into the sea, the LORD brought the waters of the sea back over them, but the Israelites walked through the sea on dry ground. ²⁰ Then Miriam the prophet, Aaron's sister, took a tambourine in her hand, and all the women followed her, with tambourines and dancing. ²¹ Miriam sang to them:

'Sing to the LORD,
   for he is highly exalted.
Both horse and driver
   he has hurled into the sea.'

²² Then Moses led Israel from the Red Sea and they went into the Desert of Shur. For three days they travelled in the desert without finding water. ²³ When they came to Marah, they could not drink its water because it was bitter. (That is why the place is called Marah.) ²⁴ So the people grumbled against Moses, saying, 'What are we to drink?' ²⁵ Then Moses cried out to the LORD, and the LORD showed him a piece of wood. He threw it into the water, and the water became fit to drink.

There the LORD issued a ruling and

instruction for them and put them to the test. [26]He said, 'If you listen carefully to the LORD your God and do what is right in his eyes, if you pay attention to his commands and keep all his decrees, I will not bring on you any of the diseases I brought on the Egyptians, for I am the LORD, who heals you.'

[27]Then they came to Elim, where there were twelve springs and seventy palm trees, and they camped there near the water.

16 The whole Israelite community set out from Elim and came to the Desert of Sin, which is between Elim and Sinai, on the fifteenth day of the second month after they had come out of Egypt. [2]In the desert the whole community grumbled against Moses and Aaron. [3]The Israelites said to them, 'If only we had died by the LORD's hand in Egypt! There we sat round pots of meat and ate all the food we wanted, but you have brought us out into this desert to starve this entire assembly to death.'

[4]Then the LORD said to Moses, 'I will rain down bread from heaven for you. The people are to go out each day and gather enough for that day. In this way I will test them and see whether they will follow my instructions. [5]On the sixth day they are to prepare what they bring in, and that is to be twice as much as they gather on the other days.'

[6]So Moses and Aaron said to all the Israelites, 'In the evening you will know that it was the LORD who brought you out of Egypt, [7]and in the morning you will see the glory of the LORD, because he has heard your grumbling against him. Who are we, that you should grumble against us?' [8]Moses also said, 'You will know that it was the LORD when he gives you meat to eat in the evening and all the bread you want in the morning, because he has heard your grumbling against him. Who are we? You are not grumbling against us, but against the LORD.'

[9]Then Moses told Aaron, 'Say to the entire Israelite community, "Come before the LORD, for he has heard your grumbling."'

[10]While Aaron was speaking to the whole Israelite community, they looked towards the desert, and there was the glory of the LORD appearing in the cloud.

[11]The LORD said to Moses, [12]'I have heard the grumbling of the Israelites. Tell them, "At twilight you will eat meat, and in the morning you will be filled with bread. Then you will know that I am the LORD your God."'

[13]That evening quail came and covered the camp, and in the morning there was a layer of dew around the camp. [14]When the dew was gone, thin flakes like frost on the ground appeared on the desert floor. [15]When the Israelites saw it, they said to each other, 'What is it?' For they did not know what it was.

Moses said to them, 'It is the bread the LORD has given you to eat. [16]This is what the LORD has commanded: "Everyone is to gather as much as they need. Take an omer for each person you have in your tent."'

[17]The Israelites did as they were told; some gathered much, some little. [18]And when they measured it by the omer, the one who gathered much did not have too much, and the one who gathered little did not have too little. Everyone had gathered just as much as they needed.

[19]Then Moses said to them, 'No one is to keep any of it until morning.'

[20]However, some of them paid no attention to Moses; they kept part of it until morning, but it was full of maggots and began to smell. So Moses was angry with them.

··

■ PSALM 18:30-36

[30]As for God, his way is perfect:
    The LORD's word is flawless;

he shields all who take refuge in him.
³¹ For who is God besides the LORD?
And who is the Rock except our God?
³² It is God who arms me with strength
and keeps my way secure.
³³ He makes my feet like the feet of a deer;
he causes me to stand on the heights.
³⁴ He trains my hands for battle;
my arms can bend a bow of bronze.
³⁵ You make your saving help my shield,
and your right hand sustains me;
your help has made me great.
³⁶ You provide a broad path for my feet,
so that my ankles do not give way.

▬ PROVERBS 4:7-9

⁷ The beginning of wisdom is this: get
wisdom.
Though it cost all you have, get
understanding.
⁸ Cherish her, and she will exalt you;
embrace her, and she will honour you.
⁹ She will give you a garland to grace your
head
and present you with a glorious crown.'

▬ MATTHEW 23:1-22

23 Then Jesus said to the crowds and
to his disciples: ² 'The teachers of
the law and the Pharisees sit in Moses' seat.
³ So you must be careful to do everything
they tell you. But do not do what they do,
for they do not practise what they preach.
⁴ They tie up heavy, cumbersome loads
and put them on other people's shoulders,
but they themselves are not willing to lift a
finger to move them.

⁵ 'Everything they do is done for people to
see: They make their phylacteries wide and
the tassels on their garments long; ⁶ they
love the place of honour at banquets and the

most important seats in the synagogues;
⁷ they love to be greeted with respect in the
market-places and to be called "Rabbi" by
others.

⁸ 'But you are not to be called "Rabbi", for
you have one Teacher, and you are all brothers. ⁹ And do not call anyone on earth "father", for you have one Father, and he is in
heaven. ¹⁰ Nor are you to be called instruc-
tors, for you have one Instructor, the Messiah. ¹¹ The greatest among you will be your
servant. ¹² For those who exalt themselves
will be humbled, and those who humble
themselves will be exalted.

¹³ 'Woe to you, teachers of the law and
Pharisees, you hypocrites! You shut the
door of the kingdom of heaven in people's
faces. You yourselves do not enter, nor will
you let those enter who are trying to. ^{[14]a}

¹⁵ 'Woe to you, teachers of the law and
Pharisees, you hypocrites! You travel over
land and sea to win a single convert, and
when you have succeeded, you make them
twice as much a child of hell as you are.

¹⁶ 'Woe to you, blind guides! You say,
"If anyone swears by the temple, it means
nothing; but anyone who swears by the
gold of the temple is bound by that oath."
¹⁷ You blind fools! Which is greater: the
gold, or the temple that makes the gold sacred? ¹⁸ You also say, "If anyone swears by
the altar, it means nothing; but anyone who
swears by the gift on the altar is bound by
that oath." ¹⁹ You blind men! Which is greater: the gift, or the altar that makes the gift
sacred? ²⁰ Therefore, anyone who swears
by the altar swears by it and by everything
on it. ²¹ And anyone who swears by the temple swears by it and by the one who dwells
in it. ²² And anyone who swears by heaven
swears by God's throne and by the one who
sits on it.

---

^a Some manuscripts include here words similar to Mark 12:40
and Luke 20:47

Spiritually Sure-Footed

'He makes my feet like the feet of a deer; he causes me to stand on the heights.' **Psalm 18:33**

I once I read the story of a man who, while holidaying on a ranch in Wyoming, was given the use of one of its horses - the fastest he had ever ridden. One day a group of the ranch cowboys invited him to join them for a ride up into the mountains. As they climbed into the hills, they came to a dangerous ascent, at which point the foreman turned to the newcomer and said, 'I think you would be well advised to take the longer but less dangerous trail to the top. Your horse is not dependable on the hills. Our horses are true climbers - their rear feet track exactly where their front feet are planted. Your horse has spent so many years on the plain that its rear feet could miss the track by inches, and one slip could mean serious injury - perhaps even death.'

When I read those words, my thoughts turned immediately to the verse before us today, for no animal has such perfect correlation of its front and rear feet as the deer. When it leaps from rock to rock, its back feet land exactly where its front feet had been placed.

If we are to climb higher with God than we have ever gone before, then more is needed than just speed. We must know spiritual sure-footedness also. Let's determine we will let nothing stand in the way of making our feet like hinds' feet and climbing with God to the 'high places.'

PRAYER

My Father and my God, hear my prayer as I begin perhaps a new chapter in my spiritual experience. Help me to climb higher with You than I have ever gone before, and do it not only with speed, but with sure-footedness also. In Jesus' name. Amen.

FURTHER STUDY

Phil. 3:1-14; Isa. 54:2; Eph. 3:17-19

- What was the deep desire of Paul's heart?
- What did he pray for the Ephesians?

February 6

■ **EXODUS 16:21–18:27**

²¹Each morning everyone gathered as much as they needed, and when the sun grew hot, it melted away. ²²On the sixth day, they gathered twice as much – two omers for each person – and the leaders of the community came and reported this to Moses. ²³He said to them, 'This is what the LORD commanded: "Tomorrow is to be

a day of sabbath rest, a holy sabbath to the LORD. So bake what you want to bake and boil what you want to boil. Save whatever is left and keep it until morning."' ²⁴So they saved it until morning, as Moses commanded, and it did not stink or get maggots in it. ²⁵'Eat it today,' Moses said, 'because today is a sabbath to the LORD. You will not find any of it on the ground today. ²⁶Six days you are to gather it, but on the seventh day, the Sabbath, there will not be any.'

²⁷Nevertheless, some of the people went out on the seventh day to gather it, but they found none. ²⁸Then the LORD said to Moses, 'How long will you refuse to keep my commands and my instructions? ²⁹Bear in mind that the LORD has given you the Sabbath; that is why on the sixth day he gives you bread for two days. Everyone is to stay where they are on the seventh day; no one is to go out.' ³⁰So the people rested on the seventh day.

³¹The people of Israel called the bread manna. It was white like coriander seed and tasted like wafers made with honey. ³²Moses said, 'This is what the LORD has commanded: "Take an omer of manna and keep it for the generations to come, so they can see the bread I gave you to eat in the wilderness when I brought you out of Egypt."'

³³So Moses said to Aaron, 'Take a jar and put an omer of manna in it. Then place it before the LORD to be kept for the generations to come.'

³⁴As the LORD commanded Moses, Aaron put the manna with the tablets of the covenant law, that it might be preserved. ³⁵The Israelites ate manna for forty years, until they came to a land that was settled; they ate manna until they reached the border of Canaan.

³⁶(An omer is one tenth of an ephah.)

17 The whole Israelite community set out from the Desert of Sin, travelling from place to place as the LORD commanded.

They camped at Rephidim, but there was no water for the people to drink. ²So they quarrelled with Moses and said, 'Give us water to drink.'

Moses replied, 'Why do you quarrel with me? Why do you put the LORD to the test?'

³But the people were thirsty for water there, and they grumbled against Moses. They said, 'Why did you bring us up out of Egypt to make us and our children and livestock die of thirst?'

⁴Then Moses cried out to the LORD, 'What am I to do with these people? They are almost ready to stone me.'

⁵The LORD answered Moses, 'Go out in front of the people. Take with you some of the elders of Israel and take in your hand the staff with which you struck the Nile, and go. ⁶I will stand there before you by the rock at Horeb. Strike the rock, and water will come out of it for the people to drink.' So Moses did this in the sight of the elders of Israel. ⁷And he called the place Massah and Meribah because the Israelites quarrelled and because they tested the LORD saying, 'Is the LORD among us or not?'

⁸The Amalekites came and attacked the Israelites at Rephidim. ⁹Moses said to Joshua, 'Choose some of our men and go out to fight the Amalekites. Tomorrow I will stand on top of the hill with the staff of God in my hands.'

¹⁰So Joshua fought the Amalekites as Moses had ordered, and Moses, Aaron and Hur went to the top of the hill. ¹¹As long as Moses held up his hands, the Israelites were winning, but whenever he lowered his hands, the Amalekites were winning. ¹²When Moses' hands grew tired, they took a stone and put it under him and he sat on it. Aaron and Hur held his hands up – one on one side, one on the other – so that his hands remained steady till sunset. ¹³So Joshua overcame the Amalekite army with the sword.

¹⁴Then the LORD said to Moses, 'Write this on a scroll as something to be remembered

and make sure that Joshua hears it, because I will completely blot out the name of Amalek from under heaven.'

[15] Moses built an altar and called it The LORD is my Banner. [16] He said, 'Because hands were lifted up against the throne of the LORD, the LORD will be at war against the Amalekites from generation to generation.'

18 Now Jethro, the priest of Midian and father-in-law of Moses, heard of everything God had done for Moses and for his people Israel, and how the LORD had brought Israel out of Egypt.

[2] After Moses had sent away his wife Zipporah, his father-in-law Jethro received her [3] and her two sons. One son was named Gershom, for Moses said, 'I have become a foreigner in a foreign land'; [4] and the other was named Eliezer, for he said, 'My father's God was my helper; he saved me from the sword of Pharaoh.'

[5] Jethro, Moses' father-in-law, together with Moses' sons and wife, came to him in the wilderness, where he was camped near the mountain of God. [6] Jethro had sent word to him, 'I, your father-in-law Jethro, am coming to you with your wife and her two sons.'

[7] So Moses went out to meet his father-in-law and bowed down and kissed him. They greeted each other and then went into the tent. [8] Moses told his father-in-law about everything the LORD had done to Pharaoh and the Egyptians for Israel's sake and about all the hardships they had met along the way and how the LORD had saved them.

[9] Jethro was delighted to hear about all the good things the LORD had done for Israel in rescuing them from the hand of the Egyptians. [10] He said, 'Praise be to the LORD, who rescued you from the hand of the Egyptians and of Pharaoh, and who rescued the people from the hand of the Egyptians. [11] Now I know that the LORD is greater than all other gods, for he did this to those who had treated Israel arrogantly.' [12] Then Jethro, Moses' father-in-law, brought a burnt offering and other sacrifices to God, and Aaron came with all the elders of Israel to eat a meal with Moses' father-in-law in the presence of God.

[13] The next day Moses took his seat to serve as judge for the people, and they stood round him from morning till evening. [14] When his father-in-law saw all that Moses was doing for the people, he said, 'What is this you are doing for the people? Why do you alone sit as judge, while all these people stand round you from morning till evening?'

[15] Moses answered him, 'Because the people come to me to seek God's will. [16] Whenever they have a dispute, it is brought to me, and I decide between the parties and inform them of God's decrees and instructions.'

[17] Moses' father-in-law replied, 'What you are doing is not good. [18] You and these people who come to you will only wear yourselves out. The work is too heavy for you; you cannot handle it alone. [19] Listen now to me and I will give you some advice, and may God be with you. You must be the people's representative before God and bring their disputes to him. [20] Teach them his decrees and instructions, and show them the way they are to live and how they are to behave. [21] But select capable men from all the people – men who fear God, trustworthy men who hate dishonest gain – and appoint them as officials over thousands, hundreds, fifties and tens. [22] Let them serve as judges for the people at all times, but let them bring every difficult case to you; the simple cases they can decide themselves. That will make your load lighter, because they will share it with you. [23] If you do this and God so commands, you will be able to stand the strain, and all these people will go home satisfied.'

[24] Moses listened to his father-in-law and did everything he said. [25] He chose capable

men from all Israel and made them leaders of the people, officials over thousands, hundreds, fifties and tens. ²⁶They served as judges for the people at all times. The difficult cases they brought to Moses, but the simple ones they decided themselves.

²⁷Then Moses sent his father-in-law on his way, and Jethro returned to his own country.

■ PSALM 18:37-42

³⁷I pursued my enemies and overtook them;
   I did not turn back till they were destroyed.
³⁸I crushed them so that they could not rise;
   they fell beneath my feet.
³⁹You armed me with strength for battle;
   you humbled my adversaries before me.
⁴⁰You made my enemies turn their backs in flight,
   and I destroyed my foes.
⁴¹They cried for help, but there was no one to save them –
   to the LORD, but he did not answer.
⁴²I beat them as fine as windblown dust;
   I trampled them like mud in the streets.

■ PROVERBS 4:10-13

¹⁰Listen, my son, accept what I say,
   and the years of your life will be many.
¹¹I instruct you in the way of wisdom
   and lead you along straight paths.
¹²When you walk, your steps will not be hampered;
   when you run, you will not stumble.
¹³Hold on to instruction, do not let it go;
   guard it well, for it is your life.

■ MATTHEW 23:23-39

²³'Woe to you, teachers of the law and Pharisees, you hypocrites! You give a tenth of your spices – mint, dill and cumin. But you have neglected the more important matters of the law – justice, mercy and faithfulness. You should have practised the latter, without neglecting the former. ²⁴You blind guides! You strain out a gnat but swallow a camel.

²⁵'Woe to you, teachers of the law and Pharisees, you hypocrites! You clean the outside of the cup and dish, but inside they are full of greed and self-indulgence. ²⁶Blind Pharisee! First clean the inside of the cup and dish, and then the outside also will be clean.

²⁷'Woe to you, teachers of the law and Pharisees, you hypocrites! You are like whitewashed tombs, which look beautiful on the outside but on the inside are full of the bones of the dead and everything unclean. ²⁸In the same way, on the outside you appear to people as righteous but on the inside you are full of hypocrisy and wickedness.

²⁹'Woe to you, teachers of the law and Pharisees, you hypocrites! You build tombs for the prophets and decorate the graves of the righteous. ³⁰And you say, "If we had lived in the days of our ancestors, we would not have taken part with them in shedding the blood of the prophets." ³¹So you testify against yourselves that you are the descendants of those who murdered the prophets. ³²Go ahead, then, and complete what your ancestors started!

³³'You snakes! You brood of vipers! How will you escape being condemned to hell? ³⁴Therefore I am sending you prophets and sages and teachers. Some of them you will kill and crucify; others you will flog in your synagogues and pursue from town to town. ³⁵And so upon you will come all the righteous blood that has been shed on earth,

from the blood of righteous Abel to the blood of Zechariah son of Berekiah, whom you murdered between the temple and the altar. ³⁶ Truly I tell you, all this will come upon this generation.

³⁷ 'Jerusalem, Jerusalem, you who kill the prophets and stone those sent to you, how often I have longed to gather your children together, as a hen gathers her chicks under her wings, and you were not willing. ³⁸ Look, your house is left to you desolate. ³⁹ For I tell you, you will not see me again until you say, "Blessed is he who comes in the name of the Lord."'

No Pretence

'You are like whitewashed tombs, which look beautiful on the outside but on the inside are full of the bones of the dead and everything unclean.'
Matthew 23:27

The Pharisees of Jesus' day specialised in looking good. Sin was defined by them in terms of visible transgressions, and as long as they did nothing to violate the standards which they so carefully defined, they regarded themselves as being free from sin. And there can be little doubt about it – they were good performers. Their level of disciplined conformity to external expectations was very high. They impressed many by their performance, but there was someone they failed to impress – Jesus. He told them that they were nothing more than 'whitewashed tombs' and called them 'blind guides' (Matt. 23:27,16).

In His rebuke to the Pharisees, our Lord established a principle that must guide us in our effort to become the people He wants us to be, and that principle is this – there must be no pretence. Christ's teaching seems to be that we can't make it as His followers unless we are willing to take an honest and straightforward look at what is going on beneath the surface of our lives. To look honestly at those parts of our being which we would rather not know about is not, as some might say, a sign of morbid introspection but a sign of healthy spirituality.

PRAYER

O Father, You know me so well – help me not to try and hide anything from You. Love me enough to overcome all my resistance, all my antipathy, and all my fear. For I don't just want to be a better person; I want to be a whole person. In Jesus' name. Amen.

FURTHER STUDY

Col. 2:1-20; Isa. 1:11-17; Gal. 4:10
• What did Paul bring to the Colossians' attention?
• How similar was it to Isaiah's word centuries before?

February 7

■ EXODUS 19:1–20:26

19 On the first day of the third month after the Israelites left Egypt – on that very day – they came to the Desert of Sinai. ²After they set out from Rephidim, they entered the Desert of Sinai, and Israel camped there in the desert in front of the mountain.

³Then Moses went up to God, and the LORD called to him from the mountain and said, 'This is what you are to say to the descendants of Jacob and what you are to tell the people of Israel: ⁴"You yourselves have seen what I did to Egypt, and how I carried you on eagles' wings and brought you to myself. ⁵Now if you obey me fully and keep my covenant, then out of all nations you will be my treasured possession. Although the whole earth is mine, ⁶you will be for me a kingdom of priests and a holy nation." These are the words you are to speak to the Israelites.'

⁷So Moses went back and summoned the elders of the people and set before them all the words the LORD had commanded him to speak. ⁸The people all responded together, 'We will do everything the LORD has said.' So Moses brought their answer back to the LORD.

⁹The LORD said to Moses, 'I am going to come to you in a dense cloud, so that the people will hear me speaking with you and will always put their trust in you.' Then Moses told the LORD what the people had said.

¹⁰And the LORD said to Moses, 'Go to the people and consecrate them today and tomorrow. Make them wash their clothes ¹¹and be ready by the third day, because on that day the LORD will come down on Mount Sinai in the sight of all the people. ¹²Put limits for the people around the mountain and tell them, "Be careful that you do not approach the mountain or touch the foot of it. Whoever touches the mountain is to be put to death. ¹³They are to be stoned or shot with arrows; not a hand is to be laid on them. No person or animal shall be permitted to live." Only when the ram's horn sounds a long blast may they approach the mountain.'

¹⁴After Moses had gone down the mountain to the people, he consecrated them, and they washed their clothes. ¹⁵Then he said to the people, 'Prepare yourselves for the third day. Abstain from sexual relations.'

¹⁶On the morning of the third day there was thunder and lightning, with a thick cloud over the mountain, and a very loud trumpet blast. Everyone in the camp trembled. ¹⁷Then Moses led the people out of the camp to meet with God, and they stood at the foot of the mountain. ¹⁸Mount Sinai was covered with smoke, because the LORD descended on it in fire. The smoke billowed up from it like smoke from a furnace, and the whole mountain trembled violently. ¹⁹As the sound of the trumpet grew louder and louder, Moses spoke and the voice of God answered him.

²⁰The LORD descended to the top of Mount Sinai and called Moses to the top of the mountain. So Moses went up ²¹and the LORD said to him, 'Go down and warn the people so they do not force their way through to see the LORD and many of them perish. ²²Even the priests, who approach the LORD, must consecrate themselves, or the LORD will break out against them.'

²³Moses said to the LORD, 'The people cannot come up Mount Sinai, because you

yourself warned us, "Put limits around the mountain and set it apart as holy."'

²⁴The LORD replied, 'Go down and bring Aaron up with you. But the priests and the people must not force their way through to come up to the LORD, or he will break out against them.'

²⁵So Moses went down to the people and told them.

20 And God spoke all these words:

²'I am the LORD your God, who brought you out of Egypt, out of the land of slavery.

³'You shall have no other gods before me.

⁴'You shall not make for yourself an image in the form of anything in heaven above or on the earth beneath or in the waters below. ⁵You shall not bow down to them or worship them; for I, the LORD your God, am a jealous God, punishing the children for the sin of the parents to the third and fourth generation of those who hate me, ⁶but showing love to a thousand generations of those who love me and keep my commandments.

⁷'You shall not misuse the name of the LORD your God, for the LORD will not hold anyone guiltless who misuses his name.

⁸'Remember the Sabbath day by keeping it holy. ⁹Six days you shall labour and do all your work, ¹⁰but the seventh day is a sabbath to the LORD your God. On it you shall not do any work, neither you, nor your son or daughter, nor your male or female servant, nor your animals, nor any foreigner residing in your towns. ¹¹For in six days the LORD made the heavens and the earth, the sea, and all that is in them,

but he rested on the seventh day. Therefore the LORD blessed the Sabbath day and made it holy.

¹²'Honour your father and your mother, so that you may live long in the land the LORD your God is giving you.

¹³'You shall not murder.

¹⁴'You shall not commit adultery.

¹⁵'You shall not steal.

¹⁶'You shall not give false testimony against your neighbour.

¹⁷'You shall not covet your neighbour's house. You shall not covet your neighbour's wife, or his male or female servant, his ox or donkey, or anything that belongs to your neighbour.'

¹⁸When the people saw the thunder and lightning and heard the trumpet and saw the mountain in smoke, they trembled with fear. They stayed at a distance ¹⁹and said to Moses, 'Speak to us yourself and we will listen. But do not let God speak to us or we will die.'

²⁰Moses said to the people, 'Do not be afraid. God has come to test you, so that the fear of God will be with you to keep you from sinning.'

²¹The people remained at a distance, while Moses approached the thick darkness where God was.

²²Then the LORD said to Moses, 'Tell the Israelites this: "You have seen for yourselves that I have spoken to you from heaven: ²³do not make any gods to be alongside me; do not make for yourselves gods of silver or gods of gold.

²⁴'"Make an altar of earth for me and sacrifice on it your burnt offerings and fellowship offerings, your sheep and goats and your cattle. Wherever I cause my name to be honoured, I will come to you and bless you. ²⁵If you make an altar of stones for me, do not build it with dressed stones, for you

will defile it if you use a tool on it. ²⁶And do not go up to my altar on steps, or your private parts may be exposed."

◼ PSALM 18:43–50

⁴³You have delivered me from the attacks
of the people;
you have made me the head of nations.
People I did not know now serve me,
⁴⁴ foreigners cower before me;
as soon as they hear of me, they obey me.
⁴⁵They all lose heart;
they come trembling from their
strongholds.

⁴⁶The LORD lives! Praise be to my Rock!
Exalted be God my Saviour!
⁴⁷He is the God who avenges me,
who subdues nations under me,
⁴⁸ who saves me from my enemies.
You exalted me above my foes;
from a violent man you rescued me.
⁴⁹Therefore I will praise you, LORD, among
the nations;
I will sing the praises of your name.

⁵⁰He gives his king great victories;
he shows unfailing love to his anointed,
to David and to his descendants for
ever.

◼ PROVERBS 4:14–17

¹⁴Do not set foot on the path of the wicked
or walk in the way of evildoers.
¹⁵Avoid it, do not travel on it;
turn from it and go on your way.
¹⁶For they cannot rest until they do evil;
they are robbed of sleep till they make
someone stumble.

¹⁷They eat the bread of wickedness
and drink the wine of violence.

◼ MATTHEW 24:1–14

24 Jesus left the temple and was walking away when his disciples came up to him to call his attention to its buildings. ²'Do you see all these things?' he asked. 'Truly I tell you, not one stone here will be left on another; every one will be thrown down.'

³As Jesus was sitting on the Mount of Olives, the disciples came to him privately. 'Tell us,' they said, 'when will this happen, and what will be the sign of your coming and of the end of the age?'

⁴Jesus answered: 'Watch out that no one deceives you. ⁵For many will come in my name, claiming, "I am the Messiah," and will deceive many. ⁶You will hear of wars and rumours of wars, but see to it that you are not alarmed. Such things must happen, but the end is still to come. ⁷Nation will rise against nation, and kingdom against kingdom. There will be famines and earthquakes in various places. ⁸All these are the beginning of birth-pains.

⁹'Then you will be handed over to be persecuted and put to death, and you will be hated by all nations because of me. ¹⁰At that time many will turn away from the faith and will betray and hate each other, ¹¹and many false prophets will appear and deceive many people. ¹²Because of the increase of wickedness, the love of most will grow cold, ¹³but the one who stands firm to the end will be saved. ¹⁴And this gospel of the kingdom will be preached in the whole world as a testimony to all nations, and then the end will come.

Three Forms of Dishonesty

'You shall not give false testimony against your neighbour.' **Exodus 20:16**

The suggestion that even mature Christians can inwardly resist truth might shock some, but the real issue is - is it true?

Among the popular defences we all use to resist truth, the first is projection. This occurs when we are to blame for something, but we project the blame onto someone else so that we can feel more comfortable about ourselves. It may sound a simple thing, but all dishonesty is destructive - even simple dishonesty.

Then take the defence of denial. How many times do we refuse to face the fact that we may be angry about something, and when someone says: 'Why are you angry?' we reply with bristling hostility, 'I'm not angry!' We fail to recognise what others can plainly see. And denial, no matter how one looks at it, is a form of inner deceit.

Another dishonest defence is rationalisation. We are guilty of this whenever we persuade ourselves that something is what it is not. C. S. Lewis points out that when our neighbour does something wrong, it is obviously because he or she is 'bad,' while if we do something wrong it is only because we did not get enough sleep, or someone gave us a rough time, or some other excuse.

All of these defence mechanisms deprive us of inner honesty, and apart from hindering our spiritual growth they also lower our defences against Satan. This is why over and over again in Scripture, we are bidden to open up to honesty. The more honest we can be, the more spiritually powerful and effective we can be.

PRAYER

Lord Jesus, help me to to open up to honesty. For I see that the more honest I am, the more authority I can wield over Satan. I want to be able to say, as You said: '... the prince of this world is coming. He has no hold over me ...' (John 14:30). I ask this for Your name's sake. Amen.

FURTHER STUDY

Rev. 3:14-22; James 1:26; Gal. 6:3
• How did the Laodiceans see themselves?
• How did God see them?

February 8

■ **EXODUS 21:1–22:20**

21 'These are the laws you are to set before them: ²'If you buy a Hebrew servant, he is to serve you for six years. But in the seventh year, he shall go free, without paying anything. ³If he comes alone, he is to go free alone; but if he has a wife when he comes, she is to go with him. ⁴If his master gives him a wife and she bears him sons or daughters, the woman and her children shall belong to her master, and only the man shall go free.

⁵'But if the servant declares, "I love my master and my wife and children and do not want to go free," ⁶then his master must take him before the judges. He shall take him to the door or the door-post and pierce his ear with an awl. Then he will be his servant for life.

⁷'If a man sells his daughter as a servant, she is not to go free as male servants do. ⁸If she does not please the master who has selected her for himself, he must let her be redeemed. He has no right to sell her to foreigners, because he has broken faith with her. ⁹If he selects her for his son, he must grant her the rights of a daughter. ¹⁰If he marries another woman, he must not deprive the first one of her food, clothing and marital rights. ¹¹If he does not provide her with these three things, she is to go free, without any payment of money.

¹²'Anyone who strikes a person with a fatal blow is to be put to death. ¹³However, if it is not done intentionally, but God lets it happen, they are to flee to a place I will designate. ¹⁴But if anyone schemes and kills someone deliberately, that person is to be taken from my altar and put to death.

¹⁵'Anyone who attacks their father or mother is to be put to death.

¹⁶'Anyone who kidnaps someone is to be put to death, whether the victim has been sold or is still in the kidnapper's possession.

¹⁷'Anyone who curses their father or mother is to be put to death.

¹⁸'If people quarrel and one person hits another with a stone or with their fist and the victim does not die but is confined to bed, ¹⁹the one who struck the blow will not be held liable if the other can get up and walk around outside with a staff; however, the guilty party must pay the injured person for any loss of time and see that the victim is completely healed.

²⁰'Anyone who beats their male or female slave with a rod must be punished if the slave dies as a direct result, ²¹but they are not to be punished if the slave recovers after a day or two, since the slave is their property.

²²'If people are fighting and hit a pregnant woman and she gives birth prematurely but there is no serious injury, the offender must be fined whatever the woman's husband demands and the court allows. ²³But if there is serious injury, you are to take life for life, ²⁴eye for eye, tooth for tooth, hand for hand, foot for foot, ²⁵burn for burn, wound for wound, bruise for bruise.

²⁶'An owner who hits a male or female slave in the eye and destroys it must let the slave go free to compensate for the eye. ²⁷And an owner who knocks out the tooth of a male or female slave must let the slave go free to compensate for the tooth.

²⁸'If a bull gores a man or woman to death, the bull is to be stoned to death, and its meat must not be eaten. But the owner of the bull will not be held responsible. ²⁹If,

however, the bull has had the habit of goring and the owner has been warned but has not kept it penned up and it kills a man or woman, the bull is to be stoned and its owner also is to be put to death. ³⁰ However, if payment is demanded, the owner may redeem his life by the payment of whatever is demanded. ³¹ This law also applies if the bull gores a son or a daughter. ³² If the bull gores a male or female slave, the owner must pay thirty shekels of silver to the master of the slave, and the bull is to be stoned to death.

³³ 'If anyone uncovers a pit or digs one and fails to cover it and an ox or a donkey falls into it, ³⁴ the one who opened the pit must pay the owner for the loss and take the dead animal in exchange.

³⁵ 'If anyone's bull injures someone else's bull and it dies, the two parties are to sell the live one and divide both the money and the dead animal equally. ³⁶ However, if it was known that the bull had the habit of goring, yet the owner did not keep it penned up, the owner must pay, animal for animal, and take the dead animal in exchange.

22 'Whoever steals an ox or a sheep and slaughters it or sells it must pay back five head of cattle for the ox and four sheep for the sheep.

² 'If a thief is caught breaking in at night and is struck a fatal blow, the defender is not guilty of bloodshed; ³ but if it happens after sunrise, the defender is guilty of bloodshed.

'Anyone who steals must certainly make restitution, but if they have nothing, they must be sold to pay for their theft. ⁴ If the stolen animal is found alive in their possession – whether ox or donkey or sheep – they must pay back double.

⁵ 'If anyone grazes their livestock in a field or vineyard and lets them stray and they graze in someone else's field, the offender must make restitution from the best

of their own field or vineyard.

⁶ 'If a fire breaks out and spreads into thorn-bushes so that it burns sheaves of corn or standing corn or the whole field, the one who started the fire must make restitution.

⁷ 'If anyone gives a neighbour silver or goods for safekeeping and they are stolen from the neighbour's house, the thief, if caught, must pay back double. ⁸ But if the thief is not found, the owner of the house must appear before the judges, and they must determine whether the owner of the house has laid hands on the other person's property. ⁹ In all cases of illegal possession of an ox, a donkey, a sheep, a garment, or any other lost property about which somebody says, "This is mine," both parties are to bring their cases before the judges. The one whom the judges declare guilty must pay back double to the other.

¹⁰ 'If anyone gives a donkey, an ox, a sheep or any other animal to their neighbour for safekeeping and it dies or is injured or is taken away while no one is looking, ¹¹ the issue between them will be settled by the taking of an oath before the LORD that the neighbour did not lay hands on the other person's property. The owner is to accept this, and no restitution is required. ¹² But if the animal was stolen from the neighbour, restitution must be made to the owner. ¹³ If it was torn to pieces by a wild animal, the neighbour shall bring in the remains as evidence and shall not be required to pay for the torn animal.

¹⁴ 'If anyone borrows an animal from their neighbour and it is injured or dies while the owner is not present, they must make restitution. ¹⁵ But if the owner is with the animal, the borrower will not have to pay. If the animal was hired, the money paid for the hire covers the loss.

¹⁶ 'If a man seduces a virgin who is not pledged to be married and sleeps with her, he must pay the bride-price, and she shall

be his wife. ¹⁷ If her father absolutely refuses to give her to him, he must still pay the bride-price for virgins.

¹⁸ 'Do not allow a sorceress to live.

¹⁹ 'Anyone who has sexual relations with an animal is to be put to death.

²⁰ 'Whoever sacrifices to any god other than the LORD must be destroyed.

■ PSALM 19:1-6

¹ The heavens declare the glory of God;
    the skies proclaim the work of his
      hands.
² Day after day they pour forth speech;
    night after night they reveal
      knowledge.
³ They have no speech, they use no words;
    no sound is heard from them.
⁴ Yet their voice goes out into all the earth,
    their words to the ends of the world.
In the heavens God has pitched a tent for
    the sun.
⁵   It is like a bridegroom coming out of
    his chamber,
    like a champion rejoicing to run his
      course.
⁶ It rises at one end of the heavens
    and makes its circuit to the other;
    nothing is deprived of its warmth.

■ PROVERBS 4:18-19

¹⁸ The path of the righteous is like the
    morning sun,
    shining ever brighter till the full light
    of day.
¹⁹ But the way of the wicked is like deep
    darkness;
    they do not know what makes them
    stumble.

■ MATTHEW 24:15-35

¹⁵ 'So when you see standing in the holy place "the abomination that causes desolation," spoken of through the prophet Daniel – let the reader understand – ¹⁶ then let those who are in Judea flee to the mountains. ¹⁷ Let no one on the housetop go down to take anything out of the house. ¹⁸ Let no one in the field go back to get their cloak. ¹⁹ How dreadful it will be in those days for pregnant women and nursing mothers! ²⁰ Pray that your flight will not take place in winter or on the Sabbath. ²¹ For then there will be great distress, unequalled from the beginning of the world until now – and never to be equalled again.

²² 'If those days had not been cut short, no one would survive, but for the sake of the elect those days will be shortened. ²³ At that time if anyone says to you, "Look, here is the Messiah!" or, "There he is!" do not believe it. ²⁴ For false messiahs and false prophets will appear and perform great signs and wonders to deceive, if possible, even the elect. ²⁵ See, I have told you in advance.

²⁶ 'So if anyone tells you, "There he is, out in the desert," do not go out; or, "Here he is, in the inner rooms," do not believe it. ²⁷ For as lightning that comes from the east is visible even in the west, so will be the coming of the Son of Man. ²⁸ Wherever there is a carcass, there the vultures will gather.

²⁹ 'Immediately after the distress of those days

    ' "the sun will be darkened,
     and the moon will not give its light;
    the stars will fall from the sky,
     and the heavenly bodies will be
      shaken."

³⁰ 'Then will appear the sign of the Son of Man in heaven. And then all the peoples of the earth will mourn when they see the Son of Man coming on the clouds of heaven, with

power and great glory. [31]And he will send his angels with a loud trumpet call, and they will gather his elect from the four winds, from one end of the heavens to the other.

[32]'Now learn this lesson from the fig-tree: as soon as its twigs become tender and its leaves come out, you know that summer is near. [33]Even so, when you see all these things, you know that it is near, right at the door. [34]Truly I tell you, this generation will certainly not pass away until all these things have happened. [35]Heaven and earth will pass away, but my words will never pass away.

The Universe Proclaims

'The heavens declare the glory of God.' **Psalm 19:1**

We must endeavour, in line with our Master's directive in the Lord's Prayer, to focus our gaze on the majesty of God. The greater the degree in which God becomes fixed in our gaze, the more realistically we will be able to evaluate the events that go on around us here on earth.

In today's passage the psalmist tells us that one way we can focus on the greatness of God is to consider His handiwork in creation. All around us in this wonderful world, we see evidence of His sublime sufficiency. Consider, for example, the vastness of the universe. Scientists tell us that in relation to the myriads of other celestial bodies in outer space, the planet we inhabit is like a tiny speck of dust in a huge railway station in relation to all the other specks of dust around it, or like a single grain of sand among all the sand on all the seashores of the world. They tell us also that if Earth were to fall out of its orbit and spin away into space, it would create no more disturbance than the dropping of a pea into the Pacific Ocean!

Such word pictures, inadequate as they are, do nevertheless help us form some idea of the greatness and power of our God. Who can meditate on the vastness of the universe without experiencing an expansion in their conception of the majesty of God? Why did God construct the universe on such a grand scale? My conclusion is: He did it to show us that He is gloriously sufficient, unchangingly adequate, and abidingly faithful. How wonderful to contemplate such creative enormity!

PRAYER

God, what a fool I am to think that Your resources might run dry. Help me to live in light of the fact that my demand will never exceed Your supply. You are the Enough. Amen.

FURTHER STUDY

Matt. 6:19-34; Luke 12:24; Psa. 45:1-17
• How did Jesus focus our attention on God's goodness?
• Of whom does the psalmist give us a picture?

February 9

■ EXODUS 22:21–24:18

²¹'Do not ill-treat or oppress a foreigner, for you were foreigners in Egypt.

²²'Do not take advantage of the widow or the fatherless. ²³If you do and they cry out to me, I will certainly hear their cry. ²⁴My anger will be aroused, and I will kill you with the sword; your wives will become widows and your children fatherless.

²⁵'If you lend money to one of my people among you who is needy, do not treat it like a business deal; charge no interest. ²⁶If you take your neighbour's cloak as a pledge, return it by sunset, ²⁷because that cloak is the only covering your neighbour has. What else can they sleep in? When they cry out to me, I will hear, for I am compassionate.

²⁸'Do not blaspheme God or curse the ruler of your people.

²⁹'Do not hold back offerings from your granaries or your vats.

'You must give me the firstborn of your sons. ³⁰Do the same with your cattle and your sheep. Let them stay with their mothers for seven days, but give them to me on the eighth day.

³¹'You are to be my holy people. So do not eat the meat of an animal torn by wild beasts; throw it to the dogs.

23 'Do not spread false reports. Do not help a guilty person by being a malicious witness.

²'Do not follow the crowd in doing wrong. When you give testimony in a lawsuit, do not pervert justice by siding with the crowd, ³and do not show favouritism to a poor person in a lawsuit.

⁴'If you come across your enemy's ox or donkey wandering off, be sure to return it. ⁵If you see the donkey of someone who

hates you fallen down under its load, do not leave it there; be sure you help them with it.

⁶'Do not deny justice to your poor people in their lawsuits. ⁷Have nothing to do with a false charge and do not put an innocent or honest person to death, for I will not acquit the guilty.

⁸'Do not accept a bribe, for a bribe blinds those who see and twists the words of the innocent.

⁹'Do not oppress a foreigner; you yourselves know how it feels to be foreigners, because you were foreigners in Egypt.

¹⁰'For six years you are to sow your fields and harvest the crops, ¹¹but during the seventh year let the land lie unploughed and unused. Then the poor among your people may get food from it, and the wild animals may eat what is left. Do the same with your vineyard and your olive grove.

¹²'Six days do your work, but on the seventh day do not work, so that your ox and your donkey may rest, and so that the slave born in your household and the foreigner living among you may be refreshed.

¹³'Be careful to do everything I have said to you. Do not invoke the names of other gods; do not let them be heard on your lips.

¹⁴'Three times a year you are to celebrate a festival to me.

¹⁵'Celebrate the Festival of Unleavened Bread; for seven days eat bread made without yeast, as I commanded you. Do this at the appointed time in the month of Aviv, for in that month you came out of Egypt.

'No one is to appear before me empty-handed.

¹⁶'Celebrate the Festival of Harvest with the firstfruits of the crops you sow in your field.

'Celebrate the Festival of Ingathering at

the end of the year, when you gather in your crops from the field.

¹⁷'Three times a year all the men are to appear before the Sovereign LORD.

¹⁸'Do not offer the blood of a sacrifice to me along with anything containing yeast.

'The fat of my festival offerings must not be kept until morning.

¹⁹'Bring the best of the firstfruits of your soil to the house of the LORD your God.

'Do not cook a young goat in its mother's milk.

²⁰'See, I am sending an angel ahead of you to guard you along the way and to bring you to the place I have prepared. ²¹Pay attention to him and listen to what he says. Do not rebel against him; he will not forgive your rebellion, since my Name is in him. ²²If you listen carefully to what he says and do all that I say, I will be an enemy to your enemies and will oppose those who oppose you. ²³My angel will go ahead of you and bring you into the land of the Amorites, Hittites, Perizzites, Canaanites, Hivites and Jebusites, and I will wipe them out. ²⁴Do not bow down before their gods or worship them or follow their practices. You must demolish them and break their sacred stones to pieces. ²⁵Worship the LORD your God, and his blessing will be on your food and water. I will take away disease from among you, ²⁶and none will miscarry or be barren in your land. I will give you a full life span.

²⁷'I will send my terror ahead of you and throw into confusion every nation you encounter. I will make all your enemies turn their backs and run. ²⁸I will send the hornet ahead of you to drive the Hivites, Canaanites and Hittites out of your way. ²⁹But I will not drive them out in a single year, because the land would become desolate and the wild animals too numerous for you. ³⁰Little by little I will drive them out before you, until you have increased enough to take possession of the land.

³¹'I will establish your borders from the Red Sea to the Mediterranean Sea, and from the desert to the Euphrates River. I will give into your hands the people who live in the land, and you will drive them out before you. ³²Do not make a covenant with them or with their gods. ³³Do not let them live in your land or they will cause you to sin against me, because the worship of their gods will certainly be a snare to you.'

24 Then the LORD said to Moses, 'Come up to the LORD, you and Aaron, Nadab and Abihu, and seventy of the elders of Israel. You are to worship at a distance, ²but Moses alone is to approach the LORD; the others must not come near. And the people may not come up with him.'

³When Moses went and told the people all the LORD's words and laws, they responded with one voice, 'Everything the LORD has said we will do.' ⁴Moses then wrote down everything the LORD had said.

He got up early the next morning and built an altar at the foot of the mountain and set up twelve stone pillars representing the twelve tribes of Israel. ⁵Then he sent young Israelite men, and they offered burnt offerings and sacrificed young bulls as fellowship offerings to the LORD. ⁶Moses took half of the blood and put it in bowls, and the other half he splashed against the altar. ⁷Then he took the Book of the Covenant and read it to the people. They responded, 'We will do everything the LORD has said; we will obey.'

⁸Moses then took the blood, sprinkled it on the people and said, 'This is the blood of the covenant that the LORD has made with you in accordance with all these words.'

⁹Moses and Aaron, Nadab and Abihu, and the seventy elders of Israel went up ¹⁰and saw the God of Israel. Under his feet was something like a pavement made of lapis lazuli, as bright blue as the sky. ¹¹But God did not raise his hand against these

leaders of the Israelites; they saw God, and they ate and drank.

¹² The LORD said to Moses, 'Come up to me on the mountain and stay here, and I will give you the tablets of stone with the law and commandments I have written for their instruction.'

¹³ Then Moses set out with Joshua his assistant, and Moses went up on the mountain of God. ¹⁴ He said to the elders, 'Wait here for us until we come back to you. Aaron and Hur are with you, and anyone involved in a dispute can go to them.'

¹⁵ When Moses went up on the mountain, the cloud covered it, ¹⁶ and the glory of the LORD settled on Mount Sinai. For six days the cloud covered the mountain, and on the seventh day the LORD called to Moses from within the cloud. ¹⁷ To the Israelites the glory of the LORD looked like a consuming fire on top of the mountain. ¹⁸ Then Moses entered the cloud as he went on up the mountain. And he stayed on the mountain forty days and forty nights.

■ PSALM 19:7-14

⁷ The law of the LORD is perfect,
    refreshing the soul.
  The statutes of the LORD are trustworthy,
    making wise the simple.
⁸ The precepts of the LORD are right,
    giving joy to the heart.
  The commands of the LORD are radiant,
    giving light to the eyes.
⁹ The fear of the LORD is pure,
    enduring for ever.
  The decrees of the LORD are firm,
    and all of them are righteous.

¹⁰ They are more precious than gold,
    than much pure gold;
  they are sweeter than honey,
    than honey from the honeycomb.
¹¹ By them your servant is warned;

  in keeping them there is great reward.
¹² But who can discern their own errors?
    Forgive my hidden faults.
¹³ Keep your servant also from wilful sins;
    may they not rule over me.
  Then I will be blameless,
    innocent of great transgression.

¹⁴ May these words of my mouth and this
    meditation of my heart
  be pleasing in your sight,
    LORD, my Rock and my Redeemer.

■ PROVERBS 4:20-22

²⁰ My son, pay attention to what I say;
    turn your ear to my words.
²¹ Do not let them out of your sight,
    keep them within your heart;
²² for they are life to those who find them
    and health to one's whole body.

■ MATTHEW 24:36-51

³⁶ 'But about that day or hour no one knows, not even the angels in heaven, nor the Son, but only the Father. ³⁷ As it was in the days of Noah, so it will be at the coming of the Son of Man. ³⁸ For in the days before the flood, people were eating and drinking, marrying and giving in marriage, up to the day Noah entered the ark; ³⁹ and they knew nothing about what would happen until the flood came and took them all away. That is how it will be at the coming of the Son of Man. ⁴⁰ Two men will be in the field; one will be taken and the other left. ⁴¹ Two women will be grinding with a hand mill; one will be taken and the other left.

⁴² 'Therefore keep watch, because you do not know on what day your Lord will come. ⁴³ But understand this: if the owner of the house had known at what time of night the thief was coming, he would have kept watch

and would not have let his house be broken into. ⁴⁴So you also must be ready, because the Son of Man will come at an hour when you do not expect him.

⁴⁵'Who then is the faithful and wise servant, whom the master has put in charge of the servants in his household to give them their food at the proper time? ⁴⁶It will be good for that servant whose master finds him doing so when he returns. ⁴⁷Truly I tell you, he will put him in charge of all his possessions. ⁴⁸But suppose that servant is wicked and says to himself, "My master is staying away a long time," ⁴⁹and he then begins to beat his fellow servants and to eat and drink with drunkards. ⁵⁰The master of that servant will come on a day when he does not expect him and at an hour he is not aware of. ⁵¹He will cut him to pieces and assign him a place with the hypocrites, where there will be weeping and gnashing of teeth.

'The Second Thought'

'My son, pay attention to what I say; turn your ear to my words. Do not let them out of your sight, keep them within your heart.' **Proverbs 4:20-21**

'To get the best out of life,' said Pascal, 'great matters have to be given a second thought.' Meditation is just that – giving biblical truths a second thought. If you have been thinking that the way to get the best out of the Bible is by reading it, studying it, or memorising it, then I urge you to think again. These are very valuable but I think meditation is more valuable still.

Reading, studying, and memorising the Bible are, in the main, intellectual exercises which bring spiritual results. Meditation is not primarily an intellectual exercise but a devotional exercise, a way by which the Word of God is carried into the spiritual digestive system so that it can be translated into spiritual nourishment and energy.

Be careful that you do not misunderstand me here. I am not saying that reading, studying, and memorising the Bible are not important spiritual exercises. I strongly advocate them. But – it is possible to do all these things and yet fail to draw from the Scriptures the spiritual nourishment that God has put within them. This comes largely from meditation.

To ensure that this matter is crystal clear, let's go over it again: meditation is the process by which we take a text, thought, or phrase from the Word of God and roll it around in our mind, passing it backward and forward, letting it go out of conscious thought, bringing it back again into consciousness, prodding it, absorbing it, admiring it over and over again until its inherent power pervades our whole personality. God has gone into His Word, and God has to come out of it. Meditation is the way.

PRAYER

O Father, if great matters need a second thought, then help me to slow down and take time to meditate on the truths that are contained in Your precious Word. For Jesus' sake. Amen.

FURTHER STUDY

Col. 3:1-16; Deut. 6:6;
Phil. 4:8; Jer. 15:16
• What does the word 'dwell' mean?
• How did Jeremiah put it?

February 10

■ EXODUS 25:1–26:14

25 The LORD said to Moses, ²'Tell the Israelites to bring me an offering. You are to receive the offering for me from everyone whose heart prompts them to give. ³These are the offerings you are to receive from them: gold, silver and bronze; ⁴blue, purple and scarlet yarn and fine linen; goat hair; ⁵ram skins dyed red and another type of durable leather; acacia wood; ⁶olive oil for the light; spices for the anointing oil and for the fragrant incense; ⁷and onyx stones and other gems to be mounted on the ephod and breastpiece.

⁸'Then let them make a sanctuary for me, and I will dwell among them. ⁹Make this tabernacle and all its furnishings exactly like the pattern I will show you.

¹⁰'Let them make an ark of acacia wood – two and a half cubits long, a cubit and a half wide, and a cubit and a half high. ¹¹Overlay it with pure gold, both inside and out, and make a gold moulding around it. ¹²Cast four gold rings for it and fasten them to its four feet, with two rings on one side and two rings on the other. ¹³Then make poles of acacia wood and overlay them with gold. ¹⁴Insert the poles into the rings on the sides of the ark to carry it. ¹⁵The poles are to remain in the rings of this ark; they are not to be removed. ¹⁶Then put in the ark the tablets of the covenant law, which I will give you.

¹⁷'Make an atonement cover of pure gold – two and a half cubits long and a cubit and a half wide. ¹⁸And make two cherubim out of hammered gold at the ends of the cover. ¹⁹Make one cherub on one end and the second cherub on the other; make the cherubim of one piece with the cover, at the two ends. ²⁰The cherubim are to have their wings spread upwards, overshadowing the cover with them. The cherubim are to face each other, looking towards the cover. ²¹Place the cover on top of the ark and put in the ark the tablets of the covenant law that I will give you. ²²There, above the cover between the two cherubim that are over the ark of the covenant law, I will meet with you and give you all my commands for the Israelites.

²³'Make a table of acacia wood – two cubits long, a cubit wide and a cubit and a half high. ²⁴Overlay it with pure gold and make a gold moulding around it. ²⁵Also make around it a rim a handbreadth wide and put a gold moulding on the rim. ²⁶Make four gold rings for the table and fasten them to the four corners, where the four legs are. ²⁷The rings are to be close to the rim to hold the poles used in carrying the table. ²⁸Make the poles of acacia wood, overlay them with gold and carry the table with them. ²⁹And make its plates and

dishes of pure gold, as well as its pitchers and bowls for the pouring out of offerings. ³⁰ Put the bread of the Presence on this table to be before me at all times.

³¹ 'Make a lampstand of pure gold. Hammer out its base and shaft, and make its flowerlike cups, buds and blossoms of one piece with them. ³² Six branches are to extend from the sides of the lampstand – three on one side and three on the other. ³³ Three cups shaped like almond flowers with buds and blossoms are to be on one branch, three on the next branch, and the same for all six branches extending from the lampstand. ³⁴ And on the lampstand there are to be four cups shaped like almond flowers with buds and blossoms. ³⁵ One bud shall be under the first pair of branches extending from the lampstand, a second bud under the second pair, and a third bud under the third pair – six branches in all. ³⁶ The buds and branches shall all be of one piece with the lampstand, hammered out of pure gold.

³⁷ 'Then make its seven lamps and set them up on it so that they light the space in front of it. ³⁸ Its wick trimmers and trays are to be of pure gold. ³⁹ A talent of pure gold is to be used for the lampstand and all these accessories. ⁴⁰ See that you make them according to the pattern shown you on the mountain.

26 'Make the tabernacle with ten curtains of finely twisted linen and blue, purple and scarlet yarn, with cherubim woven into them by a skilled worker. ² All the curtains are to be the same size – twenty-eight cubits long and four cubits wide. ³ Join five of the curtains together, and do the same with the other five. ⁴ Make loops of blue material along the edge of the end curtain in one set, and do the same with the end curtain in the other set. ⁵ Make fifty loops on one curtain and fifty loops on the end curtain of the other set, with the loops opposite each other. ⁶ Then make fifty gold clasps and use them to fasten the curtains together so that the tabernacle is a unit.

⁷ 'Make curtains of goat hair for the tent over the tabernacle – eleven altogether. ⁸ All eleven curtains are to be the same size – thirty cubits long and four cubits wide. ⁹ Join five of the curtains together into one set and the other six into another set. Fold the sixth curtain double at the front of the tent. ¹⁰ Make fifty loops along the edge of the end curtain in one set and also along the edge of the end curtain in the other set. ¹¹ Then make fifty bronze clasps and put them in the loops to fasten the tent together as a unit. ¹² As for the additional length of the tent curtains, the half curtain that is left over is to hang down at the rear of the tabernacle. ¹³ The tent curtains will be a cubit longer on both sides; what is left will hang over the sides of the tabernacle so as to cover it. ¹⁴ Make for the tent a covering of ram skins dyed red, and over that a covering of other durable leather.

▬ PSALM 20:1-9

¹ May the LORD answer you when you are
    in distress;
  may the name of the God of Jacob
    protect you.
² May he send you help from the sanctuary
    and grant you support from Zion.
³ May he remember all your sacrifices
    and accept your burnt offerings.
⁴ May he give you the desire of your heart
    and make all your plans succeed.
⁵ May we shout for joy over your victory
    and lift up our banners in the name of
    our God.

  May the LORD grant all your requests.

⁶ Now this I know:
    The LORD gives victory to his anointed.

He answers him from his heavenly
 sanctuary
with the victorious power of his right
 hand.
⁷Some trust in chariots and some in
 horses,
but we trust in the name of the LORD
 our God.
⁸They are brought to their knees and fall,
 but we rise up and stand firm.
⁹LORD, give victory to the king!
 Answer us when we call!

■ PROVERBS 4:23-24

²³Above all else, guard your heart,
 for everything you do flows from it.
²⁴Keep your mouth free of perversity;
 keep corrupt talk far from your lips.

■ MATTHEW 25:1-13

25 'At that time the kingdom of
 heaven will be like ten virgins who
took their lamps and went out to meet the
bridegroom. ²Five of them were foolish and
five were wise. ³The foolish ones took their
lamps but did not take any oil with them.
⁴The wise ones, however, took oil in jars
along with their lamps. ⁵The bridegroom
was a long time in coming, and they all became drowsy and fell asleep.

⁶'At midnight the cry rang out: "Here's
the bridegroom! Come out to meet him!"

⁷'Then all the virgins woke up and
trimmed their lamps. ⁸The foolish ones
said to the wise, "Give us some of your oil;
our lamps are going out."

⁹'"No," they replied, "there may not
be enough for both us and you. Instead,
go to those who sell oil and buy some for
yourselves."

¹⁰'But while they were on their way to buy
the oil, the bridegroom arrived. The virgins
who were ready went in with him to the
wedding banquet. And the door was shut.

¹¹'Later the others also came. "Lord,
Lord," they said, "open the door for us!"

¹²'But he replied, "Truly I tell you, I don't
know you."

¹³'Therefore keep watch, because you do
not know the day or the hour.

Not Just What You Say

'Above all else, guard your heart, for everything you
do flows from it.' **Proverbs 4:23**

I am convinced that one of the major reasons why so many of us fail to
receive from God the things which we ought to be receiving lies in the
fact that our hearts and our minds are not properly correlated.

Do you find yourself continually praying for things you never
receive? I don't mean things about which there may be some doubt,
but things you definitely know the Almighty longs to give you – love,
joy, peace, wisdom, patience, and so on. Maybe your mind is asking for
one thing and your heart another. You see, it is possible to want
something with the mind which is not supported by the heart. The
mind is a much easier part of the personality to deal with than the
heart, but, as our text for today states, '… guard your heart, for
everything you do flows from it.'

We can approach God with our minds and think that because we have a clear idea of what we want, God will give it to us, but the heart may contain hidden doubts which prevent us from being fully integrated people. We fail to receive because we are not asking out of a fully integrated personality. As someone has put it: 'God does not just answer prayer – He answers you.' Those who wish to receive from God the things He delights to give ought always to remember that who we are is just as important (if not more so) than what we ask. God is not just listening to our words; He is listening to us.

PRAYER

O Father, the more I meditate on the need for heart and mind to be in perfect coordination, the more I am set on fire to become a fully integrated person. I know You are eagerly reaching down to me; help me to be as eager to reach up to You. Amen.

FURTHER STUDY

Matt. 15:1-20; Prov. 3:5
• What did Isaiah prophesy?
• How did Jesus respond to
  Peter's request?

February 11

EXODUS 26:15–28:14

15 'Make upright frames of acacia wood for the tabernacle. 16 Each frame is to be ten cubits long and a cubit and a half wide, 17 with two projections set parallel to each other. Make all the frames of the tabernacle in this way. 18 Make twenty frames for the south side of the tabernacle 19 and make forty silver bases to go under them – two bases for each frame, one under each projection. 20 For the other side, the north side of the tabernacle, make twenty frames 21 and forty silver bases – two under each frame. 22 Make six frames for the far end, that is, the west end of the tabernacle, 23 and make two frames for the corners at the far end. 24 At these two corners they must be double from the bottom all the way to the top and fitted into a single ring; both shall be like that. 25 So there will be eight frames

and sixteen silver bases – two under each frame.

26 'Also make crossbars of acacia wood: five for the frames on one side of the tabernacle, 27 five for those on the other side, and five for the frames on the west, at the far end of the tabernacle. 28 The centre crossbar is to extend from end to end at the middle of the frames. 29 Overlay the frames with gold and make gold rings to hold the crossbars. Also overlay the crossbars with gold.

30 'Set up the tabernacle according to the plan shown you on the mountain.

31 'Make a curtain of blue, purple and scarlet yarn and finely twisted linen, with cherubim woven into it by a skilled worker. 32 Hang it with gold hooks on four posts of acacia wood overlaid with gold and standing on four silver bases. 33 Hang the curtain from the clasps and place the ark of the covenant law behind the curtain. The

curtain will separate the Holy Place from the Most Holy Place. ³⁴Put the atonement cover on the ark of the covenant law in the Most Holy Place. ³⁵Place the table outside the curtain on the north side of the tabernacle and put the lampstand opposite it on the south side.

³⁶'For the entrance to the tent make a curtain of blue, purple and scarlet yarn and finely twisted linen – the work of an embroiderer. ³⁷Make gold hooks for this curtain and five posts of acacia wood overlaid with gold. And cast five bronze bases for them.

27 'Build an altar of acacia wood, three cubits high; it is to be square, five cubits long and five cubits wide. ²Make a horn at each of the four corners, so that the horns and the altar are of one piece, and overlay the altar with bronze. ³Make all its utensils of bronze – its pots to remove the ashes, and its shovels, sprinkling bowls, meat forks and firepans. ⁴Make a grating for it, a bronze network, and make a bronze ring at each of the four corners of the network. ⁵Put it under the ledge of the altar so that it is halfway up the altar. ⁶Make poles of acacia wood for the altar and overlay them with bronze. ⁷The poles are to be inserted into the rings so they will be on two sides of the altar when it is carried. ⁸Make the altar hollow, out of boards. It is to be made just as you were shown on the mountain.

⁹'Make a courtyard for the tabernacle. The south side shall be a hundred cubits long and is to have curtains of finely twisted linen, ¹⁰with twenty posts and twenty bronze bases and with silver hooks and bands on the posts. ¹¹The north side shall also be a hundred cubits long and is to have curtains, with twenty posts and twenty bronze bases and with silver hooks and bands on the posts.

¹²'The west end of the courtyard shall be fifty cubits wide and have curtains, with ten posts and ten bases. ¹³On the east end,

towards the sunrise, the courtyard shall also be fifty cubits wide. ¹⁴Curtains fifteen cubits long are to be on one side of the entrance, with three posts and three bases, ¹⁵and curtains fifteen cubits long are to be on the other side, with three posts and three bases.

¹⁶'For the entrance to the courtyard, provide a curtain twenty cubits long, of blue, purple and scarlet yarn and finely twisted linen – the work of an embroiderer – with four posts and four bases. ¹⁷All the posts around the courtyard are to have silver bands and hooks, and bronze bases. ¹⁸The courtyard shall be a hundred cubits long and fifty cubits wide, with curtains of finely twisted linen five cubits high, and with bronze bases. ¹⁹All the other articles used in the service of the tabernacle, whatever their function, including all the tent pegs for it and those for the courtyard, are to be of bronze.

²⁰'Command the Israelites to bring you clear oil of pressed olives for the light so that the lamps may be kept burning. ²¹In the tent of meeting, outside the curtain that shields the ark of the covenant law, Aaron and his sons are to keep the lamps burning before the LORD from evening till morning. This is to be a lasting ordinance among the Israelites for the generations to come.

28 'Let Aaron your brother be brought to you from among the Israelites, with his sons Nadab and Abihu, Eleazar and Ithamar, so that they may serve me as priests. ²Make sacred garments for your brother Aaron to give him dignity and honour. ³Tell all the skilled workers to whom I have given wisdom in such matters that they are to make garments for Aaron, for his consecration, so that he may serve me as priest. ⁴These are the garments they are to make: a breastpiece, an ephod, a robe, a woven tunic, a turban and a sash. They are to make these sacred garments for your brother Aaron and his sons, so that they

may serve me as priests. [5]Make them use gold, and blue, purple and scarlet yarn, and fine linen.

[6]'Make the ephod of gold, and of blue, purple and scarlet yarn, and of finely twisted linen – the work of skilled hands. [7]It is to have two shoulder pieces attached to two of its corners, so that it can be fastened. [8]Its skilfully woven waistband is to be like it – of one piece with the ephod and made with gold, and with blue, purple and scarlet yarn, and with finely twisted linen.

[9]'Take two onyx stones and engrave on them the names of the sons of Israel [10]in the order of their birth – six names on one stone and the remaining six on the other. [11]Engrave the names of the sons of Israel on the two stones the way a gem cutter engraves a seal. Then mount the stones in gold filigree settings [12]and fasten them on the shoulder pieces of the ephod as memorial stones for the sons of Israel. Aaron is to bear the names on his shoulders as a memorial before the LORD. [13]Make gold filigree settings [14]and two braided chains of pure gold, like a rope, and attach the chains to the settings.

■ PSALM 21:1-7

[1]The king rejoices in your strength, LORD.
　How great is his joy in the victories
　　you give!

[2]You have granted him his heart's desire
　and have not withheld the request of
　　his lips.
[3]You came to greet him with rich blessings
　and placed a crown of pure gold on his
　　head.
[4]He asked you for life, and you gave it to
　　him –
　length of days, for ever and ever.
[5]Through the victories you gave, his glory
　　is great;

you have bestowed on him splendour
　and majesty.
[6]Surely you have granted him unending
　blessings
　and made him glad with the joy of
　　your presence.
[7]For the king trusts in the LORD;
　through the unfailing love of the Most
　　High
　he will not be shaken.

■ PROVERBS 4:25-27

[25]Let your eyes look straight ahead;
　fix your gaze directly before you.
[26]Give careful thought to the paths for
　　your feet
　and be steadfast in all your ways.
[27]Do not turn to the right or the left;
　keep your foot from evil.

■ MATTHEW 25:14-30

[14]'Again, it will be like a man going on a journey, who called his servants and entrusted his wealth to them. [15]To one he gave five bags of gold, to another two bags, and to another one bag, each according to his ability. Then he went on his journey. [16]The man who had received five bags of gold went at once and put his money to work and gained five bags more. [17]So also, the one with two bags of gold gained two more. [18]But the man who had received one bag went off, dug a hole in the ground and hid his master's money.

[19]'After a long time the master of those servants returned and settled accounts with them. [20]The man who had received five bags of gold brought the other five. "Master," he said, "you entrusted me with five bags of gold. See, I have gained five more."

[21]'His master replied, "Well done, good and faithful servant! You have been faithful

with a few things; I will put you in charge of many things. Come and share your master's happiness!"

²²'The man with two bags of gold also came. "Master," he said, "you entrusted me with two bags of gold: see, I have gained two more."

²³'His master replied, "Well done, good and faithful servant! You have been faithful with a few things; I will put you in charge of many things. Come and share your master's happiness!"

²⁴'Then the man who had received one bag of gold came. "Master," he said, "I knew that you are a hard man, harvesting where you have not sown and gathering where you have not scattered seed. ²⁵So I was afraid and went out and hid your gold in the ground. See, here is what belongs to you."

²⁶'His master replied, "You wicked, lazy servant! So you knew that I harvest where I have not sown and gather where I have not scattered seed? ²⁷Well then, you should have put my money on deposit with the bankers, so that when I returned I would have received it back with interest.

²⁸'"So take the bag of gold from him and give it to the one who has ten bags. ²⁹For whoever has will be given more, and they will have an abundance. Whoever does not have, even what they have will be taken from them. ³⁰And throw that worthless servant outside, into the darkness, where there will be weeping and gnashing of teeth."

Don't Go onto His Ground

'Let your eyes look straight ahead; fix your gaze directly before you.' **Proverbs 4:25**

Today we look at the issue of sexual experience and its need to be kept within marriage. Some temptations cannot be avoided; some, however, can. Anatole France has a story in which God and the devil are talking of a beautiful young girl. God asks, 'How dare you tempt such a lovely creature as that?' The devil replies, 'Well, she came on to my ground.' R. W. Everrood tells this story: A young man seeking his fortune was travelling across a desert when he came to an oasis at which a beautiful girl sat spinning on a loom. He asked for a drink and she said, 'Certainly, providing you let me put these threads around you that I am spinning.' He agreed, thinking he could easily brush away the thin gossamer threads as one would brush away a spider's web. After drinking the water, he fell asleep and awoke to find himself tied by thick, strong cords.

The best way to deal with temptation is not to go towards it. Paul's advice to young Timothy was this: 'flee from all this ...' (1 Tim. 6:11). John Ruskin says, 'No one can honestly ask to be delivered from temptation unless he has honestly and firmly determined to do the best he can to keep out of it.' My advice to every unmarried man and woman reading these lines – and married people, too – is this: Keep out of the devil's territory. Don't go on to his ground.

PRAYER

O God, make me alert to the dangers that beset my path, and when I move towards them unsuspectingly, grant that all the warning bells may ring within my heart. I know You will do Your part; help me do mine. In Jesus' name I ask it. Amen.

FURTHER STUDY

1 Thess. 4:1-12; Heb. 13:4; Eph. 5:1-5
• What instructions did Paul give concerning God's will?
• What characteristics did Paul say are proper 'for God's holy people'?

February 12

■ EXODUS 28:15–29:25

15 'Fashion a breastpiece for making decisions – the work of skilled hands. Make it like the ephod: of gold, and of blue, purple and scarlet yarn, and of finely twisted linen. 16 It is to be square – a span long and a span wide – and folded double. 17 Then mount four rows of precious stones on it. The first row shall be carnelian, chrysolite and beryl; 18 the second row shall be turquoise, lapis lazuli and emerald; 19 the third row shall be jacinth, agate and amethyst; 20 the fourth row shall be topaz, onyx and jasper. Mount them in gold filigree settings. 21 There are to be twelve stones, one for each of the names of the sons of Israel, each engraved like a seal with the name of one of the twelve tribes.

22 'For the breastpiece make braided chains of pure gold, like a rope. 23 Make two gold rings for it and fasten them to two corners of the breastpiece. 24 Fasten the two gold chains to the rings at the corners of the breastpiece, 25 and the other ends of the chains to the two settings, attaching them to the shoulder pieces of the ephod at the front. 26 Make two gold rings and attach them to the other two corners of the breastpiece on the inside edge next to the ephod. 27 Make two more gold rings and attach them to the bottom of the shoulder pieces on the front of the ephod, close to the seam just above the waistband of the ephod. 28 The rings of the breastpiece are to be tied to the rings of the ephod with blue cord, connecting it to the waistband, so that the breastpiece will not swing out from the ephod.

29 'Whenever Aaron enters the Holy Place, he will bear the names of the sons of Israel over his heart on the breastpiece of decision as a continuing memorial before the LORD. 30 Also put the Urim and the Thummim in the breastpiece, so they may be over Aaron's heart whenever he enters the presence of the LORD. Thus Aaron will always bear the means of making decisions for the Israelites over his heart before the LORD.

31 'Make the robe of the ephod entirely of blue cloth, 32 with an opening for the head in its centre. There shall be a woven edge like a collar around this opening, so that it will not tear. 33 Make pomegranates of blue, purple and scarlet yarn around the hem of the robe, with gold bells between them. 34 The gold bells and the pomegranates are to alternate round the hem of the robe. 35 Aaron must wear it when he ministers. The sound of the bells will be heard when he enters the Holy Place before the LORD and when he comes out, so that he will not die.

36 'Make a plate of pure gold and engrave

on it as on a seal: HOLY TO THE LORD. ³⁷ Fasten a blue cord to it to attach it to the turban; it is to be on the front of the turban. ³⁸ It will be on Aaron's forehead, and he will bear the guilt involved in the sacred gifts the Israelites consecrate, whatever their gifts may be. It will be on Aaron's forehead continually so that they will be acceptable to the LORD.

³⁹ 'Weave the tunic of fine linen and make the turban of fine linen. The sash is to be the work of an embroiderer. ⁴⁰ Make tunics, sashes and caps for Aaron's sons to give them dignity and honour. ⁴¹ After you put these clothes on your brother Aaron and his sons, anoint and ordain them. Consecrate them so they may serve me as priests.

⁴² 'Make linen undergarments as a covering for the body, reaching from the waist to the thigh. ⁴³ Aaron and his sons must wear them whenever they enter the tent of meeting or approach the altar to minister in the Holy Place, so that they will not incur guilt and die.

'This is to be a lasting ordinance for Aaron and his descendants.

29 'This is what you are to do to consecrate them, so that they may serve me as priests: take a young bull and two rams without defect. ² And from the finest wheat flour make round loaves without yeast, thick loaves without yeast and with olive oil mixed in, and thin loaves without yeast and brushed with olive oil. ³ Put them in a basket and present them in it – along with the bull and the two rams. ⁴ Then bring Aaron and his sons to the entrance to the tent of meeting and wash them with water. ⁵ Take the garments and dress Aaron with the tunic, the robe of the ephod, the ephod itself and the breastpiece. Fasten the ephod on him by its skilfully woven waistband. ⁶ Put the turban on his head and attach the sacred emblem to the turban. ⁷ Take the anointing oil and anoint him by pouring it on his head. ⁸ Bring his sons and dress them in tunics ⁹ and fasten caps on them. Then tie

sashes on Aaron and his sons. The priesthood is theirs by a lasting ordinance.

'Then you shall ordain Aaron and his sons.

¹⁰ 'Bring the bull to the front of the tent of meeting, and Aaron and his sons shall lay their hands on its head. ¹¹ Slaughter it in the LORD's presence at the entrance to the tent of meeting. ¹² Take some of the bull's blood and put it on the horns of the altar with your finger, and pour out the rest of it at the base of the altar. ¹³ Then take all the fat on the internal organs, the covering of the liver, and both kidneys with the fat on them, and burn them on the altar. ¹⁴ But burn the bull's flesh and its hide and its intestines outside the camp. It is a sin offering.

¹⁵ 'Take one of the rams, and Aaron and his sons shall lay their hands on its head. ¹⁶ Slaughter it and take the blood and splash it against the sides of the altar. ¹⁷ Cut the ram into pieces and wash the internal organs and the legs, putting them with the head and the other pieces. ¹⁸ Then burn the entire ram on the altar. It is a burnt offering to the LORD, a pleasing aroma, a food offering presented to the LORD.

¹⁹ 'Take the other ram, and Aaron and his sons shall lay their hands on its head. ²⁰ Slaughter it, take some of its blood and put it on the lobes of the right ears of Aaron and his sons, on the thumbs of their right hands, and on the big toes of their right feet. Then splash blood against the sides of the altar. ²¹ And take some of the blood on the altar and some of the anointing oil and sprinkle it on Aaron and his garments and on his sons and their garments. Then he and his sons and their garments will be consecrated.

²² 'Take from this ram the fat, the fat tail, the fat on the internal organs, the covering of the liver, both kidneys with the fat on them, and the right thigh. (This is the ram for the ordination.) ²³ From the basket of bread made without yeast, which is before the LORD, take one round loaf, one thick loaf

with olive oil mixed in, and one thin loaf. 24 Put all these in the hands of Aaron and his sons and wave them before the LORD as a wave offering. 25 Then take them from their hands and burn them on the altar along with the burnt offering for a pleasing aroma to the LORD, a food offering presented to the LORD.

▬ PSALM 21:8-13

8 Your hand will lay hold on all your
    enemies;
    your right hand will seize your foes.
9 When you appear for battle,
    you will burn them up as in a blazing
      furnace.
The LORD will swallow them up in his
    wrath,
    and his fire will consume them.
10 You will destroy their descendants from
    the earth,
    their posterity from mankind.
11 Though they plot evil against you
    and devise wicked schemes, they
      cannot succeed.
12 You will make them turn their backs
    when you aim at them with drawn bow.

13 Be exalted in your strength, LORD;
    we will sing and praise your might.

▬ PROVERBS 5:1-2

5 My son, pay attention to my wisdom,
    turn your ear to my words of insight,
2 that you may maintain discretion
    and your lips may preserve
      knowledge.

▬ MATTHEW 25:31-26:5

31 'When the Son of Man comes in his glory, and all the angels with him, he will sit on his glorious throne. 32 All the nations will be gathered before him, and he will separate the people one from another as a shepherd separates the sheep from the goats. 33 He will put the sheep on his right and the goats on his left.

34 'Then the King will say to those on his right, "Come, you who are blessed by my Father; take your inheritance, the kingdom prepared for you since the creation of the world. 35 For I was hungry and you gave me something to eat, I was thirsty and you gave me something to drink, I was a stranger and you invited me in, 36 I needed clothes and you clothed me, I was ill and you looked after me, I was in prison and you came to visit me."

37 'Then the righteous will answer him, "Lord, when did we see you hungry and feed you, or thirsty and give you something to drink? 38 When did we see you a stranger and invite you in, or needing clothes and clothe you? 39 When did we see you ill or in prison and go to visit you?"

40 'The King will reply, "Truly I tell you, whatever you did for one of the least of these brothers and sisters of mine, you did for me."

41 'Then he will say to those on his left, "Depart from me, you who are cursed, into the eternal fire prepared for the devil and his angels. 42 For I was hungry and you gave me nothing to eat, I was thirsty and you gave me nothing to drink, 43 I was a stranger and you did not invite me in, I needed clothes and you did not clothe me, I was ill and in prison and you did not look after me."

44 'They also will answer, "Lord, when did we see you hungry or thirsty or a stranger or needing clothes or ill or in prison, and did not help you?"

45 'He will reply, "Truly I tell you, whatever you did not do for one of the least of these, you did not do for me."

46 'Then they will go away to eternal punishment, but the righteous to eternal life.'

26 When Jesus had finished saying all these things, he said to his disciples, ²'As you know, the Passover is two days away – and the Son of Man will be handed over to be crucified.'

³Then the chief priests and the elders of the people assembled in the palace of the high priest, whose name was Caiaphas, ⁴and they schemed to arrest Jesus secretly and kill him. ⁵'But not during the festival,' they said, 'or there may be a riot among the people.'

The Great Peril of the Saints

'Truly I tell you, whatever you did for one of the least of these brothers and sisters of mine, you did for me.'
Matthew 25:40

How does kindness grow in us? It depends on how deeply we live in God. Some Christians set out to be kind, but kindness which is the fruit of the Spirit is not the result of self-effort but comes from abiding in Christ. The Christian abides in Christ and the fruit grows and ripens of its own accord.

The kindest Christians are those who have no ambition to be kind and hold no such thought. This is not to say that they do not desire to be kind, but they do not try to manufacture their kindness. Consumed with a longing to be more like Jesus every day, their thought is not on their personal sanctity but on how they can reflect their Lord. They come across as people who are so self-forgetful that it could be said of them what was said of Samuel Barnett of Toynbee Hall: 'He forgot himself even to the extent of forgetting that he had forgotten.'

The great peril of the Christian life is that we may become selfish in our consuming longing to be unselfish. Only as our roots go down daily into God through prayer and meditation in His Word can we be kept secure from the temptation to focus on growth for its own sake - rather than for His sake. The person whose kindness is an appetite for praise gives up when the praise does not come. And they give up more quickly still if people say, 'What are you getting out of this yourself?' The Christian whose kindness flows out of his relationship with God never gives up. He just can't help being kind.

PRAYER

O Father, help me to spend time with You so that in the legislature of my heart You may write the law of kindness. Help me to come under its sway forever. Amen.

FURTHER STUDY

2 Cor. 9:1-6; Deut. 15:7-8; Psa. 41:1; Acts 20:35
• How are we to sow?
• Of what did Paul remind the Ephesian elders?

February 13

■ EXODUS 29:26–30:38

26 After you take the breast of the ram for Aaron's ordination, wave it before the LORD as a wave offering, and it will be your share.

27 'Consecrate those parts of the ordination ram that belong to Aaron and his sons: the breast that was waved and the thigh that was presented. 28 This is always to be the regular share from the Israelites for Aaron and his sons. It is the contribution the Israelites are to make to the LORD from their fellowship offerings.

29 'Aaron's sacred garments will belong to his descendants so that they can be anointed and ordained in them. 30 The son who succeeds him as priest and comes to the tent of meeting to minister in the Holy Place is to wear them seven days.

31 'Take the ram for the ordination and cook the meat in a sacred place. 32 At the entrance to the tent of meeting, Aaron and his sons are to eat the meat of the ram and the bread that is in the basket. 33 They are to eat these offerings by which atonement was made for their ordination and consecration. But no one else may eat them, because they are sacred. 34 And if any of the meat of the ordination ram or any bread is left over till morning, burn it up. It must not be eaten, because it is sacred.

35 'Do for Aaron and his sons everything I have commanded you, taking seven days to ordain them. 36 Sacrifice a bull each day as a sin offering to make atonement. Purify the altar by making atonement for it, and anoint it to consecrate it. 37 For seven days make atonement for the altar and consecrate it. Then the altar will be most holy, and whatever touches it will be holy.

38 'This is what you are to offer on the altar regularly each day: two lambs a year old. 39 Offer one in the morning and the other at twilight. 40 With the first lamb offer a tenth of an ephah of the finest flour mixed with a quarter of a hin of oil from pressed olives, and a quarter of a hin of wine as a drink offering. 41 Sacrifice the other lamb at twilight with the same grain offering and its drink offering as in the morning – a pleasing aroma, a food offering presented to the LORD.

42 'For the generations to come this burnt offering is to be made regularly at the entrance to the tent of meeting, before the LORD. There I will meet you and speak to you; 43 there also I will meet with the Israelites, and the place will be consecrated by my glory.

44 'So I will consecrate the tent of meeting and the altar and will consecrate Aaron and his sons to serve me as priests. 45 Then I will dwell among the Israelites and be their God. 46 They will know that I am the LORD their God, who brought them out of Egypt so that I might dwell among them. I am the LORD their God.

30 'Make an altar of acacia wood for burning incense. 2 It is to be square, a cubit long and a cubit wide, and two cubits high – its horns of one piece with it. 3 Overlay the top and all the sides and the horns with pure gold, and make a gold moulding around it. 4 Make two gold rings for the altar below the moulding – two on each of the opposite sides – to hold the poles used to carry it. 5 Make the poles of acacia wood and overlay them with gold. 6 Put the altar in front of the curtain that shields the ark of the covenant law – before the atonement cover that is over the tablets of the covenant law – where I will meet with you.

⁷'Aaron must burn fragrant incense on the altar every morning when he tends the lamps. ⁸He must burn incense again when he lights the lamps at twilight so that incense will burn regularly before the LORD for the generations to come. ⁹Do not offer on this altar any other incense or any burnt offering or grain offering, and do not pour a drink offering on it. ¹⁰Once a year Aaron shall make atonement on its horns. This annual atonement must be made with the blood of the atoning sin offering for the generations to come. It is most holy to the LORD.'

¹¹Then the LORD said to Moses, ¹²'When you take a census of the Israelites to count them, each one must pay the LORD a ransom for his life at the time he is counted. Then no plague will come on them when you number them. ¹³Each one who crosses over to those already counted is to give a half shekel, according to the sanctuary shekel, which weighs twenty gerahs. This half shekel is an offering to the LORD. ¹⁴All who cross over, those twenty years old or more, are to give an offering to the LORD. ¹⁵The rich are not to give more than a half shekel and the poor are not to give less when you make the offering to the LORD to atone for your lives. ¹⁶Receive the atonement money from the Israelites and use it for the service of the tent of meeting. It will be a memorial for the Israelites before the LORD, making atonement for your lives.'

¹⁷Then the LORD said to Moses, ¹⁸'Make a bronze basin, with its bronze stand, for washing. Place it between the tent of meeting and the altar, and put water in it. ¹⁹Aaron and his sons are to wash their hands and feet with water from it. ²⁰Whenever they enter the tent of meeting, they shall wash with water so that they will not die. Also, when they approach the altar to minister by presenting a food offering to the LORD, ²¹they shall wash their hands and feet so that they will not die. This is to be a lasting ordinance for Aaron and his descendants for the generations to come.'

²²Then the LORD said to Moses, ²³'Take the following fine spices: 500 shekels of liquid myrrh, half as much (that is, 250 shekels) of fragrant cinnamon, 250 shekels of fragrant calamus, ²⁴500 shekels of cassia – all according to the sanctuary shekel – and a hin of olive oil. ²⁵Make these into a sacred anointing oil, a fragrant blend, the work of a perfumer. It will be the sacred anointing oil. ²⁶Then use it to anoint the tent of meeting, the ark of the covenant law, ²⁷the table and all its articles, the lampstand and its accessories, the altar of incense, ²⁸the altar of burnt offering and all its utensils, and the basin with its stand. ²⁹You shall consecrate them so they will be most holy, and whatever touches them will be holy.

³⁰'Anoint Aaron and his sons and consecrate them so they may serve me as priests. ³¹Say to the Israelites, "This is to be my sacred anointing oil for the generations to come. ³²Do not pour it on anyone else's body and do not make any other oil using the same formula. It is sacred, and you are to consider it sacred. ³³Whoever makes perfume like it and puts it on anyone other than a priest must be cut off from their people."'

³⁴Then the LORD said to Moses, 'Take fragrant spices – gum resin, onycha and galbanum – and pure frankincense, all in equal amounts, ³⁵and make a fragrant blend of incense, the work of a perfumer. It is to be salted and pure and sacred. ³⁶Grind some of it to powder and place it in front of the ark of the covenant law in the tent of meeting, where I will meet with you. It shall be most holy to you. ³⁷Do not make any incense with this formula for yourselves; consider it holy to the LORD. ³⁸Whoever makes incense like it to enjoy its fragrance must be cut off from their people.'

■ PSALM 22:1-5

¹ My God, my God, why have you forsaken
      me?
   Why are you so far from saving me,
      so far from my cries of anguish?
² My God, I cry out by day, but you do not
      answer,
   by night, but I find no rest.

³ Yet you are enthroned as the Holy One;
      you are the one Israel praises.
⁴ In you our ancestors put their trust;
      they trusted and you delivered them.
⁵ To you they cried out and were saved;
      in you they trusted and were not put to
      shame.

■ PROVERBS 5:3-6

³ For the lips of the adulterous woman
      drip honey,
   and her speech is smoother than oil;
⁴ but in the end she is bitter as gall,
      sharp as a double-edged sword.
⁵ Her feet go down to death;
      her steps lead straight to the grave.
⁶ She gives no thought to the way of life;
      her paths wander aimlessly, but she
         does not know it.

■ MATTHEW 26:6-25

⁶ While Jesus was in Bethany in the home
of Simon the Leper, ⁷ a woman came to him
with an alabaster jar of very expensive perfume, which she poured on his head as he
was reclining at the table.
⁸ When the disciples saw this, they were
indignant. 'Why this waste?' they asked.
⁹ 'This perfume could have been sold at a
high price and the money given to the poor.'

¹⁰ Aware of this, Jesus said to them, 'Why
are you bothering this woman? She has
done a beautiful thing to me. ¹¹ The poor you
will always have with you, but you will not
always have me. ¹² When she poured this
perfume on my body, she did it to prepare
me for burial. ¹³ Truly I tell you, wherever this gospel is preached throughout the
world, what she has done will also be told,
in memory of her.'
¹⁴ Then one of the Twelve – the one called
Judas Iscariot – went to the chief priests
¹⁵ and asked, 'What are you willing to give
me if I deliver him over to you?' So they
counted out for him thirty pieces of silver.
¹⁶ From then on Judas watched for an opportunity to hand him over.
¹⁷ On the first day of the Festival of Unleavened Bread, the disciples came to Jesus and
asked, 'Where do you want us to make preparations for you to eat the Passover?'
¹⁸ He replied, 'Go into the city to a certain
man and tell him, "The Teacher says: my
appointed time is near. I am going to celebrate the Passover with my disciples at your
house."' ¹⁹ So the disciples did as Jesus had
directed them and prepared the Passover.
²⁰ When evening came, Jesus was reclining at the table with the Twelve. ²¹ And while
they were eating, he said, 'Truly I tell you,
one of you will betray me.'
²² They were very sad and began to say to
him one after the other, 'Surely you don't
mean me, Lord?'
²³ Jesus replied, 'The one who has dipped
his hand into the bowl with me will betray
me. ²⁴ The Son of Man will go just as it is
written about him. But woe to that man who
betrays the Son of Man! It would be better
for him if he had not been born.'
²⁵ Then Judas, the one who would betray him, said, 'Surely you don't mean me,
Rabbi?'
   Jesus answered, 'You have said so.'

All Becomes 'All'

'... my appointed time is near. I am going to celebrate the Passover with my disciples at your house.'
Matthew 26:18

The upper room where the disciples stayed after the Ascension was associated in the minds of the disciples with the Last Supper, for it was in this room that Jesus unfolded for them the meaning of redemption. As He broke bread with them, He said, 'This is my body given for you; do this in remembrance of me.' In the same way He also took the cup after supper and said, 'This cup is the new covenant in my blood, which is poured out for you' (Luke 22:19-20).

The upper room had a double content – the cross and the Spirit. These are more closely connected than we might realise, for if we do not bear the spirit of the cross we will not bear the Spirit of God. We are to be crucified followers of a crucified Lord.

Did that upper room stand in the minds of the disciples as a symbol of Christ's self-giving? And would the whole atmosphere of the place remind them that, just as He had offered His all, so must they offer their all? I cannot help but believe that the connection between the Last Supper and the promised descent of the Holy Spirit would be much upon their minds. In that room, God, in the Person of His Son Jesus Christ, had offered His all. Now the twelve disciples were being confronted with the same challenge. Out of Christ's offering came power, for God answers self-giving by the giving of Himself. We can only conclude that something significant happened in the lives of those disciples in that ten-day waiting period between the Ascension and Pentecost, for out of that 'all' offering came 'all' power.

PRAYER

O God, in this 'upper room' where I am right now, I offer my little 'all', and I take instead Your almighty 'all'. I exchange my poverty for Your riches, my emptiness for Your fullness, my weaknesses for Your strength. Amen.

FURTHER STUDY

Acts 1:14; Eph. 2:14;
Col. 1:20; 2:14
• What was abolished by the cross?
• What is the relationship between 'Passover' and 'Pentecost'?

February 14

▬ EXODUS 31:1–32:35

31 Then the LORD said to Moses, ²'See I have chosen Bezalel son of Uri, the son of Hur, of the tribe of Judah, ³and I have filled him with the Spirit of God, with wisdom, with understanding, with knowledge and with all kinds of skills – ⁴to make artistic designs for work in gold, silver and bronze, ⁵to cut and set stones, to work in wood, and to engage in all kinds of crafts. ⁶Moreover, I have appointed Oholiab son of Ahisamak, of the tribe of Dan, to help him. Also I have given ability to all the skilled workers to make everything I have commanded you: ⁷the tent of meeting, the ark of the covenant law with the atonement cover on it, and all the other furnishings of the tent – ⁸the table and its articles, the pure gold lampstand and all its accessories, the altar of incense, ⁹the altar of burnt offering and all its utensils, the basin with its stand – ¹⁰and also the woven garments, both the sacred garments for Aaron the priest and the garments for his sons when they serve as priests, ¹¹and the anointing oil and fragrant incense for the Holy Place. They are to make them just as I commanded you.'

¹²Then the LORD said to Moses, ¹³'Say to the Israelites, "You must observe my Sabbaths. This will be a sign between me and you for the generations to come, so that you may know that I am the LORD, who makes you holy.

¹⁴'"Observe the Sabbath, because it is holy to you. Anyone who desecrates it is to be put to death; those who do any work on that day must be cut off from their people. ¹⁵For six days work is to be done, but the seventh day is a day of sabbath rest, holy to the LORD. Whoever does any work on the Sabbath day is to be put to death. ¹⁶The Israelites are to observe the Sabbath, celebrating it for the generations to come as a lasting covenant. ¹⁷It will be a sign between me and the Israelites for ever, for in six days the LORD made the heavens and the earth, and on the seventh day he rested and was refreshed."'

¹⁸When the LORD finished speaking to Moses on Mount Sinai, he gave him the two tablets of the covenant law, the tablets of stone inscribed by the finger of God.

32 When the people saw that Moses was so long in coming down from the mountain, they gathered round Aaron and said, 'Come, make us gods who will go before us. As for this fellow Moses who brought us up out of Egypt, we don't know what has happened to him.'

²Aaron answered them, 'Take off the gold earrings that your wives, your sons and your daughters are wearing, and bring them to me.' ³So all the people took off their earrings and brought them to Aaron. ⁴He took what they handed him and made it into an idol cast in the shape of a calf, fashioning it with a tool. Then they said, 'These are your gods, Israel, who brought you up out of Egypt.'

⁵When Aaron saw this, he built an altar in front of the calf and announced, 'Tomorrow there will be a festival to the LORD.' ⁶So the next day the people rose early and sacrificed burnt offerings and presented fellowship offerings. Afterwards they sat down to eat and drink and got up to indulge in revelry.

⁷Then the LORD said to Moses, 'Go down, because your people, whom you brought up out of Egypt, have become corrupt. ⁸They have been quick to turn away from what I

commanded them and have made themselves an idol cast in the shape of a calf. They have bowed down to it and sacrificed to it and have said, "These are your gods, Israel, who brought you up out of Egypt."

⁹ 'I have seen these people,' the LORD said to Moses, 'and they are a stiff-necked people. ¹⁰ Now leave me alone so that my anger may burn against them and that I may destroy them. Then I will make you into a great nation.'

¹¹ But Moses sought the favour of the LORD his God. 'LORD,' he said, 'why should your anger burn against your people, whom you brought out of Egypt with great power and a mighty hand? ¹² Why should the Egyptians say, "It was with evil intent that he brought them out, to kill them in the mountains and to wipe them off the face of the earth"? Turn from your fierce anger; relent and do not bring disaster on your people. ¹³ Remember your servants Abraham, Isaac and Israel, to whom you swore by your own self: "I will make your descendants as numerous as the stars in the sky and I will give your descendants all this land I promised them, and it will be their inheritance for ever."' ¹⁴ Then the LORD relented and did not bring on his people the disaster he had threatened.

¹⁵ Moses turned and went down the mountain with the two tablets of the covenant law in his hands. They were inscribed on both sides, front and back. ¹⁶ The tablets were the work of God; the writing was the writing of God, engraved on the tablets.

¹⁷ When Joshua heard the noise of the people shouting, he said to Moses, 'There is the sound of war in the camp.'

¹⁸ Moses replied:

'It is not the sound of victory,
    it is not the sound of defeat;
    it is the sound of singing that I hear.'

¹⁹ When Moses approached the camp and saw the calf and the dancing, his anger burned and he threw the tablets out of his hands, breaking them to pieces at the foot of the mountain. ²⁰ And he took the calf the people had made and burned it in the fire; then he ground it to powder, scattered it on the water and made the Israelites drink it.

²¹ He said to Aaron, 'What did these people do to you, that you led them into such great sin?'

²² 'Do not be angry, my lord,' Aaron answered. 'You know how prone these people are to evil. ²³ They said to me, "Make us gods who will go before us. As for this fellow Moses who brought us up out of Egypt, we don't know what has happened to him." ²⁴ So I told them, "Whoever has any gold jewellery, take it off." Then they gave me the gold, and I threw it into the fire, and out came this calf!'

²⁵ Moses saw that the people were running wild and that Aaron had let them get out of control and so become a laughing-stock to their enemies. ²⁶ So he stood at the entrance to the camp and said, 'Whoever is for the LORD, come to me.' And all the Levites rallied to him.

²⁷ Then he said to them, 'This is what the LORD, the God of Israel, says: "Each man strap a sword to his side. Go back and forth through the camp from one end to the other, each killing his brother and friend and neighbour."' ²⁸ The Levites did as Moses commanded, and that day about three thousand of the people died. ²⁹ Then Moses said, 'You have been set apart to the LORD today, for you were against your own sons and brothers, and he has blessed you this day.'

³⁰ The next day Moses said to the people, 'You have committed a great sin. But now I will go up to the LORD; perhaps I can make atonement for your sin.'

³¹ So Moses went back to the LORD and said, 'Oh, what a great sin these people have committed! They have made themselves gods of gold. ³² But now, please forgive their

sin – but if not, then blot me out of the book you have written.'

³³The LORD replied to Moses, 'Whoever has sinned against me I will blot out of my book. ³⁴Now go, lead the people to the place I spoke of, and my angel will go before you. However, when the time comes for me to punish, I will punish them for their sin.'

³⁵And the LORD struck the people with a plague because of what they did with the calf Aaron had made.

■ PSALM 22:6-10

⁶But I am a worm and not a man,
> scorned by everyone, despised by the people.
⁷All who see me mock me;
> they hurl insults, shaking their heads.
⁸'He trusts in the LORD,' they say,
> 'let the LORD rescue him.
Let him deliver him,
> since he delights in him.'

⁹Yet you brought me out of the womb;
> you made me trust in you, even at my mother's breast.
¹⁰From birth I was cast on you;
> from my mother's womb you have been my God.

■ PROVERBS 5:7-8

⁷Now then, my sons, listen to me;
> do not turn aside from what I say.
⁸Keep to a path far from her,
> do not go near the door of her house ...

■ MATTHEW 26:26-51

²⁶While they were eating, Jesus took bread, and when he had given thanks, he broke it and gave it to his disciples, saying,

'Take and eat; this is my body.'

²⁷Then he took a cup, and when he had given thanks, he gave it to them, saying, 'Drink from it, all of you. ²⁸This is my blood of the covenant, which is poured out for many for the forgiveness of sins. ²⁹I tell you, I will not drink from this fruit of the vine from now on until that day when I drink it new with you in my Father's kingdom.'

³⁰When they had sung a hymn, they went out to the Mount of Olives.

³¹Then Jesus told them, 'This very night you will all fall away on account of me, for it is written:

> '"I will strike the shepherd,
> and the sheep of the flock will be scattered."

³²But after I have risen, I will go ahead of you into Galilee.'

³³Peter replied, 'Even if all fall away on account of you, I never will.'

³⁴'Truly I tell you,' Jesus answered, 'this very night, before the cock crows, you will disown me three times.'

³⁵But Peter declared, 'Even if I have to die with you, I will never disown you.' And all the other disciples said the same.

³⁶Then Jesus went with his disciples to a place called Gethsemane, and he said to them, 'Sit here while I go over there and pray.' ³⁷He took Peter and the two sons of Zebedee along with him, and he began to be sorrowful and troubled. ³⁸Then he said to them, 'My soul is overwhelmed with sorrow to the point of death. Stay here and keep watch with me.'

³⁹Going a little farther, he fell with his face to the ground and prayed, 'My Father, if it is possible, may this cup be taken from me. Yet not as I will, but as you will.'

⁴⁰Then he returned to his disciples and found them sleeping. 'Couldn't you men keep watch with me for one hour?' he asked Peter. ⁴¹'Watch and pray so that you will not

fall into temptation. The spirit is willing, but the flesh is weak.'

⁴²He went away a second time and prayed, 'My Father, if it is not possible for this cup to be taken away unless I drink it, may your will be done.'

⁴³When he came back, he again found them sleeping, because their eyes were heavy. ⁴⁴So he left them and went away once more and prayed the third time, saying the same thing.

⁴⁵Then he returned to the disciples and said to them, 'Are you still sleeping and resting? Look, the hour has come, and the Son of Man is delivered into the hands of sinners. ⁴⁶Rise! Let us go! Here comes my betrayer!'

⁴⁷While he was still speaking, Judas, one of the Twelve, arrived. With him was a large crowd armed with swords and clubs, sent from the chief priests and the elders of the people. ⁴⁸Now the betrayer had arranged a signal with them: 'The one I kiss is the man; arrest him.' ⁴⁹Going at once to Jesus, Judas said, 'Greetings, Rabbi!' and kissed him.

⁵⁰Jesus replied, 'Do what you came for, friend.'

Then the men stepped forward, seized Jesus and arrested him. ⁵¹With that, one of Jesus' companions reached for his sword, drew it out and struck the servant of the high priest, cutting off his ear.

Coping Through Christ

'My soul is overwhelmed with sorrow to the point of death. Stay here and keep watch with me.'
Matthew 26:38

It is better to face disappointment and feel it than to pretend it is not there. And when I say 'feel it' – I mean exactly that. Most people, I find, just walk around the edges of their disappointment, in the way they would walk cautiously around the rim of a volcano, admitting they have been disappointed but working hard (often unconsciously) to blunt the feelings of disappointment with a 'let's not stay here too long' attitude.

The usual response to what I am now saying is, 'Surely there is no point in being willing to enter into all the pain of our disappointments. What is past is past; isn't it better to forget the hurts and disappointments of the past and get on with life?'

Sounds quite rational and sensible, doesn't it? However, it is not the best way to deal with life. The more deeply we are willing to face our disappointments, the readier we will be to turn to Christ and draw from Him the strength we need to cope with them.

The danger we face when we are unwilling to feel as openly as possible the disappointments that come our way is that we will come to depend on our own strategies to cope with them and turn only partially to Christ for strength. Facing and feeling disappointment is a sure way of coming to recognise that God is the only One who can help us cope. When we face and feel our disappointments, we will cling more closely to Christ.

PRAYER

Gracious and loving heavenly Father, I want to live fully and frankly. Help me to face whatever goes on inside me with complete honesty. Save me from all self-deception and subterfuges, for I would be a fit instrument for You. In Jesus' name. Amen.

FURTHER STUDY

1 Kings 19; Heb. 4:15
• What was Elijah's disappointment?
• How did he respond to it?

February 15

■ EXODUS 33:1–34:35

33 Then the LORD said to Moses, 'Leave this place, you and the people you brought up out of Egypt, and go up to the land I promised on oath to Abraham, Isaac and Jacob, saying, "I will give it to your descendants." ²I will send an angel before you and drive out the Canaanites, Amorites, Hittites, Perizzites, Hivites and Jebusites. ³Go up to the land flowing with milk and honey. But I will not go with you, because you are a stiff-necked people and I might destroy you on the way.'

⁴When the people heard these distressing words, they began to mourn and no one put on any ornaments. ⁵For the LORD had said to Moses, 'Tell the Israelites, "You are a stiff-necked people. If I were to go with you even for a moment, I might destroy you. Now take off your ornaments and I will decide what to do with you." ' ⁶So the Israelites stripped off their ornaments at Mount Horeb.

⁷Now Moses used to take a tent and pitch it outside the camp some distance away, calling it the 'tent of meeting'. Anyone enquiring of the LORD would go to the tent of meeting outside the camp. ⁸And whenever Moses went out to the tent, all the people rose and stood at the entrances to their tents, watching Moses until he entered the tent. ⁹As Moses went into the tent, the pillar of cloud would come down and stay at the entrance, while the LORD spoke with Moses. ¹⁰Whenever the people saw the pillar of cloud standing at the entrance to the tent, they all stood and worshipped, each at the entrance to their tent. ¹¹The LORD would speak to Moses face to face, as one speaks to a friend. Then Moses would return to the camp, but his young assistant Joshua son of Nun did not leave the tent.

¹²Moses said to the LORD, 'You have been telling me, "Lead these people," but you have not let me know whom you will send with me. You have said, "I know you by name and you have found favour with me." ¹³If you are pleased with me, teach me your ways so I may know you and continue to find favour with you. Remember that this nation is your people.'

¹⁴The LORD replied, 'My Presence will go with you, and I will give you rest.'

¹⁵Then Moses said to him, 'If your Presence does not go with us, do not send us up from here. ¹⁶How will anyone know that you are pleased with me and with your people unless you go with us? What else will distinguish me and your people from all the

other people on the face of the earth?'

¹⁷ And the LORD said to Moses, 'I will do the very thing you have asked, because I am pleased with you and I know you by name.'

¹⁸ Then Moses said, 'Now show me your glory.'

¹⁹ And the LORD said, 'I will cause all my goodness to pass in front of you, and I will proclaim my name, the LORD, in your presence. I will have mercy on whom I will have mercy, and I will have compassion on whom I will have compassion. ²⁰ But,' he said, 'you cannot see my face, for no one may see me and live.'

²¹ Then the LORD said, 'There is a place near me where you may stand on a rock. ²² When my glory passes by, I will put you in a cleft in the rock and cover you with my hand until I have passed by. ²³ Then I will remove my hand and you will see my back; but my face must not be seen.'

34 The LORD said to Moses, 'Chisel out two stone tablets like the first ones, and I will write on them the words that were on the first tablets, which you broke. ² Be ready in the morning, and then come up on Mount Sinai. Present yourself to me there on top of the mountain. ³ No one is to come with you or be seen anywhere on the mountain; not even the flocks and herds may graze in front of the mountain.'

⁴ So Moses chiselled out two stone tablets like the first ones and went up Mount Sinai early in the morning, as the LORD had commanded him; and he carried the two stone tablets in his hands. ⁵ Then the LORD came down in the cloud and stood there with him and proclaimed his name, the LORD. ⁶ And he passed in front of Moses, proclaiming, 'The LORD, the LORD, the compassionate and gracious God, slow to anger, abounding in love and faithfulness, ⁷ maintaining love to thousands, and forgiving wickedness, rebellion and sin. Yet he does not leave the guilty unpunished; he punishes the children and their children for the sin of the

parents to the third and fourth generation.'

⁸ Moses bowed to the ground at once and worshipped. ⁹ 'Lord,' he said, 'if I have found favour in your eyes, then let the Lord go with us. Although this is a stiff-necked people, forgive our wickedness and our sin, and take us as your inheritance.'

¹⁰ Then the LORD said: 'I am making a covenant with you. Before all your people I will do wonders never before done in any nation in all the world. The people you live among will see how awesome is the work that I, the LORD, will do for you. ¹¹ Obey what I command you today. I will drive out before you the Amorites, Canaanites, Hittites, Perizzites, Hivites and Jebusites. ¹² Be careful not to make a treaty with those who live in the land where you are going, or they will be a snare among you. ¹³ Break down their altars, smash their sacred stones and cut down their Asherah poles. ¹⁴ Do not worship any other god, for the LORD, whose name is Jealous, is a jealous God.

¹⁵ 'Be careful not to make a treaty with those who live in the land; for when they prostitute themselves to their gods and sacrifice to them, they will invite you and you will eat their sacrifices. ¹⁶ And when you choose some of their daughters as wives for your sons and those daughters prostitute themselves to their gods, they will lead your sons to do the same.

¹⁷ 'Do not make any idols.

¹⁸ 'Celebrate the Festival of Unleavened Bread. For seven days eat bread made without yeast, as I commanded you. Do this at the appointed time in the month of Aviv, for in that month you came out of Egypt.

¹⁹ 'The first offspring of every womb belongs to me, including all the firstborn males of your livestock, whether from herd or flock. ²⁰ Redeem the firstborn donkey with a lamb, but if you do not redeem it, break its neck. Redeem all your firstborn sons.

'No one is to appear before me empty-handed.

²¹'Six days you shall labour, but on the seventh day you shall rest; even during the ploughing season and harvest you must rest.
²²'Celebrate the Festival of Weeks with the firstfruits of the wheat harvest, and the Festival of Ingathering at the turn of the year. ²³Three times a year all your men are to appear before the Sovereign LORD, the God of Israel. ²⁴I will drive out nations before you and enlarge your territory, and no one will covet your land when you go up three times each year to appear before the LORD your God.
²⁵'Do not offer the blood of a sacrifice to me along with anything containing yeast, and do not let any of the sacrifice from the Passover Festival remain until morning.
²⁶'Bring the best of the firstfruits of your soil to the house of the LORD your God.
'Do not cook a young goat in its mother's milk.'
²⁷Then the LORD said to Moses, 'Write down these words, for in accordance with these words I have made a covenant with you and with Israel.' ²⁸Moses was there with the LORD forty days and forty nights without eating bread or drinking water. And he wrote on the tablets the words of the covenant – the Ten Commandments.
²⁹When Moses came down from Mount Sinai with the two tablets of the covenant law in his hands, he was not aware that his face was radiant because he had spoken with the LORD. ³⁰When Aaron and all the Israelites saw Moses, his face was radiant, and they were afraid to come near him. ³¹But Moses called to them; so Aaron and all the leaders of the community came back to him, and he spoke to them. ³²Afterwards all the Israelites came near him, and he gave them all the commands the LORD had given him on Mount Sinai.
³³When Moses finished speaking to them, he put a veil over his face. ³⁴But whenever he entered the LORD's presence to speak with him, he removed the veil until he came

out. And when he came out and told the Israelites what he had been commanded, ³⁵they saw that his face was radiant. Then Moses would put the veil back over his face until he went in to speak with the LORD.

▬ PSALM 22:11-15

¹¹Do not be far from me,
  for trouble is near
  and there is no one to help.

¹²Many bulls surround me;
  strong bulls of Bashan encircle me.
¹³Roaring lions that tear their prey
  open their mouths wide against me.
¹⁴I am poured out like water,
  and all my bones are out of joint.
  My heart has turned to wax;
  it has melted within me.
¹⁵My mouth is dried up like a potsherd,
  and my tongue sticks to the roof of my
    mouth;
  you lay me in the dust of death.

▬ PROVERBS 5:9-10

⁹... lest you lose your honour to others
  and your dignity to one who is cruel,
¹⁰lest strangers feast on your wealth
  and your toil enrich the house of
    another.

▬ MATTHEW 26:52-75

⁵²'Put your sword back in its place,' Jesus said to him, 'for all who draw the sword will die by the sword. ⁵³Do you think I cannot call on my Father, and he will at once put at my disposal more than twelve legions of angels? ⁵⁴But how then would the Scriptures be fulfilled that say it must happen in this way?'

[55] In that hour Jesus said to the crowd, 'Am I leading a rebellion, that you have come out with swords and clubs to capture me? Every day I sat in the temple courts teaching, and you did not arrest me. [56] But this has all taken place that the writings of the prophets might be fulfilled.' Then all the disciples deserted him and fled.

[57] Those who had arrested Jesus took him to Caiaphas the high priest, where the teachers of the law and the elders had assembled. [58] But Peter followed him at a distance, right up to the courtyard of the high priest. He entered and sat down with the guards to see the outcome.

[59] The chief priests and the whole Sanhedrin were looking for false evidence against Jesus so that they could put him to death. [60] But they did not find any, though many false witnesses came forward.

Finally two came forward [61] and declared, 'This fellow said, "I am able to destroy the temple of God and rebuild it in three days."'

[62] Then the high priest stood up and said to Jesus, 'Are you not going to answer? What is this testimony that these men are bringing against you?' [63] But Jesus remained silent.

The high priest said to him, 'I charge you under oath by the living God: Tell us if you are the Messiah, the Son of God.'

[64] 'You have said so,' Jesus replied. 'But I say to all of you: from now on you will see the Son of Man sitting at the right hand of the Mighty One and coming on the clouds of heaven.'

[65] Then the high priest tore his clothes and said, 'He has spoken blasphemy! Why do we need any more witnesses? Look, now you have heard the blasphemy. [66] What do you think?'

'He is worthy of death,' they answered.

[67] Then they spat in his face and struck him with their fists. Others slapped him [68] and said, 'Prophesy to us, Messiah. Who hit you?'

[69] Now Peter was sitting out in the courtyard, and a servant-girl came to him. 'You also were with Jesus of Galilee,' she said.

[70] But he denied it before them all. 'I don't know what you're talking about,' he said.

[71] Then he went out to the gateway, where another servant-girl saw him and said to the people there, 'This fellow was with Jesus of Nazareth.'

[72] He denied it again, with an oath: 'I don't know the man!'

[73] After a little while, those standing there went up to Peter and said, 'Surely you are one of them; your accent gives you away.'

[74] Then he began to call down curses, and he swore to them, 'I don't know the man!'

Immediately a cock crowed. [75] Then Peter remembered the word Jesus had spoken: 'Before the cock crows, you will disown me three times.' And he went outside and wept bitterly.

The Father God

'Then Moses said to him, "If your Presence does not go with us, do not send us up from here. How will anyone know that you are pleased with me and with your people unless you go with us?"' **Exodus 33:15-16**

Samuel Shoemaker, the American Episcopalian preacher who was instrumental in forming Alcoholics Anonymous, pointed out that the whole principle of prayer depends on what kind of Being the Creator is.

Listen to this statement made to a group of recovering alcoholics: 'If He created the universe and gave everything a primeval push, and then retired beyond where we cannot get in contact with Him, prayer is a vain effort. But if He be a personal God as Christians believe He is, then He will have a concern for the people He made and will want to involve Himself with them in all their affairs.' We are not alone in this universe; a personal God stands behind all things, waiting, longing that we might enter into a relationship with Him.

We said that one of the reasons why people desire an impersonal God is because this kind of God is easier to live with than one who is personal like themselves. It's rather nice to carry inside our hearts a subjective idea of a God of beauty, truth and goodness. That kind of God demands nothing of us. Better still a formless life-force surging through all of us, a vast power we can tap and use to our advantage. This kind of God is extremely easy to live with.

But a living God who approaches us at infinite speed – the Hunter, the King, the Lover, the Husband – this is quite another matter. Yet whether we believe it or not, this is the kind of God He is.

PRAYER

How thankful I am that You are not just a supernatural energy or a life-force, but a personal Being whom I can address as Father. Your personality engages with my personality, and we are one. In this my joy knows no bounds. Amen.

FURTHER STUDY

Gen. 3:1-8; Exod. 33:14-17; Isa. 43:2; Luke 11:2
• How did God present Himself as a personal Being?
• What did He promise Moses?

February 16

■ EXODUS 35:1–36:19

35 Moses assembled the whole Israelite community and said to them, 'These are the things the LORD has commanded you to do: ² for six days, work is to be done, but the seventh day shall be your holy day, a day of sabbath rest to the LORD. Whoever does any work on it is to be put to death. ³ Do not light a fire in any of your dwellings on the Sabbath day.'

⁴ Moses said to the whole Israelite community, 'This is what the LORD has commanded: ⁵ from what you have, take an offering for the LORD. Everyone who is willing is to bring to the LORD an offering of gold, silver and bronze; ⁶ blue, purple and scarlet yarn and fine linen; goat hair; ⁷ ram skins dyed red and another type of durable leather; acacia wood; ⁸ olive oil for the light; spices for the anointing oil and for the fragrant incense; ⁹ and onyx stones and other gems to be mounted on the ephod and breastpiece.

[10] 'All who are skilled among you are to come and make everything the LORD has commanded: [11] the tabernacle with its tent and its covering, clasps, frames, crossbars, posts and bases; [12] the ark with its poles and the atonement cover and the curtain that shields it; [13] the table with its poles and all its articles and the bread of the Presence; [14] the lampstand that is for light with its accessories, lamps and oil for the light; [15] the altar of incense with its poles, the anointing oil and the fragrant incense; the curtain for the doorway at the entrance to the tabernacle; [16] the altar of burnt offering with its bronze grating, its poles and all its utensils; the bronze basin with its stand; [17] the curtains of the courtyard with its posts and bases, and the curtain for the entrance to the courtyard; [18] the tent pegs for the tabernacle and for the courtyard, and their ropes; [19] the woven garments worn for ministering in the sanctuary – both the sacred garments for Aaron the priest and the garments for his sons when they serve as priests.'

[20] Then the whole Israelite community withdrew from Moses' presence, [21] and everyone who was willing and whose heart moved them came and brought an offering to the LORD for the work on the tent of meeting, for all its service, and for the sacred garments. [22] All who were willing, men and women alike, came and brought gold jewellery of all kinds: brooches, earrings, rings and ornaments. They all presented their gold as a wave offering to the LORD. [23] Everyone who had blue, purple or scarlet yarn or fine linen, or goat hair, ram skins dyed red or other durable leather brought them. [24] Those presenting an offering of silver or bronze brought it as an offering to the LORD, and everyone who had acacia wood for any part of the work brought it. [25] Every skilled woman spun with her hands and brought what she had spun – blue, purple or scarlet yarn or fine linen. [26] And all the women who were willing and had the skill spun the goat hair. [27] The leaders brought onyx stones and other gems to be mounted on the ephod and breastpiece. [28] They also brought spices and olive oil for the light and for the anointing oil and for the fragrant incense. [29] All the Israelite men and women who were willing brought to the LORD freewill offerings for all the work the LORD through Moses had commanded them to do.

[30] Then Moses said to the Israelites, 'See, the LORD has chosen Bezalel son of Uri, the son of Hur, of the tribe of Judah, [31] and he has filled him with the Spirit of God, with wisdom, with understanding, with knowledge and with all kinds of skills – [32] to make artistic designs for work in gold, silver and bronze, [33] to cut and set stones, to work in wood and to engage in all kinds of artistic crafts. [34] And he has given both him and Oholiab son of Ahisamak, of the tribe of Dan, the ability to teach others. [35] He has filled them with skill to do all kinds of work as engravers, designers, embroiderers in blue, purple and scarlet yarn and fine linen, and weavers – all of them skilled workers and designers.

36 [1] So Bezalel, Oholiab and every skilled person to whom the LORD has given skill and ability to know how to carry out all the work of constructing the sanctuary are to do the work just as the LORD has commanded.'

[2] Then Moses summoned Bezalel and Oholiab and every skilled person to whom the LORD had given ability and who was willing to come and do the work. [3] They received from Moses all the offerings the Israelites had brought to carry out the work of constructing the sanctuary. And the people continued to bring freewill offerings morning after morning. [4] So all the skilled workers who were doing all the work on the sanctuary left what they were doing [5] and said to Moses, 'The people are bringing more than enough for doing the work the LORD commanded to be done.'

[6] Then Moses gave an order and they sent

this word throughout the camp: 'No man or woman is to make anything else as an offering for the sanctuary.' And so the people were restrained from bringing more, ⁷because what they already had was more than enough to do all the work.

⁸All those who were skilled among the workers made the tabernacle with ten curtains of finely twisted linen and blue, purple and scarlet yarn, with cherubim woven into them by expert hands. ⁹All the curtains were the same size – twenty-eight cubits long and four cubits wide. ¹⁰They joined five of the curtains together and did the same with the other five. ¹¹Then they made loops of blue material along the edge of the end curtain in one set, and the same was done with the end curtain in the other set. ¹²They also made fifty loops on one curtain and fifty loops on the end curtain of the other set, with the loops opposite each other. ¹³Then they made fifty gold clasps and used them to fasten the two sets of curtains together so that the tabernacle was a unit.

¹⁴They made curtains of goat hair for the tent over the tabernacle – eleven altogether. ¹⁵All eleven curtains were the same size – thirty cubits long and four cubits wide. ¹⁶They joined five of the curtains into one set and the other six into another set. ¹⁷Then they made fifty loops along the edge of the end curtain in one set and also along the edge of the end curtain in the other set. ¹⁸They made fifty bronze clasps to fasten the tent together as a unit. ¹⁹Then they made for the tent a covering of ram skins dyed red, and over that a covering of other durable leather.

■ PSALM 22:16–21

¹⁶Dogs surround me,
    a pack of villains encircles me;
    they pierce my hands and my feet.

¹⁷All my bones are on display;
    people stare and gloat over me.
¹⁸They divide my clothes among them
    and cast lots for my garment.

¹⁹But you, LORD, do not be far from me.
    You are my strength; come quickly to
        help me.
²⁰Deliver me from the sword,
    my precious life from the power of the
        dogs.
²¹Rescue me from the mouth of the lions;
    save me from the horns of the wild
        oxen.

■ PROVERBS 5:11–14

¹¹At the end of your life you will groan,
    when your flesh and body are spent.
¹²You will say, 'How I hated discipline!
    How my heart spurned correction!
¹³I would not obey my teachers
    or turn my ear to my instructors.
¹⁴And I was soon in serious trouble
    in the assembly of God's people.'

■ MATTHEW 27:1–23

27 Early in the morning, all the chief priests and the elders of the people made their plans how to have Jesus executed. ²So they bound him, led him away and handed him over to Pilate the governor.

³When Judas, who had betrayed him, saw that Jesus was condemned, he was seized with remorse and returned the thirty pieces of silver to the chief priests and the elders. ⁴'I have sinned,' he said, 'for I have betrayed innocent blood.'

'What is that to us?' they replied. 'That's your responsibility.'

⁵So Judas threw the money into the temple and left. Then he went away and hanged himself.

[6] The chief priests picked up the coins and said, 'It is against the law to put this into the treasury, since it is blood money.' [7] So they decided to use the money to buy the potter's field as a burial place for foreigners. [8] That is why it has been called the Field of Blood to this day. [9] Then what was spoken by Jeremiah the prophet was fulfilled: 'They took the thirty pieces of silver, the price set on him by the people of Israel, [10] and they used them to buy the potter's field, as the Lord commanded me.'

[11] Meanwhile Jesus stood before the governor, and the governor asked him, 'Are you the king of the Jews?'

'You have said so,' Jesus replied.

[12] When he was accused by the chief priests and the elders, he gave no answer. [13] Then Pilate asked him, 'Don't you hear the testimony they are bringing against you?' [14] But Jesus made no reply, not even to a single charge – to the great amazement of the governor.

[15] Now it was the governor's custom at the festival to release a prisoner chosen by the crowd. [16] At that time they had a well-known prisoner whose name was Jesus Barabbas. [17] So when the crowd had gathered, Pilate asked them, 'Which one do you want me to release to you: Jesus Barabbas, or Jesus who is called the Messiah?' [18] For he knew it was out of self-interest that they had handed Jesus over to him.

[19] While Pilate was sitting on the judge's seat, his wife sent him this message: 'Don't have anything to do with that innocent man, for I have suffered a great deal today in a dream because of him.'

[20] But the chief priests and the elders persuaded the crowd to ask for Barabbas and to have Jesus executed.

[21] 'Which of the two do you want me to release to you?' asked the governor.

'Barabbas,' they answered.

[22] 'What shall I do, then, with Jesus who is called the Messiah?' Pilate asked.

They all answered, 'Crucify him!'

[23] 'Why? What crime has he committed?' asked Pilate.

But they shouted all the louder, 'Crucify him!'

The Way Is – Surrender

'How I hated discipline! How my heart spurned correction!' **Proverbs 5:12**

How do we go about controlling our strong urges? Do we push them under? No, for as Hadfield said, 'Repressed instincts are like bad boys who, when put out of class, retaliate by throwing stones at the windows.' It's better to keep the bad boys in class, and teach them to direct their energies to better ends.

If the answer is not to be found in repression, then is it to be found in expression? Shall we give free rein to the urges within us? No, for that would lead us into deeper bondage.

Shall we try to eliminate them? By no known process can these driving urges be eliminated. Put them out of the door and they will climb back in through the window, often in disguise. Buddhism is built on the idea that we can eliminate instincts and wipe out desire. A Buddhist monk was asked by a missionary, 'What is your desire?'

'Nothing.' 'Where are you going?' 'Nowhere.' 'Where have you come from?' 'Nowhere.' He wanted to be without desire - but not quite. He ardently desired to have no desire, so desire was still there, turned towards the absence of desire.

If we can't eliminate the driving urges, and we shouldn't repress or suppress them, or express and release them, then what can we do?

We must allow the Holy Spirit to take them over. Our urges are properly fulfilled only when they are surrendered to the will of God. When we allow the Holy Spirit to get into the driving seat of our personalities, then we are in safe hands.

PRAYER

O Father, help me to move over and let Your Holy Spirit do the steering. These urges that are within me are too strong for me to handle. From now on, You be the driver. Amen.

FURTHER STUDY

Num. 11:1-9; Eccl. 6:7; 1 Cor. 10:6; Eph. 2:3
• What was the problem of the children of Israel?
• What did they fail to see?

February 17

EXODUS 36:20–37:29

20 They made upright frames of acacia wood for the tabernacle. 21 Each frame was ten cubits long and a cubit and a half wide, 22 with two projections set parallel to each other. They made all the frames of the tabernacle in this way. 23 They made twenty frames for the south side of the tabernacle 24 and made forty silver bases to go under them – two bases for each frame, one under each projection. 25 For the other side, the north side of the tabernacle, they made twenty frames 26 and forty silver bases – two under each frame. 27 They made six frames for the far end, that is, the west end of the tabernacle, 28 and two frames were made for the corners of the tabernacle at the far end. 29 At these two corners the frames were double from the bottom all the way to the top and fitted into a single ring; both were made alike. 30 So there were eight frames and sixteen silver bases – two under each frame.

31 They also made crossbars of acacia wood: five for the frames on one side of the tabernacle, 32 five for those on the other side, and five for the frames on the west, at the far end of the tabernacle. 33 They made the centre crossbar so that it extended from end to end at the middle of the frames. 34 They overlaid the frames with gold and made gold rings to hold the crossbars. They also overlaid the crossbars with gold.

35 They made the curtain of blue, purple and scarlet yarn and finely twisted linen, with cherubim woven into it by a skilled worker. 36 They made four posts of acacia wood for it and overlaid them with gold. They made gold hooks for them and cast their four silver bases. 37 For the entrance to the tent they made a curtain of blue, purple and scarlet yarn and finely twisted linen – the work of an embroiderer; 38 and they made five posts with hooks for them. They overlaid the tops of the posts and their bands with gold and made their five bases of bronze.

37 Bezalel made the ark of acacia wood – two and a half cubits long, a cubit and a half wide, and a cubit and a half high. ²He overlaid it with pure gold, both inside and out, and made a gold moulding around it. ³He cast four gold rings for it and fastened them to its four feet, with two rings on one side and two rings on the other. ⁴Then he made poles of acacia wood and overlaid them with gold. ⁵And he inserted the poles into the rings on the sides of the ark to carry it.

⁶He made the atonement cover of pure gold – two and a half cubits long and a cubit and a half wide. ⁷Then he made two cherubim out of hammered gold at the ends of the cover. ⁸He made one cherub on one end and the second cherub on the other; at the two ends he made them of one piece with the cover. ⁹The cherubim had their wings spread upwards, overshadowing the cover with them. The cherubim faced each other, looking towards the cover.

¹⁰They made the table of acacia wood – two cubits long, a cubit wide and a cubit and a half high. ¹¹Then they overlaid it with pure gold and made a gold moulding around it. ¹²They also made around it a rim a handbreadth wide and put a gold moulding on the rim. ¹³They cast four gold rings for the table and fastened them to the four corners, where the four legs were. ¹⁴The rings were put close to the rim to hold the poles used in carrying the table. ¹⁵The poles for carrying the table were made of acacia wood and were overlaid with gold. ¹⁶And they made from pure gold the articles for the table – its plates and dishes and bowls and its pitchers for the pouring out of drink offerings.

¹⁷They made the lampstand of pure gold. They hammered out its base and shaft, and made its flowerlike cups, buds and blossoms of one piece with them. ¹⁸Six branches extended from the sides of the lampstand – three on one side and three on the other. ¹⁹Three cups shaped like almond flowers with buds and blossoms were on one branch, three on the next branch and the same for all six branches extending from the lampstand. ²⁰And on the lampstand were four cups shaped like almond flowers with buds and blossoms. ²¹One bud was under the first pair of branches extending from the lampstand, a second bud under the second pair, and a third bud under the third pair – six branches in all. ²²The buds and the branches were all of one piece with the lampstand, hammered out of pure gold.

²³They made its seven lamps, as well as its wick trimmers and trays, of pure gold. ²⁴They made the lampstand and all its accessories from one talent of pure gold.

²⁵They made the altar of incense out of acacia wood. It was square, a cubit long and a cubit wide and two cubits high – its horns of one piece with it. ²⁶They overlaid the top and all the sides and the horns with pure gold, and made a gold moulding around it. ²⁷They made two gold rings below the moulding – two on each of the opposite sides – to hold the poles used to carry it. ²⁸They made the poles of acacia wood and overlaid them with gold.

²⁹They also made the sacred anointing oil and the pure, fragrant incense – the work of a perfumer.

■ PSALM 22:22-26

²²I will declare your name to my people;
  in the assembly I will praise you.
²³You who fear the LORD, praise him!
  All you descendants of Jacob, honour
    him!
  Revere him, all you descendants of
    Israel!
²⁴For he has not despised or scorned
  the suffering of the afflicted one;
he has not hidden his face from him
  but has listened to his cry for help.

25 From you comes the theme of my praise
   in the great assembly;
   before those who fear you I will fulfil
   my vows.
26 The poor will eat and be satisfied;
   those who seek the LORD will praise
   him –
   may your hearts live for ever!

PROVERBS 5:15-17

15 Drink water from your own cistern,
   running water from your own well.
16 Should your springs overflow in the
   streets,
   your streams of water in the public
   squares?
17 Let them be yours alone,
   never to be shared with strangers.

MATTHEW 27:24-44

24 When Pilate saw that he was getting
nowhere, but that instead an uproar was
starting, he took water and washed his
hands in front of the crowd. 'I am innocent of this man's blood,' he said. 'It is your
responsibility!'

25 All the people answered, 'His blood is
on us and on our children!'

26 Then he released Barabbas to them.
But he had Jesus flogged, and handed him
over to be crucified.

27 Then the governor's soldiers took Jesus
into the Praetorium and gathered the whole
company of soldiers round him. 28 They
stripped him and put a scarlet robe on
him, 29 and then twisted together a crown
of thorns and set it on his head. They put
a staff in his right hand. Then they knelt
in front of him and mocked him. 'Hail,
king of the Jews!' they said. 30 They spat on
him, and took the staff and struck him on
the head again and again. 31 After they had
mocked him, they took off the robe and put
his own clothes on him. Then they led him
away to crucify him.

32 As they were going out, they met a
man from Cyrene, named Simon, and they
forced him to carry the cross. 33 They came
to a place called Golgotha (which means
'the place of the skull'). 34 There they offered Jesus wine to drink, mixed with gall;
but after tasting it, he refused to drink it.
35 When they had crucified him, they divided up his clothes by casting lots. 36 And sitting down, they kept watch over him there.
37 Above his head they placed the written
charge against him: THIS IS JESUS, THE KING
OF THE JEWS.

38 Two rebels were crucified with him,
one on his right and one on his left. 39 Those
who passed by hurled insults at him, shaking their heads 40 and saying, 'You who are
going to destroy the temple and build it in
three days, save yourself! Come down from
the cross, if you are the Son of God!' 41 In the
same way the chief priests, the teachers of
the law and the elders mocked him. 42 'He
saved others,' they said, 'but he can't save
himself! He's the king of Israel! Let him
come down now from the cross, and we will
believe in him. 43 He trusts in God. Let God
rescue him now if he wants him, for he said,
"I am the Son of God."' 44 In the same way
the rebels who were crucified with him also
heaped insults on him.

Self-Control

'In the same way the chief priests, the teachers of the law and the elders mocked him. "He saved others," they said, "but he can't save himself! He's the king of Israel! Let him come down now from the cross, and we will believe in him."'
Matthew 27:41-42

The last of the nine fruits of the Spirit listed in Galatians 5 is self-control. It is interesting that Paul puts self-control last. Others would put it first. Confucianism taught that self-control would help produce the 'superior' man. Hinduism thinks self-control will produce the 'realised' man. Stoicism thought self-control produced the 'detached' man. Still others believe self-control produces the 'happy' man. Yet we do not gain Christ through self-control; we gain self-control through Christ.

'Self-control' is used here as a by-product of love. When you begin with love, you end up with self-control. If you attempt it the other way around, then you end up with a nervous breakdown. The self-control that comes by the Spirit is not a nervous, anxious self-control; it is a control that is unstrained, therefore beautiful. No wonder a great thinker said, 'Love Christ and do what you like,' for when you do, then you will like what He likes. That's the kind of self-control the Spirit gives. We delight to control what needs to be controlled because we desire to please Him.

PRAYER

Blessed Holy Spirit, I am so thankful that You are working in me to produce the image of the Lord Jesus Christ. May the aspects of His nature show through me more and more every day. For His name's sake. Amen.

FURTHER STUDY

Matt. 27; Prov. 16:32;
Rom. 6:12; 2 Pet. 1:5-6
• In what ways did Jesus display self-control?
• In what ways do you show self-control?

February 18

■ **EXODUS 38:1–39:31**

38 They built the altar of burnt offering of acacia wood, three cubits high; it was square, five cubits long and five cubits wide. ²They made a horn at each of the four corners, so that the horns and the altar were of one piece, and they overlaid the altar with bronze. ³They made all its utensils of bronze – its pots, shovels, sprinkling bowls, meat forks and firepans. ⁴They made a grating for the altar, a bronze network, to be under its ledge, halfway up the altar. [5] They cast bronze rings to hold the poles for the four corners of the bronze grating. [6] They made the poles of acacia wood and overlaid them with bronze. [7] They inserted the poles into the rings so they would be on the sides of the altar for carrying it. They made it hollow, out of boards.

[8] They made the bronze basin and its bronze stand from the mirrors of the women who served at the entrance to the tent of meeting.

[9] Next they made the courtyard. The south side was a hundred cubits long and had curtains of finely twisted linen, [10] with twenty posts and twenty bronze bases, and with silver hooks and bands on the posts. [11] The north side was also a hundred cubits long and had twenty posts and twenty bronze bases, with silver hooks and bands on the posts.

[12] The west end was fifty cubits wide and had curtains, with ten posts and ten bases, with silver hooks and bands on the posts. [13] The east end, towards the sunrise, was also fifty cubits wide. [14] Curtains fifteen cubits long were on one side of the entrance, with three posts and three bases, [15] and curtains fifteen cubits long were on the other side of the entrance to the courtyard, with three posts and three bases. [16] All the curtains around the courtyard were of finely twisted linen. [17] The bases for the posts were bronze. The hooks and bands on the posts were silver, and their tops were overlaid with silver; so all the posts of the courtyard had silver bands.

[18] The curtain for the entrance to the courtyard was made of blue, purple and scarlet yarn and finely twisted linen – the work of an embroiderer. It was twenty cubits long and, like the curtains of the courtyard, five cubits high, [19] with four posts and four bronze bases. Their hooks and bands were silver, and their tops were overlaid with silver. [20] All the tent pegs of the tabernacle and of the surrounding courtyard were bronze.

[21] These are the amounts of the materials used for the tabernacle, the tabernacle of the covenant law, which were recorded at Moses' command by the Levites under the direction of Ithamar son of Aaron, the priest. [22] (Bezalel son of Uri, the son of Hur, of the tribe of Judah, made everything the LORD commanded Moses; [23] with him was Oholiab son of Ahisamak, of the tribe of Dan – an engraver and designer, and an embroiderer in blue, purple and scarlet yarn and fine linen.) [24] The total amount of the gold from the wave offering used for all the work on the sanctuary was 29 talents and 730 shekels, according to the sanctuary shekel.

[25] The silver obtained from those of the community who were counted in the census was 100 talents and 1,775 shekels, according to the sanctuary shekel – [26] one beka per person, that is, half a shekel, according to the sanctuary shekel, from everyone who had crossed over to those counted, twenty years old or more, a total of 603,550 men. [27] The 100 talents of silver were used to cast the bases for the sanctuary and for the curtain – 100 bases from the 100 talents, one talent for each base. [28] They used the 1,775 shekels to make the hooks for the posts, to overlay the tops of the posts, and to make their bands.

[29] The bronze from the wave offering was 70 talents and 2,400 shekels. [30] They used it to make the bases for the entrance to the tent of meeting, the bronze altar with its bronze grating and all its utensils, [31] the bases for the surrounding courtyard and those for its entrance and all the tent pegs for the tabernacle and those for the surrounding courtyard.

39 From the blue, purple and scarlet yarn they made woven garments for ministering in the sanctuary. They also made sacred garments for Aaron, as the LORD commanded Moses.

[2] They made the ephod of gold, and of blue,

purple and scarlet yarn, and of finely twisted linen. ³They hammered out thin sheets of gold and cut strands to be worked into the blue, purple and scarlet yarn and fine linen – the work of skilled hands. ⁴They made shoulder pieces for the ephod, which were attached to two of its corners, so that it could be fastened. ⁵Its skilfully woven waistband was like it – of one piece with the ephod and made with gold, and with blue, purple and scarlet yarn, and with finely twisted linen, as the LORD commanded Moses.

⁶They mounted the onyx stones in gold filigree settings and engraved them like a seal with the names of the sons of Israel. ⁷Then they fastened them on the shoulder pieces of the ephod as memorial stones for the sons of Israel, as the LORD commanded Moses.

⁸They fashioned the breastpiece – the work of a skilled craftsman. They made it like the ephod: of gold, and of blue, purple and scarlet yarn, and of finely twisted linen. ⁹It was square – a span long and a span wide – and folded double. ¹⁰Then they mounted four rows of precious stones on it. The first row was carnelian, chrysolite and beryl; ¹¹the second row was turquoise, lapis lazuli and emerald; ¹²the third row was jacinth, agate and amethyst; ¹³the fourth row was topaz, onyx and jasper. They were mounted in gold filigree settings. ¹⁴There were twelve stones, one for each of the names of the sons of Israel, each engraved like a seal with the name of one of the twelve tribes.

¹⁵For the breastpiece they made braided chains of pure gold, like a rope. ¹⁶They made two gold filigree settings and two gold rings, and fastened the rings to two of the corners of the breastpiece. ¹⁷They fastened the two gold chains to the rings at the corners of the breastpiece, ¹⁸and the other ends of the chains to the two settings, attaching them to the shoulder pieces of the ephod at the front. ¹⁹They made two gold rings

and attached them to the other two corners of the breastpiece on the inside edge next to the ephod. ²⁰Then they made two more gold rings and attached them to the bottom of the shoulder pieces on the front of the ephod, close to the seam just above the waistband of the ephod. ²¹They tied the rings of the breastpiece to the rings of the ephod with blue cord, connecting it to the waistband so that the breastpiece would not swing out from the ephod – as the LORD commanded Moses.

²²They made the robe of the ephod entirely of blue cloth – the work of a weaver – ²³with an opening in the centre of the robe like the opening of a collar, and a band around this opening, so that it would not tear. ²⁴They made pomegranates of blue, purple and scarlet yarn and finely twisted linen round the hem of the robe. ²⁵And they made bells of pure gold and attached them around the hem between the pomegranates. ²⁶The bells and pomegranates alternated round the hem of the robe to be worn for ministering, as the LORD commanded Moses.

²⁷For Aaron and his sons, they made tunics of fine linen – the work of a weaver – ²⁸and the turban of fine linen, the linen caps and the undergarments of finely twisted linen. ²⁹The sash was made of finely twisted linen and blue, purple and scarlet yarn – the work of an embroiderer – as the LORD commanded Moses.

³⁰They made the plate, the sacred emblem, out of pure gold and engraved on it, like an inscription on a seal: HOLY TO THE LORD. ³¹Then they fastened a blue cord to it to attach it to the turban, as the LORD commanded Moses.

▬ PSALM 22:27-31

²⁷All the ends of the earth
    will remember and turn to the LORD,

and all the families of the nations
   will bow down before him,
²⁸ for dominion belongs to the LORD
   and he rules over the nations.

²⁹ All the rich of the earth will feast and
      worship;
   all who go down to the dust will kneel
      before him –
   those who cannot keep themselves
      alive.
³⁰ Posterity will serve him;
   future generations will be told about
      the Lord.
³¹ They will proclaim his righteousness,
   declaring to a people yet unborn:
   He has done it!

▬ PROVERBS 5:18-20

¹⁸ May your fountain be blessed,
   and may you rejoice in the wife of your
      youth.
¹⁹ A loving doe, a graceful deer –
   may her breasts satisfy you always,
   may you ever be intoxicated with her
      love.
²⁰ Why, my son, be intoxicated with
   another man's wife?
   Why embrace the bosom of a wayward
      woman?

▬ MATTHEW 27:45-66

⁴⁵ From noon until three in the afternoon
darkness came over all the land. ⁴⁶ About
three in the afternoon Jesus cried out in a
loud voice, *'Eli, Eli, lema sabachthani?'*
(which means 'My God, my God, why have
you forsaken me?').

⁴⁷ When some of those standing there
heard this, they said, 'He's calling Elijah.'

⁴⁸ Immediately one of them ran and got a
sponge. He filled it with wine vinegar, put

it on a staff, and offered it to Jesus to drink.
⁴⁹ The rest said, 'Now leave him alone. Let's
see if Elijah comes to save him.'

⁵⁰ And when Jesus had cried out again in a
loud voice, he gave up his spirit.

⁵¹ At that moment the curtain of the temple was torn in two from top to bottom.
The earth shook, the rocks split ⁵² and the
tombs broke open. The bodies of many holy
people who had died were raised to life.
⁵³ They came out of the tombs after Jesus'
resurrection and went into the holy city and
appeared to many people.

⁵⁴ When the centurion and those with
him who were guarding Jesus saw the
earthquake and all that had happened, they
were terrified, and exclaimed, 'Surely he
was the Son of God!'

⁵⁵ Many women were there, watching
from a distance. They had followed Jesus
from Galilee to care for his needs. ⁵⁶ Among
them were Mary Magdalene, Mary the
mother of James and Joseph, and the mother of Zebedee's sons.

⁵⁷ As evening approached, there came a
rich man from Arimathea, named Joseph,
who had himself become a disciple of Jesus.
⁵⁸ Going to Pilate, he asked for Jesus' body,
and Pilate ordered that it be given to him.
⁵⁹ Joseph took the body, wrapped it in a
clean linen cloth, ⁶⁰ and placed it in his own
new tomb that he had cut out of the rock. He
rolled a big stone in front of the entrance to
the tomb and went away. ⁶¹ Mary Magdalene and the other Mary were sitting there
opposite the tomb.

⁶² The next day, the one after Preparation Day, the chief priests and the Pharisees went to Pilate. ⁶³ 'Sir,' they said, 'we
remember that while he was still alive that
deceiver said, "After three days I will rise
again." ⁶⁴ So give the order for the tomb to
be made secure until the third day. Otherwise, his disciples may come and steal the
body and tell the people that he has been
raised from the dead. This last deception

will be worse than the first.'

⁶⁵'Take a guard,' Pilate answered. 'Go, make the tomb as secure as you know how.'

⁶⁶So they went and made the tomb secure by putting a seal on the stone and posting the guard.

The Last Is the Best

'In the past God spoke to our ancestors through the prophets at many times and in various ways, but in these last days he has spoken to us by his Son ...'
Hebrews 1:1-2

The words of this text point out that though God spoke in times past through prophets and sages, His final Word to this world is in His Son. That is our claim as Christians. The Old Testament is just as much God breathed as the New Testament is, but it is not God's last Word to the men and women of His creation.

No other world faith claims that its great teacher was God incarnate. Yet we claim for Christ just that – and also that as God He meets every human need. He comes to us where we are and He does the work. He can relieve any plight of the human soul, and He has the power to meet every human need. Every spiritually sensitive person is aware of the presence of guilt which arises from indwelling sin, and is aware too that he or she alone can do nothing to dissolve it. Christ atoned for sin and is able to forgive it. We also stand in awe of death, knowing it is impossible to escape it. But Christ has conquered death and has opened the way to eternal life.

Christ's call is to all humanity. He does not differentiate between groups of people or races. He abides no barriers of class or creed. 'Whosoever will may come' is His constant message. There are no 'gods' or prophets equal to Him. He is unique in His Person, His mission, and in His finished work.

PRAYER

O God, how can I express my gratitude that I have found the best, or rather that the Best has found me? May I lay hold of all that is in Jesus and reflect Him to the world, not in arrogance but in humility. Amen.

FURTHER STUDY

Phil. 2:1-11; Eph. 1:22; 1 Cor. 8:6; Heb. 1:2
• Why has God exalted Christ?
• What does Paul acknowledge?

February 19

■ EXODUS 39:32–40:38

[32] So all the work on the tabernacle, the tent of meeting, was completed. The Israelites did everything just as the LORD commanded Moses. [33] Then they brought the tabernacle to Moses: the tent and all its furnishings, its clasps, frames, crossbars, posts and bases; [34] the covering of ram skins dyed red and the covering of another durable leather and the shielding curtain; [35] the ark of the covenant law with its poles and the atonement cover; [36] the table with all its articles and the bread of the Presence; [37] the pure gold lampstand with its row of lamps and all its accessories, and the olive oil for the light; [38] the gold altar, the anointing oil, the fragrant incense, and the curtain for the entrance to the tent; [39] the bronze altar with its bronze grating, its poles and all its utensils; the basin with its stand; [40] the curtains of the courtyard with its posts and bases, and the curtain for the entrance to the courtyard; the ropes and tent pegs for the courtyard; all the furnishings for the tabernacle, the tent of meeting; [41] and the woven garments worn for ministering in the sanctuary, both the sacred garments for Aaron the priest and the garments for his sons when serving as priests.

[42] The Israelites had done all the work just as the LORD had commanded Moses. [43] Moses inspected the work and saw that they had done it just as the LORD had commanded. So Moses blessed them.

40 Then the LORD said to Moses: [2] 'Set up the tabernacle, the tent of meeting, on the first day of the first month. [3] Place the ark of the covenant law in it and shield the ark with the curtain. [4] Bring in the table and set out what belongs on it. Then bring in the lampstand and set up its lamps. [5] Place the gold altar of incense in front of the ark of the covenant law and put the curtain at the entrance to the tabernacle.

[6] 'Place the altar of burnt offering in front of the entrance to the tabernacle, the tent of meeting; [7] place the basin between the tent of meeting and the altar and put water in it. [8] Set up the courtyard around it and put the curtain at the entrance to the courtyard.

[9] 'Take the anointing oil and anoint the tabernacle and everything in it; consecrate it and all its furnishings, and it will be holy. [10] Then anoint the altar of burnt offering and all its utensils; consecrate the altar, and it will be most holy. [11] Anoint the basin and its stand and consecrate them.

[12] 'Bring Aaron and his sons to the entrance to the tent of meeting and wash them with water. [13] Then dress Aaron in the sacred garments, anoint him and consecrate him so that he may serve me as priest. [14] Bring his sons and dress them in tunics. [15] Anoint them just as you anointed their father, so that they may serve me as priests. Their anointing will be to a priesthood that will continue throughout their generations.' [16] Moses did everything just as the LORD commanded him.

[17] So the tabernacle was set up on the first day of the first month in the second year. [18] When Moses set up the tabernacle, he put the bases in place, erected the frames, inserted the crossbars and set up the posts. [19] Then he spread the tent over the tabernacle and put the covering over the tent, as the LORD commanded him.

[20] He took the tablets of the covenant law and placed them in the ark, attached the poles to the ark and put the atonement cover over it. [21] Then he brought the ark into the tabernacle and hung the shielding curtain

and shielded the ark of the covenant law, as the LORD commanded him.

²²Moses placed the table in the tent of meeting on the north side of the tabernacle outside the curtain ²³and set out the bread on it before the LORD, as the LORD commanded him.

²⁴He placed the lampstand in the tent of meeting opposite the table on the south side of the tabernacle ²⁵and set up the lamps before the LORD, as the LORD commanded him.

²⁶Moses placed the gold altar in the tent of meeting in front of the curtain ²⁷and burned fragrant incense on it, as the LORD commanded him.

²⁸Then he put up the curtain at the entrance to the tabernacle. ²⁹He set the altar of burnt offering near the entrance to the tabernacle, the tent of meeting, and offered on it burnt offerings and grain offerings, as the LORD commanded him.

³⁰He placed the basin between the tent of meeting and the altar and put water in it for washing, ³¹and Moses and Aaron and his sons used it to wash their hands and feet. ³²They washed whenever they entered the tent of meeting or approached the altar, as the LORD commanded Moses.

³³Then Moses set up the courtyard around the tabernacle and altar and put up the curtain at the entrance to the courtyard. And so Moses finished the work.

³⁴Then the cloud covered the tent of meeting, and the glory of the LORD filled the tabernacle. ³⁵Moses could not enter the tent of meeting because the cloud had settled on it, and the glory of the LORD filled the tabernacle.

³⁶In all the travels of the Israelites, whenever the cloud lifted from above the tabernacle, they would set out; ³⁷but if the cloud did not lift, they did not set out – until the day it lifted. ³⁸So the cloud of the LORD was over the tabernacle by day, and fire was in the cloud by night, in the sight of all the Israelites during all their travels.

▬ PSALM 23:1-6

¹The LORD is my shepherd, I lack nothing.
² He makes me lie down in green
    pastures,
he leads me beside quiet waters,
³ he refreshes my soul.
He guides me along the right paths
    for his name's sake.
⁴Even though I walk
    through the darkest valley,
I will fear no evil,
    for you are with me;
your rod and your staff,
    they comfort me.

⁵You prepare a table before me
    in the presence of my enemies.
You anoint my head with oil;
    my cup overflows.
⁶Surely your goodness and love will
    follow me
all the days of my life,
and I will dwell in the house of the LORD
    for ever.

▬ PROVERBS 5:21-23

²¹For your ways are in full view of the
    LORD,
    and he examines all your paths.
²²The evil deeds of the wicked ensnare
    them;
    the cords of their sins hold them fast.
²³For lack of discipline they will die,
    led astray by their own great folly.

▬ MATTHEW 28:1-20

28 After the Sabbath, at dawn on the first day of the week, Mary Magdalene and the other Mary went to look at the tomb.

²There was a violent earthquake, for an

angel of the Lord came down from heaven and, going to the tomb, rolled back the stone and sat on it. ³His appearance was like lightning, and his clothes were white as snow. ⁴The guards were so afraid of him that they shook and became like dead men.

⁵The angel said to the women, 'Do not be afraid, for I know that you are looking for Jesus, who was crucified. ⁶He is not here; he has risen, just as he said. Come and see the place where he lay. ⁷Then go quickly and tell his disciples: "He has risen from the dead and is going ahead of you into Galilee. There you will see him." Now I have told you.'

⁸So the women hurried away from the tomb, afraid yet filled with joy, and ran to tell his disciples. ⁹Suddenly Jesus met them. 'Greetings,' he said. They came to him, clasped his feet and worshipped him. ¹⁰Then Jesus said to them, 'Do not be afraid. Go and tell my brothers to go to Galilee; there they will see me.'

¹¹While the women were on their way, some of the guards went into the city and reported to the chief priests everything that had happened. ¹²When the chief priests had met with the elders and devised a plan, they gave the soldiers a large sum of money, ¹³telling them, 'You are to say, "His disciples came during the night and stole him away while we were asleep." ¹⁴If this report gets to the governor, we will satisfy him and keep you out of trouble.' ¹⁵So the soldiers took the money and did as they were instructed. And this story has been widely circulated among the Jews to this very day.

¹⁶Then the eleven disciples went to Galilee, to the mountain where Jesus had told them to go. ¹⁷When they saw him, they worshipped him; but some doubted. ¹⁸Then Jesus came to them and said, 'All authority in heaven and on earth has been given to me. ¹⁹Therefore go and make disciples of all nations, baptising them in the name of the Father and of the Son and of the Holy Spirit, ²⁰and teaching them to obey everything I have commanded you. And surely I am with you always, to the very end of the age.'

The Nature of Doubt

'When they saw him, they worshipped him; but some doubted.' **Matthew 28:17**

A man whom I regarded as truly converted said to me, 'I am riddled with so many doubts that I sometimes feel I am not a Christian at all.' When I pointed out to him the nature of doubt – that it is not the same as unbelief – I saw a new expression appear on his face. He grasped me by the hands and said, 'How can I ever sufficiently thank you? You have released a pressure that has been building up inside me for years.'

I met him years later, and he told me that the simple insight I had given him concerning the nature of doubt was all he needed to face his doubts and deal with them in a spiritual way. I say again, no misunderstanding causes more anxiety to the heart of a Christian than that which concerns the nature of doubt.

Let's put unbelief under the microscope for a moment, for by doing so we will see the nature of doubt still more clearly. Unbelief is a wilful refusal to believe, resulting in a deliberate decision to disobey. It is a state of mind which is closed against God, an attitude of heart which disobeys God as much as it disbelieves the truth. It is the consequence of a settled choice.

Doubt is not a wilful decision to disbelieve but a suspension between faith and unbelief. To believe is to be in one mind; to disbelieve is also to be in one mind, but to doubt is to be caught in the halfway stage between the two – suspended between the desire to affirm and the desire to negate.

PRAYER

Father, while I am relieved to discover that doubt is not the same as unbelief, I nevertheless long to live a doubt-free existence. Break down any barriers within me that would hinder the flow of faith. In Christ's name I ask it. Amen.

FURTHER STUDY

John 11:16; 14:5; 20:24-29; 21:2; Matt. 10:3
• How did Thomas display his total commitment?
• Why then did he doubt?

February 20

■ LEVITICUS 1:1–3:17

1 The LORD called to Moses and spoke to him from the tent of meeting. He said, 2'Speak to the Israelites and say to them: "When anyone among you brings an offering to the LORD, bring as your offering an animal from either the herd or the flock.

3 "'If the offering is a burnt offering from the herd, you are to offer a male without defect. You must present it at the entrance to the tent of meeting so that it will be acceptable to the LORD. 4 You are to lay your hand on the head of the burnt offering, and it will be accepted on your behalf to make atonement for you. 5 You are to slaughter the young bull before the LORD, and then Aaron's sons the priests shall bring the blood and splash it against the sides of the altar at the entrance to the tent of meeting. 6 You are to skin the burnt offering and cut it into pieces. 7 The sons of Aaron the priest are to put fire on the altar and arrange wood on

the fire. 8 Then Aaron's sons the priests shall arrange the pieces, including the head and the fat, on the wood that is burning on the altar. 9 You are to wash the internal organs and the legs with water, and the priest is to burn all of it on the altar. It is a burnt offering, a food offering, an aroma pleasing to the LORD.

10 "'If the offering is a burnt offering from the flock, from either the sheep or the goats, you are to offer a male without defect. 11 You are to slaughter it at the north side of the altar before the LORD, and Aaron's sons the priests shall splash its blood against the sides of the altar. 12 You are to cut it into pieces, and the priest shall arrange them, including the head and the fat, on the wood that is burning on the altar. 13 You are to wash the internal organs and the legs with water, and the priest is to bring all of them and burn them on the altar. It is a burnt offering, a food offering, an aroma pleasing to the LORD.

¹⁴ "'If the offering to the LORD is a burnt offering of birds, you are to offer a dove or a young pigeon. ¹⁵ The priest shall bring it to the altar, wring off the head and burn it on the altar; its blood shall be drained out on the side of the altar. ¹⁶ He is to remove the crop and the feathers and throw them down east of the altar where the ashes are. ¹⁷ He shall tear it open by the wings, not dividing it completely, and then the priest shall burn it on the wood that is burning on the altar. It is a burnt offering, a food offering, an aroma pleasing to the LORD.

2 "'When anyone brings a grain offering to the LORD, their offering is to be of the finest flour. They are to pour olive oil on it, put incense on it ² and take it to Aaron's sons the priests. The priest shall take a handful of the flour and oil, together with all the incense, and burn this as a memorial portion on the altar, a food offering, an aroma pleasing to the LORD. ³ The rest of the grain offering belongs to Aaron and his sons; it is a most holy part of the food offerings presented to the LORD.

⁴ "'If you bring a grain offering baked in an oven, it is to consist of the finest flour: either thick loaves made without yeast and with olive oil mixed in or thin loaves made without yeast and brushed with olive oil. ⁵ If your grain offering is prepared on a griddle, it is to be made of the finest flour mixed with oil, and without yeast. ⁶ Crumble it and pour oil on it; it is a grain offering. ⁷ If your grain offering is cooked in a pan, it is to be made of the finest flour and some olive oil. ⁸ Bring the grain offering made of these things to the LORD; present it to the priest, who shall take it to the altar. ⁹ He shall take out the memorial portion from the grain offering and burn it on the altar as a food offering, an aroma pleasing to the LORD. ¹⁰ The rest of the grain offering belongs to Aaron and his sons; it is a most holy part of the food offerings presented to the LORD.

¹¹ "'Every grain offering you bring to the LORD must be made without yeast, for you are not to burn any yeast or honey in a food offering presented to the LORD. ¹² You may bring them to the LORD as an offering of the firstfruits, but they are not to be offered on the altar as a pleasing aroma. ¹³ Season all your grain offerings with salt. Do not leave the salt of the covenant of your God out of your grain offerings; add salt to all your offerings.

¹⁴ "'If you bring a grain offering of firstfruits to the LORD, offer crushed heads of new grain roasted in the fire. ¹⁵ Put oil and incense on it; it is a grain offering. ¹⁶ The priest shall burn the memorial portion of the crushed grain and the oil, together with all the incense, as a food offering presented to the LORD.

3 "'If your offering is a fellowship offering, and you offer an animal from the herd, whether male or female, you are to present before the LORD an animal without defect. ² You are to lay your hand on the head of your offering and slaughter it at the entrance to the tent of meeting. Then Aaron's sons the priests shall splash the blood against the sides of the altar. ³ From the fellowship offering you are to bring a food offering to the LORD: the internal organs and all the fat that is connected to them, ⁴ both kidneys with the fat on them near the loins, and the long lobe of the liver, which you will remove with the kidneys. ⁵ Then Aaron's sons are to burn it on the altar on top of the burnt offering that is lying on the burning wood; it is a food offering, an aroma pleasing to the LORD.

⁶ "'If you offer an animal from the flock as a fellowship offering to the LORD, you are to offer a male or female without defect. ⁷ If you offer a lamb, you are to present it before the LORD, ⁸ lay your hand on its head and slaughter it in front of the tent of meeting. Then Aaron's sons shall splash its blood against the sides of the altar. ⁹ From the fellowship offering you are to bring a food

offering to the LORD: its fat, the entire fat tail cut off close to the backbone, the internal organs and all the fat that is connected to them, ¹⁰both kidneys with the fat on them near the loins, and the long lobe of the liver, which you will remove with the kidneys. ¹¹The priest shall burn them on the altar as a food offering presented to the LORD.

¹²'"If your offering is a goat, you are to present it before the LORD, ¹³lay your hand on its head and slaughter it in front of the tent of meeting. Then Aaron's sons shall splash its blood against the sides of the altar. ¹⁴From what you offer you are to present this food offering to the LORD: the internal organs and all the fat that is connected to them, ¹⁵both kidneys with the fat on them near the loins, and the long lobe of the liver, which you will remove with the kidneys. ¹⁶The priest shall burn them on the altar as a food offering, a pleasing aroma. All the fat is the LORD's.

¹⁷'"This is a lasting ordinance for the generations to come, wherever you live: you must not eat any fat or any blood."'

PSALM 24:1-10

¹The earth is the LORD's, and everything
     in it,
the world, and all who live in it;
²for he founded it on the seas
     and established it on the waters.

³Who may ascend the mountain of the
     LORD?
Who may stand in his holy place?
⁴The one who has clean hands and a pure
     heart,
who does not trust in an idol
or swear by a false god.

⁵They will receive blessing from the LORD
     and vindication from God their
         Saviour.

⁶Such is the generation of those who seek
     him,
who seek your face, God of Jacob.

⁷Lift up your heads, you gates;
     be lifted up, you ancient doors,
     that the King of glory may come in.
⁸Who is this King of glory?
     The LORD strong and mighty,
     the LORD mighty in battle.
⁹Lift up your heads, you gates;
     lift them up, you ancient doors,
     that the King of glory may come in.
¹⁰Who is he, this King of glory?
     The LORD Almighty –
     he is the King of glory.

PROVERBS 6:1-3

6 My son, if you have put up security for
     your neighbour,
     if you have shaken hands in pledge for
         a stranger,
²you have been trapped by what you said,
     ensnared by the words of your mouth.
³So do this, my son, to free yourself,
     since you have fallen into your
         neighbour's hands:
go – to the point of exhaustion –
     and give your neighbour no rest!

MARK 1:1-20

1 The beginning of the good news about
   Jesus the Messiah, the Son of God, ²as it
is written in Isaiah the prophet:

'I will send my messenger ahead of you,
     who will prepare your way' –
³'a voice of one calling in the wilderness,
     "Prepare the way for the Lord,
     make straight paths for him."'

⁴And so John the Baptist appeared in the

wilderness, preaching a baptism of repentance for the forgiveness of sins. ⁵The whole Judean countryside and all the people of Jerusalem went out to him. Confessing their sins, they were baptised by him in the River Jordan. ⁶John wore clothing made of camel's hair, with a leather belt round his waist, and he ate locusts and wild honey. ⁷And this was his message: 'After me comes the one more powerful than I, the straps of whose sandals I am not worthy to stoop down and untie. ⁸I baptise you with water, but he will baptise you with the Holy Spirit.'

⁹At that time Jesus came from Nazareth in Galilee and was baptised by John in the Jordan. ¹⁰Just as Jesus was coming up out of the water, he saw heaven being torn open and the Spirit descending on him like a dove. ¹¹And a voice came from heaven: 'You are my Son, whom I love; with you I am well pleased.'

¹²At once the Spirit sent him out into the wilderness, ¹³and he was in the wilderness for forty days, being tempted by Satan. He was with the wild animals, and angels attended him.

¹⁴After John was put in prison, Jesus went into Galilee, proclaiming the good news of God. ¹⁵'The time has come,' he said. 'The kingdom of God has come near. Repent and believe the good news!'

¹⁶As Jesus walked beside the Sea of Galilee, he saw Simon and his brother Andrew casting a net into the lake, for they were fishermen. ¹⁷'Come, follow me,' Jesus said, 'and I will send you out to fish for people.' ¹⁸At once they left their nets and followed him.

¹⁹When he had gone a little farther, he saw James son of Zebedee and his brother John in a boat, preparing their nets. ²⁰Without delay he called them, and they left their father Zebedee in the boat with the hired men and followed him.

A Dip into the Depths

'Who may ascend the mountain of the LORD? ...
The one who has clean hands and a pure heart ...'
Psalm 24:3-4

If we take an honest and straightforward look at what is going on inside us, we must be ready for a number of strong spiritual challenges. But we must not allow ourselves to be disheartened, for in looking at our hearts we become ready to move upwards into the mountains of God.

The suggestion I want to make to you is this - recognise the subtle and insidious nature of sin. There is a view in the Christian church that as long as we focus on the sins that are obvious (sins of behaviour), then we can forget any hidden sins that may be in the heart, trusting God to deal with them in His own way. Dealing with obvious sin is extremely important - don't hear me minimising this fact. Moral discipline is part of the Christian commitment. We are expected to resist the temptations that come our way and correct any spiritual violations that may occur. But to concern ourselves only with obvious sin and avoid facing the sins of the heart will cause us to miss our footing on the slopes of God.

Someone has put it like this: 'The grime has been so embedded in the carpet that a simple vacuuming will not do the job. We need a scrubbing brush and a strong detergent.' Diligence in putting right the things that are obviously wrong is good, but without a clear understanding of how sin has penetrated our hearts, we will be nothing more than surface-copers.

PRAYER

Father, forgive me that I have been so content to live on the surface of life. Help me see that, in turning my gaze to what is going on inside me, You are not seeking to demean me but to develop me. Give me grace not to shrink from the task. Amen.

FURTHER STUDY

Jer. 17:1-11; Gen. 3:8; Prov. 28:13
• What is the tendency of the human heart?
• What is one condition for us to prosper spiritually?

February 21

■ LEVITICUS 4:1–5:19

4 The LORD said to Moses, ²'Say to the Israelites: "When anyone sins unintentionally and does what is forbidden in any of the LORD's commands –

³ "If the anointed priest sins, bringing guilt on the people, he must bring to the LORD a young bull without defect as a sin offering for the sin he has committed. ⁴He is to present the bull at the entrance to the tent of meeting before the LORD. He is to lay his hand on its head and slaughter it there before the LORD. ⁵Then the anointed priest shall take some of the bull's blood and carry it into the tent of meeting. ⁶He is to dip his finger into the blood and sprinkle some of it seven times before the LORD, in front of the curtain of the sanctuary. ⁷The priest shall then put some of the blood on the horns of the altar of fragrant incense that is before the LORD in the tent of meeting. The rest of the bull's blood he shall pour out at the base of the altar of burnt offering at the entrance to the tent of meeting. ⁸He shall remove all the fat from the bull of the sin offering – all

the fat that is connected to the internal organs, ⁹both kidneys with the fat on them near the loins, and the long lobe of the liver, which he will remove with the kidneys – ¹⁰just as the fat is removed from the ox sacrificed as a fellowship offering. Then the priest shall burn them on the altar of burnt offering. ¹¹But the hide of the bull and all its flesh, as well as the head and legs, the internal organs and the intestines – ¹²that is, all the rest of the bull – he must take outside the camp to a place ceremonially clean, where the ashes are thrown, and burn it there in a wood fire on the ash heap.

¹³ "If the whole Israelite community sins unintentionally and does what is forbidden in any of the LORD's commands, even though the community is unaware of the matter, when they realise their guilt ¹⁴and the sin they committed becomes known, the assembly must bring a young bull as a sin offering and present it before the tent of meeting. ¹⁵The elders of the community are to lay their hands on the bull's head before the LORD, and the bull shall be slaughtered before the LORD. ¹⁶Then the anointed

priest is to take some of the bull's blood into the tent of meeting. ¹⁷He shall dip his finger into the blood and sprinkle it before the LORD seven times in front of the curtain. ¹⁸He is to put some of the blood on the horns of the altar that is before the LORD in the tent of meeting. The rest of the blood he shall pour out at the base of the altar of burnt offering at the entrance to the tent of meeting. ¹⁹He shall remove all the fat from it and burn it on the altar, ²⁰and do with this bull just as he did with the bull for the sin offering. In this way the priest will make atonement for the community, and they will be forgiven. ²¹Then he shall take the bull outside the camp and burn it as he burned the first bull. This is the sin offering for the community.

²²' "When a leader sins unintentionally and does what is forbidden in any of the commands of the LORD his God, when he realises his guilt ²³and the sin he has committed becomes known, he must bring as his offering a male goat without defect. ²⁴He is to lay his hand on the goat's head and slaughter it at the place where the burnt offering is slaughtered before the LORD. It is a sin offering. ²⁵Then the priest shall take some of the blood of the sin offering with his finger and put it on the horns of the altar of burnt offering and pour out the rest of the blood at the base of the altar. ²⁶He shall burn all the fat on the altar as he burned the fat of the fellowship offering. In this way the priest will make atonement for the leader's sin, and he will be forgiven.

²⁷' "If any member of the community sins unintentionally and does what is forbidden in any of the LORD's commands, when they realise their guilt ²⁸and the sin they have committed becomes known, they must bring as their offering for the sin they committed a female goat without defect. ²⁹They are to lay their hand on the head of the sin

offering and slaughter it at the place of the burnt offering. ³⁰Then the priest is to take some of the blood with his finger and put it on the horns of the altar of burnt offering and pour out the rest of the blood at the base of the altar. ³¹They shall remove all the fat, just as the fat is removed from the fellowship offering, and the priest shall burn it on the altar as an aroma pleasing to the LORD. In this way the priest will make atonement for them, and they will be forgiven.

³²' "If someone brings a lamb as their sin offering, they are to bring a female without defect. ³³They are to lay their hand on its head and slaughter it for a sin offering at the place where the burnt offering is slaughtered. ³⁴Then the priest shall take some of the blood of the sin offering with his finger and put it on the horns of the altar of burnt offering and pour out the rest of the blood at the base of the altar. ³⁵They shall remove all the fat, just as the fat is removed from the lamb of the fellowship offering, and the priest shall burn it on the altar on top of the food offerings presented to the LORD. In this way the priest will make atonement for them for the sin they have committed, and they will be forgiven.

5 ' "If anyone sins because they do not speak up when they hear a public charge to testify regarding something they have seen or learned about, they will be held responsible.

²' "If anyone becomes aware that they are guilty – if they unwittingly touch anything ceremonially unclean (whether the carcass of an unclean animal, wild or domestic, or of any unclean creature that moves along the ground) and they are unaware that they have become unclean, but then they come to realise their guilt; ³or if they touch human uncleanness (anything that would make them unclean) even though they are unaware of it, but then they learn of it and realise their

guilt; ⁴or if anyone thoughtlessly takes an oath to do anything, whether good or evil (in any matter one might carelessly swear about) even though they are unaware of it, but then they learn of it and realise their guilt – ⁵when anyone becomes aware that they are guilty in any of these matters, they must confess in what way they have sinned. ⁶As a penalty for the sin they have committed, they must bring to the LORD a female lamb or goat from the flock as a sin offering; and the priest shall make atonement for them for their sin.

⁷"Anyone who cannot afford a lamb is to bring two doves or two young pigeons to the LORD as a penalty for their sin – one for a sin offering and the other for a burnt offering. ⁸They are to bring them to the priest, who shall first offer the one for the sin offering. He is to wring its head from its neck, not dividing it completely, ⁹and is to splash some of the blood of the sin offering against the side of the altar; the rest of the blood must be drained out at the base of the altar. It is a sin offering. ¹⁰The priest shall then offer the other as a burnt offering in the prescribed way and make atonement for them for the sin they have committed, and they will be forgiven.

¹¹"If, however, they cannot afford two doves or two young pigeons, they are to bring as an offering for their sin a tenth of an ephah of the finest flour for a sin offering. They must not put olive oil or incense on it, because it is a sin offering. ¹²They are to bring it to the priest, who shall take a handful of it as a memorial portion and burn it on the altar on top of the food offerings presented to the LORD. It is a sin offering. ¹³In this way the priest will make atonement for them for any of these sins they have committed, and they will be forgiven. The rest of the offering will belong to the priest, as in the case of the grain offering."'

¹⁴The LORD said to Moses: ¹⁵'When anyone is unfaithful to the LORD by sinning unintentionally in regard to any of the LORD's holy things, they are to bring to the LORD as a penalty a ram from the flock, one without defect and of the proper value in silver, according to the sanctuary shekel. It is a guilt offering. ¹⁶They must make restitution for what they have failed to do in regard to the holy things, pay an additional penalty of a fifth of its value and give it all to the priest. The priest will make atonement for them with the ram as a guilt offering, and they will be forgiven.

¹⁷'If anyone sins and does what is forbidden in any of the LORD's commands, even though they do not know it, they are guilty and will be held responsible. ¹⁸They are to bring to the priest as a guilt offering a ram from the flock, one without defect and of the proper value. In this way the priest will make atonement for them for the wrong they have committed unintentionally, and they will be forgiven. ¹⁹It is a guilt offering; they have been guilty of wrongdoing against the LORD.'

■ PSALM 25:1–7

¹In you, LORD my God,
  I put my trust.

²I trust in you;
  do not let me be put to shame,
  nor let my enemies triumph over me.
³No one who hopes in you
  will ever be put to shame,
but shame will come on those
  who are treacherous without cause.

⁴Show me your ways, LORD,
  teach me your paths.
⁵Guide me in your truth and teach me,
  for you are God my Saviour,
  and my hope is in you all day long.
⁶Remember, LORD, your great mercy and
    love,

for they are from of old.
⁷ Do not remember the sins of my youth
and my rebellious ways;
according to your love remember me,
for you, LORD, are good.

▬ PROVERBS 6:4-5

⁴ Allow no sleep to your eyes,
no slumber to your eyelids.
⁵ Free yourself, like a gazelle from the
hand of the hunter,
like a bird from the snare of the fowler.

▬ MARK 1:21-45

²¹ They went to Capernaum, and when the Sabbath came, Jesus went into the synagogue and began to teach. ²² The people were amazed at his teaching, because he taught them as one who had authority, not as the teachers of the law. ²³ Just then a man in their synagogue who was possessed by an impure spirit cried out, ²⁴ 'What do you want with us, Jesus of Nazareth? Have you come to destroy us? I know who you are – the Holy One of God!'

²⁵ 'Be quiet!' said Jesus sternly. 'Come out of him!' ²⁶ The impure spirit shook the man violently and came out of him with a shriek.

²⁷ The people were all so amazed that they asked each other, 'What is this? A new teaching – and with authority! He even gives orders to impure spirits and they obey him.' ²⁸ News about him spread quickly over the whole region of Galilee.

²⁹ As soon as they left the synagogue, they went with James and John to the home of Simon and Andrew. ³⁰ Simon's mother-in-law was in bed with a fever, and they

immediately told Jesus about her. ³¹ So he went to her, took her hand and helped her up. The fever left her and she began to wait on them.

³² That evening after sunset the people brought to Jesus all who were ill and demon-possessed. ³³ The whole town gathered at the door, ³⁴ and Jesus healed many who had various diseases. He also drove out many demons, but he would not let the demons speak because they knew who he was.

³⁵ Very early in the morning, while it was still dark, Jesus got up, left the house and went off to a solitary place, where he prayed. ³⁶ Simon and his companions went to look for him, ³⁷ and when they found him, they exclaimed: 'Everyone is looking for you!'

³⁸ Jesus replied, 'Let us go somewhere else – to the nearby villages – so that I can preach there also. That is why I have come.' ³⁹ So he travelled throughout Galilee, preaching in their synagogues and driving out demons.

⁴⁰ A man with leprosy came to him and begged him on his knees, 'If you are willing, you can make me clean.'

⁴¹ Jesus was indignant. He reached out his hand and touched the man. 'I am willing,' he said. 'Be clean!' ⁴² Immediately the leprosy left him and he was cleansed.

⁴³ Jesus sent him away at once with a strong warning: ⁴⁴ 'See that you don't tell this to anyone. But go, show yourself to the priest and offer the sacrifices that Moses commanded for your cleansing, as a testimony to them.' ⁴⁵ Instead he went out and began to talk freely, spreading the news. As a result, Jesus could no longer enter a town openly but stayed outside in lonely places. Yet the people still came to him from everywhere.

The Morning Watch

'Very early in the morning ... Jesus got up,
left the house and went off to a solitary place,
where he prayed.' **Mark 1:35**

It is an exciting thought that spiritual staleness need not be so. Spiritual freshness is available to us all – and on a daily basis. Maintaining it, however, does not mean that we will be exempt from having to face occasional trials and difficulties. It means, rather, that no matter how dry and difficult our circumstances, our experience of God can remain fresh and vibrant.

What, then, is the first principle of maintaining spiritual freshness? Establish a daily quiet time with God in order to replenish your spiritual resources.

Some modern-day Christians balk at this idea. They say, 'The Lord is with us all the time. Why do we need to fence off a particular part of the day to spend time with Him? A daily quiet time can soon bring one into legalism.' I am well aware of this danger, but again I say – it need not be so. There have been periods in my own life when my quiet time was nothing more than a ritual, but that was more a consequence than a cause.

The best period for a quiet time, in my opinion, is in the morning, before the day starts. Some prefer the evening or perhaps – as in the case of busy mothers and wives – the late morning is better, when the family has left and the house is quiet. Each must establish the best time according to preference or convenience. I'm merely saying that a certain time of the day ought not to belong to the day, but to the getting of resources for the day. Start the day right and you will end it right.

PRAYER

O God, help me to see that just as I need to take time out of the day to feed myself physically, so I need to take time out to feed myself spiritually. Help me not just to acknowledge this, but to act on it. In Christ's name I pray. Amen.

FURTHER STUDY

Psa. 119:137-148; 5:1-3;
Gen. 28:18; Dan. 6:10
• When did the psalmist pray?
• When do you pray?

February 22

The Mo Wa
Very early in the morning
left the house and went off to a solitary place,

◼ LEVITICUS 6:1–7:21

6 The LORD said to Moses: [2]'If anyone sins and is unfaithful to the LORD by deceiving a neighbour about something entrusted to them or left in their care or about something stolen, or if they cheat their neighbour, [3]or if they find lost property and lie about it, or if they swear falsely about any such sin that people may commit – [4]when they sin in any of these ways and realise their guilt, they must return what they have stolen or taken by extortion, or what was entrusted to them, or the lost property they found, [5]or whatever it was they swore falsely about. They must make restitution in full, add a fifth of the value to it and give it all to the owner on the day they present their guilt offering. [6]And as a penalty they must bring to the priest, that is, to the LORD, their guilt offering, a ram from the flock, one without defect and of the proper value. [7]In this way the priest will make atonement for them before the LORD, and they will be forgiven for any of the things they did that made them guilty.'

[8]The LORD said to Moses: [9]'Give Aaron and his sons this command: "These are the regulations for the burnt offering: the burnt offering is to remain on the altar hearth throughout the night, till morning, and the fire must be kept burning on the altar. [10]The priest shall then put on his linen clothes, with linen undergarments next to his body, and shall remove the ashes of the burnt offering that the fire has consumed on the altar and place them beside the altar. [11]Then he is to take off these clothes and put on others, and carry the ashes outside the camp to a place that is ceremonially clean.

[12]The fire on the altar must be kept burning; it must not go out. Every morning the priest is to add firewood and arrange the burnt offering on the fire and burn the fat of the fellowship offerings on it. [13]The fire must be kept burning on the altar continuously; it must not go out.

[14]"'These are the regulations for the grain offering: Aaron's sons are to bring it before the LORD, in front of the altar. [15]The priest is to take a handful of the finest flour and some olive oil, together with all the incense on the grain offering, and burn the memorial portion on the altar as an aroma pleasing to the LORD. [16]Aaron and his sons shall eat the rest of it, but it is to be eaten without yeast in the sanctuary area; they are to eat it in the courtyard of the tent of meeting. [17]It must not be baked with yeast; I have given it as their share of the food offerings presented to me. Like the sin offering and the guilt offering, it is most holy. [18]Any male descendant of Aaron may eat it. For all generations to come it is his perpetual share of the food offerings presented to the LORD. Whatever touches it will become holy."'

[19]The LORD also said to Moses, [20]'This is the offering Aaron and his sons are to bring to the LORD on the day he is anointed: a tenth of an ephah of the finest flour as a regular grain offering, half of it in the morning and half in the evening. [21]It must be prepared with oil on a griddle; bring it well-mixed and present the grain offering broken in pieces as an aroma pleasing to the LORD. [22]The son who is to succeed him as anointed priest shall prepare it. It is the LORD's perpetual share and is to be burned completely. [23]Every grain offering of a priest shall be burned completely; it must not be eaten.'

²⁴The LORD said to Moses, ²⁵'Say to Aaron and his sons: "These are the regulations for the sin offering: the sin offering is to be slaughtered before the LORD in the place where the burnt offering is slaughtered; it is most holy. ²⁶The priest who offers it shall eat it; it is to be eaten in the sanctuary area, in the courtyard of the tent of meeting. ²⁷Whatever touches any of the flesh will become holy, and if any of the blood is spattered on a garment, you must wash it in the sanctuary area. ²⁸The clay pot that the meat is cooked in must be broken; but if it is cooked in a bronze pot, the pot is to be scoured and rinsed with water. ²⁹Any male in a priest's family may eat it; it is most holy. ³⁰But any sin offering whose blood is brought into the tent of meeting to make atonement in the Holy Place must not be eaten; it must be burned.

7 ¹'"These are the regulations for the guilt offering, which is most holy: ²the guilt offering is to be slaughtered in the place where the burnt offering is slaughtered, and its blood is to be splashed against the sides of the altar. ³All its fat shall be offered: the fat tail and the fat that covers the internal organs, ⁴both kidneys with the fat on them near the loins, and the long lobe of the liver, which is to be removed with the kidneys. ⁵The priest shall burn them on the altar as a food offering presented to the LORD. It is a guilt offering. ⁶Any male in a priest's family may eat it, but it must be eaten in the sanctuary area; it is most holy.

⁷'"The same law applies to both the sin offering and the guilt offering: they belong to the priest who makes atonement with them. ⁸The priest who offers a burnt offering for anyone may keep its hide for himself. ⁹Every grain offering baked in an oven or cooked in a pan or on a griddle belongs to the priest who offers it, ¹⁰and every grain offering, whether mixed with olive oil or dry, belongs equally to all the sons of Aaron.

¹¹'"These are the regulations for the fellowship offering anyone may present to the LORD:

¹²'"If they offer it as an expression of thankfulness, then along with this thank-offering they are to offer thick loaves made without yeast and with olive oil mixed in, thin loaves made without yeast and brushed with oil, and thick loaves of the finest flour well-kneaded and with oil mixed in. ¹³Along with their fellowship offering of thanksgiving they are to present an offering with thick loaves of bread made with yeast. ¹⁴They are to bring one of each kind as an offering, a contribution to the LORD; it belongs to the priest who splashes the blood of the fellowship offering against the altar. ¹⁵The meat of their fellowship offering of thanksgiving must be eaten on the day it is offered; they must leave none of it till morning.

¹⁶'"If, however, their offering is the result of a vow or is a freewill offering, the sacrifice shall be eaten on the day they offer it, but anything left over may be eaten on the next day. ¹⁷Any meat of the sacrifice left over till the third day must be burned. ¹⁸If any meat of the fellowship offering is eaten on the third day, the one who offered it will not be accepted. It will not be reckoned to their credit, for it has become impure; the person who eats any of it will be held responsible.

¹⁹'"Meat that touches anything ceremonially unclean must not be eaten; it must be burned. As for other meat, anyone ceremonially clean may eat it. ²⁰But if anyone who is unclean eats any meat of the fellowship offering belonging to the LORD, they must be cut off from their people. ²¹Anyone who touches something unclean – whether human uncleanness or an unclean animal or any unclean creature that moves along the ground – and then eats any of the meat of the fellowship offering belonging to the LORD must be cut off from their people."'

◼ PSALM 25:8-15

8 Good and upright is the LORD;
   therefore he instructs sinners in his
      ways.
9 He guides the humble in what is right
   and teaches them his way.
10 All the ways of the LORD are loving and
      faithful
   toward those who keep the demands
      of his covenant.
11 For the sake of your name, LORD,
   forgive my iniquity, though it is great.

12 Who, then, are those who fear the LORD?
   He will instruct them in the ways they
      should choose.
13 They will spend their days in prosperity,
   and their descendants will inherit the
      land.
14 The LORD confides in those who fear him;
   he makes his covenant known to them.
15 My eyes are ever on the LORD,
   for only he will release my feet from
      the snare.

◼ PROVERBS 6:6-8

6 Go to the ant, you sluggard;
   consider its ways and be wise!
7 It has no commander,
   no overseer or ruler,
8 yet it stores its provisions in summer
   and gathers its food at harvest.

◼ MARK 2:1-22

2 A few days later, when Jesus again entered Capernaum, the people heard that he had come home. 2 They gathered in such large numbers that there was no room left, not even outside the door, and he preached the word to them. 3 Some men came, bringing to him a paralysed man,

carried by four of them. 4 Since they could not get him to Jesus because of the crowd, they made an opening in the roof above Jesus by digging through it and then lowered the mat the man was lying on. 5 When Jesus saw their faith, he said to the paralysed man, 'Son, your sins are forgiven.'

6 Now some teachers of the law were sitting there, thinking to themselves, 7 'Why does this fellow talk like that? He's blaspheming! Who can forgive sins but God alone?'

8 Immediately Jesus knew in his spirit that this was what they were thinking in their hearts, and he said to them, 'Why are you thinking these things? 9 Which is easier: to say to this paralysed man, "Your sins are forgiven," or to say, "Get up, take your mat and walk"? 10 But I want you to know that the Son of Man has authority on earth to forgive sins.' So he said to the man, 11 'I tell you, get up, take your mat and go home.' 12 He got up, took his mat and walked out in full view of them all. This amazed everyone and they praised God, saying, 'We have never seen anything like this!'

13 Once again Jesus went out beside the lake. A large crowd came to him, and he began to teach them. 14 As he walked along, he saw Levi son of Alphaeus sitting at the tax collector's booth. 'Follow me,' Jesus told him, and Levi got up and followed him.

15 While Jesus was having dinner at Levi's house, many tax collectors and sinners were eating with him and his disciples, for there were many who followed him. 16 When the teachers of the law who were Pharisees saw him eating with the sinners and tax collectors, they asked his disciples: 'Why does he eat with tax collectors and sinners?'

17 On hearing this, Jesus said to them, 'It is not the healthy who need a doctor, but those who are ill. I have not come to call the righteous, but sinners.'

18 Now John's disciples and the Pharisees were fasting. Some people came and asked Jesus, 'How is it that John's disciples and the

disciples of the Pharisees are fasting, but yours are not?'

¹⁹ Jesus answered, 'How can the guests of the bridegroom fast while he is with them? They cannot, so long as they have him with them. ²⁰ But the time will come when the bridegroom will be taken from them, and on that day they will fast.

²¹ 'No one sews a patch of unshrunk cloth on an old garment. Otherwise, the new piece will pull away from the old, making the tear worse. ²² And no one pours new wine into old wineskins. Otherwise, the wine will burst the skins, and both the wine and the wineskins will be ruined. No, they pour new wine into new wineskins.'

Prepare!

'Go the ant, you sluggard; consider its ways and be wise!' **Proverbs 6:6**

The vital principle of deferred satisfaction is brought out in the text that is before us today. We see it clearly in the animal kingdom: the ant doesn't spend all its time eating. It runs back and forth carrying food into the nest so that it may survive the winter when there will be no food.

Keep this picture of the ant continually in your mind. It is one of those images put into the Word of God to bring instruction to the heart. If you are young, prepare for the future in every way you can, not only by denying yourself to the things that God puts out of bounds, but also by giving yourself to the things you need to know about your chosen profession. Whatever you plan to do in life – prepare for it. Prepare by study and also by prayer.

Whatever your age – whenever you have to do anything in public, like speaking at a church meeting – prepare. Deny yourself distractions, like watching television, and give yourself to the task at hand. There are no short cuts to success. I prepared myself for years by filling my heart and mind with the Word of God, and then, when the time came, God called me to launch the *Every Day with Jesus* Bible notes. People say to me, 'How can you continue to write year after year?' I know I would not be able to do so had I not, many years ago, denied myself many things so that I could prepare. Whatever God asks you to do, don't take His blessings for granted – prepare.

PRAYER

Father, Your knife cuts deep, but Your cuts are always redemptive. Forgive me for taking so much for granted and for not giving myself to the task to which You have called me. Help me be a prepared person. In Jesus' name I ask it. Amen.

FURTHER STUDY

Matt. 16:21-28; Mark 8:34; Luke 9:23

• What did Jesus say to His disciples?
• Are there areas of your life in which you need to deny yourself?

February 23

▬ LEVITICUS 7:22–8:36

²²The LORD said to Moses, ²³'Say to the Israelites: "Do not eat any of the fat of cattle, sheep or goats. ²⁴The fat of an animal found dead or torn by wild animals may be used for any other purpose, but you must not eat it. ²⁵Anyone who eats the fat of an animal from which a food offering may be presented to the LORD must be cut off from their people. ²⁶And wherever you live, you must not eat the blood of any bird or animal. ²⁷Anyone who eats blood must be cut off from their people."'

²⁸The LORD said to Moses, ²⁹'Say to the Israelites: "Anyone who brings a fellowship offering to the LORD is to bring part of it as their sacrifice to the LORD. ³⁰With their own hands they are to present the food offering to the LORD; they are to bring the fat, together with the breast, and wave the breast before the LORD as a wave offering. ³¹The priest shall burn the fat on the altar, but the breast belongs to Aaron and his sons. ³²You are to give the right thigh of your fellowship offerings to the priest as a contribution. ³³The son of Aaron who offers the blood and the fat of the fellowship offering shall have the right thigh as his share. ³⁴From the fellowship offerings of the Israelites, I have taken the breast that is waved and the thigh that is presented and have given them to Aaron the priest and his sons as their perpetual share from the Israelites."'

³⁵This is the portion of the food offerings presented to the LORD that were allotted to Aaron and his sons on the day they were presented to serve the LORD as priests. ³⁶On the day they were anointed, the LORD commanded that the Israelites give this to them as their perpetual share for the generations to come.

³⁷These, then, are the regulations for the burnt offering, the grain offering, the sin offering, the guilt offering, the ordination offering and the fellowship offering, ³⁸which the LORD gave Moses at Mount Sinai in the Desert of Sinai on the day he commanded the Israelites to bring their offerings to the LORD.

8 The LORD said to Moses, ²'Bring Aaron and his sons, their garments, the anointing oil, the bull for the sin offering, the two rams and the basket containing bread made without yeast, ³and gather the entire assembly at the entrance to the tent of meeting.' ⁴Moses did as the LORD commanded him, and the assembly gathered at the entrance to the tent of meeting.

⁵Moses said to the assembly, 'This is what the LORD has commanded to be done.' ⁶Then Moses brought Aaron and his sons forward and washed them with water. ⁷He put the tunic on Aaron, tied the sash round him, clothed him with the robe and put the ephod on him. He also fastened the ephod with a decorative waistband, which he tied round him. ⁸He placed the breastpiece on him and put the Urim and Thummim in the breastpiece. ⁹Then he placed the turban on Aaron's head and set the gold plate, the sacred emblem, on the front of it, as the LORD commanded Moses.

¹⁰Then Moses took the anointing oil and anointed the tabernacle and everything in it, and so consecrated them. ¹¹He sprinkled some of the oil on the altar seven times, anointing the altar and all its utensils and the basin with its stand, to consecrate them. ¹²He poured some of the anointing oil on Aaron's head and anointed him to consecrate him. ¹³Then he brought Aaron's sons forward, put tunics on them, tied sashes

round them and fastened caps on them, as the LORD commanded Moses.

¹⁴ He then presented the bull for the sin offering, and Aaron and his sons laid their hands on its head. ¹⁵ Moses slaughtered the bull and took some of the blood, and with his finger he put it on all the horns of the altar to purify the altar. He poured out the rest of the blood at the base of the altar. So he consecrated it to make atonement for it. ¹⁶ Moses also took all the fat around the internal organs, the long lobe of the liver, and both kidneys and their fat, and burned it on the altar. ¹⁷ But the bull with its hide and its flesh and its intestines he burned outside the camp, as the LORD commanded Moses.

¹⁸ He then presented the ram for the burnt offering, and Aaron and his sons laid their hands on its head. ¹⁹ Then Moses slaughtered the ram and splashed the blood against the sides of the altar. ²⁰ He cut the ram into pieces and burned the head, the pieces and the fat. ²¹ He washed the internal organs and the legs with water and burned the whole ram on the altar. It was a burnt offering, a pleasing aroma, a food offering presented to the LORD, as the LORD commanded Moses.

²² He then presented the other ram, the ram for the ordination, and Aaron and his sons laid their hands on its head. ²³ Moses slaughtered the ram and took some of its blood and put it on the lobe of Aaron's right ear, on the thumb of his right hand and on the big toe of his right foot. ²⁴ Moses also brought Aaron's sons forward and put some of the blood on the lobes of their right ears, on the thumbs of their right hands and on the big toes of their right feet. Then he splashed blood against the sides of the altar. ²⁵ After that, he took the fat, the fat tail, all the fat around the internal organs, the long lobe of the liver, both kidneys and their fat and the right thigh. ²⁶ And from the basket of bread made without yeast, which was before the LORD, he took one thick loaf,

one thick loaf with olive oil mixed in, and one thin loaf, and he put these on the fat portions and on the right thigh. ²⁷ He put all these in the hands of Aaron and his sons and they waved them before the LORD as a wave offering. ²⁸ Then Moses took them from their hands and burned them on the altar on top of the burnt offering as an ordination offering, a pleasing aroma, a food offering presented to the LORD. ²⁹ Moses also took the breast, which was his share of the ordination ram, and waved it before the LORD as a wave offering, as the LORD commanded Moses.

³⁰ Then Moses took some of the anointing oil and some of the blood from the altar and sprinkled them on Aaron and his garments and on his sons and their garments. So he consecrated Aaron and his garments and his sons and their garments.

³¹ Moses then said to Aaron and his sons, 'Cook the meat at the entrance to the tent of meeting and eat it there with the bread from the basket of ordination offerings, as I was commanded: "Aaron and his sons are to eat it." ³² Then burn the rest of the meat and the bread. ³³ Do not leave the entrance to the tent of meeting for seven days, until the days of your ordination are completed, for your ordination will last seven days. ³⁴ What has been done today was commanded by the LORD to make atonement for you. ³⁵ You must stay at the entrance to the tent of meeting day and night for seven days and do what the LORD requires, so that you will not die; for that is what I have been commanded.'

³⁶ So Aaron and his sons did everything the LORD commanded through Moses.

....

▬ PSALM 25:16–22

¹⁶ Turn to me and be gracious to me,
    for I am lonely and afflicted.
¹⁷ Relieve the troubles of my heart
    and free me from my anguish.

^{18} Look on my affliction and my distress
    and take away all my sins.
^{19} See how numerous are my enemies
    and how fiercely they hate me!

^{20} Guard my life and rescue me;
    do not let me be put to shame,
    for I take refuge in you.
^{21} May integrity and uprightness protect me,
    because my hope, LORD, is in you.

^{22} Deliver Israel, O God,
    from all their troubles!

▬ PROVERBS 6:9-11

^{9} How long will you lie there, you
    sluggard?
    When will you get up from your sleep?
^{10} A little sleep, a little slumber,
    a little folding of the hands to rest –
^{11} and poverty will come on you like a thief
    and scarcity like an armed man.

▬ MARK 2:23–3:12

^{23} One Sabbath Jesus was going through the cornfields, and as his disciples walked along, they began to pick some ears of corn. ^{24} The Pharisees said to him, 'Look, why are they doing what is unlawful on the Sabbath?'

^{25} He answered, 'Have you never read what David did when he and his companions were hungry and in need? ^{26} In the days of Abiathar the high priest, he entered the house of God and ate the consecrated bread,

which is lawful only for priests to eat. And he also gave some to his companions.'

^{27} Then he said to them, 'The Sabbath was made for man, not man for the Sabbath. ^{28} So the Son of Man is Lord even of the Sabbath.'

3 Another time Jesus went into the synagogue, and a man with a shrivelled hand was there. ^{2} Some of them were looking for a reason to accuse Jesus, so they watched him closely to see if he would heal him on the Sabbath. ^{3} Jesus said to the man with the shrivelled hand, 'Stand up in front of everyone.'

^{4} Then Jesus asked them, 'Which is lawful on the Sabbath: to do good or to do evil, to save life or to kill?' But they remained silent. ^{5} He looked around at them in anger and, deeply distressed at their stubborn hearts, said to the man, 'Stretch out your hand.' He stretched it out, and his hand was completely restored. ^{6} Then the Pharisees went out and began to plot with the Herodians how they might kill Jesus.

^{7} Jesus withdrew with his disciples to the lake, and a large crowd from Galilee followed. ^{8} When they heard all he was doing, many people came to him from Judea, Jerusalem, Idumea, and the regions across the Jordan and around Tyre and Sidon. ^{9} Because of the crowd he told his disciples to have a small boat ready for him, to keep the people from crowding him. ^{10} For he had healed many, so that those with diseases were pushing forward to touch him. ^{11} Whenever the impure spirits saw him, they fell down before him and cried out, 'You are the Son of God.' ^{12} But he gave them strict orders not to tell others about him.

'God's Postal Address'?

'Guard my life and rescue me; do not let me be put to shame, for I take refuge in you.' **Psalm 25:20**

Jesus, in the opening words of the Lord's Prayer, taught us to focus first on God before presenting to Him our requests and petitions. Why did Jesus bid us pray, 'Our Father in heaven'? What is so important about the fact that God lives in heaven?

Someone has suggested that heaven is 'God's postal address' and, therefore, the place to which all prayers and petitions ought to be directed. I believe, however, that Jesus, in using the words 'in heaven,' sought to focus our minds not so much on God's location, but rather His elevation.

We are so used to living, as we say, 'in a man's world,' surrounded by limitations, that we are apt to forget that God exists in a realm where there are no shortages or restraints. Here on earth, we stagger from one crisis to another, face endless problems – such as economic recessions, strikes, political unrest – but in heaven, where God lives, such situations are non-existent. There are no shortages in the factories of His grace, no disputes on His assembly lines and no faults in His communication system. Ring 'Calvary' at any hour of the day or night, and you will be put into direct contact with the King of kings!

Can you now see what Jesus means when He bids us focus on God who is in heaven? He is telling us to elevate our spiritual vision until it breaks free of earth's gravitational pull and to remind ourselves constantly of the fact that, in our Father's presence, our greatest problems turn into possibilities.

PRAYER

O Father, this phrase 'in heaven' is like a rocket that launches me beyond earth's limitations into a realm where everything is blessedness and light. Help me never lose sight of this fact – today and every day. Amen.

FURTHER STUDY

Rev. 21; Isa. 66:1-2; Matt. 5:34; Rev. 4:2
- What is the focal point of heaven?
- How does this elevate our vision?

February 24

■ LEVITICUS 9:1–11:12

9 On the eighth day Moses summoned Aaron and his sons and the elders of Israel. ² He said to Aaron, 'Take a bull calf for your sin offering and a ram for your burnt offering, both without defect, and present them before the LORD. ³ Then say to the Israelites: "Take a male goat for a sin offering, a calf and a lamb – both a year old and without defect – for a burnt offering, ⁴ and an ox and a ram for a fellowship offering to sacrifice before the LORD, together with a grain offering mixed with olive oil. For today the LORD will appear to you."'

⁵ They took the things Moses commanded to the front of the tent of meeting, and the entire assembly came near and stood before

the LORD. ⁶Then Moses said, 'This is what the LORD has commanded you to do, so that the glory of the LORD may appear to you.'

⁷Moses said to Aaron, 'Come to the altar and sacrifice your sin offering and your burnt offering and make atonement for yourself and the people; sacrifice the offering that is for the people and make atonement for them, as the LORD has commanded.'

⁸So Aaron came to the altar and slaughtered the calf as a sin offering for himself. ⁹His sons brought the blood to him, and he dipped his finger into the blood and put it on the horns of the altar; the rest of the blood he poured out at the base of the altar. ¹⁰On the altar he burned the fat, the kidneys and the long lobe of the liver from the sin offering, as the LORD commanded Moses; ¹¹the flesh and the hide he burned outside the camp.

¹²Then he slaughtered the burnt offering. His sons handed him the blood, and he splashed it against the sides of the altar. ¹³They handed him the burnt offering piece by piece, including the head, and he burned them on the altar. ¹⁴He washed the internal organs and the legs and burned them on top of the burnt offering on the altar.

¹⁵Aaron then brought the offering that was for the people. He took the goat for the people's sin offering and slaughtered it and offered it for a sin offering as he did with the first one.

¹⁶He brought the burnt offering and offered it in the prescribed way. ¹⁷He also brought the grain offering, took a handful of it and burned it on the altar in addition to the morning's burnt offering.

¹⁸He slaughtered the ox and the ram as the fellowship offering for the people. His sons handed him the blood, and he splashed it against the sides of the altar. ¹⁹But the fat portions of the ox and the ram – the fat tail, the layer of fat, the kidneys and the long lobe of the liver – ²⁰these they laid on the breasts, and then Aaron burned the fat on the altar. ²¹Aaron waved the breasts and the right thigh before the LORD as a wave offering, as Moses commanded.

²²Then Aaron lifted his hands towards the people and blessed them. And having sacrificed the sin offering, the burnt offering and the fellowship offering, he stepped down.

²³Moses and Aaron then went into the tent of meeting. When they came out, they blessed the people; and the glory of the LORD appeared to all the people. ²⁴Fire came out from the presence of the LORD and consumed the burnt offering and the fat portions on the altar. And when all the people saw it, they shouted for joy and fell face down.

10 Aaron's sons Nadab and Abihu took their censers, put fire in them and added incense; and they offered unauthorised fire before the LORD, contrary to his command. ²So fire came out from the presence of the LORD and consumed them, and they died before the LORD. ³Moses then said to Aaron, 'This is what the LORD spoke of when he said:

'"Among those who approach me
I will be proved holy;
in the sight of all the people
I will be honoured."'

Aaron remained silent.

⁴Moses summoned Mishael and Elzaphan, sons of Aaron's uncle Uzziel, and said to them, 'Come here; carry your cousins outside the camp, away from the front of the sanctuary.' ⁵So they came and carried them, still in their tunics, outside the camp, as Moses ordered.

⁶Then Moses said to Aaron and his sons Eleazar and Ithamar, 'Do not let your hair become unkempt and do not tear your clothes or you will die and the LORD will be angry with the whole community. But your

relatives, all the Israelites, may mourn for those the LORD has destroyed by fire. ⁷Do not leave the entrance to the tent of meeting or you will die, because the LORD's anointing oil is on you.' So they did as Moses said.

⁸Then the LORD said to Aaron, ⁹'You and your sons are not to drink wine or other fermented drink whenever you go into the tent of meeting, or you will die. This is a lasting ordinance for the generations to come, ¹⁰so that you can distinguish between the holy and the common, between the unclean and the clean, ¹¹and so you can teach the Israelites all the decrees the LORD has given them through Moses.'

¹²Moses said to Aaron and his remaining sons, Eleazar and Ithamar, 'Take the grain offering left over from the food offerings prepared without yeast and presented to the LORD and eat it beside the altar, for it is most holy. ¹³Eat it in the sanctuary area, because it is your share and your sons' share of the food offerings presented to the LORD; for so I have been commanded. ¹⁴But you and your sons and your daughters may eat the breast that was waved and the thigh that was presented. Eat them in a ceremonially clean place; they have been given to you and your children as your share of the Israelites' fellowship offerings. ¹⁵The thigh that was presented and the breast that was waved must be brought with the fat portions of the food offerings, to be waved before the LORD as a wave offering. This will be the perpetual share for you and your children, as the LORD has commanded.'

¹⁶When Moses enquired about the goat of the sin offering and found that it had been burned, he was angry with Eleazar and Ithamar, Aaron's remaining sons, and asked, ¹⁷'Why didn't you eat the sin offering in the sanctuary area? It is most holy; it was given to you to take away the guilt of the community by making atonement for them before the LORD. ¹⁸Since its blood was not taken into the Holy Place, you should have

eaten the goat in the sanctuary area, as I commanded.'

¹⁹Aaron replied to Moses, 'Today they sacrificed their sin offering and their burnt offering before the LORD, but such things as this have happened to me. Would the LORD have been pleased if I had eaten the sin offering today?' ²⁰When Moses heard this, he was satisfied.

11 The LORD said to Moses and Aaron, ²'Say to the Israelites: "Of all the animals that live on land, these are the ones you may eat: ³you may eat any animal that has a divided hoof and that chews the cud.

⁴'"There are some that only chew the cud or only have a divided hoof, but you must not eat them. The camel, though it chews the cud, does not have a divided hoof; it is ceremonially unclean for you. ⁵The hyrax, though it chews the cud, does not have a divided hoof; it is unclean for you. ⁶The rabbit, though it chews the cud, does not have a divided hoof; it is unclean for you. ⁷And the pig, though it has a divided hoof, does not chew the cud; it is unclean for you. ⁸You must not eat their meat or touch their carcasses; they are unclean for you.

⁹'"Of all the creatures living in the water of the seas and the streams you may eat any that have fins and scales. ¹⁰But all creatures in the seas or streams that do not have fins and scales – whether among all the swarming things or among all the other living creatures in the water – you are to regard as unclean. ¹¹And since you are to regard them as unclean, you must not eat their meat; you must regard their carcasses as unclean. ¹²Anything living in the water that does not have fins and scales is to be regarded as unclean by you.

◼ PSALM 26:1-7

¹Vindicate me, LORD,
    for I have led a blameless life;

I have trusted in the LORD
and have not faltered.
[2] Test me, LORD, and try me,
examine my heart and my mind;
[3] for I have always been mindful of your
unfailing love
and have lived in reliance on your
faithfulness.

[4] I do not sit with the deceitful,
nor do I associate with hypocrites.
[5] I abhor the assembly of evildoers
and refuse to sit with the wicked.
[6] I wash my hands in innocence,
and go about your altar, LORD,
[7] proclaiming aloud your praise
and telling of all your wonderful
deeds.

▬ PROVERBS 6:12-15

[12] A troublemaker and a villain,
who goes about with a corrupt mouth,
[13]   who winks maliciously with his eye,
signals with his feet
and motions with his fingers,
[14]   who plots evil with deceit in his
heart –
he always stirs up conflict.
[15] Therefore disaster will overtake him in
an instant;
he will suddenly be destroyed –
without remedy.

▬ MARK 3:13-35

[13] Jesus went up on a mountainside and
called to him those he wanted, and they
came to him. [14] He appointed twelve that
they might be with him and that he might
send them out to preach [15] and to have authority to drive out demons. [16] These are the
twelve he appointed: Simon (to whom he
gave the name Peter); [17] James son of Zebedee and his brother John (to them he gave
the name Boanerges, which means 'sons of
thunder'), [18] Andrew, Philip, Bartholomew,
Matthew, Thomas, James son of Alphaeus,
Thaddaeus, Simon the Zealot [19] and Judas
Iscariot, who betrayed him.

[20] Then Jesus entered a house, and again a
crowd gathered, so that he and his disciples
were not even able to eat. [21] When his family
heard about this, they went to take charge
of him, for they said, 'He is out of his mind.'

[22] And the teachers of the law who came
down from Jerusalem said, 'He is possessed
by Beelzebul! By the prince of demons he is
driving out demons.'

[23] So Jesus called them over to him and
began to speak to them in parables: 'How
can Satan drive out Satan? [24] If a kingdom is divided against itself, that kingdom cannot stand. [25] If a house is divided
against itself, that house cannot stand.
[26] And if Satan opposes himself and is divided, he cannot stand; his end has come.
[27] In fact, no one can enter a strong man's
house without first tying him up. Then
he can plunder the strong man's house.
[28] Truly I tell you, people can be forgiven
all their sins and every slander they utter, [29] but whoever blasphemes against the
Holy Spirit will never be forgiven; they are
guilty of an eternal sin.'

[30] He said this because they were saying,
'He has an impure spirit.'

[31] Then Jesus' mother and brothers arrived. Standing outside, they sent someone
in to call him. [32] A crowd was sitting round
him, and they told him, 'Your mother and
brothers are outside looking for you.'

[33] 'Who are my mother and my brothers?'
he asked.

[34] Then he looked at those seated in a circle round him and said, 'Here are my mother and my brothers! [35] Whoever does God's
will is my brother and sister and mother.'

What Else Matters?

'Whoever does God's will is my brother and sister and mother.' **Mark 3:35**

Adoption is the highest privilege, and our entire Christian life must be understood in terms of it. Dr Martyn Lloyd-Jones said: 'The most wonderful thing of all is not that my sins have been forgiven, nor that I may enjoy certain experiences and blessings as a Christian. The thing that should astonish me ... overwhelm me is that I am a child of God, one of God's people.' The certainty that we are God's adopted children ought to be uppermost in our thoughts.

Almost every day since I became a Christian, I have reminded myself that I have been adopted into the family of God. It has become the dominant thought of my life. Some time ago, when I mentioned this fact to a fellow Christian, he looked at me blankly and said: 'So what?' So what? So not only is Jesus my Saviour, He is my Brother also. Following His resurrection our Lord said: 'Go instead to my brothers and tell them, "I am ascending to my Father and your Father, to my God and your God"' (John 20:17). Then again, the writer to the Hebrews quoting from Psalm 23 tells us that Jesus is not ashamed to call us brothers (Heb. 2:12).

When I was young I always wanted a brother. A sister came along twelve years after I was born, but I never had a brother. Not until I became a Christian, that is. Then, by virtue of the fact that I was adopted into the royal family of heaven, I found a Brother. And what a Brother! God is my Father, Jesus is my Brother ... what else matters?

PRAYER

Father God, forgive me that with such an inheritance as this I get taken up with trifling things. Help me make this the controlling thought of my life: I am a child of God. Nothing else matters. Amen.

FURTHER STUDY

Rom. 8:29; Eph. 3:14-15; 1 Tim. 5:1-2; 1 John 3:16-18
• What are the privileges of being in the family of God?
• What are the responsibilities?

February 25

▬ LEVITICUS 11:13–13:17

13 "'These are the birds you are to regard as unclean and not eat because they are unclean: the eagle, the vulture, the black vulture, 14 the red kite, any kind of black kite, 15 any kind of raven, 16 the horned owl, the screech owl, the gull, any kind of hawk, 17 the little owl, the cormorant, the great owl, 18 the white owl, the desert owl, the osprey,

¹⁹ the stork, any kind of heron, the hoopoe and the bat.

²⁰ ' "All flying insects that walk on all fours are to be regarded as unclean by you. ²¹ There are, however, some flying insects that walk on all fours that you may eat: those that have jointed legs for hopping on the ground. ²² Of these you may eat any kind of locust, cricket, cicada or grass-hopper. ²³ But all other flying insects that have four legs you are to regard as unclean.

²⁴ ' "You will make yourselves unclean by these; whoever touches their carcasses will be unclean till evening. ²⁵ Whoever picks up one of their carcasses must wash their clothes, and they will be unclean till evening.

²⁶ ' "Every animal that does not have a divided hoof or that does not chew the cud is unclean for you; whoever touches the carcass of any of them will be unclean. ²⁷ Of all the animals that walk on all fours, those that walk on their paws are unclean for you; whoever touches their carcasses will be unclean till evening. ²⁸ Anyone who picks up their carcasses must wash their clothes, and they will be unclean till evening. These animals are unclean for you.

²⁹ ' "Of the animals that move along the ground, these are unclean for you: the weasel, the rat, any kind of great lizard, ³⁰ the gecko, the monitor lizard, the wall lizard, the skink and the chameleon. ³¹ Of all those that move along the ground, these are unclean for you. Whoever touches them when they are dead will be unclean till evening. ³² When one of them dies and falls on something, that article, whatever its use, will be unclean, whether it is made of wood, cloth, hide or sackcloth. Put it in water; it will be unclean till evening, and then it will be clean. ³³ If one of them falls into a clay pot, everything in it will be unclean, and you must break the pot. ³⁴ Any food you are allowed to eat that has come into contact with water from any such pot is unclean, and any liquid that is drunk from such a pot is

unclean. ³⁵ Anything that one of their carcasses falls on becomes unclean; an oven or cooking pot must be broken up. They are unclean, and you are to regard them as unclean. ³⁶ A spring, however, or a cistern for collecting water remains clean, but anyone who touches one of these carcasses is unclean. ³⁷ If a carcass falls on any seeds that are to be planted, they remain clean. ³⁸ But if water has been put on the seed and a carcass falls on it, it is unclean for you.

³⁹ ' "If an animal that you are allowed to eat dies, anyone who touches its carcass will be unclean till evening. ⁴⁰ Anyone who eats some of its carcass must wash their clothes, and they will be unclean till evening. Anyone who picks up the carcass must wash their clothes, and they will be unclean till evening.

⁴¹ ' "Every creature that moves along the ground is to be regarded as unclean; it is not to be eaten. ⁴² You are not to eat any creature that moves along the ground, whether it moves on its belly or walks on all fours or on many feet; it is unclean. ⁴³ Do not defile yourselves by any of these creatures. Do not make yourselves unclean by means of them or be made unclean by them. ⁴⁴ I am the LORD your God; consecrate yourselves and be holy, because I am holy. Do not make yourselves unclean by any creature that moves along the ground. ⁴⁵ I am the LORD, who brought you up out of Egypt to be your God; therefore be holy, because I am holy.

⁴⁶ ' "These are the regulations concerning animals, birds, every living thing that moves about in the water and every creature that moves along the ground. ⁴⁷ You must distinguish between the unclean and the clean, between living creatures that may be eaten and those that may not be eaten." '

12 The LORD said to Moses, ² 'Say to the Israelites: "A woman who becomes pregnant and gives birth to a son will be ceremonially unclean for seven days, just as she is unclean during her monthly period. ³ On the eighth day the boy is to be circumcised.

⁴Then the woman must wait thirty-three days to be purified from her bleeding. She must not touch anything sacred or go to the sanctuary until the days of her purification are over. ⁵If she gives birth to a daughter, for two weeks the woman will be unclean, as during her period. Then she must wait sixty-six days to be purified from her bleeding.

⁶'"When the days of her purification for a son or daughter are over, she is to bring to the priest at the entrance to the tent of meeting a year-old lamb for a burnt offering and a young pigeon or a dove for a sin offering. ⁷He shall offer them before the LORD to make atonement for her, and then she will be ceremonially clean from her flow of blood.

'"These are the regulations for the woman who gives birth to a boy or a girl. ⁸But if she cannot afford a lamb, she is to bring two doves or two young pigeons, one for a burnt offering and the other for a sin offering. In this way the priest will make atonement for her, and she will be clean."'

13 The LORD said to Moses and Aaron, ²'When anyone has a swelling or a rash or a shiny spot on their skin that may be a defiling skin disease, they must be brought to Aaron the priest or to one of his sons who is a priest. ³The priest is to examine the sore on the skin, and if the hair in the sore has turned white and the sore appears to be more than skin deep, it is a defiling skin disease. When the priest examines that person, he shall pronounce them ceremonially unclean. ⁴If the shiny spot on the skin is white but does not appear to be more than skin deep and the hair in it has not turned white, the priest is to isolate the affected person for seven days. ⁵On the seventh day the priest is to examine them, and if he sees that the sore is unchanged and has not spread in the skin, he is to isolate them for another seven days. ⁶On the seventh day the priest is to examine them again, and if the sore has faded and has not spread in the skin, the priest shall pronounce them clean; it is only a rash. They must wash their clothes, and they will be clean. ⁷But if the rash does spread in their skin after they have shown themselves to the priest to be pronounced clean, they must appear before the priest again. ⁸The priest is to examine that person, and if the rash has spread in the skin, he shall pronounce them unclean; it is a defiling skin disease.

⁹'When anyone has a defiling skin disease, they must be brought to the priest. ¹⁰The priest is to examine them, and if there is a white swelling in the skin that has turned the hair white and if there is raw flesh in the swelling, ¹¹it is a chronic skin disease and the priest shall pronounce them unclean. He is not to isolate them, because they are already unclean.

¹²'If the disease breaks out all over their skin and, so far as the priest can see, it covers all the skin of the affected person from head to foot, ¹³the priest is to examine them, and if the disease has covered their whole body, he shall pronounce them clean. Since it has all turned white, they are clean. ¹⁴But whenever raw flesh appears on them, they will be unclean. ¹⁵When the priest sees the raw flesh, he shall pronounce them unclean. The raw flesh is unclean; they have a defiling disease. ¹⁶If the raw flesh changes and turns white, they must go to the priest. ¹⁷The priest is to examine them, and if the sores have turned white, the priest shall pronounce the affected person clean; then they will be clean.

▬ PSALM 26:8-12

⁸LORD, I love the house where you live,
   the place where your glory dwells.
⁹Do not take away my soul along with
    sinners,
  my life with those who are
    bloodthirsty,
¹⁰in whose hands are wicked schemes,
   whose right hands are full of bribes.

¹¹ I lead a blameless life;
   deliver me and be merciful to me.
¹² My feet stand on level ground;
   in the great congregation I will praise
   the LORD.

PROVERBS 6:16-19

¹⁶ There are six things the LORD hates,
   seven that are detestable to him:
¹⁷   haughty eyes,
     a lying tongue,
     hands that shed innocent blood,
¹⁸   a heart that devises wicked schemes,
     feet that are quick to rush into evil,
¹⁹   a false witness who pours out lies
     and a person who stirs up conflict in
     the community.

MARK 4:1-20

4 Again Jesus began to teach by the lake.
The crowd that gathered round him was
so large that he got into a boat and sat in it
out on the lake, while all the people were
along the shore at the water's edge. ²He
taught them many things by parables, and
in his teaching said: ³ 'Listen! A farmer went
out to sow his seed. ⁴As he was scattering the
seed, some fell along the path, and the birds
came and ate it up. ⁵Some fell on rocky places, where it did not have much soil. It sprang
up quickly, because the soil was shallow.
⁶But when the sun came up, the plants were
scorched, and they withered because they
had no root. ⁷Other seed fell among thorns,
which grew up and choked the plants, so

that they did not bear grain. ⁸Still other seed
fell on good soil. It came up, grew and produced a crop, some multiplying thirty, some
sixty, some a hundred times.'

⁹Then Jesus said, 'Whoever has ears to
hear, let them hear.'

¹⁰When he was alone, the Twelve and the
others around him asked him about the
parables. ¹¹He told them, 'The secret of the
kingdom of God has been given to you. But
to those on the outside everything is said in
parables ¹²so that,

' "they may be ever seeing but never
     perceiving,
   and ever hearing but never
     understanding;
   otherwise they might turn and be
     forgiven!" '

¹³Then Jesus said to them, 'Don't you understand this parable? How then will you
understand any parable? ¹⁴The farmer sows
the word. ¹⁵Some people are like seed along
the path, where the word is sown. As soon as
they hear it, Satan comes and takes away the
word that was sown in them. ¹⁶Others, like
seed sown on rocky places, hear the word
and at once receive it with joy. ¹⁷But since
they have no root, they last only a short time.
When trouble or persecution comes because
of the word, they quickly fall away. ¹⁸Still
others, like seed sown among thorns, hear
the word; ¹⁹but the worries of this life, the deceitfulness of wealth and the desires for other things come in and choke the word, making it unfruitful. ²⁰Others, like seed sown
on good soil, hear the word, accept it, and
produce a crop – some thirty, some sixty,
some a hundred times what was sown.'

The Key to Life

'... The secret of the kingdom of God has been given
to you.' **Mark 4:11**

Whenever I hear a person saying that all religions are the same, my mind runs immediately to the Cross. If what is found here is true (and I believe it is) and represents the meaning of life, then clearly all religions are not the same. No authentic note of divine self-sacrifice comes from other faiths. The Cross stands out in absolute uniqueness. As Toplady put it in his beautiful hymn:

> In the Cross of Christ I glory,
> Towering o'er the wrecks of time,
> All the light of sacred story
> Gathered round its head sublime.

For weeks and months after I became a Christian I wondered why anyone should preach anything except the Cross. The redemptive glowing mystery of it took hold of me in the early days of my conversion and I think I can honestly say it has never ceased to magnetise my heart.

Among the ancient inscriptions and paintings on the tombs of Egyptian kings, so I am told, one finds everywhere the symbol of the key of life. Strangely enough, it is in the form of a cross. Christ's cross is the only true key to life. This and this alone unlocks the doors to some of life's greatest mysteries. Other religions try, sometimes with great sincerity, to unlock the doors to these profound mysteries, but they are unsuccessful because they do not have the right key. They do not have a cross.

PRAYER

O Father, I see that if self-giving love is the meaning behind the Cross, and the meaning of the universe, then it must be the meaning behind my life too. May the Cross work itself out in all my relationships from this day forward. In Jesus' name. Amen.

FURTHER STUDY

John 19:1-15;
1 Cor. 1:1-23; 2:2-8; Gal. 6:14
• What was central to
  Paul's message?
• How was the message
  of Christ's crucifixion
  viewed?

February 26

■ LEVITICUS 13:18–14:14

[18] 'When someone has a boil on their skin and it heals, [19] and in the place where the boil was, a white swelling or reddish-white spot appears, they must present themselves to the priest. [20] The priest is to examine it, and if it appears to be more than skin deep and the hair in it has turned white, the priest shall pronounce that person unclean. It is a defiling skin disease that has broken out where the boil was. [21] But if, when the priest examines it, there is no white hair in it and it is not more than skin deep and has

faded, then the priest is to isolate them for seven days. ²²If it is spreading in the skin, the priest shall pronounce them unclean; it is a defiling disease. ²³But if the spot is unchanged and has not spread, it is only a scar from the boil, and the priest shall pronounce them clean.

²⁴'When someone has a burn on their skin and a reddish-white or white spot appears in the raw flesh of the burn, ²⁵the priest is to examine the spot, and if the hair in it has turned white, and it appears to be more than skin deep, it is a defiling disease that has broken out in the burn. The priest shall pronounce them unclean; it is a defiling skin disease. ²⁶But if the priest examines it and there is no white hair in the spot and if it is not more than skin deep and has faded, then the priest is to isolate them for seven days. ²⁷On the seventh day the priest is to examine that person, and if it is spreading in the skin, the priest shall pronounce them unclean; it is a defiling skin disease. ²⁸If, however, the spot is unchanged and has not spread in the skin but has faded, it is a swelling from the burn, and the priest shall pronounce them clean; it is only a scar from the burn.

²⁹'If a man or woman has a sore on their head or chin, ³⁰the priest is to examine the sore, and if it appears to be more than skin deep and the hair in it is yellow and thin, the priest shall pronounce them unclean; it is a defiling skin disease on the head or chin. ³¹But if, when the priest examines the sore, it does not seem to be more than skin deep and there is no black hair in it, then the priest is to isolate the affected person for seven days. ³²On the seventh day the priest is to examine the sore, and if it has not spread and there is no yellow hair in it and it does not appear to be more than skin deep, ³³then the man or woman must shave themselves, except for the affected area, and the priest is to keep them isolated another seven days. ³⁴On the seventh day

the priest is to examine the sore, and if it has not spread in the skin and appears to be no more than skin deep, the priest shall pronounce them clean. They must wash their clothes, and they will be clean. ³⁵But if the sore does spread in the skin after they are pronounced clean, ³⁶the priest is to examine them, and if he finds that the sore has spread in the skin, he does not need to look for yellow hair; they are unclean. ³⁷If, however, the sore is unchanged so far as the priest can see, and if black hair has grown in it, the affected person is healed. They are clean, and the priest shall pronounce them clean.

³⁸'When a man or woman has white spots on the skin, ³⁹the priest is to examine them, and if the spots are dull white, it is a harmless rash that has broken out on the skin; they are clean.

⁴⁰'A man who has lost his hair and is bald is clean. ⁴¹If he has lost his hair from the front of his scalp and has a bald forehead, he is clean. ⁴²But if he has a reddish-white sore on his bald head or forehead, it is a defiling disease breaking out on his head or forehead. ⁴³The priest is to examine him, and if the swollen sore on his head or forehead is reddish-white like a defiling skin disease, ⁴⁴the man is diseased and is unclean. The priest shall pronounce him unclean because of the sore on his head.

⁴⁵'Anyone with such a defiling disease must wear torn clothes, let their hair be unkempt, cover the lower part of their face and cry out, "Unclean! Unclean!" ⁴⁶As long as they have the disease they remain unclean. They must live alone; they must live outside the camp.

⁴⁷'As for any fabric that is spoiled with a defiling mould – any woollen or linen clothing, ⁴⁸any woven or knitted material of linen or wool, any leather or anything made of leather – ⁴⁹if the affected area in the fabric, the leather, the woven or knitted material, or any leather article, is greenish

or reddish, it is a defiling mould and must be shown to the priest. [50] The priest is to examine the affected area and isolate the article for seven days. [51] On the seventh day he is to examine it, and if the mould has spread in the fabric, the woven or knitted material, or the leather, whatever its use, it is a persistent defiling mould; the article is unclean. [52] He must burn the fabric, the woven or knitted material of wool or linen, or any leather article that has been spoiled, because the defiling mould is persistent; the article must be burned.

[53] 'But if, when the priest examines it, the mould has not spread in the fabric, the woven or knitted material, or the leather article, [54] he shall order that the spoiled article be washed. Then he is to isolate it for another seven days. [55] After the article has been washed, the priest is to examine it again, and if the mould has not changed its appearance, even though it has not spread, it is unclean. Burn it, no matter which side of the fabric has been spoiled. [56] If, when the priest examines it, the mould has faded after the article has been washed, he is to tear the spoiled part out of the fabric, the leather, or the woven or knitted material. [57] But if it reappears in the fabric, in the woven or knitted material, or in the leather article, it is a spreading mould; whatever has the mould must be burned. [58] Any fabric, woven or knitted material, or any leather article that has been washed and is rid of the mould, must be washed again. Then it will be clean.'

[59] These are the regulations concerning defiling moulds in woollen or linen clothing, woven or knitted material, or any leather article, for pronouncing them clean or unclean.

14 The LORD said to Moses, [2] 'These are the regulations for any diseased person at the time of their ceremonial cleansing, when they are brought to the priest: [3] the priest is to go outside the camp and examine them. If they have been healed of their defiling skin disease, [4] the priest shall order that two live clean birds and some cedar wood, scarlet yarn and hyssop be brought for the person to be cleansed. [5] Then the priest shall order that one of the birds be killed over fresh water in a clay pot. [6] He is then to take the live bird and dip it, together with the cedar wood, the scarlet yarn and the hyssop, into the blood of the bird that was killed over the fresh water. [7] Seven times he shall sprinkle the one to be cleansed of the defiling disease, and then pronounce them clean. After that, he is to release the live bird in the open fields.

[8] 'The person to be cleansed must wash their clothes, shave off all their hair and bathe with water; then they will be ceremonially clean. After this they may come into the camp, but they must stay outside their tent for seven days. [9] On the seventh day they must shave off all their hair; they must shave their head, their beard, their eyebrows and the rest of their hair. They must wash their clothes and bathe themselves with water, and they will be clean.

[10] 'On the eighth day they must bring two male lambs and one ewe lamb a year old, each without defect, along with three-tenths of an ephah of the finest flour mixed with olive oil for a grain offering, and one log of oil. [11] The priest who pronounces them clean shall present both the one to be cleansed and their offerings before the LORD at the entrance to the tent of meeting.

[12] 'Then the priest is to take one of the male lambs and offer it as a guilt offering, along with the log of oil; he shall wave them before the LORD as a wave offering. [13] He is to slaughter the lamb in the sanctuary area where the sin offering and the burnt offering are slaughtered. Like the sin offering, the guilt offering belongs to the priest; it is most holy. [14] The priest is to take some of the blood of the guilt offering and put it on the lobe of the right ear of the one to be cleansed, on the thumb of

their right hand and on the big toe of their right foot.

■ PSALM 27:1-6

¹The LORD is my light and my salvation –
  whom shall I fear?
The LORD is the stronghold of my life –
  of whom shall I be afraid?

²When the wicked advance against me
  to devour me,
it is my enemies and my foes
  who will stumble and fall.
³Though an army besiege me,
  my heart will not fear;
though war break out against me,
  even then I will be confident.

⁴One thing I ask from the LORD,
  this only do I seek:
that I may dwell in the house of the LORD
  all the days of my life,
to gaze on the beauty of the LORD
  and to seek him in his temple.
⁵For in the day of trouble
  he will keep me safe in his dwelling;
he will hide me in the shelter of his
    sacred tent
  and set me high upon a rock.

⁶Then my head will be exalted
  above the enemies who surround me;
at his sacred tent I will sacrifice with
    shouts of joy;
  I will sing and make music to the LORD.

■ PROVERBS 6:20-22

²⁰My son, keep your father's command
  and do not forsake your mother's
    teaching.
²¹Bind them always on your heart;
  fasten them round your neck.

²²When you walk, they will guide you;
  when you sleep, they will watch over
    you;
  when you awake, they will speak to you.

■ MARK 4:21-41

²¹He said to them, 'Do you bring in a lamp to put it under a bowl or a bed? Instead, don't you put it on its stand? ²²For whatever is hidden is meant to be disclosed, and whatever is concealed is meant to be brought out into the open. ²³If anyone has ears to hear, let them hear.'

²⁴'Consider carefully what you hear,' he continued. 'With the measure you use, it will be measured to you – and even more. ²⁵Whoever has will be given more; whoever does not have, even what they have will be taken from them.'

²⁶He also said, 'This is what the kingdom of God is like. A man scatters seed on the ground. ²⁷Night and day, whether he sleeps or gets up, the seed sprouts and grows, though he does not know how. ²⁸All by itself the soil produces corn – first the stalk, then the ear, then the full grain in the ear. ²⁹As soon as the corn is ripe, he puts the sickle to it, because the harvest has come.'

³⁰Again he said, 'What shall we say the kingdom of God is like, or what parable shall we use to describe it? ³¹It is like a mustard seed, which is the smallest of all seeds on earth. ³²Yet when planted, it grows and becomes the largest of all garden plants, with such big branches that the birds can perch in its shade.'

³³With many similar parables Jesus spoke the word to them, as much as they could understand. ³⁴He did not say anything to them without using a parable. But when he was alone with his own disciples, he explained everything.

³⁵That day when evening came, he said to his disciples, 'Let us go over to the other

side.' ³⁶ Leaving the crowd behind, they took him along, just as he was, in the boat. There were also other boats with him. ³⁷ A furious squall came up, and the waves broke over the boat, so that it was nearly swamped. ³⁸ Jesus was in the stern, sleeping on a cushion. The disciples woke him and said to him, 'Teacher, don't you care if we drown?'

³⁹ He got up, rebuked the wind and said to the waves, 'Quiet! Be still!' Then the wind died down and it was completely calm.

⁴⁰ He said to his disciples, 'Why are you so afraid? Do you still have no faith?'

⁴¹ They were terrified and asked each other, 'Who is this? Even the wind and the waves obey him!'

Homegrown Fears

'He said to his disciples, "Why are you so afraid? Do you still have no faith?"' **Mark 4:40**

Some social scientists maintain that there are no inherent fears except two; the rest are acquired. The two inherent fears, they say, are the fear of falling and the fear of loud noises.

I read of some psychologists who examined five hundred people and found that, between them, they had about seven thousand fears. The theory that we inherit just two fears, of course, is not a proven fact, but if that happens to be so, then those five hundred people were loading themselves down with hundreds of unnatural and paralysing fears!

Once when I was in India, I was told of a caste where the women on each of their birthdays add four rings of heavy brass - one on each ankle and one on each arm. By the time they are in middle age, they walk with great difficulty under this burden. But this is no more burdensome than weighting oneself down with paralysing fears: fear of failure, fear of rejection, fear of the future, fear of growing old, fear of what people might think, and so on. Many of our fears are homegrown - some come from past experiences. Parents who try to control their children by fear often succeed too well; their children grow up being controlled by the fears themselves.

A woman wrote to me and said, 'All my life I have been a victim of fear. My nightly prayer was: "Lord, thank You for not letting anything too bad happen to me today." You said if I turned to Christ, He would rid me of all fear. Well, I have - and He did.'

PRAYER

Father, we have filled Your world and our hearts with fear - needless, devastating fears. Help us, we pray, to find release from these fears, for they are not our real selves - they are an importation. In Jesus' name I pray. Amen.

FURTHER STUDY

Psa. 34:1-22; 23:4;
Prov. 9:10; 19:23
• What was David's testimony?
• How can we find freedom from our fears?

February 27

■ LEVITICUS 14:15–15:12

¹⁵ The priest shall then take some of the log of oil, pour it in the palm of his own left hand, ¹⁶ dip his right forefinger into the oil in his palm, and with his finger sprinkle some of it before the LORD seven times. ¹⁷ The priest is to put some of the oil remaining in his palm on the lobe of the right ear of the one to be cleansed, on the thumb of their right hand and on the big toe of their right foot, on top of the blood of the guilt offering. ¹⁸ The rest of the oil in his palm the priest shall put on the head of the one to be cleansed and make atonement for them before the LORD.

¹⁹ 'Then the priest is to sacrifice the sin offering and make atonement for the one to be cleansed from their uncleanness. After that, the priest shall slaughter the burnt offering ²⁰ and offer it on the altar, together with the grain offering, and make atonement for them, and they will be clean.

²¹ 'If, however, they are poor and cannot afford these, they must take one male lamb as a guilt offering to be waved to make atonement for them, together with a tenth of an ephah of the finest flour mixed with olive oil for a grain offering, a log of oil, ²² and two doves or two young pigeons, such as they can afford, one for a sin offering and the other for a burnt offering.

²³ 'On the eighth day they must bring them for their cleansing to the priest at the entrance to the tent of meeting, before the LORD. ²⁴ The priest is to take the lamb for the guilt offering, together with the log of oil, and wave them before the LORD as a wave offering. ²⁵ He shall slaughter the lamb for the guilt offering and take some of its blood and put it on the lobe of the right ear of the one to be cleansed, on the thumb of their right hand and on the big toe of their right foot. ²⁶ The priest is to pour some of the oil into the palm of his own left hand, ²⁷ and with his right forefinger sprinkle some of the oil from his palm seven times before the LORD. ²⁸ Some of the oil in his palm he is to put on the same places he put the blood of the guilt offering – on the lobe of the right ear of the one to be cleansed, on the thumb of their right hand and on the big toe of their right foot. ²⁹ The rest of the oil in his palm the priest shall put on the head of the one to be cleansed, to make atonement for them before the LORD. ³⁰ Then he shall sacrifice the doves or the young pigeons, such as the person can afford, ³¹ one as a sin offering and the other as a burnt offering, together with the grain offering. In this way the priest will make atonement before the LORD on behalf of the one to be cleansed.'

³² These are the regulations for anyone who has a defiling skin disease and who cannot afford the usual offerings for their cleansing.

³³ The LORD said to Moses and Aaron, ³⁴ 'When you enter the land of Canaan, which I am giving you as your possession, and I put a spreading mould in a house in that land, ³⁵ the owner of the house must go and tell the priest, "I have seen something that looks like a defiling mould in my house." ³⁶ The priest is to order the house to be emptied before he goes in to examine the mould, so that nothing in the house will be pronounced unclean. After this the priest is to go in and inspect the house. ³⁷ He is to examine the mould on the walls, and if it has greenish or reddish depressions that appear to be deeper than

the surface of the wall, [38] the priest shall go out of the doorway of the house and close it up for seven days. [39] On the seventh day the priest shall return to inspect the house. If the mould has spread on the walls, [40] he is to order that the contaminated stones be torn out and thrown into an unclean place outside the town. [41] He must have all the inside walls of the house scraped and the material that is scraped off dumped into an unclean place outside the town. [42] Then they are to take other stones to replace these and take new clay and plaster the house.

[43] 'If the defiling mould reappears in the house after the stones have been torn out and the house scraped and plastered, [44] the priest is to go and examine it and, if the mould has spread in the house, it is a persistent defiling mould; the house is unclean. [45] It must be torn down – its stones, timbers and all the plaster – and taken out of the town to an unclean place.

[46] 'Anyone who goes into the house while it is closed up will be unclean till evening. [47] Anyone who sleeps or eats in the house must wash their clothes.

[48] 'But if the priest comes to examine it and the mould has not spread after the house has been plastered, he shall pronounce the house clean, because the defiling mould is gone. [49] To purify the house he is to take two birds and some cedar wood, scarlet yarn and hyssop. [50] He shall kill one of the birds over fresh water in a clay pot. [51] Then he is to take the cedar wood, the hyssop, the scarlet yarn and the live bird, dip them into the blood of the dead bird and the fresh water, and sprinkle the house seven times. [52] He shall purify the house with the bird's blood, the fresh water, the live bird, the cedar wood, the hyssop and the scarlet yarn. [53] Then he is to release the live bird in the open fields outside the town. In this way he will make atonement for the house, and it will be clean.'

[54] These are the regulations for any defiling skin disease, for a sore, [55] for defiling moulds in fabric or in a house, [56] and for a swelling, a rash or a shiny spot, [57] to determine when something is clean or unclean.

These are the regulations for defiling skin diseases and defiling moulds.

15 The LORD said to Moses and Aaron, [2] 'Speak to the Israelites and say to them: "When any man has an unusual bodily discharge, such a discharge is unclean. [3] Whether it continues flowing from his body or is blocked, it will make him unclean. This is how his discharge will bring about uncleanness:

[4] "Any bed the man with a discharge lies on will be unclean, and anything he sits on will be unclean. [5] Anyone who touches his bed must wash their clothes and bathe with water, and they will be unclean till evening. [6] Whoever sits on anything that the man with a discharge sat on must wash their clothes and bathe with water, and they will be unclean till evening.

[7] "Whoever touches the man who has a discharge must wash their clothes and bathe with water, and they will be unclean till evening.

[8] "If the man with the discharge spits on anyone who is clean, they must wash their clothes and bathe with water, and they will be unclean till evening.

[9] "Everything the man sits on when riding will be unclean, [10] and whoever touches any of the things that were under him will be unclean till evening; whoever picks up those things must wash their clothes and bathe with water, and they will be unclean till evening.

[11] "Anyone the man with a discharge touches without rinsing his hands with water must wash their clothes and bathe with water, and they will be unclean till evening.

[12] "A clay pot that the man touches must be broken, and any wooden article is to be rinsed with water.

■ PSALM 27:7-14

⁷ Hear my voice when I call, LORD;
  be merciful to me and answer me.
⁸ My heart says of you, 'Seek his face!'
  Your face, LORD, I will seek.
⁹ Do not hide your face from me,
  do not turn your servant away in anger;
  you have been my helper.
Do not reject me or forsake me,
  God my Saviour.
¹⁰ Though my father and mother forsake me,
  the LORD will receive me.
¹¹ Teach me your way, LORD;
  lead me in a straight path
  because of my oppressors.
¹² Do not hand me over to the desire of my
    foes,
  for false witnesses rise up against me,
  spouting malicious accusations.
¹³ I remain confident of this:
  I will see the goodness of the LORD
  in the land of the living.
¹⁴ Wait for the LORD;
  be strong and take heart
  and wait for the LORD.

■ PROVERBS 6:23-26

²³ For this command is a lamp,
  this teaching is a light,
  and correction and instruction
  are the way to life,
²⁴ keeping you from your neighbour's wife,
  from the smooth talk of a wayward
    woman.

²⁵ Do not lust in your heart after her beauty
  or let her captivate you with her eyes.

²⁶ For a prostitute can be had for a loaf of
    bread,
  but another man's wife preys on your
    very life.

■ MARK 5:1-20

5 They went across the lake to the region of the Gerasenes. ²When Jesus got out of the boat, a man with an impure spirit came from the tombs to meet him. ³This man lived in the tombs, and no one could bind him anymore, not even with a chain. ⁴For he had often been chained hand and foot, but he tore the chains apart and broke the irons on his feet. No one was strong enough to subdue him. ⁵Night and day among the tombs and in the hills he would cry out and cut himself with stones.

⁶When he saw Jesus from a distance, he ran and fell on his knees in front of him. ⁷He shouted at the top of his voice, 'What do you want with me, Jesus, Son of the Most High God? In God's name don't torture me!' ⁸For Jesus had said to him, 'Come out of this man, you impure spirit!'

⁹Then Jesus asked him, 'What is your name?'

'My name is Legion,' he replied, 'for we are many.' ¹⁰And he begged Jesus again and again not to send them out of the area.

¹¹A large herd of pigs was feeding on the nearby hillside. ¹²The demons begged Jesus, 'Send us among the pigs; allow us to go into them.' ¹³He gave them permission, and the impure spirits came out and went into the pigs. The herd, about two thousand in number, rushed down the steep bank into the lake and were drowned.

¹⁴Those tending the pigs ran off and reported this in the town and countryside, and the people went out to see what had happened. ¹⁵When they came to Jesus, they saw the man who had been possessed by the legion of demons, sitting there, dressed and in his right mind; and they were afraid. ¹⁶Those who had seen it told the people what had happened to the demon-possessed man – and told about the pigs as well. ¹⁷Then the people began to plead with Jesus to leave their region.

¹⁸As Jesus was getting into the boat, the man who had been demon-possessed begged to go with him. ¹⁹Jesus did not let him, but said, 'Go home to your own people and tell them how much the Lord has done for you, and how he has had mercy on you.' ²⁰So the man went away and began to tell in the Decapolis how much Jesus had done for him. And all the people were amazed.

'Anyone Saved Lately?'

'Jesus ... said, "Go home to your own people and tell them how much the Lord has done for you, and how he has had mercy on you."' **Mark 5:19**

Christianity is not merely a conception but a contagion. And when the contagion is lost, the possibility is that the conception may also be lost.

An American pastor, an old friend of mine, says, 'Christianity is catching, and if people are not catching it from us, then perhaps it's because we do not have a sufficiently virulent case of it.' Once when he was in England, we visited Westminster Abbey. He looked around and asked in loud tones, 'Has anyone been saved here lately?' I said I was not sure, to which he replied, 'If a church is not evangelistic, then it is not evangelical.' He was right, but that didn't stop me from getting him outside as quickly as possible!

'Nothing is really ours,' said C. S. Lewis, 'until we share it.' The moment someone else shares our experience of Christ, then the faith means something more to us. The Amplified Bible translates Philippians 1:5 thus: 'I thank my God for your fellowship – your sympathetic cooperation and contributions and partnership – in advancing the good news, the Gospel, from the first day you heard it until now.' From the very first day they stepped into the kingdom of God, they began to contribute to it – to spread it. It was not something they learned; it was instinctive. It was as natural as a baby's cry at birth. Sharing Christ with others is not something we can take or leave; it is something which, if we don't take, we can easily lose. For the expression of the faith is the essence of the faith.

PRAYER

O Father, help us to be like the converts in the church at Philippi who, from the moment they saw You, wanted to share You. We ask in Christ's precious and powerful name. Amen.

FURTHER STUDY

Mark 5:15-20; Acts 1:8;
2 Tim. 1:8
• What did Jesus tell the man to do?
• What was Paul's admonition to Timothy?

February 28

■ LEVITICUS 15:13–16:34

¹³ ' "When a man is cleansed from his discharge, he is to count seven days for his ceremonial cleansing; he must wash his clothes and bathe himself with fresh water, and he will be clean. ¹⁴ On the eighth day he must take two doves or two young pigeons and come before the LORD to the entrance to the tent of meeting and give them to the priest. ¹⁵ The priest is to sacrifice them, the one for a sin offering and the other for a burnt offering. In this way he will make atonement before the LORD for the man because of his discharge.

¹⁶ ' "When a man has an emission of semen, he must bathe his whole body with water, and he will be unclean till evening. ¹⁷ Any clothing or leather that has semen on it must be washed with water, and it will be unclean till evening. ¹⁸ When a man has sexual relations with a woman and there is an emission of semen, both of them must bathe with water, and they will be unclean till evening.

¹⁹ ' "When a woman has her regular flow of blood, the impurity of her monthly period will last seven days, and anyone who touches her will be unclean till evening.

²⁰ ' "Anything she lies on during her period will be unclean, and anything she sits on will be unclean. ²¹ Anyone who touches her bed will be unclean; they must wash their clothes and bathe with water, and they will be unclean till evening. ²² Anyone who touches anything she sits on will be unclean; they must wash their clothes and bathe with water, and they will be unclean till evening. ²³ Whether it is the bed or anything she was sitting on, when anyone touches it, they will be unclean till evening.

²⁴ ' "If a man has sexual relations with her and her monthly flow touches him, he will be unclean for seven days; any bed he lies on will be unclean.

²⁵ ' "When a woman has a discharge of blood for many days at a time other than her monthly period or has a discharge that continues beyond her period, she will be unclean as long as she has the discharge, just as in the days of her period. ²⁶ Any bed she lies on while her discharge continues will be unclean, as is her bed during her monthly period, and anything she sits on will be unclean, as during her period. ²⁷ Anyone who touches them will be unclean; they must wash their clothes and bathe with water, and they will be unclean till evening.

²⁸ ' "When she is cleansed from her discharge, she must count seven days, and after that she will be ceremonially clean. ²⁹ On the eighth day she must take two doves or two young pigeons and bring them to the priest at the entrance to the tent of meeting. ³⁰ The priest is to sacrifice one for a sin offering and the other for a burnt offering. In this way he will make atonement for her before the LORD for the uncleanness of her discharge.

³¹ ' "You must keep the Israelites separate from things that make them unclean, so they will not die in their uncleanness for defiling my dwelling-place, which is among them." '

³² These are the regulations for a man with a discharge, for anyone made unclean by an emission of semen, ³³ for a woman in her monthly period, for a man or a woman with a discharge, and for a man who has sexual relations with a woman who is ceremonially unclean.

16 The LORD spoke to Moses after the death of the two sons of Aaron who died when they approached the LORD. ² The LORD said to Moses: 'Tell your brother Aaron that he is not to come whenever he chooses into the Most Holy Place behind the curtain in front of the atonement cover on the ark, or else he will die. For I will appear in the cloud over the atonement cover.

³ 'This is how Aaron is to enter the Most Holy Place: He must first bring a young bull for a sin offering and a ram for a burnt offering. ⁴ He is to put on the sacred linen tunic, with linen undergarments next to his body; he is to tie the linen sash round him and put on the linen turban. These are sacred garments; so he must bathe himself with water before he puts them on. ⁵ From the Israelite community he is to take two male goats for a sin offering and a ram for a burnt offering.

⁶ 'Aaron is to offer the bull for his own sin offering to make atonement for himself and his household. ⁷ Then he is to take the two goats and present them before the LORD at the entrance to the tent of meeting. ⁸ He is to cast lots for the two goats – one lot for the LORD and the other for the scapegoat. ⁹ Aaron shall bring the goat whose lot falls to the LORD and sacrifice it for a sin offering. ¹⁰ But the goat chosen by lot as the scapegoat shall be presented alive before the LORD to be used for making atonement by sending it into the wilderness as a scapegoat.

¹¹ 'Aaron shall bring the bull for his own sin offering to make atonement for himself and his household, and he is to slaughter the bull for his own sin offering. ¹² He is to take a censer full of burning coals from the altar before the LORD and two handfuls of finely ground fragrant incense and take them behind the curtain. ¹³ He is to put the incense on the fire before the LORD, and the smoke of the incense will conceal the atonement cover above the tablets of the covenant law, so that he will not die. ¹⁴ He is to take some of the bull's blood and with his finger sprinkle it on the front of the atonement cover; then he shall sprinkle some of it with his finger seven times before the atonement cover.

¹⁵ 'He shall then slaughter the goat for the sin offering for the people and take its blood behind the curtain and do with it as he did with the bull's blood: he shall sprinkle it on the atonement cover and in front of it. ¹⁶ In this way he will make atonement for the Most Holy Place because of the uncleanness and rebellion of the Israelites, whatever their sins have been. He is to do the same for the tent of meeting, which is among them in the midst of their uncleanness. ¹⁷ No one is to be in the tent of meeting from the time Aaron goes in to make atonement in the Most Holy Place until he comes out, having made atonement for himself, his household and the whole community of Israel.

¹⁸ 'Then he shall come out to the altar that is before the LORD and make atonement for it. He shall take some of the bull's blood and some of the goat's blood and put it on all the horns of the altar. ¹⁹ He shall sprinkle some of the blood on it with his finger seven times to cleanse it and consecrate it from the uncleanness of the Israelites.

²⁰ 'When Aaron has finished making atonement for the Most Holy Place, the tent of meeting and the altar, he shall bring forward the live goat. ²¹ He is to lay both hands on the head of the live goat and confess over it all the wickedness and rebellion of the Israelites – all their sins – and put them on the goat's head. He shall send the goat away into the wilderness in the care of someone appointed for the task. ²² The goat will carry on itself all their sins to a remote place; and the man shall release it in the wilderness.

²³ 'Then Aaron is to go into the tent of meeting and take off the linen garments he put on before he entered the Most Holy Place, and he is to leave them there. ²⁴ He shall bathe himself with water in the sanctuary area and put on his ordinary garments. Then he shall come out and sacrifice the

burnt offering for himself and the burnt offering for the people, to make atonement for himself and for the people. ²⁵He shall also burn the fat of the sin offering on the altar.

²⁶'The man who releases the goat as a scapegoat must wash his clothes and bathe himself with water; afterwards he may come into the camp. ²⁷The bull and the goat for the sin offerings, whose blood was brought into the Most Holy Place to make atonement, must be taken outside the camp; their hides, flesh and intestines are to be burned. ²⁸The man who burns them must wash his clothes and bathe himself with water; afterwards he may come into the camp.

²⁹'This is to be a lasting ordinance for you: on the tenth day of the seventh month you must deny yourselves and not do any work – whether native-born or a foreigner residing among you – ³⁰because on this day atonement will be made for you, to cleanse you. Then, before the LORD, you will be clean from all your sins. ³¹It is a day of sabbath rest, and you must deny yourselves; it is a lasting ordinance. ³²The priest who is anointed and ordained to succeed his father as high priest is to make atonement. He is to put on the sacred linen garments ³³and make atonement for the Most Holy Place, for the tent of meeting and the altar, and for the priests and all the members of the community.

³⁴'This is to be a lasting ordinance for you: atonement is to be made once a year for all the sins of the Israelites.'

And it was done, as the LORD commanded Moses.

■ PSALM 28:1-5

¹To you, LORD, I call;
   you are my Rock,
   do not turn a deaf ear to me.
For if you remain silent,
   I shall be like those who go down
      to the pit.

²Hear my cry for mercy
   as I call to you for help,
   as I lift up my hands
      towards your Most Holy Place.

³Do not drag me away with the wicked,
   with those who do evil,
who speak cordially with their
      neighbours
   but harbour malice in their hearts.
⁴Repay them for their deeds
   and for their evil work;
repay them for what their hands have
      done
   and bring back on them what they
      deserve.

⁵Because they have no regard for the
      deeds of the LORD
   and what his hands have done,
he will tear them down
   and never build them up again.

■ PROVERBS 6:27-29

²⁷Can a man scoop fire into his lap
   without his clothes being burned?
²⁸Can a man walk on hot coals
   without his feet being scorched?
²⁹So is he who sleeps with another man's
      wife;
   no one who touches her will go
      unpunished.

■ MARK 5:21-43

²¹When Jesus had again crossed over by boat to the other side of the lake, a large crowd gathered round him while he was by the lake. ²²Then one of the synagogue leaders, named Jairus, came, and when he saw Jesus, he fell at his feet. ²³He pleaded earnestly with him, 'My little daughter is dying. Please come and put your hands

on her so that she will be healed and live.' [24] So Jesus went with him.

A large crowd followed and pressed round him. [25] And a woman was there who had been subject to bleeding for twelve years. [26] She had suffered a great deal under the care of many doctors and had spent all she had, yet instead of getting better she grew worse. [27] When she heard about Jesus, she came up behind him in the crowd and touched his cloak, [28] because she thought, 'If I just touch his clothes, I will be healed.' [29] Immediately her bleeding stopped and she felt in her body that she was freed from her suffering.

[30] At once Jesus realised that power had gone out from him. He turned round in the crowd and asked, 'Who touched my clothes?'

[31] 'You see the people crowding against you,' his disciples answered, 'and yet you can ask, "Who touched me?" '

[32] But Jesus kept looking around to see who had done it. [33] Then the woman, knowing what had happened to her, came and fell at his feet and, trembling with fear, told him the whole truth. [34] He said to her, 'Daughter, your faith has healed you. Go in peace and be freed from your suffering.'

[35] While Jesus was still speaking, some people came from the house of Jairus, the synagogue leader. 'Your daughter is dead,' they said. 'Why bother the teacher anymore?'

[36] Overhearing what they said, Jesus told him, 'Don't be afraid; just believe.'

[37] He did not let anyone follow him except Peter, James and John the brother of James. [38] When they came to the home of the synagogue leader, Jesus saw a commotion, with people crying and wailing loudly. [39] He went in and said to them, 'Why all this commotion and wailing? The child is not dead but asleep.' [40] But they laughed at him.

After he put them all out, he took the child's father and mother and the disciples who were with him, and went in where the child was. [41] He took her by the hand and said to her, *'Talitha koum!'* (which means 'Little girl, I say to you, get up!'). [42] Immediately the girl stood up and began to walk around (she was twelve years old). At this they were completely astonished. [43] He gave strict orders not to let anyone know about this, and told them to give her something to eat.

Love Is Not Blind

'... I call to you for help ...' **Psalm 28:2**

If we draw back from facing and feeling our disappointments, then a part of us will experience spiritual deprivation. The more deeply we enter into our disappointment, then the more thoroughly we will see how committed we are to self-protection and turn from it in repentance to a more complete dependence on our Lord Jesus Christ.

Where have you been disappointed the most, I wonder? Many people to whom I address that question tell me: 'My parents.' It's surprising, though, how so many will not admit to being hurt or disappointed by their parents for fear they are failing to honour them or are being disloyal to them. Listen to what one writer has to say about this: 'When someone appreciates his parents only because he overlooks the pain they caused him, his appreciation is not only superficial, it is self-protective. Love is never blind to others' faults. It sees them clearly and is not threatened. It admits disappointment but forgives and continues to be warmly involved.'

Sadly, for far too many of us, love is not the bottom line – self-protection is. When we can look into the face of every disappointment and be willing to feel the pain it brings, there is no more powerful way of motivating our hearts to turn in full dependence towards the Lord. If we are unwilling to do this, then we might cling more to our own ways of handling disappointments than we do to His. And if we do, then in no way can we climb to higher and more distant spiritual peaks.

PRAYER

Father, the more I become aware of what is involved in climbing higher with You, the easier it is to become discouraged. I am a dull, blundering disciple. Help me, dear Lord. Your grace works miracles. Work one in me today. In Jesus' name. Amen.

FURTHER STUDY

2 Cor. 12:6-10; Phil. 4:11; Eph. 3:16
• What could have been a great disappointment to Paul?
• What attitude did he take instead?

March 1

■ LEVITICUS 17:1–19:10

17 The Lord said to Moses, ²'Speak to Aaron and his sons and to all the Israelites and say to them: "This is what the Lord has commanded: ³any Israelite who sacrifices an ox, a lamb or a goat in the camp or outside it ⁴instead of bringing it to the entrance to the tent of meeting to present it as an offering to the Lord in front of the tabernacle of the Lord – that person shall be considered guilty of bloodshed; they have shed blood and must be cut off from their people. ⁵This is so that the Israelites will bring to the Lord the sacrifices they are now making in the open fields. They must bring them to the priest, that is, to the Lord, at the entrance to the tent of meeting and sacrifice them as fellowship offerings. ⁶The priest is to splash the blood against the altar of the Lord at the entrance to the tent of meeting and burn the fat as an aroma pleasing to

the Lord. ⁷They must no longer offer any of their sacrifices to the goat idols to whom they prostitute themselves. This is to be a lasting ordinance for them and for the generations to come."

⁸'Say to them: "Any Israelite or any foreigner residing among them who offers a burnt offering or sacrifice ⁹and does not bring it to the entrance to the tent of meeting to sacrifice it to the Lord must be cut off from the people of Israel.

¹⁰'"I will set my face against any Israelite or any foreigner residing among them who eats blood, and I will cut them off from the people. ¹¹For the life of a creature is in the blood, and I have given it to you to make atonement for yourselves on the altar; it is the blood that makes atonement for one's life. ¹²Therefore I say to the Israelites, 'None of you may eat blood, nor may any foreigner residing among you eat blood.'

¹³'"Any Israelite or any foreigner residing

among you who hunts any animal or bird that may be eaten must drain out the blood and cover it with earth, ¹⁴because the life of every creature is its blood. That is why I have said to the Israelites, 'You must not eat the blood of any creature, because the life of every creature is its blood; anyone who eats it must be cut off.'

¹⁵'"Anyone, whether native-born or foreigner, who eats anything found dead or torn by wild animals must wash their clothes and bathe with water, and they will be ceremonially unclean till evening; then they will be clean. ¹⁶But if they do not wash their clothes and bathe themselves, they will be held responsible."'

18 The LORD said to Moses, ²'Speak to the Israelites and say to them: "I am the LORD your God. ³You must not do as they do in Egypt, where you used to live, and you must not do as they do in the land of Canaan, where I am bringing you. Do not follow their practices. ⁴You must obey my laws and be careful to follow my decrees. I am the LORD your God. ⁵Keep my decrees and laws, for the person who obeys them will live by them. I am the LORD.

⁶'"No one is to approach any close relative to have sexual relations. I am the LORD.

⁷'"Do not dishonour your father by having sexual relations with your mother. She is your mother; do not have relations with her.

⁸'"Do not have sexual relations with your father's wife; that would dishonour your father.

⁹'"Do not have sexual relations with your sister, either your father's daughter or your mother's daughter, whether she was born in the same home or elsewhere.

¹⁰'"Do not have sexual relations with your son's daughter or your daughter's daughter; that would dishonour you.

¹¹'"Do not have sexual relations with the daughter of your father's wife, born to your father; she is your sister.

¹²'"Do not have sexual relations with your father's sister; she is your father's close relative.

¹³'"Do not have sexual relations with your mother's sister, because she is your mother's close relative.

¹⁴'"Do not dishonour your father's brother by approaching his wife to have sexual relations; she is your aunt.

¹⁵'"Do not have sexual relations with your daughter-in-law. She is your son's wife; do not have relations with her.

¹⁶'"Do not have sexual relations with your brother's wife; that would dishonour your brother.

¹⁷'"Do not have sexual relations with both a woman and her daughter. Do not have sexual relations with either her son's daughter or her daughter's daughter; they are her close relatives. That is wickedness.

¹⁸'"Do not take your wife's sister as a rival wife and have sexual relations with her while your wife is living.

¹⁹'"Do not approach a woman to have sexual relations during the uncleanness of her monthly period.

²⁰'"Do not have sexual relations with your neighbour's wife and defile yourself with her.

²¹'"Do not give any of your children to be sacrificed to Molek, for you must not profane the name of your God. I am the LORD.

²²'"Do not have sexual relations with a man as one does with a woman; that is detestable.

²³'"Do not have sexual relations with an animal and defile yourself with it. A woman must not present herself to an animal to have sexual relations with it; that is a perversion.

²⁴'"Do not defile yourselves in any of these ways, because this is how the nations that I am going to drive out before you became defiled. ²⁵Even the land was defiled; so I punished it for its sin, and the land vomited out its inhabitants. ²⁶But you must

keep my decrees and my laws. The native-born and the foreigners residing among you must not do any of these detestable things, ²⁷ for all these things were done by the people who lived in the land before you, and the land became defiled. ²⁸ And if you defile the land, it will vomit you out as it vomited out the nations that were before you.

²⁹ ' "Everyone who does any of these detestable things – such persons must be cut off from their people. ³⁰ Keep my requirements and do not follow any of the detestable customs that were practised before you came and do not defile yourselves with them. I am the LORD your God." '

19 The LORD said to Moses, ²'Speak to the entire assembly of Israel and say to them: "Be holy because I, the LORD your God, am holy.

³ ' "Each of you must respect your mother and father, and you must observe my Sabbaths. I am the LORD your God.

⁴ ' "Do not turn to idols or make metal gods for yourselves. I am the LORD your God.

⁵ ' "When you sacrifice a fellowship offering to the LORD, sacrifice it in such a way that it will be accepted on your behalf. ⁶ It shall be eaten on the day you sacrifice it or on the next day; anything left over until the third day must be burned. ⁷ If any of it is eaten on the third day, it is impure and will not be accepted. ⁸ Whoever eats it will be held responsible because they have desecrated what is holy to the LORD; they must be cut off from their people.

⁹ ' "When you reap the harvest of your land, do not reap to the very edges of your field or gather the gleanings of your harvest. ¹⁰ Do not go over your vineyard a second time or pick up the grapes that have fallen. Leave them for the poor and the foreigner. I am the LORD your God.

■ PSALM 28:6-9

⁶ Praise be to the LORD,
    for he has heard my cry for mercy.
⁷ The LORD is my strength and my shield;
    my heart trusts in him, and he helps
    me.
My heart leaps for joy,
    and with my song I praise him.

⁸ The LORD is the strength of his people,
    a fortress of salvation for his anointed
    one.
⁹ Save your people and bless your
    inheritance;
    be their shepherd and carry them for
    ever.

■ PROVERBS 6:30-31

³⁰ People do not despise a thief if he steals
    to satisfy his hunger when he is
    starving.
³¹ Yet if he is caught, he must pay sevenfold,
    though it costs him all the wealth of
    his house.

■ MARK 6:1-20

6 Jesus left there and went to his home town, accompanied by his disciples. ² When the Sabbath came, he began to teach in the synagogue, and many who heard him were amazed.

'Where did this man get these things?' they asked. 'What's this wisdom that has been given him? What are these remarkable miracles he is performing? ³ Isn't this the carpenter? Isn't this Mary's son and the brother of James, Joseph, Judas and Simon? Aren't his sisters here with us?' And they took offence at him.

⁴ Jesus said to them, 'A prophet is not without honour except in his own town,

among his relatives and in his own home.'
[5] He could not do any miracles there, except lay his hands on a few people who were ill and heal them. [6] He was amazed at their lack of faith.

Then Jesus went around teaching from village to village. [7] Calling the Twelve to him, he began to send them out two by two and gave them authority over impure spirits.

[8] These were his instructions: 'Take nothing for the journey except a staff – no bread, no bag, no money in your belts. [9] Wear sandals but not an extra shirt. [10] Whenever you enter a house, stay there until you leave that town. [11] And if any place will not welcome you or listen to you, leave that place and shake the dust off your feet as a testimony against them.'

[12] They went out and preached that people should repent. [13] They drove out many demons and anointed with oil many people who were ill and healed them.

[14] King Herod heard about this, for Jesus' name had become well known. Some were saying, 'John the Baptist has been raised from the dead, and that is why miraculous powers are at work in him.'

[15] Others said, 'He is Elijah.'

And still others claimed, 'He is a prophet, like one of the prophets of long ago.'

[16] But when Herod heard this, he said, 'John, whom I beheaded, has been raised from the dead!'

[17] For Herod himself had given orders to have John arrested, and he had him bound and put in prison. He did this because of Herodias, his brother Philip's wife, whom he had married. [18] For John had been saying to Herod, 'It is not lawful for you to have your brother's wife.' [19] So Herodias nursed a grudge against John and wanted to kill him. But she was not able to, [20] because Herod feared John and protected him, knowing him to be a righteous and holy man. When Herod heard John, he was greatly puzzled; yet he liked to listen to him.

'Having' and 'Taking'

'The LORD is my strength and my shield; my heart trusts in him, and he helps me.' **Psalm 28:7**

The first three pieces of the Christian armour should be worn at all times, while the last three should be taken up and used when and where it is necessary. Evidence for this can be seen when we look at Paul's use of the words 'having' and 'taking.'

Listen to the passage: 'Stand firm then, with the belt of truth buckled round your waist, with the breastplate of righteousness in place, and with your feet fitted with the readiness that comes from the gospel of peace' (Eph. 6:14-15). Then, in the second section, the word changes: 'In addition ... take up the shield of faith ... Take the helmet of salvation and the sword of the Spirit ...' (Eph. 6:16-17). The difference between the first and last three pieces of equipment is the difference between 'having' and 'taking.'

The 'shield' referred to in Ephesians 6 was extremely large, about four feet long and about two and a half feet wide, designed to give as much protection as possible to the front of the body. More important, the front surface was covered with a sheet of fireproof metal so that the fiery darts of the enemy would have little or no effect. Clearly Paul thought that, in addition to the first three items, a further defence was needed to protect us from the devil's preliminary attacks.

When we consider the lengths to which God has gone in order to give us the protection we need against satanic attack, one wonders why we ever allow ourselves to be badgered and defeated by the devil.

PRAYER

O Father, once again I want to record my gratitude for the way in which You have provided for my defence against satanic attack. Help me to see, however, that it will do me no good just to appreciate it; I must use it. In Christ's name I will use it. Amen.

FURTHER STUDY

Heb. 11:17-40; Rom. 10:17; Phil. 3:8-9

• How does faith come?
• List some of the things accomplished through faith.

March 2

▬ LEVITICUS 19:11–20:27

11 ' "Do not steal.

' "Do not lie.

' "Do not deceive one another.

12 ' "Do not swear falsely by my name and so profane the name of your God. I am the LORD.

13 ' "Do not defraud or rob your neighbour.

' "Do not hold back the wages of a hired worker overnight.

14 ' "Do not curse the deaf or put a stumbling-block in front of the blind, but fear your God. I am the LORD.

15 ' "Do not pervert justice; do not show partiality to the poor or favouritism to the great, but judge your neighbour fairly.

16 ' "Do not go about spreading slander among your people.

' "Do not do anything that endangers your neighbour's life. I am the LORD.

17 ' "Do not hate a fellow Israelite in your heart. Rebuke your neighbour frankly so

that you will not share in their guilt.

18 ' "Do not seek revenge or bear a grudge against anyone among your people, but love your neighbour as yourself. I am the LORD.

19 ' "Keep my decrees.

' "Do not mate different kinds of animals.

' "Do not plant your field with two kinds of seed.

' "Do not wear clothing woven of two kinds of material.

20 ' "If a man sleeps with a female slave who is promised to another man but who has not been ransomed or given her freedom, there must be due punishment. Yet they are not to be put to death, because she had not been freed. 21 The man, however, must bring a ram to the entrance to the tent of meeting for a guilt offering to the LORD. 22 With the ram of the guilt offering the priest is to make atonement for him before the LORD for the sin he has committed, and his sin will be forgiven.

23 ' "When you enter the land and plant

any kind of fruit tree, regard its fruit as forbidden. For three years you are to consider it forbidden; it must not be eaten. ²⁴In the fourth year all its fruit will be holy, an offering of praise to the LORD. ²⁵But in the fifth year you may eat its fruit. In this way your harvest will be increased. I am the LORD your God.

²⁶ "Do not eat any meat with the blood still in it.

'"Do not practise divination or seek omens.

²⁷ '"Do not cut the hair at the sides of your head or clip off the edges of your beard.

²⁸ '"Do not cut your bodies for the dead or put tattoo marks on yourselves. I am the LORD.

²⁹ '"Do not degrade your daughter by making her a prostitute, or the land will turn to prostitution and be filled with wickedness.

³⁰ '"Observe my Sabbaths and have reverence for my sanctuary. I am the LORD.

³¹ '"Do not turn to mediums or seek out spiritists, for you will be defiled by them. I am the LORD your God.

³² '"Stand up in the presence of the aged, show respect for the elderly and revere your God. I am the LORD.

³³ '"When a foreigner resides among you in your land, do not ill-treat them. ³⁴The foreigner residing among you must be treated as your native-born. Love them as yourself, for you were foreigners in Egypt. I am the LORD your God.

³⁵ '"Do not use dishonest standards when measuring length, weight or quantity. ³⁶Use honest scales and honest weights, an honest ephah and an honest hin. I am the LORD your God, who brought you out of Egypt.

³⁷ '"Keep all my decrees and all my laws and follow them. I am the LORD.'"

20 The LORD said to Moses, ²'Say to the Israelites: "Any Israelite or any foreigner residing in Israel who sacrifices any of his children to Molek is to be put to death. The members of the community are to stone him. ³I myself will set my face against him and will cut him off from his people; for by sacrificing his children to Molek, he has defiled my sanctuary and profaned my holy name. ⁴If the members of the community close their eyes when that man sacrifices one of his children to Molek and if they fail to put him to death, ⁵I myself will set my face against him and his family and will cut them off from their people together with all who follow him in prostituting themselves to Molek.

⁶ "I will set my face against anyone who turns to mediums and spiritists to prostitute themselves by following them, and I will cut them off from their people.

⁷ "Consecrate yourselves and be holy, because I am the LORD your God. ⁸Keep my decrees and follow them. I am the LORD, who makes you holy.

⁹ "Anyone who curses their father or mother is to be put to death. Because they have cursed their father or mother, their blood will be on their own head.

¹⁰ "If a man commits adultery with another man's wife – with the wife of his neighbour – both the adulterer and the adulteress are to be put to death.

¹¹ "If a man has sexual relations with his father's wife, he has dishonoured his father. Both the man and the woman are to be put to death; their blood will be on their own heads.

¹² "If a man has sexual relations with his daughter-in-law, both of them are to be put to death. What they have done is a perversion; their blood will be on their own heads.

¹³ "If a man has sexual relations with a man as one does with a woman, both of them have done what is detestable. They are to be put to death; their blood will be on their own heads.

¹⁴ "If a man marries both a woman and her mother, it is wicked. Both he and

they must be burned in the fire, so that no wickedness will be among you.

¹⁵ "If a man has sexual relations with an animal, he is to be put to death, and you must kill the animal.

¹⁶ "If a woman approaches an animal to have sexual relations with it, kill both the woman and the animal. They are to be put to death; their blood will be on their own heads.

¹⁷ "If a man marries his sister, the daughter of either his father or his mother, and they have sexual relations, it is a disgrace. They are to be publicly removed from their people. He has dishonoured his sister and will be held responsible.

¹⁸ "If a man has sexual relations with a woman during her monthly period, he has exposed the source of her flow, and she has also uncovered it. Both of them are to be cut off from their people.

¹⁹ "Do not have sexual relations with the sister of either your mother or your father, for that would dishonour a close relative; both of you would be held responsible.

²⁰ "If a man has sexual relations with his aunt, he has dishonoured his uncle. They will be held responsible; they will die childless.

²¹ "If a man marries his brother's wife, it is an act of impurity; he has dishonoured his brother. They will be childless.

²² "Keep all my decrees and laws and follow them, so that the land where I am bringing you to live may not vomit you out. ²³ You must not live according to the customs of the nations I am going to drive out before you. Because they did all these things, I abhorred them. ²⁴ But I said to you, 'You will possess their land; I will give it to you as an inheritance, a land flowing with milk and honey.' I am the LORD your God, who has set you apart from the nations.

²⁵ "You must therefore make a distinction between clean and unclean animals and between unclean and clean birds. Do not defile yourselves by any animal or bird or anything that moves along the ground – those that I have set apart as unclean for you. ²⁶ You are to be holy to me because I, the LORD, am holy, and I have set you apart from the nations to be my own.

²⁷ "A man or woman who is a medium or spiritist among you must be put to death. You are to stone them; their blood will be on their own heads."'

■ PSALM 29:1-6

¹ Ascribe to the LORD, you heavenly
    beings,
  ascribe to the LORD glory and strength.
² Ascribe to the LORD the glory due to his
    name;
  worship the LORD in the splendour of
    his holiness.

³ The voice of the LORD is over the waters;
  the God of glory thunders,
  the LORD thunders over the mighty
    waters.
⁴ The voice of the LORD is powerful;
  the voice of the LORD is majestic.
⁵ The voice of the LORD breaks the cedars;
  the LORD breaks in pieces the cedars of
    Lebanon.
⁶ He makes Lebanon leap like a calf,
  Sirion like a young wild ox.

■ PROVERBS 6:32-33

³² But a man who commits adultery has no
    sense;
  whoever does so destroys himself.
³³ Blows and disgrace are his lot,
  and his shame will never be wiped
    away.

▬ MARK 6:21-46

²¹Finally the opportune time came. On his birthday Herod gave a banquet for his high officials and military commanders and the leading men of Galilee. ²²When the daughter of Herodias came in and danced, she pleased Herod and his dinner guests.

The king said to the girl, 'Ask me for anything you want, and I'll give it to you.' ²³And he promised her with an oath, 'Whatever you ask I will give you, up to half my kingdom.'

²⁴She went out and said to her mother, 'What shall I ask for?'

'The head of John the Baptist,' she answered.

²⁵At once the girl hurried in to the king with the request: 'I want you to give me right now the head of John the Baptist on a dish.'

²⁶The king was greatly distressed, but because of his oaths and his dinner guests, he did not want to refuse her. ²⁷So he immediately sent an executioner with orders to bring John's head. The man went, beheaded John in the prison, ²⁸and brought back his head on a dish. He presented it to the girl, and she gave it to her mother. ²⁹On hearing of this, John's disciples came and took his body and laid it in a tomb.

³⁰The apostles gathered round Jesus and reported to him all they had done and taught. ³¹Then, because so many people were coming and going that they did not even have a chance to eat, he said to them, 'Come with me by yourselves to a quiet place and get some rest.'

³²So they went away by themselves in a boat to a solitary place. ³³But many who saw them leaving recognised them and ran on foot from all the towns and got there ahead of them. ³⁴When Jesus landed and saw a large crowd, he had compassion on them, because they were like sheep without a shepherd. So he began teaching them many things.

³⁵By this time it was late in the day, so his disciples came to him. 'This is a remote place,' they said, 'and it's already very late. ³⁶Send the people away so that they can go to the surrounding countryside and villages and buy themselves something to eat.'

³⁷But he answered, 'You give them something to eat.'

They said to him, 'That would take more than half a year's wages! Are we to go and spend that much on bread and give it to them to eat?'

³⁸'How many loaves do you have?' he asked. 'Go and see.'

When they found out, they said, 'Five – and two fish.'

³⁹Then Jesus told them to make all the people sit down in groups on the green grass. ⁴⁰So they sat down in groups of hundreds and fifties. ⁴¹Taking the five loaves and the two fish and looking up to heaven, he gave thanks and broke the loaves. Then he gave them to his disciples to distribute to the people. He also divided the two fish among them all. ⁴²They all ate and were satisfied, ⁴³and the disciples picked up twelve basketfuls of broken pieces of bread and fish. ⁴⁴The number of the men who had eaten was five thousand.

⁴⁵Immediately Jesus made his disciples get into the boat and go on ahead of him to Bethsaida, while he dismissed the crowd. ⁴⁶After leaving them, he went up on a mountainside to pray.

Be Selective

'... he said to them, "Come with me by yourselves to a quiet place and get some rest."' **Mark 6:31**

Disregard of our physical life may affect our spiritual wellbeing, for what goes on in the body greatly influences, though it does not control, what goes on in the soul and spirit.

My suggestion in relation to this physical aspect of our lives is this: discipline your times of rest and recreation. Some recreations do not recreate; rather, they exhaust one. They leave one morally and spiritually flabby and unfit. I find that after watching some television programmes, I have been challenged or lifted, but others leave me feeling inwardly polluted. The delicacies of life seem somehow to have been invaded, the finest flowers of the spirit trampled on, and one comes out drooping. I am learning to be more selective in my recreations. One should never expose oneself to a film or television programme that is likely to leave one spiritually or morally depleted - not if you value the higher values. It is like allowing pigs into your parlour.

The same can be said of other recreations. Some pieces of literature can leave you with a sense of moral and spiritual exhaustion. Don't fall for the idea that one has to read everything that comes to hand in order to understand life. This is where many of our Christian young people need help. Does one have to wallow in a mud-hole in order to understand dirt? Does a doctor have to take germs into his own body in order to understand how they function? Recreation is extremely important to help us stay spiritually fresh, but we need to make sure our recreations really recreate.

PRAYER

Father, You have made me for health and rhythm. Help me to be sensitive to all the things I need to do so that I am at my best spiritually and physically. I want to honour You in everything I do - even in my recreations. Amen.

FURTHER STUDY

Heb. 4:1-11; Exod. 33:14; Matt. 11:29

- What are we invited to enter into?
- What does this mean in practical terms?

March 3

■ **LEVITICUS 21:1–22:33**

21 The LORD said to Moses, 'Speak to the priests, the sons of Aaron, and say to them: "A priest must not make himself ceremonially unclean for any of his people who die, ²except for a close relative, such as his mother or father, his son or daughter, his brother, ³or an unmarried sister who is dependent on him since she has no husband – for her he may make himself unclean. ⁴He must not make himself unclean for people related to him by marriage, and so defile himself.

⁵ "Priests must not shave their heads or shave off the edges of their beards or cut their bodies. ⁶They must be holy to their God and must not profane the name of their God. Because they present the food offerings to the LORD, the food of their God, they are to be holy.

⁷ "They must not marry women defiled by prostitution or divorced from their husbands, because priests are holy to their God. ⁸Regard them as holy, because they offer up the food of your God. Consider them holy, because I the LORD am holy – I who make you holy.

⁹ "If a priest's daughter defiles herself by becoming a prostitute, she disgraces her father; she must be burned in the fire.

¹⁰ "The high priest, the one among his brothers who has had the anointing oil poured on his head and who has been ordained to wear the priestly garments, must not let his hair become unkempt or tear his clothes. ¹¹He must not enter a place where there is a dead body. He must not make himself unclean, even for his father or mother, ¹²nor leave the sanctuary of his God or desecrate it, because he has been dedicated by

the anointing oil of his God. I am the LORD. ¹³ "The woman he marries must be a virgin. ¹⁴He must not marry a widow, a divorced woman, or a woman defiled by prostitution, but only a virgin from his own people, ¹⁵so that he will not defile his offspring among his people. I am the LORD, who makes him holy." '

¹⁶The LORD said to Moses, ¹⁷'Say to Aaron: "For the generations to come none of your descendants who has a defect may come near to offer the food of his God. ¹⁸No man who has any defect may come near: no man who is blind or lame, disfigured or deformed; ¹⁹no man with a crippled foot or hand, ²⁰or who is a hunchback or a dwarf, or who has any eye defect, or who has festering or running sores or damaged testicles. ²¹No descendant of Aaron the priest who has any defect is to come near to present the food offerings to the LORD. He has a defect; he must not come near to offer the food of his God. ²²He may eat the most holy food of his God, as well as the holy food; ²³yet because of his defect, he must not go near the curtain or approach the altar, and so desecrate my sanctuary. I am the LORD, who makes them holy." '

²⁴So Moses told this to Aaron and his sons and to all the Israelites.

22 The LORD said to Moses, ²'Tell Aaron and his sons to treat with respect the sacred offerings the Israelites consecrate to me, so that they will not profane my holy name. I am the LORD.

³ 'Say to them: "For the generations to come, if any of your descendants is ceremonially unclean and yet comes near the sacred offerings that the Israelites consecrate to the LORD, that person must be cut off from my presence. I am the LORD.

⁴ ' "If a descendant of Aaron has a defiling skin disease or a bodily discharge, he may not eat the sacred offerings until he is cleansed. He will also be unclean if he touches something defiled by a corpse or by anyone who has an emission of semen, ⁵ or if he touches any crawling thing that makes him unclean, or any person who makes him unclean, whatever the uncleanness may be. ⁶ The one who touches any such thing will be unclean till evening. He must not eat any of the sacred offerings unless he has bathed himself with water. ⁷ When the sun goes down, he will be clean, and after that he may eat the sacred offerings, for they are his food. ⁸ He must not eat anything found dead or torn by wild animals, and so become unclean through it. I am the LORD.

⁹ ' "The priests are to perform my service in such a way that they do not become guilty and die for treating it with contempt. I am the LORD, who makes them holy.

¹⁰ ' "No one outside a priest's family may eat the sacred offering, nor may the guest of a priest or his hired worker eat it. ¹¹ But if a priest buys a slave with money, or if slaves are born in his household, they may eat his food. ¹² If a priest's daughter marries anyone other than a priest, she may not eat any of the sacred contributions. ¹³ But if a priest's daughter becomes a widow or is divorced, yet has no children, and she returns to live in her father's household as in her youth, she may eat her father's food. No unauthorised person, however, may eat it.

¹⁴ ' "Anyone who eats a sacred offering by mistake must make restitution to the priest for the offering and add a fifth of the value to it. ¹⁵ The priests must not desecrate the sacred offerings the Israelites present to the LORD ¹⁶ by allowing them to eat the sacred offerings and so bring upon them guilt requiring payment. I am the LORD, who makes them holy." '

¹⁷ The LORD said to Moses, ¹⁸ 'Speak to Aaron and his sons and to all the Israelites and say to them: "If any of you – whether an Israelite or a foreigner residing in Israel – presents a gift for a burnt offering to the LORD, either to fulfil a vow or as a freewill offering, ¹⁹ you must present a male without defect from the cattle, sheep or goats in order that it may be accepted on your behalf. ²⁰ Do not bring anything with a defect, because it will not be accepted on your behalf. ²¹ When anyone brings from the herd or flock a fellowship offering to the LORD to fulfil a special vow or as a freewill offering, it must be without defect or blemish to be acceptable. ²² Do not offer to the LORD the blind, the injured or the maimed, or anything with warts or festering or running sores. Do not place any of these on the altar as a food offering presented to the LORD. ²³ You may, however, present as a freewill offering an ox or a sheep that is deformed or stunted, but it will not be accepted in fulfilment of a vow. ²⁴ You must not offer to the LORD an animal whose testicles are bruised, crushed, torn or cut. You must not do this in your own land, ²⁵ and you must not accept such animals from the hand of a foreigner and offer them as the food of your God. They will not be accepted on your behalf, because they are deformed and have defects." '

²⁶ The LORD said to Moses, ²⁷ 'When a calf, a lamb or a goat is born, it is to remain with its mother for seven days. From the eighth day on, it will be acceptable as a food offering presented to the LORD. ²⁸ Do not slaughter a cow or a sheep and its young on the same day.

²⁹ 'When you sacrifice a thank-offering to the LORD, sacrifice it in such a way that it will be accepted on your behalf. ³⁰ It must be eaten that same day; leave none of it till morning. I am the LORD.

³¹ 'Keep my commands and follow them. I am the LORD. ³² Do not profane my holy name, for I must be acknowledged as holy by the Israelites. I am the LORD, who made you holy ³³ and who brought you out of Egypt to be your God. I am the LORD.'

■ PSALM 29:7-11

[7] The voice of the LORD strikes
   with flashes of lightning.
[8] The voice of the LORD shakes the desert;
   the LORD shakes the Desert of Kadesh.
[9] The voice of the LORD twists the oaks
   and strips the forests bare.
   And in his temple all cry, 'Glory!'

[10] The LORD sits enthroned over the flood;
   the LORD is enthroned as King for ever.
[11] The LORD gives strength to his people;
   the LORD blesses his people with
      peace.

■ PROVERBS 6:34-35

[34] For jealousy arouses a husband's fury,
   and he will show no mercy when he
      takes revenge.
[35] He will not accept any compensation;
   he will refuse a bribe, however great
      it is.

■ MARK 6:47–7:16

[47] Later that night, the boat was in the middle of the lake, and he was alone on land. [48] He saw the disciples straining at the oars, because the wind was against them. Shortly before dawn he went out to them, walking on the lake. He was about to pass by them, [49] but when they saw him walking on the lake, they thought he was a ghost. They cried out, [50] because they all saw him and were terrified.

Immediately he spoke to them and said, 'Take courage! It is I. Don't be afraid.' [51] Then he climbed into the boat with them, and the wind died down. They were completely amazed, [52] for they had not understood about the loaves; their hearts were hardened.

[53] When they had crossed over, they landed at Gennesaret and anchored there. [54] As soon as they got out of the boat, people recognised Jesus. [55] They ran throughout that whole region and carried those who were ill on mats to wherever they heard he was. [56] And wherever he went – into villages, towns or countryside – they placed those who were ill in the market-places. They begged him to let them touch even the edge of his cloak, and all who touched it were healed.

7 The Pharisees and some of the teachers of the law who had come from Jerusalem gathered round Jesus [2] and saw some of his disciples eating food with hands that were defiled, that is, unwashed. [3] (The Pharisees and all the Jews do not eat unless they give their hands a ceremonial washing, holding to the tradition of the elders. [4] When they come from the market-place they do not eat unless they wash. And they observe many other traditions, such as the washing of cups, pitchers and kettles.) [5] So the Pharisees and teachers of the law asked Jesus, 'Why don't your disciples live according to the tradition of the elders instead of eating their food with defiled hands?'

[6] He replied, 'Isaiah was right when he prophesied about you hypocrites; as it is written:

' "These people honour me with their lips,
   but their hearts are far from me.
[7] They worship me in vain;
   their teachings are merely human
      rules."

[8] You have let go of the commands of God and are holding on to human traditions.'

[9] And he continued, 'You have a fine way of setting aside the commands of God in order to observe your own traditions! [10] For Moses said, "Honour your father and mother," and, "Anyone who curses their father or mother is to be put to death." [11] But you say that if anyone declares that what might have been used

to help their father or mother is Corban (that is, devoted to God) – ¹²then you no longer let them do anything for their father or mother. ¹³Thus you nullify the word of God by your tradition that you have handed down. And you do many things like that.'

¹⁴Again Jesus called the crowd to him and said, 'Listen to me, everyone, and understand this. ¹⁵Nothing outside a person can defile them by going into them. Rather, it is what comes out of a person that defiles them.' [16]a

---

ᵃ Some manuscripts include here the words of 4:23

Positive Thanksgiving

'The LORD gives strength to his people; the LORD blesses his people with peace.' **Psalm 29:11**

Here is a prescription for overcoming frustration. Look for something good to come out of everything that appears bad. How I wish I could hammer this thought into the mind of every Christian. Nowadays, it is almost second nature with me to look for a positive in every negative, but it was not always so. At one time, whenever anything bad happened to me, I used to say, 'Oh no, not again! Just when everything seemed to be going right! Why should this happen to me?' I learned, however, to apply this principle, and I can honestly say it has transformed my life and ministry.

This also means learning to thank God for the good that is emerging, instead of brooding over any loss that has been sustained. This positive thanksgiving will make your heart receptive to God's power. He can do anything with a thankful heart, but He will usually do little or nothing with a complaining, self-pitying heart. It is closed to grace.

Also, find someone else who is going through difficult circumstances, and help them find victory. Someone has said, 'Sorrow expands the soul for joy.' For joy? Yes – the joy of being useful and creative. God uses frustrating circumstances to prune you for fruit-bearing.

And the lessons you have learned will go even deeper as you share them with others. Expression deepens impression. If you incorporate your sorrows, they will multiply. And if you incorporate your blessings, they too will multiply. Learn this secret, and it will help you stay spiritually on top – no matter what.

PRAYER

O God, help me not to be a whiner but a worshipper. Help me to cultivate an attitude of thanksgiving in all things – for I know that all things serve. I pray in Jesus' name. Amen.

FURTHER STUDY

Rom. 8:1-7; Col. 3:15; Phil. 4:7
• What brings life and peace?
• What will the peace of God do?

March 4

■ LEVITICUS 23:1–24:23

23 The LORD said to Moses, [2] 'Speak to the Israelites and say to them: "These are my appointed festivals, the appointed festivals of the LORD, which you are to proclaim as sacred assemblies.

[3] "There are six days when you may work, but the seventh day is a day of sabbath rest, a day of sacred assembly. You are not to do any work; wherever you live, it is a sabbath to the LORD.

[4] "These are the LORD's appointed festivals, the sacred assemblies you are to proclaim at their appointed times: [5] the LORD's Passover begins at twilight on the fourteenth day of the first month. [6] On the fifteenth day of that month the LORD's Festival of Unleavened Bread begins; for seven days you must eat bread made without yeast. [7] On the first day hold a sacred assembly and do not do any of your ordinary work. [8] For seven days present a food offering to the LORD. And on the seventh day hold a sacred assembly and do not do any of your ordinary work."'

[9] The LORD said to Moses, [10] 'Speak to the Israelites and say to them: "When you enter the land I am going to give you and you reap its harvest, bring to the priest a sheaf of the first grain you harvest. [11] He is to wave the sheaf before the LORD so it will be accepted on your behalf; the priest is to wave it on the day after the Sabbath. [12] On the day you wave the sheaf, you must sacrifice as a burnt offering to the LORD a lamb a year old without defect, [13] together with its grain offering of one fifth of an ephah of the finest flour mixed with olive oil – a food offering presented to the LORD, a pleasing aroma – and its drink offering of a quarter of a hin

of wine. [14] You must not eat any bread, or roasted or new grain, until the very day you bring this offering to your God. This is to be a lasting ordinance for the generations to come, wherever you live.

[15] "From the day after the Sabbath, the day you brought the sheaf of the wave offering, count seven full weeks. [16] Count fifty days up to the day after the seventh Sabbath, and then present an offering of new grain to the LORD. [17] From wherever you live, bring two loaves made of one fifth of an ephah of the finest flour, baked with yeast, as a wave offering of firstfruits to the LORD. [18] Present with this bread seven male lambs, each a year old and without defect, one young bull and two rams. They will be a burnt offering to the LORD, together with their grain offerings and drink offerings – a food offering, an aroma pleasing to the LORD. [19] Then sacrifice one male goat for a sin offering and two lambs, each a year old, for a fellowship offering. [20] The priest is to wave the two lambs before the LORD as a wave offering, together with the bread of the firstfruits. They are a sacred offering to the LORD for the priest. [21] On that same day you are to proclaim a sacred assembly and not do any ordinary work. This is to be a lasting ordinance for the generations to come, wherever you live.

[22] "When you reap the harvest of your land, do not reap to the very edges of your field or gather the gleanings of your harvest. Leave them for the poor and for the foreigner residing among you. I am the LORD your God."'

[23] The LORD said to Moses, [24] 'Say to the Israelites: "On the first day of the seventh month you are to have a day of sabbath rest, a sacred assembly commemorated with

trumpet blasts. ²⁵Do not do any of your ordinary work, but present a food offering to the LORD." '

²⁶The LORD said to Moses, ²⁷'The tenth day of this seventh month is the Day of Atonement. Hold a sacred assembly and deny yourselves, and present a food offering to the LORD. ²⁸Do not do any work on that day, because it is the Day of Atonement, when atonement is made for you before the LORD your God. ²⁹Those who do not deny themselves on that day must be cut off from their people. ³⁰I will destroy from among their people anyone who does any work on that day. ³¹You shall do no work at all. This is to be a lasting ordinance for the generations to come, wherever you live. ³²It is a day of sabbath rest for you, and you must deny yourselves. From the evening of the ninth day of the month until the following evening you are to observe your sabbath.'

³³The LORD said to Moses, ³⁴'Say to the Israelites: "On the fifteenth day of the seventh month the LORD's Festival of Tabernacles begins, and it lasts for seven days. ³⁵The first day is a sacred assembly; do not do any of your ordinary work. ³⁶For seven days present food offerings to the LORD, and on the eighth day hold a sacred assembly and present a food offering to the LORD. It is the closing special assembly; do not do any of your ordinary work.

³⁷(' "These are the LORD's appointed festivals, which you are to proclaim as sacred assemblies for bringing food offerings to the LORD – the burnt offerings and grain offerings, sacrifices and drink offerings required for each day. ³⁸These offerings are in addition to those for the LORD's Sabbaths and in addition to your gifts and whatever you have vowed and all the freewill offerings you give to the LORD.)

³⁹' "So beginning with the fifteenth day of the seventh month, after you have gathered the crops of the land, celebrate the festival to the LORD for seven days; the first day

is a day of sabbath rest, and the eighth day also is a day of sabbath rest. ⁴⁰On the first day you are to take branches from luxuriant trees – from palms, willows and other leafy trees – and rejoice before the LORD your God for seven days. ⁴¹Celebrate this as a festival to the LORD for seven days each year. This is to be a lasting ordinance for the generations to come; celebrate it in the seventh month. ⁴²Live in temporary shelters for seven days: all native-born Israelites are to live in such shelters ⁴³so that your descendants will know that I made the Israelites live in temporary shelters when I brought them out of Egypt. I am the LORD your God." '

⁴⁴So Moses announced to the Israelites the appointed festivals of the LORD.

24 The LORD said to Moses, ²'Command the Israelites to bring you clear oil of pressed olives for the light so that the lamps may be kept burning continually. ³Outside the curtain that shields the ark of the covenant law in the tent of meeting, Aaron is to tend the lamps before the LORD from evening till morning, continually. This is to be a lasting ordinance for the generations to come. ⁴The lamps on the pure gold lampstand before the LORD must be tended continually.

⁵'Take the finest flour and bake twelve loaves of bread, using one fifth of an ephah for each loaf. ⁶Arrange them in two piles, six in each pile, on the table of pure gold before the LORD. ⁷By each pile put some pure incense as a memorial portion to represent the bread and to be a food offering presented to the LORD. ⁸This bread is to be set out before the LORD regularly, Sabbath after Sabbath, on behalf of the Israelites, as a lasting covenant. ⁹It belongs to Aaron and his sons, who are to eat it in the sanctuary area, because it is a most holy part of their perpetual share of the food offerings presented to the LORD.'

¹⁰Now the son of an Israelite mother and an Egyptian father went out among the

Israelites, and a fight broke out in the camp between him and an Israelite. [11] The son of the Israelite woman used the Name blasphemously with a curse; so they brought him to Moses. (His mother's name was Shelomith, the daughter of Dibri the Danite.) [12] They put him in custody until the will of the LORD should be made clear to them.

[13] Then the LORD said to Moses: [14] 'Take the blasphemer outside the camp. All those who heard him are to lay their hands on his head, and the entire assembly is to stone him. [15] Say to the Israelites: "Anyone who curses their God will be held responsible; [16] anyone who uses the name of the LORD blasphemously is to be put to death. The entire assembly must stone them. Whether foreigner or native-born, when they use the Name blasphemously they are to be put to death.

[17] ' "Anyone who takes the life of a human being is to be put to death. [18] Anyone who takes the life of someone's animal must make restitution – life for life. [19] Anyone who injures their neighbour is to be injured in the same manner: [20] fracture for fracture, eye for eye, tooth for tooth. The one who has inflicted the injury must suffer the same injury. [21] Whoever kills an animal must make restitution, but whoever kills a human being is to be put to death. [22] You are to have the same law for the foreigner and the native-born. I am the LORD your God." '

[23] Then Moses spoke to the Israelites, and they took the blasphemer outside the camp and stoned him. The Israelites did as the LORD commanded Moses.

■ PSALM 30:1-6

[1] I will exalt you, LORD,
    for you lifted me out of the depths
    and did not let my enemies gloat
       over me.
[2] LORD my God, I called to you for help,
    and you healed me.

[3] You, LORD, brought me up from the
    realm of the dead;
    you spared me from going down to
       the pit.

[4] Sing the praises of the LORD, you his
    faithful people;
    praise his holy name.
[5] For his anger lasts only a moment,
    but his favour lasts a lifetime;
    weeping may stay for the night,
    but rejoicing comes in the morning.

[6] When I felt secure, I said,
    'I shall never be shaken.'

■ PROVERBS 7:1-3

7 My son, keep my words
   and store up my commands within you.
[2] Keep my commands and you will live;
    guard my teachings as the apple of
       your eye.
[3] Bind them on your fingers;
    write them on the tablet of your heart.

■ MARK 7:17-37

[17] After he had left the crowd and entered the house, his disciples asked him about this parable. [18] 'Are you so dull?' he asked. 'Don't you see that nothing that enters a person from the outside can defile them? [19] For it doesn't go into their heart but into their stomach, and then out of the body.' (In saying this, Jesus declared all foods clean.)

[20] He went on: 'What comes out of a person is what defiles them. [21] For it is from within, out of a person's heart, that evil thoughts come – sexual immorality, theft, murder, [22] adultery, greed, malice, deceit, lewdness, envy, slander, arrogance and folly. [23] All these evils come from inside and defile a person.'

²⁴Jesus left that place and went to the vicinity of Tyre. He entered a house and did not want anyone to know it; yet he could not keep his presence secret. ²⁵In fact, as soon as she heard about him, a woman whose little daughter was possessed by an impure spirit came and fell at his feet. ²⁶The woman was a Greek, born in Syrian Phoenicia. She begged Jesus to drive the demon out of her daughter.

²⁷'First let the children eat all they want,' he told her, 'for it is not right to take the children's bread and toss it to the dogs.'

²⁸'Lord,' she replied, 'even the dogs under the table eat the children's crumbs.'

²⁹Then he told her, 'For such a reply, you may go; the demon has left your daughter.'

³⁰She went home and found her child lying on the bed, and the demon gone.

³¹Then Jesus left the vicinity of Tyre and went through Sidon, down to the Sea of Galilee and into the region of the Decapolis. ³²There some people brought to him a man who was deaf and could hardly talk, and they begged Jesus to place his hand on him.

³³After he took him aside, away from the crowd, Jesus put his fingers into the man's ears. Then he spat and touched the man's tongue. ³⁴He looked up to heaven and with a deep sigh said to him, 'Ephphatha!' (which means 'Be opened!'). ³⁵At this, the man's ears were opened, his tongue was loosed and he began to speak plainly.

³⁶Jesus commanded them not to tell anyone. But the more he did so, the more they kept talking about it. ³⁷People were overwhelmed with amazement. 'He has done everything well,' they said. 'He even makes the deaf hear and the mute speak.'

'Surprised by Joy'

'... weeping may stay for the night, but rejoicing comes in the morning.' **Psalm 30:5**

What a distinctive and intriguing difficulty it was for Jesus' disciples to struggle with disappointment, reluctant to believe in case what they were believing proved untrue. They were grown men whose lives had been far from sheltered and protected, yet the experience of the Crucifixion had been more harrowing than any of them ever cared to face again.

Over and over again during the days in which Jesus lay in the grave, they must have racked their brains to try to find some explanation for why His life had ended on a grisly cross. Doubtless, in the closing hours of that fateful weekend, their thoughts must have turned naturally toward how they might go about restructuring their lives. Then, suddenly, Jesus appeared to them. His appearance was everything they wanted, but such was the disappointment already in their hearts that they considered it too good to be true. Thus they protected themselves against the risk of being disappointed again.

This is the tragedy of disappointment - it can, unless looked at and dealt with, reverberate inside us and hinder us in our pursuit of God. When disappointment is put into its proper perspective and when faith comes into its own, far from being too good to be true, one discovers that there is nothing else so good and nothing else so true. God proves Himself to be not just better than our worst fears, but better than our greatest dreams. No longer believing in joy is quickly followed by being surprised by joy.

PRAYER

Gracious and loving heavenly Father, give me insight into what I have been looking at today, and show me how to press through all disappointments in the knowledge that beyond the hurts, I shall be 'surprised by joy.' Amen.

FURTHER STUDY

John 21:1-22; Psa. 126:5; Isa. 35:10

• How did Peter respond to his disappointment?

• What were Jesus' words to him?

March 5

■ LEVITICUS 25:1-55

25 The LORD said to Moses at Mount Sinai, ²'Speak to the Israelites and say to them: "When you enter the land I am going to give you, the land itself must observe a sabbath to the LORD. ³For six years sow your fields, and for six years prune your vineyards and gather their crops. ⁴But in the seventh year the land is to have a year of sabbath rest, a sabbath to the LORD. Do not sow your fields or prune your vineyards. ⁵Do not reap what grows of itself or harvest the grapes of your untended vines. The land is to have a year of rest. ⁶Whatever the land yields during the sabbath year will be food for you – for yourself, your male and female servants, and the hired worker and temporary resident who live among you, ⁷as well as for your livestock and the wild animals in your land. Whatever the land produces may be eaten.

⁸'"Count seven sabbath years – seven times seven years – so that the seven sabbath years amount to a period of forty-nine years. ⁹Then sound the trumpet everywhere on the tenth day of the seventh month; on the Day of Atonement sound the trumpet throughout your land. ¹⁰Consecrate the fiftieth year and proclaim liberty throughout the land to all its inhabitants. It shall be a jubilee for you; each of you is to return to your family property and to your own clan. ¹¹The fiftieth year shall be a jubilee for you; do not sow and do not reap what grows of itself or harvest the untended vines. ¹²For it is a jubilee and is to be holy for you; eat only what is taken directly from the fields.

¹³'"In this Year of Jubilee everyone is to return to their own property.

¹⁴'"If you sell land to any of your own people or buy land from them, do not take advantage of each other. ¹⁵You are to buy from your own people on the basis of the number of years since the Jubilee. And they are to sell to you on the basis of the number of years left for harvesting crops. ¹⁶When the years are many, you are to increase the price, and when the years are few, you are to decrease the price, because what is really being sold to you is the number of crops. ¹⁷Do not take advantage of each other, but fear your God. I am the LORD your God.

¹⁸ "'Follow my decrees and be careful to obey my laws, and you will live safely in the land. ¹⁹ Then the land will yield its fruit, and you will eat your fill and live there in safety. ²⁰ You may ask, 'What will we eat in the seventh year if we do not plant or harvest our crops?' ²¹ I will send you such a blessing in the sixth year that the land will yield enough for three years. ²² While you plant during the eighth year, you will eat from the old crop and will continue to eat from it until the harvest of the ninth year comes in.

²³ "'The land must not be sold permanently, because the land is mine and you reside in my land as foreigners and strangers. ²⁴ Throughout the land that you hold as a possession, you must provide for the redemption of the land.

²⁵ "'If one of your fellow Israelites becomes poor and sells some of their property, their nearest relative is to come and redeem what they have sold. ²⁶ If, however, there is no one to redeem it for them but later on they prosper and acquire sufficient means to redeem it themselves, ²⁷ they are to determine the value for the years since they sold it and refund the balance to the one to whom they sold it; they can then go back to their own property. ²⁸ But if they do not acquire the means to repay, what was sold will remain in the possession of the buyer until the Year of Jubilee. It will be returned in the Jubilee, and they can then go back to their property.

²⁹ "'Anyone who sells a house in a walled city retains the right of redemption a full year after its sale. During that time the seller may redeem it. ³⁰ If it is not redeemed before a full year has passed, the house in the walled city shall belong permanently to the buyer and the buyer's descendants. It is not to be returned in the Jubilee. ³¹ But houses in villages without walls round them are to be considered as belonging to the open country. They can be redeemed, and they are to be returned in the Jubilee.

³² "'The Levites always have the right to redeem their houses in the Levitical towns, which they possess. ³³ So the property of the Levites is redeemable – that is, a house sold in any town they hold – and is to be returned in the Jubilee, because the houses in the towns of the Levites are their property among the Israelites. ³⁴ But the pastureland belonging to their towns must not be sold; it is their permanent possession.

³⁵ "'If any of your fellow Israelites become poor and are unable to support themselves among you, help them as you would a foreigner and stranger, so that they can continue to live among you. ³⁶ Do not take interest or any profit from them, but fear your God, so that they may continue to live among you. ³⁷ You must not lend them money at interest or sell them food at a profit. ³⁸ I am the LORD your God, who brought you out of Egypt to give you the land of Canaan and to be your God.

³⁹ "'If any of your fellow Israelites become poor and sell themselves to you, do not make them work as slaves. ⁴⁰ They are to be treated as hired workers or temporary residents among you; they are to work for you until the Year of Jubilee. ⁴¹ Then they and their children are to be released, and they will go back to their own clans and to the property of their ancestors. ⁴² Because the Israelites are my servants, whom I brought out of Egypt, they must not be sold as slaves. ⁴³ Do not rule over them ruthlessly, but fear your God.

⁴⁴ "'Your male and female slaves are to come from the nations around you; from them you may buy slaves. ⁴⁵ You may also buy some of the temporary residents living among you and members of their clans born in your country, and they will become your property. ⁴⁶ You can bequeath them to your children as inherited property and can make them slaves for life, but you must not rule over your fellow Israelites ruthlessly.

⁴⁷ ' "If a foreigner residing among you becomes rich and any of your fellow Israelites become poor and sell themselves to the foreigner or to a member of the foreigner's clan, ⁴⁸ they retain the right of redemption after they have sold themselves. One of their relatives may redeem them: ⁴⁹ an uncle or a cousin or any blood-relative in their clan may redeem them. Or if they prosper, they may redeem themselves. ⁵⁰ They and their buyer are to count the time from the year they sold themselves up to the Year of Jubilee. The price for their release is to be based on the rate paid to a hired worker for that number of years. ⁵¹ If many years remain, they must pay for their redemption a larger share of the price paid for them. ⁵² If only a few years remain until the Year of Jubilee, they are to compute that and pay for their redemption accordingly. ⁵³ They are to be treated as workers hired from year to year; you must see to it that those to whom they owe service do not rule over them ruthlessly.

⁵⁴ ' "Even if someone is not redeemed in any of these ways, they and their children are to be released in the Year of Jubilee, ⁵⁵ for the Israelites belong to me as servants. They are my servants, whom I brought out of Egypt. I am the LORD your God.

▬ PSALM 30:7-12

⁷ LORD, when you favoured me,
    you made my royal mountain stand
      firm;
but when you hid your face,
    I was dismayed.

⁸ To you, LORD, I called;
    to the Lord I cried for mercy:
⁹ 'What is gained if I am silenced,
    if I go down to the pit?
Will the dust praise you?
    Will it proclaim your faithfulness?
¹⁰ Hear, LORD, and be merciful to me;

    LORD, be my help.'

¹¹ You turned my wailing into dancing;
    you removed my sackcloth and
      clothed me with joy,
¹² that my heart may sing your praises and
    not be silent.
LORD my God, I will praise you for
    ever.

▬ PROVERBS 7:4-5

⁴ Say to wisdom, 'You are my sister,'
    and to insight, 'You are my relative.'
⁵ They will keep you from the adulterous
    woman,
    from the wayward woman with her
      seductive words.

▬ MARK 8:1-21

8 During those days another large crowd gathered. Since they had nothing to eat, Jesus called his disciples to him and said, ² 'I have compassion for these people; they have already been with me three days and have nothing to eat. ³ If I send them home hungry, they will collapse on the way, because some of them have come a long distance.'

⁴ His disciples answered, 'But where in this remote place can anyone get enough bread to feed them?'

⁵ 'How many loaves do you have?' Jesus asked.

'Seven,' they replied.

⁶ He told the crowd to sit down on the ground. When he had taken the seven loaves and given thanks, he broke them and gave them to his disciples to distribute to the people, and they did so. ⁷ They had a few small fish as well; he gave thanks for them also and told the disciples to distribute them. ⁸ The people ate and were satisfied.

Afterwards the disciples picked up seven basketfuls of broken pieces that were left over. ⁹About four thousand were present. After he had sent them away, ¹⁰he got into the boat with his disciples and went to the region of Dalmanutha.

¹¹The Pharisees came and began to question Jesus. To test him, they asked him for a sign from heaven. ¹²He sighed deeply and said, 'Why does this generation ask for a sign? Truly I tell you, no sign will be given to it.' ¹³Then he left them, got back into the boat and crossed to the other side.

¹⁴The disciples had forgotten to bring bread, except for one loaf they had with them in the boat. ¹⁵'Be careful,' Jesus warned them. 'Watch out for the yeast of the Pharisees and that of Herod.'

¹⁶They discussed this with one another and said, 'It is because we have no bread.'

¹⁷Aware of their discussion, Jesus asked them: 'Why are you talking about having no bread? Do you still not see or understand? Are your hearts hardened? ¹⁸Do you have eyes but fail to see, and ears but fail to hear? And don't you remember? ¹⁹When I broke the five loaves for the five thousand, how many basketfuls of pieces did you pick up?'

'Twelve,' they replied.

²⁰'And when I broke the seven loaves for the four thousand, how many basketfuls of pieces did you pick up?'

They answered, 'Seven.'

²¹He said to them, 'Do you still not understand?'

Give Thanks

'Hear, LORD, and be merciful to me; LORD, be my help.'
Psalm 30:10

We pray because we have a need to tell God about our circumstances. To understand the truth of this statement, we must ask ourselves: what happens when we neglect to pray for our daily needs and thank God for providing them?

If we are honest about it and examine our lives over a period of time, we will discover a subtle change taking place in our feelings and in our thinking. If we neglect to pray for our needs, we will begin to take the blessings of life for granted, and gradually, without at first realising it, we will succumb to the senseless notion that we can provide for the necessities of life and that we are perfectly capable of managing our own affairs without any help from God.

When we think this way, it is not long before pride steps in and a kind of spiritual blindness settles upon us - a blindness which blocks our vision in relation to God, others, and even ourselves. We need, therefore, to constantly remind ourselves that everything we have comes from His hand and that at any moment, should He choose to do so, He could turn off the supplies, and we would soon become beggared and bankrupt. The only way, therefore, that we can build a barricade against this awful blight of ingratitude is to pray daily.

PRAYER

O Father, teach me the art of continual thankfulness, and help me never to become bored with acknowledging Your grace and goodness; otherwise life will begin to disintegrate. Help me, Lord Jesus. Amen.

FURTHER STUDY

1 Kings 17; Psa. 23:5;
Isa. 41:10; Mal. 3:10
• How did God test Elijah's faith?
• How did he respond?

March 6

■ LEVITICUS 26:1-46

26 ' "Do not make idols or set up an image or a sacred stone for yourselves, and do not place a carved stone in your land to bow down before it. I am the LORD your God.

[2] ' "Observe my Sabbaths and have reverence for my sanctuary. I am the LORD.

[3] ' "If you follow my decrees and are careful to obey my commands, [4] I will send you rain in its season, and the ground will yield its crops and the trees their fruit. [5] Your threshing will continue until grape harvest and the grape harvest will continue until planting, and you will eat all the food you want and live in safety in your land.

[6] ' "I will grant peace in the land, and you will lie down and no one will make you afraid. I will remove wild beasts from the land, and the sword will not pass through your country. [7] You will pursue your enemies, and they will fall by the sword before you. [8] Five of you will chase a hundred, and a hundred of you will chase ten thousand, and your enemies will fall by the sword before you.

[9] ' "I will look on you with favour and make you fruitful and increase your numbers, and I will keep my covenant with you. [10] You will still be eating last year's harvest when you will have to move it out to make room for the new. [11] I will put my dwelling-place among you, and I will not abhor you. [12] I will walk among you and be your God, and you will be my people. [13] I am the LORD your God, who brought you out of Egypt so that you would no longer be slaves to the Egyptians; I broke the bars of your yoke and enabled you to walk with heads held high.

[14] ' "But if you will not listen to me and carry out all these commands, [15] and if you reject my decrees and abhor my laws and fail to carry out all my commands and so violate my covenant, [16] then I will do this to you: I will bring on you sudden terror, wasting diseases and fever that will destroy your sight and sap your strength. You will plant seed in vain, because your enemies will eat it. [17] I will set my face against you so that you will be defeated by your enemies; those who hate you will rule over you, and you will flee even when no one is pursuing you.

[18] ' "If after all this you will not listen to me, I will punish you for your sins seven times over. [19] I will break down your stubborn pride and make the sky above you like iron and the ground beneath you like bronze. [20] Your strength will be spent in vain, because your soil will not yield its crops, nor will the trees of your land yield their fruit.

²¹ ' "If you remain hostile towards me and refuse to listen to me, I will multiply your afflictions seven times over, as your sins deserve. ²²I will send wild animals against you, and they will rob you of your children, destroy your cattle and make you so few in number that your roads will be deserted.

²³ ' "If in spite of these things you do not accept my correction but continue to be hostile towards me, ²⁴I myself will be hostile towards you and will afflict you for your sins seven times over. ²⁵And I will bring the sword on you to avenge the breaking of the covenant. When you withdraw into your cities, I will send a plague among you, and you will be given into enemy hands. ²⁶When I cut off your supply of bread, ten women will be able to bake your bread in one oven, and they will dole out the bread by weight. You will eat, but you will not be satisfied.

²⁷ ' "If in spite of this you still do not listen to me but continue to be hostile towards me, ²⁸then in my anger I will be hostile towards you, and I myself will punish you for your sins seven times over. ²⁹You will eat the flesh of your sons and the flesh of your daughters. ³⁰I will destroy your high places, cut down your incense altars and pile your dead bodies on the lifeless forms of your idols, and I will abhor you. ³¹I will turn your cities into ruins and lay waste your sanctuaries, and I will take no delight in the pleasing aroma of your offerings. ³²I myself will lay waste the land, so that your enemies who live there will be appalled. ³³I will scatter you among the nations and will draw out my sword and pursue you. Your land will be laid waste, and your cities will lie in ruins. ³⁴Then the land will enjoy its sabbath years all the time that it lies desolate and you are in the country of your enemies; then the land will rest and enjoy its sabbaths. ³⁵All the time that it lies desolate, the land will have the rest it did not have during the sabbaths you lived in it.

³⁶ ' "As for those of you who are left, I will make their hearts so fearful in the lands of their enemies that the sound of a wind-blown leaf will put them to flight. They will run as though fleeing from the sword, and they will fall, even though no one is pursuing them. ³⁷They will stumble over one another as though fleeing from the sword, even though no one is pursuing them. So you will not be able to stand before your enemies. ³⁸You will perish among the nations; the land of your enemies will devour you. ³⁹Those of you who are left will waste away in the lands of their enemies because of their sins; also because of their ancestors' sins they will waste away.

⁴⁰ ' "But if they will confess their sins and the sins of their ancestors – their unfaithfulness and their hostility towards me, ⁴¹which made me hostile towards them so that I sent them into the land of their enemies – then when their uncircumcised hearts are humbled and they pay for their sin, ⁴²I will remember my covenant with Jacob and my covenant with Isaac and my covenant with Abraham, and I will remember the land. ⁴³For the land will be deserted by them and will enjoy its sabbaths while it lies desolate without them. They will pay for their sins because they rejected my laws and abhorred my decrees. ⁴⁴Yet in spite of this, when they are in the land of their enemies, I will not reject them or abhor them so as to destroy them completely, breaking my covenant with them. I am the LORD their God. ⁴⁵But for their sake I will remember the covenant with their ancestors whom I brought out of Egypt in the sight of the nations to be their God. I am the LORD." '

⁴⁶These are the decrees, the laws and the regulations that the LORD established at Mount Sinai between himself and the Israelites through Moses.

■ PSALM 31:1-8

¹ In you, LORD, I have taken refuge;
  let me never be put to shame;
  deliver me in your righteousness.
² Turn your ear to me,
  come quickly to my rescue;
 be my rock of refuge,
  a strong fortress to save me.
³ Since you are my rock and my fortress,
  for the sake of your name lead and
    guide me.
⁴ Keep me free from the trap that is set
    for me,
  for you are my refuge.
⁵ Into your hands I commit my spirit;
  deliver me, LORD, my faithful God.

⁶ I hate those who cling to worthless idols;
  as for me, I trust in the LORD.
⁷ I will be glad and rejoice in your love,
  for you saw my affliction
  and knew the anguish of my soul.
⁸ You have not given me into the hands
    of the enemy
  but have set my feet in a spacious
    place.

■ PROVERBS 7:6-8

⁶ At the window of my house
  I looked down through the lattice.
⁷ I saw among the simple,
  I noticed among the young men,
  a youth who had no sense.
⁸ He was going down the street near her
    corner,
  walking along in the direction of her
    house

■ MARK 8:22-9:1

²² They came to Bethsaida, and some people brought a blind man and begged Jesus to touch him. ²³ He took the blind man by the hand and led him outside the village. When he had spat on the man's eyes and put his hands on him, Jesus asked, 'Do you see anything?'

²⁴ He looked up and said, 'I see people; they look like trees walking around.'

²⁵ Once more Jesus put his hands on the man's eyes. Then his eyes were opened, his sight was restored, and he saw everything clearly. ²⁶ Jesus sent him home, saying, 'Don't even go into the village.'

²⁷ Jesus and his disciples went on to the villages around Caesarea Philippi. On the way he asked them, 'Who do people say I am?'

²⁸ They replied, 'Some say John the Baptist; others say Elijah; and still others, one of the prophets.'

²⁹ 'But what about you?' he asked. 'Who do you say I am?'

Peter answered, 'You are the Messiah.'

³⁰ Jesus warned them not to tell anyone about him.

³¹ He then began to teach them that the Son of Man must suffer many things and be rejected by the elders, the chief priests and the teachers of the law, and that he must be killed and after three days rise again. ³² He spoke plainly about this, and Peter took him aside and began to rebuke him.

³³ But when Jesus turned and looked at his disciples, he rebuked Peter. 'Get behind me, Satan!' he said. 'You do not have in mind the concerns of God, but merely human concerns.'

³⁴ Then he called the crowd to him along with his disciples and said: 'Whoever wants to be my disciple must deny themselves and take up their cross and follow me. ³⁵ For whoever wants to save their life will lose it, but whoever loses their life for me and for the gospel will save it. ³⁶ What good is it for someone to gain the whole world, yet forfeit their soul? ³⁷ Or what can anyone give in exchange for their soul?

³⁸ If anyone is ashamed of me and my words in this adulterous and sinful generation, the Son of Man will be ashamed of them when he comes in his Father's glory with the holy angels.'

9 And he said to them, 'Truly I tell you, some who are standing here will not taste death before they see that the kingdom of God has come with power.'

Hallelujah – the Pressure's Off

'For whoever wants to save their life will lose it, but whoever loses their life for me and for the gospel will save it. What good is it for someone to gain the whole world, yet forfeit their soul?' **Mark 8:35-36**

Strive not so much to succeed as to do the right thing. I remember addressing a group of ministers in Atlanta, Georgia, on 'Pitfalls in the Ministry.' I told them the story of my own failures, which at that time amounted to a great many, and I said, 'The lesson I have learned from my failures is that I don't have to succeed. I have to do the right thing under God's guidance and leave success or failure in His hands.' One of the ministers came to me afterwards and said, 'I am a pastor of one of the largest churches in this area and regarded by my peers as one of the most successful ministers in my denomination. But today you have helped me overcome the greatest pressure in my life – the pressure to succeed.'

In the early years of my ministry, I was extremely success-oriented; when I succeeded, I felt good, and when I failed, I felt devastated. Then God said to me quite bluntly one day, 'Are you willing to be a failure?' The question shook me rigid. It was a whole week later before I found sufficient grace to answer that question with a 'Yes,' and when I did, I was instantly released from the two things that had crippled my life and ministry – the pressure to succeed and the fear of failure. Now, what matters is not succeeding or failing, but being true to Him. Success and failure are in His hands. I am not on the way to success; I am on the Way. What a difference!

PRAYER

Father, the more I think about this, the more excited I get. You have given me such security. I can stand anything because You can use everything, even failure. Oh glory! Amen.

FURTHER STUDY

John 10:1-10; 2 Cor. 1:21, 9:8; Eph. 3:20
• What does the thief seek to do?
• What does Christ bring us?

March 7

▬ LEVITICUS 27:1-34

27 The LORD said to Moses, ²'Speak to the Israelites and say to them: "If anyone makes a special vow to dedicate a person to the LORD by giving the equivalent value, ³set the value of a male between the ages of twenty and sixty at fifty shekels of silver, according to the sanctuary shekel; ⁴for a female, set her value at thirty shekels; ⁵for a person between the ages of five and twenty, set the value of a male at twenty shekels and of a female at ten shekels; ⁶for a person between one month and five years, set the value of a male at five shekels of silver and that of a female at three shekels of silver; ⁷for a person sixty years old or more, set the value of a male at fifteen shekels and of a female at ten shekels. ⁸If anyone making the vow is too poor to pay the specified amount, the person being dedicated is to be presented to the priest, who will set the value according to what the one making the vow can afford.

⁹'"If what they vowed is an animal that is acceptable as an offering to the LORD, such an animal given to the LORD becomes holy. ¹⁰They must not exchange it or substitute a good one for a bad one, or a bad one for a good one; if they should substitute one animal for another, both it and the substitute become holy. ¹¹If what they vowed is a ceremonially unclean animal – one that is not acceptable as an offering to the LORD – the animal must be presented to the priest, ¹²who will judge its quality as good or bad. Whatever value the priest then sets, that is what it will be. ¹³If the owner wishes to redeem the animal, a fifth must be added to its value.

¹⁴'"If anyone dedicates their house as something holy to the LORD, the priest will judge its quality as good or bad. Whatever value the priest then sets, so it will remain. ¹⁵If the one who dedicates their house wishes to redeem it, they must add a fifth to its value, and the house will again become theirs.

¹⁶'"If anyone dedicates to the LORD part of their family land, its value is to be set according to the amount of seed required for it – fifty shekels of silver to a homer of barley seed. ¹⁷If they dedicate a field during the Year of Jubilee, the value that has been set remains. ¹⁸But if they dedicate a field after the Jubilee, the priest will determine the value according to the number of years that remain until the next Year of Jubilee, and its set value will be reduced. ¹⁹If the one who dedicates the field wishes to redeem it, they must add a fifth to its value, and the field will again become theirs. ²⁰If, however, they do not redeem the field, or if they have sold it to someone else, it can never be redeemed. ²¹When the field is released in the Jubilee, it will become holy, like a field devoted to the LORD; it will become priestly property.

²²'"If anyone dedicates to the LORD a field they have bought, which is not part of their family land, ²³the priest will determine its value up to the Year of Jubilee, and the owner must pay its value on that day as something holy to the LORD. ²⁴In the Year of Jubilee the field will revert to the person from whom it was bought, the one whose land it was. ²⁵Every value is to be set according to the sanctuary shekel, twenty gerahs to the shekel.

²⁶'"No one, however, may dedicate the firstborn of an animal, since the firstborn

already belongs to the LORD; whether an ox or a sheep, it is the LORD's. ²⁷ If it is one of the unclean animals, it may be bought back at its set value, adding a fifth of the value to it. If it is not redeemed, it is to be sold at its set value.

²⁸ ' "But nothing that a person owns and devotes to the LORD – whether a human being or an animal or family land – may be sold or redeemed; everything so devoted is most holy to the LORD.

²⁹ ' "No one devoted to destruction may be ransomed; they are to be put to death.

³⁰ ' "A tithe of everything from the land, whether grain from the soil or fruit from the trees, belongs to the LORD; it is holy to the LORD. ³¹ Whoever would redeem any of their tithe must add a fifth of the value to it. ³² Every tithe of the herd and flock – every tenth animal that passes under the shepherd's rod – will be holy to the LORD. ³³ No one may pick out the good from the bad or make any substitution. If anyone does make a substitution, both the animal and its substitute become holy and cannot be redeemed." '

³⁴ These are the commands the LORD gave Moses at Mount Sinai for the Israelites.

■ PSALM 31:9-18

⁹ Be merciful to me, LORD, for I am in distress;
my eyes grow weak with sorrow,
my soul and body with grief.
¹⁰ My life is consumed by anguish
and my years by groaning;
my strength fails because of my affliction,
and my bones grow weak.
¹¹ Because of all my enemies,
I am the utter contempt of my neighbours

and an object of dread to my closest friends –
those who see me on the street flee from me.
¹² I am forgotten as though I were dead;
I have become like broken pottery.
¹³ For I hear many whispering,
'Terror on every side!'
They conspire against me
and plot to take my life.
¹⁴ But I trust in you, LORD;
I say, 'You are my God.'
¹⁵ My times are in your hands;
deliver me from the hands of my enemies,
from those who pursue me.
¹⁶ Let your face shine on your servant;
save me in your unfailing love.
¹⁷ Let me not be put to shame, LORD,
for I have cried out to you;
but let the wicked be put to shame
and be silent in the realm of the dead.
¹⁸ Let their lying lips be silenced,
for with pride and contempt
they speak arrogantly against the righteous.

■ PROVERBS 7:9-12

⁹ at twilight, as the day was fading,
as the dark of night set in.
¹⁰ Then out came a woman to meet him,
dressed like a prostitute and with crafty intent.
¹¹ (She is unruly and defiant,
her feet never stay at home;
¹² now in the street, now in the squares,
at every corner she lurks.)

■ MARK 9:2-29

² After six days Jesus took Peter, James

and John with him and led them up a high mountain, where they were all alone. There he was transfigured before them. ³His clothes became dazzling white, whiter than anyone in the world could bleach them. ⁴And there appeared before them Elijah and Moses, who were talking with Jesus.

⁵Peter said to Jesus, 'Rabbi, it is good for us to be here. Let us put up three shelters – one for you, one for Moses and one for Elijah.' ⁶(He did not know what to say, they were so frightened.)

⁷Then a cloud appeared and covered them, and a voice came from the cloud: 'This is my Son, whom I love. Listen to him!'

⁸Suddenly, when they looked around, they no longer saw anyone with them except Jesus.

⁹As they were coming down the mountain, Jesus gave them orders not to tell anyone what they had seen until the Son of Man had risen from the dead. ¹⁰They kept the matter to themselves, discussing what 'rising from the dead' meant.

¹¹And they asked him, 'Why do the teachers of the law say that Elijah must come first?'

¹²Jesus replied, 'To be sure, Elijah does come first, and restores all things. Why then is it written that the Son of Man must suffer much and be rejected? ¹³But I tell you, Elijah has come, and they have done to him everything they wished, just as it is written about him.'

¹⁴When they came to the other disciples, they saw a large crowd around them and the teachers of the law arguing with them. ¹⁵As soon as all the people saw Jesus, they were overwhelmed with wonder and ran to greet him.

¹⁶'What are you arguing with them about?' he asked.

¹⁷A man in the crowd answered, 'Teacher, I brought you my son, who is possessed by a spirit that has robbed him of speech. ¹⁸Whenever it seizes him, it throws him to the ground. He foams at the mouth, gnashes his teeth and becomes rigid. I asked your disciples to drive out the spirit, but they could not.'

¹⁹'You unbelieving generation,' Jesus replied, 'how long shall I stay with you? How long shall I put up with you? Bring the boy to me.'

²⁰So they brought him. When the spirit saw Jesus, it immediately threw the boy into a convulsion. He fell to the ground and rolled around, foaming at the mouth.

²¹Jesus asked the boy's father, 'How long has he been like this?'

'From childhood,' he answered. ²²'It has often thrown him into fire or water to kill him. But if you can do anything, take pity on us and help us.'

²³'"If you can"?' said Jesus. 'Everything is possible for one who believes.'

²⁴Immediately the boy's father exclaimed, 'I do believe; help me overcome my unbelief!'

²⁵When Jesus saw that a crowd was running to the scene, he rebuked the impure spirit. 'You deaf and mute spirit,' he said, 'I command you, come out of him and never enter him again.'

²⁶The spirit shrieked, convulsed him violently and came out. The boy looked so much like a corpse that many said, 'He's dead.' ²⁷But Jesus took him by the hand and lifted him to his feet, and he stood up.

²⁸After Jesus had gone indoors, his disciples asked him privately, 'Why couldn't we drive it out?'

²⁹He replied, 'This kind can come out only by prayer.'

Forced to Face Reality

'How abundant are the good things that you have stored up for those who fear you ...' **Psalm 31:19**

Whenever we pray, we are to pray in accordance with God's will. One Greek scholar says that the words 'Your will be done on earth as it is in heaven' can be paraphrased in this way: 'Your will, whatever You wish to happen, let it happen – as in heaven so in earth.'

In other words: 'God, do what You want.' It's not easy to pray this way. If anyone thinks it is, then it is probably because they have never really sounded the true depths of self-interest within their own hearts. It's hard sometimes to pray, 'Your will be done,' when we know that if God has His way, we will not get our way.

Has this difficulty ever presented itself to you? The basic reason for this conflict is due to the major problem of the human heart – self-centredness. Paul, when describing a self-centred life and its results in Romans 6:21, ends by asking this question: 'What benefit did you reap at that time from the things you are now ashamed of?' The end was zero. That is the inevitable end of a self-centred life – nothing. The major thing that stands in the way of God performing His will in our lives utterly and completely is just that – self-centredness.

Jesus knew, as we now do, that if we are to become effective in prayer, then we must face up to the question: whose will comes first – mine or God's? I must be willing to say: 'God, do what You want.' That is the bottom line in prayer.

PRAYER

Gracious Father, I am grateful for the gentle and loving way You are putting Your finger on the obstacles in my life. Give me the attitude that puts Your will first and my will second. For Jesus' sake. Amen.

FURTHER STUDY

1 John 5:1-15; James 4:13-17; 1 John 2:17
• What is the confidence we have?
• What ought we to say?

March 8

■ NUMBERS 1:1-54

1 The LORD spoke to Moses in the tent of meeting in the Desert of Sinai on the first day of the second month of the second year after the Israelites came out of Egypt. He said: ²'Take a census of the whole Israelite community by their clans and families, listing every man by name, one by one. ³You and Aaron are to count according to

their divisions all the men in Israel who are twenty years old or more and able to serve in the army. ⁴One man from each tribe, each of them the head of his family, is to help you. ⁵These are the names of the men who are to assist you:

from Reuben, Elizur son of Shedeur;
⁶from Simeon, Shelumiel son of Zurishaddai;
⁷from Judah, Nahshon son of Amminadab;
⁸from Issachar, Nethanel son of Zuar;
⁹from Zebulun, Eliab son of Helon;
¹⁰from the sons of Joseph:
    from Ephraim, Elishama son of Ammihud;
    from Manasseh, Gamaliel son of Pedahzur;
¹¹from Benjamin, Abidan son of Gideoni;
¹²from Dan, Ahiezer son of Ammishaddai;
¹³from Asher, Pagiel son of Okran;
¹⁴from Gad, Eliasaph son of Deuel;
¹⁵from Naphtali, Ahira son of Enan.'

¹⁶These were the men appointed from the community, the leaders of their ancestral tribes. They were the heads of the clans of Israel.

¹⁷Moses and Aaron took these men whose names had been specified, ¹⁸and they called the whole community together on the first day of the second month. The people registered their ancestry by their clans and families, and the men twenty years old or more were listed by name, one by one, ¹⁹as the Lord commanded Moses. And so he counted them in the Desert of Sinai:

²⁰From the descendants of Reuben the firstborn son of Israel:
    All the men twenty years old or more who were able to serve in the army were listed by name, one by

one, according to the records of their clans and families. ²¹The number from the tribe of Reuben was 46,500.

²²From the descendants of Simeon:
    All the men twenty years old or more who were able to serve in the army were counted and listed by name, one by one, according to the records of their clans and families. ²³The number from the tribe of Simeon was 59,300.

²⁴From the descendants of Gad:
    All the men twenty years old or more who were able to serve in the army were listed by name, according to the records of their clans and families. ²⁵The number from the tribe of Gad was 45,650.

²⁶From the descendants of Judah:
    All the men twenty years old or more who were able to serve in the army were listed by name, according to the records of their clans and families. ²⁷The number from the tribe of Judah was 74,600.

²⁸From the descendants of Issachar:
    All the men twenty years old or more who were able to serve in the army were listed by name, according to the records of their clans and families. ²⁹The number from the tribe of Issachar was 54,400.

³⁰From the descendants of Zebulun:
    All the men twenty years old or more who were able to serve in the army were listed by name, according to the records of their clans and families. ³¹The number from the tribe of Zebulun was 57,400.

³² From the sons of Joseph:

From the descendants of Ephraim:

All the men twenty years old or more who were able to serve in the army were listed by name, according to the records of their clans and families. ³³ The number from the tribe of Ephraim was 40,500

³⁴ From the descendants of Manasseh:

All the men twenty years old or more who were able to serve in the army were listed by name, according to the records of their clans and families. ³⁵ The number from the tribe of Manasseh was 32,200.

³⁶ From the descendants of Benjamin:

All the men twenty years old or more who were able to serve in the army were listed by name, according to the records of their clans and families. ³⁷ The number from the tribe of Benjamin was 35,400.

³⁸ From the descendants of Dan:

All the men twenty years old or more who were able to serve in the army were listed by name, according to the records of their clans and families. ³⁹ The number from the tribe of Dan was 62,700.

⁴⁰ From the descendants of Asher:

All the men twenty years old or more who were able to serve in the army were listed by name, according to the records of their clans and families. ⁴¹ The number from the tribe of Asher was 41,500.

⁴² From the descendants of Naphtali:

All the men twenty years old or more who were able to serve in the army were listed by name, according to the records of their clans and families. ⁴³ The number from the tribe of

Naphtali was 53,400.

⁴⁴ These were the men counted by Moses and Aaron and the twelve leaders of Israel, each one representing his family. ⁴⁵ All the Israelites twenty years old or more who were able to serve in Israel's army were counted according to their families. ⁴⁶ The total number was 603,550.

⁴⁷ The ancestral tribe of the Levites, however, was not counted along with the others. ⁴⁸ The LORD had said to Moses: ⁴⁹ 'You must not count the tribe of Levi or include them in the census of the other Israelites. ⁵⁰ Instead, appoint the Levites to be in charge of the tabernacle of the covenant law – over all its furnishings and everything belonging to it. They are to carry the tabernacle and all its furnishings; they are to take care of it and camp round it. ⁵¹ Whenever the tabernacle is to move, the Levites are to take it down, and whenever the tabernacle is to be set up, the Levites shall do it. Anyone else who approaches it is to be put to death. ⁵² The Israelites are to set up their tents by divisions, each of them in their own camp under their standard. ⁵³ The Levites, however, are to set up their tents round the tabernacle of the covenant law so that my wrath will not fall on the Israelite community. The Levites are to be responsible for the care of the tabernacle of the covenant law.'

⁵⁴ The Israelites did all this just as the LORD commanded Moses.

▬ PSALM 31:19-24

¹⁹ How abundant are the good things
  that you have stored up for those who
    fear you,
 that you bestow in the sight of all,
  on those who take refuge in you.
²⁰ In the shelter of your presence you hide
    them
  from all human intrigues;

you keep them safe in your dwelling
from accusing tongues.

²¹ Praise be to the LORD,
for he showed me the wonders of his
love
when I was in a city under siege.
²² In my alarm I said,
'I am cut off from your sight!'
Yet you heard my cry for mercy
when I called to you for help.

²³ Love the LORD, all his faithful people!
The LORD preserves those who are true
to him,
but the proud he pays back in full.
²⁴ Be strong and take heart,
all you who hope in the LORD.

▬ PROVERBS 7:13-17

¹³ She took hold of him and kissed him
and with a brazen face she said:

¹⁴ 'Today I fulfilled my vows,
and I have food from my fellowship
offering at home.
¹⁵ So I came out to meet you;
I looked for you and have found you!
¹⁶ I have covered my bed
with coloured linens from Egypt.
¹⁷ I have perfumed my bed
with myrrh, aloes and cinnamon.

▬ MARK 9:30-50

³⁰ They left that place and passed through
Galilee. Jesus did not want anyone to know
where they were, ³¹ because he was teaching
his disciples. He said to them, 'The Son of
Man is going to be delivered into the hands
of men. They will kill him, and after three
days he will rise.' ³² But they did not understand what he meant and were afraid to ask

him about it.

³³ They came to Capernaum. When he
was in the house, he asked them, 'What
were you arguing about on the road?' ³⁴ But
they kept quiet because on the way they had
argued about who was the greatest.

³⁵ Sitting down, Jesus called the Twelve
and said, 'Anyone who wants to be first
must be the very last, and the servant of all.'

³⁶ He took a little child whom he placed
among them. Taking the child in his arms,
he said to them, ³⁷ 'Whoever welcomes one
of these little children in my name welcomes me; and whoever welcomes me does
not welcome me but the one who sent me.'

³⁸ 'Teacher,' said John, 'we saw someone
driving out demons in your name and we told
him to stop, because he was not one of us.'

³⁹ 'Do not stop him,' Jesus said. 'For no one
who does a miracle in my name can in the
next moment say anything bad about me,
⁴⁰ for whoever is not against us is for us. ⁴¹ Truly I tell you, anyone who gives you a cup of
water in my name because you belong to the
Messiah will certainly not lose their reward.

⁴² 'If anyone causes one of these little
ones – those who believe in me – to stumble, it would be better for them if a large
millstone were hung round their neck and
they were thrown into the sea. ⁴³ If your
hand causes you to stumble, cut it off. It
is better for you to enter life maimed than
with two hands to go into hell, where the fire
never goes out. [44]a 45 And if your foot causes you to stumble, cut it off. It is better for
you to enter life crippled than to have two
feet and be thrown into hell. [46]a 47 And if
your eye causes you to stumble, pluck it out.
It is better for you to enter the kingdom of
God with one eye than to have two eyes and
be thrown into hell, ⁴⁸ where

' "the worms that eat them do not die,
and the fire is not quenched."

---

a Some manuscripts include here the words of verse 48

⁴⁹Everyone will be salted with fire.
⁵⁰'Salt is good, but if it loses its saltiness, how can you make it salty again? Have salt among yourselves, and be at peace with each other.'

Get on the Offensive

'If your hand causes you to stumble, cut it off ...
And if your foot causes you to stumble, cut it off ...
And if your eye causes you to stumble, pluck it out .'
Mark 9:43, 45, 47

In spite of the importance of breaking decisively with everything of which Christ cannot approve, some Christians hide sins and are not willing to get rid of them. Let there be no illusion about this - no one can maintain their spiritual freshness as long as they allow known sin to remain and take root in their lives.

This matter of spiritual freshness is decided not by living on the defensive but by living on the offensive. It involves making definite decisions - decisions such as saying 'Yes' to all that Christ offers and saying 'No' to all that sin offers.

'Christianity,' said someone, 'is not a prohibition but a privilege.' I would agree with that. But I would add that it does, however, have a prohibition in it. In our text for today, Jesus says that if your 'hand' or your 'eye' causes you to sin, then do something about it. In other words, do not tolerate anything that cuts across the central purpose of your life. From head to foot, you are to belong to Christ.

The order in these verses is important. The order is hand, foot, eye. The 'hand' represents the doing of evil, the 'foot' the approach towards evil, and the 'eye' the seeing of evil with desire from afar.

What's the message in all this? Quite clearly, the message is that sin must be cut out at every stage. The place to begin, of course, is with the 'eye' - the place of desire. Take care of that, and you won't have to worry too much about the 'hand' and the 'foot.'

PRAYER

O Father, teach me how to be a decisive and not a double-minded person - especially in relation to this matter of sin. Show me what things I need to break with in my life, and help me to do it. In Jesus' name. Amen.

FURTHER STUDY

Matt. 16:21-27;
Luke 14:26-27; Mark 10:28
• What does it mean to 'take up our cross'?
• What was Peter's declaration?

March 9

2 The LORD said to Moses and Aaron: ² 'The Israelites are to camp round the tent of meeting some distance from it, each of them under their standard and holding the banners of their family.'

³ On the east, towards the sunrise, the divisions of the camp of Judah are to camp under their standard. The leader of the people of Judah is Nahshon son of Amminadab. ⁴ His division numbers 74,600.

⁵ The tribe of Issachar will camp next to them. The leader of the people of Issachar is Nethanel son of Zuar. ⁶ His division numbers 54,400.

⁷ The tribe of Zebulun will be next. The leader of the people of Zebulun is Eliab son of Helon. ⁸ His division numbers 57,400.

⁹ All the men assigned to the camp of Judah, according to their divisions, number 186,400. They will set out first.

¹⁰ On the south will be the divisions of the camp of Reuben under their standard. The leader of the people of Reuben is Elizur son of Shedeur. ¹¹ His division numbers 46,500.

¹² The tribe of Simeon will camp next to them. The leader of the people of Simeon is Shelumiel son of Zurishaddai. ¹³ His division numbers 59,300.

¹⁴ The tribe of Gad will be next. The leader of the people of Gad is Eliasaph son of Deuel. ¹⁵ His division numbers 45,650.

¹⁶ All the men assigned to the camp of Reuben, according to their divisions, number 151,450. They will set out second.

¹⁷ Then the tent of meeting and the camp of the Levites will set out in the middle of the camps. They will set out in the same order as they set up camp, each in their own place under their standard.

¹⁸ On the west will be the divisions of the camp of Ephraim under their standard. The leader of the people of Ephraim is Elishama son of Ammihud. ¹⁹ His division numbers 40,500.

²⁰ The tribe of Manasseh will be next to them. The leader of the people of Manasseh is Gamaliel son of Pedahzur. ²¹ His division numbers 32,200.

²² The tribe of Benjamin will be next. The leader of the people of Benjamin is Abidan son of Gideoni. ²³ His division numbers 35,400.

²⁴ All the men assigned to the camp of Ephraim, according to their divisions, number 108,100. They will set out third.

²⁵ On the north will be the divisions of the camp of Dan under their standard. The leader of the people of Dan is Ahiezer son of Ammishaddai. ²⁶ His division numbers 62,700.

²⁷ The tribe of Asher will camp next to them. The leader of the people of Asher is Pagiel son of Okran. ²⁸ His division numbers 41,500.

²⁹ The tribe of Naphtali will be next. The leader of the people of Naphtali is Ahira son of Enan. ³⁰ His division numbers 53,400.

³¹ All the men assigned to the camp of Dan number 157,600. They will set out last, under their standards.

³² These are the Israelites, counted according to their families. All the men in the camps, by their divisions, number 603,550. ³³ The Levites, however, were not counted along with the other Israelites, as the LORD commanded Moses.

³⁴ So the Israelites did everything the LORD commanded Moses; that is the way they camped under their standards, and that is the way they set out, each of them with their clan and family.

3 This is the account of the family of Aaron and Moses at the time the LORD spoke to Moses at Mount Sinai.

² The names of the sons of Aaron were Nadab the firstborn and Abihu, Eleazar and Ithamar. ³ Those were the names of Aaron's sons, the anointed priests, who were ordained to serve as priests. ⁴ Nadab and Abihu, however, died before the LORD when they made an offering with unauthorised fire before him in the Desert of Sinai. They had no sons, so Eleazar and Ithamar served as priests during the lifetime of their father Aaron.

⁵ The LORD said to Moses, ⁶ 'Bring the tribe of Levi and present them to Aaron the priest to assist him. ⁷ They are to perform duties for him and for the whole community at the tent of meeting by doing the work of the tabernacle. ⁸ They are to take care of all the furnishings of the tent of meeting, fulfilling the obligations of the Israelites by doing the work of the tabernacle. ⁹ Give the Levites to Aaron and his sons; they are the Israelites who are to be given wholly to him. ¹⁰ Appoint Aaron and his sons to serve as priests; anyone else who approaches the sanctuary is to be put to death.'

¹¹ The LORD also said to Moses, ¹² 'I have taken the Levites from among the Israelites in place of the first male offspring of every Israelite woman. The Levites are mine, ¹³ for all the firstborn are mine. When I struck down all the firstborn in Egypt, I set apart for myself every firstborn in Israel, whether human or animal. They are to be mine. I am the LORD.'

¹⁴ The LORD said to Moses in the Desert of Sinai, ¹⁵ 'Count the Levites by their families and clans. Count every male a month old or more.' ¹⁶ So Moses counted them, as he was commanded by the word of the LORD.

▬ PSALM 32:1-7

¹ Blessed is the one
  whose transgressions are forgiven,
  whose sins are covered.
² Blessed is the one
  whose sin the LORD does not count
      against them
  and in whose spirit is no deceit.

³ When I kept silent,
  my bones wasted away
    through my groaning all day long.
⁴ For day and night
  your hand was heavy on me;
my strength was sapped
    as in the heat of summer.

⁵ Then I acknowledged my sin to you
  and did not cover up my iniquity.
I said, 'I will confess
  my transgressions to the LORD.'
And you forgave
  the guilt of my sin.

⁶ Therefore let all the faithful pray to you
    while you may be found;
surely the rising of the mighty waters
  will not reach them.
⁷ You are my hiding-place;

you will protect me from trouble
and surround me with songs of
deliverance.

■ PROVERBS 7:18-21

¹⁸ Come, let's drink deeply of love till
    morning;
    let's enjoy ourselves with love!
¹⁹ My husband is not at home;
    he has gone on a long journey.
²⁰ He took his purse filled with money
    and will not be home till full moon.'

²¹ With persuasive words she led him
    astray;
    she seduced him with her smooth
    talk.

■ MARK 10:1-22

10 Jesus then left that place and went
into the region of Judea and across
the Jordan. Again crowds of people came
to him, and as was his custom, he taught
them.
    ² Some Pharisees came and tested him by
asking, 'Is it lawful for a man to divorce his
wife?'
    ³ 'What did Moses command you?' he
replied.
    ⁴ They said, 'Moses permitted a man to
write a certificate of divorce and send her
away.'
    ⁵ 'It was because your hearts were hard
that Moses wrote you this law,' Jesus replied. ⁶ 'But at the beginning of creation
God "made them male and female". ⁷ "For
this reason a man will leave his father and
mother and be united to his wife, ⁸ and the
two will become one flesh." So they are

no longer two, but one flesh. ⁹ Therefore
what God has joined together, let no one
separate.'
    ¹⁰ When they were in the house again,
the disciples asked Jesus about this. ¹¹ He
answered, 'Anyone who divorces his wife
and marries another woman commits
adultery against her. ¹² And if she divorces
her husband and marries another man, she
commits adultery.'
    ¹³ People were bringing little children to
Jesus for him to place his hands on them,
but the disciples rebuked them. ¹⁴ When
Jesus saw this, he was indignant. He said
to them, 'Let the little children come to me,
and do not hinder them, for the kingdom
of God belongs to such as these. ¹⁵ Truly I tell you, anyone who will not receive
the kingdom of God like a little child will
never enter it.' ¹⁶ And he took the children
in his arms, placed his hands on them and
blessed them.
    ¹⁷ As Jesus started on his way, a man ran
up to him and fell on his knees before him.
'Good teacher,' he asked, 'what must I do to
inherit eternal life?'
    ¹⁸ 'Why do you call me good?' Jesus an-
swered. 'No one is good – except God alone.
¹⁹ You know the commandments: "You shall
not murder, you shall not commit adultery,
you shall not steal, you shall not give false
testimony, you shall not defraud, honour
your father and mother."'
    ²⁰ 'Teacher,' he declared, 'all these I have
kept since I was a boy.'
    ²¹ Jesus looked at him and loved him.
'One thing you lack,' he said. 'Go, sell everything you have and give to the poor, and you
will have treasure in heaven. Then come,
follow me.'
    ²² At this the man's face fell. He went away
sad, because he had great wealth.

The Four 'Alls'

'Therefore let all the faithful pray to you ...'
Psalm 32:6

If the effectiveness of our spiritual warfare depends not just on wearing the six pieces of armour (Eph. 6:14-17), but also on constant, believing prayer, then we must ask ourselves: what can we do to make our prayer lives more effective?

The place given to prayer in both the Old and New Testaments is remarkable. All the great saints of the Old Testament knew how to pray - Abraham, David, Daniel, Jeremiah, Isaiah, to mention just a few. The same prowess in prayer can be seen also in the New Testament saints.

But of course the greatest Person of prayer was none other than our Lord Jesus Christ. Although He possessed great knowledge and wisdom, He found it essential to turn aside time and time again to pray. On certain occasions He would spend whole nights in prayer or rise long before dawn in order to pray and maintain His communion with God.

Is it surprising, therefore, that being so dependent on prayer, He should have told His disciples to: 'Always pray and not give up' (Luke 18:1). Praying is the only alternative to fainting - we must pray or else we faint.

Paul's teaching with regard to prayer in Ephesians 6:18 revolves around four 'alls.' We are to pray at all times, with all kinds of prayers, with all perseverance, and for all the saints. Most Christians, however, pray at some times, with some prayer, and some degree of perseverance for some of God's saints.

When we replace 'some' by 'all' in these expressions, we are on our way to effective praying.

PRAYER

My Father and my God, I see that through prayer, You offer me the most breathtaking power. Help me humbly to take it and use it wisely. In Jesus' name I pray. Amen.

FURTHER STUDY

1 Sam. 1:27; 7:1-10;
Exod. 15:24-25;
1 Kings 18:37-38; Matt. 14:23
• List some prayers God answered.
• List some answers to prayer you have received.

March 10

■ NUMBERS 3:17–4:20

¹⁷ These were the names of the sons of
Levi:
   Gershon, Kohath and Merari.
¹⁸ These were the names of the Gershon-
ite clans:
   Libni and Shimei.
¹⁹ The Kohathite clans:
   Amram, Izhar, Hebron and Uzziel.
²⁰ The Merarite clans:
   Mahli and Mushi.
These were the Levite clans, according to
their families.

²¹ To Gershon belonged the clans of the
Libnites and Shimeites; these were the
Gershonite clans. ²² The number of all the
males a month old or more who were counted was 7,500. ²³ The Gershonite clans were
to camp on the west, behind the tabernacle.
²⁴ The leader of the families of the Gershonites was Eliasaph son of Lael. ²⁵ At the tent
of meeting the Gershonites were responsible for the care of the tabernacle and tent,
its coverings, the curtain at the entrance
to the tent of meeting, ²⁶ the curtains of the
courtyard, the curtain at the entrance to
the courtyard surrounding the tabernacle
and altar, and the ropes – and everything
related to their use.

²⁷ To Kohath belonged the clans of the
Amramites, Izharites, Hebronites and Uzzielites; these were the Kohathite clans.
²⁸ The number of all the males a month old
or more was 8,600. The Kohathites were
responsible for the care of the sanctuary.
²⁹ The Kohathite clans were to camp on the
south side of the tabernacle. ³⁰ The leader
of the families of the Kohathite clans was

Elizaphan son of Uzziel. ³¹ They were responsible for the care of the ark, the table,
the lampstand, the altars, the articles of the
sanctuary used in ministering, the curtain,
and everything related to their use. ³² The
chief leader of the Levites was Eleazar son
of Aaron, the priest. He was appointed over
those who were responsible for the care of
the sanctuary.

³³ To Merari belonged the clans of the
Mahlites and the Mushites; these were the
Merarite clans. ³⁴ The number of all the
males a month old or more who were counted was 6,200. ³⁵ The leader of the families of
the Merarite clans was Zuriel son of Abihail;
they were to camp on the north side of the
tabernacle. ³⁶ The Merarites were appointed
to take care of the frames of the tabernacle,
its crossbars, posts, bases, all its equipment,
and everything related to their use, ³⁷ as well
as the posts of the surrounding courtyard
with their bases, tent pegs and ropes.

³⁸ Moses and Aaron and his sons were to
camp to the east of the tabernacle, towards
the sunrise, in front of the tent of meeting.
They were responsible for the care of the
sanctuary on behalf of the Israelites. Anyone else who approached the sanctuary was
to be put to death.

³⁹ The total number of Levites counted at
the Lord's command by Moses and Aaron
according to their clans, including every
male a month old or more, was 22,000.

⁴⁰ The Lord said to Moses, 'Count all the
firstborn Israelite males who are a month
old or more and make a list of their names.
⁴¹ Take the Levites for me in place of all the

firstborn of the Israelites, and the livestock of the Levites in place of all the firstborn of the livestock of the Israelites. I am the LORD.'

⁴²So Moses counted all the firstborn of the Israelites, as the LORD commanded him. ⁴³The total number of firstborn males a month old or more, listed by name, was 22,273.

⁴⁴The LORD also said to Moses, ⁴⁵'Take the Levites in place of all the firstborn of Israel, and the livestock of the Levites in place of their livestock. The Levites are to be mine. I am the LORD. ⁴⁶To redeem the 273 firstborn Israelites who exceed the number of the Levites, ⁴⁷collect five shekels for each one, according to the sanctuary shekel, which weighs twenty gerahs. ⁴⁸Give the money for the redemption of the additional Israelites to Aaron and his sons.'

⁴⁹So Moses collected the redemption money from those who exceeded the number redeemed by the Levites. ⁵⁰From the firstborn of the Israelites he collected silver weighing 1,365 shekels, according to the sanctuary shekel. ⁵¹Moses gave the redemption money to Aaron and his sons, as he was commanded by the word of the LORD.

4 The LORD said to Moses and Aaron: ²'Take a census of the Kohathite branch of the Levites by their clans and families. ³Count all the men from thirty to fifty years of age who come to serve in the work at the tent of meeting.

⁴'This is the work of the Kohathites at the tent of meeting: the care of the most holy things. ⁵When the camp is to move, Aaron and his sons are to go in and take down the shielding curtain and put it over the ark of the covenant law. ⁶Then they are to cover the curtain with durable leather, spread a cloth of solid blue over that and put the poles in place.

⁷'Over the table of the Presence they are to spread a blue cloth and put on it the plates, dishes and bowls, and the jars for drink offerings; the bread that is continually there is

to remain on it. ⁸They are to spread a scarlet cloth over them, cover that with durable leather and put the poles in place.

⁹'They are to take a blue cloth and cover the lampstand that is for light, together with its lamps, its wick trimmers and trays, and all its jars for the oil used to supply it. ¹⁰Then they are to wrap it and all its accessories in a covering of durable leather and put it on a carrying frame.

¹¹'Over the gold altar they are to spread a blue cloth and cover that with durable leather and put the poles in place.

¹²'They are to take all the articles used for ministering in the sanctuary, wrap them in a blue cloth, cover that with durable leather and put them on a carrying frame.

¹³'They are to remove the ashes from the bronze altar and spread a purple cloth over it. ¹⁴Then they are to place on it all the utensils used for ministering at the altar, including the firepans, meat forks, shovels and sprinkling bowls. Over it they are to spread a covering of durable leather and put the poles in place.

¹⁵'After Aaron and his sons have finished covering the holy furnishings and all the holy articles, and when the camp is ready to move, only then are the Kohathites to come and do the carrying. But they must not touch the holy things or they will die. The Kohathites are to carry those things that are in the tent of meeting.

¹⁶'Eleazar son of Aaron, the priest, is to have charge of the oil for the light, the fragrant incense, the regular grain offering and the anointing oil. He is to be in charge of the entire tabernacle and everything in it, including its holy furnishings and articles.'

¹⁷The LORD said to Moses and Aaron, ¹⁸'See that the Kohathite tribal clans are not destroyed from among the Levites. ¹⁹So that they may live and not die when they come near the most holy things, do this for them: Aaron and his sons are to go into the sanctuary and assign to each man his work and

what he is to carry. ²⁰But the Kohathites must not go in to look at the holy things, even for a moment, or they will die.'

■ PSALM 32:8–11

⁸I will instruct you and teach you in the
    way you should go;
  I will counsel you with my loving eye
    on you.
⁹Do not be like the horse or the mule,
    which have no understanding
but must be controlled by bit and bridle
  or they will not come to you.
¹⁰Many are the woes of the wicked,
  but the LORD's unfailing love
  surrounds the one who trusts in him.

¹¹Rejoice in the LORD and be glad, you
    righteous;
  sing, all you who are upright in heart!

■ PROVERBS 7:22–23

²²All at once he followed her
  like an ox going to the slaughter,
like a deer stepping into a noose
²³ till an arrow pierces his liver,
like a bird darting into a snare,
  little knowing it will cost him his life.

■ MARK 10:23–45

²³Jesus looked round and said to his disciples, 'How hard it is for the rich to enter the kingdom of God!'
²⁴The disciples were amazed at his words. But Jesus said again, 'Children, how hard it is to enter the kingdom of God! ²⁵It is easier for a camel to go through the eye of a needle than for someone who is rich to enter the kingdom of God.'
²⁶The disciples were even more amazed,

and said to each other, 'Who then can be saved?'
²⁷Jesus looked at them and said, 'With man this is impossible, but not with God; all things are possible with God.'
²⁸Then Peter spoke up, 'We have left everything to follow you!'
²⁹'Truly I tell you,' Jesus replied, 'no one who has left home or brothers or sisters or mother or father or children or fields for me and the gospel ³⁰will fail to receive a hundred times as much in this present age: homes, brothers, sisters, mothers, children and fields – along with persecutions – and in the age to come eternal life. ³¹But many who are first will be last, and the last first.'
³²They were on their way up to Jerusalem, with Jesus leading the way, and the disciples were astonished, while those who followed were afraid. Again he took the Twelve aside and told them what was going to happen to him. ³³'We are going up to Jerusalem,' he said, 'and the Son of Man will be delivered over to the chief priests and the teachers of the law. They will condemn him to death and will hand him over to the Gentiles, ³⁴who will mock him and spit on him, flog him and kill him. Three days later he will rise.'
³⁵Then James and John, the sons of Zebedee, came to him. 'Teacher,' they said, 'we want you to do for us whatever we ask.'
³⁶'What do you want me to do for you?' he asked.
³⁷They replied, 'Let one of us sit at your right and the other at your left in your glory.'
³⁸'You don't know what you are asking,' Jesus said. 'Can you drink the cup I drink or be baptised with the baptism I am baptised with?'
³⁹'We can,' they answered.
Jesus said to them, 'You will drink the cup I drink and be baptised with the baptism I am baptised with, ⁴⁰but to sit at my right or left is not for me to grant. These places belong to those for whom they have been prepared.'

⁴¹When the ten heard about this, they became indignant with James and John. ⁴²Jesus called them together and said, 'You know that those who are regarded as rulers of the Gentiles lord it over them, and their high officials exercise authority over them. ⁴³Not so with you. Instead, whoever wants to become great among you must be your servant, ⁴⁴and whoever wants to be first must be slave of all. ⁴⁵For even the Son of Man did not come to be served, but to serve, and to give his life as a ransom for many.'

Suppose It Had Been 'My'?

'... whoever wants to become great among you must be your servant, and whoever wants to be first must be slave of all. For even the Son of Man did not come to be served, but to serve ...' **Mark 10:43-45**

The first word of the Lord's Prayer - 'Our' (Matt. 6:9) - determines the very nature of the Christian faith. Suppose it had been 'My'. That would have changed the whole nature of the Christian religion. Instead of our faith being 'our'-centred it would have been 'my'-centred - and that would have started us off wrong.

In the field of prayer, as in many other fields, to start wrong is to finish wrong. The word 'our' involves a shifting of emphasis from me to the Father and to my brothers and sisters in the kingdom. It implies a renunciation - a renunciation of myself. We see something similar in the first words of the Beatitudes: 'Blessed are the poor in spirit' (the renounced in spirit), 'for theirs is the kingdom of heaven' (Matt. 5:3). All the resources of God's kingdom belong to those who are renounced in spirit. So, in the first word of the Lord's Prayer, we find an implied demand that we adopt an attitude of self-surrender - to the Father and to His interests and the interests of others in His kingdom. If we do this, then everything opens to us. If not, then everything is closed. The rest of the Lord's Prayer has no meaning and dies if the 'our' is not alive.

Furthermore, this 'our' must stretch beyond our own fellowship, local church, or denomination to include the whole family of God - everywhere. We will never get very far in our walk with God unless we come to it prepared to sacrifice self-interest and willing to merge into God's greater plan for the whole.

PRAYER

O Father, cleanse my heart from any limitations I might have in relation to the word 'our.' Help me to make it a true 'our' with everybody included – those I like and those I don't like. For Jesus' sake. Amen.

FURTHER STUDY

Luke 18:9-14; Mark 10:35-45; Matt. 23:12
• How did Jesus answer James and John?
• What was wrong with the Pharisee's prayer?

March 11

■ NUMBERS 4:21–5:31

²¹ The LORD said to Moses, ²² 'Take a census also of the Gershonites by their families and clans. ²³ Count all the men from thirty to fifty years of age who come to serve in the work at the tent of meeting.

²⁴ 'This is the service of the Gershonite clans in their carrying and their other work: ²⁵ they are to carry the curtains of the tabernacle, that is, the tent of meeting, its covering and its outer covering of durable leather, the curtains for the entrance to the tent of meeting, ²⁶ the curtains of the courtyard surrounding the tabernacle and altar, the curtain for the entrance to the courtyard, the ropes and all the equipment used in the service of the tent. The Gershonites are to do all that needs to be done with these things. ²⁷ All their service, whether carrying or doing other work, is to be done under the direction of Aaron and his sons. You shall assign to them as their responsibility all they are to carry. ²⁸ This is the service of the Gershonite clans at the tent of meeting. Their duties are to be under the direction of Ithamar son of Aaron, the priest.

²⁹ 'Count the Merarites by their clans and families. ³⁰ Count all the men from thirty to fifty years of age who come to serve in the work at the tent of meeting. ³¹ As part of all their service at the tent, they are to carry the frames of the tabernacle, its crossbars, posts and bases, ³² as well as the posts of the surrounding courtyard with their bases, tent pegs, ropes, all their equipment and everything related to their use. Assign to each man the specific things he is to carry. ³³ This is the service of the Merarite clans as they work at the tent of meeting under the direction of Ithamar son of Aaron, the priest.'

³⁴ Moses, Aaron and the leaders of the community counted the Kohathites by their clans and families. ³⁵ All the men from thirty to fifty years of age who came to serve in the work at the tent of meeting, ³⁶ counted by clans, were 2,750. ³⁷ This was the total of all those in the Kohathite clans who served at the tent of meeting. Moses and Aaron counted them according to the LORD's command through Moses.

³⁸ The Gershonites were counted by their clans and families. ³⁹ All the men from thirty to fifty years of age who came to serve in the work at the tent of meeting, ⁴⁰ counted by their clans and families, were 2,630. ⁴¹ This was the total of those in the Gershonite clans who served at the tent of meeting. Moses and Aaron counted them according to the LORD's command.

⁴² The Merarites were counted by their clans and families. ⁴³ All the men from thirty to fifty years of age who came to serve in the work at the tent of meeting, ⁴⁴ counted by their clans, were 3,200. ⁴⁵ This was the total of those in the Merarite clans. Moses and Aaron counted them according to the LORD's command through Moses.

⁴⁶ So Moses, Aaron and the leaders of Israel counted all the Levites by their clans and families. ⁴⁷ All the men from thirty to fifty years of age who came to do the work of serving and carrying the tent of meeting ⁴⁸ numbered 8,580. ⁴⁹ At the LORD's command through Moses, each was assigned his work and told what to carry.

Thus they were counted, as the LORD commanded Moses.

5 The LORD said to Moses, ² 'Command the Israelites to send away from the camp anyone who has a defiling skin disease or a discharge of any kind, or who is

ceremonially unclean because of a dead body. ³Send away male and female alike; send them outside the camp so that they will not defile their camp, where I dwell among them.' ⁴The Israelites did so; they sent them outside the camp. They did just as the Lord had instructed Moses.

⁵The Lord said to Moses, ⁶'Say to the Israelites: "Any man or woman who wrongs another in any way and so is unfaithful to the Lord is guilty ⁷and must confess the sin they have committed. They must make full restitution for the wrong they have done, add a fifth of the value to it and give it all to the person they have wronged. ⁸But if that person has no close relative to whom restitution can be made for the wrong, the restitution belongs to the Lord and must be given to the priest, along with the ram with which atonement is made for the wrongdoer. ⁹All the sacred contributions the Israelites bring to a priest will belong to him. ¹⁰Sacred things belong to their owners, but what they give to the priest will belong to the priest."'

¹¹Then the Lord said to Moses, ¹²'Speak to the Israelites and say to them: "If a man's wife goes astray and is unfaithful to him ¹³so that another man has sexual relations with her, and this is hidden from her husband and her impurity is undetected (since there is no witness against her and she has not been caught in the act), ¹⁴and if feelings of jealousy come over her husband and he suspects his wife and she is impure – or if he is jealous and suspects her even though she is not impure – ¹⁵then he is to take his wife to the priest. He must also take an offering of a tenth of an ephah of barley flour on her behalf. He must not pour olive oil on it or put incense on it, because it is a grain offering for jealousy, a reminder-offering to draw attention to wrongdoing.

¹⁶'"The priest shall bring her and make her stand before the Lord. ¹⁷Then he shall take some holy water in a clay jar and put some dust from the tabernacle floor into the water. ¹⁸After the priest has made the woman stand before the Lord, he shall loosen her hair and place in her hands the reminder-offering, the grain offering for jealousy, while he himself holds the bitter water that brings a curse. ¹⁹Then the priest shall put the woman under oath and say to her, 'If no other man has had sexual relations with you and you have not gone astray and become impure while married to your husband, may this bitter water that brings a curse not harm you. ²⁰But if you have gone astray while married to your husband and you have made yourself impure by having sexual relations with a man other than your husband' – ²¹here the priest is to put the woman under this curse – 'may the Lord cause you to become a curse among your people when he makes your womb miscarry and your abdomen swell. ²²May this water that brings a curse enter your body so that your abdomen swells or your womb miscarries.'

'"Then the woman is to say, 'Amen. So be it.'

²³'"The priest is to write these curses on a scroll and then wash them off into the bitter water. ²⁴He shall make the woman drink the bitter water that brings a curse, and this water that brings a curse and causes bitter suffering will enter her. ²⁵The priest is to take from her hands the grain offering for jealousy, wave it before the Lord and bring it to the altar. ²⁶The priest is then to take a handful of the grain offering as a memorial offering and burn it on the altar; after that, he is to make the woman drink the water. ²⁷If she has made herself impure and been unfaithful to her husband, this will be the result: when she is made to drink the water that brings a curse and causes bitter suffering, it will enter her, her abdomen will swell and her womb will miscarry, and she will become a curse. ²⁸If, however, the woman has not made herself impure, but is clean, she will be cleared of guilt and will be able to have children.

²⁹‘"This, then, is the law of jealousy when a woman goes astray and makes herself impure while married to her husband, ³⁰or when feelings of jealousy come over a man because he suspects his wife. The priest is to make her stand before the LORD and is to apply this entire law to her. ³¹The husband will be innocent of any wrongdoing, but the woman will bear the consequences of her sin."'

PSALM 33:1–9

¹Sing joyfully to the LORD, you righteous;
  it is fitting for the upright to praise him.
²Praise the LORD with the harp;
  make music to him on the ten-
    stringed lyre.
³Sing to him a new song;
  play skilfully, and shout for joy.

⁴For the word of the LORD is right and
    true;
  he is faithful in all he does.
⁵The LORD loves righteousness and
    justice;
  the earth is full of his unfailing love.

⁶By the word of the LORD the heavens were
    made,
  their starry host by the breath of his
    mouth.
⁷He gathers the waters of the sea into jars;
  he puts the deep into storehouses.
⁸Let all the earth fear the LORD;
  let all the people of the world revere
    him.
⁹For he spoke, and it came to be;
  he commanded, and it stood firm.

PROVERBS 7:24–27

²⁴Now then, my sons, listen to me;
  pay attention to what I say.

²⁵Do not let your heart turn to her ways
  or stray into her paths.
²⁶Many are the victims she has brought
    down;
  her slain are a mighty throng.
²⁷Her house is a highway to the grave,
  leading down to the chambers of
    death.

MARK 10:46–11:11

⁴⁶Then they came to Jericho. As Jesus and his disciples, together with a large crowd, were leaving the city, a blind man, Bartimaeus (which means 'son of Timaeus'), was sitting by the roadside begging. ⁴⁷When he heard that it was Jesus of Nazareth, he began to shout, 'Jesus, Son of David, have mercy on me!'

⁴⁸Many rebuked him and told him to be quiet, but he shouted all the more, 'Son of David, have mercy on me!'

⁴⁹Jesus stopped and said, 'Call him.'

So they called to the blind man, 'Cheer up! On your feet! He's calling you.' ⁵⁰Throwing his cloak aside, he jumped to his feet and came to Jesus.

⁵¹'What do you want me to do for you?' Jesus asked him.

The blind man said, 'Rabbi, I want to see.'

⁵²'Go,' said Jesus, 'your faith has healed you.' Immediately he received his sight and followed Jesus along the road.

11 As they approached Jerusalem and came to Bethphage and Bethany at the Mount of Olives, Jesus sent two of his disciples, ²saying to them, 'Go to the village ahead of you, and just as you enter it, you will find a colt tied there, which no one has ever ridden. Untie it and bring it here. ³If anyone asks you, "Why are you doing this?" say, "The Lord needs it and will send it back here shortly."'

⁴They went and found a colt outside in the street, tied at a doorway. As they untied it,

⁵some people standing there asked, 'What are you doing, untying that colt?' ⁶They answered as Jesus had told them to, and the people let them go. ⁷When they brought the colt to Jesus and threw their cloaks over it, he sat on it. ⁸Many people spread their cloaks on the road, while others spread branches they had cut in the fields. ⁹Those who went ahead and those who followed shouted,

'Hosanna!'

'Blessed is he who comes in the name of the Lord!'

¹⁰'Blessed is the coming kingdom of our father David!'

'Hosanna in the highest heaven!'

¹¹Jesus entered Jerusalem and went into the temple courts. He looked around at everything, but since it was already late, he went out to Bethany with the Twelve.

'Not From Me!'

'By the word of the LORD the heavens were made, their starry host by the breath of his mouth.' **Psalm 33:6**

Many modern astronomers probing into outer space with their gigantic telescopes favour two theories as to the origin of the universe. One is the so-called Big Bang Theory, according to which 'the cosmos started with a titanic explosion, and as a consequence has been expanding ever since.' The other is the Continuous Creation Theory, which maintains that 'the universe is self-creating and is constantly making itself out of nothing and falling back into nothingness again.'

What many scientists are not prepared to admit is that the ultimate energy behind the universe is not a Big Bang, but a Big Being – an intelligent Being of indescribable majesty and power who is able to do whatever He chooses. And because what He chooses is always good, He can be trusted to have the best interest of His creation at heart.

When Joseph Haydn, the famous Austrian composer, had finished his great oratorio *The Creation*, he is said to have cried, 'Not from me! Not from me! From above it has all come!' Our text for today reminds us that by God's Word were the heavens made and by His breath the stars were formed.

I once heard my father describe the creation in this way, 'It was no harder for God to create a world than it is for my son to blow soap bubbles into the air out of his clay pipe.' I often go back to that lovely image. I find that when contemplating this awesome, mighty, all-powerful God, my soul instinctively cries, 'How great Thou art.' I hope yours does too!

PRAYER

Yes Father, as I contemplate Your majesty and Your power, my soul cries out, 'How great Thou art.' It can do nothing else, for contemplation of You inevitably leads to adoration of You. Amen.

FURTHER STUDY

Matt. 19:16–26;
1 Chron. 29:12; Psa. 62:11;
Isa. 43:12–13
• What did Jesus declare?
• What did God declare?

March 12

■ NUMBERS 6:1–7:29

6 The LORD said to Moses, ²'Speak to the Israelites and say to them: "If a man or woman wants to make a special vow, a vow of dedication to the LORD as a Nazirite, ³they must abstain from wine and other fermented drink and must not drink vinegar made from wine or other fermented drink. They must not drink grape juice or eat grapes or raisins. ⁴As long as they remain under their Nazirite vow, they must not eat anything that comes from the grapevine, not even the seeds or skins.

⁵ "During the entire period of their Nazirite vow, no razor may be used on their head. They must be holy until the period of their dedication to the LORD is over; they must let their hair grow long.

⁶ "Throughout the period of their dedication to the LORD, the Nazirite must not go near a dead body. ⁷Even if their own father or mother or brother or sister dies, they must not make themselves ceremonially unclean on account of them, because the symbol of their dedication to God is on their head. ⁸Throughout the period of their dedication, they are consecrated to the LORD.

⁹ "If someone dies suddenly in the Nazirite's presence, thus defiling the hair that symbolises their dedication, they must shave their head on the seventh day – the day of their cleansing. ¹⁰Then on the eighth day they must bring two doves or two young pigeons to the priest at the entrance to the tent of meeting. ¹¹The priest is to offer one as a sin offering and the other as a burnt offering to make atonement for the Nazirite because they sinned by being in the presence of the dead body. That same day they are to consecrate their head again. ¹²They must rededicate themselves to the LORD for the same period of dedication and must bring a year-old male lamb as a guilt offering. The previous days do not count, because they became defiled during their period of dedication.

¹³ "Now this is the law of the Nazirite when the period of their dedication is over. They are to be brought to the entrance to the tent of meeting. ¹⁴There they are to present their offerings to the LORD: a year-old male lamb without defect for a burnt offering, a year-old ewe lamb without defect for a sin offering, a ram without defect for a fellowship offering, ¹⁵together with their grain offerings and drink offerings, and a basket of bread made with the finest flour and without yeast – thick loaves with olive oil mixed in, and thin loaves brushed with olive oil.

¹⁶ "The priest is to present all these before the LORD and make the sin offering and the burnt offering. ¹⁷He is to present the basket of unleavened bread and is to

sacrifice the ram as a fellowship offering to the LORD, together with its grain offering and drink offering.

18 ' "Then at the entrance to the tent of meeting, the Nazirite must shave off the hair that symbolises their dedication. They are to take the hair and put it in the fire that is under the sacrifice of the fellowship offering.

19 ' "After the Nazirite has shaved off the hair that symbolises their dedication, the priest is to place in their hands a boiled shoulder of the ram, and one thick loaf and one thin loaf from the basket, both made without yeast. 20 The priest shall then wave these before the LORD as a wave offering; they are holy and belong to the priest, together with the breast that was waved and the thigh that was presented. After that, the Nazirite may drink wine.

21 ' "This is the law of the Nazirite who vows offerings to the LORD in accordance with their dedication, in addition to whatever else they can afford. They must fulfil the vows they have made, according to the law of the Nazirite." '

22 The LORD said to Moses, 23 'Tell Aaron and his sons, "This is how you are to bless the Israelites. Say to them:

24 ' " 'The LORD bless you
       and keep you;
25 the LORD make his face shine on you
       and be gracious to you;
26 the LORD turn his face towards you
       and give you peace.' " '

27 'So they will put my name on the Israelites, and I will bless them.'

7 When Moses finished setting up the tabernacle, he anointed and consecrated it and all its furnishings. He also anointed and consecrated the altar and all its utensils. 2 Then the leaders of Israel, the heads of families who were the tribal leaders in charge of those who were counted,

made offerings. 3 They brought as their gifts before the LORD six covered carts and twelve oxen – an ox from each leader and a cart from every two. These they presented before the tabernacle.

4 The LORD said to Moses, 5 'Accept these from them, that they may be used in the work at the tent of meeting. Give them to the Levites as each man's work requires.'

6 So Moses took the carts and oxen and gave them to the Levites. 7 He gave two carts and four oxen to the Gershonites, as their work required, 8 and he gave four carts and eight oxen to the Merarites, as their work required. They were all under the direction of Ithamar son of Aaron, the priest. 9 But Moses did not give any to the Kohathites, because they were to carry on their shoulders the holy things, for which they were responsible.

10 When the altar was anointed, the leaders brought their offerings for its dedication and presented them before the altar. 11 For the LORD had said to Moses, 'Each day one leader is to bring his offering for the dedication of the altar.'

12 The one who brought his offering on the first day was Nahshon son of Amminadab of the tribe of Judah.

13 His offering was one silver plate weighing a hundred and thirty shekels, and one silver sprinkling bowl weighing seventy shekels, both according to the sanctuary shekel, each filled with the finest flour mixed with olive oil as a grain offering; 14 one gold dish weighing ten shekels, filled with incense; 15 one young bull, one ram and one male lamb a year old for a burnt offering; 16 one male goat for a sin offering; 17 and two oxen, five rams, five male goats and five male lambs a year old to be sacrificed as a fellowship offering. This was the offering of Nahshon son of Amminadab.

18 On the second day Nethanel son of Zuar, the leader of Issachar, brought his offering.

19 The offering he brought was one silver plate weighing a hundred and thirty shekels, and one silver sprinkling bowl weighing seventy shekels, both according to the sanctuary shekel, each filled with the finest flour mixed with olive oil as a grain offering; 20 one gold dish weighing ten shekels, filled with incense; 21 one young bull, one ram and one male lamb a year old for a burnt offering; 22 one male goat for a sin offering; 23 and two oxen, five rams, five male goats and five male lambs a year old to be sacrificed as a fellowship offering. This was the offering of Nethanel son of Zuar.

24 On the third day, Eliab son of Helon, the leader of the people of Zebulun, brought his offering.

25 His offering was one silver plate weighing a hundred and thirty shekels, and one silver sprinkling bowl weighing seventy shekels, both according to the sanctuary shekel, each filled with the finest flour mixed with olive oil as a grain offering; 26 one gold dish weighing ten shekels, filled with incense; 27 one young bull, one ram and one male lamb a year old for a burnt offering; 28 one male goat for a sin offering; 29 and two oxen, five rams, five male goats and five male lambs a year old to be sacrificed as a fellowship offering. This was the offering of Eliab son of Helon.

PSALM 33:10-17

10 The LORD foils the plans of the nations;
    he thwarts the purposes of the
        peoples.

11 But the plans of the LORD stand firm for
    ever,
    the purposes of his heart through all
        generations.

12 Blessed is the nation whose God is the
    LORD,
    the people he chose for his
        inheritance.
13 From heaven the LORD looks down
    and sees all mankind;
14 from his dwelling-place he watches
    all who live on earth –
15 he who forms the hearts of all,
    who considers everything they do.

16 No king is saved by the size of his army;
    no warrior escapes by his great
        strength.
17 A horse is a vain hope for deliverance;
    despite all its great strength it cannot
        save.

PROVERBS 8:1-3

8 Does not wisdom call out?
  Does not understanding raise her
      voice?
2 At the highest point along the way,
    where the paths meet, she takes her
        stand;
3 beside the gate leading into the city,
    at the entrance, she cries aloud:

MARK 11:12-33

12 The next day as they were leaving Bethany, Jesus was hungry. 13 Seeing in the distance a fig-tree in leaf, he went to find out if it had any fruit. When he reached it, he found nothing but leaves, because it was not the season for figs. 14 Then he said to the tree, 'May no one ever eat fruit from you again.' And his disciples heard him say it.

¹⁵On reaching Jerusalem, Jesus entered the temple courts and began driving out those who were buying and selling there. He overturned the tables of the money-changers and the benches of those selling doves, ¹⁶and would not allow anyone to carry merchandise through the temple courts. ¹⁷And as he taught them, he said, 'Is it not written: "My house will be called a house of prayer for all nations"? But you have made it "a den of robbers".'

¹⁸The chief priests and the teachers of the law heard this and began looking for a way to kill him, for they feared him, because the whole crowd was amazed at his teaching.

¹⁹When evening came, Jesus and his disciples went out of the city.

²⁰In the morning, as they went along, they saw the fig-tree withered from the roots. ²¹Peter remembered and said to Jesus, 'Rabbi, look! The fig-tree you cursed has withered!'

²²'Have faith in God,' Jesus answered. ²³'Truly I tell you, if anyone says to this mountain, "Go, throw yourself into the sea," and does not doubt in their heart but believes that what they say will happen, it will be done for them. ²⁴Therefore I tell you, whatever you ask for in prayer, believe that you have received it, and it will be yours. ²⁵And when you stand praying, if you hold anything against anyone, forgive them, so that your Father in heaven may forgive you your sins.' [26]a

²⁷They arrived again in Jerusalem, and while Jesus was walking in the temple courts, the chief priests, the teachers of the law and the elders came to him. ²⁸'By what authority are you doing these things?' they asked. 'And who gave you authority to do this?'

²⁹Jesus replied, 'I will ask you one question. Answer me, and I will tell you by what authority I am doing these things. ³⁰John's baptism – was it from heaven, or of human origin? Tell me!'

³¹They discussed it among themselves and said, 'If we say, "From heaven," he will ask, "Then why didn't you believe him?" ³²But if we say, "Of human origin" ...' (They feared the people, for everyone held that John really was a prophet.)

³³So they answered Jesus, 'We don't know.'

Jesus said, 'Neither will I tell you by what authority I am doing these things.'

---

a Some manuscripts include here words similar to Matthew 6:15

Togetherness

'Truly I tell you, if anyone says to this mountain, "Go, throw yourself into the sea," and does not doubt in their heart but believes that what they say will happen, it will be done for them.' **Mark 11:23**

Just as the deer's perfect correlation between its front and rear feet allows it to make its way swiftly and safely to the mountaintop, so the Christian who has perfect coordination between the head and heart will rise to new heights with God. For you see, unless a person's head and heart are properly coordinated and move purposefully together, it is possible to miss one's step on the steep slopes of Christian experience and become a spiritual casualty.

I have known many Christians in my time who, because they lack coordination between what they ask for with their lips and what they want deep down in their hearts, stay in the same place spiritually year after year. They are not bad people; they just lack the spiritual coordination of the mature Christian, and thus they never know what it is to ascend into the mountain peaks with God.

Perhaps nowhere in Scripture is this truth more clearly portrayed than in the verse before us today. We are told that things happen in the spiritual realm when there is perfect coordination between what we ask for and what we believe. When our mind and our heart are in alignment, when they track together with the sure-footedness of a mountain deer, then nothing shall be impossible to us. How many of us, I wonder, miss our step on the slopes of the Christian life because our hearts and minds are not properly and perfectly coordinated?

PRAYER

Gracious and loving Heavenly Father, slowly I am beginning to see the truth that underlies Your promise to make my feet like deers' feet. Show me how to be as coordinated in the spiritual realm as the deer is in the natural realm. Amen.

FURTHER STUDY

Isa. 58:1-11; Matt. 23
• Why was the Lord displeased with Israel?
• How did Jesus depict the Pharisees?

March 13

■ NUMBERS 7:30-89

30 On the fourth day Elizur son of Shedeur, the leader of the people of Reuben, brought his offering.

31 His offering was one silver plate weighing a hundred and thirty shekels, and one silver sprinkling bowl weighing seventy shekels, both according to the sanctuary shekel, each filled with the finest flour mixed with olive oil as a grain offering; 32 one gold dish weighing ten shekels, filled with incense; 33 one young bull, one ram and one male lamb a year old for a burnt offering; 34 one male goat for a sin offering; 35 and two oxen, five rams, five male goats and five male lambs a year old to be sacrificed as a fellowship offering. This was the offering of Elizur son of Shedeur.

36 On the fifth day Shelumiel son of Zurishaddai, the leader of the people of Simeon, brought his offering.

37 His offering was one silver plate weighing a hundred and thirty shekels, and one silver sprinkling bowl weighing seventy shekels, both according to the sanctuary shekel, each filled with the finest flour mixed with olive oil as a grain offering; 38 one gold dish weighing ten shekels, filled with incense; 39 one young bull, one ram and one male lamb a year old for a burnt offering; 40 one male goat for a sin offering; 41 and two oxen, five rams, five male goats and five male lambs a

year old to be sacrificed as a fellowship offering. This was the offering of Shelumiel son of Zurishaddai.

⁴²On the sixth day Eliasaph son of Deuel, the leader of the people of Gad, brought his offering. ⁴³His offering was one silver plate weighing a hundred and thirty shekels, and one silver sprinkling bowl weighing seventy shekels, both according to the sanctuary shekel, each filled with the finest flour mixed with olive oil as a grain offering; ⁴⁴one gold dish weighing ten shekels, filled with incense; ⁴⁵one young bull, one ram and one male lamb a year old for a burnt offering; ⁴⁶one male goat for a sin offering; ⁴⁷and two oxen, five rams, five male goats and five male lambs a year old to be sacrificed as a fellowship offering. This was the offering of Eliasaph son of Deuel.

⁴⁸On the seventh day Elishama son of Ammihud, the leader of the people of Ephraim, brought his offering. ⁴⁹His offering was one silver plate weighing a hundred and thirty shekels, and one silver sprinkling bowl weighing seventy shekels, both according to the sanctuary shekel, each filled with the finest flour mixed with olive oil as a grain offering; ⁵⁰one gold dish weighing ten shekels, filled with incense; ⁵¹one young bull, one ram and one male lamb a year old for a burnt offering; ⁵²one male goat for a sin offering; ⁵³and two oxen, five rams, five male goats and five male lambs a year old to be sacrificed as a fellowship offering. This was the offering of Elishama son of Ammihud.

⁵⁴On the eighth day Gamaliel son of Pedahzur, the leader of the people of Manasseh, brought his offering. ⁵⁵His offering was one silver plate weighing a hundred and thirty shekels, and one silver sprinkling bowl weighing seventy shekels, both according to the sanctuary shekel, each filled with the finest flour mixed with olive oil as a grain offering; ⁵⁶one gold dish weighing ten shekels, filled with incense; ⁵⁷one young bull, one ram and one male lamb a year old for a burnt offering; ⁵⁸one male goat for a sin offering; ⁵⁹and two oxen, five rams, five male goats and five male lambs a year old to be sacrificed as a fellowship offering. This was the offering of Gamaliel son of Pedahzur.

⁶⁰On the ninth day Abidan son of Gideoni, the leader of the people of Benjamin, brought his offering. ⁶¹His offering was one silver plate weighing a hundred and thirty shekels, and one silver sprinkling bowl weighing seventy shekels, both according to the sanctuary shekel, each filled with the finest flour mixed with olive oil as a grain offering; ⁶²one gold dish weighing ten shekels, filled with incense; ⁶³one young bull, one ram and one male lamb a year old for a burnt offering; ⁶⁴one male goat for a sin offering; ⁶⁵and two oxen, five rams, five male goats and five male lambs a year old to be sacrificed as a fellowship offering. This was the offering of Abidan son of Gideoni.

⁶⁶On the tenth day Ahiezer son of Ammishaddai, the leader of the people of Dan, brought his offering. ⁶⁷His offering was one silver plate weighing a hundred and thirty shekels, and one silver sprinkling bowl weighing seventy shekels, both according to the sanctuary shekel, each

filled with the finest flour mixed with olive oil as a grain offering; [68] one gold dish weighing ten shekels, filled with incense; [69] one young bull, one ram and one male lamb a year old for a burnt offering; [70] one male goat for a sin offering; [71] and two oxen, five rams, five male goats and five male lambs a year old to be sacrificed as a fellowship offering. This was the offering of Ahiezer son of Ammishaddai.

[72] On the eleventh day Pagiel son of Okran, the leader of the people of Asher, brought his offering.

[73] His offering was one silver plate weighing a hundred and thirty shekels, and one silver sprinkling bowl weighing seventy shekels, both according to the sanctuary shekel, each filled with the finest flour mixed with olive oil as a grain offering; [74] one gold dish weighing ten shekels, filled with incense; [75] one young bull, one ram and one male lamb a year old for a burnt offering; [76] one male goat for a sin offering; [77] and two oxen, five rams, five male goats and five male lambs a year old to be sacrificed as a fellowship offering. This was the offering of Pagiel son of Okran.

[78] On the twelfth day Ahira son of Enan, the leader of the people of Naphtali, brought his offering.

[79] His offering was one silver plate weighing a hundred and thirty shekels, and one silver sprinkling bowl weighing seventy shekels, both according to the sanctuary shekel, each filled with the finest flour mixed with olive oil as a grain offering; [80] one gold dish weighing ten shekels, filled with incense; [81] one young bull, one ram and one male lamb a year old for a burnt offering; [82] one male goat for a

sin offering; [83] and two oxen, five rams, five male goats and five male lambs a year old to be sacrificed as a fellowship offering. This was the offering of Ahira son of Enan.

[84] These were the offerings of the Israelite leaders for the dedication of the altar when it was anointed: twelve silver plates, twelve silver sprinkling bowls and twelve gold dishes. [85] Each silver plate weighed a hundred and thirty shekels, and each sprinkling bowl seventy shekels. Altogether, the silver dishes weighed two thousand four hundred shekels, according to the sanctuary shekel. [86] The twelve gold dishes filled with incense weighed ten shekels each, according to the sanctuary shekel. Altogether, the gold dishes weighed a hundred and twenty shekels. [87] The total number of animals for the burnt offering came to twelve young bulls, twelve rams and twelve male lambs a year old, together with their grain offering. Twelve male goats were used for the sin offering. [88] The total number of animals for the sacrifice of the fellowship offering came to twenty-four oxen, sixty rams, sixty male goats and sixty male lambs a year old. These were the offerings for the dedication of the altar after it was anointed.

[89] When Moses entered the tent of meeting to speak with the LORD, he heard the voice speaking to him from between the two cherubim above the atonement cover on the ark of the covenant law. In this way the LORD spoke to him.

▬ PSALM 33:18-22

[18] But the eyes of the LORD are on those who
    fear him,
    on those whose hope is in his
        unfailing love,
[19] to deliver them from death
    and keep them alive in famine.

²⁰ We wait in hope for the LORD;
    he is our help and our shield.
²¹ In him our hearts rejoice,
    for we trust in his holy name.
²² May your unfailing love be with us,
    LORD,
    even as we put our hope in you.

■ PROVERBS 8:4-5

⁴ 'To you, O people, I call out;
    I raise my voice to all humanity.
⁵ You who are simple, gain prudence;
    you who are foolish, set your hearts
    on it.

■ MARK 12:1-27

12 Jesus then began to speak to them in parables: 'A man planted a vineyard. He put a wall round it, dug a pit for the winepress and built a watchtower. Then he rented the vineyard to some farmers and moved to another place. ² At harvest time he sent a servant to the tenants to collect from them some of the fruit of the vineyard. ³ But they seized him, beat him and sent him away empty-handed. ⁴ Then he sent another servant to them; they struck this man on the head and treated him shamefully. ⁵ He sent still another, and that one they killed. He sent many others; some of them they beat, others they killed.

⁶ 'He had one left to send, a son, whom he loved. He sent him last of all, saying, "They will respect my son."

⁷ 'But the tenants said to one another, "This is the heir. Come, let's kill him, and the inheritance will be ours." ⁸ So they took him and killed him, and threw him out of the vineyard.

⁹ 'What then will the owner of the vineyard do? He will come and kill those tenants and give the vineyard to others. ¹⁰ Haven't

you read this passage of Scripture:

    ' "The stone the builders rejected
      has become the cornerstone;
¹¹ the Lord has done this,
    and it is marvellous in our eyes"?'

¹² Then the chief priests, the teachers of the law and the elders looked for a way to arrest him because they knew he had spoken the parable against them. But they were afraid of the crowd; so they left him and went away.

¹³ Later they sent some of the Pharisees and Herodians to Jesus to catch him in his words. ¹⁴ They came to him and said, 'Teacher, we know that you are a man of integrity. You aren't swayed by others, because you pay no attention to who they are; but you teach the way of God in accordance with the truth. Is it right to pay the poll-tax to Caesar or not? ¹⁵ Should we pay or shouldn't we?'

But Jesus knew their hypocrisy. 'Why are you trying to trap me?' he asked. 'Bring me a denarius and let me look at it.' ¹⁶ They brought the coin, and he asked them, 'Whose image is this? And whose inscription?'

'Caesar's,' they replied.

¹⁷ Then Jesus said to them, 'Give back to Caesar what is Caesar's and to God what is God's.'

And they were amazed at him.

¹⁸ Then the Sadducees, who say there is no resurrection, came to him with a question. ¹⁹ 'Teacher,' they said, 'Moses wrote for us that if a man's brother dies and leaves a wife but no children, the man must marry the widow and raise up offspring for his brother. ²⁰ Now there were seven brothers. The first one married and died without leaving any children. ²¹ The second one married the widow, but he also died, leaving no child. It was the same with the third. ²² In fact, none of the seven left any children. Last of all, the woman died too. ²³ At the resurrection

whose wife will she be, since the seven were married to her?'

²⁴Jesus replied, 'Are you not in error because you do not know the Scriptures or the power of God? ²⁵When the dead rise, they will neither marry nor be given in marriage; they will be like the angels in heaven.

²⁶Now about the dead rising – have you not read in the Book of Moses, in the account of the burning bush, how God said to him, "I am the God of Abraham, the God of Isaac, and the God of Jacob"? ²⁷He is not the God of the dead, but of the living. You are badly mistaken!'

Overpopulation – A Myth

'But the eyes of the LORD are on those who fear him, on those whose hope is in his unfailing love ...'
Psalm 33:18

A modern writer tells how once he asked an old man how he managed to live alone in a single cottage, miles from anywhere. The old man answered cheerfully that he enjoyed it since, as he explained, 'Providence is my next-door neighbour.'

Despite what many politicians and scientists tell us, the problems of this earth are not physical but spiritual. It is not overpopulation that requires our attention, but spiritual ignorance. If people came into a knowledge of Jesus Christ as their Lord and Saviour, then they would be given the wisdom to use the earth's resources rightly. Murray Norris in his book, *The Myth of Overpopulation*, says that only 15 per cent of the arable land on the globe is being farmed, and only half of that every year. It goes without saying, of course, that although God supplies the basic necessities, people have to put some effort into harvesting them; our problem is not lack of resources, nor too many people – it is our lack of dependency upon God.

Paul, in 1 Timothy 4:3, says that God has created all food 'to be received with thanksgiving by those who believe and who know the truth.' Can you see what this verse is saying? God has provided us an incredible abundance of food so that we might express our thanks to Him.

The rest of the world indulges with little gratitude. Let's make sure that not one day passes without this prayer meaningfully crossing our lips: 'Give us today our daily bread.'

PRAYER

O Father, now that I understand the significance of Your words, 'Give us today our daily bread,' help me, every time I utter them, to make them not just a recitation, but a realisation. For Jesus' sake. Amen.

FURTHER STUDY

James 2; Rom. 12:11; Prov. 13:11; 2 Thess. 3:10
• How does James relate faith and works?
• What is Paul's exhortation?

March 14

▬ NUMBERS 8:1–10:10

8 The LORD said to Moses, ²'Speak to Aaron and say to him, "When you set up the lamps, see that all seven light up the area in front of the lampstand."'

³Aaron did so; he set up the lamps so that they faced forwards on the lampstand, just as the LORD commanded Moses. ⁴This is how the lampstand was made: it was made of hammered gold – from its base to its blossoms. The lampstand was made exactly like the pattern the LORD had shown Moses.

⁵The LORD said to Moses: ⁶'Take the Levites from among all the Israelites and make them ceremonially clean. ⁷To purify them, do this: sprinkle the water of cleansing on them; then make them shave their whole bodies and wash their clothes. And so they will purify themselves. ⁸Make them take a young bull with its grain offering of the finest flour mixed with olive oil; then you are to take a second young bull for a sin offering. ⁹Bring the Levites to the front of the tent of meeting and assemble the whole Israelite community. ¹⁰You are to bring the Levites before the LORD, and the Israelites are to lay their hands on them. ¹¹Aaron is to present the Levites before the LORD as a wave offering from the Israelites, so that they may be ready to do the work of the LORD.

¹²'Then the Levites are to lay their hands on the heads of the bulls, using one for a sin offering to the LORD and the other for a burnt offering, to make atonement for the Levites. ¹³Make the Levites stand in front of Aaron and his sons and then present them as a wave offering to the LORD. ¹⁴In this way you are to set the Levites apart from the other Israelites, and the Levites will be mine.

¹⁵'After you have purified the Levites and presented them as a wave offering, they are to come to do their work at the tent of meeting. ¹⁶They are the Israelites who are to be given wholly to me. I have taken them as my own in place of the firstborn, the first male offspring from every Israelite woman. ¹⁷Every firstborn male in Israel, whether human or animal, is mine. When I struck down all the firstborn in Egypt, I set them apart for myself. ¹⁸And I have taken the Levites in place of all the firstborn sons in Israel. ¹⁹From among all the Israelites, I have given the Levites as gifts to Aaron and his sons to do the work at the tent of meeting on behalf of the Israelites and to make atonement for them so that no plague will strike the Israelites when they go near the sanctuary.'

²⁰Moses, Aaron and the whole Israelite community did with the Levites just as the LORD commanded Moses. ²¹The Levites purified themselves and washed their clothes. Then Aaron presented them as a wave offering before the LORD and made atonement for them to purify them. ²²After that, the Levites came to do their work at the tent of meeting under the supervision of Aaron and his sons. They did with the Levites just as the LORD commanded Moses.

²³The LORD said to Moses, ²⁴'This applies to the Levites: men twenty-five years old or more shall come to take part in the work at the tent of meeting, ²⁵but at the age of fifty, they must retire from their usual duties and work no longer. ²⁶They may assist their brothers in performing their duties at the tent of meeting, but they themselves must not do the work. This, then, is how you are to assign the responsibilities of the Levites.'

9 The LORD spoke to Moses in the Desert of Sinai in the first month of the second year after they came out of Egypt.

He said, ²'Make the Israelites celebrate the Passover at the appointed time. ³Celebrate it at the appointed time, at twilight on the fourteenth day of this month, in accordance with all its rules and regulations.'

⁴So Moses told the Israelites to celebrate the Passover, ⁵and they did so in the Desert of Sinai at twilight on the fourteenth day of the first month. The Israelites did everything just as the LORD commanded Moses.

⁶But some of them could not celebrate the Passover on that day because they were ceremonially unclean on account of a dead body. So they came to Moses and Aaron that same day ⁷and said to Moses, 'We have become unclean because of a dead body, but why should we be kept from presenting the LORD's offering with the other Israelites at the appointed time?'

⁸Moses answered them, 'Wait until I find out what the LORD commands concerning you.'

⁹Then the LORD said to Moses, ¹⁰'Tell the Israelites: "When any of you or your descendants are unclean because of a dead body or are away on a journey, they are still to celebrate the LORD's Passover, ¹¹but they are to do it on the fourteenth day of the second month at twilight. They are to eat the lamb, together with unleavened bread and bitter herbs. ¹²They must not leave any of it till morning or break any of its bones. When they celebrate the Passover, they must follow all the regulations. ¹³But if anyone who is ceremonially clean and not on a journey fails to celebrate the Passover, they must be cut off from their people for not presenting the LORD's offering at the appointed time. They will bear the consequences of their sin. ¹⁴"A foreigner residing among you is also to celebrate the LORD's Passover in accordance with its rules and regulations. You must have the same regulations for both the foreigner and the native-born."'

¹⁵On the day the tabernacle, the tent of the covenant law, was set up, the cloud covered it. From evening till morning the cloud above the tabernacle looked like fire. ¹⁶That is how it continued to be; the cloud covered it, and at night it looked like fire. ¹⁷Whenever the cloud lifted from above the tent, the Israelites set out; wherever the cloud settled, the Israelites set up camp. ¹⁸At the LORD's command the Israelites set out, and at his command they set up camp. As long as the cloud stayed over the tabernacle, they remained in camp. ¹⁹When the cloud remained over the tabernacle a long time, the Israelites obeyed the LORD's order and did not set out. ²⁰Sometimes the cloud was over the tabernacle for only a few days; at the LORD's command they would set up camp, and then at his command they would set out. ²¹Sometimes the cloud stayed only from evening till morning, and when it lifted in the morning, they set out. Whether by day or by night, whenever the cloud lifted, they set out. ²²Whether the cloud stayed over the tabernacle for two days or a month or a year, the Israelites would remain in camp and not set out; but when it lifted, they would set out. ²³At the LORD's command they set up camp, and at the LORD's command they set out. They obeyed the LORD's order, in accordance with his command through Moses.

10 The LORD said to Moses: ²'Make two trumpets of hammered silver, and use them for calling the community together and for the camps to set out. ³When both are sounded, the whole community is to assemble before you at the entrance to the tent of meeting. ⁴If only one is sounded, the leaders – the heads of the clans of Israel – are to assemble before you. ⁵When a trumpet blast is sounded, the tribes camping on the east are to set out. ⁶At the sounding of a second blast, the camps on the south are to set out. The blast will be the signal for setting out. ⁷To gather the assembly, blow the trumpets, but not with the signal for setting out.

⁸'The sons of Aaron, the priests, are to blow the trumpets. This is to be a lasting ordinance

for you and the generations to come. ⁹When you go into battle in your own land against an enemy who is oppressing you, sound a blast on the trumpets. Then you will be remembered by the LORD your God and rescued from your enemies. ¹⁰ Also at your times of rejoicing – your appointed festivals and New Moon feasts – you are to sound the trumpets over your burnt offerings and fellowship offerings, and they will be a memorial for you before your God. I am the LORD your God.'

▬ PSALM 34:1–7

¹ I will extol the LORD at all times;
    his praise will always be on my lips.
² I will glory in the LORD;
    let the afflicted hear and rejoice.
³ Glorify the LORD with me:
    let us exalt his name together.

⁴ I sought the LORD, and he answered me;
    he delivered me from all my fears.
⁵ Those who look to him are radiant;
    their faces are never covered with
        shame.
⁶ This poor man called, and the LORD
        heard him;
    he saved him out of all his troubles.
⁷ The angel of the LORD encamps around
        those who fear him,
    and he delivers them.

▬ PROVERBS 8:6–7

⁶ Listen, for I have trustworthy things to say;
    I open my lips to speak what is right.
⁷ My mouth speaks what is true,
    for my lips detest wickedness.

▬ MARK 12:28–44

²⁸ One of the teachers of the law came and heard them debating. Noticing that Jesus had given them a good answer, he asked him, 'Of all the commandments, which is the most important?'

²⁹ 'The most important one,' answered Jesus, 'is this: "Hear, O Israel: the Lord our God, the Lord is one. ³⁰ Love the Lord your God with all your heart and with all your soul and with all your mind and with all your strength." ³¹ The second is this: "Love your neighbour as yourself." There is no commandment greater than these.'

³² 'Well said, teacher,' the man replied. 'You are right in saying that God is one and there is no other but him. ³³ To love him with all your heart, with all your understanding and with all your strength, and to love your neighbour as yourself is more important than all burnt offerings and sacrifices.'

³⁴ When Jesus saw that he had answered wisely, he said to him, 'You are not far from the kingdom of God.' And from then on no one dared ask him any more questions.

³⁵ While Jesus was teaching in the temple courts, he asked, 'Why do the teachers of the law say that the Messiah is the son of David? ³⁶ David himself, speaking by the Holy Spirit, declared:

' "The Lord said to my Lord:
    'Sit at my right hand
until I put your enemies
    under your feet.' "

³⁷ David himself calls him "Lord". How then can he be his son?'

The large crowd listened to him with delight.

³⁸ As he taught, Jesus said, 'Watch out for the teachers of the law. They like to walk around in flowing robes and be greeted with respect in the market-places, ³⁹ and have the most important seats in the synagogues and the places of honour at banquets. ⁴⁰ They devour widows' houses and for a show make lengthy prayers. These

men will be punished most severely.'

⁴¹Jesus sat down opposite the place where the offerings were put and watched the crowd putting their money into the temple treasury. Many rich people threw in large amounts. ⁴²But a poor widow came and put in two very small copper coins, worth only a few pence.

⁴³Calling his disciples to him, Jesus said, 'Truly I tell you, this poor widow has put more into the treasury than all the others. ⁴⁴They all gave out of their wealth; but she, out of her poverty, put in everything – all she had to live on.'

A Clear Perspective

'Glorify the LORD with me: let us exalt his name together.' **Psalm 34:3**

Honouring God's Name does not mean pronouncing the word 'God' in reverential tones. It is rather honouring all that God is, His qualities, character, and attributes – all the things embodied in His Name. When the psalmist said: 'The nations will fear the name of the LORD' (Psa. 102:15), did this mean they feared the letters in the word 'Yahweh'? No, they feared the Lord God Himself.

At the risk of over-simplifying the opening clauses of the Lord's Prayer, what Jesus is teaching us is to come before the Father with this attitude: 'Our Father, who cares for us with true tenderness, and who has in heaven the supplies to meet our every need; may Your attributes, Your nature, Your character, Your reputation, Your person, Your whole being itself be honoured.' Before we start asking for what we want from God, we need to have the right perspective of God.

I have just been reading some words of Gregory of Nyssa, who prayed: 'May I become through Thy help blameless, just, and pious. May I abstain from every evil, speak the truth, and do justice. May I walk in the straight path, shining with temperance adorned with incorruption, beautiful through wisdom and prudence. May I meditate upon the things that are above and despise what is earthly, for a man can hallow God's Name in no other way than by reflecting His character and bear witness to the fact that divine power is the cause of his goodness.'

PRAYER

Gracious Father, I see that if I am to become effective in prayer, then I must get all my values straight. Thank You for giving me a clear pattern to follow and for reminding me that when I honour Your Name, You will honour mine. Thank You, Father. Amen.

FURTHER STUDY

Psa. 111:1-10; 33:8; 34:9; 86:11
• What is the beginning of wisdom?
• What does it mean to fear the Lord?

March 15

■ NUMBERS 10:11–11:35

[11] On the twentieth day of the second month of the second year, the cloud lifted from above the tabernacle of the covenant law. [12] Then the Israelites set out from the Desert of Sinai and travelled from place to place until the cloud came to rest in the Desert of Paran. [13] They set out, this first time, at the LORD's command through Moses.

[14] The divisions of the camp of Judah went first, under their standard. Nahshon son of Amminadab was in command. [15] Nethanel son of Zuar was over the division of the tribe of Issachar, [16] and Eliab son of Helon was over the division of the tribe of Zebulun. [17] Then the tabernacle was taken down, and the Gershonites and Merarites, who carried it, set out.

[18] The divisions of the camp of Reuben went next, under their standard. Elizur son of Shedeur was in command. [19] Shelumiel son of Zurishaddai was over the division of the tribe of Simeon, [20] and Eliasaph son of Deuel was over the division of the tribe of Gad. [21] Then the Kohathites set out, carrying the holy things. The tabernacle was to be set up before they arrived.

[22] The divisions of the camp of Ephraim went next, under their standard. Elishama son of Ammihud was in command. [23] Gamaliel son of Pedahzur was over the division of the tribe of Manasseh, [24] and Abidan son of Gideoni was over the division of the tribe of Benjamin.

[25] Finally, as the rear guard for all the units, the divisions of the camp of Dan set out under their standard. Ahiezer son of Ammishaddai was in command. [26] Pagiel son of Okran was over the division of the tribe of Asher, [27] and Ahira son of Enan was over the division of the tribe of Naphtali. [28] This was the order of march for the Israelite divisions as they set out.

[29] Now Moses said to Hobab son of Reuel the Midianite, Moses' father-in-law, 'We are setting out for the place about which the LORD said, "I will give it to you." Come with us and we will treat you well, for the LORD has promised good things to Israel.'

[30] He answered, 'No, I will not go; I am going back to my own land and my own people.'

[31] But Moses said, 'Please do not leave us. You know where we should camp in the wilderness, and you can be our eyes. [32] If you come with us, we will share with you whatever good things the LORD gives us.'

[33] So they set out from the mountain of the LORD and travelled for three days. The ark of the covenant of the LORD went before them during those three days to find them a place to rest. [34] The cloud of the LORD was over them by day when they set out from the camp. [35] Whenever the ark set out, Moses said,

'Rise up, LORD!
    May your enemies be scattered;
    may your foes flee before you.'

[36] Whenever it came to rest, he said,

'Return, LORD,
    to the countless thousands of Israel.'

11 Now the people complained about their hardships in the hearing of the LORD, and when he heard them his anger was aroused. Then fire from the LORD burned among them and consumed some of the outskirts of the camp. [2] When the people cried out to Moses, he prayed to the LORD and the fire died down. [3] So that place was called Taberah, because fire from the LORD had burned among them.

⁴The rabble with them began to crave other food, and again the Israelites started wailing and said, 'If only we had meat to eat! ⁵We remember the fish we ate in Egypt at no cost – also the cucumbers, melons, leeks, onions and garlic. ⁶But now we have lost our appetite; we never see anything but this manna!'

⁷The manna was like coriander seed and looked like resin. ⁸The people went around gathering it, and then ground it in a hand-mill or crushed it in a mortar. They cooked it in a pot or made it into loaves. And it tasted like something made with olive oil. ⁹When the dew settled on the camp at night, the manna also came down.

¹⁰Moses heard the people of every family wailing at the entrance to their tents. The LORD became exceedingly angry, and Moses was troubled. ¹¹He asked the LORD, 'Why have you brought this trouble on your servant? What have I done to displease you that you put the burden of all these people on me? ¹²Did I conceive all these people? Did I give them birth? Why do you tell me to carry them in my arms, as a nurse carries an infant, to the land you promised on oath to their ancestors? ¹³Where can I get meat for all these people? They keep wailing to me, "Give us meat to eat!" ¹⁴I cannot carry all these people by myself; the burden is too heavy for me. ¹⁵If this is how you are going to treat me, please go ahead and kill me right now – if I have found favour in your eyes – and do not let me face my own ruin.'

¹⁶The LORD said to Moses: 'Bring me seventy of Israel's elders who are known to you as leaders and officials among the people. Make them come to the tent of meeting, that they may stand there with you. ¹⁷I will come down and speak with you there, and I will take some of the power of the Spirit that is on you and put it on them. They will share the burden of the people with you so that you will not have to carry it alone.

¹⁸'Tell the people: "Consecrate yourselves in preparation for tomorrow, when you will eat meat. The LORD heard you when you wailed, 'If only we had meat to eat! We were better off in Egypt!' Now the LORD will give you meat, and you will eat it. ¹⁹You will not eat it for just one day, or two days, or five, ten or twenty days, ²⁰but for a whole month – until it comes out of your nostrils and you loathe it – because you have rejected the LORD, who is among you, and have wailed before him, saying, 'Why did we ever leave Egypt?'"'

²¹But Moses said, 'Here I am among six hundred thousand men on foot, and you say, "I will give them meat to eat for a whole month!" ²²Would they have enough if flocks and herds were slaughtered for them? Would they have enough if all the fish in the sea were caught for them?'

²³The LORD answered Moses, 'Is the LORD's arm too short? Now you will see whether or not what I say will come true for you.'

²⁴So Moses went out and told the people what the LORD had said. He brought together seventy of their elders and made them stand round the tent. ²⁵Then the LORD came down in the cloud and spoke with him, and he took some of the power of the Spirit that was on him and put it on the seventy elders. When the Spirit rested on them, they prophesied – but did not do so again.

²⁶However, two men, whose names were Eldad and Medad, had remained in the camp. They were listed among the elders, but did not go out to the tent. Yet the Spirit also rested on them, and they prophesied in the camp. ²⁷A young man ran and told Moses, 'Eldad and Medad are prophesying in the camp.'

²⁸Joshua son of Nun, who had been Moses' assistant since youth, spoke up and said, 'Moses, my lord, stop them!'

²⁹But Moses replied, 'Are you jealous for my sake? I wish that all the LORD's people were prophets and that the LORD would put his Spirit on them!' ³⁰Then Moses and the elders of Israel returned to the camp.

³¹ Now a wind went out from the LORD and drove quail in from the sea. It scattered them up to two cubits deep all around the camp, as far as a day's walk in any direction. ³² All that day and night and all the next day the people went out and gathered quail. No one gathered less than ten homers. Then they spread them out all around the camp. ³³ But while the meat was still between their teeth and before it could be consumed, the anger of the LORD burned against the people, and he struck them with a severe plague. ³⁴ Therefore the place was named Kibroth Hattaavah, because there they buried the people who had craved other food.

³⁵ From Kibroth Hattaavah the people travelled to Hazeroth and stayed there.

▬ PSALM 34:8-14

⁸ Taste and see that the LORD is good;
  blessed is the one who takes refuge in
  him.
⁹ Fear the LORD, you his holy people,
  for those who fear him lack nothing.
¹⁰ The lions may grow weak and hungry,
  but those who seek the LORD lack no
  good thing.
¹¹ Come, my children, listen to me;
  I will teach you the fear of the LORD.
¹² Whoever of you loves life
  and desires to see many good days,
¹³ keep your tongue from evil
  and your lips from telling lies.
¹⁴ Turn from evil and do good;
  seek peace and pursue it.

▬ PROVERBS 8:8-9

⁸ All the words of my mouth are just;
  none of them is crooked or perverse.
⁹ To the discerning all of them are right;
  they are upright to those who have
  found knowledge.

▬ MARK 13:1-20

13 As Jesus was leaving the temple, one of his disciples said to him, 'Look, Teacher! What massive stones! What magnificent buildings!'

² 'Do you see all these great buildings?' replied Jesus. 'Not one stone here will be left on another; every one will be thrown down.'

³ As Jesus was sitting on the Mount of Olives opposite the temple, Peter, James, John and Andrew asked him privately, ⁴ 'Tell us, when will these things happen? And what will be the sign that they are all about to be fulfilled?'

⁵ Jesus said to them: 'Watch out that no one deceives you. ⁶ Many will come in my name, claiming, "I am he," and will deceive many. ⁷ When you hear of wars and rumours of wars, do not be alarmed. Such things must happen, but the end is still to come. ⁸ Nation will rise against nation, and kingdom against kingdom. There will be earthquakes in various places, and famines. These are the beginning of birth-pains.

⁹ 'You must be on your guard. You will be handed over to the local councils and flogged in the synagogues. On account of me you will stand before governors and kings as witnesses to them. ¹⁰ And the gospel must first be preached to all nations. ¹¹ Whenever you are arrested and brought to trial, do not worry beforehand about what to say. Just say whatever is given you at the time, for it is not you speaking, but the Holy Spirit.

¹² 'Brother will betray brother to death, and a father his child. Children will rebel against their parents and have them put to death. ¹³ Everyone will hate you because of me, but the one who stands firm to the end will be saved.

¹⁴ 'When you see "the abomination that causes desolation" standing where it does not belong – let the reader understand – then let those who are in Judea flee to the mountains. ¹⁵ Let no one on the housetop go

down or enter the house to take anything out. [16] Let no one in the field go back to get their cloak. [17] How dreadful it will be in those days for pregnant women and nursing mothers! [18] Pray that this will not take place in winter, [19] because those will be days of distress unequalled from the beginning, when God created the world, until now – and never to be equalled again.

[20] 'If the Lord had not cut short those days, no one would survive. But for the sake of the elect, whom he has chosen, he has shortened them.

'But God'

'... You will be handed over to the local councils and flogged in the synagogues. On account of me you will stand before governors and kings as witnesses to them.' **Mark 13:9**

We must shape the powerful and transforming thought in our minds that the goodness and faithfulness of God follow hard on our heels to turn every tragedy into a triumph and every loss into a gain. It is easy to affirm this as we look back - the challenge is to affirm it with equal conviction as we look ahead.

If you can get hold of this truth and absorb it into your life as a working principle, then it will transform your attitude toward everything. Never again will you be at the mercy of circumstances. In Acts 5:40-41 we read an astonishing statement: 'They called the apostles in and had them flogged ... the apostles left the Sanhedrin, rejoicing ...'. Rejoicing? Over injustice? How is it possible to rejoice over an injustice? Because they believed, with David, that the last word was not with men, but with God - 'goodness and faithfulness' would follow them and turn the situation to their advantage. When you can rejoice over injustice, you are indomitable.

Another verse from Acts that always intrigues me reads thus: 'Because the patriarchs were jealous of Joseph, they sold him as a slave into Egypt. But God ...' (Acts 7:9). That phrase, 'but God,' is at the end of every injustice - He has the last word. And just as God used the injustice done to Joseph to feed the Egyptian people and his own family, so He transforms every sorrow, every bereavement, every tragedy. Christianity may not explain everything, but it most certainly transforms everything.

PRAYER

O Father, I am so grateful that You are the centre of my life. Can this life within me die? Never - for it is deathless and immortal. I rest in this glad and glorious assurance. Thank You, Father. Amen.

FURTHER STUDY

2 Tim. 1:1-12; Psa. 27:1; Isa. 12:2; Rom. 10:9

• What was Paul's confession?
• What are the two requirements for assurance of salvation?

March 16

MARCH 16

■ NUMBERS 12:1–14:4

12 Miriam and Aaron began to talk against Moses because of his Cushite wife, for he had married a Cushite. ² 'Has the LORD spoken only through Moses?' they asked. 'Hasn't he also spoken through us?' And the LORD heard this.

³ (Now Moses was a very humble man, more humble than anyone else on the face of the earth.)

⁴ At once the LORD said to Moses, Aaron and Miriam, 'Come out to the tent of meeting, all three of you.' So the three of them went out. ⁵ Then the LORD came down in a pillar of cloud; he stood at the entrance to the tent and summoned Aaron and Miriam. When the two of them stepped forward, ⁶ he said, 'Listen to my words:

'When there is a prophet among you,
    I, the LORD, reveal myself to them in
        visions,
    I speak to them in dreams.
⁷ But this is not true of my servant Moses;
    he is faithful in all my house.
⁸ With him I speak face to face,
    clearly and not in riddles;
    he sees the form of the LORD.
Why then were you not afraid
    to speak against my servant Moses?'

⁹ The anger of the LORD burned against them, and he left them.

¹⁰ When the cloud lifted from above the tent, Miriam's skin was leprous – it became as white as snow. Aaron turned towards her and saw that she had a defiling skin disease, ¹¹ and he said to Moses, 'Please, my lord, I ask you not to hold against us the sin we have so foolishly committed. ¹² Do not let her be like a stillborn infant coming from its mother's womb with its flesh half eaten away.'

¹³ So Moses cried out to the LORD, 'Please, God, heal her!'

¹⁴ The LORD replied to Moses, 'If her father had spat in her face, would she not have been in disgrace for seven days? Confine her outside the camp for seven days; after that she can be brought back.' ¹⁵ So Miriam was confined outside the camp for seven days, and the people did not move on till she was brought back.

¹⁶ After that, the people left Hazeroth and camped in the Desert of Paran.

13 The LORD said to Moses, ² 'Send some men to explore the land of Canaan, which I am giving to the Israelites. From each ancestral tribe send one of its leaders.'

³ So at the LORD's command Moses sent them out from the Desert of Paran. All of them were leaders of the Israelites. ⁴ These are their names:

from the tribe of Reuben, Shammua
    son of Zakkur;
⁵ from the tribe of Simeon, Shaphat son
    of Hori;
⁶ from the tribe of Judah, Caleb son of
    Jephunneh;
⁷ from the tribe of Issachar, Igal son of
    Joseph;
⁸ from the tribe of Ephraim, Hoshea son
    of Nun;
⁹ from the tribe of Benjamin, Palti son of
    Raphu;
¹⁰ from the tribe of Zebulun, Gaddiel son
    of Sodi;
¹¹ from the tribe of Manasseh (a tribe of
    Joseph), Gaddi son of Susi;
¹² from the tribe of Dan, Ammiel son of

Gemalli;
[13] from the tribe of Asher, Sethur son of Michael;
[14] from the tribe of Naphtali, Nahbi son of Vophsi;
[15] from the tribe of Gad, Geuel son of Maki.

[16] These are the names of the men Moses sent to explore the land. (Moses gave Hoshea son of Nun the name Joshua.)

[17] When Moses sent them to explore Canaan, he said, 'Go up through the Negev and on into the hill country. [18] See what the land is like and whether the people who live there are strong or weak, few or many. [19] What kind of land do they live in? Is it good or bad? What kind of towns do they live in? Are they unwalled or fortified? [20] How is the soil? Is it fertile or poor? Are there trees in it or not? Do your best to bring back some of the fruit of the land.' (It was the season for the first ripe grapes.)

[21] So they went up and explored the land from the Desert of Zin as far as Rehob, towards Lebo Hamath. [22] They went up through the Negev and came to Hebron, where Ahiman, Sheshai and Talmai, the descendants of Anak, lived. (Hebron had been built seven years before Zoan in Egypt.) [23] When they reached the Valley of Eshkol, they cut off a branch bearing a single cluster of grapes. Two of them carried it on a pole between them, along with some pomegranates and figs. [24] That place was called the Valley of Eshkol because of the cluster of grapes the Israelites cut off there. [25] At the end of forty days they returned from exploring the land.

[26] They came back to Moses and Aaron and the whole Israelite community at Kadesh in the Desert of Paran. There they reported to them and to the whole assembly and showed them the fruit of the land. [27] They gave Moses this account: 'We went into the land to which you sent us, and it does flow with milk and honey! Here is its fruit. [28] But the people who live there are powerful, and the cities are fortified and very large. We even saw descendants of Anak there. [29] The Amalekites live in the Negev; the Hittites, Jebusites and Amorites live in the hill country; and the Canaanites live near the sea and along the Jordan.'

[30] Then Caleb silenced the people before Moses and said, 'We should go up and take possession of the land, for we can certainly do it.'

[31] But the men who had gone up with him said, 'We can't attack those people; they are stronger than we are.' [32] And they spread among the Israelites a bad report about the land they had explored. They said, 'The land we explored devours those living in it. All the people we saw there are of great size. [33] We saw the Nephilim there (the descendants of Anak come from the Nephilim). We seemed like grasshoppers in our own eyes, and we looked the same to them.'

14 That night all the members of the community raised their voices and wept aloud. [2] All the Israelites grumbled against Moses and Aaron, and the whole assembly said to them, 'If only we had died in Egypt! Or in this wilderness! [3] Why is the LORD bringing us to this land only to let us fall by the sword? Our wives and children will be taken as plunder. Wouldn't it be better for us to go back to Egypt?' [4] And they said to each other, 'We should choose a leader and go back to Egypt.'

▬ PSALM 34:15-22

[15] The eyes of the LORD are on the righteous,
and his ears are attentive to their cry;
[16] but the face of the LORD is against those who do evil,
to blot out their name from the earth.

[17] The righteous cry out, and the LORD
  hears them;
 he delivers them from all their
  troubles.
[18] The LORD is close to the broken-hearted
 and saves those who are crushed in
  spirit.

[19] The righteous person may have many
  troubles,
 but the LORD delivers him from them
  all;
[20] he protects all his bones,
 not one of them will be broken.

[21] Evil will slay the wicked;
 the foes of the righteous will be
  condemned.
[22] The LORD will rescue his servants;
 no one who takes refuge in him will be
  condemned.

▬ PROVERBS 8:10-13

[10] Choose my instruction instead of silver,
 knowledge rather than choice gold,
[11] for wisdom is more precious than rubies,
 and nothing you desire can compare
  with her.

[12] 'I, wisdom, dwell together with
  prudence;
 I possess knowledge and discretion.
[13] To fear the LORD is to hate evil;
 I hate pride and arrogance,
 evil behaviour and perverse speech.

▬ MARK 13:21-37

[21] At that time if anyone says to you,
"Look, here is the Messiah!" or, "Look, there
he is!" do not believe it. [22] For false messiahs

and false prophets will appear and perform
signs and wonders to deceive, if possible,
even the elect. [23] So be on your guard; I have
told you everything in advance.

[24] 'But in those days, following that
distress,

 ' "the sun will be darkened,
  and the moon will not give its light;
[25] the stars will fall from the sky,
  and the heavenly bodies will be
  shaken."

[26] 'At that time people will see the Son
of Man coming in clouds with great power
and glory. [27] And he will send his angels
and gather his elect from the four winds,
from the ends of the earth to the ends of the
heavens.

[28] 'Now learn this lesson from the fig-
tree: As soon as its twigs get tender and its
leaves come out, you know that summer is
near. [29] Even so, when you see these things
happening, you know that it is near, right at
the door. [30] Truly I tell you, this generation
will certainly not pass away until all these
things have happened. [31] Heaven and earth
will pass away, but my words will never
pass away.

[32] 'But about that day or hour no one
knows, not even the angels in heaven, nor
the Son, but only the Father. [33] Be on guard!
Be alert! You do not know when that time
will come. [34] It's like a man going away: he
leaves his house and puts his servants in
charge, each with their assigned task, and
tells the one at the door to keep watch.

[35] 'Therefore keep watch because you
do not know when the owner of the house
will come back – whether in the evening,
or at midnight, or when the cock crows, or
at dawn. [36] If he comes suddenly, do not let
him find you sleeping. [37] What I say to you, I
say to everyone: "Watch!" '

The Fear of God

To fear the LORD is to hate evil. - **Proverbs 8:13**

We are taught over and over again in Scripture that because God is uniquely and awesomely holy - pure, separated, and shining in His moral majesty - we are to draw near to Him with godly reverence and fear. The fear of the Lord, as we know, is the beginning of wisdom. Contemplation of His character, particularly His holiness, will lead to a reverential fear that prepares the soul (as it did for Isaiah) for more profitable service and activity.

But what does it mean to 'fear' God? There are times in the Bible when we are told to fear and times when we are told not to fear. There is a fear that helps and a fear that hinders. How do we know the difference?

The fear that helps is the fear that expresses itself in reverence, veneration, awe, a sense of the grandeur and majesty of God. The fear that hinders is described for us in 2 Timothy 1:7: 'For the Spirit God gave us does not make us timid, but gives us power, love and self-discipline.'

The Greek word *deilia*, which is translated 'fearfulness' or 'timidity' in this verse, comes from a root that means 'wretched, sorry, miserable' and implies someone lacking in courage. God is not to blame for attitudes of cowardice or timidity; they come from within our own hearts. Timid people are frightened people, and if you want to explore this thought still further, ask yourself: what kinds of things frighten me that are not related to the fear of God? If we fear them more than we fear God, then we are being ruled by the wrong kind of fear.

PRAYER

O God, I bring to You all my unhealthy fears and lay them at Your feet. Help me develop such a reverential fear for You that all other fears are quickly swallowed up. In Jesus' name. Amen.

FURTHER STUDY

Deut. 10:1-12; Josh. 24:14; Eccl. 12:13
- What did the Lord require of Israel?
- What did Joshua admonish Israel to do?

March 17

■ NUMBERS 14:5-45

⁵ Then Moses and Aaron fell face down in front of the whole Israelite assembly gathered there. ⁶ Joshua son of Nun and

Caleb son of Jephunneh, who were among those who had explored the land, tore their clothes ⁷ and said to the entire Israelite assembly, 'The land we passed through and explored is exceedingly good. ⁸ If the LORD is pleased with us, he will lead us into that land, a land flowing with milk and honey, and will give it to us. ⁹Only do not rebel against the Lord. And do not be afraid of the people of the land, because we will devour them. Their protection is gone, but the Lord is with us. Do not be afraid of them.'

¹⁰But the whole assembly talked about stoning them. Then the glory of the Lord appeared at the tent of meeting to all the Israelites. ¹¹The Lord said to Moses, 'How long will these people treat me with contempt? How long will they refuse to believe in me, in spite of all the signs I have performed among them? ¹²I will strike them down with a plague and destroy them, but I will make you into a nation greater and stronger than they.'

¹³Moses said to the Lord, 'Then the Egyptians will hear about it! By your power you brought these people up from among them. ¹⁴And they will tell the inhabitants of this land about it. They have already heard that you, Lord, are with these people and that you, Lord, have been seen face to face, that your cloud stays over them, and that you go before them in a pillar of cloud by day and a pillar of fire by night. ¹⁵If you put all these people to death, leaving none alive, the nations who have heard this report about you will say, ¹⁶"The Lord was not able to bring these people into the land he promised them on oath, so he slaughtered them in the wilderness."

¹⁷'Now may the Lord's strength be displayed, just as you have declared: ¹⁸"The Lord is slow to anger, abounding in love and forgiving sin and rebellion. Yet he does not leave the guilty unpunished; he punishes the children for the sin of the parents to the third and fourth generation." ¹⁹In accordance with your great love, forgive the sin of these people, just as you have pardoned them from the time they left Egypt until now.'

²⁰The Lord replied, 'I have forgiven them, as you asked. ²¹Nevertheless, as surely as I

live and as surely as the glory of the Lord fills the whole earth, ²²not one of those who saw my glory and the signs I performed in Egypt and in the wilderness but who disobeyed me and tested me ten times – ²³not one of them will ever see the land I promised on oath to their ancestors. No one who has treated me with contempt will ever see it. ²⁴But because my servant Caleb has a different spirit and follows me wholeheartedly, I will bring him into the land he went to, and his descendants will inherit it. ²⁵Since the Amalekites and the Canaanites are living in the valleys, turn back tomorrow and set out towards the desert along the route to the Red Sea.'

²⁶The Lord said to Moses and Aaron: ²⁷'How long will this wicked community grumble against me? I have heard the complaints of these grumbling Israelites. ²⁸So tell them, "As surely as I live, declares the Lord, I will do to you the very thing I heard you say: ²⁹in this wilderness your bodies will fall – every one of you twenty years old or more who was counted in the census and who has grumbled against me. ³⁰Not one of you will enter the land I swore with uplifted hand to make your home, except Caleb son of Jephunneh and Joshua son of Nun. ³¹As for your children that you said would be taken as plunder, I will bring them in to enjoy the land you have rejected. ³²But you – your bodies will fall in this wilderness. ³³Your children will be shepherds here for forty years, suffering for your unfaithfulness, until the last of your bodies lies in the wilderness. ³⁴For forty years – one year for each of the forty days you explored the land – you will suffer for your sins and know what it is like to have me against you." ³⁵I, the Lord, have spoken, and I will surely do these things to this whole wicked community, which has banded together against me. They will meet their end in this wilderness; here they will die.'

³⁶So the men Moses had sent to explore

the land, who returned and made the whole community grumble against him by spreading a bad report about it – ³⁷ these men who were responsible for spreading the bad report about the land were struck down and died of a plague before the Lord. ³⁸ Of the men who went to explore the land, only Joshua son of Nun and Caleb son of Jephunneh survived.

³⁹ When Moses reported this to all the Israelites, they mourned bitterly. ⁴⁰ Early the next morning they set out for the highest point in the hill country, saying, 'Now we are ready to go up to the land the Lord promised. Surely we have sinned!'

⁴¹ But Moses said, 'Why are you disobeying the Lord's command? This will not succeed! ⁴² Do not go up, because the Lord is not with you. You will be defeated by your enemies, ⁴³ for the Amalekites and the Canaanites will face you there. Because you have turned away from the Lord, he will not be with you and you will fall by the sword.'

⁴⁴ Nevertheless, in their presumption they went up towards the highest point in the hill country, though neither Moses nor the ark of the Lord's covenant moved from the camp. ⁴⁵ Then the Amalekites and the Canaanites who lived in that hill country came down and attacked them and beat them down all the way to Hormah.

■ PSALM 35:1-10

¹ Contend, Lord, with those who contend
    with me;
  fight against those who fight against
    me.
² Take up shield and armour;
  arise and come to my aid.
³ Brandish spear and javelin
  against those who pursue me.
Say to me,
  'I am your salvation.'

⁴ May those who seek my life
  be disgraced and put to shame;
may those who plot my ruin
  be turned back in dismay.
⁵ May they be like chaff before the wind,
  with the angel of the Lord driving
    them away;
⁶ may their path be dark and slippery,
  with the angel of the Lord pursuing
    them.

⁷ Since they hid their net for me without
    cause
  and without cause dug a pit for me,
⁸ may ruin overtake them by surprise –
  may the net they hid entangle them,
  may they fall into the pit, to their ruin.
⁹ Then my soul will rejoice in the Lord
  and delight in his salvation.
¹⁰ My whole being will exclaim,
  'Who is like you, Lord?
You rescue the poor from those too
    strong for them,
  the poor and needy from those who
    rob them.'

■ PROVERBS 8:14-17

¹⁴ Counsel and sound judgment are mine;
  I have insight, I have power.
¹⁵ By me kings reign
  and rulers issue decrees that are just;
¹⁶ by me princes govern,
  and nobles – all who rule on earth.
¹⁷ I love those who love me,
  and those who seek me find me.

■ MARK 14:1-21

14 Now the Passover and the Festival of Unleavened Bread were only two days away, and the chief priests and the teachers of the law were scheming to arrest Jesus secretly and kill him. ² 'But not during the festival,' they said, 'or the people may riot.'

³While he was in Bethany, reclining at the table in the home of Simon the Leper, a woman came with an alabaster jar of very expensive perfume, made of pure nard. She broke the jar and poured the perfume on his head.

⁴Some of those present were saying indignantly to one another, 'Why this waste of perfume? ⁵It could have been sold for more than a year's wages and the money given to the poor.' And they rebuked her harshly.

⁶'Leave her alone,' said Jesus. 'Why are you bothering her? She has done a beautiful thing to me. ⁷The poor you will always have with you, and you can help them any time you want. But you will not always have me. ⁸She did what she could. She poured perfume on my body beforehand to prepare for my burial. ⁹Truly I tell you, wherever the gospel is preached throughout the world, what she has done will also be told, in memory of her.'

¹⁰Then Judas Iscariot, one of the Twelve, went to the chief priests to betray Jesus to them. ¹¹They were delighted to hear this and promised to give him money. So he watched for an opportunity to hand him over.

¹²On the first day of the Festival of Unleavened Bread, when it was customary to sacrifice the Passover lamb, Jesus' disciples asked him, 'Where do you want us to go and make preparations for you to eat the Passover?'

¹³So he sent two of his disciples, telling them, 'Go into the city, and a man carrying a jar of water will meet you. Follow him. ¹⁴Say to the owner of the house he enters, "The Teacher asks: where is my guest room, where I may eat the Passover with my disciples?" ¹⁵He will show you a large room upstairs, furnished and ready. Make preparations for us there.'

¹⁶The disciples left, went into the city and found things just as Jesus had told them. So they prepared the Passover.

¹⁷When evening came, Jesus arrived with the Twelve. ¹⁸While they were reclining at the table eating, he said, 'Truly I tell you, one of you will betray me – one who is eating with me.'

¹⁹They were saddened, and one by one they said to him, 'Surely you don't mean me?'

²⁰'It is one of the Twelve,' he replied, 'one who dips bread into the bowl with me. ²¹The Son of Man will go just as it is written about him. But woe to that man who betrays the Son of Man! It would be better for him if he had not been born.'

The Safety of the Old

'I love those who love me, and those who seek me find me.' **Proverbs 8:17**

A Christian woman came to me who had an unconverted husband. She came to see that what she was asking for with her lips (his conversion) was not what she was desiring in her heart. After this revelation, she had the joy of seeing her husband become a Christian.

But this must not be taken to mean that we have a guaranteed formula for bringing a non-Christian spouse to the Lord. It is right to pray with passion for those in our families who are not converted, but we must remember that each man or woman must personally surrender his or her will to Christ in order to be converted. People are admitted into the family of God only as they give up their commitment to independence and say, in effect, 'Heavenly Father, I can do nothing to save myself; save me, in Jesus' name.'

A man came to me complaining that he was not getting what he wanted spiritually. He told me that he had a deep sense of unworthiness, and although he prayed desperately for God to take it away, it stayed with him.

After many hours of talking, praying, and heart-searching, he came to see that although in his head he was asking for God to take it away, deep down in his heart he was not desiring it. He had lived with it for so long that he was afraid of the new positive feelings he would have to face if the negative feelings were not there. He preferred the safety of the old to the adventure of the new.

PRAYER

Father, day by day I see more clearly the subtle devices of the human heart. Give me the insight I need to probe my own heart, to track down those things that may be preventing me from climbing into the heights with You. In Jesus' name I pray. Amen.

FURTHER STUDY

Luke 18:1-8; Deut. 4:29; Matt. 7:7
• What characteristic did the woman display?
• How can we be sure of finding God?

March 18

■ NUMBERS 15:1-41

15 The LORD said to Moses, [2]'Speak to the Israelites and say to them: "After you enter the land I am giving you as a home [3]and you present to the LORD food offerings from the herd or the flock, as an aroma pleasing to the LORD – whether burnt offerings or sacrifices, for special vows or freewill offerings or festival offerings – [4]then the person who brings an offering shall present to the LORD a grain offering of a tenth of an ephah of the finest flour mixed with a quarter of a hin of olive oil. [5]With each lamb for the burnt offering or the sacrifice, prepare a quarter of a hin of wine as a drink offering.

[6]"With a ram prepare a grain offering of one-fifth of an ephah of the finest flour mixed with a third of a hin of olive oil, [7]and a third of a hin of wine as a drink offering. Offer it as an aroma pleasing to the LORD.

[8]"When you prepare a young bull as a burnt offering or sacrifice, for a special vow or a fellowship offering to the LORD, [9]bring with the bull a grain offering of three-tenths of an ephah of the finest flour mixed with half a hin of olive oil, [10]and also bring half a hin of wine as a drink offering. This will be a food offering, an aroma pleasing to the LORD. [11]Each bull or ram, each lamb or young goat, is to be prepared in this manner. [12]Do this for each one, for as many as you prepare.

¹³ ' "Everyone who is native-born must do these things in this way when they present a food offering as an aroma pleasing to the LORD. ¹⁴ For the generations to come, whenever a foreigner or anyone else living among you presents a food offering as an aroma pleasing to the LORD, they must do exactly as you do. ¹⁵ The community is to have the same rules for you and for the foreigner residing among you; this is a lasting ordinance for the generations to come. You and the foreigner shall be the same before the LORD: ¹⁶ the same laws and regulations will apply both to you and to the foreigner residing among you." '

¹⁷ The LORD said to Moses, ¹⁸ 'Speak to the Israelites and say to them: "When you enter the land to which I am taking you ¹⁹ and you eat the food of the land, present a portion as an offering to the LORD. ²⁰ Present a loaf from the first of your ground meal and present it as an offering from the threshing-floor. ²¹ Throughout the generations to come you are to give this offering to the LORD from the first of your ground meal.

²² ' "Now if you as a community unintentionally fail to keep any of these commands the LORD gave Moses – ²³ any of the LORD's commands to you through him, from the day the LORD gave them and continuing through the generations to come – ²⁴ and if this is done unintentionally without the community being aware of it, then the whole community is to offer a young bull for a burnt offering as an aroma pleasing to the LORD, along with its prescribed grain offering and drink offering, and a male goat for a sin offering. ²⁵ The priest is to make atonement for the whole Israelite community, and they will be forgiven, for it was not intentional and they have presented to the LORD for their wrong a food offering and a sin offering. ²⁶ The whole Israelite community and the foreigners residing among them will be forgiven, because all the people

were involved in the unintentional wrong.

²⁷ ' "But if just one person sins unintentionally, that person must bring a year-old female goat for a sin offering. ²⁸ The priest is to make atonement before the LORD for the one who erred by sinning unintentionally, and when atonement has been made, that person will be forgiven. ²⁹ One and the same law applies to everyone who sins unintentionally, whether a native-born Israelite or a foreigner residing among you.

³⁰ ' "But anyone who sins defiantly, whether native-born or foreigner, utters blasphemy against the LORD and must be cut off from the people of Israel. ³¹ Because they have despised the LORD's word and broken his commands, they must surely be cut off; their guilt remains on them." '

³² While the Israelites were in the wilderness, a man was found gathering wood on the Sabbath day. ³³ Those who found him gathering wood brought him to Moses and Aaron and the whole assembly, ³⁴ and they kept him in custody, because it was not clear what should be done to him. ³⁵ Then the LORD said to Moses, 'The man must die. The whole assembly must stone him outside the camp.' ³⁶ So the assembly took him outside the camp and stoned him to death, as the LORD commanded Moses.

³⁷ The LORD said to Moses, ³⁸ 'Speak to the Israelites and say to them: "Throughout the generations to come you are to make tassels on the corners of your garments, with a blue cord on each tassel. ³⁹ You will have these tassels to look at and so you will remember all the commands of the LORD, that you may obey them and not prostitute yourselves by chasing after the lusts of your own hearts and eyes. ⁴⁰ Then you will remember to obey all my commands and will be consecrated to your God. ⁴¹ I am the LORD your God, who brought you out of Egypt to be your God. I am the LORD your God." '

▬ PSALM 35:11-16

11 Ruthless witnesses come forward;
　　they question me on things I know
　　　nothing about.
12 They repay me evil for good
　　and leave me like one bereaved.
13 Yet when they were ill, I put on sackcloth
　　and humbled myself with fasting.
　When my prayers returned to me
　　unanswered,
14 　I went about mourning
　　as though for my friend or brother.
　I bowed my head in grief
　　as though weeping for my mother.
15 But when I stumbled, they gathered in
　　glee;
　　assailants gathered against me
　　　without my knowledge.
　They slandered me without ceasing.
16 Like the ungodly they maliciously
　　mocked;
　　they gnashed their teeth at me.

▬ PROVERBS 8:18-19

18 With me are riches and honour,
　　enduring wealth and prosperity.
19 My fruit is better than fine gold;
　　what I yield surpasses choice silver.

▬ MARK 14:22-42

22 While they were eating, Jesus took bread, and when he had given thanks, he broke it and gave it to his disciples, saying, 'Take it; this is my body.'
23 Then he took a cup, and when he had given thanks, he gave it to them, and they all drank from it.
24 'This is my blood of the covenant, which is poured out for many,' he said to them. 25 'Truly I tell you, I will not drink again from the fruit of the vine until that day when I drink it new in the kingdom of God.'
26 When they had sung a hymn, they went out to the Mount of Olives.
27 'You will all fall away,' Jesus told them, 'for it is written:

' "I will strike the shepherd,
　　and the sheep will be scattered."

28 But after I have risen, I will go ahead of you into Galilee.'
29 Peter declared, 'Even if all fall away, I will not.'
30 'Truly I tell you,' Jesus answered, 'today – yes, tonight – before the cock crows twice you yourself will disown me three times.'
31 But Peter insisted emphatically, 'Even if I have to die with you, I will never disown you.' And all the others said the same.
32 They went to a place called Gethsemane, and Jesus said to his disciples, 'Sit here while I pray.' 33 He took Peter, James and John along with him, and he began to be deeply distressed and troubled. 34 'My soul is overwhelmed with sorrow to the point of death,' he said to them. 'Stay here and keep watch.'
35 Going a little farther, he fell to the ground and prayed that if possible the hour might pass from him. 36 'Abba, Father,' he said, 'everything is possible for you. Take this cup from me. Yet not what I will, but what you will.'
37 Then he returned to his disciples and found them sleeping. 'Simon,' he said to Peter, 'are you asleep? Couldn't you keep watch for one hour? 38 Watch and pray so that you will not fall into temptation. The spirit is willing, but the flesh is weak.'
39 Once more he went away and prayed the same thing. 40 When he came back, he again found them sleeping, because their eyes were heavy. They did not know what to say to him.

[41] Returning the third time, he said to them, 'Are you still sleeping and resting? Enough! The hour has come. Look, the Son of Man is delivered into the hands of sinners. [42] Rise! Let us go! Here comes my betrayer!'

Making Sadness Sing

'They repay me evil for good and leave me like one bereaved ... I put on sackcloth and humbled myself with fasting.' **Psalm 35:12-13**

Expect God to supply you with the strength to transform everything that comes to you, making it contribute to the central purposes for which you live. 'Expect God to supply you with strength.' That is the secret.

In the Christian life, we get what we expect. You likely have heard the story of the woman who, having heard a sermon on the text, 'If anyone says to this mountain "Be lifted up,"'(Matt. 21:21 HCSB) decided to try out her faith on a mountain near her home. Prior to going to sleep, she looked out of her window and said to the mountain, 'Be lifted up.' In the morning, as soon as she awoke, she looked out, saw that the mountain was still there, and said woefully: 'Just as I expected.' Yes, in the Christian life, we get what we expect.

Notice the remainder of the phrase from this line of advice: '... strength to transform everything that comes ...' This is what Jesus did. As the Gospel writer recorded, 'He withdrew about a stone's throw beyond them, knelt down and prayed, "Father, if you are willing, take this cup from me; yet not my will, but yours be done". An angel from heaven appeared to him and strengthened him' (Luke 22:41-43). Here, God's answer was not to take away the cup but to supply the strength to turn that bitter cup into a cup of salvation, which He would put to the thirsty lips of humanity. In the midst of your trials, don't whine to be released. Ask rather for the strength to make every sadness sing.

PRAYER

Father, don't ever let me forget this lesson – that if I cannot change my surroundings, I can change my soul. Help me see that if I am not saved from a situation, then I can be saved in the situation. I am deeply thankful. Amen.

FURTHER STUDY

Isa. 40; 41:10; 2 Cor. 12:9
• What is promised to those who wait on the Lord?
• What was Paul's testimony?

March 19

■ NUMBERS 16:1-50

16 Korah son of Izhar, the son of Kohath, the son of Levi, and certain Reubenites – Dathan and Abiram, sons of Eliab, and On son of Peleth – became insolent ²and rose up against Moses. With them were 250 Israelite men, well-known community leaders who had been appointed members of the council. ³They came as a group to oppose Moses and Aaron and said to them, 'You have gone too far! The whole community is holy, every one of them, and the LORD is with them. Why then do you set yourselves above the LORD's assembly?'

⁴When Moses heard this, he fell face down. ⁵Then he said to Korah and all his followers: 'In the morning the LORD will show who belongs to him and who is holy, and he will make that person come near him. The man he chooses he will cause to come near him. ⁶You, Korah, and all your followers are to do this: take censers ⁷and tomorrow put burning coals and incense in them before the LORD. The man the LORD chooses will be the one who is holy. You Levites have gone too far!'

⁸Moses also said to Korah, 'Now listen, you Levites! ⁹Isn't it enough for you that the God of Israel has separated you from the rest of the Israelite community and brought you near himself to do the work at the LORD's tabernacle and to stand before the community and minister to them? ¹⁰He has brought you and all your fellow Levites near himself, but now you are trying to get the priesthood too. ¹¹It is against the LORD that you and all your followers have banded together. Who is Aaron that you should grumble against him?'

¹²Then Moses summoned Dathan and Abiram, the sons of Eliab. But they said,

'We will not come! ¹³Isn't it enough that you have brought us up out of a land flowing with milk and honey to kill us in the wilderness? And now you also want to lord it over us! ¹⁴Moreover, you haven't brought us into a land flowing with milk and honey or given us an inheritance of fields and vineyards. Do you want to treat these men like slaves? No, we will not come!'

¹⁵Then Moses became very angry and said to the LORD, 'Do not accept their offering. I have not taken so much as a donkey from them, nor have I wronged any of them.'

¹⁶Moses said to Korah, 'You and all your followers are to appear before the LORD tomorrow – you and they and Aaron. ¹⁷Each man is to take his censer and put incense in it – 250 censers in all – and present it before the LORD. You and Aaron are to present your censers also.' ¹⁸So each of them took his censer, put burning coals and incense in it, and stood with Moses and Aaron at the entrance to the tent of meeting. ¹⁹When Korah had gathered all his followers in opposition to them at the entrance to the tent of meeting, the glory of the LORD appeared to the entire assembly. ²⁰The LORD said to Moses and Aaron, ²¹'Separate yourselves from this assembly so that I can put an end to them at once.'

²²But Moses and Aaron fell face down and cried out, 'O God, the God who gives breath to all living things, will you be angry with the entire assembly when only one man sins?'

²³Then the LORD said to Moses, ²⁴'Say to the assembly, "Move away from the tents of Korah, Dathan and Abiram."'

²⁵Moses got up and went to Dathan and Abiram, and the elders of Israel followed him. ²⁶He warned the assembly, 'Move back from the tents of these wicked men! Do not

touch anything belonging to them, or you will be swept away because of all their sins.' ²⁷ So they moved away from the tents of Korah, Dathan and Abiram. Dathan and Abiram had come out and were standing with their wives, children and little ones at the entrances to their tents.

²⁸ Then Moses said, 'This is how you will know that the LORD has sent me to do all these things and that it was not my idea: ²⁹ if these men die a natural death and suffer the fate of all mankind, then the LORD has not sent me. ³⁰ But if the LORD brings about something totally new, and the earth opens its mouth and swallows them, with everything that belongs to them, and they go down alive into the realm of the dead, then you will know that these men have treated the LORD with contempt.'

³¹ As soon as he finished saying all this, the ground under them split apart ³² and the earth opened its mouth and swallowed them and their households, and all those associated with Korah, together with their possessions. ³³ They went down alive into the realm of the dead, with everything they owned; the earth closed over them, and they perished and were gone from the community. ³⁴ At their cries, all the Israelites around them fled, shouting, 'The earth is going to swallow us too!'

³⁵ And fire came out from the LORD and consumed the 250 men who were offering the incense.

³⁶ The LORD said to Moses, ³⁷ 'Tell Eleazar son of Aaron, the priest, to remove the censers from the charred remains and scatter the coals some distance away, for the censers are holy – ³⁸ the censers of the men who sinned at the cost of their lives. Hammer the censers into sheets to overlay the altar, for they were presented before the LORD and have become holy. Let them be a sign to the Israelites.'

³⁹ So Eleazar the priest collected the bronze censers brought by those who had been burned to death, and he had them hammered out to overlay the altar, ⁴⁰ as the LORD directed him through Moses. This was to remind the Israelites that no one except a descendant of Aaron should come to burn incense before the LORD, or he would become like Korah and his followers.

⁴¹ The next day the whole Israelite community grumbled against Moses and Aaron. 'You have killed the LORD's people,' they said. ⁴² But when the assembly gathered in opposition to Moses and Aaron and turned towards the tent of meeting, suddenly the cloud covered it and the glory of the LORD appeared. ⁴³ Then Moses and Aaron went to the front of the tent of meeting, ⁴⁴ and the LORD said to Moses, ⁴⁵ 'Get away from this assembly so that I can put an end to them at once.' And they fell face down.

⁴⁶ Then Moses said to Aaron, 'Take your censer and put incense in it, along with burning coals from the altar, and hurry to the assembly to make atonement for them. Wrath has come out from the LORD; the plague has started.' ⁴⁷ So Aaron did as Moses said, and ran into the midst of the assembly. The plague had already started among the people, but Aaron offered the incense and made atonement for them. ⁴⁸ He stood between the living and the dead, and the plague stopped. ⁴⁹ But 14,700 people died from the plague, in addition to those who had died because of Korah. ⁵⁰ Then Aaron returned to Moses at the entrance to the tent of meeting, for the plague had stopped.

■ PSALM 35:17-21

¹⁷ How long, Lord, will you look on?
 Rescue me from their ravages,
  my precious life from these lions.
¹⁸ I will give you thanks in the great assembly;
  among the throngs I will praise you.
¹⁹ Do not let those gloat over me
  who are my enemies without cause;
 do not let those who hate me without
  reason

maliciously wink the eye.
20 They do not speak peaceably,
    but devise false accusations
    against those who live quietly in the
        land.
21 They sneer at me and say, 'Aha! Aha!
    With our own eyes we have seen it.'

▬ PROVERBS 8:20-21

20 I walk in the way of righteousness,
    along the paths of justice,
21 bestowing a rich inheritance on those
        who love me
    and making their treasuries full.

▬ MARK 14:43-72

43 Just as he was speaking, Judas, one of the Twelve, appeared. With him was a crowd armed with swords and clubs, sent from the chief priests, the teachers of the law, and the elders. 44 Now the betrayer had arranged a signal with them: 'The one I kiss is the man; arrest him and lead him away under guard.' 45 Going at once to Jesus, Judas said, 'Rabbi!' and kissed him. 46 The men seized Jesus and arrested him. 47 Then one of those standing near drew his sword and struck the servant of the high priest, cutting off his ear.

48 'Am I leading a rebellion,' said Jesus, 'that you have come out with swords and clubs to capture me? 49 Every day I was with you, teaching in the temple courts, and you did not arrest me. But the Scriptures must be fulfilled.' 50 Then everyone deserted him and fled.

51 A young man, wearing nothing but a linen garment, was following Jesus. When they seized him, 52 he fled naked, leaving his garment behind.

53 They took Jesus to the high priest, and all the chief priests, the elders and the teachers of the law came together. 54 Peter followed him at a distance, right into the courtyard of the high priest. There he sat with the guards and warmed himself at the fire.

55 The chief priests and the whole Sanhedrin were looking for evidence against Jesus so that they could put him to death, but they did not find any. 56 Many testified falsely against him, but their statements did not agree.

57 Then some stood up and gave this false testimony against him: 58 'We heard him say, "I will destroy this temple made with human hands and in three days will build another, not made with hands."' 59 Yet even then their testimony did not agree.

60 Then the high priest stood up before them and asked Jesus, 'Are you not going to answer? What is this testimony that these men are bringing against you?' 61 But Jesus remained silent and gave no answer.

Again the high priest asked him, 'Are you the Messiah, the Son of the Blessed One?'

62 'I am,' said Jesus. 'And you will see the Son of Man sitting at the right hand of the Mighty One and coming on the clouds of heaven.'

63 The high priest tore his clothes. 'Why do we need any more witnesses?' he asked. 64 'You have heard the blasphemy. What do you think?'

They all condemned him as worthy of death. 65 Then some began to spit at him; they blindfolded him, struck him with their fists, and said, 'Prophesy!' And the guards took him and beat him.

66 While Peter was below in the courtyard, one of the servant-girls of the high priest came by. 67 When she saw Peter warming himself, she looked closely at him.

'You also were with that Nazarene, Jesus,' she said.

68 But he denied it. 'I don't know or understand what you're talking about,' he said, and went out into the entrance.

69 When the servant-girl saw him there,

she said again to those standing round them, 'This fellow is one of them.' [70] Again he denied it.

After a little while, those standing near said to Peter, 'Surely you are one of them, for you are a Galilean.'

[71] He began to call down curses, and he swore to them, 'I don't know this man you're talking about.'

[72] Immediately the cock crowed the second time. Then Peter remembered the word Jesus had spoken to him: 'Before the cock crows twice you will disown me three times.' And he broke down and wept.

'Rise Up, O Men of God'

'"I am," said Jesus. "And you will see the Son of Man sitting at the right hand of the Mighty One and coming on the clouds of heaven."' **Mark 14:62**

Although the fullness of God's kingdom is yet to come, there is a sense in which the King is reigning now, and we can say with the utmost certainty, 'Our God reigns!'

A lady once wrote to me indicating her intention to withdraw from life and await the day when God would finally establish His kingdom in power and glory on the earth. I replied with a parody of a hymn that apparently got her thinking. She wrote back in a few weeks and said, 'You were right. I was waiting for God, but now I realise He is waiting for me.' She ended her letter with the words of the hymn:

> Rise up, O men of God!
> Have done with lesser things;
> Give heart and soul and mind and strength
> To serve the King of kings.

This must indicate our line of action. Yes, of course, the final ushering in of God's kingdom is yet to take place, but that does not mean that He is taking a backseat in the world's affairs. God wants to reign through us!

We need not wait for the day when spectacularly the great God of the universe demonstrates His imperial power. As He sounds forth a rallying cry, even through these pages, respond to Him, I urge you, with a fresh consecration of purpose, and dedicate yourself to letting Him reign through you.

PRAYER

God, I give myself wholly to You, not only just to live in me, but to reign through me. I gladly submit my whole being to You today. Live and reign in me. For Jesus' sake. Amen.

FURTHER STUDY

Rom. 13:1-14; 2 Cor. 10:4; 1 Tim. 1:18; 6:12; 2 Tim. 2:4
- How can we overcome the works of darkness?
- What was Paul's exhortation to Timothy?

March 20

17 The LORD said to Moses, ²'Speak to the Israelites and get twelve staffs from them, one from the leader of each of their ancestral tribes. Write the name of each man on his staff. ³On the staff of Levi write Aaron's name, for there must be one staff for the head of each ancestral tribe. ⁴Place them in the tent of meeting in front of the ark of the covenant law, where I meet with you. ⁵The staff belonging to the man I choose will sprout, and I will rid myself of this constant grumbling against you by the Israelites.'

⁶So Moses spoke to the Israelites, and their leaders gave him twelve staffs, one for the leader of each of their ancestral tribes, and Aaron's staff was among them. ⁷Moses placed the staffs before the LORD in the tent of the covenant law.

⁸The next day Moses entered the tent and saw that Aaron's staff, which represented the tribe of Levi, had not only sprouted but had budded, blossomed and produced almonds. ⁹Then Moses brought out all the staffs from the LORD's presence to all the Israelites. They looked at them, and each of the leaders took his own staff.

¹⁰The LORD said to Moses, 'Put back Aaron's staff in front of the ark of the covenant law, to be kept as a sign to the rebellious. This will put an end to their grumbling against me, so that they will not die.' ¹¹Moses did just as the LORD commanded him.

¹²The Israelites said to Moses, 'We shall die! We are lost, we are all lost! ¹³Anyone who even comes near the tabernacle of the LORD will die. Are we all going to die?'

18 The LORD said to Aaron, 'You, your sons and your family are to bear the responsibility for offences connected with the sanctuary, and you and your sons alone are to bear the responsibility for offences connected with the priesthood. ²Bring your fellow Levites from your ancestral tribe to join you and assist you when you and your sons minister before the tent of the covenant law. ³They are to be responsible to you and are to perform all the duties of the tent, but they must not go near the furnishings of the sanctuary or the altar. Otherwise both they and you will die. ⁴They are to join you and be responsible for the care of the tent of meeting – all the work at the tent – and no one else may come near where you are.

⁵'You are to be responsible for the care of the sanctuary and the altar, so that my wrath will not fall on the Israelites again. ⁶I myself have selected your fellow Levites from among the Israelites as a gift to you, dedicated to the LORD to do the work at the tent of meeting. ⁷But only you and your sons may serve as priests in connection with everything at the altar and inside the curtain. I am giving you the service of the priesthood as a gift. Anyone else who comes near the sanctuary is to be put to death.'

⁸Then the LORD said to Aaron, 'I myself have put you in charge of the offerings presented to me; all the holy offerings the Israelites give me I give to you and your sons as your portion, your perpetual share. ⁹You are to have the part of the most holy offerings that is kept from the fire. From all the gifts they bring me as most holy offerings, whether grain or sin or guilt offerings, that part belongs to you and your sons. ¹⁰Eat it as something most holy; every male shall eat it. You must regard it as holy.

¹¹'This also is yours: whatever is set aside from the gifts of all the wave offerings of

the Israelites. I give this to you and your sons and daughters as your perpetual share. Everyone in your household who is ceremonially clean may eat it.

¹²'I give you all the finest olive oil and all the finest new wine and grain they give to the LORD as the firstfruits of their harvest. ¹³All the land's firstfruits that they bring to the LORD will be yours. Everyone in your household who is ceremonially clean may eat it.

¹⁴'Everything in Israel that is devoted to the LORD is yours. ¹⁵The first offspring of every womb, both human and animal, that is offered to the LORD is yours. But you must redeem every firstborn son and every firstborn male of unclean animals. ¹⁶When they are a month old, you must redeem them at the redemption price set at five shekels of silver, according to the sanctuary shekel, which weighs twenty gerahs.

¹⁷'But you must not redeem the firstborn of an ox, a sheep or a goat; they are holy. Splash their blood against the altar and burn their fat as a food offering, an aroma pleasing to the LORD. ¹⁸Their meat is to be yours, just as the breast of the wave offering and the right thigh are yours. ¹⁹Whatever is set aside from the holy offerings the Israelites present to the LORD I give to you and your sons and daughters as your perpetual share. It is an everlasting covenant of salt before the LORD for both you and your offspring.'

²⁰The LORD said to Aaron, 'You will have no inheritance in their land, nor will you have any share among them; I am your share and your inheritance among the Israelites.

²¹'I give to the Levites all the tithes in Israel as their inheritance in return for the work they do while serving at the tent of meeting. ²²From now on the Israelites must not go near the tent of meeting, or they will bear the consequences of their sin and will die. ²³It is the Levites who are to do the work at the tent of meeting and bear the responsibility for any offences they commit against it. This is a lasting ordinance for the

generations to come. They will receive no inheritance among the Israelites. ²⁴Instead, I give to the Levites as their inheritance the tithes that the Israelites present as an offering to the LORD. That is why I said concerning them: "They will have no inheritance among the Israelites."'

²⁵The LORD said to Moses, ²⁶'Speak to the Levites and say to them: "When you receive from the Israelites the tithe I give you as your inheritance, you must present a tenth of that tithe as the LORD's offering. ²⁷Your offering will be reckoned to you as grain from the threshing-floor or juice from the winepress. ²⁸In this way you also will present an offering to the LORD from all the tithes you receive from the Israelites. From these tithes you must give the LORD's portion to Aaron the priest. ²⁹You must present as the LORD's portion the best and holiest part of everything given to you."

³⁰'Say to the Levites: "When you present the best part, it will be reckoned to you as the product of the threshing-floor or the winepress. ³¹You and your households may eat the rest of it anywhere, for it is your wages for your work at the tent of meeting. ³²By presenting the best part of it you will not be guilty in this matter; then you will not defile the holy offerings of the Israelites, and you will not die."'

19 The LORD said to Moses and Aaron: ²'This is a requirement of the law that the LORD has commanded: tell the Israelites to bring you a red heifer without defect or blemish and that has never been under a yoke. ³Give it to Eleazar the priest; it is to be taken outside the camp and slaughtered in his presence. ⁴Then Eleazar the priest is to take some of its blood on his finger and sprinkle it seven times towards the front of the tent of meeting. ⁵While he watches, the heifer is to be burned – its hide, flesh, blood and intestines. ⁶The priest is to take some cedar wood, hyssop and scarlet wool and throw them onto the burning heifer. ⁷After that, the priest must wash his clothes and bathe himself with water. He may then come into the camp, but he will be ceremonially unclean till evening. ⁸The man who burns it must also wash his clothes and bathe with water, and he too will be unclean till evening.

PSALM 35:22-28

²²Lord, you have seen this; do not be silent.
  Do not be far from me, Lord.
²³Awake, and rise to my defence!
  Contend for me, my God and Lord.
²⁴Vindicate me in your righteousness,
  Lord my God;
  do not let them gloat over me.
²⁵Do not let them think, 'Aha, just what we
    wanted!'
  or say, 'We have swallowed him up.'

²⁶May all who gloat over my distress
    be put to shame and confusion;
  may all who exalt themselves over me
    be clothed with shame and disgrace.
²⁷May those who delight in my vindication
    shout for joy and gladness;
  may they always say, 'The Lord be
    exalted,
  who delights in the well-being of his
    servant.'

²⁸My tongue will proclaim your
    righteousness,
  your praises all day long.

PROVERBS 8:22-24

²²'The Lord brought me forth as the first of
    his works,
  before his deeds of old;
²³I was formed long ages ago,
  at the very beginning, when the world
    came to be.

²⁴When there were no watery depths, I was
    given birth,
  when there were no springs
    overflowing with water;

MARK 15:1-21

15 Very early in the morning, the chief priests, with the elders, the teachers of the law and the whole Sanhedrin, made their plans. So they bound Jesus, led him away and handed him over to Pilate.

²'Are you the king of the Jews?' asked Pilate.

'You have said so,' Jesus replied.

³The chief priests accused him of many things. ⁴So again Pilate asked him, 'Aren't you going to answer? See how many things they are accusing you of.'

⁵But Jesus still made no reply, and Pilate was amazed.

⁶Now it was the custom at the festival to release a prisoner whom the people requested. ⁷A man called Barabbas was in prison with the rebels who had committed murder in the uprising. ⁸The crowd came up and asked Pilate to do for them what he usually did.

⁹'Do you want me to release to you the king of the Jews?' asked Pilate, ¹⁰knowing it was out of self-interest that the chief priests had handed Jesus over to him. ¹¹But the chief priests stirred up the crowd to get Pilate to release Barabbas instead.

¹²'What shall I do, then, with the one you call the king of the Jews?' Pilate asked them.

¹³'Crucify him!' they shouted.

¹⁴'Why? What crime has he committed?' asked Pilate.

But they shouted all the louder, 'Crucify him!'

¹⁵Wanting to satisfy the crowd, Pilate released Barabbas to them. He had Jesus flogged, and handed him over to be crucified.

¹⁶The soldiers led Jesus away into the palace (that is, the Praetorium) and called

together the whole company of soldiers. ¹⁷ They put a purple robe on him, then twisted together a crown of thorns and set it on him. ¹⁸ And they began to call out to him, 'Hail, king of the Jews!' ¹⁹ Again and again they struck him on the head with a staff and spat on him. Falling on their knees, they paid homage to him. ²⁰ And when they had mocked him, they took off the purple robe and put his own clothes on him. Then they led him out to crucify him.

²¹ A certain man from Cyrene, Simon, the father of Alexander and Rufus, was passing by on his way in from the country, and they forced him to carry the cross.

'Settling Down in God'

'My tongue will proclaim your righteousness, your praises all day long.' **Psalm 35:28**

The words 'Father in heaven' are intended to help us focus not only on God's location, but also on His elevation. The Saviour (so I believe) encourages us, when we come to God in prayer, to get our perspective right and to look above 'the ragged edges of time' to the heights of eternity where God has His royal throne.

The old Welsh preachers and theologians, such as Christmas Evans, Daniel Rowlands, and others, used to call this aspect of prayer 'settling down in God.' They taught that when we gain a right perspective of God and heavenly things, then and only then can we have a right perspective of man and earthly things. It was only when Isaiah saw the Lord 'high and exalted' (6:1) that he was able to put into focus the events that were happening around him. Our life here on earth can never be abundant until we realise that we have access to resources which are outside the realm of terrestrial things.

A good working translation of the term El-Shaddai (Gen. 17:1) is 'God – the Enough.' Actually, of course, He is more than enough, but how comforting it is to know that He is at least that. So, when coming to God in prayer, learn to settle yourself down in God. Remind yourself that His resources so infinitely exceed your requirements; His sufficiency so immeasurably surpasses every demand you may make upon it. Get the divine perspective right, and earthly things will fall into their right and proper focus.

PRAYER

My Father, gently and quietly I breathe the strength of Your Almightiness into every portion of my being. I realise that when I see You 'high and exalted,' then all of life is reduced to its proper proportions. I am so thankful. Amen.

FURTHER STUDY

Matt. 19:13-26; Eph. 3:20; 2 Cor. 9:8; Phil. 4:19
• What was the declaration of Jesus?
• How did Paul describe 'El-Shaddai'?

March 21

▬ NUMBERS 19:9–21:9

⁹'A man who is clean shall gather up the ashes of the heifer and put them in a ceremonially clean place outside the camp. They are to be kept by the Israelite community for use in the water of cleansing; it is for purification from sin. ¹⁰The man who gathers up the ashes of the heifer must also wash his clothes, and he too will be unclean till evening. This will be a lasting ordinance both for the Israelites and for the foreigners residing among them.

¹¹'Whoever touches a human corpse will be unclean for seven days. ¹²They must purify themselves with the water on the third day and on the seventh day; then they will be clean. But if they do not purify themselves on the third and seventh days, they will not be clean. ¹³If they fail to purify themselves after touching a human corpse, they defile the LORD's tabernacle. They must be cut off from Israel. Because the water of cleansing has not been sprinkled on them, they are unclean; their uncleanness remains on them.

¹⁴'This is the law that applies when a person dies in a tent: anyone who enters the tent and anyone who is in it will be unclean for seven days, ¹⁵and every open container without a lid fastened on it will be unclean.

¹⁶'Anyone out in the open who touches someone who has been killed with a sword or someone who has died a natural death, or anyone who touches a human bone or a grave, will be unclean for seven days.

¹⁷'For the unclean person, put some ashes from the burned purification offering into a jar and pour fresh water over them. ¹⁸Then a man who is ceremonially clean is to take some hyssop, dip it in the water and sprinkle the tent and all the furnishings and the people who were there. He must also sprinkle anyone who has touched a human bone or a grave or anyone who has been killed or anyone who has died a natural death. ¹⁹The man who is clean is to sprinkle those who are unclean on the third and seventh days, and on the seventh day he is to purify them. Those who are being cleansed must wash their clothes and bathe with water, and that evening they will be clean. ²⁰But if those who are unclean do not purify themselves, they must be cut off from the community, because they have defiled the sanctuary of the LORD. The water of cleansing has not been sprinkled on them, and they are unclean. ²¹This is a lasting ordinance for them.

'The man who sprinkles the water of cleansing must also wash his clothes, and anyone who touches the water of cleansing will be unclean till evening. ²²Anything that an unclean person touches becomes unclean, and anyone who touches it becomes unclean till evening.'

20 In the first month the whole Israelite community arrived at the Desert of Zin, and they stayed at Kadesh. There Miriam died and was buried.

²Now there was no water for the community, and the people gathered in opposition to Moses and Aaron. ³They quarrelled with Moses and said, 'If only we had died when our brothers fell dead before the LORD! ⁴Why did you bring the LORD's community into this wilderness, that we and our livestock should die here? ⁵Why did you bring us up out of Egypt to this terrible place? It has no corn or figs, grapevines or pomegranates. And there is no water to drink!'

⁶Moses and Aaron went from the assembly to the entrance to the tent of meeting

and fell face down, and the glory of the LORD appeared to them. ⁷The LORD said to Moses, ⁸'Take the staff, and you and your brother Aaron gather the assembly together. Speak to that rock before their eyes and it will pour out its water. You will bring water out of the rock for the community so that they and their livestock can drink.'

⁹So Moses took the staff from the LORD's presence, just as he commanded him. ¹⁰He and Aaron gathered the assembly together in front of the rock and Moses said to them, 'Listen, you rebels, must we bring you water out of this rock?' ¹¹Then Moses raised his arm and struck the rock twice with his staff. Water gushed out, and the community and their livestock drank.

¹²But the LORD said to Moses and Aaron, 'Because you did not trust in me enough to honour me as holy in the sight of the Israelites, you will not bring this community into the land I give them.'

¹³These were the waters of Meribah, where the Israelites quarrelled with the LORD and where he was proved holy among them.

¹⁴Moses sent messengers from Kadesh to the king of Edom, saying:

'This is what your brother Israel says: you know about all the hardships that have come on us. ¹⁵Our ancestors went down into Egypt, and we lived there many years. The Egyptians ill-treated us and our ancestors, ¹⁶but when we cried out to the LORD, he heard our cry and sent an angel and brought us out of Egypt.

'Now we are here at Kadesh, a town on the edge of your territory. ¹⁷Please let us pass through your country. We will not go through any field or vineyard, or drink water from any well. We will travel along the King's Highway and not turn to the right or to the left until we have passed through your territory.'

¹⁸But Edom answered:

'You may not pass through here; if you try, we will march out and attack you with the sword.'

¹⁹The Israelites replied:

'We will go along the main road, and if we or our livestock drink any of your water, we will pay for it. We only want to pass through on foot – nothing else.'

²⁰Again they answered:

'You may not pass through.'

Then Edom came out against them with a large and powerful army. ²¹Since Edom refused to let them go through their territory, Israel turned away from them.

²²The whole Israelite community set out from Kadesh and came to Mount Hor. ²³At Mount Hor, near the border of Edom, the LORD said to Moses and Aaron, ²⁴'Aaron will be gathered to his people. He will not enter the land I give the Israelites, because both of you rebelled against my command at the waters of Meribah. ²⁵Call Aaron and his son Eleazar and take them up Mount Hor. ²⁶Remove Aaron's garments and put them on his son Eleazar, for Aaron will be gathered to his people; he will die there.'

²⁷Moses did as the LORD commanded: they went up Mount Hor in the sight of the whole community. ²⁸Moses removed Aaron's garments and put them on his son Eleazar. And Aaron died there on top of the mountain. Then Moses and Eleazar came down from the mountain, ²⁹and when the whole community learned that Aaron had died, all the Israelites mourned for him thirty days.

21 When the Canaanite king of Arad, who lived in the Negev, heard that Israel was coming along the road to Atharim,

he attacked the Israelites and captured some of them. [2] Then Israel made this vow to the LORD: 'If you will deliver these people into our hands, we will totally destroy their cities.' [3] The LORD listened to Israel's plea and gave the Canaanites over to them. They completely destroyed them and their towns; so the place was named Hormah.

[4] They travelled from Mount Hor along the route to the Red Sea, to go round Edom. But the people grew impatient on the way; [5] they spoke against God and against Moses, and said, 'Why have you brought us up out of Egypt to die in the wilderness? There is no bread! There is no water! And we detest this miserable food!'

[6] Then the LORD sent venomous snakes among them; they bit the people and many Israelites died. [7] The people came to Moses and said, 'We sinned when we spoke against the LORD and against you. Pray that the LORD will take the snakes away from us.' So Moses prayed for the people.

[8] The LORD said to Moses, 'Make a snake and put it up on a pole; anyone who is bitten can look at it and live.' [9] So Moses made a bronze snake and put it up on a pole. Then when anyone was bitten by a snake and looked at the bronze snake, they lived.

■ PSALM 36:1-6

[1] I have a message from God in my heart
    concerning the sinfulness of the
    wicked:
There is no fear of God
    before their eyes.

[2] In their own eyes they flatter themselves
    too much to detect or hate their sin.
[3] The words of their mouths are wicked
    and deceitful;
they fail to act wisely or do good.
[4] Even on their beds they plot evil;

they commit themselves to a sinful
    course
and do not reject what is wrong.

[5] Your love, LORD, reaches to the heavens,
    your faithfulness to the skies.
[6] Your righteousness is like the highest
    mountains,
    your justice like the great deep.
You, LORD, preserve both people and
    animals.

■ PROVERBS 8:25-26

[25] before the mountains were settled in
    place,
    before the hills, I was given birth,
[26] before he made the world or its fields
    or any of the dust of the earth.

■ MARK 15:22-47

[22] They brought Jesus to the place called Golgotha (which means 'the place of the skull'). [23] Then they offered him wine mixed with myrrh, but he did not take it. [24] And they crucified him. Dividing up his clothes, they cast lots to see what each would get.

[25] It was nine in the morning when they crucified him. [26] The written notice of the charge against him read: THE KING OF THE JEWS. [27] They crucified two rebels with him, one on his right and one on his left. [28]a [29] Those who passed by hurled insults at him, shaking their heads and saying, 'So! You who are going to destroy the temple and build it in three days, [30] come down from the cross and save yourself!' [31] In the same way the chief priests and the teachers of the law mocked him among themselves. 'He saved others,' they said, 'but he can't save himself! [32] Let this Messiah, this king of Israel, come

a Some manuscripts include here words similat to Luke 22:37

down now from the cross, that we may see and believe.' Those crucified with him also heaped insults on him.

[33] At noon, darkness came over the whole land until three in the afternoon. [34] And at three in the afternoon Jesus cried out in a loud voice, 'Eloi, Eloi, lema sabachthani?' (which means 'My God, my God, why have you forsaken me?').

[35] When some of those standing near heard this, they said, 'Listen, he's calling Elijah.'

[36] Someone ran, filled a sponge with wine vinegar, put it on a staff, and offered it to Jesus to drink. 'Now leave him alone. Let's see if Elijah comes to take him down,' he said.

[37] With a loud cry, Jesus breathed his last.

[38] The curtain of the temple was torn in two from top to bottom. [39] And when the centurion, who stood there in front of Jesus, saw how he died, he said, 'Surely this man was the Son of God!'

[40] Some women were watching from a distance. Among them were Mary Magdalene, Mary the mother of James the younger and of Joseph, and Salome. [41] In Galilee these women had followed him and cared for his needs. Many other women who had come up with him to Jerusalem were also there.

[42] It was Preparation Day (that is, the day before the Sabbath). So as evening approached, [43] Joseph of Arimathea, a prominent member of the Council, who was himself waiting for the kingdom of God, went boldly to Pilate and asked for Jesus' body. [44] Pilate was surprised to hear that he was already dead. Summoning the centurion, he asked him if Jesus had already died. [45] When he learned from the centurion that it was so, he gave the body to Joseph. [46] So Joseph bought some linen cloth, took down the body, wrapped it in the linen, and placed it in a tomb cut out of rock. Then he rolled a stone against the entrance of the tomb. [47] Mary Magdalene and Mary the mother of Joseph saw where he was laid.

Great Faithfulness

'Your love, LORD, reaches to the heavens, your faithfulness to the skies.' **Psalm 36:5**

How wonderful it is, in an age where unfaithfulness abounds, to focus our gaze on those Scriptures that point to the trustworthiness of our God. The one before us today is quite wonderful, but consider also these:

'Who is like you, LORD God Almighty? You, LORD, are mighty, and your faithfulness surrounds you' (Psa. 89:8).

'Righteousness will be his belt and faithfulness the sash round his waist' (Isa. 11:5).

'... if we are faithless, he remains faithful, for he cannot disown himself' (2 Tim. 2:13).

Can't you just feel the energy flowing from these Scriptures, buttressing your confidence in God? For God to be unfaithful would be to act contrary to His nature, and if He ever was (we are only speculating because He could never do so), then He would cease to be God. Focus again with me on the text which heads this section. We are told God's faithfulness reaches to the skies. This is the psalmist's picturesque way of expressing the fact that far above all finite comprehension is the unchanging faithfulness of God. Everything about God is vast and incomparable, including His faithfulness. He never forgets a thing, never makes a mistake, never fails to keep a promise, never falters over a decision, never retracts a statement He has made, and has never breached a contract. Every declaration He has made, every promise He has given, every covenant He has struck is bestowed by His faithful character.

PRAYER

O God, how great Thou art. Great in power, great in majesty, great in love, great in mercy – great in so many things. But above all You are great in faithfulness. How I rejoice in that. Amen.

FURTHER STUDY

1 Cor. 1:1-9; Heb. 6:18; 1 Pet. 4:19
• What did Paul assure the Corinthians?
• What is it impossible for God to do?

March 22

■ NUMBERS 21:10–22:41

¹⁰ The Israelites moved on and camped at Oboth. ¹¹ Then they set out from Oboth and camped in Iye Abarim, in the wilderness that faces Moab towards the sunrise. ¹² From there they moved on and camped in the Zered Valley. ¹³ They set out from there and camped alongside the Arnon, which is in the wilderness extending into Amorite territory. The Arnon is the border of Moab, between Moab and the Amorites. ¹⁴ That is why the Book of the Wars of the LORD says:

'... Zahab in Suphah and the ravines,
    the Arnon ¹⁵ and the slopes of the
        ravines
that lead to the settlement of Ar
    and lie along the border of Moab.'

¹⁶ From there they continued on to Beer, the well where the LORD said to Moses, 'Gather the people together and I will give them water.'

¹⁷ Then Israel sang this song:

'Spring up, O well!
    Sing about it,
¹⁸ about the well that the princes dug,
    that the nobles of the people sank –
    the nobles with sceptres and staffs.'

Then they went from the wilderness to Mattanah, ¹⁹ from Mattanah to Nahaliel, from Nahaliel to Bamoth, ²⁰ and from Bamoth to the valley in Moab where the top of Pisgah overlooks the wasteland.

²¹ Israel sent messengers to say to Sihon king of the Amorites:

²² 'Let us pass through your country. We will not turn aside into any field or vineyard, or drink water from any well. We will travel along the King's Highway until we have passed through your territory.'

²³ But Sihon would not let Israel pass

through his territory. He mustered his entire army and marched out into the wilderness against Israel. When he reached Jahaz, he fought with Israel. ²⁴ Israel, however, put him to the sword and took over his land from the Arnon to the Jabbok, but only as far as the Ammonites, because their border was fortified. ²⁵ Israel captured all the cities of the Amorites and occupied them, including Heshbon and all its surrounding settlements. ²⁶ Heshbon was the city of Sihon king of the Amorites, who had fought against the former king of Moab and had taken from him all his land as far as the Arnon.

²⁷ That is why the poets say:

'Come to Heshbon and let it be rebuilt;
    let Sihon's city be restored.

²⁸ 'Fire went out from Heshbon,
    a blaze from the city of Sihon.
It consumed Ar of Moab,
    the citizens of Arnon's heights.
²⁹ Woe to you, Moab!
    You are destroyed, people of Chemosh!
He has given up his sons as fugitives
    and his daughters as captives
    to Sihon king of the Amorites.

³⁰ 'But we have overthrown them;
    Heshbon's dominion has been
        destroyed all the way to Dibon.
We have demolished them as far as
        Nophah,
    which extends to Medeba.'

³¹ So Israel settled in the land of the Amorites.

³² After Moses had sent spies to Jazer, the Israelites captured its surrounding settlements and drove out the Amorites who were there. ³³ Then they turned and went up along the road towards Bashan, and Og king of Bashan and his whole army marched out to meet them in battle at Edrei.

³⁴ The LORD said to Moses, 'Do not be afraid of him, for I have delivered him into your hands, along with his whole army and his land. Do to him what you did to Sihon king of the Amorites, who reigned in Heshbon.'

³⁵ So they struck him down, together with his sons and his whole army, leaving them no survivors. And they took possession of his land.

22 Then the Israelites travelled to the plains of Moab and camped along the Jordan opposite Jericho.

² Now Balak son of Zippor saw all that Israel had done to the Amorites, ³ and Moab was terrified because there were so many people. Indeed, Moab was filled with dread because of the Israelites.

⁴ The Moabites said to the elders of Midian, 'This horde is going to lick up everything around us, as an ox licks up the grass of the field.'

So Balak son of Zippor, who was king of Moab at that time, ⁵ sent messengers to summon Balaam son of Beor, who was at Pethor, near the River Euphrates, in his native land. Balak said:

'A people has come out of Egypt;
    they cover the face of the land and have
    settled next to me. ⁶ Now come and
    put a curse on these people, because
    they are too powerful for me. Perhaps
    then I will be able to defeat them and
    drive them out of the land. For I know
    that whoever you bless is blessed, and
    whoever you curse is cursed.'

⁷ The elders of Moab and Midian left, taking with them the fee for divination. When they came to Balaam, they told him what Balak had said.

⁸ 'Spend the night here,' Balaam said to them, 'and I will report back to you with the answer the LORD gives me.' So the Moabite officials stayed with him.

⁹God came to Balaam and asked, 'Who are these men with you?'

¹⁰Balaam said to God, 'Balak son of Zippor, king of Moab, sent me this message: ¹¹"A people that has come out of Egypt covers the face of the land. Now come and put a curse on them for me. Perhaps then I will be able to fight them and drive them away."'

¹²But God said to Balaam, 'Do not go with them. You must not put a curse on those people, because they are blessed.'

¹³The next morning Balaam got up and said to Balak's officials, 'Go back to your own country, for the Lord has refused to let me go with you.'

¹⁴So the Moabite officials returned to Balak and said, 'Balaam refused to come with us.'

¹⁵Then Balak sent other officials, more numerous and more distinguished than the first. ¹⁶They came to Balaam and said:

'This is what Balak son of Zippor says: do not let anything keep you from coming to me, ¹⁷because I will reward you handsomely and do whatever you say. Come and put a curse on these people for me.'

¹⁸But Balaam answered them, 'Even if Balak gave me all the silver and gold in his palace, I could not do anything great or small to go beyond the command of the Lord my God. ¹⁹Now spend the night here so that I can find out what else the Lord will tell me.'

²⁰That night God came to Balaam and said, 'Since these men have come to summon you, go with them, but do only what I tell you.'

²¹Balaam got up in the morning, saddled his donkey and went with the Moabite officials. ²²But God was very angry when he went, and the angel of the Lord stood in the road to oppose him. Balaam was riding on his donkey, and his two servants were with

him. ²³When the donkey saw the angel of the Lord standing in the road with a drawn sword in his hand, it turned off the road into a field. Balaam beat it to get it back on the road.

²⁴Then the angel of the Lord stood in a narrow path through the vineyards, with walls on both sides. ²⁵When the donkey saw the angel of the Lord, it pressed close to the wall, crushing Balaam's foot against it. So he beat the donkey again.

²⁶Then the angel of the Lord moved on ahead and stood in a narrow place where there was no room to turn, either to the right or to the left. ²⁷When the donkey saw the angel of the Lord, it lay down under Balaam, and he was angry and beat it with his staff. ²⁸Then the Lord opened the donkey's mouth, and it said to Balaam, 'What have I done to you to make you beat me these three times?'

²⁹Balaam answered the donkey, 'You have made a fool of me! If only I had a sword in my hand, I would kill you here and now.'

³⁰The donkey said to Balaam, 'Am I not your own donkey, which you have always ridden, to this day? Have I been in the habit of doing this to you?'

'No,' he said.

³¹Then the Lord opened Balaam's eyes, and he saw the angel of the Lord standing in the road with his sword drawn. So he bowed low and fell face down.

³²The angel of the Lord asked him, 'Why have you beaten your donkey these three times? I have come here to oppose you because your path is a reckless one before me. ³³The donkey saw me and turned away from me these three times. If it had not turned away, I would certainly have killed you by now, but I would have spared it.'

³⁴Balaam said to the angel of the Lord, 'I have sinned. I did not realise you were standing in the road to oppose me. Now if you are displeased, I will go back.'

³⁵The angel of the Lord said to Balaam,

'Go with the men, but speak only what I tell you.' So Balaam went with Balak's officials.

36 When Balak heard that Balaam was coming, he went out to meet him at the Moabite town on the Arnon border, at the edge of his territory. 37 Balak said to Balaam, 'Did I not send you an urgent summons? Why didn't you come to me? Am I really not able to reward you?'

38 'Well, I have come to you now,' Balaam replied. 'But I can't say whatever I please. I must speak only what God puts in my mouth.'

39 Then Balaam went with Balak to Kiriath Huzoth. 40 Balak sacrificed cattle and sheep, and gave some to Balaam and the officials who were with him. 41 The next morning Balak took Balaam up to Bamoth Baal, and from there he could see the outskirts of the Israelite camp.

▬ PSALM 36:7-12

7 How priceless is your unfailing love,
    O God!
  People take refuge in the shadow of
    your wings.
8 They feast in the abundance of your
    house;
  you give them drink from your river of
    delights.
9 For with you is the fountain of life;
  in your light we see light.

10 Continue your love to those who know
    you,
  your righteousness to the upright in
    heart.
11 May the foot of the proud not come
    against me,
  nor the hand of the wicked drive me
    away.
12 See how the evildoers lie fallen –
  thrown down, not able to rise!

▬ PROVERBS 8:27-29

27 I was there when he set the heavens in
    place,
  when he marked out the horizon on
    the face of the deep,
28 when he established the clouds above
  and fixed securely the fountains of the
    deep,
29 when he gave the sea its boundary
  so that the waters would not overstep
    his command,
  and when he marked out the foundations
    of the earth.

▬ MARK 16:1-20

16 When the Sabbath was over, Mary Magdalene, Mary the mother of James, and Salome bought spices so that they might go to anoint Jesus' body. 2 Very early on the first day of the week, just after sunrise, they were on their way to the tomb 3 and they asked each other, 'Who will roll the stone away from the entrance of the tomb?'

4 But when they looked up, they saw that the stone, which was very large, had been rolled away. 5 As they entered the tomb, they saw a young man dressed in a white robe sitting on the right side, and they were alarmed.

6 'Don't be alarmed,' he said. 'You are looking for Jesus the Nazarene, who was crucified. He has risen! He is not here. See the place where they laid him. 7 But go, tell his disciples and Peter, "He is going ahead of you into Galilee. There you will see him, just as he told you."'

8 Trembling and bewildered, the women went out and fled from the tomb. They said nothing to anyone, because they were afraid.

[The earliest manuscripts and some other ancient witnesses do not have verses 9 – 20.]

9 When Jesus rose early on the first day of the week,

he appeared first to Mary Magdalene, out of whom he had driven seven demons. [10] She went and told those who had been with him and who were mourning and weeping. [11] When they heard that Jesus was alive and that she had seen him, they did not believe it.

[12] Afterwards Jesus appeared in a different form to two of them while they were walking in the country. [13] These returned and reported it to the rest; but they did not believe them either.

[14] Later Jesus appeared to the Eleven as they were eating; he rebuked them for their lack of faith and their stubborn refusal to believe those who had seen him after he had risen.

[15] He said to them, 'Go into all the world and preach the gospel to all creation. [16] Whoever believes and is baptised will be saved, but whoever does not believe will be condemned. [17] And these signs will accompany those who believe: in my name they will drive out demons; they will speak in new tongues; [18] they will pick up snakes with their hands; and when they drink deadly poison, it will not hurt them at all; they will place their hands on people who are ill, and they will get well.'

[19] After the Lord Jesus had spoken to them, he was taken up into heaven and he sat at the right hand of God. [20] Then the disciples went out and preached everywhere, and the Lord worked with them and confirmed his word by the signs that accompanied it.

Step Out in Faith

'... they will place their hands on people who are ill, and they will get well.' **Mark 16:18**

Becoming intimately acquainted with the power aspect of the Holy Spirit's ministry is vital if we are to move out into the world and share with people the message of new life in Christ.

We have usually taken the words, 'But you will receive power when the Holy Spirit comes on you' (Acts 1:8), as power to talk about Jesus. It is - but it is much more. It is power in general. Under that general power is the specific power to witness; but the power itself is for the total personality - the strengthening of faith, the heightening of expectancy, the flushing out of fear, the daring to believe. And one of the ways in which God seems to be leading His children to witness to their non-Christian friends in these days is by praying, in the power of the Spirit, for their physical as well as spiritual needs. Our aim in doing this should not be to try to convince those who have a 'prove-it-to-me' mentality, as many of those who were eyewitnesses of Christ's healing ministry were not persuaded. It is rather to show them that Jesus Christ and the Christian faith are concerned about the physical as well as the spiritual needs of people.

If you have not yet experienced the empowering work of the Holy Spirit in your life, then be assured that such an experience awaits you as you take a step of faith towards what, up until now, has been a vast spiritual unknown. Just one more step - and you are there!

March 23

■ NUMBERS 23:1-24:25

23 Balaam said, 'Build me seven altars here, and prepare seven bulls and seven rams for me.' ²Balak did as Balaam said, and the two of them offered a bull and a ram on each altar.

³Then Balaam said to Balak, 'Stay here beside your offering while I go aside. Perhaps the LORD will come to meet with me. Whatever he reveals to me I will tell you.' Then he went off to a barren height.

⁴God met with him, and Balaam said, 'I have prepared seven altars, and on each altar I have offered a bull and a ram.'

⁵The LORD put a word in Balaam's mouth and said, 'Go back to Balak and give him this word.'

⁶So he went back to him and found him standing beside his offering, with all the Moabite officials. ⁷Then Balaam spoke his message:

'Balak brought me from Aram,
    the king of Moab from the eastern
        mountains.
"Come," he said, "curse Jacob for me;
    come, denounce Israel."
⁸How can I curse
    those whom God has not cursed?
How can I denounce

those whom the LORD has not
    denounced?
⁹From the rocky peaks I see them,
    from the heights I view them.
I see people who live apart
    and do not consider themselves one of
        the nations.
¹⁰Who can count the dust of Jacob
    or number even a fourth of Israel?
Let me die the death of the righteous,
    and may my final end be like theirs!'

¹¹Balak said to Balaam, 'What have you done to me? I brought you to curse my enemies, but you have done nothing but bless them!'

¹²He answered, 'Must I not speak what the LORD puts in my mouth?'

¹³Then Balak said to him, 'Come with me to another place where you can see them; you will not see them all but only the outskirts of their camp. And from there, curse them for me.' ¹⁴So he took him to the field of Zophim on the top of Pisgah, and there he built seven altars and offered a bull and a ram on each altar.

¹⁵Balaam said to Balak, 'Stay here beside your offering while I meet with him over there.'

¹⁶The LORD met with Balaam and put a word in his mouth and said, 'Go back to Balak and give him this word.'

¹⁷ So he went to him and found him standing beside his offering, with the Moabite officials. Balak asked him, 'What did the LORD say?'
¹⁸ Then he spoke his message:

'Arise, Balak, and listen;
hear me, son of Zippor.
¹⁹ God is not human, that he should lie,
not a human being, that he should change his mind.
Does he speak and then not act?
Does he promise and not fulfil?
²⁰ I have received a command to bless;
he has blessed, and I cannot change it.

²¹ 'No misfortune is seen in Jacob,
no misery observed in Israel.
The LORD their God is with them;
the shout of the King is among them.
²² God brought them out of Egypt;
they have the strength of a wild ox.
²³ There is no divination against Jacob,
no evil omens against Israel.
It will now be said of Jacob
and of Israel, "See what God has done!"
²⁴ The people rise like a lioness;
they rouse themselves like a lion
that does not rest till it devours its prey
and drinks the blood of its victims.'

²⁵ Then Balak said to Balaam, 'Neither curse them at all nor bless them at all!'
²⁶ Balaam answered, 'Did I not tell you I must do whatever the LORD says?'
²⁷ Then Balak said to Balaam, 'Come, let me take you to another place. Perhaps it will please God to let you curse them for me from there.' ²⁸ And Balak took Balaam to the top of Peor, overlooking the wasteland.
²⁹ Balaam said, 'Build me seven altars here, and prepare seven bulls and seven rams for me.' ³⁰ Balak did as Balaam had said, and offered a bull and a ram on each altar.

24 Now when Balaam saw that it pleased the LORD to bless Israel, he did not resort to divination as at other times, but turned his face towards the wilderness. ² When Balaam looked out and saw Israel encamped tribe by tribe, the Spirit of God came on him ³ and he spoke his message:

'The prophecy of Balaam son of Beor,
the prophecy of one whose eye sees clearly,
⁴ the prophecy of one who hears the words of God,
who sees a vision from the Almighty,
who falls prostrate, and whose eyes are opened:

⁵ 'How beautiful are your tents, Jacob,
your dwelling-places, Israel!

⁶ 'Like valleys they spread out,
like gardens beside a river,
like aloes planted by the LORD,
like cedars beside the waters.
⁷ Water will flow from their buckets;
their seed will have abundant water.

'Their king will be greater than Agag;
their kingdom will be exalted.

⁸ 'God brought them out of Egypt;
they have the strength of a wild ox.
They devour hostile nations
and break their bones in pieces;
with their arrows they pierce them.
⁹ Like a lion they crouch and lie down,
like a lioness – who dares to rouse them?

'May those who bless you be blessed
and those who curse you be cursed!'

¹⁰ Then Balak's anger burned against Balaam. He struck his hands together and

said to him, 'I summoned you to curse my enemies, but you have blessed them these three times. ¹¹Now leave at once and go home! I said I would reward you handsomely, but the LORD has kept you from being rewarded.'

¹²Balaam answered Balak, 'Did I not tell the messengers you sent me, ¹³ "Even if Balak gave me all the silver and gold in his palace, I could not do anything of my own accord, good or bad, to go beyond the command of the LORD – and I must say only what the LORD says"? ¹⁴Now I am going back to my people, but come, let me warn you of what this people will do to your people in days to come.'

¹⁵Then he spoke his message:

'The prophecy of Balaam son of Beor,
  the prophecy of one whose eye sees
    clearly,
¹⁶ the prophecy of one who hears the words
    of God,
  who has knowledge from the Most
    High,
  who sees a vision from the Almighty,
  who falls prostrate, and whose eyes
    are opened:

¹⁷ 'I see him, but not now;
  I behold him, but not near.
A star will come out of Jacob;
  a sceptre will rise out of Israel.
He will crush the foreheads of Moab,
  the skulls of all the people of Sheth.
¹⁸ Edom will be conquered;
  Seir, his enemy, will be conquered,
  but Israel will grow strong.
¹⁹ A ruler will come out of Jacob
  and destroy the survivors of the
    city.'
²⁰Then Balaam saw Amalek and spoke his message:

'Amalek was first among the nations,
  but their end will be utter destruction.'

²¹Then he saw the Kenites and spoke his message:

'Your dwelling-place is secure,
  your nest is set in a rock;
²² yet you Kenites will be destroyed
  when Ashur takes you captive.'
²³ Then he spoke his message:

'Alas! Who can live when God does this?
²⁴   Ships will come from the shores of
    Cyprus;
  they will subdue Ashur and Eber,
  but they too will come to ruin.'

²⁵Then Balaam got up and returned home, and Balak went his own way.

■ PSALM 37:1-6

¹Do not fret because of those who are evil
  or be envious of those who do wrong;
² for like the grass they will soon wither,
  like green plants they will soon die
    away.

³ Trust in the LORD and do good;
  dwell in the land and enjoy safe
    pasture.
⁴ Take delight in the LORD,
  and he will give you the desires of your
    heart.

⁵ Commit your way to the LORD;
  trust in him and he will do this:
⁶ He will make your righteous reward
    shine like the dawn,
  your vindication like the noonday
    sun.

■ PROVERBS 8:30-31

³⁰   Then I was constantly at his side.
  I was filled with delight day after day,

rejoicing always in his presence,
³¹ rejoicing in his whole world
and delighting in the human race.

....

▬ LUKE 1:1-23

1 Many have undertaken to draw up an account of the things that have been fulfilled among us, ² just as they were handed down to us by those who from the first were eyewitnesses and servants of the word. ³ With this in mind, since I myself have carefully investigated everything from the beginning, I too decided to write an orderly account for you, most excellent Theophilus, ⁴ so that you may know the certainty of the things you have been taught.

⁵ In the time of Herod king of Judea there was a priest named Zechariah, who belonged to the priestly division of Abijah; his wife Elizabeth was also a descendant of Aaron. ⁶ Both of them were righteous in the sight of God, observing all the Lord's commands and decrees blamelessly. ⁷ But they were childless because Elizabeth was not able to conceive, and they were both very old.

⁸ Once when Zechariah's division was on duty and he was serving as priest before God, ⁹ he was chosen by lot, according to the custom of the priesthood, to go into the temple of the Lord and burn incense. ¹⁰ And when the time for the burning of incense came, all the assembled worshippers were praying outside.

¹¹ Then an angel of the Lord appeared to him, standing at the right side of the altar of incense. ¹² When Zechariah saw him, he was startled and was gripped with fear. ¹³ But the angel said to him: 'Do not be afraid, Zechariah; your prayer has been heard. Your wife Elizabeth will bear you a son, and you are to call him John. ¹⁴ He will be a joy and delight to you, and many will rejoice because of his birth, ¹⁵ for he will be great in the sight of the Lord. He is never to take wine or other fermented drink, and he will be filled with the Holy Spirit even before he is born. ¹⁶ He will bring back many of the people of Israel to the Lord their God. ¹⁷ And he will go on before the Lord, in the spirit and power of Elijah, to turn the hearts of the parents to their children and the disobedient to the wisdom of the righteous – to make ready a people prepared for the Lord.'

¹⁸ Zechariah asked the angel, 'How can I be sure of this? I am an old man and my wife is well on in years.'

¹⁹ The angel said to him, 'I am Gabriel. I stand in the presence of God, and I have been sent to speak to you and to tell you this good news. ²⁰ And now you will be silent and not able to speak until the day this happens, because you did not believe my words, which will come true at their appointed time.'

²¹ Meanwhile, the people were waiting for Zechariah and wondering why he stayed so long in the temple. ²² When he came out, he could not speak to them. They realised he had seen a vision in the temple, for he kept making signs to them but remained unable to speak.

²³ When his time of service was completed, he returned home.

Faithfulness, Meekness

'Trust in the LORD and do good; dwell in the land and enjoy safe pasture.' **Psalm 37:3**

One of the fruits of the Spirit is faithfulness. A Christian in whom this fruit has developed will be completely dependable. Someone has said, 'The ultimate test of a man's character is this: are there any cir-cumstances under which he will not speak the truth? If so, the rest of his character is worthless, for basically he is unsound.' Strong words. How many of us, I wonder, could pass this test? I knew a Christian worker who worked herself almost to a standstill in the cause of Christ, but she couldn't refrain from telling lies.

Is it ever right to lie? 'God is not human, that he should lie ...' (Num. 23:19). If God cannot lie, then He won't delegate to us the privilege of doing it for Him! Let's go over our lives today in the light of the Holy Spirit's presence and check to see if there are any loose ends, unfulfilled promises, or half-fulfilled tasks. If there are, let's decide to complete them.

Another fruit of the Spirit is gentleness or meekness. This word is greatly misunderstood in Christian circles, for meekness is seen by many as weakness. It brings to mind (for many) the cringing spirit of Uriah Heap, who said, 'I am so very 'umble, Master Copperfield, so very 'umble.' I once saw a powerful steam hammer come down so gently on an egg that it just cracked its top. That is meekness. It is divine strength and power projected in the gentlest manner.

PRAYER

O Father, how I long for this quality to be seen in my life. Too often I am either too assertive or too unassertive. Give me, by the Spirit, a meekness that lets others know I am a follower of Yours. For Jesus' sake. Amen.

FURTHER STUDY

Luke 19:1-27; Rev. 2:10; Heb. 10:23; 1 Pet. 4:19; 1 Cor. 4:2; James 3:13
- What was the master's response to the faithful steward?
- How did he deal with the unfaithful one?

March 24

■ **NUMBERS 25:1-26:22**

25 While Israel was staying in Shittim, the men began to indulge in sexual immorality with Moabite women, ²who invited them to the sacrifices to their gods. The people ate the sacrificial meal and bowed down before these gods. ³So Israel

yoked themselves to the Baal of Peor. And the LORD's anger burned against them.

⁴The LORD said to Moses, 'Take all the leaders of these people, kill them and expose them in broad daylight before the LORD, so that the LORD's fierce anger may turn away from Israel.'

⁵So Moses said to Israel's judges, 'Each of you must put to death those of your people who have yoked themselves to the Baal of Peor.'

⁶Then an Israelite man brought into the camp a Midianite woman right before the eyes of Moses and the whole assembly of Israel while they were weeping at the entrance to the tent of meeting. ⁷When Phinehas son of Eleazar, the son of Aaron, the priest, saw this, he left the assembly, took a spear in his hand ⁸and followed the Israelite into the tent. He drove the spear into both of them, right through the Israelite man and into the woman's stomach. Then the plague against the Israelites was stopped; ⁹but those who died in the plague numbered 24,000.

¹⁰The LORD said to Moses, ¹¹'Phinehas son of Eleazar, the son of Aaron, the priest, has turned my anger away from the Israelites. Since he was as zealous for my honour among them as I am, I did not put an end to them in my zeal. ¹²Therefore tell him I am making my covenant of peace with him. ¹³He and his descendants will have a covenant of a lasting priesthood, because he was zealous for the honour of his God and made atonement for the Israelites.'

¹⁴The name of the Israelite who was killed with the Midianite woman was Zimri son of Salu, the leader of a Simeonite family. ¹⁵And the name of the Midianite woman who was put to death was Kozbi daughter of Zur, a tribal chief of a Midianite family.

¹⁶The LORD said to Moses, ¹⁷'Treat the Midianites as enemies and kill them. ¹⁸They treated you as enemies when they deceived you in the Peor incident involving their sister Kozbi, the daughter of a Midianite

leader, the woman who was killed when the plague came as a result of that incident.'

26 After the plague the LORD said to Moses and Eleazar son of Aaron, the priest, ²'Take a census of the whole Israelite community by families – all those twenty years old or more who are able to serve in the army of Israel.' ³So on the plains of Moab by the Jordan opposite Jericho, Moses and Eleazar the priest spoke with them and said, ⁴'Take a census of men twenty years old or more, as the LORD commanded Moses.'

These were the Israelites who came out of Egypt:

⁵The descendants of Reuben, the firstborn son of Israel, were:

through Hanok, the Hanokite clan;
through Pallu, the Palluite clan;
⁶through Hezron, the Hezronite clan;
through Karmi, the Karmite clan.

⁷These were the clans of Reuben; those numbered were 43,730.

⁸The son of Pallu was Eliab, ⁹and the sons of Eliab were Nemuel, Dathan and Abiram. The same Dathan and Abiram were the community officials who rebelled against Moses and Aaron and were among Korah's followers when they rebelled against the LORD. ¹⁰The earth opened its mouth and swallowed them along with Korah, whose followers died when the fire devoured the 250 men. And they served as a warning sign. ¹¹The line of Korah, however, did not die out.

¹²The descendants of Simeon by their clans were:

through Nemuel, the Nemuelite clan;
through Jamin, the Jaminite clan;
through Jakin, the Jakinite clan;
¹³through Zerah, the Zerahite clan;
through Shaul, the Shaulite clan.

¹⁴These were the clans of Simeon; those numbered were 22,200.

¹⁵ The descendants of Gad by their clans were:

through Zephon, the Zephonite clan;
through Haggi, the Haggite clan;
through Shuni, the Shunite clan;
¹⁶ through Ozni, the Oznite clan;
through Eri, the Erite clan;
¹⁷ through Arodi, the Arodite clan;
through Areli, the Arelite clan.
¹⁸ These were the clans of Gad; those numbered were 40,500.

¹⁹ Er and Onan were sons of Judah, but they died in Canaan.
²⁰ The descendants of Judah by their clans were:

through Shelah, the Shelanite clan;
through Perez, the Perezite clan;
through Zerah, the Zerahite clan.
²¹ The descendants of Perez were:
through Hezron, the Hezronite clan;
through Hamul, the Hamulite clan.
²² These were the clans of Judah; those numbered were 76,500.

▬ PSALM 37:7-13

⁷ Be still before the LORD
and wait patiently for him;
do not fret when people succeed in their
ways,
when they carry out their wicked
schemes.

⁸ Refrain from anger and turn from
wrath;
do not fret – it leads only to evil.
⁹ For those who are evil will be destroyed,
but those who hope in the LORD will
inherit the land.

¹⁰ A little while, and the wicked will be no
more;
though you look for them, they will
not be found.

¹¹ But the meek will inherit the land
and enjoy peace and prosperity.

¹² The wicked plot against the righteous
and gnash their teeth at them;
¹³ but the Lord laughs at the wicked,
for he knows their day is coming.

▬ PROVERBS 8:32-33

³² 'Now then, my children, listen to me;
blessed are those who keep my ways.
³³ Listen to my instruction and be wise;
do not disregard it.

▬ LUKE 1:24-56

²⁴ After this his wife Elizabeth became pregnant and for five months remained in seclusion. ²⁵ 'The Lord has done this for me,' she said. 'In these days he has shown his favour and taken away my disgrace among the people.'

²⁶ In the sixth month of Elizabeth's pregnancy, God sent the angel Gabriel to Nazareth, a town in Galilee, ²⁷ to a virgin pledged to be married to a man named Joseph, a descendant of David. The virgin's name was Mary. ²⁸ The angel went to her and said, 'Greetings, you who are highly favoured! The Lord is with you.'

²⁹ Mary was greatly troubled at his words and wondered what kind of greeting this might be. ³⁰ But the angel said to her, 'Do not be afraid, Mary, you have found favour with God. ³¹ You will conceive and give birth to a son, and you are to call him Jesus. ³² He will be great and will be called the Son of the Most High. The Lord God will give him the throne of his father David, ³³ and he will reign over Jacob's descendants for ever; his kingdom will never end.'

³⁴ 'How will this be,' Mary asked the angel, 'since I am a virgin?'

³⁵The angel answered, 'The Holy Spirit will come on you, and the power of the Most High will overshadow you. So the holy one to be born will be called the Son of God. ³⁶Even Elizabeth your relative is going to have a child in her old age, and she who was said to be unable to conceive is in her sixth month. ³⁷For no word from God will ever fail.'

³⁸'I am the Lord's servant,' Mary answered. 'May your word to me be fulfilled.' Then the angel left her.

³⁹At that time Mary got ready and hurried to a town in the hill country of Judea, ⁴⁰where she entered Zechariah's home and greeted Elizabeth. ⁴¹When Elizabeth heard Mary's greeting, the baby leaped in her womb, and Elizabeth was filled with the Holy Spirit. ⁴²In a loud voice she exclaimed: 'Blessed are you among women, and blessed is the child you will bear! ⁴³But why am I so favoured, that the mother of my Lord should come to me? ⁴⁴As soon as the sound of your greeting reached my ears, the baby in my womb leaped for joy. ⁴⁵Blessed is she who has believed that the Lord would fulfil his promises to her!'

⁴⁶And Mary said:

'My soul glorifies the Lord

⁴⁷   and my spirit rejoices in God my
        Saviour,
⁴⁸for he has been mindful
        of the humble state of his servant.
    From now on all generations will call me
        blessed,
⁴⁹   for the Mighty One has done great
        things for me –
        holy is his name.
⁵⁰His mercy extends to those who fear
        him,
        from generation to generation.
⁵¹He has performed mighty deeds with his
        arm;
    he has scattered those who are proud
        in their inmost thoughts.
⁵²He has brought down rulers from their
        thrones
    but has lifted up the humble.
⁵³He has filled the hungry with good
        things
    but has sent the rich away empty.
⁵⁴He has helped his servant Israel,
        remembering to be merciful
⁵⁵to Abraham and his descendants for
        ever,
    just as he promised our ancestors.'

⁵⁶Mary stayed with Elizabeth for about three months and then returned home.

'The Ground Is Level'

'"I am the Lord's servant," Mary answered. "May your word to me be fulfilled."' **Luke 1:38**

The coming of the Holy Spirit not only made all places and persons equal, but cancelled out all distinctions based on blood or special privilege. Acts 1:14 says that among those who devoted themselves to prayer were 'Mary the mother of Jesus, and His brothers.' How easy it would have been to have established a privileged line through those who were closely related to the Lord. If the Holy Spirit had set these people aside in a certain way and had come to them and them alone, then Christianity would have merely followed the family line for all succeeding generations. However, Mary, blessed though she was, waited together with the others for the coming of the Holy Spirit. And when she received Him, she received Him on the same basis as the others – by faith in Christ as Saviour and Lord. At the great moment of the Holy Spirit's coming, no one was singled out for special favour, no distinctions were made based on blood, and no one was identified as being superior or inferior. All were equal.

'At the foot of the cross,' said Dr Abernathy, when a judge and a Chinese laundryman stood before him to be received into the membership of his church, 'the ground is level.' In Christianity, no special hierarchy was ever attempted. Why? Because it was cancelled out by the coming of the Spirit. A new hierarchy came into being. The blood of God's Son has made it possible for us all to become sons of God.

PRAYER

O God, my Father, in giving Your Holy Spirit to me, You have opened the Highest to the lowest, the Greatest to the least. I belong to the twice-born nobility. Hallelujah!

FURTHER STUDY

Luke 1:38-55; 2:51;
John 2:3-5,19-25
• List some of the characteristics of Jesus' mother.
• Does she have a special place within the Church?

March 25

■ NUMBERS 26:23-65

23 The descendants of Issachar by their clans were:
    through Tola, the Tolaite clan;
    through Puah, the Puite clan;
24 through Jashub, the Jashubite clan;
    through Shimron, the Shimronite clan.
25 These were the clans of Issachar; those numbered were 64,300.

26 The descendants of Zebulun by their clans were:
    through Sered, the Seredite clan;
    through Elon, the Elonite clan;
    through Jahleel, the Jahleelite clan.
27 These were the clans of Zebulun; those numbered were 60,500.

28 The descendants of Joseph by their clans through Manasseh and Ephraim were:

29 The descendants of Manasseh:
    through Makir, the Makirite clan (Makir was the father of Gilead);
    through Gilead, the Gileadite clan.
30 These were the descendants of Gilead:
    through Iezer, the Iezerite clan;
    through Helek, the Helekite clan;
31 through Asriel, the Asrielite clan;
    through Shechem, the Shechemite clan;
32 through Shemida, the Shemidaite clan;
    through Hepher, the Hepherite clan.
33 (Zelophehad son of Hepher had no sons; he had only daughters, whose names were Mahlah, Noah, Hoglah,

Milkah and Tirzah.)

³⁴ These were the clans of Manasseh; those numbered were 52,700.

³⁵ These were the descendants of Ephraim by their clans:

through Shuthelah, the Shuthelahite clan;

through Beker, the Bekerite clan;

through Tahan, the Tahanite clan.

³⁶ These were the descendants of Shuthelah:

through Eran, the Eranite clan.

³⁷ These were the clans of Ephraim; those numbered were 32,500.

These were the descendants of Joseph by their clans.

³⁸ The descendants of Benjamin by their clans were:

through Bela, the Belaite clan;

through Ashbel, the Ashbelite clan;

through Ahiram, the Ahiramite clan;

³⁹ through Shupham, the Shuphamite clan;

through Hupham, the Huphamite clan.

⁴⁰ The descendants of Bela through Ard and Naaman were:

through Ard, the Ardite clan;

through Naaman, the Naamite clan.

⁴¹ These were the clans of Benjamin; those numbered were 45,600.

⁴² These were the descendants of Dan by their clans:

through Shuham, the Shuhamite clan.

These were the clans of Dan: ⁴³ all of them were Shuhamite clans; and those numbered were 64,400.

⁴⁴ The descendants of Asher by their clans were:

through Imnah, the Imnite clan;

through Ishvi, the Ishvite clan;

through Beriah, the Beriite clan;

⁴⁵ and through the descendants of Beriah:

through Heber, the Heberite clan;

through Malkiel, the Malkielite clan.

⁴⁶ (Asher had a daughter named Serah.)

⁴⁷ These were the clans of Asher; those numbered were 53,400.

⁴⁸ The descendants of Naphtali by their clans were:

through Jahzeel, the Jahzeelite clan;

through Guni, the Gunite clan;

⁴⁹ through Jezer, the Jezerite clan;

through Shillem, the Shillemite clan.

⁵⁰ These were the clans of Naphtali; those numbered were 45,400.

⁵¹ The total number of the men of Israel was 601,730.

⁵² The LORD said to Moses, ⁵³ 'The land is to be allotted to them as an inheritance based on the number of names. ⁵⁴ To a larger group give a larger inheritance, and to a smaller group a smaller one; each is to receive its inheritance according to the number of those listed. ⁵⁵ Be sure that the land is distributed by lot. What each group inherits will be according to the names for its ancestral tribe. ⁵⁶ Each inheritance is to be distributed by lot among the larger and smaller groups.'

⁵⁷ These were the Levites who were counted by their clans:

through Gershon, the Gershonite clan;

through Kohath, the Kohathite clan;

through Merari, the Merarite clan.

⁵⁸ These also were Levite clans:

the Libnite clan,

the Hebronite clan,

the Mahlite clan,

the Mushite clan,

the Korahite clan.

(Kohath was the forefather of Amram; ⁵⁹ the name of Amram's wife was Jochebed, a descendant of Levi, who was born to the Levites in Egypt. To Amram she bore Aaron, Moses and their sister Miriam. ⁶⁰ Aaron was the father of Nadab and Abihu, Eleazar and Ithamar. ⁶¹ But Nadab and Abihu died when they made an offering before the LORD with unauthorised fire.)

⁶² All the male Levites a month old or more numbered 23,000. They were not counted along with the other Israelites because they received no inheritance among them.

⁶³ These are the ones counted by Moses and Eleazar the priest when they counted the Israelites on the plains of Moab by the Jordan opposite Jericho. ⁶⁴ Not one of them was among those counted by Moses and Aaron the priest when they counted the Israelites in the Desert of Sinai. ⁶⁵ For the LORD had told those Israelites they would surely die in the wilderness, and not one of them was left except Caleb son of Jephunneh and Joshua son of Nun.

■ PSALM 37:14-20

¹⁴ The wicked draw the sword
    and bend the bow
to bring down the poor and needy,
    to slay those whose ways are upright.
¹⁵ But their swords will pierce their own
    hearts,
    and their bows will be broken.

¹⁶ Better the little that the righteous have
    than the wealth of many wicked;
¹⁷ for the power of the wicked will be
    broken,
    but the LORD upholds the righteous.

¹⁸ The blameless spend their days under
    the LORD's care,
    and their inheritance will endure for
    ever.
¹⁹ In times of disaster they will not wither;
    in days of famine they will enjoy plenty.

²⁰ But the wicked will perish:
    Though the LORD's enemies are like
      the flowers of the field,
    they will be consumed, they will go up
    in smoke.

■ PROVERBS 8:34-36

³⁴ Blessed are those who listen to me,
    watching daily at my doors,
    waiting at my doorway.
³⁵ For those who find me find life
    and receive favour from the LORD.
³⁶ But those who fail to find me harm
    themselves;
    all who hate me love death.'

■ LUKE 1:57-80

⁵⁷ When it was time for Elizabeth to have her baby, she gave birth to a son. ⁵⁸ Her neighbours and relatives heard that the Lord had shown her great mercy, and they shared her joy.

⁵⁹ On the eighth day they came to circumcise the child, and they were going to name him after his father Zechariah, ⁶⁰ but his mother spoke up and said, 'No! He is to be called John.'

⁶¹ They said to her, 'There is no one among your relatives who has that name.'

⁶² Then they made signs to his father, to find out what he would like to name the child. ⁶³ He asked for a writing tablet, and to everyone's astonishment he wrote, 'His name is John.' ⁶⁴ Immediately his mouth was opened and his tongue set free, and

he began to speak, praising God. ⁶⁵All the neighbours were filled with awe, and throughout the hill country of Judea people were talking about all these things. ⁶⁶Everyone who heard this wondered about it, asking, 'What then is this child going to be?' For the Lord's hand was with him.

⁶⁷His father Zechariah was filled with the Holy Spirit and prophesied:

⁶⁸ 'Praise be to the Lord, the God of Israel,
because he has come to his people and redeemed them.
⁶⁹He has raised up a horn of salvation for us
in the house of his servant David
⁷⁰(as he said through his holy prophets of long ago),
⁷¹salvation from our enemies
and from the hand of all who hate us –
⁷²to show mercy to our ancestors
and to remember his holy covenant,
⁷³ the oath he swore to our father Abraham:

⁷⁴to rescue us from the hand of our enemies,
and to enable us to serve him without fear
⁷⁵ in holiness and righteousness before him all our days.

⁷⁶And you, my child, will be called a prophet of the Most High;
for you will go on before the Lord to prepare the way for him,
⁷⁷to give his people the knowledge of salvation
through the forgiveness of their sins,
⁷⁸because of the tender mercy of our God,
by which the rising sun will come to us from heaven
⁷⁹to shine on those living in darkness
and in the shadow of death,
to guide our feet into the path of peace.'

⁸⁰And the child grew and became strong in spirit; and he lived in the wilderness until he appeared publicly to Israel.

They Will Be Satisfied

'... in days of famine they will enjoy plenty.'
Psalm 37:19

Jesus directs us to ask God for our daily bread because we have a need to ask Him. It does us good to ask, for asking increases our awareness of our dependency upon God and builds a defence against ingratitude.

I find it greatly encouraging that the God of creation, who is infinitely holy and who holds the universe in His hand, cares that my physical needs are met. This implies that God regards our bodies as important. He designed them and is interested in the way they function.

Some Christians regard it as 'unspiritual' to pray about the needs of the body, but, as Jesus pointed out, this is really where our personal petitions ought to begin. While Jesus endeavoured to get His hearers to keep their values straight by saying that the spiritual was all important - 'seek first the kingdom of God' (Matt. 6:33, HSCB) - He nevertheless put the body in its rightful place, as being a matter of great concern. The Father, we are told, guarantees our physical needs if we seek first the kingdom of God.

Most of the promises in the Bible have to do with spiritual truth, but never to the exclusion of the physical. How much spiritual use would we be to our heavenly Father if He didn't meet our basic physical needs? This is why I do not fear the future. In whatever way people might mismanage the resources which God has placed in the earth, I have confidence in the truth of the verse before us today: '... in days of famine they will enjoy plenty.'

PRAYER

Father, help me not to get bogged down in wrong attitudes about the physical factors of my life, for they are a part of me. Teach me to live, physically and spiritually, as one. For Jesus' sake. Amen.

FURTHER STUDY

John 6:1-15; Psa. 37:25; Joel 2:24; Luke 12:27-31
• What was the disciples' attitude?
• How did Jesus show interest in physical needs?

March 26

■ NUMBERS 27:1–28:31

27 The daughters of Zelophehad son of Hepher, the son of Gilead, the son of Makir, the son of Manasseh, belonged to the clans of Manasseh son of Joseph. The names of the daughters were Mahlah, Noah, Hoglah, Milkah and Tirzah. They came forward ² and stood before Moses, Eleazar the priest, the leaders and the whole assembly at the entrance to the tent of meeting and said, ³ 'Our father died in the wilderness. He was not among Korah's followers, who banded together against the LORD, but he died for his own sin and left no sons. ⁴ Why should our father's name disappear from his clan because he had no son? Give us property among our father's relatives.'

⁵ So Moses brought their case before the LORD, ⁶ and the LORD said to him, ⁷ 'What Zelophehad's daughters are saying is right. You must certainly give them property as an inheritance among their father's relatives and give their father's inheritance to them.

⁸ 'Say to the Israelites, "If a man dies and leaves no son, give his inheritance to his daughter. ⁹ If he has no daughter, give his inheritance to his brothers. ¹⁰ If he has no brothers, give his inheritance to his father's brothers. ¹¹ If his father had no brothers, give his inheritance to the nearest relative in his clan, that he may possess it. This is to have the force of law for the Israelites, as the LORD commanded Moses." '

¹² Then the LORD said to Moses, 'Go up this mountain in the Abarim Range and see the land I have given the Israelites. ¹³ After you have seen it, you too will be gathered to your people, as your brother Aaron was, ¹⁴ for when the community rebelled at the waters in the Desert of Zin, both of you disobeyed my command to honour me as holy before their eyes.' (These were the waters of Meribah Kadesh, in the Desert of Zin.)

¹⁵ Moses said to the LORD, ¹⁶ 'May the LORD, the God who gives breath to all living things, appoint someone over this community ¹⁷ to go out and come in before them,

one who will lead them out and bring them in, so that the LORD's people will not be like sheep without a shepherd.'

¹⁸ So the LORD said to Moses, 'Take Joshua son of Nun, a man in whom is the spirit of leadership, and lay your hand on him. ¹⁹ Make him stand before Eleazar the priest and the entire assembly and commission him in their presence. ²⁰ Give him some of your authority so that the whole Israelite community will obey him. ²¹ He is to stand before Eleazar the priest, who will obtain decisions for him by enquiring of the Urim before the LORD. At his command he and the entire community of the Israelites will go out, and at his command they will come in.'

²² Moses did as the LORD commanded him. He took Joshua and made him stand before Eleazar the priest and the whole assembly. ²³ Then he laid his hands on him and commissioned him, as the LORD instructed through Moses.

28 The LORD said to Moses, ² 'Give this command to the Israelites and say to them: "Make sure that you present to me at the appointed time my food offerings, as an aroma pleasing to me." ³ Say to them: "This is the food offering you are to present to the LORD: two lambs a year old without defect, as a regular burnt offering each day. ⁴ Offer one lamb in the morning and the other at twilight, ⁵ together with a grain offering of a tenth of an ephah of the finest flour mixed with a quarter of a hin of oil from pressed olives. ⁶ This is the regular burnt offering instituted at Mount Sinai as a pleasing aroma, a food offering presented to the LORD. ⁷ The accompanying drink offering is to be a quarter of a hin of fermented drink with each lamb. Pour out the drink offering to the LORD at the sanctuary. ⁸ Offer the second lamb at twilight, along with the same kind of grain offering and drink offering that you offer in the morning. This is a food offering, an aroma pleasing to the LORD.

⁹ "On the Sabbath day, make an offering of two lambs a year old without defect, together with its drink offering and a grain offering of one-fifth of an ephah of the finest flour mixed with olive oil. ¹⁰ This is the burnt offering for every Sabbath, in addition to the regular burnt offering and its drink offering.

¹¹ "On the first of every month, present to the LORD a burnt offering of two young bulls, one ram and seven male lambs a year old, all without defect. ¹² With each bull there is to be a grain offering of three-tenths of an ephah of the finest flour mixed with oil; with the ram, a grain offering of one-fifth of an ephah of the finest flour mixed with oil; ¹³ and with each lamb, a grain offering of a tenth of an ephah of the finest flour mixed with oil. This is for a burnt offering, a pleasing aroma, a food offering presented to the LORD. ¹⁴ With each bull there is to be a drink offering of half a hin of wine; with the ram, a third of a hin; and with each lamb, a quarter of a hin. This is the monthly burnt offering to be made at each new moon during the year. ¹⁵ Besides the regular burnt offering with its drink offering, one male goat is to be presented to the LORD as a sin offering.

¹⁶ "On the fourteenth day of the first month the LORD's Passover is to be held. ¹⁷ On the fifteenth day of this month there is to be a festival; for seven days eat bread made without yeast. ¹⁸ On the first day hold a sacred assembly and do not do any of your ordinary work. ¹⁹ Present to the LORD a food offering consisting of a burnt offering of two young bulls, one ram and seven male lambs a year old, all without defect. ²⁰ With each bull offer a grain offering of three-tenths of an ephah of the finest flour mixed with oil; with the ram, one-fifth; ²¹ and with each of the seven lambs, one-tenth. ²² Include one male goat as a sin offering to make atonement for you. ²³ Offer these in addition to the regular morning burnt offering. ²⁴ In this way present the food offering every

day for seven days as an aroma pleasing to the LORD; it is to be offered in addition to the regular burnt offering and its drink offering. ²⁵On the seventh day hold a sacred assembly and do not do any ordinary work.

²⁶'"On the day of firstfruits, when you present to the LORD an offering of new grain during the Festival of Weeks, hold a sacred assembly and do not do any of your ordinary work. ²⁷Present a burnt offering of two young bulls, one ram and seven male lambs a year old as an aroma pleasing to the LORD. ²⁸With each bull there is to be a grain offering of three-tenths of an ephah of the finest flour mixed with oil; with the ram, one-fifth; ²⁹and with each of the seven lambs, one-tenth. ³⁰Include one male goat to make atonement for you. ³¹Offer these together with their drink offerings, in addition to the regular burnt offering and its grain offering. Be sure the animals are without defect.

PSALM 37:21-26

²¹The wicked borrow and do not repay,
    but the righteous give generously;
²²those the LORD blesses will inherit the
        land,
    but those he curses will be destroyed.

²³The LORD makes firm the steps
    of the one who delights in him;
²⁴though he may stumble, he will not fall,
    for the LORD upholds him with his
        hand.

²⁵I was young and now I am old,
    yet I have never seen the righteous
        forsaken
    or their children begging bread.
²⁶They are always generous and lend
        freely;
    their children will be a blessing.

PROVERBS 9:1-2

9 Wisdom has built her house;
    she has set up its seven pillars.
²She has prepared her meat and mixed
        her wine;
    she has also set her table.

LUKE 2:1-20

2 In those days Caesar Augustus issued a
    decree that a census should be taken of the entire Roman world. ²(This was the first census that took place while Quirinius was governor of Syria.) ³And everyone went to their own town to register.

⁴So Joseph also went up from the town of Nazareth in Galilee to Judea, to Bethlehem the town of David, because he belonged to the house and line of David. ⁵He went there to register with Mary, who was pledged to be married to him and was expecting a child. ⁶While they were there, the time came for the baby to be born, ⁷and she gave birth to her firstborn, a son. She wrapped him in cloths and placed him in a manger, because there was no guest room available for them.

⁸And there were shepherds living out in the fields near by, keeping watch over their flocks at night. ⁹An angel of the Lord appeared to them, and the glory of the Lord shone around them, and they were terrified. ¹⁰But the angel said to them, 'Do not be afraid. I bring you good news that will cause great joy for all the people. ¹¹Today in the town of David a Saviour has been born to you; he is the Messiah, the Lord. ¹²This will be a sign to you: you will find a baby wrapped in cloths and lying in a manger.'

¹³Suddenly a great company of the heavenly host appeared with the angel, praising God and saying,

¹⁴'Glory to God in the highest heaven,

and on earth peace to those on whom his favour rests.'

[15] When the angels had left them and gone into heaven, the shepherds said to one another, 'Let's go to Bethlehem and see this thing that has happened, which the Lord has told us about.' [16] So they hurried off and found Mary and Joseph, and the baby, who was lying in the manger. [17] When they had seen him, they spread the word concerning what had been told them about this child, [18] and all who heard it were amazed at what the shepherds said to them. [19] But Mary treasured up all these things and pondered them in her heart. [20] The shepherds returned, glorifying and praising God for all the things they had heard and seen, which were just as they had been told.

Come into My House

'Wisdom has built her house; she has set up its seven pillars.' **Proverbs 9:1**

Our text for today tells us that wisdom is like a house built on seven pillars. There are two ways of interpreting this text. One view says that both wisdom and folly have a house to which humankind is invited. Wisdom has a much larger house than folly, being built upon 'seven pillars' - a sign in ancient times of wealth, status and prestige. There is no doubt that this is one meaning of the text, but the other view is that wisdom has seven major aspects.

The human race is overrun with many problems, much confusion, and so many conflicting philosophies of how to live. Those who lack wisdom do not have the perspectives that enable them to discern the connection between cause and effect, and therefore they don't understand what they are stumbling over, or, if they do avoid problems, they don't understand why they avoid them. We need wisdom to live, and Proverbs shows us how.

PRAYER

Gracious and loving heavenly Father, grant that as I expose myself day by day to the truths of Your Word, wisdom may be more deeply imprinted into my spirit. In Jesus' name I pray. Amen.

FURTHER STUDY

Job 28; 42:1-3; Psa. 119:169; Eccl. 1:13; 8:16-17
• What question did Job ponder?
• What conclusion did he come to?

March 27

■ NUMBERS 29:1–30:16

29 ¹"On the first day of the seventh month hold a sacred assembly and do not do any of your ordinary work. It is a day for you to sound the trumpets. ²As an aroma pleasing to the LORD, offer a burnt offering of one young bull, one ram and seven male lambs a year old, all without defect. ³With the bull offer a grain offering of three-tenths of an ephah of the finest flour mixed with olive oil; with the ram, one-fifth; ⁴and with each of the seven lambs, one-tenth. ⁵Include one male goat as a sin offering to make atonement for you. ⁶These are in addition to the monthly and daily burnt offerings with their grain offerings and drink offerings as specified. They are food offerings presented to the LORD, a pleasing aroma.

⁷"On the tenth day of this seventh month hold a sacred assembly. You must deny yourselves and do no work. ⁸Present as an aroma pleasing to the LORD a burnt offering of one young bull, one ram and seven male lambs a year old, all without defect. ⁹With the bull offer a grain offering of three-tenths of an ephah of the finest flour mixed with oil; with the ram, one-fifth; ¹⁰and with each of the seven lambs, one-tenth. ¹¹Include one male goat as a sin offering, in addition to the sin offering for atonement and the regular burnt offering with its grain offering, and their drink offerings.

¹²"On the fifteenth day of the seventh month, hold a sacred assembly and do not do any of your ordinary work. Celebrate a festival to the LORD for seven days. ¹³Present as an aroma pleasing to the LORD a food offering consisting of a burnt offering of thirteen young bulls, two rams and fourteen

male lambs a year old, all without defect. ¹⁴With each of the thirteen bulls offer a grain offering of three-tenths of an ephah of the finest flour mixed with oil; with each of the two rams, one-fifth; ¹⁵and with each of the fourteen lambs, one-tenth. ¹⁶Include one male goat as a sin offering, in addition to the regular burnt offering with its grain offering and drink offering.

¹⁷"On the second day offer twelve young bulls, two rams and fourteen male lambs a year old, all without defect. ¹⁸With the bulls, rams and lambs, offer their grain offerings and drink offerings according to the number specified. ¹⁹Include one male goat as a sin offering, in addition to the regular burnt offering with its grain offering, and their drink offerings.

²⁰"On the third day offer eleven bulls, two rams and fourteen male lambs a year old, all without defect. ²¹With the bulls, rams and lambs, offer their grain offerings and drink offerings according to the number specified. ²²Include one male goat as a sin offering, in addition to the regular burnt offering with its grain offering and drink offering.

²³"On the fourth day offer ten bulls, two rams and fourteen male lambs a year old, all without defect. ²⁴With the bulls, rams and lambs, offer their grain offerings and drink offerings according to the number specified. ²⁵Include one male goat as a sin offering, in addition to the regular burnt offering with its grain offering and drink offering.

²⁶"On the fifth day offer nine bulls, two rams and fourteen male lambs a year old, all without defect. ²⁷With the bulls, rams and lambs, offer their grain offerings and drink offerings according to the number specified.

²⁸ Include one male goat as a sin offering, in addition to the regular burnt offering with its grain offering and drink offering.

²⁹ ' "On the sixth day offer eight bulls, two rams and fourteen male lambs a year old, all without defect. ³⁰ With the bulls, rams and lambs, offer their grain offerings and drink offerings according to the number specified. ³¹ Include one male goat as a sin offering, in addition to the regular burnt offering with its grain offering and drink offering.

³² ' "On the seventh day offer seven bulls, two rams and fourteen male lambs a year old, all without defect. ³³ With the bulls, rams and lambs, offer their grain offerings and drink offerings according to the number specified. ³⁴ Include one male goat as a sin offering, in addition to the regular burnt offering with its grain offering and drink offering.

³⁵ ' "On the eighth day hold a closing special assembly and do not do any of your ordinary work. ³⁶ Present as an aroma pleasing to the LORD a food offering consisting of a burnt offering of one bull, one ram and seven male lambs a year old, all without defect. ³⁷ With the bull, the ram and the lambs, offer their grain offerings and drink offerings according to the number specified. ³⁸ Include one male goat as a sin offering, in addition to the regular burnt offering with its grain offering and drink offering.

³⁹ ' "In addition to what you vow and your freewill offerings, offer these to the LORD at your appointed festivals: your burnt offerings, grain offerings, drink offerings and fellowship offerings." '

⁴⁰ Moses told the Israelites all that the LORD commanded him.

30 Moses said to the heads of the tribes of Israel: 'This is what the LORD commands: ² when a man makes a vow to the LORD or takes an oath to bind himself by a pledge, he must not break his word but must do everything he said.

³ 'When a young woman still living in her father's household makes a vow to the LORD or binds herself by a pledge ⁴ and her father hears about her vow or pledge but says nothing to her, then all her vows and every pledge by which she bound herself will stand. ⁵ But if her father forbids her when he hears about it, none of her vows or the pledges by which she bound herself will stand; the LORD will release her because her father has forbidden her.

⁶ 'If she marries after she makes a vow or after her lips utter a rash promise by which she binds herself ⁷ and her husband hears about it but says nothing to her, then her vows or the pledges by which she bound herself will stand. ⁸ But if her husband forbids her when he hears about it, he nullifies the vow that binds her or the rash promise by which she binds herself, and the LORD will release her.

⁹ 'Any vow or obligation taken by a widow or divorced woman will be binding on her.

¹⁰ 'If a woman living with her husband makes a vow or binds herself by a pledge under oath ¹¹ and her husband hears about it but says nothing to her and does not forbid her, then all her vows or the pledges by which she bound herself will stand. ¹² But if her husband nullifies them when he hears about them, then none of the vows or pledges that came from her lips will stand. Her husband has nullified them, and the LORD will release her. ¹³ Her husband may confirm or nullify any vow she makes or any sworn pledge to deny herself. ¹⁴ But if her husband says nothing to her about it from day to day, then he confirms all her vows or the pledges binding on her. He confirms them by saying nothing to her when he hears about them. ¹⁵ If, however, he nullifies them some time after he hears about them, then he must bear the consequences of her wrongdoing.'

¹⁶ These are the regulations the LORD gave Moses concerning relationships between a man and his wife, and between a father and his young daughter still living at home.

▬ PSALM 37:27-33

²⁷ Turn from evil and do good;
   then you will dwell in the land for ever.
²⁸ For the LORD loves the just
   and will not forsake his faithful ones.

Wrongdoers will be completely destroyed;
   the offspring of the wicked will perish.
²⁹ The righteous will inherit the land
   and dwell in it for ever.

³⁰ The mouths of the righteous utter
      wisdom,
   and their tongues speak what is just.
³¹ The law of their God is in their hearts;
   their feet do not slip.

³² The wicked lie in wait for the righteous,
   intent on putting them to death;
³³ but the LORD will not leave them in the
      power of the wicked
   or let them be condemned when
      brought to trial.

▬ PROVERBS 9:3-6

³ She has sent out her servants, and she
      calls
   from the highest point of the city,
⁴ 'Let all who are simple come to my
      house!'
   To those who have no sense she says,
⁵ 'Come, eat my food
   and drink the wine I have mixed.
⁶ Leave your simple ways and you will live;
   walk in the way of insight.'

▬ LUKE 2:21-38

²¹ On the eighth day, when it was time to
circumcise the child, he was named Jesus,
the name the angel had given him before he
was conceived.

²² When the time came for the purification rites required by the Law of Moses, Joseph and Mary took him to Jerusalem to present him to the Lord ²³ (as it is written in the Law of the Lord, 'Every firstborn male is to be consecrated to the Lord'), ²⁴ and to offer a sacrifice in keeping with what is said in the Law of the Lord: 'a pair of doves or two young pigeons'.

²⁵ Now there was a man in Jerusalem called Simeon, who was righteous and devout. He was waiting for the consolation of Israel, and the Holy Spirit was on him. ²⁶ It had been revealed to him by the Holy Spirit that he would not die before he had seen the Lord's Messiah. ²⁷ Moved by the Spirit, he went into the temple courts. When the parents brought in the child Jesus to do for him what the custom of the Law required, ²⁸ Simeon took him in his arms and praised God, saying:

²⁹ 'Sovereign Lord, as you have promised,
   you may now dismiss your servant in
      peace.
³⁰ For my eyes have seen your salvation,
³¹   which you have prepared in the sight
         of all nations:
³² a light for revelation to the Gentiles,
   and the glory of your people Israel.'

³³ The child's father and mother marvelled at what was said about him. ³⁴ Then Simeon blessed them and said to Mary, his mother: 'This child is destined to cause the falling and rising of many in Israel, and to be a sign that will be spoken against, ³⁵ so that the thoughts of many hearts will be revealed. And a sword will pierce your own soul too.'

³⁶ There was also a prophet, Anna, the daughter of Penuel, of the tribe of Asher. She was very old; she had lived with her husband seven years after her marriage, ³⁷ and then was a widow until she was eighty-four. She never left the temple but worshipped

night and day, fasting and praying. [38] Coming up to them at that very moment, she gave thanks to God and spoke about the child to all who were looking forward to the redemption of Jerusalem.

The 'Inner-Stances'

'For the LORD loves the just and will not forsake his faithful ones.' **Psalm 37:28**

Why is it that while the same things can happen to us all, they may not have the same effect upon us all? The same thing happening to two different people may have entirely different effects. Why should this be so? It depends not so much on the circumstances, but on the 'inner-stances' - or, in other words, our inner attitudes. As someone has said, 'What life does to us in the long run depends on what life finds in us.' Life's blows can make some people irritable and bitter; others they sweeten and refine - the same events, but with opposite effects.

The Gospels tell us that there were three crosses set up on Calvary on the first Good Friday. The same event happened to three different people, but look at the different results. One thief complained and blamed Jesus for not saving Himself and them; the other thief recognised his own unworthiness, repented of it and found an open door to Paradise. Jesus, of course, saw it as the climax of His earthly achievements and made it the fulcrum on which He moved the world.

What counts, therefore, is not so much what happens to us, but what we do with it. The same sunshine falling on two different plants can cause one to wither and die, while the other will blossom and flourish. And why? It all depends on the response the plants make. Although, of course, they both need water, one plant is more suited to hot sunshine than the other and therefore responds with more life and growth, while the other shrivels.

PRAYER

Gracious heavenly Father, write this precept upon my heart so that I shall never forget it: it's not so much what happens to me, but what I do with it that is important. Thank You, Father. Amen.

FURTHER STUDY

2 Cor. 11:21-29; 2 Tim. 4:7;
Prov. 2:8; 2 Cor. 12:8-9
• What was Paul's testimony?
• How did he sum up his life?

March 28

▬ NUMBERS 31:1-54

31 The LORD said to Moses, ²'Take vengeance on the Midianites for the Israelites. After that, you will be gathered to your people.'

³So Moses said to the people, 'Arm some of your men to go to war against the Midianites so that they may carry out the LORD's vengeance on them. ⁴Send into battle a thousand men from each of the tribes of Israel.' ⁵So twelve thousand men armed for battle, a thousand from each tribe, were supplied from the clans of Israel. ⁶Moses sent them into battle, a thousand from each tribe, along with Phinehas son of Eleazar, the priest, who took with him articles from the sanctuary and the trumpets for signalling.

⁷They fought against Midian, as the LORD commanded Moses, and killed every man. ⁸Among their victims were Evi, Rekem, Zur, Hur and Reba – the five kings of Midian. They also killed Balaam son of Beor with the sword. ⁹The Israelites captured the Midianite women and children and took all the Midianite herds, flocks and goods as plunder. ¹⁰They burned all the towns where the Midianites had settled, as well as all their camps. ¹¹They took all the plunder and spoils, including the people and animals, ¹²and brought the captives, spoils and plunder to Moses and Eleazar the priest and the Israelite assembly at their camp on the plains of Moab, by the Jordan opposite Jericho.

¹³Moses, Eleazar the priest and all the leaders of the community went to meet them outside the camp. ¹⁴Moses was angry with the officers of the army – the commanders of thousands and commanders of hundreds – who returned from the battle.

¹⁵'Have you allowed all the women to live?' he asked them. ¹⁶'They were the ones who followed Balaam's advice and enticed the Israelites to be unfaithful to the LORD in the Peor incident, so that a plague struck the LORD's people. ¹⁷Now kill all the boys. And kill every woman who has slept with a man, ¹⁸but save for yourselves every girl who has never slept with a man.

¹⁹'Anyone who has killed someone or touched someone who was killed must stay outside the camp seven days. On the third and seventh days you must purify yourselves and your captives. ²⁰Purify every garment as well as everything made of leather, goat hair or wood.'

²¹Then Eleazar the priest said to the soldiers who had gone into battle, 'This is what is required by the law that the LORD gave Moses: ²²gold, silver, bronze, iron, tin, lead ²³and anything else that can withstand fire must be put through the fire, and then it will be clean. But it must also be purified with the water of cleansing. And whatever cannot withstand fire must be put through that water. ²⁴On the seventh day wash your clothes and you will be clean. Then you may come into the camp.'

²⁵The LORD said to Moses, ²⁶'You and Eleazar the priest and the family heads of the community are to count all the people and animals that were captured. ²⁷Divide the spoils equally between the soldiers who took part in the battle and the rest of the community. ²⁸From the soldiers who fought in the battle, set apart as tribute for the LORD one out of every five hundred, whether people, cattle, donkeys or sheep. ²⁹Take this tribute from their half share and give it to Eleazar the priest as the LORD's

part. ³⁰From the Israelites' half, select one out of every fifty, whether people, cattle, donkeys, sheep or other animals. Give them to the Levites, who are responsible for the care of the LORD's tabernacle.' ³¹So Moses and Eleazar the priest did as the LORD commanded Moses.

³²The plunder remaining from the spoils that the soldiers took was 675,000 sheep, ³³72,000 cattle, ³⁴61,000 donkeys ³⁵and 32,000 women who had never slept with a man.

³⁶The half share of those who fought in the battle was:

> 337,500 sheep, ³⁷of which the tribute for the LORD was 675;
> ³⁸36,000 cattle, of which the tribute for the LORD was 72;
> ³⁹30,500 donkeys, of which the tribute for the LORD was 61;
> ⁴⁰16,000 people, of whom the tribute for the LORD was 32.

⁴¹Moses gave the tribute to Eleazar the priest as the LORD's part, as the LORD commanded Moses.

⁴²The half belonging to the Israelites, which Moses set apart from that of the fighting men – ⁴³the community's half – was 337,500 sheep, ⁴⁴36,000 cattle, ⁴⁵30,500 donkeys ⁴⁶and 16,000 people. ⁴⁷From the Israelites' half, Moses selected one out of every fifty people and animals, as the LORD commanded him, and gave them to the Levites, who were responsible for the care of the LORD's tabernacle.

⁴⁸Then the officers who were over the units of the army – the commanders of thousands and commanders of hundreds – went to Moses ⁴⁹and said to him, 'Your servants have counted the soldiers under our command, and not one is missing. ⁵⁰So we have brought as an offering to the LORD the gold articles each of us acquired – armlets, bracelets, signet rings, earrings and necklaces – to make atonement for ourselves before the LORD.'

⁵¹Moses and Eleazar the priest accepted from them the gold – all the handcrafted articles. ⁵²All the gold from the commanders of thousands and commanders of hundreds that Moses and Eleazar presented as a gift to the LORD weighed 16,750 shekels. ⁵³Each soldier had taken plunder for himself. ⁵⁴Moses and Eleazar the priest accepted the gold from the commanders of thousands and commanders of hundreds and brought it into the tent of meeting as a memorial for the Israelites before the LORD.

··

■ PSALM 37:34-40

³⁴Hope in the LORD
> and keep his way.
> He will exalt you to inherit the land;
> > when the wicked are destroyed, you
> > > will see it.

³⁵I have seen a wicked and ruthless man
> flourishing like a luxuriant native
> > tree,
³⁶but he soon passed away and was no
> > more;
> > though I looked for him, he could not
> > > be found.

³⁷Consider the blameless, observe the
> > upright;
> a future awaits those who seek peace.
³⁸But all sinners will be destroyed;
> > there will be no future for the wicked.

³⁹The salvation of the righteous comes
> > from the LORD;
> he is their stronghold in time of
> > trouble.
⁴⁰The LORD helps them and delivers them;
> > he delivers them from the wicked and
> > > saves them,
> > because they take refuge in him.

■ PROVERBS 9:7-9

⁷ Whoever corrects a mocker invites insults;
   whoever rebukes the wicked incurs
      abuse.
⁸ Do not rebuke mockers or they will hate
      you;
   rebuke the wise and they will love you.
⁹ Instruct the wise and they will be wiser
      still;
   teach the righteous and they will add
      to their learning.

■ LUKE 2:39-52

³⁹ When Joseph and Mary had done everything required by the Law of the Lord, they returned to Galilee to their own town of Nazareth. ⁴⁰ And the child grew and became strong; he was filled with wisdom, and the grace of God was on him.

⁴¹ Every year Jesus' parents went to Jerusalem for the Festival of the Passover. ⁴² When he was twelve years old, they went up to the festival, according to the custom. ⁴³ After the festival was over, while his parents were returning home, the boy Jesus stayed behind in Jerusalem, but they were unaware of it. ⁴⁴ Thinking he was in their company, they travelled on for a day. Then they began looking for him among their relatives and friends. ⁴⁵ When they did not find him, they went back to Jerusalem to look for him. ⁴⁶ After three days they found him in the temple courts, sitting among the teachers, listening to them and asking them questions. ⁴⁷ Everyone who heard him was amazed at his understanding and his answers. ⁴⁸ When his parents saw him, they were astonished. His mother said to him, 'Son, why have you treated us like this? Your father and I have been anxiously searching for you.'

⁴⁹ 'Why were you searching for me?' he asked. 'Didn't you know I had to be in my Father's house?' ⁵⁰ But they did not understand what he was saying to them.

⁵¹ Then he went down to Nazareth with them and was obedient to them. But his mother treasured all these things in her heart. ⁵² And Jesus grew in wisdom and stature, and in favour with God and man.

The Tenses of Salvation

'The salvation of the righteous comes from the LORD;
he is their stronghold in time of trouble.' **Psalm 37:39**

Satan will take advantage of every situation that comes his way in order to disable a Christian, and he will not hesitate to use chaotic world conditions and problems to oppose the mind. But God's answer to this is the helmet of salvation.

In 1 Thessalonians 5:8, Paul is not talking about the salvation of the soul when he says, '... let us be sober, putting on faith and love as a breastplate, and the hope of salvation as a helmet.' He is not referring to salvation as regeneration or conversion. This is the mistake that many make when attempting to interpret this verse. They say, 'Whenever the devil attacks your mind and seeks to oppress it, remind yourself that you have been saved.' Well, there is nothing wrong with that, of course. This explanation is mistaken, however, not because it is untrue, but because it does not go far enough.

The best way to interpret any verse of Scripture is with another verse of Scripture. Thus this text from 1 Thessalonians throws a shaft of light on Paul's statement in Ephesians 6:17: 'Take the helmet of salvation,' for it shows salvation, not just as something in the past, but something that is also a future 'hope'. He uses the word salvation the same way in Romans when he writes: 'Our salvation is nearer now than when we first believed' (Rom. 13:11).

In the Bible, the word salvation has three distinct tenses – past, present and future. At conversion, we are saved from the penalty of sin. At present, day by day, we are being saved from the power of sin. And one day in the future, we will be saved from the presence of sin. It is to the future Paul is looking when he invites us to put on the helmet of salvation.

PRAYER

O Father, thank You for reminding me of the tenses of salvation. I see that in order to live effectively, I must view the present tense by the future tense. Help me lay hold on this. In Jesus' name. Amen.

FURTHER STUDY

Psa. 27:1-14; Isa. 12:2; 25:9
• What was the psalmist's conviction?
• What was the prophet proclaiming?

March 29

■ NUMBERS 32:1-42

32 The Reubenites and Gadites, who had very large herds and flocks, saw that the lands of Jazer and Gilead were suitable for livestock. ²So they came to Moses and Eleazar the priest and to the leaders of the community, and said, ³'Ataroth, Dibon, Jazer, Nimrah, Heshbon, Elealeh, Sebam, Nebo and Beon – ⁴the land the LORD subdued before the people of Israel – are suitable for livestock, and your servants have livestock. ⁵If we have found favour in your eyes,' they said, 'let this land be given to your servants as our possession. Do not make us cross the Jordan.'

⁶Moses said to the Gadites and Reubenites, 'Should your fellow Israelites go to war while you sit here? ⁷Why do you discourage the Israelites from crossing over into the land the LORD has given them? ⁸This is what your fathers did when I sent them from Kadesh Barnea to look over the land. ⁹After they went up to the Valley of Eshkol and viewed the land, they discouraged the Israelites from entering the land the LORD had given them. ¹⁰The LORD's anger was aroused that day and he swore this oath: ¹¹"Because they have not followed me wholeheartedly, not one of those who were twenty years old or more when they came up out of Egypt will see the land I promised on oath to Abraham, Isaac and Jacob – ¹²not one except Caleb son of Jephunneh the Kenizzite and Joshua son of Nun, for they followed the LORD wholeheartedly." ¹³The LORD's anger burned against Israel and he made them wander in the wilderness for forty years,

until the whole generation of those who had done evil in his sight was gone.

¹⁴'And here you are, a brood of sinners, standing in the place of your fathers and making the LORD even more angry with Israel. ¹⁵ If you turn away from following him, he will again leave all this people in the wilderness, and you will be the cause of their destruction.'

¹⁶ Then they came up to him and said, 'We would like to build pens here for our livestock and cities for our women and children. ¹⁷ But we will arm ourselves for battle and go ahead of the Israelites until we have brought them to their place. Meanwhile our women and children will live in fortified cities, for protection from the inhabitants of the land. ¹⁸ We will not return to our homes until each of the Israelites has received their inheritance. ¹⁹ We will not receive any inheritance with them on the other side of the Jordan, because our inheritance has come to us on the east side of the Jordan.'

²⁰ Then Moses said to them, 'If you will do this – if you will arm yourselves before the LORD for battle ²¹ and if all of you who are armed cross over the Jordan before the LORD until he has driven his enemies out before him – ²² then when the land is subdued before the LORD, you may return and be free from your obligation to the LORD and to Israel. And this land will be your possession before the LORD.

²³ 'But if you fail to do this, you will be sinning against the LORD; and you may be sure that your sin will find you out. ²⁴ Build cities for your women and children, and pens for your flocks, but do what you have promised.'

²⁵ The Gadites and Reubenites said to Moses, 'We your servants will do as our lord commands. ²⁶ Our children and wives, our flocks and herds will remain here in the cities of Gilead. ²⁷ But your servants, every man who is armed for battle, will cross over to fight before the LORD, just as our lord says.'

²⁸ Then Moses gave orders about them to Eleazar the priest and Joshua son of Nun and to the family heads of the Israelite tribes. ²⁹ He said to them, 'If the Gadites and Reubenites, every man armed for battle, cross over the Jordan with you before the LORD, then when the land is subdued before you, you must give them the land of Gilead as their possession. ³⁰ But if they do not cross over with you armed, they must accept their possession with you in Canaan.'

³¹ The Gadites and Reubenites answered, 'Your servants will do what the LORD has said. ³² We will cross over before the LORD into Canaan armed, but the property we inherit will be on this side of the Jordan.'

³³ Then Moses gave to the Gadites, the Reubenites and the half-tribe of Manasseh son of Joseph the kingdom of Sihon king of the Amorites and the kingdom of Og king of Bashan – the whole land with its cities and the territory around them.

³⁴ The Gadites built up Dibon, Ataroth, Aroer, ³⁵ Atroth Shophan, Jazer, Jogbehah, ³⁶ Beth Nimrah and Beth Haran as fortified cities, and built pens for their flocks. ³⁷ And the Reubenites rebuilt Heshbon, Elealeh and Kiriathaim, ³⁸ as well as Nebo and Baal Meon (these names were changed) and Sibmah. They gave names to the cities they rebuilt.

³⁹ The descendants of Makir son of Manasseh went to Gilead, captured it and drove out the Amorites who were there. ⁴⁰ So Moses gave Gilead to the Makirites, the descendants of Manasseh, and they settled there. ⁴¹ Jair, a descendant of Manasseh, captured their settlements and called them Havvoth Jair. ⁴² And Nobah captured Kenath and its surrounding settlements and called it Nobah after himself.

··

■ PSALM 38:1–8

¹ LORD, do not rebuke me in your anger
    or discipline me in your wrath.

² Your arrows have pierced me,
   and your hand has come down on me.
³ Because of your wrath there is no health
      in my body;
   there is no soundness in my bones
      because of my sin.
⁴ My guilt has overwhelmed me
   like a burden too heavy to bear.

⁵ My wounds fester and are loathsome
   because of my sinful folly.
⁶ I am bowed down and brought very low;
   all day long I go about mourning.
⁷ My back is filled with searing pain;
   there is no health in my body.
⁸ I am feeble and utterly crushed;
   I groan in anguish of heart.

▬ PROVERBS 9:10-12

¹⁰ The fear of the LORD is the beginning of
      wisdom,
   and knowledge of the Holy One is
      understanding.
¹¹ For through wisdom your days will be
      many,
   and years will be added to your life.
¹² If you are wise, your wisdom will reward
      you;
   if you are a mocker, you alone will
      suffer.

▬ LUKE 3:1-20

3 In the fifteenth year of the reign of Tiberius Caesar – when Pontius Pilate was governor of Judea, Herod tetrarch of Galilee, his brother Philip tetrarch of Iturea and Traconitis, and Lysanias tetrarch of Abilene – ²during the high-priesthood of Annas and Caiaphas, the word of God came to John son of Zechariah in the wilderness. ³He went into all the country around the Jordan, preaching a baptism of repentance

for the forgiveness of sins. ⁴As it is written in the book of the words of Isaiah the prophet:

   'A voice of one calling in the wilderness,
   "Prepare the way for the Lord,
      make straight paths for him.
⁵ Every valley shall be filled in,
      every mountain and hill made low.
   The crooked roads shall become straight,
      the rough ways smooth.
⁶ And all people will see God's salvation." '

⁷ John said to the crowds coming out to be baptised by him, 'You brood of vipers! Who warned you to flee from the coming wrath? ⁸Produce fruit in keeping with repentance. And do not begin to say to yourselves, "We have Abraham as our father." For I tell you that out of these stones God can raise up children for Abraham. ⁹The axe has been laid to the root of the trees, and every tree that does not produce good fruit will be cut down and thrown into the fire.'

¹⁰ 'What should we do then?' the crowd asked.

¹¹ John answered, 'Anyone who has two shirts should share with the one who has none, and anyone who has food should do the same.'

¹² Even tax collectors came to be baptised. 'Teacher,' they asked, 'what should we do?'

¹³ 'Don't collect any more than you are required to,' he told them.

¹⁴ Then some soldiers asked him, 'And what should we do?'

He replied, 'Don't extort money and don't accuse people falsely – be content with your pay.'

¹⁵ The people were waiting expectantly and were all wondering in their hearts if John might possibly be the Messiah. ¹⁶John answered them all, 'I baptise you with water. But one who is more powerful than I will come, the straps of whose sandals I am not worthy to untie. He will baptise you

with the Holy Spirit and fire. [17] His winnowing fork is in his hand to clear his threshing-floor and to gather the wheat into his barn, but he will burn up the chaff with unquenchable fire.' [18] And with many other words John exhorted the people and proclaimed the good news to them.

[19] But when John rebuked Herod the tetrarch because of his marriage to Herodias, his brother's wife, and all the other evil things he had done, [20] Herod added this to them all: he locked John up in prison.

The Place to Kill a Cobra

'The fear of the LORD is the beginning of wisdom, and knowledge of the Holy One is understanding.'
Proverbs 9:10

The most effective place to deal with sin is at the 'eye' stage. That may mean the actual seeing of evil with the physical eye, or seeing it in imagination with the mental eye. 'The best place to kill a cobra,' runs an old Indian proverb, 'is in its egg.'

Most sin follows on from a failure to kill it at the place of desire – the 'eye'. Matthew 6:22 says, 'The eye is the lamp of the body. If your eyes are healthy, your whole body will be full of light.' When an evil thought comes, try blinking your eyes very rapidly and you will discover that the thought is broken up. It is a voluntary act demanding the attention of the will, and thus draws attention away from the evil thought. Add to this action the simple prayer that Peter prayed when he was about to sink into the waters of the Sea of Galilee, 'Lord, save me!'

Another thing you can do when a sinful thought or desire invades your mind is to change whatever you are doing in order to focus your attention elsewhere. An old Welsh miner I knew told me many years ago that when he was a young man, he was out walking one day and was attacked with an evil thought. He deliberately picked up a heavy stone and carried it back home. The attention necessary to carry the load made him forget the thought.

These ideas may not work for everyone, but they have certainly worked for some. Another way to deal with an evil thought or desire is to focus your attention on a mental picture of Christ on the cross. It is hard to think of evil and Him at the same time. They are incompatibilities.

PRAYER

O Lord, help me to outmanoeuvre any sinful thoughts that come into my mind. Give me the kind of mind in which You can be at home. This I ask in Jesus' peerless and precious name. Amen.

FURTHER STUDY

Isa. 33:10-17; Psa. 119:59; Prov. 15:26; Rom. 8:6
• What is the result of refusing to contemplate evil?
• How will you guard your eyes today?

March 30

■ NUMBERS 33:1-56

33 Here are the stages in the journey of the Israelites when they came out of Egypt by divisions under the leadership of Moses and Aaron. ²At the LORD's command Moses recorded the stages in their journey. This is their journey by stages:

³The Israelites set out from Rameses on the fifteenth day of the first month, the day after the Passover. They marched out defiantly in full view of all the Egyptians, ⁴who were burying all their firstborn, whom the LORD had struck down among them; for the LORD had brought judgment on their gods.

⁵The Israelites left Rameses and camped at Sukkoth.

⁶They left Sukkoth and camped at Etham, on the edge of the desert.

⁷They left Etham, turned back to Pi Hahiroth, to the east of Baal Zephon, and camped near Migdol.

⁸They left Pi Hahiroth and passed through the sea into the desert, and when they had travelled for three days in the Desert of Etham, they camped at Marah.

⁹They left Marah and went to Elim, where there were twelve springs and seventy palm trees, and they camped there.

¹⁰They left Elim and camped by the Red Sea.

¹¹They left the Red Sea and camped in the Desert of Sin.

¹²They left the Desert of Sin and camped at Dophkah.

¹³They left Dophkah and camped at Alush.

¹⁴They left Alush and camped at Rephidim, where there was no water for the people to drink.

¹⁵They left Rephidim and camped in the Desert of Sinai.

¹⁶They left the Desert of Sinai and camped at Kibroth Hattaavah.

¹⁷They left Kibroth Hattaavah and camped at Hazeroth.

¹⁸They left Hazeroth and camped at Rithmah.

¹⁹They left Rithmah and camped at Rimmon Perez.

²⁰They left Rimmon Perez and camped at Libnah.

²¹They left Libnah and camped at Rissah.

²²They left Rissah and camped at Kehelathah.

²³They left Kehelathah and camped at Mount Shepher.

²⁴They left Mount Shepher and camped at Haradah.

²⁵They left Haradah and camped at Makheloth.

²⁶They left Makheloth and camped at Tahath.

²⁷They left Tahath and camped at Terah.

²⁸They left Terah and camped at Mithkah.

²⁹They left Mithkah and camped at Hashmonah.

³⁰They left Hashmonah and camped at Moseroth.

³¹They left Moseroth and camped at Bene Jaakan.

³²They left Bene Jaakan and camped at Hor Haggidgad.

³³They left Hor Haggidgad and

camped at Jotbathah.

[34] They left Jotbathah and camped at Abronah.

[35] They left Abronah and camped at Ezion Geber.

[36] They left Ezion Geber and camped at Kadesh, in the Desert of Zin.

[37] They left Kadesh and camped at Mount Hor, on the border of Edom. [38] At the LORD's command Aaron the priest went up Mount Hor, where he died on the first day of the fifth month of the fortieth year after the Israelites came out of Egypt. [39] Aaron was a hundred and twenty-three years old when he died on Mount Hor.

[40] The Canaanite king of Arad, who lived in the Negev of Canaan, heard that the Israelites were coming.

[41] They left Mount Hor and camped at Zalmonah.

[42] They left Zalmonah and camped at Punon.

[43] They left Punon and camped at Oboth.

[44] They left Oboth and camped at Iye Abarim, on the border of Moab.

[45] They left Iye Abarim and camped at Dibon Gad.

[46] They left Dibon Gad and camped at Almon Diblathaim.

[47] They left Almon Diblathaim and camped in the mountains of Abarim, near Nebo.

[48] They left the mountains of Abarim and camped on the plains of Moab by the Jordan opposite Jericho. [49] There on the plains of Moab they camped along the Jordan from Beth Jeshimoth to Abel Shittim.

[50] On the plains of Moab by the Jordan opposite Jericho the LORD said to Moses, [51] 'Speak to the Israelites and say to them: "When you cross the Jordan into Canaan, [52] drive out all the inhabitants of the land before you. Destroy all their carved images and their cast idols, and demolish all their high places. [53] Take possession of the land and settle in it, for I have given you the land to possess. [54] Distribute the land by lot, according to your clans. To a larger group give a larger inheritance, and to a smaller group a smaller one. Whatever falls to them by lot will be theirs. Distribute it according to your ancestral tribes.

[55] ' "But if you do not drive out the inhabitants of the land, those you allow to remain will become barbs in your eyes and thorns in your sides. They will give you trouble in the land where you will live. [56] And then I will do to you what I plan to do to them." '

■ PSALM 38:9-14

[9] All my longings lie open before you,
    Lord:
    my sighing is not hidden from you.
[10] My heart pounds, my strength fails me;
    even the light has gone from my eyes.
[11] My friends and companions avoid me
    because of my wounds;
    my neighbours stay far away.
[12] Those who want to kill me set their traps,
    those who would harm me talk of my
      ruin;
    all day long they scheme and lie.

[13] I am like the deaf, who cannot hear,
    like the mute, who cannot speak;
[14] I have become like one who does not
    hear,
    whose mouth can offer no reply.

■ PROVERBS 9:13-15

[13] Folly is an unruly woman;
    she is simple and knows nothing.
[14] She sits at the door of her house,
    on a seat at the highest point of the city,

[15] calling out to those who pass by,
who go straight on their way,

··

■ LUKE 3:21-38

[21] When all the people were being baptised, Jesus was baptised too. And as he was praying, heaven was opened [22] and the Holy Spirit descended on him in bodily form like a dove. And a voice came from heaven: 'You are my Son, whom I love; with you I am well pleased.'

[23] Now Jesus himself was about thirty years old when he began his ministry. He was the son, so it was thought, of Joseph,

the son of Heli, [24] the son of Matthat,
the son of Levi, the son of Melki,
the son of Jannai, the son of Joseph,
[25] the son of Mattathias, the son of Amos,
the son of Nahum, the son of Esli,
the son of Naggai, [26] the son of Maath,
the son of Mattathias, the son of Semein,
the son of Josek, the son of Joda,
[27] the son of Joanan, the son of Rhesa,
the son of Zerubbabel, the son of Shealtiel,

the son of Neri, [28] the son of Melki,
the son of Addi, the son of Cosam,
the son of Elmadam, the son of Er,
[29] the son of Joshua, the son of Eliezer,
the son of Jorim, the son of Matthat,
the son of Levi, [30] the son of Simeon,
the son of Judah, the son of Joseph,
the son of Jonam, the son of Eliakim,
[31] the son of Melea, the son of Menna,
the son of Mattatha, the son of Nathan,
the son of David, [32] the son of Jesse,
the son of Obed, the son of Boaz,
the son of Salmon, the son of Nahshon,
[33] the son of Amminadab, the son of Ram,
the son of Hezron, the son of Perez,
the son of Judah, [34] the son of Jacob,
the son of Isaac, the son of Abraham,
the son of Terah, the son of Nahor,
[35] the son of Serug, the son of Reu,
the son of Peleg, the son of Eber,
the son of Shelah, [36] the son of Cainan,
the son of Arphaxad, the son of Shem,
the son of Noah, the son of Lamech,
[37] the son of Methuselah, the son of Enoch,
the son of Jared, the son of Mahalalel,
the son of Kenan, [38] the son of Enosh,
the son of Seth, the son of Adam,
the son of God.

The Lyre Pine

'My heart pounds, my strength fails me ... My friends and companions avoid me because of my wounds ...'
Psalm 38:10-11

I want to share with you the lessons taught me by a radiant Christian woman on how to overcome frustration. In case of doubt, let me make clear that the woman concerned was not a thick-skinned individual who cared for nothing and nobody, but rather a highly sensitive person who knew how to turn every test into a testimony.

Here is her prescription for overcoming frustration.

First, realise that Christians aren't exempt from facing problems. It is true that Christians may avoid many self-inflicted pains which non-Christians bring on themselves through wrong attitudes, wrong moral choices, wrong behaviour, and so on. But apart from this, every Christian is as subject as a non-Christian to accidents, sickness, and even death. Some years ago a plane full of non-Christian Indian seamen crashed into the Alps; a few days later, fifty-eight Christians, fresh from a conference, crashed in the same Alps.

Secondly, fix in your mind that the Christian answer is along the line of using whatever comes - justice or injustice, pain or pleasure, compliment or criticism. Ever heard of a lyre pine? The lyre pine is a pine tree whose top is shaped like a harp, with a number of branches forming the top, instead of one straight branch. It is produced, they say, by a calamity such as a storm or a lightning flash striking off the original top. Frustrated, it then puts up a whole series of tops stretched on a more or less horizontal bar. This, too, can happen to us - if we let it. Calamity can turn dullness into music, a lone top into a lyre.

PRAYER

Father, let this truth sink deeply into my spirit so that I will be able to turn all my lone tops into lyres. Quicken within me today the sense that with You, I can overcome everything - including frustration. Amen.

FURTHER STUDY

1 Pet. 1:1-7; 4:12-13;
Matt. 5:45; John 16:33;
2 Cor. 4:17; Rom. 5:3
• What is the sequence of God's dealings in our lives?
• How is this working out in your life?

March 31

■ NUMBERS 34:1–35:34

34 The LORD said to Moses, [2] 'Command the Israelites and say to them: "When you enter Canaan, the land that will be allotted to you as an inheritance is to have these boundaries:

[3] "'Your southern side will include some of the Desert of Zin along the border of Edom. Your southern boundary will start in the east from the southern end of the Dead Sea, [4] cross south of Scorpion Pass, continue on to Zin and go south of Kadesh Barnea. Then it will go to Hazar Addar and over to Azmon, [5] where it will turn, join the Wadi of Egypt and end at the Mediterranean Sea.

[6] "'Your western boundary will be the coast of the Mediterranean Sea. This will be your boundary on the west.

[7] "'For your northern boundary, run a line from the Mediterranean Sea to Mount Hor [8] and from Mount Hor to Lebo Hamath. Then the boundary will go to Zedad, [9] continue to Ziphron and end at Hazar Enan. This will be your boundary on the north.

[10] "'For your eastern boundary, run a line from Hazar Enan to Shepham. [11] The boundary will go down from Shepham to Riblah on the east side of Ain and continue along the slopes east of the Sea of Galilee.

¹²Then the boundary will go down along the Jordan and end at the Dead Sea.

'"This will be your land, with its boundaries on every side."'

¹³Moses commanded the Israelites: 'Assign this land by lot as an inheritance. The LORD has ordered that it be given to the nine-and-a-half tribes, ¹⁴because the families of the tribe of Reuben, the tribe of Gad and the half-tribe of Manasseh have received their inheritance. ¹⁵These two-and-a-half tribes have received their inheritance east of the Jordan opposite Jericho, towards the sunrise.'

¹⁶The LORD said to Moses, ¹⁷'These are the names of the men who are to assign the land for you as an inheritance: Eleazar the priest and Joshua son of Nun. ¹⁸And appoint one leader from each tribe to help assign the land. ¹⁹These are their names:

Caleb son of Jephunneh,
    from the tribe of Judah;
²⁰Shemuel son of Ammihud,
    from the tribe of Simeon;
²¹Elidad son of Kislon,
    from the tribe of Benjamin;
²²Bukki son of Jogli,
    the leader from the tribe of Dan;
²³Hanniel son of Ephod,
    the leader from the tribe of Manasseh son of Joseph;
²⁴Kemuel son of Shiphtan,
    the leader from the tribe of Ephraim son of Joseph;
²⁵Elizaphan son of Parnak,
    the leader from the tribe of Zebulun;
²⁶Paltiel son of Azzan,
    the leader from the tribe of Issachar;
²⁷Ahihud son of Shelomi,
    the leader from the tribe of Asher;
²⁸Pedahel son of Ammihud,
    the leader from the tribe of Naphtali.'

²⁹These are the men the LORD commanded to assign the inheritance to the Israelites in the land of Canaan.

35 On the plains of Moab by the Jordan opposite Jericho, the LORD said to Moses, ²'Command the Israelites to give the Levites towns to live in from the inheritance the Israelites will possess. And give them pasture-lands around the towns. ³Then they will have towns to live in and pasture-lands for the cattle they own and all their other animals.

⁴'The pasture-lands around the towns that you give the Levites will extend a thousand cubits from the town wall. ⁵Outside the town, measure two thousand cubits on the east side, two thousand on the south side, two thousand on the west and two thousand on the north, with the town in the centre. They will have this area as pasture-land for the towns.

⁶'Six of the towns you give the Levites will be cities of refuge, to which a person who has killed someone may flee. In addition, give them forty-two other towns. ⁷In all you must give the Levites forty-eight towns, together with their pasture-lands. ⁸The towns you give the Levites from the land the Israelites possess are to be given in proportion to the inheritance of each tribe: take many towns from a tribe that has many, but few from one that has few.'

⁹Then the LORD said to Moses: ¹⁰'Speak to the Israelites and say to them: "When you cross the Jordan into Canaan, ¹¹select some towns to be your cities of refuge, to which a person who has killed someone accidentally may flee. ¹²They will be places of refuge from the avenger, so that anyone accused of murder may not die before they stand trial before the assembly. ¹³These six towns you give will be your cities of refuge. ¹⁴Give three on this side of the Jordan and three in Canaan as cities of refuge. ¹⁵These six towns will be a place of refuge for Israelites and for foreigners residing among them, so that anyone who has killed another accidentally can flee there.

¹⁶'"If anyone strikes someone a fatal blow with an iron object, that person is

a murderer; the murderer is to be put to death. ¹⁷ Or if anyone is holding a stone and strikes someone a fatal blow with it, that person is a murderer; the murderer is to be put to death. ¹⁸ Or if anyone is holding a wooden object and strikes someone a fatal blow with it, that person is a murderer; the murderer is to be put to death. ¹⁹ The avenger of blood shall put the murderer to death; when the avenger comes upon the murderer, the avenger shall put the murderer to death. ²⁰ If anyone with malice aforethought pushes another or throws something at them intentionally so that they die ²¹ or if out of enmity one person hits another with their fist so that the other dies, that person is to be put to death; that person is a murderer. The avenger of blood shall put the murderer to death when they meet.

²² ' "But if without enmity someone suddenly pushes another or throws something at them unintentionally ²³ or, without seeing them, drops on them a stone heavy enough to kill them, and they die, then since that other person was not an enemy and no harm was intended, ²⁴ the assembly must judge between the accused and the avenger of blood according to these regulations. ²⁵ The assembly must protect the one accused of murder from the avenger of blood and send the accused back to the city of refuge to which they fled. The accused must stay there until the death of the high priest, who was anointed with holy oil.

²⁶ ' "But if the accused ever goes outside the limits of the city of refuge to which they fled ²⁷ and the avenger of blood finds them outside the city, the avenger of blood may kill the accused without being guilty of murder. ²⁸ The accused must stay in the city of refuge until the death of the high priest; only after the death of the high priest may they return to their own property.

²⁹ ' "This is to have the force of law for you throughout the generations to come, wherever you live.

³⁰ ' "Anyone who kills a person is to be put to death as a murderer only on the testimony of witnesses. But no one is to be put to death on the testimony of only one witness.

³¹ ' "Do not accept a ransom for the life of a murderer, who deserves to die. They are to be put to death.

³² ' "Do not accept a ransom for anyone who has fled to a city of refuge and so allow them to go back and live on their own land before the death of the high priest.

³³ ' "Do not pollute the land where you are. Bloodshed pollutes the land, and atonement cannot be made for the land on which blood has been shed, except by the blood of the one who shed it. ³⁴ Do not defile the land where you live and where I dwell, for I, the LORD, dwell among the Israelites." '

- ## ▬ PSALM 38:15-22

¹⁵ LORD, I wait for you;
    you will answer, Lord my God.
¹⁶ For I said, 'Do not let them gloat
    or exalt themselves over me when my
        feet slip.'

¹⁷ For I am about to fall,
    and my pain is ever with me.
¹⁸ I confess my iniquity;
    I am troubled by my sin.
¹⁹ Many have become my enemies without
        cause;
    those who hate me without reason are
        numerous.
²⁰ Those who repay my good with evil
    lodge accusations against me,
    though I seek only to do what is good.

²¹ LORD, do not forsake me;
    do not be far from me, my God.
²² Come quickly to help me,
    my Lord and my Saviour.

■ PROVERBS 9:16–18

16 'Let all who are simple come to my
     house!'
   To those who have no sense she says,
17 'Stolen water is sweet;
     food eaten in secret is delicious!'
18 But little do they know that the dead
     are there,
     that her guests are deep in the realm
     of the dead.

■ LUKE 4:1-21

4 Jesus, full of the Holy Spirit, left the Jordan and was led by the Spirit into the wilderness, ²where for forty days he was tempted by the devil. He ate nothing during those days, and at the end of them he was hungry.

³The devil said to him, 'If you are the Son of God, tell this stone to become bread.'

⁴Jesus answered, 'It is written: "Man shall not live on bread alone."'

⁵The devil led him up to a high place and showed him in an instant all the kingdoms of the world. ⁶And he said to him, 'I will give you all their authority and splendour; it has been given to me, and I can give it to anyone I want to. ⁷If you worship me, it will all be yours.'

⁸Jesus answered, 'It is written: "Worship the Lord your God and serve him only."'

⁹The devil led him to Jerusalem and had him stand on the highest point of the temple. 'If you are the Son of God,' he said, 'throw yourself down from here. ¹⁰For it is written:

' "He will command his angels
     concerning you
   to guard you carefully;
¹¹ they will lift you up in their hands,
     so that you will not strike your foot
     against a stone." '

¹²Jesus answered, 'It is said: "Do not put the Lord your God to the test."'

¹³When the devil had finished all this tempting, he left him until an opportune time.

¹⁴Jesus returned to Galilee in the power of the Spirit, and news about him spread through the whole countryside. ¹⁵He was teaching in their synagogues, and everyone praised him.

¹⁶He went to Nazareth, where he had been brought up, and on the Sabbath day he went into the synagogue, as was his custom. He stood up to read, ¹⁷and the scroll of the prophet Isaiah was handed to him. Unrolling it, he found the place where it is written:

¹⁸ 'The Spirit of the Lord is on me,
     because he has anointed me
     to proclaim good news to the poor.
   He has sent me to proclaim freedom for
     the prisoners
     and recovery of sight for the blind,
   to set the oppressed free,
¹⁹   to proclaim the year of the Lord's
     favour.'

²⁰Then he rolled up the scroll, gave it back to the attendant and sat down. The eyes of everyone in the synagogue were fastened on him. ²¹He began by saying to them, 'Today this scripture is fulfilled in your hearing.'

Leave Vengeance to God

'The Spirit of the Lord is on me ... to proclaim the year of the Lord's favour.' **Luke 4:18-19**

N ow and again I stress heavily this matter of grudges because I have found that this is the truth which always brings a positive response.

Following some remarks I made concerning an unforgiving spirit, a woman wrote: 'I had often read in *Every Day with Jesus* your words about forgiveness, and I knew that one day I would have to face up to this challenge. Today's reading demolished all my defences.

'Intellectually I had always accepted what you said about the need to forgive and that I could not be whole until I had completely forgiven those who had hurt me, but I wouldn't get down to actually putting it into words. I kept holding back my feelings, saying subconsciously: "I will forgive someday, and then my troubles will be over - but not yet."

'Your words today came like a bolt from the blue: "There is usually a reason why we don't want to give up our grudges and resentments. One reason is that we use them to feel sorry for ourselves." I certainly had done my share of that, but suddenly I let go. It was like a boil bursting. All the pent-up poisons gushed out of me, and I was a new person. I'm in the midst of a campaign now to overcome the misunderstandings of years.' What happened to this woman can happen now, today, to you. No matter how wronged you have been - forgive.

When Jesus announced His mission in Nazareth, He read from Isaiah's prophecy, but stopped just before He came to the words, 'the day of vengeance of our God.' Then He closed the book. You do the same. Leave vengeance to God. Use only redemptive goodwill.

PRAYER

Father, help me to realise that nothing anyone has ever done against me compares to what I have done against You. You have forgiven me - help me to forgive others. And not grudgingly, but graciously. In Jesus' name. Amen

FURTHER STUDY

Mark 11:18-25; Luke 11:4; 17:4; Matt. 18:21-22
• What are we to do when we pray?
• How many times should we forgive?

April 1

NUMBERS 36:1–DEUTERONOMY 1:46

36 The family heads of the clan of Gilead son of Makir, the son of Manasseh, who were from the clans of the descendants of Joseph, came and spoke before Moses and the leaders, the heads of the Israelite families. ²They said, 'When the LORD commanded my lord to give the land as an inheritance to the Israelites by lot, he ordered you to give the inheritance of our brother Zelophehad to his daughters. ³Now suppose they marry men from other

Israelite tribes; then their inheritance will be taken from our ancestral inheritance and added to that of the tribe they marry into. And so part of the inheritance allotted to us will be taken away. ⁴When the Year of Jubilee for the Israelites comes, their inheritance will be added to that of the tribe into which they marry, and their property will be taken from the tribal inheritance of our ancestors.'

⁵Then at the LORD's command Moses gave this order to the Israelites: 'What the tribe of the descendants of Joseph is saying is right. ⁶This is what the LORD commands for Zelophehad's daughters: they may marry anyone they please as long as they marry within their father's tribal clan. ⁷No inheritance in Israel is to pass from one tribe to another, for every Israelite shall keep the tribal inheritance of their ancestors. ⁸Every daughter who inherits land in any Israelite tribe must marry someone in her father's tribal clan, so that every Israelite will possess the inheritance of their ancestors. ⁹No inheritance may pass from one tribe to another, for each Israelite tribe is to keep the land it inherits.'

¹⁰So Zelophehad's daughters did as the LORD commanded Moses. ¹¹Zelophehad's daughters – Mahlah, Tirzah, Hoglah, Milkah and Noah – married their cousins on their father's side. ¹²They married within the clans of the descendants of Manasseh son of Joseph, and their inheritance remained in their father's tribe and clan.

¹³These are the commands and regulations the LORD gave through Moses to the Israelites on the plains of Moab by the Jordan opposite Jericho.

1 These are the words Moses spoke to all Israel in the wilderness east of the Jordan – that is, in the Arabah – opposite Suph, between Paran and Tophel, Laban, Hazeroth and Dizahab. ²(It takes eleven days to go from Horeb to Kadesh Barnea by the Mount Seir road.)

³In the fortieth year, on the first day of the eleventh month, Moses proclaimed to the Israelites all that the LORD had commanded him concerning them. ⁴This was after he had defeated Sihon king of the Amorites, who reigned in Heshbon, and at Edrei had defeated Og king of Bashan, who reigned in Ashtaroth.

⁵East of the Jordan in the territory of Moab, Moses began to expound this law, saying:

⁶The LORD our God said to us at Horeb, 'You have stayed long enough at this mountain. ⁷Break camp and advance into the hill country of the Amorites; go to all the neighbouring peoples in the Arabah, in the mountains, in the western foothills, in the Negev and along the coast, to the land of the Canaanites and to Lebanon, as far as the great river, the Euphrates. ⁸See, I have given you this land. Go in and take possession of the land that the LORD swore he would give to your fathers – to Abraham, Isaac and Jacob – and to their descendants after them.'

⁹At that time I said to you, 'You are too heavy a burden for me to carry alone. ¹⁰The LORD your God has increased your numbers so that today you are as numerous as the stars in the sky. ¹¹May the LORD, the God of your ancestors, increase you a thousand times and bless you as he has promised! ¹²But how can I bear your problems and your burdens and your disputes all by myself? ¹³Choose some wise, understanding and respected men from each of your tribes, and I will set them over you.'

¹⁴You answered me, 'What you propose to do is good.'

¹⁵So I took the leading men of your tribes, wise and respected men, and appointed them to have authority over you – as commanders of thousands, of hundreds, of fifties and of tens and as tribal officials. ¹⁶And I charged your judges at that time, 'Hear the disputes between your people and judge

fairly, whether the case is between two Israelites or between an Israelite and a foreigner residing among you. ¹⁷ Do not show partiality in judging; hear both small and great alike. Do not be afraid of anyone, for judgment belongs to God. Bring me any case too hard for you, and I will hear it.' ¹⁸ And at that time I told you everything you were to do.

¹⁹ Then, as the LORD our God commanded us, we set out from Horeb and went towards the hill country of the Amorites through all that vast and dreadful wilderness that you have seen, and so we reached Kadesh Barnea. ²⁰ Then I said to you, 'You have reached the hill country of the Amorites, which the LORD our God is giving us. ²¹ See, the LORD your God has given you the land. Go up and take possession of it as the LORD, the God of your ancestors, told you. Do not be afraid; do not be discouraged.'

²² Then all of you came to me and said, 'Let us send men ahead to spy out the land for us and bring back a report about the route we are to take and the towns we will come to.'

²³ The idea seemed good to me; so I selected twelve of you, one man from each tribe. ²⁴ They left and went up into the hill country, and came to the Valley of Eshkol and explored it. ²⁵ Taking with them some of the fruit of the land, they brought it down to us and reported, 'It is a good land that the LORD our God is giving us.'

²⁶ But you were unwilling to go up; you rebelled against the command of the LORD your God. ²⁷ You grumbled in your tents and said, 'The LORD hates us; so he brought us out of Egypt to deliver us into the hands of the Amorites to destroy us. ²⁸ Where can we go? Our brothers have made our hearts melt in fear. They say, "The people are stronger and taller than we are; the cities are large, with walls up to the sky. We even saw the Anakites there."'

²⁹ Then I said to you, 'Do not be terrified; do not be afraid of them. ³⁰ The LORD your God, who is going before you, will fight for you, as he did for you in Egypt, before your very eyes, ³¹ and in the wilderness. There you saw how the LORD your God carried you, as a father carries his son, all the way you went until you reached this place.'

³² In spite of this, you did not trust in the LORD your God, ³³ who went ahead of you on your journey, in fire by night and in a cloud by day, to search out places for you to camp and to show you the way you should go.

³⁴ When the LORD heard what you said, he was angry and solemnly swore: ³⁵ 'No one from this evil generation shall see the good land I swore to give your ancestors, ³⁶ except Caleb son of Jephunneh. He will see it, and I will give him and his descendants the land he set his feet on, because he followed the LORD wholeheartedly.'

³⁷ Because of you the LORD became angry with me also and said, 'You shall not enter it, either. ³⁸ But your assistant, Joshua son of Nun, will enter it. Encourage him, because he will lead Israel to inherit it. ³⁹ And the little ones that you said would be taken captive, your children who do not yet know good from bad – they will enter the land. I will give it to them and they will take possession of it. ⁴⁰ But as for you, turn round and set out towards the desert along the route to the Red Sea.'

⁴¹ Then you replied, 'We have sinned against the LORD. We will go up and fight, as the LORD our God commanded us.' So every one of you put on his weapons, thinking it easy to go up into the hill country.

⁴² But the LORD said to me, 'Tell them, "Do not go up and fight, because I will not be with you. You will be defeated by your enemies."'

⁴³ So I told you, but you would not listen. You rebelled against the LORD's command and in your arrogance you marched up into the hill country. ⁴⁴ The Amorites who lived in those hills came out against you; they chased you like a swarm of bees and beat

you down from Seir all the way to Hormah. ⁴⁵You came back and wept before the Lord, but he paid no attention to your weeping and turned a deaf ear to you. ⁴⁶And so you stayed in Kadesh many days – all the time you spent there.

■ PSALM 39:1-6

¹I said, 'I will watch my ways
  and keep my tongue from sin;
I will put a muzzle on my mouth
  while in the presence of the wicked.'
²So I remained utterly silent,
  not even saying anything good.
But my anguish increased;
³ my heart grew hot within me.
While I meditated, the fire burned;
  then I spoke with my tongue:

⁴'Show me, Lord, my life's end
  and the number of my days;
  let me know how fleeting my life is.
⁵You have made my days a mere
  handbreadth;
  the span of my years is as nothing
  before you.
Everyone is but a breath,
  even those who seem secure.

⁶'Surely everyone goes around like a mere
  phantom;
  in vain they rush about, heaping up
  wealth
  without knowing whose it will
  finally be.

■ PROVERBS 10:1-2

10 The proverbs of Solomon:

A wise son brings joy to his father,
  but a foolish son brings grief to his
  mother.

²Ill-gotten treasures have no lasting value,
  but righteousness delivers from death.

■ LUKE 4:22-44

²²All spoke well of him and were amazed at the gracious words that came from his lips. 'Isn't this Joseph's son?' they asked. ²³Jesus said to them, 'Surely you will quote this proverb to me: "Physician, heal yourself!" And you will tell me, "Do here in your home town what we have heard that you did in Capernaum."' ²⁴'Truly I tell you,' he continued, 'no prophet is accepted in his home town. ²⁵I assure you that there were many widows in Israel in Elijah's time, when the sky was shut for three and a half years and there was a severe famine throughout the land. ²⁶Yet Elijah was not sent to any of them, but to a widow in Zarephath in the region of Sidon. ²⁷And there were many in Israel with leprosy in the time of Elisha the prophet, yet not one of them was cleansed – only Naaman the Syrian.' ²⁸All the people in the synagogue were furious when they heard this. ²⁹They got up, drove him out of the town, and took him to the brow of the hill on which the town was built, in order to throw him off the cliff. ³⁰But he walked right through the crowd and went on his way.

³¹Then he went down to Capernaum, a town in Galilee, and on the Sabbath he taught the people. ³²They were amazed at his teaching, because his words had authority. ³³In the synagogue there was a man possessed by a demon, an impure spirit. He cried out at the top of his voice, ³⁴'Go away! What do you want with us, Jesus of Nazareth? Have you come to destroy us? I know who you are – the Holy One of God!' ³⁵'Be quiet!' Jesus said sternly. 'Come out of him!' Then the demon threw the man

down before them all and came out without injuring him.

³⁶ All the people were amazed and said to each other, 'What words these are! With authority and power he gives orders to impure spirits and they come out!' ³⁷ And the news about him spread throughout the surrounding area.

³⁸ Jesus left the synagogue and went to the home of Simon. Now Simon's mother-in-law was suffering from a high fever, and they asked Jesus to help her. ³⁹ So he bent over her and rebuked the fever, and it left her. She got up at once and began to wait on them.

⁴⁰ At sunset, the people brought to Jesus all who had various kinds of illness, and laying his hands on each one, he healed them. ⁴¹ Moreover, demons came out of many people, shouting, 'You are the Son of God!' But he rebuked them and would not allow them to speak, because they knew he was the Messiah.

⁴² At daybreak, Jesus went out to a solitary place. The people were looking for him and when they came to where he was, they tried to keep him from leaving them. ⁴³ But he said, 'I must proclaim the good news of the kingdom of God to the other towns also, because that is why I was sent.' ⁴⁴ And he kept on preaching in the synagogues of Judea.

'The Unseen Sculptor'

'While I meditated, the fire burned ...' **Psalm 39:3**

What are the benefits of Scripture meditation? They are beyond telling. Here, however, are just some of the benefits the Bible offers to those of us who will take the time to meditate: (1) success – Joshua 1:8, (2) understanding – Psalm 119:99, (3) the ability to wisely discern between right and wrong – Psalm 119:11.

But the one that is most pivotal occurs in Psalm 1 – spiritual freshness. This psalm makes it clear that one of the secrets of staying spiritually fresh is to send one's roots down into the Word of God by meditation.

In my teens I knew a man, a miner by trade, whose spiritual freshness and radiance were responsible for turning many people to Jesus Christ. Just before he died, and in the company of several other Christians, I asked him, 'What is the secret of your spiritual freshness? You always seem to be on top of things, always radiant. Tell me how you maintain this inner poise and power.' He replied in one word – meditation.

I pressed him for some further thoughts on the subject. This is not a verbatim quotation, but as far as I can remember, this is what he said: 'Meditation is letting your heart become the workshop of the unseen Sculptor who chisels in its secret chambers the living forms that contribute to character development and an increasing likeness to Jesus Christ.' That old man, now in heaven, was one of the greatest illustrations I have ever known of the spiritual freshness and fruitfulness that comes from meditating on God's Word. His experience can be ours – if we meditate.

PRAYER

O Father, help me to master the art of Scripture meditation, so that through the written Word and by the meditated Word, those around me may see the Living Word. Amen.

FURTHER STUDY

Rom. 10:1-9; Deut. 11:18; Prov. 6:23; 2 Cor. 3:3
• What happens when the Word is in our hearts?
• What was Paul's testimony of the Corinthians?

April 2

▬ DEUTERONOMY 2:1–3:29

2 Then we turned back and set out towards the wilderness along the route to the Red Sea, as the LORD had directed me. For a long time we made our way around the hill country of Seir.

² Then the LORD said to me, ³ 'You have made your way around this hill country long enough; now turn north. ⁴ Give the people these orders: "You are about to pass through the territory of your relatives the descendants of Esau, who live in Seir. They will be afraid of you, but be very careful. ⁵ Do not provoke them to war, for I will not give you any of their land, not even enough to put your foot on. I have given Esau the hill country of Seir as his own. ⁶ You are to pay them in silver for the food you eat and the water you drink."'

⁷ The LORD your God has blessed you in all the work of your hands. He has watched over your journey through this vast wilderness. These forty years the LORD your God has been with you, and you have not lacked anything.

⁸ So we went on past our relatives the descendants of Esau, who live in Seir. We turned from the Arabah road, which comes up from Elath and Ezion Geber, and travelled along the desert road of Moab.

⁹ Then the LORD said to me, 'Do not harass the Moabites or provoke them to war, for I will not give you any part of their land. I have given Ar to the descendants of Lot as a possession.'

¹⁰ (The Emites used to live there – a people strong and numerous, and as tall as the Anakites. ¹¹ Like the Anakites, they too were considered Rephaites, but the Moabites called them Emites. ¹² Horites used to live in Seir, but the descendants of Esau drove them out. They destroyed the Horites from before them and settled in their place, just as Israel did in the land the LORD gave them as their possession.)

¹³ And the LORD said, 'Now get up and cross the Zered Valley.' So we crossed the valley.

¹⁴ Thirty-eight years passed from the time we left Kadesh Barnea until we crossed the Zered Valley. By then, that entire generation of fighting men had perished from the camp, as the LORD had sworn to them. ¹⁵ The LORD's hand was against them until he had completely eliminated them from the camp.

¹⁶ Now when the last of these fighting men among the people had died, ¹⁷ the LORD said to me, ¹⁸ 'Today you are to pass by the region of Moab at Ar. ¹⁹ When you come to the Ammonites, do not harass them or provoke them to war, for I will not give you possession of any land belonging to the

Ammonites. I have given it as a possession to the descendants of Lot.'

²⁰ (That too was considered a land of the Rephaites, who used to live there; but the Ammonites called them Zamzummites. ²¹ They were a people strong and numerous, and as tall as the Anakites. The LORD destroyed them from before the Ammonites, who drove them out and settled in their place. ²² The LORD had done the same for the descendants of Esau, who lived in Seir, when he destroyed the Horites from before them. They drove them out and have lived in their place to this day. ²³ And as for the Avvites who lived in villages as far as Gaza, the Caphtorites coming out from Caphtor destroyed them and settled in their place.)

²⁴ 'Set out now and cross the Arnon Gorge. See, I have given into your hand Sihon the Amorite, king of Heshbon, and his country. Begin to take possession of it and engage him in battle. ²⁵ This very day I will begin to put the terror and fear of you on all the nations under heaven. They will hear reports of you and will tremble and be in anguish because of you.'

²⁶ From the Desert of Kedemoth I sent messengers to Sihon king of Heshbon offering peace and saying, ²⁷ 'Let us pass through your country. We will stay on the main road; we will not turn aside to the right or to the left. ²⁸ Sell us food to eat and water to drink for their price in silver. Only let us pass through on foot – ²⁹ as the descendants of Esau, who live in Seir, and the Moabites, who live in Ar, did for us – until we cross the Jordan into the land the LORD our God is giving us.' ³⁰ But Sihon king of Heshbon refused to let us pass through. For the LORD your God had made his spirit stubborn and his heart obstinate in order to give him into your hands, as he has now done.

³¹ The LORD said to me, 'See, I have begun to deliver Sihon and his country over to you. Now begin to conquer and possess his land.'

³² When Sihon and all his army came out to meet us in battle at Jahaz, ³³ the LORD our God delivered him over to us and we struck him down, together with his sons and his whole army. ³⁴ At that time we took all his towns and completely destroyed them – men, women and children. We left no survivors. ³⁵ But the livestock and the plunder from the towns we had captured we carried off for ourselves. ³⁶ From Aroer on the rim of the Arnon Gorge, and from the town in the gorge, even as far as Gilead, not one town was too strong for us. The LORD our God gave us all of them. ³⁷ But in accordance with the command of the LORD our God, you did not encroach on any of the land of the Ammonites, neither the land along the course of the Jabbok nor that around the towns in the hills.

3 Next we turned and went up along the road towards Bashan, and Og king of Bashan with his whole army marched out to meet us in battle at Edrei. ² The LORD said to me, 'Do not be afraid of him, for I have delivered him into your hands, along with his whole army and his land. Do to him what you did to Sihon king of the Amorites, who reigned in Heshbon.'

³ So the LORD our God also gave into our hands Og king of Bashan and all his army. We struck them down, leaving no survivors. ⁴ At that time we took all his cities. There was not one of the sixty cities that we did not take from them – the whole region of Argob, Og's kingdom in Bashan. ⁵ All these cities were fortified with high walls and with gates and bars, and there were also a great many unwalled villages. ⁶ We completely destroyed them, as we had done with Sihon king of Heshbon, destroying every city – men, women and children. ⁷ But all the livestock and the plunder from their cities we carried off for ourselves.

⁸ So at that time we took from these two kings of the Amorites the territory east of the Jordan, from the Arnon Gorge as far as Mount Hermon. ⁹ (Hermon is called Sirion

by the Sidonians; the Amorites call it Senir.) [10] We took all the towns on the plateau, and all Gilead, and all Bashan as far as Salekah and Edrei, towns of Og's kingdom in Bashan. [11] (Og king of Bashan was the last of the Rephaites. His bed was decorated with iron and was more than nine cubits long and four cubits wide. It is still in Rabbah of the Ammonites.)

[12] Of the land that we took over at that time, I gave the Reubenites and the Gadites the territory north of Aroer by the Arnon Gorge, including half the hill country of Gilead, together with its towns. [13] The rest of Gilead and also all of Bashan, the kingdom of Og, I gave to the half-tribe of Manasseh. (The whole region of Argob in Bashan used to be known as a land of the Rephaites. [14] Jair, a descendant of Manasseh, took the whole region of Argob as far as the border of the Geshurites and the Maakathites; it was named after him, so that to this day Bashan is called Havvoth Jair.) [15] And I gave Gilead to Makir. [16] But to the Reubenites and the Gadites I gave the territory extending from Gilead down to the Arnon Gorge (the middle of the gorge being the border) and out to the River Jabbok, which is the border of the Ammonites. [17] Its western border was the Jordan in the Arabah, from Kinnereth to the Sea of the Arabah (that is, the Dead Sea), below the slopes of Pisgah.

[18] I commanded you at that time: 'The LORD your God has given you this land to take possession of it. But all your able-bodied men, armed for battle, must cross over ahead of the other Israelites. [19] However, your wives, your children and your livestock (I know you have much livestock) may stay in the towns I have given you, [20] until the LORD gives rest to your fellow Israelites as he has to you, and they too have taken over the land that the LORD your God is giving them across the Jordan. After that, each of you may go back to the possession I have given you.'

[21] At that time I commanded Joshua: 'You have seen with your own eyes all that the LORD your God has done to these two kings. The LORD will do the same to all the kingdoms over there where you are going. [22] Do not be afraid of them; the LORD your God himself will fight for you.'

[23] At that time I pleaded with the LORD: [24] 'Sovereign LORD, you have begun to show to your servant your greatness and your strong hand. For what god is there in heaven or on earth who can do the deeds and mighty works you do? [25] Let me go over and see the good land beyond the Jordan – that fine hill country and Lebanon.'

[26] But because of you the LORD was angry with me and would not listen to me. 'That is enough,' the LORD said. 'Do not speak to me any more about this matter. [27] Go up to the top of Pisgah and look west and north and south and east. Look at the land with your own eyes, since you are not going to cross this Jordan. [28] But commission Joshua, and encourage and strengthen him, for he will lead this people across and will cause them to inherit the land that you will see.' [29] So we stayed in the valley near Beth Peor.

··

▬ PSALM 39:7-13

[7] 'But now, Lord, what do I look for?
     My hope is in you.
[8] Save me from all my transgressions;
     do not make me the scorn of fools.
[9] I was silent; I would not open my mouth,
     for you are the one who has done this.
[10] Remove your scourge from me;
     I am overcome by the blow of your
         hand.
[11] When you rebuke and discipline anyone
         for their sin,
     you consume their wealth like a moth –
     surely everyone is but a breath.

[12] 'Hear my prayer, LORD,
     listen to my cry for help;

do not be deaf to my weeping.
I dwell with you as a foreigner,
a stranger, as all my ancestors were.
[13] Look away from me, that I may enjoy life
again
before I depart and am no more.'

PROVERBS 10:3-5

[3] The LORD does not let the righteous go
hungry,
but he thwarts the craving of the
wicked.

[4] Lazy hands make for poverty,
but diligent hands bring wealth.

[5] He who gathers crops in summer is a
prudent son,
but he who sleeps during harvest is a
disgraceful son.

LUKE 5:1-20

5 One day as Jesus was standing by the
Lake of Gennesaret, the people were
crowding round him and listening to the
word of God. [2] He saw at the water's edge
two boats, left there by the fishermen, who
were washing their nets. [3] He got into one of
the boats, the one belonging to Simon, and
asked him to put out a little from the shore.
Then he sat down and taught the people
from the boat.
[4] When he had finished speaking, he said
to Simon, 'Put out into deep water, and let
down the nets for a catch.'
[5] Simon answered, 'Master, we've worked
hard all night and haven't caught anything.
But because you say so, I will let down
the nets.'
[6] When they had done so, they caught
such a large number of fish that their nets
began to break. [7] So they signalled to their

partners in the other boat to come and help
them, and they came and filled both boats
so full that they began to sink.
[8] When Simon Peter saw this, he fell at
Jesus' knees and said, 'Go away from me,
Lord; I am a sinful man!' [9] For he and all his
companions were astonished at the catch
of fish they had taken, [10] and so were James
and John, the sons of Zebedee, Simon's
partners.
Then Jesus said to Simon, 'Don't be
afraid; from now on you will fish for people.' [11] So they pulled their boats up on shore,
left everything and followed him.
[12] While Jesus was in one of the towns,
a man came along who was covered with
leprosy. When he saw Jesus, he fell with his
face to the ground and begged him, 'Lord,
if you are willing, you can make me clean.'
[13] Jesus reached out his hand and touched
the man. 'I am willing,' he said. 'Be clean!'
And immediately the leprosy left him.
[14] Then Jesus ordered him, 'Don't tell anyone, but go, show yourself to the priest and
offer the sacrifices that Moses commanded
for your cleansing, as a testimony to them.'
[15] Yet the news about him spread all the
more, so that crowds of people came to hear
him and to be healed of their illnesses. [16] But
Jesus often withdrew to lonely places and
prayed.
[17] One day Jesus was teaching, and Pharisees and teachers of the law were sitting
there. They had come from every village
of Galilee and from Judea and Jerusalem.
And the power of the Lord was with Jesus
to heal those who were ill. [18] Some men came
carrying a paralysed man on a mat and
tried to take him into the house to lay him
before Jesus. [19] When they could not find a
way to do this because of the crowd, they
went up on the roof and lowered him on his
mat through the tiles into the middle of the
crowd, right in front of Jesus.
[20] When Jesus saw their faith, he said,
'Friend, your sins are forgiven.'

First Principles

'... "Put out into deep water ..."' **Luke 5:4**

I find myself compelled to discuss Paul's pregnant phrase: 'praying in the Spirit.'

There are times in my own life, as I am sure there are in yours, when I struggle in prayer and find it difficult to concentrate, only to discover that suddenly I am taken out of myself and given a freedom that transforms my prayer time from that point on. When this happens, I know I have been praying in the Spirit. This is the kind of thing about which the apostle Paul is exhorting us in Ephesians 6:18. Formal prayer is fine and has its place, but oh, how we need to experience more times of praying in the Spirit.

But how do we attain these times? Is it the Spirit's responsibility to bring us there, or do we have some responsibility in the matter, too? I believe we can learn to pray in the Spirit.

Some first principles are these: (1) Come to God in an attitude of dependence. This means recognising that your greatest need in prayer is not an ability to put words together or form fine phrases, but the Holy Spirit's empowerment. (2) Yield yourself totally to the Spirit, letting Him guide and direct your praying. Be continually aware that He wants to have the bigger part in your prayer life. Start with these two principles, learning to depend less and less on your own experience or ability and more and more on the Spirit's enabling. Once you experience what it means to 'pray in the Spirit,' you will long to experience it more and more.

PRAYER

O Father, my appetite is being whetted. Help me to 'put out into deep water' and give myself to You in the way that You are willing to give Yourself to me. In Christ's name I ask it. Amen.

FURTHER STUDY

John 3:22-27;
2 Chron. 20:12; 2 Cor. 3:3-5
• What was John's declaration?
• How did Paul express his dependence on God?

April 3

■ DEUTERONOMY 4:1-49

4 Now, Israel, hear the decrees and laws I am about to teach you. Follow them so that you may live and may go in and take possession of the land that the LORD, the God of your ancestors, is giving you. ²Do not add to what I command you and do not subtract from it, but keep the commands of the LORD your God that I give you.

³You saw with your own eyes what the LORD did at Baal Peor. The LORD your God destroyed from among you everyone who followed the Baal of Peor, ⁴but all of you who held fast to the LORD your God are still alive today.

⁵See, I have taught you decrees and laws as the LORD my God commanded me, so that you may follow them in the land you are entering to take possession of it. ⁶Observe them carefully, for this will show your wisdom and understanding to the nations, who will hear about all these decrees and say, 'Surely this great nation is a wise and understanding people.' ⁷What other nation is so great as to have their gods near them the way the LORD our God is near us whenever we pray to him? ⁸And what other nation is so great as to have such righteous decrees and laws as this body of laws I am setting before you today?

⁹Only be careful, and watch yourselves closely so that you do not forget the things your eyes have seen or let them fade from your heart as long as you live. Teach them to your children and to their children after them. ¹⁰Remember the day you stood before the LORD your God at Horeb, when he said to me, 'Assemble the people before me to hear my words so that they may learn to revere me as long as they live in the land and may teach them to their children.' ¹¹You came near and stood at the foot of the mountain while it blazed with fire to the very heavens, with black clouds and deep darkness. ¹²Then the LORD spoke to you out of the fire. You heard the sound of words but saw no form; there was only a voice. ¹³He declared to you his covenant, the Ten Commandments, which he commanded you to follow and then wrote them on two stone tablets. ¹⁴And the LORD directed me at that time to teach you the decrees and laws you are to follow in the land that you are crossing the Jordan to possess.

¹⁵You saw no form of any kind the day the LORD spoke to you at Horeb out of the fire.

Therefore watch yourselves very carefully, ¹⁶so that you do not become corrupt and make for yourselves an idol, an image of any shape, whether formed like a man or a woman, ¹⁷or like any animal on earth or any bird that flies in the air, ¹⁸or like any creature that moves along the ground or any fish in the waters below. ¹⁹And when you look up to the sky and see the sun, the moon and the stars – all the heavenly array – do not be enticed into bowing down to them and worshipping things the LORD your God has apportioned to all the nations under heaven. ²⁰But as for you, the LORD took you and brought you out of the iron-smelting furnace, out of Egypt, to be the people of his inheritance, as you now are.

²¹The LORD was angry with me because of you, and he solemnly swore that I would not cross the Jordan and enter the good land the LORD your God is giving you as your inheritance. ²²I will die in this land; I will not cross the Jordan; but you are about to cross over and take possession of that good land. ²³Be careful not to forget the covenant of the LORD your God that he made with you; do not make for yourselves an idol in the form of anything the LORD your God has forbidden. ²⁴For the LORD your God is a consuming fire, a jealous God.

²⁵After you have had children and grandchildren and have lived in the land a long time – if you then become corrupt and make any kind of idol, doing evil in the eyes of the LORD your God and arousing his anger, ²⁶I call the heavens and the earth as witnesses against you this day that you will quickly perish from the land that you are crossing the Jordan to possess. You will not live there long but will certainly be destroyed. ²⁷The LORD will scatter you among the peoples, and only a few of you will survive among the nations to which the LORD will drive you. ²⁸There you will worship man-made gods of wood and stone, which cannot see or hear or eat or smell. ²⁹But if from there you seek the LORD your God, you

will find him if you seek him with all your heart and with all your soul. ³⁰When you are in distress and all these things have happened to you, then in later days you will return to the LORD your God and obey him. ³¹For the LORD your God is a merciful God; he will not abandon or destroy you or forget the covenant with your ancestors, which he confirmed to them by oath.

³²Ask now about the former days, long before your time, from the day God created human beings on the earth; ask from one end of the heavens to the other. Has anything so great as this ever happened, or has anything like it ever been heard of? ³³Has any other people heard the voice of God speaking out of fire, as you have, and lived? ³⁴Has any god ever tried to take for himself one nation out of another nation, by testings, by signs and wonders, by war, by a mighty hand and an outstretched arm, or by great and awesome deeds, like all the things the LORD your God did for you in Egypt before your very eyes?

³⁵You were shown these things so that you might know that the LORD is God; besides him there is no other. ³⁶From heaven he made you hear his voice to discipline you. On earth he showed you his great fire, and you heard his words from out of the fire. ³⁷Because he loved your ancestors and chose their descendants after them, he brought you out of Egypt by his Presence and his great strength, ³⁸to drive out before you nations greater and stronger than you and to bring you into their land to give it to you for your inheritance, as it is today.

³⁹Acknowledge and take to heart this day that the LORD is God in heaven above and on the earth below. There is no other. ⁴⁰Keep his decrees and commands, which I am giving you today, so that it may go well with you and your children after you and that you may live long in the land the LORD your God gives you for all time.

⁴¹Then Moses set aside three cities east of the Jordan, ⁴²to which anyone who had killed a person could flee if they had unintentionally killed a neighbour without malice aforethought. They could flee into one of these cities and save their life. ⁴³The cities were these: Bezer in the wilderness plateau, for the Reubenites; Ramoth in Gilead, for the Gadites; and Golan in Bashan, for the Manassites.

⁴⁴This is the law Moses set before the Israelites. ⁴⁵These are the stipulations, decrees and laws Moses gave them when they came out of Egypt ⁴⁶and were in the valley near Beth Peor east of the Jordan, in the land of Sihon king of the Amorites, who reigned in Heshbon and was defeated by Moses and the Israelites as they came out of Egypt. ⁴⁷They took possession of his land and the land of Og king of Bashan, the two Amorite kings east of the Jordan. ⁴⁸This land extended from Aroer on the rim of the Arnon Gorge to Mount Sirion (that is, Hermon), ⁴⁹and included all the Arabah east of the Jordan, as far as the Dead Sea, below the slopes of Pisgah.

PSALM 40:1-5

¹I waited patiently for the LORD;
 he turned to me and heard my cry.
²He lifted me out of the slimy pit,
 out of the mud and mire;
 he set my feet on a rock
 and gave me a firm place to stand.
³He put a new song in my mouth,
 a hymn of praise to our God.
Many will see and fear the LORD
 and put their trust in him.

⁴Blessed is the one
 who trusts in the LORD,
who does not look to the proud,
 to those who turn aside to false gods.
⁵Many, LORD my God,
 are the wonders you have done,
 the things you planned for us.

None can compare with you;
were I to speak and tell of your deeds,
they would be too many to declare.

....

▬ PROVERBS 10:6-8

⁶ Blessings crown the head of the
     righteous,
   but violence overwhelms the mouth of
     the wicked.

⁷ The name of the righteous is used in
     blessings,
   but the name of the wicked will rot.

⁸ The wise in heart accept commands,
   but a chattering fool comes to ruin.

....

▬ LUKE 5:21-6:11

²¹ The Pharisees and the teachers of the law began thinking to themselves, 'Who is this fellow who speaks blasphemy? Who can forgive sins but God alone?' ²² Jesus knew what they were thinking and asked, 'Why are you thinking these things in your hearts? ²³ Which is easier: to say, "Your sins are forgiven," or to say, "Get up and walk"? ²⁴ But I want you to know that the Son of Man has authority on earth to forgive sins.' So he said to the paralysed man, 'I tell you, get up, take your mat and go home.' ²⁵ Immediately he stood up in front of them, took what he had been lying on and went home praising God. ²⁶ Everyone was amazed and gave praise to God. They were filled with awe and said, 'We have seen remarkable things today.'

²⁷ After this, Jesus went out and saw a tax collector by the name of Levi sitting at his tax booth. 'Follow me,' Jesus said to him, ²⁸ and Levi got up, left everything and followed him.

²⁹ Then Levi held a great banquet for Jesus at his house, and a large crowd of tax collectors and others were eating with them. ³⁰ But the Pharisees and the teachers of the law who belonged to their sect complained to his disciples, 'Why do you eat and drink with tax collectors and sinners?'

³¹ Jesus answered them, 'It is not the healthy who need a doctor, but those who are ill. ³² I have not come to call the righteous, but sinners to repentance.'

³³ They said to him, 'John's disciples often fast and pray, and so do the disciples of the Pharisees, but yours go on eating and drinking.'

³⁴ Jesus answered, 'Can you make the friends of the bridegroom fast while he is with them? ³⁵ But the time will come when the bridegroom will be taken from them; in those days they will fast.'

³⁶ He told them this parable: 'No one tears a piece out of a new garment to patch an old one. Otherwise, they will have torn the new garment, and the patch from the new will not match the old. ³⁷ And no one pours new wine into old wineskins. Otherwise, the new wine will burst the skins; the wine will run out and the wineskins will be ruined. ³⁸ No, new wine must be poured into new wineskins. ³⁹ And no one after drinking old wine wants the new, for they say, "The old is better."'

6 One Sabbath Jesus was going through the cornfields, and his disciples began to pick some ears of corn, rub them in their hands and eat the grain. ² Some of the Pharisees asked, 'Why are you doing what is unlawful on the Sabbath?'

³ Jesus answered them, 'Have you never read what David did when he and his companions were hungry? ⁴ He entered the house of God, and taking the consecrated bread, he ate what is lawful only for priests to eat. And he also gave some to his companions.' ⁵ Then Jesus said to them, 'The Son of Man is Lord of the Sabbath.'

⁶ On another Sabbath he went into the synagogue and was teaching, and a man was

there whose right hand was shrivelled. [7] The Pharisees and the teachers of the law were looking for a reason to accuse Jesus, so they watched him closely to see if he would heal on the Sabbath. [8] But Jesus knew what they were thinking and said to the man with the shrivelled hand, 'Get up and stand in front of everyone.' So he got up and stood there. [9] Then Jesus said to them, 'I ask you, which is lawful on the Sabbath: to do good or to do evil, to save life or to destroy it?'

[10] He looked round at them all, and then said to the man, 'Stretch out your hand.' He did so, and his hand was completely restored. [11] But the Pharisees and the teachers of the law were furious and began to discuss with one another what they might do to Jesus.

God Has the Biggest Part

'... he set my feet on a rock and gave me a firm place to stand.' **Psalm 40:2**

The more we are acquainted with the way a deer functions in its natural habitat, the more clearly we can see the spiritual lessons that God wants us to learn. While the male deer, the hart, is a wonderful example of sure-footedness, still more wonderful is the female, the hind. Those who have watched it leading its young into the hidden fastnesses of the mountain peaks say it is the most perfect example of physical coordination that God ever made.

Why is this physical coordination so important?

When a deer moves upwards over a steep mountain slope, it proceeds by leaping from one spot to another. So it needs to be certain that its back feet will land on something solid. By positioning its front feet on something secure, it instinctively knows that if its rear feet land there also, it will proceed upwards in safety. If this were not so, and the deer's back feet were to land on a loose rock, then it would slip and meet with serious injury – perhaps even death. This sense of perfect coordination is not something the deer learns; it is an instinctive ability given to it by its Creator.

And what God has done for the deer in the natural realm, He is able to do for us in the spiritual realm. Listen to the words of the psalmist: 'He makes my feet like the feet of a deer' (Psa. 18:33). Note the word 'makes.' I find that deeply encouraging. It is not something I have to achieve on my own; He has a part in it too. And, may I add – the biggest part.

PRAYER

O Father, help me understand that although You have the biggest part in making my feet like hinds' feet, it cannot be accomplished unless I, too, do my part. Thus I willingly surrender to Your divine purposes. In Jesus' name I pray. Amen.

FURTHER STUDY

Isa. 26:1–4; Psa. 92:15; 61:2; Matt. 7:24–29
• What did Isaiah declare?
• What was Jesus' teaching?

April 4

■ DEUTERONOMY 5:1– 6:25

5 Moses summoned all Israel and said: Hear, Israel, the decrees and the laws I declare in your hearing today. Learn them and be sure to follow them. ² The LORD our God made a covenant with us at Horeb. ³ It was not with our ancestors that the LORD made this covenant, but with us, with all of us who are alive here today. ⁴ The LORD spoke to you face to face out of the fire on the mountain. ⁵ (At that time I stood between the LORD and you to declare to you the word of the LORD, because you were afraid of the fire and did not go up the mountain.) And he said:

⁶ 'I am the LORD your God, who brought you out of Egypt, out of the land of slavery.
⁷ 'You shall have no other gods before me.
⁸ 'You shall not make for yourself an image in the form of anything in heaven above or on the earth beneath or in the waters below. ⁹ You shall not bow down to them or worship them; for I, the LORD your God, am a jealous God, punishing the children for the sin of the parents to the third and fourth generation of those who hate me, ¹⁰ but showing love to a thousand generations of those who love me and keep my commandments.
¹¹ 'You shall not misuse the name of the LORD your God, for the LORD will not hold anyone guiltless who misuses his name.
¹² 'Observe the Sabbath day by keeping it holy, as the LORD your God has

commanded you. ¹³ Six days you shall labour and do all your work, ¹⁴ but the seventh day is a sabbath to the LORD your God. On it you shall not do any work, neither you, nor your son or daughter, nor your male or female servant, nor your ox, your donkey or any of your animals, nor any foreigner residing in your towns, so that your male and female servants may rest, as you do. ¹⁵ Remember that you were slaves in Egypt and that the LORD your God brought you out of there with a mighty hand and an outstretched arm. Therefore the LORD your God has commanded you to observe the Sabbath day.
¹⁶ 'Honour your father and your mother, as the LORD your God has commanded you, so that you may live long and that it may go well with you in the land the LORD your God is giving you.
¹⁷ 'You shall not murder.
¹⁸ 'You shall not commit adultery.
¹⁹ 'You shall not steal.
²⁰ 'You shall not give false testimony against your neighbour.
²¹ 'You shall not covet your neighbour's wife. You shall not set your desire on your neighbour's house or land, his male or female servant, his ox or donkey, or anything that belongs to your neighbour.'

²² These are the commandments the LORD proclaimed in a loud voice to your whole assembly there on the mountain from out of the fire, the cloud and the deep darkness;

and he added nothing more. Then he wrote them on two stone tablets and gave them to me.

²³When you heard the voice out of the darkness, while the mountain was ablaze with fire, all the leaders of your tribes and your elders came to me. ²⁴And you said, 'The LORD our God has shown us his glory and his majesty, and we have heard his voice from the fire. Today we have seen that a person can live even if God speaks with them. ²⁵But now, why should we die? This great fire will consume us, and we will die if we hear the voice of the LORD our God any longer. ²⁶For what mortal has ever heard the voice of the living God speaking out of fire, as we have, and survived? ²⁷Go near and listen to all that the LORD our God says. Then tell us whatever the LORD our God tells you. We will listen and obey.'

²⁸The LORD heard you when you spoke to me, and the LORD said to me, 'I have heard what this people said to you. Everything they said was good. ²⁹Oh, that their hearts would be inclined to fear me and keep all my commands always, so that it might go well with them and their children for ever!

³⁰'Go, tell them to return to their tents. ³¹But you stay here with me so that I may give you all the commands, decrees and laws that you are to teach them to follow in the land I am giving them to possess.'

³²So be careful to do what the LORD your God has commanded you; do not turn aside to the right or to the left. ³³Walk in obedience to all that the LORD your God has commanded you, so that you may live and prosper and prolong your days in the land that you will possess.

6 These are the commands, decrees and laws the LORD your God directed me to teach you to observe in the land that you are crossing the Jordan to possess, ²so that you, your children and their children after them may fear the LORD your God as long as you live by keeping all his decrees and commands that I give you, and so that you may enjoy long life. ³Hear, Israel, and be careful to obey so that it may go well with you and that you may increase greatly in a land flowing with milk and honey, just as the LORD, the God of your ancestors, promised you.

⁴Hear, O Israel: the LORD our God, the LORD is one. ⁵Love the LORD your God with all your heart and with all your soul and with all your strength. ⁶These commandments that I give you today are to be on your hearts. ⁷Impress them on your children. Talk about them when you sit at home and when you walk along the road, when you lie down and when you get up. ⁸Tie them as symbols on your hands and bind them on your foreheads. ⁹Write them on the doorframes of your houses and on your gates.

¹⁰When the LORD your God brings you into the land he swore to your fathers, to Abraham, Isaac and Jacob, to give you – a land with large, flourishing cities you did not build, ¹¹houses filled with all kinds of good things you did not provide, wells you did not dig, and vineyards and olive groves you did not plant – then when you eat and are satisfied, ¹²be careful that you do not forget the LORD, who brought you out of Egypt, out of the land of slavery.

¹³Fear the LORD your God, serve him only and take your oaths in his name. ¹⁴Do not follow other gods, the gods of the peoples around you; ¹⁵for the LORD your God, who is among you, is a jealous God and his anger will burn against you, and he will destroy you from the face of the land. ¹⁶Do not put the LORD your God to the test as you did at Massah. ¹⁷Be sure to keep the commands of the LORD your God and the stipulations and decrees he has given you. ¹⁸Do what is right and good in the LORD's sight, so that it may go well with you and you may go in and take over the good land that the LORD promised on oath to your ancestors, ¹⁹thrusting out all your enemies before you, as the LORD said.

²⁰In the future, when your son asks you, 'What is the meaning of the stipulations, decrees and laws the LORD our God has commanded you?' ²¹tell him: 'We were slaves of Pharaoh in Egypt, but the LORD brought us out of Egypt with a mighty hand. ²²Before our eyes the LORD sent signs and wonders – great and terrible – on Egypt and Pharaoh and his whole household. ²³But he brought us out from there to bring us in and give us the land that he promised on oath to our ancestors. ²⁴The LORD commanded us to obey all these decrees and to fear the LORD our God, so that we might always prosper and be kept alive, as is the case today. ²⁵And if we are careful to obey all this law before the LORD our God, as he has commanded us, that will be our righteousness.'

▪ PSALM 40:6-10

⁶Sacrifice and offering you did not
   desire –
   but my ears you have opened; –
   burnt offerings and sin offerings you
     did not require.
⁷Then I said, 'Here I am, I have come –
   it is written about me in the scroll.
⁸I desire to do your will, my God;
   your law is within my heart.'

⁹I proclaim your saving acts in the great
   assembly;
   I do not seal my lips, LORD,
   as you know.
¹⁰I do not hide your righteousness in my
   heart;
   I speak of your faithfulness and your
   saving help.
I do not conceal your love and your
   faithfulness
from the great assembly.

▪ PROVERBS 10:9-11

⁹Whoever walks in integrity walks
   securely,
   but whoever takes crooked paths will
   be found out.

¹⁰Whoever winks maliciously causes grief,
   and a chattering fool comes to ruin.

¹¹The mouth of the righteous is a fountain
   of life,
   but the mouth of the wicked conceals
   violence.

▪ LUKE 6:12-36

¹²One of those days Jesus went out to a mountainside to pray, and spent the night praying to God. ¹³When morning came, he called his disciples to him and chose twelve of them, whom he also designated apostles: ¹⁴Simon (whom he named Peter), his brother Andrew, James, John, Philip, Bartholomew, ¹⁵Matthew, Thomas, James son of Alphaeus, Simon who was called the Zealot, ¹⁶Judas son of James, and Judas Iscariot, who became a traitor.

¹⁷He went down with them and stood on a level place. A large crowd of his disciples was there and a great number of people from all over Judea, from Jerusalem, and from the coastal region around Tyre and Sidon, ¹⁸who had come to hear him and to be healed of their diseases. Those troubled by impure spirits were cured, ¹⁹and the people all tried to touch him, because power was coming from him and healing them all.

²⁰Looking at his disciples, he said:

'Blessed are you who are poor,
   for yours is the kingdom of God.
²¹Blessed are you who hunger now,
   for you will be satisfied.
Blessed are you who weep now,

for you will laugh.

²² Blessed are you when people hate you,
   when they exclude you and insult you
   and reject your name as evil,
      because of the Son of Man.

²³ 'Rejoice in that day and leap for joy, because great is your reward in heaven. For that is how their ancestors treated the prophets.

²⁴ 'But woe to you who are rich,
   for you have already received your
      comfort.
²⁵ Woe to you who are well fed now,
   for you will go hungry.
   Woe to you who laugh now,
      for you will mourn and weep.
²⁶ Woe to you when everyone speaks well of
      you,
   for that is how their ancestors treated
      the false prophets.

²⁷ 'But to you who are listening I say: love your enemies, do good to those who hate you, ²⁸ bless those who curse you, pray for those who ill-treat you. ²⁹ If someone slaps you on one cheek, turn to them the other also. If someone takes your coat, do not withhold your shirt from them. ³⁰ Give to everyone who asks you, and if anyone takes what belongs to you, do not demand it back. ³¹ Do to others as you would have them do to you.

³² 'If you love those who love you, what credit is that to you? Even sinners love those who love them. ³³ And if you do good to those who are good to you, what credit is that to you? Even sinners do that. ³⁴ And if you lend to those from whom you expect repayment, what credit is that to you? Even sinners lend to sinners, expecting to be repaid in full. ³⁵ But love your enemies, do good to them, and lend to them without expecting to get anything back. Then your reward will be great, and you will be children of the Most High, because he is kind to the ungrateful and wicked. ³⁶ Be merciful, just as your Father is merciful.

Louder Than 'Amen'

'I desire to do your will, my God; your law is within my heart.' **Psalm 40:8**

To pray the words 'Your will be done' sometimes creates a conflict in us, particularly when we know that God's will is the opposite of what we ourselves want. We must consider whose will is to have precedence - ours or God's.

There are some Christians who pray, 'Your will be done,' but they do it with an attitude of rebellion and resentment. They believe that they cannot escape the inevitable, and they become angry about it. They say the words 'Your will be done' almost through clenched teeth. Other people say the words with an attitude of passive resignation. They say, 'Your will be done,' but what they mean is something like this: 'Lord, I'm not very happy about the way things are turning out, but I suppose You know best. So I'll go along with it, and I'll try hard to believe it's for the best.'

The proper attitude to the will of God, and the goal for which we should aim, is one of rejoicing. It's not easy to arrive at such an attitude,

I know, but nevertheless we must have it before us as the desired end.

David, as we see in the passage before us today, prayed this way. If we can cultivate this attitude as our normal and characteristic reaction to everything that happens around us – sorrow, disappointment, disillusionment, frustration, disaster, loss, bereavement – then such a spirit is more than a match for anything. As someone has said: 'The Hallelujah of triumph is louder than the Amen of resignation.' It is!

PRAYER

God, help me drop my anchor into the depths of Your eternal love and ride out my storms in the assurance that You are willing my highest good. Help me to accept it joyously. For Jesus' sake. Amen.

FURTHER STUDY

Psa. 100; John 5:30; Eph. 6:6; Heb. 13:21
• What is the psalmist's exhortation?
• What should be our heart attitude?

April 5

■ DEUTERONOMY 7:1–8:20

7 When the LORD your God brings you into the land you are entering to possess and drives out before you many nations – the Hittites, Girgashites, Amorites, Canaanites, Perizzites, Hivites and Jebusites, seven nations larger and stronger than you – ²and when the LORD your God has delivered them over to you and you have defeated them, then you must destroy them totally. Make no treaty with them, and show them no mercy. ³Do not intermarry with them. Do not give your daughters to their sons or take their daughters for your sons, ⁴for they will turn your children away from following me to serve other gods, and the LORD's anger will burn against you and will quickly destroy you. ⁵This is what you are to do to them: break down their altars, smash their sacred stones, cut down their Asherah poles and burn their idols in the fire. ⁶For you are a people holy to the LORD your God. The LORD your God has chosen you out of all the peoples on the face of the earth to be his

people, his treasured possession.

⁷The LORD did not set his affection on you and choose you because you were more numerous than other peoples, for you were the fewest of all peoples. ⁸But it was because the LORD loved you and kept the oath he swore to your ancestors that he brought you out with a mighty hand and redeemed you from the land of slavery, from the power of Pharaoh king of Egypt. ⁹Know therefore that the LORD your God is God; he is the faithful God, keeping his covenant of love to a thousand generations of those who love him and keep his commandments. ¹⁰But

those who hate him he will repay to their face by destruction;
he will not be slow to repay to their face those who hate him.

¹¹Therefore, take care to follow the commands, decrees and laws I give you today.

¹²If you pay attention to these laws and are careful to follow them, then the LORD your God will keep his covenant of love with

you, as he swore to your ancestors. [13] He will love you and bless you and increase your numbers. He will bless the fruit of your womb, the crops of your land – your corn, new wine and oil – the calves of your herds and the lambs of your flocks in the land that he swore to your ancestors to give you. [14] You will be blessed more than any other people; none of your men or women will be childless, nor any of your livestock without young. [15] The LORD will keep you free from every disease. He will not inflict on you the horrible diseases you knew in Egypt, but he will inflict them on all who hate you. [16] You must destroy all the peoples the LORD your God gives over to you. Do not look on them with pity and do not serve their gods, for that will be a snare to you.

[17] You may say to yourselves, 'These nations are stronger than we are. How can we drive them out?' [18] But do not be afraid of them; remember well what the LORD your God did to Pharaoh and to all Egypt. [19] You saw with your own eyes the great trials, the signs and wonders, the mighty hand and outstretched arm, with which the LORD your God brought you out. The LORD your God will do the same to all the peoples you now fear. [20] Moreover, the LORD your God will send the hornet among them until even the survivors who hide from you have perished. [21] Do not be terrified by them, for the LORD your God, who is among you, is a great and awesome God. [22] The LORD your God will drive out those nations before you, little by little. You will not be allowed to eliminate them all at once, or the wild animals will multiply around you. [23] But the LORD your God will deliver them over to you, throwing them into great confusion until they are destroyed. [24] He will give their kings into your hand, and you will wipe out their names from under heaven. No one will be able to stand up against you; you will destroy them. [25] The images of their gods you are to burn in the fire. Do not covet the silver and

gold on them, and do not take it for yourselves, or you will be ensnared by it, for it is detestable to the LORD your God. [26] Do not bring a detestable thing into your house or you, like it, will be set apart for destruction. Regard it as vile and utterly detest it, for it is set apart for destruction.

8 Be careful to follow every command I am giving you today, so that you may live and increase and may enter and possess the land that the LORD promised on oath to your ancestors. [2] Remember how the LORD your God led you all the way in the wilderness these forty years, to humble and test you in order to know what was in your heart, whether or not you would keep his commands. [3] He humbled you, causing you to hunger and then feeding you with manna, which neither you nor your ancestors had known, to teach you that man does not live on bread alone but on every word that comes from the mouth of the LORD. [4] Your clothes did not wear out and your feet did not swell during these forty years. [5] Know then in your heart that as a man disciplines his son, so the LORD your God disciplines you.

[6] Observe the commands of the LORD your God, walking in obedience to him and revering him. [7] For the LORD your God is bringing you into a good land – a land with brooks, streams, and deep springs gushing out into the valleys and hills; [8] a land with wheat and barley, vines and fig-trees, pomegranates, olive oil and honey; [9] a land where bread will not be scarce and you will lack nothing; a land where the rocks are iron and you can dig copper out of the hills.

[10] When you have eaten and are satisfied, praise the LORD your God for the good land he has given you. [11] Be careful that you do not forget the LORD your God, failing to observe his commands, his laws and his decrees that I am giving you this day. [12] Otherwise, when you eat and are satisfied, when you build fine houses and settle down, [13] and when your herds and flocks grow large and

your silver and gold increase and all you have is multiplied, ¹⁴then your heart will become proud and you will forget the LORD your God, who brought you out of Egypt, out of the land of slavery. ¹⁵He led you through the vast and dreadful wilderness, that thirsty and waterless land, with its venomous snakes and scorpions. He brought you water out of hard rock. ¹⁶He gave you manna to eat in the wilderness, something your ancestors had never known, to humble and test you so that in the end it might go well with you. ¹⁷You may say to yourself, 'My power and the strength of my hands have produced this wealth for me.' ¹⁸But remember the LORD your God, for it is he who gives you the ability to produce wealth, and so confirms his covenant, which he swore to your ancestors, as it is today.

¹⁹If you ever forget the LORD your God and follow other gods and worship and bow down to them, I testify against you today that you will surely be destroyed. ²⁰Like the nations the LORD destroyed before you, so you will be destroyed for not obeying the LORD your God.

■ **PSALM 40:11-17**

¹¹Do not withhold your mercy from me,
    LORD;
        may your love and faithfulness always
        protect me.
¹²For troubles without number surround
        me;
    my sins have overtaken me, and I
        cannot see.
    They are more than the hairs of my head,
        and my heart fails within me.
¹³Be pleased to save me, LORD;
    come quickly, LORD, to help me.

¹⁴May all who want to take my life
    be put to shame and confusion;
    may all who desire my ruin

be turned back in disgrace.
¹⁵May those who say to me, 'Aha! Aha!'
    be appalled at their own shame.
¹⁶But may all who seek you
    rejoice and be glad in you;
    may those who long for your saving help
        always say,
    'The LORD is great!'

¹⁷But as for me, I am poor and needy;
    may the Lord think of me.
    You are my help and my deliverer;
        you are my God, do not delay.

■ **PROVERBS 10:12-14**

¹²Hatred stirs up conflict,
    but love covers over all wrongs.

¹³Wisdom is found on the lips of the
        discerning,
    but a rod is for the back of one who has
        no sense.

¹⁴The wise store up knowledge,
    but the mouth of a fool invites ruin.

■ **LUKE 6:37–7:10**

³⁷'Do not judge, and you will not be judged. Do not condemn, and you will not be condemned. Forgive, and you will be forgiven. ³⁸Give, and it will be given to you. A good measure, pressed down, shaken together and running over, will be poured into your lap. For with the measure you use, it will be measured to you.'

³⁹He also told them this parable: 'Can the blind lead the blind? Will they not both fall into a pit? ⁴⁰The student is not above the teacher, but everyone who is fully trained will be like their teacher.

⁴¹'Why do you look at the speck of sawdust in your brother's eye and pay no attention to

the plank in your own eye? ⁴²How can you say to your brother, "Brother, let me take the speck out of your eye," when you yourself fail to see the plank in your own eye? You hypocrite, first take the plank out of your eye, and then you will see clearly to remove the speck from your brother's eye.

⁴³'No good tree bears bad fruit, nor does a bad tree bear good fruit. ⁴⁴Each tree is recognised by its own fruit. People do not pick figs from thorn-bushes, or grapes from briers. ⁴⁵A good man brings good things out of the good stored up in his heart, and an evil man brings evil things out of the evil stored up in his heart. For the mouth speaks what the heart is full of.

⁴⁶'Why do you call me, "Lord, Lord," and do not do what I say? ⁴⁷As for everyone who comes to me and hears my words and puts them into practice, I will show you what they are like. ⁴⁸They are like a man building a house, who dug down deep and laid the foundation on rock. When the flood came, the torrent struck that house but could not shake it, because it was well built. ⁴⁹But the one who hears my words and does not put them into practice is like a man who built a house on the ground without a foundation. The moment the torrent struck that house, it collapsed and its destruction was complete.'

7 When Jesus had finished saying all this to the people who were listening, he entered Capernaum. ²There a centurion's servant, whom his master valued highly, was ill and about to die. ³The centurion heard of Jesus and sent some elders of the Jews to him, asking him to come and heal his servant. ⁴When they came to Jesus, they pleaded earnestly with him, 'This man deserves to have you do this, ⁵because he loves our nation and has built our synagogue.' ⁶So Jesus went with them.

He was not far from the house when the centurion sent friends to say to him: 'Lord, don't trouble yourself, for I do not deserve to have you come under my roof. ⁷That is why I did not even consider myself worthy to come to you. But say the word, and my servant will be healed. ⁸For I myself am a man under authority, with soldiers under me. I tell this one, "Go", and he goes; and that one, "Come", and he comes. I say to my servant, "Do this", and he does it.'

⁹When Jesus heard this, he was amazed at him, and turning to the crowd following him, he said, 'I tell you, I have not found such great faith even in Israel.' ¹⁰Then the men who had been sent returned to the house and found the servant well.

Amazing Love!

'The LORD did not ... choose you because you were more numerous than other peoples ... But it was because the LORD loved you ...' **Deuteronomy 7:7-8**

When the Bible says God is love, it is saying more than the fact that God loves, or that God is loving, or even that God is lovely; it is saying that love is the power behind everything He does. Love is not merely one of His attributes but His whole nature. God is not only the Author of loving acts; He is love in the very core of His being. Our thoughts of God's love must be built on God's revelation about Himself in the Scriptures, not by projecting our own ideas about love onto Him. Let's focus, therefore, on what the Bible has to say about the God who is love.

First, God's love is uninfluenced. By this I mean that nothing in us can give rise to it and nothing in us can extinguish it. It is 'love for nothing,' as someone once put it.

The love which we humans have for one another is drawn out of us by something in the object of our love. But God's love is not like that; His love is free, spontaneous, and uncaused. The passage before us today makes clear that there is no reason behind the love of God for His people. If you look for a reason, you just won't find one. He loves because ... He loves.

No man or woman can ever explain why God loves us. To explain it would require that He loves us for something outside of Himself. And as we have seen, He loves us for ourselves alone. His love has its beginning not in us but in Himself. He is love's source, as well as its river.

PRAYER

O God, what security this gives me to know that Your love for me will never be diminished and never be taken away. Help me reflect on this and draw from it the inspiration I need to walk tall and strong through every day. In Jesus' name. Amen.

FURTHER STUDY

Eph. 2:1–10; 1 John 3:1
• How does Paul describe God's reason for saving us?
• How does John put it?

April 6

■ DEUTERONOMY 9:1–10:22

9 Hear, Israel: you are now about to cross the Jordan to go in and dispossess nations greater and stronger than you, with large cities that have walls up to the sky. ²The people are strong and tall – Anakites! You know about them and have heard it said: 'Who can stand up against the Anakites?' ³But be assured today that the LORD your God is the one who goes across ahead of you like a devouring fire. He will destroy them; he will subdue them before you. And you will drive them out and annihilate them quickly, as the LORD has promised you.

⁴After the LORD your God has driven them out before you, do not say to yourself, 'The LORD has brought me here to

take possession of this land because of my righteousness.' No, it is on account of the wickedness of these nations that the LORD is going to drive them out before you. ⁵It is not because of your righteousness or your integrity that you are going in to take possession of their land; but on account of the wickedness of these nations, the LORD your God will drive them out before you, to accomplish what he swore to your fathers, to Abraham, Isaac and Jacob. ⁶Understand, then, that it is not because of your righteousness that the LORD your God is giving you this good land to possess, for you are a stiff-necked people.

⁷Remember this and never forget how you aroused the anger of the LORD your God in the wilderness. From the day you

left Egypt until you arrived here, you have been rebellious against the LORD. ⁸At Horeb you aroused the LORD's wrath so that he was angry enough to destroy you. ⁹When I went up on the mountain to receive the tablets of stone, the tablets of the covenant that the LORD had made with you, I stayed on the mountain for forty days and forty nights; I ate no bread and drank no water. ¹⁰The LORD gave me two stone tablets inscribed by the finger of God. On them were all the commandments the LORD proclaimed to you on the mountain out of the fire, on the day of the assembly.

¹¹At the end of the forty days and forty nights, the LORD gave me the two stone tablets, the tablets of the covenant. ¹²Then the LORD told me, 'Go down from here at once, because your people whom you brought out of Egypt have become corrupt. They have turned away quickly from what I commanded them and have made an idol for themselves.'

¹³And the LORD said to me, 'I have seen this people, and they are a stiff-necked people indeed! ¹⁴Let me alone, so that I may destroy them and blot out their name from under heaven. And I will make you into a nation stronger and more numerous than they.'

¹⁵So I turned and went down from the mountain while it was ablaze with fire. And the two tablets of the covenant were in my hands. ¹⁶When I looked, I saw that you had sinned against the LORD your God; you had made for yourselves an idol cast in the shape of a calf. You had turned aside quickly from the way that the LORD had commanded you. ¹⁷So I took the two tablets and threw them out of my hands, breaking them to pieces before your eyes.

¹⁸Then once again I fell prostrate before the LORD for forty days and forty nights; I ate no bread and drank no water, because of all the sin you had committed, doing what was evil in the LORD's sight and so arousing his anger. ¹⁹I feared the anger and wrath of the LORD, for he was angry enough with you to destroy you. But again the LORD listened to me. ²⁰And the LORD was angry enough with Aaron to destroy him, but at that time I prayed for Aaron too. ²¹Also I took that sinful thing of yours, the calf you had made, and burned it in the fire. Then I crushed it and ground it to powder as fine as dust and threw the dust into a stream that flowed down the mountain.

²²You also made the LORD angry at Taberah, at Massah and at Kibroth Hattaavah.

²³And when the LORD sent you out from Kadesh Barnea, he said, 'Go up and take possession of the land I have given you.' But you rebelled against the command of the LORD your God. You did not trust him or obey him. ²⁴You have been rebellious against the LORD ever since I have known you.

²⁵I lay prostrate before the LORD those forty days and forty nights because the LORD had said he would destroy you. ²⁶I prayed to the LORD and said, 'Sovereign LORD, do not destroy your people, your own inheritance that you redeemed by your great power and brought out of Egypt with a mighty hand. ²⁷Remember your servants Abraham, Isaac and Jacob. Overlook the stubbornness of this people, their wickedness and their sin. ²⁸Otherwise, the country from which you brought us will say, "Because the LORD was not able to take them into the land he had promised them, and because he hated them, he brought them out to put them to death in the wilderness." ²⁹But they are your people, your inheritance that you brought out by your great power and your outstretched arm.'

10 At that time the LORD said to me, 'Chisel out two stone tablets like the first ones and come up to me on the mountain. Also make a wooden ark. ²I will write on the tablets the words that were on the first tablets, which you broke. Then you are to put them in the ark.'

³So I made the ark out of acacia wood and chiselled out two stone tablets like the first ones, and I went up on the mountain with the two tablets in my hands. ⁴The LORD wrote on these tablets what he had written before, the Ten Commandments he had proclaimed to you on the mountain, out of the fire, on the day of the assembly. And the LORD gave them to me. ⁵Then I came back down the mountain and put the tablets in the ark I had made, as the LORD commanded me, and they are there now.

⁶(The Israelites travelled from the wells of Bene Jaakan to Moserah. There Aaron died and was buried, and Eleazar his son succeeded him as priest. ⁷From there they travelled to Gudgodah and on to Jotbathah, a land with streams of water. ⁸At that time the LORD set apart the tribe of Levi to carry the ark of the covenant of the LORD, to stand before the LORD to minister and to pronounce blessings in his name, as they still do today. ⁹That is why the Levites have no share or inheritance among their fellow Israelites; the LORD is their inheritance, as the LORD your God told them.)

¹⁰Now I had stayed on the mountain for forty days and forty nights, as I did the first time, and the LORD listened to me at this time also. It was not his will to destroy you. ¹¹'Go,' the LORD said to me, 'and lead the people on their way, so that they may enter and possess the land that I swore to their ancestors to give them.'

¹²And now, Israel, what does the LORD your God ask of you but to fear the LORD your God, to walk in obedience to him, to love him, to serve the LORD your God with all your heart and with all your soul, ¹³and to observe the LORD's commands and decrees that I am giving you today for your own good?

¹⁴To the LORD your God belong the heavens, even the highest heavens, the earth and everything in it. ¹⁵Yet the LORD set his affection on your ancestors and loved

them, and he chose you, their descendants, above all the nations – as it is today. ¹⁶Circumcise your hearts, therefore, and do not be stiff-necked any longer. ¹⁷For the LORD your God is God of gods and Lord of lords, the great God, mighty and awesome, who shows no partiality and accepts no bribes. ¹⁸He defends the cause of the fatherless and the widow, and loves the foreigner residing among you, giving them food and clothing. ¹⁹And you are to love those who are foreigners, for you yourselves were foreigners in Egypt. ²⁰Fear the LORD your God and serve him. Hold fast to him and take your oaths in his name. ²¹He is your praise; he is your God, who performed for you those great and awesome wonders you saw with your own eyes. ²²Your ancestors who went down into Egypt were seventy in all, and now the LORD your God has made you as numerous as the stars in the sky.

■ PSALM 41:1-6

¹Blessed are those who have regard for the
    weak;
    the LORD delivers them in times of
        trouble.
²The LORD protects and preserves them –
    they are counted among the blessed in
        the land –
    he does not give them over to the
        desire of their foes.
³The LORD sustains them on their
        sick-bed
    and restores them from their bed of
        illness.

⁴I said, 'Have mercy on me, LORD;
    heal me, for I have sinned against you.'
⁵My enemies say of me in malice,
    'When will he die and his name
        perish?'
⁶When one of them comes to see me,

he speaks falsely, while his heart
    gathers slander;
then he goes out and spreads it
    around.

■ PROVERBS 10:15-17

[15] The wealth of the rich is their fortified
    city,
    but poverty is the ruin of the poor.

[16] The wages of the righteous is life,
    but the earnings of the wicked are sin
      and death.

[17] Whoever heeds discipline shows the way
    to life,
    but whoever ignores correction leads
      others astray.

■ LUKE 7:11-35

[11] Soon afterwards, Jesus went to a town called Nain, and his disciples and a large crowd went along with him. [12] As he approached the town gate, a dead person was being carried out – the only son of his mother, and she was a widow. And a large crowd from the town was with her. [13] When the Lord saw her, his heart went out to her and he said, 'Don't cry.' [14] Then he went up and touched the bier they were carrying him on, and the bearers stood still. He said, 'Young man, I say to you, get up!' [15] The dead man sat up and began to talk, and Jesus gave him back to his mother.

[16] They were all filled with awe and praised God. 'A great prophet has appeared among us,' they said. 'God has come to help his people.' [17] This news about Jesus spread throughout Judea and the surrounding country.

[18] John's disciples told him about all these things. Calling two of them, [19] he sent them to the Lord to ask, 'Are you the one who is to come, or should we expect someone else?'

[20] When the men came to Jesus, they said, 'John the Baptist sent us to you to ask, "Are you the one who is to come, or should we expect someone else?"'

[21] At that very time Jesus cured many who had diseases, illnesses and evil spirits, and gave sight to many who were blind. [22] So he replied to the messengers, 'Go back and report to John what you have seen and heard: the blind receive sight, the lame walk, those who have leprosy are cleansed, the deaf hear, the dead are raised, and the good news is proclaimed to the poor. [23] Blessed is anyone who does not stumble on account of me.'

[24] After John's messengers left, Jesus began to speak to the crowd about John: 'What did you go out into the wilderness to see? A reed swayed by the wind? [25] If not, what did you go out to see? A man dressed in fine clothes? No, those who wear expensive clothes and indulge in luxury are in palaces. [26] But what did you go out to see? A prophet? Yes, I tell you, and more than a prophet. [27] This is the one about whom it is written:

'"I will send my messenger ahead of you,
    who will prepare your way before you."

[28] I tell you, among those born of women there is no one greater than John; yet the one who is least in the kingdom of God is greater than he.'

[29] (All the people, even the tax collectors, when they heard Jesus' words, acknowledged that God's way was right, because they had been baptised by John. [30] But the Pharisees and the experts in the law rejected God's purpose for themselves, because they had not been baptised by John.)

[31] Jesus went on to say, 'To what, then, can I compare the people of this generation? What are they like? [32] They are like children

sitting in the market-place and calling out to each other:

¹'"We played the pipe for you,
    and you did not dance;
we sang a dirge,
    and you did not cry."

³³For John the Baptist came neither eating bread nor drinking wine, and you say, "He has a demon." ³⁴The Son of Man came eating and drinking, and you say, "Here is a glutton and a drunkard, a friend of tax collectors and sinners." ³⁵But wisdom is proved right by all her children.'

Toward Perfection

'... what does the LORD your God ask of you but to fear the LORD your God ...' **Deuteronomy 10:12**

The first thing God called Israel to do - when He announced that they were to be His special people and to live the way He wanted them to live - was to fear Him. Loving Him, serving Him, and keeping His laws were of great importance, of course, but the very first things God asked of them were reverence and fear.

How does all this relate to the love of God? When thinking about God, it is wise to see love and holiness as intertwined; not to do so can sometimes lead to serious error.

Many in today's church present the love of God in such a way that it has given rise to the saying 'God loves me as I am.' The idea in many minds is, 'God loves me as I am, and whether I go on from here or whether I stay the same, it makes no difference to His love for me'. This is entirely true, but it is not the entire truth. Because God is love, He loves us as we are, but because He is holy love, He loves us too much to let us stay as we are. Yes, we can be secure in the fact that God loves us just the way we are, but the holy love of God calls us to move ever closer to Him. It cries out: 'Be holy as I am holy.'

Error is truth out of balance. We need to rejoice in the fact that we are loved because of who we are and not for what we do, but we must see also that God's love is a holy love and thus will inevitably prod us toward perfection.

PRAYER

O Father, help me keep these two things in balance - both Your love and Your holiness. Don't let the security I feel as I rest in Your love turn to smugness and complacency. Show me that though I am accepted 'in the Beloved,' that does not mean You don't want me to come closer. Amen.

FURTHER STUDY

1 Sam. 6:1-21; Rev. 15:4
• What question did the men of Beth-shemesh ask?
• What truth was revealed to John in the song of the Lamb?

April 7

■ DEUTERONOMY 11:1–12:19

11 Love the LORD your God and keep his requirements, his decrees, his laws and his commands always. ²Remember today that your children were not the ones who saw and experienced the discipline of the LORD your God: his majesty, his mighty hand, his outstretched arm; ³the signs he performed and the things he did in the heart of Egypt, both to Pharaoh king of Egypt and to his whole country; ⁴what he did to the Egyptian army, to its horses and chariots, how he overwhelmed them with the waters of the Red Sea as they were pursuing you, and how the LORD brought lasting ruin on them. ⁵It was not your children who saw what he did for you in the wilderness until you arrived at this place, ⁶and what he did to Dathan and Abiram, sons of Eliab the Reubenite, when the earth opened its mouth right in the middle of all Israel and swallowed them up with their households, their tents and every living thing that belonged to them. ⁷But it was your own eyes that saw all these great things the LORD has done.

⁸Observe therefore all the commands I am giving you today, so that you may have the strength to go in and take over the land that you are crossing the Jordan to possess, ⁹and so that you may live long in the land that the LORD swore to your ancestors to give to them and their descendants, a land flowing with milk and honey. ¹⁰The land you are entering to take over is not like the land of Egypt, from which you have come, where you planted your seed and irrigated it by foot as in a vegetable garden. ¹¹But the land you are crossing the Jordan to take possession of is a land of mountains and valleys that drinks rain from heaven. ¹²It is a land the LORD your God cares for; the eyes of the LORD your God are continually on it from the beginning of the year to its end.

¹³So if you faithfully obey the commands I am giving you today – to love the LORD your God and to serve him with all your heart and with all your soul – ¹⁴then I will send rain on your land in its season, both autumn and spring rains, so that you may gather in your corn, new wine and olive oil. ¹⁵I will provide grass in the fields for your cattle, and you will eat and be satisfied.

¹⁶Be careful, or you will be enticed to turn away and worship other gods and bow down to them. ¹⁷Then the LORD's anger will burn against you, and he will shut the heavens so that it will not rain and the ground will yield no produce, and you will soon perish from the good land the LORD is giving you. ¹⁸Fix these words of mine in your hearts and minds; tie them as symbols on your hands and bind them on your foreheads. ¹⁹Teach them to your children, talking about them when you sit at home and when you walk along the road, when you lie down and when you get up. ²⁰Write them on the door-frames of your houses and on your gates, ²¹so that your days and the days of your children may be many in the land that the LORD swore to give your ancestors, as many as the days that the heavens are above the earth.

²²If you carefully observe all these commands I am giving you to follow – to love the LORD your God, to walk in obedience to him and to hold fast to him – ²³then the LORD will drive out all these nations before you, and you will dispossess nations larger and stronger than you. ²⁴Every place where you set your foot will be yours: your

territory will extend from the desert to Lebanon, and from the River Euphrates to the Mediterranean Sea. ²⁵No one will be able to stand against you. The LORD your God, as he promised you, will put the terror and fear of you on the whole land, wherever you go.

²⁶See, I am setting before you today a blessing and a curse – ²⁷the blessing if you obey the commands of the LORD your God that I am giving you today; ²⁸the curse if you disobey the commands of the LORD your God and turn from the way that I command you today by following other gods, which you have not known. ²⁹When the LORD your God has brought you into the land you are entering to possess, you are to proclaim on Mount Gerizim the blessings, and on Mount Ebal the curses. ³⁰As you know, these mountains are across the Jordan, westward, towards the setting sun, near the great trees of Moreh, in the territory of those Canaanites living in the Arabah in the vicinity of Gilgal. ³¹You are about to cross the Jordan to enter and take possession of the land the LORD your God is giving you. When you have taken it over and are living there, ³²be sure that you obey all the decrees and laws I am setting before you today.

12 These are the decrees and laws you must be careful to follow in the land that the LORD, the God of your ancestors, has given you to possess – as long as you live in the land. ²Destroy completely all the places on the high mountains, on the hills and under every spreading tree, where the nations you are dispossessing worship their gods. ³Break down their altars, smash their sacred stones and burn their Asherah poles in the fire; cut down the idols of their gods and wipe out their names from those places.

⁴You must not worship the LORD your God in their way. ⁵But you are to seek the place the LORD your God will choose from among all your tribes to put his Name there

for his dwelling. To that place you must go; ⁶there bring your burnt offerings and sacrifices, your tithes and special gifts, what you have vowed to give and your freewill offerings, and the firstborn of your herds and flocks. ⁷There, in the presence of the LORD your God, you and your families shall eat and shall rejoice in everything you have put your hand to, because the LORD your God has blessed you.

⁸You are not to do as we do here today, everyone doing as they see fit, ⁹since you have not yet reached the resting place and the inheritance the LORD your God is giving you. ¹⁰But you will cross the Jordan and settle in the land the LORD your God is giving you as an inheritance, and he will give you rest from all your enemies around you so that you will live in safety. ¹¹Then to the place the LORD your God will choose as a dwelling for his Name – there you are to bring everything I command you: your burnt offerings and sacrifices, your tithes and special gifts, and all the choice possessions you have vowed to the LORD. ¹²And there rejoice before the LORD your God – you, your sons and daughters, your male and female servants, and the Levites from your towns who have no land allotted to them or any inheritance of their own. ¹³Be careful not to sacrifice your burnt offerings anywhere you please. ¹⁴Offer them only at the place the LORD will choose in one of your tribes, and there observe everything I command you.

¹⁵Nevertheless, you may slaughter your animals in any of your towns and eat as much of the meat as you want, as if it were gazelle or deer, according to the blessing the LORD your God gives you. Both the ceremonially unclean and the clean may eat it. ¹⁶But you must not eat the blood; pour it out on the ground like water. ¹⁷You must not eat in your own towns the tithe of your corn and new wine and olive oil, or the firstborn of your herds and flocks, or whatever you have vowed to give, or your freewill offerings or

special gifts. ¹⁸ Instead, you are to eat them in the presence of the LORD your God at the place the LORD your God will choose – you, your sons and daughters, your male and female servants, and the Levites from your towns – and you are to rejoice before the LORD your God in everything you put your hand to. ¹⁹ Be careful not to neglect the Levites as long as you live in your land.

▬ PSALM 41:7-13

⁷ All my enemies whisper together against
   me;
   they imagine the worst for me, saying,
⁸ 'A vile disease has afflicted him;
   he will never get up from the place
      where he lies.'
⁹ Even my close friend,
   someone I trusted,
   one who shared my bread,
   has turned against me.

¹⁰ But may you have mercy on me, LORD;
   raise me up, that I may repay them.
¹¹ I know that you are pleased with me,
   for my enemy does not triumph over
      me.
¹² Because of my integrity you uphold me
   and set me in your presence for ever.

¹³ Praise be to the LORD, the God of Israel,
   from everlasting to everlasting.
      Amen and Amen.

▬ PROVERBS 10:18-21

¹⁸ Whoever conceals hatred with lying lips
   and spreads slander is a fool.

¹⁹ Sin is not ended by multiplying words,
   but the prudent hold their tongues.

²⁰ The tongue of the righteous is choice
   silver,
   but the heart of the wicked is of little
      value.

²¹ The lips of the righteous nourish many,
   but fools die for lack of sense.

▬ LUKE 7:36–8:3

³⁶ When one of the Pharisees invited Jesus to have dinner with him, he went to the Pharisee's house and reclined at the table. ³⁷ A woman in that town who lived a sinful life learned that Jesus was eating at the Pharisee's house, so she came there with an alabaster jar of perfume. ³⁸ As she stood behind him at his feet weeping, she began to wet his feet with her tears. Then she wiped them with her hair, kissed them and poured perfume on them.

³⁹ When the Pharisee who had invited him saw this, he said to himself, 'If this man were a prophet, he would know who is touching him and what kind of woman she is – that she is a sinner.'

⁴⁰ Jesus answered him, 'Simon, I have something to tell you.'

'Tell me, teacher,' he said.

⁴¹ 'Two people owed money to a certain money-lender. One owed him five hundred denarii, and the other fifty. ⁴² Neither of them had the money to pay him back, so he forgave the debts of both. Now which of them will love him more?'

⁴³ Simon replied, 'I suppose the one who had the bigger debt forgiven.'

'You have judged correctly,' Jesus said.

⁴⁴ Then he turned towards the woman and said to Simon, 'Do you see this woman? I came into your house. You did not give me any water for my feet, but she wet my feet with her tears and wiped them with her hair. ⁴⁵ You did not give me a kiss, but this woman, from the time I entered, has not

stopped kissing my feet. ⁴⁶You did not put oil on my head, but she has poured perfume on my feet. ⁴⁷Therefore, I tell you, her many sins have been forgiven – as her great love has shown. But whoever has been forgiven little loves little.'

⁴⁸Then Jesus said to her, 'Your sins are forgiven.'

⁴⁹The other guests began to say among themselves, 'Who is this who even forgives sins?'

⁵⁰Jesus said to the woman, 'Your faith has saved you; go in peace.'

8 After this, Jesus travelled about from one town and village to another, proclaiming the good news of the kingdom of God. The Twelve were with him, ²and also some women who had been cured of evil spirits and diseases: Mary (called Magdalene) from whom seven demons had come out; ³Joanna the wife of Chuza, the manager of Herod's household; Susanna; and many others. These women were helping to support them out of their own means.

An Inspired Book

'Fix these words of mine in your hearts and minds; tie them as symbols on your hands and bind them on your foreheads.' **Deuteronomy 11:18**

Why are the Scriptures described as a sword provided by the Holy Spirit? Quite simply, it is the Holy Spirit who has given us the Scriptures. They come altogether from Him.

It was the Holy Spirit who inspired men to write them: '... prophets, though human, spoke from God as they were carried along by the Holy Spirit' (2 Pet. 1:21). Again in 2 Timothy 3:16 we read: 'All Scripture is God-breathed' - a statement which assures us that the Scriptures come from the Holy Spirit.

The Bible is not a mere human document. The Holy Spirit breathed into men and inspired them to write the way they did. This does not mean that the people who wrote the Scriptures did so mechanically, in the way that a dictating machine would record someone's dictation. The Holy Spirit used their natural way of expression but gave them an additional ability to write without error.

It is vital, if you are to win the battle against Satan, that you not only see this truth but believe it. When you consider how powerful Satan is, you need something that is even more powerful. The Bible, the inspired Word of God, is your strength.

One step further - only the Holy Spirit can enable us truly to understand God's Word: 'What we have received is not the spirit of the world, but the Spirit who is from God, so that we may understand what God has freely given us' (1 Cor. 2:12). Without the Holy Spirit, we would be no more able to understand the Scriptures than a blind man could judge a beauty contest.

PRAYER

Gracious Holy Spirit, just as You breathed into the Bible to give it its life and power, breathe also into my heart today so that I might know and understand its truth. I ask this in Jesus' name. Amen.

FURTHER STUDY

Col. 3:1-16; Deut. 6:6; Heb. 10:15-16

• What does the word 'dwell' mean?

• Where must God's Word be written?

April 8

▬ DEUTERONOMY 12:20–14:21

20 When the LORD your God has enlarged your territory as he promised you, and you crave meat and say, 'I would like some meat,' then you may eat as much of it as you want. 21 If the place where the LORD your God chooses to put his Name is too far away from you, you may slaughter animals from the herds and flocks the LORD has given you, as I have commanded you, and in your own towns you may eat as much of them as you want. 22 Eat them as you would gazelle or deer. Both the ceremonially unclean and the clean may eat. 23 But be sure you do not eat the blood, because the blood is the life, and you must not eat the life with the meat. 24 You must not eat the blood; pour it out on the ground like water. 25 Do not eat it, so that it may go well with you and your children after you, because you will be doing what is right in the eyes of the LORD. 26 But take your consecrated things and whatever you have vowed to give, and go to the place the LORD will choose. 27 Present your burnt offerings on the altar of the LORD your God, both the meat and the blood. The blood of your sacrifices must be poured beside the altar of the LORD your God, but you may eat the meat. 28 Be careful to obey all these regulations I am giving you, so that

it may always go well with you and your children after you, because you will be doing what is good and right in the eyes of the LORD your God.

29 The LORD your God will cut off before you the nations you are about to invade and dispossess. But when you have driven them out and settled in their land, 30 and after they have been destroyed before you, be careful not to be ensnared by enquiring about their gods, saying, 'How do these nations serve their gods? We will do the same.' 31 You must not worship the LORD your God in their way, because in worshipping their gods, they do all kinds of detestable things the LORD hates. They even burn their sons and daughters in the fire as sacrifices to their gods.

32 See that you do all I command you; do not add to it or take away from it.

13 If a prophet, or one who foretells by dreams, appears among you and announces to you a sign or wonder, 2 and if the sign or wonder spoken of takes place, and the prophet says, 'Let us follow other gods' (gods you have not known) 'and let us worship them,' 3 you must not listen to the words of that prophet or dreamer. The LORD your God is testing you to find out whether you love him with all your heart and with all your soul. 4 It is the LORD your God you must follow, and him you must revere. Keep his

commands and obey him; serve him and hold fast to him. [5] That prophet or dreamer must be put to death for inciting rebellion against the LORD your God, who brought you out of Egypt and redeemed you from the land of slavery. That prophet or dreamer tried to turn you from the way the LORD your God commanded you to follow. You must purge the evil from among you.

[6] If your very own brother, or your son or daughter, or the wife you love, or your closest friend secretly entices you, saying, 'Let us go and worship other gods' (gods that neither you nor your ancestors have known, [7] gods of the peoples around you, whether near or far, from one end of the land to the other), [8] do not yield to them or listen to them. Show them no pity. Do not spare them or shield them. [9] You must certainly put them to death. Your hand must be the first in putting them to death, and then the hands of all the people. [10] Stone them to death, because they tried to turn you away from the LORD your God, who brought you out of Egypt, out of the land of slavery. [11] Then all Israel will hear and be afraid, and no one among you will do such an evil thing again.

[12] If you hear it said about one of the towns the LORD your God is giving you to live in [13] that troublemakers have arisen among you and have led the people of their town astray, saying, 'Let us go and worship other gods' (gods you have not known), [14] then you must enquire, probe and investigate it thoroughly. And if it is true and it has been proved that this detestable thing has been done among you, [15] you must certainly put to the sword all who live in that town. You must destroy it completely, both its people and its livestock. [16] You are to gather all the plunder of the town into the middle of the public square and completely burn the town and all its plunder as a whole burnt offering to the LORD your God. That town is to remain a ruin for ever, never to be rebuilt,

[17] and none of the condemned things are to be found in your hands. Then the LORD will turn from his fierce anger, will show you mercy, and will have compassion on you. He will increase your numbers, as he promised on oath to your ancestors – [18] because you obey the LORD your God by keeping all his commands that I am giving you today and doing what is right in his eyes.

14 You are the children of the LORD your God. Do not cut yourselves or shave the front of your heads for the dead, [2] for you are a people holy to the LORD your God. Out of all the peoples on the face of the earth, the LORD has chosen you to be his treasured possession.

[3] Do not eat any detestable thing. [4] These are the animals you may eat: the ox, the sheep, the goat, [5] the deer, the gazelle, the roe deer, the wild goat, the ibex, the antelope and the mountain sheep. [6] You may eat any animal that has a divided hoof and that chews the cud. [7] However, of those that chew the cud or that have a divided hoof you may not eat the camel, the hare or the hyrax. Although they chew the cud, they do not have a divided hoof; they are ceremonially unclean for you. [8] The pig is also unclean; although it has a divided hoof, it does not chew the cud. You are not to eat their meat or touch their carcasses.

[9] Of all the creatures living in the water, you may eat any that has fins and scales. [10] But anything that does not have fins and scales you may not eat; for you it is unclean.

[11] You may eat any clean bird. [12] But these you may not eat: the eagle, the vulture, the black vulture, [13] the red kite, the black kite, any kind of falcon, [14] any kind of raven, [15] the horned owl, the screech owl, the gull, any kind of hawk, [16] the little owl, the great owl, the white owl, [17] the desert owl, the osprey, the cormorant, [18] the stork, any kind of heron, the hoopoe and the bat.

[19] All flying insects are unclean to you; do not eat them. [20] But any winged creature

that is clean you may eat.

²¹ Do not eat anything you find already dead. You may give it to the foreigner residing in any of your towns, and they may eat it, or you may sell it to any other foreigner. But you are a people holy to the LORD your God.

Do not cook a young goat in its mother's milk.

▬ PSALM 42:1-11

¹ As the deer pants for streams of water,
    so my soul pants for you, my God.
² My soul thirsts for God, for the living
        God.
    When can I go and meet with God?
³ My tears have been my food
        day and night,
    while people say to me all day long,
        'Where is your God?'
⁴ These things I remember
        as I pour out my soul:
    how I used to go to the house of God
        under the protection of the Mighty
            One
    with shouts of joy and praise
        among the festive throng.

⁵ Why, my soul, are you downcast?
    Why so disturbed within me?
Put your hope in God,
    for I will yet praise him,
        my Saviour and my God.

⁶ My soul is downcast within me;
    therefore I will remember you
from the land of the Jordan,
    the heights of Hermon – from
        Mount Mizar.
⁷ Deep calls to deep
    in the roar of your waterfalls;
all your waves and breakers
    have swept over me.

⁸ By day the LORD directs his love,
    at night his song is with me –
    a prayer to the God of my life.

⁹ I say to God my Rock,
    'Why have you forgotten me?
Why must I go about mourning,
    oppressed by the enemy?'
¹⁰ My bones suffer mortal agony
    as my foes taunt me,
saying to me all day long,
    'Where is your God?'

¹¹ Why, my soul, are you downcast?
    Why so disturbed within me?
Put your hope in God,
    for I will yet praise him,
        my Saviour and my God.

▬ PROVERBS 10:22-25

²² The blessing of the LORD brings wealth,
    without painful toil for it.

²³ A fool finds pleasure in wicked schemes,
    but a person of understanding
        delights in wisdom.

²⁴ What the wicked dread will overtake
        them;
    what the righteous desire will be
        granted.

²⁵ When the storm has swept by, the wicked
        are gone,
    but the righteous stand firm for ever.

▬ LUKE 8:4-25

⁴ While a large crowd was gathering and people were coming to Jesus from town after town, he told this parable: ⁵ 'A farmer went out to sow his seed. As he was scattering the seed, some fell along the path;

it was trampled on, and the birds ate it up. [6]Some fell on rocky ground, and when it came up, the plants withered because they had no moisture. [7]Other seed fell among thorns, which grew up with it and choked the plants. [8]Still other seed fell on good soil. It came up and yielded a crop, a hundred times more than was sown.'

When he said this, he called out, 'Whoever has ears to hear, let them hear.'

[9]His disciples asked him what this parable meant. [10]He said, 'The knowledge of the secrets of the kingdom of God has been given to you, but to others I speak in parables, so that,

'"though seeing, they may not see;
    though hearing, they may not
        understand."'

[11]'This is the meaning of the parable: the seed is the word of God. [12]Those along the path are the ones who hear, and then the devil comes and takes away the word from their hearts, so that they may not believe and be saved. [13]Those on the rocky ground are the ones who receive the word with joy when they hear it, but they have no root. They believe for a while, but in the time of testing they fall away. [14]The seed that fell among thorns stands for those who hear, but as they go on their way they are choked by life's worries, riches and pleasures, and they do not mature. [15]But the seed on good soil stands for those with a noble and good heart, who hear the word, retain it, and by persevering produce a crop.

[16]'No one lights a lamp and hides it in a clay jar or puts it under a bed. Instead, they put it on a stand, so that those who come in can see the light. [17]For there is nothing hidden that will not be disclosed, and nothing concealed that will not be known or brought out into the open. [18]Therefore consider carefully how you listen. Whoever has will be given more; whoever does not have, even what they think they have will be taken from them.'

[19]Now Jesus' mother and brothers came to see him, but they were not able to get near him because of the crowd. [20]Someone told him, 'Your mother and brothers are standing outside, wanting to see you.'

[21]He replied, 'My mother and brothers are those who hear God's word and put it into practice.'

[22]One day Jesus said to his disciples, 'Let us go over to the other side of the lake.' So they got into a boat and set out. [23]As they sailed, he fell asleep. A squall came down on the lake, so that the boat was being swamped, and they were in great danger.

[24]The disciples went and woke him, saying, 'Master, Master, we're going to drown!'

He got up and rebuked the wind and the raging waters; the storm subsided, and all was calm. [25]'Where is your faith?' he asked his disciples.

In fear and amazement they asked one another, 'Who is this? He commands even the winds and the water, and they obey him.'

A Heart Panting for God

'As the deer pants for streams of water, so my soul pants for you, my God.' **Psalm 42:1**

If we are to be able to pursue God with a coordinated heart and mind, we must be willing to get in touch with the deep thirst for God which resides at the core of our being. You will never pursue God 'with all four feet' until you become intensely aware of this deep inner thirst.

The thought underlying the word picture in our text today is that of a deer craving for water during a prolonged drought or after having been chased. The psalmist said his heart longed, or panted, for God, and the strong Hebrew word used here suggests a desire so intense that it is audible.

Do you pant after God in the way the psalmist described? Do you pursue Him in such a way that everything else in your life takes second place? I have to confess that I don't. Oh yes, I long after God. But I know I don't pant after Him in the way the psalmist described. And neither, I am convinced, do most other Christians.

Now don't react defensively and say, 'Whatever does he mean? My heart pants after God, and I will not let anyone try to tell me differently.' Reflect on the fact that although you have a deep desire to know God, you still might not have reached a place where your heart pants after Him in the way the psalmist described. But take heart – you can.

PRAYER

God my Father, I would be rid of all that hinders my pursuit of You. Help me to see clearly into my heart, for I am so prone to defend myself. If there is something here that I need to know, then help me to look at it – openly and honestly. Amen.

FURTHER STUDY

Psa. 73:15-28; 27:4; 2 Chron. 15:15

• What was the psalmist's confession?
• What happened when Israel sought the Lord eagerly?

April 9

■ DEUTERONOMY 14:22–16:22

²²Be sure to set aside a tenth of all that your fields produce each year. ²³Eat the tithe of your corn, new wine and olive oil, and the firstborn of your herds and flocks in the presence of the LORD your God at the place he will choose as a dwelling for his Name, so that you may learn to revere the LORD your God always. ²⁴But if that place is too distant and you have been blessed by the LORD your God and cannot carry your tithe (because the place where the LORD will choose to put his Name is so far away), ²⁵then exchange your tithe for silver, and take the silver with you and go to the place the LORD your God will choose. ²⁶Use the silver to buy whatever you like: cattle, sheep, wine or other fermented drink, or anything you wish. Then you and your household shall eat there in the presence of the LORD your God and rejoice. ²⁷And do not neglect the Levites living in your towns, for they have no land allotted to them or any inheritance of their own.

²⁸At the end of every three years, bring all the tithes of that year's produce and store it in your towns, ²⁹so that the Levites (who have no land allotted to them or any inheritance of their own) and the foreigners, the fatherless and the widows who live in your

towns may come and eat and be satisfied, and so that the LORD your God may bless you in all the work of your hands.

15 At the end of every seven years you must cancel debts. ²This is how it is to be done: every creditor shall cancel any loan they have made to a fellow Israelite. They shall not require payment from anyone among their own people, because the LORD's time for cancelling debts has been proclaimed. ³You may require payment from a foreigner, but you must cancel any debt your fellow Israelite owes you. ⁴However, there need be no poor people among you, for in the land the LORD your God is giving you to possess as your inheritance, he will richly bless you, ⁵if only you fully obey the LORD your God and are careful to follow all these commands I am giving you today. ⁶For the LORD your God will bless you as he has promised, and you will lend to many nations but will borrow from none. You will rule over many nations but none will rule over you.

⁷If anyone is poor among your fellow Israelites in any of the towns of the land that the LORD your God is giving you, do not be hardhearted or tight-fisted towards them. ⁸Rather, be open-handed and freely lend them whatever they need. ⁹Be careful not to harbour this wicked thought: 'The seventh year, the year for cancelling debts, is near,' so that you do not show ill will towards the needy among your fellow Israelites and give them nothing. They may then appeal to the LORD against you, and you will be found guilty of sin. ¹⁰Give generously to them and do so without a grudging heart; then because of this the LORD your God will bless you in all your work and in everything you put your hand to. ¹¹There will always be poor people in the land. Therefore I command you to be open-handed towards your fellow Israelites who are poor and needy in your land.

¹²If any of your people – Hebrew men or women – sell themselves to you and serve you for six years, in the seventh year you must let them go free. ¹³And when you release them, do not send them away empty-handed. ¹⁴Supply them liberally from your flock, your threshing-floor and your winepress. Give to them as the LORD your God has blessed you. ¹⁵Remember that you were slaves in Egypt and the LORD your God redeemed you. That is why I give you this command today.

¹⁶But if your servant says to you, 'I do not want to leave you,' because he loves you and your family and is well off with you, ¹⁷then take an awl and push it through his ear lobe into the door, and he will become your servant for life. Do the same for your female servant.

¹⁸Do not consider it a hardship to set your servant free, because their service to you these six years has been worth twice as much as that of a hired hand. And the LORD your God will bless you in everything you do.

¹⁹Set apart for the LORD your God every firstborn male of your herds and flocks. Do not put the firstborn of your oxen to work, and do not shear the firstborn of your sheep. ²⁰Each year you and your family are to eat them in the presence of the LORD your God at the place he will choose. ²¹If an animal has a defect, is lame or blind, or has any serious flaw, you must not sacrifice it to the LORD your God. ²²You are to eat it in your own towns. Both the ceremonially unclean and the clean may eat it, as if it were gazelle or deer. ²³But you must not eat the blood; pour it out on the ground like water.

16 Observe the month of Aviv and celebrate the Passover of the LORD your God, because in the month of Aviv he brought you out of Egypt by night. ²Sacrifice as the Passover to the LORD your God an animal from your flock or herd at the place the LORD will choose as a dwelling for his Name. ³Do not eat it with bread made with yeast, but for seven days eat unleavened bread, the bread of affliction, because you left Egypt in haste – so that all the days of your life you may remember the time of your departure from Egypt. ⁴Let no yeast be found in your possession in all your land for seven days. Do not let any of the meat you sacrifice on the evening of the first day remain until morning.

⁵You must not sacrifice the Passover in any town the LORD your God gives you ⁶except in the place he will choose as a dwelling for his Name. There you must sacrifice the Passover in the evening, when the sun goes down, on the anniversary of your departure from Egypt. ⁷Roast it and eat it at the place the LORD your God will choose. Then in the morning return to your tents. ⁸For six days eat unleavened bread and on the seventh day hold an assembly to the LORD your God and do no work.

⁹Count seven weeks from the time you begin to put the sickle to the standing corn. ¹⁰Then celebrate the Festival of Weeks to the LORD your God by giving a freewill offering in proportion to the blessings the LORD your God has given you. ¹¹And rejoice before the LORD your God at the place he will choose as a dwelling for his Name – you, your sons and daughters, your male and female servants, the Levites in your towns, and the foreigners, the fatherless and the widows living among you. ¹²Remember that you were slaves in Egypt, and follow carefully these decrees.

¹³Celebrate the Festival of Tabernacles for seven days after you have gathered the produce of your threshing-floor and your winepress. ¹⁴Be joyful at your festival – you, your sons and daughters, your male and female servants, and the Levites, the foreigners, the fatherless and the widows who live in your towns. ¹⁵For seven days celebrate the festival to the LORD your God at the place the LORD will choose. For the LORD your God will bless you in all your harvest and in all the work of your hands, and your joy will be complete.

¹⁶Three times a year all your men must appear before the LORD your God at the place he will choose: at the Festival of Unleavened Bread, the Festival of Weeks and the Festival of Tabernacles. No one should appear before the LORD empty-handed: ¹⁷each of you must bring a gift in proportion to the way the LORD your God has blessed you.

¹⁸Appoint judges and officials for each of your tribes in every town the LORD your God is giving you, and they shall judge the people fairly. ¹⁹Do not pervert justice or show partiality. Do not accept a bribe, for a bribe blinds the eyes of the wise and twists the words of the innocent. ²⁰Follow justice and justice alone, so that you may live and possess the land the LORD your God is giving you.

²¹Do not set up any wooden Asherah pole beside the altar you build to the LORD your God, ²²and do not erect a sacred stone, for these the LORD your God hates.

■ PSALM 43:1-5

¹Vindicate me, my God,
   and plead my cause
      against an unfaithful nation.
Rescue me from those who are
   deceitful and wicked.
²You are God my stronghold.
   Why have you rejected me?
Why must I go about mourning,
   oppressed by the enemy?
³Send me your light and your faithful
      care,
   let them lead me;
let them bring me to your holy
      mountain,
   to the place where you dwell.
⁴Then I will go to the altar of God,
   to God, my joy and my delight.
I will praise you with the lyre,
   O God, my God.

⁵ Why, my soul, are you downcast?
Why so disturbed within me?
Put your hope in God,
for I will yet praise him,
my Saviour and my God.

▬ PROVERBS 10:26–27

²⁶ As vinegar to the teeth and smoke to the
eyes,
so are sluggards to those who send
them.

²⁷ The fear of the LORD adds length to life,
but the years of the wicked are cut
short.

▬ LUKE 8:26–56

²⁶ They sailed to the region of the Gera-senes, which is across the lake from Gal-ilee. ²⁷ When Jesus stepped ashore, he was met by a demon-possessed man from the town. For a long time this man had not worn clothes or lived in a house, but had lived in the tombs. ²⁸ When he saw Jesus, he cried out and fell at his feet, shouting at the top of his voice, 'What do you want with me, Jesus, Son of the Most High God? I beg you, don't torture me!' ²⁹ For Jesus had commanded the impure spirit to come out of the man. Many times it had seized him, and though he was chained hand and foot and kept under guard, he had broken his chains and had been driven by the demon into solitary places.

³⁰ Jesus asked him, 'What is your name?'

'Legion,' he replied, because many de-mons had gone into him. ³¹ And they begged Jesus repeatedly not to order them to go into the Abyss.

³² A large herd of pigs was feeding there on the hillside. The demons begged Jesus to let them go into the pigs, and he gave them

permission. ³³ When the demons came out of the man, they went into the pigs, and the herd rushed down the steep bank into the lake and was drowned.

³⁴ When those tending the pigs saw what had happened, they ran off and reported this in the town and countryside, ³⁵ and the people went out to see what had happened. When they came to Jesus, they found the man from whom the demons had gone out, sitting at Jesus' feet, dressed and in his right mind; and they were afraid. ³⁶ Those who had seen it told the people how the demon-possessed man had been cured. ³⁷ Then all the people of the region of the Gerasenes asked Jesus to leave them, because they were overcome with fear. So he got into the boat and left.

³⁸ The man from whom the demons had gone out begged to go with him, but Jesus sent him away, saying, ³⁹ 'Return home and tell how much God has done for you.' So the man went away and told all over the town how much Jesus had done for him.

⁴⁰ Now when Jesus returned, a crowd wel-comed him, for they were all expecting him. ⁴¹ Then a man named Jairus, a synagogue leader, came and fell at Jesus' feet, pleading with him to come to his house ⁴² because his only daughter, a girl of about twelve, was dying.

As Jesus was on his way, the crowds almost crushed him. ⁴³ And a woman was there who had been subject to bleeding for twelve years, but no one could heal her. ⁴⁴ She came up behind him and touched the edge of his cloak, and immediately her bleeding stopped.

⁴⁵ 'Who touched me?' Jesus asked.

When they all denied it, Peter said, 'Mas-ter, the people are crowding and pressing against you.'

⁴⁶ But Jesus said, 'Someone touched me; I know that power has gone out from me.'

⁴⁷ Then the woman, seeing that she could not go unnoticed, came trembling and fell

at his feet. In the presence of all the people, she told why she had touched him and how she had been instantly healed. [48]Then he said to her, 'Daughter, your faith has healed you. Go in peace.'

[49]While Jesus was still speaking, someone came from the house of Jairus, the synagogue leader. 'Your daughter is dead,' he said. 'Don't bother the teacher anymore.'

[50]Hearing this, Jesus said to Jairus, 'Don't be afraid; just believe, and she will be healed.'

[51]When he arrived at the house of Jairus, he did not let anyone go in with him except Peter, John and James, and the child's father and mother. [52]Meanwhile, all the people were wailing and mourning for her. 'Stop wailing,' Jesus said. 'She is not dead but asleep.'

[53]They laughed at him, knowing that she was dead. [54]But he took her by the hand and said, 'My child, get up!' [55]Her spirit returned, and at once she stood up. Then Jesus told them to give her something to eat. [56]Her parents were astonished, but he ordered them not to tell anyone what had happened.

Disappointment

'You are God my stronghold. Why have you rejected me?' **Psalm 43:2**

A deep hurt that may come is disappointment. We expect things to happen in a certain way, and when they don't we feel let down. We can be disappointed by people, or even by God if He chooses to direct our lives in a way other than we had hoped.

A woman wrote to me that during a meeting where I spoke on 'The Healing of Life's Hurts,' the Lord had ministered to her deep feelings of disappointment. Her disappointment was with God (as she put it) for 'not healing my husband and for taking him to be with Himself'. On the way home from the meeting, she narrowly missed being involved in a serious accident, and the Lord whispered to her heart: 'And you have been doubting My love for you?' Within hours the bitter pain she had been carrying for a number of years was healed.

Are you in the throes of disappointment at this moment? Have others let you down? Or perhaps you feel God has let you down, and, because He is God, you feel you ought not to feel that way; therefore, you are repressing your disappointment and pushing it down into your subconscious. Bring it to Him now. God is not going to get mad at you for telling Him that you are disappointed with Him. If you feel upset with God, then confess the hurt; tell Him exactly how you feel. Then, when it is all out and you admit you were wrong – and not He – surrender the hurt into His hands and experience the healing that the divine Comforter brings.

PRAYER

Father, I am thankful that I can bring all my disappointments to You. Some earthly fathers won't permit their children to be upset with them, but You accept me as I am. I am so grateful. Heal every disappointment in me now. For Jesus' sake. Amen.

FURTHER STUDY

John 11:6-22;
Psa. 13:1-6; 69:3; 2 Pet. 3:9
• How did David express his disappointment?
• What did Martha do about her disappointment?

April 10

▬ DEUTERONOMY 17:1–19:13

17 Do not sacrifice to the LORD your God an ox or a sheep that has any defect or flaw in it, for that would be detestable to him.

² If a man or woman living among you in one of the towns the LORD gives you is found doing evil in the eyes of the LORD your God in violation of his covenant, ³ and contrary to my command has worshipped other gods, bowing down to them or to the sun or the moon or the stars in the sky, ⁴ and this has been brought to your attention, then you must investigate it thoroughly. If it is true and it has been proved that this detestable thing has been done in Israel, ⁵ take the man or woman who has done this evil deed to your city gate and stone that person to death. ⁶ On the testimony of two or three witnesses a person is to be put to death, but no one is to be put to death on the testimony of only one witness. ⁷ The hands of the witnesses must be the first in putting that person to death, and then the hands of all the people. You must purge the evil from among you.

⁸ If cases come before your courts that are too difficult for you to judge – whether bloodshed, lawsuits or assaults – take them to the place the LORD your God will choose. ⁹ Go to the Levitical priests and to the judge who is in office at that time. Enquire of them and they will give you the verdict. ¹⁰ You must act according to the decisions they give you at the place the LORD will choose. Be careful to do everything they instruct you to do. ¹¹ Act according to whatever they teach you and the decisions they give you. Do not turn aside from what they tell you, to the right or to the left. ¹² Anyone who shows contempt for the judge or for the priest who stands ministering there to the LORD your God is to be put to death. You must purge the evil from Israel. ¹³ All the people will hear and be afraid, and will not be contemptuous again.

¹⁴ When you enter the land the LORD your God is giving you and have taken possession of it and settled in it, and you say, 'Let us set a king over us like all the nations around us,' ¹⁵ be sure to appoint over you a king the LORD your God chooses. He must be from among your fellow Israelites. Do not place a foreigner over you, one who is not an Israelite. ¹⁶ The king, moreover, must not acquire great numbers of horses for himself or make the people return to Egypt to get more of them, for the LORD has told you, 'You are not to go back that way again.' ¹⁷ He must not take many wives, or his heart will be led astray. He must not accumulate large amounts of silver and gold.

[18] When he takes the throne of his kingdom, he is to write for himself on a scroll a copy of this law, taken from that of the Levitical priests. [19] It is to be with him, and he is to read it all the days of his life so that he may learn to revere the LORD his God and follow carefully all the words of this law and these decrees [20] and not consider himself better than his fellow Israelites and turn from the law to the right or to the left. Then he and his descendants will reign a long time over his kingdom in Israel.

18 The Levitical priests – indeed, the whole tribe of Levi – are to have no land allotted to them or any inheritance with Israel. They shall live on the food offerings presented to the LORD, for that is their inheritance. [2] They shall have no inheritance among their fellow Israelites; the LORD is their inheritance, as he promised them.

[3] This is the share due to the priests from the people who sacrifice a bull or a sheep: the shoulder, the internal organs and the meat from the head. [4] You are to give them the firstfruits of your corn, new wine and olive oil, and the first wool from the shearing of your sheep, [5] for the LORD your God has chosen them and their descendants out of all your tribes to stand and minister in the LORD's name always.

[6] If a Levite moves from one of your towns anywhere in Israel where he is living, and comes in all earnestness to the place the LORD will choose, [7] he may minister in the name of the LORD his God like all his fellow Levites who serve there in the presence of the LORD. [8] He is to share equally in their benefits even though he has received money from the sale of family possessions.

[9] When you enter the land the LORD your God is giving you, do not learn to imitate the detestable ways of the nations there. [10] Let no one be found among you who sacrifices their son or daughter in the fire, who practises divination or sorcery, interprets omens, engages in witchcraft, [11] or casts spells, or who is a medium or spiritist or who consults the dead. [12] Anyone who does these things is detestable to the LORD; because of these same detestable practices the LORD your God will drive out those nations before you. [13] You must be blameless before the LORD your God.

[14] The nations you will dispossess listen to those who practise sorcery or divination. But as for you, the LORD your God has not permitted you to do so. [15] The LORD your God will raise up for you a prophet like me from among you, from your fellow Israelites. You must listen to him. [16] For this is what you asked of the LORD your God at Horeb on the day of the assembly when you said, 'Let us not hear the voice of the LORD our God nor see this great fire any more, or we will die.'

[17] The LORD said to me: 'What they say is good. [18] I will raise up for them a prophet like you from among their fellow Israelites, and I will put my words in his mouth. He will tell them everything I command him. [19] I myself will call to account anyone who does not listen to my words that the prophet speaks in my name. [20] But a prophet who presumes to speak in my name anything I have not commanded, or a prophet who speaks in the name of other gods, is to be put to death.'

[21] You may say to yourselves, 'How can we know when a message has not been spoken by the LORD?' [22] If what a prophet proclaims in the name of the LORD does not take place or come true, that is a message the LORD has not spoken. That prophet has spoken presumptuously, so do not be alarmed.

19 When the LORD your God has destroyed the nations whose land he is giving you, and when you have driven them out and settled in their towns and houses, [2] then set aside for yourselves three cities in the land the LORD your God is giving you to possess. [3] Determine the distances involved and divide into three parts the land the

LORD your God is giving you as an inheritance, so that a person who kills someone may flee for refuge to one of these cities.

⁴ This is the rule concerning anyone who kills a person and flees there for safety – anyone who kills a neighbour unintentionally, without malice aforethought. ⁵ For instance, a man may go into the forest with his neighbour to cut wood, and as he swings his axe to fell a tree, the head may fly off and hit his neighbour and kill him. That man may flee to one of these cities and save his life. ⁶ Otherwise, the avenger of blood might pursue him in a rage, overtake him if the distance is too great, and kill him even though he is not deserving of death, since he did it to his neighbour without malice aforethought. ⁷ This is why I command you to set aside for yourselves three cities.

⁸ If the LORD your God enlarges your territory, as he promised on oath to your ancestors, and gives you the whole land he promised them, ⁹ because you carefully follow all these laws I command you today – to love the LORD your God and to walk always in obedience to him – then you are to set aside three more cities. ¹⁰ Do this so that innocent blood will not be shed in your land, which the LORD your God is giving you as your inheritance, and so that you will not be guilty of bloodshed.

¹¹ But if out of hate someone lies in wait, assaults and kills a neighbour, and then flees to one of these cities, ¹² the killer shall be sent for by the town elders, be brought back from the city, and be handed over to the avenger of blood to die. ¹³ Show no pity. You must purge from Israel the guilt of shedding innocent blood, so that it may go well with you.

■ PSALM 44:1-8

¹ We have heard it with our ears, O God;
    our ancestors have told us

what you did in their days,
    in days long ago.
² With your hand you drove out the nations
    and planted our ancestors;
  you crushed the peoples
    and made our ancestors flourish.
³ It was not by their sword that they won
        the land,
    nor did their arm bring them victory;
  it was your right hand, your arm,
    and the light of your face, for you loved
        them.

⁴ You are my King and my God,
    who decrees victories for Jacob.
⁵ Through you we push back our enemies;
    through your name we trample our
        foes.
⁶ I put no trust in my bow,
    my sword does not bring me victory;
⁷ but you give us victory over our enemies,
    you put our adversaries to shame.
⁸ In God we make our boast all day long,
    and we will praise your name for ever.

■ PROVERBS 10:28-30

²⁸ The prospect of the righteous is joy,
    but the hopes of the wicked come to
        nothing.

²⁹ The way of the LORD is a refuge for the
        blameless,
    but it is the ruin of those who do evil.
³⁰ The righteous will never be uprooted,
    but the wicked will not remain in the
        land.

■ LUKE 9:1-22

9 When Jesus had called the Twelve together, he gave them power and authority to drive out all demons and to cure

diseases, ²and he sent them out to proclaim the kingdom of God and to heal those who were ill. ³He told them: 'Take nothing for the journey – no staff, no bag, no bread, no money, no extra shirt. ⁴Whatever house you enter, stay there until you leave that town. ⁵If people do not welcome you, leave their town and shake the dust off your feet as a testimony against them.' ⁶So they set out and went from village to village, proclaiming the good news and healing people everywhere.

⁷Now Herod the tetrarch heard about all that was going on. And he was perplexed because some were saying that John had been raised from the dead, ⁸others that Elijah had appeared, and still others that one of the prophets of long ago had come back to life. ⁹But Herod said, 'I beheaded John. Who, then, is this I hear such things about?' And he tried to see him.

¹⁰When the apostles returned, they reported to Jesus what they had done. Then he took them with him and they withdrew by themselves to a town called Bethsaida, ¹¹but the crowds learned about it and followed him. He welcomed them and spoke to them about the kingdom of God, and healed those who needed healing.

¹²Late in the afternoon the Twelve came to him and said, 'Send the crowd away so they can go to the surrounding villages and countryside and find food and lodging, because we are in a remote place here.'

¹³He replied, 'You give them something to eat.'

They answered, 'We have only five loaves of bread and two fish – unless we go and buy food for all this crowd.' ¹⁴(About five thousand men were there.)

But he said to his disciples, 'Make them sit down in groups of about fifty each.' ¹⁵The disciples did so, and everyone sat down. ¹⁶Taking the five loaves and the two fish and looking up to heaven, he gave thanks and broke them. Then he gave them to the disciples to distribute to the people. ¹⁷They all ate and were satisfied, and the disciples picked up twelve basketfuls of broken pieces that were left over.

¹⁸Once when Jesus was praying in private and his disciples were with him, he asked them, 'Who do the crowds say I am?'

¹⁹They replied, 'Some say John the Baptist; others say Elijah; and still others, that one of the prophets of long ago has come back to life.'

²⁰'But what about you?' he asked. 'Who do you say I am?'

Peter answered, 'God's Messiah.'

²¹Jesus strictly warned them not to tell this to anyone. ²²And he said, 'The Son of Man must suffer many things and be rejected by the elders, the chief priests and the teachers of the law, and he must be killed and on the third day be raised to life.'

Christ's Righteousness

'I put no trust in my bow, my sword does not bring me victory; but you give us victory over our enemies ...'
Psalm 44:6–7

When Paul talks about the 'breastplate of righteousness in place' in Ephesians 6:14, is he talking about our righteousness or Christ's righteousness?

I believe he is talking about Christ's righteousness. That is not to say, of course, that our own righteousness (our moral uprightness) is unimportant, for as Paul points out in 2 Corinthians 6:7, our righteousness can be a definite defence against Satan. In Ephesians 6, however, the emphasis is not on our righteousness in Christ, but Christ's righteousness imputed to us.

So how does putting on the breastplate of righteousness act as a spiritual defence against the wiles of the devil? Take, for example, those people who have definitely surrendered their lives to Christ but whom Satan afflicts with a feeling that they are not good enough to be saved. Why do they have such feelings? The answer is simple – they have taken their eyes off Christ and His righteousness and have focused on themselves and their righteousness. And in doing that, they have played right into the Devil's hands.

You see, the Devil can find all kinds of flaws and blemishes in your righteousness, but he can find nothing wrong with the righteousness of Christ. The way to withstand an attack like this, then, is to put on the breastplate of righteousness. In other words, remind yourself and Satan that you stand not on your own merits but on Christ's. This may sound simple, even simplistic to some, but I have lived long enough to see people latch on to it and come from the depths of emotional distress to the heights of spiritual elation.

PRAYER

Lord Jesus, help me to latch onto it. Make it crystal clear to my spirit that although the Devil can find many flaws in my righteousness, he cannot find a single flaw in Yours. I rest my case – on You. Thank You, dear Lord. Amen.

FURTHER STUDY

1 Cor. 1:19-31; Isa. 64:6; Rom. 8:34; Phil. 3:9
• What is our righteousness like?
• What was Paul's declaration?

April 11

▬ DEUTERONOMY 19:14–21:23

¹⁴ Do not move your neighbour's boundary stone set up by your predecessors in the inheritance you receive in the land the LORD your God is giving you to possess.

¹⁵ One witness is not enough to convict anyone accused of any crime or offence they may have committed. A matter must be established by the testimony of two or three witnesses.

¹⁶ If a malicious witness takes the stand to accuse someone of a crime, ¹⁷ the two people involved in the dispute must stand in the presence of the LORD before the priests and the judges who are in office at the time. ¹⁸ The judges must make a thorough investigation, and if the witness proves to be a liar, giving false testimony against a fellow Israelite, ¹⁹ then do to the false witness as that witness intended to do to the other party.

You must purge the evil from among you. ²⁰ The rest of the people will hear of this and be afraid, and never again will such an evil thing be done among you. ²¹ Show no pity: life for life, eye for eye, tooth for tooth, hand for hand, foot for foot.

20 When you go to war against your enemies and see horses and chariots and an army greater than yours, do not be afraid of them, because the LORD your God, who brought you up out of Egypt, will be with you. ² When you are about to go into battle, the priest shall come forward and address the army. ³ He shall say: 'Hear, Israel: today you are going into battle against your enemies. Do not be faint-hearted or afraid; do not panic or be terrified by them. ⁴ For the LORD your God is the one who goes with you to fight for you against your enemies to give you victory.'

⁵ The officers shall say to the army: 'Has anyone built a new house and not yet begun to live in it? Let him go home, or he may die in battle and someone else may begin to live in it. ⁶ Has anyone planted a vineyard and not begun to enjoy it? Let him go home, or he may die in battle and someone else enjoy it. ⁷ Has anyone become pledged to a woman and not married her? Let him go home, or he may die in battle and someone else marry her.' ⁸ Then the officers shall add, 'Is anyone afraid or faint-hearted? Let him go home so that his fellow soldiers will not become disheartened too.' ⁹ When the officers have finished speaking to the army, they shall appoint commanders over it.

¹⁰ When you march up to attack a city, make its people an offer of peace. ¹¹ If they accept and open their gates, all the people in it shall be subject to forced labour and shall work for you. ¹² If they refuse to make peace and they engage you in battle, lay siege to that city. ¹³ When the LORD your God delivers it into your hand, put to the sword all the men in it. ¹⁴ As for the women, the children, the livestock and everything else in the city, you may take these as plunder for yourselves. And you may use the plunder the LORD your God gives you from your enemies. ¹⁵ This is how you are to treat all the cities that are at a distance from you and do not belong to the nations nearby.

¹⁶ However, in the cities of the nations the LORD your God is giving you as an inheritance, do not leave alive anything that breathes. ¹⁷ Completely destroy them – the Hittites, Amorites, Canaanites, Perizzites, Hivites and Jebusites – as the LORD your God has commanded you. ¹⁸ Otherwise, they will teach you to follow all the detestable things they do in worshipping their gods, and you will sin against the LORD your God.

¹⁹ When you lay siege to a city for a long time, fighting against it to capture it, do not destroy its trees by putting an axe to them, because you can eat their fruit. Do not cut them down. Are the trees people, that you should besiege them? ²⁰ However, you may cut down trees that you know are not fruit trees and use them to build siege works until the city at war with you falls.

21 If someone is found slain, lying in a field in the land the LORD your God is giving you to possess, and it is not known who the killer was, ² your elders and judges shall go out and measure the distance from the body to the neighbouring towns. ³ Then the elders of the town nearest the body shall take a heifer that has never been worked and has never worn a yoke ⁴ and lead it down to a valley that has not been ploughed or planted and where there is a flowing stream. There in the valley they are to break the heifer's neck. ⁵ The Levitical priests shall step forward, for the LORD your God has chosen them to minister and to pronounce blessings in the name of the LORD and to decide all cases of dispute and assault. ⁶ Then all the elders of the town nearest the body shall wash their hands over the heifer whose neck was broken in the valley, ⁷ and they shall declare: 'Our hands did not shed this blood, nor did our eyes see it done. ⁸ Accept this atonement for your people Israel, whom you have redeemed, LORD, and do not hold your people guilty of the blood of an innocent person.' Then the bloodshed will be atoned for, ⁹ and you will have purged from yourselves the guilt of shedding innocent blood, since you have done what is right in the eyes of the LORD.

¹⁰ When you go to war against your enemies and the LORD your God delivers them into your hands and you take captives, ¹¹ if you notice among the captives a beautiful woman and are attracted to her, you may take her as your wife. ¹² Bring her into your home and make her shave her head, trim her nails ¹³ and put aside the clothes she was wearing when captured. After she has lived in your house and mourned her father and mother for a full month, then you may go to her and be her husband and she shall be your wife. ¹⁴ If you are not pleased with her, let her go wherever she wishes. You must not sell her or treat her as a slave, since you have dishonoured her.

¹⁵ If a man has two wives, and he loves one but not the other, and both bear him sons but the firstborn is the son of the wife he does not love, ¹⁶ when he wills his property to his sons, he must not give the rights of the firstborn to the son of the wife he loves in preference to his actual firstborn, the son of the wife he does not love. ¹⁷ He must acknowledge the son of his unloved wife as the firstborn by giving him a double share of all he has. That son is the first sign of his father's strength. The right of the firstborn belongs to him.

¹⁸ If someone has a stubborn and rebellious son who does not obey his father and mother and will not listen to them when they discipline him, ¹⁹ his father and mother shall take hold of him and bring him to the elders at the gate of his town. ²⁰ They shall say to the elders, 'This son of ours is stubborn and rebellious. He will not obey us.

He is a glutton and a drunkard.' ²¹ Then all the men of his town are to stone him to death. You must purge the evil from among you. All Israel will hear of it and be afraid.

²² If someone guilty of a capital offence is put to death and their body is exposed on a pole, ²³ you must not leave the body hanging on the pole overnight. Be sure to bury it that same day, because anyone who is hung on a pole is under God's curse. You must not desecrate the land the LORD your God is giving you as an inheritance.

▬ PSALM 44:9-16

⁹ But now you have rejected and humbled us;
    you no longer go out with our armies.
¹⁰ You made us retreat before the enemy,
    and our adversaries have plundered us.
¹¹ You gave us up to be devoured like sheep
    and have scattered us among the
       nations.
¹² You sold your people for a pittance,
    gaining nothing from their sale.
¹³ You have made us a reproach to our
       neighbours,
    the scorn and derision of those around
       us.
¹⁴ You have made us a byword among the
       nations;
    the peoples shake their heads at us.
¹⁵ I live in disgrace all day long,
    and my face is covered with shame
¹⁶ at the taunts of those who reproach and
       revile me,
    because of the enemy, who is bent on
       revenge.

▬ PROVERBS 10:31-32

³¹ From the mouth of the righteous comes
    the fruit of wisdom,

but a perverse tongue will be silenced.

32 The lips of the righteous know what
finds favour,
but the mouth of the wicked only what
is perverse.

■ LUKE 9:23-45

23 Then he said to them all: 'Whoever wants to be my disciple must deny themselves and take up their cross daily and follow me. 24 For whoever wants to save their life will lose it, but whoever loses their life for me will save it. 25 What good is it for someone to gain the whole world, and yet lose or forfeit their very self? 26 Whoever is ashamed of me and my words, the Son of Man will be ashamed of them when he comes in his glory and in the glory of the Father and of the holy angels.

27 'Truly I tell you, some who are standing here will not taste death before they see the kingdom of God.'

28 About eight days after Jesus said this, he took Peter, John and James with him and went up onto a mountain to pray. 29 As he was praying, the appearance of his face changed, and his clothes became as bright as a flash of lightning. 30 Two men, Moses and Elijah, appeared in glorious splendour, talking with Jesus. 31 They spoke about his departure, which he was about to bring to fulfilment at Jerusalem. 32 Peter and his companions were very sleepy, but when they became fully awake, they saw his glory and the two men standing with him. 33 As the men were leaving Jesus, Peter said to him, 'Master, it is good for us to be here.

Let us put up three shelters – one for you, one for Moses and one for Elijah.' (He did not know what he was saying.)

34 While he was speaking, a cloud appeared and covered them, and they were afraid as they entered the cloud. 35 A voice came from the cloud, saying, 'This is my Son, whom I have chosen; listen to him.' 36 When the voice had spoken, they found that Jesus was alone. The disciples kept this to themselves and did not tell anyone at that time what they had seen.

37 The next day, when they came down from the mountain, a large crowd met him. 38 A man in the crowd called out, 'Teacher, I beg you to look at my son, for he is my only child. 39 A spirit seizes him and he suddenly screams; it throws him into convulsions so that he foams at the mouth. It scarcely ever leaves him and is destroying him. 40 I begged your disciples to drive it out, but they could not.'

41 'You unbelieving and perverse generation,' Jesus replied, 'how long shall I stay with you and put up with you? Bring your son here.'

42 Even while the boy was coming, the demon threw him to the ground in a convulsion. But Jesus rebuked the impure spirit, healed the boy and gave him back to his father. 43 And they were all amazed at the greatness of God.

While everyone was marvelling at all that Jesus did, he said to his disciples, 44 'Listen carefully to what I am about to tell you: the Son of Man is going to be delivered into the hands of men.' 45 But they did not understand what this meant. It was hidden from them, so that they did not grasp it, and they were afraid to ask him about it.

God Speaks

'A voice came from the clouds saying, "This is my Son, whom I have chosen; listen to him"' **Luke 9:35**

Peter's Jewish heart is divided – wanting to keep Moses, representing the Law; Elijah, representing the Prophets; and Jesus, representing the new revelation, all on the same level. He said: 'Let us put up three shelters.' This was serious, for the whole future was bound up with the question of whether Jesus was final and whether supreme allegiance should be given to Him. It is significant that immediately following this statement, a cloud descended and 'they were afraid as they entered the cloud.'

Where there is division, there will always be clouds. There are clouds over our churches, and we fear as we enter those clouds. Why are we afraid? The answer is simple – division. Each denomination is thinking in terms of itself, is losing a sense of the collective unity. But out of the cloud comes a Voice. God speaks! The voice is one of evaluation and invitation: 'This is my Son, whom I have chosen; listen to him' (Luke 9:35). The clouds will never lift and the fears will never depart until we listen to Christ. And what is He saying? This: '... that all of them may be one, Father, just as you are in me and I am in you' (John 17:21). Christ must be first, and the unity of His Body must take priority over any denominational allegiance.

As the Divine Eagle nudges His Church toward the edge of the nest in an effort to cause it to soar above denominational divides, I pray that it will not be long before we who share Christ's Name truly become one.

PRAYER

O Father, I am so thankful that I am part of Your glorious Family. Make me a good member of that Family. May the Family spirit be in all I do and say, for I want others to come into this Family. In Jesus' name. Amen.

FURTHER STUDY

Matt. 5:21-26; Isa. 11:13; 52:7; John 10:16
• What steps will you take to build Christian unity?
• Is there anyone you need to be reconciled to?

April 12

DEUTERONOMY 22:1–23:25

22 If you see your fellow Israelite's ox or sheep straying, do not ignore it but be sure to take it back to its owner. ²If they do not live near you or if you do not know who owns it, take it home with you and keep it until they come looking for it. Then give it back. ³Do the same if you find their donkey or cloak or anything else they have lost. Do not ignore it.

⁴If you see your fellow Israelite's donkey or ox fallen on the road, do not ignore it. Help the owner to get it to its feet.

⁵A woman must not wear men's clothing, nor a man wear women's clothing, for the LORD your God detests anyone who does this.

⁶If you come across a bird's nest beside the road, either in a tree or on the ground, and the mother is sitting on the young or

on the eggs, do not take the mother with the young. ⁷You may take the young, but be sure to let the mother go, so that it may go well with you and you may have a long life.

⁸When you build a new house, make a parapet around your roof so that you may not bring the guilt of bloodshed on your house if someone falls from the roof.

⁹Do not plant two kinds of seed in your vineyard; if you do, not only the crops you plant but also the fruit of the vineyard will be defiled.

¹⁰Do not plough with an ox and a donkey yoked together.

¹¹Do not wear clothes of wool and linen woven together.

¹²Make tassels on the four corners of the cloak you wear.

¹³If a man takes a wife and, after sleeping with her, dislikes her ¹⁴and slanders her and gives her a bad name, saying, 'I married this woman, but when I approached her, I did not find proof of her virginity,' ¹⁵then the young woman's father and mother shall bring to the town elders at the gate proof that she was a virgin. ¹⁶Her father will say to the elders, 'I gave my daughter in marriage to this man, but he dislikes her. ¹⁷Now he has slandered her and said, "I did not find your daughter to be a virgin." But here is the proof of my daughter's virginity.' Then her parents shall display the cloth before the elders of the town, ¹⁸and the elders shall take the man and punish him. ¹⁹They shall fine him a hundred shekels of silver and give them to the young woman's father, because this man has given an Israelite virgin a bad name. She shall continue to be his wife; he must not divorce her as long as he lives.

²⁰If, however, the charge is true and no proof of the young woman's virginity can be found, ²¹she shall be brought to the door of her father's house and there the men of her town shall stone her to death. She has done an outrageous thing in Israel by being promiscuous while still in her father's house.

You must purge the evil from among you.

²²If a man is found sleeping with another man's wife, both the man who slept with her and the woman must die. You must purge the evil from Israel.

²³If a man happens to meet in a town a virgin pledged to be married and he sleeps with her, ²⁴you shall take both of them to the gate of that town and stone them to death – the young woman because she was in a town and did not scream for help, and the man because he violated another man's wife. You must purge the evil from among you.

²⁵But if out in the country a man happens to meet a young woman pledged to be married and rapes her, only the man who has done this shall die. ²⁶Do nothing to the woman; she has committed no sin deserving death. This case is like that of someone who attacks and murders a neighbour, ²⁷for the man found the young woman out in the country, and though the betrothed woman screamed, there was no one to rescue her.

²⁸If a man happens to meet a virgin who is not pledged to be married and rapes her and they are discovered, ²⁹he shall pay her father fifty shekels of silver. He must marry the young woman, for he has violated her. He can never divorce her as long as he lives.

³⁰A man is not to marry his father's wife; he must not dishonour his father's bed.

23 No one who has been emasculated by crushing or cutting may enter the assembly of the Lord.

²No one born of a forbidden marriage nor any of their descendants may enter the assembly of the LORD, not even in the tenth generation.

³No Ammonite or Moabite or any of their descendants may enter the assembly of the LORD, not even in the tenth generation. ⁴For they did not come to meet you with bread and water on your way when you came out of Egypt, and they hired Balaam son of Beor from Pethor in Aram Naharaim to

pronounce a curse on you. ⁵However, the LORD your God would not listen to Balaam but turned the curse into a blessing for you, because the LORD your God loves you. ⁶Do not seek a treaty of friendship with them as long as you live.

⁷Do not despise an Edomite, for the Edomites are related to you. Do not despise an Egyptian, because you resided as foreigners in their country. ⁸The third generation of children born to them may enter the assembly of the LORD.

⁹When you set up camp against your enemies, keep away from everything impure. ¹⁰If one of your men is unclean because of a nocturnal emission, he is to go outside the camp and stay there. ¹¹But as evening approaches he is to wash himself, and at sunset he may return to the camp.

¹²Designate a place outside the camp where you can go to relieve yourself. ¹³As part of your equipment have something to dig with, and when you relieve yourself, dig a hole and cover up your excrement. ¹⁴For the LORD your God moves about in your camp to protect you and to deliver your enemies to you. Your camp must be holy, so that he will not see among you anything indecent and turn away from you.

¹⁵If a slave has taken refuge with you, do not hand them over to their master. ¹⁶Let them live among you wherever they like and in whatever town they choose. Do not oppress them.

¹⁷No Israelite man or woman is to become a shrine-prostitute. ¹⁸You must not bring the earnings of a female prostitute or of a male prostitute into the house of the LORD your God to pay any vow, because the LORD your God detests them both.

¹⁹Do not charge a fellow Israelite interest, whether on money or food or anything else that may earn interest. ²⁰You may charge a foreigner interest, but not a fellow Israelite, so that the LORD your God may bless you in everything you put your hand to in the land

you are entering to possess.

²¹If you make a vow to the LORD your God, do not be slow to pay it, for the LORD your God will certainly demand it of you and you will be guilty of sin. ²²But if you refrain from making a vow, you will not be guilty. ²³Whatever your lips utter you must be sure to do, because you made your vow freely to the LORD your God with your own mouth.

²⁴If you enter your neighbour's vineyard, you may eat all the grapes you want, but do not put any in your basket. ²⁵If you enter your neighbour's cornfield, you may pick the ears with your hands, but you must not put a sickle to their standing corn.

▬ PSALM 44:17-26

¹⁷All this came upon us,
    though we had not forgotten you;
    we had not been false to your
        covenant.
¹⁸Our hearts had not turned back;
    our feet had not strayed from your
        path.
¹⁹But you crushed us and made us a haunt
        for jackals;
    you covered us over with deep
        darkness.

²⁰If we had forgotten the name of our God
    or spread out our hands to a foreign
        god,
²¹would not God have discovered it,
    since he knows the secrets of the
        heart?
²²Yet for your sake we face death all day
        long;
    we are considered as sheep to be
        slaughtered.

²³Awake, Lord! Why do you sleep?
    Rouse yourself! Do not reject us for
        ever.

²⁴ Why do you hide your face
    and forget our misery and oppression?

²⁵ We are brought down to the dust;
    our bodies cling to the ground.
²⁶ Rise up and help us;
    rescue us because of your unfailing
    love.

■ PROVERBS 11:1-4

11 The LORD detests dishonest scales,
    but accurate weights find favour with
him.

² When pride comes, then comes disgrace,
    but with humility comes wisdom.

³ The integrity of the upright guides them,
    but the unfaithful are destroyed by
    their duplicity.

⁴ Wealth is worthless in the day of wrath,
    but righteousness delivers from death.

■ LUKE 9:46-62

⁴⁶ An argument started among the disciples as to which of them would be the greatest. ⁴⁷ Jesus, knowing their thoughts, took a little child and made him stand beside him. ⁴⁸ Then he said to them, 'Whoever welcomes this little child in my name welcomes me; and whoever welcomes me welcomes the one who sent me. For it is the one who is least among you all who is the greatest.'

⁴⁹ 'Master,' said John, 'we saw someone driving out demons in your name and we tried to stop him, because he is not one of us.'

⁵⁰ 'Do not stop him,' Jesus said, 'for whoever is not against you is for you.'

⁵¹ As the time approached for him to be taken up to heaven, Jesus resolutely set out for Jerusalem. ⁵² And he sent messengers on ahead, who went into a Samaritan village to get things ready for him; ⁵³ but the people there did not welcome him, because he was heading for Jerusalem. ⁵⁴ When the disciples James and John saw this, they asked, 'Lord, do you want us to call fire down from heaven to destroy them?' ⁵⁵ But Jesus turned and rebuked them. ⁵⁶ Then he and his disciples went to another village.

⁵⁷ As they were walking along the road, a man said to him, 'I will follow you wherever you go.'

⁵⁸ Jesus replied, 'Foxes have dens and birds have nests, but the Son of Man has nowhere to lay his head.'

⁵⁹ He said to another man, 'Follow me.'

But he replied, 'Lord, first let me go and bury my father.'

⁶⁰ Jesus said to him, 'Let the dead bury their own dead, but you go and proclaim the kingdom of God.'

⁶¹ Still another said, 'I will follow you, Lord; but first let me go back and say goodbye to my family.'

⁶² Jesus replied, 'No one who puts a hand to the plough and looks back is fit for service in the kingdom of God.'

The Measure of Maturity

'... we saw someone driving out demons in your name
and we tried to stop him, because he is not one of us.'
Luke 9:49

Our fellowship with other Christians heightens our understanding of God and helps us stay spiritually fresh. I have no doubt that my fellowship with other Christians has helped more than words can convey in keeping me spiritually alert and topped up. When for some reason I am not able to fellowship with other Christians, my spiritual life tends to sag. This is one of the laws of the Christian life, and we ignore it to our peril.

Dr. E. Stanley Jones said: 'The measure of our spiritual maturity can be and is measured by the breadth and depth of our capacity and willingness for fellowship.' Note the words 'capacity' and 'willingness.' This doesn't mean working at enlarging our circle of fellowship - though for some it may mean that - but that we have the capacity and willingness to do it if God should so lead.

I know there are Christians in churches, fellowships, and denominations whom I will never meet down here on earth, but I have the capacity and willingness to fellowship with them if God were to make it possible. We are only as mature as our willingness and capacity for fellowship. Therefore, if we cannot or do not want to fellowship with others who are truly Christ's, then we are immature Christians. Churches and denominations have different rules and guidelines in relation to mixing with others of different groups, but as far as individual fellowship is concerned, our basis ought to be this: everyone who belongs to Christ should belong to everyone else who belongs to Christ.

PRAYER

Father, I see that if I shut out my brother, I shut out You, and my life will soon become stale. Help me deepen all the areas of my fellowship - my fellowship with You and my fellowship with others. In Jesus' name. Amen.

FURTHER STUDY

John 13:31-35; Rom. 12:5; 1 Cor. 10:17; Gal. 3:28
- What is the greatest testimony of Christ to the world?
- To what does Paul liken the body of Christ?

April 13

■ DEUTERONOMY 24:1–26:19

24 If a man marries a woman who becomes displeasing to him because he finds something indecent about her, and he writes her a certificate of divorce, gives it to her and sends her from his house, [2]and if after she leaves his house she becomes the wife of another man, [3]and her second husband dislikes her and writes her a certificate of divorce, gives it to her and sends her from his house, or if he dies, [4]then her first husband, who divorced her, is not allowed to marry her again after she has been defiled. That would be detestable in the eyes of the LORD. Do not bring sin upon the land the LORD your God is giving you as an inheritance.

⁵ If a man has recently married, he must not be sent to war or have any other duty laid on him. For one year he is to be free to stay at home and bring happiness to the wife he has married.

⁶ Do not take a pair of millstones – not even the upper one – as security for a debt, because that would be taking a person's livelihood as security.

⁷ If someone is caught kidnapping a fellow Israelite and treating or selling them as a slave, the kidnapper must die. You must purge the evil from among you.

⁸ In cases of defiling skin diseases, be very careful to do exactly as the Levitical priests instruct you. You must follow carefully what I have commanded them. ⁹ Remember what the LORD your God did to Miriam along the way after you came out of Egypt.

¹⁰ When you make a loan of any kind to your neighbour, do not go into their house to get what is offered to you as a pledge. ¹¹ Stay outside and let the neighbour to whom you are making the loan bring the pledge out to you. ¹² If the neighbour is poor, do not go to sleep with their pledge in your possession. ¹³ Return their cloak by sunset so that your neighbour may sleep in it. Then they will thank you, and it will be regarded as a righteous act in the sight of the LORD your God.

¹⁴ Do not take advantage of a hired worker who is poor and needy, whether that worker is a fellow Israelite or a foreigner residing in one of your towns. ¹⁵ Pay them their wages each day before sunset, because they are poor and are counting on it. Otherwise they may cry to the LORD against you, and you will be guilty of sin.

¹⁶ Parents are not to be put to death for their children, nor children put to death for their parents; each will die for their own sin.

¹⁷ Do not deprive the foreigner or the fatherless of justice, or take the cloak of the widow as a pledge. ¹⁸ Remember that you were slaves in Egypt and the LORD your God

redeemed you from there. That is why I command you to do this.

¹⁹ When you are harvesting in your field and you overlook a sheaf, do not go back to get it. Leave it for the foreigner, the fatherless and the widow, so that the LORD your God may bless you in all the work of your hands. ²⁰ When you beat the olives from your trees, do not go over the branches a second time. Leave what remains for the foreigner, the fatherless and the widow. ²¹ When you harvest the grapes in your vineyard, do not go over the vines again. Leave what remains for the foreigner, the fatherless and the widow. ²² Remember that you were slaves in Egypt. That is why I command you to do this.

25 When people have a dispute, they are to take it to court and the judges will decide the case, acquitting the innocent and condemning the guilty. ² If the guilty person deserves to be beaten, the judge shall make them lie down and have them flogged in his presence with the number of lashes the crime deserves, ³ but the judge must not impose more than forty lashes. If the guilty party is flogged more than that, your fellow Israelite will be degraded in your eyes.

⁴ Do not muzzle an ox while it is treading out the grain.

⁵ If brothers are living together and one of them dies without a son, his widow must not marry outside the family. Her husband's brother shall take her and marry her and fulfil the duty of a brother-in-law to her. ⁶ The first son she bears shall carry on the name of the dead brother so that his name will not be blotted out from Israel.

⁷ However, if a man does not want to marry his brother's wife, she shall go to the elders at the town gate and say, 'My husband's brother refuses to carry on his brother's name in Israel. He will not fulfil the duty of a brother-in-law to me.' ⁸ Then the elders of his town shall summon him and talk to him. If he persists in saying, 'I do not want

to marry her,' ⁹his brother's widow shall go up to him in the presence of the elders, take off one of his sandals, spit in his face and say, 'This is what is done to the man who will not build up his brother's family line.' ¹⁰That man's line shall be known in Israel as The Family of the Unsandalled.

¹¹If two men are fighting and the wife of one of them comes to rescue her husband from his assailant, and she reaches out and seizes him by his private parts, ¹²you shall cut off her hand. Show her no pity.

¹³Do not have two differing weights in your bag – one heavy, one light. ¹⁴Do not have two differing measures in your house – one large, one small. ¹⁵You must have accurate and honest weights and measures, so that you may live long in the land the LORD your God is giving you. ¹⁶For the LORD your God detests anyone who does these things, anyone who deals dishonestly.

¹⁷Remember what the Amalekites did to you along the way when you came out of Egypt. ¹⁸When you were weary and worn out, they met you on your journey and attacked all who were lagging behind; they had no fear of God. ¹⁹When the LORD your God gives you rest from all the enemies around you in the land he is giving you to possess as an inheritance, you shall blot out the name of Amalek from under heaven. Do not forget!

26 When you have entered the land that the LORD your God is giving you as an inheritance and have taken possession of it and settled in it, ²take some of the firstfruits of all that you produce from the soil of the land that the LORD your God is giving you and put them in a basket. Then go to the place that the LORD your God will choose as a dwelling for his Name ³and say to the priest in office at the time, 'I declare today to the LORD your God that I have come to the land the LORD swore to our ancestors to give us.' ⁴The priest shall take the basket from your hands and set it down in front of the altar of the LORD your God. ⁵Then you

shall declare before the LORD your God: 'My father was a wandering Aramean, and he went down into Egypt with a few people and lived there and became a great nation, powerful and numerous. ⁶But the Egyptians ill-treated us and made us suffer, subjecting us to harsh labour. ⁷Then we cried out to the LORD, the God of our ancestors, and the LORD heard our voice and saw our misery, toil and oppression. ⁸So the LORD brought us out of Egypt with a mighty hand and an outstretched arm, with great terror and with signs and wonders. ⁹He brought us to this place and gave us this land, a land flowing with milk and honey; ¹⁰and now I bring the firstfruits of the soil that you, LORD, have given me.' Place the basket before the LORD your God and bow down before him. ¹¹Then you and the Levites and the foreigners residing among you shall rejoice in all the good things the LORD your God has given to you and your household.

¹²When you have finished setting aside a tenth of all your produce in the third year, the year of the tithe, you shall give it to the Levite, the foreigner, the fatherless and the widow, so that they may eat in your towns and be satisfied. ¹³Then say to the LORD your God: 'I have removed from my house the sacred portion and have given it to the Levite, the foreigner, the fatherless and the widow, according to all you commanded. I have not turned aside from your commands nor have I forgotten any of them. ¹⁴I have not eaten any of the sacred portion while I was in mourning, nor have I removed any of it while I was unclean, nor have I offered any of it to the dead. I have obeyed the LORD my God; I have done everything you commanded me. ¹⁵Look down from heaven, your holy dwelling-place, and bless your people Israel and the land you have given us as you promised on oath to our ancestors, a land flowing with milk and honey.'

¹⁶The LORD your God commands you this day to follow these decrees and laws;

carefully observe them with all your heart and with all your soul. ¹⁷ You have declared this day that the LORD is your God and that you will walk in obedience to him, that you will keep his decrees, commands and laws – that you will listen to him. ¹⁸ And the LORD has declared this day that you are his people, his treasured possession as he promised, and that you are to keep all his commands. ¹⁹ He has declared that he will set you in praise, fame and honour high above all the nations he has made and that you will be a people holy to the LORD your God, as he promised.

PSALM 45:1-5

¹ My heart is stirred by a noble theme
     as I recite my verses for the king;
     my tongue is the pen of a skilful writer.

² You are the most excellent of men
     and your lips have been anointed with
       grace,
     since God has blessed you for ever.

³ Gird your sword on your side, you
       mighty one;
     clothe yourself with splendour and
       majesty.
⁴ In your majesty ride forth victoriously
     in the cause of truth, humility and
       justice;
     let your right hand achieve awesome
       deeds.
⁵ Let your sharp arrows pierce the hearts
     of the king's enemies;
     let the nations fall beneath your feet.

PROVERBS 11:5-6

⁵ The righteousness of the blameless
     makes their paths straight,
     but the wicked are brought down by
       their own wickedness.

⁶ The righteousness of the upright delivers
     them,
     but the unfaithful are trapped by evil
       desires.

LUKE 10:1-24

10 After this the Lord appointed seventy-two others and sent them two by two ahead of him to every town and place where he was about to go. ² He told them, 'The harvest is plentiful, but the workers are few. Ask the Lord of the harvest, therefore, to send out workers into his harvest field. ³ Go! I am sending you out like lambs among wolves. ⁴ Do not take a purse or bag or sandals; and do not greet anyone on the road.

⁵ 'When you enter a house, first say, "Peace to this house." ⁶ If someone who promotes peace is there, your peace will rest on them; if not, it will return to you. ⁷ Stay there, eating and drinking whatever they give you, for the worker deserves his wages. Do not move around from house to house.

⁸ 'When you enter a town and are welcomed, eat what is offered to you. ⁹ Heal those there who are ill and tell them, "The kingdom of God has come near to you." ¹⁰ But when you enter a town and are not welcomed, go into its streets and say, ¹¹ "Even the dust of your town we wipe from our feet as a warning to you. Yet be sure of this: the kingdom of God has come near." ¹² I tell you, it will be more bearable on that day for Sodom than for that town.

¹³ 'Woe to you, Chorazin! Woe to you, Bethsaida! For if the miracles that were performed in you had been performed in Tyre and Sidon, they would have repented long ago, sitting in sackcloth and ashes. ¹⁴ But it will be more bearable for Tyre and Sidon at the judgment than for you. ¹⁵ And you, Capernaum, will you be lifted to the heavens? No, you will go down to Hades.

¹⁶ 'Whoever listens to you listens to me;

whoever rejects you rejects me; but whoever rejects me rejects him who sent me.'

¹⁷ The seventy-two returned with joy and said, 'Lord, even the demons submit to us in your name.'

¹⁸ He replied, 'I saw Satan fall like lightning from heaven. ¹⁹ I have given you authority to trample on snakes and scorpions and to overcome all the power of the enemy; nothing will harm you. ²⁰ However, do not rejoice that the spirits submit to you, but rejoice that your names are written in heaven.'

²¹ At that time Jesus, full of joy through the Holy Spirit, said, 'I praise you, Father, Lord of heaven and earth, because you have hidden these things from the wise and learned, and revealed them to little children. Yes, Father, for this is what you were pleased to do.

²² 'All things have been committed to me by my Father. No one knows who the Son is except the Father, and no one knows who the Father is except the Son and those to whom the Son chooses to reveal him.'

²³ Then he turned to his disciples and said privately, 'Blessed are the eyes that see what you see. ²⁴ For I tell you that many prophets and kings wanted to see what you see but did not see it, and to hear what you hear but did not hear it.'

The Sword of the Spirit

'... I am sending you out like lambs among wolves.'
Luke 10:3

The last of the six pieces of the Christian's armour listed in Ephesians 6 is 'the sword of the Spirit, which is the word of God' (Eph. 6:17). John Stott points out that 'of all the six pieces of armour or weaponry listed, the sword is the only one which can clearly be used for attack as well as defence.' And the kind of attack envisaged here is one that involves a close encounter, for the word used for sword is *machaira*, meaning a short sword or dagger.

There is much more to spiritual warfare than standing up to the Devil. We possess, according to James 4:7, the potential to make him 'flee': 'Resist the devil, and he will flee from you.' The word 'flee' is a very strong word in the original Greek. It means much more than just a strategic withdrawal; it means beating a swift retreat. What an amazing truth! It is possible for a Christian so to resist the Devil that he races away as fast as he can.

This truth must not be seen in any way as limiting the Devil's power, for he is a strong and determined foe. It means rather that a Christian able to wield the sword of the Spirit can ensure that Satan is overpowered. We are right to develop a healthy respect for the Devil's wiles, but we are wrong when we allow him to terrorize us.

We must have the assurance, given everywhere in the New Testament, that to engage in conflict with the Devil is not a hopeless task. We are not to indulge in overconfidence, but, at the same time, we are not to be frightened by him.

PRAYER

O Father, the thought that I, a sinner saved by grace, am able to send Satan into retreat almost overwhelms me. Yet I must believe it, for Your Word tells me so. Help me understand even more clearly the authority I have in Christ. In His name I ask it. Amen.

FURTHER STUDY

Luke 10:1-20; Acts 3:6-8; 16:16-18; 1 Pet. 5:8-9
• How much authority over Satan have we been given?
• How did the early church exercise this authority?

April 14

▬ DEUTERONOMY 27:1–28:14

27 Moses and the elders of Israel commanded the people: 'Keep all these commands that I give you today. ² When you have crossed the Jordan into the land the LORD your God is giving you, set up some large stones and coat them with plaster. ³ Write on them all the words of this law when you have crossed over to enter the land the LORD your God is giving you, a land flowing with milk and honey, just as the LORD, the God of your ancestors, promised you. ⁴ And when you have crossed the Jordan, set up these stones on Mount Ebal, as I command you today, and coat them with plaster. ⁵ Build there an altar to the LORD your God, an altar of stones. Do not use any iron tool on them. ⁶ Build the altar of the LORD your God with stones from the field and offer burnt offerings on it to the LORD your God. ⁷ Sacrifice fellowship offerings there, eating them and rejoicing in the presence of the LORD your God. ⁸ And you shall write very clearly all the words of this law on these stones you have set up.'

⁹ Then Moses and the Levitical priests said to all Israel, 'Be silent, Israel, and listen! You have now become the people of the LORD your God. ¹⁰ Obey the LORD your God and follow his commands and decrees that I give you today.'

¹¹ On the same day Moses commanded the people:

¹² When you have crossed the Jordan, these tribes shall stand on Mount Gerizim to bless the people: Simeon, Levi, Judah, Issachar, Joseph and Benjamin. ¹³ And these tribes shall stand on Mount Ebal to pronounce curses: Reuben, Gad, Asher, Zebulun, Dan and Naphtali.

¹⁴ The Levites shall recite to all the people of Israel in a loud voice:

¹⁵ 'Cursed is anyone who makes an idol – a thing detestable to the LORD, the work of skilled hands – and sets it up in secret.'

Then all the people shall say, 'Amen!'
¹⁶ 'Cursed is anyone who dishonours their father or mother.'

Then all the people shall say, 'Amen!'
¹⁷ 'Cursed is anyone who moves their neighbour's boundary stone.'

Then all the people shall say, 'Amen!'

¹⁸'Cursed is anyone who leads the blind astray on the road.'

Then all the people shall say, 'Amen!'

¹⁹'Cursed is anyone who withholds justice from the foreigner, the fatherless or the widow.'

Then all the people shall say, 'Amen!'

²⁰'Cursed is anyone who sleeps with his father's wife, for he dishonours his father's bed.'

Then all the people shall say, 'Amen!'

²¹'Cursed is anyone who has sexual relations with any animal.'

Then all the people shall say, 'Amen!'

²²'Cursed is anyone who sleeps with his sister, the daughter of his father or the daughter of his mother.'

Then all the people shall say, 'Amen!'

²³'Cursed is anyone who sleeps with his mother-in-law.'

Then all the people shall say, 'Amen!'

²⁴'Cursed is anyone who kills their neighbour secretly.'

Then all the people shall say, 'Amen!'

²⁵'Cursed is anyone who accepts a bribe to kill an innocent person.'

Then all the people shall say, 'Amen!'

²⁶'Cursed is anyone who does not uphold the words of this law by carrying them out.'

Then all the people shall say, 'Amen!'

28 If you fully obey the LORD your God and carefully follow all his commands that I give you today, the LORD your God will set you high above all the nations on earth. ²All these blessings will come on you and accompany you if you obey the LORD your God:

³You will be blessed in the city and blessed in the country.

⁴The fruit of your womb will be blessed, and the crops of your land and the young of your livestock – the calves of your herds and the lambs of your flocks.

⁵Your basket and your kneading trough will be blessed.

⁶You will be blessed when you come in and blessed when you go out.

⁷The LORD will grant that the enemies who rise up against you will be defeated before you. They will come at you from one direction but flee from you in seven.

⁸The LORD will send a blessing on your barns and on everything you put your hand to. The LORD your God will bless you in the land he is giving you.

⁹The LORD will establish you as his holy people, as he promised you on oath, if you keep the commands of the LORD your God and walk in obedience to him. ¹⁰Then all the peoples on earth will see that you are called by the name of the LORD, and they will fear you. ¹¹The LORD will grant you abundant prosperity – in the fruit of your womb, the young of your livestock and the crops of your ground – in the land he swore to your ancestors to give you.

¹²The LORD will open the heavens, the storehouse of his bounty, to send rain on your land in season and to bless all the work of your hands. You will lend to many nations but will borrow from none. ¹³The LORD will make you the head, not the tail. If you pay attention to the commands of the LORD your God that I give you this day and carefully follow them, you will always be at the top, never at the bottom. ¹⁴Do not turn aside from any of the commands I give you today, to the right or to the left, following other gods and serving them.

■ PSALM 45:6–12

6 Your throne, O God, will last for ever and
ever;
    a sceptre of justice will be the sceptre
    of your kingdom.
7 You love righteousness and hate
wickedness;
    therefore God, your God, has set you
    above your companions
    by anointing you with the oil of joy.
8 All your robes are fragrant with myrrh
    and aloes and cassia;
    from palaces adorned with ivory
    the music of the strings makes you
    glad.
9 Daughters of kings are among your
    honoured women;
    at your right hand is the royal bride in
    gold of Ophir.

10 Listen, daughter, and pay careful attention:
    Forget your people and your father's
    house.
11 Let the king be enthralled by your beauty;
    honour him, for he is your lord.
12 The city of Tyre will come with a gift,
    people of wealth will seek your favour.

■ PROVERBS 11:7–8

7 Hopes placed in mortals die with them;
    all the promise of their power comes
    to nothing.

8 The righteous person is rescued from
    trouble,
    and it falls on the wicked instead.

■ LUKE 10:25–11:4

25 On one occasion an expert in the law
stood up to test Jesus. 'Teacher,' he asked,
'what must I do to inherit eternal life?'

26 'What is written in the Law?' he
replied. 'How do you read it?'

27 He answered, '"Love the Lord your
God with all your heart and with all your
soul and with all your strength and with all
your mind"; and, "Love your neighbour as
yourself."'

28 'You have answered correctly,' Jesus
replied. 'Do this and you will live.'

29 But he wanted to justify himself, so he
asked Jesus, 'And who is my neighbour?'

30 In reply Jesus said: 'A man was going
down from Jerusalem to Jericho, when he
was attacked by robbers. They stripped
him of his clothes, beat him and went away,
leaving him half-dead. 31 A priest happened
to be going down the same road, and when
he saw the man, he passed by on the other
side. 32 So too, a Levite, when he came to the
place and saw him, passed by on the other side. 33 But a Samaritan, as he travelled,
came where the man was; and when he saw
him, he took pity on him. 34 He went to him
and bandaged his wounds, pouring on oil
and wine. Then he put the man on his own
donkey, brought him to an inn and took
care of him. 35 The next day he took out
two denarii and gave them to the innkeep-
er. "Look after him," he said, "and when I
return, I will reimburse you for any extra
expense you may have."

36 'Which of these three do you think was
a neighbour to the man who fell into the
hands of robbers?'

37 The expert in the law replied, 'The one
who had mercy on him.'
Jesus told him, 'Go and do likewise.'

38 As Jesus and his disciples were on their
way, he came to a village where a woman
named Martha opened her home to him.
39 She had a sister called Mary, who sat at
the Lord's feet listening to what he said.
40 But Martha was distracted by all the
preparations that had to be made. She
came to him and asked, 'Lord, don't you
care that my sister has left me to do the

work by myself? Tell her to help me!'

⁴¹'Martha, Martha,' the Lord answered, 'you are worried and upset about many things, ⁴²but few things are needed – or indeed only one. Mary has chosen what is better, and it will not be taken away from her.'

11 One day Jesus was praying in a certain place. When he finished, one of his disciples said to him, 'Lord, teach us to pray, just as John taught his disciples.'

²He said to them, 'When you pray, say:

' "Father,
hallowed be your name,
your kingdom come.
³Give us each day our daily bread.
⁴Forgive us our sins,
    for we also forgive everyone who sins
        against us.
And lead us not into temptation." '

The Purpose of Living

'Love the Lord your God with all your heart and ... your neighbour as yourself.' **Luke 10:27**

The energy behind most of our behaviour (particularly strange or abnormal behaviour) is an independent attempt to satiate the deep longings which God – and God alone – can satisfy. If you want to know a biblical reason why people do the things they do, then keep these thoughts in mind.

A man said to me some time ago, 'Why do I browbeat my wife and make demands on her which I know are not loving? And why, despite my best efforts to change, do I fall back into my usual patterns?' I told him, 'Your legitimate longings for impact and respect are not being met by God, and as you can't function very well when these longings go unmet, you set about trying to get your wife to meet them.' He saw the point, asked God to forgive him for drinking at the wrong well, and turned in a fresh way to Christ for life and power and reality.

But what about the person who goes in the other direction and withdraws from others, manifesting such symptoms as extreme shyness and some forms of depression? This person is someone who has little awareness of their thirst being quenched by God – hence a degree of inner emptiness – and is motivated to avoid moving toward involvement with others for fear he or she might be rejected.

Self-enhancement (a selfish attempt to quench our own thirst) or self-rejection – these are the two styles of relationship which characterise many Christians' lives. And both are a violation of the law of love.

PRAYER

Loving Lord, Your Word is crystal clear – the purpose of living is simply to love as I am loved. If I am not loving others, then quite simply I am not allowing You to love me. I am sinning in both directions. Help me, my Saviour. Amen.

FURTHER STUDY

John 13:1-35; 15:12;
Matt. 22:39; 1 Thess. 3:12
• How do we show that we belong to Jesus?
• What was Paul's desire for the Thessalonians?

April 15

■ DEUTERONOMY 28:15-68

15 However, if you do not obey the LORD your God and do not carefully follow all his commands and decrees I am giving you today, all these curses will come on you and overtake you:

16 You will be cursed in the city and cursed in the country.

17 Your basket and your kneading trough will be cursed.

18 The fruit of your womb will be cursed, and the crops of your land, and the calves of your herds and the lambs of your flocks.

19 You will be cursed when you come in and cursed when you go out.

20 The LORD will send on you curses, confusion and rebuke in everything you put your hand to, until you are destroyed and come to sudden ruin because of the evil you have done in forsaking him. 21 The LORD will plague you with diseases until he has destroyed you from the land you are entering to possess. 22 The LORD will strike you with wasting disease, with fever and inflammation, with scorching heat and drought, with blight and mildew, which will plague you until you perish. 23 The sky over your head will be bronze, the ground beneath you iron. 24 The LORD will turn the rain of your country into dust and powder; it will come down from the skies until you are destroyed.

25 The LORD will cause you to be defeated before your enemies. You will come at them from one direction but flee from them in seven, and you will become a thing of horror to all the kingdoms on earth. 26 Your carcasses will be food for all the birds and the wild animals, and there will be no one to frighten them away. 27 The LORD will afflict you with the boils of Egypt and with tumours, festering sores and the itch, from which you cannot be cured. 28 The LORD will afflict you with madness, blindness and confusion of mind. 29 At midday you will grope about like a blind person in the dark. You will be unsuccessful in everything you do; day after day you will be oppressed and robbed, with no one to rescue you.

30 You will be pledged to be married to a woman, but another will take her and rape her. You will build a house, but you will not live in it. You will plant a vineyard, but you will not even begin to enjoy its fruit. 31 Your ox will be slaughtered before your eyes, but you will eat none of it. Your donkey will be forcibly taken from you and will not be returned. Your sheep will be given to your

enemies, and no one will rescue them. [32] Your sons and daughters will be given to another nation, and you will wear out your eyes watching for them day after day, powerless to lift a hand. [33] A people that you do not know will eat what your land and labour produce, and you will have nothing but cruel oppression all your days. [34] The sights you see will drive you mad. [35] The LORD will afflict your knees and legs with painful boils that cannot be cured, spreading from the soles of your feet to the top of your head.

[36] The LORD will drive you and the king you set over you to a nation unknown to you or your ancestors. There you will worship other gods, gods of wood and stone. [37] You will become a thing of horror, a byword and an object of ridicule among all the peoples where the LORD will drive you.

[38] You will sow much seed in the field but you will harvest little, because locusts will devour it. [39] You will plant vineyards and cultivate them but you will not drink the wine or gather the grapes, because worms will eat them. [40] You will have olive trees throughout your country but you will not use the oil, because the olives will drop off. [41] You will have sons and daughters but you will not keep them, because they will go into captivity. [42] Swarms of locusts will take over all your trees and the crops of your land.

[43] The foreigners who reside among you will rise above you higher and higher, but you will sink lower and lower. [44] They will lend to you, but you will not lend to them. They will be the head, but you will be the tail.

[45] All these curses will come on you. They will pursue you and overtake you until you are destroyed, because you did not obey the LORD your God and observe the commands and decrees he gave you. [46] They will be a sign and a wonder to you and your descendants for ever. [47] Because you did not serve the LORD your God joyfully and gladly in the time of prosperity, [48] therefore in hunger and thirst, in nakedness and dire poverty, you will serve the enemies the LORD sends against you. He will put an iron yoke on your neck until he has destroyed you.

[49] The LORD will bring a nation against you from far away, from the ends of the earth, like an eagle swooping down, a nation whose language you will not understand, [50] a fierce-looking nation without respect for the old or pity for the young. [51] They will devour the young of your livestock and the crops of your land until you are destroyed. They will leave you no corn, new wine or olive oil, nor any calves of your herds or lambs of your flocks until you are ruined. [52] They will lay siege to all the cities throughout your land until the high fortified walls in which you trust fall down. They will besiege all the cities throughout the land the LORD your God is giving you.

[53] Because of the suffering your enemy will inflict on you during the siege, you will eat the fruit of the womb, the flesh of the sons and daughters the LORD your God has given you. [54] Even the most gentle and sensitive man among you will have no compassion on his own brother or the wife he loves or his surviving children, [55] and he will not give to one of them any of the flesh of his children that he is eating. It will be all he has left because of the suffering that your enemy will inflict on you during the siege of all your cities. [56] The most gentle and sensitive woman among you – so sensitive and gentle that she would not venture to touch the ground with the sole of her foot – will begrudge the husband she loves and her own son or daughter [57] the afterbirth from her womb and the children she bears. For in her dire need she intends to eat them secretly because of the suffering your enemy will inflict on you during the siege of your cities.

[58] If you do not carefully follow all the words of this law, which are written in this book, and do not revere this glorious and awesome name – the LORD your God – [59] the

LORD will send fearful plagues on you and your descendants, harsh and prolonged disasters, and severe and lingering illnesses. ⁶⁰He will bring on you all the diseases of Egypt that you dreaded, and they will cling to you. ⁶¹The LORD will also bring on you every kind of sickness and disaster not recorded in this Book of the Law, until you are destroyed. ⁶²You who were as numerous as the stars in the sky will be left but few in number, because you did not obey the LORD your God. ⁶³Just as it pleased the LORD to make you prosper and increase in number, so it will please him to ruin and destroy you. You will be uprooted from the land you are entering to possess.

⁶⁴Then the LORD will scatter you among all nations, from one end of the earth to the other. There you will worship other gods – gods of wood and stone, which neither you nor your ancestors have known. ⁶⁵Among those nations you will find no repose, no resting place for the sole of your foot. There the LORD will give you an anxious mind, eyes weary with longing, and a despairing heart. ⁶⁶You will live in constant suspense, filled with dread both night and day, never sure of your life. ⁶⁷In the morning you will say, 'If only it were evening!' and in the evening, 'If only it were morning!' – because of the terror that will fill your hearts and the sights that your eyes will see. ⁶⁸The LORD will send you back in ships to Egypt on a journey I said you should never make again. There you will offer yourselves for sale to your enemies as male and female slaves, but no one will buy you.

▬ PSALM 45:13-17

¹³All glorious is the princess within her chamber;
  her gown is interwoven with gold.
¹⁴In embroidered garments she is led to the king;

her virgin companions follow her –
  those brought to be with her.
¹⁵Led in with joy and gladness,
  they enter the palace of the king.

¹⁶Your sons will take the place of your fathers;
  you will make them princes throughout the land.

¹⁷I will perpetuate your memory through all generations;
  therefore the nations will praise you for ever and ever.

▬ PROVERBS 11:9-11

⁹With their mouths the godless destroy their neighbours,
  but through knowledge the righteous escape.

¹⁰When the righteous prosper, the city rejoices;
  when the wicked perish, there are shouts of joy.

¹¹Through the blessing of the upright a city is exalted,
  but by the mouth of the wicked it is destroyed.

▬ LUKE 11:5-28

⁵Then Jesus said to them, 'Suppose you have a friend, and you go to him at midnight and say, "Friend, lend me three loaves of bread; ⁶a friend of mine on a journey has come to me, and I have no food to offer him." ⁷And suppose the one inside answers, "Don't bother me. The door is already locked, and my children and I are in bed. I can't get up and give you anything." ⁸I tell you, even though he will not get up

and give you the bread because of friendship, yet because of your shameless audacity he will surely get up and give you as much as you need.

⁹'So I say to you: ask and it will be given to you; seek and you will find; knock and the door will be opened to you. ¹⁰For everyone who asks receives; the one who seeks finds; and to the one who knocks, the door will be opened.

¹¹'Which of you fathers, if your son asks for a fish, will give him a snake instead? ¹²Or if he asks for an egg, will give him a scorpion? ¹³If you then, though you are evil, know how to give good gifts to your children, how much more will your Father in heaven give the Holy Spirit to those who ask him!'

¹⁴Jesus was driving out a demon that was mute. When the demon left, the man who had been mute spoke, and the crowd was amazed. ¹⁵But some of them said, 'By Beelzebul, the prince of demons, he is driving out demons.' ¹⁶Others tested him by asking for a sign from heaven.

¹⁷Jesus knew their thoughts and said to them: 'Any kingdom divided against itself will be ruined, and a house divided against itself will fall. ¹⁸If Satan is divided against himself, how can his kingdom stand? I say this because you claim that I drive out demons by Beelzebul. ¹⁹Now if I drive out demons by Beelzebul, by whom do your followers drive them out? So then, they will be your judges. ²⁰But if I drive out demons by the finger of God, then the kingdom of God has come upon you.

²¹'When a strong man, fully armed, guards his own house, his possessions are safe. ²²But when someone stronger attacks and overpowers him, he takes away the armour in which the man trusted and divides up his plunder.

²³'Whoever is not with me is against me, and whoever does not gather with me scatters.

²⁴'When an impure spirit comes out of a person, it goes through arid places seeking rest and does not find it. Then it says, "I will return to the house I left." ²⁵When it arrives, it finds the house swept clean and put in order. ²⁶Then it goes and takes seven other spirits more wicked than itself, and they go in and live there. And the final condition of that person is worse than the first.'

²⁷As Jesus was saying these things, a woman in the crowd called out, 'Blessed is the mother who gave you birth and nursed you.'

²⁸He replied, 'Blessed rather are those who hear the word of God and obey it.'

Proper Priorities

'... how much more will your Father in heaven give the Holy Spirit to those who ask him!' **Luke 11:13**

In the passage before us today, Jesus spends some time sharing with His hearers that God is both a Father and a Friend. It is vitally important that we realise that God wants to give us the Holy Spirit, for if we are not absolutely sure of this, then our asking will be shot through with indecision and uncertainty.

The great Archbishop William Temple said, 'We ask for the Holy Spirit, yet in the depth of our hearts we are not sure whether He wants to give it to us, and this one single doubt negates the object of the exercise.' So stop wishing to receive the Spirit in all His fullness and start expecting.

You can be positive in asking because God is positive in giving.

Bring the whole matter to a crisis. One great preacher said that 'the soul grows by a series of crises'. Make it a matter of priority to spend some time in prayer to receive more of His Spirit and become desperate over the issue. Treat it as if God dropped a letter into your mailbox this morning that said, 'I would like to see you as soon as possible over a matter of a very important gift I want to give you'.

If that happened, I wonder how you would handle your schedule over the next few days? Things you thought were top priority would become of secondary importance. When you decide to give God top priority in your plans, then, believe me, God will give you His top priority – the Holy Spirit.

PRAYER

Lord, I wonder, am I thirsty or desperate enough to make this matter of being filled with the Spirit my top priority? Help me to face up to the challenge – now. For Jesus' sake. Amen.

FURTHER STUDY

Matt. 6:1-15; 14:23;
2 Kings 4:33; Luke 6:12
• What did Jesus teach
  about prayer?
• What was His example?

April 16

▬ DEUTERONOMY 29:1–30:20

29 These are the terms of the covenant the LORD commanded Moses to make with the Israelites in Moab, in addition to the covenant he had made with them at Horeb.

² Moses summoned all the Israelites and said to them:

Your eyes have seen all that the LORD did in Egypt to Pharaoh, to all his officials and to all his land. ³ With your own eyes you saw those great trials, those signs and great wonders. ⁴ But to this day the LORD has not given you a mind that understands or eyes that see or ears that hear. ⁵ Yet the LORD says, 'During the forty years that I led you through the wilderness, your clothes did not wear out, nor did the sandals on your feet. ⁶ You ate no bread and drank no wine or other fermented drink. I did this so that you might know that I am the LORD your God.'

⁷ When you reached this place, Sihon king of Heshbon and Og king of Bashan came out to fight against us, but we defeated them. ⁸ We took their land and gave it as an inheritance to the Reubenites, the Gadites and the half-tribe of Manasseh.

⁹ Carefully follow the terms of this covenant, so that you may prosper in everything you do. ¹⁰ All of you are standing today in the presence of the LORD your God – your leaders and chief men, your elders and officials, and all the other men of Israel, ¹¹ together with your children and your wives, and the foreigners living in your camps who chop your wood and carry your water. ¹² You are standing here in order to enter into a covenant with the LORD your

God, a covenant the LORD is making with you this day and sealing with an oath, [13] to confirm you this day as his people, that he may be your God as he promised you and as he swore to your fathers, Abraham, Isaac and Jacob. [14] I am making this covenant, with its oath, not only with you [15] who are standing here with us today in the presence of the LORD our God but also with those who are not here today.

[16] You yourselves know how we lived in Egypt and how we passed through the countries on the way here. [17] You saw among them their detestable images and idols of wood and stone, of silver and gold. [18] Make sure there is no man or woman, clan or tribe among you today whose heart turns away from the LORD our God to go and worship the gods of those nations; make sure there is no root among you that produces such bitter poison.

[19] When such a person hears the words of this oath and they invoke a blessing on themselves, thinking, 'I will be safe, even though I persist in going my own way,' they will bring disaster on the watered land as well as the dry. [20] The LORD will never be willing to forgive them; his wrath and zeal will burn against them. All the curses written in this book will fall on them, and the LORD will blot out their names from under heaven. [21] The LORD will single them out from all the tribes of Israel for disaster, according to all the curses of the covenant written in this Book of the Law.

[22] Your children who follow you in later generations and foreigners who come from distant lands will see the calamities that have fallen on the land and the diseases with which the LORD has afflicted it. [23] The whole land will be a burning waste of salt and sulphur – nothing planted, nothing sprouting, no vegetation growing on it. It will be like the destruction of Sodom and Gomorrah, Admah and Zeboyim, which the LORD overthrew in fierce anger. [24] All the

nations will ask: 'Why has the LORD done this to this land? Why this fierce, burning anger?'

[25] And the answer will be: 'It is because this people abandoned the covenant of the LORD, the God of their ancestors, the covenant he made with them when he brought them out of Egypt. [26] They went off and worshipped other gods and bowed down to them, gods they did not know, gods he had not given them. [27] Therefore the LORD's anger burned against this land, so that he brought on it all the curses written in this book. [28] In furious anger and in great wrath the LORD uprooted them from their land and thrust them into another land, as it is now.'

[29] The secret things belong to the LORD our God, but the things revealed belong to us and to our children for ever, that we may follow all the words of this law.

30 When all these blessings and curses I have set before you come on you and you take them to heart wherever the LORD your God disperses you among the nations, [2] and when you and your children return to the LORD your God and obey him with all your heart and with all your soul according to everything I command you today, [3] then the LORD your God will restore your fortunes and have compassion on you and gather you again from all the nations where he scattered you. [4] Even if you have been banished to the most distant land under the heavens, from there the LORD your God will gather you and bring you back. [5] He will bring you to the land that belonged to your ancestors, and you will take possession of it. He will make you more prosperous and numerous than your ancestors. [6] The LORD your God will circumcise your hearts and the hearts of your descendants, so that you may love him with all your heart and with all your soul, and live. [7] The LORD your God will put all these curses on your enemies who hate and persecute you. [8] You will again

obey the LORD and follow all his commands I am giving you today. ⁹Then the LORD your God will make you most prosperous in all the work of your hands and in the fruit of your womb, the young of your livestock and the crops of your land. The LORD will again delight in you and make you prosperous, just as he delighted in your ancestors, ¹⁰if you obey the LORD your God and keep his commands and decrees that are written in this Book of the Law and turn to the LORD your God with all your heart and with all your soul.

¹¹Now what I am commanding you today is not too difficult for you or beyond your reach. ¹²It is not up in heaven, so that you have to ask, 'Who will ascend into heaven to get it and proclaim it to us so that we may obey it?' ¹³Nor is it beyond the sea, so that you have to ask, 'Who will cross the sea to get it and proclaim it to us so that we may obey it?' ¹⁴No, the word is very near you; it is in your mouth and in your heart so that you may obey it.

¹⁵See, I set before you today life and prosperity, death and destruction. ¹⁶For I command you today to love the LORD your God, to walk in obedience to him, and to keep his commands, decrees and laws; then you will live and increase, and the LORD your God will bless you in the land you are entering to possess.

¹⁷But if your heart turns away and you are not obedient, and if you are drawn away to bow down to other gods and worship them, ¹⁸I declare to you this day that you will certainly be destroyed. You will not live long in the land you are crossing the Jordan to enter and possess.

¹⁹This day I call the heavens and the earth as witnesses against you that I have set before you life and death, blessings and curses. Now choose life, so that you and your children may live ²⁰and that you may love the LORD your God, listen to his voice, and hold fast to him. For the LORD is your

life, and he will give you many years in the land he swore to give to your fathers, Abraham, Isaac and Jacob.

▬ PSALM 46:1-11

¹God is our refuge and strength,
    an ever-present help in trouble.
²Therefore we will not fear, though the
        earth give way
    and the mountains fall into the heart
        of the sea,
³though its waters roar and foam
    and the mountains quake with their
        surging.

⁴There is a river whose streams make glad
        the city of God,
    the holy place where the Most High
        dwells.
⁵God is within her, she will not fall;
    God will help her at break of day.
⁶Nations are in uproar, kingdoms fall;
    he lifts his voice, the earth melts.

⁷The LORD Almighty is with us;
    the God of Jacob is our fortress.

⁸Come and see what the LORD has done,
    the desolations he has brought on the
        earth.
⁹He makes wars cease
    to the ends of the earth.
    He breaks the bow and shatters the
        spear;
    he burns the shields with fire.
¹⁰He says, 'Be still, and know that I am
        God;
    I will be exalted among the nations,
    I will be exalted in the earth.'

¹¹The LORD Almighty is with us;
    the God of Jacob is our fortress.

■ PROVERBS 11:12-13

¹² Whoever derides their neighbour has no sense,
> but the one who has understanding holds their tongue.

¹³ A gossip betrays a confidence,
> but a trustworthy person keeps a secret.

■ LUKE 11:29-54

²⁹ As the crowds increased, Jesus said, 'This is a wicked generation. It asks for a sign, but none will be given it except the sign of Jonah. ³⁰ For as Jonah was a sign to the Ninevites, so also will the Son of Man be to this generation. ³¹ The Queen of the South will rise at the judgment with the people of this generation and condemn them, for she came from the ends of the earth to listen to Solomon's wisdom; and now something greater than Solomon is here. ³² The men of Nineveh will stand up at the judgment with this generation and condemn it, for they repented at the preaching of Jonah; and now something greater than Jonah is here.

³³ 'No one lights a lamp and puts it in a place where it will be hidden, or under a bowl. Instead they put it on its stand, so that those who come in may see the light. ³⁴ Your eye is the lamp of your body. When your eyes are healthy, your whole body also is full of light. But when they are unhealthy, your body also is full of darkness. ³⁵ See to it, then, that the light within you is not darkness. ³⁶ Therefore, if your whole body is full of light, and no part of it dark, it will be just as full of light as when a lamp shines its light on you.'

³⁷ When Jesus had finished speaking, a Pharisee invited him to eat with him; so he went in and reclined at the table. ³⁸ But the Pharisee was surprised when he noticed that Jesus did not first wash before the meal.

³⁹ Then the Lord said to him, 'Now then, you Pharisees clean the outside of the cup and dish, but inside you are full of greed and wickedness. ⁴⁰ You foolish people! Did not the one who made the outside make the inside also? ⁴¹ But now as for what is inside you – be generous to the poor, and everything will be clean for you.

⁴² 'Woe to you Pharisees, because you give God a tenth of your mint, rue and all other kinds of garden herbs, but you neglect justice and the love of God. You should have practised the latter without leaving the former undone.

⁴³ 'Woe to you Pharisees, because you love the most important seats in the synagogues and respectful greetings in the market-places.

⁴⁴ 'Woe to you, because you are like unmarked graves, which people walk over without knowing it.'

⁴⁵ One of the experts in the law answered him, 'Teacher, when you say these things, you insult us also.'

⁴⁶ Jesus replied, 'And you experts in the law, woe to you, because you load people down with burdens they can hardly carry, and you yourselves will not lift one finger to help them.

⁴⁷ 'Woe to you, because you build tombs for the prophets, and it was your ancestors who killed them. ⁴⁸ So you testify that you approve of what your ancestors did; they killed the prophets, and you build their tombs. ⁴⁹ Because of this, God in his wisdom said, "I will send them prophets and apostles, some of whom they will kill and others they will persecute." ⁵⁰ Therefore this generation will be held responsible for the blood of all the prophets that has been shed since the beginning of the world, ⁵¹ from the blood of Abel to the blood of Zechariah, who was killed between the altar and the sanctuary. Yes, I tell you, this generation will be held responsible for it all.

[52]'Woe to you experts in the law, because you have taken away the key to knowledge. You yourselves have not entered, and you have hindered those who were entering.'

[53]When Jesus went outside, the Pharisees and the teachers of the law began to oppose him fiercely and to besiege him with questions, [54]waiting to catch him in something he might say.

Why Fear to Meditate?

'Be still, and know that I am God ...' **Psalm 46:10**

In our age of increasing uncertainty, one sure way of staying on top is by the continuous activity of Scripture meditation. Many Christians, however, are afraid of the word 'meditation.' They view it as something to be practised by gurus, mystics, or the devotees of Eastern religions. They look askance at those who advocate its usefulness and power in the Christian life.

Scripture meditation in the Christian's life, however, is as different from that practised in Eastern religions as chalk is from cheese. Those who practise these other faiths advocate emptying the mind, while the Bible advocates filling it – with the truths of God's holy Word.

David Ray, an American author and pastor of a large church, says: 'I, for one, looked with suspicion on any Christian who advocated the practice of meditation. I thought to myself, "They are out of touch with reality. Give me action and work, lots of work. Let somebody else waste his time by staring at the end of his nose."' Then somebody introduced him to the principles of Scripture meditation. He was shown how to place a verse of Scripture on the tip of his spiritual tongue and slowly suck from it the refreshment it contained.

The verse he chose as the focus of his meditation was the one before us today: 'Be still, and know that I am God.' Take this text now and begin to focus on it. Place it on the tip of your spiritual tongue and draw from it hour by hour the spiritual refreshment that it contains. In your spare moments, pull it to the centre of your mind and begin to experience the joy of drawing from God's Word the power He has placed within it.

PRAYER

Father, I sense that here I am at the crux of the matter of spiritual freshness. Help me not to miss out on any of the lessons You are trying to teach me at this moment in my life. In Jesus' name. Amen.

FURTHER STUDY

1 Pet. 3:1-4; Job 37:14; Psa. 131:2; Isa. 32:17
• What is of great worth?
• What advice was given to Job?

April 17

■ DEUTERONOMY 31:1-29

31 Then Moses went out and spoke these words to all Israel: ²'I am now a hundred and twenty years old and I am no longer able to lead you. The LORD has said to me, "You shall not cross the Jordan." ³The LORD your God himself will cross over ahead of you. He will destroy these nations before you, and you will take possession of their land. Joshua also will cross over ahead of you, as the LORD said. ⁴And the LORD will do to them what he did to Sihon and Og, the kings of the Amorites, whom he destroyed along with their land. ⁵The LORD will deliver them to you, and you must do to them all that I have commanded you. ⁶Be strong and courageous. Do not be afraid or terrified because of them, for the LORD your God goes with you; he will never leave you nor forsake you.'

⁷Then Moses summoned Joshua and said to him in the presence of all Israel, 'Be strong and courageous, for you must go with this people into the land that the LORD swore to their ancestors to give them, and you must divide it among them as their inheritance. ⁸The LORD himself goes before you and will be with you; he will never leave you nor forsake you. Do not be afraid; do not be discouraged.'

⁹So Moses wrote down this law and gave it to the Levitical priests, who carried the ark of the covenant of the LORD, and to all the elders of Israel. ¹⁰Then Moses commanded them: 'At the end of every seven years, in the year for cancelling debts, during the Festival of Tabernacles, ¹¹when all Israel comes to appear before the LORD your God at the place he will choose, you shall read this law before them in their hearing.

¹²Assemble the people – men, women and children, and the foreigners residing in your towns – so that they can listen and learn to fear the LORD your God and follow carefully all the words of this law. ¹³Their children, who do not know this law, must hear it and learn to fear the LORD your God as long as you live in the land you are crossing the Jordan to possess.'

¹⁴The LORD said to Moses, 'Now the day of your death is near. Call Joshua and present yourselves at the tent of meeting, where I will commission him.' So Moses and Joshua came and presented themselves at the tent of meeting.

¹⁵Then the LORD appeared at the tent in a pillar of cloud, and the cloud stood over the entrance to the tent. ¹⁶And the LORD said to Moses: 'You are going to rest with your ancestors, and these people will soon prostitute themselves to the foreign gods of the land they are entering. They will forsake me and break the covenant I made with them. ¹⁷And in that day I will become angry with them and forsake them; I will hide my face from them, and they will be destroyed. Many disasters and calamities will come on them, and in that day they will ask, "Have not these disasters come on us because our God is not with us?" ¹⁸And I will certainly hide my face in that day because of all their wickedness in turning to other gods.

¹⁹'Now write down this song and teach it to the Israelites and make them sing it, so that it may be a witness for me against them. ²⁰When I have brought them into the land flowing with milk and honey, the land I promised on oath to their ancestors, and when they eat their fill and thrive, they will turn to other gods and worship them, rejecting me and breaking my covenant.

²¹ And when many disasters and calamities come on them, this song will testify against them, because it will not be forgotten by their descendants. I know what they are disposed to do, even before I bring them into the land I promised them on oath.' ²² So Moses wrote down this song that day and taught it to the Israelites.

²³ The LORD gave this command to Joshua son of Nun: 'Be strong and courageous, for you will bring the Israelites into the land I promised them on oath, and I myself will be with you.'

²⁴ After Moses finished writing in a book the words of this law from beginning to end, ²⁵ he gave this command to the Levites who carried the ark of the covenant of the LORD: ²⁶ 'Take this Book of the Law and place it beside the ark of the covenant of the LORD your God. There it will remain as a witness against you. ²⁷ For I know how rebellious and stiff-necked you are. If you have been rebellious against the LORD while I am still alive and with you, how much more will you rebel after I die! ²⁸ Assemble before me all the elders of your tribes and all your officials, so that I can speak these words in their hearing and call the heavens and the earth to testify against them. ²⁹ For I know that after my death you are sure to become utterly corrupt and to turn from the way I have commanded you. In days to come, disaster will fall on you because you will do evil in the sight of the LORD and arouse his anger by what your hands have made.'

▪ PSALM 47:1-9

¹ Clap your hands, all you nations;
    shout to God with cries of joy.

² For the LORD Most High is awesome,
    the great King over all the earth.

³ He subdued nations under us,

peoples under our feet.

⁴ He chose our inheritance for us,
    the pride of Jacob, whom he loved.

⁵ God has ascended amid shouts of joy,
    the LORD amid the sounding of
        trumpets.

⁶ Sing praises to God, sing praises;
    sing praises to our King, sing praises.

⁷ For God is the King of all the earth;
    sing to him a psalm of praise.

⁸ God reigns over the nations;
    God is seated on his holy throne.

⁹ The nobles of the nations assemble
    as the people of the God of Abraham,
    for the kings of the earth belong to God;
        he is greatly exalted.

▪ PROVERBS 11:14-15

¹⁴ For lack of guidance a nation falls,
    but victory is won through many
        advisors.

¹⁵ Whoever puts up security for a stranger
        will surely suffer,
    but whoever refuses to shake hands in
        pledge is safe.

▪ LUKE 12:1-21

12 Meanwhile, when a crowd of many thousands had gathered, so that they were trampling on one another, Jesus began to speak first to his disciples, saying: 'Be on your guard against the yeast of the Pharisees, which is hypocrisy. ² There is nothing concealed that will not be disclosed, or hidden that will not be made known. ³ What you have said in the dark will be heard in the daylight, and what you have whispered in the ear in the inner rooms will be proclaimed from the roofs.

⁴'I tell you, my friends, do not be afraid of those who kill the body and after that can do no more. ⁵But I will show you whom you should fear: fear him who, after your body has been killed, has authority to throw you into hell. Yes, I tell you, fear him. ⁶Are not five sparrows sold for two pennies? Yet not one of them is forgotten by God. ⁷Indeed, the very hairs of your head are all numbered. Don't be afraid; you are worth more than many sparrows.

⁸'I tell you, whoever publicly acknowledges me before others, the Son of Man will also acknowledge before the angels of God. ⁹But whoever disowns me before others will be disowned before the angels of God. ¹⁰And everyone who speaks a word against the Son of Man will be forgiven, but anyone who blasphemes against the Holy Spirit will not be forgiven.

¹¹'When you are brought before synagogues, rulers and authorities, do not worry about how you will defend yourselves or what you will say, ¹²for the Holy Spirit will teach you at that time what you should say.'

¹³Someone in the crowd said to him, 'Teacher, tell my brother to divide the inheritance with me.'

¹⁴Jesus replied, 'Man, who appointed me a judge or an arbiter between you?' ¹⁵Then he said to them, 'Watch out! Be on your guard against all kinds of greed; life does not consist in an abundance of possessions.'

¹⁶And he told them this parable: 'The ground of a certain rich man yielded an abundant harvest. ¹⁷He thought to himself, "What shall I do? I have no place to store my crops."

¹⁸'Then he said, "This is what I'll do. I will tear down my barns and build bigger ones, and there I will store my surplus grain. ¹⁹And I'll say to myself, 'You have plenty of grain laid up for many years. Take life easy; eat, drink and be merry.' "

²⁰'But God said to him, "You fool! This very night your life will be demanded from you. Then who will get what you have prepared for yourself?"

²¹'This is how it will be with whoever stores up things for themselves but is not rich towards God.'

Jittery Theologians

'But God said to him, "You fool!" This very night your life will be demanded from you.' **Luke 12:20**

Why is it that so many in our day and age are attracted to the notion of a God who is impersonal? New Age theories seem to be infiltrating all parts of society in almost every country of the world.

I think there is a very subtle reason why men and women prefer to think of God as a power rather than as a person. If God is merely a power, or a formless life-force flowing through the universe, He can make no demands. One is not challenged to relate to an energy in the same way that one is challenged to relate to a person. When we believe God is a Person, the next question we have to face is, 'How do I relate to Him?' It is the idea of meeting a personal God which causes men and women to tremble.

But deep down in every human heart, placed there by the Almighty, is a conviction that a personal God exists. We have all been made in His image, and His stamp is upon us whether we like it or not. In reality there are very few atheists; most people believe in some kind of God.

Someone has described an atheist as 'a theologian with the jitters.' A good way of dealing with those jitters is to expunge from the heart the idea that God may be personal and that one might be accountable to Him. Better a life-force or a celestial energy – a power that can be tapped – rather than a Person one might some day have to meet. How foolish it all is – settling for short-term comfort but facing eternal loss.

PRAYER

Father, I am saddened when I realise how so many want to run from You when their best interests lie in running to You. Draw many to You this very day, dear Lord. In Jesus' name. Amen.

FURTHER STUDY

Gen. 1:26-30; 5:1; 1 Cor. 11:7; James 3:9; Eccl. 3:11
- What are the implications of being created in God's image?
- What has God set within us?

April 18

◼ DEUTERONOMY 31:30 –32:52

³⁰ And Moses recited the words of this song from beginning to end in the hearing of the whole assembly of Israel:

32 Listen, you heavens, and I will speak;
hear, you earth, the words of my mouth.
² Let my teaching fall like rain
and my words descend like dew,
like showers on new grass,
like abundant rain on tender plants.

³ I will proclaim the name of the LORD.
Oh, praise the greatness of our God!
⁴ He is the Rock, his works are perfect,
and all his ways are just.
A faithful God who does no wrong,
upright and just is he.

⁵ They are corrupt and not his children;
to their shame they are a warped
and crooked generation.
⁶ Is this the way you repay the LORD,
you foolish and unwise people?
Is he not your Father, your Creator,
who made you and formed you?

⁷ Remember the days of old;
consider the generations long past.
Ask your father and he will tell you,
your elders, and they will explain to
you.
⁸ When the Most High gave the nations
their inheritance,
when he divided all mankind,
he set up boundaries for the peoples
according to the number of the sons
of Israel.
⁹ For the LORD's portion is his people,
Jacob his allotted inheritance.

¹⁰ In a desert land he found him,

in a barren and howling waste.
He shielded him and cared for him;
   he guarded him as the apple of his
     eye,
[11] like an eagle that stirs up its nest
   and hovers over its young,
that spreads its wings to catch them
   and carries them on its pinions.
[12] The LORD alone led him;
   no foreign god was with him.

[13] He made him ride on the heights of the
    land
   and fed him with the fruit of the
     fields.
He nourished him with honey from
    the rock,
   and with oil from the flinty crag,
[14] with curds and milk from herd and
    flock
   and with fattened lambs and goats,
with choice rams of Bashan
   and the finest grains of wheat.
You drank the foaming blood of the
    grape.

[15] Jeshurun grew fat and kicked;
   filled with food, they became heavy
    and sleek.
They abandoned the God who made
    them
   and rejected the Rock their Saviour.
[16] They made him jealous with their
    foreign gods
   and angered him with their
    detestable idols.
[17] They sacrificed to false gods, which
    are not God –
   gods they had not known,
   gods that recently appeared,
   gods your ancestors did not fear.
[18] You deserted the Rock, who fathered
    you;
   you forgot the God who gave you
    birth.

[19] The LORD saw this and rejected them
   because he was angered by his sons
    and daughters.
[20] 'I will hide my face from them,' he
    said,
   'and see what their end will be;
for they are a perverse generation,
   children who are unfaithful.
[21] They made me jealous by what is no
    god
   and angered me with their
    worthless idols.
I will make them envious by those
   who are not a people;
I will make them angry by a nation
   that has no understanding.
[22] For a fire will be kindled by my wrath,
   one that burns down to the realm of
    the dead below.
It will devour the earth and its
    harvests
   and set on fire the foundations of
    the mountains.

[23] 'I will heap calamities on them
   and expend my arrows against
    them.
[24] I will send wasting famine against
    them,
   consuming pestilence and deadly
    plague;
I will send against them the fangs of
    wild beasts,
   the venom of vipers that glide in the
    dust.
[25] In the street the sword will make them
    childless;
   in their homes terror will reign.
The young men and young women
    will perish,
   the infants and those with grey hair.
[26] I said I would scatter them
   and erase their name from human
    memory,
[27] but I dreaded the taunt of the enemy,
   lest the adversary misunderstand

and say, "Our hand has triumphed;
the LORD has not done all this."'

²⁸ They are a nation without sense,
there is no discernment in them.
²⁹ If only they were wise and would
understand this
and discern what their end will be!
³⁰ How could one man chase a thousand,
or two put ten thousand to flight,
unless their Rock had sold them,
unless the LORD had given them up?
³¹ For their rock is not like our Rock,
as even our enemies concede.
³² Their vine comes from the vine of
Sodom
and from the fields of Gomorrah.
Their grapes are filled with poison,
and their clusters with bitterness.
³³ Their wine is the venom of serpents,
the deadly poison of cobras.

³⁴ 'Have I not kept this in reserve
and sealed it in my vaults?
³⁵ It is mine to avenge; I will repay.
In due time their foot will slip;
their day of disaster is near
and their doom rushes upon them.'

³⁶ The LORD will vindicate his people
and relent concerning his servants
when he sees their strength is gone
and no one is left, slave or free.
³⁷ He will say: 'Now where are their gods,
the rock they took refuge in,
³⁸ the gods who ate the fat of their
sacrifices
and drank the wine of their drink
offerings?
Let them rise up to help you!
Let them give you shelter!

³⁹ 'See now that I myself am he!
There is no god besides me.
I put to death and I bring to life,
I have wounded and I will heal,

and no one can deliver out of my
hand.
⁴⁰ I lift my hand to heaven and solemnly
swear:
As surely as I live for ever,
⁴¹ when I sharpen my flashing sword
and my hand grasps it in judgment,
I will take vengeance on my
adversaries
and repay those who hate me.
⁴² I will make my arrows drunk with
blood,
while my sword devours flesh:
the blood of the slain and the captives,
the heads of the enemy leaders.'

⁴³ Rejoice, you nations, with his people,
for he will avenge the blood of his
servants;
he will take vengeance on his enemies
and make atonement for his land
and people.

⁴⁴ Moses came with Joshua son of Nun and spoke all the words of this song in the hearing of the people. ⁴⁵ When Moses had finished reciting all these words to all Israel, ⁴⁶ he said to them, 'Take to heart all the words I have solemnly declared to you this day, so that you may command your children to obey carefully all the words of this law. ⁴⁷ They are not just idle words for you – they are your life. By them you will live long in the land you are crossing the Jordan to possess.'

⁴⁸ On that same day the LORD told Moses, ⁴⁹ 'Go up into the Abarim Range to Mount Nebo in Moab, opposite Jericho, and view Canaan, the land I am giving the Israelites as their own possession. ⁵⁰ There on the mountain that you have climbed you will die and be gathered to your people, just as your brother Aaron died on Mount Hor and was gathered to his people. ⁵¹ This is because both of you broke faith with me in the presence of the Israelites at the waters

of Meribah Kadesh in the Desert of Zin and because you did not uphold my holiness among the Israelites. ⁵²Therefore, you will see the land only from a distance; you will not enter the land I am giving to the people of Israel.'

PSALM 48:1-7

¹Great is the LORD, and most worthy of praise,
  in the city of our God, his holy mountain.

²Beautiful in its loftiness,
  the joy of the whole earth,
like the heights of Zaphon is Mount Zion,
  the city of the Great King.
³God is in her citadels;
  he has shown himself to be her fortress.

⁴When the kings joined forces,
  when they advanced together,
⁵they saw her and were astounded;
  they fled in terror.
⁶Trembling seized them there,
  pain like that of a woman in labour.
⁷You destroyed them like ships of Tarshish
  shattered by an east wind.

PROVERBS 11:16-18

¹⁶A kind-hearted woman gains honour,
  but ruthless men gain only wealth.

¹⁷Those who are kind benefit themselves,
  but the cruel bring ruin on themselves.

¹⁸A wicked person earns deceptive wages,
  but the one who sows righteousness reaps a sure reward.

LUKE 12:22-40

²²Then Jesus said to his disciples: 'Therefore I tell you, do not worry about your life, what you will eat; or about your body, what you will wear. ²³For life is more than food, and the body more than clothes. ²⁴Consider the ravens: they do not sow or reap, they have no storeroom or barn; yet God feeds them. And how much more valuable you are than birds! ²⁵Who of you by worrying can add a single hour to your life? ²⁶Since you cannot do this very little thing, why do you worry about the rest?

²⁷'Consider how the wild flowers grow. They do not labour or spin. Yet I tell you, not even Solomon in all his splendour was dressed like one of these. ²⁸If that is how God clothes the grass of the field, which is here today, and tomorrow is thrown into the fire, how much more will he clothe you – you of little faith! ²⁹And do not set your heart on what you will eat or drink; do not worry about it. ³⁰For the pagan world runs after all such things, and your Father knows that you need them. ³¹But seek his kingdom, and these things will be given to you as well.

³²'Do not be afraid, little flock, for your Father has been pleased to give you the kingdom. ³³Sell your possessions and give to the poor. Provide purses for yourselves that will not wear out, a treasure in heaven that will never fail, where no thief comes near and no moth destroys. ³⁴For where your treasure is, there your heart will be also.

³⁵'Be dressed ready for service and keep your lamps burning, ³⁶like servants waiting for their master to return from a wedding banquet, so that when he comes and knocks they can immediately open the door for him. ³⁷It will be good for those servants whose master finds them watching when he comes. Truly I tell you, he will dress himself to serve, will make them recline at the table and will come and wait on

them. [38] It will be good for those servants whose master finds them ready, even if he comes in the middle of the night or towards daybreak. [39] But understand this: if the owner of the house had known at what hour the thief was coming, he would not have let his house be broken into. [40] You also must be ready, because the Son of Man will come at an hour when you do not expect him.'

No Blemish in God

'... I will take vengeance on my adversaries and repay those who hate me.' **Deuteronomy 32:41**

There is one aspect of God's character that for some reason many see as a blotch or blemish in the divine nature. I refer to the matter of God's wrath. Though the subject may be missing from many modern-day pulpits, it is not missing from the Bible. If you look up in a Bible concordance all the texts that refer to the wrath, anger, or the severity of God, you will find that there are more references to these than there are to His love, graciousness, or tenderness. A proper study of God can never be complete unless consideration is given to the fact that God is not only a God of love but a God of wrath and anger also.

I remember in the early days of my Christian experience that whenever I heard any reference to the wrath of God, I would feel a deep resentment arise within me, and instead of regarding this aspect of God's nature with delight, I looked upon it with disdain. Later, however, when I came to understand it and saw it in its proper light - as something to rejoice in rather than to be resented - I found my love for God and my awe of God swell to new proportions.

In his book *The Attributes of God*, Arthur W. Pink describes the wrath of God as the 'eternal detestation of all unrighteousness ... the displeasure and indignation of Divine equity against evil ... the holiness of God stirred into activity against sin.' Never view the wrath of God as a moral blemish or a blotch on His character. It would be a blemish if wrath were absent from Him.

PRAYER

Father, I would face all reality - even those aspects that do not fit into my preconceived ideas. Help me not to balk at the idea that You are a God of wrath as well as a God of wonder. In Jesus' name I pray. Amen.

FURTHER STUDY

2 Kings 22:1-13; Psa. 90:11
- Why did God's anger burn?
- What did the psalmist say about God's wrath?

April 19

■ **DEUTERONOMY**
33:1–34:12

33 This is the blessing that Moses the man of God pronounced on the Israelites before his death. [2] He said:

'The LORD came from Sinai
    and dawned over them from Seir;
he shone forth from Mount Paran.
He came with myriads of holy ones
    from the south, from his mountain
      slopes.
[3] Surely it is you who love the people;
    all the holy ones are in your hand.
At your feet they all bow down,
    and from you receive instruction,
[4] the law that Moses gave us,
    the possession of the assembly of
      Jacob.
[5] He was king over Jeshurun
    when the leaders of the people
      assembled,
    along with the tribes of Israel.

[6] 'Let Reuben live and not die,
    nor his people be few.'

[7] And this he said about Judah:

'Hear, LORD, the cry of Judah;
    bring him to his people.
With his own hands he defends his
      cause.
    Oh, be his help against his foes!'

[8] About Levi he said:

'Your Thummim and Urim belong
    to your faithful servant.
You tested him at Massah;

you contended with him at the
      waters of Meribah.
[9] He said of his father and mother,
    "I have no regard for them."
He did not recognise his brothers
    or acknowledge his own children,
but he watched over your word
    and guarded your covenant.
[10] He teaches your precepts to Jacob
    and your law to Israel.
He offers incense before you
    and whole burnt offerings on your
      altar.
[11] Bless all his skills, LORD,
    and be pleased with the work of his
      hands.
Strike down those who rise against
      him,
    his foes till they rise no more.'

[12] About Benjamin he said:

'Let the beloved of the LORD rest secure
    in him,
for he shields him all day long,
    and the one the LORD loves rests
      between his shoulders.'

[13] About Joseph he said:

'May the LORD bless his land
    with the precious dew from heaven
      above
    and with the deep waters that lie
      below;
[14] with the best the sun brings forth
    and the finest the moon can yield;
[15] with the choicest gifts of the ancient
      mountains
    and the fruitfulness of the
      everlasting hills;

[16] with the best gifts of the earth and its
fulness
and the favour of him who dwelt in
the burning bush.
Let all these rest on the head of Joseph,
on the brow of the prince among his
brothers.
[17] In majesty he is like a firstborn bull;
his horns are the horns of a wild ox.
With them he will gore the nations,
even those at the ends of the earth.
Such are the ten thousands of Ephraim;
such are the thousands of Manasseh.'

[18] About Zebulun he said:

'Rejoice, Zebulun, in your going out,
and you, Issachar, in your tents.
[19] They will summon peoples to the
mountain
and there offer the sacrifices of the
righteous;
they will feast on the abundance of the
seas,
on the treasures hidden in the sand.'

[20] About Gad he said:

'Blessed is he who enlarges Gad's
domain!
Gad lives there like a lion,
tearing at arm or head.
[21] He chose the best land for himself;
the leader's portion was kept for him.
When the heads of the people
assembled,
he carried out the LORD's righteous
will,
and his judgments concerning Israel.'

[22] About Dan he said:

'Dan is a lion's cub,
springing out of Bashan.'

[23] About Naphtali he said:

'Naphtali is abounding with the favour
of the LORD
and is full of his blessing;
he will inherit southward to the lake.'

[24] About Asher he said:

'Most blessed of sons is Asher;
let him be favoured by his brothers,
and let him bathe his feet in oil.
[25] The bolts of your gates will be iron and
bronze,
and your strength will equal your
days.

[26] 'There is no one like the God of
Jeshurun,
who rides across the heavens to help
you
and on the clouds in his majesty.
[27] The eternal God is your refuge,
and underneath are the everlasting
arms.
He will drive out your enemies before
you,
saying, "Destroy them!"
[28] So Israel will live in safety;
Jacob will dwell secure
in a land of grain and new wine,
where the heavens drop dew.
[29] Blessed are you, Israel!
Who is like you,
a people saved by the LORD?
He is your shield and helper
and your glorious sword.
Your enemies will cower before you,
and you will tread on their heights.'

34

Then Moses climbed Mount Nebo
from the plains of Moab to the top
of Pisgah, opposite Jericho. There the Lord
showed him the whole land – from Gilead to Dan, [2] all of Naphtali, the territory of
Ephraim and Manasseh, all the land of Judah as far as the Mediterranean Sea, [3] the
Negev and the whole region from the Valley

of Jericho, the City of Palms, as far as Zoar. ⁴Then the Lord said to him, 'This is the land I promised on oath to Abraham, Isaac and Jacob when I said, "I will give it to your descendants." I have let you see it with your eyes, but you will not cross over into it.'

⁵And Moses the servant of the LORD died there in Moab, as the LORD had said. ⁶He buried him in Moab, in the valley opposite Beth Peor, but to this day no one knows where his grave is. ⁷Moses was a hundred and twenty years old when he died, yet his eyes were not weak nor his strength gone. ⁸The Israelites grieved for Moses in the plains of Moab thirty days, until the time of weeping and mourning was over.

⁹Now Joshua son of Nun was filled with the spirit of wisdom because Moses had laid his hands on him. So the Israelites listened to him and did what the LORD had commanded Moses.

¹⁰Since then, no prophet has risen in Israel like Moses, whom the LORD knew face to face, ¹¹who did all those signs and wonders the LORD sent him to do in Egypt – to Pharaoh and to all his officials and to his whole land. ¹²For no one has ever shown the mighty power or performed the awesome deeds that Moses did in the sight of all Israel.

■ PSALM 48:8-14

⁸As we have heard,
   so we have seen
in the city of the LORD Almighty,
   in the city of our God:
God makes her secure
   for ever.

⁹Within your temple, O God,
   we meditate on your unfailing love.
¹⁰Like your name, O God,
   your praise reaches to the ends of the earth;

your right hand is filled with
   righteousness.
¹¹Mount Zion rejoices,
   the villages of Judah are glad
   because of your judgments.

¹²Walk about Zion, go round her,
   count her towers,
¹³consider well her ramparts,
   view her citadels,
that you may tell of them
   to the next generation.

¹⁴For this God is our God for ever and ever;
   he will be our guide even to the end.

■ PROVERBS 11:19-21

¹⁹Truly the righteous attain life,
   but whoever pursues evil finds death.

²⁰The LORD detests those whose hearts are
      perverse,
   but he delights in those whose ways
      are blameless.

²¹Be sure of this: the wicked will not go
      unpunished,
   but those who are righteous will go
      free.

■ LUKE 12:41-59

⁴¹Peter asked, 'Lord, are you telling this parable to us, or to everyone?'

⁴²The Lord answered, 'Who then is the faithful and wise manager, whom the master puts in charge of his servants to give them their food allowance at the proper time? ⁴³It will be good for that servant whom the master finds doing so when he returns. ⁴⁴Truly I tell you, he will put him in charge of all his possessions. ⁴⁵But suppose the servant says to himself, "My master is

taking a long time in coming," and he then begins to beat the other servants, both men and women, and to eat and drink and get drunk. [46]The master of that servant will come on a day when he does not expect him and at an hour he is not aware of. He will cut him to pieces and assign him a place with the unbelievers.

[47]'The servant who knows the master's will and does not get ready or does not do what the master wants will be beaten with many blows. [48]But the one who does not know and does things deserving punishment will be beaten with few blows. From everyone who has been given much, much will be demanded; and from the one who has been entrusted with much, much more will be asked.

[49]'I have come to bring fire on the earth, and how I wish it were already kindled! [50]But I have a baptism to undergo, and what constraint I am under until it is completed! [51]Do you think I came to bring peace on earth? No, I tell you, but division. [52]From now on there will be five in one family divided against each other, three against two and two against three. [53]They will be divided, father against son and son against father, mother against daughter and daughter against mother, mother-in-law against daughter-in-law and daughter-in-law against mother-in-law.'

[54]He said to the crowd: 'When you see a cloud rising in the west, immediately you say, "It's going to rain," and it does. [55]And when the south wind blows, you say, "It's going to be hot," and it is. [56]Hypocrites! You know how to interpret the appearance of the earth and the sky. How is it that you don't know how to interpret this present time?

[57]'Why don't you judge for yourselves what is right? [58]As you are going with your adversary to the magistrate, try hard to be reconciled on the way, or your adversary may drag you off to the judge, and the judge turn you over to the officer, and the officer throw you into prison. [59]I tell you, you will not get out until you have paid the last penny.'

Pluralism's Persuasiveness

'For this God is our God for ever and ever; he will be our guide even to the end.' **Psalm 48:14**

The argument presented by pluralists that Christians must view their religion as one among many, and Jesus as only one Saviour among others, must be firmly resisted. It may sound arrogant to say so but it is nevertheless a fact that Christianity is unique, absolute, definitive, ultimate, and final.

Critics of the uniqueness of Christianity can be very persuasive. 'The world is under great threat,' they tell us, 'because of environmental pollution, economic injustice, and many other problems. Nothing that divides us, including our religions, should be considered as important as the need to live together in harmony.' Another emphasis is on the need to study comparative faiths. There is a sense in which understanding what other people believe is useful, but not until the claims of Christianity are seen to be definitive and final. Christianity is not a comparative religion; it reveals God's one and only way of entering into a personal relationship with Him.

Galatians 2:20 in the *Amplified Bible* reads: 'The life I now live ... I live by faith - by adherence to and reliance on and [complete] trust - in the Son of God, Who loved me and gave Himself up for me.' Bishop Lesslie Newbigin put it well: 'If it is really true, as it is, that "the Son of God loved me and gave Himself up for me," how can I agree that this amazing act of matchless grace should merely become part of a syllabus for the "comparative study of religions"?' Christ is not first in a class; He occupies the category all by Himself.

PRAYER

My Father and my God, may the Person of Your Son become as real and as precious to me as He is to You. And teach me more about Him so that I can make clear to others why He is a Saviour beyond compare. For His own dear name's sake. Amen.

FURTHER STUDY

Acts 4:1-12; 1 Tim. 2:1-6; 1 Cor. 3:11

• What did Peter declare to the Sanhedrin?
• What did Paul declare to Timothy?

April 20

■ JOSHUA 1:1–3:17

1 After the death of Moses the servant of the LORD, the LORD said to Joshua son of Nun, Moses' assistant: ² 'Moses my servant is dead. Now then, you and all these people, get ready to cross the River Jordan into the land I am about to give to them – to the Israelites. ³ I will give you every place where you set your foot, as I promised Moses. ⁴ Your territory will extend from the desert to Lebanon, and from the great river, the Euphrates – all the Hittite country – to the Mediterranean Sea in the west. ⁵ No one will be able to stand against you all the days of your life. As I was with Moses, so I will be with you; I will never leave you nor forsake you. ⁶ Be strong and courageous, because you will lead these people to inherit the land I swore to their ancestors to give them.

⁷ 'Be strong and very courageous. Be careful to obey all the law my servant Moses gave you; do not turn from it to the right or to the left, that you may be successful wherever you go. ⁸ Keep this Book of the Law always on your lips; meditate on it day and night, so that you may be careful to do everything written in it. Then you will be prosperous and successful. ⁹ Have I not commanded you? Be strong and courageous. Do not be afraid; do not be discouraged, for the LORD your God will be with you wherever you go.'

¹⁰ So Joshua ordered the officers of the people: ¹¹ 'Go through the camp and tell the people, "Get your provisions ready. Three days from now you will cross the Jordan here to go in and take possession of the land the LORD your God is giving you for your own."'

¹² But to the Reubenites, the Gadites and the half-tribe of Manasseh, Joshua said, ¹³ 'Remember the command that Moses the servant of the LORD gave you after he said, "The LORD your God will give you rest by giving you this land." ¹⁴ Your wives, your

children and your livestock may stay in the land that Moses gave you east of the Jordan, but all your fighting men, ready for battle, must cross over ahead of your fellow Israelites. You are to help them ¹⁵ until the LORD gives them rest, as he has done for you, and until they too have taken possession of the land that the LORD your God is giving them. After that, you may go back and occupy your own land, which Moses the servant of the LORD gave you east of the Jordan towards the sunrise.'

¹⁶ Then they answered Joshua, 'Whatever you have commanded us we will do, and wherever you send us we will go. ¹⁷ Just as we fully obeyed Moses, so we will obey you. Only may the LORD your God be with you as he was with Moses. ¹⁸ Whoever rebels against your word and does not obey it, whatever you may command them, will be put to death. Only be strong and courageous!'

2 Then Joshua son of Nun secretly sent two spies from Shittim. 'Go, look over the land,' he said, 'especially Jericho.' So they went and entered the house of a prostitute named Rahab and stayed there.

² The king of Jericho was told, 'Look, some of the Israelites have come here tonight to spy out the land.' ³ So the king of Jericho sent this message to Rahab: 'Bring out the men who came to you and entered your house, because they have come to spy out the whole land.'

⁴ But the woman had taken the two men and hidden them. She said, 'Yes, the men came to me, but I did not know where they had come from. ⁵ At dusk, when it was time to close the city gate, they left. I don't know which way they went. Go after them quickly. You may catch up with them.' ⁶ (But she had taken them up to the roof and hidden them under the stalks of flax she had laid out on the roof.) ⁷ So the men set out in pursuit of the spies on the road that leads to the fords of the Jordan, and as soon as the pursuers

had gone out, the gate was shut.

⁸ Before the spies lay down for the night, she went up on the roof ⁹ and said to them, 'I know that the LORD has given this land to you and that a great fear of you has fallen on us, so that all who live in this country are melting in fear because of you. ¹⁰ We have heard how the LORD dried up the water of the Red Sea for you when you came out of Egypt, and what you did to Sihon and Og, the two kings of the Amorites east of the Jordan, whom you completely destroyed. ¹¹ When we heard of it, our hearts sank and everyone's courage failed because of you, for the LORD your God is God in heaven above and on the earth below.

¹² 'Now then, please swear to me by the LORD that you will show kindness to my family, because I have shown kindness to you. Give me a sure sign ¹³ that you will spare the lives of my father and mother, my brothers and sisters, and all who belong to them – and that you will save us from death.'

¹⁴ 'Our lives for your lives!' the men assured her. 'If you don't tell what we are doing, we will treat you kindly and faithfully when the LORD gives us the land.'

¹⁵ So she let them down by a rope through the window, for the house she lived in was part of the city wall. ¹⁶ She said to them, 'Go to the hills so that the pursuers will not find you. Hide yourselves there for three days until they return, and then go on your way.'

¹⁷ Now the men had said to her, 'This oath you made us swear will not be binding on us ¹⁸ unless, when we enter the land, you have tied this scarlet cord in the window through which you let us down, and unless you have brought your father and mother, your brothers and all your family into your house. ¹⁹ If any of them go outside your house into the street, their blood will be on their own heads; we will not be responsible. As for those who are in the house with you, their blood will be on our head if a hand is

laid on them. ²⁰ But if you tell what we are doing, we will be released from the oath you made us swear.'

²¹ 'Agreed,' she replied. 'Let it be as you say.'

So she sent them away, and they departed. And she tied the scarlet cord in the window.

²² When they left, they went into the hills and stayed there three days, until the pursuers had searched all along the road and returned without finding them. ²³ Then the two men started back. They went down out of the hills, forded the river and came to Joshua son of Nun and told him everything that had happened to them. ²⁴ They said to Joshua, 'The LORD has surely given the whole land into our hands; all the people are melting in fear because of us.'

3 Early in the morning Joshua and all the Israelites set out from Shittim and went to the Jordan, where they camped before crossing over. ² After three days the officers went throughout the camp, ³ giving orders to the people: 'When you see the ark of the covenant of the LORD your God, and the Levitical priests carrying it, you are to move out from your positions and follow it. ⁴ Then you will know which way to go, since you have never been this way before. But keep a distance of about two thousand cubits between you and the ark; do not go near it.'

⁵ Joshua told the people, 'Consecrate yourselves, for tomorrow the LORD will do amazing things among you.'

⁶ Joshua said to the priests, 'Take up the ark of the covenant and pass on ahead of the people.' So they took it up and went ahead of them.

⁷ And the LORD said to Joshua, 'Today I will begin to exalt you in the eyes of all Israel, so that they may know that I am with you as I was with Moses. ⁸ Tell the priests who carry the ark of the covenant: "When you reach the edge of the Jordan's waters, go and stand in the river."'

⁹ Joshua said to the Israelites, 'Come here and listen to the words of the LORD your God. ¹⁰ This is how you will know that the living God is among you and that he will certainly drive out before you the Canaanites, Hittites, Hivites, Perizzites, Girgashites, Amorites and Jebusites. ¹¹ See, the ark of the covenant of the Lord of all the earth will go into the Jordan ahead of you. ¹² Now then, choose twelve men from the tribes of Israel, one from each tribe. ¹³ And as soon as the priests who carry the ark of the LORD – the Lord of all the earth – set foot in the Jordan, its waters flowing downstream will be cut off and stand up in a heap.'

¹⁴ So when the people broke camp to cross the Jordan, the priests carrying the ark of the covenant went ahead of them. ¹⁵ Now the Jordan is in flood all during harvest. Yet as soon as the priests who carried the ark reached the Jordan and their feet touched the water's edge, ¹⁶ the water from upstream stopped flowing. It piled up in a heap a great distance away, at a town called Adam in the vicinity of Zarethan, while the water flowing down to the Sea of the Arabah (that is, the Dead Sea) was completely cut off. So the people crossed over opposite Jericho. ¹⁷ The priests who carried the ark of the covenant of the LORD stopped in the middle of the Jordan and stood on dry ground, while all Israel passed by until the whole nation had completed the crossing on dry ground.

▬ PSALM 49:1-9

¹ Hear this, all you peoples;
    listen, all who live in this world,
² both low and high,
    rich and poor alike:
³ My mouth will speak words of wisdom;
    the meditation of my heart will give
        you understanding.
⁴ I will turn my ear to a proverb;

with the harp I will expound my riddle:

5 Why should I fear when evil days come,
   when wicked deceivers surround me –
6 those who trust in their wealth
   and boast of their great riches?
7 No one can redeem the life of another
   or give to God a ransom for them –
8 the ransom for a life is costly,
   no payment is ever enough –
9 so that they should live on for ever
   and not see decay.

■ PROVERBS 11:22-23

22 Like a gold ring in a pig's snout
   is a beautiful woman who shows no
    discretion.

23 The desire of the righteous ends only in
    good,
   but the hope of the wicked only in
    wrath.

■ LUKE 13:1-21

13 Now there were some present at that time who told Jesus about the Galileans whose blood Pilate had mixed with their sacrifices. 2 Jesus answered, 'Do you think that these Galileans were worse sinners than all the other Galileans because they suffered this way? 3 I tell you, no! But unless you repent, you too will all perish. 4 Or those eighteen who died when the tower in Siloam fell on them – do you think they were more guilty than all the others living in Jerusalem? 5 I tell you, no! But unless you repent, you too will all perish.'

6 Then he told this parable: 'A man had a fig-tree growing in his vineyard, and he went to look for fruit on it but did not find any. 7 So he said to the man who took care of the vineyard, "For three years now I've been coming to look for fruit on this fig-tree and haven't found any. Cut it down! Why should it use up the soil?"

8 ' "Sir," the man replied, "leave it alone for one more year, and I'll dig round it and fertilise it. 9 If it bears fruit next year, fine! If not, then cut it down." '

10 On a Sabbath Jesus was teaching in one of the synagogues, 11 and a woman was there who had been crippled by a spirit for eighteen years. She was bent over and could not straighten up at all. 12 When Jesus saw her, he called her forward and said to her, 'Woman, you are set free from your infirmity.' 13 Then he put his hands on her, and immediately she straightened up and praised God.

14 Indignant because Jesus had healed on the Sabbath, the synagogue leader said to the people, 'There are six days for work. So come and be healed on those days, not on the Sabbath.'

15 The Lord answered him, 'You hypocrites! Doesn't each of you on the Sabbath untie your ox or donkey from the stall and lead it out to give it water? 16 Then should not this woman, a daughter of Abraham, whom Satan has kept bound for eighteen long years, be set free on the Sabbath day from what bound her?'

17 When he said this, all his opponents were humiliated, but the people were delighted with all the wonderful things he was doing.

18 Then Jesus asked, 'What is the kingdom of God like? What shall I compare it to? 19 It is like a mustard seed, which a man took and planted in his garden. It grew and became a tree, and the birds perched in its branches.'

20 Again he asked, 'What shall I compare the kingdom of God to? 21 It is like yeast that a woman took and mixed into about thirty kilograms of flour until it worked all through the dough.'

The Mantle of Power

'Be strong and very courageous ...' **Joshua 1:7**

The Holy Spirit clothes His people with supernatural power. It is one thing to be unified on the inside; it is another to be fortified to meet whatever happens on the outside. The Holy Spirit - if we let Him - can do both. Jesus, when speaking of the Holy Spirit in John's Gospel (14:17), used two different prepositions to describe His work. He said, 'He lives *with* you and will be *in* you' (italics added). In Acts 1:8 he uses a different preposition: 'the Holy Spirit comes *on* you' (italics added). The word 'on' gives us a picture of the Holy Spirit wrapping a mantle of divine omnipotence around the shoulders of Jesus' disciples, which would enable them to do great exploits in His Name.

The story of Elijah and Elisha in the Old Testament illustrates this particular aspect. Elijah, you remember, wore a mantle that was invested with supernatural power. Elijah's servant Elisha no doubt greatly coveted that supernatural mantle. Elijah promised him that if he saw him when he returned to heaven, the mantle (the double share of his spirit) would be his. On the day of Elijah's departure to heaven, Elisha fulfilled the condition and received the desired mantle. He then went out and performed twice as many miracles as his master.

The mantle of power Jesus used when He was here on earth, He has now given to us. Now, hold your breath, for this is what Jesus said of those who have faith in Him: 'they will do even greater things than these' (John 14:12).

PRAYER

O Father, what a challenge this puts before me and everyone else in the church today. We are hardly performing a tenth of what You did, let alone twice as much. Something is wrong. Show me how to put it right in my life. In Jesus' name. Amen.

FURTHER STUDY

2 Kings 2; Zech. 4:6;
Luke 4:14; Acts 19:11-12
• What characteristics did
  Elisha show in obtaining
  the mantle?
• What is said of Jesus
  when He returned from
  the wilderness?

April 21

■ **JOSHUA 4:1–6:27**

4 When the whole nation had finished crossing the Jordan, the LORD said to Joshua, ²'Choose twelve men from among the people, one from each tribe, ³and tell them to take up twelve stones from the middle of the Jordan, from right where the priests are standing, and carry them over with you and put them down at the place where you stay tonight.'

⁴So Joshua called together the twelve men he had appointed from the Israelites, one from each tribe, ⁵and said to them, 'Go over before the ark of the LORD your God into the middle of the Jordan. Each of you is to take up a stone on his shoulder, according to the number of the tribes of the Israelites, ⁶to serve as a sign among you. In the future, when your children ask you, "What do these stones mean?" ⁷tell them that the flow of the Jordan was cut off before the ark of the covenant of the LORD. When it crossed the Jordan, the waters of the Jordan were cut off. These stones are to be a memorial to the people of Israel for ever.'

⁸So the Israelites did as Joshua commanded them. They took twelve stones from the middle of the Jordan, according to the number of the tribes of the Israelites, as the LORD had told Joshua; and they carried them over with them to their camp, where they put them down. ⁹Joshua set up the twelve stones that had been in the middle of the Jordan at the spot where the priests who carried the ark of the covenant had stood. And they are there to this day.

¹⁰Now the priests who carried the ark remained standing in the middle of the Jordan until everything the LORD had commanded Joshua was done by the people, just

as Moses had directed Joshua. The people hurried over, ¹¹and as soon as all of them had crossed, the ark of the LORD and the priests came to the other side while the people watched. ¹²The men of Reuben, Gad and the half-tribe of Manasseh crossed over, ready for battle, in front of the Israelites, as Moses had directed them. ¹³About forty thousand armed for battle crossed over before the LORD to the plains of Jericho for war.

¹⁴That day the LORD exalted Joshua in the sight of all Israel; and they stood in awe of him all the days of his life, just as they had stood in awe of Moses.

¹⁵Then the LORD said to Joshua, ¹⁶'Command the priests carrying the ark of the covenant law to come up out of the Jordan.'

¹⁷So Joshua commanded the priests, 'Come up out of the Jordan.'

¹⁸And the priests came up out of the river carrying the ark of the covenant of the LORD. No sooner had they set their feet on the dry ground than the waters of the Jordan returned to their place and ran in flood as before.

¹⁹On the tenth day of the first month the people went up from the Jordan and camped at Gilgal on the eastern border of Jericho. ²⁰And Joshua set up at Gilgal the twelve stones they had taken out of the Jordan. ²¹He said to the Israelites, 'In the future when your descendants ask their parents, "What do these stones mean?" ²²tell them, "Israel crossed the Jordan on dry ground." ²³For the LORD your God dried up the Jordan before you until you had crossed over. The LORD your God did to the Jordan what he had done to the Red Sea when he dried it up before us until we had crossed over. ²⁴He did this so that all the peoples of the earth might know that the

hand of the LORD is powerful and so that you might always fear the LORD your God.'

5 Now when all the Amorite kings west of the Jordan and all the Canaanite kings along the coast heard how the LORD had dried up the Jordan before the Israelites until they had crossed over, their hearts melted in fear and they no longer had the courage to face the Israelites.

² At that time the LORD said to Joshua, 'Make flint knives and circumcise the Israelites again.' ³ So Joshua made flint knives and circumcised the Israelites at Gibeath Haaraloth.

⁴ Now this is why he did so: all those who came out of Egypt – all the men of military age – died in the wilderness on the way after leaving Egypt. ⁵ All the people that came out had been circumcised, but all the people born in the wilderness during the journey from Egypt had not. ⁶ The Israelites had moved about in the wilderness for forty years until all the men who were of military age when they left Egypt had died, since they had not obeyed the LORD. For the LORD had sworn to them that they would not see the land that he had solemnly promised their ancestors to give us, a land flowing with milk and honey. ⁷ So he raised up their sons in their place, and these were the ones Joshua circumcised. They were still uncircumcised because they had not been circumcised on the way. ⁸ And after the whole nation had been circumcised, they remained where they were in camp until they were healed.

⁹ Then the LORD said to Joshua, 'Today I have rolled away the reproach of Egypt from you.' So the place has been called Gilgal to this day.

¹⁰ On the evening of the fourteenth day of the month, while camped at Gilgal on the plains of Jericho, the Israelites celebrated the Passover. ¹¹ The day after the Passover, that very day, they ate some of the produce of the land: unleavened bread and roasted grain. ¹² The manna stopped the day after they ate this food from the land; there was no longer any manna for the Israelites, but that year they ate the produce of Canaan.

¹³ Now when Joshua was near Jericho, he looked up and saw a man standing in front of him with a drawn sword in his hand. Joshua went up to him and asked, 'Are you for us or for our enemies?'

¹⁴ 'Neither,' he replied, 'but as commander of the army of the LORD I have now come.' Then Joshua fell face down to the ground in reverence, and asked him, 'What message does my Lord have for his servant?'

¹⁵ The commander of the LORD's army replied, 'Take off your sandals, for the place where you are standing is holy.' And Joshua did so.

6 Now the gates of Jericho were securely barred because of the Israelites. No one went out and no one came in.

² Then the LORD said to Joshua, 'See, I have delivered Jericho into your hands, along with its king and its fighting men. ³ March round the city once with all the armed men. Do this for six days. ⁴ Make seven priests carry trumpets of rams' horns in front of the ark. On the seventh day, march round the city seven times, with the priests blowing the trumpets. ⁵ When you hear them sound a long blast on the trumpets, make the whole army give a loud shout; then the wall of the city will collapse and the army will go up, everyone straight in.'

⁶ So Joshua son of Nun called the priests and said to them, 'Take up the ark of the covenant of the LORD and make seven priests carry trumpets in front of it.' ⁷ And he ordered the army, 'Advance! March round the city, with an armed guard going ahead of the ark of the LORD.'

⁸ When Joshua had spoken to the people, the seven priests carrying the seven trumpets before the LORD went forwards, blowing their trumpets, and the ark of the LORD's covenant followed them. ⁹ The armed guard

marched ahead of the priests who blew the trumpets, and the rear guard followed the ark. All this time the trumpets were sounding. ¹⁰But Joshua had commanded the army, 'Do not give a war cry, do not raise your voices, do not say a word until the day I tell you to shout. Then shout!' ¹¹So he had the ark of the LORD carried round the city, circling it once. Then the army returned to camp and spent the night there.

¹²Joshua got up early the next morning and the priests took up the ark of the LORD. ¹³The seven priests carrying the seven trumpets went forwards, marching before the ark of the LORD and blowing the trumpets. The armed men went ahead of them and the rear guard followed the ark of the LORD, while the trumpets kept sounding. ¹⁴So on the second day they marched round the city once and returned to the camp. They did this for six days.

¹⁵On the seventh day, they got up at daybreak and marched round the city seven times in the same manner, except that on that day they circled the city seven times. ¹⁶The seventh time round, when the priests sounded the trumpet blast, Joshua commanded the army, 'Shout! For the LORD has given you the city! ¹⁷The city and all that is in it are to be devoted to the LORD. Only Rahab the prostitute and all who are with her in her house shall be spared, because she hid the spies we sent. ¹⁸But keep away from the devoted things, so that you will not bring about your own destruction by taking any of them. Otherwise you will make the camp of Israel liable to destruction and bring trouble on it. ¹⁹All the silver and gold and the articles of bronze and iron are sacred to the LORD and must go into his treasury.'

²⁰When the trumpets sounded, the army shouted, and at the sound of the trumpet, when the men gave a loud shout, the wall collapsed; so everyone charged straight in, and they took the city. ²¹They devoted the city to the LORD and destroyed with the sword every living thing in it – men and women, young and old, cattle, sheep and donkeys.

²²Joshua said to the two men who had spied out the land, 'Go into the prostitute's house and bring her out and all who belong to her, in accordance with your oath to her.' ²³So the young men who had done the spying went in and brought out Rahab, her father and mother, her brothers and sisters and all who belonged to her. They brought out her entire family and put them in a place outside the camp of Israel.

²⁴Then they burned the whole city and everything in it, but they put the silver and gold and the articles of bronze and iron into the treasury of the LORD's house. ²⁵But Joshua spared Rahab the prostitute, with her family and all who belonged to her, because she hid the men Joshua had sent as spies to Jericho – and she lives among the Israelites to this day.

²⁶At that time Joshua pronounced this solemn oath: 'Cursed before the LORD is the one who undertakes to rebuild this city, Jericho:

'At the cost of his firstborn son
    he will lay its foundations;
at the cost of his youngest
    he will set up its gates.'

²⁷So the LORD was with Joshua, and his fame spread throughout the land.

▬ PSALM 49:10-15

¹⁰For all can see that the wise die,
    that the foolish and the senseless also
        perish,
    leaving their wealth to others.
¹¹Their tombs will remain their houses for
        ever,

their dwellings for endless
generations,
though they had named lands after
themselves.

12 People, despite their wealth, do not
endure;
they are like the beasts that perish.

13 This is the fate of those who trust in
themselves,
and of their followers, who approve
their sayings.
14 They are like sheep and are destined to
die;
death will be their shepherd
(but the upright will prevail over them
in the morning).
Their forms will decay in the grave,
far from their princely mansions.
15 But God will redeem me from the realm
of the dead;
he will surely take me to himself.

■ PROVERBS 11:24-26

24 One person gives freely, yet gains even
more;
another withholds unduly, but comes
to poverty.

25 A generous person will prosper;
whoever refreshes others will be
refreshed.

26 People curse the one who hoards grain,
but they pray God's blessing on the
one who is willing to sell.

■ LUKE 13:22–14:6

22 Then Jesus went through the towns and
villages, teaching as he made his way to Jerusalem. 23 Someone asked him, 'Lord, are

only a few people going to be saved?'

He said to them, 24 'Make every effort to
enter through the narrow door, because
many, I tell you, will try to enter and will not
be able to. 25 Once the owner of the house
gets up and closes the door, you will stand
outside knocking and pleading, "Sir, open
the door for us."

'But he will answer, "I don't know you or
where you come from."

26 'Then you will say, "We ate and drank
with you, and you taught in our streets."

27 'But he will reply, "I don't know you or
where you come from. Away from me, all
you evildoers!"

28 'There will be weeping there, and
gnashing of teeth, when you see Abraham,
Isaac and Jacob and all the prophets in the
kingdom of God, but you yourselves thrown
out. 29 People will come from east and west
and north and south, and will take their
places at the feast in the kingdom of God.
30 Indeed there are those who are last who
will be first, and first who will be last.'

31 At that time some Pharisees came to
Jesus and said to him, 'Leave this place and
go somewhere else. Herod wants to kill you.'

32 He replied, 'Go and tell that fox, "I will
keep on driving out demons and healing
people today and tomorrow, and on the
third day I will reach my goal." 33 In any
case, I must press on today and tomorrow
and the next day – for surely no prophet can
die outside Jerusalem!

34 'Jerusalem, Jerusalem, you who kill the
prophets and stone those sent to you, how
often I have longed to gather your children
together, as a hen gathers her chicks under her wings, and you were not willing.
35 Look, your house is left to you desolate. I
tell you, you will not see me again until you
say, "Blessed is he who comes in the name
of the Lord."'

14 One Sabbath, when Jesus went to eat
in the house of a prominent Pharisee, he was being carefully watched. 2 There

in front of him was a man suffering from abnormal swelling of his body. ³Jesus asked the Pharisees and experts in the law, 'Is it lawful to heal on the Sabbath or not?' ⁴But they remained silent. So taking hold of the man, he healed him and sent him on his way.

⁵Then he asked them, 'If one of you has a child or an ox that falls into a well on the Sabbath day, will you not immediately pull it out?' ⁶And they had nothing to say.

Divine Mathematics

'One person gives freely, yet gains even more; another withholds unduly, but comes to poverty.'
Proverbs 11:24

What all the passages in Proverbs which talk about generosity are really teaching us is that selfishness short-circuits human happiness and that the route to joy is liberality - liberality with our talents, our treasure, and our time.

Today's text is, of course, difficult for some to accept because it violates all the rules of mathematics. How can it be that the more you give away, the more you have? It doesn't seem logical! Well, one of the greatest mathematicians of the twentieth century commented that, 'Mathematics and logic have nothing to do with reality.' David Rivett, a chartered accountant and one of the founding directors of CWR said that when he joined the organisation he found that God has a quite different arithmetic from what he as an accountant had been used to. For example - what do five and two make? Seven? Yes, in man's arithmetic, but not in God's. In God's arithmetic five and two make five thousand. How come? Well, five loaves and two fish - the little lunch which a boy once gave to Jesus - were taken by Him and turned into enough food to feed five thousand. And just to add to the point - twelve baskets of fragments were gathered up after everyone had eaten their fill!

Nature, we are told, abhors a vacuum; it is the same in the spiritual realm. Liberality and generosity create a vacuum into which God flows, enabling us to give and to go on giving. I cannot explain it, but I have seen it happen again and again.

PRAYER

O God, You who are always reaching out to me in generosity and love, help me this day to do the same. May You use my generosity to touch the lives of others. For Your own dear name's sake. Amen.

FURTHER STUDY

Matt. 26:1-13; 25:34-40;
Eccl. 5:13
• How did the disciples view this extravagant act?
• How did Jesus view it?

April 22

■ JOSHUA 7:1–8:35

7 But the Israelites were unfaithful in regard to the devoted things; Achan son of Karmi, the son of Zimri, the son of Zerah, of the tribe of Judah, took some of them. So the LORD's anger burned against Israel.

² Now Joshua sent men from Jericho to Ai, which is near Beth Aven to the east of Bethel, and told them, 'Go up and spy out the region.' So the men went up and spied out Ai.

³ When they returned to Joshua, they said, 'Not all the army will have to go up against Ai. Send two or three thousand men to take it and do not weary the whole army, for only a few people live there.' ⁴ So about three thousand went up; but they were routed by the men of Ai, ⁵ who killed about thirty-six of them. They chased the Israelites from the city gate as far as the stone quarries and struck them down on the slopes. At this the hearts of the people melted in fear and became like water.

⁶ Then Joshua tore his clothes and fell face down to the ground before the ark of the LORD, remaining there till evening. The elders of Israel did the same, and sprinkled dust on their heads. ⁷ And Joshua said, 'Alas, Sovereign LORD, why did you ever bring this people across the Jordan to deliver us into the hands of the Amorites to destroy us? If only we had been content to stay on the other side of the Jordan! ⁸ Pardon your servant, Lord. What can I say, now that Israel has been routed by its enemies? ⁹ The Canaanites and the other people of the country will hear about this and they will surround us and wipe out our name from the earth. What then will you do for your own great name?'

¹⁰ The LORD said to Joshua, 'Stand up! What are you doing down on your face?

¹¹ Israel has sinned; they have violated my covenant, which I commanded them to keep. They have taken some of the devoted things; they have stolen, they have lied, they have put them with their own possessions. ¹² That is why the Israelites cannot stand against their enemies; they turn their backs and run because they have been made liable to destruction. I will not be with you any more unless you destroy whatever among you is devoted to destruction.

¹³ 'Go, consecrate the people. Tell them, "Consecrate yourselves in preparation for tomorrow; for this is what the LORD, the God of Israel, says: there are devoted things among you, Israel. You cannot stand against your enemies until you remove them.

¹⁴ '"In the morning, present yourselves tribe by tribe. The tribe that the LORD chooses shall come forward clan by clan; the clan that the LORD chooses shall come forward family by family; and the family that the LORD chooses shall come forward man by man. ¹⁵ Whoever is caught with the devoted things shall be destroyed by fire, along with all that belongs to him. He has violated the covenant of the LORD and has done an outrageous thing in Israel!"'

¹⁶ Early the next morning Joshua made Israel come forward by tribes, and Judah was chosen. ¹⁷ The clans of Judah came forward, and the Zerahites were chosen. He made the clan of the Zerahites come forward by families, and Zimri was chosen. ¹⁸ Joshua made his family come forward man by man, and Achan son of Karmi, the son of Zimri, the son of Zerah, of the tribe of Judah, was chosen.

¹⁹ Then Joshua said to Achan, 'My son, give glory to the LORD, the God of Israel, and honour him. Tell me what you have done; do

not hide it from me.'

²⁰Achan replied, 'It is true! I have sinned against the Lord, the God of Israel. This is what I have done: ²¹when I saw in the plunder a beautiful robe from Babylonia, two hundred shekels of silver and a bar of gold weighing fifty shekels, I coveted them and took them. They are hidden in the ground inside my tent, with the silver underneath.'

²²So Joshua sent messengers, and they ran to the tent, and there it was, hidden in his tent, with the silver underneath. ²³They took the things from the tent, brought them to Joshua and all the Israelites and spread them out before the Lord.

²⁴Then Joshua, together with all Israel, took Achan son of Zerah, the silver, the robe, the gold bar, his sons and daughters, his cattle, donkeys and sheep, his tent and all that he had, to the Valley of Achor. ²⁵Joshua said, 'Why have you brought this trouble on us? The Lord will bring trouble on you today.'

Then all Israel stoned him, and after they had stoned the rest, they burned them. ²⁶Over Achan they heaped up a large pile of rocks, which remains to this day. Then the Lord turned from his fierce anger. Therefore that place has been called the Valley of Achor ever since.

8 Then the Lord said to Joshua, 'Do not be afraid; do not be discouraged. Take the whole army with you, and go up and attack Ai. For I have delivered into your hands the king of Ai, his people, his city and his land. ²You shall do to Ai and its king as you did to Jericho and its king, except that you may carry off their plunder and livestock for yourselves. Set an ambush behind the city.'

³So Joshua and the whole army moved out to attack Ai. He chose thirty thousand of his best fighting men and sent them out at night ⁴with these orders: 'Listen carefully. You are to set an ambush behind the city. Don't go very far from it. All of you be on the alert. ⁵I and all those with me will advance on the city, and when the men come out against us, as they did before, we will flee from them. ⁶They will pursue us until we have lured them away from the city, for they will say, "They are running away from us as they did before." So when we flee from them, ⁷you are to rise up from ambush and take the city. The Lord your God will give it into your hand. ⁸When you have taken the city, set it on fire. Do what the Lord has commanded. See to it; you have my orders.'

⁹Then Joshua sent them off, and they went to the place of ambush and lay in wait between Bethel and Ai, to the west of Ai – but Joshua spent that night with the people.

¹⁰Early the next morning Joshua mustered his army, and he and the leaders of Israel marched before them to Ai. ¹¹The entire force that was with him marched up and approached the city and arrived in front of it. They set up camp north of Ai, with the valley between them and the city. ¹²Joshua had taken about five thousand men and set them in ambush between Bethel and Ai, to the west of the city. ¹³So the soldiers took up their positions – with the main camp to the north of the city and the ambush to the west of it. That night Joshua went into the valley.

¹⁴When the king of Ai saw this, he and all the men of the city hurried out early in the morning to meet Israel in battle at a certain place overlooking the Arabah. But he did not know that an ambush had been set against him behind the city. ¹⁵Joshua and all Israel let themselves be driven back before them, and they fled towards the wilderness. ¹⁶All the men of Ai were called to pursue them, and they pursued Joshua and were lured away from the city. ¹⁷Not a man remained in Ai or Bethel who did not go after Israel. They left the city open and went in pursuit of Israel.

¹⁸Then the Lord said to Joshua, 'Hold out towards Ai the javelin that is in your hand, for into your hand I will deliver the city.' So

Joshua held out towards the city the javelin that was in his hand. ¹⁹As soon as he did this, the men in the ambush rose quickly from their position and rushed forward. They entered the city and captured it and quickly set it on fire.

²⁰The men of Ai looked back and saw the smoke of the city rising up into the sky, but they had no chance to escape in any direction; the Israelites who had been fleeing towards the wilderness had turned back against their pursuers. ²¹For when Joshua and all Israel saw that the ambush had taken the city and that smoke was going up from the city, they turned round and attacked the men of Ai. ²²Those in the ambush also came out of the city against them, so that they were caught in the middle, with Israelites on both sides. Israel cut them down, leaving them neither survivors nor fugitives. ²³But they took the king of Ai alive and brought him to Joshua.

²⁴When Israel had finished killing all the men of Ai in the fields and in the wilderness where they had chased them, and when every one of them had been put to the sword, all the Israelites returned to Ai and killed those who were in it. ²⁵Twelve thousand men and women fell that day – all the people of Ai. ²⁶For Joshua did not draw back the hand that held out his javelin until he had destroyed all who lived in Ai. ²⁷But Israel did carry off for themselves the livestock and plunder of this city, as the LORD had instructed Joshua.

²⁸So Joshua burned Ai and made it a permanent heap of ruins, a desolate place to this day. ²⁹He impaled the body of the king of Ai on a pole and left it there until evening. At sunset, Joshua ordered them to take the body from the pole and throw it down at the entrance of the city gate. And they raised a large pile of rocks over it, which remains to this day.

³⁰Then Joshua built on Mount Ebal an altar to the LORD, the God of Israel, ³¹as Moses the servant of the LORD had commanded the Israelites. He built it according to what is written in the Book of the Law of Moses – an altar of uncut stones, on which no iron tool had been used. On it they offered to the LORD burnt offerings and sacrificed fellowship offerings. ³²There, in the presence of the Israelites, Joshua wrote on stones a copy of the law of Moses. ³³All the Israelites, with their elders, officials and judges, were standing on both sides of the ark of the covenant of the LORD, facing the Levitical priests who carried it. Both the foreigners living among them and the native-born were there. Half of the people stood in front of Mount Gerizim and half of them in front of Mount Ebal, as Moses the servant of the LORD had formerly commanded when he gave instructions to bless the people of Israel.

³⁴Afterwards, Joshua read all the words of the law – the blessings and the curses – just as it is written in the Book of the Law. ³⁵There was not a word of all that Moses had commanded that Joshua did not read to the whole assembly of Israel, including the women and children, and the foreigners who lived among them.

■ PSALM 49:16-20

¹⁶Do not be overawed when others grow
  rich,
    when the splendour of their houses
      increases;
¹⁷for they will take nothing with them
    when they die,
    their splendour will not descend with
      them.
¹⁸Though while they live they count
      themselves blessed –
    and people praise you when you
      prosper –
¹⁹they will join those who have gone before
      them,

who will never again see the light of life.

²⁰ People who have wealth but lack
     understanding
are like the beasts that perish.

- -

■ PROVERBS 11:27-29

²⁷ Whoever seeks good finds favour,
     but evil comes to one who searches
         for it.

²⁸ Those who trust in their riches will fall,
     but the righteous will thrive like a
         green leaf.

²⁹ Whoever brings ruin on their family will
     inherit only wind,
and the fool will be servant to the
     wise.

- -

■ LUKE 14:7-24

⁷ When he noticed how the guests picked the places of honour at the table, he told them this parable: ⁸ 'When someone invites you to a wedding feast, do not take the place of honour, for a person more distinguished than you may have been invited. ⁹ If so, the host who invited both of you will come and say to you, "Give this person your seat." Then, humiliated, you will have to take the least important place. ¹⁰ But when you are invited, take the lowest place, so that when your host comes, he will say to you, "Friend, move up to a better place." Then you will be honoured in the presence of all the other guests. ¹¹ For all those who exalt themselves will be humbled, and those who humble themselves will be exalted.'

¹² Then Jesus said to his host, 'When you give a luncheon or dinner, do not invite your friends, your brothers or sisters, your relatives, or your rich neighbours; if you do, they may invite you back and so you will be repaid. ¹³ But when you give a banquet, invite the poor, the crippled, the lame, the blind, ¹⁴ and you will be blessed. Although they cannot repay you, you will be repaid at the resurrection of the righteous.'

¹⁵ When one of those at the table with him heard this, he said to Jesus, 'Blessed is the one who will eat at the feast in the kingdom of God.'

¹⁶ Jesus replied: 'A certain man was preparing a great banquet and invited many guests. ¹⁷ At the time of the banquet he sent his servant to tell those who had been invited, "Come, for everything is now ready."

¹⁸ 'But they all alike began to make excuses. The first said, "I have just bought a field, and I must go and see it. Please excuse me."

¹⁹ 'Another said, "I have just bought five yoke of oxen, and I'm on my way to try them out. Please excuse me."

²⁰ 'Still another said, "I have just got married, so I can't come."

²¹ 'The servant came back and reported this to his master. Then the owner of the house became angry and ordered his servant, "Go out quickly into the streets and alleys of the town and bring in the poor, the crippled, the blind and the lame."

²² ' "Sir," the servant said, "what you ordered has been done, but there is still room."

²³ 'Then the master told his servant, "Go out to the roads and country lanes and compel them to come in, so that my house will be full. ²⁴ I tell you, not one of those who were invited will get a taste of my banquet." '

A Little of Eternity

'For all those who exalt themselves will be humbled,
and those who humble themselves will be exalted.'
Luke 14:11

Why does Jesus insist that our first consideration in prayer
should be the honour of God's Name? Is this a device (as some
have suggested) to appeal to the vanity and egotism of the Almighty?
Can it be that our loving heavenly Father wants us to give Him what He
wants (admiration and praise) before He gives us what we want?

No, of course not! God encourages us to focus on Himself because He
knows that in contemplating Him, we complete ourselves and bring all
parts of our personality to health. To admire, appreciate, respect, and
venerate the character of God is to awaken ourselves to reality. Not to
do so is to deprive ourselves and bring about a depletion of spiritual
power. We are designed for the worship and contemplation of God, and
when, therefore, we stand before Him and gaze at His majesty and glory,
the machinery of our inner being whirs into activity, and our characters
take on the features of His character.

God, therefore, has our interests at heart more than His own when He
asks us to venerate Him. We 'hallow' His Name, and our own name (our
character) is hallowed. We gaze at His character, and our own character
is made better for the gazing. Someone put it this way: 'I just go quiet
and empty into His presence, gaze at His glory and loveliness, and give
myself time for His disposition to get through to mine.'

Yes, that's the secret. Give God a little of your time, and He will give
you a little of eternity.

PRAYER

O Father, forgive me for the times I
rush into Your presence intent only
on getting my needs met. Slow me
down and make me a more
contemplative person. Then Your
character can rub off on mine. In
Jesus' name I pray. Amen.

FURTHER STUDY

2 Pet. 1; Rom. 8:29;
Phil. 3:21; 1 John 3:2
• How do we become
  partakers of the divine
  nature?
• List some of these
  characteristics.

April 23

▬ JOSHUA 9:1–10:28

9 Now when all the kings west of the Jordan heard about these things – the kings in the hill country, in the western foothills, and along the entire coast of the Mediterranean Sea as far as Lebanon (the kings of the Hittites, Amorites, Canaanites, Perizzites, Hivites and Jebusites) – ²they came together to wage war against Joshua and Israel.

³However, when the people of Gibeon heard what Joshua had done to Jericho and Ai, ⁴they resorted to a ruse: they went as a delegation whose donkeys were loaded with worn-out sacks and old wineskins, cracked and mended. ⁵They put worn and patched sandals on their feet and wore old clothes. All the bread of their food supply was dry and mouldy. ⁶Then they went to Joshua in the camp at Gilgal and said to him and the Israelites, 'We have come from a distant country; make a treaty with us.'

⁷The Israelites said to the Hivites, 'But perhaps you live near us, so how can we make a treaty with you?'

⁸'We are your servants,' they said to Joshua.

But Joshua asked, 'Who are you and where do you come from?'

⁹They answered: 'Your servants have come from a very distant country because of the fame of the LORD your God. For we have heard reports of him: all that he did in Egypt, ¹⁰and all that he did to the two kings of the Amorites east of the Jordan – Sihon king of Heshbon, and Og king of Bashan, who reigned in Ashtaroth. ¹¹And our elders and all those living in our country said to us, "Take provisions for your journey; go and meet them and say to them, 'We are

your servants; make a treaty with us.' "

¹²This bread of ours was warm when we packed it at home on the day we left to come to you. But now see how dry and mouldy it is. ¹³And these wineskins that we filled were new, but see how cracked they are. And our clothes and sandals are worn out by the very long journey.'

¹⁴The Israelites sampled their provisions but did not enquire of the LORD. ¹⁵Then Joshua made a treaty of peace with them to let them live, and the leaders of the assembly ratified it by oath.

¹⁶Three days after they made the treaty with the Gibeonites, the Israelites heard that they were neighbours, living near them. ¹⁷So the Israelites set out and on the third day came to their cities: Gibeon, Kephirah, Beeroth and Kiriath Jearim. ¹⁸But the Israelites did not attack them, because the leaders of the assembly had sworn an oath to them by the LORD, the God of Israel.

The whole assembly grumbled against the leaders, ¹⁹but all the leaders answered, 'We have given them our oath by the LORD, the God of Israel, and we cannot touch them now. ²⁰This is what we will do to them: we will let them live, so that God's wrath will not fall on us for breaking the oath we swore to them.' ²¹They continued, 'Let them live, but let them be woodcutters and water-carriers in the service of the whole assembly.' So the leaders' promise to them was kept.

²²Then Joshua summoned the Gibeonites and said, 'Why did you deceive us by saying, "We live a long way from you," while actually you live near us? ²³You are now under a curse: you will never be released from service as woodcutters and water-carriers for the house of my God.'

²⁴They answered Joshua, 'Your servants

were clearly told how the LORD your God had commanded his servant Moses to give you the whole land and to wipe out all its inhabitants from before you. So we feared for our lives because of you, and that is why we did this. ²⁵ We are now in your hands. Do to us whatever seems good and right to you.'

²⁶ So Joshua saved them from the Israelites, and they did not kill them. ²⁷ That day he made the Gibeonites woodcutters and water-carriers for the assembly, to provide for the needs of the altar of the LORD at the place the LORD would choose. And that is what they are to this day.

10 Now Adoni-Zedek king of Jerusalem heard that Joshua had taken Ai and totally destroyed it, doing to Ai and its king as he had done to Jericho and its king, and that the people of Gibeon had made a treaty of peace with Israel and had become their allies. ² He and his people were very much alarmed at this, because Gibeon was an important city, like one of the royal cities; it was larger than Ai, and all its men were good fighters. ³ So Adoni-Zedek king of Jerusalem appealed to Hoham king of Hebron, Piram king of Jarmuth, Japhia king of Lachish and Debir king of Eglon. ⁴ 'Come up and help me attack Gibeon,' he said, 'because it has made peace with Joshua and the Israelites.'

⁵ Then the five kings of the Amorites – the kings of Jerusalem, Hebron, Jarmuth, Lachish and Eglon – joined forces. They moved up with all their troops and took up positions against Gibeon and attacked it.

⁶ The Gibeonites then sent word to Joshua in the camp at Gilgal: 'Do not abandon your servants. Come up to us quickly and save us! Help us, because all the Amorite kings from the hill country have joined forces against us.'

⁷ So Joshua marched up from Gilgal with his entire army, including all the best fighting men. ⁸ The LORD said to Joshua, 'Do not be afraid of them; I have given them into your hand. Not one of them will be able to withstand you.'

⁹ After an all-night march from Gilgal, Joshua took them by surprise. ¹⁰ The LORD threw them into confusion before Israel, so Joshua and the Israelites defeated them completely at Gibeon. Israel pursued them along the road going up to Beth Horon and cut them down all the way to Azekah and Makkedah. ¹¹ As they fled before Israel on the road down from Beth Horon to Azekah, the LORD hurled large hailstones down on them, and more of them died from the hail than were killed by the swords of the Israelites.

¹² On the day the LORD gave the Amorites over to Israel, Joshua said to the LORD in the presence of Israel:

'Sun, stand still over Gibeon,
    and you, moon, over the Valley of
        Aijalon.'
¹³ So the sun stood still,
    and the moon stopped,
        till the nation avenged itself on its
            enemies,

as it is written in the Book of Jashar.

The sun stopped in the middle of the sky and delayed going down about a full day. ¹⁴ There has never been a day like it before or since, a day when the LORD listened to a human being. Surely the LORD was fighting for Israel!

¹⁵ Then Joshua returned with all Israel to the camp at Gilgal.

¹⁶ Now the five kings had fled and hidden in the cave at Makkedah. ¹⁷ When Joshua was told that the five kings had been found hiding in the cave at Makkedah, ¹⁸ he said, 'Roll large rocks up to the mouth of the cave, and post some men there to guard it. ¹⁹ But don't stop; pursue your enemies! Attack them from the rear and don't let them reach their cities, for the LORD your God has given them into your hand.'

²⁰ So Joshua and the Israelites defeated

them completely, but a few survivors managed to reach their fortified cities. ²¹ The whole army then returned safely to Joshua in the camp at Makkedah, and no one uttered a word against the Israelites.

²² Joshua said, 'Open the mouth of the cave and bring those five kings out to me.' ²³ So they brought the five kings out of the cave – the kings of Jerusalem, Hebron, Jarmuth, Lachish and Eglon. ²⁴ When they had brought these kings to Joshua, he summoned all the men of Israel and said to the army commanders who had come with him, 'Come here and put your feet on the necks of these kings.' So they came forward and placed their feet on their necks.

²⁵ Joshua said to them, 'Do not be afraid; do not be discouraged. Be strong and courageous. This is what the LORD will do to all the enemies you are going to fight.' ²⁶ Then Joshua put the kings to death and exposed their bodies on five poles, and they were left hanging on the poles until evening.

²⁷ At sunset Joshua gave the order and they took them down from the poles and threw them into the cave where they had been hiding. At the mouth of the cave they placed large rocks, which are there to this day.

²⁸ That day Joshua took Makkedah. He put the city and its king to the sword and totally destroyed everyone in it. He left no survivors. And he did to the king of Makkedah as he had done to the king of Jericho.

PSALM 50:1-6

¹ The Mighty One, God, the LORD,
   speaks and summons the earth
   from the rising of the sun to where
      it sets.
² From Zion, perfect in beauty,
   God shines forth.
³ Our God comes
   and will not be silent;
   a fire devours before him,

and around him a tempest rages.
⁴ He summons the heavens above,
   and the earth, that he may judge his
      people:
⁵ 'Gather to me this consecrated people,
   who made a covenant with me by
      sacrifice.'
⁶ And the heavens proclaim his
      righteousness,
   for he is a God of justice.

PROVERBS 11:30-31

³⁰ The fruit of the righteous is a tree of life,
   and the one who is wise saves lives.

³¹ If the righteous receive their due on
      earth,
   how much more the ungodly and the
      sinner!

LUKE 14:25–15:10

²⁵ Large crowds were travelling with Jesus, and turning to them he said: ²⁶ 'If anyone comes to me and does not hate father and mother, wife and children, brothers and sisters – yes, even their own life – such a person cannot be my disciple. ²⁷ And whoever does not carry their cross and follow me cannot be my disciple.

²⁸ 'Suppose one of you wants to build a tower. Won't you first sit down and estimate the cost to see if you have enough money to complete it? ²⁹ For if you lay the foundation and are not able to finish it, everyone who sees it will ridicule you, ³⁰ saying, "This person began to build and wasn't able to finish."

³¹ 'Or suppose a king is about to go to war against another king. Won't he first sit down and consider whether he is able with ten thousand men to oppose the one coming against him with twenty thousand? ³² If he is not able, he will send a delegation

while the other is still a long way off and will ask for terms of peace. ³³In the same way, those of you who do not give up everything you have cannot be my disciples.

³⁴'Salt is good, but if it loses its saltiness, how can it be made salty again? ³⁵It is fit neither for the soil nor for the manure heap; it is thrown out.

'Whoever has ears to hear, let them hear.'

15 Now the tax collectors and sinners were all gathering round to hear Jesus. ²But the Pharisees and the teachers of the law muttered, 'This man welcomes sinners, and eats with them.'

³Then Jesus told them this parable: ⁴'Suppose one of you has a hundred sheep and loses one of them. Doesn't he leave the ninety-nine in the open country and go after the lost sheep until he finds it? ⁵And when he finds it, he joyfully puts it on his shoulders ⁶and goes home. Then he calls his friends and neighbours together and says, "Rejoice with me; I have found my lost sheep." ⁷I tell you that in the same way there will be more rejoicing in heaven over one sinner who repents than over ninety-nine righteous people who do not need to repent.

⁸'Or suppose a woman has ten silver coins and loses one. Doesn't she light a lamp, sweep the house and search carefully until she finds it? ⁹And when she finds it, she calls her friends and neighbours together and says, "Rejoice with me; I have found my lost coin." ¹⁰In the same way, I tell you, there is rejoicing in the presence of the angels of God over one sinner who repents.'

The God Who Seeks

'Rejoice with me; I have found my lost sheep.'
Luke 15:6

One of the aspects that makes Christianity unique is the issue of personal salvation. The vocabulary of salvation is distasteful to those of other religions, and many insist we should give it up. They say, 'It smacks of spiritual smugness and arrogance.'

But before we answer this criticism we must realise what Christianity is all about. Christianity is essentially a rescue religion; it is the announcement of the good news that God has come in the Person of His Son to save us from the power of sin, the penalty of sin, and one day in the future, the presence of sin. In the passage before us today we see that God likens Himself to a shepherd who leaves the rest of the sheep in order to go after one sheep that is lost. The Divine Shepherd, far from abandoning the sheep in the hope that, bleating and stumbling, it may find its own way home, puts His own life on the line to search it out.

Judaism denies that Jesus is the Messiah and that His sin-bearing death is the only ground on which divine forgiveness can be offered. One Jewish scholar, C. G. Montefiore, refers to the 'greatness and originality' of Jesus in His attitude to sinners that 'instead of avoiding them he actively sought them out'. However, although this recognises that God receives sinners who return to Him, it fails to see that He also seeks them out. How utterly amazing. The One who *seeks* and saves is God.

PRAYER

O Father, what a thought: You did not send an angel to seek us out and save us. You came Yourself in the Person of Your Son. I can never put my gratitude into mere words. Help me to show it by my life. In Jesus' name. Amen.

FURTHER STUDY

Luke 19:1-10; Matt. 18:10-14; John 1:43; 5:14; 9:35
• What was Jesus' message to Zacchaeus?
• How did Jesus illustrate the heart of the shepherd?

April 24

■ JOSHUA 10:29–12:24

²⁹ Then Joshua and all Israel with him moved on from Makkedah to Libnah and attacked it. ³⁰ The LORD also gave that city and its king into Israel's hand. The city and everyone in it Joshua put to the sword. He left no survivors there. And he did to its king as he had done to the king of Jericho.

³¹ Then Joshua and all Israel with him moved on from Libnah to Lachish; he took up positions against it and attacked it. ³² The LORD gave Lachish into Israel's hands, and Joshua took it on the second day. The city and everyone in it he put to the sword, just as he had done to Libnah. ³³ Meanwhile, Horam king of Gezer had come up to help Lachish, but Joshua defeated him and his army – until no survivors were left.

³⁴ Then Joshua and all Israel with him moved on from Lachish to Eglon; they took up positions against it and attacked it. ³⁵ They captured it that same day and put it to the sword and totally destroyed everyone in it, just as they had done to Lachish.

³⁶ Then Joshua and all Israel with him went up from Eglon to Hebron and attacked it. ³⁷ They took the city and put it to the sword, together with its king, its villages and everyone in it. They left no survivors. Just as at Eglon, they totally destroyed it

and everyone in it.

³⁸ Then Joshua and all Israel with him turned round and attacked Debir. ³⁹ They took the city, its king and its villages, and put them to the sword. Everyone in it they totally destroyed. They left no survivors. They did to Debir and its king as they had done to Libnah and its king and to Hebron.

⁴⁰ So Joshua subdued the whole region, including the hill country, the Negev, the western foothills and the mountain slopes, together with all their kings. He left no survivors. He totally destroyed all who breathed, just as the LORD, the God of Israel, had commanded. ⁴¹ Joshua subdued them from Kadesh Barnea to Gaza and from the whole region of Goshen to Gibeon. ⁴² All these kings and their lands Joshua conquered in one campaign, because the LORD, the God of Israel, fought for Israel.

⁴³ Then Joshua returned with all Israel to the camp at Gilgal.

11 When Jabin king of Hazor heard of this, he sent word to Jobab king of Madon, to the kings of Shimron and Akshaph, ² and to the northern kings who were in the mountains, in the Arabah south of Kinnereth, in the western foothills and in Naphoth Dor on the west; ³ to the Canaanites in the east and west; to the Amorites, Hittites, Perizzites and Jebusites in the hill

country; and to the Hivites below Hermon in the region of Mizpah. ⁴They came out with all their troops and a large number of horses and chariots – a huge army, as numerous as the sand on the seashore. ⁵All these kings joined forces and made camp together at the Waters of Merom to fight against Israel.

⁶The LORD said to Joshua, 'Do not be afraid of them, because by this time tomorrow I will hand all of them, slain, over to Israel. You are to hamstring their horses and burn their chariots.'

⁷So Joshua and his whole army came against them suddenly at the Waters of Merom and attacked them, ⁸and the LORD gave them into the hand of Israel. They defeated them and pursued them all the way to Greater Sidon, to Misrephoth Maim, and to the Valley of Mizpah on the east, until no survivors were left. ⁹Joshua did to them as the LORD had directed: he hamstrung their horses and burned their chariots.

¹⁰At that time Joshua turned back and captured Hazor and put its king to the sword. (Hazor had been the head of all these kingdoms.) ¹¹Everyone in it they put to the sword. They totally destroyed them, not sparing anyone that breathed, and he burned Hazor itself.

¹²Joshua took all these royal cities and their kings and put them to the sword. He totally destroyed them, as Moses the servant of the LORD had commanded. ¹³Yet Israel did not burn any of the cities built on their mounds – except Hazor, which Joshua burned. ¹⁴The Israelites carried off for themselves all the plunder and livestock of these cities, but all the people they put to the sword until they completely destroyed them, not sparing anyone that breathed. ¹⁵As the LORD commanded his servant Moses, so Moses commanded Joshua, and Joshua did it; he left nothing undone of all that the LORD commanded Moses.

¹⁶So Joshua took this entire land: the hill country, all the Negev, the whole region of Goshen, the western foothills, the Arabah and the mountains of Israel with their foothills, ¹⁷from Mount Halak, which rises towards Seir, to Baal Gad in the Valley of Lebanon below Mount Hermon. He captured all their kings and put them to death. ¹⁸Joshua waged war against all these kings for a long time. ¹⁹Except for the Hivites living in Gibeon, not one city made a treaty of peace with the Israelites, who took them all in battle. ²⁰For it was the LORD himself who hardened their hearts to wage war against Israel, so that he might destroy them totally, exterminating them without mercy, as the LORD had commanded Moses.

²¹At that time Joshua went and destroyed the Anakites from the hill country: from Hebron, Debir and Anab, from all the hill country of Judah, and from all the hill country of Israel. Joshua totally destroyed them and their towns. ²²No Anakites were left in Israelite territory; only in Gaza, Gath and Ashdod did any survive.

²³So Joshua took the entire land, just as the LORD had directed Moses, and he gave it as an inheritance to Israel according to their tribal divisions. Then the land had rest from war.

12 These are the kings of the land whom the Israelites had defeated and whose territory they took over east of the Jordan, from the Arnon Gorge to Mount Hermon, including all the eastern side of the Arabah:

²Sihon king of the Amorites, who reigned in Heshbon.

He ruled from Aroer on the rim of the Arnon Gorge – from the middle of the gorge – to the River Jabbok, which is the border of the Ammonites. This included half of Gilead. ³He also ruled over the eastern Arabah from the Sea of Galilee to the Sea of the Arabah (that is, the Dead Sea),

to Beth Jeshimoth, and then southward below the slopes of Pisgah.

⁴And the territory of Og king of
Bashan, one of the last of the Rephaites, who reigned in Ashtaroth and
Edrei.
  ⁵He ruled over Mount Hermon, Salekah, all of Bashan to the border of
  the people of Geshur and Maakah,
  and half of Gilead to the border of
  Sihon king of Heshbon.

⁶Moses, the servant of the LORD, and the
Israelites conquered them. And Moses the
servant of the LORD gave their land to the
Reubenites, the Gadites and the half-tribe of
Manasseh to be their possession.
  ⁷Here is a list of the kings of the land that
Joshua and the Israelites conquered on the
west side of the Jordan, from Baal Gad in the
Valley of Lebanon to Mount Halak, which
rises towards Seir. Joshua gave their lands
as an inheritance to the tribes of Israel according to their tribal divisions. ⁸The lands
included the hill country, the western foothills, the Arabah, the mountain slopes, the
wilderness and the Negev. These were the
lands of the Hittites, Amorites, Canaanites, Perizzites, Hivites and Jebusites. These
were the kings:

  ⁹the king of Jericho   one
  the king of Ai (near Bethel)   one
  ¹⁰the king of Jerusalem   one
  the king of Hebron   one
  ¹¹the king of Jarmuth   one
  the king of Lachish   one
  ¹²the king of Eglon   one
  the king of Gezer   one
  ¹³the king of Debir   one
  the king of Geder   one
  ¹⁴the king of Hormah   one
  the king of Arad   one
  ¹⁵the king of Libnah   one
  the king of Adullam   one

  ¹⁶the king of Makkedah   one
  the king of Bethel   one
  ¹⁷the king of Tappuah   one
  the king of Hepher   one
  ¹⁸the king of Aphek   one
  the king of Lasharon   one
  ¹⁹the king of Madon   one
  the king of Hazor   one
  ²⁰the king of Shimron Meron   one
  the king of Akshaph   one
  ²¹the king of Taanach   one
  the king of Megiddo   one
  ²²the king of Kedesh   one
  the king of Jokneam in
    Carmel   one
  ²³the king of Dor (in Naphoth
    Dor)   one
  the king of Goyim in Gilgal   one
  ²⁴the king of Tirzah   one
       thirty-one kings in all.

▬ PSALM 50:7-15

⁷'Listen, my people, and I will speak;
    I will testify against you, Israel:
    I am God, your God.
⁸I bring no charges against you
      concerning your sacrifices
    or concerning your burnt offerings,
      which are ever before me.
⁹I have no need of a bull from your stall
    or of goats from your pens,
¹⁰for every animal of the forest is mine,
    and the cattle on a thousand hills.
¹¹I know every bird in the mountains,
    and the insects in the fields are mine.
¹²If I were hungry I would not tell you,
    for the world is mine, and all that is in
      it.
¹³Do I eat the flesh of bulls
    or drink the blood of goats?

¹⁴'Sacrifice thank-offerings to God,
    fulfil your vows to the Most High,
¹⁵and call on me in the day of trouble;

I will deliver you, and you will honour me.'

PROVERBS 12:1-3

12 Whoever loves discipline loves knowledge,
but whoever hates correction is stupid.

² Good people obtain favour from the LORD,
but he condemns those who devise wicked schemes.

³ No one can be established through wickedness,
but the righteous cannot be uprooted.

LUKE 15:11-32

¹¹ Jesus continued: 'There was a man who had two sons. ¹² The younger one said to his father, "Father, give me my share of the estate." So he divided his property between them.

¹³ 'Not long after that, the younger son got together all he had, set off for a distant country and there squandered his wealth in wild living. ¹⁴ After he had spent everything, there was a severe famine in that whole country, and he began to be in need. ¹⁵ So he went and hired himself out to a citizen of that country, who sent him to his fields to feed pigs. ¹⁶ He longed to fill his stomach with the pods that the pigs were eating, but no one gave him anything.

¹⁷ 'When he came to his senses, he said, "How many of my father's hired servants have food to spare, and here I am starving to death! ¹⁸ I will set out and go back to my father and say to him: Father, I have sinned against heaven and against you. ¹⁹ I am no longer worthy to be called your son; make me like one of your hired servants." ²⁰ So he got up and went to his father.

'But while he was still a long way off, his father saw him and was filled with compassion for him; he ran to his son, threw his arms round him and kissed him.

²¹ 'The son said to him, "Father, I have sinned against heaven and against you. I am no longer worthy to be called your son."

²² 'But the father said to his servants, "Quick! Bring the best robe and put it on him. Put a ring on his finger and sandals on his feet. ²³ Bring the fattened calf and kill it. Let's have a feast and celebrate. ²⁴ For this son of mine was dead and is alive again; he was lost and is found." So they began to celebrate.

²⁵ 'Meanwhile, the elder son was in the field. When he came near the house, he heard music and dancing. ²⁶ So he called one of the servants and asked him what was going on. ²⁷ "Your brother has come," he replied, "and your father has killed the fattened calf because he has him back safe and sound."

²⁸ 'The elder brother became angry and refused to go in. So his father went out and pleaded with him. ²⁹ But he answered his father, "Look! All these years I've been slaving for you and never disobeyed your orders. Yet you never gave me even a young goat so I could celebrate with my friends. ³⁰ But when this son of yours who has squandered your property with prostitutes comes home, you kill the fattened calf for him!"

³¹ ' "My son," the father said, "you are always with me, and everything I have is yours. ³² But we had to celebrate and be glad, because this brother of yours was dead and is alive again; he was lost and is found." '

The Hurt of Rejection

'The younger [son] said to his father, "Father, give me my share of the estate." So he divided his property between them ... the younger son got together all he had, set off for a distant country ...' **Luke 15:12-13**

One of the greatest, most encouraging ministries of the Holy Spirit within our lives is that of a Comforter.

During my ministry, I have observed that there are five main hurts which people experience in life. The first is the hurt of rejection. Can the Holy Spirit comfort us when we feel rejected? He most certainly can. Sooner or later in this mixed-up world, everyone feels rejected. Indeed, some go through so much rejection, they cease to expect anything else.

Rejection often happens in childhood: the child may have been unwanted by his parents, or may have been the wrong sex, or for some reason doesn't please her parents. These feelings of rejection are recorded in our system on a kind of tape recorder, and later in life, whenever we feel rejected, we not only experience the present rejection, but in some strange way it triggers the 'tape recorder' inside us, and we play back all the feelings of rejection we felt in earlier years.

Past feelings of rejection that have never been healed may put a weight on the personality that is too heavy for it to bear, and this is why, as we say, a person breaks down. People rarely break down because of one event; it is usually the one event that becomes the last straw.

Are you carrying deep feelings of rejection from the past within you? Or have you been rejected in recent days or weeks? Then draw near to God. The Spirit is with you to heal your hurts – right now.

PRAYER

Gracious Holy Spirit, I am so thankful that You come alongside to help in my hour of need. I offer You every feeling of rejection and hurt that lies within my heart. Heal me now in Jesus' name. Thank You, Father. It's done. Amen.

FURTHER STUDY

Luke 15:11-32; Eph. 1:6;
2 Cor. 5:9; Acts 10:35
• What is the message of
  the parable?
• What three things did the
  younger son receive to
  verify this?

April 25

■ JOSHUA 13:1–14:15

13 When Joshua had grown old, the LORD said to him, 'You are now very old, and there are still very large areas of land to be taken over.

² 'This is the land that remains: all the regions of the Philistines and Geshurites, ³ from the River Shihor on the east of Egypt to the territory of Ekron on the north, all of it counted as Canaanite though held by the five Philistine rulers in Gaza, Ashdod, Ashkelon, Gath and Ekron; the territory of the Avvites ⁴ on the south; all the land of the Canaanites, from Arah of the Sidonians as far as Aphek and the border of the Amorites; ⁵ the area of Byblos; and all Lebanon to the east, from Baal Gad below Mount Hermon to Lebo Hamath.

⁶ 'As for all the inhabitants of the mountain regions from Lebanon to Misrephoth Maim, that is, all the Sidonians, I myself will drive them out before the Israelites. Be sure to allocate this land to Israel for an inheritance, as I have instructed you, ⁷ and divide it as an inheritance among the nine tribes and half of the tribe of Manasseh.'

⁸ The other half of Manasseh, the Reubenites and the Gadites had received the inheritance that Moses had given them east of the Jordan, as he, the servant of the LORD, had assigned it to them.

⁹ It extended from Aroer on the rim of the Arnon Gorge, and from the town in the middle of the gorge, and included the whole plateau of Medeba as far as Dibon, ¹⁰ and all the towns of Sihon king of the Amorites, who ruled in Heshbon, out to the border of the Ammonites. ¹¹ It also included Gilead, the territory of the people of Geshur and Maakah, all of Mount Hermon and all Bashan as far as Salekah – ¹² that is, the whole kingdom of Og in Bashan, who had reigned in Ashtaroth and Edrei. (He was the last of the Rephaites.) Moses had defeated them and taken over their land. ¹³ But the Israelites did not drive out the people of Geshur and Maakah, so they continue to live among the Israelites to this day.

¹⁴ But to the tribe of Levi he gave no inheritance, since the food offerings presented to the LORD, the God of Israel, are their inheritance, as he promised them.

¹⁵ This is what Moses had given to the tribe of Reuben, according to its clans:

¹⁶ The territory from Aroer on the rim of the Arnon Gorge, and from the town in the middle of the gorge, and the whole plateau past Medeba ¹⁷ to Heshbon and all its towns on the plateau, including Dibon, Bamoth Baal, Beth Baal Meon, ¹⁸ Jahaz, Kedemoth, Mephaath, ¹⁹ Kiriathaim, Sibmah, Zereth Shahar on the hill in the valley, ²⁰ Beth Peor, the slopes of Pisgah, and Beth Jeshimoth ²¹ – all the towns on the plateau and the entire realm of Sihon king of the Amorites, who ruled at Heshbon. Moses had defeated him and the Midianite chiefs, Evi, Rekem, Zur, Hur and Reba – princes allied with Sihon – who lived in that country. ²² In addition to those

slain in battle, the Israelites had put to the sword Balaam son of Beor, who practised divination. ²³ The boundary of the Reubenites was the bank of the Jordan. These towns and their villages were the inheritance of the Reubenites, according to their clans.

²⁴ This is what Moses had given to the tribe of Gad, according to its clans:

²⁵ The territory of Jazer, all the towns of Gilead and half the Ammonite country as far as Aroer, near Rabbah; ²⁶ and from Heshbon to Ramath Mizpah and Betonim, and from Mahanaim to the territory of Debir; ²⁷ and in the valley, Beth Haram, Beth Nimrah, Sukkoth and Zaphon with the rest of the realm of Sihon king of Heshbon (the east side of the Jordan, the territory up to the end of the Sea of Galilee). ²⁸ These towns and their villages were the inheritance of the Gadites, according to their clans.

²⁹ This is what Moses had given to the half-tribe of Manasseh, that is, to half the family of the descendants of Manasseh, according to its clans:

³⁰ The territory extending from Mahanaim and including all of Bashan, the entire realm of Og king of Bashan – all the settlements of Jair in Bashan, sixty towns, ³¹ half of Gilead, and Ashtaroth and Edrei (the royal cities of Og in Bashan). This was for the descendants of Makir son of Manasseh – for half of the sons of Makir, according to their clans.

³² This is the inheritance Moses had given when he was in the plains of Moab across the Jordan east of Jericho. ³³ But to the tribe of Levi, Moses had given no inheritance; the LORD, the God of Israel, is their inheritance, as he promised them.

14 Now these are the areas the Israelites received as an inheritance in the land of Canaan, which Eleazar the priest, Joshua son of Nun and the heads of the tribal clans of Israel allotted to them. ² Their inheritances were assigned by lot to the nine-and-a-half tribes, as the LORD had commanded through Moses. ³ Moses had granted the two-and-a-half tribes their inheritance east of the Jordan but had not granted the Levites an inheritance among the rest, ⁴ for Joseph's descendants had become two tribes – Manasseh and Ephraim. The Levites received no share of the land but only towns to live in, with pasture-lands for their flocks and herds. ⁵ So the Israelites divided the land, just as the LORD had commanded Moses.

⁶ Now the people of Judah approached Joshua at Gilgal, and Caleb son of Jephunneh the Kenizzite said to him, 'You know what the LORD said to Moses the man of God at Kadesh Barnea about you and me. ⁷ I was forty years old when Moses the servant of the LORD sent me from Kadesh Barnea to explore the land. And I brought him back a report according to my convictions, ⁸ but my fellow Israelites who went up with me made the hearts of the people sink. I, however, followed the LORD my God wholeheartedly. ⁹ So on that day Moses swore to me, "The land on which your feet have walked will be your inheritance and that of your children for ever, because you have followed the LORD my God wholeheartedly."

¹⁰ 'Now then, just as the LORD promised, he has kept me alive for forty-five years since the time he said this to Moses, while Israel moved about in the wilderness. So here I am today, eighty-five years old! ¹¹ I am still as strong today as the day Moses sent me out; I'm just as vigorous to go out to battle now as I was then. ¹² Now give me this hill country that the LORD promised me that day. You yourself heard then that the Anakites were there and their cities were large

and fortified, but, the LORD helping me, I will drive them out just as he said.'

¹³ Then Joshua blessed Caleb son of Jephunneh and gave him Hebron as his inheritance. ¹⁴ So Hebron has belonged to Caleb son of Jephunneh the Kenizzite ever since, because he followed the LORD, the God of Israel, wholeheartedly. ¹⁵ (Hebron used to be called Kiriath Arba after Arba, who was the greatest man among the Anakites.)

Then the land had rest from war.

▬ PSALM 50:16-23

¹⁶ But to the wicked person, God says:

'What right have you to recite my laws
    or take my covenant on your lips?
¹⁷ You hate my instruction
    and cast my words behind you.
¹⁸ When you see a thief, you join with him;
    you throw in your lot with adulterers.
¹⁹ You use your mouth for evil
    and harness your tongue to deceit.
²⁰ You sit and testify against your brother
    and slander your own mother's son.
²¹ When you did these things and I kept
        silent,
    you thought I was exactly like you.
But I now arraign you
    and set my accusations before you.

²² 'Consider this, you who forget God,
    or I will tear you to pieces, with no one
        to rescue you:
²³ Those who sacrifice thank-offerings
        honour me,
    and to the blameless I will show my
        salvation.'

▬ PROVERBS 12:4-5

⁴ A wife of noble character is her
    husband's crown,

but a disgraceful wife is like decay in
    his bones.

⁵ The plans of the righteous are just,
    but the advice of the wicked is
        deceitful.

▬ LUKE 16:1-18

16 Jesus told his disciples: 'There was a rich man whose manager was accused of wasting his possessions. ² So he called him in and asked him, "What is this I hear about you? Give an account of your management, because you cannot be manager any longer."

³ 'The manager said to himself, "What shall I do now? My master is taking away my job. I'm not strong enough to dig, and I'm ashamed to beg – ⁴ I know what I'll do so that, when I lose my job here, people will welcome me into their houses."

⁵ 'So he called in each one of his master's debtors. He asked the first, "How much do you owe my master?"

⁶ ' "Three thousand litres of olive oil," he replied.

'The manager told him, "Take your bill, sit down quickly, and make it fifteen hundred."

⁷ 'Then he asked the second, "And how much do you owe?"

' "Thirty tons of wheat," he replied.

'He told him, "Take your bill and make it twenty-four."

⁸ 'The master commended the dishonest manager because he had acted shrewdly. For the people of this world are more shrewd in dealing with their own kind than are the people of the light. ⁹ I tell you, use worldly wealth to gain friends for yourselves, so that when it is gone, you will be welcomed into eternal dwellings.

¹⁰ 'Whoever can be trusted with very little can also be trusted with much, and whoever

is dishonest with very little will also be dishonest with much. [11] So if you have not been trustworthy in handling worldly wealth, who will trust you with true riches? [12] And if you have not been trustworthy with someone else's property, who will give you property of your own?

[13] 'No one can serve two masters. Either you will hate the one and love the other, or you will be devoted to the one and despise the other. You cannot serve both God and Money.'

[14] The Pharisees, who loved money, heard all this and were sneering at Jesus. [15] He said to them, 'You are the ones who justify yourselves in the eyes of others, but God knows your hearts. What people value highly is detestable in God's sight.

[16] 'The Law and the Prophets were proclaimed until John. Since that time, the good news of the kingdom of God is being preached, and everyone is forcing their way into it. [17] It is easier for heaven and earth to disappear than for the least stroke of a pen to drop out of the Law.

[18] 'Anyone who divorces his wife and marries another woman commits adultery, and the man who marries a divorced woman commits adultery.

The Choice Facing Us

'Whoever can be trusted with very little can also be trusted with much ...' **Luke 16:10**

What is denial? It is the attitude that avoids looking realistically at issues and pretends that things are not the way they are.

Most Christians (myself included) are to varying degrees held together by denial. Deep down we sense that if we were to face the realities of life openly and honestly, we might not be able to cope, and so we pretend things are not what they are.

I know Christians who pretend that what they have in life satisfies more than it does, or pretend they haven't been hurt as badly as they have. They refuse to face and feel what is going on inside them, due to the strange belief that it is lack of faith on their part to admit to anything that is negative.

This faulty teaching – that we ought to ignore what is going on inside us instead of facing it and dealing with it – is responsible for more casualties in the Christian life than anything I know. A Christian psychologist says: 'I am convinced that much of what we admire as spiritual maturity is a fragile adjustment to life based on the foundation of denial.' I would agree. My own observation would lead me to say that I have found some non-Christians to be more open and honest in facing what is going on inside them than some Christians.

Is denial a wise plan for life? Absolutely not. The choice, then, is stark: either to deny and live comfortably or to face every painful issue – and go on to climb the heights with God.

PRAYER

Father, help me to see that I need never be afraid to face anything, for in You I have the resources to resolve all problems, not just skirt them. Show me how to blast denial right out of my life – once and for all. In Jesus' name. Amen.

FURTHER STUDY

Eccl. 5:1-7; Isa. 29:13; Matt. 15:1-9

- What do fools do?
- What prophecy was fulfilled by the Pharisees?

April 26

▬ JOSHUA 15:1-63

15 The land allotted to the tribe of Judah, according to its clans, extended down to the territory of Edom, to the Desert of Zin in the extreme south.

² Their southern boundary started from the bay at the southern end of the Dead Sea, ³ crossed south of Scorpion Pass, continued on to Zin and went over to the south of Kadesh Barnea. Then it ran past Hezron up to Addar and curved around to Karka. ⁴ It then passed along to Azmon and joined the Wadi of Egypt, ending at the Mediterranean Sea. This is their southern boundary.

⁵ The eastern boundary is the Dead Sea as far as the mouth of the Jordan.

The northern boundary started from the bay of the sea at the mouth of the Jordan, ⁶ went up to Beth Hoglah and continued north of Beth Arabah to the Stone of Bohan son of Reuben. ⁷ The boundary then went up to Debir from the Valley of Achor and turned north to Gilgal, which faces the Pass of Adummim south of the gorge. It continued along to the waters of En Shemesh and came out at En Rogel. ⁸ Then it ran up the Valley of Ben Hinnom along the southern slope of the Jebusite city (that is, Jerusalem). From there it climbed to the top of the hill west of the Hinnom Valley at the northern end of the Valley of Rephaim. ⁹ From the hilltop the boundary headed towards the spring of the waters of Nephtoah, came out at the towns of Mount Ephron and went down towards Baalah (that is, Kiriath Jearim). ¹⁰ Then it curved westward from Baalah to Mount Seir, ran along the northern slope of Mount Jearim (that is, Kesalon), continued down to Beth Shemesh and crossed to Timnah. ¹¹ It went to the northern slope of Ekron, turned toward Shikkeron, passed along to Mount Baalah and reached Jabneel. The boundary ended at the sea.

¹² The western boundary is the coastline of the Mediterranean Sea.

These are the boundaries around the people of Judah by their clans.

¹³ In accordance with the LORD's command to him, Joshua gave to Caleb son of Jephunneh a portion in Judah – Kiriath Arba, that is, Hebron. (Arba was the forefather of Anak.) ¹⁴ From Hebron Caleb drove out the three Anakites – Sheshai, Ahiman and

Talmai, the sons of Anak. [15] From there he marched against the people living in Debir (formerly called Kiriath Sepher). [16] And Caleb said, 'I will give my daughter Aksah in marriage to the man who attacks and captures Kiriath Sepher.' [17] Othniel son of Kenaz, Caleb's brother, took it; so Caleb gave his daughter Aksah to him in marriage.

[18] One day when she came to Othniel, she urged him to ask her father for a field. When she got off her donkey, Caleb asked her, 'What can I do for you?'

[19] She replied, 'Do me a special favour. Since you have given me land in the Negev, give me also springs of water.' So Caleb gave her the upper and lower springs.

[20] This is the inheritance of the tribe of Judah, according to its clans:

[21] The southernmost towns of the tribe of Judah in the Negev towards the boundary of Edom were:

Kabzeel, Eder, Jagur, [22] Kinah, Dimonah, Adadah, [23] Kedesh, Hazor, Ithnan, [24] Ziph, Telem, Bealoth, [25] Hazor Hadattah, Kerioth Hezron (that is, Hazor), [26] Amam, Shema, Moladah, [27] Hazar Gaddah, Heshmon, Beth Pelet, [28] Hazar Shual, Beersheba, Biziothiah, [29] Baalah, Iyim, Ezem, [30] Eltolad, Kesil, Hormah, [31] Ziklag, Madmannah, Sansannah, [32] Lebaoth, Shilhim, Ain and Rimmon – a total of twenty-nine towns and their villages.

[33] In the western foothills:

Eshtaol, Zorah, Ashnah, [34] Zanoah, En Gannim, Tappuah, Enam, [35] Jarmuth, Adullam, Sokoh, Azekah, [36] Shaaraim, Adithaim and Gederah (or Gederothaim) – fourteen towns and their villages.

[37] Zenan, Hadashah, Migdal Gad, [38] Dilean, Mizpah, Joktheel, [39] Lachish, Bozkath, Eglon, [40] Kabbon,

Lahmas, Kitlish, [41] Gederoth, Beth Dagon, Naamah and Makkedah – sixteen towns and their villages.

[42] Libnah, Ether, Ashan, [43] Iphtah, Ashnah, Nezib, [44] Keilah, Akzib and Mareshah – nine towns and their villages.

[45] Ekron, with its surrounding settlements and villages; [46] west of Ekron, all that were in the vicinity of Ashdod, together with their villages; [47] Ashdod, its surrounding settlements and villages; and Gaza, its settlements and villages, as far as the Wadi of Egypt and the coastline of the Mediterranean Sea.

[48] In the hill country:

Shamir, Jattir, Sokoh, [49] Dannah, Kiriath Sannah (that is, Debir), [50] Anab, Eshtemoh, Anim, [51] Goshen, Holon and Giloh – eleven towns and their villages.

[52] Arab, Dumah, Eshan, [53] Janim, Beth Tappuah, Aphekah, [54] Humtah, Kiriath Arba (that is, Hebron) and Zior – nine towns and their villages.

[55] Maon, Carmel, Ziph, Juttah, [56] Jezreel, Jokdeam, Zanoah, [57] Kain, Gibeah and Timnah – ten towns and their villages.

[58] Halhul, Beth Zur, Gedor, [59] Maarath, Beth Anoth and Eltekon – six towns and their villages.

[60] Kiriath Baal (that is, Kiriath Jearim) and Rabbah – two towns and their villages.

[61] In the wilderness:

Beth Arabah, Middin, Sekakah, [62] Nibshan, the City of Salt and En Gedi – six towns and their villages.

[63] Judah could not dislodge the Jebusites, who were living in Jerusalem; to this day the Jebusites live there with the people of Judah.

PSALM 51:1–5

[1] Have mercy on me, O God,
    according to your unfailing love;
    according to your great compassion
    blot out my transgressions.
[2] Wash away all my iniquity
    and cleanse me from my sin.

[3] For I know my transgressions,
    and my sin is always before me.
[4] Against you, you only, have I sinned
    and done what is evil in your sight;
so you are right in your verdict
    and justified when you judge.
[5] Surely I was sinful at birth,
    sinful from the time my mother
        conceived me.

PROVERBS 12:6–7

[6] The words of the wicked lie in wait for
        blood,
    but the speech of the upright rescues
        them.

[7] The wicked are overthrown and are no
        more,
    but the house of the righteous stands
        firm.

LUKE 16:19–17:10

[19] 'There was a rich man who was dressed in purple and fine linen and lived in luxury every day. [20] At his gate was laid a beggar named Lazarus, covered with sores [21] and longing to eat what fell from the rich man's table. Even the dogs came and licked his sores.

[22] 'The time came when the beggar died and the angels carried him to Abraham's side. The rich man also died and was buried. [23] In Hades, where he was in torment, he looked up and saw Abraham far away, with Lazarus by his side. [24] So he called to him, "Father Abraham, have pity on me and send Lazarus to dip the tip of his finger in water and cool my tongue, because I am in agony in this fire."

[25] 'But Abraham replied, "Son, remember that in your lifetime you received your good things, while Lazarus received bad things, but now he is comforted here and you are in agony. [26] And besides all this, between us and you a great chasm has been set in place, so that those who want to go from here to you cannot, nor can anyone cross over from there to us."

[27] 'He answered, "Then I beg you, father, send Lazarus to my family, [28] for I have five brothers. Let him warn them, so that they will not also come to this place of torment."

[29] 'Abraham replied, "They have Moses and the Prophets; let them listen to them."

[30] ' "No, father Abraham," he said, "but if someone from the dead goes to them, they will repent."

[31] 'He said to him, "If they do not listen to Moses and the Prophets, they will not be convinced even if someone rises from the dead." '

17 Jesus said to his disciples: 'Things that cause people to stumble are bound to come, but woe to anyone through whom they come. [2] It would be better for them to be thrown into the sea with a millstone tied round their neck than to cause one of these little ones to stumble. [3] So watch yourselves.

'If your brother or sister sins against you, rebuke them; and if they repent, forgive them. [4] Even if they sin against you seven times in a day and seven times come back to you saying "I repent," you must forgive them.'

[5] The apostles said to the Lord, 'Increase our faith!'

[6] He replied, 'If you have faith as small as a mustard seed, you can say to this mulberry

tree, "Be uprooted and planted in the sea," and it will obey you.

7 'Suppose one of you has a servant ploughing or looking after the sheep. Will he say to the servant when he comes in from the field, "Come along now and sit down to eat"? 8 Won't he rather say, "Prepare my supper, get yourself ready and wait on me while I eat and drink; after that you may eat and drink"? 9 Will he thank the servant because he did what he was told to do? 10 So you also, when you have done everything you were told to do, should say, "We are unworthy servants; we have only done our duty." '

Heaven or Hell

'In Hades, where he was in torment, he looked up and saw Abraham far away ...' **Luke 16:23**

The final state of those who die without availing themselves of God's freely offered forgiveness is eternal banishment from God's presence. The Bible calls this 'hell'. 'There is no heaven with a little of hell in it,' said George MacDonald, meaning that the God who is passionately for righteousness and implacably against sin must ensure that the two are finally separated.

However, hell is always something that people choose for themselves. It is a state for which men and women opt. Before hell is experienced as eternal, it is always experienced as something temporary in the sense that, as men and women retreat from the light God shines into their hearts to lead them to Himself, they experience in a small way what they will experience in full when they are banished 'outside, into the darkness' (Matt. 25:30). Dorothy Sayers described hell as 'the enjoyment of one's own way forever'. God says to those who die impenitent: 'You preferred your own way to mine; you shall have it – forever'. God is a God of justice and in consigning people to hell He is allowing them to face the full consequences of the choice they have made.

Those of you reading these lines who have never surrendered your lives to Christ, I urge you to surrender your hearts to Him today. Christ has died to save you from hell. Pray this prayer with me now.

PRAYER

Father God, I come to You now through Your Son, the Lord Jesus Christ. I repent of my sin, ask Your forgiveness, and receive You into my life as Saviour and Lord. Thank You, dear Lord. Amen.

FURTHER STUDY

Matt. 5:27–30; 18:7–9; 25:34–43
- How did Jesus illustrate the importance of avoiding hell?
- How can we be sure of avoiding hell?

April 27

■ JOSHUA 16:1–18:28

16 The land allotted to Joseph began at the Jordan, east of the springs of Jericho, and went up from there through the desert into the hill country of Bethel. ²It went on from Bethel (that is, Luz), crossed over to the territory of the Arkites in Ataroth, ³descended westward to the territory of the Japhletites as far as the region of Lower Beth Horon and on to Gezer, ending at the Mediterranean Sea. ⁴So Manasseh and Ephraim, the descendants of Joseph, received their inheritance.

⁵This was the territory of Ephraim, according to its clans:

The boundary of their inheritance went from Ataroth Addar in the east to Upper Beth Horon ⁶and continued to the Mediterranean Sea. From Mikmethath on the north it curved eastward to Taanath Shiloh, passing by it to Janoah on the east. ⁷Then it went down from Janoah to Ataroth and Naarah, touched Jericho and came out at the Jordan. ⁸From Tappuah the border went west to the Kanah Ravine and ended at the Mediterranean Sea. This was the inheritance of the tribe of the Ephraimites, according to its clans. ⁹It also included all the towns and their villages that were set aside for the Ephraimites within the inheritance of the Manassites.
¹⁰They did not dislodge the Canaanites living in Gezer; to this day the Canaanites live among the people of Ephraim but are required to do forced labour.

17 This was the land allotted to the tribe of Manasseh as Joseph's firstborn, that is, for Makir, Manasseh's firstborn. Makir was the ancestor of the Gileadites, who had received Gilead and Bashan because the Makirites were great soldiers. ²So this land was allotted to the rest of the people of Manasseh – the clans of Abiezer, Helek, Asriel, Shechem, Hepher and Shemida. These are the other male descendants of Manasseh son of Joseph by their clans.

³Now Zelophehad son of Hepher, the son of Gilead, the son of Makir, the son of Manasseh, had no sons but only daughters, whose names were Mahlah, Noah, Hoglah, Milkah and Tirzah. ⁴They went to Eleazar the priest, Joshua son of Nun, and the leaders and said, 'The LORD commanded Moses to give us an inheritance among our relatives.' So Joshua gave them an inheritance along with the brothers of their father, according to the LORD's command. ⁵Manasseh's share consisted of ten tracts of land besides Gilead and Bashan east of the Jordan, ⁶because the daughters of the tribe of Manasseh received an inheritance among the sons. The land of Gilead belonged to the rest of the descendants of Manasseh.

⁷The territory of Manasseh extended from Asher to Mikmethath east of Shechem. The boundary ran southward from there to include the people living at En Tappuah. ⁸(Manasseh had the land of Tappuah, but Tappuah itself, on the boundary of Manasseh, belonged to the Ephraimites.) ⁹Then the boundary continued south to the Kanah Ravine. There were towns belonging to Ephraim lying among the towns of Manasseh, but the boundary of Manasseh was the northern side of

the ravine and ended at the Mediterranean Sea. ¹⁰On the south the land belonged to Ephraim, on the north to Manasseh. The territory of Manasseh reached the Mediterranean Sea and bordered Asher on the north and Issachar on the east.

¹¹Within Issachar and Asher, Manasseh also had Beth Shan, Ibleam and the people of Dor, Endor, Taanach and Megiddo, together with their surrounding settlements (the third in the list is Naphoth).

¹²Yet the Manassites were not able to occupy these towns, for the Canaanites were determined to live in that region. ¹³However, when the Israelites grew stronger, they subjected the Canaanites to forced labour but did not drive them out completely.

¹⁴The people of Joseph said to Joshua, 'Why have you alloted us only one portion of land and one share for an inheritance? We are a numerous people, and the LORD has blessed us abundantly.'

¹⁵'If you are so numerous,' Joshua answered, 'and if the hill country of Ephraim is too small for you, go up into the forest and clear land for yourselves there in the land of the Perizzites and Rephaites.'

¹⁶The people of Joseph replied, 'The hill country is not enough for us, and all the Canaanites who live in the plain have chariots fitted with iron, both those in Beth Shan and its settlements and those in the Valley of Jezreel.'

¹⁷But Joshua said to the tribes of Joseph – to Ephraim and Manasseh – 'You are numerous and very powerful. You will have not only one portion of land allotted to you ¹⁸but the forested hill country as well. Clear it, and its farthest limits will be yours; though the Canaanites have chariots fitted with iron and though they are strong, you can drive them out.'

18 The whole assembly of the Israelites gathered at Shiloh and set up the tent of meeting there. The country was brought under their control, ²but there were still seven Israelite tribes who had not yet received their inheritance.

³So Joshua said to the Israelites: 'How long will you wait before you begin to take possession of the land that the LORD, the God of your ancestors, has given you? ⁴Appoint three men from each tribe. I will send them out to make a survey of the land and to write a description of it, according to the inheritance of each. Then they will return to me. ⁵You are to divide the land into seven parts. Judah is to remain in its territory on the south and the tribes of Joseph in their territory on the north. ⁶After you have written descriptions of the seven parts of the land, bring them here to me and I will cast lots for you in the presence of the LORD our God. ⁷The Levites, however, do not get a portion among you, because the priestly service of the LORD is their inheritance. And Gad, Reuben and the half-tribe of Manasseh have already received their inheritance on the east side of the Jordan. Moses the servant of the LORD gave it to them.'

⁸As the men started on their way to map out the land, Joshua instructed them, 'Go and make a survey of the land and write a description of it. Then return to me, and I will cast lots for you here at Shiloh in the presence of the LORD.' ⁹So the men left and went through the land. They wrote its description on a scroll, town by town, in seven parts, and returned to Joshua in the camp at Shiloh. ¹⁰Joshua then cast lots for them in Shiloh in the presence of the LORD, and there he distributed the land to the Israelites according to their tribal divisions.

¹¹The first lot came up for the tribe of Benjamin according to its clans. Their allotted territory lay between the tribes of Judah and Joseph:

¹²On the north side their boundary began at the Jordan, passed the

northern slope of Jericho and headed west into the hill country, coming out at the wilderness of Beth Aven. [13] From there it crossed to the south slope of Luz (that is, Bethel) and went down to Ataroth Addar on the hill south of Lower Beth Horon.

[14] From the hill facing Beth Horon on the south the boundary turned south along the western side and came out at Kiriath Baal (that is, Kiriath Jearim), a town of the people of Judah. This was the western side.

[15] The southern side began at the outskirts of Kiriath Jearim on the west, and the boundary came out at the spring of the waters of Nephtoah. [16] The boundary went down to the foot of the hill facing the Valley of Ben Hinnom, north of the Valley of Rephaim. It continued down the Hinnom Valley along the southern slope of the Jebusite city and so to En Rogel. [17] It then curved north, went to En Shemesh, continued to Geliloth, which faces the Pass of Adummim, and ran down to the Stone of Bohan son of Reuben. [18] It continued to the northern slope of Beth Arabah and on down into the Arabah. [19] It then went to the northern slope of Beth Hoglah and came out at the northern bay of the Dead Sea, at the mouth of the Jordan in the south. This was the southern boundary.

[20] The Jordan formed the boundary on the eastern side.

These were the boundaries that marked out the inheritance of the clans of Benjamin on all sides.

[21] The tribe of Benjamin, according to its clans, had the following cities:

Jericho, Beth Hoglah, Emek Keziz, [22] Beth Arabah, Zemaraim, Bethel, [23] Avvim, Parah, Ophrah, [24] Kephar Ammoni, Ophni and Geba – twelve towns and their villages.

[25] Gibeon, Ramah, Beeroth, [26] Mizpah, Kephirah, Mozah, [27] Rekem, Irpeel, Taralah, [28] Zelah, Haeleph, the Jebusite city (that is, Jerusalem), Gibeah and Kiriath – fourteen towns and their villages.

This was the inheritance of Benjamin for its clans.

■ PSALM 51:6-9

[6] Yet you desired faithfulness even in the womb;
    you taught me wisdom in that secret place.

[7] Cleanse me with hyssop, and I shall be clean;
    wash me, and I shall be whiter than snow.
[8] Let me hear joy and gladness;
    let the bones you have crushed rejoice.
[9] Hide your face from my sins
    and blot out all my iniquity.

■ PROVERBS 12:8-10

[8] A person is praised according to their prudence,
    and one with a warped mind is despised.

[9] Better to be a nobody and yet have a servant
    than pretend to be somebody and have no food.

[10] The righteous care for the needs of their animals,
    but the kindest acts of the wicked are cruel.

■ LUKE 17:11-37

[11] Now on his way to Jerusalem, Jesus travelled along the border between Samaria and Galilee. [12] As he was going into a village, ten men who had leprosy met him. They stood at a distance [13] and called out in a loud voice, 'Jesus, Master, have pity on us!'

[14] When he saw them, he said, 'Go, show yourselves to the priests.' And as they went, they were cleansed.

[15] One of them, when he saw he was healed, came back, praising God in a loud voice. [16] He threw himself at Jesus' feet and thanked him – and he was a Samaritan.

[17] Jesus asked, 'Were not all ten cleansed? Where are the other nine? [18] Has no one returned to give praise to God except this foreigner?' [19] Then he said to him, 'Rise and go; your faith has made you well.'

[20] Once, on being asked by the Pharisees when the kingdom of God would come, Jesus replied, 'The coming of the kingdom of God is not something that can be observed, [21] nor will people say, "Here it is," or "There it is," because the kingdom of God is in your midst.'

[22] Then he said to his disciples, 'The time is coming when you will long to see one of the days of the Son of Man, but you will not see it. [23] People will tell you, "There he is!" or "Here he is!" Do not go running off after them. [24] For the Son of Man in his day will be like the lightning, which flashes and lights up the sky from one end to the other. [25] But first he must suffer many things and be rejected by this generation.

[26] 'Just as it was in the days of Noah, so also will it be in the days of the Son of Man. [27] People were eating, drinking, marrying and being given in marriage up to the day Noah entered the ark. Then the flood came and destroyed them all.

[28] 'It was the same in the days of Lot. People were eating and drinking, buying and selling, planting and building. [29] But the day Lot left Sodom, fire and sulphur rained down from heaven and destroyed them all.

[30] 'It will be just like this on the day the Son of Man is revealed. [31] On that day no one who is on the housetop, with possessions inside, should go down to get them. Likewise, no one in the field should go back for anything. [32] Remember Lot's wife! [33] Whoever tries to keep their life will lose it, and whoever loses their life will preserve it. [34] I tell you, on that night two people will be in one bed; one will be taken and the other left. [35] Two women will be grinding corn together; one will be taken and the other left.' [36]a

[37] 'Where, Lord?' they asked.

He replied, 'Where there is a dead body, there the vultures will gather.'

---

a Some manuscripts include here words similar to Matt. 24:40

Below the Waterline

'Yet you desired faithfulness even in the womb ...'
Psalm 51:6

When considering the proposition that a balanced, honest look at what is going on beneath the surface of your life can contribute greatly to your spiritual health, think of your life as an iceberg.

We are told that the visible part of an iceberg – that is, the part we see above the water – is about one-tenth of its total size. Its bulk lies beneath the surface and is revealed only to those who are equipped to go down below the waterline. Our lives are like that; there is much more to them than we see on the surface.

Think of the visible part above the waterline as representing the things you do, the thoughts you consciously think, and the feelings you sense going on within you. Let the mass below the waterline represent the things that go on inside you that cannot be clearly seen or understood, such as motives, attitudes, impulses and so on. Facing what goes on above the waterline - our visible behaviours and actions - is a whole lot easier than delving below the surface, and this is why many Christians (not all, of course) concern themselves only with what they can see, know and understand.

These people can be described as 'surface copers,' who cope with life by dealing with whatever they can see and ignoring all the rest. If, however, we are to enjoy a deeper relationship with God, then we will do so only as we come to grips with the tough issues that lie beneath the surface of our lives.

PRAYER

God, help me this day to stand before You in complete and utter honesty. Save me from becoming a 'surface coper', and give me the grace I need to face the things that I would normally avoid. In Jesus' name I pray. Amen.

FURTHER STUDY

Isa. 11; 1 Kings 3:1-10; John 5:30

• How does Jesus judge and reprove?
• What did Solomon ask for?

April 28

■ JOSHUA 19:1-51

19 The second lot came out for the tribe of Simeon according to its clans. Their inheritance lay within the territory of Judah. ² It included:

Beersheba (or Sheba), Moladah, ³ Hazar Shual, Balah, Ezem, ⁴ Eltolad, Bethul, Hormah, ⁵ Ziklag, Beth Markaboth, Hazar Susah, ⁶ Beth Lebaoth and Sharuhen – thirteen towns and their villages;

⁷ Ain, Rimmon, Ether and Ashan – four towns and their villages – ⁸ and all the villages around these towns as far as Baalath Beer (Ramah in the Negev).

This was the inheritance of the tribe of the Simeonites, according to its clans. ⁹ The inheritance of the Simeonites was taken from the share of Judah, because Judah's portion was more than they needed. So the Simeonites received their inheritance within the territory of Judah.

¹⁰ The third lot came up for Zebulun according to its clans:

The boundary of their inheritance went as far as Sarid. ¹¹ Going west it ran to Maralah, touched Dabbesheth, and extended to the ravine near Jokneam. ¹² It turned east from Sarid towards the sunrise to the territory of Kisloth Tabor and went on to Daberath and up to

Japhia. [13] Then it continued eastward to Gath Hepher and Eth Kazin; it came out at Rimmon and turned towards Neah. [14] There the boundary went round on the north to Hannathon and ended at the Valley of Iphtah El. [15] Included were Kattath, Nahalal, Shimron, Idalah and Bethlehem. There were twelve towns and their villages.

[16] These towns and their villages were the inheritance of Zebulun, according to its clans.

[17] The fourth lot came out for Issachar according to its clans. [18] Their territory included:

Jezreel, Kesulloth, Shunem, [19] Hapharaim, Shion, Anaharath, [20] Rabbith, Kishion, Ebez, [21] Remeth, En Gannim, En Haddah and Beth Pazzez. [22] The boundary touched Tabor, Shahazumah and Beth Shemesh, and ended at the Jordan. There were sixteen towns and their villages.

[23] These towns and their villages were the inheritance of the tribe of Issachar, according to its clans.

[24] The fifth lot came out for the tribe of Asher according to its clans. [25] Their territory included:

Helkath, Hali, Beten, Akshaph, [26] Allammelek, Amad and Mishal. On the west the boundary touched Carmel and Shihor Libnath. [27] It then turned east towards Beth Dagon, touched Zebulun and the Valley of Iphtah El, and went north to Beth Emek and Neiel, passing Kabul on the left. [28] It went to Abdon, Rehob, Hammon and Kanah, as far as Greater Sidon. [29] The boundary then turned back towards Ramah and went to the fortified city of Tyre, turned towards Hosah and came out at the Mediterranean Sea in the region of Akzib, [30] Ummah, Aphek and Rehob. There were twenty-two towns and their villages.

[31] These towns and their villages were the inheritance of the tribe of Asher, according to its clans.

[32] The sixth lot came out for Naphtali according to its clans:

[33] Their boundary went from Heleph and the large tree in Zaanannim, passing Adami Nekeb and Jabneel to Lakkum and ending at the Jordan. [34] The boundary ran west through Aznoth Tabor and came out at Hukkok. It touched Zebulun on the south, Asher on the west and the Jordan on the east. [35] The fortified cities were Ziddim, Zer, Hammath, Rakkath, Kinnereth, [36] Adamah, Ramah, Hazor, [37] Kedesh, Edrei, En Hazor, [38] Iron, Migdal El, Horem, Beth Anath and Beth Shemesh. There were nineteen towns and their villages.

[39] These towns and their villages were the inheritance of the tribe of Naphtali, according to its clans.

[40] The seventh lot came out for the tribe of Dan according to its clans. [41] The territory of their inheritance included:

Zorah, Eshtaol, Ir Shemesh, [42] Shaalabbin, Aijalon, Ithlah, [43] Elon, Timnah, Ekron, [44] Eltekeh, Gibbethon, Baalath, [45] Jehud, Bene Berak, Gath Rimmon, [46] Me Jarkon and Rakkon, with the area facing Joppa.

[47] (When the territory of the Danites was lost to them, they went up and attacked Leshem, took it, put it to the sword and occupied it. They settled in Leshem and named it Dan after their ancestor.)

[48] These towns and their villages were the inheritance of the tribe of Dan, according to its clans.

[49] When they had finished dividing the land into its allotted portions, the Israelites gave Joshua son of Nun an inheritance among them, [50] as the LORD had commanded. They gave him the town he asked for – Timnath Serah in the hill country of

Ephraim. And he built up the town and settled there.

⁵¹These are the territories that Eleazar the priest, Joshua son of Nun and the heads of the tribal clans of Israel assigned by lot at Shiloh in the presence of the LORD at the entrance to the tent of meeting. And so they finished dividing the land.

■ PSALM 51:10-13

¹⁰Create in me a pure heart, O God,
    and renew a steadfast spirit within me.
¹¹Do not cast me from your presence
    or take your Holy Spirit from me.
¹²Restore to me the joy of your salvation
    and grant me a willing spirit, to
        sustain me.

¹³Then I will teach transgressors your
        ways,
    so that sinners will turn back to you.

■ PROVERBS 12:11-12

¹¹Those who work their land will have
        abundant food,
    but those who chase fantasies have no
        sense.

¹²The wicked desire the stronghold of
        evildoers,
    but the root of the righteous endures.

■ LUKE 18:1-23

18 Then Jesus told his disciples a parable to show them that they should always pray and not give up. ²He said: 'In a certain town there was a judge who neither feared God nor cared what people thought. ³And there was a widow in that town who kept coming to him with the plea, "Grant me justice against my adversary."

⁴'For some time he refused. But finally he said to himself, "Even though I don't fear God or care what people think, ⁵yet because this widow keeps bothering me, I will see that she gets justice, so that she won't eventually come and attack me!"'

⁶And the Lord said, 'Listen to what the unjust judge says. ⁷And will not God bring about justice for his chosen ones, who cry out to him day and night? Will he keep putting them off? ⁸I tell you, he will see that they get justice, and quickly. However, when the Son of Man comes, will he find faith on the earth?'

⁹To some who were confident of their own righteousness and looked down on everyone else, Jesus told this parable: ¹⁰'Two men went up to the temple to pray, one a Pharisee and the other a tax collector. ¹¹The Pharisee stood by himself and prayed: "God, I thank you that I am not like other people – robbers, evildoers, adulterers – or even like this tax collector. ¹²I fast twice a week and give a tenth of all I get."

¹³'But the tax collector stood at a distance. He would not even look up to heaven, but beat his breast and said, "God, have mercy on me, a sinner."

¹⁴'I tell you that this man, rather than the other, went home justified before God. For all those who exalt themselves will be humbled, and those who humble themselves will be exalted.'

¹⁵People were also bringing babies to Jesus for him to place his hands on them. When the disciples saw this, they rebuked them. ¹⁶But Jesus called the children to him and said, 'Let the little children come to me, and do not hinder them, for the kingdom of God belongs to such as these. ¹⁷Truly I tell you, anyone who will not receive the kingdom of God like a little child will never enter it.'

¹⁸A certain ruler asked him, 'Good teacher, what must I do to inherit eternal life?'

¹⁹'Why do you call me good?' Jesus

answered. 'No one is good – except God alone. [20]You know the commandments: "You shall not commit adultery, you shall not murder, you shall not steal, you shall not give false testimony, honour your father and mother."'

[21]'All these I have kept since I was a boy,'

he said.

[22]When Jesus heard this, he said to him, 'You still lack one thing. Sell everything you have and give to the poor, and you will have treasure in heaven. Then come, follow me.'

[23]When he heard this, he became very sad, because he was very wealthy.

Our Biggest Problem

'Create in me a pure heart, O God, and renew a steadfast spirit within me.' **Psalm 51:10**

What is the biggest problem we face? Some would say ill health; others, lack of money; still others, uncertainty about the future or fear of dying. My own view is that the biggest problem with which human beings have to grapple is the problem of guilt. It is the most powerfully destructive force in the personality. We cannot live with guilt – that is, truly live.

When I was a young Christian, I heard some great preaching in my native Wales, most of which focused on how God was able to release us from the guilt of inbred sin. Nowadays, apart from a few exceptions, that message is hardly heard in pulpits. The emphasis ceased to appeal to the modern mind and so was discarded. However, it is now coming back to us through the science of psychology. Someone said that the point at which psychology and religion meet is at the point of guilt. Christianity and the social sciences underline what the human heart knows so well: it cannot live comfortably with guilt.

In this simple prayer of Jesus, however, we have an adequate answer: 'Forgive us our debts, as we also have forgiven our debtors.' If we have fully accepted the forgiveness of God and we know that our sins have been forgiven, then the result is a pervading sense of peace. The human heart cannot be put off by subterfuge; it needs reconciliation, forgiveness, and assurance.

PRAYER

O God, my Father, I see that within the ways of men, You have a way – a way that is written into the nature of reality, and that way is the way of forgiveness. May I ever walk in it. For Jesus' sake. Amen.

FURTHER STUDY

John 8:1-11;
Psa. 40:12; 38:4; 73:21
• What made the Pharisees leave?
• How did Jesus respond to the woman?

April 29

▬ JOSHUA 20:1–21:45

20 Then the LORD said to Joshua: ² 'Tell the Israelites to designate the cities of refuge, as I instructed you through Moses, ³ so that anyone who kills a person accidentally and unintentionally may flee there and find protection from the avenger of blood. ⁴ When they flee to one of these cities, they are to stand in the entrance of the city gate and state their case before the elders of that city. Then the elders are to admit the fugitive into their city and provide a place to live among them. ⁵ If the avenger of blood comes in pursuit, the elders must not surrender the fugitive, because the fugitive killed their neighbour unintentionally and without malice aforethought. ⁶ They are to stay in that city until they have stood trial before the assembly and until the death of the high priest who is serving at that time. Then they may go back to their own home in the town from which they fled.'

⁷ So they set apart Kedesh in Galilee in the hill country of Naphtali, Shechem in the hill country of Ephraim, and Kiriath Arba (that is, Hebron) in the hill country of Judah. ⁸ East of the Jordan (on the other side from Jericho) they designated Bezer in the wilderness on the plateau in the tribe of Reuben, Ramoth in Gilead in the tribe of Gad, and Golan in Bashan in the tribe of Manasseh. ⁹ Any of the Israelites or any foreigner residing among them who killed someone accidentally could flee to these designated cities and not be killed by the avenger of blood prior to standing trial before the assembly.

21 Now the family heads of the Levites approached Eleazar the priest, Joshua son of Nun, and the heads of the other tribal families of Israel ² at Shiloh in Canaan and said to them, 'The LORD commanded through Moses that you give us towns to live in, with pasture-lands for our livestock.' ³ So, as the LORD had commanded, the Israelites gave the Levites the following towns and pasture-lands out of their own inheritance:

⁴ The first lot came out for the Kohathites, according to their clans. The Levites who were descendants of Aaron the priest were allotted thirteen towns from the tribes of Judah, Simeon and Benjamin. ⁵ The rest of Kohath's descendants were allotted ten towns from the clans of the tribes of Ephraim, Dan and half of Manasseh.

⁶ The descendants of Gershon were allotted thirteen towns from the clans of the tribes of Issachar, Asher, Naphtali and the half-tribe of Manasseh in Bashan.

⁷ The descendants of Merari, according to their clans, received twelve towns from the tribes of Reuben, Gad and Zebulun.

⁸ So the Israelites allotted to the Levites these towns and their pasture-lands, as the LORD had commanded through Moses.

⁹ From the tribes of Judah and Simeon they allotted the following towns by name ¹⁰ (these towns were assigned to the descendants of Aaron who were from the Kohathite clans of the Levites, because the first lot fell to them):

¹¹ They gave them Kiriath Arba (that is, Hebron), with its surrounding pasture-land, in the hill country of Judah. (Arba was the forefather of Anak.) ¹² But the fields and villages around the city they had given to Caleb son of Jephunneh as his possession.

¹³ So to the descendants of Aaron the

priest they gave Hebron (a city of refuge for one accused of murder), Libnah, [14] Jattir, Eshtemoa, [15] Holon, Debir, [16] Ain, Juttah and Beth Shemesh, together with their pasture-lands – nine towns from these two tribes.

[17] And from the tribe of Benjamin they gave them Gibeon, Geba, [18] Anathoth and Almon, together with their pasture-lands – four towns.

[19] The total number of towns for the priests, the descendants of Aaron, came to thirteen, together with their pasture-lands.

[20] The rest of the Kohathite clans of the Levites were allotted towns from the tribe of Ephraim:

[21] In the hill country of Ephraim they were given Shechem (a city of refuge for one accused of murder) and Gezer, [22] Kibzaim and Beth Horon, together with their pasture-lands – four towns.

[23] Also from the tribe of Dan they received Eltekeh, Gibbethon, [24] Aijalon and Gath Rimmon, together with their pasture-lands – four towns.

[25] From half the tribe of Manasseh they received Taanach and Gath Rimmon, together with their pasture-lands – two towns.

[26] All these ten towns and their pasture-lands were given to the rest of the Kohathite clans.

[27] The Levite clans of the Gershonites were given:

from the half-tribe of Manasseh,
Golan in Bashan (a city of refuge for one accused of murder) and Be Eshterah, together with their pasture-lands – two towns;

[28] from the tribe of Issachar,
Kishion, Daberath, [29] Jarmuth and En Gannim, together with their pasture-lands – four towns;

[30] from the tribe of Asher,

Mishal, Abdon, [31] Helkath and Rehob, together with their pasture-lands – four towns;

[32] from the tribe of Naphtali,
Kedesh in Galilee (a city of refuge for one accused of murder), Hammoth Dor and Kartan, together with their pasture-lands – three towns.

[33] The total number of towns of the Gershonite clans came to thirteen, together with their pasture-lands.

[34] The Merarite clans (the rest of the Levites) were given:

from the tribe of Zebulun,
Jokneam, Kartah, [35] Dimnah and Nahalal, together with their pasture-lands – four towns;

[36] from the tribe of Reuben,
Bezer, Jahaz, [37] Kedemoth and Mephaath, together with their pasture-lands – four towns;

[38] from the tribe of Gad,
Ramoth in Gilead (a city of refuge for one accused of murder), Mahanaim, [39] Heshbon and Jazer, together with their pasture-lands – four towns in all.

[40] The total number of towns allotted to the Merarite clans, who were the rest of the Levites, came to twelve.

[41] The towns of the Levites in the territory held by the Israelites were forty-eight in all, together with their pasture-lands. [42] Each of these towns had pasture-lands surrounding it; this was true for all these towns.

[43] So the LORD gave Israel all the land he had sworn to give their ancestors, and they took possession of it and settled there. [44] The LORD gave them rest on every side, just as he had sworn to their ancestors. Not one of their enemies withstood them; the LORD gave all their enemies into their hands. [45] Not one of all the LORD's good promises to Israel failed; every one was fulfilled.

▬ PSALM 51:14-19

14 Deliver me from the guilt of bloodshed,
O God,
you who are God my Saviour,
and my tongue will sing of your
righteousness.
15 Open my lips, Lord,
and my mouth will declare your
praise.
16 You do not delight in sacrifice, or I would
bring it;
you do not take pleasure in burnt
offerings.
17 My sacrifice, O God, is a broken spirit;
a broken and contrite heart
you, God, will not despise.

18 May it please you to prosper Zion,
to build up the walls of Jerusalem.
19 Then you will delight in the sacrifices of
the righteous,
in burnt offerings offered whole;
then bulls will be offered on your
altar.

▬ PROVERBS 12:13-14

13 Evildoers are trapped by their sinful talk,
and so the innocent escape trouble.

14 From the fruit of their lips people are
filled with good things,
and the work of their hands brings
them reward.

▬ LUKE 18:24-43

24 Jesus looked at him and said, 'How hard
it is for the rich to enter the kingdom of
God! 25 Indeed, it is easier for a camel to go
through the eye of a needle than for someone who is rich to enter the kingdom of God.'

26 Those who heard this asked, 'Who then
can be saved?'

27 Jesus replied, 'What is impossible with
man is possible with God.'

28 Peter said to him, 'We have left all we
had to follow you!'

29 'Truly I tell you,' Jesus said to them, 'no
one who has left home or wife or brothers
or sisters or parents or children for the sake
of the kingdom of God 30 will fail to receive
many times as much in this age, and in the
age to come eternal life.'

31 Jesus took the Twelve aside and told
them, 'We are going up to Jerusalem, and
everything that is written by the prophets
about the Son of Man will be fulfilled. 32 He
will be handed over to the Gentiles. They
will mock him, insult him and spit on him;
33 they will flog him and kill him. On the
third day he will rise again.'

34 The disciples did not understand any
of this. Its meaning was hidden from them,
and they did not know what he was talking
about.

35 As Jesus approached Jericho, a blind
man was sitting by the roadside begging.
36 When he heard the crowd going by, he
asked what was happening. 37 They told
him, 'Jesus of Nazareth is passing by.'

38 He called out, 'Jesus, Son of David, have
mercy on me!'

39 Those who led the way rebuked him
and told him to be quiet, but he shouted all
the more, 'Son of David, have mercy on me!'

40 Jesus stopped and ordered the man
to be brought to him. When he came near,
Jesus asked him, 41 'What do you want me to
do for you?'

'Lord, I want to see,' he replied.

42 Jesus said to him, 'Receive your sight;
your faith has healed you.' 43 Immediately he received his sight and followed Jesus,
praising God. When all the people saw it,
they also praised God.

The Spirit of Holiness

'My sacrifice, O God, is a broken spirit; a broken and contrite heart you, God, will not despise.' **Psalm 51:17**

Here are two important steps toward greater openness to the work of the Holy Spirit in your life:

(1) Ask yourself, 'Is there any unresolved conflict, unrepented sin, or anything I must put right in order that God can flood my life with His Holy Spirit?' We must not forget that the Spirit of God is called the Holy Spirit. Holy symbolises purity; Spirit symbolises power. The Holy Spirit is completely holy, searching, convicting, cleansing, yet at the same time immensely powerful to support, strengthen, and sustain. If there is anything in your life that needs to be put right, then talk to God about it now. Remember at this point that you are not just reading a page – you are ridding yourself of a plague. You cannot have the Holy Spirit flowing through your life and hold onto unrepented sin. One or the other must go.

(2) Remind yourself that God is more eager to give you His Holy Spirit than you are to receive. Jesus called the giving of the Spirit 'the gift my Father promised' (Acts 1:4). This is the promise of promises. For God to go back on a promise would be the very reverse of His nature; it is impossible. The character of God is behind this promise. You can bank on it. If you could part the clouds for a moment and look into heaven you would see in the heart of God such an intense longing and yearning for you to be filled with His Spirit that it would completely overwhelm and overawe you. He aches to give you the fullness of His Spirit – He really does.

PRAYER

O Father, what You want for my life, I want too – for my will and Your will to coincide. Make me as eager to be filled as You are to fill me. For Jesus' sake. Amen.

FURTHER STUDY

Acts 2:14-38; Psa. 34:18; Isa. 66:2; Eph. 4:24
• How did Peter exhort the people to receive the Spirit?
• What was the result?

April 30

■ JOSHUA 22:1–23:16

22 Then Joshua summoned the Reubenites, the Gadites and the half-tribe of Manasseh ²and said to them, 'You have done all that Moses the servant of the LORD commanded, and you have obeyed me in everything I commanded. ³For a long time now – to this very day – you have not deserted your fellow Israelites but have

carried out the mission the LORD your God gave you. ⁴Now that the LORD your God has given them rest as he promised, return to your homes in the land that Moses the servant of the LORD gave you on the other side of the Jordan. ⁵But be very careful to keep the commandment and the law that Moses the servant of the LORD gave you: to love the LORD your God, to walk in obedience to him, to keep his commands, to hold fast to him and to serve him with all your heart and with all your soul.'

⁶Then Joshua blessed them and sent them away, and they went to their homes. ⁷(To the half-tribe of Manasseh Moses had given land in Bashan, and to the other half of the tribe Joshua gave land on the west side of the Jordan along with their fellow Israelites.) When Joshua sent them home, he blessed them, ⁸saying, 'Return to your homes with your great wealth – with large herds of livestock, with silver, gold, bronze and iron, and a great quantity of clothing – and divide the plunder from your enemies with your fellow Israelites.'

⁹So the Reubenites, the Gadites and the half-tribe of Manasseh left the Israelites at Shiloh in Canaan to return to Gilead, their own land, which they had acquired in accordance with the command of the LORD through Moses.

¹⁰When they came to Geliloth near the Jordan in the land of Canaan, the Reubenites, the Gadites and the half-tribe of Manasseh built an imposing altar there by the Jordan. ¹¹And when the Israelites heard that they had built the altar on the border of Canaan at Geliloth near the Jordan on the Israelite side, ¹²the whole assembly of Israel gathered at Shiloh to go to war against them.

¹³So the Israelites sent Phinehas son of Eleazar, the priest, to the land of Gilead – to Reuben, Gad and the half-tribe of Manasseh. ¹⁴With him they sent ten of the chief men, one from each of the tribes of Israel,

each the head of a family division among the Israelite clans.

¹⁵When they went to Gilead – to Reuben, Gad and the half-tribe of Manasseh – they said to them: ¹⁶'The whole assembly of the LORD says: "How could you break faith with the God of Israel like this? How could you turn away from the LORD and build yourselves an altar in rebellion against him now? ¹⁷Was not the sin of Peor enough for us? Up to this very day we have not cleansed ourselves from that sin, even though a plague fell on the community of the LORD! ¹⁸And are you now turning away from the LORD?

'"If you rebel against the LORD today, tomorrow he will be angry with the whole community of Israel. ¹⁹If the land you possess is defiled, come over to the LORD's land, where the LORD's tabernacle stands, and share the land with us. But do not rebel against the LORD or against us by building an altar for yourselves, other than the altar of the LORD our God. ²⁰When Achan son of Zerah was unfaithful in regard to the devoted things, did not wrath come on the whole community of Israel? He was not the only one who died for his sin."'

²¹Then Reuben, Gad and the half-tribe of Manasseh replied to the heads of the clans of Israel: ²²'The Mighty One, God, the LORD! The Mighty One, God, the LORD! He knows! And let Israel know! If this has been in rebellion or disobedience to the LORD, do not spare us this day. ²³If we have built our own altar to turn away from the LORD and to offer burnt offerings and grain offerings, or to sacrifice fellowship offerings on it, may the LORD himself call us to account.

²⁴'No! We did it for fear that some day your descendants might say to ours, "What do you have to do with the LORD, the God of Israel? ²⁵The LORD has made the Jordan a boundary between us and you – you Reubenites and Gadites! You have no share in the LORD." So your descendants might cause ours to stop fearing the LORD.

26'That is why we said, "Let us get ready and build an altar – but not for burnt offerings or sacrifices." 27On the contrary, it is to be a witness between us and you and the generations that follow, that we will worship the LORD at his sanctuary with our burnt offerings, sacrifices and fellowship offerings. Then in the future your descendants will not be able to say to ours, "You have no share in the LORD."

28'And we said, "If they ever say this to us, or to our descendants, we will answer: look at the replica of the LORD's altar, which our ancestors built, not for burnt offerings and sacrifices, but as a witness between us and you."

29'Far be it from us to rebel against the LORD and turn away from him today by building an altar for burnt offerings, grain offerings and sacrifices, other than the altar of the LORD our God that stands before his tabernacle.'

30When Phinehas the priest and the leaders of the community – the heads of the clans of the Israelites – heard what Reuben, Gad and Manasseh had to say, they were pleased. 31And Phinehas son of Eleazar, the priest, said to Reuben, Gad and Manasseh, 'Today we know that the LORD is with us, because you have not been unfaithful to the LORD in this matter. Now you have rescued the Israelites from the LORD's hand.'

32Then Phinehas son of Eleazar, the priest, and the leaders returned to Canaan from their meeting with the Reubenites and Gadites in Gilead and reported to the Israelites. 33They were glad to hear the report and praised God. And they talked no more about going to war against them to devastate the country where the Reubenites and the Gadites lived.

34And the Reubenites and the Gadites gave the altar this name: A Witness Between Us – that the LORD is God.

23 After a long time had passed and the LORD had given Israel rest from all their enemies around them, Joshua, by then a very old man, 2summoned all Israel – their elders, leaders, judges and officials – and said to them: 'I am very old. 3You yourselves have seen everything the LORD your God has done to all these nations for your sake; it was the LORD your God who fought for you. 4Remember how I have allotted as an inheritance for your tribes all the land of the nations that remain – the nations I conquered – between the Jordan and the Mediterranean Sea in the west. 5The LORD your God himself will push them out for your sake. He will drive them out before you, and you will take possession of their land, as the LORD your God promised you.

6'Be very strong; be careful to obey all that is written in the Book of the Law of Moses, without turning aside to the right or to the left. 7Do not associate with these nations that remain among you; do not invoke the names of their gods or swear by them. You must not serve them or bow down to them. 8But you are to hold fast to the LORD your God, as you have until now.

9'The LORD has driven out before you great and powerful nations; to this day no one has been able to withstand you. 10One of you routs a thousand, because the LORD your God fights for you, just as he promised. 11So be very careful to love the LORD your God.

12'But if you turn away and ally yourselves with the survivors of these nations that remain among you and if you intermarry with them and associate with them, 13then you may be sure that the LORD your God will no longer drive out these nations before you. Instead, they will become snares and traps for you, whips on your backs and thorns in your eyes, until you perish from this good land, which the LORD your God has given you.

14'Now I am about to go the way of all the earth. You know with all your heart and soul that not one of all the good promises the LORD your God gave you has failed. Every promise has been fulfilled; not one has failed. [15] But just as all the good things the LORD your God has promised you have come to you, so he will bring on you all the evil things he has threatened, until the LORD your God has destroyed you from this good land he has given you. [16] If you violate the covenant of the LORD your God, which he commanded you, and go and serve other gods and bow down to them, the LORD's anger will burn against you, and you will quickly perish from the good land he has given you.'

▬ PSALM 52:1-9

[1] Why do you boast of evil, you mighty
   hero?
   Why do you boast all day long,
   you who are a disgrace in the eyes of
   God?
[2] You who practise deceit,
   your tongue plots destruction;
   it is like a sharpened razor.
[3] You love evil rather than good,
   falsehood rather than speaking the
   truth.
[4] You love every harmful word,
   you deceitful tongue!

[5] Surely God will bring you down to
   everlasting ruin:
   He will snatch you up and pluck you
   from your tent;
   he will uproot you from the land of the
   living.
[6] The righteous will see and fear;
   they will laugh at you, saying,
[7] 'Here now is the man
   who did not make God his stronghold
   but trusted in his great wealth
   and grew strong by destroying
   others!'

[8] But I am like an olive tree
   flourishing in the house of God;
   I trust in God's unfailing love
   for ever and ever.
[9] For what you have done I will always
   praise you
   in the presence of your faithful people.
   And I will hope in your name,
   for your name is good.

▬ PROVERBS 12:15-16

[15] The way of fools seems right to them,
   but the wise listen to advice.

[16] Fools show their annoyance at once,
   but the prudent overlook an
   insult.

▬ LUKE 19:1-27

19 Jesus entered Jericho and was passing through. [2] A man was there by the name of Zacchaeus; he was a chief tax collector and was wealthy. [3] He wanted to see who Jesus was, but because he was short he could not see over the crowd. [4] So he ran ahead and climbed a sycamore-fig tree to see him, since Jesus was coming that way.

[5] When Jesus reached the spot, he looked up and said to him, 'Zacchaeus, come down immediately. I must stay at your house today.' [6] So he came down at once and welcomed him gladly.

[7] All the people saw this and began to mutter, 'He has gone to be the guest of a sinner.'

[8] But Zacchaeus stood up and said to the Lord, 'Look, Lord! Here and now I give half of my possessions to the poor, and if I have cheated anybody out of anything, I will pay back four times the amount.'

[9] Jesus said to him, 'Today salvation has come to this house, because this man, too,

is a son of Abraham. ¹⁰ For the Son of Man came to seek and to save the lost.'

¹¹ While they were listening to this, he went on to tell them a parable, because he was near Jerusalem and the people thought that the kingdom of God was going to appear at once. ¹² He said: 'A man of noble birth went to a distant country to have himself appointed king and then to return. ¹³ So he called ten of his servants and gave them ten minas. "Put this money to work," he said, "until I come back."

¹⁴ 'But his subjects hated him and sent a delegation after him to say, "We don't want this man to be our king."

¹⁵ 'He was made king, however, and returned home. Then he sent for the servants to whom he had given the money, in order to find out what they had gained with it.

¹⁶ 'The first one came and said, "Sir, your mina has earned ten more."

¹⁷ ' "Well done, my good servant!" his master replied. "Because you have been trustworthy in a very small matter, take charge of ten cities."

¹⁸ 'The second came and said, "Sir, your mina has earned five more."

¹⁹ 'His master answered, "You take charge of five cities."

²⁰ 'Then another servant came and said, "Sir, here is your mina; I have kept it laid away in a piece of cloth. ²¹ I was afraid of you, because you are a hard man. You take out what you did not put in and reap what you did not sow."

²² 'His master replied, "I will judge you by your own words, you wicked servant! You knew, did you, that I am a hard man, taking out what I did not put in, and reaping what I did not sow? ²³ Why then didn't you put my money on deposit, so that when I came back, I could have collected it with interest?"

²⁴ 'Then he said to those standing by, "Take his mina away from him and give it to the one who has ten minas."

²⁵ ' "Sir," they said, "he already has ten!"

²⁶ 'He replied, "I tell you that to everyone who has, more will be given, but as for the one who has nothing, even what they have will be taken away. ²⁷ But those enemies of mine who did not want me to be king over them – bring them here and kill them in front of me." '

No Matter What ...

'But I am like an olive tree flourishing in the house of God; I trust in God's unfailing love for ever and ever.'
Psalm 52:8

As he encourages himself in God, David utters: 'The LORD is my shepherd, I lack nothing' (Psa. 23:1). What a bold and positive statement to make! At first glance, however, the words seem quite absurd. Here is David in the midst of intense privation, hunted and hounded by hostile enemy forces, deserted by many of his former supporters – yet quietly affirming, 'I lack nothing'. In the past I have known many Christians who have had great difficulty in understanding this phrase. They have said, 'How can I recite this verse with any meaning when I want so many things? I want a happy family/better living conditions/an adequate supply of money/employment/a wife/a husband' and so on.

David's meaning becomes clear when we dig a little deeper into the original Hebrew words that are used. Our translation says: 'There is nothing I lack.' Another puts it like this: 'I shall not lack any good thing.' 'The main thought,' says one commentator, 'is that of not lacking - not being deficient - in proper care, management or husbandry.'

So what David is really saying is this: no matter what hardships or privations come my way, I am confident of this one thing - that I shall not lack the expert care and tender supervision of my Master and my Shepherd. There were many things that David lacked - he lacked the comforts of life, family affection, physical security, and so on. What he did not lack, however, was the assurance that God was with him in his difficulties, managing his affairs and turning all his stumbling blocks into stepping-stones.

PRAYER

Dear Lord Jesus, You who took everything that men threw at You and made it work toward Your ends – teach me how to do the same. Impress this truth deeply upon my spirit: that it is not what happens to me, but what I do with it, that determines the result. Amen.

FURTHER STUDY

Isa. 40:11; 41:1-10;
Deut. 33:27; Psa. 18:35-36
• What was God's assurance to the children of Israel?
• What was the psalmist's affirmation?

May 1

■ JOSHUA 24:1-33

24 Then Joshua assembled all the tribes of Israel at Shechem. He summoned the elders, leaders, judges and officials of Israel, and they presented themselves before God.

² Joshua said to all the people, 'This is what the LORD, the God of Israel, says: "Long ago your ancestors, including Terah the father of Abraham and Nahor, lived beyond the River Euphrates and worshipped other gods. ³ But I took your father Abraham from the land beyond the Euphrates and led him throughout Canaan and gave him many descendants. I gave him Isaac, ⁴ and to Isaac I gave Jacob and Esau. I assigned the hill country of Seir to Esau, but Jacob and his

family went down to Egypt.

⁵ ' "Then I sent Moses and Aaron, and I afflicted the Egyptians by what I did there, and I brought you out. ⁶ When I brought your people out of Egypt, you came to the sea, and the Egyptians pursued them with chariots and horsemen as far as the Red Sea. ⁷ But they cried to the LORD for help, and he put darkness between you and the Egyptians; he brought the sea over them and covered them. You saw with your own eyes what I did to the Egyptians. Then you lived in the wilderness for a long time.

⁸ ' "I brought you to the land of the Amorites who lived east of the Jordan. They fought against you, but I gave them into your hands. I destroyed them from before you, and you took possession of their land. ⁹ When Balak

son of Zippor, the king of Moab, prepared to fight against Israel, he sent for Balaam son of Beor to put a curse on you. ¹⁰But I would not listen to Balaam, so he blessed you again and again, and I delivered you out of his hand.

¹¹ ' "Then you crossed the Jordan and came to Jericho. The citizens of Jericho fought against you, as did also the Amorites, Perizzites, Canaanites, Hittites, Girgashites, Hivites and Jebusites, but I gave them into your hands. ¹²I sent the hornet ahead of you, which drove them out before you – also the two Amorite kings. You did not do it with your own sword and bow. ¹³So I gave you a land on which you did not toil and cities you did not build; and you live in them and eat from vineyards and olive groves that you did not plant."

¹⁴'Now fear the LORD and serve him with all faithfulness. Throw away the gods your ancestors worshipped beyond the River Euphrates and in Egypt, and serve the LORD. ¹⁵But if serving the LORD seems undesirable to you, then choose for yourselves this day whom you will serve, whether the gods your ancestors served beyond the Euphrates, or the gods of the Amorites, in whose land you are living. But as for me and my household, we will serve the LORD.'

¹⁶Then the people answered, 'Far be it from us to forsake the LORD to serve other gods! ¹⁷It was the LORD our God himself who brought us and our parents up out of Egypt, from that land of slavery, and performed those great signs before our eyes. He protected us on our entire journey and among all the nations through which we travelled. ¹⁸And the LORD drove out before us all the nations, including the Amorites, who lived in the land. We too will serve the LORD, because he is our God.'

¹⁹Joshua said to the people, 'You are not able to serve the LORD. He is a holy God; he is a jealous God. He will not forgive your rebellion and your sins. ²⁰If you forsake the LORD and serve foreign gods, he will turn and bring disaster on you and make an end of you, after he has been good to you.'

²¹But the people said to Joshua, 'No! We will serve the LORD.'

²²Then Joshua said, 'You are witnesses against yourselves that you have chosen to serve the LORD.'

'Yes, we are witnesses,' they replied.

²³'Now then,' said Joshua, 'throw away the foreign gods that are among you and yield your hearts to the LORD, the God of Israel.'

²⁴And the people said to Joshua, 'We will serve the LORD our God and obey him.'

²⁵On that day Joshua made a covenant for the people, and there at Shechem he reaffirmed for them decrees and laws. ²⁶And Joshua recorded these things in the Book of the Law of God. Then he took a large stone and set it up there under the oak near the holy place of the LORD.

²⁷'See!' he said to all the people. 'This stone will be a witness against us. It has heard all the words the LORD has said to us. It will be a witness against you if you are untrue to your God.'

²⁸Then Joshua dismissed the people, each to their own inheritance.

²⁹After these things, Joshua son of Nun, the servant of the LORD, died at the age of a hundred and ten. ³⁰And they buried him in the land of his inheritance, at Timnath Serah in the hill country of Ephraim, north of Mount Gaash.

³¹Israel served the LORD throughout the lifetime of Joshua and of the elders who outlived him and who had experienced everything the LORD had done for Israel.

³²And Joseph's bones, which the Israelites had brought up from Egypt, were buried at Shechem in the tract of land that Jacob bought for a hundred pieces of silver from the sons of Hamor, the father of Shechem. This became the inheritance of Joseph's descendants.

³³And Eleazar son of Aaron died and was buried at Gibeah, which had been allotted to his son Phinehas in the hill country of Ephraim.

▬ PSALM 53:1–6

¹ The fool says in his heart,
  'There is no God.'
  They are corrupt, and their ways are vile;
    there is no one who does good.

² God looks down from heaven
    on all mankind
  to see if there are any who understand,
    any who seek God.
³ Everyone has turned away, all have
      become corrupt;
    there is no one who does good,
    not even one.

⁴ Do all these evildoers know nothing?

  They devour my people as though eating
      bread;
    they never call on God.
⁵ But there they are, overwhelmed with
      dread,
    where there was nothing to dread.
  God scattered the bones of those who
      attacked you;
    you put them to shame, for God
      despised them.

⁶ Oh, that salvation for Israel would come
    out of Zion!
  When God restores his people,
    let Jacob rejoice and Israel be glad!

▬ PROVERBS 12:17–18

¹⁷ An honest witness tells the truth,
    but a false witness tells lies.

¹⁸ The words of the reckless pierce like
      swords,
    but the tongue of the wise brings
      healing.

▬ LUKE 19:28–48

²⁸ After Jesus had said this, he went on ahead, going up to Jerusalem. ²⁹ As he approached Bethphage and Bethany at the hill called the Mount of Olives, he sent two of his disciples, saying to them, ³⁰ 'Go to the village ahead of you, and as you enter it, you will find a colt tied there, which no one has ever ridden. Untie it and bring it here. ³¹ If anyone asks you, "Why are you untying it?" say, "The Lord needs it." '

³² Those who were sent ahead went and found it just as he had told them. ³³ As they were untying the colt, its owners asked them, 'Why are you untying the colt?'

³⁴ They replied, 'The Lord needs it.'

³⁵ They brought it to Jesus, threw their cloaks on the colt and put Jesus on it. ³⁶ As he went along, people spread their cloaks on the road.

³⁷ When he came near the place where the road goes down the Mount of Olives, the whole crowd of disciples began joyfully to praise God in loud voices for all the miracles they had seen:

³⁸ 'Blessed is the king who comes in the
      name of the Lord!'

  'Peace in heaven and glory in the highest!'

³⁹ Some of the Pharisees in the crowd said to Jesus, 'Teacher, rebuke your disciples!'

⁴⁰ 'I tell you,' he replied, 'if they keep quiet, the stones will cry out.'

⁴¹ As he approached Jerusalem and saw the city, he wept over it ⁴² and said, 'If you, even you, had only known on this day what would bring you peace – but now it is hidden from your eyes. ⁴³ The days will come upon you when your enemies will build an embankment against you and encircle you and hem you in on every side. ⁴⁴ They will dash you to the ground, you and the children within your walls. They will not leave

one stone on another, because you did not recognise the time of God's coming to you.'

⁴⁵When Jesus entered the temple courts, he began to drive out those who were selling. ⁴⁶'It is written,' he said to them, ' "My house will be a house of prayer"; but you have made it "a den of robbers".'

⁴⁷Every day he was teaching at the temple. But the chief priests, the teachers of the law and the leaders among the people were trying to kill him. ⁴⁸Yet they could not find any way to do it, because all the people hung on his words.

The Worst Thing ...

'An honest witness tells the truth, but a false witness tells lies.' **Proverbs 12:17**

Both we and the universe are made for integrity, and both the universe and we are alien to untruth and dishonesty. The whole thrust of the universe which God designed and created is simple, uncomplicated, and built on truth. There are great mysteries, of course, but no lies. Scientific laws are upheld by truth. Gravity, for example, will not lie; it is as true in one country as it is in another, as reliable in Jerusalem as it is in Japan.

It has often been pointed out that the word 'evil' is the word 'live' spelled backwards. Satan delights to take what God does and try to reverse it – to move life in the opposite way to that in which it was designed to go. Satan is a liar (John 8:44), and lies are always roundabout, complicated, and deceiving.

The fact that the universe is built on truth can be verified by the simple device known as a 'lie detector.' The lie detector test works on the basis that people who tell lies and know they are telling lies become extremely anxious and uncomfortable, and this anxiety is then picked up by the machine. But why does telling a lie make a person anxious? Because we are built for truth, and any departure from it registers on the inside in a way that can be picked up on the outside. A lie detector is not infallible and can sometimes (though not often) be fooled. But what cannot be fooled is the soul of the person who is lying. The worst thing about being a liar is to be the person telling the lie.

PRAYER

Father, help me lay hold of the fact that a lie demeans me, but the truth develops me. I cannot live successfully by a lie any more than I can fling myself out of the window and defy gravity. May I be a person of truth. In Jesus' name I pray. Amen.

FURTHER STUDY

Psa. 10:1-8; Matt. 17:17;
1 Tim. 6:3-10; Prov. 28:18-28

• List some of the aspects of integrity to which David committed himself.
• What did Paul highlight as one area where integrity is compromised?

May 2

■ JUDGES 1:1-2:23

1 After the death of Joshua, the Israelites asked the LORD, 'Who of us is to go up first to fight against the Canaanites?'

² The LORD answered, 'Judah shall go up; I have given the land into their hands.'

³ The men of Judah then said to the Simeonites their fellow Israelites, 'Come up with us into the territory allotted to us, to fight against the Canaanites. We in turn will go with you into yours.' So the Simeonites went with them.

⁴ When Judah attacked, the LORD gave the Canaanites and Perizzites into their hands, and they struck down ten thousand men at Bezek. ⁵ It was there that they found Adoni-Bezek and fought against him, putting to rout the Canaanites and Perizzites. ⁶ Adoni-Bezek fled, but they chased him and caught him, and cut off his thumbs and big toes.

⁷ Then Adoni-Bezek said, 'Seventy kings with their thumbs and big toes cut off have picked up scraps under my table. Now God has paid me back for what I did to them.' They brought him to Jerusalem, and he died there.

⁸ The men of Judah attacked Jerusalem also and took it. They put the city to the sword and set it on fire.

⁹ After that, Judah went down to fight against the Canaanites living in the hill country, the Negev and the western foothills. ¹⁰ They advanced against the Canaanites living in Hebron (formerly called Kiriath Arba) and defeated Sheshai, Ahiman and Talmai. ¹¹ From there they advanced against the people living in Debir (formerly called Kiriath Sepher).

¹² And Caleb said, 'I will give my daughter Aksah in marriage to the man who attacks and captures Kiriath Sepher.' ¹³ Othniel son of Kenaz, Caleb's younger brother, took it; so Caleb gave his daughter Aksah to him in marriage.

¹⁴ One day when she came to Othniel, she urged him to ask her father for a field. When she got off her donkey, Caleb asked her, 'What can I do for you?'

¹⁵ She replied, 'Do me a special favour. Since you have given me land in the Negev, give me also springs of water.' So Caleb gave her the upper and lower springs.

¹⁶ The descendants of Moses' father-in-law, the Kenite, went up from the City of Palms with the people of Judah to live among the inhabitants of the Desert of Judah in the Negev near Arad.

¹⁷ Then the men of Judah went with the Simeonites their fellow Israelites and attacked the Canaanites living in Zephath, and they totally destroyed the city. Therefore it was called Hormah. ¹⁸ Judah also took Gaza, Ashkelon and Ekron – each city with its territory.

¹⁹ The LORD was with the men of Judah. They took possession of the hill country, but they were unable to drive the people from the plains, because they had chariots fitted with iron. ²⁰ As Moses had promised, Hebron was given to Caleb, who drove from it the three sons of Anak. ²¹ The Benjaminites, however, did not drive out the Jebusites, who were living in Jerusalem; to this day the Jebusites live there with the Benjaminites.

²² Now the tribes of Joseph attacked Bethel, and the LORD was with them. ²³ When they sent men to spy out Bethel (formerly called Luz), ²⁴ the spies saw a man coming out of the city and they said to him, 'Show us how to get into the city and we will see

that you are treated well.' ²⁵So he showed them, and they put the city to the sword but spared the man and his whole family. ²⁶He then went to the land of the Hittites, where he built a city and called it Luz, which is its name to this day.

²⁷But Manasseh did not drive out the people of Beth Shan or Taanach or Dor or Ibleam or Megiddo and their surrounding settlements, for the Canaanites were determined to live in that land. ²⁸When Israel became strong, they pressed the Canaanites into forced labour but never drove them out completely. ²⁹Nor did Ephraim drive out the Canaanites living in Gezer, but the Canaanites continued to live there among them. ³⁰Neither did Zebulun drive out the Canaanites living in Kitron or Nahalol, so these Canaanites lived among them, but Zebulun did subject them to forced labour. ³¹Nor did Asher drive out those living in Akko or Sidon or Ahlab or Akzib or Helbah or Aphek or Rehob. ³²The Asherites lived among the Canaanite inhabitants of the land because they did not drive them out. ³³Neither did Naphtali drive out those living in Beth Shemesh or Beth Anath; but the Naphtalites too lived among the Canaanite inhabitants of the land, and those living in Beth Shemesh and Beth Anath became forced labourers for them. ³⁴The Amorites confined the Danites to the hill country, not allowing them to come down into the plain. ³⁵And the Amorites were determined also to hold out in Mount Heres, Aijalon and Shaalbim, but when the power of the tribes of Joseph increased, they too were pressed into forced labour. ³⁶The boundary of the Amorites was from Scorpion Pass to Sela and beyond.

2 The angel of the LORD went up from Gilgal to Bokim and said, 'I brought you up out of Egypt and led you into the land that I swore to give to your ancestors. I said, "I will never break my covenant with you, ²and you shall not make a covenant with the people of this land, but you shall break down their altars." Yet you have disobeyed me. Why have you done this? ³And I have also said, "I will not drive them out before you; they will become traps for you, and their gods will become snares to you."'

⁴When the angel of the LORD had spoken these things to all the Israelites, the people wept aloud, ⁵and they called that place Bokim. There they offered sacrifices to the LORD.

⁶After Joshua had dismissed the Israelites, they went to take possession of the land, each to their own inheritance. ⁷The people served the LORD throughout the lifetime of Joshua and of the elders who outlived him and who had seen all the great things the LORD had done for Israel.

⁸Joshua son of Nun, the servant of the LORD, died at the age of a hundred and ten. ⁹And they buried him in the land of his inheritance, at Timnath Heres in the hill country of Ephraim, north of Mount Gaash.

¹⁰After that whole generation had been gathered to their ancestors, another generation grew up who knew neither the LORD nor what he had done for Israel. ¹¹Then the Israelites did evil in the eyes of the LORD and served the Baals. ¹²They forsook the LORD, the God of their ancestors, who had brought them out of Egypt. They followed and worshipped various gods of the peoples around them. They aroused the LORD's anger ¹³because they forsook him and served Baal and the Ashtoreths. ¹⁴In his anger against Israel the LORD gave them into the hands of raiders who plundered them. He sold them into the hands of their enemies all around, whom they were no longer able to resist. ¹⁵Whenever Israel went out to fight, the hand of the LORD was against them to defeat them, just as he had sworn to them. They were in great distress.

¹⁶Then the LORD raised up judges, who saved them out of the hands of these raiders. ¹⁷Yet they would not listen to their judges but prostituted themselves to other gods and worshipped them. They quickly turned

from the ways of their ancestors, who had been obedient to the LORD's commands. ¹⁸ Whenever the LORD raised up a judge for them, he was with the judge and saved them out of the hands of their enemies as long as the judge lived; for the LORD relented because of their groaning under those who oppressed and afflicted them. ¹⁹ But when the judge died, the people returned to ways even more corrupt than those of their ancestors, following other gods and serving and worshipping them. They refused to give up their evil practices and stubborn ways.

²⁰ Therefore the LORD was very angry with Israel and said, 'Because this nation has violated the covenant I ordained for their ancestors and has not listened to me, ²¹ I will no longer drive out before them any of the nations Joshua left when he died. ²² I will use them to test Israel and see whether they will keep the way of the LORD and walk in it as their ancestors did.' ²³ The LORD had allowed those nations to remain; he did not drive them out at once by giving them into the hands of Joshua.

■ PSALM 54:1-7

¹ Save me, O God, by your name;
  vindicate me by your might.
² Hear my prayer, O God;
  listen to the words of my mouth.

³ Arrogant foes are attacking me;
  ruthless people are trying to kill me –
  people without regard for God.

⁴ Surely God is my help;
  the Lord is the one who sustains me.

⁵ Let evil recoil on those who slander me;
  in your faithfulness destroy them.

⁶ I will sacrifice a freewill offering to you;

I will praise your name, LORD, for it is good.
⁷ You have delivered me from all my troubles,
  and my eyes have looked in triumph on my foes.

■ PROVERBS 12:19-22

¹⁹ Truthful lips endure for ever,
  but a lying tongue lasts only a moment.

²⁰ Deceit is in the hearts of those who plot evil,
  but those who promote peace have joy.

²¹ No harm overtakes the righteous,
  but the wicked have their fill of trouble.

²² The LORD detests lying lips,
  but he delights in people who are trustworthy.

■ LUKE 20:1-19

20 One day as Jesus was teaching the people in the temple courts and proclaiming the good news, the chief priests and the teachers of the law, together with the elders, came up to him. ² 'Tell us by what authority you are doing these things,' they said. 'Who gave you this authority?'

³ He replied, 'I will also ask you a question. Tell me: ⁴ John's baptism – was it from heaven, or of human origin?'

⁵ They discussed it among themselves and said, 'If we say, "From heaven," he will ask, "Why didn't you believe him?" ⁶ But if we say, "Of human origin," all the people will stone us, because they are persuaded that John was a prophet.'

⁷ So they answered, 'We don't know where it was from.'

⁸Jesus said, 'Neither will I tell you by what authority I am doing these things.'

⁹He went on to tell the people this parable: 'A man planted a vineyard, rented it to some farmers and went away for a long time. ¹⁰At harvest time he sent a servant to the tenants so they would give him some of the fruit of the vineyard. But the tenants beat him and sent him away empty-handed. ¹¹He sent another servant, but that one also they beat and treated shamefully and sent away empty-handed. ¹²He sent still a third, and they wounded him and threw him out.

¹³'Then the owner of the vineyard said, "What shall I do? I will send my son, whom I love; perhaps they will respect him."

¹⁴'But when the tenants saw him, they talked the matter over. "This is the heir," they said. "Let's kill him, and the inheritance will be ours." ¹⁵So they threw him out of the vineyard and killed him.

'What then will the owner of the vineyard do to them? ¹⁶He will come and kill those tenants and give the vineyard to others.'

When the people heard this, they said, 'God forbid!'

¹⁷Jesus looked directly at them and asked, 'Then what is the meaning of that which is written:

'"The stone the builders rejected
    has become the cornerstone"?

¹⁸Everyone who falls on that stone will be broken to pieces; anyone on whom it falls will be crushed.'

¹⁹The teachers of the law and the chief priests looked for a way to arrest him immediately, because they knew he had spoken this parable against them. But they were afraid of the people.

Before You Can Say 'Yes'

'Save me, O God, by your name ... ruthless people are trying to kill me - people without regard for God.'
Psalm 54:1,3

The more disillusioned we are with the world, the more motivated we will be to pursue the Christian way. If we are not willing to face the reality that we live in a fallen world, that the latest invention is not going to bring us Utopia, that possessions fail to give any lasting happiness, then we are not going to move along the rugged road of faith with a steady tread.

My favourite word to summarise the message of this, the first of the Songs of Ascents, is renunciation. The psalmist seems to have made a decision to move away from the lies he has heard, and we too must make a similar decision. We must renounce lies such as that human beings are basically good, we are not responsible for the way we are, we can find happiness independently of God. The truth of God does not begin to dawn upon us until we realise that what we have assumed was the truth - that we are the masters of our fate - is in fact a lie. It is painful to admit that we have been taken in by the world's lies, but until we accept that we have and confess it, we are not ready to move on into all that God has for us.

If the psalmist were writing today, he might have worded his prayer like this: 'Save me, O Lord, from the lies of those who think they know the answer to life but don't.' We must discover that before we can say 'yes' to God we must first learn to say 'no' to the world.

PRAYER

Father, I would make the prayer of the psalmist my prayer also. Rescue me from those who would represent the world to me in terms that are not entirely true. I turn from the untrue to the True. Help me dear Lord. In Jesus' name. Amen.

FURTHER STUDY

Luke 21:29-36; Rom. 12:1-2; Col. 3:2
- How does Paul admonish the Romans?
- What did he encourage the Colossians to do?

May 3

■ JUDGES 3:1– 4:24

3 These are the nations the LORD left to test all those Israelites who had not experienced any of the wars in Canaan ²(he did this only to teach warfare to the descendants of the Israelites who had not had previous battle experience): ³the five rulers of the Philistines, all the Canaanites, the Sidonians, and the Hivites living in the Lebanon mountains from Mount Baal Hermon to Lebo Hamath. ⁴They were left to test the Israelites to see whether they would obey the LORD's commands, which he had given their ancestors through Moses.

⁵The Israelites lived among the Canaanites, Hittites, Amorites, Perizzites, Hivites and Jebusites. ⁶They took their daughters in marriage and gave their own daughters to their sons, and served their gods.

⁷The Israelites did evil in the eyes of the LORD; they forgot the LORD their God and served the Baals and the Asherahs. ⁸The anger of the LORD burned against Israel so that he sold them into the hands of Cushan-Rishathaim king of Aram Naharaim, to whom the Israelites were subject for eight years. ⁹But when they cried out to the LORD, he raised up for them a deliverer, Othniel son of Kenaz, Caleb's younger brother, who saved them. ¹⁰The Spirit of the LORD came on him, so that he became Israel's judge and went to war. The LORD gave Cushan-Rishathaim king of Aram into the hands of Othniel, who overpowered him. ¹¹So the land had peace for forty years, until Othniel son of Kenaz died.

¹²Again the Israelites did evil in the eyes of the LORD, and because they did this evil the LORD gave Eglon king of Moab power over Israel. ¹³Getting the Ammonites and Amalekites to join him, Eglon came and attacked Israel, and they took possession of the City of Palms. ¹⁴The Israelites were subject to Eglon king of Moab for eighteen years.

¹⁵Again the Israelites cried out to the LORD, and he gave them a deliverer – Ehud, a left-handed man, the son of Gera the Benjaminite. The Israelites sent him with tribute to Eglon king of Moab. ¹⁶Now Ehud had made a double-edged sword about a cubit long, which he strapped to his right thigh under his clothing. ¹⁷He presented the tribute to Eglon king of Moab, who was a very

fat man. [18] After Ehud had presented the tribute, he sent on their way those who had carried it. [19] But on reaching the stone images near Gilgal he himself went back to Eglon and said, 'Your majesty, I have a secret message for you.'

The king said to his attendants, 'Leave us!' And they all left.

[20] Ehud then approached him while he was sitting alone in the upper room of his palace and said, 'I have a message from God for you.' As the king rose from his seat, [21] Ehud reached with his left hand, drew the sword from his right thigh and plunged it into the king's belly. [22] Even the handle sank in after the blade, and his bowels discharged. Ehud did not pull the sword out, and the fat closed in over it. [23] Then Ehud went out to the porch; he shut the doors of the upper room behind him and locked them.

[24] After he had gone, the servants came and found the doors of the upper room locked. They said, 'He must be relieving himself in the inner room of the palace.' [25] They waited to the point of embarrassment, but when he did not open the doors of the room, they took a key and unlocked them. There they saw their lord fallen to the floor, dead.

[26] While they waited, Ehud got away. He passed by the stone images and escaped to Seirah. [27] When he arrived there, he blew a trumpet in the hill country of Ephraim, and the Israelites went down with him from the hills, with him leading them.

[28] 'Follow me,' he ordered, 'for the LORD has given Moab, your enemy, into your hands.' So they followed him down and took possession of the fords of the Jordan that led to Moab; they allowed no one to cross over. [29] At that time they struck down about ten thousand Moabites, all vigorous and strong; not one escaped. [30] That day Moab was made subject to Israel, and the land had peace for eighty years.

[31] After Ehud came Shamgar son of Anath, who struck down six hundred Philistines with an ox-goad. He too saved Israel.

4 Again the Israelites did evil in the eyes of the LORD, now that Ehud was dead. [2] So the LORD sold them into the hands of Jabin king of Canaan, who reigned in Hazor. Sisera, the commander of his army, was based in Harosheth Haggoyim. [3] Because he had nine hundred chariots fitted with iron and had cruelly oppressed the Israelites for twenty years, they cried to the LORD for help.

[4] Now Deborah, a prophet, the wife of Lappidoth, was leading Israel at that time. [5] She held court under the Palm of Deborah between Ramah and Bethel in the hill country of Ephraim, and the Israelites went up to her to have their disputes decided. [6] She sent for Barak son of Abinoam from Kedesh in Naphtali and said to him, 'The LORD, the God of Israel, commands you: "Go, take with you ten thousand men of Naphtali and Zebulun and lead them up to Mount Tabor. [7] I will lead Sisera, the commander of Jabin's army, with his chariots and his troops to the River Kishon and give him into your hands."'

[8] Barak said to her, 'If you go with me, I will go; but if you don't go with me, I won't go.'

[9] 'Certainly I will go with you,' said Deborah. 'But because of the course you are taking, the honour will not be yours, for the LORD will deliver Sisera into the hands of a woman.' So Deborah went with Barak to Kedesh. [10] There Barak summoned Zebulun and Naphtali, and ten thousand men went up under his command. Deborah also went up with him.

[11] Now Heber the Kenite had left the other Kenites, the descendants of Hobab, Moses' brother-in-law, and pitched his tent by the great tree in Zaanannim near Kedesh.

[12] When they told Sisera that Barak son of Abinoam had gone up to Mount Tabor, [13] Sisera summoned from Harosheth Haggoyim

to the River Kishon all his men and his nine hundred chariots fitted with iron.

¹⁴ Then Deborah said to Barak, 'Go! This is the day the LORD has given Sisera into your hands. Has not the LORD gone ahead of you?' So Barak went down Mount Tabor, with ten thousand men following him. ¹⁵ At Barak's advance, the LORD routed Sisera and all his chariots and army by the sword, and Sisera got down from his chariot and fled on foot.

¹⁶ Barak pursued the chariots and army as far as Harosheth Haggoyim, and all Sisera's troops fell by the sword; not a man was left. ¹⁷ Sisera, meanwhile, fled on foot to the tent of Jael, the wife of Heber the Kenite, because there was an alliance between Jabin king of Hazor and the family of Heber the Kenite.

¹⁸ Jael went out to meet Sisera and said to him, 'Come, my lord, come right in. Don't be afraid.' So he entered her tent, and she covered him with a blanket.

¹⁹ 'I'm thirsty,' he said. 'Please give me some water.' She opened a skin of milk, gave him a drink, and covered him up.

²⁰ 'Stand in the doorway of the tent,' he told her. 'If someone comes and asks you, "Is anyone in there?" say "No."'

²¹ But Jael, Heber's wife, picked up a tent peg and a hammer and went quietly to him while he lay fast asleep, exhausted. She drove the peg through his temple into the ground, and he died.

²² Just then Barak came by in pursuit of Sisera, and Jael went out to meet him. 'Come,' she said, 'I will show you the man you're looking for.' So he went in with her, and there lay Sisera with the tent peg through his temple – dead.

²³ On that day God subdued Jabin king of Canaan before the Israelites. ²⁴ And the hand of the Israelites pressed harder and harder against Jabin king of Canaan until they destroyed him.

■ PSALM 55:1-8

¹ Listen to my prayer, O God,
   do not ignore my plea;
² hear me and answer me.
My thoughts trouble me and I am
      distraught
³   because of what my enemy is saying,
   because of the threats of the wicked;
for they bring down suffering on me
   and assail me in their anger.

⁴ My heart is in anguish within me;
   the terrors of death have fallen on me.
⁵ Fear and trembling have beset me;
   horror has overwhelmed me.
⁶ I said, 'Oh, that I had the wings of a dove!
   I would fly away and be at rest.
⁷ I would flee far away
   and stay in the desert;
⁸ I would hurry to my place of shelter,
   far from the tempest and storm.'

■ PROVERBS 12:23-24

²³ The prudent keep their knowledge to
      themselves,
   but a fool's heart blurts out folly.

²⁴ Diligent hands will rule,
   but laziness ends in forced
      labour.

■ LUKE 20:20-40

²⁰ Keeping a close watch on him, they sent spies, who pretended to be sincere. They hoped to catch Jesus in something he said, so that they might hand him over to the power and authority of the governor. ²¹ So the spies questioned him: 'Teacher, we know that you speak and teach what is right, and that you do not show partiality but teach the way of God in accordance with

the truth. [22]Is it right for us to pay taxes to Caesar or not?'

[23]He saw through their duplicity and said to them, [24]'Show me a denarius. Whose image and inscription are on it?'

'Caesar's,' they replied.

[25]He said to them, 'Then give back to Caesar what is Caesar's, and to God what is God's.'

[26]They were unable to trap him in what he had said there in public. And astonished by his answer, they became silent.

[27]Some of the Sadducees, who say there is no resurrection, came to Jesus with a question. [28]'Teacher,' they said, 'Moses wrote for us that if a man's brother dies and leaves a wife but no children, the man must marry the widow and raise up offspring for his brother. [29]Now there were seven brothers. The first one married a woman and died childless. [30]The second [31]and then the third married her, and in the same way the seven died, leaving no children. [32]Finally, the woman died too. [33]Now then, at the resurrection whose wife will she be, since the seven were married to her?'

[34]Jesus replied, 'The people of this age marry and are given in marriage. [35]But those who are considered worthy of taking part in the age to come and in the resurrection from the dead will neither marry nor be given in marriage, [36]and they can no longer die; for they are like the angels. They are God's children, since they are children of the resurrection. [37]But in the account of the burning bush, even Moses showed that the dead rise, for he calls the Lord "the God of Abraham, and the God of Isaac, and the God of Jacob". [38]He is not the God of the dead, but of the living, for to him all are alive.'

[39]Some of the teachers of the law responded, 'Well said, teacher!' [40]And no one dared to ask him any more questions.

The Secret of Survival

'Diligent hands will rule, but laziness ends in forced labour.' **Proverbs 12:24**

We need to make clear the difference between diligence and obstinacy. I know people who have experienced spiritual shipwreck because they didn't know the difference between these two things. When asked to clarify the difference between perseverance and obstinacy, a student wrote: 'One is a strong will and the other is a strong won't.' Diligence is dogged perseverance; obstinacy is dogged inflexibility and self-will.

A man whose life was full of promise as far as the Christian ministry was concerned now spends his days in depression because he did not know the difference between these two things. He set out on a project that he thought was God's will for him, and when things started to go wrong, instead of checking his guidance, he continued to press on and ended up in failure. Those who loved him, and were more objective, urged him to give up as what he was doing was clearly not the will of God. However, he did not have the wisdom to realise that what he was doing was not being diligent but obstinate. Now he lives in perpetual disillusionment.

When Jesus came to Calvary, He said, 'I have brought you glory on earth by finishing the work you gave me to do' (John 17:4). Note the word 'You'. There were many who would have liked Jesus to do this and that, to go here and go there, but He did only what the Father required Him to do. Saying 'yes' to God's will and pursuing it is diligence. Saying 'yes' to a thing that is not God's will and pursuing that is obstinacy. We had better learn the difference.

PRAYER

Father, I see how important it is to be clear about these two issues. Help me differentiate between diligence and obstinacy so that at the end of my time here on earth I, too, will be able to say, 'I have finished the work which You have given me to do'. Amen.

FURTHER STUDY

Matt. 25:14-30; 7:26; James 2:14
• What was Jesus' teaching in the parable of the talents?
• Why were the two who multiplied the talents successful?

May 4

■ JUDGES 5:1–6:10

5 On that day Deborah and Barak son of Abinoam sang this song:

2 'When the princes in Israel take the lead,
    when the people willingly offer
        themselves –
    praise the LORD!

3 'Hear this, you kings! Listen, you rulers!
    I, even I, will sing to the LORD;
    I will praise the LORD, the God of
        Israel, in song.

4 'When you, LORD, went out from Seir,
    when you marched from the land of
        Edom,
    the earth shook, the heavens poured,
    the clouds poured down water.
5 The mountains quaked before the LORD,
    the One of Sinai,
    before the LORD, the God of Israel.

6 'In the days of Shamgar son of Anath,
    in the days of Jael, the highways were
        abandoned;
    travellers took to winding paths.
7 Villagers in Israel would not fight;
    they held back until I, Deborah, arose,
    until I arose, a mother in Israel.
8 God chose new leaders
    when war came to the city gates,
    but not a shield or spear was seen
        among forty thousand in Israel.
9 My heart is with Israel's princes,
    with the willing volunteers among
        the people.
    Praise the LORD!

10 'You who ride on white donkeys,
    sitting on your saddle blankets,
    and you who walk along the road,
    consider 11 the voice of the singers at the
        watering places.
    They recite the victories of the LORD,
    the victories of his villagers in Israel.

'Then the people of the LORD
went down to the city gates.
¹² "Wake up, wake up, Deborah!
Wake up, wake up, break out in song!
Arise, Barak!
Take captive your captives, son of
Abinoam."

¹³ 'The remnant of the nobles came down;
the people of the LORD came down to
me against the mighty.
¹⁴ Some came from Ephraim, whose roots
were in Amalek;
Benjamin was with the people who
followed you.
From Makir captains came down,
from Zebulun those who bear a
commander's staff.
¹⁵ The princes of Issachar were with
Deborah;
yes, Issachar was with Barak,
sent under his command into the
valley.
In the districts of Reuben
there was much searching of heart.
¹⁶ Why did you stay among the sheepfolds
to hear the whistling for the flocks?
In the districts of Reuben
there was much searching of heart.
¹⁷ Gilead stayed beyond the Jordan.
And Dan, why did he linger by the
ships?
Asher remained on the coast
and stayed in his coves.
¹⁸ The people of Zebulun risked their very
lives;
so did Naphtali on the terraced fields.

¹⁹ 'Kings came, they fought,
the kings of Canaan fought.
At Taanach, by the waters of Megiddo,
they took no plunder of silver.
²⁰ From the heavens the stars fought,
from their courses they fought against
Sisera.
²¹ The River Kishon swept them away,

the age-old river, the River Kishon.
March on, my soul; be strong!
²² Then thundered the horses' hooves –
galloping, galloping go his mighty
steeds.
²³ "Curse Meroz," said the angel of the
LORD.
"Curse its people bitterly,
because they did not come to help the
LORD,
to help the LORD against the mighty."

²⁴ 'Most blessed of women be Jael,
the wife of Heber the Kenite,
most blessed of tent-dwelling women.
²⁵ He asked for water, and she gave him
milk;
in a bowl fit for nobles she brought
him curdled milk.
²⁶ Her hand reached for the tent peg,
her right hand for the workman's
hammer.
She struck Sisera, she crushed his head,
she shattered and pierced his temple.
²⁷ At her feet he sank,
he fell; there he lay.
At her feet he sank, he fell;
where he sank, there he fell – dead.

²⁸ 'Through the window peered Sisera's
mother;
behind the lattice she cried out,
"Why is his chariot so long in coming?
Why is the clatter of his chariots
delayed?"
²⁹ The wisest of her ladies answer her;
indeed, she keeps saying to herself,
³⁰ "Are they not finding and dividing the
spoils:
a woman or two for each man,
colourful garments as plunder for Sisera,
colourful garments embroidered,
highly embroidered garments for my
neck –
all this as plunder?"

³¹'So may all your enemies perish, O LORD!
But may all who love you be like the
sun
when it rises in its strength.'

Then the land had peace for forty years.

6 The Israelites did evil in the eyes of
the LORD, and for seven years he gave
them into the hands of the Midianites.
²Because the power of Midian was so op-
pressive, the Israelites prepared shelters
for themselves in mountain clefts, caves
and strongholds. ³Whenever the Israelites
planted their crops, the Midianites, Amalekites and other eastern peoples invaded
the country. ⁴They camped on the land
and ruined the crops all the way to Gaza
and did not spare a living thing for Israel, neither sheep nor cattle nor donkeys.
⁵They came up with their livestock and
their tents like swarms of locusts. It was
impossible to count them or their camels;
they invaded the land to ravage it. ⁶Midi-
an so impoverished the Israelites that they
cried out to the LORD for help.

⁷When the Israelites cried out to the LORD
because of Midian, ⁸he sent them a prophet,
who said, 'This is what the LORD, the God of
Israel, says: I brought you up out of Egypt,
out of the land of slavery. ⁹I rescued you from
the hand of the Egyptians. And I delivered
you from the hand of all your oppressors; I
drove them out before you and gave you their
land. ¹⁰I said to you, "I am the LORD your
God; do not worship the gods of the Amorites, in whose land you live." But you have
not listened to me.'

■ PSALM 55:9-14

⁹Lord, confuse the wicked, confound
their words,
for I see violence and strife in the city.
¹⁰Day and night they prowl about on its
walls;

malice and abuse are within it.
¹¹Destructive forces are at work in the city;
threats and lies never leave its streets.

¹²If an enemy were insulting me,
I could endure it;
if a foe were rising against me,
I could hide.
¹³But it is you, a man like myself,
my companion, my close friend,
¹⁴with whom I once enjoyed sweet
fellowship
at the house of God,
as we walked about
among the worshippers.

■ PROVERBS 12:25-26

²⁵Anxiety weighs down the heart,
but a kind word cheers it up.

²⁶The righteous choose their friends
carefully,
but the way of the wicked leads them
astray.

■ LUKE 20:41–21:19

⁴¹Then Jesus said to them, 'Why is it said
that the Messiah is the son of David? ⁴²Da-
vid himself declares in the Book of Psalms:

'"The Lord said to my Lord:
'Sit at my right hand
⁴³until I make your enemies
a footstool for your feet.'"

⁴⁴David calls him "Lord." How then can he
be his son?'

⁴⁵While all the people were listening,
Jesus said to his disciples, ⁴⁶'Beware of
the teachers of the law. They like to walk
around in flowing robes and love to be
greeted with respect in the market-places

and have the most important seats in the synagogues and the places of honour at banquets. [47] They devour widows' houses and for a show make lengthy prayers. These men will be punished most severely.'

21 As Jesus looked up, he saw the rich putting their gifts into the temple treasury. [2] He also saw a poor widow put in two very small copper coins. [3] 'Truly I tell you,' he said, 'this poor widow has put in more than all the others. [4] All these people gave their gifts out of their wealth; but she out of her poverty put in all she had to live on.'

[5] Some of his disciples were remarking about how the temple was adorned with beautiful stones and with gifts dedicated to God. But Jesus said, [6] 'As for what you see here, the time will come when not one stone will be left on another; every one of them will be thrown down.'

[7] 'Teacher,' they asked, 'when will these things happen? And what will be the sign that they are about to take place?'

[8] He replied: 'Watch out that you are not deceived. For many will come in my name, claiming, "I am he," and, "The time is near." Do not follow them. [9] When you hear of wars and uprisings, do not be frightened. These things must happen first, but the end will not come right away.'

[10] Then he said to them: 'Nation will rise against nation, and kingdom against kingdom. [11] There will be great earthquakes, famines and pestilences in various places, and fearful events and great signs from heaven.

[12] 'But before all this, they will seize you and persecute you. They will hand you over to synagogues and put you in prison, and you will be brought before kings and governors, and all on account of my name. [13] And so you will bear testimony to me. [14] But make up your mind not to worry beforehand how you will defend yourselves. [15] For I will give you words and wisdom that none of your adversaries will be able to resist or contradict. [16] You will be betrayed even by parents, brothers and sisters, relatives and friends, and they will put some of you to death. [17] Everyone will hate you because of me. [18] But not a hair of your head will perish. [19] Stand firm, and you will win life.

'Clinging to His Creeks'

'... Asher remained on the coast and stayed in his coves.' **Judges 5:17**

One of the greatest mistakes we can make in life is to block the efforts of the Divine Eagle when He attempts to push us out of the nest of the accustomed into the world of the adventurous. Asher did this – the account in the Moffatt translation reads: 'Asher sat still by the seaboard clinging to his creeks.' Although the metaphor is changed, the principle is still the same. There was Asher sitting by the seaboard, clinging to his creeks, when he could have launched out into the ocean and experienced the joy of a great adventure. In the face of the big, he settled for the little. They were 'his' creeks and he wasn't going to let the accustomed go to venture into the unaccustomed no matter how great the possibilities.

Asher is a type of Christian who wants to stay by the safe and secure and finishes up by doing nothing and getting nowhere. I am not advocating spiritual recklessness, nor am I arguing for an unmindful approach to the Christian life; I am simply saying that we ought to be ocean-minded and not creek-minded Christians. The people who try to find inner security by clinging to the creeks are invariably unfulfilled, for we are inwardly made for growth and creativity.

A turtle doesn't get anywhere until he sticks his neck out! To cling to our creeks for safety and security is to be upset at every call of the big. We are made for the big and are restless in our littleness. We cannot be content this side of God's purpose.

PRAYER

O Father, You are calling and I must come. I come from my littleness and watch it sink into the bigness of Your purpose for me. The great calls and I must come – at any price. Amen.

FURTHER STUDY

1 Sam. 17; Matt. 21:22; Mark 11:24; 1 John 5:14-15
• In what ways was David adventurous?
• On what was his adventurous spirit based?

May 5

▬ JUDGES 6:11–7:25

[11] The angel of the LORD came and sat down under the oak in Ophrah that belonged to Joash the Abiezrite, where his son Gideon was threshing wheat in a winepress to keep it from the Midianites. [12] When the angel of the LORD appeared to Gideon, he said, 'The LORD is with you, mighty warrior.'

[13] 'Pardon me, my lord,' Gideon replied, 'but if the LORD is with us, why has all this happened to us? Where are all his wonders that our ancestors told us about when they said, "Did not the LORD bring us up out of Egypt?" But now the LORD has abandoned us and given us into the hand of Midian.'

[14] The LORD turned to him and said, 'Go in the strength you have and save Israel out of Midian's hand. Am I not sending you?'

[15] 'Pardon me, my lord,' Gideon replied, 'but how can I save Israel? My clan is the weakest in Manasseh, and I am the least in my family.'

[16] The LORD answered, 'I will be with you, and you will strike down all the Midianites, leaving none alive.'

[17] Gideon replied, 'If now I have found favour in your eyes, give me a sign that it is really you talking to me. [18] Please do not go away until I come back and bring my offering and set it before you.'

And the LORD said, 'I will wait until you return.'

[19] Gideon went inside, prepared a young goat, and from an ephah of flour he made bread without yeast. Putting the meat in a basket and its broth in a pot, he brought them out and offered them to him under the oak.

[20] The angel of God said to him, 'Take the meat and the unleavened bread, place them on this rock, and pour out the broth.' And Gideon did so. [21] Then the angel of the LORD touched the meat and the unleavened bread with the tip of the staff that was in his hand. Fire flared from the rock, consuming the meat and the bread. And the angel of the

LORD disappeared. ²²When Gideon realised that it was the angel of the LORD, he exclaimed, 'Alas, Sovereign LORD! I have seen the angel of the LORD face to face!'

²³But the LORD said to him, 'Peace! Do not be afraid. You are not going to die.'

²⁴So Gideon built an altar to the LORD there and called it The LORD Is Peace. To this day it stands in Ophrah of the Abiezrites.

²⁵That same night the LORD said to him, 'Take the second bull from your father's herd, the one seven years old. Tear down your father's altar to Baal and cut down the Asherah pole beside it. ²⁶Then build a proper kind of altar to the LORD your God on the top of this height. Using the wood of the Asherah pole that you cut down, offer the second bull as a burnt offering.'

²⁷So Gideon took ten of his servants and did as the LORD told him. But because he was afraid of his family and the townspeople, he did it at night rather than in the daytime.

²⁸In the morning when the people of the town got up, there was Baal's altar, demolished, with the Asherah pole beside it cut down and the second bull sacrificed on the newly-built altar!

²⁹They asked each other, 'Who did this?'

When they carefully investigated, they were told, 'Gideon son of Joash did it.'

³⁰The people of the town demanded of Joash, 'Bring out your son. He must die, because he has broken down Baal's altar and cut down the Asherah pole beside it.'

³¹But Joash replied to the hostile crowd around him, 'Are you going to plead Baal's cause? Are you trying to save him? Whoever fights for him shall be put to death by morning! If Baal really is a god, he can defend himself when someone breaks down his altar.' ³²So because Gideon broke down Baal's altar, they gave him the name Jerub-Baal that day, saying, 'Let Baal contend with him.'

³³Now all the Midianites, Amalekites and other eastern peoples joined forces and crossed over the Jordan and camped in the Valley of Jezreel. ³⁴Then the Spirit of the LORD came on Gideon, and he blew a trumpet, summoning the Abiezrites to follow him. ³⁵He sent messengers throughout Manasseh, calling them to arms, and also into Asher, Zebulun and Naphtali, so that they too went up to meet them.

³⁶Gideon said to God, 'If you will save Israel by my hand as you have promised – ³⁷look, I will place a wool fleece on the threshing-floor. If there is dew only on the fleece and all the ground is dry, then I will know that you will save Israel by my hand, as you said.' ³⁸And that is what happened. Gideon rose early the next day; he squeezed the fleece and wrung out the dew – a bowlful of water.

³⁹Then Gideon said to God, 'Do not be angry with me. Let me make just one more request. Allow me one more test with the fleece, but this time make the fleece dry and let the ground be covered with dew.' ⁴⁰That night God did so. Only the fleece was dry; all the ground was covered with dew.

7 Early in the morning, Jerub-Baal (that is, Gideon) and all his men camped at the spring of Harod. The camp of Midian was north of them in the valley near the hill of Moreh. ²The LORD said to Gideon, 'You have too many men. I cannot deliver Midian into their hands, or Israel would boast against me, "My own strength has saved me." ³Now announce to the army, "Anyone who trembles with fear may turn back and leave Mount Gilead."' So twenty-two thousand men left, while ten thousand remained.

⁴But the LORD said to Gideon, 'There are still too many men. Take them down to the water, and I will thin them out for you there. If I say, "This one shall go with you," he shall go; but if I say, "This one shall not go with you," he shall not go.'

⁵So Gideon took the men down to the water. There the LORD told him, 'Separate those who lap the water with their tongues as a dog laps from those who kneel down to drink.' ⁶Three hundred of them drank from

cupped hands, lapping like dogs. All the rest got down on their knees to drink.

[7] The LORD said to Gideon, 'With the three hundred men that lapped I will save you and give the Midianites into your hands. Let all the others go home.' [8] So Gideon sent the rest of the Israelites home but kept the three hundred, who took over the provisions and trumpets of the others.

Now the camp of Midian lay below him in the valley. [9] During that night the LORD said to Gideon, 'Get up, go down against the camp, because I am going to give it into your hands. [10] If you are afraid to attack, go down to the camp with your servant Purah [11] and listen to what they are saying. Afterwards, you will be encouraged to attack the camp.' So he and Purah his servant went down to the outposts of the camp. [12] The Midianites, the Amalekites and all the other eastern peoples had settled in the valley, thick as locusts. Their camels could no more be counted than the sand on the seashore.

[13] Gideon arrived just as a man was telling a friend his dream. 'I had a dream,' he was saying. 'A round loaf of barley bread came tumbling into the Midianite camp. It struck the tent with such force that the tent overturned and collapsed.'

[14] His friend responded, 'This can be nothing other than the sword of Gideon son of Joash, the Israelite. God has given the Midianites and the whole camp into his hands.'

[15] When Gideon heard the dream and its interpretation, he bowed down and worshipped. He returned to the camp of Israel and called out, 'Get up! The LORD has given the Midianite camp into your hands.' [16] Dividing the three hundred men into three companies, he placed trumpets and empty jars in the hands of all of them, with torches inside.

[17] 'Watch me,' he told them. 'Follow my lead. When I get to the edge of the camp, do exactly as I do. [18] When I and all who are with me blow our trumpets, then from all round the camp blow yours and shout,

"For the LORD and for Gideon."'

[19] Gideon and the hundred men with him reached the edge of the camp at the beginning of the middle watch, just after they had changed the guard. They blew their trumpets and broke the jars that were in their hands. [20] The three companies blew the trumpets and smashed the jars. Grasping the torches in their left hands and holding in their right hands the trumpets they were to blow, they shouted, 'A sword for the LORD and for Gideon!' [21] While each man held his position round the camp, all the Midianites ran, crying out as they fled.

[22] When the three hundred trumpets sounded, the LORD caused the men throughout the camp to turn on each other with their swords. The army fled to Beth Shittah towards Zererah as far as the border of Abel Meholah near Tabbath. [23] Israelites from Naphtali, Asher and all Manasseh were called out, and they pursued the Midianites. [24] Gideon sent messengers throughout the hill country of Ephraim, saying, 'Come down against the Midianites and seize the waters of the Jordan ahead of them as far as Beth Barah.'

So all the men of Ephraim were called out and they seized the waters of the Jordan as far as Beth Barah. [25] They also captured two of the Midianite leaders, Oreb and Zeeb. They killed Oreb at the rock of Oreb, and Zeeb at the winepress of Zeeb. They pursued the Midianites and brought the heads of Oreb and Zeeb to Gideon, who was by the Jordan.

■ PSALM 55:15-23

[15] Let death take my enemies by surprise;
 let them go down alive to the realm of
  the dead,
  for evil finds lodging among them.

[16] As for me, I call to God,
 and the LORD saves me.

¹⁷ Evening, morning and noon
     I cry out in distress,
     and he hears my voice.
¹⁸ He rescues me unharmed
     from the battle waged against me,
     even though many oppose me.
¹⁹ God, who is enthroned from of old,
     who does not change –
     he will hear them and humble them,
     because they have no fear of God.

²⁰ My companion attacks his friends;
     he violates his covenant.
²¹ His talk is smooth as butter,
     yet war is in his heart;
     his words are more soothing than oil,
     yet they are drawn swords.

²² Cast your cares on the LORD
     and he will sustain you;
     he will never let
     the righteous be shaken.
²³ But you, God, will bring down the wicked
     into the pit of decay;
     the bloodthirsty and deceitful
     will not live out half their days.

But as for me, I trust in you.

■ PROVERBS 12:27-28

²⁷ The lazy do not roast any game,
     but the diligent feed on the riches of
     the hunt.

²⁸ In the way of righteousness there is life;
     along that path is immortality.

■ LUKE 21:20-38

²⁰ 'When you see Jerusalem being sur-
rounded by armies, you will know that its
desolation is near. ²¹ Then let those who are
in Judea flee to the mountains, let those in
the city get out, and let those in the coun-
try not enter the city. ²² For this is the time
of punishment in fulfilment of all that has
been written. ²³ How dreadful it will be in
those days for pregnant women and nurs-
ing mothers! There will be great distress
in the land and wrath against this people.
²⁴ They will fall by the sword and will be
taken as prisoners to all the nations. Jerusalem will be trampled on by the Gentiles
until the times of the Gentiles are fulfilled.

²⁵ 'There will be signs in the sun, moon
and stars. On the earth, nations will be in
anguish and perplexity at the roaring and
tossing of the sea. ²⁶ People will faint from
terror, apprehensive of what is coming on
the world, for the heavenly bodies will be
shaken. ²⁷ At that time they will see the Son
of Man coming in a cloud with power and
great glory. ²⁸ When these things begin to
take place, stand up and lift up your heads,
because your redemption is drawing near.'

²⁹ He told them this parable: 'Look at
the fig-tree and all the trees. ³⁰ When they
sprout leaves, you can see for yourselves
and know that summer is near. ³¹ Even so,
when you see these things happening, you
know that the kingdom of God is near.

³² 'Truly I tell you, this generation will cer-
tainly not pass away until all these things
have happened. ³³ Heaven and earth will pass
away, but my words will never pass away.

³⁴ 'Be careful, or your hearts will be
weighed down with carousing, drunkenness and the anxieties of life, and that day
will close on you suddenly like a trap. ³⁵ For
it will come on all those who live on the face
of the whole earth. ³⁶ Be always on the watch,
and pray that you may be able to escape all
that is about to happen, and that you may be
able to stand before the Son of Man.'

³⁷ Each day Jesus was teaching at the tem-
ple, and each evening he went out to spend
the night on the hill called the Mount of Olives, ³⁸ and all the people came early in the
morning to hear him at the temple.

A Spiritual Adventure

'The LORD said to Gideon, "With the three hundred men that lapped I will save you ..."' **Judges 7:7**

This passage illustrates an important point: God is looking for people who will 'stand'. When the hosts of Midian came against the Israelites, Gideon gathered together a large army of 32,000 men. Then God reduced them to a mere handful. Of the 32,000, there were only three hundred whom God could trust. He saw that they were men who would stand and never quit, so He dismissed the rest. And with just a small army of three hundred, He proceeded to discomfit and rout the Midianites.

God has always done His greatest work in and through a comparatively small number of people. This is why, when it comes to spiritual victories, we forget the idea of numbers. What God wants is men and women who are prepared to 'stand,' whose feet are 'shod with the preparation of the gospel of peace' (Eph. 6:15, AV). He will not entrust great responsibility to people whom He knows will not 'stand', for that would be an exercise in fruitlessness.

Are you standing for God – in the environment in which God has put you? Or are you ready to stand? You cannot stand until you are prepared to stand. It begins with a firm attitude which then issues into resolute action. As in Gideon's day, the Lord is looking for people who will take their stand on His Word, come what may, and commit themselves to doing what He asks even though they may not feel like it or see the sense of it. Are you such a one? If you are, then I predict that ahead of you is an exciting spiritual adventure.

PRAYER

O God, help me not to miss the highest because of my spiritual unpreparedness. Help me to be ready for all that You have for me – even before I see it. In Jesus' name. Amen.

FURTHER STUDY

Gal. 6:1-9; 1 Cor. 15:58; Eph. 4:15
• What is the result of remaining steadfast?
• What can hinder our spiritual success?

May 6

■ **JUDGES 8:1–9:21**

8 Now the Ephraimites asked Gideon, 'Why have you treated us like this? Why didn't you call us when you went to fight Midian?' And they challenged him vigorously.

²But he answered them, 'What have I accomplished compared to you? Aren't the gleanings of Ephraim's grapes better than

the full grape harvest of Abiezer? ³God gave Oreb and Zeeb, the Midianite leaders, into your hands. What was I able to do compared to you?' At this, their resentment against him subsided.

⁴Gideon and his three hundred men, exhausted yet keeping up the pursuit, came to the Jordan and crossed it. ⁵He said to the men of Sukkoth, 'Give my troops some bread; they are worn out, and I am still pursuing Zebah and Zalmunna, the kings of Midian.'

⁶But the officials of Sukkoth said, 'Do you already have the hands of Zebah and Zalmunna in your possession? Why should we give bread to your troops?'

⁷Then Gideon replied, 'Just for that, when the LORD has given Zebah and Zalmunna into my hand, I will tear your flesh with desert thorns and briers.'

⁸From there he went up to Peniel and made the same request of them, but they answered as the men of Sukkoth had. ⁹So he said to the men of Peniel, 'When I return in triumph, I will tear down this tower.'

¹⁰Now Zebah and Zalmunna were in Karkor with a force of about fifteen thousand men, all that were left of the armies of the eastern peoples; a hundred and twenty thousand swordsmen had fallen. ¹¹Gideon went up by the route of the nomads east of Nobah and Jogbehah and attacked the unsuspecting army. ¹²Zebah and Zalmunna, the two kings of Midian, fled, but he pursued them and captured them, routing their entire army.

¹³Gideon son of Joash then returned from the battle by the Pass of Heres. ¹⁴He caught a young man of Sukkoth and questioned him, and the young man wrote down for him the names of the seventy-seven officials of Sukkoth, the elders of the town. ¹⁵Then Gideon came and said to the men of Sukkoth, 'Here are Zebah and Zalmunna, about whom you taunted me by saying, "Do you already have the hands of Zebah and Zalmunna in your possession? Why should we give bread to your exhausted men?"'

¹⁶He took the elders of the town and taught the men of Sukkoth a lesson by punishing them with desert thorns and briers. ¹⁷He also pulled down the tower of Peniel and killed the men of the town.

¹⁸Then he asked Zebah and Zalmunna, 'What kind of men did you kill at Tabor?'

'Men like you,' they answered, 'each one with the bearing of a prince.'

¹⁹Gideon replied, 'Those were my brothers, the sons of my own mother. As surely as the LORD lives, if you had spared their lives, I would not kill you.' ²⁰Turning to Jether, his eldest son, he said, 'Kill them!' But Jether did not draw his sword, because he was only a boy and was afraid.

²¹Zebah and Zalmunna said, 'Come, do it yourself. "As is the man, so is his strength."' So Gideon stepped forward and killed them, and took the ornaments off their camels' necks.

²²The Israelites said to Gideon, 'Rule over us – you, your son and your grandson – because you have saved us from the hand of Midian.'

²³But Gideon told them, 'I will not rule over you, nor will my son rule over you. The LORD will rule over you.' ²⁴And he said, 'I do have one request, that each of you give me an earring from your share of the plunder.' (It was the custom of the Ishmaelites to wear gold earrings.)

²⁵They answered, 'We'll be glad to give them.' So they spread out a garment, and each of them threw a ring from his plunder onto it. ²⁶The weight of the gold rings he asked for came to seventeen hundred shekels, not counting the ornaments, the pendants and the purple garments worn by the kings of Midian or the chains that were on their camels' necks. ²⁷Gideon made the gold into an ephod, which he placed in Ophrah, his town. All Israel prostituted themselves by worshipping it there, and it became a snare to Gideon and his family.

²⁸Thus Midian was subdued before the

Israelites and did not raise its head again. During Gideon's lifetime, the land had peace for forty years.

²⁹ Jerub-Baal son of Joash went back home to live. ³⁰ He had seventy sons of his own, for he had many wives. ³¹ His concubine, who lived in Shechem, also bore him a son, whom he named Abimelek. ³² Gideon son of Joash died at a good old age and was buried in the tomb of his father Joash in Ophrah of the Abiezrites.

³³ No sooner had Gideon died than the Israelites again prostituted themselves to the Baals. They set up Baal-Berith as their god ³⁴ and did not remember the LORD their God, who had rescued them from the hands of all their enemies on every side. ³⁵ They also failed to show any loyalty to the family of Jerub-Baal (that is, Gideon) in spite of all the good things he had done for them.

9 Abimelek son of Jerub-Baal went to his mother's brothers in Shechem and said to them and to all his mother's clan, ² 'Ask all the citizens of Shechem, "Which is better for you: to have all seventy of Jerub-Baal's sons rule over you, or just one man?" Remember, I am your flesh and blood.'

³ When the brothers repeated all this to the citizens of Shechem, they were inclined to follow Abimelek, for they said, 'He is related to us.' ⁴ They gave him seventy shekels of silver from the temple of Baal-Berith, and Abimelek used it to hire reckless scoundrels, who became his followers. ⁵ He went to his father's home in Ophrah and on one stone murdered his seventy brothers, the sons of Jerub-Baal. But Jotham, the youngest son of Jerub-Baal, escaped by hiding. ⁶ Then all the citizens of Shechem and Beth Millo gathered beside the great tree at the pillar in Shechem to crown Abimelek king.

⁷ When Jotham was told about this, he climbed up on the top of Mount Gerizim and shouted to them, 'Listen to me, citizens of Shechem, so that God may listen to you. ⁸ One day the trees went out to anoint a king for themselves. They said to the olive tree, "Be our king."

⁹ 'But the olive tree answered, "Should I give up my oil, by which both gods and humans are honoured, to hold sway over the trees?"

¹⁰ 'Next, the trees said to the fig-tree, "Come and be our king."

¹¹ 'But the fig-tree replied, "Should I give up my fruit, so good and sweet, to hold sway over the trees?"

¹² 'Then the trees said to the vine, "Come and be our king."

¹³ 'But the vine answered, "Should I give up my wine, which cheers both gods and humans, to hold sway over the trees?"

¹⁴ 'Finally all the trees said to the thornbush, "Come and be our king."

¹⁵ 'The thorn-bush said to the trees, "If you really want to anoint me king over you, come and take refuge in my shade; but if not, then let fire come out of the thorn-bush and consume the cedars of Lebanon!"

¹⁶ 'Have you acted honourably and in good faith by making Abimelek king? Have you been fair to Jerub-Baal and his family? Have you treated him as he deserves? ¹⁷ Remember that my father fought for you and risked his life to rescue you from the hand of Midian. ¹⁸ But today you have revolted against my father's family. You have murdered his seventy sons on a single stone and have made Abimelek, the son of his female slave, king over the citizens of Shechem because he is related to you. ¹⁹ So have you acted honourably and in good faith towards Jerub-Baal and his family today? If you have, may Abimelek be your joy, and may you be his, too! ²⁰ But if you have not, let fire come out from Abimelek and consume you, the citizens of Shechem and Beth Millo, and let fire come out from you, the citizens of Shechem and Beth Millo, and consume Abimelek!'

²¹ Then Jotham fled, escaping to Beer, and he lived there because he was afraid of his brother Abimelek.

PSALM 56:1-7

[1] Be merciful to me, my God,
    for my enemies are in hot pursuit;
    all day long they press their attack.
[2] My adversaries pursue me all day long;
    in their pride many are attacking me.

[3] When I am afraid, I put my trust in you.
[4]   In God, whose word I praise –
    in God I trust and am not afraid.
    What can mere mortals do to me?

[5] All day long they twist my words;
    all their schemes are for my ruin.
[6] They conspire, they lurk,
    they watch my steps,
    hoping to take my life.
[7] Because of their wickedness do not let
        them escape;
    in your anger, God, bring the nations
        down.

PROVERBS 13:1-2

13 A wise son heeds his father's
    instruction,
    but a mocker does not respond to
    rebukes.

[2] From the fruit of their lips people enjoy
        good things,
    but the unfaithful have an appetite for
        violence.

LUKE 22:1-23

22 Now the Festival of Unleavened
    Bread, called the Passover, was ap-
proaching, [2] and the chief priests and the
teachers of the law were looking for some way
to get rid of Jesus, for they were afraid of the
people. [3] Then Satan entered Judas, called Iscariot, one of the Twelve. [4] And Judas went to
the chief priests and the officers of the temple guard and discussed with them how he
might betray Jesus. [5] They were delighted and
agreed to give him money. [6] He consented,
and watched for an opportunity to hand Jesus
over to them when no crowd was present.

[7] Then came the day of Unleavened Bread
on which the Passover lamb had to be sacrificed. [8] Jesus sent Peter and John, saying,
'Go and make preparations for us to eat the
Passover.'

[9] 'Where do you want us to prepare for it?'
they asked.

[10] He replied, 'As you enter the city, a man
carrying a jar of water will meet you. Follow
him to the house that he enters, [11] and say to
the owner of the house, "The Teacher asks:
where is the guest room, where I may eat the
Passover with my disciples?" [12] He will show
you a large room upstairs, all furnished.
Make preparations there.'

[13] They left and found things just as Jesus
had told them. So they prepared the Passover.

[14] When the hour came, Jesus and his
apostles reclined at the table. [15] And he said
to them, 'I have eagerly desired to eat this
Passover with you before I suffer. [16] For I
tell you, I will not eat it again until it finds
fulfilment in the kingdom of God.'

[17] After taking the cup, he gave thanks
and said, 'Take this and divide it among
you. [18] For I tell you I will not drink again
from the fruit of the vine until the kingdom
of God comes.'

[19] And he took bread, gave thanks and broke
it, and gave it to them, saying, 'This is my body
given for you; do this in remembrance of me.'

[20] In the same way, after the supper he
took the cup, saying, 'This cup is the new
covenant in my blood, which is poured out
for you. [21] But the hand of him who is going
to betray me is with mine on the table. [22] The
Son of Man will go as it has been decreed. But
woe to that man who betrays him!' [23] They
began to question among themselves which
of them it might be who would do this.

The Three Elements of Fear

'... in God I trust and am not afraid. What can mere mortals do to me?' **Psalm 56:4**

Many people, some Christians included, see death as an intruder. Gandhi, the great Indian leader and politician, said that he started his Swaraj movement to help people overcome the fear of death. Politics was only a minor part of his purpose. 'My aim,' he said, 'was the abandonment of the fear of death. So long as we let ourselves be influenced by the fear of death, we can never attain freedom.'

When we come to analyse the fear of death, three elements can be seen to be present: the fear of the physical act of dying, the fear of finality, and the fear of judgment. Let's look first at the fear of the physical act of dying. This is very real to some people. Perhaps they have suffered and know, through bitter experience, how pain lacerates and hurts.

Doctors assure us that what people normally call 'the agony of death' is felt much more by those who are watching than by the one who is passing away. Sir Frederick Treves, the eminent surgeon, said: 'A last illness may be long, wearisome and painful, but the closing moments of it are, as a rule, free from suffering. There may appear to be a terrible struggle at the end, but of this struggle the subject is unconscious. It is the onlooker who bears the misery of it.' Add to this natural phenomenon the supporting power of God's never-failing grace, and it is possible to look even this physical aspect of death quietly in the face and say, 'My enemy - you are not really the terror that you seem'.

PRAYER

Lord Jesus, You who are Master of life and death, I am so grateful that in You I see the death of death and the defeat of defeat. In You everything is alive - alive with meaning, destiny, goal - alive forevermore. Hallelujah!

FURTHER STUDY

Isa. 43:2-3; 1 Cor. 15:1-21; John 11:11; Acts 13:36
- Of what is Christ the firstfruits?
- What is the difference between sleep and death?

May 7

■ JUDGES 9:22–10:18

²²After Abimelek had governed Israel for three years, ²³God stirred up animosity between Abimelek and the citizens of Shechem so that they acted treacherously against Abimelek. ²⁴God did this in order that the crime against Jerub-Baal's seventy sons,

the shedding of their blood, might be avenged on their brother Abimelek and on the citizens of Shechem, who had helped him murder his brothers. ²⁵In opposition to him these citizens of Shechem set men on the hilltops to ambush and rob everyone who passed by, and this was reported to Abimelek.

²⁶Now Gaal son of Ebed moved with his clan into Shechem, and its citizens put their confidence in him. ²⁷After they had gone out into the fields and gathered the grapes and trodden them, they held a festival in the temple of their god. While they were eating and drinking, they cursed Abimelek. ²⁸Then Gaal son of Ebed said, 'Who is Abimelek, and why should we Shechemites be subject to him? Isn't he Jerub-Baal's son, and isn't Zebul his deputy? Serve the family of Hamor, Shechem's father! Why should we serve Abimelek? ²⁹If only this people were under my command! Then I would get rid of him. I would say to Abimelek, "Call out your whole army!"'

³⁰When Zebul the governor of the city heard what Gaal son of Ebed said, he was very angry. ³¹Under cover he sent messengers to Abimelek, saying, 'Gaal son of Ebed and his clan have come to Shechem and are stirring up the city against you. ³²Now then, during the night you and your men should come and lie in wait in the fields. ³³In the morning at sunrise, advance against the city. When Gaal and his men come out against you, seize the opportunity to attack them.'

³⁴So Abimelek and all his troops set out by night and took up concealed positions near Shechem in four companies. ³⁵Now Gaal son of Ebed had gone out and was standing at the entrance of the city gate just as Abimelek and his troops came out from their hiding-place.

³⁶When Gaal saw them, he said to Zebul, 'Look, people are coming down from the tops of the mountains!'

Zebul replied, 'You mistake the shadows of the mountains for men.'

³⁷But Gaal spoke up again: 'Look, people are coming down from the central hill, and a company is coming from the direction of the diviners' tree.'

³⁸Then Zebul said to him, 'Where is your big talk now, you who said, "Who is Abimelek that we should be subject to him?" Aren't these the men you ridiculed? Go out and fight them!'

³⁹So Gaal led out the citizens of Shechem and fought Abimelek. ⁴⁰Abimelek chased him all the way to the entrance of the gate, and many were killed as they fled. ⁴¹Then Abimelek stayed in Arumah, and Zebul drove Gaal and his clan out of Shechem.

⁴²The next day the people of Shechem went out to the fields, and this was reported to Abimelek. ⁴³So he took his men, divided them into three companies and set an ambush in the fields. When he saw the people coming out of the city, he rose to attack them. ⁴⁴Abimelek and the companies with him rushed forward to a position at the entrance of the city gate. Then two companies attacked those in the fields and struck them down. ⁴⁵All that day Abimelek pressed his attack against the city until he had captured it and killed its people. Then he destroyed the city and scattered salt over it.

⁴⁶On hearing this, the citizens in the tower of Shechem went into the stronghold of the temple of El-Berith. ⁴⁷When Abimelek heard that they had assembled there, ⁴⁸he and all his men went up Mount Zalmon. He took an axe and cut off some branches, which he lifted to his shoulders. He ordered the men with him, 'Quick! Do what you have seen me do!' ⁴⁹So all the men cut branches and followed Abimelek. They piled them against the stronghold and set it on fire with the people still inside. So all the people in the tower of Shechem, about a thousand men and women, also died.

⁵⁰Next Abimelek went to Thebez and besieged it and captured it. ⁵¹Inside the city, however, was a strong tower, to which all

the men and women – all the people of the city – had fled. They had locked themselves in and climbed up on the tower roof. [52] Abimelek went to the tower and attacked it. But as he approached the entrance to the tower to set it on fire, [53] a woman dropped an upper millstone on his head and cracked his skull.

[54] Hurriedly he called to his armour-bearer, 'Draw your sword and kill me, so that they can't say, "A woman killed him." ' So his servant ran him through, and he died. [55] When the Israelites saw that Abimelek was dead, they went home.

[56] Thus God repaid the wickedness that Abimelek had done to his father by murdering his seventy brothers. [57] God also made the people of Shechem pay for all their wickedness. The curse of Jotham son of Jerub-Baal came on them.

10 After the time of Abimelek, a man of Issachar named Tola son of Puah, the son of Dodo, rose to save Israel. He lived in Shamir, in the hill country of Ephraim. [2] He led Israel for twenty-three years; then he died, and was buried in Shamir.

[3] He was followed by Jair of Gilead, who led Israel for twenty-two years. [4] He had thirty sons, who rode thirty donkeys. They controlled thirty towns in Gilead, which to this day are called Havvoth Jair. [5] When Jair died, he was buried in Kamon.

[6] Again the Israelites did evil in the eyes of the LORD. They served the Baals and the Ashtoreths, and the gods of Aram, the gods of Sidon, the gods of Moab, the gods of the Ammonites and the gods of the Philistines. And because the Israelites forsook the LORD and no longer served him, [7] he became angry with them. He sold them into the hands of the Philistines and the Ammonites, [8] who that year shattered and crushed them. For eighteen years they oppressed all the Israelites on the east side of the Jordan in Gilead, the land of the Amorites. [9] The Ammonites also crossed the Jordan to fight against Judah, Benjamin and Ephraim;

Israel was in great distress. [10] Then the Israelites cried out to the LORD, 'We have sinned against you, forsaking our God and serving the Baals.'

[11] The LORD replied, 'When the Egyptians, the Amorites, the Ammonites, the Philistines, [12] the Sidonians, the Amalekites and the Maonites oppressed you and you cried to me for help, did I not save you from their hands? [13] But you have forsaken me and served other gods, so I will no longer save you. [14] Go and cry out to the gods you have chosen. Let them save you when you are in trouble!'

[15] But the Israelites said to the LORD, 'We have sinned. Do with us whatever you think best, but please rescue us now.' [16] Then they got rid of the foreign gods among them and served the LORD. And he could bear Israel's misery no longer.

[17] When the Ammonites were called to arms and camped in Gilead, the Israelites assembled and camped at Mizpah. [18] The leaders of the people of Gilead said to each other, 'Whoever will take the lead in attacking the Ammonites will be head over all who live in Gilead.'

··

■ PSALM 56:8-13

[8] Record my misery;
    list my tears on your scroll –
    are they not in your record?
[9] Then my enemies will turn back
    when I call for help.
    By this I will know that God is for me.

[10] In God, whose word I praise,
    in the LORD, whose word I praise –
[11] in God I trust and am not afraid.
    What can man do to me?

[12] I am under vows to you, my God;
    I will present my thank-offerings to you.
[13] For you have delivered me from death

and my feet from stumbling,
that I may walk before God
in the light of life.

▬ PROVERBS 13:3-4

3 Those who guard their lips preserve
their lives,
but those who speak rashly will come
to ruin.

4 A sluggard's appetite is never filled,
but the desires of the diligent are fully
satisfied.

▬ LUKE 22:24-46

24 A dispute also arose among them as to which of them was considered to be greatest. 25 Jesus said to them, 'The kings of the Gentiles lord it over them; and those who exercise authority over them call themselves Benefactors. 26 But you are not to be like that. Instead, the greatest among you should be like the youngest, and the one who rules like the one who serves. 27 For who is greater, the one who is at the table or the one who serves? Is it not the one who is at the table? But I am among you as one who serves. 28 You are those who have stood by me in my trials. 29 And I confer on you a kingdom, just as my Father conferred one on me, 30 so that you may eat and drink at my table in my kingdom and sit on thrones, judging the twelve tribes of Israel.

31 'Simon, Simon, Satan has asked to sift all of you as wheat. 32 But I have prayed for you, Simon, that your faith may not fail. And when you have turned back, strengthen your brothers.'

33 But he replied, 'Lord, I am ready to go with you to prison and to death.'

34 Jesus answered, 'I tell you, Peter, before the cock crows today, you will deny three times that you know me.'

35 Then Jesus asked them, 'When I sent you without purse, bag or sandals, did you lack anything?'

'Nothing,' they answered.

36 He said to them, 'But now if you have a purse, take it, and also a bag; and if you don't have a sword, sell your cloak and buy one. 37 It is written: "And he was numbered with the transgressors"; and I tell you that this must be fulfilled in me. Yes, what is written about me is reaching its fulfilment.'

38 The disciples said, 'See, Lord, here are two swords.'

'That's enough!' he replied.

39 Jesus went out as usual to the Mount of Olives, and his disciples followed him. 40 On reaching the place, he said to them, 'Pray that you will not fall into temptation.' 41 He withdrew about a stone's throw beyond them, knelt down and prayed, 42 'Father, if you are willing, take this cup from me; yet not my will, but yours be done.' 43 An angel from heaven appeared to him and strengthened him. 44 And being in anguish, he prayed more earnestly, and his sweat was like drops of blood falling to the ground.

45 When he rose from prayer and went back to the disciples, he found them asleep, exhausted from sorrow. 46 'Why are you sleeping?' he asked them. 'Get up and pray so that you will not fall into temptation.'

Satan's Pincer Movement

'Simon, Simon, Satan has asked to sift all of you as wheat. But I have prayed for you, Simon, that your faith may not fail.' **Luke 22:31-32**

One of the reasons the Apostle Paul bids us pray for one another is this: the failure of any one of us is going to have some effect upon the spiritual campaign which God is waging against the Devil through the church.

All those who have committed themselves to Jesus Christ should know that the forces of two kingdoms – the kingdoms of God and of the Devil – are locked together in mortal combat. And Christians, whether they like it or not, are thrust right onto the cutting edge of this conflict.

The battle line between the forces of God and the forces of Satan is the church – and that means you and me. What is Satan's best tactic in attempting to bring about the church's spiritual defeat? He probes at every point he can, looking for the weakest part. When he finds a weak Christian (or a group of weak Christians), he calls for reinforcements. Then, using what military strategists call 'a pincer movement', he attempts to break through at that point. And when one Christian fails, all of us to some extent are affected, for we are all part of the one line of defence.

How the Devil rejoices when an individual Christian falls – especially a church leader. Therefore, we are called to a ministry of prayer – not just for ourselves but for one another also – that we might stand perfect and complete in the will of God and that our faith will not fail when under attack by the Devil.

PRAYER

Father, I am encouraged as I think that today, many Christians around the world will be praying for me. Help me never to fail in my responsibility to pray for them. In Christ's peerless and precious name. Amen.

FURTHER STUDY

Gal. 6:1-10; 1 Cor. 9:27; Phil. 3:12; James 5:16
- What are we to carry in prayer?
- Of what was Paul conscious?

May 8

■ JUDGES 11:1–12:15

11 Jephthah the Gileadite was a mighty warrior. His father was Gilead; his mother was a prostitute. ²Gilead's wife also bore him sons, and when they were grown up, they drove Jephthah away. 'You are not going to get any inheritance in our family,' they said, 'because you are the son of another woman.' ³So Jephthah fled from his brothers and settled in the land of Tob, where a gang of scoundrels gathered around him and followed him.

⁴Some time later, when the Ammonites were fighting against Israel, ⁵the elders of Gilead went to get Jephthah from the land of Tob. ⁶'Come,' they said, 'be our commander, so we can fight the Ammonites.'

⁷Jephthah said to them, 'Didn't you hate me and drive me from my father's house?

Why do you come to me now, when you're in trouble?'

⁸ The elders of Gilead said to him, 'Nevertheless, we are turning to you now; come with us to fight the Ammonites, and you will be head over all of us who live in Gilead.'

⁹ Jephthah answered, 'Suppose you take me back to fight the Ammonites and the LORD gives them to me – will I really be your head?'

¹⁰ The elders of Gilead replied, 'The LORD is our witness; we will certainly do as you say.' ¹¹ So Jephthah went with the elders of Gilead, and the people made him head and commander over them. And he repeated all his words before the LORD in Mizpah.

¹² Then Jephthah sent messengers to the Ammonite king with the question: 'What do you have against me that you have attacked my country?'

¹³ The king of the Ammonites answered Jephthah's messengers, 'When Israel came up out of Egypt, they took away my land from the Arnon to the Jabbok, all the way to the Jordan. Now give it back peaceably.'

¹⁴ Jephthah sent back messengers to the Ammonite king, ¹⁵ saying:

'This is what Jephthah says: Israel did not take the land of Moab or the land of the Ammonites. ¹⁶ But when they came up out of Egypt, Israel went through the wilderness to the Red Sea and on to Kadesh. ¹⁷ Then Israel sent messengers to the king of Edom, saying, "Give us permission to go through your country," but the king of Edom would not listen. They sent also to the king of Moab, and he refused. So Israel stayed at Kadesh.

¹⁸ 'Next they travelled through the wilderness, skirted the lands of Edom and Moab, passed along the eastern side of the country of Moab, and camped on the other side of the Arnon. They did not enter the territory of Moab, for the Arnon was its border.

¹⁹ 'Then Israel sent messengers to Sihon king of the Amorites, who ruled in Heshbon, and said to him, "Let us pass through your country to our own place." ²⁰ Sihon, however, did not trust Israel to pass through his territory. He mustered all his troops and encamped at Jahaz and fought with Israel.

²¹ 'Then the LORD, the God of Israel, gave Sihon and his whole army into Israel's hands, and they defeated them. Israel took over all the land of the Amorites who lived in that country, ²² capturing all of it from the Arnon to the Jabbok and from the desert to the Jordan.

²³ 'Now since the LORD, the God of Israel, has driven the Amorites out before his people Israel, what right have you to take it over? ²⁴ Will you not take what your god Chemosh gives you? Likewise, whatever the LORD our God has given us, we will possess. ²⁵ Are you any better than Balak son of Zippor, king of Moab? Did he ever quarrel with Israel or fight with them? ²⁶ For three hundred years Israel occupied Heshbon, Aroer, the surrounding settlements and all the towns along the Arnon. Why didn't you retake them during that time? ²⁷ I have not wronged you, but you are doing me wrong by waging war against me. Let the LORD, the Judge, decide the dispute this day between the Israelites and the Ammonites.'

²⁸ The king of Ammon, however, paid no attention to the message Jephthah sent him.

²⁹ Then the Spirit of the LORD came on Jephthah. He crossed Gilead and Manasseh, passed through Mizpah of Gilead, and from there he advanced against the Ammonites. ³⁰ And Jephthah made a vow to the LORD: 'If you give the Ammonites into my hands, ³¹ whatever comes out of the door of my house to meet me when I return in triumph from the Ammonites will be the LORD's, and

I will sacrifice it as a burnt offering.'

³²Then Jephthah went over to fight the Ammonites, and the LORD gave them into his hands. ³³He devastated twenty towns from Aroer to the vicinity of Minnith, as far as Abel Keramim. Thus Israel subdued Ammon.

³⁴When Jephthah returned to his home in Mizpah, who should come out to meet him but his daughter, dancing to the sound of tambourines! She was an only child. Except for her he had neither son nor daughter. ³⁵When he saw her, he tore his clothes and cried, 'Oh no, my daughter! You have brought me down and I am devastated. I have made a vow to the LORD that I cannot break.'

³⁶'My father,' she replied, 'you have given your word to the LORD. Do to me just as you promised, now that the LORD has avenged you of your enemies, the Ammonites. ³⁷But grant me this one request,' she said. 'Give me two months to roam the hills and weep with my friends, because I will never marry.'

³⁸'You may go,' he said. And he let her go for two months. She and her friends went into the hills and wept because she would never marry. ³⁹After the two months, she returned to her father, and he did to her as he had vowed. And she was a virgin.

From this comes the Israelite tradition ⁴⁰that each year the young women of Israel go out for four days to commemorate the daughter of Jephthah the Gileadite.

12 The Ephraimite forces were called out, and they crossed over to Zaphon. They said to Jephthah, 'Why did you go to fight the Ammonites without calling us to go with you? We're going to burn down your house over your head.'

²Jephthah answered, 'I and my people were engaged in a great struggle with the Ammonites, and although I called, you didn't save me out of their hands. ³When I saw that you wouldn't help, I took my life in my hands and crossed over to fight the Ammonites, and the LORD gave me the victory

over them. Now why have you come up today to fight me?'

⁴Jephthah then called together the men of Gilead and fought against Ephraim. The Gileadites struck them down because the Ephraimites had said, 'You Gileadites are renegades from Ephraim and Manasseh.' ⁵The Gileadites captured the fords of the Jordan leading to Ephraim, and whenever a survivor of Ephraim said, 'Let me cross over,' the men of Gilead asked him, 'Are you an Ephraimite?' If he replied, 'No,' ⁶they said, 'All right, say "Shibboleth".' If he said, 'Sibboleth', because he could not pronounce the word correctly, they seized him and killed him at the fords of the Jordan. Forty-two thousand Ephraimites were killed at that time.

⁷Jephthah led Israel for six years. Then Jephthah the Gileadite died and was buried in a town in Gilead.

⁸After him, Ibzan of Bethlehem led Israel. ⁹He had thirty sons and thirty daughters. He gave his daughters away in marriage to those outside his clan, and for his sons he brought in thirty young women as wives from outside his clan. Ibzan led Israel for seven years. ¹⁰Then Ibzan died and was buried in Bethlehem.

¹¹After him, Elon the Zebulunite led Israel for ten years. ¹²Then Elon died and was buried in Aijalon in the land of Zebulun.

¹³After him, Abdon son of Hillel, from Pirathon, led Israel. ¹⁴He had forty sons and thirty grandsons, who rode on seventy donkeys. He led Israel for eight years. ¹⁵Then Abdon son of Hillel died and was buried at Pirathon in Ephraim, in the hill country of the Amalekites.

■ PSALM 57:1-6

¹Have mercy on me, my God, have mercy on me,
    for in you I take refuge.

I will take refuge in the shadow of your
  wings
    until the disaster has passed.

² I cry out to God Most High,
    to God, who vindicates me.
³ He sends from heaven and saves me,
    rebuking those who hotly pursue me –
    God sends forth his love and his
      faithfulness.

⁴ I am in the midst of lions;
    I am forced to dwell among ravenous
      beasts –
  men whose teeth are spears and arrows,
    whose tongues are sharp swords.

⁵ Be exalted, O God, above the heavens;
    let your glory be over all the earth.

⁶ They spread a net for my feet –
    I was bowed down in distress.
  They dug a pit in my path –
    but they have fallen into it themselves.

▬ PROVERBS 13:5-6

⁵ The righteous hate what is false,
    but the wicked make themselves
      obnoxious
    and bring shame on themselves.

⁶ Righteousness guards the person of
    integrity,
  but wickedness overthrows the sinner.

▬ LUKE 22:47-71

⁴⁷ While he was still speaking a crowd
came up, and the man who was called Judas, one of the Twelve, was leading them.
He approached Jesus to kiss him, ⁴⁸ but
Jesus asked him, 'Judas, are you betraying
the Son of Man with a kiss?'

⁴⁹ When Jesus' followers saw what was
going to happen, they said, 'Lord, should we
strike with our swords?' ⁵⁰ And one of them
struck the servant of the high priest, cutting
off his right ear.

⁵¹ But Jesus answered, 'No more of this!'
And he touched the man's ear and healed
him.

⁵² Then Jesus said to the chief priests,
the officers of the temple guard, and the elders, who had come for him, 'Am I leading
a rebellion, that you have come with swords
and clubs? ⁵³ Every day I was with you in
the temple courts, and you did not lay a
hand on me. But this is your hour – when
darkness reigns.'

⁵⁴ Then seizing him, they led him away
and took him into the house of the high
priest. Peter followed at a distance. ⁵⁵ And
when some there had kindled a fire in the
middle of the courtyard and had sat down
together, Peter sat down with them. ⁵⁶ A
servant-girl saw him seated there in the
firelight. She looked closely at him and said,
'This man was with him.'

⁵⁷ But he denied it. 'Woman, I don't know
him,' he said.

⁵⁸ A little later someone else saw him and
said, 'You also are one of them.'

'Man, I am not!' Peter replied.

⁵⁹ About an hour later another asserted,
'Certainly this fellow was with him, for he
is a Galilean.'

⁶⁰ Peter replied, 'Man, I don't know what
you're talking about!' Just as he was speaking, the cock crowed. ⁶¹ The Lord turned
and looked straight at Peter. Then Peter
remembered the word the Lord had spoken
to him: 'Before the cock crows today, you
will disown me three times.' ⁶² And he went
outside and wept bitterly.

⁶³ The men who were guarding Jesus
began mocking and beating him. ⁶⁴ They
blindfolded him and demanded, 'Prophesy!
Who hit you?' ⁶⁵ And they said many other
insulting things to him.

⁶⁶At daybreak the council of the elders of the people, both the chief priests and the teachers of the law, met together, and Jesus was led before them. ⁶⁷'If you are the Messiah,' they said, 'tell us.'

Jesus answered, 'If I tell you, you will not believe me, ⁶⁸and if I asked you, you would not answer. ⁶⁹But from now on, the Son of Man will be seated at the right hand of the mighty God.'

⁷⁰They all asked, 'Are you then the Son of God?'

He replied, 'You say that I am.'

⁷¹Then they said, 'Why do we need any more testimony? We have heard it from his own lips.'

'Stupid'

'Peter replied, "Man, I don't know what you're talking about!"' Luke 22:60

Today we look at a game called 'Stupid'. Simon Peter played this game. Picture the scene. Peter, the big fisherman, strong, resolute, determined, firm in his declaration of love for Christ, denies all knowledge of the Master. Why? He had walked with the Master for three whole years, heard Him speak the most wonderful words, seen Him heal the sick, raise the dead, cleanse the lepers, and work other amazing miracles. Yet when he is asked if he knows Jesus, his response is one of withdrawal. In other words, he plays stupid.

Eric Berne claims that we always play games for a reward. What was Peter's reward? It was the reinforcement of his fear. Why should the reinforcement of his fear be a reward? Well, the more deeply he believed that he was afraid and the more he did to reinforce that fear, the easier it would be to excuse himself for his failure to stand up for Jesus when confronted. The final pay-off was to be protected from danger.

A Christian schoolteacher told me that at an educational conference, someone happened to remark that the Bible was a fable. The man then turned to the schoolteacher and said: 'What do you think?' He told me that his first impulse was to play stupid and say: 'I am not sure', or 'I don't know'. He caught himself just about to play the game but instead accepted the challenge of the situation and responded with some positive comments. To play the game of 'Stupid' may bring temporary benefits, but the dishonesty involved greatly upsets one's spiritual balance.

PRAYER

O Father, help me to be an honest person. Help me to absorb Your love in such a measure that it will dissolve every fear. Then strengthen me to face life – fearless and unafraid. Amen.

FURTHER STUDY

Acts 5:1-10; Psa. 63:11;
Prov. 19:5; Jer. 9:5
• When we play 'Stupid', what are we really doing?
• How serious is it?

May 9

◼ JUDGES 13:1–15:8

13 Again the Israelites did evil in the eyes of the LORD, so the LORD delivered them into the hands of the Philistines for forty years.

² A certain man of Zorah, named Manoah, from the clan of the Danites, had a wife who was childless, unable to give birth. ³ The angel of the LORD appeared to her and said, 'You are barren and childless, but you are going to become pregnant and give birth to a son. ⁴ Now see to it that you drink no wine or other fermented drink and that you do not eat anything unclean. ⁵ You will become pregnant and have a son whose head is never to be touched by a razor because the boy is to be a Nazirite, dedicated to God from the womb. He will take the lead in delivering Israel from the hands of the Philistines.'

⁶ Then the woman went to her husband and told him, 'A man of God came to me. He looked like an angel of God, very awesome. I didn't ask him where he came from, and he didn't tell me his name. ⁷ But he said to me, "You will become pregnant and have a son. Now then, drink no wine or other fermented drink and do not eat anything unclean, because the boy will be a Nazirite of God from the womb until the day of his death."'

⁸ Then Manoah prayed to the LORD: 'Pardon your servant, Lord. I beg you to let the man of God you sent to us come again to teach us how to bring up the boy who is to be born.'

⁹ God heard Manoah, and the angel of God came again to the woman while she was out in the field; but her husband Manoah was not with her. ¹⁰ The woman hurried to tell her husband, 'He's here! The man who appeared to me the other day!'

¹¹ Manoah got up and followed his wife. When he came to the man, he said, 'Are you the man who talked to my wife?'

'I am,' he said.

¹² So Manoah asked him, 'When your words are fulfilled, what is to be the rule that governs the boy's life and work?'

¹³ The angel of the LORD answered, 'Your wife must do all that I have told her. ¹⁴ She must not eat anything that comes from the grapevine, nor drink any wine or other fermented drink nor eat anything unclean. She must do everything I have commanded her.'

¹⁵ Manoah said to the angel of the LORD, 'We would like you to stay until we prepare a young goat for you.'

¹⁶ The angel of the LORD replied, 'Even though you detain me, I will not eat any of your food. But if you prepare a burnt offering, offer it to the LORD.' (Manoah did not realise that it was the angel of the LORD.)

¹⁷ Then Manoah enquired of the angel of the LORD, 'What is your name, so that we may honour you when your word comes true?'

¹⁸ He replied, 'Why do you ask my name? It is beyond understanding.' ¹⁹ Then Manoah took a young goat, together with the grain offering, and sacrificed it on a rock to the LORD. And the LORD did an amazing thing while Manoah and his wife watched: ²⁰ as the flame blazed up from the altar towards heaven, the angel of the LORD ascended in the flame. Seeing this, Manoah and his wife fell with their faces to the ground. ²¹ When the angel of the LORD did not show himself again to Manoah and his wife, Manoah realised that it was the angel of the LORD.

²² 'We are doomed to die!' he said to his wife. 'We have seen God!'

²³But his wife answered, 'If the LORD had meant to kill us, he would not have accepted a burnt offering and grain offering from our hands, nor shown us all these things or now told us this.'

²⁴The woman gave birth to a boy and named him Samson. He grew and the LORD blessed him, ²⁵and the Spirit of the LORD began to stir him while he was in Mahaneh Dan, between Zorah and Eshtaol.

14 Samson went down to Timnah and saw there a young Philistine woman. ²When he returned, he said to his father and mother, 'I have seen a Philistine woman in Timnah; now get her for me as my wife.'

³His father and mother replied, 'Isn't there an acceptable woman among your relatives or among all our people? Must you go to the uncircumcised Philistines to get a wife?'

But Samson said to his father, 'Get her for me. She's the right one for me.' ⁴(His parents did not know that this was from the LORD, who was seeking an occasion to confront the Philistines; for at that time they were ruling over Israel.)

⁵Samson went down to Timnah together with his father and mother. As they approached the vineyards of Timnah, suddenly a young lion came roaring towards him. ⁶The Spirit of the LORD came powerfully upon him so that he tore the lion apart with his bare hands as he might have torn a young goat. But he told neither his father nor his mother what he had done. ⁷Then he went down and talked with the woman, and he liked her.

⁸Some time later, when he went back to marry her, he turned aside to look at the lion's carcass, and in it he saw a swarm of bees and some honey. ⁹He scooped out the honey with his hands and ate as he went along. When he rejoined his parents, he gave them some, and they too ate it. But he did not tell them that he had taken the honey from the lion's carcass.

¹⁰Now his father went down to see the woman. And there Samson held a feast, as was customary for young men. ¹¹When the people saw him, they chose thirty men to be his companions.

¹²'Let me tell you a riddle,' Samson said to them. 'If you can give me the answer within the seven days of the feast, I will give you thirty linen garments and thirty sets of clothes. ¹³If you can't tell me the answer, you must give me thirty linen garments and thirty sets of clothes.'

'Tell us your riddle,' they said. 'Let's hear it.'

¹⁴He replied,

'Out of the eater, something to eat;
   out of the strong, something sweet.'

For three days they could not give the answer.

¹⁵On the fourth day, they said to Samson's wife, 'Coax your husband into explaining the riddle for us, or we will burn you and your father's household to death. Did you invite us here to steal our property?'

¹⁶Then Samson's wife threw herself on him, sobbing, 'You hate me! You don't really love me. You've given my people a riddle, but you haven't told me the answer.'

'I haven't even explained it to my father or mother,' he replied, 'so why should I explain it to you?' ¹⁷She cried the whole seven days of the feast. So on the seventh day he finally told her, because she continued to press him. She in turn explained the riddle to her people.

¹⁸Before sunset on the seventh day the men of the town said to him,

'What is sweeter than honey?
   What is stronger than a lion?'

Samson said to them,

'If you had not ploughed with my heifer,
   you would not have solved my riddle.'

19 Then the Spirit of the LORD came powerfully upon him. He went down to Ashkelon, struck down thirty of their men, stripped them of everything and gave their clothes to those who had explained the riddle. Burning with anger, he returned to his father's home. 20 And Samson's wife was given to one of his companions who had attended him at the feast.

15 Later on, at the time of wheat harvest, Samson took a young goat and went to visit his wife. He said, 'I'm going to my wife's room.' But her father would not let him go in.

2 'I was so sure you hated her,' he said, 'that I gave her to your companion. Isn't her younger sister more attractive? Take her instead.'

3 Samson said to them, 'This time I have a right to get even with the Philistines; I will really harm them.' 4 So he went out and caught three hundred foxes and tied them tail to tail in pairs. He then fastened a torch to every pair of tails, 5 lit the torches and let the foxes loose in the standing corn of the Philistines. He burned up the shocks and standing corn, together with the vineyards and olive groves.

6 When the Philistines asked, 'Who did this?' they were told, 'Samson, the Timnite's son-in-law, because his wife was given to his companion.'

So the Philistines went up and burned her and her father to death. 7 Samson said to them, 'Since you've acted like this, I swear that I won't stop until I get my revenge on you.' 8 He attacked them viciously and slaughtered many of them. Then he went down and stayed in a cave in the rock of Etam.

▬ PSALM 57:7-11

7 My heart, O God, is steadfast,
   my heart is steadfast;
   I will sing and make music.

8 Awake, my soul!
   Awake, harp and lyre!
   I will awaken the dawn.

9 I will praise you, Lord, among the nations;
   I will sing of you among the peoples.
10 For great is your love, reaching to the
     heavens;
   your faithfulness reaches to the skies.

11 Be exalted, O God, above the heavens;
   let your glory be over all the earth.

▬ PROVERBS 13:7-8

7 One person pretends to be rich, yet has
     nothing;
   another pretends to be poor, yet has
     great wealth.

8 A person's riches may ransom their life,
   but the poor cannot respond to
     threatening rebukes.

▬ LUKE 23:1-19

23 Then the whole assembly rose and led him off to Pilate. 2 And they began to accuse him, saying, 'We have found this man subverting our nation. He opposes payment of taxes to Caesar and claims to be Messiah, a king.'

3 So Pilate asked Jesus, 'Are you the king of the Jews?'

'You have said so,' Jesus replied.

4 Then Pilate announced to the chief priests and the crowd, 'I find no basis for a charge against this man.'

5 But they insisted, 'He stirs up the people all over Judea by his teaching. He started in Galilee and has come all the way here.'

6 On hearing this, Pilate asked if the man was a Galilean. 7 When he learned that Jesus was under Herod's jurisdiction,

he sent him to Herod, who was also in Jerusalem at that time.

8 When Herod saw Jesus, he was greatly pleased, because for a long time he had been wanting to see him. From what he had heard about him, he hoped to see him perform a sign of some sort. 9 He plied him with many questions, but Jesus gave him no answer. 10 The chief priests and the teachers of the law were standing there, vehemently accusing him. 11 Then Herod and his soldiers ridiculed and mocked him. Dressing him in an elegant robe, they sent him back to Pilate. 12 That day Herod and Pilate became friends – before this they had been enemies.

13 Pilate called together the chief priests, the rulers and the people, 14 and said to them, 'You brought me this man as one who was inciting the people to rebellion. I have examined him in your presence and have found no basis for your charges against him. 15 Neither has Herod, for he sent him back to us; as you can see, he has done nothing to deserve death. 16 Therefore, I will punish him and then release him.' [17] a

18 But the whole crowd shouted, 'Away with this man! Release Barabbas to us!' 19 (Barabbas had been thrown into prison for an insurrection in the city, and for murder.)

---

a Some manuscripts here include words similar to Matt. 27:15 and Mark 15:16.

The High-Water Mark

'For great is your love, reaching to the heavens; your faithfulness reaches to the skies.' **Psalm 57:10**

Let us consider an important aspect of God's nature and character – love. There are at least three things that are told us in Scripture concerning the nature of God.

First, 'God is spirit' (John 4:24), which means He has no visible substance.

Second, 'God is light' (1 John 1:5), which means no darkness can dwell in Him. In Scripture darkness stands for sin, death, and so on.

Third, 'God is love' (1 John 4:16), which means that the energy which flows out from His being is that of infinite, eternal beneficence.

When John wrote the words 'God is love', it was no slick statement, since it was the first time in history that the phrase had been used in that way. People had believed God was love and had speculated about His benevolence, but now the categorical statement was laid down for all to behold. These words, in my judgment, are the high-water mark of divine revelation; nothing more needs to be said, for nothing greater can be said.

I often create a mental picture for myself of the angels peering over the battlements of heaven as John wrote these words. And then, when they had been written down, I imagine them breaking into rapturous applause and saying to each other: 'They've got it. They've got it! At last they see that God is love.' A sigh of deep satisfaction and great joy would have filled the portals of heaven in the knowledge that the greatest truth about God was now finally made crystal clear. The implied was now inscribed.

PRAYER

Father, I am so thankful that You have demonstrated categorically that the greatest thing about You is love. My heart gladly rests upon that glorious fact. I look forward to exploring it forever. In Jesus' name. Amen.

FURTHER STUDY

Jer. 31:1-4; John 3:16;
Rom. 5:8
• What did the Lord say
 to Israel?
• How did He demonstrate
 this?

May 10

▬ JUDGES 15:9–17:13

⁹ The Philistines went up and camped in Judah, spreading out near Lehi. ¹⁰ The people of Judah asked, 'Why have you come to fight us?'

'We have come to take Samson prisoner,' they answered, 'to do to him as he did to us.'

¹¹ Then three thousand men from Judah went down to the cave in the rock of Etam and said to Samson, 'Don't you realise that the Philistines are rulers over us? What have you done to us?'

He answered, 'I merely did to them what they did to me.'

¹² They said to him, 'We've come to tie you up and hand you over to the Philistines.'

Samson said, 'Swear to me that you won't kill me yourselves.'

¹³ 'Agreed,' they answered. 'We will only tie you up and hand you over to them. We will not kill you.' So they bound him with two new ropes and led him up from the rock. ¹⁴ As he approached Lehi, the Philistines came towards him shouting. The Spirit of the LORD came powerfully upon him. The ropes on his arms became like charred flax, and the bindings dropped from his hands. ¹⁵ Finding a fresh jawbone of a donkey, he grabbed it and struck down a thousand men.

¹⁶ Then Samson said,

'With a donkey's jawbone
 I have made donkeys of them.
With a donkey's jawbone
 I have killed a thousand men.'

¹⁷ When he finished speaking, he threw away the jawbone; and the place was called Ramath Lehi.

¹⁸ Because he was very thirsty, he cried out to the LORD, 'You have given your servant this great victory. Must I now die of thirst and fall into the hands of the uncircumcised?' ¹⁹ Then God opened up the hollow place in Lehi, and water came out of it. When Samson drank, his strength returned and he revived. So the spring was called En Hakkore, and it is still there in Lehi.

²⁰ Samson led Israel for twenty years in the days of the Philistines.

16 One day Samson went to Gaza, where he saw a prostitute. He went in to spend the night with her. ² The people of Gaza were told, 'Samson is here!' So they surrounded the place and lay in wait for him all night at the city gate. They made no move during the night, saying, 'At dawn we'll kill him.'

³ But Samson lay there only until the middle of the night. Then he got up and took hold of the doors of the city gate, together with the two posts, and tore them loose, bar and all. He lifted them to his shoulders and carried them to the top of the hill that faces Hebron.

⁴Some time later, he fell in love with a woman in the Valley of Sorek whose name was Delilah. ⁵The rulers of the Philistines went to her and said, 'See if you can lure him into showing you the secret of his great strength and how we can overpower him so that we may tie him up and subdue him. Each one of us will give you eleven hundred shekels of silver.'

⁶So Delilah said to Samson, 'Tell me the secret of your great strength and how you can be tied up and subdued.'

⁷Samson answered her, 'If anyone ties me with seven fresh bow-strings that have not been dried, I'll become as weak as any other man.'

⁸Then the rulers of the Philistines brought her seven fresh bow-strings that had not been dried, and she tied him with them. ⁹With men hidden in the room, she called to him, 'Samson, the Philistines are upon you!' But he snapped the bow-strings as easily as a piece of string snaps when it comes close to a flame. So the secret of his strength was not discovered.

¹⁰Then Delilah said to Samson, 'You have made a fool of me; you lied to me. Come now, tell me how you can be tied.'

¹¹He said, 'If anyone ties me securely with new ropes that have never been used, I'll become as weak as any other man.'

¹²So Delilah took new ropes and tied him with them. Then, with men hidden in the room, she called to him, 'Samson, the Philistines are upon you!' But he snapped the ropes off his arms as if they were threads.

¹³Delilah then said to Samson, 'All this time you have been making a fool of me and lying to me. Tell me how you can be tied.'

He replied, 'If you weave the seven braids of my head into the fabric on the loom and tighten it with the pin, I'll become as weak as any other man.' So while he was sleeping, Delilah took the seven braids of his head, wove them into the fabric ¹⁴and tightened it with the pin.

Again she called to him, 'Samson, the Philistines are upon you!' He awoke from his sleep and pulled up the pin and the loom, with the fabric.

¹⁵Then she said to him, 'How can you say, "I love you," when you won't confide in me? This is the third time you have made a fool of me and haven't told me the secret of your great strength.' ¹⁶With such nagging she prodded him day after day until he was sick to death of it.

¹⁷So he told her everything. 'No razor has ever been used on my head,' he said, 'because I have been a Nazirite dedicated to God from my mother's womb. If my head were shaved, my strength would leave me, and I would become as weak as any other man.'

¹⁸When Delilah saw that he had told her everything, she sent word to the rulers of the Philistines, 'Come back once more; he has told me everything.' So the rulers of the Philistines returned with the silver in their hands. ¹⁹After putting him to sleep on her lap, she called for someone to shave off the seven braids of his hair, and so began to subdue him. And his strength left him.

²⁰Then she called, 'Samson, the Philistines are upon you!'

He awoke from his sleep and thought, 'I'll go out as before and shake myself free.' But he did not know that the LORD had left him.

²¹Then the Philistines seized him, gouged out his eyes and took him down to Gaza. Binding him with bronze shackles, they set him to grinding corn in the prison. ²²But the hair on his head began to grow again after it had been shaved.

²³Now the rulers of the Philistines assembled to offer a great sacrifice to Dagon their god and to celebrate, saying, 'Our god has delivered Samson, our enemy, into our hands.' ²⁴When the people saw him, they praised their god, saying,

'Our god has delivered our enemy
    into our hands,
the one who laid waste our land

and multiplied our slain.'

²⁵While they were in high spirits, they shouted, 'Bring out Samson to entertain us.' So they called Samson out of the prison, and he performed for them.

When they stood him among the pillars, ²⁶Samson said to the servant who held his hand, 'Put me where I can feel the pillars that support the temple, so that I may lean against them.' ²⁷Now the temple was crowded with men and women; all the rulers of the Philistines were there, and on the roof were about three thousand men and women watching Samson perform. ²⁸Then Samson prayed to the Lord, 'Sovereign Lord, remember me. Please, God, strengthen me just once more, and let me with one blow get revenge on the Philistines for my two eyes.' ²⁹Then Samson reached towards the two central pillars on which the temple stood. Bracing himself against them, his right hand on the one and his left hand on the other, ³⁰Samson said, 'Let me die with the Philistines!' Then he pushed with all his might, and down came the temple on the rulers and all the people in it. Thus he killed many more when he died than while he lived.

³¹Then his brothers and his father's whole family went down to get him. They brought him back and buried him between Zorah and Eshtaol in the tomb of Manoah his father. He had led Israel for twenty years.

17 Now a man named Micah from the hill country of Ephraim ²said to his mother, 'The eleven hundred shekels of silver that were taken from you and about which I heard you utter a curse – I have that silver with me; I took it.'

Then his mother said, 'The Lord bless you, my son!'

³When he returned the eleven hundred shekels of silver to his mother, she said, 'I solemnly consecrate my silver to the Lord for my son to make an image overlaid with silver. I will give it back to you.'

⁴So after he returned the silver to his mother, she took two hundred shekels of silver and gave them to a silversmith, who used them to make the idol. And it was put in Micah's house.

⁵Now this man Micah had a shrine, and he made an ephod and some household gods and installed one of his sons as his priest. ⁶In those days Israel had no king; everyone did as they saw fit.

⁷A young Levite from Bethlehem in Judah, who had been living within the clan of Judah, ⁸left that town in search of some other place to stay. On his way he came to Micah's house in the hill country of Ephraim.

⁹Micah asked him, 'Where are you from?'

'I'm a Levite from Bethlehem in Judah,' he said, 'and I'm looking for a place to stay.'

¹⁰Then Micah said to him, 'Live with me and be my father and priest, and I'll give you ten shekels of silver a year, your clothes and your food.' ¹¹So the Levite agreed to live with him, and the young man became like one of his sons to him. ¹²Then Micah installed the Levite, and the young man became his priest and lived in his house. ¹³And Micah said, 'Now I know that the Lord will be good to me, since this Levite has become my priest.'

- **PSALM 58:1-5**

¹Do you rulers indeed speak justly?
  Do you judge people with equity?
²No, in your heart you devise injustice,
  and your hands mete out violence on
    the earth.

³Even from birth the wicked go astray;
  from the womb they are wayward,
    spreading lies.
⁴Their venom is like the venom of a snake,
  like that of a cobra that has stopped its
    ears,
⁵that will not heed the tune of the charmer,
  however skilful the enchanter may be.

▬ PROVERBS 13:9-10

⁹ The light of the righteous shines brightly,
   but the lamp of the wicked is snuffed
   out.

¹⁰ Where there is strife, there is pride,
   but wisdom is found in those who take
   advice.

▬ LUKE 23:20-38

²⁰ Wanting to release Jesus, Pilate appealed to them again. ²¹ But they kept shouting, 'Crucify him! Crucify him!'

²² For the third time he spoke to them: 'Why? What crime has this man committed? I have found in him no grounds for the death penalty. Therefore I will have him punished and then release him.'

²³ But with loud shouts they insistently demanded that he be crucified, and their shouts prevailed. ²⁴ So Pilate decided to grant their demand. ²⁵ He released the man who had been thrown into prison for insurrection and murder, the one they asked for, and surrendered Jesus to their will.

²⁶ As the soldiers led him away, they seized Simon from Cyrene, who was on his way in from the country, and put the cross on him and made him carry it behind Jesus. ²⁷ A large number of people followed him,

including women who mourned and wailed for him. ²⁸ Jesus turned and said to them, 'Daughters of Jerusalem, do not weep for me; weep for yourselves and for your children. ²⁹ For the time will come when you will say, "Blessed are the childless women, the wombs that never bore and the breasts that never nursed!" ³⁰ Then

'"they will say to the mountains, 'Fall
   on us!'
   and to the hills, 'Cover us!'"'

³¹ For if people do these things when the tree is green, what will happen when it is dry?'

³² Two other men, both criminals, were also led out with him to be executed. ³³ When they came to the place called the Skull, they crucified him there, along with the criminals – one on his right, the other on his left. ³⁴ Jesus said, 'Father, forgive them, for they do not know what they are doing.' And they divided up his clothes by casting lots.

³⁵ The people stood watching, and the rulers even sneered at him. They said, 'He saved others; let him save himself if he is God's Messiah, the Chosen One.'

³⁶ The soldiers also came up and mocked him. They offered him wine vinegar ³⁷ and said, 'If you are the king of the Jews, save yourself.'

³⁸ There was a written notice above him, which read: THIS IS THE KING OF THE JEWS.

The Divine Example

'Jesus said, "Father, forgive them, for they do not
know what they are doing"' **Luke 23:34**

We can only ask God to forgive us our sins when we are willing to forgive those who have sinned against us.

Does this mean that before we can be converted to Christ and have our sins forgiven, we have to search our hearts in order to make sure that we hold no bitterness or resentment against anyone? No. There is nothing in Scripture that states that a non-Christian receives forgiveness from God on the basis of claiming to forgive everyone else. Jesus is referring here, so I believe, to those who are already His followers. They have been forgiven for their sins, but they now need a principle by which they can deal with guilt that arises, subsequent to conversion, through the violation of some biblical standard. Paul says in Ephesians 1:7: 'In him we have redemption through his blood, the forgiveness of our sins in accordance with the riches of God's grace.' Grace - that's the basis of our forgiveness when we first come to Christ. But although we have received that forgiveness, we can never enjoy freedom from defilement in our Christian walk unless we are ready to extend the forgiveness God has given us to those who have hurt us.

This is an extremely important issue, for if we fail to forgive those who have offended us, we break the bridge over which God's forgiveness flows into us.

PRAYER

Blessed Lord Jesus, You who hung upon a cross, tortured in every nerve, yet prayed, 'Father, forgive them', help me this day to forgive all those who have wronged me in a lesser way. For Your own dear name's sake. Amen.

FURTHER STUDY

Luke 17:1-10; Mark 11:25;
Col. 3:13; Eph. 4:32
- What did Jesus teach on forgiveness?
- What was the disciples' response?

May 11

■ JUDGES 18:1-31

18 In those days Israel had no king. And in those days the tribe of the Danites was seeking a place of their own where they might settle, because they had not yet come into an inheritance among the tribes of Israel. [2] So the Danites sent five of their leading men from Zorah and Eshtaol to spy out the land and explore it. These men represented all the Danites. They told them, 'Go, explore the land.'

So they entered the hill country of Ephraim and came to the house of Micah, where they spent the night. [3] When they were near Micah's house, they recognised the voice of the young Levite; so they turned in there and asked him, 'Who brought you here? What are

you doing in this place? Why are you here?'

[4] He told them what Micah had done for him, and said, 'He has hired me and I am his priest.'

[5] Then they said to him, 'Please enquire of God to learn whether our journey will be successful.'

[6] The priest answered them, 'Go in peace. Your journey has the LORD's approval.'

[7] So the five men left and came to Laish, where they saw that the people were living in safety, like the Sidonians, at peace and secure. And since their land lacked nothing, they were prosperous. Also, they lived a long way from the Sidonians and had no relationship with anyone else.

[8] When they returned to Zorah and Eshtaol, their fellow Danites asked them,

'How did you find things?'

⁹They answered, 'Come on, let's attack them! We have seen the land, and it is very good. Aren't you going to do something? Don't hesitate to go there and take it over. ¹⁰When you get there, you will find an unsuspecting people and a spacious land that God has put into your hands, a land that lacks nothing whatever.'

¹¹Then six hundred men of the Danites, armed for battle, set out from Zorah and Eshtaol. ¹²On their way they set up camp near Kiriath Jearim in Judah. This is why the place west of Kiriath Jearim is called Mahaneh Dan to this day. ¹³From there they went on to the hill country of Ephraim and came to Micah's house.

¹⁴Then the five men who had spied out the land of Laish said to their fellow Danites, 'Do you know that one of these houses has an ephod, some household gods and an image overlaid with silver? Now you know what to do.' ¹⁵So they turned in there and went to the house of the young Levite at Micah's place and greeted him. ¹⁶The six hundred Danites, armed for battle, stood at the entrance of the gate. ¹⁷The five men who had spied out the land went inside and took the idol, the ephod and the household gods while the priest and the six hundred armed men stood at the entrance of the gate.

¹⁸When the five men went into Micah's house and took the idol, the ephod and the household gods, the priest said to them, 'What are you doing?'

¹⁹They answered him, 'Be quiet! Don't say a word. Come with us, and be our father and priest. Isn't it better that you serve a tribe and clan in Israel as priest rather than just one man's household?' ²⁰The priest was very pleased. He took the ephod, the household gods and the idol and went along with the people. ²¹Putting their little children, their livestock and their possessions in front of them, they turned away and left.

²²When they had gone some distance from Micah's house, the men who lived near Micah were called together and overtook the Danites. ²³As they shouted after them, the Danites turned and said to Micah, 'What's the matter with you that you called out your men to fight?'

²⁴He replied, 'You took the gods I made, and my priest, and went away. What else do I have? How can you ask, "What's the matter with you?"'

²⁵The Danites answered, 'Don't argue with us, or some of the men may get angry and attack you, and you and your family will lose your lives.' ²⁶So the Danites went their way, and Micah, seeing that they were too strong for him, turned round and went back home.

²⁷Then they took what Micah had made, and his priest, and went on to Laish, against a people at peace and secure. They attacked them with the sword and burned down their city. ²⁸There was no one to rescue them because they lived a long way from Sidon and had no relationship with anyone else. The city was in a valley near Beth Rehob.

The Danites rebuilt the city and settled there. ²⁹They named it Dan after their ancestor Dan, who was born to Israel – though the city used to be called Laish. ³⁰There the Danites set up for themselves the idol, and Jonathan son of Gershom, the son of Moses, and his sons were priests for the tribe of Dan until the time of the captivity of the land. ³¹They continued to use the idol Micah had made, all the time the house of God was in Shiloh.

■ PSALM 58:6-11

⁶Break the teeth in their mouths, O God;
    LORD, tear out the fangs of those lions!
⁷Let them vanish like water that flows
        away;
    when they draw the bow, let their
        arrows fall short.
⁸May they be like a slug that melts away
        as it moves along,

like a stillborn child that never sees
the sun.

⁹ Before your pots can feel the heat of the
thorns –
whether they be green or dry – the
wicked will be swept away.
¹⁰ The righteous will be glad when they are
avenged,
when they dip their feet in the blood of
the wicked.
¹¹ Then people will say,
'Surely the righteous still are rewarded;
surely there is a God who judges the
earth.'

■ PROVERBS 13:11-12

¹¹ Dishonest money dwindles away,
but whoever gathers money little by
little makes it grow.

¹² Hope deferred makes the heart sick,
but a longing fulfilled is a tree of life.

■ LUKE 23:39-56

³⁹ One of the criminals who hung there
hurled insults at him: 'Aren't you the Messiah? Save yourself and us!'
⁴⁰ But the other criminal rebuked him.
'Don't you fear God,' he said, 'since you
are under the same sentence? ⁴¹ We are
punished justly, for we are getting what
our deeds deserve. But this man has done
nothing wrong.'

⁴² Then he said, 'Jesus, remember me
when you come into your kingdom.'
⁴³ Jesus answered him, 'Truly I tell you,
today you will be with me in paradise.'
⁴⁴ It was now about noon, and darkness
came over the whole land until three in the
afternoon, ⁴⁵ for the sun stopped shining.
And the curtain of the temple was torn in
two. ⁴⁶ Jesus called out with a loud voice,
'Father, into your hands I commit my spirit.'
When he had said this, he breathed his last.
⁴⁷ The centurion, seeing what had happened, praised God and said, 'Surely this
was a righteous man.' ⁴⁸ When all the people
who had gathered to witness this sight saw
what took place, they beat their breasts and
went away. ⁴⁹ But all those who knew him,
including the women who had followed him
from Galilee, stood at a distance, watching
these things.
⁵⁰ Now there was a man named Joseph, a
member of the Council, a good and upright
man, ⁵¹ who had not consented to their decision and action. He came from the Judean town of Arimathea, and he himself was
waiting for the kingdom of God. ⁵² Going
to Pilate, he asked for Jesus' body. ⁵³ Then
he took it down, wrapped it in linen cloth
and placed it in a tomb cut in the rock,
one in which no one had yet been laid. ⁵⁴ It
was Preparation Day, and the Sabbath was
about to begin.
⁵⁵ The women who had come with Jesus
from Galilee followed Joseph and saw the
tomb and how his body was laid in it. ⁵⁶ Then
they went home and prepared spices and
perfumes. But they rested on the Sabbath in
obedience to the commandment.

The Patience of God

'The righteous will be glad when they are avenged ...
Then people will say, "Surely the righteous still are
rewarded; surely there is a God who judges the
earth."' **Psalm 58:10-11**

Ever found yourself feeling frustrated because of the way in which wickedness seems to win over justice? Then you know something of how Solomon felt when he said, 'God will bring into judgment both the righteous and the wicked' (Eccl. 3:17). Every generation, throughout time, has had to face this problem. James Russell Lowell put it this way:

> Truth forever on the scaffold,
> Wrong forever on the throne.

Solomon struggles, as no doubt you have done (and perhaps still do), with the fact that in the very place where you would expect to see justice, you find wickedness and corruption prevailing. In the days when I was a pastor, I sometimes went to court with people who had a genuine case to be heard, only to see it broken down by tactics that were dishonest and unjust. I have seen enough injustice in my time to share something of Solomon's cynicism.

Are you at this moment a victim of judicial injustice? Then don't allow yourself to become cynical, for, as Solomon said: 'God will bring into judgment both the righteous and the wicked'. Wrong will not continue forever. The day is coming when all corruption and injustice will be called to judgment before the throne of God's truth. But of course, being human, we wish the injustices we have received could be put right - now. God seems to be much more patient than we are, and what we must do is to ask for grace to be patient with the patience of God.

PRAYER

O God my Father, give me the divine perspective on things so that present injustices may be swallowed up in Your long-term purposes. Help me see that I will have my day in court - Your court. In Jesus' name I ask it. Amen.

FURTHER STUDY

Psa. 58:1-11; Gen. 18:25; Psa. 96:13
- What was the view of the psalmist?
- How does God judge?

May 12

■ JUDGES 19:1–20:25

19 In those days Israel had no king. Now a Levite who lived in a remote area in the hill country of Ephraim took a concubine from Bethlehem in Judah. ²But she was unfaithful to him. She left him and went back to her parents' home in Bethlehem, Judah. After she had been there for four months, ³her husband went to her to persuade her to return. He had with him his servant and two donkeys. She took him into her parents' home, and when her father saw him, he gladly welcomed him. ⁴His father-in-law, the woman's father, prevailed on him to stay; so he remained with him three days, eating and drinking, and sleeping there.

⁵ On the fourth day they got up early and he prepared to leave, but the woman's father said to his son-in-law, 'Refresh yourself with something to eat; then you can go.' ⁶ So the two of them sat down to eat and drink together. Afterwards the woman's father said, 'Please stay tonight and enjoy yourself.' ⁷ And when the man got up to go, his father-in-law persuaded him, so he stayed there that night. ⁸ On the morning of the fifth day, when he rose to go, the woman's father said, 'Refresh yourself. Wait till afternoon!' So the two of them ate together.

⁹ Then when the man, with his concubine and his servant, got up to leave, his father-in-law, the woman's father, said, 'Now look, it's almost evening. Spend the night here; the day is nearly over. Stay and enjoy yourself. Early tomorrow morning you can get up and be on your way home.' ¹⁰ But, unwilling to stay another night, the man left and went towards Jebus (that is, Jerusalem), with his two saddled donkeys and his concubine.

¹¹ When they were near Jebus and the day was almost gone, the servant said to his master, 'Come, let's stop at this city of the Jebusites and spend the night.'

¹² His master replied, 'No. We won't go into any city whose people are not Israelites. We will go on to Gibeah.' ¹³ He added, 'Come, let's try to reach Gibeah or Ramah and spend the night in one of those places.' ¹⁴ So they went on, and the sun set as they neared Gibeah in Benjamin. ¹⁵ There they stopped to spend the night. They went and sat in the city square, but no one took them in for the night.

¹⁶ That evening an old man from the hill country of Ephraim, who was living in Gibeah (the inhabitants of the place were Benjaminites), came in from his work in the fields. ¹⁷ When he looked and saw the traveller in the city square, the old man asked, 'Where are you going? Where did you come from?'

¹⁸ He answered, 'We are on our way from Bethlehem in Judah to a remote area in the hill country of Ephraim where I live. I have been to Bethlehem in Judah and now I am going to the house of the LORD. No one has taken me in for the night. ¹⁹ We have both straw and fodder for our donkeys and bread and wine for ourselves your servants – me, the woman and the young man with us. We don't need anything.'

²⁰ 'You are welcome at my house,' the old man said. 'Let me supply whatever you need. Only don't spend the night in the square.' ²¹ So he took him into his house and fed his donkeys. After they had washed their feet, they had something to eat and drink.

²² While they were enjoying themselves, some of the wicked men of the city surrounded the house. Pounding on the door, they shouted to the old man who owned the house, 'Bring out the man who came to your house so we can have sex with him.'

²³ The owner of the house went outside and said to them, 'No, my friends, don't be so vile. Since this man is my guest, don't do this outrageous thing. ²⁴ Look, here is my virgin daughter, and his concubine. I will bring them out to you now, and you can use them and do to them whatever you wish. But as for this man, don't do such an outrageous thing.'

²⁵ But the men would not listen to him. So the man took his concubine and sent her outside to them, and they raped her and abused her throughout the night, and at dawn they let her go. ²⁶ At daybreak the woman went back to the house where her master was staying, fell down at the door and lay there until daylight.

²⁷ When her master got up in the morning and opened the door of the house and stepped out to continue on his way, there lay his concubine, fallen in the doorway of the house, with her hands on the threshold. ²⁸ He said to her, 'Get up; let's go.' But there was no answer. Then the man put her on his donkey and set out for home.

²⁹ When he reached home, he took a knife

and cut up his concubine, limb by limb, into twelve parts and sent them into all the areas of Israel. ³⁰ Everyone who saw it was saying to one another, 'Such a thing has never been seen or done, not since the day the Israelites came up out of Egypt. Just imagine! We must do something! So speak up!'

20 Then all Israel from Dan to Beersheba and from the land of Gilead came together as one and assembled before the LORD in Mizpah. ² The leaders of all the people of the tribes of Israel took their places in the assembly of God's people, four hundred thousand men armed with swords. ³ (The Benjaminites heard that the Israelites had gone up to Mizpah.) Then the Israelites said, 'Tell us how this awful thing happened.'

⁴ So the Levite, the husband of the murdered woman, said, 'I and my concubine came to Gibeah in Benjamin to spend the night. ⁵ During the night the men of Gibeah came after me and surrounded the house, intending to kill me. They raped my concubine, and she died. ⁶ I took my concubine, cut her into pieces and sent one piece to each region of Israel's inheritance, because they committed this lewd and outrageous act in Israel. ⁷ Now, all you Israelites, speak up and tell me what you have decided to do.'

⁸ All the men rose up together as one, saying, 'None of us will go home. No, not one of us will return to his house. ⁹ But now this is what we'll do to Gibeah: we'll go up against it in the order decided by casting lots. ¹⁰ We'll take ten men out of every hundred from all the tribes of Israel, and a hundred from a thousand, and a thousand from ten thousand, to get provisions for the army. Then, when the army arrives at Gibeah in Benjamin, it can give them what they deserve for this outrageous act done in Israel.' ¹¹ So all the Israelites got together and united as one against the city.

¹² The tribes of Israel sent messengers throughout the tribe of Benjamin, saying,

'What about this awful crime that was committed among you? ¹³ Now turn those wicked men of Gibeah over to us so that we may put them to death and purge the evil from Israel.'

But the Benjaminites would not listen to their fellow Israelites. ¹⁴ From their towns they came together at Gibeah to fight against the Israelites. ¹⁵ At once the Benjaminites mobilised twenty-six thousand swordsmen from their towns, in addition to seven hundred able young men from those living in Gibeah. ¹⁶ Among all these soldiers there were seven hundred select troops who were left-handed, each of whom could sling a stone at a hair and not miss.

¹⁷ Israel, apart from Benjamin, mustered four hundred thousand swordsmen, all of them fit for battle.

¹⁸ The Israelites went up to Bethel and enquired of God. They said, 'Who of us is to go up first to fight against the Benjaminites?'

The LORD replied, 'Judah shall go first.'

¹⁹ The next morning the Israelites got up and pitched camp near Gibeah. ²⁰ The Israelites went out to fight the Benjaminites and took up battle positions against them at Gibeah. ²¹ The Benjaminites came out of Gibeah and cut down twenty-two thousand Israelites on the battlefield that day. ²² But the Israelites encouraged one another and again took up their positions where they had stationed themselves the first day. ²³ The Israelites went up and wept before the LORD until evening, and they enquired of the LORD. They said, 'Shall we go up again to fight against the Benjaminites, our fellow Israelites?'

The LORD answered, 'Go up against them.'

²⁴ Then the Israelites drew near to Benjamin the second day. ²⁵ This time, when the Benjaminites came out from Gibeah to oppose them, they cut down another eighteen thousand Israelites, all of them armed with swords.

▬ PSALM 59:1-10

[1] Deliver me from my enemies, O God;
    be my fortress against those who are
       attacking me.
[2] Deliver me from evildoers
    and save me from those who are after
       my blood.

[3] See how they lie in wait for me!
    Fierce men conspire against me
    for no offence or sin of mine, LORD.
[4] I have done no wrong, yet they are ready
       to attack me.
    Arise to help me; look on my plight!
[5] You, LORD God Almighty,
    you who are the God of Israel,
    rouse yourself to punish all the nations;
    show no mercy to wicked traitors.

[6] They return at evening,
    snarling like dogs,
    and prowl about the city.
[7] See what they spew from their mouths –
    the words from their lips are sharp
       as swords,
    and they think, 'Who can hear us?'
[8] But you laugh at them, LORD;
    you scoff at all those nations.

[9] You are my strength, I watch for you;
    you, God, are my fortress,
[10]   my God on whom I can rely.

    God will go before me
    and will let me gloat over those who
       slander me.

▬ PROVERBS 13:13

[13] Whoever scorns instruction will pay
       for it,
    but whoever respects a command is
       rewarded.

▬ LUKE 24:1-24

24 On the first day of the week, very early in the morning, the women took the spices they had prepared and went to the tomb. [2] They found the stone rolled away from the tomb, [3] but when they entered, they did not find the body of the Lord Jesus. [4] While they were wondering about this, suddenly two men in clothes that gleamed like lightning stood beside them. [5] In their fright the women bowed down with their faces to the ground, but the men said to them, 'Why do you look for the living among the dead? [6] He is not here; he has risen! Remember how he told you, while he was still with you in Galilee: [7] "The Son of Man must be delivered over to the hands of sinners, be crucified and on the third day be raised again."' [8] Then they remembered his words.

[9] When they came back from the tomb, they told all these things to the Eleven and to all the others. [10] It was Mary Magdalene, Joanna, Mary the mother of James, and the others with them who told this to the apostles. [11] But they did not believe the women, because their words seemed to them like nonsense. [12] Peter, however, got up and ran to the tomb. Bending over, he saw the strips of linen lying by themselves, and he went away, wondering to himself what had happened.

[13] Now that same day two of them were going to a village called Emmaus, about seven miles from Jerusalem. [14] They were talking with each other about everything that had happened. [15] As they talked and discussed these things with each other, Jesus himself came up and walked along with them; [16] but they were kept from recognising him. [17] He asked them, 'What are you discussing together as you walk along?'

They stood still, their faces downcast. [18] One of them, named Cleopas, asked him, 'Are you the only one visiting Jerusalem who does not know the things that have happened there in these days?'

[19] 'What things?' he asked.

'About Jesus of Nazareth,' they replied. 'He was a prophet, powerful in word and deed before God and all the people. ²⁰The chief priests and our rulers handed him over to be sentenced to death, and they crucified him; ²¹but we had hoped that he was the one who was going to redeem Israel. And what is more, it is the third day since all this took place. ²²In addition, some of our women amazed us. They went to the tomb early this morning ²³but didn't find his body. They came and told us that they had seen a vision of angels, who said he was alive. ²⁴Then some of our companions went to the tomb and found it just as the women had said, but they did not see Jesus.'

Worship Is Central

'You are my strength, I watch for you; you, God, are my fortress, my God on whom I can rely.'
Psalm 59:9-10

If we are to go deeper with God, then we must understand both the importance and meaning of worship. Dr. Dick Averby, professor of the Old Testament at Dallas Seminary, claims that the antidote to every human problem is worship. I am sure he is thinking of personality problems, not physical problems, and allowing for this caveat, I would agree with him. Dr. Larry Crabb, professor of counselling at Colorado Christian University, says something similar: 'Worship means, in the middle of life as it is experienced, that you find some way to be caught up in God's character and purpose so that His will becomes central.'

Mature Christians are people who think of themselves first and foremost as worshippers. They will see their other roles in life - as fathers, mothers, factory workers, business people, farmers, doctors, evangelists, pastors, and so on - as secondary.

Some worship the servants of God more than they worship God Himself. A story is told of an occasion when Christmas Evans, the great Welsh preacher of a past century, was due to preach. Prior to the service the church was packed with people eager to hear the great orator. As the service was about to begin, it was announced that Christmas Evans was unable to keep the engagement and a lesser-known preacher would take his place. People began to show signs of leaving until the moderator said, 'All those who have come to worship Christmas Evans may leave. All those who have come to worship God may stay'. No one left.

PRAYER

O God, my soul is too big to be satisfied with the writings of a mere man. I can be inspired by human words, but I can be fed only by Your words. May I continually seek You. Amen.

FURTHER STUDY

John 6:25-58; Psa. 132:7; Isa. 55:2; 1 Cor. 10:3-4
- What did Jesus declare?
- Why did the Jews stumble over it?

May 13

■ JUDGES 20:26–21:25

²⁶ Then all the Israelites, the whole army, went up to Bethel, and there they sat weeping before the LORD. They fasted that day until evening and presented burnt offerings and fellowship offerings to the LORD. ²⁷ And the Israelites enquired of the LORD. (In those days the ark of the covenant of God was there, ²⁸ with Phinehas son of Eleazar, the son of Aaron, ministering before it.) They asked, 'Shall we go up again to fight against the Benjaminites, our fellow Israelites, or not?'

The LORD responded, 'Go, for tomorrow I will give them into your hands.'

²⁹ Then Israel set an ambush around Gibeah. ³⁰ They went up against the Benjaminites on the third day and took up positions against Gibeah as they had done before. ³¹ The Benjaminites came out to meet them and were drawn away from the city. They began to inflict casualties on the Israelites as before, so that about thirty men fell in the open field and on the roads – the one leading to Bethel and the other to Gibeah. ³² While the Benjaminites were saying, 'We are defeating them as before,' the Israelites were saying, 'Let's retreat and draw them away from the city to the roads.'

³³ All the men of Israel moved from their places and took up positions at Baal Tamar, and the Israelite ambush charged out of its place on the west of Gibeah. ³⁴ Then ten thousand of Israel's able young men made a frontal attack on Gibeah. The fighting was so heavy that the Benjaminites did not realise how near disaster was. ³⁵ The LORD defeated Benjamin before Israel, and on that day the Israelites struck down 25,100 Benjaminites, all armed with swords. ³⁶ Then the Benjaminites saw that they were beaten.

Now the men of Israel had given way before Benjamin, because they relied on the ambush they had set near Gibeah. ³⁷ Those who had been in ambush made a sudden dash into Gibeah, spread out and put the whole city to the sword. ³⁸ The Israelites had arranged with the ambush that they should send up a great cloud of smoke from the city, ³⁹ and then the Israelites would counterattack.

The Benjaminites had begun to inflict casualties on the Israelites (about thirty), and they said, 'We are defeating them as in the first battle.' ⁴⁰ But when the column of smoke began to rise from the city, the Benjaminites turned and saw the whole city going up in smoke. ⁴¹ Then the Israelites counter-attacked, and the Benjaminites were terrified, because they realised that disaster had come on them. ⁴² So they fled before the Israelites in the direction of the wilderness, but they could not escape the battle. And the Israelites who came out of the towns cut them down there. ⁴³ They surrounded the Benjaminites, chased them and easily overran them in the vicinity of Gibeah on the east. ⁴⁴ Eighteen thousand Benjaminites fell, all of them valiant fighters. ⁴⁵ As they turned and fled towards the wilderness to the rock of Rimmon, the Israelites cut down five thousand men along the roads. They kept pressing after the Benjaminites as far as Gidom and struck down two thousand more.

⁴⁶ On that day twenty-five thousand Benjaminite swordsmen fell, all of them valiant fighters. ⁴⁷ But six hundred of them turned and fled into the wilderness to the rock of Rimmon, where they stayed for four months. ⁴⁸ The men of Israel went back to Benjamin and put all the towns to the sword, including the animals and everything else they found. All the towns they came across they set on fire.

21 The men of Israel had taken an oath at Mizpah: 'Not one of us will give his daughter in marriage to a Benjaminite.'

² The people went to Bethel, where they sat before God until evening, raising their voices and weeping bitterly. ³ 'LORD, God of Israel,' they cried, 'why has this happened to Israel? Why should one tribe be missing from Israel today?'

⁴ Early the next day the people built an altar and presented burnt offerings and fellowship offerings.

⁵ Then the Israelites asked, 'Who from all the tribes of Israel has failed to assemble before the LORD?' For they had taken a solemn oath that anyone who failed to assemble before the LORD at Mizpah was to be put to death.

⁶ Now the Israelites grieved for the tribe of Benjamin, their fellow Israelites. 'Today one tribe is cut off from Israel,' they said. ⁷ 'How can we provide wives for those who are left, since we have taken an oath by the LORD not to give them any of our daughters in marriage?' ⁸ Then they asked, 'Which one of the tribes of Israel failed to assemble before the LORD at Mizpah?' They discovered that no one from Jabesh Gilead had come to the camp for the assembly. ⁹ For when they counted the people, they found that none of the people of Jabesh Gilead were there.

¹⁰ So the assembly sent twelve thousand fighting men with instructions to go to Jabesh Gilead and put to the sword those living there, including the women and children. ¹¹ 'This is what you are to do,' they said. 'Kill every male and every woman who is not a virgin.' ¹² They found among the people living in Jabesh Gilead four hundred young women who had never slept with a man, and they took them to the camp at Shiloh in Canaan.

¹³ Then the whole assembly sent an offer of peace to the Benjaminites at the rock of Rimmon. ¹⁴ So the Benjaminites returned at that time and were given the women of Jabesh Gilead who had been spared. But there were not enough for all of them.

¹⁵ The people grieved for Benjamin, because the LORD had made a gap in the tribes of Israel. ¹⁶ And the elders of the assembly said, 'With the women of Benjamin destroyed, how shall we provide wives for the men who are left?' ¹⁷ The Benjaminite survivors must have heirs,' they said, 'so that a tribe of Israel will not be wiped out. ¹⁸ We can't give them our daughters as wives, since we Israelites have taken this oath: "Cursed be anyone who gives a wife to a Benjaminite." ¹⁹ But look, there is the annual festival of the LORD in Shiloh, which lies north of Bethel, east of the road that goes from Bethel to Shechem, and south of Lebonah.'

²⁰ So they instructed the Benjaminites, saying, 'Go and hide in the vineyards ²¹ and watch. When the young women of Shiloh come out to join in the dancing, rush from the vineyards and each of you seize one of them to be your wife. Then return to the land of Benjamin. ²² When their fathers or brothers complain to us, we will say to them, "Do us the favour of helping them, because we did not get wives for them during the war. You will not be guilty of breaking your oath because you did not give your daughters to them."'

²³ So that is what the Benjaminites did. While the young women were dancing, each man caught one and carried her off to be his wife. Then they returned to their inheritance and rebuilt the towns and settled in them.

²⁴ At that time the Israelites left that place and went home to their tribes and clans, each to his own inheritance.

²⁵ In those days Israel had no king; everyone did as they saw fit.

••

■ PSALM 59:11-17

¹¹ But do not kill them, Lord our shield,
    or my people will forget.
In your might uproot them
    and bring them down.

12 For the sins of their mouths,
  for the words of their lips,
  let them be caught in their pride.
For the curses and lies they utter,
13   consume them in your wrath,
  consume them till they are no more.
Then it will be known to the ends of the
    earth
  that God rules over Jacob.

14 They return at evening,
  snarling like dogs,
  and prowl about the city.
15 They wander about for food
  and howl if not satisfied.
16 But I will sing of your strength,
  in the morning I will sing of your love;
for you are my fortress,
  my refuge in times of trouble.

17 You are my strength, I sing praise to you;
  you, God, are my fortress,
  my God on whom I can rely.

PROVERBS 13:14-15

14 The teaching of the wise is a fountain of
    life,
  turning a person from the snares of
    death.

15 Good judgment wins favour,
  but the way of the unfaithful leads to
    their destruction.

LUKE 24:25-53

25 He said to them, 'How foolish you are,
and how slow to believe all that the prophets
have spoken! 26 Did not the Messiah have to
suffer these things and then enter his glory?' 27 And beginning with Moses and all
the Prophets, he explained to them what was
said in all the Scriptures concerning himself.

28 As they approached the village to
which they were going, Jesus continued on
as if he were going further. 29 But they urged
him strongly, 'Stay with us, for it is nearly
evening; the day is almost over.' So he went
in to stay with them.

30 When he was at the table with them, he
took bread, gave thanks, broke it and began
to give it to them. 31 Then their eyes were
opened and they recognised him, and he
disappeared from their sight. 32 They asked
each other, 'Were not our hearts burning
within us while he talked with us on the
road and opened the Scriptures to us?'

33 They got up and returned at once to
Jerusalem. There they found the Eleven
and those with them, assembled together
34 and saying, 'It is true! The Lord has ris-
en and has appeared to Simon.' 35 Then the
two told what had happened on the way, and
how Jesus was recognised by them when he
broke the bread.

36 While they were still talking about this,
Jesus himself stood among them and said to
them, 'Peace be with you.'

37 They were startled and frightened,
thinking they saw a ghost. 38 He said to
them, 'Why are you troubled, and why do
doubts rise in your minds? 39 Look at my
hands and my feet. It is I myself! Touch me
and see; a ghost does not have flesh and
bones, as you see I have.'

40 When he had said this, he showed them
his hands and feet. 41 And while they still
did not believe it because of joy and amazement, he asked them, 'Do you have anything here to eat?' 42 They gave him a piece
of broiled fish, 43 and he took it and ate it in
their presence.

44 He said to them, 'This is what I told you
while I was still with you: everything must
be fulfilled that is written about me in the
Law of Moses, the Prophets and the Psalms.'

45 Then he opened their minds so they
could understand the Scriptures. 46 He told
them, 'This is what is written: the Messiah

will suffer and rise from the dead on the third day, [47] and repentance for the forgiveness of sins will be preached in his name to all nations, beginning at Jerusalem. [48] You are witnesses of these things. [49] I am going to send you what my Father has promised; but stay in the city until you have been clothed with power from on high.'

[50] When he had led them out to the vicinity of Bethany, he lifted up his hands and blessed them. [51] While he was blessing them, he left them and was taken up into heaven. [52] Then they worshipped him and returned to Jerusalem with great joy. [53] And they stayed continually at the temple, praising God.

'Too Good to Be True'

'And while they still did not believe it because of joy and amazement, he asked of them, "Do you have anything here to eat?"' **Luke 24:41**

If we are to let nothing stand between us and the making of our feet into 'hinds' feet,' we must understand the nature of disappointment and how it hinders our pursuit of God.

All of us have been disappointed. Living in a fallen world means we have been subjected to experiences where we have been let down by others, even our loved ones at times. But this is not the problem – the problem occurs when we allow the hurts of the past to prevent us from reaching out to God and to others in an attitude of love.

A dramatic illustration of this is found in the passage before us today. It is the evening of the day of the Resurrection, and, without warning, Jesus suddenly enters the room where His disciples are assembled and makes Himself known to them. How did they respond? 'They were still unconvinced, still wondering, for it seemed too good to be true' (v.41, NEB). It was obvious that the disappointment of Christ's crucifixion and death still reverberated within them. And now, faced with the reality of the Resurrection, they did not want to believe it in case it was not true – and they would be disappointed again.

They wanted to believe, but they had difficulty in doing so because they knew they could not cope with what would happen in their hearts if it turned out to be untrue. Rather than take the risk of faith, they preferred – for a little while at least – to withdraw into the safety of disappointment.

PRAYER

God, forgive me that so often I allow the disappointments of life to deter me from moving towards You – in case something might happen that would disappoint me again. Help me to put everything I am and have in Your hands – with nothing held back. Amen.

FURTHER STUDY

Luke 24:13-35; Job 30:26
· How did the disciples express their disappointment?
· How did Jesus deal with them?

May 14

■ RUTH 1:1–2:23

1 In the days when the judges ruled, there was a famine in the land. So a man from Bethlehem in Judah, together with his wife and two sons, went to live for a while in the country of Moab. ²The man's name was Elimelek, his wife's name was Naomi, and the names of his two sons were Mahlon and Kilion. They were Ephrathites from Bethlehem, Judah. And they went to Moab and lived there.

³Now Elimelek, Naomi's husband, died, and she was left with her two sons. ⁴They married Moabite women, one named Orpah and the other Ruth. After they had lived there about ten years, ⁵both Mahlon and Kilion also died, and Naomi was left without her two sons and her husband.

⁶When Naomi heard in Moab that the LORD had come to the aid of his people by providing food for them, she and her daughters-in-law prepared to return home from there. ⁷With her two daughters-in-law she left the place where she had been living and set out on the road that would take them back to the land of Judah.

⁸Then Naomi said to her two daughters-in-law, 'Go back, each of you, to your mother's home. May the LORD show you kindness, as you have shown kindness to your dead husbands and to me. ⁹May the LORD grant that each of you will find rest in the home of another husband.'

Then she kissed them goodbye and they wept aloud ¹⁰and said to her, 'We will go back with you to your people.'

¹¹But Naomi said, 'Return home, my daughters. Why would you come with me? Am I going to have any more sons, who could become your husbands? ¹²Return home, my daughters; I am too old to have another husband. Even if I thought there was still hope for me – even if I had a husband tonight and then gave birth to sons – ¹³would you wait until they grew up? Would you remain unmarried for them? No, my daughters. It is more bitter for me than for you, because the LORD's hand has turned against me!'

¹⁴At this they wept aloud again. Then Orpah kissed her mother-in-law goodbye, but Ruth clung to her.

¹⁵'Look,' said Naomi, 'your sister-in-law is going back to her people and her gods. Go back with her.'

¹⁶But Ruth replied, 'Don't urge me to leave you or to turn back from you. Where you go I will go, and where you stay I will stay. Your people will be my people and your God my God. ¹⁷Where you die I will die, and there I will be buried. May the LORD deal with me, be it ever so severely, if even death separates you and me.' ¹⁸When Naomi realised that Ruth was determined to go with her, she stopped urging her.

¹⁹So the two women went on until they came to Bethlehem. When they arrived in Bethlehem, the whole town was stirred because of them, and the women exclaimed, 'Can this be Naomi?'

²⁰'Don't call me Naomi,' she told them. 'Call me Mara, because the Almighty has made my life very bitter. ²¹I went away full, but the LORD has brought me back empty. Why call me Naomi? The LORD has afflicted me; the Almighty has brought misfortune upon me.'

²²So Naomi returned from Moab accompanied by Ruth the Moabite, her daughter-in-law, arriving in Bethlehem as the barley harvest was beginning.

2 Now Naomi had a relative on her husband's side, a man of standing from the clan of Elimelek, whose name was Boaz.

² And Ruth the Moabite said to Naomi, 'Let me go to the fields and pick up the leftover grain behind anyone in whose eyes I find favour.'

Naomi said to her, 'Go ahead, my daughter.' ³ So she went out, entered a field and began to glean behind the harvesters. As it turned out, she was working in a field belonging to Boaz, who was from the clan of Elimelek.

⁴ Just then Boaz arrived from Bethlehem and greeted the harvesters, 'The LORD be with you!'

'The LORD bless you!' they answered.

⁵ Boaz asked the overseer of his harvesters, 'Who does that young woman belong to?'

⁶ The overseer replied, 'She is the Moabite who came back from Moab with Naomi. ⁷ She said, "Please let me glean and gather among the sheaves behind the harvesters." She came into the field and has remained here from morning till now, except for a short rest in the shelter.'

⁸ So Boaz said to Ruth, 'My daughter, listen to me. Don't go and glean in another field and don't go away from here. Stay here with the women who work for me. ⁹ Watch the field where the men are harvesting, and follow along after the women. I have told the men not to lay a hand on you. And whenever you are thirsty, go and get a drink from the water jars the men have filled.'

¹⁰ At this, she bowed down with her face to the ground. She asked him, 'Why have I found such favour in your eyes that you notice me – a foreigner?'

¹¹ Boaz replied, 'I've been told all about what you have done for your mother-in-law since the death of your husband – how you left your father and mother and your homeland and came to live with a people you did not know before. ¹² May the LORD repay you for what you have done. May you be richly rewarded by the LORD, the God of Israel, under whose wings you have come to take refuge.'

¹³ 'May I continue to find favour in your eyes, my lord,' she said. 'You have put me at ease by speaking kindly to your servant – though I do not have the standing of one of your servants.'

¹⁴ At mealtime Boaz said to her, 'Come over here. Have some bread and dip it in the wine vinegar.'

When she sat down with the harvesters, he offered her some roasted grain. She ate all she wanted and had some left over. ¹⁵ As she got up to glean, Boaz gave orders to his men, 'Let her gather among the sheaves and don't reprimand her. ¹⁶ Even pull out some stalks for her from the bundles and leave them for her to pick up, and don't rebuke her.'

¹⁷ So Ruth gleaned in the field until evening. Then she threshed the barley she had gathered, and it amounted to about an ephah. ¹⁸ She carried it back to town, and her mother-in-law saw how much she had gathered. Ruth also brought out and gave her what she had left over after she had eaten enough.

¹⁹ Her mother-in-law asked her, 'Where did you glean today? Where did you work? Blessed be the man who took notice of you!'

Then Ruth told her mother-in-law about the one at whose place she had been working. 'The name of the man I worked with today is Boaz,' she said.

²⁰ 'The LORD bless him!' Naomi said to her daughter-in-law. 'He has not stopped showing his kindness to the living and the dead.' She added, 'That man is our close relative; he is one of our guardian-redeemers.'

²¹ Then Ruth the Moabite said, 'He even said to me, "Stay with my workers until they finish harvesting all my grain."'

²² Naomi said to Ruth her daughter-in-law, 'It will be good for you, my daughter, to go with the women who work for him, because in someone else's field you might be harmed.'

²³ So Ruth stayed close to the women of Boaz to glean until the barley and wheat

harvests were finished. And she lived with her mother-in-law.

▬ PSALM 60:1–5

¹ You have rejected us, God, and burst
    upon us;
  you have been angry – now restore us!
² You have shaken the land and torn it open;
  mend its fractures, for it is quaking.
³ You have shown your people desperate
    times;
  you have given us wine that makes us
    stagger.
⁴ But for those who fear you, you have
    raised a banner
  to be unfurled against the bow.

⁵ Save us and help us with your right hand,
  that those you love may be delivered.

▬ PROVERBS 13:16–17

¹⁶ All who are prudent act with knowledge,
  but fools expose their folly.

¹⁷ A wicked messenger falls into trouble,
  but a trustworthy envoy brings healing.

▬ JOHN 1:1–23

1 In the beginning was the Word, and the Word was with God, and the Word was God. ² He was with God in the beginning. ³ Through him all things were made; without him nothing was made that has been made. ⁴ In him was life, and that life was the light of all mankind. ⁵ The light shines in the darkness, and the darkness has not overcome it.

⁶ There was a man sent from God whose name was John. ⁷ He came as a witness to testify concerning that light, so that through him all might believe. ⁸ He himself was not the light; he came only as a witness to the light.

⁹ The true light that gives light to everyone was coming into the world. ¹⁰ He was in the world, and though the world was made through him, the world did not recognise him. ¹¹ He came to that which was his own, but his own did not receive him. ¹² Yet to all who did receive him, to those who believed in his name, he gave the right to become children of God – ¹³ children born not of natural descent, nor of human decision or a husband's will, but born of God.

¹⁴ The Word became flesh and made his dwelling among us. We have seen his glory, the glory of the one and only Son, who came from the Father, full of grace and truth.

¹⁵ (John testified concerning him. He cried out, saying, 'This is the one I spoke about when I said, "He who comes after me has surpassed me because he was before me."') ¹⁶ Out of his fullness we have all received grace in place of grace already given. ¹⁷ For the law was given through Moses; grace and truth came through Jesus Christ. ¹⁸ No one has ever seen God, but the one and only Son, who is himself God and is in the closest relationship with the Father, has made him known.

¹⁹ Now this was John's testimony when the Jewish leaders in Jerusalem sent priests and Levites to ask him who he was. ²⁰ He did not fail to confess, but confessed freely, 'I am not the Messiah.'

²¹ They asked him, 'Then who are you? Are you Elijah?'

He said, 'I am not.'

'Are you the Prophet?'

He answered, 'No.'

²² Finally they said, 'Who are you? Give us an answer to take back to those who sent us. What do you say about yourself?'

²³ John replied in the words of Isaiah the prophet, 'I am the voice of one calling in the wilderness, "Make straight the way for the Lord."'

The Great Triune God

'The Word became flesh and made his dwelling among us.' **John 1:14**

Dr W. E. Sangster tells the story of following three children out of church. One remarked to the others, 'I can't understand all this "Three in One and One in Three" business'.

'I can't either,' said another child, 'but I think of it like this: my mother is Mummy to me, she is Mabel to Daddy, and Mrs Douglas to lots of other people.'

Is that the answer? Is it just a question of names? Are we right in finding the doctrine of the Trinity in the text of Matthew 28:19, where the word 'name' is singular, but three names are given – Father, Son, and Holy Spirit?

No, that is just part of it; there is much more to it than that. God, we know, is one God. But there stepped into the world someone who claimed also to be God. His name was Jesus. He forgave sins, claimed to have existence before Abraham, and accepted worship as His right. Worship, remember, is for God alone. After Jesus was resurrected and returned to heaven, He sent back the Holy Spirit, who was also seen as God (2 Cor. 13:14). He – the Holy Spirit – came into the disciples and brought with Him the resources of the Godhead, breaking the sin in their nature, pleading in prayer, and exalting the Saviour.

Thus we see God is One but also Three in One: God above us, God among us, God within us. The Father in majesty, the Son in suffering, the Spirit in striving. This is the central mystery of our most holy faith. Together, and with all our hearts, let us adore the great triune God.

PRAYER

Father, Son, and Holy Spirit, though I cannot comprehend Your essential oneness and unity, I can worship You nevertheless. This I do now, in humble adoration. Glory, honour and power be unto Your name forever and ever. Amen.

FURTHER STUDY

John 1:1-14; 8:58; 10:30; 17:5
- How did John describe Jesus?
- What did Jesus declare of Himself?

May 15

■ RUTH 3:1–4:22

3 One day Ruth's mother-in-law Naomi said to her, 'My daughter, I must find a home for you, where you will be well provided for. ²Now Boaz, with whose women you have worked, is a relative of ours. Tonight he will be winnowing barley on the

threshing-floor. ³Wash, put on perfume, and get dressed in your best clothes. Then go down to the threshing-floor, but don't let him know you are there until he has finished eating and drinking. ⁴When he lies down, note the place where he is lying. Then go and uncover his feet and lie down. He will tell you what to do.'

⁵'I will do whatever you say,' Ruth answered. ⁶So she went down to the threshing-floor and did everything her mother-in-law told her to do.

⁷When Boaz had finished eating and drinking and was in good spirits, he went over to lie down at the far end of the grain pile. Ruth approached quietly, uncovered his feet and lay down. ⁸In the middle of the night something startled the man; he turned – and there was a woman lying at his feet!

⁹'Who are you?' he asked.

'I am your servant Ruth,' she said. 'Spread the corner of your garment over me, since you are a guardian-redeemer of our family.'

¹⁰'The LORD bless you, my daughter,' he replied. 'This kindness is greater than that which you showed earlier: you have not run after the younger men, whether rich or poor. ¹¹And now, my daughter, don't be afraid. I will do for you all you ask. All the people of my town know that you are a woman of noble character. ¹²Although it is true that I am a guardian-redeemer of our family, there is another who is more closely related than I. ¹³Stay here for the night, and in the morning if he wants to do his duty as your guardian-redeemer, good; let him redeem you. But if he is not willing, as surely as the LORD lives I will do it. Lie here until morning.'

¹⁴So she lay at his feet until morning, but got up before anyone could be recognised; and he said, 'No one must know that a woman came to the threshing-floor.'

¹⁵He also said, 'Bring me the shawl you are wearing and hold it out.' When she did so, he poured into it six measures of barley and placed the bundle on her. Then he went back to town.

¹⁶When Ruth came to her mother-in-law, Naomi asked, 'How did it go, my daughter?'

Then she told her everything Boaz had done for her ¹⁷and added, 'He gave me these six measures of barley, saying, "Don't go back to your mother-in-law empty-handed."'

¹⁸Then Naomi said, 'Wait, my daughter, until you find out what happens. For the man will not rest until the matter is settled today.'

4 Meanwhile Boaz went up to the town gate and sat down there just as the guardian-redeemer he had mentioned came along. Boaz said, 'Come over here, my friend, and sit down.' So he went over and sat down.

²Boaz took ten of the elders of the town and said, 'Sit here,' and they did so. ³Then he said to the guardian-redeemer, 'Naomi, who has come back from Moab, is selling the piece of land that belonged to our relative Elimelek. ⁴I thought I should bring the matter to your attention and suggest that you buy it in the presence of these seated here and in the presence of the elders of my people. If you will redeem it, do so. But if you will not, tell me, so I will know. For no one has the right to do it except you, and I am next in line.'

'I will redeem it,' he said.

⁵Then Boaz said, 'On the day you buy the land from Naomi, you also acquire Ruth the Moabite, the dead man's widow, in order to maintain the name of the dead with his property.'

⁶At this, the guardian-redeemer said, 'Then I cannot redeem it because I might endanger my own estate. You redeem it yourself. I cannot do it.'

⁷(Now in earlier times in Israel, for the redemption and transfer of property to become final, one party took off his sandal and gave it to the other. This was the method of legalising transactions in Israel.)

⁸So the guardian-redeemer said to Boaz, 'Buy it yourself.' And he removed his sandal.

⁹Then Boaz announced to the elders and

all the people, 'Today you are witnesses that I have bought from Naomi all the property of Elimelek, Kilion and Mahlon. [10] I have also acquired Ruth the Moabite, Mahlon's widow, as my wife, in order to maintain the name of the dead with his property, so that his name will not disappear from among his family or from his home town. Today you are witnesses!'

[11] Then the elders and all the people at the gate said, 'We are witnesses. May the LORD make the woman who is coming into your home like Rachel and Leah, who together built up the family of Israel. May you have standing in Ephrathah and be famous in Bethlehem. [12] Through the offspring the LORD gives you by this young woman, may your family be like that of Perez, whom Tamar bore to Judah.'

[13] So Boaz took Ruth and she became his wife. When he made love to her, the LORD enabled her to conceive, and she gave birth to a son. [14] The women said to Naomi: 'Praise be to the LORD, who this day has not left you without a guardian-redeemer. May he become famous throughout Israel! [15] He will renew your life and sustain you in your old age. For your daughter-in-law, who loves you and who is better to you than seven sons, has given him birth.'

[16] Then Naomi took the child in her arms and cared for him. [17] The women living there said, 'Naomi has a son!' And they named him Obed. He was the father of Jesse, the father of David.

[18] This, then, is the family line of Perez:

Perez was the father of Hezron,
[19] Hezron the father of Ram,
Ram the father of Amminadab,
[20] Amminadab the father of Nahshon,
Nahshon the father of Salmon,
[21] Salmon the father of Boaz,
Boaz the father of Obed,
[22] Obed the father of Jesse,
and Jesse the father of David.

PSALM 60:6-12

[6] God has spoken from his sanctuary:
'In triumph I will parcel out Shechem
and measure off the Valley of Sukkoth.
[7] Gilead is mine, and Manasseh is mine;
Ephraim is my helmet,
Judah is my sceptre.
[8] Moab is my washbasin,
on Edom I toss my sandal;
over Philistia I shout in triumph.'

[9] Who will bring me to the fortified city?
Who will lead me to Edom?
[10] Is it not you, God, you who have now rejected us
and no longer go out with our armies?
[11] Give us aid against the enemy,
for human help is worthless.
[12] With God we shall gain the victory,
and he will trample down our enemies.

PROVERBS 13:18-20

[18] Whoever disregards discipline comes to poverty and shame,
but whoever heeds correction is honoured.

[19] A longing fulfilled is sweet to the soul,
but fools detest turning from evil.

[20] Walk with the wise and become wise,
for a companion of fools suffers harm.

JOHN 1:24-51

[24] Now the Pharisees who had been sent [25] questioned him, 'Why then do you baptise if you are not the Messiah, nor Elijah, nor the Prophet?'

[26] 'I baptise with water,' John replied, 'but among you stands one you do not know. [27] He is the one who comes after me, the straps of

whose sandals I am not worthy to untie.'

[28] This all happened at Bethany on the other side of the Jordan, where John was baptising.

[29] The next day John saw Jesus coming towards him and said, 'Look, the Lamb of God, who takes away the sin of the world! [30] This is the one I meant when I said, "A man who comes after me has surpassed me because he was before me." [31] I myself did not know him, but the reason I came baptising with water was that he might be revealed to Israel.'

[32] Then John gave this testimony: 'I saw the Spirit come down from heaven as a dove and remain on him. [33] And I myself did not know him, but the one who sent me to baptise with water told me, "The man on whom you see the Spirit come down and remain is the one who will baptise with the Holy Spirit." [34] I have seen and I testify that this is God's Chosen One.'

[35] The next day John was there again with two of his disciples. [36] When he saw Jesus passing by, he said, 'Look, the Lamb of God!'

[37] When the two disciples heard him say this, they followed Jesus. [38] Turning round, Jesus saw them following and asked, 'What do you want?'

They said, 'Rabbi' (which means 'Teacher'), 'where are you staying?'

[39] 'Come,' he replied, 'and you will see.'

So they went and saw where he was staying, and they spent that day with him. It was about four in the afternoon.

[40] Andrew, Simon Peter's brother, was one of the two who heard what John had said and who had followed Jesus. [41] The first thing Andrew did was to find his brother Simon and tell him, 'We have found the Messiah' (that is, the Christ). [42] And he brought him to Jesus.

Jesus looked at him and said, 'You are Simon son of John. You will be called Cephas' (which, when translated, is Peter).

[43] The next day Jesus decided to leave for Galilee. Finding Philip, he said to him, 'Follow me.'

[44] Philip, like Andrew and Peter, was from the town of Bethsaida. [45] Philip found Nathanael and told him, 'We have found the one Moses wrote about in the Law, and about whom the prophets also wrote – Jesus of Nazareth, the son of Joseph.'

[46] 'Nazareth! Can anything good come from there?' Nathanael asked.

'Come and see,' said Philip.

[47] When Jesus saw Nathanael approaching, he said of him, 'Here truly is an Israelite in whom there is no deceit.'

[48] 'How do you know me?' Nathanael asked.

Jesus answered, 'I saw you while you were still under the fig-tree before Philip called you.'

[49] Then Nathanael declared, 'Rabbi, you are the Son of God; you are the king of Israel.'

[50] Jesus said, 'You believe because I told you I saw you under the fig-tree. You will see greater things than that.' [51] He then added, 'Very truly I tell you, you will see "heaven open, and the angels of God ascending and descending on" the Son of Man.'

He Reigns – Now

'With God we shall gain the victory ...' **Psalm 60:12**

The final part of the Lord's Prayer, which is really a doxology, contains a categorical assertion that God reigns through His kingdom – now. It manifestly requires a measure of faith and courage to affirm this truth in our modern society, when so many things seem positively to shout against it – so many wrongs that clamour for redress, so many problems that demand a solution, and so many social evils whose existence appears utterly incompatible with the reign of God. Yet affirm it we must.

A dear Christian, in a letter to me some time ago, said, 'I look around the world and am appalled. My only comfort is the hymn "Jesus Shall Reign Where'er the Sun." I, therefore, sit back and watch and wait the day'. I told her that her letter reminded me of some words I once heard someone put together in a conference:

> *Sit down, O men of God!*
> *His kingdom He will bring.*
> *Whenever it shall please His will.*
> *You need not do a thing!*

In my reply I said, 'Yes, it's true that one day the kingdom of God shall "stretch from shore to shore," but let us not ignore the fact that God is reigning now. Given our cooperation, the Almighty can greatly affect the world through our committed lives. If we fail to see this, then it is possible that we struggle and stumble through life, waiting for Him, while all the time He is waiting for us.'

PRAYER

O God, deliver me from a view of life that says, 'Look what the world is coming to'. Help me to look at You; then I can say: 'Look what has come to the world'. Thank You, Father. Amen.

FURTHER STUDY

Rev. 7:9-17; Exod. 24:17; 40:34; Psa. 19:1; John 1:14; Rom. 11:36

• How can we behold His glory?
• How is our vision of God enlarged?

May 16

■ 1 SAMUEL 1:1–2:36

1 There was a certain man from Ramathaim, a Zuphite from the hill country of Ephraim, whose name was Elkanah son of Jeroham, the son of Elihu, the son of Tohu, the son of Zuph, an Ephraimite. ²He had two wives; one was called Hannah and the other Peninnah. Peninnah had children, but Hannah had none.

³Year after year this man went up from his town to worship and sacrifice to the LORD Almighty at Shiloh, where Hophni and Phinehas, the two sons of Eli, were priests of the LORD. ⁴Whenever the day came for Elkanah to sacrifice, he would give portions of the meat to his wife Peninnah and to all her sons and daughters. ⁵But to Hannah he gave a double portion because he loved her, and the LORD had closed her womb. ⁶Because

the Lord had closed Hannah's womb, her rival kept provoking her in order to irritate her. ⁷This went on year after year. Whenever Hannah went up to the house of the Lord, her rival provoked her till she wept and would not eat. ⁸Her husband Elkanah would say to her, 'Hannah, why are you weeping? Why don't you eat? Why are you downhearted? Don't I mean more to you than ten sons?'

⁹Once when they had finished eating and drinking in Shiloh, Hannah stood up. Now Eli the priest was sitting on his chair by the doorpost of the Lord's house. ¹⁰In her deep anguish Hannah prayed to the Lord, weeping bitterly. ¹¹And she made a vow, saying, 'Lord Almighty, if you will only look on your servant's misery and remember me, and not forget your servant but give her a son, then I will give him to the Lord for all the days of his life, and no razor will ever be used on his head.'

¹²As she kept on praying to the Lord, Eli observed her mouth. ¹³Hannah was praying in her heart, and her lips were moving but her voice was not heard. Eli thought she was drunk ¹⁴and said to her, 'How long are you going to stay drunk? Put away your wine.'

¹⁵'Not so, my lord,' Hannah replied, 'I am a woman who is deeply troubled. I have not been drinking wine or beer; I was pouring out my soul to the Lord. ¹⁶Do not take your servant for a wicked woman; I have been praying here out of my great anguish and grief.'

¹⁷Eli answered, 'Go in peace, and may the God of Israel grant you what you have asked of him.'

¹⁸She said, 'May your servant find favour in your eyes.' Then she went her way and ate something, and her face was no longer downcast.

¹⁹Early the next morning they arose and worshipped before the Lord and then went back to their home at Ramah. Elkanah made love to his wife Hannah, and the Lord remembered her. ²⁰So in the course of time Hannah became pregnant and gave birth

to a son. She named him Samuel, saying, 'Because I asked the Lord for him.'

²¹When her husband Elkanah went up with all his family to offer the annual sacrifice to the Lord and to fulfil his vow, ²²Hannah did not go. She said to her husband, 'After the boy is weaned, I will take him and present him before the Lord, and he will live there always.'

²³'Do what seems best to you,' her husband Elkanah told her. 'Stay here until you have weaned him; only may the Lord make good his word.' So the woman stayed at home and nursed her son until she had weaned him.

²⁴After he was weaned, she took the boy with her, young as he was, along with a three-year-old bull, an ephah of flour and a skin of wine, and brought him to the house of the Lord at Shiloh. ²⁵When the bull had been sacrificed, they brought the boy to Eli, ²⁶and she said to him, 'Pardon me, my lord. As surely as you live, I am the woman who stood here beside you praying to the Lord. ²⁷I prayed for this child, and the Lord has granted me what I asked of him. ²⁸So now I give him to the Lord. For his whole life he shall be given over to the Lord.' And he worshipped the Lord there.

2 Then Hannah prayed and said:

'My heart rejoices in the Lord;
    in the Lord my horn is lifted high.
My mouth boasts over my enemies,
    for I delight in your deliverance.

² 'There is no one holy like the Lord;
    there is no one besides you;
    there is no Rock like our God.

³ 'Do not keep talking so proudly
    or let your mouth speak such arrogance,
for the Lord is a God who knows,
    and by him deeds are weighed.

⁴ 'The bows of the warriors are broken,

but those who stumbled are armed
   with strength.
5 Those who were full hire themselves out
   for food,
   but those who were hungry are hungry
     no more.
She who was barren has borne seven
   children,
   but she who has had many sons pines
     away.

6 'The LORD brings death and makes alive;
   he brings down to the grave and raises
     up.
7 The LORD sends poverty and wealth;
   he humbles and he exalts.
8 He raises the poor from the dust
   and lifts the needy from the ash heap;
he seats them with princes
   and makes them inherit a throne of
     honour.

'For the foundations of the earth are the
   LORD's;
   on them he has set the world.
9 He will guard the feet of his faithful
   servants,
   but the wicked will be silenced in the
     place of darkness.

'It is not by strength that one prevails;
10   those who oppose the LORD will be
     broken.
The Most High will thunder from heaven;
   the LORD will judge the ends of the earth.

'He will give strength to his king
   and exalt the horn of his anointed.'

11 Then Elkanah went home to Ramah, but
the boy ministered before the LORD under
Eli the priest.

12 Eli's sons were scoundrels; they had no
regard for the LORD. 13 Now it was the practice of the priests that, whenever any of the
people offered a sacrifice, the priest's servant
would come with a three-pronged fork in
his hand while the meat was being boiled
14 and would plunge the fork into the pan or
kettle or cauldron or pot. Whatever the fork
brought up the priest would take for himself. This is how they treated all the Israelites
who came to Shiloh. 15 But even before the fat
was burned, the priest's servant would come
and say to the person who was sacrificing,
'Give the priest some meat to roast; he won't
accept boiled meat from you, but only raw.'
16 If the person said to him, 'Let the fat be
burned first, and then take whatever you
want,' the servant would answer, 'No, hand
it over now; if you don't, I'll take it by force.'

17 This sin of the young men was very
great in the LORD's sight, for they were
treating the LORD's offering with contempt.

18 But Samuel was ministering before
the LORD – a boy wearing a linen ephod.
19 Each year his mother made him a little
robe and took it to him when she went up
with her husband to offer the annual sacrifice. 20 Eli would bless Elkanah and his wife,
saying, 'May the LORD give you children by
this woman to take the place of the one she
prayed for and gave to the LORD.' Then they
would go home. 21 And the LORD was gracious to Hannah; she gave birth to three
sons and two daughters. Meanwhile, the boy
Samuel grew up in the presence of the LORD.

22 Now Eli, who was very old, heard about
everything his sons were doing to all Israel and how they slept with the women who
served at the entrance to the tent of meeting.
23 So he said to them, 'Why do you do such
things? I hear from all the people about these
wicked deeds of yours. 24 No, my sons; the report I hear spreading among the LORD's people is not good. 25 If one person sins against
another, God may mediate for the offender;
but if anyone sins against the LORD, who will
intercede for them?' His sons, however, did
not listen to their father's rebuke, for it was
the LORD's will to put them to death.

26 And the boy Samuel continued to grow

in stature and in favour with the LORD and with people.

²⁷Now a man of God came to Eli and said to him, 'This is what the LORD says: "Did I not clearly reveal myself to your ancestor's family when they were in Egypt under Pharaoh? ²⁸I chose your ancestor out of all the tribes of Israel to be my priest, to go up to my altar, to burn incense, and to wear an ephod in my presence. I also gave your ancestor's family all the food offerings presented by the Israelites. ²⁹Why do you scorn my sacrifice and offering that I prescribed for my dwelling? Why do you honour your sons more than me by fattening yourselves on the choice parts of every offering made by my people Israel?"

³⁰'Therefore the LORD, the God of Israel, declares: "I promised that members of your family would minister before me for ever." But now the LORD declares: "Far be it from me! Those who honour me I will honour, but those who despise me will be disdained. ³¹The time is coming when I will cut short your strength and the strength of your priestly house, so that no one in it will reach old age, ³²and you will see distress in my dwelling. Although good will be done to Israel, no one in your family line will ever reach old age. ³³Every one of you that I do not cut off from serving at my altar I will spare only to destroy your sight and sap your strength, and all your descendants will die in the prime of life.

³⁴' "And what happens to your two sons, Hophni and Phinehas, will be a sign to you – they will both die on the same day. ³⁵I will raise up for myself a faithful priest, who will do according to what is in my heart and mind. I will firmly establish his priestly house, and they will minister before my anointed one always. ³⁶Then everyone left in your family line will come and bow down before him for a piece of silver and a loaf of bread and plead, 'Appoint me to some priestly office so that I can have food to eat.'"'

■ PSALM 61:1-8

¹Hear my cry, O God;
  listen to my prayer.

²From the ends of the earth I call to you,
  I call as my heart grows faint;
  lead me to the rock that is higher than I.
³For you have been my refuge,
  a strong tower against the foe.

⁴I long to dwell in your tent for ever
  and take refuge in the shelter of your
    wings.
⁵For you, God, have heard my vows;
  you have given me the heritage of
    those who fear your name.

⁶Increase the days of the king's life,
  his years for many generations.
⁷May he be enthroned in God's presence
    for ever;
  appoint your love and faithfulness to
    protect him.

⁸Then I will ever sing in praise of your name
  and fulfil my vows day after day.

■ PROVERBS 13:21-22

²¹Trouble pursues the sinner,
  but the righteous are rewarded with
    good things.

²²A good person leaves an inheritance for
    their children's children,
  but a sinner's wealth is stored up for
    the righteous.

■ JOHN 2:1-25

2 On the third day a wedding took place at Cana in Galilee. Jesus' mother was there, ²and Jesus and his disciples had also

been invited to the wedding. ³When the wine was gone, Jesus' mother said to him, 'They have no more wine.'

⁴'Woman, why do you involve me?' Jesus replied. 'My hour has not yet come.'

⁵His mother said to the servants, 'Do whatever he tells you.'

⁶Nearby stood six stone water jars, the kind used by the Jews for ceremonial washing, each holding from eighty to a hundred and twenty litres.

⁷Jesus said to the servants, 'Fill the jars with water'; so they filled them to the brim.

⁸Then he told them, 'Now draw some out and take it to the master of the banquet.'

They did so, ⁹and the master of the banquet tasted the water that had been turned into wine. He did not realise where it had come from, though the servants who had drawn the water knew. Then he called the bridegroom aside ¹⁰and said, 'Everyone brings out the choice wine first and then the cheaper wine after the guests have had too much to drink; but you have saved the best till now.'

¹¹What Jesus did here in Cana of Galilee was the first of the signs through which he revealed his glory; and his disciples believed in him.

¹²After this he went down to Capernaum with his mother and brothers and his disciples. There they stayed for a few days.

¹³When it was almost time for the Jewish Passover, Jesus went up to Jerusalem. ¹⁴In the temple courts he found people selling cattle, sheep and doves, and others sitting at tables exchanging money. ¹⁵So he made a whip out of cords, and drove all from the temple courts, both sheep and cattle; he scattered the coins of the money-changers and overturned their tables. ¹⁶To those who sold doves he said, 'Get these out of here! Stop turning my Father's house into a market!' ¹⁷His disciples remembered that it is written: 'Zeal for your house will consume me.'

¹⁸The Jews then responded to him, 'What sign can you show us to prove your authority to do all this?'

¹⁹Jesus answered them, 'Destroy this temple, and I will raise it again in three days.'

²⁰They replied, 'It has taken forty-six years to build this temple, and you are going to raise it in three days?' ²¹But the temple he had spoken of was his body. ²²After he was raised from the dead, his disciples recalled what he had said. Then they believed the Scripture and the words that Jesus had spoken.

²³Now while he was in Jerusalem at the Passover Festival, many people saw the signs he was performing and believed in his name. ²⁴But Jesus would not entrust himself to them, for he knew all people. ²⁵He did not need any testimony about mankind, for he knew what was in each person.

Have a Great Childhood

'Trouble pursues the sinner, but the righteous are rewarded with good things.' **Proverbs 13:21**

Solomon's comments in Ecclesiastes 11:9 are aimed at the young: 'Let your heart give you joy in the days of your youth.' Enjoy your days one by one, he is saying, because before you know it, you will be an adult.

The words that come next have sent some Christians into apoplexy: 'Follow the ways of your heart and whatever your eyes see' (v.9). I remember a youth leader in a church I pastored who set out to teach the Book of Ecclesiastes to the young people. But he deliberately left out these words. When I asked him why, he said, 'That's bad advice for young people. They are inclined that way already so I thought it best not to draw attention to it.' I drew his attention to the words that follow: 'but know that for all these things God will bring you into judgment.' This is what Solomon is really saying: 'Relax and have a super time when you are young. There will be many impulses and many things that appeal to your eyes. Follow them, but keep in mind there will be a day of accountability. So don't let your impulses go wild.'

Some believe that warning takes the joy out of living, but it shouldn't. If we ignore the God to whom we must all answer, then we leave ourselves open to experiencing not life but unrestricted liberty. And that kind of freedom is bad for us. So banish all worries, Solomon tells the young, and avoid those things that bring pain to your body. Young person, you are only young once. Stay close to God and you'll get the most out of it.

PRAYER

O God my Father, while I am thankful for all the books that help me learn of You and know about You, help me never to put these ahead of Your Word, the Bible, but always behind it. Make me a person of the Book. In Jesus' name. Amen.

FURTHER STUDY

Josh. 1:1-8; 2 Kings 22:1-20
- What was God's command to Joshua?
- Why did the king tear his robes?

May 17

■ 1 SAMUEL 3:1–5:12

3 The boy Samuel ministered before the LORD under Eli. In those days the word of the LORD was rare; there were not many visions.

² One night Eli, whose eyes were becoming so weak that he could barely see, was lying down in his usual place. ³ The lamp of God had not yet gone out, and Samuel was lying down in the house of the LORD, where the ark of God was. ⁴ Then the LORD called Samuel.

Samuel answered, 'Here I am.' ⁵ And he ran to Eli and said, 'Here I am; you called me.'

But Eli said, 'I did not call; go back and lie down.' So he went and lay down.

⁶ Again the LORD called, 'Samuel!' And Samuel got up and went to Eli and said, 'Here I am; you called me.'

'My son,' Eli said, 'I did not call; go back and lie down.'

⁷ Now Samuel did not yet know the LORD: the word of the LORD had not yet been revealed to him.

⁸ A third time the LORD called, 'Samuel!' And Samuel got up and went to Eli and said, 'Here I am; you called me.'

Then Eli realised that the LORD was calling the boy. ⁹ So Eli told Samuel, 'Go and lie down, and if he calls you, say, "Speak, LORD, for your servant is listening."' So Samuel went and lay down in his place.

¹⁰ The LORD came and stood there, calling

as at the other times, 'Samuel! Samuel!'

Then Samuel said, 'Speak, for your servant is listening.'

[11] And the LORD said to Samuel: 'See, I am about to do something in Israel that will make the ears of everyone who hears about it tingle. [12] At that time I will carry out against Eli everything I spoke against his family – from beginning to end. [13] For I told him that I would judge his family for ever because of the sin he knew about; his sons uttered blasphemies against God, and he failed to restrain them. [14] Therefore I swore to the house of Eli, "The guilt of Eli's house will never be atoned for by sacrifice or offering."'

[15] Samuel lay down until morning and then opened the doors of the house of the LORD. He was afraid to tell Eli the vision, [16] but Eli called him and said, 'Samuel, my son.'

Samuel answered, 'Here I am.'

[17] 'What was it he said to you?' Eli asked. 'Do not hide it from me. May God deal with you, be it ever so severely, if you hide from me anything he told you.' [18] So Samuel told him everything, hiding nothing from him. Then Eli said, 'He is the LORD; let him do what is good in his eyes.'

[19] The LORD was with Samuel as he grew up, and he let none of Samuel's words fall to the ground. [20] And all Israel from Dan to Beersheba recognised that Samuel was attested as a prophet of the LORD. [21] The LORD continued to appear at Shiloh, and there he revealed himself to Samuel through his word.

4 And Samuel's word came to all Israel.

Now the Israelites went out to fight against the Philistines. The Israelites camped at Ebenezer, and the Philistines at Aphek. [2] The Philistines deployed their forces to meet Israel, and as the battle spread, Israel was defeated by the Philistines, who killed about four thousand of them on the battlefield. [3] When the soldiers returned to camp, the elders of Israel asked, 'Why did the Lord bring defeat on us today before the Philistines? Let us bring the ark of the Lord's covenant from Shiloh, so that he may go with us and save us from the hand of our enemies.'

[4] So the people sent men to Shiloh, and they brought back the ark of the covenant of the LORD Almighty, who is enthroned between the cherubim. And Eli's two sons, Hophni and Phinehas, were there with the ark of the covenant of God.

[5] When the ark of the LORD's covenant came into the camp, all Israel raised such a great shout that the ground shook. [6] Hearing the uproar, the Philistines asked, 'What's all this shouting in the Hebrew camp?'

When they learned that the ark of the LORD had come into the camp, [7] the Philistines were afraid. 'A god has come into the camp,' they said. 'Oh no! Nothing like this has happened before. [8] We're doomed! Who will deliver us from the hand of these mighty gods? They are the gods who struck the Egyptians with all kinds of plagues in the wilderness. [9] Be strong, Philistines! Be men, or you will be subject to the Hebrews, as they have been to you. Be men, and fight!'

[10] So the Philistines fought, and the Israelites were defeated and every man fled to his tent. The slaughter was very great; Israel lost thirty thousand foot soldiers. [11] The ark of God was captured, and Eli's two sons, Hophni and Phinehas, died.

[12] That same day a Benjaminite ran from the battle line and went to Shiloh with his clothes torn and dust on his head. [13] When he arrived, there was Eli sitting on his chair by the side of the road, watching, because his heart feared for the ark of God. When the man entered the town and told what had happened, the whole town sent up a cry.

[14] Eli heard the outcry and asked, 'What is the meaning of this uproar?'

The man hurried over to Eli, [15] who was ninety-eight years old and whose eyes had failed so that he could not see. [16] He told Eli, 'I have just come from the battle line; I fled from it this very day.'

Eli asked, 'What happened, my son?'

[17] The man who brought the news replied, 'Israel fled before the Philistines, and the army has suffered heavy losses. Also your two sons, Hophni and Phinehas, are dead, and the ark of God has been captured.'

[18] When he mentioned the ark of God, Eli fell backwards off his chair by the side of the gate. His neck was broken and he died, for he was an old man, and he was heavy. He had led Israel for forty years.

[19] His daughter-in-law, the wife of Phinehas, was pregnant and near the time of delivery. When she heard the news that the ark of God had been captured and that her father-in-law and her husband were dead, she went into labour and gave birth, but was overcome by her labour pains. [20] As she was dying, the women attending her said, 'Don't despair; you have given birth to a son.' But she did not respond or pay any attention.

[21] She named the boy Ichabod, saying, 'The Glory has departed from Israel' – because of the capture of the ark of God and the deaths of her father-in-law and her husband. [22] She said, 'The Glory has departed from Israel, for the ark of God has been captured.'

5 After the Philistines had captured the ark of God, they took it from Ebenezer to Ashdod. [2] Then they carried the ark into Dagon's temple and set it beside Dagon. [3] When the people of Ashdod rose early the next day, there was Dagon, fallen on his face on the ground before the ark of the LORD! They took Dagon and put him back in his place. [4] But the following morning when they rose, there was Dagon, fallen on his face on the ground before the ark of the LORD! His head and hands had been broken off and were lying on the threshold; only his body remained. [5] That is why to this day neither the priests of Dagon nor any others who enter Dagon's temple at Ashdod step on the threshold.

[6] The LORD's hand was heavy on the people of Ashdod and its vicinity; he brought devastation on them and afflicted them with tumours. [7] When the people of Ashdod saw what was happening, they said, 'The ark of the god of Israel must not stay here with us, because his hand is heavy on us and on Dagon our god.' [8] So they called together all the rulers of the Philistines and asked them, 'What shall we do with the ark of the god of Israel?'

They answered, 'Let the ark of the god of Israel be moved to Gath.' So they moved the ark of the God of Israel.

[9] But after they had moved it, the LORD's hand was against that city, throwing it into a great panic. He afflicted the people of the city, both young and old, with an outbreak of tumours. [10] So they sent the ark of God to Ekron.

As the ark of God was entering Ekron, the people of Ekron cried out, 'They have brought the ark of the god of Israel round to us to kill us and our people.' [11] So they called together all the rulers of the Philistines and said, 'Send the ark of the god of Israel away; let it go back to its own place, or it will kill us and our people.' For death had filled the city with panic; God's hand was very heavy on it. [12] Those who did not die were afflicted with tumours, and the outcry of the city went up to heaven.

- -

▬ PSALM 62:1-8

[1] Truly my soul finds rest in God;
  my salvation comes from him.
[2] Truly he is my rock and my salvation;
  he is my fortress, I shall never be
    shaken.

[3] How long will you assault me?
  Would all of you throw me down –
    this leaning wall, this tottering fence?
[4] Surely they intend to topple me
  from my lofty place;
    they take delight in lies.

With their mouths they bless,
　　but in their hearts they curse.

[5] Yes, my soul, find rest in God;
　　my hope comes from him.
[6] Truly he is my rock and my salvation;
　　he is my fortress, I shall not be shaken.
[7] My salvation and my honour depend on
　　　God;
　　he is my mighty rock, my refuge.
[8] Trust in him at all times, you people;
　　pour out your hearts to him,
　　for God is our refuge.

▰ PROVERBS 13:23-25

[23] An unploughed field produces food for
　　　the poor,
　　but injustice sweeps it away.

[24] Whoever spares the rod hates their
　　　children,
　　but the one who loves their children is
　　careful to discipline them.

[25] The righteous eat to their hearts'
　　　content,
　　but the stomach of the wicked goes
　　hungry.

▰ JOHN 3:1-21

3 Now there was a Pharisee, a man named Nicodemus who was a member of the Jewish ruling council. [2] He came to Jesus at night and said, 'Rabbi, we know that you are a teacher who has come from God. For no one could perform the signs you are doing if God were not with him.'

[3] Jesus replied, 'Very truly I tell you, no one can see the kingdom of God unless they are born again.'

[4] 'How can someone be born when they are old?' Nicodemus asked. 'Surely they cannot enter a second time into their mother's womb to be born!'

[5] Jesus answered, 'Very truly I tell you, no one can enter the kingdom of God unless they are born of water and the Spirit. [6] Flesh gives birth to flesh, but the Spirit gives birth to spirit. [7] You should not be surprised at my saying, "You must be born again." [8] The wind blows wherever it pleases. You hear its sound, but you cannot tell where it comes from or where it is going. So it is with everyone born of the Spirit.'

[9] 'How can this be?' Nicodemus asked.

[10] 'You are Israel's teacher,' said Jesus, 'and do you not understand these things? [11] Very truly I tell you, we speak of what we know, and we testify to what we have seen, but still you people do not accept our testimony. [12] I have spoken to you of earthly things and you do not believe; how then will you believe if I speak of heavenly things? [13] No one has ever gone into heaven except the one who came from heaven – the Son of Man. [14] Just as Moses lifted up the snake in the wilderness, so the Son of Man must be lifted up, [15] that everyone who believes may have eternal life in him.'

[16] For God so loved the world that he gave his one and only Son, that whoever believes in him shall not perish but have eternal life. [17] For God did not send his Son into the world to condemn the world, but to save the world through him. [18] Whoever believes in him is not condemned, but whoever does not believe stands condemned already because they have not believed in the name of God's one and only Son. [19] This is the verdict: light has come into the world, but people loved darkness instead of light because their deeds were evil. [20] Everyone who does evil hates the light, and will not come into the light for fear that their deeds will be exposed. [21] But whoever lives by the truth comes into the light, so that it may be seen plainly that what they have done has been done in the sight of God.

The Birth of the Spirit

'... no one can enter the kingdom of God unless they are born of water and the Spirit.' **John 3:5**

Jesus prepared His disciples for the reception of the Holy Spirit. This course of training is best revealed in John's Gospel.

It is through the ministry of the Holy Spirit that we are born again into the kingdom of God. John makes clear what the new birth is not: 'children born not of natural descent, nor of human decision or a husband's will, but born of God' (1:13). The new birth is brought about by the Holy Spirit, and unless He is involved in it, then it is not a new birth at all.

Someone has described the new birth as 'the change, gradual or sudden, by which we, who are the children of the first birth, through a physical birth into a physical world, become children of the second birth, through a spiritual birth into a spiritual world'. Just as you have to have brains to enter the kingdom of knowledge, an aesthetic nature to enter the kingdom of beauty, a musical sensitivity to enter the kingdom of music, an emotional nature to enter the kingdom of love, so you have to have a spiritual birth to enter the kingdom of God.

Jesus, in His first reference to the Holy Spirit in John's Gospel, put His finger on the first step of the Spirit's ministry in human life - the birth of the Spirit. Jesus said these words, not to a down-and-out, but to a member of the Jewish ruling council, a Pharisee. If Nicodemus, a morally upright religious leader, needed the Spirit, then we all need Him.

PRAYER

O Father, I am grateful for this new life within - the new birth - and now I want more. This that I have experienced sets my heart on fire for life in all its fullness. Amen.

FURTHER STUDY

Gal. 5; John 1:13; Titus 3:5; 1 Pet. 1:23
- What are the characteristics of those born of the Spirit?
- What does it mean to 'walk in the Spirit'?

May 18

■ 1 SAMUEL 6:1–8:22

6 When the ark of the LORD had been in Philistine territory for seven months, ²the Philistines called for the priests and the diviners and said, 'What shall we do with the ark of the LORD? Tell us how we should send it back to its place.'

³They answered, 'If you return the ark of the god of Israel, do not send it back to him

without a gift; by all means send a guilt offering to him. Then you will be healed, and
you will know why his hand has not been
lifted from you.'

⁴The Philistines asked, 'What guilt
offering should we send to him?'

They replied, 'Five gold tumours and five
gold rats, according to the number of the
Philistine rulers, because the same plague
has struck both you and your rulers. ⁵Make
models of the tumours and of the rats that are
destroying the country, and give glory to Israel's god. Perhaps he will lift his hand from
you and your gods and your land. ⁶Why do
you harden your hearts as the Egyptians and
Pharaoh did? When Israel's god dealt harshly with them, did they not send the Israelites
out so that they could go on their way?

⁷'Now then, get a new cart ready, with two
cows that have calved and have never been
yoked. Hitch the cows to the cart, but take
their calves away and pen them up. ⁸Take the
ark of the LORD and put it on the cart, and in
a chest beside it put the gold objects you are
sending back to him as a guilt offering. Send
it on its way, ⁹but keep watching it. If it goes
up to its own territory, towards Beth Shemesh, then the LORD has brought this great
disaster on us. But if it does not, then we shall
know that it was not his hand that struck us
but that it happened to us by chance.'

¹⁰So they did this. They took two such
cows and hitched them to the cart and
penned up their calves. ¹¹They placed the
ark of the LORD on the cart and along with
it the chest containing the gold rats and the
models of the tumours. ¹²Then the cows went
straight up towards Beth Shemesh, keeping
on the road and lowing all the way; they did
not turn to the right or to the left. The rulers
of the Philistines followed them as far as the
border of Beth Shemesh.

¹³Now the people of Beth Shemesh were
harvesting their wheat in the valley, and when
they looked up and saw the ark, they rejoiced
at the sight. ¹⁴The cart came to the field of

Joshua of Beth Shemesh, and there it stopped
beside a large rock. The people chopped up
the wood of the cart and sacrificed the cows
as a burnt offering to the LORD. ¹⁵The Levites
took down the ark of the LORD, together with
the chest containing the gold objects, and
placed them on the large rock. On that day the
people of Beth Shemesh offered burnt offerings and made sacrifices to the LORD. ¹⁶The
five rulers of the Philistines saw all this and
then returned that same day to Ekron.

¹⁷These are the gold tumours the Philistines sent as a guilt offering to the LORD –
one each for Ashdod, Gaza, Ashkelon, Gath
and Ekron. ¹⁸And the number of the gold
rats was according to the number of Philistine towns belonging to the five rulers – the
fortified towns with their country villages.
The large rock on which the Levites set the
ark of the LORD is a witness to this day in the
field of Joshua of Beth Shemesh.

¹⁹But God struck down some of the inhabitants of Beth Shemesh, putting seventy
of them to death because they looked into
the ark of the LORD. The people mourned
because of the heavy blow the LORD had
dealt them. ²⁰And the people of Beth Shemesh asked, 'Who can stand in the presence
of the LORD, this holy God? To whom will the
ark go up from here?'

²¹Then they sent messengers to the people of Kiriath Jearim, saying, 'The Philistines have returned the ark of the LORD.
Come down and take it up to your town.'
7 ¹So the men of Kiriath Jearim came
and took up the ark of the LORD. They
brought it to Abinadab's house on the hill
and consecrated Eleazar his son to guard the
ark of the LORD. ²The ark remained at Kiriath Jearim a long time – twenty years in all.

Then all the people of Israel turned back
to the LORD. ³So Samuel said to all the Israelites, 'If you are returning to the LORD
with all your hearts, then rid yourselves of
the foreign gods and the Ashtoreths and
commit yourselves to the LORD and serve

him only, and he will deliver you out of the hand of the Philistines.' ⁴ So the Israelites put away their Baals and Ashtoreths, and served the LORD only.

⁵ Then Samuel said, 'Assemble all Israel at Mizpah, and I will intercede with the LORD for you.' ⁶ When they had assembled at Mizpah, they drew water and poured it out before the LORD. On that day they fasted and there they confessed, 'We have sinned against the LORD.' Now Samuel was serving as leader of Israel at Mizpah.

⁷ When the Philistines heard that Israel had assembled at Mizpah, the rulers of the Philistines came up to attack them. When the Israelites heard of it, they were afraid because of the Philistines. ⁸ They said to Samuel, 'Do not stop crying out to the LORD our God for us, that he may rescue us from the hand of the Philistines.' ⁹ Then Samuel took a suckling lamb and sacrificed it as a whole burnt offering to the LORD. He cried out to the LORD on Israel's behalf, and the LORD answered him.

¹⁰ While Samuel was sacrificing the burnt offering, the Philistines drew near to engage Israel in battle. But that day the LORD thundered with loud thunder against the Philistines and threw them into such a panic that they were routed before the Israelites. ¹¹ The men of Israel rushed out of Mizpah and pursued the Philistines, slaughtering them along the way to a point below Beth Kar.

¹² Then Samuel took a stone and set it up between Mizpah and Shen. He named it Ebenezer, saying, 'Thus far the LORD has helped us.' ¹³ So the Philistines were subdued and they stopped invading Israel's territory. Throughout Samuel's lifetime, the hand of the LORD was against the Philistines. ¹⁴ The towns from Ekron to Gath that the Philistines had captured from Israel were restored to Israel, and Israel delivered the neighbouring territory from the hands of the Philistines. And there was peace between Israel and the Amorites.

¹⁵ Samuel continued as Israel's leader all the days of his life. ¹⁶ From year to year he went on a circuit from Bethel to Gilgal to Mizpah, judging Israel in all those places. ¹⁷ But he always went back to Ramah, where his home was, and there he also held court for Israel. And he built an altar there to the LORD.

8 When Samuel grew old, he appointed his sons as Israel's leaders. ² The name of his firstborn was Joel and the name of his second was Abijah, and they served at Beersheba. ³ But his sons did not follow his ways. They turned aside after dishonest gain and accepted bribes and perverted justice.

⁴ So all the elders of Israel gathered together and came to Samuel at Ramah. ⁵ They said to him, 'You are old, and your sons do not follow your ways; now appoint a king to lead us, such as all the other nations have.'

⁶ But when they said, 'Give us a king to lead us,' this displeased Samuel; so he prayed to the LORD. ⁷ And the LORD told him: 'Listen to all that the people are saying to you; it is not you they have rejected, but they have rejected me as their king. ⁸ As they have done from the day I brought them up out of Egypt until this day, forsaking me and serving other gods, so they are doing to you. ⁹ Now listen to them; but warn them solemnly and let them know what the king who will reign over them will claim as his rights.'

¹⁰ Samuel told all the words of the LORD to the people who were asking him for a king. ¹¹ He said, 'This is what the king who will reign over you will claim as his rights: he will take your sons and make them serve with his chariots and horses, and they will run in front of his chariots. ¹² Some he will assign to be commanders of thousands and commanders of fifties, and others to plough his ground and reap his harvest, and still others to make weapons of war and equipment for his chariots. ¹³ He will take your daughters to be perfumers and cooks and bakers. ¹⁴ He will take the best of your fields and vineyards and olive groves and give them to his attendants. ¹⁵ He will take a tenth

of your grain and of your vintage and give it to his officials and attendants. ¹⁶ Your male and female servants and the best of your cattle and donkeys he will take for his own use. ¹⁷ He will take a tenth of your flocks, and you yourselves will become his slaves. ¹⁸ When that day comes, you will cry out for relief from the king you have chosen, but the LORD will not answer you in that day.'

¹⁹ But the people refused to listen to Samuel. 'No!' they said. 'We want a king over us. ²⁰ Then we shall be like all the other nations, with a king to lead us and to go out before us and fight our battles.'

²¹ When Samuel heard all that the people said, he repeated it before the LORD. ²² The LORD answered, 'Listen to them and give them a king.'

Then Samuel said to the Israelites, 'Everyone go back to your own town.'

■ PSALM 62:9-12

⁹ Surely the lowborn are but a breath,
    the highborn are but a lie.
If weighed on a balance, they are nothing;
    together they are only a breath.
¹⁰ Do not trust in extortion
    or put vain hope in stolen goods;
though your riches increase,
    do not set your heart on them.

¹¹ One thing God has spoken,
    two things I have heard:
'Power belongs to you, God,
¹²   and with you, Lord, is unfailing love';
and, 'You reward everyone
    according to what they have done.'

■ PROVERBS 14:1-2

14 The wise woman builds her house,
    but with her own hands the foolish
    one tears hers down.

² Whoever fears the LORD walks uprightly,
    but those who despise him are devious
    in their ways.

■ JOHN 3:22–4:6

²² After this, Jesus and his disciples went out into the Judean countryside, where he spent some time with them, and baptised. ²³ Now John also was baptising at Aenon near Salim, because there was plenty of water, and people were coming and being baptised. ²⁴ (This was before John was put in prison.) ²⁵ An argument developed between some of John's disciples and a certain Jew over the matter of ceremonial washing. ²⁶ They came to John and said to him, 'Rabbi, that man who was with you on the other side of the Jordan – the one you testified about – look, he is baptising, and everyone is going to him.'

²⁷ To this John replied, 'A person can receive only what is given them from heaven. ²⁸ You yourselves can testify that I said, "I am not the Messiah but am sent ahead of him." ²⁹ The bride belongs to the bridegroom. The friend who attends the bridegroom waits and listens for him, and is full of joy when he hears the bridegroom's voice. That joy is mine, and it is now complete. ³⁰ He must become greater; I must become less.'

³¹ The one who comes from above is above all; the one who is from the earth belongs to the earth, and speaks as one from the earth. The one who comes from heaven is above all. ³² He testifies to what he has seen and heard, but no one accepts his testimony. ³³ Whoever has accepted it has certified that God is truthful. ³⁴ For the one whom God has sent speaks the words of God, for God gives the Spirit without limit. ³⁵ The Father loves the Son and has placed everything in his hands. ³⁶ Whoever believes in the Son has eternal life, but whoever rejects the Son will not see life, for God's wrath remains on them.

4 Now Jesus learned that the Pharisees had heard that he was gaining and baptising more disciples than John – [2] although in fact it was not Jesus who baptised, but his disciples. [3] So he left Judea and went back once more to Galilee.

[4] Now he had to go through Samaria. [5] So he came to a town in Samaria called Sychar, near the plot of ground Jacob had given to his son Joseph. [6] Jacob's well was there, and Jesus, tired as he was from the journey, sat down by the well. It was about noon.

'A Time Exposure to God'

'... two things I have heard: "Power belongs to you, God and with you, Lord, is unfailing love ..."' **Psalm 62:11-12**

It is futile to present our requests to God before pausing to reflect on His unchanging adequacy and sufficiency. One reason why Jesus directed us to use the words 'Our Father in heaven' was to encourage us to focus our gaze on a God who is unaffected by the restrictions and limitations of earth and who dwells in a place where the resources never run dry. Those who plunge into the areas of petition and intercession before reflecting on the abundant resources that lie in God will find their praying ineffective. They are praying contrary to God's pattern. As the poet Lascelles Abercrombie says:

What a frail soul he gave me, and a heart
Lame, and unlikely for the large events.

However, I wonder if, more often than not, we haven't given ourselves 'a heart lame, and unlikely for the large events' because we rush into God's presence to present our petitions before taking stock of our spiritual resources.

God offers us infinite resources for the asking and the taking – Himself. The first moments of prayer should, therefore, be contemplative, reflective, meditative. As we gaze upon God and His infinite resources, we take, as someone put it, 'a time exposure to God.' His adequacy and sufficiency are printed indelibly upon us. No matter, then, what difficulties and problems face us – He is more than a match for them. The vision of His greatness puts the whole of life into its proper perspective. 'We kneel, how weak – we rise, how full of power.'

PRAYER

O Father, I am so thankful that Your resources are so near at hand. I reflect on Your greatness and Your wonder in the depths of my heart, and my praying takes on new strength and power. I am so grateful. Amen.

FURTHER STUDY

Eph. 1; Psa. 5:3; 65:5-7; 1 Chron. 29:12
- What was Paul's prayer for the Ephesians?
- Ask God to enlarge your vision in this way.

May 19

■ **1 SAMUEL 9:1–10:27**

9 There was a Benjaminite, a man of standing, whose name was Kish son of Abiel, the son of Zeror, the son of Bekorath, the son of Aphiah of Benjamin. ² Kish had a son named Saul, as handsome a young man as could be found anywhere in Israel, and he was a head taller than anyone else.

³ Now the donkeys belonging to Saul's father Kish were lost, and Kish said to his son Saul, 'Take one of the servants with you and go and look for the donkeys.' ⁴ So he passed through the hill country of Ephraim and through the area around Shalisha, but they did not find them. They went on into the district of Shaalim, but the donkeys were not there. Then he passed through the territory of Benjamin, but they did not find them.

⁵ When they reached the district of Zuph, Saul said to the servant who was with him, 'Come, let's go back, or my father will stop thinking about the donkeys and start worrying about us.'

⁶ But the servant replied, 'Look, in this town there is a man of God; he is highly respected, and everything he says comes true. Let's go there now. Perhaps he will tell us what way to take.'

⁷ Saul said to his servant, 'If we go, what can we give the man? The food in our sacks is gone. We have no gift to take to the man of God. What do we have?'

⁸ The servant answered him again. 'Look,' he said, 'I have a quarter of a shekel of silver. I will give it to the man of God so that he will tell us what way to take.' ⁹ (Formerly in Israel, if someone went to enquire of God, they would say, 'Come, let us go to the seer,' because the prophet of today used to be called a seer.)

¹⁰ 'Good,' Saul said to his servant. 'Come, let's go.' So they set out for the town where the man of God was.

¹¹ As they were going up the hill to the town, they met some young women coming out to draw water, and they asked them, 'Is the seer here?'

¹² 'He is,' they answered. 'He's ahead of you. Hurry now; he has just come to our town today, for the people have a sacrifice at the high place. ¹³ As soon as you enter the town, you will find him before he goes up to the high place to eat. The people will not begin eating until he comes, because he must bless the sacrifice; afterwards, those who are invited will eat. Go up now; you should find him about this time.'

¹⁴ They went up to the town, and as they were entering it, there was Samuel, coming towards them on his way up to the high place.

¹⁵ Now the day before Saul came, the LORD had revealed this to Samuel: ¹⁶ 'About this time tomorrow I will send you a man from the land of Benjamin. Anoint him ruler over my people Israel; he will deliver them from the hand of the Philistines. I have looked on my people, for their cry has reached me.'

¹⁷ When Samuel caught sight of Saul, the LORD said to him, 'This is the man I spoke to you about; he will govern my people.'

¹⁸ Saul approached Samuel in the gateway and asked, 'Would you please tell me where the seer's house is?'

¹⁹ 'I am the seer,' Samuel replied. 'Go up ahead of me to the high place, for today you are to eat with me, and in the morning I will send you on your way and will tell you all that is in your heart. ²⁰ As for the donkeys you lost three days ago, do not worry about them; they have been found. And to whom is all the desire of Israel turned, if not to you

and your whole family line?'

²¹Saul answered, 'But am I not a Benjaminite, from the smallest tribe of Israel, and is not my clan the least of all the clans of the tribe of Benjamin? Why do you say such a thing to me?'

²²Then Samuel brought Saul and his servant into the hall and seated them at the head of those who were invited – about thirty in number. ²³Samuel said to the cook, 'Bring the piece of meat I gave you, the one I told you to lay aside.'

²⁴So the cook took up the thigh with what was on it and set it in front of Saul. Samuel said, 'Here is what has been kept for you. Eat, because it was set aside for you for this occasion from the time I said, "I have invited guests."' And Saul dined with Samuel that day.

²⁵After they came down from the high place to the town, Samuel talked with Saul on the roof of his house. ²⁶They rose about daybreak, and Samuel called to Saul on the roof, 'Get ready, and I will send you on your way.' When Saul got ready, he and Samuel went outside together. ²⁷As they were going down to the edge of the town, Samuel said to Saul, 'Tell the servant to go on ahead of us' – and the servant did so – 'but you stay here for a while, so that I may give you a message from God.'

10 Then Samuel took a flask of olive oil and poured it on Saul's head and kissed him, saying, 'Has not the LORD anointed you ruler over his inheritance? ²When you leave me today, you will meet two men near Rachel's tomb, at Zelzah on the border of Benjamin. They will say to you, "The donkeys you set out to look for have been found. And now your father has stopped thinking about them and is worried about you. He is asking, 'What shall I do about my son?'"

³'Then you will go on from there until you reach the great tree of Tabor. Three men going up to worship God at Bethel will meet you there. One will be carrying three young goats, another three loaves of bread, and another a skin of wine. ⁴They will greet you and offer you two loaves of bread, which you will accept from them.

⁵'After that you will go to Gibeah of God, where there is a Philistine outpost. As you approach the town, you will meet a procession of prophets coming down from the high place with lyres, tambourines, pipes and harps being played before them, and they will be prophesying. ⁶The Spirit of the LORD will come powerfully upon you, and you will prophesy with them; and you will be changed into a different person. ⁷Once these signs are fulfilled, do whatever your hand finds to do, for God is with you.

⁸'Go down ahead of me to Gilgal. I will surely come down to you to sacrifice burnt offerings and fellowship offerings, but you must wait seven days until I come to you and tell you what you are to do.'

⁹As Saul turned to leave Samuel, God changed Saul's heart, and all these signs were fulfilled that day. ¹⁰When he and his servant arrived at Gibeah, a procession of prophets met him; the Spirit of God came powerfully upon him, and he joined in their prophesying. ¹¹When all those who had formerly known him saw him prophesying with the prophets, they asked each other, 'What is this that has happened to the son of Kish? Is Saul also among the prophets?'

¹²A man who lived there answered, 'And who is their father?' So it became a saying: 'Is Saul also among the prophets?' ¹³After Saul stopped prophesying, he went to the high place.

¹⁴Now Saul's uncle asked him and his servant, 'Where have you been?'

'Looking for the donkeys,' he said. 'But when we saw they were not to be found, we went to Samuel.'

¹⁵Saul's uncle said, 'Tell me what Samuel said to you.'

¹⁶Saul replied, 'He assured us that the donkeys had been found.' But he did not tell his uncle what Samuel had said about the kingship.

[17] Samuel summoned the people of Israel to the LORD at Mizpah [18] and said to them, 'This is what the LORD, the God of Israel, says: "I brought Israel up out of Egypt, and I delivered you from the power of Egypt and all the kingdoms that oppressed you." [19] But you have now rejected your God, who saves you out of all your disasters and calamities. And you have said, "No, appoint a king over us." So now present yourselves before the LORD by your tribes and clans.'

[20] When Samuel had made all Israel come forward by tribes, the tribe of Benjamin was taken by lot. [21] Then he brought forward the tribe of Benjamin, clan by clan, and Matri's clan was taken. Finally Saul son of Kish was taken. But when they looked for him, he was not to be found. [22] So they enquired further of the LORD, 'Has the man come here yet?'

And the LORD said, 'Yes, he has hidden himself among the supplies.'

[23] They ran and brought him out, and as he stood among the people he was a head taller than any of the others. [24] Samuel said to all the people, 'Do you see the man the LORD has chosen? There is no one like him among all the people.'

Then the people shouted, 'Long live the king!'

[25] Samuel explained to the people the rights and duties of kingship. He wrote them down on a scroll and deposited it before the LORD. Then Samuel dismissed the people to go to their own homes.

[26] Saul also went to his home in Gibeah, accompanied by valiant men whose hearts God had touched. [27] But some scoundrels said, 'How can this fellow save us?' They despised him and brought him no gifts. But Saul kept silent.

PSALM 63:1-5

[1] You, God, are my God,
  earnestly I seek you;
I thirst for you,
  my whole being longs for you,
in a dry and parched land
  where there is no water.

[2] I have seen you in the sanctuary
  and beheld your power and your glory.
[3] Because your love is better than life,
  my lips will glorify you.
[4] I will praise you as long as I live,
  and in your name I will lift up my hands.
[5] I will be satisfied as with the richest of
    foods;
  with singing lips my mouth will praise
    you.

PROVERBS 14:3

[3] A fool's mouth lashes out with pride,
  but the lips of the wise protect them.

JOHN 4:7-26

[7] When a Samaritan woman came to draw water, Jesus said to her, 'Will you give me a drink?' [8] (His disciples had gone into the town to buy food.)

[9] The Samaritan woman said to him, 'You are a Jew and I am a Samaritan woman. How can you ask me for a drink?' (For Jews do not associate with Samaritans.)

[10] Jesus answered her, 'If you knew the gift of God and who it is that asks you for a drink, you would have asked him and he would have given you living water.'

[11] 'Sir,' the woman said, 'you have nothing to draw with and the well is deep. Where can you get this living water? [12] Are you greater than our father Jacob, who gave us the well and drank from it himself, as did also his sons and his livestock?'

[13] Jesus answered, 'Everyone who drinks this water will be thirsty again, [14] but whoever drinks the water I give them will never

thirst. Indeed, the water I give them will become in them a spring of water welling up to eternal life.'

[15] The woman said to him, 'Sir, give me this water so that I won't get thirsty and have to keep coming here to draw water.'

[16] He told her, 'Go, call your husband and come back.'

[17] 'I have no husband,' she replied.

Jesus said to her, 'You are right when you say you have no husband. [18] The fact is, you have had five husbands, and the man you now have is not your husband. What you have just said is quite true.'

[19] 'Sir,' the woman said, 'I can see that you are a prophet. [20] Our ancestors worshipped on this mountain, but you Jews claim that the place where we must worship is in Jerusalem.'

[21] 'Woman,' Jesus replied, 'believe me, a time is coming when you will worship the Father neither on this mountain nor in Jerusalem. [22] You Samaritans worship what you do not know; we worship what we do know, for salvation is from the Jews. [23] Yet a time is coming and has now come when the true worshippers will worship the Father in the Spirit and in truth, for they are the kind of worshippers the Father seeks. [24] God is spirit, and his worshippers must worship in the Spirit and in truth.'

[25] The woman said, 'I know that Messiah' (called Christ) 'is coming. When he comes, he will explain everything to us.'

[26] Then Jesus declared, 'I, the one speaking to you – I am he.'

Living Water

'... whoever drinks the water I give them will never thirst. Indeed, the water I give them will become in them a spring of water welling up to eternal life.' **John 4:14**

John 7:38 says, 'Whoever believes in me ... rivers of living water will flow from within them.' *The Amplified Bible* translates this passage: 'He who believes in Me ... From his innermost being shall flow continuously springs and rivers of living water. But He was speaking here of the Spirit, whom those who believe in Him were afterward to receive.'

Are our lives truly like this? Do fresh springs flow out of us day after day? If not, why not? The answer is simple - there can be no outflow unless there is an inflow. This is the rhythm of the Holy Spirit - intake and outflow. If there is more intake than outflow, then the intake stops; if there is more outflow than intake, then the outflow stops. The doors open inward to receive, only to open outward to give.

When we come to talk about life in the Spirit, we are not to think in terms of a reservoir which has only limited resources. Life is a channel, attached to infinite resources. The more we draw on these resources, the more we have. There is no danger of exhausting one's resources. We do not have to hold back - for the more we give, the more we have.

Living on the overflow is what many of us lack today. A sign could be put up over our individual and collective lives saying, 'Life Limited'. According to Jesus' promise, however, when the Spirit comes, life is unlimited: 'rivers of living water will flow from within them.'

Not rivulets, not trickles, not brooks, not streams – but rivers. Rivers!

PRAYER

O God, help me to link my channel to Your infinite resources. Flow through me until I become a flowing river – no, an overflowing river. In Jesus' name. Amen.

FURTHER STUDY

Acts 10:34-38; 1 Cor. 3:16; 6:19; 2 Tim. 1:14
• How did Peter link Christ's work with that of the Spirit?
• What has God made us to be?

May 20

1 SAMUEL 11:1–13:22

11 Nahash the Ammonite went up and besieged Jabesh Gilead. And all the men of Jabesh said to him, 'Make a treaty with us, and we will be subject to you.'

² But Nahash the Ammonite replied, 'I will make a treaty with you only on the condition that I gouge out the right eye of every one of you and so bring disgrace on all Israel.'

³ The elders of Jabesh said to him, 'Give us seven days so that we can send messengers throughout Israel; if no one comes to rescue us, we will surrender to you.'

⁴ When the messengers came to Gibeah of Saul and reported these terms to the people, they all wept aloud. ⁵ Just then Saul was returning from the fields, behind his oxen, and he asked, 'What is wrong with everyone? Why are they weeping?' Then they repeated to him what the men of Jabesh had said.

⁶ When Saul heard their words, the Spirit of God came powerfully upon him, and he burned with anger. ⁷ He took a pair of oxen, cut them into pieces, and sent the pieces by messengers throughout Israel, proclaiming, 'This is what will be done to the oxen of anyone who does not follow Saul and Samuel.' Then the terror of the LORD fell on the people, and they came out together as one. ⁸ When Saul mustered them at Bezek, the men of Israel numbered three hundred thousand and those of Judah thirty thousand.

⁹ They told the messengers who had come, 'Say to the men of Jabesh Gilead, "By the time the sun is hot tomorrow, you will be rescued."' When the messengers went and reported this to the men of Jabesh, they were elated. ¹⁰ They said to the Ammonites, 'Tomorrow we will surrender to you, and you can do to us whatever you like.'

¹¹ The next day Saul separated his men into three divisions; during the last watch of the night they broke into the camp of the Ammonites and slaughtered them until the heat of the day. Those who survived were scattered, so that no two of them were left together.

¹² The people then said to Samuel, 'Who was it that asked, "Shall Saul reign over us?" Turn these men over to us so that we may put them to death.'

¹³ But Saul said, 'No one will be put to death today, for this day the LORD has rescued Israel.'

¹⁴ Then Samuel said to the people, 'Come, let us go to Gilgal and there renew the kingship.' ¹⁵ So all the people went to Gilgal and made Saul king in the presence of the LORD. There they sacrificed fellowship offerings before the LORD, and Saul and all the Israelites held a great celebration.

12 Samuel said to all Israel, 'I have listened to everything you said to me and have set a king over you. ² Now you have

a king as your leader. As for me, I am old and grey, and my sons are here with you. I have been your leader from my youth until this day. ³Here I stand. Testify against me in the presence of the Lord and his anointed. Whose ox have I taken? Whose donkey have I taken? Whom have I cheated? Whom have I oppressed? From whose hand have I accepted a bribe to make me shut my eyes? If I have done any of these things, I will make it right.'

⁴'You have not cheated or oppressed us,' they replied. 'You have not taken anything from anyone's hand.'

⁵Samuel said to them, 'The Lord is witness against you, and also his anointed is witness this day, that you have not found anything in my hand.'

'He is witness,' they said.

⁶Then Samuel said to the people, 'It is the Lord who appointed Moses and Aaron and brought your ancestors up out of Egypt. ⁷Now then, stand here, because I am going to confront you with evidence before the Lord as to all the righteous acts performed by the Lord for you and your ancestors.

⁸'After Jacob entered Egypt, they cried to the Lord for help, and the Lord sent Moses and Aaron, who brought your ancestors out of Egypt and settled them in this place.

⁹'But they forgot the Lord their God; so he sold them into the hands of Sisera, the commander of the army of Hazor, and into the hands of the Philistines and the king of Moab, who fought against them. ¹⁰They cried out to the Lord and said, "We have sinned; we have forsaken the Lord and served the Baals and the Ashtoreths. But now deliver us from the hands of our enemies, and we will serve you." ¹¹Then the Lord sent Jerub-Baal, Barak, Jephthah and Samuel, and he delivered you from the hands of your enemies all around you, so that you lived in safety.

¹²'But when you saw that Nahash king of the Ammonites was moving against you, you said to me, "No, we want a king to rule over us" – even though the Lord your God

was your king. ¹³Now here is the king you have chosen, the one you asked for; see, the Lord has set a king over you. ¹⁴If you fear the Lord and serve and obey him and do not rebel against his commands, and if both you and the king who reigns over you follow the Lord your God – good! ¹⁵But if you do not obey the Lord, and if you rebel against his commands, his hand will be against you, as it was against your ancestors.

¹⁶'Now then, stand still and see this great thing the Lord is about to do before your eyes! ¹⁷Is it not wheat harvest now? I will call on the Lord to send thunder and rain. And you will realise what an evil thing you did in the eyes of the Lord when you asked for a king.'

¹⁸Then Samuel called on the Lord, and that same day the Lord sent thunder and rain. So all the people stood in awe of the Lord and of Samuel.

¹⁹The people all said to Samuel, 'Pray to the Lord your God for your servants so that we will not die, for we have added to all our other sins the evil of asking for a king.'

²⁰'Do not be afraid,' Samuel replied. 'You have done all this evil; yet do not turn away from the Lord, but serve the Lord with all your heart. ²¹Do not turn away after useless idols. They can do you no good, nor can they rescue you, because they are useless. ²²For the sake of his great name the Lord will not reject his people, because the Lord was pleased to make you his own. ²³As for me, far be it from me that I should sin against the Lord by failing to pray for you. And I will teach you the way that is good and right. ²⁴But be sure to fear the Lord and serve him faithfully with all your heart; consider what great things he has done for you. ²⁵Yet if you persist in doing evil, both you and your king will perish.'

13 Saul was thirty years old when he became king, and he reigned over Israel for forty-two years. ²Saul chose three thousand men from

Israel; two thousand were with him at Michmash and in the hill country of Bethel, and a thousand were with Jonathan at Gibeah in Benjamin. The rest of the men he sent back to their homes.

³ Jonathan attacked the Philistine outpost at Geba, and the Philistines heard about it. Then Saul had the trumpet blown throughout the land and said, 'Let the Hebrews hear!' ⁴ So all Israel heard the news: 'Saul has attacked the Philistine outpost, and now Israel has become obnoxious to the Philistines.' And the people were summoned to join Saul at Gilgal.

⁵ The Philistines assembled to fight Israel, with three thousand chariots, six thousand charioteers, and soldiers as numerous as the sand on the seashore. They went up and camped at Michmash, east of Beth Aven. ⁶ When the Israelites saw that their situation was critical and that their army was hard pressed, they hid in caves and thickets, among the rocks, and in pits and cisterns. ⁷ Some Hebrews even crossed the Jordan to the land of Gad and Gilead.

Saul remained at Gilgal, and all the troops with him were quaking with fear. ⁸ He waited for seven days, the time set by Samuel; but Samuel did not come to Gilgal, and Saul's men began to scatter. ⁹ So he said, 'Bring me the burnt offering and the fellowship offerings.' And Saul offered up the burnt offering. ¹⁰ Just as he finished making the offering, Samuel arrived, and Saul went out to greet him.

¹¹ 'What have you done?' asked Samuel.

Saul replied, 'When I saw that the men were scattering, and that you did not come at the set time, and that the Philistines were assembling at Michmash, ¹² I thought, "Now the Philistines will come down against me at Gilgal, and I have not sought the LORD's favour." So I felt compelled to offer the burnt offering.'

¹³ 'You have done a foolish thing,' Samuel said. 'You have not kept the command the LORD your God gave you; if you had, he would have established your kingdom over Israel for all time. ¹⁴ But now your kingdom will not endure; the LORD has sought out a man after his own heart and appointed him ruler of his people, because you have not kept the LORD's command.'

¹⁵ Then Samuel left Gilgal and went up to Gibeah in Benjamin, and Saul counted the men who were with him. They numbered about six hundred.

¹⁶ Saul and his son Jonathan and the men with them were staying in Gibeah of Benjamin, while the Philistines camped at Michmash. ¹⁷ Raiding parties went out from the Philistine camp in three detachments. One turned towards Ophrah in the vicinity of Shual, ¹⁸ another towards Beth Horon, and the third towards the borderland overlooking the Valley of Zeboyim facing the wilderness.

¹⁹ Not a blacksmith could be found in the whole land of Israel, because the Philistines had said, 'Otherwise the Hebrews will make swords or spears!' ²⁰ So all Israel went down to the Philistines to have their ploughshares, mattocks, axes and sickles sharpened. ²¹ The price was two-thirds of a shekel for sharpening ploughshares and mattocks, and a third of a shekel for sharpening forks and axes and for repointing goads.

²² So on the day of the battle not a soldier with Saul and Jonathan had a sword or spear in his hand; only Saul and his son Jonathan had them.

◼ PSALM 63:6-11

⁶ On my bed I remember you;
  I think of you through the watches of
    the night.
⁷ Because you are my help,
  I sing in the shadow of your wings.
⁸ I cling to you;
  your right hand upholds me.

⁹ Those who want to kill me will be
    destroyed;

they will go down to the depths of the
earth.
¹⁰ They will be given over to the sword
and become food for jackals.

¹¹ But the king will rejoice in God;
all who swear by God will glory in him,
while the mouths of liars will be silenced.

....

▬ PROVERBS 14:4

⁴ Where there are no oxen, the manger is
empty,
but from the strength of an ox come
abundant harvests.

....

▬ JOHN 4:27-54

²⁷ Just then his disciples returned and
were surprised to find him talking with
a woman. But no one asked, 'What do you
want?' or 'Why are you talking with her?'
²⁸ Then, leaving her water jar, the woman
went back to the town and said to the people, ²⁹ 'Come, see a man who told me everything I've ever done. Could this be the
Messiah?' ³⁰ They came out of the town and
made their way towards him.
³¹ Meanwhile his disciples urged him,
'Rabbi, eat something.'
³² But he said to them, 'I have food to eat
that you know nothing about.'
³³ Then his disciples said to each other,
'Could someone have brought him food?'
³⁴ 'My food,' said Jesus, 'is to do the will
of him who sent me and to finish his work.
³⁵ Don't you have a saying, "It's still four
months until harvest"? I tell you, open your
eyes and look at the fields! They are ripe
for harvest. ³⁶ Even now the one who reaps
draws a wage and harvests a crop for eternal
life, so that the sower and the reaper may be
glad together. ³⁷ Thus the saying "One sows
and another reaps" is true. ³⁸ I sent you to

reap what you have not worked for. Others have done the hard work, and you have
reaped the benefits of their labour.'
³⁹ Many of the Samaritans from that town
believed in him because of the woman's testimony, 'He told me everything I've ever
done.' ⁴⁰ So when the Samaritans came to
him, they urged him to stay with them, and
he stayed two days. ⁴¹ And because of his
words many more became believers.
⁴² They said to the woman, 'We no longer
believe just because of what you said; now we
have heard for ourselves, and we know that
this man really is the Saviour of the world.'
⁴³ After the two days he left for Galilee.
⁴⁴ (Now Jesus himself had pointed out that a
prophet has no honour in his own country.)
⁴⁵ When he arrived in Galilee, the Galileans welcomed him. They had seen all that
he had done in Jerusalem at the Passover
Festival, for they also had been there.
⁴⁶ Once more he visited Cana in Galilee,
where he had turned the water into wine. And
there was a certain royal official whose son
lay ill at Capernaum. ⁴⁷ When this man heard
that Jesus had arrived in Galilee from Judea,
he went to him and begged him to come and
heal his son, who was close to death.
⁴⁸ 'Unless you people see signs and wonders,' Jesus told him, 'you will never believe.'
⁴⁹ The royal official said, 'Sir, come down
before my child dies.'
⁵⁰ 'Go,' Jesus replied, 'your son will live.'
The man took Jesus at his word and departed. ⁵¹ While he was still on the way, his servants
met him with the news that his boy was living.
⁵² When he enquired as to the time when his
son got better, they said to him, 'Yesterday, at
one in the afternoon, the fever left him.'
⁵³ Then the father realised that this was
the exact time at which Jesus had said to
him, 'Your son will live.' So he and his whole
household believed.
⁵⁴ This was the second sign Jesus performed after coming from Judea to Galilee.

Four Simple Words

'... the woman went back to the town and said to the people, "Come, see a man who told me everything I've ever done ..."' **John 4:28-29**

In the true Christian heart, sharing is instinctive. What was the instinct of the woman at the well as soon as she had received salvation? It was to share what she had found with others.

What I am saying will cause some people to feel guilty, especially those who do not find it easy to share their faith. It is not that we should go out and accost everyone we meet with the message of salvation, but we do need to be alert for every opportunity and to take advantage of it.

The four words which most succinctly summarise the gospel are each found in the Scripture passage before us today. They are these: 'come ... see ... went ... told.' We get a firsthand knowledge – 'come and see' – and then the instinctive impulse takes over – 'go and tell'. And if there is no 'go and tell' impulse, then perhaps the 'come and see' impulse is not ours, or at least it has ceased to hold a commanding place in our lives.

A woman once wrote to me following something I had written in *Every Day with Jesus* and said, 'I had a real experience of God and refused to share it with anyone, so it died'. How sad. J. B. Phillips' translation of 2 Corinthians 9:10 is luminous: 'He who gives the seed to the sower ...' See the inference? He gives seed only to the one who uses it – the sower. If we won't use the seed, then we won't get it. Our powers are either dead or dedicated. If they are dedicated, they are alive with God. If they are saved up or conserved, they die.

PRAYER

O Father, I ask not for an experience of You – I already have that. I ask rather for the courage to share it with others. Give me some seed today, and help me to sow it in prepared hearts. For Your own dear name's sake. Amen.

FURTHER STUDY

1 Pet. 3:1-16; Psa. 66:16; Isa. 63:7
- What must we always be prepared to do?
- How did Isaiah and the psalmist do this?

May 21

■ 1 SAMUEL 13:23–14:52

23 Now a detachment of Philistines had

14 gone out to the pass at Michmash. 1 One day Jonathan son of Saul said to his young armour-bearer, 'Come, let's go over to the Philistine outpost on the other

side.' But he did not tell his father.

² Saul was staying on the outskirts of Gibeah under a pomegranate tree in Migron. With him were about six hundred men, ³ among whom was Ahijah, who was wearing an ephod. He was a son of Ichabod's brother Ahitub son of Phinehas, the son of Eli, the LORD's priest in Shiloh. No one was aware that Jonathan had left.

⁴ On each side of the pass that Jonathan intended to cross to reach the Philistine outpost was a cliff; one was called Bozez and the other Seneh. ⁵ One cliff stood to the north towards Michmash, the other to the south towards Geba.

⁶ Jonathan said to his young armour-bearer, 'Come, let's go over to the outpost of those uncircumcised men. Perhaps the LORD will act on our behalf. Nothing can hinder the LORD from saving, whether by many or by few.'

⁷ 'Do all that you have in mind,' his armour-bearer said. 'Go ahead; I am with you heart and soul.'

⁸ Jonathan said, 'Come on, then; we will cross over towards them and let them see us. ⁹ If they say to us, "Wait there until we come to you," we will stay where we are and not go up to them. ¹⁰ But if they say, "Come up to us," we will climb up, because that will be our sign that the LORD has given them into our hands.'

¹¹ So both of them showed themselves to the Philistine outpost. 'Look!' said the Philistines. 'The Hebrews are crawling out of the holes they were hiding in.' ¹² The men of the outpost shouted to Jonathan and his armour-bearer, 'Come up to us and we'll teach you a lesson.'

So Jonathan said to his armour-bearer, 'Climb up after me; the LORD has given them into the hand of Israel.'

¹³ Jonathan climbed up, using his hands and feet, with his armour-bearer right behind him. The Philistines fell before Jonathan, and his armour-bearer followed and killed behind him. ¹⁴ In that first attack Jonathan and his armour-bearer killed some twenty men in an area of about half an acre.

¹⁵ Then panic struck the whole army – those in the camp and field, and those in the outposts and raiding parties – and the ground shook. It was a panic sent by God.

¹⁶ Saul's lookouts at Gibeah in Benjamin saw the army melting away in all directions. ¹⁷ Then Saul said to the men who were with him, 'Muster the forces and see who has left us.' When they did, it was Jonathan and his armour-bearer who were not there.

¹⁸ Saul said to Ahijah, 'Bring the ark of God.' (At that time it was with the Israelites.) ¹⁹ While Saul was talking to the priest, the tumult in the Philistine camp increased more and more. So Saul said to the priest, 'Withdraw your hand.'

²⁰ Then Saul and all his men assembled and went to the battle. They found the Philistines in total confusion, striking each other with their swords. ²¹ Those Hebrews who had previously been with the Philistines and had gone up with them to their camp went over to the Israelites who were with Saul and Jonathan. ²² When all the Israelites who had hidden in the hill country of Ephraim heard that the Philistines were on the run, they joined the battle in hot pursuit. ²³ So on that day the LORD saved Israel, and the battle moved on beyond Beth Aven.

²⁴ Now the Israelites were in distress that day, because Saul had bound the people under an oath, saying, 'Cursed be anyone who eats food before evening comes, before I have avenged myself on my enemies!' So none of the troops tasted food.

²⁵ The entire army entered the woods, and there was honey on the ground. ²⁶ When they went into the woods, they saw the honey oozing out; yet no one put his hand to his mouth, because they feared the oath. ²⁷ But Jonathan had not heard that his father had bound the people with the oath, so he reached out the end of the staff that was in his hand and dipped it into the honeycomb. He raised his hand to his mouth, and his eyes brightened.

²⁸ Then one of the soldiers told him, 'Your father bound the army under a strict oath, saying, "Cursed be anyone who eats food today!" That is why the men are faint.'

²⁹ Jonathan said, 'My father has made trouble for the country. See how my eyes brightened when I tasted a little of this honey. ³⁰ How much better it would have been if the men had eaten today some of the plunder they took from their enemies. Would not the slaughter of the Philistines have been even greater?'

³¹ That day, after the Israelites had struck down the Philistines from Michmash to Aijalon, they were exhausted. ³² They pounced on the plunder and, taking sheep, cattle and calves, they butchered them on the ground and ate them, together with the blood. ³³ Then someone said to Saul, 'Look, the men are sinning against the LORD by eating meat that has blood in it.'

'You have broken faith,' he said. 'Roll a large stone over here at once.' ³⁴ Then he said, 'Go out among the men and tell them, "Each of you bring me your cattle and sheep, and slaughter them here and eat them. Do not sin against the LORD by eating meat with blood still in it."'

So everyone brought his ox that night and slaughtered it there. ³⁵ Then Saul built an altar to the LORD; it was the first time he had done this.

³⁶ Saul said, 'Let us go down and pursue the Philistines by night and plunder them till dawn, and let us not leave one of them alive.'

'Do whatever seems best to you,' they replied.

But the priest said, 'Let us enquire of God here.'

³⁷ So Saul asked God, 'Shall I go down and pursue the Philistines? Will you give them into Israel's hand?' But God did not answer him that day.

³⁸ Saul therefore said, 'Come here, all you who are leaders of the army, and let us find out what sin has been committed today. ³⁹ As surely as the LORD who rescues Israel lives, even if the guilt lies with my son Jonathan, he must die.' But not one of them said a word.

⁴⁰ Saul then said to all the Israelites, 'You stand over there; I and Jonathan my son will stand over here.'

'Do what seems best to you,' they replied.

⁴¹ Then Saul prayed to the LORD, the God of Israel, 'Why have you not answered your servant today? If the fault is in me or my son Jonathan, respond with Urim, but if the men of Israel are at fault, respond with Thummim.' Jonathan and Saul were taken by lot, and the men were cleared. ⁴² Saul said, 'Cast the lot between me and Jonathan my son.' And Jonathan was taken.

⁴³ Then Saul said to Jonathan, 'Tell me what you have done.'

So Jonathan told him, 'I tasted a little honey with the end of my staff. And now I must die!'

⁴⁴ Saul said, 'May God deal with me, be it ever so severely, if you do not die, Jonathan.'

⁴⁵ But the men said to Saul, 'Should Jonathan die – he who has brought about this great deliverance in Israel? Never! As surely as the LORD lives, not a hair of his head shall fall to the ground, for he did this today with God's help.' So the men rescued Jonathan, and he was not put to death.

⁴⁶ Then Saul stopped pursuing the Philistines, and they withdrew to their own land.

⁴⁷ After Saul had assumed rule over Israel, he fought against their enemies on every side: Moab, the Ammonites, Edom, the kings of Zobah, and the Philistines. Wherever he turned, he inflicted punishment on them. ⁴⁸ He fought valiantly and defeated the Amalekites, delivering Israel from the hands of those who had plundered them.

⁴⁹ Saul's sons were Jonathan, Ishvi and Malki-Shua. The name of his elder daughter was Merab, and that of the younger was Michal. ⁵⁰ His wife's name was Ahinoam daughter of Ahimaaz. The name of the commander of Saul's army was Abner son of Ner, and Ner was Saul's uncle. ⁵¹ Saul's father Kish and Abner's father Ner were sons of Abiel.

52 All the days of Saul there was bitter war with the Philistines, and whenever Saul saw a mighty or brave man, he took him into his service.

■ PSALM 64:1-6

1 Hear me, my God, as I voice my complaint;
   protect my life from the threat of the
   enemy.

2 Hide me from the conspiracy of the wicked,
   from the plots of evildoers.
3 They sharpen their tongues like swords
   and aim cruel words like deadly arrows.
4 They shoot from ambush at the innocent;
   they shoot suddenly, without fear.

5 They encourage each other in evil plans,
   they talk about hiding their snares;
   they say, 'Who will see it?'
6 They plot injustice and say,
   'We have devised a perfect plan!'
   Surely the human mind and heart are
   cunning.

■ PROVERBS 14:5-7

5 An honest witness does not deceive,
   but a false witness pours out lies.

6 The mocker seeks wisdom and finds none,
   but knowledge comes easily to the
   discerning.

7 Stay away from a fool,
   for you will not find knowledge on
   their lips.

■ JOHN 5:1-23

5 Some time later, Jesus went up to Jerusalem for one of the Jewish festivals. 2 Now there is in Jerusalem near the Sheep Gate a pool, which in Aramaic is called Bethesda and which is surrounded by five covered colonnades. 3 Here a great number of disabled people used to lie – the blind, the lame, the paralysed. [4]a 5 One who was there had been an invalid for thirty-eight years. 6 When Jesus saw him lying there and learned that he had been in this condition for a long time, he asked him, 'Do you want to get well?'

7 'Sir,' the invalid replied, 'I have no one to help me into the pool when the water is stirred. While I am trying to get in, someone else goes down ahead of me.'

8 Then Jesus said to him, 'Get up! Pick up your mat and walk.' 9 At once the man was cured; he picked up his mat and walked.

The day on which this took place was a Sabbath, 10 and so the Jewish leaders said to the man who had been healed, 'It is the Sabbath; the law forbids you to carry your mat.'

11 But he replied, 'The man who made me well said to me, "Pick up your mat and walk."'

12 So they asked him, 'Who is this fellow who told you to pick it up and walk?'

13 The man who was healed had no idea who it was, for Jesus had slipped away into the crowd that was there.

14 Later Jesus found him at the temple and said to him, 'See, you are well again. Stop sinning or something worse may happen to you.'
15 The man went away and told the Jewish leaders that it was Jesus who had made him well.

16 So, because Jesus was doing these things on the Sabbath, the Jewish leaders began to persecute him. 17 In his defence Jesus said to them, 'My Father is always at his work to this very day, and I too am working.' 18 For this reason they tried all the more to kill him; not only was he breaking the Sabbath, but he was even calling God his own Father,

---

a 3,4 Some manuscripts include here, wholly or in part, *paralysed – and they waited for the moving of the waters.* 4 *From time to time an angel of the Lord would come down and stir up the waters. The first one into the pool after each disturbance would be cured of whatever disease they had.*

making himself equal with God.

[19] Jesus gave them this answer: 'Very truly I tell you, the Son can do nothing by himself; he can do only what he sees his Father doing, because whatever the Father does the Son also does. [20] For the Father loves the Son and shows him all he does. Yes, and he will show him even greater works than these, so that you will be amazed. [21] For just as the Father raises the dead and gives them life, even so the Son gives life to whom he is pleased to give it. [22] Moreover, the Father judges no one, but has entrusted all judgment to the Son, [23] that all may honour the Son just as they honour the Father. Whoever does not honour the Son does not honour the Father, who sent him.

Safe and Sealed

'... he will show him even greater works than these, so that you will be amazed.' **John 5:20**

In Ephesians 1:13-14, we see that those who 'heard' were 'sealed': 'And you also were included in Christ when you heard the message of truth ... when you believed, you were marked in him with a seal, the promised Holy Spirit.' Does the 'sealing' take place at conversion or at some point beyond it? I believe it takes place at conversion. A seal is a mark of ownership, and when the Holy Spirit comes in to regenerate our beings at conversion, He produces the assurance in our hearts that we are heirs of God and joint heirs with Christ.

I know that some believe that the 'sealing' takes place subsequent to conversion, such as at one's baptism by total immersion, or at a crisis point of sanctification, or, as some would describe it, when we are baptised in the Holy Spirit. But how insecure life would be if we had to wait for 'this' or 'that' experience in order to know that we are safe in Christ.

One historian says that it was customary in Ephesus for certain traders to send their slaves into the marketplace to make purchases for them and, once the transaction was complete, the slaves would mark the item with their master's seal, whereupon it was delivered to the master's home. In something of the same way, the Holy Spirit in our own hearts seals, once and for all, the question of His ownership over our lives, and also acts as a pledge, or guarantee, that one day we will be safely delivered to our Father's home in glory. In Wales, many years ago, I heard a frail old Christian say, 'The envelope [meaning his body] may be a bit tattered, but the letter inside is quite safe'. It is!

PRAYER

O Father, what endless blessings follow the coming of Your Spirit into my life. I am saved by grace, sealed by the Spirit, and supported by eternal love. What more could I ask for this side of glory! Amen.

FURTHER STUDY

John 5; Rom. 8:16; Gal. 4:6; 1 John 4:13
• How does the Holy Spirit 'bear witness'?
• What confidence does this give us?

May 22

■ 1 SAMUEL 15:1–16:23

15 Samuel said to Saul, 'I am the one the LORD sent to anoint you king over his people Israel; so listen now to the message from the LORD. ²This is what the LORD Almighty says: "I will punish the Amalekites for what they did to Israel when they waylaid them as they came up from Egypt. ³Now go, attack the Amalekites and totally destroy all that belongs to them. Do not spare them; put to death men and women, children and infants, cattle and sheep, camels and donkeys."'

⁴So Saul summoned the men and mustered them at Telaim – two hundred thousand foot soldiers and ten thousand from Judah. ⁵Saul went to the city of Amalek and set an ambush in the ravine. ⁶Then he said to the Kenites, 'Go away, leave the Amalekites so that I do not destroy you along with them; for you showed kindness to all the Israelites when they came up out of Egypt.' So the Kenites moved away from the Amalekites.

⁷Then Saul attacked the Amalekites all the way from Havilah to Shur, near the eastern border of Egypt. ⁸He took Agag king of the Amalekites alive, and all his people he totally destroyed with the sword. ⁹But Saul and the army spared Agag and the best of the sheep and cattle, the fat calves and lambs – everything that was good. These they were unwilling to destroy completely, but everything that was despised and weak they totally destroyed.

¹⁰Then the word of the LORD came to Samuel: ¹¹'I regret that I have made Saul king, because he has turned away from me and has not carried out my instructions.' Samuel was angry, and he cried out to the LORD all that night.

¹²Early in the morning Samuel got up and went to meet Saul, but he was told, 'Saul has gone to Carmel. There he has set up a monument in his own honour and has turned and gone on down to Gilgal.'

¹³When Samuel reached him, Saul said, 'The LORD bless you! I have carried out the LORD's instructions.'

¹⁴But Samuel said, 'What then is this bleating of sheep in my ears? What is this lowing of cattle that I hear?'

¹⁵Saul answered, 'The soldiers brought them from the Amalekites; they spared the best of the sheep and cattle to sacrifice to the LORD your God, but we totally destroyed the rest.'

¹⁶'Enough!' Samuel said to Saul. 'Let me tell you what the LORD said to me last night.'

'Tell me,' Saul replied.

¹⁷Samuel said, 'Although you were once small in your own eyes, did you not become the head of the tribes of Israel? The LORD anointed you king over Israel. ¹⁸And he sent you on a mission, saying, "Go and completely destroy those wicked people, the Amalekites; wage war against them until you have wiped them out." ¹⁹Why did you not obey the LORD? Why did you pounce on the plunder and do evil in the eyes of the LORD?'

²⁰'But I did obey the LORD,' Saul said. 'I went on the mission the LORD assigned me. I completely destroyed the Amalekites and brought back Agag their king. ²¹The soldiers took sheep and cattle from the plunder, the best of what was devoted to God, in order to sacrifice them to the LORD your God at Gilgal.'

²²But Samuel replied:

'Does the LORD delight in burnt offerings
and sacrifices
as much as in obeying the LORD?

To obey is better than sacrifice,
  and to heed is better than the fat of
    rams.
²³For rebellion is like the sin of divination,
  and arrogance like the evil of idolatry.
Because you have rejected the word of
    the LORD,
  he has rejected you as king.'

²⁴Then Saul said to Samuel, 'I have sinned. I violated the LORD's command and your instructions. I was afraid of the men and so I gave in to them. ²⁵Now I beg you, forgive my sin and come back with me, so that I may worship the LORD.'

²⁶But Samuel said to him, 'I will not go back with you. You have rejected the word of the LORD, and the LORD has rejected you as king over Israel!'

²⁷As Samuel turned to leave, Saul caught hold of the hem of his robe, and it tore. ²⁸Samuel said to him, 'The LORD has torn the kingdom of Israel from you today and has given it to one of your neighbours – to one better than you. ²⁹He who is the Glory of Israel does not lie or change his mind; for he is not a human being, that he should change his mind.'

³⁰Saul replied, 'I have sinned. But please honour me before the elders of my people and before Israel; come back with me, so that I may worship the LORD your God.' ³¹So Samuel went back with Saul, and Saul worshipped the LORD.

³²Then Samuel said, 'Bring me Agag king of the Amalekites.'

Agag came to him in chains. And he thought, 'Surely the bitterness of death is past.'

³³But Samuel said,

'As your sword has made women childless,
  so will your mother be childless
    among women.'

And Samuel put Agag to death before the LORD at Gilgal.

³⁴Then Samuel left for Ramah, but Saul went up to his home in Gibeah of Saul. ³⁵Until the day Samuel died, he did not go to see Saul again, though Samuel mourned for him. And the LORD regretted that he had made Saul king over Israel.

16 The LORD said to Samuel, 'How long will you mourn for Saul, since I have rejected him as king over Israel? Fill your horn with oil and be on your way; I am sending you to Jesse of Bethlehem. I have chosen one of his sons to be king.'

²But Samuel said, 'How can I go? If Saul hears about it, he will kill me.'

The LORD said, 'Take a heifer with you and say, "I have come to sacrifice to the LORD." ³Invite Jesse to the sacrifice, and I will show you what to do. You are to anoint for me the one I indicate.'

⁴Samuel did what the LORD said. When he arrived at Bethlehem, the elders of the town trembled when they met him. They asked, 'Do you come in peace?'

⁵Samuel replied, 'Yes, in peace; I have come to sacrifice to the LORD. Consecrate yourselves and come to the sacrifice with me.' Then he consecrated Jesse and his sons and invited them to the sacrifice.

⁶When they arrived, Samuel saw Eliab and thought, 'Surely the LORD's anointed stands here before the LORD.'

⁷But the LORD said to Samuel, 'Do not consider his appearance or his height, for I have rejected him. The LORD does not look at the things people look at. People look at the outward appearance, but the LORD looks at the heart.'

⁸Then Jesse called Abinadab and made him pass in front of Samuel. But Samuel said, 'The LORD has not chosen this one either.' ⁹Jesse then made Shammah pass by, but Samuel said, 'Nor has the LORD chosen this one.' ¹⁰Jesse made seven of his sons pass before Samuel, but Samuel said to him, 'The LORD has not chosen these.' ¹¹So he asked Jesse, 'Are these all the sons you have?'

'There is still the youngest,' Jesse answered. 'He is tending the sheep.'

Samuel said, 'Send for him; we will not sit down until he arrives.'

¹² So he sent for him and had him brought in. He was glowing with health and had a fine appearance and handsome features.

Then the LORD said, 'Rise and anoint him; this is the one.'

¹³ So Samuel took the horn of oil and anointed him in the presence of his brothers, and from that day on the Spirit of the LORD came powerfully upon David. Samuel then went to Ramah.

¹⁴ Now the Spirit of the LORD had departed from Saul, and an evil spirit from the LORD tormented him.

¹⁵ Saul's attendants said to him, 'See, an evil spirit from God is tormenting you. ¹⁶ Let our lord command his servants here to search for someone who can play the lyre. He will play when the evil spirit from God comes on you, and you will feel better.'

¹⁷ So Saul said to his attendants, 'Find someone who plays well and bring him to me.'

¹⁸ One of the servants answered, 'I have seen a son of Jesse of Bethlehem who knows how to play the lyre. He is a brave man and a warrior. He speaks well and is a fine-looking man. And the LORD is with him.'

¹⁹ Then Saul sent messengers to Jesse and said, 'Send me your son David, who is with the sheep.' ²⁰ So Jesse took a donkey loaded with bread, a skin of wine and a young goat and sent them with his son David to Saul.

²¹ David came to Saul and entered his service. Saul liked him very much, and David became one of his armour-bearers. ²² Then Saul sent word to Jesse, saying, 'Allow David to remain in my service, for I am pleased with him.'

²³ Whenever the spirit from God came on Saul, David would take up his lyre and play. Then relief would come to Saul; he would feel better, and the evil spirit would leave him.

▬ PSALM 64:7-10

⁷ But God will shoot them with his arrows;
  they will suddenly be struck down.
⁸ He will turn their own tongues against
  them
  and bring them to ruin;
  all who see them will shake their
  heads in scorn.
⁹ All people will fear;
  they will proclaim the works of God
  and ponder what he has done.

¹⁰ The righteous will rejoice in the LORD
  and take refuge in him;
  all the upright in heart will glory in him!

▬ PROVERBS 14:8-9

⁸ The wisdom of the prudent is to give
  thought to their ways,
  but the folly of fools is deception.

⁹ Fools mock at making amends for sin,
  but goodwill is found among the
  upright.

▬ JOHN 5:24-47

²⁴ 'Very truly I tell you, whoever hears my word and believes him who sent me has eternal life and will not be judged but has crossed over from death to life. ²⁵ Very truly I tell you, a time is coming and has now come when the dead will hear the voice of the Son of God and those who hear will live. ²⁶ For as the Father has life in himself, so he has granted the Son also to have life in himself. ²⁷ And he has given him authority to judge because he is the Son of Man.

²⁸ 'Do not be amazed at this, for a time is coming when all who are in their graves will hear his voice ²⁹ and come out – those who have done what is good will rise to live, and

those who have done what is evil will rise to be condemned. [30]By myself I can do nothing; I judge only as I hear, and my judgment is just, for I seek not to please myself but him who sent me.

[31]'If I testify about myself, my testimony is not true. [32]There is another who testifies in my favour, and I know that his testimony about me is true.

[33]'You have sent to John and he has testified to the truth. [34]Not that I accept human testimony; but I mention it that you may be saved. [35]John was a lamp that burned and gave light, and you chose for a time to enjoy his light.

[36]'I have testimony weightier than that of John. For the works that the Father has given me to finish – the very works that I am doing – testify that the Father has sent me. [37]And the Father who sent me has himself testified concerning me. You have never heard his voice nor seen his form,

[38]nor does his word dwell in you, for you do not believe the one he sent. [39]You study the Scriptures diligently because you think that in them you have eternal life. These are the very Scriptures that testify about me, [40]yet you refuse to come to me to have life.

[41]'I do not accept glory from human beings, [42]but I know you. I know that you do not have the love of God in your hearts. [43]I have come in my Father's name, and you do not accept me; but if someone else comes in his own name, you will accept him. [44]How can you believe since you accept glory from one another but do not seek the glory that comes from the only God?

[45]'But do not think I will accuse you before the Father. Your accuser is Moses, on whom your hopes are set. [46]If you believed Moses, you would believe me, for he wrote about me. [47]But since you do not believe what he wrote, how are you going to believe what I say?'

Easier to Pretend

'... you refuse to come to me to have life.' **John 5:40**

In Psalm 42:1, the psalmist states, 'As the deer pants for streams of water, so my soul pants for you, my God.' Why do most Christians not long for God in this way? Because to long for God means we must get in touch with the deep thirst that is at the centre of our being and acknowledge our basic helplessness – a feeling which our fallen human nature deeply dislikes.

Most of us instinctively draw back from dealing with this stubborn commitment to independence, pretending we are all right as we are. It is much easier to pretend we are thirsting after God than it is to face the challenge of giving up our commitment to independence.

I am conscious that the challenge I am putting before you is one I want to deny in my own life. There is something in me that would like to think – and would like you to think – that I have a heart that thirsts for God. But I know that if I stop short of identifying my independent strategies for finding life on my own and giving them up, I will never get in touch with the deep thirst for God that exists at the core of my being.

What is the answer? I must ask God to search my heart, expose my self-centred motivations, and help me see just where it is that I stop short of panting after Him.

You see, the more deeply we sense our thirst, the more passionately we will pursue water. But we will never sense that thirst until we are willing to face the fact that we may be drinking more from our own self-constructed wells than from the wells of God.

PRAYER

Father, I tremble as I recognise this tendency within me to walk right past the fountain of living water and drink from a well of my own making. But help me to recognise it for what it really is – not just a terrible tendency, but a terrible sin. Amen.

FURTHER STUDY

Exod. 32:1–9; Isa. 28:12; 30:15; 2 Chron. 24:19
• How did God describe the children of Israel?
• What is said of them time and time again?

May 23

■ 1 SAMUEL 17:1–58

17 Now the Philistines gathered their forces for war and assembled at Sokoh in Judah. They pitched camp at Ephes Dammim, between Sokoh and Azekah. ² Saul and the Israelites assembled and camped in the Valley of Elah and drew up their battle line to meet the Philistines. ³ The Philistines occupied one hill and the Israelites another, with the valley between them.

⁴ A champion named Goliath, who was from Gath, came out of the Philistine camp. His height was six cubits and a span. ⁵ He had a bronze helmet on his head and wore a coat of scale armour of bronze weighing five thousand shekels; ⁶ on his legs he wore bronze greaves, and a bronze javelin was slung on his back. ⁷ His spear shaft was like a weaver's rod, and its iron point weighed six hundred shekels. His shield-bearer went ahead of him.

⁸ Goliath stood and shouted to the ranks of Israel, 'Why do you come out and line up for battle? Am I not a Philistine, and are you not the servants of Saul? Choose a man and let him come down to me. ⁹ If he is able to fight and kill me, we will become your subjects; but if I overcome him and kill him, you will become our subjects and serve us.' ¹⁰ Then the Philistine said, 'This day I defy the armies of Israel! Give me a man and let us fight each other.' ¹¹ On hearing the Philistine's words, Saul and all the Israelites were dismayed and terrified.

¹² Now David was the son of an Ephrathite named Jesse, who was from Bethlehem in Judah. Jesse had eight sons, and in Saul's time he was very old. ¹³ Jesse's three eldest sons had followed Saul to the war: the firstborn was Eliab; the second, Abinadab; and the third, Shammah. ¹⁴ David was the youngest. The three eldest followed Saul, ¹⁵ but David went back and forth from Saul to tend his father's sheep at Bethlehem.

¹⁶ For forty days the Philistine came forward every morning and evening and took his stand.

¹⁷ Now Jesse said to his son David, 'Take this ephah of roasted grain and these ten loaves of bread for your brothers and hurry to their camp. ¹⁸ Take along these ten cheeses to the commander of their unit. See how your brothers are and bring back some

assurance from them. ¹⁹They are with Saul and all the men of Israel in the Valley of Elah, fighting against the Philistines.'

²⁰Early in the morning David left the flock in the care of a shepherd, loaded up and set out, as Jesse had directed. He reached the camp as the army was going out to its battle positions, shouting the war cry. ²¹Israel and the Philistines were drawing up their lines facing each other. ²²David left his things with the keeper of supplies, ran to the battle lines and asked his brothers how they were. ²³As he was talking with them, Goliath, the Philistine champion from Gath, stepped out from his lines and shouted his usual defiance, and David heard it. ²⁴Whenever the Israelites saw the man, they all fled from him in great fear.

²⁵Now the Israelites had been saying, 'Do you see how this man keeps coming out? He comes out to defy Israel. The king will give great wealth to the man who kills him. He will also give him his daughter in marriage and will exempt his family from taxes in Israel.'

²⁶David asked the men standing near him, 'What will be done for the man who kills this Philistine and removes this disgrace from Israel? Who is this uncircumcised Philistine that he should defy the armies of the living God?'

²⁷They repeated to him what they had been saying and told him, 'This is what will be done for the man who kills him.'

²⁸When Eliab, David's eldest brother, heard him speaking with the men, he burned with anger at him and asked, 'Why have you come down here? And with whom did you leave those few sheep in the wilderness? I know how conceited you are and how wicked your heart is; you came down only to watch the battle.'

²⁹'Now what have I done?' said David. 'Can't I even speak?' ³⁰He then turned away to someone else and brought up the same matter, and the men answered him as before. ³¹What David said was overheard and reported to Saul, and Saul sent for him.

³²David said to Saul, 'Let no one lose heart on account of this Philistine; your servant will go and fight him.'

³³Saul replied, 'You are not able to go out against this Philistine and fight him; you are only a young man, and he has been a warrior from his youth.'

³⁴But David said to Saul, 'Your servant has been keeping his father's sheep. When a lion or a bear came and carried off a sheep from the flock, ³⁵I went after it, struck it and rescued the sheep from its mouth. When it turned on me, I seized it by its hair, struck it and killed it. ³⁶Your servant has killed both the lion and the bear; this uncircumcised Philistine will be like one of them, because he has defied the armies of the living God. ³⁷The LORD who rescued me from the paw of the lion and the paw of the bear will rescue me from the hand of this Philistine.'

Saul said to David, 'Go, and the LORD be with you.'

³⁸Then Saul dressed David in his own tunic. He put a coat of armour on him and a bronze helmet on his head. ³⁹David fastened on his sword over the tunic and tried walking around, because he was not used to them.

'I cannot go in these,' he said to Saul, 'because I am not used to them.' So he took them off. ⁴⁰Then he took his staff in his hand, chose five smooth stones from the stream, put them in the pouch of his shepherd's bag and, with his sling in his hand, approached the Philistine.

⁴¹Meanwhile, the Philistine, with his shield-bearer in front of him, kept coming closer to David. ⁴²He looked David over and saw that he was little more than a boy, glowing with health and handsome, and he despised him. ⁴³He said to David, 'Am I a dog, that you come at me with sticks?' And the Philistine cursed David by his gods. ⁴⁴'Come here,' he said, 'and I'll give your flesh to the birds and the wild animals!'

⁴⁵David said to the Philistine, 'You come against me with sword and spear and javelin, but I come against you in the name of

the LORD Almighty, the God of the armies of Israel, whom you have defied. ⁴⁶This day the LORD will deliver you into my hands, and I'll strike you down and cut off your head. This very day I will give the carcasses of the Philistine army to the birds and the wild animals, and the whole world will know that there is a God in Israel. ⁴⁷All those gathered here will know that it is not by sword or spear that the LORD saves; for the battle is the LORD's, and he will give all of you into our hands.'

⁴⁸As the Philistine moved closer to attack him, David ran quickly towards the battle line to meet him. ⁴⁹Reaching into his bag and taking out a stone, he slung it and struck the Philistine on the forehead. The stone sank into his forehead, and he fell face down on the ground.

⁵⁰So David triumphed over the Philistine with a sling and a stone; without a sword in his hand he struck down the Philistine and killed him.

⁵¹David ran and stood over him. He took hold of the Philistine's sword and drew it from the sheath. After he killed him, he cut off his head with the sword.

When the Philistines saw that their hero was dead, they turned and ran. ⁵²Then the men of Israel and Judah surged forward with a shout and pursued the Philistines to the entrance of Gath and to the gates of Ekron. Their dead were strewn along the Shaaraim road to Gath and Ekron. ⁵³When the Israelites returned from chasing the Philistines, they plundered their camp.

⁵⁴David took the Philistine's head and brought it to Jerusalem; he put the Philistine's weapons in his own tent.

⁵⁵As Saul watched David going out to meet the Philistine, he said to Abner, commander of the army, 'Abner, whose son is that young man?'

Abner replied, 'As surely as you live, Your Majesty, I don't know.'

⁵⁶The king said, 'Find out whose son this young man is.'

⁵⁷As soon as David returned from killing the Philistine, Abner took him and brought him before Saul, with David still holding the Philistine's head.

⁵⁸'Whose son are you, young man?' Saul asked him.

David said, 'I am the son of your servant Jesse of Bethlehem.'

■ PSALM 65:1-8

¹Praise awaits you, our God, in Zion;
   to you our vows will be fulfilled.
²You who answer prayer,
   to you all people will come.
³When we were overwhelmed by sins,
   you forgave our transgressions.
⁴Blessed are those you choose
   and bring near to live in your courts!
We are filled with the good things of
      your house,
   of your holy temple.

⁵You answer us with awesome and
      righteous deeds,
   God our Saviour,
the hope of all the ends of the earth
   and of the farthest seas,
⁶who formed the mountains by your
      power,
   having armed yourself with strength,
⁷who stilled the roaring of the seas,
   the roaring of their waves,
   and the turmoil of the nations.
⁸The whole earth is filled with awe at your
      wonders;
   where morning dawns, where evening
      fades,
   you call forth songs of joy.

■ PROVERBS 14:10-12

¹⁰Each heart knows its own bitterness,
   and no one else can share its joy.

[11] The house of the wicked will be
destroyed,
   but the tent of the upright will
   flourish.

[12] There is a way that appears to be right,
   but in the end it leads to death.

- -

▬ JOHN 6:1-21

6 Some time after this, Jesus crossed to
the far shore of the Sea of Galilee (that
is, the Sea of Tiberias), [2] and a great crowd
of people followed him because they saw
the signs he had performed by healing those
who were ill. [3] Then Jesus went up on a mountainside and sat down with his disciples.
[4] The Jewish Passover Festival was near.

[5] When Jesus looked up and saw a great
crowd coming towards him, he said to
Philip, 'Where shall we buy bread for these
people to eat?' [6] He asked this only to test
him, for he already had in mind what he was
going to do.

[7] Philip answered him, 'It would take
more than half a year's wages to buy enough
bread for each one to have a bite!'

[8] Another of his disciples, Andrew, Simon
Peter's brother, spoke up, [9] 'Here is a boy with
five small barley loaves and two small fish,
but how far will they go among so many?'

[10] Jesus said, 'Make the people sit down.'
There was plenty of grass in that place, and
they sat down (about five thousand men
were there). [11] Jesus then took the loaves,
gave thanks, and distributed to those who
were seated as much as they wanted. He did
the same with the fish.

[12] When they had all had enough to eat, he
said to his disciples, 'Gather the pieces that
are left over. Let nothing be wasted.' [13] So
they gathered them and filled twelve baskets with the pieces of the five barley loaves
left over by those who had eaten.

[14] After the people saw the sign Jesus performed, they began to say, 'Surely this is
the Prophet who is to come into the world.'
[15] Jesus, knowing that they intended to come
and make him king by force, withdrew
again to a mountain by himself.

[16] When evening came, his disciples went
down to the lake, [17] where they got into a
boat and set off across the lake for Capernaum. By now it was dark, and Jesus had not
yet joined them. [18] A strong wind was blowing and the waters grew rough. [19] When they
had rowed about three or four miles, they
saw Jesus approaching the boat, walking on
the water; and they were frightened. [20] But
he said to them, 'It is I; don't be afraid.'
[21] Then they were willing to take him into
the boat, and immediately the boat reached
the shore where they were heading.

Two Opposite Pairs

'There is a way that appears to be right, but in the end
it leads to death.' **Proverbs 14:12**

I have met many people who have experienced such deep hurt in their
early relationships that they cannot rid themselves of negative ideas
about having God as their Father, and by God's grace I have been able to
help some of them. But the route to healing is not an easy one and
involves walking a path that is quite different from the one a secular
counsellor might suggest.

The route which the world usually advises victims of parental abuse to take consists of three steps: self-discovery, self-expression, and self-protection. Self-discovery is where the victim is encouraged to get in touch with his or her repressed emotions. Self-expression is the release and expression of those emotions. Self-protection is the establishment of boundaries around one's life so that one will never have to endure or experience serious hurt again.

The biblical route to healing, while recognising some truth in these ideas, starts from a different base and leads to a different goal. It begins with the question: Do I believe that a God who allowed me to be as deeply hurt as I was is good? And it ends with the question: Am I willing to give myself to those I am called to love and to be more interested in loving well than in protecting myself against hurt?

Which sounds like the easier path of these two? Undoubtedly, the way of the world. The way of Christ may seem as if it is the route to death, but really it is the route to life. To live we must be willing to die; to find we must be willing to lose.

PRAYER

Father, help me take Your way in everything I pray. I don't want symptom relief; I want a complete cure. And if I don't need help on this particular issue, help me learn how to be of help to others. Amen.

FURTHER STUDY

Matt. 5:43-48; 7:13-14; 16:24-25; John 12:24-25
• What is the biblical way to life?
• What makes the narrow way narrow?

May 24

▬ 1 SAMUEL 18:1–19:24

18 After David had finished talking with Saul, Jonathan became one in spirit with David, and he loved him as himself. ²From that day Saul kept David with him and did not let him return home to his family. ³And Jonathan made a covenant with David because he loved him as himself. ⁴Jonathan took off the robe he was wearing and gave it to David, along with his tunic, and even his sword, his bow and his belt.

⁵Whatever mission Saul sent him on, David was so successful that Saul gave him a high rank in the army. This pleased all the troops, and Saul's officers as well.

⁶When the men were returning home after David had killed the Philistine, the women came out from all the towns of Israel to meet King Saul with singing and dancing, with joyful songs and with tambourines and lyres. ⁷As they danced, they sang:

'Saul has slain his thousands,
and David his tens of thousands.'

⁸Saul was very angry; this refrain displeased him greatly. 'They have credited David with tens of thousands,' he thought, 'but me with only thousands. What more can he get but the kingdom?' ⁹And from that time on Saul kept a close eye on David.

¹⁰The next day an evil spirit from God came forcefully on Saul. He was prophesying in his house, while David was playing the lyre, as he usually did. Saul had a spear in his hand ¹¹and he hurled it, saying to himself, 'I'll pin David to the wall.' But David eluded him twice.

¹²Saul was afraid of David, because the LORD was with David but had departed from Saul. ¹³So he sent David away from him and gave him command over a thousand men, and David led the troops in their campaigns. ¹⁴In everything he did he had great success, because the LORD was with him. ¹⁵When Saul saw how successful he was, he was afraid of him. ¹⁶But all Israel and Judah loved David, because he led them in their campaigns.

¹⁷Saul said to David, 'Here is my elder daughter Merab. I will give her to you in marriage; only serve me bravely and fight the battles of the LORD.' For Saul said to himself, 'I will not raise a hand against him. Let the Philistines do that!'

¹⁸But David said to Saul, 'Who am I, and what is my family or my clan in Israel, that I should become the king's son-in-law?' ¹⁹So when the time came for Merab, Saul's daughter, to be given to David, she was given in marriage to Adriel of Meholah.

²⁰Now Saul's daughter Michal was in love with David, and when they told Saul about it, he was pleased. ²¹'I will give her to him,' he thought, 'so that she may be a snare to him and so that the hand of the Philistines may be against him.' So Saul said to David, 'Now you have a second opportunity to become my son-in-law.'

²²Then Saul ordered his attendants: 'Speak to David privately and say, "Look, the king likes you, and his attendants all love you; now become his son-in-law."'

²³They repeated these words to David. But David said, 'Do you think it is a small matter to become the king's son-in-law? I'm only a poor man and little known.'

²⁴When Saul's servants told him what David had said, ²⁵Saul replied, 'Say to David, "The king wants no other price for the bride than a hundred Philistine foreskins, to take revenge on his enemies."' Saul's plan was for David to fall by the hands of the Philistines.

²⁶When the attendants told David these things, he was pleased to become the king's son-in-law. So before the allotted time elapsed, ²⁷David took his men with him and went out and killed two hundred Philistines and brought back their foreskins. They counted out the full number to the king so that David might become the king's son-in-law. Then Saul gave him his daughter Michal in marriage.

²⁸When Saul realised that the LORD was with David and that his daughter Michal loved David, ²⁹Saul became still more afraid of him, and he remained his enemy for the rest of his days.

³⁰The Philistine commanders continued to go out to battle, and as often as they did, David met with more success than the rest of Saul's officers, and his name became well known.

19 Saul told his son Jonathan and all the attendants to kill David. But Jonathan had taken a great liking to David ²and warned him, 'My father Saul is looking for a chance to kill you. Be on your guard tomorrow morning; go into hiding and stay there. ³I will go out and stand with my father in the field where you are. I'll speak to him about you and will tell you what I find out.'

⁴Jonathan spoke well of David to Saul his father and said to him, 'Let not the king do wrong to his servant David; he has not wronged you, and what he has done has benefited you greatly. ⁵He took his life in his hands when he killed the Philistine. The LORD won a great victory for all Israel, and you saw it and were glad. Why then would you do wrong to an innocent man like David by killing him for no reason?'

⁶Saul listened to Jonathan and took this oath: 'As surely as the LORD lives, David will

not be put to death.'

⁷So Jonathan called David and told him the whole conversation. He brought him to Saul, and David was with Saul as before.

⁸Once more war broke out, and David went out and fought the Philistines. He struck them with such force that they fled before him.

⁹But an evil spirit from the Lord came on Saul as he was sitting in his house with his spear in his hand. While David was playing the lyre, ¹⁰Saul tried to pin him to the wall with his spear, but David eluded him as Saul drove the spear into the wall. That night David made good his escape.

¹¹Saul sent men to David's house to watch it and to kill him in the morning. But Michal, David's wife, warned him, 'If you don't run for your life tonight, tomorrow you'll be killed.' ¹²So Michal let David down through a window, and he fled and escaped. ¹³Then Michal took an idol and laid it on the bed, covering it with a garment and putting some goats' hair at the head.

¹⁴When Saul sent the men to capture David, Michal said, 'He is ill.'

¹⁵Then Saul sent the men back to see David and told them, 'Bring him up to me in his bed so that I may kill him.' ¹⁶But when the men entered, there was the idol in the bed, and at the head was some goats' hair.

¹⁷Saul said to Michal, 'Why did you deceive me like this and send my enemy away so that he escaped?'

Michal told him, 'He said to me, "Let me get away. Why should I kill you?"'

¹⁸When David had fled and made his escape, he went to Samuel at Ramah and told him all that Saul had done to him. Then he and Samuel went to Naioth and stayed there. ¹⁹Word came to Saul: 'David is in Naioth at Ramah'; ²⁰so he sent men to capture him. But when they saw a group of prophets prophesying, with Samuel standing there as their leader, the Spirit of God came on Saul's men, and they also prophesied. ²¹Saul was told about

it, and he sent more men, and they prophesied too. Saul sent men a third time, and they also prophesied. ²²Finally, he himself left for Ramah and went to the great cistern at Seku. And he asked, 'Where are Samuel and David?'

'Over in Naioth at Ramah,' they said.

²³So Saul went to Naioth at Ramah. But the Spirit of God came even on him, and he walked along prophesying until he came to Naioth. ²⁴He stripped off his garments, and he too prophesied in Samuel's presence. He lay naked all that day and all that night. This is why people say, 'Is Saul also among the prophets?'

▬ Psalm 65:9-13

⁹You care for the land and water it;
  you enrich it abundantly.
The streams of God are filled with water
  to provide the people with corn,
  for so you have ordained it.
¹⁰You drench its furrows and level its
    ridges;
  you soften it with showers and bless its
    crops.
¹¹You crown the year with your bounty,
  and your carts overflow with
    abundance.
¹²The grasslands of the wilderness
    overflow;
  the hills are clothed with gladness.
¹³The meadows are covered with flocks
  and the valleys are mantled with corn;
  they shout for joy and sing.

▬ Proverbs 14:13-14

¹³Even in laughter the heart may ache,
  and rejoicing may end in grief.

¹⁴The faithless will be fully repaid for their
    ways,
  and the good rewarded for theirs.

■ JOHN 6:22-40

²²The next day the crowd that had stayed on the opposite shore of the lake realised that only one boat had been there, and that Jesus had not entered it with his disciples, but that they had gone away alone. ²³Then some boats from Tiberias landed near the place where the people had eaten the bread after the Lord had given thanks. ²⁴Once the crowd realised that neither Jesus nor his disciples were there, they got into the boats and went to Capernaum in search of Jesus.

²⁵When they found him on the other side of the lake, they asked him, 'Rabbi, when did you get here?'

²⁶Jesus answered, 'Very truly I tell you, you are looking for me, not because you saw the signs I performed but because you ate the loaves and had your fill. ²⁷Do not work for food that spoils, but for food that endures to eternal life, which the Son of Man will give you. For on him God the Father has placed his seal of approval.'

²⁸Then they asked him, 'What must we do to do the works God requires?'

²⁹Jesus answered, 'The work of God is this: to believe in the one he has sent.'

³⁰So they asked him, 'What sign then will you give that we may see it and believe you? What will you do? ³¹Our ancestors ate the manna in the wilderness; as it is written: "He gave them bread from heaven to eat." '

³²Jesus said to them, 'Very truly I tell you, it is not Moses who has given you the bread from heaven, but it is my Father who gives you the true bread from heaven. ³³For the bread of God is the bread that comes down from heaven and gives life to the world.'

³⁴'Sir,' they said, 'always give us this bread.'

³⁵Then Jesus declared, 'I am the bread of life. Whoever comes to me will never go hungry, and whoever believes in me will never be thirsty. ³⁶But as I told you, you have seen me and still you do not believe. ³⁷All those the Father gives me will come to me, and whoever comes to me I will never drive away. ³⁸For I have come down from heaven not to do my will but to do the will of him who sent me. ³⁹And this is the will of him who sent me, that I shall lose none of all those he has given me, but raise them up at the last day. ⁴⁰For my Father's will is that everyone who looks to the Son and believes in him shall have eternal life, and I will raise them up at the last day.'

He Can't Forget!

'Jesus answered, "The work of God is this: to believe in the one he has sent."' **John 6:29**

In this passage, our Lord is asked, 'What must we do to do the works God requires?' (v.28). His answer was entirely different from that which you would receive if you posed the question to adherents of different religious systems today. A Buddhist would answer, 'We must follow the eightfold path of Buddhism.' A Muslim would answer, 'We must fast and pray and make a trip to Mecca.' Some followers of the Christian way might answer, 'We must engage in regular Bible study, prayer, tithing, and Christian fellowship.' But the answer Jesus gave was, 'This is the work of God: that you believe ...'

George Watson, a devotional writer, said, 'To trust the Origin of our existence is the fundamental grace of life. There is one virtue [in God] that stands out forever more conspicuously than friendship, or love, or knowledge, or wisdom. It is fidelity. God's fidelity is in Him what trust is in us.'

Understanding that God is utterly trustworthy will deliver us from such incapacitating emotions as worry, anxiety and fear. To be overwhelmed by the concerns of this life reflects poorly upon the faithfulness of God.

An old saint who was dying became concerned that he couldn't remember any of God's promises. His pastor said, 'Do you think God will forget any of them?' A smile came over the face of the dying Christian as he exclaimed joyfully, 'No, no, He won't.' This, too, is our confidence. He won't forget, because being God, He can't forget.

PRAYER

O God my Father, if fidelity in You is what trust is in us, then help us come to a place where our trust matches Your fidelity. We confess we are not there yet, but we long to arrive. Help us, dear Father. In Jesus' name. Amen.

FURTHER STUDY

2 Tim. 2:1-13; Heb. 2:17; 10:23
- What did Paul assure Timothy?
- Why was Jesus made like His brothers?

May 25

■ 1 SAMUEL 20:1–21:15

20 Then David fled from Naioth at Ramah and went to Jonathan and asked, 'What have I done? What is my crime? How have I wronged your father, that he is trying to kill me?'

² 'Never!' Jonathan replied. 'You are not going to die! Look, my father doesn't do anything, great or small, without letting me know. Why should he hide this from me? It isn't so!'

³ But David took an oath and said, 'Your father knows very well that I have found favour in your eyes, and he has said to himself, "Jonathan must not know this or he will be grieved." Yet as surely as the LORD lives and as you live, there is only a step between me and death.'

⁴ Jonathan said to David, 'Whatever you want me to do, I'll do for you.'

⁵ So David said, 'Look, tomorrow is the New Moon feast, and I am supposed to dine with the king; but let me go and hide in the field until the evening of the day after tomorrow. ⁶ If your father misses me at all, tell him, "David earnestly asked my permission to hurry to Bethlehem, his home town, because an annual sacrifice is being made there for his whole clan." ⁷ If he says, "Very well," then your servant is safe. But if he loses his temper, you can be sure that he is determined to harm me. ⁸ As for you, show kindness to your servant, for you have brought him into a covenant with you before the LORD. If I am guilty, then kill me yourself! Why hand me over to your father?'

⁹ 'Never!' Jonathan said. 'If I had the least inkling that my father was determined to harm you, wouldn't I tell you?'

¹⁰ David asked, 'Who will tell me if your father answers you harshly?'

11 'Come,' Jonathan said, 'let's go out into the field.' So they went there together.

12 Then Jonathan said to David, 'I swear by the LORD, the God of Israel, that I will surely sound out my father by this time the day after tomorrow! If he is favourably disposed towards you, will I not send you word and let you know? 13 But if my father intends to harm you, may the LORD deal with me, be it ever so severely, if I do not let you know and send you away in peace. May the LORD be with you as he has been with my father. 14 But show me unfailing kindness like the LORD's kindness as long as I live, so that I may not be killed, 15 and do not ever cut off your kindness from my family – not even when the LORD has cut off every one of David's enemies from the face of the earth.'

16 So Jonathan made a covenant with the house of David, saying, 'May the LORD call David's enemies to account.' 17 And Jonathan made David reaffirm his oath out of love for him, because he loved him as he loved himself.

18 Then Jonathan said to David, 'Tomorrow is the New Moon feast. You will be missed, because your seat will be empty. 19 The day after tomorrow, towards evening, go to the place where you hid when this trouble began, and wait by the stone Ezel. 20 I will shoot three arrows to the side of it, as though I were shooting at a target. 21 Then I will send a boy and say, "Go, find the arrows." If I say to him, "Look, the arrows are on this side of you; bring them here," then come, because, as surely as the LORD lives, you are safe; there is no danger. 22 But if I say to the boy, "Look, the arrows are beyond you," then you must go, because the LORD has sent you away. 23 And about the matter you and I discussed – remember, the LORD is witness between you and me for ever.'

24 So David hid in the field, and when the New Moon feast came, the king sat down to eat. 25 He sat in his customary place by the wall, opposite Jonathan, and Abner sat next to Saul, but David's place was empty. 26 Saul said nothing that day, for he thought, 'Something must have happened to David to make him ceremonially unclean – surely he is unclean.' 27 But the next day, the second day of the month, David's place was empty again. Then Saul said to his son Jonathan, 'Why hasn't the son of Jesse come to the meal, either yesterday or today?'

28 Jonathan answered, 'David earnestly asked me for permission to go to Bethlehem. 29 He said, "Let me go, because our family is observing a sacrifice in the town and my brother has ordered me to be there. If I have found favour in your eyes, let me go to see my brothers." That is why he has not come to the king's table.'

30 Saul's anger flared up at Jonathan and he said to him, 'You son of a perverse and rebellious woman! Don't I know that you have sided with the son of Jesse to your own shame and to the shame of the mother who bore you? 31 As long as the son of Jesse lives on this earth, neither you nor your kingdom will be established. Now send someone to bring him to me, for he must die!'

32 'Why should he be put to death? What has he done?' Jonathan asked his father. 33 But Saul hurled his spear at him to kill him. Then Jonathan knew that his father intended to kill David.

34 Jonathan got up from the table in fierce anger; on that second day of the feast he did not eat, because he was grieved at his father's shameful treatment of David.

35 In the morning Jonathan went out to the field for his meeting with David. He had a small boy with him, 36 and he said to the boy, 'Run and find the arrows I shoot.' As the boy ran, he shot an arrow beyond him. 37 When the boy came to the place where Jonathan's arrow had fallen, Jonathan called out after him, 'Isn't the arrow beyond you?' 38 Then he shouted, 'Hurry! Go quickly! Don't stop!' The boy picked up the arrow and returned to his master.

³⁹(The boy knew nothing about all this; only Jonathan and David knew.) ⁴⁰Then Jonathan gave his weapons to the boy and said, 'Go, carry them back to town.'

⁴¹After the boy had gone, David got up from the south side of the stone and bowed down before Jonathan three times, with his face to the ground. Then they kissed each other and wept together – but David wept the most.

⁴²Jonathan said to David, 'Go in peace, for we have sworn friendship with each other in the name of the LORD, saying, "The LORD is witness between you and me, and between your descendants and my descendants for ever."' Then David left, and Jonathan went back to the town.

21 David went to Nob, to Ahimelek the priest. Ahimelek trembled when he met him, and asked, 'Why are you alone? Why is no one with you?'

²David answered Ahimelek the priest, 'The king sent me on a mission and said to me, "No one is to know anything about the mission I am sending you on." As for my men, I have told them to meet me at a certain place. ³Now then, what have you to hand? Give me five loaves of bread, or whatever you can find.'

⁴But the priest answered David, 'I don't have any ordinary bread to hand; however, there is some consecrated bread here – provided the men have kept themselves from women.'

⁵David replied, 'Indeed women have been kept from us, as usual whenever I set out. The men's bodies are holy even on missions that are not holy. How much more so today!' ⁶So the priest gave him the consecrated bread, since there was no bread there except the bread of the Presence that had been removed from before the LORD and replaced by hot bread on the day it was taken away.

⁷Now one of Saul's servants was there that day, detained before the LORD; he was Doeg the Edomite, Saul's chief shepherd.

⁸David asked Ahimelek, 'Don't you have a spear or sword here? I haven't brought my sword or any other weapon, because the king's mission was urgent.'

⁹The priest replied, 'The sword of Goliath the Philistine, whom you killed in the Valley of Elah, is here; it is wrapped in a cloth behind the ephod. If you want it, take it; there is no sword here but that one.'

David said, 'There is none like it; give it to me.'

¹⁰That day David fled from Saul and went to Achish king of Gath. ¹¹But the servants of Achish said to him, 'Isn't this David, the king of the land? Isn't he the one they sing about in their dances:

'"Saul has slain his thousands,
    and David his tens of thousands"?'

¹²David took these words to heart and was very much afraid of Achish king of Gath. ¹³So he feigned insanity in their presence; and while he was in their hands he acted like a madman, making marks on the doors of the gate and letting saliva run down his beard.

¹⁴Achish said to his servants, 'Look at the man! He is insane! Why bring him to me? ¹⁵Am I so short of madmen that you have to bring this fellow here to carry on like this in front of me? Must this man come into my house?'

··

■ **PSALM 66:1-7**

¹Shout for joy to God, all the earth!
²   Sing the glory of his name;
        make his praise glorious.
³Say to God, 'How awesome are your deeds!
        So great is your power
        that your enemies cringe before you.
⁴All the earth bows down to you;
        they sing praise to you,
        they sing the praises of your name.'

⁵ Come and see what God has done,
his awesome deeds for mankind!
⁶ He turned the sea into dry land,
they passed through the waters on
foot –
come, let us rejoice in him.
⁷ He rules for ever by his power,
his eyes watch the nations –
let not the rebellious rise up against him.

PROVERBS 14:15-16

¹⁵ The simple believe anything,
but the prudent give thought to their
steps.

¹⁶ The wise fear the LORD and shun evil,
but a fool is hotheaded and yet feels
secure.

JOHN 6:41-59

⁴¹ At this the Jews there began to grumble about him because he said, 'I am the bread that came down from heaven.' ⁴² They said, 'Is this not Jesus, the son of Joseph, whose father and mother we know? How can he now say, "I came down from heaven"?' ⁴³ 'Stop grumbling among yourselves,' Jesus answered. ⁴⁴ 'No one can come to me unless the Father who sent me draws them, and I will raise them up at the last day.

⁴⁵ It is written in the Prophets: "They will all be taught by God." Everyone who has heard the Father and learned from him comes to me. ⁴⁶ No one has seen the Father except the one who is from God; only he has seen the Father. ⁴⁷ Very truly I tell you, the one who believes has eternal life. ⁴⁸ I am the bread of life. ⁴⁹ Your ancestors ate the manna in the wilderness, yet they died. ⁵⁰ But here is the bread that comes down from heaven, which anyone may eat and not die. ⁵¹ I am the living bread that came down from heaven. Whoever eats this bread will live for ever. This bread is my flesh, which I will give for the life of the world.'

⁵² Then the Jews began to argue sharply among themselves, 'How can this man give us his flesh to eat?'

⁵³ Jesus said to them, 'Very truly I tell you, unless you eat the flesh of the Son of Man and drink his blood, you have no life in you. ⁵⁴ Whoever eats my flesh and drinks my blood has eternal life, and I will raise them up at the last day. ⁵⁵ For my flesh is real food and my blood is real drink. ⁵⁶ Whoever eats my flesh and drinks my blood remains in me, and I in them. ⁵⁷ Just as the living Father sent me and I live because of the Father, so the one who feeds on me will live because of me. ⁵⁸ This is the bread that came down from heaven. Your ancestors ate manna and died, but whoever feeds on this bread will live for ever.' ⁵⁹ He said this while teaching in the synagogue in Capernaum.

'As Good as Your Book'

'I am the living bread that came down from heaven. Whoever eats this bread will live for ever.' **John 6:51**

A Hindu said to a missionary in India, 'Sir, I do not want to appear presumptuous, but have you found out what the Acts of the Apostles records? I see there a strange power, making weak, ineffective men into strong, effective, radiant men. That seems new and central – have you found that?' And that is the central question we must ask ourselves. We are taken up with so many little and marginal things in church life that we miss the central power.

A group of children, on the way to see the ocean, got occupied with a pond that one of them had made by blocking the flow of a tiny stream. One little fellow, seeing the ocean in the distance, said, 'Come on, Billy, that ain't the ocean – that's only a pond!'

Sometimes I feel like calling to the thousands of Christians who are gathered around their little denominational pools, thinking them to be the ocean, 'Come on, brothers and sisters, that isn't the whole thing. Look over there. The ocean awaits us – God's ocean of power and plenty. I'll race you to it!'

A Christian who gave a Bible to an acquaintance asked him some time later if he had read it. 'Yes,' said the man, 'and what is more, I have found you out. You are not as good as your Book! The Book says there is power for human weakness, joy instead of sorrow, victory instead of defeat – but I see little of this in you.' What an indictment! Could the same be said of you and me?

PRAYER

O Father, help me to be as good as the Book. Show me the way to power and poise, so that I will represent the highest qualities of life to those I live with or work with. For Jesus' sake. Amen.

FURTHER STUDY

John 6:44-71; Rev. 2:4, 3:16; Matt. 24:12; Acts 5:13
• How did some of Jesus' disciples respond?
• What did Simon Peter say?

May 26

■ 1 SAMUEL 22:1–23:29

22 David left Gath and escaped to the cave of Adullam. When his brothers and his father's household heard about it, they went down to him there. ²All those who were in distress or in debt or discontented gathered round him, and he became their commander. About four hundred men were with him.

³From there David went to Mizpah in Moab and said to the king of Moab, 'Would you let my father and mother come and stay with you until I learn what God will do for me?' ⁴So he left them with the king of Moab,

and they stayed with him as long as David was in the stronghold.

⁵But the prophet Gad said to David, 'Do not stay in the stronghold. Go into the land of Judah.' So David left and went to the forest of Hereth.

⁶Now Saul heard that David and his men had been discovered. And Saul was seated, spear in hand, under the tamarisk tree on the hill at Gibeah, with all his officials standing at his side. ⁷He said to them, 'Listen, men of Benjamin! Will the son of Jesse give all of you fields and vineyards? Will he make all of you commanders of thousands and commanders of hundreds? ⁸Is that why

you have all conspired against me? No one tells me when my son makes a covenant with the son of Jesse. None of you is concerned about me or tells me that my son has incited my servant to lie in wait for me, as he does today.'

⁹But Doeg the Edomite, who was standing with Saul's officials, said, 'I saw the son of Jesse come to Ahimelek son of Ahitub at Nob. ¹⁰Ahimelek enquired of the LORD for him; he also gave him provisions and the sword of Goliath the Philistine.'

¹¹Then the king sent for the priest Ahimelek son of Ahitub and all the men of his family, who were the priests at Nob, and they all came to the king. ¹²Saul said, 'Listen now, son of Ahitub.'

'Yes, my lord,' he answered.

¹³Saul said to him, 'Why have you conspired against me, you and the son of Jesse, giving him bread and a sword and enquiring of God for him, so that he has rebelled against me and lies in wait for me, as he does today?'

¹⁴Ahimelek answered the king, 'Who of all your servants is as loyal as David, the king's son-in-law, captain of your bodyguard and highly respected in your household? ¹⁵Was that day the first time I enquired of God for him? Of course not! Let not the king accuse your servant or any of his father's family, for your servant knows nothing at all about this whole affair.'

¹⁶But the king said, 'You shall surely die, Ahimelek, you and your whole family.'

¹⁷Then the king ordered the guards at his side: 'Turn and kill the priests of the LORD, because they too have sided with David. They knew he was fleeing, yet they did not tell me.'

But the king's officials were unwilling to raise a hand to strike the priests of the LORD.

¹⁸The king then ordered Doeg, 'You turn and strike down the priests.' So Doeg the Edomite turned and struck them down. That day he killed eighty-five men who wore the linen ephod. ¹⁹He also put to the sword Nob, the town of the priests, with its men and women, its children and infants, and its cattle, donkeys and sheep.

²⁰But one son of Ahimelek son of Ahitub, named Abiathar, escaped and fled to join David. ²¹He told David that Saul had killed the priests of the LORD. ²²Then David said to Abiathar, 'That day, when Doeg the Edomite was there, I knew he would be sure to tell Saul. I am responsible for the death of your whole family. ²³Stay with me; don't be afraid. The man who wants to kill you is trying to kill me too. You will be safe with me.'

23 When David was told, 'Look, the Philistines are fighting against Keilah and are looting the threshing-floors,' ²he enquired of the LORD, saying, 'Shall I go and attack these Philistines?'

The LORD answered him, 'Go, attack the Philistines and save Keilah.'

³But David's men said to him, 'Here in Judah we are afraid. How much more, then, if we go to Keilah against the Philistine forces!'

⁴Once again David enquired of the LORD, and the LORD answered him, 'Go down to Keilah, for I am going to give the Philistines into your hand.' ⁵So David and his men went to Keilah, fought the Philistines and carried off their livestock. He inflicted heavy losses on the Philistines and saved the people of Keilah. ⁶(Now Abiathar son of Ahimelek had brought the ephod down with him when he fled to David at Keilah.)

⁷Saul was told that David had gone to Keilah, and he said, 'God has delivered him into my hands, for David has imprisoned himself by entering a town with gates and bars.' ⁸And Saul called up all his forces for battle, to go down to Keilah to besiege David and his men.

⁹When David learned that Saul was plotting against him, he said to Abiathar the priest, 'Bring the ephod.' ¹⁰David said, 'LORD,

God of Israel, your servant has heard definitely that Saul plans to come to Keilah and destroy the town on account of me. ¹¹ Will the citizens of Keilah surrender me to him? Will Saul come down, as your servant has heard? Lord, God of Israel, tell your servant.'

And the Lord said, 'He will.'

¹² Again David asked, 'Will the citizens of Keilah surrender me and my men to Saul?'

And the Lord said, 'They will.'

¹³ So David and his men, about six hundred in number, left Keilah and kept moving from place to place. When Saul was told that David had escaped from Keilah, he did not go there.

¹⁴ David stayed in the wilderness strongholds and in the hills of the Desert of Ziph. Day after day Saul searched for him, but God did not give David into his hands.

¹⁵ While David was at Horesh in the Desert of Ziph, he learned that Saul had come out to take his life. ¹⁶ And Saul's son Jonathan went to David at Horesh and helped him to find strength in God. ¹⁷ 'Don't be afraid,' he said. 'My father Saul will not lay a hand on you. You shall be king over Israel, and I will be second to you. Even my father Saul knows this.' ¹⁸ The two of them made a covenant before the Lord. Then Jonathan went home, but David remained at Horesh.

¹⁹ The Ziphites went up to Saul at Gibeah and said, 'Is not David hiding among us in the strongholds at Horesh, on the hill of Hakilah, south of Jeshimon? ²⁰ Now, Your Majesty, come down whenever it pleases you to do so, and we will be responsible for giving him into your hands.'

²¹ Saul replied, 'The Lord bless you for your concern for me. ²² Go and get more information. Find out where David usually goes and who has seen him there. They tell me he is very crafty. ²³ Find out about all the hiding-places he uses and come back to me with definite information. Then I will go with you; if he is in the area, I will track him down among all the clans of Judah.'

²⁴ So they set out and went to Ziph ahead of Saul. Now David and his men were in the Desert of Maon, in the Arabah south of Jeshimon. ²⁵ Saul and his men began the search, and when David was told about it, he went down to the rock and stayed in the Desert of Maon. When Saul heard this, he went into the Desert of Maon in pursuit of David.

²⁶ Saul was going along one side of the mountain, and David and his men were on the other side, hurrying to get away from Saul. As Saul and his forces were closing in on David and his men to capture them, ²⁷ a messenger came to Saul, saying, 'Come quickly! The Philistines are raiding the land.' ²⁸ Then Saul broke off his pursuit of David and went to meet the Philistines. That is why they call this place Sela Hammahlekoth. ²⁹ And David went up from there and lived in the strongholds of En Gedi.

··

▬ Psalm 66:8-15

⁸ Praise our God, all peoples,
    let the sound of his praise be heard;
⁹ he has preserved our lives
    and kept our feet from slipping.
¹⁰ For you, God, tested us;
    you refined us like silver.
¹¹ You brought us into prison
    and laid burdens on our backs.
¹² You let people ride over our heads;
    we went through fire and water,
    but you brought us to a place of
       abundance.

¹³ I will come to your temple with burnt
       offerings
    and fulfil my vows to you –
¹⁴ vows my lips promised and my mouth
       spoke
    when I was in trouble.
¹⁵ I will sacrifice fat animals to you
    and an offering of rams;
    I will offer bulls and goats.

■ PROVERBS 14:17-19

¹⁷ A quick-tempered person does foolish
    things,
    and the one who devises evil schemes
        is hated.

¹⁸ The simple inherit folly,
    but the prudent are crowned with
        knowledge.

¹⁹ Evildoers will bow down in the presence
        of the good,
    and the wicked at the gates of the
        righteous.

■ JOHN 6:60-7:9

⁶⁰ On hearing it, many of his disciples
said, 'This is a hard teaching. Who can
accept it?'
    ⁶¹ Aware that his disciples were grum-
bling about this, Jesus said to them, 'Does
this offend you? ⁶² Then what if you see the
Son of Man ascend to where he was before!
⁶³ The Spirit gives life; the flesh counts for
nothing. The words I have spoken to you –
they are full of the Spirit and life. ⁶⁴ Yet there
are some of you who do not believe.' For
Jesus had known from the beginning which
of them did not believe and who would betray him. ⁶⁵ He went on to say, 'This is why I
told you that no one can come to me unless

the Father has enabled them.'
    ⁶⁶ From this time many of his disciples
turned back and no longer followed him.
    ⁶⁷ 'You do not want to leave too, do you?'
Jesus asked the Twelve.
    ⁶⁸ Simon Peter answered him, 'Lord, to
whom shall we go? You have the words of
eternal life. ⁶⁹ We have come to believe and
to know that you are the Holy One of God.'
    ⁷⁰ Then Jesus replied, 'Have I not chosen
you, the Twelve? Yet one of you is a devil!'
⁷¹ (He meant Judas, the son of Simon Iscariot, who, though one of the Twelve, was later
to betray him.)

7 After this, Jesus went around in Galilee. He did not want to go about in Judea because the Jewish leaders there were
looking for a way to kill him. ² But when the
Jewish Festival of Tabernacles was near,
³ Jesus' brothers said to him, 'Leave Galilee
and go to Judea, so that your disciples there
may see the works you do. ⁴ No one who
wants to become a public figure acts in secret. Since you are doing these things, show
yourself to the world.' ⁵ For even his own
brothers did not believe in him.
    ⁶ Therefore Jesus told them, 'My time is
not yet here; for you any time will do. ⁷ The
world cannot hate you, but it hates me because I testify that its works are evil. ⁸ You
go to the festival. I am not going up to this
festival, because my time has not yet fully
come.' ⁹ After he had said this, he stayed in
Galilee.

Spirit-Aided Praying

'The Spirit gives life ...' **John 6:63**

The more I consider 'praying in the Spirit', the more convinced I am
that the majority of Christians do not know what it means to pray in
this particular way. Many are content to recite prayers and know nothing
of the thrill of entering a dimension of prayer in which the Holy Spirit has
full control.
    Not that there is anything wrong with liturgical or written prayers –

they can be a wonderful primer for one's spiritual pump. Many people tell me that the prayers I frame at the end of each devotion in *Every Day with Jesus* have sometimes helped them more than the actual notes I have written. Using written prayers can be helpful, but we must heed the apostle's exhortation to move on into that dimension which he calls 'praying in the Spirit'. The best description of this I have ever heard is that given by some of the old Welsh preachers, like Daniel Rowlands, Christmas Evans and others. They describe it as 'praying with unusual liberty and freedom'.

There is hardly anything more wonderful in the Christian life than to experience this 'liberty and freedom' in prayer. I can remember the minister and elders of the church in which I was converted in South Wales saying after a prayer meeting in which there had been great liberty and power, 'Tonight we have prayed in the Spirit'.

Have you not experienced moments when, after struggling and halting in prayer, you were suddenly taken out of yourself and words just poured out of you? At that moment, you were 'praying in the Spirit'.

PRAYER

O Father, forgive me that I try to do so much in my own strength instead of learning how to let You do it in me. Teach me how to let go and let You take over in everything – particularly my praying. In Jesus' name. Amen.

FURTHER STUDY

2 Cor. 3:6-18; Matt. 6:7-8; 1 Cor. 14:15; Jude 20
- What does the Spirit of the Lord bring?
- What are we to avoid when we pray?

May 27

▬ 1 SAMUEL 24:1-25:44

24 After Saul returned from pursuing the Philistines, he was told, 'David is in the Desert of En Gedi.' ²So Saul took three thousand able young men from all Israel and set out to look for David and his men near the Crags of the Wild Goats.

³He came to the sheepfolds along the way; a cave was there, and Saul went in to relieve himself. David and his men were far back in the cave. ⁴The men said, 'This is the day the LORD spoke of when he said to you, "I will give your enemy into your hands for you to

deal with as you wish."' Then David crept up unnoticed and cut off a corner of Saul's robe.

⁵Afterwards, David was conscience-stricken for having cut off a corner of his robe. ⁶He said to his men, 'The LORD forbid that I should do such a thing to my master, the LORD's anointed, or lay my hand on him; for he is the anointed of the LORD.' ⁷With these words David sharply rebuked his men and did not allow them to attack Saul. And Saul left the cave and went his way.

⁸Then David went out of the cave and called out to Saul, 'My lord the king!' When Saul looked behind him, David bowed down

and prostrated himself with his face to the ground. [9] He said to Saul, 'Why do you listen when men say, "David is bent on harming you"? [10] This day you have seen with your own eyes how the LORD gave you into my hands in the cave. Some urged me to kill you, but I spared you; I said, "I will not lay my hand on my lord, because he is the LORD's anointed." [11] See, my father, look at this piece of your robe in my hand! I cut off the corner of your robe but did not kill you. See that there is nothing in my hand to indicate that I am guilty of wrongdoing or rebellion. I have not wronged you, but you are hunting me down to take my life. [12] May the LORD judge between you and me. And may the LORD avenge the wrongs you have done to me, but my hand will not touch you. [13] As the old saying goes, "From evildoers come evil deeds," so my hand will not touch you.

[14] 'Against whom has the king of Israel come out? Who are you pursuing? A dead dog? A flea? [15] May the LORD be our judge and decide between us. May he consider my cause and uphold it; may he vindicate me by delivering me from your hand.'

[16] When David finished saying this, Saul asked, 'Is that your voice, David my son?' And he wept aloud. [17] 'You are more righteous than I,' he said. 'You have treated me well, but I have treated you badly. [18] You have just now told me about the good you did to me; the LORD gave me into your hands, but you did not kill me. [19] When a man finds his enemy, does he let him get away unharmed? May the LORD reward you well for the way you treated me today. [20] I know that you will surely be king and that the kingdom of Israel will be established in your hands. [21] Now swear to me by the LORD that you will not kill off my descendants or wipe out my name from my father's family.'

[22] So David gave his oath to Saul. Then Saul returned home, but David and his men went up to the stronghold.

25

Now Samuel died, and all Israel assembled and mourned for him; and they buried him at his home in Ramah. Then David moved down into the Desert of Paran.

[2] A certain man in Maon, who had property there at Carmel, was very wealthy. He had a thousand goats and three thousand sheep, which he was shearing in Carmel. [3] His name was Nabal and his wife's name was Abigail. She was an intelligent and beautiful woman, but her husband was surly and mean in his dealings – he was a Calebite.

[4] While David was in the wilderness, he heard that Nabal was shearing sheep. [5] So he sent ten young men and said to them, 'Go up to Nabal at Carmel and greet him in my name. [6] Say to him: "Long life to you! Good health to you and your household! And good health to all that is yours!

[7] '"Now I hear that it is sheep-shearing time. When your shepherds were with us, we did not ill-treat them, and the whole time they were at Carmel nothing of theirs was missing. [8] Ask your own servants and they will tell you. Therefore be favourable towards my men, since we come at a festive time. Please give your servants and your son David whatever you can find for them."'

[9] When David's men arrived, they gave Nabal this message in David's name. Then they waited.

[10] Nabal answered David's servants, 'Who is this David? Who is this son of Jesse? Many servants are breaking away from their masters these days. [11] Why should I take my bread and water, and the meat I have slaughtered for my shearers, and give it to men coming from who knows where?'

[12] David's men turned round and went back. When they arrived, they reported every word. [13] David said to his men, 'Each of you strap on your sword!' So they did, and David strapped his on as well. About four hundred men went up with David, while

two hundred stayed with the supplies.

¹⁴ One of the servants told Abigail, Nabal's wife, 'David sent messengers from the wilderness to give our master his greetings, but he hurled insults at them. ¹⁵ Yet these men were very good to us. They did not ill-treat us, and the whole time we were out in the fields near them nothing was missing. ¹⁶ Night and day they were a wall around us the whole time we were herding our sheep near them. ¹⁷ Now think it over and see what you can do, because disaster is hanging over our master and his whole household. He is such a wicked man that no one can talk to him.'

¹⁸ Abigail acted quickly. She took two hundred loaves of bread, two skins of wine, five dressed sheep, five seahs of roasted grain, a hundred cakes of raisins and two hundred cakes of pressed figs, and loaded them on donkeys. ¹⁹ Then she told her servants, 'Go on ahead; I'll follow you.' But she did not tell her husband Nabal.

²⁰ As she came riding her donkey into a mountain ravine, there were David and his men descending towards her, and she met them. ²¹ David had just said, 'It's been useless – all my watching over this fellow's property in the wilderness so that nothing of his was missing. He has paid me back evil for good. ²² May God deal with David, be it ever so severely, if by morning I leave alive one male of all who belong to him!'

²³ When Abigail saw David, she quickly got off her donkey and bowed down before David with her face to the ground. ²⁴ She fell at his feet and said: 'Pardon your servant, my lord, and let me speak to you; hear what your servant has to say. ²⁵ Please pay no attention, my lord, to that wicked man Nabal. He is just like his name – his name means Fool, and folly goes with him. And as for me, your servant, I did not see the men my lord sent. ²⁶ And now, my lord, as surely as the LORD your God lives and as you live, since the LORD has kept you from bloodshed

and from avenging yourself with your own hands, may your enemies and all who are intent on harming my lord be like Nabal. ²⁷ And let this gift, which your servant has brought to my lord, be given to the men who follow you.

²⁸ 'Please forgive your servant's presumption. The LORD your God will certainly make a lasting dynasty for my lord, because you fight the LORD's battles, and no wrongdoing will be found in you as long as you live. ²⁹ Even though someone is pursuing you to take your life, the life of my lord will be bound securely in the bundle of the living by the LORD your God, but the lives of your enemies he will hurl away as from the pocket of a sling. ³⁰ When the LORD has fulfilled for my lord every good thing he promised concerning him and has appointed him ruler over Israel, ³¹ my lord will not have on his conscience the staggering burden of needless bloodshed or of having avenged himself. And when the LORD your God has brought my lord success, remember your servant.'

³² David said to Abigail, 'Praise be to the LORD, the God of Israel, who has sent you today to meet me. ³³ May you be blessed for your good judgment and for keeping me from bloodshed this day and from avenging myself with my own hands. ³⁴ Otherwise, as surely as the LORD, the God of Israel, lives, who has kept me from harming you, if you had not come quickly to meet me, not one male belonging to Nabal would have been left alive by daybreak.'

³⁵ Then David accepted from her hand what she had brought to him and said, 'Go home in peace. I have heard your words and granted your request.'

³⁶ When Abigail went to Nabal, he was in the house holding a banquet like that of a king. He was in high spirits and very drunk. So she told him nothing at all until daybreak. ³⁷ Then in the morning, when Nabal was sober, his wife told him all these things,

and his heart failed him and he became like a stone. ³⁸ About ten days later, the LORD struck Nabal and he died.

³⁹ When David heard that Nabal was dead, he said, 'Praise be to the LORD, who has upheld my cause against Nabal for treating me with contempt. He has kept his servant from doing wrong and has brought Nabal's wrongdoing down on his own head.' Then David sent word to Abigail, asking her to become his wife. ⁴⁰ His servants went to Carmel and said to Abigail, 'David has sent us to you to take you to become his wife.'

⁴¹ She bowed down with her face to the ground and said, 'I am your servant and am ready to serve you and wash the feet of my lord's servants.' ⁴² Abigail quickly got on a donkey and, attended by her five female servants, went with David's messengers and became his wife. ⁴³ David had also married Ahinoam of Jezreel, and they both were his wives. ⁴⁴ But Saul had given his daughter Michal, David's wife, to Paltiel son of Laish, who was from Gallim.

■ PSALM 66:16-20

¹⁶ Come and hear, all you who fear God;
　　let me tell you what he has done for me.
¹⁷ I cried out to him with my mouth;
　　his praise was on my tongue.
¹⁸ If I had cherished sin in my heart,
　　the Lord would not have listened;
¹⁹ but God has surely listened
　　and has heard my prayer.
²⁰ Praise be to God,
　　who has not rejected my prayer
　　or withheld his love from me!

■ PROVERBS 14:20-22

²⁰ The poor are shunned even by their
　　neighbours,

　　but the rich have many friends.
²¹ It is a sin to despise one's neighbour,
　　but blessed is the one who is kind to
　　the needy.
²² Do not those who plot evil go astray?
　　But those who plan what is good find
　　love and faithfulness.

■ JOHN 7:10-29

¹⁰ However, after his brothers had left for the festival, he went also, not publicly, but in secret. ¹¹ Now at the festival the Jewish leaders were watching for Jesus and asking, 'Where is he?'

¹² Among the crowds there was widespread whispering about him. Some said, 'He is a good man.'

Others replied, 'No, he deceives the people.' ¹³ But no one would say anything publicly about him for fear of the leaders.

¹⁴ Not until halfway through the festival did Jesus go up to the temple courts and begin to teach. ¹⁵ The Jews there were amazed and asked, 'How did this man get such learning without having been taught?'

¹⁶ Jesus answered, 'My teaching is not my own. It comes from the one who sent me. ¹⁷ Anyone who chooses to do the will of God will find out whether my teaching comes from God or whether I speak on my own. ¹⁸ Whoever speaks on their own does so to gain personal glory, but he who seeks the glory of the one who sent him is a man of truth; there is nothing false about him. ¹⁹ Has not Moses given you the law? Yet not one of you keeps the law. Why are you trying to kill me?'

²⁰ 'You are demon-possessed,' the crowd answered. 'Who is trying to kill you?'

²¹ Jesus said to them, 'I did one miracle, and you are all amazed. ²² Yet, because Moses gave you circumcision (though actually

it did not come from Moses, but from the patriarchs), you circumcise a boy on the Sabbath. ²³Now if a boy can be circumcised on the Sabbath so that the law of Moses may not be broken, why are you angry with me for healing a man's whole body on the Sabbath? ²⁴Stop judging by mere appearances, but instead judge correctly.'

²⁵At that point some of the people of Jerusalem began to ask, 'Isn't this the man they are trying to kill? ²⁶Here he is, speaking publicly, and they are not saying a word to him. Have the authorities really concluded that he is the Messiah? ²⁷But we know where this man is from; when the Messiah comes, no one will know where he is from.'

²⁸Then Jesus, still teaching in the temple courts, cried out, 'Yes, you know me, and you know where I am from. I am not here on my own authority, but he who sent me is true. You do not know him, ²⁹but I know him because I am from him and he sent me.'

Why Many Slip and Fail

'If I had cherished sin in my heart, the Lord would not have listened.' **Psalm 66:18**

A Christian woman begged God to deliver her from an unforgiving spirit, yet deep down in her heart she held onto it because of the way in which it served her unconscious purposes.

I want to suggest that you read the next sentence carefully, for in it lies the secret of the failure of many Christians to walk with 'hinds' feet' to the high places which God has prepared for them.

If you harbour resentment or hatred towards just one individual in the world, by that much you are separated from God Himself.

By just that much do your rear feet fail to track with your front feet and, in the pursuit of God, you are in danger of slipping over the edge to spiritual failure. Let me put it even more clearly - if anyone has sinned against you and you have not forgiven them from the depths of your heart, then your attitude of unwillingness is a sin against God.

Listen to what the Apostle John says about this: 'Whoever claims to love God yet hates a brother or sister is a liar. For whoever does not love their brother and sister, whom they have seen, cannot love God, whom they have not seen' (1 John 4:20).

The very first thing we must do if we are to climb higher with God is make sure there is no bitterness or resentment lingering in our hearts. If you have not done so before, turn now in thought to all those who have trespassed against you, and forgive them - fully and completely.

May 28

▬ 1 SAMUEL 26:1–28:25

26 The Ziphites went to Saul at Gibeah and said, 'Is not David hiding on the hill of Hakilah, which faces Jeshimon?'

² So Saul went down to the Desert of Ziph, with his three thousand select Israelite troops, to search there for David. ³ Saul made his camp beside the road on the hill of Hakilah facing Jeshimon, but David stayed in the wilderness. When he saw that Saul had followed him there, ⁴ he sent out scouts and learned that Saul had definitely arrived.

⁵ Then David set out and went to the place where Saul had camped. He saw where Saul and Abner son of Ner, the commander of the army, had lain down. Saul was lying inside the camp, with the army camped around him.

⁶ David then asked Ahimelek the Hittite and Abishai son of Zeruiah, Joab's brother, 'Who will go down into the camp with me to Saul?'

'I'll go with you,' said Abishai.

⁷ So David and Abishai went to the army by night, and there was Saul, lying asleep inside the camp with his spear stuck in the ground near his head. Abner and the soldiers were lying round him.

⁸ Abishai said to David, 'Today God has given your enemy into your hands. Now let me pin him to the ground with one thrust of the spear; I won't strike him twice.'

⁹ But David said to Abishai, 'Don't destroy him! Who can lay a hand on the LORD's anointed and be guiltless? ¹⁰ As surely as the LORD lives,' he said, 'the LORD himself will strike him, or his time will come and he will die, or he will go into battle and perish. ¹¹ But the LORD forbid that I should lay a hand on the LORD's anointed. Now get the spear and water jug that are near his head, and let's go.'

¹² So David took the spear and water jug near Saul's head, and they left. No one saw or knew about it, nor did anyone wake up. They were all sleeping, because the LORD had put them into a deep sleep.

¹³ Then David crossed over to the other side and stood on top of the hill some distance away; there was a wide space between them. ¹⁴ He called out to the army and to Abner son of Ner, 'Aren't you going to answer me, Abner?'

Abner replied, 'Who are you who calls to the king?'

¹⁵ David said, 'You're a man, aren't you? And who is like you in Israel? Why didn't you guard your lord the king? Someone came to destroy your lord the king. ¹⁶ What you have done is not good. As surely as the LORD lives, you and your men must die, because you did not guard your master, the LORD's anointed. Look around you. Where are the king's spear

and water jug that were near his head?'
¹⁷ Saul recognised David's voice and said, 'Is that your voice, David my son?'

David replied, 'Yes it is, my lord the king.' ¹⁸ And he added, 'Why is my lord pursuing his servant? What have I done, and what wrong am I guilty of? ¹⁹ Now let my lord the king listen to his servant's words. If the LORD has incited you against me, then may he accept an offering. If, however, people have done it, may they be cursed before the LORD! They have driven me today from my share in the LORD's inheritance and have said, "Go, serve other gods." ²⁰ Now do not let my blood fall to the ground far from the presence of the LORD. The king of Israel has come out to look for a flea – as one hunts a partridge in the mountains.'

²¹ Then Saul said, 'I have sinned. Come back, David my son. Because you considered my life precious today, I will not try to harm you again. Surely I have acted like a fool and have been terribly wrong.'

²² 'Here is the king's spear,' David answered. 'Let one of your young men come over and get it. ²³ The LORD rewards everyone for their righteousness and faithfulness. The LORD gave you into my hands today, but I would not lay a hand on the LORD's anointed. ²⁴ As surely as I valued your life today, so may the LORD value my life and deliver me from all trouble.'

²⁵ Then Saul said to David, 'May you be blessed, David my son; you will do great things and surely triumph.'

So David went on his way, and Saul returned home.

27 But David thought to himself, 'One of these days I shall be destroyed by the hand of Saul. The best thing I can do is to escape to the land of the Philistines. Then Saul will give up searching for me anywhere in Israel, and I will slip out of his hand.'

² So David and the six hundred men with him left and went over to Achish son of Maok king of Gath. ³ David and his men settled in Gath with Achish. Each man had

his family with him, and David had his two wives: Ahinoam of Jezreel and Abigail of Carmel, the widow of Nabal. ⁴ When Saul was told that David had fled to Gath, he no longer searched for him.

⁵ Then David said to Achish, 'If I have found favour in your eyes, let a place be assigned to me in one of the country towns, that I may live there. Why should your servant live in the royal city with you?'

⁶ So on that day Achish gave him Ziklag, and it has belonged to the kings of Judah ever since. ⁷ David lived in Philistine territory for a year and four months.

⁸ Now David and his men went up and raided the Geshurites, the Girzites and the Amalekites. (From ancient times these peoples had lived in the land extending to Shur and Egypt.) ⁹ Whenever David attacked an area, he did not leave a man or woman alive, but took sheep and cattle, donkeys and camels, and clothes. Then he returned to Achish.

¹⁰ When Achish asked, 'Where did you go raiding today?' David would say, 'Against the Negev of Judah' or 'Against the Negev of Jerahmeel' or 'Against the Negev of the Kenites.' ¹¹ He did not leave a man or woman alive to be brought to Gath, for he thought, 'They might inform on us and say, "This is what David did."' And such was his practice as long as he lived in Philistine territory. ¹² Achish trusted David and said to himself, 'He has become so obnoxious to his people, the Israelites, that he will be my servant for life.'

28 In those days the Philistines gathered their forces to fight against Israel. Achish said to David, 'You must understand that you and your men will accompany me in the army.'

² David said, 'Then you will see for yourself what your servant can do.'

Achish replied, 'Very well, I will make you my bodyguard for life.'

³ Now Samuel was dead, and all Israel had mourned for him and buried him in his own town of Ramah. Saul had expelled the

mediums and spiritists from the land.

⁴The Philistines assembled and came and set up camp at Shunem, while Saul gathered all Israel and set up camp at Gilboa. ⁵When Saul saw the Philistine army, he was afraid; terror filled his heart. ⁶He enquired of the LORD, but the LORD did not answer him by dreams or Urim or prophets. ⁷Saul then said to his attendants, 'Find me a woman who is a medium, so that I may go and enquire of her.'

'There is one in Endor,' they said.

⁸So Saul disguised himself, putting on other clothes, and at night he and two men went to the woman. 'Consult a spirit for me,' he said, 'and bring up for me the one I name.'

⁹But the woman said to him, 'Surely you know what Saul has done. He has cut off the mediums and spiritists from the land. Why have you set a trap for my life to bring about my death?'

¹⁰Saul swore to her by the LORD, 'As surely as the LORD lives, you will not be punished for this.'

¹¹Then the woman asked, 'Whom shall I bring up for you?'

'Bring up Samuel,' he said.

¹²When the woman saw Samuel, she cried out at the top of her voice and said to Saul, 'Why have you deceived me? You are Saul!'

¹³The king said to her, 'Don't be afraid. What do you see?'

The woman said, 'I see a ghostly figure coming up out of the earth.'

¹⁴'What does he look like?' he asked.

'An old man wearing a robe is coming up,' she said.

Then Saul knew it was Samuel, and he bowed down and prostrated himself with his face to the ground.

¹⁵Samuel said to Saul, 'Why have you disturbed me by bringing me up?'

'I am in great distress,' Saul said. 'The Philistines are fighting against me, and God has departed from me. He no longer answers me, either by prophets or by dreams. So I have called on you to tell me what to do.'

¹⁶Samuel said, 'Why do you consult me, now that the LORD has departed from you and become your enemy? ¹⁷The LORD has done what he predicted through me. The LORD has torn the kingdom out of your hands and given it to one of your neighbours – to David. ¹⁸Because you did not obey the LORD or carry out his fierce wrath against the Amalekites, the LORD has done this to you today. ¹⁹The LORD will deliver both Israel and you into the hands of the Philistines, and tomorrow you and your sons will be with me. The LORD will also give the army of Israel into the hands of the Philistines.'

²⁰Immediately Saul fell full length on the ground, filled with fear because of Samuel's words. His strength was gone, for he had eaten nothing all that day and all that night.

²¹When the woman came to Saul and saw that he was greatly shaken, she said, 'Look, your servant has obeyed you. I took my life in my hands and did what you told me to do. ²²Now please listen to your servant and let me give you some food so that you may eat and have the strength to go on your way.'

²³He refused and said, 'I will not eat.'

But his men joined the woman in urging him, and he listened to them. He got up from the ground and sat on the couch.

²⁴The woman had a fattened calf at the house, which she slaughtered at once. She took some flour, kneaded it and baked bread without yeast. ²⁵Then she set it before Saul and his men, and they ate. That same night they got up and left.

■ PSALM 67:1-7

¹May God be gracious to us and bless us
  and make his face shine on us –
²so that your ways may be known on earth,
  your salvation among all nations.

³ May the peoples praise you, God;
    may all the peoples praise you.
⁴ May the nations be glad and sing for joy,
    for you rule the peoples with equity
    and guide the nations of the earth.
⁵ May the peoples praise you, God;
    may all the peoples praise you.

⁶ The land yields its harvest;
    God, our God, blesses us.
⁷ May God bless us still,
    so that all the ends of the earth will
    fear him.

▬ PROVERBS 14:23-25

²³ All hard work brings a profit,
    but mere talk leads only to poverty.

²⁴ The wealth of the wise is their crown,
    but the folly of fools yields folly.

²⁵ A truthful witness saves lives,
    but a false witness is deceitful.

▬ JOHN 7:30-52

³⁰ At this they tried to seize him, but no one laid a hand on him, because his hour had not yet come. ³¹ Still, many in the crowd believed in him. They said, 'When the Messiah comes, will he perform more signs than this man?'

³² The Pharisees heard the crowd whispering such things about him. Then the chief priests and the Pharisees sent temple guards to arrest him.

³³ Jesus said, 'I am with you for only a short time, and then I am going to the one who sent me. ³⁴ You will look for me, but you will not find me; and where I am, you cannot come.'

³⁵ The Jews said to one another, 'Where does this man intend to go that we cannot find him? Will he go where our people live scattered among the Greeks, and teach the Greeks? ³⁶ What did he mean when he said, "You will look for me, but you will not find me," and "Where I am, you cannot come"?'

³⁷ On the last and greatest day of the festival, Jesus stood and said in a loud voice, 'Let anyone who is thirsty come to me and drink. ³⁸ Whoever believes in me, as Scripture has said, rivers of living water will flow from within them.' ³⁹ By this he meant the Spirit, whom those who believed in him were later to receive. Up to that time the Spirit had not been given, since Jesus had not yet been glorified.

⁴⁰ On hearing his words, some of the people said, 'Surely this man is the Prophet.' ⁴¹ Others said, 'He is the Messiah.'

Still others asked, 'How can the Messiah come from Galilee? ⁴² Does not Scripture say that the Messiah will come from David's descendants and from Bethlehem, the town where David lived?' ⁴³ Thus the people were divided because of Jesus. ⁴⁴ Some wanted to seize him, but no one laid a hand on him.

⁴⁵ Finally the temple guards went back to the chief priests and the Pharisees, who asked them, 'Why didn't you bring him in?'

⁴⁶ 'No one ever spoke the way this man does,' the guards replied.

⁴⁷ 'You mean he has deceived you also?' the Pharisees retorted. ⁴⁸ 'Have any of the rulers or of the Pharisees believed in him? ⁴⁹ No! But this mob that knows nothing of the law – there is a curse on them.'

⁵⁰ Nicodemus, who had gone to Jesus earlier and who was one of their own number, asked, ⁵¹ 'Does our law condemn a man without first hearing him to find out what he has been doing?'

⁵² They replied, 'Are you from Galilee, too? Look into it, and you will find that a prophet does not come out of Galilee.'

How Problems Occur

'Let anyone who is thirsty come to me and drink.'
John 7:37

In my opinion, the biggest single preventative to us having feet like 'hinds' feet' is a stubborn commitment to independence. This reflects itself in the lives of every one of us - even those who have been on the Way for several decades. In the garden of Eden, Adam and Eve, who were designed to experience fulfilment by being dependent on God, decided to act independently of Him. Sin can be summed up as a 'Declaration of Independence' - an attempt to do for ourselves what only God can do for us.

What happened in the garden of Eden is duplicated millions of times daily, not only in the lives of unbelievers but in the lives of Christians also - Christians who use self-centred strategies to satisfy the deep thirst that is in their heart for God. Almost every spiritual or psychological problem has at its roots this condition - the person is failing in some way to let God satisfy his deep inner thirst.

This might sound simplistic to some, but after many years of experience working in the field of counselling, I am convinced that this is what underlies many conditions. You see, if we are not conscious that God is meeting the deep thirst we have for Him on the inside of our being, then the inner emptiness will move us in one of two directions - to fill the emptiness in any way we can or to withdraw and protect ourselves from the possibility of any further pain.

PRAYER

Father, I see yet again that until and unless my deep thirst for You is being quenched, I am in deep trouble and vulnerable to all kinds of problems. I simply must get this issue straightened out. Help me, dear Father. In Jesus' name. Amen.

FURTHER STUDY

Matt. 5:1-6; John 4:1-42
• What was the message of Jesus to the woman?
• How was this reinforced through the Sermon on the Mount?

May 29

■ 1 SAMUEL 29:1–31:13

29 The Philistines gathered all their forces at Aphek, and Israel camped by the spring in Jezreel. ²As the Philistine rulers marched with their units of hundreds and thousands, David and his men were marching at the rear with Achish. ³The commanders of the Philistines asked, 'What about these Hebrews?'

Achish replied, 'Is this not David, who was an officer of Saul king of Israel? He has already been with me for over a year, and from the day he left Saul until now, I have found no fault in him.'

⁴But the Philistine commanders were angry with Achish and said, 'Send the man back, that he may return to the place you assigned him. He must not go with us into battle, or he will turn against us during the fighting. How better could he regain his master's favour than by taking the heads of our own men? ⁵Isn't this the David they sang about in their dances:

'"Saul has slain his thousands,
    and David his tens of thousands"?'

⁶So Achish called David and said to him, 'As surely as the LORD lives, you have been reliable, and I would be pleased for you to serve with me in the army. From the day you came to me until today, I have found no fault in you, but the rulers don't approve of you. ⁷Now turn back and go in peace; do nothing to displease the Philistine rulers.'

⁸'But what have I done?' asked David. 'What have you found against your servant from the day I came to you until now? Why can't I go and fight against the enemies of my lord the king?'

⁹Achish answered, 'I know that you have been as pleasing in my eyes as an angel of God; nevertheless, the Philistine commanders have said, "He must not go up with us into battle." ¹⁰Now get up early, along with your master's servants who have come with you, and leave in the morning as soon as it is light.'

¹¹So David and his men got up early in the morning to go back to the land of the Philistines, and the Philistines went up to Jezreel.

30 David and his men reached Ziklag on the third day. Now the Amalekites had raided the Negev and Ziklag. They had attacked Ziklag and burned it, ²and

had taken captive the women and everyone else in it, both young and old. They killed none of them, but carried them off as they went on their way.

³When David and his men reached Ziklag, they found it destroyed by fire and their wives and sons and daughters taken captive. ⁴So David and his men wept aloud until they had no strength left to weep. ⁵David's two wives had been captured – Ahinoam of Jezreel and Abigail, the widow of Nabal of Carmel. ⁶David was greatly distressed because the men were talking of stoning him; each one was bitter in spirit because of his sons and daughters. But David found strength in the LORD his God.

⁷Then David said to Abiathar the priest, the son of Ahimelek, 'Bring me the ephod.' Abiathar brought it to him, ⁸and David enquired of the LORD, 'Shall I pursue this raiding party? Will I overtake them?'

'Pursue them,' he answered. 'You will certainly overtake them and succeed in the rescue.'

⁹David and the six hundred men with him came to the Besor Valley, where some stayed behind. ¹⁰Two hundred of them were too exhausted to cross the valley, but David and the other four hundred continued the pursuit.

¹¹They found an Egyptian in a field and brought him to David. They gave him water to drink and food to eat – ¹²part of a cake of pressed figs and two cakes of raisins. He ate and was revived, for he had not eaten any food or drunk any water for three days and three nights.

¹³David asked him, 'Who do you belong to? Where do you come from?'

He said, 'I am an Egyptian, the slave of an Amalekite. My master abandoned me when I became ill three days ago. ¹⁴We raided the Negev of the Kerethites, some territory belonging to Judah and the Negev of Caleb. And we burned Ziklag.'

¹⁵David asked him, 'Can you lead me

down to this raiding party?'

He answered, 'Swear to me before God that you will not kill me or hand me over to my master, and I will take you down to them.'

¹⁶ He led David down, and there they were, scattered over the countryside, eating, drinking and revelling because of the great amount of plunder they had taken from the land of the Philistines and from Judah. ¹⁷ David fought them from dusk until the evening of the next day, and none of them got away, except four hundred young men who rode off on camels and fled. ¹⁸ David recovered everything the Amalekites had taken, including his two wives. ¹⁹ Nothing was missing: young or old, boy or girl, plunder or anything else they had taken. David brought everything back. ²⁰ He took all the flocks and herds, and his men drove them ahead of the other livestock, saying, 'This is David's plunder.'

²¹ Then David came to the two hundred men who had been too exhausted to follow him and who were left behind at the Besor Valley. They came out to meet David and the men with him. As David and his men approached, he asked them how they were. ²² But all the evil men and troublemakers among David's followers said, 'Because they did not go out with us, we will not share with them the plunder we recovered. However, each man may take his wife and children and go.'

²³ David replied, 'No, my brothers, you must not do that with what the LORD has given us. He has protected us and delivered into our hands the raiding party that came against us. ²⁴ Who will listen to what you say? The share of the man who stayed with the supplies is to be the same as that of him who went down to the battle. All shall share alike.' ²⁵ David made this a statute and ordinance for Israel from that day to this.

²⁶ When David reached Ziklag, he sent some of the plunder to the elders of Judah, who were his friends, saying, 'Here is a gift for you from the plunder of the LORD's enemies.'

²⁷ David sent it to those who were in Bethel, Ramoth Negev and Jattir; ²⁸ to those in Aroer, Siphmoth, Eshtemoa ²⁹ and Rakal; to those in the towns of the Jerahmeelites and the Kenites; ³⁰ to those in Hormah, Bor Ashan, Athak ³¹ and Hebron; and to those in all the other places where he and his men had roamed.

31 Now the Philistines fought against Israel; the Israelites fled before them, and many fell dead on Mount Gilboa. ² The Philistines were in hot pursuit of Saul and his sons, and they killed his sons Jonathan, Abinadab and Malki-Shua. ³ The fighting grew fierce around Saul, and when the archers overtook him, they wounded him critically.

⁴ Saul said to his armour-bearer, 'Draw your sword and run me through, or these uncircumcised fellows will come and run me through and abuse me.'

But the armour-bearer was terrified and would not do it; so Saul took his own sword and fell on it. ⁵ When the armour-bearer saw that Saul was dead, he too fell on his sword and died with him. ⁶ So Saul and his three sons and his armour-bearer and all his men died together that same day.

⁷ When the Israelites along the valley and those across the Jordan saw that the Israelite army had fled and that Saul and his sons had died, they abandoned their towns and fled. And the Philistines came and occupied them.

⁸ The next day, when the Philistines came to strip the dead, they found Saul and his three sons fallen on Mount Gilboa. ⁹ They cut off his head and stripped off his armour, and they sent messengers throughout the land of the Philistines to proclaim the news in the temple of their idols and among their people. ¹⁰ They put his armour in the temple of the Ashtoreths and fastened his body to the wall of Beth Shan.

¹¹ When the people of Jabesh Gilead heard what the Philistines had done to Saul, ¹² all their valiant men marched through the night to Beth Shan. They took down the

bodies of Saul and his sons from the wall of Beth Shan and went to Jabesh, where they burned them. ¹³ Then they took their bones and buried them under a tamarisk tree at Jabesh, and they fasted seven days.

PSALM 68:1-6

¹ May God arise, may his enemies be
scattered;
    may his foes flee before him.
² May you blow them away like smoke –
as wax melts before the fire,
    may the wicked perish before God.
³ But may the righteous be glad
and rejoice before God;
    may they be happy and joyful.

⁴ Sing to God, sing in praise of his name,
extol him who rides on the clouds;
    rejoice before him – his name is the
    LORD.
⁵ A father to the fatherless, a defender of
widows,
    is God in his holy dwelling.
⁶ God sets the lonely in families,
he leads out the prisoners with singing;
    but the rebellious live in a sun-
    scorched land.

PROVERBS 14:26-28

²⁶ Whoever fears the LORD has a secure
fortress,
    and for their children it will be a refuge.

²⁷ The fear of the LORD is a fountain of life,
turning a person from the snares of
death.

²⁸ A large population is a king's glory,
but without subjects a prince is ruined.

JOHN 8:1-20

The earliest manuscripts and many other ancient witnesses do not have John 7:53 – 8:11. A few manuscripts include these verses, wholly or in part, after John 7:36, John 21:25, Luke 21:38 or Luke 24:53.

8 ⁵³ Then they all went home, ¹ but Jesus went to the Mount of Olives.

² At dawn he appeared again in the temple courts, where all the people gathered round him, and he sat down to teach them. ³ The teachers of the law and the Pharisees brought in a woman caught in adultery. They made her stand before the group ⁴ and said to Jesus, 'Teacher, this woman was caught in the act of adultery. ⁵ In the Law Moses commanded us to stone such women. Now what do you say?' ⁶ They were using this question as a trap, in order to have a basis for accusing him.

But Jesus bent down and started to write on the ground with his finger. ⁷ When they kept on questioning him, he straightened up and said to them, 'Let any one of you who is without sin be the first to throw a stone at her.' ⁸ Again he stooped down and wrote on the ground.

⁹ At this, those who heard began to go away one at a time, the older ones first, until only Jesus was left, with the woman still standing there. ¹⁰ Jesus straightened up and asked her, 'Woman, where are they? Has no one condemned you?'

¹¹ 'No one, sir,' she said.

'Then neither do I condemn you,' Jesus declared. 'Go now and leave your life of sin.'

¹² When Jesus spoke again to the people, he said, 'I am the light of the world. Whoever follows me will never walk in darkness, but will have the light of life.'

¹³ The Pharisees challenged him, 'Here you are, appearing as your own witness; your testimony is not valid.'

¹⁴ Jesus answered, 'Even if I testify on my own behalf, my testimony is valid, for I know where I came from and where I am going. But you have no idea where I come from or where I am going. ¹⁵ You judge by human standards; I pass judgment on no one. ¹⁶ But

if I do judge, my decisions are true, because I am not alone. I stand with the Father, who sent me. [17] In your own Law it is written that the testimony of two witnesses is true. [18] I am one who testifies for myself; my other witness is the Father, who sent me.'

[19] Then they asked him, 'Where is your father?'

'You do not know me or my Father,' Jesus replied. 'If you knew me, you would know my Father also.' [20] He spoke these words while teaching in the temple courts near the place where the offerings were put. Yet no one seized him, because his hour had not yet come.

Family Within a Family

'A father to the fatherless, a defender of widows, is God in his holy dwelling.' **Psalm 68:5**

The second word in our Master's model of prayer is 'Father.' In Christian circles the term 'Father' is probably the most common term used when addressing God, and rightly so, for this is the pattern Jesus set when teaching His disciples the art of effective praying.

This raises the much debated question: Is God a Father to all men and women everywhere or only to those who are committed members of the Christian church? For many years now liberally minded theologians have taught that God is everyone's Father, so we are all His children and thus all brothers and sisters. This teaching, known as the universal brotherhood of man, makes conversion unnecessary and puts to one side the redemptive sufferings of Christ on the cross.

The Bible teaches that God is a Father in two senses. Firstly, He is the Father of the human family by virtue of creation. Malachi 2:10 says: 'Do we not all have one Father? Did not one God create us?' In Acts 17:28 Paul, quoting from an ancient poet, said: 'We are his offspring'. In the sense of creation, yes, God is our Father.

In the sense of a familial relationship, He is not. Jesus said to the Jewish leaders: 'You belong to your father, the devil' (John 8:44). Quite clearly, the fatherhood of God is seen in the Bible in two senses. He is the Father of all as their Creator, but He has another family – a family within a family – consisting of those who have committed themselves to Jesus Christ, the Son.

PRAYER

O God, I am so grateful that I know You as my Father – not only in the creative sense, but in the familial sense. May the wonder of this closer relationship grow within me hour by hour and day by day. For Jesus' sake. Amen.

FURTHER STUDY

Rom. 8:1-17; Isa. 64:8; John 1:12
• How has 'the Spirit you received brought about your adoption'?
• What is our cry?

May 30

MAY 30

▬ 2 SAMUEL 1:1–2:32

1 After the death of Saul, David returned from striking down the Amalekites and stayed in Ziklag two days. ² On the third day a man arrived from Saul's camp with his clothes torn and dust on his head. When he came to David, he fell to the ground to pay him honour.

³ 'Where have you come from?' David asked him.

He answered, 'I have escaped from the Israelite camp.'

⁴ 'What happened?' David asked. 'Tell me.'

'The men fled from the battle,' he replied. 'Many of them fell and died. And Saul and his son Jonathan are dead.'

⁵ Then David said to the young man who brought him the report, 'How do you know that Saul and his son Jonathan are dead?'

⁶ 'I happened to be on Mount Gilboa,' the young man said, 'and there was Saul, leaning on his spear, with the chariots and their drivers in hot pursuit. ⁷ When he turned round and saw me, he called out to me, and I said, "What can I do?"

⁸ 'He asked me, "Who are you?"

' "An Amalekite," I answered.

⁹ 'Then he said to me, "Stand here by me and kill me! I'm in the throes of death, but I'm still alive."

¹⁰ 'So I stood beside him and killed him, because I knew that after he had fallen he could not survive. And I took the crown that was on his head and the band on his arm and have brought them here to my lord.'

¹¹ Then David and all the men with him took hold of their clothes and tore them. ¹² They mourned and wept and fasted till evening for Saul and his son Jonathan, and for the army of the LORD and for the nation of Israel, because they had fallen by the sword.

¹³ David said to the young man who brought him the report, 'Where are you from?'

'I am the son of a foreigner, an Amalekite,' he answered.

¹⁴ David asked him, 'Why weren't you afraid to lift your hand to destroy the LORD's anointed?'

¹⁵ Then David called one of his men and said, 'Go, strike him down!' So he struck him down, and he died. ¹⁶ For David had said to him, 'Your blood be on your own head. Your own mouth testified against you when you said, "I killed the LORD's anointed." '

¹⁷ David took up this lament concerning Saul and his son Jonathan, ¹⁸ and he ordered that the people of Judah be taught this lament of the bow (it is written in the Book of Jashar):

¹⁹ 'A gazelle lies slain on your heights,
    Israel.
    How the mighty have fallen!

²⁰ 'Tell it not in Gath,
    proclaim it not in the streets of
        Ashkelon,
lest the daughters of the Philistines be
        glad,
    lest the daughters of the
        uncircumcised rejoice.

²¹ 'Mountains of Gilboa,
    may you have neither dew nor rain,
    may no showers fall on your terraced
        fields.
For there the shield of the mighty was
        despised,

the shield of Saul – no longer rubbed
with oil.

²² 'From the blood of the slain,
    from the flesh of the mighty,
  the bow of Jonathan did not turn back,
    the sword of Saul did not return
      unsatisfied.
²³ Saul and Jonathan –
    in life they were loved and admired,
    and in death they were not parted.
  They were swifter than eagles,
    they were stronger than lions.

²⁴ 'Daughters of Israel,
    weep for Saul,
  who clothed you in scarlet and finery,
    who adorned your garments with
      ornaments of gold.

²⁵ 'How the mighty have fallen in battle!
    Jonathan lies slain on your heights.
²⁶ I grieve for you, Jonathan my brother;
    you were very dear to me.
  Your love for me was wonderful,
    more wonderful than that of women.

²⁷ 'How the mighty have fallen!
    The weapons of war have perished!'

2 In the course of time, David enquired
  of the LORD. 'Shall I go up to one of the
towns of Judah?' he asked.
  The LORD said, 'Go up.'
  David asked, 'Where shall I go?'
  'To Hebron,' the LORD answered.
  ² So David went up there with his two
wives, Ahinoam of Jezreel and Abigail, the
widow of Nabal of Carmel. ³ David also took
the men who were with him, each with his
family, and they settled in Hebron and its
towns. ⁴ Then the men of Judah came to Hebron, and there they anointed David king
over the tribe of Judah.
  When David was told that it was the
men from Jabesh Gilead who had buried

Saul, ⁵ he sent messengers to them to say to
them, 'The LORD bless you for showing this
kindness to Saul your master by burying
him. ⁶ May the LORD now show you kindness and faithfulness, and I too will show
you the same favour because you have done
this. ⁷ Now then, be strong and brave, for
Saul your master is dead, and the people of
Judah have anointed me king over them.'

⁸ Meanwhile, Abner son of Ner, the
commander of Saul's army, had taken Ish-
Bosheth son of Saul and brought him over
to Mahanaim. ⁹ He made him king over
Gilead, Ashuri and Jezreel, and also over
Ephraim, Benjamin and all Israel.

¹⁰ Ish-Bosheth son of Saul was forty years
old when he became king over Israel, and he
reigned two years. The tribe of Judah, however, remained loyal to David. ¹¹ The length
of time David was king in Hebron over
Judah was seven years and six months.

¹² Abner son of Ner, together with the men
of Ish-Bosheth son of Saul, left Mahanaim
and went to Gibeon. ¹³ Joab son of Zeruiah
and David's men went out and met them at
the pool of Gibeon. One group sat down on
one side of the pool and one group on the
other side.

¹⁴ Then Abner said to Joab, 'Let's have
some of the young men get up and fight
hand to hand in front of us.'

'All right, let them do it,' Joab said.

¹⁵ So they stood up and were counted –
twelve men for Benjamin and Ish-Bosheth
son of Saul, and twelve for David. ¹⁶ Then each
man grabbed his opponent by the head and
thrust his dagger into his opponent's side,
and they fell down together. So that place in
Gibeon was called Helkath Hazzurim.

¹⁷ The battle that day was very fierce, and
Abner and the Israelites were defeated by
David's men.

¹⁸ The three sons of Zeruiah were there:
Joab, Abishai and Asahel. Now Asahel was
as fleet-footed as a wild gazelle. ¹⁹ He chased
Abner, turning neither to the right nor to

the left as he pursued him. ²⁰ Abner looked behind him and asked, 'Is that you, Asahel?'

'It is,' he answered.

²¹ Then Abner said to him, 'Turn aside to the right or to the left; take on one of the young men and strip him of his weapons.' But Asahel would not stop chasing him.

²² Again Abner warned Asahel, 'Stop chasing me! Why should I strike you down? How could I look your brother Joab in the face?'

²³ But Asahel refused to give up the pursuit; so Abner thrust the butt of his spear into Asahel's stomach, and the spear came out through his back. He fell there and died on the spot. And every man stopped when he came to the place where Asahel had fallen and died.

²⁴ But Joab and Abishai pursued Abner, and as the sun was setting, they came to the hill of Ammah, near Giah on the way to the wasteland of Gibeon. ²⁵ Then the men of Benjamin rallied behind Abner. They formed themselves into a group and took their stand on top of a hill.

²⁶ Abner called out to Joab, 'Must the sword devour for ever? Don't you realise that this will end in bitterness? How long before you order your men to stop pursuing their fellow Israelites?'

²⁷ Joab answered, 'As surely as God lives, if you had not spoken, the men would have continued pursuing them until morning.'

²⁸ So Joab blew the trumpet, and all the troops came to a halt; they no longer pursued Israel, nor did they fight any more.

²⁹ All that night Abner and his men marched through the Arabah. They crossed the Jordan, continued through the morning hours and came to Mahanaim.

³⁰ Then Joab stopped pursuing Abner and assembled the whole army. Besides Asahel, nineteen of David's men were found missing. ³¹ But David's men had killed 360 Benjaminites who were with Abner. ³² They took Asahel and buried him in his father's tomb at Bethlehem. Then Joab and his men marched all night and arrived at Hebron by daybreak.

■ PSALM 68:7-14

⁷ When you, God, went out before your people,
  when you marched through the wilderness,
⁸ the earth shook, the heavens poured down rain,
  before God, the One of Sinai,
  before God, the God of Israel.
⁹ You gave abundant showers, O God;
  you refreshed your weary inheritance.
¹⁰ Your people settled in it,
  and from your bounty, God, you provided for the poor.

¹¹ The Lord announces the word,
  and the women who proclaim it are a mighty throng:
¹² 'Kings and armies flee in haste;
  the women at home divide the plunder.
¹³ Even while you sleep among the sheepfolds,
  the wings of my dove are sheathed with silver,
  its feathers with shining gold.'
¹⁴ When the Almighty scattered the kings in the land,
  it was like snow fallen on Mount Zalmon.

■ PROVERBS 14:29-30

²⁹ Whoever is patient has great understanding,
  but one who is quick-tempered displays folly.

³⁰ A heart at peace gives life to the body,
  but envy rots the bones.

JOHN 8:21-41

[21] Once more Jesus said to them, 'I am going away, and you will look for me, and you will die in your sin. Where I go, you cannot come.'

[22] This made the Jews ask, 'Will he kill himself? Is that why he says, "Where I go, you cannot come"?'

[23] But he continued, 'You are from below; I am from above. You are of this world; I am not of this world. [24] I told you that you would die in your sins; if you do not believe that I am he, you will indeed die in your sins.'

[25] 'Who are you?' they asked.

'Just what I have been telling you from the beginning,' Jesus replied. [26] 'I have much to say in judgment of you. But he who sent me is trustworthy, and what I have heard from him I tell the world.'

[27] They did not understand that he was telling them about his Father. [28] So Jesus said, 'When you have lifted up the Son of Man, then you will know that I am he and that I do nothing on my own but speak just what the Father has taught me. [29] The one who sent me is with me; he has not left me alone, for I always do what pleases him.' [30] Even as he spoke, many believed in him.

[31] To the Jews who had believed him, Jesus said, 'If you hold to my teaching, you are really my disciples. [32] Then you will know the truth, and the truth will set you free.'

[33] They answered him, 'We are Abraham's descendants and have never been slaves of anyone. How can you say that we shall be set free?'

[34] Jesus replied, 'Very truly I tell you, everyone who sins is a slave to sin. [35] Now a slave has no permanent place in the family, but a son belongs to it for ever. [36] So if the Son sets you free, you will be free indeed. [37] I know you are Abraham's descendants. Yet you are looking for a way to kill me, because you have no room for my word. [38] I am telling you what I have seen in the Father's presence, and you are doing what you have heard from your father.'

[39] 'Abraham is our father,' they answered.

'If you were Abraham's children,' said Jesus, 'then you would do what Abraham did. [40] As it is, you are looking for a way to kill me, a man who has told you the truth that I heard from God. Abraham did not do such things. [41] You are doing the works of your own father.'

'We are not illegitimate children,' they protested. 'The only Father we have is God himself.'

The Danger of Denial

'... you will know the truth, and the truth will set you free.' **John 8:32**

It may be difficult for you to admit that perhaps your heart and your head are not spiritually coordinated. Many Christians are content to live above the waterline and insist that it is quite unnecessary to wrestle and struggle with the things that go on deep inside us. Their motto is: just trust, persevere and obey. This is fine as far as it goes, but in my opinion it does not go far enough.

The effect of this teaching is to blunt the painful reality of what the Bible says about the condition of the human heart: 'The heart is deceitful above all things and beyond cure. Who can understand it? I, the LORD, search the heart and examine the mind' (Jer. 17:9-10). It is possible for even mature Christians to be self-deceived, to not really know their own hearts. This is why we must live in constant dependence on God, inviting Him from time to time, as did the psalmist, to 'search me, God, and know my heart' (Psa. 139:23).

There is a word to describe the attitude of those who ignore what may be going on deep inside them and concentrate only on what they can see above the waterline, and that word is denial. In many Christian circles, maintaining a comfortable distance from what may be going on deep down inside is strongly encouraged. But nothing can be gained from denial. In fact, I would say it is one of the major reasons why our feet are not like 'hinds' feet' and why we slip and slide on the slopes that lead upward to a deeper understanding and knowledge of God.

PRAYER

God, I realise I am dealing with something too devastating to pass over quickly or lightly. Help me be aware of the tendency that is in me to deny that I deny. Stay close to me at this moment, dear Father, for without You I can do nothing. Amen.

FURTHER STUDY

Gal. 6; Rom. 6:16-23
• What was Paul's word to the Galatians?
• How are we to walk?

May 31

■ 2 SAMUEL 3:1–4:12

3 The war between the house of Saul and the house of David lasted a long time. David grew stronger and stronger, while the house of Saul grew weaker and weaker.
2 Sons were born to David in Hebron:
his firstborn was Amnon the son of Ahinoam of Jezreel;
3 his second, Kileab the son of Abigail the widow of Nabal of Carmel;
the third, Absalom the son of Maakah daughter of Talmai king of Geshur;
4 the fourth, Adonijah the son of Haggith;
the fifth, Shephatiah the son of Abital;
5 and the sixth, Ithream the son of David's wife Eglah.

These were born to David in Hebron.
6 During the war between the house of Saul and the house of David, Abner had been strengthening his own position in the house of Saul. 7 Now Saul had had a concubine named Rizpah daughter of Aiah. And Ish-Bosheth said to Abner, 'Why did you sleep with my father's concubine?'
8 Abner was very angry because of what Ish-Bosheth said. So he answered, 'Am I a dog's head – on Judah's side? This very day I am loyal to the house of your father Saul and to his family and friends. I haven't handed you over to David. Yet now you accuse me of an offence involving this woman! 9 May God deal with Abner, be it ever so severely, if I do not do for David what the LORD promised him on oath 10 and transfer the kingdom from the

house of Saul and establish David's throne over Israel and Judah from Dan to Beersheba.' ¹¹Ish-Bosheth did not dare to say another word to Abner, because he was afraid of him.

¹²Then Abner sent messengers on his behalf to say to David, 'Whose land is it? Make an agreement with me, and I will help you bring all Israel over to you.'

¹³'Good,' said David. 'I will make an agreement with you. But I demand one thing of you: do not come into my presence unless you bring Michal daughter of Saul when you come to see me.' ¹⁴Then David sent messengers to Ish-Bosheth son of Saul, demanding, 'Give me my wife Michal, whom I betrothed to myself for the price of a hundred Philistine foreskins.'

¹⁵So Ish-Bosheth gave orders and had her taken away from her husband Paltiel son of Laish. ¹⁶Her husband, however, went with her, weeping behind her all the way to Bahurim. Then Abner said to him, 'Go back home!' So he went back.

¹⁷Abner conferred with the elders of Israel and said, 'For some time you have wanted to make David your king. ¹⁸Now do it! For the LORD promised David, "By my servant David I will rescue my people Israel from the hand of the Philistines and from the hand of all their enemies."'

¹⁹Abner also spoke to the Benjaminites in person. Then he went to Hebron to tell David everything that Israel and the whole tribe of Benjamin wanted to do. ²⁰When Abner, who had twenty men with him, came to David at Hebron, David prepared a feast for him and his men. ²¹Then Abner said to David, 'Let me go at once and assemble all Israel for my lord the king, so that they may make a covenant with you, and that you may rule over all that your heart desires.' So David sent Abner away, and he went in peace.

²²Just then David's men and Joab returned from a raid and brought with them a great deal of plunder. But Abner was no longer with David in Hebron, because David had sent him away, and he had gone in peace. ²³When Joab and all the soldiers with him arrived, he was told that Abner son of Ner had come to the king and that the king had sent him away and that he had gone in peace.

²⁴So Joab went to the king and said, 'What have you done? Look, Abner came to you. Why did you let him go? Now he is gone! ²⁵You know Abner son of Ner; he came to deceive you and observe your movements and find out everything you are doing.'

²⁶Joab then left David and sent messengers after Abner, and they brought him back from the cistern at Sirah. But David did not know it. ²⁷Now when Abner returned to Hebron, Joab took him aside into an inner chamber, as if to speak with him privately. And there, to avenge the blood of his brother Asahel, Joab stabbed him in the stomach, and he died.

²⁸Later, when David heard about this, he said, 'I and my kingdom are for ever innocent before the LORD concerning the blood of Abner son of Ner. ²⁹May his blood fall on the head of Joab and on his whole family! May Joab's family never be without someone who has a running sore or leprosy or who leans on a crutch or who falls by the sword or who lacks food.'

³⁰(Joab and his brother Abishai murdered Abner because he had killed their brother Asahel in the battle of Gibeon.)

³¹Then David said to Joab and all the people with him, 'Tear your clothes and put on sackcloth and walk in mourning in front of Abner.' King David himself walked behind the bier. ³²They buried Abner in Hebron, and the king wept aloud at Abner's tomb. All the people wept also.

³³The king sang this lament for Abner:

'Should Abner have died as the lawless
    die?

³⁴ Your hands were not bound,
     your feet were not fettered.
You fell as one falls before the wicked.'

And all the people wept over him again.

³⁵ Then they all came and urged David to eat something while it was still day; but David took an oath, saying, 'May God deal with me, be it ever so severely, if I taste bread or anything else before the sun sets!'

³⁶ All the people took note and were pleased; indeed, everything the king did pleased them. ³⁷ So on that day all the people there and all Israel knew that the king had no part in the murder of Abner son of Ner.

³⁸ Then the king said to his men, 'Do you not realise that a commander and a great man has fallen in Israel this day? ³⁹ And today, though I am the anointed king, I am weak, and these sons of Zeruiah are too strong for me. May the LORD repay the evildoer according to his evil deeds!'

4 When Ish-Bosheth son of Saul heard that Abner had died in Hebron, he lost courage, and all Israel became alarmed. ² Now Saul's son had two men who were leaders of raiding bands. One was named Baanah and the other Rekab; they were sons of Rimmon the Beerothite from the tribe of Benjamin – Beeroth is considered part of Benjamin, ³ because the people of Beeroth fled to Gittaim and have resided there as foreigners to this day.

⁴ (Jonathan son of Saul had a son who was lame in both feet. He was five years old when the news about Saul and Jonathan came from Jezreel. His nurse picked him up and fled, but as she hurried to leave, he fell and became disabled. His name was Mephibosheth.)

⁵ Now Rekab and Baanah, the sons of Rimmon the Beerothite, set out for the house of Ish-Bosheth, and they arrived there in the heat of the day while he was taking his noonday rest. ⁶ They went into the inner part of the house as if to get some wheat, and they stabbed him in the stomach. Then Rekab and his brother Baanah slipped away.

⁷ They had gone into the house while he was lying on the bed in his bedroom. After they stabbed and killed him, they cut off his head. Taking it with them, they travelled all night by way of the Arabah. ⁸ They brought the head of Ish-Bosheth to David at Hebron and said to the king, 'Here is the head of Ish-Bosheth son of Saul, your enemy, who tried to kill you. This day the LORD has avenged my lord the king against Saul and his offspring.'

⁹ David answered Rekab and his brother Baanah, the sons of Rimmon the Beerothite, 'As surely as the LORD lives, who has delivered me out of every trouble, ¹⁰ when someone told me, "Saul is dead," and thought he was bringing good news, I seized him and put him to death in Ziklag. That was the reward I gave him for his news! ¹¹ How much more – when wicked men have killed an innocent man in his own house and on his own bed – should I not now demand his blood from your hand and rid the earth of you!'

¹² So David gave an order to his men, and they killed them. They cut off their hands and feet and hung the bodies by the pool in Hebron. But they took the head of Ish-Bosheth and buried it in Abner's tomb at Hebron.

··

◼ PSALM 68:15-19

¹⁵ Mount Bashan, majestic mountain,
     Mount Bashan, rugged mountain,
¹⁶ why gaze in envy, you rugged mountain,
     at the mountain where God chooses to
         reign,
     where the LORD himself will dwell for
         ever?
¹⁷ The chariots of God are tens of
         thousands
     and thousands of thousands;
     the Lord has come from Sinai into his
         sanctuary.

[18] When you ascended on high,
    you took many captives;
    you received gifts from people,
even from the rebellious –
    that you, LORD God, might dwell there.

[19] Praise be to the Lord, to God our Saviour,
    who daily bears our burdens.

■ PROVERBS 14:31-32

[31] Whoever oppresses the poor shows
        contempt for their Maker,
    but whoever is kind to the needy
        honours God.

[32] When calamity comes, the wicked are
        brought down,
    but even in death the righteous seek
        refuge in God.

■ JOHN 8:42–9:7

[42] Jesus said to them, 'If God were your Father, you would love me, for I have come here from God. I have not come on my own; God sent me. [43] Why is my language not clear to you? Because you are unable to hear what I say. [44] You belong to your father, the devil, and you want to carry out your father's desires. He was a murderer from the beginning, not holding to the truth, for there is no truth in him. When he lies, he speaks his native language, for he is a liar and the father of lies. [45] Yet because I tell the truth, you do not believe me! [46] Can any of you prove me guilty of sin? If I am telling the truth, why don't you believe me? [47] Whoever belongs to God hears what God says. The reason you do not hear is that you do not belong to God.'

[48] The Jews answered him, 'Aren't we right in saying that you are a Samaritan and demon-possessed?'

[49] 'I am not possessed by a demon,' said Jesus, 'but I honour my Father and you dishonour me. [50] I am not seeking glory for myself; but there is one who seeks it, and he is the judge. [51] Very truly I tell you, whoever obeys my word will never see death.'

[52] At this they exclaimed, 'Now we know that you are demon-possessed! Abraham died and so did the prophets, yet you say that whoever obeys your word will never taste death. [53] Are you greater than our father Abraham? He died, and so did the prophets. Who do you think you are?'

[54] Jesus replied, 'If I glorify myself, my glory means nothing. My Father, whom you claim as your God, is the one who glorifies me. [55] Though you do not know him, I know him. If I said I did not, I would be a liar like you, but I do know him and obey his word. [56] Your father Abraham rejoiced at the thought of seeing my day; he saw it and was glad.'

[57] 'You are not yet fifty years old,' they said to him, 'and you have seen Abraham!'

[58] 'Very truly I tell you,' Jesus answered, 'before Abraham was born, I am!' [59] At this, they picked up stones to stone him, but Jesus hid himself, slipping away from the temple grounds.

9 As he went along, he saw a man blind from birth. [2] His disciples asked him, 'Rabbi, who sinned, this man or his parents, that he was born blind?'

[3] 'Neither this man nor his parents sinned,' said Jesus, 'but this happened so that the works of God might be displayed in him. [4] As long as it is day, we must do the works of him who sent me. Night is coming, when no one can work. [5] While I am in the world, I am the light of the world.'

[6] After saying this, he spat on the ground, made some mud with the saliva, and put it on the man's eyes. [7] 'Go,' he told him, 'wash in the Pool of Siloam' (this word means 'Sent'). So the man went and washed, and came home seeing.

Keeping Our Faith Trim

'... he is a liar and the father of lies.' **John 8:44**

There are many things in life that at first glance appear to have no point. Fear is one such thing; doubt is another. I have heard it argued that all fear is of the Devil and can serve no useful purpose in human life – but this is not true. Fear of being burned, for example, helps us avoid coming in contact with hot metals. Fear can have a positive purpose – and so can doubt.

Doubt, for one, can be used to help us detect error. We live in a world of which Satan is temporarily 'prince', and he tries his utmost to get us to believe his lies. Jesus was not merely being poetic when He described Satan as the 'father of liars'. Half-truths and half-lies that masquerade as the whole truth are the Devil's stock-in-trade. So because all things are not true, not everything should be believed. Some things clearly ought to be doubted.

One writer says: 'The inescapable presence of doubt is a constant reminder of our responsibility to truth in a twilight world of truth and half-truth'. It acts like a spur to challenge us to find out the truth about a situation. It is precisely because all is not certain that we have to make certain.

Francis Bacon put it like this: 'If a man will begin with certainties, he shall end in doubts; but if he will be content to begin with doubts, he shall end in certainties'. Doubt can act as a sparring partner both to truth and error; it keeps faith trim and assists us in shedding the paunchiness of false ideas.

PRAYER

Gracious and loving Father, thank You for reminding me yet again that I can take anything that comes and use it to positive ends – even doubt. Help me to use my doubts as a sparring partner to keep my faith trim. In Jesus' name I pray. Amen.

FURTHER STUDY

2 Pet. 2:1-10; Titus 1:9-11; 2 Tim. 4:1-5
• What will come in the last days?
• How did Paul exhort Timothy?

June 1

■ **2 SAMUEL 5:1-6:23**

5 All the tribes of Israel came to David at Hebron and said, 'We are your own flesh and blood. ² In the past, while Saul was king over us, you were the one who led Israel on their military campaigns. And the LORD said to you, "You shall shepherd my people

Israel, and you shall become their ruler." '

³When all the elders of Israel had come to King David at Hebron, the king made a covenant with them at Hebron before the LORD, and they anointed David king over Israel.

⁴David was thirty years old when he became king, and he reigned for forty years. ⁵In Hebron he reigned over Judah for seven years and six months, and in Jerusalem he reigned over all Israel and Judah for thirty-three years.

⁶The king and his men marched to Jerusalem to attack the Jebusites, who lived there. The Jebusites said to David, 'You will not get in here; even the blind and the lame can ward you off.' They thought, 'David cannot get in here.' ⁷Nevertheless, David captured the fortress of Zion – which is the City of David.

⁸On that day David had said, 'Anyone who conquers the Jebusites will have to use the water shaft to reach those "lame and blind" who are David's enemies.' That is why they say, 'The "blind and lame" will not enter the palace.'

⁹David then took up residence in the fortress and called it the City of David. He built up the area around it, from the terraces inwards. ¹⁰And he became more and more powerful, because the LORD God Almighty was with him.

¹¹Now Hiram king of Tyre sent envoys to David, along with cedar logs and carpenters and stonemasons, and they built a palace for David. ¹²Then David knew that the LORD had established him as king over Israel and had exalted his kingdom for the sake of his people Israel.

¹³After he left Hebron, David took more concubines and wives in Jerusalem, and more sons and daughters were born to him. ¹⁴These are the names of the children born to him there: Shammua, Shobab, Nathan, Solomon, ¹⁵Ibhar, Elishua, Nepheg, Japhia, ¹⁶Elishama, Eliada and Eliphelet.

¹⁷When the Philistines heard that David

had been anointed king over Israel, they went up in full force to search for him, but David heard about it and went down to the stronghold. ¹⁸Now the Philistines had come and spread out in the Valley of Rephaim; ¹⁹so David enquired of the LORD, 'Shall I go and attack the Philistines? Will you deliver them into my hands?'

The LORD answered him, 'Go, for I will surely deliver the Philistines into your hands.'

²⁰So David went to Baal Perazim, and there he defeated them. He said, 'As waters break out, the LORD has broken out against my enemies before me.' So that place was called Baal Perazim. ²¹The Philistines abandoned their idols there, and David and his men carried them off.

²²Once more the Philistines came up and spread out in the Valley of Rephaim; ²³so David enquired of the LORD, and he answered, 'Do not go straight up, but circle round behind them and attack them in front of the poplar trees. ²⁴As soon as you hear the sound of marching in the tops of the poplar trees, move quickly, because that will mean the LORD has gone out in front of you to strike the Philistine army.' ²⁵So David did as the LORD commanded him, and he struck down the Philistines all the way from Gibeon to Gezer.

6 David again brought together all the able young men of Israel – thirty thousand. ²He and all his men went to Baalah in Judah to bring up from there the ark of God, which is called by the Name, the name of the LORD Almighty, who is enthroned between the cherubim on the ark. ³They set the ark of God on a new cart and brought it from the house of Abinadab, which was on the hill. Uzzah and Ahio, sons of Abinadab, were guiding the new cart ⁴with the ark of God on it, and Ahio was walking in front of it. ⁵David and all Israel were celebrating with all their might before the LORD, with castanets, harps, lyres, tambourines, rattles and cymbals.

⁶When they came to the threshing-floor of Nakon, Uzzah reached out and took hold of the ark of God, because the oxen stumbled. ⁷The LORD's anger burned against Uzzah because of his irreverent act; therefore God struck him down, and he died there beside the ark of God.

⁸Then David was angry because the LORD's wrath had broken out against Uzzah, and to this day that place is called Perez Uzzah.

⁹David was afraid of the LORD that day and said, 'How can the ark of the LORD ever come to me?' ¹⁰He was not willing to take the ark of the LORD to be with him in the City of David. Instead, he took it to the house of Obed-Edom the Gittite. ¹¹The ark of the LORD remained in the house of Obed-Edom the Gittite for three months, and the LORD blessed him and his entire household.

¹²Now King David was told, 'The LORD has blessed the household of Obed-Edom and everything he has, because of the ark of God.' So David went to bring up the ark of God from the house of Obed-Edom to the City of David with rejoicing. ¹³When those who were carrying the ark of the LORD had taken six steps, he sacrificed a bull and a fattened calf. ¹⁴Wearing a linen ephod, David was dancing before the LORD with all his might, ¹⁵while he and all Israel were bringing up the ark of the LORD with shouts and the sound of trumpets.

¹⁶As the ark of the LORD was entering the City of David, Michal daughter of Saul watched from a window. And when she saw King David leaping and dancing before the LORD, she despised him in her heart.

¹⁷They brought the ark of the LORD and set it in its place inside the tent that David had pitched for it, and David sacrificed burnt offerings and fellowship offerings before the LORD. ¹⁸After he had finished sacrificing the burnt offerings and fellowship offerings, he blessed the people in the name of the LORD Almighty. ¹⁹Then he gave a loaf of bread, a cake of dates and a cake of raisins to each person in the whole crowd of Israelites, both men and women. And all the people went to their homes.

²⁰When David returned home to bless his household, Michal daughter of Saul came out to meet him and said, 'How the king of Israel has distinguished himself today, going around half-naked in full view of the slave girls of his servants as any vulgar fellow would!'

²¹David said to Michal, 'It was before the LORD, who chose me rather than your father or anyone from his house when he appointed me ruler over the LORD's people Israel – I will celebrate before the LORD. ²²I will become even more undignified than this, and I will be humiliated in my own eyes. But by these slave girls you spoke of, I will be held in honour.'

²³And Michal daughter of Saul had no children to the day of her death.

■ PSALM 68:20-27

²⁰Our God is a God who saves;
from the Sovereign LORD comes escape
from death.
²¹Surely God will crush the heads of his
enemies,
the hairy crowns of those who go on in
their sins.
²²The Lord says, 'I will bring them from
Bashan;
I will bring them from the depths of
the sea,
²³that your feet may wade in the blood of
your foes,
while the tongues of your dogs have
their share.'

²⁴Your procession, God, has come into
view,
the procession of my God and King
into the sanctuary.

²⁵ In front are the singers, after them the
   musicians;
   with them are the young women
      playing the tambourines.
²⁶ Praise God in the great congregation;
   praise the LORD in the assembly of
      Israel.
²⁷ There is the little tribe of Benjamin,
      leading them,
   there the great throng of Judah's
      princes,
   and there the princes of Zebulun and
      of Naphtali.

▬ PROVERBS 14:33-35

³³ Wisdom reposes in the heart of the
      discerning
   and even among fools she lets herself
      be known.

³⁴ Righteousness exalts a nation,
   but sin condemns any people.

³⁵ A king delights in a wise servant,
   but a shameful servant arouses his
      fury.

▬ JOHN 9:8-27

⁸ His neighbours and those who had formerly seen him begging asked, 'Isn't this
the same man who used to sit and beg?'
⁹ Some claimed that he was.

Others said, 'No, he only looks like him.'

But he himself insisted, 'I am the man.'

¹⁰ 'How then were your eyes opened?' they
asked.

¹¹ He replied, 'The man they call Jesus
made some mud and put it on my eyes. He
told me to go to Siloam and wash. So I went
and washed, and then I could see.'

¹² 'Where is this man?' they asked him.

'I don't know,' he said.

¹³ They brought to the Pharisees the man
who had been blind. ¹⁴ Now the day on
which Jesus had made the mud and opened
the man's eyes was a Sabbath. ¹⁵ Therefore the Pharisees also asked him how he
had received his sight. 'He put mud on my
eyes,' the man replied, 'and I washed, and
now I see.'

¹⁶ Some of the Pharisees said, 'This man
is not from God, for he does not keep the
Sabbath.'

But others asked, 'How can a sinner
perform such signs?' So they were divided.

¹⁷ Then they turned again to the blind
man, 'What have you to say about him? It
was your eyes he opened.'

The man replied, 'He is a prophet.'

¹⁸ They still did not believe that he had
been blind and had received his sight until
they sent for the man's parents. ¹⁹ 'Is this your
son?' they asked. 'Is this the one you say was
born blind? How is it that now he can see?'

²⁰ 'We know he is our son,' the parents
answered, 'and we know he was born blind.
²¹ But how he can see now, or who opened
his eyes, we don't know. Ask him. He is of
age; he will speak for himself.' ²² His parents said this because they were afraid of
the Jewish leaders, who already had decided that anyone who acknowledged that
Jesus was the Messiah would be put out of
the synagogue. ²³ That was why his parents
said, 'He is of age; ask him.'

²⁴ A second time they summoned the
man who had been blind. 'Give glory to God
by telling the truth,' they said. 'We know
this man is a sinner.'

²⁵ He replied, 'Whether he is a sinner or
not, I don't know. One thing I do know. I was
blind but now I see!'

²⁶ Then they asked him, 'What did he do
to you? How did he open your eyes?'

²⁷ He answered, 'I have told you already
and you did not listen. Why do you want to
hear it again? Do you want to become his
disciples too?'

Completing the Framework

'Wisdom reposes in the heart of the discerning and even among fools she lets herself be known.' **Proverbs 14:33**

It is important to build a biblical framework for generosity. First, give at least a tithe of your earnings to the Lord's work. The giving of a tithe is seen by many as legalistic, but the tithe is really a symbol of acknowledgment that the nine-tenths belongs to God. The Hebrews waved the firstfruits of the harvest before the Lord as an acknowledgment that the coming harvest belonged to Him. Some will be able to give far more than a tithe, but the tithe is a good place to begin.

Next, make your will under God's direction and maintain a balance between responsibility for your family and the continuing work of God. Make sure your relatives don't waste what God has given you to invest in His kingdom. You might need advice here from a wise Christian.

Also, remember that the principle of generosity applies not only to your treasure but also to your talents and your time. Each day ask God to show you ways of using your talents and time for Him. John Wesley's advice is worth repeating: 'Make all you can; save all you can; give all you can'.

Finally, accept the smallest opportunity to be generous as a proving ground for faithfulness. 'You have been faithful with a few things; I will put you in charge of many things' (Matt. 25:21). Don't wait for the big opportunities to be generous but start with the next opportunity that comes your way – no matter how small it may be. Get ready for the bigger by doing the little well. Why does the Bible make much of generosity? Because the truly generous are the truly wise.

PRAYER

Father, just like Simon Peter, who gave Your Son his boat from which to preach, I give You my treasure, my talents, and my time for You to use as Your pulpit – today and every day. In Christ's name. Amen.

FURTHER STUDY

Gen. 14:20; Lev. 27:30;
2 Chron. 31:5; Matt. 3:1-10
• What principle did Abram follow?
• What is your response to the biblical principle expressed by the tithe?

June 2

7 After the king was settled in his palace and the LORD had given him rest from all his enemies around him, ²he said to Nathan the prophet, 'Here I am, living in a house of cedar, while the ark of God remains in a tent.'

³Nathan replied to the king, 'Whatever you have in mind, go ahead and do it, for the LORD is with you.'

⁴But that night the word of the LORD came to Nathan, saying:

⁵'Go and tell my servant David, "This is what the LORD says: are you the one to build me a house to dwell in? ⁶I have not dwelt in a house from the day I brought the Israelites up out of Egypt to this day. I have been moving from place to place with a tent as my dwelling. ⁷Wherever I have moved with all the Israelites, did I ever say to any of their rulers whom I commanded to shepherd my people Israel, 'Why have you not built me a house of cedar?'"

⁸'Now then, tell my servant David, "This is what the LORD Almighty says: I took you from the pasture, from tending the flock, and appointed you ruler over my people Israel. ⁹I have been with you wherever you have gone, and I have cut off all your enemies from before you. Now I will make your name great, like the names of the greatest men on earth. ¹⁰And I will provide a place for my people Israel and will plant them so that they can have a home of their own and no longer be disturbed. Wicked people shall not oppress them any more, as they did

at the beginning ¹¹and have done ever since the time I appointed leaders over my people Israel. I will also give you rest from all your enemies.

'"The LORD declares to you that the LORD himself will establish a house for you: ¹²when your days are over and you rest with your ancestors, I will raise up your offspring to succeed you, your own flesh and blood, and I will establish his kingdom. ¹³He is the one who will build a house for my Name, and I will establish the throne of his kingdom for ever. ¹⁴I will be his father, and he shall be my son. When he does wrong, I will punish him with a rod wielded by men, with floggings inflicted by human hands. ¹⁵But my love will never be taken away from him, as I took it away from Saul, whom I removed from before you. ¹⁶Your house and your kingdom shall endure for ever before me; your throne shall be established for ever."'

¹⁷Nathan reported to David all the words of this entire revelation.

¹⁸Then King David went in and sat before the LORD, and he said:

'Who am I, Sovereign LORD, and what is my family, that you have brought me this far? ¹⁹And as if this were not enough in your sight, Sovereign LORD, you have also spoken about the future of the house of your servant – and this decree, Sovereign LORD, is for a mere human!

²⁰'What more can David say to you? For you know your servant, Sovereign LORD. ²¹For the sake of your word and

according to your will, you have done this great thing and made it known to your servant.

²²'How great you are, Sovereign Lord! There is no one like you, and there is no God but you, as we have heard with our own ears. ²³And who is like your people Israel – the one nation on earth that God went out to redeem as a people for himself, and to make a name for himself, and to perform great and awesome wonders by driving out nations and their gods from before your people, whom you redeemed from Egypt? ²⁴You have established your people Israel as your very own for ever, and you, Lord, have become their God.

²⁵'And now, Lord God, keep for ever the promise you have made concerning your servant and his house. Do as you promised, ²⁶so that your name will be great for ever. Then people will say, "The Lord Almighty is God over Israel!" And the house of your servant David will be established in your sight. ²⁷Lord Almighty, God of Israel, you have revealed this to your servant, saying, "I will build a house for you." So your servant has found courage to pray this prayer to you. ²⁸Sovereign Lord, you are God! Your covenant is trustworthy, and you have promised these good things to your servant. ²⁹Now be pleased to bless the house of your servant, that it may continue for ever in your sight; for you, Sovereign Lord, have spoken, and with your blessing the house of your servant will be blessed for ever.'

8 In the course of time, David defeated the Philistines and subdued them, and he took Metheg Ammah from the control of the Philistines.

²David also defeated the Moabites. He made them lie down on the ground and measured them off with a length of cord.

Every two lengths of them were put to death, and the third length was allowed to live. So the Moabites became subject to David and brought him tribute.

³Moreover, David defeated Hadadezer son of Rehob, king of Zobah, when he went to restore his monument at the River Euphrates. ⁴David captured a thousand of his chariots, seven thousand charioteers and twenty thousand foot soldiers. He hamstrung all but a hundred of the chariot horses.

⁵When the Arameans of Damascus came to help Hadadezer king of Zobah, David struck down twenty-two thousand of them. ⁶He put garrisons in the Aramean kingdom of Damascus, and the Arameans became subject to him and brought tribute. The Lord gave David victory wherever he went.

⁷David took the gold shields that belonged to the officers of Hadadezer and brought them to Jerusalem. ⁸From Tebah and Berothai, towns that belonged to Hadadezer, King David took a great quantity of bronze.

⁹When Tou king of Hamath heard that David had defeated the entire army of Hadadezer, ¹⁰he sent his son Joram to King David to greet him and congratulate him on his victory in battle over Hadadezer, who had been at war with Tou. Joram brought with him articles of silver, of gold and of bronze.

¹¹King David dedicated these articles to the Lord, as he had done with the silver and gold from all the nations he had subdued: ¹²Edom and Moab, the Ammonites and the Philistines, and Amalek. He also dedicated the plunder taken from Hadadezer son of Rehob, king of Zobah.

¹³And David became famous after he returned from striking down eighteen thousand Edomites in the Valley of Salt.

¹⁴He put garrisons throughout Edom, and all the Edomites became subject to David. The Lord gave David victory wherever he went.

¹⁵ David reigned over all Israel, doing what was just and right for all his people. ¹⁶ Joab son of Zeruiah was over the army; Jehoshaphat son of Ahilud was recorder; ¹⁷ Zadok son of Ahitub and Ahimelek son of Abiathar were priests; Seraiah was secretary; ¹⁸ Benaiah son of Jehoiada was over the Kerethites and Pelethites; and David's sons were priests.

9 David asked, 'Is there anyone still left of the house of Saul to whom I can show kindness for Jonathan's sake?'

² Now there was a servant of Saul's household named Ziba. They summoned him to appear before David, and the king said to him, 'Are you Ziba?'

'At your service,' he replied.

³ The king asked, 'Is there no one still alive from the house of Saul to whom I can show God's kindness?'

Ziba answered the king, 'There is still a son of Jonathan; he is lame in both feet.'

⁴ 'Where is he?' the king asked.

Ziba answered, 'He is at the house of Makir son of Ammiel in Lo Debar.'

⁵ So King David had him brought from Lo Debar, from the house of Makir son of Ammiel.

⁶ When Mephibosheth son of Jonathan, the son of Saul, came to David, he bowed down to pay him honour.

David said, 'Mephibosheth!'

'At your service,' he replied.

⁷ 'Don't be afraid,' David said to him, 'for I will surely show you kindness for the sake of your father Jonathan. I will restore to you all the land that belonged to your grandfather Saul, and you will always eat at my table.'

⁸ Mephibosheth bowed down and said, 'What is your servant, that you should notice a dead dog like me?'

⁹ Then the king summoned Ziba, Saul's steward, and said to him, 'I have given your master's grandson everything that belonged to Saul and his family. ¹⁰ You and your sons and your servants are to farm the land for him and bring in the crops, so that your master's grandson may be provided for. And Mephibosheth, grandson of your master, will always eat at my table.' (Now Ziba had fifteen sons and twenty servants.)

¹¹ Then Ziba said to the king, 'Your servant will do whatever my lord the king commands his servant to do.' So Mephibosheth ate at David's table like one of the king's sons.

¹² Mephibosheth had a young son named Mika, and all the members of Ziba's household were servants of Mephibosheth. ¹³ And Mephibosheth lived in Jerusalem, because he always ate at the king's table; he was lame in both feet.

PSALM 68:28–31

²⁸ Summon your power, God;
    show us your strength, our God, as
        you have done before.
²⁹ Because of your temple at Jerusalem
        kings will bring you gifts.
³⁰ Rebuke the beast among the reeds,
    the herd of bulls among the calves of
        the nations.
Humbled, may the beast bring bars of
        silver.
Scatter the nations who delight in war.
³¹ Envoys will come from Egypt;
    Cush will submit herself to God.

PROVERBS 15:1–3

15 A gentle answer turns away wrath,
    but a harsh word stirs up anger.

² The tongue of the wise adorns
        knowledge,
    but the mouth of the fool gushes folly.

³ The eyes of the LORD are everywhere,

keeping watch on the wicked and the good.

··

■ JOHN 9:28–10:6

²⁸Then they hurled insults at him and said, 'You are this fellow's disciple! We are disciples of Moses! ²⁹We know that God spoke to Moses, but as for this fellow, we don't even know where he comes from.'

³⁰The man answered, 'Now that is remarkable! You don't know where he comes from, yet he opened my eyes. ³¹We know that God does not listen to sinners. He listens to the godly person who does his will. ³²Nobody has ever heard of opening the eyes of a man born blind. ³³If this man were not from God, he could do nothing.'

³⁴To this they replied, 'You were steeped in sin at birth; how dare you lecture us!' And they threw him out.

³⁵Jesus heard that they had thrown him out, and when he found him, he said, 'Do you believe in the Son of Man?'

³⁶'Who is he, sir?' the man asked. 'Tell me so that I may believe in him.'

³⁷Jesus said, 'You have now seen him; in fact, he is the one speaking with you.'

³⁸Then the man said, 'Lord, I believe,' and he worshipped him.

³⁹Jesus said, 'For judgment I have come into this world, so that the blind will see and those who see will become blind.'

⁴⁰Some Pharisees who were with him heard him say this and asked, 'What? Are we blind too?'

⁴¹Jesus said, 'If you were blind, you would not be guilty of sin; but now that you claim you can see, your guilt remains.

10 'Very truly I tell you Pharisees, anyone who does not enter the sheepfold by the gate, but climbs in by some other way, is a thief and a robber. ²The one who enters by the gate is the shepherd of the sheep. ³The gatekeeper opens the gate for him, and the sheep listen to his voice. He calls his own sheep by name and leads them out. ⁴When he has brought out all his own, he goes on ahead of them, and his sheep follow him because they know his voice. ⁵But they will never follow a stranger; in fact, they will run away from him because they do not recognise a stranger's voice.' ⁶Jesus used this figure of speech, but the Pharisees did not understand what he was telling them.

We Become What We Say

'The tongue of the wise adorns knowledge, but the mouth of the fool gushes folly.' **Proverbs 15:2**

Why is the tongue so important? Because the expression of a thing deepens the impression. A word uttered becomes a word made flesh - in us. We become the incarnation of what we express. Jesus said, 'For by your words you will be acquitted, and by your words you will be condemned' (Matt. 12:37). After I saw that a person becomes what he says, I have looked at this verse in a different light. If you tell a lie, you become a lie. The deepest punishment of a lie is to be the one who tells the lie. That person has to live with someone he cannot trust.

Now look at what I am saying from the opposite perspective. When we express good things, positive things, loving things, scriptural things, these things go deeper into us. Clear expression deepens impression.

A brilliant young physicist tells how he often discusses complex issues relating to physics with his wife who doesn't know the first thing about the subject. He told a friend, 'I describe in detail what I am doing and she doesn't understand a word. But sometimes when I'm through – I do'.

If it is true – and I believe it is – that we become the incarnation of what we express, then how careful we ought to be to ensure that what we say is guarded and governed by truth, integrity, and kindness. Always remember: every word you utter becomes flesh – in you.

PRAYER

O Father, how awesome is this thought – I become the incarnation of what I express. Cleanse me deep within so that I may be pure in soul as well as speech. I would be a clarified person. Grant it please, dear Father. In Jesus' name. Amen.

FURTHER STUDY

1 Tim. 4:1-12; Psa. 34:13; Phil. 4:8; Prov. 21:16-31
• In what areas was Timothy to set a good example?
• What should our thoughts be focused on?

June 3

2 SAMUEL 10:1–11:27

10 In the course of time, the king of the Ammonites died, and his son Hanun succeeded him as king. ²David thought, 'I will show kindness to Hanun son of Nahash, just as his father showed kindness to me.' So David sent a delegation to express his sympathy to Hanun concerning his father.

When David's men came to the land of the Ammonites, ³the Ammonite commanders said to Hanun their lord, 'Do you think David is honouring your father by sending envoys to you to express sympathy? Hasn't David sent them to you only to explore the city and spy it out and overthrow it?' ⁴So Hanun seized David's envoys, shaved off half of each man's beard, cut off their garments at the buttocks, and sent them away.

⁵When David was told about this, he sent messengers to meet the men, for they were greatly humiliated. The king said, 'Stay at

Jericho till your beards have grown, and then come back.'

⁶When the Ammonites realised that they had become obnoxious to David, they hired twenty thousand Aramean foot soldiers from Beth Rehob and Zobah, as well as the king of Maakah with a thousand men, and also twelve thousand men from Tob.

⁷On hearing this, David sent Joab out with the entire army of fighting men. ⁸The Ammonites came out and drew up in battle formation at the entrance of their city gate, while the Arameans of Zobah and Rehob and the men of Tob and Maakah were by themselves in the open country.

⁹Joab saw that there were battle lines in front of him and behind him; so he selected some of the best troops in Israel and deployed them against the Arameans. ¹⁰He put the rest of the men under the command of Abishai his brother and deployed them against the Ammonites. ¹¹Joab said, 'If the Arameans are too strong for me, then you

are to come to my rescue; but if the Ammonites are too strong for you, then I will come to rescue you. ¹²Be strong, and let us fight bravely for our people and the cities of our God. The LORD will do what is good in his sight.'

¹³Then Joab and the troops with him advanced to fight the Arameans, and they fled before him. ¹⁴When the Ammonites realised that the Arameans were fleeing, they fled before Abishai and went inside the city. So Joab returned from fighting the Ammonites and came to Jerusalem.

¹⁵After the Arameans saw that they had been routed by Israel, they regrouped. ¹⁶Hadadezer had Arameans brought from beyond the River Euphrates; they went to Helam, with Shobak the commander of Hadadezer's army leading them.

¹⁷When David was told of this, he gathered all Israel, crossed the Jordan and went to Helam. The Arameans formed their battle lines to meet David and fought against him. ¹⁸But they fled before Israel, and David killed seven hundred of their charioteers and forty thousand of their foot soldiers. He also struck down Shobak the commander of their army, and he died there. ¹⁹When all the kings who were vassals of Hadadezer saw that they had been routed by Israel, they made peace with the Israelites and became subject to them.

So the Arameans were afraid to help the Ammonites any more.

11 In the spring, at the time when kings go off to war, David sent Joab out with the king's men and the whole Israelite army. They destroyed the Ammonites and besieged Rabbah. But David remained in Jerusalem.

²One evening David got up from his bed and walked around on the roof of the palace. From the roof he saw a woman washing. The woman was very beautiful, ³and David sent someone to find out about her. The man said, 'She is Bathsheba, the daughter of Eliam and the wife of Uriah the Hittite.' ⁴Then David sent messengers to get her. She came to him, and he slept with her. (Now she was purifying herself from her monthly uncleanness.) Then she went back home. ⁵The woman conceived and sent word to David, saying, 'I am pregnant.'

⁶So David sent this word to Joab: 'Send me Uriah the Hittite.' And Joab sent him to David. ⁷When Uriah came to him, David asked him how Joab was, how the soldiers were and how the war was going. ⁸Then David said to Uriah, 'Go down to your house and wash your feet.' So Uriah left the palace, and a gift from the king was sent after him. ⁹But Uriah slept at the entrance to the palace with all his master's servants and did not go down to his house.

¹⁰David was told, 'Uriah did not go home.' So he asked Uriah, 'Haven't you just come from a military campaign? Why didn't you go home?'

¹¹Uriah said to David, 'The ark and Israel and Judah are staying in tents, and my commander Joab and my lord's men are camped in the open country. How could I go to my house to eat and drink and make love to my wife? As surely as you live, I will not do such a thing!'

¹²Then David said to him, 'Stay here one more day, and tomorrow I will send you back.' So Uriah remained in Jerusalem that day and the next. ¹³At David's invitation, he ate and drank with him, and David made him drunk. But in the evening Uriah went out to sleep on his mat among his master's servants; he did not go home.

¹⁴In the morning David wrote a letter to Joab and sent it with Uriah. ¹⁵In it he wrote, 'Put Uriah out in front where the fighting is fiercest. Then withdraw from him so that he will be struck down and die.'

¹⁶So while Joab had the city under siege, he put Uriah at a place where he knew the strongest defenders were. ¹⁷When the men of the city came out and fought against Joab,

some of the men in David's army fell; moreover, Uriah the Hittite died.

[18] Joab sent David a full account of the battle. [19] He instructed the messenger: 'When you have finished giving the king this account of the battle, [20] the king's anger may flare up, and he may ask you, "Why did you get so close to the city to fight? Didn't you know they would shoot arrows from the wall? [21] Who killed Abimelek son of Jerub-Besheth? Didn't a woman drop an upper millstone on him from the wall, so that he died in Thebez? Why did you get so close to the wall?" If he asks you this, then say to him, "Moreover, your servant Uriah the Hittite is dead."'

[22] The messenger set out, and when he arrived he told David everything Joab had sent him to say. [23] The messenger said to David, 'The men overpowered us and came out against us in the open, but we drove them back to the entrance of the city gate. [24] Then the archers shot arrows at your servants from the wall, and some of the king's men died. Moreover, your servant Uriah the Hittite is dead.'

[25] David told the messenger, 'Say this to Joab: "Don't let this upset you; the sword devours one as well as another. Press the attack against the city and destroy it." Say this to encourage Joab.'

[26] When Uriah's wife heard that her husband was dead, she mourned for him. [27] After the time of mourning was over, David had her brought to his house, and she became his wife and bore him a son. But the thing David had done displeased the LORD.

▬ PSALM 68:32-35

[32] Sing to God, you kingdoms of the earth,
    sing praise to the Lord,
[33] to him who rides across the highest
    heavens, the ancient heavens,
    who thunders with mighty voice.

[34] Proclaim the power of God,
    whose majesty is over Israel,
    whose power is in the heavens.
[35] You, God, are awesome in your
    sanctuary;
    the God of Israel gives power and
    strength to his people.

Praise be to God!

▬ PROVERBS 15:4-5

[4] The soothing tongue is a tree of life,
    but a perverse tongue crushes the
    spirit.

[5] A fool spurns a parent's discipline,
    but whoever heeds correction shows
    prudence.

▬ JOHN 10:7-30

[7] Therefore Jesus said again, 'Very truly I tell you, I am the gate for the sheep. [8] All who have come before me are thieves and robbers, but the sheep have not listened to them. [9] I am the gate; whoever enters through me will be saved. They will come in and go out, and find pasture. [10] The thief comes only to steal and kill and destroy; I have come that they may have life, and have it to the full.

[11] 'I am the good shepherd. The good shepherd lays down his life for the sheep. [12] The hired hand is not the shepherd and does not own the sheep. So when he sees the wolf coming, he abandons the sheep and runs away. Then the wolf attacks the flock and scatters it. [13] The man runs away because he is a hired hand and cares nothing for the sheep.

[14] 'I am the good shepherd; I know my sheep and my sheep know me – [15] just as the Father knows me and I know the

Father – and I lay down my life for the sheep. [16] I have other sheep that are not of this sheepfold. I must bring them also. They too will listen to my voice, and there shall be one flock and one shepherd. [17] The reason my Father loves me is that I lay down my life – only to take it up again. [18] No one takes it from me, but I lay it down of my own accord. I have authority to lay it down and authority to take it up again. This command I received from my Father.'

[19] The Jews who heard these words were again divided. [20] Many of them said, 'He is demon-possessed and raving mad. Why listen to him?'

[21] But others said, 'These are not the sayings of a man possessed by a demon. Can a demon open the eyes of the blind?'

[22] Then came the Festival of Dedication at Jerusalem. It was winter, [23] and Jesus was in the temple courts walking in Solomon's Colonnade. [24] The Jews who were there gathered round him, saying, 'How long will you keep us in suspense? If you are the Messiah, tell us plainly.'

[25] Jesus answered, 'I did tell you, but you do not believe. The works I do in my Father's name testify about me, [26] but you do not believe because you are not my sheep. [27] My sheep listen to my voice; I know them, and they follow me. [28] I give them eternal life, and they shall never perish; no one will snatch them out of my hand. [29] My Father, who has given them to me, is greater than all; no one can snatch them out of my Father's hand. [30] I and the Father are one.'

Life to its Fullest

'... I have come that they may have life, and have it to the full.' **John 10:10**

A nest which God seeks to overturn in our lives is spiritual complacency. Many Christians are content to live at a level far below the best. It might be comfortable in the nest, but it is far better to expand one's wings, launch out into the clear, blue sky, and live life to its fullest potential. God's desire is to get you out of the nest and up into the air.

I am thinking particularly of those Christians who, although soundly saved and fully committed to Jesus Christ, have never experienced all the fullness of the Holy Spirit. Although every Christian has the Holy Spirit (1 Cor. 12:3), the Holy Spirit does not have every Christian. When you surrendered your life to Jesus Christ, the Holy Spirit came in to regenerate you, give you a new birth, but now you need to experience another encounter with the Spirit that lifts you clean out of the nest and up into the air.

The text before us today claims that Jesus came not merely to give us life but to give it – abundantly. One writer says of this verse: 'At conversion, Christ gives us life, but when we experience the fullness of the Spirit, we encounter not merely life but life that is abundant. In conversion, God's life is imparted to us. In the fullness of the Spirit, God's life inundates us.' A sign over a shop read: 'Life Ltd'. A sign could be put over our individual and collective lives: 'Life Ltd'. And yet Jesus said that the purpose of His coming was to give life to the full.

PRAYER

O Father, take me from life limited to Life Unlimited. I have lived far too long in the nest. Now I want to get up into the air. Amen.

FURTHER STUDY

Acts 1-2; John 7:38-39; 1 Cor. 3:16; Rom. 8:11
• What caused the disciples to soar to new heights?
• What does the word 'quicken' (Rom 8:11, AV) mean?

June 4

■ 2 SAMUEL 12:1–13:39

12 The LORD sent Nathan to David. When he came to him, he said, 'There were two men in a certain town, one rich and the other poor. ²The rich man had a very large number of sheep and cattle, ³but the poor man had nothing except one little ewe lamb that he had bought. He raised it, and it grew up with him and his children. It shared his food, drank from his cup and even slept in his arms. It was like a daughter to him.

⁴'Now a traveller came to the rich man, but the rich man refrained from taking one of his own sheep or cattle to prepare a meal for the traveller who had come to him. Instead, he took the ewe lamb that belonged to the poor man and prepared it for the one who had come to him.'

⁵David burned with anger against the man and said to Nathan, 'As surely as the LORD lives, the man who did this must die! ⁶He must pay for that lamb four times over, because he did such a thing and had no pity.'

⁷Then Nathan said to David, 'You are the man! This is what the LORD, the God of Israel, says: "I anointed you king over Israel, and I delivered you from the hand of Saul. ⁸I gave your master's house to you, and your master's wives into your arms. I gave you all Israel and Judah. And if all this had been too little, I would have given you even more. ⁹Why did you despise the word of the LORD by doing what is evil in his eyes? You struck down Uriah the Hittite with the sword and took his wife to be your own. You killed him with the sword of the Ammonites. ¹⁰Now, therefore, the sword shall never depart from your house, because you despised me and took the wife of Uriah the Hittite to be your own."

¹¹'This is what the LORD says: "Out of your own household I am going to bring calamity on you. Before your very eyes I will take your wives and give them to one who is close to you, and he will sleep with your wives in broad daylight. ¹²You did it in secret, but I will do this thing in broad daylight before all Israel."'

¹³Then David said to Nathan, 'I have sinned against the LORD.'

Nathan replied, 'The LORD has taken away your sin. You are not going to die. ¹⁴But because by doing this you have shown utter contempt for the LORD, the son born to you will die.'

¹⁵After Nathan had gone home, the LORD struck the child that Uriah's wife had borne to David, and he became ill. ¹⁶David pleaded with God for the child. He fasted and spent the nights lying in sackcloth on the ground. ¹⁷The elders of his household stood beside him to

get him up from the ground, but he refused, and he would not eat any food with them.

¹⁸ On the seventh day the child died. David's attendants were afraid to tell him that the child was dead, for they thought, 'While the child was still living, he wouldn't listen to us when we spoke to him. How can we now tell him the child is dead? He may do something desperate.'

¹⁹ David noticed that his attendants were whispering among themselves, and he realised that the child was dead. 'Is the child dead?' he asked.

'Yes,' they replied, 'he is dead.'

²⁰ Then David got up from the ground. After he had washed, put on lotions and changed his clothes, he went into the house of the LORD and worshipped. Then he went to his own house, and at his request they served him food, and he ate.

²¹ His attendants asked him, 'Why are you acting in this way? While the child was alive, you fasted and wept, but now that the child is dead, you get up and eat!'

²² He answered, 'While the child was still alive, I fasted and wept. I thought, "Who knows? The LORD may be gracious to me and let the child live." ²³ But now that he is dead, why should I go on fasting? Can I bring him back again? I will go to him, but he will not return to me.'

²⁴ Then David comforted his wife Bathsheba, and he went to her and made love to her. She gave birth to a son, and they named him Solomon. The LORD loved him; ²⁵ and because the LORD loved him, he sent word through Nathan the prophet to name him Jedidiah.

²⁶ Meanwhile Joab fought against Rabbah of the Ammonites and captured the royal citadel. ²⁷ Joab then sent messengers to David, saying, 'I have fought against Rabbah and taken its water supply. ²⁸ Now muster the rest of the troops and besiege the city and capture it. Otherwise I shall take the city, and it will be named after me.'

²⁹ So David mustered the entire army and went to Rabbah, and attacked and captured it. ³⁰ David took the crown from their king's head, and it was placed on his own head. It weighed a talent of gold, and it was set with precious stones. David took a great quantity of plunder from the city ³¹ and brought out the people who were there, consigning them to labour with saws and with iron picks and axes, and he made them work at brickmaking. David did this to all the Ammonite towns. Then he and his entire army returned to Jerusalem.

13 In the course of time, Amnon son of David fell in love with Tamar, the beautiful sister of Absalom son of David.

² Amnon became so obsessed with his sister Tamar that he made himself ill. She was a virgin, and it seemed impossible for him to do anything to her.

³ Now Amnon had an advisor named Jonadab son of Shimeah, David's brother. Jonadab was a very shrewd man. ⁴ He asked Amnon, 'Why do you, the king's son, look so haggard morning after morning? Won't you tell me?'

Amnon said to him, 'I'm in love with Tamar, my brother Absalom's sister.'

⁵ 'Go to bed and pretend to be ill,' Jonadab said. 'When your father comes to see you, say to him, "I would like my sister Tamar to come and give me something to eat. Let her prepare the food in my sight so that I may watch her and then eat it from her hand."'

⁶ So Amnon lay down and pretended to be ill. When the king came to see him, Amnon said to him, 'I would like my sister Tamar to come and make some special bread in my sight, so that I may eat from her hand.'

⁷ David sent word to Tamar at the palace: 'Go to the house of your brother Amnon and prepare some food for him.' ⁸ So Tamar went to the house of her brother Amnon, who was lying down. She took some dough, kneaded it, made the bread in his sight and baked it. ⁹ Then she took the pan and served

him the bread, but he refused to eat.

'Send everyone out of here,' Amnon said. So everyone left him. ¹⁰Then Amnon said to Tamar, 'Bring the food here into my bedroom so that I may eat from your hand.' And Tamar took the bread she had prepared and brought it to her brother Amnon in his bedroom. ¹¹But when she took it to him to eat, he grabbed her and said, 'Come to bed with me, my sister.'

¹²'No, my brother!' she said to him. 'Don't force me! Such a thing should not be done in Israel! Don't do this wicked thing. ¹³What about me? Where could I get rid of my disgrace? And what about you? You would be like one of the wicked fools in Israel. Please speak to the king; he will not keep me from being married to you.' ¹⁴But he refused to listen to her, and since he was stronger than she, he raped her.

¹⁵Then Amnon hated her with intense hatred. In fact, he hated her more than he had loved her. Amnon said to her, 'Get up and get out!'

¹⁶'No!' she said to him. 'Sending me away would be a greater wrong than what you have already done to me.'

But he refused to listen to her. ¹⁷He called his personal servant and said, 'Get this woman out of my sight and bolt the door after her.' ¹⁸So his servant put her out and bolted the door after her. She was wearing an ornate robe, for this was the kind of garment the virgin daughters of the king wore. ¹⁹Tamar put ashes on her head and tore the ornate robe she was wearing. She put her hands on her head and went away, weeping aloud as she went.

²⁰Her brother Absalom said to her, 'Has that Amnon, your brother, been with you? Be quiet for now, my sister; he is your brother. Don't take this thing to heart.' And Tamar lived in her brother Absalom's house, a desolate woman.

²¹When King David heard all this, he was furious. ²²And Absalom never said a word

to Amnon, either good or bad; he hated Amnon because he had disgraced his sister Tamar.

²³Two years later, when Absalom's sheepshearers were at Baal Hazor near the border of Ephraim, he invited all the king's sons to come there. ²⁴Absalom went to the king and said, 'Your servant has had shearers come. Will the king and his attendants please join me?'

²⁵'No, my son,' the king replied. 'All of us should not go; we would only be a burden to you.' Although Absalom urged him, he still refused to go but gave him his blessing.

²⁶Then Absalom said, 'If not, please let my brother Amnon come with us.'

The king asked him, 'Why should he go with you?' ²⁷But Absalom urged him, so he sent with him Amnon and the rest of the king's sons.

²⁸Absalom ordered his men, 'Listen! When Amnon is in high spirits from drinking wine and I say to you, "Strike Amnon down," then kill him. Don't be afraid. Haven't I given you this order? Be strong and brave.' ²⁹So Absalom's men did to Amnon what Absalom had ordered. Then all the king's sons got up, mounted their mules and fled.

³⁰While they were on their way, the report came to David: 'Absalom has struck down all the king's sons; not one of them is left.' ³¹The king stood up, tore his clothes and lay down on the ground; and all his attendants stood by with their clothes torn.

³²But Jonadab son of Shimeah, David's brother, said, 'My lord should not think that they killed all the princes; only Amnon is dead. This has been Absalom's express intention ever since the day that Amnon raped his sister Tamar. ³³My lord the king should not be concerned about the report that all the king's sons are dead. Only Amnon is dead.'

³⁴Meanwhile, Absalom had fled.

Now the man standing watch looked up

and saw many people on the road west of him, coming down the side of the hill. The watchman went and told the king, 'I see men in the direction of Horonaim, on the side of the hill.'

³⁵ Jonadab said to the king, 'See, the king's sons have come; it has happened just as your servant said.'

³⁶ As he finished speaking, the king's sons came in, wailing loudly. The king, too, and all his attendants wept very bitterly.

³⁷ Absalom fled and went to Talmai son of Ammihud, the king of Geshur. But King David mourned many days for his son.

³⁸ After Absalom fled and went to Geshur, he stayed there for three years. ³⁹ And King David longed to go to Absalom, for he was consoled concerning Amnon's death.

▬ PSALM 69:1–4

¹ Save me, O God,
    for the waters have come up to my neck.
² I sink in the miry depths,
    where there is no foothold.
I have come into the deep waters;
    the floods engulf me.
³ I am worn out calling for help;
    my throat is parched.
My eyes fail,
    looking for my God.
⁴ Those who hate me without reason
    outnumber the hairs of my head;
many are my enemies without cause,
    those who seek to destroy me.
I am forced to restore
    what I did not steal.

▬ PROVERBS 15:6–7

⁶ The house of the righteous contains
        great treasure,
    but the income of the wicked brings
        ruin.

⁷ The lips of the wise spread knowledge,
    but the hearts of fools are not upright.

▬ JOHN 10:31–11:6

³¹ Again his Jewish opponents picked up stones to stone him, ³² but Jesus said to them, 'I have shown you many good works from the Father. For which of these do you stone me?'

³³ 'We are not stoning you for any good work,' they replied, 'but for blasphemy, because you, a mere man, claim to be God.'

³⁴ Jesus answered them, 'Is it not written in your Law, "I have said you are 'gods' "? ³⁵ If he called them "gods", to whom the word of God came – and Scripture cannot be set aside – ³⁶ what about the one whom the Father set apart as his very own and sent into the world? Why then do you accuse me of blasphemy because I said, "I am God's Son"? ³⁷ Do not believe me unless I do the works of my Father. ³⁸ But if I do them, even though you do not believe me, believe the works, that you may know and understand that the Father is in me, and I in the Father.' ³⁹ Again they tried to seize him, but he escaped their grasp.

⁴⁰ Then Jesus went back across the Jordan to the place where John had been baptising in the early days. There he stayed, ⁴¹ and many people came to him. They said, 'Though John never performed a sign, all that John said about this man was true.' ⁴² And in that place many believed in Jesus.

11 Now a man named Lazarus was ill. He was from Bethany, the village of Mary and her sister Martha. ² (This Mary, whose brother Lazarus now lay ill, was the same one who poured perfume on the Lord and wiped his feet with her hair.) ³ So the sisters sent word to Jesus, 'Lord, the one you love is ill.'

⁴ When he heard this, Jesus said, 'This illness will not end in death. No, it is for

God's glory so that God's Son may be glorified through it.' ⁵Now Jesus loved Martha and her sister and Lazarus. ⁶So when he heard that Lazarus was ill, he stayed where he was two more days ...

God's Great Masterpiece

'... and Scripture cannot be set aside ...' **John 10:35**

I subscribe to the supervisal inspiration of the Bible. I believe God led the minds and hearts of the writers of Scripture to go to the right sources for information, to come up with the required data, and in the process protected them from exposure to error, deceit, or imposture. He supervised them in their research, in their reporting, and when He spoke directly to them, He was there also to make sure that they received clearly the message He wanted to convey. Ian Macpherson puts this truth most powerfully in his book *The Faith Once Delivered* when he says: 'As in the mystery of the Incarnation, God linked Himself to humanity, so in the mystery of the inspiration of the Holy Scripture, God made use of human channels, yet He never surrendered His Divine authorship or permitted the Book to become the word of man rather than the word of God'.

Another writer, H. O. Mackey, put it like this: 'Who built St. Paul's Cathedral? So many masons, carpenters, iron-workers, carvers, painters – and then there was Wren. He was not a mason, or a carpenter ... and never laid a stone. What did he do? He did it all. He planned it, inspired it with his thought'. Mackey does not intend to dishonour the workmen who toiled hard and long, but simply to make the point that in the final analysis St. Paul's Cathedral is Sir Christopher Wren's masterpiece.

Who wrote the Bible? Moses, David, Isaiah, Jeremiah, John, Peter, Paul, and many others. But whose book is it really? It is God's.

PRAYER

O God, it is the entrance of Your Word that brings light, and the neglect of Your Word that brings darkness. Help me to expose myself more and more to that light, so that I may walk through life with a sure and steady tread. In Jesus' name. Amen.

FURTHER STUDY

Rev. 22:12-21;
Deut. 4:2; 12:32; Prov. 30:5-6
• What was the conclusion of the writer of Proverbs?
• What was John's warning?

June 5

JUNE 5

■ 2 SAMUEL 14:1–15:37

14 Joab son of Zeruiah knew that the king's heart longed for Absalom. ² So Joab sent someone to Tekoa and had a wise woman brought from there. He said to her, 'Pretend you are in mourning. Dress in mourning clothes, and don't use any cosmetic lotions. Act like a woman who has spent many days grieving for the dead. ³ Then go to the king and speak these words to him.' And Joab put the words in her mouth.

⁴ When the woman from Tekoa went to the king, she fell with her face to the ground to pay him honour, and she said, 'Help me, Your Majesty!'

⁵ The king asked her, 'What is troubling you?'

She said, 'I am a widow; my husband is dead. ⁶ I your servant had two sons. They got into a fight with each other in the field, and no one was there to separate them. One struck the other and killed him. ⁷ Now the whole clan has risen up against your servant; they say, "Hand over the one who struck his brother down, so that we may put him to death for the life of his brother whom he killed; then we will get rid of the heir as well." They would put out the only burning coal I have left, leaving my husband neither name nor descendant on the face of the earth.'

⁸ The king said to the woman, 'Go home, and I will issue an order on your behalf.'

⁹ But the woman from Tekoa said to him, 'Let my lord the king pardon me and my family, and let the king and his throne be without guilt.'

¹⁰ The king replied, 'If anyone says anything to you, bring them to me, and they will not bother you again.'

¹¹ She said, 'Then let the king invoke the LORD his God to prevent the avenger of blood from adding to the destruction, so that my son shall not be destroyed.'

'As surely as the LORD lives,' he said, 'not one hair of your son's head will fall to the ground.'

¹² Then the woman said, 'Let your servant speak a word to my lord the king.'

'Speak,' he replied.

¹³ The woman said, 'Why then have you devised a thing like this against the people of God? When the king says this, does he not convict himself, for the king has not brought back his banished son? ¹⁴ Like water spilled on the ground, which cannot be recovered, so we must die. But that is not what God desires; rather, he devises ways so that a banished person does not remain banished from him.

¹⁵ 'And now I have come to say this to my lord the king because the people have made me afraid. Your servant thought, "I will speak to the king; perhaps he will grant his servant's request. ¹⁶ Perhaps the king will agree to deliver his servant from the hand of the man who is trying to cut off both me and my son from God's inheritance."

¹⁷ 'And now your servant says, "May the word of my lord the king secure my inheritance, for my lord the king is like an angel of God in discerning good and evil. May the LORD your God be with you."'

¹⁸ Then the king said to the woman, 'Don't keep from me the answer to what I am going to ask you.'

'Let my lord the king speak,' the woman said.

¹⁹ The king asked, 'Isn't the hand of Joab with you in all this?'

The woman answered, 'As surely as you

live, my lord the king, no one can turn to the right or to the left from anything my lord the king says. Yes, it was your servant Joab who instructed me to do this and who put all these words into the mouth of your servant. ²⁰Your servant Joab did this to change the present situation. My lord has wisdom like that of an angel of God – he knows everything that happens in the land.'

²¹The king said to Joab, 'Very well, I will do it. Go, bring back the young man Absalom.'

²²Joab fell with his face to the ground to pay him honour, and he blessed the king. Joab said, 'Today your servant knows that he has found favour in your eyes, my lord the king, because the king has granted his servant's request.'

²³Then Joab went to Geshur and brought Absalom back to Jerusalem. ²⁴But the king said, 'He must go to his own house; he must not see my face.' So Absalom went to his own house and did not see the face of the king.

²⁵In all Israel there was not a man so highly praised for his handsome appearance as Absalom. From the top of his head to the sole of his foot there was no blemish in him. ²⁶Whenever he cut the hair of his head – he used to cut his hair once a year because it became too heavy for him – he would weigh it, and its weight was two hundred shekels by the royal standard.

²⁷Three sons and a daughter were born to Absalom. His daughter's name was Tamar, and she became a beautiful woman.

²⁸Absalom lived for two years in Jerusalem without seeing the king's face. ²⁹Then Absalom sent for Joab in order to send him to the king, but Joab refused to come to him. So he sent a second time, but he refused to come. ³⁰Then he said to his servants, 'Look, Joab's field is next to mine, and he has barley there. Go and set it on fire.' So Absalom's servants set the field on fire.

³¹Then Joab did go to Absalom's house, and he said to him, 'Why have your servants set my field on fire?'

³²Absalom said to Joab, 'Look, I sent word to you and said, "Come here so that I can send you to the king to ask, 'Why have I come from Geshur? It would be better for me if I were still there!' " Now then, I want to see the king's face, and if I am guilty of anything, let him put me to death.'

³³So Joab went to the king and told him this. Then the king summoned Absalom, and he came in and bowed down with his face to the ground before the king. And the king kissed Absalom.

15 In the course of time, Absalom provided himself with a chariot and horses and with fifty men to run ahead of him. ²He would get up early and stand by the side of the road leading to the city gate. Whenever anyone came with a complaint to be placed before the king for a decision, Absalom would call out to him, 'What town are you from?' He would answer, 'Your servant is from one of the tribes of Israel.' ³Then Absalom would say to him, 'Look, your claims are valid and proper, but there is no representative of the king to hear you.' ⁴And Absalom would add, 'If only I were appointed judge in the land! Then everyone who has a complaint or case could come to me and I would see that they receive justice.'

⁵Also, whenever anyone approached him to bow down before him, Absalom would reach out his hand, take hold of him and kiss him. ⁶Absalom behaved in this way towards all the Israelites who came to the king asking for justice, and so he stole the hearts of the people of Israel.

⁷At the end of four years, Absalom said to the king, 'Let me go to Hebron and fulfil a vow I made to the LORD. ⁸While your servant was living at Geshur in Aram, I made this vow: "If the LORD takes me back to Jerusalem, I will worship the LORD in Hebron." '

⁹The king said to him, 'Go in peace.' So he went to Hebron.

¹⁰Then Absalom sent secret messengers

throughout the tribes of Israel to say, 'As soon as you hear the sound of the trumpets, then say, "Absalom is king in Hebron."' [11] Two hundred men from Jerusalem had accompanied Absalom. They had been invited as guests and went quite innocently, knowing nothing about the matter. [12] While Absalom was offering sacrifices, he also sent for Ahithophel the Gilonite, David's counsellor, to come from Giloh, his home town. And so the conspiracy gained strength, and Absalom's following kept on increasing.

[13] A messenger came and told David, 'The hearts of the people of Israel are with Absalom.'

[14] Then David said to all his officials who were with him in Jerusalem, 'Come! We must flee, or none of us will escape from Absalom. We must leave immediately, or he will move quickly to overtake us and bring ruin on us and put the city to the sword.'

[15] The king's officials answered him, 'Your servants are ready to do whatever our lord the king chooses.'

[16] The king set out, with his entire household following him; but he left ten concubines to take care of the palace. [17] So the king set out, with all the people following him, and they halted at the edge of the city. [18] All his men marched past him, along with all the Kerethites and Pelethites; and all the six hundred Gittites who had accompanied him from Gath marched before the king.

[19] The king said to Ittai the Gittite, 'Why should you come along with us? Go back and stay with King Absalom. You are a foreigner, an exile from your homeland. [20] You came only yesterday. And today shall I make you wander about with us, when I do not know where I am going? Go back, and take your people with you. May the LORD show you kindness and faithfulness.'

[21] But Ittai replied to the king, 'As surely as the LORD lives, and as my lord the king lives, wherever my lord the king may be, whether it means life or death, there will

your servant be.'

[22] David said to Ittai, 'Go ahead, march on.' So Ittai the Gittite marched on with all his men and the families that were with him.

[23] The whole countryside wept aloud as all the people passed by. The king also crossed the Kidron Valley, and all the people moved on towards the wilderness.

[24] Zadok was there, too, and all the Levites who were with him were carrying the ark of the covenant of God. They set down the ark of God, and Abiathar offered sacrifices until all the people had finished leaving the city.

[25] Then the king said to Zadok, 'Take the ark of God back into the city. If I find favour in the LORD's eyes, he will bring me back and let me see it and his dwelling-place again. [26] But if he says, "I am not pleased with you," then I am ready; let him do to me whatever seems good to him.'

[27] The king also said to Zadok the priest, 'Do you understand? Go back to the city with my blessing. Take your son Ahimaaz with you, and also Abiathar's son Jonathan. You and Abiathar return with your two sons. [28] I will wait at the fords in the wilderness until word comes from you to inform me.' [29] So Zadok and Abiathar took the ark of God back to Jerusalem and stayed there.

[30] But David continued up the Mount of Olives, weeping as he went; his head was covered and he was barefoot. All the people with him covered their heads too and were weeping as they went up. [31] Now David had been told, 'Ahithophel is among the conspirators with Absalom.' So David prayed, 'LORD, turn Ahithophel's counsel into foolishness.'

[32] When David arrived at the summit, where people used to worship God, Hushai the Arkite was there to meet him, his robe torn and dust on his head. [33] David said to him, 'If you go with me, you will be a burden to me. [34] But if you return to the city and say

to Absalom, "Your Majesty, I will be your servant; I was your father's servant in the past, but now I will be your servant," then you can help me by frustrating Ahithophel's advice. ³⁵ Won't the priests Zadok and Abiathar be there with you? Tell them anything you hear in the king's palace. ³⁶ Their two sons, Ahimaaz son of Zadok and Jonathan son of Abiathar, are there with them. Send them to me with anything you hear.'

³⁷ So Hushai, David's confidant, arrived at Jerusalem as Absalom was entering the city.

■ PSALM 69:5-12

⁵ You, God, know my folly;
my guilt is not hidden from you.

⁶ Lord, the LORD Almighty,
may those who hope in you
not be disgraced because of me;
God of Israel,
may those who seek you
not be put to shame because of me.
⁷ For I endure scorn for your sake,
and shame covers my face.
⁸ I am a foreigner to my own family,
a stranger to my own mother's
children;
⁹ for zeal for your house consumes me,
and the insults of those who insult you
fall on me.
¹⁰ When I weep and fast,
I must endure scorn;
¹¹ when I put on sackcloth,
people make sport of me.
¹² Those who sit at the gate mock me,
and I am the song of the drunkards.

■ PROVERBS 15:8-9

⁸ The LORD detests the sacrifice of the
wicked,

but the prayer of the upright pleases
him.

⁹ The LORD detests the way of the
wicked,
but he loves those who pursue
righteousness.

■ JOHN 11:7-20

⁷ ... and then he said to his disciples, 'Let us go back to Judea.'

⁸ 'But Rabbi,' they said, 'a short while ago the Jews there tried to stone you, and yet you are going back?'

⁹ Jesus answered, 'Are there not twelve hours of daylight? Anyone who walks in the day-time will not stumble, for they see by this world's light. ¹⁰ It is when a person walks at night that they stumble, for they have no light.'

¹¹ After he had said this, he went on to tell them, 'Our friend Lazarus has fallen asleep; but I am going there to wake him up.'

¹² His disciples replied, 'Lord, if he sleeps, he will get better.' ¹³ Jesus had been speaking of his death, but his disciples thought he meant natural sleep.

¹⁴ So then he told them plainly, 'Lazarus is dead, ¹⁵ and for your sake I am glad I was not there, so that you may believe. But let us go to him.'

¹⁶ Then Thomas (also known as Didymus) said to the rest of the disciples, 'Let us also go, that we may die with him.'

¹⁷ On his arrival, Jesus found that Lazarus had already been in the tomb for four days. ¹⁸ Now Bethany was less than two miles from Jerusalem, ¹⁹ and many Jews had come to Martha and Mary to comfort them in the loss of their brother. ²⁰ When Martha heard that Jesus was coming, she went out to meet him, but Mary stayed at home.

Worship - Expected of All

'... the prayer of the upright pleases him.'
Proverbs 15:8

When you can stop in the midst of life's most pressing problems and give yourself eagerly to worshipping God, then you are moving along the road to knowing God more intimately. Sometimes when I have had the occasion to talk face to face with people who were going through difficult circumstances, I have asked them, 'How does all this affect your ability to worship God?' Most have responded something like this, 'I find it very difficult to give my heart in worship as I struggle with these problems.' And some have said, 'I find it utterly impossible'.

Are we justified in refusing to worship God because life has dealt us some hard blows? Those who are at a standstill spiritually might react like this, 'Yes, how can God expect me to worship Him when He has allowed these troubles to weigh me down?' Those moving slowly along the road of discipleship might say, 'I know I should worship Him, but my preoccupation with my problems makes it almost impossible to do so'. The spiritually mature will affirm, 'Nothing is more important than the worship of the One who holds my life in His hands. Because He is God then I know that no matter how things might look to the contrary, all will be well. Thus my heart delights to worship Him'.

Christian counselling ought to be seen (though in some parts of the church it isn't) as restoring people to worship. This may be hard for some to accept, but it is true nevertheless - nothing that ever happens to us can justify a Christian's refusal to worship God.

PRAYER

My Father and my God, may this emphasis on worship remain undiminished as I turn to other things. I see it is so central. Help me not only to remember it but to apply it. In Jesus' name. Amen.

FURTHER STUDY

1 Cor. 1:1-17; Acts 3:11-16; 14:11-15

• What was a problem in the early church?
• How did Peter and John deal with this problem?

June 6

16 When David had gone a short distance beyond the summit, there

was Ziba, the steward of Mephibosheth, waiting to meet him. He had a string of donkeys saddled and loaded with two hundred loaves of bread, a hundred cakes of raisins, a hundred cakes of figs and a skin of wine.

²The king asked Ziba, 'Why have you brought these?'

Ziba answered, 'The donkeys are for the king's household to ride on, the bread and fruit are for the men to eat, and the wine is to refresh those who become exhausted in the wilderness.'

³The king then asked, 'Where is your master's grandson?'

Ziba said to him, 'He is staying in Jerusalem, because he thinks, "Today the Israelites will restore to me my grandfather's kingdom."'

⁴Then the king said to Ziba, 'All that belonged to Mephibosheth is now yours.'

'I humbly bow,' Ziba said. 'May I find favour in your eyes, my lord the king.'

⁵As King David approached Bahurim, a man from the same clan as Saul's family came out from there. His name was Shimei son of Gera, and he cursed as he came out. ⁶He pelted David and all the king's officials with stones, though all the troops and the special guard were on David's right and left. ⁷As he cursed, Shimei said, 'Get out, get out, you murderer, you scoundrel! ⁸The LORD has repaid you for all the blood you shed in the household of Saul, in whose place you have reigned. The LORD has given the kingdom into the hands of your son Absalom. You have come to ruin because you are a murderer!'

⁹Then Abishai son of Zeruiah said to the king, 'Why should this dead dog curse my lord the king? Let me go over and cut off his head.'

¹⁰But the king said, 'What does this have to do with you, you sons of Zeruiah? If he is cursing because the LORD said to him, "Curse David," who can ask, "Why do you do this?"'

¹¹David then said to Abishai and all his officials, 'My son, my own flesh and blood, is trying to kill me. How much more, then, this Benjaminite! Leave him alone; let him

curse, for the LORD has told him to. ¹²It may be that the LORD will look upon my misery and restore to me his covenant blessing instead of his curse today.'

¹³So David and his men continued along the road while Shimei was going along the hillside opposite him, cursing as he went and throwing stones at him and showering him with dirt. ¹⁴The king and all the people with him arrived at their destination exhausted. And there he refreshed himself.

¹⁵Meanwhile, Absalom and all the men of Israel came to Jerusalem, and Ahithophel was with him. ¹⁶Then Hushai the Arkite, David's confidant, went to Absalom and said to him, 'Long live the king! Long live the king!'

¹⁷Absalom said to Hushai, 'So this is the love you show your friend? If he's your friend, why didn't you go with him?'

¹⁸Hushai said to Absalom, 'No, the one chosen by the LORD, by these people and by all the men of Israel – his I will be, and I will remain with him. ¹⁹Furthermore, whom should I serve? Should I not serve the son? Just as I served your father, so I will serve you.'

²⁰Absalom said to Ahithophel, 'Give us your advice. What should we do?'

²¹Ahithophel answered, 'Sleep with your father's concubines whom he left to take care of the palace. Then all Israel will hear that you have made yourself obnoxious to your father, and the hands of everyone with you will be more resolute.' ²²So they pitched a tent for Absalom on the roof, and he slept with his father's concubines in the sight of all Israel.

²³Now in those days the advice Ahithophel gave was like that of one who enquires of God. That was how both David and Absalom regarded all of Ahithophel's advice.

17 Ahithophel said to Absalom, 'I would choose twelve thousand men and set out tonight in pursuit of David. ²I would attack him while he is weary and weak. I would strike him with terror,

and then all the people with him will flee. I would strike down only the king ³and bring all the people back to you. The death of the man you seek will mean the return of all; all the people will be unharmed.' ⁴This plan seemed good to Absalom and to all the elders of Israel.

⁵But Absalom said, 'Summon also Hushai the Arkite, so that we can hear what he has to say as well.' ⁶When Hushai came to him, Absalom said, 'Ahithophel has given this advice. Should we do what he says? If not, give us your opinion.'

⁷Hushai replied to Absalom, 'The advice Ahithophel has given is not good this time. ⁸You know your father and his men; they are fighters, and as fierce as a wild bear robbed of her cubs. Besides, your father is an experienced fighter; he will not spend the night with the troops. ⁹Even now, he is hidden in a cave or some other place. If he should attack your troops first, whoever hears about it will say, "There has been a slaughter among the troops who follow Absalom." ¹⁰Then even the bravest soldier, whose heart is like the heart of a lion, will melt with fear, for all Israel knows that your father is a fighter and that those with him are brave.

¹¹'So I advise you: let all Israel, from Dan to Beersheba – as numerous as the sand on the seashore – be gathered to you, with you yourself leading them into battle. ¹²Then we will attack him wherever he may be found, and we will fall on him as dew settles on the ground. Neither he nor any of his men will be left alive. ¹³If he withdraws into a city, then all Israel will bring ropes to that city, and we will drag it down to the valley until not so much as a pebble is left.'

¹⁴Absalom and all the men of Israel said, 'The advice of Hushai the Arkite is better than that of Ahithophel.' For the LORD had determined to frustrate the good advice of Ahithophel in order to bring disaster on Absalom.

¹⁵Hushai told Zadok and Abiathar, the priests, 'Ahithophel has advised Absalom and the elders of Israel to do such and such, but I have advised them to do so and so. ¹⁶Now send a message at once and tell David, "Do not spend the night at the fords in the wilderness; cross over without fail, or the king and all the people with him will be swallowed up."'

¹⁷Jonathan and Ahimaaz were staying at En Rogel. A female servant was to go and inform them, and they were to go and tell King David, for they could not risk being seen entering the city. ¹⁸But a young man saw them and told Absalom. So the two of them left at once and went to the house of a man in Bahurim. He had a well in his courtyard, and they climbed down into it. ¹⁹His wife took a covering and spread it out over the opening of the well and scattered corn over it. No one knew anything about it.

²⁰When Absalom's men came to the woman at the house, they asked, 'Where are Ahimaaz and Jonathan?'

The woman answered them, 'They crossed over the brook.' The men searched but found no one, so they returned to Jerusalem.

²¹After they had gone, the two climbed out of the well and went to inform King David. They said to him, 'Set out and cross the river at once; Ahithophel has advised such and such against you.' ²²So David and all the people with him set out and crossed the Jordan. By daybreak, no one was left who had not crossed the Jordan.

²³When Ahithophel saw that his advice had not been followed, he saddled his donkey and set out for his house in his home town. He put his house in order and then hanged himself. So he died and was buried in his father's tomb.

²⁴David went to Mahanaim, and Absalom crossed the Jordan with all the men of Israel. ²⁵Absalom had appointed Amasa over the army in place of Joab. Amasa was

the son of Jether, an Ishmaelite who had married Abigail, the daughter of Nahash and sister of Zeruiah the mother of Joab. ²⁶ The Israelites and Absalom camped in the land of Gilead.

²⁷ When David came to Mahanaim, Shobi son of Nahash from Rabbah of the Ammonites, and Makir son of Ammiel from Lo Debar, and Barzillai the Gileadite from Rogelim ²⁸ brought bedding and bowls and articles of pottery. They also brought wheat and barley, flour and roasted grain, beans and lentils, ²⁹ honey and curds, sheep, and cheese from cows' milk for David and his people to eat. For they said, 'The people have become exhausted and hungry and thirsty in the wilderness.'

▬ PSALM 69:13-18

¹³ But I pray to you, LORD,
in the time of your favour;
in your great love, O God,
answer me with your sure salvation.
¹⁴ Rescue me from the mire,
do not let me sink;
deliver me from those who hate me,
from the deep waters.
¹⁵ Do not let the floodwaters engulf me
or the depths swallow me up
or the pit close its mouth over me.

¹⁶ Answer me, LORD, out of the goodness of
your love;
in your great mercy turn to me.
¹⁷ Do not hide your face from your servant;
answer me quickly, for I am in trouble.
¹⁸ Come near and rescue me;
deliver me because of my foes.

▬ PROVERBS 15:10-11

¹⁰ Stern discipline awaits anyone who
leaves the path;

the one who hates correction will die.
¹¹ Death and Destruction lie open before
the LORD –
how much more do human hearts!

▬ JOHN 11:21-44

²¹ 'Lord,' Martha said to Jesus, 'if you had been here, my brother would not have died. ²² But I know that even now God will give you whatever you ask.'

²³ Jesus said to her, 'Your brother will rise again.'

²⁴ Martha answered, 'I know he will rise again in the resurrection at the last day.'

²⁵ Jesus said to her, 'I am the resurrection and the life. The one who believes in me will live, even though they die; ²⁶ and whoever lives by believing in me will never die. Do you believe this?'

²⁷ 'Yes, Lord,' she replied, 'I believe that you are the Messiah, the Son of God, who is to come into the world.'

²⁸ After she had said this, she went back and called her sister Mary aside. 'The Teacher is here,' she said, 'and is asking for you.' ²⁹ When Mary heard this, she got up quickly and went to him. ³⁰ Now Jesus had not yet entered the village, but was still at the place where Martha had met him. ³¹ When the Jews who had been with Mary in the house, comforting her, noticed how quickly she got up and went out, they followed her, supposing she was going to the tomb to mourn there.

³² When Mary reached the place where Jesus was and saw him, she fell at his feet and said, 'Lord, if you had been here, my brother would not have died.'

³³ When Jesus saw her weeping, and the Jews who had come along with her also weeping, he was deeply moved in spirit and troubled. ³⁴ 'Where have you laid him?' he asked.

'Come and see, Lord,' they replied.

[35] Jesus wept.

[36] Then the Jews said, 'See how he loved him!'

[37] But some of them said, 'Could not he who opened the eyes of the blind man have kept this man from dying?'

[38] Jesus, once more deeply moved, came to the tomb. It was a cave with a stone laid across the entrance. [39] 'Take away the stone,' he said.

'But, Lord,' said Martha, the sister of the dead man, 'by this time there is a bad odour, for he has been there four days.'

[40] Then Jesus said, 'Did I not tell you that if you believe, you will see the glory of God?'

[41] So they took away the stone. Then Jesus looked up and said, 'Father, I thank you that you have heard me. [42] I knew that you always hear me, but I said this for the benefit of the people standing here, that they may believe that you sent me.'

[43] When he had said this, Jesus called in a loud voice, 'Lazarus, come out!' [44] The dead man came out, his hands and feet wrapped with strips of linen, and a cloth round his face.

Jesus said to them, 'Take off the grave clothes and let him go.'

Blessings – Not Just for Now

'They also brought wheat and barley, flour and roasted grain, beans and lentils, honey and curds, sheep, and cheese from cows' milk for David and his people to eat.'
2 Samuel 17:28-29

Some commentators believe that when David wrote the words, 'You prepare a table before me in the presence of my enemies' (Psa. 23:5), he had in mind the events about which we read in today's passage. Driven into the wilderness by his son Absalom's rebellion, David and his followers became desperately hungry, thirsty, and weary. God came to his aid, however, and directed to him three men who 'brought bedding and and bowls' (so that David could wash and refresh himself) as well as 'articles of pottery ... wheat and barley, flour and roasted grain, beans and lentils, honey and curds, sheep and cheese ... '.

How David must have rubbed his eyes in astonishment as he saw God provide for him a table 'in the presence of [his] enemies'. Can you cast your mind back at this moment to something 'special' that God did for you to demonstrate His tender love and care? I can. Every Christian has these times – how sad that we forget them so soon.

God never does anything 'special' in our lives just for the sake of the passing hour – it is done also as a pledge for the future. It is as though God is saying, 'I'll do this for you now, not only to meet your need, but also that you might *always* know you are the object of My love'.

If new dangers startle us with fear, we have forgotten the past mercies. I believe that David's confidence in God was due to the fact that whenever he faced a new problem, he remembered vividly the past hour of deliverance.

PRAYER

O Father, forgive me for taking so
much for granted – rather than taking
it with gratitude. I recall the words of
Your servant John Newton and make
them my own this day: 'His love in
time past forbids me to think, He'll
leave me at last in trouble to sink'.
Thank You, Father – thank You. Amen.

FURTHER STUDY

1 Kings 17; Ezek. 34:14;
Isa. 25:6; John 6:51
• How did Elijah experience
  God's provision?
• What are we to feed on?

June 7

■ 2 SAMUEL 18:1–19:23

18 David mustered the men who were
with him and appointed over them
commanders of thousands and commanders of hundreds. ² David sent out his troops,
a third under the command of Joab, a third
under Joab's brother Abishai son of Zeruiah, and a third under Ittai the Gittite. The
king told the troops, 'I myself will surely
march out with you.'

³ But the men said, 'You must not go out;
if we are forced to flee, they won't care about
us. Even if half of us die, they won't care; but
you are worth ten thousand of us. It would
be better now for you to give us support
from the city.'

⁴ The king answered, 'I will do whatever
seems best to you.'

So the king stood beside the gate while
all his men marched out in units of hundreds and of thousands. ⁵ The king commanded Joab, Abishai and Ittai, 'Be gentle
with the young man Absalom for my sake.'
And all the troops heard the king giving
orders concerning Absalom to each of the
commanders.

⁶ David's army marched out of the city
to fight Israel, and the battle took place in
the forest of Ephraim. ⁷ There Israel's troops

were routed by David's men, and the casualties that day were great – twenty thousand
men. ⁸ The battle spread out over the whole
countryside, and the forest swallowed up
more men that day than the sword.

⁹ Now Absalom happened to meet David's men. He was riding his mule, and as
the mule went under the thick branches of a
large oak, Absalom's hair got caught in the
tree. He was left hanging in mid-air, while
the mule he was riding kept on going.

¹⁰ When one of the men saw what had
happened, he told Joab, 'I have just seen
Absalom hanging in an oak tree.'

¹¹ Joab said to the man who had told him
this, 'What! You saw him? Why didn't you
strike him to the ground right there? Then
I would have had to give you ten shekels of
silver and a warrior's belt.'

¹² But the man replied, 'Even if a thousand
shekels were weighed out into my hands, I
would not lay a hand on the king's son. In
our hearing the king commanded you and
Abishai and Ittai, "Protect the young man
Absalom for my sake." ¹³ And if I had put
my life in jeopardy – and nothing is hidden
from the king – you would have kept your
distance from me.'

¹⁴ Joab said, 'I am not going to wait like
this for you.' So he took three javelins in

his hand and plunged them into Absalom's heart while Absalom was still alive in the oak tree. ¹⁵And ten of Joab's armour-bearers surrounded Absalom, struck him and killed him.

¹⁶Then Joab sounded the trumpet, and the troops stopped pursuing Israel, for Joab halted them. ¹⁷They took Absalom, threw him into a big pit in the forest and piled up a large heap of rocks over him. Meanwhile, all the Israelites fled to their homes.

¹⁸During his life-time Absalom had taken a pillar and erected it in the King's Valley as a monument to himself, for he thought, 'I have no son to carry on the memory of my name.' He named the pillar after himself, and it is called Absalom's Monument to this day.

¹⁹Now Ahimaaz son of Zadok said, 'Let me run and take the news to the king that the LORD has vindicated him by delivering him from the hand of his enemies.'

²⁰'You are not the one to take the news today,' Joab told him. 'You may take the news another time, but you must not do so today, because the king's son is dead.'

²¹Then Joab said to a Cushite, 'Go, tell the king what you have seen.' The Cushite bowed down before Joab and ran off.

²²Ahimaaz son of Zadok again said to Joab, 'Come what may, please let me run behind the Cushite.'

But Joab replied, 'My son, why do you want to go? You don't have any news that will bring you a reward.'

²³He said, 'Come what may, I want to run.'

So Joab said, 'Run!' Then Ahimaaz ran by way of the plain and outran the Cushite.

²⁴While David was sitting between the inner and outer gates, the watchman went up to the roof of the gateway by the wall. As he looked out, he saw a man running alone. ²⁵The watchman called out to the king and reported it.

The king said, 'If he is alone, he must have good news.' And the runner came closer and closer.

²⁶Then the watchman saw another runner, and he called down to the gatekeeper, 'Look, another man running alone!'

The king said, 'He must be bringing good news, too.'

²⁷The watchman said, 'It seems to me that the first one runs like Ahimaaz son of Zadok.'

'He's a good man,' the king said. 'He comes with good news.'

²⁸Then Ahimaaz called out to the king, 'All is well!' He bowed down before the king with his face to the ground and said, 'Praise be to the LORD your God! He has delivered up those who lifted their hands against my lord the king.'

²⁹The king asked, 'Is the young man Absalom safe?'

Ahimaaz answered, 'I saw great confusion just as Joab was about to send the king's servant and me, your servant, but I don't know what it was.'

³⁰The king said, 'Stand aside and wait here.' So he stepped aside and stood there.

³¹Then the Cushite arrived and said, 'My lord the king, hear the good news! The LORD has vindicated you today by delivering you from the hand of all who rose up against you.'

³²The king asked the Cushite, 'Is the young man Absalom safe?'

The Cushite replied, 'May the enemies of my lord the king and all who rise up to harm you be like that young man.'

³³The king was shaken. He went up to the room over the gateway and wept. As he went, he said: 'O my son Absalom! My son, my son Absalom! If only I had died instead of you – O Absalom, my son, my son!'

19 Joab was told, 'The king is weeping and mourning for Absalom.' ²And for the whole army the victory that day was turned into mourning, because on that day the troops heard it said, 'The king is grieving for his son.' ³The men stole into the city that day as men steal in who are ashamed when they flee from battle. ⁴The king covered his face and cried aloud, 'O my son Absalom! O Absalom, my son, my son!'

⁵Then Joab went into the house to the king and said, 'Today you have humiliated all your men, who have just saved your life and the lives of your sons and daughters and the lives of your wives and concubines. ⁶You love those who hate you and hate those who love you. You have made it clear today that the commanders and their men mean nothing to you. I see that you would be pleased if Absalom were alive today and all of us were dead. ⁷Now go out and encourage your men. I swear by the LORD that if you don't go out, not a man will be left with you by nightfall. This will be worse for you than all the calamities that have come on you from your youth till now.'

⁸So the king got up and took his seat in the gateway. When the men were told, 'The king is sitting in the gateway,' they all came before him.

Meanwhile, the Israelites had fled to their homes.

⁹Throughout the tribes of Israel, all the people were arguing among themselves, saying, 'The king delivered us from the hand of our enemies; he is the one who rescued us from the hand of the Philistines. But now he has fled the country to escape from Absalom; ¹⁰and Absalom, whom we anointed to rule over us, has died in battle. So why do you say nothing about bringing the king back?'

¹¹King David sent this message to Zadok and Abiathar, the priests: 'Ask the elders of Judah, "Why should you be the last to bring the king back to his palace, since what is being said throughout Israel has reached the king at his quarters? ¹²You are my relatives, my own flesh and blood. So why should you be the last to bring back the king?" ¹³And say to Amasa, "Are you not my own flesh and blood? May God deal with me, be it ever so severely, if you are not the commander of my army for life in place of Joab."'

¹⁴He won over the hearts of the men of Judah so that they were all of one mind. They sent word to the king, 'Return, you and all your men.' ¹⁵Then the king returned and went as far as the Jordan.

Now the men of Judah had come to Gilgal to go out and meet the king and bring him across the Jordan. ¹⁶Shimei son of Gera, the Benjaminite from Bahurim, hurried down with the men of Judah to meet King David. ¹⁷With him were a thousand Benjaminites, along with Ziba, the steward of Saul's household, and his fifteen sons and twenty servants. They rushed to the Jordan, where the king was. ¹⁸They crossed at the ford to take the king's household over and to do whatever he wished.

When Shimei son of Gera crossed the Jordan, he fell prostrate before the king ¹⁹and said to him, 'May my lord not hold me guilty. Do not remember how your servant did wrong on the day my lord the king left Jerusalem. May the king put it out of his mind. ²⁰For I your servant know that I have sinned, but today I have come here as the first from the tribes of Joseph to come down and meet my lord the king.'

²¹Then Abishai son of Zeruiah said, 'Shouldn't Shimei be put to death for this? He cursed the LORD's anointed.'

²²David replied, 'What does this have to do with you, you sons of Zeruiah? What right do you have to interfere? Should anyone be put to death in Israel today? Don't I know that today I am king over Israel?' ²³So the king said to Shimei, 'You shall not die.' And the king promised him on oath.

■ PSALM 69:19-28

¹⁹You know how I am scorned, disgraced and shamed;
   all my enemies are before you.
²⁰Scorn has broken my heart
   and has left me helpless;

I looked for sympathy, but there was
none,
for comforters, but I found none.
²¹ They put gall in my food
and gave me vinegar for my thirst.

²² May the table set before them become a
snare;
may it become retribution and a trap.
²³ May their eyes be darkened so that they
cannot see,
and their backs be bent for ever.
²⁴ Pour out your wrath on them;
let your fierce anger overtake them.
²⁵ May their place be deserted;
let there be no one to dwell in their
tents.
²⁶ For they persecute those you wound
and talk about the pain of those you
hurt.
²⁷ Charge them with crime upon crime;
do not let them share in your
salvation.
²⁸ May they be blotted out of the book of life
and not be listed with the righteous.

PROVERBS 15:12-13

¹² Mockers resent correction,
so they avoid the wise.

¹³ A happy heart makes the face cheerful,
but heartache crushes the spirit.

JOHN 11:45–12:11

⁴⁵ Therefore many of the Jews who had
come to visit Mary, and had seen what Jesus
did, believed in him. ⁴⁶ But some of them
went to the Pharisees and told them what
Jesus had done. ⁴⁷ Then the chief priests
and the Pharisees called a meeting of the
Sanhedrin.

'What are we accomplishing?' they

asked. 'Here is this man performing many
signs. ⁴⁸ If we let him go on like this, everyone will believe in him, and then the Romans will come and take away both our
temple and our nation.'

⁴⁹ Then one of them, named Caiaphas,
who was high priest that year, spoke up,
'You know nothing at all! ⁵⁰ You do not realise that it is better for you that one man
die for the people than that the whole nation
perish.'

⁵¹ He did not say this on his own, but as
high priest that year he prophesied that
Jesus would die for the Jewish nation, ⁵² and
not only for that nation but also for the scattered children of God, to bring them together and make them one. ⁵³ So from that day
on they plotted to take his life.

⁵⁴ Therefore Jesus no longer moved about
publicly among the people of Judea. Instead
he withdrew to a region near the wilderness, to a village called Ephraim, where he
stayed with his disciples.

⁵⁵ When it was almost time for the Jewish
Passover, many went up from the country
to Jerusalem for their ceremonial cleansing
before the Passover. ⁵⁶ They kept looking
for Jesus, and as they stood in the temple
courts they asked one another, 'What do
you think? Isn't he coming to the festival at
all?' ⁵⁷ But the chief priests and the Pharisees had given orders that anyone who
found out where Jesus was should report it
so that they might arrest him.

12 Six days before the Passover, Jesus
came to Bethany, where Lazarus
lived, whom Jesus had raised from the dead.
² Here a dinner was given in Jesus' honour.
Martha served, while Lazarus was among
those reclining at the table with him. ³ Then
Mary took about half a litre of pure nard, an
expensive perfume; she poured it on Jesus'
feet and wiped his feet with her hair. And
the house was filled with the fragrance of
the perfume.

⁴ But one of his disciples, Judas

Iscariot, who was later to betray him, objected, ⁵'Why wasn't this perfume sold and the money given to the poor? It was worth a year's wages.' ⁶He did not say this because he cared about the poor but because he was a thief; as keeper of the money bag, he used to help himself to what was put into it.

⁷'Leave her alone,' Jesus replied. 'It was intended that she should save this perfume for the day of my burial. ⁸You will always have the poor among you, but you will not always have me.'

⁹Meanwhile a large crowd of Jews found out that Jesus was there and came, not only because of him but also to see Lazarus, whom he had raised from the dead. ¹⁰So the chief priests made plans to kill Lazarus as well, ¹¹for on account of him many of the Jews were going over to Jesus and believing in him.

Joy – Always There

'A happy heart makes the face cheerful, but heartache crushes the spirit.' **Proverbs 15:13**

Joy is a central characteristic of the Christian – and yet so many know nothing of it. They are under the lash of duty and not unabashed delight. They are artificial, not artesian. Someone once described such Christians as 'creaking in body and soul as they limp along the highway toward glory'. They walk the road to glory, but they are certainly not walking the glory road.

The word 'joy' (Greek: *chara*) is a strong and robust word. It is not resignation wearing a wan smile. It means a joy that is exuberant and overflowing. The summons to rejoice is sounded no less than seventy times in the New Testament, and the word *chara* occurs close to sixty times. The New Testament is a book of joy. Dr. William Barclay says that joy is the distinguishing atmosphere of the Christian life. He wrote: 'We may put it this way – whatever the ingredients of Christian experience and in whatever proportions they are mixed together, joy is one of them'.

Even in the first year after the death of my wife, I was wonderfully conscious of Christ's joy quietly breaking through the layers of my sadness and grief. Joy is always present in the heart of a Christian. It may not always be felt or recognised – but it is always there. And eventually it will break the surface, no matter what our situation or our circumstances. I have always maintained that joy is an inevitable part of the Christian life. Now I am sure. Oh, so very sure.

PRAYER

Father, thank You for reminding me that when joy has its roots in You, then its fruits will eventually appear – no matter what happens. Eternal honour and praise be to Your wonderful name. Amen.

FURTHER STUDY

Psa. 16:11; 30:1-12; 126:1-6; Neh. 8:10

• What does joy bring to our beings?
• How are tears linked with joy?

June 8

▬ 2 SAMUEL 19:24–21:22

²⁴Mephibosheth, Saul's grandson, also went down to meet the king. He had not taken care of his feet or trimmed his moustache or washed his clothes from the day the king left until the day he returned safely. ²⁵When he came from Jerusalem to meet the king, the king asked him, 'Why didn't you go with me, Mephibosheth?'

²⁶He said, 'My lord the king, since I your servant am lame, I said, "I will have my donkey saddled and will ride on it, so that I can go with the king." But Ziba my servant betrayed me. ²⁷And he has slandered your servant to my lord the king. My lord the king is like an angel of God; so do whatever you wish. ²⁸All my grandfather's descendants deserved nothing but death from my lord the king, but you gave your servant a place among those who eat at your table. So what right do I have to make any more appeals to the king?'

²⁹The king said to him, 'Why say more? I order you and Ziba to divide the land.'

³⁰Mephibosheth said to the king, 'Let him take everything, now that my lord the king has returned home safely.'

³¹Barzillai the Gileadite also came down from Rogelim to cross the Jordan with the king and to send him on his way from there. ³²Now Barzillai was very old, eighty years of age. He had provided for the king during his stay in Mahanaim, for he was a very wealthy man. ³³The king said to Barzillai, 'Cross over with me and stay with me in Jerusalem, and I will provide for you.'

³⁴But Barzillai answered the king, 'How many more years shall I live, that I should go up to Jerusalem with the king? ³⁵I am now eighty years old. Can I tell the difference between what is enjoyable and what is not? Can your servant taste what he eats and drinks? Can I still hear the voices of male and female singers? Why should your servant be an added burden to my lord the king? ³⁶Your servant will cross over the Jordan with the king for a short distance, but why should the king reward me in this way? ³⁷Let your servant return, that I may die in my own town near the tomb of my father and mother. But here is your servant Kimham. Let him cross over with my lord the king. Do for him whatever you wish.'

³⁸The king said, 'Kimham shall cross over with me, and I will do for him whatever you wish. And anything you desire from me I will do for you.'

³⁹So all the people crossed the Jordan, and then the king crossed over. The king kissed Barzillai and bade him farewell, and Barzillai returned to his home.

⁴⁰When the king crossed over to Gilgal, Kimham crossed with him. All the troops of Judah and half the troops of Israel had taken the king over.

⁴¹Soon all the men of Israel were coming to the king and saying to him, 'Why did our brothers, the men of Judah, steal the king away and bring him and his household across the Jordan, together with all his men?'

⁴²All the men of Judah answered the men of Israel, 'We did this because the king is closely related to us. Why are you angry about it? Have we eaten any of the king's provisions? Have we taken anything for ourselves?'

⁴³Then the men of Israel answered the men of Judah, 'We have ten shares in the king; so we have a greater claim on David than you have. Why then do you treat us

with contempt? Weren't we the first to speak of bringing back our king?'

But the men of Judah pressed their claims even more forcefully than the men of Israel.

20 Now a troublemaker named Sheba son of Bikri, a Benjaminite, happened to be there. He sounded the trumpet and shouted,

'We have no share in David,
    no part in Jesse's son!
Every man to his tent, Israel!'

²So all the men of Israel deserted David to follow Sheba son of Bikri. But the men of Judah stayed by their king all the way from the Jordan to Jerusalem.

³When David returned to his palace in Jerusalem, he took the ten concubines he had left to take care of the palace and put them in a house under guard. He provided for them but had no sexual relations with them. They were kept in confinement till the day of their death, living as widows.

⁴Then the king said to Amasa, 'Summon the men of Judah to come to me within three days, and be here yourself.' ⁵But when Amasa went to summon Judah, he took longer than the time the king had set for him.

⁶David said to Abishai, 'Now Sheba son of Bikri will do us more harm than Absalom did. Take your master's men and pursue him, or he will find fortified cities and escape from us.' ⁷So Joab's men and the Kerethites and Pelethites and all the mighty warriors went out under the command of Abishai. They marched out from Jerusalem to pursue Sheba son of Bikri.

⁸While they were at the great rock in Gibeon, Amasa came to meet them. Joab was wearing his military tunic, and strapped over it at his waist was a belt with a dagger in its sheath. As he stepped forward, it dropped out of its sheath.

⁹Joab said to Amasa, 'How are you, my brother?' Then Joab took Amasa by the beard with his right hand to kiss him. ¹⁰Amasa was not on his guard against the dagger in Joab's hand, and Joab plunged it into his belly, and his intestines spilled out on the ground. Without being stabbed again, Amasa died. Then Joab and his brother Abishai pursued Sheba son of Bikri.

¹¹One of Joab's men stood beside Amasa and said, 'Whoever favours Joab, and whoever is for David, let him follow Joab!' ¹²Amasa lay wallowing in his blood in the middle of the road, and the man saw that all the troops came to a halt there. When he realised that everyone who came up to Amasa stopped, he dragged him from the road into a field and threw a garment over him. ¹³After Amasa had been removed from the road, everyone went on with Joab to pursue Sheba son of Bikri.

¹⁴Sheba passed through all the tribes of Israel to Abel Beth Maakah and through the entire region of the Bikrites, who gathered together and followed him. ¹⁵All the troops with Joab came and besieged Sheba in Abel Beth Maakah. They built a siege ramp up to the city, and it stood against the outer fortifications. While they were battering the wall to bring it down, ¹⁶a wise woman called from the city, 'Listen! Listen! Tell Joab to come here so that I can speak to him.' ¹⁷He went towards her, and she asked, 'Are you Joab?'

'I am,' he answered.

She said, 'Listen to what your servant has to say.'

'I'm listening,' he said.

¹⁸She continued, 'Long ago they used to say, "Get your answer at Abel," and that settled it. ¹⁹We are the peaceful and faithful in Israel. You are trying to destroy a city that is a mother in Israel. Why do you want to swallow up the LORD's inheritance?'

²⁰'Far be it from me!' Joab replied, 'Far be it from me to swallow up or destroy! ²¹That is not the case. A man named Sheba son of Bikri, from the hill country of Ephraim, has

lifted up his hand against the king, against David. Hand over this one man, and I'll withdraw from the city.'

The woman said to Joab, 'His head will be thrown to you from the wall.'

²²Then the woman went to all the people with her wise advice, and they cut off the head of Sheba son of Bikri and threw it to Joab. So he sounded the trumpet, and his men dispersed from the city, each returning to his home. And Joab went back to the king in Jerusalem.

²³Joab was over Israel's entire army; Benaiah son of Jehoiada was over the Kerethites and Pelethites; ²⁴Adoniram was in charge of forced labour; Jehoshaphat son of Ahilud was recorder; ²⁵Sheva was secretary; Zadok and Abiathar were priests; ²⁶and Ira the Jairite was David's priest.

21 During the reign of David, there was a famine for three successive years; so David sought the face of the LORD. The LORD said, 'It is on account of Saul and his blood-stained house; it is because he put the Gibeonites to death.'

²The king summoned the Gibeonites and spoke to them. (Now the Gibeonites were not a part of Israel but were survivors of the Amorites; the Israelites had sworn to spare them, but Saul in his zeal for Israel and Judah had tried to annihilate them.) ³David asked the Gibeonites, 'What shall I do for you? How shall I make atonement so that you will bless the LORD's inheritance?'

⁴The Gibeonites answered him, 'We have no right to demand silver or gold from Saul or his family, nor do we have the right to put anyone in Israel to death.'

'What do you want me to do for you?' David asked.

⁵They answered the king, 'As for the man who destroyed us and plotted against us so that we have been decimated and have no place anywhere in Israel, ⁶let seven of his male descendants be given to us to be killed and their bodies exposed before the LORD at Gibeah of Saul – the LORD's chosen one.'

So the king said, 'I will give them to you.'

⁷The king spared Mephibosheth son of Jonathan, the son of Saul, because of the oath before the LORD between David and Jonathan son of Saul. ⁸But the king took Armoni and Mephibosheth, the two sons of Aiah's daughter Rizpah, whom she had borne to Saul, together with the five sons of Saul's daughter Merab, whom she had borne to Adriel son of Barzillai the Meholathite. ⁹He handed them over to the Gibeonites, who killed them and exposed their bodies on a hill before the LORD. All seven of them fell together; they were put to death during the first days of harvest, just as the barley harvest was beginning.

¹⁰Rizpah daughter of Aiah took sackcloth and spread it out for herself on a rock. From the beginning of the harvest till the rain poured down from the heavens on the bodies, she did not let the birds touch them by day or the wild animals by night. ¹¹When David was told what Aiah's daughter Rizpah, Saul's concubine, had done, ¹²he went and took the bones of Saul and his son Jonathan from the citizens of Jabesh Gilead. (They had stolen their bodies from the public square at Beth Shan, where the Philistines had hung them after they struck Saul down on Gilboa.) ¹³David brought the bones of Saul and his son Jonathan from there, and the bones of those who had been killed and exposed were gathered up.

¹⁴They buried the bones of Saul and his son Jonathan in the tomb of Saul's father Kish, at Zela in Benjamin, and did everything the king commanded. After that, God answered prayer on behalf of the land.

¹⁵Once again there was a battle between the Philistines and Israel. David went down with his men to fight against the Philistines, and he became exhausted. ¹⁶And Ishbi-Benob, one of the descendants of Rapha, whose bronze spearhead weighed three hundred shekels and who was armed with

a new sword, said he would kill David. [17] But Abishai son of Zeruiah came to David's rescue; he struck the Philistine down and killed him. Then David's men swore to him, saying, 'Never again will you go out with us to battle, so that the lamp of Israel will not be extinguished.'

[18] In the course of time, there was another battle with the Philistines, at Gob. At that time Sibbekai the Hushathite killed Saph, one of the descendants of Rapha.

[19] In another battle with the Philistines at Gob, Elhanan son of Jair the Bethlehemite killed the brother of Goliath the Gittite, who had a spear with a shaft like a weaver's rod.

[20] In still another battle, which took place at Gath, there was a huge man with six fingers on each hand and six toes on each foot – twenty-four in all. He also was descended from Rapha. [21] When he taunted Israel, Jonathan son of Shimeah, David's brother, killed him.

[22] These four were descendants of Rapha in Gath, and they fell at the hands of David and his men.

PSALM 69:29-36

[29] But as for me, afflicted and in pain –
    may your salvation, God, protect me.

[30] I will praise God's name in song
    and glorify him with thanksgiving.
[31] This will please the LORD more than
      an ox,
    more than a bull with its horns and
      hooves.
[32] The poor will see and be glad –
    you who seek God, may your hearts
      live!
[33] The LORD hears the needy
    and does not despise his captive people.

[34] Let heaven and earth praise him,
    the seas and all that move in them,

[35] for God will save Zion
    and rebuild the cities of Judah.
Then people will settle there and
      possess it;
[36]   the children of his servants will
      inherit it,
    and those who love his name will
      dwell there.

PROVERBS 15:14-15

[14] The discerning heart seeks knowledge,
    but the mouth of a fool feeds on folly.

[15] All the days of the oppressed are
      wretched,
    but the cheerful heart has a continual
      feast.

JOHN 12:12-33

[12] The next day the great crowd that had come for the festival heard that Jesus was on his way to Jerusalem. [13] They took palm branches and went out to meet him, shouting,

'Hosanna!'

'Blessed is he who comes in the name of
      the Lord!'

'Blessed is the king of Israel!'

[14] Jesus found a young donkey and sat upon it, as it is written:

[15] 'Do not be afraid, Daughter Zion;
    see, your king is coming,
    seated on a donkey's colt.'

[16] At first his disciples did not understand all this. Only after Jesus was glorified did they realise that these things had been

written about him and that these things had been done to him.

¹⁷ Now the crowd that was with him when he called Lazarus from the tomb and raised him from the dead continued to spread the word. ¹⁸ Many people, because they had heard that he had performed this sign, went out to meet him. ¹⁹ So the Pharisees said to one another, 'See, this is getting us nowhere. Look how the whole world has gone after him!'

²⁰ Now there were some Greeks among those who went up to worship at the festival. ²¹ They came to Philip, who was from Bethsaida in Galilee, with a request. 'Sir,' they said, 'we would like to see Jesus.' ²² Philip went to tell Andrew; Andrew and Philip in turn told Jesus.

²³ Jesus replied, 'The hour has come for the Son of Man to be glorified. ²⁴ Very truly I tell you, unless a grain of wheat falls to the ground and dies, it remains only a single seed. But if it dies, it produces many seeds.

²⁵ Anyone who loves their life will lose it, while anyone who hates their life in this world will keep it for eternal life. ²⁶ Whoever serves me must follow me; and where I am, my servant also will be. My Father will honour the one who serves me.

²⁷ 'Now my soul is troubled, and what shall I say? "Father, save me from this hour"? No, it was for this very reason I came to this hour. ²⁸ Father, glorify your name!'

Then a voice came from heaven, 'I have glorified it, and will glorify it again.' ²⁹ The crowd that was there and heard it said it had thundered; others said an angel had spoken to him.

³⁰ Jesus said, 'This voice was for your benefit, not mine. ³¹ Now is the time for judgment on this world; now the prince of this world will be driven out. ³² And I, when I am lifted up from the earth, will draw all people to myself.' ³³ He said this to show the kind of death he was going to die.

The Cross's Magnetism

'And I, when I am lifted up from the earth, will draw all people to myself.' **John 12:32**

The love for God that burns in our hearts must never be seen as the fruit of our labour, as if it is something we manufacture. Seeing the love of God for us, our own hearts respond with love. We give love for love. We cannot help it. Let's be done with the idea that love for God is something we work at. It issues forth in good works, of course, but it begins in contemplation of how much we are loved.

I often tell my students that they cannot love until they have been loved. By this I mean that love is a response. Our souls must receive love before we can give out love. Those who did not receive much love from their parents complain at this stage, 'I can't love God because my soul was never properly prepared to love; my parents didn't love me'.

This is a problem, I agree, but it must never be seen as an insoluble problem. No one who stands at Calvary and sees God dying for them on that tree can ever argue that because they were not loved by their parents, they cannot now receive God's love. If they really believe that, then they are saying that God's love is balked by the adverse influence of human conditioning.

God's love will only flow into us if we let it and if we really want it. To desire it is like the touch of the hand on a spring blind: the blind is released and the sunlight flows in. Just to want His love is enough; He will do the rest.

PRAYER

O God, forgive me if I have used excuses to barricade my heart against Your love. I gaze once more on Calvary and open my heart to allow its mighty magnetism to draw my soul toward You in a way it has never been drawn before. Amen.

FURTHER STUDY

2 Thess. 3:1-5; Jude 21; Eph. 3:17-19
• What was Paul's desire for the Thessalonians?
• What was Paul's prayer for the Ephesians?

June 9

▪ 2 SAMUEL 22:1–23:7

22 David sang to the LORD the words of this song when the LORD delivered him from the hand of all his enemies and from the hand of Saul. ²He said:

'The LORD is my rock, my fortress and
my deliverer;
³   my God is my rock, in whom I take
refuge,
my shield and the horn of my
salvation.
He is my stronghold, my refuge and my
saviour –
from violent people you save me.

⁴'I called to the LORD, who is worthy of
praise,
and have been saved from my
enemies.
⁵The waves of death swirled about me;
the torrents of destruction
overwhelmed me.
⁶The cords of the grave coiled around me;
the snares of death confronted me.

⁷'In my distress I called to the LORD;
I called out to my God.
From his temple he heard my voice;
my cry came to his ears.
⁸The earth trembled and quaked,
the foundations of the heavens shook;
they trembled because he was angry.
⁹Smoke rose from his nostrils;
consuming fire came from his mouth,
burning coals blazed out of it.
¹⁰He parted the heavens and came down;
dark clouds were under his feet.
¹¹He mounted the cherubim and flew;
he soared on the wings of the wind.
¹²He made darkness his canopy around
him –
the dark rain clouds of the sky.
¹³Out of the brightness of his presence
bolts of lightning blazed forth.
¹⁴The LORD thundered from heaven;
the voice of the Most High resounded.
¹⁵He shot his arrows and scattered the
enemy,
with great bolts of lightning he routed
them.
¹⁶The valleys of the sea were exposed

and the foundations of the earth laid
bare
at the rebuke of the LORD,
at the blast of breath from his nostrils.

¹⁷ 'He reached down from on high and took
hold of me;
he drew me out of deep waters.
¹⁸ He rescued me from my powerful enemy,
from my foes, who were too strong
for me.
¹⁹ They confronted me in the day of my
disaster,
but the LORD was my support.
²⁰ He brought me out into a spacious place;
he rescued me because he delighted
in me.

²¹ 'The LORD has dealt with me according to
my righteousness;
according to the cleanness of my
hands he has rewarded me.
²² For I have kept the ways of the LORD;
I am not guilty of turning from my
God.
²³ All his laws are before me;
I have not turned away from his
decrees.
²⁴ I have been blameless before him
and have kept myself from sin.
²⁵ The LORD has rewarded me according to
my righteousness,
according to my cleanness in his sight.

²⁶ 'To the faithful you show yourself
faithful,
to the blameless you show yourself
blameless,
²⁷ to the pure you show yourself pure,
but to the devious you show yourself
shrewd.
²⁸ You save the humble,
but your eyes are on the haughty to
bring them low.
²⁹ You, LORD, are my lamp;
the LORD turns my darkness into light.

³⁰ With your help I can advance against a
troop;
with my God I can scale a wall.

³¹ 'As for God, his way is perfect:
the LORD's word is flawless;
he shields all who take refuge in him.
³² For who is God besides the LORD?
And who is the Rock except our God?
³³ It is God who arms me with strength
and keeps my way secure.
³⁴ He makes my feet like the feet of a deer;
he causes me to stand on the heights.
³⁵ He trains my hands for battle;
my arms can bend a bow of bronze.
³⁶ You make your saving help my shield;
your help has made me great.
³⁷ You provide a broad path for my feet,
so that my ankles do not give way.

³⁸ 'I pursued my enemies and crushed
them;
I did not turn back till they were
destroyed.
³⁹ I crushed them completely, and they
could not rise;
they fell beneath my feet.
⁴⁰ You armed me with strength for battle;
you humbled my adversaries before
me.
⁴¹ You made my enemies turn their backs
in flight,
and I destroyed my foes.
⁴² They cried for help, but there was no one
to save them –
to the LORD, but he did not answer.
⁴³ I beat them as fine as the dust of the
earth;
I pounded and trampled them like
mud in the streets.

⁴⁴ 'You have delivered me from the attacks
of the peoples;
you have preserved me as the head of
nations.
People I did not know now serve me,

45 foreigners cower before me;
as soon as they hear of me, they obey
me.
46 They all lose heart;
they come trembling from their
strongholds.

47 'The Lord lives! Praise be to my Rock!
Exalted be my God, the Rock, my
Saviour!
48 He is the God who avenges me,
who puts the nations under me,
49 who sets me free from my enemies.
You exalted me above my foes;
from a violent man you rescued me.
50 Therefore I will praise you, Lord, among
the nations;
I will sing the praises of your name.

51 'He gives his king great victories;
he shows unfailing kindness to his
anointed,
to David and his descendants for ever.'

23 These are the last words of David:

'The inspired utterance of David son of
Jesse,
the utterance of the man exalted by
the Most High,
the man anointed by the God of Jacob,
the hero of Israel's songs:

2 'The Spirit of the Lord spoke through
me;
his word was on my tongue.
3 The God of Israel spoke,
the Rock of Israel said to me:
"When one rules over people in
righteousness,
when he rules in the fear of God,
4 he is like the light of morning at sunrise
on a cloudless morning,
like the brightness after rain
that brings grass from the earth."

5 'If my house were not right with God,
surely he would not have made with
me an everlasting covenant,
arranged and secured in every part;
surely he would not bring to fruition my
salvation
and grant me my every desire.
6 But evil men are all to be cast aside like
thorns,
which are not gathered with the hand.
7 Whoever touches thorns
uses a tool of iron or the shaft of a
spear;
they are burned up where they lie.'

■ PSALM 70:1–5

1 Hasten, O God, to save me;
come quickly, Lord, to help me.

2 May those who want to take my life
be put to shame and confusion;
may all who desire my ruin
be turned back in disgrace.
3 May those who say to me, 'Aha! Aha!'
turn back because of their shame.
4 But may all who seek you
rejoice and be glad in you;
may those who long for your saving help
always say,
'The Lord is great!'

5 But as for me, I am poor and needy;
come quickly to me, O God.
You are my help and my deliverer;
Lord, do not delay.

■ PROVERBS 15:16–17

16 Better a little with the fear of the Lord
than great wealth with turmoil.

17 Better a dish of vegetables with love
than a fattened calf with hatred.

■ JOHN 12:34–13:11

³⁴The crowd spoke up, 'We have heard from the Law that the Messiah will remain for ever, so how can you say, "The Son of Man must be lifted up"? Who is this "Son of Man"?'

³⁵Then Jesus told them, 'You are going to have the light just a little while longer. Walk while you have the light, before darkness overtakes you. Whoever walks in the dark does not know where they are going. ³⁶Believe in the light while you have the light, so that you may become children of light.' When he had finished speaking, Jesus left and hid himself from them.

³⁷Even after Jesus had performed so many signs in their presence, they still would not believe in him. ³⁸This was to fulfil the word of Isaiah the prophet:

'Lord, who has believed our message
and to whom has the arm of the Lord
been revealed?'

³⁹For this reason they could not believe, because, as Isaiah says elsewhere:

⁴⁰'He has blinded their eyes
and hardened their hearts,
so they can neither see with their eyes,
nor understand with their hearts,
nor turn – and I would heal them.'

⁴¹Isaiah said this because he saw Jesus' glory and spoke about him.

⁴²Yet at the same time many even among the leaders believed in him. But because of the Pharisees they would not openly acknowledge their faith for fear they would be put out of the synagogue; ⁴³for they loved human praise more than praise from God.

⁴⁴Then Jesus cried out, 'Whoever believes in me does not believe in me only, but in the one who sent me. ⁴⁵The one who looks at me is seeing the one who sent me.

⁴⁶I have come into the world as a light, so that no one who believes in me should stay in darkness.

⁴⁷'If anyone hears my words but does not keep them, I do not judge that person. For I did not come to judge the world, but to save the world. ⁴⁸There is a judge for the one who rejects me and does not accept my words; the very words I have spoken will condemn them at the last day. ⁴⁹For I did not speak on my own, but the Father who sent me commanded me to say all that I have spoken. ⁵⁰I know that his command leads to eternal life. So whatever I say is just what the Father has told me to say.'

13 It was just before the Passover Festival. Jesus knew that the hour had come for him to leave this world and go to the Father. Having loved his own who were in the world, he loved them to the end.

²The evening meal was in progress, and the devil had already prompted Judas, the son of Simon Iscariot, to betray Jesus. ³Jesus knew that the Father had put all things under his power, and that he had come from God and was returning to God; ⁴so he got up from the meal, took off his outer clothing, and wrapped a towel round his waist. ⁵After that, he poured water into a basin and began to wash his disciples' feet, drying them with the towel that was wrapped round him.

⁶He came to Simon Peter, who said to him, 'Lord, are you going to wash my feet?'

⁷Jesus replied, 'You do not realise now what I am doing, but later you will understand.'

⁸'No,' said Peter, 'you shall never wash my feet.'

Jesus answered, 'Unless I wash you, you have no part with me.'

⁹'Then, Lord,' Simon Peter replied, 'not just my feet but my hands and my head as well!'

¹⁰Jesus answered, 'Those who have had a bath need only to wash their feet; their

whole body is clean. And you are clean, though not every one of you.' ¹¹ For he knew who was going to betray him, and that was why he said not every one was clean.

The Satanic Strategy

'... the devil had already prompted Judas ... to betray Jesus.' **John 13:2**

The 'fiery darts' of the Devil are quite different from the thoughts that are generated by our carnal nature. These 'fiery darts' come at us rather than from within us. A satanic attack can usually be differentiated from something that arises within by the force with which the thought hits us. Thoughts that arise out of the carnal nature are offensive, but the thoughts that come as 'fiery darts' from the Devil burn.

Many Christians have told me that they often experience these attacks when they go to read their Bibles or to pray. When they read a newspaper, nothing seems to happen. But when they turn their attention to something spiritual, they find it almost impossible to concentrate, by reason of the shameful thoughts that occupy their minds.

The other thing one notices about these attacks is that they seem to come in cycles. They are not there permanently, but they come at certain times and seasons. I once counselled a man for one hour a week over a period of a whole year and got him to write down in his diary the times and dates when he felt under satanic attack. When we looked through his diary together at the end of the year, we discovered an amazing thing – every single attack took place immediately prior to his doing something special for the Lord, like leading a Bible study, conducting a service, visiting the sick, or giving a public testimony. I shall never forget the expression on his face as he looked at me and said, 'Who says that Satan isn't a strategist?'

PRAYER

My Father and my God, I realise that even though Satan is a strategist, he is no match for You. You know how to outmanoeuvre his every move. Help me to stay close to You, that I might experience Your strategy and not his. Amen.

FURTHER STUDY

Gen. 3; Matt. 4:1-10
• How did Satan seek to penetrate Eve's mind?
• How does this correlate with the temptation of Christ?

June 10

■ **2 SAMUEL 23:8–24:25**

⁸These are the names of David's mighty warriors:

Josheb-Basshebeth, a Tahkemonite,was chief of the Three; he raised his spear against eight hundred men, whom he killed in one encounter.

⁹Next to him was Eleazar son of Dodai the Ahohite. As one of the three mighty warriors, he was with David when they taunted the Philistines gathered at Pas Dammim for battle. Then the Israelites retreated, ¹⁰but Eleazar stood his ground and struck down the Philistines till his hand grew tired and froze to the sword. The LORD brought about a great victory that day. The troops returned to Eleazar, but only to strip the dead.

¹¹Next to him was Shammah son of Agee the Hararite. When the Philistines banded together at a place where there was a field full of lentils, Israel's troops fled from them. ¹²But Shammah took his stand in the middle of the field. He defended it and struck the Philistines down, and the LORD brought about a great victory.

¹³During harvest time, three of the thirty chief warriors came down to David at the cave of Adullam, while a band of Philistines was encamped in the Valley of Rephaim. ¹⁴At that time David was in the stronghold, and the Philistine garrison was at Bethlehem. ¹⁵David longed for water and said, 'Oh, that someone would get me a drink of water from the well near the gate of Bethlehem!' ¹⁶So the three mighty warriors broke through the Philistine lines, drew water from the well near the gate of Bethlehem and carried it back to David. But he refused to drink it; instead, he poured it out before the LORD.

¹⁷'Far be it from me, LORD, to do this!' he said. 'Is it not the blood of men who went at the risk of their lives?' And David would not drink it.

Such were the exploits of the three mighty warriors.

¹⁸Abishai the brother of Joab son of Zeruiah was chief of the Three. He raised his spear against three hundred men, whom he killed, and so he became as famous as the Three. ¹⁹Was he not held in greater honour than the Three? He became their commander, even though he was not included among them.

²⁰Benaiah son of Jehoiada, a valiant fighter from Kabzeel, performed great exploits. He struck down Moab's two mightiest warriors. He also went down into a pit on a snowy day and killed a lion. ²¹And he struck down a huge Egyptian. Although the Egyptian had a spear in his hand, Benaiah went against him with a club. He snatched the spear from the Egyptian's hand and killed him with his own spear. ²²Such were the exploits of Benaiah son of Jehoiada; he too was as famous as the three mighty warriors. ²³He was held in greater honour than any of the Thirty, but he was not included among the Three. And David put him in charge of his bodyguard.

²⁴Among the Thirty were:
Asahel the brother of Joab,
Elhanan son of Dodo from
    Bethlehem,
²⁵Shammah the Harodite,
Elika the Harodite,
²⁶Helez the Paltite,
Ira son of Ikkesh from Tekoa,
²⁷Abiezer from Anathoth,
Sibbekai the Hushathite,

²⁸ Zalmon the Ahohite,
Maharai the Netophathite,
²⁹ Heled son of Baanah the Netophathite,
Ithai son of Ribai from Gibeah in Benjamin,
³⁰ Benaiah the Pirathonite,
Hiddai from the ravines of Gaash,
³¹ Abi-Albon the Arbathite,
Azmaveth the Barhumite,
³² Eliahba the Shaalbonite,
the sons of Jashen,
Jonathan ³³ son of Shammah the Hararite,
Ahiam son of Sharar the Hararite,
³⁴ Eliphelet son of Ahasbai the Maakathite,
Eliam son of Ahithophel the Gilonite,
³⁵ Hezro the Carmelite,
Paarai the Arbite,
³⁶ Igal son of Nathan from Zobah,
the son of Hagri,
³⁷ Zelek the Ammonite,
Naharai the Beerothite, the armour-bearer of Joab son of Zeruiah,
³⁸ Ira the Ithrite,
Gareb the Ithrite
³⁹ and Uriah the Hittite.
There were thirty-seven in all.

24 Again the anger of the Lord burned against Israel, and he incited David against them, saying, 'Go and take a census of Israel and Judah.'

² So the king said to Joab and the army commanders with him, 'Go throughout the tribes of Israel from Dan to Beersheba and enrol the fighting men, so that I may know how many there are.'

³ But Joab replied to the king, 'May the LORD your God multiply the troops a hundred times over, and may the eyes of my lord the king see it. But why does my lord the king want to do such a thing?'

⁴ The king's word, however, overruled Joab and the army commanders; so they left the presence of the king to enrol the fighting men of Israel.

⁵ After crossing the Jordan, they camped near Aroer, south of the town in the gorge, and then went through Gad and on to Jazer. ⁶ They went to Gilead and the region of Tahtim Hodshi, and on to Dan Jaan and around towards Sidon. ⁷ Then they went towards the fortress of Tyre and all the towns of the Hivites and Canaanites. Finally, they went on to Beersheba in the Negev of Judah.

⁸ After they had gone through the entire land, they came back to Jerusalem at the end of nine months and twenty days.

⁹ Joab reported the number of the fighting men to the king: in Israel there were eight hundred thousand able-bodied men who could handle a sword, and in Judah five hundred thousand.

¹⁰ David was conscience-stricken after he had counted the fighting men, and he said to the LORD, 'I have sinned greatly in what I have done. Now, LORD, I beg you, take away the guilt of your servant. I have done a very foolish thing.'

¹¹ Before David got up the next morning, the word of the LORD had come to Gad the prophet, David's seer: ¹² 'Go and tell David, "This is what the LORD says: I am giving you three options. Choose one of them for me to carry out against you."'

¹³ So Gad went to David and said to him, 'Shall there come on you three years of famine in your land? Or three months of fleeing from your enemies while they pursue you? Or three days of plague in your land? Now then, think it over and decide how I should answer the one who sent me.'

¹⁴ David said to Gad, 'I am in deep distress. Let us fall into the hands of the LORD, for his mercy is great; but do not let me fall into human hands.'

¹⁵ So the LORD sent a plague on Israel from that morning until the end of the time designated, and seventy thousand of the people

from Dan to Beersheba died. ¹⁶When the angel stretched out his hand to destroy Jerusalem, the LORD relented concerning the disaster and said to the angel who was afflicting the people, 'Enough! Withdraw your hand.' The angel of the LORD was then at the threshing-floor of Araunah the Jebusite.

¹⁷When David saw the angel who was striking down the people, he said to the LORD, 'I have sinned; I, the shepherd, have done wrong. These are but sheep. What have they done? Let your hand fall on me and my family.'

¹⁸On that day Gad went to David and said to him, 'Go up and build an altar to the LORD on the threshing floor of Araunah the Jebusite.' ¹⁹So David went up, as the LORD had commanded through Gad. ²⁰When Araunah looked and saw the king and his officials coming towards him, he went out and bowed down before the king with his face to the ground.

²¹Araunah said, 'Why has my lord the king come to his servant?'

'To buy your threshing-floor,' David answered, 'so that I can build an altar to the LORD, that the plague on the people may be stopped.'

²²Araunah said to David, 'Let my lord the king take whatever he wishes and offer it up. Here are oxen for the burnt offering, and here are threshing-sledges and ox yokes for the wood. ²³Your Majesty, Araunah gives all this to the king.' Araunah also said to him, 'May the LORD your God accept you.'

²⁴But the king replied to Araunah, 'No, I insist on paying you for it. I will not sacrifice to the LORD my God burnt offerings that cost me nothing.'

So David bought the threshing-floor and the oxen and paid fifty shekels of silver for them. ²⁵David built an altar to the LORD there and sacrificed burnt offerings and fellowship offerings. Then the LORD answered his prayer on behalf of the land, and the plague on Israel was stopped.

■ PSALM 71:1-8

¹ In you, LORD, I have taken refuge;
    let me never be put to shame.
² In your righteousness, rescue me and
    deliver me;
    turn your ear to me and save me.
³ Be my rock of refuge,
    to which I can always go;
give the command to save me,
    for you are my rock and my fortress.
⁴ Deliver me, my God, from the hand of
    the wicked,
    from the grasp of those who are evil
    and cruel.

⁵ For you have been my hope, Sovereign
    LORD,
    my confidence since my youth.
⁶ From my birth I have relied on you;
    you brought me forth from my
    mother's womb.
    I will ever praise you.
⁷ I have become a sign to many;
    you are my strong refuge.
⁸ My mouth is filled with your praise,
    declaring your splendour all day long.

■ PROVERBS 15:18-19

¹⁸ A hot-tempered person stirs up conflict,
    but the one who is patient calms a
    quarrel.

¹⁹ The way of the sluggard is blocked with
    thorns,
    but the path of the upright is a highway.

■ JOHN 13:12-38

¹²When he had finished washing their feet, he put on his clothes and returned to his place. 'Do you understand what I have done for you?' he asked them. ¹³'You call me

"Teacher" and "Lord", and rightly so, for that is what I am. [14] Now that I, your Lord and Teacher, have washed your feet, you also should wash one another's feet. [15] I have set you an example that you should do as I have done for you. [16] Very truly I tell you, no servant is greater than his master, nor is a messenger greater than the one who sent him. [17] Now that you know these things, you will be blessed if you do them.

[18] 'I am not referring to all of you; I know those I have chosen. But this is to fulfil this passage of Scripture: "He who shared my bread has turned against me."

[19] 'I am telling you now before it happens, so that when it does happen you will believe that I am who I am. [20] Very truly I tell you, whoever accepts anyone I send accepts me; and whoever accepts me accepts the one who sent me.'

[21] After he had said this, Jesus was troubled in spirit and testified, 'Very truly I tell you, one of you is going to betray me.'

[22] His disciples stared at one another, at a loss to know which of them he meant. [23] One of them, the disciple whom Jesus loved, was reclining next to him. [24] Simon Peter motioned to this disciple and said, 'Ask him which one he means.'

[25] Leaning back against Jesus, he asked him, 'Lord, who is it?'

[26] Jesus answered, 'It is the one to whom I will give this piece of bread when I have dipped it in the dish.' Then, dipping the piece of bread, he gave it to Judas, the son of Simon Iscariot. [27] As soon as Judas took the bread, Satan entered into him.

So Jesus told him, 'What you are about to do, do quickly.' [28] But no one at the meal understood why Jesus said this to him. [29] Since Judas had charge of the money, some thought Jesus was telling him to buy what was needed for the festival, or to give something to the poor. [30] As soon as Judas had taken the bread, he went out. And it was night.

[31] When he was gone, Jesus said, 'Now the Son of Man is glorified and God is glorified in him. [32] If God is glorified in him, God will glorify the Son in himself, and will glorify him at once.

[33] 'My children, I will be with you only a little longer. You will look for me, and just as I told the Jews, so I tell you now: where I am going, you cannot come.

[34] 'A new command I give you: love one another. As I have loved you, so you must love one another. [35] By this everyone will know that you are my disciples, if you love one another.'

[36] Simon Peter asked him, 'Lord, where are you going?'

Jesus replied, 'Where I am going, you cannot follow now, but you will follow later.'

[37] Peter asked, 'Lord, why can't I follow you now? I will lay down my life for you.'

[38] Then Jesus answered, 'Will you really lay down your life for me? Very truly I tell you, before the cock crows, you will disown me three times!

Our Code Is a Character

'A new command I give you: love one another. As I have loved you, so you must love one another.' **John 13:34**

What other teacher has taken the Ten Commandments and had the right to add another commandment to them? But this is precisely what Jesus did, as we see from our text today. 'A new command I give you' He says. 'Love one another. As I have loved you, so you must love one another'.

The Old Testament and other religious writings enjoined loving one another. What was new was this: 'As I have loved you.' Our Lord's conduct – 'as I have loved you' – produced a new code for those who are His disciples. Paul, writing to the Philippians, catches the spirit of it when he says: 'Treat one another with the same spirit as you experience in Christ Jesus' (Phil. 2:5, Moffatt). Here morality reaches its high-water mark. From the moment Jesus uttered the words that are occupying our attention, there came into human life something more than a code – there came a Character. Now, therefore, our code is a Character – the Character of Jesus.

When someone asks me if I believe in the Ten Commandments, I say, 'Yes, and very much more besides. I believe in Jesus'. The Ten Commandments are an injunction – and a God-given one. But Jesus is an injunction plus an inspiration. To follow an injunction is to obey imposed morality, but to follow a Person and do the things He does is an inspired morality. One is legalism, the other love. One binds you, the other frees you. One makes you feel trammelled, the other relaxed and spontaneous. Our code is not a commandment but a Character. One greater than the commandments is here.

PRAYER

O Christ, Your law lays upon me an injunction, but Your life entering into my life inspires me to live up to that injunction. It is this that makes Your yoke so easy. I am deeply, deeply grateful. Amen.

FURTHER STUDY

John 15:1-17; James 2:8; Matt. 7:12
- What was the basis of Christ's love?
- What is the basis of our being able to fulfil the royal law?

June 11

■ 1 KINGS 1:1-53

1 When King David was very old, he could not keep warm even when they put covers over him. ²So his attendants said to him, 'Let us look for a young virgin to serve the king and take care of him. She can lie beside him so that our lord the king may keep warm.'

³Then they searched throughout Israel for a beautiful young woman and found Abishag, a Shunammite, and brought her to the king. ⁴The woman was very beautiful; she took care of the king and waited on him, but the king had no sexual relations with her.

⁵Now Adonijah, whose mother was Haggith, put himself forward and said, 'I will be king.' So he got chariots and horses ready, with fifty men to run ahead of him. ⁶(His father had never rebuked him by asking, 'Why do you behave as you do?' He was also very handsome and was born next after Absalom.)

⁷Adonijah conferred with Joab son of Zeruiah and with Abiathar the priest, and

they gave him their support. ⁸But Zadok the priest, Benaiah son of Jehoiada, Nathan the prophet, Shimei and Rei and David's special guard did not join Adonijah.

⁹Adonijah then sacrificed sheep, cattle and fattened calves at the Stone of Zoheleth near En Rogel. He invited all his brothers, the king's sons, and all the royal officials of Judah, ¹⁰but he did not invite Nathan the prophet or Benaiah or the special guard or his brother Solomon.

¹¹Then Nathan asked Bathsheba, Solomon's mother, 'Have you not heard that Adonijah, the son of Haggith, has become king, and our lord David knows nothing about it? ¹²Now then, let me advise you how you can save your own life and the life of your son Solomon. ¹³Go in to King David and say to him, "My lord the king, did you not swear to me your servant: 'Surely Solomon your son shall be king after me, and he will sit on my throne'? Why then has Adonijah become king?" ¹⁴While you are still there talking to the king, I will come in and add my word to what you have said.'

¹⁵So Bathsheba went to see the aged king in his room, where Abishag the Shunammite was attending him. ¹⁶Bathsheba bowed down, prostrating herself before the king.

'What is it you want?' the king asked.

¹⁷She said to him, 'My lord, you yourself swore to me your servant by the LORD your God: "Solomon your son shall become king after me, and he will sit on my throne." ¹⁸But now Adonijah has become king, and you, my lord the king, do not know about it. ¹⁹He has sacrificed great numbers of cattle, fattened calves, and sheep, and has invited all the king's sons, Abiathar the priest and Joab the commander of the army, but he has not invited Solomon your servant. ²⁰My lord the king, the eyes of all Israel are on you, to learn from you who will sit on the throne of my lord the king after him. ²¹Otherwise, as soon as my lord the king is laid to rest with

his ancestors, I and my son Solomon will be treated as criminals.'

²²While she was still speaking with the king, Nathan the prophet arrived. ²³And the king was told, 'Nathan the prophet is here.' So he went before the king and bowed with his face to the ground.

²⁴Nathan said, 'Have you, my lord the king, declared that Adonijah shall be king after you, and that he will sit on your throne? ²⁵Today he has gone down and sacrificed great numbers of cattle, fattened calves, and sheep. He has invited all the king's sons, the commanders of the army and Abiathar the priest. At this very moment they are eating and drinking with him and saying, "Long live King Adonijah!" ²⁶But me your servant, and Zadok the priest, and Benaiah son of Jehoiada, and your servant Solomon he did not invite. ²⁷Is this something my lord the king has done without letting his servants know who should sit on the throne of my lord the king after him?'

²⁸Then King David said, 'Call in Bathsheba.' So she came into the king's presence and stood before him.

²⁹The king then took an oath: 'As surely as the LORD lives, who has delivered me out of every trouble, ³⁰I will surely carry out this very day what I swore to you by the LORD, the God of Israel: Solomon your son shall be king after me, and he will sit on my throne in my place.'

³¹Then Bathsheba bowed down with her face to the ground, prostrating herself before the king, and said, 'May my lord King David live for ever!'

³²King David said, 'Call in Zadok the priest, Nathan the prophet and Benaiah son of Jehoiada.' When they came before the king, ³³he said to them: 'Take your lord's servants with you and put Solomon my son on my own mule and take him down to Gihon. ³⁴There shall Zadok the priest and Nathan the prophet anoint him king over Israel. Blow the trumpet and shout, "Long

live King Solomon!" ³⁵Then you are to go up with him, and he is to come and sit on my throne and reign in my place. I have appointed him ruler over Israel and Judah.'

³⁶Benaiah son of Jehoiada answered the king, 'Amen! May the LORD, the God of my lord the king, so declare it. ³⁷As the LORD was with my lord the king, so may he be with Solomon to make his throne even greater than the throne of my lord King David!'

³⁸So Zadok the priest, Nathan the prophet, Benaiah son of Jehoiada, the Kerethites and the Pelethites went down and put Solomon on King David's mule, and they escorted him to Gihon. ³⁹Zadok the priest took the horn of oil from the sacred tent and anointed Solomon. Then they sounded the trumpet and all the people shouted, 'Long live King Solomon!' ⁴⁰And all the people went up after him, playing pipes and rejoicing greatly, so that the ground shook with the sound.

⁴¹Adonijah and all the guests who were with him heard it as they were finishing their feast. On hearing the sound of the trumpet, Joab asked, 'What's the meaning of all the noise in the city?'

⁴²Even as he was speaking, Jonathan son of Abiathar the priest arrived. Adonijah said, 'Come in. A worthy man like you must be bringing good news.'

⁴³'Not at all!' Jonathan answered. 'Our lord King David has made Solomon king. ⁴⁴The king has sent with him Zadok the priest, Nathan the prophet, Benaiah son of Jehoiada, the Kerethites and the Pelethites, and they have put him on the king's mule, ⁴⁵and Zadok the priest and Nathan the prophet have anointed him king at Gihon. From there they have gone up cheering, and the city resounds with it. That's the noise you hear. ⁴⁶Moreover, Solomon has taken his seat on the royal throne. ⁴⁷Also, the royal officials have come to congratulate our lord King David, saying, "May your God make Solomon's name more famous than

yours and his throne greater than yours!" And the king bowed in worship on his bed ⁴⁸and said, "Praise be to the LORD, the God of Israel, who has allowed my eyes to see a successor on my throne today."'

⁴⁹At this, all Adonijah's guests rose in alarm and dispersed. ⁵⁰But Adonijah, in fear of Solomon, went and took hold of the horns of the altar. ⁵¹Then Solomon was told, 'Adonijah is afraid of King Solomon and is clinging to the horns of the altar. He says, "Let King Solomon swear to me today that he will not put his servant to death with the sword."'

⁵²Solomon replied, 'If he shows himself to be worthy, not a hair of his head will fall to the ground; but if evil is found in him, he will die.' ⁵³Then King Solomon sent men, and they brought him down from the altar. And Adonijah came and bowed down to King Solomon, and Solomon said, 'Go to your home.'

···

▬ PSALM 71:9-16

⁹Do not cast me away when I am old;
  do not forsake me when my strength
    is gone.
¹⁰For my enemies speak against me;
  those who wait to kill me conspire
    together.
¹¹They say, 'God has forsaken him;
  pursue him and seize him,
  for no one will rescue him.'
¹²Do not be far from me, my God;
  come quickly, God, to help me.
¹³May my accusers perish in shame;
  may those who want to harm me
  be covered with scorn and disgrace.

¹⁴As for me, I shall always have hope;
  I will praise you more and more.

¹⁵My mouth will tell of your righteous
    deeds,

of your saving acts all day long –
though I know not how to relate them
all.
¹⁶ I will come and proclaim your mighty
acts, Sovereign LORD;
I will proclaim your righteous deeds,
yours alone.

■ PROVERBS 15:20-21

²⁰ A wise son brings joy to his father,
but a foolish man despises his mother.

²¹ Folly brings joy to one who has no sense,
but whoever has understanding keeps
a straight course.

■ JOHN 14:1-21

14 'Do not let your hearts be troubled.
You believe in God; believe also in
me. ² My Father's house has many rooms; if
that were not so, would I have told you that
I am going there to prepare a place for you?
³ And if I go and prepare a place for you, I
will come back and take you to be with me
that you also may be where I am. ⁴ You know
the way to the place where I am going.'

⁵ Thomas said to him, 'Lord, we don't
know where you are going, so how can we
know the way?'

⁶ Jesus answered, 'I am the way and the
truth and the life. No one comes to the Father except through me. ⁷ If you really know
me, you will know my Father as well. From
now on, you do know him and have seen
him.'

⁸ Philip said, 'Lord, show us the Father
and that will be enough for us.'

⁹ Jesus answered: 'Don't you know me,
Philip, even after I have been among you
such a long time? Anyone who has seen me
has seen the Father. How can you say, "Show
us the Father"? ¹⁰ Don't you believe that I am
in the Father, and that the Father is in me?
The words I say to you I do not speak on my
own authority. Rather, it is the Father, living in me, who is doing his work. ¹¹ Believe
me when I say that I am in the Father and
the Father is in me; or at least believe on the
evidence of the works themselves. ¹² Very
truly I tell you, whoever believes in me will
do the works I have been doing, and they
will do even greater things than these, because I am going to the Father. ¹³ And I will
do whatever you ask in my name, so that the
Father may be glorified in the Son. ¹⁴ You
may ask me for anything in my name, and
I will do it.

¹⁵ 'If you love me, keep my commands.
¹⁶ And I will ask the Father, and he will give
you another advocate to help you and be
with you for ever – ¹⁷ the Spirit of truth. The
world cannot accept him, because it neither
sees him nor knows him. But you know
him, for he lives with you and will be in you.
¹⁸ I will not leave you as orphans; I will come
to you. ¹⁹ Before long, the world will not see
me any more, but you will see me. Because
I live, you also will live. ²⁰ On that day you
will realise that I am in my Father, and you
are in me, and I am in you. ²¹ Whoever has
my commands and keeps them is the one
who loves me. The one who loves me will be
loved by my Father, and I too will love them
and show myself to them.'

A Permanent Guest

'... he will give you another advocate to help you and be
with you for ever – the Spirit of truth ...' **John 14:16-17**

One of the lessons Jesus gave His disciples when preparing them to receive the Holy Spirit was that the Spirit's coming would not be a temporary visitation – He would abide in them forever. In the Old Testament, the Holy Spirit provided temporary supplies of power to individual people for certain tasks. When these purposes were accomplished, He returned to heaven. The disciples were no doubt aware of this aspect of the Spirit's ministry, but now Jesus gives them the breathtaking news that the Holy Spirit's coming would be permanent: 'He will help you and be with you forever'. What a revelation this must have been to the disciples! The occasional would give place to the permanent; the special would give way to the general. Jesus was saying, in effect, that the Holy Spirit would not come and go – a kind of 'hide-and-seek' experience – but He would move within the inner recesses of their beings and abide with them forever.

This is probably one of the most important truths we can grasp from the Scripture, for there are many Christians who think of the possession of the Holy Spirit as tentative and momentary. However, that would defeat the very point and purpose of redemption, for as someone said: 'The Holy Spirit is the applied point of redemption'. His coming into our lives must be permanent, or our redemption (at least its application) will be temporary. The Holy Ghost becomes a Holy Guest! And, thank God, a permanent guest!

PRAYER

Blessed Holy Spirit, I am so grateful that You are willing to take up a permanent abode within my heart. With You abiding in me, I want for nothing and am equipped for every task. I am so thankful. Amen.

FURTHER STUDY

Gen. 1; Ezek. 36:27;
1 John 3:24; Heb. 9:14;
Rev. 22:17

• What was the Holy Spirit's ministry in the beginning?
• What is His ministry since Pentecost?

June 12

▬ 1 KINGS 2:1-46

2 When the time drew near for David to die, he gave a charge to Solomon his son.

² 'I am about to go the way of all the earth,' he said. 'So be strong, act like a man, ³ and observe what the LORD your God requires: walk in obedience to him, and keep his decrees and commands, his laws and regulations, as written in the Law of Moses. Do this so that you may prosper in all you do and wherever you go ⁴ and that the LORD may keep his promise to me: "If your descendants watch how they live, and if they walk faithfully before me with all their heart and soul, you will never fail to have a successor on the throne of Israel."

⁵'Now you yourself know what Joab son of Zeruiah did to me – what he did to the two commanders of Israel's armies, Abner son of Ner and Amasa son of Jether. He killed them, shedding their blood in peacetime as if in battle, and with that blood he stained the belt round his waist and the sandals on his feet. ⁶Deal with him according to your wisdom, but do not let his grey head go down to the grave in peace.

⁷'But show kindness to the sons of Barzillai of Gilead and let them be among those who eat at your table. They stood by me when I fled from your brother Absalom.

⁸"And remember, you have with you Shimei son of Gera, the Benjaminite from Bahurim, who called down bitter curses on me the day I went to Mahanaim. When he came down to meet me at the Jordan, I swore to him by the LORD: "I will not put you to death by the sword." ⁹But now, do not consider him innocent. You are a man of wisdom; you will know what to do to him. Bring his grey head down to the grave in blood.'

¹⁰Then David rested with his ancestors and was buried in the City of David. ¹¹He had reigned for forty years over Israel – seven years in Hebron and thirty-three in Jerusalem. ¹²So Solomon sat on the throne of his father David, and his rule was firmly established.

¹³Now Adonijah, the son of Haggith, went to Bathsheba, Solomon's mother. Bathsheba asked him, 'Do you come peacefully?'

He answered, 'Yes, peacefully.' ¹⁴Then he added, 'I have something to say to you.'

'You may say it,' she replied.

¹⁵'As you know,' he said, 'the kingdom was mine. All Israel looked to me as their king. But things changed, and the kingdom has gone to my brother; for it has come to him from the LORD. ¹⁶Now I have one request to make of you. Do not refuse me.'

'You may make it,' she said.

¹⁷So he continued, 'Please ask King Solomon – he will not refuse you – to give me Abishag the Shunammite as my wife.'

¹⁸'Very well,' Bathsheba replied, 'I will speak to the king for you.'

¹⁹When Bathsheba went to King Solomon to speak to him for Adonijah, the king stood up to meet her, bowed down to her and sat down on his throne. He had a throne brought for the king's mother, and she sat down at his right hand.

²⁰'I have one small request to make of you,' she said. 'Do not refuse me.'

The king replied, 'Make it, my mother; I will not refuse you.'

²¹So she said, 'Let Abishag the Shunammite be given in marriage to your brother Adonijah.'

²²King Solomon answered his mother, 'Why do you request Abishag the Shunammite for Adonijah? You might as well request the kingdom for him – after all, he is my older brother – yes, for him and for Abiathar the priest and Joab son of Zeruiah!'

²³Then King Solomon swore by the LORD: 'May God deal with me, be it ever so severely, if Adonijah does not pay with his life for this request! ²⁴And now, as surely as the LORD lives – he who has established me securely on the throne of my father David and has founded a dynasty for me as he promised – Adonijah shall be put to death today!' ²⁵So King Solomon gave orders to Benaiah son of Jehoiada, and he struck down Adonijah and he died.

²⁶To Abiathar the priest the king said, 'Go back to your fields in Anathoth. You deserve to die, but I will not put you to death now, because you carried the ark of the Sovereign LORD before my father David and shared all my father's hardships.' ²⁷So Solomon removed Abiathar from the priesthood of the LORD, fulfilling the word the LORD had spoken at Shiloh about the house of Eli.

²⁸When the news reached Joab, who had conspired with Adonijah though not with Absalom, he fled to the tent of the LORD and

took hold of the horns of the altar. ²⁹King Solomon was told that Joab had fled to the tent of the LORD and was beside the altar. Then Solomon ordered Benaiah son of Jehoiada, 'Go, strike him down!'

³⁰So Benaiah entered the tent of the LORD and said to Joab, 'The king says, "Come out!"'

But he answered, 'No, I will die here.'

Benaiah reported to the king, 'This is how Joab answered me.'

³¹Then the king commanded Benaiah, 'Do as he says. Strike him down and bury him, and so clear me and my whole family of the guilt of the innocent blood that Joab shed. ³²The LORD will repay him for the blood he shed, because without my father David knowing it he attacked two men and killed them with the sword. Both of them – Abner son of Ner, commander of Israel's army, and Amasa son of Jether, commander of Judah's army – were better men and more upright than he. ³³May the guilt of their blood rest on the head of Joab and his descendants for ever. But on David and his descendants, his house and his throne, may there be the LORD's peace for ever.'

³⁴So Benaiah son of Jehoiada went up and struck down Joab and killed him, and he was buried at his home out in the country. ³⁵The king put Benaiah son of Jehoiada over the army in Joab's position and replaced Abiathar with Zadok the priest.

³⁶Then the king sent for Shimei and said to him, 'Build yourself a house in Jerusalem and live there, but do not go anywhere else. ³⁷The day you leave and cross the Kidron Valley, you can be sure you will die; your blood will be on your own head.'

³⁸Shimei answered the king, 'What you say is good. Your servant will do as my lord the king has said.' And Shimei stayed in Jerusalem for a long time.

³⁹But three years later, two of Shimei's slaves ran off to Achish son of Maakah, king of Gath, and Shimei was told, 'Your slaves

are in Gath.' ⁴⁰At this, he saddled his donkey and went to Achish at Gath in search of his slaves. So Shimei went away and brought the slaves back from Gath.

⁴¹When Solomon was told that Shimei had gone from Jerusalem to Gath and had returned, ⁴²the king summoned Shimei and said to him, 'Did I not make you swear by the LORD and warn you, "On the day you leave to go anywhere else, you can be sure you will die"? At that time you said to me, "What you say is good. I will obey." ⁴³Why then did you not keep your oath to the LORD and obey the command I gave you?'

⁴⁴The king also said to Shimei, 'You know in your heart all the wrong you did to my father David. Now the LORD will repay you for your wrongdoing. ⁴⁵But King Solomon will be blessed, and David's throne will remain secure before the LORD for ever.'

⁴⁶Then the king gave the order to Benaiah son of Jehoiada, and he went out and struck Shimei down and he died.

The kingdom was now established in Solomon's hands.

■ PSALM 71:17-24

¹⁷Since my youth, God, you have taught
    me,
    and to this day I declare your
        marvellous deeds.
¹⁸Even when I am old and grey,
    do not forsake me, my God,
    till I declare your power to the next
        generation,
    your mighty acts to all who are to
        come.

¹⁹Your righteousness, God, reaches to the
        heavens,
    you who have done great things.
    Who is like you, God?
²⁰Though you have made me see troubles,
    many and bitter,

you will restore my life again;
from the depths of the earth
    you will again bring me up.
²¹ You will increase my honour
    and comfort me once more.

²² I will praise you with the harp
    for your faithfulness, my God;
I will sing praise to you with the lyre,
    Holy One of Israel.
²³ My lips will shout for joy
    when I sing praise to you –
    I whom you have delivered.
²⁴ My tongue will tell of your righteous acts
    all day long,
    for those who wanted to harm me
    have been put to shame and
        confusion.

▬ PROVERBS 15:22-23

²² Plans fail for lack of counsel,
    but with many advisors they succeed.

²³ A person finds joy in giving an apt
        reply –
    and how good is a timely word!

▬ JOHN 14:22–15:10

²² Then Judas (not Judas Iscariot) said, 'But, Lord, why do you intend to show yourself to us and not to the world?'

²³ Jesus replied, 'Anyone who loves me will obey my teaching. My Father will love them, and we will come to them and make our home with them. ²⁴ Anyone who does not love me will not obey my teaching. These words you hear are not my own; they belong to the Father who sent me.

²⁵ 'All this I have spoken while still with you. ²⁶ But the Advocate, the Holy Spirit, whom the Father will send in my name, will teach you all things and will remind you of everything I have said to you. ²⁷ Peace I leave with you; my peace I give you. I do not give to you as the world gives. Do not let your hearts be troubled and do not be afraid.

²⁸ 'You heard me say, "I am going away and I am coming back to you." If you loved me, you would be glad that I am going to the Father, for the Father is greater than I. ²⁹ I have told you now before it happens, so that when it does happen you will believe. ³⁰ I will not say much more to you, for the prince of this world is coming. He has no hold over me, ³¹ but he comes so that the world may learn that I love the Father and do exactly what my Father has commanded me.

'Come now; let us leave.

15 'I am the true vine, and my Father is the gardener. ² He cuts off every branch in me that bears no fruit, while every branch that does bear fruit he prunes so that it will be even more fruitful. ³ You are already clean because of the word I have spoken to you. ⁴ Remain in me, as I also remain in you. No branch can bear fruit by itself; it must remain in the vine. Neither can you bear fruit unless you remain in me.

⁵ 'I am the vine; you are the branches. If you remain in me and I in you, you will bear much fruit; apart from me you can do nothing. ⁶ If you do not remain in me, you are like a branch that is thrown away and withers; such branches are picked up, thrown into the fire and burned. ⁷ If you remain in me and my words remain in you, ask whatever you wish, and it will be done for you. ⁸ This is to my Father's glory, that you bear much fruit, showing yourselves to be my disciples.

⁹ 'As the Father has loved me, so have I loved you. Now remain in my love. ¹⁰ If you keep my commands, you will remain in my love, just as I have kept my Father's commands and remain in his love.

The Whole Truth

'... the Holy Spirit, whom the Father will send in my name, will teach you all things and will remind you of everything I have said to you.' **John 14:26**

Another lesson given by Jesus to His disciples when preparing them to receive the Holy Spirit was that the Holy Spirit would teach them and remind them of all that Jesus had said. A famous agnostic once said that the irreconcilable conflict between science and religion is that science is never fixed - it is open and progressive: religion, on the other hand, is fixed on absolutes and dogmas.

Well, it is true that Christianity is fixed, but it also provides for a continuing revelation: 'The Holy Spirit ... will teach you all things'. Jesus is God's final and complete revelation, but because of the limitations in us, this revelation must be gradually unfolding. Notice, however, that the teaching of the Spirit is according to a fixed pattern: '[He] will ... remind you of everything I have said to you' (v. 26). He will teach us more than Jesus taught but not other than Jesus taught. Someone said of this approach that it is both conservative and radical because it conserves all that Jesus taught and because it applies to new areas of life the universal aspect of Jesus.

'[He] will ... remind you of everything I have said to you'. Note that word 'everything'. When we are not under the Holy Spirit's tutelage, we tend to focus on just one thing Jesus said and neglect the 'everything'. Then what happens? We produce a lopsided type of Christianity, with an overemphasis on one thing and an underemphasis on another. Christian communities who concentrate on one truth can easily miss the whole truth. Christians under the Spirit's control give heed to the 'everything'.

PRAYER

O Father, I don't want to live on a truth, or even a cluster of truths - I want to live on the Truth. In Jesus' name. Amen.

FURTHER STUDY

1 Cor. 2; Neh. 9:20; Luke 12:12; 1 John 2:27
• What has God revealed to us by His Spirit?
• What does the Holy Spirit bring to us?

June 13

3 Solomon made an alliance with Pharaoh king of Egypt and married his daughter. He brought her to the City of David until he finished building his palace and the temple of the LORD, and the wall around Jerusalem. ²The people, however, were still sacrificing at the high places, because a temple had not yet been built for the Name of the LORD. ³Solomon showed his love for the LORD by walking according to the instructions given him by his father David, except that he offered sacrifices and burned incense on the high places.

⁴The king went to Gibeon to offer sacrifices, for that was the most important high place, and Solomon offered a thousand burnt offerings on that altar. ⁵At Gibeon the LORD appeared to Solomon during the night in a dream, and God said, 'Ask for whatever you want me to give you.'

⁶Solomon answered, 'You have shown great kindness to your servant, my father David, because he was faithful to you and righteous and upright in heart. You have continued this great kindness to him and have given him a son to sit on his throne this very day.

⁷'Now, LORD my God, you have made your servant king in place of my father David. But I am only a little child and do not know how to carry out my duties. ⁸Your servant is here among the people you have chosen, a great people, too numerous to count or number. ⁹So give your servant a discerning heart to govern your people and to distinguish between right and wrong. For who is able to govern this great people of yours?'

¹⁰The Lord was pleased that Solomon had asked for this. ¹¹So God said to him, 'Since you have asked for this and not for long life or wealth for yourself, nor have asked for the death of your enemies but for discernment in administering justice, ¹²I will do what you have asked. I will give you a wise and discerning heart, so that there will never have been anyone like you, nor will there ever be. ¹³Moreover, I will give you what you have not asked for – both wealth and honour – so that in your lifetime you will have no equal among kings. ¹⁴And if you walk in obedience to me and keep my decrees and commands as David your father did, I will give you a long life.' ¹⁵Then Solomon awoke – and he realised it had been a dream.

He returned to Jerusalem, stood before the ark of the Lord's covenant and sacrificed burnt offerings and fellowship offerings. Then he gave a feast for all his court.

¹⁶Now two prostitutes came to the king and stood before him. ¹⁷One of them said, 'Pardon me, my lord. This woman and I live in the same house. I had a baby while she was there with me. ¹⁸The third day after my child was born, this woman also had a baby. We were alone; there was no one in the house but the two of us.

¹⁹'During the night this woman's son died because she lay on him. ²⁰So she got up in the middle of the night and took my son from my side while I your servant was asleep. She put him by her breast and put her dead son by my breast. ²¹The next morning, I got up to nurse my son – and he was dead! But when I looked at him closely in the morning light, I saw that it wasn't the son I had borne.'

²²The other woman said, 'No! The living one is my son; the dead one is yours.'

But the first one insisted, 'No! The dead one is yours; the living one is mine.' And so they argued before the king.

²³ The king said, 'This one says, "My son is alive and your son is dead," while that one says, "No! Your son is dead and mine is alive."'

²⁴ Then the king said, 'Bring me a sword.' So they brought a sword for the king. ²⁵ He then gave an order: 'Cut the living child in two and give half to one and half to the other.'

²⁶ The woman whose son was alive was deeply moved out of love for her son and said to the king, 'Please, my lord, give her the living baby! Don't kill him!'

But the other said, 'Neither I nor you shall have him. Cut him in two!'

²⁷ Then the king gave his ruling: 'Give the living baby to the first woman. Do not kill him; she is his mother.'

²⁸ When all Israel heard the verdict the king had given, they held the king in awe, because they saw that he had wisdom from God to administer justice.

4 So King Solomon ruled over all Israel. ² And these were his chief officials:

Azariah son of Zadok – the priest;
³ Elihoreph and Ahijah, sons of Shisha – secretaries;
Jehoshaphat son of Ahilud – recorder;
⁴ Benaiah son of Jehoiada – commander -in-chief;
Zadok and Abiathar – priests;
⁵ Azariah son of Nathan – in charge of the district governors;
Zabud son of Nathan – a priest and advisor to the king;
⁶ Ahishar – palace administrator;
Adoniram son of Abda – in charge of forced labour.

⁷ Solomon had twelve district governors over all Israel, who supplied provisions for the king and the royal household. Each one had to provide supplies for one month in the year. ⁸ These are their names:

Ben-Hur – in the hill country of Ephraim;
⁹ Ben-Deker – in Makaz, Shaalbim, Beth Shemesh and Elon Bethhanan;
¹⁰ Ben-Hesed – in Arubboth (Sokoh and all the land of Hepher were his);
¹¹ Ben-Abinadab – in Naphoth Dor (he was married to Taphath daughter of Solomon);
¹² Baana son of Ahilud – in Taanach and Megiddo, and in all of Beth Shan next to Zarethan below Jezreel, from Beth Shan to Abel Meholah across to Jokmeam;
¹³ Ben-Geber – in Ramoth Gilead (the settlements of Jair son of Manasseh in Gilead were his, as well as the region of Argob in Bashan and its sixty large walled cities with bronze gate bars);
¹⁴ Ahinadab son of Iddo – in Mahanaim;
¹⁵ Ahimaaz – in Naphtali (he had married Basemath daughter of Solomon);
¹⁶ Baana son of Hushai – in Asher and in Aloth;
¹⁷ Jehoshaphat son of Paruah – in Issachar;
¹⁸ Shimei son of Ela – in Benjamin;
¹⁹ Geber son of Uri – in Gilead (the country of Sihon king of the Amorites and the country of Og king of Bashan). He was the only governor over the district.

²⁰ The people of Judah and Israel were as numerous as the sand on the seashore; they ate, they drank and they were happy. ²¹ And Solomon ruled over all the kingdoms from the River Euphrates to the land of the Philistines, as far as the border of Egypt. These countries brought tribute and were Solomon's subjects all his life.

²² Solomon's daily provisions were thirty cors of the finest flour and sixty cors of meal, ²³ ten head of stall-fed cattle, twenty of pasture-fed cattle and a hundred sheep

and goats, as well as deer, gazelles, roe-bucks and choice fowl. [24]For he ruled over all the kingdoms west of the River Euphrates, from Tiphsah to Gaza, and had peace on all sides. [25]During Solomon's lifetime Judah and Israel, from Dan to Beersheba, lived in safety, everyone under their own vine and under their own fig-tree.

[26]Solomon had four thousand stalls for chariot horses, and twelve thousand horses.

[27]The district governors, each in his month, supplied provisions for King Solomon and all who came to the king's table. They saw to it that nothing was lacking. [28]They also brought to the proper place their quotas of barley and straw for the chariot horses and the other horses.

[29]God gave Solomon wisdom and very great insight, and a breadth of understanding as measureless as the sand on the seashore. [30]Solomon's wisdom was greater than the wisdom of all the people of the East, and greater than all the wisdom of Egypt. [31]He was wiser than anyone else, including Ethan the Ezrahite – wiser than Heman, Kalkol and Darda, the sons of Mahol. And his fame spread to all the surrounding nations. [32]He spoke three thousand proverbs and his songs numbered a thousand and five. [33]He spoke about plant life, from the cedar of Lebanon to the hyssop that grows out of walls. He also spoke about animals and birds, reptiles and fish. [34]From all nations people came to listen to Solomon's wisdom, sent by all the kings of the world, who had heard of his wisdom.

▬ PSALM 72:1-7

[1]Endow the king with your justice, O God,
  the royal son with your righteousness.
[2]May he judge your people in
    righteousness,
  your afflicted ones with justice.

[3]May the mountains bring prosperity to
    the people,
  the hills the fruit of righteousness.
[4]May he defend the afflicted among the
    people
  and save the children of the needy;
  may he crush the oppressor.
[5]May he endure as long as the sun,
  as long as the moon, through all
    generations.
[6]May he be like rain falling on a mown
    field,
  like showers watering the earth.
[7]In his days may the righteous flourish
  and prosperity abound till the moon is
    no more.

▬ PROVERBS 15:24-25

[24]The path of life leads upward for the
    prudent
  to keep them from going down to the
    realm of the dead.

[25]The LORD tears down the house of the
    proud,
  but he sets the widow's boundary
    stones in place.

▬ JOHN 15:11–16:4

[11]I have told you this so that my joy may be in you and that your joy may be complete. [12]My command is this: love each other as I have loved you. [13]Greater love has no one than this: to lay down one's life for one's friends. [14]You are my friends if you do what I command. [15]I no longer call you servants, because a servant does not know his master's business. Instead, I have called you friends, for everything that I learned from my Father I have made known to you. [16]You did not choose me, but I chose you and appointed you so that you might go and bear

fruit – fruit that will last – and so that whatever you ask in my name the Father will give you. [17] This is my command: love each other.

[18] 'If the world hates you, keep in mind that it hated me first. [19] If you belonged to the world, it would love you as its own. As it is, you do not belong to the world, but I have chosen you out of the world. That is why the world hates you. [20] Remember what I told you: "A servant is not greater than his master." If they persecuted me, they will persecute you also. If they obeyed my teaching, they will obey yours also. [21] They will treat you this way because of my name, for they do not know the one who sent me. [22] If I had not come and spoken to them, they would not be guilty of sin; but now they have no excuse for their sin. [23] Whoever hates me hates my Father as well. [24] If I had not done among them the works no one else did, they would

not be guilty of sin. As it is, they have seen, and yet they have hated both me and my Father. [25] But this is to fulfil what is written in their Law: "They hated me without reason."

[26] 'When the Advocate comes, whom I will send to you from the Father – the Spirit of truth who goes out from the Father – he will testify about me. [27] And you also must testify, for you have been with me from the beginning.

16 'All this I have told you so that you will not fall away. [2] They will put you out of the synagogue; in fact, the time is coming when anyone who kills you will think they are offering a service to God. [3] They will do such things because they have not known the Father or me. [4] I have told you this, so that when their time comes you will remember that I warned you about them. I did not tell you this from the beginning because I was with you ...

Believing – We Receive

'... whatever you ask in my name the Father will give you.' **John 15:16**

An important step to help you access the power of the Spirit is to reach out in faith and receive the fullness of all that God has for you. We enter into all God's blessing by faith. As a child of God, you are heir to all that the Father has – Himself. So reach out and take Him now. Jesus said, 'Let anyone who is thirsty come to me and drink' (John 7:37).

Are you thirsty? Then drink. 'This is the confidence we have in approaching God: that if we ask anything according to his will, he hears us. And if we know that he hears us – whatever we ask – we know that we have what we asked of him' (1 John 5:14-15). Here are the principles:

Confidence – 'the confidence we have in approaching God'.
Conversing – 'we ask anything'.
Condition – 'according to his will'.
Conviction – 'we know that he hears us – whatever we ask'.
Consequence – 'we know that we have.'

Follow the principles one by one. Have confidence in the character of God. Converse with Him and tell Him your need – to be filled to overflowing with His Holy Spirit. Believe that the condition is met and your asking is in harmony with His will. Remind yourself that He hears your request and that He is flooding your whole being with His power. Have the boldness to take what is there. Faith will turn it to fact; fact will turn it to feeling. Welcome His coming in whatever manner He comes. You are thirsty – so drink ... and drink ... and drink.

PRAYER

O Father, how can I thank You enough for bringing me to this moment? It is an end, yet it is a beginning. I know that life is ahead of me, for life is within me. I am grateful beyond words. Amen.

FURTHER STUDY

Acts 7:42-56; John 20:22; Eph. 5:18; 3:19
· What was said of Stephen?
· What is Paul's exhortation?

June 14

■ 1 KINGS 5:1–6:38

5 When Hiram king of Tyre heard that Solomon had been anointed king to succeed his father David, he sent his envoys to Solomon, because he had always been on friendly terms with David. ²Solomon sent back this message to Hiram:

³'You know that because of the wars waged against my father David from all sides, he could not build a temple for the Name of the LORD his God until the LORD put his enemies under his feet. ⁴But now the LORD my God has given me rest on every side, and there is no adversary or disaster. ⁵I intend, therefore, to build a temple for the Name of the LORD my God, as the LORD told my father David, when he said, "Your son whom I will put on the throne in your place will build the temple for my Name."

⁶'So give orders that cedars of Lebanon be cut for me. My men will work with yours, and I will pay you for your men whatever wages you set. You know that we have no one so skilled in felling timber as the Sidonians.'

⁷When Hiram heard Solomon's message, he was greatly pleased and said, 'Praise be to the LORD today, for he has given David a wise son to rule over this great nation.'

⁸So Hiram sent word to Solomon:

'I have received the message you sent me and will do all you want in providing the cedar and juniper logs. ⁹My men will haul them down from Lebanon to the Mediterranean Sea, and I will float them as rafts by sea to the place you specify. There I will separate them and you can take them away. And you are to grant my wish by providing food for my royal household.'

¹⁰In this way Hiram kept Solomon supplied with all the cedar and juniper logs he wanted, ¹¹and Solomon gave Hiram twenty thousand cors of wheat as food for his household, in addition to twenty thousand

baths of pressed olive oil. Solomon continued to do this for Hiram year after year. ¹²The LORD gave Solomon wisdom, just as he had promised him. There were peaceful relations between Hiram and Solomon, and the two of them made a treaty.

¹³King Solomon conscripted labourers from all Israel – thirty thousand men. ¹⁴He sent them off to Lebanon in shifts of ten thousand a month, so that they spent one month in Lebanon and two months at home. Adoniram was in charge of the forced labour. ¹⁵Solomon had seventy thousand carriers and eighty thousand stonecutters in the hills, ¹⁶as well as thirty-three hundred foremen who supervised the project and directed the workers. ¹⁷At the king's command they removed from the quarry large blocks of high-grade stone to provide a foundation of dressed stone for the temple. ¹⁸The craftsmen of Solomon and Hiram and workers from Byblos cut and prepared the timber and stone for the building of the temple.

6 In the four hundred and eightieth year after the Israelites came out of Egypt, in the fourth year of Solomon's reign over Israel, in the month of Ziv, the second month, he began to build the temple of the LORD.

²The temple that King Solomon built for the LORD was sixty cubits long, twenty wide and thirty high. ³The portico at the front of the main hall of the temple extended the width of the temple, that is twenty cubits, and projected ten cubits from the front of the temple. ⁴He made narrow windows high up in the temple walls. ⁵Against the walls of the main hall and inner sanctuary he built a structure around the building, in which there were side rooms. ⁶The lowest floor was five cubits wide, the middle floor six cubits and the third floor seven. He made offset ledges around the outside of the temple so that nothing would be inserted into the temple walls.

⁷In building the temple, only blocks dressed at the quarry were used, and no hammer, chisel or any other iron tool was heard at the temple site while it was being built.

⁸The entrance to the lowest floor was on the south side of the temple; a stairway led up to the middle level and from there to the third. ⁹So he built the temple and completed it, roofing it with beams and cedar planks. ¹⁰And he built the side rooms all along the temple. The height of each was five cubits, and they were attached to the temple by beams of cedar.

¹¹The word of the LORD came to Solomon: ¹²'As for this temple you are building, if you follow my decrees, observe my laws and keep all my commands and obey them, I will fulfil through you the promise I gave to David your father. ¹³And I will live among the Israelites and will not abandon my people Israel.'

¹⁴So Solomon built the temple and completed it. ¹⁵He lined its interior walls with cedar boards, panelling them from the floor of the temple to the ceiling, and covered the floor of the temple with planks of juniper. ¹⁶He partitioned off twenty cubits at the rear of the temple with cedar boards from floor to ceiling to form within the temple an inner sanctuary, the Most Holy Place. ¹⁷The main hall in front of this room was forty cubits long. ¹⁸The inside of the temple was cedar, carved with gourds and open flowers. Everything was cedar; no stone was to be seen.

¹⁹He prepared the inner sanctuary within the temple to set the ark of the covenant of the LORD there. ²⁰The inner sanctuary was twenty cubits long, twenty wide and twenty high. He overlaid the inside with pure gold, and he also overlaid the altar of cedar. ²¹Solomon covered the inside of the temple with pure gold, and he extended gold chains across the front of the inner sanctuary, which was overlaid with gold.

²²So he overlaid the whole interior with gold. He also overlaid with gold the altar that belonged to the inner sanctuary.

²³For the inner sanctuary he made a pair of cherubim out of olive wood, each ten cubits high. ²⁴One wing of the first cherub was five cubits long, and the other wing five cubits – ten cubits from wing tip to wing tip. ²⁵The second cherub also measured ten cubits, for the two cherubim were identical in size and shape. ²⁶The height of each cherub was ten cubits. ²⁷He placed the cherubim inside the innermost room of the temple, with their wings spread out. The wing of one cherub touched one wall, while the wing of the other touched the other wall, and their wings touched each other in the middle of the room. ²⁸He overlaid the cherubim with gold.

²⁹On the walls all round the temple, in both the inner and outer rooms, he carved cherubim, palm trees and open flowers. ³⁰He also covered the floors of both the inner and outer rooms of the temple with gold. ³¹For the entrance to the inner sanctuary he made doors out of olive wood that were one fifth of the width of the sanctuary. ³²And on the two olive-wood doors he carved cherubim, palm trees and open flowers, and overlaid the cherubim and palm trees with hammered gold. ³³In the same way, for the entrance to the main hall he made doorframes out of olive wood that were one quarter of the width of the hall. ³⁴He also made two doors out of juniper wood, each having two leaves that turned in sockets. ³⁵He carved cherubim, palm trees and open flowers on them and overlaid them with gold hammered evenly over the carvings.

³⁶And he built the inner courtyard of three courses of dressed stone and one course of trimmed cedar beams.

³⁷The foundation of the temple of the LORD was laid in the fourth year, in the month of Ziv. ³⁸In the eleventh year in the month of Bul, the eighth month, the temple was finished in all its details

according to its specifications. He had spent seven years building it.

▬ PSALM 72:8-14

⁸ May he rule from sea to sea
    and from the River to the ends of the
        earth.
⁹ May the desert tribes bow before him
    and his enemies lick the dust.
¹⁰ May the kings of Tarshish and of distant
        shores
    bring tribute to him.
  May the kings of Sheba and Seba
    present him with gifts.
¹¹ May all kings bow down to him
    and all nations serve him.

¹² For he will deliver the needy who cry out,
    the afflicted who have no one to help.
¹³ He will take pity on the weak and the
        needy
    and save the needy from death.
¹⁴ He will rescue them from oppression and
        violence,
    for precious is their blood in his sight.

▬ PROVERBS 15:26-27

²⁶ The LORD detests the thoughts of the
        wicked,
    but gracious words are pure in his sight.

²⁷ The greedy bring ruin to their
        households,
    but the one who hates bribes will live.

▬ JOHN 16:5-33

⁵... but now I am going to him who sent me. None of you asks me, "Where are you going?" ⁶Rather, you are filled with grief because I have said these things. ⁷But very

truly I tell you, it is for your good that I am going away. Unless I go away, the Advocate will not come to you; but if I go, I will send him to you. [8] When he comes, he will prove the world to be in the wrong about sin and righteousness and judgment: [9] about sin, because people do not believe in me; [10] about righteousness, because I am going to the Father, where you can see me no longer; [11] and about judgment, because the prince of this world now stands condemned.

[12] 'I have much more to say to you, more than you can now bear. [13] But when he, the Spirit of truth, comes, he will guide you into all the truth. He will not speak on his own; he will speak only what he hears, and he will tell you what is yet to come. [14] He will glorify me because it is from me that he will receive what he will make known to you. [15] All that belongs to the Father is mine. That is why I said the Spirit will receive from me what he will make known to you.'

[16] Jesus went on to say, 'In a little while you will see me no more, and then after a little while you will see me.'

[17] At this, some of his disciples said to one another, 'What does he mean by saying, "In a little while you will see me no more, and then after a little while you will see me," and "Because I am going to the Father"?' [18] They kept asking, 'What does he mean by "a little while"? We don't understand what he is saying.'

[19] Jesus saw that they wanted to ask him about this, so he said to them, 'Are you asking one another what I meant when I said, "In a little while you will see me no more, and then after a little while you will see me"? [20] Very truly I tell you, you will weep and mourn while the world rejoices.

You will grieve, but your grief will turn to joy. [21] A woman giving birth to a child has pain because her time has come; but when her baby is born she forgets the anguish because of her joy that a child is born into the world. [22] So with you: now is your time of grief, but I will see you again and you will rejoice, and no one will take away your joy. [23] In that day you will no longer ask me anything. Very truly I tell you, my Father will give you whatever you ask in my name. [24] Until now you have not asked for anything in my name. Ask and you will receive, and your joy will be complete.

[25] 'Though I have been speaking figuratively, a time is coming when I will no longer use this kind of language but will tell you plainly about my Father. [26] In that day you will ask in my name. I am not saying that I will ask the Father on your behalf. [27] No, the Father himself loves you because you have loved me and have believed that I came from God. [28] I came from the Father and entered the world; now I am leaving the world and going back to the Father.'

[29] Then Jesus' disciples said, 'Now you are speaking clearly and without figures of speech. [30] Now we can see that you know all things and that you do not even need to have anyone ask you questions. This makes us believe that you came from God.'

[31] 'Do you now believe?' Jesus replied. [32] 'A time is coming and in fact has come when you will be scattered, each to your own home. You will leave me all alone. Yet I am not alone, for my Father is with me.

[33] 'I have told you these things, so that in me you may have peace. In this world you will have trouble. But take heart! I have overcome the world.'

Who Is the Holy Spirit?

'... he will guide you into all the truth. He will not speak on his own ...' **John 16:13**

The Christian faith is a religion of the Spirit, and unless we are continually filled with His divine resources, then our lives are largely ineffective. If the Scripture places so much emphasis on being possessed by the Holy Spirit, then it follows that we ought to find out everything we can about the One who seeks to indwell us.

I say 'who,' for the Holy Spirit is not just an impersonal influence, nor is He just a sense of fellowship when we get together, nor an enthusiasm over ideas or causes. It is evident from the personal pronouns used of Him in the Scriptures that the writers viewed Him as a member of the Trinity, equal in honour and status to the Father and the Son. However, the Holy Spirit does not like to draw attention to Himself. In the Old Testament, the Spirit turns the spotlight fully upon the face of the Father. In the New Testament, He turns it fully upon the face of the Son. Never does He focus attention on Himself.

We owe a great deal of our understanding of the Holy Spirit to what Christ said of Him in the Gospels, for there Jesus returns the compliment and occasionally turns the spotlight upon the Holy Spirit, revealing His nature and His ministry. Jesus, in fact, put His disciples through a deliberate course of mental and spiritual training to prepare them for the reception of the Spirit. If we are to understand the Spirit's ministry in our lives, then we must enroll in this course, too.

PRAYER

Gracious Father, as I seek to understand who the Holy Spirit is and what He wants to do in my life, give me an eager mind and a receptive spirit. In Jesus' name I pray. Amen.

FURTHER STUDY

John 14:16-31; 15:26-27; Luke 24:49; 11:13
- What did Jesus teach about the Holy Spirit?
- What does the word 'comforter' mean?

June 15

■ 1 KINGS 7:1-51

7 It took Solomon thirteen years, however, to complete the construction of his palace. ²He built the Palace of the Forest of Lebanon a hundred cubits long, fifty wide and thirty high, with four rows of cedar columns supporting trimmed cedar beams. ³It was roofed with cedar above the beams that rested on the columns – forty-five beams, fifteen to a row. ⁴Its windows were

placed high in sets of three, facing each other. ⁵All the doorways had rectangular frames; they were in the front part in sets of three, facing each other.

⁶He made a colonnade fifty cubits long and thirty wide. In front of it was a portico, and in front of that were pillars and an overhanging roof.

⁷He built the throne hall, the Hall of Justice, where he was to judge, and he covered it with cedar from floor to ceiling. ⁸And the

palace in which he was to live, set farther back, was similar in design. Solomon also made a palace like this hall for Pharaoh's daughter, whom he had married.

⁹All these structures, from the outside to the great courtyard and from foundation to eaves, were made of blocks of high-grade stone cut to size and smoothed on their inner and outer faces. ¹⁰The foundations were laid with large stones of good quality, some measuring ten cubits and some eight. ¹¹Above were high-grade stones, cut to size, and cedar beams. ¹²The great courtyard was surrounded by a wall of three courses of dressed stone and one course of trimmed cedar beams, as was the inner courtyard of the temple of the LORD with its portico.

¹³King Solomon sent to Tyre and brought Huram, ¹⁴whose mother was a widow from the tribe of Naphtali and whose father was from Tyre and a skilled craftsman in bronze. Huram was filled with wisdom, with understanding and with knowledge to do all kinds of bronze work. He came to King Solomon and did all the work assigned to him.

¹⁵He cast two bronze pillars, each eighteen cubits high and twelve cubits in circumference. ¹⁶He also made two capitals of cast bronze to set on the tops of the pillars; each capital was five cubits high. ¹⁷A network of interwoven chains adorned the capitals on top of the pillars, seven for each capital. ¹⁸He made pomegranates in two rows encircling each network to decorate the capitals on top of the pillars. He did the same for each capital. ¹⁹The capitals on top of the pillars in the portico were in the shape of lilies, four cubits high. ²⁰On the capitals of both pillars, above the bowl-shaped part next to the network, were the two hundred pomegranates in rows all around. ²¹He erected the pillars at the portico of the temple. The pillar to the south he named Jakin and the one to the north Boaz. ²²The capitals on top were in the shape of lilies. And so the work on the pillars was completed.

²³He made the Sea of cast metal, circular in shape, measuring ten cubits from rim to rim and five cubits high. It took a line of thirty cubits to measure round it. ²⁴Below the rim, gourds encircled it – ten to a cubit. The gourds were cast in two rows in one piece with the Sea.

²⁵The Sea stood on twelve bulls, three facing north, three facing west, three facing south and three facing east. The Sea rested on top of them, and their hindquarters were towards the centre. ²⁶It was a handbreadth in thickness, and its rim was like the rim of a cup, like a lily blossom. It held two thousand baths.

²⁷He also made ten movable stands of bronze; each was four cubits long, four wide and three high. ²⁸This is how the stands were made: they had side panels attached to uprights. ²⁹On the panels between the uprights were lions, bulls and cherubim – and on the uprights as well. Above and below the lions and bulls were wreaths of hammered work. ³⁰Each stand had four bronze wheels with bronze axles, and each had a basin resting on four supports, cast with wreaths on each side. ³¹On the inside of the stand there was an opening that had a circular frame one cubit deep. This opening was round, and with its basework it measured a cubit and a half. Around its opening there was engraving. The panels of the stands were square, not round. ³²The four wheels were under the panels, and the axles of the wheels were attached to the stand. The diameter of each wheel was a cubit and a half. ³³The wheels were made like chariot wheels; the axles, rims, spokes and hubs were all of cast metal.

³⁴Each stand had four handles, one on each corner, projecting from the stand. ³⁵At the top of the stand there was a circular band half a cubit deep. The supports and panels were attached to the top of the stand. ³⁶He engraved cherubim, lions and palm trees on the surfaces of the supports and on the panels, in every available space,

with wreaths all around. ³⁷This is the way he made the ten stands. They were all cast in the same moulds and were identical in size and shape.

³⁸He then made ten bronze basins, each holding forty baths and measuring four cubits across, one basin to go on each of the ten stands. ³⁹He placed five of the stands on the south side of the temple and five on the north. He placed the Sea on the south side, at the south-east corner of the temple. ⁴⁰He also made the pots and shovels and sprinkling bowls.

So Huram finished all the work he had undertaken for King Solomon in the temple of the LORD:

⁴¹the two pillars;

the two bowl-shaped capitals on top of the pillars;

the two sets of network decorating the two bowl-shaped capitals on top of the pillars;

⁴²the four hundred pomegranates for the two sets of network (two rows of pomegranates for each network decorating the bowl-shaped capitals on top of the pillars);

⁴³the ten stands with their ten basins;

⁴⁴the Sea and the twelve bulls under it;

⁴⁵the pots, shovels and sprinkling bowls.

All these objects that Huram made for King Solomon for the temple of the LORD were of burnished bronze. ⁴⁶The king had them cast in clay moulds in the plain of the Jordan between Sukkoth and Zarethan. ⁴⁷Solomon left all these things unweighed, because there were so many; the weight of the bronze was not determined.

⁴⁸Solomon also made all the furnishings that were in the LORD's temple:

the golden altar;

the golden table on which was the bread of the Presence;

⁴⁹the lampstands of pure gold (five on the right and five on the left, in front of the inner sanctuary);

the gold floral work and lamps and tongs;

⁵⁰the pure gold dishes, wick trimmers, sprinkling bowls, dishes and censers;

and the gold sockets for the doors of the innermost room, the Most Holy Place, and also for the doors of the main hall of the temple.

⁵¹When all the work King Solomon had done for the temple of the LORD was finished, he brought in the things his father David had dedicated – the silver and gold and the furnishings – and he placed them in the treasuries of the LORD's temple.

▬ PSALM 72:15-20

¹⁵Long may he live!
    May gold from Sheba be given to him.
May people ever pray for him
    and bless him all day long.
¹⁶May corn abound throughout the land;
    on the tops of the hills may it sway.
May the crops flourish like Lebanon
    and thrive like the grass of the field.
¹⁷May his name endure for ever;
    may it continue as long as the sun.

Then all nations will be blessed through him,
    and they will call him blessed.

¹⁸Praise be to the LORD God, the God of Israel,
    who alone does marvellous deeds.
¹⁹Praise be to his glorious name for ever;
    may the whole earth be filled with his glory.
        Amen and Amen.

²⁰ This concludes the prayers of David son of Jesse.

▬ PROVERBS 15:28-29

²⁸ The heart of the righteous weighs its
        answers,
    but the mouth of the wicked gushes
        evil.

²⁹ The LORD is far from the wicked,
    but he hears the prayer of the
        righteous.

▬ JOHN 17:1-26

17 After Jesus said this, he looked towards heaven and prayed:

'Father, the hour has come. Glorify your Son, that your Son may glorify you. ² For you granted him authority over all people that he might give eternal life to all those you have given him. ³ Now this is eternal life: that they know you, the only true God, and Jesus Christ, whom you have sent. ⁴ I have brought you glory on earth by finishing the work you gave me to do. ⁵ And now, Father, glorify me in your presence with the glory I had with you before the world began.

⁶ 'I have revealed you to those whom you gave me out of the world. They were yours; you gave them to me and they have obeyed your word. ⁷ Now they know that everything you have given me comes from you. ⁸ For I gave them the words you gave me and they accepted them. They knew with certainty that I came from you, and they believed that you sent me. ⁹ I pray for them. I am not praying for the world, but for those you have given me,

for they are yours. ¹⁰ All I have is yours, and all you have is mine. And glory has come to me through them. ¹¹ I will remain in the world no longer, but they are still in the world, and I am coming to you. Holy Father, protect them by the power of your name, the name you gave me, so that they may be one as we are one. ¹² While I was with them, I protected them and kept them safe by that name you gave me. None has been lost except the one doomed to destruction so that Scripture would be fulfilled.

¹³ 'I am coming to you now, but I say these things while I am still in the world, so that they may have the full measure of my joy within them. ¹⁴ I have given them your word and the world has hated them, for they are not of the world any more than I am of the world. ¹⁵ My prayer is not that you take them out of the world but that you protect them from the evil one. ¹⁶ They are not of the world, even as I am not of it. ¹⁷ Sanctify them by the truth; your word is truth. ¹⁸ As you sent me into the world, I have sent them into the world. ¹⁹ For them I sanctify myself, that they too may be truly sanctified.

²⁰ 'My prayer is not for them alone. I pray also for those who will believe in me through their message, ²¹ that all of them may be one, Father, just as you are in me and I am in you. May they also be in us so that the world may believe that you have sent me. ²² I have given them the glory that you gave me, that they may be one as we are one – ²³ I in them and you in me – so that they may be brought to complete unity. Then the world will know that you sent me and have loved them even as you have loved me.

²⁴ 'Father, I want those you have given me to be with me where I am, and to

see my glory, the glory you have given me because you loved me before the creation of the world.

²⁵'Righteous Father, though the world does not know you, I know you, and they know that you have sent me.

²⁶I have made you known to them, and will continue to make you known in order that the love you have for me may be in them and that I myself may be in them.'

Not Just a 'Father'

'Holy Father, protect them by the power of your name ...'
John 17:11

John Calvin said, 'That God's name should be hallowed is to say that God should have His own honour of which He is so worthy, so that men should never think or speak of Him without the greatest veneration'.

One of the things that saddens me about the contemporary Christian church is the way that some believers refer to the Almighty in terms that drag Him down to a 'good buddy' relationship. They refer to the great God of creation as 'The Man Upstairs' or 'My Partner in the Sky'. When people talk about God in such low-level terms, they do Him an injustice. And it's not so much the terms but the image of God that lies behind those terms which is the real problem.

We must, of course, strike a balanced note on this issue, for Paul himself teaches us that the Holy Spirit in our hearts prompts us to call God not merely 'Father,' but 'Daddy' (Rom. 8:15). Too much of the 'Daddy' however, can lead us, if we are not careful, into sloppy sentimentalism. I believe this is why, after the phrase 'Our Father,' Jesus introduces us to another aspect of God - hallowed, holy, reverenced be His Name. It is right that we think of God in familiar terms such as 'Daddy', but it is right also that we remember that our heavenly Father is a God of majestic holiness and unsullied purity. A. W. Tozer was right in his book *The Knowledge of the Holy* when he said, 'No religion has been greater than its idea of God'. Jesus put it into proper focus when He addressed God, not only as Father, but Holy Father.

PRAYER

My Father and my God, help me gain a healthy and balanced view of Your person, so that while I enjoy the familiarity of Your Fatherhood, I am exceedingly conscious also of Your holiness. In Jesus' name. Amen.

FURTHER STUDY

Heb. 12:1-14; Exod. 15:11;
1 Sam. 6:20; Isa. 6:3;
Rev. 15:4
• Where are we to look?
• How do we become holy?

June 16

■ 1 KINGS 8:1-66

8 Then King Solomon summoned into his presence at Jerusalem the elders of Israel, all the heads of the tribes and the chiefs of the Israelite families, to bring up the ark of the LORD's covenant from Zion, the City of David. ²All the Israelites came together to King Solomon at the time of the festival in the month of Ethanim, the seventh month.

³When all the elders of Israel had arrived, the priests took up the ark, ⁴and they brought up the ark of the LORD and the tent of meeting and all the sacred furnishings in it. The priests and Levites carried them up, ⁵and King Solomon and the entire assembly of Israel that had gathered about him were before the ark, sacrificing so many sheep and cattle that they could not be recorded or counted.

⁶The priests then brought the ark of the LORD's covenant to its place in the inner sanctuary of the temple, the Most Holy Place, and put it beneath the wings of the cherubim. ⁷The cherubim spread their wings over the place of the ark and overshadowed the ark and its carrying poles. ⁸These poles were so long that their ends could be seen from the Holy Place in front of the inner sanctuary, but not from outside the Holy Place; and they are still there today. ⁹There was nothing in the ark except the two stone tablets that Moses had placed in it at Horeb, where the LORD made a covenant with the Israelites after they came out of Egypt.

¹⁰When the priests withdrew from the Holy Place, the cloud filled the temple of the LORD. ¹¹And the priests could not perform their service because of the cloud, for the glory of the LORD filled his temple.

¹²Then Solomon said, 'The LORD has said that he would dwell in a dark cloud; ¹³I have indeed built a magnificent temple for you, a place for you to dwell for ever.'

¹⁴While the whole assembly of Israel was standing there, the king turned round and blessed them. ¹⁵Then he said:

'Praise be to the LORD, the God of Israel, who with his own hand has fulfilled what he promised with his own mouth to my father David. For he said, ¹⁶"Since the day I brought my people Israel out of Egypt, I have not chosen a city in any tribe of Israel to have a temple built so that my Name might be there, but I have chosen David to rule my people Israel."

¹⁷'My father David had it in his heart to build a temple for the Name of the LORD, the God of Israel. ¹⁸But the LORD said to my father David, "You did well to have it in your heart to build a temple for my Name. ¹⁹Nevertheless, you are not the one to build the temple, but your son, your own flesh and blood – he is the one who will build the temple for my Name."

²⁰'The LORD has kept the promise he made: I have succeeded David my father and now I sit on the throne of Israel, just as the LORD promised, and I have built the temple for the Name of the LORD, the God of Israel. ²¹I have provided a place there for the ark, in which is the covenant of the LORD that he made with our ancestors when he brought them out of Egypt.'

²²Then Solomon stood before the altar of the Lord in front of the whole assembly of

Israel, spread out his hands towards heaven ²³ and said:

'LORD, the God of Israel, there is no God like you in heaven above or on earth below – you who keep your covenant of love with your servants who continue wholeheartedly in your way. ²⁴ You have kept your promise to your servant David my father; with your mouth you have promised and with your hand you have fulfilled it – as it is today.

²⁵ 'Now LORD, the God of Israel, keep for your servant David my father the promises you made to him when you said, "You shall never fail to have a successor to sit before me on the throne of Israel, if only your descendants are careful in all they do to walk before me faithfully as you have done." ²⁶ And now, God of Israel, let your word that you promised your servant David my father come true.

²⁷ 'But will God really dwell on earth? The heavens, even the highest heaven, cannot contain you. How much less this temple I have built! ²⁸ Yet give attention to your servant's prayer and his plea for mercy, LORD my God. Hear the cry and the prayer that your servant is praying in your presence this day. ²⁹ May your eyes be open towards this temple night and day, this place of which you said, "My Name shall be there," so that you will hear the prayer your servant prays towards this place. ³⁰ Hear the supplication of your servant and of your people Israel when they pray towards this place. Hear from heaven, your dwelling place, and when you hear, forgive.

³¹ 'When anyone wrongs their neighbour and is required to take an oath and they come and swear the oath before your altar in this temple, ³² then

hear from heaven and act. Judge between your servants, condemning the guilty by bringing down on their heads what they have done, and vindicating the innocent by treating them in accordance with their innocence.

³³ 'When your people Israel have been defeated by an enemy because they have sinned against you, and when they turn back to you and give praise to your name, praying and making supplication to you in this temple, ³⁴ then hear from heaven and forgive the sin of your people Israel and bring them back to the land you gave to their ancestors.

³⁵ 'When the heavens are shut up and there is no rain because your people have sinned against you, and when they pray towards this place and give praise to your name and turn from their sin because you have afflicted them, ³⁶ then hear from heaven and forgive the sin of your servants, your people Israel. Teach them the right way to live, and send rain on the land you gave your people for an inheritance.

³⁷ 'When famine or plague comes to the land, or blight or mildew, locusts or grasshoppers, or when an enemy besieges them in any of their cities, whatever disaster or disease may come, ³⁸ and when a prayer or plea is made by anyone among your people Israel – being aware of the afflictions of their own hearts, and spreading out their hands towards this temple – ³⁹ then hear from heaven, your dwelling-place. Forgive and act; deal with everyone according to all they do, since you know their hearts (for you alone know every human heart), ⁴⁰ so that they will fear you all the time they live in the land you gave our ancestors.

⁴¹ 'As for the foreigner who does not belong to your people Israel but has

come from a distant land because of your name – ⁴²for they will hear of your great name and your mighty hand and your outstretched arm – when they come and pray towards this temple, ⁴³then hear from heaven, your dwelling-place. Do whatever the foreigner asks of you, so that all the peoples of the earth may know your name and fear you, as do your own people Israel, and may know that this house I have built bears your Name.

⁴⁴'When your people go to war against their enemies, wherever you send them, and when they pray to the LORD towards the city you have chosen and the temple I have built for your Name, ⁴⁵then hear from heaven their prayer and their plea, and uphold their cause.

⁴⁶'When they sin against you – for there is no one who does not sin – and you become angry with them and give them over to their enemies, who take them captive to their own lands, far away or near; ⁴⁷and if they have a change of heart in the land where they are held captive, and repent and plead with you in the land of their captors and say, "We have sinned, we have done wrong, we have acted wickedly"; ⁴⁸and if they turn back to you with all their heart and soul in the land of their enemies who took them captive, and pray to you towards the land you gave their ancestors, towards the city you have chosen and the temple I have built for your Name; ⁴⁹then from heaven, your dwelling-place, hear their prayer and their plea, and uphold their cause. ⁵⁰And forgive your people, who have sinned against you; forgive all the offences they have committed against you, and cause their captors to show them mercy; ⁵¹for they are your people and your inheritance, whom you

brought out of Egypt, out of that iron-smelting furnace.

⁵²'May your eyes be open to your servant's plea and to the plea of your people Israel, and may you listen to them whenever they cry out to you. ⁵³For you singled them out from all the nations of the world to be your own inheritance, just as you declared through your servant Moses when you, Sovereign LORD, brought our ancestors out of Egypt.'

⁵⁴When Solomon had finished all these prayers and supplications to the LORD, he rose from before the altar of the LORD, where he had been kneeling with his hands spread out towards heaven. ⁵⁵He stood and blessed the whole assembly of Israel in a loud voice, saying:

⁵⁶'Praise be to the LORD, who has given rest to his people Israel just as he promised. Not one word has failed of all the good promises he gave through his servant Moses. ⁵⁷May the LORD our God be with us as he was with our ancestors; may he never leave us nor forsake us. ⁵⁸May he turn our hearts to him, to walk in obedience to him and keep the commands, decrees and laws he gave our ancestors. ⁵⁹And may these words of mine, which I have prayed before the LORD, be near to the LORD our God day and night, that he may uphold the cause of his servant and the cause of his people Israel according to each day's need, ⁶⁰so that all the peoples of the earth may know that the LORD is God and that there is no other. ⁶¹And may your hearts be fully committed to the LORD our God, to live by his decrees and obey his commands, as at this time.'

⁶²Then the king and all Israel with him offered sacrifices before the Lord.

⁶³ Solomon offered a sacrifice of fellowship offerings to the Lord: twenty-two thousand cattle and a hundred and twenty thousand sheep and goats. So the king and all the Israelites dedicated the temple of the Lord.

⁶⁴ On that same day the king consecrated the middle part of the courtyard in front of the temple of the LORD, and there he offered burnt offerings, grain offerings and the fat of the fellowship offerings, because the bronze altar that stood before the LORD was too small to hold the burnt offerings, the grain offerings and the fat of the fellowship offerings.

⁶⁵ So Solomon observed the festival at that time, and all Israel with him – a vast assembly, people from Lebo Hamath to the Wadi of Egypt. They celebrated it before the LORD our God for seven days and seven days more, fourteen days in all. ⁶⁶ On the following day he sent the people away. They blessed the king and then went home, joyful and glad in heart for all the good things the LORD had done for his servant David and his people Israel.

▬ PSALM 73:1-6

¹ Surely God is good to Israel,
   to those who are pure in heart.

² But as for me, my feet had almost
      slipped;
   I had nearly lost my foothold.
³ For I envied the arrogant
   when I saw the prosperity of the
      wicked.

⁴ They have no struggles;
   their bodies are healthy and strong.
⁵ They are free from common human
      burdens;
   they are not plagued by human ills.
⁶ Therefore pride is their necklace;
   they clothe themselves with violence.

▬ PROVERBS 15:30-31

³⁰ Light in a messenger's eyes brings joy to
      the heart,
   and good news gives health to the
      bones.

³¹ Whoever heeds life-giving correction
   will be at home among the wise.

▬ JOHN 18:1-24

18 When he had finished praying, Jesus left with his disciples and crossed the Kidron Valley. On the other side there was a garden, and he and his disciples went into it.

² Now Judas, who betrayed him, knew the place, because Jesus had often met there with his disciples. ³ So Judas came to the garden, guiding a detachment of soldiers and some officials from the chief priests and the Pharisees. They were carrying torches, lanterns and weapons.

⁴ Jesus, knowing all that was going to happen to him, went out and asked them, 'Who is it you want?'

⁵ 'Jesus of Nazareth,' they replied.

'I am he,' Jesus said. (And Judas the traitor was standing there with them.) ⁶ When Jesus said, 'I am he,' they drew back and fell to the ground.

⁷ Again he asked them, 'Who is it you want?'

'Jesus of Nazareth,' they said.

⁸ Jesus answered, 'I told you that I am he. If you are looking for me, then let these men go.' ⁹ This happened so that the words he had spoken would be fulfilled: 'I have not lost one of those you gave me.'

¹⁰ Then Simon Peter, who had a sword, drew it and struck the high priest's servant, cutting off his right ear. (The servant's name was Malchus.)

¹¹ Jesus commanded Peter, 'Put your

sword away! Shall I not drink the cup the Father has given me?'

¹²Then the detachment of soldiers with its commander and the Jewish officials arrested Jesus. They bound him ¹³ and brought him first to Annas, who was the father-in-law of Caiaphas, the high priest that year. ¹⁴Caiaphas was the one who had advised the Jewish leaders that it would be good if one man died for the people.

¹⁵Simon Peter and another disciple were following Jesus. Because this disciple was known to the high priest, he went with Jesus into the high priest's courtyard, ¹⁶but Peter had to wait outside at the door. The other disciple, who was known to the high priest, came back, spoke to the servant-girl on duty there and brought Peter in.

¹⁷'You aren't one of this man's disciples too, are you?' she asked Peter.

He replied, 'I am not.'

¹⁸It was cold, and the servants and officials stood round a fire they had made to keep warm. Peter also was standing with them, warming himself.

¹⁹Meanwhile, the high priest questioned Jesus about his disciples and his teaching.

²⁰'I have spoken openly to the world,' Jesus replied. 'I always taught in synagogues or at the temple, where all the Jews come together. I said nothing in secret. ²¹Why question me? Ask those who heard me. Surely they know what I said.'

²²When Jesus said this, one of the officials near by slapped him in the face. 'Is this the way you answer the high priest?' he demanded.

²³'If I said something wrong,' Jesus replied, 'testify as to what is wrong. But if I spoke the truth, why did you strike me?' ²⁴Then Annas sent him bound to Caiaphas the high priest.

Paul's Breastplate

'Jesus answered, " I told you that I am he."' **John 18:8**

A feeling, which Satan can arouse in a heart that is unprotected by a spiritual breastplate, is that of a subtle form of discouragement, in which he draws our attention to what other Christians may be saying or thinking about us.

The Apostle Paul was a particular target of Satan in this respect, but see how he used the breastplate of righteousness as his spiritual defence. Paul's background was anti-Christian, and he could never get completely away from that. He had been the most hostile persecutor of the church, and he must therefore have constantly run across families whose loved ones he had put to death. Perhaps there were many who doubted his claim to be an apostle. Some commentators claim that in 1 Corinthians 15:10 he was replying to such an accusation.

How does Paul react to this criticism? Does he succumb to discouragement? Does he say, 'What's the use of working my fingers to the bone for these unappreciative people? They don't do anything but hurl recriminations in my face!' This is what the Devil would have liked him to do. But look at what he does. He says: 'But by the grace of God I am what I am' (1 Cor. 15:10). Can you see what he is doing? He is using the breastplate of righteousness. He is saying, in other words: 'I don't need to do anything to protect myself; what I am is what Christ has made me. I am not standing in my own righteousness, I am standing in His.'

What a lesson this is in how to use the spiritual breastplate. You and I need to learn this lesson, too.

PRAYER

O God, day by day I am catching little glimpses of what You are trying to teach me - that the more I depend on Your righteousness and the less I depend on my own, the better off I will be. Help me to learn it - and learn it completely. Amen.

FURTHER STUDY

Psa. 73:1-28; 2 Cor. 5:7-21
• What brought discouragement to the psalmist?
• How did Paul encourage the Corinthians?

June 17

1 KINGS 9:1–10:29

9 When Solomon had finished building the temple of the LORD and the royal palace, and had achieved all he had desired to do, ²the LORD appeared to him a second time, as he had appeared to him at Gibeon. ³The LORD said to him:

'I have heard the prayer and plea you have made before me; I have consecrated this temple, which you have built, by putting my Name there for ever. My eyes and my heart will always be there.

⁴'As for you, if you walk before me faithfully with integrity of heart and uprightness, as David your father did, and do all I command and observe my decrees and laws, ⁵I will establish your royal throne over Israel for ever, as I promised David your father when I said, "You shall never fail to have a successor on the throne of Israel."

⁶'But if you or your descendants turn away from me and do not observe the commands and decrees I have given

you and go off to serve other gods and worship them, ⁷then I will cut off Israel from the land I have given them and will reject this temple I have consecrated for my Name. Israel will then become a byword and an object of ridicule among all peoples. ⁸This temple will become a heap of rubble. All who pass by will be appalled and will scoff and say, "Why has the LORD done such a thing to this land and to this temple?" ⁹People will answer, "Because they have forsaken the LORD their God, who brought their ancestors out of Egypt, and have embraced other gods, worshipping and serving them – that is why the LORD brought all this disaster on them."'

¹⁰At the end of twenty years, during which Solomon built these two buildings – the temple of the Lord and the royal palace – ¹¹King Solomon gave twenty towns in Galilee to Hiram king of Tyre, because Hiram had supplied him with all the cedar and juniper and gold he wanted. ¹²But when Hiram went from Tyre to see the towns that Solomon had given him, he was not pleased

with them. ¹³'What kind of towns are these you have given me, my brother?' he asked. And he called them the Land of Kabul, a name they have to this day. ¹⁴Now Hiram had sent to the king 120 talents of gold.

¹⁵Here is the account of the forced labour King Solomon conscripted to build the LORD's temple, his own palace, the terraces, the wall of Jerusalem, and Hazor, Megiddo and Gezer. ¹⁶(Pharaoh king of Egypt had attacked and captured Gezer. He had set it on fire. He killed its Canaanite inhabitants and then gave it as a wedding gift to his daughter, Solomon's wife. ¹⁷And Solomon rebuilt Gezer.) He built up Lower Beth Horon, ¹⁸Baalath, and Tadmor in the desert, within his land, ¹⁹as well as all his store cities and the towns for his chariots and for his horses – whatever he desired to build in Jerusalem, in Lebanon and throughout all the territory he ruled.

²⁰There were still people left from the Amorites, Hittites, Perizzites, Hivites and Jebusites (these peoples were not Israelites). ²¹Solomon conscripted the descendants of all these peoples remaining in the land – whom the Israelites could not exterminate – to serve as slave labour, as it is to this day. ²²But Solomon did not make slaves of any of the Israelites; they were his fighting men, his government officials, his officers, his captains, and the commanders of his chariots and charioteers. ²³They were also the chief officials in charge of Solomon's projects – 550 officials supervising those who did the work.

²⁴After Pharaoh's daughter had come up from the City of David to the palace Solomon had built for her, he constructed the terraces.

²⁵Three times a year Solomon sacrificed burnt offerings and fellowship offerings on the altar he had built for the LORD, burning incense before the LORD along with them, and so fulfilled the temple obligations.

²⁶King Solomon also built ships at Ezion Geber, which is near Elath in Edom, on the shore of the Red Sea. ²⁷And Hiram sent his men – sailors who knew the sea – to serve in the fleet with Solomon's men. ²⁸They sailed to Ophir and brought back 420 talents of gold, which they delivered to King Solomon.

10 When the queen of Sheba heard about the fame of Solomon and his relationship to the LORD, she came to test Solomon with hard questions. ²Arriving at Jerusalem with a very great caravan – with camels carrying spices, large quantities of gold, and precious stones – she came to Solomon and talked with him about all that she had on her mind. ³Solomon answered all her questions; nothing was too hard for the king to explain to her. ⁴When the queen of Sheba saw all the wisdom of Solomon and the palace he had built, ⁵the food on his table, the seating of his officials, the attending servants in their robes, his cupbearers, and the burnt offerings he made at the temple of the LORD, she was overwhelmed.

⁶She said to the king, 'The report I heard in my own country about your achievements and your wisdom is true. ⁷But I did not believe these things until I came and saw with my own eyes. Indeed, not even half was told me; in wisdom and wealth you have far exceeded the report I heard. ⁸How happy your people must be! How happy your officials, who continually stand before you and hear your wisdom! ⁹Praise be to the LORD your God, who has delighted in you and placed you on the throne of Israel. Because of the LORD's eternal love for Israel, he has made you king to maintain justice and righteousness.'

¹⁰And she gave the king 120 talents of gold, large quantities of spices, and precious stones. Never again were so many spices brought in as those the queen of Sheba gave to King Solomon.

¹¹(Hiram's ships brought gold from Ophir; and from there they brought great cargoes of almug-wood and precious stones. ¹²The king used the almug-wood to make supports for the temple of the LORD

and for the royal palace, and to make harps and lyres for the musicians. So much almug-wood has never been imported or seen since that day.)

¹³ King Solomon gave the queen of Sheba all she desired and asked for, besides what he had given her out of his royal bounty. Then she left and returned with her retinue to her own country.

¹⁴ The weight of the gold that Solomon received yearly was 666 talents, ¹⁵ not including the revenues from merchants and traders and from all the Arabian kings and the governors of the territories.

¹⁶ King Solomon made two hundred large shields of hammered gold; six hundred shekels of gold went into each shield. ¹⁷ He also made three hundred small shields of hammered gold, with three minas of gold in each shield. The king put them in the Palace of the Forest of Lebanon.

¹⁸ Then the king made a great throne covered with ivory and overlaid with fine gold. ¹⁹ The throne had six steps, and its back had a rounded top. On both sides of the seat were armrests, with a lion standing beside each of them. ²⁰ Twelve lions stood on the six steps, one at either end of each step. Nothing like it had ever been made for any other kingdom. ²¹ All King Solomon's goblets were gold, and all the household articles in the Palace of the Forest of Lebanon were pure gold. Nothing was made of silver, because silver was considered of little value in Solomon's days. ²² The king had a fleet of trading ships at sea along with the ships of Hiram. Once every three years it returned carrying gold, silver and ivory, and apes and baboons.

²³ King Solomon was greater in riches and wisdom than all the other kings of the earth. ²⁴ The whole world sought audience with Solomon to hear the wisdom God had put in his heart. ²⁵ Year after year, everyone who came brought a gift – articles of silver and gold, robes, weapons and spices, and horses and mules.

²⁶ Solomon accumulated chariots and horses; he had fourteen hundred chariots and twelve thousand horses, which he kept in the chariot cities and also with him in Jerusalem. ²⁷ The king made silver as common in Jerusalem as stones, and cedar as plentiful as sycamore-fig trees in the foothills. ²⁸ Solomon's horses were imported from Egypt and from Kue – the royal merchants purchased them from Kue at the current price. ²⁹ They imported a chariot from Egypt for six hundred shekels of silver, and a horse for a hundred and fifty. They also exported them to all the kings of the Hittites and of the Arameans.

■ PSALM 73:7–12

⁷ From their callous hearts comes iniquity;
 their evil imaginations have no limits.
⁸ They scoff, and speak with malice;
 with arrogance they threaten
  oppression.
⁹ Their mouths lay claim to heaven,
 and their tongues take possession of
  the earth.
¹⁰ Therefore their people turn to them
 and drink up waters in abundance.
¹¹ They say, 'How would God know?
 Does the Most High know anything?'

¹² This is what the wicked are like –
 always free of care, they go on
  amassing wealth.

■ PROVERBS 15:32–33

³² Those who disregard discipline despise
  themselves,
 but the one who heeds correction
  gains understanding.

³³ Wisdom's instruction is to fear the LORD,
 and humility comes before honour.

■ JOHN 18:25–19:4

²⁵Meanwhile, Simon Peter was still standing there warming himself. So they asked him, 'You aren't one of his disciples too, are you?'

He denied it, saying, 'I am not.'

²⁶One of the high priest's servants, a relative of the man whose ear Peter had cut off, challenged him, 'Didn't I see you with him in the garden?' ²⁷Again Peter denied it, and at that moment a cock began to crow.

²⁸Then the Jewish leaders took Jesus from Caiaphas to the palace of the Roman governor. By now it was early morning, and to avoid ceremonial uncleanness they did not enter the palace, because they wanted to be able to eat the Passover. ²⁹So Pilate came out to them and asked, 'What charges are you bringing against this man?'

³⁰'If he were not a criminal,' they replied, 'we would not have handed him over to you.'

³¹Pilate said, 'Take him yourselves and judge him by your own law.'

'But we have no right to execute anyone,' they objected. ³²This took place to fulfil what Jesus had said about the kind of death he was going to die.

³³Pilate then went back inside the palace, summoned Jesus and asked him, 'Are you the king of the Jews?'

³⁴'Is that your own idea,' Jesus asked, 'or did others talk to you about me?'

³⁵'Am I a Jew?' Pilate replied. 'Your own people and chief priests handed you over to me. What is it you have done?'

³⁶Jesus said, 'My kingdom is not of this world. If it were, my servants would fight to prevent my arrest by the Jewish leaders. But now my kingdom is from another place.'

³⁷'You are a king, then!' said Pilate.

Jesus answered, 'You say that I am a king. In fact, the reason I was born and came into the world is to testify to the truth. Everyone on the side of truth listens to me.'

³⁸'What is truth?' retorted Pilate. With this he went out again to the Jews gathered there and said, 'I find no basis for a charge against him. ³⁹But it is your custom for me to release to you one prisoner at the time of the Passover. Do you want me to release "the king of the Jews"?'

⁴⁰They shouted back, 'No, not him! Give us Barabbas!' Now Barabbas had taken part in an uprising.

19 Then Pilate took Jesus and had him flogged. ²The soldiers twisted together a crown of thorns and put it on his head. They clothed him in a purple robe ³and went up to him again and again, saying, 'Hail, king of the Jews!' And they slapped him in the face.

⁴Once more Pilate came out and said to the Jews gathered there, 'Look, I am bringing him out to you to let you know that I find no basis for a charge against him.'

Our God Reigns

'Jesus said, "My kingdom is not of this world ..."'
John 18:36

The kingdom of God was the motif running through everything Jesus taught. However, I pick up many Christian books and magazines today and find that, with one or two exceptions, the kingdom of God is not mentioned. Yet Jesus made it the central note of His preaching and also His praying.

It is time now to ask ourselves, 'What exactly does Jesus mean when He uses the word "kingdom"? The word for kingdom (*basileia* in the Greek) means 'rule' or 'reign.' The kingdom of God, then, is the rule or reign of God, His sovereignty, for which we are to pray. Jesus spoke of the kingdom as being in the present as well as in the future. In Luke 17:21 He said, 'The kingdom of God is in your midst'. Wherever there is a heart that is surrendered to the claims and demands of Jesus Christ, there the kingdom exists. But there is a day coming, says Jesus in Matthew 8:11, when both small and great will sit side by side in the kingdom and realise that in God's order of things there are no favourites.

The Scripture tells us also that God has a kingdom that is established in the heavens (Heb. 12:22-28), and the phrase from the Lord's Prayer 'Your kingdom come' is a petition for God to let that kingdom extend to every area of the universe where His rule is resisted. We are thus introduced to another great purpose of prayer - transporting to all parts of the universe, across the bridge of prayer, the power that overcomes all sin, all rebellion, and all evil.

PRAYER

Father, what can I say? When I see that You have given me the privilege of helping You usher in Your kingdom through prayer, my heart is overwhelmed. What confidence You place in Your redeemed children. May we be worthy of it. For Jesus' sake. Amen.

FURTHER STUDY

Psa. 93; 47:8; Exod. 15:18; Micah 4:7; Rom. 5:17
• What does the psalmist conclude?
• What is Paul's expectation?

June 18

▬ 1 KINGS 11:1–12:11

11 King Solomon, however, loved many foreign women besides Pharaoh's daughter – Moabites, Ammonites, Edomites, Sidonians and Hittites. ²They were from nations about which the LORD had told the Israelites, 'You must not intermarry with them, because they will surely turn your hearts after their gods.' Nevertheless, Solomon held fast to them in love. ³He had seven hundred wives of royal birth and three hundred concubines, and his wives

led him astray. ⁴As Solomon grew old, his wives turned his heart after other gods, and his heart was not fully devoted to the LORD his God, as the heart of David his father had been. ⁵He followed Ashtoreth the goddess of the Sidonians, and Molek the detestable god of the Ammonites. ⁶So Solomon did evil in the eyes of the LORD; he did not follow the LORD completely, as David his father had done.

⁷On a hill east of Jerusalem, Solomon built a high place for Chemosh the detestable god of Moab, and for Molek the detestable god

of the Ammonites. ⁸He did the same for all his foreign wives, who burned incense and offered sacrifices to their gods.

⁹The LORD became angry with Solomon because his heart had turned away from the LORD, the God of Israel, who had appeared to him twice. ¹⁰Although he had forbidden Solomon to follow other gods, Solomon did not keep the LORD's command. ¹¹So the LORD said to Solomon, 'Since this is your attitude and you have not kept my covenant and my decrees, which I commanded you, I will most certainly tear the kingdom away from you and give it to one of your subordinates. ¹²Nevertheless, for the sake of David your father, I will not do it during your lifetime. I will tear it out of the hand of your son. ¹³Yet I will not tear the whole kingdom from him, but will give him one tribe for the sake of David my servant and for the sake of Jerusalem, which I have chosen.'

¹⁴Then the LORD raised up against Solomon an adversary, Hadad the Edomite, from the royal line of Edom. ¹⁵Earlier when David was fighting with Edom, Joab the commander of the army, who had gone up to bury the dead, had struck down all the men in Edom. ¹⁶Joab and all the Israelites stayed there for six months, until they had destroyed all the men in Edom. ¹⁷But Hadad, still only a boy, fled to Egypt with some Edomite officials who had served his father. ¹⁸They set out from Midian and went to Paran. Then taking people from Paran with them, they went to Egypt, to Pharaoh king of Egypt, who gave Hadad a house and land and provided him with food.

¹⁹Pharaoh was so pleased with Hadad that he gave him a sister of his own wife, Queen Tahpenes, in marriage. ²⁰The sister of Tahpenes bore him a son named Genubath, whom Tahpenes brought up in the royal palace. There Genubath lived with Pharaoh's own children.

²¹While he was in Egypt, Hadad heard that David rested with his ancestors and that Joab the commander of the army was also dead. Then Hadad said to Pharaoh, 'Let me go, so that I may return to my own country.'

²²'What have you lacked here that you want to go back to your own country?' Pharaoh asked.

'Nothing,' Hadad replied, 'but do let me go!'

²³And God raised up against Solomon another adversary, Rezon son of Eliada, who had fled from his master, Hadadezer king of Zobah. ²⁴When David destroyed Zobah's army, Rezon gathered a band of men around him and became their leader; they went to Damascus, where they settled and took control. ²⁵Rezon was Israel's adversary as long as Solomon lived, adding to the trouble caused by Hadad. So Rezon ruled in Aram and was hostile towards Israel.

²⁶Also, Jeroboam son of Nebat rebelled against the king. He was one of Solomon's officials, an Ephraimite from Zeredah, and his mother was a widow named Zeruah.

²⁷Here is the account of how he rebelled against the king: Solomon had built the terraces and had filled in the gap in the wall of the city of David his father. ²⁸Now Jeroboam was a man of standing, and when Solomon saw how well the young man did his work, he put him in charge of the whole labour force of the tribes of Joseph.

²⁹About that time Jeroboam was going out of Jerusalem, and Ahijah the prophet of Shiloh met him on the way, wearing a new cloak. The two of them were alone out in the country, ³⁰and Ahijah took hold of the new cloak he was wearing and tore it into twelve pieces. ³¹Then he said to Jeroboam, 'Take ten pieces for yourself, for this is what the LORD, the God of Israel, says: "See, I am going to tear the kingdom out of Solomon's hand and give you ten tribes. ³²But for the sake of my servant David and the city of Jerusalem, which I have chosen out of all the tribes of Israel, he will have one tribe.

³³ I will do this because they have forsaken me and worshipped Ashtoreth the goddess of the Sidonians, Chemosh the god of the Moabites, and Molek the god of the Ammonites, and have not walked in obedience to me, nor done what is right in my eyes, nor kept my decrees and laws as David, Solomon's father, did.

³⁴ ' "But I will not take the whole kingdom out of Solomon's hand; I have made him ruler all the days of his life for the sake of David my servant, whom I chose and who obeyed my commands and decrees. ³⁵ I will take the kingdom from his son's hands and give you ten tribes. ³⁶ I will give one tribe to his son so that David my servant may always have a lamp before me in Jerusalem, the city where I chose to put my Name. ³⁷ However, as for you, I will take you, and you will rule over all that your heart desires; you will be king over Israel. ³⁸ If you do whatever I command you and walk in obedience to me and do what is right in my eyes by obeying my decrees and commands, as David my servant did, I will be with you. I will build you a dynasty as enduring as the one I built for David and will give Israel to you. ³⁹ I will humble David's descendants because of this, but not for ever." '

⁴⁰ Solomon tried to kill Jeroboam, but Jeroboam fled to Egypt, to Shishak the king, and stayed there until Solomon's death.

⁴¹ As for the other events of Solomon's reign – all he did and the wisdom he displayed – are they not written in the book of the annals of Solomon? ⁴² Solomon reigned in Jerusalem over all Israel for forty years. ⁴³ Then he rested with his ancestors and was buried in the city of David his father. And Rehoboam his son succeeded him as king.

12 Rehoboam went to Shechem, for all Israel had gone there to make him king. ² When Jeroboam son of Nebat heard this (he was still in Egypt, where he had fled from King Solomon), he returned from Egypt. ³ So they sent for Jeroboam, and he and the whole assembly of Israel went to Rehoboam and said to him: ⁴ 'Your father put a heavy yoke on us, but now lighten the harsh labour and the heavy yoke he put on us, and we will serve you.'

⁵ Rehoboam answered, 'Go away for three days and then come back to me.' So the people went away.

⁶ Then King Rehoboam consulted the elders who had served his father Solomon during his lifetime. 'How would you advise me to answer these people?' he asked.

⁷ They replied, 'If today you will be a servant to these people and serve them and give them a favourable answer, they will always be your servants.'

⁸ But Rehoboam rejected the advice the elders gave him and consulted the young men who had grown up with him and were serving him. ⁹ He asked them, 'What is your advice? How should we answer these people who say to me, "Lighten the yoke your father put on us"?'

¹⁰ The young men who had grown up with him replied, 'These people have said to you, "Your father put a heavy yoke on us, but make our yoke lighter." Now tell them, "My little finger is thicker than my father's waist. ¹¹ My father laid on you a heavy yoke; I will make it even heavier. My father scourged you with whips; I will scourge you with scorpions." '

···

■ **PSALM 73:13-20**

¹³ Surely in vain I have kept my heart pure
    and have washed my hands in
        innocence.
¹⁴ All day long I have been afflicted,
    and every morning brings new
        punishments.

¹⁵ If I had spoken out like that,
    I would have betrayed your children.
¹⁶ When I tried to understand all this,
    it troubled me deeply

[17] till I entered the sanctuary of God;
　　then I understood their final destiny.

[18] Surely you place them on slippery
　　　ground;
　　you cast them down to ruin.
[19] How suddenly are they destroyed,
　　completely swept away by terrors!
[20] They are like a dream when one awakes;
　　when you arise, Lord,
　　you will despise them as fantasies.

▬ PROVERBS 16:1-2

16 To humans belong the plans of the
　　heart,
　　but from the LORD comes the proper
　　　answer of the tongue.

[2] All a person's ways seem pure to them,
　　but motives are weighed by the LORD.

▬ JOHN 19:5-24

[5] When Jesus came out wearing the crown
of thorns and the purple robe, Pilate said to
them, 'Here is the man!'
　　[6] As soon as the chief priests and their
officials saw him, they shouted, 'Crucify!
Crucify!'
　　But Pilate answered, 'You take him and
crucify him. As for me, I find no basis for a
charge against him.'
　　[7] The Jewish leaders insisted, 'We have a
law, and according to that law he must die,
because he claimed to be the Son of God.'
　　[8] When Pilate heard this, he was even
more afraid, [9] and he went back inside
the palace. 'Where do you come from?' he
asked Jesus, but Jesus gave him no answer.
[10] 'Do you refuse to speak to me?' Pilate said.
'Don't you realise I have power either to free
you or to crucify you?'
　　[11] Jesus answered, 'You would have no

power over me if it were not given to you
from above. Therefore the one who handed
me over to you is guilty of a greater sin.'
　　[12] From then on, Pilate tried to set Jesus
free, but the Jewish leaders kept shouting,
'If you let this man go, you are no friend
of Caesar. Anyone who claims to be a king
opposes Caesar.'
　　[13] When Pilate heard this, he brought
Jesus out and sat down on the judge's seat
at a place known as the Stone Pavement
(which in Aramaic is Gabbatha). [14] It was
the day of Preparation of the Passover; it
was about noon.
　　'Here is your king,' Pilate said to the Jews.
　　[15] But they shouted, 'Take him away! Take
him away! Crucify him!'
　　'Shall I crucify your king?' Pilate asked.
　　'We have no king but Caesar,' the chief
priests answered.
　　[16] Finally Pilate handed him over to them
to be crucified.
　　So the soldiers took charge of Jesus.
[17] Carrying his own cross, he went out to
the place of the Skull (which in Aramaic
is called Golgotha). [18] There they crucified
him, and with him two others – one on each
side and Jesus in the middle.
　　[19] Pilate had a notice prepared and fastened to the cross. It read: JESUS OF NAZA-
RETH, THE KING OF THE JEWS. [20] Many of the
Jews read this sign, for the place where Jesus
was crucified was near the city, and the sign
was written in Aramaic, Latin and Greek.
[21] The chief priests of the Jews protested to
Pilate, 'Do not write "The King of the Jews",
but that this man claimed to be king of
the Jews.'
　　[22] Pilate answered, 'What I have written,
I have written.'
　　[23] When the soldiers crucified Jesus, they
took his clothes, dividing them into four
shares, one for each of them, with the un-
dergarment remaining. This garment was
seamless, woven in one piece from top to
bottom.

²⁴'Let's not tear it,' they said to one another. 'Let's decide by lot who will get it.'

This happened that the scripture might be fulfilled that said,

'They divided my clothes among them
and cast lots for my garment.'

So this is what the soldiers did.

Love Creating Love

'Carrying his own cross, he went out to the place of the skull ... There they crucified him ...' **John 19:17-18**

Although the love of God is clearly laid out in the Old Testament, why did humankind have to wait so long to have the message spelled out in such clear terms as John uses: 'God is love' (1 John 4:8)? People could not see this sufficiently clearly until they had looked into the face of Jesus. In the life of Jesus is the clearest revelation that God is love.

So few of us open ourselves to the love of God. We have more fear of Him than we have love for Him. There is, of course, a godly fear (or reverence), but that is not what I mean. If we fail to comprehend how much we are loved by God, then there will be no energy to turn the machinery of our lives in the way they were meant to turn.

Whenever I doubted the love of God as a young Christian, I was told I should go to Calvary. I never quite understood what that meant until one day I complained to God that He could not really love me; if He did, He wouldn't let such things happen as were befalling me. He gave me no answer but showed me the Cross. And as I saw His Son dying there for me, the scales fell from my eyes and I found love for Him flowing out of His love for me. I discovered what 1 John 4:19 means: 'We love because he first loved us'.

Love for God is not the fruit of labour but the response of our hearts to being loved. It is not something we manufacture; it is something we receive.

PRAYER

O God my Father, save me from believing that my problem is 'I don't love You enough,' when the real problem is 'I don't know how much I am loved by You'. Let the scales fall from my eyes right now and let me see – really see. In Jesus' name. Amen.

FURTHER STUDY

John 19:16-30; Eph. 2:15-16; Col. 1:19-22

• What is the result of the Cross?
• Spend some moments in prayer contemplating the Cross.

June 19

■ **1 KINGS 12:12–13:34**

¹²Three days later Jeroboam and all the people returned to Rehoboam, as the king had said, 'Come back to me in three days.' ¹³The king answered the people harshly. Rejecting the advice given him by the elders, ¹⁴he followed the advice of the young men and said, 'My father made your yoke heavy; I will make it even heavier. My father scourged you with whips; I will scourge you with scorpions.' ¹⁵So the king did not listen to the people, for this turn of events was from the LORD, to fulfil the word the LORD had spoken to Jeroboam son of Nebat through Ahijah the Shilonite.

¹⁶When all Israel saw that the king refused to listen to them, they answered the king:

'What share do we have in David,
    what part in Jesse's son?
To your tents, Israel!
Look after your own house, David!'

So the Israelites went home. ¹⁷But as for the Israelites who were living in the towns of Judah, Rehoboam still ruled over them.

¹⁸King Rehoboam sent out Adoniram, who was in charge of forced labour, but all Israel stoned him to death. King Rehoboam, however, managed to get into his chariot and escape to Jerusalem. ¹⁹So Israel has been in rebellion against the house of David to this day.

²⁰When all the Israelites heard that Jeroboam had returned, they sent and called him to the assembly and made him king over all Israel. Only the tribe of Judah remained loyal to the house of David.

²¹When Rehoboam arrived in Jerusalem, he mustered all Judah and the tribe of Benjamin – a hundred and eighty thousand able young men – to go to war against Israel and to regain the kingdom for Rehoboam son of Solomon.

²²But this word of God came to Shemaiah the man of God: ²³'Say to Rehoboam son of Solomon king of Judah, to all Judah and Benjamin, and to the rest of the people, ²⁴"This is what the LORD says: do not go up to fight against your brothers, the Israelites. Go home, every one of you, for this is my doing."' So they obeyed the word of the LORD and went home again, as the LORD had ordered.

²⁵Then Jeroboam fortified Shechem in the hill country of Ephraim and lived there. From there he went out and built up Peniel.

²⁶Jeroboam thought to himself, 'The kingdom is now likely to revert to the house of David. ²⁷If these people go up to offer sacrifices at the temple of the LORD in Jerusalem, they will again give their allegiance to their lord, Rehoboam king of Judah. They will kill me and return to King Rehoboam.'

²⁸After seeking advice, the king made two golden calves. He said to the people, 'It is too much for you to go up to Jerusalem. Here are your gods, Israel, who brought you up out of Egypt.' ²⁹One he set up in Bethel, and the other in Dan. ³⁰And this thing became a sin; the people came to worship the one at Bethel and went as far as Dan to worship the other.

³¹Jeroboam built shrines on high places and appointed priests from all sorts of people, even though they were not Levites. ³²He instituted a festival on the fifteenth day of the eighth month, like the festival held in Judah, and offered sacrifices on the altar. This he did in Bethel, sacrificing to the

calves he had made. And at Bethel he also installed priests at the high places he had made. ³³ On the fifteenth day of the eighth month, a month of his own choosing, he offered sacrifices on the altar he had built at Bethel. So he instituted the festival for the Israelites and went up to the altar to make offerings.

13 By the word of the LORD a man of God came from Judah to Bethel, as Jeroboam was standing by the altar to make an offering. ² By the word of the LORD he cried out against the altar: 'Altar, altar! This is what the LORD says: "A son named Josiah will be born to the house of David. On you he will sacrifice the priests of the high places who make offerings here, and human bones will be burned on you."' ³ That same day the man of God gave a sign: 'This is the sign the LORD has declared: the altar will be split apart and the ashes on it will be poured out.'

⁴ When King Jeroboam heard what the man of God cried out against the altar at Bethel, he stretched out his hand from the altar and said, 'Seize him!' But the hand he stretched out towards the man shrivelled up, so that he could not pull it back. ⁵ Also, the altar was split apart and its ashes poured out according to the sign given by the man of God by the word of the LORD.

⁶ Then the king said to the man of God, 'Intercede with the LORD your God and pray for me that my hand may be restored.' So the man of God interceded with the LORD, and the king's hand was restored and became as it was before.

⁷ The king said to the man of God, 'Come home with me for a meal, and I will give you a gift.'

⁸ But the man of God answered the king, 'Even if you were to give me half your possessions, I would not go with you, nor would I eat bread or drink water here. ⁹ For I was commanded by the word of the LORD: "You must not eat bread or drink water or return

by the way you came."' ¹⁰ So he took another road and did not return by the way he had come to Bethel.

¹¹ Now there was a certain old prophet living in Bethel, whose sons came and told him all that the man of God had done there that day. They also told their father what he had said to the king. ¹² Their father asked them, 'Which way did he go?' And his sons showed him which road the man of God from Judah had taken. ¹³ So he said to his sons, 'Saddle the donkey for me.' And when they had saddled the donkey for him, he mounted it ¹⁴ and rode after the man of God. He found him sitting under an oak tree and asked, 'Are you the man of God who came from Judah?'

'I am,' he replied.

¹⁵ So the prophet said to him, 'Come home with me and eat.'

¹⁶ The man of God said, 'I cannot turn back and go with you, nor can I eat bread or drink water with you in this place. ¹⁷ I have been told by the word of the LORD: "You must not eat bread or drink water there or return by the way you came."'

¹⁸ The old prophet answered, 'I too am a prophet, as you are. And an angel said to me by the word of the LORD: "Bring him back with you to your house so that he may eat bread and drink water."' (But he was lying to him.) ¹⁹ So the man of God returned with him and ate and drank in his house.

²⁰ While they were sitting at the table, the word of the LORD came to the old prophet who had brought him back. ²¹ He cried out to the man of God who had come from Judah, 'This is what the LORD says: "You have defied the word of the LORD and have not kept the command the LORD your God gave you. ²² You came back and ate bread and drank water in the place where he told you not to eat or drink. Therefore your body will not be buried in the tomb of your ancestors."'

²³ When the man of God had finished eating and drinking, the prophet who had

brought him back saddled his donkey for him. ²⁴As he went on his way, a lion met him on the road and killed him, and his body was left lying on the road, with both the donkey and the lion standing beside it. ²⁵Some people who passed by saw the body lying there, with the lion standing beside the body, and they went and reported it in the city where the old prophet lived.

²⁶When the prophet who had brought him back from his journey heard of it, he said, 'It is the man of God who defied the word of the LORD. The LORD has given him over to the lion, which has mauled him and killed him, as the word of the LORD had warned him.'

²⁷The prophet said to his sons, 'Saddle the donkey for me,' and they did so. ²⁸Then he went out and found the body lying on the road, with the donkey and the lion standing beside it. The lion had neither eaten the body nor mauled the donkey. ²⁹So the prophet picked up the body of the man of God, laid it on the donkey, and brought it back to his own city to mourn for him and bury him. ³⁰Then he laid the body in his own tomb, and they mourned over him and said, 'Alas, my brother!'

³¹After burying him, he said to his sons, 'When I die, bury me in the grave where the man of God is buried; lay my bones beside his bones. ³²For the message he declared by the word of the LORD against the altar in Bethel and against all the shrines on the high places in the towns of Samaria will certainly come true.'

³³Even after this, Jeroboam did not change his evil ways, but once more appointed priests for the high places from all sorts of people. Anyone who wanted to become a priest he consecrated for the high places. ³⁴This was the sin of the house of Jeroboam that led to its downfall and to its destruction from the face of the earth.

■ PSALM 73:21-28

²¹When my heart was grieved
  and my spirit embittered,
²²I was senseless and ignorant;
  I was a brute beast before you.

²³Yet I am always with you;
  you hold me by my right hand.
²⁴You guide me with your counsel,
  and afterwards you will take me into
    glory.
²⁵Whom have I in heaven but you?
  And earth has nothing I desire besides
    you.
²⁶My flesh and my heart may fail,
  but God is the strength of my heart
  and my portion for ever.

²⁷Those who are far from you will perish;
  you destroy all who are unfaithful to
    you.
²⁸But as for me, it is good to be near God.
  I have made the Sovereign LORD my
    refuge;
  I will tell of all your deeds.

■ PROVERBS 16:3-4

³Commit to the LORD whatever you do,
  and he will establish your plans.

⁴The LORD works out everything to its
    proper end –
  even the wicked for a day of disaster.

■ JOHN 19:25-42

²⁵Near the cross of Jesus stood his mother, his mother's sister, Mary the wife of Clopas, and Mary Magdalene. ²⁶When Jesus saw his mother there, and the disciple whom he loved standing near by, he said to her, 'Woman, here is your son,' ²⁷and to

the disciple, 'Here is your mother.' From that time on, this disciple took her into his home.

²⁸ Later, knowing that everything had now been finished, and so that Scripture would be fulfilled, Jesus said, 'I am thirsty.' ²⁹ A jar of wine vinegar was there, so they soaked a sponge in it, put the sponge on a stalk of the hyssop plant, and lifted it to Jesus' lips. ³⁰ When he had received the drink, Jesus said, 'It is finished.' With that, he bowed his head and gave up his spirit.

³¹ Now it was the day of Preparation, and the next day was to be a special Sabbath. Because the Jewish leaders did not want the bodies left on the crosses during the Sabbath, they asked Pilate to have the legs broken and the bodies taken down. ³² The soldiers therefore came and broke the legs of the first man who had been crucified with Jesus, and then those of the other. ³³ But when they came to Jesus and found that he was already dead, they did not break his legs. ³⁴ Instead, one of the soldiers pierced Jesus' side with a spear, bringing a sudden flow of blood and water. ³⁵ The man who saw

it has given testimony, and his testimony is true. He knows that he tells the truth, and he testifies so that you also may believe. ³⁶ These things happened so that the scripture would be fulfilled: 'Not one of his bones will be broken,' ³⁷ and, as another scripture says, 'They will look on the one they have pierced.'

³⁸ Later, Joseph of Arimathea asked Pilate for the body of Jesus. Now Joseph was a disciple of Jesus, but secretly because he feared the Jewish leaders. With Pilate's permission, he came and took the body away. ³⁹ He was accompanied by Nicodemus, the man who earlier had visited Jesus at night. Nicodemus brought a mixture of myrrh and aloes, about thirty-five kilograms. ⁴⁰ Taking Jesus' body, the two of them wrapped it, with the spices, in strips of linen. This was in accordance with Jewish burial customs. ⁴¹ At the place where Jesus was crucified, there was a garden, and in the garden a new tomb, in which no one had ever been laid. ⁴² Because it was the Jewish day of Preparation and since the tomb was near by, they laid Jesus there.

Is There an Answer?

'Yet I am always with you; you hold me by my right hand. You guide me with your counsel ...' **Psalm 73:23-24**

A devoted Christian man I knew married a widow who had a teenage son. The son was deeply rebellious, and the man, now his stepfather, grew very resentful towards him. One night, while the mother was away, they shared the same bedroom, and the man woke up in the middle of the night, finding himself trying to push the young man out of the bedroom window. Another push, and he would have fallen and been seriously injured. What had happened? The man told me that he had gone to sleep that night with a great bitterness in his heart towards his stepson. The subconscious mind is very receptive at the moment one drops into sleep, and the resentment his subconscious mind received precipitated an act which would have horrified him when conscious.

A little girl said, 'I want to be good, but I don't want to be obedient'. Her conscious mind wanted her to be known as good, but her subconscious mind, where self-centredness was the driving urge, did not want to obey anything except itself. The minister who preaches full surrender to God yet yearns to be praised and complimented is suffering from a division between the conscious and the subconscious mind. The person who works hard at helping others but does it to meet some inner need rather than truly giving himself to the needs of others is inwardly divided. The question is, can the subconscious be reached by the Holy Spirit? With all my heart, I say it can. In the Holy Spirit, we are provided with a divine presence that redeems and unifies the whole personality.

PRAYER

Father, I am tired of inward division that threatens to tear me apart. Tame these wild horses within me that I might know Your perfect peace in every part of my being. For Jesus' sake. Amen.

FURTHER STUDY

James 1; Rom. 7:22-23, 8:6; Isa. 26:3; Phil. 4:8
• What makes a man unstable?
• What brings stability and peace?

June 20

▬ 1 KINGS 14:1–15:34

14 At that time Abijah son of Jeroboam became ill, ²and Jeroboam said to his wife, 'Go, disguise yourself, so that you won't be recognised as the wife of Jeroboam. Then go to Shiloh. Ahijah the prophet is there – the one who told me I would be king over this people. ³Take ten loaves of bread with you, some cakes and a jar of honey, and go to him. He will tell you what will happen to the boy.' ⁴So Jeroboam's wife did what he said and went to Ahijah's house in Shiloh.

Now Ahijah could not see; his sight was gone because of his age. ⁵But the LORD had told Ahijah, 'Jeroboam's wife is coming to ask you about her son, for he is ill, and you are to give her such and such an answer. When she arrives, she will pretend to be someone else.'

⁶So when Ahijah heard the sound of her footsteps at the door, he said, 'Come in, wife of Jeroboam. Why this pretence?

I have been sent to you with bad news. ⁷Go, tell Jeroboam that this is what the LORD, the God of Israel, says: "I raised you up from among the people and appointed you ruler over my people Israel. ⁸I tore the kingdom away from the house of David and gave it to you, but you have not been like my servant David, who kept my commands and followed me with all his heart, doing only what was right in my eyes. ⁹You have done more evil than all who lived before you. You have made for yourself other gods, idols made of metal; you have aroused my anger and turned your back on me.

¹⁰ "Because of this, I am going to bring disaster on the house of Jeroboam. I will cut off from Jeroboam every last male in Israel – slave or free. I will burn up the house of Jeroboam as one burns dung, until it is all gone. ¹¹Dogs will eat those belonging to Jeroboam who die in the city, and the birds will feed on those who die in the country. The LORD has spoken!"

¹² 'As for you, go back home. When you set foot in your city, the boy will die. ¹³ All Israel will mourn for him and bury him. He is the only one belonging to Jeroboam who will be buried, because he is the only one in the house of Jeroboam in whom the LORD, the God of Israel, has found anything good.

¹⁴ 'The LORD will raise up for himself a king over Israel who will cut off the family of Jeroboam. Even now this is beginning to happen. ¹⁵ And the LORD will strike Israel, so that it will be like a reed swaying in the water. He will uproot Israel from this good land that he gave to their ancestors and scatter them beyond the River Euphrates, because they aroused the LORD's anger by making Asherah poles. ¹⁶ And he will give Israel up because of the sins Jeroboam has committed and has caused Israel to commit.'

¹⁷ Then Jeroboam's wife got up and left and went to Tirzah. As soon as she stepped over the threshold of the house, the boy died. ¹⁸ They buried him, and all Israel mourned for him, as the LORD had said through his servant the prophet Ahijah.

¹⁹ The other events of Jeroboam's reign, his wars and how he ruled, are written in the book of the annals of the kings of Israel. ²⁰ He reigned for twenty-two years and then rested with his ancestors. And Nadab his son succeeded him as king.

²¹ Rehoboam son of Solomon was king in Judah. He was forty-one years old when he became king, and he reigned for seventeen years in Jerusalem, the city the LORD had chosen out of all the tribes of Israel in which to put his Name. His mother's name was Naamah; she was an Ammonite.

²² Judah did evil in the eyes of the LORD. By the sins they committed they stirred up his jealous anger more than those who were before them had done. ²³ They also set up for themselves high places, sacred stones and Asherah poles on every high hill and under every spreading tree. ²⁴ There were even male shrine-prostitutes in the land;

the people engaged in all the detestable practices of the nations the LORD had driven out before the Israelites.

²⁵ In the fifth year of King Rehoboam, Shishak king of Egypt attacked Jerusalem. ²⁶ He carried off the treasures of the temple of the LORD and the treasures of the royal palace. He took everything, including all the gold shields Solomon had made. ²⁷ So King Rehoboam made bronze shields to replace them and assigned these to the commanders of the guard on duty at the entrance to the royal palace. ²⁸ Whenever the king went to the LORD's temple, the guards bore the shields, and afterwards they returned them to the guardroom.

²⁹ As for the other events of Rehoboam's reign, and all he did, are they not written in the book of the annals of the kings of Judah? ³⁰ There was continual warfare between Rehoboam and Jeroboam. ³¹ And Rehoboam rested with his ancestors and was buried with them in the City of David. His mother's name was Naamah; she was an Ammonite. And Abijah his son succeeded him as king.

15 In the eighteenth year of the reign of Jeroboam son of Nebat, Abijah became king of Judah, ² and he reigned in Jerusalem for three years. His mother's name was Maakah daughter of Abishalom.

³ He committed all the sins his father had done before him; his heart was not fully devoted to the LORD his God, as the heart of David his forefather had been. ⁴ Nevertheless, for David's sake the LORD his God gave him a lamp in Jerusalem by raising up a son to succeed him and by making Jerusalem strong. ⁵ For David had done what was right in the eyes of the LORD and had not failed to keep any of the LORD's commands all the days of his life – except in the case of Uriah the Hittite.

⁶ There was war between Abijah and Jeroboam throughout Abijah's lifetime. ⁷ As for the other events of Abijah's reign, and all he did, are they not written in the book of

the annals of the kings of Judah? There was war between Abijah and Jeroboam. ⁸And Abijah rested with his ancestors and was buried in the City of David. And Asa his son succeeded him as king.

⁹In the twentieth year of Jeroboam king of Israel, Asa became king of Judah, ¹⁰and he reigned in Jerusalem for forty-one years. His grandmother's name was Maakah daughter of Abishalom.

¹¹Asa did what was right in the eyes of the LORD, as his father David had done. ¹²He expelled the male shrine-prostitutes from the land and got rid of all the idols his ancestors had made. ¹³He even deposed his grandmother Maakah from her position as queen mother, because she had made a repulsive image for the worship of Asherah. Asa cut it down and burned it in the Kidron Valley. ¹⁴Although he did not remove the high places, Asa's heart was fully committed to the LORD all his life. ¹⁵He brought into the temple of the LORD the silver and gold and the articles that he and his father had dedicated.

¹⁶There was war between Asa and Baasha king of Israel throughout their reigns. ¹⁷Baasha king of Israel went up against Judah and fortified Ramah to prevent anyone from leaving or entering the territory of Asa king of Judah.

¹⁸Asa then took all the silver and gold that was left in the treasuries of the LORD's temple and of his own palace. He entrusted it to his officials and sent them to Ben-Hadad son of Tabrimmon, the son of Hezion, the king of Aram, who was ruling in Damascus. ¹⁹'Let there be a treaty between me and you,' he said, 'as there was between my father and your father. See, I am sending you a gift of silver and gold. Now break your treaty with Baasha king of Israel so that he will withdraw from me.'

²⁰Ben-Hadad agreed with King Asa and sent the commanders of his forces against the towns of Israel. He conquered Ijon, Dan,

Abel Beth Maakah and all Kinnereth in addition to Naphtali. ²¹When Baasha heard this, he stopped building Ramah and withdrew to Tirzah. ²²Then King Asa issued an order to all Judah – no one was exempt – and they carried away from Ramah the stones and timber Baasha had been using there. With them King Asa built up Geba in Benjamin, and also Mizpah.

²³As for all the other events of Asa's reign, all his achievements, all he did and the cities he built, are they not written in the book of the annals of the kings of Judah? In his old age, however, his feet became diseased. ²⁴Then Asa rested with his ancestors and was buried with them in the city of his father David. And Jehoshaphat his son succeeded him as king.

²⁵Nadab son of Jeroboam became king of Israel in the second year of Asa king of Judah, and he reigned over Israel for two years. ²⁶He did evil in the eyes of the LORD, following the ways of his father and committing the same sin his father had caused Israel to commit.

²⁷Baasha son of Ahijah from the tribe of Issachar plotted against him, and he struck him down at Gibbethon, a Philistine town, while Nadab and all Israel were besieging it. ²⁸Baasha killed Nadab in the third year of Asa king of Judah and succeeded him as king.

²⁹As soon as he began to reign, he killed Jeroboam's whole family. He did not leave Jeroboam anyone that breathed, but destroyed them all, according to the word of the LORD given through his servant Ahijah the Shilonite. ³⁰This happened because of the sins Jeroboam had committed and had caused Israel to commit, and because he aroused the anger of the LORD, the God of Israel.

³¹As for the other events of Nadab's reign, and all he did, are they not written in the book of the annals of the kings of Israel? ³²There was war between Asa and Baasha

king of Israel throughout their reigns.

³³ In the third year of Asa king of Judah, Baasha son of Ahijah became king of all Israel in Tirzah, and he reigned for twenty-four years. ³⁴ He did evil in the eyes of the LORD, following the ways of Jeroboam and committing the same sin Jeroboam had caused Israel to commit.

■ PSALM 74:1-6

¹ O God, why have you rejected us for ever?
    Why does your anger smoulder
        against the sheep of your
        pasture?
² Remember the nation you purchased
        long ago,
    the people of your inheritance, whom
        you redeemed –
    Mount Zion, where you dwelt.
³ Turn your steps towards these
        everlasting ruins,
    all this destruction the enemy has
        brought on the sanctuary.

⁴ Your foes roared in the place where you
        met with us;
    they set up their standards as signs.
⁵ They behaved like men wielding axes
    to cut through a thicket of trees.
⁶ They smashed all the carved panelling
    with their axes and hatchets.

■ PROVERBS 16:5-7

⁵ The LORD detests all the proud of heart.
    Be sure of this: they will not go
        unpunished.

⁶ Through love and faithfulness sin is
        atoned for;
    through the fear of the LORD evil is
        avoided.

⁷ When the LORD takes pleasure in
        anyone's way,
    he causes their enemies to make peace
        with them.

■ JOHN 20:1-20

20 Early on the first day of the week, while it was still dark, Mary Magdalene went to the tomb and saw that the stone had been removed from the entrance. ² So she came running to Simon Peter and the other disciple, the one Jesus loved, and said, 'They have taken the Lord out of the tomb, and we don't know where they have put him!'

³ So Peter and the other disciple started for the tomb. ⁴ Both were running, but the other disciple outran Peter and reached the tomb first. ⁵ He bent over and looked in at the strips of linen lying there but did not go in. ⁶ Then Simon Peter came along behind him and went straight into the tomb. He saw the strips of linen lying there, ⁷ as well as the cloth that had been wrapped round Jesus' head. The cloth was still lying in its place, separate from the linen. ⁸ Finally the other disciple, who had reached the tomb first, also went inside. He saw and believed. ⁹ (They still did not understand from Scripture that Jesus had to rise from the dead.) ¹⁰ Then the disciples went back to where they were staying.

¹¹ Now Mary stood outside the tomb crying. As she wept, she bent over to look into the tomb ¹² and saw two angels in white, seated where Jesus' body had been, one at the head and the other at the foot.

¹³ They asked her, 'Woman, why are you crying?'

'They have taken my Lord away,' she said, 'and I don't know where they have put him.' ¹⁴ At this, she turned round and saw Jesus standing there, but she did not realise that it was Jesus.

¹⁵He asked her, 'Woman, why are you crying? Who is it you are looking for?'

Thinking he was the gardener, she said, 'Sir, if you have carried him away, tell me where you have put him, and I will get him.'

¹⁶Jesus said to her, 'Mary.'

She turned towards him and cried out in Aramaic, 'Rabboni!' (which means 'Teacher').

¹⁷Jesus said, 'Do not hold on to me, for I have not yet ascended to the Father. Go instead to my brothers and tell them, "I am ascending to my Father and your Father, to my God and your God."'

¹⁸Mary Magdalene went to the disciples with the news: 'I have seen the Lord!' And she told them that he had said these things to her.

¹⁹On the evening of that first day of the week, when the disciples were together, with the doors locked for fear of the Jewish leaders, Jesus came and stood among them and said, 'Peace be with you!' ²⁰After he said this, he showed them his hands and side. The disciples were overjoyed when they saw the Lord.

The Forgotten Father

'"I am ascending to my Father and your Father, to my God and your God."' **John 20:17**

The theme in this verse – my Father and your Father – is one that I view as among the greatest I have ever tackled, and I approach it with the earnest prayer that as the Father revealed Himself through the 'Word made flesh' (God's most perfect self-revelation), so He might reveal Himself also through the words that are being written about Him here.

It has been said that the Christian faith is essentially a Father movement. Yet theologian Tom Smail suggested that in today's church the Father is forgotten in precisely the same way that the Spirit was forgotten before the growth of the Pentecostal and charismatic movements. Can this be true? Are we in danger of focusing so much on the work of the Holy Spirit that we forget the Father? I think that in some sections of the church there are evidences that this is the case. We hear much about the Son and much about the Spirit, but how much do we hear about the Father? When our Lord Jesus Christ lived on this earth, He fulfilled many roles – Saviour, Shepherd, Deliverer, Healer, Prophet, Life-giver – but the overall purpose of His being here was to restore us to relationship with the Father. Some of the greatest words He ever uttered are the words of our text for today, 'I am ascending to My Father and your Father'. Your Father.

Let those words sink their way into your consciousness. Through our Lord's redemptive work on the cross, God is not just the Father of Jesus. He is our Father too.

PRAYER

O God my Father, give me a new understanding of what it means to have You as my Father. I am standing on the shore of a great and wondrous truth. Help me launch out into the deep. In Jesus' name. Amen.

FURTHER STUDY

Acts 17:22-30; Deut. 32:18; Psa. 44:20-21; Isa. 17:10-11
• In what way is God unknown today?
• What are our modern-day idol substitutes?

June 21

▬ 1 KINGS 16:1–17:24

16 Then the word of the LORD came to Jehu son of Hanani concerning Baasha: ²'I lifted you up from the dust and appointed you ruler over my people Israel, but you followed the ways of Jeroboam and caused my people Israel to sin and to arouse my anger by their sins. ³So I am about to wipe out Baasha and his house, and I will make your house like that of Jeroboam son of Nebat. ⁴Dogs will eat those belonging to Baasha who die in the city, and birds will feed on those who die in the country.'

⁵As for the other events of Baasha's reign, what he did and his achievements, are they not written in the book of the annals of the kings of Israel? ⁶Baasha rested with his ancestors and was buried in Tirzah. And Elah his son succeeded him as king.

⁷Moreover, the word of the LORD came through the prophet Jehu son of Hanani to Baasha and his house, because of all the evil he had done in the eyes of the LORD, arousing his anger by the things he did, becoming like the house of Jeroboam – and also because he destroyed it.

⁸In the twenty-sixth year of Asa king of Judah, Elah son of Baasha became king of Israel, and he reigned in Tirzah for two years.

⁹Zimri, one of his officials, who had command of half his chariots, plotted against him. Elah was in Tirzah at the time, getting drunk in the home of Arza, the palace administrator at Tirzah. ¹⁰Zimri came in, struck him down and killed him in the twenty-seventh year of Asa king of Judah. Then he succeeded him as king.

¹¹As soon as he began to reign and was seated on the throne, he killed off Baasha's whole family. He did not spare a single male, whether relative or friend. ¹²So Zimri destroyed the whole family of Baasha, in accordance with the word of the LORD spoken against Baasha through the prophet Jehu – ¹³because of all the sins Baasha and his son Elah had committed and had caused Israel to commit, so that they aroused the anger of the LORD, the God of Israel, by their worthless idols.

¹⁴As for the other events of Elah's reign, and all he did, are they not written in the book of the annals of the kings of Israel?

¹⁵In the twenty-seventh year of Asa king of Judah, Zimri reigned in Tirzah for seven days. The army was encamped near Gibbethon, a Philistine town. ¹⁶When the Israelites in the camp heard that Zimri had plotted against the king and murdered him, they proclaimed Omri, the commander of the army, king over Israel that very day there in the camp. ¹⁷Then Omri and all the

Israelites with him withdrew from Gibbethon and laid siege to Tirzah. ¹⁸When Zimri saw that the city was taken, he went into the citadel of the royal palace and set the palace on fire around him. So he died, ¹⁹because of the sins he had committed, doing evil in the eyes of the LORD and following the ways of Jeroboam and committing the same sin Jeroboam had caused Israel to commit.

²⁰As for the other events of Zimri's reign, and the rebellion he carried out, are they not written in the book of the annals of the kings of Israel?

²¹Then the people of Israel were split into two factions; half supported Tibni son of Ginath for king, and the other half supported Omri. ²²But Omri's followers proved stronger than those of Tibni son of Ginath. So Tibni died and Omri became king.

²³In the thirty-first year of Asa king of Judah, Omri became king of Israel, and he reigned for twelve years, six of them in Tirzah. ²⁴He bought the hill of Samaria from Shemer for two talents of silver and built a city on the hill, calling it Samaria, after Shemer, the name of the former owner of the hill.

²⁵But Omri did evil in the eyes of the LORD and sinned more than all those before him. ²⁶He followed completely the ways of Jeroboam son of Nebat, committing the same sin Jeroboam had caused Israel to commit, so that they aroused the anger of the LORD, the God of Israel, by their worthless idols.

²⁷As for the other events of Omri's reign, what he did and the things he achieved, are they not written in the book of the annals of the kings of Israel? ²⁸Omri rested with his ancestors and was buried in Samaria. And Ahab his son succeeded him as king.

²⁹In the thirty-eighth year of Asa king of Judah, Ahab son of Omri became king of Israel, and he reigned in Samaria over Israel for twenty-two years. ³⁰Ahab son of Omri did more evil in the eyes of the LORD than any of those before him. ³¹He not only

considered it trivial to commit the sins of Jeroboam son of Nebat, but he also married Jezebel daughter of Ethbaal king of the Sidonians, and began to serve Baal and worship him. ³²He set up an altar for Baal in the temple of Baal that he built in Samaria. ³³Ahab also made an Asherah pole and did more to arouse the anger of the LORD, the God of Israel, than did all the kings of Israel before him.

³⁴In Ahab's time, Hiel of Bethel rebuilt Jericho. He laid its foundations at the cost of his firstborn son Abiram, and he set up its gates at the cost of his youngest son Segub, in accordance with the word of the LORD spoken by Joshua son of Nun.

17 Now Elijah the Tishbite, from Tishbe in Gilead, said to Ahab, 'As the LORD, the God of Israel, lives, whom I serve, there will be neither dew nor rain in the next few years except at my word.'

²Then the word of the LORD came to Elijah: ³'Leave here, turn eastward and hide in the Kerith Ravine, east of the Jordan. ⁴You will drink from the brook, and I have instructed the ravens to supply you with food there.'

⁵So he did what the LORD had told him. He went to the Kerith Ravine, east of the Jordan, and stayed there. ⁶The ravens brought him bread and meat in the morning and bread and meat in the evening, and he drank from the brook.

⁷Some time later the brook dried up because there had been no rain in the land. ⁸Then the word of the LORD came to him: ⁹'Go at once to Zarephath in the region of Sidon and stay there. I have instructed a widow there to supply you with food.' ¹⁰So he went to Zarephath. When he came to the town gate, a widow was there gathering sticks. He called to her and asked, 'Would you bring me a little water in a jar so I may have a drink?' ¹¹As she was going to get it, he called, 'And bring me, please, a piece of bread.'

¹²'As surely as the LORD your God lives,'

she replied, 'I don't have any bread – only a handful of flour in a jar and a little olive oil in a jug. I am gathering a few sticks to take home and make a meal for myself and my son, that we may eat it – and die.'

¹³ Elijah said to her, 'Don't be afraid. Go home and do as you have said. But first make a small loaf of bread for me from what you have and bring it to me, and then make something for yourself and your son. ¹⁴ For this is what the LORD, the God of Israel, says: "The jar of flour will not be used up and the jug of oil will not run dry until the day the LORD sends rain on the land."'

¹⁵ She went away and did as Elijah had told her. So there was food every day for Elijah and for the woman and her family. ¹⁶ For the jar of flour was not used up and the jug of oil did not run dry, in keeping with the word of the LORD spoken by Elijah.

¹⁷ Some time later the son of the woman who owned the house became ill. He grew worse and worse, and finally stopped breathing. ¹⁸ She said to Elijah, 'What do you have against me, man of God? Did you come to remind me of my sin and kill my son?'

¹⁹ 'Give me your son,' Elijah replied. He took him from her arms, carried him to the upper room where he was staying, and laid him on his bed. ²⁰ Then he cried out to the LORD, 'LORD my God, have you brought tragedy even on this widow I am staying with, by causing her son to die?' ²¹ Then he stretched himself out on the boy three times and cried out to the LORD, 'LORD my God, let this boy's life return to him!'

²² The LORD heard Elijah's cry, and the boy's life returned to him, and he lived. ²³ Elijah picked up the child and carried him down from the room into the house. He gave him to his mother and said, 'Look, your son is alive!'

²⁴ Then the woman said to Elijah, 'Now I know that you are a man of God and that the word of the LORD from your mouth is the truth.'

▬ PSALM 74:7–11

⁷ They burned your sanctuary to the ground;
    they defiled the dwelling-place of your Name.
⁸ They said in their hearts, 'We will crush them completely!'
    They burned every place where God was worshipped in the land.

⁹ We are given no signs from God;
    no prophets are left,
    and none of us knows how long this will be.
¹⁰ How long will the enemy mock you, God?
    Will the foe revile your name for ever?
¹¹ Why do you hold back your hand, your right hand?
    Take it from the folds of your garment and destroy them!

▬ PROVERBS 16:8–10

⁸ Better a little with righteousness
    than much gain with injustice.

⁹ In their hearts humans plan their course,
    but the LORD establishes their steps.

¹⁰ The lips of a king speak as an oracle,
    and his mouth does not betray justice.

▬ JOHN 20:21–21:9

²¹ Again Jesus said, 'Peace be with you! As the Father has sent me, I am sending you.' ²² And with that he breathed on them and said, 'Receive the Holy Spirit. ²³ If you forgive anyone's sins, their sins are forgiven; if you do not forgive them, they are not forgiven.'

²⁴ Now Thomas (also known as Didymus),

one of the Twelve, was not with the disciples when Jesus came. ²⁵So the other disciples told him, 'We have seen the Lord!'

But he said to them, 'Unless I see the nail marks in his hands and put my finger where the nails were, and put my hand into his side, I will not believe.'

²⁶A week later his disciples were in the house again, and Thomas was with them. Though the doors were locked, Jesus came and stood among them and said, 'Peace be with you!' ²⁷Then he said to Thomas, 'Put your finger here; see my hands. Reach out your hand and put it into my side. Stop doubting and believe.'

²⁸Thomas said to him, 'My Lord and my God!'

²⁹Then Jesus told him, 'Because you have seen me, you have believed; blessed are those who have not seen and yet have believed.'

³⁰Jesus performed many other signs in the presence of his disciples, which are not recorded in this book. ³¹But these are written that you may believe that Jesus is the Messiah, the Son of God, and that by believing you may have life in his name.

21 Afterwards Jesus appeared again to his disciples, by the Sea of Galilee. It happened this way: ²Simon Peter, Thomas (also known as Didymus), Nathanael from Cana in Galilee, the sons of Zebedee, and two other disciples were together. ³'I'm going out to fish,' Simon Peter told them, and they said, 'We'll go with you.' So they went out and got into the boat, but that night they caught nothing.

⁴Early in the morning, Jesus stood on the shore, but the disciples did not realise that it was Jesus.

⁵He called out to them, 'Friends, haven't you any fish?'

'No,' they answered.

⁶He said, 'Throw your net on the right side of the boat and you will find some.' When they did, they were unable to haul the net in because of the large number of fish.

⁷Then the disciple whom Jesus loved said to Peter, 'It is the Lord!' As soon as Simon Peter heard him say, 'It is the Lord,' he wrapped his outer garment round him (for he had taken it off) and jumped into the water. ⁸The other disciples followed in the boat, towing the net full of fish, for they were not far from shore, about a hundred metres. ⁹When they landed, they saw a fire of burning coals there with fish on it, and some bread.

'The Doubter's Prayer'

'"Stop doubting and believe."' **John 20:27**

If your doubts still persist after facing them, praying about them, and developing the habit of talking to yourself with a Scripture passage that refutes them, then seek the help of a minister or a Christian counsellor. God has given us three resources to help us whenever we get into spiritual difficulties: the Word of God, the Spirit of God, and the people of God. The final answer to doubt may come as you share with an experienced Christian the things that are going on in your heart.

If you are not able to get the kind of help I am suggesting, then get in touch with your nearest Christian bookshop and ask them to recommend some helpful reading on the subject. Whatever you do, don't allow yourself to settle down into a complacent attitude about your doubts.

Adopt a positive approach and determine to do something about resolving them. This will ensure that even though your doubts may take a certain amount of time to be cleared away, they will not be able to degenerate into unbelief.

Let me remind you of 'The Doubter's Prayer' compiled by Martin Luther:

Dear Lord, although I am sure of my position,
I am unable to sustain it without Thee.
Help me or I am lost.

If the only thing you are able to do is pray, then that by itself will prevent doubt from becoming unbelief. If you also adopt the principle of 'talking to yourself' from the Word of God, then you have in your hands the strategy for overcoming doubt.

PRAYER

Father, help me, whenever I don't know what to do, to turn naturally to prayer. Then no moment will be empty or fruitless. But help me also to utilise the power of Your Word, the Bible. Let these two things become my central strategy. Amen.

FURTHER STUDY

Mark 9:14-29;
Matt. 9:29-30; 21:21
• What was the father's request?
• Do you need to pray that prayer today?

June 22

■ 1 KINGS 18:1-46

18 After a long time, in the third year, the word of the LORD came to Elijah: 'Go and present yourself to Ahab, and I will send rain on the land.' ²So Elijah went to present himself to Ahab.

Now the famine was severe in Samaria, ³and Ahab had summoned Obadiah, his palace administrator. (Obadiah was a devout believer in the LORD. ⁴While Jezebel was killing off the LORD's prophets, Obadiah had taken a hundred prophets and hidden them in two caves, fifty in each, and had supplied them with food and water.) ⁵Ahab had said to Obadiah, 'Go through the land

to all the springs and valleys. Maybe we can find some grass to keep the horses and mules alive so we will not have to kill any of our animals.' ⁶So they divided the land they were to cover, Ahab going in one direction and Obadiah in another.

⁷As Obadiah was walking along, Elijah met him. Obadiah recognised him, bowed down to the ground, and said, 'Is it really you, my lord Elijah?'

⁸'Yes,' he replied. 'Go tell your master, "Elijah is here."'

⁹'What have I done wrong,' asked Obadiah, 'that you are handing your servant over to Ahab to be put to death? ¹⁰As surely as the LORD your God lives, there is not a

nation or kingdom where my master has not sent someone to look for you. And whenever a nation or kingdom claimed you were not there, he made them swear they could not find you. ¹¹But now you tell me to go to my master and say, "Elijah is here." ¹²I don't know where the Spirit of the LORD may carry you when I leave you. If I go and tell Ahab and he doesn't find you, he will kill me. Yet I your servant have worshipped the LORD since my youth. ¹³Haven't you heard, my lord, what I did while Jezebel was killing the prophets of the LORD? I hid a hundred of the LORD's prophets in two caves, fifty in each, and supplied them with food and water. ¹⁴And now you tell me to go to my master and say, "Elijah is here." He will kill me!'

¹⁵Elijah said, 'As the LORD Almighty lives, whom I serve, I will surely present myself to Ahab today.'

¹⁶So Obadiah went to meet Ahab and told him, and Ahab went to meet Elijah. ¹⁷When he saw Elijah, he said to him, 'Is that you, you troubler of Israel?'

¹⁸'I have not made trouble for Israel,' Elijah replied. 'But you and your father's family have. You have abandoned the LORD's commands and have followed the Baals. ¹⁹Now summon the people from all over Israel to meet me on Mount Carmel. And bring the four hundred and fifty prophets of Baal and the four hundred prophets of Asherah, who eat at Jezebel's table.'

²⁰So Ahab sent word throughout all Israel and assembled the prophets on Mount Carmel. ²¹Elijah went before the people and said, 'How long will you waver between two opinions? If the LORD is God, follow him; but if Baal is God, follow him.'

But the people said nothing. ²²Then Elijah said to them, 'I am the only one of the LORD's prophets left, but Baal has four hundred and fifty prophets. ²³Get two bulls for us. Let Baal's prophets choose one for themselves, and let them cut it into

pieces and put it on the wood but not set fire to it. I will prepare the other bull and put it on the wood but not set fire to it. ²⁴Then you call on the name of your god, and I will call on the name of the LORD. The god who answers by fire – he is God.'

Then all the people said, 'What you say is good.'

²⁵Elijah said to the prophets of Baal, 'Choose one of the bulls and prepare it first, since there are so many of you. Call on the name of your god, but do not light the fire.' ²⁶So they took the bull that was given to them and prepared it.

Then they called on the name of Baal from morning till noon. 'Baal, answer us!' they shouted. But there was no response; no one answered. And they danced around the altar they had made.

²⁷At noon Elijah began to taunt them. 'Shout louder!' he said. 'Surely he is a god! Perhaps he is deep in thought, or busy, or travelling. Maybe he is sleeping and must be awakened.' ²⁸So they shouted louder and slashed themselves with swords and spears, as was their custom, until their blood flowed. ²⁹Midday passed, and they continued their frantic prophesying until the time for the evening sacrifice. But there was no response, no one answered, no one paid attention.

³⁰Then Elijah said to all the people, 'Come here to me.' They came to him, and he repaired the altar of the LORD, which had been torn down. ³¹Elijah took twelve stones, one for each of the tribes descended from Jacob, to whom the word of the LORD had come, saying, 'Your name shall be Israel.' ³²With the stones he built an altar in the name of the LORD, and he dug a trench round it large enough to hold two seahs of seed. ³³He arranged the wood, cut the bull into pieces and laid it on the wood. Then he said to them, 'Fill four large jars with water and pour it on the offering and on the wood.'

³⁴ 'Do it again,' he said, and they did it again.

'Do it a third time,' he ordered, and they did it the third time. ³⁵ The water ran down around the altar and even filled the trench.

³⁶ At the time of sacrifice, the prophet Elijah stepped forward and prayed: 'LORD, the God of Abraham, Isaac and Israel, let it be known today that you are God in Israel and that I am your servant and have done all these things at your command. ³⁷ Answer me, LORD, answer me, so these people will know that you, LORD, are God, and that you are turning their hearts back again.'

³⁸ Then the fire of the LORD fell and burned up the sacrifice, the wood, the stones and the soil, and also licked up the water in the trench.

³⁹ When all the people saw this, they fell prostrate and cried, 'The LORD – he is God! The LORD – he is God!'

⁴⁰ Then Elijah commanded them, 'Seize the prophets of Baal. Don't let anyone get away!' They seized them, and Elijah had them brought down to the Kishon Valley and slaughtered there.

⁴¹ And Elijah said to Ahab, 'Go, eat and drink, for there is the sound of a heavy rain.' ⁴² So Ahab went off to eat and drink, but Elijah climbed to the top of Carmel, bent down to the ground and put his face between his knees.

⁴³ 'Go and look toward the sea,' he told his servant. And he went up and looked.

'There is nothing there,' he said.

Seven times Elijah said, 'Go back.'

⁴⁴ The seventh time the servant reported, 'A cloud as small as a man's hand is rising from the sea.'

So Elijah said, 'Go and tell Ahab, "Hitch up your chariot and go down before the rain stops you."'

⁴⁵ Meanwhile, the sky grew black with clouds, the wind rose, a heavy rainstorm came on and Ahab rode off to Jezreel. ⁴⁶ The power of the LORD came on Elijah and,

tucking his cloak into his belt, he ran ahead of Ahab all the way to Jezreel.

▬ PSALM 74:12-17

¹² But God is my King from long ago;
    he brings salvation on the earth.

¹³ It was you who split open the sea by your
        power;
    you broke the heads of the monster in
        the waters.
¹⁴ It was you who crushed the heads of
        Leviathan
    and gave it as food to the creatures of
        the desert.
¹⁵ It was you who opened up springs and
        streams;
    you dried up the ever-flowing rivers.
¹⁶ The day is yours, and yours also the
        night;
    you established the sun and moon.
¹⁷ It was you who set all the boundaries of
        the earth;
    you made both summer and winter.

▬ PROVERBS 16:11-12

¹¹ Honest scales and balances belong to the
        LORD;
    all the weights in the bag are of his
        making.

¹² Kings detest wrongdoing,
    for a throne is established through
        righteousness.

▬ JOHN 21:10-25

¹⁰ Jesus said to them, 'Bring some of the fish you have just caught.' ¹¹ So Simon Peter climbed back into the boat and dragged the net ashore. It was full of large fish, 153,

but even with so many the net was not torn. [12] Jesus said to them, 'Come and have breakfast.' None of the disciples dared ask him, 'Who are you?' They knew it was the Lord. [13] Jesus came, took the bread and gave it to them, and did the same with the fish. [14] This was now the third time Jesus appeared to his disciples after he was raised from the dead.

[15] When they had finished eating, Jesus said to Simon Peter, 'Simon son of John, do you love me more than these?'

'Yes, Lord,' he said, 'you know that I love you.'

Jesus said, 'Feed my lambs.'

[16] Again Jesus said, 'Simon son of John, do you love me?'

He answered, 'Yes, Lord, you know that I love you.'

Jesus said, 'Take care of my sheep.'

[17] The third time he said to him, 'Simon son of John, do you love me?'

Peter was hurt because Jesus asked him the third time, 'Do you love me?' He said, 'Lord, you know all things; you know that I love you.'

Jesus said, 'Feed my sheep. [18] Very truly I tell you, when you were younger you dressed yourself and went where you wanted; but when you are old you will stretch out your hands, and someone else will dress you and lead you where you do not want to go.' [19] Jesus said this to indicate the kind of death by which Peter would glorify God. Then he said to him, 'Follow me!'

[20] Peter turned and saw that the disciple whom Jesus loved was following them. (This was the one who had leaned back against Jesus at the supper and had said, 'Lord, who is going to betray you?') [21] When Peter saw him, he asked, 'Lord, what about him?'

[22] Jesus answered, 'If I want him to remain alive until I return, what is that to you? You must follow me.' [23] Because of this, the rumour spread among the believers that this disciple would not die. But Jesus did not say that he would not die; he only said, 'If I want him to remain alive until I return, what is that to you?'

[24] This is the disciple who testifies to these things and who wrote them down. We know that his testimony is true.

[25] Jesus did many other things as well. If every one of them were written down, I suppose that even the whole world would not have room for the books that would be written.

Devout Realists

'Kings detest wrongdoing for a throne is established through righteousness.' **Proverbs 16:12**

The confession and acknowledgement of God's goodness is evident when we consider the time when the Israelites first settled in Canaan - the period of the judges - and the monarchy. Throughout these years the same pattern repeated itself over and over again - disobedience led to warnings, repentance, and appeals to God for mercy. The words 'You' and 'them' draw attention to the interaction between God and His people in Nehemiah 9:31: 'You did not put an end to them or abandon them'.

This review of their national history provides every one of the Jews listening with encouraging evidences of what God has done in the past, the awesome consequences of ingratitude, and the inevitability of punishment if sin goes unconfessed. But most important of all, there is hope for the future. And that hope is based on the unchanging character of God. They see in the present a product of the past and the seed of the future. Their anticipation now is that the knowledge of past events will help them avoid the evil and follow the good, which is Paul's message in 1 Corinthians 10:6 and 11.

One person has said, 'We have no light to illuminate the pathway of the future save that which falls over our shoulder from the past'. Reflecting on what God has done for us in the past enables us to have a clearer perspective on the present and the future. A biblical approach to history makes us neither wide-eyed optimists nor downhearted pessimists. We become devout realists, for we see God at work in all things and triumphing over everything.

PRAYER

O God, help me build into my life times for reflection on the way in which Your goodness has been with me in the past. For I see that by contemplating this I draw hope and encouragement for the future. Answer my prayer. In Jesus' name. Amen.

FURTHER STUDY

Psa. 23:1-6; Luke 22:35-38; Neh. 9:26-31

- As you read the psalm, reflect on God's dealings with you.
- How will devout realists react to different situations?

June 23

■ 1 KINGS 19:1–20:43

19 Now Ahab told Jezebel everything Elijah had done and how he had killed all the prophets with the sword. ²So Jezebel sent a messenger to Elijah to say, 'May the gods deal with me, be it ever so severely, if by this time tomorrow I do not make your life like that of one of them.'

³Elijah was afraid and ran for his life. When he came to Beersheba in Judah, he left his servant there, ⁴while he himself went a day's journey into the wilderness. He came to a broom bush, sat down under it and prayed that he might die. 'I have had enough, LORD,' he said. 'Take my life; I am no better than my ancestors.' ⁵Then he lay down under the bush and fell asleep.

All at once an angel touched him and said, 'Get up and eat.' ⁶He looked around, and there by his head was some bread baked over hot coals, and a jar of water. He ate and drank and then lay down again.

⁷The angel of the LORD came back a second time and touched him and said, 'Get up and eat, for the journey is too much for you.' ⁸So he got up and ate and drank. Strengthened by that food, he travelled for forty days and forty nights until he reached Horeb, the mountain of God. ⁹There he went into a cave and spent the night.

And the word of the LORD came to him: 'What are you doing here, Elijah?'

¹⁰He replied, 'I have been very zealous for

the LORD God Almighty. The Israelites have rejected your covenant, torn down your altars, and put your prophets to death with the sword. I am the only one left, and now they are trying to kill me too.'

[11] The LORD said, 'Go out and stand on the mountain in the presence of the LORD, for the LORD is about to pass by.'

Then a great and powerful wind tore the mountains apart and shattered the rocks before the LORD, but the LORD was not in the wind. After the wind there was an earthquake, but the LORD was not in the earthquake. [12] After the earthquake came a fire, but the LORD was not in the fire. And after the fire came a gentle whisper. [13] When Elijah heard it, he pulled his cloak over his face and went out and stood at the mouth of the cave.

Then a voice said to him, 'What are you doing here, Elijah?'

[14] He replied, 'I have been very zealous for the LORD God Almighty. The Israelites have rejected your covenant, torn down your altars, and put your prophets to death with the sword. I am the only one left, and now they are trying to kill me too.'

[15] The LORD said to him, 'Go back the way you came, and go to the Desert of Damascus. When you get there, anoint Hazael king over Aram. [16] Also, anoint Jehu son of Nimshi king over Israel, and anoint Elisha son of Shaphat from Abel Meholah to succeed you as prophet. [17] Jehu will put to death any who escape the sword of Hazael, and Elisha will put to death any who escape the sword of Jehu. [18] Yet I reserve seven thousand in Israel – all whose knees have not bowed down to Baal and whose mouths have not kissed him.'

[19] So Elijah went from there and found Elisha son of Shaphat. He was ploughing with twelve yoke of oxen, and he himself was driving the twelfth pair. Elijah went up to him and threw his cloak around him. [20] Elisha then left his oxen and ran after Elijah. 'Let me kiss my father and mother goodbye,' he said, 'and then I will come with you.'

'Go back,' Elijah replied. 'What have I done to you?'

[21] So Elisha left him and went back. He took his yoke of oxen and slaughtered them. He burned the ploughing equipment to cook the meat and gave it to the people, and they ate. Then he set out to follow Elijah and became his servant.

20 Now Ben-Hadad king of Aram mustered his entire army. Accompanied by thirty-two kings with their horses and chariots, he went up and besieged Samaria and attacked it. [2] He sent messengers into the city to Ahab king of Israel, saying, 'This is what Ben-Hadad says: [3] "Your silver and gold are mine, and the best of your wives and children are mine."'

[4] The king of Israel answered, 'Just as you say, my lord the king. I and all I have are yours.'

[5] The messengers came again and said, 'This is what Ben-Hadad says: "I sent to demand your silver and gold, your wives and your children. [6] But about this time tomorrow I am going to send my officials to search your palace and the houses of your officials. They will seize everything you value and carry it away."'

[7] The king of Israel summoned all the elders of the land and said to them, 'See how this man is looking for trouble! When he sent for my wives and my children, my silver and my gold, I did not refuse him.'

[8] The elders and the people all answered, 'Don't listen to him or agree to his demands.'

[9] So he replied to Ben-Hadad's messengers, 'Tell my lord the king, "Your servant will do all you demanded the first time, but this demand I cannot meet."' They left and took the answer back to Ben-Hadad.

[10] Then Ben-Hadad sent another message to Ahab: 'May the gods deal with me, be it ever so severely, if enough dust remains in Samaria to give each of my men a handful.'

[11] The king of Israel answered, 'Tell him: "One who puts on his armour should not

boast like one who takes it off."'

¹²Ben-Hadad heard this message while he and the kings were drinking in their tents, and he ordered his men: 'Prepare to attack.' So they prepared to attack the city.

¹³Meanwhile a prophet came to Ahab king of Israel and announced, 'This is what the LORD says: "Do you see this vast army? I will give it into your hand today, and then you will know that I am the LORD."'

¹⁴'But who will do this?' asked Ahab.

The prophet replied, 'This is what the LORD says: "The junior officers under the provincial commanders will do it."'

'And who will start the battle?' he asked.

The prophet answered, 'You will.'

¹⁵So Ahab summoned the 232 junior officers under the provincial commanders. Then he assembled the rest of the Israelites, 7,000 in all. ¹⁶They set out at noon while Ben-Hadad and the 32 kings allied with him were in their tents getting drunk. ¹⁷The junior officers under the provincial commanders went out first.

Now Ben-Hadad had dispatched scouts, who reported, 'Men are advancing from Samaria.'

¹⁸He said, 'If they have come out for peace, take them alive; if they have come out for war, take them alive.'

¹⁹The junior officers under the provincial commanders marched out of the city with the army behind them ²⁰and each one struck down his opponent. At that, the Arameans fled, with the Israelites in pursuit. But Ben-Hadad king of Aram escaped on horseback with some of his horsemen. ²¹The king of Israel advanced and overpowered the horses and chariots and inflicted heavy losses on the Arameans.

²²Afterwards, the prophet came to the king of Israel and said, 'Strengthen your position and see what must be done, because next spring the king of Aram will attack you again.'

²³Meanwhile, the officials of the king of Aram advised him, 'Their gods are gods of the hills. That is why they were too strong for us. But if we fight them on the plains, surely we will be stronger than they. ²⁴Do this: remove all the kings from their commands and replace them with other officers. ²⁵You must also raise an army like the one you lost – horse for horse and chariot for chariot – so we can fight Israel on the plains. Then surely we will be stronger than they.' He agreed with them and acted accordingly.

²⁶The next spring Ben-Hadad mustered the Arameans and went up to Aphek to fight against Israel. ²⁷When the Israelites were also mustered and given provisions, they marched out to meet them. The Israelites camped opposite them like two small flocks of goats, while the Arameans covered the countryside.

²⁸The man of God came up and told the king of Israel, 'This is what the LORD says: "Because the Arameans think the LORD is a god of the hills and not a god of the valleys, I will deliver this vast army into your hands, and you will know that I am the LORD."'

²⁹For seven days they camped opposite each other, and on the seventh day the battle was joined. The Israelites inflicted a hundred thousand casualties on the Aramean foot soldiers in one day. ³⁰The rest of them escaped to the city of Aphek, where the wall collapsed on twenty-seven thousand of them. And Ben-Hadad fled to the city and hid in an inner room.

³¹His officials said to him, 'Look, we have heard that the kings of Israel are merciful. Let us go to the king of Israel with sackcloth round our waists and ropes round our heads. Perhaps he will spare your life.'

³²Wearing sackcloth round their waists and ropes round their heads, they went to the king of Israel and said, 'Your servant Ben-Hadad says: "Please let me live."'

The king answered, 'Is he still alive? He is my brother.'

³³The men took this as a good sign and were quick to pick up his word. 'Yes, your brother Ben-Hadad!' they said.

'Go and get him,' the king said. When Ben-Hadad came out, Ahab brought him up into his chariot.

³⁴'I will return the cities my father took from your father,' Ben-Hadad offered. 'You may set up your own market areas in Damascus, as my father did in Samaria.'

Ahab said, 'On the basis of a treaty I will set you free.' So he made a treaty with him, and let him go.

³⁵By the word of the LORD one of the company of the prophets said to his companion, 'Strike me with your weapon,' but he refused.

³⁶So the prophet said, 'Because you have not obeyed the LORD, as soon as you leave me a lion will kill you.' And after the man went away, a lion found him and killed him.

³⁷The prophet found another man and said, 'Strike me, please.' So the man struck him and wounded him. ³⁸Then the prophet went and stood by the road waiting for the king. He disguised himself with his headband down over his eyes. ³⁹As the king passed by, the prophet called out to him, 'Your servant went into the thick of the battle, and someone came to me with a captive and said, "Guard this man. If he is missing, it will be your life for his life, or you must pay a talent of silver." ⁴⁰While your servant was busy here and there, the man disappeared.'

'That is your sentence,' the king of Israel said. 'You have pronounced it yourself.'

⁴¹Then the prophet quickly removed the headband from his eyes, and the king of Israel recognised him as one of the prophets. ⁴²He said to the king, 'This is what the LORD says: "You have set free a man I had determined should die. Therefore it is your life for his life, your people for his people."' ⁴³Sullen and angry, the king of Israel went to his palace in Samaria.

PSALM 74:18-23

¹⁸Remember how the enemy has mocked you, LORD,
    how foolish people have reviled your name.
¹⁹Do not hand over the life of your dove to wild beasts;
    do not forget the lives of your afflicted people for ever.
²⁰Have regard for your covenant,
    because haunts of violence fill the dark places of the land.
²¹Do not let the oppressed retreat in disgrace;
    may the poor and needy praise your name.
²²Rise up, O God, and defend your cause;
    remember how fools mock you all day long.
²³Do not ignore the clamour of your adversaries,
    the uproar of your enemies, which rises continually.

PROVERBS 16:13-15

¹³Kings take pleasure in honest lips;
    they value the one who speaks what is right.

¹⁴A king's wrath is a messenger of death,
    but the wise will appease it.

¹⁵When a king's face brightens, it means life;
    his favour is like a rain cloud in spring.

ACTS 1:1-26

1 In my former book, Theophilus, I wrote about all that Jesus began to do and to teach ²until the day he was taken up to heaven, after giving instructions through

the Holy Spirit to the apostles he had chosen. ³After his suffering, he presented himself to them and gave many convincing proofs that he was alive. He appeared to them over a period of forty days and spoke about the kingdom of God. ⁴On one occasion, while he was eating with them, he gave them this command: 'Do not leave Jerusalem, but wait for the gift my Father promised, which you have heard me speak about. ⁵For John baptised with water, but in a few days you will be baptised with the Holy Spirit.'

⁶Then they gathered round him and asked him, 'Lord, are you at this time going to restore the kingdom to Israel?'

⁷He said to them: 'It is not for you to know the times or dates the Father has set by his own authority. ⁸But you will receive power when the Holy Spirit comes on you; and you will be my witnesses in Jerusalem, and in all Judea and Samaria, and to the ends of the earth.'

⁹After he said this, he was taken up before their very eyes, and a cloud hid him from their sight.

¹⁰They were looking intently up into the sky as he was going, when suddenly two men dressed in white stood beside them. ¹¹'Men of Galilee,' they said, 'why do you stand here looking into the sky? This same Jesus, who has been taken from you into heaven, will come back in the same way you have seen him go into heaven.'

¹²Then the apostles returned to Jerusalem from the hill called the Mount of Olives, a Sabbath day's walk from the city. ¹³When they arrived, they went upstairs to the room where they were staying. Those present were Peter, John, James and Andrew; Philip and Thomas, Bartholomew and Matthew; James son of Alphaeus and Simon the Zealot, and Judas son of James. ¹⁴They all joined together constantly in prayer, along with the women and Mary the mother of Jesus, and with his brothers.

¹⁵In those days Peter stood up among the believers (a group numbering about a hundred and twenty) ¹⁶and said, 'Brothers and sisters, the Scripture had to be fulfilled in which the Holy Spirit spoke long ago through David concerning Judas, who served as guide for those who arrested Jesus. ¹⁷He was one of our number and shared in our ministry.'

¹⁸(With the payment he received for his wickedness, Judas bought a field; there he fell headlong, his body burst open and all his intestines spilled out. ¹⁹Everyone in Jerusalem heard about this, so they called that field in their language Akeldama, that is, Field of Blood.)

²⁰'For,' said Peter, 'it is written in the Book of Psalms:

' "May his place be deserted;
    let there be no one to dwell in it,"

and,

' "May another take his place of
        leadership."

²¹Therefore it is necessary to choose one of the men who have been with us the whole time the Lord Jesus was living among us, ²²beginning from John's baptism to the time when Jesus was taken up from us. For one of these must become a witness with us of his resurrection.'

²³So they nominated two men: Joseph called Barsabbas (also known as Justus) and Matthias. ²⁴Then they prayed, 'Lord, you know everyone's heart. Show us which of these two you have chosen ²⁵to take over this apostolic ministry, which Judas left to go where he belongs.' ²⁶Then they cast lots, and the lot fell to Matthias; so he was added to the eleven apostles.

'With' – or 'In' and 'Upon'

'... you will receive power when the Holy Spirit comes on you ...' **Acts 1:8**

The Holy Spirit is a resident counsellor. The Greek word here is interesting: *parakletos* – *para* (beside), *kletos* (call) – one who is called alongside to help. There isn't a single thing needed in the Christian life that He isn't there to provide. Note the difference in the prepositions that are found in these passages: 'He lives with you and will be in you' (John 14:17) and 'You will receive power when the Holy Spirit comes on you' (Acts 1:8). Jesus said that the Spirit was 'with' them, but later would be 'in' them and 'on' them. I take these prepositions to mean that the Holy Spirit was 'with' them prior to Pentecost but was 'in' them and 'upon' them subsequent to Pentecost. Prior to Pentecost their lives lacked character and consistency. They cast out devils, but, on other occasions, they seemed to be somewhat influenced by them.

Simon Peter is a case in point (Matt. 16:23). The disciples were loud in their assertions of loyalty and loud in their blunderings and misunderstandings. The Spirit was most certainly 'with' them – helping, encouraging, and revealing – but He was most certainly not 'in' them or 'on' them. When the Spirit came 'in' and 'on' them at a later date, then fitful living became faithful living; erratic loyalty became everlasting loyalty.

Today, in the lives of many Christians, the Holy Spirit seems to be working on the outside rather than on the inside. Actually, of course, the Holy Spirit is resident 'in' every Christian, but He wants to be more than just resident – He wants also to be president! How is it in your life and experience? Is the Spirit a passing guest or a permanent guest?

PRAYER

God, forgive me for not utilising the resources of the Holy Spirit You have placed within me. Help me see that the Spirit within makes for adequacy without if I avail myself of Him. Amen.

FURTHER STUDY

1 Cor. 2; Neh. 9:20; Luke 12:12; 1 John 2:27
• What has God revealed to us by His Spirit?
• What does the Holy Spirit bring to us?

June 24

24

▬ 1 KINGS 21:1–22:23

21 Some time later there was an incident involving a vineyard belonging to Naboth the Jezreelite. The vineyard was in Jezreel, close to the palace of Ahab king of Samaria. ²Ahab said to Naboth, 'Let me have your vineyard to use for a vegetable garden, since it is close to my palace. In exchange I will give you a better vineyard or, if you prefer, I will pay you whatever it is worth.'

³But Naboth replied, 'The LORD forbid that I should give you the inheritance of my ancestors.'

⁴So Ahab went home, sullen and angry because Naboth the Jezreelite had said, 'I will not give you the inheritance of my ancestors.' He lay on his bed sulking and refused to eat.

⁵His wife Jezebel came in and asked him, 'Why are you so sullen? Why won't you eat?'

⁶He answered her, 'Because I said to Naboth the Jezreelite, "Sell me your vineyard; or if you prefer, I will give you another vineyard in its place." But he said, "I will not give you my vineyard."'

⁷Jezebel his wife said, 'Is this how you act as king over Israel? Get up and eat! Cheer up. I'll get you the vineyard of Naboth the Jezreelite.'

⁸So she wrote letters in Ahab's name, placed his seal on them, and sent them to the elders and nobles who lived in Naboth's city with him. ⁹In those letters she wrote:

'Proclaim a day of fasting and give Naboth a prominent seat among the people. ¹⁰But put two scoundrels opposite him and get them to bring charges that he has cursed both God and the king. Then take him out and stone him to death.'

¹¹So the elders and nobles who lived in Naboth's city did as Jezebel directed in the letters she had written to them. ¹²They proclaimed a fast and seated Naboth in a prominent place among the people. ¹³Then two scoundrels came and sat opposite him and brought charges against Naboth before the people, saying, 'Naboth has cursed both God and the king.' So they took him outside the city and stoned him to death. ¹⁴Then they sent word to Jezebel: 'Naboth has been stoned to death.'

¹⁵As soon as Jezebel heard that Naboth had been stoned to death, she said to Ahab, 'Get up and take possession of the vineyard of Naboth the Jezreelite that he refused to sell you. He is no longer alive, but dead.' ¹⁶When Ahab heard that Naboth was dead, he got up and went down to take possession of Naboth's vineyard.

¹⁷Then the word of the LORD came to Elijah the Tishbite: ¹⁸'Go down to meet Ahab king of Israel, who rules in Samaria. He is now in Naboth's vineyard, where he has gone to take possession of it. ¹⁹Say to him, "This is what the LORD says: have you not murdered a man and seized his property?" Then say to him, "This is what the LORD says: in the place where dogs licked up Naboth's blood, dogs will lick up your blood – yes, yours!"'

²⁰Ahab said to Elijah, 'So you have found me, my enemy!'

'I have found you,' he answered, 'because you have sold yourself to do evil in the eyes of the LORD. ²¹He says, "I am going to bring disaster on you. I will wipe out your descendants and cut off from Ahab every last male in Israel – slave or free. ²²I will make your house like that of Jeroboam son of Nebat and that of Baasha son of Ahijah, because you have aroused my anger and have caused Israel to sin."

²³'And also concerning Jezebel the LORD says: "Dogs will devour Jezebel by the wall of Jezreel."

²⁴'Dogs will eat those belonging to Ahab who die in the city, and the birds will feed on those who die in the country.'

²⁵(There was never anyone like Ahab, who sold himself to do evil in the eyes of the LORD, urged on by Jezebel his wife. ²⁶He behaved in the vilest manner by going after idols, like the Amorites the LORD drove out before Israel.)

²⁷When Ahab heard these words, he tore his clothes, put on sackcloth and fasted. He lay in sackcloth and went around meekly.

²⁸Then the word of the LORD came to Elijah the Tishbite: ²⁹'Have you noticed how Ahab has humbled himself before me? Because he has humbled himself, I will not bring this disaster in his day, but I will bring it on his house in the days of his son.'

22 For three years there was no war between Aram and Israel. ²But in the third year Jehoshaphat king of Judah went down to see the king of Israel. ³The king of Israel had said to his officials, 'Don't you know that Ramoth Gilead belongs to us and yet we are doing nothing to retake it from the king of Aram?'

⁴So he asked Jehoshaphat, 'Will you go with me to fight against Ramoth Gilead?'

Jehoshaphat replied to the king of Israel, 'I am as you are, my people as your people, my horses as your horses.' ⁵But Jehoshaphat also said to the king of Israel, 'First seek the counsel of the LORD.'

⁶So the king of Israel brought together the prophets – about four hundred men – and asked them, 'Shall I go to war against Ramoth Gilead, or shall I refrain?'

'Go,' they answered, 'for the Lord will give it into the king's hand.'

⁷But Jehoshaphat asked, 'Is there no longer a prophet of the LORD here whom we can enquire of?'

⁸The king of Israel answered Jehoshaphat, 'There is still one prophet through whom we can enquire of the LORD, but I hate him because he never prophesies anything good about me, but always bad. He is Micaiah son of Imlah.'

'The king should not say such a thing,' Jehoshaphat replied.

⁹So the king of Israel called one of his officials and said, 'Bring Micaiah son of Imlah at once.'

¹⁰Dressed in their royal robes, the king of Israel and Jehoshaphat king of Judah were sitting on their thrones at the threshing-floor by the entrance of the gate of Samaria, with all the prophets prophesying before them. ¹¹Now Zedekiah son of Kenaanah had made iron horns and he declared, 'This is what the LORD says: "With these you will gore the Arameans until they are destroyed."'

¹²All the other prophets were prophesying the same thing. 'Attack Ramoth Gilead and be victorious,' they said, 'for the LORD will give it into the king's hand.'

¹³The messenger who had gone to summon Micaiah said to him, 'Look, the other prophets without exception are predicting success for the king. Let your word agree with theirs, and speak favourably.'

¹⁴But Micaiah said, 'As surely as the LORD lives, I can tell him only what the LORD tells me.'

¹⁵When he arrived, the king asked him, 'Micaiah, shall we go to war against Ramoth Gilead, or not?'

'Attack and be victorious,' he answered, 'for the LORD will give it into the king's hand.'

¹⁶The king said to him, 'How many times must I make you swear to tell me nothing but the truth in the name of the LORD?'

[17] Then Micaiah answered, 'I saw all Israel scattered on the hills like sheep without a shepherd, and the LORD said, "These people have no master. Let each one go home in peace."'

[18] The king of Israel said to Jehoshaphat, 'Didn't I tell you that he never prophesies anything good about me, but only bad?'

[19] Micaiah continued, 'Therefore hear the word of the LORD: I saw the LORD sitting on his throne with all the multitudes of heaven standing round him on his right and on his left. [20] And the LORD said, "Who will entice Ahab into attacking Ramoth Gilead and going to his death there?"

'One suggested this, and another that. [21] Finally, a spirit came forward, stood before the LORD and said, "I will entice him."

[22] '"By what means?" the LORD asked.

'"I will go out and be a deceiving spirit in the mouths of all his prophets," he said.

'"You will succeed in enticing him," said the LORD. "Go and do it."

[23] 'So now the LORD has put a deceiving spirit in the mouths of all these prophets of yours. The LORD has decreed disaster for you.'

PSALM 75:1-10

[1] We praise you, God,
  we praise you, for your Name is near;
  people tell of your wonderful deeds.

[2] You say, 'I choose the appointed time;
  it is I who judge with equity.
[3] When the earth and all its people quake,
  it is I who hold its pillars firm.
[4] To the arrogant I say, "Boast no more,"
  and to the wicked, "Do not lift up your horns.
[5] Do not lift your horns against heaven;
  do not speak so defiantly."'

[6] No one from the east or the west

or from the desert can exalt
  themselves.
[7] It is God who judges:
  He brings one down, he exalts another.
[8] In the hand of the LORD is a cup
  full of foaming wine mixed with
    spices;
  he pours it out, and all the wicked of the
    earth
  drink it down to its very dregs.

[9] As for me, I will declare this for ever;
  I will sing praise to the God of Jacob,
[10] who says, 'I will cut off the horns of all
    the wicked,
  but the horns of the righteous shall be
    lifted up.'

PROVERBS 16:16-17

[16] How much better to get wisdom than
    gold,
  to get insight rather than silver!

[17] The highway of the upright avoids evil;
  those who guard their ways preserve
    their lives.

ACTS 2:1-21

2 When the day of Pentecost came, they were all together in one place. [2] Suddenly a sound like the blowing of a violent wind came from heaven and filled the whole house where they were sitting. [3] They saw what seemed to be tongues of fire that separated and came to rest on each of them. [4] All of them were filled with the Holy Spirit and began to speak in other tongues as the Spirit enabled them.

[5] Now there were staying in Jerusalem God-fearing Jews from every nation under heaven. [6] When they heard this sound, a crowd came together in bewilderment,

because each one heard their own language being spoken. ⁷Utterly amazed, they asked: 'Aren't all these who are speaking Galileans? ⁸Then how is it that each of us hears them in our native language? ⁹Parthians, Medes and Elamites; residents of Mesopotamia, Judea and Cappadocia, Pontus and Asia, ¹⁰Phrygia and Pamphylia, Egypt and the parts of Libya near Cyrene; visitors from Rome ¹¹(both Jews and converts to Judaism); Cretans and Arabs – we hear them declaring the wonders of God in our own tongues!' ¹²Amazed and perplexed, they asked one another, 'What does this mean?'

¹³Some, however, made fun of them and said, 'They have had too much wine.'

¹⁴Then Peter stood up with the Eleven, raised his voice and addressed the crowd: 'Fellow Jews and all of you who live in Jerusalem, let me explain this to you; listen carefully to what I say. ¹⁵These people are not drunk, as you suppose. It's only nine in the morning! ¹⁶No, this is what was spoken by the prophet Joel:

¹⁷'"In the last days, God says,
    I will pour out my Spirit on all people.
Your sons and daughters will prophesy,
    your young men will see visions,
    your old men will dream dreams.
¹⁸Even on my servants, both men and
        women,
    I will pour out my Spirit in those days,
    and they will prophesy.
¹⁹I will show wonders in the heavens above
    and signs on the earth below,
    blood and fire and billows of smoke.
²⁰The sun will be turned to darkness
    and the moon to blood
    before the coming of the great and
        glorious day of the Lord.
²¹And everyone who calls
    on the name of the Lord will be saved."'

The Young and the Old

'"... I will pour out my Spirit on all people. Your sons and daughters will prophesy, your young men will see visions, your old men will dream dreams."' **Acts 2:17**

A barrier that went down in the upper room was that between the young and the old. Peter pointed out that what had happened in the upper room was the fulfilment of Joel's prophecy, in which the prophet had declared that the day would come when young and old alike would receive the gift of the Holy Spirit. 'This is the day the prophet spoke about!' said Peter. 'It's arrived!'

'There has always been a sacred age,' said someone, ' - old age.' In almost all religions, power and sanctity have been associated with the old. This is why many religions tend to be backward-looking rather than forward-looking. In the upper room there were young men (I think we can assume this) who received the gift of the Holy Spirit in the same way as their elders. What a dynamic this produced. Young and old, moving together in the power of the Spirit. The old would naturally want to conserve the values and good things they had come to love and respect, while the young would want to move these values into greater realms and make them more widely operative.

One writer said, 'The Christian faith demands radicalism as well as conservatism to fully express itself'. Young and old combine to fully express the nature of the Christian faith, for conservatism or radicalism on their own are weak. Together, however, they become strong and powerful.

PRAYER

Heavenly Father, I am thankful that both young and old can be used in the kingdom. Blend the conservatism of the old with the radicalism of the young, so that this generation might see a new Pentecost. For Jesus' sake. Amen.

FURTHER STUDY

1 Tim. 5; 4:12; 1 John 2:13-14; 1 Pet. 5:5; Rom. 12:10
• What was Paul teaching Timothy?
• What does Paul mean: 'Honour one another above yourselves'?

June 25

1 KINGS 22:24– 2 KINGS 1:18

²⁴ Then Zedekiah son of Kenaanah went up and slapped Micaiah in the face. 'Which way did the spirit from the LORD go when he went from me to speak to you?' he asked.

²⁵ Micaiah replied, 'You will find out on the day you go to hide in an inner room.'

²⁶ The king of Israel then ordered, 'Take Micaiah and send him back to Amon the ruler of the city and to Joash the king's son ²⁷ and say, "This is what the king says: put this fellow in prison and give him nothing but bread and water until I return safely."'

²⁸ Micaiah declared, 'If you ever return safely, the LORD has not spoken through me.' Then he added, 'Mark my words, all you people!'

²⁹ So the king of Israel and Jehoshaphat king of Judah went up to Ramoth Gilead. ³⁰ The king of Israel said to Jehoshaphat, 'I will enter the battle in disguise, but you wear your royal robes.' So the king of Israel disguised himself and went into battle.

³¹ Now the king of Aram had ordered his thirty-two chariot commanders, 'Do not fight with anyone, small or great, except the king of Israel.' ³² When the chariot commanders saw Jehoshaphat, they thought, 'Surely this is the king of Israel.' So they turned to attack him, but when Jehoshaphat cried out, ³³ the chariot commanders saw that he was not the king of Israel and stopped pursuing him.

³⁴ But someone drew his bow at random and hit the king of Israel between the sections of his armour. The king told his chariot driver, 'Wheel around and get me out of the fighting. I've been wounded.' ³⁵ All day long the battle raged, and the king was propped up in his chariot facing the Arameans. The blood from his wound ran onto the floor of the chariot, and that evening he died. ³⁶ As the sun was setting, a cry spread through the army: 'Every man to his town. Every man to his land!'

³⁷ So the king died and was brought to Samaria, and they buried him there. ³⁸ They washed the chariot at a pool in Samaria (where the prostitutes bathed), and the dogs licked up his blood, as the word of the

LORD had declared.

³⁹ As for the other events of Ahab's reign, including all he did, the palace he built and adorned with ivory, and the cities he fortified, are they not written in the book of the annals of the kings of Israel? ⁴⁰ Ahab rested with his ancestors. And Ahaziah his son succeeded him as king.

⁴¹ Jehoshaphat son of Asa became king of Judah in the fourth year of Ahab king of Israel. ⁴² Jehoshaphat was thirty-five years old when he became king, and he reigned in Jerusalem for twenty-five years. His mother's name was Azubah daughter of Shilhi. ⁴³ In everything he followed the ways of his father Asa and did not stray from them; he did what was right in the eyes of the LORD. The high places, however, were not removed, and the people continued to offer sacrifices and burn incense there. ⁴⁴ Jehoshaphat was also at peace with the king of Israel.

⁴⁵ As for the other events of Jehoshaphat's reign, the things he achieved and his military exploits, are they not written in the book of the annals of the kings of Judah? ⁴⁶ He rid the land of the rest of the male-shrine prostitutes who remained there even after the reign of his father Asa. ⁴⁷ There was then no king in Edom; a provincial governor ruled.

⁴⁸ Now Jehoshaphat built a fleet of trading ships to go to Ophir for gold, but they never set sail – they were wrecked at Ezion Geber. ⁴⁹ At that time Ahaziah son of Ahab said to Jehoshaphat, 'Let my men sail with yours,' but Jehoshaphat refused.

⁵⁰ Then Jehoshaphat rested with his ancestors and was buried with them in the city of David his father. And Jehoram his son succeeded him as king.

⁵¹ Ahaziah son of Ahab became king of Israel in Samaria in the seventeenth year of Jehoshaphat king of Judah, and he reigned over Israel for two years. ⁵² He did evil in the eyes of the LORD, because he followed the ways of his father and mother and of

Jeroboam son of Nebat, who caused Israel to sin. ⁵³ He served and worshipped Baal and aroused the anger of the LORD, the God of Israel, just as his father had done.

1 After Ahab's death, Moab rebelled against Israel. ² Now Ahaziah had fallen through the lattice of his upper room in Samaria and injured himself. So he sent messengers, saying to them, 'Go and consult Baal-Zebub, the god of Ekron, to see if I will recover from this injury.'

³ But the angel of the LORD said to Elijah the Tishbite, 'Go up and meet the messengers of the king of Samaria and ask them, "Is it because there is no God in Israel that you are going off to consult Baal-Zebub, the god of Ekron?" ⁴ Therefore this is what the LORD says: "You will not leave the bed you are lying on. You will certainly die!"' So Elijah went.

⁵ When the messengers returned to the king, he asked them, 'Why have you come back?'

⁶ 'A man came to meet us,' they replied. 'And he said to us, "Go back to the king who sent you and tell him, 'This is what the LORD says: is it because there is no God in Israel that you are sending messengers to consult Baal-Zebub, the god of Ekron? Therefore you will not leave the bed you are lying on. You will certainly die!'"'

⁷ The king asked them, 'What kind of man was it who came to meet you and told you this?'

⁸ They replied, 'He had a garment of hair and had a leather belt round his waist.'

The king said, 'That was Elijah the Tishbite.'

⁹ Then he sent to Elijah a captain with his company of fifty men. The captain went up to Elijah, who was sitting on the top of a hill, and said to him, 'Man of God, the king says, "Come down!"'

¹⁰ Elijah answered the captain, 'If I am a man of God, may fire come down from

heaven and consume you and your fifty men!' Then the fire fell from heaven and consumed the captain and his men.

¹¹ At this the king sent to Elijah another captain with his fifty men. The captain said to him, 'Man of God, this is what the king says, "Come down at once!"'

¹² 'If I am a man of God,' Elijah replied, 'may fire come down from heaven and consume you and your fifty men!' Then the fire of God fell from heaven and consumed him and his fifty men.

¹³ So the king sent a third captain with his fifty men. This third captain went up and fell on his knees before Elijah. 'Man of God,' he begged, 'please have respect for my life and the lives of these fifty men, your servants! ¹⁴ See, fire has fallen from heaven and consumed the first two captains and all their men. But now have respect for my life!'

¹⁵ The angel of the LORD said to Elijah, 'Go down with him; do not be afraid of him.' So Elijah got up and went down with him to the king.

¹⁶ He told the king, 'This is what the LORD says: is it because there is no God in Israel for you to consult that you have sent messengers to consult Baal-Zebub, the god of Ekron? Because you have done this, you will never leave the bed you are lying on. You will certainly die!' ¹⁷ So he died, according to the word of the LORD that Elijah had spoken.

Because Ahaziah had no son, Joram succeeded him as king in the second year of Jehoram son of Jehoshaphat king of Judah. ¹⁸ As for all the other events of Ahaziah's reign, and what he did, are they not written in the book of the annals of the kings of Israel?

▬ PSALM 76:1-6

¹ God is renowned in Judah;
in Israel his name is great.

² His tent is in Salem,
his dwelling-place in Zion.
³ There he broke the flashing arrows,
the shields and the swords, the
weapons of war.

⁴ You are radiant with light,
more majestic than mountains rich
with game.
⁵ The valiant lie plundered,
they sleep their last sleep;
not one of the warriors
can lift his hands.
⁶ At your rebuke, God of Jacob,
both horse and chariot lie still.

▬ PROVERBS 16:18-19

¹⁸ Pride goes before destruction,
a haughty spirit before a fall.

¹⁹ Better to be lowly in spirit along with the
oppressed
than to share plunder with the proud.

▬ ACTS 2:22-47

²² 'Fellow Israelites, listen to this: Jesus of Nazareth was a man accredited by God to you by miracles, wonders and signs, which God did among you through him, as you yourselves know. ²³ This man was handed over to you by God's deliberate plan and foreknowledge; and you, with the help of wicked men, put him to death by nailing him to the cross. ²⁴ But God raised him from the dead, freeing him from the agony of death, because it was impossible for death to keep its hold on him. ²⁵ David said about him:

' "I saw the Lord always before me.
Because he is at my right hand,
I will not be shaken.

26 Therefore my heart is glad and my
tongue rejoices;
my body also will rest in hope,
27 because you will not abandon me to the
realm of the dead,
you will not let your holy one see
decay.
28 You have made known to me the paths
of life;
you will fill me with joy in your
presence."

29 'Fellow Israelites, I can tell you confidently that the patriarch David died and was buried, and his tomb is here to this day. 30 But he was a prophet and knew that God had promised him on oath that he would place one of his descendants on his throne. 31 Seeing what was to come, he spoke of the resurrection of the Messiah, that he was not abandoned to the realm of the dead, nor did his body see decay. 32 God has raised this Jesus to life, and we are all witnesses of it. 33 Exalted to the right hand of God, he has received from the Father the promised Holy Spirit and has poured out what you now see and hear. 34 For David did not ascend to heaven, and yet he said,

' "The Lord said to my Lord:
'Sit at my right hand
35 until I make your enemies
a footstool for your feet.' "

36 'Therefore let all Israel be assured of this: God has made this Jesus, whom you crucified, both Lord and Messiah.'

37 When the people heard this, they were cut to the heart and said to Peter and the other apostles, 'Brothers, what shall we do?'

38 Peter replied, 'Repent and be baptised, every one of you, in the name of Jesus Christ for the forgiveness of your sins. And you will receive the gift of the Holy Spirit. 39 The promise is for you and your children and for all who are far off – for all whom the Lord our God will call.'

40 With many other words he warned them; and he pleaded with them, 'Save yourselves from this corrupt generation.' 41 Those who accepted his message were baptised, and about three thousand were added to their number that day.

42 They devoted themselves to the apostles' teaching and to fellowship, to the breaking of bread and to prayer. 43 Everyone was filled with awe at the many wonders and signs performed by the apostles. 44 All the believers were together and had everything in common. 45 They sold property and possessions to give to anyone who had need. 46 Every day they continued to meet together in the temple courts. They broke bread in their homes and ate together with glad and sincere hearts, 47 praising God and enjoying the favour of all the people. And the Lord added to their number daily those who were being saved.

Made for Fellowship

'They devoted themselves to the apostles' teaching and to fellowship ...' **Acts 2:42**

I read a passage in a book that said: 'We can only get to know ourselves and others to the extent that we tune in to the heartbeat of the universe'.

Here is a psychologist, a non-Christian, attempting to put into words one of the greatest truths of Scripture - namely, that it is only as we have fellowship with God that we can experience fellowship with ourselves and others. What a pity he could not see that what he calls 'the heartbeat of the universe' is the heart that was broken on the cross.

Isn't it sad that so many philosophers and scientists come so close to seeing the reality that lies behind the universe and yet, for some reason, sidestep the great issue of entering into a personal relationship with God? They struggle to know the secrets of the cosmos, and yet miss the 'open secret' of God's revelation through Christ which He laid bare at Calvary. Instead, they try to achieve fellowship through psychological processes that leave the heart estranged.

The popularity of group therapy testifies to the need of the human heart for fellowship. In most countries of the world small groups meet together to encourage, confront, and stimulate one another towards good emotional health and maturity. The world is waking up to the fact that we are made for fellowship. Oh, if only they could see that fellowship which does not begin with God, does not begin.

PRAYER

Father, I am so thankful for the discovery that fellowship cannot be produced by trying but by trusting. It begins and ends with You. Take me deeper into Your heart that I might take others deeper into mine. For Jesus' sake. Amen.

FURTHER STUDY

1 John 1:1-7; Rom. 1:11-12; 12:5
· What is the purpose of fellowship?
· Whom do you have fellowship with?

June 26

■ 2 KINGS 2:1–3:27

2 When the LORD was about to take Elijah up to heaven in a whirlwind, Elijah and Elisha were on their way from Gilgal. ² Elijah said to Elisha, 'Stay here; the LORD has sent me to Bethel.'

But Elisha said, 'As surely as the LORD lives and as you live, I will not leave you.' So they went down to Bethel.

³ The company of the prophets at Bethel came out to Elisha and asked, 'Do you know that the LORD is going to take your master from you today?'

'Yes, I know,' Elisha replied, 'so be quiet.'

⁴ Then Elijah said to him, 'Stay here, Elisha; the LORD has sent me to Jericho.'

And he replied, 'As surely as the LORD lives and as you live, I will not leave you.' So they went to Jericho.

⁵ The company of the prophets at Jericho went up to Elisha and asked him, 'Do you know that the LORD is going to take your master from you today?'

'Yes, I know,' he replied, 'so be quiet.'

⁶ Then Elijah said to him, 'Stay here; the LORD has sent me to the Jordan.'

And he replied, 'As surely as the LORD lives and as you live, I will not leave you.' So the two of them walked on.

⁷Fifty men from the company of the prophets went and stood at a distance, facing the place where Elijah and Elisha had stopped at the Jordan. ⁸Elijah took his cloak, rolled it up and struck the water with it. The water divided to the right and to the left, and the two of them crossed over on dry ground.

⁹When they had crossed, Elijah said to Elisha, 'Tell me, what can I do for you before I am taken from you?'

'Let me inherit a double portion of your spirit,' Elisha replied.

¹⁰'You have asked a difficult thing,' Elijah said, 'yet if you see me when I am taken from you, it will be yours – otherwise, it will not.'

¹¹As they were walking along and talking together, suddenly a chariot of fire and horses of fire appeared and separated the two of them, and Elijah went up to heaven in a whirlwind. ¹²Elisha saw this and cried out, 'My father! My father! The chariots and horsemen of Israel!' And Elisha saw him no more. Then he took hold of his garment and tore it in two.

¹³Elisha then picked up Elijah's cloak that had fallen from him and went back and stood on the bank of the Jordan. ¹⁴He took the cloak that had fallen from Elijah and struck the water with it. 'Where now is the LORD, the God of Elijah?' he asked. When he struck the water, it divided to the right and to the left, and he crossed over.

¹⁵The company of the prophets from Jericho, who were watching, said, 'The spirit of Elijah is resting on Elisha.' And they went to meet him and bowed to the ground before him. ¹⁶'Look,' they said, 'we your servants have fifty able men. Let them go and look for your master. Perhaps the Spirit of the LORD has picked him up and set him down on some mountain or in some valley.'

'No,' Elisha replied, 'do not send them.'

¹⁷But they persisted until he was too embarrassed to refuse. So he said, 'Send them.'

And they sent fifty men, who searched for three days but did not find him. ¹⁸When they returned to Elisha, who was staying in Jericho, he said to them, 'Didn't I tell you not to go?'

¹⁹The people of the city said to Elisha, 'Look, our lord, this town is well situated, as you can see, but the water is bad and the land is unproductive.'

²⁰'Bring me a new bowl,' he said, 'and put salt in it.' So they brought it to him.

²¹Then he went out to the spring and threw the salt into it, saying, 'This is what the LORD says: "I have healed this water. Never again will it cause death or make the land unproductive."' ²²And the water has remained pure to this day, according to the word Elisha had spoken.

²³From there Elisha went up to Bethel. As he was walking along the road, some boys came out of the town and jeered at him. 'Get out of here, baldy!' they said. 'Get out of here, baldy!' ²⁴He turned round, looked at them and called down a curse on them in the name of the LORD. Then two bears came out of the woods and mauled forty-two of the boys. ²⁵And he went on to Mount Carmel and from there returned to Samaria.

3 Joram son of Ahab became king of Israel in Samaria in the eighteenth year of Jehoshaphat king of Judah, and he reigned for twelve years. ²He did evil in the eyes of the LORD, but not as his father and mother had done. He got rid of the sacred stone of Baal that his father had made. ³Nevertheless he clung to the sins of Jeroboam son of Nebat, which he had caused Israel to commit; he did not turn away from them.

⁴Now Mesha king of Moab raised sheep, and he had to pay the king of Israel a tribute of a hundred thousand lambs and the wool of a hundred thousand rams. ⁵But after Ahab died, the king of Moab rebelled against the king of Israel. ⁶So at that time King Joram set out from Samaria and mobilised all Israel. ⁷He also sent this message

to Jehoshaphat king of Judah: 'The king of Moab has rebelled against me. Will you go with me to fight against Moab?'

'I will go with you,' he replied. 'I am as you are, my people as your people, my horses as your horses.'

⁸'By what route shall we attack?' he asked.

'Through the Desert of Edom,' he answered.

⁹So the king of Israel set out with the king of Judah and the king of Edom. After a roundabout march of seven days, the army had no more water for themselves or for the animals with them.

¹⁰'What!' exclaimed the king of Israel. 'Has the LORD called us three kings together only to deliver us into the hands of Moab?'

¹¹But Jehoshaphat asked, 'Is there no prophet of the LORD here, through whom we may enquire of the LORD?'

An officer of the king of Israel answered, 'Elisha son of Shaphat is here. He used to pour water on the hands of Elijah.'

¹²Jehoshaphat said, 'The word of the LORD is with him.' So the king of Israel and Jehoshaphat and the king of Edom went down to him.

¹³Elisha said to the king of Israel, 'Why do you want to involve me? Go to the prophets of your father and the prophets of your mother.'

'No,' the king of Israel answered, 'because it was the LORD who called us three kings together to deliver us into the hands of Moab.'

¹⁴Elisha said, 'As surely as the LORD Almighty lives, whom I serve, if I did not have respect for the presence of Jehoshaphat king of Judah, I would not pay any attention to you. ¹⁵But now bring me a harpist.'

While the harpist was playing, the hand of the LORD came on Elisha ¹⁶and he said, 'This is what the LORD says: I will fill this valley with pools of water. ¹⁷For this is what the LORD says: you will see neither wind nor rain, yet this valley will be filled with water, and you, your cattle and your other animals will drink. ¹⁸This is an easy thing in the eyes of the LORD; he will also deliver Moab into your hands. ¹⁹You will overthrow every fortified city and every major town. You will cut down every good tree, block up all the springs, and ruin every good field with stones.'

²⁰The next morning, about the time for offering the sacrifice, there it was – water flowing from the direction of Edom! And the land was filled with water.

²¹Now all the Moabites had heard that the kings had come to fight against them; so every man, young and old, who could bear arms was called up and stationed on the border. ²²When they got up early in the morning, the sun was shining on the water. To the Moabites across the way, the water looked red – like blood. ²³'That's blood!' they said. 'Those kings must have fought and slaughtered each other. Now to the plunder, Moab!'

²⁴But when the Moabites came to the camp of Israel, the Israelites rose up and fought them until they fled. And the Israelites invaded the land and slaughtered the Moabites. ²⁵They destroyed the towns, and each man threw a stone on every good field until it was covered. They stopped up all the springs and cut down every good tree. Only Kir Hareseth was left with its stones in place, but men armed with slings surrounded it and attacked it.

²⁶When the king of Moab saw that the battle had gone against him, he took with him seven hundred swordsmen to break through to the king of Edom, but they failed. ²⁷Then he took his firstborn son, who was to succeed him as king, and offered him as a sacrifice on the city wall. The fury against Israel was great; they withdrew and returned to their own land.

■ PSALM 76:7–12

⁷ It is you alone who are to be feared.
　　Who can stand before you when you
　　　are angry?
⁸ From heaven you pronounced judgment,
　　and the land feared and was quiet –
⁹ when you, God, rose up to judge,
　　to save all the afflicted of the land.
¹⁰ Surely your wrath against mankind
　　　brings you praise,
　　and the survivors of your wrath are
　　　restrained.

¹¹ Make vows to the LORD your God and
　　　fulfil them;
　　let all the neighbouring lands
　　　bring gifts to the One to be feared.
¹² He breaks the spirit of rulers;
　　he is feared by the kings of the earth.

■ PROVERBS 16:20

²⁰ Whoever gives heed to instruction
　　　prospers,
　　and blessed is the one who trusts in
　　　the LORD.

■ ACTS 3:1–26

3 One day Peter and John were going up to the temple at the time of prayer – at three in the afternoon. ² Now a man who was lame from birth was being carried to the temple gate called Beautiful, where he was put every day to beg from those going into the temple courts. ³ When he saw Peter and John about to enter, he asked them for money. ⁴ Peter looked straight at him, as did John. Then Peter said, 'Look at us!' ⁵ So the man gave them his attention, expecting to get something from them.

⁶ Then Peter said, 'Silver or gold I do not have, but what I do have I give you. In the name of Jesus Christ of Nazareth, walk.' ⁷ Taking him by the right hand, he helped him up, and instantly the man's feet and ankles became strong. ⁸ He jumped to his feet and began to walk. Then he went with them into the temple courts, walking and jumping, and praising God. ⁹ When all the people saw him walking and praising God, ¹⁰ they recognised him as the same man who used to sit begging at the temple gate called Beautiful, and they were filled with wonder and amazement at what had happened to him.

¹¹ While the man held on to Peter and John, all the people were astonished and came running to them in the place called Solomon's Colonnade. ¹² When Peter saw this, he said to them: 'Fellow Israelites, why does this surprise you? Why do you stare at us as if by our own power or godliness we had made this man walk? ¹³ The God of Abraham, Isaac and Jacob, the God of our fathers, has glorified his servant Jesus. You handed him over to be killed, and you disowned him before Pilate, though he had decided to let him go. ¹⁴ You disowned the Holy and Righteous One and asked that a murderer be released to you. ¹⁵ You killed the author of life, but God raised him from the dead. We are witnesses of this. ¹⁶ By faith in the name of Jesus, this man whom you see and know was made strong. It is Jesus' name and the faith that comes through him that has completely healed him, as you can all see.

¹⁷ 'Now, fellow Israelites, I know that you acted in ignorance, as did your leaders. ¹⁸ But this is how God fulfilled what he had foretold through all the prophets, saying that his Messiah would suffer. ¹⁹ Repent, then, and turn to God, so that your sins may be wiped out, that times of refreshing may come from the Lord, ²⁰ and that he may send the Messiah, who has been appointed for you – even Jesus. ²¹ Heaven must receive him until the time comes for God to restore everything, as he promised long ago through his holy prophets. ²² For Moses said, "The Lord your

God will raise up for you a prophet like me from among your own people; you must listen to everything he tells you. ²³Anyone who does not listen to him will be completely cut off from their people."

²⁴'Indeed, beginning with Samuel, all the prophets who have spoken have foretold these days. ²⁵And you are heirs of the prophets and of the covenant God made with your fathers. He said to Abraham, "Through your offspring all peoples on earth will be blessed." ²⁶When God raised up his servant, he sent him first to you to bless you by turning each of you from your wicked ways.'

'But Your Head Is Gone'

'Repent, then, and turn to God, so that your sins may be wiped out, that times of refreshing may come from the Lord ...' Acts 3:19

One of the things we must do if we are to stay spiritually fresh is to break decisively with everything that Christ cannot approve.

When we are fighting sin and evil, we are fighting a defeated foe, because Jesus met and conquered every sin on the cross. You will never meet a single sin that has not been defeated by Christ. So if sin is bullying you, do what E. Stanley Jones advised. He said, 'When sin intimidates me, I quietly ask it to bend its neck. When it does, I joyfully point to the footprints of the Son of God on its neck. My inferiority complex is gone. I am on the winning side'. This language may be picturesque, but the truth is powerful – because of what Christ has accomplished on Calvary, we walk the earth amid conquered foes.

A far-fetched but illustrative story from the ancient battles of Africa tells how a warrior was beheaded during a skirmish, but he fought on even though his head was gone. He succeeded in killing many until someone said, 'But your head has gone! You're dead,' whereupon he fell down and died. When sin comes against you, point and say, 'Look, your head has gone. My Master conquered you on the cross. Begone! You are headless'. Evil fights on, but it is brainless. It depends on prejudices, old habits, and perhaps above all on our lack of decisiveness. So if there are still any sins in your life that need to be dealt with, face them in the assurance that they are conquered foes, and break decisively with everything that Christ cannot approve.

PRAYER

O God, thank You for reminding me that I need not develop an inferiority complex in relation to sin – it is a conquered foe. Help me to accept and enter into the great victory of Calvary. In Christ's powerful name. Amen.

FURTHER STUDY

1 John 1; Prov. 28:13; Col. 2:14
• What prevents us from prospering?
• How are we to deal with sin?

June 27

■ **2 KINGS 4:1–5:14**

4 The wife of a man from the company of the prophets cried out to Elisha, 'Your servant my husband is dead, and you know that he revered the LORD. But now his creditor is coming to take my two boys as his slaves.'

[2] Elisha replied to her, 'How can I help you? Tell me, what do you have in your house?'

'Your servant has nothing there at all,' she said, 'except a small jar of olive oil.'

[3] Elisha said, 'Go round and ask all your neighbours for empty jars. Don't ask for just a few. [4] Then go inside and shut the door behind you and your sons. Pour oil into all the jars, and as each is filled, put it to one side.'

[5] She left him and shut the door behind her and her sons. They brought the jars to her and she kept pouring. [6] When all the jars were full, she said to her son, 'Bring me another one.'

But he replied, 'There is not a jar left.' Then the oil stopped flowing.

[7] She went and told the man of God, and he said, 'Go, sell the oil and pay your debts. You and your sons can live on what is left.'

[8] One day Elisha went to Shunem. And a well-to-do woman was there, who urged him to stay for a meal. So whenever he passed by, he stopped there to eat. [9] She said to her husband, 'I know that this man who often comes our way is a holy man of God. [10] Let's make a small room on the roof and put in it a bed and a table, a chair and a lamp for him. Then he can stay there whenever he comes to us.'

[11] One day when Elisha came, he went up to his room and lay down there. [12] He said to his servant Gehazi, 'Call the Shunammite.' So he called her, and she stood before him.

[13] Elisha said to him, 'Tell her, "You have gone to all this trouble for us. Now what can be done for you? Can we speak on your behalf to the king or the commander of the army?"'

She replied, 'I have a home among my own people.'

[14] 'What can be done for her?' Elisha asked.

Gehazi said, 'She has no son, and her husband is old.'

[15] Then Elisha said, 'Call her.' So he called her, and she stood in the doorway. [16] 'About this time next year,' Elisha said, 'you will hold a son in your arms.'

'No, my lord!' she objected. 'Please, man of God, don't mislead your servant!'

[17] But the woman became pregnant, and the next year about that same time she gave birth to a son, just as Elisha had told her.

[18] The child grew, and one day he went out to his father, who was with the reapers. [19] He said to his father, 'My head! My head!'

His father told a servant, 'Carry him to his mother.' [20] After the servant had lifted him up and carried him to his mother, the boy sat on her lap until noon, and then he died. [21] She went up and laid him on the bed of the man of God, then shut the door and went out.

[22] She called her husband and said, 'Please send me one of the servants and a donkey so I can go to the man of God quickly and return.'

[23] 'Why go to him today?' he asked. 'It's not the New Moon or the Sabbath.'

'That's all right,' she said.

[24] She saddled the donkey and said to her servant, 'Lead on; don't slow down for me unless I tell you.' [25] So she set out and came to the man of God at Mount Carmel.

When he saw her in the distance, the man of God said to his servant Gehazi, 'Look! There's the Shunammite! ²⁶Run to meet her and ask her, "Are you all right? Is your husband all right? Is your child all right?"'

'Everything is all right,' she said.

²⁷When she reached the man of God at the mountain, she took hold of his feet. Gehazi came over to push her away, but the man of God said, 'Leave her alone! She is in bitter distress, but the LORD has hidden it from me and has not told me why.'

²⁸'Did I ask you for a son, my lord?' she said. 'Didn't I tell you, "Don't raise my hopes"?'

²⁹Elisha said to Gehazi, 'Tuck your cloak into your belt, take my staff in your hand and run. Don't greet anyone you meet, and if anyone greets you, do not answer. Lay my staff on the boy's face.'

³⁰But the child's mother said, 'As surely as the LORD lives and as you live, I will not leave you.' So he got up and followed her.

³¹Gehazi went on ahead and laid the staff on the boy's face, but there was no sound or response. So Gehazi went back to meet Elisha and told him, 'The boy has not awakened.'

³²When Elisha reached the house, there was the boy lying dead on his couch. ³³He went in, shut the door on the two of them and prayed to the LORD. ³⁴Then he got on the bed and lay on the boy, mouth to mouth, eyes to eyes, hands to hands. As he stretched himself out on him, the boy's body grew warm. ³⁵Elisha turned away and walked back and forth in the room and then got onto the bed and stretched out on him once more. The boy sneezed seven times and opened his eyes.

³⁶Elisha summoned Gehazi and said, 'Call the Shunammite.' And he did. When she came, he said, 'Take your son.' ³⁷She came in, fell at his feet and bowed to the ground. Then she took her son and went out.

³⁸Elisha returned to Gilgal and there was a famine in that region. While the company of the prophets was meeting with him, he said to his servant, 'Put on the large pot and cook some stew for these prophets.'

³⁹One of them went out into the fields to gather herbs and found a wild gourd plant and picked as many of its gourds as his garment could hold. When he returned, he cut them up into the pot of stew, though no one knew what they were. ⁴⁰The stew was poured out for the men, but as they began to eat it, they cried out, 'Man of God, there is death in the pot!' And they could not eat it.

⁴¹Elisha said, 'Get some flour.' He put it into the pot and said, 'Serve it to the people to eat.' And there was nothing harmful in the pot.

⁴²A man came from Baal Shalishah, bringing the man of God twenty loaves of barley bread baked from the first ripe corn, along with some ears of new corn. 'Give it to the people to eat,' Elisha said.

⁴³'How can I set this before a hundred men?' his servant asked.

But Elisha answered, 'Give it to the people to eat. For this is what the LORD says: "They will eat and have some left over."' ⁴⁴Then he set it before them, and they ate and had some left over, according to the word of the LORD.

5 Now Naaman was commander of the army of the king of Aram. He was a great man in the sight of his master and highly regarded, because through him the LORD had given victory to Aram. He was a valiant soldier, but he had leprosy.

²Now bands of raiders from Aram had gone out and had taken captive a young girl from Israel, and she served Naaman's wife. ³She said to her mistress, 'If only my master would see the prophet who is in Samaria! He would cure him of his leprosy.'

⁴Naaman went to his master and told him what the girl from Israel had said. ⁵'By all means, go,' the king of Aram replied. 'I will send a letter to the king of Israel.' So Naaman left, taking with him ten talents of

silver, six thousand shekels of gold and ten sets of clothing. ⁶The letter that he took to the king of Israel read: 'With this letter I am sending my servant Naaman to you so that you may cure him of his leprosy.'

⁷As soon as the king of Israel read the letter, he tore his robes and said, 'Am I God? Can I kill and bring back to life? Why does this fellow send someone to me to be cured of his leprosy? See how he is trying to pick a quarrel with me!'

⁸When Elisha the man of God heard that the king of Israel had torn his robes, he sent him this message: 'Why have you torn your robes? Make the man come to me and he will know that there is a prophet in Israel.' ⁹So Naaman went with his horses and chariots and stopped at the door of Elisha's house. ¹⁰Elisha sent a messenger to say to him, 'Go, wash yourself seven times in the Jordan, and your flesh will be restored and you will be cleansed.'

¹¹But Naaman went away angry and said, 'I thought that he would surely come out to me and stand and call on the name of the LORD his God, wave his hand over the spot and cure me of my leprosy. ¹²Are not Abana and Pharpar, the rivers of Damascus, better than all the waters of Israel? Couldn't I wash in them and be cleansed?' So he turned and went off in a rage.

¹³Naaman's servants went to him and said, 'My father, if the prophet had told you to do some great thing, would you not have done it? How much more, then, when he tells you, "Wash and be cleansed"!' ¹⁴So he went down and dipped himself in the Jordan seven times, as the man of God had told him, and his flesh was restored and became clean like that of a young boy.

▬ PSALM 77:1-6

¹I cried out to God for help;
  I cried out to God to hear me.

²When I was in distress, I sought the
    Lord;
  at night I stretched out untiring hands,
  and I would not be comforted.

³I remembered you, God, and I groaned;
  I meditated, and my spirit grew faint.
⁴You kept my eyes from closing;
  I was too troubled to speak.
⁵I thought about the former days,
  the years of long ago;
⁶I remembered my songs in the night.
  My heart meditated and my spirit
    asked ...

▬ PROVERBS 16:21-22

²¹The wise in heart are called discerning,
  and gracious words promote
    instruction.

²²Prudence is a fountain of life to the
    prudent,
  but folly brings punishment to fools.

▬ ACTS 4:1-22

4 The priests and the captain of the temple guard and the Sadducees came up to Peter and John while they were speaking to the people. ²They were greatly disturbed because the apostles were teaching the people, proclaiming in Jesus the resurrection of the dead. ³They seized Peter and John and, because it was evening, they put them in jail until the next day. ⁴But many who heard the message believed; so the number of men who believed grew to about five thousand.

⁵The next day the rulers, the elders and the teachers of the law met in Jerusalem. ⁶Annas the high priest was there, and so were Caiaphas, John, Alexander and others of the high priest's family. ⁷They had Peter and John brought before them and began

to question them: 'By what power or what name did you do this?'

⁸Then Peter, filled with the Holy Spirit, said to them: 'Rulers and elders of the people! ⁹If we are being called to account today for an act of kindness shown to a man who was lame and are being asked how he was healed, ¹⁰then know this, you and all the people of Israel: it is by the name of Jesus Christ of Nazareth, whom you crucified but whom God raised from the dead, that this man stands before you healed. ¹¹Jesus is

' "the stone you builders rejected,
    which has become the cornerstone."

¹²Salvation is found in no one else, for there is no other name under heaven given to mankind by which we must be saved.'

¹³When they saw the courage of Peter and John and realised that they were unschooled, ordinary men, they were astonished and they took note that these men had been with Jesus. ¹⁴But since they could see the man who had been healed standing there with them, there was nothing they could say. ¹⁵So they ordered them to withdraw from the Sanhedrin and then conferred together. ¹⁶'What are we going to do with these men?' they asked. 'Everyone living in Jerusalem knows they have performed a notable sign, and we cannot deny it. ¹⁷But to stop this thing from spreading any further among the people, we must warn them to speak no longer to anyone in this name.'

¹⁸Then they called them in again and commanded them not to speak or teach at all in the name of Jesus. ¹⁹But Peter and John replied, 'Which is right in God's eyes: to listen to you, or to him? You be the judges! ²⁰As for us, we cannot help speaking about what we have seen and heard.'

²¹After further threats they let them go. They could not decide how to punish them, because all the people were praising God for what had happened. ²²For the man who was miraculously healed was over forty years old.

No Other Name

'Salvation is found in no one else ...' **Acts 4:12**

We must continually watch out for statements that assert that all religions are the same, for when they are repeated over and over again, and by seemingly sincere people, we can be brainwashed into accepting them.

In 1966, when the first multi-faith service was held in an Anglican church in London, in which Hindus, Buddhists, Muslims and Christians took part on equal terms, some Christian newspapers described it as a 'betrayal of the faith'. Nowadays there is hardly a mention of such services although they take place regularly in different parts of our nation and also in other countries. People seem to have given up the idea of syncretism – the idea that all religions can be fused into one – and are focusing more on pluralism – the recognition of each faith as being of equal value. I take my stand with Dr. Visser't Hooft, who said: 'It is high time that Christians should rediscover that Jesus Christ did not come to make a contribution to the religious storehouse of mankind, but that in Him God reconciled the world unto Himself'.

The words of our text for today were displayed outside a church in London until the minister was told by the local authority to take the poster down as it offended some local inhabitants who were adherents of other faiths. 'It is not the best way to love one's neighbour as oneself' was how one critic put it. But how can we love our neighbour as ourselves if we make no attempt to share with them the knowledge of salvation in Jesus Christ?

PRAYER

O Father, in an age when the faith once delivered to the saints is being watered down, deepen my understanding of it so that I may contend for it without being contentious. In Christ's name I pray. Amen.

FURTHER STUDY

John 3:1-17; 6:35; 14:6
- What Old Testament example shows there is only one way to salvation?
- What did Jesus declare about Himself?

June 28

2 KINGS 5:15–7:9

15 Then Naaman and all his attendants went back to the man of God. He stood before him and said, 'Now I know that there is no God in all the world except in Israel. So please accept a gift from your servant.'

16 The prophet answered, 'As surely as the LORD lives, whom I serve, I will not accept a thing.' And even though Naaman urged him, he refused.

17 'If you will not,' said Naaman, 'please let me, your servant, be given as much earth as a pair of mules can carry, for your servant will never again make burnt offerings and sacrifices to any other god but the LORD. 18 But may the LORD forgive your servant for this one thing: when my master enters the temple of Rimmon to bow down and he is leaning on my arm and I have to bow there also – when I bow down in the temple of Rimmon, may the LORD forgive your servant for this.'

19 'Go in peace,' Elisha said.

After Naaman had travelled some distance, 20 Gehazi, the servant of Elisha the man of God, said to himself, 'My master was too easy on Naaman, this Aramean, by not accepting from him what he brought. As surely as the LORD lives, I will run after him and get something from him.'

21 So Gehazi hurried after Naaman. When Naaman saw him running towards him, he got down from the chariot to meet him. 'Is everything all right?' he asked.

22 'Everything is all right,' Gehazi answered. 'My master sent me to say, "Two young men from the company of the prophets have just come to me from the hill country of Ephraim. Please give them a talent of silver and two sets of clothing."'

23 'By all means, take two talents,' said Naaman. He urged Gehazi to accept them, and then tied up the two talents of silver in two bags, with two sets of clothing. He gave them to two of his servants, and they carried them ahead of Gehazi. 24 When Gehazi came to the hill, he took the things from the servants and put them away in the house.

He sent the men away and they left.

²⁵When he went in and stood before his master, Elisha asked him, 'Where have you been, Gehazi?'

'Your servant didn't go anywhere,' Gehazi answered.

²⁶But Elisha said to him, 'Was not my spirit with you when the man got down from his chariot to meet you? Is this the time to take money or to accept clothes – or olive groves and vineyards, or flocks and herds, or male and female slaves? ²⁷Naaman's leprosy will cling to you and to your descendants for ever.' Then Gehazi went from Elisha's presence and his skin was leprous – it had become as white as snow.

6 The company of the prophets said to Elisha, 'Look, the place where we meet with you is too small for us. ²Let us go to the Jordan, where each of us can get a pole; and let us build a place there for us to meet.'

And he said, 'Go.'

³Then one of them said, 'Won't you please come with your servants?'

'I will,' Elisha replied. ⁴And he went with them.

They went to the Jordan and began to cut down trees. ⁵As one of them was cutting down a tree, the iron axe-head fell into the water. 'Oh no, my lord!' he cried out. 'It was borrowed!'

⁶The man of God asked, 'Where did it fall?' When he showed him the place, Elisha cut a stick and threw it there, and made the iron float. ⁷'Lift it out,' he said. Then the man reached out his hand and took it.

⁸Now the king of Aram was at war with Israel. After conferring with his officers, he said, 'I will set up my camp in such and such a place.'

⁹The man of God sent word to the king of Israel: 'Beware of passing that place, because the Arameans are going down there.' ¹⁰So the king of Israel checked on the place indicated by the man of God. Time and again Elisha warned the king, so that he was on his guard in such places.

¹¹This enraged the king of Aram. He summoned his officers and demanded of them, 'Tell me! Which of us is on the side of the king of Israel?'

¹²'None of us, my lord the king,' said one of his officers, 'but Elisha, the prophet who is in Israel, tells the king of Israel the very words you speak in your bedroom.'

¹³'Go, find out where he is,' the king ordered, 'so that I can send men and capture him.' The report came back: 'He is in Dothan.' ¹⁴Then he sent horses and chariots and a strong force there. They went by night and surrounded the city.

¹⁵When the servant of the man of God got up and went out early the next morning, an army with horses and chariots had surrounded the city. 'Oh no, my lord! What shall we do?' the servant asked.

¹⁶'Don't be afraid,' the prophet answered. 'Those who are with us are more than those who are with them.'

¹⁷And Elisha prayed, 'Open his eyes, LORD, so that he may see.' Then the LORD opened the servant's eyes, and he looked and saw the hills full of horses and chariots of fire all round Elisha.

¹⁸As the enemy came down towards him, Elisha prayed to the LORD, 'Strike this army with blindness.' So he struck them with blindness, as Elisha had asked.

¹⁹Elisha told them, 'This is not the road and this is not the city. Follow me, and I will lead you to the man you are looking for.' And he led them to Samaria.

²⁰After they entered the city, Elisha said, 'LORD, open the eyes of these men so that they can see.' Then the LORD opened their eyes and they looked, and there they were, inside Samaria.

²¹When the king of Israel saw them, he asked Elisha, 'Shall I kill them, my father? Shall I kill them?'

²²'Do not kill them,' he answered. 'Would you kill those you have captured with your

own sword or bow? Set food and water before them so that they may eat and drink and then go back to their master.' 23 So he prepared a great feast for them, and after they had finished eating and drinking, he sent them away, and they returned to their master. So the bands from Aram stopped raiding Israel's territory.

24 Some time later, Ben-Hadad king of Aram mobilised his entire army and marched up and laid siege to Samaria. 25 There was a great famine in the city; the siege lasted so long that a donkey's head sold for eighty shekels of silver, and a quarter of a cab of seed pods for five shekels.

26 As the king of Israel was passing by on the wall, a woman cried to him, 'Help me, my lord the king!'

27 The king replied, 'If the LORD does not help you, where can I get help for you? From the threshing floor? From the winepress?' 28 Then he asked her, 'What's the matter?'

She answered, 'This woman said to me, "Give up your son so that we may eat him today, and tomorrow we'll eat my son." 29 So we cooked my son and ate him. The next day I said to her, "Give up your son so that we may eat him," but she had hidden him.'

30 When the king heard the woman's words, he tore his robes. As he went along the wall, the people looked, and they saw that, under his robes, he had sackcloth on his body. 31 He said, 'May God deal with me, be it ever so severely, if the head of Elisha son of Shaphat remains on his shoulders today!'

32 Now Elisha was sitting in his house, and the elders were sitting with him. The king sent a messenger ahead, but before he arrived, Elisha said to the elders, 'Don't you see how this murderer is sending someone to cut off my head? Look, when the messenger comes, shut the door and hold it shut against him. Is not the sound of his master's footsteps behind him?' 33 While he was still talking to them, the messenger came down to him.

The king said, 'This disaster is from the LORD. Why should I wait for the LORD any longer?'

7 Elisha replied, 'Hear the word of the LORD. This is what the LORD says: about this time tomorrow, a seah of the finest flour will sell for a shekel and two seahs of barley for a shekel at the gate of Samaria.'

2 The officer on whose arm the king was leaning said to the man of God, 'Look, even if the LORD should open the floodgates of the heavens, could this happen?'

'You will see it with your own eyes,' answered Elisha, 'but you will not eat any of it!'

3 Now there were four men with leprosy at the entrance of the city gate. They said to each other, 'Why stay here until we die? 4 If we say, "We'll go into the city" – the famine is there, and we will die. And if we stay here, we will die. So let's go over to the camp of the Arameans and surrender. If they spare us, we live; if they kill us, then we die.'

5 At dusk they got up and went to the camp of the Arameans. When they reached the edge of the camp, no one was there, 6 for the Lord had caused the Arameans to hear the sound of chariots and horses and a great army, so that they said to one another, 'Look, the king of Israel has hired the Hittite and Egyptian kings to attack us!' 7 So they got up and fled in the dusk and abandoned their tents and their horses and donkeys. They left the camp as it was and ran for their lives.

8 The men who had leprosy reached the edge of the camp, entered one of the tents and ate and drank. Then they took silver, gold and clothes, and went off and hid them. They returned and entered another tent and took some things from it and hid them also.

9 Then they said to each other, 'What we're doing is not right. This is a day of good news and we are keeping it to ourselves. If we wait until daylight, punishment will

overtake us. Let's go at once and report this to the royal palace.'

■ PSALM 77:7-12

7 'Will the Lord reject for ever?
   Will he never show his favour again?
8 Has his unfailing love vanished for ever?
   Has his promise failed for all time?
9 Has God forgotten to be merciful?
   Has he in anger withheld his
      compassion?'

10 Then I thought, 'To this I will appeal:
   the years when the Most High
      stretched out his right hand.
11 I will remember the deeds of the LORD;
   yes, I will remember your miracles of
      long ago.
12 I will consider all your works
   and meditate on all your mighty
      deeds.'

■ PROVERBS 16:23-24

23 The hearts of the wise make their
      mouths prudent,
   and their lips promote instruction.

24 Gracious words are a honeycomb,
   sweet to the soul and healing to the
      bones.

■ ACTS 4:23–5:11

23 On their release, Peter and John went back to their own people and reported all that the chief priests and the elders had said to them. 24 When they heard this, they raised their voices together in prayer to God. 'Sovereign Lord,' they said, 'you made the heavens and the earth and the sea, and everything in them. 25 You spoke by the Holy Spirit through the mouth of your servant, our father David:

"'Why do the nations rage
   and the peoples plot in vain?
26 The kings of the earth rise up
   and the rulers band together
   against the Lord
   and against his anointed one."

27 Indeed Herod and Pontius Pilate met together with the Gentiles and the people of Israel in this city to conspire against your holy servant Jesus, whom you anointed. 28 They did what your power and will had decided beforehand should happen. 29 Now, Lord, consider their threats and enable your servants to speak your word with great boldness. 30 Stretch out your hand to heal and perform signs and wonders through the name of your holy servant Jesus.' 31 After they prayed, the place where they were meeting was shaken. And they were all filled with the Holy Spirit and spoke the word of God boldly.

32 All the believers were one in heart and mind. No one claimed that any of their possessions was their own, but they shared everything they had. 33 With great power the apostles continued to testify to the resurrection of the Lord Jesus. And God's grace was so powerfully at work in them all 34 that there was no needy person among them. For from time to time those who owned land or houses sold them, brought the money from the sales 35 and put it at the apostles' feet, and it was distributed to anyone who had need.

36 Joseph, a Levite from Cyprus, whom the apostles called Barnabas (which means 'son of encouragement'), 37 sold a field he owned and brought the money and put it at the apostles' feet.

5 Now a man named Ananias, together with his wife Sapphira, also sold a piece of property. 2 With his wife's full knowledge he kept back part of the money for

himself, but brought the rest and put it at the apostles' feet.

³ Then Peter said, 'Ananias, how is it that Satan has so filled your heart that you have lied to the Holy Spirit and have kept for yourself some of the money you received for the land? ⁴ Didn't it belong to you before it was sold? And after it was sold, wasn't the money at your disposal? What made you think of doing such a thing? You have not lied just to human beings but to God.'

⁵ When Ananias heard this, he fell down and died. And great fear seized all who heard what had happened. ⁶ Then some young men came forward, wrapped up his body, and carried him out and buried him.

⁷ About three hours later his wife came in, not knowing what had happened. ⁸ Peter asked her, 'Tell me, is this the price you and Ananias got for the land?'

'Yes,' she said, 'that is the price.'

⁹ Peter said to her, 'How could you conspire to test the Spirit of the Lord? Listen! The feet of the men who buried your husband are at the door, and they will carry you out also.'

¹⁰ At that moment she fell down at his feet and died. Then the young men came in and, finding her dead, carried her out and buried her beside her husband. ¹¹ Great fear seized the whole church and all who heard about these events.

Pretence, Consequence

'When Ananias heard this, he fell down and died. And great fear seized all who heard what had happened.'
Acts 5:5

Consider this story about a couple from the Bible who forfeited their lives because they pretended to be more spiritual than they really were.

Ananias and Sapphira were highly respected members of the early church and appeared on the surface to be deeply committed disciples of the Lord Jesus Christ. Doubtless, they had a fairly high degree of dedication, and they easily went along with the idea of selling their possessions and putting the proceeds into the treasury of the church. Their mistake, of course, was in pretending they had given their all when in reality they hadn't, and the consequences that fell to them because of their pretences were swift and dramatic.

God deals harshly with dishonesty, but He is compassionate to those who see themselves as they really are, who confess this to Him, and who request His help in becoming the people they know He wants them to be.

I have known people who have stood up in front of a Christian audience and talked about how wonderful it is to live a victorious Christian life, when in reality they were inwardly messed up. And I have known of others getting up before their brothers and sisters, confessing that though they love the Lord, they are experiencing great struggles and difficulties in seeking to live for Him. Who do you think is the closer to God? I will tell you – it is the one who is honest and open. Pretence repels God; openness and honesty draw Him quickly to our side.

June 29

■ 2 KINGS 7:10–9:13

¹⁰ So they went and called out to the city gatekeepers and told them, 'We went into the Aramean camp and no one was there – not a sound of anyone – only tethered horses and donkeys, and the tents left just as they were.' ¹¹ The gatekeepers shouted the news, and it was reported within the palace.

¹² The king got up in the night and said to his officers, 'I will tell you what the Arameans have done to us. They know we are starving; so they have left the camp to hide in the countryside, thinking, "They will surely come out, and then we will take them alive and get into the city."'

¹³ One of his officers answered, 'Make some men take five of the horses that are left in the city. Their plight will be like that of all the Israelites left here – yes, they will only be like all these Israelites who are doomed. So let us send them to find out what happened.'

¹⁴ So they selected two chariots with their horses, and the king sent them after the Aramean army. He commanded the drivers, 'Go and find out what has happened.' ¹⁵ They followed them as far as the Jordan, and they found the whole road strewn with the clothing and equipment the Arameans had thrown away in their headlong flight. So the messengers returned and reported to the king. ¹⁶ Then the people went out and plundered the camp of the Arameans. So a seah of the finest flour sold for a shekel, and two seahs of barley sold for a shekel, as the LORD had said.

¹⁷ Now the king had put the officer on whose arm he leaned in charge of the gate, and the people trampled him in the gateway, and he died, just as the man of God had foretold when the king came down to his house. ¹⁸ It happened as the man of God had said to the king: 'About this time tomorrow, a seah of the finest flour will sell for a shekel and two seahs of barley for a shekel at the gate of Samaria.'

¹⁹ The officer had said to the man of God, 'Look, even if the LORD should open the floodgates of the heavens, could this happen?' The man of God had replied, 'You will see it with your own eyes, but you will not eat any of it!' ²⁰ And that is exactly what happened to him, for the people trampled him in the gateway, and he died.

8 Now Elisha had said to the woman whose son he had restored to life, 'Go away with your family and stay for a while wherever you can, because the LORD has decreed a famine in the land that will last seven years.' ² The woman proceeded to do as the man of God said. She and her family went away and stayed in the land of

the Philistines for seven years.

³ At the end of the seven years she came back from the land of the Philistines and went to appeal to the king for her house and land. ⁴ The king was talking to Gehazi, the servant of the man of God, and had said, 'Tell me about all the great things Elisha has done.' ⁵ Just as Gehazi was telling the king how Elisha had restored the dead to life, the woman whose son Elisha had brought back to life came to appeal to the king for her house and land.

Gehazi said, 'This is the woman, my lord the king, and this is her son whom Elisha restored to life.' ⁶ The king asked the woman about it, and she told him.

Then he assigned an official to her case and said to him, 'Give back everything that belonged to her, including all the income from her land from the day she left the country until now.'

⁷ Elisha went to Damascus, and Ben-Hadad king of Aram was ill. When the king was told, 'The man of God has come all the way up here,' ⁸ he said to Hazael, 'Take a gift with you and go to meet the man of God. Consult the LORD through him; ask him, "Will I recover from this illness?"'

⁹ Hazael went to meet Elisha, taking with him as a gift forty camel-loads of all the finest wares of Damascus. He went in and stood before him, and said, 'Your son Ben-Hadad king of Aram has sent me to ask, "Will I recover from this illness?"'

¹⁰ Elisha answered, 'Go and say to him, "You will certainly recover." Nevertheless, the LORD has revealed to me that he will in fact die.' ¹¹ He stared at him with a fixed gaze until Hazael was embarrassed. Then the man of God began to weep.

¹² 'Why is my lord weeping?' asked Hazael.

'Because I know the harm you will do to the Israelites,' he answered. 'You will set fire to their fortified places, kill their young men with the sword, dash their little children to the ground, and rip open their pregnant women.'

¹³ Hazael said, 'How could your servant, a mere dog, accomplish such a feat?'

'The LORD has shown me that you will become king of Aram,' answered Elisha.

¹⁴ Then Hazael left Elisha and returned to his master. When Ben-Hadad asked, 'What did Elisha say to you?' Hazael replied, 'He told me that you would certainly recover.' ¹⁵ But the next day he took a thick cloth, soaked it in water and spread it over the king's face, so that he died. Then Hazael succeeded him as king.

¹⁶ In the fifth year of Joram son of Ahab king of Israel, when Jehoshaphat was king of Judah, Jehoram son of Jehoshaphat began his reign as king of Judah. ¹⁷ He was thirty-two years old when he became king, and he reigned in Jerusalem for eight years. ¹⁸ He followed the ways of the kings of Israel, as the house of Ahab had done, for he married a daughter of Ahab. He did evil in the eyes of the LORD. ¹⁹ Nevertheless, for the sake of his servant David, the LORD was not willing to destroy Judah. He had promised to maintain a lamp for David and his descendants for ever.

²⁰ In the time of Jehoram, Edom rebelled against Judah and set up its own king. ²¹ So Jehoram went to Zair with all his chariots. The Edomites surrounded him and his chariot commanders, but he rose up and broke through by night; his army, however, fled back home. ²² To this day Edom has been in rebellion against Judah. Libnah revolted at the same time.

²³ As for the other events of Jehoram's reign, and all he did, are they not written in the book of the annals of the kings of Judah? ²⁴ Jehoram rested with his ancestors and was buried with them in the City of David. And Ahaziah his son succeeded him as king.

²⁵ In the twelfth year of Joram son of Ahab king of Israel, Ahaziah son of Jehoram

king of Judah began to reign. ²⁶Ahaziah was twenty-two years old when he became king, and he reigned in Jerusalem for one year. His mother's name was Athaliah, a granddaughter of Omri king of Israel. ²⁷He followed the ways of the house of Ahab and did evil in the eyes of the LORD, as the house of Ahab had done, for he was related by marriage to Ahab's family.

²⁸Ahaziah went with Joram son of Ahab to war against Hazael king of Aram at Ramoth Gilead. The Arameans wounded Joram; ²⁹so King Joram returned to Jezreel to recover from the wounds the Arameans had inflicted on him at Ramoth in his battle with Hazael king of Aram.

Then Ahaziah son of Jehoram king of Judah went down to Jezreel to see Joram son of Ahab, because he had been wounded.

9 The prophet Elisha summoned a man from the company of the prophets and said to him, 'Tuck your cloak into your belt, take this flask of olive oil with you and go to Ramoth Gilead. ²When you get there, look for Jehu son of Jehoshaphat, the son of Nimshi. Go to him, get him away from his companions and take him into an inner room. ³Then take the flask and pour the oil on his head and declare, "This is what the LORD says: I anoint you king over Israel." Then open the door and run; don't delay!'

⁴So the young prophet went to Ramoth Gilead. ⁵When he arrived, he found the army officers sitting together. 'I have a message for you, commander,' he said.

'For which of us?' asked Jehu.

'For you, commander,' he replied.

⁶Jehu got up and went into the house. Then the prophet poured the oil on Jehu's head and declared, 'This is what the LORD, the God of Israel, says: "I anoint you king over the LORD's people Israel. ⁷You are to destroy the house of Ahab your master, and I will avenge the blood of my servants the prophets and the blood of all the LORD's servants shed by Jezebel. ⁸The whole house of Ahab will perish. I will cut off from Ahab every last male in Israel – slave or free. ⁹I will make the house of Ahab like the house of Jeroboam son of Nebat and like the house of Baasha son of Ahijah. ¹⁰As for Jezebel, dogs will devour her on the plot of ground at Jezreel, and no one will bury her."' Then he opened the door and ran.

¹¹When Jehu went out to his fellow officers, one of them asked him, 'Is everything all right? Why did this maniac come to you?'

'You know the man and the sort of things he says,' Jehu replied.

¹²'That's not true!' they said. 'Tell us.'

Jehu said, 'Here is what he told me: "This is what the LORD says: I anoint you king over Israel."'

¹³They quickly took their cloaks and spread them under him on the bare steps. Then they blew the trumpet and shouted, 'Jehu is king!'

▬ PSALM 77:13-20

¹³Your ways, God, are holy.
    What god is as great as our God?
¹⁴You are the God who performs miracles;
        you display your power among the
        peoples.
¹⁵With your mighty arm you redeemed
            your people,
    the descendants of Jacob and Joseph.

¹⁶The waters saw you, God,
    the waters saw you and writhed;
    the very depths were convulsed.
¹⁷The clouds poured down water,
    the heavens resounded with thunder;
    your arrows flashed back and forth.
¹⁸Your thunder was heard in the
            whirlwind,
    your lightning lit up the world;
    the earth trembled and quaked.

¹⁹ Your path led through the sea,
　　your way through the mighty waters,
　　though your footprints were not seen.

²⁰ You led your people like a flock
　　by the hand of Moses and Aaron.

....

▪ PROVERBS 16:25-26

²⁵ There is a way that appears to be right,
　　but in the end it leads to death.

²⁶ The appetite of labourers works for them;
　　their hunger drives them on.

....

▪ ACTS 5:12-32

¹² The apostles performed many signs and wonders among the people. And all the believers used to meet together in Solomon's Colonnade. ¹³ No one else dared join them, even though they were highly regarded by the people. ¹⁴ Nevertheless, more and more men and women believed in the Lord and were added to their number. ¹⁵ As a result, people brought those who were ill into the streets and laid them on beds and mats so that at least Peter's shadow might fall on some of them as he passed by. ¹⁶ Crowds gathered also from the towns around Jerusalem, bringing those who were ill and those tormented by impure spirits, and all of them were healed.

¹⁷ Then the high priest and all his associates, who were members of the party of the Sadducees, were filled with jealousy. ¹⁸ They arrested the apostles and put them in the public jail. ¹⁹ But during the night an angel of the Lord opened the doors of the jail and brought them out. ²⁰ 'Go, stand in the temple courts,' he said, 'and tell the people all about this new life.'

²¹ At daybreak they entered the temple courts, as they had been told, and began to teach the people.

When the high priest and his associates arrived, they called together the Sanhedrin – the full assembly of the elders of Israel – and sent to the jail for the apostles. ²² But on arriving at the jail, the officers did not find them there. So they went back and reported, ²³ 'We found the jail securely locked, with the guards standing at the doors; but when we opened them, we found no one inside.' ²⁴ On hearing this report, the captain of the temple guard and the chief priests were at a loss, wondering what this might lead to.

²⁵ Then someone came and said, 'Look! The men you put in jail are standing in the temple courts teaching the people.' ²⁶ At that, the captain went with his officers and brought the apostles. They did not use force, because they feared that the people would stone them.

²⁷ The apostles were brought in and made to appear before the Sanhedrin to be questioned by the high priest. ²⁸ 'We gave you strict orders not to teach in this name,' he said. 'Yet you have filled Jerusalem with your teaching and are determined to make us guilty of this man's blood.'

²⁹ Peter and the other apostles replied: 'We must obey God rather than human beings! ³⁰ The God of our ancestors raised Jesus from the dead – whom you killed by hanging him on a cross. ³¹ God exalted him to his own right hand as Prince and Saviour that he might bring Israel to repentance and forgive their sins. ³² We are witnesses of these things, and so is the Holy Spirit, whom God has given to those who obey him.'

The Final Emphasis – Jesus

'We are witnesses of these things, and so is the Holy Spirit, whom God has given to those who obey him.'
Acts 5:32

The Holy Spirit will glorify Jesus. The promise of John 16:14 – 'He will glorify me' – was fulfilled after the Holy Spirit came on the disciples at Pentecost, for we read: 'We are witnesses of these things, and so is the Holy Spirit, whom God has given to those who obey him' (Acts 5:32). This shows that the divine Spirit and human spirits were working together for the same end – the glorification of Jesus.

The statement that the Holy Spirit would glorify Jesus was one of the most important lessons in the process of spiritual education. The whole purpose of the Spirit's coming was not to glorify Himself or the person who receives Him, but to glorify Jesus. That puts the emphasis in the proper place. If the Holy Spirit glorified the person who received Him, then that would make Christianity an eccentric religion – off centre. If He glorified Himself, then it would make Christianity Spirit-centred rather than Christ-centred. Christianity that is not linked to the Incarnation can have no fixed idea as to what God is really like. Spirit-centred Christianity would leave us going off on a tangent into subjectivity.

There are some Christians who are more Spirit-oriented than Christ-oriented. They hear what they describe as the 'voice of the Spirit' telling them to do things. Every 'voice' we hear must be tested against the character of Jesus, and if it doesn't come up to His standard, then it has to be rejected. The Holy Spirit will always glorify Jesus.

PRAYER

O God, my Father, I am conscious that I am thinking through a delicate issue here. Give me such a clear vision of Jesus that I shall always decide according to Him. Amen.

FURTHER STUDY

Matt. 3; Isa. 11:2; 42:1; 61:1; John 1:32, 16:14; Acts 10:38
• What did Isaiah prophesy?
• How was this fulfilled?

June 30

▬ 2 KINGS 9:14–10:36

¹⁴So Jehu son of Jehoshaphat, the son of Nimshi, conspired against Joram. (Now Joram and all Israel had been defending Ramoth Gilead against Hazael king of Aram, ¹⁵but King Joram had returned to Jezreel to recover from the wounds the Arameans

had inflicted on him in the battle with Hazael king of Aram.) Jehu said, 'If you desire to make me king, don't let anyone slip out of the city to go and tell the news in Jezreel.' ¹⁶ Then he got into his chariot and rode to Jezreel, because Joram was resting there and Ahaziah king of Judah had gone down to see him.

¹⁷ When the lookout standing on the tower in Jezreel saw Jehu's troops approaching, he called out, 'I see some troops coming.'

'Get a horseman,' Joram ordered. 'Send him to meet them and ask, "Do you come in peace?"'

¹⁸ The horseman rode off to meet Jehu and said, 'This is what the king says: "Do you come in peace?"'

'What do you have to do with peace?' Jehu replied. 'Fall in behind me.'

The lookout reported, 'The messenger has reached them, but he isn't coming back.'

¹⁹ So the king sent out a second horseman. When he came to them he said, 'This is what the king says: "Do you come in peace?"'

Jehu replied, 'What do you have to do with peace? Fall in behind me.'

²⁰ The lookout reported, 'He has reached them, but he isn't coming back either. The driving is like that of Jehu son of Nimshi – he drives like a maniac.'

²¹ 'Hitch up my chariot,' Joram ordered. And when it was hitched up, Joram king of Israel and Ahaziah king of Judah rode out, each in his own chariot, to meet Jehu. They met him at the plot of ground that had belonged to Naboth the Jezreelite. ²² When Joram saw Jehu he asked, 'Have you come in peace, Jehu?'

'How can there be peace,' Jehu replied, 'as long as all the idolatry and witchcraft of your mother Jezebel abound?'

²³ Joram turned about and fled, calling out to Ahaziah, 'Treachery, Ahaziah!'

²⁴ Then Jehu drew his bow and shot Joram between the shoulders. The arrow pierced his heart and he slumped down in his chariot. ²⁵ Jehu said to Bidkar, his chariot officer,

'Pick him up and throw him on the field that belonged to Naboth the Jezreelite. Remember how you and I were riding together in chariots behind Ahab his father when the LORD spoke this prophecy against him: ²⁶ "Yesterday I saw the blood of Naboth and the blood of his sons, declares the LORD, and I will surely make you pay for it on this plot of ground, declares the LORD." Now then, pick him up and throw him on that plot, in accordance with the word of the LORD.'

²⁷ When Ahaziah king of Judah saw what had happened, he fled up the road to Beth Haggan. Jehu chased him, shouting, 'Kill him too!' They wounded him in his chariot on the way up to Gur near Ibleam, but he escaped to Megiddo and died there. ²⁸ His servants took him by chariot to Jerusalem and buried him with his ancestors in his tomb in the City of David. ²⁹ (In the eleventh year of Joram son of Ahab, Ahaziah had become king of Judah.)

³⁰ Then Jehu went to Jezreel. When Jezebel heard about it, she put on eye makeup, arranged her hair and looked out of a window. ³¹ As Jehu entered the gate, she asked, 'Have you come in peace, you Zimri, you murderer of your master?'

³² He looked up at the window and called out, 'Who is on my side? Who?' Two or three eunuchs looked down at him. ³³ 'Throw her down!' Jehu said. So they threw her down, and some of her blood spattered the wall and the horses as they trampled her underfoot.

³⁴ Jehu went in and ate and drank. 'Take care of that cursed woman,' he said, 'and bury her, for she was a king's daughter.' ³⁵ But when they went out to bury her, they found nothing except her skull, her feet and her hands. ³⁶ They went back and told Jehu, who said, 'This is the word of the LORD that he spoke through his servant Elijah the Tishbite: on the plot of ground at Jezreel dogs will devour Jezebel's flesh. ³⁷ Jezebel's body will be like dung on the ground in the

plot at Jezreel, so that no one will be able to say, "This is Jezebel." '

10 Now there were in Samaria seventy sons of the house of Ahab. So Jehu wrote letters and sent them to Samaria: to the officials of Jezreel, to the elders and to the guardians of Ahab's children. He said, ²'You have your master's sons with you and you have chariots and horses, a fortified city and weapons. Now as soon as this letter reaches you, ³choose the best and most worthy of your master's sons and set him on his father's throne. Then fight for your master's house.'

⁴But they were terrified and said, 'If two kings could not resist him, how can we?'

⁵So the palace administrator, the city governor, the elders and the guardians sent this message to Jehu: 'We are your servants and we will do anything you say. We will not appoint anyone as king; you do whatever you think best.'

⁶Then Jehu wrote them a second letter, saying, 'If you are on my side and will obey me, take the heads of your master's sons and come to me in Jezreel by this time tomorrow.'

Now the royal princes, seventy of them, were with the leading men of the city, who were bringing them up. ⁷When the letter arrived, these men took the princes and slaughtered all seventy of them. They put their heads in baskets and sent them to Jehu in Jezreel. ⁸When the messenger arrived, he told Jehu, 'They have brought the heads of the princes.'

Then Jehu ordered, 'Put them in two piles at the entrance of the city gate until morning.'

⁹The next morning Jehu went out. He stood before all the people and said, 'You are innocent. It was I who conspired against my master and killed him, but who killed all these? ¹⁰Know, then, that not a word the LORD has spoken against the house of Ahab will fail. The LORD has done what he announced through his servant Elijah.' ¹¹So Jehu killed everyone in Jezreel who

remained of the house of Ahab, as well as all his chief men, his close friends and his priests, leaving him no survivor.

¹²Jehu then set out and went towards Samaria. At Beth Eked of the Shepherds, ¹³he met some relatives of Ahaziah king of Judah and asked, 'Who are you?'

They said, 'We are relatives of Ahaziah, and we have come down to greet the families of the king and of the queen mother.'

¹⁴'Take them alive!' he ordered. So they took them alive and slaughtered them by the well of Beth Eked – forty-two of them. He left no survivor.

¹⁵After he left there, he came upon Jehonadab son of Rekab, who was on his way to meet him. Jehu greeted him and said, 'Are you in accord with me, as I am with you?'

'I am,' Jehonadab answered.

'If so,' said Jehu, 'give me your hand.' So he did, and Jehu helped him up into the chariot. ¹⁶Jehu said, 'Come with me and see my zeal for the LORD.' Then he made him ride in his chariot.

¹⁷When Jehu came to Samaria, he killed all who were left there of Ahab's family; he destroyed them, according to the word of the LORD spoken to Elijah.

¹⁸Then Jehu brought all the people together and said to them, 'Ahab served Baal a little; Jehu will serve him much. ¹⁹Now summon all the prophets of Baal, all his servants and all his priests. See that no one is missing, because I am going to hold a great sacrifice for Baal. Anyone who fails to come will no longer live.' But Jehu was acting deceptively in order to destroy the servants of Baal.

²⁰Jehu said, 'Call an assembly in honour of Baal.' So they proclaimed it. ²¹Then he sent word throughout Israel, and all the servants of Baal came; not one stayed away. They crowded into the temple of Baal until it was full from one end to the other. ²²And Jehu said to the keeper of the wardrobe, 'Bring robes for all the servants of Baal.' So he brought out robes for them.

²³Then Jehu and Jehonadab son of Rekab went into the temple of Baal. Jehu said to the servants of Baal, 'Look around and see that no one who serves the LORD is here with you – only servants of Baal.' ²⁴So they went in to make sacrifices and burnt offerings. Now Jehu had posted eighty men outside with this warning: 'If one of you lets any of the men I am placing in your hands escape, it will be your life for his life.'

²⁵As soon as Jehu had finished making the burnt offering, he ordered the guards and officers: 'Go in and kill them; let no one escape.' So they cut them down with the sword. The guards and officers threw the bodies out and then entered the inner shrine of the temple of Baal. ²⁶They brought the sacred stone out of the temple of Baal and burned it. ²⁷They demolished the sacred stone of Baal and tore down the temple of Baal, and people have used it for a latrine to this day.

²⁸So Jehu destroyed Baal worship in Israel. ²⁹However, he did not turn away from the sins of Jeroboam son of Nebat, which he had caused Israel to commit – the worship of the golden calves at Bethel and Dan.

³⁰The LORD said to Jehu, 'Because you have done well in accomplishing what is right in my eyes and have done to the house of Ahab all I had in mind to do, your descendants will sit on the throne of Israel to the fourth generation.' ³¹Yet Jehu was not careful to keep the law of the LORD, the God of Israel, with all his heart. He did not turn away from the sins of Jeroboam, which he had caused Israel to commit.

³²In those days the LORD began to reduce the size of Israel. Hazael overpowered the Israelites throughout their territory ³³east of the Jordan in all the land of Gilead (the region of Gad, Reuben and Manasseh), from Aroer by the Arnon Gorge through Gilead to Bashan.

³⁴As for the other events of Jehu's reign, all he did, and all his achievements, are they not written in the book of the annals of the kings of Israel?

³⁵Jehu rested with his ancestors and was buried in Samaria. And Jehoahaz his son succeeded him as king. ³⁶The time that Jehu reigned over Israel in Samaria was twenty-eight years.

■ PSALM 78:1-8

¹My people, hear my teaching;
    listen to the words of my mouth.
²I will open my mouth with a parable;
    I will utter hidden things, things from
        of old –
³things we have heard and known,
    things our ancestors have told us.
⁴We will not hide them from their
        descendants;
    we will tell the next generation
    the praiseworthy deeds of the LORD,
    his power, and the wonders he has
        done.
⁵He decreed statutes for Jacob
    and established the law in Israel,
    which he commanded our ancestors
    to teach their children,
⁶so that the next generation would know
        them,
    even the children yet to be born,
    and they in turn would tell their
        children.
⁷Then they would put their trust in God
    and would not forget his deeds
    but would keep his commands.
⁸They would not be like their ancestors –
    a stubborn and rebellious generation,
    whose hearts were not loyal to God,
    whose spirits were not faithful to him.

■ PROVERBS 16:27-28

²⁷A scoundrel plots evil,
    and on their lips it is like a scorching
        fire.

28 A perverse person stirs up conflict,
   and a gossip separates close friends.

....

■ ACTS 5:33–6:15

33 When they heard this, they were furious and wanted to put them to death. 34 But a Pharisee named Gamaliel, a teacher of the law, who was honoured by all the people, stood up in the Sanhedrin and ordered that the men be put outside for a little while. 35 Then he addressed the Sanhedrin: 'Men of Israel, consider carefully what you intend to do to these men. 36 Some time ago Theudas appeared, claiming to be somebody, and about four hundred men rallied to him. He was killed, all his followers were dispersed, and it all came to nothing. 37 After him, Judas the Galilean appeared in the days of the census and led a band of people in revolt. He too was killed, and all his followers were scattered. 38 Therefore, in the present case I advise you: leave these men alone! Let them go! For if their purpose or activity is of human origin, it will fail. 39 But if it is from God, you will not be able to stop these men; you will only find yourselves fighting against God.'

40 His speech persuaded them. They called the apostles in and had them flogged. Then they ordered them not to speak in the name of Jesus, and let them go.

41 The apostles left the Sanhedrin, rejoicing because they had been counted worthy of suffering disgrace for the Name. 42 Day after day, in the temple courts and from house to house, they never stopped teaching and proclaiming the good news that Jesus is the Messiah.

6 In those days when the number of disciples was increasing, the Hellenistic Jews among them complained against the Hebraic Jews because their widows were being overlooked in the daily distribution of food. 2 So the Twelve gathered all the disciples together and said, 'It would not be right for us to neglect the ministry of the word of God in order to wait on tables. 3 Brothers and sisters, choose seven men from among you who are known to be full of the Spirit and wisdom. We will turn this responsibility over to them 4 and will give our attention to prayer and the ministry of the word.'

5 This proposal pleased the whole group. They chose Stephen, a man full of faith and of the Holy Spirit; also Philip, Procorus, Nicanor, Timon, Parmenas, and Nicolas from Antioch, a convert to Judaism. 6 They presented these men to the apostles, who prayed and laid their hands on them.

7 So the word of God spread. The number of disciples in Jerusalem increased rapidly, and a large number of priests became obedient to the faith.

8 Now Stephen, a man full of God's grace and power, performed great wonders and signs among the people. 9 Opposition arose, however, from members of the Synagogue of the Freedmen (as it was called) – Jews of Cyrene and Alexandria as well as the provinces of Cilicia and Asia – who began to argue with Stephen. 10 But they could not stand up against the wisdom the Spirit gave him as he spoke.

11 Then they secretly persuaded some men to say, 'We have heard Stephen speak blasphemous words against Moses and against God.'

12 So they stirred up the people and the elders and the teachers of the law. They seized Stephen and brought him before the Sanhedrin. 13 They produced false witnesses, who testified, 'This fellow never stops speaking against this holy place and against the law. 14 For we have heard him say that this Jesus of Nazareth will destroy this place and change the customs Moses handed down to us.'

15 All who were sitting in the Sanhedrin looked intently at Stephen, and they saw that his face was like the face of an angel.

Creative Commonplace

'They chose Stephen, a man full of faith and of the Holy Spirit; also Philip ...' **Acts 6:5**

No matter what happens to you or when it happens to you, it is never too late to become creative. Pray as one man did who was on the verge of a breakdown, 'O Jesus, come into my soul, my mind, my body, into every brain cell, and help me to be a contributive person'. Jesus did come into every brain cell, and that man is now well and contributing to the kingdom of God in an astonishing way.

I wonder, am I talking today to someone who feels they are caught up in so many routines that they are in the rut? Routines often become (if I might coin a word) 'rut'-ines. They make us into grooved, non-creative individuals unless – and this is the point – unless we make the commonplace a creative place. And how do we do that? By the creative spirit we bring to it.

Someone has described Philip the evangelist as 'a third-rate man in a second-rate task who did a first-rate job'. He was quite different from the Philip who was one of Christ's group of twelve disciples. He didn't have the privilege of having been chosen as one of the apostolic band. He was instead one of 'the seven' whose task was 'to wait on tables'. He might have folded up under these limitations and said, 'I am in a rut.' Instead, he accepted the commonplace as a consecrated place and gently pushed against the barriers until they broke. His creativity marks him out as one of the greatest characters of the New Testament.

PRAYER

O God, help me to turn all common places into creative places. Give me the attitude of Your servant Philip, who turned a routine task into a redemptive one. In Jesus' name I pray this. Amen.

FURTHER STUDY

Col. 3:1-10; 2 Cor. 5:17; Rom. 12:2
- In what image is the new self made?
- What are you creating at present?

July 1

■ 2 KINGS 11:1–13:9

11 When Athaliah the mother of Ahaziah saw that her son was dead, she proceeded to destroy the whole royal family. ²But Jehosheba, the daughter of King Jehoram and sister of Ahaziah, took Joash son of Ahaziah and stole him away from among the royal princes, who were about to be murdered. She put him and his nurse in a bedroom to hide him from Athaliah; so he was not killed. ³He remained hidden with his nurse at the temple of the LORD for six years while Athaliah ruled the land.

⁴In the seventh year Jehoiada sent for the commanders of units of a hundred, the Carites and the guards and had them brought to him at the temple of the LORD. He made a covenant with them and put them under oath at the temple of the LORD. Then he showed them the king's son. ⁵He commanded them, saying, 'This is what you are to do: you who are in the three companies that are going on duty on the Sabbath – a third of you guarding the royal palace, ⁶a third at the Sur Gate, and a third at the gate behind the guard, who take turns guarding the temple – ⁷and you who are in the other two companies that normally go off Sabbath duty are all to guard the temple for the king. ⁸Station yourselves round the king, each of you with weapon in hand. Anyone who approaches your ranks is to be put to death. Stay close to the king wherever he goes.'

⁹The commanders of units of a hundred did just as Jehoiada the priest ordered. Each one took his men – those who were going on duty on the Sabbath and those who were going off duty – and came to Jehoiada the priest. ¹⁰Then he gave the commanders the spears and shields that had belonged to King David and that were in the temple of the LORD. ¹¹The guards, each with weapon in hand, stationed themselves round the king – near the altar and the temple, from the south side to the north side of the temple.

¹²Jehoiada brought out the king's son and put the crown on him; he presented him with a copy of the covenant and proclaimed him king. They anointed him, and the people clapped their hands and shouted, 'Long live the king!'

¹³When Athaliah heard the noise made by the guards and the people, she went to the people at the temple of the LORD. ¹⁴She looked and there was the king, standing by the pillar, as the custom was. The officers and the trumpeters were beside the king, and all the people of the land were rejoicing and blowing trumpets. Then Athaliah tore her robes and called out, 'Treason! Treason!'

¹⁵Jehoiada the priest ordered the commanders of units of a hundred, who were in charge of the troops: 'Bring her out between the ranks and put to the sword anyone who follows her.' For the priest had said, 'She must not be put to death in the temple of the LORD.' ¹⁶So they seized her as she reached the place where the horses enter the palace grounds, and there she was put to death.

¹⁷Jehoiada then made a covenant between the LORD and the king and people that they would be the LORD's people. He also made a covenant between the king and the people. ¹⁸All the people of the land went to the temple of Baal and tore it down. They smashed the altars and idols to pieces and killed Mattan the priest of Baal in front of the altars.

Then Jehoiada the priest posted guards at the temple of the LORD. ¹⁹He took with him the commanders of hundreds, the Carites, the guards and all the people of the land, and together they brought the king down from the temple of the LORD and went into the palace, entering by way of the gate of the guards. The king then took his place on the royal throne. ²⁰All the people of the land rejoiced, and the city was calm, because Athaliah had been slain with the sword at the palace.

²¹Joash was seven years old when he began his reign.

12 In the seventh year of Jehu, Joash became king, and he reigned in Jerusalem for forty years. His mother's name was Zibiah; she was from Beersheba. ²Joash did what was right in the eyes of the Lord all the years Jehoiada the priest instructed

him. ³The high places, however, were not removed; the people continued to offer sacrifices and burn incense there.

⁴Joash said to the priests, 'Collect all the money that is brought as sacred offerings to the temple of the LORD – the money collected in the census, the money received from personal vows and the money brought voluntarily to the temple. ⁵Let every priest receive the money from one of the treasurers, then use it to repair whatever damage is found in the temple.'

⁶But by the twenty-third year of King Joash the priests still had not repaired the temple. ⁷Therefore King Joash summoned Jehoiada the priest and the other priests and asked them, 'Why aren't you repairing the damage done to the temple? Take no more money from your treasurers, but hand it over for repairing the temple.' ⁸The priests agreed that they would not collect any more money from the people and that they would not repair the temple themselves.

⁹Jehoiada the priest took a chest and bored a hole in its lid. He placed it beside the altar, on the right side as one enters the temple of the LORD. The priests who guarded the entrance put into the chest all the money that was brought to the temple of the LORD. ¹⁰Whenever they saw that there was a large amount of money in the chest, the royal secretary and the high priest came, counted the money that had been brought into the temple of the LORD and put it into bags. ¹¹When the amount had been determined, they gave the money to the men appointed to supervise the work on the temple. With it they paid those who worked on the temple of the LORD – the carpenters and builders, ¹²the masons and stonecutters. They purchased timber and blocks of dressed stone for the repair of the temple of the LORD, and met all the other expenses of restoring the temple.

¹³The money brought into the temple was not spent for making silver basins, wick trimmers, sprinkling bowls, trumpets or any other articles of gold or silver for the temple of the LORD; ¹⁴it was paid to the workers, who used it to repair the temple. ¹⁵They did not require an accounting from those to whom they gave the money to pay the workers, because they acted with complete honesty. ¹⁶The money from the guilt offerings and sin offerings was not brought into the temple of the LORD; it belonged to the priests.

¹⁷About this time Hazael king of Aram went up and attacked Gath and captured it. Then he turned to attack Jerusalem. ¹⁸But Joash king of Judah took all the sacred objects dedicated by his predecessors – Jehoshaphat, Jehoram and Ahaziah, the kings of Judah – and the gifts he himself had dedicated and all the gold found in the treasuries of the temple of the LORD and of the royal palace, and he sent them to Hazael king of Aram, who then withdrew from Jerusalem.

¹⁹As for the other events of the reign of Joash, and all he did, are they not written in the book of the annals of the kings of Judah? ²⁰His officials conspired against him and assassinated him at Beth Millo, on the road down to Silla. ²¹The officials who murdered him were Jozabad son of Shimeath and Jehozabad son of Shomer. He died and was buried with his ancestors in the City of David. And Amaziah his son succeeded him as king.

13 In the twenty-third year of Joash son of Ahaziah king of Judah, Jehoahaz son of Jehu became king of Israel in Samaria, and he reigned for seventeen years. ²He did evil in the eyes of the LORD by following the sins of Jeroboam son of Nebat, which he had caused Israel to commit, and he did not turn away from them. ³So the LORD's anger burned against Israel, and for a long time he kept them under the power of Hazael king of Aram and Ben-Hadad his son.

⁴Then Jehoahaz sought the LORD's favour, and the LORD listened to him, for he

saw how severely the king of Aram was oppressing Israel. ⁵ The LORD provided a deliverer for Israel, and they escaped from the power of Aram. So the Israelites lived in their own homes as they had before. ⁶ But they did not turn away from the sins of the house of Jeroboam, which he had caused Israel to commit; they continued in them. Also, the Asherah pole remained standing in Samaria.

⁷ Nothing had been left of the army of Jehoahaz except fifty horsemen, ten chariots and ten thousand foot soldiers, for the king of Aram had destroyed the rest and made them like the dust at threshing time.

⁸ As for the other events of the reign of Jehoahaz, all he did and his achievements, are they not written in the book of the annals of the kings of Israel? ⁹ Jehoahaz rested with his ancestors and was buried in Samaria. And Jehoash his son succeeded him as king.

■ PSALM 78:9-16

⁹ The men of Ephraim, though armed with bows,
  turned back on the day of battle;
¹⁰ they did not keep God's covenant
  and refused to live by his law.
¹¹ They forgot what he had done,
  the wonders he had shown them.
¹² He did miracles in the sight of their
    ancestors
  in the land of Egypt, in the region of
    Zoan.
¹³ He divided the sea and led them
    through;
  he made the water stand up like a wall.
¹⁴ He guided them with the cloud by day
  and with light from the fire all night.
¹⁵ He split the rocks in the wilderness
  and gave them water as abundant as
    the seas;
¹⁶ he brought streams out of a rocky crag
  and made water flow down like rivers.

■ PROVERBS 16:29-30

²⁹ A violent person entices their neighbour
  and leads them down a path that is not
    good.

³⁰ Whoever winks with their eye is plotting
    perversity;
  whoever purses their lips is bent on evil.

■ ACTS 7:1-22

7 Then the high priest asked Stephen, 'Are these charges true?'
  ² To this he replied: 'Brothers and fathers, listen to me! The God of glory appeared to our father Abraham while he was still in Mesopotamia, before he lived in Harran. ³ "Leave your country and your people," God said, "and go to the land I will show you."

⁴ 'So he left the land of the Chaldeans and settled in Harran. After the death of his father, God sent him to this land where you are now living. ⁵ He gave him no inheritance here, not even enough ground to set his foot on. But God promised him that he and his descendants after him would possess the land, even though at that time Abraham had no child. ⁶ God spoke to him in this way: "For four hundred years your descendants will be strangers in a country not their own, and they will be enslaved and ill-treated. ⁷ But I will punish the nation they serve as slaves," God said, "and afterwards they will come out of that country and worship me in this place." ⁸ Then he gave Abraham the covenant of circumcision. And Abraham became the father of Isaac and circumcised him eight days after his birth. Later Isaac became the father of Jacob, and Jacob became the father of the twelve patriarchs.

⁹ 'Because the patriarchs were jealous of Joseph, they sold him as a slave into Egypt. But God was with him ¹⁰ and rescued him from all his troubles. He gave Joseph wisdom

and enabled him to gain the goodwill of Pharaoh king of Egypt. So Pharaoh made him ruler over Egypt and all his palace.

[11] 'Then a famine struck all Egypt and Canaan, bringing great suffering, and our ancestors could not find food. [12] When Jacob heard that there was grain in Egypt, he sent our forefathers on their first visit. [13] On their second visit, Joseph told his brothers who he was, and Pharaoh learned about Joseph's family. [14] After this, Joseph sent for his father Jacob and his whole family, seventy-five in all. [15] Then Jacob went down to Egypt, where he and our ancestors died. [16] Their bodies were brought back to Shechem and placed in the tomb that Abraham had bought from the sons of Hamor at Shechem

for a certain sum of money.

[17] 'As the time drew near for God to fulfil his promise to Abraham, the number of our people in Egypt had greatly increased. [18] Then "a new king, to whom Joseph meant nothing, came to power in Egypt". [19] He dealt treacherously with our people and oppressed our ancestors by forcing them to throw out their newborn babies so that they would die.

[20] 'At that time Moses was born, and he was no ordinary child. For three months he was cared for by his family. [21] When he was placed outside, Pharaoh's daughter took him and brought him up as her own son. [22] Moses was educated in all the wisdom of the Egyptians and was powerful in speech and action.

The Original Quitters

'They forgot what he had done, the wonders he had shown them.' **Psalm 78:11**

The psalm before us today begins by commanding us to listen: 'My people, hear my teaching; listen to the words of my mouth' (Psa. 78:1). You have only to read a few verses of this psalm to see that the psalmist Asaph is recalling the disobedience that characterised the Jews during their forty years' wandering in the wilderness. Then a strange verse appears: 'The men of Ephraim, though armed with bows, turned back on the day of battle' (v.9).

These Ephraimites were equipped with all they needed for warfare, but on the day of battle – that is, the first day of the fray – they 'turned back'. Although well armed, in the moment of testing they were overcome by fear. Doubtless they paraded well and looked fine as they marched out to battle, but when they came face to face with the enemy, the only weapon they used was a cloud of dust as they retreated en masse – and in a hurry.

A preacher I once heard referred to the Ephraimites in this verse as 'the original quitters'. What an indictment. The Ephraimites live on, you know; they are to be found in the rank and file of many a modern-day congregation. They look fine in church on Sunday mornings with a hymn book and a Bible in their hands, but let the hot rays of temptation beat upon them – and they run. They surrender to temptation because they have never learned how to surrender to God. When we surrender to God, then we need not surrender to anything else.

PRAYER

Lord Jesus, help me clarify to myself whether I am surrendered or not. For I see that if I do not fall at Your feet, then I fall at the feet of things and circumstances. Show me at whose feet I am lying. For Your own name's sake. Amen.

FURTHER STUDY

Dan. 1:1-21; Rom. 6:13; Eph. 6:13
• How did Daniel resist the temptation to compromise?
• What are the results of resisting temptation?

July 2

■ 2 KINGS 13:10–15:15

¹⁰ In the thirty-seventh year of Joash king of Judah, Jehoash son of Jehoahaz became king of Israel in Samaria, and he reigned for sixteen years. ¹¹ He did evil in the eyes of the LORD and did not turn away from any of the sins of Jeroboam son of Nebat, which he had caused Israel to commit; he continued in them.

¹² As for the other events of the reign of Jehoash, all he did and his achievements, including his war against Amaziah king of Judah, are they not written in the book of the annals of the kings of Israel? ¹³ Jehoash rested with his ancestors, and Jeroboam succeeded him on the throne. Jehoash was buried in Samaria with the kings of Israel.

¹⁴ Now Elisha had been suffering from the illness from which he died. Jehoash king of Israel went down to see him and wept over him. 'My father! My father!' he cried. 'The chariots and horsemen of Israel!'

¹⁵ Elisha said, 'Get a bow and some arrows,' and he did so. ¹⁶ 'Take the bow in your hands,' he said to the king of Israel. When he had taken it, Elisha put his hands on the king's hands.

¹⁷ 'Open the east window,' he said, and he opened it. 'Shoot!' Elisha said, and he shot. 'The LORD's arrow of victory, the arrow of victory over Aram!' Elisha declared. 'You will completely destroy the Arameans at Aphek.'

¹⁸ Then he said, 'Take the arrows,' and the king took them. Elisha told him, 'Strike the ground.' He struck it three times and stopped. ¹⁹ The man of God was angry with him and said, 'You should have struck the ground five or six times; then you would have defeated Aram and completely destroyed it. But now you will defeat it only three times.'

²⁰ Elisha died and was buried.

Now Moabite raiders used to enter the country every spring. ²¹ Once while some Israelites were burying a man, suddenly they saw a band of raiders; so they threw the man's body into Elisha's tomb. When the body touched Elisha's bones, the man came to life and stood up on his feet.

²² Hazael king of Aram oppressed Israel throughout the reign of Jehoahaz. ²³ But the LORD was gracious to them and had compassion and showed concern for them because of his covenant with Abraham, Isaac and Jacob. To this day he has been unwilling to destroy them or banish them from his presence.

²⁴ Hazael king of Aram died, and Ben-Hadad his son succeeded him as king. ²⁵ Then Jehoash son of Jehoahaz recaptured

from Ben-Hadad son of Hazael the towns he had taken in battle from his father Jehoahaz. Three times Jehoash defeated him, and so he recovered the Israelite towns.

14 In the second year of Jehoash son of Jehoahaz king of Israel, Amaziah son of Joash king of Judah began to reign. ²He was twenty-five years old when he became king, and he reigned in Jerusalem for twenty-nine years. His mother's name was Jehoaddan; she was from Jerusalem. ³He did what was right in the eyes of the LORD, but not as his father David had done. In everything he followed the example of his father Joash. ⁴The high places, however, were not removed; the people continued to offer sacrifices and burn incense there.

⁵After the kingdom was firmly in his grasp, he executed the officials who had murdered his father the king. ⁶Yet he did not put the children of the assassins to death, in accordance with what is written in the Book of the Law of Moses where the LORD commanded: 'Parents are not to be put to death for their children, nor children put to death for their parents; each will die for their own sin.'

⁷He was the one who defeated ten thousand Edomites in the Valley of Salt and captured Sela in battle, calling it Joktheel, the name it has to this day.

⁸Then Amaziah sent messengers to Jehoash son of Jehoahaz, the son of Jehu, king of Israel, with the challenge: 'Come, let us face each other in battle.'

⁹But Jehoash king of Israel replied to Amaziah king of Judah: 'A thistle in Lebanon sent a message to a cedar in Lebanon, "Give your daughter to my son in marriage." Then a wild beast in Lebanon came along and trampled the thistle underfoot. ¹⁰You have indeed defeated Edom and now you are arrogant. Glory in your victory, but stay at home! Why ask for trouble and cause your own downfall and that of Judah also?'

¹¹Amaziah, however, would not listen,

so Jehoash king of Israel attacked. He and Amaziah king of Judah faced each other at Beth Shemesh in Judah. ¹²Judah was routed by Israel, and every man fled to his home. ¹³Jehoash king of Israel captured Amaziah king of Judah, the son of Joash, the son of Ahaziah, at Beth Shemesh. Then Jehoash went to Jerusalem and broke down the wall of Jerusalem from the Ephraim Gate to the Corner Gate – a section about four hundred cubits long. ¹⁴He took all the gold and silver and all the articles found in the temple of the LORD and in the treasuries of the royal palace. He also took hostages and returned to Samaria.

¹⁵As for the other events of the reign of Jehoash, what he did and his achievements, including his war against Amaziah king of Judah, are they not written in the book of the annals of the kings of Israel? ¹⁶Jehoash rested with his ancestors and was buried in Samaria with the kings of Israel. And Jeroboam his son succeeded him as king.

¹⁷Amaziah son of Joash king of Judah lived for fifteen years after the death of Jehoash son of Jehoahaz king of Israel. ¹⁸As for the other events of Amaziah's reign, are they not written in the book of the annals of the kings of Judah?

¹⁹They conspired against him in Jerusalem, and he fled to Lachish, but they sent men after him to Lachish and killed him there. ²⁰He was brought back by horse and was buried in Jerusalem with his ancestors, in the City of David.

²¹Then all the people of Judah took Azariah, who was sixteen years old, and made him king in place of his father Amaziah. ²²He was the one who rebuilt Elath and restored it to Judah after Amaziah rested with his ancestors.

²³In the fifteenth year of Amaziah son of Joash king of Judah, Jeroboam son of Jehoash king of Israel became king in Samaria, and he reigned for forty-one years. ²⁴He did evil in the eyes of the LORD and did not

turn away from any of the sins of Jeroboam son of Nebat, which he had caused Israel to commit. ²⁵He was the one who restored the boundaries of Israel from Lebo Hamath to the Dead Sea, in accordance with the word of the LORD, the God of Israel, spoken through his servant Jonah son of Amittai, the prophet from Gath Hepher.

²⁶The LORD had seen how bitterly everyone in Israel, whether slave or free, was suffering; there was no one to help them. ²⁷And since the LORD had not said he would blot out the name of Israel from under heaven, he saved them by the hand of Jeroboam son of Jehoash.

²⁸As for the other events of Jeroboam's reign, all he did, and his military achievements, including how he recovered for Israel both Damascus and Hamath, which had belonged to Judah, are they not written in the book of the annals of the kings of Israel? ²⁹Jeroboam rested with his ancestors, the kings of Israel. And Zechariah his son succeeded him as king.

15 In the twenty-seventh year of Jeroboam king of Israel, Azariah son of Amaziah king of Judah began to reign. ²He was sixteen years old when he became king, and he reigned in Jerusalem for fifty-two years. His mother's name was Jekoliah; she was from Jerusalem. ³He did what was right in the eyes of the LORD, just as his father Amaziah had done. ⁴The high places, however, were not removed; the people continued to offer sacrifices and burn incense there.

⁵The LORD afflicted the king with leprosy until the day he died, and he lived in a separate house. Jotham the king's son had charge of the palace and governed the people of the land.

⁶As for the other events of Azariah's reign, and all he did, are they not written in the book of the annals of the kings of Judah? ⁷Azariah rested with his ancestors and was buried near them in the City of David. And Jotham his son succeeded him as king.

⁸In the thirty-eighth year of Azariah king of Judah, Zechariah son of Jeroboam became king of Israel in Samaria, and he reigned for six months. ⁹He did evil in the eyes of the LORD, as his predecessors had done. He did not turn away from the sins of Jeroboam son of Nebat, which he had caused Israel to commit.

¹⁰Shallum son of Jabesh conspired against Zechariah. He attacked him in front of the people, assassinated him and succeeded him as king. ¹¹The other events of Zechariah's reign are written in the book of the annals of the kings of Israel. ¹²So the word of the LORD spoken to Jehu was fulfilled: 'Your descendants will sit on the throne of Israel to the fourth generation.'

¹³Shallum son of Jabesh became king in the thirty-ninth year of Uzziah king of Judah, and he reigned in Samaria for one month. ¹⁴Then Menahem son of Gadi went from Tirzah up to Samaria. He attacked Shallum son of Jabesh in Samaria, assassinated him and succeeded him as king.

¹⁵The other events of Shallum's reign, and the conspiracy he led, are written in the book of the annals of the kings of Israel.

■ PSALM 78:17-22

¹⁷But they continued to sin against him,
    rebelling in the wilderness against the
        Most High.
¹⁸They wilfully put God to the test
    by demanding the food they craved.
¹⁹They spoke against God;
    they said, 'Can God really
      spread a table in the wilderness?
²⁰True, he struck the rock,
    and water gushed out,
      streams flowed abundantly,
    but can he also give us bread?
    Can he supply meat for his people?'

21 When the LORD heard them, he was
furious;
  his fire broke out against Jacob,
    and his wrath rose against Israel,
22 for they did not believe in God
  or trust in his deliverance.

▬ PROVERBS 16:31-33

31 Grey hair is a crown of splendour;
  it is attained in the way of
    righteousness.

32 Better a patient person than a warrior,
  one with self-control than one who
    takes a city.

33 The lot is cast into the lap,
  but its every decision is from the LORD.

▬ ACTS 7:23-43

23 'When Moses was forty years old, he
decided to visit his own people, the Israelites. 24 He saw one of them being ill-treated
by an Egyptian, so he went to his defence
and avenged him by killing the Egyptian.
25 Moses thought that his own people would
realise that God was using him to rescue
them, but they did not. 26 The next day
Moses came upon two Israelites who were
fighting. He tried to reconcile them by saying, "Men, you are brothers; why do you
want to hurt each other?"

27 'But the man who was ill-treating the
other pushed Moses aside and said, "Who
made you ruler and judge over us? 28 Are
you thinking of killing me as you killed the
Egyptian yesterday?" 29 When Moses heard
this, he fled to Midian, where he settled as a
foreigner and had two sons.

30 'After forty years had passed, an angel
appeared to Moses in the flames of a burning bush in the desert near Mount Sinai.

31 When he saw this, he was amazed at the
sight. As he went over to get a closer look, he
heard the Lord say: 32 "I am the God of your
fathers, the God of Abraham, Isaac and Jacob." Moses trembled with fear and did not
dare to look.

33 'Then the Lord said to him, "Take off
your sandals, for the place where you are
standing is holy ground. 34 I have indeed
seen the oppression of my people in Egypt.
I have heard their groaning and have come
down to set them free. Now come, I will
send you back to Egypt."

35 'This is the same Moses they had rejected with the words, "Who made you
ruler and judge?" He was sent to be their
ruler and deliverer by God himself, through
the angel who appeared to him in the bush.
36 He led them out of Egypt and performed
wonders and signs in Egypt, at the Red Sea
and for forty years in the wilderness.

37 'This is the Moses who told the Israelites, "God will raise up for you a prophet
like me from your own people." 38 He was in
the assembly in the wilderness, with the angel who spoke to him on Mount Sinai, and
with our ancestors; and he received living
words to pass on to us.

39 'But our ancestors refused to obey him.
Instead, they rejected him and in their
hearts turned back to Egypt. 40 They told
Aaron, "Make us gods who will go before
us. As for this fellow Moses who led us out of
Egypt – we don't know what has happened
to him!" 41 That was the time they made
an idol in the form of a calf. They brought
sacrifices to it and revelled in what their
own hands had made. 42 But God turned
away from them and gave them over to the
worship of the sun, moon and stars. This
agrees with what is written in the book of
the prophets:

  ' "Did you bring me sacrifices and
    offerings

for forty years in the wilderness,
people of Israel?
[43] You have taken up the tabernacle of
Molek

and the star of your god Rephan,
the idols you made to worship.
Therefore I will send you into exile"
beyond Babylon.

Good Temper

'Better is a patient person than a warrior, one with self-control than one who takes a city.' **Proverbs 16:32**

One of the fruits of the Spirit is patience. The central meaning of this word (Greek: *makrothumia*) is 'good temper'. It denotes a person who does not easily 'fly off the handle'. He maintains good temper amid the flux and flow of human events.

William Barclay says of this word, 'This . . . fruit of the Spirit expresses the attitude to people which never loses hope for them, however unlovely and unteachable they may be'. Archbishop Trench defined the word as 'a long holding out of the mind before it gives room to action or to passion, the self-restraint which does not hastily retaliate a wrong'. And Moffatt describes it as 'the tenacity with which faith holds out'.

Good temper must not, however, be confused with apathy. In the days of the Early Church, the group called the Stoics made indifference a virtue. They said, 'Nothing is worth suffering for, so build a wall around your heart and keep out all sense of feeling.' The Early Christians did not share that view, however, for Christians care – and because they cared, they suffered. Through the ministry of the Spirit in their lives, they found poise and good temper amidst their sufferings. The more we cared, the more sensitive we will be to things that tend to block our goal of caring – that is why the quality of patience is so essential. An evangelist addressing a meeting was subjected to persistent heckling. Unfortunately, he lost his temper – and also his audience. They saw he had little to offer except words.

PRAYER

O Father, help me to become a person of good temper. Dwell deep in me so that I shall be the peaceful exception amid the disturbed surroundings that I encounter day by day. Amen.

FURTHER STUDY

Eccl. 7:1-12; Num. 20:1-13;
Luke 21:19; Rom. 12:12
• What was the result of Moses' impatience?
• What will be the result of our impatience?

July 3

■ **2 KINGS 15:16–16:20**

¹⁶ At that time Menahem, starting out from Tirzah, attacked Tiphsah and everyone in the city and its vicinity, because they refused to open their gates. He sacked Tiphsah and ripped open all the pregnant women.

¹⁷ In the thirty-ninth year of Azariah king of Judah, Menahem son of Gadi became king of Israel, and he reigned in Samaria for ten years. ¹⁸ He did evil in the eyes of the LORD. During his entire reign he did not turn away from the sins of Jeroboam son of Nebat, which he had caused Israel to commit.

¹⁹ Then Pul king of Assyria invaded the land, and Menahem gave him a thousand talents of silver to gain his support and strengthen his own hold on the kingdom. ²⁰ Menahem exacted this money from Israel. Every wealthy person had to contribute fifty shekels of silver to be given to the king of Assyria. So the king of Assyria withdrew and stayed in the land no longer.

²¹ As for the other events of Menahem's reign, and all he did, are they not written in the book of the annals of the kings of Israel? ²² Menahem rested with his ancestors. And Pekahiah his son succeeded him as king.

²³ In the fiftieth year of Azariah king of Judah, Pekahiah son of Menahem became king of Israel in Samaria, and he reigned for two years. ²⁴ Pekahiah did evil in the eyes of the LORD. He did not turn away from the sins of Jeroboam son of Nebat, which he had caused Israel to commit. ²⁵ One of his chief officers, Pekah son of Remaliah, conspired against him. Taking fifty men of Gilead with him, he assassinated Pekahiah, along with Argob and Arieh, in the citadel of the royal palace at Samaria. So Pekah killed Pekahiah and succeeded him as king.

²⁶ The other events of Pekahiah's reign, and all he did, are written in the book of the annals of the kings of Israel.

²⁷ In the fifty-second year of Azariah king of Judah, Pekah son of Remaliah became king of Israel in Samaria, and he reigned for twenty years. ²⁸ He did evil in the eyes of the LORD. He did not turn away from the sins of Jeroboam son of Nebat, which he had caused Israel to commit.

²⁹ In the time of Pekah king of Israel, Tiglath-Pileser king of Assyria came and took Ijon, Abel Beth Maakah, Janoah, Kedesh and Hazor. He took Gilead and Galilee, including all the land of Naphtali, and deported the people to Assyria. ³⁰ Then Hoshea son of Elah conspired against Pekah son of Remaliah. He attacked and assassinated him, and then succeeded him as king in the twentieth year of Jotham son of Uzziah.

³¹ As for the other events of Pekah's reign, and all he did, are they not written in the book of the annals of the kings of Israel?

³² In the second year of Pekah son of Remaliah king of Israel, Jotham son of Uzziah king of Judah began to reign. ³³ He was twenty-five years old when he became king, and he reigned in Jerusalem for sixteen years. His mother's name was Jerusha daughter of Zadok. ³⁴ He did what was right in the eyes of the LORD, just as his father Uzziah had done. ³⁵ The high places, however, were not removed; the people continued to offer sacrifices and burn incense there. Jotham rebuilt the Upper Gate of the temple of the LORD.

³⁶ As for the other events of Jotham's reign, and what he did, are they not written in the book of the annals of the kings of Judah?

³⁷(In those days the LORD began to send Rezin king of Aram and Pekah son of Remaliah against Judah.) ³⁸Jotham rested with his ancestors and was buried with them in the City of David, the city of his father. And Ahaz his son succeeded him as king.

16 In the seventeenth year of Pekah son of Remaliah, Ahaz son of Jotham king of Judah began to reign. ²Ahaz was twenty years old when he became king, and he reigned in Jerusalem for sixteen years. Unlike David his father, he did not do what was right in the eyes of the LORD his God. ³He followed the ways of the kings of Israel and even sacrificed his son in the fire, engaging in the detestable practices of the nations the LORD had driven out before the Israelites. ⁴He offered sacrifices and burned incense at the high places, on the hilltops and under every spreading tree.

⁵Then Rezin king of Aram and Pekah son of Remaliah king of Israel marched up to fight against Jerusalem and besieged Ahaz, but they could not overpower him. ⁶At that time, Rezin king of Aram recovered Elath for Aram by driving out the people of Judah. Edomites then moved into Elath and have lived there to this day.

⁷Ahaz sent messengers to say to Tiglath-Pileser king of Assyria, 'I am your servant and vassal. Come up and save me out of the hand of the king of Aram and of the king of Israel, who are attacking me.' ⁸And Ahaz took the silver and gold found in the temple of the LORD and in the treasuries of the royal palace and sent it as a gift to the king of Assyria. ⁹The king of Assyria complied by attacking Damascus and capturing it. He deported its inhabitants to Kir and put Rezin to death.

¹⁰Then King Ahaz went to Damascus to meet Tiglath-Pileser king of Assyria. He saw an altar in Damascus and sent to Uriah the priest a sketch of the altar, with detailed plans for its construction. ¹¹So Uriah the priest built an altar in accordance with all the plans that King Ahaz had sent from Damascus and finished it before King Ahaz returned. ¹²When the king came back from Damascus and saw the altar, he approached it and presented offerings on it. ¹³He offered up his burnt offering and grain offering, poured out his drink offering, and splashed the blood of his fellowship offerings against the altar. ¹⁴The bronze altar that stood before the LORD he brought from the front of the temple – from between the new altar and the temple of the LORD – and put it on the north side of the new altar.

¹⁵King Ahaz then gave these orders to Uriah the priest: 'On the large new altar, offer the morning burnt offering and the evening grain offering, the king's burnt offering and his grain offering, and the burnt offering of all the people of the land, and their grain offering and their drink offering. Splash against this altar the blood of all the burnt offerings and sacrifices. But I will use the bronze altar for seeking guidance.' ¹⁶And Uriah the priest did just as King Ahaz had ordered.

¹⁷King Ahaz cut off the side panels and removed the basins from the movable stands. He removed the Sea from the bronze bulls that supported it and set it on a stone base. ¹⁸He took away the Sabbath canopy that had been built at the temple and removed the royal entrance outside the temple of the LORD, in deference to the king of Assyria.

¹⁹As for the other events of the reign of Ahaz, and what he did, are they not written in the book of the annals of the kings of Judah? ²⁰Ahaz rested with his ancestors and was buried with them in the City of David. And Hezekiah his son succeeded him as king.

─ **PSALM 78:23-31**

²³Yet he gave a command to the skies
  above
    and opened the doors of the heavens;

²⁴ he rained down manna for the people
to eat,
    he gave them the grain of heaven.
²⁵ Human beings ate the bread of angels;
    he sent them all the food they could
        eat.
²⁶ He let loose the east wind from the
        heavens
    and by his power made the south wind
        blow.
²⁷ He rained meat down on them like dust,
    birds like sand on the seashore.
²⁸ He made them come down inside their
        camp,
    all around their tents.
²⁹ They ate till they were gorged –
    he had given them what they craved.
³⁰ But before they turned from what they
        craved,
    even while the food was still in their
        mouths,
³¹ God's anger rose against them;
    he put to death the sturdiest among
        them,
    cutting down the young men of Israel.

■ PROVERBS 17:1-2

17 Better a dry crust with peace and
quiet
    than a house full of feasting, with
        strife.

² A prudent servant will rule over a
        disgraceful son,
    and will share the inheritance as one
        of the family.

■ ACTS 7:44–8:3

⁴⁴ 'Our ancestors had the tabernacle of
the covenant law with them in the wilderness. It had been made as God directed
Moses, according to the pattern he had seen.

⁴⁵ After receiving the tabernacle, our ancestors under Joshua brought it with them
when they took the land from the nations
God drove out before them. It remained in
the land until the time of David, ⁴⁶ who enjoyed God's favour and asked that he might
provide a dwelling-place for the God of Jacob. ⁴⁷ But it was Solomon who built a house
for him.

⁴⁸ 'However, the Most High does not live
in houses made by human hands. As the
prophet says:

⁴⁹ ' "Heaven is my throne,
    and the earth is my footstool.
What kind of house will you build for
        me?
                    says the Lord.
Or where will my resting place be?
⁵⁰ Has not my hand made all these things?" '

⁵¹ 'You stiff-necked people! Your hearts
and ears are still uncircumcised. You are
just like your ancestors: you always resist
the Holy Spirit! ⁵² Was there ever a prophet
your ancestors did not persecute? They
even killed those who predicted the coming
of the Righteous One. And now you have betrayed and murdered him – ⁵³ you who have
received the law that was given through
angels but have not obeyed it.'

⁵⁴ When the members of the Sanhedrin
heard this, they were furious and gnashed
their teeth at him. ⁵⁵ But Stephen, full of the
Holy Spirit, looked up to heaven and saw the
glory of God, and Jesus standing at the right
hand of God. ⁵⁶ 'Look,' he said, 'I see heav-
en open and the Son of Man standing at the
right hand of God.'

⁵⁷ At this they covered their ears and,
yelling at the top of their voices, they all
rushed at him, ⁵⁸ dragged him out of the
city and began to stone him. Meanwhile,
the witnesses laid their coats at the feet of a
young man named Saul.

⁵⁹ While they were stoning him, Stephen

prayed, 'Lord Jesus, receive my spirit.'
60 Then he fell on his knees and cried out,
'Lord, do not hold this sin against them.'
When he had said this, he fell asleep.

8 And Saul approved of their killing him.
    On that day a great persecution broke
out against the church in Jerusalem, and all
except the apostles were scattered throughout Judea and Samaria. 2 Godly men buried
Stephen and mourned deeply for him. 3 But
Saul began to destroy the church. Going
from house to house, he dragged off both
men and women and put them in prison.

The First Christian Martyr

'Lord, do not hold this sin against them.' **Acts 7:60**

If Jesus lives in you then He can love in you. You too can forgive injuries, pray for your enemies and do not keep a record of their wrongs.

The first man ever to die for Christ was Stephen. Our reading makes it clear that he was unjustly murdered. But Christ lived in him. His last words were a magnificent echo of Calvary: 'Lord, do not hold this sin against them.' Remember Stephen was stoned to death. Imagine how painful that must have been. It was almost as cruel as crucifixion. One by one the stones pounded the life from his body, but though they battered the life out of him they could not batter the love out of him. Like his Lord he kept on loving to the end. Christ was in his mind up until his last moments. 'Lord,' he said, 'do not hold this sin against them.'

The chapter ends with a lovely sentence: 'When he had said this, he fell asleep.' But don't let these words lead you to think there was no hurt, no pain, no physical agony. He would have felt it all; you can be certain of that. But the love of Jesus poured into him and through him, and, taken up with Him in his heart and mind, his soul was taken up to be with Him. Some words ring in my mind as I write – words spoken by one who stood holding the coats of those who threw the stones: '... have the same mindset as Christ Jesus' (Phil. 2:5).

PRAYER

Heavenly Father, I must not perpetuate the treatment people give to me. I must echo Your words and treat people as You do. But I can't do this except by Your grace. May Your love melt all my resentments and heal all my hurts. Amen.

FURTHER STUDY

1 Sam. 24:1-22; Acts 22:19-21; Rom. 12:14-21

• How did David have the mind of Christ?

• How are we to treat those who treat us badly?

July 4

17 In the twelfth year of Ahaz king of Judah, Hoshea son of Elah became king of Israel in Samaria, and he reigned for nine years. ² He did evil in the eyes of the LORD, but not like the kings of Israel who preceded him.

³ Shalmaneser king of Assyria came up to attack Hoshea, who had been Shalmaneser's vassal and had paid him tribute. ⁴ But the king of Assyria discovered that Hoshea was a traitor, for he had sent envoys to So king of Egypt, and he no longer paid tribute to the king of Assyria, as he had done year by year. Therefore Shalmaneser seized him and put him in prison. ⁵ The king of Assyria invaded the entire land, marched against Samaria and laid siege to it for three years. ⁶ In the ninth year of Hoshea, the king of Assyria captured Samaria and deported the Israelites to Assyria. He settled them in Halah, in Gozan on the River Habor and in the towns of the Medes.

⁷ All this took place because the Israelites had sinned against the LORD their God, who had brought them up out of Egypt from under the power of Pharaoh king of Egypt. They worshipped other gods ⁸ and followed the practices of the nations the LORD had driven out before them, as well as the practices that the kings of Israel had introduced. ⁹ The Israelites secretly did things against the LORD their God that were not right. From watchtower to fortified city they built themselves high places in all their towns. ¹⁰ They set up sacred stones and Asherah poles on every high hill and under every spreading tree. ¹¹ At every high place they burned incense, as the nations whom the LORD had driven out before them had done. They

did wicked things that aroused the LORD's anger. ¹² They worshipped idols, though the LORD had said, 'You shall not do this.' ¹³ The LORD warned Israel and Judah through all his prophets and seers: 'Turn from your evil ways. Observe my commands and decrees, in accordance with the entire Law that I commanded your ancestors to obey and that I delivered to you through my servants the prophets.'

¹⁴ But they would not listen and were as stiff-necked as their ancestors, who did not trust in the LORD their God. ¹⁵ They rejected his decrees and the covenant he had made with their ancestors and the statutes he had warned them to keep. They followed worthless idols and themselves became worthless. They imitated the nations around them although the LORD had ordered them, 'Do not do as they do.'

¹⁶ They forsook all the commands of the LORD their God and made for themselves two idols cast in the shape of calves, and an Asherah pole. They bowed down to all the starry hosts, and they worshipped Baal. ¹⁷ They sacrificed their sons and daughters in the fire. They practised divination and sought omens and sold themselves to do evil in the eyes of the LORD, arousing his anger.

¹⁸ So the LORD was very angry with Israel and removed them from his presence. Only the tribe of Judah was left, ¹⁹ and even Judah did not keep the commands of the LORD their God. They followed the practices Israel had introduced. ²⁰ Therefore the LORD rejected all the people of Israel; he afflicted them and gave them into the hands of plunderers, until he thrust them from his presence.

²¹ When he tore Israel away from the

house of David, they made Jeroboam son of Nebat their king. Jeroboam enticed Israel away from following the LORD and caused them to commit a great sin. ²² The Israelites persisted in all the sins of Jeroboam and did not turn away from them ²³ until the LORD removed them from his presence, as he had warned through all his servants the prophets. So the people of Israel were taken from their homeland into exile in Assyria, and they are still there.

²⁴ The king of Assyria brought people from Babylon, Kuthah, Avva, Hamath and Sepharvaim and settled them in the towns of Samaria to replace the Israelites. They took over Samaria and lived in its towns. ²⁵ When they first lived there, they did not worship the LORD; so he sent lions among them and they killed some of the people. ²⁶ It was reported to the king of Assyria: 'The people you deported and resettled in the towns of Samaria do not know what the god of that country requires. He has sent lions among them, which are killing them off, because the people do not know what he requires.'

²⁷ Then the king of Assyria gave this order: 'Make one of the priests you took captive from Samaria go back to live there and teach the people what the god of the land requires.' ²⁸ So one of the priests who had been exiled from Samaria came to live in Bethel and taught them how to worship the LORD.

²⁹ Nevertheless, each national group made its own gods in the several towns where they settled, and set them up in the shrines the people of Samaria had made at the high places. ³⁰ The people from Babylon made Sukkoth Benoth, those from Kuthah made Nergal, and those from Hamath made Ashima; ³¹ the Avvites made Nibhaz and Tartak, and the Sepharvites burned their children in the fire as sacrifices to Adrammelek and Anammelek, the gods of Sepharvaim. ³² They worshipped the LORD, but they also appointed all sorts of their own people to officiate for them as priests in the shrines

at the high places. ³³ They worshipped the LORD, but they also served their own gods in accordance with the customs of the nations from which they had been brought.

³⁴ To this day they persist in their former practices. They neither worship the LORD nor adhere to the decrees and regulations, the laws and commands that the LORD gave the descendants of Jacob, whom he named Israel. ³⁵ When the LORD made a covenant with the Israelites, he commanded them: 'Do not worship any other gods or bow down to them, serve them or sacrifice to them. ³⁶ But the LORD, who brought you up out of Egypt with mighty power and outstretched arm, is the one you must worship. To him you shall bow down and to him offer sacrifices. ³⁷ You must always be careful to keep the decrees and regulations, the laws and commands he wrote for you. Do not worship other gods. ³⁸ Do not forget the covenant I have made with you, and do not worship other gods. ³⁹ Rather, worship the LORD your God; it is he who will deliver you from the hand of all your enemies.'

⁴⁰ They would not listen, however, but persisted in their former practices. ⁴¹ Even while these people were worshipping the LORD, they were serving their idols. To this day their children and grandchildren continue to do as their ancestors did.

▬ PSALM 78:32-39

³² In spite of all this, they kept on sinning;
    in spite of his wonders, they did not
        believe.
³³ So he ended their days in futility
    and their years in terror.
³⁴ Whenever God slew them, they would
        seek him;
    they eagerly turned to him again.
³⁵ They remembered that God was their
        Rock,
    that God Most High was their
        Redeemer.

³⁶ But then they would flatter him with
    their mouths,
  lying to him with their tongues;
³⁷ their hearts were not loyal to him,
  they were not faithful to his covenant.
³⁸ Yet he was merciful;
  he forgave their iniquities
  and did not destroy them.
Time after time he restrained his anger
  and did not stir up his full wrath.
³⁹ He remembered that they were but flesh,
  a passing breeze that does not return.

■ PROVERBS 17:3-4

³ The crucible for silver and the furnace
    for gold,
  but the LORD tests the heart.

⁴ A wicked person listens to deceitful lips;
  a liar pays attention to a destructive
    tongue.

■ ACTS 8:4-40

⁴ Those who had been scattered preached the word wherever they went. ⁵ Philip went down to a city in Samaria and proclaimed the Messiah there. ⁶ When the crowds heard Philip and saw the signs he performed, they all paid close attention to what he said. ⁷ For with shrieks, impure spirits came out of many, and many who were paralysed or lame were healed. ⁸ So there was great joy in that city.

⁹ Now for some time a man named Simon had practised sorcery in the city and amazed all the people of Samaria. He boasted that he was someone great, ¹⁰ and all the people, both high and low, gave him their attention and exclaimed, 'This man is rightly called the Great Power of God.' ¹¹ They followed him because he had amazed them for a long time with his sorcery. ¹² But when

they believed Philip as he proclaimed the good news of the kingdom of God and the name of Jesus Christ, they were baptised, both men and women. ¹³ Simon himself believed and was baptised. And he followed Philip everywhere, astonished by the great signs and miracles he saw.

¹⁴ When the apostles in Jerusalem heard that Samaria had accepted the word of God, they sent Peter and John to Samaria. ¹⁵ When they arrived, they prayed for the new believers there that they might receive the Holy Spirit, ¹⁶ because the Holy Spirit had not yet come on any of them; they had simply been baptised in the name of the Lord Jesus. ¹⁷ Then Peter and John placed their hands on them, and they received the Holy Spirit.

¹⁸ When Simon saw that the Spirit was given at the laying on of the apostles' hands, he offered them money ¹⁹ and said, 'Give me also this ability so that everyone on whom I lay my hands may receive the Holy Spirit.'

²⁰ Peter answered: 'May your money perish with you, because you thought you could buy the gift of God with money! ²¹ You have no part or share in this ministry, because your heart is not right before God. ²² Repent of this wickedness and pray to the Lord in the hope that he may forgive you for having such a thought in your heart. ²³ For I see that you are full of bitterness and captive to sin.'

²⁴ Then Simon answered, 'Pray to the Lord for me so that nothing you have said may happen to me.'

²⁵ After they had further proclaimed the word of the Lord and testified about Jesus, Peter and John returned to Jerusalem, preaching the gospel in many Samaritan villages.

²⁶ Now an angel of the Lord said to Philip, 'Go south to the road – the desert road – that goes down from Jerusalem to Gaza.' ²⁷ So he started out, and on his way he met an Ethiopian eunuch, an important official in charge of all the treasury of the Kandake

(which means 'queen of the Ethiopians'). This man had gone to Jerusalem to worship, [28] and on his way home was sitting in his chariot reading the Book of Isaiah the prophet. [29] The Spirit told Philip, 'Go to that chariot and stay near it.'

[30] Then Philip ran up to the chariot and heard the man reading Isaiah the prophet. 'Do you understand what you are reading?' Philip asked.

[31] 'How can I,' he said, 'unless someone explains it to me?' So he invited Philip to come up and sit with him.

[32] This is the passage of Scripture the eunuch was reading:

'He was led like a sheep to the slaughter,
    and as a lamb before its shearer is
        silent,
    so he did not open his mouth.
[33] In his humiliation he was deprived of
        justice.
Who can speak of his descendants?
For his life was taken from the earth.'

[34] The eunuch asked Philip, 'Tell me, please, who is the prophet talking about, himself or someone else?' [35] Then Philip began with that very passage of Scripture and told him the good news about Jesus.

[36] As they travelled along the road, they came to some water and the eunuch said, 'Look, here is water. What can stand in the way of my being baptised?' [37]a [38] And he gave orders to stop the chariot. Then both Philip and the eunuch went down into the water and Philip baptised him. [39] When they came up out of the water, the Spirit of the Lord suddenly took Philip away, and the eunuch did not see him again, but went on his way rejoicing. [40] Philip, however, appeared at Azotus and travelled about, preaching the gospel in all the towns until he reached Caesarea.

---

a Some manuscripts include here *Philip said, 'If you believe with all your heart, you may.' The eunuch answered, 'I believe that Jesus Christ is the Son of God.'*

Amazing!

'Yet he was merciful; he forgave their iniquities ...'
Psalm 78:38

If we are to go deeper with God, we need to know how to avail ourselves of God's grace. Romans 5:17 talks about 'those who receive God's abundant provision of grace'. Though God's grace may be abundant, it is only effective in our lives if it is received. But what do we mean by 'grace'?

Grace is spoken of in both the Old and New Testaments, and the root meaning of the word is that of kindness and favour. In the New Testament it is used chiefly in connection with God's undeserved mercy in redeeming humankind. Grace, as undeserved favour, is a term still used in business – especially the world of insurance. Sometimes a representative of a firm will write to a client and say something like this: 'In the circumstances you have no claim, we will give you a certain sum as an act of grace.' They acknowledge no indebtedness, but out of their kindness (and in hope of business to come) they give the client something to which he has no legal right.

A definition of grace I like very much is this: 'Grace is the strength God gives us to obey His commands.' Grace is not just a kindly attitude but an impartation of power, too. We can be sure that the people who seem to know God in a much deeper way than we do have received more of that power that God imparts 'unmerited and free'. It is by grace that they leap over all the impediments on their onward way. Grace truly is amazing!

PRAYER

O God, help me look at the values of earth in the light of heaven. Show me the folly of accumulating riches, the absurdity of heaping together the treasures of earth. May I come to recognise what has the highest value of all – Your matchless grace. Amen.

FURTHER STUDY

2 Cor. 8:9; 12:9; 2 Tim. 2:1-10
• How did Paul describe grace at work?
• What was Paul's admonition to Timothy?

July 5

▬ 2 KINGS 18:1–19:19

18 In the third year of Hoshea son of Elah king of Israel, Hezekiah son of Ahaz king of Judah began to reign. ²He was twenty-five years old when he became king, and he reigned in Jerusalem for twenty-nine years. His mother's name was Abijah daughter of Zechariah. ³He did what was right in the eyes of the LORD, just as his father David had done. ⁴He removed the high places, smashed the sacred stones and cut down the Asherah poles. He broke into pieces the bronze snake Moses had made, for up to that time the Israelites had been burning incense to it. (It was called Nehushtan.)

⁵Hezekiah trusted in the LORD, the God of Israel. There was no one like him among all the kings of Judah, either before him or after him. ⁶He held fast to the LORD and did not stop following him; he kept the commands the LORD had given Moses. ⁷And the LORD was with him; he was successful in

whatever he undertook. He rebelled against the king of Assyria and did not serve him. ⁸From watchtower to fortified city, he defeated the Philistines, as far as Gaza and its territory.

⁹In King Hezekiah's fourth year, which was the seventh year of Hoshea son of Elah king of Israel, Shalmaneser king of Assyria marched against Samaria and laid siege to it. ¹⁰At the end of three years the Assyrians took it. So Samaria was captured in Hezekiah's sixth year, which was the ninth year of Hoshea king of Israel. ¹¹The king of Assyria deported Israel to Assyria and settled them in Halah, in Gozan on the River Habor and in towns of the Medes. ¹²This happened because they had not obeyed the LORD their God, but had violated his covenant – all that Moses the servant of the LORD commanded. They neither listened to the commands nor carried them out.

¹³In the fourteenth year of King Hezekiah's reign, Sennacherib king of Assyria

attacked all the fortified cities of Judah and captured them. ¹⁴ So Hezekiah king of Judah sent this message to the king of Assyria at Lachish: 'I have done wrong. Withdraw from me, and I will pay whatever you demand of me.' The king of Assyria exacted from Hezekiah king of Judah three hundred talents of silver and thirty talents of gold. ¹⁵ So Hezekiah gave him all the silver that was found in the temple of the LORD and in the treasuries of the royal palace.

¹⁶ At this time Hezekiah king of Judah stripped off the gold with which he had covered the doors and doorposts of the temple of the LORD, and gave it to the king of Assyria.

¹⁷ The king of Assyria sent his supreme commander, his chief officer and his field commander with a large army, from Lachish to King Hezekiah at Jerusalem. They came up to Jerusalem and stopped at the aqueduct of the Upper Pool, on the road to the Washerman's Field. ¹⁸ They called for the king; and Eliakim son of Hilkiah the palace administrator, Shebna the secretary, and Joah son of Asaph the recorder went out to them.

¹⁹ The field commander said to them, 'Tell Hezekiah:

' "This is what the great king, the king of Assyria, says: on what are you basing this confidence of yours? ²⁰ You say you have the counsel and the might for war – but you speak only empty words. On whom are you depending, that you rebel against me? ²¹ Look, I know you are depending on Egypt, that splintered reed of a staff, which pierces the hand of anyone who leans on it! Such is Pharaoh king of Egypt to all who depend on him. ²² But if you say to me, 'We are depending on the LORD our God' – isn't he the one whose high places and altars Hezekiah removed, saying to Judah and Jerusalem,

'You must worship before this altar in Jerusalem'?

²³ ' "Come now, make a bargain with my master, the king of Assyria: I will give you two thousand horses – if you can put riders on them! ²⁴ How can you repulse one officer of the least of my master's officials, even though you are depending on Egypt for chariots and horsemen? ²⁵ Furthermore, have I come to attack and destroy this place without word from the LORD? The LORD himself told me to march against this country and destroy it." '

²⁶ Then Eliakim son of Hilkiah, and Shebna and Joah said to the field commander, 'Please speak to your servants in Aramaic, since we understand it. Don't speak to us in Hebrew in the hearing of the people on the wall.'

²⁷ But the commander replied, 'Was it only to your master and you that my master sent me to say these things, and not to the people sitting on the wall – who, like you, will have to eat their own excrement and drink their own urine?'

²⁸ Then the commander stood and called out in Hebrew, 'Hear the word of the great king, the king of Assyria! ²⁹ This is what the king says: do not let Hezekiah deceive you. He cannot deliver you from my hand. ³⁰ Do not let Hezekiah persuade you to trust in the LORD when he says, "The LORD will surely deliver us; this city will not be given into the hand of the king of Assyria."

³¹ 'Do not listen to Hezekiah. This is what the king of Assyria says: make peace with me and come out to me. Then each of you will eat fruit from your own vine and fig-tree and drink water from your own cistern, ³² until I come and take you to a land like your own – a land of grain and new wine, a land of bread and vineyards, a land of olive trees and honey. Choose life and not death!

'Do not listen to Hezekiah, for he is

misleading you when he says, "The LORD will deliver us." ³³ Has the god of any nation ever delivered his land from the hand of the king of Assyria? ³⁴ Where are the gods of Hamath and Arpad? Where are the gods of Sepharvaim, Hena and Ivvah? Have they rescued Samaria from my hand? ³⁵ Who of all the gods of these countries has been able to save his land from me? How then can the LORD deliver Jerusalem from my hand?'

³⁶ But the people remained silent and said nothing in reply, because the king had commanded, 'Do not answer him.'

³⁷ Then Eliakim son of Hilkiah the palace administrator, Shebna the secretary, and Joah son of Asaph the recorder went to Hezekiah, with their clothes torn, and told him what the field commander had said.

19 When King Hezekiah heard this, he tore his clothes and put on sackcloth and went into the temple of the LORD. ² He sent Eliakim the palace administrator, Shebna the secretary and the leading priests, all wearing sackcloth, to the prophet Isaiah son of Amoz. ³ They told him, 'This is what Hezekiah says: this day is a day of distress and rebuke and disgrace, as when children come to the moment of birth and there is no strength to deliver them. ⁴ It may be that the LORD your God will hear all the words of the field commander, whom his master, the king of Assyria, has sent to ridicule the living God, and that he will rebuke him for the words the LORD your God has heard. Therefore pray for the remnant that still survives.'

⁵ When King Hezekiah's officials came to Isaiah, ⁶ Isaiah said to them, 'Tell your master, "This is what the LORD says: do not be afraid of what you have heard – those words with which the underlings of the king of Assyria have blasphemed me. ⁷ Listen! When he hears a certain report, I will make him want to return to his own country, and there I will have him cut down with the sword." '

⁸ When the field commander heard that the king of Assyria had left Lachish,

he withdrew and found the king fighting against Libnah.

⁹ Now Sennacherib received a report that Tirhakah, the king of Cush, was marching out to fight against him. So he again sent messengers to Hezekiah with this word: ¹⁰ 'Say to Hezekiah king of Judah: do not let the god you depend on deceive you when he says, "Jerusalem will not be given into the hands of the king of Assyria." ¹¹ Surely you have heard what the kings of Assyria have done to all the countries, destroying them completely. And will you be delivered? ¹² Did the gods of the nations that were destroyed by my predecessors deliver them – the gods of Gozan, Harran, Rezeph and the people of Eden who were in Tel Assar? ¹³ Where is the king of Hamath or the king of Arpad? Where are the kings of Lair, Sepharvaim, Hena and Ivvah?'

¹⁴ Hezekiah received the letter from the messengers and read it. Then he went up to the temple of the LORD and spread it out before the LORD. ¹⁵ And Hezekiah prayed to the LORD: 'LORD, the God of Israel, enthroned between the cherubim, you alone are God over all the kingdoms of the earth. You have made heaven and earth. ¹⁶ Give ear, LORD, and hear; open your eyes, LORD, and see; listen to the words Sennacherib has sent to ridicule the living God.

¹⁷ 'It is true, LORD, that the Assyrian kings have laid waste these nations and their lands. ¹⁸ They have thrown their gods into the fire and destroyed them, for they were not gods but only wood and stone, fashioned by human hands. ¹⁹ Now, LORD our God, deliver us from his hand, so that all the kingdoms of the earth may know that you alone, LORD, are God.'

··

■ **PSALM 78:40-47**

⁴⁰ How often they rebelled against him in the wilderness
and grieved him in the wasteland!

⁴¹ Again and again they put God to the test;
   they vexed the Holy One of Israel.
⁴² They did not remember his power –
   the day he redeemed them from the
   oppressor,
⁴³ the day he displayed his signs in Egypt,
   his wonders in the region of Zoan.
⁴⁴ He turned their river into blood;
   they could not drink from their
   streams.
⁴⁵ He sent swarms of flies that devoured
   them,
   and frogs that devastated them.
⁴⁶ He gave their crops to the grasshopper,
   their produce to the locust.
⁴⁷ He destroyed their vines with hail
   and their sycamore-figs with sleet.

■ PROVERBS 17:5-6

⁵ Whoever mocks the poor shows
   contempt for their Maker;
   whoever gloats over disaster will not
   go unpunished.

⁶ Children's children are a crown to the
   aged,
   and parents are the pride of their
   children.

■ ACTS 9:1-22

9 Meanwhile, Saul was still breathing out
   murderous threats against the Lord's
disciples. He went to the high priest ²and
asked him for letters to the synagogues in
Damascus, so that if he found any there
who belonged to the Way, whether men or
women, he might take them as prisoners
to Jerusalem. ³ As he neared Damascus on
his journey, suddenly a light from heaven
flashed around him. ⁴ He fell to the ground
and heard a voice say to him, 'Saul, Saul,
why do you persecute me?'

⁵ 'Who are you, Lord?' Saul asked.
   'I am Jesus, whom you are persecuting,'
he replied. ⁶ 'Now get up and go into the city,
and you will be told what you must do.'

⁷ The men travelling with Saul stood
there speechless; they heard the sound
but did not see anyone. ⁸ Saul got up from
the ground, but when he opened his eyes
he could see nothing. So they led him by
the hand into Damascus. ⁹ For three days
he was blind, and did not eat or drink
anything.

¹⁰ In Damascus there was a disciple
named Ananias. The Lord called to him in a
vision, 'Ananias!'

'Yes, Lord,' he answered.

¹¹ The Lord told him, 'Go to the house of
Judas on Straight Street and ask for a man
from Tarsus named Saul, for he is praying.
¹² In a vision he has seen a man named Ananias come and place his hands on him to
restore his sight.'

¹³ 'Lord,' Ananias answered, 'I have heard
many reports about this man and all the
harm he has done to your holy people in
Jerusalem. ¹⁴ And he has come here with
authority from the chief priests to arrest all
who call on your name.'

¹⁵ But the Lord said to Ananias, 'Go! This
man is my chosen instrument to proclaim
my name to the Gentiles and their kings
and to the people of Israel. ¹⁶ I will show him
how much he must suffer for my name.'

¹⁷ Then Ananias went to the house and
entered it. Placing his hands on Saul, he
said, 'Brother Saul, the Lord – Jesus, who
appeared to you on the road as you were
coming here – has sent me so that you may
see again and be filled with the Holy Spirit.' ¹⁸ Immediately, something like scales fell
from Saul's eyes, and he could see again. He
got up and was baptised, ¹⁹ and after taking
some food, he regained his strength.

Saul spent several days with the disciples
in Damascus. ²⁰ At once he began to preach
in the synagogues that Jesus is the Son of

God. [21] All those who heard him were astonished and asked, 'Isn't he the man who caused havoc in Jerusalem among those who call on this name? And hasn't he come here to take them as prisoners to the chief priests?' [22] Yet Saul grew more and more powerful and baffled the Jews living in Damascus by proving that Jesus is the Messiah.

Nothing!

'Who are you, Lord?' **Acts 9:5**

When reflecting on belief, we look at the fact that God has appeared in this world in the Person of His eternal Son. Our faith is not man's words but the Word of the Son Himself. No other world faith even attempts to represent its great teacher as God incarnate. Yet we claim for Christ just that. As God, He comes to us from the highest, and He comes all the way.

I remember hearing a missionary to India say that he was forced to rethink his faith in the light of other faiths and other ways of life. 'All the old shibboleths and modes of expression and accepted outlooks on life are challenged,' he said, 'and one begins to see where the relevant lies.' He started discussions with Hindu, Buddhist and Muslim leaders, as well as representatives of India's many other religions. The gatherings were called 'Round Table' discussions to suggest that everyone could present what they considered to be the distinctives of their faith. One could see scintillations of truth, the missionary recalled, as people spoke from experience or from their sacred books. But whenever a Christian spoke and unfolded the truth of the Incarnation, the meeting would lapse into silence. Sometimes the silence would last for many minutes, only to be broken with the remark, 'We have nothing in our faith that compares to that. Nothing!'

PRAYER

Dear God and Father, if You hadn't come down to us, how could we have ever come up to You? What condescension. Yet what love. Our hearts sing with gratitude. Blessed be Your name forever. Amen.

FURTHER STUDY

Acts 1:1-5; 1 Cor. 15:1-8; Acts 9:1-6; 1 Tim. 3:16

• What was Paul's testimony?
• How did he substantiate it?

July 6

■ **2 KINGS 19:20–21:26**

[20] Then Isaiah son of Amoz sent a message to Hezekiah: 'This is what the LORD, the God of Israel, says: I have heard your prayer concerning Sennacherib king of Assyria. [21] This is the word that the LORD has spoken against him:

' "Virgin Daughter Zion
    despises you and mocks you.
Daughter Jerusalem
    tosses her head as you flee.
²² Who is it you have ridiculed and
        blasphemed?
    Against whom have you raised your
        voice
    and lifted your eyes in pride?
    Against the Holy One of Israel!
²³ By your messengers
    you have ridiculed the Lord.
And you have said,
    'With my many chariots
I have ascended the heights of the
        mountains,
    the utmost heights of Lebanon.
I have cut down its tallest cedars,
    the choicest of its junipers.
I have reached its remotest parts,
    the finest of its forests.
²⁴ I have dug wells in foreign lands
    and drunk the water there.
With the soles of my feet
    I have dried up all the streams of Egypt.'

²⁵ ' "Have you not heard?
    Long ago I ordained it.
In days of old I planned it;
    now I have brought it to pass,
that you have turned fortified cities
    into piles of stone.
²⁶ Their people, drained of power,
    are dismayed and put to shame.
They are like plants in the field,
    like tender green shoots,
like grass sprouting on the roof,
    scorched before it grows up.

²⁷ ' "But I know where you are
    and when you come and go
    and how you rage against me.
²⁸ Because you rage against me
    and because your insolence has
        reached my ears,
I will put my hook in your nose

and my bit in your mouth,
    and I will make you return
    by the way you came." '

²⁹ 'This will be the sign for you, Hezekiah:

'This year you will eat what grows by
        itself,
    and the second year what springs
        from that.
But in the third year sow and reap,
    plant vineyards and eat their fruit.
³⁰ Once more a remnant of the kingdom of
        Judah
    will take root below and bear fruit
        above.
³¹ For out of Jerusalem will come a
        remnant,
    and out of Mount Zion a band of
        survivors.

'The zeal of the LORD Almighty will
accomplish this.

³² 'Therefore this is what the LORD says
concerning the king of Assyria:

' "He will not enter this city
    or shoot an arrow here.
He will not come before it with shield
    or build a siege ramp against it.
³³ By the way that he came he will return;
    he will not enter this city
                    declares the LORD.
³⁴ I will defend this city and save it,
    for my sake and for the sake of David
        my servant." '

³⁵ That night the angel of the LORD
went out and put to death a hundred and
eighty-five thousand in the Assyrian camp.
When the people got up the next morning – there were all the dead bodies! ³⁶ So
Sennacherib king of Assyria broke camp
and withdrew. He returned to Nineveh and
stayed there.

³⁷One day, while he was worshipping in the temple of his god Nisrok, his sons Adrammelek and Sharezer killed him with the sword, and they escaped to the land of Ararat. And Esarhaddon his son succeeded him as king.

20 In those days Hezekiah became ill and was at the point of death. The prophet Isaiah son of Amoz went to him and said, 'This is what the LORD says: put your house in order, because you are going to die; you will not recover.'

²Hezekiah turned his face to the wall and prayed to the LORD, ³'Remember, LORD, how I have walked before you faithfully and with wholehearted devotion and have done what is good in your eyes.' And Hezekiah wept bitterly.

⁴Before Isaiah had left the middle court, the word of the LORD came to him: ⁵'Go back and tell Hezekiah, the ruler of my people, "This is what the LORD, the God of your father David, says: I have heard your prayer and seen your tears; I will heal you. On the third day from now you will go up to the temple of the LORD. ⁶I will add fifteen years to your life. And I will deliver you and this city from the hand of the king of Assyria. I will defend this city for my sake and for the sake of my servant David."'

⁷Then Isaiah said, 'Prepare a poultice of figs.' They did so and applied it to the boil, and he recovered.

⁸Hezekiah had asked Isaiah, 'What will be the sign that the LORD will heal me and that I will go up to the temple of the LORD on the third day from now?'

⁹Isaiah answered, 'This is the LORD's sign to you that the LORD will do what he has promised: shall the shadow go forward ten steps, or shall it go back ten steps?'

¹⁰'It is a simple matter for the shadow to go forward ten steps,' said Hezekiah. 'Rather, let it go back ten steps.'

¹¹Then the prophet Isaiah called on the LORD, and the LORD made the shadow go back the ten steps it had gone down on the stairway of Ahaz.

¹²At that time Marduk-Baladan son of Baladan king of Babylon sent Hezekiah letters and a gift, because he had heard of Hezekiah's illness. ¹³Hezekiah received the envoys and showed them all that was in his storehouses – the silver, the gold, the spices and the fine oil – his armoury and everything found among his treasures. There was nothing in his palace or in all his kingdom that Hezekiah did not show them.

¹⁴Then Isaiah the prophet went to King Hezekiah and asked, 'What did those men say, and where did they come from?'

'From a distant land,' Hezekiah replied. 'They came from Babylon.'

¹⁵The prophet asked, 'What did they see in your palace?'

'They saw everything in my palace,' Hezekiah said. 'There is nothing among my treasures that I did not show them.'

¹⁶Then Isaiah said to Hezekiah, 'Hear the word of the LORD: ¹⁷the time will surely come when everything in your palace, and all that your predecessors have stored up until this day, will be carried off to Babylon. Nothing will be left, says the LORD. ¹⁸And some of your descendants, your own flesh and blood who will be born to you, will be taken away, and they will become eunuchs in the palace of the king of Babylon.'

¹⁹'The word of the LORD you have spoken is good,' Hezekiah replied. For he thought, 'Will there not be peace and security in my lifetime?'

²⁰As for the other events of Hezekiah's reign, all his achievements and how he made the pool and the tunnel by which he brought water into the city, are they not written in the book of the annals of the kings of Judah? ²¹Hezekiah rested with his ancestors. And Manasseh his son succeeded him as king.

21 Manasseh was twelve years old when he became king, and he reigned in

Jerusalem for fifty-five years. His mother's name was Hephzibah. [2] He did evil in the eyes of the LORD, following the detestable practices of the nations the LORD had driven out before the Israelites. [3] He rebuilt the high places his father Hezekiah had destroyed; he also erected altars to Baal and made an Asherah pole, as Ahab king of Israel had done. He bowed down to all the starry hosts and worshipped them. [4] He built altars in the temple of the LORD, of which the LORD had said, 'In Jerusalem I will put my Name.' [5] In the two courts of the temple of the LORD, he built altars to all the starry hosts. [6] He sacrificed his own son in the fire, practised divination, sought omens, and consulted mediums and spiritists. He did much evil in the eyes of the LORD, arousing his anger.

[7] He took the carved Asherah pole he had made and put it in the temple, of which the LORD had said to David and to his son Solomon, 'In this temple and in Jerusalem, which I have chosen out of all the tribes of Israel, I will put my Name for ever. [8] I will not again make the feet of the Israelites wander from the land I gave their ancestors, if only they will be careful to do everything I commanded them and will keep the whole Law that my servant Moses gave them.' [9] But the people did not listen. Manasseh led them astray, so that they did more evil than the nations the LORD had destroyed before the Israelites.

[10] The LORD said through his servants the prophets: [11] 'Manasseh king of Judah has committed these detestable sins. He has done more evil than the Amorites who preceded him and has led Judah into sin with his idols. [12] Therefore this is what the LORD, the God of Israel, says: I am going to bring such disaster on Jerusalem and Judah that the ears of everyone who hears of it will tingle. [13] I will stretch out over Jerusalem the measuring line used against Samaria and the plumb-line used against the house of Ahab. I will wipe out Jerusalem as one wipes out a dish, wiping it and turning it upside-down. [14] I will forsake the remnant of my inheritance and give them into the hands of enemies. They will be looted and plundered by all their enemies; [15] they have done evil in my eyes and have aroused my anger from the day their ancestors came out of Egypt until this day.'

[16] Moreover, Manasseh also shed so much innocent blood that he filled Jerusalem from end to end – besides the sin that he had caused Judah to commit, so that they did evil in the eyes of the LORD.

[17] As for the other events of Manasseh's reign, and all he did, including the sin he committed, are they not written in the book of the annals of the kings of Judah? [18] Manasseh rested with his ancestors and was buried in his palace garden, the garden of Uzza. And Amon his son succeeded him as king.

[19] Amon was twenty-two years old when he became king, and he reigned in Jerusalem for two years. His mother's name was Meshullemeth daughter of Haruz; she was from Jotbah. [20] He did evil in the eyes of the LORD, as his father Manasseh had done. [21] He followed completely the ways of his father, worshipped the idols his father had worshipped, and bowing down to them. [22] He forsook the LORD, the God of his ancestors, and did not walk in obedience to him.

[23] Amon's officials conspired against him and assassinated the king in his palace. [24] Then the people of the land killed all who had plotted against King Amon, and they made Josiah his son king in his place.

[25] As for the other events of Amon's reign, and what he did, are they not written in the book of the annals of the kings of Judah? [26] He was buried in his tomb in the garden of Uzza. And Josiah his son succeeded him as king.

▬ PSALM 78:48-55

[48] He gave over their cattle to the hail,

their livestock to bolts of lightning.
⁴⁹ He unleashed against them his hot
    anger,
  his wrath, indignation and hostility –
    a band of destroying angels.
⁵⁰ He prepared a path for his anger;
  he did not spare them from death
    but gave them over to the plague.
⁵¹ He struck down all the firstborn of Egypt,
  the firstfruits of manhood in the tents
    of Ham.
⁵² But he brought his people out like a flock;
  he led them like sheep through the
    wilderness.
⁵³ He guided them safely, so they were
    unafraid;
  but the sea engulfed their enemies.
⁵⁴ And so he brought them to the border of
    his holy land,
  to the hill country his right hand had
    taken.
⁵⁵ He drove out nations before them
  and allotted their lands to them as an
    inheritance;
  he settled the tribes of Israel in their
    homes.

■ PROVERBS 17:7-8

⁷ Eloquent lips are unsuited to a godless
    fool –
  how much worse lying lips to a ruler!

⁸ A bribe is seen as a charm by the one
    who gives it;
  they think success will come at every
    turn.

■ ACTS 9:23-43

²³ After many days had gone by, there was
a conspiracy among the Jews to kill him,
²⁴ but Saul learned of their plan. Day and
night they kept close watch on the city gates

in order to kill him. ²⁵ But his followers took
him by night and lowered him in a basket
through an opening in the wall.

²⁶ When he came to Jerusalem, he tried to
join the disciples, but they were all afraid of
him, not believing that he really was a disciple. ²⁷ But Barnabas took him and brought
him to the apostles. He told them how Saul
on his journey had seen the Lord and that
the Lord had spoken to him, and how in
Damascus he had preached fearlessly in
the name of Jesus. ²⁸ So Saul stayed with
them and moved about freely in Jerusalem,
speaking boldly in the name of the Lord.
²⁹ He talked and debated with the Hellenistic Jews, but they tried to kill him. ³⁰ When
the believers learned of this, they took
him down to Caesarea and sent him off to
Tarsus.

³¹ Then the church throughout Judea,
Galilee and Samaria enjoyed a time of peace
and was strengthened. Living in the fear of
the Lord and encouraged by the Holy Spirit,
it increased in numbers.

³² As Peter travelled about the country,
he went to visit the Lord's people who lived
in Lydda. ³³ There he found a man named
Aeneas, who was paralysed and had been
bedridden for eight years. ³⁴ 'Aeneas,' Peter
said to him, 'Jesus Christ heals you. Get up
and roll up your mat.' Immediately Aeneas
got up. ³⁵ All those who lived in Lydda and
Sharon saw him and turned to the Lord.

³⁶ In Joppa there was a disciple named
Tabitha (in Greek her name is Dorcas);
she was always doing good and helping the
poor. ³⁷ About that time she became ill and
died, and her body was washed and placed
in an upstairs room. ³⁸ Lydda was near Joppa; so when the disciples heard that Peter
was in Lydda, they sent two men to him and
urged him, 'Please come at once!'

³⁹ Peter went with them, and when he arrived he was taken upstairs to the room. All
the widows stood round him, crying and
showing him the robes and other clothing

that Dorcas had made while she was still with them.

⁴⁰ Peter sent them all out of the room; then he got down on his knees and prayed. Turning towards the dead woman, he said, 'Tabitha, get up.' She opened her eyes, and seeing Peter she sat up. ⁴¹ He took her by the hand and helped her to her feet. Then he called for the believers, especially the widows, and presented her to them alive. ⁴² This became known all over Joppa, and many people believed in the Lord. ⁴³ Peter stayed in Joppa for some time with a tanner named Simon.

Righteous Indignation

'He unleashed against them his hot anger, his wrath, indignation and hostility ...' **Psalm 78:49**

For many of us, 'wrath' conjures up the idea of being out of control, an outburst of 'seeing red', a sense of wounded pride or just downright petulance. But it is quite wrong to take these ideas or feelings and impose them on God. God's wrath is never out of control, never capricious, never self-indulgent, never irritable and never ignoble. These may be indicative of human anger but never of the divine. God is angry only when anger is called for.

Even among men and women, there is such a thing as righteous indignation, though (in my opinion) it is more rare than we think.

I used to believe the difference between righteous indignation and carnal hostility was this: when someone was angry with me, that was carnal hostility; when I was angry with someone else, that was righteous indignation! I have 'grown out' of that opinion now, I hasten to add.

All God's indignation is righteous. It is grief at what is happening to others, not a grudge because of what is happening to Him. Would a God who took as much pleasure in evil as He did in good be a God we could love? Would a God who did not react adversely to evil be morally perfect? Of course not. It is precisely this adverse reaction to evil that the Bible has in mind when it talks about God's wrath. God cannot treat good and evil alike. He can look over it - look over it to the cross where it can be forgiven - but He cannot overlook it.

PRAYER

O God, the more I see the reason behind Your wrath and the more I consider the purity of its motive, the more praise and adoration I want to give. What a great and wonderful God You are. And how glad I am that You looked over my sin. Amen.

FURTHER STUDY

Isa. 13:1-22; Psa. 78:40-55; Isa. 30:27; Rom. 1:18

• How does the psalmist describe God's wrath?
• How did Isaiah depict God's anger towards Babylon?

July 7

22 Josiah was eight years old when he became king, and he reigned in Jerusalem for thirty-one years. His mother's name was Jedidah daughter of Adaiah; she was from Bozkath. ²He did what was right in the eyes of the LORD and followed completely the ways of his father David, not turning aside to the right or to the left.

³In the eighteenth year of his reign, King Josiah sent the secretary, Shaphan son of Azaliah, the son of Meshullam, to the temple of the LORD. He said: ⁴'Go up to Hilkiah the high priest and make him get ready the money that has been brought into the temple of the LORD, which the doorkeepers have collected from the people. ⁵Make them entrust it to the men appointed to supervise the work on the temple. And make these men pay the workers who repair the temple of the LORD – ⁶the carpenters, the builders and the masons. Also make them purchase timber and dressed stone to repair the temple. ⁷But they need not account for the money entrusted to them, because they are honest in their dealings.'

⁸Hilkiah the high priest said to Shaphan the secretary, 'I have found the Book of the Law in the temple of the LORD.' He gave it to Shaphan, who read it. ⁹Then Shaphan the secretary went to the king and reported to him: 'Your officials have paid out the money that was in the temple of the LORD and have entrusted it to the workers and supervisors at the temple.' ¹⁰Then Shaphan the secretary informed the king, 'Hilkiah the priest has given me a book.' And Shaphan read from it in the presence of the king.

¹¹When the king heard the words of the Book of the Law, he tore his robes. ¹²He gave these orders to Hilkiah the priest, Ahikam son of Shaphan, Akbor son of Micaiah, Shaphan the secretary and Asaiah the king's attendant: ¹³'Go and enquire of the LORD for me and for the people and for all Judah about what is written in this book that has been found. Great is the LORD's anger that burns against us because those who have gone before us have not obeyed the words of this book; they have not acted in accordance with all that is written there concerning us.'

¹⁴Hilkiah the priest, Ahikam, Akbor, Shaphan and Asaiah went to speak to the prophet Huldah, who was the wife of Shallum son of Tikvah, the son of Harhas, keeper of the wardrobe. She lived in Jerusalem, in the New Quarter.

¹⁵She said to them, 'This is what the LORD, the God of Israel, says: tell the man who sent you to me, ¹⁶"This is what the LORD says: I am going to bring disaster on this place and its people, according to everything written in the book the king of Judah has read. ¹⁷Because they have forsaken me and burned incense to other gods and aroused my anger by all the idols their hands have made, my anger will burn against this place and will not be quenched." ¹⁸Tell the king of Judah, who sent you to enquire of the LORD, "This is what the LORD, the God of Israel, says concerning the words you heard: ¹⁹because your heart was responsive and you humbled yourself before the LORD when you heard what I have spoken against this place and its people – that they would become a curse and be laid waste – and because you tore your robes and wept in my presence, I also have heard you, declares the LORD. ²⁰Therefore I will gather you to your ancestors, and you will be buried in peace.

Your eyes will not see all the disaster I am going to bring on this place."'

So they took her answer back to the king.

23 Then the king called together all the elders of Judah and Jerusalem. ²He went up to the temple of the LORD with the people of Judah, the inhabitants of Jerusalem, the priests and the prophets – all the people from the least to the greatest. He read in their hearing all the words of the Book of the Covenant, which had been found in the temple of the LORD. ³The king stood by the pillar and renewed the covenant in the presence of the LORD – to follow the LORD and keep his commands, statutes and decrees with all his heart and all his soul, thus confirming the words of the covenant written in this book. Then all the people pledged themselves to the covenant.

⁴The king ordered Hilkiah the high priest, the priests next in rank and the doorkeepers to remove from the temple of the LORD all the articles made for Baal and Asherah and all the starry hosts. He burned them outside Jerusalem in the fields of the Kidron Valley and took the ashes to Bethel. ⁵He did away with the idolatrous priests appointed by the kings of Judah to burn incense on the high places of the towns of Judah and on those around Jerusalem – those who burned incense to Baal, to the sun and moon, to the constellations and to all the starry hosts. ⁶He took the Asherah pole from the temple of the LORD to the Kidron Valley outside Jerusalem and burned it there. He ground it to powder and scattered the dust over the graves of the common people. ⁷He also tore down the quarters of the male shrine-prostitutes that were in the temple of the LORD, the quarters where women did weaving for Asherah.

⁸Josiah brought all the priests from the towns of Judah and desecrated the high places, from Geba to Beersheba, where the priests had burned incense. He broke down the gateway at the entrance of the Gate of Joshua, the city governor, which was on the left of the city gate. ⁹Although the priests of the high places did not serve at the altar of the LORD in Jerusalem, they ate unleavened bread with their fellow priests.

¹⁰He desecrated Topheth, which was in the Valley of Ben Hinnom, so no one could use it to sacrifice their son or daughter in the fire to Molek. ¹¹He removed from the entrance to the temple of the LORD the horses that the kings of Judah had dedicated to the sun. They were in the court near the room of an official named Nathan-Melek. Josiah then burned the chariots dedicated to the sun.

¹²He pulled down the altars the kings of Judah had erected on the roof near the upper room of Ahaz, and the altars Manasseh had built in the two courts of the temple of the LORD. He removed them from there, smashed them to pieces and threw the rubble into the Kidron Valley. ¹³The king also desecrated the high places that were east of Jerusalem on the south of the Hill of Corruption – the ones Solomon king of Israel had built for Ashtoreth the vile goddess of the Sidonians, for Chemosh the vile god of Moab, and for Molek the detestable god of the people of Ammon. ¹⁴Josiah smashed the sacred stones and cut down the Asherah poles and covered the sites with human bones.

¹⁵Even the altar at Bethel, the high place made by Jeroboam son of Nebat, who had caused Israel to sin – even that altar and high place he demolished. He burned the high place and ground it to powder, and burned the Asherah pole also. ¹⁶Then Josiah looked around, and when he saw the tombs that were there on the hillside, he had the bones removed from them and burned on the altar to defile it, in accordance with the word of the LORD proclaimed by the man of God who foretold these things.

¹⁷The king asked, 'What is that tombstone I see?'

The people of the city said, 'It marks the

tomb of the man of God who came from Judah and pronounced against the altar of Bethel the very things you have done to it.'

[18] 'Leave it alone,' he said. 'Don't let anyone disturb his bones.' So they spared his bones and those of the prophet who had come from Samaria.

[19] Just as he had done at Bethel, Josiah removed all the shrines at the high places that the kings of Israel had built in the towns of Samaria and that had aroused the LORD's anger. [20] Josiah slaughtered all the priests of those high places on the altars and burned human bones on them. Then he went back to Jerusalem.

[21] The king gave this order to all the people: 'Celebrate the Passover to the LORD your God, as it is written in this Book of the Covenant.' [22] Neither in the days of the judges who led Israel nor in the days of the kings of Israel and the kings of Judah had any such Passover been observed. [23] But in the eighteenth year of King Josiah, this Passover was celebrated to the LORD in Jerusalem.

[24] Furthermore, Josiah got rid of the mediums and spiritists, the household gods, the idols and all the other detestable things seen in Judah and Jerusalem. This he did to fulfil the requirements of the law written in the book that Hilkiah the priest had discovered in the temple of the LORD. [25] Neither before nor after Josiah was there a king like him who turned to the LORD as he did – with all his heart and with all his soul and with all his strength, in accordance with all the Law of Moses.

[26] Nevertheless, the LORD did not turn away from the heat of his fierce anger, which burned against Judah because of all that Manasseh had done to arouse his anger. [27] So the LORD said, 'I will remove Judah also from my presence as I removed Israel, and I will reject Jerusalem, the city I chose, and this temple, about which I said, "My Name shall be there."'

[28] As for the other events of Josiah's reign,

and all he did, are they not written in the book of the annals of the kings of Judah?

[29] While Josiah was king, Pharaoh Necho king of Egypt went up to the River Euphrates to help the king of Assyria. King Josiah marched out to meet him in battle, but Necho faced him and killed him at Megiddo. [30] Josiah's servants brought his body in a chariot from Megiddo to Jerusalem and buried him in his own tomb. And the people of the land took Jehoahaz son of Josiah and anointed him and made him king in place of his father.

[31] Jehoahaz was twenty-three years old when he became king, and he reigned in Jerusalem for three months. His mother's name was Hamutal daughter of Jeremiah; she was from Libnah. [32] He did evil in the eyes of the LORD, just as his predecessors had done. [33] Pharaoh Necho put him in chains at Riblah in the land of Hamath so that he might not reign in Jerusalem, and he imposed on Judah a levy of a hundred talents of silver and a talent of gold. [34] Pharaoh Necho made Eliakim son of Josiah king in place of his father Josiah and changed Eliakim's name to Jehoiakim. But he took Jehoahaz and carried him off to Egypt, and there he died. [35] Jehoiakim paid Pharaoh Necho the silver and gold he demanded. In order to do so, he taxed the land and exacted the silver and gold from the people of the land according to their assessments.

[36] Jehoiakim was twenty-five years old when he became king, and he reigned in Jerusalem for eleven years. His mother's name was Zebidah daughter of Pedaiah; she was from Rumah. [37] And he did evil in the eyes of the LORD, just as his predecessors had done.

....

■ PSALM 78:56-64

[56] But they put God to the test
and rebelled against the Most High;

they did not keep his statutes.
⁵⁷ Like their ancestors they were disloyal
     and faithless,
     as unreliable as a faulty bow.
⁵⁸ They angered him with their high places;
     they aroused his jealousy with their
          idols.
⁵⁹ When God heard them, he was furious;
     he rejected Israel completely.
⁶⁰ He abandoned the tabernacle of Shiloh,
     the tent he had set up among humans.
⁶¹ He sent the ark of his might into
          captivity,
     his splendour into the hands of the
          enemy.
⁶² He gave his people over to the sword;
     he was furious with his inheritance.
⁶³ Fire consumed their young men,
     and their young women had no
          wedding songs;
⁶⁴ their priests were put to the sword,
     and their widows could not weep.

··

▬ PROVERBS 17:9-10

⁹ Whoever would foster love covers over
     an offence,
     but whoever repeats the matter
          separates close friends.

¹⁰ A rebuke impresses a discerning person
     more than a hundred lashes a fool.

··

▬ ACTS 10:1-23ᵃ

10 At Caesarea there was a man named
Cornelius, a centurion in what was
known as the Italian Regiment. ²He and all
his family were devout and God-fearing; he
gave generously to those in need and prayed
to God regularly. ³One day at about three in
the afternoon he had a vision. He distinctly
saw an angel of God, who came to him and
said, 'Cornelius!'

⁴ Cornelius stared at him in fear. 'What is
it, Lord?' he asked.

The angel answered, 'Your prayers and
gifts to the poor have come up as a memorial
offering before God. ⁵Now send men to Joppa to bring back a man named Simon who
is called Peter. ⁶He is staying with Simon
the tanner, whose house is by the sea.'

⁷ When the angel who spoke to him had
gone, Cornelius called two of his servants
and a devout soldier who was one of his
attendants. ⁸He told them everything that
had happened and sent them to Joppa.

⁹ About noon the following day as they
were on their journey and approaching the
city, Peter went up on the roof to pray. ¹⁰He
became hungry and wanted something to
eat, and while the meal was being prepared,
he fell into a trance. ¹¹He saw heaven opened
and something like a large sheet being let
down to earth by its four corners. ¹²It contained all kinds of four-footed animals, as
well as reptiles and birds. ¹³Then a voice
told him, 'Get up, Peter. Kill and eat.'

¹⁴ 'Surely not, Lord!' Peter replied. 'I have
never eaten anything impure or unclean.'

¹⁵ The voice spoke to him a second time,
'Do not call anything impure that God has
made clean.'

¹⁶ This happened three times, and immediately the sheet was taken back to heaven.

¹⁷ While Peter was wondering about the
meaning of the vision, the men sent by Cornelius found out where Simon's house was
and stopped at the gate. ¹⁸They called out,
asking if Simon who was known as Peter
was staying there.

¹⁹ While Peter was still thinking about the
vision, the Spirit said to him, 'Simon, three
men are looking for you. ²⁰So get up and go
downstairs. Do not hesitate to go with them,
for I have sent them.'

²¹ Peter went down and said to the men,
'I'm the one you're looking for. Why have
you come?'

²² The men replied, 'We have come from

Cornelius the centurion. He is a righteous and God-fearing man, who is respected by all the Jewish people. A holy angel told him to ask you to come to his house so that he could hear what you have to say.' ²³Then Peter invited the men into the house to be his guests.

Choose to Forgive

'Whoever would foster love covers over an offence, but whoever repeats the matter separates close friends.' **Proverbs 17:9**

Jesus gives us stern and uncompromising warnings about forgiveness. But if forgiveness is so important and yet so difficult, how do we go about it? We must do several things.

First, we must not try to minimise or dismiss the offence as if it never happened. If it hurts, then we must face it and feel it. A common misconception that keeps people from forgiving is that they think in order to forgive they must come to the place where they look upon the things done to them as being really not that bad. That is excusing, not forgiving. C. S. Lewis says, 'Real forgiveness means looking steadily at the sin, the sin that is left over without any excuse after all allowances have been made, and seeing it in all its horror, dirt, meanness and malice, and nevertheless being wholly reconciled to the man who has done it. That, and only that, is forgiveness.'

Second, we must see that forgiveness is not an emotional thing (though it can affect the emotions), but a matter of the will. It is making the decision that the wrong done against you will not count or cause a separation. In making that decision, remember you have all the resources of God available to you. This applies not just to minor matters like snubs, but to major matters too.

The task of forgiving must be more than a match for the magnitude of the pain involved. A choice has to be made. No matter how we are wronged, we can choose out of a desire for love to forgive.

PRAYER

Lord Jesus Christ, You looked into the eyes of those who hammered You to a cross and cried, 'Father, forgive them!' Help me do the same when I am confronted with lesser injury or hurt. For Your own dear name's sake. Amen.

FURTHER STUDY

Micah 6:1-8; 7:18; Isa. 43:25
• What does God delight to do?
• What are we to love?

July 8

■ 2 KINGS 24:1–25:30

24 During Jehoiakim's reign, Nebuchadnezzar king of Babylon invaded the land, and Jehoiakim became his vassal for three years. But then he turned against Nebuchadnezzar and rebelled. ²The LORD sent Babylonian, Aramean, Moabite and Ammonite raiders against him to destroy Judah, in accordance with the word of the LORD proclaimed by his servants the prophets. ³Surely these things happened to Judah according to the LORD's command, in order to remove them from his presence because of the sins of Manasseh and all he had done, ⁴including the shedding of innocent blood. For he had filled Jerusalem with innocent blood, and the LORD was not willing to forgive.

⁵As for the other events of Jehoiakim's reign, and all he did, are they not written in the book of the annals of the kings of Judah? ⁶Jehoiakim rested with his ancestors. And Jehoiachin his son succeeded him as king.

⁷The king of Egypt did not march out from his own country again, because the king of Babylon had taken all his territory, from the Wadi of Egypt to the River Euphrates.

⁸Jehoiachin was eighteen years old when he became king, and he reigned in Jerusalem for three months. His mother's name was Nehushta daughter of Elnathan; she was from Jerusalem. ⁹He did evil in the eyes of the LORD, just as his father had done.

¹⁰At that time the officers of Nebuchadnezzar king of Babylon advanced on Jerusalem and laid siege to it, ¹¹and Nebuchadnezzar himself came up to the city while his officers were besieging it. ¹²Jehoiachin king of Judah, his mother, his attendants, his nobles and his officials all surrendered to him.

In the eighth year of the reign of the king of Babylon, he took Jehoiachin prisoner. ¹³As the LORD had declared, Nebuchadnezzar removed the treasures from the temple of the LORD and from the royal palace, and cut up the gold articles that Solomon king of Israel had made for the temple of the LORD. ¹⁴He carried all Jerusalem into exile: all the officers and fighting men, and all the skilled workers and artisans – a total of ten thousand. Only the poorest people of the land were left.

¹⁵Nebuchadnezzar took Jehoiachin captive to Babylon. He also took from Jerusalem to Babylon the king's mother, his wives, his officials and the prominent people of the land. ¹⁶The king of Babylon also deported to Babylon the entire force of seven thousand fighting men, strong and fit for war, and a thousand skilled workers and artisans. ¹⁷He made Mattaniah, Jehoiachin's uncle, king in his place and changed his name to Zedekiah.

¹⁸Zedekiah was twenty-one years old when he became king, and he reigned in Jerusalem for eleven years. His mother's name was Hamutal daughter of Jeremiah; she was from Libnah. ¹⁹He did evil in the eyes of the LORD, just as Jehoiakim had done. ²⁰It was because of the LORD's anger that all this happened to Jerusalem and Judah, and in the end he thrust them from his presence.

Now Zedekiah rebelled against the king of Babylon.

25 So in the ninth year of Zedekiah's reign, on the tenth day of the tenth month, Nebuchadnezzar king of Babylon marched against Jerusalem with his whole

army. He camped outside the city and built siege works all around it. ²The city was kept under siege until the eleventh year of King Zedekiah.

³By the ninth day of the fourth month the famine in the city had become so severe that there was no food for the people to eat. ⁴Then the city wall was broken through, and the whole army fled at night through the gate between the two walls near the king's garden, though the Babylonians were surrounding the city. They fled towards the Arabah, ⁵but the Babylonian army pursued the king and overtook him in the plains of Jericho. All his soldiers were separated from him and scattered, ⁶and he was captured.

He was taken to the king of Babylon at Riblah, where sentence was pronounced on him. ⁷They killed the sons of Zedekiah before his eyes. Then they put out his eyes, bound him with bronze shackles and took him to Babylon.

⁸On the seventh day of the fifth month, in the nineteenth year of Nebuchadnezzar king of Babylon, Nebuzaradan commander of the imperial guard, an official of the king of Babylon, came to Jerusalem. ⁹He set fire to the temple of the LORD, the royal palace and all the houses of Jerusalem. Every important building he burned down. ¹⁰The whole Babylonian army under the commander of the imperial guard broke down the walls around Jerusalem. ¹¹Nebuzaradan the commander of the guard carried into exile the people who remained in the city, along with the rest of the populace and those who had deserted to the king of Babylon. ¹²But the commander left behind some of the poorest people of the land to work the vineyards and fields.

¹³The Babylonians broke up the bronze pillars, the movable stands and the bronze Sea that were at the temple of the LORD and they carried the bronze to Babylon. ¹⁴They also took away the pots, shovels, wick trimmers, dishes and all the bronze articles used in the temple service. ¹⁵The commander of the imperial guard took away the censers and sprinkling bowls – all that were made of pure gold or silver.

¹⁶The bronze from the two pillars, the Sea and the movable stands, which Solomon had made for the temple of the LORD, was more than could be weighed. ¹⁷Each pillar was eighteen cubits high. The bronze capital on top of one pillar was three cubits high and was decorated with a network and pomegranates of bronze all around. The other pillar, with its network, was similar.

¹⁸The commander of the guard took as prisoners Seraiah the chief priest, Zephaniah the priest next in rank and the three doorkeepers. ¹⁹Of those still in the city, he took the officer in charge of the fighting men, and five royal advisors. He also took the secretary who was chief officer in charge of conscripting the people of the land and sixty of the conscripts who were found in the city. ²⁰Nebuzaradan the commander took them all and brought them to the king of Babylon at Riblah. ²¹There at Riblah, in the land of Hamath, the king had them executed.

So Judah went into captivity, away from her land.

²²Nebuchadnezzar king of Babylon appointed Gedaliah son of Ahikam, the son of Shaphan, to be over the people he had left behind in Judah. ²³When all the army officers and their men heard that the king of Babylon had appointed Gedaliah as governor, they came to Gedaliah at Mizpah – Ishmael son of Nethaniah, Johanan son of Kareah, Seraiah son of Tanhumeth the Netophathite, Jaazaniah the son of the Maakathite, and their men. ²⁴Gedaliah took an oath to reassure them and their men. 'Do not be afraid of the Babylonian officials,' he said. 'Settle down in the land and serve the king of Babylon, and it will go well with you.'

²⁵In the seventh month, however, Ishmael son of Nethaniah, the son of Elishama,

who was of royal blood, came with ten men and assassinated Gedaliah and also the men of Judah and the Babylonians who were with him at Mizpah. ²⁶At this, all the people from the least to the greatest, together with the army officers, fled to Egypt for fear of the Babylonians.

²⁷In the thirty-seventh year of the exile of Jehoiachin king of Judah, in the year Awel-Marduk became king of Babylon, he released Jehoiachin king of Judah from prison. He did this on the twenty-seventh day of the twelfth month. ²⁸He spoke kindly to him and gave him a seat of honour higher than those of the other kings who were with him in Babylon. ²⁹So Jehoiachin put aside his prison clothes and for the rest of his life ate regularly at the king's table. ³⁰Day by day the king gave Jehoiachin a regular allowance as long as he lived.

▬ PSALM 78:65-72

⁶⁵ Then the Lord awoke as from sleep,
    as a warrior wakes from the stupor
      of wine.
⁶⁶ He beat back his enemies;
    he put them to everlasting shame.
⁶⁷ Then he rejected the tents of Joseph,
    he did not choose the tribe of
      Ephraim;
⁶⁸ but he chose the tribe of Judah,
    Mount Zion, which he loved.
⁶⁹ He built his sanctuary like the heights,
    like the earth that he established for
      ever.
⁷⁰ He chose David his servant
    and took him from the sheepfolds;
⁷¹ from tending the sheep he brought him
    to be the shepherd of his people Jacob,
    of Israel his inheritance.
⁷² And David shepherded them with
    integrity of heart;
    with skilful hands he led them.

▬ PROVERBS 17:11-12

¹¹ Evildoers foster rebellion against God;
    the messenger of death will be sent
      against them.

¹² Better to meet a bear robbed of her cubs
    than a fool bent on folly.

▬ ACTS 10:23ᵇ-48

The next day Peter started out with them, and some of the believers from Joppa went along. ²⁴The following day he arrived in Caesarea. Cornelius was expecting them and had called together his relatives and close friends. ²⁵As Peter entered the house, Cornelius met him and fell at his feet in reverence. ²⁶But Peter made him get up. 'Stand up,' he said, 'I am only a man myself.'

²⁷While talking with him, Peter went inside and found a large gathering of people. ²⁸He said to them: 'You are well aware that it is against our law for a Jew to associate with or visit a Gentile. But God has shown me that I should not call anyone impure or unclean. ²⁹So when I was sent for, I came without raising any objection. May I ask why you sent for me?'

³⁰Cornelius answered: 'Three days ago I was in my house praying at this hour, at three in the afternoon. Suddenly a man in shining clothes stood before me ³¹and said, "Cornelius, God has heard your prayer and remembered your gifts to the poor. ³²Send to Joppa for Simon who is called Peter. He is a guest in the home of Simon the tanner, who lives by the sea." ³³So I sent for you immediately, and it was good of you to come. Now we are all here in the presence of God to listen to everything the Lord has commanded you to tell us.'

³⁴Then Peter began to speak: 'I now realise how true it is that God does not show favouritism ³⁵but accepts from every nation

the one who fears him and does what is right. ³⁶You know the message God sent to the people of Israel, announcing the good news of peace through Jesus Christ, who is Lord of all. ³⁷You know what has happened throughout the province of Judea, beginning in Galilee after the baptism that John preached – ³⁸how God anointed Jesus of Nazareth with the Holy Spirit and power, and how he went around doing good and healing all who were under the power of the devil, because God was with him.

³⁹'We are witnesses of everything he did in the country of the Jews and in Jerusalem. They killed him by hanging him on a cross, ⁴⁰but God raised him from the dead on the third day and caused him to be seen. ⁴¹He was not seen by all the people, but by witnesses whom God had already chosen – by us who ate and drank with him after he rose from the dead. ⁴²He commanded us to preach to the people and to testify that he is the one whom God appointed as judge of the living and the dead. ⁴³All the prophets testify about him that everyone who believes in him receives forgiveness of sins through his name.'

⁴⁴While Peter was still speaking these words, the Holy Spirit came on all who heard the message. ⁴⁵The circumcised believers who had come with Peter were astonished that the gift of the Holy Spirit had been poured out even on Gentiles. ⁴⁶For they heard them speaking in tongues and praising God.

Then Peter said, ⁴⁷'Surely no one can stand in the way of their being baptised with water. They have received the Holy Spirit just as we have.' ⁴⁸So he ordered that they be baptised in the name of Jesus Christ. Then they asked Peter to stay with them for a few days.

Channels of Blessing

'... God anointed Jesus of Nazareth with the Holy Spirit and with power, and ... he went around doing good and healing all who were under the power of the devil ...'
Acts 10:38

How much spiritual power is projected from our lives into a lost and dying world? If we are honest, we will be compelled to say, 'Very little.'

A sign on the door of the electricity company stated: 'The electric bell is not working - please knock.' All our signs, making great claims for the gospel, are cancelled out if power is not apparent in our everyday lives. The Holy Spirit's power is not confined to delighting Christians with manifestations of the gifts of the Spirit in our church gatherings, but in empowering them for effective witness in the world. We must watch that we do not degenerate into being simply consumers of blessing rather than channels of blessing.

Over the years I have had a stream of letters telling me how God has been leading people to pray for healing from sickness for their non-Christian friends - and remarkable things have happened as a result. Some would regard it as doctrinally incorrect to pray for a person's healing if that person is not a Christian. Jesus did it, and so did Paul.

I feel that the Holy Spirit is nudging me to say that, in the future, one of the ways by which we will see multitudes won to Christ is by allowing the Holy Spirit to work through us in supernatural signs and wonders. God is calling us to launch out into the deep.

PRAYER

O Father, something within me seems to draw back at the borders of the supernatural. Give me the faith and expectancy, however, to step over that line and demonstrate to others that I am not just a consumer, but a channel of Your blessings. Amen.

FURTHER STUDY

Acts 3:1–13; Isa. 53:5; Luke 4:18; 1 Cor. 12:9
• What were Peter and John doing after the Spirit's coming?
• How did they respond to the lame man?

July 9

▪ 1 CHRONICLES 1:1–2:2

1 Adam, Seth, Enosh, ²Kenan, Mahalalel, Jared, ³Enoch, Methuselah, Lamech, Noah.

⁴ The sons of Noah:
Shem, Ham and Japheth.

⁵ The sons of Japheth:
Gomer, Magog, Madai, Javan, Tubal, Meshek and Tiras.
⁶ The sons of Gomer:
Ashkenaz, Riphath and Togarmah.
⁷ The sons of Javan:
Elishah, Tarshish, the Kittites and the Rodanites.

⁸ The sons of Ham:
Cush, Egypt, Put and Canaan.
⁹ The sons of Cush:
Seba, Havilah, Sabta, Raamah and Sabteka.
The sons of Raamah:
Sheba and Dedan.
¹⁰ Cush was the father of

Nimrod, who became a mighty warrior on earth.

¹¹ Egypt was the father of
the Ludites, Anamites, Lehabites, Naphtuhites, ¹²Pathrusites, Kasluhites (from whom the Philistines came) and Caphtorites.
¹³ Canaan was the father of
Sidon his firstborn, and of the Hittites, ¹⁴Jebusites, Amorites, Girgashites, ¹⁵Hivites, Arkites, Sinites, ¹⁶Arvadites, Zemarites and Hamathites.

¹⁷ The sons of Shem:
Elam, Ashur, Arphaxad, Lud and Aram.
The sons of Aram:
Uz, Hul, Gether and Meshek.
¹⁸ Arphaxad was the father of Shelah, and Shelah the father of Eber.
¹⁹ Two sons were born to Eber:
one was named Peleg, because in his time the earth was divided; his brother was named Joktan.
²⁰ Joktan was the father of

Almodad, Sheleph, Hazarmaveth, Jerah, ²¹Hadoram, Uzal, Diklah, ²²Obal, Abimael, Sheba, ²³Ophir, Havilah and Jobab. All these were sons of Joktan.

²⁴Shem, Arphaxad, Shelah,
²⁵Eber, Peleg, Reu,
²⁶Serug, Nahor, Terah
²⁷and Abram (that is, Abraham).

²⁸The sons of Abraham:
　Isaac and Ishmael.

²⁹These were their descendants:
　Nebaioth the firstborn of Ishmael, Kedar, Adbeel, Mibsam, ³⁰Mishma, Dumah, Massa, Hadad, Tema, ³¹Jetur, Naphish and Kedemah. These were the sons of Ishmael.

³²The sons born to Keturah, Abraham's concubine:
　Zimran, Jokshan, Medan, Midian, Ishbak and Shuah.
　The sons of Jokshan:
　Sheba and Dedan.
³³The sons of Midian:
　Ephah, Epher, Hanok, Abida and Eldaah.
All these were descendants of Keturah.

³⁴Abraham was the father of Isaac.
　The sons of Isaac:
　Esau and Israel.

³⁵The sons of Esau:
　Eliphaz, Reuel, Jeush, Jalam and Korah.
³⁶The sons of Eliphaz:
　Teman, Omar, Zepho, Gatam and Kenaz;
　by Timna: Amalek.
³⁷The sons of Reuel:
　Nahath, Zerah, Shammah and Mizzah.

³⁸The sons of Seir:
　Lotan, Shobal, Zibeon, Anah, Dishon, Ezer and Dishan.
³⁹The sons of Lotan:
　Hori and Homam. Timna was Lotan's sister.
⁴⁰The sons of Shobal:
　Alvan, Manahath, Ebal, Shepho and Onam.
　The sons of Zibeon:
　Aiah and Anah.
⁴¹The son of Anah:
　Dishon.
　The sons of Dishon:
　Hemdan, Eshban, Ithran and Keran.
⁴²The sons of Ezer:
　Bilhan, Zaavan and Akan.
　The sons of Dishan:
　Uz and Aran.

⁴³These were the kings who reigned in Edom before any Israelite king reigned:
　Bela son of Beor, whose city was named Dinhabah.
⁴⁴When Bela died, Jobab son of Zerah from Bozrah succeeded him as king.
⁴⁵When Jobab died, Husham from the land of the Temanites succeeded him as king.
⁴⁶When Husham died, Hadad son of Bedad, who defeated Midian in the country of Moab, succeeded him as king. His city was named Avith.
⁴⁷When Hadad died, Samlah from Masrekah succeeded him as king.
⁴⁸When Samlah died, Shaul from Rehoboth on the river succeeded him as king.
⁴⁹When Shaul died, Baal-Hanan son of Akbor succeeded him as king.
⁵⁰When Baal-Hanan died, Hadad succeeded him as king. His city was named Pau, and his wife's name was Mehetabel daughter of Matred, the daughter of Me-Zahab. ⁵¹Hadad also died.

The chiefs of Edom were:
Timna, Alvah, Jetheth, ⁵²Oholiba-
mah, Elah, Pinon, ⁵³Kenaz, Teman,
Mibzar, ⁵⁴Magdiel and Iram. These
were the chiefs of Edom.

2 These were the sons of Israel:
Reuben, Simeon, Levi, Judah, Is-
sachar, Zebulun, ²Dan, Joseph,
Benjamin, Naphtali, Gad and Asher.

■ PSALM 79:1–8

¹O God, the nations have invaded your
inheritance;
they have defiled your holy temple,
they have reduced Jerusalem to
rubble.
²They have left the dead bodies of your
servants
as food for the birds of the sky,
the flesh of your own people for the
animals of the wild.
³They have poured out blood like water
all around Jerusalem,
and there is no one to bury the dead.
⁴We are objects of contempt to our
neighbours,
of scorn and derision to those around us.

⁵How long, LORD? Will you be angry for
ever?
How long will your jealousy burn like
fire?
⁶Pour out your wrath on the nations
that do not acknowledge you,
on the kingdoms
that do not call on your name;
⁷for they have devoured Jacob
and devastated his homeland.

⁸Do not hold against us the sins of past
generations;
may your mercy come quickly to
meet us,
for we are in desperate need.

■ PROVERBS 17:13–14

¹³Evil will never leave the house
of one who pays back evil for good.

¹⁴Starting a quarrel is like breaching a dam;
so drop the matter before a dispute
breaks out.

■ ACTS 11:1–30

11 The apostles and the believers
throughout Judea heard that the Gentiles also had received the word of God. ²So
when Peter went up to Jerusalem, the circumcised believers criticised him ³and said,
'You went into the house of uncircumcised
men and ate with them.'

⁴Starting from the beginning, Peter told
them the whole story: ⁵'I was in the city of
Joppa praying, and in a trance I saw a vision. I saw something like a large sheet
being let down from heaven by its four corners, and it came down to where I was. ⁶I
looked into it and saw four-footed animals
of the earth, wild beasts, reptiles and birds.
⁷Then I heard a voice telling me, "Get up,
Peter. Kill and eat."

⁸'I replied, "Surely not, Lord! Nothing
impure or unclean has ever entered my
mouth."

⁹'The voice spoke from heaven a second
time, "Do not call anything impure that
God has made clean." ¹⁰This happened
three times, and then it was all pulled up to
heaven again.

¹¹'Right then three men who had been
sent to me from Caesarea stopped at the
house where I was staying. ¹²The Spirit told
me to have no hesitation about going with
them. These six brothers also went with me,
and we entered the man's house. ¹³He told
us how he had seen an angel appear in his
house and say, "Send to Joppa for Simon
who is called Peter. ¹⁴He will bring you a

message through which you and all your household will be saved."

¹⁵'As I began to speak, the Holy Spirit came on them as he had come on us at the beginning. ¹⁶Then I remembered what the Lord had said: "John baptised with water, but you will be baptised with the Holy Spirit." ¹⁷So if God gave them the same gift he gave us who believed in the Lord Jesus Christ, who was I to think that I could stand in God's way?'

¹⁸When they heard this, they had no further objections and praised God, saying, 'So then, even to Gentiles God has granted repentance that leads to life.'

¹⁹Now those who had been scattered by the persecution that broke out when Stephen was killed travelled as far as Phoenicia, Cyprus and Antioch, spreading the word only among Jews. ²⁰Some of them, however, men from Cyprus and Cyrene, went to Antioch and began to speak to Greeks also, telling them the good news about the Lord Jesus. ²¹The Lord's hand was with them, and a great number of people believed and turned to the Lord.

²²News of this reached the church in Jerusalem, and they sent Barnabas to Antioch. ²³When he arrived and saw what the grace of God had done, he was glad and encouraged them all to remain true to the Lord with all their hearts. ²⁴He was a good man, full of the Holy Spirit and faith, and a great number of people were brought to the Lord.

²⁵Then Barnabas went to Tarsus to look for Saul, ²⁶and when he found him, he brought him to Antioch. So for a whole year Barnabas and Saul met with the church and taught great numbers of people. The disciples were called Christians first at Antioch.

²⁷During this time some prophets came down from Jerusalem to Antioch. ²⁸One of them, named Agabus, stood up and through the Spirit predicted that a severe famine would spread over the entire Roman world. (This happened during the reign of Claudius.) ²⁹The disciples, as each one was able, decided to provide help for the brothers and sisters living in Judea. ³⁰This they did, sending their gift to the elders by Barnabas and Saul.

All Persons Sacred

'... the Holy Spirit came on them as he had come on us at the beginning.' **Acts 11:15**

An interesting thing to notice about the upper room is that the Holy Spirit came, not just on the Twelve, but on the one hundred and twenty (see Acts 1:15ff).

Suppose the Spirit had come on the Twelve and had bypassed the others who were waiting in that room – what would that have done to Christianity? It would have limited the Spirit's power and presence to special people, called to a specially sacred task. Someone has remarked that the addition of a zero to the Twelve, making 120, is one of the greatest additions in history. It is! The coming of the Holy Spirit on the 120 meant that all distinctions based on a special class or group were gone. Some have different gifts, of course, such as are described in Romans 12, 1 Corinthians 12, and Ephesians 4:11. As far as receiving the gift of the Holy Spirit is concerned, however, all who are redeemed are eligible.

If we think this through carefully, it might enable us to regain a sense of mission in life. Some occupations are considered sacred and some secular. This produces a sag in every so-called secular occupation – the layman is in a secular occupation and so is excused if he lives a half-hearted Christian life. This impoverishes life because it removes any sense of divine calling. A minister can be holy and a layman can be holy – all on the same conditions with no special favours. Sacredness is found in character, not in a collar; in values, not in vestments.

PRAYER

O Father, I am grateful that I, as a person, can receive the greatest gift of all – the Holy Spirit – and live out my life where You have placed me, with a sense of divine vocation. Thank You, dear Father. Amen.

FURTHER STUDY

Acts 11:5-10; 16-18
• What problem did some of the Early Christians have?
• How did God overcome this?

July 10

■ 1 CHRONICLES 2:3-55

³ The sons of Judah:
Er, Onan and Shelah. These three were born to him by a Canaanite woman, the daughter of Shua. Er, Judah's firstborn, was wicked in the LORD's sight; so the LORD put him to death. ⁴ Judah's daughter-in-law Tamar bore Perez and Zerah to Judah. He had five sons in all.

⁵ The sons of Perez:
Hezron and Hamul.
⁶ The sons of Zerah:
Zimri, Ethan, Heman, Kalkol and Darda – five in all.
⁷ The son of Karmi:
Achar, who brought trouble on Israel by violating the ban on taking devoted things.
⁸ The son of Ethan:
Azariah.
⁹ The sons born to Hezron were:

Jerahmeel, Ram and Caleb.

¹⁰ Ram was the father of
Amminadab, and Amminadab the father of Nahshon, the leader of the people of Judah. ¹¹ Nahshon was the father of Salmon, Salmon the father of Boaz, ¹² Boaz the father of Obed and Obed the father of Jesse.
¹³ Jesse was the father of
Eliab his firstborn; the second son was Abinadab, the third Shimea, ¹⁴ the fourth Nethanel, the fifth Raddai, ¹⁵ the sixth Ozem and the seventh David. ¹⁶ Their sisters were Zeruiah and Abigail. Zeruiah's three sons were Abishai, Joab and Asahel. ¹⁷ Abigail was the mother of Amasa, whose father was Jether the Ishmaelite.

¹⁸ Caleb son of Hezron had children by his wife Azubah (and by Jerioth). These were her sons: Jesher, Shobab

and Ardon. ¹⁹When Azubah died, Caleb married Ephrath, who bore him Hur. ²⁰Hur was the father of Uri, and Uri the father of Bezalel.

²¹Later, Hezron, when he was sixty years old, married the daughter of Makir the father of Gilead. He made love to her, and she bore him Segub. ²²Segub was the father of Jair, who controlled twenty-three towns in Gilead. ²³(But Geshur and Aram captured Havvoth Jair, as well as Kenath with its surrounding settlements – sixty towns.) All these were descendants of Makir the father of Gilead.

²⁴After Hezron died in Caleb Ephrathah, Abijah the wife of Hezron bore him Ashhur the father of Tekoa.

²⁵The sons of Jerahmeel the firstborn of Hezron:
Ram his firstborn, Bunah, Oren, Ozem and Ahijah. ²⁶Jerahmeel had another wife, whose name was Atarah; she was the mother of Onam.
²⁷The sons of Ram the firstborn of Jerahmeel:
Maaz, Jamin and Eker.
²⁸The sons of Onam:
Shammai and Jada.
The sons of Shammai:
Nadab and Abishur.
²⁹Abishur's wife was named Abihail, who bore him Ahban and Molid.
³⁰The sons of Nadab:
Seled and Appaim. Seled died without children.
³¹The son of Appaim:
Ishi, who was the father of Sheshan. Sheshan was the father of Ahlai.
³²The sons of Jada, Shammai's brother:
Jether and Jonathan. Jether died without children.

³³The sons of Jonathan:
Peleth and Zaza.
These were the descendants of Jerahmeel.
³⁴Sheshan had no sons – only daughters. He had an Egyptian servant named Jarha. ³⁵Sheshan gave his daughter in marriage to his servant Jarha, and she bore him Attai.
³⁶Attai was the father of Nathan, Nathan the father of Zabad,
³⁷Zabad the father of Ephlal, Ephlal the father of Obed,
³⁸Obed the father of Jehu, Jehu the father of Azariah,
³⁹Azariah the father of Helez, Helez the father of Eleasah,
⁴⁰Eleasah the father of Sismai, Sismai the father of Shallum,
⁴¹Shallum the father of Jekamiah, and Jekamiah the father of Elishama.

⁴²The sons of Caleb the brother of Jerahmeel:
Mesha his firstborn, who was the father of Ziph, and his son Mareshah, who was the father of Hebron.
⁴³The sons of Hebron:
Korah, Tappuah, Rekem and Shema. ⁴⁴Shema was the father of Raham, and Raham the father of Jorkeam. Rekem was the father of Shammai. ⁴⁵The son of Shammai was Maon, and Maon was the father of Beth Zur.
⁴⁶Caleb's concubine Ephah was the mother of Haran, Moza and Gazez. Haran was the father of Gazez.
⁴⁷The sons of Jahdai:
Regem, Jotham, Geshan, Pelet, Ephah and Shaaph.
⁴⁸Caleb's concubine Maakah was the mother of Sheber and Tirhanah. ⁴⁹She also gave birth to Shaaph the father of Madmannah and to Sheva

the father of Makbenah and Gibea. Caleb's daughter was Aksah. ⁵⁰These were the descendants of Caleb.

The sons of Hur the firstborn of Ephrathah:
Shobal the father of Kiriath Jearim,
⁵¹Salma the father of Bethlehem,
and Hareph the father of Beth Gader.
⁵²The descendants of Shobal the father of Kiriath Jearim were:
Haroeh, half the Manahathites, ⁵³and the clans of Kiriath Jearim: the Ithrites, Puthites, Shumathites and Mishraites. From these descended the Zorathites and Eshtaolites.
⁵⁴The descendants of Salma:
Bethlehem, the Netophathites, Atroth Beth Joab, half the Manahathites, the Zorites, ⁵⁵and the clans of scribes who lived at Jabez: the Tirathites, Shimeathites and Sucathites. These are the Kenites who came from Hammath, the father of the Rekabites.

▬ PSALM 79:9-13

⁹Help us, God our Saviour,
for the glory of your name;
deliver us and forgive our sins
for your name's sake.
¹⁰Why should the nations say,
'Where is their God?'

Before our eyes, make known among the nations
that you avenge the outpoured blood of your servants.
¹¹May the groans of the prisoners come before you;
with your strong arm preserve those condemned to die.

¹²Pay back into the laps of our neighbours seven times
the contempt they have hurled at you, Lord.
¹³Then we your people, the sheep of your pasture,
will praise you for ever;
from generation to generation
we will proclaim your praise.

▬ PROVERBS 17:15-16

¹⁵Acquitting the guilty and condemning the innocent –
the LORD detests them both.

¹⁶Why should fools have money in hand to buy wisdom,
when they are not able to understand it?

▬ ACTS 12:1-25

12 It was about this time that King Herod arrested some who belonged to the church, intending to persecute them. ²He had James, the brother of John, put to death with the sword. ³When he saw that this met with approval among the Jews, he proceeded to seize Peter also. This happened during the Festival of Unleavened Bread. ⁴After arresting him, he put him in prison, handing him over to be guarded by four squads of four soldiers each. Herod intended to bring him out for public trial after the Passover.

⁵So Peter was kept in prison, but the church was earnestly praying to God for him.

⁶The night before Herod was to bring him to trial, Peter was sleeping between two soldiers, bound with two chains, and sentries stood guard at the entrance. ⁷Suddenly an angel of the Lord appeared and a light shone

in the cell. He struck Peter on the side and woke him up. 'Quick, get up!' he said, and the chains fell off Peter's wrists.

⁸ Then the angel said to him, 'Put on your clothes and sandals.' And Peter did so. 'Wrap your cloak round you and follow me,' the angel told him. ⁹ Peter followed him out of the prison, but he had no idea that what the angel was doing was really happening; he thought he was seeing a vision. ¹⁰ They passed the first and second guards and came to the iron gate leading to the city. It opened for them by itself, and they went through it. When they had walked the length of one street, suddenly the angel left him.

¹¹ Then Peter came to himself and said, 'Now I know without a doubt that the Lord has sent his angel and rescued me from Herod's clutches and from everything the Jewish people were hoping would happen.'

¹² When this had dawned on him, he went to the house of Mary the mother of John, also called Mark, where many people had gathered and were praying. ¹³ Peter knocked at the outer entrance, and a servant named Rhoda came to answer the door. ¹⁴ When she recognised Peter's voice, she was so overjoyed she ran back without opening it and exclaimed, 'Peter is at the door!'

¹⁵ 'You're out of your mind,' they told her. When she kept insisting that it was so, they said, 'It must be his angel.'

¹⁶ But Peter kept on knocking, and when they opened the door and saw him, they were astonished. ¹⁷ Peter motioned with his hand for them to be quiet and described how the Lord had brought him out of prison. 'Tell James and the other brothers and sisters about this,' he said, and then he left for another place.

¹⁸ In the morning, there was no small commotion among the soldiers as to what had become of Peter. ¹⁹ After Herod had a thorough search made for him and did not find him, he cross-examined the guards and ordered that they be executed.

Then Herod went from Judea to Caesarea and stayed there. ²⁰ He had been quarrelling with the people of Tyre and Sidon; they now joined together and sought an audience with him. After securing the support of Blastus, a trusted personal servant of the king, they asked for peace, because they depended on the king's country for their food supply.

²¹ On the appointed day Herod, wearing his royal robes, sat on his throne and delivered a public address to the people. ²² They shouted, 'This is the voice of a god, not of a man.' ²³ Immediately, because Herod did not give praise to God, an angel of the Lord struck him down, and he was eaten by worms and died.

²⁴ But the word of God continued to spread and flourish.

²⁵ When Barnabas and Saul had finished their mission, they returned from Jerusalem, taking with them John, also called Mark.

Our Only Protection

'Help us, God our Saviour, for the glory of your name; deliver us ...' **Psalm 79:9**

The armour of God is our only protection against the wiles of Satan, but it will do us no good unless we avail ourselves of it in its entirety. In considering this matter, we must constantly keep before us the fact that such is the might and power of Satan that nothing apart from the armour of God will protect us from his onslaughts. Mark this and mark it well, for there are many Christians who have tried to stand against Satan in their own strength and have found themselves not victors but victims. One of the 'wiles' of Satan is to get us to believe that we can resist him in our own strength. But the moment we think this – we are in danger!

In my time I have seen many believers lulled by Satan into thinking that their long experience in the faith and their understanding of Christian doctrine were all they needed in order to be protected from satanic attack. But they found to their great cost that this was inadequate and insufficient. We never live more dangerously than when we depend on our spiritual experience and understanding to protect us from the flaming arrows of the enemy.

One thing and one thing only can protect us from the attacks of Satan, and that is the spiritual armour that God has provided to His people. In the devil, you see, we are dealing with a foe who is inferior in power only to the Almighty Himself. Therefore, nothing less than the protection that God provides is adequate for our need.

PRAYER

O Father, I need to get this matter straight, for I see that if my dependence is on anything other than You, then I am sunk. Drive this truth deep into my spirit this day. In Jesus' name. Amen.

FURTHER STUDY

Rom. 13:1-12; 1 Thess. 5:8; 2 Tim. 2:4; Eph. 6:11
• What are we to put aside?
• What are we to put on?

July 11

▬ 1 CHRONICLES 3:1–4:43

3 These were the sons of David born to him in Hebron:

the firstborn was Amnon the son of Ahinoam of Jezreel;

the second, Daniel the son of Abigail of Carmel;

²the third, Absalom the son of Maakah daughter of Talmai king of Geshur;

the fourth, Adonijah the son of Haggith;

³the fifth, Shephatiah the son of Abital;

and the sixth, Ithream, by his wife Eglah.

⁴These six were born to David in Hebron, where he reigned seven years and six months.

David reigned in Jerusalem for thirty-three years, ⁵and these were the children born to him there:

Shammua, Shobab, Nathan and Solomon. These four were by Bathsheba daughter of Ammiel. ⁶There were also Ibhar, Elishua, Eliphelet, ⁷Nogah, Nepheg, Japhia, ⁸Elishama, Eliada and Eliphelet – nine in all. ⁹All these were the sons of David, besides his sons by his concubines. And Tamar was their sister.

¹⁰ Solomon's son was Rehoboam,
  Abijah his son,
  Asa his son,
  Jehoshaphat his son,
¹¹ Jehoram his son,
  Ahaziah his son,
  Joash his son,
¹² Amaziah his son,
  Azariah his son,
  Jotham his son,
¹³ Ahaz his son,
  Hezekiah his son,
  Manasseh his son,
¹⁴ Amon his son,
  Josiah his son.
¹⁵ The sons of Josiah:
  Johanan the firstborn,
  Jehoiakim the second son,
  Zedekiah the third,
  Shallum the fourth.
¹⁶ The successors of Jehoiakim:
  Jehoiachin his son,
  and Zedekiah.

¹⁷ The descendants of Jehoiachin the
  captive:
  Shealtiel his son, ¹⁸ Malkiram, Pedaiah, Shenazzar, Jekamiah, Hoshama
  and Nedabiah.
¹⁹ The sons of Pedaiah:
  Zerubbabel and Shimei.
  The sons of Zerubbabel:
  Meshullam and Hananiah.
  Shelomith was their sister.
²⁰ There were also five others:
  Hashubah, Ohel, Berekiah, Hasadiah
  and Jushab-Hesed.
²¹ The descendants of Hananiah:
  Pelatiah and Jeshaiah, and the sons
  of Rephaiah, of Arnan, of Obadiah
  and of Shekaniah.
²² The descendants of Shekaniah:
  Shemaiah and his sons:
  Hattush, Igal, Bariah, Neariah and
  Shaphat – six in all.
²³ The sons of Neariah:

Elioenai, Hizkiah and Azrikam –
  three in all.
²⁴ The sons of Elioenai:
  Hodaviah, Eliashib, Pelaiah, Akkub,
  Johanan, Delaiah and Anani – seven
  in all.

4 The descendants of Judah:
  Perez, Hezron, Karmi, Hur and
  Shobal.
² Reaiah son of Shobal was the father
  of Jahath, and Jahath the father of
  Ahumai and Lahad. These were the
  clans of the Zorathites.
³ These were the sons of Etam:
  Jezreel, Ishma and Idbash. Their sister was named Hazzelelponi. ⁴ Penuel was the father of Gedor, and Ezer
  the father of Hushah.
  These were the descendants of Hur, the
  firstborn of Ephrathah and father of
  Bethlehem.
⁵ Ashhur the father of Tekoa had two
  wives, Helah and Naarah.
⁶ Naarah bore him Ahuzzam, Hepher,
  Temeni and Haahashtari. These
  were the descendants of Naarah.
⁷ The sons of Helah:
  Zereth, Zohar, Ethnan, ⁸ and Koz,
  who was the father of Anub and
  Hazzobebah and of the clans of
  Aharhel son of Harum.

⁹ Jabez was more honourable than his
brothers. His mother had named him Jabez,
saying, 'I gave birth to him in pain.' ¹⁰ Jabez
cried out to the God of Israel, 'Oh, that you
would bless me and enlarge my territory!
Let your hand be with me, and keep me
from harm so that I will be free from pain.'
And God granted his request.

¹¹ Kelub, Shuhah's brother, was the fa-
ther of Mehir, who was the father of
Eshton. ¹² Eshton was the father of
Beth Rapha, Paseah and Tehinnah

the father of Ir Nahash. These were the men of Rekah.

[13] The sons of Kenaz:
Othniel and Seraiah.
The sons of Othniel:
Hathath and Meonothai. [14] Meonothai was the father of Ophrah.
Seraiah was the father of Joab,
the father of Ge Harashim. It was called this because its people were skilled workers.

[15] The sons of Caleb son of Jephunneh:
Iru, Elah and Naam.
The son of Elah:
Kenaz.

[16] The sons of Jehallelel:
Ziph, Ziphah, Tiria and Asarel.

[17] The sons of Ezrah:
Jether, Mered, Epher and Jalon. One of Mered's wives gave birth to Miriam, Shammai and Ishbah the father of Eshtemoa. [18] (His wife from the tribe of Judah gave birth to Jered the father of Gedor, Heber the father of Soko, and Jekuthiel the father of Zanoah.) These were the children of Pharaoh's daughter Bithiah, whom Mered had married.

[19] The sons of Hodiah's wife, the sister of Naham:
the father of Keilah the Garmite, and Eshtemoa the Maakathite.

[20] The sons of Shimon:
Amnon, Rinnah, Ben-Hanan and Tilon.
The descendants of Ishi:
Zoheth and Ben-Zoheth.

[21] The sons of Shelah son of Judah:
Er the father of Lekah, Laadah the father of Mareshah and the clans of the linen workers at Beth Ashbea, [22] Jokim, the men of Kozeba, and Joash and Saraph, who ruled in Moab and Jashubi Lehem. (These records are from ancient times.) [23] They

were the potters who lived at Netaim and Gederah; they stayed there and worked for the king.

[24] The descendants of Simeon:
Nemuel, Jamin, Jarib, Zerah and Shaul;
[25] Shallum was Shaul's son, Mibsam his son and Mishma his son.

[26] The descendants of Mishma:
Hammuel his son, Zakkur his son and Shimei his son.

[27] Shimei had sixteen sons and six daughters, but his brothers did not have many children; so their entire clan did not become as numerous as the people of Judah. [28] They lived in Beersheba, Moladah, Hazar Shual, [29] Bilhah, Ezem, Tolad, [30] Bethuel, Hormah, Ziklag, [31] Beth Markaboth, Hazar Susim, Beth Biri and Shaaraim. These were their towns until the reign of David. [32] Their surrounding villages were Etam, Ain, Rimmon, Token and Ashan – five towns – [33] and all the villages around these towns as far as Baalath. These were their settlements. And they kept a genealogical record.

[34] Meshobab, Jamlech, Joshah son of Amaziah, [35] Joel, Jehu son of Joshibiah, the son of Seraiah, the son of Asiel, [36] also Elioenai, Jaakobah, Jeshohaiah, Asaiah, Adiel, Jesimiel, Benaiah, [37] and Ziza son of Shiphi, the son of Allon, the son of Jedaiah, the son of Shimri, the son of Shemaiah.

[38] The men listed above by name were leaders of their clans. Their families increased greatly, [39] and they went to the outskirts of Gedor to the east of the valley in search of pasture for their flocks. [40] They found rich, good pasture, and the land was spacious, peaceful and quiet. Some Hamites had lived there formerly.

[41] The men whose names were listed came in the days of Hezekiah king of Judah. They attacked the Hamites in their dwellings

and also the Meunites who were there and completely destroyed them, as is evident to this day. Then they settled in their place, because there was pasture for their flocks. [42] And five hundred of these Simeonites, led by Pelatiah, Neariah, Rephaiah and Uzziel, the sons of Ishi, invaded the hill country of Seir. [43] They killed the remaining Amalekites who had escaped, and they have lived there to this day.

■ PSALM 80:1-7

[1] Hear us, Shepherd of Israel,
    you who lead Joseph like a flock.
You who sit enthroned between the
    cherubim,
    shine forth [2] before Ephraim,
       Benjamin and Manasseh.
Awaken your might;
    come and save us.

[3] Restore us, O God;
    make your face shine on us,
    that we may be saved.

[4] How long, LORD God Almighty,
    will your anger smoulder
    against the prayers of your people?
[5] You have fed them with the bread of
       tears;
    you have made them drink tears by
       the bowlful.
[6] You have made us an object of derision
       to our neighbours,
    and our enemies mock us.

[7] Restore us, God Almighty;
    make your face shine on us,
    that we may be saved.

■ PROVERBS 17:17

[17] A friend loves at all times,
and a brother is born for a time of
    adversity.

■ ACTS 13:1-22

13 [1] Now in the church at Antioch there were prophets and teachers: Barnabas, Simeon called Niger, Lucius of Cyrene, Manaen (who had been brought up with Herod the tetrarch) and Saul. [2] While they were worshipping the Lord and fasting, the Holy Spirit said, 'Set apart for me Barnabas and Saul for the work to which I have called them.' [3] So after they had fasted and prayed, they placed their hands on them and sent them off.

[4] The two of them, sent on their way by the Holy Spirit, went down to Seleucia and sailed from there to Cyprus. [5] When they arrived at Salamis, they proclaimed the word of God in the Jewish synagogues. John was with them as their helper.

[6] They travelled through the whole island until they came to Paphos. There they met a Jewish sorcerer and false prophet named Bar-Jesus, [7] who was an attendant of the proconsul, Sergius Paulus. The proconsul, an intelligent man, sent for Barnabas and Saul because he wanted to hear the word of God. [8] But Elymas the sorcerer (for that is what his name means) opposed them and tried to turn the proconsul from the faith. [9] Then Saul, who was also called Paul, filled with the Holy Spirit, looked straight at Elymas and said, [10] 'You are a child of the devil and an enemy of everything that is right! You are full of all kinds of deceit and trickery. Will you never stop perverting the right ways of the Lord? [11] Now the hand of the Lord is against you. You are going to be blind for a time, not even able to see the light of the sun.'

Immediately mist and darkness came over him, and he groped about, seeking someone to lead him by the hand. [12] When the proconsul saw what had happened, he believed, for he was amazed at the teaching about the Lord.

[13] From Paphos, Paul and his companions sailed to Perga in Pamphylia, where John left them to return to Jerusalem. [14] From Perga they went on to Pisidian Antioch. On the Sabbath they entered the synagogue and sat down. [15] After the reading from the Law and the Prophets, the leaders of the synagogue sent word to them, saying, 'Brothers, if you have a word of exhortation for the people, please speak.'

[16] Standing up, Paul motioned with his hand and said: 'Fellow Israelites and you Gentiles who worship God, listen to me! [17] The God of the people of Israel chose our ancestors; he made the people prosper during their stay in Egypt; with mighty power he led them out of that country; [18] for about forty years he endured their conduct in the wilderness; [19] and he overthrew seven nations in Canaan, giving their land to his people as their inheritance. [20] All this took about 450 years.

'After this, God gave them judges until the time of Samuel the prophet. [21] Then the people asked for a king, and he gave them Saul son of Kish, of the tribe of Benjamin, who ruled for forty years. [22] After removing Saul, he made David their king. God testified concerning him: "I have found David son of Jesse, a man after my own heart; he will do everything I want him to do."

Our Primary View of Him

'Hear us, Shepherd of Israel, you who lead Joseph like a flock.' **Psalm 80:1**

Why did David choose to think of God as his Shepherd? The picture of God we carry deep in our hearts is the one we relate to whenever we find ourselves surrounded by trouble or difficulties. But perhaps what is more important is this - we will interpret every event of our lives in accordance with the inner picture that we have of Him.

When I have asked people during counselling to describe to me their *primary* view of God, I have been surprised that so often they see Him not as a loving Shepherd but as an austere and stern Judge. God *is* a Judge, of course - as David discovered when he committed adultery with Bathsheba - but that is not His *primary* relationship to His children. Someone has pointed out that the two most beautiful illustrations of God's relationship to His people given in Scripture are those of a Father and a Shepherd. It is interesting also that the two best-known passages in the whole of God's Word - the Lord's Prayer and Psalm 23 - use these analogies.

What kind of picture of God, I wonder, do you carry deep down in your heart? If your *primary* view of God is as a Judge, then you will tend to interpret your problems as God's judgment upon you, rather than an opportunity to experience in your troubles His tender love and care. Make no mistake about it - the image of God that you carry deep in your heart is the one that you will relate to in a moment of crisis.

PRAYER

O Father, help me develop a true image of You in my heart: a picture that is exposed, not from my own feelings and ideas about You, but from the principles that lie hidden in Your precious Word. In Jesus' name I ask it. Amen.

FURTHER STUDY

Col. 1:1-15; 2:9; John 1:1-2
• How has God revealed Himself to us?
• What is your picture of God?

July 12

1 CHRONICLES 5:1–6:32

5 The sons of Reuben the firstborn of Israel (he was the firstborn, but when he defiled his father's marriage bed, his rights as firstborn were given to the sons of Joseph son of Israel; so he could not be listed in the genealogical record in accordance with his birthright, ²and though Judah was the strongest of his brothers and a ruler came from him, the rights of the firstborn belonged to Joseph) – ³the sons of Reuben the firstborn of Israel:

Hanok, Pallu, Hezron and Karmi.

⁴ The descendants of Joel:

Shemaiah his son, Gog his son, Shimei his son, ⁵Micah his son, Reaiah his son, Baal his son, ⁶and Beerah his son, whom Tiglath-Pileser king of Assyria took into exile. Beerah was a leader of the Reubenites.

⁷ Their relatives by clans, listed according to their genealogical records:

Jeiel the chief, Zechariah, ⁸and Bela son of Azaz, the son of Shema, the son of Joel. They settled in the area from Aroer to Nebo and Baal Meon. ⁹To the east they occupied the land up to the edge of the desert that extends to the River Euphrates, because their livestock had increased in Gilead.

¹⁰During Saul's reign they waged war against the Hagrites, who were defeated at their hands; they occupied the dwellings of the Hagrites throughout the entire region east of Gilead.

¹¹The Gadites lived next to them in Bashan, as far as Salekah:

¹²Joel was the chief, Shapham the second, then Janai and Shaphat, in Bashan.

¹³ Their relatives, by families, were:

Michael, Meshullam, Sheba, Jorai, Jakan, Zia and Eber – seven in all.

¹⁴These were the sons of Abihail son of Huri, the son of Jaroah, the son of Gilead, the son of Michael, the son of Jeshishai, the son of Jahdo, the son of Buz.

¹⁵Ahi son of Abdiel, the son of Guni, was head of their family.

¹⁶The Gadites lived in Gilead, in Bashan and its outlying villages, and on all the pasture-lands of Sharon as far as they extended.

¹⁷All these were entered in the genealogical records during the reigns of Jotham king of Judah and Jeroboam king of Israel.

¹⁸The Reubenites, the Gadites and the

half-tribe of Manasseh had 44,760 men ready for military service – able-bodied men who could handle shield and sword, who could use a bow, and who were trained for battle. ¹⁹They waged war against the Hagrites, Jetur, Naphish and Nodab. ²⁰They were helped in fighting them, and God delivered the Hagrites and all their allies into their hands, because they cried out to him during the battle. He answered their prayers, because they trusted in him. ²¹They seized the livestock of the Hagrites – fifty thousand camels, two hundred and fifty thousand sheep and two thousand donkeys. They also took one hundred thousand people captive, ²²and many others fell slain, because the battle was God's. And they occupied the land until the exile.

²³The people of the half-tribe of Manasseh were numerous; they settled in the land from Bashan to Baal Hermon, that is, to Senir (Mount Hermon).

²⁴These were the heads of their families: Epher, Ishi, Eliel, Azriel, Jeremiah, Hodaviah and Jahdiel. They were brave warriors, famous men, and heads of their families. ²⁵But they were unfaithful to the God of their ancestors and prostituted themselves to the gods of the peoples of the land, whom God had destroyed before them. ²⁶So the God of Israel stirred up the spirit of Pul king of Assyria (that is, Tiglath-Pileser king of Assyria), who took the Reubenites, the Gadites and the half-tribe of Manasseh into exile. He took them to Halah, Habor, Hara and the river of Gozan, where they are to this day.

6 The sons of Levi:
Gershon, Kohath and Merari.
²The sons of Kohath:
Amram, Izhar, Hebron and Uzziel.
³The children of Amram:
Aaron, Moses and Miriam.
The sons of Aaron:
Nadab, Abihu, Eleazar and Ithamar.
⁴Eleazar was the father of Phinehas,

Phinehas the father of Abishua,
⁵Abishua the father of Bukki,
Bukki the father of Uzzi,
⁶Uzzi the father of Zerahiah,
Zerahiah the father of Meraioth,
⁷Meraioth the father of Amariah,
Amariah the father of Ahitub,
⁸Ahitub the father of Zadok,
Zadok the father of Ahimaaz,
⁹Ahimaaz the father of Azariah,
Azariah the father of Johanan,
¹⁰Johanan the father of Azariah (it was he who served as priest in the temple Solomon built in Jerusalem),
¹¹Azariah the father of Amariah,
Amariah the father of Ahitub,
¹²Ahitub the father of Zadok,
Zadok the father of Shallum,
¹³Shallum the father of Hilkiah,
Hilkiah the father of Azariah,
¹⁴Azariah the father of Seraiah,
and Seraiah the father of Jozadak.
¹⁵Jozadak was deported when the LORD sent Judah and Jerusalem into exile by the hand of Nebuchadnezzar.
¹⁶The sons of Levi:
Gershon, Kohath and Merari.
¹⁷These are the names of the sons of Gershon:
Libni and Shimei.
¹⁸The sons of Kohath:
Amram, Izhar, Hebron and Uzziel.
¹⁹The sons of Merari:
Mahli and Mushi.
These are the clans of the Levites listed according to their fathers:
²⁰of Gershon:
Libni his son, Jahath his son,
Zimmah his son, ²¹Joah his son,
Iddo his son, Zerah his son
and Jeatherai his son.
²²The descendants of Kohath:
Amminadab his son, Korah his son,
Assir his son, ²³Elkanah his son,
Ebiasaph his son, Assir his son,
²⁴Tahath his son, Uriel his son,

Uzziah his son and Shaul his son.
25 The descendants of Elkanah:
Amasai, Ahimoth,
    26 Elkanah his son, Zophai his son,
Nahath his son, 27 Eliab his son,
Jeroham his son, Elkanah his son
and Samuel his son.
28 The sons of Samuel:
Joel the firstborn
and Abijah the second son.
29 The descendants of Merari:
Mahli, Libni his son,
Shimei his son, Uzzah his son,
    30 Shimea his son, Haggiah his son
and Asaiah his son.

31 These are the men David put in charge of the music in the house of the Lord after the ark came to rest there. 32 They ministered with music before the tabernacle, the tent of meeting, until Solomon built the temple of the Lord in Jerusalem. They performed their duties according to the regulations laid down for them.

■ PSALM 80:8-13

8 You transplanted a vine from Egypt;
    you drove out the nations and
        planted it.
9 You cleared the ground for it,
    and it took root and filled the land.
10 The mountains were covered with its
        shade,
    the mighty cedars with its branches.
11 Its branches reached as far as the Sea,
    its shoots as far as the River.

12 Why have you broken down its walls
    so that all who pass by pick its grapes?
13 Boars from the forest ravage it,
    and insects from the fields feed on it.

■ PROVERBS 17:18-19

18 One who has no sense shakes hands in
        pledge
    and puts up security for a neighbour.

19 Whoever loves a quarrel loves sin;
    whoever builds a high gate invites
        destruction.

■ ACTS 13:23-41

23 'From this man's descendants God has brought to Israel the Saviour Jesus, as he promised. 24 Before the coming of Jesus, John preached repentance and baptism to all the people of Israel. 25 As John was completing his work, he said: "Who do you suppose I am? I am not the one you are looking for. But there is one coming after me whose sandals I am not worthy to untie."

26 'Fellow children of Abraham and you God-fearing Gentiles, it is to us that this message of salvation has been sent. 27 The people of Jerusalem and their rulers did not recognise Jesus, yet in condemning him they fulfilled the words of the prophets that are read every Sabbath. 28 Though they found no proper ground for a death sentence, they asked Pilate to have him executed. 29 When they had carried out all that was written about him, they took him down from the cross and laid him in a tomb. 30 But God raised him from the dead, 31 and for many days he was seen by those who had travelled with him from Galilee to Jerusalem. They are now his witnesses to our people.

32 'We tell you the good news: what God promised our ancestors 33 he has fulfilled for us, their children, by raising up Jesus. As it is written in the second Psalm:

' "You are my son;
    today I have become your father."

³⁴God raised him from the dead so that he will never be subject to decay. As God has said,

'"I will give you the holy and sure blessings promised to David."

³⁵So it is also stated elsewhere:

'"You will not let your holy one see decay."

³⁶'Now when David had served God's purpose in his own generation, he fell asleep; he was buried with his ancestors and his body decayed. ³⁷But the one whom God raised from the dead did not see decay.

³⁸'Therefore, my friends, I want you to know that through Jesus the forgiveness of sins is proclaimed to you. ³⁹Through him everyone who believes is set free from every sin, a justification you were not able to obtain under the law of Moses. ⁴⁰Take care that what the prophets have said does not happen to you:

⁴¹'"Look, you scoffers,
    wonder and perish,
for I am going to do something in your
    days
that you would never believe,
    even if someone told you."'

Rejected by God?

'... I want you to know that through Jesus the forgiveness of sins is proclaimed to you. Through him everyone who believes is set free from every sin ...'
Acts 13:38

A feeling that the devil likes to arouse in an unguarded heart is the feeling that when we have committed a sin, we will be rejected by God and have to forfeit our salvation. The Hebrew name 'Satan' means 'adversary', and the Greek name for 'devil' means 'slanderer'. This gives us a pretty good idea of the nature of the evil one. He is never happier than when he is engaged in pointing the finger of scorn at us whenever we have failed.

It is part of the doctrine of the Church that a Christian may sometimes fall into sin. We are saved, but we are still fallible. God forbid that we should fall into sin, but when we do, we must remember that we have 'an advocate with the Father – Jesus Christ, the Righteous One' (1 John 2:1).

You can be sure, however, that when you fall into sin, the devil will come to you and say, 'You were forgiven when you became a Christian because you sinned in ignorance, but now that you are a Christian, you have sinned against the light. There can be no forgiveness for you now because of what you have done. You are lost – forever!'

The answer to this, as with all of Satan's accusations, is to put on the 'armour of righteousness'. You must remind him that God's righteousness not only covers us at our salvation but continues to cover us for time and eternity. Never allow the devil to use a particular sin to call into question your whole standing before God. This is something that has been settled in heaven, not in the debating chamber of the devil.

PRAYER

My Father and my God, my heart overflows at the revelation of Your full and free forgiveness. Help me not to take it for granted but to take it with gratitude. In Jesus' name I pray. Amen.

FURTHER STUDY

Isa. 55:1-7; 43:25; Eph. 1:7-8; Acts 13:38; 1 John 1:9
- What does God do when He blots out our sin?
- How does the Lord respond when we return to Him?

July 13

1 CHRONICLES 6:33-81

33 Here are the men who served, together with their sons:

from the Kohathites:

Heman, the musician,

the son of Joel, the son of Samuel,

34 the son of Elkanah, the son of Jeroham,

the son of Eliel, the son of Toah,

35 the son of Zuph, the son of Elkanah,

the son of Mahath, the son of Amasai,

36 the son of Elkanah, the son of Joel,

the son of Azariah, the son of Zephaniah,

37 the son of Tahath, the son of Assir,

the son of Ebiasaph, the son of Korah,

38 the son of Izhar, the son of Kohath,

the son of Levi, the son of Israel;

39 and Heman's associate Asaph, who served at his right hand:

Asaph son of Berekiah, the son of Shimea,

40 the son of Michael, the son of Baaseiah,

the son of Malkijah, 41 the son of Ethni,

the son of Zerah, the son of Adaiah,

42 the son of Ethan, the son of Zimmah,

the son of Shimei, 43 the son of Jahath,

the son of Gershon, the son of Levi;

44 and from their associates, the Merarites, at his left hand:

Ethan son of Kishi, the son of Abdi,

the son of Malluk, 45 the son of Hashabiah,

the son of Amaziah, the son of Hilkiah,

46 the son of Amzi, the son of Bani,

the son of Shemer, 47 the son of Mahli,

the son of Mushi, the son of Merari,

the son of Levi.

48 Their fellow Levites were assigned to all the other duties of the tabernacle, the house of God. 49 But Aaron and his descendants were the ones who presented offerings on the altar of burnt offering and on the altar of incense in connection with all that was done in the Most Holy Place, making atonement for Israel, in accordance with all that Moses the servant of God had commanded.

50 These were the descendants of Aaron:

Eleazar his son, Phinehas his son,

Abishua his son, 51 Bukki his son,

Uzzi his son, Zerahiah his son,

⁵² Meraioth his son, Amariah his son, Ahitub his son, ⁵³ Zadok his son and Ahimaaz his son.

⁵⁴ These were the locations of their settlements allotted as their territory (they were assigned to the descendants of Aaron who were from the Kohathite clan, because the first lot was for them):
⁵⁵ they were given Hebron in Judah with its surrounding pasture-lands. ⁵⁶ But the fields and villages around the city were given to Caleb son of Jephunneh.
⁵⁷ So the descendants of Aaron were given Hebron (a city of refuge), and Libnah, Jattir, Eshtemoa, ⁵⁸ Hilen, Debir, ⁵⁹ Ashan, Juttah and Beth Shemesh, together with their pasture-lands. ⁶⁰ And from the tribe of Benjamin they were given Gibeon, Geba, Alemeth and Anathoth, together with their pasture-lands.

The total number of towns distributed among the Kohathite clans came to thirteen.
⁶¹ The rest of Kohath's descendants were allotted ten towns from the clans of half the tribe of Manasseh.
⁶² The descendants of Gershon, clan by clan, were allotted thirteen towns from the tribes of Issachar, Asher and Naphtali, and from the part of the tribe of Manasseh that is in Bashan.
⁶³ The descendants of Merari, clan by clan, were allotted twelve towns from the tribes of Reuben, Gad and Zebulun.
⁶⁴ So the Israelites gave the Levites these towns and their pasture-lands. ⁶⁵ From the tribes of Judah, Simeon and Benjamin they allotted the previously named towns.
⁶⁶ Some of the Kohathite clans were given as their territory towns from the tribe of Ephraim.
⁶⁷ In the hill country of Ephraim they were given Shechem (a city of refuge), and Gezer, ⁶⁸ Jokmeam, Beth Horon, ⁶⁹ Aijalon and Gath Rimmon, together with their pasture-lands.
⁷⁰ And from half the tribe of Manasseh the Israelites gave Aner and Bileam, together with their pasture-lands, to the rest of the Kohathite clans.

⁷¹ The Gershonites received the following:
from the clan of the half-tribe of Manasseh
they received Golan in Bashan and also Ashtaroth, together with their pasture-lands;
⁷² from the tribe of Issachar
they received Kedesh, Daberath, ⁷³ Ramoth and Anem, together with their pasture-lands;
⁷⁴ from the tribe of Asher
they received Mashal, Abdon, ⁷⁵ Hukok and Rehob, together with their pasture-lands;
⁷⁶ and from the tribe of Naphtali
they received Kedesh in Galilee, Hammon and Kiriathaim, together with their pasture-lands.

⁷⁷ The Merarites (the rest of the Levites) received the following:
from the tribe of Zebulun
they received Jokneam, Kartah, Rimmono and Tabor, together with their pasture-lands;
⁷⁸ from the tribe of Reuben across the Jordan east of Jericho
they received Bezer in the wilderness, Jahzah, ⁷⁹ Kedemoth and Mephaath, together with their pasture-lands;
⁸⁰ and from the tribe of Gad
they received Ramoth in Gilead, Mahanaim, ⁸¹ Heshbon and Jazer, together with their pasture-lands.

▬ PSALM 80:14-19

¹⁴ Return to us, God Almighty!
>   Look down from heaven and see!
>   Watch over this vine,
¹⁵   the root your right hand has planted,
>   the son you have raised up for
>   yourself.

¹⁶ Your vine is cut down, it is burned with
>   fire;
>   at your rebuke your people perish.
¹⁷ Let your hand rest on the man at your
>   right hand,
>   the son of man you have raised up for
>   yourself.
¹⁸ Then we will not turn away from you;
>   revive us, and we will call on your
>   name.

¹⁹ Restore us, LORD God Almighty;
>   make your face shine on us,
>   that we may be saved.

▬ PROVERBS 17:20-21

²⁰ One whose heart is corrupt does not
>   prosper;
>   one whose tongue is perverse falls
>   into trouble.

²¹ To have a fool for a child brings grief;
>   there is no joy for the parent of a
>   godless fool.

▬ ACTS 13:42–14:7

⁴² As Paul and Barnabas were leaving the synagogue, the people invited them to speak further about these things on the next Sabbath. ⁴³ When the congregation was dismissed, many of the Jews and devout converts to Judaism followed Paul and Barnabas, who talked with them and urged them to continue in the grace of God.

⁴⁴ On the next Sabbath almost the whole city gathered to hear the word of the Lord. ⁴⁵ When the Jews saw the crowds, they were filled with jealousy. They began to contradict what Paul was saying and heaped abuse on him.

⁴⁶ Then Paul and Barnabas answered them boldly: 'We had to speak the word of God to you first. Since you reject it and do not consider yourselves worthy of eternal life, we now turn to the Gentiles. ⁴⁷ For this is what the Lord has commanded us:

> ' "I have made you a light for the
>   Gentiles,
>   that you may bring salvation to the
>   ends of the earth." '

⁴⁸ When the Gentiles heard this, they were glad and honoured the word of the Lord; and all who were appointed for eternal life believed.

⁴⁹ The word of the Lord spread through the whole region. ⁵⁰ But the Jewish leaders incited the God-fearing women of high standing and the leading men of the city. They stirred up persecution against Paul and Barnabas, and expelled them from their region. ⁵¹ So they shook the dust off their feet as a warning to them and went to Iconium. ⁵² And the disciples were filled with joy and with the Holy Spirit.

14 At Iconium Paul and Barnabas went as usual into the Jewish synagogue. There they spoke so effectively that a great number of Jews and Greeks believed. ² But the Jews who refused to believe stirred up the other Gentiles and poisoned their minds against the brothers. ³ So Paul and Barnabas spent considerable time there, speaking boldly for the Lord, who confirmed the message of his grace by enabling them to perform signs and wonders. ⁴ The people of the city were divided; some sided with the Jews, others with the apostles. ⁵ There was a plot afoot among both Gentiles and Jews, together with their leaders, to ill-treat them and stone them. ⁶But they found out about it and fled to the Lycaonian cities of Lystra and Derbe and to the surrounding country, ⁷where they continued to preach the gospel.

'Lies Have Short Legs'

'One whose heart is corrupt does not prosper; one whose tongue is perverse falls into trouble.'
Proverbs 17:20

Both the universe and ourselves are made for truth and honesty, and both the universe and ourselves are alien to untruth and dishonesty. The universe is made for the same thing as we are – namely, righteousness. Not only the face of the Lord but the face of the universe is set against those who live below its standards.

I know that this may sound somewhat hollow in an age that appears to thrive on dishonesty and corruption, but I stand by it nevertheless. The universe is not built for the success of dishonesty and corruption. A lie breaks itself upon the moral universe, perhaps not today, not tomorrow – but certainly at some point in the future. The Tamils of South India have a saying: 'The life of the cleverest lie is only eight days.' The Germans have a saying: 'Lies have short legs.' During the Second World War, they adapted that saying to, 'Lies have one leg.' That was because Goebbels, the Propaganda Minister, had one short leg.

A passionate antagonist of Communism is reported to have said, 'In our fight against Communism we are handicapped by our decency and honesty.' Since when were honesty and decency handicaps? Rather, indecency and dishonesty are handicaps; they bring us into bondage – inwardly and outwardly. Governments, organisations and institutions that practise dishonesty will be broken from within. History has proved that. The Roman Empire collapsed not from without but from within – broken upon the rock of its own corruption. Believe me, no one gets away with anything in a moral universe. No one.

PRAYER

Gracious Father, I don't want my moral joints to creak with dishonesty, so dwell deeply within me by Your Spirit and lubricate them with the oil of Your honesty. In Jesus' name I ask it. Amen.

FURTHER STUDY

Luke 12:1-12; 1 Cor. 4:1-5; Num. 32:23; Eccl. 12:14
• What will happen when the Lord comes?
• Of what can we be sure?

July 14

■ 1 CHRONICLES 7:1–8:28

7 The sons of Issachar:
Tola, Puah, Jashub and Shimron – four in all. ²The sons of Tola:
Uzzi, Rephaiah, Jeriel, Jahmai, Ibsam and Samuel – heads of their families. During the reign of David, the descendants of Tola listed as fighting men in their genealogy numbered 22,600. ³The son of Uzzi:
Izrahiah.

The sons of Izrahiah:
Michael, Obadiah, Joel and Ishiah. All five of them were chiefs. ⁴According to their family genealogy, they had 36,000 men ready for battle, for they had many wives and children.

⁵The relatives who were fighting men belonging to all the clans of Issachar, as listed in their genealogy, were 87,000 in all.

⁶Three sons of Benjamin:
Bela, Beker and Jediael.

⁷The sons of Bela:
Ezbon, Uzzi, Uzziel, Jerimoth and Iri, heads of families – five in all. Their genealogical record listed 22,034 fighting men.

⁸The sons of Beker:
Zemirah, Joash, Eliezer, Elioenai, Omri, Jeremoth, Abijah, Anathoth and Alemeth. All these were the sons of Beker. ⁹Their genealogical record listed the heads of families and 20,200 fighting men.

¹⁰The son of Jediael:
Bilhan.

The sons of Bilhan:
Jeush, Benjamin, Ehud, Kenaanah, Zethan, Tarshish and Ahishahar. ¹¹All these sons of Jediael were heads of families. There were 17,200 fighting men ready to go out to war.

¹²The Shuppites and Huppites were the descendants of Ir, and the Hushites the descendants of Aher.

¹³The sons of Naphtali:
Jahziel, Guni, Jezer and Shillem – the descendants of Bilhah.

¹⁴The descendants of Manasseh:
Asriel was his descendant through his Aramean concubine. She gave birth to Makir the father of Gilead. ¹⁵Makir took a wife from among the Huppites and Shuppites. His sister's name was Maakah.

Another descendant was named Zelophehad, who had only daughters.

¹⁶Makir's wife Maakah gave birth to a son and named him Peresh. His brother was named Sheresh, and his sons were Ulam and Rakem.

¹⁷The son of Ulam:
Bedan.

These were the sons of Gilead son of Makir, the son of Manasseh. ¹⁸His sister Hammoleketh gave birth to Ishhod, Abiezer and Mahlah.

¹⁹The sons of Shemida were:
Ahian, Shechem, Likhi and Aniam.

²⁰The descendants of Ephraim:
Shuthelah, Bered his son,
Tahath his son, Eleadah his son,
Tahath his son, ²¹Zabad his son
and Shuthelah his son.

Ezer and Elead were killed by the native-born men of Gath, when they went down to seize their livestock.

22 Their father Ephraim mourned for them many days, and his relatives came to comfort him. 23 Then he made love to his wife again, and she became pregnant and gave birth to a son. He named him Beriah, because there had been misfortune in his family. 24 His daughter was Sheerah, who built Lower and Upper Beth Horon as well as Uzzen Sheerah.

25 Rephah was his son, Resheph his son,
Telah his son, Tahan his son,
26 Ladan his son, Ammihud his son,
Elishama his son, 27 Nun his son
and Joshua his son.

28 Their lands and settlements included Bethel and its surrounding villages, Naaran to the east, Gezer and its villages to the west, and Shechem and its villages all the way to Ayyah and its villages. 29 Along the borders of Manasseh were Beth Shan, Taanach, Megiddo and Dor, together with their villages. The descendants of Joseph son of Israel lived in these towns.

30 The sons of Asher:
Imnah, Ishvah, Ishvi and Beriah.
Their sister was Serah.
31 The sons of Beriah:
Heber and Malkiel, who was the father of Birzaith.
32 Heber was the father of Japhlet, Shomer and Hotham and of their sister Shua.
33 The sons of Japhlet:
Pasak, Bimhal and Ashvath.
These were Japhlet's sons.
34 The sons of Shomer:
Ahi, Rohgah, Hubbah and Aram.
35 The sons of his brother Helem:
Zophah, Imna, Shelesh and Amal.
36 The sons of Zophah:
Suah, Harnepher, Shual, Beri, Imrah, 37 Bezer, Hod, Shamma, Shilshah, Ithran and Beera.
38 The sons of Jether:
Jephunneh, Pispah and Ara.

39 The sons of Ulla:
Arah, Hanniel and Rizia.

40 All these were descendants of Asher – heads of families, choice men, brave warriors and outstanding leaders. The number of men ready for battle, as listed in their genealogy, was 26,000.

8 Benjamin was the father of Bela his firstborn,
Ashbel the second son, Aharah the third,
2 Nohah the fourth and Rapha the fifth.
3 The sons of Bela were:
Addar, Gera, Abihud, 4 Abishua, Naaman, Ahoah, 5 Gera, Shephuphan and Huram.
6 These were the descendants of Ehud, who were heads of families of those living in Geba and were deported to Manahath:
7 Naaman, Ahijah and Gera, who deported them and who was the father of Uzza and Ahihud.

8 Sons were born to Shaharaim in Moab after he had divorced his wives Hushim and Baara. 9 By his wife Hodesh he had Jobab, Zibia, Mesha, Malkam, 10 Jeuz, Sakia and Mirmah. These were his sons, heads of families. 11 By Hushim he had Abitub and Elpaal.
12 The sons of Elpaal:
Eber, Misham, Shemed (who built Ono and Lod with its surrounding villages), 13 and Beriah and Shema, who were heads of families of those living in Aijalon and who drove out the inhabitants of Gath.

14 Ahio, Shashak, Jeremoth, 15 Zebadiah, Arad, Eder, 16 Michael, Ishpah and Joha were the sons of Beriah.
17 Zebadiah, Meshullam, Hizki, Heber, 18 Ishmerai, Izliah and Jobab were the sons of Elpaal.
19 Jakim, Zikri, Zabdi, 20 Elienai,

Zillethai, Eliel, ²¹Adaiah, Berai-
ah and Shimrath were the sons of
Shimei.
²²Ishpan, Eber, Eliel, ²³Abdon, Zikri,
Hanan, ²⁴Hananiah, Elam, Antho-
thijah, ²⁵Iphdeiah and Penuel were
the sons of Shashak.
²⁶Shamsherai, Shehariah, Athaliah,
²⁷Jaareshiah, Elijah and Zikri were
the sons of Jeroham.
²⁸All these were heads of families, chiefs
as listed in their genealogy, and they lived
in Jerusalem.

■ PSALM 81:1-7

¹Sing for joy to God our strength;
    shout aloud to the God of Jacob!
²Begin the music, strike the tambourine,
    play the melodious harp and lyre.

³Sound the ram's horn at the New Moon,
    and when the moon is full, on the day
        of our Feast;
⁴this is a decree for Israel,
    an ordinance of the God of Jacob.
⁵When God went out against Egypt,
    he established it as a statute for Joseph.

I heard an unknown voice say:

⁶'I removed the burden from their
        shoulders;
    their hands were set free from the
        basket.
⁷In your distress you called and I rescued
        you,
    I answered you out of a thundercloud;
    I tested you at the waters of Meribah.

■ PROVERBS 17:22-23

²²A cheerful heart is good medicine,
    but a crushed spirit dries up the bones.

²³The wicked accept bribes in secret
    to pervert the course of justice.

■ ACTS 14:8-28

⁸In Lystra there sat a man who was lame.
He had been that way from birth and had
never walked. ⁹He listened to Paul as he was
speaking. Paul looked directly at him, saw
that he had faith to be healed ¹⁰and called
out, 'Stand up on your feet!' At that, the
man jumped up and began to walk.

¹¹When the crowd saw what Paul had
done, they shouted in the Lycaonian language, 'The gods have come down to us in
human form!' ¹²Barnabas they called Zeus,
and Paul they called Hermes because he
was the chief speaker. ¹³The priest of Zeus,
whose temple was just outside the city,
brought bulls and wreaths to the city gates
because he and the crowd wanted to offer
sacrifices to them.

¹⁴But when the apostles Barnabas and
Paul heard of this, they tore their clothes
and rushed out into the crowd, shouting:
¹⁵'Friends, why are you doing this? We too
are only human, like you. We are bringing
you good news, telling you to turn from
these worthless things to the living God,
who made the heavens and the earth and
the sea and everything in them. ¹⁶In the
past, he let all nations go their own way.
¹⁷Yet he has not left himself without testimony: he has shown kindness by giving
you rain from heaven and crops in their
seasons; he provides you with plenty of food
and fills your hearts with joy.' ¹⁸Even with
these words, they had difficulty keeping the
crowd from sacrificing to them.

¹⁹Then some Jews came from Antioch
and Iconium and won the crowd over. They
stoned Paul and dragged him outside the
city, thinking he was dead. ²⁰But after the
disciples had gathered round him, he got up
and went back into the city. The next day he

and Barnabas left for Derbe. ²¹They preached the gospel in that city and won a large number of disciples. Then they returned to Lystra, Iconium and Antioch, ²²strengthening the disciples and encouraging them to remain true to the faith. 'We must go through many hardships to enter the kingdom of God,' they said. ²³Paul and Barnabas appointed elders for them in each church and, with prayer and fasting, committed them to the Lord, in whom they had put their trust. ²⁴After going through Pisidia, they came into Pamphylia, ²⁵and when they had preached the word in Perga, they went down to Attalia.

²⁶From Attalia they sailed back to Antioch, where they had been committed to the grace of God for the work they had now completed. ²⁷On arriving there, they gathered the church together and reported all that God had done through them and how he had opened a door of faith to the Gentiles. ²⁸And they stayed there a long time with the disciples.

'No Reason to Smile'

'A cheerful heart is good medicine, but a crushed spirit dries up the bones.' Proverbs 17:22

A surprising thing takes place in those whose temper is tempered by the Holy Spirit – bad temper is replaced by a growing sense of humour. God has given us the power of humour, not only to laugh at things, but to laugh off things. I am not suggesting that we ought to use laughter to deny realities, but humour often reduces things to their proper size.

I once heard a preacher say, 'There is no good in a movement or a person where there is no good humour, for goodness has laughter as a corollary.' There is something basically wrong with a person who, at appropriate times, cannot break out into hearty laughter. I heard of a member of the Irish Republican Army who was wonderfully converted. He spent the first month after his conversion in the home of a minister who said of him, 'It was two weeks before I saw him smile, and when I spoke to him about this, he said, "I have been in a grim business, plotting against people – and the way I was living, there was just no reason to smile".' How tragic – 'just no reason to smile'. Depend on it, where you cannot smile, you cannot live – you just exist.

Over the years, I have watched many groups come to the CWR courses in Christian Counselling. Many are tied up with fears, guilt and apprehension. We invite them to share their fears and get them up and out. They do. Then the laughter begins. They grow progressively happier as the week goes on. By the end of the week, they are ready to laugh at anything – themselves included.

PRAYER

Lord Jesus, it is said of You that You were anointed 'above your companions ... with the oil of joy'. (Psa. 45:7) Let that same anointing rest and remain upon me today – and every day. For Your own dear name's sake. Amen.

FURTHER STUDY

Prov. 15:1-15; James 5:13; Psa. 126:2
• What does a happy heart enjoy?
• How is this expressed?

July 15

■ 1 CHRONICLES 8:29–9:44

²⁹ Jeiel the father of Gibeon lived in Gibeon.

His wife's name was Maakah, ³⁰ and his firstborn son was Abdon, followed by Zur, Kish, Baal, Ner, Nadab, ³¹ Gedor, Ahio, Zeker ³² and Mikloth, who was the father of Shimeah. They too lived near their relatives in Jerusalem.

³³ Ner was the father of Kish, Kish the father of Saul, and Saul the father of Jonathan, Malki-Shua, Abinadab and Esh-Baal.

³⁴ The son of Jonathan:
Merib-Baal, who was the father of Micah.

³⁵ The sons of Micah:
Pithon, Melek, Tarea and Ahaz.

³⁶ Ahaz was the father of Jehoaddah, Jehoaddah was the father of Alemeth, Azmaveth and Zimri, and Zimri was the father of Moza.

³⁷ Moza was the father of Binea; Raphah was his son, Eleasah his son and Azel his son.

³⁸ Azel had six sons, and these were their names:
Azrikam, Bokeru, Ishmael, Sheariah, Obadiah and Hanan. All these were the sons of Azel.

³⁹ The sons of his brother Eshek:
Ulam his firstborn, Jeush the second son and Eliphelet the third. ⁴⁰ The sons of Ulam were brave warriors who could handle the bow. They had many sons and grandsons – 150 in all.

All these were the descendants of Benjamin.

9 All Israel was listed in the genealogies in the book of the kings of Israel and Judah. They were taken captive to Babylon because of their unfaithfulness.

² Now the first to resettle on their own property in their own towns were some Israelites, priests, Levites and temple servants.

³ Those from Judah, from Benjamin, and from Ephraim and Manasseh who lived in Jerusalem were:

⁴ Uthai son of Ammihud, the son of Omri, the son of Imri, the son of Bani, a descendant of Perez son of Judah.

⁵ Of the Shelanites:
Asaiah the firstborn and his sons.

⁶ Of the Zerahites:
Jeuel.

The people from Judah numbered 690.

[7] Of the Benjaminites:

Sallu son of Meshullam, the son of Hodaviah, the son of Hassenuah;

[8] Ibneiah son of Jeroham; Elah son of Uzzi, the son of Mikri; and Meshullam son of Shephatiah, the son of Reuel, the son of Ibnijah.

[9] The people from Benjamin, as listed in their genealogy, numbered 956. All these men were heads of their families.

[10] Of the priests:

Jedaiah; Jehoiarib; Jakin;

[11] Azariah son of Hilkiah, the son of Meshullam, the son of Zadok, the son of Meraioth, the son of Ahitub, the official in charge of the house of God;

[12] Adaiah son of Jeroham, the son of Pashhur, the son of Malkijah; and Maasai son of Adiel, the son of Jahzerah, the son of Meshullam, the son of Meshillemith, the son of Immer.

[13] The priests, who were heads of families, numbered 1,760. They were able men, responsible for ministering in the house of God.

[14] Of the Levites:

Shemaiah son of Hasshub, the son of Azrikam, the son of Hashabiah, a Merarite; [15] Bakbakkar, Heresh, Galal and Mattaniah son of Mika, the son of Zikri, the son of Asaph; [16] Obadiah son of Shemaiah, the son of Galal, the son of Jeduthun; and Berekiah son of Asa, the son of Elkanah, who lived in the villages of the Netophathites.

[17] The gatekeepers:

Shallum, Akkub, Talmon, Ahiman and their fellow Levites, Shallum their chief [18] being stationed at the King's Gate on the east, up to the present time. These were the gatekeepers belonging to the camp of the Levites. [19] Shallum son of Kore, the son of Ebiasaph, the son of Korah, and his fellow gatekeepers from his family (the Korahites) were responsible for guarding the thresholds of the tent just as their ancestors had been responsible for guarding the entrance to the dwelling of the LORD. [20] In earlier times Phinehas son of Eleazar was the official in charge of the gatekeepers, and the LORD was with him. [21] Zechariah son of Meshelemiah was the gatekeeper at the entrance to the tent of meeting.

[22] Altogether, those chosen to be gatekeepers at the thresholds numbered 212. They were registered by genealogy in their villages. The gatekeepers had been assigned to their positions of trust by David and Samuel the seer. [23] They and their descendants were in charge of guarding the gates of the house of the Lord – the house called the tent of meeting. [24] The gatekeepers were on the four sides: east, west, north and south. [25] Their fellow Levites in their villages had to come from time to time and share their duties for seven-day periods. [26] But the four principal gatekeepers, who were Levites, were entrusted with the responsibility for the rooms and treasuries in the house of God. [27] They would spend the night stationed round the house of God, because they had to guard it; and they had charge of the key for opening it each morning.

[28] Some of them were in charge of the articles used in the temple service; they counted them when they were brought in and when they were taken out. [29] Others were assigned to take care of the furnishings and all the other articles of the sanctuary, as well as the special flour and wine, and the olive oil, incense and spices. [30] But some of the priests took care of mixing the spices. [31] A Levite named Mattithiah, the firstborn son of Shallum the Korahite, was entrusted with the responsibility for baking

the offering bread. ³²Some of the Kohathites, their fellow Levites, were in charge of preparing for every Sabbath the bread set out on the table.

³³Those who were musicians, heads of Levite families, stayed in the rooms of the temple and were exempt from other duties because they were responsible for the work day and night.

³⁴All these were heads of Levite families, chiefs as listed in their genealogy, and they lived in Jerusalem.

³⁵Jeiel the father of Gibeon lived in Gibeon.

His wife's name was Maakah, ³⁶and his firstborn son was Abdon, followed by Zur, Kish, Baal, Ner, Nadab, ³⁷Gedor, Ahio, Zechariah and Mikloth. ³⁸Mikloth was the father of Shimeam. They too lived near their relatives in Jerusalem.

³⁹Ner was the father of Kish, Kish the father of Saul, and Saul the father of Jonathan, Malki-Shua, Abinadab and Esh-Baal.

⁴⁰The son of Jonathan:

Merib-Baal, who was the father of Micah.

⁴¹The sons of Micah:

Pithon, Melek, Tahrea and Ahaz.

⁴²Ahaz was the father of Jadah, Jadah was the father of Alemeth, Azmaveth and Zimri, and Zimri was the father of Moza. ⁴³Moza was the father of Binea; Rephaiah was his son, Eleasah his son and Azel his son.

⁴⁴Azel had six sons, and these were their names:

Azrikam, Bokeru, Ishmael, Sheariah, Obadiah and Hanan. These were the sons of Azel.

■ PSALM 81:8-16

⁸Hear me, my people, and I will warn you –
   if you would only listen to me, Israel!
⁹You shall have no foreign god among you;
   you shall not worship any god other than me.
¹⁰I am the LORD your God,
   who brought you up out of Egypt.
   Open wide your mouth and I will fill it.

¹¹'But my people would not listen to me;
   Israel would not submit to me.
¹²So I gave them over to their stubborn hearts
   to follow their own devices.

¹³'If my people would only listen to me,
   if Israel would only follow my ways,
¹⁴how quickly I would subdue their enemies
   and turn my hand against their foes!
¹⁵Those who hate the LORD would cringe before him,
   and their punishment would last for ever.
¹⁶But you would be fed with the finest of wheat;
   with honey from the rock I would satisfy you.'

■ PROVERBS 17:24-25

²⁴A discerning person keeps wisdom in view,
   but a fool's eyes wander to the ends of the earth.

²⁵A foolish son brings grief to his father
   and bitterness to the mother who bore him.

ACTS 15:1-21

15 Certain people came down from Judea to Antioch and were teaching the believers: 'Unless you are circumcised, according to the custom taught by Moses, you cannot be saved.' ²This brought Paul and Barnabas into sharp dispute and debate with them. So Paul and Barnabas were appointed, along with some other believers, to go up to Jerusalem to see the apostles and elders about this question. ³The church sent them on their way, and as they travelled through Phoenicia and Samaria, they told how the Gentiles had been converted. This news made all the believers very glad. ⁴When they came to Jerusalem, they were welcomed by the church and the apostles and elders, to whom they reported everything God had done through them.

⁵Then some of the believers who belonged to the party of the Pharisees stood up and said, 'The Gentiles must be circumcised and required to keep the law of Moses.'

⁶The apostles and elders met to consider this question. ⁷After much discussion, Peter got up and addressed them: 'Brothers, you know that some time ago God made a choice among you that the Gentiles should hear from my lips the message of the gospel and believe. ⁸God, who knows the heart, showed that he accepted them by giving the Holy Spirit to them, just as he did to us. ⁹He did not discriminate between us and them, for he purified their hearts by faith. ¹⁰Now then, why do you try to test God by putting

on the necks of Gentiles a yoke that neither we nor our ancestors have been able to bear? ¹¹No! We believe it is through the grace of our Lord Jesus that we are saved, just as they are.'

¹²The whole assembly became silent as they listened to Barnabas and Paul telling about the signs and wonders God had done among the Gentiles through them. ¹³When they finished, James spoke up. 'Brothers,' he said, 'listen to me. ¹⁴Simon has described to us how God first intervened to choose a people for his name from the Gentiles. ¹⁵The words of the prophets are in agreement with this, as it is written:

¹⁶ ' "After this I will return
    and rebuild David's fallen tent.
  Its ruins I will rebuild,
    and I will restore it,
¹⁷ that the rest of mankind may seek the
      Lord,
    even all the Gentiles who bear my
      name,
  says the Lord, who does these things" –
¹⁸ things known from long ago.

¹⁹'It is my judgment, therefore, that we should not make it difficult for the Gentiles who are turning to God. ²⁰Instead we should write to them, telling them to abstain from food polluted by idols, from sexual immorality, from the meat of strangled animals and from blood. ²¹For the law of Moses has been preached in every city from the earliest times and is read in the synagogues on every Sabbath.'

Purity - Not a Popular Thought

'He did not discriminate between us and them, for he purified their hearts by faith.' **Acts 15:9**

If we understand what Scripture means by the term 'heart' - the core of our being - we can ask ourselves an important question: what does our Lord mean when He uses the word 'pure'? 'Blessed are the pure in heart, for they will see God' (Matt. 5:8). The word 'pure' (Greek: *katharos*) means a heart that is clean or clear. Unfortunately, purity does not always seem to be popular in contemporary Christianity. The emphasis nowadays seems to be more on power than on purity. Many Christians I talk to want to know how they can possess and develop spiritual gifts. Few, generally speaking, want to know how to experience the blessing of what our text today calls a heart purified by faith.

Sixteen hundred years ago St Augustine expressed a sentiment in words which might well sum up the thoughts of many – thankfully, not all – in today's Church: 'Lord, make me pure … but not just yet.' Most of us would be willing to identify ourselves with the conditions laid down in the first five of our Lord's Beatitudes, but how do we feel about the condition of being pure in heart? Are we ready and willing to pray:

> I want, dear Lord, a heart that's true and clean
> A sunlit heart, with not a cloud between.
> A heart like Thine, a heart divine.
> A heart as white as snow.
> On me, dear Lord, a heart like this bestow.

George Galloway Jackson (1866-1893)

PRAYER

O yes, dear Father, from the depths of my being I cry out make me clean. I have come so far with You – how can I turn back now? I'm a candidate for both power and purity. Give me the deep inner cleansing I need – today. For Jesus' sake. Amen.

FURTHER STUDY

John 13:1-17; 2 Cor. 7:1; James 4:8; 1 John 3:3
• What was Peter's request?
• Make your request today.

July 16

■ 1 CHRONICLES 10:1–11:47

10 Now the Philistines fought against Israel; the Israelites fled before them, and many fell dead on Mount Gilboa. ²The Philistines were in hot pursuit of Saul and his sons, and they killed his sons Jonathan, Abinadab and Malki-Shua. ³The fighting grew fierce around Saul, and when the archers overtook him, they wounded him.

⁴Saul said to his armour-bearer, 'Draw your sword and run me through, or these uncircumcised fellows will come and abuse me.'

But his armour-bearer was terrified and would not do it; so Saul took his own sword and fell on it. ⁵When the armour-bearer saw that Saul was dead, he too fell on his sword and died. ⁶So Saul and his three sons died, and all his house died together.

[7] When all the Israelites in the valley saw that the army had fled and that Saul and his sons had died, they abandoned their towns and fled. And the Philistines came and occupied them.

[8] The next day, when the Philistines came to strip the dead, they found Saul and his sons fallen on Mount Gilboa. [9] They stripped him and took his head and his armour, and sent messengers throughout the land of the Philistines to proclaim the news among their idols and their people. [10] They put his armour in the temple of their gods and hung up his head in the temple of Dagon.

[11] When all the inhabitants of Jabesh Gilead heard what the Philistines had done to Saul, [12] all their valiant men went and took the bodies of Saul and his sons and brought them to Jabesh. Then they buried their bones under the great tree in Jabesh, and they fasted seven days.

[13] Saul died because he was unfaithful to the LORD; he did not keep the word of the LORD and even consulted a medium for guidance, [14] and did not enquire of the LORD. So the LORD put him to death and turned the kingdom over to David son of Jesse.

11 All Israel came together to David at Hebron and said, 'We are your own flesh and blood. [2] In the past, even while Saul was king, you were the one who led Israel on their military campaigns. And the LORD your God said to you, "You will shepherd my people Israel, and you will become their ruler." '

[3] When all the elders of Israel had come to King David at Hebron, he made a covenant with them at Hebron before the LORD, and they anointed David king over Israel, as the LORD had promised through Samuel.

[4] David and all the Israelites marched to Jerusalem (that is, Jebus). The Jebusites who lived there [5] said to David, 'You will not get in here.' Nevertheless, David captured the fortress of Zion – which is the City of David.

[6] David had said, 'Whoever leads the attack on the Jebusites will become commander-in-chief.' Joab son of Zeruiah went up first, and so he received the command.

[7] David then took up residence in the fortress, and so it was called the City of David. [8] He built up the city around it, from the terraces to the surrounding wall, while Joab restored the rest of the city. [9] And David became more and more powerful, because the LORD Almighty was with him.

[10] These were the chiefs of David's mighty warriors – they, together with all Israel, gave his kingship strong support to extend it over the whole land, as the LORD had promised – [11] this is the list of David's mighty warriors:

Jashobeam, a Hakmonite, was chief of the officers; he raised his spear against three hundred men, whom he killed in one encounter. [12] Next to him was Eleazar son of Dodai the Ahohite, one of the three mighty warriors. [13] He was with David at Pas Dammim when the Philistines gathered there for battle. At a place where there was a field full of barley, the troops fled from the Philistines. [14] But they took their stand in the middle of the field. They defended it and struck the Philistines down, and the LORD brought about a great victory.

[15] Three of the thirty chiefs came down to David to the rock at the cave of Adullam, while a band of Philistines was encamped in the Valley of Rephaim. [16] At that time David was in the stronghold, and the Philistine garrison was at Bethlehem. [17] David longed for water and said, 'Oh, that someone would get me a drink of water from the well near the gate of Bethlehem!' [18] So the Three broke through the Philistine lines, drew water from the well near the gate of Bethlehem and carried it back to David. But he refused to drink it; instead, he poured it out to the LORD. [19] 'God forbid that I should do this!' he said. 'Should I drink the blood of these men who went at the risk of their lives?'

Because they risked their lives to bring it back, David would not drink it.

Such were the exploits of the three mighty warriors.

²⁰ Abishai the brother of Joab was chief of the Three. He raised his spear against three hundred men, whom he killed, and so he became as famous as the Three. ²¹ He was doubly honoured above the Three and became their commander, even though he was not included among them.

²² Benaiah son of Jehoiada, a valiant fighter from Kabzeel, performed great exploits. He struck down Moab's two mightiest warriors. He also went down into a pit on a snowy day and killed a lion. ²³ And he struck down an Egyptian who was five cubits tall. Although the Egyptian had a spear like a weaver's rod in his hand, Benaiah went against him with a club. He snatched the spear from the Egyptian's hand and killed him with his own spear. ²⁴ Such were the exploits of Benaiah son of Jehoiada; he too was as famous as the three mighty warriors. ²⁵ He was held in greater honour than any of the Thirty, but he was not included among the Three. And David put him in charge of his bodyguard.

²⁶ The mighty warriors were:
Asahel the brother of Joab,
Elhanan son of Dodo from Bethlehem,
²⁷ Shammoth the Harorite,
Helez the Pelonite,
²⁸ Ira son of Ikkesh from Tekoa,
Abiezer from Anathoth,
²⁹ Sibbekai the Hushathite,
Ilai the Ahohite,
³⁰ Maharai the Netophathite,
Heled son of Baanah the Netophathite,
³¹ Ithai son of Ribai from Gibeah in Benjamin,
Benaiah the Pirathonite,
³² Hurai from the ravines of Gaash,

Abiel the Arbathite,
³³ Azmaveth the Baharumite,
Eliahba the Shaalbonite,
³⁴ the sons of Hashem the Gizonite,
Jonathan son of Shagee the Hararite,
³⁵ Ahiam son of Sakar the Hararite,
Eliphal son of Ur,
³⁶ Hepher the Mekerathite,
Ahijah the Pelonite,
³⁷ Hezro the Carmelite,
Naarai son of Ezbai,
³⁸ Joel the brother of Nathan,
Mibhar son of Hagri,
³⁹ Zelek the Ammonite,
Naharai the Berothite, the armourbearer of Joab son of Zeruiah,
⁴⁰ Ira the Ithrite,
Gareb the Ithrite,
⁴¹ Uriah the Hittite,
Zabad son of Ahlai,
⁴² Adina son of Shiza the Reubenite, who was chief of the Reubenites, and the thirty with him,
⁴³ Hanan son of Maakah,
Joshaphat the Mithnite,
⁴⁴ Uzzia the Ashterathite,
Shama and Jeiel the sons of Hotham the Aroerite,
⁴⁵ Jediael son of Shimri,
his brother Joha the Tizite,
⁴⁶ Eliel the Mahavite,
Jeribai and Joshaviah the sons of Elnaam,
Ithmah the Moabite,
⁴⁷ Eliel, Obed and Jaasiel the Mezobaite.

....

■ PSALM 82:1-8

¹ God presides in the great assembly;
he renders judgment among the 'gods':

² 'How long will you defend the unjust
and show partiality to the wicked?

³ Defend the weak and the fatherless;
    uphold the cause of the poor and the
        oppressed.
⁴ Rescue the weak and the needy;
    deliver them from the hand of the
        wicked.

⁵ 'The "gods" know nothing, they
        understand nothing.
    They walk about in darkness;
    all the foundations of the earth are
        shaken.

⁶ 'I said, "You are 'gods';
    you are all sons of the Most High."
⁷ But you will die like mere mortals;
    you will fall like every other ruler.'

⁸ Rise up, O God, judge the earth,
    for all the nations are your
        inheritance.

■ PROVERBS 17:26

²⁶ If imposing a fine on the innocent is not
        good,
    surely to flog honest officials is not
        right.

■ ACTS 15:22-41

²² Then the apostles and elders, with the whole church, decided to choose some of their own men and send them to Antioch with Paul and Barnabas. They chose Judas (called Barsabbas) and Silas, men who were leaders among the believers. ²³ With them they sent the following letter:

The apostles and elders, your brothers,

To the Gentile believers in Antioch, Syria and Cilicia:

Greetings.

²⁴ We have heard that some went out from us without our authorisation and disturbed you, troubling your minds by what they said. ²⁵ So we all agreed to choose some men and send them to you with our dear friends Barnabas and Paul – ²⁶ men who have risked their lives for the name of our Lord Jesus Christ. ²⁷ Therefore we are sending Judas and Silas to confirm by word of mouth what we are writing. ²⁸ It seemed good to the Holy Spirit and to us not to burden you with anything beyond the following requirements: ²⁹ You are to abstain from food sacrificed to idols, from blood, from the meat of strangled animals and from sexual immorality. You will do well to avoid these things.

Farewell.

³⁰ So the men were sent off and went down to Antioch, where they gathered the church together and delivered the letter. ³¹ The people read it and were glad for its encouraging message. ³² Judas and Silas, who themselves were prophets, said much to encourage and strengthen the believers. ³³ After spending some time there, they were sent off by the believers with the blessing of peace to return to those who had sent them. [34]a ³⁵ But Paul and Barnabas remained in Antioch, where they and many others taught and preached the word of the Lord.

³⁶ Some time later Paul said to Barnabas, 'Let us go back and visit the believers in all the towns where we preached the word of the Lord and see how they are doing.' ³⁷ Barnabas wanted to take John, also called Mark, with them, ³⁸ but Paul did not think it wise to take him, because he had deserted them in Pamphylia and had not continued with them in the work. ³⁹ They had such a

sharp disagreement that they parted company. Barnabas took Mark and sailed for Cyprus, [40]but Paul chose Silas and left, commended by the believers to the grace of the Lord. [41]He went through Syria and Cilicia, strengthening the churches.

---

[a] Some manuscripts include here *But Silas decided to remain there.*

It's All Under Control

'Rise up, O God, judge the earth, for all the nations are your inheritance.' **Psalm 82:8**

The salvation spoken of in the phrase 'the helmet of salvation' is the salvation we are going to enjoy when God works out His eternal purposes.

The Christian has a hope for the future. He has an understanding that God is working out His purposes in history, and therefore we need not be disturbed when human programmes appear to be going wrong. We hear about 'new deals' and 'fair deals' and 'better deals', yet they end up in disappointment for all concerned.

The Christian expects the world to get worse and worse, for this is what the Bible tells us will happen. He expects false teachings to abound. He expects the world's systems to fail, for anything that is not built on Christ has no guarantee of success. The Christian knows that wars and international tension are unavoidable, even though every effort is made to avoid them. The world is in such a state and such a condition that the more attention we give it, the more weary our minds become.

What is a Christian to do in such a world as ours? How are we to react when the devil takes advantage of our sensitivities to world conditions and focuses our thoughts upon them? Shall we give up? Shall we withdraw from life?

No, we put on the helmet of salvation and remind ourselves that in the face of everything that appears contrary, God is working out His eternal plan and purpose. History remains His story! Almighty God is at work in the very events that appear to be filled with darkness and confusion.

PRAYER

O God, help me see that although You are apart from the events of history, You are also in the events of history. Ultimately all things are going to glorify You. Thank You, Father. Amen.

FURTHER STUDY

Heb. 6; 1 Pet. 1:3; 1 John 3:3; Eph. 1:11
• What does this hope provide for us?
• How does Peter describe our hope?

July 17

■ 1 CHRONICLES 12:1–13:14

12 These were the men who came to David at Ziklag, while he was banished from the presence of Saul son of Kish (they were among the warriors who helped him in battle; ²they were armed with bows and were able to shoot arrows or to sling stones right-handed or left-handed; they were relatives of Saul from the tribe of Benjamin):

³Ahiezer their chief and Joash the sons of Shemaah the Gibeathite; Jeziel and Pelet the sons of Azmaveth; Berakah, Jehu the Anathothite, ⁴and Ishmaiah the Gibeonite, a mighty warrior among the Thirty, who was a leader of the Thirty; Jeremiah, Jahaziel, Johanan, Jozabad the Gederathite, ⁵Eluzai, Jerimoth, Bealiah, Shemariah and Shephatiah the Haruphite; ⁶Elkanah, Ishiah, Azarel, Joezer and Jashobeam the Korahites; ⁷and Joelah and Zebadiah the sons of Jeroham from Gedor.

⁸Some Gadites defected to David at his stronghold in the wilderness. They were brave warriors, ready for battle and able to handle the shield and spear. Their faces were the faces of lions, and they were as swift as gazelles in the mountains.
⁹Ezer was the chief,
  Obadiah the second in command,
    Eliab the third,
¹⁰Mishmannah the fourth, Jeremiah the
    fifth,
¹¹Attai the sixth, Eliel the seventh,
¹²Johanan the eighth, Elzabad the ninth,
¹³Jeremiah the tenth and Makbannai the
    eleventh.
¹⁴These Gadites were army commanders;

the least was a match for a hundred, and the greatest for a thousand. ¹⁵It was they who crossed the Jordan in the first month when it was overflowing all its banks, and they put to flight everyone living in the valleys, to the east and to the west.

¹⁶Other Benjaminites and some men from Judah also came to David in his stronghold. ¹⁷David went out to meet them and said to them, 'If you have come to me in peace to help me, I am ready for you to join me. But if you have come to betray me to my enemies when my hands are free from violence, may the God of our ancestors see it and judge you.'

¹⁸Then the Spirit came on Amasai, chief of the Thirty, and he said:

'We are yours, David!
  We are with you, son of Jesse!
Success, success to you,
    and success to those who help you,
    for your God will help you.'

So David received them and made them leaders of his raiding bands.

¹⁹Some of the tribe of Manasseh defected to David when he went with the Philistines to fight against Saul. (He and his men did not help the Philistines because, after consultation, their rulers sent him away. They said, 'It will cost us our heads if he deserts to his master Saul.') ²⁰When David went to Ziklag, these were the men of Manasseh who defected to him: Adnah, Jozabad, Jediael, Michael, Jozabad, Elihu and Zillethai, leaders of units of a thousand in Manasseh. ²¹They helped David against raiding bands, for all of them were brave warriors, and they were commanders in his army. ²²Day after day men came to help David, until he

had a great army, like the army of God.

²³These are the numbers of the men armed for battle who came to David at Hebron to turn Saul's kingdom over to him, as the Lord had said:

²⁴from Judah, carrying shield and spear – 6,800 armed for battle;

²⁵from Simeon, warriors ready for battle – 7,100;

²⁶from Levi – 4,600, ²⁷including Jehoiada, leader of the family of Aaron, with 3,700 men, ²⁸and Zadok, a brave young warrior, with 22 officers from his family;

²⁹from Benjamin, Saul's tribe – 3,000, most of whom had remained loyal to Saul's house until then;

³⁰from Ephraim, brave warriors, famous in their own clans – 20,800;

³¹from half the tribe of Manasseh, designated by name to come and make David king – 18,000;

³²from Issachar, men who understood the times and knew what Israel should do – 200 chiefs, with all their relatives under their command;

³³from Zebulun, experienced soldiers prepared for battle with every type of weapon, to help David with undivided loyalty – 50,000;

³⁴from Naphtali – 1,000 officers, together with 37,000 men carrying shields and spears;

³⁵from Dan, ready for battle – 28,600;

³⁶from Asher, experienced soldiers prepared for battle – 40,000;

³⁷and from east of the Jordan, from Reuben, Gad and the half-tribe of Manasseh, armed with every type of weapon – 120,000.

³⁸All these were fighting men who volunteered to serve in the ranks. They came to Hebron fully determined to make David king over all Israel. All the rest of the Israelites were also of one mind to make David king. ³⁹The men spent three days there with David, eating and drinking, for their families had supplied provisions for them. ⁴⁰Also, their neighbours from as far away as Issachar, Zebulun and Naphtali came bringing food on donkeys, camels, mules and oxen. There were plentiful supplies of flour, fig cakes, raisin cakes, wine, olive oil, cattle and sheep, for there was joy in Israel.

13 David conferred with each of his officers, the commanders of thousands and commanders of hundreds. ²He then said to the whole assembly of Israel, 'If it seems good to you and if it is the will of the Lord our God, let us send word far and wide to the rest of our people throughout the territories of Israel, and also to the priests and Levites who are with them in their towns and pasture-lands, to come and join us. ³Let us bring the ark of our God back to us, for we did not enquire of it during the reign of Saul.' ⁴The whole assembly agreed to do this, because it seemed right to all the people.

⁵So David assembled all Israel, from the River Shihor in Egypt to Lebo Hamath, to bring the ark of God from Kiriath Jearim. ⁶David and all Israel went to Baalah of Judah (Kiriath Jearim) to bring up from there the ark of God the Lord, who is enthroned between the cherubim – the ark that is called by the Name.

⁷They moved the ark of God from Abinadab's house on a new cart, with Uzzah and Ahio guiding it. ⁸David and all the Israelites were celebrating with all their might before God, with songs and with harps, lyres, tambourines, cymbals and trumpets.

⁹When they came to the threshing-floor of Kidon, Uzzah reached out his hand to steady the ark, because the oxen stumbled. ¹⁰The Lord's anger burned against Uzzah, and he struck him down because he had put his hand on the ark. So he died there before God.

¹¹Then David was angry because the Lord's wrath had broken out against Uzzah, and to this day that place is called Perez Uzzah.

¹²David was afraid of God that day and asked, 'How can I ever bring the ark of God to me?' ¹³He did not take the ark to be with him in the City of David. Instead, he took it to the house of Obed-Edom the Gittite. ¹⁴The ark of God remained with the family of Obed-Edom in his house for three months, and the LORD blessed his household and everything he had.

■ PSALM 83:1–8

¹O God, do not remain silent;
　do not turn a deaf ear,
　do not stand aloof, O God.
²See how your enemies growl,
　how your foes rear their heads.
³With cunning they conspire against your
　people;
　they plot against those you cherish.
⁴'Come,' they say, 'let us destroy them as a
　nation,
　so that Israel's name is remembered
　no more.'

⁵With one mind they plot together;
　they form an alliance against you –
⁶the tents of Edom and the
　Ishmaelites,
　of Moab and the Hagrites,
⁷Byblos, Ammon and Amalek,
　Philistia, with the people of Tyre.
⁸Even Assyria has joined them
　to reinforce Lot's descendants.

■ PROVERBS 17:27–28

²⁷The one who has knowledge uses words
　with restraint,
　and whoever has understanding is
　even-tempered.

²⁸Even fools are thought wise if they keep
　silent,

and discerning if they hold their
　tongues.

■ ACTS 16:1–24

16 Paul came to Derbe and then to Lystra, where a disciple named Timothy lived, whose mother was Jewish and a believer but whose father was a Greek. ²The believers at Lystra and Iconium spoke well of him. ³Paul wanted to take him along on the journey, so he circumcised him because of the Jews who lived in that area, for they all knew that his father was a Greek. ⁴As they travelled from town to town, they delivered the decisions reached by the apostles and elders in Jerusalem for the people to obey. ⁵So the churches were strengthened in the faith and grew daily in numbers.

⁶Paul and his companions travelled throughout the region of Phrygia and Galatia, having been kept by the Holy Spirit from preaching the word in the province of Asia. ⁷When they came to the border of Mysia, they tried to enter Bithynia, but the Spirit of Jesus would not allow them to. ⁸So they passed by Mysia and went down to Troas. ⁹During the night Paul had a vision of a man of Macedonia standing and begging him, 'Come over to Macedonia and help us.' ¹⁰After Paul had seen the vision, we got ready at once to leave for Macedonia, concluding that God had called us to preach the gospel to them.

¹¹From Troas we put out to sea and sailed straight for Samothrace, and the next day we went on to Neapolis. ¹²From there we travelled to Philippi, a Roman colony and the leading city of that district of Macedonia. And we stayed there several days.

¹³On the Sabbath we went outside the city gate to the river, where we expected to find a place of prayer. We sat down and began to speak to the women who had gathered there. ¹⁴One of those listening was a woman from

the city of Thyatira named Lydia, a dealer in purple cloth. She was a worshipper of God. The Lord opened her heart to respond to Paul's message. [15] When she and the members of her household were baptised, she invited us to her home. 'If you consider me a believer in the Lord,' she said, 'come and stay at my house.' And she persuaded us.

[16] Once when we were going to the place of prayer, we were met by a female slave who had a spirit by which she predicted the future. She earned a great deal of money for her owners by fortune-telling. [17] She followed Paul and the rest of us, shouting, 'These men are servants of the Most High God, who are telling you the way to be saved.' [18] She kept this up for many days. Finally Paul became so annoyed that he turned round and said to the spirit, 'In the name of Jesus Christ I command you to come out of her!' At that moment the spirit left her.

[19] When her owners realised that their hope of making money was gone, they seized Paul and Silas and dragged them into the market-place to face the authorities. [20] They brought them before the magistrates and said, 'These men are Jews, and are throwing our city into an uproar [21] by advocating customs unlawful for us Romans to accept or practise.'

[22] The crowd joined in the attack against Paul and Silas, and the magistrates ordered them to be stripped and beaten with rods. [23] After they had been severely flogged, they were thrown into prison, and the jailer was commanded to guard them carefully. [24] When he received these orders, he put them in the inner cell and fastened their feet in the stocks.

The Spirit Guides

'When they came to the border of Mysia, they tried to enter Bithynia, but the Spirit of Jesus would not allow them to.' **Acts 16:7**

The Holy Spirit seeks to bring us around to accepting God's guidance for our lives. 'For those who are led by the Spirit of God are the children of God' (Rom. 8:14).

This is a stage in life which many Christians never attain - they are not Spirit-led Christians. They are led by self-interest, physical impulses or by the opinions of others. They have not put themselves at the disposal of the Spirit to be led of Him in the details of their lives. Hence they lack direction and, therefore, a goal.

When Christians say to me, 'The Spirit never seems to guide me,' I usually reply, 'How well do you listen?' The problem we face over guidance is not because the Spirit fails to lead us, but because we are not listening. We must be prepared to stop talking and wait before Him so that He can talk to us.

In this frenzied age many Christians have lost the art of listening. They are willing to spend time in prayer talking to God, but are not willing to spend very much of the time listening to God. We must stop, wait and tune ourselves in to the Holy Spirit's wavelength if we are to hear His voice in our hearts and feel His gentle impressions.

A Quaker woman inquired of a young man, 'Hast thou heard God speak lately?' 'No,' said the young man. 'Then thou hast forgotten to be still,' said the woman. 'Be still ... and know ...' says the Scripture (Psa. 46:10). Be restless and you will not know. God guides everyone who wants to be guided.

PRAYER

O Spirit of the living God, help me tune my heart so that I can hear Your voice, for without Your guidance my life lacks mission and direction. Take the reins of my life and guide me. For Jesus' sake, I pray. Amen.

FURTHER STUDY

Acts 16; 13:2; John 16:13
• How did the Holy Spirit guide Paul?
• What was the result?

July 18

▬ 1 CHRONICLES 14:1–16:6

14 Now Hiram king of Tyre sent messengers to David, along with cedar logs, stonemasons and carpenters to build a palace for him. ² And David knew that the LORD had established him as king over Israel and that his kingdom had been highly exalted for the sake of his people Israel.

³ In Jerusalem David took more wives and became the father of more sons and daughters. ⁴ These are the names of the children born to him there: Shammua, Shobab, Nathan, Solomon, ⁵ Ibhar, Elishua, Elpelet, ⁶ Nogah, Nepheg, Japhia, ⁷ Elishama, Beeliada and Eliphelet.

⁸ When the Philistines heard that David had been anointed king over all Israel, they went up in full force to search for him, but David heard about it and went out to meet them. ⁹ Now the Philistines had come and raided the Valley of Rephaim; ¹⁰ so David enquired of God: 'Shall I go and attack the Philistines? Will you deliver them into my hands?'

The LORD answered him, 'Go, I will deliver them into your hands.'

¹¹ So David and his men went up to Baal Perazim, and there he defeated them. He said, 'As waters break out, God has broken out against my enemies by my hand.' So that place was called Baal Perazim. ¹² The Philistines had abandoned their gods there, and David gave orders to burn them in the fire.

¹³ Once more the Philistines raided the valley; ¹⁴ so David enquired of God again, and God answered him, 'Do not go directly after them, but circle round them and attack them in front of the poplar trees. ¹⁵ As soon as you hear the sound of marching in the tops of the poplar trees, move out to battle, because that will mean God has gone out in front of you to strike the Philistine army.' ¹⁶ So David did as God commanded him, and they struck down the Philistine army, all the way from Gibeon to Gezer.

¹⁷ So David's fame spread throughout every land, and the LORD made all the nations fear him.

15 After David had constructed buildings for himself in the City of David,

he prepared a place for the ark of God and pitched a tent for it. ²Then David said, 'No one but the Levites may carry the ark of God, because the LORD chose them to carry the ark of the LORD and to minister before him for ever.'

³David assembled all Israel in Jerusalem to bring up the ark of the LORD to the place he had prepared for it. ⁴He called together the descendants of Aaron and the Levites:

⁵from the descendants of Kohath,
  Uriel the leader and 120 relatives;
⁶from the descendants of Merari,
  Asaiah the leader and 220 relatives;
⁷from the descendants of Gershon,
  Joel the leader and 130 relatives;
⁸from the descendants of Elizaphan,
  Shemaiah the leader and 200 relatives;
⁹from the descendants of Hebron,
  Eliel the leader and 80 relatives;
¹⁰from the descendants of Uzziel,
  Amminadab the leader and 112 relatives.

¹¹Then David summoned Zadok and Abiathar the priests, and Uriel, Asaiah, Joel, Shemaiah, Eliel and Amminadab the Levites. ¹²He said to them, 'You are the heads of the Levitical families; you and your fellow Levites are to consecrate yourselves and bring up the ark of the LORD, the God of Israel, to the place I have prepared for it. ¹³It was because you, the Levites, did not bring it up the first time that the LORD our God broke out in anger against us. We did not enquire of him about how to do it in the prescribed way.' ¹⁴So the priests and Levites consecrated themselves in order to bring up the ark of the LORD, the God of Israel. ¹⁵And the Levites carried the ark of God with the poles on their shoulders, as Moses had commanded in accordance with the word of the LORD.

¹⁶David told the leaders of the Levites to appoint their fellow Levites as musicians to make a joyful sound with musical instruments: lyres, harps and cymbals.

¹⁷So the Levites appointed Heman son of Joel; from his relatives, Asaph son of Berekiah; and from their relatives the Merarites, Ethan son of Kushaiah; ¹⁸and with them their relatives next in rank: Zechariah, Jaaziel, Shemiramoth, Jehiel, Unni, Eliab, Benaiah, Maaseiah, Mattithiah, Eliphelehu, Mikneiah, Obed-Edom and Jeiel, the gatekeepers.

¹⁹The musicians Heman, Asaph and Ethan were to sound the bronze cymbals; ²⁰Zechariah, Jaaziel, Shemiramoth, Jehiel, Unni, Eliab, Maaseiah and Benaiah were to play the lyres according to *alamoth,* ²¹and Mattithiah, Eliphelehu, Mikneiah, Obed-Edom, Jeiel and Azaziah were to play the harps, directing according to *sheminith.* ²²Kenaniah the head Levite was in charge of the singing; that was his responsibility because he was skilful at it.

²³Berekiah and Elkanah were to be doorkeepers for the ark. ²⁴Shebaniah, Joshaphat, Nethanel, Amasai, Zechariah, Benaiah and Eliezer the priests were to blow trumpets before the ark of God. Obed-Edom and Jehiah were also to be doorkeepers for the ark.

²⁵So David and the elders of Israel and the commanders of units of a thousand went to bring up the ark of the covenant of the LORD from the house of Obed-Edom, with rejoicing. ²⁶Because God had helped the Levites who were carrying the ark of the covenant of the LORD, seven bulls and seven rams were sacrificed. ²⁷Now David was clothed in a robe of fine linen, as were all the Levites who were carrying the ark, and as were the musicians, and Kenaniah, who was in charge of the singing of the choirs. David also wore a linen ephod. ²⁸So all Israel brought up the ark of the covenant of the LORD with shouts, with the sounding of rams' horns and trumpets, and of cymbals, and the playing of lyres and harps.

²⁹As the ark of the covenant of the LORD was entering the City of David, Michal

daughter of Saul watched from a window. And when she saw King David dancing and celebrating, she despised him in her heart.

16 They brought the ark of God and set it inside the tent that David had pitched for it, and they presented burnt offerings and fellowship offerings before God. ²After David had finished sacrificing the burnt offerings and fellowship offerings, he blessed the people in the name of the LORD. ³Then he gave a loaf of bread, a cake of dates and a cake of raisins to each Israelite man and woman.

⁴He appointed some of the Levites to minister before the ark of the LORD, to extol, thank, and praise the LORD, the God of Israel: ⁵Asaph was the chief, and next to him in rank were Zechariah, then Jaaziel, Shemiramoth, Jehiel, Mattithiah, Eliab, Benaiah, Obed-Edom and Jeiel. They were to play the lyres and harps, Asaph was to sound the cymbals, ⁶and Benaiah and Jahaziel the priests were to blow the trumpets regularly before the ark of the covenant of God.

■ PSALM 83:9-18

⁹Do to them as you did to Midian,
  as you did to Sisera and Jabin at the
    River Kishon,
¹⁰who perished at Endor
  and became like dung on the ground.
¹¹Make their nobles like Oreb and Zeeb,
  all their princes like Zebah and
    Zalmunna,
¹²who said, 'Let us take possession
  of the pasture-lands of God.'

¹³Make them like tumble-weed, my God,
  like chaff before the wind.
¹⁴As fire consumes the forest
  or a flame sets the mountains ablaze,
¹⁵so pursue them with your tempest
  and terrify them with your storm.
¹⁶Cover their faces with shame, LORD,

so that they will seek your name.

¹⁷May they ever be ashamed and dismayed;
  may they perish in disgrace.
¹⁸Let them know that you, whose name is
    the LORD –
  that you alone are the Most High over
    all the earth.

■ PROVERBS 18:1-3

18 An unfriendly person pursues
    selfish ends
  and against all sound judgment starts
    quarrels.

²Fools find no pleasure in understanding
  but delight in airing their own
    opinions.

³When wickedness comes, so does
    contempt,
  and with shame comes reproach.

■ ACTS 16:25–17:9

²⁵About midnight Paul and Silas were praying and singing hymns to God, and the other prisoners were listening to them. ²⁶Suddenly there was such a violent earthquake that the foundations of the prison were shaken. At once all the prison doors flew open, and everyone's chains came loose. ²⁷The jailer woke up, and when he saw the prison doors open, he drew his sword and was about to kill himself because he thought the prisoners had escaped. ²⁸But Paul shouted, 'Don't harm yourself! We are all here!'

²⁹The jailer called for lights, rushed in and fell trembling before Paul and Silas. ³⁰He then brought them out and asked, 'Sirs, what must I do to be saved?' ³¹They replied, 'Believe in the Lord

Jesus, and you will be saved – you and your household.' ³²Then they spoke the word of the Lord to him and to all the others in his house. ³³At that hour of the night the jailer took them and washed their wounds; then immediately he and all his household were baptised. ³⁴The jailer brought them into his house and set a meal before them; he was filled with joy because he had come to believe in God – he and his whole household.

³⁵When it was daylight, the magistrates sent their officers to the jailer with the order: 'Release those men.' ³⁶The jailer told Paul, 'The magistrates have ordered that you and Silas be released. Now you can leave. Go in peace.'

³⁷But Paul said to the officers: 'They beat us publicly without a trial, even though we are Roman citizens, and threw us into prison. And now do they want to get rid of us quietly? No! Let them come themselves and escort us out.'

³⁸The officers reported this to the magistrates, and when they heard that Paul and Silas were Roman citizens, they were alarmed. ³⁹They came to appease them and escorted them from the prison, requesting them to leave the city. ⁴⁰After Paul and Silas came out of the prison, they went to Lydia's house, where they met with the brothers and sisters and encouraged them. Then they left.

17 When Paul and his companions had passed through Amphipolis and Apollonia, they came to Thessalonica, where there was a Jewish synagogue. ²As was his custom, Paul went into the synagogue, and on three Sabbath days he reasoned with them from the Scriptures, ³explaining and proving that the Messiah had to suffer and rise from the dead. 'This Jesus I am proclaiming to you is the Messiah,' he said. ⁴Some of the Jews were persuaded and joined Paul and Silas, as did a large number of God-fearing Greeks and quite a few prominent women.

⁵But other Jews were jealous; so they rounded up some bad characters from the market-place, formed a mob and started a riot in the city. They rushed to Jason's house in search of Paul and Silas in order to bring them out to the crowd. ⁶But when they did not find them, they dragged Jason and some other believers before the city officials, shouting: 'These men who have caused trouble all over the world have now come here, ⁷and Jason has welcomed them into his house. They are all defying Caesar's decrees, saying that there is another king, one called Jesus.' ⁸When they heard this, the crowd and the city officials were thrown into turmoil. ⁹Then they put Jason and the others on bail and let them go.

The Cement of Society

'When wickedness comes, so does contempt, and with shame comes reproach.' **Proverbs 18:3**

Nobody gets away with anything in a moral universe if that 'anything' is dishonest and untrue. The whole history of humanity is a commentary on this. Remember the first lie uttered by Satan – 'You will not die'? He keeps on repeating that well-worn but discredited lie to every member of Adam's race. Something dies in us the moment we are dishonest – not the least, our self-respect. Death eats away at our hearts the moment dishonesty is let in. We are not so much punished for sin as by sin. I came across a statement in a book in which the writer said, 'There are two major principles for getting and keeping political power: (1) let nothing, least of all truth and honour, interfere with success; (2) be honest and trustworthy in the little things, but boldly dishonest in the large ones.' What would be the result of someone getting political power by following those two principles? I will tell you. Like blind Samson, they would pull down the pillars of society around their heads and the heads of others also.

It is the ten righteous men who spare the Sodoms of this world. Fidelity is the cement that holds society together; take it away and it destroys itself. I may be stretching imagination too far by saying this, but in my opinion the Christian presence, especially as it represents fidelity, holds the world on its course. Civilisation would have disintegrated long ago were it not for the moral and Christian character that flows out of the Church into the world.

PRAYER

Father, help me to be one who holds the world together by my character. And let the hallmark of my character be fidelity to truth and righteousness. In Jesus' name I ask it. Amen.

FURTHER STUDY

Matt. 5:13-30; Mark 9:38-50; 1 Thess. 1:8; Heb. 11:4

• When is salt useless?
• For what did Paul commend the Thessalonians?

July 19

■ 1 CHRONICLES 16:7–17:15

7 That day David first appointed Asaph and his associates to give praise to the LORD in this manner:

8 Give praise to the LORD, proclaim his name;
    make known among the nations what he has done.
9 Sing to him, sing praise to him;
    tell of all his wonderful acts.
10 Glory in his holy name;
    let the hearts of those who seek the LORD rejoice.
11 Look to the LORD and his strength;
    seek his face always.

12 Remember the wonders he has done,
    his miracles, and the judgments he pronounced,
13 you his servants, the descendants of Israel,
    his chosen ones, the children of Jacob.
14 He is the LORD our God;
    his judgments are in all the earth.
15 He remembers his covenant for ever,
    the promise he made, for a thousand generations,
16 the covenant he made with Abraham,
    the oath he swore to Isaac.
17 He confirmed it to Jacob as a decree,
    to Israel as an everlasting covenant:
18 'To you I will give the land of Canaan

as the portion you will inherit.'
¹⁹ When they were but few in number,
    few indeed, and strangers in it,
²⁰ they wandered from nation to nation,
    from one kingdom to another.
²¹ He allowed no one to oppress them;
    for their sake he rebuked kings:
²² 'Do not touch my anointed ones;
    do my prophets no harm.'

²³ Sing to the LORD, all the earth;
    proclaim his salvation day after day.
²⁴ Declare his glory among the nations,
    his marvellous deeds among all
    peoples.

²⁵ For great is the LORD and most worthy of
    praise;
    he is to be feared above all gods.
²⁶ For all the gods of the nations are idols,
    but the LORD made the heavens.
²⁷ Splendour and majesty are before
    him;
    strength and joy are in his
    dwelling-place.

²⁸ Ascribe to the LORD, all you families of
    nations,
    ascribe to the LORD glory and strength.
²⁹ Ascribe to the LORD the glory due to his
    name;
    bring an offering and come before
    him.
    Worship the LORD in the splendour of his
    holiness.
³⁰   Tremble before him, all the earth!
    The world is firmly established; it
    cannot be moved.

³¹ Let the heavens rejoice, let the earth be
    glad;
    let them say among the nations, 'The
    LORD reigns!'
³² Let the sea resound, and all that is
    in it;

let the fields be jubilant, and
    everything in them!
³³ Let the trees of the forest sing,
    let them sing for joy before the LORD,
    for he comes to judge the earth.

³⁴ Give thanks to the LORD, for he is good;
    his love endures for ever.
³⁵ Cry out, 'Save us, God our Saviour;
    gather us and deliver us from the
    nations,
    that we may give thanks to your holy
    name,
    and glory in your praise.'
³⁶ Praise be to the LORD, the God of Israel,
    from everlasting to everlasting.

Then all the people said 'Amen' and 'Praise
the LORD.'

³⁷ David left Asaph and his associates before the ark of the covenant of the LORD to
minister there regularly, according to each
day's requirements. ³⁸ He also left Obed-
Edom and his sixty-eight associates to
minister with them. Obed-Edom son of Jeduthun, and also Hosah, were gatekeepers.

³⁹ David left Zadok the priest and his
fellow priests before the tabernacle of the
LORD at the high place in Gibeon ⁴⁰ to present burnt offerings to the LORD on the altar
of burnt offering regularly, morning and
evening, in accordance with everything
written in the Law of the LORD, which he had
given Israel. ⁴¹ With them were Heman and
Jeduthun and the rest of those chosen and
designated by name to give thanks to the
LORD, 'for his love endures for ever.' ⁴² Heman and Jeduthun were responsible for the
sounding of the trumpets and cymbals and
for the playing of the other instruments
for sacred song. The sons of Jeduthun were
stationed at the gate.

⁴³ Then all the people left, each for their
own home, and David returned home to
bless his family.

17 After David was settled in his palace, he said to Nathan the prophet, 'Here I am, living in a house of cedar, while the ark of the covenant of the LORD is under a tent.'

² Nathan replied to David, 'Whatever you have in mind, do it, for God is with you.'

³ But that night the word of God came to Nathan, saying:

⁴ 'Go and tell my servant David, "This is what the LORD says: you are not the one to build me a house to dwell in. ⁵ I have not dwelt in a house from the day I brought Israel up out of Egypt to this day. I have moved from one tent site to another, from one dwelling-place to another. ⁶ Wherever I have moved with all the Israelites, did I ever say to any of their leaders whom I commanded to shepherd my people, 'Why have you not built me a house of cedar?'"

⁷ 'Now then, tell my servant David, "This is what the LORD Almighty says: I took you from the pasture, from tending the flock, and appointed you ruler over my people Israel. ⁸ I have been with you wherever you have gone, and I have cut off all your enemies from before you. Now I will make your name like the names of the greatest men on earth. ⁹ And I will provide a place for my people Israel and will plant them so that they can have a home of their own and no longer be disturbed. Wicked people will not oppress them any more, as they did at the beginning ¹⁰ and have done ever since the time I appointed leaders over my people Israel. I will also subdue all your enemies.

' "I declare to you that the LORD will build a house for you: ¹¹ when your days are over and you go to be with your ancestors, I will raise up your offspring to succeed you, one of your own sons, and I will establish his kingdom. ¹² He is the one who will build a house for me, and I will establish his throne for ever. ¹³ I will be his father, and he will be my son. I will never take my love away from him, as I took it away from your predecessor. ¹⁴ I will set him over my house and my kingdom for ever; his throne will be established for ever." '

¹⁵ Nathan reported to David all the words of this entire revelation.

▬ PSALM 84:1-12

¹ How lovely is your dwelling-place,
    LORD Almighty!
² My soul yearns, even faints,
    for the courts of the LORD;
  my heart and my flesh cry out
    for the living God.
³ Even the sparrow has found a home,
    and the swallow a nest for herself,
    where she may have her young –
  a place near your altar,
    LORD Almighty, my King and my God.
⁴ Blessed are those who dwell in your house;
    they are ever praising you.

⁵ Blessed are those whose strength is in you,
    whose hearts are set on pilgrimage.
⁶ As they pass through the Valley of Baka,
    they make it a place of springs;
    the autumn rains also cover it with
        pools.
⁷ They go from strength to strength,
    till each appears before God in Zion.

⁸ Hear my prayer, LORD God Almighty;
    listen to me, God of Jacob.
⁹ Look on our shield, O God;
    look with favour on your anointed one.

¹⁰ Better is one day in your courts
    than a thousand elsewhere;

I would rather be a doorkeeper in the
house of my God
than dwell in the tents of the wicked.
[11] For the LORD God is a sun and shield;
the LORD bestows favour and honour;
no good thing does he withhold
from those whose way of life is
blameless.

[12] LORD Almighty,
blessed is the one who trusts in you.

▰ PROVERBS 18:4–5

[4] The words of the mouth are deep waters,
but the fountain of wisdom is a
rushing stream.

[5] It is not good to be partial to the wicked
and so deprive the innocent of justice.

▰ ACTS 17:10–34

[10] As soon as it was night, the believers
sent Paul and Silas away to Berea. On arriving there, they went to the Jewish synagogue. [11] Now the Berean Jews were of more
noble character than those in Thessalonica,
for they received the message with great eagerness and examined the Scriptures every
day to see if what Paul said was true. [12] As
a result, many of them believed, as did also
a number of prominent Greek women and
many Greek men.

[13] But when the Jews in Thessalonica
learned that Paul was preaching the word of
God at Berea, some of them went there too,
agitating the crowds and stirring them up.
[14] The believers immediately sent Paul to
the coast, but Silas and Timothy stayed at
Berea. [15] Those who escorted Paul brought
him to Athens and then left with instructions for Silas and Timothy to join him as
soon as possible.

[16] While Paul was waiting for them in Athens, he was greatly distressed to see that the
city was full of idols. [17] So he reasoned in the
synagogue with both Jews and God-fearing
Greeks, as well as in the market-place day by
day with those who happened to be there. [18] A
group of Epicurean and Stoic philosophers
began to debate with him. Some of them
asked, 'What is this babbler trying to say?'
Others remarked, 'He seems to be advocating foreign gods.' They said this because
Paul was preaching the good news about
Jesus and the resurrection. [19] Then they took
him and brought him to a meeting of the
Areopagus, where they said to him, 'May we
know what this new teaching is that you are
presenting? [20] You are bringing some strange
ideas to our ears, and we would like to know
what they mean.' [21] (All the Athenians and
the foreigners who lived there spent their
time doing nothing but talking about and
listening to the latest ideas.)

[22] Paul then stood up in the meeting of
the Areopagus and said: 'People of Athens!
I see that in every way you are very religious. [23] For as I walked around and looked
carefully at your objects of worship, I even
found an altar with this inscription: TO AN
UNKNOWN GOD. So you are ignorant of the
very thing you worship – and this is what I
am going to proclaim to you.

[24] 'The God who made the world and
everything in it is the Lord of heaven and
earth and does not live in temples built by
human hands. [25] And he is not served by human hands, as if he needed anything. Rather, he himself gives everyone life and breath
and everything else. [26] From one man he
made all the nations, that they should inhabit the whole earth; and he marked out
their appointed times in history and the
boundaries of their lands. [27] God did this
so that they would seek him and perhaps
reach out for him and find him, though
he is not far from any one of us. [28] 'For in
him we live and move and have our being.'

As some of your own poets have said, "We are his offspring."

²⁹'Therefore since we are God's offspring, we should not think that the divine being is like gold or silver or stone – an image made by human design and skill. ³⁰In the past God overlooked such ignorance, but now he commands all people everywhere to repent. ³¹For he has set a day when he will judge the world with justice by the man he has appointed. He has given proof of this to everyone by raising him from the dead.'

³²When they heard about the resurrection of the dead, some of them sneered, but others said, 'We want to hear you again on this subject.' ³³At that, Paul left the Council. ³⁴Some of the people became followers of Paul and believed. Among them was Dionysius, a member of the Areopagus, also a woman named Damaris, and a number of others.

Go Still Deeper

'Now the Berean Jews ... received the message with great eagerness and examined the Scriptures every day to see if what Paul said was true.' **Acts 17:11**

Christians who do not accept the authority of the Scriptures have no effective weapon with which to overcome Satan. It is as simple as that. If you are not certain that the Bible is the Word of God, if you do not believe that it is without error in all that it affirms, then you are like a soldier with a broken sword.

To use the sword of the Spirit effectively, we need to have as wide a knowledge of the Bible as possible. Let me take you back to Christ's encounter with Satan in the wilderness of temptation. When Satan advanced, Jesus took up the sword of the Spirit and knew exactly which particular Scriptures to use to rebut each of the three separate temptations of the devil.

If we are to conquer Satan in the same way that Jesus conquered him, then we need to know our Bibles well.

You need a deep, intensive programme of study if you are to become proficient in the use of the Scriptures against Satan. Decide right now to commit yourself to exploring the Bible more deeply and thoroughly than you have ever done before.*

PRAYER

O Father, I see that the more I know of Your Word, the more effective I will be in resisting Satan. Show me how to go more deeply into the Scriptures than I have ever done before. In Jesus' name I pray. Amen.

FURTHER STUDY

Ezek. 37:1-10; John 17:17; Rom. 10:8
• What was the result of the spoken Word through Ezekiel?
• What did Paul say of the Bereans?

*There are many resources available to help you, from themed devotional notes like *Every Day with Jesus* to programmes to help you read through the entire Bible in a year.

July 20

■ 1 CHRONICLES 17:16–20:8

16 Then King David went in and sat before the LORD, and he said:

'Who am I, LORD God, and what is my family, that you have brought me this far? 17 And as if this were not enough in your sight, my God, you have spoken about the future of the house of your servant. You, LORD God, have looked on me as though I were the most exalted of men.

18 'What more can David say to you for honouring your servant? For you know your servant, 19 LORD. For the sake of your servant and according to your will, you have done this great thing and made known all these great promises.

20 'There is no one like you, LORD, and there is no God but you, as we have heard with our own ears. 21 And who is like your people Israel – the one nation on earth whose God went out to redeem a people for himself, and to make a name for yourself, and to perform great and awesome wonders by driving out nations from before your people, whom you redeemed from Egypt? 22 You made your people Israel your very own for ever, and you, LORD, have become their God.

23 'And now, LORD, let the promise you have made concerning your servant and his house be established for ever. Do as you promised, 24 so that it will be established and that your name will be great for ever. Then people will say, "The LORD Almighty, the God over Israel, is Israel's God!" And the house of your servant David will be established before you.

25 'You, my God, have revealed to your servant that you will build a house for him. So your servant has found courage to pray to you. 26 You, LORD, are God! You have promised these good things to your servant. 27 Now you have been pleased to bless the house of your servant, that it may continue for ever in your sight; for you, LORD, have blessed it, and it will be blessed for ever.'

18 In the course of time, David defeated the Philistines and subdued them, and he took Gath and its surrounding villages from the control of the Philistines.

2 David also defeated the Moabites, and they became subject to him and brought him tribute.

3 Moreover, David defeated Hadadezer king of Zobah, in the vicinity of Hamath, when he went to set up his monument at the River Euphrates. 4 David captured a thousand of his chariots, seven thousand charioteers and twenty thousand foot soldiers. He hamstrung all but a hundred of the chariot horses.

5 When the Arameans of Damascus came to help Hadadezer king of Zobah, David struck down twenty-two thousand of them. 6 He put garrisons in the Aramean kingdom of Damascus, and the Arameans became subject to him and brought him tribute. The LORD gave David victory wherever he went.

7 David took the gold shields carried by the officers of Hadadezer and brought them to Jerusalem. 8 From Tebah and Kun, towns that belonged to Hadadezer, David took a great quantity of bronze, which Solomon used to make the bronze Sea, the pillars and various bronze articles.

⁹When Tou king of Hamath heard that David had defeated the entire army of Hadadezer king of Zobah, ¹⁰he sent his son Hadoram to King David to greet him and congratulate him on his victory in battle over Hadadezer, who had been at war with Tou. Hadoram brought all kinds of articles of gold, of silver and of bronze.

¹¹King David dedicated these articles to the Lord, as he had done with the silver and gold he had taken from all these nations: Edom and Moab, the Ammonites and the Philistines, and Amalek.

¹²Abishai son of Zeruiah struck down eighteen thousand Edomites in the Valley of Salt. ¹³He put garrisons in Edom, and all the Edomites became subject to David. The Lord gave David victory wherever he went.

¹⁴David reigned over all Israel, doing what was just and right for all his people. ¹⁵Joab son of Zeruiah was over the army; Jehoshaphat son of Ahilud was recorder; ¹⁶Zadok son of Ahitub and Ahimelek son of Abiathar were priests; Shavsha was secretary; ¹⁷Benaiah son of Jehoiada was over the Kerethites and Pelethites; and David's sons were chief officials at the king's side.

19 In the course of time, Nahash king of the Ammonites died, and his son succeeded him as king. ²David thought, 'I will show kindness to Hanun son of Nahash, because his father showed kindness to me.' So David sent a delegation to express his sympathy to Hanun concerning his father.

When David's envoys came to Hanun in the land of the Ammonites to express sympathy to him, ³the Ammonite commanders said to Hanun, 'Do you think David is honouring your father by sending envoys to you to express sympathy? Haven't his envoys come to you only to explore and spy out the country and overthrow it?' ⁴So Hanun seized David's envoys, shaved them, cut off their garments at the buttocks, and sent them away.

⁵When someone came and told David about the men, he sent messengers to meet them, for they were greatly humiliated. The king said, 'Stay at Jericho till your beards have grown, and then come back.'

⁶When the Ammonites realised that they had become obnoxious to David, Hanun and the Ammonites sent a thousand talents of silver to hire chariots and charioteers from Aram Naharaim, Aram Maakah and Zobah. ⁷They hired thirty-two thousand chariots and charioteers, as well as the king of Maakah with his troops, who came and camped near Medeba, while the Ammonites were mustered from their towns and moved out for battle.

⁸On hearing this, David sent Joab out with the entire army of fighting men. ⁹The Ammonites came out and drew up in battle formation at the entrance to their city, while the kings who had come were by themselves in the open country.

¹⁰Joab saw that there were battle lines in front of him and behind him; so he selected some of the best troops in Israel and deployed them against the Arameans. ¹¹He put the rest of the men under the command of Abishai his brother, and they were deployed against the Ammonites. ¹²Joab said, 'If the Arameans are too strong for me, then you are to rescue me; but if the Ammonites are too strong for you, then I will rescue you. ¹³Be strong, and let us fight bravely for our people and the cities of our God. The Lord will do what is good in his sight.'

¹⁴Then Joab and the troops with him advanced to fight the Arameans, and they fled before him. ¹⁵When the Ammonites realised that the Arameans were fleeing, they too fled before his brother Abishai and went inside the city. So Joab went back to Jerusalem.

¹⁶After the Arameans saw that they had been routed by Israel, they sent messengers and had Arameans brought from beyond the River Euphrates, with Shophak the

commander of Hadadezer's army leading them.

¹⁷When David was told of this, he gathered all Israel and crossed the Jordan; he advanced against them and formed his battle lines opposite them. David formed his lines to meet the Arameans in battle, and they fought against him. ¹⁸But they fled before Israel, and David killed seven thousand of their charioteers and forty thousand of their foot soldiers. He also killed Shophak the commander of their army.

¹⁹When the vassals of Hadadezer saw that they had been routed by Israel, they made peace with David and became subject to him.

So the Arameans were not willing to help the Ammonites any more.

20 In the spring, at the time when kings go off to war, Joab led out the armed forces. He laid waste the land of the Ammonites and went to Rabbah and besieged it, but David remained in Jerusalem. Joab attacked Rabbah and left it in ruins. ²David took the crown from the head of their king – its weight was found to be a talent of gold, and it was set with precious stones – and it was placed on David's head. He took a great quantity of plunder from the city ³and brought out the people who were there, consigning them to labour with saws and with iron picks and axes. David did this to all the Ammonite towns. Then David and his entire army returned to Jerusalem.

⁴In the course of time, war broke out with the Philistines, at Gezer. At that time Sibbekai the Hushathite killed Sippai, one of the descendants of the Rephaites, and the Philistines were subjugated.

⁵In another battle with the Philistines, Elhanan son of Jair killed Lahmi the brother of Goliath the Gittite, who had a spear with a shaft like a weaver's rod.

⁶In still another battle, which took place at Gath, there was a huge man with six fingers on each hand and six toes on each

foot – twenty-four in all. He also was descended from Rapha. ⁷When he taunted Israel, Jonathan son of Shimea, David's brother, killed him.

⁸These were descendants of Rapha in Gath, and they fell at the hands of David and his men.

◼ PSALM 85:1-7

¹You, LORD, showed favour to your land;
    you restored the fortunes of Jacob.
²You forgave the iniquity of your people
    and covered all their sins.
³You set aside all your wrath
    and turned from your fierce anger.

⁴Restore us again, God our Saviour,
    and put away your displeasure
        towards us.
⁵Will you be angry with us for ever?
    Will you prolong your anger through
        all generations?
⁶Will you not revive us again,
    that your people may rejoice in you?
⁷Show us your unfailing love, LORD,
    and grant us your salvation.

◼ PROVERBS 18:6-8

⁶The lips of fools bring them strife,
    and their mouths invite a beating.

⁷The mouths of fools are their undoing,
    and their lips are a snare to their very
        lives.

⁸The words of a gossip are like choice
        morsels;
    they go down to the inmost parts.

■ ACTS 18:1-23

18 After this, Paul left Athens and went to Corinth. ²There he met a Jew named Aquila, a native of Pontus, who had recently come from Italy with his wife Priscilla, because Claudius had ordered all Jews to leave Rome. Paul went to see them, ³and because he was a tentmaker as they were, he stayed and worked with them. ⁴Every Sabbath he reasoned in the synagogue, trying to persuade Jews and Greeks.

⁵When Silas and Timothy came from Macedonia, Paul devoted himself exclusively to preaching, testifying to the Jews that Jesus was the Messiah. ⁶But when they opposed Paul and became abusive, he shook out his clothes in protest and said to them, 'Your blood be on your own heads! I am innocent of it. From now on I will go to the Gentiles.'

⁷Then Paul left the synagogue and went next door to the house of Titius Justus, a worshipper of God. ⁸Crispus, the synagogue leader, and his entire household believed in the Lord; and many of the Corinthians who heard Paul believed and were baptised.

⁹One night the Lord spoke to Paul in a vision: 'Do not be afraid; keep on speaking, do not be silent. ¹⁰For I am with you, and no one is going to attack and harm you, because I have many people in this city.' ¹¹So Paul stayed in Corinth for a year and a half, teaching them the word of God.

¹²While Gallio was proconsul of Achaia, the Jews of Corinth made a united attack on Paul and brought him to the place of judgment. ¹³'This man,' they charged, 'is persuading the people to worship God in ways contrary to the law.'

¹⁴Just as Paul was about to speak, Gallio said to them, 'If you Jews were making a complaint about some misdemeanour or serious crime, it would be reasonable for me to listen to you. ¹⁵But since it involves questions about words and names and your own law – settle the matter yourselves. I will not be a judge of such things.' ¹⁶So he drove them off. ¹⁷Then the crowd there turned on Sosthenes the synagogue leader and beat him in front of the proconsul; and Gallio showed no concern whatever.

¹⁸Paul stayed on in Corinth for some time. Then he left the brothers and sisters and sailed for Syria, accompanied by Priscilla and Aquila. Before he sailed, he had his hair cut off at Cenchreae because of a vow he had taken. ¹⁹They arrived at Ephesus, where Paul left Priscilla and Aquila. He himself went into the synagogue and reasoned with the Jews. ²⁰When they asked him to spend more time with them, he declined. ²¹But as he left, he promised, 'I will come back if it is God's will.' Then he set sail from Ephesus. ²²When he landed at Caesarea, he went up to Jerusalem and greeted the church and then went down to Antioch.

²³After spending some time in Antioch, Paul set out from there and travelled from place to place throughout the region of Galatia and Phrygia, strengthening all the disciples.

Build on the Rock

'There is no one like you, Lord, and there is no God but you, as we have heard with our own ears.'
1 Chronicles 17:20

'The biggest problem we face in the Christian life,' said Dr Cynddylan Jones, a famous Welsh preacher, 'is distance.' He continued, 'The only way that distance can be overcome is by having the perspective of Job who said: "Though He slay me yet will I trust Him."'

When I talk to counsellors in training I tell them that what they should be listening for as a counsellee tells his or her story is distance. That's what underlies most problems that bring people into counselling. This does not mean we should ignore or make light of the surface problems with which people may be struggling. But the plain fact is this – when we are close to God and have a deep and intimate relationship with Him, we may feel downcast but not destroyed. Therefore, every Christian counsellor's ultimate goal should be to close any distance there may be between the person and God and to develop spiritual oneness. Counselling is not effective or complete until this is accomplished.

How does distance come between ourselves and God? There are many causes – bitterness and resentment against another, persistent sin, failure to establish a devotional life – but largely it arises through a lack of trust. If you cut your way through the maze of human problems, that's what you find – an inability to trust. That's what happened in the Garden of Eden, and that's what happens in our personal Garden of Eden also. To try to develop a close relationship with God and fail to deal with this most basic issue is about as effective as building a skyscraper on an acre of sand.

PRAYER

O God, bring us closer day by day to that place of deep confidence and absolute trust. May we know You so deeply that nothing we see around us will shake or shatter our belief in Your unchanging goodness. In our Lord's name we pray. Amen.

FURTHER STUDY

Dan. 3:13-30; Hab. 3:16-18; Psa. 46:2; Matt. 7:26
• How did the Hebrew youths demonstrate faith in God?
• What does Habakkuk declare?

July 21

■ 1 CHRONICLES 21:1–23:13

21 Satan rose up against Israel and incited David to take a census of Israel. ²So David said to Joab and the commanders of the troops, 'Go and count the Israelites from Beersheba to Dan. Then report back to me so that I may know how many there are.'

³But Joab replied, 'May the LORD multiply his troops a hundred times over. My lord the king, are they not all my lord's subjects? Why does my lord want to do this? Why should he bring guilt on Israel?'

⁴The king's word, however, overruled Joab; so Joab left and went throughout Israel and then came back to Jerusalem. ⁵Joab reported the number of the fighting men to David: in all Israel there were one million one hundred thousand men who could handle a sword, including four hundred and

seventy thousand in Judah.

⁶But Joab did not include Levi and Benjamin in the numbering, because the king's command was repulsive to him. ⁷This command was also evil in the sight of God; so he punished Israel.

⁸Then David said to God, 'I have sinned greatly by doing this. Now, I beg you, take away the guilt of your servant. I have done a very foolish thing.'

⁹The Lord said to Gad, David's seer, ¹⁰'Go and tell David, "This is what the Lord says: I am giving you three options. Choose one of them for me to carry out against you."'

¹¹So Gad went to David and said to him, 'This is what the Lord says: "Take your choice: ¹²three years of famine, three months of being swept away before your enemies, with their swords overtaking you, or three days of the sword of the Lord – days of plague in the land, with the angel of the Lord ravaging every part of Israel." Now then, decide how I should answer the one who sent me.'

¹³David said to Gad, 'I am in deep distress. Let me fall into the hands of the Lord, for his mercy is very great; but do not let me fall into human hands.'

¹⁴So the Lord sent a plague on Israel, and seventy thousand men of Israel fell dead. ¹⁵And God sent an angel to destroy Jerusalem. But as the angel was doing so, the Lord saw it and relented concerning the disaster and said to the angel who was destroying the people, 'Enough! Withdraw your hand.' The angel of the Lord was then standing at the threshing-floor of Araunah the Jebusite.

¹⁶David looked up and saw the angel of the Lord standing between heaven and earth, with a drawn sword in his hand extended over Jerusalem. Then David and the elders, clothed in sackcloth, fell face down.

¹⁷David said to God, 'Was it not I who ordered the fighting men to be counted? I, the shepherd, have sinned and done wrong. These are but sheep. What have they done?

Lord my God, let your hand fall on me and my family, but do not let this plague remain on your people.'

¹⁸Then the angel of the Lord ordered Gad to tell David to go up and build an altar to the Lord on the threshing-floor of Araunah the Jebusite. ¹⁹So David went up in obedience to the word that Gad had spoken in the name of the Lord.

²⁰While Araunah was threshing wheat, he turned and saw the angel; his four sons who were with him hid themselves. ²¹Then David approached, and when Araunah looked and saw him, he left the threshing-floor and bowed down before David with his face to the ground.

²²David said to him, 'Let me have the site of your threshing-floor so that I can build an altar to the Lord, that the plague on the people may be stopped. Sell it to me at the full price.'

²³Araunah said to David, 'Take it! Let my lord the king do whatever pleases him. Look, I will give the oxen for the burnt offerings, the threshing-sledges for the wood, and the wheat for the grain offering. I will give all this.'

²⁴But King David replied to Araunah, 'No, I insist on paying the full price. I will not take for the Lord what is yours, or sacrifice a burnt offering that costs me nothing.'

²⁵So David paid Araunah six hundred shekels of gold for the site. ²⁶David built an altar to the Lord there and sacrificed burnt offerings and fellowship offerings. He called on the Lord, and the Lord answered him with fire from heaven on the altar of burnt offering.

²⁷Then the Lord spoke to the angel, and he put his sword back into its sheath. ²⁸At that time, when David saw that the Lord had answered him on the threshing-floor of Araunah the Jebusite, he offered sacrifices there. ²⁹The tabernacle of the Lord, which Moses had made in the wilderness, and the altar of burnt offering were at that time on

the high place at Gibeon. ³⁰But David could not go before it to enquire of God, because he was afraid of the sword of the angel of the Lord.

22 Then David said, 'The house of the Lord God is to be here, and also the altar of burnt offering for Israel.'

²So David gave orders to assemble the foreigners residing in Israel, and from among them he appointed stonecutters to prepare dressed stone for building the house of God. ³He provided a large amount of iron to make nails for the doors of the gateways and for the fittings, and more bronze than could be weighed. ⁴He also provided more cedar logs than could be counted, for the Sidonians and Tyrians had brought large numbers of them to David.

⁵David said, 'My son Solomon is young and inexperienced, and the house to be built for the Lord should be of great magnificence and fame and splendour in the sight of all the nations. Therefore I will make preparations for it.' So David made extensive preparations before his death.

⁶Then he called for his son Solomon and charged him to build a house for the Lord, the God of Israel. ⁷David said to Solomon: 'My son, I had it in my heart to build a house for the Name of the Lord my God. ⁸But this word of the Lord came to me: "You have shed much blood and have fought many wars. You are not to build a house for my Name, because you have shed much blood on the earth in my sight. ⁹But you will have a son who will be a man of peace and rest, and I will give him rest from all his enemies on every side. His name will be Solomon, and I will grant Israel peace and quiet during his reign. ¹⁰He is the one who will build a house for my Name. He will be my son, and I will be his father. And I will establish the throne of his kingdom over Israel for ever."

¹¹'Now, my son, the Lord be with you, and may you have success and build the house of the Lord your God, as he said you would.

¹²May the Lord give you discretion and understanding when he puts you in command over Israel, so that you may keep the law of the Lord your God. ¹³Then you will have success if you are careful to observe the decrees and laws that the Lord gave to Moses for Israel. Be strong and courageous. Do not be afraid or discouraged.

¹⁴'I have taken great pains to provide for the temple of the Lord a hundred thousand talents of gold, a million talents of silver, quantities of bronze and iron too great to be weighed, and wood and stone. And you may add to them. ¹⁵You have many workers: stonecutters, masons and carpenters, as well as those skilled in every kind of work ¹⁶in gold and silver, bronze and iron – craftsmen beyond number. Now begin the work, and the Lord be with you.'

¹⁷Then David ordered all the leaders of Israel to help his son Solomon. ¹⁸He said to them, 'Is not the Lord your God with you? And has he not granted you rest on every side? For he has given the inhabitants of the land into my hands, and the land is subject to the Lord and to his people. ¹⁹Now devote your heart and soul to seeking the Lord your God. Begin to build the sanctuary of the Lord God, so that you may bring the ark of the covenant of the Lord and the sacred articles belonging to God into the temple that will be built for the Name of the Lord.'

23 When David was old and full of years, he made his son Solomon king over Israel.

²He also gathered together all the leaders of Israel, as well as the priests and Levites. ³The Levites thirty years old or more were counted, and the total number of men was thirty-eight thousand. ⁴David said, 'Of these, twenty-four thousand are to be in charge of the work of the temple of the Lord and six thousand are to be officials and judges. ⁵Four thousand are to be gatekeepers and four thousand are to praise the Lord with the musical instruments I have

provided for that purpose.'

⁶David separated the Levites into divisions corresponding to the sons of Levi: Gershon, Kohath and Merari.

⁷Belonging to the Gershonites:
Ladan and Shimei.

⁸The sons of Ladan:
Jehiel the first, Zetham and Joel – three in all.

⁹The sons of Shimei:
Shelomoth, Haziel and Haran – three in all.
These were the heads of the families of Ladan.

¹⁰And the sons of Shimei:
Jahath, Ziza, Jeush and Beriah.
These were the sons of Shimei – four in all.

¹¹Jahath was the first and Ziza the second, but Jeush and Beriah did not have many sons; so they were counted as one family with one assignment.

¹²The sons of Kohath:
Amram, Izhar, Hebron and Uzziel – four in all.

¹³The sons of Amram:
Aaron and Moses.
Aaron was set apart, he and his descendants for ever, to consecrate the most holy things, to offer sacrifices before the LORD, to minister before him and to pronounce blessings in his name for ever.

▬ PSALM 85:8-13

⁸I will listen to what God the LORD says;
he promises peace to his people, his faithful servants –
but let them not turn to folly.

⁹Surely his salvation is near those who fear him,
that his glory may dwell in our land.

¹⁰Love and faithfulness meet together;
righteousness and peace kiss each other.

¹¹Faithfulness springs forth from the earth,
and righteousness looks down from heaven.

¹²The LORD will indeed give what is good,
and our land will yield its harvest.

¹³Righteousness goes before him
and prepares the way for his steps.

▬ PROVERBS 18:9-11

⁹One who is slack in his work
is brother to one who destroys.

¹⁰The name of the LORD is a fortified tower;
the righteous run to it and are safe.

¹¹The wealth of the rich is their fortified city;
they imagine it a wall too high to scale.

▬ ACTS 18:24–19:20

²⁴Meanwhile a Jew named Apollos, a native of Alexandria, came to Ephesus. He was a learned man, with a thorough knowledge of the Scriptures. ²⁵He had been instructed in the way of the Lord, and he spoke with great fervour and taught about Jesus accurately, though he knew only the baptism of John. ²⁶He began to speak boldly in the synagogue. When Priscilla and Aquila heard him, they invited him to their home and explained to him the way of God more adequately.

²⁷When Apollos wanted to go to Achaia, the brothers and sisters encouraged him and wrote to the disciples there to welcome him. When he arrived, he was a great help to those who by grace had believed. ²⁸For he

vigorously refuted his Jewish opponents in public debate, proving from the Scriptures that Jesus was the Messiah.

19 While Apollos was at Corinth, Paul took the road through the interior and arrived at Ephesus. There he found some disciples ²and asked them, 'Did you receive the Holy Spirit when you believed?'

They answered, 'No, we have not even heard that there is a Holy Spirit.'

³So Paul asked, 'Then what baptism did you receive?'

'John's baptism,' they replied.

⁴Paul said, 'John's baptism was a baptism of repentance. He told the people to believe in the one coming after him, that is, in Jesus.' ⁵On hearing this, they were baptised in the name of the Lord Jesus. ⁶When Paul placed his hands on them, the Holy Spirit came on them, and they spoke in tongues and prophesied. ⁷There were about twelve men in all.

⁸Paul entered the synagogue and spoke boldly there for three months, arguing persuasively about the kingdom of God. ⁹But some of them became obstinate; they refused to believe and publicly maligned the Way. So Paul left them. He took the disciples with him and had discussions daily in the lecture hall of Tyrannus. ¹⁰This went on for two years, so that all the Jews and Greeks who lived in the province of Asia heard the word of the Lord.

¹¹God did extraordinary miracles through Paul, ¹²so that even handkerchiefs and aprons that had touched him were taken to those who were ill, and their illnesses were cured and the evil spirits left them.

¹³Some Jews who went around driving out evil spirits tried to invoke the name of the Lord Jesus over those who were demon-possessed. They would say, 'In the name of the Jesus whom Paul preaches, I command you to come out.' ¹⁴Seven sons of Sceva, a Jewish chief priest, were doing this. ¹⁵One day the evil spirit answered them, 'Jesus I know, and Paul I know about, but who are you?' ¹⁶Then the man who had the evil spirit jumped on them and overpowered them all. He gave them such a beating that they ran out of the house naked and bleeding.

¹⁷When this became known to the Jews and Greeks living in Ephesus, they were all seized with fear, and the name of the Lord Jesus was held in high honour. ¹⁸Many of those who believed now came and openly confessed what they had done. ¹⁹A number who had practised sorcery brought their scrolls together and burned them publicly. When they calculated the value of the scrolls, the total came to fifty thousand drachmas. ²⁰In this way the word of the Lord spread widely and grew in power.

Having Your Own Way

'I will listen to what God the LORD says ... let [his people] not turn to folly.' **Psalm 85:8**

Although our divine Shepherd seeks to lead us in the paths that are right, often we are so stubborn and self-centred that we decline to follow. We prefer our own way even though it may lead us straight into trouble.

When challenged about this issue, many of us, of course, strongly deny it. Yet in actual fact, comparatively few of God's people follow continually in His path. We say, 'I want to do God's will and be led by Him in all that I do' - and then promptly proceed to follow our own self- determined desires. We sing beautiful hymns and choruses about trusting in God's guidance and following Him obediently - then take the path that we think is best.

This is an issue that we must come to grips with right now, for unless we learn how to give up our self-centredness, we will fall into serious trouble - no matter how loving and concerned is our Shepherd. I recognise that this is a difficult issue for many Christians, for our civilisation teaches us self-interest as the primary motivating force in life - 'every man for himself and the devil take the hindmost'. Actually if self-interest is primary, then the result is self-destruction, for the self-centred soon become the self-disrupted. They are making themselves God, and they are not God, so the universe won't back their way of life.

PRAYER

Blessed Lord Jesus, You show me how to truly live – help me to live Your way. I want to abound, not drag leaden feet to dead tasks. Purge me of self and make me a committed follower of Your Way. For Your own name's sake. Amen.

FURTHER STUDY

Prov. 14:12; Col. 3; Gal. 2:20; Rom. 6:11
• What was Paul's confession?
• List some characteristics of the unselfish life.

July 22

1 CHRONICLES 23:14–24:31

¹⁴ The sons of Moses the man of God were counted as part of the tribe of Levi.
¹⁵ The sons of Moses:
Gershom and Eliezer.
¹⁶ The descendants of Gershom:
Shubael was the first.
¹⁷ The descendants of Eliezer:
Rehabiah was the first.
Eliezer had no other sons, but the sons of Rehabiah were very numerous.
¹⁸ The sons of Izhar:
Shelomith was the first.
¹⁹ The sons of Hebron:
Jeriah the first, Amariah the second, Jahaziel the third and Jekameam the fourth.

²⁰ The sons of Uzziel:
Micah the first and Ishiah the second.
²¹ The sons of Merari:
Mahli and Mushi.
The sons of Mahli:
Eleazar and Kish.
²² Eleazar died without having sons: he had only daughters. Their cousins, the sons of Kish, married them.
²³ The sons of Mushi:
Mahli, Eder and Jerimoth – three in all.

²⁴ These were the descendants of Levi by their families – the heads of families as they were registered under their names and counted individually, that is, the workers twenty years old or more who served in the

temple of the LORD. ²⁵For David had said, 'Since the LORD, the God of Israel, has granted rest to his people and has come to dwell in Jerusalem for ever, ²⁶the Levites no longer need to carry the tabernacle or any of the articles used in its service.' ²⁷According to the last instructions of David, the Levites were counted from those twenty years old or more.

²⁸The duty of the Levites was to help Aaron's descendants in the service of the temple of the LORD: to be in charge of the courtyards, the side rooms, the purification of all sacred things and the performance of other duties at the house of God. ²⁹They were in charge of the bread set out on the table, the special flour for the grain offerings, the thin loaves made without yeast, the baking and the mixing, and all measurements of quantity and size. ³⁰They were also to stand every morning to thank and praise the LORD. They were to do the same in the evening ³¹and whenever burnt offerings were presented to the LORD on the Sabbaths, at the New Moon feasts and at the appointed festivals. They were to serve before the LORD regularly in the proper number and in the way prescribed for them.

³²And so the Levites carried out their responsibilities for the tent of meeting, for the Holy Place and, under their relatives the descendants of Aaron, for the service of the temple of the LORD.

24 These were the divisions of the descendants of Aaron:

The sons of Aaron were Nadab, Abihu, Eleazar and Ithamar. ²But Nadab and Abihu died before their father did, and they had no sons; so Eleazar and Ithamar served as the priests. ³With the help of Zadok a descendant of Eleazar and Ahimelek a descendant of Ithamar, David separated them into divisions for their appointed order of ministering. ⁴A larger number of leaders were found among Eleazar's descendants than among Ithamar's, and they were divided accordingly: sixteen heads of families from Eleazar's descendants and eight heads of families from Ithamar's descendants. ⁵They divided them impartially by casting lots, for there were officials of the sanctuary and officials of God among the descendants of both Eleazar and Ithamar.

⁶The scribe Shemaiah son of Nethanel, a Levite, recorded their names in the presence of the king and of the officials: Zadok the priest, Ahimelek son of Abiathar and the heads of families of the priests and of the Levites – one family being taken from Eleazar and then one from Ithamar.

⁷The first lot fell to Jehoiarib,
    the second to Jedaiah,
⁸the third to Harim,
    the fourth to Seorim,
⁹the fifth to Malkijah,
    the sixth to Mijamin,
¹⁰the seventh to Hakkoz,
    the eighth to Abijah,
¹¹the ninth to Jeshua,
    the tenth to Shekaniah,
¹²the eleventh to Eliashib,
    the twelfth to Jakim,
¹³the thirteenth to Huppah,
    the fourteenth to Jeshebeab,
¹⁴the fifteenth to Bilgah,
    the sixteenth to Immer,
¹⁵the seventeenth to Hezir,
    the eighteenth to Happizzez,
¹⁶the nineteenth to Pethahiah,
    the twentieth to Jehezkel,
¹⁷the twenty-first to Jakin,
    the twenty-second to Gamul,
¹⁸the twenty-third to Delaiah
    and the twenty-fourth to Maaziah.

¹⁹This was their appointed order of ministering when they entered the temple of the LORD, according to the regulations prescribed for them by their ancestor Aaron, as the LORD, the God of Israel, had commanded him.

²⁰As for the rest of the descendants of Levi:

from the sons of Amram: Shubael;
from the sons of Shubael: Jehdeiah.
²¹As for Rehabiah, from his sons:
Ishiah was the first.
²²From the Izharites: Shelomoth;
from the sons of Shelomoth: Jahath.
²³The sons of Hebron: Jeriah the first,
Amariah the second, Jahaziel the
third and Jekameam the fourth.
²⁴The son of Uzziel: Micah;
from the sons of Micah: Shamir.
²⁵The brother of Micah: Ishiah;
from the sons of Ishiah: Zechariah.
²⁶The sons of Merari: Mahli and Mushi.
The son of Jaaziah: Beno.
²⁷The sons of Merari:
from Jaaziah: Beno, Shoham, Zakkur and Ibri.
²⁸From Mahli: Eleazar, who had no sons.
²⁹From Kish: the son of Kish:
Jerahmeel.
³⁰And the sons of Mushi: Mahli, Eder
and Jerimoth.

These were the Levites, according to their families. ³¹They also cast lots, just as their relatives the descendants of Aaron did, in the presence of King David and of Zadok, Ahimelek, and the heads of families of the priests and of the Levites. The families of the eldest brother were treated the same as those of the youngest.

PSALM 86:1-10

¹Hear me, LORD, and answer me,
for I am poor and needy.
²Guard my life, for I am faithful to you;
save your servant who trusts in you.
You are my God; ³have mercy on me,
Lord,
for I call to you all day long.
⁴Bring joy to your servant, Lord,

for I put my trust in you.

⁵You, Lord, are forgiving and good,
abounding in love to all who call to
you.
⁶Hear my prayer, LORD;
listen to my cry for mercy.
⁷When I am in distress, I call to you,
because you answer me.

⁸Among the gods there is none like you,
Lord;
no deeds can compare with yours.
⁹All the nations you have made
will come and worship before you,
Lord;
they will bring glory to your name.
¹⁰For you are great and do marvellous
deeds;
you alone are God.

PROVERBS 18:12-13

¹²Before a downfall the heart is haughty,
but humility comes before honour.

¹³To answer before listening –
that is folly and shame.

ACTS 19:21-41

²¹After all this had happened, Paul decided to go to Jerusalem, passing through Macedonia and Achaia. 'After I have been there,' he said, 'I must visit Rome also.' ²²He sent two of his helpers, Timothy and Erastus, to Macedonia, while he stayed in the province of Asia a little longer.

²³About that time there arose a great disturbance about the Way. ²⁴A silversmith named Demetrius, who made silver shrines of Artemis, brought in a lot of business for the craftsmen there. ²⁵He called them together, along with the workers in related

trades, and said: 'You know, my friends, that we receive a good income from this business. [26] And you see and hear how this fellow Paul has convinced and led astray large numbers of people here in Ephesus and in practically the whole province of Asia. He says that gods made by human hands are no gods at all. [27] There is danger not only that our trade will lose its good name, but also that the temple of the great goddess Artemis will be discredited; and the goddess herself, who is worshipped throughout the province of Asia and the world, will be robbed of her divine majesty.'

[28] When they heard this, they were furious and began shouting: 'Great is Artemis of the Ephesians!' [29] Soon the whole city was in an uproar. The people seized Gaius and Aristarchus, Paul's travelling companions from Macedonia, and all of them rushed into the theatre together. [30] Paul wanted to appear before the crowd, but the disciples would not let him. [31] Even some of the officials of the province, friends of Paul, sent him a message begging him not to venture into the theatre.

[32] The assembly was in confusion: some were shouting one thing, some another. Most of the people did not even know why they were there. [33] The Jews in the crowd pushed Alexander to the front, and they shouted instructions to him. He motioned for silence in order to make a defence before the people. [34] But when they realised he was a Jew, they all shouted in unison for about two hours: 'Great is Artemis of the Ephesians!'

[35] The city clerk quietened the crowd and said: 'Fellow Ephesians, doesn't all the world know that the city of Ephesus is the guardian of the temple of the great Artemis and of her image, which fell from heaven? [36] Therefore, since these facts are undeniable, you ought to calm down and not do anything rash. [37] You have brought these men here, though they have neither robbed temples nor blasphemed our goddess. [38] If, then, Demetrius and his fellow craftsmen have a grievance against anybody, the courts are open and there are proconsuls. They can press charges. [39] If there is anything further you want to bring up, it must be settled in a legal assembly. [40] As it is, we are in danger of being charged with rioting because of what happened today. In that case we would not be able to account for this commotion, since there is no reason for it.' [41] After he had said this, he dismissed the assembly.

The Wonder of Forgiveness

'You, Lord, are forgiving and good, abounding in love to all who call to you.' **Psalm 86:5**

Psalm 130:3 says, 'If you, LORD, kept a record of sins ... who could stand?' The psalmist is conscious of a great gulf that divides people from God, particularly himself, and he makes the assertion that if God kept a strict tally of mankind's sins, there would be no hope for anyone. But then come the most beautiful and wondrous words in the Old Testament: 'But with you there is forgiveness, so that we can, with reverence, serve you' (Psa. 130:4). The Living Bible paraphrases the verse like this: 'But you forgive! What an awesome thing this is!'

Eight times the divine name 'LORD' is used in this psalm, and as we observe how God is addressed we see what a difference knowing Him makes whatever plight we find ourselves in. He is addressed in the first couple of verses as the God who hears, and then, in verses 3 to 4, as the God who forgives. What a wonderful thing it is that God forgives. It is, as the Living Bible puts it, awesome.

As Christians we are so used to hearing about God's forgiveness that we are in danger of taking it for granted. Heinrich Heine, when lying on his deathbed, was asked by a friend, 'Do you think God has forgiven you?' Heine replied, 'Of course God will forgive me. That's His job.' I hope none of my readers will approach the subject of divine forgiveness with such cynicism. The fact that God forgives and forgets is something we will never fully understand, but it must never be taken for granted.

PRAYER

O Father, forgive me if I have thought that divine forgiveness is just the result of Your doing Your job. Grant that my reaction to being forgiven will not be one of complacency but of constant reverence and holy awe. In Jesus' name I ask it. Amen.

FURTHER STUDY

Psa. 104:1-35; Eph. 1:7; 1 John 1:9
• Why was the psalmist filled with praise?
• How did he describe the removal of sins?

July 23

■ 1 CHRONICLES 25:1–26:32

25 David, together with the commanders of the army, set apart some of the sons of Asaph, Heman and Jeduthun for the ministry of prophesying, accompanied by harps, lyres and cymbals. Here is the list of the men who performed this service:

2 from the sons of Asaph:
Zakkur, Joseph, Nethaniah and Asarelah. The sons of Asaph were under the supervision of Asaph, who prophesied under the king's supervision.
3 As for Jeduthun, from his sons:
Gedaliah, Zeri, Jeshaiah, Shimei, Hashabiah and Mattithiah, six in all,

under the supervision of their father Jeduthun, who prophesied, using the harp in thanking and praising the LORD.
4 As for Heman, from his sons:
Bukkiah, Mattaniah, Uzziel, Shubael and Jerimoth; Hananiah, Hanani, Eliathah, Giddalti and Romamti-Ezer; Joshbekashah, Mallothi, Hothir and Mahazioth. 5(All these were sons of Heman the king's seer. They were given to him through the promises of God to exalt him. God gave Heman fourteen sons and three daughters.)

6 All these men were under the supervision of their father for the music of the

temple of the LORD, with cymbals, lyres and harps, for the ministry at the house of God.

Asaph, Jeduthun and Heman were under the supervision of the king. [7] Along with their relatives – all of them trained and skilled in music for the LORD – they numbered 288. [8] Young and old alike, teacher as well as student, cast lots for their duties.

[9] The first lot, which was for Asaph,
  fell to Joseph,
    his sons and relatives   12
  the second to Gedaliah,
    him and his relatives and
    sons   12
[10] the third to Zakkur,
    his sons and relatives   12
[11] the fourth to Izri,
    his sons and relatives   12
[12] the fifth to Nethaniah,
    his sons and relatives   12
[13] the sixth to Bukkiah,
    his sons and relatives   12
[14] the seventh to Jesarelah,
    his sons and relatives   12
[15] the eighth to Jeshaiah,
    his sons and relatives   12
[16] the ninth to Mattaniah,
    his sons and relatives   12
[17] the tenth to Shimei,
    his sons and relatives   12
[18] the eleventh to Azarel,
    his sons and relatives   12
[19] the twelfth to Hashabiah,
    his sons and relatives   12
[20] the thirteenth to Shubael,
    his sons and relatives   12
[21] the fourteenth to Mattithiah,
    his sons and relatives   12
[22] the fifteenth to Jerimoth,
    his sons and relatives   12
[23] the sixteenth to Hananiah,
    his sons and relatives   12
[24] the seventeenth to Joshbekashah,
    his sons and relatives   12
[25] the eighteenth to Hanani,

    his sons and relatives   12
[26] the nineteenth to Mallothi,
    his sons and relatives   12
[27] the twentieth to Eliathah,
    his sons and relatives   12
[28] the twenty-first to Hothir,
    his sons and relatives   12
[29] the twenty-second to Giddalti,
    his sons and relatives   12
[30] the twenty-third to Mahazioth,
    his sons and relatives   12
[31] the twenty-fourth to Romamti-Ezer,
    his sons and relatives.   12

26

The divisions of the gatekeepers: from the Korahites: Meshelemiah son of Kore, one of the sons of Asaph.

[2] Meshelemiah had sons:
  Zechariah the firstborn,
  Jediael the second,
  Zebadiah the third,
  Jathniel the fourth,
[3] Elam the fifth,
  Jehohanan the sixth
  and Eliehoenai the seventh.
[4] Obed-Edom also had sons:
  Shemaiah the firstborn,
  Jehozabad the second,
  Joah the third,
  Sakar the fourth,
  Nethanel the fifth,
[5] Ammiel the sixth,
  Issachar the seventh
  and Peullethai the eighth.
  (For God had blessed Obed-Edom.)

[6] Obed-Edom's son Shemaiah also had sons, who were leaders in their father's family because they were very capable men. [7] The sons of Shemaiah: Othni, Rephael, Obed and Elzabad; his relatives Elihu and Semakiah were also able men. [8] All these were descendants of Obed-Edom; they and their sons and their relatives were capable men with the strength to do the

work – descendants of Obed-Edom, 62 in all.

⁹Meshelemiah had sons and relatives, who were able men – 18 in all.

¹⁰Hosah the Merarite had sons: Shimri the first (although he was not the firstborn, his father had appointed him the first), ¹¹Hilkiah the second, Tabaliah the third and Zechariah the fourth. The sons and relatives of Hosah were 13 in all.

¹²These divisions of the gatekeepers, through their leaders, had duties for ministering in the temple of the LORD, just as their relatives had. ¹³Lots were cast for each gate, according to their families, young and old alike.

¹⁴The lot for the East Gate fell to Shelemiah. Then lots were cast for his son Zechariah, a wise counsellor, and the lot for the North Gate fell to him. ¹⁵The lot for the South Gate fell to Obed-Edom, and the lot for the storehouse fell to his sons. ¹⁶The lots for the West Gate and the Shalleketh Gate on the upper road fell to Shuppim and Hosah.

Guard was alongside guard: ¹⁷there were six Levites a day on the east, four a day on the north, four a day on the south and two at a time at the storehouse. ¹⁸As for the court to the west, there were four at the road and two at the court itself.

¹⁹These were the divisions of the gatekeepers who were descendants of Korah and Merari.

²⁰Their fellow Levites were in charge of the treasuries of the house of God and the treasuries for the dedicated things.

²¹The descendants of Ladan, who were Gershonites through Ladan and who were heads of families belonging to Ladan the Gershonite, were Jehieli, ²²the sons of Jehieli, Zetham and his brother Joel. They were in charge of the treasuries of the temple of the LORD.

²³From the Amramites, the Izharites, the Hebronites and the Uzzielites:

²⁴Shubael, a descendant of Gershom son of Moses, was the official in charge of the treasuries. ²⁵His relatives through Eliezer: Rehabiah his son, Jeshaiah his son, Joram his son, Zikri his son and Shelomith his son. ²⁶Shelomith and his relatives were in charge of all the treasuries for the things dedicated by King David, by the heads of families who were the commanders of thousands and commanders of hundreds, and by the other army commanders. ²⁷Some of the plunder taken in battle they dedicated for the repair of the temple of the LORD. ²⁸And everything dedicated by Samuel the seer and by Saul son of Kish, Abner son of Ner and Joab son of Zeruiah, and all the other dedicated things were in the care of Shelomith and his relatives.

²⁹From the Izharites: Kenaniah and his sons were assigned duties away from the temple, as officials and judges over Israel.

³⁰From the Hebronites: Hashabiah and his relatives – seventeen hundred able men – were responsible in Israel west of the Jordan for all the work of the LORD and for the king's service. ³¹As for the Hebronites, Jeriah was their chief according to the genealogical records of their families. In the fortieth year of David's reign a search was made in the records, and capable men among the Hebronites were found at Jazer in Gilead. ³²Jeriah had two thousand seven hundred relatives, who were able men and heads of families, and King David put them in charge of the Reubenites, the Gadites and the half-tribe of Manasseh for every matter pertaining to God and for the affairs of the king.

■ PSALM 86:11-17

¹¹ Teach me your way, LORD,
　　that I may rely on your faithfulness;
give me an undivided heart,
　　that I may fear your name.
¹² I will praise you, Lord my God, with all
　　my heart;
　　I will glorify your name for ever.
¹³ For great is your love towards me;
　　you have delivered me from the
　　　depths,
　　from the realm of the dead.

¹⁴ Arrogant foes are attacking me, O God;
　　ruthless people are trying to kill me –
　　they have no regard for you.
¹⁵ But you, Lord, are a compassionate and
　　gracious God,
　　slow to anger, abounding in love and
　　faithfulness.
¹⁶ Turn to me and have mercy on me;
　　show your strength on behalf of your
　　　servant;
　　save me, because I serve you
　　just as my mother did.
¹⁷ Give me a sign of your goodness,
　　that my enemies may see it and be put
　　　to shame,
　　for you, LORD, have helped me and
　　comforted me.

■ PROVERBS 18:14-15

¹⁴ The human spirit can endure in times of
　　illness,
　　but a crushed spirit who can bear?

¹⁵ The heart of the discerning acquires
　　knowledge,
　　for the ears of the wise seek it out.

■ ACTS 20:1-21

20 When the uproar had ended, Paul sent for the disciples and, after encouraging them, said goodbye and set out for Macedonia. ²He travelled through that area, speaking many words of encouragement to the people, and finally arrived in Greece, ³where he stayed three months. Because some Jews had plotted against him just as he was about to sail for Syria, he decided to go back through Macedonia. ⁴He was accompanied by Sopater son of Pyrrhus from Berea, Aristarchus and Secundus from Thessalonica, Gaius from Derbe, Timothy also, and Tychicus and Trophimus from the province of Asia. ⁵These men went on ahead and waited for us at Troas. ⁶But we sailed from Philippi after the Festival of Unleavened Bread, and five days later joined the others at Troas, where we stayed seven days.

⁷On the first day of the week we came together to break bread. Paul spoke to the people and, because he intended to leave the next day, kept on talking until midnight. ⁸There were many lamps in the upstairs room where we were meeting. ⁹Seated in a window was a young man named Eutychus, who was sinking into a deep sleep as Paul talked on and on. When he was sound asleep, he fell to the ground from the third storey and was picked up dead. ¹⁰Paul went down, threw himself on the young man and put his arms round him. 'Don't be alarmed,' he said. 'He's alive!' ¹¹Then he went upstairs again and broke bread and ate. After talking until daylight, he left. ¹²The people took the young man home alive and were greatly comforted.

¹³We went on ahead to the ship and sailed for Assos, where we were going to take Paul aboard. He had made this arrangement because he was going there on foot. ¹⁴When he met us at Assos, we took him aboard and went on to Mitylene. ¹⁵The next day we set

sail from there and arrived off Chios. The day after that we crossed over to Samos, and on the following day arrived at Miletus. [16] Paul had decided to sail past Ephesus to avoid spending time in the province of Asia, for he was in a hurry to reach Jerusalem, if possible, by the day of Pentecost.

[17] From Miletus, Paul sent to Ephesus for the elders of the church. [18] When they arrived, he said to them: 'You know how I lived the whole time I was with you, from the first day I came into the province of Asia. [19] I served the Lord with great humility and with tears and in the midst of severe testing by the plots of my Jewish opponents. [20] You know that I have not hesitated to preach anything that would be helpful to you but have taught you publicly and from house to house. [21] I have declared to both Jews and Greeks that they must turn to God in repentance and have faith in our Lord Jesus.

Clinging to Unforgiveness

'... give me an undivided heart, that I may fear your name.' **Psalm 86:11**

A friend of mine who is a minister and Christian counsellor shared with me about a woman who told him that she spent thirty to forty-five minutes every day asking God to take away from her an unforgiving spirit. She told Him that what she wanted more than anything in the world was the ability to forgive those in her family who had brought her hurt.

The minister joined her in prayer, but the Holy Spirit spoke to his heart and showed him that deep down, the woman did not want a forgiving spirit. The minister waited for the Spirit to show more, but nothing came. Realising that he had enough information to pursue the matter, the minister invited the woman to explore the possibility that what she was asking for with her lips was not what she was asking for in her heart.

At first the woman seemed annoyed and upset by the suggestion that deep down she might not really want what she was asking for, but gradually she agreed to take an inside look. In the hour or two that followed, this came out - despite her claim that she wanted to forgive, deep down in her heart she clung to an unforgiving spirit. This gave her the justification she felt she needed when she was the cause of hurt to someone else. In other words, she was saying to herself, 'Other people have hurt me, so it won't matter so much when I hurt them.' When she saw what she was doing, however, she immediately surrendered it to God and found inner release and freedom.

PRAYER

God, I am deeply challenged by this yet deeply relieved to know that whatever might elude me can never elude You. I open up my heart right now for inspection and examination. Search me and make me whole. In Jesus' name. Amen.

FURTHER STUDY

Luke 17:1-5; Mark 11:25; Eph. 4:32
• How did the apostles respond to Christ's challenge?
• What did Paul encourage the Ephesians to do?

July 24

1 CHRONICLES 27:1–28:21

27 This is the list of the Israelites – heads of families, commanders of thousands and commanders of hundreds, and their officers, who served the king in all that concerned the army divisions that were on duty month by month throughout the year. Each division consisted of 24,000 men.

² In charge of the first division, for the first month, was Jashobeam son of Zabdiel. There were 24,000 men in his division. ³ He was a descendant of Perez and chief of all the army officers for the first month.
⁴ In charge of the division for the second month was Dodai the Ahohite; Mikloth was the leader of his division. There were 24,000 men in his division.
⁵ The third army commander, for the third month, was Benaiah son of Jehoiada the priest. He was chief and there were 24,000 men in his division. ⁶ This was the Benaiah who was a mighty warrior among the Thirty and was over the Thirty. His son Ammizabad was in charge of his division.
⁷ The fourth, for the fourth month, was Asahel the brother of Joab; his son Zebadiah was his successor. There were

24,000 men in his division.
⁸ The fifth, for the fifth month, was the commander Shamhuth the Izrahite. There were 24,000 men in his division.
⁹ The sixth, for the sixth month, was Ira the son of Ikkesh the Tekoite. There were 24,000 men in his division.
¹⁰ The seventh, for the seventh month, was Helez the Pelonite, an Ephraimite. There were 24,000 men in his division.
¹¹ The eighth, for the eighth month, was Sibbekai the Hushathite, a Zerahite. There were 24,000 men in his division.
¹² The ninth, for the ninth month, was Abiezer the Anathothite, a Benjaminite. There were 24,000 men in his division.
¹³ The tenth, for the tenth month, was Maharai the Netophathite, a Zerahite. There were 24,000 men in his division.
¹⁴ The eleventh, for the eleventh month, was Benaiah the Pirathonite, an Ephraimite. There were 24,000 men in his division.
¹⁵ The twelfth, for the twelfth month, was Heldai the Netophathite, from the family of Othniel. There were 24,000 men in his division.
¹⁶ The leaders of the tribes of Israel:

over the Reubenites: Eliezer son of Zikri;

over the Simeonites: Shephatiah son of
Maakah;
¹⁷ over Levi: Hashabiah son of Kemuel;
over Aaron: Zadok;
¹⁸ over Judah: Elihu, a brother of David;
over Issachar: Omri son of Michael;
¹⁹ over Zebulun: Ishmaiah son of
Obadiah;
over Naphtali: Jerimoth son of Azriel;
²⁰ over the Ephraimites: Hoshea son of
Azaziah;
over half the tribe of Manasseh: Joel
son of Pedaiah;
²¹ over the half-tribe of Manasseh in Gilead: Iddo son of Zechariah;
over Benjamin: Jaasiel son of Abner;
²² over Dan: Azarel son of Jeroham.
These were the leaders of the tribes of
Israel.

²³ David did not take the number of the
men twenty years old or less, because the
LORD had promised to make Israel as numerous as the stars in the sky. ²⁴ Joab son
of Zeruiah began to count the men but did
not finish. God's wrath came on Israel on
account of this numbering, and the number
was not entered in the book of the annals of
King David.
²⁵ Azmaveth son of Adiel was in charge of
the royal storehouses.
Jonathan son of Uzziah was in charge of
the storehouses in the outlying districts, in
the towns, the villages and the watchtowers.
²⁶ Ezri son of Kelub was in charge of the
workers who farmed the land.
²⁷ Shimei the Ramathite was in charge of
the vineyards.
Zabdi the Shiphmite was in charge of the
produce of the vineyards for the wine vats.
²⁸ Baal-Hanan the Gederite was in charge
of the olive and sycamore-fig trees in the
western foothills.
Joash was in charge of the supplies of
olive oil.
²⁹ Shitrai the Sharonite was in charge of

the herds grazing in Sharon.
Shaphat son of Adlai was in charge of the
herds in the valleys.
³⁰ Obil the Ishmaelite was in charge of the
camels.
Jehdeiah the Meronothite was in charge
of the donkeys.
³¹ Jaziz the Hagrite was in charge of the
flocks.
All these were the officials in charge of
King David's property.

³² Jonathan, David's uncle, was a counsellor, a man of insight and a scribe. Jehiel
son of Hakmoni took care of the king's sons.
³³ Ahithophel was the king's counsellor.
Hushai the Arkite was the king's confidant. ³⁴ Ahithophel was succeeded by
Jehoiada son of Benaiah and by Abiathar.
Joab was the commander of the royal
army.

28 David summoned all the officials of
Israel to assemble at Jerusalem: the
officers over the tribes, the commanders of
the divisions in the service of the king, the
commanders of thousands and commanders of hundreds, and the officials in charge
of all the property and livestock belonging
to the king and his sons, together with the
palace officials, the warriors and all the
brave fighting men.
² King David rose to his feet and said:
'Listen to me, my fellow Israelites, my people. I had it in my heart to build a house as
a place of rest for the ark of the covenant of
the LORD, for the footstool of our God, and I
made plans to build it. ³ But God said to me,
"You are not to build a house for my Name,
because you are a warrior and have shed
blood."
⁴ 'Yet the LORD, the God of Israel, chose
me from my whole family to be king over Israel for ever. He chose Judah as leader, and
from the tribe of Judah he chose my family,
and from my father's sons he was pleased
to make me king over all Israel. ⁵ Of all my

sons – and the LORD has given me many – he has chosen my son Solomon to sit on the throne of the kingdom of the LORD over Israel. [6] He said to me, "Solomon your son is the one who will build my house and my courts, for I have chosen him to be my son, and I will be his father. [7] I will establish his kingdom for ever if he is unswerving in carrying out my commands and laws, as is being done at this time."

[8] 'So now I charge you in the sight of all Israel and of the assembly of the LORD, and in the hearing of our God: be careful to follow all the commands of the LORD your God, that you may possess this good land and pass it on as an inheritance to your descendants for ever.

[9] 'And you, my son Solomon, acknowledge the God of your father, and serve him with wholehearted devotion and with a willing mind, for the LORD searches every heart and understands every desire and every thought. If you seek him, he will be found by you; but if you forsake him, he will reject you for ever. [10] Consider now, for the LORD has chosen you to build a house as the sanctuary. Be strong and do the work.'

[11] Then David gave his son Solomon the plans for the portico of the temple, its buildings, its storerooms, its upper parts, its inner rooms and the place of atonement. [12] He gave him the plans of all that the Spirit had put in his mind for the courts of the temple of the LORD and all the surrounding rooms, for the treasuries of the temple of God and for the treasuries for the dedicated things. [13] He gave him instructions for the divisions of the priests and Levites, and for all the work of serving in the temple of the LORD, as well as for all the articles to be used in its service. [14] He designated the weight of gold for all the gold articles to be used in various kinds of service, and the weight of silver for all the silver articles to be used in various kinds of service: [15] the weight of gold for the gold lampstands and their lamps, with the weight for each lampstand and its lamps; and the weight of silver for each silver lampstand and its lamps, according to the use of each lampstand; [16] the weight of gold for each table for consecrated bread; the weight of silver for the silver tables; [17] the weight of pure gold for the forks, sprinkling bowls and pitchers; the weight of gold for each gold dish; the weight of silver for each silver dish; [18] and the weight of the refined gold for the altar of incense. He also gave him the plan for the chariot, that is, the cherubim of gold that spread their wings and overshadow the ark of the covenant of the LORD.

[19] 'All this,' David said, 'I have in writing as a result of the LORD's hand on me, and he enabled me to understand all the details of the plan.'

[20] David also said to Solomon his son, 'Be strong and courageous, and do the work. Do not be afraid or discouraged, for the LORD God, my God, is with you. He will not fail you or forsake you until all the work for the service of the temple of the LORD is finished. [21] The divisions of the priests and Levites are ready for all the work on the temple of God, and every willing person skilled in any craft will help you in all the work. The officials and all the people will obey your every command.'

....

▬ PSALM 87:1-7

[1] He has founded his city on the holy
    mountain.
[2] The LORD loves the gates of Zion
    more than all the other dwellings of
    Jacob.

[3] Glorious things are said of you,
    city of God:
[4] 'I will record Rahab and Babylon
    among those who acknowledge me –
    Philistia too, and Tyre, along with Cush –

and will say, "This one was born in
Zion."'
5 Indeed, of Zion it will be said,
'This one and that one were born in her,
and the Most High himself will
establish her.'
6 The LORD will write in the register of the
peoples:
'This one was born in Zion.'

7 As they make music they will sing,
'All my fountains are in you.'

■ PROVERBS 18:16-17

16 A gift opens the way
and ushers the giver into the presence
of the great.

17 In a lawsuit the first to speak seems right,
until someone comes forward and
cross-examines.

■ ACTS 20:22–21:6

22 'And now, compelled by the Spirit, I
am going to Jerusalem, not knowing what
will happen to me there. 23 I only know that
in every city the Holy Spirit warns me that
prison and hardships are facing me. 24 However, I consider my life worth nothing to
me; my only aim is to finish the race and
complete the task the Lord Jesus has given
me – the task of testifying to the good news
of God's grace.

25 'Now I know that none of you among
whom I have gone about preaching the
kingdom will ever see me again. 26 Therefore, I declare to you today that I am innocent of the blood of any of you. 27 For I have
not hesitated to proclaim to you the whole
will of God. 28 Keep watch over yourselves
and all the flock of which the Holy Spirit has
made you overseers. Be shepherds of the
church of God, which he bought with his
own blood. 29 I know that after I leave, savage wolves will come in among you and will
not spare the flock. 30 Even from your own
number men will arise and distort the truth
in order to draw away disciples after them.
31 So be on your guard! Remember that for
three years I never stopped warning each of
you night and day with tears.

32 'Now I commit you to God and to the
word of his grace, which can build you up
and give you an inheritance among all those
who are sanctified. 33 I have not coveted
anyone's silver or gold or clothing. 34 You
yourselves know that these hands of mine
have supplied my own needs and the needs
of my companions. 35 In everything I did, I
showed you that by this kind of hard work
we must help the weak, remembering the
words the Lord Jesus himself said: "It is
more blessed to give than to receive."'

36 When Paul had finished speaking, he
knelt down with all of them and prayed.
37 They all wept as they embraced him and
kissed him. 38 What grieved them most was
his statement that they would never see his
face again. Then they accompanied him to
the ship.

21 After we had torn ourselves away
from them, we put out to sea and
sailed straight to Kos. The next day we went
to Rhodes and from there to Patara. 2 We
found a ship crossing over to Phoenicia, went
on board and set sail. 3 After sighting Cyprus
and passing to the south of it, we sailed on
to Syria. We landed at Tyre, where our ship
was to unload its cargo. 4 We sought out the
disciples there and stayed with them seven
days. Through the Spirit they urged Paul not
to go on to Jerusalem. 5 When it was time to
leave, we left and continued on our way. All
of them, including wives and children, accompanied us out of the city, and there on
the beach we knelt to pray. 6 After saying
goodbye to each other, we went aboard the
ship, and they returned home.

Deliverance from Fear

'"Be strong and courageous ... Do not be afraid or discouraged, for the Lord God, my God, is with you."'
1 Chronicles 28:20

If we are to have feet like 'hinds' feet', we must ask God to rid our hearts of all and every fear. I am convinced that perhaps millions of Christians are held back from pursuing God by fear.

Not all fears are harmful. When fear is spelled with a small 'f', it can have useful, biological ends. It makes the frightened deer alert and fleet of foot; it makes the surgeon skilful, for he sees the dangers that beset him if he does the wrong thing. Fear harnessed to constructive ends may be constructive. When we use fear and control it, then it is good.

But when fear uses and controls us, it is bad. When fear becomes Fear with a capital 'F', it becomes fearsome. I am sure that you have known times, as I have, when God beckons to you, as He did with John in the Revelation, to 'Come up here' (Rev. 4:1), only to find that as your mind got ready to begin the journey, your heart suddenly became gripped with fear. You wanted to move upward, but your progress was halted because you could not mount 'with all four feet'.

Overcoming fear ought to be one of our greatest objectives. The first spoken word of Luke's Gospel was the voice of the angel: 'Do not be afraid' (Luke 1:13). The first word of Jesus after His resurrection was, 'Do not be afraid' (Matt. 28:10). Between that first word and the last, the constant endeavour of Jesus was to help us get rid of fear. We must learn His secret.

PRAYER

O God, give me deliverance from every harmful and unproductive fear. I know this is a prayer that You delight to answer, for You have fashioned me for faith, not for fear. Help me, then, to surrender to what I am made for. Amen.

FURTHER STUDY

1 Chron. 28:20;
Matt. 14:22-33; 17:1-8
• What caused Peter to sink?
• What did Jesus say to the disciples on the mountain?

July 25

▬ 1 CHRONICLES 29:1–2 CHRONICLES 1:17

29 Then King David said to the whole assembly: 'My son Solomon, the one whom God has chosen, is young and inexperienced. The task is great, because this palatial structure is not for man but for the LORD God. ² With all my resources I have provided for the temple of my God – gold for the gold work, silver for the silver, bronze for the bronze, iron for the iron and wood for the wood, as well as onyx for the settings, turquoise, stones of various colours, and all kinds of fine stone and marble – all of these in large quantities. ³ Besides, in my devotion to the temple of my God I now give my personal treasures of gold and silver for the temple of my God, over and above everything I have provided for this holy temple: ⁴ three thousand talents of gold (gold of Ophir) and seven thousand talents of refined silver, for the overlaying of the walls of the buildings, ⁵ for the gold work and the silver work, and for all the work to be done by the craftsmen. Now, who is willing to consecrate themselves to the LORD today?'

⁶ Then the leaders of families, the officers of the tribes of Israel, the commanders of thousands and commanders of hundreds, and the officials in charge of the king's work gave willingly. ⁷ They gave towards the work on the temple of God five thousand talents and ten thousand darics of gold, ten thousand talents of silver, eighteen thousand talents of bronze and a hundred thousand talents of iron. ⁸ Anyone who had precious stones gave them to the treasury of the temple of the LORD in the custody of Jehiel the Gershonite. ⁹ The people rejoiced at the willing response of their leaders, for they had given freely and wholeheartedly to the LORD. David the king also rejoiced greatly.

¹⁰ David praised the LORD in the presence of the whole assembly, saying,

'Praise be to you, LORD,
    the God of our father Israel,
    from everlasting to everlasting.
¹¹ Yours, LORD, is the greatness and the power
    and the glory and the majesty and the splendour,
    for everything in heaven and earth is yours.
Yours, LORD, is the kingdom;
    you are exalted as head over all.
¹² Wealth and honour come from you;
    you are the ruler of all things.
In your hands are strength and power
    to exalt and give strength to all.
¹³ Now, our God, we give you thanks,
    and praise your glorious name.

¹⁴ 'But who am I, and who are my people, that we should be able to give as generously as this? Everything comes from you, and we have given you only what comes from your hand. ¹⁵ We are foreigners and strangers in your sight, as were all our ancestors. Our days on earth are like a shadow, without hope. ¹⁶ LORD our God, all this abundance that we have provided for building you a temple for your Holy Name comes from your hand, and all of it belongs to you. ¹⁷ I know, my God, that you test the heart and are pleased with integrity. All these things I have given willingly and with honest intent. And now I have seen with joy how willingly your people who are here have given to you. ¹⁸ LORD, the God of our fathers Abraham,

Isaac and Israel, keep these desires and thoughts in the hearts of your people for ever, and keep their hearts loyal to you. [19] And give my son Solomon the wholehearted devotion to keep your commands, statutes and decrees and to do everything to build the palatial structure for which I have provided.'

[20] Then David said to the whole assembly, 'Praise the LORD your God.' So they all praised the LORD, the God of their fathers; they bowed down, prostrating themselves before the LORD and the king.

[21] The next day they made sacrifices to the LORD and presented burnt offerings to him: a thousand bulls, a thousand rams and a thousand male lambs, together with their drink offerings, and other sacrifices in abundance for all Israel. [22] They ate and drank with great joy in the presence of the LORD that day.

Then they acknowledged Solomon son of David as king a second time, anointing him before the LORD to be ruler and Zadok to be priest. [23] So Solomon sat on the throne of the LORD as king in place of his father David. He prospered and all Israel obeyed him. [24] All the officers and warriors, as well as all of King David's sons, pledged their submission to King Solomon.

[25] The LORD highly exalted Solomon in the sight of all Israel and bestowed on him royal splendour such as no king over Israel ever had before.

[26] David son of Jesse was king over all Israel. [27] He ruled over Israel for forty years – seven in Hebron and thirty-three in Jerusalem. [28] He died at a good old age, having enjoyed long life, wealth and honour. His son Solomon succeeded him as king.

[29] As for the events of King David's reign, from beginning to end, they are written in the records of Samuel the seer, the records of Nathan the prophet and the records of Gad the seer, [30] together with the details of his reign and power, and the circumstances that surrounded him and Israel and the kingdoms of all the other lands.

1 Solomon son of David established himself firmly over his kingdom, for the Lord his God was with him and made him exceedingly great.

[2] Then Solomon spoke to all Israel – to the commanders of thousands and commanders of hundreds, to the judges and to all the leaders in Israel, the heads of families – [3] and Solomon and the whole assembly went to the high place at Gibeon, for God's tent of meeting was there, which Moses the LORD's servant had made in the wilderness. [4] Now David had brought up the ark of God from Kiriath Jearim to the place he had prepared for it, because he had pitched a tent for it in Jerusalem. [5] But the bronze altar that Bezalel son of Uri, the son of Hur, had made was in Gibeon in front of the tabernacle of the LORD; so Solomon and the assembly enquired of him there. [6] Solomon went up to the bronze altar before the LORD in the tent of meeting and offered a thousand burnt offerings on it.

[7] That night God appeared to Solomon and said to him, 'Ask for whatever you want me to give you.'

[8] Solomon answered God, 'You have shown great kindness to David my father and have made me king in his place. [9] Now, LORD God, let your promise to my father David be confirmed, for you have made me king over a people who are as numerous as the dust of the earth. [10] Give me wisdom and knowledge, that I may lead this people, for who is able to govern this great people of yours?'

[11] God said to Solomon, 'Since this is your heart's desire and you have not asked for wealth, possessions or honour, nor for the death of your enemies, and since you have not asked for a long life but for wisdom and knowledge to govern my people over whom I have made you king, [12] therefore wisdom

and knowledge will be given you. And I will also give you wealth, possessions and honour, such as no king who was before you ever had and none after you will have.'

¹³ Then Solomon went to Jerusalem from the high place at Gibeon, from before the tent of meeting. And he reigned over Israel.

¹⁴ Solomon accumulated chariots and horses; he had fourteen hundred chariots and twelve thousand horses, which he kept in the chariot cities and also with him in Jerusalem. ¹⁵ The king made silver and gold as common in Jerusalem as stones, and cedar as plentiful as sycamore-fig trees in the foothills. ¹⁶ Solomon's horses were imported from Egypt and from Kue – the royal merchants purchased them from Kue at the current price. ¹⁷ They imported a chariot from Egypt for six hundred shekels of silver, and a horse for a hundred and fifty. They also exported them to all the kings of the Hittites and of the Arameans.

■ PSALM 88:1-9

¹ LORD, you are the God who saves me;
    day and night I cry out to you.
² May my prayer come before you;
    turn your ear to my cry.

³ I am overwhelmed with troubles
    and my life draws near to death.
⁴ I am counted among those who go down
        to the pit;
    I am like one without strength.
⁵ I am set apart with the dead,
    like the slain who lie in the grave,
  whom you remember no more,
    who are cut off from your care.

⁶ You have put me in the lowest pit,
    in the darkest depths.
⁷ Your wrath lies heavily on me;
    you have overwhelmed me with all
        your waves.

⁸ You have taken from me my closest
        friends
    and have made me repulsive to them.
  I am confined and cannot escape;
⁹   my eyes are dim with grief.

  I call to you, LORD, every day;
    I spread out my hands to you.

■ PROVERBS 18:18-19

¹⁸ Casting the lot settles disputes
    and keeps strong opponents apart.

¹⁹ A brother wronged is more unyielding
        than a fortified city;
    disputes are like the barred gates of a
        citadel.

■ ACTS 21:7-29

⁷ We continued our voyage from Tyre and landed at Ptolemais, where we greeted the brothers and sisters and stayed with them for a day. ⁸ Leaving the next day, we reached Caesarea and stayed at the house of Philip the evangelist, one of the Seven. ⁹ He had four unmarried daughters who prophesied.

¹⁰ After we had been there a number of days, a prophet named Agabus came down from Judea. ¹¹ Coming over to us, he took Paul's belt, tied his own hands and feet with it and said, 'The Holy Spirit says, "In this way the Jewish leaders in Jerusalem will bind the owner of this belt and will hand him over to the Gentiles."'

¹² When we heard this, we and the people there pleaded with Paul not to go up to Jerusalem. ¹³ Then Paul answered, 'Why are you weeping and breaking my heart? I am ready not only to be bound, but also to die in Jerusalem for the name of the Lord Jesus.' ¹⁴ When he would not be dissuaded, we gave up and said, 'The Lord's will be done.'

¹⁵After this, we started on our way up to Jerusalem. ¹⁶Some of the disciples from Caesarea accompanied us and brought us to the home of Mnason, where we were to stay. He was a man from Cyprus and one of the early disciples.

¹⁷When we arrived at Jerusalem, the brothers and sisters received us warmly. ¹⁸The next day Paul and the rest of us went to see James, and all the elders were present. ¹⁹Paul greeted them and reported in detail what God had done among the Gentiles through his ministry.

²⁰When they heard this, they praised God. Then they said to Paul: 'You see, brother, how many thousands of Jews have believed, and all of them are zealous for the law. ²¹They have been informed that you teach all the Jews who live among the Gentiles to turn away from Moses, telling them not to circumcise their children or live according to our customs. ²²What shall we do? They will certainly hear that you have come, ²³so do what we tell you. There are four men with us who have made a vow. ²⁴Take these men, join in their purification rites and pay their expenses, so that they can have their heads shaved. Then everyone will know there is no truth in these reports about you, but that you yourself are living in obedience to the law. ²⁵As for the Gentile believers, we have written to them our decision that they should abstain from food sacrificed to idols, from blood, from the meat of strangled animals and from sexual immorality.'

²⁶The next day Paul took the men and purified himself along with them. Then he went to the temple to give notice of the date when the days of purification would end and the offering would be made for each of them.

²⁷When the seven days were nearly over, some Jews from the province of Asia saw Paul at the temple. They stirred up the whole crowd and seized him, ²⁸shouting, 'Fellow Israelites, help us! This is the man who teaches everyone everywhere against our people and our law and this place. And besides, he has brought Greeks into the temple and defiled this holy place.' ²⁹(They had previously seen Trophimus the Ephesian in the city with Paul and assumed that Paul had brought him into the temple.)

Creativity Is Contagious

'He had four unmarried daughters who prophesied.'
Acts 21:9

Philip's creative spirit heightened everything he touched. We find no evidence of spiritual staleness in his life. He was spiritually alert, spiritually alive, and spiritually creative.

Our text today tells us that he had four unmarried daughters who prophesied. We must not, of course, ignore the evident work of the Holy Spirit in the lives of these four women, but we must also recognise their father Philip's creative influence in their lives. We often say, 'Like father, like son'. Here it was a case of 'Like father, like daughters'. Creativity is contagious.

When you consider that the society in which these daughters were born and brought up was a male-dominated one, the statement that Philip had 'four daughters who prophesied' comes as a surprise.

What caused these unmarried women to break the mould in which they found themselves and exercise their prophetic gifts? Popular opinion at the time said that women should remain in the background and take no part in public ministry. It was the Holy Spirit, of course, who inspired them to prophesy, but I think I see some of the marks of Philip's creativity rubbing off on them also.

These young women did not stay at home and lament the fact that they were not married. They used the gifts God had given them for His glory. Some of the greatest work in the kingdom of God has been done by the spiritual descendants of the daughters of Philip – women who are open to God using them whatever their situation.

PRAYER

Father, I want to thank You today for the ministry of those in Your kingdom who, have not let their circumstances prevent them from being open to Your calling. We appreciate them, but as You have taught us, we give all the honour to You. Amen.

FURTHER STUDY

1 Cor. 7; Matt. 19:12
• What does Jesus teach about singleness?
• How did Paul reinforce this?

July 26

■ 2 CHRONICLES 2:1–4:22

2 Solomon gave orders to build a temple for the Name of the Lord and a royal palace for himself. ²He conscripted 70,000 men as carriers and 80,000 as stonecutters in the hills and 3,600 as foremen over them.

³Solomon sent this message to Hiram king of Tyre:

'Send me cedar logs as you did for my father David when you sent him cedar to build a palace to live in. ⁴Now I am about to build a temple for the Name of the LORD my God and to dedicate it to him for burning fragrant incense before him, for setting out the consecrated bread regularly, and for making burnt offerings every morning and evening and on the Sabbaths,

at the New Moons and at the appointed festivals of the LORD our God. This is a lasting ordinance for Israel.

⁵'The temple I am going to build will be great, because our God is greater than all other gods. ⁶But who is able to build a temple for him, since the heavens, even the highest heavens, cannot contain him? Who then am I to build a temple for him, except as a place to burn sacrifices before him?

⁷'Send me, therefore, a man skilled to work in gold and silver, bronze and iron, and in purple, crimson and blue yarn, and experienced in the art of engraving, to work in Judah and Jerusalem with my skilled workers, whom my father David provided.

⁸'Send me also cedar, juniper and algum logs from Lebanon, for I know

that your servants are skilled in cutting timber there. My servants shall work with yours ⁹to provide me with plenty of timber, because the temple I build must be large and magnificent. ¹⁰I will give your servants, the woodsmen who cut the timber, twenty thousand cors of ground wheat, twenty thousand cors of barley, twenty thousand baths of wine and twenty thousand baths of olive oil.'

¹¹Hiram king of Tyre replied by letter to Solomon:

'Because the LORD loves his people, he has made you their king.'

¹²And Hiram added:

'Praise be to the LORD, the God of Israel, who made heaven and earth! He has given King David a wise son, endowed with intelligence and discernment, who will build a temple for the LORD and a palace for himself. ¹³I am sending you Huram-Abi, a man of great skill, ¹⁴whose mother was from Dan and whose father was from Tyre. He is trained to work in gold and silver, bronze and iron, stone and wood, and with purple and blue and crimson yarn and fine linen. He is experienced in all kinds of engraving and can execute any design given to him. He will work with your skilled workers and with those of my lord, David your father.

¹⁵'Now let my lord send his servants the wheat and barley and the olive oil and wine he promised, ¹⁶and we will cut all the logs from Lebanon that you need and will float them as rafts by sea down to Joppa. You can then take them up to Jerusalem.'

¹⁷Solomon took a census of all the foreigners residing in Israel, after the census his father David had taken; and they were found to be 153,600. ¹⁸He assigned 70,000 of them to be carriers and 80,000 to be stonecutters in the hills, with 3,600 foremen over them to keep the people working.

3 Then Solomon began to build the temple of the LORD in Jerusalem on Mount Moriah, where the LORD had appeared to his father David. It was on the threshing-floor of Araunah the Jebusite, the place provided by David. ²He began building on the second day of the second month in the fourth year of his reign.

³The foundation Solomon laid for building the temple of God was sixty cubits long and twenty cubits wide (using the cubit of the old standard). ⁴The portico at the front of the temple was twenty cubits long across the width of the building and twenty cubits high.

He overlaid the inside with pure gold. ⁵He panelled the main hall with juniper and covered it with fine gold and decorated it with palm tree and chain designs. ⁶He adorned the temple with precious stones. And the gold he used was gold of Parvaim. ⁷He overlaid the ceiling beams, doorframes, walls and doors of the temple with gold, and he carved cherubim on the walls.

⁸He built the Most Holy Place, its length corresponding to the width of the temple – twenty cubits long and twenty cubits wide. He overlaid the inside with six hundred talents of fine gold. ⁹The gold nails weighed fifty shekels. He also overlaid the upper parts with gold.

¹⁰For the Most Holy Place he made a pair of sculptured cherubim and overlaid them with gold. ¹¹The total wing-span of the cherubim was twenty cubits. One wing of the first cherub was five cubits long and touched the temple wall, while its other wing, also five cubits long, touched the wing of the other cherub. ¹²Similarly one wing of the second cherub was five cubits long and

touched the other temple wall, and its other wing, also five cubits long, touched the wing of the first cherub. ¹³ The wings of these cherubim extended twenty cubits. They stood on their feet, facing the main hall.

¹⁴ He made the curtain of blue, purple and crimson yarn and fine linen, with cherubim worked into it.

¹⁵ For the front of the temple he made two pillars, which together were thirty-five cubits long, each with a capital five cubits high. ¹⁶ He made interwoven chains and put them on top of the pillars. He also made a hundred pomegranates and attached them to the chains. ¹⁷ He erected the pillars in the front of the temple, one to the south and one to the north. The one to the south he named Jakin and the one to the north Boaz.

4 He made a bronze altar twenty cubits long, twenty cubits wide and ten cubits high. ² He made the Sea of cast metal, circular in shape, measuring ten cubits from rim to rim and five cubits high. It took a line of thirty cubits to measure round it. ³ Below the rim, figures of bulls encircled it – ten to a cubit. The bulls were cast in two rows in one piece with the Sea.

⁴ The Sea stood on twelve bulls, three facing north, three facing west, three facing south and three facing east. The Sea rested on top of them, and their hindquarters were towards the centre. ⁵ It was a handbreadth in thickness, and its rim was like the rim of a cup, like a lily blossom. It held three thousand baths.

⁶ He then made ten basins for washing and placed five on the south side and five on the north. In them the things to be used for the burnt offerings were rinsed, but the Sea was to be used by the priests for washing.

⁷ He made ten gold lampstands according to the specifications for them and placed them in the temple, five on the south side and five on the north.

⁸ He made ten tables and placed them in the temple, five on the south side and five on the north. He also made a hundred gold sprinkling bowls.

⁹ He made the courtyard of the priests, and the large court and the doors for the court, and overlaid the doors with bronze. ¹⁰ He placed the Sea on the south side, at the south-east corner.

¹¹ And Huram also made the pots and shovels and sprinkling bowls.

So Huram finished the work he had undertaken for King Solomon in the temple of God:

¹² the two pillars;

    the two bowl-shaped capitals on top of the pillars;

    the two sets of network decorating the two bowl-shaped capitals on top of the pillars;

¹³ the four hundred pomegranates for the two sets of network (two rows of pomegranates for each network, decorating the bowl-shaped capitals on top of the pillars);

¹⁴ the stands with their basins;

¹⁵ the Sea and the twelve bulls under it;

¹⁶ the pots, shovels, meat forks and all related articles.

All the objects that Huram-Abi made for King Solomon for the temple of the LORD were of polished bronze. ¹⁷ The king had them cast in clay moulds in the plain of the Jordan between Sukkoth and Zarethan. ¹⁸ All these things that Solomon made amounted to so much that the weight of the bronze could not be calculated.

¹⁹ Solomon also made all the furnishings that were in God's temple:

    the golden altar;

    the tables on which was the bread of the Presence;

²⁰ the lampstands of pure gold with their lamps, to burn in front of the inner

sanctuary as prescribed;
²¹ the gold floral work and lamps and tongs (they were solid gold);
²² the pure gold wick trimmers, sprinkling bowls, dishes and censers; and the gold doors of the temple: the inner doors to the Most Holy Place and the doors of the main hall.

■ PSALM 88:10-18

¹⁰ Do you show your wonders to the dead?
    Do their spirits rise up and praise you?
¹¹ Is your love declared in the grave,
    your faithfulness in Destruction?
¹² Are your wonders known in the place of darkness,
    or your righteous deeds in the land of oblivion?

¹³ But I cry to you for help, Lord;
    in the morning my prayer comes before you.
¹⁴ Why, Lord, do you reject me
    and hide your face from me?

¹⁵ From my youth I have suffered and been close to death;
    I have borne your terrors and am in despair.
¹⁶ Your wrath has swept over me;
    your terrors have destroyed me.
¹⁷ All day long they surround me like a flood;
    they have completely engulfed me.
¹⁸ You have taken from me friend and neighbour –
    darkness is my closest friend.

■ PROVERBS 18:20-21

²⁰ From the fruit of their mouth a person's stomach is filled;
    with the harvest of their lips they are satisfied.
²¹ The tongue has the power of life and death,
    and those who love it will eat its fruit.

■ ACTS 21:30–22:10

³⁰ The whole city was aroused, and the people came running from all directions. Seizing Paul, they dragged him from the temple, and immediately the gates were shut. ³¹ While they were trying to kill him, news reached the commander of the Roman troops that the whole city of Jerusalem was in an uproar. ³² He at once took some officers and soldiers and ran down to the crowd. When the rioters saw the commander and his soldiers, they stopped beating Paul.

³³ The commander came up and arrested him and ordered him to be bound with two chains. Then he asked who he was and what he had done. ³⁴ Some in the crowd shouted one thing and some another, and since the commander could not get at the truth because of the uproar, he ordered that Paul be taken into the barracks. ³⁵ When Paul reached the steps, the violence of the mob was so great he had to be carried by the soldiers. ³⁶ The crowd that followed kept shouting, 'Get rid of him!'

³⁷ As the soldiers were about to take Paul into the barracks, he asked the commander, 'May I say something to you?'

'Do you speak Greek?' he replied. ³⁸ 'Aren't you the Egyptian who started a revolt and led four thousand terrorists out into the wilderness some time ago?'

³⁹ Paul answered, 'I am a Jew, from Tarsus in Cilicia, a citizen of no ordinary city. Please let me speak to the people.'

⁴⁰ After receiving the commander's permission, Paul stood on the steps and motioned to the crowd. When they were all

22 silent, he said to them in Aramaic: [1]'Brothers and fathers, listen now to my defence.'

[2]When they heard him speak to them in Aramaic, they became very quiet.

Then Paul said: [3]'I am a Jew, born in Tarsus of Cilicia, but brought up in this city. I studied under Gamaliel and was thoroughly trained in the law of our ancestors. I was just as zealous for God as any of you are today. [4]I persecuted the followers of this Way to their death, arresting both men and women and throwing them into prison, [5]as the high priest and all the Council can themselves testify. I even obtained letters from them to their associates in Damascus,

and went there to bring these people as prisoners to Jerusalem to be punished.

[6]'About noon as I came near Damascus, suddenly a bright light from heaven flashed around me. [7]I fell to the ground and heard a voice say to me, "Saul! Saul! Why do you persecute me?"

[8]'"Who are you, Lord?" I asked.

'"I am Jesus of Nazareth, whom you are persecuting," he replied. [9]My companions saw the light, but they did not understand the voice of him who was speaking to me.

[10]'"What shall I do, Lord?" I asked.

'"Get up," the Lord said, "and go into Damascus. There you will be told all that you have been assigned to do."

Children of the Dawn

'But I cry to you for help, LORD; in the morning my prayer comes before you.' **Psalm 88:13**

Those who do not provide for a set-aside time during the day – preferably in the morning, when they can replenish their spiritual resources – may find that they have to provide a time at the end of the day for regret, for repentance and for eating humble pie.

A traveller in the Himalayas told how he arose very early one morning to watch the sun rise on the towering peaks. He said, 'There, as the day began to dawn, we saw arise before our enraptured gaze, within a complete semicircle, twenty peaks each above twenty thousand feet in height, snow-capped with virgin snow. For half an hour the curtain was lifted and we inwardly worshipped. Then the mists began to fill the valleys between, and the view was gone. Gone? No, not really – it was forever laid up in our green and grateful memories.'

That is what a quiet time in the early part of the day does for you. Before the mists of worldly happenings blot out your view of God, you can take a time-exposure of Him which is indelibly imprinted on your mind. Then, after the mists close in, the vision is still there within. You live in two worlds at once – drawing physical strength from the world around you while drawing spiritual sustenance from the world above you.

Pascal, the great French philosopher and Christian, once said, 'Nearly all the ills of life spring from this simple source: that we are not able to sit still in a room.' But what if in the stillness, we were to meet with God? How healing that would be! We would arise with what Stevenson calls 'happy morning faces'. We would become children of the dawn.

PRAYER

Heavenly Father, give me the wisdom to be able to take 'the pause that refreshes', to drink every day from the living Fountain, the eternal Spring. In Jesus' name I pray. Amen.

FURTHER STUDY

Lam. 3:22-26; Psa. 40:1; Isa. 26:8; 33:2
- What was the psalmist's testimony?
- What did the writer of Lamentations say he would do?

July 27

▬ 2 CHRONICLES 5:1–6:42

5 When all the work Solomon had done for the temple of the LORD was finished, he brought in the things his father David had dedicated – the silver and gold and all the furnishings – and he placed them in the treasuries of God's temple.

²Then Solomon summoned to Jerusalem the elders of Israel, all the heads of the tribes and the chiefs of the Israelite families, to bring up the ark of the LORD's covenant from Zion, the City of David. ³And all the Israelites came together to the king at the time of the festival in the seventh month.

⁴When all the elders of Israel had arrived, the Levites took up the ark, ⁵and they brought up the ark and the tent of meeting and all the sacred furnishings in it. The Levitical priests carried them up; ⁶and King Solomon and the entire assembly of Israel that had gathered about him were before the ark, sacrificing so many sheep and cattle that they could not be recorded or counted.

⁷The priests then brought the ark of the LORD's covenant to its place in the inner sanctuary of the temple, the Most Holy Place, and put it beneath the wings of the cherubim. ⁸The cherubim spread their wings over the place of the ark and covered the ark and its carrying poles.

⁹These poles were so long that their ends, extending from the ark, could be seen from in front of the inner sanctuary, but not from outside the Holy Place; and they are still there today. ¹⁰There was nothing in the ark except the two tablets that Moses had placed in it at Horeb, where the LORD made a covenant with the Israelites after they came out of Egypt.

¹¹The priests then withdrew from the Holy Place. All the priests who were there had consecrated themselves, regardless of their divisions. ¹²All the Levites who were musicians – Asaph, Heman, Jeduthun and their sons and relatives – stood on the east side of the altar, dressed in fine linen and playing cymbals, harps and lyres. They were accompanied by 120 priests sounding trumpets. ¹³The trumpeters and musicians joined in unison to give praise and thanks to the LORD. Accompanied by trumpets, cymbals and other instruments, the singers raised their voices in praise to the LORD and sang:

'He is good;
    his love endures for ever.'

Then the temple of the LORD was filled with the cloud, ¹⁴and the priests could not perform their service because of the cloud, for the glory of the LORD filled the temple of God.

6 Then Solomon said, 'The LORD has said that he would dwell in a dark cloud; ²I have built a magnificent temple for you, a place for you to dwell for ever.'

³While the whole assembly of Israel was standing there, the king turned round and blessed them. ⁴Then he said:

'Praise be to the LORD, the God of Israel, who with his hands has fulfilled what he promised with his mouth to my father David. For he said, ⁵"Since the day I brought my people out of Egypt, I have not chosen a city in any tribe of Israel to have a temple built so that my Name might be there, nor have I chosen anyone to be ruler over my people Israel. ⁶But now I have chosen Jerusalem for my Name to be there, and I have chosen David to rule my people Israel."

⁷'My father David had it in his heart to build a temple for the Name of the LORD, the God of Israel. ⁸But the LORD said to my father David, "You did well to have it in your heart to build a temple for my Name. ⁹Nevertheless, you are not the one to build the temple, but your son, your own flesh and blood – he is the one who will build the temple for my Name."

¹⁰'The LORD has kept the promise he made. I have succeeded David my father and now I sit on the throne of Israel, just as the LORD promised, and I have built the temple for the Name of the LORD, the God of Israel. ¹¹There I have placed the ark, in which is the covenant of the LORD that he made with the people of Israel.'

¹²Then Solomon stood before the altar of the Lord in front of the whole assembly of Israel and spread out his hands. ¹³Now he had made a bronze platform, five cubits long, five cubits wide and three cubits high, and had placed it in the centre of the outer court. He stood on the platform and then knelt down before the whole assembly of Israel and spread out his hands towards heaven. ¹⁴He said:

'LORD, the God of Israel, there is no God like you in heaven or on earth – you who keep your covenant of love with your servants who continue wholeheartedly in your way. ¹⁵You have kept your promise to your servant David my father; with your mouth you have promised and with your hand you have fulfilled it – as it is today.

¹⁶'Now, LORD, the God of Israel, keep for your servant David my father the promises you made to him when you said, "You shall never fail to have a successor to sit before me on the throne of Israel, if only your descendants are careful in all they do to walk before me according to my law, as you have done." ¹⁷And now, LORD, the God of Israel, let your word that you promised your servant David come true.

¹⁸'But will God really dwell on earth with humans? The heavens, even the highest heavens, cannot contain you. How much less this temple that I have built! ¹⁹Yet, LORD my God, give attention to your servant's prayer and his plea for mercy. Hear the cry and the prayer that your servant is praying in your presence. ²⁰May your eyes be open towards this temple day and night, this place of which you said you would put your Name there. May you hear the prayer your servant prays towards this place. ²¹Hear the supplications of your servant and of your people Israel when they pray towards this place. Hear from heaven, your dwelling-place; and when you hear, forgive.

22 'When anyone wrongs their neighbour and is required to take an oath and they come and swear the oath before your altar in this temple, 23 then hear from heaven and act. Judge between your servants, condemning the guilty and bringing down on their heads what they have done, and vindicating the innocent by treating them in accordance with their innocence.

24 'When your people Israel have been defeated by an enemy because they have sinned against you and when they turn back and give praise to your name, praying and making supplication before you in this temple, 25 then hear from heaven and forgive the sin of your people Israel and bring them back to the land you gave to them and their ancestors.

26 'When the heavens are shut up and there is no rain because your people have sinned against you, and when they pray towards this place and give praise to your name and turn from their sin because you have afflicted them, 27 then hear from heaven and forgive the sin of your servants, your people Israel. Teach them the right way to live, and send rain on the land that you gave your people for an inheritance.

28 'When famine or plague comes to the land, or blight or mildew, locusts or grasshoppers, or when enemies besiege them in any of their cities, whatever disaster or disease may come, 29 and when a prayer or plea is made by anyone among your people Israel – being aware of their afflictions and pains, and spreading out their hands towards this temple – 30 then hear from heaven, your dwelling-place. Forgive, and deal with everyone according to all they do, since you know their hearts (for you alone know the human heart), 31 so that they will fear you and walk in obedience to you all the time they live in the land that you gave our ancestors.

32 'As for the foreigner who does not belong to your people Israel but has come from a distant land because of your great name and your mighty hand and your outstretched arm – when they come and pray towards this temple, 33 then hear from heaven, your dwelling-place. Do whatever the foreigner asks of you, so that all the peoples of the earth may know your name and fear you, as do your own people Israel, and may know that this house that I have built bears your Name.

34 'When your people go to war against their enemies, wherever you send them, and when they pray to you towards this city you have chosen and the temple I have built for your Name, 35 then hear from heaven their prayer and their plea, and uphold their cause.

36 'When they sin against you – for there is no one who does not sin – and you become angry with them and give them over to the enemy, who takes them captive to a land far away or near; 37 and if they have a change of heart in the land where they are held captive, and repent and plead with you in the land of their captivity and say, "We have sinned, we have done wrong and acted wickedly"; 38 and if they turn back to you with all their heart and soul in the land of their captivity where they were taken, and pray towards the land that you gave their ancestors, towards the city you have chosen and towards the temple that I have built for your Name; 39 then from heaven, your dwelling-place, hear their prayer and their pleas, and uphold their cause. And forgive your people, who have sinned against you.

40 'Now, my God, may your eyes be open and your ears attentive to the prayers offered in this place.

41 'Now arise, LORD God, and come
 to your resting place,
 you and the ark of your might.
May your priests, LORD God, be
 clothed with salvation,
 may your faithful people
  rejoice in your goodness.
42 LORD God, do not reject your
 anointed one.
 Remember the great love
 promised to David your
 servant.'

■ PSALM 89:1-10

1 I will sing of the LORD's great love for
 ever;
 with my mouth I will make your
  faithfulness known
 through all generations.
2 I will declare that your love stands firm
 for ever,
 that you have established your
 faithfulness in heaven itself.
3 You said, 'I have made a covenant with
 my chosen one,
 I have sworn to David my servant,
4 "I will establish your line for ever
 and make your throne firm through
  all generations." '

5 The heavens praise your wonders, LORD,
 your faithfulness too, in the assembly
 of the holy ones.
6 For who in the skies above can compare
 with the LORD?
 Who is like the LORD among the
  heavenly beings?
7 In the council of the holy ones God is
 greatly feared;
 he is more awesome than all who
 surround him.
8 Who is like you, LORD God Almighty?
 You, LORD, are mighty, and your
 faithfulness surrounds you.

9 You rule over the surging sea;
 when its waves mount up, you still
  them.
10 You crushed Rahab like one of the slain;
 with your strong arm you scattered
  your enemies.

■ PROVERBS 18:22

22 He who finds a wife finds what is good
 and receives favour from the LORD.

■ ACTS 22:11-30

11 My companions led me by the hand into Damascus, because the brilliance of the light had blinded me.

12 'A man named Ananias came to see me. He was a devout observer of the law and highly respected by all the Jews living there. 13 He stood beside me and said, "Brother Saul, receive your sight!" And at that very moment I was able to see him.

14 'Then he said: "The God of our ancestors has chosen you to know his will and to see the Righteous One and to hear words from his mouth. 15 You will be his witness to all people of what you have seen and heard. 16 And now what are you waiting for? Get up, be baptised and wash your sins away, calling on his name."

17 'When I returned to Jerusalem and was praying at the temple, I fell into a trance 18 and saw the Lord speaking to me. "Quick!" he said. "Leave Jerusalem immediately, because the people here will not accept your testimony about me."

19 ' "Lord," I replied, "these people know that I went from one synagogue to another to imprison and beat those who believe in you. 20 And when the blood of your martyr Stephen was shed, I stood there giving my approval and guarding the clothes of those who were killing him." '

21 'Then the Lord said to me, "Go; I will send you far away to the Gentiles."'

22 The crowd listened to Paul until he said this. Then they raised their voices and shouted, 'Rid the earth of him! He's not fit to live!'

23 As they were shouting and throwing off their cloaks and flinging dust into the air, 24 the commander ordered that Paul be taken into the barracks. He directed that he be flogged and interrogated in order to find out why the people were shouting at him like this. 25 As they stretched him out to flog him, Paul said to the centurion standing there, 'Is it legal for you to flog a Roman citizen who hasn't even been found guilty?'

26 When the centurion heard this, he went to the commander and reported it. 'What are you going to do?' he asked. 'This man is a Roman citizen.'

27 The commander went to Paul and asked, 'Tell me, are you a Roman citizen?'

'Yes, I am,' he answered.

28 Then the commander said, 'I had to pay a lot of money for my citizenship.'

'But I was born a citizen,' Paul replied.

29 Those who were about to interrogate him withdrew immediately. The commander himself was alarmed when he realised that he had put Paul, a Roman citizen, in chains.

30 The commander wanted to find out exactly why Paul was being accused by the Jews. So the next day he released him and ordered the chief priests and all the members of the Sanhedrin to assemble. Then he brought Paul and set him before them.

Our Trustworthy God

'I will sing of the LORD's great love for ever; with my mouth I will make your faithfulness known through all generations.' **Psalm 89:1**

God is utterly trustworthy in all He says and does, and this is the rock-bottom reality on which everything in the universe depends. In an age when so much unfaithfulness abounds, how good it is to realise that we have One who will never let us down, never have to apologise for failing us, and never go back on His Word.

Am I speaking to someone who has just discovered unfaithfulness in a marriage partner, or experienced the break-up of a relationship because a person you trusted did not keep their word? It's a sad moment when we get a revelation of the inconsistency of the human heart. But we need to look into our own hearts also, for none of us can claim complete immunity to the sin of unfaithfulness. We may not have broken a contract or violated the marriage covenant, but we have been unfaithful to Christ in other ways - to the light and privileges that God has entrusted to us, perhaps.

How refreshing it is, then, to read today's text and focus our gaze on the One who is faithful at all times and in all things. We may let Him down, but He will never let us down.

A chorus I learned as a young Christian comes back to me when I am tempted to doubt the faithfulness of God:

He cannot fail for He is God,
He cannot fail, He pledged His Word,
He cannot fail, He'll see you through,
He cannot fail, He'll answer you.
C.E Mason, Jr

PRAYER

Gracious and loving God, what inspiration it brings to my soul to realise that of all the things You can do, the one thing You can't do is fail. May the reality of this be the pavement on which I tread this day and every day. In Jesus' name. Amen.

FURTHER STUDY

Deut. 7:9; 1 Kings 8:54-61;
Psa. 89:1-8
• What did Solomon testify?
• What did the psalmist
  promise to do?

July 28

■ 2 CHRONICLES 7:1–8:18

7 When Solomon finished praying, fire came down from heaven and consumed the burnt offering and the sacrifices, and the glory of the LORD filled the temple. ²The priests could not enter the temple of the LORD because the glory of the LORD filled it. ³When all the Israelites saw the fire coming down and the glory of the LORD above the temple, they knelt on the pavement with their faces to the ground, and they worshipped and gave thanks to the LORD, saying,

'He is good;
    his love endures for ever.'

⁴Then the king and all the people offered sacrifices before the LORD. ⁵And King Solomon offered a sacrifice of twenty-two thousand head of cattle and a hundred and twenty thousand sheep and goats. So the king and all the people dedicated the temple of God. ⁶The priests took up their positions,

as did the Levites with the LORD's musical instruments, which King David had made for praising the LORD and which were used when he gave thanks, saying, 'His love endures for ever.' Opposite the Levites, the priests blew their trumpets, and all the Israelites were standing.

⁷Solomon consecrated the middle part of the courtyard in front of the temple of the LORD, and there he offered burnt offerings and the fat of the fellowship offerings, because the bronze altar he had made could not hold the burnt offerings, the grain offerings and the fat portions.

⁸So Solomon observed the festival at that time for seven days, and all Israel with him – a vast assembly, people from Lebo Hamath to the Wadi of Egypt. ⁹On the eighth day they held an assembly, for they had celebrated the dedication of the altar for seven days and the festival for seven days more. ¹⁰On the twenty-third day of the seventh month he sent the people to their homes, joyful and glad in heart for the good things the LORD had done for David and

Solomon and for his people Israel.

[11] When Solomon had finished the temple of the LORD and the royal palace, and had succeeded in carrying out all he had in mind to do in the temple of the LORD and in his own palace, [12] the LORD appeared to him at night and said:

'I have heard your prayer and have chosen this place for myself as a temple for sacrifices.

[13] 'When I shut up the heavens so that there is no rain, or command locusts to devour the land or send a plague among my people, [14] if my people, who are called by my name, will humble themselves and pray and seek my face and turn from their wicked ways, then I will hear from heaven, and I will forgive their sin and will heal their land. [15] Now my eyes will be open and my ears attentive to the prayers offered in this place. [16] I have chosen and consecrated this temple so that my Name may be there for ever. My eyes and my heart will always be there.

[17] 'As for you, if you walk before me faithfully as David your father did, and do all I command, and observe my decrees and laws, [18] I will establish your royal throne, as I covenanted with David your father when I said, "You shall never fail to have a successor to rule over Israel."

[19] 'But if you turn away and forsake the decrees and commands I have given you and go off to serve other gods and worship them, [20] then I will uproot Israel from my land, which I have given them, and will reject this temple which I have consecrated for my Name. I will make it a byword and an object of ridicule among all peoples. [21] This temple will become a heap of rubble. All who pass by will be appalled and say, "Why has the LORD done such a thing to this land and to this temple?" [22] People will answer, "Because they have forsaken the LORD, the God of their ancestors, who brought them out of Egypt, and have embraced other gods, worshipping and serving them – that is why he brought all this disaster on them."'

[8] At the end of twenty years, during which Solomon built the temple of the Lord and his own palace, [2] Solomon rebuilt the villages that Hiram had given him, and settled Israelites in them. [3] Solomon then went to Hamath Zobah and captured it. [4] He also built up Tadmor in the desert and all the store cities he had built in Hamath. [5] He rebuilt Upper Beth Horon and Lower Beth Horon as fortified cities, with walls and with gates and bars, [6] as well as Baalath and all his store cities, and all the cities for his chariots and for his horses – whatever he desired to build in Jerusalem, in Lebanon and throughout all the territory that he ruled.

[7] There were still people left from the Hittites, Amorites, Perizzites, Hivites and Jebusites (these people were not Israelites). [8] Solomon conscripted the descendants of all these people remaining in the land – whom the Israelites had not destroyed – to serve as slave labour, as it is to this day. [9] But Solomon did not make slaves of the Israelites for his work; they were his fighting men, commanders of his captains, and commanders of his chariots and charioteers. [10] They were also King Solomon's chief officials – two hundred and fifty officials supervising the men.

[11] Solomon brought Pharaoh's daughter up from the City of David to the palace he had built for her, for he said, 'My wife must not live in the palace of David king of Israel, because the places the ark of the LORD has entered are holy.'

[12] On the altar of the LORD that he had built in front of the portico, Solomon sacrificed burnt offerings to the LORD, [13] according to

the daily requirement for offerings commanded by Moses for the Sabbaths, the New Moons and the three annual festivals – the Festival of Unleavened Bread, the Festival of Weeks and the Festival of Tabernacles. [14] In keeping with the ordinance of his father David, he appointed the divisions of the priests for their duties and the Levites to lead the praise and to assist the priests according to each day's requirement. He also appointed the gatekeepers by divisions for the various gates, because this was what David the man of God had ordered. [15] They did not deviate from the king's commands to the priests or to the Levites in any matter, including that of the treasuries.

[16] All Solomon's work was carried out, from the day the foundation of the temple of the LORD was laid until its completion. So the temple of the LORD was finished.

[17] Then Solomon went to Ezion Geber and Elath on the coast of Edom. [18] And Hiram sent him ships commanded by his own men, sailors who knew the sea. These, with Solomon's men, sailed to Ophir and brought back four hundred and fifty talents of gold, which they delivered to King Solomon.

■ PSALM 89:11-18

[11] The heavens are yours, and yours also
    the earth;
    you founded the world and all that is
    in it.
[12] You created the north and the south;
    Tabor and Hermon sing for joy at your
    name.
[13] Your arm is endowed with power;
    your hand is strong, your right hand
    exalted.

[14] Righteousness and justice are the
    foundation of your throne;
    love and faithfulness go before you.

[15] Blessed are those who have learned to
    acclaim you,
    who walk in the light of your presence,
    LORD.
[16] They rejoice in your name all day long;
    they celebrate your righteousness.
[17] For you are their glory and strength,
    and by your favour you exalt our horn.
[18] Indeed, our shield belongs to the LORD,
    our king to the Holy One of Israel.

■ PROVERBS 18:23-24

[23] The poor plead for mercy,
    but the rich answer harshly.

[24] One who has unreliable friends soon
    comes to ruin,
    but there is a friend who sticks closer
    than a brother.

■ ACTS 23:1-22

23 Paul looked straight at the Sanhedrin and said, 'My brothers, I have fulfilled my duty to God in all good conscience to this day.' [2] At this the high priest Ananias ordered those standing near Paul to strike him on the mouth. [3] Then Paul said to him, 'God will strike you, you whitewashed wall! You sit there to judge me according to the law, yet you yourself violate the law by commanding that I be struck!'

[4] Those who were standing near Paul said, 'How dare you insult God's high priest!'

[5] Paul replied, 'Brothers, I did not realise that he was the high priest; for it is written: "Do not speak evil about the ruler of your people."'

[6] Then Paul, knowing that some of them were Sadducees and the others Pharisees, called out in the Sanhedrin, 'My brothers, I am a Pharisee, descended from Pharisees. I stand on trial because of the hope of the

resurrection of the dead.' ⁷When he said this, a dispute broke out between the Pharisees and the Sadducees, and the assembly was divided. ⁸(The Sadducees say that there is no resurrection, and that there are neither angels nor spirits, but the Pharisees believe all these things.)

⁹There was a great uproar, and some of the teachers of the law who were Pharisees stood up and argued vigorously. 'We find nothing wrong with this man,' they said. 'What if a spirit or an angel has spoken to him?' ¹⁰The dispute became so violent that the commander was afraid Paul would be torn to pieces by them. He ordered the troops to go down and take him away from them by force and bring him into the barracks.

¹¹The following night the Lord stood near Paul and said, 'Take courage! As you have testified about me in Jerusalem, so you must also testify in Rome.'

¹²The next morning some Jews formed a conspiracy and bound themselves with an oath not to eat or drink until they had killed Paul. ¹³More than forty men were involved in this plot. ¹⁴They went to the chief priests and the elders and said, 'We have taken a solemn oath not to eat anything until we have killed Paul. ¹⁵Now then, you and the Sanhedrin petition the commander

to bring him before you on the pretext of wanting more accurate information about his case. We are ready to kill him before he gets here.'

¹⁶But when the son of Paul's sister heard of this plot, he went into the barracks and told Paul.

¹⁷Then Paul called one of the centurions and said, 'Take this young man to the commander; he has something to tell him.' ¹⁸So he took him to the commander.

The centurion said, 'Paul, the prisoner, sent for me and asked me to bring this young man to you because he has something to tell you.'

¹⁹The commander took the young man by the hand, drew him aside and asked, 'What is it you want to tell me?'

²⁰He said: 'Some Jews have agreed to ask you to bring Paul before the Sanhedrin tomorrow on the pretext of wanting more accurate information about him. ²¹Don't give in to them, because more than forty of them are waiting in ambush for him. They have taken an oath not to eat or drink until they have killed him. They are ready now, waiting for your consent to their request.'

²²The commander dismissed the young man with this warning: 'Don't tell anyone that you have reported this to me.'

The Word That Irritates

'... if my people ... humble themselves ... and turn from their wicked ways, them I will ... forgive their sin and will heal their land.' **2 Chronicles 7:14**

Most Christians never allow themselves to come too close to the deep thirst for God that exists at the core of their being, for if they did, they would be compelled to get in touch with their basic helplessness.

Why would we want to deny this? Because to recognise our helplessness puts us in a position where we have to repent of it - and that is something our fallen human nature pulls back from doing. Believe me, the one word that grates and irritates our human nature is the word 'repent'.

It is much easier to be given advice like, 'Read more of the Bible every day', 'Add extra minutes to your prayer time', or 'Seize more opportunities to share your faith', than to be told to repent. All these things I have just mentioned may be excellent in themselves, but more is required if we are to get in touch with our deep thirst for God.

We must repent!

But repent of what? Our stubborn commitment to independence, as well as the awful desire and practice of choosing to dig our own wells (see Jer. 2:13).

A passionate pursuit of God demands this. Believe me, no matter what we say with our lips, we will never begin to pant after God until we repent of the self-sufficiency that has made its home deep within our hearts. This, in my opinion, is the biggest single step we can take in our pursuit of God and the experience of having feet like 'hinds' feet'.

PRAYER

Gracious and loving heavenly Father, help me to repent deeply. May I know at this moment a turning from self-dependence to God-dependence. I give You my willingness – now give me Your power. In Jesus' name I ask it. Amen.

FURTHER STUDY

Psa. 34:1-18; Joel 2:12; Luke 13:1-3

- What was the central message of Jesus?
- How does the psalmist express it?

July 29

▬ 2 CHRONICLES 9:1–10:19

9 When the queen of Sheba heard of Solomon's fame, she came to Jerusalem to test him with hard questions. Arriving with a very great caravan – with camels carrying spices, large quantities of gold, and precious stones – she came to Solomon and talked with him about all she had on her mind. ²Solomon answered all her questions; nothing was too hard for him to explain to her. ³When the queen of Sheba saw the wisdom of Solomon, as well as the palace he had built, ⁴the food on his table, the seating of his officials, the attending servants in their robes, the cupbearers in their robes and the burnt offerings he made at the temple of the LORD, she was overwhelmed.

⁵She said to the king, 'The report I heard in my own country about your achievements and your wisdom is true. ⁶But I did not believe what they said until I came and saw with my own eyes. Indeed, not even half the greatness of your wisdom was told me; you have far exceeded the report I heard. ⁷How happy your people must be! How happy your officials, who continually stand before you and hear your wisdom! ⁸Praise be to the LORD your God, who has delighted in you and placed you on his throne as king to rule for the LORD your God. Because of the love of your God for Israel and his desire to uphold them for ever, he has made you king over them, to maintain justice and righteousness.'

⁹Then she gave the king 120 talents of gold, large quantities of spices, and precious stones. There had never been such spices as those the queen of Sheba gave to King Solomon.

¹⁰(The servants of Hiram and the servants of Solomon brought gold from Ophir; they also brought algum-wood and precious stones. ¹¹The king used the algum-wood to make steps for the temple of the LORD and for the royal palace, and to make harps and lyres for the musicians. Nothing like them had ever been seen in Judah.)

¹²King Solomon gave the queen of Sheba all she desired and asked for; he gave her more than she had brought to him. Then she left and returned with her retinue to her own country.

¹³The weight of the gold that Solomon received yearly was 666 talents, ¹⁴not including the revenues brought in by merchants and traders. Also all the kings of Arabia and the governors of the territories brought gold and silver to Solomon.

¹⁵King Solomon made two hundred large shields of hammered gold; six hundred shekels of hammered gold went into each shield. ¹⁶He also made three hundred small shields of hammered gold, with three hundred shekels of gold in each shield. The king put them in the Palace of the Forest of Lebanon.

¹⁷Then the king made a great throne covered with ivory and overlaid with pure gold. ¹⁸The throne had six steps, and a footstool of gold was attached to it. On both sides of the seat were armrests, with a lion standing beside each of them. ¹⁹Twelve lions stood on the six steps, one at either end of each step. Nothing like it had ever been made for any other kingdom. ²⁰All King Solomon's goblets were gold, and all the household articles in the Palace of the Forest of Lebanon were pure gold. Nothing was made of silver, because silver was considered of little value in Solomon's day. ²¹The king had a fleet of trading ships manned by Hiram's servants. Once every three years it returned, carrying gold, silver and ivory, and apes and baboons.

²²King Solomon was greater in riches and wisdom than all the other kings of the earth. ²³All the kings of the earth sought audience with Solomon to hear the wisdom God had put in his heart. ²⁴Year after year, everyone who came brought a gift – articles of silver and gold, and robes, weapons and spices, and horses and mules.

²⁵Solomon had four thousand stalls for horses and chariots, and twelve thousand horses, which he kept in the chariot cities and also with him in Jerusalem. ²⁶He ruled over all the kings from the River Euphrates to the land of the Philistines, as far as the border of Egypt. ²⁷The king made silver as common in Jerusalem as stones, and cedar as plentiful as sycamore-fig trees in the foothills. ²⁸Solomon's horses were imported from Egypt and from all other countries.

²⁹As for the other events of Solomon's reign, from beginning to end, are they not written in the records of Nathan the prophet, in the prophecy of Ahijah the Shilonite and in the visions of Iddo the seer concerning Jeroboam son of Nebat? ³⁰Solomon reigned in Jerusalem over all Israel for forty years. ³¹Then he rested with his ancestors and was buried in the city of David his father. And Rehoboam his son succeeded him as king.

10 Rehoboam went to Shechem, for all Israel had gone there to make him king. ²When Jeroboam son of Nebat heard this (he was in Egypt, where he had fled from King Solomon), he returned from Egypt. ³So they sent for Jeroboam, and he and all Israel went to Rehoboam and said to him: ⁴'Your father put a heavy yoke on us, but now lighten the harsh labour and the heavy yoke he put on us, and we will serve you.'

⁵Rehoboam answered, 'Come back to me in three days.' So the people went away.

⁶Then King Rehoboam consulted the elders who had served his father Solomon during his lifetime. 'How would you advise me to answer these people?' he asked.

⁷They replied, 'If you will be kind to these people and please them and give them a favourable answer, they will always be your servants.'

⁸But Rehoboam rejected the advice the elders gave him and consulted the young men who had grown up with him and were serving him. ⁹He asked them, 'What is your advice? How should we answer these people who say to me, "Lighten the yoke your father put on us"?'

¹⁰The young men who had grown up with him replied, 'The people have said to you, "Your father put a heavy yoke on us, but make our yoke lighter." Now tell them, "My little finger is thicker than my father's waist. ¹¹My father laid on you a heavy yoke; I will make it even heavier. My father scourged you with whips; I will scourge you with scorpions."'

¹²Three days later Jeroboam and all the people returned to Rehoboam, as the king had said, 'Come back to me in three days.' ¹³The king answered them harshly. Rejecting the advice of the elders, ¹⁴he followed the advice of the young men and said, 'My father made your yoke heavy; I will make it even heavier. My father scourged you with whips; I will scourge you with scorpions.' ¹⁵So the king did not listen to the people, for this turn of events was from God, to fulfil the word that the LORD had spoken to Jeroboam son of Nebat through Ahijah the Shilonite.

¹⁶When all Israel saw that the king refused to listen to them, they answered the king:

'What share do we have in David,
    what part in Jesse's son?
To your tents, Israel!
    Look after your own house, David!'

So all the Israelites went home. ¹⁷But as for the Israelites who were living in the towns of Judah, Rehoboam still ruled over them.

¹⁸King Rehoboam sent out Adoniram, who was in charge of forced labour, but the Israelites stoned him to death. King Rehoboam, however, managed to get into his chariot and escape to Jerusalem. ¹⁹So Israel has been in rebellion against the house of David to this day.

....

■ PSALM 89:19-29

¹⁹Once you spoke in a vision,
    to your faithful people you said:
'I have bestowed strength on a warrior;
    I have raised up a young man from
        among the people.
²⁰I have found David my servant;
    with my sacred oil I have anointed
        him.
²¹My hand will sustain him;
    surely my arm will strengthen him.
²²The enemy will not get the better of him;
    the wicked will not oppress him.
²³I will crush his foes before him
    and strike down his adversaries.
²⁴My faithful love will be with him,
    and through my name his horn will be
        exalted.
²⁵I will set his hand over the sea,
    his right hand over the rivers.
²⁶He will call out to me, "You are my
        Father,
    my God, the Rock my Saviour."
²⁷And I will appoint him to be my
        firstborn,
    the most exalted of the kings of the
        earth.
²⁸I will maintain my love to him for ever,
    and my covenant with him will never
        fail.
²⁹I will establish his line for ever,
    his throne as long as the heavens
        endure.

■ PROVERBS 19:1-3

19 Better the poor whose way of life is
blameless
than a fool whose lips are perverse.

² Desire without knowledge is not good –
how much more will hasty feet miss
the way!

³ A person's own folly leads to their ruin,
yet their heart rages against the LORD.

■ ACTS 23:23–24:9

²³ Then he called two of his centurions
and ordered them, 'Get ready a detachment
of two hundred soldiers, seventy horsemen and two hundred spearmen to go to
Caesarea at nine tonight. ²⁴ Provide horses
for Paul so that he may be taken safely to
Governor Felix.'

²⁵ He wrote a letter as follows:

²⁶ Claudius Lysias,

To His Excellency, Governor Felix:

Greetings.

²⁷ This man was seized by the Jews
and they were about to kill him, but
I came with my troops and rescued
him, for I had learned that he is a Roman citizen. ²⁸ I wanted to know why
they were accusing him, so I brought
him to their Sanhedrin. ²⁹ I found that
the accusation had to do with questions about their law, but there was
no charge against him that deserved
death or imprisonment. ³⁰ When I
was informed of a plot to be carried
out against the man, I sent him to you

at once. I also ordered his accusers to
present to you their case against him.

³¹ So the soldiers, carrying out their orders, took Paul with them during the night
and brought him as far as Antipatris. ³² The
next day they let the cavalry go on with him,
while they returned to the barracks. ³³ When
the cavalry arrived in Caesarea, they delivered the letter to the governor and handed
Paul over to him. ³⁴ The governor read the
letter and asked what province he was from.
Learning that he was from Cilicia, ³⁵ he said,
'I will hear your case when your accusers
get here.' Then he ordered that Paul be kept
under guard in Herod's palace.

24 Five days later the high priest Ananias went down to Caesarea with
some of the elders and a lawyer named
Tertullus, and they brought their charges
against Paul before the governor. ² When
Paul was called in, Tertullus presented his
case before Felix: 'We have enjoyed a long
period of peace under you, and your fore-
sight has brought about reforms in this nation. ³ Everywhere and in every way, most
excellent Felix, we acknowledge this with
profound gratitude. ⁴ But in order not to
weary you further, I would request that you
be kind enough to hear us briefly.

⁵ 'We have found this man to be a
troublemaker, stirring up riots among the
Jews all over the world. He is a ringleader of
the Nazarene sect ⁶ and even tried to desecrate the temple; so we seized him. [7]ᵃ ⁸ By
examining him yourself you will be able to
learn the truth about all these charges we
are bringing against him.'

⁹ The other Jews joined in the accusation,
asserting that these things were true.

ᵃ Some manuscripts include here *him, and we would have judged
him in accordance with our law.* ⁷ *But the commander Lysias came and
took him from us with much violence,* ⁸ *ordering his accusers to come
before you.*

Satan - Angel of Light

'My faithful love will be with him ...' **Psalm 89:24**

A feeling that the devil delights to arouse in an unguarded heart is the feeling that God does not love us. He usually times his attack to coincide with those moments when everything is going wrong and we are beset by all kinds of difficulties. Then he whispers in our ear, 'Do you still believe that God is love?'

When you respond by saying that you do, he transforms himself into an angel of light and tries another of his deceitful tactics. 'Well,' he says, 'it is obvious that He does not love you, for if He did, then He would not allow you to go through these difficult situations.'

There is only one protection against such an assault; it is to put firmly in place the 'armour of righteousness'. Nothing else will avail at this point. You must point him to the truth of Romans 8:28: 'And we know that in all things God works for the good of those who love him ...'. Paul does not say 'we understand,' but 'we know'.

This brings you directly to the theme of justification by faith, which is in fact the righteousness of Christ. You rest on this established truth, and that is all you need. You must say to yourself, 'He would never have clothed me with His righteousness if He had not also set His love upon me and saved me. I will have courage. I do not know what is happening to me now. I cannot fathom it. But if He has begun His work in me, then I know He will go on to complete it.'

PRAYER

O God, what wondrous power there is in Your Word. I can feel it doing me good even as I read and ponder it. Give me a greater knowledge of Your Word, for only through its truth can I maintain an advantage over the devil. Amen.

FURTHER STUDY

Jer. 31:1-3; Eph. 2:1-7; 3:16-19; Phil. 1:6; Rom. 5:8
• How has God demonstrated His love?
• What was Paul's desire for the Ephesians?

July 30

■ 2 CHRONICLES 11:1–13:22

11 When Rehoboam arrived in Jerusalem, he mustered Judah and Benjamin – a hundred and eighty thousand able young men – to go to war against Israel and to regain the kingdom for Rehoboam.

²But this word of the LORD came to Shemaiah the man of God: ³'Say to Rehoboam son of Solomon king of Judah and to all

Israel in Judah and Benjamin, ⁴"This is what the LORD says: do not go up to fight against your fellow Israelites. Go home, every one of you, for this is my doing."' So they obeyed the words of the LORD and turned back from marching against Jeroboam.

⁵Rehoboam lived in Jerusalem and built up towns for defence in Judah: ⁶Bethlehem, Etam, Tekoa, ⁷Beth Zur, Soko, Adullam, ⁸Gath, Mareshah, Ziph, ⁹Adoraim, Lachish, Azekah, ¹⁰Zorah, Aijalon and Hebron. These were fortified cities in Judah and Benjamin. ¹¹He strengthened their defences and put commanders in them, with supplies of food, olive oil and wine. ¹²He put shields and spears in all the cities, and made them very strong. So Judah and Benjamin were his.

¹³The priests and Levites from all their districts throughout Israel sided with him. ¹⁴The Levites even abandoned their pasture-lands and property and came to Judah and Jerusalem, because Jeroboam and his sons had rejected them as priests of the LORD ¹⁵when he appointed his own priests for the high places and for the goat and calf idols he had made. ¹⁶Those from every tribe of Israel who set their hearts on seeking the LORD, the God of Israel, followed the Levites to Jerusalem to offer sacrifices to the LORD, the God of their ancestors. ¹⁷They strengthened the kingdom of Judah and supported Rehoboam son of Solomon for three years, following the ways of David and Solomon during this time.

¹⁸Rehoboam married Mahalath, who was the daughter of David's son Jerimoth and of Abihail, the daughter of Jesse's son Eliab. ¹⁹She bore him sons: Jeush, Shemariah and Zaham. ²⁰Then he married Maakah daughter of Absalom, who bore him Abijah, Attai, Ziza and Shelomith. ²¹Rehoboam loved Maakah daughter of Absalom more than any of his other wives and concubines. In all, he had eighteen wives and sixty concubines, twenty-eight sons and sixty daughters.

²²Rehoboam appointed Abijah son of Maakah as crown prince among his brothers, in order to make him king. ²³He acted wisely, dispersing some of his sons throughout the districts of Judah and Benjamin, and to all the fortified cities. He gave them abundant provisions and took many wives for them.

12 After Rehoboam's position as king was established and he had become strong, he and all Israel with him abandoned the law of the LORD. ²Because they had been unfaithful to the LORD, Shishak king of Egypt attacked Jerusalem in the fifth year of King Rehoboam. ³With twelve hundred chariots and sixty thousand horsemen and the innumerable troops of Libyans, Sukkites and Cushites that came with him from Egypt, ⁴he captured the fortified cities of Judah and came as far as Jerusalem.

⁵Then the prophet Shemaiah came to Rehoboam and to the leaders of Judah who had assembled in Jerusalem for fear of Shishak, and he said to them, 'This is what the LORD says: "You have abandoned me; therefore, I now abandon you to Shishak."'

⁶The leaders of Israel and the king humbled themselves and said, 'The LORD is just.'

⁷When the LORD saw that they humbled themselves, this word of the LORD came to Shemaiah: 'Since they have humbled themselves, I will not destroy them but will soon give them deliverance. My wrath will not be poured out on Jerusalem through Shishak. ⁸They will, however, become subject to him, so that they may learn the difference between serving me and serving the kings of other lands.'

⁹When Shishak king of Egypt attacked Jerusalem, he carried off the treasures of the temple of the LORD and the treasures of the royal palace. He took everything, including the gold shields that Solomon had made. ¹⁰So King Rehoboam made bronze shields to replace them and assigned these to the commanders of the guard on duty at

the entrance to the royal palace. [11] Whenever the king went to the LORD's temple, the guards went with him, bearing the shields, and afterwards they returned them to the guardroom.

[12] Because Rehoboam humbled himself, the LORD's anger turned from him, and he was not totally destroyed. Indeed, there was some good in Judah.

[13] King Rehoboam established himself firmly in Jerusalem and continued as king. He was forty-one years old when he became king, and he reigned for seventeen years in Jerusalem, the city the LORD had chosen out of all the tribes of Israel in which to put his Name. His mother's name was Naamah; she was an Ammonite. [14] He did evil because he had not set his heart on seeking the LORD.

[15] As for the events of Rehoboam's reign, from beginning to end, are they not written in the records of Shemaiah the prophet and of Iddo the seer that deal with genealogies? There was continual warfare between Rehoboam and Jeroboam. [16] Rehoboam rested with his ancestors and was buried in the City of David. And Abijah his son succeeded him as king.

13 In the eighteenth year of the reign of Jeroboam, Abijah became king of Judah, [2] and he reigned in Jerusalem for three years. His mother's name was Maakah, a daughter of Uriel of Gibeah.

There was war between Abijah and Jeroboam. [3] Abijah went into battle with an army of four hundred thousand able fighting men, and Jeroboam drew up a battle line against him with eight hundred thousand able troops.

[4] Abijah stood on Mount Zemaraim, in the hill country of Ephraim, and said, 'Jeroboam and all Israel, listen to me! [5] Don't you know that the LORD, the God of Israel, has given the kingship of Israel to David and his descendants for ever by a covenant of salt? [6] Yet Jeroboam son of Nebat, an official of Solomon son of David, rebelled against

his master. [7] Some worthless scoundrels gathered around him and opposed Rehoboam son of Solomon when he was young and indecisive and not strong enough to resist them.

[8] 'And now you plan to resist the kingdom of the LORD, which is in the hands of David's descendants. You are indeed a vast army and have with you the golden calves that Jeroboam made to be your gods. [9] But didn't you drive out the priests of the LORD, the sons of Aaron, and the Levites, and make priests of your own as the peoples of other lands do? Whoever comes to consecrate himself with a young bull and seven rams may become a priest of what are not gods.

[10] 'As for us, the LORD is our God, and we have not forsaken him. The priests who serve the LORD are sons of Aaron, and the Levites assist them. [11] Every morning and evening they present burnt offerings and fragrant incense to the LORD. They set out the bread on the ceremonially clean table and light the lamps on the gold lampstand every evening. We are observing the requirements of the LORD our God. But you have forsaken him. [12] God is with us; he is our leader. His priests with their trumpets will sound the battle cry against you. People of Israel, do not fight against the LORD, the God of your ancestors, for you will not succeed.'

[13] Now Jeroboam had sent troops round to the rear, so that while he was in front of Judah the ambush was behind them. [14] Judah turned and saw that they were being attacked at both front and rear. Then they cried out to the LORD. The priests blew their trumpets [15] and the men of Judah raised the battle cry. At the sound of their battle cry, God routed Jeroboam and all Israel before Abijah and Judah. [16] The Israelites fled before Judah, and God delivered them into their hands. [17] Abijah and his troops inflicted heavy losses on them, so that there were five hundred thousand casualties among

Israel's able men. [18] The Israelites were subdued on that occasion, and the people of Judah were victorious because they relied on the LORD, the God of their ancestors.

[19] Abijah pursued Jeroboam and took from him the towns of Bethel, Jeshanah and Ephron, with their surrounding villages. [20] Jeroboam did not regain power during the time of Abijah. And the LORD struck him down and he died.

[21] But Abijah grew in strength. He married fourteen wives and had twenty-two sons and sixteen daughters.

[22] The other events of Abijah's reign, what he did and what he said, are written in the annotations of the prophet Iddo.

PSALM 89:30-37

[30] 'If his sons forsake my law
     and do not follow my statutes,
[31] if they violate my decrees
     and fail to keep my commands,
[32] I will punish their sin with the rod,
     their iniquity with flogging;
[33] but I will not take my love from him,
     nor will I ever betray my faithfulness.
[34] I will not violate my covenant
     or alter what my lips have uttered.
[35] Once for all, I have sworn by my
         holiness –
     and I will not lie to David –
[36] that his line will continue for ever
     and his throne endure before me like
         the sun;
[37] it will be established for ever like the
         moon,
     the faithful witness in the sky.'

PROVERBS 19:4-5

[4] Wealth attracts many friends,
     but even the closest friend of the poor
         person deserts them.

[5] A false witness will not go unpunished,
     and whoever pours out lies will not
         go free.

ACTS 24:10-27

[10] When the governor motioned for him to speak, Paul replied: 'I know that for a number of years you have been a judge over this nation; so I gladly make my defence. [11] You can easily verify that no more than twelve days ago I went up to Jerusalem to worship. [12] My accusers did not find me arguing with anyone at the temple, or stirring up a crowd in the synagogues or anywhere else in the city. [13] And they cannot prove to you the charges they are now making against me. [14] However, I admit that I worship the God of our ancestors as a follower of the Way, which they call a sect. I believe everything that is in accordance with the Law and that is written in the Prophets, [15] and I have the same hope in God as these men themselves have, that there will be a resurrection of both the righteous and the wicked. [16] So I strive always to keep my conscience clear before God and man.

[17] 'After an absence of several years, I came to Jerusalem to bring my people gifts for the poor and to present offerings. [18] I was ceremonially clean when they found me in the temple courts doing this. There was no crowd with me, nor was I involved in any disturbance. [19] But there are some Jews from the province of Asia, who ought to be here before you and bring charges if they have anything against me. [20] Or these who are here should state what crime they found in me when I stood before the Sanhedrin – [21] unless it was this one thing I shouted as I stood in their presence: "It is concerning the resurrection of the dead that I am on trial before you today." '

[22] Then Felix, who was well acquainted with the Way, adjourned the proceedings.

'When Lysias the commander comes,' he said, 'I will decide your case.' 23 He ordered the centurion to keep Paul under guard but to give him some freedom and permit his friends to take care of his needs.

24 Several days later Felix came with his wife Drusilla, who was Jewish. He sent for Paul and listened to him as he spoke about faith in Christ Jesus. 25 As Paul talked about righteousness, self-control and the judgment to come, Felix was afraid and said, 'That's enough for now! You may leave. When I find it convenient, I will send for you.' 26 At the same time he was hoping that Paul would offer him a bribe, so he sent for him frequently and talked with him.

27 When two years had passed, Felix was succeeded by Porcius Festus, but because Felix wanted to grant a favour to the Jews, he left Paul in prison.

'Creative disobedience'

'A false witness will not go unpunished, and whoever pours out lies will perish.' **Proverbs 19:5**

One of the great truths of Scripture - and one we must hold on to in these days when there is so much resistance against the things of God - is this: His purposes will not be blocked by manmade barriers. Ultimately God will bring His plans to fruition despite every form of resistance, often by utilising the very opposition of men - and even their anger! The psalmist understood this for he wrote, 'Surely the wrath of man shall praise you ...' (Psa. 76:10, NKJV).

So it was in the story of the midwives in Egypt (see Exod. 1:15-22). Some rush to say that these women clearly lied to Pharaoh, and yet God blessed them. But I believe the Hebrew midwives practised 'passive resistance' or, as someone has put it, 'creative disobedience'. As God's people, it needs to be said, we are under no obligation to cooperate with the unjust or violent, be they husbands, bosses or rulers! These midwives were fearless before men because they 'feared God'. 'Fear God,' it has been said, 'and you will fear nothing else.'

We can take comfort from two things here: one is the fact that, I believe, nothing can happen to us that cannot, in turn, bless us and be turned to our good. Everything that happened to Job first had to pass through God's hands, as we see from the opening chapters. Second, small acts of courage have a big impact on the world. It was C.S. Lewis who commented that cowardice and Christ do not fit together. Wherever you are today and whatever you do, stand up and be counted if that is what is needed. Have the courage of your convictions and be assured of this: it can and will make a difference to the big picture of what God is achieving on the earth!

PRAYER

O Father, let me grasp these two simple but sublime truths, namely that nothing can ever happen to me that cannot be turned to good, and that my stand for truth really does make a difference. I am so thankful. In Jesus' name. Amen.

FURTHER STUDY

Dan. 1:1-17; Rom. 1:16-17
• How did Daniel practise creative disobedience?
• What was Paul's conviction?

July 31

▬ 2 CHRONICLES 14:1–16:14

14 And Abijah rested with his ancestors and was buried in the City of David. Asa his son succeeded him as king, and in his days the country was at peace for ten years.

² Asa did what was good and right in the eyes of the LORD his God. ³ He removed the foreign altars and the high places, smashed the sacred stones and cut down the Asherah poles. ⁴ He commanded Judah to seek the LORD, the God of their ancestors, and to obey his laws and commands. ⁵ He removed the high places and incense altars in every town in Judah, and the kingdom was at peace under him. ⁶ He built up the fortified cities of Judah, since the land was at peace. No one was at war with him during those years, for the LORD gave him rest.

⁷ 'Let us build up these towns,' he said to Judah, 'and put walls round them, with towers, gates and bars. The land is still ours, because we have sought the LORD our God; we sought him and he has given us rest on every side.' So they built and prospered.

⁸ Asa had an army of three hundred thousand men from Judah, equipped with large shields and with spears, and two hundred and eighty thousand from Benjamin, armed with small shields and with bows.

All these were brave fighting men.

⁹ Zerah the Cushite marched out against them with an army of thousands upon thousands and three hundred chariots, and came as far as Mareshah. ¹⁰ Asa went out to meet him, and they took up battle positions in the Valley of Zephathah near Mareshah.

¹¹ Then Asa called to the LORD his God and said, 'LORD, there is no one like you to help the powerless against the mighty. Help us, LORD our God, for we rely on you, and in your name we have come against this vast army. LORD, you are our God; do not let mere mortals prevail against you.'

¹² The LORD struck down the Cushites before Asa and Judah. The Cushites fled, ¹³ and Asa and his army pursued them as far as Gerar. Such a great number of Cushites fell that they could not recover; they were crushed before the LORD and his forces. The men of Judah carried off a large amount of plunder. ¹⁴ They destroyed all the villages around Gerar, for the terror of the LORD had fallen on them. They looted all these villages, since there was much plunder there. ¹⁵ They also attacked the camps of the herdsmen and carried off droves of sheep and goats and camels. Then they returned to Jerusalem.

15 The Spirit of God came on Azariah son of Oded. ² He went out to meet Asa and said to him, 'Listen to me, Asa and all Judah and Benjamin. The LORD is with you when you are with him. If you seek him, he will be found by you, but if you forsake him, he will forsake you. ³For a long time Israel was without the true God, without a priest to teach and without the law. ⁴But in their distress they turned to the LORD, the God of Israel, and sought him, and he was found by them. ⁵In those days it was not safe to travel about, for all the inhabitants of the lands were in great turmoil. ⁶One nation was being crushed by another and one city by another, because God was troubling them with every kind of distress. ⁷But as for you, be strong and do not give up, for your work will be rewarded.'

⁸When Asa heard these words and the prophecy of Azariah son of Oded the prophet, he took courage. He removed the detestable idols from the whole land of Judah and Benjamin and from the towns he had captured in the hills of Ephraim. He repaired the altar of the LORD that was in front of the portico of the LORD's temple.

⁹Then he assembled all Judah and Benjamin and the people from Ephraim, Manasseh and Simeon who had settled among them, for large numbers had come over to him from Israel when they saw that the LORD his God was with him.

¹⁰They assembled at Jerusalem in the third month of the fifteenth year of Asa's reign. ¹¹At that time they sacrificed to the LORD seven hundred head of cattle and seven thousand sheep and goats from the plunder they had brought back. ¹²They entered into a covenant to seek the LORD, the God of their ancestors, with all their heart and soul. ¹³All who would not seek the LORD, the God of Israel, were to be put to death, whether small or great, man or woman. ¹⁴They took an oath to the LORD with loud acclamation, with shouting and with trumpets and horns. ¹⁵All Judah rejoiced about the oath because they had sworn it

wholeheartedly. They sought God eagerly, and he was found by them. So the LORD gave them rest on every side.

¹⁶King Asa also deposed his grandmother Maakah from her position as queen mother, because she had made a repulsive image for the worship of Asherah. Asa cut it down, broke it up and burned it in the Kidron Valley. ¹⁷Although he did not remove the high places from Israel, Asa's heart was fully committed to the LORD all his life. ¹⁸He brought into the temple of God the silver and gold and the articles that he and his father had dedicated.

¹⁹There was no more war until the thirty-fifth year of Asa's reign.

16 In the thirty-sixth year of Asa's reign Baasha king of Israel went up against Judah and fortified Ramah to prevent anyone from leaving or entering the territory of Asa king of Judah.

²Asa then took the silver and gold out of the treasuries of the LORD's temple and of his own palace and sent it to Ben-Hadad king of Aram, who was ruling in Damascus. ³'Let there be a treaty between me and you,' he said, 'as there was between my father and your father. See, I am sending you silver and gold. Now break your treaty with Baasha king of Israel so that he will withdraw from me.'

⁴Ben-Hadad agreed with King Asa and sent the commanders of his forces against the towns of Israel. They conquered Ijon, Dan, Abel Maim and all the store cities of Naphtali. ⁵When Baasha heard this, he stopped building Ramah and abandoned his work. ⁶Then King Asa brought all the men of Judah, and they carried away from Ramah the stones and timber Baasha had been using. With them he built up Geba and Mizpah.

⁷At that time Hanani the seer came to Asa king of Judah and said to him: 'Because you relied on the king of Aram and not on the LORD your God, the army of the king of Aram has escaped from your hand. ⁸Were

not the Cushites and Libyans a mighty army with great numbers of chariots and horsemen? Yet when you relied on the LORD, he delivered them into your hand. ⁹ For the eyes of the LORD range throughout the earth to strengthen those whose hearts are fully committed to him. You have done a foolish thing, and from now on you will be at war.'

¹⁰ Asa was angry with the seer because of this; he was so enraged that he put him in prison. At the same time Asa brutally oppressed some of the people.

¹¹ The events of Asa's reign, from beginning to end, are written in the book of the kings of Judah and Israel. ¹² In the thirty-ninth year of his reign Asa was afflicted with a disease in his feet. Though his disease was severe, even in his illness he did not seek help from the LORD, but only from the doctors. ¹³ Then in the forty-first year of his reign Asa died and rested with his ancestors. ¹⁴ They buried him in the tomb that he had cut out for himself in the City of David. They laid him on a bier covered with spices and various blended perfumes, and they made a huge fire in his honour.

▬ PSALM 89:38-45

³⁸ But you have rejected, you have spurned,
    you have been very angry with your
        anointed one.
³⁹ You have renounced the covenant with
        your servant
    and have defiled his crown in the dust.
⁴⁰ You have broken through all his walls
    and reduced his strongholds to ruins.
⁴¹ All who pass by have plundered him;
    he has become the scorn of his
        neighbours.
⁴² You have exalted the right hand of his
        foes;
    you have made all his enemies rejoice.
⁴³ Indeed, you have turned back the edge of
        his sword

and have not supported him in battle.
⁴⁴ You have put an end to his splendour
    and cast his throne to the ground.
⁴⁵ You have cut short the days of his youth;
    you have covered him with a mantle
        of shame.

▬ PROVERBS 19:6-7

⁶ Many curry favour with a ruler,
    and everyone is the friend of one who
        gives gifts.

⁷ The poor are shunned by all their
        relatives –
    how much more do their friends avoid
        them!
Though the poor pursue them with
        pleading,
    they are nowhere to be found.

▬ ACTS 25:1-22

25 Three days after arriving in the province, Festus went up from Caesarea to Jerusalem, ² where the chief priests and the Jewish leaders appeared before him and presented the charges against Paul. ³ They requested Festus, as a favour to them, to have Paul transferred to Jerusalem, for they were preparing an ambush to kill him along the way. ⁴ Festus answered, 'Paul is being held at Caesarea, and I myself am going there soon. ⁵ Let some of your leaders come with me, and if the man has done anything wrong, they can press charges against him there.'

⁶ After spending eight or ten days with them, Festus went down to Caesarea. The next day he convened the court and ordered that Paul be brought before him. ⁷ When Paul came in, the Jews who had come down from Jerusalem stood round him. They brought many serious charges against him, but they could not prove them.

[8]Then Paul made his defence: 'I have done nothing wrong against the Jewish law or against the temple or against Caesar.'

[9]Festus, wishing to do the Jews a favour, said to Paul, 'Are you willing to go up to Jerusalem and stand trial before me there on these charges?'

[10]Paul answered: 'I am now standing before Caesar's court, where I ought to be tried. I have not done any wrong to the Jews, as you yourself know very well. [11]If, however, I am guilty of doing anything deserving death, I do not refuse to die. But if the charges brought against me by these Jews are not true, no one has the right to hand me over to them. I appeal to Caesar!'

[12]After Festus had conferred with his council, he declared: 'You have appealed to Caesar. To Caesar you will go!'

[13]A few days later King Agrippa and Bernice arrived at Caesarea to pay their respects to Festus. [14]Since they were spending many days there, Festus discussed Paul's case with the king. He said: 'There is a man here whom Felix left as a prisoner. [15]When I went to Jerusalem, the chief priests and the elders of the Jews brought charges against him and asked that he be condemned.

[16]'I told them that it is not the Roman custom to hand over anyone before they have faced their accusers and have had an opportunity to defend themselves against the charges. [17]When they came here with me, I did not delay the case, but convened the court the next day and ordered the man to be brought in. [18]When his accusers got up to speak, they did not charge him with any of the crimes I had expected. [19]Instead, they had some points of dispute with him about their own religion and about a dead man named Jesus whom Paul claimed was alive. [20]I was at a loss how to investigate such matters; so I asked if he would be willing to go to Jerusalem and stand trial there on these charges. [21]But when Paul made his appeal to be held over for the Emperor's decision, I ordered him to be held until I could send him to Caesar.'

[22]Then Agrippa said to Festus, 'I would like to hear this man myself.'

He replied, 'Tomorrow you will hear him.'

Where Is Our Trust?

'... you have been very angry with your anointed one.'
Psalm 89:38

Giving God glory should be our greatest priority. The serious problem is not the pain that others have inflicted upon us, but the pain we have inflicted (and continue to inflict) upon God. Let me spell out as clearly as I can exactly what I mean.

Many Christians are far more interested in focusing on how they can get God to comfort them when they have been hurt than considering how much they have hurt Him. Not that it is wrong to seek His comfort – Scripture encourages us to do this – but it is only one side of the picture. The most popular books in our bookshops today are titles such as these: *How to Be Healed of Life's Hurts* or *How to Overcome the Pains of the Past*. I repeat that this is a legitimate emphasis, but we must not lose sight of the fact that the important issue is not how badly people have behaved towards us, but how badly we have behaved (and continue to behave) towards God.

Take this for example: someone hurts us or upsets us, and we decide to become the architects of their judgment. But what does God say? 'Do not take revenge, my dear friends, but leave room for God's wrath, for it is written: "It is mine to avenge; I will repay ..."' (Rom. 12:19). Don't you think God is hurt when He sees us ignoring His Word? We may have been sinned against, but is that any justification for sinning against God? Let's not mince words here, for any violation of a divine principle must be called by its rightful name - sin. And no sin ought to be treated lightly - especially a sin against God.

PRAYER

O God, forgive me that so often I am more concerned about how others have treated me than the way I treat You. I see that a failure to trust You is a failure in love. I say, 'I love You,' but only so far. Forgive me and help me. In Jesus' name. Amen.

FURTHER STUDY

Psa. 62:1-12; Matt. 21:12-13; 23:37-39; Luke 19:41
• What pain was inflicted on Jesus as He observed the Temple area?
• What pain did Jesus feel as He approached the city?

August 1

■ 2 CHRONICLES 17:1–18:34

17 Jehoshaphat his son succeeded him as king and strengthened himself against Israel. ²He stationed troops in all the fortified cities of Judah and put garrisons in Judah and in the towns of Ephraim that his father Asa had captured.

³The LORD was with Jehoshaphat because he followed the ways of his father David before him. He did not consult the Baals ⁴but sought the God of his father and followed his commands rather than the practices of Israel. ⁵The LORD established the kingdom under his control; and all Judah brought gifts to Jehoshaphat, so that he had great wealth and honour. ⁶His heart was devoted to the ways of the LORD; furthermore, he removed the high places and the Asherah poles from Judah.

⁷In the third year of his reign he sent his officials Ben-Hail, Obadiah, Zechariah,

Nethanel and Micaiah to teach in the towns of Judah. ⁸With them were certain Levites – Shemaiah, Nethaniah, Zebadiah, Asahel, Shemiramoth, Jehonathan, Adonijah, Tobijah and Tob-Adonijah – and the priests Elishama and Jehoram. ⁹They taught throughout Judah, taking with them the Book of the Law of the LORD; they went round to all the towns of Judah and taught the people.

¹⁰The fear of the LORD fell on all the kingdoms of the lands surrounding Judah, so that they did not go to war against Jehoshaphat. ¹¹Some Philistines brought Jehoshaphat gifts and silver as tribute, and the Arabs brought him flocks: seven thousand seven hundred rams and seven thousand seven hundred goats.

¹²Jehoshaphat became more and more powerful; he built forts and store cities in Judah ¹³and had large supplies in the towns of Judah. He also kept experienced fighting

men in Jerusalem. ¹⁴ Their enrolment by families was as follows:

from Judah, commanders of units of 1,000:

Adnah the commander, with 300,000 fighting men;

¹⁵ next, Jehohanan the commander, with 280,000;

¹⁶ next, Amasiah son of Zikri, who volunteered himself for the service of the LORD, with 200,000.

¹⁷ From Benjamin:

Eliada, a valiant soldier, with 200,000 men armed with bows and shields;

¹⁸ next, Jehozabad, with 180,000 men armed for battle.

¹⁹ These were the men who served the king, besides those he stationed in the fortified cities throughout Judah.

18 Now Jehoshaphat had great wealth and honour, and he allied himself with Ahab by marriage. ² Some years later he went down to see Ahab in Samaria. Ahab slaughtered many sheep and cattle for him and the people with him and urged him to attack Ramoth Gilead. ³ Ahab king of Israel asked Jehoshaphat king of Judah, 'Will you go with me against Ramoth Gilead?'

Jehoshaphat replied, 'I am as you are, and my people as your people; we will join you in the war.' ⁴ But Jehoshaphat also said to the king of Israel, 'First seek the counsel of the LORD.'

⁵ So the king of Israel brought together the prophets – four hundred men – and asked them, 'Shall we go to war against Ramoth Gilead, or shall I not?'

'Go,' they answered, 'for God will give it into the king's hand.'

⁶ But Jehoshaphat asked, 'Is there no longer a prophet of the LORD here whom we can enquire of?'

⁷ The king of Israel answered Jehoshaphat,

'There is still one prophet through whom we can enquire of the LORD, but I hate him because he never prophesies anything good about me, but always bad. He is Micaiah son of Imlah.'

'The king should not say such a thing,' Jehoshaphat replied.

⁸ So the king of Israel called one of his officials and said, 'Bring Micaiah son of Imlah at once.'

⁹ Dressed in their royal robes, the king of Israel and Jehoshaphat king of Judah were sitting on their thrones at the threshing-floor by the entrance of the gate of Samaria, with all the prophets prophesying before them. ¹⁰ Now Zedekiah son of Kenaanah had made iron horns, and he declared, 'This is what the LORD says: "With these you will gore the Arameans until they are destroyed."'

¹¹ All the other prophets were prophesying the same thing. 'Attack Ramoth Gilead and be victorious,' they said, 'for the LORD will give it into the king's hand.'

¹² The messenger who had gone to summon Micaiah said to him, 'Look, the other prophets without exception are predicting success for the king. Let your word agree with theirs, and speak favourably.'

¹³ But Micaiah said, 'As surely as the LORD lives, I can tell him only what my God says.'

¹⁴ When he arrived, the king asked him, 'Micaiah, shall we go to war against Ramoth Gilead, or shall I not?'

'Attack and be victorious,' he answered, 'for they will be given into your hand.'

¹⁵ The king said to him, 'How many times must I make you swear to tell me nothing but the truth in the name of the LORD?'

¹⁶ Then Micaiah answered, 'I saw all Israel scattered on the hills like sheep without a shepherd, and the LORD said, "These people have no master. Let each one go home in peace."'

¹⁷ The king of Israel said to Jehoshaphat, 'Didn't I tell you that he never prophesies

anything good about me, but only bad?'

¹⁸ Micaiah continued, 'Therefore hear the word of the LORD: I saw the LORD sitting on his throne with all the multitudes of heaven standing on his right and on his left. ¹⁹ And the LORD said, "Who will entice Ahab king of Israel into attacking Ramoth Gilead and going to his death there?"

'One suggested this, and another that. ²⁰ Finally, a spirit came forward, stood before the LORD and said, "I will entice him."

'"By what means?" the LORD asked.

²¹ '"I will go and be a deceiving spirit in the mouths of all his prophets," he said.

'"You will succeed in enticing him," said the LORD. "Go and do it."

²² 'So now the LORD has put a deceiving spirit in the mouths of these prophets of yours. The LORD has decreed disaster for you.'

²³ Then Zedekiah son of Kenaanah went up and slapped Micaiah in the face. 'Which way did the spirit from the LORD go when he went from me to speak to you?' he asked.

²⁴ Micaiah replied, 'You will find out on the day you go to hide in an inner room.'

²⁵ The king of Israel then ordered, 'Take Micaiah and send him back to Amon the ruler of the city and to Joash the king's son, ²⁶ and say, "This is what the king says: put this fellow in prison and give him nothing but bread and water until I return safely."'

²⁷ Micaiah declared, 'If you ever return safely, the LORD has not spoken through me.' Then he added, 'Mark my words, all you people!'

²⁸ So the king of Israel and Jehoshaphat king of Judah went up to Ramoth Gilead. ²⁹ The king of Israel said to Jehoshaphat, 'I will enter the battle in disguise, but you wear your royal robes.' So the king of Israel disguised himself and went into battle.

³⁰ Now the king of Aram had ordered his chariot commanders, 'Do not fight with anyone, small or great, except the king of Israel.' ³¹ When the chariot commanders

saw Jehoshaphat, they thought, 'This is the king of Israel.' So they turned to attack him, but Jehoshaphat cried out, and the LORD helped him. God drew them away from him, ³² for when the chariot commanders saw that he was not the king of Israel, they stopped pursuing him.

³³ But someone drew his bow at random and hit the king of Israel between the breastplate and the scale armour. The king told the chariot driver, 'Wheel round and get me out of the fighting. I've been wounded.' ³⁴ All day long the battle raged, and the king of Israel propped himself up in his chariot facing the Arameans until evening. Then at sunset he died.

■ PSALM 89:46-52

⁴⁶ How long, LORD? Will you hide yourself
    for ever?
  How long will your wrath burn like
    fire?
⁴⁷ Remember how fleeting is my life.
  For what futility you have created all
    humanity!
⁴⁸ Who can live and not see death,
  or who can escape the power of the
    grave?
⁴⁹ Lord, where is your former great love,
  which in your faithfulness you swore
    to David?
⁵⁰ Remember, Lord, how your servant has
    been mocked,
  how I bear in my heart the taunts of all
    the nations,
⁵¹ the taunts with which your enemies,
  LORD, have mocked,
  with which they have mocked every
    step of your anointed one.

⁵² Praise be to the LORD for ever!
    Amen and Amen.

PROVERBS 19:8-9

[8] The one who gets wisdom loves life;
     the one who cherishes understanding
          will soon prosper.

[9] A false witness will not go unpunished,
     and whoever pours out lies will perish.

ACTS 25:23–26:18

[23] The next day Agrippa and Bernice came with great pomp and entered the audience room with the high-ranking military officers and the prominent men of the city. At the command of Festus, Paul was brought in. [24] Festus said: 'King Agrippa, and all who are present with us, you see this man! The whole Jewish community has petitioned me about him in Jerusalem and here in Caesarea, shouting that he ought not to live any longer. [25] I found he had done nothing deserving of death, but because he made his appeal to the Emperor I decided to send him to Rome. [26] But I have nothing definite to write to His Majesty about him. Therefore I have brought him before all of you, and especially before you, King Agrippa, so that as a result of this investigation I may have something to write. [27] For I think it is unreasonable to send a prisoner on to Rome without specifying the charges against him.'

26 Then Agrippa said to Paul, 'You have permission to speak for yourself.'

So Paul motioned with his hand and began his defence: [2] 'King Agrippa, I consider myself fortunate to stand before you today as I make my defence against all the accusations of the Jews, [3] and especially so because you are well acquainted with all the Jewish customs and controversies. Therefore, I beg you to listen to me patiently.

[4] 'The Jewish people all know the way I have lived ever since I was a child, from the beginning of my life in my own country, and also in Jerusalem. [5] They have known me for a long time and can testify, if they are willing, that I conformed to the strictest sect of our religion, living as a Pharisee. [6] And now it is because of my hope in what God has promised our ancestors that I am on trial today. [7] This is the promise our twelve tribes are hoping to see fulfilled as they earnestly serve God day and night. King Agrippa, it is because of this hope that these Jews are accusing me. [8] Why should any of you consider it incredible that God raises the dead?

[9] 'I too was convinced that I ought to do all that was possible to oppose the name of Jesus of Nazareth. [10] And that is just what I did in Jerusalem. On the authority of the chief priests I put many of the Lord's people in prison, and when they were put to death, I cast my vote against them. [11] Many a time I went from one synagogue to another to have them punished, and I tried to force them to blaspheme. I was so obsessed with persecuting them that I even hunted them down in foreign cities.

[12] 'On one of these journeys I was going to Damascus with the authority and commission of the chief priests. [13] About noon, King Agrippa, as I was on the road, I saw a light from heaven, brighter than the sun, blazing around me and my companions. [14] We all fell to the ground, and I heard a voice saying to me in Aramaic, "Saul, Saul, why do you persecute me? It is hard for you to kick against the goads."

[15] 'Then I asked, "Who are you, Lord?"

' "I am Jesus, whom you are persecuting," the Lord replied. [16] "Now get up and stand on your feet. I have appeared to you to appoint you as a servant and as a witness of what you have seen and will see of me. [17] I will rescue you from your own people and from the Gentiles. I am sending you to them [18] to open their eyes and turn them from darkness to light, and from the power of Satan to God, so that they may receive forgiveness of sins and a place among those who are sanctified by faith in me."

No Need for Dead Reckoning

'I too was convinced that I ought to do all that was possible to oppose the name of Jesus of Nazareth.'
Acts 26:9

The place where we can see life as a whole is in the sanctuary of God, or, if you prefer, in the presence of God. There we are reminded of things we have forgotten or ignored. See how the Good News Bible translates Acts 26:9: 'I myself thought that I should do everything I could against the cause of Jesus of Nazareth.' Here you see the root of Paul's problem: 'I myself thought.' And is not that the underlying cause of many of our problems too? We say, 'I myself thought ...' instead of asking, 'What does God think?'

Sometimes sailors will attempt to establish the position of their ships by estimating the distance and direction they have travelled, rather than by astronomical observation. This is called 'dead reckoning'. It is sometimes necessary in foul weather, but it is fraught with peril. One mariner has said, 'Undue trust in the dead reckoning has produced more disastrous shipwrecks of seaworthy ships than all other causes put together.'

There are people who attempt the voyage of life by dead reckoning, but there is no need. God has charted the map for us with loving care in the Scriptures, and our plain duty is to study the chart so that we might become better acquainted with His purposes and His ways. For the better we know the Scriptures, the better we will know God. We cannot ignore the facts of history or science - they help - but if our perspective is not drawn from the Scriptures it will lead us astray. We must not rely on dead reckoning but on divine reckoning.

PRAYER

O Father, just as the art of navigation requires definite and fixed points from which to take a bearing, so does my voyage through life. I am grateful, dear Father, that in You I have all the fixed points I need. Amen.

FURTHER STUDY

Judg. 17:1-6; 21:25
• What was said of the children of Israel?
• Can the same be said of us?

August 2

■ 2 CHRONICLES 19:1–21:11

19 When Jehoshaphat king of Judah returned safely to his palace in Jerusalem, ²Jehu the seer, the son of Hanani, went out to meet him and said to the king, 'Should you help the wicked and love those who hate the LORD? Because of this, the wrath of the LORD is on you. ³There is, however, some good in you, for you have rid the land of the Asherah poles and have set your heart on seeking God.'

⁴Jehoshaphat lived in Jerusalem, and he went out again among the people from Beersheba to the hill country of Ephraim and turned them back to the LORD, the God of their ancestors. ⁵He appointed judges in the land, in each of the fortified cities of Judah. ⁶He told them, 'Consider carefully what you do, because you are not judging for mere mortals but for the LORD, who is with you whenever you give a verdict. ⁷Now let the fear of the LORD be on you. Judge carefully, for with the LORD our God there is no injustice or partiality or bribery.'

⁸In Jerusalem also, Jehoshaphat appointed some of the Levites, priests and heads of Israelite families to administer the law of the LORD and to settle disputes. And they lived in Jerusalem. ⁹He gave them these orders: 'You must serve faithfully and wholeheartedly in the fear of the LORD. ¹⁰In every case that comes before you from your people who live in the cities – whether bloodshed or other concerns of the law, commands, decrees or regulations – you are to warn them not to sin against the LORD; otherwise his wrath will come on you and your people. Do this, and you will not sin.

¹¹'Amariah the chief priest will be over you in any matter concerning the LORD, and Zebadiah son of Ishmael, the leader of the tribe of Judah, will be over you in any matter concerning the king, and the Levites will serve as officials before you. Act with courage, and may the LORD be with those who do well.'

20 After this, the Moabites and Ammonites with some of the Meunites came to wage war against Jehoshaphat.

²Some people came and told Jehoshaphat, 'A vast army is coming against you from Edom, from the other side of the Dead Sea. It is already in Hazezon Tamar' (that is, En Gedi). ³Alarmed, Jehoshaphat resolved to enquire of the LORD, and he proclaimed a fast for all Judah. ⁴The people of Judah came together to seek help from the LORD; indeed, they came from every town in Judah to seek him.

⁵Then Jehoshaphat stood up in the assembly of Judah and Jerusalem at the temple of the LORD in the front of the new courtyard ⁶and said:

'LORD, the God of our ancestors, are you not the God who is in heaven? You rule over all the kingdoms of the nations. Power and might are in your hand, and no one can withstand you. ⁷Our God, did you not drive out the inhabitants of this land before your people Israel and give it for ever to the descendants of Abraham your friend? ⁸They have lived in it and have built in it a sanctuary for your Name, saying, ⁹"If calamity comes upon us, whether the sword of judgment, or plague or famine, we will stand in your presence before this temple that bears your Name and will cry out to you in our distress, and you will hear us and save us."

¹⁰'But now here are men from Ammon, Moab and Mount Seir, whose territory you would not allow Israel to invade when they came from Egypt; so they turned away from them and did not destroy them. ¹¹See how they are repaying us by coming to drive us out of the possession you gave us as an inheritance. ¹²Our God, will you not judge them? For we have no power to face this vast army that is attacking us. We do not know what to do, but our eyes are on you.'

¹³All the men of Judah, with their wives and children and little ones, stood there before the LORD.

¹⁴Then the Spirit of the LORD came on Jahaziel son of Zechariah, the son of Benaiah, the son of Jeiel, the son of Mattaniah, a Levite and descendant of Asaph, as he stood in the assembly.

¹⁵He said: 'Listen, King Jehoshaphat and all who live in Judah and Jerusalem! This is what the LORD says to you: "Do not be afraid or discouraged because of this vast army. For the battle is not yours, but God's. ¹⁶Tomorrow march down against them. They will be climbing up by the Pass of Ziz, and you will find them at the end of the gorge in the Desert of Jeruel. ¹⁷You will not have to fight this battle. Take up your positions; stand firm and see the deliverance the LORD will give you, Judah and Jerusalem. Do not be afraid; do not be discouraged. Go out to face them tomorrow, and the LORD will be with you."'

¹⁸Jehoshaphat bowed down with his face to the ground, and all the people of Judah and Jerusalem fell down in worship before the LORD. ¹⁹Then some Levites from the Kohathites and Korahites stood up and praised the LORD, the God of Israel, with a very loud voice.

²⁰Early in the morning they left for the Desert of Tekoa. As they set out,

Jehoshaphat stood and said, 'Listen to me, Judah and people of Jerusalem! Have faith in the LORD your God and you will be upheld; have faith in his prophets and you will be successful.' ²¹After consulting the people, Jehoshaphat appointed men to sing to the LORD and to praise him for the splendour of his holiness as they went out at the head of the army, saying:

'Give thanks to the LORD,
    for his love endures for ever.'

²²As they began to sing and praise, the LORD set ambushes against the men of Ammon and Moab and Mount Seir who were invading Judah, and they were defeated. ²³The Ammonites and Moabites rose up against the men from Mount Seir to destroy and annihilate them. After they finished slaughtering the men from Seir, they helped to destroy one another.

²⁴When the men of Judah came to the place that overlooks the desert and looked towards the vast army, they saw only dead bodies lying on the ground; no one had escaped. ²⁵So Jehoshaphat and his men went to carry off their plunder, and they found among them a great amount of equipment and clothing and also articles of value – more than they could take away. There was so much plunder that it took three days to collect it. ²⁶On the fourth day they assembled in the Valley of Berakah, where they praised the LORD. This is why it is called the Valley of Berakah to this day.

²⁷Then, led by Jehoshaphat, all the men of Judah and Jerusalem returned joyfully to Jerusalem, for the LORD had given them cause to rejoice over their enemies. ²⁸They entered Jerusalem and went to the temple of the LORD with harps and lyres and trumpets.

²⁹The fear of God came on all the surrounding kingdoms when they heard how the LORD had fought against the enemies of

Israel. ³⁰ And the kingdom of Jehoshaphat was at peace, for his God had given him rest on every side.

³¹ So Jehoshaphat reigned over Judah. He was thirty-five years old when he became king of Judah, and he reigned in Jerusalem for twenty-five years. His mother's name was Azubah daughter of Shilhi. ³² He followed the ways of his father Asa and did not stray from them; he did what was right in the eyes of the LORD. ³³ The high places, however, were not removed, and the people still had not set their hearts on the God of their ancestors.

³⁴ The other events of Jehoshaphat's reign, from beginning to end, are written in the annals of Jehu son of Hanani, which are recorded in the book of the kings of Israel.

³⁵ Later, Jehoshaphat king of Judah made an alliance with Ahaziah king of Israel, whose ways were wicked. ³⁶ He agreed with him to construct a fleet of trading ships. After these were built at Ezion Geber, ³⁷ Eliezer son of Dodavahu of Mareshah prophesied against Jehoshaphat, saying, 'Because you have made an alliance with Ahaziah, the LORD will destroy what you have made.' The ships were wrecked and were not able to set sail to trade.

21 Then Jehoshaphat rested with his ancestors and was buried with them in the City of David. And Jehoram his son succeeded him as king. ² Jehoram's brothers, the sons of Jehoshaphat, were Azariah, Jehiel, Zechariah, Azariahu, Michael and Shephatiah. All these were sons of Jehoshaphat king of Israel. ³ Their father had given them many gifts of silver and gold and articles of value, as well as fortified cities in Judah, but he had given the kingdom to Jehoram because he was his firstborn son.

⁴ When Jehoram established himself firmly over his father's kingdom, he put all his brothers to the sword along with some of the officials of Israel. ⁵ Jehoram was thirty-two years old when he became king, and he reigned in Jerusalem for eight years. ⁶ He followed the ways of the kings of Israel, as the house of Ahab had done, for he married a daughter of Ahab. He did evil in the eyes of the LORD. ⁷ Nevertheless, because of the covenant the LORD had made with David, the LORD was not willing to destroy the house of David. He had promised to maintain a lamp for him and his descendants for ever.

⁸ In the time of Jehoram, Edom rebelled against Judah and set up its own king. ⁹ So Jehoram went there with his officers and all his chariots. The Edomites surrounded him and his chariot commanders, but he rose up and broke through by night. ¹⁰ To this day Edom has been in rebellion against Judah.

Libnah revolted at the same time, because Jehoram had forsaken the LORD, the God of his ancestors. ¹¹ He had also built high places on the hills of Judah and had caused the people of Jerusalem to prostitute themselves and had led Judah astray.

■ PSALM 90:1-12

¹ Lord, you have been our dwelling-place
    throughout all generations.
² Before the mountains were born
    or you brought forth the whole world,
    from everlasting to everlasting you
      are God.

³ You turn people back to dust,
    saying, 'Return to dust, you mortals.'
⁴ A thousand years in your sight
    are like a day that has just gone by,
    or like a watch in the night.
⁵ Yet you sweep people away in the sleep
      of death –
    they are like the new grass of the
      morning:
⁶ In the morning it springs up new,
    but by evening it is dry and withered.

⁷ We are consumed by your anger
    and terrified by your indignation.
⁸ You have set our iniquities before you,
    our secret sins in the light of your
        presence.
⁹ All our days pass away under your wrath;
    we finish our years with a moan.
¹⁰ Our days may come to seventy years,
    or eighty, if our strength endures;
    yet the best of them are but trouble and
        sorrow,
    for they quickly pass, and we fly away.
¹¹ If only we knew the power of your anger!
    Your wrath is as great as the fear that
        is your due.
¹² Teach us to number our days,
    that we may gain a heart of wisdom.

▬ PROVERBS 19:10-12

¹⁰ It is not fitting for a fool to live in
        luxury –
    how much worse for a slave to rule
        over princes!

¹¹ A person's wisdom yields patience;
    it is to one's glory to overlook an
        offence.

¹² A king's rage is like the roar of a lion,
    but his favour is like dew on the grass.

▬ ACTS 26:19–27:8

¹⁹ 'So then, King Agrippa, I was not disobedient to the vision from heaven. ²⁰ First
to those in Damascus, then to those in Jerusalem and in all Judea, and then to the
Gentiles, I preached that they should repent
and turn to God and demonstrate their repentance by their deeds. ²¹ That is why some
Jews seized me in the temple courts and
tried to kill me. ²² But God has helped me
to this very day; so I stand here and testify

to small and great alike. I am saying nothing beyond what the prophets and Moses
said would happen – ²³ that the Messiah
would suffer and, as the first to rise from the
dead, would bring the message of light to
his own people and to the Gentiles.'
²⁴ At this point Festus interrupted Paul's
defence. 'You are out of your mind, Paul!' he
shouted. 'Your great learning is driving you
insane.'
²⁵ 'I am not insane, most excellent Festus,' Paul replied. 'What I am saying is true
and reasonable. ²⁶ The king is familiar with
these things, and I can speak freely to him.
I am convinced that none of this has escaped his notice, because it was not done in
a corner. ²⁷ King Agrippa, do you believe the
prophets? I know you do.'
²⁸ Then Agrippa said to Paul, 'Do you
think that in such a short time you can
persuade me to be a Christian?'
²⁹ Paul replied, 'Short time or long – I
pray to God that not only you but all who
are listening to me today may become what
I am, except for these chains.'
³⁰ The king rose, and with him the governor and Bernice and those sitting with
them. ³¹ After they left the room, they began saying to one another, 'This man is
not doing anything that deserves death or
imprisonment.'
³² Agrippa said to Festus, 'This man
could have been set free if he had not
appealed to Caesar.'

27 When it was decided that we would
sail for Italy, Paul and some other
prisoners were handed over to a centurion
named Julius, who belonged to the Imperial
Regiment. ² We boarded a ship from Adra-
myttium about to sail for ports along the
coast of the province of Asia, and we put
out to sea. Aristarchus, a Macedonian from
Thessalonica, was with us.
³ The next day we landed at Sidon; and
Julius, in kindness to Paul, allowed him to
go to his friends so they might provide for

his needs. ⁴From there we put out to sea again and passed to the lee of Cyprus because the winds were against us. ⁵When we had sailed across the open sea off the coast of Cilicia and Pamphylia, we landed at Myra in Lycia. ⁶There the centurion found an Alexandrian ship sailing for Italy and put us on board. ⁷We made slow headway for many days and had difficulty arriving off Cnidus. When the wind did not allow us to hold our course, we sailed to the lee of Crete, opposite Salmone. ⁸We moved along the coast with difficulty and came to a place called Fair Havens, near the town of Lasea.

Not a Private Fight

'"Do not be afraid or discouraged ... For the battle is not yours, but God's'". **2 Chronicles 20:15**

The spiritual application of the helmet of salvation is not so much the enjoyment of our present salvation (though it includes that) as it is the assurance that a sure salvation is coming - and is even now at work.

This is what we need to know if we are to prevent the Devil from bringing us into a state of mental distress - not merely that things will finally end right, but that God's plan is being worked out now. 'History,' writes Ray Stedman, an American Bible teacher, 'is not a meaningless jumble but a controlled pattern, and the Lord Jesus Christ is the one who is directing these events.'

The attack of Satan on the mind proceeds differently. He says to us: 'Just look around you at the state of the world. God seems powerless to put things right. He has given lots of promises that things will one day get better, but none has come to pass. Hadn't you better give up this foolish idea that it's all going to work out right?'

If you were to let your mind dwell on that kind of argument, you would soon find yourself in distress. The answer is to put on the helmet, the hope of salvation. You must remind yourself that things are not as they appear. The battle is not ours, but the Lord's. We may be individual soldiers fighting in the army of God, but the ultimate cause is sure and the end is certain. We need not be unduly troubled by what is happening in the world, for our commander is not just winning - He has already won!

PRAYER

Lord Jesus, I am grateful that the Cross is the guarantee that neither sin nor Satan will ever defeat You. Your victory at Calvary has settled forever the question of who has the final word in the universe. I am so deeply, deeply thankful. Amen.

FURTHER STUDY

Luke 21:10-28; John 14:1-4; 16:33
• How did Jesus describe the world?
• What did He say to His disciples?

August 3

■ 2 Chronicles 21:12–24:16

¹²Jehoram received a letter from Elijah the prophet, which said:

'This is what the LORD, the God of your father David, says: "You have not followed the ways of your father Jehoshaphat or of Asa king of Judah. ¹³But you have followed the ways of the kings of Israel, and you have led Judah and the people of Jerusalem to prostitute themselves, just as the house of Ahab did. You have also murdered your own brothers, members of your own family, men who were better than you. ¹⁴So now the LORD is about to strike your people, your sons, your wives and everything that is yours, with a heavy blow. ¹⁵You yourself will be very ill with a lingering disease of the bowels, until the disease causes your bowels to come out."'

¹⁶The LORD aroused against Jehoram the hostility of the Philistines and of the Arabs who lived near the Cushites. ¹⁷They attacked Judah, invaded it and carried off all the goods found in the king's palace, together with his sons and wives. Not a son was left to him except Ahaziah, the youngest.

¹⁸After all this, the LORD afflicted Jehoram with an incurable disease of the bowels. ¹⁹In the course of time, at the end of the second year, his bowels came out because of the disease, and he died in great pain. His people made no funeral fire in his honour, as they had for his predecessors.

²⁰Jehoram was thirty-two years old when he became king, and he reigned in Jerusalem for eight years. He passed away, to no one's regret, and was buried in the City of David, but not in the tombs of the kings.

22 The people of Jerusalem made Ahaziah, Jehoram's youngest son, king in his place, since the raiders, who came with the Arabs into the camp, had killed all the older sons. So Ahaziah son of Jehoram king of Judah began to reign.

²Ahaziah was twenty-two years old when he became king, and he reigned in Jerusalem for one year. His mother's name was Athaliah, a granddaughter of Omri.

³He too followed the ways of the house of Ahab, for his mother encouraged him to act wickedly. ⁴He did evil in the eyes of the LORD, as the house of Ahab had done, for after his father's death they became his advisors, to his undoing. ⁵He also followed their counsel when he went with Joram son of Ahab king of Israel to wage war against Hazael king of Aram at Ramoth Gilead. The Arameans wounded Joram; ⁶so he returned to Jezreel to recover from the wounds they had inflicted on him at Ramoth in his battle with Hazael king of Aram.

Then Ahaziah son of Jehoram king of Judah went down to Jezreel to see Joram son of Ahab because he had been wounded.

⁷Through Ahaziah's visit to Joram, God brought about Ahaziah's downfall. When Ahaziah arrived, he went out with Joram to meet Jehu son of Nimshi, whom the LORD had anointed to destroy the house of Ahab. ⁸While Jehu was executing judgment on the house of Ahab, he found the officials of Judah and the sons of Ahaziah's relatives, who had been attending Ahaziah, and he killed them. ⁹He then went in search of Ahaziah, and his men captured him while he was hiding in Samaria. He was brought to Jehu and put to death. They

buried him, for they said, 'He was a son of Jehoshaphat, who sought the LORD with all his heart.' So there was no one in the house of Ahaziah powerful enough to retain the kingdom.

¹⁰When Athaliah the mother of Ahaziah saw that her son was dead, she proceeded to destroy the whole royal family of the house of Judah. ¹¹But Jehosheba, the daughter of King Jehoram, took Joash son of Ahaziah and stole him away from among the royal princes who were about to be murdered and put him and his nurse in a bedroom. Because Jehosheba, the daughter of King Jehoram and wife of the priest Jehoiada, was Ahaziah's sister, she hid the child from Athaliah so that she could not kill him. ¹²He remained hidden with them at the temple of God for six years while Athaliah ruled the land.

23 In the seventh year Jehoiada showed his strength. He made a covenant with the commanders of units of a hundred: Azariah son of Jeroham, Ishmael son of Jehohanan, Azariah son of Obed, Maaseiah son of Adaiah, and Elishaphat son of Zikri. ²They went throughout Judah and gathered the Levites and the heads of Israelite families from all the towns. When they came to Jerusalem, ³the whole assembly made a covenant with the king at the temple of God.

Jehoiada said to them, 'The king's son shall reign, as the LORD promised concerning the descendants of David. ⁴Now this is what you are to do: a third of you priests and Levites who are going on duty on the Sabbath are to keep watch at the doors, ⁵a third of you at the royal palace and a third at the Foundation Gate, and all the others are to be in the courtyards of the temple of the LORD. ⁶No one is to enter the temple of the LORD except the priests and Levites on duty; they may enter because they are consecrated, but all the others are to observe the LORD's command not to enter. ⁷The Levites are to

station themselves round the king, each with weapon in hand. Anyone who enters the temple is to be put to death. Stay close to the king wherever he goes.'

⁸The Levites and all the men of Judah did just as Jehoiada the priest ordered. Each one took his men – those who were going on duty on the Sabbath and those who were going off duty – for Jehoiada the priest had not released any of the divisions. ⁹Then he gave the commanders of units of a hundred the spears and the large and small shields that had belonged to King David and that were in the temple of God. ¹⁰He stationed all the men, each with his weapon in his hand, round the king – near the altar and the temple, from the south side to the north side of the temple.

¹¹Jehoiada and his sons brought out the king's son and put the crown on him; they presented him with a copy of the covenant and proclaimed him king. They anointed him and shouted, 'Long live the king!'

¹²When Athaliah heard the noise of the people running and cheering the king, she went to them at the temple of the LORD. ¹³She looked, and there was the king, standing by his pillar at the entrance. The officers and the trumpeters were beside the king, and all the people of the land were rejoicing and blowing trumpets, and musicians with their instruments were leading the praises. Then Athaliah tore her robes and shouted, 'Treason! Treason!'

¹⁴Jehoiada the priest sent out the commanders of units of a hundred, who were in charge of the troops, and said to them: 'Bring her out between the ranks and put to the sword anyone who follows her.' For the priest had said, 'Do not put her to death at the temple of the LORD.' ¹⁵So they seized her as she reached the entrance of the Horse Gate on the palace grounds, and there they put her to death.

¹⁶Jehoiada then made a covenant that he, the people and the king would be the LORD's

people. **17** All the people went to the temple of Baal and tore it down. They smashed the altars and idols and killed Mattan the priest of Baal in front of the altars.

18 Then Jehoiada placed the oversight of the temple of the LORD in the hands of the Levitical priests, to whom David had made assignments in the temple, to present the burnt offerings of the LORD as written in the Law of Moses, with rejoicing and singing, as David had ordered. **19** He also stationed gatekeepers at the gates of the LORD's temple so that no one who was in any way unclean might enter.

20 He took with him the commanders of hundreds, the nobles, the rulers of the people and all the people of the land and brought the king down from the temple of the LORD. They went into the palace through the Upper Gate and seated the king on the royal throne. **21** All the people of the land rejoiced, and the city was calm, because Athaliah had been slain with the sword.

24 Joash was seven years old when he became king, and he reigned in Jerusalem for forty years. His mother's name was Zibiah; she was from Beersheba. **2** Joash did what was right in the eyes of the LORD all the years of Jehoiada the priest. **3** Jehoiada chose two wives for him, and he had sons and daughters.

4 Some time later Joash decided to restore the temple of the LORD. **5** He called together the priests and Levites and said to them, 'Go to the towns of Judah and collect the money due annually from all Israel, to repair the temple of your God. Do it now.' But the Levites did not act at once.

6 Therefore the king summoned Jehoiada the chief priest and said to him, 'Why haven't you required the Levites to bring in from Judah and Jerusalem the tax imposed by Moses the servant of the LORD and by the assembly of Israel for the tent of the covenant law?'

7 Now the sons of that wicked woman Athaliah had broken into the temple of God and had used even its sacred objects for the Baals.

8 At the king's command, a chest was made and placed outside, at the gate of the temple of the LORD. **9** A proclamation was then issued in Judah and Jerusalem that they should bring to the LORD the tax that Moses the servant of God had required of Israel in the wilderness. **10** All the officials and all the people brought their contributions gladly, dropping them into the chest until it was full. **11** Whenever the chest was brought in by the Levites to the king's officials and they saw that there was a large amount of money, the royal secretary and the officer of the chief priest would come and empty the chest and carry it back to its place. They did this regularly and collected a great amount of money. **12** The king and Jehoiada gave it to those who carried out the work required for the temple of the LORD. They hired masons and carpenters to restore the LORD's temple, and also workers in iron and bronze to repair the temple.

13 The men in charge of the work were diligent, and the repairs progressed under them. They rebuilt the temple of God according to its original design and reinforced it. **14** When they had finished, they brought the rest of the money to the king and Jehoiada, and with it were made articles for the LORD's temple: articles for the service and for the burnt offerings, and also dishes and other objects of gold and silver. As long as Jehoiada lived, burnt offerings were presented continually in the temple of the LORD.

15 Now Jehoiada was old and full of years, and he died at the age of a hundred and thirty. **16** He was buried with the kings in the City of David, because of the good he had done in Israel for God and his temple.

▬ PSALM 90:13-17

¹³ Relent, LORD! How long will it be?
    Have compassion on your servants.
¹⁴ Satisfy us in the morning with your
        unfailing love,
    that we may sing for joy and be glad all
        our days.
¹⁵ Make us glad for as many days as you
        have afflicted us,
    for as many years as we have seen
        trouble.
¹⁶ May your deeds be shown to your
        servants,
    your splendour to their children.

¹⁷ May the favour of the Lord our God rest
        on us;
    establish the work of our hands for
        us –
    yes, establish the work of our hands.

▬ PROVERBS 19:13-14

¹³ A foolish child is a father's ruin,
    and a quarrelsome wife is like
        the constant dripping of a leaky roof.

¹⁴ Houses and wealth are inherited from
        parents,
    but a prudent wife is from the LORD.

▬ ACTS 27:9-29

⁹ Much time had been lost, and sailing had already become dangerous because by now it was after the Day of Atonement. So Paul warned them, ¹⁰ 'Men, I can see that our voyage is going to be disastrous and bring great loss to ship and cargo, and to our own lives also.' ¹¹ But the centurion, instead of listening to what Paul said, followed the advice of the pilot and of the owner of the ship. ¹² Since the harbour was unsuitable to winter in, the majority decided that we should sail on, hoping to reach Phoenix and winter there. This was a harbour in Crete, facing both south-west and north-west.

¹³ When a gentle south wind began to blow, they saw their opportunity; so they weighed anchor and sailed along the shore of Crete. ¹⁴ Before very long, a wind of hurricane force, called the 'North-Easter', swept down from the island. ¹⁵ The ship was caught by the storm and could not head into the wind; so we gave way to it and were driven along. ¹⁶ As we passed to the lee of a small island called Cauda, we were hardly able to make the lifeboat secure, ¹⁷ so the men hoisted it aboard. Then they passed ropes under the ship itself to hold it together. Because they were afraid they would run aground on the sand-bars of Syrtis, they lowered the sea anchor and let the ship be driven along. ¹⁸ We took such a violent battering from the storm that the next day they began to throw the cargo overboard. ¹⁹ On the third day, they threw the ship's tackle overboard with their own hands. ²⁰ When neither sun nor stars appeared for many days and the storm continued raging, we finally gave up all hope of being saved.

²¹ After they had gone a long time without food, Paul stood up before them and said: 'Men, you should have taken my advice not to sail from Crete; then you would have spared yourselves this damage and loss. ²² But now I urge you to keep up your courage, because not one of you will be lost; only the ship will be destroyed. ²³ Last night an angel of the God to whom I belong and whom I serve stood beside me ²⁴ and said, "Do not be afraid, Paul. You must stand trial before Caesar; and God has graciously given you the lives of all who sail with you." ²⁵ So keep up your courage, men, for I have faith in God that it will happen just as he told me. ²⁶ Nevertheless, we must run aground on some island.'

²⁷ On the fourteenth night we were still

being driven across the Adriatic Sea, when about midnight the sailors sensed they were approaching land. ²⁸They took soundings and found that the water was forty metres deep. A short time later they took soundings again and found it was thirty metres deep. ²⁹Fearing that we would be dashed against the rocks, they dropped four anchors from the stern and prayed for daylight.

Joy - More Than Pleasure

'Satisfy us in the morning with your unfailing love, that we may sing for joy and be glad all our days.'
Psalm 90:14

One of the reasons why so many Christians do not experience the delights of spiritual joy is that they do not expect to. A woman who came into the experience of Christian conversion said, 'Strange, but I never associated joy with God before.' How sad that many do not expect their faith to make them basically and fully joyful now. They think that joy is reserved for the hereafter. Our Lord pointed out to the disciples that it was for the present.

We can better understand this supernatural joy if we distinguish it from the pleasures of life with which it is sometimes confused. Spiritual or supernatural joy is quite different from pleasure or happiness. A worldling can experience pleasure and happiness, but he cannot experience supernatural joy. Indeed, worldly people often pride themselves in knowing how to experience pleasure.

Yet pleasure and Christian joy cannot be equated. Look with me at some of the differences. Pleasure depends on circumstances. It requires a measure of health and wealth. It demands that the life conditions be kindly, and thus it can be stolen from us by things like lack of money - or even a toothache. Christian joy is completely independent of circumstances. It is there in the believer even when 'strength and health and friends' are gone; when circumstances are not only unkind but savage. Out of all the miracles I have witnessed in my life, none is more wonderful than the miracle of seeing Christ's exuberant joy burst forth in those who are caught up in pain or persecution. The springs of Christian joy are deep within and can exist, no matter what the circumstances.

PRAYER

O Father, how can I thank You enough for imparting into my sadness Your unconquerable gladness? No matter what happens - all is well with my soul. I am so grateful. Amen.

FURTHER STUDY

John 16:17-33; Acts 5:12-42; 15:23-25; 2 Cor. 6:10
• How did the apostles respond to persecution?
• How did Paul express it?

August 4

▬ 2 CHRONICLES
24:17–26:23

¹⁷ After the death of Jehoiada, the officials of Judah came and paid homage to the king, and he listened to them. ¹⁸ They abandoned the temple of the LORD, the God of their ancestors, and worshipped Asherah poles and idols. Because of their guilt, God's anger came on Judah and Jerusalem. ¹⁹ Although the LORD sent prophets to the people to bring them back to him, and though they testified against them, they would not listen.

²⁰ Then the Spirit of God came on Zechariah son of Jehoiada the priest. He stood before the people and said, 'This is what God says: "Why do you disobey the LORD's commands? You will not prosper. Because you have forsaken the LORD, he has forsaken you."'

²¹ But they plotted against him, and by order of the king they stoned him to death in the courtyard of the LORD's temple. ²² King Joash did not remember the kindness Zechariah's father Jehoiada had shown him but killed his son, who said as he lay dying, 'May the LORD see this and call you to account.'

²³ At the turn of the year, the army of Aram marched against Joash; it invaded Judah and Jerusalem and killed all the leaders of the people. They sent all the plunder to their king in Damascus. ²⁴ Although the Aramean army had come with only a few men, the LORD delivered into their hands a much larger army. Because Judah had forsaken the LORD, the God of their ancestors, judgment was executed on Joash. ²⁵ When the Arameans withdrew, they left Joash severely wounded. His officials conspired against him for murdering the son of Jehoiada the priest, and they killed him in his bed. So he

died and was buried in the City of David, but not in the tombs of the kings.

²⁶ Those who conspired against him were Zabad, son of Shimeath an Ammonite woman, and Jehozabad, son of Shimrith a Moabite woman. ²⁷ The account of his sons, the many prophecies about him, and the record of the restoration of the temple of God are written in the annotations on the book of the kings. And Amaziah his son succeeded him as king.

25 Amaziah was twenty-five years old when he became king, and he reigned in Jerusalem for twenty-nine years. His mother's name was Jehoaddan; she was from Jerusalem. ² He did what was right in the eyes of the LORD, but not wholeheartedly. ³ After the kingdom was firmly in his control, he executed the officials who had murdered his father the king. ⁴ Yet he did not put their children to death, but acted in accordance with what is written in the Law, in the Book of Moses, where the LORD commanded: 'Parents shall not be put to death for their children, nor children be put to death for their parents; each will die for their own sin.'

⁵ Amaziah called the people of Judah together and assigned them according to their families to commanders of thousands and commanders of hundreds for all Judah and Benjamin. He then mustered those twenty years old or more and found that there were three hundred thousand men fit for military service, able to handle the spear and shield. ⁶ He also hired a hundred thousand fighting men from Israel for a hundred talents of silver.

⁷ But a man of God came to him and said, 'Your Majesty, these troops from Israel must not march with you, for the LORD is not

with Israel – not with any of the people of Ephraim. ⁸Even if you go and fight courageously in battle, God will overthrow you before the enemy, for God has the power to help or to overthrow.'

⁹Amaziah asked the man of God, 'But what about the hundred talents I paid for these Israelite troops?'

The man of God replied, 'The LORD can give you much more than that.'

¹⁰So Amaziah dismissed the troops who had come to him from Ephraim and sent them home. They were furious with Judah and left for home in a great rage.

¹¹Amaziah then marshalled his strength and led his army to the Valley of Salt, where he killed ten thousand men of Seir. ¹²The army of Judah also captured ten thousand men alive, took them to the top of a cliff and threw them down so that all were dashed to pieces.

¹³Meanwhile the troops that Amaziah had sent back and had not allowed to take part in the war raided towns belonging to Judah from Samaria to Beth Horon. They killed three thousand people and carried off great quantities of plunder.

¹⁴When Amaziah returned from slaughtering the Edomites, he brought back the gods of the people of Seir. He set them up as his own gods, bowed down to them and burned sacrifices to them. ¹⁵The anger of the LORD burned against Amaziah, and he sent a prophet to him, who said, 'Why do you consult this people's gods, which could not save their own people from your hand?'

¹⁶While he was still speaking, the king said to him, 'Have we appointed you an advisor to the king? Stop! Why be struck down?'

So the prophet stopped but said, 'I know that God has determined to destroy you, because you have done this and have not listened to my counsel.'

¹⁷After Amaziah king of Judah consulted his advisors, he sent this challenge to Jehoash son of Jehoahaz, the son of Jehu, king of Israel: 'Come, let us face each other in battle.'

¹⁸But Jehoash king of Israel replied to Amaziah king of Judah, 'A thistle in Lebanon sent a message to a cedar in Lebanon, "Give your daughter to my son in marriage." Then a wild beast in Lebanon came along and trampled the thistle underfoot. ¹⁹You say to yourself that you have defeated Edom, and now you are arrogant and proud. But stay at home! Why ask for trouble and cause your own downfall and that of Judah also?'

²⁰Amaziah, however, would not listen, for God so worked that he might deliver them into the hands of Jehoash, because they sought the gods of Edom. ²¹So Jehoash king of Israel attacked. He and Amaziah king of Judah faced each other at Beth Shemesh in Judah. ²²Judah was routed by Israel, and every man fled to his home. ²³Jehoash king of Israel captured Amaziah king of Judah, the son of Joash, the son of Ahaziah, at Beth Shemesh. Then Jehoash brought him to Jerusalem and broke down the wall of Jerusalem from the Ephraim Gate to the Corner Gate – a section about four hundred cubits long. ²⁴He took all the gold and silver and all the articles found in the temple of God that had been in the care of Obed-Edom, together with the palace treasures and the hostages, and returned to Samaria.

²⁵Amaziah son of Joash king of Judah lived for fifteen years after the death of Jehoash son of Jehoahaz king of Israel. ²⁶As for the other events of Amaziah's reign, from beginning to end, are they not written in the book of the kings of Judah and Israel? ²⁷From the time that Amaziah turned away from following the LORD, they conspired against him in Jerusalem and he fled to Lachish, but they sent men after him to Lachish and killed him there. ²⁸He was brought back by horse and was buried with his ancestors in the City of Judah.

26 Then all the people of Judah took Uzziah, who was sixteen years old, and made him king in place of his father Amaziah. ²He was the one who rebuilt Elath and restored it to Judah after Amaziah rested with his ancestors.

³Uzziah was sixteen years old when he became king, and he reigned in Jerusalem for fifty-two years. His mother's name was Jekoliah; she was from Jerusalem. ⁴He did what was right in the eyes of the LORD, just as his father Amaziah had done. ⁵He sought God during the days of Zechariah, who instructed him in the fear of God. As long as he sought the LORD, God gave him success.

⁶He went to war against the Philistines and broke down the walls of Gath, Jabneh and Ashdod. He then rebuilt towns near Ashdod and elsewhere among the Philistines. ⁷God helped him against the Philistines and against the Arabs who lived in Gur Baal and against the Meunites. ⁸The Ammonites brought tribute to Uzziah, and his fame spread as far as the border of Egypt, because he had become very powerful.

⁹Uzziah built towers in Jerusalem at the Corner Gate, at the Valley Gate and at the angle of the wall, and he fortified them. ¹⁰He also built towers in the wilderness and dug many cisterns, because he had much livestock in the foothills and in the plain. He had people working his fields and vineyards in the hills and in the fertile lands, for he loved the soil.

¹¹Uzziah had a well-trained army, ready to go out by divisions according to their numbers as mustered by Jeiel the secretary and Maaseiah the officer under the direction of Hananiah, one of the royal officials. ¹²The total number of family leaders over the fighting men was 2,600. ¹³Under their command was an army of 307,500 men trained for war, a powerful force to support the king against his enemies. ¹⁴Uzziah provided shields, spears, helmets, coats of armour, bows and slingstones for the entire army. ¹⁵In Jerusalem he made devices invented for use on the towers and on the corner defences so that soldiers could shoot arrows and hurl large stones from the walls. His fame spread far and wide, for he was greatly helped until he became powerful.

¹⁶But after Uzziah became powerful, his pride led to his downfall. He was unfaithful to the LORD his God, and entered the temple of the LORD to burn incense on the altar of incense. ¹⁷Azariah the priest with eighty other courageous priests of the LORD followed him in. ¹⁸They confronted King Uzziah and said, 'It is not right for you, Uzziah, to burn incense to the LORD. That is for the priests, the descendants of Aaron, who have been consecrated to burn incense. Leave the sanctuary, for you have been unfaithful; and you will not be honoured by the LORD God.'

¹⁹Uzziah, who had a censer in his hand ready to burn incense, became angry. While he was raging at the priests in their presence before the incense altar in the LORD's temple, leprosy broke out on his forehead. ²⁰When Azariah the chief priest and all the other priests looked at him, they saw that he had leprosy on his forehead, so they hurried him out. Indeed, he himself was eager to leave, because the LORD had afflicted him.

²¹King Uzziah had leprosy until the day he died. He lived in a separate house – leprous, and excluded from the temple of the LORD. Jotham his son had charge of the palace and governed the people of the land.

²²The other events of Uzziah's reign, from beginning to end, are recorded by the prophet Isaiah son of Amoz. ²³Uzziah rested with his ancestors and was buried near them in a cemetery that belonged to the kings, for people said, 'He had leprosy.' And Jotham his son succeeded him as king.

PSALM 91:1-8

¹ Whoever dwells in the shelter of the
   Most High
   will rest in the shadow of the
   Almighty.
² I will say of the LORD, 'He is my refuge
   and my fortress,
   my God, in whom I trust.'

³ Surely he will save you
   from the fowler's snare
   and from the deadly pestilence.
⁴ He will cover you with his feathers,
   and under his wings you will find
   refuge;
   his faithfulness will be your shield
   and rampart.
⁵ You will not fear the terror of night,
   nor the arrow that flies by day,
⁶ nor the pestilence that stalks in the
   darkness,
   nor the plague that destroys at
   midday.
⁷ A thousand may fall at your side,
   ten thousand at your right hand,
   but it will not come near you.
⁸ You will only observe with your eyes
   and see the punishment of the wicked.

PROVERBS 19:15-16

¹⁵ Laziness brings on deep sleep,
   and the shiftless go hungry.

¹⁶ Whoever keeps commandments keeps
   their life,
   but whoever shows contempt for their
   ways will die.

ACTS 27:30–28:10

³⁰ In an attempt to escape from the ship, the
sailors let the lifeboat down into the sea,
pretending they were going to lower some
anchors from the bow. ³¹ Then Paul said
to the centurion and the soldiers, 'Unless
these men stay with the ship, you cannot be
saved.' ³² So the soldiers cut the ropes that
held the lifeboat and let it drift away.

³³ Just before dawn Paul urged them all
to eat. 'For the last fourteen days,' he said,
'you have been in constant suspense and
have gone without food – you haven't eaten
anything. ³⁴ Now I urge you to take some
food. You need it to survive. Not one of you
will lose a single hair from his head.' ³⁵ After
he said this, he took some bread and gave
thanks to God in front of them all. Then
he broke it and began to eat. ³⁶ They were
all encouraged and ate some food themselves. ³⁷ Altogether there were 276 of us
on board. ³⁸ When they had eaten as much
as they wanted, they lightened the ship by
throwing the grain into the sea.

³⁹ When daylight came, they did not recognise the land, but they saw a bay with a
sandy beach, where they decided to run the
ship aground if they could. ⁴⁰ Cutting loose
the anchors, they left them in the sea and at
the same time untied the ropes that held the
rudders. Then they hoisted the foresail to
the wind and made for the beach. ⁴¹ But the
ship struck a sand-bar and ran aground.
The bow stuck fast and would not move,
and the stern was broken to pieces by the
pounding of the surf.

⁴² The soldiers planned to kill the prisoners to prevent any of them from swimming
away and escaping. ⁴³ But the centurion
wanted to spare Paul's life and kept them
from carrying out their plan. He ordered
those who could swim to jump overboard
first and get to land. ⁴⁴ The rest were to get
there on planks or on other pieces of the ship.
In this way everyone reached land safely.

28 Once safely on shore, we found out
that the island was called Malta.
² The islanders showed us unusual kindness. They built a fire and welcomed us all

because it was raining and cold. ³ Paul gathered a pile of brushwood and, as he put it on the fire, a viper, driven out by the heat, fastened itself on his hand. ⁴ When the islanders saw the snake hanging from his hand, they said to each other, 'This man must be a murderer; for though he escaped from the sea, the goddess Justice has not allowed him to live.' ⁵ But Paul shook the snake off into the fire and suffered no ill effects. ⁶ The people expected him to swell up or suddenly fall dead; but after waiting a long time and seeing nothing unusual happen to him, they

changed their minds and said he was a god.

⁷ There was an estate near by that belonged to Publius, the chief official of the island. He welcomed us to his home and showed us generous hospitality for three days. ⁸ His father was ill in bed, suffering from fever and dysentery. Paul went in to see him and, after prayer, placed his hands on him and healed him. ⁹ When this had happened, the rest of those on the island who were ill came and were cured. ¹⁰ They honoured us in many ways; and when we were ready to sail, they furnished us with the supplies we needed.

Inner Cohesion

'He did what was right in the eyes of the LORD, but not wholeheartedly.' **2 Chronicles 25:2**

One scriptural example that illustrates the need for a proper correlation between heart and mind is the Old Testament character, Amaziah. Second Chronicles 25:2 tells us: 'He did what was right in the eyes of the LORD, but not wholeheartedly.' His mind gave itself to doing right in the sight of the Lord, but his heart did not support his actions.

This lack of coordination proved to be his undoing: 'When Amaziah returned from slaughtering the Edomites, he brought back the gods of the people of Seir. He set them up as his own gods, bowed down to them and burned sacrifices to them' (25:14). Now look at how the life of Amaziah ends: 'From the time that Amaziah turned away from following the LORD, they conspired against him in Jerusalem ... they sent men after him to Lachish and killed him there' (25:27). Notice the steps:

(1) He was outwardly correct but inwardly uncoordinated.

(2) His inner disunity showed itself in outer disloyalty.

(3) This disunity resulted in his failure and death.

At the beginning, Amaziah does not appear to be a particularly bad individual – he just failed to be wholehearted in his commitment. He did all the right things outwardly, but his heart was not in them – hence, his spiritual ruin. We could say he missed his step by inches, but his fall was one of the worst ever recorded. If we are not held together by a single-minded devotion, our spiritual life can quickly go to pieces. Commitment to God demands cohesion – the cohesion of heart and mind.

August 5

▬ 2 CHRONICLES 27:1–29:17

27 Jotham was twenty-five years old when he became king, and he reigned in Jerusalem for sixteen years. His mother's name was Jerusha daughter of Zadok. ²He did what was right in the eyes of the LORD, just as his father Uzziah had done, but unlike him he did not enter the temple of the LORD. The people, however, continued their corrupt practices. ³Jotham rebuilt the Upper Gate of the temple of the LORD and did extensive work on the wall at the hill of Ophel. ⁴He built towns in the hill country of Judah and forts and towers in the wooded areas.

⁵Jotham waged war against the king of the Ammonites and conquered them. That year the Ammonites paid him a hundred talents of silver, ten thousand cors of wheat and ten thousand cors of barley. The Ammonites brought him the same amount also in the second and third years.

⁶Jotham grew powerful because he walked steadfastly before the LORD his God. ⁷The other events in Jotham's reign, including all his wars and the other things he did, are written in the book of the kings of Israel and Judah. ⁸He was twenty-five years old when he became king, and he reigned in Jerusalem for sixteen years. ⁹Jotham rested with his ancestors and was buried in the City of David. And Ahaz his son succeeded him as king.

28 Ahaz was twenty years old when he became king, and he reigned in Jerusalem for sixteen years. Unlike David his father, he did not do what was right in the eyes of the LORD. ²He followed the ways of the kings of Israel and also made idols for worshipping the Baals. ³He burned sacrifices in the Valley of Ben Hinnom and sacrificed his children in the fire, engaging in the detestable practices of the nations that the LORD had driven out before the Israelites. ⁴He offered sacrifices and burned incense at the high places, on the hilltops and under every spreading tree.

⁵Therefore the LORD his God delivered him into the hands of the king of Aram. The Arameans defeated him and took many of his people as prisoners and brought them to Damascus.

He was also given into the hands of the king of Israel, who inflicted heavy casualties on him. ⁶In one day Pekah son of Remaliah killed a hundred and twenty thousand soldiers in Judah – because Judah had forsaken the LORD, the God of their ancestors. ⁷Zikri, an Ephraimite warrior, killed Maaseiah the king's son, Azrikam the officer in charge of the palace, and Elkanah, second to the king. ⁸The men of Israel took captive from their fellow Israelites who were from Judah two hundred thousand wives, sons and daughters. They also took a great deal of plunder, which they carried back to Samaria.

⁹ But a prophet of the LORD named Oded was there, and he went out to meet the army when it returned to Samaria. He said to them, 'Because the LORD, the God of your ancestors, was angry with Judah, he gave them into your hand. But you have slaughtered them in a rage that reaches to heaven. ¹⁰ And now you intend to make the men and women of Judah and Jerusalem your slaves. But aren't you also guilty of sins against the LORD your God? ¹¹ Now listen to me! Send back your fellow Israelites that you have taken as prisoners, for the LORD's fierce anger rests on you.'

¹² Then some of the leaders in Ephraim – Azariah son of Jehohanan, Berekiah son of Meshillemoth, Jehizkiah son of Shallum, and Amasa son of Hadlai – confronted those who were arriving from the war. ¹³ 'You must not bring those prisoners here,' they said, 'or we will be guilty before the LORD. Do you intend to add to our sin and guilt? For our guilt is already great, and his fierce anger rests on Israel.'

¹⁴ So the soldiers gave up the prisoners and plunder in the presence of the officials and all the assembly. ¹⁵ The men designated by name took the prisoners, and from the plunder they clothed all who were naked. They provided them with clothes and sandals, food and drink, and healing balm. All those who were weak they put on donkeys. So they took them back to their fellow Israelites at Jericho, the City of Palms, and returned to Samaria.

¹⁶ At that time King Ahaz sent to the kings of Assyria for help. ¹⁷ The Edomites had again come and attacked Judah and carried away prisoners, ¹⁸ while the Philistines had raided towns in the foothills and in the Negev of Judah. They captured and occupied Beth Shemesh, Aijalon and Gederoth, as well as Soko, Timnah and Gimzo, with their surrounding villages. ¹⁹ The LORD had humbled Judah because of Ahaz king of Israel, for he had promoted wickedness in Judah and had been most unfaithful to the LORD. ²⁰ Tiglath-Pileser king of Assyria came to him, but gave him trouble instead of help. ²¹ Ahaz took some of the things from the temple of the LORD and from the royal palace and from the officials and presented them to the king of Assyria, but that did not help him.

²² In his time of trouble King Ahaz became even more unfaithful to the LORD. ²³ He offered sacrifices to the gods of Damascus, who had defeated him; for he thought, 'Since the gods of the kings of Aram have helped them, I will sacrifice to them so that they will help me.' But they were his downfall and the downfall of all Israel.

²⁴ Ahaz gathered together the furnishings from the temple of God and cut them in pieces. He shut the doors of the LORD's temple and set up altars at every street corner in Jerusalem. ²⁵ In every town in Judah he built high places to burn sacrifices to other gods and aroused the anger of the LORD, the God of his ancestors.

²⁶ The other events of his reign and all his ways, from beginning to end, are written in the book of the kings of Judah and Israel. ²⁷ Ahaz rested with his ancestors and was buried in the city of Jerusalem, but he was not placed in the tombs of the kings of Israel. And Hezekiah his son succeeded him as king.

29 Hezekiah was twenty-five years old when he became king, and he reigned in Jerusalem for twenty-nine years. His mother's name was Abijah daughter of Zechariah. ² He did what was right in the eyes of the LORD, just as his father David had done.

³ In the first month of the first year of his reign, he opened the doors of the temple of the LORD and repaired them. ⁴ He brought in the priests and the Levites, assembled them in the square on the east side ⁵ and said, 'Listen to me, Levites! Consecrate yourselves now and consecrate the temple

of the Lord, the God of your ancestors. Remove all defilement from the sanctuary. ⁶Our parents were unfaithful; they did evil in the eyes of the Lord our God and forsook him. They turned their faces away from the Lord's dwelling-place and turned their backs on him. ⁷They also shut the doors of the portico and put out the lamps. They did not burn incense or present any burnt offerings at the sanctuary to the God of Israel. ⁸Therefore, the anger of the Lord has fallen on Judah and Jerusalem; he has made them an object of dread and horror and scorn, as you can see with your own eyes. ⁹This is why our fathers have fallen by the sword and why our sons and daughters and our wives are in captivity. ¹⁰Now I intend to make a covenant with the Lord, the God of Israel, so that his fierce anger will turn away from us. ¹¹My sons, do not be negligent now, for the Lord has chosen you to stand before him and serve him, to minister before him and to burn incense.'

¹²Then these Levites set to work:

from the Kohathites,
Mahath son of Amasai and Joel son of Azariah;
from the Merarites,
Kish son of Abdi and Azariah son of Jehallelel;
from the Gershonites,
Joah son of Zimmah and Eden son of Joah;
¹³from the descendants of Elizaphan,
Shimri and Jeiel;
from the descendants of Asaph,
Zechariah and Mattaniah;
¹⁴from the descendants of Heman,
Jehiel and Shimei;
from the descendants of Jeduthun,
Shemaiah and Uzziel.

¹⁵When they had assembled their fellow Levites and consecrated themselves, they went in to purify the temple of the Lord, as the king had ordered, following the word of the Lord. ¹⁶The priests went into the sanctuary of the Lord to purify it. They brought out to the courtyard of the Lord's temple everything unclean that they found in the temple of the Lord. The Levites took it and carried it out to the Kidron Valley. ¹⁷They began the consecration on the first day of the first month, and by the eighth day of the month they reached the portico of the Lord. For eight more days they consecrated the temple of the Lord itself, finishing on the sixteenth day of the first month.

- **PSALM 91:9-16**

⁹If you say, 'The Lord is my refuge,'
and you make the Most High your dwelling,
¹⁰no harm will overtake you,
no disaster will come near your tent.
¹¹For he will command his angels concerning you
to guard you in all your ways;
¹²they will lift you up in their hands,
so that you will not strike your foot against a stone.
¹³You will tread on the lion and the cobra;
you will trample the great lion and the serpent.

¹⁴'Because he loves me,' says the Lord, 'I will rescue him;
I will protect him, for he acknowledges my name.
¹⁵He will call on me, and I will answer him;
I will be with him in trouble,
I will deliver him and honour him.
¹⁶With long life I will satisfy him
and show him my salvation.'

- **PROVERBS 19:17**

¹⁷Whoever is kind to the poor lends to the Lord,

and he will reward them for what they have done.

··

■ ACTS 28:11-31

[11] After three months we put out to sea in a ship that had wintered in the island – it was an Alexandrian ship with the figurehead of the twin gods Castor and Pollux. [12] We put in at Syracuse and stayed there three days. [13] From there we set sail and arrived at Rhegium. The next day the south wind came up, and on the following day we reached Puteoli. [14] There we found some brothers and sisters who invited us to spend a week with them. And so we came to Rome. [15] The brothers and sisters there had heard that we were coming, and they travelled as far as the Forum of Appius and the Three Taverns to meet us. At the sight of these people Paul thanked God and was encouraged. [16] When we got to Rome, Paul was allowed to live by himself, with a soldier to guard him.

[17] Three days later he called together the local Jewish leaders. When they had assembled, Paul said to them: 'My brothers, although I have done nothing against our people or against the customs of our ancestors, I was arrested in Jerusalem and handed over to the Romans. [18] They examined me and wanted to release me, because I was not guilty of any crime deserving death. [19] The Jews objected, so I was compelled to make an appeal to Caesar. I certainly did not intend to bring any charge against my own people. [20] For this reason I have asked to see you and talk with you. It is because of the hope of Israel that I am bound with this chain.'

[21] They replied, 'We have not received any letters from Judea concerning you, and none of our people who have come from there has reported or said anything bad about you. [22] But we want to hear what your views are, for we know that people everywhere are talking against this sect.'

[23] They arranged to meet Paul on a certain day, and came in even larger numbers to the place where he was staying. He witnessed to them from morning till evening, explaining about the kingdom of God, and from the Law of Moses and from the Prophets he tried to persuade them about Jesus. [24] Some were convinced by what he said, but others would not believe. [25] They disagreed among themselves and began to leave after Paul had made this final statement: 'The Holy Spirit spoke the truth to your ancestors when he said through Isaiah the prophet:

[26] ' "Go to this people and say,
  'You will be ever hearing but never
      understanding;
    you will be ever seeing but never
      perceiving.'
[27] For this people's heart has become
      calloused;
    they hardly hear with their ears,
    and they have closed their eyes.
  Otherwise they might see with their
      eyes,
    hear with their ears,
    understand with their hearts
  and turn, and I would heal them." "

[28] 'Therefore I want you to know that God's salvation has been sent to the Gentiles, and they will listen!' [29] a

[30] For two whole years Paul stayed there in his own rented house and welcomed all who came to see him. [31] He proclaimed the kingdom of God and taught about the Lord Jesus Christ – with all boldness and without hindrance!

---

a Some manuscripts include here *After he said this, the Jews left, arguing vigorously among themselves.*

Generosity Generates

Whoever is kind to the poor lends to the LORD, and he will reward them for what they have done.
Proverbs 19:17

One of God's purposes for money is to bless and enrich other Christians. One of the characteristics which God wants to develop in us is that of generosity, for our generosity will determine how much spiritual light we have in our being. Take this verse: 'The eye is the lamp of the body. If your eyes are healthy, your whole body will be full of light' (Matt. 6:22). If your 'eye' – your outlook on life, your whole way of looking at things and people – is generous, then your whole personality is illuminated. If you have a greedy or selfish 'eye', your whole being will be filled with darkness.

In Acts 11:27-30 we read about a severe famine that caused suffering to many Jewish Christians. The church at Antioch – made up mostly of Gentiles – sent an offering to their fellow believers in Jerusalem, and that offering was an important means of tearing down national and cultural barriers between them and building bonds of genuine Christian love. God likens generous giving to reaping a harvest: '... whoever sows sparingly will also reap sparingly, and whoever sows generously will also reap generously' (2 Cor. 9:6).

Perhaps the greatest benefit of generous giving to other Christians, however, is this – it results in 'overflowing in many expressions of thanks to God' (2 Cor. 9:12). Yes, God will give you much so that you can give away much, and when you take your gifts to those who need them, they will break out in thanksgiving and praise of God for your help. Giving to the needs of fellow Christians means that many will thank God and fill His church with praise.

PRAYER

O God, help me to become a truly generous person, for I see that when I am generous, then my generosity generates generosity in others. I ask this in the peerless and exalted name of the Lord Jesus. Amen.

FURTHER STUDY

Rom. 12:9-21; 1 Kings 17:8-16; Prov. 25:21; 11:25; Eccl. 11:1
• What is the lesson of the widow of Zarephath?
• How will you be generous today?

August 6

■ 2 CHRONICLES 29:18–31:10

¹⁸ Then they went in to King Hezekiah and reported: 'We have purified the entire temple of the LORD, the altar of burnt offering with all its utensils, and the table for setting out the consecrated bread, with all its articles. ¹⁹ We have prepared and consecrated all the articles that King Ahaz removed in his unfaithfulness while he was king. They are now in front of the LORD's altar.'

²⁰ Early the next morning King Hezekiah gathered the city officials together and went up to the temple of the LORD. ²¹ They brought seven bulls, seven rams, seven male lambs and seven male goats as a sin offering for the kingdom, for the sanctuary and for Judah. The king commanded the priests, the descendants of Aaron, to offer these on the altar of the LORD. ²² So they slaughtered the bulls, and the priests took the blood and splashed it against the altar; next they slaughtered the rams and splashed their blood against the altar; then they slaughtered the lambs and splashed their blood against the altar. ²³ The goats for the sin offering were brought before the king and the assembly, and they laid their hands on them. ²⁴ The priests then slaughtered the goats and presented their blood on the altar for a sin offering to atone for all Israel, because the king had ordered the burnt offering and the sin offering for all Israel.

²⁵ He stationed the Levites in the temple of the LORD with cymbals, harps and lyres in the way prescribed by David and Gad the king's seer and Nathan the prophet; this was commanded by the LORD through his prophets. ²⁶ So the Levites stood ready with David's instruments, and the priests with their trumpets.

²⁷ Hezekiah gave the order to sacrifice the burnt offering on the altar. As the offering began, singing to the LORD began also, accompanied by trumpets and the instruments of David king of Israel. ²⁸ The whole assembly bowed in worship, while the musicians played and the trumpets sounded. All this continued until the sacrifice of the burnt offering was completed.

²⁹ When the offerings were finished, the king and everyone present with him knelt down and worshipped. ³⁰ King Hezekiah and his officials ordered the Levites to praise the LORD with the words of David and of Asaph the seer. So they sang praises with gladness and bowed down and worshipped.

³¹ Then Hezekiah said, 'You have now dedicated yourselves to the LORD. Come and bring sacrifices and thank-offerings to the temple of the LORD.' So the assembly brought sacrifices and thank-offerings, and all whose hearts were willing brought burnt offerings.

³² The number of burnt offerings the assembly brought was seventy bulls, a hundred rams and two hundred male lambs – all of them for burnt offerings to the LORD. ³³ The animals consecrated as sacrifices amounted to six hundred bulls and three thousand sheep and goats. ³⁴ The priests, however, were too few to skin all the burnt offerings; so their relatives the Levites helped them until the task was finished and until other priests had been consecrated, for the Levites had been more conscientious in consecrating themselves than the priests had been. ³⁵ There were burnt offerings in abundance, together with the fat of the fellowship offerings and the drink offerings that accompanied the burnt offerings.

So the service of the temple of the LORD

was re-established. [36] Hezekiah and all the people rejoiced at what God had brought about for his people, because it was done so quickly.

30 Hezekiah sent word to all Israel and Judah and also wrote letters to Ephraim and Manasseh, inviting them to come to the temple of the LORD in Jerusalem and celebrate the Passover to the LORD, the God of Israel. [2] The king and his officials and the whole assembly in Jerusalem decided to celebrate the Passover in the second month. [3] They had not been able to celebrate it at the regular time because not enough priests had consecrated themselves and the people had not assembled in Jerusalem. [4] The plan seemed right both to the king and to the whole assembly. [5] They decided to send a proclamation throughout Israel, from Beersheba to Dan, calling the people to come to Jerusalem and celebrate the Passover to the LORD, the God of Israel. It had not been celebrated in large numbers according to what was written.

[6] At the king's command, couriers went throughout Israel and Judah with letters from the king and from his officials, which read:

'People of Israel, return to the LORD, the God of Abraham, Isaac and Israel, that he may return to you who are left, who have escaped from the hand of the kings of Assyria. [7] Do not be like your parents and your fellow Israelites, who were unfaithful to the LORD, the God of their ancestors, so that he made them an object of horror, as you see. [8] Do not be stiff-necked, as your ancestors were; submit to the LORD. Come to his sanctuary, which he has consecrated for ever. Serve the LORD your God, so that his fierce anger will turn away from you. [9] If you return to the LORD, then your fellow Israelites and your children will be shown compassion

by their captors and will return to this land, for the LORD your God is gracious and compassionate. He will not turn his face from you if you return to him.'

[10] The couriers went from town to town in Ephraim and Manasseh, as far as Zebulun, but people scorned and ridiculed them. [11] Nevertheless, some from Asher, Manasseh and Zebulun humbled themselves and went to Jerusalem. [12] Also in Judah the hand of God was on the people to give them unity of mind to carry out what the king and his officials had ordered, following the word of the LORD.

[13] A very large crowd of people assembled in Jerusalem to celebrate the Festival of Unleavened Bread in the second month. [14] They removed the altars in Jerusalem and cleared away the incense altars and threw them into the Kidron Valley.

[15] They slaughtered the Passover lamb on the fourteenth day of the second month. The priests and the Levites were ashamed and consecrated themselves and brought burnt offerings to the temple of the LORD. [16] Then they took up their usual positions as prescribed in the Law of Moses the man of God. The priests splashed against the altar the blood handed to them by the Levites. [17] Since many in the crowd had not consecrated themselves, the Levites had to kill the Passover lambs for all those who were not ceremonially clean and could not consecrate their lambs to the LORD. [18] Although most of the many people who came from Ephraim, Manasseh, Issachar and Zebulun had not purified themselves, yet they ate the Passover, contrary to what was written. But Hezekiah prayed for them, saying, 'May the LORD, who is good, pardon everyone [19] who sets their heart on seeking God – the LORD, the God of their ancestors – even if they are not clean according to the rules of the sanctuary.' [20] And the LORD heard Hezekiah and healed the people.

²¹ The Israelites who were present in Jerusalem celebrated the Festival of Unleavened Bread for seven days with great rejoicing, while the Levites and priests praised the LORD every day with resounding instruments dedicated to the LORD.

²² Hezekiah spoke encouragingly to all the Levites, who showed good understanding of the service of the LORD. For the seven days they ate their assigned portion and offered fellowship offerings and praised the LORD, the God of their ancestors.

²³ The whole assembly then agreed to celebrate the festival seven more days; so for another seven days they celebrated joyfully. ²⁴ Hezekiah king of Judah provided a thousand bulls and seven thousand sheep and goats for the assembly, and the officials provided them with a thousand bulls and ten thousand sheep and goats. A great number of priests consecrated themselves. ²⁵ The entire assembly of Judah rejoiced, along with the priests and Levites and all who had assembled from Israel, including the foreigners who had come from Israel and also those who resided in Judah. ²⁶ There was great joy in Jerusalem, for since the days of Solomon son of David king of Israel there had been nothing like this in Jerusalem. ²⁷ The priests and the Levites stood to bless the people, and God heard them, for their prayer reached heaven, his holy dwelling-place.

31 When all this had ended, the Israelites who were there went out to the towns of Judah, smashed the sacred stones and cut down the Asherah poles. They destroyed the high places and the altars throughout Judah and Benjamin and in Ephraim and Manasseh. After they had destroyed all of them, the Israelites returned to their own towns and to their own property.

² Hezekiah assigned the priests and Levites to divisions – each of them according to their duties as priests or Levites – to offer burnt offerings and fellowship offerings, to minister, to give thanks and to sing praises at the gates of the LORD's dwelling. ³ The king contributed from his own possessions for the morning and evening burnt offerings and for the burnt offerings on the Sabbaths, at the New Moons and at the appointed festivals as written in the Law of the LORD. ⁴ He ordered the people living in Jerusalem to give the portion due to the priests and Levites so that they could devote themselves to the Law of the LORD. ⁵ As soon as the order went out, the Israelites generously gave the firstfruits of their grain, new wine, olive oil and honey and all that the fields produced. They brought a great amount, a tithe of everything. ⁶ The people of Israel and Judah who lived in the towns of Judah also brought a tithe of their herds and flocks and a tithe of the holy things dedicated to the LORD their God, and they piled them in heaps. ⁷ They began doing this in the third month and finished in the seventh month. ⁸ When Hezekiah and his officials came and saw the heaps, they praised the LORD and blessed his people Israel.

⁹ Hezekiah asked the priests and Levites about the heaps; ¹⁰ and Azariah the chief priest, from the family of Zadok, answered, 'Since the people began to bring their contributions to the temple of the LORD, we have had enough to eat and plenty to spare, because the LORD has blessed his people, and this great amount is left over.'

■ PSALM 92:1-7

¹ It is good to praise the LORD
　　and make music to your name, O Most High,
² proclaiming your love in the morning
　　and your faithfulness at night,
³ to the music of the ten-stringed lyre
　　and the melody of the harp.

⁴ For you make me glad by your deeds,
    LORD;
    I sing for joy at what your hands have
        done.
⁵ How great are your works, LORD,
    how profound your thoughts!
⁶ Senseless people do not know,
    fools do not understand,
⁷ that though the wicked spring up like
        grass
    and all evildoers flourish,
    they will be destroyed for ever.

■ PROVERBS 19:18-19

¹⁸ Discipline your children, for in that there
        is hope;
    do not be a willing party to their death.

¹⁹ A hot-tempered person must pay the
        penalty;
    rescue them, and you will have to do it
        again.

■ ROMANS 1:1-23

1 Paul, a servant of Christ Jesus, called
  to be an apostle and set apart for the
gospel of God – ² the gospel he promised
beforehand through his prophets in the
Holy Scriptures ³ regarding his Son, who as
to his earthly life was a descendant of David, ⁴ and who through the Spirit of holiness
was appointed the Son of God in power by
his resurrection from the dead: Jesus Christ
our Lord. ⁵ Through him we received grace
and apostleship to call all the Gentiles to
the obedience that comes from faith for
his name's sake. ⁶ And you also are among
those Gentiles who are called to belong to
Jesus Christ.

⁷ To all in Rome who are loved by God and
called to be his holy people:

Grace and peace to you from God our Father and from the Lord Jesus Christ.

⁸ First, I thank my God through Jesus
Christ for all of you, because your faith is
being reported all over the world. ⁹ God,
whom I serve in my spirit in preaching the
gospel of his Son, is my witness how constantly I remember you ¹⁰ in my prayers
at all times; and I pray that now at last by
God's will the way may be opened for me to
come to you.

¹¹ I long to see you so that I may impart to
you some spiritual gift to make you strong –
¹² that is, that you and I may be mutually
encouraged by each other's faith. ¹³ I do not
want you to be unaware, brothers and sisters, that I planned many times to come to
you (but have been prevented from doing so
until now) in order that I might have a harvest among you, just as I have had among
the other Gentiles.

¹⁴ I am a debtor both to Greeks and non-
Greeks, both to the wise and the foolish.
¹⁵ That is why I am so eager to preach the
gospel also to you who are in Rome.

¹⁶ For I am not ashamed of the gospel,
because it is the power of God that brings
salvation to everyone who believes: first to
the Jew, then to the Gentile. ¹⁷ For in the gospel the righteousness of God is revealed – a
righteousness that is by faith from first to
last, just as it is written: 'The righteous will
live by faith.'

¹⁸ The wrath of God is being revealed from
heaven against all the godlessness and wickedness of people, who suppress the truth
by their wickedness, ¹⁹ since what may be
known about God is plain to them, because
God has made it plain to them. ²⁰ For since
the creation of the world God's invisible
qualities – his eternal power and divine
nature – have been clearly seen, being understood from what has been made, so that
people are without excuse.

²¹ For although they knew God, they neither glorified him as God nor gave thanks

to him, but their thinking became futile and their foolish hearts were darkened. ²²Although they claimed to be wise, they became fools ²³and exchanged the glory of the immortal God for images made to look like a mortal human being and birds and animals and reptiles.

Quiet Contemplation

'For you make me glad by your deeds, LORD; I sing for joy at what your hands have done.' Psalm 92:4

The contemplation of God humbles the mind, expands the soul, and consoles the heart.

How does it expand the soul? 'The soul,' says one theologian, 'is at home only when it is in God.' He meant, of course, that as the soul was made for God, it can only function effectively when indwelt by God. Contemplation of God is like breath to the soul; it inflates it and causes it to be fully actualised. 'My body and my whole physiology functions better when God is in it', said a doctor to me some years ago. I replied, 'And so it is also with the soul, dear doctor, so it is also with the soul.'

Another benefit of contemplating God is that it consoles the heart. But how? It does so by focusing the heart's attention on the greatness and goodness of the Eternal and also on His tender mercies and compassion. The more we know of God, the more we realise that when He permits us to pass through deep and dark waters, it is not because He is powerless to deliver us, but because a beneficent and eternal purpose is being worked out in that process. And what is more, we discover that God is not interested merely in working out His purposes in us, but in imparting to us a richer sense of His presence. In God there is a balm for every wound, a comfort for every sorrow, and healing for every heartache.

All kinds of nostrums are on offer in today's church to help the hurting (some of them more secular than sacred), but I know of nothing that calms the swelling billows of sorrow and grief as does the quiet contemplation of the Godhead.

PRAYER

My Father and my God, forgive me if in times of trial and distress I look for comfort in the wrong places. You and You alone are able to meet my soul's deepest needs. Help me to see this not merely as an opinion but as a conviction. In Jesus' name. Amen.

FURTHER STUDY

Psa. 145:1-21; Deut. 32:1-4; 1 Chron. 29:10-13
• How did David express the feelings of his soul?
• How did Moses put it?

August 7

■ 2 CHRONICLES 31:11–33:13

¹¹Hezekiah gave orders to prepare store-rooms in the temple of the LORD, and this was done. ¹²Then they faithfully brought in the contributions, tithes and dedicated gifts. Konaniah, a Levite, was the overseer in charge of these things, and his brother Shimei was next in rank. ¹³Jehiel, Azaziah, Nahath, Asahel, Jerimoth, Jozabad, Eliel, Ismakiah, Mahath and Benaiah were assistants of Konaniah and Shimei his brother. All these served by appointment of King Hezekiah and Azariah the official in charge of the temple of God.

¹⁴Kore son of Imnah the Levite, keeper of the East Gate, was in charge of the free-will offerings given to God, distributing the contributions made to the LORD and also the consecrated gifts. ¹⁵Eden, Miniamin, Jeshua, Shemaiah, Amariah and Shekaniah assisted him faithfully in the towns of the priests, distributing to their fellow priests according to their divisions, old and young alike.

¹⁶In addition, they distributed to the males three years old or more whose names were in the genealogical records – all who would enter the temple of the LORD to perform the daily duties of their various tasks, according to their responsibilities and their divisions. ¹⁷And they distributed to the priests enrolled by their families in the genealogical records and likewise to the Levites twenty years old or more, according to their responsibilities and their divisions. ¹⁸They included all the little ones, the wives, and the sons and daughters of the whole community listed in these genealogical records. For they were faithful in consecrating themselves.

¹⁹As for the priests, the descendants of Aaron, who lived on the farmlands around their towns or in any other towns, men were designated by name to distribute portions to every male among them and to all who were recorded in the genealogies of the Levites.

²⁰This is what Hezekiah did throughout Judah, doing what was good and right and faithful before the LORD his God. ²¹In everything that he undertook in the service of God's temple and in obedience to the law and the commands, he sought his God and worked wholeheartedly. And so he prospered.

32 After all that Hezekiah had so faithfully done, Sennacherib king of Assyria came and invaded Judah. He laid siege to the fortified cities, thinking to conquer them for himself. ²When Hezekiah saw that Sennacherib had come and that he intended to wage war against Jerusalem, ³he consulted with his officials and military staff about blocking off the water from the springs outside the city, and they helped him. ⁴They gathered a large group of people who blocked all the springs and the stream that flowed through the land. 'Why should the kings of Assyria come and find plenty of water?' they said. ⁵Then he worked hard repairing all the broken sections of the wall and building towers on it. He built another wall outside that one and reinforced the terraces of the City of David. He also made large numbers of weapons and shields.

⁶He appointed military officers over the people and assembled them before him in the square at the city gate and encouraged them with these words: ⁷'Be strong and courageous. Do not be afraid or discouraged because of the king of Assyria and the

vast army with him, for there is a greater power with us than with him. ⁸With him is only the arm of flesh, but with us is the LORD our God to help us and to fight our battles.' And the people gained confidence from what Hezekiah the king of Judah said.

⁹Later, when Sennacherib king of Assyria and all his forces were laying siege to Lachish, he sent his officers to Jerusalem with this message for Hezekiah king of Judah and for all the people of Judah who were there:

¹⁰'This is what Sennacherib king of Assyria says: on what are you basing your confidence, that you remain in Jerusalem under siege? ¹¹When Hezekiah says, "The LORD our God will save us from the hand of the king of Assyria," he is misleading you, to let you die of hunger and thirst. ¹²Did not Hezekiah himself remove this god's high places and altars, saying to Judah and Jerusalem, "You must worship before one altar and burn sacrifices on it"?

¹³'Do you not know what I and my predecessors have done to all the peoples of the other lands? Were the gods of those nations ever able to deliver their land from my hand? ¹⁴Who of all the gods of these nations that my predecessors destroyed has been able to save his people from me? How then can your god deliver you from my hand? ¹⁵Now do not let Hezekiah deceive you and mislead you like this. Do not believe him, for no god of any nation or kingdom has been able to deliver his people from my hand or the hand of my predecessors. How much less will your god deliver you from my hand!'

¹⁶Sennacherib's officers spoke further against the LORD God and against his servant Hezekiah. ¹⁷The king also wrote letters ridiculing the LORD, the God of Israel, and saying this against him: 'Just as the gods of the peoples of the other lands did not rescue their people from my hand, so the god of Hezekiah will not rescue his people from my hand.' ¹⁸Then they called out in Hebrew to the people of Jerusalem who were on the wall, to terrify them and make them afraid in order to capture the city. ¹⁹They spoke about the God of Jerusalem as they did about the gods of the other peoples of the world – the work of human hands.

²⁰King Hezekiah and the prophet Isaiah son of Amoz cried out in prayer to heaven about this. ²¹And the LORD sent an angel, who annihilated all the fighting men and the commanders and officers in the camp of the Assyrian king. So he withdrew to his own land in disgrace. And when he went into the temple of his god, some of his sons, his own flesh and blood, cut him down with the sword.

²²So the LORD saved Hezekiah and the people of Jerusalem from the hand of Sennacherib king of Assyria and from the hand of all others. He took care of them on every side. ²³Many brought offerings to Jerusalem for the LORD and valuable gifts for Hezekiah king of Judah. From then on he was highly regarded by all the nations.

²⁴In those days Hezekiah became ill and was at the point of death. He prayed to the LORD, who answered him and gave him a miraculous sign. ²⁵But Hezekiah's heart was proud and he did not respond to the kindness shown him; therefore the LORD's wrath was on him and on Judah and Jerusalem. ²⁶Then Hezekiah repented of the pride of his heart, as did the people of Jerusalem; therefore the LORD's wrath did not come on them during the days of Hezekiah.

²⁷Hezekiah had very great wealth and honour, and he made treasuries for his silver and gold and for his precious stones, spices, shields and all kinds of valuables. ²⁸He also made buildings to store the

harvest of grain, new wine and olive oil; and he made stalls for various kinds of cattle, and pens for the flocks. ²⁹ He built villages and acquired great numbers of flocks and herds, for God had given him very great riches.

³⁰ It was Hezekiah who blocked the upper outlet of the Gihon spring and channelled the water down to the west side of the City of David. He succeeded in everything he undertook. ³¹ But when envoys were sent by the rulers of Babylon to ask him about the miraculous sign that had occurred in the land, God left him to test him and to know everything that was in his heart.

³² The other events of Hezekiah's reign and his acts of devotion are written in the vision of the prophet Isaiah son of Amoz in the book of the kings of Judah and Israel. ³³ Hezekiah rested with his ancestors and was buried on the hill where the tombs of David's descendants are. All Judah and the people of Jerusalem honoured him when he died. And Manasseh his son succeeded him as king.

33 Manasseh was twelve years old when he became king, and he reigned in Jerusalem for fifty-five years. ² He did evil in the eyes of the LORD, following the detestable practices of the nations the LORD had driven out before the Israelites. ³ He rebuilt the high places his father Hezekiah had demolished; he also erected altars to the Baals and made Asherah poles. He bowed down to all the starry hosts and worshipped them. ⁴ He built altars in the temple of the LORD, of which the LORD had said, 'My Name will remain in Jerusalem for ever.' ⁵ In both courts of the temple of the LORD, he built altars to all the starry hosts. ⁶ He sacrificed his children in the fire in the Valley of Ben Hinnom, practised divination and witchcraft, sought omens, and consulted mediums and spiritists. He did much evil in the eyes of the LORD, arousing his anger.

⁷ He took the image he had made and put it in God's temple, of which God had said to David and to his son Solomon, 'In this temple and in Jerusalem, which I have chosen out of all the tribes of Israel, I will put my Name for ever. ⁸ I will not again make the feet of the Israelites leave the land I assigned to your ancestors, if only they will be careful to do everything that I commanded them concerning all the laws, decrees and regulations given through Moses.' ⁹ But Manasseh led Judah and the people of Jerusalem astray, so that they did more evil than the nations the LORD had destroyed before the Israelites.

¹⁰ The LORD spoke to Manasseh and his people, but they paid no attention. ¹¹ So the LORD brought against them the army commanders of the king of Assyria, who took Manasseh prisoner, put a hook in his nose, bound him with bronze shackles and took him to Babylon. ¹² In his distress he sought the favour of the LORD his God and humbled himself greatly before the God of his ancestors. ¹³ And when he prayed to him, the LORD was moved by his entreaty and listened to his plea; so he brought him back to Jerusalem and to his kingdom. Then Manasseh knew that the LORD is God.

··

▬ PSALM 92:8-15

⁸ But you, LORD, are for ever exalted.

⁹ For surely your enemies, LORD,
   surely your enemies will perish;
   all evildoers will be scattered.
¹⁰ You have exalted my horn like that of a
   wild ox;
   fine oils have been poured on me.
¹¹ My eyes have seen the defeat of my
   adversaries;
   my ears have heard the rout of my
   wicked foes.

12 The righteous will flourish like a palm
    tree,
    they will grow like a cedar of Lebanon;
13 planted in the house of the LORD,
    they will flourish in the courts of our
    God.
14 They will still bear fruit in old age,
    they will stay fresh and green,
15 proclaiming, 'The LORD is upright;
    he is my Rock, and there is no
    wickedness in him.'

▬ PROVERBS 19:20-21

20 Listen to advice and accept discipline,
    and at the end you will be counted
    among the wise.

21 Many are the plans in a person's heart,
    but it is the LORD's purpose that
    prevails.

▬ ROMANS 1:24-2:16

24 Therefore God gave them over in the sinful desires of their hearts to sexual impurity for the degrading of their bodies with one another. 25 They exchanged the truth about God for a lie, and worshipped and served created things rather than the Creator – who is for ever praised. Amen.

26 Because of this, God gave them over to shameful lusts. Even their women exchanged natural sexual relations for unnatural ones. 27 In the same way the men also abandoned natural relations with women and were inflamed with lust for one another. Men committed shameful acts with other men, and received in themselves the due penalty for their error.

28 Furthermore, just as they did not think it worth while to retain the knowledge of God, so God gave them over to a depraved mind, so that they do what ought

not to be done. 29 They have become filled with every kind of wickedness, evil, greed and depravity. They are full of envy, murder, strife, deceit and malice. They are gossips, 30 slanderers, God-haters, insolent, arrogant and boastful; they invent ways of doing evil; they disobey their parents; 31 they have no understanding, no fidelity, no love, no mercy. 32 Although they know God's righteous decree that those who do such things deserve death, they not only continue to do these very things but also approve of those who practise them.

2 You, therefore, have no excuse, you who pass judgment on someone else, for at whatever point you judge another, you are condemning yourself, because you who pass judgment do the same things. 2 Now we know that God's judgment against those who do such things is based on truth. 3 So when you, a mere human being, pass judgment on them and yet do the same things, do you think you will escape God's judgment? 4 Or do you show contempt for the riches of his kindness, forbearance and patience, not realising that God's kindness is intended to lead you to repentance?

5 But because of your stubbornness and your unrepentant heart, you are storing up wrath against yourself for the day of God's wrath, when his righteous judgment will be revealed. 6 God 'will repay each person according to what they have done.' 7 To those who by persistence in doing good seek glory, honour and immortality, he will give eternal life. 8 But for those who are self-seeking and who reject the truth and follow evil, there will be wrath and anger. 9 There will be trouble and distress for every human being who does evil: first for the Jew, then for the Gentile; 10 but glory, honour and peace for everyone who does good: first for the Jew, then for the Gentile. 11 For God does not show favouritism.

12 All who sin apart from the law will also perish apart from the law, and all who sin

under the law will be judged by the law. [13] For it is not those who hear the law who are righteous in God's sight, but it is those who obey the law who will be declared righteous. [14] (Indeed, when Gentiles, who do not have the law, do by nature things required by the law, they are a law for themselves, even though they do not have the law. [15] They show that the requirements of the law are written on their hearts, their consciences also bearing witness, and their thoughts sometimes accusing them and at other times even defending them.) [16] This will take place on the day when God judges people's secrets through Jesus Christ, as my gospel declares.

Too Close to the Ground

'But you, LORD, are for ever exalted.' **Psalm 92:8**

The reason our personal problems and difficulties seem so large and ominous is due mainly to the fact that we have not brought God into proper focus. When we are able to see Him as He really is – 'high and lofty' – then all our troubles and anxieties are reduced to their proper proportions.

A minister looked through his study window one day into the garden next door. He saw a little boy there, holding in his hand two pieces of wood, each about eighteen inches long. He heard him ask his mother if he could make a weathercock. After getting her permission, he proceeded to nail one piece of wood upright on the low garden wall, then nailed the other piece loosely on top. Soon the loosely nailed piece of wood turned and twisted, first this way and then that, and the little boy danced with delight. He thought he had made a weathercock that registered the winds, but all it did was register the draughts. 'It turned half a circle,' said the minister, 'when the back door banged.'

From where the minister sat in his study, he could see a real weathercock on the church steeple. It was as steady as a rock in the constant winds that blew in from the sea. There are many Christians, however, who are like the little boy's weathercock, always living at the mercy of every gust of circumstance, their thoughts of God fluctuating with their personal experiences. They take their direction from a weathercock that is too close to the ground.

PRAYER

O God, my Father, forgive me that my life is taken up more with the immediate than the ultimate. I have been glancing at You and gazing at my circumstances. From today it will be different – I will glance at my circumstances and gaze at You. Amen.

FURTHER STUDY

Psa. 8:1-9; 1 Cor. 13:12; 2 Cor. 3:18
• How did the psalmist focus his gaze on God?
• How did Paul describe it?

August 8

■ 2 CHRONICLES 33:14–35:15

¹⁴ Afterwards he rebuilt the outer wall of the City of David, west of the Gihon spring in the valley, as far as the entrance of the Fish Gate and encircling the hill of Ophel; he also made it much higher. He stationed military commanders in all the fortified cities in Judah.

¹⁵ He got rid of the foreign gods and removed the image from the temple of the LORD, as well as all the altars he had built on the temple hill and in Jerusalem; and he threw them out of the city. ¹⁶ Then he restored the altar of the LORD and sacrificed fellowship offerings and thank-offerings on it, and told Judah to serve the LORD, the God of Israel. ¹⁷ The people, however, continued to sacrifice at the high places, but only to the LORD their God.

¹⁸ The other events of Manasseh's reign, including his prayer to his God and the words the seers spoke to him in the name of the LORD, the God of Israel, are written in the annals of the kings of Israel. ¹⁹ His prayer and how God was moved by his entreaty, as well as all his sins and unfaithfulness, and the sites where he built high places and set up Asherah poles and idols before he humbled himself – all these are written in the records of the seers. ²⁰ Manasseh rested with his ancestors and was buried in his palace. And Amon his son succeeded him as king.

²¹ Amon was twenty-two years old when he became king, and he reigned in Jerusalem for two years. ²² He did evil in the eyes of the LORD, as his father Manasseh had done. Amon worshipped and offered sacrifices to all the idols Manasseh had made. ²³ But unlike his father Manasseh, he did

not humble himself before the LORD; Amon increased his guilt.

²⁴ Amon's officials conspired against him and assassinated him in his palace. ²⁵ Then the people of the land killed all who had plotted against King Amon, and they made Josiah his son king in his place.

34 Josiah was eight years old when he became king, and he reigned in Jerusalem for thirty-one years. ² He did what was right in the eyes of the LORD and followed the ways of his father David, not turning aside to the right or to the left.

³ In the eighth year of his reign, while he was still young, he began to seek the God of his father David. In his twelfth year he began to purge Judah and Jerusalem of high places, Asherah poles and idols. ⁴ Under his direction the altars of the Baals were torn down; he cut to pieces the incense altars that were above them, and smashed the Asherah poles and the idols. These he broke to pieces and scattered over the graves of those who had sacrificed to them. ⁵ He burned the bones of the priests on their altars, and so he purged Judah and Jerusalem. ⁶ In the towns of Manasseh, Ephraim and Simeon, as far as Naphtali, and in the ruins around them, ⁷ he tore down the altars and the Asherah poles and crushed the idols to powder and cut to pieces all the incense altars throughout Israel. Then he went back to Jerusalem.

⁸ In the eighteenth year of Josiah's reign, to purify the land and the temple, he sent Shaphan son of Azaliah and Maaseiah the ruler of the city, with Joah son of Joahaz, the recorder, to repair the temple of the LORD his God.

⁹ They went to Hilkiah the high priest and gave him the money that had been brought

into the temple of God, which the Levites who were the gatekeepers had collected from the people of Manasseh, Ephraim and the entire remnant of Israel and from all the people of Judah and Benjamin and the inhabitants of Jerusalem. ¹⁰Then they entrusted it to the men appointed to supervise the work on the LORD's temple. These men paid the workers who repaired and restored the temple. ¹¹They also gave money to the carpenters and builders to purchase dressed stone, and timber for joists and beams for the buildings that the kings of Judah had allowed to fall into ruin.

¹²The workers laboured faithfully. Over them to direct them were Jahath and Obadiah, Levites descended from Merari, and Zechariah and Meshullam, descended from Kohath. The Levites – all who were skilled in playing musical instruments – ¹³had charge of the labourers and supervised all the workers from job to job. Some of the Levites were secretaries, scribes and gatekeepers.

¹⁴While they were bringing out the money that had been taken into the temple of the LORD, Hilkiah the priest found the Book of the Law of the LORD that had been given through Moses. ¹⁵Hilkiah said to Shaphan the secretary, 'I have found the Book of the Law in the temple of the LORD.' He gave it to Shaphan.

¹⁶Then Shaphan took the book to the king and reported to him: 'Your officials are doing everything that has been committed to them. ¹⁷They have paid out the money that was in the temple of the LORD and have entrusted it to the supervisors and workers.' ¹⁸Then Shaphan the secretary informed the king, 'Hilkiah the priest has given me a book.' And Shaphan read from it in the presence of the king.

¹⁹When the king heard the words of the Law, he tore his robes. ²⁰He gave these orders to Hilkiah, Ahikam son of Shaphan, Abdon son of Micah, Shaphan the secretary and Asaiah the king's attendant: ²¹'Go and enquire of the LORD for me and for the remnant in Israel and Judah about what is written in this book that has been found. Great is the LORD's anger that is poured out on us because those who have gone before us have not kept the word of the LORD; they have not acted in accordance with all that is written in this book.'

²²Hilkiah and those the king had sent with him went to speak to the prophet Huldah, who was the wife of Shallum son of Tokhath, the son of Hasrah, keeper of the wardrobe. She lived in Jerusalem, in the New Quarter.

²³She said to them, 'This is what the LORD, the God of Israel, says: tell the man who sent you to me, ²⁴"This is what the LORD says: I am going to bring disaster on this place and its people – all the curses written in the book that has been read in the presence of the king of Judah. ²⁵Because they have forsaken me and burned incense to other gods and aroused my anger by all that their hands have made, my anger will be poured out on this place and will not be quenched." ²⁶Tell the king of Judah, who sent you to enquire of the LORD, "This is what the LORD, the God of Israel, says concerning the words you heard: ²⁷because your heart was responsive and you humbled yourself before God when you heard what he spoke against this place and its people, and because you humbled yourself before me and tore your robes and wept in my presence, I have heard you, declares the LORD. ²⁸Now I will gather you to your ancestors, and you will be buried in peace. Your eyes will not see all the disaster I am going to bring on this place and on those who live here." '

So they took her answer back to the king.

²⁹Then the king called together all the elders of Judah and Jerusalem. ³⁰He went up to the temple of the LORD with the people of Judah, the inhabitants of Jerusalem, the priests and the Levites – all the people from the least to the greatest. He read in their

hearing all the words of the Book of the Covenant, which had been found in the temple of the LORD. ³¹The king stood by his pillar and renewed the covenant in the presence of the LORD – to follow the LORD and keep his commands, statutes and decrees with all his heart and all his soul, and to obey the words of the covenant written in this book.

³²Then he made everyone in Jerusalem and Benjamin pledge themselves to it; the people of Jerusalem did this in accordance with the covenant of God, the God of their ancestors.

³³Josiah removed all the detestable idols from all the territory belonging to the Israelites, and he made all who were present in Israel serve the LORD their God. As long as he lived, they did not fail to follow the LORD, the God of their ancestors.

35 Josiah celebrated the Passover to the LORD in Jerusalem, and the Passover lamb was slaughtered on the fourteenth day of the first month. ²He appointed the priests to their duties and encouraged them in the service of the LORD's temple. ³He said to the Levites, who instructed all Israel and who had been consecrated to the LORD: 'Put the sacred ark in the temple that Solomon son of David king of Israel built. It is not to be carried about on your shoulders. Now serve the LORD your God and his people Israel. ⁴Prepare yourselves by families in your divisions, according to the instructions written by David king of Israel and by his son Solomon.

⁵'Stand in the holy place with a group of Levites for each sub-division of the families of your fellow Israelites, the lay people. ⁶Slaughter the Passover lambs, consecrate yourselves and prepare the lambs for your fellow Israelites, doing what the LORD commanded through Moses.'

⁷Josiah provided for all the lay people who were there a total of thirty thousand lambs and goats for the Passover offerings, and also three thousand cattle – all from the king's own possessions.

⁸His officials also contributed voluntarily to the people and the priests and Levites. Hilkiah, Zechariah and Jehiel, the officials in charge of God's temple, gave the priests two thousand six hundred Passover offerings and three hundred cattle. ⁹Also Konaniah along with Shemaiah and Nethanel, his brothers, and Hashabiah, Jeiel and Jozabad, the leaders of the Levites, provided five thousand Passover offerings and five hundred head of cattle for the Levites.

¹⁰The service was arranged and the priests stood in their places with the Levites in their divisions as the king had ordered. ¹¹The Passover lambs were slaughtered, and the priests splashed against the altar the blood handed to them, while the Levites skinned the animals. ¹²They set aside the burnt offerings to give them to the sub-divisions of the families of the people to offer to the LORD, as it is written in the Book of Moses. They did the same with the cattle. ¹³They roasted the Passover animals over the fire as prescribed, and boiled the holy offerings in pots, cauldrons and pans and served them quickly to all the people. ¹⁴After this, they made preparations for themselves and for the priests, because the priests, the descendants of Aaron, were sacrificing the burnt offerings and the fat portions until nightfall. So the Levites made preparations for themselves and for the Aaronic priests.

¹⁵The musicians, the descendants of Asaph, were in the places prescribed by David, Asaph, Heman and Jeduthun the king's seer. The gatekeepers at each gate did not need to leave their posts, because their fellow Levites made the preparations for them.

▬ PSALM 93:1-5

¹The LORD reigns, he is robed in majesty;
the LORD is robed in majesty and
armed with strength;

indeed, the world is established,
    firm and secure.
[2] Your throne was established long ago;
    you are from all eternity.

[3] The seas have lifted up, LORD,
    the seas have lifted up their voice;
    the seas have lifted up their pounding
        waves.
[4] Mightier than the thunder of the great
        waters,
    mightier than the breakers of the sea –
    the LORD on high is mighty.

[5] Your statutes, LORD, stand firm;
    holiness adorns your house
    for endless days.

PROVERBS 19:22–23

[22] What a person desires is unfailing love;
    better to be poor than a liar.

[23] The fear of the LORD leads to life;
    then one rests content, untouched by
        trouble.

ROMANS 2:17–3:8

[17] Now you, if you call yourself a Jew; if
you rely on the law and boast in God; [18] if you
know his will and approve of what is superior because you are instructed by the law;
[19] if you are convinced that you are a guide
for the blind, a light for those who are in
the dark, [20] an instructor of the foolish, a
teacher of little children, because you have
in the law the embodiment of knowledge
and truth – [21] you, then, who teach others,
do you not teach yourself? You who preach
against stealing, do you steal? [22] You who say
that people should not commit adultery, do
you commit adultery? You who abhor idols,
do you rob temples? [23] You who boast in the
law, do you dishonour God by breaking the
law? [24] As it is written: 'God's name is blasphemed among the Gentiles because of you.'
[25] Circumcision has value if you observe the
law, but if you break the law, you have become
as though you had not been circumcised.
[26] So then, if those who are not circumcised
keep the law's requirements, will they not be
regarded as though they were circumcised?
[27] The one who is not circumcised physically
and yet obeys the law will condemn you who,
even though you have the written code and
circumcision, are a law-breaker.

[28] A person is not a Jew who is one only
outwardly, nor is circumcision merely outward and physical. [29] No, a person is a Jew
who is one inwardly; and circumcision is
circumcision of the heart, by the Spirit, not
by the written code. Such a person's praise
is not from other people, but from God.

[3] What advantage, then, is there in being a Jew, or what value is there in circumcision? [2] Much in every way! First of all,
the Jews have been entrusted with the very
words of God.

[3] What if some were unfaithful? Will
their unfaithfulness nullify God's faithfulness? [4] Not at all! Let God be true, and every
human being a liar. As it is written:

'So that you may be proved right when
        you speak
    and prevail when you judge.'

[5] But if our unrighteousness brings out
God's righteousness more clearly, what shall
we say? That God is unjust in bringing his
wrath on us? (I am using a human argument.) [6] Certainly not! If that were so, how
could God judge the world? [7] Someone might
argue, 'If my falsehood enhances God's
truthfulness and so increases his glory, why
am I still condemned as a sinner?' [8] Why not
say – as some slanderously claim that we
say – 'Let us do evil that good may result'?
Their condemnation is just!

Unassailable – but Accessible

'The LORD reigns, he is robed in majesty … Your throne was established long ago; you are from all eternity.'
Psalm 93:1-2

Ultimate authority rests with God who sits upon His throne. Years ago congregations frequently sang a chorus that goes like this:

God is still on the throne,
And He will remember His own;
Though trials may press us
And burdens distress us
He never will leave us alone.

The story is told of a little boy who, when introduced to this chorus for the first time in his Sunday school, came home and told his mother, 'We learned a new song in Sunday school today.' 'Oh yes', said his mother, 'what was it?' 'God is still on the phone', said the little lad. Well that wasn't exactly what he had been taught, but the thought contained in those words was equally true. Though God reigns from a majestic throne, He is accessible to us at all times of day and night. The lines of communication that lead from us to Him are never blocked and never 'down'. When a man or woman, boy or girl says, 'God be merciful to me a sinner', the message goes straight through to the throne, and they receive His personal reply, 'You are forgiven, redeemed, and set free from your sin.'

The throne of God, you see, is not only a throne of righteousness but also a throne of grace! Righteousness says: 'Stay back until you are good enough to approach.' Grace says: 'I will put on you the robes of righteousness that are provided for you by Christ – now you are good enough.' Too good to be true? Too good not to be true!

PRAYER

Father, I draw near again today to Your throne of grace and with the redeemed all around the world sing: 'How marvellous, how wonderful, this my song shall ever be; how marvellous, how wonderful is my Saviour's love to me.' Amen.

FURTHER STUDY

Heb. 4:1-6; Eph. 1:1-7; 2:7; Phil. 4:19; 1 Tim. 1:14
• What will God meet according to His riches?
• What was Paul's testimony?

August 9

▬ 2 CHRONICLES 35:16–EZRA 1:11

[16] So at that time the entire service of the LORD was carried out for the celebration of the Passover and the offering of burnt offerings on the altar of the LORD, as King Josiah had ordered. [17] The Israelites who were present celebrated the Passover at that time and observed the Festival of Unleavened Bread for seven days. [18] The Passover had not been observed like this in Israel since the days of the prophet Samuel; and none of the kings of Israel had ever celebrated such a Passover as did Josiah, with the priests, the Levites and all Judah and Israel who were there with the people of Jerusalem. [19] This Passover was celebrated in the eighteenth year of Josiah's reign.

[20] After all this, when Josiah had set the temple in order, Necho king of Egypt went up to fight at Carchemish on the Euphrates, and Josiah marched out to meet him in battle. [21] But Necho sent messengers to him saying, 'What quarrel is there, king of Judah, between you and me? It is not you I am attacking at this time, but the house with which I am at war. God has told me to hurry; so stop opposing God, who is with me, or he will destroy you.'

[22] Josiah, however, would not turn away from him, but disguised himself to engage him in battle. He would not listen to what Necho had said at God's command but went to fight him on the plain of Megiddo.

[23] Archers shot King Josiah, and he told his officers, 'Take me away; I am badly wounded.' [24] So they took him out of his chariot, put him in his other chariot and brought him to Jerusalem, where he died. He was buried in the tombs of his ancestors, and all Judah and Jerusalem mourned for him.

[25] Jeremiah composed laments for Josiah, and to this day all the male and female singers commemorate Josiah in the laments. These became a tradition in Israel and are written in the Laments.

[26] The other events of Josiah's reign and his acts of devotion in accordance with what is written in the Law of the LORD – [27] all the events, from beginning to end, are written in the book of the kings of Israel and Judah.

36 [1] And the people of the land took Jehoahaz son of Josiah and made him king in Jerusalem in place of his father.

[2] Jehoahaz was twenty-three years old when he became king, and he reigned in Jerusalem for three months. [3] The king of Egypt dethroned him in Jerusalem and imposed on Judah a levy of a hundred talents of silver and a talent of gold. [4] The king of Egypt made Eliakim, a brother of Jehoahaz, king over Judah and Jerusalem and changed Eliakim's name to Jehoiakim. But Necho took Eliakim's brother Jehoahaz and carried him off to Egypt.

[5] Jehoiakim was twenty-five years old when he became king, and he reigned in Jerusalem for eleven years. He did evil in the eyes of the LORD his God. [6] Nebuchadnezzar king of Babylon attacked him and bound him with bronze shackles to take him to Babylon. [7] Nebuchadnezzar also took to Babylon articles from the temple of the LORD and put them in his temple there.

[8] The other events of Jehoiakim's reign, the detestable things he did and all that was found against him, are written in the book of the kings of Israel and Judah. And Jehoiachin his son succeeded him as king.

⁹ Jehoiachin was eighteen years old when he became king, and he reigned in Jerusalem for three months and ten days. He did evil in the eyes of the LORD. ¹⁰ In the spring, King Nebuchadnezzar sent for him and brought him to Babylon, together with articles of value from the temple of the LORD, and he made Jehoiachin's uncle, Zedekiah, king over Judah and Jerusalem.

¹¹ Zedekiah was twenty-one years old when he became king, and he reigned in Jerusalem for eleven years. ¹² He did evil in the eyes of the LORD his God and did not humble himself before Jeremiah the prophet, who spoke the word of the LORD. ¹³ He also rebelled against King Nebuchadnezzar, who had made him take an oath in God's name. He became stiff-necked and hardened his heart and would not turn to the LORD, the God of Israel. ¹⁴ Furthermore, all the leaders of the priests and the people became more and more unfaithful, following all the detestable practices of the nations and defiling the temple of the LORD, which he had consecrated in Jerusalem.

¹⁵ The LORD, the God of their ancestors, sent word to them through his messengers again and again, because he had pity on his people and on his dwelling-place. ¹⁶ But they mocked God's messengers, despised his words and scoffed at his prophets until the wrath of the LORD was aroused against his people and there was no remedy. ¹⁷ He brought up against them the king of the Babylonians, who killed their young men with the sword in the sanctuary, and did not spare young men or young women, the elderly or the infirm. God gave them all into the hands of Nebuchadnezzar. ¹⁸ He carried to Babylon all the articles from the temple of God, both large and small, and the treasures of the LORD's temple and the treasures of the king and his officials. ¹⁹ They set fire to God's temple and broke down the wall of Jerusalem; they burned all the palaces and destroyed everything of value there.

²⁰ He carried into exile to Babylon the remnant, who escaped from the sword, and they became servants to him and his successors until the kingdom of Persia came to power. ²¹ The land enjoyed its sabbath rests; all the time of its desolation it rested, until the seventy years were completed in fulfilment of the word of the LORD spoken by Jeremiah.

²² In the first year of Cyrus king of Persia, in order to fulfil the word of the LORD spoken by Jeremiah, the LORD moved the heart of Cyrus king of Persia to make a proclamation throughout his realm and also to put it in writing:

²³ 'This is what Cyrus king of Persia says:

'"The LORD, the God of heaven, has given me all the kingdoms of the earth and he has appointed me to build a temple for him at Jerusalem in Judah. Any of his people among you may go up, and may the LORD their God be with them."'

1 In the first year of Cyrus king of Persia, in order to fulfil the word of the Lord spoken by Jeremiah, the Lord moved the heart of Cyrus king of Persia to make a proclamation throughout his realm and also to put it in writing:

² 'This is what Cyrus king of Persia says:

'"The LORD, the God of heaven, has given me all the kingdoms of the earth and he has appointed me to build a temple for him at Jerusalem in Judah. ³ Any of his people among you may go up to Jerusalem in Judah and build the temple of the LORD, the God of Israel, the God who is in Jerusalem, and may their God be with them. ⁴ And in any locality where survivors may now be living, the people are to provide them with silver and gold, with goods and livestock, and with freewill offerings for the temple of God in Jerusalem.'"'

⁵Then the family heads of Judah and Benjamin, and the priests and Levites – everyone whose heart God had moved – prepared to go up and build the house of the LORD in Jerusalem. ⁶All their neighbours assisted them with articles of silver and gold, with goods and livestock, and with valuable gifts, in addition to all the freewill offerings.

⁷Moreover, King Cyrus brought out the articles belonging to the temple of the LORD, which Nebuchadnezzar had carried away from Jerusalem and had placed in the temple of his god. ⁸Cyrus king of Persia had them brought by Mithredath the treasurer, who counted them out to Sheshbazzar the prince of Judah.

⁹This was the inventory:

gold dishes	30
silver dishes	1,000
silver pans	29
¹⁰gold bowls	30
matching silver bowls	410
other articles	1,000

¹¹In all, there were 5,400 articles of gold and of silver. Sheshbazzar brought all these along with the exiles when they came up from Babylon to Jerusalem.

■ PSALM 94:1-11

¹The LORD is a God who avenges.
O God who avenges, shine forth.
²Rise up, Judge of the earth;
pay back to the proud what they deserve.
³How long, LORD, will the wicked,
how long will the wicked be jubilant?

⁴They pour out arrogant words;

all the evildoers are full of boasting.
⁵They crush your people, LORD;
they oppress your inheritance.
⁶They slay the widow and the foreigner;
they murder the fatherless.
⁷They say, 'The LORD does not see;
the God of Jacob takes no notice.'

⁸Take notice, you senseless ones among the people;
you fools, when will you become wise?
⁹Does he who fashioned the ear not hear?
Does he who formed the eye not see?
¹⁰Does he who disciplines nations not punish?
Does he who teaches mankind lack knowledge?
¹¹The LORD knows all human plans;
he knows that they are futile.

■ PROVERBS 19:24-25

²⁴A sluggard buries his hand in the dish;
he will not even bring it back to his mouth!

²⁵Flog a mocker, and the simple will learn prudence;
rebuke the discerning, and they will gain knowledge.

■ ROMANS 3:9-31

⁹What shall we conclude then? Do we have any advantage? Not at all! For we have already made the charge that Jews and Gentiles alike are all under the power of sin. ¹⁰As it is written:

'There is no one righteous, not even one;
¹¹   there is no one who understands;
there is no one who seeks God.
¹²All have turned away,
they have together become worthless;

there is no one who does good,
not even one.'
[13] 'Their throats are open graves;
their tongues practise deceit.'
'The poison of vipers is on their lips.'
[14]   'Their mouths are full of cursing and
bitterness.'
[15] 'Their feet are swift to shed blood;
[16]   ruin and misery mark their ways,
[17] and the way of peace they do not know.'
[18]   'There is no fear of God before their eyes.'

[19] Now we know that whatever the law says, it says to those who are under the law, so that every mouth may be silenced and the whole world held accountable to God. [20] Therefore no one will be declared righteous in God's sight by the works of the law; rather, through the law we become conscious of our sin.

[21] But now apart from the law the righteousness of God has been made known, to which the Law and the Prophets testify. [22] This righteousness is given through faith in Jesus Christ to all who believe. There is no difference between Jew and Gentile, [23] for all have sinned and fall short of the glory of God, [24] and all are justified freely by his grace through the redemption that came by Christ Jesus. [25] God presented Christ as a sacrifice of atonement, through the shedding of his blood – to be received by faith. He did this to demonstrate his righteousness, because in his forbearance he had left the sins committed beforehand unpunished [26] – he did it to demonstrate his righteousness at the present time, so as to be just and the one who justifies those who have faith in Jesus.

[27] Where, then, is boasting? It is excluded. Because of what law? The law that requires works? No, because of the 'law' that requires faith. [28] For we maintain that a person is justified by faith apart from the works of the law. [29] Or is God the God of Jews only? Is he not the God of Gentiles too? Yes, of Gentiles too, [30] since there is only one God, who will justify the circumcised by faith and the uncircumcised through that same faith. [31] Do we, then, nullify the law by this faith? Not at all! Rather, we uphold the law.

God's Thorn Hedges

'... in his forbearance he had left the sins committed beforehand unpunished ...' **Romans 3:25**

There are some psychiatrists who take the attitude that guilt is dangerous to the personality, and so they persuade their clients that there is no basis for their guilt feelings, that conscience and the moral universe are man-made concepts and must be eliminated. There is nothing, they say, to feel guilty about, so, as some put it: 'Let bygones be bygones, and wave goodbye to guilt.'

It must be acknowledged that some ideas regarding guilt have to be dealt with in that way, for some guilt is false and needlessly torments many sincere people. However, I am not talking here about false guilt. I am talking about real guilt – the guilt that the human heart carries because it has offended a holy God. You cannot get rid of that by waving your hand and saying, 'Let bygones be bygones.' Nor can you get away from sin by joking about it. Oscar Wilde said, 'The only way to get rid of a temptation is to yield to it.' But you do not get rid of temptation by yielding to it. It becomes an act, and then a habit, and then part of you.

No, we are hedged in - thorn hedges on either side. The only open door is the mercy of God. And these thorn hedges are His provision, too. They are God's creation enabling us not to live comfortably with evil, for evil is bad for us. God has so arranged the universe that we can only be truly comfortable with that which is good for us. Guilt cannot be banished by subterfuge. Only God can redeem us.

PRAYER

O God, I know that although men might be able to help me with my false guilt, only You can help me with my real guilt. I bring my guilty heart to You for cleansing, forgiveness, and reconciliation. In Jesus' name. Amen.

FURTHER STUDY

Psa. 32; Acts 2:37; Ezra 9:6; John 16:8
• What was the result of guilt?
• What did confession produce?

August 10

■ EZRA 2:1-70

2 Now these are the people of the province who came up from the captivity of the exiles, whom Nebuchadnezzar king of Babylon had taken captive to Babylon (they returned to Jerusalem and Judah, each to their own town, ²in company with Zerubbabel, Joshua, Nehemiah, Seraiah, Reelaiah, Mordecai, Bilshan, Mispar, Bigvai, Rehum and Baanah):

The list of the men of the people of Israel:

³the descendants of Parosh	2,172
⁴of Shephatiah	372
⁵of Arah	775
⁶of Pahath-Moab (through the line of Jeshua and Joab)	2,812
⁷of Elam	1,254
⁸of Zattu	945
⁹of Zakkai	760
¹⁰of Bani	642
¹¹of Bebai	623
¹²of Azgad	1,222
¹³of Adonikam	666
¹⁴of Bigvai	2,056
¹⁵of Adin	454
¹⁶of Ater (through Hezekiah)	98
¹⁷of Bezai	323
¹⁸of Jorah	112
¹⁹of Hashum	223
²⁰of Gibbar	95
²¹the men of Bethlehem	123
²²of Netophah	56
²³of Anathoth	128
²⁴of Azmaveth	42
²⁵of Kiriath Jearim, Kephirah and Beeroth	743
²⁶of Ramah and Geba	621
²⁷of Mikmash	122
²⁸of Bethel and Ai	223
²⁹of Nebo	52

³⁰ of Magbish   156
³¹ of the other Elam   1,254
³² of Harim   320
³³ of Lod, Hadid and Ono   725
³⁴ of Jericho   345
³⁵ of Senaah   3,630

³⁶ The priests:

the descendants of Jedaiah
   (through the family of
   Jeshua)   973
³⁷ of Immer   1,052
³⁸ of Pashhur   1,247
³⁹ of Harim   1,017

⁴⁰ The Levites:

the descendants of Jeshua and
   Kadmiel (of the line of
   Hodaviah)   74

⁴¹ The musicians:

the descendants of Asaph   128

⁴² The gatekeepers of the temple:

the descendants of
   Shallum, Ater, Talmon,
   Akkub, Hatita and Shobai   139

⁴³ The temple servants:

the descendants of
   Ziha, Hasupha, Tabbaoth,
⁴⁴ Keros, Siaha, Padon,
⁴⁵ Lebanah, Hagabah, Akkub,
⁴⁶ Hagab, Shalmai, Hanan,
⁴⁷ Giddel, Gahar, Reaiah,
⁴⁸ Rezin, Nekoda, Gazzam,
⁴⁹ Uzza, Paseah, Besai,
⁵⁰ Asnah, Meunim, Nephussim,
⁵¹ Bakbuk, Hakupha, Harhur,
⁵² Bazluth, Mehida, Harsha,
⁵³ Barkos, Sisera, Temah,

⁵⁴ Neziah and Hatipha

⁵⁵ The descendants of the servants of
Solomon:

the descendants of
   Sotai, Hassophereth, Peruda,
⁵⁶ Jaala, Darkon, Giddel,
⁵⁷ Shephatiah, Hattil,
   Pokereth-Hazzebaim and
   Ami

⁵⁸ The temple servants and the
   descendants of the servants
   of Solomon   392

⁵⁹ The following came up from the
towns of Tel Melah, Tel Harsha, Kerub,
Addon and Immer, but they could not
show that their families were descended from Israel:

⁶⁰ The descendants of
   Delaiah, Tobiah and
   Nekoda   652

⁶¹ And from among the priests:

The descendants of
   Hobaiah, Hakkoz and Barzillai (a
   man who had married a daughter
   of Barzillai the Gileadite and was
   called by that name).

⁶² These searched for their fam-
ily records, but they could not find
them and so were excluded from the
priesthood as unclean. ⁶³ The governor ordered them not to eat any of
the most sacred food until there was a
priest ministering with the Urim and
Thummim.

⁶⁴ The whole company numbered
42,360, ⁶⁵ besides their 7,337 male and
female slaves; and they also had 200
male and female singers. ⁶⁶ They had

736 horses, 245 mules, [67]435 camels and 6,720 donkeys.

[68]When they arrived at the house of the LORD in Jerusalem, some of the heads of the families gave freewill offerings towards the rebuilding of the house of God on its site. [69]According to their ability they gave to the treasury for this work 61,000 darics of gold, 5,000 minas of silver and 100 priestly garments.

[70]The priests, the Levites, the musicians, the gatekeepers and the temple servants settled in their own towns, along with some of the other people, and the rest of the Israelites settled in their towns.

PSALM 94:12-23

[12]Blessed is the one you discipline, LORD,
    the one you teach from your law;
[13]you grant them relief from days of
        trouble,
    till a pit is dug for the wicked.
[14]For the LORD will not reject his people;
    he will never forsake his inheritance.
[15]Judgment will again be founded on
        righteousness,
    and all the upright in heart will
        follow it.

[16]Who will rise up for me against the
        wicked?
    Who will take a stand for me against
        evildoers?
[17]Unless the LORD had given me help,
    I would soon have dwelt in the silence
        of death.
[18]When I said, 'My foot is slipping,'
    your unfailing love, LORD, supported
        me.
[19]When anxiety was great within me,
    your consolation brought me joy.

[20]Can a corrupt throne be allied with you –

a throne that brings on misery by its
        decrees?
[21]The wicked band together against the
        righteous
    and condemn the innocent to death.
[22]But the LORD has become my fortress,
    and my God the rock in whom I take
        refuge.
[23]He will repay them for their sins
    and destroy them for their
        wickedness;
    the LORD our God will destroy them.

PROVERBS 19:26-27

[26]Whoever robs their father and drives out
        their mother
    is a child who brings shame and
        disgrace.

[27]Stop listening to instruction, my son,
    and you will stray from the words of
        knowledge.

ROMANS 4:1-25

4 What then shall we say that Abraham, our forefather according to the flesh, discovered in this matter? [2]If, in fact, Abraham was justified by works, he had something to boast about – but not before God. [3]What does Scripture say? 'Abraham believed God, and it was credited to him as righteousness.'

[4]Now to the one who works, wages are not credited as a gift but as an obligation. [5]However, to the one who does not work but trusts God who justifies the ungodly, their faith is credited as righteousness. [6]David says the same thing when he speaks of the blessedness of the one to whom God credits righteousness apart from works:

7 'Blessed are those
 whose transgressions are forgiven,
 whose sins are covered.
8 Blessed is the one
 whose sin the Lord will never count
 against them.'

9 Is this blessedness only for the circumcised, or also for the uncircumcised? We have been saying that Abraham's faith was credited to him as righteousness. 10 Under what circumstances was it credited? Was it after he was circumcised, or before? It was not after, but before! 11 And he received circumcision as a sign, a seal of the righteousness that he had by faith while he was still uncircumcised. So then, he is the father of all who believe but have not been circumcised, in order that righteousness might be credited to them. 12 And he is then also the father of the circumcised who not only are circumcised but who also follow in the footsteps of the faith that our father Abraham had before he was circumcised.

13 It was not through the law that Abraham and his offspring received the promise that he would be heir of the world, but through the righteousness that comes by faith. 14 For if those who depend on the law are heirs, faith means nothing and the promise is worthless, 15 because the law brings wrath. And where there is no law there is no transgression.

16 Therefore, the promise comes by faith, so that it may be by grace and may be guaranteed to all Abraham's offspring – not only to those who are of the law but also to those who have the faith of Abraham. He is the father of us all. 17 As it is written: 'I have made you a father of many nations.' He is our father in the sight of God, in whom he believed – the God who gives life to the dead and calls into being things that were not.

18 Against all hope, Abraham in hope believed and so became the father of many nations, just as it had been said to him, 'So shall your offspring be.' 19 Without weakening in his faith, he faced the fact that his body was as good as dead – since he was about a hundred years old – and that Sarah's womb was also dead. 20 Yet he did not waver through unbelief regarding the promise of God, but was strengthened in his faith and gave glory to God, 21 being fully persuaded that God had power to do what he had promised. 22 This is why 'it was credited to him as righteousness.' 23 The words 'it was credited to him' were written not for him alone, 24 but also for us, to whom God will credit righteousness – for us who believe in him who raised Jesus our Lord from the dead. 25 He was delivered over to death for our sins and was raised to life for our justification.

The Elements of Prophecy

'... being fully persuaded that God had power to do
what he had promised.' **Romans 4:21**

Prophecy is a revelation of God to humankind. It will take place at exactly the right time: 'For the revelation awaits an appointed time; it speaks of the end and will not prove false' (Hab. 2:3). The time for the fulfilment is fixed by God, and it will come to pass at the exact moment that God foreordains.

   Yet another element is that of foretelling the future. Here again, some Bible teachers object to this and say that prophecy is forth-telling rather foretelling. It is quite true, of course, that prophecy is a form of teaching and therefore contains an element of forth-telling (speaking out the truth), but the true nature of prophecy lies in the fact that it is predictive. God told Habakkuk things that would happen long before they came to pass.

The last element of prophecy is that it will be fulfilled: 'Write down the revelation and make it plain on tablets ... For the revelation awaits an appointed time ...' (Hab. 2:2-3). The events God foretells are certain to take place – and in God's time. The revelation may seem to be delayed, but nothing can prevent or frustrate its fulfilment.

How does all this relate to the more practical aspects of daily Christian living? Let me put the answer in the form of two questions: Has God given you a word or promise that is yet to be fulfilled? And does the delay cause you to wonder whether or not He has forgotten His promise? Then take heart – there are trains on His line until 11:59. What God has promised, He will most certainly perform.

PRAYER

O God, I bring to You my doubts and uncertainties for You to put them to rest – forever. Today I want You to burn deep into me the conviction that nothing can ever stop Your Word from being fulfilled. Nothing. I am so thankful. Amen.

FURTHER STUDY

Matt. 5:1-18; 1 Kings 8:56; Psa. 111:7-8; Ezek. 12:25
• What did Christ promise concerning God's Word?
• Reaffirm your trust in His ability to fulfil His promise to you.

August 11

■ EZRA 3:1–5:17

3 When the seventh month came and the Israelites had settled in their towns, the people assembled together as one in Jerusalem. ²Then Joshua son of Jozadak and his fellow priests and Zerubbabel son of Shealtiel and his associates began to build the altar of the God of Israel to sacrifice burnt offerings on it, in accordance with what is written in the Law of Moses the man of God. ³Despite their fear of the peoples around them, they built the altar on its foundation and sacrificed burnt offerings on it to the LORD, both the morning and evening sacrifices. ⁴Then in accordance with what is written, they celebrated the Festival of Tabernacles with the required number of burnt offerings prescribed for each day. ⁵After that, they presented the regular burnt offerings, the New Moon sacrifices and the sacrifices for all the appointed sacred festivals of the LORD, as well as those brought as freewill offerings to the LORD. ⁶On the first day of the seventh month they began to offer burnt offerings to the LORD, though the foundation of the LORD's temple had not yet been laid.

⁷Then they gave money to the masons and carpenters, and gave food and drink

and olive oil to the people of Sidon and Tyre, so that they would bring cedar logs by sea from Lebanon to Joppa, as authorised by Cyrus king of Persia.

⁸ In the second month of the second year after their arrival at the house of God in Jerusalem, Zerubbabel son of Shealtiel, Joshua son of Jozadak and the rest of the people (the priests and the Levites and all who had returned from the captivity to Jerusalem) began the work. They appointed Levites twenty years old and older to supervise the building of the house of the LORD. ⁹ Joshua and his sons and brothers and Kadmiel and his sons (descendants of Hodaviah) and the sons of Henadad and their sons and brothers – all Levites – joined together in supervising those working on the house of God.

¹⁰ When the builders laid the foundation of the temple of the LORD, the priests in their vestments and with trumpets, and the Levites (the sons of Asaph) with cymbals, took their places to praise the LORD, as prescribed by David king of Israel. ¹¹ With praise and thanksgiving they sang to the LORD:

'He is good;
    his love towards Israel endures for
        ever.'

And all the people gave a great shout of praise to the LORD, because the foundation of the house of the LORD was laid. ¹² But many of the older priests and Levites and family heads, who had seen the former temple, wept aloud when they saw the foundation of this temple being laid, while many others shouted for joy. ¹³ No one could distinguish the sound of the shouts of joy from the sound of weeping, because the people made so much noise. And the sound was heard far away.

4 When the enemies of Judah and Benjamin heard that the exiles were building

a temple for the LORD, the God of Israel, ² they came to Zerubbabel and to the heads of the families and said, 'Let us help you build because, like you, we seek your God and have been sacrificing to him since the time of Esarhaddon king of Assyria, who brought us here.'

³ But Zerubbabel, Joshua and the rest of the heads of the families of Israel answered, 'You have no part with us in building a temple to our God. We alone will build it for the LORD, the God of Israel, as King Cyrus, the king of Persia, commanded us.'

⁴ Then the peoples around them set out to discourage the people of Judah and make them afraid to go on building. ⁵ They bribed officials to work against them and frustrate their plans during the entire reign of Cyrus king of Persia and down to the reign of Darius king of Persia.

⁶ At the beginning of the reign of Xerxes, they lodged an accusation against the people of Judah and Jerusalem.

⁷ And in the days of Artaxerxes king of Persia, Bishlam, Mithredath, Tabeel and the rest of his associates wrote a letter to Artaxerxes. The letter was written in Aramaic script and in the Aramaic language.

⁸ Rehum the commanding officer and Shimshai the secretary wrote a letter against Jerusalem to Artaxerxes the king as follows:

⁹ Rehum the commanding officer and Shimshai the secretary, together with the rest of their associates – the judges, officials and administrators over the people from Persia, Uruk and Babylon, the Elamites of Susa, ¹⁰ and the other people whom the great and honourable Ashurbanipal deported and settled in the city of Samaria and elsewhere in Trans-Euphrates.

¹¹ (This is a copy of the letter they sent him.)

To King Artaxerxes,

From your servants, the men of Trans-Euphrates:

¹²The king should know that the people who came up to us from you have gone to Jerusalem and are rebuilding that rebellious and wicked city. They are restoring the walls and repairing the foundations.

¹³Furthermore, the king should know that if this city is built and its walls are restored, no more taxes, tribute or duty will be paid, and eventually the royal revenues will suffer. ¹⁴Now since we are under obligation to the palace and it is not proper for us to see the king dishonoured, we are sending this message to inform the king, ¹⁵so that a search may be made in the archives of your predecessors. In these records you will find that this city is a rebellious city, troublesome to kings and provinces, a place with a long history of sedition. That is why this city was destroyed. ¹⁶We inform the king that if this city is built and its walls are restored, you will be left with nothing in Trans-Euphrates.

¹⁷The king sent this reply:

To Rehum the commanding officer, Shimshai the secretary and the rest of their associates living in Samaria and elsewhere in Trans-Euphrates:

Greetings.

¹⁸The letter you sent us has been read and translated in my presence. ¹⁹I issued an order and a search was made, and it was found that this city has a long history of revolt against kings and has been a place of rebellion

and sedition. ²⁰Jerusalem has had powerful kings ruling over the whole of Trans-Euphrates, and taxes, tribute and duty were paid to them. ²¹Now issue an order to these men to stop work, so that this city will not be rebuilt until I so order. ²²Be careful not to neglect this matter. Why let this threat grow, to the detriment of the royal interests?

²³As soon as the copy of the letter of King Artaxerxes was read to Rehum and Shimshai the secretary and their associates, they went immediately to the Jews in Jerusalem and compelled them by force to stop.

²⁴Thus the work on the house of God in Jerusalem came to a standstill until the second year of the reign of Darius king of Persia.

5 Now Haggai the prophet and Zechariah the prophet, a descendant of Iddo, prophesied to the Jews in Judah and Jerusalem in the name of the God of Israel, who was over them. ²Then Zerubbabel son of Shealtiel and Joshua son of Jozadak set to work to rebuild the house of God in Jerusalem. And the prophets of God were with them, supporting them.

³At that time Tattenai, governor of Trans-Euphrates, and Shethar-Bozenai and their associates went to them and asked, 'Who authorised you to rebuild this temple and to finish it?' ⁴They also asked, 'What are the names of those who are constructing this building?' ⁵But the eye of their God was watching over the elders of the Jews, and they were not stopped until a report could go to Darius and his written reply be received.

⁶This is a copy of the letter that Tattenai, governor of Trans-Euphrates, and Shethar-Bozenai and their associates, the officials of Trans-Euphrates, sent to King Darius. ⁷The report they sent him read as follows:

To King Darius:

Cordial greetings.

⁸ The king should know that we went to the district of Judah, to the temple of the great God. The people are building it with large stones and placing the timbers in the walls. The work is being carried on with diligence and is making rapid progress under their direction.
⁹ We questioned the elders and asked them, 'Who authorised you to rebuild this temple and to finish it?' ¹⁰ We also asked them their names, so that we could write down the names of their leaders for your information.
¹¹ This is the answer they gave us:

'We are the servants of the God of heaven and earth, and we are rebuilding the temple that was built many years ago, one that a great king of Israel built and finished. ¹² But because our ancestors angered the God of heaven, he gave them into the hands of Nebuchadnezzar the Chaldean, king of Babylon, who destroyed this temple and deported the people to Babylon.
¹³ 'However, in the first year of Cyrus king of Babylon, King Cyrus issued a decree to rebuild this house of God. ¹⁴ He even removed from the temple of Babylon the gold and silver articles of the house of God, which Nebuchadnezzar had taken from the temple in Jerusalem and brought to the temple in Babylon. Then King Cyrus gave them to a man named Sheshbazzar, whom he had appointed governor, ¹⁵ and he told him, "Take these articles and go and deposit them in the temple in Jerusalem. And rebuild the house of God on its site."
¹⁶ 'So this Sheshbazzar came and laid the foundations of the house of God in Jerusalem. From that day to the present it has been under construction but is not yet finished.'

¹⁷ Now if it pleases the king, let a search be made in the royal archives of Babylon to see if King Cyrus did in fact issue a decree to rebuild this house of God in Jerusalem. Then let the king send us his decision in this matter.

■ PSALM 95:1-11

¹ Come, let us sing for joy to the LORD;
  let us shout aloud to the Rock of our
    salvation.
² Let us come before him with
    thanksgiving
  and extol him with music and song.

³ For the LORD is the great God,
  the great King above all gods.
⁴ In his hand are the depths of the earth,
  and the mountain peaks belong to
    him.
⁵ The sea is his, for he made it,
  and his hands formed the dry land.

⁶ Come, let us bow down in worship,
  let us kneel before the LORD our
    Maker;
⁷ for he is our God
  and we are the people of his pasture,
  the flock under his care.

Today, if only you would hear his
    voice,
⁸ 'Do not harden your hearts as you did at
    Meribah,
  as you did that day at Massah in the
    wilderness,
⁹ where your ancestors tested me;
  they tried me, though they had seen
    what I did.

¹⁰ For forty years I was angry with that
    generation;
    I said, "They are a people whose
      hearts go astray,
    and they have not known my ways."
¹¹ So I declared on oath in my anger,
    "They shall never enter my rest." '

▬ PROVERBS 19:28-29

²⁸ A corrupt witness mocks at justice,
    and the mouth of the wicked gulps
      down evil.

²⁹ Penalties are prepared for mockers,
    and beatings for the backs of fools.

▬ ROMANS 5:1-21

5 Therefore, since we have been justified
   through faith, we have peace with God
through our Lord Jesus Christ, ² through
whom we have gained access by faith into
this grace in which we now stand. And we
boast in the hope of the glory of God. ³ Not
only so, but we also glory in our sufferings,
because we know that suffering produces
perseverance; ⁴ perseverance, character;
and character, hope. ⁵ And hope does not
put us to shame, because God's love has
been poured out into our hearts through
the Holy Spirit, who has been given to us.

⁶ You see, at just the right time, when we
were still powerless, Christ died for the ungodly. ⁷ Very rarely will anyone die for a
righteous person, though for a good person
someone might possibly dare to die. ⁸ But
God demonstrates his own love for us in this:
while we were still sinners, Christ died for us.

⁹ Since we have now been justified by his
blood, how much more shall we be saved
from God's wrath through him! ¹⁰ For if,
while we were God's enemies, we were reconciled to him through the death of his Son,
how much more, having been reconciled,
shall we be saved through his life! ¹¹ Not only
is this so, but we also boast in God through
our Lord Jesus Christ, through whom we
have now received reconciliation.

¹² Therefore, just as sin entered the world
through one man, and death through sin,
and in this way death came to all people,
because all sinned –

¹³ To be sure, sin was in the world before
the law was given, but sin is not charged
against anyone's account where there is no
law. ¹⁴ Nevertheless, death reigned from the
time of Adam to the time of Moses, even
over those who did not sin by breaking a
command, as did Adam, who is a pattern of
the one to come.

¹⁵ But the gift is not like the trespass. For
if the many died by the trespass of the one
man, how much more did God's grace and
the gift that came by the grace of the one
man, Jesus Christ, overflow to the many!
¹⁶ Nor can the gift of God be compared with
the result of one man's sin: the judgment followed one sin and brought condemnation,
but the gift followed many trespasses and
brought justification. ¹⁷ For if, by the trespass
of the one man, death reigned through that
one man, how much more will those who
receive God's abundant provision of grace
and of the gift of righteousness reign in life
through the one man, Jesus Christ!

¹⁸ Consequently, just as one trespass resulted in condemnation for all people, so
also one righteous act resulted in justification and life for all people. ¹⁹ For just
as through the disobedience of the one
man the many were made sinners, so also
through the obedience of the one man the
many will be made righteous.

²⁰ The law was brought in so that the trespass might increase. But where sin increased,
grace increased all the more, ²¹ so that, just
as sin reigned in death, so also grace might
reign through righteousness to bring eternal
life through Jesus Christ our Lord.

Tyranny of the Shoulds

'Therefore, since we have been justified through faith, we have peace with God through our Lord Jesus Christ.' **Romans 5:1**

The breastplate of righteousness protects us from the feeling that we are not good enough to be saved. We now look at a feeling which Satan delights to whip up in the heart of a Christian – the feeling that we are only accepted by God when we are doing everything perfectly. The feeling gives rise to *perfectionism* – a condition which afflicts multitudes of Christians.

The chief characteristic of perfectionism is a constant overall feeling of never doing enough to be thought well of by God. The psychoanalyst Karen Horney describes it as 'the tyranny of the shoulds'. Here are some typical statements of those who are afflicted in this way: 'I should do better', 'I should have done better', 'I should be able to do better.' There is nothing wrong with wanting to do better, but in the twisted thinking of a perfectionist, a person believes that because he or she could or should have done better, they will not be accepted or thought well of by God. They come to believe that their acceptance by God depends on their performance. They constantly try to develop a righteousness of their own rather than resting in the righteousness that Christ has provided for them.

If you suffer from this condition, then it's time to put on your spiritual breastplate. You need to remind yourself that the way you came into the Christian life is the same way you are enabled to go on in it – by depending on Christ and His righteousness, not on yourself and your righteousness. You are not working to be saved; you are working because you are saved.

PRAYER

Lord Jesus, I see that when I stand in Your righteousness, I stand in God's smile. But when I stand in my own righteousness, I stand in God's frown. Help me move over from frown to smile. In Your dear name. Amen.

FURTHER STUDY

Gal. 3; Gen. 15:6; Acts 13:39
- What was the purpose of the law?
- What does it mean to be 'justified'?

August 12

▬ EZRA 6:1–7:28

6 King Darius then issued an order, and they searched in the archives stored in the treasury at Babylon. ²A scroll was found in the citadel of Ecbatana in the province of Media, and this was written on it:

Memorandum:

³In the first year of King Cyrus, the king issued a decree concerning the temple of God in Jerusalem:

Let the temple be rebuilt as a place to present sacrifices, and let its foundations be laid. It is to be sixty cubits high and sixty cubits wide, ⁴with three courses of large stones and one of timber. The costs are to be paid by the royal treasury. ⁵Also, the gold and silver articles of the house of God, which Nebuchadnezzar took from the temple in Jerusalem and brought to Babylon, are to be returned to their places in the temple in Jerusalem; they are to be deposited in the house of God.

⁶Now then, Tattenai, governor of Trans-Euphrates, and Shethar-Bozenai and you other officials of that province, stay away from there. ⁷Do not interfere with the work on this temple of God. Let the governor of the Jews and the Jewish elders rebuild this house of God on its site.

⁸Moreover, I hereby decree what you are to do for these elders of the Jews in the construction of this house of God:

Their expenses are to be fully paid out of the royal treasury, from the revenues of Trans-Euphrates, so that the work will not stop. ⁹Whatever is needed – young bulls, rams, male lambs for burnt offerings to the God of heaven, and wheat, salt, wine and olive oil, as requested by the priests in Jerusalem – must be given them daily without fail, ¹⁰so that they may offer sacrifices pleasing to the God of heaven and pray for the well-being of the king and his sons.

¹¹Furthermore, I decree that if anyone defies this edict, a beam is to be pulled from their house and they are to be impaled on it. And for this crime their house is to be made a pile of rubble. ¹²May God, who has caused his Name to dwell there, overthrow any king or people who lifts a hand to change this decree or to destroy this temple in Jerusalem.

I Darius have decreed it. Let it be carried out with diligence.

¹³Then, because of the decree King Darius had sent, Tattenai, governor of Trans-Euphrates, and Shethar-Bozenai and their associates carried it out with diligence. ¹⁴So the elders of the Jews continued to build and prosper under the preaching of Haggai the prophet and Zechariah, a descendant of Iddo. They finished building the temple according to the command of the God of Israel and the decrees of Cyrus, Darius and Artaxerxes, kings of Persia. ¹⁵The temple was completed on the third day of the month Adar, in the sixth year of the reign of King Darius.

¹⁶Then the people of Israel – the priests, the Levites and the rest of the exiles – celebrated the dedication of the house of God

with joy. ¹⁷ For the dedication of this house of God they offered a hundred bulls, two hundred rams, four hundred male lambs and, as a sin offering for all Israel, twelve male goats, one for each of the tribes of Israel. ¹⁸ And they installed the priests in their divisions and the Levites in their groups for the service of God at Jerusalem, according to what is written in the Book of Moses.

¹⁹ On the fourteenth day of the first month, the exiles celebrated the Passover. ²⁰ The priests and Levites had purified themselves and were all ceremonially clean. The Levites slaughtered the Passover lamb for all the exiles, for their relatives the priests and for themselves. ²¹ So the Israelites who had returned from the exile ate it, together with all who had separated themselves from the unclean practices of their Gentile neighbours in order to seek the LORD, the God of Israel. ²² For seven days they celebrated with joy the Festival of Unleavened Bread, because the LORD had filled them with joy by changing the attitude of the king of Assyria so that he assisted them in the work on the house of God, the God of Israel.

7 After these things, during the reign of Artaxerxes king of Persia, Ezra son of Seraiah, the son of Azariah, the son of Hilkiah, ² the son of Shallum, the son of Zadok, the son of Ahitub, ³ the son of Amariah, the son of Azariah, the son of Meraioth, ⁴ the son of Zerahiah, the son of Uzzi, the son of Bukki, ⁵ the son of Abishua, the son of Phinehas, the son of Eleazar, the son of Aaron the chief priest – ⁶ this Ezra came up from Babylon. He was a teacher well versed in the Law of Moses, which the LORD, the God of Israel, had given. The king had granted him everything he asked, for the hand of the LORD his God was on him. ⁷ Some of the Israelites, including priests, Levites, musicians, gatekeepers and temple servants, also came up to Jerusalem in the seventh year of King Artaxerxes.

⁸ Ezra arrived in Jerusalem in the fifth month of the seventh year of the king. ⁹ He had begun his journey from Babylon on the first day of the first month, and he arrived in Jerusalem on the first day of the fifth month, for the gracious hand of his God was on him. ¹⁰ For Ezra had devoted himself to the study and observance of the Law of the LORD, and to teaching its decrees and laws in Israel.

¹¹ This is a copy of the letter King Artaxerxes had given to Ezra the priest, a teacher of the Law, a man learned in matters concerning the commands and decrees of the LORD for Israel:

¹² Artaxerxes, king of kings,

To Ezra the priest, teacher of the Law of the God of heaven:

Greetings.

¹³ Now I decree that any of the Israelites in my kingdom, including priests and Levites, who volunteer to go to Jerusalem with you, may go. ¹⁴ You are sent by the king and his seven advisors to enquire about Judah and Jerusalem with regard to the Law of your God, which is in your hand. ¹⁵ Moreover, you are to take with you the silver and gold that the king and his advisors have freely given to the God of Israel, whose dwelling is in Jerusalem, ¹⁶ together with all the silver and gold you may obtain from the province of Babylon, as well as the freewill offerings of the people and priests for the temple of their God in Jerusalem. ¹⁷ With this money be sure to buy bulls, rams and male lambs, together with their grain offerings and drink offerings, and sacrifice them on the altar of the temple of your God in Jerusalem.

¹⁸ You and your fellow Israelites may

then do whatever seems best with the rest of the silver and gold, in accordance with the will of your God. ¹⁹ Deliver to the God of Jerusalem all the articles entrusted to you for worship in the temple of your God. ²⁰ And anything else needed for the temple of your God that you are responsible to supply, you may provide from the royal treasury.

²¹ Now I, King Artaxerxes, decree that all the treasurers of Trans-Euphrates are to provide with diligence whatever Ezra the priest, the teacher of the Law of the God of heaven, may ask of you – ²² up to a hundred talents of silver, a hundred cors of wheat, a hundred baths of wine, a hundred baths of olive oil, and salt without limit. ²³ Whatever the God of heaven has prescribed, let it be done with diligence for the temple of the God of heaven. Why should his wrath fall on the realm of the king and of his sons? ²⁴ You are also to know that you have no authority to impose taxes, tribute or duty on any of the priests, Levites, musicians, gatekeepers, temple servants or other workers at this house of God.

²⁵ And you, Ezra, in accordance with the wisdom of your God, which you possess, appoint magistrates and judges to administer justice to all the people of Trans-Euphrates – all who know the laws of your God. And you are to teach any who do not know them. ²⁶ Whoever does not obey the law of your God and the law of the king must surely be punished by death, banishment, confiscation of property, or imprisonment.

²⁷ Praise be to the LORD, the God of our ancestors, who has put it into the king's heart to bring honour to the house of the LORD in Jerusalem in this way ²⁸ and who

has extended his good favour to me before the king and his advisors and all the king's powerful officials. Because the hand of the LORD my God was on me, I took courage and gathered leaders from Israel to go up with me.

PSALM 96:1–9

¹ Sing to the LORD a new song;
  sing to the LORD, all the earth.
² Sing to the LORD, praise his name;
  proclaim his salvation day after day.
³ Declare his glory among the nations,
  his marvellous deeds among all
    peoples.

⁴ For great is the LORD and most worthy of
    praise;
  he is to be feared above all gods.
⁵ For all the gods of the nations are
    idols,
  but the LORD made the heavens.
⁶ Splendour and majesty are before him;
  strength and glory are in his
    sanctuary.

⁷ Ascribe to the LORD, all you families of
    nations,
  ascribe to the LORD glory and strength.
⁸ Ascribe to the LORD the glory due to his
    name;
  bring an offering and come into his
    courts.
⁹ Worship the LORD in the splendour of his
    holiness;
  tremble before him, all the earth.

PROVERBS 20:1

20 Wine is a mocker and beer a
   brawler;
  whoever is led astray by them is not
    wise.

▬ ROMANS 6:1-23

6 What shall we say, then? Shall we go on sinning, so that grace may increase? ²By no means! We are those who have died to sin; how can we live in it any longer? ³Or don't you know that all of us who were baptised into Christ Jesus were baptised into his death? ⁴We were therefore buried with him through baptism into death in order that, just as Christ was raised from the dead through the glory of the Father, we too may live a new life.

⁵For if we have been united with him in a death like his, we will certainly also be united with him in a resurrection like his. ⁶For we know that our old self was crucified with him so that the body ruled by sin might be done away with, that we should no longer be slaves to sin – ⁷because anyone who has died has been set free from sin.

⁸Now if we died with Christ, we believe that we will also live with him. ⁹For we know that since Christ was raised from the dead, he cannot die again; death no longer has mastery over him. ¹⁰The death he died, he died to sin once for all; but the life he lives, he lives to God.

¹¹In the same way, count yourselves dead to sin but alive to God in Christ Jesus. ¹²Therefore do not let sin reign in your mortal body so that you obey its evil desires. ¹³Do not offer any part of yourself to sin as an instrument of wickedness, but rather offer yourselves to God as those who have been brought from death to life; and offer every part of yourself to him as an instrument of righteousness. ¹⁴For sin shall no longer be your master, because you are not under the law, but under grace.

¹⁵What then? Shall we sin because we are not under the law but under grace? By no means! ¹⁶Don't you know that when you offer yourselves to someone as obedient slaves, you are slaves of the one you obey – whether you are slaves to sin, which leads to death, or to obedience, which leads to righteousness? ¹⁷But thanks be to God that, though you used to be slaves to sin, you have come to obey from your heart the pattern of teaching that has now claimed your allegiance. ¹⁸You have been set free from sin and have become slaves to righteousness.

¹⁹I am using an example from everyday life because of your human limitations. Just as you used to offer yourselves as slaves to impurity and to ever-increasing wickedness, so now offer yourselves as slaves to righteousness leading to holiness. ²⁰When you were slaves to sin, you were free from the control of righteousness. ²¹What benefit did you reap at that time from the things you are now ashamed of? Those things result in death! ²²But now that you have been set free from sin and have become slaves of God, the benefit you reap leads to holiness, and the result is eternal life. ²³For the wages of sin is death, but the gift of God is eternal life in Christ Jesus our Lord.

Leave Nothing Behind

'We are those who have died to sin; how can we live in it any longer?' **Romans 6:2**

If we are to stay spiritually fresh we must break decisively with everything of which Christ cannot approve. We must get rid of everything that mars our relationship with the Master. This means that we must make up our minds that anything the Lord speaks to us about must go. There is to be no trifling with Him.

A gardener who works in an evangelical conference centre tells how, during the first two or three days of a conference, Christians are keen to obey the signs that say, 'Do not litter'. They go out of their way to carry unwanted paper to the litter bins. After four or five days have passed, however, he finds that people grow tired of looking for the bins and hide their unwanted paper under the bushes. They have enough conscience to hide the paper, but not enough to get rid of it.

Do not let this matter of getting rid of the things of which Christ disapproves end in a compromise or a stalemate. Look down into the hidden recesses where your sins may have been tucked away, and bring them all out - every one. They will plead to be left alone, but bring them all out. Not a thing must be left behind. Don't be content with a conscience that will hide sins but not get rid of sins. If I had to put into one word the biggest single barrier to maintaining spiritual freshness, it would be procrastination. So be decisive - beginning today.

PRAYER

Father, I have put my hand to the plough, and I do not intend to look back. This shall be no halfway business. Help me to bring to You everything that needs to be dealt with today. Amen.

FURTHER STUDY

Acts 24:1-25; Jer. 8:20;
Heb. 3:7-15
• What was Felix's mistake?
• What lesson must we
learn from the children
of Israel?

August 13

■ EZRA 8:1–9:15

8 These are the family heads and those registered with them who came up with me from Babylon during the reign of King Artaxerxes:

² of the descendants of Phinehas, Gershom;
of the descendants of Ithamar, Daniel;
of the descendants of David, Hattush
³ of the descendants of Shekaniah;

of the descendants of Parosh, Zecha- riah, and with him were registered 150 men;
⁴ of the descendants of Pahath-Moab,

Eliehoenai son of Zerahiah, and with him 200 men;
⁵ of the descendants of Zattu, Shekani- ah son of Jahaziel, and with him 300 men;
⁶ of the descendants of Adin, Ebed son of Jonathan, and with him 50 men;
⁷ of the descendants of Elam, Jeshaiah son of Athaliah, and with him 70 men;
⁸ of the descendants of Shephatiah, Zeb- adiah son of Michael, and with him 80 men;
⁹ of the descendants of Joab, Obadiah son of Jehiel, and with him 218 men;
¹⁰ of the descendants of Bani, Shelomith son of Josiphiah, and with him 160 men;

¹¹ of the descendants of Bebai, Zechariah son of Bebai, and with him 28 men; ¹² of the descendants of Azgad, Johanan son of Hakkatan, and with him 110 men; ¹³ of the descendants of Adonikam, the last ones, whose names were Eliphelet, Jeuel and Shemaiah, and with them 60 men; ¹⁴ of the descendants of Bigvai, Uthai and Zakkur, and with them 70 men.

¹⁵ I assembled them at the canal that flows towards Ahava, and we camped there three days. When I checked among the people and the priests, I found no Levites there. ¹⁶ So I summoned Eliezer, Ariel, Shemaiah, Elnathan, Jarib, Elnathan, Nathan, Zechariah and Meshullam, who were leaders, and Joiarib and Elnathan, who were men of learning, ¹⁷ and I ordered them to go to Iddo, the leader in Kasiphia. I told them what to say to Iddo and his fellow Levites, the temple servants in Kasiphia, so that they might bring attendants to us for the house of our God. ¹⁸ Because the gracious hand of our God was on us, they brought us Sherebiah, a capable man, from the descendants of Mahli son of Levi, the son of Israel, and Sherebiah's sons and brothers, 18 in all; ¹⁹ and Hashabiah, together with Jeshaiah from the descendants of Merari, and his brothers and nephews, 20 men in all. ²⁰ They also brought 220 of the temple servants – a body that David and the officials had established to assist the Levites. All were registered by name.

²¹ There, by the Ahava Canal, I proclaimed a fast, so that we might humble ourselves before our God and ask him for a safe journey for us and our children, with all our possessions. ²² I was ashamed to ask the king for soldiers and horsemen to protect us from enemies on the road, because we had told the king, 'The gracious hand of our God is on everyone who looks to him, but his great anger is against all who forsake him.' ²³ So we fasted and petitioned our God

about this, and he answered our prayer.

²⁴ Then I set apart twelve of the leading priests, namely, Sherebiah, Hashabiah and ten of their brothers, ²⁵ and I weighed out to them the offering of silver and gold and the articles that the king, his advisors, his officials and all Israel present there had donated for the house of our God. ²⁶ I weighed out to them 650 talents of silver, silver articles weighing 100 talents, 100 talents of gold, ²⁷ 20 bowls of gold valued at 1,000 darics, and two fine articles of polished bronze, as precious as gold.

²⁸ I said to them, 'You as well as these articles are consecrated to the LORD. The silver and gold are a freewill offering to the LORD, the God of your ancestors. ²⁹ Guard them carefully until you weigh them out in the chambers of the house of the LORD in Jerusalem before the leading priests and the Levites and the family heads of Israel.' ³⁰ Then the priests and Levites received the silver and gold and sacred articles that had been weighed out to be taken to the house of our God in Jerusalem.

³¹ On the twelfth day of the first month we set out from the Ahava Canal to go to Jerusalem. The hand of our God was on us, and he protected us from enemies and bandits along the way. ³² So we arrived in Jerusalem, where we rested three days.

³³ On the fourth day, in the house of our God, we weighed out the silver and gold and the sacred articles into the hands of Meremoth son of Uriah, the priest. Eleazar son of Phinehas was with him, and so were the Levites Jozabad son of Jeshua and Noadiah son of Binnui. ³⁴ Everything was accounted for by number and weight, and the entire weight was recorded at that time.

³⁵ Then the exiles who had returned from captivity sacrificed burnt offerings to the God of Israel: twelve bulls for all Israel, ninety-six rams, seventy-seven male lambs and, as a sin offering, twelve male goats. All this was a burnt offering to the LORD.

³⁶They also delivered the king's orders to the royal satraps and to the governors of Trans-Euphrates, who then gave assistance to the people and to the house of God.

9 After these things had been done, the leaders came to me and said, 'The people of Israel, including the priests and the Levites, have not kept themselves separate from the neighbouring peoples with their detestable practices, like those of the Canaanites, Hittites, Perizzites, Jebusites, Ammonites, Moabites, Egyptians and Amorites. ²They have taken some of their daughters as wives for themselves and their sons, and have mingled the holy race with the peoples around them. And the leaders and officials have led the way in this unfaithfulness.'

³When I heard this, I tore my tunic and cloak, pulled hair from my head and beard and sat down appalled. ⁴Then everyone who trembled at the words of the God of Israel gathered round me because of this unfaithfulness of the exiles. And I sat there appalled until the evening sacrifice.

⁵Then, at the evening sacrifice, I rose from my self-abasement, with my tunic and cloak torn, and fell on my knees with my hands spread out to the LORD my God ⁶and prayed:

'I am too ashamed and disgraced,
my God, to lift up my face to you, because our sins are higher than our heads and our guilt has reached to the heavens. ⁷From the days of our ancestors until now, our guilt has been great. Because of our sins, we and our kings and our priests have been subjected to the sword and captivity, to pillage and humiliation at the hand of foreign kings, as it is today.

⁸'But now, for a brief moment, the LORD our God has been gracious in leaving us a remnant and giving us a firm place in his sanctuary, and so our God gives light to our eyes and a little relief in our bondage. ⁹Though we are slaves, our God has not forsaken us in our bondage. He has shown us kindness in the sight of the kings of Persia: he has granted us new life to rebuild the house of our God and repair its ruins, and he has given us a wall of protection in Judah and Jerusalem.

¹⁰'But now, our God, what can we say after this? For we have forsaken the commands ¹¹you gave through your servants the prophets when you said: "The land you are entering to possess is a land polluted by the corruption of its peoples. By their detestable practices they have filled it with their impurity from one end to the other. ¹²Therefore, do not give your daughters in marriage to their sons or take their daughters for your sons. Do not seek a treaty of friendship with them at any time, that you may be strong and eat the good things of the land and leave it to your children as an everlasting inheritance."

¹³'What has happened to us is a result of our evil deeds and our great guilt, and yet, our God, you have punished us less than our sins have deserved and have given us a remnant like this. ¹⁴Shall we then break your commands again and intermarry with the peoples who commit such detestable practices? Would you not be angry enough with us to destroy us, leaving us no remnant or survivor? ¹⁵LORD, the God of Israel, you are righteous! We are left this day as a remnant. Here we are before you in our guilt, though because of it not one of us can stand in your presence.'

◼ PSALM 96:10-13

¹⁰ Say among the nations, 'The LORD reigns.'

The world is firmly established, it
   cannot be moved;
   he will judge the peoples with equity.

[11] Let the heavens rejoice, let the earth be
   glad;
   let the sea resound, and all that is in it.
[12] Let the fields be jubilant, and everything
   in them;
   let all the trees of the forest sing for joy.
[13] Let all creation rejoice before the LORD,
   for he comes,
   he comes to judge the earth.
He will judge the world in righteousness
   and the peoples in his faithfulness.

▬ PROVERBS 20:2-3

[2] A king's wrath strikes terror like the roar
   of a lion;
   those who anger him forfeit their lives.

[3] It is to one's honour to avoid strife,
   but every fool is quick to quarrel.

▬ ROMANS 7:1-25

7 Do you not know, brothers and sisters –
  for I am speaking to those who know
the law – that the law has authority over
someone only as long as that person lives?
[2] For example, by law a married woman is
bound to her husband as long as he is alive,
but if her husband dies, she is released from
the law that binds her to him. [3] So then, if
she has sexual relations with another man
while her husband is still alive, she is called
an adulteress. But if her husband dies,
she is released from that law and is not an
adulteress if she marries another man.

[4] So, my brothers and sisters, you also
died to the law through the body of Christ,
that you might belong to another, to him
who was raised from the dead, in order that

we might bear fruit for God. [5] For when we
were in the realm of the flesh, the sinful passions aroused by the law were at work in us,
so that we bore fruit for death. [6] But now, by
dying to what once bound us, we have been
released from the law so that we serve in the
new way of the Spirit, and not in the old way
of the written code.

[7] What shall we say, then? Is the law sinful? Certainly not! Nevertheless, I would not
have known what sin was had it not been for
the law. For I would not have known what
coveting really was if the law had not said,
'You shall not covet.' [8] But sin, seizing the
opportunity afforded by the commandment, produced in me every kind of coveting. For apart from the law, sin was dead.
[9] Once I was alive apart from the law; but
when the commandment came, sin sprang
to life and I died. [10] I found that the very
commandment that was intended to bring
life actually brought death. [11] For sin, seizing the opportunity afforded by the commandment, deceived me, and through the
commandment put me to death. [12] So then,
the law is holy, and the commandment is
holy, righteous and good.
[13] Did that which is good, then, become
death to me? By no means! Nevertheless, in
order that sin might be recognised as sin, it
used what is good to bring about my death,
so that through the commandment sin
might become utterly sinful.

[14] We know that the law is spiritual; but I
am unspiritual, sold as a slave to sin. [15] I do
not understand what I do. For what I want
to do I do not do, but what I hate I do. [16] And
if I do what I do not want to do, I agree that
the law is good. [17] As it is, it is no longer I myself who do it, but it is sin living in me. [18] For
I know that good itself does not dwell in me,
that is, in my sinful nature. For I have the desire to do what is good, but I cannot carry it
out. [19] For I do not do the good I want to do,
but the evil I do not want to do – this I keep
on doing. [20] Now if I do what I do not want to

do, it is no longer I who do it, but it is sin living in me that does it.

²¹ So I find this law at work: although I want to do good, evil is right there with me. ²² For in my inner being I delight in God's law; ²³ but I see another law at work in me, waging war against the law of my mind and making me a prisoner of the law of sin at

work within me. ²⁴ What a wretched man I am! Who will rescue me from this body that is subject to death? ²⁵ Thanks be to God, who delivers me through Jesus Christ our Lord!

So then, I myself in my mind am a slave to God's law, but in my sinful nature a slave to the law of sin.

Two Ways to Sound a Horn

'It is to one's honour to avoid strife, but every fool is quick to quarrel.' **Proverbs 20:3**

'Temper', someone has said, 'turns to bad or good according to what is behind it.' Remember that the word 'temper' simply means 'a disposition of mind' and really requires the words 'good' or 'bad' to be prefixed to it if it is to be clearly identified.

Dr Stanley Jones says that there are two ways to sound a horn – the Christian way and the non-Christian way. The Christian way calls attention to a situation; the non-Christian way not only calls attention to the situation but it also calls attention to what the person feels about it. In the USA I once saw a sign on a car that said: 'Honk away – it's your ulcer.' Ulcers are usually visible signs of an ulcerated spirit – ulcerated by irritation and bad temper.

Whenever we lose our temper and take it out on people around us, we do the utmost harm, not to them, but to ourselves. The one who is out of sorts with someone else is usually out of sorts with himself. He projects his inner problems onto others and fails to see the cause and remedy are in himself. I once witnessed a Sunday School superintendent lose his temper in a committee meeting, and when reprimanded by another for his bad spirit, he said, 'I have to lose my temper in order to get anything done around here.' James 1:20 contradicts that view: '... human anger does not produce the righteousness that God desires.' Listen to it again, this time in the Phillips translation: 'For man's temper is never the means of achieving God's true goodness.' Wrong means lead to wrong ends – inevitably.

PRAYER

O Father, help me to meet all impatience with patience, all hate with love, all grumpiness with joy, and all bad temper with good temper. In Jesus' name I ask it. Amen.

FURTHER STUDY

Matt. 5:1-26; Psa. 37:8; Prov. 14:17
• What did Jesus teach about anger?
• Are you angry with anyone?

August 14

▪ EZRA 10:1– NEHEMIAH 1:11

10 While Ezra was praying and confessing, weeping and throwing himself down before the house of God, a large crowd of Israelites – men, women and children – gathered round him. They too wept bitterly. ²Then Shekaniah son of Jehiel, one of the descendants of Elam, said to Ezra, 'We have been unfaithful to our God by marrying foreign women from the peoples around us. But in spite of this, there is still hope for Israel. ³Now let us make a covenant before our God to send away all these women and their children, in accordance with the counsel of my lord and of those who fear the commands of our God. Let it be done according to the Law. ⁴Rise up; this matter is in your hands. We will support you, so take courage and do it.'

⁵So Ezra rose up and put the leading priests and Levites and all Israel under oath to do what had been suggested. And they took the oath. ⁶Then Ezra withdrew from before the house of God and went to the room of Jehohanan son of Eliashib. While he was there, he ate no food and drank no water, because he continued to mourn over the unfaithfulness of the exiles.

⁷A proclamation was then issued throughout Judah and Jerusalem for all the exiles to assemble in Jerusalem. ⁸Anyone who failed to appear within three days would forfeit all his property, in accordance with the decision of the officials and elders, and would himself be expelled from the assembly of the exiles.

⁹Within the three days, all the men of Judah and Benjamin had gathered in Jerusalem. And on the twentieth day of the ninth month, all the people were sitting in the square before the house of God, greatly distressed by the occasion and because of the rain. ¹⁰Then Ezra the priest stood up and said to them, 'You have been unfaithful; you have married foreign women, adding to Israel's guilt. ¹¹Now honour the LORD, the God of your ancestors, and do his will. Separate yourselves from the peoples around you and from your foreign wives.'

¹²The whole assembly responded with a loud voice: 'You are right! We must do as you say. ¹³But there are many people here and it is the rainy season; so we cannot stand outside. Besides, this matter cannot be taken care of in a day or two, because we have sinned greatly in this thing. ¹⁴Let our officials act for the whole assembly. Then let everyone in our towns who has married a foreign woman come at a set time, along with the elders and judges of each town, until the fierce anger of our God in this matter is turned away from us.' ¹⁵Only Jonathan son of Asahel and Jahzeiah son of Tikvah, supported by Meshullam and Shabbethai the Levite, opposed this.

¹⁶So the exiles did as was proposed. Ezra the priest selected men who were family heads, one from each family division, and all of them designated by name. On the first day of the tenth month they sat down to investigate the cases, ¹⁷and by the first day of the first month they finished dealing with all the men who had married foreign women.

¹⁸Among the descendants of the priests, the following had married foreign women:

From the descendants of Joshua son of Jozadak, and his brothers Maaseiah,

Eliezer, Jarib and Gedaliah. [19](They all gave their hands in pledge to put away their wives, and for their guilt they each presented a ram from the flock as a guilt offering.)

[20] From the descendants of Immer:
Hanani and Zebadiah.

[21] From the descendants of Harim:
Maaseiah, Elijah, Shemaiah, Jehiel and Uzziah.

[22] From the descendants of Pashhur:
Elioenai, Maaseiah, Ishmael, Nethanel, Jozabad and Elasah.

[23] Among the Levites:

Jozabad, Shimei, Kelaiah (that is Kelita), Pethahiah, Judah and Eliezer.

[24] From the musicians:
Eliashib.
From the gatekeepers:
Shallum, Telem and Uri.

[25] And among the other Israelites:

From the descendants of Parosh:
Ramiah, Izziah, Malkijah, Mijamin, Eleazar, Malkijah and Benaiah.

[26] From the descendants of Elam:
Mattaniah, Zechariah, Jehiel, Abdi, Jeremoth and Elijah.

[27] From the descendants of Zattu:
Elioenai, Eliashib, Mattaniah, Jeremoth, Zabad and Aziza.

[28] From the descendants of Bebai:
Jehohanan, Hananiah, Zabbai and Athlai.

[29] From the descendants of Bani:
Meshullam, Malluk, Adaiah, Jashub, Sheal and Jeremoth.

[30] From the descendants of Pahath-Moab:
Adna, Kelal, Benaiah, Maaseiah, Mattaniah, Bezalel, Binnui and Manasseh.

[31] From the descendants of Harim:
Eliezer, Ishijah, Malkijah, Shemaiah, Shimeon, [32] Benjamin, Malluk and Shemariah.

[33] From the descendants of Hashum:
Mattenai, Mattattah, Zabad, Eliphelet, Jeremai, Manasseh and Shimei.

[34] From the descendants of Bani:
Maadai, Amram, Uel, [35] Benaiah, Bedeiah, Keluhi, [36] Vaniah, Meremoth, Eliashib, [37] Mattaniah, Mattenai and Jaasu.

[38] From the descendants of Binnui:
Shimei, [39] Shelemiah, Nathan, Adaiah, [40] Maknadebai, Shashai, Sharai, [41] Azarel, Shelemiah, Shemariah, [42] Shallum, Amariah and Joseph.

[43] From the descendants of Nebo:
Jeiel, Mattithiah, Zabad, Zebina, Jaddai, Joel and Benaiah.

[44] All these had married foreign women, and some of them had children by these wives.

1 The words of Nehemiah son of Hakaliah:

In the month of Kislev in the twentieth year, while I was in the citadel of Susa, [2] Hanani, one of my brothers, came from Judah with some other men, and I questioned them about the Jewish remnant that had survived the exile, and also about Jerusalem.

[3] They said to me, 'Those who survived the exile and are back in the province are in great trouble and disgrace. The wall of Jerusalem is broken down, and its gates have been burned with fire.'

[4] When I heard these things, I sat down and wept. For some days I mourned and fasted and prayed before the God of heaven. [5] Then I said:

'LORD, the God of heaven, the great and awesome God, who keeps his covenant of love with those who love him and keep his commandments, [6] let your ear be attentive and your eyes open to hear the prayer your servant is praying before you day and night for your servants, the people of Israel. I confess the sins we Israelites, including myself and my father's family, have committed against you. [7] We have acted very wickedly towards you. We have not obeyed the commands, decrees and laws you gave your servant Moses.

[8] 'Remember the instruction you gave your servant Moses, saying, "If you are unfaithful, I will scatter you among the nations, [9] but if you return to me and obey my commands, then even if your exiled people are at the farthest horizon, I will gather them from there and bring them to the place I have chosen as a dwelling for my Name."

[10] 'They are your servants and your people, whom you redeemed by your great strength and your mighty hand. [11] Lord, let your ear be attentive to the prayer of this your servant and to the prayer of your servants who delight in revering your name. Give your servant success today by granting him favour in the presence of this man.'

I was cupbearer to the king.

■ PSALM 97:1-6

[1] The LORD reigns, let the earth be glad;
   let the distant shores rejoice.
[2] Clouds and thick darkness surround
      him;
   righteousness and justice are the
      foundation of his throne.
[3] Fire goes before him
   and consumes his foes on every side.
[4] His lightning lights up the world;
   the earth sees and trembles.

[5] The mountains melt like wax before the
      LORD,
   before the Lord of all the earth.
[6] The heavens proclaim his righteousness,
   and all peoples see his glory.

■ PROVERBS 20:4-6

[4] Sluggards do not plough in season;
   so at harvest time they look but find
      nothing.

[5] The purposes of a person's heart are
      deep waters,
   but one who has insight draws
      them out.

[6] Many claim to have unfailing love,
   but a faithful person who can find?

■ ROMANS 8:1-25

8 Therefore, there is now no condemnation for those who are in Christ Jesus, [2] because through Christ Jesus the law of the Spirit who gives life has set you free from the law of sin and death. [3] For what the law was powerless to do because it was weakened by the flesh, God did by sending his own Son in the likeness of sinful flesh to be a sin offering. And so he condemned sin in the flesh, [4] in order that the righteous requirement of the law might be fully met in us, who do not live according to the flesh but according to the Spirit.

[5] Those who live according to the flesh have their minds set on what the flesh desires; but those who live in accordance with the Spirit have their minds set on what the Spirit desires. [6] The mind governed by the flesh is death, but the mind governed by the Spirit is life and peace. [7] The mind governed by the flesh is hostile to God; it does not submit to God's law, nor can it do so. [8] Those

who are in the realm of the flesh cannot please God.

⁹You, however, are not in the realm of the flesh but are in the realm of the Spirit, if indeed the Spirit of God lives in you. And if anyone does not have the Spirit of Christ, they do not belong to Christ. ¹⁰But if Christ is in you, then even though your body is subject to death because of sin, the Spirit gives life because of righteousness. ¹¹And if the Spirit of him who raised Jesus from the dead is living in you, he who raised Christ from the dead will also give life to your mortal bodies because of his Spirit who lives in you.

¹²Therefore, brothers and sisters, we have an obligation – but it is not to the flesh, to live according to it. ¹³For if you live according to the flesh, you will die; but if by the Spirit you put to death the misdeeds of the body, you will live.

¹⁴For those who are led by the Spirit of God are the children of God. ¹⁵The Spirit you received does not make you slaves, so that you live in fear again; rather, the Spirit you received brought about your adoption to sonship. And by him we cry, 'Abba, Father.' ¹⁶The Spirit himself testifies with our spirit that we are God's children. ¹⁷Now if we are children, then we are heirs – heirs of God and co-heirs with Christ, if indeed we share in his sufferings in order that we may also share in his glory.

¹⁸I consider that our present sufferings are not worth comparing with the glory that will be revealed in us. ¹⁹For the creation waits in eager expectation for the children of God to be revealed. ²⁰For the creation was subjected to frustration, not by its own choice, but by the will of the one who subjected it, in hope ²¹that the creation itself will be liberated from its bondage to decay and brought into the freedom and glory of the children of God.

²²We know that the whole creation has been groaning as in the pains of childbirth right up to the present time. ²³Not only so, but we ourselves, who have the firstfruits of the Spirit, groan inwardly as we wait eagerly for our adoption to sonship, the redemption of our bodies. ²⁴For in this hope we were saved. But hope that is seen is no hope at all. Who hopes for what they already have? ²⁵But if we hope for what we do not yet have, we wait for it patiently.

It's OK to Feel It

'When I heard these things, I sat down and wept.'
Nehemiah 1:4

Why is it necessary to know how to cope with disappointment? Because if it is allowed to reverberate in our hearts, however much we pretend with our minds that we do not care, our true feelings will prevent us from moving upward toward the peaks of God 'with all four feet'. Our back feet will not track where our front feet have been positioned, and thus we will miss our step on the steep slopes that lead us upward to closer fellowship with God.

The first thing we should learn about disappointment is this – it's OK to feel it. The worst possible thing we can do with any problem that arises in our lives is to refuse to face it and feel it. Yet this is a typical response made by many Christians to life's problems.

I once counselled a young, unmarried woman who had gone through some bitter disappointments both in her childhood and in her adolescent years. Such was the pain these disappointments brought that the only way she could cope with them was to turn her mind to something else. She toyed with the idea of drink, sensual pleasures, and several other things, but because she possessed a deep commitment to Christ, she decided to enroll in a Bible correspondence course. As we talked, it became clear to me that in doing this, her primary goal was not to learn more about Scripture but to relieve the pain of disappointment that was reverberating in her heart. Bible study became a way to escape from her problems rather than what it should have been – a way to confront them.

PRAYER

Father, help me to see that You have made me in such a way that I function best when I go through problems rather than around them. Show me that maturity means being in charge of my feelings, not my feelings being in charge of me. Amen.

FURTHER STUDY

Jonah 1-4; Prov. 16:32; Eccl. 7:9
• Why was Jonah disappointed?
• How did demandingness come into it?

August 15

■ NEHEMIAH 2:1–3:32

2 In the month of Nisan in the twentieth year of King Artaxerxes, when wine was brought for him, I took the wine and gave it to the king. I had not been sad in his presence before, ²so the king asked me, 'Why does your face look so sad when you are not ill? This can be nothing but sadness of heart.'

I was very much afraid, ³but I said to the king, 'May the king live forever! Why should my face not look sad when the city where my ancestors are buried lies in ruins, and its gates have been destroyed by fire?'

⁴The king said to me, 'What is it you want?'

Then I prayed to the God of heaven, ⁵and I answered the king, 'If it pleases the king and if your servant has found favour in his

sight, let him send me to the city in Judah where my ancestors are buried so that I can rebuild it.'

⁶Then the king, with the queen sitting beside him, asked me, 'How long will your journey take, and when will you get back?' It pleased the king to send me; so I set a time.

⁷I also said to him, 'If it pleases the king, may I have letters to the governors of Trans-Euphrates, so that they will provide me safe-conduct until I arrive in Judah? ⁸And may I have a letter to Asaph, keeper of the royal park, so he will give me timber to make beams for the gates of the citadel by the temple and for the city wall and for the residence I will occupy?' And because the gracious hand of my God was on me, the king granted my requests. ⁹So I went to the governors of Trans-Euphrates and gave

them the king's letters. The king had also sent army officers and cavalry with me.

[10] When Sanballat the Horonite and Tobiah the Ammonite official heard about this, they were very much disturbed that someone had come to promote the welfare of the Israelites.

[11] I went to Jerusalem, and after staying there three days [12] I set out during the night with a few others. I had not told anyone what my God had put in my heart to do for Jerusalem. There were no mounts with me except the one I was riding on.

[13] By night I went out through the Valley Gate towards the Jackal Well and the Dung Gate, examining the walls of Jerusalem, which had been broken down, and its gates, which had been destroyed by fire. [14] Then I moved on towards the Fountain Gate and the King's Pool, but there was not enough room for my mount to get through; [15] so I went up the valley by night, examining the wall. Finally, I turned back and re-entered through the Valley Gate. [16] The officials did not know where I had gone or what I was doing, because as yet I had said nothing to the Jews or the priests or nobles or officials or any others who would be doing the work.

[17] Then I said to them, 'You see the trouble we are in: Jerusalem lies in ruins, and its gates have been burned with fire. Come, let us rebuild the wall of Jerusalem, and we will no longer be in disgrace.' [18] I also told them about the gracious hand of my God on me and what the king had said to me.

They replied, 'Let us start rebuilding.' So they began this good work.

[19] But when Sanballat the Horonite, Tobiah the Ammonite official and Geshem the Arab heard about it, they mocked and ridiculed us. 'What is this you are doing?' they asked. 'Are you rebelling against the king?'

[20] I answered them by saying, 'The God of heaven will give us success. We his servants will start rebuilding, but as for you, you have no share in Jerusalem or any claim or historic right to it.'

3 Eliashib the high priest and his fellow priests went to work and rebuilt the Sheep Gate. They dedicated it and set its doors in place, building as far as the Tower of the Hundred, which they dedicated, and as far as the Tower of Hananel. [2] The men of Jericho built the adjoining section, and Zakkur son of Imri built next to them.

[3] The Fish Gate was rebuilt by the sons of Hassenaah. They laid its beams and put its doors and bolts and bars in place. [4] Meremoth son of Uriah, the son of Hakkoz, repaired the next section. Next to him Meshullam son of Berekiah, the son of Meshezabel, made repairs, and next to him Zadok son of Baana also made repairs. [5] The next section was repaired by the men of Tekoa, but their nobles would not put their shoulders to the work under their supervisors.

[6] The Jeshanah Gate was repaired by Joiada son of Paseah and Meshullam son of Besodeiah. They laid its beams and put its doors with their bolts and bars in place. [7] Next to them, repairs were made by men from Gibeon and Mizpah – Melatiah of Gibeon and Jadon of Meronoth – places under the authority of the governor of Trans-Euphrates. [8] Uzziel son of Harhaiah, one of the goldsmiths, repaired the next section; and Hananiah, one of the perfume-makers, made repairs next to that. They restored Jerusalem as far as the Broad Wall. [9] Rephaiah son of Hur, ruler of a half-district of Jerusalem, repaired the next section. [10] Adjoining this, Jedaiah son of Harumaph made repairs opposite his house, and Hattush son of Hashabneiah made repairs next to him. [11] Malkijah son of Harim and Hasshub son of Pahath-Moab repaired another section and the Tower of the Ovens. [12] Shallum son of Hallohesh, ruler of a half-district of Jerusalem, repaired the next section with the help of his daughters.

¹³ The Valley Gate was repaired by Hanun and the residents of Zanoah. They rebuilt it and put its doors with their bolts and bars in place. They also repaired a thousand cubits of the wall as far as the Dung Gate.

¹⁴ The Dung Gate was repaired by Malkijah son of Rekab, ruler of the district of Beth Hakkerem. He rebuilt it and put its doors with their bolts and bars in place.

¹⁵ The Fountain Gate was repaired by Shallun son of Kol-Hozeh, ruler of the district of Mizpah. He rebuilt it, roofing it over and putting its doors and bolts and bars in place. He also repaired the wall of the Pool of Siloam, by the King's Garden, as far as the steps going down from the City of David. ¹⁶ Beyond him, Nehemiah son of Azbuk, ruler of a half-district of Beth Zur, made repairs up to a point opposite the tombs of David, as far as the artificial pool and the House of the Heroes.

¹⁷ Next to him, the repairs were made by the Levites under Rehum son of Bani. Beside him, Hashabiah, ruler of half the district of Keilah, carried out repairs for his district. ¹⁸ Next to him, the repairs were made by their fellow Levites under Binnui son of Henadad, ruler of the other half-district of Keilah. ¹⁹ Next to him, Ezer son of Jeshua, ruler of Mizpah, repaired another section, from a point facing the ascent to the armoury as far as the angle of the wall. ²⁰ Next to him, Baruch son of Zabbai zealously repaired another section, from the angle to the entrance of the house of Eliashib the high priest. ²¹ Next to him, Meremoth son of Uriah, the son of Hakkoz, repaired another section, from the entrance of Eliashib's house to the end of it.

²² The repairs next to him were made by the priests from the surrounding region. ²³ Beyond them, Benjamin and Hasshub made repairs in front of their house; and next to them, Azariah son of Maaseiah, the son of Ananiah, made repairs beside his house. ²⁴ Next to him, Binnui son of Henadad repaired another section, from Azariah's house to the angle and the corner, ²⁵ and Palal son of Uzai worked opposite the angle and the tower projecting from the upper palace near the court of the guard. Next to him, Pedaiah son of Parosh ²⁶ and the temple servants living on the hill of Ophel made repairs up to a point opposite the Water Gate towards the east and the projecting tower. ²⁷ Next to them, the men of Tekoa repaired another section, from the great projecting tower to the wall of Ophel.

²⁸ Above the Horse Gate, the priests made repairs, each in front of his own house. ²⁹ Next to them, Zadok son of Immer made repairs opposite his house. Next to him, Shemaiah son of Shekaniah, the guard at the East Gate, made repairs. ³⁰ Next to him, Hananiah son of Shelemiah, and Hanun, the sixth son of Zalaph, repaired another section. Next to them, Meshullam son of Berekiah made repairs opposite his living quarters. ³¹ Next to him, Malkijah, one of the goldsmiths, made repairs as far as the house of the temple servants and the merchants, opposite the Inspection Gate, and as far as the room above the corner; ³² and between the room above the corner and the Sheep Gate the goldsmiths and merchants made repairs.

....

■ PSALM 97:7-12

⁷ All who worship images are put to
     shame,
   those who boast in idols –
   worship him, all you gods!

⁸ Zion hears and rejoices
   and the villages of Judah are glad
   because of your judgments, LORD.

⁹ For you, LORD, are the Most High over all
the earth;
you are exalted far above all gods.
¹⁰ Let those who love the LORD hate evil,
for he guards the lives of his faithful
ones
and delivers them from the hand of
the wicked.
¹¹ Light shines on the righteous
and joy on the upright in heart.
¹² Rejoice in the LORD, you who are
righteous,
and praise his holy name.

▬ PROVERBS 20:7-9

⁷ The righteous lead blameless lives;
blessed are their children after them.

⁸ When a king sits on his throne to judge,
he winnows out all evil with his
eyes.

⁹ Who can say, 'I have kept my heart pure;
I am clean and without sin'?

▬ ROMANS 8:26–9:5

²⁶ In the same way, the Spirit helps us in
our weakness. We do not know what we
ought to pray for, but the Spirit himself intercedes for us through wordless groans.
²⁷ And he who searches our hearts knows
the mind of the Spirit, because the Spirit
intercedes for God's people in accordance
with the will of God.

²⁸ And we know that in all things God
works for the good of those who love him,
who have been called according to his purpose. ²⁹ For those God foreknew he also
predestined to be conformed to the image of his Son, that he might be the firstborn among many brothers and sisters.
³⁰ And those he predestined, he also called;

those he called, he also justified; those he
justified, he also glorified.

³¹ What, then, shall we say in response to
these things? If God is for us, who can be
against us? ³² He who did not spare his own
Son, but gave him up for us all – how will
he not also, along with him, graciously give
us all things? ³³ Who will bring any charge
against those whom God has chosen? It is
God who justifies. ³⁴ Who then is the one
who condemns? No one. Christ Jesus who
died – more than that, who was raised to
life – is at the right hand of God and is also
interceding for us. ³⁵ Who shall separate
us from the love of Christ? Shall trouble
or hardship or persecution or famine or
nakedness or danger or sword? ³⁶ As it is
written:

'For your sake we face death all day long;
we are considered as sheep to be
slaughtered.'

³⁷ No, in all these things we are more than
conquerors through him who loved us.
³⁸ For I am convinced that neither death
nor life, neither angels nor demons, neither
the present nor the future, nor any powers,
³⁹ neither height nor depth, nor anything
else in all creation, will be able to separate
us from the love of God that is in Christ
Jesus our Lord.

9 I speak the truth in Christ – I am not lying, my conscience confirms it through
the Holy Spirit – ² I have great sorrow and
unceasing anguish in my heart. ³ For I could
wish that I myself were cursed and cut off
from Christ for the sake of my people, those
of my own race, ⁴ the people of Israel. Theirs
is the adoption to sonship; theirs the divine
glory, the covenants, the receiving of the
law, the temple worship and the promises.
⁵ Theirs are the patriarchs, and from them
is traced the human ancestry of the Messiah, who is God over all, for ever praised!
Amen.

God's One Great Goal

'For those God foreknew he also predestined to be
conformed to the image of his Son ...' **Romans 8:29**

What is God's great goal in the universe to which His energies are
devoted? We have it in our text for today. The Living Bible puts this
best, and I have no hesitation in saying that although it is not regarded as
a true translation (it is, rather, a paraphrase), its rendering of Romans 8:29
is one of the most exciting things I have ever read. This is what it says: 'For
from the very beginning God decided that those who came to him ... should
become like his Son.' God's great energy and wisdom, working on behalf of
all Christians, is directed to making us like His Son Jesus Christ. Of course
this purpose will only be fully realised in the world to come, but while we
are here, He is pursuing this same purpose nevertheless.

It is only when we comprehend this that we will be able to understand
the purpose that lies behind all our trials and difficulties. Romans 8:28
- 'And we know that in all things God works for the good of those who
love him ...' - must be read in connection with Romans 8:29. Because God
is committed to making us like His Son, His wisdom goes to work on
every trial that comes our way in order to bring from it something that
will enrich our character and make us more like Jesus Christ.

Infinite power is ruled by infinite wisdom. He could deliver us and
make our lives comfortable, but in a fallen world this is not the best
purpose. Understanding this is crucial if we are to live our lives the way
God desires.

PRAYER

Father, forgive me that so often my
goals are diametrically opposed to
Yours. Help me bring my goals in line
with Your goals. I shall need Your help
to adjust. Whatever happens, keep me
ever moving towards becoming more
and more like Jesus. Amen.

FURTHER STUDY

1 Cor. 1:1-31; Col. 2:3
• How does Paul describe
  the foolishness of God?
• What is hidden in Christ?

August 16

■ **NEHEMIAH 4:1–6:19**

4 When Sanballat heard that we were
rebuilding the wall, he became angry

and was greatly incensed. He ridiculed
the Jews, 2and in the presence of his associates and the army of Samaria, he said,
'What are those feeble Jews doing? Will they

restore their wall? Will they offer sacrifices? Will they finish in a day? Can they bring the stones back to life from those heaps of rubble – burned as they are?'

³Tobiah the Ammonite, who was at his side, said, 'What they are building – even a fox climbing up on it would break down their wall of stones!'

⁴Hear us, our God, for we are despised. Turn their insults back on their own heads. Give them over as plunder in a land of captivity. ⁵Do not cover up their guilt or blot out their sins from your sight, for they have thrown insults in the face of the builders.

⁶So we rebuilt the wall till all of it reached half its height, for the people worked with all their heart.

⁷But when Sanballat, Tobiah, the Arabs, the Ammonites and the people of Ashdod heard that the repairs to Jerusalem's walls had gone ahead and that the gaps were being closed, they were very angry. ⁸They all plotted together to come and fight against Jerusalem and stir up trouble against it. ⁹But we prayed to our God and posted a guard day and night to meet this threat.

¹⁰Meanwhile, the people in Judah said, 'The strength of the labourers is giving out, and there is so much rubble that we cannot rebuild the wall.'

¹¹Also our enemies said, 'Before they know it or see us, we will be right there among them and will kill them and put an end to the work.'

¹²Then the Jews who lived near them came and told us ten times over, 'Wherever you turn, they will attack us.'

¹³Therefore I stationed some of the people behind the lowest points of the wall at the exposed places, posting them by families, with their swords, spears and bows. ¹⁴After I looked things over, I stood up and said to the nobles, the officials and the rest of the people, 'Don't be afraid of them. Remember the Lord, who is great and awesome, and fight for your families, your sons and your daughters, your wives and your homes.'

¹⁵When our enemies heard that we were aware of their plot and that God had frustrated it, we all returned to the wall, each to our work.

¹⁶From that day on, half of my men did the work, while the other half were equipped with spears, shields, bows and armour. The officers posted themselves behind all the people of Judah ¹⁷who were building the wall. Those who carried materials did their work with one hand and held a weapon in the other, ¹⁸and each of the builders wore his sword at his side as he worked. But the man who sounded the trumpet stayed with me.

¹⁹Then I said to the nobles, the officials and the rest of the people, 'The work is extensive and spread out, and we are widely separated from each other along the wall. ²⁰Wherever you hear the sound of the trumpet, join us there. Our God will fight for us!'

²¹So we continued the work with half the men holding spears, from the first light of dawn till the stars came out. ²²At that time I also said to the people, 'Let every man and his helper stay inside Jerusalem at night, so that they can serve us as guards by night and as workers by day.' ²³Neither I nor my brothers nor my men nor the guards with me took off our clothes; each had his weapon, even when he went for water.

5 Now the men and their wives raised a great outcry against their fellow Jews. ²Some were saying, 'We and our sons and daughters are numerous; in order for us to eat and stay alive, we must get grain.'

³Others were saying, 'We are mortgaging our fields, our vineyards and our homes to get grain during the famine.'

⁴Still others were saying, 'We have had to borrow money to pay the king's tax on our fields and vineyards. ⁵Although we are of the same flesh and blood as our fellow

Jews and though our children are as good as theirs, yet we have to subject our sons and daughters to slavery. Some of our daughters have already been enslaved, but we are powerless, because our fields and our vineyards belong to others.'

⁶When I heard their outcry and these charges, I was very angry. ⁷I pondered them in my mind and then accused the nobles and officials. I told them, 'You are charging your own people interest!' So I called together a large meeting to deal with them ⁸and said: 'As far as possible, we have bought back our fellow Jews who were sold to the Gentiles. Now you are selling your own people, only for them to be sold back to us!' They kept quiet, because they could find nothing to say.

⁹So I continued, 'What you are doing is not right. Shouldn't you walk in the fear of our God to avoid the reproach of our Gentile enemies? ¹⁰I and my brothers and my men are also lending the people money and grain. But let us stop charging interest! ¹¹Give back to them immediately their fields, vineyards, olive groves and houses, and also the interest you are charging them – one per cent of the money, grain, new wine and olive oil.'

¹²'We will give it back,' they said. 'And we will not demand anything more from them. We will do as you say.'

Then I summoned the priests and made the nobles and officials take an oath to do what they had promised. ¹³I also shook out the folds of my robe and said, 'In this way may God shake out of their house and possessions anyone who does not keep this promise. So may such a person be shaken out and emptied!'

At this the whole assembly said, 'Amen,' and praised the LORD. And the people did as they had promised.

¹⁴Moreover, from the twentieth year of King Artaxerxes, when I was appointed to be their governor in the land of Judah, until his thirty-second year – twelve years – neither I nor my brothers ate the food allotted to the governor. ¹⁵But the earlier governors – those preceding me – placed a heavy burden on the people and took forty shekels of silver from them in addition to food and wine. Their assistants also lorded it over the people. But out of reverence for God I did not act like that. ¹⁶Instead, I devoted myself to the work on this wall. All my men were assembled there for the work; we did not acquire any land.

¹⁷Furthermore, a hundred and fifty Jews and officials ate at my table, as well as those who came to us from the surrounding nations. ¹⁸Each day one ox, six choice sheep and some poultry were prepared for me, and every ten days an abundant supply of wine of all kinds. In spite of all this, I never demanded the food allotted to the governor, because the demands were heavy on these people.

¹⁹Remember me with favour, my God, for all I have done for these people.

6 When word came to Sanballat, Tobiah, Geshem the Arab and the rest of our enemies that I had rebuilt the wall and not a gap was left in it – though up to that time I had not set the doors in the gates – ²Sanballat and Geshem sent me this message: 'Come, let us meet together in one of the villages on the plain of Ono.'

But they were scheming to harm me; ³so I sent messengers to them with this reply: 'I am carrying on a great project and cannot go down. Why should the work stop while I leave it and go down to you?' ⁴Four times they sent me the same message, and each time I gave them the same answer.

⁵Then, the fifth time, Sanballat sent his assistant to me with the same message, and in his hand was an unsealed letter ⁶in which was written:

'It is reported among the nations –
and Geshem says it is true – that

you and the Jews are plotting to revolt, and therefore you are building the wall. Moreover, according to these reports you are about to become their king ⁷and have even appointed prophets to make this proclamation about you in Jerusalem: "There is a king in Judah!" Now this report will get back to the king; so come, let us meet together.'

⁸I sent him this reply: 'Nothing like what you are saying is happening; you are just making it up out of your head.'

⁹They were all trying to frighten us, thinking, 'Their hands will get too weak for the work, and it will not be completed.'

But I prayed, 'Now strengthen my hands.'

¹⁰One day I went to the house of Shemaiah son of Delaiah, the son of Mehetabel, who was shut in at his home. He said, 'Let us meet in the house of God, inside the temple, and let us close the temple doors, because men are coming to kill you – by night they are coming to kill you.'

¹¹But I said, 'Should a man like me run away? Or should someone like me go into the temple to save his life? I will not go!' ¹²I realised that God had not sent him, but that he had prophesied against me because Tobiah and Sanballat had hired him. ¹³He had been hired to intimidate me so that I would commit a sin by doing this, and then they would give me a bad name to discredit me.

¹⁴Remember Tobiah and Sanballat, my God, because of what they have done; remember also the prophet Noadiah and how she and the rest of the prophets have been trying to intimidate me. ¹⁵So the wall was completed on the twenty-fifth of Elul, in fifty-two days.

¹⁶When all our enemies heard about this, all the surrounding nations were afraid and lost their self-confidence, because they realised that this work had been done with the help of our God.

¹⁷Also, in those days the nobles of Judah were sending many letters to Tobiah, and replies from Tobiah kept coming to them. ¹⁸For many in Judah were under oath to him, since he was son-in-law to Shekaniah son of Arah, and his son Jehohanan had married the daughter of Meshullam son of Berekiah. ¹⁹Moreover, they kept reporting to me his good deeds and then telling him what I said. And Tobiah sent letters to intimidate me.

▬ PSALM 98:1-9

¹Sing to the Lord a new song,
   for he has done marvellous things;
his right hand and his holy arm
   have worked salvation for him.
²The Lord has made his salvation known
   and revealed his righteousness to the
      nations.
³He has remembered his love
   and his faithfulness to Israel;
all the ends of the earth have seen
   the salvation of our God.

⁴Shout for joy to the Lord, all the earth,
   burst into jubilant song with music;
⁵make music to the Lord with the harp,
   with the harp and the sound of
      singing,
⁶with trumpets and the blast of the ram's
      horn –
   shout for joy before the Lord, the King.

⁷Let the sea resound, and everything in it,
   the world, and all who live in it.
⁸Let the rivers clap their hands,
   let the mountains sing together for
      joy;
⁹let them sing before the Lord,
   for he comes to judge the earth.
He will judge the world in righteousness
   and the peoples with equity.

■ PROVERBS 20:10-12

¹⁰ Differing weights and differing
    measures –
    the LORD detests them both.

¹¹ Even small children are known by their
    actions,
    so is their conduct really pure and
    upright?

¹² Ears that hear and eyes that see –
    the LORD has made them both.

■ ROMANS 9:6-26

⁶ It is not as though God's word had
failed. For not all who are descended from
Israel are Israel. ⁷ Nor because they are his
descendants are they all Abraham's children. On the contrary, 'It is through Isaac
that your offspring will be reckoned.' ⁸ In
other words, it is not the children by physical descent who are God's children, but it
is the children of the promise who are regarded as Abraham's offspring. ⁹ For this
was how the promise was stated: 'At the appointed time I will return, and Sarah will
have a son.'

¹⁰ Not only that, but Rebekah's children
were conceived at the same time by our father Isaac. ¹¹ Yet, before the twins were born
or had done anything good or bad – in order
that God's purpose in election might stand:
¹² not by works but by him who calls – she
was told, 'The older will serve the younger.'
¹³ Just as it is written: 'Jacob I loved, but Esau
I hated.'

¹⁴ What then shall we say? Is God unjust?
Not at all! ¹⁵ For he says to Moses,

'I will have mercy on whom I have mercy,
    and I will have compassion on whom I
        have compassion.'

¹⁶ It does not, therefore, depend on human
desire or effort, but on God's mercy. ¹⁷ For
Scripture says to Pharaoh: 'I raised you up
for this very purpose, that I might display
my power in you and that my name might be
proclaimed in all the earth.' ¹⁸ Therefore God
has mercy on whom he wants to have mercy,
and he hardens whom he wants to harden.

¹⁹ One of you will say to me: 'Then why
does God still blame us? For who is able to
resist his will?' ²⁰ But who are you, a human
being, to talk back to God? 'Shall what is
formed say to the one who formed it, "Why
did you make me like this?"' ²¹ Does not
the potter have the right to make out of the
same lump of clay some pottery for special
purposes and some for common use?

²² What if God, although choosing to show
his wrath and make his power known, bore
with great patience the objects of his wrath –
prepared for destruction? ²³ What if he did
this to make the riches of his glory known to
the objects of his mercy, whom he prepared
in advance for glory – ²⁴ even us, whom he
also called, not only from the Jews but also
from the Gentiles? ²⁵ As he says in Hosea:

'I will call them "my people" who are not
    my people;
    and I will call her "my loved one" who
        is not my loved one,'

²⁶ and,

'In the very place where it was said to them,
    "You are not my people,"
    there they will be called "children of
        the living God."'

The Conscience Corrected

'Even small children are known by their actions, so is their conduct really pure and upright?' **Proverbs 20:11**

One way that the Holy Spirit exercises His convincing ministry in our lives is by addressing our consciences, prevailing upon them to take the way of Christ in every issue. Romans 9:1 brings together the objective standard, 'the truth in Christ', and the subjective standard, 'my conscience confirms it through the Holy Spirit'.

Some people say, 'I'm living in accordance with my conscience – isn't that enough?' No, for conscience by itself is not a safe guide. Conscience is the capacity to distinguish between right and wrong – according to the standards you uphold. It can be taught to approve directly opposite things.

For example, a missionary intervened to stop an Indian woman from throwing her child into the Ganges River as a human sacrifice. 'But my conscience tells me to do it', she said. 'Yes', said the missionary, 'and my conscience tells me to stop you from doing it.'

Conscience is not an infallible guide unless it has in it the highest content possible – the Holy Spirit. He can be relied upon to act as Jesus would act in every situation, for the Spirit is a Christlike Spirit. I am bold to say that there is not one of you reading these lines (if you are a Christian) who, by the mercy of God, doesn't know something in your conscience of the work of the Holy Spirit as Convincer. He pleads in you and with you to bring your conscience to the highest place possible, 'I strive always to keep my conscience clear before God and man' (Acts 24:16).

PRAYER

O Father, I surrender myself and my standards to You for cleansing and correction. Teach me the standards of Christ so that my conscience may bear a true witness. For Jesus' sake. Amen.

FURTHER STUDY

Rom. 14; 15:1-13; Acts 24:16; 2 Cor. 1:12; 1 Tim. 1:5
• What is Paul teaching about our conscience?
• How does he relate it to the ministry of the Holy Spirit?

August 17

■ NEHEMIAH 7:1-60

7 After the wall had been rebuilt and I had set the doors in place, the gatekeepers, the musicians and the Levites were appointed. ²I put in charge of Jerusalem my brother Hanani, along with Hananiah the commander of the citadel, because he was a

man of integrity and feared God more than most people do. ³I said to them, 'The gates of Jerusalem are not to be opened until the sun is hot. While the gatekeepers are still on duty, make them shut the doors and bar them. Also appoint residents of Jerusalem as guards, some at their posts and some near their own houses.'

⁴Now the city was large and spacious, but there were few people in it, and the houses had not yet been rebuilt. ⁵So my God put it into my heart to assemble the nobles, the officials and the common people for registration by families. I found the genealogical record of those who had been the first to return. This is what I found written there:

⁶These are the people of the province who came up from the captivity of the exiles whom Nebuchadnezzar king of Babylon had taken captive (they returned to Jerusalem and Judah, each to his own town, ⁷in company with Zerubbabel, Joshua, Nehemiah, Azariah, Raamiah, Nahamani, Mordecai, Bilshan, Mispereth, Bigvai, Nehum and Baanah):

The list of the men of Israel:

⁸the descendants of Parosh		2,172
⁹of Shephatiah		372
¹⁰of Arah		652
¹¹of Pahath-Moab (through the line of Joshua and Joab)		2,818
¹²of Elam		1,254
¹³of Zattu		845
¹⁴of Zakkai		760
¹⁵of Binnui		648
¹⁶of Bebai		628
¹⁷of Azgad		2,322
¹⁸of Adonikam		667
¹⁹of Bigvai		2,067
²⁰of Adin		655
²¹of Ater (through Hezekiah)		98
²²of Hashum		328
²³of Bezai		324
²⁴of Hariph		112
²⁵of Gibeon		95
²⁶the men of Bethlehem and Netophah		188
²⁷of Anathoth		128
²⁸of Beth Azmaveth		42
²⁹of Kiriath Jearim, Kephirah and Beeroth		743
³⁰of Ramah and Geba		621
³¹of Mikmash		122
³²of Bethel and Ai		123
³³of the other Nebo		52
³⁴of the other Elam		1,254
³⁵of Harim		320
³⁶of Jericho		345
³⁷of Lod, Hadid and Ono		721
³⁸of Senaah		3,930

³⁹The priests:

the descendants of Jedaiah (through the family of Jeshua)		973
⁴⁰of Immer		1,052
⁴¹of Pashhur		1,247
⁴²of Harim		1,017

⁴³The Levites:

the descendants of Jeshua (through Kadmiel through the line of Hodaviah)		74

⁴⁴The musicians:

the descendants of Asaph		148

⁴⁵The gatekeepers:

the descendants of Shallum, Ater, Talmon, Akkub, Hatita and Shobai		138

⁴⁶The temple servants:

the descendants of
Ziha, Hasupha, Tabbaoth,
⁴⁷Keros, Sia, Padon,
⁴⁸Lebana, Hagaba, Shalmai,
⁴⁹Hanan, Giddel, Gahar,
⁵⁰Reaiah, Rezin, Nekoda,
⁵¹Gazzam, Uzza, Paseah,
⁵²Besai, Meunim, Nephussim,
⁵³Bakbuk, Hakupha, Harhur,
⁵⁴Bazluth, Mehida, Harsha,
⁵⁵Barkos, Sisera, Temah,
⁵⁶Neziah and Hatipha

⁵⁷The descendants of the servants of
Solomon:

the descendants of
Sotai, Sophereth, Perida,
⁵⁸Jaala, Darkon, Giddel,
⁵⁹Shephatiah, Hattil,
Pokereth-Hazzebaim and Amon

⁶⁰The temple servants and the
descendants of the servants of
Solomon   392

■ PSALM 99:1–9

¹The LORD reigns,
let the nations tremble;
he sits enthroned between the cherubim,
let the earth shake.
²Great is the LORD in Zion;
he is exalted over all the nations.
³Let them praise your great and awesome
name –
he is holy.

⁴The King is mighty, he loves justice –
you have established equity;
in Jacob you have done
what is just and right.
⁵Exalt the LORD our God

and worship at his footstool;
he is holy.

⁶Moses and Aaron were among his
priests,
Samuel was among those who called
on his name;
they called on the LORD
and he answered them.
⁷He spoke to them from the pillar of
cloud;
they kept his statutes and the decrees
he gave them.

⁸LORD our God,
you answered them;
you were to Israel a forgiving God,
though you punished their misdeeds.
⁹Exalt the LORD our God
and worship at his holy mountain,
for the LORD our God is holy.

■ PROVERBS 20:13–15

¹³Do not love sleep or you will grow poor;
stay awake and you will have food to
spare.

¹⁴'It's no good, it's no good!' says the
buyer –
then goes off and boasts about the
purchase.

¹⁵Gold there is, and rubies in abundance,
but lips that speak knowledge are a
rare jewel.

■ ROMANS 9:27–10:15

²⁷Isaiah cries out concerning Israel:

'Though the number of the Israelites be
like the sand by the sea,
only the remnant will be saved.

28 For the Lord will carry out
   his sentence on earth with speed and
      finality.'

29 It is just as Isaiah said previously:

'Unless the Lord Almighty
   had left us descendants,
we would have become like Sodom,
   we would have been like Gomorrah.'

30 What then shall we say? That the Gentiles, who did not pursue righteousness, have obtained it, a righteousness that is by faith; 31 but the people of Israel, who pursued the law as the way of righteousness, have not attained their goal. 32 Why not? Because they pursued it not by faith but as if it were by works. They stumbled over the 'stumbling stone.' 33 As it is written:

'See, I lay in Zion a stone that causes
   people to stumble
and a rock that makes them fall,
and the one who believes in him will
   never be put to shame.'

10 Brothers and sisters, my heart's desire and prayer to God for the Israelites is that they may be saved. 2 For I can testify about them that they are zealous for God, but their zeal is not based on knowledge. 3 Since they did not know the righteousness of God and sought to establish their own, they did not submit to God's

righteousness. 4 Christ is the culmination of the law so that there may be righteousness for everyone who believes.

5 Moses writes this about the righteousness that is by the law: 'The person who does these things will live by them.' 6 But the righteousness that is by faith says: 'Do not say in your heart, "Who will ascend into heaven?"' (that is, to bring Christ down) 7 'or "Who will descend into the deep?"' (that is, to bring Christ up from the dead). 8 But what does it say? 'The word is near you; it is in your mouth and in your heart,' that is, the message concerning faith that we proclaim: 9 if you declare with your mouth, 'Jesus is Lord,' and believe in your heart that God raised him from the dead, you will be saved. 10 For it is with your heart that you believe and are justified, and it is with your mouth that you profess your faith and are saved. 11 As Scripture says, 'Anyone who believes in him will never be put to shame.' 12 For there is no difference between Jew and Gentile – the same Lord is Lord of all and richly blesses all who call on him, 13 for, 'Everyone who calls on the name of the Lord will be saved.'

14 How, then, can they call on the one they have not believed in? And how can they believe in the one of whom they have not heard? And how can they hear without someone preaching to them? 15 And how can anyone preach unless they are sent? As it is written: 'How beautiful are the feet of those who bring good news!'

The Power of Holiness

'Exalt the LORD our God and worship at his footstool;
he is holy.' **Psalm 99:5**

'No one can know the true grace of God', said the great Bible teacher A. W. Tozer, 'who has not first known the fear of God.' He continued: 'Always there was about any manifestation of God something that dismayed the onlookers, that daunted and overawed them ...

I do not believe any lasting good can come from religious activities that are not rooted in this fear. Until we have been gripped by that nameless terror that results when an unholy creature is suddenly confronted by the One who is holiest of all, we are not likely to be affected by the doctrine of love and grace.'

There was a time when the nature and character of God was a constant theme in Christian pulpits. Generally speaking, today's preachers (and writers) tend to give people what they want rather than what they need. This is why we must stop every time we come across a reference to God's character in our Bibles and pause to consider it. No one has done anything mighty for God without a new vision of God's holiness. Ezekiel tells us of the 'rims' in his vision that were 'high and awesome' (Ezek. 1:18), and Jacob, rising from his sleep, said: 'How awesome is this place!' (Gen. 28:17).

We will be of little use to God unless we know how to tremble before Him, for otherwise our own ideas and feelings of self-sufficiency will soon take over. Have we lost the sense of awe when we come into God's presence which seemed to characterise the saints of the past? I am afraid we have.

PRAYER

O God, I am afraid as I draw near to You, but I draw near because I am afraid. Nothing or no one can dissolve the fears that hinder me but You. Draw me closer, for in You and You alone lie both my salvation and sanctification. Amen.

FURTHER STUDY

Exod. 3:1–5; Josh. 5:15;
Psa. 33:8; 89:7
• What was Moses and
  Joshua's experience?
• What did the psalmist
  admonish?

August 18

■ NEHEMIAH 7:61–9:38

⁶¹ The following came up from the towns of Tel Melah, Tel Harsha, Kerub, Addon and Immer, but they could not show that their families were descended from Israel:

⁶² the descendants of
Delaiah, Tobiah and Nekoda   642

⁶³ And from among the priests:

the descendants of
Hobaiah, Hakkoz and Barzillai (a man who had married a daughter of Barzillai the Gileadite and was called by that name).

⁶⁴ These searched for their family records, but they could not find them and so were excluded from the priesthood as unclean. ⁶⁵ The governor, therefore, ordered them not to eat any of the most sacred food until there should be a priest ministering with the Urim and Thummim.

66 The whole company numbered 42,360, 67 besides their 7,337 male and female slaves; and they also had 245 male and female singers. 68 There were 736 horses, 245 mules, 69 435 camels and 6,720 donkeys.

70 Some of the heads of the families contributed to the work. The governor gave to the treasury 1,000 darics of gold, 50 bowls and 530 garments for priests. 71 Some of the heads of the families gave to the treasury for the work 20,000 darics of gold and 2,200 minas of silver. 72 The total given by the rest of the people was 20,000 darics of gold, 2,000 minas of silver and 67 garments for priests.

73 The priests, the Levites, the gatekeepers, the musicians and the temple servants, along with certain of the people and the rest of the Israelites, settled in their own towns.

When the seventh month came and the Israelites had settled in their towns, 8 1 all the people came together as one in the square before the Water Gate. They told Ezra the teacher of the Law to bring out the Book of the Law of Moses, which the LORD had commanded for Israel.

2 So on the first day of the seventh month Ezra the priest brought the Law before the assembly, which was made up of men and women and all who were able to understand. 3 He read it aloud from daybreak till noon as he faced the square before the Water Gate in the presence of the men, women and others who could understand. And all the people listened attentively to the Book of the Law.

4 Ezra the teacher of the Law stood on a high wooden platform built for the occasion. Beside him on his right stood Mattithiah, Shema, Anaiah, Uriah, Hilkiah and Maaseiah; and on his left were Pedaiah, Mishael, Malkijah, Hashum,

Hashbaddanah, Zechariah and Meshullam. 5 Ezra opened the book. All the people could see him because he was standing above them; and as he opened it, the people all stood up. 6 Ezra praised the LORD, the great God; and all the people lifted their hands and responded, 'Amen! Amen!' Then they bowed down and worshipped the LORD with their faces to the ground.

7 The Levites – Jeshua, Bani, Sherebiah, Jamin, Akkub, Shabbethai, Hodiah, Maaseiah, Kelita, Azariah, Jozabad, Hanan and Pelaiah – instructed the people in the Law while the people were standing there. 8 They read from the Book of the Law of God, making it clear and giving the meaning so that the people understood what was being read.

9 Then Nehemiah the governor, Ezra the priest and teacher of the Law, and the Levites who were instructing the people said to them all, 'This day is holy to the LORD your God. Do not mourn or weep.' For all the people had been weeping as they listened to the words of the Law.

10 Nehemiah said, 'Go and enjoy choice food and sweet drinks, and send some to those who have nothing prepared. This day is holy to our Lord. Do not grieve, for the joy of the LORD is your strength.'

11 The Levites calmed all the people, saying, 'Be still, for this is a holy day. Do not grieve.'

12 Then all the people went away to eat and drink, to send portions of food and to celebrate with great joy, because they now understood the words that had been made known to them.

13 On the second day of the month, the heads of all the families, along with the priests and the Levites, gathered round Ezra the teacher of the Law to give attention to the words of the Law. 14 They found written in the Law, which the LORD had commanded through Moses, that the Israelites were to live in temporary shelters during the festival of the seventh month 15 and that they should

proclaim this word and spread it throughout their towns and in Jerusalem: 'Go out into the hill country and bring back branches from olive and wild olive trees, and from myrtles, palms and other leafy trees, to make temporary shelters' – as it is written.

[16] So the people went out and brought back branches and built themselves temporary shelters on their own roofs, in their courtyards, in the courts of the house of God and in the square by the Water Gate and the one by the Gate of Ephraim. [17] The whole company that had returned from exile built temporary shelters and lived in them. From the days of Joshua son of Nun until that day, the Israelites had not celebrated it like this. And their joy was very great.

[18] Day after day, from the first day to the last, Ezra read from the Book of the Law of God. They celebrated the festival for seven days, and on the eighth day, in accordance with the regulation, there was an assembly.

9 On the twenty-fourth day of the same month, the Israelites gathered together, fasting and wearing sackcloth and putting dust on their heads. [2] Those of Israelite descent had separated themselves from all foreigners. They stood in their places and confessed their sins and the sins of their ancestors. [3] They stood where they were and read from the Book of the Law of the LORD their God for a quarter of the day, and spent another quarter in confession and in worshipping the LORD their God. [4] Standing on the stairs of the Levites were Jeshua, Bani, Kadmiel, Shebaniah, Bunni, Sherebiah, Bani and Kenani. They cried out with loud voices to the LORD their God. [5] And the Levites – Jeshua, Kadmiel, Bani, Hashabneiah, Sherebiah, Hodiah, Shebaniah and Pethahiah – said: 'Stand up and praise the LORD your God, who is from everlasting to everlasting.'

'Blessed be your glorious name, and may it be exalted above all blessing and praise. [6] You alone are the LORD.

You made the heavens, even the highest heavens, and all their starry host, the earth and all that is on it, the seas and all that is in them. You give life to everything, and the multitudes of heaven worship you.

[7] 'You are the LORD God, who chose Abram and brought him out of Ur of the Chaldeans and named him Abraham. [8] You found his heart faithful to you, and you made a covenant with him to give to his descendants the land of the Canaanites, Hittites, Amorites, Perizzites, Jebusites and Girgashites. You have kept your promise because you are righteous.

[9] 'You saw the suffering of our ancestors in Egypt; you heard their cry at the Red Sea. [10] You sent signs and wonders against Pharaoh, against all his officials and all the people of his land, for you knew how arrogantly the Egyptians treated them. You made a name for yourself, which remains to this day. [11] You divided the sea before them, so that they passed through it on dry ground, but you hurled their pursuers into the depths, like a stone into mighty waters. [12] By day you led them with a pillar of cloud, and by night with a pillar of fire to give them light on the way they were to take.

[13] 'You came down on Mount Sinai; you spoke to them from heaven. You gave them regulations and laws that are just and right, and decrees and commands that are good. [14] You made known to them your holy Sabbath and gave them commands, decrees and laws through your servant Moses. [15] In their hunger you gave them bread from heaven and in their thirst you brought them water from the rock; you told them to go in and take possession of the land you had sworn with uplifted hand to give them.

16 'But they, our ancestors, became arrogant and stiff-necked, and they did not obey your commands. 17 They refused to listen and failed to remember the miracles you performed among them. They became stiff-necked and in their rebellion appointed a leader in order to return to their slavery. But you are a forgiving God, gracious and compassionate, slow to anger and abounding in love. Therefore you did not desert them, 18 even when they cast for themselves an image of a calf and said, "This is your god, who brought you up out of Egypt," or when they committed awful blasphemies.

19 'Because of your great compassion you did not abandon them in the wilderness. By day the pillar of cloud did not fail to guide them on their path, nor the pillar of fire by night to shine on the way they were to take. 20 You gave your good Spirit to instruct them. You did not withhold your manna from their mouths, and you gave them water for their thirst. 21 For forty years you sustained them in the wilderness; they lacked nothing, their clothes did not wear out nor did their feet become swollen.

22 'You gave them kingdoms and nations, allotting to them even the remotest frontiers. They took over the country of Sihon king of Heshbon and the country of Og king of Bashan. 23 You made their children as numerous as the stars in the sky, and you brought them into the land that you told their parents to enter and possess. 24 Their children went in and took possession of the land. You subdued before them the Canaanites, who lived in the land; you gave the Canaanites into their hands, along with their kings and the peoples of the land, to deal with them as they pleased. 25 They captured fortified cities and fertile land; they took possession of houses filled with all kinds of good things, wells already dug, vineyards, olive groves and fruit trees in abundance. They ate to the full and were well-nourished; they revelled in your great goodness.

26 'But they were disobedient and rebelled against you; they turned their backs on your law. They killed your prophets, who had warned them in order to turn them back to you; they committed awful blasphemies. 27 So you delivered them into the hands of their enemies, who oppressed them. But when they were oppressed they cried out to you. From heaven you heard them, and in your great compassion you gave them deliverers, who rescued them from the hand of their enemies.

28 'But as soon as they were at rest, they again did what was evil in your sight. Then you abandoned them to the hand of their enemies so that they ruled over them. And when they cried out to you again, you heard from heaven, and in your compassion you delivered them time after time.

29 'You warned them in order to turn them back to your law, but they became arrogant and disobeyed your commands. They sinned against your ordinances, of which you said, "The person who obeys them will live by them." Stubbornly they turned their backs on you, became stiff-necked and refused to listen. 30 For many years you were patient with them. By your Spirit you warned them through your prophets. Yet they paid no attention, so you gave them into the hands of the neighbouring peoples. 31 But in your great mercy you did not put an end to them or abandon them, for you are a gracious and merciful God.

³²'Now therefore, our God, the great God, mighty and awesome, who keeps his covenant of love, do not let all this hardship seem trifling in your eyes – the hardship that has come on us, on our kings and leaders, on our priests and prophets, on our ancestors and all your people, from the days of the kings of Assyria until today. ³³In all that has happened to us, you have remained righteous; you have acted faithfully, while we acted wickedly. ³⁴Our kings, our leaders, our priests and our ancestors did not follow your law; they did not pay attention to your commands or the statutes you warned them to keep. ³⁵Even while they were in their kingdom, enjoying your great goodness to them in the spacious and fertile land you gave them, they did not serve you or turn from their evil ways.

³⁶'But see, we are slaves today, slaves in the land you gave our ancestors so that they could eat its fruit and the other good things it produces. ³⁷Because of our sins, its abundant harvest goes to the kings you have placed over us. They rule over our bodies and our cattle as they please. We are in great distress.

³⁸'In view of all this, we are making a binding agreement, putting it in writing, and our leaders, our Levites and our priests are affixing their seals to it.'

▬ PSALM 100:1-5

¹Shout for joy to the LORD, all the earth.
² Worship the LORD with gladness;
     come before him with joyful songs.
³Know that the LORD is God.
     It is he who made us, and we are his;
     we are his people, the sheep of his
          pasture.

⁴Enter his gates with thanksgiving
     and his courts with praise;
     give thanks to him and praise his
          name.
⁵For the LORD is good and his love endures
          for ever;
     his faithfulness continues through all
          generations.

▬ PROVERBS 20:16-18

¹⁶Take the garment of one who puts up
          security for a stranger;
     hold it in pledge if it is done for an
          outsider.

¹⁷Food gained by fraud tastes sweet,
     but one ends up with a mouth full
          of gravel.

¹⁸Plans are established by seeking advice;
     so if you wage war, obtain guidance.

▬ ROMANS 10:16–11:10

¹⁶But not all the Israelites accepted the good news. For Isaiah says, 'Lord, who has believed our message?' ¹⁷Consequently, faith comes from hearing the message, and the message is heard through the word about Christ. ¹⁸But I ask: did they not hear? Of course they did:

'Their voice has gone out into all the
          earth,
     their words to the ends of the world.'

¹⁹Again I ask: did Israel not understand? First, Moses says,

'I will make you envious by those who
          are not a nation;
     I will make you angry by a nation that
          has no understanding.'

²⁰ And Isaiah boldly says,

'I was found by those who did not seek me;
    I revealed myself to those who did not
        ask for me.'

²¹ But concerning Israel he says,

'All day long I have held out my hands
    to a disobedient and obstinate people.'

11 I ask then: did God reject his people? By no means! I am an Israelite myself, a descendant of Abraham, from the tribe of Benjamin. ²God did not reject his people, whom he foreknew. Don't you know what Scripture says in the passage about Elijah – how he appealed to God against Israel: ³'Lord, they have killed your prophets and torn down your altars; I am the only one left, and they are trying to kill me'? ⁴And what was God's answer to him? 'I have reserved for myself seven thousand who have not bowed

the knee to Baal.' ⁵So too, at the present time there is a remnant chosen by grace. ⁶And if by grace, then it cannot be based on works; if it were, grace would no longer be grace.

⁷What then? What the people of Israel sought so earnestly they did not obtain. The elect among them did, but the others were hardened, ⁸as it is written:

'God gave them a spirit of stupor,
    eyes that could not see
    and ears that could not hear,
to this very day.'

⁹And David says:

'May their table become a snare and a
        trap,
    a stumbling-block and a retribution
        for them.
¹⁰ May their eyes be darkened so they
        cannot see,
    and their backs be bent for ever.'

Prompt Action

'Consequently, faith comes from hearing the message, and the message is heard through the word about Christ.' **Romans 10:17**

In Ephesians 6:16, Paul refers to 'the shield of faith'. Prayerfully, we must ask ourselves this question: How does faith act as a protective shield? First of all, we must understand what faith is and how the word is being used here by Paul.

A little boy, when asked to give a definition of faith, said, 'Faith is believing something you know isn't true.' Well, that is precisely what faith is not! Faith is believing what you know to be true! But it is even more than that – it is acting on what you know to be true.

Some people see faith as something vague and mysterious, but faith is one of the Christian's most practical commodities. Take this verse, for example: '... faith without deeds is dead' (James 2:26). There is always the element of activity in faith; it prompts us to action. 'Now faith is confidence in what we hope for and assurance about what we do not see' (Heb. 11:1).

Taking the shield of faith, then, is responding to the things the Devil hurls at us by the quick application of what we believe about God and His Word, the Bible. When Satan sends his 'flaming arrows' in our direction, we can either stand and lament the fact that we are being attacked, or quickly raise the shield of faith and remind ourselves that the Devil is a liar from the very beginning. We affirm that because we are redeemed by the blood of Christ, the Devil has no legal or moral right to taunt us. But believing this is not enough; it must be acted on – and acted on quickly.

PRAYER

Father, I see that when Satan throws his 'flaming arrows' at me, I must act and act quickly. Help my faith to be so strong that it will not need a 'jump start' to get it going. This I ask in Jesus' name. Amen.

FURTHER STUDY

James 2:14-26; Heb. 11:1; 1 John 5:4
• How are we justified?
• Write out your definition of faith.

August 19

■ NEHEMIAH 10:1–11:19

10 Those who sealed it were:

Nehemiah the governor, the son of Hakaliah.

Zedekiah, ²Seraiah, Azariah, Jeremiah,
³Pashhur, Amariah, Malkijah,
⁴Hattush, Shebaniah, Malluk,
⁵Harim, Meremoth, Obadiah,
⁶Daniel, Ginnethon, Baruch,
⁷Meshullam, Abijah, Mijamin,
⁸Maaziah, Bilgai and Shemaiah.
These were the priests.

⁹The Levites:

Jeshua son of Azaniah, Binnui of the sons of Henadad, Kadmiel,
¹⁰and their associates: Shebaniah, Hodiah, Kelita, Pelaiah, Hanan,

¹¹Mika, Rehob, Hashabiah,
¹²Zakkur, Sherebiah, Shebaniah,
¹³Hodiah, Bani and Beninu.

¹⁴The leaders of the people:

Parosh, Pahath-Moab, Elam, Zattu, Bani,
¹⁵Bunni, Azgad, Bebai,
¹⁶Adonijah, Bigvai, Adin,
¹⁷Ater, Hezekiah, Azzur,
¹⁸Hodiah, Hashum, Bezai,
¹⁹Hariph, Anathoth, Nebai,
²⁰Magpiash, Meshullam, Hezir,
²¹Meshezabel, Zadok, Jaddua,
²²Pelatiah, Hanan, Anaiah,
²³Hoshea, Hananiah, Hasshub,
²⁴Hallohesh, Pilha, Shobek,
²⁵Rehum, Hashabnah, Maaseiah,
²⁶Ahiah, Hanan, Anan,
²⁷Malluk, Harim and Baanah.

²⁸'The rest of the people – priests,

Levites, gatekeepers, musicians, temple servants and all who separated themselves from the neighbouring peoples for the sake of the Law of God, together with their wives and all their sons and daughters who are able to understand – ²⁹ all these now join their fellow Israelites the nobles, and bind themselves with a curse and an oath to follow the Law of God given through Moses the servant of God and to obey carefully all the commands, regulations and decrees of the LORD our Lord.

³⁰ 'We promise not to give our daughters in marriage to the peoples around us or take their daughters for our sons.

³¹ 'When the neighbouring peoples bring merchandise or grain to sell on the Sabbath, we will not buy from them on the Sabbath or on any holy day. Every seventh year we will forgo working the land and will cancel all debts.

³² 'We assume the responsibility for carrying out the commands to give a third of a shekel each year for the service of the house of our God: ³³ for the bread set out on the table; for the regular grain offerings and burnt offerings; for the offerings on the Sabbaths, at the New Moon feasts and at the appointed festivals; for the holy offerings; for sin offerings to make atonement for Israel; and for all the duties of the house of our God.

³⁴ 'We – the priests, the Levites and the people – have cast lots to determine when each of our families is to bring to the house of our God at set times each year a contribution of wood to burn on the altar of the LORD our God, as it is written in the Law.

³⁵ 'We also assume responsibility for bringing to the house of the LORD each year the firstfruits of our crops and of every fruit tree.

³⁶ 'As it is also written in the Law, we will bring the firstborn of our sons and of our cattle, of our herds and of our flocks to the house of our God, to the priests ministering there.

³⁷ 'Moreover, we will bring to the storerooms of the house of our God, to the priests, the first of our ground meal, of our grain offerings, of the fruit of all our trees and of our new wine and olive oil. And we will bring a tithe of our crops to the Levites, for it is the Levites who collect the tithes in all the towns where we work. ³⁸ A priest descended from Aaron is to accompany the Levites when they receive the tithes, and the Levites are to bring a tenth of the tithes up to the house of our God, to the storerooms of the treasury. ³⁹ The people of Israel, including the Levites, are to bring their contributions of grain, new wine and olive oil to the storerooms, where the articles for the sanctuary and for the ministering priests, the gatekeepers and the musicians are also kept.

'We will not neglect the house of our God.'

11 Now the leaders of the people settled in Jerusalem. The rest of the people cast lots to bring one out of every ten of them to live in Jerusalem, the holy city, while the remaining nine were to stay in their own towns. ² The people commended all who volunteered to live in Jerusalem.

³ These are the provincial leaders who settled in Jerusalem (now some Israelites, priests, Levites, temple servants and descendants of Solomon's servants lived in the towns of Judah, each on their own property in the various towns, ⁴ while other people from both Judah and Benjamin lived in Jerusalem):

From the descendants of Judah:

Athaiah son of Uzziah, the son of Zechariah, the son of Amariah, the son of Shephatiah, the son of Mahalalel, a descendant of Perez; ⁵and Maaseiah son of Baruch, the son of Kol-Hozeh, the son of Hazaiah, the son of Adaiah, the son of Joiarib, the son of Zechariah, a descendant of Shelah. ⁶The descendants of Perez who lived in Jerusalem totalled 468 men of standing.

⁷From the descendants of Benjamin:

Sallu son of Meshullam, the son of Joed, the son of Pedaiah, the son of Kolaiah, the son of Maaseiah, the son of Ithiel, the son of Jeshaiah, ⁸and his followers, Gabbai and Sallai – 928 men. ⁹Joel son of Zikri was their chief officer, and Judah son of Hassenuah was over the New Quarter of the city.

¹⁰From the priests:

Jedaiah; the son of Joiarib; Jakin; ¹¹Seraiah son of Hilkiah, the son of Meshullam, the son of Zadok, the son of Meraioth, the son of Ahitub, the official in charge of the house of God, ¹²and their associates, who carried on work for the temple – 822 men; Adaiah son of Jeroham, the son of Pelaliah, the son of Amzi, the son of Zechariah, the son of Pashhur, the son of Malkijah, ¹³and his associates, who were heads of families – 242 men; Amashsai son of Azarel, the son of Ahzai, the son of Meshillemoth, the son of Immer, ¹⁴and his associates, who were men of standing – 128. Their chief officer was Zabdiel son of Haggedolim.

¹⁵From the Levites:

Shemaiah son of Hasshub, the son of Azrikam, the son of Hashabiah, the son of Bunni; ¹⁶Shabbethai and Jozabad, two of the heads of the Levites, who had charge of the outside work of the house of God; ¹⁷Mattaniah son of Mika, the son of Zabdi, the son of Asaph, the director who led in thanksgiving and prayer; Bakbukiah, second among his associates; and Abda son of Shammua, the son of Galal, the son of Jeduthun. ¹⁸The Levites in the holy city totalled 284.

¹⁹The gatekeepers:

Akkub, Talmon and their associates, who kept watch at the gates – 172 men.

◼ PSALM 101:1-8

¹I will sing of your love and justice;
　to you, LORD, I will sing praise.
²I will be careful to lead a blameless life –
　when will you come to me?

I will conduct the affairs of my
　house
　with a blameless heart.
³I will not look with approval
　on anything that is vile.

I hate what faithless people do;
　I will have no part in it.
⁴The perverse of heart shall be far from
　me;
　I will have nothing to do with what
　is evil.

⁵Whoever slanders their neighbour in
　secret,
　I will put to silence;
whoever has haughty eyes and a proud
　heart,
　I will not tolerate.

⁶ My eyes will be on the faithful in the
land,
that they may dwell with me;
the one whose way of life is blameless
will minister to me.

⁷ No one who practises deceit
will dwell in my house;
no one who speaks falsely
will stand in my presence.

⁸ Every morning I will put to silence
all the wicked in the land;
I will cut off every evildoer
from the city of the LORD.

▬ PROVERBS 20:19-21

¹⁹ A gossip betrays a confidence;
so avoid anyone who talks too much.

²⁰ If someone curses their father or mother,
their lamp will be snuffed out in pitch
darkness.

²¹ An inheritance claimed too soon
will not be blessed at the end.

▬ ROMANS 11:11-36

¹¹ Again I ask: did they stumble so as to
fall beyond recovery? Not at all! Rather,
because of their transgression, salvation
has come to the Gentiles to make Israel envious. ¹² But if their transgression means
riches for the world, and their loss means
riches for the Gentiles, how much greater
riches will their full inclusion bring!

¹³ I am talking to you Gentiles. Inasmuch
as I am the apostle to the Gentiles, I take
pride in my ministry ¹⁴ in the hope that I
may somehow arouse my own people to
envy and save some of them. ¹⁵ For if their
rejection brought reconciliation to the

world, what will their acceptance be but life
from the dead? ¹⁶ If the part of the dough
offered as firstfruits is holy, then the whole
batch is holy; if the root is holy, so are the
branches.

¹⁷ If some of the branches have been broken off, and you, though a wild olive shoot,
have been grafted in among the others and
now share in the nourishing sap from the
olive root, ¹⁸ do not consider yourself to be
superior to those other branches. If you
do, consider this: you do not support the
root, but the root supports you. ¹⁹ You will
say then, 'Branches were broken off so that
I could be grafted in.' ²⁰ Granted. But they
were broken off because of unbelief, and
you stand by faith. Do not be arrogant, but
tremble. ²¹ For if God did not spare the natural branches, he will not spare you either.

²² Consider therefore the kindness and
sternness of God: sternness to those who fell,
but kindness to you, provided that you continue in his kindness. Otherwise, you also will be
cut off. ²³ And if they do not persist in unbelief,
they will be grafted in, for God is able to graft
them in again. ²⁴ After all, if you were cut out
of an olive tree that is wild by nature, and contrary to nature were grafted into a cultivated
olive tree, how much more readily will these,
the natural branches, be grafted into their
own olive tree!

²⁵ I do not want you to be ignorant of
this mystery, brothers and sisters, so that
you may not be conceited: Israel has experienced a hardening in part until the full
number of the Gentiles has come in, ²⁶ and
in this way all Israel will be saved. As it is
written:

'The deliverer will come from Zion;
he will turn godlessness away from
Jacob.
²⁷ And this is my covenant with them
when I take away their sins.'

²⁸ As far as the gospel is concerned, they

are enemies for your sake; but as far as election is concerned, they are loved on account of the patriarchs, [29] for God's gifts and his call are irrevocable. [30] Just as you who were at one time disobedient to God have now received mercy as a result of their disobedience, [31] so they too have now become disobedient in order that they too may now receive mercy as a result of God's mercy to you. [32] For God has bound everyone over to disobedience so that he may have mercy on them all.

[33] Oh, the depth of the riches of the wisdom
    and knowledge of God!
How unsearchable his judgments,
    and his paths beyond tracing out!
[34] 'Who has known the mind of the Lord?
    Or who has been his counsellor?'
[35] 'Who has ever given to God,
    that God should repay them?'
[36] For from him and through him and for
    him are all things.
To him be the glory for ever! Amen.

A Lost Art

'Who has known the mind of the Lord? Or who has been his counsellor?' **Romans 11:34**

A subject which is of great interest to many today is anthropology: the study of man. Although this subject is of great importance, for a Christian there is something far more important: the study of God. The great preacher A. W. Pink in his book *The Attributes of God* said: 'The highest science, the loftiest speculation, the mightiest philosophy which can engage the attention of a child of God is the name, the nature, the person, the work, the doings, and the existence of the great God whom he calls his Father.'

The contemplation of God seems to be a lost art today. We appear to be more concerned about subjects such as church growth, the end times, signs, wonders, and miracles. I am not suggesting these issues are unimportant, but they must not be allowed to replace the supremely important matter of the constant, earnest, and continued investigation of the great subject of the Deity. The more we know of God, the more effective will be our lives here on earth. Those who have given themselves to the study of God tell us that it humbles the mind, expands the soul, and consoles the heart.

It humbles the mind. When our minds grapple with other subjects, we feel a degree of self-content and come away thinking, 'Behold, I am wise.' But when our minds engage with thoughts of God, we discover that there is no plumb line that can sound His depth, and we come away thinking, 'Behold, I know nothing.' In an age that stresses the supremacy of the human ego, it is no bad thing to learn that there is something far greater.

PRAYER

Gracious and loving heavenly Father, teach me how to focus on You and contemplate You so that all vanity and pride dies within me, and I go on my way no longer caught up with how wise I am but how wonderful You are. In Jesus' name. Amen.

FURTHER STUDY

Isa. 40:18-26; Job 11:7-9
• What probing question does Isaiah ask?
• What conclusion had Zophar come to?

August 20

▬ NEHEMIAH 11:20–12:47

²⁰ The rest of the Israelites, with the priests and Levites, were in all the towns of Judah, each on their ancestral property.

²¹ The temple servants lived on the hill of Ophel, and Ziha and Gishpa were in charge of them.

²² The chief officer of the Levites in Jerusalem was Uzzi son of Bani, the son of Hashabiah, the son of Mattaniah, the son of Mika. Uzzi was one of Asaph's descendants, who were the musicians responsible for the service of the house of God. ²³ The musicians were under the king's orders, which regulated their daily activity.

²⁴ Pethahiah son of Meshezabel, one of the descendants of Zerah son of Judah, was the king's agent in all affairs relating to the people.

²⁵ As for the villages with their fields, some of the people of Judah lived in Kiriath Arba and its surrounding settlements, in Dibon and its settlements, in Jekabzeel and its villages, ²⁶ in Jeshua, in Moladah, in Beth Pelet, ²⁷ in Hazar Shual, in Beersheba and its settlements, ²⁸ in Ziklag, in Mekonah and its settlements, ²⁹ in En Rimmon, in Zorah, in Jarmuth, ³⁰ Zanoah, Adullam and their villages, in Lachish and its fields, and in Azekah and its settlements. So they were

living all the way from Beersheba to the Valley of Hinnom.

³¹ The descendants of the Benjaminites from Geba lived in Mikmash, Aija, Bethel and its settlements, ³² in Anathoth, Nob and Ananiah, ³³ in Hazor, Ramah and Gittaim, ³⁴ in Hadid, Zeboim and Neballat, ³⁵ in Lod and Ono, and in Ge Harashim.

³⁶ Some of the divisions of the Levites of Judah settled in Benjamin.

12 These were the priests and Levites who returned with Zerubbabel son of Shealtiel and with Joshua:

Seraiah, Jeremiah, Ezra,
² Amariah, Malluk, Hattush,
³ Shekaniah, Rehum, Meremoth,
⁴ Iddo, Ginnethon, Abijah,
⁵ Mijamin, Moadiah, Bilgah,
⁶ Shemaiah, Joiarib, Jedaiah,
⁷ Sallu, Amok, Hilkiah and Jedaiah.

These were the leaders of the priests and their associates in the days of Joshua.

⁸ The Levites were Jeshua, Binnui, Kadmiel, Sherebiah, Judah, and also Mattaniah, who, together with his associates, was in charge of the songs of thanksgiving. ⁹ Bakbukiah and Unni, their associates, stood opposite them in the services.

¹⁰ Joshua was the father of Joiakim, Joiakim the father of Eliashib, Eliashib the father of Joiada, ¹¹ Joiada the father

of Jonathan, and Jonathan the father of Jaddua.

¹² In the days of Joiakim, these were the heads of the priestly families:

of Seraiah's family, Meraiah;

of Jeremiah's, Hananiah;

¹³ of Ezra's, Meshullam;

of Amariah's, Jehohanan;

¹⁴ of Malluk's, Jonathan;

of Shekaniah's, Joseph;

¹⁵ of Harim's, Adna;

of Meremoth's, Helkai;

¹⁶ of Iddo's, Zechariah;

of Ginnethon's, Meshullam;

¹⁷ of Abijah's, Zikri;

of Miniamin's and of Moadiah's, Piltai;

¹⁸ of Bilgah's, Shammua;

of Shemaiah's, Jehonathan;

¹⁹ of Joiarib's, Mattenai;

of Jedaiah's, Uzzi;

²⁰ of Sallu's, Kallai;

of Amok's, Eber;

²¹ of Hilkiah's, Hashabiah;

of Jedaiah's, Nethanel.

²² The family heads of the Levites in the days of Eliashib, Joiada, Johanan and Jaddua, as well as those of the priests, were recorded in the reign of Darius the Persian. ²³ The family heads among the descendants of Levi up to the time of Johanan son of Eliashib were recorded in the book of the annals. ²⁴ And the leaders of the Levites were Hashabiah, Sherebiah, Jeshua son of Kadmiel, and their associates, who stood opposite them to give praise and thanksgiving, one section responding to the other, as prescribed by David the man of God.

²⁵ Mattaniah, Bakbukiah, Obadiah, Meshullam, Talmon and Akkub were gatekeepers who guarded the storerooms at the gates. ²⁶ They served in the days of Joiakim son of Joshua, the son of Jozadak, and in the days of Nehemiah the governor and of Ezra the priest, the teacher of the Law.

²⁷ At the dedication of the wall of Jerusalem, the Levites were sought out from where they lived and were brought to Jerusalem to celebrate joyfully the dedication with songs of thanksgiving and with the music of cymbals, harps and lyres. ²⁸ The musicians also were brought together from the region around Jerusalem – from the villages of the Netophathites, ²⁹ from Beth Gilgal, and from the area of Geba and Azmaveth, for the musicians had built villages for themselves around Jerusalem. ³⁰ When the priests and Levites had purified themselves ceremonially, they purified the people, the gates and the wall.

³¹ I had the leaders of Judah go up on top of the wall. I also assigned two large choirs to give thanks. One was to proceed on top of the wall to the right, towards the Dung Gate. ³² Hoshaiah and half the leaders of Judah followed them, ³³ along with Azariah, Ezra, Meshullam, ³⁴ Judah, Benjamin, Shemaiah, Jeremiah, ³⁵ as well as some priests with trumpets, and also Zechariah son of Jonathan, the son of Shemaiah, the son of Mattaniah, the son of Micaiah, the son of Zakkur, the son of Asaph, ³⁶ and his associates – Shemaiah, Azarel, Milalai, Gilalai, Maai, Nethanel, Judah and Hanani – with musical instruments prescribed by David the man of God. Ezra the teacher of the Law led the procession. ³⁷ At the Fountain Gate they continued directly up the steps of the City of David on the ascent to the wall and passed above the site of David's palace to the Water Gate on the east.

³⁸ The second choir proceeded in the opposite direction. I followed them on top of the wall, together with half the people – past the Tower of the Ovens to the Broad Wall, ³⁹ over the Gate of Ephraim, the Jeshanah Gate, the Fish Gate, the Tower of Hananel and the Tower of the Hundred, as far as the Sheep Gate. At the Gate of the Guard they stopped.

⁴⁰ The two choirs that gave thanks then took their places in the house of God; so did

I, together with half the officials, [41] as well as the priests – Eliakim, Maaseiah, Miniamin, Micaiah, Elioenai, Zechariah and Hananiah with their trumpets – [42] and also Maaseiah, Shemaiah, Eleazar, Uzzi, Jehohanan, Malkijah, Elam and Ezer. The choirs sang under the direction of Jezrahiah. [43] And on that day they offered great sacrifices, rejoicing because God had given them great joy. The women and children also rejoiced. The sound of rejoicing in Jerusalem could be heard far away.

[44] At that time men were appointed to be in charge of the storerooms for the contributions, firstfruits and tithes. From the fields around the towns they were to bring into the storerooms the portions required by the Law for the priests and the Levites, for Judah was pleased with the ministering priests and Levites. [45] They performed the service of their God and the service of purification, as did also the musicians and gatekeepers, according to the commands of David and his son Solomon. [46] For long ago, in the days of David and Asaph, there had been directors for the musicians and for the songs of praise and thanksgiving to God. [47] So in the days of Zerubbabel and of Nehemiah, all Israel contributed the daily portions for the musicians and the gatekeepers. They also set aside the portion for the other Levites, and the Levites set aside the portion for the descendants of Aaron.

⸺ **PSALM 102:1-11**

[1] Hear my prayer, LORD;
    let my cry for help come to you.
[2] Do not hide your face from me
    when I am in distress.
Turn your ear to me;
    when I call, answer me quickly.

[3] For my days vanish like smoke;
    my bones burn like glowing embers.

[4] My heart is blighted and withered like
    grass;
    I forget to eat my food.
[5] In my distress I groan aloud
    and am reduced to skin and bones.
[6] I am like a desert owl,
    like an owl among the ruins.
[7] I lie awake; I have become
    like a bird alone on a roof.
[8] All day long my enemies taunt me;
    those who rail against me use my
    name as a curse.
[9] For I eat ashes as my food
    and mingle my drink with tears
[10] because of your great wrath,
    for you have taken me up and thrown
    me aside.
[11] My days are like the evening shadow;
    I wither away like grass.

⸺ **PROVERBS 20:22-23**

[22] Do not say, 'I'll pay you back for this
    wrong!'
    Wait for the LORD, and he will avenge
    you.

[23] The LORD detests differing weights,
    and dishonest scales do not please
    him.

⸺ **ROMANS 12:1-21**

12 Therefore, I urge you, brothers and sisters, in view of God's mercy, to offer your bodies as a living sacrifice, holy and pleasing to God – this is your true and proper worship. [2] Do not conform to the pattern of this world, but be transformed by the renewing of your mind. Then you will be able to test and approve what God's will is – his good, pleasing and perfect will.

[3] For by the grace given me I say to every one of you: do not think of yourself more

highly than you ought, but rather think of yourself with sober judgment, in accordance with the faith God has distributed to each of you. ⁴For just as each of us has one body with many members, and these members do not all have the same function, ⁵so in Christ we, though many, form one body, and each member belongs to all the others. ⁶We have different gifts, according to the grace given to each of us. If your gift is prophesying, then prophesy in accordance with your faith; ⁷if it is serving, then serve; if it is teaching, then teach; ⁸if it is to encourage, then give encouragement; if it is giving, then give generously; if it is to lead, do it diligently; if it is to show mercy, do it cheerfully.

⁹Love must be sincere. Hate what is evil; cling to what is good. ¹⁰Be devoted to one another in love. Honour one another above yourselves. ¹¹Never be lacking in zeal, but keep your spiritual fervour, serving the Lord. ¹²Be joyful in hope, patient in affliction, faithful in prayer. ¹³Share with the Lord's people who are in need. Practise hospitality.

¹⁴Bless those who persecute you; bless and do not curse. ¹⁵Rejoice with those who rejoice; mourn with those who mourn. ¹⁶Live in harmony with one another. Do not be proud, but be willing to associate with people of low position. Do not be conceited.

¹⁷Do not repay anyone evil for evil. Be careful to do what is right in the eyes of everyone. ¹⁸If it is possible, as far as it depends on you, live at peace with everyone. ¹⁹Do not take revenge, my dear friends, but leave room for God's wrath, for it is written: 'It is mine to avenge; I will repay,' says the Lord. ²⁰On the contrary:

'If your enemy is hungry, feed him;
    if he is thirsty, give him something to
        drink.
In doing this, you will heap burning
    coals on his head.'

²¹Do not be overcome by evil, but overcome evil with good.

Evil Is Bad for Us

'Love must be sincere. Hate what is evil; cling to what is good.' **Romans 12:9**

In considering the words 'Lead us not into temptation, but deliver us from the evil one', here we concentrate on 'deliver us from the evil one'. Notice it is not a prayer for deliverance from this or that type of evil, but from evil itself. To Jesus, evil was evil in whatever form it came – whether in the evil of the flesh or the evil of the disposition, whether in the individual will or in the corporate will. Evil was never good, and good was never evil.

Someone has pointed out that the word 'evil' is the word 'live' spelled backwards. Evil, then, could be said to be anti-life. Some people find out how not to live the hard way. They think they know better than God and follow a way of their own choosing, only to find, like the rats in the scientific experiments who go down the wrong path, that there are wires at the end which carry electric shocks. These shocks are of various kinds: neuroses, inner conflicts, as well as some forms of physical illness.

Society is concerned about sexual diseases which are spread through sexual permissiveness. God has made it impossible for us to live against His design or harm ourselves without His protest. And He protests because He loves us.

We can decide to have done with evil. The best way to deal with evil is to keep away from it, hence the prayer 'Lead us not into temptation, but deliver us from the evil one.' I say again, evil is bad for us, and good is good for us.

PRAYER

My Father, You who made me for good, because goodness is good for me, help me to abstain, not only from evil, but from the very appearance of it. For Your own dear name's sake. Amen.

FURTHER STUDY

Gen. 39; 1 Cor. 10:6;
1 Thess. 5:22; 1 Pet. 3:11;
2 Tim. 2:22
• How did Joseph resist temptation?
• What did Paul advise Timothy?

August 21

■ NEHEMIAH 13:1– ESTHER 1:22

13 On that day the Book of Moses was read aloud in the hearing of the people and there it was found written that no Ammonite or Moabite should ever be admitted into the assembly of God, ²because they had not met the Israelites with food and water but had hired Balaam to call a curse down on them. (Our God, however, turned the curse into a blessing.) ³When the people heard this law, they excluded from Israel all who were of foreign descent.

⁴Before this, Eliashib the priest had been put in charge of the storerooms of the house of our God. He was closely associated with Tobiah, ⁵and he had provided him with a large room formerly used to store the grain offerings and incense and temple articles, and also the tithes of grain, new wine and olive oil prescribed for the Levites, musicians and gatekeepers, as well as the contributions for the priests.

⁶But while all this was going on, I was not in Jerusalem, for in the thirty-second year of Artaxerxes king of Babylon I had returned to the king. Some time later I asked his permission ⁷and came back to Jerusalem. Here I learned about the evil thing Eliashib had done in providing Tobiah a room in the courts of the house of God. ⁸I was greatly displeased and threw all Tobiah's household goods out of the room. ⁹I gave orders to purify the rooms, and then I put back into them the equipment of the house of God, with the grain offerings and the incense.

¹⁰I also learned that the portions assigned to the Levites had not been given to them, and that all the Levites and musicians responsible for the service had gone back to their own fields. ¹¹So I rebuked the officials and asked them, 'Why is the house of God neglected?' Then I called them together and stationed them at their posts.

¹² All Judah brought the tithes of grain, new wine and olive oil into the storerooms. ¹³ I put Shelemiah the priest, Zadok the scribe, and a Levite named Pedaiah in charge of the storerooms and made Hanan son of Zakkur, the son of Mattaniah, their assistant, because they were considered trustworthy. They were made responsible for distributing the supplies to their fellow Levites.

¹⁴ Remember me for this, my God, and do not blot out what I have so faithfully done for the house of my God and its services.

¹⁵ In those days I saw people in Judah treading winepresses on the Sabbath and bringing in grain and loading it on donkeys, together with wine, grapes, figs and all other kinds of loads. And they were bringing all this into Jerusalem on the Sabbath. Therefore I warned them against selling food on that day. ¹⁶ People from Tyre who lived in Jerusalem were bringing in fish and all kinds of merchandise and selling them in Jerusalem on the Sabbath to the people of Judah. ¹⁷ I rebuked the nobles of Judah and said to them, 'What is this wicked thing you are doing – desecrating the Sabbath day? ¹⁸ Didn't your ancestors do the same things, so that our God brought all this calamity on us and on this city? Now you are stirring up more wrath against Israel by desecrating the Sabbath.'

¹⁹ When evening shadows fell on the gates of Jerusalem before the Sabbath, I ordered the doors to be shut and not opened until the Sabbath was over. I stationed some of my own men at the gates so that no load could be brought in on the Sabbath day. ²⁰ Once or twice the merchants and sellers of all kinds of goods spent the night outside Jerusalem. ²¹ But I warned them and said, 'Why do you spend the night by the wall? If you do this again, I will arrest you.' From that time on they no longer came on the Sabbath. ²² Then I commanded the Levites to purify themselves and go and guard the gates in order to keep the Sabbath day holy.

Remember me for this also, my God, and show mercy to me according to your great love.

²³ Moreover, in those days I saw men of Judah who had married women from Ashdod, Ammon and Moab. ²⁴ Half of their children spoke the language of Ashdod or the language of one of the other peoples, and did not know how to speak the language of Judah. ²⁵ I rebuked them and called curses down on them. I beat some of the men and pulled out their hair. I made them take an oath in God's name and said: 'You are not to give your daughters in marriage to their sons, nor are you to take their daughters in marriage for your sons or for yourselves. ²⁶ Was it not because of marriages like these that Solomon king of Israel sinned? Among the many nations there was no king like him. He was loved by his God, and God made him king over all Israel, but even he was led into sin by foreign women. ²⁷ Must we hear now that you too are doing all this terrible wickedness and are being unfaithful to our God by marrying foreign women?'

²⁸ One of the sons of Joiada son of Eliashib the high priest was son-in-law to Sanballat the Horonite. And I drove him away from me.

²⁹ Remember them, my God, because they defiled the priestly office and the covenant of the priesthood and of the Levites.

³⁰ So I purified the priests and the Levites of everything foreign, and assigned them duties, each to his own task. ³¹ I also made provision for contributions of wood at designated times, and for the firstfruits.

Remember me with favour, my God.

1 This is what happened during the time of Xerxes, the Xerxes who ruled over 127 provinces stretching from India to Cush: ²At that time King Xerxes reigned from his royal throne in the citadel of Susa, ³and in the third year of his reign he gave a banquet for all his nobles and officials. The military leaders of Persia and Media, the princes, and the nobles of the provinces were present.

⁴For a full 180 days he displayed the vast wealth of his kingdom and the splendour and glory of his majesty. ⁵When these days were over, the king gave a banquet, lasting seven days, in the enclosed garden of the king's palace, for all the people from the least to the greatest who were in the citadel of Susa. ⁶The garden had hangings of white and blue linen, fastened with cords of white linen and purple material to silver rings on marble pillars. There were couches of gold and silver on a mosaic pavement of porphyry, marble, mother-of-pearl and other costly stones. ⁷Wine was served in goblets of gold, each one different from the other, and the royal wine was abundant, in keeping with the king's liberality. ⁸By the king's command each guest was allowed to drink without restriction, for the king instructed all the wine stewards to serve each man what he wished.

⁹Queen Vashti also gave a banquet for the women in the royal palace of King Xerxes.

¹⁰On the seventh day, when King Xerxes was in high spirits from wine, he commanded the seven eunuchs who served him – Mehuman, Biztha, Harbona, Bigtha, Abagtha, Zethar and Karkas – ¹¹to bring before him Queen Vashti, wearing her royal crown, in order to display her beauty to the people and nobles, for she was lovely to look at. ¹²But when the attendants delivered the king's command, Queen Vashti refused to come. Then the king became furious and burned with anger.

¹³Since it was customary for the king to consult experts in matters of law and justice, he spoke with the wise men who understood the times ¹⁴and were closest to the king – Karshena, Shethar, Admatha, Tarshish, Meres, Marsena and Memukan, the seven nobles of Persia and Media who had special access to the king and were highest in the kingdom.

¹⁵'According to law, what must be done to Queen Vashti?' he asked. 'She has not obeyed the command of King Xerxes that the eunuchs have taken to her.'

¹⁶Then Memukan replied in the presence of the king and the nobles, 'Queen Vashti has done wrong, not only against the king but also against all the nobles and the peoples of all the provinces of King Xerxes. ¹⁷For the queen's conduct will become known to all the women, and so they will despise their husbands and say, "King Xerxes commanded Queen Vashti to be brought before him, but she would not come." ¹⁸This very day the Persian and Median women of the nobility who have heard about the queen's conduct will respond to all the king's nobles in the same way. There will be no end of disrespect and discord.

¹⁹'Therefore, if it pleases the king, let him issue a royal decree and let it be written in the laws of Persia and Media, which cannot be repealed, that Vashti is never again to enter the presence of King Xerxes. Also let the king give her royal position to someone else who is better than she. ²⁰Then when the king's edict is proclaimed throughout all his vast realm, all the women will respect their husbands, from the least to the greatest.'

²¹The king and his nobles were pleased with this advice, so the king did as Memukan proposed. ²²He sent dispatches to all parts of the kingdom, to each province in its own script and to each people in their own language, proclaiming that every man should be ruler over his own household, using his native tongue.

■ PSALM 102:12-17

¹² But you, LORD, sit enthroned for ever;
　　your renown endures through all
　　　generations.
¹³ You will arise and have compassion on
　　　Zion,
　　for it is time to show favour to her;
　　　the appointed time has come.
¹⁴ For her stones are dear to your servants;
　　her very dust moves them to pity.
¹⁵ The nations will fear the name of the
　　　LORD,
　　all the kings of the earth will revere
　　　your glory.
¹⁶ For the LORD will rebuild Zion
　　and appear in his glory.
¹⁷ He will respond to the prayer of the
　　　destitute;
　　he will not despise their plea.

■ PROVERBS 20:24-25

²⁴ A person's steps are directed by the LORD.
　　How then can anyone understand
　　　their own way?

²⁵ It is a trap to dedicate something rashly
　　and only later to consider one's vows.

■ ROMANS 13:1–14:12

13 Let everyone be subject to the governing authorities, for there is no authority except that which God has established. The authorities that exist have been established by God. ² Consequently, whoever rebels against the authority is rebelling against what God has instituted, and those who do so will bring judgment on themselves. ³ For rulers hold no terror for those who do right, but for those who do wrong. Do you want to be free from fear of the one in authority? Then do what is right and you

will be commended. ⁴ For the one in authority is God's servant for your good. But if you do wrong, be afraid, for rulers do not bear the sword for no reason. They are God's servants, agents of wrath to bring punishment on the wrongdoer. ⁵ Therefore, it is necessary to submit to the authorities, not only because of possible punishment but also as a matter of conscience.

⁶ This is also why you pay taxes, for the authorities are God's servants, who give their full time to governing. ⁷ Give to everyone what you owe them: if you owe taxes, pay taxes; if revenue, then revenue; if respect, then respect; if honour, then honour.

⁸ Let no debt remain outstanding, except the continuing debt to love one another, for whoever loves others has fulfilled the law. ⁹ The commandments, 'You shall not commit adultery,' 'You shall not murder,' 'You shall not steal,' 'You shall not covet,' and whatever other command there may be, are summed up in this one command: 'Love your neighbour as yourself.' ¹⁰ Love does no harm to a neighbour. Therefore love is the fulfilment of the law.

¹¹ And do this, understanding the present time: the hour has already come for you to wake up from your slumber, because our salvation is nearer now than when we first believed. ¹² The night is nearly over; the day is almost here. So let us put aside the deeds of darkness and put on the armour of light. ¹³ Let us behave decently, as in the daytime, not in carousing and drunkenness, not in sexual immorality and debauchery, not in dissension and jealousy. ¹⁴ Rather, clothe yourselves with the Lord Jesus Christ, and do not think about how to gratify the desires of the flesh.

14 Accept the one whose faith is weak, without quarrelling over disputable matters. ² One person's faith allows them to eat anything, but another, whose faith is weak, eats only vegetables. ³ The one who eats everything must not treat with

contempt the one who does not, and the one who does not eat everything must not judge the one who does, for God has accepted them. ⁴Who are you to judge someone else's servant? To their own master, servants stand or fall. And they will stand, for the Lord is able to make them stand.

⁵One person considers one day more sacred than another; another considers every day alike. Each of them should be fully convinced in their own mind. ⁶Whoever regards one day as special does so to the Lord. Whoever eats meat does so to the Lord, for they give thanks to God; and whoever abstains does so to the Lord and gives thanks to God. ⁷For none of us lives for ourselves alone, and none of us dies for ourselves alone. ⁸If we live, we live for the Lord; and if we die, we die for the Lord. So, whether we live or die, we belong to the Lord. ⁹For this very reason, Christ died and returned to life so that he might be the Lord of both the dead and the living.

¹⁰You, then, why do you judge your brother or sister? Or why do you treat them with contempt? For we will all stand before God's judgment seat. ¹¹It is written:

' "As surely as I live," says the Lord,
  "Every knee will bow before me;
    every tongue will acknowledge God." '

¹²So then, each of us will give an account of ourselves to God.

'Wobbly Christians'

'So let us put aside the deeds of darkness and put on the armour of light.' **Romans 13:12**

The armour of God will not do us any good unless it is worn in its entirety. We must put on the whole armour of God, not just a few of the pieces we think are most suitable for us.

This again is something of crucial importance. If we are to be steadfast soldiers in the Lord's army, if we are to avoid becoming what John Stott calls 'wobbly Christians who have no firm foothold in Christ', then we must put on the entire equipment which God provides for us. We cannot - we dare not - select parts of the armour and say: 'I don't really like the helmet of salvation, but I don't mind wearing the breastplate of righteousness.' You can do that, of course, but if you do, then you must know exactly what will happen to you - you risk being overcome by Satan. You cannot say, 'I need the breastplate, but I don't need the helmet'. You need it all - the whole armour of God.

You see, our understanding of what is involved in spiritual defence against Satan is extremely inadequate. We just don't have sufficient knowledge of what is involved. It is God alone who knows our enemy, and it is God alone who knows exactly how to protect us so that we remain firm and steadfast when Satan and his forces hurl themselves against us. So learn this lesson now before going any further - every single piece of God's armour is essential, and to select some and leave out the others is to take the route to failure and defeat.

PRAYER

O God, deliver me from the attitude of pride that seeks to put my ideas ahead of Your ideas. You know more about what I need to protect me from the enemy than I do. Help me ever to trust Your judgment. In Jesus' name I ask it. Amen.

FURTHER STUDY

2 Cor. 6:1-10; Phil. 1:27;
1 Pet. 5:9
• What was a necessary requirement for Paul's ministry?
• What are we called to do?

August 22

▬ ESTHER 2:1–4:17

2 Later when King Xerxes' fury had subsided, he remembered Vashti and what she had done and what he had decreed about her. ²Then the king's personal attendants proposed, 'Let a search be made for beautiful young virgins for the king. ³Let the king appoint commissioners in every province of his realm to bring all these beautiful young women into the harem at the citadel of Susa. Let them be placed under the care of Hegai, the king's eunuch, who is in charge of the women; and let beauty treatments be given to them. ⁴Then let the young woman who pleases the king be queen instead of Vashti.' This advice appealed to the king, and he followed it.

⁵Now there was in the citadel of Susa a Jew of the tribe of Benjamin, named Mordecai son of Jair, the son of Shimei, the son of Kish, ⁶who had been carried into exile from Jerusalem by Nebuchadnezzar king of Babylon, among those taken captive with Jehoiachin king of Judah. ⁷Mordecai had a cousin named Hadassah, whom he had brought up because she had neither father nor mother. This young woman, who was also known as Esther, had a lovely figure and was beautiful. Mordecai had taken her as his own daughter when her father and mother died.

⁸When the king's order and edict had been proclaimed, many young women were brought to the citadel of Susa and put under the care of Hegai. Esther also was taken to the king's palace and entrusted to Hegai, who had charge of the harem. ⁹She pleased him and won his favour. Immediately he provided her with her beauty treatments and special food. He assigned to her seven female attendants selected from the king's palace and moved her and her attendants into the best place in the harem.

¹⁰Esther had not revealed her nationality and family background, because Mordecai had forbidden her to do so. ¹¹Every day he walked to and fro near the courtyard of the harem to find out how Esther was and what was happening to her.

¹²Before a young woman's turn came to go in to King Xerxes, she had to complete twelve months of beauty treatments prescribed for the women, six months with oil of myrrh and six with perfumes and cosmetics. ¹³And this is how she would go to the king: anything she wanted was given to her to take with her from the harem to the king's palace. ¹⁴In the evening she would go there and in the morning return to another part of the harem to the care of Shaashgaz, the king's eunuch who was in charge of the concubines. She would not return to

the king unless he was pleased with her and summoned her by name.

¹⁵ When the turn came for Esther (the young woman Mordecai had adopted, the daughter of his uncle Abihail) to go to the king, she asked for nothing other than what Hegai, the king's eunuch who was in charge of the harem, suggested. And Esther won the favour of everyone who saw her. ¹⁶ She was taken to King Xerxes in the royal residence in the tenth month, the month of Tebeth, in the seventh year of his reign.

¹⁷ Now the king was attracted to Esther more than to any of the other women, and she won his favour and approval more than any of the other virgins. So he set a royal crown on her head and made her queen instead of Vashti. ¹⁸ And the king gave a great banquet, Esther's banquet, for all his nobles and officials. He proclaimed a holiday throughout the provinces and distributed gifts with royal liberality.

¹⁹ When the virgins were assembled a second time, Mordecai was sitting at the king's gate. ²⁰ But Esther had kept secret her family background and nationality just as Mordecai had told her to do, for she continued to follow Mordecai's instructions as she had done when he was bringing her up.

²¹ During the time Mordecai was sitting at the king's gate, Bigthana and Teresh, two of the king's officers who guarded the doorway, became angry and conspired to assassinate King Xerxes. ²² But Mordecai found out about the plot and told Queen Esther, who in turn reported it to the king, giving credit to Mordecai. ²³ And when the report was investigated and found to be true, the two officials were impaled on poles. All this was recorded in the book of the annals in the presence of the king.

3 After these events, King Xerxes honoured Haman son of Hammedatha, the Agagite, elevating him and giving him a seat of honour higher than that of all the other nobles. ² All the royal officials at the king's gate knelt down and paid honour to Haman, for the king had commanded this concerning him. But Mordecai would not kneel down or pay him honour.

³ Then the royal officials at the king's gate asked Mordecai, 'Why do you disobey the king's command?' ⁴ Day after day they spoke to him but he refused to comply. Therefore they told Haman about it to see whether Mordecai's behaviour would be tolerated, for he had told them he was a Jew.

⁵ When Haman saw that Mordecai would not kneel down or pay him honour, he was enraged. ⁶ Yet having learned who Mordecai's people were, he scorned the idea of killing only Mordecai. Instead Haman looked for a way to destroy all Mordecai's people, the Jews, throughout the whole kingdom of Xerxes.

⁷ In the twelfth year of King Xerxes, in the first month, the month of Nisan, the *pur* (that is, the lot) was cast in the presence of Haman to select a day and month. And the lot fell on the twelfth month, the month of Adar.

⁸ Then Haman said to King Xerxes, 'There is a certain people dispersed among the peoples in all the provinces of your kingdom who keep themselves separate. Their customs are different from those of all other people, and they do not obey the king's laws; it is not in the king's best interest to tolerate them. ⁹ If it pleases the king, let a decree be issued to destroy them, and I will give ten thousand talents of silver to the king's administrators for the royal treasury.'

¹⁰ So the king took his signet ring from his finger and gave it to Haman son of Hammedatha, the Agagite, the enemy of the Jews. ¹¹ 'Keep the money,' the king said to Haman, 'and do with the people as you please.'

¹² Then on the thirteenth day of the first month the royal secretaries were summoned. They wrote out in the script of each province and in the language of each people

all Haman's orders to the king's satraps, the governors of the various provinces and the nobles of the various peoples. These were written in the name of King Xerxes himself and sealed with his own ring. [13] Dispatches were sent by couriers to all the king's provinces with the order to destroy, kill and annihilate all the Jews – young and old, women and children – on a single day, the thirteenth day of the twelfth month, the month of Adar, and to plunder their goods. [14] A copy of the text of the edict was to be issued as law in every province and made known to the people of every nationality so that they would be ready for that day.

[15] The couriers went out, spurred on by the king's command, and the edict was issued in the citadel of Susa. The king and Haman sat down to drink, but the city of Susa was bewildered.

4 When Mordecai learned of all that had been done, he tore his clothes, put on sackcloth and ashes, and went out into the city, wailing loudly and bitterly. [2] But he went only as far as the king's gate, because no one clothed in sackcloth was allowed to enter it. [3] In every province to which the edict and order of the king came, there was great mourning among the Jews, with fasting, weeping and wailing. Many lay in sackcloth and ashes.

[4] When Esther's eunuchs and female attendants came and told her about Mordecai, she was in great distress. She sent clothes for him to put on instead of his sackcloth, but he would not accept them. [5] Then Esther summoned Hathak, one of the king's eunuchs assigned to attend her, and ordered him to find out what was troubling Mordecai and why.

[6] So Hathak went out to Mordecai in the open square of the city in front of the king's gate. [7] Mordecai told him everything that had happened to him, including the exact amount of money Haman had promised to pay into the royal treasury for the destruction of the Jews. [8] He also gave him a copy of the text of the edict for their annihilation, which had been published in Susa, to show to Esther and explain it to her, and he told him to instruct her to go into the king's presence to beg for mercy and plead with him for her people.

[9] Hathak went back and reported to Esther what Mordecai had said. [10] Then she instructed him to say to Mordecai, [11] 'All the king's officials and the people of the royal provinces know that for any man or woman who approaches the king in the inner court without being summoned the king has but one law: that they be put to death unless the king extends the gold sceptre to them and spares their lives. But thirty days have passed since I was called to go to the king.'

[12] When Esther's words were reported to Mordecai, [13] he sent back this answer: 'Do not think that because you are in the king's house you alone of all the Jews will escape. [14] For if you remain silent at this time, relief and deliverance for the Jews will arise from another place, but you and your father's family will perish. And who knows but that you have come to your royal position for such a time as this?'

[15] Then Esther sent this reply to Mordecai: [16] 'Go, gather together all the Jews who are in Susa, and fast for me. Do not eat or drink for three days, night or day. I and my attendants will fast as you do. When this is done, I will go to the king, even though it is against the law. And if I perish, I perish.'

[17] So Mordecai went away and carried out all of Esther's instructions.

▬ PSALM 102:18–22

[18] Let this be written for a future generation,
    that a people not yet created may
        praise the LORD:

¹⁹ 'The LORD looked down from his
    sanctuary on high,
    from heaven he viewed the earth,
²⁰ to hear the groans of the prisoners
    and release those condemned to
    death.'
²¹ So the name of the LORD will be declared
    in Zion
    and his praise in Jerusalem
²² when the peoples and the kingdoms
    assemble to worship the LORD.

■ PROVERBS 20:26-27

²⁶A wise king winnows out the wicked;
    he drives the threshing wheel over them.

²⁷ The human spirit is the lamp of the LORD
    that sheds light on one's inmost being.

■ ROMANS 14:13–15:13

¹³ Therefore let us stop passing judgment on one another. Instead, make up your mind not to put any stumbling-block or obstacle in the way of a brother or sister. ¹⁴ I am convinced, being fully persuaded in the Lord Jesus, that nothing is unclean in itself. But if anyone regards something as unclean, then for that person it is unclean. ¹⁵ If your brother or sister is distressed because of what you eat, you are no longer acting in love. Do not by your eating destroy someone for whom Christ died. ¹⁶ Therefore do not let what you know is good be spoken of as evil. ¹⁷ For the kingdom of God is not a matter of eating and drinking, but of righteousness, peace and joy in the Holy Spirit, ¹⁸ because anyone who serves Christ in this way is pleasing to God and receives human approval.

¹⁹ Let us therefore make every effort to do what leads to peace and to mutual edification. ²⁰ Do not destroy the work of God for the sake of food. All food is clean, but it is wrong for a person to eat anything that causes someone else to stumble. ²¹ It is better not to eat meat or drink wine or to do anything else that will cause your brother or sister to fall.

²² So whatever you believe about these things keep between yourself and God. Blessed is the one who does not condemn himself by what he approves. ²³ But whoever has doubts is condemned if they eat, because their eating is not from faith; and everything that does not come from faith is sin.

15 We who are strong ought to bear with the failings of the weak and not to please ourselves. ² Each of us should please our neighbours for their good, to build them up. ³ For even Christ did not please himself but, as it is written: 'The insults of those who insult you have fallen on me.' ⁴ For everything that was written in the past was written to teach us, so that through the endurance taught in the Scriptures and the encouragement they provide we might have hope.

⁵ May the God who gives endurance and encouragement give you the same attitude of mind toward each other that Christ Jesus had, ⁶ so that with one mind and one voice you may glorify the God and Father of our Lord Jesus Christ.

⁷ Accept one another, then, just as Christ accepted you, in order to bring praise to God. ⁸ For I tell you that Christ has become a servant of the Jews on behalf of God's truth, so that the promises made to the patriarchs might be confirmed ⁹ and, moreover, that the Gentiles might glorify God for his mercy. As it is written:

'Therefore I will praise you among the
    Gentiles;
    I will sing the praises of your name.'

¹⁰ Again, it says,

'Rejoice, you Gentiles, with his people.'

¹¹ And again,

'Praise the Lord, all you Gentiles;
let all the peoples extol him.'

¹² And again, Isaiah says,

'The Root of Jesse will spring up,

one who will arise to rule over the
nations;
in him the Gentiles will hope.'

¹³ May the God of hope fill you with all joy
and peace as you trust in him, so that you
may overflow with hope by the power of the
Holy Spirit.

Ostrich Christians

**'The human spirit is the lamp of the LORD that sheds
light on one's inmost being.' Proverbs 20:27**

Most of us (myself included) are not good at observing ourselves
and reflecting honestly on what goes on beneath the surface of
our lives. Why is this so? I think one of the reasons is fear – fear of the
unknown, fear of losing control, fear of spoiling a comfortable existence,
or fear of having to face some unpleasant discoveries about ourselves.
I have met many Christians in my time who adopt this attitude: however
things are, good or bad, they could be worse, so it is better to leave well
enough alone.

When we read the Bible, however, we discover texts like the one before
us today, showing us that God has designed us with the ability to explore
our deepest parts. We also hear men like the psalmist crying out to God:
'Search me, God, and know my heart; test me and know my anxious
thoughts. See if there is any offensive way in me, and lead me in the way
everlasting' (Psa. 139:23-24).

I want to stress that too much introspection is unhealthy, but
occasionally and in proper doses it is 'good medicine'. Those who resist
this and pretend everything is well when it isn't are what a friend of mine
calls 'ostrich Christians'. They have peace, but it is a peace built on
unreality. When they lift their heads out of the sand, the peace they
possess somehow falls to pieces. God's peace can keep our hearts and
minds intact while we face whatever is true – outside and inside.

PRAYER

Father, save me from becoming an
'ostrich Christian' – someone who
pretends everything is well when it
isn't. Nothing must be allowed to
hinder the work that You want to do
in my heart. Corner my soul and
make me what You want me to be.
Amen.

FURTHER STUDY

Mark 2:1-8; Matt. 12:25;
Luke 6:8; John 2:25
• How deeply did Jesus see
  into people's lives?
• How deeply do you let
  Him penetrate into your
  life?

August 23

▬ ESTHER 5:1–7:10

5 On the third day Esther put on her royal robes and stood in the inner court of the palace, in front of the king's hall. The king was sitting on his royal throne in the hall, facing the entrance. ²When he saw Queen Esther standing in the court, he was pleased with her and held out to her the gold sceptre that was in his hand. So Esther approached and touched the tip of the sceptre.

³Then the king asked, 'What is it, Queen Esther? What is your request? Even up to half the kingdom, it will be given you.'

⁴'If it pleases the king,' replied Esther, 'let the king, together with Haman, come today to a banquet I have prepared for him.'

⁵'Bring Haman at once,' the king said, 'so that we may do what Esther asks.'

So the king and Haman went to the banquet Esther had prepared. ⁶As they were drinking wine, the king again asked Esther, 'Now what is your petition? It will be given you. And what is your request? Even up to half the kingdom, it will be granted.'

⁷Esther replied, 'My petition and my request is this: ⁸If the king regards me with favour and if it pleases the king to grant my petition and fulfil my request, let the king and Haman come tomorrow to the banquet I will prepare for them. Then I will answer the king's question.'

⁹Haman went out that day happy and in high spirits. But when he saw Mordecai at the king's gate and observed that he neither rose nor showed fear in his presence, he was filled with rage against Mordecai. ¹⁰Nevertheless, Haman restrained himself and went home.

Calling together his friends and Zeresh, his wife, ¹¹Haman boasted to them about his vast wealth, his many sons, and all the ways the king had honoured him and how he had elevated him above the other nobles and officials. ¹²'And that's not all,' Haman added. 'I'm the only person Queen Esther invited to accompany the king to the banquet she gave. And she has invited me along with the king tomorrow. ¹³But all this gives me no satisfaction as long as I see that Jew Mordecai sitting at the king's gate.'

¹⁴His wife Zeresh and all his friends said to him, 'Have a pole set up, reaching to a height of fifty cubits, and ask the king in the morning to have Mordecai impaled on it. Then go with the king to the banquet and enjoy yourself.' This suggestion delighted Haman, and he had the pole set up.

6 That night the king could not sleep; so he ordered the book of the chronicles, the record of his reign, to be brought in and read to him. ²It was found recorded there that Mordecai had exposed Bigthana and Teresh, two of the king's officers who guarded the doorway, who had conspired to assassinate King Xerxes.

³'What honour and recognition has Mordecai received for this?' the king asked.

'Nothing has been done for him,' his attendants answered.

⁴The king said, 'Who is in the court?' Now Haman had just entered the outer court of the palace to speak to the king about impaling Mordecai on the pole he had set up for him.

⁵His attendants answered, 'Haman is standing in the court.'

'Bring him in,' the king ordered.

⁶When Haman entered, the king asked him, 'What should be done for the man the king delights to honour?'

Now Haman thought to himself, 'Who

is there that the king would rather honour than me?' ⁷So he answered the king, 'For the man the king delights to honour, ⁸let them bring a royal robe the king has worn and a horse the king has ridden, one with a royal crest placed on its head. ⁹Then let the robe and horse be entrusted to one of the king's most noble princes. Let them robe the man the king delights to honour, and lead him on the horse through the city streets, proclaiming before him, "This is what is done for the man the king delights to honour!"'

¹⁰'Go at once,' the king commanded Haman. 'Get the robe and the horse and do just as you have suggested for Mordecai the Jew, who sits at the king's gate. Do not neglect anything you have recommended.'

¹¹So Haman got the robe and the horse. He robed Mordecai, and led him on horseback through the city streets, proclaiming before him, 'This is what is done for the man the king delights to honour!'

¹²Afterwards Mordecai returned to the king's gate. But Haman rushed home, with his head covered in grief, ¹³and told Zeresh his wife and all his friends everything that had happened to him.

His advisors and his wife Zeresh said to him, 'Since Mordecai, before whom your downfall has started, is of Jewish origin, you cannot stand against him – you will surely come to ruin!' ¹⁴While they were still talking with him, the king's eunuchs arrived and hurried Haman away to the banquet Esther had prepared.

7 So the king and Haman went to Queen Esther's banquet, ²and as they were drinking wine on the second day, the king again asked, 'Queen Esther, what is your petition? It will be given you. What is your request? Even up to half the kingdom, it will be granted.'

³Then Queen Esther answered, 'If I have found favour with you, Your Majesty, and if it pleases you, grant me my life – this is my petition. And spare my people – this is my request. ⁴For I and my people have been sold to be destroyed, killed and annihilated. If we had merely been sold as male and female slaves, I would have kept quiet, because no such distress would justify disturbing the king.'

⁵King Xerxes asked Queen Esther, 'Who is he? Where is he – the man who has dared to do such a thing?'

⁶Esther said, 'An adversary and enemy! This vile Haman!'

Then Haman was terrified before the king and queen. ⁷The king got up in a rage, left his wine and went out into the palace garden. But Haman, realising that the king had already decided his fate, stayed behind to beg Queen Esther for his life.

⁸Just as the king returned from the palace garden to the banqueting hall, Haman was falling on the couch where Esther was reclining.

The king exclaimed, 'Will he even molest the queen while she is with me in the house?'

As soon as the word left the king's mouth, they covered Haman's face. ⁹Then Harbona, one of the eunuchs attending the king, said, 'A pole reaching to a height of fifty cubits stands by Haman's house. He had it set up for Mordecai, who spoke up to help the king.'

The king said, 'Impale him on it!' ¹⁰So they impaled Haman on the pole he had set up for Mordecai. Then the king's fury subsided.

....

■ **PSALM 102:23–28**

²³In the course of my life he broke my
    strength;
    he cut short my days.
²⁴So I said:
  'Do not take me away, my God, in the
    midst of my days;

your years go on through all
    generations.

25 In the beginning you laid the
    foundations of the earth,
    and the heavens are the work of your
    hands.

26 They will perish, but you remain;
    they will all wear out like a garment.
    Like clothing you will change them
    and they will be discarded.

27 But you remain the same,
    and your years will never end.

28 The children of your servants will live in
    your presence;
    their descendants will be established
    before you.'

PROVERBS 20:28-30

28 Love and faithfulness keep a king safe;
    through love his throne is made
    secure.

29 The glory of young men is their strength,
    grey hair the splendour of the old.

30 Blows and wounds scrub away evil,
    and beatings purge the inmost being.

ROMANS 15:14-33

14 I myself am convinced, my brothers
and sisters, that you yourselves are full of
goodness, filled with knowledge and competent to instruct one another. 15 Yet I have
written to you quite boldly on some points
to remind you of them again, because of
the grace God gave me 16 to be a minister of
Christ Jesus to the Gentiles. He gave me the
priestly duty of proclaiming the gospel of
God, so that the Gentiles might become an
offering acceptable to God, sanctified by the
Holy Spirit.
17 Therefore I glory in Christ Jesus in my

service to God. 18 I will not venture to speak
of anything except what Christ has accomplished through me in leading the Gentiles to obey God by what I have said and
done – 19 by the power of signs and wonders,
through the power of the Spirit of God. So
from Jerusalem all the way round to Illyr-
icum, I have fully proclaimed the gospel of
Christ. 20 It has always been my ambition
to preach the gospel where Christ was not
known, so that I would not be building on
someone else's foundation. 21 Rather, as it is
written:

'Those who were not told about him will
    see,
    and those who have not heard will
    understand.'

22 This is why I have often been hindered
from coming to you.
23 But now that there is no more place for
me to work in these regions, and since I have
been longing for many years to visit you, 24 I
plan to do so when I go to Spain. I hope to
see you while passing through and that you
will assist me on my journey there, after I
have enjoyed your company for a while.
25 Now, however, I am on my way to Jerusalem in the service of the Lord's people there.
26 For Macedonia and Achaia were pleased
to make a contribution for the poor among
the Lord's people in Jerusalem. 27 They
were pleased to do it, and indeed they owe
it to them. For if the Gentiles have shared in
the Jews' spiritual blessings, they owe it to
the Jews to share with them their material
blessings. 28 So after I have completed this
task and have made sure that they have received this contribution, I will go to Spain
and visit you on the way. 29 I know that
when I come to you, I will come in the full
measure of the blessing of Christ.
30 I urge you, brothers and sisters, by our
Lord Jesus Christ and by the love of the Spirit, to join me in my struggle by praying to

God for me. ³¹Pray that I may be kept safe from the unbelievers in Judea and that the contribution I take to Jerusalem may be favourably received by the Lord's people there, ³²so that I may come to you with joy, by God's will, and in your company be refreshed. ³³The God of peace be with you all. Amen.

Three Great Errors

'I urge you ... by our Lord Jesus Christ and by the love of the Spirit, to join me in my struggle by praying to God for me.' **Romans 15:30**

'God is One, yet God is Three. How can such a strange thing be?' These are the lines of a ditty that supposedly was sung by troops on the march in World War I. Theologians down the ages have tried to illuminate this doctrine for us, but it is an issue that will never be fully clarified until we arrive in heaven (1 Cor. 13:12). Basically the doctrine of the Trinity is God is One but with three distinct Persons. Around this truth a number of errors have been propounded.

The first was the teaching that there are three gods. Jehovah's Witnesses think that present-day Christians believe this and say that we conceive of God as a body with three heads. That might be true of ancient heresy, but it is not true of classic Trinitarianism. The second heresy taught that God is unipersonal and the other two Persons in the Trinity are simply manifestations of the one God. The third main error denied the equality of the divine Persons and regarded them as being of different rank.

The historic church formulated the Athanasian Creed, which states that we worship one God in Trinity and Trinity in unity. What we must see, however, is that no words can fully explain the truth of the Trinity. 'The creed is a safety net to keep us from falling into error', says one preacher, 'rather than a verbal net in which to trap the truth.' We use the term 'Trinity' expecting not so much that in that one word the truth may be spoken, but that it may not be left unspoken.

PRAYER

Father, I see that life often presents me with facts which seem irreconcilable at one stage of knowledge, though better understood at another. Perhaps one day this great mystery of the Trinity may be cleared up. Meanwhile I simply worship and adore. Amen.

FURTHER STUDY

1 Pet. 1:1-6; 1 Tim. 2:5
- How did Peter distinguish the members of the Trinity?
- What did Paul confirm to Timothy?

August 24

■ ESTHER 8:1–10:3

8 That same day King Xerxes gave Queen Esther the estate of Haman, the enemy of the Jews. And Mordecai came into the presence of the king, for Esther had told how he was related to her. ²The king took off his signet ring, which he had reclaimed from Haman, and presented it to Mordecai. And Esther appointed him over Haman's estate.

³Esther again pleaded with the king, falling at his feet and weeping. She begged him to put an end to the evil plan of Haman the Agagite, which he had devised against the Jews. ⁴Then the king extended the gold sceptre to Esther and she arose and stood before him.

⁵'If it pleases the king,' she said, 'and if he regards me with favour and thinks it the right thing to do, and if he is pleased with me, let an order be written overruling the dispatches that Haman son of Hammedatha, the Agagite, devised and wrote to destroy the Jews in all the king's provinces. ⁶For how can I bear to see disaster fall on my people? How can I bear to see the destruction of my family?'

⁷King Xerxes replied to Queen Esther and to Mordecai the Jew, 'Because Haman attacked the Jews, I have given his estate to Esther, and they have impaled him on the pole he set up. ⁸Now write another decree in the king's name on behalf of the Jews as seems best to you, and seal it with the king's signet ring – for no document written in the king's name and sealed with his ring can be revoked.'

⁹At once the royal secretaries were summoned – on the twenty-third day of the third month, the month of Sivan. They wrote out all Mordecai's orders to the Jews, and to the satraps, governors and nobles of the 127 provinces stretching from India to Cush. These orders were written in the script of each province and the language of each people and also to the Jews in their own script and language. ¹⁰Mordecai wrote in the name of King Xerxes, sealed the dispatches with the king's signet ring, and sent them by mounted couriers, who rode fast horses especially bred for the king.

¹¹The king's edict granted the Jews in every city the right to assemble and protect themselves; to destroy, kill and annihilate the armed men of any nationality or province who might attack them and their women and children, and to plunder the property of their enemies. ¹²The day appointed for the Jews to do this in all the provinces of King Xerxes was the thirteenth day of the twelfth month, the month of Adar. ¹³A copy of the text of the edict was to be issued as law in every province and made known to the people of every nationality so that the Jews would be ready on that day to avenge themselves on their enemies.

¹⁴The couriers, riding the royal horses, went out, spurred on by the king's command, and the edict was issued in the citadel of Susa.

¹⁵When Mordecai left the king's presence, he was wearing royal garments of blue and white, a large crown of gold and a purple robe of fine linen. And the city of Susa held a joyous celebration. ¹⁶For the Jews it was a time of happiness and joy, gladness and honour. ¹⁷In every province and in every city to which the edict of the king came, there was joy and gladness among the Jews, with feasting and celebrating. And many people of other nationalities became Jews because fear of the Jews had seized them.

9 On the thirteenth day of the twelfth month, the month of Adar, the edict commanded by the king was to be carried out. On this day the enemies of the Jews had hoped to overpower them, but now the tables were turned and the Jews got the upper hand over those who hated them. ² The Jews assembled in their cities in all the provinces of King Xerxes to attack those determined to destroy them. No one could stand against them, because the people of all the other nationalities were afraid of them. ³ And all the nobles of the provinces, the satraps, the governors and the king's administrators helped the Jews, because fear of Mordecai had seized them. ⁴ Mordecai was prominent in the palace; his reputation spread throughout the provinces, and he became more and more powerful.

⁵ The Jews struck down all their enemies with the sword, killing and destroying them, and they did what they pleased to those who hated them. ⁶ In the citadel of Susa, the Jews killed and destroyed five hundred men. ⁷ They also killed Parshandatha, Dalphon, Aspatha, ⁸ Poratha, Adalia, Aridatha, ⁹ Parmashta, Arisai, Aridai and Vaizatha, ¹⁰ the ten sons of Haman son of Hammedatha, the enemy of the Jews. But they did not lay their hands on the plunder.

¹¹ The number of those killed in the citadel of Susa was reported to the king that same day. ¹² The king said to Queen Esther, 'The Jews have killed and destroyed five hundred men and the ten sons of Haman in the citadel of Susa. What have they done in the rest of the king's provinces? Now what is your petition? It will be given you. What is your request? It will also be granted.'

¹³ 'If it pleases the king,' Esther answered, 'give the Jews in Susa permission to carry out this day's edict tomorrow also, and let Haman's ten sons be impaled on poles.'

¹⁴ So the king commanded that this be done. An edict was issued in Susa, and they impaled the ten sons of Haman. ¹⁵ The Jews in Susa came together on the fourteenth day of the month of Adar, and they put to death in Susa three hundred men, but they did not lay their hands on the plunder.

¹⁶ Meanwhile, the remainder of the Jews who were in the king's provinces also assembled to protect themselves and get relief from their enemies. They killed seventy-five thousand of them but did not lay their hands on the plunder. ¹⁷ This happened on the thirteenth day of the month of Adar, and on the fourteenth they rested and made it a day of feasting and joy.

¹⁸ The Jews in Susa, however, had assembled on the thirteenth and fourteenth, and then on the fifteenth they rested and made it a day of feasting and joy.

¹⁹ That is why rural Jews – those living in villages – observe the fourteenth of the month of Adar as a day of joy and feasting, a day for giving presents to each other.

²⁰ Mordecai recorded these events, and he sent letters to all the Jews throughout the provinces of King Xerxes, near and far, ²¹ that they should celebrate annually the fourteenth and fifteenth days of the month of Adar ²² as the time when the Jews got relief from their enemies, and as the month when their sorrow was turned into joy and their mourning into a day of celebration. He wrote to them to observe the days as days of feasting and joy and giving presents of food to one another and gifts to the poor.

²³ So the Jews agreed to continue the celebration they had begun, doing what Mordecai had written to them. ²⁴ For Haman son of Hammedatha, the Agagite, the enemy of all the Jews, had plotted against the Jews to destroy them and had cast the *pur* (that is, the lot) for their ruin and destruction. ²⁵ But when the plot came to the king's attention, he issued written orders that the evil scheme Haman had devised against the Jews should come back on to his own head, and that he and his sons should be impaled on poles. ²⁶ (Therefore these

days were called Purim, from the word *pur.*) Because of everything written in this letter and because of what they had seen and what had happened to them, ²⁷ the Jews took it on themselves to establish the custom that they and their descendants and all who join them should without fail observe these two days every year, in the way prescribed and at the time appointed. ²⁸ These days should be remembered and observed in every generation by every family, and in every province and in every city. And these days of Purim should never fail to be celebrated by the Jews – nor should the memory of these days die out among their descendants.

²⁹ So Queen Esther, daughter of Abihail, along with Mordecai the Jew, wrote with full authority to confirm this second letter concerning Purim. ³⁰ And Mordecai sent letters to all the Jews in the 127 provinces of Xerxes's kingdom – words of goodwill and assurance – ³¹ to establish these days of Purim at their designated times, as Mordecai the Jew and Queen Esther had decreed for them, and as they had established for themselves and their descendants in regard to their times of fasting and lamentation. ³² Esther's decree confirmed these regulations about Purim, and it was written down in the records.

10 King Xerxes imposed tribute throughout the empire, to its distant shores. ² And all his acts of power and might, together with a full account of the greatness of Mordecai, whom the king had promoted, are they not written in the book of the annals of the kings of Media and Persia? ³ Mordecai the Jew was second in rank to King Xerxes, pre-eminent among the Jews, and held in high esteem by his many fellow Jews, because he worked for the good of his people and spoke up for the welfare of all the Jews.

■ PSALM 103:1–5

¹ Praise the LORD, my soul;
   all my inmost being, praise his holy
      name.
² Praise the LORD, my soul,
   and forget not all his benefits –
³ who forgives all your sins
   and heals all your diseases,
⁴ who redeems your life from the pit
   and crowns you with love and
      compassion,
⁵ who satisfies your desires with good
      things
   so that your youth is renewed like the
      eagle's.

■ PROVERBS 21:1–3

21 In the LORD's hand the king's heart
   is a stream of water
that he channels towards all who
      please him.

² A person may think their own ways are
      right,
   but the LORD weighs the heart.

³ To do what is right and just
   is more acceptable to the LORD than
      sacrifice.

■ ROMANS 16:1–27

16 I commend to you our sister Phoebe, a deacon of the church in Cenchreae. ² I ask you to receive her in the Lord in a way worthy of his people and to give her any help she may need from you, for she has been the benefactor of many people, including me.

³ Greet Priscilla and Aquila, my fellow workers in Christ Jesus. ⁴ They risked their lives for me. Not only I but all the

churches of the Gentiles are grateful to them.

5 Greet also the church that meets at their house.

Greet my dear friend Epenetus, who was the first convert to Christ in the province of Asia. 6 Greet Mary, who worked very hard for you. 7 Greet Andronicus and Junia, my fellow Jews who have been in prison with me. They are outstanding among the apostles, and they were in Christ before I was. 8 Greet Ampliatus, my dear friend in the Lord. 9 Greet Urbanus, our fellow worker in Christ, and my dear friend Stachys. 10 Greet Apelles, whose fidelity to Christ has stood the test.

Greet those who belong to the household of Aristobulus. 11 Greet Herodion, my fellow Jew.

Greet those in the household of Narcissus who are in the Lord. 12 Greet Tryphena and Tryphosa, those women who work hard in the Lord.

Greet my dear friend Persis, another woman who has worked very hard in the Lord. 13 Greet Rufus, chosen in the Lord, and his mother, who has been a mother to me, too. 14 Greet Asyncritus, Phlegon, Hermes, Patrobas, Hermas and the other brothers and sisters with them. 15 Greet Philologus, Julia, Nereus and his sister, and Olympas and all the Lord's people who are with them.

16 Greet one another with a holy kiss.

All the churches of Christ send greetings.

17 I urge you, brothers and sisters, to watch out for those who cause divisions and put obstacles in your way that are contrary to the teaching you have learned. Keep away from them. 18 For such people are not serving our Lord Christ, but their own appetites. By smooth talk and flattery they deceive the minds of naïve people. 19 Everyone has heard about your obedience, so I rejoice because of you; but I want you to be wise about what is good, and innocent about what is evil.

20 The God of peace will soon crush Satan under your feet.

The grace of our Lord Jesus be with you.

21 Timothy, my co-worker, sends his greetings to you, as do Lucius, Jason and Sosipater, my fellow Jews.

22 I, Tertius, who wrote down this letter, greet you in the Lord.

23 Gaius, whose hospitality I and the whole church here enjoy, sends you his greetings.

Erastus, who is the city's director of public works, and our brother Quartus send you their greetings. [24] a

25 Now to him who is able to establish you in accordance with my gospel, the message I proclaim about Jesus Christ, in keeping with the revelation of the mystery hidden for long ages past, 26 but now revealed and made known through the prophetic writings by the command of the eternal God, so that all the Gentiles might come to the obedience that comes from faith – 27 to the only wise God be glory for ever through Jesus Christ! Amen.

---

a Some manuscripts include here *May the grace of our Lord Jesus Christ be with all of you. Amen.*

Fullness – Only in God

'... to the only wise God be glory for ever through Jesus Christ!' **Romans 16:27**

The subject of God's knowledge must be linked to His wisdom, and it is this aspect of the divine nature that we consider now. What does the Bible mean when it describes God as wise? Wisdom is the ability to use knowledge to the best possible ends. This ability is found in its fullness only in God. God is never other than wise in everything He does. Knowledge without wisdom would be pathetic, a broken reed. Wisdom without knowledge would be inoperative and quite frightening. God's boundless knowledge and wisdom are perfect in every way and it is this that makes Him utterly worthy of our trust.

One of the great difficulties we have in the Christian life is trusting the divine wisdom. We can recognise wisdom only when we see the end to which it is moving. Yet God often calls us to trust Him when we can't see the end that He is pursuing. And then in such times we have to ask ourselves, 'How much do I trust Him?'

Before I began speaking to a Christian youth group once, I asked if someone could offer a definition of God's wisdom. One young man said, 'God's wisdom is the ability to get us through scrapes and difficulties without getting hurt.' I gave the young man full marks for attempting a definition, but I had to show him that this was not what divine wisdom is all about. The goal behind divine wisdom is not to make us happy but to make us holy. And sometimes pursuing that goal may involve us in considerable pain.

PRAYER

Father, here I am again – at the road less travelled. Help me tread the road ahead knowing that whatever pain You allow me to feel is for my good. I do not welcome it, but I do not run from it either, as long as You stay with me. Amen.

FURTHER STUDY

Psa. 104:1-24; Prov. 3:19; Rom. 11:33
• Where is God's wisdom evidenced?
• What was Paul's conclusion?

August 25

■ JOB 1:1–3:26

1 In the land of Uz there lived a man whose name was Job. This man was blameless and upright; he feared God and shunned evil. ²He had seven sons and three daughters, ³and he owned seven thousand sheep, three thousand camels, five

hundred yoke of oxen and five hundred donkeys, and had a large number of servants. He was the greatest man among all the people of the East.

⁴His sons used to hold feasts in their homes on their birthdays, and they would invite their three sisters to eat and drink with them. ⁵When a period of feasting had run its course, Job would make arrangements for them to be purified. Early in the morning he would sacrifice a burnt offering for each of them, thinking, 'Perhaps my children have sinned and cursed God in their hearts.' This was Job's regular custom.

⁶One day the angels came to present themselves before the LORD, and Satan also came with them. ⁷The LORD said to Satan, 'Where have you come from?'

Satan answered the LORD, 'From roaming throughout the earth, going to and fro on it.'

⁸Then the LORD said to Satan, 'Have you considered my servant Job? There is no one on earth like him; he is blameless and upright, a man who fears God and shuns evil.'

⁹'Does Job fear God for nothing?' Satan replied. ¹⁰'Have you not put a hedge around him and his household and everything he has? You have blessed the work of his hands, so that his flocks and herds are spread throughout the land. ¹¹But now stretch out your hand and strike everything he has, and he will surely curse you to your face.'

¹²The LORD said to Satan, 'Very well, then, everything he has is in your power, but on the man himself do not lay a finger.'

Then Satan went out from the presence of the LORD.

¹³One day when Job's sons and daughters were feasting and drinking wine at the eldest brother's house, ¹⁴a messenger came to Job and said, 'The oxen were ploughing and the donkeys were grazing nearby, ¹⁵and the Sabeans attacked and made off with them. They put the servants to the sword, and I am the only one who has escaped to tell you!'

¹⁶While he was still speaking, another messenger came and said, 'The fire of God fell from the heavens and burned up the sheep and the servants, and I am the only one who has escaped to tell you!'

¹⁷While he was still speaking, another messenger came and said, 'The Chaldeans formed three raiding parties and swept down on your camels and made off with them. They put the servants to the sword, and I am the only one who has escaped to tell you!'

¹⁸While he was still speaking, yet another messenger came and said, 'Your sons and daughters were feasting and drinking wine at the eldest brother's house, ¹⁹when suddenly a mighty wind swept in from the desert and struck the four corners of the house. It collapsed on them and they are dead, and I am the only one who has escaped to tell you!'

²⁰At this, Job got up and tore his robe and shaved his head. Then he fell to the ground in worship ²¹and said:

'Naked I came from my mother's womb,
    and naked I shall depart.
The LORD gave and the LORD has taken
        away;
    may the name of the LORD be praised.'

²²In all this, Job did not sin by charging God with wrongdoing.

2 On another day the angels came to present themselves before the Lord, and Satan also came with them to present himself before him. ²And the Lord said to Satan, 'Where have you come from?'

Satan answered the LORD, 'From roaming throughout the earth, going to and fro on it.'

³Then the LORD said to Satan, 'Have you considered my servant Job? There is no one on earth like him; he is blameless and upright, a man who fears God and shuns evil. And he still maintains his integrity, though you incited me against him to ruin him without any reason.'

⁴'Skin for skin!' Satan replied. 'A man

will give all he has for his own life. [5] But now stretch out your hand and strike his flesh and bones, and he will surely curse you to your face.'

[6] The LORD said to Satan, 'Very well, then, he is in your hands; but you must spare his life.'

[7] So Satan went out from the presence of the LORD and afflicted Job with painful sores from the soles of his feet to the crown of his head. [8] Then Job took a piece of broken pottery and scraped himself with it as he sat among the ashes.

[9] His wife said to him, 'Are you still maintaining your integrity? Curse God and die!'

[10] He replied, 'You are talking like a foolish woman. Shall we accept good from God, and not trouble?'

In all this, Job did not sin in what he said.

[11] When Job's three friends, Eliphaz the Temanite, Bildad the Shuhite and Zophar the Naamathite, heard about all the troubles that had come upon him, they set out from their homes and met together by agreement to go and sympathise with him and comfort him. [12] When they saw him from a distance, they could hardly recognise him; they began to weep aloud, and they tore their robes and sprinkled dust on their heads. [13] Then they sat on the ground with him for seven days and seven nights. No one said a word to him, because they saw how great his suffering was.

3 After this, Job opened his mouth and cursed the day of his birth. [2] He said:

[3] 'May the day of my birth perish,
    and the night that said, "A boy is
        conceived!"
[4] That day – may it turn to darkness;
    may God above not care about it;
    may no light shine on it.
[5] May gloom and utter darkness claim it
        once more;
    may a cloud settle over it;
    may blackness overwhelm it.

[6] That night – may thick darkness seize it;
    may it not be included among the days
        of the year
    nor be entered in any of the months.
[7] May that night be barren;
    may no shout of joy be heard in it.
[8] May those who curse days curse that day,
    those who are ready to rouse Leviathan.
[9] May its morning stars become dark;
    may it wait for daylight in vain
    and not see the first rays of dawn,
[10] for it did not shut the doors of the womb
        on me
    to hide trouble from my eyes.

[11] 'Why did I not perish at birth,
    and die as I came from the womb?
[12] Why were there knees to receive me
    and breasts that I might be nursed?
[13] For now I would be lying down in peace;
    I would be asleep and at rest
[14] with kings and rulers of the earth,
    who built for themselves places now
        lying in ruins,
[15] with princes who had gold,
    who filled their houses with silver.
[16] Or why was I not hidden away in the
        ground like a stillborn child,
    like an infant who never saw the light
        of day?
[17] There the wicked cease from turmoil,
    and there the weary are at rest.
[18] Captives also enjoy their ease;
    they no longer hear the slave driver's
        shout.
[19] The small and the great are there,
    and the slaves are freed from their
        owners.

[20] 'Why is light given to those in misery,
    and life to the bitter of soul,
[21] to those who long for death that does not
        come,
    who search for it more than for hidden
        treasure,
[22] who are filled with gladness

and rejoice when they reach the grave?
²³ Why is life given to a man
  whose way is hidden,
  whom God has hedged in?
²⁴ For sighing has become my daily food;
  my groans pour out like water.
²⁵ What I feared has come upon me;
  what I dreaded has happened to me.
²⁶ I have no peace, no quietness;
  I have no rest, but only turmoil.'

PSALM 103:6-14

⁶ The LORD works righteousness
  and justice for all the oppressed.

⁷ He made known his ways to Moses,
  his deeds to the people of Israel:
⁸ the LORD is compassionate and gracious,
  slow to anger, abounding in love.
⁹ He will not always accuse,
  nor will he harbour his anger for ever;
¹⁰ he does not treat us as our sins deserve
  or repay us according to our iniquities.
¹¹ For as high as the heavens are above the
    earth,
  so great is his love for those who fear
    him;
¹² as far as the east is from the west,
  so far has he removed our
    transgressions from us.

¹³ As a father has compassion on his
    children,
  so the LORD has compassion on those
    who fear him;
¹⁴ for he knows how we are formed,
  he remembers that we are dust.

PROVERBS 21:4-5

⁴ Haughty eyes and a proud heart –
  the unploughed field of the wicked –
  produce sin.

⁵ The plans of the diligent lead to profit
  as surely as haste leads to poverty.

1 CORINTHIANS 1:1-19

1 Paul, called to be an apostle of Christ Jesus by the will of God, and our brother Sosthenes,

² To the church of God in Corinth, to those sanctified in Christ Jesus and called to be his holy people, together with all those everywhere who call on the name of our Lord Jesus Christ – their Lord and ours:

³ Grace and peace to you from God our Father and the Lord Jesus Christ.

⁴ I always thank my God for you because of his grace given you in Christ Jesus. ⁵ For in him you have been enriched in every way – with all kinds of speech and with all knowledge – ⁶ God thus confirming our testimony about Christ among you. ⁷ Therefore you do not lack any spiritual gift as you eagerly wait for our Lord Jesus Christ to be revealed. ⁸ He will also keep you firm to the end, so that you will be blameless on the day of our Lord Jesus Christ. ⁹ God is faithful, who has called you into fellowship with his Son, Jesus Christ our Lord.

¹⁰ I appeal to you, brothers and sisters, in the name of our Lord Jesus Christ, that all of you agree with one another in what you say and that there be no divisions among you, but that you be perfectly united in mind and thought. ¹¹ My brothers and sisters, some from Chloe's household have informed me that there are quarrels among you. ¹² What I mean is this: one of you says, 'I follow Paul'; another, 'I follow Apollos'; another, 'I follow Cephas'; still another, 'I follow Christ.'
¹³ Is Christ divided? Was Paul crucified for you? Were you baptised in the name of Paul? ¹⁴ I thank God that I did not baptise any of you except Crispus and Gaius,

¹⁵ so no one can say that you were baptised in my name. ¹⁶ (Yes, I also baptised the household of Stephanas; beyond that, I don't remember if I baptised anyone else.) ¹⁷ For Christ did not send me to baptise, but to preach the gospel – not with wisdom and eloquence, lest the cross of Christ be emptied of its power.

¹⁸ For the message of the cross is foolishness to those who are perishing, but to us who are being saved it is the power of God. ¹⁹ For it is written:

'I will destroy the wisdom of the wise;
    the intelligence of the intelligent I will
        frustrate.'

Fellowship

'God is faithful, who has called you into fellowship with his Son, Jesus Christ our Lord.' **1 Corinthians 1:9**

Seek fellowship with other Christians. Daniel Rowlands, a famous Welsh revivalist of a past century, said, 'The whole purpose of the Christian message can be summarised in a single word - fellowship.'

What did he mean? 1 John 1:3 spells it out clearly: 'And our fellowship is with the Father and with His Son, Jesus Christ.' Listen to it as it appears in *The Amplified Bible*: 'What we have seen and ourselves heard, we are also telling you, so that you too may realise and enjoy fellowship as partners and partakers with us. And this fellowship that we have ... is with the Father and with His Son Jesus Christ, the Messiah.' At first, John seems to say that the fellowship is 'with us', but he hastens to add that our fellowship 'is with the Father and with His Son, Jesus Christ'.

Follow me carefully now, for what I am about to say can be easily misunderstood: the person who does not know fellowship with God will struggle to know fellowship with anyone else. It must be noted that I am here using the word 'fellowship' in its highest possible sense. The one who does not know fellowship with God may feel, consciously or unconsciously, that he is cut off from the very roots of his being. He will feel like a spiritual orphan. This is why our horizontal relationships - that is, our relationship with ourselves and with others - are limited until we experience a vertical relationship, a relationship with God. When we are reconciled with God we have the potential for experiencing true fellowship with ourselves and with others.

PRAYER

Father, I see that I cannot experience true fellowship with myself or with others until I have known it with You. Help me to deepen my fellowship with You so that I might deepen it with others. In Jesus' name. Amen.

FURTHER STUDY

Exod. 19:1-22; 20:21; 24:2; 25:22; 33:9
• What was the key to Moses' ministry?
• What was the effect?

August 26

■ **JOB 4:1–6:10**

4 Then Eliphaz the Temanite replied:

² 'If someone ventures a word with you,
    will you be impatient?
    But who can keep from speaking?
³ Think how you have instructed many,
    how you have strengthened feeble
        hands.
⁴ Your words have supported those who
        stumbled;
    you have strengthened faltering
        knees.
⁵ But now trouble comes to you, and you
        are discouraged;
    it strikes you, and you are dismayed.
⁶ Should not your piety be your confidence
    and your blameless ways your hope?

⁷ 'Consider now: who, being innocent, has
        ever perished?
    Where were the upright ever
        destroyed?
⁸ As I have observed, those who plough
        evil
    and those who sow trouble reap it.
⁹ At the breath of God they perish;
    at the blast of his anger they are no
        more.
¹⁰ The lions may roar and growl,
    yet the teeth of the great lions are
        broken.
¹¹ The lion perishes for lack of prey,
    and the cubs of the lioness are
        scattered.

¹² 'A word was secretly brought to me,
    my ears caught a whisper of it.
¹³ Amid disquieting dreams in the night,
    when deep sleep falls on people,
¹⁴ fear and trembling seized me
    and made all my bones shake.
¹⁵ A spirit glided past my face,
    and the hair on my body stood on end.
¹⁶ It stopped,
    but I could not tell what it was.
    A form stood before my eyes,
    and I heard a hushed voice:
¹⁷ "Can a mortal be more righteous than
        God?
    Can even a strong man be more pure
        than his Maker?
¹⁸ If God places no trust in his servants,
    if he charges his angels with error,
¹⁹ how much more those who live in houses
        of clay,
    whose foundations are in the dust,
    who are crushed more readily than a
        moth!
²⁰ Between dawn and dusk they are broken
        to pieces;
    unnoticed, they perish for ever.
²¹ Are not the cords of their tent pulled up,
    so that they die without wisdom?"

5 'Call if you will, but who will answer
        you?
    To which of the holy ones will you
        turn?
² Resentment kills a fool,
    and envy slays the simple.
³ I myself have seen a fool taking root,
    but suddenly his house was cursed.
⁴ His children are far from safety,
    crushed in court without a defender.
⁵ The hungry consume his harvest,
    taking it even from among thorns,
    and the thirsty pant after his wealth.
⁶ For hardship does not spring from the
        soil,

nor does trouble sprout from the
   ground.
7 Yet man is born to trouble
   as surely as sparks fly upwards.

8 'But if I were you, I would appeal to God;
   I would lay my cause before him.
9 He performs wonders that cannot be
      fathomed,
   miracles that cannot be counted.
10 He provides rain for the earth;
   he sends water on the countryside.
11 The lowly he sets on high,
   and those who mourn are lifted to safety.
12 He thwarts the plans of the crafty,
   so that their hands achieve no success.
13 He catches the wise in their craftiness,
   and the schemes of the wily are swept
      away.
14 Darkness comes upon them in the
      daytime;
   at noon they grope as in the night.
15 He saves the needy from the sword in
      their mouth;
   he saves them from the clutches of the
      powerful.
16 So the poor have hope,
   and injustice shuts its mouth.

17 'Blessed is the one whom God corrects;
   so do not despise the discipline of the
      Almighty.
18 For he wounds, but he also binds up;
   he injures, but his hands also heal.
19 From six calamities he will rescue you;
   in seven no harm will touch you.
20 In famine he will deliver you from death,
   and in battle from the stroke of the
      sword.
21 You will be protected from the lash of the
      tongue,
   and need not fear when destruction
      comes.
22 You will laugh at destruction and
      famine,
   and need not fear the wild animals.

23 For you will have a covenant with the
      stones of the field,
   and the wild animals will be at peace
      with you.
24 You will know that your tent is secure;
   you will take stock of your property
   and find nothing missing.
25 You will know that your children will be
      many,
   and your descendants like the grass of
      the earth.
26 You will come to the grave in full vigour,
   like sheaves gathered in season.

27 'We have examined this, and it is true.
   So hear it and apply it to yourself.'

6 Then Job replied:

2 'If only my anguish could be weighed
   and all my misery be placed on the
      scales!
3 It would surely outweigh the sand of the
      seas –
   no wonder my words have been
      impetuous.
4 The arrows of the Almighty are in me,
   my spirit drinks in their poison;
   God's terrors are marshalled against
      me.
5 Does a wild donkey bray when it has grass,
   or an ox bellow when it has fodder?
6 Is tasteless food eaten without salt,
   or is there flavour in the sap of the
      mallow?
7 I refuse to touch it;
   such food makes me ill.

8 'Oh, that I might have my request,
   that God would grant what I hope for,
9 that God would be willing to crush me,
   to let loose his hand and cut off my
      life!
10 Then I would still have this consolation –
   my joy in unrelenting pain –
   that I had not denied the words of the
      Holy One.

■ PSALM 103:15-22

¹⁵ The life of mortals is like grass,
  they flourish like a flower of the field;
¹⁶ the wind blows over it and it is gone,
  and its place remembers it no more.
¹⁷ But from everlasting to everlasting
  the LORD's love is with those who fear
    him,
  and his righteousness with their
    children's children –
¹⁸ with those who keep his covenant
  and remember to obey his precepts.

¹⁹ The LORD has established his throne in
    heaven,
  and his kingdom rules over all.

²⁰ Praise the LORD, you his angels,
  you mighty ones who do his bidding,
  who obey his word.
²¹ Praise the LORD, all his heavenly hosts,
  you his servants who do his will.
²² Praise the LORD, all his works
  everywhere in his dominion.

Praise the LORD, my soul.

■ PROVERBS 21:6-7

⁶ A fortune made by a lying tongue
  is a fleeting vapour and a deadly snare.

⁷ The violence of the wicked will drag
    them away,
  for they refuse to do what is right.

■ 1 CORINTHIANS 1:20–2:9

²⁰ Where is the wise person? Where is
the teacher of the law? Where is the philosopher of this age? Has not God made foolish the wisdom of the world? ²¹ For since
in the wisdom of God the world through
its wisdom did not know him, God was
pleased through the foolishness of what
was preached to save those who believe.
²² Jews demand signs and Greeks look for
wisdom, ²³ but we preach Christ crucified:
a stumbling-block to Jews and foolishness
to Gentiles, ²⁴ but to those whom God has
called, both Jews and Greeks, Christ the
power of God and the wisdom of God. ²⁵ For
the foolishness of God is wiser than human wisdom, and the weakness of God is
stronger than human strength.

²⁶ Brothers and sisters, think of what you
were when you were called. Not many of you
were wise by human standards; not many
were influential; not many were of noble
birth. ²⁷ But God chose the foolish things
of the world to shame the wise; God chose
the weak things of the world to shame the
strong. ²⁸ God chose the lowly things of this
world and the despised things – and the
things that are not – to nullify the things
that are, ²⁹ so that no one may boast before
him. ³⁰ It is because of him that you are in
Christ Jesus, who has become for us wisdom from God – that is, our righteousness,
holiness and redemption. ³¹ Therefore, as it
is written: 'Let the one who boasts boast in
the Lord.'

2 And so it was with me, brothers and
sisters. When I came to you, I did not
come with eloquence or human wisdom as
I proclaimed to you the testimony about
God. ² For I resolved to know nothing while
I was with you except Jesus Christ and him
crucified. ³ I came to you in weakness with
great fear and trembling. ⁴ My message and
my preaching were not with wise and persuasive words, but with a demonstration of
the Spirit's power, ⁵ so that your faith might
not rest on human wisdom, but on God's
power.

⁶ We do, however, speak a message of
wisdom among the mature, but not the wisdom of this age or of the rulers of this age,
who are coming to nothing. ⁷ No, we declare

God's wisdom, a mystery that has been hidden and that God destined for our glory before time began. [8] None of the rulers of this age understood it, for if they had, they would not have crucified the Lord of glory. [9] However, as it is written:

'What no eye has seen,

what no ear has heard,
and what no human mind has
    conceived' –
the things God has prepared for those
    who love him –

[10] these are the things God has revealed to us by his Spirit.

It Lacks That

'My message and my preaching were not with wise and persuasive words, but with a demonstration of the Spirit's power.' **1 Corinthians 2:4**

Much of modern-day Christianity is lacking power and conviction because it lacks a close encounter with this aspect of the Spirit's resources. If we are to experience the fullness of the Spirit in our lives, then we must open ourselves to everything He wants to give us. We must not pick and choose and say, 'I'll take this but not that', for in order to be God's true representatives in this world, we must know Him in all His fullness.

I watched a man on television one day examine a beautiful painting. He studied it for a few moments and said, 'Its perspective is good, the colouring is fine, the tones are excellent, the idea behind it is to be commended, but it lacks ... that.'

The same can be said of a lot of Christian activity in this generation. Our preaching is correct, our worship services are well-structured, our music is fine, our organisation is superb, but it lacks one thing – the throbbing power of the Holy Spirit. Without the power of the Spirit in our midst, we are preaching unquickened truth – truth that doesn't fall upon the soul with convicting, sobering, awakening, converting power. Our Christianity is not bad – it is just dull. The Holy Spirit, when accepted and obeyed, turns insipidity into inspiration, dullness into dancing, and mediocrity into magnificence. If we are not careful, we may find ourselves in court one of these days accused of contravening the Trade Descriptions Act!

PRAYER

Ouch, Lord, this hurts! But I know from experience that You hurt me in order to heal me. Begin with me today, and set me on fire that others may catch it, too! Amen.

FURTHER STUDY

Acts 19:21-41; Eph. 5:18; 3:19
• How did the Holy Spirit give Paul holy boldness?
• What was Paul's exhortation to the Ephesian church?

August 27

■ JOB 6:11–8:22

¹¹ 'What strength do I have, that I should
      still hope?
    What prospects, that I should be
      patient?
¹² Do I have the strength of stone?
      Is my flesh bronze?
¹³ Do I have any power to help myself,
      now that success has been driven
        from me?

¹⁴ 'Anyone who withholds kindness from a
      friend
    forsakes the fear of the Almighty.
¹⁵ But my brothers are as undependable as
      intermittent streams,
    as the streams that overflow
¹⁶ when darkened by thawing ice
      and swollen with melting snow,
¹⁷ but that stop flowing in the dry season,
      and in the heat vanish from their
        channels.
¹⁸ Caravans turn aside from their routes;
      they go off into the wasteland and
        perish.
¹⁹ The caravans of Tema look for water,
      the travelling merchants of Sheba look
        in hope.
²⁰ They are distressed, because they had
      been confident;
    they arrive there, only to be
        disappointed.
²¹ Now you too have proved to be of no
      help;
    you see something dreadful and are
        afraid.
²² Have I ever said, "Give something on my
      behalf,
    pay a ransom for me from your
        wealth,

²³ deliver me from the hand of the enemy,
      rescue me from the clutches of the
        ruthless"?

²⁴ 'Teach me, and I will be quiet;
      show me where I have been wrong.
²⁵ How painful are honest words!
      But what do your arguments prove?
²⁶ Do you mean to correct what I say,
      and treat my desperate words as
        wind?
²⁷ You would even cast lots for the
      fatherless
    and barter away your friend.

²⁸ 'But now be so kind as to look at me.
      Would I lie to your face?
²⁹ Relent, do not be unjust;
      reconsider, for my integrity is at stake.
³⁰ Is there any wickedness on my lips?
      Can my mouth not discern malice?

7 'Do not mortals have hard service on
      earth?
    Are not their days like those of hired
        labourers?
² Like a slave longing for the evening
      shadows,
    or a hired labourer waiting to be paid,
³ so I have been allotted months of futility,
      and nights of misery have been
        assigned to me.
⁴ When I lie down I think, "How long
      before I get up?"
    The night drags on, and I toss and
        turn until dawn.
⁵ My body is clothed with worms and
      scabs,
    my skin is broken and festering.

⁶ 'My days are swifter than a weaver's
    shuttle,
    and they come to an end without hope.
⁷ Remember, O God, that my life is but a
    breath;
    my eyes will never see happiness
        again.
⁸ The eye that now sees me will see me no
    longer;
    you will look for me, but I will be no
        more.
⁹ As a cloud vanishes and is gone,
    so one who goes down to the grave
        does not return.
¹⁰ He will never come to his house again;
    his place will know him no more.

¹¹ 'Therefore I will not keep silent;
    I will speak out in the anguish of my
        spirit,
    I will complain in the bitterness of my
        soul.
¹² Am I the sea, or the monster of the deep,
    that you put me under guard?
¹³ When I think my bed will comfort me
    and my couch will ease my complaint,
¹⁴ even then you frighten me with dreams
    and terrify me with visions,
¹⁵ so that I prefer strangling and death,
    rather than this body of mine.
¹⁶ I despise my life; I would not live for
    ever.
    Let me alone; my days have no
        meaning.

¹⁷ 'What is mankind that you make so
    much of them,
    that you give them so much attention,
¹⁸ that you examine them every morning
    and test them every moment?
¹⁹ Will you never look away from me,
    or let me alone even for an instant?
²⁰ If I have sinned, what have I done to you,
    you who see everything we do?
    Why have you made me your target?
    Have I become a burden to you?

²¹ Why do you not pardon my offences
    and forgive my sins?
    For I shall soon lie down in the dust;
    you will search for me, but I shall be
        no more.'

8 Then Bildad the Shuhite replied:

² 'How long will you say such things?
    Your words are a blustering wind.
³ Does God pervert justice?
    Does the Almighty pervert what is
        right?
⁴ When your children sinned against him,
    he gave them over to the penalty of
        their sin.
⁵ But if you will seek God earnestly
    and plead with the Almighty,
⁶ if you are pure and upright,
    even now he will rouse himself on
        your behalf
    and restore you to your prosperous
        state.
⁷ Your beginnings will seem humble,
    so prosperous will your future be.

⁸ 'Ask the former generations
    and find out what their ancestors
        learned,
⁹ for we were born only yesterday and
        know nothing,
    and our days on earth are but a
        shadow.
¹⁰ Will they not instruct you and tell you?
    Will they not bring forth words from
        their understanding?
¹¹ Can papyrus grow tall where there is no
        marsh?
    Can reeds thrive without water?
¹² While still growing and uncut,
    they wither more quickly than grass.
¹³ Such is the destiny of all who forget God;
    so perishes the hope of the godless.
¹⁴ What they trust in is fragile;
    what they rely on is a spider's web.
¹⁵ They lean on the web, but it gives way;

they cling to it, but it does not hold.
16 They are like a well-watered plant in the
    sunshine,
    spreading its shoots over the garden;
17 it entwines its roots round a pile of rocks
    and looks for a place among the
    stones.
18 But when it is torn from its spot,
    that place disowns it and says, "I never
    saw you."
19 Surely its life withers away,
    and from the soil other plants grow.

20 'Surely God does not reject one who is
    blameless
    or strengthen the hands of evildoers.
21 He will yet fill your mouth with laughter
    and your lips with shouts of joy.
22 Your enemies will be clothed in shame,
    and the tents of the wicked will be no
    more.'

▬ Psalm 104:1-9

1 Praise the Lord, my soul.

Lord my God, you are very great;
    you are clothed with splendour and
    majesty.

2 The Lord wraps himself in light as with a
    garment;
    he stretches out the heavens like a tent
3   and lays the beams of his upper
        chambers on their waters.
He makes the clouds his chariot
    and rides on the wings of the wind.
4 He makes winds his messengers,
    flames of fire his servants.

5 He set the earth on its foundations;
    it can never be moved.
6 You covered it with the watery depths as
    with a garment;
    the waters stood above the mountains.

7 But at your rebuke the waters fled,
    at the sound of your thunder they took
        to flight;
8 they flowed over the mountains,
    they went down into the valleys,
    to the place you assigned for them.
9 You set a boundary they cannot cross;
    never again will they cover the earth.

▬ Proverbs 21:8-9

8 The way of the guilty is devious,
    but the conduct of the innocent is
        upright.

9 Better to live on a corner of the roof
    than share a house with a quarrelsome
        wife.

▬ 1 Corinthians 2:10–3:15

The Spirit searches all things, even the
deep things of God. 11 For who knows a person's thoughts except their own spirit within them? In the same way no one knows the
thoughts of God except the Spirit of God.
12 What we have received is not the spirit of
the world, but the Spirit who is from God,
so that we may understand what God has
freely given us. 13 This is what we speak, not
in words taught us by human wisdom but
in words taught by the Spirit, explaining
spiritual realities with Spirit-taught words.
14 The person without the Spirit does not
accept the things that come from the Spirit
of God but considers them foolishness, and
cannot understand them because they are
discerned only through the Spirit. 15 The
person with the Spirit makes judgments
about all things, but such a person is not
subject to merely human judgments, 16 for,

'Who has known the mind of the Lord
    so as to instruct him?'

But we have the mind of Christ.

3 Brothers and sisters, I could not address you as people who live by the Spirit but as people who are still worldly – mere infants in Christ. ²I gave you milk, not solid food, for you were not yet ready for it. Indeed, you are still not ready. ³You are still worldly. For since there is jealousy and quarrelling among you, are you not worldly? Are you not acting like mere humans? ⁴For when one says, 'I follow Paul,' and another, 'I follow Apollos,' are you not mere human beings?

⁵What, after all, is Apollos? And what is Paul? Only servants, through whom you came to believe – as the Lord has assigned to each his task. ⁶I planted the seed, Apollos watered it, but God has been making it grow. ⁷So neither the one who plants nor the one who waters is anything, but only God, who makes things grow. ⁸The one who plants and the one who waters have one purpose, and they will each be rewarded according to their own labour. ⁹For we are fellow workers in God's service; you are God's field, God's building.

¹⁰By the grace God has given me, I laid a foundation as a wise builder, and someone else is building on it. But each one should build with care. ¹¹For no one can lay any foundation other than the one already laid, which is Jesus Christ. ¹²If anyone builds on this foundation using gold, silver, costly stones, wood, hay or straw, ¹³their work will be shown for what it is, because the Day will bring it to light. It will be revealed with fire, and the fire will test the quality of each person's work. ¹⁴If what has been built survives, the builder will receive a reward. ¹⁵If it is burned up, the builder will suffer loss but yet will be saved – even though only as one escaping through the flames.

Divide and Conquer

'... the things that come from the Spirit of God ... are discerned only through the Spirit.' **1 Corinthians 2:14**

Only the Holy Spirit can help us properly to interpret the Word of God. A person may have a fine mind, a good seminary training, even a theological degree, but none of these is a sufficient foundation on which to attempt to interpret the Word of God. Truth, as the above text tells us, is 'discerned spiritually'.

But there is one more thing we need to understand – only the Holy Spirit can show us how to use it aright. Doubtless, this was the consideration in the mind of the apostle when he penned this statement: 'the sword of the Spirit which is the word of God' (Eph. 6:17). It is one thing to know the contents of Scripture; it is another thing to know how to use those contents in a way that defeats the devil. Only the Holy Spirit can enable us to do this.

The relationship between the Holy Spirit and the Word of God is an important one. Some tend to put the emphasis on one side or the other. But the moment we separate the Spirit and the Word, we are in trouble. The late Donald Gee once said: 'All Spirit and no Word, you blow up. All Word and no Spirit, you dry up. Word and Spirit – you grow up.'

Without the Spirit, the Word is a dead letter; with the Spirit, it is a living and powerful force. The devil has a policy of 'divide and conquer'. And if he can get us to separate the Word from the Spirit, then he has us just where he wants us.

PRAYER

My Father, I see that when I separate the Spirit from the Word and the Word from the Spirit, I am in trouble. Help me to be as open to the Spirit as I am to the Bible, and as open to the Bible as I am to the Spirit. In Jesus' name. Amen.

FURTHER STUDY

2 Cor. 3:1-6; John 6:63; 1 Pet. 3:18
• What 'gives life'?
• What made Paul an able minister of truth?

August 28

■ JOB 9:1–10:22

9 Then Job replied:

2 'Indeed, I know that this is true.
   But how can mere mortals prove their innocence before God?
3 Though they wished to dispute with him,
   they could not answer him once in a thousand times.
4 His wisdom is profound, his power is vast.
   Who has resisted him and come out unscathed?
5 He moves mountains without their knowing it
   and overturns them in his anger.
6 He shakes the earth from its place
   and makes its pillars tremble.
7 He speaks to the sun and it does not shine;
   he seals off the light of the stars.
8 He alone stretches out the heavens
   and treads on the waves of the sea.
9 He is the Maker of the Bear and Orion,

the Pleiades and the constellations of the south.
10 He performs wonders that cannot be fathomed,
   miracles that cannot be counted.
11 When he passes me, I cannot see him;
   when he goes by, I cannot perceive him.
12 If he snatches away, who can stop him?
   Who can say to him, "What are you doing?"
13 God does not restrain his anger;
   even the cohorts of Rahab cowered at his feet.

14 'How then can I dispute with him?
   How can I find words to argue with him?
15 Though I were innocent, I could not answer him;
   I could only plead with my Judge for mercy.
16 Even if I summoned him and he responded,
   I do not believe he would give me a hearing.
17 He would crush me with a storm

and multiply my wounds for no
reason.
¹⁸ He would not let me catch my breath
but would overwhelm me with misery.
¹⁹ If it is a matter of strength, he is mighty!
And if it is a matter of justice, who can
challenge him?
²⁰ Even if I were innocent, my mouth would
condemn me;
if I were blameless, it would
pronounce me guilty.

²¹ 'Although I am blameless,
I have no concern for myself;
I despise my own life.
²² It is all the same; that is why I say,
"He destroys both the blameless and
the wicked."
²³ When a scourge brings sudden death,
he mocks the despair of the innocent.
²⁴ When a land falls into the hands of the
wicked,
he blindfolds its judges.
If it is not he, then who is it?

²⁵ 'My days are swifter than a runner;
they fly away without a glimpse of joy.
²⁶ They skim past like boats of papyrus,
like eagles swooping down on their
prey.
²⁷ If I say, "I will forget my complaint,
I will change my expression, and smile,"
²⁸ I still dread all my sufferings,
for I know you will not hold me
innocent.
²⁹ Since I am already found guilty,
why should I struggle in vain?
³⁰ Even if I washed myself with soap
and my hands with cleansing powder,
³¹ you would plunge me into a slime pit
so that even my clothes would detest
me.

³² 'He is not a mere mortal like me that I
might answer him,

that we might confront each other in
court.
³³ If only there were someone to mediate
between us,
someone to bring us together,
³⁴ someone to remove God's rod from me,
so that his terror would frighten me no
more.
³⁵ Then I would speak up without fear of
him,
but as it now stands with me, I cannot.

10 'I loathe my very life;
therefore I will give free rein to my
complaint
and speak out in the bitterness of my
soul.
² I say to God: do not declare me guilty,
but tell me what charges you have
against me.
³ Does it please you to oppress me,
to spurn the work of your hands,
while you smile on the plans of the
wicked?
⁴ Do you have eyes of flesh?
Do you see as a mortal sees?
⁵ Are your days like those of a mortal
or your years like those of a strong
man,
⁶ that you must search out my faults
and probe after my sin –
⁷ though you know that I am not guilty
and that no one can rescue me from
your hand?

⁸ 'Your hands shaped me and made me.
Will you now turn and destroy me?
⁹ Remember that you moulded me like
clay.
Will you now turn me to dust again?
¹⁰ Did you not pour me out like milk
and curdle me like cheese,
¹¹ clothe me with skin and flesh
and knit me together with bones and
sinews?

¹²You gave me life and showed me
kindness,
and in your providence watched over
my spirit.

¹³'But this is what you concealed in your
heart,
and I know that this was in your mind:
¹⁴if I sinned, you would be watching me
and would not let my offence go
unpunished.
¹⁵If I am guilty – woe to me!
Even if I am innocent, I cannot lift my
head,
for I am full of shame
and drowned in my affliction.
¹⁶If I hold my head high, you stalk me like
a lion
and again display your awesome
power against me.
¹⁷You bring new witnesses against me
and increase your anger towards me;
your forces come against me wave
upon wave.

¹⁸'Why then did you bring me out of the
womb?
I wish I had died before any eye saw
me.
¹⁹If only I had never come into being,
or had been carried straight from the
womb to the grave!
²⁰Are not my few days almost over?
Turn away from me so that I can have
a moment's joy
²¹before I go to the place of no return,
to the land of gloom and utter darkness,
²²to the land of deepest night,
of utter darkness and disorder,
where even the light is like darkness.'

▬ PSALM 104:10-15

¹⁰He makes springs pour water into the
ravines;

it flows between the mountains.
¹¹They give water to all the beasts of the
field;
the wild donkeys quench their thirst.
¹²The birds of the sky nest by the waters;
they sing among the branches.
¹³He waters the mountains from his upper
chambers;
the land is satisfied by the fruit of his
work.
¹⁴He makes grass grow for the cattle,
and plants for people to cultivate –
bringing forth food from the earth:
¹⁵wine that gladdens human hearts,
oil to make their faces shine,
and bread that sustains their hearts.

▬ PROVERBS 21:10-11

¹⁰The wicked crave evil;
their neighbours get no mercy from
them.

¹¹When a mocker is punished, the simple
gain wisdom;
by paying attention to the wise they
get knowledge.

▬ 1 CORINTHIANS 3:16–4:13

¹⁶Don't you know that you yourselves
are God's temple and that God's Spirit lives
among you? ¹⁷If anyone destroys God's temple, God will destroy that person; for God's
temple is sacred, and you together are that
temple.

¹⁸Do not deceive yourselves. If any of
you think you are wise by the standards of
this age, you should become 'fools' so that
you may become wise. ¹⁹For the wisdom of
this world is foolishness in God's sight. As
it is written: 'He catches the wise in their
craftiness'; ²⁰and again, 'The Lord knows
that the thoughts of the wise are futile.'

²¹So then, no more boasting about human leaders! All things are yours, ²²whether Paul or Apollos or Cephas or the world or life or death or the present or the future – all are yours, ²³and you are of Christ, and Christ is of God.

4 This, then, is how you ought to regard us: as servants of Christ and as those entrusted with the mysteries God has revealed. ²Now it is required that those who have been given a trust must prove faithful. ³I care very little if I am judged by you or by any human court; indeed, I do not even judge myself. ⁴My conscience is clear, but that does not make me innocent. It is the Lord who judges me. ⁵Therefore judge nothing before the appointed time; wait until the Lord comes. He will bring to light what is hidden in darkness and will expose the motives of the heart. At that time each will receive their praise from God.

⁶Now, brothers and sisters, I have applied these things to myself and Apollos for your benefit, so that you may learn from us the meaning of the saying, 'Do not go beyond what is written.' Then you will not be puffed up in being a follower of one of us

over against the other. ⁷For who makes you different from anyone else? What do you have that you did not receive? And if you did receive it, why do you boast as though you did not?

⁸Already you have all you want! Already you have become rich! You have begun to reign – and that without us! How I wish that you really had begun to reign so that we also might reign with you! ⁹For it seems to me that God has put us apostles on display at the end of the procession, like those condemned to die in the arena. We have been made a spectacle to the whole universe, to angels as well as to human beings. ¹⁰We are fools for Christ, but you are so wise in Christ! We are weak, but you are strong! You are honoured, we are dishonoured! ¹¹To this very hour we go hungry and thirsty, we are in rags, we are brutally treated, we are homeless. ¹²We work hard with our own hands. When we are cursed, we bless; when we are persecuted, we endure it; ¹³when we are slandered, we answer kindly. We have become the scum of the earth, the garbage of the world – right up to this moment.

Body and Soul - United

'Don't you know that you yourselves are God's temple and that God's Spirit lives among you ... God's temple is sacred, and you together are that temple.'
1 Corinthians 3:16-17

Many centuries of misunderstanding have brought about a division between body and soul. This division is in evidence in some parts of the church today. Jesus, however, did not see His body as something to be ignored but as something to be used. As He said, '... a body you prepared for me' (Heb. 10:5).

His body and soul were attuned. He neither neglected His body nor pampered it, but offered it as the vehicle of God's will and purpose. And He kept it fit for God. There is no mention of His ever being sick. Tired, yes, but never ill.

It is accepted today that body and soul are a unity, that a sick soul can produce a sick body, just as a healthy spirit contributes to a healthy body. It also works the other way around – a healthy body can contribute to good emotional and mental health. We Christians tend to overemphasise the spiritual side of life while underestimating the importance of physical facts like body chemistry, weather, water, air pollution, and nutrition. But through ignorance of the way in which body and soul are related, we succeed only in tearing them apart. I believe what is said about husband and wife in the marriage service can also be applied to the body and the soul: 'Therefore what God has joined together, let no one separate' (Matt. 19:6).

A good pianist may be able to get a lot out of a poor instrument, but he cannot give full expression to the music if the piano is out of tune. You cannot ignore the physical if you want to stay spiritually fresh.

PRAYER

O Father, help me see that my body is not something over which to be offended, but something to be offered. Give me a balanced understanding of this matter so that I can be at my best for You – spirit, soul, and body. Amen.

FURTHER STUDY

1 Kings 19; Rom. 8:11; 1 Cor. 3:16
- What was part of Elijah's problem?
- How did the angel minister to Elijah?

August 29

■ JOB 11:1–13:12

11 Then Zophar the Naamathite replied:

² 'Are all these words to go unanswered?
   Is this talker to be vindicated?
³ Will your idle talk reduce others to
      silence?
   Will no one rebuke you when you
      mock?
⁴ You say to God, "My beliefs are flawless
   and I am pure in your sight."
⁵ Oh, how I wish that God would speak,
   that he would open his lips against you
⁶ and disclose to you the secrets of
      wisdom,
   for true wisdom has two sides.

Know this: God has even forgotten
   some of your sin.

⁷ 'Can you fathom the mysteries of God?
   Can you probe the limits of the
      Almighty?
⁸ They are higher than the heavens
      above – what can you do?
   They are deeper than the depths
      below – what can you know?
⁹ Their measure is longer than the earth
   and wider than the sea.

¹⁰ 'If he comes along and confines you in
      prison
   and convenes a court, who can oppose
      him?

¹¹ Surely he recognises deceivers;
    and when he sees evil, does he not take
        note?
¹² But the witless can no more become wise
    than a wild donkey's colt can be born
        human.

¹³ 'Yet if you devote your heart to him
    and stretch out your hands to him,
¹⁴ if you put away the sin that is in your
        hand
    and allow no evil to dwell in your tent,
¹⁵ then, free of fault, you will lift up your
        face;
    you will stand firm and without fear.
¹⁶ You will surely forget your trouble,
    recalling it only as waters gone by.
¹⁷ Life will be brighter than noonday,
    and darkness will become like
        morning.
¹⁸ You will be secure, because there is hope;
    you will look about you and take your
        rest in safety.
¹⁹ You will lie down, with no one to make
        you afraid,
    and many will court your favour.
²⁰ But the eyes of the wicked will fail,
    and escape will elude them;
    their hope will become a dying gasp.'

12

Then Job replied:

² 'Doubtless you are the only people who
        matter,
    and wisdom will die with you!
³ But I have a mind as well as you;
    I am not inferior to you.
    Who does not know all these things?

⁴ 'I have become a laughing-stock to my
        friends,
    though I called on God and he
        answered –
    a mere laughing-stock, though
        righteous and blameless!
⁵ Those who are at ease have contempt for
        misfortune

as the fate of those whose feet are
        slipping.
⁶ The tents of marauders are undisturbed,
    and those who provoke God are
        secure –
    those whom God has in his hand.

⁷ 'But ask the animals, and they will teach
        you,
    or the birds in the sky, and they will
        tell you;
⁸ or speak to the earth, and it will teach
        you,
    or let the fish in the sea inform you.
⁹ Which of all these does not know
    that the hand of the LORD has done
        this?
¹⁰ In his hand is the life of every creature
    and the breath of all mankind.
¹¹ Does not the ear test words
    as the tongue tastes food?
¹² Is not wisdom found among the aged?
    Does not long life bring
        understanding?

¹³ 'To God belong wisdom and power;
    counsel and understanding are his.
¹⁴ What he tears down cannot be rebuilt;
    those he imprisons cannot be
        released.
¹⁵ If he holds back the waters, there is
        drought;
    if he lets them loose, they devastate
        the land.
¹⁶ To him belong strength and insight;
    both deceived and deceiver are his.
¹⁷ He leads rulers away stripped
    and makes fools of judges.
¹⁸ He takes off the shackles put on by kings
    and ties a loincloth round their waist.
¹⁹ He leads priests away stripped
    and overthrows officials long
        established.
²⁰ He silences the lips of trusted advisors
    and takes away the discernment of
        elders.

²¹ He pours contempt on nobles
   and disarms the mighty.
²² He reveals the deep things of darkness
   and brings utter darkness into the
      light.
²³ He makes nations great, and destroys
      them;
   he enlarges nations, and disperses
      them.
²⁴ He deprives the leaders of the earth of
      their reason;
   he makes them wander in a trackless
      waste.
²⁵ They grope in darkness with no light;
   he makes them stagger like
      drunkards.

13 'My eyes have seen all this,
   my ears have heard and understood
      it.
² What you know, I also know;
   I am not inferior to you.
³ But I desire to speak to the Almighty
   and to argue my case with God.
⁴ You, however, smear me with lies;
   you are worthless physicians, all of
      you!
⁵ If only you would be altogether silent!
   For you, that would be wisdom.
⁶ Hear now my argument;
   listen to the pleas of my lips.
⁷ Will you speak wickedly on God's
      behalf?
   Will you speak deceitfully for him?
⁸ Will you show him partiality?
   Will you argue the case for God?
⁹ Would it turn out well if he examined
      you?
   Could you deceive him as you might
      deceive a mortal?
¹⁰ He would surely call you to account
   if you secretly showed partiality.
¹¹ Would not his splendour terrify you?
   Would not the dread of him fall on you?
¹² Your maxims are proverbs of ashes;
   your defences are defences of clay.

▬ PSALM 104:16-23

¹⁶ The trees of the Lord are well watered,
   the cedars of Lebanon that he planted.
¹⁷ There the birds make their nests;
   the stork has its home in the junipers.
¹⁸ The high mountains belong to the wild
      goats;
   the crags are a refuge for the hyrax.

¹⁹ He made the moon to mark the seasons,
   and the sun knows when to go down.
²⁰ You bring darkness, it becomes night,
   and all the beasts of the forest prowl.
²¹ The lions roar for their prey
   and seek their food from God.
²² The sun rises, and they steal away;
   they return and lie down in their dens.
²³ Then people go out to their work,
   to their labour until evening.

▬ PROVERBS 21:12-14

¹² The Righteous One takes note of the
      house of the wicked
   and brings the wicked to ruin.

¹³ Whoever shuts their ears to the cry of the
      poor
   will also cry out and not be answered.

¹⁴ A gift given in secret soothes anger,
   and a bribe concealed in the cloak
      pacifies great wrath.

▬ 1 CORINTHIANS 4:14–5:13

¹⁴ I am writing this not to shame you but
to warn you as my dear children. ¹⁵ Even if
you had ten thousand guardians in Christ,
you do not have many fathers, for in Christ
Jesus I became your father through the gospel. ¹⁶ Therefore I urge you to imitate me.
¹⁷ For this reason I have sent to you Timothy,

my son whom I love, who is faithful in the Lord. He will remind you of my way of life in Christ Jesus, which agrees with what I teach everywhere in every church.

¹⁸ Some of you have become arrogant, as if I were not coming to you. ¹⁹ But I will come to you very soon, if the Lord is willing, and then I will find out not only how these arrogant people are talking, but what power they have. ²⁰ For the kingdom of God is not a matter of talk but of power. ²¹ What do you prefer? Shall I come to you with a rod of discipline, or shall I come in love and with a gentle spirit?

5 It is actually reported that there is sexual immorality among you, and of a kind that even pagans do not tolerate: a man is sleeping with his father's wife. ² And you are proud! Shouldn't you rather have gone into mourning and have put out of your fellowship the man who has been doing this? ³ For my part, even though I am not physically present, I am with you in spirit. As one who is present with you in this way, I have already passed judgment in the name of our Lord Jesus on the one who has been doing this. ⁴ So when you are assembled and I am with you in spirit, and the power of our Lord Jesus is present, ⁵ hand this man over

to Satan for the destruction of the flesh, so that his spirit may be saved on the day of the Lord.

⁶ Your boasting is not good. Don't you know that a little yeast leavens the whole batch of dough? ⁷ Get rid of the old yeast, so that you may be a new unleavened batch – as you really are. For Christ, our Passover lamb, has been sacrificed. ⁸ Therefore let us keep the Festival, not with the old bread leavened with malice and wickedness, but with the unleavened bread of sincerity and truth.

⁹ I wrote to you in my letter not to associate with sexually immoral people – ¹⁰ not at all meaning the people of this world who are immoral, or the greedy and swindlers, or idolaters. In that case you would have to leave this world. ¹¹ But now I am writing to you that you must not associate with anyone who claims to be a brother or sister but is sexually immoral or greedy, an idolater or slanderer, a drunkard or swindler. Do not even eat with such people.

¹² What business is it of mine to judge those outside the church? Are you not to judge those inside? ¹³ God will judge those outside. 'Expel the wicked person from among you.'

He Burns Me Up

'Therefore let us keep the Festival, not with ... malice and wickedness, but with the unleavened bread of sincerity and truth.' **1 Corinthians 5:8**

Is it true that nursing a grudge can cause physical illness? A man I knew became enraged over something another Christian had done to him. I advised him to forgive and forget. He replied, 'But every time I see him, he burns me up.' I said, 'That's because you want to burn him up, and all you succeed in doing is burning yourself up.' I told him about the sadistic farmer who tied a stick of dynamite to a hawk, lit the fuse, and then turned the bird loose, expecting it to blow itself up in mid-air. Instead, the hawk flew into the man's barn, and the explosion wrecked not only the barn but part of his house also.

He listened, but I could see my words had not gone in. He could think and talk of nothing else but getting even with his fellow Christian. His wife told me that his breath became foul, his appetite left him, his digestion became bad, he suffered loss of sleep and, after a few months, he dropped down dead.

In case someone says, 'But there could have been other reasons for his death', I can tell you that I talked to his doctor, who was a close personal friend of mine, and he told me that the man had died of an 'undrained grudge'. Of course, you can't put that on a death certificate, but many doctors know that 'undrained grudges' play a major role in creating physical disorders. A missionary suffered a breakdown because of a grudge he had held against his ministry organisation for not supplying him with enough money. Apparently, grudges are just as deadly in the godly as the ungodly.

PRAYER

Father, I see so clearly that my hurts harm me even more when I harbour them. Help me not to hold on stubbornly to my wounded pride, but consent for You to work in my life, no matter how much it may hurt. In Jesus' name. Amen.

FURTHER STUDY

1 John 2:1-11; Prov. 10:12; Isa. 59:9-10

• What brings us back into darkness?
• What is the result of walking in darkness?

August 30

■ JOB 13:13–15:13

13 'Keep silent and let me speak;
    then let come to me what may.
14 Why do I put myself in jeopardy
    and take my life in my hands?
15 Though he slay me, yet will I hope in
       him;
    I will surely defend my ways to his
       face.
16 Indeed, this will turn out for my
       deliverance,
    for no godless person would dare
       come before him!
17 Listen carefully to what I say;
    let my words ring in your ears.
18 Now that I have prepared my case,

    I know I will be vindicated.
19 Can anyone bring charges against me?
    If so, I will be silent and die.
20 'Only grant me these two things, God,
    and then I will not hide from you:
21 Withdraw your hand far from me,
    and stop frightening me with your
       terrors.
22 Then summon me and I will answer,
    or let me speak, and you reply to me.
23 How many wrongs and sins have I
       committed?
    Show me my offence and my sin.
24 Why do you hide your face
    and consider me your enemy?
25 Will you torment a wind-blown leaf?

Will you chase after dry chaff?
26 For you write down bitter things against
me
and make me reap the sins of my
youth.
27 You fasten my feet in shackles;
you keep close watch on all my paths
by putting marks on the soles of my
feet.

28 'So man wastes away like something
rotten,
like a garment eaten by moths.

14 'Mortals, born of woman,
are of few days and full of trouble.
2 They spring up like flowers and wither
away;
like fleeting shadows, they do not
endure.
3 Do you fix your eye on them?
Will you bring them before you for
judgment?
4 Who can bring what is pure from the
impure?
No one!
5 A person's days are determined;
you have decreed the number of his
months
and have set limits he cannot exceed.
6 So look away from him and let him
alone,
till he has put in his time like a hired
labourer.

7 'At least there is hope for a tree:
if it is cut down, it will sprout again,
and its new shoots will not fail.
8 Its roots may grow old in the ground
and its stump die in the soil,
9 yet at the scent of water it will bud
and put forth shoots like a plant.
10 But a man dies and is laid low;
he breathes his last and is no more.
11 As the water of a lake dries up

or a river bed becomes parched and
dry,
12 so he lies down and does not rise;
till the heavens are no more, people
will not awake
or be roused from their sleep.

13 'If only you would hide me in the grave
and conceal me till your anger has
passed!
If only you would set me a time
and then remember me!
14 If someone dies, will they live again?
All the days of my hard service
I will wait for my renewal to come.
15 You will call and I will answer you;
you will long for the creature your
hands have made.
16 Surely then you will count my steps
but not keep track of my sin.
17 My offences will be sealed up in a bag;
you will cover over my sin.

18 'But as a mountain erodes and crumbles
and as a rock is moved from its place,
19 as water wears away stones
and torrents wash away the soil,
so you destroy a person's hope.
20 You overpower them once for all, and
they are gone;
you change their countenance and
send them away.
21 If their children are honoured, they do
not know it;
if their children are brought low, they
do not see it.
22 They feel but the pain of their own
bodies
and mourn only for themselves.'

15 Then Eliphaz the Temanite replied:

2 'Would a wise person answer with empty
notions
or fill their belly with the hot east
wind?
3 Would they argue with useless words,

with speeches that have no value?
4 But you even undermine piety
    and hinder devotion to God.
5 Your sin prompts your mouth;
    you adopt the tongue of the crafty.
6 Your own mouth condemns you, not
        mine;
    your own lips testify against you.

7 'Are you the first man ever born?
    Were you brought forth before the
        hills?
8 Do you listen in on God's council?
    Do you have a monopoly on wisdom?
9 What do you know that we do not know?
    What insights do you have that we do
        not have?
10 The grey-haired and the aged are on our
        side,
    men even older than your father.
11 Are God's consolations not enough for
        you,
    words spoken gently to you?
12 Why has your heart carried you away,
    and why do your eyes flash,
13 so that you vent your rage against God
    and pour out such words from your
        mouth?

■ PSALM 104:24–30

24 How many are your works, LORD!
    In wisdom you made them all;
    the earth is full of your creatures.
25 There is the sea, vast and spacious,
    teeming with creatures beyond
        number –
    living things both large and small.
26 There the ships go to and fro,
    and Leviathan, which you formed to
        frolic there.

27 All creatures look to you
    to give them their food at the proper
        time.

28 When you give it to them,
    they gather it up;
    when you open your hand,
    they are satisfied with good things.
29 When you hide your face,
    they are terrified;
    when you take away their breath,
    they die and return to the dust.
30 When you send your Spirit,
    they are created,
    and you renew the face of the ground.

■ PROVERBS 21:15–16

15 When justice is done, it brings joy to the
        righteous
    but terror to evildoers.

16 Whoever strays from the path of
        prudence
    comes to rest in the company of the
        dead.

■ 1 CORINTHIANS 6:1–20

6 If any of you has a dispute with another, do you dare to take it before the
ungodly for judgment instead of before the
Lord's people? 2 Or do you not know that the
Lord's people will judge the world? And if
you are to judge the world, are you not competent to judge trivial cases? 3 Do you not
know that we will judge angels? How much
more the things of this life! 4 Therefore, if
you have disputes about such matters, do
you ask for a ruling from those whose way
of life is scorned in the church? 5 I say this
to shame you. Is it possible that there is nobody among you wise enough to judge a dispute between believers? 6 But instead, one
brother takes another to court – and this in
front of unbelievers!

7 The very fact that you have lawsuits
among you means you have been completely

defeated already. Why not rather be wronged? Why not rather be cheated? [8] Instead, you yourselves cheat and do wrong, and you do this to your brothers and sisters. [9] Or do you not know that wrongdoers will not inherit the kingdom of God? Do not be deceived: neither the sexually immoral nor idolaters nor adulterers nor men who have sex with men [10] nor thieves nor the greedy nor drunkards nor slanderers nor swindlers will inherit the kingdom of God. [11] And that is what some of you were. But you were washed, you were sanctified, you were justified in the name of the Lord Jesus Christ and by the Spirit of our God.

[12] 'I have the right to do anything,' you say – but not everything is beneficial. 'I have the right to do anything' – but I will not be mastered by anything. [13] You say, 'Food for the stomach and the stomach for food, and God will destroy them both.' The body, however, is not meant for sexual immorality but for the Lord, and the Lord for the body. [14] By his power God raised the Lord from the dead, and he will raise us also. [15] Do you not know that your bodies are members of Christ himself? Shall I then take the members of Christ and unite them with a prostitute? Never! [16] Do you not know that he who unites himself with a prostitute is one with her in body? For it is said, 'The two will become one flesh.' [17] But whoever is united with the Lord is one with him in spirit.

[18] Flee from sexual immorality. All other sins a person commits are outside the body, but whoever sins sexually, sins against their own body. [19] Do you not know that your bodies are temples of the Holy Spirit, who is in you, whom you have received from God? You are not your own; [20] you were bought at a price. Therefore honour God with your bodies.

Sustained and Secure

'All creatures look to you to give them their food at the proper time.' **Psalm 104:27**

No creature has the power to preserve itself. 'Can papyrus grow tall where there is no marsh?' asked Job (Job 8:11). Both man and beast would perish if there were no food, and there would be no food if the earth were not refreshed with fruitful showers. As one preacher put it: 'We came from God's hand, and we remain in His hand.'

Think of the marvel of life in the womb. How an infant can live for so many months in such a cramped environment – and without breathing – is unaccountable except for the power of God in preservation. It was divine preservation Daniel was thinking of when he said to the godless Belshazzar: 'But you did not honour the God who holds in his hand your life and all your ways' (Dan. 5:23). Everywhere in the Scriptures God is presented not only as the Creator of the world but as its Sustainer and Preserver also. God has not wound up the universe like a clock and then separated Himself from it; rather, He is active in sustaining it, and were He to remove Himself from it, it would cease to exist.

The writer to the Hebrews reminds us that 'the Son is ... sustaining all things by his powerful word' (1:3). If the maker of some artifact were to die, his death would make no difference to it. It would continue to exist just as it did before. Not so with God and His world, however. If God were to die, the universe would fall to pieces. But don't worry – God cannot die. The universe is quite secure.

PRAYER

O God, when I consider how You are my Sustainer and my Preserver, my heart is humbled before You. You cannot die, and because I am linked to You, I cannot die. I know my body will die, but my soul is Yours forever. Thank You, dear Father. Amen.

FURTHER STUDY

Isa. 46:1-13; Psa. 18:35; 147:6
• What did the Lord underline to the children of Israel?
• What did the psalmist testify?

August 31

■ JOB 15:14–17:16

14 'What are mortals, that they could be pure,
    or those born of woman, that they could be righteous?
15 If God places no trust in his holy ones,
    if even the heavens are not pure in his eyes,
16 how much less mortals, who are vile and corrupt,
    who drink up evil like water!

17 'Listen to me and I will explain to you;
    let me tell you what I have seen,
18 what the wise have declared,
    hiding nothing received from their ancestors
19 (to whom alone the land was given
    when no foreigners moved among them):
20 all his days the wicked man suffers torment,
    the ruthless man through all the years stored up for him.
21 Terrifying sounds fill his ears;
    when all seems well, marauders attack him.

22 He despairs of escaping the realm of darkness;
    he is marked for the sword.
23 He wanders about for food like a vulture;
    he knows the day of darkness is at hand.
24 Distress and anguish fill him with terror;
    troubles overwhelm him, like a king poised to attack,
25 because he shakes his fist at God
    and vaunts himself against the Almighty,
26 defiantly charging against him
    with a thick, strong shield.

27 'Though his face is covered with fat
    and his waist bulges with flesh,
28 he will inhabit ruined towns
    and houses where no one lives,
    houses crumbling to rubble.
29 He will no longer be rich and his wealth will not endure,
    nor will his possessions spread over the land.
30 He will not escape the darkness;
    a flame will wither his shoots,
    and the breath of God's mouth will carry him away.

31 Let him not deceive himself by trusting
    what is worthless,
  for he will get nothing in return.
32 Before his time he will wither,
    and his branches will not flourish.
33 He will be like a vine stripped of its
      unripe grapes,
    like an olive tree shedding its
      blossoms.
34 For the company of the godless will be
      barren,
    and fire will consume the tents of
      those who love bribes.
35 They conceive trouble and give birth to
      evil;
    their womb fashions deceit.'

16 Then Job replied:

2 'I have heard many things like these;
    you are miserable comforters, all of
      you!
3 Will your long-winded speeches never
      end?
  What ails you that you keep on
      arguing?
4 I also could speak like you,
    if you were in my place;
  I could make fine speeches against you
    and shake my head at you.
5 But my mouth would encourage you;
    comfort from my lips would bring you
      relief.

6 'Yet if I speak, my pain is not relieved;
    and if I refrain, it does not go away.
7 Surely, God, you have worn me out;
    you have devastated my entire
      household.
8 You have shrivelled me up – and it has
      become a witness;
    my gauntness rises up and testifies
      against me.
9 God assails me and tears me in his anger
    and gnashes his teeth at me;
    my opponent fastens on me his
      piercing eyes.

10 People open their mouths to jeer at me;
    they strike my cheek in scorn
    and unite together against me.
11 God has turned me over to the ungodly
    and thrown me into the clutches of the
      wicked.
12 All was well with me, but he shattered me;
    he seized me by the neck and crushed
      me.
  He has made me his target;
13   his archers surround me.
  Without pity, he pierces my kidneys
    and spills my gall on the ground.
14 Again and again he bursts upon me;
    he rushes at me like a warrior.

15 'I have sewed sackcloth over my skin
    and buried my brow in the dust.
16 My face is red with weeping,
    dark shadows ring my eyes;
17 yet my hands have been free of violence
    and my prayer is pure.

18 'Earth, do not cover my blood;
    may my cry never be laid to rest!
19 Even now my witness is in heaven;
    my advocate is on high.
20 My intercessor is my friend
    as my eyes pour out tears to God;
21 on behalf of a man he pleads with God
    as one pleads for a friend.

22 'Only a few years will pass
    before I take the path of no return.

17 1 My spirit is broken,
    my days are cut short,
    the grave awaits me.
2 Surely mockers surround me;
    my eyes must dwell on their hostility.

3 'Give me, O God, the pledge you demand.
    Who else will put up security for me?
4 You have closed their minds to
      understanding;
    therefore you will not let them
      triumph.

⁵ If anyone denounces their friends for
reward,
    the eyes of their children will fail.

⁶ 'God has made me a byword to everyone,
    a man in whose face people spit.
⁷ My eyes have grown dim with grief;
    my whole frame is but a shadow.
⁸ The upright are appalled at this;
    the innocent are aroused against the
    ungodly.
⁹ Nevertheless, the righteous will hold to
    their ways,
    and those with clean hands will grow
    stronger.

¹⁰ 'But come on, all of you, try again!
    I will not find a wise man among you.
¹¹ My days have passed, my plans are
    shattered.
    Yet the desires of my heart
¹² turn night into day;
    in the face of the darkness light is near.
¹³ If the only home I hope for is the grave,
    if I spread out my bed in the realm of
    darkness,
¹⁴ if I say to corruption, "You are my
    father,"
    and to the worm, "My mother" or
    "My sister",
¹⁵ where then is my hope –
    who can see any hope for me?
¹⁶ Will it go down to the gates of death?
    Will we descend together into the dust?'

▬ PSALM 104:31-35

³¹ May the glory of the LORD endure for ever;
    may the LORD rejoice in his works –
³² he who looks at the earth, and it
    trembles,
    who touches the mountains, and they
    smoke.

³³ I will sing to the LORD all my life;

I will sing praise to my God as long as
    I live.
³⁴ May my meditation be pleasing to him,
    as I rejoice in the LORD.
³⁵ But may sinners vanish from the earth
    and the wicked be no more.

Praise the LORD, my soul.

Praise the LORD.

▬ PROVERBS 21:17-19

¹⁷ Whoever loves pleasure will become
    poor;
    whoever loves wine and olive oil will
    never be rich.

¹⁸ The wicked become a ransom for the
    righteous,
    and the unfaithful for the upright.

¹⁹ Better to live in a desert
    than with a quarrelsome and nagging
    wife.

▬ 1 CORINTHIANS 7:1-24

7 Now for the matters you wrote about:
'It is good for a man not to have sexual
relations with a woman.' ² But since sexual
immorality is occurring, each man should
have sexual relations with his own wife, and
each woman with her own husband. ³ The
husband should fulfil his marital duty to his
wife, and likewise the wife to her husband.
⁴ The wife does not have authority over her
own body but yields it to her husband. In
the same way, the husband does not have
authority over his own body but yields it to
his wife. ⁵ Do not deprive each other except
perhaps by mutual consent and for a time,
so that you may devote yourselves to prayer.
Then come together again so that Satan will

not tempt you because of your lack of self-control. ⁶I say this as a concession, not as a command. ⁷I wish that all of you were as I am. But each of you has your own gift from God; one has this gift, another has that.

⁸Now to the unmarried and the widows I say: it is good for them to stay unmarried, as I do. ⁹But if they cannot control themselves, they should marry, for it is better to marry than to burn with passion.

¹⁰To the married I give this command (not I, but the Lord): a wife must not separate from her husband. ¹¹But if she does, she must remain unmarried or else be reconciled to her husband. And a husband must not divorce his wife.

¹²To the rest I say this (I, not the Lord): If any brother has a wife who is not a believer and she is willing to live with him, he must not divorce her. ¹³And if a woman has a husband who is not a believer and he is willing to live with her, she must not divorce him. ¹⁴For the unbelieving husband has been sanctified through his wife, and the unbelieving wife has been sanctified through her believing husband. Otherwise your children would be unclean, but as it is, they are holy.

¹⁵But if the unbeliever leaves, let it be so. The brother or the sister is not bound in such circumstances; God has called us to live in peace. ¹⁶How do you know, wife, whether you will save your husband? Or, how do you know, husband, whether you will save your wife?

¹⁷Nevertheless, each person should live as a believer in whatever situation the Lord has assigned to them, just as God has called them. This is the rule I lay down in all the churches. ¹⁸Was a man already circumcised when he was called? He should not become uncircumcised. Was a man uncircumcised when he was called? He should not be circumcised. ¹⁹Circumcision is nothing and uncircumcision is nothing. Keeping God's commands is what counts. ²⁰Each person should remain in the situation they were in when God called them.

²¹Were you a slave when you were called? Don't let it trouble you – although if you can gain your freedom, do so. ²²For the one who was a slave when called to faith in the Lord is the Lord's freed person; similarly, the one who was free when called is Christ's slave. ²³You were bought at a price; do not become slaves of human beings. ²⁴Brothers and sisters, each person, as responsible to God, should remain in the situation they were in when God called them.

The Ceaseless Creator

'May my meditation be pleasing to him, as I rejoice in the LORD.' **Psalm 104:34**

Dr Douglas Speere says that with advancing years, 'Our greatest danger is not hardening of the arteries but hardening of the attitudes.' We harden our viewpoint, refusing to look at anything beyond it. We groove our thinking and acting, and the grooves get deeper until they become graves that bury us. As someone put it: 'You don't grow old; you get old by not growing.' Some people are dead at 40, although their funerals are postponed until they are 60. For many Christians, life has settled into ruts – mental, physical, and spiritual ruts. 'And a rut,' said someone, 'is a grave with ends knocked out.' In Canada I saw a dirt road leading off the main highway which had a sign on it that read:

'Choose your rut - you will be in it for the next 20 miles.' When New Year's Day comes, many could say to themselves, 'I'd better choose my rut, for I'll be in it for the next 365 days.' Life for them is not an adventure. It holds no surprises, offers no excitement, and is uncreative. My friend, I beg you, open your mind to God today and don't resist the Divine Eagle as He prepares to push you out into a more creative way of thinking, acting, and living. Someone has said that the last words of the church when it is taken up to heaven will be these, 'It has never been done like this before.' Focus your mind once again on today's psalm, and keep in mind that the God who created all things desires to live, move, and think in you.

PRAYER

O Father, You who are a ceaseless Creator, make me a ceaseless creator. Break the moulds of my thinking patterns, and give me new ones. In Jesus' name. Amen.

FURTHER STUDY

Col. 2; Isa. 11:2; Matt. 13:15; 1 Cor. 1:25; Rom. 11:33
- What are the characteristics of Christ's thoughts?
- How are they opposed to human philosophy and tradition?

September 1

■ JOB 18:1–20:11

18 Then Bildad the Shuhite replied:

² 'When will you end these speeches?
    Be sensible, and then we can talk.
³ Why are we regarded as cattle
    and considered stupid in your sight?
⁴ You who tear yourself to pieces in your anger,
    is the earth to be abandoned for your sake?
    Or must the rocks be moved from their place?

⁵ 'The lamp of a wicked man is snuffed out;
    the flame of his fire stops burning.
⁶ The light in his tent becomes dark;
    the lamp beside him goes out.
⁷ The vigour of his step is weakened;
    his own schemes throw him down.
⁸ His feet thrust him into a net;
    he wanders into its mesh.
⁹ A trap seizes him by the heel;
    a snare holds him fast.
¹⁰ A noose is hidden for him on the ground;
    a trap lies in his path.
¹¹ Terrors startle him on every side
    and dog his every step.
¹² Calamity is hungry for him;
    disaster is ready for him when he falls.
¹³ It eats away parts of his skin;
    death's firstborn devours his limbs.
¹⁴ He is torn from the security of his tent
    and marched off to the king of terrors.
¹⁵ Fire resides in his tent;

burning sulphur is scattered over his
dwelling.
¹⁶ His roots dry up below
and his branches wither above.
¹⁷ The memory of him perishes from the
earth;
he has no name in the land.
¹⁸ He is driven from light into the realm of
darkness
and is banished from the world.
¹⁹ He has no offspring or descendants
among his people,
no survivor where once he lived.
²⁰ People of the west are appalled at his
fate;
those of the east are seized with
horror.
²¹ Surely such is the dwelling of an evil man;
such is the place of one who does not
know God.'

19 Then Job replied:

² 'How long will you torment me
and crush me with words?
³ Ten times now you have reproached me;
shamelessly you attack me.
⁴ If it is true that I have gone astray,
my error remains my concern alone.
⁵ If indeed you would exalt yourselves
above me
and use my humiliation against me,
⁶ then know that God has wronged me
and drawn his net around me.

⁷ 'Though I cry, "Violence!" I get no
response;
though I call for help, there is no
justice.
⁸ He has blocked my way so that I cannot
pass;
he has shrouded my paths in
darkness.
⁹ He has stripped me of my honour
and removed the crown from my
head.

¹⁰ He tears me down on every side till I
am gone;
he uproots my hope like a tree.
¹¹ His anger burns against me;
he counts me among his enemies.
¹² His troops advance in force;
they build a siege ramp against me
and encamp around my tent.

¹³ 'He has alienated my family from me;
my acquaintances are completely
estranged from me.
¹⁴ My relatives have gone away;
my closest friends have forgotten me.
¹⁵ My guests and my female servants count
me a foreigner;
they look upon me as a stranger.
¹⁶ I summon my servant, but he does not
answer,
though I beg him with my own mouth.
¹⁷ My breath is offensive to my wife;
I am loathsome to my own family.
¹⁸ Even the little boys scorn me;
when I appear, they ridicule me.
¹⁹ All my intimate friends detest me;
those I love have turned against me.
²⁰ I am nothing but skin and bones;
I have escaped only by the skin of my
teeth.

²¹ 'Have pity on me, my friends, have pity,
for the hand of God has struck me.
²² Why do you pursue me as God does?
Will you never get enough of my flesh?

²³ 'Oh, that my words were recorded,
that they were written on a scroll,
²⁴ that they were inscribed with an iron
tool on lead,
or engraved in rock for ever!
²⁵ I know that my redeemer lives,
and that in the end he will stand on
the earth.
²⁶ And after my skin has been destroyed,
yet in my flesh I will see God;
²⁷ I myself will see him

with my own eyes – I, and not another.
How my heart yearns within me!

²⁸ 'If you say, "How we will hound him,
  since the root of the trouble lies in him,"
²⁹ you should fear the sword yourselves;
  for wrath will bring punishment by
    the sword,
  and then you will know that there is
    judgment.'

20 Then Zophar the Naamathite
replied:

² 'My troubled thoughts prompt me to
    answer
  because I am greatly disturbed.
³ I hear a rebuke that dishonours me,
  and my understanding inspires me
    to reply.

⁴ 'Surely you know how it has been from
    of old,
  ever since mankind was placed on the
    earth,
⁵ that the mirth of the wicked is brief,
  the joy of the godless lasts but a
    moment.
⁶ Though the pride of the godless person
    reaches to the heavens
  and his head touches the clouds,
⁷ he will perish for ever, like his own dung;
  those who have seen him will say,
    "Where is he?"
⁸ Like a dream he flies away, no more to
    be found,
  banished like a vision of the night.
⁹ The eye that saw him will not see him
    again;
  his place will look on him no more.
¹⁰ His children must make amends to the
    poor;
  his own hands must give back his
    wealth.
¹¹ The youthful vigour that fills his bones
  will lie with him in the dust.

▬ PSALM 105:1-6

¹ Give praise to the LORD, proclaim his
    name;
  make known among the nations what
    he has done.
² Sing to him, sing praise to him;
  tell of all his wonderful acts.
³ Glory in his holy name;
  let the hearts of those who seek the
    LORD rejoice.
⁴ Look to the LORD and his strength;
  seek his face always.
⁵ Remember the wonders he has done,
  his miracles, and the judgments he
    pronounced,
⁶ you his servants, the descendants of
    Abraham,
  his chosen ones, the children of Jacob.

▬ PROVERBS 21:20-21

²⁰ The wise store up choice food and olive
    oil,
  but fools gulp theirs down.

²¹ Whoever pursues righteousness and love
  finds life, prosperity and honour.

▬ 1 CORINTHIANS 7:25-40

²⁵ Now about virgins: I have no command
from the Lord, but I give a judgment as one
who by the Lord's mercy is trustworthy.
²⁶ Because of the present crisis, I think that
it is good for a man to remain as he is. ²⁷ Are
you pledged to a woman? Do not seek to be
released. Are you free from such a commit-
ment? Do not look for a wife. ²⁸ But if you do
marry, you have not sinned; and if a virgin
marries, she has not sinned. But those who
marry will face many troubles in this life,
and I want to spare you this.

²⁹ What I mean, brothers and sisters, is that the time is short. From now on those who have wives should live as if they do not; ³⁰ those who mourn, as if they did not; those who are happy, as if they were not; those who buy something, as if it were not theirs to keep; ³¹ those who use the things of the world, as if not engrossed in them. For this world in its present form is passing away.

³² I would like you to be free from concern. An unmarried man is concerned about the Lord's affairs – how he can please the Lord. ³³ But a married man is concerned about the affairs of this world – how he can please his wife – ³⁴ and his interests are divided. An unmarried woman or virgin is concerned about the Lord's affairs: her aim is to be devoted to the Lord in both body and spirit. But a married woman is concerned about the affairs of this world – how she can please her husband. ³⁵ I am saying this for your own good, not to restrict you, but that you may live in a right way in undivided devotion to the Lord.

³⁶ If anyone is worried that he might not be acting honourably towards the virgin he is engaged to, and if his passions are too strong and he feels he ought to marry, he should do as he wants. He is not sinning. They should get married. ³⁷ But the man who has settled the matter in his own mind, who is under no compulsion but has control over his own will, and who has made up his mind not to marry the virgin – this man also does the right thing. ³⁸ So then, he who marries the virgin does right, but he who does not marry her does better.

³⁹ A woman is bound to her husband as long as he lives. But if her husband dies, she is free to marry anyone she wishes, but he must belong to the Lord. ⁴⁰ In my judgment, she is happier if she stays as she is – and I think that I too have the Spirit of God.

Always a Reason to Rejoice

'Glory in his holy name; let the hearts of those who seek the LORD rejoice.' **Psalm 105:3**

The second fruit of the Spirit listed by Paul is joy (Gal. 5:22). It is no mere accident that 'joy' follows the first, love. Joy is a byproduct of love. If you concentrate on getting joy, it will elude you. But if you concentrate on getting love, then joy will seek you out – you will be automatically joyful.

The nine qualities of the fruit of the Spirit are not natural attributes, but supernatural ones. You cannot manufacture them – they just appear in our lives as we allow the Holy Spirit to have His way within us. I know many Christians who find it difficult to embrace the fact that the fruit of the Spirit is joy. They not only don't expect joy – they don't want it. One grim Christian said to me once, 'At the heart of our faith is a cross. This means we ought to be spending our time weeping, not laughing.'

Well, it is true that there is a cross at the heart of the Christian faith and that following Christ involves some rigorous self-denials, but it does not alter – and cannot alter – the fact that the fruit of the Spirit is joy. We cannot deny that there is a good deal of suffering in Christianity, but beneath the suffering is a joy that will, if we allow it, burst upward through everything. I am bound to say that if there is no joy, there is no Christianity, for Christianity is inherent joy. The empty tomb takes away our empty gloom. We have an Easter morning in our faith, and that means there is always a reason to rejoice.

PRAYER

Father, I am so thankful that Your Holy Spirit applies redemption right to the roots of my being. Thus I can be glad even when I am sad. Thank You, dear Father. Amen.

FURTHER STUDY

Luke 10:17-22; 15:4-6; Heb. 12:2
- How did Christ relate joy to the Cross?
- What brings joy to His heart?

September 2

■ JOB 20:12–21:34

12 'Though evil is sweet in his mouth
　and he hides it under his tongue,
13 though he cannot bear to let it go
　and lets it linger in his mouth,
14 yet his food will turn sour in his
　　stomach;
　it will become the venom of serpents
　　within him.
15 He will spit out the riches he swallowed;
　God will make his stomach vomit
　　them up.
16 He will suck the poison of serpents;
　the fangs of an adder will kill him.
17 He will not enjoy the streams,
　the rivers flowing with honey and
　　cream.
18 What he toiled for he must give back
　　uneaten;
　he will not enjoy the profit from his
　　trading.
19 For he has oppressed the poor and left
　　them destitute;
　he has seized houses he did not build.

20 'Surely he will have no respite from his
　　craving;

he cannot save himself by his treasure.
21 Nothing is left for him to devour;
　his prosperity will not endure.
22 In the midst of his plenty, distress will
　　overtake him;
　the full force of misery will come upon
　　him.
23 When he has filled his belly,
　God will vent his burning anger
　　against him
　and rain down his blows on him.
24 Though he flees from an iron weapon,
　a bronze-tipped arrow pierces him.
25 He pulls it out of his back,
　the gleaming point out of his liver.
　Terrors will come over him;
26 　total darkness lies in wait for his
　　treasures.
　A fire unfanned will consume him
　　and devour what is left in his tent.
27 The heavens will expose his guilt;
　the earth will rise up against him.
28 A flood will carry off his house,
　rushing waters on the day of God's
　　wrath.
29 Such is the fate God allots the wicked,
　the heritage appointed for them by
　　God.'

21

Then Job replied:

² 'Listen carefully to my words;
  let this be the consolation you give me.
³ Bear with me while I speak,
  and after I have spoken, mock on.

⁴ 'Is my complaint directed to a human
    being?
  Why should I not be impatient?
⁵ Look at me and be appalled;
  clap your hand over your mouth.
⁶ When I think about this, I am terrified;
  trembling seizes my body.
⁷ Why do the wicked live on,
  growing old and increasing in power?
⁸ They see their children established
    around them,
  their offspring before their eyes.
⁹ Their homes are safe and free from fear;
  the rod of God is not on them.
¹⁰ Their bulls never fail to breed;
  their cows calve and do not miscarry.
¹¹ They send forth their children as a flock;
  their little ones dance about.
¹² They sing to the music of tambourine
    and lyre;
  they make merry to the sound of the
    pipe.
¹³ They spend their years in prosperity
  and go down to the grave in peace.
¹⁴ Yet they say to God, "Leave us alone!
  We have no desire to know your ways.
¹⁵ Who is the Almighty, that we should
    serve him?
  What would we gain by praying to
    him?"
¹⁶ But their prosperity is not in their own
    hands,
  so I stand aloof from the plans of the
    wicked.

¹⁷ 'Yet how often is the lamp of the wicked
    snuffed out?
  How often does calamity come upon
    them,

the fate God allots in his anger?
¹⁸ How often are they like straw before the
    wind,
  like chaff swept away by a gale?
¹⁹ It is said, "God stores up the punishment
    of the wicked for their children."
  Let him repay the wicked, so that they
    themselves will experience it!
²⁰ Let their own eyes see their destruction;
  let them drink the cup of the wrath of
    the Almighty.
²¹ For what do they care about the families
    they leave behind
  when their allotted months come to an
    end?

²² 'Can anyone teach knowledge to God,
  since he judges even the highest?
²³ One person dies in full vigour,
  completely secure and at ease,
²⁴ well nourished in body,
  bones rich with marrow.
²⁵ Another dies in bitterness of soul,
  never having enjoyed anything good.
²⁶ Side by side they lie in the dust,
  and worms cover them both.

²⁷ 'I know full well what you are thinking,
  the schemes by which you would
    wrong me.
²⁸ You say, "Where now is the house of the
    great,
  the tents where the wicked lived?"
²⁹ Have you never questioned those who
    travel?
  Have you paid no regard to their
    accounts –
³⁰ that the wicked are spared from the day
    of calamity,
  that they are delivered from the day of
    wrath?
³¹ Who denounces their conduct to their
    face?
  Who repays them for what they have
    done?
³² They are carried to the grave,

and watch is kept over their tombs.
³³ The soil in the valley is sweet to them;
everyone follows after them,
and a countless throng goes before
them.

³⁴ 'So how can you console me with your
nonsense?
Nothing is left of your answers but
falsehood!'

▬ PSALM 105:7-15

⁷ He is the LORD our God;
his judgments are in all the earth.

⁸ He remembers his covenant for ever,
the promise he made, for a thousand
generations,
⁹ the covenant he made with Abraham,
the oath he swore to Isaac.
¹⁰ He confirmed it to Jacob as a decree,
to Israel as an everlasting covenant:
¹¹ 'To you I will give the land of Canaan
as the portion you will inherit.'

¹² When they were but few in number,
few indeed, and strangers in it,
¹³ they wandered from nation to nation,
from one kingdom to another.
¹⁴ He allowed no one to oppress them;
for their sake he rebuked kings:
¹⁵ 'Do not touch my anointed ones;
do my prophets no harm.'

▬ PROVERBS 21:22-24

²² One who is wise can go up against the
city of the mighty
and pull down the stronghold in
which they trust.

²³ Those who guard their mouths and their
tongues

keep themselves from calamity.

²⁴ The proud and arrogant person –
'Mocker' is his name –
behaves with insolent fury.

▬ 1 CORINTHIANS 8:1–9:12

8 Now about food sacrificed to idols: we
know that 'We all possess knowledge.'
But knowledge puffs up while love builds
up. ² Those who think they know something
do not yet know as they ought to know. ³ But
whoever loves God is known by God.

⁴ So then, about eating food sacrificed to
idols: we know that 'An idol is nothing at all
in the world' and that 'There is no God but
one.' ⁵ For even if there are so-called gods,
whether in heaven or on earth (as indeed
there are many 'gods' and many 'lords'),
⁶ yet for us there is but one God, the Father,
from whom all things came and for whom
we live; and there is but one Lord, Jesus
Christ, through whom all things came and
through whom we live.

⁷ But not everyone possesses this knowl-
edge. Some people are still so accustomed
to idols that when they eat sacrificial food
they think of it as having been sacrificed to
a god, and since their conscience is weak, it
is defiled. ⁸ But food does not bring us near
to God; we are no worse if we do not eat, and
no better if we do.

⁹ Be careful, however, that the exercise of
your rights does not become a stumbling-
block to the weak. ¹⁰ For if someone with a
weak conscience sees you, with all your
knowledge, eating in an idol's temple, won't
that person be emboldened to eat what is
sacrificed to idols? ¹¹ So this weak brother
or sister, for whom Christ died, is destroyed
by your knowledge. ¹² When you sin against
them in this way and wound their weak
conscience, you sin against Christ. ¹³ Therefore, if what I eat causes my brother or sister

to fall into sin, I will never eat meat again, so that I will not cause them to fall.

9 Am I not free? Am I not an apostle? Have I not seen Jesus our Lord? Are you not the result of my work in the Lord? [2]Even though I may not be an apostle to others, surely I am to you! For you are the seal of my apostleship in the Lord.

[3]This is my defence to those who sit in judgment on me. [4]Don't we have the right to food and drink? [5]Don't we have the right to take a believing wife along with us, as do the other apostles and the Lord's brothers and Cephas? [6]Or is it only I and Barnabas who lack the right to not work for a living?

[7]Who serves as a soldier at his own expense? Who plants a vineyard and does not eat its grapes? Who tends a flock and does not drink the milk? [8]Do I say this merely on human authority? Doesn't the Law say the same thing? [9]For it is written in the Law of Moses: 'Do not muzzle an ox while it is treading out the grain.' Is it about oxen that God is concerned? [10]Surely he says this for us, doesn't he? Yes, this was written for us, because whoever ploughs and threshes should be able to do so in the hope of sharing in the harvest. [11]If we have sown spiritual seed among you, is it too much if we reap a material harvest from you? [12]If others have this right of support from you, shouldn't we have it all the more?

But we did not use this right. On the contrary, we put up with anything rather than hinder the gospel of Christ.

The Great Creator

'... there is but one God, the Father, from whom all things came ... there is but one Lord, Jesus Christ, through whom all things came ...' **1 Corinthians 8:6**

In order to remain spiritually vibrant we must strive to be creative and outgoing. It is never too late to acquire this characteristic. We are made in the image of our Creator, and when we cease to be creative, we cease to be.

Kagawa, the famous Japanese Christian, used to refer to Jesus as 'the great Stimulator'. One day some students asked him why he was so fond of this phrase, and he replied, 'Because He stimulates the creative centre in each one of us, making us first aware of God, and then aware of the infinite possibilities in God'.

When I was at school, I struggled with my studies, and although I passed all my examinations and went to college, my passes were always on the borderline. Then I found Christ – and what a change. He stimulated the creative centre within me, and He so transformed my attitude toward work that within months I had moved from near the bottom of my classes to near the top.

When taking a seminar in Birmingham, I met a friend who had recently come to live there. 'What do you think of Birmingham?' I asked. His reply was, 'I have lived here for three months, and every day I keep seeing new horizons'. This is what happens when we stay close to Jesus – every day we keep seeing new horizons. In His company we begin to see farther, feel for people on a wider scale, act more decisively, and live on the growing edge of adventure. Why? Because a creative God gives to His creation the same creative impulses.

PRAYER

O God, stimulate my whole being, I pray, so that every day I shall see new horizons. Help me never to walk with my eyes focused on the ground, but with my eyes fixed on You. For Your own dear name's sake I ask it. Amen.

FURTHER STUDY

John 1:1-18; Col. 1:16; Phil. 2:1
• Who is at the centre of creation?
• What happens if He is the centre of our lives?

September 3

JOB 22:1–24:12

22 Then Eliphaz the Temanite replied:

2 'Can a man be of benefit to God?
   Can even a wise person benefit him?
3 What pleasure would it give the
      Almighty if you were righteous?
   What would he gain if your ways were
      blameless?

4 'Is it for your piety that he rebukes you
   and brings charges against you?
5 Is not your wickedness great?
   Are not your sins endless?
6 You demanded security from your
      relatives for no reason;
   you stripped people of their clothing,
      leaving them naked.
7 You gave no water to the weary
   and you withheld food from the
      hungry,
8 though you were a powerful man,
      owning land –
   an honoured man, living on it.
9 And you sent widows away
      empty-handed

and broke the strength of the
      fatherless.
10 That is why snares are all around you,
   why sudden peril terrifies you,
11 why it is so dark that you cannot see,
   and why a flood of water covers you.

12 'Is not God in the heights of heaven?
   And see how lofty are the highest
      stars!
13 Yet you say, "What does God know?
   Does he judge through such darkness?
14 Thick clouds veil him, so he does not see us
   as he goes about in the vaulted
      heavens."
15 Will you keep to the old path
   that the wicked have trod?
16 They were carried off before their time,
   their foundations washed away by a
      flood.
17 They said to God, "Leave us alone!
   What can the Almighty do to us?"
18 Yet it was he who filled their houses with
      good things,
   so I stand aloof from the plans of the
      wicked.
19 The righteous see their ruin and rejoice;
   the innocent mock them, saying,

20 "Surely our foes are destroyed,
    and fire devours their wealth."

21 'Submit to God and be at peace with him;
    in this way prosperity will come to
    you.
22 Accept instruction from his mouth
    and lay up his words in your heart.
23 If you return to the Almighty, you will be
    restored:
    if you remove wickedness far from
    your tent
24 and assign your nuggets to the dust,
    your gold of Ophir to the rocks in the
    ravines,
25 then the Almighty will be your gold,
    the choicest silver for you.
26 Surely then you will find delight in the
    Almighty
    and will lift up your face to God.
27 You will pray to him, and he will hear
    you,
    and you will fulfil your vows.
28 What you decide on will be done,
    and light will shine on your ways.
29 When people are brought low and you
    say, "Lift them up!"
    then he will save the downcast.
30 He will deliver even one who is not
    innocent,
    who will be delivered through the
    cleanness of your hands.'

23

Then Job replied:

2 'Even today my complaint is bitter;
    his hand is heavy in spite of my
    groaning.
3 If only I knew where to find him;
    if only I could go to his dwelling!
4 I would state my case before him
    and fill my mouth with arguments.
5 I would find out what he would answer
    me,
    and consider what he would say to me.

6 Would he vigorously oppose me with
    great power?
    No, he would not press charges against
    me.
7 There the upright can establish their
    innocence before him,
    and there I would be delivered for ever
    from my judge.

8 'But if I go to the east, he is not there;
    if I go to the west, I do not find him.
9 When he is at work in the north, I do not
    see him;
    when he turns to the south, I catch no
    glimpse of him.
10 But he knows the way that I take;
    when he has tested me, I shall come
    forth as gold.
11 My feet have closely followed his steps;
    I have kept to his way without turning
    aside.
12 I have not departed from the commands
    of his lips;
    I have treasured the words of his
    mouth more than my daily bread.

13 'But he stands alone, and who can
    oppose him?
    He does whatever he pleases.
14 He carries out his decree against me,
    and many such plans he still has in
    store.
15 That is why I am terrified before him;
    when I think of all this, I fear him.
16 God has made my heart faint;
    the Almighty has terrified me.
17 Yet I am not silenced by the darkness,
    by the thick darkness that covers my
    face.

24

'Why does the Almighty not set
times for judgment?
    Why must those who know him look
    in vain for such days?
2 There are those who move boundary
    stones;

they pasture flocks they have stolen.
³ They drive away the orphan's donkey
and take the widow's ox in pledge.
⁴ They thrust the needy from the path
and force all the poor of the land into
hiding.
⁵ Like wild donkeys in the desert,
the poor go about their labour of
foraging food;
the wasteland provides food for their
children.
⁶ They gather fodder in the fields
and glean in the vineyards of the
wicked.
⁷ Lacking clothes, they spend the night
naked;
they have nothing to cover themselves
in the cold.
⁸ They are drenched by mountain rains
and hug the rocks for lack of shelter.
⁹ The fatherless child is snatched from the
breast;
the infant of the poor is seized for a
debt.
¹⁰ Lacking clothes, they go about naked;
they carry the sheaves, but still go
hungry.
¹¹ They crush olives among the terraces;
they tread the winepresses, yet suffer
thirst.
¹² The groans of the dying rise from the
city,
and the souls of the wounded cry out
for help.
But God charges no one with
wrongdoing.

PSALM 105:16-27

¹⁶ He called down famine on the land
and destroyed all their supplies of
food;
¹⁷ and he sent a man before them –
Joseph, sold as a slave.
¹⁸ They bruised his feet with shackles,

his neck was put in irons,
¹⁹ till what he foretold came to pass,
till the word of the LORD proved him
true.
²⁰ The king sent and released him,
the ruler of peoples set him free.
²¹ He made him master of his household,
ruler over all he possessed,
²² to instruct his princes as he pleased
and teach his elders wisdom.
²³ Then Israel entered Egypt;
Jacob resided as a foreigner in the land
of Ham.
²⁴ The LORD made his people very fruitful;
he made them too numerous for their
foes,
²⁵ whose hearts he turned to hate his
people,
to conspire against his servants.
²⁶ He sent Moses his servant,
and Aaron, whom he had chosen.
²⁷ They performed his signs among them,
his wonders in the land of Ham.

PROVERBS 21:25-26

²⁵ The craving of a sluggard will be the
death of him,
because his hands refuse to work.
²⁶ All day long he craves for more,
but the righteous give without
sparing.

1 CORINTHIANS 9:13–10:5

¹³ Don't you know that those who serve in
the temple get their food from the temple,
and that those who serve at the altar share
in what is offered on the altar? ¹⁴ In the same
way, the Lord has commanded that those
who preach the gospel should receive their
living from the gospel.
¹⁵ But I have not used any of these rights.

And I am not writing this in the hope that you will do such things for me, for I would rather die than allow anyone to deprive me of this boast. ¹⁶For when I preach the gospel, I cannot boast, since I am compelled to preach. Woe to me if I do not preach the gospel! ¹⁷If I preach voluntarily, I have a reward; if not voluntarily, I am simply discharging the trust committed to me. ¹⁸What then is my reward? Just this: that in preaching the gospel I may offer it free of charge, and so not make full use of my rights as a preacher of the gospel.

¹⁹Though I am free and belong to no one, I have made myself a slave to everyone, to win as many as possible. ²⁰To the Jews I became like a Jew, to win the Jews. To those under the law I became like one under the law (though I myself am not under the law), so as to win those under the law. ²¹To those not having the law I became like one not having the law (though I am not free from God's law but am under Christ's law), so as to win those not having the law. ²²To the weak I became weak, to win the weak. I have become all things to all people so that by all possible means I might save some.

²³I do all this for the sake of the gospel, that I may share in its blessings.

²⁴Do you not know that in a race all the runners run, but only one gets the prize? Run in such a way as to get the prize. ²⁵Everyone who competes in the games goes into strict training. They do it to get a crown that will not last; but we do it to get a crown that will last for ever. ²⁶Therefore I do not run like someone running aimlessly; I do not fight like a boxer beating the air. ²⁷No, I strike a blow to my body and make it my slave so that after I have preached to others, I myself will not be disqualified for the prize.

10 For I do not want you to be ignorant of the fact, brothers and sisters, that our ancestors were all under the cloud and that they all passed through the sea. ²They were all baptised into Moses in the cloud and in the sea. ³They all ate the same spiritual food ⁴and drank the same spiritual drink; for they drank from the spiritual rock that accompanied them, and that rock was Christ. ⁵Nevertheless, God was not pleased with most of them; their bodies were scattered in the wilderness.

Like a Finely-Tuned Violin

'Do you not know that in a race all the runners run, but only one gets the prize? Run in such a way as to get the prize.' **1 Corinthians 9:24**

What and how much we eat can greatly affect the way we feel. If the nerves are starved on account of a lack of vitamins, they will kick back in physical depression - exactly the same way that a starved soul or spirit will kick back in psychological depression. So discipline yourself to eat correctly and nutritionally.

Next, discipline yourself to take appropriate physical exercise. God designed our bodies for movement, and if they don't move, they get sluggish. Then what happens? A sluggish body contributes to a sluggish spirit.

Time and time again, when counselling people who are suffering with depression, I have recommended (along with other suggestions) that they take up physical exercise. One should not, of course, embark upon vigorous exercise, like playing squash or jogging, without having a medical check-up. But I have been surprised at how even a short, brisk walk can do wonders for the soul.

I feel a word of caution may be needed here, because many people in our culture are fast becoming exercise 'freaks'. It is possible to regulate the body too much! You should get enough exercise to remain fit, but also keep in mind that too much attention to exercise or sports may drain higher interests. Everything must be kept in balance: just enough food to keep you fit and not enough to make you fat; just enough sleep to keep you fresh and a little less than that which would make you lazy. We must keep our bodies like a finely-tuned violin, and then the music of God will come out from every fibre of our being.

PRAYER

O God of my mind and my body, I come to You to have both of these brought under the control of Your redemption and Your guidance. May I pass on the health of my mind to my body and the health of my body to my mind. Amen.

FURTHER STUDY

1 Kings 19:8; Phil. 3:1-16; Gal. 2:2; Heb. 12:1
• What picture did Paul use in illustrating truth?
• How much exercise do you take?

September 4

■ JOB 24:13–27:23

13 'There are those who rebel against the light,
who do not know its ways
or stay in its paths.
14 When daylight is gone, the murderer
rises up,
kills the poor and needy,
and in the night steals forth like a
thief.
15 The eye of the adulterer watches for
dusk;
he thinks, "No eye will see me,"
and he keeps his face concealed.
16 In the dark, thieves break into houses,
but by day they shut themselves in;
they want nothing to do with the light.

17 For all of them, midnight is their
morning;
they make friends with the terrors
of darkness.

18 'Yet they are foam on the surface of the
water;
their portion of the land is cursed,
so that no one goes to the vineyards.
19 As heat and drought snatch away the
melted snow,
so the grave snatches away those who
have sinned.
20 The womb forgets them,
the worm feasts on them;
the wicked are no longer remembered
but are broken like a tree.
21 They prey on the barren and childless
woman,

and to the widow they show no
kindness.
²² But God drags away the mighty by his
power;
though they become established, they
have no assurance of life.
²³ He may let them rest in a feeling of
security,
but his eyes are on their ways.
²⁴ For a little while they are exalted, and
then they are gone;
they are brought low and gathered up
like all others;
they are cut off like ears of corn.

²⁵ 'If this is not so, who can prove me false
and reduce my words to nothing?'

25 Then Bildad the Shuhite replied:

² 'Dominion and awe belong to God;
he establishes order in the heights of
heaven.
³ Can his forces be numbered?
On whom does his light not rise?
⁴ How then can a mortal be righteous
before God?
How can one born of woman be pure?
⁵ If even the moon is not bright
and the stars are not pure in his eyes,
⁶ how much less a mortal, who is but a
maggot –
a human being, who is only a worm!'

26 Then Job replied:

² 'How you have helped the powerless!
How you have saved the arm that is
feeble!
³ What advice you have offered to one
without wisdom!
And what great insight you have
displayed!
⁴ Who has helped you utter these words?
And whose spirit spoke from your
mouth?

⁵ 'The dead are in deep anguish,
those beneath the waters and all that
live in them.
⁶ The realm of the dead is naked before
God;
Destruction lies uncovered.
⁷ He spreads out the northern skies over
empty space;
he suspends the earth over nothing.
⁸ He wraps up the waters in his clouds,
yet the clouds do not burst under their
weight.
⁹ He covers the face of the full moon,
spreading his clouds over it.
¹⁰ He marks out the horizon on the face of
the waters
for a boundary between light and
darkness.
¹¹ The pillars of the heavens quake,
aghast at his rebuke.
¹² By his power he churned up the sea;
by his wisdom he cut Rahab to pieces.
¹³ By his breath the skies became fair;
his hand pierced the gliding serpent.
¹⁴ And these are but the outer fringe of his
works;
how faint the whisper we hear of him!
Who then can understand the thunder
of his power?'

27 And Job continued his discourse:

² 'As surely as God lives, who has denied
me justice,
the Almighty, who has made my life
bitter,
³ as long as I have life within me,
the breath of God in my nostrils,
⁴ my lips will not say anything wicked,
and my tongue will not utter lies.
⁵ I will never admit you are in the right;
till I die, I will not deny my integrity.
⁶ I will maintain my innocence and never
let go of it;
my conscience will not reproach me as
long as I live.

⁷ 'May my enemy be like the wicked,
    my adversary like the unjust!
⁸ For what hope have the godless when
        they are cut off,
    when God takes away their life?
⁹ Does God listen to their cry
    when distress comes upon them?
¹⁰ Will they find delight in the Almighty?
    Will they call on God at all times?

¹¹ 'I will teach you about the power of God;
    the ways of the Almighty I will not
        conceal.
¹² You have all seen this yourselves.
    Why then this meaningless talk?

¹³ 'Here is the fate God allots to the wicked,
    the heritage a ruthless man receives
        from the Almighty:
¹⁴ However many his children, their fate is
        the sword;
    his offspring will never have enough
        to eat.
¹⁵ The plague will bury those who survive
        him,
    and their widows will not weep for them.
¹⁶ Though he heaps up silver like dust
    and clothes like piles of clay,
¹⁷ what he lays up the righteous will wear,
    and the innocent will divide his silver.
¹⁸ The house he builds is like a moth's
        cocoon,
    like a hut made by a watchman.
¹⁹ He lies down wealthy, but will do so no
        more;
    when he opens his eyes, all is gone.
²⁰ Terrors overtake him like a flood;
    a tempest snatches him away in the
        night.
²¹ The east wind carries him off, and he is
        gone;
    it sweeps him out of his place.
²² It hurls itself against him without mercy
    as he flees headlong from its power.
²³ It claps its hands in derision
    and hisses him out of his place.'

■ PSALM 105:28-36

²⁸ He sent darkness and made the land
        dark –
    for had they not rebelled against his
        words?
²⁹ He turned their waters into blood,
    causing their fish to die.
³⁰ Their land teemed with frogs,
    which went up into the bedrooms of
        their rulers.
³¹ He spoke, and there came swarms of
        flies,
    and gnats throughout their country.
³² He turned their rain into hail,
    with lightning throughout their land;
³³ he struck down their vines and fig-trees
    and shattered the trees of their
        country.
³⁴ He spoke, and the locusts came,
    grasshoppers without number;
³⁵ they ate up every green thing in their
        land,
    ate up the produce of their soil.
³⁶ Then he struck down all the firstborn in
        their land,
    the firstfruits of all their manhood.

■ PROVERBS 21:27-28

²⁷ The sacrifice of the wicked is detestable –
    how much more so when brought with
        evil intent!

²⁸ A false witness will perish,
    but a careful listener will testify
        successfully.

■ 1 CORINTHIANS 10:6-24

⁶ Now these things occurred as examples
to keep us from setting our hearts on evil
things as they did. ⁷ Do not be idolaters,
as some of them were; as it is written:

'The people sat down to eat and drink and got up to indulge in revelry.' [8]We should not commit sexual immorality, as some of them did – and in one day twenty-three thousand of them died. [9]We should not test Christ, as some of them did – and were killed by snakes. [10]And do not grumble, as some of them did – and were killed by the destroying angel.

[11]These things happened to them as examples and were written down as warnings for us, on whom the culmination of the ages has come. [12]So, if you think you are standing firm, be careful that you don't fall! [13]No temptation has overtaken you except what is common to mankind. And God is faithful; he will not let you be tempted beyond what you can bear. But when you are tempted, he will also provide a way out so that you can endure it.

[14]Therefore, my dear friends, flee from idolatry. [15]I speak to sensible people; judge for yourselves what I say. [16]Is not the cup of thanksgiving for which we give thanks a participation in the blood of Christ? And is not the bread that we break a participation in the body of Christ? [17]Because there is one loaf, we, who are many, are one body, for we all share the one loaf.

[18]Consider the people of Israel: do not those who eat the sacrifices participate in the altar? [19]Do I mean then that food sacrificed to an idol is anything, or that an idol is anything? [20]No, but the sacrifices of pagans are offered to demons, not to God, and I do not want you to be participants with demons. [21]You cannot drink the cup of the Lord and the cup of demons too; you cannot have a part in both the Lord's table and the table of demons. [22]Are we trying to arouse the Lord's jealousy? Are we stronger than he?

[23]'I have the right to do anything,' you say – but not everything is beneficial. 'I have the right to do anything' – but not everything is constructive. [24]No one should seek their own good, but the good of others.

'Lord, Help Me'

'... God is faithful; he will not let you be tempted beyond what you can bear.' **1 Corinthians 10:13**

One perspective on the phrase 'Lead us not into temptation' tells us that if we pray for the ability to recognise temptation when it comes our way, then we will be able to confront it and turn it to advantage.

Another interpretation explains that this is a prayer for us to be kept back from more temptation than we can cope with. It's like saying, 'Lord, help us not to get involved in more temptation than we can handle'. This view, as I am sure you can see at once, makes good sense and could well be what Jesus meant.

One of the biographers of an intrepid missionary tells how, in his early days in China, Hudson Taylor met with several great disappointments. One day, after a spate of troubles, he took hold of a guide who had demanded an outrageous fee from him and shook him violently. A few hours later, he realised he had denied his Lord by this action and after searching his heart for the reason why he had succumbed to anger and violence, he realised that he had been so preoccupied with his problems that he had failed to commit his ways to the Lord. His biographer says:

'If Hudson Taylor had prayed the prayer, "Lead us not into temptation", and committed his ways to the Lord, then perhaps the Spirit would have been able to direct his path so that he would not have faced more temptation than he could bear.'

It is an intriguing thought.

PRAYER

Father, though the meaning of this phrase is not yet clear, one thing is – I need Your help at every stage of my earthly pilgrimage, for I cannot face temptation alone. So stay with me, every day and every hour. For Jesus' sake. Amen.

FURTHER STUDY

Acts 5:1-11; Prov. 1:10; 4:14; Rom. 6:13
- Why did Ananias and Sapphira yield to temptation?
- What is Paul's antidote?

September 5

■ JOB 28:1–30:8

28 There is a mine for silver
and a place where gold is refined.
² Iron is taken from the earth,
and copper is smelted from ore.
³ Mortals put an end to the darkness;
they search out the farthest recesses
for ore in the blackest darkness.
⁴ Far from human dwellings they cut a
shaft,
in places untouched by human feet;
far from other people they dangle and
sway.
⁵ The earth, from which food comes,
is transformed below as by fire;
⁶ lapis lazuli comes from its rocks,
and its dust contains nuggets of gold.
⁷ No bird of prey knows that hidden path,
no falcon's eye has seen it.
⁸ Proud beasts do not set foot on it,
and no lion prowls there.
⁹ People assault the flinty rock with their
hands
and lay bare the roots of the
mountains.

¹⁰ They tunnel through the rock;
their eyes see all its treasures.
¹¹ They search the sources of the rivers
and bring hidden things to light.

¹² But where can wisdom be found?
Where does understanding dwell?
¹³ No mortal comprehends its worth;
it cannot be found in the land of the
living.
¹⁴ The deep says, 'It is not in me';
the sea says, 'It is not with me.'
¹⁵ It cannot be bought with the finest gold,
nor can its price be weighed out in
silver.
¹⁶ It cannot be bought with the gold of Ophir,
with precious onyx or lapis lazuli.
¹⁷ Neither gold nor crystal can compare
with it,
nor can it be had for jewels of gold.
¹⁸ Coral and jasper are not worthy of
mention;
the price of wisdom is beyond rubies.
¹⁹ The topaz of Cush cannot compare
with it;
it cannot be bought with pure gold.

²⁰ Where then does wisdom come from?
  Where does understanding dwell?
²¹ It is hidden from the eyes of every living
    thing,
  concealed even from the birds in the
    sky.
²² Destruction and Death say,
  'Only a rumour of it has reached our
    ears.'
²³ God understands the way to it
  and he alone knows where it dwells,
²⁴ for he views the ends of the earth
  and sees everything under the
    heavens.
²⁵ When he established the force of the
    wind
  and measured out the waters,
²⁶ when he made a decree for the rain
  and a path for the thunderstorm,
²⁷ then he looked at wisdom and appraised
    it;
  he confirmed it and tested it.
²⁸ And he said to the human race,
  'The fear of the Lord – that is wisdom,
  and to shun evil is understanding.'

29 Job continued his discourse:

² 'How I long for the months gone by,
  for the days when God watched over
    me,
³ when his lamp shone on my head
  and by his light I walked through
    darkness!
⁴ Oh, for the days when I was in my prime,
  when God's intimate friendship
    blessed my house,
⁵ when the Almighty was still with me
  and my children were around me,
⁶ when my path was drenched with cream
  and the rock poured out for me
    streams of olive oil.

⁷ 'When I went to the gate of the city
  and took my seat in the public square,
⁸ the young men saw me and stepped aside

and the old men rose to their feet;
⁹ the chief men refrained from speaking
  and covered their mouths with their
    hands;
¹⁰ the voices of the nobles were hushed,
  and their tongues stuck to the roof of
    their mouths.
¹¹ Whoever heard me spoke well of me,
  and those who saw me commended
    me,
¹² because I rescued the poor who cried for
    help,
  and the fatherless who had none to
    assist them.
¹³ The one who was dying blessed me;
  I made the widow's heart sing.
¹⁴ I put on righteousness as my clothing;
  justice was my robe and my turban.
¹⁵ I was eyes to the blind
  and feet to the lame.
¹⁶ I was a father to the needy;
  I took up the case of the stranger.
¹⁷ I broke the fangs of the wicked
  and snatched the victims from their
    teeth.

¹⁸ 'I thought, "I shall die in my own house,
  my days as numerous as the grains of
    sand.
¹⁹ My roots will reach to the water,
  and the dew will lie all night on my
    branches.
²⁰ My glory will not fade;
  the bow will be ever new in my hand."

²¹ 'People listened to me expectantly,
  waiting in silence for my counsel.
²² After I had spoken, they spoke no more;
  my words fell gently on their ears.
²³ They waited for me as for showers
  and drank in my words as the spring
    rain.
²⁴ When I smiled at them, they scarcely
    believed it;
  the light of my face was precious to
    them.

²⁵ I chose the way for them and sat as their
 chief;
 I dwelt as a king among his troops;
 I was like one who comforts
  mourners.

30

 'But now they mock me,
  men younger than I,
 whose fathers I would have disdained
  to put with my sheep dogs.
² Of what use was the strength of their
  hands to me,
 since their vigour had gone from them?
³ Haggard from want and hunger,
 they roamed the parched land
 in desolate wastelands at night.
⁴ In the brush they gathered salt herbs,
 and their food was the root of the
  broom bush.
⁵ They were banished from human
  society,
 shouted at as if they were thieves.
⁶ They were forced to live in the dry
  stream beds,
 among the rocks and in holes in the
  ground.
⁷ They brayed among the bushes
 and huddled in the undergrowth.
⁸ A base and nameless brood,
 they were driven out of the land.

PSALM 105:37-45

³⁷ He brought out Israel, laden with silver
  and gold,
 and from among their tribes no one
  faltered.
³⁸ Egypt was glad when they left,
 because dread of Israel had fallen on
  them.

³⁹ He spread out a cloud as a covering,
 and a fire to give light at night.
⁴⁰ They asked, and he brought them quail;

he fed them well with the bread of
 heaven.
⁴¹ He opened the rock, and water gushed
 out;
 it flowed like a river in the desert.

⁴² For he remembered his holy promise
 given to his servant Abraham.
⁴³ He brought out his people with rejoicing,
 his chosen ones with shouts of joy;
⁴⁴ he gave them the lands of the nations,
 and they fell heir to what others had
  toiled for –
⁴⁵ that they might keep his precepts
 and observe his laws.

Praise the LORD.

PROVERBS 21:29-31

²⁹ The wicked put up a bold front,
 but the upright give thought to their
  ways.

³⁰ There is no wisdom, no insight, no plan
 that can succeed against the LORD.

³¹ The horse is made ready for the day of
  battle,
 but victory rests with the LORD.

1 CORINTHIANS 10:25–11:16

²⁵ Eat anything sold in the meat market
without raising questions of conscience,
²⁶ for, 'The earth is the Lord's, and every-
thing in it.'

²⁷ If an unbeliever invites you to a meal
and you want to go, eat whatever is put before you without raising questions of conscience. ²⁸ But if someone says to you, 'This
has been offered in sacrifice,' then do not
eat it, both for the sake of the one who told

you and for the sake of conscience. [29] I am referring to the other person's conscience, not yours. For why is my freedom being judged by another's conscience? [30] If I take part in the meal with thankfulness, why am I denounced because of something I thank God for?

[31] So whether you eat or drink or whatever you do, do it all for the glory of God. [32] Do not cause anyone to stumble, whether Jews, Greeks or the church of God – [33] even as I try to please everyone in every way. For I am not seeking my own good but the good of many, so that they may be saved. [1] Follow my example, as I follow the example of Christ.

11 [2] I praise you for remembering me in everything and for holding to the traditions just as I passed them on to you. [3] But I want you to realise that the head of every man is Christ, and the head of the woman is man, and the head of Christ is God. [4] Every man who prays or prophesies with his head covered dishonours his head. [5] But every woman who prays or prophesies with her head uncovered dishonours her head – it is the same as having her head shaved. [6] For if a woman does not cover her head, she might

as well have her hair cut off; but if it is a disgrace for a woman to have her hair cut off or her head shaved, then she should cover her head.

[7] A man ought not to cover his head, since he is the image and glory of God; but woman is the glory of man. [8] For man did not come from woman, but woman from man; [9] neither was man created for woman, but woman for man. [10] It is for this reason that a woman ought to have authority over her own head, because of the angels. [11] Nevertheless, in the Lord woman is not independent of man, nor is man independent of woman. [12] For as woman came from man, so also man is born of woman. But everything comes from God.

[13] Judge for yourselves: is it proper for a woman to pray to God with her head uncovered? [14] Does not the very nature of things teach you that if a man has long hair, it is a disgrace to him, [15] but that if a woman has long hair, it is her glory? For long hair is given to her as a covering. [16] If anyone wants to be contentious about this, we have no other practice – nor do the churches of God.

Deadly Weapons

'So whether you eat or drink or whatever you do, do it all for the glory of God.' **1 Corinthians 10:31**

Disregard for the physical aspect of life can greatly contribute to spiritual dryness. This means that a certain amount of discipline must be introduced into our lives. But what kind of discipline?

Firstly, we need discipline in what and how much we eat. Every meal should be a sacrament offered on the altar of fitter and finer living. Doctors tell us that excess food – as well as too little food – destroys brain power. What is in the stomach often determines what is in the head. Scripture says, '... the kingdom of God is not a matter of eating and drinking ...' (Rom. 14:17). But it is not a contradiction of that verse to say that often our food and drink determine our fitness for the kingdom of God.

Seneca, in an exaggerated statement made for the sake of emphasis, said, 'Man does not die: he kills himself'. Dr. R. L. Greene, a professor of chemistry and a specialist in nutrition, says, 'The most deadly weapons used by man in committing suicide are the knife, fork, and spoon.' You may be repelled at the idea of committing suicide – and so you should be – but you may well be contributing to your death by choosing wrong ways of eating.

We need discipline also to ensure that we get at least the minimum amount of vitamins. Vitamins are necessary to vitality; they are God's gift to us. The divine Chemist has designed our bodies to work in a certain way. And if we ignore His prescription for health, we reduce our physical effectiveness, which can also reduce our spiritual effectiveness.

PRAYER

O Father, help me recognise that physical vitality contributes to spiritual vitality. May I respect the body You have given me and pay attention to the laws of health that You have built into the universe. In Jesus' name I pray. Amen.

FURTHER STUDY

Prov. 23:1-21; Eccl. 6:7; Phil. 3:19
• How does the Scripture regard gluttony?
• What is gluttony?

September 6

■ JOB 30:9–31:40

9 'And now those young men mock me in song;
    I have become a byword among them.
10 They detest me and keep their distance;
    they do not hesitate to spit in my face.
11 Now that God has unstrung my bow and afflicted me,
    they throw off restraint in my presence.
12 On my right the tribe attacks;
    they lay snares for my feet,
    they build their siege ramps against me.
13 They break up my road;
    they succeed in destroying me.
    "No one can help him," they say.

14 They advance as through a gaping breach;
    amid the ruins they come rolling in.
15 Terrors overwhelm me;
    my dignity is driven away as by the wind,
    my safety vanishes like a cloud.

16 'And now my life ebbs away;
    days of suffering grip me.
17 Night pierces my bones;
    my gnawing pains never rest.
18 In his great power God becomes like clothing to me;
    he binds me like the neck of my garment.
19 He throws me into the mud,
    and I am reduced to dust and ashes.

²⁰ 'I cry out to you, God, but you do not
answer;
I stand up, but you merely look at me.
²¹ You turn on me ruthlessly;
with the might of your hand you
attack me.
²² You snatch me up and drive me before
the wind;
you toss me about in the storm.
²³ I know you will bring me down to death,
to the place appointed for all the
living.

²⁴ 'Surely no one lays a hand on a broken
man
when he cries for help in his distress.
²⁵ Have I not wept for those in trouble?
Has not my soul grieved for the poor?
²⁶ Yet when I hoped for good, evil came;
when I looked for light, then came
darkness.
²⁷ The churning inside me never stops;
days of suffering confront me.
²⁸ I go about blackened, but not by the sun;
I stand up in the assembly and cry
for help.
²⁹ I have become a brother of jackals,
a companion of owls.
³⁰ My skin grows black and peels;
my body burns with fever.
³¹ My lyre is tuned to mourning,
and my pipe to the sound of wailing.

31 'I made a covenant with my eyes
not to look lustfully at a young
woman.
² For what is our lot from God above,
our heritage from the Almighty on
high?
³ Is it not ruin for the wicked,
disaster for those who do wrong?
⁴ Does he not see my ways
and count my every step?

⁵ 'If I have walked with falsehood
or my foot has hurried after deceit –

⁶ let God weigh me in honest scales
and he will know that I am
blameless –
⁷ if my steps have turned from the path,
if my heart has been led by my eyes,
or if my hands have been defiled,
⁸ then may others eat what I have sown,
and may my crops be uprooted.

⁹ 'If my heart has been enticed by a
woman,
or if I have lurked at my neighbour's
door,
¹⁰ then may my wife grind another man's
grain,
and may other men sleep with her.
¹¹ For that would have been wicked,
a sin to be judged.
¹² It is a fire that burns to Destruction;
it would have uprooted my harvest.

¹³ 'If I have denied justice to any of my
servants,
whether male or female,
when they had a grievance against me,
¹⁴ what will I do when God confronts me?
What will I answer when called to
account?
¹⁵ Did not he who made me in the womb
make them?
Did not the same one form us both
within our mothers?

¹⁶ 'If I have denied the desires of the poor
or let the eyes of the widow grow
weary,
¹⁷ if I have kept my bread to myself,
not sharing it with the fatherless –
¹⁸ but from my youth I reared them as a
father would,
and from my birth I guided the
widow –
¹⁹ if I have seen anyone perishing for lack
of clothing,
or the needy without garments,
²⁰ and their hearts did not bless me

for warming them with the fleece from
my sheep,
²¹ if I have raised my hand against the
fatherless,
knowing that I had influence in court,
²² then let my arm fall from the shoulder,
let it be broken off at the joint.
²³ For I dreaded destruction from God,
and for fear of his splendour I could
not do such things.

²⁴ 'If I have put my trust in gold
or said to pure gold, "You are my
security,"
²⁵ if I have rejoiced over my great wealth,
the fortune my hands had gained,
²⁶ if I have regarded the sun in its radiance
or the moon moving in splendour,
²⁷ so that my heart was secretly enticed
and my hand offered them a kiss of
homage,
²⁸ then these also would be sins to be
judged,
for I would have been unfaithful to
God on high.

²⁹ 'If I have rejoiced at my enemy's
misfortune
or gloated over the trouble that came
to him –
³⁰ I have not allowed my mouth to sin
by invoking a curse against their life –
³¹ if those of my household have never said,
"Who has not been filled with Job's
meat?" –
³² but no stranger had to spend the night in
the street,
for my door was always open to the
traveller –
³³ if I have concealed my sin as people do,
by hiding my guilt in my heart
³⁴ because I so feared the crowd
and so dreaded the contempt of the
clans
that I kept silent and would not go
outside –

³⁵ ('Oh, that I had someone to hear me!
I sign now my defence – let the
Almighty answer me;
let my accuser put his indictment in
writing.
³⁶ Surely I would wear it on my shoulder,
I would put it on like a crown.
³⁷ I would give him an account of my every
step;
I would present it to him as to a ruler.) –

³⁸ 'if my land cries out against me
and all its furrows are wet with tears,
³⁹ if I have devoured its yield without
payment
or broken the spirit of its tenants,
⁴⁰ then let briers come up instead of wheat
and stinkweed instead of barley.'

The words of Job are ended.

▬ PSALM 106:1-12

¹ Praise the LORD.

Give thanks to the LORD, for he is good;
his love endures for ever.

² Who can proclaim the mighty acts of the
LORD
or fully declare his praise?
³ Blessed are those who act justly,
who always do what is right.

⁴ Remember me, LORD, when you show
favour to your people,
come to my aid when you save them,
⁵ that I may enjoy the prosperity of your
chosen ones,
that I may share in the joy of your nation
and join your inheritance in giving
praise.

⁶ We have sinned, even as our ancestors
did;

we have done wrong and acted
wickedly.
[7] When our ancestors were in Egypt,
they gave no thought to your miracles;
they did not remember your many
kindnesses,
and they rebelled by the sea, the Red
Sea.
[8] Yet he saved them for his name's sake,
to make his mighty power known.
[9] He rebuked the Red Sea, and it dried up;
he led them through the depths as
through a desert.
[10] He saved them from the hand of the foe;
from the hand of the enemy he
redeemed them.
[11] The waters covered their adversaries;
not one of them survived.
[12] Then they believed his promises
and sang his praise.

....

▬ PROVERBS 22:1-2

22 A good name is more desirable
than great riches;
to be esteemed is better than silver
or gold.

[2] Rich and poor have this in common:
The LORD is the Maker of them all.

....

▬ 1 CORINTHIANS 11:17-34

[17] In the following directives I have no
praise for you, for your meetings do more
harm than good. [18] In the first place, I hear
that when you come together as a church,
there are divisions among you, and to some
extent I believe it. [19] No doubt there have to
be differences among you to show which
of you have God's approval. [20] So then,
when you come together, it is not the Lord's
Supper you eat, [21] for when you are eating,
some of you go ahead with your own private
suppers. As a result, one person remains
hungry and another gets drunk. [22] Don't
you have homes to eat and drink in? Or do
you despise the church of God by humiliat-
ing those who have nothing? What shall I
say to you? Shall I praise you? Certainly not
in this matter!

[23] For I received from the Lord what I also
passed on to you: the Lord Jesus, on the
night he was betrayed, took bread, [24] and
when he had given thanks, he broke it and
said, 'This is my body, which is for you; do
this in remembrance of me.' [25] In the same
way, after supper he took the cup, saying,
'This cup is the new covenant in my blood;
do this, whenever you drink it, in remembrance of me.' [26] For whenever you eat this
bread and drink this cup, you proclaim the
Lord's death until he comes.

[27] So then, whoever eats the bread or
drinks the cup of the Lord in an unworthy
manner will be guilty of sinning against
the body and blood of the Lord. [28] Everyone ought to examine themselves before
they eat of the bread and drink from the
cup. [29] For those who eat and drink without discerning the body of Christ eat and
drink judgment on themselves. [30] That is
why many among you are weak and ill, and
a number of you have fallen asleep. [31] But
if we were more discerning with regard to
ourselves, we would not come under such
judgment. [32] Nevertheless, when we are
judged in this way by the Lord, we are being disciplined so that we will not be finally
condemned with the world.

[33] So then, my brothers and sisters, when
you gather to eat, you should all eat together. [34] Anyone who is hungry should eat
something at home, so that when you meet
together it may not result in judgment.

And when I come I will give further
instructions.

An Honest Look

'Everyone ought to examine themselves ...'
1 Corinthians 11:28

An important step in bringing about a more perfect coordination between heart and mind is to take an honest, straightforward look at what is going on beneath the surface of your life.

I have often invited my readers to spend a few days taking an honest look at themselves. The reactions I have received to this suggestion have been quite interesting. Some Christians hear in my words a call to self-preoccupation and become concerned that I am pushing them towards becoming engrossed with their aches and pains.

One of my readers put it like this: 'What people need is to forget about themselves and concentrate on reaching out to others; then their personal problems will quickly be forgotten.' Others have taken an opposite position and said, 'We need more of this, for our hearts are so self-deceived that unless we are constantly challenged in this way, we will never get through to a close relationship with God.' I am unhappy about both those reactions, for both are unbalanced positions.

The first one fears that taking a look beneath the surface of our lives leads to unhealthy self-preoccupation. And the second opinion assumes that constant self-examination is the only way forward. But I believe an occasional, honest, straightforward look at what is going on beneath the surface of our lives contributes greatly to our spiritual progress, providing it is done in a proper and balanced way.

PRAYER

O God, help me to see that in inviting me to examine myself, You are not seeking to demean me but to develop me; not to take away from my spiritual stature but to add to it. Make me an honest person – with You, with myself, with others. Amen.

FURTHER STUDY

Luke 8:1-15; Psa. 51:1-6; 15:1-2; Rom. 8:27
• Where does God require truth?
• What must we allow God to do?

September 7

■ JOB 32:1–33:33

32 So these three men stopped answering Job, because he was righteous in his own eyes. ²But Elihu son of Barakel the Buzite, of the family of Ram, became very angry with Job for justifying himself rather than God. ³He was also angry with the

three friends, because they had found no
way to refute Job, and yet had condemned
him. ⁴Now Elihu had waited before speaking to Job because they were older than he.
⁵But when he saw that the three men had
nothing more to say, his anger was aroused.

⁶So Elihu son of Barakel the Buzite said:

'I am young in years,
    and you are old;
that is why I was fearful,
    not daring to tell you what I know.
⁷I thought, "Age should speak;
    advanced years should teach
        wisdom."
⁸But it is the spirit in a person,
    the breath of the Almighty, that gives
        them understanding.
⁹It is not only the old who are wise,
    not only the aged who understand
        what is right.

¹⁰'Therefore I say: listen to me;
    I too will tell you what I know.
¹¹I waited while you spoke,
    I listened to your reasoning;
while you were searching for words,
¹²   I gave you my full attention.
But not one of you has proved Job wrong;
    none of you has answered his
        arguments.
¹³Do not say, "We have found wisdom;
    let God, not a man, refute him."
¹⁴But Job has not marshalled his words
        against me,
    and I will not answer him with your
        arguments.

¹⁵'They are dismayed and have no more
        to say;
    words have failed them.
¹⁶Must I wait, now that they are silent,
    now that they stand there with no
        reply?
¹⁷I too will have my say;
    I too will tell what I know.

¹⁸For I am full of words,
    and the spirit within me compels me;
¹⁹inside I am like bottled-up wine,
    like new wineskins ready to burst.
²⁰I must speak and find relief;
    I must open my lips and reply.
²¹I will show no partiality,
    nor will I flatter anyone;
²²for if I were skilled in flattery,
    my Maker would soon take me away.

33 'But now, Job, listen to my words;
        pay attention to everything I say.
²I am about to open my mouth;
    my words are on the tip of my tongue.
³My words come from an upright heart;
    my lips sincerely speak what I know.
⁴The Spirit of God has made me;
    the breath of the Almighty gives me
        life.
⁵Answer me then, if you can;
    stand up and argue your case before
        me.
⁶I am the same as you; in God's sight;
    I too am a piece of clay.
⁷No fear of me should alarm you,
    nor should my hand be heavy on you.

⁸'But you have said in my hearing –
    I heard the very words –
⁹"I am pure, I have done no wrong;
    I am clean and free from sin.
¹⁰Yet God has found fault with me;
    he considers me his enemy.
¹¹He fastens my feet in shackles;
    he keeps close watch on all my paths."

¹²'But I tell you, in this you are not right,
    for God is greater than any mortal.
¹³Why do you complain to him
    that he responds to no one's words?
¹⁴For God does speak – now one way,
        now another –
    though no one perceives it.
¹⁵In a dream, in a vision of the night,
    when deep sleep falls on people

as they slumber in their beds,
¹⁶ he may speak in their ears
    and terrify them with warnings,
¹⁷ to turn them from wrongdoing
    and keep them from pride,
¹⁸ to preserve them from the pit,
    their lives from perishing by the
        sword.

¹⁹ 'Or someone may be chastened on a bed
        of pain
    with constant distress in their bones,
²⁰ so that their body finds food repulsive
    and their soul loathes the choicest
        meal.
²¹ Their flesh wastes away to nothing,
    and their bones, once hidden, now
        stick out.
²² They draw near to the pit,
    and their life to the messengers of
        death.
²³ Yet if there is an angel at their side,
    a messenger, one out of a thousand,
    sent to tell them how to be upright,
²⁴ and he is gracious to that person and
        says to God,
    "Spare them from going down to the
        pit;
    I have found a ransom for them –
²⁵ let their flesh be renewed like a child's;
    let them be restored as in the days of
        their youth" –
²⁶ then that person can pray to God and
        find favour with him,
    they will see God's face and shout for
        joy;
    he will restore them to full well-being.
²⁷ And they will go to others and say,
    "I have sinned, and I have perverted
        what is right,
    but I did not get what I deserved.
²⁸ God has delivered me from going down
        to the pit,
    and I shall live to enjoy the light of
        life."

²⁹ 'God does all these things to a person –
    twice, even three times –
³⁰ to turn them back from the pit,
    that the light of life may shine on
        them.

³¹ 'Pay attention, Job, and listen to me;
    be silent, and I will speak.
³² If you have anything to say, answer me;
    speak up, for I want to vindicate you.
³³ But if not, then listen to me;
    be silent, and I will teach you wisdom.'

....

▬ PSALM 106:13-23

¹³ But they soon forgot what he had done
    and did not wait for his plan to unfold.
¹⁴ In the desert they gave in to their
        craving;
    in the wilderness they put God to the
        test.
¹⁵ So he gave them what they asked for,
    but sent a wasting disease among
        them.

¹⁶ In the camp they grew envious of Moses
    and of Aaron, who was consecrated to
        the LORD.
¹⁷ The earth opened up and swallowed
        Dathan;
    it buried the company of Abiram.
¹⁸ Fire blazed among their followers;
    a flame consumed the wicked.
¹⁹ At Horeb they made a calf
    and worshipped an idol cast from
        metal.
²⁰ They exchanged their glorious God
    for an image of a bull, which eats
        grass.
²¹ They forgot the God who saved them,
    who had done great things in Egypt,
²² miracles in the land of Ham
    and awesome deeds by the Red Sea.
²³ So he said he would destroy them –
    had not Moses, his chosen one,

stood in the breach before him
    to keep his wrath from destroying them.

▬ PROVERBS 22:3-4

3 The prudent see danger and take refuge,
    but the simple keep going and pay the
      penalty.

4 Humility is the fear of the LORD;
    its wages are riches and honour and
      life.

▬ 1 CORINTHIANS 12:1-20

12 Now about the gifts of the Spirit, brothers and sisters, I do not want you to be uninformed. 2 You know that when you were pagans, somehow or other you were influenced and led astray to dumb idols. 3 Therefore I want you to know that no one who is speaking by the Spirit of God says, 'Jesus be cursed,' and no one can say, 'Jesus is Lord,' except by the Holy Spirit.

4 There are different kinds of gifts, but the same Spirit distributes them. 5 There are different kinds of service, but the same Lord. 6 There are different kinds of working, but in all of them and in everyone it is the same God at work.

7 Now to each one the manifestation of the Spirit is given for the common good. 8 To one there is given through the Spirit a message of wisdom, to another a message of knowledge by means of the same Spirit, 9 to another faith by the same Spirit, to another gifts of healing by that one Spirit, 10 to another miraculous powers, to another prophecy, to another distinguishing between spirits, to another speaking in different kinds of tongues, and to still another the interpretation of tongues. 11 All these are the work of one and the same Spirit, and he distributes them to each one, just as he determines.

12 Just as a body, though one, has many parts, but all its many parts form one body, so it is with Christ. 13 For we were all baptised by one Spirit so as to form one body – whether Jews or Gentiles, slave or free – and we were all given the one Spirit to drink. 14 And so the body is not made up of one part but of many.

15 Now if the foot should say, 'Because I am not a hand, I do not belong to the body,' it would not for that reason stop being part of the body. 16 And if the ear should say, 'Because I am not an eye, I do not belong to the body,' it would not for that reason stop being part of the body. 17 If the whole body were an eye, where would the sense of hearing be? If the whole body were an ear, where would the sense of smell be? 18 But in fact God has placed the parts in the body, every one of them, just as he wanted them to be. 19 If they were all one part, where would the body be? 20 As it is, there are many parts, but one body.

Purity and Power

'Now to each one the manifestation of the Spirit is
given for the common good.' **1 Corinthians 12:7**

A lthough Jesus told us that through the Holy Spirit's power, we
would do greater works than He had performed, the truth is that
we are just not availing ourselves of the divine resources. There are
notable exceptions to what I am saying, but, by and large, this is the

way it is in today's church. Paul says in 1 Thessalonians 1:5: '... our gospel came to you not simply with words but also with power, with the Holy Spirit and deep conviction.' At the centre of that 'power' and 'conviction' was the Holy Spirit. These traits are largely lacking in much of modern Christianity, because too many of us lack a full encounter with the Holy Spirit.

Some years ago, when I was a pastor in the north of England, another minister in the town (a good friend of mine) said, 'You preach about the Spirit's power, and I'll preach about the Spirit's purity. That way we will keep a balance in the lives of Christians in this town.' I pondered what he said and came to the conclusion that such a procedure would produce lopsided Christians, for both congregations needed to hear of the Spirit's purity and power.

Today's churches can be divided into two camps – those where the purity aspect is emphasised and those where the power aspect is emphasised. If every church focused with equal emphasis on both these characteristics of the Spirit, we would witness a healthier body of believers. Purity is essential, but so is power. The Holy Spirit supplies both.

PRAYER

O Spirit of purity and power, live in Your church as both. For I need purity to see my destiny and power to follow it. Give me equal measure. In Jesus' name. Amen.

FURTHER STUDY

Acts 5:1-16; 1 Cor. 12; Gal. 5:22-26
• How did the early church learn about this power and purity?
• What was the result?

September 8

▬ JOB 34:1–35:16

34 Then Elihu said:
² 'Hear my words, you wise men;
    listen to me, you men of learning.
³ For the ear tests words
    as the tongue tastes food.
⁴ Let us discern for ourselves what is right;
    let us learn together what is good.

⁵ 'Job says, "I am innocent,
    but God denies me justice.
⁶ Although I am right,

I am considered a liar;
although I am guiltless,
    his arrow inflicts an incurable
        wound."
⁷ Is there anyone like Job,
    who drinks scorn like water?
⁸ He keeps company with evildoers;
    he associates with the wicked.
⁹ For he says, "There is no profit
    in trying to please God."

¹⁰ 'So listen to me, you men of
        understanding.
    Far be it from God to do evil,

from the Almighty to do wrong.

¹¹ He repays everyone for what they have done;

he brings on them what their conduct deserves.

¹² It is unthinkable that God would do wrong,

that the Almighty would pervert justice.

¹³ Who appointed him over the earth?

Who put him in charge of the whole world?

¹⁴ If it were his intention

and he withdrew his spirit and breath,

¹⁵ all humanity would perish together

and mankind would return to the dust.

¹⁶ 'If you have understanding, hear this;

listen to what I say.

¹⁷ Can someone who hates justice govern?

Will you condemn the just and mighty One?

¹⁸ Is he not the One who says to kings, "You are worthless,"

and to nobles, "You are wicked,"

¹⁹ who shows no partiality to princes

and does not favour the rich over the poor,

for they are all the work of his hands?

²⁰ They die in an instant, in the middle of the night;

the people are shaken and they pass away;

the mighty are removed without human hand.

²¹ 'His eyes are on the ways of mortals;

he sees their every step.

²² There is no deep shadow, no utter darkness,

where evildoers can hide.

²³ God has no need to examine men further,

that they should come before him for judgment.

²⁴ Without enquiry he shatters the mighty

and sets up others in their place.

²⁵ Because he takes note of their deeds,

he overthrows them in the night and they are crushed.

²⁶ He punishes them for their wickedness

where everyone can see them,

²⁷ because they turned from following him

and had no regard for any of his ways.

²⁸ They caused the cry of the poor to come before him,

so that he heard the cry of the needy.

²⁹ But if he remains silent, who can condemn him?

If he hides his face, who can see him?

Yet he is over individual and nation alike,

³⁰ to keep the godless from ruling,

from laying snares for the people.

³¹ 'Suppose someone says to God,

"I am guilty but will offend no more.

³² Teach me what I cannot see;

if I have done wrong, I will not do so again."

³³ Should God then reward you on your terms,

when you refuse to repent?

You must decide, not I;

so tell me what you know.

³⁴ 'Men of understanding declare,

wise men who hear me say to me,

³⁵ "Job speaks without knowledge;

his words lack insight."

³⁶ Oh, that Job might be tested to the utmost

for answering like a wicked man!

³⁷ To his sin he adds rebellion;

scornfully he claps his hands among us

and multiplies his words against God.'

35

Then Elihu said:

² 'Do you think this is just?

You say, "I am in the right, not God."

³ Yet you ask him, "What profit is it to me,
and what do I gain by not sinning?"

⁴ 'I would like to reply to you
and to your friends with you.
⁵ Look up at the heavens and see;
gaze at the clouds so high above you.
⁶ If you sin, how does that affect him?
If your sins are many, what does that
do to him?
⁷ If you are righteous, what do you give to
him,
or what does he receive from your
hand?
⁸ Your wickedness only affects humans
like yourself,
and your righteousness only other
people.

⁹ 'People cry out under a load of
oppression;
they plead for relief from the arm of
the powerful.
¹⁰ But no one says, "Where is God my Maker,
who gives songs in the night,
¹¹ who teaches us more than he teaches the
beasts of the earth
and makes us wiser than the birds in
the sky?"
¹² He does not answer when people cry out
because of the arrogance of the
wicked.
¹³ Indeed, God does not listen to their
empty plea;
the Almighty pays no attention to it.
¹⁴ How much less, then, will he listen
when you say that you do not see him,
that your case is before him
and you must wait for him,
¹⁵ and further, that his anger never
punishes
and he does not take the least notice of
wickedness.
¹⁶ So Job opens his mouth with empty talk;
without knowledge he multiplies
words.'

PSALM 106:24–31

²⁴ Then they despised the pleasant land;
they did not believe his promise.
²⁵ They grumbled in their tents
and did not obey the LORD.
²⁶ So he swore to them with uplifted hand
that he would make them fall in the
wilderness,
²⁷ make their descendants fall among the
nations
and scatter them throughout the
lands.

²⁸ They yoked themselves to the Baal of
Peor
and ate sacrifices offered to lifeless
gods;
²⁹ they aroused the LORD's anger by their
wicked deeds,
and a plague broke out among them.
³⁰ But Phinehas stood up and intervened,
and the plague was checked.
³¹ This was credited to him as
righteousness
for endless generations to come.

PROVERBS 22:5–6

⁵ In the paths of the wicked are snares and
pitfalls,
but those who would preserve their
life stay far from them.

⁶ Start children off on the way they should
go,
and even when they are old they will
not turn from it.

1 CORINTHIANS
12:21–13:13

²¹ The eye cannot say to the hand, 'I don't
need you!' And the head cannot say to the

feet, 'I don't need you!' [22] On the contrary, those parts of the body that seem to be weaker are indispensable, [23] and the parts that we think are less honourable we treat with special honour. And the parts that are unpresentable are treated with special modesty, [24] while our presentable parts need no special treatment. But God has put the body together, giving greater honour to the parts that lacked it, [25] so that there should be no division in the body, but that its parts should have equal concern for each other. [26] If one part suffers, every part suffers with it; if one part is honoured, every part rejoices with it.

[27] Now you are the body of Christ, and each one of you is a part of it. [28] And God has placed in the church first of all apostles, second prophets, third teachers, then miracles, then gifts of healing, of helping, of guidance, and of different kinds of tongues. [29] Are all apostles? Are all prophets? Are all teachers? Do all work miracles? [30] Do all have gifts of healing? Do all speak in tongues? Do all interpret? [31] Now eagerly desire the greater gifts.

And yet I will show you the most excellent way.

13 If I speak in the tongues of men or of angels, but do not have love, I am only a resounding gong or a clanging cymbal. [2] If I have the gift of prophecy and can fathom all mysteries and all knowledge, and if I have a faith that can move mountains, but do not have love, I am nothing. [3] If I give all I possess to the poor and give over my body to hardship that I may boast, but do not have love, I gain nothing.

[4] Love is patient, love is kind. It does not envy, it does not boast, it is not proud. [5] It does not dishonour others, it is not self-seeking, it is not easily angered, it keeps no record of wrongs. [6] Love does not delight in evil but rejoices with the truth. [7] It always protects, always trusts, always hopes, always perseveres.

[8] Love never fails. But where there are prophecies, they will cease; where there are tongues, they will be stilled; where there is knowledge, it will pass away. [9] For we know in part and we prophesy in part, [10] but when completeness comes, what is in part disappears. [11] When I was a child, I talked like a child, I thought like a child, I reasoned like a child. When I became a man, I put the ways of childhood behind me. [12] For now we see only a reflection as in a mirror; then we shall see face to face. Now I know in part; then I shall know fully, even as I am fully known.

[13] And now these three remain: faith, hope and love. But the greatest of these is love.

Katargeo

'When I was a child … I thought like a child, I reasoned like a child. When I became a man, I put the ways of childhood behind me.' **1 Corinthians 13:11**

Today we ask ourselves: how do we deal with those issues from our past which tend to influence and control our present attitudes and reactions?

We must find how and where they began. They come especially from the early formative years of childhood. There we were subjected to influences, ideas, and experiences that helped to shape our expectations and attitudes to life. Many of these influences, ideas, and experiences were good – and this point must not be overlooked – but by the same token, many were bad. These negative things sometimes stay inside us and can become dictating forces in our lives. We need the help of the Holy Spirit to track down some of these hidden agendas and we then need to deal with them in a mature and adult manner.

How do we do this? Look once again at the verse before us today: 'When I became a man, I put the ways of childhood behind me'. The Greek word for 'put away' is *katargeo*. It is an extremely strong word, meaning 'to put away, to break a hold, finish it off, have done with, render inoperative'.

Childhood agendas don't just fall away like the leaves fall off the trees in the autumn; we have to 'put them away' – we have to *katargeo* them – and be finished with childish things. If the Holy Spirit has identified any hidden agendas in your life, then bring them to Him now and lay them at His feet. Decide to have done with them. Get out of the passenger seat and into the driving seat. Remember – with God, all things are possible.

PRAYER

O Father, give me the victory over all the enemies that may be within me. *Katargeo* them – render them inoperative – once and for all. In Jesus' name. Amen.

FURTHER STUDY

Heb. 12:1-13; Isa. 55:7; Eph. 4:22
• What are we to throw off?
• What does 'forsake' mean?

September 9

■ JOB 36:1–37:24

36 Elihu continued:

2 'Bear with me a little longer and I will show you
   that there is more to be said on God's behalf.
3 I get my knowledge from afar;
   I will ascribe justice to my Maker.
4 Be assured that my words are not false;
   one who has perfect knowledge is with you.

5 'God is mighty, but despises no one;
   he is mighty, and firm in his purpose.
6 He does not keep the wicked alive
   but gives the afflicted their rights.

7 He does not take his eyes off the righteous;
   he enthrones them with kings
   and exalts them for ever.
8 But if people are bound in chains,
   held fast by cords of affliction,
9 he tells them what they have done –
   that they have sinned arrogantly.
10 He makes them listen to correction
   and commands them to repent of their evil.
11 If they obey and serve him,
   they will spend the rest of their days in prosperity
   and their years in contentment.
12 But if they do not listen,
   they will perish by the sword
   and die without knowledge.

13 'The godless in heart harbour
      resentment;
   even when he fetters them, they do not
      cry for help.
14 They die in their youth,
   among male prostitutes of the shrines.
15 But those who suffer he delivers in their
      suffering;
   he speaks to them in their affliction.

16 'He is wooing you from the jaws of
      distress
   to a spacious place free from
      restriction,
   to the comfort of your table laden with
      choice food.
17 But now you are laden with the judgment
      due to the wicked;
   judgment and justice have taken hold
      of you.
18 Be careful that no one entices you by
      riches;
   do not let a large bribe turn you aside.
19 Would your wealth or even all your
      mighty efforts
   sustain you so you would not be in
      distress?
20 Do not long for the night,
   to drag people away from their homes.
21 Beware of turning to evil,
   which you seem to prefer to affliction.

22 'God is exalted in his power.
   Who is a teacher like him?
23 Who has prescribed his ways for him,
   or said to him, "You have done
      wrong"?
24 Remember to extol his work,
   which people have praised in song.
25 All humanity has seen it;
   mortals gaze on it from afar.
26 How great is God – beyond our
      understanding!
   The number of his years is past
      finding out.

27 'He draws up the drops of water,
   which distil as rain to the streams;
28 the clouds pour down their moisture
   and abundant showers fall on
      mankind.
29 Who can understand how he spreads out
      the clouds,
   how he thunders from his pavilion?
30 See how he scatters his lightning about
      him,
   bathing the depths of the sea.
31 This is the way he governs the nations
   and provides food in abundance.
32 He fills his hands with lightning
   and commands it to strike its mark.
33 His thunder announces the coming
      storm;
   even the cattle make known its
      approach.

37 'At this my heart pounds
      and leaps from its place.
2 Listen! Listen to the roar of his voice,
   to the rumbling that comes from his
      mouth.
3 He unleashes his lightning beneath the
      whole heaven
   and sends it to the ends of the earth.
4 After that comes the sound of his roar;
   he thunders with his majestic voice.
   When his voice resounds,
   he holds nothing back.
5 God's voice thunders in marvellous
      ways;
   he does great things beyond our
      understanding.
6 He says to the snow, "Fall on the earth,"
   and to the rain shower, "Be a mighty
      downpour."
7 So that everyone he has made may know
      his work,
   he stops all people from their labour.
8 The animals take cover;
   they remain in their dens.
9 The tempest comes out from its
      chamber,

the cold from the driving winds.
¹⁰ The breath of God produces ice,
    and the broad waters become frozen.
¹¹ He loads the clouds with moisture;
    he scatters his lightning through
        them.
¹² At his direction they swirl around
    over the face of the whole earth
    to do whatever he commands them.
¹³ He brings the clouds to punish people,
    or to water his earth and show his
        love.

¹⁴ 'Listen to this, Job;
    stop and consider God's wonders.
¹⁵ Do you know how God controls the
        clouds
    and makes his lightning flash?
¹⁶ Do you know how the clouds hang
        poised,
        those wonders of him who is perfect in
            knowledge?
¹⁷ You who swelter in your clothes
    when the land lies hushed under the
        south wind,
¹⁸ can you join him in spreading out the
        skies,
    hard as a mirror of cast bronze?

¹⁹ 'Tell us what we should say to him;
    we cannot draw up our case because
        of our darkness.
²⁰ Should he be told that I want to speak?
    Would anyone ask to be swallowed
        up?
²¹ Now no one can look at the sun,
    bright as it is in the skies
    after the wind has swept them clean.
²² Out of the north he comes in golden
        splendour;
    God comes in awesome majesty.
²³ The Almighty is beyond our reach and
        exalted in power;
    in his justice and great righteousness,
        he does not oppress.
²⁴ Therefore, people revere him,

for does he not have regard for all the
    wise in heart?'

━ PSALM 106:32-39

³² By the waters of Meribah they angered
        the LORD,
    and trouble came to Moses because of
        them;
³³ for they rebelled against the Spirit of
        God,
    and rash words came from Moses'
        lips.

³⁴ They did not destroy the peoples
    as the LORD had commanded them,
³⁵ but they mingled with the nations
    and adopted their customs.
³⁶ They worshipped their idols,
    which became a snare to them.
³⁷ They sacrificed their sons
    and their daughters to false gods.
³⁸ They shed innocent blood,
    the blood of their sons and daughters,
    whom they sacrificed to the idols of
        Canaan,
    and the land was desecrated by their
        blood.
³⁹ They defiled themselves by what they
        did;
    by their deeds they prostituted
        themselves.

━ PROVERBS 22:7-8

⁷ The rich rule over the poor,
    and the borrower is slave to the lender.

⁸ Whoever sows injustice reaps calamity,
    and the rod they wield in fury will be
        broken.

▬ 1 CORINTHIANS 14:1-25

14 Follow the way of love and eagerly desire gifts of the Spirit, especially prophecy. ²For anyone who speaks in a tongue does not speak to people but to God. Indeed, no one understands them; they utter mysteries by the Spirit. ³But the one who prophesies speaks to people for their strengthening, encouraging and comfort. ⁴Anyone who speaks in a tongue edifies themselves, but the one who prophesies edifies the church. ⁵I would like every one of you to speak in tongues, but even more to prophesy. The one who prophesies is greater than the one who speaks in tongues, unless someone interprets, so that the church may be edified.

⁶Now, brothers and sisters, if I come to you and speak in tongues, what good will I be to you, unless I bring you some revelation or knowledge or prophecy or word of instruction? ⁷Even in the case of lifeless things that make sounds, such as the pipe or harp, how will anyone know what tune is being played unless there is a distinction in the notes? ⁸Again, if the trumpet does not sound a clear call, who will get ready for battle? ⁹So it is with you. Unless you speak intelligible words with your tongue, how will anyone know what you are saying? You will just be speaking into the air. ¹⁰Undoubtedly there are all sorts of languages in the world, yet none of them is without meaning. ¹¹If then I do not grasp the meaning of what someone is saying, I am a foreigner to the speaker, and the speaker is a foreigner to me. ¹²So it is with you. Since you are eager for gifts of the Spirit, try to excel in those that build up the church.

¹³For this reason the one who speaks in a tongue should pray that they may interpret what they say. ¹⁴For if I pray in a tongue, my spirit prays, but my mind is unfruitful. ¹⁵So what shall I do? I will pray with my spirit, but I will also pray with my understanding; I will sing with my spirit, but I will also sing with my understanding. ¹⁶Otherwise when you are praising God in the Spirit, how can someone else, who is now put in the position of an enquirer, say 'Amen' to your thanksgiving, since they do not know what you are saying? ¹⁷You are giving thanks well enough, but no one else is edified.

¹⁸I thank God that I speak in tongues more than all of you. ¹⁹But in the church I would rather speak five intelligible words to instruct others than ten thousand words in a tongue.

²⁰Brothers and sisters, stop thinking like children. In regard to evil be infants, but in your thinking be adults. ²¹In the Law it is written:

'With other tongues
  and through the lips of foreigners
I will speak to this people,
    but even then they will not listen to me,
      says the Lord.'

²²Tongues, then, are a sign, not for believers but for unbelievers; prophecy, however, is not for unbelievers but for believers. ²³So if the whole church comes together and everyone speaks in tongues, and enquirers or unbelievers come in, will they not say that you are out of your mind? ²⁴But if an unbeliever or an enquirer comes in while everyone is prophesying, they are convicted of sin and are brought under judgment by all, ²⁵as the secrets of their hearts are laid bare. So they will fall down and worship God, exclaiming, 'God is really among you!'

'Praying in the Spirit'

'And pray in the Spirit on all occasions ...' **Ephesians 6:18**

W hat does it mean to pray 'in the Spirit'? Here again, there is a good deal of misunderstanding among Christians as to the true meaning of this phrase.

There are times when one feels deeply affected emotionally as one prays, but this is not the meaning of the phrase 'praying in the Spirit'. It has no relationship to the emotions that we feel in prayer. I am not saying that feelings are unimportant in prayer; I am simply saying that I do not believe this is what Paul had in mind when he used the phrase 'praying in the Spirit'.

The 'Spirit' spoken of here is not the human spirit but the Holy Spirit. Some believe that 'praying in the Spirit' takes place when we pray in other tongues, and although it can include that, I believe it is much more than that.

Prayer that is 'in the Spirit' is prayer that is prompted and guided by the Spirit. One commentator puts it this way: 'It means that the Holy Spirit directs the prayer, creates the prayer within us, and empowers us to offer it and to pray it'.

Dr Martyn Lloyd-Jones calls praying in the Spirit 'the secret of true prayer' and goes on to say, 'If we do not pray in the Spirit, we do not really pray'. If we do not know what it means to pray in the Spirit, our prayers will have little impact upon Satan and his forces.

PRAYER

Dear Father, I have so much to learn about prayer that unless You take my hand and guide me, I can soon lose my way. Teach me how to enter the deeper levels of prayer. In Jesus' name. Amen.

FURTHER STUDY

Rom. 8:1-17, 26;
Luke 11:13; 24:49
• To what does the Spirit bear witness?
• What was Christ's promise to His disciples?

September 10

■ JOB 38:1–39:12

38 Then the LORD spoke to Job out of the storm. He said:

² 'Who is this that obscures my plans with words without knowledge?
³ Brace yourself like a man;

I will question you,
and you shall answer me.

⁴ 'Where were you when I laid the earth's foundation?
Tell me, if you understand.
⁵ Who marked off its dimensions? Surely you know!

Who stretched a measuring line
　　across it?
⁶ On what were its footings set,
　　or who laid its cornerstone –
⁷ while the morning stars sang together
　　and all the angels shouted for joy?

⁸ 'Who shut up the sea behind doors
　　when it burst forth from the womb,
⁹ when I made the clouds its garment
　　and wrapped it in thick darkness,
¹⁰ when I fixed limits for it
　　and set its doors and bars in place,
¹¹ when I said, "This far you may come and
　　no farther;
　　here is where your proud waves halt"?

¹² 'Have you ever given orders to the morning,
　　or shown the dawn its place,
¹³ that it might take the earth by the edges
　　and shake the wicked out of it?
¹⁴ The earth takes shape like clay under a
　　seal;
　　its features stand out like those of a
　　garment.
¹⁵ The wicked are denied their light,
　　and their upraised arm is broken.

¹⁶ 'Have you journeyed to the springs of the
　　sea
　　or walked in the recesses of the deep?
¹⁷ Have the gates of death been shown to you?
　　Have you seen the gates of the deepest
　　darkness?
¹⁸ Have you comprehended the vast
　　expanses of the earth?
　　Tell me, if you know all this.

¹⁹ 'What is the way to the abode of light?
　　And where does darkness reside?
²⁰ Can you take them to their places?
　　Do you know the paths to their
　　dwellings?
²¹ Surely you know, for you were already
　　born!
　　You have lived so many years!

²² 'Have you entered the storehouses of the
　　snow
　　or seen the storehouses of the hail,
²³ which I reserve for times of trouble,
　　for days of war and battle?
²⁴ What is the way to the place where the
　　lightning is dispersed,
　　or the place where the east winds are
　　scattered over the earth?
²⁵ Who cuts a channel for the torrents of
　　rain,
　　and a path for the thunderstorm,
²⁶ to water a land where no one lives,
　　an uninhabited desert,
²⁷ to satisfy a desolate wasteland
　　and make it sprout with grass?
²⁸ Does the rain have a father?
　　Who fathers the drops of dew?
²⁹ From whose womb comes the ice?
　　Who gives birth to the frost from the
　　heavens
³⁰ when the waters become hard as stone,
　　when the surface of the deep is frozen?

³¹ 'Can you bind the chains of the Pleiades?
　　Can you loosen Orion's belt?
³² Can you bring forth the constellations in
　　their seasons
　　or lead out the Bear with its cubs?
³³ Do you know the laws of the heavens?
　　Can you set up God's dominion over
　　the earth?

³⁴ 'Can you raise your voice to the clouds
　　and cover yourself with a flood of
　　water?
³⁵ Do you send the lightning bolts on their
　　way?
　　Do they report to you, "Here we are"?
³⁶ Who gives the ibis wisdom
　　or gives the cockerel understanding?
³⁷ Who has the wisdom to count the clouds?
　　Who can tip over the water jars of the
　　heavens
³⁸ when the dust becomes hard
　　and the clods of earth stick together?

³⁹ 'Do you hunt the prey for the lioness
    and satisfy the hunger of the lions
⁴⁰ when they crouch in their dens
    or lie in wait in a thicket?
⁴¹ Who provides food for the raven
    when its young cry out to God
    and wander about for lack of food?

39 'Do you know when the mountain
       goats give birth?
    Do you watch when the doe bears her
       fawn?
² Do you count the months till they bear?
    Do you know the time they give birth?
³ They crouch down and bring forth their
       young;
    their labour pains are ended.
⁴ Their young thrive and grow strong in
       the wilds;
    they leave and do not return.

⁵ 'Who let the wild donkey go free?
    Who untied its ropes?
⁶ I gave it the wasteland as its home,
    the salt flats as its habitat.
⁷ It laughs at the commotion in the town;
    it does not hear a driver's shout.
⁸ It ranges the hills for its pasture
    and searches for any green thing.

⁹ 'Will the wild ox consent to serve you?
    Will it stay by your manger at night?
¹⁰ Can you hold it to the furrow with a
       harness?
    Will it till the valleys behind you?
¹¹ Will you rely on it for its great strength?
    Will you leave your heavy work to it?
¹² Can you trust it to haul in your grain
    and bring it to your threshing-floor?

▬ PSALM 106:40-48

⁴⁰ Therefore the LORD was angry with his
       people
    and abhorred his inheritance.

⁴¹ He gave them into the hands of the nations,
    and their foes ruled over them.
⁴² Their enemies oppressed them
    and subjected them to their power.
⁴³ Many times he delivered them,
    but they were bent on rebellion
    and they wasted away in their sin.
⁴⁴ Yet he took note of their distress
    when he heard their cry;
⁴⁵ for their sake he remembered his covenant
    and out of his great love he relented.
⁴⁶ He caused all who held them captive
    to show them mercy.

⁴⁷ Save us, LORD our God,
    and gather us from the nations,
    that we may give thanks to your holy
       name
    and glory in your praise.

⁴⁸ Praise be to the LORD, the God of Israel,
    from everlasting to everlasting.

    Let all the people say, 'Amen!'

    Praise the LORD.

▬ PROVERBS 22:9-10

⁹ The generous will themselves be blessed,
    for they share their food with the poor.

¹⁰ Drive out the mocker, and out goes strife;
    quarrels and insults are ended.

▬ 1 CORINTHIANS 14:26–15:11

²⁶ What then shall we say, brothers and
sisters? When you come together, each of
you has a hymn, or a word of instruction,
a revelation, a tongue or an interpretation.
Everything must be done so that the church
may be built up. ²⁷ If anyone speaks in a

tongue, two – or at the most three – should speak, one at a time, and someone must interpret. ²⁸If there is no interpreter, the speaker should keep quiet in the church and speak to himself and to God.

²⁹Two or three prophets should speak, and the others should weigh carefully what is said. ³⁰And if a revelation comes to someone who is sitting down, the first speaker should stop. ³¹For you can all prophesy in turn so that everyone may be instructed and encouraged. ³²The spirits of prophets are subject to the control of prophets. ³³For God is not a God of disorder but of peace – as in all the congregations of the Lord's people.

³⁴Women should remain silent in the churches. They are not allowed to speak, but must be in submission, as the law says. ³⁵If they want to enquire about something, they should ask their own husbands at home; for it is disgraceful for a woman to speak in the church.

³⁶Or did the word of God originate with you? Or are you the only people it has reached? ³⁷If anyone thinks they are a prophet or otherwise gifted by the Spirit, let them acknowledge that what I am writing to you is the Lord's command. ³⁸But if anyone ignores this, they will themselves be ignored.

³⁹Therefore, my brothers and sisters, be eager to prophesy, and do not forbid speaking in tongues. ⁴⁰But everything should be done in a fitting and orderly way.

15 Now, brothers and sisters, I want to remind you of the gospel I preached to you, which you received and on which you have taken your stand. ²By this gospel you are saved, if you hold firmly to the word I preached to you. Otherwise, you have believed in vain.

³For what I received I passed on to you as of first importance: that Christ died for our sins according to the Scriptures, ⁴that he was buried, that he was raised on the third day according to the Scriptures, ⁵and that he appeared to Cephas, and then to the Twelve. ⁶After that, he appeared to more than five hundred of the brothers and sisters at the same time, most of whom are still living, though some have fallen asleep. ⁷Then he appeared to James, then to all the apostles, ⁸and last of all he appeared to me also, as to one abnormally born.

⁹For I am the least of the apostles and do not even deserve to be called an apostle, because I persecuted the church of God. ¹⁰But by the grace of God I am what I am, and his grace to me was not without effect. No, I worked harder than all of them – yet not I, but the grace of God that was with me. ¹¹Whether, then, it is I or they, this is what we preach, and this is what you believed.

The God of All Grace

'But by the grace of God, I am what I am ...'
1 Corinthians 15:10

Is it any wonder that throughout the history of the Christian church, men and women have found the thought of grace so overwhelmingly wonderful that they seemed unable to get over it? Grace was the constant theme of their prayers, their preaching, their writing – and their hymns. Take this for example:

Great God of wonders, all Thy ways
Display the attributes divine;

> *But countless acts of pardoning grace*
> *Beyond Thine other wonders shine;*
> *Who is a pardoning God like Thee?*
> *Or who has grace so rich and free?*

Many have fought to uphold the truth of God's grace, accepting ridicule and loss of privilege as the price of their stand. Paul waged war against the legalists in the Galatian churches over this matter, and the battle to uphold this great truth has gone on ever since. Augustine fought it in the fourth and fifth centuries, as did the Reformers in the sixteenth.

I sense that the church once again is in danger of losing out to legalism as more and more Christians get caught up with doing rather than being. Talk to people about what they are doing, and they are with you at once; talk to them about who they are being (who they really are), and their attitude is one of deferential blankness.

The church of Jesus Christ is in a sad state when it can't say with conviction and meaning, as did the apostle Paul: 'By the grace of God I am what I am.'

PRAYER

God of all grace, give me grace to feel my need of grace. And give me grace to ask for grace. Then give me grace to receive grace. And when grace is given to me, give me grace to use that grace. In Jesus' name I pray. Amen.

FURTHER STUDY

2 Cor. 1:1–12; 6:1; Gal. 2:21
- Where was Paul's boast rooted?
- What was Paul's warning to the Corinthians?

September 11

◼ JOB 39:13–40:24

13 'The wings of the ostrich flap joyfully,
    though they cannot compare
    with the wings and feathers of the stork.
14 She lays her eggs on the ground
    and lets them warm in the sand,
15 unmindful that a foot may crush them,
    that some wild animal may trample
    them.
16 She treats her young harshly, as if they
    were not hers;
    she cares not that her labour was in
    vain,

17 for God did not endow her with wisdom
    or give her a share of good sense.
18 Yet when she spreads her feathers to run,
    she laughs at horse and rider.

19 'Do you give the horse its strength
    or clothe its neck with a flowing mane?
20 Do you make it leap like a locust,
    striking terror with its proud
      snorting?
21 It paws fiercely, rejoicing in its strength,
    and charges into the fray.
22 It laughs at fear, afraid of nothing;
    it does not shy away from the sword.

23 The quiver rattles against its side,
      along with the flashing spear and
      lance.
24 In frenzied excitement it eats up the
      ground;
   it cannot stand still when the trumpet
      sounds.
25 At the blast of the trumpet it snorts, "Aha!"
   It catches the scent of battle from afar,
      the shout of commanders and the
      battle cry.

26 'Does the hawk take flight by your
      wisdom
   and spread its wings towards the
      south?
27 Does the eagle soar at your command
      and build its nest on high?
28 It dwells on a cliff and stays there at
      night;
   a rocky crag is its stronghold.
29 From there it looks for food;
   its eyes detect it from afar.
30 Its young ones feast on blood,
   and where the slain are, there it is.'

40

The LORD said to Job:

2 'Will the one who contends with the
      Almighty correct him?
   Let him who accuses God answer
      him!'

3 Then Job answered the LORD:

4 'I am unworthy – how can I reply to you?
   I put my hand over my mouth.
5 I spoke once, but I have no answer –
   twice, but I will say no more.'

6 Then the LORD spoke to Job out of the
storm:

7 'Brace yourself like a man;
   I will question you,
   and you shall answer me.

8 'Would you discredit my justice?
   Would you condemn me to justify
      yourself?
9 Do you have an arm like God's,
   and can your voice thunder like his?
10 Then adorn yourself with glory and
      splendour,
   and clothe yourself in honour and
      majesty.
11 Unleash the fury of your wrath,
   look at all who are proud and bring
      them low,
12 look at all who are proud and humble
      them,
   crush the wicked where they stand.
13 Bury them all in the dust together;
   shroud their faces in the grave.
14 Then I myself will admit to you
   that your own right hand can save
      you.

15 'Look at Behemoth,
   which I made along with you
   and which feeds on grass like an ox.
16 What strength it has in its loins,
   what power in the muscles of its belly!
17 Its tail sways like a cedar;
   the sinews of its thighs are close-knit.
18 Its bones are tubes of bronze,
   its limbs like rods of iron.
19 It ranks first among the works of God,
   yet its Maker can approach it with his
      sword.
20 The hills bring it their produce,
   and all the wild animals play nearby.
21 Under the lotus plant it lies,
   hidden among the reeds in the marsh.
22 The lotuses conceal it in their shadow;
   the poplars by the stream surround it.
23 A raging river does not alarm it;
   it is secure, though the Jordan should
      surge against its mouth.
24 Can anyone capture it by the eyes,
   or trap it and pierce its nose?

PSALM 107:1–9

¹ Give thanks to the LORD, for he is good;
  his love endures for ever.

² Let the redeemed of the LORD tell their
    story –
  those he redeemed from the hand of
    the foe,
³ those he gathered from the lands,
  from east and west, from north and
    south.

⁴ Some wandered in desert wastelands,
  finding no way to a city where they
    could settle.
⁵ They were hungry and thirsty,
  and their lives ebbed away.
⁶ Then they cried out to the LORD in their
    trouble,
  and he delivered them from their
    distress.
⁷ He led them by a straight way
  to a city where they could settle.
⁸ Let them give thanks to the LORD for his
    unfailing love
  and his wonderful deeds for mankind,
⁹ for he satisfies the thirsty
  and fills the hungry with good things.

PROVERBS 22:11–12

¹¹ One who loves a pure heart and who
    speaks with grace
  will have the king for a friend.

¹² The eyes of the LORD keep watch over
    knowledge,
  but he frustrates the words of the
    unfaithful.

1 CORINTHIANS 15:12–34

¹² But if it is preached that Christ has been
raised from the dead, how can some of you
say that there is no resurrection of the dead?
¹³ If there is no resurrection of the dead, then
not even Christ has been raised. ¹⁴ And if
Christ has not been raised, our preaching is
useless and so is your faith. ¹⁵ More than that,
we are then found to be false witnesses about
God, for we have testified about God that he
raised Christ from the dead. But he did not
raise him if in fact the dead are not raised.
¹⁶ For if the dead are not raised, then Christ
has not been raised either. ¹⁷ And if Christ
has not been raised, your faith is futile; you
are still in your sins. ¹⁸ Then those also who
have fallen asleep in Christ are lost. ¹⁹ If only
for this life we have hope in Christ, we are of
all people most to be pitied.

²⁰ But Christ has indeed been raised
from the dead, the firstfruits of those who
have fallen asleep. ²¹ For since death came
through a man, the resurrection of the
dead comes also through a man. ²² For
as in Adam all die, so in Christ all will be
made alive. ²³ But each in turn: Christ, the
firstfruits; then, when he comes, those who
belong to him. ²⁴ Then the end will come,
when he hands over the kingdom to God the
Father after he has destroyed all dominion,
authority and power. ²⁵ For he must reign
until he has put all his enemies under his
feet. ²⁶ The last enemy to be destroyed is
death. ²⁷ For he 'has put everything under
his feet'. Now when it says that 'everything'
has been put under him, it is clear that this
does not include God himself, who put everything under Christ. ²⁸ When he has done
this, then the Son himself will be made subject to him who put everything under him,
so that God may be all in all.

²⁹ Now if there is no resurrection, what
will those do who are baptised for the dead?
If the dead are not raised at all, why are
people baptised for them? ³⁰ And as for us,
why do we endanger ourselves every hour?
³¹ I face death every day – yes, just as surely as I boast about you in Christ Jesus our

Lord. [32]If I fought wild beasts in Ephesus with no more than human hopes, what have I gained? If the dead are not raised,

'Let us eat and drink,
for tomorrow we die.'

[33]Do not be misled: 'Bad company corrupts good character.' [34]Come back to your senses as you ought, and stop sinning; for there are some who are ignorant of God – I say this to your shame.

A Position of Strength

'Then the end will come, when he hands over the kingdom to God the Father after he has destroyed all dominion, authority and power.' **1 Corinthians 15:24**

If people are to live securely in this world, then they must cultivate a worldview. They must see the 'big picture'. Is this why Jesus, when laying down a pattern for prayer, taught His disciples to focus on the 'big picture' of the kingdom of God? Whether it is or not, one thing is certain – when we start off in prayer, gripped by the certainty of God's coming kingdom, our prayers are launched from a position of strength.

Just as I was about to begin this page, a sales bulletin came in the mail, and on it were the words: 'Get the idea – and all else follows.' I thought to myself: When the idea is God's idea (the kingdom) then, indeed, all else follows. What if we were to begin our prayers, however, by focusing, not on the kingdom of God, but on the kingdoms of this world? We would receive very little motivation from such an action. Man-made empires come and go. Egypt came and went. Assyria came and went. Babylon came and went. Greece came and went. Historians tell us that at least twenty-one former great civilisations are extinct. Earthly kingdoms go the way of all flesh.

The kingdom of God, however, unlike earthly kingdoms, is destined for success. Call it triumphalism if you like, but the eventual accomplishment of God's kingdom has more reliability about it than tomorrow's dawn. When our minds are permitted to focus on such a tremendous truth, it will not be long before the heart leaps up in confident, believing prayer.

PRAYER

Father, I think I get the idea. When I focus my mind on the glory of Your coming kingdom, then, against such a wonderful backdrop, my prayers take on a new boldness and authority. 'Get the idea, then all else follows.' Thank You, Father. Amen.

FURTHER STUDY

Psa. 115:1-18; Phil. 2:10;
Heb. 1:8; Rev. 11:15

• How does the psalmist relate heaven and earth?
• How can we help to bring the kingdom of heaven to earth?

September 12

▬ JOB 41:1–42:17

41 ¹'Can you pull in Leviathan with a
fishhook
   or tie down its tongue with a rope?
²Can you put a cord through its nose
   or pierce its jaw with a hook?
³Will it keep begging you for mercy?
   Will it speak to you with gentle words?
⁴Will it make an agreement with you
   for you to take it as your slave for life?
⁵Can you make a pet of it like a bird
   or put it on a leash for the young
      women in your house?
⁶Will traders barter for it?
   Will they divide it up among the
      merchants?
⁷Can you fill its hide with harpoons
   or its head with fishing spears?
⁸If you lay a hand on it,
   you will remember the struggle and
      never do it again!
⁹Any hope of subduing it is false;
   the mere sight of it is overpowering.
¹⁰No one is fierce enough to rouse it.
   Who then is able to stand against me?
¹¹Who has a claim against me that I must
     pay?
   Everything under heaven belongs to me.

¹²'I will not fail to speak of Leviathan's
    limbs,
   its strength and its graceful form.
¹³Who can strip off its outer coat?
   Who can penetrate its double coat of
      armour?
¹⁴Who dares open the doors of its mouth,
   ringed about with its fearsome teeth?
¹⁵Its back has rows of shields
   tightly sealed together;
¹⁶each is so close to the next
   that no air can pass between.
¹⁷They are joined fast to one another;
   they cling together and cannot be
      parted.
¹⁸Its snorting throws out flashes of light;
   its eyes are like the rays of dawn.
¹⁹Flames stream from its mouth;
   sparks of fire shoot out.
²⁰Smoke pours from its nostrils
   as from a boiling pot over burning
      reeds.
²¹Its breath sets coals ablaze,
   and flames dart from its mouth.
²²Strength resides in its neck;
   dismay goes before it.
²³The folds of its flesh are tightly joined;
   they are firm and immovable.
²⁴Its chest is hard as rock,
   hard as a lower millstone.
²⁵When it rises up, the mighty are
     terrified;
   they retreat before its thrashing.
²⁶The sword that reaches it has no effect,
   nor does the spear or the dart or the
      javelin.
²⁷Iron it treats like straw
   and bronze like rotten wood.
²⁸Arrows do not make it flee;
   slingstones are like chaff to it.
²⁹A club seems to it but a piece of straw;
   it laughs at the rattling of the lance.
³⁰Its undersides are jagged potsherds,
   leaving a trail in the mud like a
      threshing-sledge.
³¹It makes the depths churn like a boiling
     cauldron
   and stirs up the sea like a pot of
      ointment.
³²It leaves a glistening wake behind it;
   one would think the deep had white
      hair.

[33] Nothing on earth is its equal –
a creature without fear.
[34] It looks down on all that are haughty;
it is king over all that are proud.'

42

Then Job replied to the LORD:

[2] 'I know that you can do all things;
no purpose of yours can be thwarted.
[3] You asked, "Who is this that obscures
my plans without knowledge?"
Surely I spoke of things I did not
understand,
things too wonderful for me to know.

[4] 'You said, "Listen now, and I will speak;
I will question you,
and you shall answer me."
[5] My ears had heard of you
but now my eyes have seen you.
[6] Therefore I despise myself
and repent in dust and ashes.'

[7] After the LORD had said these things to Job, he said to Eliphaz the Temanite, 'I am angry with you and your two friends, because you have not spoken the truth about me, as my servant Job has. [8] So now take seven bulls and seven rams and go to my servant Job and sacrifice a burnt offering for yourselves. My servant Job will pray for you, and I will accept his prayer and not deal with you according to your folly. You have not spoken the truth about me, as my servant Job has.' [9] So Eliphaz the Temanite, Bildad the Shuhite and Zophar the Naamathite did what the LORD told them; and the LORD accepted Job's prayer.

[10] After Job had prayed for his friends, the LORD restored his fortunes and gave him twice as much as he had before. [11] All his brothers and sisters and everyone who had known him before came and ate with him in his house. They comforted and consoled him over all the trouble the LORD had brought on him, and each one gave him a piece of silver and a gold ring.

[12] The LORD blessed the latter part of Job's life more than the former part. He had fourteen thousand sheep, six thousand camels, a thousand yoke of oxen and a thousand donkeys. [13] And he also had seven sons and three daughters. [14] The first daughter he named Jemimah, the second Keziah and the third Keren-Happuch. [15] Nowhere in all the land were there found women as beautiful as Job's daughters, and their father granted them an inheritance along with their brothers.

[16] After this, Job lived a hundred and forty years; he saw his children and their children to the fourth generation. [17] And so Job died, an old man and full of years.

▬ PSALM 107:10–16

[10] Some sat in darkness, in utter darkness,
prisoners suffering in iron chains,
[11] because they rebelled against God's
commands
and despised the plans of the Most
High.
[12] So he subjected them to bitter labour;
they stumbled, and there was no one
to help.
[13] Then they cried to the LORD in their
trouble,
and he saved them from their distress.
[14] He brought them out of darkness, the
utter darkness,
and broke away their chains.
[15] Let them give thanks to the LORD for his
unfailing love
and his wonderful deeds for mankind,
[16] for he breaks down gates of bronze
and cuts through bars of iron.

▬ PROVERBS 22:13–14

[13] The sluggard says, 'There's a lion
outside!

I'll be killed in the public square!'

¹⁴ The mouth of an adulterous woman is a
deep pit;
a man who is under the LORD's wrath
falls into it.

■ 1 CORINTHIANS 15:35-58

³⁵ But someone will ask, 'How are the
dead raised? With what kind of body will
they come?' ³⁶ How foolish! What you sow
does not come to life unless it dies. ³⁷ When
you sow, you do not plant the body that will
be, but just a seed, perhaps of wheat or of
something else. ³⁸ But God gives it a body
as he has determined, and to each kind of
seed he gives its own body. ³⁹ Not all flesh is
the same: people have one kind of flesh, animals have another, birds another and fish
another. ⁴⁰ There are also heavenly bodies
and there are earthly bodies; but the splendour of the heavenly bodies is one kind, and
the splendour of the earthly bodies is another. ⁴¹ The sun has one kind of splendour,
the moon another and the stars another;
and star differs from star in splendour.

⁴² So will it be with the resurrection of the
dead. The body that is sown is perishable, it
is raised imperishable; ⁴³ it is sown in dishonour, it is raised in glory; it is sown in
weakness, it is raised in power; ⁴⁴ it is sown
a natural body, it is raised a spiritual body.

If there is a natural body, there is also a
spiritual body. ⁴⁵ So it is written: 'The first
man Adam became a living being'; the last
Adam, a life-giving spirit. ⁴⁶ The spiritual

did not come first, but the natural, and after
that the spiritual. ⁴⁷ The first man was of the
dust of the earth; the second man is of heav-
en. ⁴⁸ As was the earthly man, so are those
who are of the earth; and as is the heavenly
man, so also are those who are of heaven.
⁴⁹ And just as we have borne the image of
the earthly man, so shall we bear the image
of the heavenly man.

⁵⁰ I declare to you, brothers and sisters,
that flesh and blood cannot inherit the kingdom of God, nor does the perishable inherit
the imperishable. ⁵¹ Listen, I tell you a mystery: we will not all sleep, but we will all be
changed – ⁵² in a flash, in the twinkling of
an eye, at the last trumpet. For the trumpet
will sound, the dead will be raised imperishable, and we will be changed. ⁵³ For the
perishable must clothe itself with the imperishable, and the mortal with immortality. ⁵⁴ When the perishable has been clothed
with the imperishable, and the mortal with
immortality, then the saying that is written
will come true: 'Death has been swallowed
up in victory.'

⁵⁵ 'Where, O death, is your victory?
Where, O death, is your sting?'

⁵⁶ The sting of death is sin, and the power
of sin is the law. ⁵⁷ But thanks be to God! He
gives us the victory through our Lord Jesus
Christ.

⁵⁸ Therefore, my dear brothers and sisters, stand firm. Let nothing move you. Always give yourselves fully to the work of the
Lord, because you know that your labour in
the Lord is not in vain.

Deep Trauma

'The LORD blessed the latter part of Job's life more than the former part.' **Job 42:12**

There are many 'walking wounded' in the Christian church who have experienced some deep horror, such as physical beating, sexual abuse, or serious injury. The Holy Spirit yearns to heal you of these hurts, but He can only do so when you let Him.

For the Holy Spirit to be able to heal our deep hurts, we must be willing to part with the resentment that is often mixed up in them. When something traumatic happens to us, more often than not, we respond to it with a measure of self-pity and say, 'Why should that have happened to me?' In whatever way you might justify the bitterness at the time, there must be a willingness to abandon all resentment before there can be a deep healing.

This is what I mean when I say that the Holy Spirit will heal your hurts – if you let Him. He can't bring healing where there is bitterness. That would be like healing over a boil. When you truly part with the bitterness, however, then I assure you, a deep healing will begin.

Have you heard the story of Joni Eareckson Tada? Young, beautiful, vivacious, she had a diving accident that resulted in paralysis. She is now a quadriplegic. She paints pictures with a brush held between her teeth. Her witness has become worldwide. At first she was angry and bitter, but one day she let go of the bitterness and experienced inner healing. Outside she remained the same, but inside she was made anew.

PRAYER

Blessed Holy Spirit, I see that when I hold onto bitterness and resentment, I succeed only in blocking Your healing power. I surrender every resentment, every ounce of self-pity, into Your hands, and receive in its place complete healing. Amen.

FURTHER STUDY

Gen. 41:51; Job 42; Heb. 12:15; Eph. 4:31; Deut. 32:32; Acts 8:23

• What was Job's confession?
• When did God bring good out of Job's calamity?

September 13

1 The words of the Teacher, son of David, king of Jerusalem:

[2] 'Meaningless! Meaningless!'
says the Teacher.
'Utterly meaningless!
Everything is meaningless.'

³ What do people gain from all their
   labours
   at which they toil under the sun?
⁴ Generations come and generations go,
   but the earth remains for ever.
⁵ The sun rises and the sun sets,
   and hurries back to where it rises.
⁶ The wind blows to the south
   and turns to the north;
   round and round it goes,
   ever returning on its course.
⁷ All streams flow into the sea,
   yet the sea is never full.
   To the place the streams come from,
   there they return again.
⁸ All things are wearisome,
   more than one can say.
   The eye never has enough of seeing,
   nor the ear its fill of hearing.
⁹ What has been will be again,
   what has been done will be done again;
   there is nothing new under the sun.
¹⁰ Is there anything of which one can say,
   'Look! This is something new'?
   It was here already, long ago;
   it was here before our time.
¹¹ No one remembers the former
   generations,
   and even those yet to come
   will not be remembered
   by those who follow them.

¹² I, the Teacher, was king over Israel in
Jerusalem. ¹³ I applied my mind to study
and to explore by wisdom all that is done
under the heavens. What a heavy burden
God has laid on mankind! ¹⁴ I have seen all
the things that are done under the sun; all
of them are meaningless, a chasing after the
wind.

¹⁵ What is crooked cannot be straightened;
   what is lacking cannot be counted.

¹⁶ I said to myself, 'Look, I have increased
in wisdom more than anyone who has ruled

over Jerusalem before me; I have experienced much of wisdom and knowledge.'
¹⁷ Then I applied myself to the understanding of wisdom, and also of madness and folly, but I learned that this, too, is a chasing
after the wind.

¹⁸ For with much wisdom comes much
   sorrow;
   the more knowledge, the more grief.

2 I said to myself, 'Come now, I will test
you with pleasure to find out what is
good.' But that also proved to be meaningless. ² 'Laughter,' I said, 'is madness. And
what does pleasure accomplish?' ³ I tried
cheering myself with wine, and embracing
folly – my mind still guiding me with wisdom. I wanted to see what was good for people to do under the heavens during the few
days of their lives.

⁴ I undertook great projects: I built houses for myself and planted vineyards. ⁵ I
made gardens and parks and planted all
kinds of fruit trees in them. ⁶ I made reservoirs to water groves of flourishing trees.
⁷ I bought male and female slaves and had
other slaves who were born in my house.
I also owned more herds and flocks than
anyone in Jerusalem before me. ⁸ I amassed
silver and gold for myself, and the treasure
of kings and provinces. I acquired male and
female singers, and a harem as well – the
delights of a man's heart. ⁹ I became greater
by far than anyone in Jerusalem before me.
In all this my wisdom stayed with me.

¹⁰ I denied myself nothing my eyes desired;
   I refused my heart no pleasure.
   My heart took delight in all my labour,
   and this was the reward for all my toil.
¹¹ Yet when I surveyed all that my hands
      had done
   and what I had toiled to achieve,
   everything was meaningless, a chasing
      after the wind;
   nothing was gained under the sun.

¹² Then I turned my thoughts to consider
wisdom,
and also madness and folly.
What more can the king's successor do
than what has already been done?
¹³ I saw that wisdom is better than folly,
just as light is better than darkness.
¹⁴ The wise have eyes in their heads,
while the fool walks in the darkness;
but I came to realise
that the same fate overtakes them
both.

¹⁵ Then I said to myself,

'The fate of the fool will overtake me
also.
What then do I gain by being wise?'
I said to myself,
'This too is meaningless.'
¹⁶ For the wise, like the fool, will not be
long remembered;
the days have already come when both
have been forgotten.
Like the fool, the wise too must die!

¹⁷ So I hated life, because the work that
is done under the sun was grievous to me.
All of it is meaningless, a chasing after the
wind. ¹⁸ I hated all the things I had toiled for
under the sun, because I must leave them
to the one who comes after me. ¹⁹ And who
knows whether that person will be wise or
foolish? Yet they will have control over all
the fruit of my toil into which I have poured
my effort and skill under the sun. This too
is meaningless. ²⁰ So my heart began to despair over all my toilsome labour under the
sun. ²¹ For a person may labour with wisdom, knowledge and skill, and then they
must leave all they own to another who has
not toiled for it. This too is meaningless
and a great misfortune. ²² What do people get for all the toil and anxious striving
with which they labour under the sun? ²³ All
their days their work is grief and pain; even

at night their minds do not rest. This too is
meaningless.
²⁴ A person can do nothing better than to
eat and drink and find satisfaction in their
own toil. This too, I see, is from the hand
of God, ²⁵ for without him, who can eat or
find enjoyment? ²⁶ To the person who pleases him, God gives wisdom, knowledge and
happiness, but to the sinner he gives the
task of gathering and storing up wealth to
hand it over to the one who pleases God.
This too is meaningless, a chasing after
the wind.

3 There is a time for everything,
and a season for every activity under
the heavens:

²   a time to be born and a time to die,
a time to plant and a time to uproot,
³   a time to kill and a time to heal,
a time to tear down and a time to
build,
⁴   a time to weep and a time to laugh,
a time to mourn and a time to dance,
⁵   a time to scatter stones and a time to
gather them,
a time to embrace and a time to
refrain from embracing,
⁶   a time to search and a time to give up,
a time to keep and a time to throw
away,
⁷   a time to tear and a time to mend,
a time to be silent and a time to speak,
⁸   a time to love and a time to hate,
a time for war and a time for peace.

▬ PSALM 107:17-22

¹⁷ Some became fools through their
rebellious ways
and suffered affliction because of their
iniquities.
¹⁸ They loathed all food
and drew near the gates of death.

[19] Then they cried to the LORD in their
     trouble,
   and he saved them from their distress.
[20] He sent out his word and healed them;
   he rescued them from the grave.
[21] Let them give thanks to the LORD for his
     unfailing love
   and his wonderful deeds for mankind.
[22] Let them sacrifice thank-offerings
   and tell of his works with songs of joy.

▬ PROVERBS 22:15–16

[15] Folly is bound up in the heart of a child,
   but the rod of discipline will drive it
     far away.

[16] One who oppresses the poor to increase
     his wealth
   and one who gives gifts to the rich –
     both come to poverty.

▬ 1 CORINTHIANS 16:1–24

16 Now about the collection for the
Lord's people: do what I told the
Galatian churches to do. [2] On the first day
of every week, each one of you should set
aside a sum of money in keeping with your
income, saving it up, so that when I come
no collections will have to be made. [3] Then,
when I arrive, I will give letters of introduction to the men you approve and send
them with your gift to Jerusalem. [4] If it
seems advisable for me to go also, they will
accompany me.

[5] After I go through Macedonia, I will
come to you – for I will be going through
Macedonia. [6] Perhaps I will stay with you
for a while, or even spend the winter, so that
you can help me on my journey, wherever I
go. [7] For I do not want to see you now and
make only a passing visit; I hope to spend

some time with you, if the Lord permits.
[8] But I will stay on at Ephesus until Pentecost, [9] because a great door for effective
work has opened to me, and there are many
who oppose me.

[10] When Timothy comes, see to it that he
has nothing to fear while he is with you,
for he is carrying on the work of the Lord,
just as I am. [11] No one, then, should treat
him with contempt. Send him on his way
in peace so that he may return to me. I am
expecting him along with the brothers.

[12] Now about our brother Apollos: I
strongly urged him to go to you with the
brothers. He was quite unwilling to go now,
but he will go when he has the opportunity.

[13] Be on your guard; stand firm in the
faith; be courageous; be strong. [14] Do everything in love.

[15] You know that the household of Stephanas were the first converts in Achaia, and
they have devoted themselves to the service
of the Lord's people. I urge you, brothers
and sisters, [16] to submit to such people and
to everyone who joins in the work and labours at it. [17] I was glad when Stephanas,
Fortunatus and Achaicus arrived, because
they have supplied what was lacking from
you. [18] For they refreshed my spirit and
yours also. Such men deserve recognition.

[19] The churches in the province of Asia
send you greetings. Aquila and Priscilla greet you warmly in the Lord, and so
does the church that meets at their house.
[20] All the brothers and sisters here send you
greetings. Greet one another with a holy
kiss.

[21] I, Paul, write this greeting in my own
hand.

[22] If anyone does not love the Lord, let
that person be cursed! Come, Lord!

[23] The grace of the Lord Jesus be with you.

[24] My love to all of you in Christ Jesus.
Amen.

'Don't Adjust Your Life'

'... there is nothing new under the sun.'
Ecclesiastes 1:9

It is surprising how many Christians have never read the book of Ecclesiastes. One woman told me that Ecclesiastes was the one book in the Bible she could not read. 'I am put off by all that pessimism and gloom', she explained. There is, however, a purpose behind this pessimism and gloom. Dr Cynddylan Jones, a famous Welsh preacher, put it like this: 'No Christian will be ready to open himself up to God until he has been gripped, as Ecclesiastes was gripped, by the emptiness and pointlessness of life. It is only when we see, and see clearly, that life is not to be found in the world that we will be ready to move closer toward God.'

It is interesting to observe that most philosophers, when they look reality in the face, come to the same conclusion as Solomon. Malcolm Muggeridge, for example, in the days before he found God, saw the world as 'an interminable soap opera.' Some graffiti found on the walls of Bath University was even more to the point: 'Do not adjust your life, the fault lies in reality.'

One of the reasons, I believe, that Solomon used such vivid illustrations is in order to break through our defensive attempts to avoid reality. Life 'under the sun', he has told us, can be boring, fleeting, repetitive, and empty. Life will never be meaningful 'under the sun' until we make contact with the One who is above the sun. Those who try to find meaning without living their lives to the Creator inevitably see life as an 'interminable soap opera'. Is it any wonder?

PRAYER

Gracious and loving Father, wean me off any idea I may have that life can be found 'under the sun'. Grant that I might be gripped by the truth that life, real life, is never found in the horizontal but in the vertical. In You. Amen.

FURTHER STUDY

Isa. 55:1-13; John 4:13-14
• What question does Isaiah ask?
• What remedy does he advocate?

September 14

■ ECCLESIASTES 3:9–6:12

⁹What do workers gain from their toil? ¹⁰I have seen the burden God has laid on the human race. ¹¹He has made everything beautiful in its time. He has also set eternity in the human heart; yet no one can fathom what God has done from beginning to end.

¹²I know that there is nothing better for people than to be happy and to do good while they live. ¹³That each of them may eat and drink, and find satisfaction in all their toil – this is the gift of God. ¹⁴I know that everything God does will endure for ever; nothing can be added to it and nothing taken from it. God does it so that people will fear him.

¹⁵Whatever is has already been,
and what will be has been before;
and God will call the past to account.

¹⁶And I saw something else under the sun:

In the place of judgment – wickedness
was there,
in the place of justice – wickedness
was there.

¹⁷I said to myself,

'God will bring into judgment
both the righteous and the wicked,
for there will be a time for every activity,
a time to judge every deed.'

¹⁸I also said to myself, 'As for humans, God tests them so that they may see that they are like the animals. ¹⁹Surely the fate of human beings is like that of the animals; the same fate awaits them both: As one dies, so dies the other. All have the same breath; humans have no advantage over animals. Everything is meaningless. ²⁰All go to the same place; all come from dust, and to dust all return. ²¹Who knows if the human spirit rises upward and if the spirit of the animal goes down into the earth?'

²²So I saw that there is nothing better for a person than to enjoy their work, because that is their lot. For who can bring them to see what will happen after them?

4 Again I looked and saw all the oppression that was taking place under the sun:

I saw the tears of the oppressed –

and they have no comforter;
power was on the side of their oppressors –
and they have no comforter.
²And I declared that the dead,
who had already died,
are happier than the living,
who are still alive.
³But better than both
is the one who has never been born,
who has not seen the evil
that is done under the sun.

⁴And I saw that all toil and all achievement spring from one person's envy of another. This too is meaningless, a chasing after the wind.

⁵Fools fold their hands
and ruin themselves.
⁶Better one handful with tranquillity
than two handfuls with toil
and chasing after the wind.

⁷Again I saw something meaningless under the sun:

⁸There was a man all alone;
he had neither son nor brother.
There was no end to his toil,
yet his eyes were not content with his
wealth.
'For whom am I toiling,' he asked,
'and why am I depriving myself of
enjoyment?'
This too is meaningless –
a miserable business!

⁹Two are better than one,
because they have a good return for
their labour:
¹⁰If either of them falls down,
one can help the other up.
But pity anyone who falls
and has no one to help them up.
¹¹Also, if two lie down together, they will
keep warm.

But how can one keep warm alone?
¹² Though one may be overpowered,
    two can defend themselves.
A cord of three strands is not quickly
    broken.

¹³ Better a poor but wise youth than an old but foolish king who no longer knows how to heed a warning. ¹⁴ The youth may have come from prison to the kingship, or he may have been born in poverty within his kingdom. ¹⁵ I saw that all who lived and walked under the sun followed the youth, the king's successor. ¹⁶ There was no end to all the people who were before them. But those who came later were not pleased with the successor. This too is meaningless, a chasing after the wind.

5 Guard your steps when you go to the house of God. Go near to listen rather than to offer the sacrifice of fools, who do not know that they do wrong.

² Do not be quick with your mouth,
    do not be hasty in your heart
    to utter anything before God.
God is in heaven
    and you are on earth,
    so let your words be few.
³ A dream comes when there are many cares,
    and many words mark the speech of a
        fool.

⁴ When you make a vow to God, do not delay to fulfil it. He has no pleasure in fools; fulfil your vow. ⁵ It is better not to make a vow than to make one and not fulfil it. ⁶ Do not let your mouth lead you into sin. And do not protest to the temple messenger, 'My vow was a mistake.' Why should God be angry at what you say and destroy the work of your hands? ⁷ Much dreaming and many words are meaningless. Therefore fear God.

⁸ If you see the poor oppressed in a district, and justice and rights denied, do not be surprised at such things; for one official is eyed by a higher one, and over them both are others higher still. ⁹ The increase from the land is taken by all; the king himself profits from the fields.

¹⁰ Whoever loves money never has enough;
    whoever loves wealth is never satisfied
        with their income.
This too is meaningless.

¹¹ As goods increase,
    so do those who consume them.
And what benefit are they to the owners
    except to feast their eyes on them?

¹² The sleep of a labourer is sweet,
    whether they eat little or much,
but as for the rich, their abundance
    permits them no sleep.

¹³ I have seen a grievous evil under the sun:

wealth hoarded to the harm of its
        owners,
¹⁴   or wealth lost through some
        misfortune,
so that when they have children
    there is nothing left for them to
        inherit.
¹⁵ Everyone comes naked from their
        mother's womb,
    and as everyone comes, so they depart.
They take nothing from their toil
    that they can carry in their hands.

¹⁶ This too is a grievous evil:

As everyone comes, so they depart,
    and what do they gain,
    since they toil for the wind?
¹⁷ All their days they eat in darkness,
    with great frustration, affliction and
        anger.

¹⁸ This is what I have observed to be good: that it is appropriate for a person to eat, to drink and to find satisfaction in their

toilsome labour under the sun during the few days of life God has given them – for this is their lot. ¹⁹ Moreover, when God gives someone wealth and possessions, and the ability to enjoy them, to accept their lot and be happy in their toil – this is a gift of God. ²⁰ They seldom reflect on the days of their life, because God keeps them occupied with gladness of heart.

6 I have seen another evil under the sun, and it weighs heavily on mankind: ² God gives some people wealth, possessions and honour, so that they lack nothing their hearts desire, but God does not grant them the ability to enjoy them, and strangers enjoy them instead. This is meaningless, a grievous evil.

³ A man may have a hundred children and live many years; yet no matter how long he lives, if he cannot enjoy his prosperity and does not receive proper burial, I say that a stillborn child is better off than he. ⁴ It comes without meaning, it departs in darkness, and in darkness its name is shrouded. ⁵ Though it never saw the sun or knew anything, it has more rest than does that man – ⁶ even if he lives a thousand years twice over but fails to enjoy his prosperity. Do not all go to the same place?

⁷ Everyone's toil is for their mouth,
  yet their appetite is never satisfied.
⁸ What advantage have the wise over fools?
  What do the poor gain
  by knowing how to conduct
    themselves before others?
⁹ Better what the eye sees
  than the roving of the appetite.
  This too is meaningless,
  a chasing after the wind.

¹⁰ Whatever exists has already been named,
  and what humanity is has been known;
  no one can contend
  with someone who is stronger.
¹¹ The more the words,
  the less the meaning,

and how does that profit anyone?

¹² For who knows what is good for a person in life, during the few and meaningless days they pass through like a shadow? Who can tell them what will happen under the sun after they are gone?

▬ PSALM 107:23–32

²³ Some went out on the sea in ships;
  they were merchants on the mighty
    waters.
²⁴ They saw the works of the LORD,
  his wonderful deeds in the deep.
²⁵ For he spoke and stirred up a tempest
  that lifted high the waves.
²⁶ They mounted up to the heavens and
    went down to the depths;
  in their peril their courage melted
    away.
²⁷ They reeled and staggered like drunkards;
  they were at their wits' end.
²⁸ Then they cried out to the LORD in their
    trouble,
  and he brought them out of their
    distress.
²⁹ He stilled the storm to a whisper;
  the waves of the sea were hushed.
³⁰ They were glad when it grew calm,
  and he guided them to their desired
    haven.
³¹ Let them give thanks to the LORD for his
    unfailing love
  and his wonderful deeds for mankind.
³² Let them exalt him in the assembly of the
    people
  and praise him in the council of the
    elders.

▬ PROVERBS 22:17-19

¹⁷ Pay attention and turn your ear to the
    sayings of the wise;

apply your heart to what I teach,
[18] for it is pleasing when you keep them in
your heart
and have all of them ready on your
lips.
[19] So that your trust may be in the LORD,
I teach you today, even you.

....

■ 2 CORINTHIANS 1:1-22

1 Paul, an apostle of Christ Jesus by the
will of God, and Timothy our brother,

To the church of God in Corinth, together
with all his holy people throughout Achaia:

[2] Grace and peace to you from God our
Father and the Lord Jesus Christ.

[3] Praise be to the God and Father of our
Lord Jesus Christ, the Father of compassion
and the God of all comfort, [4] who comforts
us in all our troubles, so that we can comfort those in any trouble with the comfort
we ourselves receive from God. [5] For just
as we share abundantly in the sufferings
of Christ, so also our comfort abounds
through Christ. [6] If we are distressed, it is
for your comfort and salvation; if we are
comforted, it is for your comfort, which
produces in you patient endurance of the
same sufferings we suffer. [7] And our hope
for you is firm, because we know that just
as you share in our sufferings, so also you
share in our comfort.

[8] We do not want you to be uninformed,
brothers and sisters, about the troubles we
experienced in the province of Asia. We
were under great pressure, far beyond our
ability to endure, so that we despaired of
life itself. [9] Indeed, we felt we had received
the sentence of death. But this happened
that we might not rely on ourselves but on
God, who raises the dead. [10] He has delivered us from such a deadly peril, and he
will deliver us again. On him we have set
our hope that he will continue to deliver
us, [11] as you help us by your prayers. Then
many will give thanks on our behalf for the
gracious favour granted us in answer to the
prayers of many.

[12] Now this is our boast: our conscience
testifies that we have conducted ourselves
in the world, and especially in our relations
with you, with integrity and godly sincerity. We have done so, relying not on worldly
wisdom but on God's grace. [13] For we do not
write to you anything you cannot read or
understand. And I hope that, [14] as you have
understood us in part, you will come to
understand fully that you can boast of us
just as we will boast of you in the day of the
Lord Jesus.

[15] Because I was confident of this, I wanted
to visit you first so that you might benefit
twice. [16] I wanted to visit you on my way to
Macedonia and to come back to you from
Macedonia, and then to let you send me on
my way to Judea. [17] Was I fickle when I intended to do this? Or do I make my plans in
a worldly manner so that in the same breath I
say both 'Yes, yes' and 'No, no'?

[18] But as surely as God is faithful, our
message to you is not 'Yes' and 'No'. [19] For
the Son of God, Jesus Christ, who was
preached among you by us – by me, Silas
and Timothy – was not 'Yes' and 'No', but in
him it has always been 'Yes'. [20] For no matter how many promises God has made, they
are 'Yes' in Christ. And so through him the
'Amen' is spoken by us to the glory of God.
[21] Now it is God who makes both us and you
stand firm in Christ. He anointed us, [22] set
his seal of ownership on us, and put his Spirit in our hearts as a deposit, guaranteeing
what is to come.

The Irreducible Minimum

'For no matter how many promises God has made, they are "Yes" in Christ.' **2 Corinthians 1:20**

It is time to face some very personal and pointed questions. Do you believe the Bible is the Word of God, divinely and uniquely inspired and reliable in all it affirms? Do you believe that Jesus Christ is the Son of God, born of a virgin, and the only way to God? Do you believe that He was crucified for your sins, raised again on the third day, and is now sitting on the right hand of God?

I could go on raising more questions, but the ones I have mentioned are what I consider to be the irreducible minimum of Christianity. In other words, these are the basic truths of the gospel, and if you don't take your stand on these truths, then you cannot call yourself a Christian.

This is what is meant by having your feet shod with the preparation of the gospel of peace – that you are ready to stand for the authority of Scripture, the deity of Christ, His substitutionary death, His resurrection from the dead, and His return to earth in power and glory.

Do you know where you stand on these matters? Are you sure of your spiritual position? How can you fight the enemy if you do not know what you believe? As I write, some of the daily newspapers here in Britain are calling on church leaders to give a spiritual lead. But many of our leaders do not have a high view of Scripture. How can they give a lead when they don't know where they are going? They don't know where they stand, and no one else knows either.

PRAYER

O Father, Your Word promises to be a lamp to our feet and a light for our path. Bring those whose feet are slipping and sliding in the faith back to an unshakeable confidence in Your gospel. In Jesus' name I ask it. Amen.

FURTHER STUDY

2 Pet. 1; Col. 2:7; 1 Cor. 3:11
- Why are we given so many great and precious promises?
- What should our foundation be?

September 15

ECCLESIASTES 7:1–9:10

7 A good name is better than fine perfume,

and the day of death better than the day of birth.
² It is better to go to a house of mourning than to go to a house of feasting, for death is the destiny of everyone;

the living should take this to heart.
³ Frustration is better than laughter,
     because a sad face is good for the
          heart.
⁴ The heart of the wise is in the house of
          mourning,
     but the heart of fools is in the house of
          pleasure.
⁵ It is better to heed the rebuke of a wise
          person
     than to listen to the song of fools.
⁶ Like the crackling of thorns under the
          pot,
     so is the laughter of fools.
          This too is meaningless.

⁷ Extortion turns a wise person into a fool,
     and a bribe corrupts the heart.

⁸ The end of a matter is better than its
          beginning,
     and patience is better than pride.
⁹ Do not be quickly provoked in your
          spirit,
     for anger resides in the lap of fools.

¹⁰ Do not say, 'Why were the old days better
          than these?'
     For it is not wise to ask such questions.

¹¹ Wisdom, like an inheritance, is a good
          thing
     and benefits those who see the sun.
¹² Wisdom is a shelter
     as money is a shelter,
     but the advantage of knowledge is this:
          Wisdom preserves those who have it.

¹³ Consider what God has done:

Who can straighten
     what he has made crooked?
¹⁴ When times are good, be happy;
     but when times are bad, consider this:
God has made the one
     as well as the other.

Therefore, no one can discover
     anything about their future.

¹⁵ In this meaningless life of mine I have
seen both of these:

the righteous perishing in their
     righteousness,
     and the wicked living long in their
          wickedness.
¹⁶ Do not be over-righteous,
     neither be overwise –
     why destroy yourself?
¹⁷ Do not be overwicked,
     and do not be a fool –
     why die before your time?
¹⁸ It is good to grasp the one
     and not let go of the other.
     Whoever fears God will avoid all
          extremes.

¹⁹ Wisdom makes one wise person more
     powerful
     than ten rulers in a city.

²⁰ Indeed, there is no one on earth who is
     righteous,
     no one who does what is right and
          never sins.

²¹ Do not pay attention to every word
          people say,
     or you may hear your servant cursing
          you –
²² for you know in your heart
     that many times you yourself have
          cursed others.

²³ All this I tested by wisdom and I said,

'I am determined to be wise' –
     but this was beyond me.
²⁴ Whatever exists is far off and most
          profound –
     who can discover it?
²⁵ So I turned my mind to understand,

to investigate and to search out
    wisdom and the scheme of things
and to understand the stupidity of
    wickedness
    and the madness of folly.

²⁶ I find more bitter than death
    the woman who is a snare,
whose heart is a trap
    and whose hands are chains.
The man who pleases God will escape
    her,
    but the sinner she will ensnare.

²⁷ 'Look,' says the Teacher, 'this is what I
have discovered:

    'Adding one thing to another to discover
        the scheme of things –
²⁸   while I was still searching
      but not finding –
I found one upright man among a
      thousand,
    but not one upright woman among
      them all.
²⁹ This only have I found:
    God created mankind upright,
    but they have gone in search of many
      schemes.'

8 Who is like the wise?
    Who knows the explanation of things?
A person's wisdom brightens their face
    and changes its hard appearance.

² Obey the king's command, I say, because you took an oath before God. ³ Do not
be in a hurry to leave the king's presence. Do
not stand up for a bad cause, for he will do
whatever he pleases. ⁴ Since a king's word is
supreme, who can say to him, 'What are you
doing?'

⁵ Whoever obeys his command will come
    to no harm,
    and the wise heart will know the
      proper time and procedure.

⁶ For there is a proper time and procedure
    for every matter,
    though a person may be weighed
      down by misery.

⁷ Since no one knows the future,
    who can tell someone else what is to
      come?
⁸ As no one has power over the wind to
    contain it,
    so no one has power over the time of
      their death.
As no one is discharged in time of war,
    so wickedness will not release those
      who practise it.

⁹ All this I saw, as I applied my mind to
everything done under the sun. There is
a time when a man lords it over others to
his own hurt. ¹⁰ Then too, I saw the wicked
buried – those who used to come and go
from the holy place and receive praise in
the city where they did this. This too is
meaningless.

¹¹ When the sentence for a crime is not
quickly carried out, people's hearts are
filled with schemes to do wrong. ¹² Although
a wicked person who commits a hundred
crimes may live a long time, I know that it
will go better with those who fear God, who
are reverent before him. ¹³ Yet because the
wicked do not fear God, it will not go well
with them, and their days will not lengthen
like a shadow.

¹⁴ There is something else meaningless
that occurs on earth: the righteous who get
what the wicked deserve, and the wicked
who get what the righteous deserve. This
too, I say, is meaningless. ¹⁵ So I commend
the enjoyment of life, because there is nothing better for a person under the sun than
to eat and drink and be glad. Then joy will
accompany them in their toil all the days of
the life God has given them under the sun.

¹⁶ When I applied my mind to know wisdom and to observe the labour that is done

on earth – people getting no sleep day or night – ¹⁷ then I saw all that God has done. No one can comprehend what goes on under the sun. Despite all their efforts to search it out, no one can discover its meaning. Even if the wise claim they know, they cannot really comprehend it.

9 So I reflected on all this and concluded that the righteous and the wise and what they do are in God's hands, but no one knows whether love or hate awaits them. ² All share a common destiny – the righteous and the wicked, the good and the bad, the clean and the unclean, those who offer sacrifices and those who do not.

As it is with the good,
  so with the sinful;
as it is with those who take oaths,
  so with those who are afraid to take
    them.

³ This is the evil in everything that happens under the sun: The same destiny overtakes all. The hearts of people, moreover, are full of evil and there is madness in their hearts while they live, and afterwards they join the dead. ⁴ Anyone who is among the living has hope – even a live dog is better off than a dead lion!

⁵ For the living know that they will die,
  but the dead know nothing;
they have no further reward,
  and even their name is forgotten.
⁶ Their love, their hate
  and their jealousy have long since
    vanished;
never again will they have a part
  in anything that happens under the
    sun.

⁷ Go, eat your food with gladness, and drink your wine with a joyful heart, for God has already approved what you do. ⁸ Always be clothed in white, and always anoint your head with oil. ⁹ Enjoy life with your wife, whom you love, all the days of this meaningless life that God has given you under the sun – all your meaningless days. For this is your lot in life and in your toilsome labour under the sun. ¹⁰ Whatever your hand finds to do, do it with all your might, for in the realm of the dead, where you are going, there is neither working nor planning nor knowledge nor wisdom.

■ PSALM 107:33-38

³³ He turned rivers into a desert,
  flowing springs into thirsty ground,
³⁴ and fruitful land into a salt waste,
  because of the wickedness of those
    who lived there.
³⁵ He turned the desert into pools of water
  and the parched ground into flowing
    springs;
³⁶ there he brought the hungry to live,
  and they founded a city where they
    could settle.
³⁷ They sowed fields and planted vineyards
  that yielded a fruitful harvest;
³⁸ he blessed them, and their numbers
    greatly increased,
  and he did not let their herds diminish.

■ PROVERBS 22:20-21

²⁰ Have I not written thirty sayings for you,
  sayings of counsel and knowledge,
²¹ teaching you to be honest and to speak
    the truth,
  so that you bring back truthful reports
    to those you serve?

■ 2 CORINTHIANS 1:23–3:3

²³ I call God as my witness – and I stake my life on it – that it was in order to spare

you that I did not return to Corinth. [24]Not that we lord it over your faith, but we work with you for your joy, because it is by faith you stand firm. [1]So I made up my mind that I would not make another painful visit to you. [2]For if I grieve you, who is left to make me glad but you whom I have grieved? [3]I wrote as I did, so that when I came I would not be distressed by those who should have made me rejoice. I had confidence in all of you, that you would all share my joy. [4]For I wrote to you out of great distress and anguish of heart and with many tears, not to grieve you but to let you know the depth of my love for you.

[5]If anyone has caused grief, he has not so much grieved me as he has grieved all of you to some extent – not to put it too severely. [6]The punishment inflicted on him by the majority is sufficient. [7]Now instead, you ought to forgive and comfort him, so that he will not be overwhelmed by excessive sorrow. [8]I urge you, therefore, to reaffirm your love for him. [9]Another reason I wrote to you was to see if you would stand the test and be obedient in everything. [10]Anyone you forgive, I also forgive. And what I have forgiven – if there was anything to forgive – I have forgiven in the sight of Christ for your sake, [11]in order that Satan might not outwit

us. For we are not unaware of his schemes.

[12]Now when I went to Troas to preach the gospel of Christ and found that the Lord had opened a door for me, [13]I still had no peace of mind, because I did not find my brother Titus there. So I said goodbye to them and went on to Macedonia.

[14]But thanks be to God, who always leads us as captives in Christ's triumphal procession and uses us to spread the aroma of the knowledge of him everywhere. [15]For we are to God the pleasing aroma of Christ among those who are being saved and those who are perishing. [16]To the one we are an aroma that brings death; to the other, an aroma that brings life. And who is equal to such a task? [17]Unlike so many, we do not peddle the word of God for profit. On the contrary, in Christ we speak before God with sincerity, as those sent from God.

[3] Are we beginning to commend ourselves again? Or do we need, like some people, letters of recommendation to you or from you? [2]You yourselves are our letter, written on our hearts, known and read by everyone. [3]You show that you are a letter from Christ, the result of our ministry, written not with ink but with the Spirit of the living God, not on tablets of stone but on tablets of human hearts.

Blasphemous Thoughts

'... in order that Satan might not outwit us. For we are not unaware of his schemes.' **2 Corinthians 2:11**

The form of satanic attack that is possibly the most difficult of all to endure is having blasphemous thoughts. Dr Martyn Lloyd-Jones said on this: 'The devil has often plagued some of the noblest saints with blasphemous thoughts - blasphemous thoughts about God, blasphemous thoughts about the Lord Jesus Christ, and blasphemous thoughts about the Holy Spirit.'

How difficult such thoughts can be. Sometimes the Devil hurls the most awful words and phrases into the mind; but again, it is important to see that these do not arise from within the heart of the believer - they come from the Devil, who is trying to confuse and demoralise you.

How grateful we should be to the saints down the ages who have recorded these satanic attacks, for otherwise we would be tempted when experiencing them to believe that they have never happened to anyone else. Many masters of the spiritual life have described these satanic attacks in great detail - John Bunyan and Martin Luther being the two best examples.

But how do we deal with these 'flaming arrows' of Satan? What action must we take to repel these attacks? There is only one answer - we must take and use the shield of faith. Faith alone enables us to meet and overcome this particular type of attack. What we must not do is expose our chests, expecting the breastplate of righteousness to deal with this problem. Each piece of the equipment is designed to deal with a particular attack. And the answer here is - faith.

PRAYER

Heavenly Father, I understand the problem - now show me how to apply the answer. The answer, I see, is faith. But how does it work? How can I apply it? Teach me more. In Jesus' name. Amen.

FURTHER STUDY

2 Cor. 10:1-5; Matt. 22:37-38; Eph. 1:22-23; James 4:7-8
• In what ways does Satan attack the mind?
• What is the scriptural antidote?

September 16

▪ ECCLESIASTES 9:11–12:14

[11] I have seen something else under the sun:

The race is not to the swift
    or the battle to the strong,
nor does food come to the wise
    or wealth to the brilliant
    or favour to the learned;
but time and chance happen to them all.

[12] Moreover, no one knows when their hour will come:

As fish are caught in a cruel net,
    or birds are taken in a snare,

so people are trapped by evil times
    that fall unexpectedly upon them.

[13] I also saw under the sun this example of wisdom that greatly impressed me: [14] there was once a small city with only a few people in it. And a powerful king came against it, surrounded it and built huge siege works against it. [15] Now there lived in that city a man poor but wise, and he saved the city by his wisdom. But nobody remembered that poor man. [16] So I said, 'Wisdom is better than strength.' But the poor man's wisdom is despised, and his words are no longer heeded.

[17] The quiet words of the wise are more to be heeded

than the shouts of a ruler of fools.
¹⁸ Wisdom is better than weapons of war,
    but one sinner destroys much good.

10

As dead flies give perfume a bad
    smell,
    so a little folly outweighs wisdom and
      honour.
² The heart of the wise inclines to the
    right,
    but the heart of the fool to the left.
³ Even as fools walk along the road,
    they lack sense
    and show everyone how stupid they
      are.
⁴ If a ruler's anger rises against you,
    do not leave your post;
    calmness can lay great offences to
      rest.

⁵ There is an evil I have seen under the sun,
    the sort of error that arises from a
      ruler:
⁶ fools are put in many high positions,
    while the rich occupy the low ones.
⁷ I have seen slaves on horseback,
    while princes go on foot like slaves.

⁸ Whoever digs a pit may fall into it;
    whoever breaks through a wall may be
      bitten by a snake.
⁹ Whoever quarries stones may be injured
    by them;
    whoever splits logs may be
      endangered by them.

¹⁰ If the axe is dull
    and its edge unsharpened,
    more strength is needed,
    but skill will bring success.
¹¹ If a snake bites before it is charmed,
    the charmer receives no fee.

¹² Words from the mouth of the wise are
    gracious,

but fools are consumed by their own
    lips.
¹³ At the beginning their words are folly;
    at the end they are wicked madness –
¹⁴   and fools multiply words.

No one knows what is coming –
    who can tell someone else what will
      happen after them?

¹⁵ The toil of fools wearies them;
    they do not know the way to town.

¹⁶ Woe to the land whose king was a
    servant
    and whose princes feast in the
      morning.
¹⁷ Blessed is the land whose king is of noble
    birth
    and whose princes eat at a proper
      time –
    for strength and not for drunkenness.

¹⁸ Through laziness, the rafters sag;
    because of idle hands, the house leaks.

¹⁹ A feast is made for laughter,
    wine makes life merry,
    and money is the answer for everything.

²⁰ Do not revile the king even in your
    thoughts,
    or curse the rich in your bedroom,
    because a bird in the sky may carry your
      words,
    and a bird on the wing may report
      what you say.

11

Ship your grain across the sea;
    after many days you may receive a
      return.
² Invest in seven ventures, yes, in eight;
    you do not know what disaster may
      come upon the land.

³ If clouds are full of water,
    they pour rain on the earth.

Whether a tree falls to the south or to the
north,
in the place where it falls, there it will
lie.
[4] Whoever watches the wind will not
plant;
whoever looks at the clouds will not
reap.

[5] As you do not know the path of the wind,
or how the body is formed in a
mother's womb,
so you cannot understand the work of
God,
the Maker of all things.

[6] Sow your seed in the morning,
and at evening let your hands not be
idle,
for you do not know which will succeed,
whether this or that,
or whether both will do equally well.
[7] Light is sweet,
and it pleases the eyes to see the sun.
[8] However many years anyone may live,
let them enjoy them all.
But let them remember the days of
darkness,
for there will be many.
Everything to come is meaningless.

[9] You who are young, be happy while you
are young,
and let your heart give you joy in the
days of your youth.
Follow the ways of your heart
and whatever your eyes see,
but know that for all these things
God will bring you into judgment.
[10] So then, banish anxiety from your heart
and cast off the troubles of your body,
for youth and vigour are meaningless.

12 Remember your Creator
in the days of your youth,
before the days of trouble come

and the years approach when you will
say,
'I find no pleasure in them' –
[2] before the sun and the light
and the moon and the stars grow dark,
and the clouds return after the rain;
[3] when the keepers of the house tremble,
and the strong men stoop,
when the grinders cease because they
are few,
and those looking through the
windows grow dim;
[4] when the doors to the street are closed
and the sound of grinding fades;
when people rise up at the sound of
birds,
but all their songs grow faint;
[5] when people are afraid of heights
and of dangers in the streets;
when the almond tree blossoms
and the grasshopper drags itself along
and desire no longer is stirred.
Then people go to their eternal home
and mourners go about the streets.

[6] Remember him – before the silver cord
is severed,
and the golden bowl is broken;
before the pitcher is shattered at the
spring,
and the wheel broken at the well,
[7] and the dust returns to the ground it
came from,
and the spirit returns to God who
gave it.

[8] 'Meaningless! Meaningless!' says the
Teacher.
'Everything is meaningless!'

[9] Not only was the Teacher wise, but also
he imparted knowledge to the people. He
pondered and searched out and set in order
many proverbs. [10] The Teacher searched to
find just the right words, and what he wrote
was upright and true.

¹¹The words of the wise are like goads, their collected sayings like firmly embedded nails – given by one shepherd. ¹²Be warned, my son, of anything in addition to them.

Of making many books there is no end, and much study wearies the body.

¹³Now all has been heard;
here is the conclusion of the matter:
Fear God and keep his commandments,
for this is the duty of all mankind.
¹⁴For God will bring every deed into judgment,
including every hidden thing,
whether it is good or evil.

PSALM 107:39-43

³⁹Then their numbers decreased, and they were humbled
by oppression, calamity and sorrow;
⁴⁰he who pours contempt on nobles
made them wander in a trackless waste.
⁴¹But he lifted the needy out of their affliction
and increased their families like flocks.
⁴²The upright see and rejoice,
but all the wicked shut their mouths.

⁴³Let the one who is wise heed these things
and ponder the loving deeds of the LORD.

PROVERBS 22:22-23

²²Do not exploit the poor because they are poor
and do not crush the needy in court,
²³for the LORD will take up their case
and will exact life for life.

2 CORINTHIANS 3:4–4:6

⁴Such confidence we have through Christ before God. ⁵Not that we are competent in ourselves to claim anything for ourselves, but our competence comes from God. ⁶He has made us competent as ministers of a new covenant – not of the letter but of the Spirit; for the letter kills, but the Spirit gives life.

⁷Now if the ministry that brought death, which was engraved in letters on stone, came with glory, so that the Israelites could not look steadily at the face of Moses because of its glory, transitory though it was, ⁸will not the ministry of the Spirit be even more glorious? ⁹If the ministry that brought condemnation was glorious, how much more glorious is the ministry that brings righteousness! ¹⁰For what was glorious has no glory now in comparison with the surpassing glory. ¹¹And if what was transitory came with glory, how much greater is the glory of that which lasts!

¹²Therefore, since we have such a hope, we are very bold. ¹³We are not like Moses, who would put a veil over his face to prevent the Israelites from seeing the end of what was passing away. ¹⁴But their minds were made dull, for to this day the same veil remains when the old covenant is read. It has not been removed, because only in Christ is it taken away. ¹⁵Even to this day when Moses is read, a veil covers their hearts. ¹⁶But whenever anyone turns to the Lord, the veil is taken away. ¹⁷Now the Lord is the Spirit, and where the Spirit of the Lord is, there is freedom. ¹⁸And we all, who with unveiled faces contemplate the Lord's glory, are being transformed into his image with ever-increasing glory, which comes from the Lord, who is the Spirit.

4 Therefore, since through God's mercy we have this ministry, we do not lose heart. ²Rather, we have renounced secret and shameful ways; we do not use deception, nor do we distort the word of God. On the contrary, by setting forth the truth

plainly we commend ourselves to everyone's conscience in the sight of God. ³And even if our gospel is veiled, it is veiled to those who are perishing. ⁴The god of this age has blinded the minds of unbelievers, so that they cannot see the light of the gospel that displays the glory of Christ, who is the image of God. ⁵For what we preach is not ourselves, but Jesus Christ as Lord, and ourselves as your servants for Jesus' sake. ⁶For God, who said, 'Let light shine out of darkness,' made his light shine in our hearts to give us the light of the knowledge of God's glory displayed in the face of Christ.

Full Surrender

'Now the Lord is the Spirit, and where the Spirit of the Lord is, there is freedom.' **2 Corinthians 3:17**

M odern approaches to the subconscious can do no more than throw the pale light of information into it. The message of the Bible, however, is not merely information but transformation: 'Where the Spirit of the Lord is, there is freedom.' So if the Spirit of the Lord is within us, there is freedom from the conflict between the conscious and the subconscious.

If such a freedom is possible, why do so many live out their lives in conflict? Because they have never appropriated the power and presence of the Spirit available to them and channelled Him into the deeper regions of their personality through self-surrender. God, Christ, or the Holy Spirit will never barge their way into any area of the personality. They come in when we put up the white flag of surrender and, by a conscious act, agree to their residing and presiding within us.

It's surprising how many Christians say with the conscious mind, 'I surrender all', and yet with the subconscious say, 'I want some areas for myself'. We must take ourselves in hand and decide whether or not we want the Holy Spirit simply to evangelise certain areas of our personality, or whether we want Him to occupy our entire being. If you haven't properly settled this issue, then ask yourself today, 'Am I just kidding myself when I say I want to be filled with God? Is there a part of me that says, "Come in", while another part of me says at the same time, "Keep out"?' The Holy Spirit only comes into the areas where He is freely admitted.

PRAYER

O Father, I think You have put Your finger right on my problem. Perhaps the reason I have never felt the Holy Spirit's full control is because deep down I never wanted it. But now I do. My whole being cries out for its rightful Lord. I surrender now. Amen.

FURTHER STUDY

James 4; Gal. 2:20; Rom. 6:6; 2 Tim. 2:11
• Where does strife come from?
• What was Paul's testimony?

September 17

▪ Song of Songs 1:1–4:16

1 Solomon's Song of Songs.

She[a]

² Let him kiss me with the kisses of his
mouth –
for your love is more delightful than
wine.
³ Pleasing is the fragrance of your
perfumes;
your name is like perfume poured out.
No wonder the young women love you!
⁴ Take me away with you – let us hurry!
Let the king bring me into his
chambers.

Friends

We rejoice and delight in you;
we will praise your love more than
wine.

She

How right they are to adore you!

⁵ Dark am I, yet lovely,
daughters of Jerusalem,
dark like the tents of Kedar,
like the tent curtains of Solomon.
⁶ Do not stare at me because I am dark,
because I am darkened by the sun.
My mother's sons were angry with me
and made me take care of the
vineyards;
my own vineyard I had to neglect.
⁷ Tell me, you whom I love,
where you graze your flock
and where you rest your sheep at
midday.
Why should I be like a veiled woman
beside the flocks of your friends?

Friends

⁸ If you do not know, most beautiful of
women,
follow the tracks of the sheep
and graze your young goats
by the tents of the shepherds.

He

⁹ I liken you, my darling, to a mare
among Pharaoh's chariot horses.
¹⁰ Your cheeks are beautiful with earrings,
your neck with strings of jewels.
¹¹ We will make you earrings of gold,
studded with silver.

She

¹² While the king was at his table,
my perfume spread its fragrance.
¹³ My beloved is to me a sachet of myrrh
resting between my breasts.
¹⁴ My beloved is to me a cluster of henna
blossoms
from the vineyards of En Gedi.

He

¹⁵ How beautiful you are, my darling!
Oh, how beautiful!
Your eyes are doves.

She

¹⁶ How handsome you are, my beloved!
Oh, how charming!
And our bed is verdant.

He

¹⁷ The beams of our house are cedars;
our rafters are firs.

---

[a] The main male and female speakers (identified primarily on the basis of the gender of the relevant Hebrew forms) are indicated by the captions *He* and *She* respectively. The words of others are marked *Friends*. In some instances, the divisions and their captions are debatable.

She

2 I am a rose of Sharon,
   a lily of the valleys.

He

[2] Like a lily among thorns
   is my darling among the young
      women.

She

[3] Like an apple tree among the trees of the
      forest
   is my beloved among the young men.
   I delight to sit in his shade,
      and his fruit is sweet to my taste.
[4] Let him lead me to the banquet hall,
   and let his banner over me be love.
[5] Strengthen me with raisins,
      refresh me with apples,
   for I am faint with love.
[6] His left arm is under my head,
   and his right arm embraces me.
[7] Daughters of Jerusalem, I charge you
      by the gazelles and by the does of the
         field:
   Do not arouse or awaken love
      until it so desires.

[8] Listen! My beloved!
   Look! Here he comes,
   leaping across the mountains,
      bounding over the hills.
[9] My beloved is like a gazelle or a young
      stag.
   Look! There he stands behind our wall,
   gazing through the windows,
      peering through the lattice.
[10] My beloved spoke and said to me,
   'Arise, my darling,
      my beautiful one, come with me.
[11] See! The winter is past;
      the rains are over and gone.
[12] Flowers appear on the earth;
      the season of singing has come,
   the cooing of doves
      is heard in our land.
[13] The fig-tree forms its early fruit;

the blossoming vines spread their
   fragrance.
Arise, come, my darling;
   my beautiful one, come with me.'

He

[14] My dove in the clefts of the rock,
   in the hiding-places on the
      mountainside,
   show me your face,
   let me hear your voice;
   for your voice is sweet,
      and your face is lovely.
[15] Catch for us the foxes,
   the little foxes
   that ruin the vineyards,
      our vineyards that are in bloom.

She

[16] My beloved is mine and I am his;
   he browses among the lilies.
[17] Until the day breaks
   and the shadows flee,
   turn, my beloved,
      and be like a gazelle
   or like a young stag
      on the rugged hills.

3 All night long on my bed
   I looked for the one my heart loves;
   I looked for him but did not find him.
[2] I will get up now and go about the city,
      through its streets and squares;
   I will search for the one my heart loves.
      So I looked for him but did not find him.
[3] The watchmen found me
      as they made their rounds in the city.
   'Have you seen the one my heart loves?'
[4] Scarcely had I passed them
      when I found the one my heart loves.
   I held him and would not let him go
      till I had brought him to my mother's
         house,
      to the room of the one who conceived
         me.
[5] Daughters of Jerusalem, I charge you

by the gazelles and by the does of the
    field:
do not arouse or awaken love
    until it so desires.

⁶ Who is this coming up from the
    wilderness
    like a column of smoke,
perfumed with myrrh and incense
    made from all the spices of the
    merchant?
⁷ Look! It is Solomon's carriage,
    escorted by sixty warriors,
    the noblest of Israel,
⁸ all of them wearing the sword,
    all experienced in battle,
each with his sword at his side,
    prepared for the terrors of the night.
⁹ King Solomon made for himself the
    carriage;
    he made it of wood from Lebanon.
¹⁰ Its posts he made of silver,
    its base of gold.
Its seat was upholstered with purple,
    its interior inlaid with love.
Daughters of Jerusalem, ¹¹ come out,
    and look, you daughters of Zion.
Look on King Solomon wearing a crown,
    the crown with which his mother
    crowned him
on the day of his wedding,
    the day his heart rejoiced.

He

4 How beautiful you are, my darling!
    Oh, how beautiful!
    Your eyes behind your veil are doves.
    Your hair is like a flock of goats
    descending from the hills of Gilead.
² Your teeth are like a flock of sheep just
    shorn,
    coming up from the washing.
Each has its twin;
    not one of them is alone.
³ Your lips are like a scarlet ribbon;
    your mouth is lovely.

Your temples behind your veil
    are like the halves of a pomegranate.
⁴ Your neck is like the tower of David,
    built with courses of stone;
on it hang a thousand shields,
    all of them shields of warriors.
⁵ Your breasts are like two fawns,
    like twin fawns of a gazelle
    that browse among the lilies.
⁶ Until the day breaks
    and the shadows flee,
I will go to the mountain of myrrh
    and to the hill of incense.
⁷ You are altogether beautiful, my darling;
    there is no flaw in you.

⁸ Come with me from Lebanon, my bride,
    come with me from Lebanon.
Descend from the crest of Amana,
    from the top of Senir, the summit of
    Hermon,
from the lions' dens
    and the mountain haunts of leopards.
⁹ You have stolen my heart, my sister, my
    bride;
    you have stolen my heart
with one glance of your eyes,
    with one jewel of your necklace.
¹⁰ How delightful is your love, my sister,
    my bride!
How much more pleasing is your love
    than wine,
and the fragrance of your perfume
    more than any spice!
¹¹ Your lips drop sweetness as the
    honeycomb, my bride;
    milk and honey are under your tongue.
The fragrance of your garments
    is like the fragrance of Lebanon.
¹² You are a garden locked up, my sister, my
    bride;
    you are a spring enclosed, a sealed
    fountain.
¹³ Your plants are an orchard of
    pomegranates
    with choice fruits,

with henna and nard,
14 nard and saffron,
   calamus and cinnamon,
   with every kind of incense tree,
   with myrrh and aloes
   and all the finest spices.
15 You are a garden fountain,
   a well of flowing water
   streaming down from Lebanon.

She
16 Awake, north wind,
   and come, south wind!
Blow on my garden,
   that its fragrance may spread
      everywhere.
Let my beloved come into his garden
   and taste its choice fruits.

▬ PSALM 108:1-6

1 My heart, O God, is steadfast;
   I will sing and make music with all my
      soul.
2 Awake, harp and lyre!
   I will awaken the dawn.
3 I will praise you, LORD, among the nations;
   I will sing of you among the peoples.
4 For great is your love, higher than the
      heavens;
   your faithfulness reaches to the skies.
5 Be exalted, O God, above the heavens;
   let your glory be over all the earth.

6 Save us and help us with your right hand,
   that those you love may be delivered.

▬ PROVERBS 22:24-25

24 Do not make friends with a
      hot-tempered person,
   do not associate with one easily angered,
25 or you may learn their ways
   and get yourself ensnared.

▬ 2 CORINTHIANS 4:7–5:10

7 But we have this treasure in jars of clay to show that this all-surpassing power is from God and not from us. 8 We are hard pressed on every side, but not crushed; perplexed, but not in despair; 9 persecuted, but not abandoned; struck down, but not destroyed. 10 We always carry around in our body the death of Jesus, so that the life of Jesus may also be revealed in our body. 11 For we who are alive are always being given over to death for Jesus' sake, so that his life may also be revealed in our mortal body. 12 So then, death is at work in us, but life is at work in you.

13 It is written: 'I believed; therefore I have spoken.' Since we have that same spirit of faith, we also believe and therefore speak, 14 because we know that the one who raised the Lord Jesus from the dead will also raise us with Jesus and present us with you to himself. 15 All this is for your benefit, so that the grace that is reaching more and more people may cause thanksgiving to overflow to the glory of God.

16 Therefore we do not lose heart. Though outwardly we are wasting away, yet inwardly we are being renewed day by day. 17 For our light and momentary troubles are achieving for us an eternal glory that far outweighs them all. 18 So we fix our eyes not on what is seen, but on what is unseen, since what is seen is temporary, but what is unseen is eternal.

5 For we know that if the earthly tent we live in is destroyed, we have a building from God, an eternal house in heaven, not built by human hands. 2 Meanwhile we groan, longing to be clothed instead with our heavenly dwelling, 3 because when we are clothed, we will not be found naked. 4 For while we are in this tent, we groan and are burdened, because we do not wish to be unclothed but to be clothed instead with our heavenly dwelling, so that what is mortal may be swallowed up by life. 5 Now the one who has fashioned us for this very

purpose is God, who has given us the Spirit as a deposit, guaranteeing what is to come.

[6] Therefore we are always confident and know that as long as we are at home in the body we are away from the Lord. [7] For we live by faith, not by sight. [8] We are confident, I say, and would prefer to be away from the body and at home with the Lord. [9] So we make it our goal to please him, whether we are at home in the body or away from it. [10] For we must all appear before the judgment seat of Christ, so that each of us may receive what is due to us for the things done while in the body, whether good or bad.

Overcoming Frustration

'We are hard pressed on every side, but not crushed; perplexed, but not in despair ... Therefore we do not lose heart. Thought outwardly we are wasting away, yet inwardly we are being renewed day by day.'
2 Corinthians 4:8,16

Learn how to deal with frustration. Time and time again, I have sat with people who have said: 'What's wrong with me? I feel so low spiritually. I am not involved in sin. Why does my Christian life feel so stale?' On many of these occasions, I have observed that the problem contributing to their feelings of spiritual staleness was an inability to cope with frustration.

One of the most radiant Christians I have ever met was a seed salesman in West Wales whose name was Mordecai Price. Crippled in both his lower limbs by poliomyelitis, he drove a hand-controlled car and would make his way to outlying farms to sell seed to the farmers. Sometimes it would take him an hour just to get out of his car and open a farm gate - but he persevered nevertheless.

One day I said to him: 'Don't you get frustrated by your condition? How do you keep going like this when many others would have settled for a lifetime of invalidism and inactivity?' My friend has gone to be with the Lord now, but his reply has lived on in my heart for over thirty years, 'I take every project prisoner to make it obey Christ - even the project of poliomyelitis'. He had learned how to make his frustration fruitful. When you and I can learn how to turn the ugly into the beautiful, and the evil into the good, then frustration will never get a hold on us. The secret of living is the secret of using. Learn this, and you will never be frustrated again.

PRAYER

O Father, teach me how to turn the ugly into the beautiful, the evil into the good, and take every project prisoner for Christ. I ask this for Your own dear name's sake. Amen.

FURTHER STUDY

2 Cor. 4:1-10; 10:5; Psa. 44:5; Rom. 8:35-37
• What was Paul's testimony?
• What does it mean to be 'more than conquerors'?

September 18

■ SONG OF SONGS 5:1–8:14

He

5 I have come into my garden, my sister,
   my bride;
 I have gathered my myrrh with my
   spice.
 I have eaten my honeycomb and my
   honey;
 I have drunk my wine and my milk.

Friends

 Eat, friends, and drink;
   drink your fill of love.

She

2 I slept but my heart was awake.
 Listen! My beloved is knocking:
 'Open to me, my sister, my darling,
   my dove, my flawless one.
 My head is drenched with dew,
   my hair with the dampness of the
   night.'
3 I have taken off my robe –
   must I put it on again?
 I have washed my feet –
   must I soil them again?
4 My beloved thrust his hand through the
   latch-opening;
 my heart began to pound for him.
5 I arose to open for my beloved,
   and my hands dripped with myrrh,
 my fingers with flowing myrrh,
   on the handles of the bolt.
6 I opened for my beloved,
   but my beloved had left; he was gone.
 My heart sank at his departure.
 I looked for him but did not find him.
 I called him but he did not answer.
7 The watchmen found me
   as they made their rounds in the city.

They beat me, they bruised me;
   they took away my cloak,
 those watchmen of the walls!
8 Daughters of Jerusalem, I charge you –
 if you find my beloved,
 what will you tell him?
 Tell him I am faint with love.

Friends

9 How is your beloved better than others,
   most beautiful of women?
 How is your beloved better than others,
   that you so charge us?

She

10 My beloved is radiant and ruddy,
   outstanding among ten thousand.
11 His head is purest gold;
   his hair is wavy
   and black as a raven.
12 His eyes are like doves
   by the water streams,
 washed in milk,
   mounted like jewels.
13 His cheeks are like beds of spice
   yielding perfume.
 His lips are like lilies
   dripping with myrrh.
14 His arms are rods of gold
   set with topaz.
 His body is like polished ivory
   decorated with lapis lazuli.
15 His legs are pillars of marble
   set on bases of pure gold.
 His appearance is like Lebanon,
   choice as its cedars.
16 His mouth is sweetness itself;
   he is altogether lovely.
 This is my beloved, this is my friend,
   daughters of Jerusalem.

Friends

6 Where has your beloved gone,
   most beautiful of women?
Which way did your beloved turn,
   that we may look for him with you?

She

²My beloved has gone down to his garden,
   to the beds of spices,
to browse in the gardens
   and to gather lilies.
³I am my beloved's and my beloved is
      mine;
   he browses among the lilies.

He

⁴You are as beautiful as Tirzah, my
      darling,
   as lovely as Jerusalem,
   as majestic as troops with banners.
⁵Turn your eyes from me;
   they overwhelm me.
Your hair is like a flock of goats
   descending from Gilead.
⁶Your teeth are like a flock of sheep
   coming up from the washing.
Each has its twin,
   not one of them is missing.
⁷Your temples behind your veil
   are like the halves of a pomegranate.
⁸Sixty queens there may be,
   and eighty concubines,
   and virgins beyond number;
⁹but my dove, my perfect one, is unique,
   the only daughter of her mother,
   the favourite of the one who bore her.
The young women saw her and called her
      blessed;
   the queens and concubines praised
      her.

Friends

¹⁰Who is this that appears like the dawn,
   fair as the moon, bright as the sun,
   majestic as the stars in procession?

He

¹¹I went down to the grove of nut trees
   to look at the new growth in the valley,
to see if the vines had budded
   or the pomegranates were in bloom.
¹²Before I realised it,
   my desire set me among the royal
      chariots of my people.

Friends

¹³Come back, come back, O Shulammite;
   come back, come back, that we may
      gaze on you!

He

Why would you gaze on the Shulammite
   as on the dance of Mahanaim?

7 How beautiful your sandalled feet,
   O prince's daughter!
Your graceful legs are like jewels,
   the work of an artist's hands.
²Your navel is a rounded goblet
   that never lacks blended wine.
Your waist is a mound of wheat
   encircled by lilies.
³Your breasts are like two fawns,
   like twin fawns of a gazelle.
⁴Your neck is like an ivory tower.
Your eyes are the pools of Heshbon
   by the gate of Bath Rabbim.
Your nose is like the tower of Lebanon
   looking towards Damascus.
⁵Your head crowns you like Mount
      Carmel.
Your hair is like royal tapestry;
   the king is held captive by its tresses.
⁶How beautiful you are and how pleasing,
   my love, with your delights!
⁷Your stature is like that of the palm,
   and your breasts like clusters of fruit.
⁸I said, 'I will climb the palm tree;
   I will take hold of its fruit.'
May your breasts be like clusters of
      grapes on the vine,
   the fragrance of your breath like apples,
⁹   and your mouth like the best wine.

She

May the wine go straight to my beloved,
   flowing gently over lips and teeth.
¹⁰ I belong to my beloved,
   and his desire is for me.
¹¹ Come, my beloved, let us go to the
     countryside,
   let us spend the night in the villages.
¹² Let us go early to the vineyards
   to see if the vines have budded,
   if their blossoms have opened,
   and if the pomegranates are in
     bloom –
   there I will give you my love.
¹³ The mandrakes send out their fragrance,
   and at our door is every delicacy,
   both new and old,
   that I have stored up for you, my
     beloved.

8 If only you were to me like a brother,
   who was nursed at my mother's
   breasts!
Then, if I found you outside,
   I would kiss you,
   and no one would despise me.
² I would lead you
   and bring you to my mother's house –
   she who has taught me.
I would give you spiced wine to drink,
   the nectar of my pomegranates.
³ His left arm is under my head
   and his right arm embraces me.
⁴ Daughters of Jerusalem, I charge you:
   do not arouse or awaken love
   until it so desires.

Friends

⁵ Who is this coming up from the
     wilderness
   leaning on her beloved?

She

Under the apple tree I roused you;
   there your mother conceived you,
   there she who was in labour gave you
     birth.

⁶ Place me like a seal over your heart,
   like a seal on your arm;
for love is as strong as death,
   its jealousy unyielding as the grave.
It burns like blazing fire,
   like a mighty flame.
⁷ Many waters cannot quench love;
   rivers cannot sweep it away.
If one were to give
   all the wealth of one's house for love,
   it would be utterly scorned.

Friends

⁸ We have a little sister,
   and her breasts are not yet grown.
What shall we do for our sister
   on the day she is spoken for?
⁹ If she is a wall,
   we will build towers of silver on her.
If she is a door,
   we will enclose her with panels of
     cedar.

She

¹⁰ I am a wall,
   and my breasts are like towers.
Thus I have become in his eyes
   like one bringing contentment.
¹¹ Solomon had a vineyard in Baal Hamon;
   he let out his vineyard to tenants.
Each was to bring for its fruit
   a thousand shekels of silver.
¹² But my own vineyard is mine to give;
   the thousand shekels are for you,
     Solomon,
   and two hundred are for those who
     tend its fruit.

He

¹³ You who dwell in the gardens
   with friends in attendance,
   let me hear your voice!

She

¹⁴ Come away, my beloved,
   and be like a gazelle

or like a young stag
on the spice-laden mountains.

■ PSALM 108:7-13

⁷ God has spoken from his sanctuary:
  'In triumph I will parcel out Shechem
  and measure off the Valley of Sukkoth.
⁸ Gilead is mine, Manasseh is mine;
  Ephraim is my helmet,
  Judah is my sceptre.
⁹ Moab is my washbasin,
  on Edom I toss my sandal;
  over Philistia I shout in triumph.'

¹⁰ Who will bring me to the fortified city?
  Who will lead me to Edom?
¹¹ Is it not you, God, you who have rejected
    us
  and no longer go out with our armies?
¹² Give us aid against the enemy,
  for human help is worthless.
¹³ With God we shall gain the victory,
  and he will trample down our
    enemies.

■ PROVERBS 22:26-27

²⁶ Do not be one who shakes hands in
    pledge
  or puts up security for debts;
²⁷ if you lack the means to pay,
  your very bed will be snatched from
    under you.

■ 2 CORINTHIANS 5:11–6:13

¹¹ Since, then, we know what it is to fear
the Lord, we try to persuade others. What
we are is plain to God, and I hope it is also
plain to your conscience. ¹² We are not trying to commend ourselves to you again, but
are giving you an opportunity to take pride

in us, so that you can answer those who take
pride in what is seen rather than in what is
in the heart. ¹³ If we are 'out of our mind,' as
some say, it is for God; if we are in our right
mind, it is for you. ¹⁴ For Christ's love compels us, because we are convinced that one
died for all, and therefore all died. ¹⁵ And he
died for all, that those who live should no
longer live for themselves but for him who
died for them and was raised again.

¹⁶ So from now on we regard no one from
a worldly point of view. Though we once regarded Christ in this way, we do so no longer. ¹⁷ Therefore, if anyone is in Christ, the
new creation has come: the old has gone,
the new is here! ¹⁸ All this is from God, who
reconciled us to himself through Christ and
gave us the ministry of reconciliation: ¹⁹ that
God was reconciling the world to himself in
Christ, not counting people's sins against
them. And he has committed to us the message of reconciliation. ²⁰ We are therefore
Christ's ambassadors, as though God were
making his appeal through us. We implore
you on Christ's behalf: be reconciled to God.
²¹ God made him who had no sin to be sin
for us, so that in him we might become the
righteousness of God.

6 As God's fellow workers we urge you
not to receive God's grace in vain. ² For
he says,

'In the time of my favour I heard you,
  and in the day of salvation I helped you.'

I tell you, now is the time of God's favour,
now is the day of salvation.

³ We put no stumbling-block in anyone's
path, so that our ministry will not be discredited. ⁴ Rather, as servants of God we
commend ourselves in every way: in great
endurance; in troubles, hardships and dis-
tresses; ⁵ in beatings, imprisonments and
riots; in hard work, sleepless nights and
hunger; ⁶ in purity, understanding, patience and kindness; in the Holy Spirit and

in sincere love; [7] in truthful speech and in the power of God; with weapons of righteousness in the right hand and in the left; [8] through glory and dishonour, bad report and good report; genuine, yet regarded as impostors; [9] known, yet regarded as unknown; dying, and yet we live on; beaten, and yet not killed; [10] sorrowful, yet always rejoicing; poor, yet making many rich; having nothing, and yet possessing everything.

[11] We have spoken freely to you, Corinthians, and opened wide our hearts to you. [12] We are not withholding our affection from you, but you are withholding yours from us. [13] As a fair exchange – I speak as to my children – open wide your hearts also.

When God's People Share

'We are therefore Christ's ambassadors, as though God were making his appeal through us ...'
2 Corinthians 5:20

The aspects of experience and expression are extremely important in the Christian life: if experience gets low, then expression gets low; if expression gets low, then experience gets low.

We focus now on expression. If this side of the Christian life is not transformed from a bottled-up, non-contagious type of outflowing, then spiritual staleness is the inevitable result.

Two young men, both fairly new converts, had been listening to a sermon on evangelism. Afterwards, they approached their pastor and said, 'We have never shared with anyone the experience we have had in Christ. How do we do it?' He suggested that they could go out, knock on a few doors, and just begin to share their experience of Christ. The next night, in fear and trembling, they knocked on the first door of the street that they had decided to evangelise and found it to be the home of a well-known lawyer. They were a little nonplussed when they discovered this and blurted out: 'We have come to invite you to join our church.' The lawyer said, 'A lot of people have asked me to join the church over the years. Haven't you anything better than that to say to me?' They said, 'Well, how about committing your life to Jesus Christ?'

The lawyer invited them in, and within an hour had surrendered to Christ. 'Now, where are you going next', he said, 'because I want to go with you.' Before the end of the evening, the lawyer had the joy of witnessing another conversion like his own. Things happen when people share.

PRAYER

O Father, help me to come to such a place in my Christian life that in every situation where You want someone to pass on a special word from You, You will hear me say, 'Here am I, Lord – send me.' Amen.

FURTHER STUDY

Acts 2; 5:20; 18:9; 22:15
• What was the hallmark of the early church?
• Witness to someone today.

September 19

■ ISAIAH 1:1–2:22

1 The vision concerning Judah and Jerusalem that Isaiah son of Amoz saw during the reigns of Uzziah, Jotham, Ahaz and Hezekiah, kings of Judah.

² Hear me, you heavens! Listen, earth!
    For the LORD has spoken:
'I reared children and brought them up,
    but they have rebelled against me.
³ The ox knows its master,
    the donkey its owner's manger,
but Israel does not know,
    my people do not understand.'

⁴ Woe to the sinful nation,
    a people whose guilt is great,
a brood of evildoers,
    children given to corruption!
They have forsaken the LORD;
    they have spurned the Holy One of
        Israel
and turned their backs on him.

⁵ Why should you be beaten any more?
    Why do you persist in rebellion?
Your whole head is injured,
    your whole heart afflicted.
⁶ From the sole of your foot to the top of
        your head
    there is no soundness –
only wounds and bruises
    and open sores,
not cleansed or bandaged
    or soothed with oil.

⁷ Your country is desolate,
    your cities burned with fire;
your fields are being stripped by
    foreigners
right before you,
    laid waste as when overthrown by
        strangers.
⁸ Daughter Zion is left
    like a shelter in a vineyard,
    like a hut in a cucumber field,
    like a city under siege.
⁹ Unless the LORD Almighty
    had left us some survivors,
we would have become like Sodom,
    we would have been like Gomorrah.

¹⁰ Hear the word of the LORD,
    you rulers of Sodom;
listen to the instruction of our God,
    you people of Gomorrah!
¹¹ 'The multitude of your sacrifices –
    what are they to me?' says the LORD.
'I have more than enough of burnt
        offerings,
    of rams and the fat of fattened animals;
I have no pleasure
    in the blood of bulls and lambs and
        goats.
¹² When you come to appear before me,
    who has asked this of you,
    this trampling of my courts?
¹³ Stop bringing meaningless offerings!
    Your incense is detestable to me.
New Moons, Sabbaths and convocations –
    I cannot bear your worthless
        assemblies.
¹⁴ Your New Moon feasts and your
        appointed festivals
    I hate with all my being.
They have become a burden to me;
    I am weary of bearing them.
¹⁵ When you spread out your hands in
        prayer,
    I hide my eyes from you;
even when you offer many prayers,

I am not listening.

Your hands are full of blood!

¹⁶ Wash and make yourselves clean.
Take your evil deeds out of my sight;
stop doing wrong.
¹⁷ Learn to do right; seek justice.
Defend the oppressed.
Take up the cause of the fatherless;
plead the case of the widow.

¹⁸ 'Come now, let us settle the matter,'
says the LORD.
'Though your sins are like scarlet,
they shall be as white as snow;
though they are red as crimson,
they shall be like wool.
¹⁹ If you are willing and obedient,
you will eat the good things of the
land;
²⁰ but if you resist and rebel,
you will be devoured by the sword.'
For the mouth of the LORD
has spoken.

²¹ See how the faithful city
has become a prostitute!
She once was full of justice;
righteousness used to dwell in her –
but now murderers!
²² Your silver has become dross,
your choice wine is diluted with water.
²³ Your rulers are rebels,
partners with thieves;
they all love bribes
and chase after gifts.
They do not defend the cause of the
fatherless;
the widow's case does not come before
them.

²⁴ Therefore the Lord, the LORD Almighty,
the Mighty One of Israel, declares:
'Ah! I will vent my wrath on my foes
and avenge myself on my enemies.

²⁵ I will turn my hand against you;
I will thoroughly purge away your
dross
and remove all your impurities.
²⁶ I will restore your leaders as in days of
old,
your rulers as at the beginning.
Afterwards you will be called
the City of Righteousness,
the Faithful City.'

²⁷ Zion will be delivered with justice,
her penitent ones with righteousness.
²⁸ But rebels and sinners will both be
broken,
and those who forsake the LORD will
perish.

²⁹ 'You will be ashamed because of the
sacred oaks
in which you have delighted;
you will be disgraced because of the
gardens
that you have chosen.
³⁰ You will be like an oak with fading
leaves,
like a garden without water.
³¹ The mighty man will become tinder
and his work a spark;
both will burn together,
with no one to quench the fire.'

2 This is what Isaiah son of Amoz saw
concerning Judah and Jerusalem:

² in the last days

the mountain of the LORD's temple will
be established
as the highest of the mountains;
it will be exalted above the hills,
and all nations will stream to it.

³ Many peoples will come and say,

'Come, let us go up to the mountain of
the LORD,
to the temple of the God of Jacob.
He will teach us his ways,
so that we may walk in his paths.'
The law will go out from Zion,
the word of the LORD from Jerusalem.
⁴ He will judge between the nations
and will settle disputes for many
peoples.
They will beat their swords into
ploughshares
and their spears into pruning hooks.
Nation will not take up sword against
nation,
nor will they train for war any more.

⁵ Come, descendants of Jacob,
let us walk in the light of the LORD.

⁶ You, Lord, have abandoned your people,
the descendants of Jacob.
They are full of superstitions from the
East;
they practise divination like the
Philistines
and embrace pagan customs.
⁷ Their land is full of silver and gold;
there is no end to their treasures.
Their land is full of horses;
there is no end to the chariots.
⁸ Their land is full of idols;
they bow down to the work of their
hands,
to what their fingers have made.
⁹ So people will be brought low
and everyone humbled –
do not forgive them.

¹⁰ Go into the rocks, hide in the ground
from the fearful presence of the LORD
and the splendour of his majesty!
¹¹ The eyes of the arrogant will be humbled
and human pride brought low;
the LORD alone will be exalted in that day.

¹² The LORD Almighty has a day in store
for all the proud and lofty,
for all that is exalted
(and they will be humbled),
¹³ for all the cedars of Lebanon, tall and
lofty,
and all the oaks of Bashan,
¹⁴ for all the towering mountains
and all the high hills,
¹⁵ for every lofty tower
and every fortified wall,
¹⁶ for every trading ship
and every stately vessel.
¹⁷ The arrogance of man will be brought
low
and human pride humbled;
the LORD alone will be exalted in that
day,
¹⁸ and the idols will totally disappear.

¹⁹ People will flee to caves in the rocks
and to holes in the ground
from the fearful presence of the LORD
and the splendour of his majesty,
when he rises to shake the earth.
²⁰ In that day people will throw away
to the moles and bats
their idols of silver and idols of gold,
which they made to worship.
²¹ They will flee to caverns in the rocks
and to the overhanging crags
from the fearful presence of the LORD
and the splendour of his majesty,
when he rises to shake the earth.

²² Stop trusting in mere humans,
who have but a breath in their nostrils.
Why hold them in esteem?

······································

▬ PSALM 109:1-7

¹ My God, whom I praise,
do not remain silent,
² for people who are wicked and deceitful
have opened their mouths against me;

they have spoken against me with
lying tongues.
³ With words of hatred they surround me;
they attack me without cause.
⁴ In return for my friendship they accuse
me,
but I am a man of prayer.
⁵ They repay me evil for good,
and hatred for my friendship.

⁶ Appoint someone evil to oppose my
enemy;
let an accuser stand at his right hand.
⁷ When he is tried, let him be found guilty,
and may his prayers condemn him.

PROVERBS 22:28-29

²⁸ Do not move an ancient boundary stone
set up by your ancestors.
²⁹ Do you see someone skilled in their
work?
They will serve before kings;
they will not serve before officials of
low rank.

2 CORINTHIANS 6:14–7:16

¹⁴ Do not be yoked together with unbelievers. For what do righteousness and wickedness have in common? Or what fellowship
can light have with darkness? ¹⁵ What harmony is there between Christ and Belial? Or
what does a believer have in common with
an unbeliever? ¹⁶ What agreement is there
between the temple of God and idols? For
we are the temple of the living God. As God
has said:

'I will live with them
and walk among them,
and I will be their God,
and they will be my people.'

¹⁷ Therefore,

'Come out from them
and be separate,
                          says the Lord.
Touch no unclean thing,
and I will receive you.'

¹⁸ And,

'I will be a Father to you,
and you will be my sons and
daughters,
                    says the Lord Almighty.'

7 Therefore, since we have these
promises, dear friends, let us purify
ourselves from everything that contaminates body and spirit, perfecting holiness
out of reverence for God.

² Make room for us in your hearts. We
have wronged no one, we have corrupted no
one, we have exploited no one. ³ I do not say
this to condemn you; I have said before that
you have such a place in our hearts that we
would live or die with you. ⁴ I have spoken to
you with great frankness; I take great pride
in you. I am greatly encouraged; in all our
troubles my joy knows no bounds.

⁵ For when we came into Macedonia, we
had no rest, but we were harassed at every
turn – conflicts on the outside, fears within.
⁶ But God, who comforts the downcast,
comforted us by the coming of Titus, ⁷ and
not only by his coming but also by the comfort you had given him. He told us about
your longing for me, your deep sorrow, your
ardent concern for me, so that my joy was
greater than ever.

⁸ Even if I caused you sorrow by my letter, I do not regret it. Though I did regret
it – I see that my letter hurt you, but only
for a little while – ⁹ yet now I am happy, not
because you were made sorry, but because
your sorrow led you to repentance. For you
became sorrowful as God intended and so

were not harmed in any way by us. [10]Godly sorrow brings repentance that leads to salvation and leaves no regret, but worldly sorrow brings death. [11]See what this godly sorrow has produced in you: what earnestness, what eagerness to clear yourselves, what indignation, what alarm, what longing, what concern, what readiness to see justice done. At every point you have proved yourselves to be innocent in this matter. [12]So even though I wrote to you, it was neither on account of the one who did the wrong nor on account of the injured party, but rather that before God you could see for yourselves how devoted to us you are. [13]By all this we are encouraged.

In addition to our own encouragement, we were especially delighted to see how happy Titus was, because his spirit has been refreshed by all of you. [14]I had boasted to him about you, and you have not embarrassed me. But just as everything we said to you was true, so our boasting about you to Titus has proved to be true as well. [15]And his affection for you is all the greater when he remembers that you were all obedient, receiving him with fear and trembling. [16]I am glad I can have complete confidence in you.

Holiness Is Healthiness

'... let us purify ourselves from everything that contaminates body and spirit, perfecting holiness out of reverence for God.' **2 Corinthians 7:1**

When we study the Scriptures, particularly the Old Testament, we find that those who got closest to God thought more of His holiness than any other thing. Why should this be? I think in the nature of things it cannot be any other way because, more than anything else, God wants us to be holy. Over and over again in the Bible we are told: 'Be holy because I am holy.' We are not directed to be omnipotent (all-powerful) or omniscient (all-wise) as God is, but we are to be holy. This is the prime way of honouring God. We do not glorify Him by eloquent expressions of pompous service but by aspiring to converse with Him with unstained spirits and live to Him in living *like* Him.

Are you seeking to be holy? God has made holiness the moral condition necessary to the health of His universe. Sin's temporary presence in the world only accentuates this. Whatever is holy is healthy, and evil is a moral sickness that must ultimately end in death. The formation of the language itself suggests this, the English word 'holy' deriving from the Anglo-Saxon *halig*, meaning 'well' or 'whole'. To be whole in Christian terms means to be holy. Can you say 'I am holy – truly holy'? I am afraid I can't. I don't think any honest Christian would say 'yes' to that question. But neither would any honest Christian ignore these solemn words: 'Make every effort to live in peace with everyone and to be holy; without holiness no one will see the Lord' (Heb. 12:14).

PRAYER

O Father, help me to be as concerned for the moral health of the universe as You are. But more, help me to focus first on my own moral health and to be rid of all in my life that is contrary to You and Your nature. In Jesus' name I ask it. Amen.

FURTHER STUDY

Luke 1:67-80; 2 Pet. 3:11;
2 Cor. 7:1
• Why has God raised up a horn of salvation?
• What kind of people ought we to be?

September 20

■ ISAIAH 3:1–5:23

3 See now, the Lord,
 the LORD Almighty,
 is about to take from Jerusalem and
  Judah
  both supply and support:
 all supplies of food and all supplies of
  water,
² the hero and the warrior,
 the judge and the prophet,
 the diviner and the elder,
³ the captain of fifty and the man of rank,
 the counsellor, skilled craftsman and
  clever enchanter.

⁴ 'I will make mere youths their officials;
 children will rule over them.'

⁵ People will oppress each other –
 man against man, neighbour against
  neighbour.
 The young will rise up against the old,
 the nobody against the honoured.

⁶ A man will seize one of his brothers
 in his father's house, and say,
 'You have a cloak, you be our leader;
 take charge of this heap of ruins!'
⁷ But in that day he will cry out,

'I have no remedy.
 I have no food or clothing in my house;
 do not make me the leader of the
  people.'

⁸ Jerusalem staggers,
 Judah is falling;
 their words and deeds are against the
  LORD,
 defying his glorious presence.
⁹ The look on their faces testifies against
  them;
 they parade their sin like Sodom;
 they do not hide it.
 Woe to them!
 They have brought disaster upon
  themselves.

¹⁰ Tell the righteous it will be well with
  them,
 for they will enjoy the fruit of their
  deeds.
¹¹ Woe to the wicked!
 Disaster is upon them!
 They will be paid back
 for what their hands have done.

¹² Youths oppress my people,
 women rule over them.
 My people, your guides lead you astray;

they turn you from the path.

13 The LORD takes his place in court;
    he rises to judge the people.
14 The LORD enters into judgment
    against the elders and leaders of his
        people:
'It is you who have ruined my vineyard;
    the plunder from the poor is in your
        houses.
15 What do you mean by crushing my
        people
    and grinding the faces of the poor?'
                declares the Lord,
                the LORD Almighty.

16 The LORD says,
'The women of Zion are haughty,
    walking along with outstretched necks,
    flirting with their eyes,
    strutting along with swaying hips,
    with ornaments jingling on their ankles.
17 Therefore the Lord will bring sores on
        the heads of the women of Zion;
    the LORD will make their scalps bald.'

18 In that day the Lord will snatch away
their finery: the bangles and headbands
and crescent necklaces, 19 the earrings and
bracelets and veils, 20 the head-dresses and
anklets and sashes, the perfume bottles
and charms, 21 the signet rings and nose
rings, 22 the fine robes and the capes and
cloaks, the purses 23 and mirrors, and the
linen garments and tiaras and shawls.

24 Instead of fragrance there will be a
        stench;
    instead of a sash, a rope;
    instead of well-dressed hair, baldness;
    instead of fine clothing, sackcloth;
    instead of beauty, branding.
25 Your men will fall by the sword,
    your warriors in battle.
26 The gates of Zion will lament and mourn;
    destitute, she will sit on the ground.

4 ¹In that day seven women
    will take hold of one man
and say, 'We will eat our own food
    and provide our own clothes;
only let us be called by your name.
    Take away our disgrace!'

² In that day the Branch of the Lord will
be beautiful and glorious, and the fruit of
the land will be the pride and glory of the
survivors in Israel. ³ Those who are left in
Zion, who remain in Jerusalem, will be
called holy, all who are recorded among the
living in Jerusalem. ⁴ The Lord will wash
away the filth of the women of Zion; he will
cleanse the bloodstains from Jerusalem
by a spirit of judgment and a spirit of fire.
⁵ Then the Lord will create over all of Mount
Zion and over those who assemble there a
cloud of smoke by day and a glow of flaming
fire by night; over everything the glory will
be a canopy. ⁶ It will be a shelter and shade
from the heat of the day, and a refuge and
hiding-place from the storm and rain.

5 I will sing for the one I love
    a song about his vineyard:
my loved one had a vineyard
    on a fertile hillside.
² He dug it up and cleared it of stones
    and planted it with the choicest vines.
He built a watchtower in it
    and cut out a winepress as well.
Then he looked for a crop of good grapes,
    but it yielded only bad fruit.

³ 'Now you dwellers in Jerusalem and
        people of Judah,
    judge between me and my vineyard.
⁴ What more could have been done for my
        vineyard
    than I have done for it?
When I looked for good grapes,
    why did it yield only bad?
⁵ Now I will tell you
    what I am going to do to my vineyard:

I will take away its hedge,
and it will be destroyed;
I will break down its wall,
and it will be trampled.
⁶ I will make it a wasteland,
neither pruned nor cultivated,
and briers and thorns will grow there.
I will command the clouds
not to rain on it.'

⁷ The vineyard of the LORD Almighty
is the nation of Israel,
and the people of Judah
are the vines he delighted in.
And he looked for justice, but saw
bloodshed;
for righteousness, but heard cries of
distress.
⁸ Woe to you who add house to house
and join field to field
till no space is left
and you live alone in the land.

⁹ The LORD Almighty has declared in my
hearing:

'Surely the great houses will become
desolate,
the fine mansions left without
occupants.
¹⁰ A ten-acre vineyard will produce only a
bath of wine;
a homer of seed will yield only an
ephah of grain.'

¹¹ Woe to those who rise early in the
morning
to run after their drinks,
who stay up late at night
till they are inflamed with wine.
¹² They have harps and lyres at their
banquets,
pipes and tambourines and wine,
but they have no regard for the deeds of
the LORD,
no respect for the work of his hands.

¹³ Therefore my people will go into exile
for lack of understanding;
those of high rank will die of hunger
and the common people will be
parched with thirst.
¹⁴ Therefore Death expands its jaws,
opening wide its mouth;
into it will descend their nobles and
masses
with all their brawlers and revellers.
¹⁵ So people will be brought low
and everyone humbled,
the eyes of the arrogant humbled.
¹⁶ But the LORD Almighty will be exalted by
his justice,
and the holy God will be proved holy
by his righteous acts.
¹⁷ Then sheep will graze as in their own
pasture;
lambs will feed among the ruins of the
rich.

¹⁸ Woe to those who draw sin along with
cords of deceit,
and wickedness as with cart ropes,
¹⁹ to those who say, 'Let God hurry;
let him hasten his work
so that we may see it.
The plan of the Holy One of Israel –
let it approach, let it come into view,
so that we may know it.'

²⁰ Woe to those who call evil good
and good evil,
who put darkness for light
and light for darkness,
who put bitter for sweet
and sweet for bitter.

²¹ Woe to those who are wise in their own
eyes
and clever in their own sight.

²² Woe to those who are heroes at drinking
wine
and champions at mixing drinks,

²³ who acquit the guilty for a bribe,
    but deny justice to the innocent.

▬ PSALM 109:8-15

⁸ May his days be few;
    may another take his place of leadership.
⁹ May his children be fatherless
    and his wife a widow.
¹⁰ May his children be wandering beggars;
    may they be driven from their ruined
        homes.
¹¹ May a creditor seize all he has;
    may strangers plunder the fruits of his
        labour.
¹² May no one extend kindness to him
    or take pity on his fatherless children.
¹³ May his descendants be cut off,
    their names blotted out from the next
        generation.
¹⁴ May the iniquity of his fathers be
    remembered before the LORD;
    may the sin of his mother never be
        blotted out.
¹⁵ May their sins always remain before the
        LORD,
    that he may blot out their name from
        the earth.

▬ PROVERBS 23:1-3

23 When you sit to dine with a ruler,
    note well what is before you,
² and put a knife to your throat
    if you are given to gluttony.
³ Do not crave his delicacies,
    for that food is deceptive.

▬ 2 CORINTHIANS 8:1-24

8 And now, brothers and sisters, we want
    you to know about the grace that God
has given the Macedonian churches. ² In the

midst of a very severe trial, their overflowing joy and their extreme poverty welled up in rich generosity. ³ For I testify that they gave as much as they were able, and even beyond their ability. Entirely on their own, ⁴ they urgently pleaded with us for the privilege of sharing in this service to the Lord's people. ⁵ And they exceeded our expectations: they gave themselves first of all to the Lord, and then by the will of God also to us. ⁶ So we urged Titus, just as he had earlier made a beginning, to bring also to completion this act of grace on your part. ⁷ But since you excel in everything – in faith, in speech, in knowledge, in complete earnestness and in the love we have kindled in you – see that you also excel in this grace of giving.

⁸ I am not commanding you, but I want to test the sincerity of your love by comparing it with the earnestness of others. ⁹ For you know the grace of our Lord Jesus Christ, that though he was rich, yet for your sake he became poor, so that you through his poverty might become rich.

¹⁰ And here is my judgment about what is best for you in this matter. Last year you were the first not only to give but also to have the desire to do so. ¹¹ Now finish the work, so that your eager willingness to do it may be matched by your completion of it, according to your means. ¹² For if the willingness is there, the gift is acceptable according to what one has, not according to what one does not have.

¹³ Our desire is not that others might be relieved while you are hard pressed, but that there might be equality. ¹⁴ At the present time your plenty will supply what they need, so that in turn their plenty will supply what you need. The goal is equality, ¹⁵ as it is written: 'The one who gathered much did not have too much, and the one who gathered little did not have too little.'

¹⁶ Thanks be to God, who put into the heart of Titus the same concern I have for you. ¹⁷ For Titus not only welcomed our

appeal, but he is coming to you with much enthusiasm and on his own initiative. [18] And we are sending along with him the brother who is praised by all the churches for his service to the gospel. [19] What is more, he was chosen by the churches to accompany us as we carry the offering, which we administer in order to honour the Lord himself and to show our eagerness to help. [20] We want to avoid any criticism of the way we administer this liberal gift. [21] For we are taking pains to do what is right, not only in the eyes of the Lord but also in the eyes of man.

[22] In addition, we are sending with them our brother who has often proved to us in many ways that he is zealous, and now even more so because of his great confidence in you. [23] As for Titus, he is my partner and fellow worker among you; as for our brothers, they are representatives of the churches and an honour to Christ. [24] Therefore show these men the proof of your love and the reason for our pride in you, so that the churches can see it.

Some Things Bitter to Digest

'Woe to them! They have brought disaster upon themselves.' **Isaiah 3:9**

The fifth Beatitude, (Matt. 5:7) when practised, engenders within us good mental and spiritual health. Psychologists have shown that those who lack the qualities of mercy and compassion are more likely to develop physical problems. Harsh, judgmental attitudes may bring a sense of satisfaction to the person who does not know the meaning of mercy, but it is a false sense of satisfaction.

A verse that, strictly speaking, does not apply to what I am saying here, but nevertheless has some application is this: 'It tasted as sweet as honey in my mouth, but when I had eaten it, my stomach turned sour' (Rev. 10:10). That is what happens whenever we adopt any attitude that is not in harmony with Jesus Christ. At first it is 'as sweet as honey' - its beginnings are apparently sweet - but it '[becomes] bitter' - it cannot be assimilated. Our human constitution is not made to function effectively on any attitude that is foreign to the spirit of Jesus Christ.

A Christian doctor says, 'We are allergic to wrong attitudes just as some people are allergic to shrimps.' I am physically allergic to red and green peppers. I have tried them scores of times, but the result has always been the same - I get sick. I am just as allergic to harsh, judgmental attitudes. I can't assimilate them. They disrupt me - body, soul and spirit. And what goes for me goes also for you. When we fail to practise the principles which our Lord outlined for us in the Beatitudes, then our sense of well-being is lowered, depleted, and poisoned. Goodness is good for us - spiritually, mentally, and physically.

PRAYER

Father, something is being burned into my consciousness: there is only one healthy way to live – Your Way. When I break with You, I break with life. Help me always to maintain a close connection with You. In Jesus' name. Amen.

FURTHER STUDY

Psa. 23:1-6; 31:9; Exod. 34:6; Gal. 5:22; Eph. 5:9
• Of what is goodness a characteristic?
• Can you make the same declaration as the psalmist?

September 21

■ ISAIAH 5:24–7:25

24 Therefore, as tongues of fire lick up straw
   and as dry grass sinks down in the
      flames,
so their roots will decay
   and their flowers blow away like dust;
for they have rejected the law of the LORD
      Almighty
   and spurned the word of the Holy One
      of Israel.
25 Therefore the LORD's anger burns against
      his people;
   his hand is raised and he strikes them
      down.
The mountains shake,
   and the dead bodies are like refuse in
      the streets.

Yet for all this, his anger is not turned
      away,
   his hand is still upraised.

26 He lifts up a banner for the distant
      nations,
   he whistles for those at the ends of the
      earth.
Here they come,
   swiftly and speedily!
27 Not one of them grows tired or stumbles,
   not one slumbers or sleeps;

not a belt is loosened at the waist,
   not a sandal strap is broken.
28 Their arrows are sharp,
   all their bows are strung;
their horses' hooves seem like flint,
   their chariot wheels like a whirlwind.
29 Their roar is like that of the lion,
   they roar like young lions;
they growl as they seize their prey
   and carry it off with no one to rescue.
30 In that day they will roar over it
   like the roaring of the sea.
And if one looks at the land,
   there is only darkness and distress;
   even the sun will be darkened by clouds.

6 In the year that King Uzziah died, I saw the Lord, high and exalted, seated on a throne; and the train of his robe filled the temple. 2 Above him were seraphim, each with six wings: with two wings they covered their faces, with two they covered their feet, and with two they were flying. 3 And they were calling to one another:

'Holy, holy, holy is the LORD Almighty;
   the whole earth is full of his glory.'

4 At the sound of their voices the doorposts and thresholds shook and the temple was filled with smoke.

⁵'Woe to me!' I cried. 'I am ruined! For I am a man of unclean lips, and I live among a people of unclean lips, and my eyes have seen the King, the LORD Almighty.'

⁶Then one of the seraphim flew to me with a live coal in his hand, which he had taken with tongs from the altar. ⁷With it he touched my mouth and said, 'See, this has touched your lips; your guilt is taken away and your sin atoned for.'

⁸Then I heard the voice of the Lord saying, 'Whom shall I send? And who will go for us?'

And I said, 'Here am I. Send me!'

⁹He said, 'Go and tell this people:

' "Be ever hearing, but never
        understanding;
    be ever seeing, but never perceiving."
¹⁰ Make the heart of this people calloused;
    make their ears dull
    and close their eyes.
Otherwise they might see with their eyes,
    hear with their ears,
    understand with their hearts,
    and turn and be healed.'

¹¹ Then I said, 'For how long, Lord?'
And he answered:

'Until the cities lie ruined
    and without inhabitant,
until the houses are left deserted
    and the fields ruined and ravaged,
¹² until the LORD has sent everyone far away
    and the land is utterly forsaken.
¹³ And though a tenth remains in the land,
    it will again be laid waste.
But as the terebinth and oak
    leave stumps when they are cut down,
    so the holy seed will be the stump in
        the land.'

7 When Ahaz son of Jotham, the son of Uzziah, was king of Judah, King Rezin of Aram and Pekah son of Remaliah king of Israel marched up to fight against Jerusalem, but they could not overpower it.

² Now the house of David was told, 'Aram has allied itself with Ephraim'; so the hearts of Ahaz and his people were shaken, as the trees of the forest are shaken by the wind.

³ Then the LORD said to Isaiah, 'Go out, you and your son Shear-Jashub, to meet Ahaz at the end of the aqueduct of the Upper Pool, on the road to the Launderer's Field. ⁴ Say to him, "Be careful, keep calm and don't be afraid. Do not lose heart because of these two smouldering stubs of firewood – because of the fierce anger of Rezin and Aram and of the son of Remaliah. ⁵ Aram, Ephraim and Remaliah's son have plotted your ruin, saying, ⁶ 'Let us invade Judah; let us tear it apart and divide it among ourselves, and make the son of Tabeel king over it.' ⁷ Yet this is what the Sovereign LORD says:

' "It will not take place,
    it will not happen,
⁸ for the head of Aram is Damascus,
    and the head of Damascus is only
        Rezin.
Within sixty-five years
    Ephraim will be too shattered to be a
        people.
⁹ The head of Ephraim is Samaria,
    and the head of Samaria is only
        Remaliah's son.
If you do not stand firm in your faith,
    you will not stand at all." '

¹⁰ Again the LORD spoke to Ahaz, ¹¹ 'Ask the LORD your God for a sign, whether in the deepest depths or in the highest heights.'

¹² But Ahaz said, 'I will not ask; I will not put the LORD to the test.'

¹³ Then Isaiah said, 'Hear now, you house of David! Is it not enough to try the patience of humans? Will you try the patience of my God also? ¹⁴ Therefore the Lord himself will give you a sign: the virgin will conceive and give birth to a son, and will call him

Immanuel. ¹⁵He will be eating curds and honey when he knows enough to reject the wrong and choose the right, ¹⁶for before the boy knows enough to reject the wrong and choose the right, the land of the two kings you dread will be laid waste. ¹⁷The LORD will bring on you and on your people and on the house of your father a time unlike any since Ephraim broke away from Judah – he will bring the king of Assyria.'

¹⁸In that day the LORD will whistle for flies from the Nile delta in Egypt and for bees from the land of Assyria. ¹⁹They will all come and settle in the steep ravines and in the crevices in the rocks, on all the thornbushes and at all the water holes. ²⁰In that day the Lord will use a razor hired from beyond the River Euphrates – the king of Assyria – to shave your heads and private parts, and to cut off your beards also. ²¹In that day, a person will keep alive a young cow and two goats. ²²And because of the abundance of the milk they give, there will be curds to eat. All who remain in the land will eat curds and honey. ²³In that day, in every place where there were a thousand vines worth a thousand silver shekels, there will be only briers and thorns. ²⁴Hunters will go there with bow and arrow, for the land will be covered with briers and thorns. ²⁵As for all the hills once cultivated by the hoe, you will no longer go there for fear of the briers and thorns; they will become places where cattle are turned loose and where sheep run.

■ PSALM 109:16-25

¹⁶For he never thought of doing a
   kindness,
   but hounded to death the poor
   and the needy and the
    broken-hearted.
¹⁷He loved to pronounce a curse –
   may it come back on him.
He found no pleasure in blessing –

may it be far from him.
¹⁸He wore cursing as his garment;
   it entered into his body like water,
   into his bones like oil.
¹⁹May it be like a cloak wrapped about
   him,
   like a belt tied for ever round him.
²⁰May this be the LORD's payment to my
   accusers,
   to those who speak evil of me.

²¹But you, Sovereign LORD,
   help me for your name's sake;
   out of the goodness of your love,
    deliver me.
²²For I am poor and needy,
   and my heart is wounded within me.
²³I fade away like an evening shadow;
   I am shaken off like a locust.
²⁴My knees give way from fasting;
   my body is thin and gaunt.
²⁵I am an object of scorn to my accusers;
   when they see me, they shake their
    heads.

■ PROVERBS 23:4-5

⁴Do not wear yourself out to get rich;
   do not trust your own cleverness.
⁵Cast but a glance at riches, and they are
   gone,
   for they will surely sprout wings
   and fly off to the sky like an eagle.

■ 2 CORINTHIANS 9:1–10:11

9 There is no need for me to write to you about this service to the Lord's people. ²For I know your eagerness to help, and I have been boasting about it to the Macedonians, telling them that since last year you in Achaia were ready to give; and your enthusiasm has stirred most of them to action. ³But I am sending the brothers in order

that our boasting about you in this matter should not prove hollow, but that you may be ready, as I said you would be. ⁴For if any Macedonians come with me and find you unprepared, we – not to say anything about you – would be ashamed of having been so confident. ⁵So I thought it necessary to urge the brothers to visit you in advance and finish the arrangements for the generous gift you had promised. Then it will be ready as a generous gift, not as one grudgingly given.

⁶Remember this: whoever sows sparingly will also reap sparingly, and whoever sows generously will also reap generously. ⁷Each of you should give what you have decided in your heart to give, not reluctantly or under compulsion, for God loves a cheerful giver. ⁸And God is able to bless you abundantly, so that in all things at all times, having all that you need, you will abound in every good work. ⁹As it is written:

'They have freely scattered their gifts to
the poor;
their righteousness endures for ever.'

¹⁰Now he who supplies seed to the sower and bread for food will also supply and increase your store of seed and will enlarge the harvest of your righteousness. ¹¹You will be enriched in every way so that you can be generous on every occasion, and through us your generosity will result in thanksgiving to God.

¹²This service that you perform is not only supplying the needs of the Lord's people but is also overflowing in many expressions of thanks to God. ¹³Because of the service by which you have proved yourselves, others will praise God for the obedience that accompanies your confession of the gospel of Christ, and for your generosity in sharing with them and with everyone else. ¹⁴And in their prayers for you their hearts will go out to you, because of the surpassing grace God has given you. ¹⁵Thanks be to God for his indescribable gift!

10 By the humility and gentleness of Christ, I appeal to you – I, Paul, who am 'timid' when face to face with you, but 'bold' towards you when away! ²I beg you that when I come I may not have to be as bold as I expect to be towards some people who think that we live by the standards of this world. ³For though we live in the world, we do not wage war as the world does. ⁴The weapons we fight with are not the weapons of the world. On the contrary, they have divine power to demolish strongholds. ⁵We demolish arguments and every pretension that sets itself up against the knowledge of God, and we take captive every thought to make it obedient to Christ. ⁶And we will be ready to punish every act of disobedience, once your obedience is complete.

⁷You are judging by appearances. If anyone is confident that they belong to Christ, they should consider again that we belong to Christ just as much as they do. ⁸So even if I boast somewhat freely about the authority the Lord gave us for building you up rather than tearing you down, I will not be ashamed of it. ⁹I do not want to seem to be trying to frighten you with my letters. ¹⁰For some say, 'His letters are weighty and forceful, but in person he is unimpressive and his speaking amounts to nothing.' ¹¹Such people should realise that what we are in our letters when we are absent, we will be in our actions when we are present.

Quality Par Excellence

'Holy, holy, holy is the LORD Almighty ...' **Isaiah 6:3**

Even the most casual reader of the Scriptures cannot help but notice that God is portrayed in the Bible as uniquely and awesomely holy. In fact, there are more references to the holiness of God in Scripture than to any other aspect of His character. This ought to give us some indication of how important it is.

But what do we mean when we say God is 'holy'? There are three thoughts underlying the word 'holy'.

First, the idea of separation, being withdrawn or apart.

Second, brightness or brilliance.

Third, moral majesty, purity, or cleanliness.

It is interesting that those who came into direct contact with the Almighty in the Old Testament were inevitably overwhelmed by His moral majesty.

Isaiah went into the temple to pray at a time when his people were in grave difficulties. Uzziah, the king who had ruled for half a century, was dying, and Assyria, a terrible and evil force, stood threateningly to the north. Whatever answer Isaiah thought he would get as he opened up his heart to God, it was not the one he received. He was given instead a vision of a holy God that shook him to the core of his being.

Why should this be? I think it was because the concept of God's holiness is the main lesson in His school, the divine prerequisite for admission to the inner heart of God, the most important qualification for learning from the Lord.

PRAYER

Father, I must search my heart this day and ask myself: Do I know what it is to serve a holy God? Have I ever received a vision of the moral majesty and purity of the divine? Deepen my understanding of all this I pray. In Jesus' name. Amen.

FURTHER STUDY

Exod. 15:1–11; Psa. 99:9
• What question did Moses pose?
• What did the psalmist affirm?

September 22

■ ISAIAH 8:1–10:11

8 The LORD said to me, 'Take a large scroll and write on it with an ordinary pen: Maher-Shalal-Hash-Baz.' ²So I called in Uriah the priest and Zechariah son of Jeberekiah as reliable witnesses for me. ³Then I made love to the prophetess,

and she conceived and gave birth to a son. And the LORD said to me, 'Name him Maher-Shalal-Hash-Baz. ⁴For before the boy knows how to say "My father" or "My mother", the wealth of Damascus and the plunder of Samaria will be carried off by the king of Assyria.'

⁵The LORD spoke to me again:

6 'Because this people has rejected
   the gently flowing waters of Shiloah
and rejoices over Rezin
   and the son of Remaliah,
7 therefore the Lord is about to bring
      against them
   the mighty floodwaters of the
      Euphrates –
   the king of Assyria with all his pomp.
It will overflow all its channels,
   run over all its banks
8 and sweep on into Judah, swirling
      over it,
   passing through it and reaching up to
      the neck.
Its outspread wings will cover the
      breadth of your land,
   Immanuel!'

9 Raise the war cry, you nations, and be
      shattered!
   Listen, all you distant lands.
Prepare for battle, and be shattered!
Prepare for battle, and be shattered!
10 Devise your strategy, but it will be
      thwarted;
   propose your plan, but it will not
      stand,
   for God is with us.

11 This is what the LORD says to me with
his strong hand upon me, warning me not
to follow the way of this people:

12 'Do not call conspiracy
   everything this people calls a
      conspiracy;
   do not fear what they fear,
      and do not dread it.
13 The LORD Almighty is the one you are to
      regard as holy,
   he is the one you are to fear,
   he is the one you are to dread.
14 He will be a holy place;
   for both Israel and Judah he will be
      a stone that causes people to stumble

and a rock that makes them fall.
   And for the people of Jerusalem he
      will be
   a trap and a snare.
15 Many of them will stumble;
   they will fall and be broken,
   they will be snared and captured.'

16 Bind up this testimony of warning
   and seal up God's instruction among
      my disciples.
17 I will wait for the LORD,
   who is hiding his face from the
      descendants of Jacob.
I will put my trust in him.

18 Here am I, and the children the LORD
has given me. We are signs and symbols in
Israel from the LORD Almighty, who dwells
on Mount Zion.

19 When someone tells you to consult
mediums and spiritists, who whisper and
mutter, should not a people enquire of their
God? Why consult the dead on behalf of the
living? 20 Consult God's instruction and the
testimony of warning. If anyone does not
speak according to this word, they have no
light of dawn. 21 Distressed and hungry, they
will roam through the land; when they are
famished, they will become enraged and,
looking upwards, will curse their king and
their God. 22 Then they will look towards
the earth and see only distress and darkness and fearful gloom, and they will be
thrust into utter darkness.

9 Nevertheless, there will be no more
gloom for those who were in distress.
In the past he humbled the land of Zebulun
and the land of Naphtali, but in the future
he will honour Galilee of the nations, by the
Way of the Sea, beyond the Jordan –

2 The people walking in darkness
   have seen a great light;
   on those living in the land of deep
      darkness

a light has dawned.
³ You have enlarged the nation
   and increased their joy;
they rejoice before you
   as people rejoice at the harvest,
   as warriors rejoice
   when dividing the plunder.
⁴ For as in the day of Midian's defeat,
   you have shattered
the yoke that burdens them,
   the bar across their shoulders,
   the rod of their oppressor.
⁵ Every warrior's boot used in battle
   and every garment rolled in blood
will be destined for burning,
   will be fuel for the fire.
⁶ For to us a child is born,
   to us a son is given,
   and the government will be on his
      shoulders.
And he will be called
   Wonderful Counsellor, Mighty God,
   Everlasting Father, Prince of Peace.
⁷ Of the greatness of his government and
      peace
   there will be no end.
He will reign on David's throne
   and over his kingdom,
establishing and upholding it
   with justice and righteousness
   from that time on and for ever.
The zeal of the LORD Almighty
   will accomplish this.
⁸ The Lord has sent a message against
      Jacob;
   it will fall on Israel.
⁹ All the people will know it –
   Ephraim and the inhabitants of
      Samaria –
who say with pride
   and arrogance of heart,
¹⁰ 'The bricks have fallen down,
   but we will rebuild with dressed stone;
   the fig trees have been felled,
   but we will replace them with cedars.'

¹¹ But the LORD has strengthened Rezin's
      foes against them
   and has spurred their enemies on.
¹² Arameans from the east and Philistines
      from the west
   have devoured Israel with open
      mouth.

Yet for all this, his anger is not turned
      away,
   his hand is still upraised.

¹³ But the people have not returned to him
      who struck them,
   nor have they sought the LORD
      Almighty.
¹⁴ So the LORD will cut off from Israel both
      head and tail,
   both palm branch and reed in a single
      day;
¹⁵ the elders and dignitaries are the head,
   the prophets who teach lies are the
      tail.
¹⁶ Those who guide this people mislead
      them,
   and those who are guided are led
      astray.
¹⁷ Therefore the Lord will take no pleasure
      in the young men,
   nor will he pity the fatherless and
      widows,
for everyone is ungodly and wicked,
   every mouth speaks folly.

Yet for all this, his anger is not turned
      away,
   his hand is still upraised.

¹⁸ Surely wickedness burns like a fire;
   it consumes briers and thorns,
it sets the forest thickets ablaze,
   so that it rolls upwards in a column of
      smoke.
¹⁹ By the wrath of the LORD Almighty
   the land will be scorched
and the people will be fuel for the fire;

they will not spare one another.
²⁰ On the right they will devour,
    but still be hungry;
on the left they will eat,
    but not be satisfied.
Each will feed on the flesh of their own
    offspring:
²¹   Manasseh will feed on Ephraim, and
    Ephraim on Manasseh;
    together they will turn against Judah.

Yet for all this, his anger is not turned
    away,
    his hand is still upraised.

10 Woe to those who make unjust laws,
    to those who issue oppressive
    decrees,
² to deprive the poor of their rights
    and withhold justice from the
    oppressed of my people,
making widows their prey
    and robbing the fatherless.
³ What will you do on the day of
    reckoning,
    when disaster comes from afar?
To whom will you run for help?
    Where will you leave your riches?
⁴ Nothing will remain but to cringe among
    the captives
    or fall among the slain.

Yet for all this, his anger is not turned
    away,
    his hand is still upraised.
⁵ 'Woe to the Assyrian, the rod of my
    anger,
    in whose hand is the club of my wrath!
⁶ I send him against a godless nation,
    I dispatch him against a people who
    anger me,
to seize loot and snatch plunder,
    and to trample them down like mud
    in the streets.
⁷ But this is not what he intends,
    this is not what he has in mind;

his purpose is to destroy,
    to put an end to many nations.
⁸ "Are not my commanders all kings?" he
    says.
⁹   "Has not Kalno fared like Carchemish?
Is not Hamath like Arpad,
    and Samaria like Damascus?
¹⁰ As my hand seized the kingdoms of the
    idols,
    kingdoms whose images excelled those
    of Jerusalem and Samaria –
¹¹ shall I not deal with Jerusalem and her
    images
    as I dealt with Samaria and her idols?" '

▬ PSALM 109:26-31

²⁶ Help me, LORD my God;
    save me according to your unfailing
    love.
²⁷ Let them know that it is your hand,
    that you, LORD, have done it.
²⁸ While they curse, may you bless;
    may those who attack me be put to
    shame,
    but may your servant rejoice.
²⁹ May my accusers be clothed with
    disgrace
    and wrapped in shame as in a cloak.

³⁰ With my mouth I will greatly extol the
    LORD;
    in the great throng of worshippers I
    will praise him.
³¹ For he stands at the right hand of the
    needy,
    to save their lives from those who
    would condemn them.

▬ PROVERBS 23:6-8

⁶ Do not eat the food of a stingy host,
    do not crave his delicacies;
⁷ for he is the kind of person

who is always thinking about the
cost.[a]
'Eat and drink,' he says to you,
but his heart is not with you.
[8] You will vomit up the little you have
eaten
and will have wasted your
compliments.

---

[a] Or *for as he thinks within himself, / so he is; or for as he puts on a
feast, / so he is*

....

■ 2 CORINTHIANS 10:12–11:15

[12] We do not dare to classify or compare ourselves with some who commend
themselves. When they measure themselves by themselves and compare themselves with themselves, they are not wise.
[13] We, however, will not boast beyond
proper limits, but will confine our boasting to the sphere of service God himself
has assigned to us, a sphere that also includes you. [14] We are not going too far in
our boasting, as would be the case if we
had not come to you, for we did get as far
as you with the gospel of Christ. [15] Neither
do we go beyond our limits by boasting of
work done by others. Our hope is that, as
your faith continues to grow, our sphere
of activity among you will greatly expand,
[16] so that we can preach the gospel in the
regions beyond you. For we do not want to
boast about work already done in someone else's territory. [17] But, 'Let the one
who boasts boast in the Lord.' [18] For it is
not the one who commends himself who
is approved, but the one whom the Lord
commends.

11 I hope you will put up with me in a
little foolishness. Yes, please put up
with me! [2] I am jealous for you with a godly
jealousy. I promised you to one husband, to
Christ, so that I might present you as a pure
virgin to him. [3] But I am afraid that just as
Eve was deceived by the snake's cunning,
your minds may somehow be led astray
from your sincere and pure devotion to
Christ. [4] For if someone comes to you and
preaches a Jesus other than the Jesus we
preached, or if you receive a different spirit
from the Spirit you received, or a different
gospel from the one you accepted, you put
up with it easily enough.

[5] I do not think I am in the least inferi-
or to those 'super-apostles'. [6] I may indeed
be untrained as a speaker, but I do have
knowledge. We have made this perfectly
clear to you in every way. [7] Was it a sin for
me to lower myself in order to elevate you
by preaching the gospel of God to you free
of charge? [8] I robbed other churches by receiving support from them so as to serve
you. [9] And when I was with you and needed
something, I was not a burden to anyone,
for the brothers who came from Macedonia
supplied what I needed. I have kept myself
from being a burden to you in any way, and
will continue to do so. [10] As surely as the
truth of Christ is in me, nobody in the regions of Achaia will stop this boasting of
mine. [11] Why? Because I do not love you?
God knows I do!

[12] And I will keep on doing what I am doing in order to cut the ground from under
those who want an opportunity to be considered equal with us in the things they
boast about. [13] For such people are false
apostles, deceitful workers, masquerad-
ing as apostles of Christ. [14] And no wonder,
for Satan himself masquerades as an angel
of light. [15] It is not surprising, then, if his
servants also masquerade as servants of
righteousness. Their end will be what their
actions deserve.

The Helmet of Salvation

'But I am afraid that just as Eve was deceived by the snake's cunning, your minds may somehow be led astray from your sincere and pure devotion to Christ.'
2 Corinthians 11:3

The second piece of armour that is not tied or fixed to the body but that a Christian soldier has to take up and put on is 'the helmet of salvation' (Eph. 6:17). The helmet worn by a Roman soldier was usually made of bronze or iron with an inside lining of felt or sponge. In some cases a hinged visor added frontal protection. When a Roman soldier saw an enemy coming, he would take hold of his shield, put on his helmet, take his sword in hand, and stand alert and ready to do battle.

The figure of a helmet immediately suggests to us that this is something designed to protect the mind, the intelligence, the ability to think and reason. Just as the breastplate of righteousness protects us from emotional distress, the helmet of salvation protects us from mental distress. This helmet can help us keep our thinking straight and preserve us from mental confusion.

Has there ever been a time in history when we needed something to keep our thinking straight more than we do now? Politicians vacillate and oscillate between despairing pessimism and unrealistic optimism. Just think of the staggering complexities of the issues we face in our current generation – AIDS, violence, nuclear weapons, international tensions, economic instability, inner-city deprivation and so on. The intelligentsia of our day confess to being utterly baffled in dealing with the problems with which human society is confronted. Where can we turn to ease the pressure on our minds? The only answer is God – in the helmet of salvation that He provides.

PRAYER

O Father, I am so grateful that You have provided freedom from that most terrifying of human problems – mental distress. Teach me all I need to know in applying Your truth to the important area of my mind. In Jesus' name. Amen.

FURTHER STUDY

Eph. 4:1–17; Rom. 8:7; Col. 1:21

• How were the Ephesians not to live?
• How powerful is the influence of the mind?

September 23

▬ Isaiah 10:12–12:6

¹²When the Lord has finished all his work against Mount Zion and Jerusalem, he will say, 'I will punish the king of Assyria for the wilful pride of his heart and the haughty look in his eyes. ¹³For he says:

'"By the strength of my hand I have done this,
　and by my wisdom, because I have understanding.
I removed the boundaries of nations,
　I plundered their treasures;
like a mighty one I subdued their kings.
¹⁴As one reaches into a nest,
　so my hand reached for the wealth of the nations;
as people gather abandoned eggs,
　so I gathered all the countries;
not one flapped a wing,
　or opened its mouth to chirp."'

¹⁵Does the axe raise itself above the person who swings it,
　or the saw boast against the one who uses it?
As if a rod were to wield the person who lifts it up,
　or a club brandish the one who is not wood!
¹⁶Therefore, the Lord, the Lord Almighty,
　will send a wasting disease upon his sturdy warriors;
under his pomp a fire will be kindled
　like a blazing flame.
¹⁷The Light of Israel will become a fire,
　their Holy One a flame;
in a single day it will burn and consume
　his thorns and his briers.

¹⁸The splendour of his forests and fertile fields
　it will completely destroy,
　as when one who is ill wastes away.
¹⁹And the remaining trees of his forests
　will be so few
　that a child could write them down.
²⁰In that day the remnant of Israel,
　the survivors of Jacob,
will no longer rely on him
　who struck them down
but will truly rely on the Lord,
　the Holy One of Israel.
²¹A remnant will return, a remnant of Jacob
　will return to the Mighty God.
²²Though your people be like the sand by the sea, Israel,
　only a remnant will return.
Destruction has been decreed,
　overwhelming and righteous.
²³The Lord, the Lord Almighty, will carry out
　the destruction decreed upon the whole land.

²⁴Therefore this is what the Lord, the Lord Almighty, says:

'My people who live in Zion,
　do not be afraid of the Assyrians,
who beat you with a rod
　and lift up a club against you, as Egypt did.
²⁵Very soon my anger against you will end
　and my wrath will be directed to their destruction.'

²⁶The Lord Almighty will lash them with a whip,

as when he struck down Midian at the
    rock of Oreb;
and he will raise his staff over the waters,
    as he did in Egypt.
²⁷ In that day their burden will be lifted
      from your shoulders,
    their yoke from your neck;
the yoke will be broken
    because you have grown so fat.

²⁸ They enter Aiath;
    they pass through Migron;
    they store supplies at Michmash.
²⁹ They go over the pass, and say,
    'We will camp overnight at Geba.'
Ramah trembles;
    Gibeah of Saul flees.
³⁰ Cry out, Daughter Gallim!
    Listen, Laishah!
    Poor Anathoth!
³¹ Madmenah is in flight;
    the people of Gebim take cover.
³² This day they will halt at Nob;
    they will shake their fist
at the mount of Daughter Zion,
    at the hill of Jerusalem.

³³ See, the Lord, the LORD Almighty,
    will lop off the boughs with great
      power.
The lofty trees will be felled,
    the tall ones will be brought low.
³⁴ He will cut down the forest thickets with
      an axe;
Lebanon will fall before the Mighty
    One.

11 A shoot will come up from the stump
      of Jesse;
    from his roots a Branch will bear fruit.
² The Spirit of the LORD will rest on him –
    the Spirit of wisdom and of
      understanding,
    the Spirit of counsel and of might,
    the Spirit of the knowledge and fear of
      the LORD –

³ and he will delight in the fear of the
    LORD.

He will not judge by what he sees with
    his eyes,
    or decide by what he hears with his
      ears;
⁴ but with righteousness he will judge the
    needy,
    with justice he will give decisions for
      the poor of the earth.
He will strike the earth with the rod of
    his mouth;
    with the breath of his lips he will slay
      the wicked.
⁵ Righteousness will be his belt
    and faithfulness the sash round his
      waist.

⁶ The wolf will live with the lamb,
    the leopard will lie down with the
      goat,
the calf and the lion and the yearling
      together;
    and a little child will lead them.
⁷ The cow will feed with the bear,
    their young will lie down together,
    and the lion will eat straw like the ox.
⁸ The infant will play near the cobra's den,
    and the young child will put its hand
      into the viper's nest.
⁹ They will neither harm nor destroy
    on all my holy mountain,
for the earth will be filled with the
      knowledge of the LORD
    as the waters cover the sea.

¹⁰ In that day the Root of Jesse will stand as
a banner for the peoples; the nations will rally to him, and his resting place will be glorious. ¹¹ In that day the Lord will reach out his
hand a second time to reclaim the surviving
remnant of his people from Assyria, from
Lower Egypt, from Upper Egypt, from Cush,
from Elam, from Babylonia, from Hamath
and from the islands of the Mediterranean.

¹² He will raise a banner for the nations
    and gather the exiles of Israel;
he will assemble the scattered people of
    Judah
    from the four quarters of the earth.
¹³ Ephraim's jealousy will vanish,
    and Judah's enemies will be
    destroyed;
Ephraim will not be jealous of Judah,
    nor Judah hostile towards Ephraim.
¹⁴ They will swoop down on the slopes of
    Philistia to the west;
    together they will plunder the people
    to the east.
They will subdue Edom and Moab,
    and the Ammonites will be subject to
    them.
¹⁵ The LORD will dry up
    the gulf of the Egyptian sea;
with a scorching wind he will sweep his
    hand
    over the River Euphrates.
He will break it up into seven streams
    so that anyone can cross over in
    sandals.
¹⁶ There will be a highway for the remnant
    of his people
    that is left from Assyria,
as there was for Israel
    when they came up from Egypt.

12 In that day you will say:

'I will praise you, LORD.
    Although you were angry with me,
your anger has turned away
    and you have comforted me.
² Surely God is my salvation;
    I will trust and not be afraid.
The LORD, the LORD himself, is my
    strength and my defence;
he has become my salvation.'
³ With joy you will draw water
    from the wells of salvation.

⁴ In that day you will say:

'Give praise to the LORD, proclaim his
    name;
make known among the nations what
    he has done,
and proclaim that his name is exalted.
⁵ Sing to the LORD, for he has done glorious
    things;
let this be known to all the world.
⁶ Shout aloud and sing for joy, people of
    Zion,
for great is the Holy One of Israel
    among you.'

▬ PSALM 110:1–7

¹ The LORD says to my lord:

'Sit at my right hand
    until I make your enemies
    a footstool for your feet.'

² The LORD will extend your mighty
    sceptre from Zion, saying,
    'Rule in the midst of your enemies!'
³ Your troops will be willing
    on your day of battle.
Arrayed in holy splendour,
    your young men will come to you
    like dew from the morning's womb.

⁴ The LORD has sworn
    and will not change his mind:
'You are a priest for ever,
    in the order of Melchizedek.'

⁵ The Lord is at your right hand;
    he will crush kings on the day of his
    wrath.
⁶ He will judge nations, heaping up the
    dead
    and crushing the rulers of the whole
    earth.
⁷ He will drink from a brook along the
    way;
    and so he will lift his head high.

▬ PROVERBS 23:9-11

⁹ Do not speak to fools,
   for they will scorn your prudent
      words.
¹⁰ Do not move an ancient boundary stone
   or encroach on the fields of the
      fatherless,
¹¹ for their Defender is strong;
   he will take up their case against you.

▬ 2 CORINTHIANS
   11:16–12:10

¹⁶ I repeat: let no one take me for a fool. But if you do, then tolerate me just as you would a fool, so that I may do a little boasting. ¹⁷ In this self-confident boasting I am not talking as the Lord would, but as a fool. ¹⁸ Since many are boasting in the way the world does, I too will boast. ¹⁹ You gladly put up with fools since you are so wise! ²⁰ In fact, you even put up with anyone who enslaves you or exploits you or takes advantage of you or puts on airs or slaps you in the face. ²¹ To my shame I admit that we were too weak for that!

Whatever anyone else dares to boast about – I am speaking as a fool – I also dare to boast about. ²² Are they Hebrews? So am I. Are they Israelites? So am I. Are they Abraham's descendants? So am I. ²³ Are they servants of Christ? (I am out of my mind to talk like this.) I am more. I have worked much harder, been in prison more frequently, been flogged more severely, and been exposed to death again and again. ²⁴ Five times I received from the Jews the forty lashes minus one. ²⁵ Three times I was beaten with rods, once I was pelted with stones, three times I was shipwrecked, I spent a night and a day in the open sea, ²⁶ I have been constantly on the move. I have been in danger from rivers, in danger from bandits, in danger from my fellow Jews, in danger from Gentiles; in danger in the city, in danger in the country, in danger at sea; and in danger from false believers. ²⁷ I have laboured and toiled and have often gone without sleep; I have known hunger and thirst and have often gone without food; I have been cold and naked. ²⁸ Besides everything else, I face daily the pressure of my concern for all the churches. ²⁹ Who is weak, and I do not feel weak? Who is led into sin, and I do not inwardly burn?

³⁰ If I must boast, I will boast of the things that show my weakness. ³¹ The God and Father of the Lord Jesus, who is to be praised for ever, knows that I am not lying. ³² In Damascus the governor under King Aretas had the city of the Damascenes guarded in order to arrest me. ³³ But I was lowered in a basket from a window in the wall and slipped through his hands.

12 I must go on boasting. Although there is nothing to be gained, I will go on to visions and revelations from the Lord. ² I know a man in Christ who fourteen years ago was caught up to the third heaven. Whether it was in the body or out of the body I do not know – God knows. ³ And I know that this man – whether in the body or apart from the body I do not know, but God knows – ⁴ was caught up to paradise and heard inexpressible things, things that no one is permitted to tell. ⁵ I will boast about a man like that, but I will not boast about myself, except about my weaknesses. ⁶ Even if I should choose to boast, I would not be a fool, because I would be speaking the truth. But I refrain, so no one will think more of me than is warranted by what I do or say, ⁷ or because of these surpassingly great revelations. Therefore, in order to keep me from becoming conceited, I was given a thorn in my flesh, a messenger of Satan, to torment me. ⁸ Three times I pleaded with the Lord to take it away from me. ⁹ But he said to me, 'My grace is sufficient for you, for my power is made perfect in weakness.'

Therefore I will boast all the more gladly about my weaknesses, so that Christ's power may rest on me. [10] That is why, for Christ's sake, I delight in weaknesses, in insults, in hardships, in persecutions, in difficulties. For when I am weak, then I am strong.

'Keep Your Eyes on the Tide'

'Your troops will be willing on your day of battle ...'
Psalm 110:3

Has God something bigger for us than we are at present seeing? I hope you are convinced that He has! How can we be open to receiving it? It comes at the precise moment God appoints but it is carried down from heaven on the wings of fervent, believing prayer. Dr A. T. Pierson said: 'From the Day of Pentecost until now, there has not been one great spiritual awakening in any land which has not begun in a union of prayer though only among two or three, and no such outward or upward movement has continued after such prayer meetings have declined.' Revivals are born in prayer and sustained by prayer.

Just as there are signs concerning the second coming, so there are signs that the Lord is not far from reviving His whole church. In the early days of the Salvation Army in France, the eldest daughter of General Booth, known by her French rank as the 'Marechale', found herself at one point in an extremely discouraging situation. She wrote to General Booth asking for his advice, which came in these words: 'Take your eyes off the waves and fix them on the tide.'

I give you now that same advice. Don't let your eyes become focused on the waves, with their advances and retreats. Keep your eyes on the tide and ask yourself: is it rising? If you look with the eye of faith I think you will see that it is. When it breaks I pray that it will not find you or me unprepared but that we shall be a people who are willing in the day of God's power.

PRAYER

Father, I don't know whether I will live to see a world-wide revival, but I want to live to experience a personal revival. Take me on from this point to know You in a much greater way. In Christ's name I ask it. Amen.

FURTHER STUDY

Ezek. 37:1-14; 2 Kings 3:16-17; Isa. 40:3-5; Rev. 22:1
- What was God's message to Ezekiel?
- What will you do to bring about revival?

September 24

■ ISAIAH 13:1–14:32

13 A prophecy against Babylon that Isaiah son of Amoz saw:

2 Raise a banner on a bare hilltop,
   shout to them;
beckon to them
   to enter the gates of the nobles.
3 I have commanded those I prepared for
      battle;
   I have summoned my warriors to
      carry out my wrath –
   those who rejoice in my triumph.

4 Listen, a noise on the mountains,
   like that of a great multitude!
Listen, an uproar among the kingdoms,
   like nations massing together!
The LORD Almighty is mustering
   an army for war.
5 They come from faraway lands,
   from the ends of the heavens –
the LORD and the weapons of his wrath –
   to destroy the whole country.

6 Wail, for the day of the LORD is near;
   it will come like destruction from the
      Almighty.
7 Because of this, all hands will go limp,
   every heart will melt with fear.
8 Terror will seize them,
   pain and anguish will grip them;
   they will writhe like a woman in
      labour.
They will look aghast at each other,
   their faces aflame.

9 See, the day of the LORD is coming
   – a cruel day, with wrath and fierce
      anger –

to make the land desolate
   and destroy the sinners within it.
10 The stars of heaven and their
      constellations
   will not show their light.
The rising sun will be darkened
   and the moon will not give its light.
11 I will punish the world for its evil,
   the wicked for their sins.
I will put an end to the arrogance of the
      haughty
   and will humble the pride of the
      ruthless.
12 I will make people scarcer than pure
      gold,
   more rare than the gold of Ophir.
13 Therefore I will make the heavens
      tremble;
   and the earth will shake from its place
at the wrath of the LORD Almighty,
   in the day of his burning anger.

14 Like a hunted gazelle,
   like sheep without a shepherd,
they will all return to their own people,
   they will flee to their native land.
15 Whoever is captured will be thrust
      through;
   all who are caught will fall by the
      sword.
16 Their infants will be dashed to pieces
      before their eyes;
   their houses will be looted and their
      wives violated.

17 See, I will stir up against them the
      Medes,
   who do not care for silver
   and have no delight in gold.
18 Their bows will strike down the young
      men;

they will have no mercy on infants
　nor will they look with compassion on
　　children.
¹⁹ Babylon, the jewel of kingdoms,
　the pride and glory of the
　　Babylonians,
will be overthrown by God
　like Sodom and Gomorrah.
²⁰ She will never be inhabited
　or lived in through all generations;
there no nomads will pitch their tents,
　there no shepherds will rest their
　　flocks.
²¹ But desert creatures will lie there,
　jackals will fill her houses;
there the owls will dwell,
　and there the wild goats will leap
　　about.
²² Hyenas will inhabit her strongholds,
　jackals her luxurious palaces.
Her time is at hand,
　and her days will not be prolonged.

14 The LORD will have compassion on
　Jacob;
　once again he will choose Israel
　and will settle them in their own land.
Foreigners will join them
　and unite with the descendants of
　　Jacob.
² Nations will take them
　and bring them to their own place.
And Israel will take possession of the
　nations
　and make them male and female
　　servants in the LORD's land.
They will make captives of their captors
　and rule over their oppressors.

³ On the day the LORD gives you relief from
your suffering and turmoil and from the
harsh labour forced on you, ⁴ you will take
up this taunt against the king of Babylon:

How the oppressor has come to an end!
　How his fury has ended!

⁵ The LORD has broken the rod of the
　wicked,
　the sceptre of the rulers,
⁶ which in anger struck down peoples
　with unceasing blows,
and in fury subdued nations
　with relentless aggression.
⁷ All the lands are at rest and at peace;
　they break into singing.
⁸ Even the junipers and the cedars of
　　Lebanon
gloat over you and say,
　'Now that you have been laid low,
　no one comes to cut us down.'

⁹ The realm of the dead below is all astir
　to meet you at your coming;
it rouses the spirits of the departed to
　　greet you –
all those who were leaders in the
　　world;
it makes them rise from their thrones –
　all those who were kings over the
　　nations.
¹⁰ They will all respond,
　they will say to you,
'You also have become weak, as we are;
　you have become like us.'
¹¹ All your pomp has been brought down to
　　the grave,
　along with the noise of your harps;
maggots are spread out beneath you
　and worms cover you.

¹² How you have fallen from heaven,
　morning star, son of the dawn!
You have been cast down to the earth,
　you who once laid low the nations!
¹³ You said in your heart,
　'I will ascend to the heavens;
I will raise my throne
　above the stars of God;
I will sit enthroned on the mount of
　　assembly,
　on the utmost heights of Mount
　　Zaphon.

¹⁴ I will ascend above the tops of the clouds;
     I will make myself like the Most High.'
¹⁵ But you are brought down to the realm of
         the dead,
     to the depths of the pit.

¹⁶ Those who see you stare at you,
     they ponder your fate:
   'Is this the man who shook the earth
     and made kingdoms tremble,
¹⁷ the man who made the world a
         wilderness,
     who overthrew its cities
     and would not let his captives go
         home?'

¹⁸ All the kings of the nations lie in state,
     each in his own tomb.
¹⁹ But you are cast out of your tomb
     like a rejected branch;
   you are covered with the slain,
     with those pierced by the sword,
     those who descend to the stones of the
         pit.
   Like a corpse trampled underfoot,
²⁰   you will not join them in burial,
   for you have destroyed your land
     and killed your people.

   Let the offspring of the wicked
     never be mentioned again.
²¹ Prepare a place to slaughter his children
     for the sins of their ancestors;
   they are not to rise to inherit the land
     and cover the earth with their cities.

²² 'I will rise up against them,'
     declares the LORD Almighty.
   'I will wipe out Babylon's name and
         survivors,
     her offspring and descendants,'
                         declares the LORD.
²³ 'I will turn her into a place for owls
     and into swampland;
   I will sweep her with the broom of
         destruction,'

declares the LORD Almighty.

²⁴ The LORD Almighty has sworn,

   'Surely, as I have planned, so it will be,
     and as I have purposed, so it will
         happen.
²⁵ I will crush the Assyrian in my land;
     on my mountains I will trample him
         down.
   His yoke will be taken from my people,
     and his burden removed from their
         shoulders.'

²⁶ This is the plan determined for the whole
         world;
     this is the hand stretched out over all
         nations.
²⁷ For the LORD Almighty has purposed,
     and who can thwart him?
   His hand is stretched out, and who can
         turn it back?

²⁸ This prophecy came in the year King
Ahaz died:

²⁹ Do not rejoice, all you Philistines,
     that the rod that struck you is broken;
   from the root of that snake will spring up
         a viper,
     its fruit will be a darting, venomous
         serpent.
³⁰ The poorest of the poor will find pasture,
     and the needy will lie down in safety.
   But your root I will destroy by famine;
     it will slay your survivors.

³¹ Wail, you gate! Howl, you city!
     Melt away, all you Philistines!
   A cloud of smoke comes from the north,
     and there is not a straggler in its ranks.
³² What answer shall be given
     to the envoys of that nation?
   'The LORD has established Zion,
     and in her his afflicted people will find
         refuge.'

PSALM 111:1–5

¹ Praise the LORD.

I will extol the LORD with all my
heart
   in the council of the upright and in the
   assembly.

² Great are the works of the LORD;
   they are pondered by all who delight
   in them.
³ Glorious and majestic are his deeds,
   and his righteousness endures for
   ever.
⁴ He has caused his wonders to be
   remembered;
   the LORD is gracious and
   compassionate.
⁵ He provides food for those who fear him;
   he remembers his covenant for ever.

PROVERBS 23:12–14

¹² Apply your heart to instruction
   and your ears to words of knowledge.
¹³ Do not withhold discipline from a child;
   if you punish them with the rod, they
   will not die.
¹⁴ Punish them with the rod
   and save them from death.

2 CORINTHIANS 12:11–13:13

¹¹ I have made a fool of myself, but
you drove me to it. I ought to have been
commended by you, for I am not in the least
inferior to the 'super-apostles', even though
I am nothing. ¹² I persevered in demonstrat-
ing among you the marks of a true apostle,
including signs, wonders and miracles.
¹³ How were you inferior to the other churches, except that I was never a burden to you?

Forgive me this wrong!

¹⁴ Now I am ready to visit you for the third
time, and I will not be a burden to you, because what I want is not your possessions
but you. After all, children should not have
to save up for their parents, but parents for
their children. ¹⁵ So I will very gladly spend
for you everything I have and expend myself as well. If I love you more, will you love
me less? ¹⁶ Be that as it may, I have not been
a burden to you. Yet, crafty fellow that I
am, I caught you by trickery! ¹⁷ Did I exploit you through any of the men I sent to
you? ¹⁸ I urged Titus to go to you and I sent
our brother with him. Titus did not exploit
you, did he? Did we not walk in the same
footsteps by the same Spirit?

¹⁹ Have you been thinking all along that
we have been defending ourselves to you?
We have been speaking in the sight of God
as those in Christ; and everything we do,
dear friends, is for your strengthening.
²⁰ For I am afraid that when I come I may
not find you as I want you to be, and you
may not find me as you want me to be. I fear
that there may be discord, jealousy, fits of
rage, selfish ambition, slander, gossip, arrogance and disorder. ²¹ I am afraid that when
I come again my God will humble me before
you, and I will be grieved over many who
have sinned earlier and have not repented of
the impurity, sexual sin and debauchery in
which they have indulged.

13 This will be my third visit to you.
'Every matter must be established
by the testimony of two or three witnesses.'
² I already gave you a warning when I was
with you the second time. I now repeat it
while absent: on my return I will not spare
those who sinned earlier or any of the others, ³ since you are demanding proof that
Christ is speaking through me. He is not
weak in dealing with you, but is powerful
among you. ⁴ For to be sure, he was crucified
in weakness, yet he lives by God's power.
Likewise, we are weak in him, yet by God's

power we will live with him in our dealing with you.

⁵Examine yourselves to see whether you are in the faith; test yourselves. Do you not realise that Christ Jesus is in you – unless, of course, you fail the test? ⁶And I trust that you will discover that we have not failed the test. ⁷Now we pray to God that you will not do anything wrong – not so that people will see that we have stood the test but so that you will do what is right even though we may seem to have failed. ⁸For we cannot do anything against the truth, but only for the truth. ⁹We are glad whenever we are weak but you are strong; and our prayer is that you may be fully restored. ¹⁰This is why I write these things when I am absent, that when I come I may not have to be harsh in my use of authority – the authority the Lord gave me for building you up, not for tearing you down.

¹¹Finally, brothers and sisters, rejoice! Strive for full restoration, encourage one another, be of one mind, live in peace. And the God of love and peace will be with you.

¹²Greet one another with a holy kiss. ¹³All God's people here send their greetings.

¹⁴May the grace of the Lord Jesus Christ, and the love of God, and the fellowship of the Holy Spirit be with you all.

A Watershed Truth

'May the grace of the Lord Jesus Christ, and the love of God, and the fellowship of the Holy Spirit be with you all.' **2 Corinthians 13:14**

That great Christian, Francis Schaeffer, said that he would have remained an agnostic if it weren't for the doctrine of the Trinity. It was this, he claimed, that gave him the answer - the only answer - to the theme of unity and diversity.

The question I have been asked most often about the Trinity is this: Why did not God make clear the truth of the Trinity in the Old Testament, rather than leaving it as something to be deduced in the New Testament? I usually answer like this: Before God could entrust His people with the knowledge of His essential Threeness, He had to lay deep in their minds a piercing conviction of His Oneness. The Bible begins in monotheism (belief in one God), but soon after the Fall comes polytheism (belief in many gods). Which god is the real God? Not until belief in one God was laid deep in the consciousness of the Jewish nation was God ready to reveal more clearly to mankind the sublime truth of the Trinity.

Dr George Smeaton says: 'The biblical idea of the Trinity is the heart of the unique message of Christianity. To explain this mystery is not our province. Ours is simply to conserve the mystery.' Those who call themselves Christians yet reject the doctrine of the Trinity will soon latch onto some other error. It is a strange thing, but I have observed it as a fact of the Christian life that when this truth is modified or pushed aside, it is as if the door is opened to the inrush of all kinds of absurd ideas, bizarre theories and half-truths.

PRAYER

Father, help me hold fast to this sublime truth, and enable me to see that though something is above reason, it is not necessarily against reason. Blessed Trinity – Father, Son, and Holy Spirit – I worship You. Amen.

FURTHER STUDY

John 14:8-21; 17:22
- How did Jesus depict the Trinity?
- What did Jesus confirm?

September 25

■ ISAIAH 15:1–18:7

15 A prophecy against Moab:

Ar in Moab is ruined,
　destroyed in a night!
Kir in Moab is ruined,
　destroyed in a night!
[2] Dibon goes up to its temple,
　to its high places to weep;
　Moab wails over Nebo and Medeba.
Every head is shaved
　and every beard cut off.
[3] In the streets they wear sackcloth;
　on the roofs and in the public squares
they all wail,
　prostrate with weeping.
[4] Heshbon and Elealeh cry out,
　their voices are heard all the way to
　　Jahaz.
Therefore the armed men of Moab cry
　　out,
　and their hearts are faint.

[5] My heart cries out over Moab;
　her fugitives flee as far as Zoar,
　as far as Eglath Shelishiyah.
They go up the hill to Luhith,
　weeping as they go;
on the road to Horonaim
　they lament their destruction.

[6] The waters of Nimrim are dried up
　and the grass is withered;
the vegetation is gone
　and nothing green is left.
[7] So the wealth they have acquired and
　　stored up
　they carry away over the Ravine of the
　　Poplars.
[8] Their outcry echoes along the border of
　　Moab;
　their wailing reaches as far as Eglaim,
　their lamentation as far as Beer Elim.
[9] The waters of Dimon are full of blood,
　but I will bring still more upon
　　Dimon –
a lion upon the fugitives of Moab
　and upon those who remain in the
　　land.

16 Send lambs as tribute
　to the ruler of the land,
from Sela, across the desert,
　to the mount of Daughter Zion.
[2] Like fluttering birds
　pushed from the nest,
so are the women of Moab
　at the fords of the Arnon.

[3] 'Make up your mind,' Moab says.
　'Render a decision.
Make your shadow like night –

at high noon.
Hide the fugitives,
    do not betray the refugees.
⁴ Let the Moabite fugitives stay with you;
    be their shelter from the destroyer.'

The oppressor will come to an end,
    and destruction will cease;
    the aggressor will vanish from the
        land.
⁵ In love a throne will be established;
    in faithfulness a man will sit on it –
    one from the house of David –
one who in judging seeks justice
    and speeds the cause of righteousness.

⁶ We have heard of Moab's pride –
    how great is her arrogance! –
of her conceit, her pride and her
        insolence;
    but her boasts are empty.
⁷ Therefore the Moabites wail,
    they wail together for Moab.
Lament and grieve
    for the raisin cakes of Kir Hareseth.
⁸ The fields of Heshbon wither,
    the vines of Sibmah also.
The rulers of the nations
    have trampled down the choicest
        vines,
which once reached Jazer
    and spread towards the desert.
Their shoots spread out
    and went as far as the sea.
⁹ So I weep, as Jazer weeps,
    for the vines of Sibmah.
Heshbon and Elealeh,
    I drench you with tears!
The shouts of joy over your ripened fruit
    and over your harvests have been
        stilled.
¹⁰ Joy and gladness are taken away from
        the orchards;
    no one sings or shouts in the
        vineyards;
    no one treads out wine at the presses,

for I have put an end to the shouting.
¹¹ My heart laments for Moab like a harp,
    my inmost being for Kir Hareseth.
¹² When Moab appears at her high place,
    she only wears herself out;
when she goes to her shrine to pray,
    it is to no avail.

¹³ This is the word the LORD has already spoken concerning Moab. ¹⁴ But now the LORD says: 'Within three years, as a servant bound by contract would count them, Moab's splendour and all her many people will be despised, and her survivors will be very few and feeble.'

17 A prophecy against Damascus:

'See, Damascus will no longer be a city
    but will become a heap of ruins.
² The cities of Aroer will be deserted
    and left to flocks, which will lie down,
    with no one to make them afraid.
³ The fortified city will disappear from
        Ephraim,
    and royal power from Damascus;
the remnant of Aram will be
    like the glory of the Israelites,'
                declares the LORD Almighty.

⁴ 'In that day the glory of Jacob will fade;
    the fat of his body will waste away.
⁵ It will be as when reapers harvest the
        standing corn,
    gathering the corn in their arms –
as when someone gleans ears of corn
    in the Valley of Rephaim.
⁶ Yet some gleanings will remain,
    as when an olive tree is beaten,
leaving two or three olives on the
        topmost branches,
    four or five on the fruitful boughs,'
                declares the LORD,
                the God of Israel.

⁷ In that day people will look to their
        Maker

and turn their eyes to the Holy One of
   Israel.
⁸ They will not look to the altars,
   the work of their hands,
and they will have no regard for the
   Asherah poles
and the incense altars their fingers
   have made.

⁹ In that day their strong cities, which
they left because of the Israelites, will be
like places abandoned to thickets and
undergrowth. And all will be desolation.

¹⁰ You have forgotten God your Saviour;
   you have not remembered the Rock,
      your fortress.
Therefore, though you set out the finest
   plants
   and plant imported vines,
¹¹ though on the day you set them out, you
      make them grow,
   and on the morning when you plant
      them, you bring them to bud,
yet the harvest will be as nothing
   in the day of disease and incurable
      pain.

¹² Woe to the many nations that rage –
   they rage like the raging sea!
Woe to the peoples who roar –
   they roar like the roaring of great
      waters!
¹³ Although the peoples roar like the roar
      of surging waters,
   when he rebukes them they flee far
      away,
   driven before the wind like chaff on the
      hills,
   like tumble-weed before a gale.
¹⁴ In the evening, sudden terror!
   Before the morning, they are gone!
This is the portion of those who
      loot us,
   the lot of those who plunder us.

18 Woe to the land of whirring wings
   along the rivers of Cush,
² which sends envoys by sea
   in papyrus boats over the water.

Go, swift messengers,
to a people tall and smooth-skinned,
   to a people feared far and wide,
an aggressive nation of strange speech,
   whose land is divided by rivers.

³ All you people of the world,
   you who live on the earth,
when a banner is raised on the
      mountains,
   you will see it,
and when a trumpet sounds,
   you will hear it.
⁴ This is what the LORD says to me:
   'I will remain quiet and will look on
      from my dwelling-place,
   like shimmering heat in the sunshine,
   like a cloud of dew in the heat of
      harvest.'
⁵ For, before the harvest, when the
      blossom is gone
   and the flower becomes a ripening
      grape,
he will cut off the shoots with pruning
      knives,
   and cut down and take away the
      spreading branches.
⁶ They will all be left to the mountain
      birds of prey
   and to the wild animals;
the birds will feed on them all summer,
   the wild animals all winter.

⁷ At that time gifts will be brought to the
LORD Almighty

from a people tall and smooth-skinned,
   from a people feared far and wide,
an aggressive nation of strange speech,
   whose land is divided by rivers –

the gifts will be brought to Mount Zion, the place of the Name of the LORD Almighty.

■ PSALM 111:6-10

⁶ He has shown his people the power of his works,
    giving them the lands of other nations.
⁷ The works of his hands are faithful and just;
    all his precepts are trustworthy.
⁸ They are established for ever and ever,
    enacted in faithfulness and uprightness.
⁹ He provided redemption for his people;
    he ordained his covenant for ever –
    holy and awesome is his name.

¹⁰ The fear of the LORD is the beginning of wisdom;
    all who follow his precepts have good understanding.
    To him belongs eternal praise.

■ PROVERBS 23:15-16

¹⁵ My son, if your heart is wise,
    then my heart will be glad indeed;
¹⁶ my inmost being will rejoice
    when your lips speak what is right.

■ GALATIANS 1:1-24

1 Paul, an apostle – sent not from men nor by a man, but by Jesus Christ and God the Father, who raised him from the dead – ²and all the brothers and sisters with me,

To the churches in Galatia:

³Grace and peace to you from God our Father and the Lord Jesus Christ, ⁴who gave himself for our sins to rescue us from the present evil age, according to the will of our God and Father, ⁵to whom be glory for ever and ever. Amen.

⁶I am astonished that you are so quickly deserting the one who called you to live in the grace of Christ and are turning to a different gospel – ⁷which is really no gospel at all. Evidently some people are throwing you into confusion and are trying to pervert the gospel of Christ. ⁸But even if we or an angel from heaven should preach a gospel other than the one we preached to you, let them be under God's curse! ⁹As we have already said, so now I say again: if anybody is preaching to you a gospel other than what you accepted, let them be under God's curse!

¹⁰Am I now trying to win the approval of human beings, or of God? Or am I trying to please people? If I were still trying to please people, I would not be a servant of Christ.

¹¹I want you to know, brothers and sisters, that the gospel I preached is not of human origin. ¹²I did not receive it from any man, nor was I taught it; rather, I received it by revelation from Jesus Christ.

¹³For you have heard of my previous way of life in Judaism, how intensely I persecuted the church of God and tried to destroy it. ¹⁴I was advancing in Judaism beyond many of my own age among my people and was extremely zealous for the traditions of my fathers. ¹⁵But when God, who set me apart from my mother's womb and called me by his grace, was pleased ¹⁶to reveal his Son in me so that I might preach him among the Gentiles, my immediate response was not to consult any human being. ¹⁷I did not go up to Jerusalem to see those who were apostles before I was, but I went into Arabia. Later I returned to Damascus.

¹⁸Then after three years, I went up to Jerusalem to get acquainted with Cephas and stayed with him fifteen days. ¹⁹I saw none of the other apostles – only James, the Lord's

brother. [20] I assure you before God that what I am writing to you is no lie.

[21] Then I went to Syria and Cilicia. [22] I was personally unknown to the churches of Judea that are in Christ. [23] They only heard the report: 'The man who formerly persecuted us is now preaching the faith he once tried to destroy.' [24] And they praised God because of me.

What Is Faith?

'My son, if your heart is wise, then my heart will be glad indeed.' Proverbs 23:15

'A man's belief', says Dr Albert Ellis, a well-known psychologist, 'determines both his conduct and his character.' Proverbs 23:7, written almost 3,000 years before Ellis, puts the truth in an even more succinct form: 'For as he thinks within himself, so he is.'[a]

There are two possibilities before each of us as we look at life: we can base our conclusions about the meaning of life on what the humanistic philosophers, poets, and historians tell us, or we can base them on what God tells us in His Word. Either we take the Word of God and live by it – or we do not. If we take the attitude that the prophets didn't know what they were talking about and there are no such things as miracles in the universe, then we do what the writer to the Hebrews tells us – we draw back from the godly way of life (Heb. 10:39). The biblical way is living by faith.

Listen to the word given to Habakkuk: 'The righteous person will live by his faithfulness' (Hab. 2:4). Faith is taking the Word of God and relying on it. It involves believing what God says, simply and solely because He said it. The heroes of faith listed in Hebrews 11 did just that – they had no real reason for believing what God told them, other than the fact that He had spoken. Why did Abraham take his son Isaac to Mount Moriah? Why did he prepare to offer him as a sacrifice? Simply because God had spoken. A little boy, when invited to comment on the statement, 'Faith is having confidence in what God has spoken', said: 'God has confidence in what He has said – so must we.'

PRAYER

O Father, forgive my doubts and hesitancies – and help me to have an unshakeable confidence in the truth and power of Your Word. Show me how to link my littleness to Your greatness. In Jesus' name I ask it. Amen.

FURTHER STUDY

Heb. 11:1-40; Gal. 3:6; Phil. 3:8-9
• How does Hebrews 11 describe faith?
• Write out your definition of faith.

---

[a] Or *for as he thinks within himself,/so he is*; or *for as he puts on a feast,/ so he is*

September 26

■ ISAIAH 19:1–22:8

19 A prophecy against Egypt:

See, the LORD rides on a swift cloud
    and is coming to Egypt.
The idols of Egypt tremble before him,
    and the hearts of the Egyptians melt
        with fear.

2 'I will stir up Egyptian against
        Egyptian –
    brother will fight against brother,
    neighbour against neighbour,
    city against city,
    kingdom against kingdom.
3 The Egyptians will lose heart,
    and I will bring their plans to nothing;
they will consult the idols and the spirits
        of the dead,
    the mediums and the spiritists.
4 I will hand the Egyptians over
    to the power of a cruel master,
and a fierce king will rule over them,'
    declares the Lord, the LORD Almighty.

5 The waters of the river will dry up,
    and the river bed will be parched and
        dry.
6 The canals will stink;
    the streams of Egypt will dwindle and
        dry up.
The reeds and rushes will wither,
7   also the plants along the Nile,
    at the mouth of the river.
Every sown field along the Nile
    will become parched, will blow away
        and be no more.
8 The fishermen will groan and lament,
    all who cast hooks into the Nile;
those who throw nets on the water

will pine away.
9 Those who work with combed flax will
        despair,
    the weavers of fine linen will lose
        hope.
10 The workers in cloth will be dejected,
    and all the wage earners will be sick at
        heart.

11 The officials of Zoan are nothing but
        fools;
    the wise counsellors of Pharaoh give
        senseless advice.
How can you say to Pharaoh,
    'I am one of the wise men,
    a disciple of the ancient kings'?

12 Where are your wise men now?
    Let them show you and make known
    what the LORD Almighty
    has planned against Egypt.
13 The officials of Zoan have become fools,
    the leaders of Memphis are deceived;
    the cornerstones of her peoples
    have led Egypt astray.
14 The LORD has poured into them
    a spirit of dizziness;
    they make Egypt stagger in all that she
        does,
    as a drunkard staggers around in his
        vomit.
15 There is nothing Egypt can do –
    head or tail, palm branch or reed.

16 In that day the Egyptians will become
weaklings. They will shudder with fear at
the uplifted hand that the LORD Almighty
raises against them. 17 And the land of Judah
will bring terror to the Egyptians; everyone
to whom Judah is mentioned will be terrified, because of what the LORD Almighty is

planning against them.

¹⁸ In that day five cities in Egypt will speak the language of Canaan and swear allegiance to the LORD Almighty. One of them will be called the City of the Sun.

¹⁹ In that day there will be an altar to the LORD in the heart of Egypt, and a monument to the LORD at its border. ²⁰ It will be a sign and witness to the LORD Almighty in the land of Egypt. When they cry out to the LORD because of their oppressors, he will send them a saviour and defender, and he will rescue them. ²¹ So the LORD will make himself known to the Egyptians, and in that day they will acknowledge the LORD. They will worship with sacrifices and grain offerings; they will make vows to the LORD and keep them. ²² The LORD will strike Egypt with a plague; he will strike them and heal them. They will turn to the LORD, and he will respond to their pleas and heal them.

²³ In that day there will be a highway from Egypt to Assyria. The Assyrians will go to Egypt and the Egyptians to Assyria. The Egyptians and Assyrians will worship together. ²⁴ In that day Israel will be the third, along with Egypt and Assyria, a blessing on the earth. ²⁵ The LORD Almighty will bless them, saying, 'Blessed be Egypt my people, Assyria my handiwork, and Israel my inheritance.'

20 In the year that the supreme commander, sent by Sargon king of Assyria, came to Ashdod and attacked and captured it – ² at that time the LORD spoke through Isaiah son of Amoz. He said to him, 'Take off the sackcloth from your body and the sandals from your feet.' And he did so, going around stripped and barefoot.

³ Then the LORD said, 'Just as my servant Isaiah has gone stripped and barefoot for three years, as a sign and portent against Egypt and Cush, ⁴ so the king of Assyria will lead away stripped and barefoot the Egyptian captives and Cushite exiles, young and old, with buttocks bared – to Egypt's shame. ⁵ Those who trusted in Cush and boasted in Egypt will be dismayed and put to shame.

⁶ In that day the people who live on this coast will say, "See what has happened to those we relied on, those we fled to for help and deliverance from the king of Assyria! How then can we escape?"'

21 A prophecy against the Desert by the Sea:

Like whirlwinds sweeping through the
    southland,
  an invader comes from the desert,
  from a land of terror.

² A dire vision has been shown to me:
  the traitor betrays, the looter takes
    loot.
Elam, attack! Media, lay siege!
  I will bring to an end all the groaning
    she caused.

³ At this my body is racked with pain,
  pangs seize me, like those of a woman
    in labour;
I am staggered by what I hear,
  I am bewildered by what I see.
⁴ My heart falters,
  fear makes me tremble;
the twilight I longed for
  has become a horror to me.

⁵ They set the tables,
  they spread the rugs,
  they eat, they drink!
Get up, you officers,
  oil the shields!

⁶ This is what the Lord says to me:

'Go, post a lookout
  and let him report what he sees.
⁷ When he sees chariots
  with teams of horses,
riders on donkeys
  or riders on camels,
let him be alert,
  fully alert.'

[8] And the lookout shouted,

'Day after day, my lord, I stand on the
    watchtower;
  every night I stay at my post.
[9] Look, here comes a man in a chariot
    with a team of horses.
  And he gives back the answer:
    "Babylon has fallen, has fallen!
  All the images of its gods
    lie shattered on the ground!"'

[10] My people who are crushed on the
    threshing-floor,
  I tell you what I have heard
  from the LORD Almighty,
    from the God of Israel.

[11] A prophecy against Dumah:

Someone calls to me from Seir,
  'Watchman, what is left of the night?
  Watchman, what is left of the night?'
[12] The watchman replies,
  'Morning is coming, but also the
    night.
  If you would ask, then ask;
    and come back yet again.'

[13] A prophecy against Arabia:

You caravans of Dedanites,
  who camp in the thickets of Arabia,
[14]   bring water for the thirsty;
  you who live in Tema,
    bring food for the fugitives.
[15] They flee from the sword,
    from the drawn sword,
  from the bent bow
    and from the heat of battle.

[16] This is what the Lord says to me:
'Within one year, as a servant bound by
contract would count it, all the splendour
of Kedar will come to an end. [17] The survivors of the archers, the warriors of Kedar,

will be few.' The LORD, the God of Israel, has
spoken.

22 A prophecy against the Valley of Vision:

What troubles you now,
  that you have all gone up on the roofs,
[2] you town so full of commotion,
  you city of tumult and revelry?
Your slain were not killed by the sword,
  nor did they die in battle.
[3] All your leaders have fled together;
  they have been captured without
    using the bow.
All you who were caught were taken
    prisoner together,
  having fled while the enemy was still
    far away.
[4] Therefore I said, 'Turn away from me;
  let me weep bitterly.
Do not try to console me
  over the destruction of my people.'

[5] The Lord, the LORD Almighty, has a day
  of tumult and trampling and terror
  in the Valley of Vision,
a day of battering down walls
  and of crying out to the mountains.
[6] Elam takes up the quiver,
  with her charioteers and horses;
  Kir uncovers the shield.
[7] Your choicest valleys are full of chariots,
  and horsemen are posted at the city
    gates.

[8] The Lord stripped away the defences of
    Judah,
  and you looked in that day
  to the weapons in the Palace of the
    Forest.

....

■ PSALM 112:1–5

[1] Praise the LORD.

Blessed are those who fear the LORD,
who find great delight in his
commands.

2 Their children will be mighty in the
land;
the generation of the upright will be
blessed.
3 Wealth and riches are in their houses,
and their righteousness endures for
ever.
4 Even in darkness light dawns for the
upright,
for those who are gracious and
compassionate and righteous.
5 Good will come to those who are
generous and lend freely,
who conduct their affairs with justice.

▬ PROVERBS 23:17-18

17 Do not let your heart envy sinners,
but always be zealous for the fear of
the LORD.
18 There is surely a future hope for you,
and your hope will not be cut off.

▬ GALATIANS 2:1-21

2 Then after fourteen years, I went up
again to Jerusalem, this time with
Barnabas. I took Titus along also. 2 I went
in response to a revelation and, meeting
privately with those esteemed as leaders, I
presented to them the gospel that I preach
among the Gentiles. I wanted to be sure I
was not running and had not been running
my race in vain. 3 Yet not even Titus, who
was with me, was compelled to be circumcised, even though he was a Greek. 4 This
matter arose because some false believers
had infiltrated our ranks to spy on the freedom we have in Christ Jesus and to make
us slaves. 5 We did not give in to them for

a moment, so that the truth of the gospel
might be preserved for you.

6 As for those who were held in high esteem – whatever they were makes no difference to me; God does not show favouritism – they added nothing to my message.
7 On the contrary, they recognised that I had
been entrusted with the task of preaching
the gospel to the uncircumcised, just as Peter had been to the circumcised. 8 For God,
who was at work in Peter as an apostle to
the circumcised, was also at work in me as
an apostle to the Gentiles. 9 James, Cephas
and John, those esteemed as pillars, gave
me and Barnabas the right hand of fellowship when they recognised the grace given
to me. They agreed that we should go to the
Gentiles, and they to the circumcised. 10 All
they asked was that we should continue to
remember the poor, the very thing I had
been eager to do all along.

11 When Cephas came to Antioch, I opposed him to his face, because he stood
condemned. 12 For before certain men came
from James, he used to eat with the Gentiles.
But when they arrived, he began to draw
back and separate himself from the Gentiles
because he was afraid of those who belonged
to the circumcision group. 13 The other Jews
joined him in his hypocrisy, so that by their
hypocrisy even Barnabas was led astray.

14 When I saw that they were not acting
in line with the truth of the gospel, I said to
Cephas in front of them all, 'You are a Jew,
yet you live like a Gentile and not like a Jew.
How is it, then, that you force Gentiles to
follow Jewish customs?

15 'We who are Jews by birth and not sinful Gentiles 16 know that a person is not justified by the works of the law, but by faith in
Jesus Christ. So we, too, have put our faith
in Christ Jesus that we may be justified by
faith in Christ and not by the works of the
law, because by the works of the law no one
will be justified.

17 'But if, in seeking to be justified in

Christ, we Jews find ourselves also among the sinners, doesn't that mean that Christ promotes sin? Absolutely not! **18** If I rebuild what I destroyed, then I really would be a law-breaker.

19 'For through the law I died to the law so that I might live for God. **20** I have been crucified with Christ and I no longer live, but Christ lives in me. The life I now live in the body, I live by faith in the Son of God, who loved me and gave himself for me. **21** I do not set aside the grace of God, for if righteousness could be gained through the law, Christ died for nothing!'

Touching the Intangible

'James, Cephas and John … gave me and Barnabas the right hand of fellowship when they recognised the grace given to me. They agreed that we should go to the Gentiles and they to the circumcised.' **Galatians 2:9**

Truly, in making an effort to go outside of ourselves and relate to others, we receive a wider awareness and a deeper understanding of God. This has been one of the greatest and most exciting discoveries of my life. The more I have given myself to my brothers and sisters in Christ, the greater has been my awareness and understanding of God.

I am not saying that in order to know God, we first have to get to know each other. That would be blatant error. We can know *about* Him through such means as creation, providence, and so on, but we can only know Him through His Son Jesus Christ. 'No one has ever seen God, but the one and only Son, who is himself God and is in the closest relationship with the Father, has made him known' (John 1:18). However, once we know Him in this way, our fellowship with Him and our understanding of Him can be deepened by our relationship with others who know Him.

How does this work? The more I have focused on learning to listen - really listen - to my brothers and sisters in Christ, the more I have found that the effort I have made to do this has resulted in a heightening of my ability to listen to God. And the more I have sought to understand the mystery of His dealings in their lives, the more I have come to know the depth and beauty of His character. Although down the years I have come to know Him intimately in prayer, I believe I can say that I know Him even better because I have met Him in others.

PRAYER

O Father, how can I sufficiently thank You for the fellowship we have with one another in Christ. In the tangible I see the Intangible, and through the visible I see the Invisible. I am eternally grateful. Amen.

FURTHER STUDY

John 14:20; Gal. 2:1-20; Col. 1:27; 1 John 3:24
• How does God make His riches known?
• Are those riches being made known to others through you?

September 27

■ ISAIAH 22:9–24:23

⁹ You saw that the walls of the City of
    David
    were broken through in many places;
  you stored up water
    in the Lower Pool.
¹⁰ You counted the buildings in Jerusalem
    and tore down houses to strengthen
      the wall.
¹¹ You built a reservoir between the two
    walls
    for the water of the Old Pool,
  but you did not look to the One who
    made it,
  or have regard for the One who
    planned it long ago.

¹² The Lord, the LORD Almighty,
    called you on that day
to weep and to wail,
    to tear out your hair and put on
      sackcloth.
¹³ But see, there is joy and revelry,
    slaughtering of cattle and killing of
      sheep,
    eating of meat and drinking of wine!
'Let us eat and drink,' you say,
    'for tomorrow we die!'

¹⁴ The LORD Almighty has revealed this
in my hearing: 'Till your dying day this sin
will not be atoned for,' says the Lord, the
LORD Almighty.

¹⁵ This is what the Lord, the LORD
Almighty, says:

'Go, say to this steward,
    to Shebna the palace administrator:

¹⁶ what are you doing here and who gave
    you permission
  to cut out a grave for yourself here,
hewing your grave on the height
    and chiselling your resting place in
      the rock?

¹⁷ 'Beware, the LORD is about to take firm
    hold of you
  and hurl you away, you mighty man.
¹⁸ He will roll you up tightly like a ball
    and throw you into a large country.
There you will die
    and there the chariots you were so
      proud of
  will become a disgrace to your
    master's house.
¹⁹ I will depose you from your office,
    and you will be ousted from your
      position.

²⁰ 'In that day I will summon my servant,
Eliakim son of Hilkiah. ²¹ I will clothe him
with your robe and fasten your sash around
him and hand your authority over to him.
He will be a father to those who live in Jerusalem and to the people of Judah. ²² I will
place on his shoulder the key to the house of
David; what he opens no one can shut, and
what he shuts no one can open. ²³ I will drive
him like a peg into a firm place; he will become a seat of honour for the house of his
father. ²⁴ All the glory of his family will hang
on him: its offspring and offshoots – all its
lesser vessels, from the bowls to all the jars.

²⁵ 'In that day,' declares the LORD
Almighty, 'the peg driven into the firm
place will give way; it will be sheared off and
will fall, and the load hanging on it will be
cut down.' The LORD has spoken.

23

A prophecy against Tyre:

Wail, you ships of Tarshish!
  For Tyre is destroyed
  and left without house or harbour.
From the land of Cyprus
  word has come to them.

2 Be silent, you people of the island
    and you merchants of Sidon,
    whom the seafarers have enriched.
3 On the great waters
    came the grain of the Shihor;
  the harvest of the Nile was the revenue
      of Tyre,
    and she became the market-place of
      the nations.

4 Be ashamed, Sidon, and you fortress of
      the sea,
    for the sea has spoken:
'I have neither been in labour nor given
      birth;
    I have neither reared sons nor brought
      up daughters.'
5 When word comes to Egypt,
    they will be in anguish at the report
      from Tyre.

6 Cross over to Tarshish;
    wail, you people of the island.
7 Is this your city of revelry,
    the old, old city,
  whose feet have taken her
    to settle in far-off lands?
8 Who planned this against Tyre,
    the bestower of crowns,
  whose merchants are princes,
    whose traders are renowned in the
      earth?
9 The LORD Almighty planned it,
    to bring down her pride in all her
      splendour
    and to humble all who are renowned
      on the earth.

10 Till your land as they do along the Nile,
      Daughter Tarshish,
    for you no longer have a harbour.
11 The LORD has stretched out his hand over
      the sea
    and made its kingdoms tremble.
  He has given an order concerning
      Phoenicia
    that her fortresses be destroyed.
12 He said, 'No more of your revelling,
    Virgin Daughter Sidon, now crushed!

'Up, cross over to Cyprus;
    even there you will find no rest.'
13 Look at the land of the Babylonians,
    this people that is now of no account!
The Assyrians have made it
    a place for desert creatures;
  they raised up their siege towers,
    they stripped its fortresses bare
    and turned it into a ruin.

14 Wail, you ships of Tarshish;
    your fortress is destroyed!

15 At that time Tyre will be forgotten for
seventy years, the span of a king's life. But at
the end of these seventy years, it will happen
to Tyre as in the song of the prostitute:

16 'Take up a harp, walk through the city,
    you forgotten prostitute;
  play the harp well, sing many a song,
    so that you will be remembered.'

17 At the end of seventy years, the LORD
will deal with Tyre. She will return to her
lucrative prostitution and will ply her
trade with all the kingdoms on the face of
the earth. 18 Yet her profit and her earnings
will be set apart for the LORD; they will not
be stored up or hoarded. Her profits will
go to those who live before the LORD, for
abundant food and fine clothes.

24

See, the LORD is going to lay waste
  the earth

and devastate it;
he will ruin its face
and scatter its inhabitants –
² it will be the same
for priest as for people,
for the master as for his servant,
for the mistress as for her servant,
for seller as for buyer,
for borrower as for lender,
for debtor as for creditor.
³ The earth will be completely laid waste
and totally plundered.
           The Lord has spoken this word.

⁴ The earth dries up and withers,
the world languishes and withers,
the heavens languish with the earth.
⁵ The earth is defiled by its people;
they have disobeyed the laws,
violated the statutes
and broken the everlasting covenant.
⁶ Therefore a curse consumes the earth;
its people must bear their guilt.
Therefore earth's inhabitants are burned
up,
and very few are left.
⁷ The new wine dries up and the vine
withers;
all the merrymakers groan.
⁸ The joyful tambourines are stilled,
the noise of the revellers has stopped,
the joyful harp is silent.
⁹ No longer do they drink wine with a song;
the beer is bitter to its drinkers.
¹⁰ The ruined city lies desolate;
the entrance to every house is barred.
¹¹ In the streets they cry out for wine;
all joy turns to gloom,
all joyful sounds are banished from
the earth.
¹² The city is left in ruins,
its gate is battered to pieces.
¹³ So will it be on the earth
and among the nations,
as when an olive tree is beaten,

or as when gleanings are left after the
grape harvest.

¹⁴ They raise their voices, they shout for joy;
from the west they acclaim the Lord's
majesty.
¹⁵ Therefore in the east give glory to the
Lord;
exalt the name of the Lord, the God of
Israel,
in the islands of the sea.
¹⁶ From the ends of the earth we hear
singing:
'Glory to the Righteous One.'

But I said, 'I waste away, I waste away!
Woe to me!
The treacherous betray!
With treachery the treacherous betray!'
¹⁷ Terror and pit and snare await you,
people of the earth.
¹⁸ Whoever flees at the sound of terror
will fall into a pit;
whoever climbs out of the pit
will be caught in a snare.

The floodgates of the heavens are opened,
the foundations of the earth shake.
¹⁹ The earth is broken up,
the earth is split asunder,
the earth is violently shaken.
²⁰ The earth reels like a drunkard,
it sways like a hut in the wind;
so heavy upon it is the guilt of its rebellion
that it falls – never to rise again.

²¹ In that day the Lord will punish
the powers in the heavens above
and the kings on the earth below.
²² They will be herded together
like prisoners bound in a dungeon;
they will be shut up in prison
and be punished after many days.
²³ The moon will be dismayed,
the sun ashamed;
for the Lord Almighty will reign

on Mount Zion and in Jerusalem,
and before its elders – with great glory.

▬ PSALM 112:6-10

⁶ Surely the righteous will never be
shaken;
they will be remembered for ever.
⁷ They will have no fear of bad news;
their hearts are steadfast, trusting in
the LORD.
⁸ Their hearts are secure, they will have no
fear;
in the end they will look in triumph on
their foes.
⁹ They have freely scattered their gifts to
the poor,
their righteousness endures for ever;
their horn will be lifted high in
honour.

¹⁰ The wicked will see and be vexed,
they will gnash their teeth and waste
away;
the longings of the wicked will come
to nothing.

▬ PROVERBS 23:19-21

¹⁹ Listen, my son, and be wise,
and set your heart on the right path:
²⁰ do not join those who drink too much
wine
or gorge themselves on meat,
²¹ for drunkards and gluttons become
poor,
and drowsiness clothes them in rags.

▬ GALATIANS 3:1-18

3 You foolish Galatians! Who has be-
witched you? Before your very eyes
Jesus Christ was clearly portrayed as
crucified. ²I would like to learn just one
thing from you: did you receive the Spirit by the works of the law, or by believing
what you heard? ³Are you so foolish? After
beginning by means of the Spirit, are you
now trying to finish by means of the flesh?
⁴Have you experienced so much in vain – if
it really was in vain? ⁵So again I ask, does
God give you his Spirit and work miracles
among you by the works of the law, or by
your believing what you heard? ⁶So also
Abraham 'believed God, and it was credited
to him as righteousness.'

⁷Understand, then, that those who have
faith are children of Abraham. ⁸Scripture
foresaw that God would justify the Gentiles by faith, and announced the gospel in
advance to Abraham: 'All nations will be
blessed through you.' ⁹So those who rely on
faith are blessed along with Abraham, the
man of faith.

¹⁰For all who rely on the works of the law
are under a curse, as it is written: 'Cursed
is everyone who does not continue to do
everything written in the Book of the Law.'
¹¹Clearly no one who relies on the law is justified before God, because 'the righteous
will live by faith.' ¹²The law is not based on
faith; on the contrary, it says, 'The person
who does these things will live by them.'
¹³Christ redeemed us from the curse of
the law by becoming a curse for us, for it
is written: 'Cursed is everyone who is hung
on a pole.' ¹⁴He redeemed us in order that
the blessing given to Abraham might come
to the Gentiles through Christ Jesus, so
that by faith we might receive the promise
of the Spirit.

¹⁵Brothers and sisters, let me take an example from everyday life. Just as no one can
set aside or add to a human covenant that
has been duly established, so it is in this
case. ¹⁶The promises were spoken to Abraham and to his seed. Scripture does not say
'and to seeds', meaning many people, but
'and to your seed', meaning one person,

who is Christ. ¹⁷What I mean is this: the law, introduced 430 years later, does not set aside the covenant previously established by God and thus do away with the promise. ¹⁸For if the inheritance depends on the law, then it no longer depends on the promise; but God in his grace gave it to Abraham through a promise.

Balanced Christianity

'After beginning by means of the Spirit, are you now trying to finish by means of the flesh?' **Galatians 3:3**

The Christian church has always struggled to get the balance right between faith and works. Romans is the great book on 'faith', while James is the great book on 'works'. I know some Christians who never read the book of James, taking sides with Martin Luther who called it a 'book of straw'. Martin Luther may have been right about many things, but he was wrong when he referred to the Epistle of James in this way. We need to study both Romans and James if we want to be properly balanced Christians.

The difficulty with faith and works is this: we come into the Christian life by depending on Jesus' innocent sufferings on Calvary as sufficient ground for our acceptance with God, and then when we learn the principles of Christian living, we turn from dependency on Christ to dependency on them. This was the great problem in the Galatian churches, and it is still a problem here in the church of the current century. Bringing forth the fruit of repentance by good works is terribly important, but we are not to depend on works for our salvation.

We tend to focus more on works than faith because it is something visible and tangible. We can see what we are doing and assess it or measure it. Faith is different. It requires of us a degree of helplessness (something the carnal nature detests), but if we are to know God better and avoid falling into the trap of pursuing godliness more keenly than pursuing God, then faith must be seen as the primary virtue.

PRAYER

O Father, help me get this right. I am saved to good works, but I am not saved by good works. Prevent me from falling into the trap of being more preoccupied with Your principles than with You Yourself. In Jesus' name. Amen.

FURTHER STUDY

Eph. 2:1-9; Gal. 2:16; Rom. 9:32
• What did Paul remind the Ephesians?
• What did he emphasise to the Galatians?

September 28

■ ISAIAH 25:1–27:13

25 LORD, you are my God;
I will exalt you and praise your
name,
for in perfect faithfulness
you have done wonderful things,
things planned long ago.
² You have made the city a heap of rubble,
the fortified town a ruin,
the foreigners' stronghold a city no more;
it will never be rebuilt.
³ Therefore strong peoples will honour
you;
cities of ruthless nations will revere
you.
⁴ You have been a refuge for the poor,
a refuge for the needy in their distress,
a shelter from the storm
and a shade from the heat.
For the breath of the ruthless
is like a storm driving against a wall
⁵ and like the heat of the desert.
You silence the uproar of foreigners;
as heat is reduced by the shadow of a
cloud,
so the song of the ruthless is stilled.

⁶ On this mountain the LORD Almighty
will prepare
a feast of rich food for all peoples,
a banquet of aged wine –
the best of meats and the finest of
wines.
⁷ On this mountain he will destroy
the shroud that enfolds all peoples,
the sheet that covers all nations;
⁸ he will swallow up death for ever.
The Sovereign LORD will wipe away the
tears
from all faces;

he will remove his people's disgrace
from all the earth.
The LORD has spoken.

⁹ In that day they will say,

'Surely this is our God;
we trusted in him, and he saved us.
This is the LORD, we trusted in him;
let us rejoice and be glad in his
salvation.'

¹⁰ The hand of the LORD will rest on this
mountain;
but Moab will be trampled in their
land
as straw is trampled down in the
manure.
¹¹ They will stretch out their hands in it,
as swimmers stretch out their hands
to swim.
God will bring down their pride
despite the cleverness of their hands.
¹² He will bring down your high fortified
walls
and lay them low;
he will bring them down to the ground,
to the very dust.

26 In that day this song will be sung in
the land of Judah:

We have a strong city;
God makes salvation
its walls and ramparts.
² Open the gates
that the righteous nation may enter,
the nation that keeps faith.
³ You will keep in perfect peace
those whose minds are steadfast,
because they trust in you.

⁴ Trust in the LORD for ever,
for the LORD, the LORD himself, is the
Rock eternal.
⁵ He humbles those who dwell on high,
he lays the lofty city low;
he levels it to the ground
and casts it down to the dust.
⁶ Feet trample it down –
the feet of the oppressed,
the footsteps of the poor.

⁷ The path of the righteous is level;
you, the Upright One, make the way of
the righteous smooth.
⁸ Yes, LORD, walking in the way of your
laws,
we wait for you;
your name and renown
are the desire of our hearts.
⁹ My soul yearns for you in the night;
in the morning my spirit longs for you.
When your judgments come upon the
earth,
the people of the world learn
righteousness.
¹⁰ But when grace is shown to the wicked,
they do not learn righteousness;
even in a land of uprightness they go on
doing evil
and do not regard the majesty of the
LORD.
¹¹ LORD, your hand is lifted high,
but they do not see it.
Let them see your zeal for your people
and be put to shame;
let the fire reserved for your enemies
consume them.

¹² LORD, you establish peace for us;
all that we have accomplished you
have done for us.
¹³ LORD our God, other lords besides you
have ruled over us,
but your name alone do we honour.
¹⁴ They are now dead, they live no more;
their spirits do not rise.

You punished them and brought them to
ruin;
you wiped out all memory of them.
¹⁵ You have enlarged the nation, LORD;
you have enlarged the nation.
You have gained glory for yourself;
you have extended all the borders of
the land.

¹⁶ LORD, they came to you in their distress;
when you disciplined them,
they could barely whisper a prayer.
¹⁷ As a pregnant woman about to give birth
writhes and cries out in her pain,
so were we in your presence, LORD.
¹⁸ We were with child, we writhed in labour,
but we gave birth to wind.
We have not brought salvation to the
earth,
and the people of the world have not
come to life.

¹⁹ But your dead will live, LORD;
their bodies will rise –
let those who dwell in the dust
wake up and shout for joy –
your dew is like the dew of the morning;
the earth will give birth to her dead.

²⁰ Go, my people, enter your rooms
and shut the doors behind you;
hide yourselves for a little while
until his wrath has passed by.
²¹ See, the LORD is coming out of his
dwelling
to punish the people of the earth for
their sins.
The earth will disclose the blood shed
on it;
the earth will conceal its slain no
longer.

27 In that day,

the LORD will punish with his sword –
his fierce, great and powerful sword –

Leviathan the gliding serpent,
   Leviathan the coiling serpent;
he will slay the monster of the sea.

²In that day –

'Sing about a fruitful vineyard:
³   I, the LORD, watch over it;
   I water it continually.
I guard it day and night
   so that no one may harm it.
⁴   I am not angry.
If only there were briers and thorns
      confronting me!
   I would march against them in battle;
   I would set them all on fire.
⁵Or else let them come to me for refuge;
   let them make peace with me,
   yes, let them make peace with me.'

⁶In days to come Jacob will take root,
   Israel will bud and blossom
   and fill all the world with fruit.

⁷Has the LORD struck her
   as he struck down those who struck
      her?
Has she been killed
   as those were killed who killed her?
⁸By warfare and exile you contend with
      her –
   with his fierce blast he drives her out,
   as on a day the east wind blows.
⁹By this, then, will Jacob's guilt be atoned
      for,
   and this will be the full fruit of the
      removal of his sin:
when he makes all the altar stones
   to be like limestone crushed to pieces,
   no Asherah poles or incense altars
   will be left standing.
¹⁰The fortified city stands desolate,
   an abandoned settlement, forsaken
      like the wilderness;
there the calves graze,
   there they lie down;

they strip its branches bare.
¹¹When its twigs are dry, they are broken
      off
   and women come and make fires with
      them.
For this is a people without
      understanding;
   so their Maker has no compassion on
      them,
   and their Creator shows them no
      favour.

¹²In that day the LORD will thresh from
the flowing Euphrates to the Wadi of Egypt,
and you, Israel, will be gathered up one by
one. ¹³And in that day a great trumpet will
sound. Those who were perishing in Assyria and those who were exiled in Egypt
will come and worship the LORD on the holy
mountain in Jerusalem.

....

■ PSALM 113:1-9

¹Praise the LORD.

Praise the LORD, you his servants;
   praise the name of the LORD.
²Let the name of the LORD be praised,
   both now and for evermore.
³From the rising of the sun to the place
      where it sets,
   the name of the LORD is to be praised.

⁴The LORD is exalted over all the nations,
   his glory above the heavens.
⁵Who is like the LORD our God,
   the One who sits enthroned on high,
⁶who stoops down to look
   on the heavens and the earth?

⁷He raises the poor from the dust
   and lifts the needy from the ash heap;
⁸he seats them with princes,
   with the princes of his people.

[9] He settles the childless woman in her
home
as a happy mother of children.

Praise the LORD.

■ PROVERBS 23:22-23

[22] Listen to your father, who gave you life,
and do not despise your mother when
she is old.
[23] Buy the truth and do not sell it –
wisdom, instruction and insight as
well.

■ GALATIANS 3:19–4:11

[19] Why, then, was the law given at all? It
was added because of transgressions until
the Seed to whom the promise referred had
come. The law was given through angels
and entrusted to a mediator. [20] A mediator,
however, implies more than one party; but
God is one.

[21] Is the law, therefore, opposed to the
promises of God? Absolutely not! For if a
law had been given that could impart life,
then righteousness would certainly have
come by the law. [22] But Scripture has locked
up everything under the control of sin,
so that what was promised, being given
through faith in Jesus Christ, might be
given to those who believe.

[23] Before the coming of this faith, we were
held in custody under the law, locked up
until the faith that was to come would be revealed. [24] So the law was our guardian until

Christ came that we might be justified by
faith. [25] Now that this faith has come, we are
no longer under a guardian.

[26] So in Christ Jesus you are all children of
God through faith, [27] for all of you who were
baptised into Christ have clothed yourselves
with Christ. [28] There is neither Jew nor Gentile, neither slave nor free, nor is there male
and female, for you are all one in Christ
Jesus. [29] If you belong to Christ, then you
are Abraham's seed, and heirs according
to the promise.

4 What I am saying is that as long as an
heir is under age, he is no different
from a slave, although he owns the whole
estate. [2] The heir is subject to guardians and
trustees until the time set by his father. [3] So
also, when we were under age, we were in
slavery under the elemental spiritual forces
of the world. [4] But when the set time had fully come, God sent his Son, born of a woman,
born under the law, [5] to redeem those under
the law, that we might receive adoption to
sonship. [6] Because you are his sons, God
sent the Spirit of his Son into our hearts, the
Spirit who calls out, 'Abba, Father.' [7] So you
are no longer a slave, but God's child; and
since you are his child, God has made you
also an heir.

[8] Formerly, when you did not know God,
you were slaves to those who by nature are
not gods. [9] But now that you know God – or
rather are known by God – how is it that
you are turning back to those weak and
miserable forces? Do you wish to be enslaved
by them all over again? [10] You are observing
special days and months and seasons and
years! [11] I fear for you, that somehow I have
wasted my efforts on you.

'Imagineering'

'You will keep in perfect peace those whose minds are
steadfast, because they trust in you.' **Isaiah 26:3**

How many times, when making an approach to God in prayer, have we gone immediately into a series of petitions that have to do with our problems, our difficulties, our circumstances? And so, by focusing our attention on what is troubling us, we end up wondering whether or not God is big enough or strong enough to help us.

In the first six words of the Lord's Prayer, Jesus shows us a better way. He tells us to take a slow, calm, reassuring gaze at God – at His tenderness, His eagerness to give, His unwearying patience and untiring love. The result of this, of course, is that we develop a calmness and tranquility in our spirit which means we will find it no longer necessary to plunge into a panicky flood of words.

In some parts of the world one can enrol in courses called 'Imagineering' – courses that are designed to stimulate creative imagination. Most of our problems begin in the imagination – hence the instruction in the words of our text for today. 'One can never become proficient in prayer', said one great writer, 'until the imagination has been redeemed.' He meant that when the imagination is redeemed from self-concentration, sex-concentration, and sin-concentration, and makes God its primary focus, then it becomes creative-conscious, since its attention is concentrated on the Creator and the Re-Creator. And when the imagination is redeemed, all the doors of the personality fly open.

PRAYER

O God, how can I be calm and tranquil when my imagination is more self-centred than God-centred? Help me to be a God-focused person, not only at prayer times, but at all times. Amen.

FURTHER STUDY

1 Cor. 2:1-16; Gen. 6:5; Rom. 1:21; 2 Cor. 10:5
• How can we 'demolish arguments and every pretension'?
• What has God given to us?

September 29

■ ISAIAH 28:1–29:24

28 Woe to that wreath, the pride of Ephraim's drunkards,
to the fading flower, his glorious beauty,
set on the head of a fertile valley –
to that city, the pride of those laid low by wine!
² See, the Lord has one who is powerful and strong.

Like a hailstorm and a destructive wind,
like a driving rain and a flooding downpour,
he will throw it forcefully to the ground.
³ That wreath, the pride of Ephraim's drunkards,
will be trampled underfoot.
⁴ That fading flower, his glorious beauty,
set on the head of a fertile valley,

will be like figs ripe before harvest –
    as soon as people see them and take
        them in hand,
    they swallow them.

⁵ In that day the Lord Almighty
    will be a glorious crown,
a beautiful wreath
    for the remnant of his people.
⁶ He will be a spirit of justice
    to the one who sits in judgment,
a source of strength
    to those who turn back the battle at
        the gate.

⁷ And these also stagger from wine
    and reel from beer:
priests and prophets stagger from beer
    and are befuddled with wine;
they reel from beer,
    they stagger when seeing visions,
    they stumble when rendering
        decisions.
⁸ All the tables are covered with vomit
    and there is not a spot without filth.

⁹ 'Who is it he is trying to teach?
    To whom is he explaining his
        message?
To children weaned from their milk,
    to those just taken from the breast?
¹⁰ For it is:
    do this, do that,
    a rule for this, a rule for that;
    a little here, a little there.'

¹¹ Very well then, with foreign lips and
        strange tongues
    God will speak to this people,
¹² to whom he said,
    'This is the resting-place, let the weary
        rest';
    and, 'This is the place of repose' –
    but they would not listen.
¹³ So then, the word of the Lord to them
    will become:

do this, do that,
    a rule for this, a rule for that;
    a little here, a little there –
so that as they go they will fall
        backwards;
    they will be injured and snared and
        captured.

¹⁴ Therefore hear the word of the Lord, you
        scoffers
    who rule this people in Jerusalem.
¹⁵ You boast, 'We have entered into a
        covenant with death,
    with the realm of the dead we have
        made an agreement.
When an overwhelming scourge sweeps
        by,
    it cannot touch us,
for we have made a lie our refuge
    and falsehood our hiding-place.'

¹⁶ So this is what the Sovereign Lord says:

'See, I lay a stone in Zion, a tested stone,
    a precious cornerstone for a sure
        foundation;
the one who relies on it
    will never be stricken with panic.
¹⁷ I will make justice the measuring line
    and righteousness the plumb-line;
hail will sweep away your refuge, the lie,
    and water will overflow your
        hiding-place.
¹⁸ Your covenant with death will be
        annulled;
    your agreement with the realm of the
        dead will not stand.
When the overwhelming scourge sweeps
        by,
    you will be beaten down by it.
¹⁹ As often as it comes it will carry you
        away;
    morning after morning, by day and by
        night,
    it will sweep through.'

The understanding of this message
will bring sheer terror.
²⁰ The bed is too short to stretch out on,
the blanket too narrow to wrap
around you.
²¹ The LORD will rise up as he did at Mount
Perazim,
he will rouse himself as in the Valley
of Gibeon –
to do his work, his strange work,
and perform his task, his alien task.
²² Now stop your mocking,
or your chains will become heavier;
the Lord, the LORD Almighty, has told me
of the destruction decreed against the
whole land.

²³ Listen and hear my voice;
pay attention and hear what I say.
²⁴ When a farmer ploughs for planting,
does he plough continually?
Does he keep on breaking up and
working the soil?
²⁵ When he has levelled the surface,
does he not sow caraway and scatter
cummin?
Does he not plant wheat in its place,
barley in its plot,
and spelt in its field?
²⁶ His God instructs him
and teaches him the right way.

²⁷ Caraway is not threshed with a sledge,
nor is the cartwheel rolled over
cummin;
caraway is beaten out with a rod,
and cummin with a stick.
²⁸ Grain must be ground to make bread;
so one does not go on threshing it for
ever.
The wheels of a threshing-cart may be
rolled over it,
but one does not use horses to grind
grain.
²⁹ All this also comes from the LORD
Almighty,

whose plan is wonderful,
whose wisdom is magnificent.

29
Woe to you, Ariel, Ariel,
the city where David settled!
Add year to year
and let your cycle of festivals go on.
² Yet I will besiege Ariel;
she will mourn and lament,
she will be to me like an altar hearth.
³ I will encamp against you on all sides;
I will encircle you with towers
and set up my siege works against you.
⁴ Brought low, you will speak from the
ground;
your speech will mumble out of the
dust.
Your voice will come ghostlike from the
earth;
out of the dust your speech will
whisper.

⁵ But your many enemies will become like
fine dust,
the ruthless hordes like blown chaff.
Suddenly, in an instant,
⁶   the LORD Almighty will come
with thunder and earthquake and great
noise,
with whirlwind and tempest and
flames of a devouring fire.
⁷ Then the hordes of all the nations that
fight against Ariel,
that attack her and her fortress and
besiege her,
will be as it is with a dream,
with a vision in the night –
⁸ as when a hungry person dreams of
eating,
but awakens hungry still;
as when a thirsty person dreams of
drinking,
but awakens faint and thirsty still.
So will it be with the hordes of all the
nations
that fight against Mount Zion.

⁹ Be stunned and amazed,
    blind yourselves and be sightless;
    be drunk, but not from wine,
        stagger, but not from beer.
¹⁰ The LORD has brought over you a deep
        sleep:
    he has sealed your eyes (the prophets);
    he has covered your heads (the seers).

¹¹ For you this whole vision is nothing
but words sealed in a scroll. And if you give
the scroll to someone who can read, and
say, 'Read this, please,' they will answer, 'I
can't; it is sealed.' ¹² Or if you give the scroll
to someone who cannot read, and say, 'Read
this, please,' they will answer, 'I don't know
how to read.'

¹³ The Lord says:

'These people come near to me with their
        mouth
    and honour me with their lips,
    but their hearts are far from me.
Their worship of me
    is based on merely human rules they
        have been taught.
¹⁴ Therefore once more I will astound these
        people
    with wonder upon wonder;
    the wisdom of the wise will perish,
    the intelligence of the intelligent will
        vanish.'
¹⁵ Woe to those who go to great depths
    to hide their plans from the LORD,
who do their work in darkness and think,
    'Who sees us? Who will know?'
¹⁶ You turn things upside down,
    as if the potter were thought to be like
        the clay!
Shall what is formed say to the one who
        formed it,
    'You did not make me'?
Can the pot say to the potter,
    'You know nothing'?

¹⁷ In a very short time, will not Lebanon be
        turned into a fertile field
    and the fertile field seem like a forest?
¹⁸ In that day the deaf will hear the words
        of the scroll,
    and out of gloom and darkness
    the eyes of the blind will see.
¹⁹ Once more the humble will rejoice in the
        LORD;
    the needy will rejoice in the Holy One
        of Israel.
²⁰ The ruthless will vanish,
    the mockers will disappear,
    and all who have an eye for evil will be
        cut down –
²¹ those who with a word make someone
        out to be guilty,
    who ensnare the defender in court
    and with false testimony deprive the
        innocent of justice.

²² Therefore this is what the LORD, who redeemed Abraham, says to the descendants
of Jacob:

'No longer will Jacob be ashamed;
    no longer will their faces grow pale.
²³ When they see among them their children,
    the work of my hands,
they will keep my name holy;
    they will acknowledge the holiness of
        the Holy One of Jacob,
    and will stand in awe of the God of
        Israel.
²⁴ Those who are wayward in spirit will
        gain understanding;
    those who complain will accept
        instruction.'

▬ **PSALM 114:1–8**

¹ When Israel came out of Egypt,
    Jacob from a people of foreign tongue,
² Judah became God's sanctuary,
    Israel his dominion.

³ The sea looked and fled,
  the Jordan turned back;
⁴ the mountains leaped like rams,
  the hills like lambs.

⁵ Why was it, sea, that you fled?
  Why, Jordan, did you turn back?
⁶ Why, mountains, did you leap like rams,
  you hills, like lambs?

⁷ Tremble, earth, at the presence of the
  Lord,
  at the presence of the God of Jacob,
⁸ who turned the rock into a pool,
  the hard rock into springs of water.

▬ PROVERBS 23:24-25

²⁴ The father of a righteous child has great
  joy;
  a man who fathers a wise son rejoices
  in him.
²⁵ May your father and mother rejoice;
  may she who gave you birth be joyful!

▬ GALATIANS 4:12-31

¹² I plead with you, brothers and sisters,
become like me, for I became like you. You
did me no wrong. ¹³ As you know, it was because of an illness that I first preached the
gospel to you, ¹⁴ and even though my illness
was a trial to you, you did not treat me with
contempt or scorn. Instead, you welcomed
me as if I were an angel of God, as if I were
Christ Jesus himself. ¹⁵ Where, then, is your
blessing of me now? I can testify that, if you
could have done so, you would have torn
out your eyes and given them to me. ¹⁶ Have
I now become your enemy by telling you
the truth?

¹⁷ Those people are zealous to win you
over, but for no good. What they want is
to alienate you from us, so that you may

have zeal for them. ¹⁸ It is fine to be zealous,
provided the purpose is good, and to be so
always, not just when I am with you. ¹⁹ My
dear children, for whom I am again in the
pains of childbirth until Christ is formed
in you, ²⁰ how I wish I could be with you
now and change my tone, because I am
perplexed about you!

²¹ Tell me, you who want to be under the
law, are you not aware of what the law says?
²² For it is written that Abraham had two
sons, one by the slave woman and the other by the free woman. ²³ His son by the slave
woman was born according to the flesh, but
his son by the free woman was born as the
result of a divine promise.

²⁴ These things are being taken figuratively: the women represent two covenants.
One covenant is from Mount Sinai and
bears children who are to be slaves: this is
Hagar. ²⁵ Now Hagar stands for Mount Sinai
in Arabia and corresponds to the present
city of Jerusalem, because she is in slavery with her children. ²⁶ But the Jerusalem
that is above is free, and she is our mother.
²⁷ For it is written:

'Be glad, barren woman,
  you who never bore a child;
break forth and cry aloud,
  you who were never in labour;
because more are the children of the
    desolate woman
  than of her who has a husband.'

²⁸ Now you, brothers and sisters, like
Isaac, are children of promise. ²⁹ At that
time the son born according to the flesh
persecuted the son born by the power of the
Spirit. It is the same now. ³⁰ But what does
Scripture say? 'Get rid of the slave woman and her son, for the slave woman's son
will never share in the inheritance with the
free woman's son.' ³¹ Therefore, brothers
and sisters, we are not children of the slave
woman, but of the free woman.

More Than a Recitation

'... "These people come near to me with their mouth and honour me with their lips, but their hearts are far from me."' **Isaiah 29:13**

Some Christians think that prayer consists solely of reciting the words of the Lord's Prayer, but, as the great preacher C. H. Spurgeon once said, 'To recite the Lord's Prayer and believe that you have then prayed is the height of foolishness.' This does not mean, of course, that there is no spiritual value in reciting it, providing we realise that it is not just a prayer to be recited. Personally, I would not want to deprive Christian congregations of the pleasure and joy of reciting together the Lord's Prayer, but I do want to encourage them to view it as a departure point rather than an arrival platform.

If Jesus advised His disciples to avoid 'babbling like pagans' (Matt. 6:7), would He then immediately follow it by giving us a prayer to simply recite? Obviously, as I have said, one can derive great spiritual pleasure from repeating the words that Jesus gave us, but if we are to obtain the greatest value from the Lord's Prayer, then we must view it as a skeleton on which we have to put flesh. If we view these words not merely as something to recite but as an outline from which we must work our way when praying, no matter what we are praying about, then we will experience a growing confidence that we are praying the way Jesus taught.

You see, it's one thing to recite a prayer; it's another thing to know how to pray.

PRAYER

Heavenly Father, I see there can be great value in reciting a prayer, but I want to be able to do more than repeat a prayer – I want to pray. Help me, for without You I can do nothing. For Jesus' sake. Amen.

FURTHER STUDY

Gal. 4:1-11; Luke 20:47
• What is Paul saying about ritualism?
• When does prayer become hypocritical?

September 30

■ ISAIAH 30:1–32:10

30 'Woe to the obstinate children,'
declares the LORD,

'to those who carry out plans that are not mine,
forming an alliance, but not by my Spirit,
heaping sin upon sin;

² who go down to Egypt
without consulting me;
who look for help to Pharaoh's
protection,
to Egypt's shade for refuge.
³ But Pharaoh's protection will be to your
shame,
Egypt's shade will bring you disgrace.
⁴ Though they have officials in Zoan
and their envoys have arrived in
Hanes,
⁵ everyone will be put to shame
because of a people useless to them,
who bring neither help nor advantage,
but only shame and disgrace.'

⁶ A prophecy concerning the animals of
the Negev:

Through a land of hardship and distress,
of lions and lionesses,
of adders and darting snakes,
the envoys carry their riches on donkeys'
backs,
their treasures on the humps of
camels,
to that unprofitable nation,
⁷   to Egypt, whose help is utterly useless.
Therefore I call her
Rahab the Do-Nothing.

⁸ Go now, write it on a tablet for them,
inscribe it on a scroll,
that for the days to come
it may be an everlasting witness.
⁹ For these are rebellious people, deceitful
children,
children unwilling to listen to the
LORD's instruction.
¹⁰ They say to the seers,
'See no more visions!'
and to the prophets,
'Give us no more visions of what is
right!
Tell us pleasant things,
prophesy illusions.

¹¹ Leave this way,
get off this path,
and stop confronting us
with the Holy One of Israel!'

¹² Therefore this is what the Holy One of
Israel says:

'Because you have rejected this message,
relied on oppression
and depended on deceit,
¹³ this sin will become for you
like a high wall, cracked and bulging,
that collapses suddenly, in an instant.
¹⁴ It will break in pieces like pottery,
shattered so mercilessly
that among its pieces not a fragment will
be found
for taking coals from a hearth
or scooping water out of a cistern.'

¹⁵ This is what the Sovereign LORD, the
Holy One of Israel, says:

'In repentance and rest is your salvation,
in quietness and trust is your strength,
but you would have none of it.
¹⁶ You said, "No, we will flee on horses."
Therefore you will flee!
You said, "We will ride off on swift
horses."
Therefore your pursuers will be swift!
¹⁷ A thousand will flee
at the threat of one;
at the threat of five
you will all flee away,
till you are left
like a flagstaff on a mountaintop,
like a banner on a hill.'

¹⁸ Yet the LORD longs to be gracious to you;
therefore he will rise up to show you
compassion.
For the LORD is a God of justice.
Blessed are all who wait for him!

¹⁹People of Zion, who live in Jerusalem, you will weep no more. How gracious he will be when you cry for help! As soon as he hears, he will answer you. ²⁰Although the Lord gives you the bread of adversity and the water of affliction, your teachers will be hidden no more; with your own eyes you will see them. ²¹Whether you turn to the right or to the left, your ears will hear a voice behind you, saying, 'This is the way; walk in it.' ²²Then you will desecrate your idols overlaid with silver and your images covered with gold; you will throw them away like a menstrual cloth and say to them, 'Away with you!'

²³He will also send you rain for the seed you sow in the ground, and the food that comes from the land will be rich and plentiful. In that day your cattle will graze in broad meadows. ²⁴The oxen and donkeys that work the soil will eat fodder and mash, spread out with fork and shovel. ²⁵In the day of great slaughter, when the towers fall, streams of water will flow on every high mountain and every lofty hill. ²⁶The moon will shine like the sun, and the sunlight will be seven times brighter, like the light of seven full days, when the Lord binds up the bruises of his people and heals the wounds he inflicted.

²⁷See, the Name of the Lord comes from
    afar,
  with burning anger and dense clouds
    of smoke;
his lips are full of wrath,
  and his tongue is a consuming fire.
²⁸His breath is like a rushing torrent,
  rising up to the neck.
He shakes the nations in the sieve of
    destruction;
  he places in the jaws of the peoples
  a bit that leads them astray.
²⁹And you will sing

as on the night you celebrate a holy
    festival;
your hearts will rejoice
  as when people playing pipes go up
to the mountain of the Lord,
  to the Rock of Israel.
³⁰The Lord will cause people to hear his
    majestic voice
  and will make them see his arm
    coming down
with raging anger and consuming fire,
  with cloudburst, thunderstorm and
    hail.
³¹The voice of the Lord will shatter
    Assyria;
  with his rod he will strike them down.
³²Every stroke the Lord lays on them
  with his punishing club
will be to the music of tambourines and
    harps,
  as he fights them in battle with the
    blows of his arm.
³³Topheth has long been prepared;
  it has been made ready for the king.
Its fire pit has been made deep and wide,
  with an abundance of fire and wood;
the breath of the Lord,
  like a stream of burning sulphur,
    sets it ablaze.

31 Woe to those who go down to Egypt
  for help,
who rely on horses,
who trust in the multitude of their
    chariots
  and in the great strength of their
    horsemen,
but do not look to the Holy One of Israel,
  or seek help from the Lord.
²Yet he too is wise and can bring disaster;
  he does not take back his words.
He will rise up against that wicked
    nation,
  against those who help evildoers.
³But the Egyptians are mere mortals and
    not God;

their horses are flesh and not spirit.
When the LORD stretches out his hand,
　those who help will stumble,
　those who are helped will fall;
　all will perish together.

⁴ This is what the LORD says to me:

'As a lion growls,
　a great lion over its prey –
and though a whole band of shepherds
　is called together against it,
it is not frightened by their shouts
　or disturbed by their clamour –
so the LORD Almighty will come down
　to do battle on Mount Zion and on its
　　heights.
⁵ Like birds hovering overhead,
　the LORD Almighty will shield
　　Jerusalem;
he will shield it and deliver it,
　he will "pass over" it and will
　　rescue it.'

⁶ Return, you Israelites, to the One you
have so greatly revolted against. ⁷ For in
that day every one of you will reject the
idols of silver and gold your sinful hands
have made.

⁸ 'Assyria will fall by no human sword;
　a sword, not of mortals, will devour
　　them.
They will flee before the sword
　and their young men will be put to
　　forced labour.
⁹ Their stronghold will fall because of
　　terror;
　at the sight of the battle standard their
　　commanders will panic,'
declares the LORD,
　whose fire is in Zion,
　whose furnace is in Jerusalem.

32 See, a king will reign in
righteousness

and rulers will rule with justice.
² Each one will be like a shelter from the
　　wind
　and a refuge from the storm,
like streams of water in the desert
　and the shadow of a great rock in a
　　thirsty land.

³ Then the eyes of those who see will no
　longer be closed,
　and the ears of those who hear will
　　listen.
⁴ The fearful heart will know and
　　understand,
　and the stammering tongue will be
　　fluent and clear.
⁵ No longer will the fool be called noble
　nor the scoundrel be highly respected.
⁶ For fools speak folly,
　their hearts are bent on evil:
they practise ungodliness
　and spread error concerning the LORD;
the hungry they leave empty
　and from the thirsty they withhold
　　water.
⁷ Scoundrels use wicked methods,
　they make up evil schemes
to destroy the poor with lies,
　even when the plea of the needy is just.
⁸ But the noble make noble plans,
　and by noble deeds they stand.
⁹ You women who are so complacent,
　rise up and listen to me;
you daughters who feel secure,
　hear what I have to say!
¹⁰ In little more than a year
　you who feel secure will tremble;
the grape harvest will fail,
　and the harvest of fruit will not come.

▬ PSALM 115:1-8

¹ Not to us, LORD, not to us
　but to your name be the glory,
　because of your love and faithfulness.

2 Why do the nations say,
  'Where is their God?'
3 Our God is in heaven;
  he does whatever pleases him.
4 But their idols are silver and gold,
  made by human hands.
5 They have mouths, but cannot speak,
  eyes, but cannot see.
6 They have ears, but cannot hear,
  noses, but cannot smell.
7 They have hands, but cannot feel,
  feet, but cannot walk,
  nor can they utter a sound with their
    throats.
8 Those who make them will be like them,
  and so will all who trust in them.

▬ PROVERBS 23:26-28

26 My son, give me your heart
  and let your eyes delight in my ways,
27 for an adulterous woman is a deep pit,
  and a wayward wife is a narrow well.
28 Like a bandit she lies in wait
  and multiplies the unfaithful among
    men.

▬ GALATIANS 5:1-18

5 It is for freedom that Christ has set us
free. Stand firm, then, and do not let
yourselves be burdened again by a yoke of
slavery.

2 Mark my words! I, Paul, tell you that if
you let yourselves be circumcised, Christ
will be of no value to you at all. 3 Again I
declare to every man who lets himself be
circumcised that he is required to obey the
whole law. 4 You who are trying to be justified by the law have been alienated from
Christ; you have fallen away from grace.
5 For through the Spirit we eagerly await by
faith the righteousness for which we hope.
6 For in Christ Jesus neither circumcision
nor uncircumcision has any value. The only
thing that counts is faith expressing itself
through love.

7 You were running a good race. Who
cut in on you to keep you from obeying the
truth? 8 That kind of persuasion does not
come from the one who calls you. 9 'A little yeast works through the whole batch of
dough.' 10 I am confident in the Lord that
you will take no other view. The one who
is throwing you into confusion, whoever
that may be, will have to pay the penalty.
11 Brothers and sisters, if I am still preaching
circumcision, why am I still being persecuted? In that case the offence of the cross
has been abolished. 12 As for those agitators,
I wish they would go the whole way and
emasculate themselves!

13 You, my brothers and sisters, were called
to be free. But do not use your freedom to
indulge the flesh; rather, serve one another
humbly in love. 14 For the entire law is fulfilled in keeping this one command: 'Love
your neighbour as yourself.' 15 If you bite and
devour each other, watch out or you will be
destroyed by each other.

16 So I say, live by the Spirit, and you will
not gratify the desires of the flesh. 17 For the
flesh desires what is contrary to the Spirit,
and the Spirit what is contrary to the flesh.
They are in conflict with each other, so
that you are not to do whatever you want.
18 But if you are led by the Spirit, you are not
under the law.

More Than Performance

'My son, give me your heart and let your eyes delight in my ways.' **Proverbs 23:26**

Many Christians live on the surface of life and rarely, if ever, look below the waterline. They do have inner longings sometimes to climb higher with God, but their response to these feelings is to focus their attention on what goes on above the waterline - the area of performance and behaviour. So they try harder in terms of more Bible reading, more prayer, more giving, more Christian activities.

I would be the last person to view greater obedience as unimportant, but it is not the only, or indeed the final, answer. A great mistake made by many Christians who recognise they are not receiving from God the things they ought to be receiving is to think that the solution lies solely in more spiritual effort, the assumption being that as we do more above the waterline, the problems that lie below the waterline will all come right.

Now sometimes greater obedience and more responsible effort do have this result. I have often found, for example, that when a man who falls out of love with his wife chooses a change in behaviour and deliberately sets out to do loving things for her, the loving behaviour can trigger loving feelings.

There is more to spiritual change, however, than a change on the surface. It can begin there, but it is not complete until the focus moves from the surface down into the depths. Those who remain above the waterline in their Christian living and resist the invitation to look beneath the surface will soon become legalists - good at performing but bad at being.

PRAYER

My Father and my God, I see that if change is to take place in me, then it must take place in all of me. Help me to see even more clearly that while what I do is important, what I am in the depth of my being is even more important. In Jesus' name. Amen.

FURTHER STUDY

2 Tim. 3:1-5; Isa. 29:1-13
· What did Paul say would be a characteristic of the last days?
· What was the Lord's complaint against the children of Israel?

October 1

[11] Tremble, you complacent women;
    shudder, you daughters who feel secure!
    Strip off your fine clothes
    and wrap yourselves in rags.
[12] Beat your breasts for the pleasant fields,
    for the fruitful vines

¹³ and for the land of my people,
   a land overgrown with thorns and
      briers –
   yes, mourn for all houses of merriment
   and for this city of revelry.
¹⁴ The fortress will be abandoned,
   the noisy city deserted;
   citadel and watchtower will become a
      wasteland for ever,
   the delight of donkeys, a pasture for
      flocks,
¹⁵ till the Spirit is poured on us from on
      high,
   and the desert becomes a fertile field,
   and the fertile field seems like a forest.
¹⁶ The Lord's justice will dwell in the
      desert,
   his righteousness live in the fertile
      field.
¹⁷ The fruit of that righteousness will be
      peace;
   its effect will be quietness and
      confidence for ever.
¹⁸ My people will live in peaceful
      dwelling-places,
   in secure homes,
   in undisturbed places of rest.
¹⁹ Though hail flattens the forest
   and the city is levelled completely,
²⁰ how blessed you will be,
   sowing your seed by every stream,
   and letting your cattle and donkeys
      range free.

33 Woe to you, destroyer,
      you who have not been destroyed!
   Woe to you, betrayer,
   you who have not been betrayed!
   When you stop destroying,
   you will be destroyed;
   when you stop betraying,
   you will be betrayed.

² Lord, be gracious to us;
   we long for you.
   Be our strength every morning,
   our salvation in time of distress.

³ At the uproar of your army, the peoples
      flee;
   when you rise up, the nations scatter.
⁴ Your plunder, O nations, is harvested as
      by young locusts;
   like a swarm of locusts people pounce
      on it.

⁵ The Lord is exalted, for he dwells on high;
   he will fill Zion with his justice and
      righteousness.
⁶ He will be the sure foundation for your
      times,
   a rich store of salvation and wisdom
      and knowledge;
   the fear of the Lord is the key to this
      treasure.

⁷ Look, their brave men cry aloud in the
      streets;
   the envoys of peace weep bitterly.
⁸ The highways are deserted,
   no travellers are on the roads.
   The treaty is broken,
   its witnesses are despised,
   no one is respected.
⁹ The land dries up and wastes away,
   Lebanon is ashamed and withers;
   Sharon is like the Arabah,
   and Bashan and Carmel drop their
      leaves.

¹⁰ 'Now will I arise,' says the Lord.
   'Now will I be exalted;
   now will I be lifted up.
¹¹ You conceive chaff,
   you give birth to straw;
   your breath is a fire that consumes you.
¹² The peoples will be burned to ashes;
   like cut thorn-bushes they will be set
      ablaze.'

¹³ You who are far away, hear what I have
      done;
   you who are near, acknowledge my
      power!

¹⁴ The sinners in Zion are terrified;
   trembling grips the godless:
'Who of us can dwell with the
      consuming fire?
   Who of us can dwell with everlasting
      burning?'
¹⁵ Those who walk righteously
   and speak what is right,
who reject gain from extortion
   and keep their hands from accepting
      bribes,
who stop their ears against plots of
      murder
   and shut their eyes against
      contemplating evil –
¹⁶ they are the ones who will dwell on the
      heights,
   whose refuge will be the mountain
      fortress.
Their bread will be supplied,
   and water will not fail them.

¹⁷ Your eyes will see the king in his beauty
   and view a land that stretches afar.
¹⁸ In your thoughts you will ponder the
      former terror:
   'Where is that chief officer?
Where is the one who took the revenue?
   Where is the officer in charge of the
      towers?'
¹⁹ You will see those arrogant people no
      more,
   people whose speech is obscure,
   whose language is strange and
      incomprehensible.

²⁰ Look on Zion, the city of our festivals;
   your eyes will see Jerusalem,
   a peaceful abode, a tent that will not
      be moved;
its stakes will never be pulled up,
   nor any of its ropes broken.
²¹ There the LORD will be our Mighty One.
   It will be like a place of broad rivers
      and streams.
No galley with oars will ride them,

no mighty ship will sail them.
²² For the LORD is our judge,
   the LORD is our lawgiver,
   the LORD is our king;
   it is he who will save us.

²³ Your rigging hangs loose:
   the mast is not held secure,
   the sail is not spread.
Then an abundance of spoils will be
      divided
   and even the lame will carry off
      plunder.
²⁴ No one living in Zion will say, 'I am ill';
   and the sins of those who dwell there
      will be forgiven.

34 Come near, you nations, and listen;
   pay attention, you peoples!
Let the earth hear, and all that is in it,
   the world, and all that comes out of it!
² The LORD is angry with all nations;
   his wrath is on all their armies.
He will totally destroy them,
   he will give them over to slaughter.
³ Their slain will be thrown out,
   their dead bodies will stink;
   the mountains will be soaked with
      their blood.
⁴ All the stars in the sky will be dissolved
   and the heavens rolled up like a scroll;
all the starry host will fall
   like withered leaves from the vine,
   like shrivelled figs from the fig-tree.

⁵ My sword has drunk its fill in the heavens;
   see, it descends in judgment on Edom,
   the people I have totally destroyed.
⁶ The sword of the LORD is bathed in blood,
   it is covered with fat –
the blood of lambs and goats,
   fat from the kidneys of rams.
For the LORD has a sacrifice in Bozrah
   and a great slaughter in the land of
      Edom.
⁷ And the wild oxen will fall with them,
   the bull calves and the great bulls.

Their land will be drenched with blood,
and the dust will be soaked with fat.

[8] For the LORD has a day of vengeance,
a year of retribution, to uphold Zion's
cause.
[9] Edom's streams will be turned into pitch,
her dust into burning sulphur;
her land will become blazing pitch!
[10] It will not be quenched night or day;
its smoke will rise for ever.
From generation to generation it will lie
desolate;
no one will ever pass through it again.
[11] The desert owl and screech owl will
possess it;
the great owl and the raven will nest
there.
God will stretch out over Edom
the measuring line of chaos
and the plumb-line of desolation.
[12] Her nobles will have nothing there to be
called a kingdom,
all her princes will vanish away.
[13] Thorns will overrun her citadels,
nettles and brambles her strongholds.
She will become a haunt for jackals,
a home for owls.
[14] Desert creatures will meet with hyenas,
and wild goats will bleat to each other;
there the night creatures will also lie
down
and find for themselves places of rest.
[15] The owl will nest there and lay eggs,
she will hatch them, and care for her
young
under the shadow of her wings;
there also the falcons will gather,
each with its mate.

[16] Look in the scroll of the LORD and read:

None of these will be missing,
not one will lack her mate.
For it is his mouth that has given the order,
and his Spirit will gather them together.

[17] He allots their portions;
his hand distributes them by measure.
They will possess it for ever
and dwell there from generation to
generation.

▬ PSALM 115:9-13

[9] All you Israelites, trust in the LORD –
he is their help and shield.
[10] House of Aaron, trust in the LORD –
he is their help and shield.
[11] You who fear him, trust in the LORD –
he is their help and shield.

[12] The LORD remembers us and will bless us:
he will bless his people Israel,
he will bless the house of Aaron,
[13] he will bless those who fear the LORD –
small and great alike.

▬ PROVERBS 23:29-30

[29] Who has woe? Who has sorrow?
Who has strife? Who has complaints?
Who has needless bruises? Who has
bloodshot eyes?
[30] Those who linger over wine,
who go to sample bowls of mixed wine.

▬ GALATIANS 5:19–6:18

[19] The acts of the flesh are obvious: sexual immorality, impurity and debauchery; [20] idolatry and witchcraft; hatred, discord, jealousy, fits of rage, selfish ambition, dissensions, factions [21] and envy; drunkenness, orgies, and the like. I warn you, as I did before, that those who live like this will not inherit the kingdom of God.

[22] But the fruit of the Spirit is love, joy, peace, forbearance, kindness, goodness, faithfulness, [23] gentleness and self-control.

Against such things there is no law. ²⁴Those who belong to Christ Jesus have crucified the flesh with its passions and desires. ²⁵Since we live by the Spirit, let us keep in step with the Spirit. ²⁶Let us not become conceited, provoking and envying each other.

6 Brothers and sisters, if someone is caught in a sin, you who live by the Spirit should restore that person gently. But watch yourselves, or you also may be tempted. ²Carry each other's burdens, and in this way you will fulfil the law of Christ. ³If anyone thinks they are something when they are not, they deceive themselves. ⁴Each one should test their own actions. Then they can take pride in themselves alone, without comparing themselves to someone else, ⁵for each one should carry their own load. ⁶Nevertheless, the one who receives instruction in the word should share all good things with their instructor.

⁷Do not be deceived: God cannot be mocked. A man reaps what he sows. ⁸Whoever sows to please their flesh, from the flesh will reap destruction; whoever sows to please the Spirit, from the Spirit will reap eternal life. ⁹Let us not become weary in doing good, for at the proper time we will reap a harvest if we do not give up. ¹⁰Therefore, as we have opportunity, let us do good to all people, especially to those who belong to the family of believers.

¹¹See what large letters I use as I write to you with my own hand!

¹²Those who want to impress people by means of the flesh are trying to compel you to be circumcised. The only reason they do this is to avoid being persecuted for the cross of Christ. ¹³Not even those who are circumcised keep the law, yet they want you to be circumcised that they may boast about your circumcision in the flesh. ¹⁴May I never boast except in the cross of our Lord Jesus Christ, through which the world has been crucified to me, and I to the world. ¹⁵Neither circumcision nor uncircumcision means anything; what counts is the new creation. ¹⁶Peace and mercy to all who follow this rule – to the Israel of God.

¹⁷From now on, let no one cause me trouble, for I bear on my body the marks of Jesus.

¹⁸The grace of our Lord Jesus Christ be with your spirit, brothers and sisters. Amen.

Why an Inside Look?

'... they are the ones who will dwell on the heights, whose refuge will be the mountain fortress.'
Isaiah 33:16

Before we can dwell on the heights, we must be prepared to take an honest look at what is going on beneath the surface of our lives. Doing this, of course, can be dangerous unless it is approached in the right attitude. Some Christians use the process of self-examination as a means of avoiding rather than assuming responsibility. They look at what is going on inside themselves and allow what they discover there to develop into a cynical negativism, which hinders rather than helps their Christian life.

Those who do this fail to understand the purpose of godly self-examination: to bring what is discovered to the Lord so that He can deal with it. Many commentators have pointed out, in the incident when the Israelites in the wilderness were bitten by the snakes, that when they looked at themselves and recognised their condition, they were then highly motivated to look to the brass serpent for help (see Num. 21:4-9).

The purpose of taking such an honest look at what is going on beneath the surface of our lives is to promote a deeper dependence on the Lord and thus contribute to our spiritual effectiveness. Recognition of our true condition provides a strong motivation to look away from ourselves and turn in simple faith to the Lord Jesus Christ. As you take this journey into the core of your being, be willing to face yourself in a way that you have never done before. I cannot promise you it will be painless, but I can promise you it will be profitable.

PRAYER

Father, give me the courage to overcome the fears that would rise within me saying, 'I am not sure that I can face it'. Deepen the conviction within me that with You, I can face anything. Amen.

FURTHER STUDY

1 Cor. 11:23-33; Lam. 3:40; Gal. 6:4

- How does Paul admonish us?
- How does the writer of Lamentations put it?

October 2

■ ISAIAH 35:1–37:20

35 The desert and the parched land will be glad;
the wilderness will rejoice and blossom.
Like the crocus, ²it will burst into bloom;
it will rejoice greatly and shout for joy.
The glory of Lebanon will be given to it,
the splendour of Carmel and Sharon;
they will see the glory of the LORD,
the splendour of our God.

³Strengthen the feeble hands,
steady the knees that give way;
⁴say to those with fearful hearts,
'Be strong, do not fear;
your God will come,
he will come with vengeance;
with divine retribution
he will come to save you.'

⁵Then will the eyes of the blind be opened
and the ears of the deaf unstopped.

⁶Then will the lame leap like a deer,
and the mute tongue shout for joy.
Water will gush forth in the wilderness
and streams in the desert.
⁷The burning sand will become a pool,
the thirsty ground bubbling springs.
In the haunts where jackals once lay,
grass and reeds and papyrus will grow.

⁸And a highway will be there;
it will be called the Way of Holiness;
it will be for those who walk on that
Way.
The unclean will not journey on it;
wicked fools will not go about on it.
⁹No lion will be there,
nor any ravenous beast;
they will not be found there.
But only the redeemed will walk there,
¹⁰ and those the LORD has rescued will
return.
They will enter Zion with singing;
everlasting joy will crown their heads.

Gladness and joy will overtake them,
and sorrow and sighing will flee away.

36 In the fourteenth year of King Hezekiah's reign, Sennacherib king of Assyria attacked all the fortified cities of Judah and captured them. ²Then the king of Assyria sent his field commander with a large army from Lachish to King Hezekiah at Jerusalem. When the commander stopped at the aqueduct of the Upper Pool, on the road to the Launderer's Field, ³Eliakim son of Hilkiah the palace administrator, Shebna the secretary, and Joah son of Asaph the recorder went out to him.

⁴The field commander said to them, 'Tell Hezekiah:

'"This is what the great king, the king of Assyria, says: on what are you basing this confidence of yours? ⁵You say you have counsel and might for war – but you speak only empty words. On whom are you depending, that you rebel against me? ⁶Look, I know you are depending on Egypt, that splintered reed of a staff, which pierces the hand of anyone who leans on it! Such is Pharaoh king of Egypt to all who depend on him. ⁷But if you say to me, 'We are depending on the LORD our God' – isn't he the one whose high places and altars Hezekiah removed, saying to Judah and Jerusalem, 'You must worship before this altar'?

⁸'"Come now, make a bargain with my master, the king of Assyria: I will give you two thousand horses – if you can put riders on them! ⁹How then can you repulse one officer of the least of my master's officials, even though you are depending on Egypt for chariots and horsemen? ¹⁰Furthermore, have I come to attack and destroy this land without the LORD? The LORD himself told me to march against this country and destroy it."'

¹¹Then Eliakim, Shebna and Joah said to the field commander, 'Please speak to your servants in Aramaic, since we understand it. Don't speak to us in Hebrew in the hearing of the people on the wall.'

¹²But the commander replied, 'Was it only to your master and you that my master sent me to say these things, and not to the people sitting on the wall – who, like you, will have to eat their own excrement and drink their own urine?'

¹³Then the commander stood and called out in Hebrew, 'Hear the words of the great king, the king of Assyria! ¹⁴This is what the king says: do not let Hezekiah deceive you. He cannot deliver you! ¹⁵Do not let Hezekiah persuade you to trust in the LORD when he says, "The LORD will surely deliver us; this city will not be given into the hand of the king of Assyria."

¹⁶'Do not listen to Hezekiah. This is what the king of Assyria says: make peace with me and come out to me. Then each of you will eat fruit from your own vine and fig-tree and drink water from your own cistern, ¹⁷until I come and take you to a land like your own – a land of corn and new wine, a land of bread and vineyards.

¹⁸'Do not let Hezekiah mislead you when he says, "The LORD will deliver us." Have the gods of any nations ever delivered their lands from the hand of the king of Assyria? ¹⁹Where are the gods of Hamath and Arpad? Where are the gods of Sepharvaim? Have they rescued Samaria from my hand? ²⁰Who of all the gods of these countries have been able to save their lands from me? How then can the LORD deliver Jerusalem from my hand?'

²¹But the people remained silent and said nothing in reply, because the king had commanded, 'Do not answer him.'

²²Then Eliakim son of Hilkiah the palace administrator, Shebna the secretary and Joah son of Asaph the recorder went to Hezekiah, with their clothes torn, and told

him what the field commander had said.

37 When King Hezekiah heard this, he tore his clothes and put on sackcloth and went into the temple of the LORD. ²He sent Eliakim the palace administrator, Shebna the secretary, and the leading priests, all wearing sackcloth, to the prophet Isaiah son of Amoz. ³They told him, 'This is what Hezekiah says: this day is a day of distress and rebuke and disgrace, as when children come to the moment of birth and there is no strength to deliver them. ⁴It may be that the LORD your God will hear the words of the field commander, whom his master, the king of Assyria, has sent to ridicule the living God, and that he will rebuke him for the words the LORD your God has heard. Therefore pray for the remnant that still survives.'

⁵When King Hezekiah's officials came to Isaiah, ⁶Isaiah said to them, 'Tell your master, "This is what the LORD says: do not be afraid of what you have heard – those words with which the underlings of the king of Assyria have blasphemed me. ⁷Listen! When he hears a certain report, I will make him want to return to his own country, and there I will have him cut down with the sword."'

⁸When the field commander heard that the king of Assyria had left Lachish, he withdrew and found the king fighting against Libnah.

⁹Now Sennacherib received a report that Tirhakah, the king of Cush, was marching out to fight against him. When he heard it, he sent messengers to Hezekiah with this word: ¹⁰'Say to Hezekiah king of Judah: do not let the god you depend on deceive you when he says, "Jerusalem will not be given into the hands of the king of Assyria." ¹¹Surely you have heard what the kings of Assyria have done to all the countries, destroying them completely. And will you be delivered? ¹²Did the gods of the nations that were destroyed by my predecessors deliver them – the gods of Gozan, Harran, Rezeph

and the people of Eden who were in Tel Assar? ¹³Where is the king of Hamath or the king of Arpad? Where are the kings of Lair, Sepharvaim, Hena and Ivvah?'

¹⁴Hezekiah received the letter from the messengers and read it. Then he went up to the temple of the LORD and spread it out before the LORD. ¹⁵And Hezekiah prayed to the LORD: ¹⁶'LORD Almighty, the God of Israel, enthroned between the cherubim, you alone are God over all the kingdoms of the earth. You have made heaven and earth. ¹⁷Give ear, LORD, and hear; open your eyes, LORD, and see; listen to all the words Sennacherib has sent to ridicule the living God.

¹⁸'It is true, LORD, that the Assyrian kings have laid waste all these peoples and their lands. ¹⁹They have thrown their gods into the fire and destroyed them, for they were not gods but only wood and stone, fashioned by human hands. ²⁰Now, LORD our God, deliver us from his hand, so that all the kingdoms of the earth may know that you, LORD, are the only God.'

··

■ **PSALM 115:14-18**

¹⁴ May the LORD cause you to flourish,
    both you and your children.
¹⁵ May you be blessed by the LORD,
    the Maker of heaven and earth.

¹⁶ The highest heavens belong to the LORD,
    but the earth he has given to the
      human race.
¹⁷ It is not the dead who praise the LORD,
    those who go down to the place of
      silence;
¹⁸ it is we who extol the LORD,
    both now and for evermore.

Praise the LORD.

■ PROVERBS 23:31-32

³¹ Do not gaze at wine when it is red,
  when it sparkles in the cup,
  when it goes down smoothly!
³² In the end it bites like a snake
  and poisons like a viper.

■ EPHESIANS 1:1-23

1 Paul, an apostle of Christ Jesus by the
  will of God,

To God's holy people in Ephesus, the
faithful in Christ Jesus:

²Grace and peace to you from God our
Father and the Lord Jesus Christ.

³Praise be to the God and Father of our
Lord Jesus Christ, who has blessed us in the
heavenly realms with every spiritual blessing in Christ. ⁴For he chose us in him before the creation of the world to be holy and
blameless in his sight. In love ⁵he predestined us for adoption to sonship through
Jesus Christ, in accordance with his pleasure and will – ⁶to the praise of his glorious
grace, which he has freely given us in the
One he loves. ⁷In him we have redemption
through his blood, the forgiveness of sins,
in accordance with the riches of God's grace
⁸that he lavished on us. With all wisdom
and understanding, ⁹he made known to us
the mystery of his will according to his good
pleasure, which he purposed in Christ, ¹⁰to
be put into effect when the times reach their
fulfilment – to bring unity to all things in
heaven and on earth under Christ.

¹¹In him we were also chosen, having been
predestined according to the plan of him
who works out everything in conformity
with the purpose of his will, ¹²in order that
we, who were the first to put our hope in
Christ, might be for the praise of his glory.
¹³And you also were included in Christ when
you heard the message of truth, the gospel
of your salvation. When you believed, you
were marked in him with a seal, the promised Holy Spirit, ¹⁴who is a deposit guaranteeing our inheritance until the redemption
of those who are God's possession – to the
praise of his glory.

¹⁵For this reason, ever since I heard about
your faith in the Lord Jesus and your love
for all God's people, ¹⁶I have not stopped
giving thanks for you, remembering you in
my prayers. ¹⁷I keep asking that the God of
our Lord Jesus Christ, the glorious Father,
may give you the Spirit of wisdom and revelation, so that you may know him better.
¹⁸I pray that the eyes of your heart may be
enlightened in order that you may know the
hope to which he has called you, the riches
of his glorious inheritance in his holy people, ¹⁹and his incomparably great power for
us who believe. That power is the same as
the mighty strength ²⁰he exerted when he
raised Christ from the dead and seated him
at his right hand in the heavenly realms,
²¹far above all rule and authority, power and
dominion, and every name that is invoked,
not only in the present age but also in the
one to come. ²²And God placed all things
under his feet and appointed him to be head
over everything for the church, ²³which
is his body, the fullness of him who fills
everything in every way.

'We've Won a Holiday'

'In him we have redemption through his blood, the
forgiveness of sins, in accordance with the riches of
God's grace.' **Ephesians 1:7**

What is it in the heart of most men and women that rejects the idea of God's free and generous offer of salvation? It is pride, the deadliest of all the deadly sins. As playwright George Bernard Shaw wrote in his play *Major Barbara:* 'Forgiveness is a beggar's refuge. We must pay our debts.' But we cannot pay our debts. As our spiritual fathers saw so clearly, the only language we can use in the presence of a God who demands so much and whose demands we are unable to meet is expressed by hymn writer Charlotte Elliott:

> *Just as I am without one plea*
> *But that Thy blood was shed for me,*
> *And that Thou bidd'st me come to Thee,*
> *O Lamb of God, I come, I come.*

In response to our coming, the free unmerited favour of God flows down to us, cancels our debt and imputes and imparts Christ's righteousness to us. How can Christ's righteousness be imputed and imparted to us? It's His righteousness, not ours.

A simple illustration may help to illuminate this point. A little boy came home from school one day and said to his mother, 'We've won a holiday.' The truth was, another boy had come top of the region in some examinations, and the head teacher had decided to give the whole school a holiday. Yet the little lad said, 'We've won a holiday.'

Grace is like that. God permits the righteousness of Jesus to cover us and then - as we open ourselves to it - to enter us. He did it, but we benefit from it. Isn't grace really amazing?

PRAYER

O Father, as I contemplate still further the 'riches' of Your grace, once again I have to confess it's truly amazing. No wonder men and women use that term to describe Your grace. No other adjective will do! Amen.

FURTHER STUDY

Phil. 4:1-19; 1 Tim. 1:14; Titus 3:6
• What has God promised?
• What did Paul testify to Timothy?

October 3

■ ISAIAH 37:21–39:8

²¹Then Isaiah son of Amoz sent a message to Hezekiah: 'This is what the LORD, the God of Israel, says: because you have prayed to me concerning Sennacherib king of Assyria, ²²this is the word the LORD has spoken against him:

'Virgin Daughter Zion
  despises and mocks you.
Daughter Jerusalem

tosses her head as you flee.

²³ Who is it you have ridiculed and
      blasphemed?
  Against whom have you raised your
      voice
  and lifted your eyes in pride?
  Against the Holy One of Israel!
²⁴ By your messengers
      you have ridiculed the Lord.
  And you have said,
  "With my many chariots
  I have ascended the heights of the
      mountains,
      the utmost heights of Lebanon.
  I have cut down its tallest cedars,
      the choicest of its junipers.
  I have reached its remotest heights,
      the finest of its forests.
²⁵ I have dug wells in foreign lands
      and drunk the water there.
  With the soles of my feet
  I have dried up all the streams of Egypt."

²⁶ 'Have you not heard?
      Long ago I ordained it.
  In days of old I planned it;
      now I have brought it to pass,
  that you have turned fortified cities
      into piles of stone.
²⁷ Their people, drained of power,
      are dismayed and put to shame.
  They are like plants in the field,
      like tender green shoots,
  like grass sprouting on the roof,
      scorched before it grows up.

²⁸ 'But I know where you are
      and when you come and go
      and how you rage against me.
²⁹ Because you rage against me
      and because your insolence has
          reached my ears,
  I will put my hook in your nose
      and my bit in your mouth,
  and I will make you return
      by the way you came.

³⁰ 'This will be the sign for you, Hezekiah:

'This year you will eat what grows by
      itself,
  and the second year what springs
      from that.
  But in the third year sow and reap,
      plant vineyards and eat their fruit.
³¹ Once more a remnant of the kingdom of
      Judah
  will take root below and bear fruit
      above.
³² For out of Jerusalem will come a remnant,
      and out of Mount Zion a band of
          survivors.
  The zeal of the LORD Almighty
      will accomplish this.

³³ 'Therefore this is what the LORD says
concerning the king of Assyria:

'He will not enter this city
      or shoot an arrow here.
  He will not come before it with shield
      or build a siege ramp against it.
³⁴ By the way that he came he will return;
      he will not enter this city,'
                    declares the LORD.
³⁵ 'I will defend this city and save it,
      for my sake and for the sake of David
          my servant!'

³⁶ Then the angel of the LORD went out and put to death a hundred and eighty-five thousand in the Assyrian camp. When the people got up the next morning – there were all the dead bodies! ³⁷ So Sennacherib king of Assyria broke camp and withdrew. He returned to Nineveh and stayed there.

³⁸ One day, while he was worshipping in the temple of his god Nisrok, his sons Adrammelek and Sharezer killed him with the sword, and they escaped to the land of Ararat. And Esarhaddon his son succeeded him as king.

38 In those days Hezekiah became ill and was at the point of death. The prophet Isaiah son of Amoz went to him and said, 'This is what the LORD says: put your house in order, because you are going to die; you will not recover.'

² Hezekiah turned his face to the wall and prayed to the LORD, ³ 'Remember, LORD, how I have walked before you faithfully and with wholehearted devotion and have done what is good in your eyes.' And Hezekiah wept bitterly.

⁴ Then the word of the LORD came to Isaiah: ⁵ 'Go and tell Hezekiah, "This is what the LORD, the God of your father David, says: I have heard your prayer and seen your tears; I will add fifteen years to your life. ⁶ And I will deliver you and this city from the hand of the king of Assyria. I will defend this city.

⁷ ' "This is the LORD's sign to you that the LORD will do what he has promised: ⁸ I will make the shadow cast by the sun go back the ten steps it has gone down on the stairway of Ahaz." ' So the sunlight went back the ten steps it had gone down.

⁹ A writing of Hezekiah king of Judah after his illness and recovery:

¹⁰ I said, 'In the prime of my life
    must I go through the gates of death
    and be robbed of the rest of my years?'
¹¹ I said, 'I will not again see the LORD
        himself
    in the land of the living;
no longer will I look on my fellow man,
    or be with those who now dwell in this
        world.
¹² Like a shepherd's tent my house
    has been pulled down and taken from
        me.
Like a weaver I have rolled up my life,
    and he has cut me off from the loom;
    day and night you made an end of me.
¹³ I waited patiently till dawn,

but like a lion he broke all my bones;
    day and night you made an end of me.
¹⁴ I cried like a swift or thrush,
    I moaned like a mourning dove.
My eyes grew weak as I looked to the
        heavens.
    I am being threatened; Lord, come to
        my aid!'

¹⁵ But what can I say?
    He has spoken to me, and he himself
        has done this.
I will walk humbly all my years
    because of this anguish of my soul.
¹⁶ Lord, by such things people live;
    and my spirit finds life in them too.
You restored me to health
    and let me live.
¹⁷ Surely it was for my benefit
    that I suffered such anguish.
In your love you kept me
    from the pit of destruction;
you have put all my sins
    behind your back.
¹⁸ For the grave cannot praise you,
    death cannot sing your praise;
those who go down to the pit
    cannot hope for your faithfulness.
¹⁹ The living, the living – they praise you,
    as I am doing today;
parents tell their children
    about your faithfulness.

²⁰ The LORD will save me,
    and we will sing with stringed
        instruments
all the days of our lives
    in the temple of the LORD.

²¹ Isaiah had said, 'Prepare a poultice of figs and apply it to the boil, and he will recover.'

²² Hezekiah had asked, 'What will be the sign that I will go up to the temple of the LORD?'

39

At that time Marduk-Baladan son of Baladan king of Babylon sent Hezekiah letters and a gift, because he had heard of his illness and recovery. ²Hezekiah received the envoys gladly and showed them what was in his storehouses – the silver, the gold, the spices, the fine olive oil – his entire armoury and everything found among his treasures. There was nothing in his palace or in all his kingdom that Hezekiah did not show them.

³Then Isaiah the prophet went to King Hezekiah and asked, 'What did those men say, and where did they come from?'

'From a distant land,' Hezekiah replied. 'They came to me from Babylon.'

⁴The prophet asked, 'What did they see in your palace?'

'They saw everything in my palace,' Hezekiah said. 'There is nothing among my treasures that I did not show them.'

⁵Then Isaiah said to Hezekiah, 'Hear the word of the LORD Almighty: ⁶the time will surely come when everything in your palace, and all that your predecessors have stored up until this day, will be carried off to Babylon. Nothing will be left, says the LORD. ⁷And some of your descendants, your own flesh and blood who will be born to you, will be taken away, and they will become eunuchs in the palace of the king of Babylon.'

⁸'The word of the LORD you have spoken is good,' Hezekiah replied. For he thought, 'There will be peace and security in my lifetime.'

■ PSALM 116:1-7

¹I love the LORD, for he heard my voice;
  he heard my cry for mercy.
²Because he turned his ear to me,
  I will call on him as long as I live.

³The cords of death entangled me,
  the anguish of the grave came over
    me;
  I was overcome by distress and
    sorrow.
⁴Then I called on the name of the LORD:
  'LORD, save me!'

⁵The LORD is gracious and righteous;
  our God is full of compassion.
⁶The LORD protects the unwary;
  when I was brought low, he saved me.

⁷Return to your rest, my soul,
  for the LORD has been good to you.

■ PROVERBS 23:33-35

³³Your eyes will see strange sights,
  and your mind will imagine confusing
    things.
³⁴You will be like one sleeping on the high
    seas,
  lying on top of the rigging.
³⁵'They hit me,' you will say, 'but I'm not
    hurt!
  They beat me, but I don't feel it!
When will I wake up
  so I can find another drink?'

■ EPHESIANS 2:1-22

2

As for you, you were dead in your transgressions and sins, ²in which you used to live when you followed the ways of this world and of the ruler of the kingdom of the air, the spirit who is now at work in those who are disobedient. ³All of us also lived among them at one time, gratifying the cravings of our flesh and following its desires and thoughts. Like the rest, we were by nature deserving of wrath. ⁴But because of his great love for us, God, who is rich in mercy, ⁵made us alive with Christ even when we were dead in transgressions – it is by grace you have been saved. [6] And God raised us up with Christ and seated us with him in the heavenly realms in Christ Jesus, [7] in order that in the coming ages he might show the incomparable riches of his grace, expressed in his kindness to us in Christ Jesus. [8] For it is by grace you have been saved, through faith – and this is not from yourselves, it is the gift of God – [9] not by works, so that no one can boast. [10] For we are God's handiwork, created in Christ Jesus to do good works, which God prepared in advance for us to do.

[11] Therefore, remember that formerly you who are Gentiles by birth and called 'uncircumcised' by those who call themselves 'the circumcision' (which is done in the body by human hands) – [12] remember that at that time you were separate from Christ, excluded from citizenship in Israel and foreigners to the covenants of the promise, without hope and without God in the world. [13] But now in Christ Jesus you who once were far away have been brought near by the blood of Christ.

[14] For he himself is our peace, who has made the two groups one and has destroyed the barrier, the dividing wall of hostility, [15] by setting aside in his flesh the law with its commands and regulations. His purpose was to create in himself one new humanity out of the two, thus making peace, [16] and in one body to reconcile both of them to God through the cross, by which he put to death their hostility. [17] He came and preached peace to you who were far away and peace to those who were near. [18] For through him we both have access to the Father by one Spirit.

[19] Consequently, you are no longer foreigners and strangers, but fellow citizens with God's people and also members of his household, [20] built on the foundation of the apostles and prophets, with Christ Jesus himself as the chief cornerstone. [21] In him the whole building is joined together and rises to become a holy temple in the Lord. [22] And in him you too are being built together to become a dwelling in which God lives by his Spirit.

Sovereign Grace

'For it is by grace you have been saved, through faith ... it is the gift of God.' **Ephesians 2:8**

In order to understand grace, we must see it in relation to the Sovereign. As one writer puts it: 'Grace is bound to be sovereign since it cannot by its very nature be subject to compulsion.' This is why we often refer to it as free grace. There is no reason for grace but grace.

I believe the old definition of grace cannot be improved upon: 'Grace is the free, unmerited favour of God.' At the heart of all true communion with God there lies this gripping truth: God took the initiative. He is more inclined towards us than we are towards Him. We cannot earn His affection. We have simply to receive it. Always the initiative is from God.

When you originally came to Him, you came because He first drew you. The very faith by which you lay hold of Him is not of yourself; it is, as our text says, 'the gift of God'. Every step you make on your spiritual pilgrimage is possible because of His grace.

I know this teaching affronts some people because they like to feel that they can work their own way to heaven. This is like someone in debt for a million pounds trying to get the one to whom he is indebted to accept his resources of a few pence as being sufficient to clear the debt. Listen to the Word of God again and let it sink deep into your soul: 'For it is by grace you have been saved, through faith ... it is the gift of God.' Grace is a gift. You do not have to achieve but simply receive.

PRAYER

O Father, once again my heart is moved as I realise it was not my merit but Your mercy, acting in grace, that drew You to me and me to You. All honour and glory be to Your mighty and everlasting name. Amen.

FURTHER STUDY

Rom. 5:1-21; Titus 3:7
• How does Paul define grace?
• Write out your own definition of grace.

October 4

ISAIAH 40:1–41:20

40 Comfort, comfort my people, says your God.
² Speak tenderly to Jerusalem,
and proclaim to her
that her hard service has been completed,
that her sin has been paid for,
that she has received from the LORD's
hand
double for all her sins.

³ A voice of one calling:
'In the wilderness prepare
the way for the LORD;
make straight in the desert
a highway for our God.
⁴ Every valley shall be raised up,
every mountain and hill made low;
the rough ground shall become level,
the rugged places a plain.
⁵ And the glory of the LORD will be revealed,
and all people will see it together.
For the mouth of the LORD
has spoken.'

⁶ A voice says, 'Cry out.'
And I said, 'What shall I cry?'

'All people are like grass,
and all their faithfulness is like the
flowers of the field.
⁷ The grass withers and the flowers fall,
because the breath of the LORD blows
on them.
Surely the people are grass.
⁸ The grass withers and the flowers fall,
but the word of our God endures for
ever.'

⁹ You who bring good news to Zion,
go up on a high mountain.
You who bring good news to Jerusalem,
lift up your voice with a shout,
lift it up, do not be afraid;
say to the towns of Judah,
'Here is your God!'
¹⁰ See, the Sovereign LORD comes with
power,
and he rules with a mighty arm.
See, his reward is with him,

and his recompense accompanies
    him.
[11] He tends his flock like a shepherd:
    he gathers the lambs in his arms
and carries them close to his heart;
    he gently leads those that have young.

[12] Who has measured the waters in the
    hollow of his hand,
    or with the breadth of his hand
      marked off the heavens?
Who has held the dust of the earth in a
    basket,
    or weighed the mountains on the
      scales
    and the hills in a balance?
[13] Who can fathom the Spirit of the LORD,
    or instruct the LORD as his counsellor?
[14] Whom did the LORD consult to enlighten
    him,
    and who taught him the right way?
Who was it that taught him knowledge,
    or showed him the path of
      understanding?

[15] Surely the nations are like a drop in a
    bucket;
    they are regarded as dust on the
      scales;
he weighs the islands as though they
    were fine dust.
[16] Lebanon is not sufficient for altar fires,
    nor its animals enough for burnt
      offerings.
[17] Before him all the nations are as
    nothing;
    they are regarded by him as worthless
    and less than nothing.

[18] With whom, then, will you compare
    God?
    To what image will you liken him?
[19] As for an idol, a metalworker casts it,
    and a goldsmith overlays it with gold
    and fashions silver chains for it.

[20] A person too poor to present such an
    offering
    selects wood that will not rot;
they look for a skilled worker
    to set up an idol that will not topple.

[21] Do you not know?
    Have you not heard?
Has it not been told you from the
    beginning?
    Have you not understood since the
      earth was founded?
[22] He sits enthroned above the circle of the
    earth,
    and its people are like grasshoppers.
He stretches out the heavens like a
    canopy,
    and spreads them out like a tent to live
      in.
[23] He brings princes to naught
    and reduces the rulers of this world to
      nothing.
[24] No sooner are they planted,
    no sooner are they sown,
    no sooner do they take root in the
      ground,
than he blows on them and they wither,
    and a whirlwind sweeps them away
      like chaff.

[25] 'To whom will you compare me?
    Or who is my equal?' says the Holy
      One.
[26] Lift up your eyes and look to the heavens:
    who created all these?
He who brings out the starry host one by
    one
    and calls forth each of them by name.
Because of his great power and mighty
    strength,
    not one of them is missing.

[27] Why do you complain, Jacob?
    Why do you say, Israel,
'My way is hidden from the LORD;
    my cause is disregarded by my God'?

²⁸ Do you not know?
   Have you not heard?
The LORD is the everlasting God,
   the Creator of the ends of the earth.
He will not grow tired or weary,
   and his understanding no one can
      fathom.
²⁹ He gives strength to the weary
   and increases the power of the weak.
³⁰ Even youths grow tired and weary,
   and young men stumble and fall;
³¹ but those who hope in the LORD
   will renew their strength.
They will soar on wings like eagles;
   they will run and not grow weary,
   they will walk and not be faint.

41 'Be silent before me, you islands!
   Let the nations renew their strength!
Let them come forward and speak;
   let us meet together at the place of
      judgment.

² 'Who has stirred up one from the east,
   calling him in righteousness to his
      service?
He hands nations over to him
   and subdues kings before him.
He turns them to dust with his sword,
   to wind-blown chaff with his bow.
³ He pursues them and moves on
      unscathed,
   by a path his feet have not travelled
      before.
⁴ Who has done this and carried it
      through,
   calling forth the generations from the
      beginning?
I, the LORD – with the first of them
   and with the last – I am he.'

⁵ The islands have seen it and fear;
   the ends of the earth tremble.
They approach and come forward;
⁶   they help each other
   and say to their companions, 'Be
      strong!'

⁷ The metalworker encourages the
      goldsmith,
   and the one who smooths with the
      hammer
spurs on the one who strikes the anvil.
One says of the welding, 'It is good.'
   The other nails down the idol so that it
      will not topple.

⁸ 'But you, Israel, my servant,
   Jacob, whom I have chosen,
   you descendants of Abraham my
      friend,
⁹ I took you from the ends of the earth,
   from its farthest corners I called you.
I said, "You are my servant";
   I have chosen you and have not
      rejected you.
¹⁰ So do not fear, for I am with you;
   do not be dismayed, for I am your
      God.
I will strengthen you and help you;
   I will uphold you with my righteous
      right hand.

¹¹ 'All who rage against you
   will surely be ashamed and disgraced;
those who oppose you
   will be as nothing and perish.
¹² Though you search for your enemies,
   you will not find them.
Those who wage war against you
   will be as nothing at all.
¹³ For I am the LORD your God
   who takes hold of your right hand
and says to you, Do not fear;
   I will help you.
¹⁴ Do not be afraid, you worm Jacob,
   little Israel, do not fear,
for I myself will help you,' declares the
      LORD,
   your Redeemer, the Holy One of Israel.
¹⁵ 'See, I will make you into a
      threshing-sledge,
   new and sharp, with many teeth.

You will thresh the mountains and crush
them,
and reduce the hills to chaff.
[16] You will winnow them, the wind will
pick them up,
and a gale will blow them away.
But you will rejoice in the LORD
and glory in the Holy One of Israel.

[17] 'The poor and needy search for water,
but there is none;
their tongues are parched with thirst.
But I the LORD will answer them;
I, the God of Israel, will not forsake
them.
[18] I will make rivers flow on barren heights,
and springs within the valleys.
I will turn the desert into pools of water,
and the parched ground into springs.
[19] I will put in the desert
the cedar and the acacia, the myrtle
and the olive.
I will set junipers in the wasteland,
the fir and the cypress together,
[20] so that people may see and know,
may consider and understand,
that the hand of the LORD has done this,
that the Holy One of Israel has
created it.

▬ PSALM 116:8-14

[8] For you, LORD, have delivered me from
death,
my eyes from tears,
my feet from stumbling,
[9] that I may walk before the LORD
in the land of the living.

[10] I trusted in the LORD when I said,
'I am greatly afflicted';
[11] in my alarm I said,
'Everyone is a liar.'

[12] What shall I return to the LORD

for all his goodness to me?
[13] I will lift up the cup of salvation
and call on the name of the LORD.
[14] I will fulfil my vows to the LORD
in the presence of all his people.

▬ PROVERBS 24:1-2

24 Do not envy the wicked,
do not desire their company;
[2] for their hearts plot violence,
and their lips talk about making
trouble.

▬ EPHESIANS 3:1-21

3 For this reason I, Paul, the prisoner
of Christ Jesus for the sake of you
Gentiles –
[2] Surely you have heard about the admin-
istration of God's grace that was given to me
for you, [3] that is, the mystery made known to
me by revelation, as I have already written
briefly. [4] In reading this, then, you will be
able to understand my insight into the mystery of Christ, [5] which was not made known
to people in other generations as it has now
been revealed by the Spirit to God's holy
apostles and prophets. [6] This mystery is that
through the gospel the Gentiles are heirs together with Israel, members together of one
body, and sharers together in the promise in
Christ Jesus.
[7] I became a servant of this gospel by
the gift of God's grace given me through
the working of his power. [8] Although I am
less than the least of all the Lord's people,
this grace was given me: to preach to the
Gentiles the boundless riches of Christ,
[9] and to make plain to everyone the ad-
ministration of this mystery, which for
ages past was kept hidden in God, who created all things. [10] His intent was that now,

through the church, the manifold wisdom of God should be made known to the rulers and authorities in the heavenly realms, [11] according to his eternal purpose that he accomplished in Christ Jesus our Lord. [12] In him and through faith in him we may approach God with freedom and confidence. [13] I ask you, therefore, not to be discouraged because of my sufferings for you, which are your glory.

[14] For this reason I kneel before the Father, [15] from whom every family in heaven and on earth derives its name. [16] I pray that out of his glorious riches he may strengthen you with power through his Spirit in your inner being, [17] so that Christ may dwell in your hearts through faith. And I pray that you, being rooted and established in love, [18] may have power, together with all the Lord's holy people, to grasp how wide and long and high and deep is the love of Christ, [19] and to know this love that surpasses knowledge – that you may be filled to the measure of all the fulness of God.

[20] Now to him who is able to do immeasurably more than all we ask or imagine, according to his power that is at work within us, [21] to him be glory in the church and in Christ Jesus throughout all generations, for ever and ever! Amen.

'Eccentric' Christians

'He sits enthroned above the circle of the earth, and its people are like grasshoppers.' **Isaiah 40:22**

The man-centred focus that is creeping into the church must be resisted at all costs. Such matters as disciplining children, dealing with marital problems, and establishing proper priorities should be addressed also, but we must be careful that 'market forces' do not mould our theology.

It could be argued that our problems are so acute because we are deficient in our knowledge of God. The context in which we think and feel is so limited that it is no wonder our souls feel stifled and claustrophobic. One preacher describes our condition in this way: 'We are like Peter trying to walk on the water but becoming so engrossed in the winds and the waves that we lose sight of the all-sufficient Christ who is right there beside us. The immediate environment has blotted out the sense of the eternal.'

This is why I have chosen today's reading from the magnificent book of Isaiah. The prophet does what a doctor would do upon visiting a patient with a minor sickness and finding the windows shut fast and the room lacking in oxygen. He would throw open the windows and invite the patient to inhale the purer air. 'Take a deep breath of the oxygen of the Spirit,' Isaiah is saying in effect. 'See how great and powerful God is. Set your problems in the context of His omnipotence.'

We become like the thing we focus on. If we centre on man rather than God, then we ought not be surprised if we finish up off centre - eccentric.

PRAYER

O God, save me from being an off-centre Christian and thus an eccentric Christian – the true meaning of that term. May my primary focus be always on You. Grant it, dear Lord. In Jesus' name I pray. Amen.

FURTHER STUDY

2 Cor. 4:13-18; Heb. 3:1; 12:2; Psa. 141:8
• What was Paul's focus?
• What is the exhortation of the writer of Hebrews?

October 5

■ ISAIAH 41:21–43:13

²¹ 'Present your case,' says the LORD.
'Set forth your arguments,' says
Jacob's King.
²² 'Tell us, you idols,
what is going to happen.
Tell us what the former things were,
so that we may consider them
and know their final outcome.
Or declare to us the things to come,
²³ tell us what the future holds,
so that we may know you are gods.
Do something, whether good or bad,
so that we will be dismayed and filled
with fear.
²⁴ But you are less than nothing
and your works are utterly worthless;
whoever chooses you is detestable.

²⁵ 'I have stirred up one from the north,
and he comes –
one from the rising sun who calls on
my name.
He treads on rulers as if they were
mortar,
as if he were a potter treading the clay.
²⁶ Who told of this from the beginning, so
that we could know,
or beforehand, so that we could say,
"He was right"?
No one told of this,
no one foretold it,
no one heard any words from you.
²⁷ I was the first to tell Zion, "Look, here
they are!"
I gave to Jerusalem a messenger of
good news.
²⁸ I look but there is no one –
no one among the gods to give
counsel,
no one to give answer when I ask
them.
²⁹ See, they are all false!
Their deeds amount to nothing;
their images are but wind and
confusion.

42 'Here is my servant, whom I
uphold,
my chosen one in whom I delight;
I will put my Spirit on him,
and he will bring justice to the
nations.
² He will not shout or cry out,
or raise his voice in the streets.
³ A bruised reed he will not break,
and a smouldering wick he will not
snuff out.
In faithfulness he will bring forth
justice;
⁴ he will not falter or be discouraged
till he establishes justice on earth.
In his teaching the islands will put
their hope.'

⁵ This is what God the LORD says –
  the Creator of the heavens, who stretches
      them out,
    who spreads out the earth with all that
      springs from it,
    who gives breath to its people,
    and life to those who walk on it:
⁶ 'I, the LORD, have called you in
      righteousness;
    I will take hold of your hand.
  I will keep you and will make you
    to be a covenant for the people
    and a light for the Gentiles,
⁷ to open eyes that are blind,
    to free captives from prison
    and to release from the dungeon those
      who sit in darkness.

⁸ 'I am the LORD; that is my name!
  I will not yield my glory to another
    or my praise to idols.
⁹ See, the former things have taken place,
    and new things I declare;
  before they spring into being
    I announce them to you.'
¹⁰ Sing to the LORD a new song,
    his praise from the ends of the earth,
  you who go down to the sea, and all that
      is in it,
    you islands, and all who live in them.
¹¹ Let the wilderness and its towns raise
      their voices;
    let the settlements where Kedar lives
      rejoice.
  Let the people of Sela sing for joy;
    let them shout from the
      mountaintops.
¹² Let them give glory to the LORD
    and proclaim his praise in the islands.
¹³ The LORD will march out like a
      champion,
    like a warrior he will stir up his zeal;
  with a shout he will raise the battle cry
    and will triumph over his enemies.

¹⁴ 'For a long time I have kept silent,
    I have been quiet and held myself
      back.
  But now, like a woman in childbirth,
    I cry out, I gasp and pant.
¹⁵ I will lay waste the mountains and hills
    and dry up all their vegetation;
  I will turn rivers into islands
    and dry up the pools.
¹⁶ I will lead the blind by ways they have
      not known,
    along unfamiliar paths I will guide
      them;
  I will turn the darkness into light before
      them
    and make the rough places smooth.
  These are the things I will do;
    I will not forsake them.
¹⁷ But those who trust in idols,
    who say to images, "You are our gods,"
    will be turned back in utter shame.

¹⁸ 'Hear, you deaf;
    look, you blind, and see!
¹⁹ Who is blind but my servant,
    and deaf like the messenger I send?
  Who is blind like the one in covenant
      with me,
    blind like the servant of the LORD?
²⁰ You have seen many things, but you pay
      no attention;
    your ears are open, but you do not
      listen.'
²¹ It pleased the LORD
    for the sake of his righteousness
    to make his law great and glorious.
²² But this is a people plundered and
      looted,
    all of them trapped in pits
    or hidden away in prisons.
  They have become plunder,
    with no one to rescue them;
  they have been made loot,
    with no one to say, 'Send them back.'

²³ Which of you will listen to this
    or pay close attention in time to come?

²⁴ Who handed Jacob over to become loot,
      and Israel to the plunderers?
   Was it not the LORD,
      against whom we have sinned?
   For they would not follow his ways;
      they did not obey his law.
²⁵ So he poured out on them his burning
      anger,
      the violence of war.
   It enveloped them in flames, yet they did
      not understand;
      it consumed them, but they did not
      take it to heart.

43 But now, this is what the LORD
      says –
   he who created you, Jacob,
   he who formed you, Israel:
   'Do not fear, for I have redeemed you;
      I have summoned you by name; you
      are mine.
² When you pass through the waters,
      I will be with you;
   and when you pass through the rivers,
      they will not sweep over you.
   When you walk through the fire,
      you will not be burned;
      the flames will not set you ablaze.
³ For I am the LORD your God,
      the Holy One of Israel, your Saviour;
   I give Egypt for your ransom,
      Cush and Seba in your stead.
⁴ Since you are precious and honoured in
      my sight,
      and because I love you,
   I will give people in exchange for you,
      nations in exchange for your life.
⁵ Do not be afraid, for I am with you;
      I will bring your children from the
      east
   and gather you from the west.
⁶ I will say to the north, "Give them up!"
      and to the south, "Do not hold them
      back."
   Bring my sons from afar
      and my daughters from the ends of the
      earth –

⁷ everyone who is called by my name,
      whom I created for my glory,
      whom I formed and made.'

⁸ Lead out those who have eyes but are
      blind,
      who have ears but are deaf.
⁹ All the nations gather together
      and the peoples assemble.
   Which of their gods foretold this
      and proclaimed to us the former
      things?
   Let them bring in their witnesses to
      prove they were right,
      so that others may hear and say, 'It is
      true.'
¹⁰ 'You are my witnesses,' declares the
      LORD,
      'and my servant whom I have chosen,
   so that you may know and believe me
      and understand that I am he.
   Before me no god was formed,
      nor will there be one after me.
¹¹ I, even I, am the LORD,
      and apart from me there is no saviour.
¹² I have revealed and saved and
      proclaimed –
      I, and not some foreign god among
      you.
   You are my witnesses,' declares the LORD,
      'that I am God.
¹³   Yes, and from ancient days I am he.
   No one can deliver out of my hand.
      When I act, who can reverse it?'

....

■ **PSALM 116:15-19**

¹⁵ Precious in the sight of the LORD
      is the death of his faithful servants.
¹⁶ Truly I am your servant, LORD;
      I serve you just as my mother did;
      you have freed me from my chains.

¹⁷ I will sacrifice a thank-offering to you
      and call on the name of the LORD.

[18] I will fulfil my vows to the LORD
    in the presence of all his people,
[19] in the courts of the house of the LORD –
    in your midst, Jerusalem.

Praise the LORD.

PROVERBS 24:3-4

[3] By wisdom a house is built,
    and through understanding it is
        established;
[4] through knowledge its rooms are filled
    with rare and beautiful treasures.

EPHESIANS 4:1-24

4 As a prisoner for the Lord, then, I urge
you to live a life worthy of the calling
you have received. [2] Be completely humble
and gentle; be patient, bearing with one
another in love. [3] Make every effort to keep
the unity of the Spirit through the bond of
peace. [4] There is one body and one Spirit,
just as you were called to one hope when you
were called; [5] one Lord, one faith, one baptism; [6] one God and Father of all, who is over
all and through all and in all.

[7] But to each one of us grace has been
given as Christ apportioned it. [8] This is
why it says:

'When he ascended on high,
    he took many captives
    and gave gifts to his people.'

[9] (What does 'he ascended' mean except
that he also descended to the lower, earthly regions? [10] He who descended is the
very one who ascended higher than all the

heavens, in order to fill the whole universe.)
[11] So Christ himself gave the apostles, the
prophets, the evangelists, the pastors and
teachers, [12] to equip his people for works
of service, so that the body of Christ may
be built up [13] until we all reach unity in the
faith and in the knowledge of the Son of God
and become mature, attaining to the whole
measure of the fulness of Christ.

[14] Then we will no longer be infants,
tossed back and forth by the waves, and
blown here and there by every wind of
teaching and by the cunning and craftiness
of people in their deceitful scheming. [15] Instead, speaking the truth in love, we will
grow to become in every respect the mature
body of him who is the head, that is, Christ.
[16] From him the whole body, joined and held
together by every supporting ligament,
grows and builds itself up in love, as each
part does its work.

[17] So I tell you this, and insist on it in the
Lord, that you must no longer live as the
Gentiles do, in the futility of their thinking. [18] They are darkened in their understanding and separated from the life of
God because of the ignorance that is in
them due to the hardening of their hearts.
[19] Having lost all sensitivity, they have
given themselves over to sensuality so as to
indulge in every kind of impurity, and they
are full of greed.

[20] That, however, is not the way of life you
learned [21] when you heard about Christ and
were taught in him in accordance with the
truth that is in Jesus. [22] You were taught,
with regard to your former way of life, to put
off your old self, which is being corrupted
by its deceitful desires; [23] to be made new in
the attitude of your minds; [24] and to put on
the new self, created to be like God in true
righteousness and holiness.

The Great Creator

'... the LORD ... the Creator of the heavens, who stretches them out, who spreads out the earth with all that springs from it ...' **Isaiah 42:5**

The Bible never argues that there is a God; everywhere it assumes and asserts the fact. Majestically the opening verse of Scripture says: 'In the beginning God ...' Its paramount concern is not to persuade us that God is but to tell us *who* God is and what He does. This is why the first thing we see Him do in the Scriptures is to act creatively, to show His might and omnipotence.

I love the story about a group of researchers who set out to discover what really happened when the earth was created. They spent months gathering information and feeding data into a computer. Finally they hit the print-out key and waited. Soon a message appeared with these words: 'See Genesis 1:1.'

Many think the only reference to God's creative act is the one that appears in the first two chapters of Genesis, but this truth is woven inextricably into the very texture of both the Old and New Testaments. One example of this is found in our text for today. We cannot have a right conception of God or contemplate Him correctly unless we think of Him as being all-powerful. He who cannot do what He wills and pleases cannot be God. As God has a will to do good, so He has the necessary power to execute that will. Who can look upward to the midnight sky, behold its wonders, and not exclaim, 'Of what were these mighty orbs formed?' A great and powerful God brought them into being simply by saying, 'Let them be.' This kind of God can have my heart any time.

PRAYER

Father, I sense that the more enlightened my understanding, the more my soul responds to that enlightenment with thanksgiving, adoration, and praise. Enlighten me still more, dear Father. In Jesus' name I pray. Amen.

FURTHER STUDY

Acts 14:8-15; Neh. 9:5-6; Psa. 102:25; Heb. 11:3
- What did Paul and Barnabas declare?
- How do we understand that God formed the universe?

October 6

◼ ISAIAH 43:14 – 45:10

14 This is what the LORD says –
  your Redeemer, the Holy One of Israel:

'For your sake I will send to Babylon
  and bring down as fugitives all the
    Babylonians,
  in the ships in which they took pride.

¹⁵ I am the LORD, your Holy One,
  Israel's Creator, your King.'

¹⁶ This is what the LORD says –
  he who made a way through the sea,
  a path through the mighty waters,
¹⁷ who drew out the chariots and horses,
  the army and reinforcements together,
  and they lay there, never to rise again,
  extinguished, snuffed out like a wick:
¹⁸ 'Forget the former things;
  do not dwell on the past.
¹⁹ See, I am doing a new thing!
  Now it springs up; do you not perceive
    it?
  I am making a way in the wilderness
  and streams in the wasteland.
²⁰ The wild animals honour me,
  the jackals and the owls,
  because I provide water in the
    wilderness
  and streams in the wasteland,
  to give drink to my people, my chosen,
²¹   the people I formed for myself
  that they may proclaim my praise.

²² 'Yet you have not called on me, Jacob,
  you have not wearied yourselves for
    me, Israel.
²³ You have not brought me sheep for burnt
    offerings,
  nor honoured me with your sacrifices.
  I have not burdened you with grain
    offerings
  nor wearied you with demands for
    incense.
²⁴ You have not bought any fragrant
    calamus for me,
  or lavished on me the fat of your
    sacrifices.
  But you have burdened me with your
    sins
  and wearied me with your offences.

²⁵ 'I, even I, am he who blots out
  your transgressions, for my own sake,

and remembers your sins no more.
²⁶ Review the past for me,
  let us argue the matter together;
  state the case for your innocence.
²⁷ Your first father sinned;
  those I sent to teach you rebelled
    against me.
²⁸ So I disgraced the dignitaries of your
    temple;
  I consigned Jacob to destruction
  and Israel to scorn.

44 'But now listen, Jacob, my servant,
  Israel, whom I have chosen.
² This is what the LORD says –
  he who made you, who formed you in
    the womb,
  and who will help you:
  do not be afraid, Jacob, my servant,
  Jeshurun, whom I have chosen.
³ For I will pour water on the thirsty land,
  and streams on the dry ground;
  I will pour out my Spirit on your
    offspring,
  and my blessing on your descendants.
⁴ They will spring up like grass in a
    meadow,
  like poplar trees by flowing streams.
⁵ Some will say, "I belong to the LORD";
  others will call themselves by the
    name of Jacob;
  still others will write on their hand, "The
    LORD'S,"
  and will take the name Israel.

⁶ 'This is what the Lord says –
  Israel's King and Redeemer, the LORD
    Almighty:
  I am the first and I am the last;
  apart from me there is no God.
⁷ Who then is like me? Let him proclaim
    it.
  Let him declare and lay out before me
  what has happened since I established
    my ancient people,
  and what is yet to come –

yes, let them foretell what will come.
⁸ Do not tremble, do not be afraid.
  Did I not proclaim this and foretell it
    long ago?
  You are my witnesses. Is there any God
    besides me?
  No, there is no other Rock; I know not
    one.'

⁹ All who make idols are nothing,
  and the things they treasure are
    worthless.
  Those who would speak up for them are
    blind;
  they are ignorant, to their own shame.
¹⁰ Who shapes a god and casts an idol,
  which can profit nothing?
¹¹ People who do that will be put to shame;
  such craftsmen are only human
    beings.
  Let them all come together and take
    their stand;
  they will be brought down to terror
    and shame.

¹² The blacksmith takes a tool
  and works with it in the coals;
  he shapes an idol with hammers,
    he forges it with the might of his arm.
  He gets hungry and loses his strength;
    he drinks no water and grows faint.
¹³ The carpenter measures with a line
  and makes an outline with a marker;
  he roughs it out with chisels
    and marks it with compasses.
  He shapes it in human form,
    human form in all its glory,
    that it may dwell in a shrine.
¹⁴ He cut down cedars,
  or perhaps took a cypress or oak.
  He let it grow among the trees of the
    forest,
  or planted a pine, and the rain made it
    grow.
¹⁵ It is used as fuel for burning;
  some of it he takes and warms himself,

he kindles a fire and bakes bread.
  But he also fashions a god and worships
    it;
  he makes an idol and bows down
    to it.
¹⁶ Half of the wood he burns in the fire;
  over it he prepares his meal,
  he roasts his meat and eats his fill.
  He also warms himself and says,
    'Ah! I am warm; I see the fire.'
¹⁷ From the rest he makes a god, his idol;
  he bows down to it and worships.
  He prays to it and says,
    'Save me! You are my god!'
¹⁸ They know nothing, they understand
    nothing;
  their eyes are plastered over so that
    they cannot see,
  and their minds closed so that they
    cannot understand.
¹⁹ No one stops to think,
  no one has the knowledge or
    understanding to say,
  'Half of it I used for fuel;
  I even baked bread over its coals,
  I roasted meat and I ate.
  Shall I make a detestable thing from
    what is left?
  Shall I bow down to a block of wood?'
²⁰ Such a person feeds on ashes; a deluded
    heart misleads him;
  he cannot save himself, or say,
    'Is not this thing in my right hand a
    lie?'

²¹ 'Remember these things, Jacob,
  for you, Israel, are my servant.
  I have made you, you are my servant;
  Israel, I will not forget you.
²² I have swept away your offences like a
    cloud,
  your sins like the morning mist.
  Return to me,
  for I have redeemed you.'

23 Sing for joy, you heavens, for the LORD
        has done this;
    shout aloud, you earth beneath.
    Burst into song, you mountains,
        you forests and all your trees,
    for the LORD has redeemed Jacob,
        he displays his glory in Israel.
24 'This is what the LORD says –
        your Redeemer, who formed you in
        the womb:

    I am the LORD,
        the Maker of all things,
    who stretches out the heavens,
    who spreads out the earth by myself,
25 who foils the signs of false prophets
        and makes fools of diviners,
    who overthrows the learning of the wise
        and turns it into nonsense,
26 who carries out the words of his servants
        and fulfils the predictions of his
        messengers,

    who says of Jerusalem, "It shall be
        inhabited,"
    of the towns of Judah, "They shall be
        rebuilt,"
    and of their ruins, "I will restore
        them,"
27 who says to the watery deep, "Be dry,
        and I will dry up your streams,"
28 who says of Cyrus, "He is my shepherd
        and will accomplish all that I please;
    he will say of Jerusalem, 'Let it be rebuilt,'
        and of the temple, 'Let its foundations
        be laid.' "

45 'This is what the LORD says to his
        anointed,
    to Cyrus, whose right hand I take hold
        of
    to subdue nations before him
        and to strip kings of their armour,
    to open doors before him
        so that gates will not be shut:
2 I will go before you

    and will level the mountains;
    I will break down gates of bronze
        and cut through bars of iron.
3 I will give you hidden treasures,
        riches stored in secret places,
    so that you may know that I am the LORD,
        the God of Israel, who summons you
        by name.
4 For the sake of Jacob my servant,
        of Israel my chosen,
    I summon you by name
        and bestow on you a title of honour,
        though you do not acknowledge me.
5 I am the LORD, and there is no other;
        apart from me there is no God.
    I will strengthen you,
        though you have not acknowledged me,
6 so that from the rising of the sun
        to the place of its setting
    people may know there is none besides
        me.
    I am the LORD, and there is no other.
7 I form the light and create darkness,
        I bring prosperity and create disaster;
    I, the LORD, do all these things.

8 'You heavens above, rain down my
        righteousness;
        let the clouds shower it down.
    Let the earth open wide,
        let salvation spring up,
    let righteousness flourish with it;
        I, the LORD, have created it.

9 'Woe to those who quarrel with their
        Maker,
    those who are nothing but potsherds
        among the potsherds on the ground.
    Does the clay say to the potter,
        "What are you making?"
    Does your work say,
        "The potter has no hands"?
10 Woe to the one who says to a father,
        "What have you begotten?"
    or to a mother,
        "What have you brought to birth?"

▬ PSALM 117:1–118:4

¹ Praise the LORD, all you nations;
    extol him, all you peoples.
² For great is his love towards us,
    and the faithfulness of the LORD
       endures for ever.

Praise the LORD.

¹ Give thanks to the Lord, for he is good;
    his love endures for ever.

² Let Israel say:
    'His love endures for ever.'
³ Let the house of Aaron say:
    'His love endures for ever.'
⁴ Let those who fear the LORD say:
    'His love endures for ever.'

▬ PROVERBS 24:5-6

⁵ The wise prevail through great power,
    and those who have knowledge muster
       their strength.
⁶ Surely you need guidance to wage war,
    and victory is won through many
       advisors.

▬ EPHESIANS 4:25–5:14

²⁵ Therefore each of you must put off falsehood and speak truthfully to your neighbour, for we are all members of one body. ²⁶ 'In your anger do not sin': do not let the sun go down while you are still angry, ²⁷ and do not give the devil a foothold. ²⁸ Anyone who has been stealing must steal no longer, but must work, doing something useful with their own hands, that they may have something to share with those in need.

²⁹ Do not let any unwholesome talk come out of your mouths, but only what is helpful for building others up according to their needs, that it may benefit those who listen. ³⁰ And do not grieve the Holy Spirit of God, with whom you were sealed for the day of redemption. ³¹ Get rid of all bitterness, rage and anger, brawling and slander, along with every form of malice. ³² Be kind and compassionate to one another, forgiving each other, just as in Christ God forgave you. ¹ Follow God's example, therefore, as dearly loved children ² and live a life of love, just as Christ loved us and gave himself up for us as a fragrant offering and sacrifice to God.

³ But among you there must not be even a hint of sexual immorality, or of any kind of impurity, or of greed, because these are improper for God's holy people. ⁴ Nor should there be obscenity, foolish talk or coarse joking, which are out of place, but rather thanksgiving. ⁵ For of this you can be sure: no immoral, impure or greedy person – such a person is an idolater – has any inheritance in the kingdom of Christ and of God. ⁶ Let no one deceive you with empty words, for because of such things God's wrath comes on those who are disobedient. ⁷ Therefore do not be partners with them.

⁸ For you were once darkness, but now you are light in the Lord. Live as children of light ⁹ (for the fruit of the light consists in all goodness, righteousness and truth) ¹⁰ and find out what pleases the Lord. ¹¹ Have nothing to do with the fruitless deeds of darkness, but rather expose them. ¹² It is shameful even to mention what the disobedient do in secret. ¹³ But everything exposed by the light becomes visible – and everything that is illuminated becomes a light. ¹⁴ This is why it is said:

'Wake up, sleeper,
    rise from the dead,
       and Christ will shine on you.'

For the Sake of Christ

'Be kind and compassionate to one another, forgiving each another, just as in Christ God forgave you.'
Ephesians 4:32

W e experience divine forgiveness for our sins which we are then to extend to those who have offended us.

This cuts deep.

Perhaps you might be saying at this moment, 'But I can't forgive; I have been hurt too deeply.' Then, may I say it very tenderly, but very solemnly, you can never, never be forgiven. 'But if you do not forgive others their sins,' says Jesus, 'your Father will not forgive your sins' (Matt. 6:15). In refusing to forgive others you break the bridge over which you yourself must pass.

A man once said to me, 'I know I'm a Christian, but someone did such an awful thing to me that I find I can't forgive him.' After spending a good deal of time with him, and getting nowhere, I said, 'If it is really true that you can't forgive this person, it suggests that you yourself have not been forgiven, and you may be deluding yourself that you are a Christian.' He looked at me aghast and went white in the face. My counselling methods are not always as abrupt as that; however, this brought him face to face with reality – and it worked. He got down on his knees, right where he was, and said, 'Father, because You have forgiven me, I offer Your forgiveness and my forgiveness to my brother who has offended me, and I absolve him of his offence in Jesus' name.' Then what happened? Instantly the joy of the Lord streamed right into the centre of his being, and he laughed and laughed, literally, for almost an hour.

PRAYER

Lord Jesus, You who forgave those who spat in Your face and nailed You to a cross, help me to open my heart now and forgive all those who have hurt me. I do it in Your strength and power. Thank You, Lord Jesus. Amen.

FURTHER STUDY

Matt. 5:7; 18:21-35;
Luke 6:36; Prov. 3:3
• How does the parable of
  the unmerciful servant
  apply to us?
• What is the basis of
  forgiving others?

October 7

■ ISAIAH 45:11– 48:11

11 'This is what the LORD says –

the Holy One of Israel, and its Maker:
concerning things to come,
  do you question me about my children,

or give me orders about the work of
    my hands?
¹² It is I who made the earth
    and created mankind on it.
My own hands stretched out the heavens;
    I marshalled their starry hosts.
¹³ I will raise up Cyrus in my
    righteousness:
    I will make all his ways straight.
He will rebuild my city
    and set my exiles free,
but not for a price or reward,
    says the LORD Almighty.'

¹⁴ This is what the LORD says:

'The products of Egypt and the
    merchandise of Cush,
    and those tall Sabeans –
they will come over to you
    and will be yours;
they will trudge behind you,
    coming over to you in chains.
They will bow down before you
    and plead with you, saying,
"Surely God is with you, and there is no
    other;
    there is no other god."'

¹⁵ Truly you are a God who has been hiding
    himself,
    the God and Saviour of Israel.
¹⁶ All the makers of idols will be put to
    shame and disgraced;
    they will go off into disgrace together.
¹⁷ But Israel will be saved by the LORD
    with an everlasting salvation;
you will never be put to shame or
    disgraced,
    to ages everlasting.

¹⁸ For this is what the LORD says –
he who created the heavens,
    he is God;
he who fashioned and made the earth,
    he founded it;

he did not create it to be empty,
    but formed it to be inhabited –
he says:
'I am the LORD,
    and there is no other.
¹⁹ I have not spoken in secret,
    from somewhere in a land of
    darkness;
I have not said to Jacob's descendants,
    "Seek me in vain."
I, the LORD, speak the truth;
    I declare what is right.

²⁰ 'Gather together and come;
    assemble, you fugitives from the
    nations.
Ignorant are those who carry about idols
    of wood,
who pray to gods that cannot save.
²¹ Declare what is to be, present it –
    let them take counsel together.
Who foretold this long ago,
    who declared it from the distant past?
Was it not I, the LORD?
    And there is no God apart from me,
a righteous God and a Saviour;
    there is none but me.

²² 'Turn to me and be saved,
    all you ends of the earth;
    for I am God, and there is no other.
²³ By myself I have sworn,
    my mouth has uttered in all integrity
    a word that will not be revoked:
before me every knee will bow;
    by me every tongue will swear.
²⁴ They will say of me, "In the LORD alone
    are deliverance and strength."'
All who have raged against him
    will come to him and be put to shame.
²⁵ But all the descendants of Israel
    will find deliverance in the LORD
    and will make their boast in him.

46 Bel bows down, Nebo stoops low;
    their idols are borne by beasts of
    burden.

The images that are carried about are
        burdensome,
    a burden for the weary.
² They stoop and bow down together;
    unable to rescue the burden,
    they themselves go off into captivity.

³ 'Listen to me, you descendants of Jacob,
    all the remnant of the people of Israel,
you whom I have upheld since your
        birth,
    and have carried since you were born.
⁴ Even to your old age and grey hairs
    I am he, I am he who will sustain you.
I have made you and I will carry you;
    I will sustain you and I will rescue you.

⁵ 'With whom will you compare me or
        count me equal?
    To whom will you liken me that we
        may be compared?
⁶ Some pour out gold from their bags
    and weigh out silver on the scales;
they hire a goldsmith to make it into a
        god,
    and they bow down and worship it.
⁷ They lift it to their shoulders and carry it;
    they set it up in its place, and there it
        stands.
    From that spot it cannot move.
Even though someone cries out to it, it
        cannot answer;
    it cannot save them from their
        troubles.

⁸ 'Remember this, keep it in mind,
    take it to heart, you rebels.
⁹ Remember the former things, those of
        long ago;
    I am God, and there is no other;
    I am God, and there is none like me.
¹⁰ I make known the end from the
        beginning,
    from ancient times, what is still to
        come.
I say, "My purpose will stand,

and I will do all that I please."
¹¹ From the east I summon a bird of prey;
    from a far-off land, a man to fulfil my
        purpose.
What I have said, that I will bring about;
    what I have planned, that I will do.
¹² Listen to me, you stubborn-hearted,
    you who are now far from my
        righteousness.
¹³ I am bringing my righteousness near,
    it is not far away;
    and my salvation will not be delayed.
I will grant salvation to Zion,
    my splendour to Israel.

47 'Go down, sit in the dust,
        Virgin Daughter Babylon;
    sit on the ground without a throne,
        queen city of the Babylonians.
No more will you be called
    tender or delicate.
² Take millstones and grind flour;
    take off your veil.
Lift up your skirts, bare your legs,
    and wade through the streams.
³ Your nakedness will be exposed
    and your shame uncovered.
I will take vengeance;
    I will spare no one.'

⁴ Our Redeemer – the LORD Almighty is
        his name –
    is the Holy One of Israel.

⁵ 'Sit in silence, go into darkness,
    queen city of the Babylonians;
no more will you be called
    queen of kingdoms.
⁶ I was angry with my people
    and desecrated my inheritance;
I gave them into your hand,
    and you showed them no mercy.
Even on the aged
    you laid a very heavy yoke.
⁷ You said, "I am for ever –
    the eternal queen!"

But you did not consider these things
  or reflect on what might happen.

8 'Now then, listen, you lover of pleasure,
  lounging in your security
and saying to yourself,
  "I am, and there is none besides me.
I will never be a widow
  or suffer the loss of children."
9 Both of these will overtake you
  in a moment, on a single day:
  loss of children and widowhood.
They will come upon you in full measure,
  in spite of your many sorceries
  and all your potent spells.
10 You have trusted in your wickedness
  and have said, "No one sees me."
Your wisdom and knowledge mislead you
  when you say to yourself,
  "I am, and there is none besides me."
11 Disaster will come upon you,
  and you will not know how to conjure
    it away.
A calamity will fall upon you
  that you cannot ward off with a
    ransom;
a catastrophe you cannot foresee
  will suddenly come upon you.

12 'Keep on, then, with your magic spells
  and with your many sorceries,
  which you have laboured at since
    childhood.
Perhaps you will succeed,
  perhaps you will cause terror.
13 All the counsel you have received has
    only worn you out!
Let your astrologers come forward,
  those stargazers who make predictions
    month by month,
let them save you from what is coming
    upon you.
14 Surely they are like stubble;
  the fire will burn them up.
They cannot even save themselves
  from the power of the flame.

These are not coals for warmth;
  this is not a fire to sit by.
15 That is all they are to you –
  these you have dealt with
  and laboured with since childhood.
All of them go on in their error;
  there is not one that can save you.

48 'Listen to this, you descendants of
    Jacob,
you who are called by the name of
    Israel
and come from the line of Judah,
you who take oaths in the name of the
    LORD
and invoke the God of Israel –
  but not in truth or righteousness –
2 you who call yourselves citizens of the
    holy city
and claim to rely on the God of Israel –
  the LORD Almighty is his name:
3 I foretold the former things long ago,
  my mouth announced them and I
    made them known;
  then suddenly I acted, and they came
    to pass.
4 For I knew how stubborn you were;
  your neck muscles were iron,
  your forehead was bronze.
5 Therefore I told you these things long
    ago;
  before they happened I announced
    them to you
so that you could not say,
  "My images brought them about;
  my wooden image and metal god
    ordained them."
6 You have heard these things; look at
    them all.
  Will you not admit them?

'From now on I will tell you of new things,
  of hidden things unknown to you.
7 They are created now, and not long ago;
  you have not heard of them before
    today.

So you cannot say,
"Yes, I knew of them."
[8] You have neither heard nor understood;
from of old your ears have not been
open.
Well do I know how treacherous you are;
you were called a rebel from birth.
[9] For my own name's sake I delay my
wrath;
for the sake of my praise I hold it back
from you,
so as not to destroy you completely.
[10] See, I have refined you, though not as
silver;
I have tested you in the furnace of
affliction.
[11] For my own sake, for my own sake, I do
this.
How can I let myself be defamed?
I will not yield my glory to another.

▪ PSALM 118:5-9

[5] When hard pressed, I cried to the LORD;
he brought me into a spacious place.
[6] The LORD is with me; I will not be afraid.
What can mere mortals do to me?
[7] The LORD is with me; he is my helper.
I look in triumph on my enemies.

[8] It is better to take refuge in the LORD
than to trust in humans.
[9] It is better to take refuge in the LORD
than to trust in princes.

▪ PROVERBS 24:7-9

[7] Wisdom is too high for fools;
in the assembly at the gate they must
not open their mouths.
[8] Whoever plots evil
will be known as a schemer.
[9] The schemes of folly are sin,
and people detest a mocker.

▪ EPHESIANS 5:15-33

[15] Be very careful, then, how you live –
not as unwise but as wise, [16] making the
most of every opportunity, because the
days are evil. [17] Therefore do not be foolish, but understand what the Lord's will
is. [18] Do not get drunk on wine, which leads
to debauchery. Instead, be filled with the
Spirit, [19] speaking to one another with
psalms, hymns, and songs from the Spirit.
Sing and make music from your heart to
the Lord, [20] always giving thanks to God
the Father for everything, in the name of
our Lord Jesus Christ.

[21] Submit to one another out of reverence
for Christ.

[22] Wives, submit yourselves to your own
husbands as you do to the Lord. [23] For the
husband is the head of the wife as Christ is
the head of the church, his body, of which
he is the Saviour. [24] Now as the church sub-
mits to Christ, so also wives should submit
to their husbands in everything.

[25] Husbands, love your wives, just as
Christ loved the church and gave himself up
for her [26] to make her holy, cleansing her by
the washing with water through the word,
[27] and to present her to himself as a radiant church, without stain or wrinkle or any
other blemish, but holy and blameless. [28] In
this same way, husbands ought to love their
wives as their own bodies. He who loves his
wife loves himself. [29] After all, no one ever
hated their own body, but they feed and
care for their body, just as Christ does the
church – [30] for we are members of his body.
[31] 'For this reason a man will leave his father and mother and be united to his wife,
and the two will become one flesh.' [32] This
is a profound mystery – but I am talking
about Christ and the church. [33] However,
each one of you also must love his wife as
he loves himself, and the wife must respect
her husband.

A Command to Be Obeyed

'Do not get drunk on wine ... Instead, be filled with the Spirit ...' **Ephesians 5:18**

In *The Amplified Bible* this text reads: 'And do not get drunk with wine ... but ever be filled and stimulated with the (Holy) Spirit.'

However we may view the doctrine of the Holy Spirit, or whatever experience we may have had of Him in the past, if we do not enjoy an ever-present flow of His power in our lives, then we are living below the New Testament standard. This text, as many commentators have pointed out, is a command to be obeyed. If we are not experiencing what the Bible commands, then our lives are not in harmony with God's purposes.

I meet many Christians who are sighing over lost ecstasies, mourning over lost victories, and who are downcast because they have lost touch with God. It is largely because they are living not 'the life of the Spirit', but the life of following an ideal with their own resources, stirred by emotion through a special sermon or something they read in a book. They grow tired and are on the point of giving up.

A translator in India, working on a piece of writing on the Holy Spirit, wrote: 'I'd like another subject. I'm tired of working on the Holy Spirit.' A lot of Christians have that problem; they grow tired of working on the Holy Spirit, instead of letting the Holy Spirit work on them. Let's stop working on the Spirit, and allow Him to work on us!

PRAYER

Blessed Holy Spirit, help me as I thread my way through the maze of thoughts and attitudes about You. Help me to come out with Your thoughts and attitudes. I want to be filled with the Spirit – today and always. For Jesus' sake. Amen.

FURTHER STUDY

Rom. 8:1-17; Ezek. 36:27; John 14:17; Heb. 10:15-16
• What is the result of 'the law of the Spirit who gives life'?
• What is Paul teaching about the Holy Spirit?

October 8

■ ISAIAH 48:12–50:11

12 'Listen to me, Jacob,
     Israel, whom I have called:
I am he;
     I am the first and I am the last.

13 My own hand laid the foundations of
       the earth,
     and my right hand spread out the
       heavens;
when I summon them,
     they all stand up together.

14 'Come together, all of you, and listen:
    which of the idols has foretold these
        things?
The LORD's chosen ally
    will carry out his purpose against
        Babylon;
    his arm will be against the
        Babylonians.
15 I, even I, have spoken;
    yes, I have called him.
I will bring him,
    and he will succeed in his mission.

16 'Come near me and listen to this:

'From the first announcement I have not
        spoken in secret;
    at the time it happens, I am there.'

And now the Sovereign LORD has sent me,
    endowed with his Spirit.

17 This is what the LORD says –
    your Redeemer, the Holy One of Israel:
'I am the LORD your God,
    who teaches you what is best for you,
    who directs you in the way you should
        go.
18 If only you had paid attention to my
        commands,
    your peace would have been like a
        river,
    your well-being like the waves of the
        sea.
19 Your descendants would have been like
        the sand,
    your children like its numberless
        grains;
    their name would never be blotted out
        nor destroyed from before me.'

20 Leave Babylon,
    flee from the Babylonians!
Announce this with shouts of joy
    and proclaim it.
Send it out to the ends of the earth;

say, 'The LORD has redeemed his
        servant Jacob.'
21 They did not thirst when he led them
        through the deserts;
    he made water flow for them from the
        rock;
he split the rock
    and water gushed out.

22 'There is no peace,' says the LORD, 'for
        the wicked.'

49 Listen to me, you islands;
    hear this, you distant nations:
before I was born the LORD called me;
    from my mother's womb he has
        spoken my name.
2 He made my mouth like a sharpened
        sword,
    in the shadow of his hand he hid me;
he made me into a polished arrow
    and concealed me in his quiver.
3 He said to me, 'You are my servant,
    Israel, in whom I will display my
        splendour.'
4 But I said, 'I have laboured in vain;
    I have spent my strength for nothing
        at all.
Yet what is due to me is in the LORD's
        hand,
    and my reward is with my God.'

5 And now the LORD says –
    he who formed me in the womb to be
        his servant
to bring Jacob back to him
    and gather Israel to himself,
for I am honoured in the eyes of the LORD
    and my God has been my strength –
6 he says:
'It is too small a thing for you to be my
        servant
    to restore the tribes of Jacob
    and bring back those of Israel I have
        kept.
I will also make you a light for the
        Gentiles,

that my salvation may reach to the
ends of the earth.'

⁷ This is what the LORD says –
the Redeemer and Holy One of Israel –
to him who was despised and abhorred
by the nation,
to the servant of rulers:
'Kings will see you and stand up,
princes will see and bow down,
because of the LORD, who is faithful,
the Holy One of Israel, who has chosen
you.'
⁸ This is what the LORD says:

'In the time of my favour I will answer
you,
and in the day of salvation I will help
you;
I will keep you and will make you
to be a covenant for the people,
to restore the land
and to reassign its desolate
inheritances,
⁹ to say to the captives, "Come out,"
and to those in darkness, "Be free!"

'They will feed beside the roads
and find pasture on every barren hill.
¹⁰ They will neither hunger nor thirst,
nor will the desert heat or the sun beat
down on them.
He who has compassion on them will
guide them
and lead them beside springs of water.
¹¹ I will turn all my mountains into roads,
and my highways will be raised up.
¹² See, they will come from afar –
some from the north, some from the
west,
some from the region of Aswan.'

¹³ Shout for joy, you heavens;
rejoice, you earth;
burst into song, you mountains!
For the LORD comforts his people

and will have compassion on his
afflicted ones.

¹⁴ But Zion said, 'The LORD has forsaken
me,
the Lord has forgotten me.'

¹⁵ 'Can a mother forget the baby at her
breast
and have no compassion on the child
she has borne?
Though she may forget,
I will not forget you!
¹⁶ See, I have engraved you on the palms of
my hands;
your walls are ever before me.
¹⁷ Your children hasten back,
and those who laid you waste depart
from you.
¹⁸ Lift up your eyes and look around;
all your children gather and come to
you.
As surely as I live,' declares the LORD,
'you will wear them all as ornaments;
you will put them on, like a bride.

¹⁹ 'Though you were ruined and made
desolate
and your land laid waste,
now you will be too small for your
people,
and those who devoured you will be
far away.
²⁰ The children born during your
bereavement
will yet say in your hearing,
"This place is too small for us;
give us more space to live in."
²¹ Then you will say in your heart,
"Who bore me these?
I was bereaved and barren;
I was exiled and rejected.
Who brought these up?
I was left all alone,
but these – where have they come
from?"'

²² This is what the Sovereign LORD says:

'See, I will beckon to the nations,
    I will lift up my banner to the peoples;
they will bring your sons in their arms
    and carry your daughters on their
        hips.
²³ Kings will be your foster fathers,
    and their queens your nursing
        mothers.
They will bow down before you with
        their faces to the ground;
    they will lick the dust at your feet.
Then you will know that I am the LORD;
    those who hope in me will not be
        disappointed.'

²⁴ Can plunder be taken from warriors,
    or captives be rescued from the fierce?

²⁵ But this is what the LORD says:

'Yes, captives will be taken from warriors,
    and plunder retrieved from the fierce;
I will contend with those who contend
        with you,
    and your children I will save.
²⁶ I will make your oppressors eat their
        own flesh;
    they will be drunk on their own blood,
        as with wine.
Then all mankind will know
    that I, the LORD, am your Saviour,
    your Redeemer, the Mighty One of
        Jacob.'

50 This is what the Lord says:

'Where is your mother's certificate of
        divorce
    with which I sent her away?
Or to which of my creditors
    did I sell you?
Because of your sins you were sold;
    because of your transgressions your
        mother was sent away.

² When I came, why was there no one?
    When I called, why was there no one
        to answer?
Was my arm too short to deliver you?
    Do I lack the strength to rescue you?
By a mere rebuke I dry up the sea,
    I turn rivers into a desert;
their fish rot for lack of water
    and die of thirst.
³ I clothe the heavens with darkness
    and make sackcloth its covering.'

⁴ The Sovereign LORD has given me a well-
        instructed tongue,
    to know the word that sustains the
        weary.
He wakens me morning by morning,
    wakens my ear to listen like one being
        instructed.
⁵ The Sovereign LORD has opened my ears;
    I have not been rebellious,
    I have not turned away.
⁶ I offered my back to those who beat me,
    my cheeks to those who pulled out my
        beard;
    I did not hide my face
        from mocking and spitting.
⁷ Because the Sovereign LORD helps me,
    I will not be disgraced.
Therefore have I set my face like flint,
    and I know I will not be put to shame.
⁸ He who vindicates me is near.
    Who then will bring charges against
        me?
    Let us face each other!
Who is my accuser?
    Let him confront me!
⁹ It is the Sovereign LORD who helps me.
    Who will condemn me?
They will all wear out like a garment;
    the moths will eat them up.

¹⁰ Who among you fears the LORD
    and obeys the word of his servant?
Let the one who walks in the dark,
    who has no light,

trust in the name of the LORD
  and rely on their God.
[11] But now, all you who light fires
  and provide yourselves with flaming
    torches,
go, walk in the light of your fires
  and of the torches you have set ablaze.
This is what you shall receive from my
    hand:
  you will lie down in torment.

▬ PSALM 118:10-14

[10] All the nations surrounded me,
  but in the name of the LORD I cut them
    down.
[11] They surrounded me on every side,
  but in the name of the LORD I cut them
    down.
[12] They swarmed around me like bees,
  but they were consumed as quickly as
    burning thorns;
  in the name of the LORD I cut them
    down.
[13] I was pushed back and about to fall,
  but the LORD helped me.
[14] The LORD is my strength and my defence;
  he has become my salvation.

▬ PROVERBS 24:10-12

[10] If you falter in a time of trouble,
  how small is your strength!
[11] Rescue those being led away to death;
  hold back those staggering towards
    slaughter.
[12] If you say, 'But we knew nothing about
    this,'
  does not he who weighs the heart
    perceive it?
  Does not he who guards your life know
    it?
  Will he not repay everyone according
    to what they have done?

▬ EPHESIANS 6:1-24

6 Children, obey your parents in the
  Lord, for this is right. [2] 'Honour your
father and mother' – which is the first commandment with a promise – [3] 'so that it may
go well with you and that you may enjoy
long life on the earth.'

[4] Fathers, do not exasperate your children; instead, bring them up in the training
and instruction of the Lord.

[5] Slaves, obey your earthly masters with
respect and fear, and with sincerity of heart,
just as you would obey Christ. [6] Obey them
not only to win their favour when their eye
is on you, but as slaves of Christ, doing the
will of God from your heart. [7] Serve wholeheartedly, as if you were serving the Lord,
not people, [8] because you know that the
Lord will reward each one for whatever
good they do, whether they are slave or free.

[9] And masters, treat your slaves in the same
way. Do not threaten them, since you know
that he who is both their Master and yours is in
heaven, and there is no favouritism with him.

[10] Finally, be strong in the Lord and in his
mighty power. [11] Put on the full armour of
God, so that you can take your stand against
the devil's schemes. [12] For our struggle is not
against flesh and blood, but against the rulers,
against the authorities, against the powers of
this dark world and against the spiritual forces
of evil in the heavenly realms. [13] Therefore put
on the full armour of God, so that when the day
of evil comes, you may be able to stand your
ground, and after you have done everything, to
stand. [14] Stand firm then, with the belt of truth
buckled round your waist, with the breastplate
of righteousness in place, [15] and with your feet
fitted with the readiness that comes from the
gospel of peace. [16] In addition to all this, take
up the shield of faith, with which you can extinguish all the flaming arrows of the evil one.
[17] Take the helmet of salvation and the sword of
the Spirit, which is the word of God.

[18] And pray in the Spirit on all occasions

with all kinds of prayers and requests. With this in mind, be alert and always keep on praying for all the Lord's people. [19] Pray also for me, that whenever I speak, words may be given me so that I will fearlessly make known the mystery of the gospel, [20] for which I am an ambassador in chains. Pray that I may declare it fearlessly, as I should.

[21] Tychicus, the dear brother and faithful servant in the Lord, will tell you everything, so that you also may know how I am and what I am doing. [22] I am sending him to you for this very purpose, that you may know how we are, and that he may encourage you.

[23] Peace to the brothers and sisters, and love with faith from God the Father and the Lord Jesus Christ. [24] Grace to all who love our Lord Jesus Christ with an undying love.

A Call to Arms

'For our struggle is not against flesh and blood ...'
Ephesians 6:12

Ephesians 6:10-20 concerns the spiritual protection that is available to every Christian when doing battle with the Devil. All those who have committed their lives to Jesus Christ know (or should know) that the kingdoms of God and the Devil are locked together in mortal combat. And Christians, whether they like it or not, are thrust right onto the cutting edge of that conflict.

Many Christians are pacifists when it comes to the matter of earthly warfare, but no one can be a pacifist when it comes to the matter of spiritual warfare. Once we enlist in the army of God, we are then expected to train in the art of offensive and defensive spiritual warfare. At certain times and occasions in the Christian life, we find ourselves in a battle that demands fierce hand-to-hand combat with the forces of darkness, and unless we know how to handle these trying situations, we shall easily be overthrown.

The Bible shows us that the Devil and his minions are bitter enemies of God, but because they are powerless against the Almighty, they turn their concentrated attention on those who are His followers – you and me. Notice how many times the word 'against' appears in Ephesians 6:10-13. It occurs six times in all, showing that when anyone comes over to the side of Jesus Christ, they are immediately identified as being for God and against the Devil. There can be no compromise on this issue, no peaceful coexistence pact. To be for God is to be against the Devil.

PRAYER

Gracious and loving Father, help me get my perspectives clear. Train me in the art of spiritual warfare so that I will be able to resist every onslaught of the Devil and come through every conflict victoriously. In Jesus' name. Amen.

FURTHER STUDY

2 Cor. 10:1-5; 1 Tim. 1:18; 6:12
• What does Paul say about our weapons of warfare?
• What was Paul's charge to Timothy?

October 9

■ ISAIAH 51:1–54:3

51 ¹'Listen to me, you who pursue
righteousness
and who seek the LORD:
look to the rock from which you were cut
and to the quarry from which you
were hewn;
²look to Abraham, your father,
and to Sarah, who gave you birth.
When I called him he was only one man,
and I blessed him and made him
many.
³The LORD will surely comfort Zion
and will look with compassion on all
her ruins;
he will make her deserts like Eden,
her wastelands like the garden of the
LORD.
Joy and gladness will be found in her,
thanksgiving and the sound of
singing.

⁴'Listen to me, my people;
hear me, my nation:
instruction will go out from me;
my justice will become a light to the
nations.
⁵My righteousness draws near speedily,
my salvation is on the way,
and my arm will bring justice to the
nations.
The islands will look to me
and wait in hope for my arm.
⁶Lift up your eyes to the heavens,
look at the earth beneath;
the heavens will vanish like smoke,
the earth will wear out like a garment
and its inhabitants die like flies.
But my salvation will last for ever,
my righteousness will never fail.

⁷'Hear me, you who know what is right,
you people who have taken my
instruction to heart:
do not fear the reproach of mere mortals
or be terrified by their insults.
⁸For the moth will eat them up like a
garment;
the worm will devour them like wool.
But my righteousness will last for ever,
my salvation through all generations.'

⁹Awake, awake, arm of the LORD,
clothe yourself with strength!
Awake, as in days gone by,
as in generations of old.
Was it not you who cut Rahab to pieces,
who pierced that monster through?
¹⁰Was it not you who dried up the sea,
the waters of the great deep,
who made a road in the depths of the sea
so that the redeemed might cross over?
¹¹Those the LORD has rescued will return.
They will enter Zion with singing;
everlasting joy will crown their heads.
Gladness and joy will overtake them,
and sorrow and sighing will flee away.

¹²'I, even I, am he who comforts you.
Who are you that you fear mere
mortals,
human beings who are but grass,
¹³that you forget the LORD your Maker,
who stretches out the heavens
and who lays the foundations of the
earth,
that you live in constant terror every day
because of the wrath of the oppressor,
who is bent on destruction?
For where is the wrath of the oppressor?
¹⁴   The cowering prisoners will soon be
set free;

they will not die in their dungeon,
    nor will they lack bread.
[15] For I am the LORD your God,
    who stirs up the sea so that its waves
        roar –
    the LORD Almighty is his name.
[16] I have put my words in your mouth
    and covered you with the shadow of
        my hand –
    I who set the heavens in place,
    who laid the foundations of the earth,
    and who say to Zion, "You are my
        people."'
[17] Awake, awake!
    Rise up, Jerusalem,
you who have drunk from the hand of
        the LORD
    the cup of his wrath,
you who have drained to its dregs
    the goblet that makes people stagger.
[18] Among all the children she bore
    there was none to guide her;
among all the children she brought up
    there was none to take her by the
        hand.
[19] These double calamities have come upon
        you –
    who can comfort you? –
ruin and destruction, famine and sword –
    who can console you?
[20] Your children have fainted;
    they lie at every street corner,
    like antelope caught in a net.
They are filled with the wrath of the LORD,
    with the rebuke of your God.

[21] Therefore hear this, you afflicted one,
    made drunk, but not with wine.
[22] This is what your Sovereign LORD says,
    your God, who defends his people:
'See, I have taken out of your hand
    the cup that made you stagger;
from that cup, the goblet of my wrath,
    you will never drink again.
[23] I will put it into the hands of your
        tormentors,

who said to you,
    "Fall prostrate that we may walk on you."
And you made your back like the ground,
    like a street to be walked on.'

52

Awake, awake, Zion,
    clothe yourself with strength!
Put on your garments of splendour,
    Jerusalem, the holy city.
The uncircumcised and defiled
    will not enter you again.
[2] Shake off your dust;
    rise up, sit enthroned, Jerusalem.
Free yourself from the chains on your
        neck,
    Daughter Zion, now a captive.

[3] For this is what the LORD says:

'You were sold for nothing,
    and without money you will be
        redeemed.'

[4] For this is what the Sovereign LORD says:

'At first my people went down to Egypt to
        live;
    lately, Assyria has oppressed them.

[5] 'And now what do I have here?' declares
the LORD.

'For my people have been taken away for
        nothing,
    and those who rule them mock,'
                    declares the LORD.
'And all day long
    my name is constantly blasphemed.
[6] Therefore my people will know my name;
    therefore in that day they will know
that it is I who foretold it.
        Yes, it is I.'

[7] How beautiful on the mountains
    are the feet of those who bring good
        news,

who proclaim peace,
who bring good tidings,
who proclaim salvation,
who say to Zion,
'Your God reigns!'
⁸ Listen! Your watchmen lift up their voices;
together they shout for joy.
When the Lord returns to Zion,
they will see it with their own eyes.
⁹ Burst into songs of joy together,
you ruins of Jerusalem,
for the Lord has comforted his people,
he has redeemed Jerusalem.
¹⁰ The Lord will lay bare his holy arm
in the sight of all the nations,
and all the ends of the earth will see
the salvation of our God.

¹¹ Depart, depart, go out from there!
Touch no unclean thing!
Come out from it and be pure,
you who carry the articles of the
Lord's house.
¹² But you will not leave in haste
or go in flight;
for the Lord will go before you,
the God of Israel will be your rear guard.
¹³ See, my servant will act wisely;
he will be raised and lifted up and
highly exalted.
¹⁴ Just as there were many who were
appalled at him –
his appearance was so disfigured
beyond that of any human being
and his form marred beyond human
likeness –
¹⁵ so he will sprinkle many nations,
and kings will shut their mouths
because of him.
For what they were not told, they will see,
and what they have not heard, they
will understand.

53

Who has believed our message
and to whom has the arm of the
Lord been revealed?

² He grew up before him like a tender
shoot,
and like a root out of dry ground.
He had no beauty or majesty to attract us
to him,
nothing in his appearance that we
should desire him.
³ He was despised and rejected by
mankind,
a man of suffering, and familiar with
pain.
Like one from whom people hide their
faces
he was despised, and we held him in
low esteem.

⁴ Surely he took up our pain
and bore our suffering,
yet we considered him punished by God,
stricken by him, and afflicted.
⁵ But he was pierced for our
transgressions,
he was crushed for our iniquities;
the punishment that brought us peace
was on him,
and by his wounds we are healed.
⁶ We all, like sheep, have gone astray,
each of us has turned to our own way;
and the Lord has laid on him
the iniquity of us all.

⁷ He was oppressed and afflicted,
yet he did not open his mouth;
he was led like a lamb to the slaughter,
and as a sheep before its shearers is
silent,
so he did not open his mouth.
⁸ By oppression and judgment he was
taken away.
Yet who of his generation protested?
For he was cut off from the land of the
living;
for the transgression of my people he
was punished.
⁹ He was assigned a grave with the wicked,
and with the rich in his death,

though he had done no violence,
nor was any deceit in his mouth.

[10] Yet it was the LORD's will to crush him
and cause him to suffer,
and though the LORD makes his life an
offering for sin,
he will see his offspring and prolong his
days,
and the will of the LORD will prosper in
his hand.
[11] After he has suffered,
he will see the light of life and be
satisfied;
by his knowledge my righteous servant
will justify many,
and he will bear their iniquities.
[12] Therefore I will give him a portion
among the great,
and he will divide the spoils with the
strong,
because he poured out his life unto death,
and was numbered with the
transgressors.
For he bore the sin of many,
and made intercession for the
transgressors.
54 'Sing, barren woman,
you who never bore a child;
burst into song, shout for joy,
you who were never in labour;
because more are the children of the
desolate woman
than of her who has a husband,'
says the LORD.
[2] 'Enlarge the place of your tent,
stretch your tent curtains wide,
do not hold back;
lengthen your cords,
strengthen your stakes.
[3] For you will spread out to the right and
to the left;
your descendants will dispossess
nations
and settle in their desolate cities.

PSALM 118:15-21

[15] Shouts of joy and victory
resound in the tents of the righteous:
'The LORD's right hand has done mighty
things!
[16] The LORD's right hand is lifted high;
the LORD's right hand has done mighty
things!'
[17] I will not die but live,
and will proclaim what the LORD has
done.
[18] The LORD has chastened me severely,
but he has not given me over to death.
[19] Open for me the gates of the righteous;
I will enter and give thanks to the
LORD.
[20] This is the gate of the LORD
through which the righteous may
enter.
[21] I will give you thanks, for you answered
me;
you have become my salvation.

PROVERBS 24:13-14

[13] Eat honey, my son, for it is good;
honey from the comb is sweet to your
taste.
[14] Know also that wisdom is like honey for
you:
if you find it, there is a future hope for
you,
and your hope will not be cut off.

PHILIPPIANS 1:1-20

1 Paul and Timothy, servants of Christ
Jesus,

To all God's holy people in Christ Jesus
at Philippi, together with the overseers and
deacons:

[2]Grace and peace to you from God our Father and the Lord Jesus Christ.

[3]I thank my God every time I remember you. [4]In all my prayers for all of you, I always pray with joy [5]because of your partnership in the gospel from the first day until now, [6]being confident of this, that he who began a good work in you will carry it on to completion until the day of Christ Jesus.

[7]It is right for me to feel this way about all of you, since I have you in my heart and, whether I am in chains or defending and confirming the gospel, all of you share in God's grace with me. [8]God can testify how I long for all of you with the affection of Christ Jesus.

[9]And this is my prayer: that your love may abound more and more in knowledge and depth of insight, [10]so that you may be able to discern what is best and may be pure and blameless for the day of Christ, [11]filled with the fruit of righteousness that comes through Jesus Christ – to the glory and praise of God.

[12]Now I want you to know, brothers and sisters, that what has happened to me has actually served to advance the gospel.

[13]As a result, it has become clear throughout the whole palace guard and to everyone else that I am in chains for Christ. [14]And because of my chains, most of the brothers and sisters have become confident in the Lord and dare all the more to proclaim the gospel without fear.

[15]It is true that some preach Christ out of envy and rivalry, but others out of goodwill. [16]The latter do so out of love, knowing that I am put here for the defence of the gospel. [17]The former preach Christ out of selfish ambition, not sincerely, supposing that they can stir up trouble for me while I am in chains. [18]But what does it matter? The important thing is that in every way, whether from false motives or true, Christ is preached. And because of this I rejoice.

Yes, and I will continue to rejoice, [19]for I know that through your prayers and God's provision of the Spirit of Jesus Christ what has happened to me will turn out for my deliverance. [20]I eagerly expect and hope that I will in no way be ashamed, but will have sufficient courage so that now as always Christ will be exalted in my body, whether by life or by death.

Enter at Your Own Risk

'I eagerly expect and hope that I will in no way be ashamed ... so that now as always Christ will be exalted in my body, whether by life or by death.'
Philippians 1:20

Jesus is the supreme example of living without fear of being disappointed by others: '... he made himself nothing by taking the very nature of a servant ... he humbled himself by becoming obedient to death – even death on a cross' (Phil. 2:7-8).

Disappointed people sometimes find it difficult to move out towards others. After all, people – even Christian people – can be rude, uncouth and unkind. And I have lived long enough to know that Christians can hurt! What are we supposed to do when we know that to move towards another person in love exposes us to the risk of being disappointed? We move forwards in love: easy to say, but more difficult to do.

Making ourselves vulnerable to disappointment is frightening, but this has to happen if we are to love as we are loved.

Mature Christians are those who are willing to look fully into the face of disappointment and feel it, knowing that because they do, they will come to a deeper awareness that no one can comfort the heart like Jesus Christ. In the presence of such pain, one more easily sees the uselessness of every attempt to find solace in one's own independent strategies. Facing and feeling the pain of disappointment underlies more than anything else the gripping truth that only in God can we trust.

PRAYER

Father, at times Your purposes seem to run diametrically opposite to my interests, but the more I ponder them, the more I see that You always have my highest interests at heart. Help me to trust You more – and myself less. In Jesus' name. Amen.

FURTHER STUDY

Matt. 26; 2 Tim. 2:13; Phil. 2:3

- What disappointments must Jesus have felt?
- How often do you disappoint Him?

October 10

■ ISAIAH 54:4–57:13

4 'Do not be afraid; you will not be put to shame.
 Do not fear disgrace; you will not be humiliated.
You will forget the shame of your youth
 and remember no more the reproach of your widowhood.
5 For your Maker is your husband –
 the LORD Almighty is his name –
the Holy One of Israel is your Redeemer;
 he is called the God of all the earth.
6 The LORD will call you back
 as if you were a wife deserted and distressed in spirit –
a wife who married young,
 only to be rejected,' says your God.
7 'For a brief moment I abandoned you,
 but with deep compassion I will bring you back.
8 In a surge of anger

I hid my face from you for a moment,
 but with everlasting kindness
 I will have compassion on you,'
 says the LORD your Redeemer.

9 'To me this is like the days of Noah,
 when I swore that the waters of Noah
 would never again cover the earth.
So now I have sworn not to be angry with you,
 never to rebuke you again.
10 Though the mountains be shaken
 and the hills be removed,
yet my unfailing love for you will not be shaken
 nor my covenant of peace be removed,'
 says the LORD, who has compassion on you.

11 'Afflicted city, lashed by storms and not comforted,

I will rebuild you with stones of
turquoise,
your foundations with lapis lazuli.
¹² I will make your battlements of rubies,
your gates of sparkling jewels,
and all your walls of precious stones.
¹³ All your children will be taught by the
LORD,
and great will be their peace.
¹⁴ In righteousness you will be established:
tyranny will be far from you;
you will have nothing to fear.
Terror will be far removed;
it will not come near you.
¹⁵ If anyone does attack you, it will not be
my doing;
whoever attacks you will surrender to
you.

¹⁶ 'See, it is I who created the blacksmith
who fans the coals into flame
and forges a weapon fit for its work.
And it is I who have created the destroyer
to wreak havoc;
¹⁷   no weapon forged against you will
prevail,
and you will refute every tongue that
accuses you.
This is the heritage of the servants of the
LORD,
and this is their vindication from me,'
declares the LORD.

55 'Come, all you who are thirsty,
come to the waters;
and you who have no money,
come, buy and eat!
Come, buy wine and milk
without money and without cost.
² Why spend money on what is not bread,
and your labour on what does not
satisfy?
Listen, listen to me, and eat what is good,
and you will delight in the richest of
fare.
³ Give ear and come to me;

listen, that you may live.
I will make an everlasting covenant with
you,
my faithful love promised to David.
⁴ See, I have made him a witness to the
peoples,
a ruler and commander of the peoples.
⁵ Surely you will summon nations you
know not,
and nations you do not know will
come running to you,
because of the LORD your God,
the Holy One of Israel,
for he has endowed you with
splendour.'

⁶ Seek the LORD while he may be found;
call on him while he is near.
⁷ Let the wicked forsake their ways
and the unrighteous their thoughts.
Let them turn to the LORD, and he will
have mercy on them,
and to our God, for he will freely
pardon.

⁸ 'For my thoughts are not your thoughts,
neither are your ways my ways,'
declares the LORD.
⁹ 'As the heavens are higher than the earth,
so are my ways higher than your ways
and my thoughts than your thoughts.
¹⁰ As the rain and the snow
come down from heaven,
and do not return to it
without watering the earth
and making it bud and flourish,
so that it yields seed for the sower and
bread for the eater,
¹¹ so is my word that goes out from my
mouth:
it will not return to me empty,
but will accomplish what I desire
and achieve the purpose for which I
sent it.
¹² You will go out in joy
and be led forth in peace;

the mountains and hills
　will burst into song before you,
　and all the trees of the field
　will clap their hands.
¹³ Instead of the thorn-bush will grow the
　　juniper,
　　and instead of briers the myrtle will
　　grow.
This will be for the LORD's renown,
　for an everlasting sign,
　that will endure for ever.'

56

This is what the Lord says:

'Maintain justice
　and do what is right,
for my salvation is close at hand
　and my righteousness will soon be
　　revealed.
² Blessed is the one who does this –
　the person who holds it fast,
who keeps the Sabbath without
　　desecrating it,
　and keeps their hands from doing any
　　evil.'

³ Let no foreigner who is bound to the
　　LORD say,
　'The LORD will surely exclude me from
　　his people.'
And let no eunuch complain,
　'I am only a dry tree.'

⁴ For this is what the LORD says:

'To the eunuchs who keep my Sabbaths,
　who choose what pleases me
　and hold fast to my covenant –
⁵ to them I will give within my temple and
　　its walls
　a memorial and a name
　better than sons and daughters;
I will give them an everlasting name
　that will endure for ever.
⁶ And foreigners who bind themselves to
　　the LORD

to minister to him,
to love the name of the LORD,
　and to be his servants,
all who keep the Sabbath without
　　desecrating it
　and who hold fast to my covenant –
⁷ these I will bring to my holy mountain
　and give them joy in my house of
　　prayer.
Their burnt offerings and sacrifices
　will be accepted on my altar;
for my house will be called
　a house of prayer for all nations.'
⁸ The Sovereign LORD declares –
　he who gathers the exiles of Israel:
'I will gather still others to them
　besides those already gathered.'
⁹ Come, all you beasts of the field,
　come and devour, all you beasts of the
　　forest!
¹⁰ Israel's watchmen are blind,
　they all lack knowledge;
they are all mute dogs,
　they cannot bark;
they lie around and dream,
　they love to sleep.
¹¹ They are dogs with mighty appetites;
　they never have enough.
They are shepherds who lack
　　understanding;
　they all turn to their own way,
　they seek their own gain.
¹² 'Come,' each one cries, 'let me get wine!
　Let us drink our fill of beer!
And tomorrow will be like today,
　or even far better.'

57

The righteous perish,
　and no one takes it to heart;
the devout are taken away,
　and no one understands
that the righteous are taken away
　to be spared from evil.
² Those who walk uprightly
　enter into peace;
　they find rest as they lie in death.

³ 'But you – come here, you children of a
     sorceress,
   you offspring of adulterers and
     prostitutes!
⁴ Who are you mocking?
   At whom do you sneer
   and stick out your tongue?
   Are you not a brood of rebels,
     the offspring of liars?
⁵ You burn with lust among the oaks
   and under every spreading tree;
   you sacrifice your children in the ravines
     and under the overhanging crags.
⁶ The idols among the smooth stones of
     the ravines are your portion;
     indeed, they are your lot.
   Yes, to them you have poured out drink
     offerings
     and offered grain offerings.
     In view of all this, should I relent?
⁷ You have made your bed on a high and
     lofty hill;
     there you went up to offer your
     sacrifices.
⁸ Behind your doors and your doorposts
     you have put your pagan symbols.
   Forsaking me, you uncovered your bed,
     you climbed into it and opened it
     wide;
   you made a pact with those whose beds
     you love,
     and you looked with lust on their
     naked bodies.
⁹ You went to Molek with olive oil
   and increased your perfumes.
   You sent your ambassadors far away;
     you descended to the very realm of the
     dead!
¹⁰ You wearied yourself by such going
     about,
     but you would not say, "It is hopeless."
   You found renewal of your strength,
     and so you did not faint.

¹¹ 'Whom have you so dreaded and feared
     that you have not been true to me,

   and have neither remembered me
     nor taken this to heart?
   Is it not because I have long been silent
     that you do not fear me?
¹² I will expose your righteousness and
     your works,
     and they will not benefit you.
¹³ When you cry out for help,
     let your collection of idols save you!
   The wind will carry all of them off,
     a mere breath will blow them away.
   But whoever takes refuge in me
     will inherit the land
     and possess my holy mountain.'

■ PSALM 118:22-29

²² The stone the builders rejected
     has become the cornerstone;
²³ the LORD has done this,
     and it is marvellous in our eyes.
²⁴ The LORD has done it this very day;
     let us rejoice today and be glad.

²⁵ LORD, save us!
   LORD, grant us success!

²⁶ Blessed is he who comes in the name of
     the LORD.
   From the house of the LORD we bless
     you.
²⁷ The LORD is God,
     and he has made his light shine on us.
   With boughs in hand, join in the festal
     procession
     up to the horns of the altar.

²⁸ You are my God, and I will praise you;
     you are my God, and I will exalt you.

²⁹ Give thanks to the LORD, for he is good;
     his love endures for ever.

▬ PROVERBS 24:15–16

¹⁵ Do not lurk like a thief near the house of
the righteous,
    do not plunder their dwelling-place;
¹⁶ for though the righteous fall seven times,
    they rise again,
    but the wicked stumble when calamity
    strikes.

▬ PHILIPPIANS 1:21–2:11

²¹ For to me, to live is Christ and to die is
gain. ²² If I am to go on living in the body,
this will mean fruitful labour for me. Yet
what shall I choose? I do not know! ²³ I am
torn between the two: I desire to depart and
be with Christ, which is better by far; ²⁴ but
it is more necessary for you that I remain in
the body. ²⁵ Convinced of this, I know that I
will remain, and I will continue with all of
you for your progress and joy in the faith,
²⁶ so that through my being with you again
your boasting in Christ Jesus will abound
on account of me.

²⁷ Whatever happens, conduct yourselves
in a manner worthy of the gospel of Christ.
Then, whether I come and see you or only hear
about you in my absence, I will know that you
stand firm in the one Spirit, striving together as one for the faith of the gospel ²⁸ without
being frightened in any way by those who oppose you. This is a sign to them that they will
be destroyed, but that you will be saved – and
that by God. ²⁹ For it has been granted to you
on behalf of Christ not only to believe in him,
but also to suffer for him, ³⁰ since you are going through the same struggle you saw I had,
and now hear that I still have.

2 Therefore if you have any encouragement from being united with Christ, if
any comfort from his love, if any common
sharing in the Spirit, if any tenderness and
compassion, ² then make my joy complete
by being like-minded, having the same
love, being one in spirit and of one mind.
³ Do nothing out of selfish ambition or vain
conceit. Rather, in humility value others
above yourselves, ⁴ not looking to your own
interests but each of you to the interests of
the others.

⁵ In your relationships with one another,
have the same mindset as Christ Jesus:

⁶ who, being in very nature God,
    did not consider equality with God
        something to be used to his own
        advantage;
⁷ rather, he made himself nothing
    by taking the very nature of a servant,
    being made in human likeness.
⁸ And being found in appearance as a
    man,
    he humbled himself
    by becoming obedient to death –
        even death on a cross!

⁹ Therefore God exalted him to the highest
    place
    and gave him the name that is above
        every name,
¹⁰ that at the name of Jesus every knee
        should bow,
    in heaven and on earth and under the
        earth,
¹¹ and every tongue acknowledge that Jesus
        Christ is Lord,
    to the glory of God the Father.

The God Who Speaks

'"... so are my ways higher than your ways and my
thoughts than your thoughts."' **Isaiah 55:9**

Although we know that God is all-powerful, we also know that He is personal. But what does it mean to be a person? What predicates personality?

The best definition of personality I know is the one given to me by the tutor who taught me theology: 'To be a person, we have to be able to think, to reason, to feel, to judge, to choose, and to communicate in words that constitute a language.' Richard Swinburne, a theologian, observes that people use language not only to communicate and for private thought, but to argue, to raise a consideration or to object to another. Unlike animals that show evidence only of wanting food and drink, people can want not to want something – like a fasting man, for example, wanting not to want food.

Now with that in mind – that one of the constituents of personality is the ability to think and speak – read the first chapter of Genesis. Notice how many times the words appear: 'God said.' Count them. God is portrayed to us as a speaking God. And because speech is one of the constituent parts of personality, this proves to us that the Deity is a personal Being. We are not far into Genesis before we are brought face-to-face with the fact that there is more to God than mere power; the Almighty is a Person. This means, among other things, that the Almighty cannot be studied from a 'safe' distance. Because He is a Person, He is someone who wants and waits to be known.

PRAYER

Loving heavenly Father, how thankful I am that You made me like Yourself – to know and be known. May my strongest desire be to know You, not merely to know myself. For it is only when I know You that I can most truly know myself. Amen.

FURTHER STUDY

Gen. 1:1-31; Job 33:13-14; 1 Kings 19:12; Ezek. 43:2
• How many times does it say 'God said'?
• How did Ezekiel describe God's voice?

October 11

◼ ISAIAH 57:14 – 60:16

¹⁴ And it will be said:

'Build up, build up, prepare the road!
    Remove the obstacles out of the way of
        my people.'
¹⁵ For this is what the high and exalted One
    says –

he who lives for ever, whose name is
        holy:
'I live in a high and holy place,
    but also with the one who is contrite
        and lowly in spirit,
to revive the spirit of the lowly
    and to revive the heart of the contrite.
¹⁶ I will not accuse them for ever,
    nor will I always be angry,

for then they would faint away because
    of me –
  the very people I have created.
¹⁷ I was enraged by their sinful greed;
  I punished them, and hid my face in
      anger,
  yet they kept on in their wilful ways.
¹⁸ I have seen their ways, but I will heal
      them;
  I will guide them and restore comfort
      to Israel's mourners,
¹⁹   creating praise on their lips.
  Peace, peace, to those far and near,'
    says the LORD. 'And I will heal them.'
²⁰ But the wicked are like the tossing sea,
    which cannot rest,
  whose waves cast up mire and mud.
²¹ 'There is no peace,' says my God, 'for the
      wicked.'

58 'Shout it aloud, do not hold back.
      Raise your voice like a trumpet.
  Declare to my people their rebellion
    and to the descendants of Jacob their
      sins.
² For day after day they seek me out;
    they seem eager to know my ways,
  as if they were a nation that does what is
      right
    and has not forsaken the commands
      of its God.
  They ask me for just decisions
    and seem eager for God to come near
      them.
³ "Why have we fasted," they say,
    "and you have not seen it?
  Why have we humbled ourselves,
    and you have not noticed?"

'Yet on the day of your fasting, you do as
      you please
  and exploit all your workers.
⁴ Your fasting ends in quarrelling and
      strife,
    and in striking each other with wicked
      fists.
  You cannot fast as you do today

and expect your voice to be heard on
    high.
⁵ Is this the kind of fast I have chosen,
  only a day for people to humble
      themselves?
  Is it only for bowing one's head like a
      reed
    and for lying in sackcloth and ashes?
  Is that what you call a fast,
    a day acceptable to the LORD?

⁶ 'Is not this the kind of fasting I have
      chosen:
  to loose the chains of injustice
    and untie the cords of the yoke,
  to set the oppressed free
    and break every yoke?
⁷ Is it not to share your food with the
      hungry
    and to provide the poor wanderer with
      shelter –
  when you see the naked, to clothe them,
    and not to turn away from your own
      flesh and blood?
⁸ Then your light will break forth like the
      dawn,
    and your healing will quickly appear;
  then your righteousness will go before
      you,
    and the glory of the LORD will be your
      rear guard.
⁹ Then you will call, and the LORD will
      answer;
    you will cry for help, and he will say:
      here am I.

'If you do away with the yoke of
      oppression,
    with the pointing finger and malicious
      talk,
¹⁰ and if you spend yourselves on behalf of
      the hungry
    and satisfy the needs of the oppressed,
  then your light will rise in the darkness,
    and your night will become like the
      noonday.

¹¹ The LORD will guide you always;
    he will satisfy your needs in a sun-
        scorched land
    and will strengthen your frame.
You will be like a well-watered garden,
    like a spring whose waters never fail.
¹² Your people will rebuild the ancient
        ruins
    and will raise up the age-old
        foundations;
you will be called Repairer of Broken
        Walls,
    Restorer of Streets with Dwellings.

¹³ 'If you keep your feet from breaking the
        Sabbath
    and from doing as you please on my
        holy day,
if you call the Sabbath a delight
    and the LORD's holy day honourable,
and if you honour it by not going your
        own way
    and not doing as you please or
        speaking idle words,
¹⁴ then you will find your joy in the LORD,
    and I will cause you to ride in triumph
        on the heights of the land
    and to feast on the inheritance of your
        father Jacob.'
        For the mouth of the LORD
        has spoken.

59 Surely the arm of the LORD is not
        too short to save,
    nor his ear too dull to hear.
² But your iniquities have separated
    you from your God;
your sins have hidden his face from you,
    so that he will not hear.
³ For your hands are stained with blood,
    your fingers with guilt.
Your lips have spoken falsely,
    and your tongue mutters wicked
        things.
⁴ No one calls for justice;
    no one pleads a case with integrity.

They rely on empty arguments, they
        utter lies;
    they conceive trouble and give birth to
        evil.
⁵ They hatch the eggs of vipers
    and spin a spider's web.
Whoever eats their eggs will die,
    and when one is broken, an adder is
        hatched.
⁶ Their cobwebs are useless for clothing;
    they cannot cover themselves with
        what they make.
Their deeds are evil deeds,
    and acts of violence are in their hands.
⁷ Their feet rush into sin;
    they are swift to shed innocent blood.
They pursue evil schemes;
    acts of violence mark their ways.
⁸ The way of peace they do not know;
    there is no justice in their paths.
They have turned them into crooked
        roads;
    no one who walks along them will
        know peace.

⁹ So justice is far from us,
    and righteousness does not reach us.
We look for light, but all is darkness;
    for brightness, but we walk in deep
        shadows.
¹⁰ Like the blind we grope along the wall,
    feeling our way like people without
        eyes.
At midday we stumble as if it were
        twilight;
    among the strong, we are like the
        dead.
¹¹ We all growl like bears;
    we moan mournfully like doves.
We look for justice, but find none;
    for deliverance, but it is far away.

¹² For our offences are many in your sight,
    and our sins testify against us.
Our offences are ever with us,
    and we acknowledge our iniquities:

¹³ rebellion and treachery against the LORD,
        turning our backs on our God,
    inciting revolt and oppression,
        uttering lies our hearts have
            conceived.
¹⁴ So justice is driven back,
        and righteousness stands at a distance;
    truth has stumbled in the streets,
        honesty cannot enter.
¹⁵ Truth is nowhere to be found,
        and whoever shuns evil becomes a
            prey.

    The LORD looked and was displeased
        that there was no justice.
¹⁶ He saw that there was no one,
        he was appalled that there was no one
            to intervene;
    so his own arm achieved salvation for
            him,
        and his own righteousness sustained
            him.
¹⁷ He put on righteousness as his
            breastplate,
        and the helmet of salvation on his
            head;
    he put on the garments of vengeance
        and wrapped himself in zeal as in a
            cloak.
¹⁸ According to what they have done,
        so will he repay
    wrath to his enemies
        and retribution to his foes;
    he will repay the islands their due.
¹⁹ From the west, people will fear the name
            of the LORD,
        and from the rising of the sun, they
            will revere his glory.
    For he will come like a pent-up flood
        that the breath of the LORD drives
            along.

²⁰ 'The Redeemer will come to Zion,
        to those in Jacob who repent of their
            sins,'
                declares the LORD.

²¹ 'As for me, this is my covenant with
    them,' says the LORD. 'My Spirit, who is on
    you, will not depart from you, and my words
    that I have put in your mouth will always be
    on your lips, on the lips of your children and
    on the lips of their descendants – from this
    time on and for ever,' says the LORD.

60 'Arise, shine, for your light has
        come,
        and the glory of the LORD rises upon
            you.
² See, darkness covers the earth
        and thick darkness is over the peoples,
    but the LORD rises upon you
        and his glory appears over you.
³ Nations will come to your light,
        and kings to the brightness of your
            dawn.

⁴ 'Lift up your eyes and look about you:
        all assemble and come to you;
    your sons come from afar,
        and your daughters are carried on the
            hip.
⁵ Then you will look and be radiant,
        your heart will throb and swell with
            joy;
    the wealth on the seas will be brought to
            you,
        to you the riches of the nations will
            come.
⁶ Herds of camels will cover your land,
        young camels of Midian and Ephah.
    And all from Sheba will come,
        bearing gold and incense
        and proclaiming the praise of the
            LORD.
⁷ All Kedar's flocks will be gathered to you,
        the rams of Nebaioth will serve you;
    they will be accepted as offerings on my
            altar,
        and I will adorn my glorious temple.

⁸ 'Who are these that fly along like clouds,
        like doves to their nests?

⁹ Surely the islands look to me;
    in the lead are the ships of Tarshish,
bringing your children from afar,
    with their silver and gold,
to the honour of the Lord your God,
    the Holy One of Israel,
for he has endowed you with
    splendour.

¹⁰ 'Foreigners will rebuild your walls,
    and their kings will serve you.
Though in anger I struck you,
    in favour I will show you compassion.
¹¹ Your gates will always stand open,
    they will never be shut, day or night,
so that people may bring you the wealth
    of the nations –
    their kings led in triumphal
    procession.
¹² For the nation or kingdom that will not
    serve you will perish;
    it will be utterly ruined.

¹³ 'The glory of Lebanon will come to you,
    the juniper, the fir and the cypress
    together,
to adorn my sanctuary;
    and I will glorify the place for my feet.
¹⁴ The children of your oppressors will
    come bowing before you;
all who despise you will bow down at
    your feet
and will call you the City of the Lord,
    Zion of the Holy One of Israel.

¹⁵ 'Although you have been forsaken and
    hated,
    with no one travelling through,
I will make you the everlasting pride
    and the joy of all generations.
¹⁶ You will drink the milk of nations
    and be nursed at royal breasts.
Then you will know that I, the Lord, am
    your Saviour,
    your Redeemer, the Mighty One of
    Jacob.

■ PSALM 119:1-4

¹ Blessed are those whose ways are
    blameless,
    who walk according to the law of the
    Lord.
² Blessed are those who keep his statutes
    and seek him with all their heart –
³ they do no wrong
    but follow his ways.
⁴ You have laid down precepts
    that are to be fully obeyed.

■ PROVERBS 24:17-18

¹⁷ Do not gloat when your enemy falls;
    when they stumble, do not let your
    heart rejoice,
¹⁸ or the Lord will see and disapprove
    and turn his wrath away from them.

■ PHILIPPIANS 2:12-30

¹² Therefore, my dear friends, as you have always obeyed – not only in my presence, but now much more in my absence – continue to work out your salvation with fear and trembling, ¹³ for it is God who works in you to will and to act in order to fulfil his good purpose.

¹⁴ Do everything without grumbling or arguing, ¹⁵ so that you may become blameless and pure, 'children of God without fault in a warped and crooked generation.' Then you will shine among them like stars in the sky ¹⁶ as you hold firmly to the word of life. And then I will be able to boast on the day of Christ that I did not run or labour in vain. ¹⁷ But even if I am being poured out like a drink offering on the sacrifice and service coming from your faith, I am glad and rejoice with all of you. ¹⁸ So you too should be glad and rejoice with me.

¹⁹ I hope in the Lord Jesus to send Timothy to you soon, that I also may be cheered when I receive news about you. ²⁰ I have no one else like him, who will show genuine concern for your welfare. ²¹ For everyone looks out for their own interests, not those of Jesus Christ. ²² But you know that Timothy has proved himself, because as a son with his father he has served with me in the work of the gospel. ²³ I hope, therefore, to send him as soon as I see how things go with me. ²⁴ And I am confident in the Lord that I myself will come soon.

²⁵ But I think it is necessary to send back to you Epaphroditus, my brother, co-worker and fellow soldier, who is also your messenger, whom you sent to take care of my needs. ²⁶ For he longs for all of you and is distressed because you heard he was ill. ²⁷ Indeed he was ill, and almost died. But God had mercy on him, and not on him only but also on me, to spare me sorrow upon sorrow. ²⁸ Therefore I am all the more eager to send him, so that when you see him again you may be glad and I may have less anxiety. ²⁹ So then, welcome him in the Lord with great joy, and honour people like him, ³⁰ because he almost died for the work of Christ. He risked his life to make up for the help you yourselves could not give me.

Doing His Will - Now

'... for it is God who works in you to will and to act in order to fulfil his good purpose.' **Philippians 2:13**

Theologians are divided about whether the statement of Jesus in the Lord's Prayer should be translated 'in earth as it is in heaven' or 'on earth as it is in heaven'. Today we look at the words 'on earth'.

Most commentators believe the phrase has reference to the world of human beings who have their home on this earth. In other words - us. Fantastic as it may sound, a day will dawn when this earth will be peopled with those who will do the will of God, not with resentment or resignation, but with rejoicing. That day may not be as far distant as we may think, so we ought to double our efforts in prayer and joyously become involved in bringing our lives in line with His will. One thing is sure - the more you and I conform to His will, the more quickly can His purposes for this earth be realised. John Wesley famously said: 'God does nothing redemptively in this world except by prayer.' Can you see what he is saying? The purposes of God for the future will have to cross the bridge of prayer.

This raises the question: how committed are you and I to doing the will of God? Are we hindering or are we promoting the interests of His future kingdom? It is vital that we Christians, both individually and corporately, focus our prayers on this issue with fervency and passion, remembering as we do so that the more abandoned we are to the divine will, the more speedily will His purposes come to pass for the world.

PRAYER

O Father, in the light of this challenge today, I feel like praying: 'Your will be done, on earth in me as it is done in heaven.' Grant it, I pray, for the honour and glory of Your peerless name. Amen.

FURTHER STUDY

Matt. 3; John 8:29; 1 Thess. 4:1; Heb. 13:16
• What was the pronouncement from heaven?
• Could this be said of your life?

October 12

▬ ISAIAH 60:17–63:19

¹⁷ Instead of bronze I will bring you gold,
and silver in place of iron.
Instead of wood I will bring you bronze,
and iron in place of stones.
I will make peace your governor
and well-being your ruler.
¹⁸ No longer will violence be heard in your
land,
nor ruin or destruction within your
borders,
but you will call your walls Salvation
and your gates Praise.
¹⁹ The sun will no more be your light by
day,
nor will the brightness of the moon
shine on you,
for the LORD will be your everlasting
light,
and your God will be your glory.
²⁰ Your sun will never set again,
and your moon will wane no more;
the LORD will be your everlasting light,
and your days of sorrow will end.
²¹ Then all your people will be righteous
and they will possess the land for ever.
They are the shoot I have planted,
the work of my hands,
for the display of my splendour.
²² The least of you will become a thousand,
the smallest a mighty nation.
I am the LORD;
in its time I will do this swiftly.'

61 The Spirit of the Sovereign Lord is
on me,
because the LORD has anointed me
to proclaim good news to the poor.
He has sent me to bind up the
broken-hearted,
to proclaim freedom for the captives
and release from darkness for the
prisoners,
² to proclaim the year of the LORD's favour
and the day of vengeance of our God,
to comfort all who mourn,
³   and provide for those who grieve in
Zion –
to bestow on them a crown of beauty
instead of ashes,
the oil of joy
instead of mourning,
and a garment of praise
instead of a spirit of despair.
They will be called oaks of righteousness,
a planting of the LORD
for the display of his splendour.

⁴ They will rebuild the ancient ruins
and restore the places long devastated;
they will renew the ruined cities

that have been devastated for
   generations.
⁵ Strangers will shepherd your flocks;
   foreigners will work your fields and
      vineyards.
⁶ And you will be called priests of the
      LORD,
   you will be named ministers of our
      God.
You will feed on the wealth of nations,
   and in their riches you will boast.

⁷ Instead of your shame
   you will receive a double portion,
and instead of disgrace
   you will rejoice in your inheritance.
And so you will inherit a double portion
      in your land,
   and everlasting joy will be yours.

⁸ 'For I, the LORD, love justice;
   I hate robbery and wrongdoing.
In my faithfulness I will reward my
      people
   and make an everlasting covenant
      with them.
⁹ Their descendants will be known among
      the nations
   and their offspring among the
      peoples.
All who see them will acknowledge
   that they are a people the LORD has
      blessed.'

¹⁰ I delight greatly in the LORD;
   my soul rejoices in my God.
For he has clothed me with garments of
      salvation
   and arrayed me in a robe of his
      righteousness,
as a bridegroom adorns his head like a
      priest,
   and as a bride adorns herself with her
      jewels.
¹¹ For as the soil makes the young plant
      come up

and a garden causes seeds to grow,
   so the Sovereign LORD will make
      righteousness
   and praise spring up before all
      nations.

62 For Zion's sake I will not keep
      silent,
   for Jerusalem's sake I will not remain
      quiet,
till her vindication shines out like the
      dawn,
   her salvation like a blazing torch.
² The nations will see your vindication,
   and all kings your glory;
you will be called by a new name
   that the mouth of the LORD will
      bestow.
³ You will be a crown of splendour in the
      LORD's hand,
   a royal diadem in the hand of your
      God.
⁴ No longer will they call you Deserted,
   or name your land Desolate.
But you will be called Hephzibah,
   and your land Beulah;
for the LORD will take delight in you,
   and your land will be married.
⁵ As a young man marries a young
      woman,
   so will your Builder marry you;
as a bridegroom rejoices over his bride,
   so will your God rejoice over you.

⁶ I have posted watchmen on your walls,
      Jerusalem;
   they will never be silent day or night.
You who call on the LORD,
   give yourselves no rest,
⁷ and give him no rest till he establishes
      Jerusalem
   and makes her the praise of the earth.

⁸ The LORD has sworn by his right hand
   and by his mighty arm:
'Never again will I give your grain
   as food for your enemies,

and never again will foreigners drink the
new wine
for which you have toiled;
⁹ but those who harvest it will eat it
and praise the LORD,
and those who gather the grapes will
drink it
in the courts of my sanctuary.'

¹⁰ Pass through, pass through the gates!
Prepare the way for the people.
Build up, build up the highway!
Remove the stones.
Raise a banner for the nations.

¹¹ The LORD has made proclamation
to the ends of the earth:
'Say to Daughter Zion,
"See, your Saviour comes!
See, his reward is with him,
and his recompense accompanies
him."'
¹² They will be called the Holy People,
the Redeemed of the LORD;
and you will be called Sought After,
the City No Longer Deserted.

63 Who is this coming from Edom,
from Bozrah, with his garments
stained crimson?
Who is this, robed in splendour,
striding forward in the greatness of
his strength?

'It is I, proclaiming victory,
mighty to save.'

² Why are your garments red,
like those of one treading the
winepress?

³ 'I have trodden the winepress alone;
from the nations no one was with me.
I trampled them in my anger
and trod them down in my wrath;
their blood spattered my garments,
and I stained all my clothing.

⁴ It was for me the day of vengeance;
the year for me to redeem had come.
⁵ I looked, but there was no one to help,
I was appalled that no one gave
support;
so my own arm achieved salvation for
me,
and my own wrath sustained me.
⁶ I trampled the nations in my anger;
in my wrath I made them drunk
and poured their blood on the
ground.'

⁷ I will tell of the kindnesses of the LORD,
the deeds for which he is to be praised,
according to all the LORD has done for
us –
yes, the many good things
he has done for Israel,
according to his compassion and
many kindnesses.
⁸ He said, 'Surely they are my people,
children who will be true to me';
and so he became their Saviour.
⁹ In all their distress he too was distressed,
and the angel of his presence saved
them.
In his love and mercy he redeemed them;
he lifted them up and carried them
all the days of old.
¹⁰ Yet they rebelled
and grieved his Holy Spirit.
So he turned and became their enemy
and he himself fought against them.

¹¹ Then his people recalled the days of old,
the days of Moses and his people –
where is he who brought them through
the sea,
with the shepherd of his flock?
Where is he who set
his Holy Spirit among them,
¹² who sent his glorious arm of power
to be at Moses' right hand,
who divided the waters before them,
to gain for himself everlasting
renown,

¹³ who led them through the depths?
   Like a horse in open country,
      they did not stumble;
¹⁴ like cattle that go down to the plain,
      they were given rest by the Spirit of the
   LORD.
   This is how you guided your people
      to make for yourself a glorious name.

¹⁵ Look down from heaven and see,
      from your lofty throne, holy and
         glorious.
   Where are your zeal and your might?
      Your tenderness and compassion are
         withheld from us.
¹⁶ But you are our Father,
      though Abraham does not know us
      or Israel acknowledge us;
   you, LORD, are our Father,
      our Redeemer from of old is your
         name.
¹⁷ Why, LORD, do you make us wander from
         your ways
      and harden our hearts so we do not
         revere you?
   Return for the sake of your servants,
      the tribes that are your inheritance.
¹⁸ For a little while your people possessed
         your holy place,
      but now our enemies have trampled
         down your sanctuary.
¹⁹ We are yours from of old;
      but you have not ruled over them,
      they have not been called by your name.

■ PSALM 119:5–8

⁵ Oh, that my ways were steadfast
      in obeying your decrees!
⁶ Then I would not be put to shame
      when I consider all your commands.
⁷ I will praise you with an upright heart
      as I learn your righteous laws.
⁸ I will obey your decrees;
      do not utterly forsake me.

■ PROVERBS 24:19–20

¹⁹ Do not fret because of evildoers
      or be envious of the wicked,
²⁰ for the evildoer has no future hope,
      and the lamp of the wicked will be
         snuffed out.

■ PHILIPPIANS 3:1–21

3 Further, my brothers and sisters, rejoice in the Lord! It is no trouble for me
to write the same things to you again, and it
is a safeguard for you. ² Watch out for those
dogs, those evildoers, those mutilators of
the flesh. ³ For it is we who are the circumcision, we who serve God by his Spirit, who
boast in Christ Jesus, and who put no confidence in the flesh – ⁴ though I myself have
reasons for such confidence.

If someone else thinks they have reasons
to put confidence in the flesh, I have more:
⁵ circumcised on the eighth day, of the people
of Israel, of the tribe of Benjamin, a Hebrew
of Hebrews; in regard to the law, a Pharisee;
⁶ as for zeal, persecuting the church; as for
righteousness based on the law, faultless.

⁷ But whatever were gains to me I now
consider loss for the sake of Christ. ⁸ What
is more, I consider everything a loss because of the surpassing worth of knowing
Christ Jesus my Lord, for whose sake I have
lost all things. I consider them garbage,
that I may gain Christ ⁹ and be found in
him, not having a righteousness of my own
that comes from the law, but that which is
through faith in Christ – the righteousness
that comes from God on the basis of faith.
¹⁰ I want to know Christ – yes, to know the
power of his resurrection and participation
in his sufferings, becoming like him in his
death, ¹¹ and so, somehow, attaining to the
resurrection from the dead.

¹² Not that I have already obtained all
this, or have already arrived at my goal,

but I press on to take hold of that for which Christ Jesus took hold of me. [13] Brothers and sisters, I do not consider myself yet to have taken hold of it. But one thing I do: forgetting what is behind and straining towards what is ahead, [14] I press on towards the goal to win the prize for which God has called me heavenwards in Christ Jesus.

[15] All of us, then, who are mature should take such a view of things. And if on some point you think differently, that too God will make clear to you. [16] Only let us live up to what we have already attained.

[17] Join together in following my example, brothers and sisters, and just as you have us as a model, keep your eyes on those who live as we do. [18] For, as I have often told you before and now tell you again even with tears, many live as enemies of the cross of Christ. [19] Their destiny is destruction, their god is their stomach, and their glory is in their shame. Their mind is set on earthly things. [20] But our citizenship is in heaven. And we eagerly await a Saviour from there, the Lord Jesus Christ, [21] who, by the power that enables him to bring everything under his control, will transform our lowly bodies so that they will be like his glorious body.

Meeting the Person

'I want to know Christ – yes, to know the power of his resurrection ...' **Philippians 3:10**

It must not be assumed that the study of Scripture and the contemplation of the principles that God has built into His Word are unimportant. They most certainly are. But let us be on our guard that we do not fall into the trap of contemplating the principles that God has built into the universe more than God Himself.

I have often seen students of Scripture fall into this trap when, in reading their Bible, the only things that get their attention are the principles that relate to godliness. They underline them in their Bible, mark alongside them other Scriptural references, and think that by doing this they are growing spiritually. The problem, however, is that only the principles of daily personal godliness capture their interest; their heavenly Father does not.

Imagine treating a love letter that way: identifying and underlining the principles, reflecting on the profundity of some of the insights, marvelling at the clarity of the language and yet missing the main purpose of the letter – romantic passion and love. Yet this is the way some people approach the Bible. Our aim in studying the nature and character of God must be to know God better (not merely know His Word better), and we must seek to enlarge our acquaintance not simply with the characteristics of His nature, but with the living God whose characteristics they are.

PRAYER

O God, help me never to approach the Bible content to know only the written Word. Give me a passion that never remains satisfied until, through the written Word, I discover more of the living Word. In Jesus' name. Amen.

FURTHER STUDY

Rev. 2:1-7; 2 Cor. 5:14
• What was the church in Ephesus commended for?
• Why was this insufficient?

October 13

ISAIAH 64:1–66:24

64 Oh, that you would rend the heavens
    and come down,
that the mountains would tremble
    before you!
² As when fire sets twigs ablaze
    and causes water to boil,
come down to make your name known
    to your enemies
and cause the nations to quake before
    you!
³ For when you did awesome things that
    we did not expect,
you came down, and the mountains
    trembled before you.
⁴ Since ancient times no one has heard,
    no ear has perceived,
no eye has seen any God besides you,
    who acts on behalf of those who wait
    for him.
⁵ You come to the help of those who gladly
    do right,
who remember your ways.
But when we continued to sin against
    them,
    you were angry.
How then can we be saved?
⁶ All of us have become like one who is
    unclean,
and all our righteous acts are like
    filthy rags;

we all shrivel up like a leaf,
    and like the wind our sins sweep us
    away.
⁷ No one calls on your name
    or strives to lay hold of you;
for you have hidden your face from us
    and have given us over to our sins.

⁸ Yet you, LORD, are our Father.
    We are the clay, you are the potter;
    we are all the work of your hand.
⁹ Do not be angry beyond measure, LORD;
    do not remember our sins for ever.
Oh, look upon us we pray,
    for we are all your people.
¹⁰ Your sacred cities have become a
    wasteland;
even Zion is a wasteland, Jerusalem a
    desolation.
¹¹ Our holy and glorious temple, where our
    ancestors praised you,
has been burned with fire,
    and all that we treasured lies in ruins.
¹² After all this, LORD, will you hold
    yourself back?
Will you keep silent and punish us
    beyond measure?

65 'I revealed myself to those who did
    not ask for me;
I was found by those who did not seek
    me.
To a nation that did not call on my name,

I said, "Here am I, here am I."
² All day long I have held out my hands
    to an obstinate people,
who walk in ways not good,
    pursuing their own imaginations –
³ a people who continually provoke me
    to my very face,
offering sacrifices in gardens
    and burning incense on altars of brick;
⁴ who sit among the graves
    and spend their nights keeping secret
        vigil;
who eat the flesh of pigs,
    and whose pots hold broth of impure
        meat;
⁵ who say, "Keep away; don't come near me,
    for I am too sacred for you!"
Such people are smoke in my nostrils,
    a fire that keeps burning all day.

⁶ 'See, it stands written before me;
    I will not keep silent but will pay back
        in full;
    I will pay it back into their laps –
⁷ both your sins and the sins of your
        ancestors,'
    says the LORD.
'Because they burned sacrifices on the
        mountains
    and defied me on the hills,
I will measure into their laps
    the full payment for their former
        deeds.'

⁸ This is what the LORD says:

'As when juice is still found in a cluster of
        grapes
    and people say, "Don't destroy it,
    there is still a blessing in it,"
so will I do on behalf of my servants;
    I will not destroy them all.
⁹ I will bring forth descendants from
        Jacob,
    and from Judah those who will
        possess my mountains;

my chosen people will inherit them,
    and there will my servants live.
¹⁰ Sharon will become a pasture for flocks,
    and the Valley of Achor a resting place
        for herds,
    for my people who seek me.

¹¹ 'But as for you who forsake the LORD
    and forget my holy mountain,
who spread a table for Fortune
    and fill bowls of mixed wine for
        Destiny,
¹² I will destine you for the sword,
    and all of you will fall in the slaughter;
for I called but you did not answer,
    I spoke but you did not listen.
You did evil in my sight
    and chose what displeases me.'

¹³ Therefore this is what the Sovereign
LORD says:

'My servants will eat,
    but you will go hungry;
my servants will drink,
    but you will go thirsty;
my servants will rejoice,
    but you will be put to shame.
¹⁴ My servants will sing
    out of the joy of their hearts,
but you will cry out
    from anguish of heart
    and wail in brokenness of spirit.
¹⁵ You will leave your name
    for my chosen ones to use in their
        curses;
the Sovereign LORD will put you to death,
    but to his servants he will give another
        name.
¹⁶ Whoever invokes a blessing in the land
    will do so by the one true God;
whoever takes an oath in the land
    will swear by the one true God.
For the past troubles will be forgotten
    and hidden from my eyes.
¹⁷ 'See, I will create

new heavens and a new earth.
The former things will not be
    remembered,
    nor will they come to mind.
18 But be glad and rejoice for ever
    in what I will create,
for I will create Jerusalem to be a delight
    and its people a joy.
19 I will rejoice over Jerusalem
    and take delight in my people;
the sound of weeping and of crying
    will be heard in it no more.

20 'Never again will there be in it
    an infant who lives but a few days,
    or an old man who does not live out
      his years;
the one who dies at a hundred
    will be thought a mere child;
the one who fails to reach a hundred
    will be considered accursed.
21 They will build houses and dwell in them;
    they will plant vineyards and eat their
      fruit.
22 No longer will they build houses and
      others live in them,
    or plant and others eat.
For as the days of a tree,
    so will be the days of my people;
my chosen ones will long enjoy
    the work of their hands.
23 They will not labour in vain,
    nor will they bear children doomed to
      misfortune;
for they will be a people blessed by the
    LORD,
    they and their descendants with them.
24 Before they call I will answer;
    while they are still speaking I will hear.
25 The wolf and the lamb will feed together,
    and the lion will eat straw like the ox,
    and dust will be the serpent's food.
They will neither harm nor destroy
    on all my holy mountain,'
                  says the LORD.

66 This is what the LORD says:

'Heaven is my throne,
    and the earth is my footstool.
Where is the house you will build for me?
    Where will my resting place be?
2 Has not my hand made all these things,
    and so they came into being?'
                  declares the LORD.

'These are the ones I look on with favour:
    those who are humble and contrite in
      spirit,
    and who tremble at my word.
3 But whoever sacrifices a bull
    is like one who kills a person,
and whoever offers a lamb
    is like one who breaks a dog's neck;
whoever makes a grain offering
    is like one who presents pig's blood,
and whoever burns memorial incense
    is like one who worships an idol.
They have chosen their own ways,
    and they delight in their
      abominations;
4 so I also will choose harsh treatment for
      them
    and will bring on them what they
      dread.
For when I called, no one answered,
    when I spoke, no one listened.
They did evil in my sight
    and chose what displeases me.'

5 Hear the word of the LORD,
    you who tremble at his word;
'Your own people who hate you,
    and exclude you because of my name,
      have said,
"Let the LORD be glorified,
    that we may see your joy!"
    Yet they will be put to shame.
6 Hear that uproar from the city,
    hear that noise from the temple!
It is the sound of the LORD
    repaying his enemies all they deserve.

7 'Before she goes into labour,
   she gives birth;
 before the pains come upon her,
   she delivers a son.
8 Who has ever heard of such things?
   Who has ever seen things like this?
 Can a country be born in a day
   or a nation be brought forth in a
     moment?
 Yet no sooner is Zion in labour
   than she gives birth to her children.
9 Do I bring to the moment of birth
   and not give delivery?' says the LORD.
 'Do I close up the womb
   when I bring to delivery?' says your
     God.
10 'Rejoice with Jerusalem and be glad for
     her,
   all you who love her;
 rejoice greatly with her,
   all you who mourn over her.
11 For you will feed and be satisfied
   at her comforting breasts;
 you will drink deeply
   and delight in her overflowing
     abundance.'

12 For this is what the LORD says:

 'I will extend peace to her like a river,
   and the wealth of nations like a
     flooding stream;
 you will feed and be carried on her arm
   and dandled on her knees.
13 As a mother comforts her child,
   so will I comfort you;
 and you will be comforted over
     Jerusalem.'

14 When you see this, your heart will
     rejoice
   and you will flourish like grass;
 the hand of the LORD will be made known
   to his servants,
   but his fury will be shown to his foes.
15 See, the LORD is coming with fire,

and his chariots are like a whirlwind;
 he will bring down his anger with fury,
   and his rebuke with flames of fire.
16 For with fire and with his sword
   the LORD will execute judgment on all
     people,
 and many will be those slain by the
     LORD.

17 'Those who consecrate and purify
themselves to go into the gardens, following
one who is among those who eat the flesh of
pigs, rats and other unclean things – they
will meet their end together with the one
they follow,' declares the LORD.

18 'And I, because of what they have
planned and done, am about to come
and gather the people of all nations and
languages, and they will come and see my
glory.

19 'I will set a sign among them, and I
will send some of those who survive to the
nations – to Tarshish, to the Libyans and
Lydians (famous as archers), to Tubal and
Greece, and to the distant islands that have
not heard of my fame or seen my glory. They
will proclaim my glory among the nations.
20 And they will bring all your people, from
all the nations, to my holy mountain in Jerusalem as an offering to the LORD – on
horses, in chariots and wagons, and on
mules and camels,' says the LORD. 'They
will bring them, as the Israelites bring their
grain offerings, to the temple of the LORD
in ceremonially clean vessels. 21 And I will
select some of them also to be priests and
Levites,' says the LORD.

22 'As the new heavens and the new earth
that I make will endure before me,' declares
the LORD, 'so will your name and descendants endure. 23 From one New Moon to
another and from one Sabbath to another,
all mankind will come and bow down before me,' says the LORD. 24 'And they will go
out and look on the dead bodies of those

who rebelled against me; the worms that eat them will not die, the fire that burns them will not be quenched, and they will be loathsome to all mankind.'

▬ PSALM 119:9-11

⁹ How can a young person stay on the path of purity?
  By living according to your word.
¹⁰ I seek you with all my heart;
  do not let me stray from your commands.
¹¹ I have hidden your word in my heart
  that I might not sin against you.

▬ PROVERBS 24:21-22

²¹ Fear the LORD and the king, my son,
  and do not join with rebellious officials,
²² for those two will send sudden destruction on them,
  and who knows what calamities they can bring?

▬ PHILIPPIANS 4:1-23

4 Therefore, my brothers and sisters, you whom I love and long for, my joy and crown, stand firm in the Lord in this way, dear friends!

² I plead with Euodia and I plead with Syntyche to be of the same mind in the Lord. ³ Yes, and I ask you, my true companion, help these women since they have contended at my side in the cause of the gospel, along with Clement and the rest of my co-workers, whose names are in the book of life.

⁴ Rejoice in the Lord always. I will say it again: rejoice! ⁵ Let your gentleness be evident to all. The Lord is near. ⁶ Do not be anxious about anything, but in every situation, by prayer and petition, with thanksgiving, present your requests to God. ⁷ And the peace of God, which transcends all understanding, will guard your hearts and your minds in Christ Jesus.

⁸ Finally, brothers and sisters, whatever is true, whatever is noble, whatever is right, whatever is pure, whatever is lovely, whatever is admirable – if anything is excellent or praiseworthy – think about such things. ⁹ Whatever you have learned or received or heard from me, or seen in me – put it into practice. And the God of peace will be with you.

¹⁰ I rejoiced greatly in the Lord that at last you renewed your concern for me. Indeed, you were concerned, but you had no opportunity to show it. ¹¹ I am not saying this because I am in need, for I have learned to be content whatever the circumstances. ¹² I know what it is to be in need, and I know what it is to have plenty. I have learned the secret of being content in any and every situation, whether well fed or hungry, whether living in plenty or in want. ¹³ I can do all this through him who gives me strength.

¹⁴ Yet it was good of you to share in my troubles. ¹⁵ Moreover, as you Philippians know, in the early days of your acquaintance with the gospel, when I set out from Macedonia, not one church shared with me in the matter of giving and receiving, except you only; ¹⁶ for even when I was in Thessalonica, you sent me aid more than once when I was in need. ¹⁷ Not that I desire your gifts; what I desire is that more be credited to your account. ¹⁸ I have received full payment and have more than enough. I am amply supplied, now that I have received from Epaphroditus the gifts you sent. They are a fragrant offering, an acceptable sacrifice, pleasing to God. ¹⁹ And my God will meet all your needs according to the riches of his glory in Christ Jesus.

²⁰To our God and Father be glory for ever and ever. Amen.

²¹Greet all God's people in Christ Jesus. The brothers and sisters who are with me send greetings. ²²All God's people here send you greetings, especially those who belong to Caesar's household.

²³The grace of the Lord Jesus Christ be with your spirit. Amen.

We Need to Tell Him

'... in every situation, by prayer and petition, with thanksgiving, present your requests to God.'
Philippians 4:6

One of the reasons Jesus taught us to pray 'Give us today our daily bread' was because He wanted to build in us a barrier against ingratitude.

Do you pray daily for your physical needs? Do you ask God daily for things like food, shelter, and the other physical necessities of life? I must confess that when I asked myself this question before writing this page, I had to admit that I did not. Now I have made a decision to apply myself to this part of the Lord's Prayer with greater sincerity.

Of course some people argue that because Jesus said: 'Your Father knows what you need before you ask him' (Matt. 6:8), then it is pointless to inform God of our physical needs because He knows them already. But the central value of prayer is that prayer is not something by which we inform God of our needs and thus influence Him to give things to us. Prayer is designed to influence us; it is we who are in need of this kind of prayer, not God. Of course God knows what we are in need of, but He also knows that unless we come face to face daily with the fact that we are creatures of need, then we can soon develop a spirit of independence and withdraw ourselves from close contact with Him.

Prayer, then, is something we need. God may not need to be told, but we need to tell Him. That's the point. And unless we grasp it, we can miss one of the primary purposes of prayer.

PRAYER

O Father, thank You for showing me that prayer is not begging for blessings. It is becoming a blessing – to myself. I pray, not to change Your attitude towards me, but to change my attitude towards You. Thank You, Father. Amen.

FURTHER STUDY

Matt. 6:19-34;
Psa. 37:5; 118:8; 125:1
• What should be our attitude to worldly cares?
• What should be our first priority?

October 14

1 The words of Jeremiah son of Hilkiah, one of the priests at Anathoth in the territory of Benjamin. ²The word of the LORD came to him in the thirteenth year of the reign of Josiah son of Amon king of Judah, ³and through the reign of Jehoiakim son of Josiah king of Judah, down to the fifth month of the eleventh year of Zedekiah son of Josiah king of Judah, when the people of Jerusalem went into exile.

⁴The word of the LORD came to me, saying,

⁵'Before I formed you in the womb I knew
   you,
   before you were born I set you apart;
   I appointed you as a prophet to the
   nations.'

⁶'Alas, Sovereign LORD,' I said, 'I do not know how to speak; I am too young.'

⁷But the LORD said to me, 'Do not say, "I am too young." You must go to everyone I send you to and say whatever I command you. ⁸Do not be afraid of them, for I am with you and will rescue you,' declares the LORD.

⁹Then the LORD reached out his hand and touched my mouth and said to me, 'I have put my words in your mouth. ¹⁰See, today I appoint you over nations and kingdoms to uproot and tear down, to destroy and overthrow, to build and to plant.'

¹¹The word of the LORD came to me: 'What do you see, Jeremiah?'

'I see the branch of an almond tree,' I replied.

¹²The LORD said to me, 'You have seen correctly, for I am watching to see that my word is fulfilled.'

¹³The word of the LORD came to me again: 'What do you see?'

'I see a pot that is boiling,' I answered. 'It is tilting towards us from the north.'

¹⁴The LORD said to me, 'From the north disaster will be poured out on all who live in the land. ¹⁵I am about to summon all the peoples of the northern kingdoms,' declares the LORD.

'Their kings will come and set up their
   thrones
   in the entrance of the gates of
   Jerusalem;
they will come against all her
   surrounding walls
   and against all the towns of Judah.
¹⁶I will pronounce my judgments on my
   people
   because of their wickedness in
   forsaking me,
in burning incense to other gods
   and in worshipping what their hands
   have made.

¹⁷'Get yourself ready! Stand up and say to them whatever I command you. Do not be terrified by them, or I will terrify you before them. ¹⁸Today I have made you a fortified city, an iron pillar and a bronze wall to stand against the whole land – against the kings of Judah, its officials, its priests and the people of the land. ¹⁹They will fight against you but will not overcome you, for I am with you and will rescue you,' declares the LORD.

2 The word of the LORD came to me: ²'Go and proclaim in the hearing of Jerusalem:

'This is what the LORD says:

' "I remember the devotion of your
     youth,
how as a bride you loved me
and followed me through the wilderness,
     through a land not sown.
³ Israel was holy to the Lord,
     the firstfruits of his harvest;
all who devoured her were held guilty,
     and disaster overtook them," '
                     declares the Lord.

⁴ Hear the word of the Lord, you
     descendants of Jacob,
     all you clans of Israel.

⁵ This is what the Lord says:

'What fault did your ancestors find in
     me,
     that they strayed so far from me?
They followed worthless idols
     and became worthless themselves.
⁶ They did not ask, "Where is the Lord,
     who brought us up out of Egypt
and led us through the barren
     wilderness,
     through a land of deserts and ravines,
a land of drought and utter darkness,
     a land where no one travels and no one
     lives?"
⁷ I brought you into a fertile land
     to eat its fruit and rich produce.
But you came and defiled my land
     and made my inheritance detestable.
⁸ The priests did not ask,
     "Where is the Lord?"
Those who deal with the law did not
     know me;
     the leaders rebelled against me.
The prophets prophesied by Baal,
     following worthless idols.

⁹ 'Therefore I bring charges against you
     again,'
                     declares the Lord.

'And I will bring charges against your
     children's children.
¹⁰ Cross over to the coasts of Cyprus and
     look,
     send to Kedar and observe closely;
     see if there has ever been anything like
     this:
¹¹ has a nation ever changed its gods?
     (Yet they are not gods at all.)
But my people have exchanged their
     glorious God
     for worthless idols.
¹² Be appalled at this, you heavens,
     and shudder with great horror,'
                     declares the Lord.
¹³ 'My people have committed two sins:
They have forsaken me,
     the spring of living water,
and have dug their own cisterns,
     broken cisterns that cannot hold
     water.
¹⁴ Is Israel a servant, a slave by birth?
     Why then has he become plunder?
¹⁵ Lions have roared;
     they have growled at him.
They have laid waste his land;
     his towns are burned and deserted.
¹⁶ Also, the men of Memphis and
     Tahpanhes
     have cracked your skull.
¹⁷ Have you not brought this on yourselves
     by forsaking the Lord your God
     when he led you in the way?
¹⁸ Now why go to Egypt
     to drink water from the Nile?
And why go to Assyria
     to drink water from the Euphrates?
¹⁹ Your wickedness will punish you;
     your backsliding will rebuke you.
Consider then and realise
     how evil and bitter it is for you
when you forsake the Lord your God
     and have no awe of me,'
                     declares the Lord,
                     the Lord Almighty.

²⁰ 'Long ago you broke off your yoke
and tore off your bonds;
you said, "I will not serve you!"
Indeed, on every high hill
and under every spreading tree
you lay down as a prostitute.
²¹ I had planted you like a choice vine
of sound and reliable stock.
How then did you turn against me
into a corrupt, wild vine?
²² Although you wash yourself with soap
and use an abundance of cleansing
powder,
the stain of your guilt is still before me,'
declares the Sovereign LORD.
²³ 'How can you say, "I am not defiled;
I have not run after the Baals"?
See how you behaved in the valley;
consider what you have done.
You are a swift she-camel
running here and there,
²⁴ a wild donkey accustomed to the desert,
sniffing the wind in her craving –
in her heat who can restrain her?
Any males that pursue her need not tire
themselves;
at mating time they will find her.
²⁵ Do not run until your feet are bare
and your throat is dry.
But you said, "It's no use!
I love foreign gods,
and I must go after them."

²⁶ 'As a thief is disgraced when he is caught,
so the people of Israel are disgraced –
they, their kings and their officials,
their priests and their prophets.
²⁷ They say to wood, "You are my father,"
and to stone, "You gave me birth."
They have turned their backs to me
and not their faces;
yet when they are in trouble, they say,
"Come and save us!"
²⁸ Where then are the gods you made for
yourselves?
Let them come if they can save you

when you are in trouble!
For you, Judah, have as many gods
as you have towns.

²⁹ 'Why do you bring charges against me?
You have all rebelled against me,'
declares the LORD.
³⁰ 'In vain I punished your people;
they did not respond to correction.
Your sword has devoured your prophets
like a ravenous lion.

³¹ 'You of this generation, consider the
word of the LORD:

'Have I been a desert to Israel
or a land of great darkness?
Why do my people say, "We are free to
roam;
we will come to you no more"?
³² Does a young woman forget her
jewellery,
a bride her wedding ornaments?
Yet my people have forgotten me,
days without number.
³³ How skilled you are at pursuing love!
Even the worst of women can learn
from your ways.
³⁴ On your clothes is found
the lifeblood of the innocent poor,
though you did not catch them
breaking in.
Yet in spite of all this
³⁵   you say, "I am innocent;
he is not angry with me."
But I will pass judgment on you
because you say, "I have not sinned."
³⁶ Why do you go about so much,
changing your ways?
You will be disappointed by Egypt
as you were by Assyria.
³⁷ You will also leave that place
with your hands on your head,
for the LORD has rejected those you trust;
you will not be helped by them.

▬ PSALM 119:12-16

¹²Praise be to you, LORD;
    teach me your decrees.
¹³With my lips I recount
    all the laws that come from your
      mouth.
¹⁴I rejoice in following your statutes
    as one rejoices in great riches.
¹⁵I meditate on your precepts
    and consider your ways.
¹⁶I delight in your decrees;
    I will not neglect your word.

▬ PROVERBS 24:23-25

²³These also are sayings of the wise:

To show partiality in judging is not good:
²⁴whoever says to the guilty, 'You are
      innocent,'
    will be cursed by peoples and
    denounced by nations.
²⁵But it will go well with those who convict
      the guilty,
    and rich blessing will come on them.

▬ COLOSSIANS 1:1-20

1 Paul, an apostle of Christ Jesus by the will of God, and Timothy our brother,

²To God's holy people in Colossae, the faithful brothers and sisters in Christ:

Grace and peace to you from God our Father.

³We always thank God, the Father of our Lord Jesus Christ, when we pray for you, ⁴because we have heard of your faith in Christ Jesus and of the love you have for all God's people – ⁵the faith and love that spring from the hope stored up for you in heaven and about which you have already heard in the true message of the gospel ⁶that has come to you. In the same way, the gospel is bearing fruit and growing throughout the whole world – just as it has been doing among you since the day you heard it and truly understood God's grace. ⁷You learned it from Epaphras, our dear fellow servant, who is a faithful minister of Christ on our behalf, ⁸and who also told us of your love in the Spirit.

⁹For this reason, since the day we heard about you, we have not stopped praying for you. We continually ask God to fill you with the knowledge of his will through all the wisdom and understanding that the Spirit gives, ¹⁰so that you may live a life worthy of the Lord and please him in every way: bearing fruit in every good work, growing in the knowledge of God, ¹¹being strengthened with all power according to his glorious might so that you may have great endurance and patience, ¹²and giving joyful thanks to the Father, who has qualified you to share in the inheritance of his holy people in the kingdom of light. ¹³For he has rescued us from the dominion of darkness and brought us into the kingdom of the Son he loves, ¹⁴in whom we have redemption, the forgiveness of sins.

¹⁵The Son is the image of the invisible God, the firstborn over all creation. ¹⁶For in him all things were created: things in heaven and on earth, visible and invisible, whether thrones or powers or rulers or authorities; all things have been created through him and for him. ¹⁷He is before all things, and in him all things hold together. ¹⁸And he is the head of the body, the church; he is the beginning and the firstborn from among the dead, so that in everything he might have the supremacy. ¹⁹For God was pleased to have all his fulness dwell in him, ²⁰and through him to reconcile to himself all things, whether things on earth or things in heaven, by making peace through his blood, shed on the cross.

Wrong Places

'My people have committed two sins: They have forsaken me, the spring of living water, and have dug ... broken cisterns that cannot hold water.' **Jeremiah 2:13**

One of the major problems with which we are all confronted is that we have at the core of our being a deep thirst for God, which makes us entirely dependent on Him for satisfaction. Our sinful human nature resents this, because it dislikes the feeling of helplessness that such dependence brings; it prefers to have a hand in bringing about its own satisfaction.

This terrible tendency of the human heart to try to satisfy its own thirst independently of God is brought out clearly in the passage before us today. The Prophet Jeremiah indicts Israel – the people of God – for depending on 'broken cisterns' in their efforts to quench their spiritual thirst (cisterns which they themselves made but which can hold no water).

Note the two observations our text for today suggests. First, the people were thirsty, and second, they moved in the wrong direction to satisfy their thirst.

God said it was as if they walked right past the clear waters He provided and chose instead to dig their own well. They wanted to run their own lives and refused to come to God, allowing Him to quench their deep thirst. This stubborn commitment to independence is responsible more than anything else for preventing us from having feet like 'hinds' feet'.

PRAYER

Gracious Father, I see that the problem You had with the nation of Israel is my problem, too. For far too often I try to dig my own well. You are searching deeply into my life. Help me not to evade or avoid any issue. In Jesus' name. Amen.

FURTHER STUDY

Judg. 17:1-6; 21:25; Prov. 28:26; 1 Cor. 10:12
• How does the book of Judges sum up the human heart?
• What was Paul's admonition to the Corinthians?

October 15

■ **JEREMIAH 3:1–4:31**

3 'If a man divorces his wife and she leaves him and marries another man,

should he return to her again?
Would not the land be completely defiled?
But you have lived as a prostitute with many lovers –

would you now return to me?'
declares the LORD.

²'Look up to the barren heights and see.
   Is there any place where you have not
     been ravished?
By the roadside you sat waiting for lovers,
   sat like a nomad in the desert.
You have defiled the land
   with your prostitution and
     wickedness.
³Therefore the showers have been withheld,
   and no spring rains have fallen.
Yet you have the brazen look of a prostitute;
   you refuse to blush with shame.
⁴Have you not just called to me:
   "My Father, my friend from my youth,
⁵will you always be angry?
   Will your wrath continue for ever?"
This is how you talk,
   but you do all the evil you can.'

⁶During the reign of King Josiah, the Lord said to me, 'Have you seen what faithless Israel has done? She has gone up on every high hill and under every spreading tree and has committed adultery there. ⁷I thought that after she had done all this she would return to me but she did not, and her unfaithful sister Judah saw it. ⁸I gave faithless Israel her certificate of divorce and sent her away because of all her adulteries. Yet I saw that her unfaithful sister Judah had no fear; she also went out and committed adultery. ⁹Because Israel's immorality mattered so little to her, she defiled the land and committed adultery with stone and wood. ¹⁰In spite of all this, her unfaithful sister Judah did not return to me with all her heart, but only in pretence,' declares the Lord.

¹¹The LORD said to me, 'Faithless Israel is more righteous than unfaithful Judah. ¹²Go, proclaim this message towards the north:

'"Return, faithless Israel," declares the
   LORD,

"I will frown on you no longer,
   for I am faithful," declares the LORD,
   "I will not be angry for ever.
¹³Only acknowledge your guilt –
   you have rebelled against the LORD
     your God,
you have scattered your favours to
     foreign gods
under every spreading tree,
   and have not obeyed me,"'
declares the LORD.

¹⁴'Return, faithless people,' declares the LORD, 'for I am your husband. I will choose you – one from a town and two from a clan – and bring you to Zion. ¹⁵Then I will give you shepherds after my own heart, who will lead you with knowledge and understanding. ¹⁶In those days, when your numbers have increased greatly in the land,' declares the LORD, 'people will no longer say, "The ark of the covenant of the LORD." It will never enter their minds or be remembered; it will not be missed, nor will another one be made. ¹⁷At that time they will call Jerusalem The Throne of the LORD, and all nations will gather in Jerusalem to honour the name of the LORD. No longer will they follow the stubbornness of their evil hearts. ¹⁸In those days the people of Judah will join the people of Israel, and together they will come from a northern land to the land I gave your ancestors as an inheritance.

¹⁹'I myself said,

'"How gladly would I treat you like my
   children
   and give you a pleasant land,
   the most beautiful inheritance of any
     nation."
I thought you would call me "Father"
   and not turn away from following me.
²⁰But like a woman unfaithful to her
     husband,
   so you, Israel, have been unfaithful to
     me,'
declares the LORD.

²¹ A cry is heard on the barren heights,
 the weeping and pleading of the
  people of Israel,
because they have perverted their ways
 and have forgotten the LORD their God.

²² 'Return, faithless people;
 I will cure you of backsliding.'

'Yes, we will come to you,
 for you are the LORD our God.
²³ Surely the idolatrous commotion on the
  hills
 and mountains is a deception;
surely in the LORD our God
 is the salvation of Israel.
²⁴ From our youth shameful gods have
  consumed
 the fruits of our ancestors' labour –
their flocks and herds,
 their sons and daughters.
²⁵ Let us lie down in our shame,
 and let our disgrace cover us.
We have sinned against the LORD our
  God,
 both we and our ancestors;
from our youth till this day
 we have not obeyed the LORD our God.'

4 'If you, Israel, will return,
 then return to me,'
       declares the LORD.
'If you put your detestable idols out of my
  sight
 and no longer go astray,
² and if in a truthful, just and righteous
  way
 you swear, "As surely as the LORD lives,"
then the nations will invoke blessings by
  him
 and in him they will boast.'

³ This is what the LORD says to the people
of Judah and to Jerusalem:

'Break up your unploughed ground

and do not sow among thorns.
⁴ Circumcise yourselves to the LORD,
 circumcise your hearts,
 you people of Judah and inhabitants of
  Jerusalem,
or my wrath will flare up and burn like
  fire
because of the evil you have done –
 burn with no one to quench it.
⁵ 'Announce in Judah and proclaim in
  Jerusalem and say:
 "Sound the trumpet throughout the
  land!"
Cry aloud and say:
 "Gather together!
 Let us flee to the fortified cities!"
⁶ Raise the signal to go to Zion!
 Flee for safety without delay!
For I am bringing disaster from the north,
 even terrible destruction.'

⁷ A lion has come out of his lair;
 a destroyer of nations has set out.
He has left his place
 to lay waste your land.
Your towns will lie in ruins
 without inhabitant.
⁸ So put on sackcloth,
 lament and wail,
for the fierce anger of the LORD
 has not turned away from us.

⁹ 'In that day,' declares the LORD,
 'the king and the officials will lose
  heart,
the priests will be horrified,
 and the prophets will be appalled.'

¹⁰ Then I said, 'Alas, Sovereign LORD! How
completely you have deceived this people
and Jerusalem by saying, "You will have
peace," when the sword is at our throats!'

¹¹ At that time this people and Jerusalem
will be told, 'A scorching wind from the barren heights in the desert blows towards my
people, but not to winnow or cleanse; ¹²a

wind too strong for that comes from me. Now I pronounce my judgments against them.'

13 Look! He advances like the clouds,
    his chariots come like a whirlwind,
his horses are swifter than eagles.
    Woe to us! We are ruined!
14 Jerusalem, wash the evil from your heart
        and be saved.
    How long will you harbour wicked
        thoughts?
15 A voice is announcing from Dan,
    proclaiming disaster from the hills of
        Ephraim.
16 'Tell this to the nations,
    proclaim concerning Jerusalem:
"A besieging army is coming from a
        distant land,
    raising a war cry against the cities of
        Judah.
17 They surround her like men guarding a
        field,
    because she has rebelled against me,"'
            declares the Lord.
18 'Your own conduct and actions
    have brought this on you.
This is your punishment.
    How bitter it is!
    How it pierces to the heart!'

19 Oh, my anguish, my anguish!
    I writhe in pain.
Oh, the agony of my heart!
    My heart pounds within me,
    I cannot keep silent.
For I have heard the sound of the trumpet;
    I have heard the battle cry.
20 Disaster follows disaster;
    the whole land lies in ruins.
In an instant my tents are destroyed,
    my shelter in a moment.
21 How long must I see the battle standard
    and hear the sound of the trumpet?

22 'My people are fools;
    they do not know me.

They are senseless children;
    they have no understanding.
They are skilled in doing evil;
    they know not how to do good.'

23 I looked at the earth,
    and it was formless and empty;
and at the heavens,
    and their light was gone.
24 I looked at the mountains,
    and they were quaking;
all the hills were swaying.
25 I looked, and there were no people;
    every bird in the sky had flown away.
26 I looked, and the fruitful land was a
        desert;
    all its towns lay in ruins
    before the Lord, before his fierce anger.

27 This is what the Lord says:

'The whole land will be ruined,
    though I will not destroy it completely.
28 Therefore the earth will mourn
    and the heavens above grow dark,
because I have spoken and will not
        relent,
    I have decided and will not turn back.'

29 At the sound of horsemen and archers
    every town takes to flight.
Some go into the thickets;
    some climb up among the rocks.
All the towns are deserted;
    no one lives in them.

30 What are you doing, you devastated one?
    Why dress yourself in scarlet
    and put on jewels of gold?
Why highlight your eyes with makeup?
    You adorn yourself in vain.
Your lovers despise you;
    they want to kill you.

31 I hear a cry as of a woman in labour,
    a groan as of one bearing her first child –

the cry of Daughter Zion gasping for
    breath,
  stretching out her hands and saying,
  'Alas! I am fainting;
    my life is given over to murderers.'

■ PSALM 119:17-20

[17] Be good to your servant while I live,
    that I may obey your word.
[18] Open my eyes that I may see
    wonderful things in your law.
[19] I am a stranger on earth;
    do not hide your commands from me.
[20] My soul is consumed with longing
    for your laws at all times.

■ PROVERBS 24:26-27

[26] An honest answer
    is like a kiss on the lips.

[27] Put your outdoor work in order
    and get your fields ready;
    after that, build your house.

■ COLOSSIANS 1:21-2:15

[21] Once you were alienated from God and were enemies in your minds because of your evil behaviour. [22] But now he has reconciled you by Christ's physical body through death to present you holy in his sight, without blemish and free from accusation – [23] if you continue in your faith, established and firm, and do not move from the hope held out in the gospel. This is the gospel that you heard and that has been proclaimed to every creature under heaven, and of which I, Paul, have become a servant.

[24] Now I rejoice in what I am suffering for you, and I fill up in my flesh what is still lacking in regard to Christ's afflictions, for the sake of his body, which is the church. [25] I have become its servant by the commission God gave me to present to you the word of God in its fulness – [26] the mystery that has been kept hidden for ages and generations, but is now disclosed to the Lord's people. [27] To them God has chosen to make known among the Gentiles the glorious riches of this mystery, which is Christ in you, the hope of glory.

[28] He is the one we proclaim, admonishing and teaching everyone with all wisdom, so that we may present everyone fully mature in Christ. [29] To this end I strenuously contend with all the energy Christ so powerfully works in me.

2 I want you to know how hard I am contending for you and for those at Laodicea, and for all who have not met me personally. [2] My goal is that they may be encouraged in heart and united in love, so that they may have the full riches of complete understanding, in order that they may know the mystery of God, namely, Christ, [3] in whom are hidden all the treasures of wisdom and knowledge. [4] I tell you this so that no one may deceive you by fine-sounding arguments. [5] For though I am absent from you in body, I am present with you in spirit and delight to see how disciplined you are and how firm your faith in Christ is.

[6] So then, just as you received Christ Jesus as Lord, continue to live your lives in him, [7] rooted and built up in him, strengthened in the faith as you were taught, and overflowing with thankfulness.

[8] See to it that no one takes you captive through hollow and deceptive philosophy, which depends on human tradition and the elemental spiritual forces of this world rather than on Christ.

[9] For in Christ all the fulness of the Deity lives in bodily form, [10] and in Christ you have been brought to fulness. He is the head over every power and authority. [11] In him you were also circumcised with a circumcision not performed by human hands.

Your whole self ruled by the flesh was put off when you were circumcised by Christ, [12] having been buried with him in baptism, in which you were also raised with him through your faith in the working of God, who raised him from the dead.

[13] When you were dead in your sins and in the uncircumcision of your flesh, God made you alive with Christ. He forgave us all our sins, [14] having cancelled the charge of our legal indebtedness, which stood against us and condemned us; he has taken it away, nailing it to the cross. [15] And having disarmed the powers and authorities, he made a public spectacle of them, triumphing over them by the cross.

In the Right Direction

'He is the one we proclaim, admonishing and teaching everyone with all wisdom, so that we may present everyone fully mature in Christ.' **Colossians 1:28**

In the Spirit-controlled life, self is still there, but now it is not self-centred but God-centred, and therefore, rhythmic and harmonious. The self functions perfectly and is, therefore, perfectly healthy; it is a self you can live with. The sex drive is still there, but now, being God-centred, it functions as God intended it to function. If one is married, then it can be expressed in a physical relationship, but if one is unmarried, then it can be sublimated and channelled into creativity in other directions. The herd instinct is still there, but now it is fastened on the kingdom of God, and one moves with the rest of the church towards the unity of the faith and of the Spirit.

The life of the Spirit is not one of asceticism but one of assertion. We get rid of unacceptable desires in the only way possible, by replacing them with higher desires. We get rid of self-centredness by God-centredness, through surrender. We get rid of sex domination by surrendering the drive to God and the controls He places upon it, so that sex serves us and makes us creative in the whole of life – not just within the physical relationship of marriage. We get rid of the herd dominance by surrender to God and, when surrendered, we love people more because we are no longer dominated or intimidated by them. The expulsive power of a new affection casts out 'lower loves' by focusing them on higher objectives.

PRAYER

Holy Spirit, I am beginning to learn that when You have control, everything is a perfect cosmos; when I have control, it is chaos. As life is for living, I want to live it to the brim. Help me not just to surrender, but to stay surrendered. Amen.

FURTHER STUDY

Heb. 6; Matt. 5:48;
2 Cor. 13:11
• What did Paul mean by 'perfection'?
• What was Paul's desire?

October 16

■ JEREMIAH 5:1–6:21

5 'Go up and down the streets of
Jerusalem,
look around and consider,
search through her squares.
If you can find but one person
who deals honestly and seeks the
truth,
I will forgive this city.
² Although they say, "As surely as the LORD
lives,"
still they are swearing falsely.'

³ LORD, do not your eyes look for truth?
You struck them, but they felt no pain;
you crushed them but they refused
correction.
They made their faces harder than stone
and refused to repent.
⁴ I thought, 'These are only the poor;
they are foolish,
for they do not know the way of the LORD,
the requirements of their God.
⁵ So I will go to the leaders
and speak to them;
surely they know the way of the LORD,
the requirements of their God.'
But with one accord they too had broken
off the yoke
and torn off the bonds.
⁶ Therefore a lion from the forest will
attack them,
a wolf from the desert will ravage
them,
a leopard will lie in wait near their towns
to tear to pieces any who venture out,
for their rebellion is great
and their backslidings many.

⁷ 'Why should I forgive you?

Your children have forsaken me
and sworn by gods that are not gods.
I supplied all their needs,
yet they committed adultery
and thronged to the houses of
prostitutes.
⁸ They are well-fed, lusty stallions,
each neighing for another man's wife.
⁹ Should I not punish them for this?'
declares the LORD.
'Should I not avenge myself
on such a nation as this?

¹⁰ 'Go through her vineyards and ravage
them,
but do not destroy them completely.
Strip off her branches,
for these people do not belong to the
LORD.
¹¹ The people of Israel and the people of
Judah
have been utterly unfaithful to me,'
declares the LORD.
¹² They have lied about the LORD;
they said, 'He will do nothing!
No harm will come to us;
we will never see sword or famine.
¹³ The prophets are but wind
and the word is not in them;
so let what they say be done to them.'

¹⁴ Therefore this is what the LORD God
Almighty says:

'Because the people have spoken these
words,
I will make my words in your mouth a
fire
and these people the wood it
consumes.

¹⁵ People of Israel,' declares the Lord,
'I am bringing a distant nation against
you –
an ancient and enduring nation,
a people whose language you do not
know,
whose speech you do not understand.
¹⁶ Their quivers are like an open grave;
all of them are mighty warriors.
¹⁷ They will devour your harvests and food,
devour your sons and daughters;
they will devour your flocks and herds,
devour your vines and fig trees.
With the sword they will destroy
the fortified cities in which you trust.

¹⁸ 'Yet even in those days,' declares the
Lord, 'I will not destroy you completely.
¹⁹ And when the people ask, "Why has the
Lord our God done all this to us?" you will
tell them, "As you have forsaken me and
served foreign gods in your own land, so
now you will serve foreigners in a land not
your own."

²⁰ 'Announce this to the descendants of
Jacob
and proclaim it in Judah:
²¹ Hear this, you foolish and senseless
people,
who have eyes but do not see,
who have ears but do not hear:
²² Should you not fear me?' declares the
Lord.
'Should you not tremble in my
presence?
I made the sand a boundary for the sea,
an everlasting barrier it cannot cross.
The waves may roll, but they cannot
prevail;
they may roar, but they cannot cross
it.
²³ But these people have stubborn and
rebellious hearts;
they have turned aside and gone away.
²⁴ They do not say to themselves,

"Let us fear the Lord our God,
who gives autumn and spring rains in
season,
who assures us of the regular weeks of
harvest."
²⁵ Your wrongdoings have kept these away;
your sins have deprived you of good.

²⁶ 'Among my people are the wicked
who lie in wait like men who snare
birds
and like those who set traps to catch
people.
²⁷ Like cages full of birds,
their houses are full of deceit;
they have become rich and powerful
²⁸ and have grown fat and sleek.
Their evil deeds have no limit;
they do not seek justice.
They do not promote the case of the
fatherless;
they do not defend the just cause of the
poor.
²⁹ Should I not punish them for this?'
declares the Lord.
'Should I not avenge myself
on such a nation as this?

³⁰ 'A horrible and shocking thing
has happened in the land:
³¹ The prophets prophesy lies,
the priests rule by their own authority,
and my people love it this way.
But what will you do in the end?

6 'Flee for safety, people of Benjamin!
Flee from Jerusalem!
Sound the trumpet in Tekoa!
Raise the signal over Beth Hakkerem!
For disaster looms out of the north,
even terrible destruction.
² I will destroy Daughter Zion,
so beautiful and delicate.
³ Shepherds with their flocks will come
against her;
they will pitch their tents round her,
each tending his own portion.'

⁴ 'Prepare for battle against her!
    Arise, let us attack at noon!
But, alas, the daylight is fading,
    and the shadows of evening grow long.
⁵ So arise, let us attack at night
    and destroy her fortresses!'

⁶ This is what the LORD Almighty says:

'Cut down the trees
    and build siege ramps against
        Jerusalem.
This city must be punished;
    it is filled with oppression.
⁷ As a well pours out its water,
    so she pours out her wickedness.
Violence and destruction resound in her;
    her sickness and wounds are ever
        before me.
⁸ Take warning, Jerusalem,
    or I will turn away from you
and make your land desolate
    so that no one can live in it.'

⁹ This is what the LORD Almighty says:

'Let them glean the remnant of Israel
    as thoroughly as a vine;
pass your hand over the branches again,
    like one gathering grapes.'

¹⁰ To whom can I speak and give warning?
    Who will listen to me?
Their ears are closed
    so that they cannot hear.
The word of the LORD is offensive to
        them;
    they find no pleasure in it.
¹¹ But I am full of the wrath of the LORD,
    and I cannot hold it in.

'Pour it out on the children in the street
    and on the young men gathered
        together;
both husband and wife will be caught
    in it,

and the old, those weighed down with
        years.
¹² Their houses will be turned over to
        others,
    together with their fields and their
        wives,
when I stretch out my hand
    against those who live in the land,'
            declares the LORD.
¹³ 'From the least to the greatest,
    all are greedy for gain;
prophets and priests alike,
    all practise deceit.
¹⁴ They dress the wound of my people
    as though it were not serious.
"Peace, peace," they say,
    when there is no peace.
¹⁵ Are they ashamed of their detestable
        conduct?
    No, they have no shame at all;
    they do not even know how to blush.
So they will fall among the fallen;
    they will be brought down when I
        punish them,'
            says the LORD.

¹⁶ This is what the LORD says:

'Stand at the crossroads and look;
    ask for the ancient paths,
ask where the good way is, and walk
    in it,
    and you will find rest for your souls.
    But you said, "We will not walk in it."
¹⁷ I appointed watchmen over you and said,
    "Listen to the sound of the trumpet!"
    But you said, "We will not listen."
¹⁸ Therefore hear, you nations;
    you who are witnesses,
    observe what will happen to them.
¹⁹ Hear, you earth:
    I am bringing disaster on this people,
    the fruit of their schemes,
because they have not listened to my
        words
    and have rejected my law.

²⁰ What do I care about incense from Sheba
   or sweet calamus from a distant land?
Your burnt offerings are not acceptable;
   your sacrifices do not please me.'

²¹ Therefore this is what the LORD says:

'I will put obstacles before this people.
Parents and children alike will
      stumble over them;
   neighbours and friends will perish.'

▬ PSALM 119:21-24

²¹ You rebuke the arrogant, who are
      accursed,
   those who stray from your commands.
²² Remove from me scorn and contempt,
   for I keep your statutes.
²³ Though rulers sit together and slander
      me,
   your servant will meditate on your
      decrees.
²⁴ Your statutes are my delight;
   they are my counsellors.

▬ PROVERBS 24:28-29

²⁸ Do not testify against your neighbour
      without cause –
   would you use your lips to mislead?
²⁹ Do not say, 'I'll do to them as they have
      done to me;
   I'll pay them back for what they did.'

▬ COLOSSIANS 2:16–3:17

¹⁶ Therefore do not let anyone judge you
by what you eat or drink, or with regard to
a religious festival, a New Moon celebration
or a Sabbath day. ¹⁷ These are a shadow of
the things that were to come; the reality,
however, is found in Christ. ¹⁸ Do not let
anyone who delights in false humility and
the worship of angels disqualify you. Such
a person also goes into great detail about
what they have seen; they are puffed up
with idle notions by their unspiritual mind.
¹⁹ They have lost connection with the head,
from whom the whole body, supported and
held together by its ligaments and sinews,
grows as God causes it to grow.

²⁰ Since you died with Christ to the elemental spiritual forces of this world, why,
as though you still belonged to the world,
do you submit to its rules: ²¹ 'Do not handle!
Do not taste! Do not touch!'? ²² These rules,
which have to do with things that are all destined to perish with use, are based on merely human commands and teachings. ²³ Such
regulations indeed have an appearance of
wisdom, with their self-imposed worship,
their false humility and their harsh treatment of the body, but they lack any value in
restraining sensual indulgence.

3 Since, then, you have been raised with
   Christ, set your hearts on things above,
where Christ is, seated at the right hand
of God. ² Set your minds on things above,
not on earthly things. ³ For you died, and
your life is now hidden with Christ in God.
⁴ When Christ, who is your life, appears,
then you also will appear with him in glory.

⁵ Put to death, therefore, whatever belongs to your earthly nature: sexual immorality, impurity, lust, evil desires and greed,
which is idolatry. ⁶ Because of these, the
wrath of God is coming. ⁷ You used to walk
in these ways, in the life you once lived. ⁸ But
now you must also rid yourselves of all such
things as these: anger, rage, malice, slander,
and filthy language from your lips. ⁹ Do not
lie to each other, since you have taken off
your old self with its practices ¹⁰ and have put
on the new self, which is being renewed in
knowledge in the image of its Creator. ¹¹ Here
there is no Gentile or Jew, circumcised or
uncircumcised, barbarian, Scythian, slave
or free, but Christ is all, and is in all.

[12] Therefore, as God's chosen people, holy and dearly loved, clothe yourselves with compassion, kindness, humility, gentleness and patience. [13] Bear with each other and forgive one another if any of you has a grievance against someone. Forgive as the Lord forgave you. [14] And over all these virtues put on love, which binds them all together in perfect unity. [15] Let the peace of Christ rule in your hearts, since as members of one body you were called to peace. And be thankful. [16] Let the message of Christ dwell among you richly as you teach and admonish one another with all wisdom through psalms, hymns, and songs from the Spirit, singing to God with gratitude in your hearts. [17] And whatever you do, whether in word or deed, do it all in the name of the Lord Jesus, giving thanks to God the Father through him.

Patience and Kindness

'Therefore as God's chosen people ... clothe yourselves with ... kindness ... and patience.' **Colossians 3:12**

The fourth fruit of the Spirit listed by Paul is patience. The King James Version uses the word 'longsuffering'. Someone has suggested that longsuffering is 'love stretched out'. It is so elastic and tough that it doesn't break up into impatience. It maintains a patient attitude amidst the flux of human events.

Patience, however, must not be confused with indifference. One group of people in ancient history – the Stoics – made indifference a virtue. Some people in the early centuries of the church tried to Christianise this characteristic, but it couldn't be done. A Christian is someone who cares. Because we care, we suffer, but in the midst of suffering, we discover the Spirit's enabling patience.

A woman, after finding Christ, went through a time of great persecution from her family. She said, 'I have never been a patient woman, but since Christ and the Holy Spirit came into my life, He has turned me upside down and inside out. I always had to have the last word, but my last word is silence.' Now, whenever she says something, her family listens, because she speaks out of the depth of silence. *The Amplified Bible* presents Galatians 5:22 as, 'But the fruit of the ... Spirit [the work which His presence within accomplishes] is ... patience.'

The next fruit is kindness. This may seem a very ordinary virtue, but yet, without it, the other virtues are incomplete. It is not by chance that this virtue is in the middle of the nine, for it puts flavour in all the others.

PRAYER

Father, I want all the other virtues to be flavoured with kindness, so that the spirit of kindness pervades everything I do and everything I am. For Jesus' sake. Amen.

FURTHER STUDY

1 Thess. 1; Rom. 5:3; 12:12; Luke 21:19; James 1:4

• How did Paul relate patience to tribulation?
• In what did Paul rejoice?

October 17

▬ JEREMIAH 6:22–8:13

²² This is what the LORD says:

'Look, an army is coming
    from the land of the north;
a great nation is being stirred up
    from the ends of the earth.
²³ They are armed with bow and spear;
    they are cruel and show no mercy.
They sound like the roaring sea
    as they ride on their horses;
they come like men in battle formation
    to attack you, Daughter Zion.'

²⁴ We have heard reports about them,
    and our hands hang limp.
Anguish has gripped us,
    pain like that of a woman in labour.
²⁵ Do not go out to the fields
    or walk on the roads,
for the enemy has a sword,
    and there is terror on every side.
²⁶ Put on sackcloth, my people,
    and roll in ashes;
mourn with bitter wailing
    as for an only son,
for suddenly the destroyer
    will come upon us.

²⁷ 'I have made you a tester of metals
    and my people the ore,
that you may observe
    and test their ways.
²⁸ They are all hardened rebels,
    going about to slander.
They are bronze and iron;
    they all act corruptly.
²⁹ The bellows blow fiercely
    to burn away the lead with fire,
but the refining goes on in vain;

the wicked are not purged out.
³⁰ They are called rejected silver,
    because the LORD has rejected them.'

7 This is the word that came to Jeremiah from the Lord: ² 'Stand at the gate of the Lord's house and there proclaim this message:

' "Hear the word of the LORD, all you people of Judah who come through these gates to worship the LORD. ³ This is what the LORD Almighty, the God of Israel, says: reform your ways and your actions, and I will let you live in this place. ⁴ Do not trust in deceptive words and say, 'This is the temple of the LORD, the temple of the LORD, the temple of the LORD!' ⁵ If you really change your ways and your actions and deal with each other justly, ⁶ if you do not oppress the foreigner, the fatherless or the widow and do not shed innocent blood in this place, and if you do not follow other gods to your own harm, ⁷ then I will let you live in this place, in the land I gave to your ancestors for ever and ever. ⁸ But look, you are trusting in deceptive words that are worthless.

⁹ ' "Will you steal and murder, commit adultery and perjury, burn incense to Baal and follow other gods you have not known, ¹⁰ and then come and stand before me in this house, which bears my Name, and say, 'We are safe' – safe to do all these detestable things? ¹¹ Has this house, which bears my Name, become a den of robbers to you? But I have been watching! declares the LORD.

¹² ' "Go now to the place in Shiloh where I first made a dwelling for my Name, and see what I did to it because of the wickedness of my people Israel. ¹³ While you were doing all these things, declares the LORD, I spoke to you again and again, but you did not listen; I called you, but you did not answer.

¹⁴ Therefore, what I did to Shiloh I will now do to the house that bears my Name, the temple you trust in, the place I gave to you and your ancestors. ¹⁵ I will thrust you from my presence, just as I did all your fellow Israelites, the people of Ephraim."

¹⁶ "So do not pray for this people nor offer any plea or petition for them; do not plead with me, for I will not listen to you. ¹⁷ Do you not see what they are doing in the towns of Judah and in the streets of Jerusalem? ¹⁸ The children gather wood, the fathers light the fire, and the women knead the dough and make cakes to offer to the Queen of Heaven. They pour out drink offerings to other gods to arouse my anger. ¹⁹ But am I the one they are provoking? declares the LORD. Are they not rather harming themselves, to their own shame?

²⁰ "Therefore this is what the Sovereign LORD says: my anger and my wrath will be poured out on this place – on man and beast, on the trees of the field and on the crops of your land – and it will burn and not be quenched.

²¹ "This is what the LORD Almighty, the God of Israel, says: go ahead, add your burnt offerings to your other sacrifices and eat the meat yourselves! ²² For when I brought your ancestors out of Egypt and spoke to them, I did not just give them commands about burnt offerings and sacrifices, ²³ but I gave them this command: obey me, and I will be your God and you will be my people. Walk in obedience to all I command you, that it may go well with you. ²⁴ But they did not listen or pay attention; instead, they followed the stubborn inclinations of their evil hearts. They went backwards and not forwards. ²⁵ From the time your ancestors left Egypt until now, day after day, again and again I sent you my servants the prophets. ²⁶ But they did not listen to me or pay attention. They were stiff-necked and did more evil than their ancestors."

²⁷ 'When you tell them all this, they will not listen to you; when you call to them, they will not answer. ²⁸ Therefore say to them, "This is the nation that has not obeyed the LORD its God or responded to correction. Truth has perished; it has vanished from their lips.

²⁹ '"Cut off your hair and throw it away; take up a lament on the barren heights, for the LORD has rejected and abandoned this generation that is under his wrath.

³⁰ '"The people of Judah have done evil in my eyes, declares the LORD. They have set up their detestable idols in the house that bears my Name and have defiled it. ³¹ They have built the high places of Topheth in the Valley of Ben Hinnom to burn their sons and daughters in the fire – something I did not command, nor did it enter my mind. ³² So beware, the days are coming, declares the LORD, when people will no longer call it Topheth or the Valley of Ben Hinnom, but the Valley of Slaughter, for they will bury the dead in Topheth until there is no more room. ³³ Then the carcasses of this people will become food for the birds and the wild animals, and there will be no one to frighten them away. ³⁴ I will bring an end to the sounds of joy and gladness and to the voices of bride and bridegroom in the towns of Judah and the streets of Jerusalem, for the land will become desolate.

8 '"At that time, declares the LORD, the bones of the kings and officials of Judah, the bones of the priests and prophets, and the bones of the people of Jerusalem will be removed from their graves. ² They will be exposed to the sun and the moon and all the stars of the heavens, which they have loved and served and which they have followed and consulted and worshipped. They will not be gathered up or buried, but will be like dung lying on the ground. ³ Wherever I banish them, all the survivors of this evil nation will prefer death to life, declares the LORD Almighty."

⁴ 'Say to them, "This is what the LORD says:

' "When people fall down, do they not get
       up?
   When someone turns away, do they
       not return?
⁵ Why then have these people turned
       away?
   Why does Jerusalem always turn
       away?
   They cling to deceit;
       they refuse to return.
⁶ I have listened attentively,
       but they do not say what is right.
   None of them repent of their wickedness,
       saying, 'What have I done?'
   Each pursues their own course
       like a horse charging into battle.
⁷ Even the stork in the sky
       knows her appointed seasons,
   and the dove, the swift and the thrush
       observe the time of their migration.
   But my people do not know
       the requirements of the LORD.

⁸ ' "How can you say, 'We are wise,
       for we have the law of the LORD,'
   when actually the lying pen of the
       scribes
       has handled it falsely?
⁹ The wise will be put to shame;
       they will be dismayed and trapped.
   Since they have rejected the word of the
       LORD,
       what kind of wisdom do they have?
¹⁰ Therefore I will give their wives to other
       men
       and their fields to new owners.
   From the least to the greatest,
       all are greedy for gain;
   prophets and priests alike,
       all practise deceit.
¹¹ They dress the wound of my people
       as though it were not serious.
   'Peace, peace,' they say,
       when there is no peace.
¹² Are they ashamed of their detestable
       conduct?

No, they have no shame at all;
       they do not even know how to blush.
   So they will fall among the fallen;
       they will be brought down when they
       are punished,
                              says the LORD.

¹³ ' "I will take away their harvest,
                              declares the LORD.
   There will be no grapes on the vine.
   There will be no figs on the tree,
       and their leaves will wither.
   What I have given them
       will be taken from them." ' "

▬ PSALM 119:25–27

²⁵ I am laid low in the dust;
       preserve my life according to your
       word.
²⁶ I gave an account of my ways and you
       answered me;
       teach me your decrees.
²⁷ Cause me to understand the way of your
       precepts,
       that I may meditate on your wonderful
       deeds.

▬ PROVERBS 24:30–34

³⁰ I went past the field of a sluggard,
       past the vineyard of someone who has
       no sense;
³¹ thorns had come up everywhere,
       the ground was covered with weeds,
       and the stone wall was in ruins.
³² I applied my heart to what I observed
       and learned a lesson from what I saw:
³³ a little sleep, a little slumber,
       a little folding of the hands to rest –
³⁴ and poverty will come on you like a thief
       and scarcity like an armed man.

■ COLOSSIANS 3:18–4:18

¹⁸Wives, submit yourselves to your husbands, as is fitting in the Lord.

¹⁹Husbands, love your wives and do not be harsh with them.

²⁰Children, obey your parents in everything, for this pleases the Lord.

²¹Fathers, do not embitter your children, or they will become discouraged.

²²Slaves, obey your earthly masters in everything; and do it, not only when their eye is on you and to curry their favour, but with sincerity of heart and reverence for the Lord. ²³Whatever you do, work at it with all your heart, as working for the Lord, not for human masters, ²⁴since you know that you will receive an inheritance from the Lord as a reward. It is the Lord Christ you are serving. ²⁵Anyone who does wrong will be repaid for their wrongs, and there is no favouritism.

4 Masters, provide your slaves with what is right and fair, because you know that you also have a Master in heaven.

²Devote yourselves to prayer, being watchful and thankful. ³And pray for us, too, that God may open a door for our message, so that we may proclaim the mystery of Christ, for which I am in chains. ⁴Pray that I may proclaim it clearly, as I should. ⁵Be wise in the way you act towards outsiders; make the most of every opportunity. ⁶Let your conversation be always full of grace, seasoned with salt, so that you may know how to answer everyone.

⁷Tychicus will tell you all the news about me. He is a dear brother, a faithful minister and fellow servant in the Lord. ⁸I am sending him to you for the express purpose that you may know about our circumstances and that he may encourage your hearts. ⁹He is coming with Onesimus, our faithful and dear brother, who is one of you. They will tell you everything that is happening here.

¹⁰My fellow prisoner Aristarchus sends you his greetings, as does Mark, the cousin of Barnabas. (You have received instructions about him; if he comes to you, welcome him.) ¹¹Jesus, who is called Justus, also sends greetings. These are the only Jews among my fellow workers for the kingdom of God, and they have proved a comfort to me. ¹²Epaphras, who is one of you and a servant of Christ Jesus, sends greetings. He is always wrestling in prayer for you, that you may stand firm in all the will of God, mature and fully assured. ¹³I vouch for him that he is working hard for you and for those at Laodicea and Hierapolis. ¹⁴Our dear friend Luke, the doctor, and Demas send greetings. ¹⁵Give my greetings to the brothers and sisters at Laodicea, and to Nympha and the church in her house.

¹⁶After this letter has been read to you, see that it is also read in the church of the Laodiceans and that you in turn read the letter from Laodicea.

¹⁷Tell Archippus: 'See to it that you complete the ministry you have received in the Lord.'

¹⁸I, Paul, write this greeting in my own hand. Remember my chains. Grace be with you.

Various Forms of Prayer

'Devote yourselves to prayer, being watchful and thankful.' **Colossians 4:2**

Today we ask ourselves: what does it mean to 'pray on all occasions with all kinds of prayers and requests' (Eph. 6:18)? The phrase 'pray on all occasions' presents no difficulty; quite clearly, this means praying as often as possible, regularly and constantly. But what does it mean to pray 'with all prayer and supplication'? Paul means, I believe, that we should pray with all forms or kinds of prayer.

You see, there are many different forms of prayer that are available to us. First, there is verbal prayer when we present our prayer to God in carefully chosen words and phrases. Second, there is silent prayer, when no words cross our lips, but prayer flows directly from our hearts. Third, there is wordless prayer, when we express sounds rather than words, as when we sigh or groan in prayer. Then there is public prayer, common prayer, or 'praying together' - or, as some prefer to call it, 'praying in concert'. So praying with 'all kinds of prayer' means using every form of prayer available to us, praying in every way and manner we can. We are to be at it always and in endless ways.

But there is a certain form of prayer to which the apostle refers which deserves our closer examination: when we pray with regard to special requests and needs. We must not overlook this, for it is so easy to be caught up in adoration and praise that we neglect to focus our prayers on the various needs that arise from time to time, not only in our own lives, but also in the lives of others. This, too, is a necessary kind of prayer.

PRAYER

Father, help me to see the senselessness of trying to muddle through life in my own strength when You have made Your power and resources available to me through prayer. Help me grow in prayer. In Jesus' name. Amen.

FURTHER STUDY

Matt. 7:1-12; Acts 1:14; 4:24; 12:12; 21:5
- What is evident about the early church?
- How does Jesus relate fatherhood to prayer?

October 18

■ JEREMIAH 8:14–10:17

14 Why are we sitting here?
    Gather together!
Let us flee to the fortified cities
    and perish there!
For the LORD our God has doomed us to perish
    and given us poisoned water to drink,
    because we have sinned against him.
15 We hoped for peace
    but no good has come,

for a time of healing
    but there is only terror.
16 The snorting of the enemy's horses
    is heard from Dan;
at the neighing of their stallions
    the whole land trembles.
They have come to devour
    the land and everything in it,
    the city and all who live there.

17 'See, I will send venomous snakes among you,

vipers that cannot be charmed,
　and they will bite you,'
　　　　declares the LORD.

¹⁸ You who are my Comforter in sorrow,
　my heart is faint within me.
¹⁹ Listen to the cry of my people
　from a land far away:
'Is the LORD not in Zion?
　Is her King no longer there?'

'Why have they aroused my anger with
　　their images,
　with their worthless foreign idols?'

²⁰ 'The harvest is past,
　the summer has ended,
　and we are not saved.'

²¹ Since my people are crushed, I am
　　crushed;
　I mourn, and horror grips me.
²² Is there no balm in Gilead?
　Is there no physician there?
Why then is there no healing
　for the wound of my people?

9 ¹ Oh, that my head were a spring of
　　water
　and my eyes a fountain of tears!
I would weep day and night
　for the slain of my people.
² Oh, that I had in the desert
　a lodging place for travellers,
so that I might leave my people
　and go away from them;
for they are all adulterers,
　a crowd of unfaithful people.

³ 'They make ready their tongue
　like a bow, to shoot lies;
it is not by truth
　that they triumph in the land.
They go from one sin to another;
　they do not acknowledge me,'
　　　　declares the LORD.
⁴ 'Beware of your friends;

do not trust anyone in your clan.
For every one of them is a deceiver,
　and every friend a slanderer.
⁵ Friend deceives friend,
　and no one speaks the truth.
They have taught their tongues to lie;
　they weary themselves with sinning.
⁶ You live in the midst of deception;
　in their deceit they refuse to
　　acknowledge me,'
　　　　declares the LORD.

⁷ Therefore this is what the LORD
Almighty says:

'See, I will refine and test them,
　for what else can I do
　because of the sin of my people?
⁸ Their tongue is a deadly arrow;
　it speaks deceitfully.
With their mouths they all speak
　cordially to their neighbours,
　but in their hearts they set traps for
　　them.
⁹ Should I not punish them for this?'
　declares the LORD.
'Should I not avenge myself
　on such a nation as this?'

¹⁰ I will weep and wail for the mountains
　and take up a lament concerning the
　　wilderness grasslands.
They are desolate and untravelled,
　and the lowing of cattle is not heard.
The birds have all fled
　and the animals are gone.

¹¹ 'I will make Jerusalem a heap of ruins,
　a haunt of jackals;
and I will lay waste the towns of Judah
　so that no one can live there.'

¹² Who is wise enough to understand
this? Who has been instructed by the LORD
and can explain it? Why has the land been
ruined and laid waste like a desert that no

one can cross?

¹³ The LORD said, 'It is because they have forsaken my law, which I set before them; they have not obeyed me or followed my law. ¹⁴ Instead, they have followed the stubbornness of their hearts; they have followed the Baals, as their ancestors taught them.' ¹⁵ Therefore this is what the LORD Almighty, the God of Israel, says: 'See, I will make this people eat bitter food and drink poisoned water. ¹⁶ I will scatter them among nations that neither they nor their ancestors have known, and I will pursue them with the sword until I have made an end of them.'

¹⁷ This is what the LORD Almighty says:

'Consider now! Call for the wailing
  women to come;
 send for the most skilful of them.
¹⁸ Let them come quickly
 and wail over us
till our eyes overflow with tears
 and water streams from our eyelids.
¹⁹ The sound of wailing is heard from Zion:
 "How ruined we are!
How great is our shame!
We must leave our land
 because our houses are in ruins."'

²⁰ Now, you women, hear the word of the
 LORD;
 open your ears to the words of his
  mouth.
Teach your daughters how to wail;
 teach one another a lament.
²¹ Death has climbed in through our
 windows
 and has entered our fortresses;
it has removed the children from the
 streets
 and the young men from the public
 squares.

²² Say, 'This is what the LORD declares:

' "Dead bodies will lie
 like dung on the open field,
like cut corn behind the reaper,
 with no one to gather them." '

²³ This is what the LORD says:

'Let not the wise boast of their wisdom
 or the strong boast of their strength
 or the rich boast of their riches,
²⁴ but let the one who boasts boast about
 this:
 that they have the understanding to
  know me,
that I am the LORD, who exercises
 kindness,
 justice and righteousness on earth,
 for in these I delight,'
       declares the LORD.

²⁵ 'The days are coming,' declares the LORD, 'when I will punish all who are circumcised only in the flesh – ²⁶ Egypt, Judah, Edom, Ammon, Moab and all who live in the wilderness in distant places. For all these nations are really uncircumcised, and even the whole house of Israel is uncircumcised in heart.'

10 Hear what the LORD says to you, people of Israel. ² This is what the LORD says:

'Do not learn the ways of the nations
 or be terrified by signs in the heavens,
 though the nations are terrified by
  them.
³ For the practices of the peoples are
 worthless;
 they cut a tree out of the forest,
 and a craftsman shapes it with his
  chisel.
⁴ They adorn it with silver and gold;
 they fasten it with hammer and nails
 so that it will not totter.
⁵ Like a scarecrow in a cucumber field,
 their idols cannot speak;

they must be carried
  because they cannot walk.
Do not fear them;
  they can do no harm
  nor can they do any good.'

⁶ No one is like you, LORD;
  you are great,
  and your name is mighty in power.
⁷ Who should not fear you,
  King of the nations?
  This is your due.
Among all the wise leaders of the nations
  and in all their kingdoms,
  there is no one like you.

⁸ They are all senseless and foolish;
  they are taught by worthless wooden
    idols.
⁹ Hammered silver is brought from
    Tarshish
  and gold from Uphaz.
What the craftsman and goldsmith have
    made
  is then dressed in blue and purple –
  all made by skilled workers.
¹⁰ But the LORD is the true God;
  he is the living God, the eternal King.
When he is angry, the earth trembles;
  the nations cannot endure his wrath.

¹¹ 'Tell them this: "These gods, who did
not make the heavens and the earth, will
perish from the earth and from under the
heavens."'

¹² But God made the earth by his power;
  he founded the world by his wisdom
  and stretched out the heavens by his
    understanding.
¹³ When he thunders, the waters in the
    heavens roar;
  he makes clouds rise from the ends of
    the earth.
He sends lightning with the rain

and brings out the wind from his
  storehouses.

¹⁴ Everyone is senseless and without
    knowledge;
  every goldsmith is shamed by his
    idols.
The images he makes are a fraud;
  they have no breath in them.
¹⁵ They are worthless, the objects of
    mockery;
  when their judgment comes, they will
    perish.
¹⁶ He who is the Portion of Jacob is not like
    these,
  for he is the Maker of all things,
including Israel, the people of his
    inheritance –
  the LORD Almighty is his name.
¹⁷ Gather up your belongings to leave the
    land,
  you who live under siege.

··

■ **PSALM 119:28-32**

²⁸ My soul is weary with sorrow;
  strengthen me according to your
    word.
²⁹ Keep me from deceitful ways;
  be gracious to me and teach me your
    law.
³⁰ I have chosen the way of faithfulness;
  I have set my heart on your laws.
³¹ I hold fast to your statutes, LORD;
  do not let me be put to shame.
³² I run in the path of your commands,
  for you have broadened my
    understanding.

··

■ **PROVERBS 25:1-3**

25 These are more proverbs of Solomon, compiled by the men of
Hezekiah king of Judah:

²It is the glory of God to conceal a matter;
to search out a matter is the glory of
kings.
³As the heavens are high and the earth is
deep,
so the hearts of kings are
unsearchable.

....

▬ 1 THESSALONIANS
1:1–2:12

1 Paul, Silas and Timothy,

To the church of the Thessalonians in
God the Father and the Lord Jesus Christ:

Grace and peace to you.
²We always thank God for all of you and
continually mention you in our prayers.
³We remember before our God and Father
your work produced by faith, your labour
prompted by love, and your endurance inspired by hope in our Lord Jesus Christ.

⁴For we know, brothers and sisters loved
by God, that he has chosen you, ⁵because
our gospel came to you not simply with
words but also with power, with the Holy
Spirit and deep conviction. You know how
we lived among you for your sake. ⁶You became imitators of us and of the Lord, for
you welcomed the message in the midst of
severe suffering with the joy given by the
Holy Spirit. ⁷And so you became a model to
all the believers in Macedonia and Achaia.
⁸The Lord's message rang out from you not
only in Macedonia and Achaia – your faith
in God has become known everywhere.
Therefore we do not need to say anything
about it, ⁹for they themselves report what
kind of reception you gave us. They tell how

you turned to God from idols to serve the
living and true God, ¹⁰and to wait for his
Son from heaven, whom he raised from
the dead – Jesus, who rescues us from the
coming wrath.

2 You know, brothers and sisters, that
our visit to you was not without results.
²We had previously suffered and been
treated outrageously in Philippi, as you
know, but with the help of our God we dared
to tell you his gospel in the face of strong opposition. ³For the appeal we make does not
spring from error or impure motives, nor
are we trying to trick you. ⁴On the contrary,
we speak as those approved by God to be entrusted with the gospel. We are not trying to
please people but God, who tests our hearts.
⁵You know we never used flattery, nor did
we put on a mask to cover up greed – God
is our witness. ⁶We were not looking for
praise from people, not from you or anyone
else, even though as apostles of Christ we
could have asserted our authority. ⁷Instead,
we were like young children among you.

Just as a nursing mother cares for her
children, ⁸so we cared for you. Because
we loved you so much, we were delighted
to share with you not only the gospel of
God but our lives as well. ⁹Surely you remember, brothers and sisters, our toil and
hardship; we worked night and day in order not to be a burden to anyone while we
preached the gospel of God to you. ¹⁰You
are witnesses, and so is God, of how holy,
righteous and blameless we were among
you who believed. ¹¹For you know that we
dealt with each of you as a father deals
with his own children, ¹²encouraging,
comforting and urging you to live lives
worthy of God, who calls you into his
kingdom and glory.

Our Only Hope

'... I am the LORD, who exercises kindness, justice and righteousness on earth ...' **Jeremiah 9:24**

In today's church, we seem more interested in knowing about ourselves than in knowing God. The result of this is increased anxiety, depression, and a hundred other ills. However, God has revealed Himself through the Scripture in many different ways: as powerful, personal, plural, having holy love, a God of wrath, trustworthy, gracious, all-knowing, and all-wise.

It's interesting, isn't it, as our passage for today shows, that when the Lord talks about Himself in the Scriptures, it is usually in terms of His attributes or character traits: kindness, justice, righteousness, and so on. And there is a clear and definite purpose in this: the more we know of God, the more established our lives will be here on the earth.

I myself am convinced that there is nothing more important than knowing God through contemplation of Him. I am not talking about mere intellectual knowledge. I speak of the knowledge of God that comes through contemplation of Him, the ability to see life from His perspective, through His eyes. It means to look out at life's circumstances through the lens of faith, bearing in mind God's plan, to accept that whatever is happening is allowed by God and that everything comes under His personal surveillance. This kind of God-understanding and God-awareness is our only hope for coping with the problems of our day.

PRAYER

Father, I am convinced. I see that if I am to operate in a context of confidence, I can only do so as I look out at life through Your eyes. Help me to do more than glance at You occasionally. Help me to gaze on You continually. Amen.

FURTHER STUDY

Phil. 3:1-11; Col. 1:9-10
• What was Paul's desire?
• What did Paul pray for the Colossians?

October 19

▬ JEREMIAH 10:18–12:17

[18] For this is what the LORD says:
'At this time I will hurl out
those who live in this land;

I will bring distress on them
so that they may be captured.'

[19] Woe to me because of my injury!
My wound is incurable!

Yet I said to myself,
      'This is my sickness, and I must
            endure it.'
²⁰ My tent is destroyed;
      all its ropes are snapped.
My children are gone from me and are
      no more;
      no one is left now to pitch my tent
      or to set up my shelter.
²¹ The shepherds are senseless
      and do not enquire of the LORD;
so they do not prosper
      and all their flock is scattered.
²² Listen! The report is coming –
      a great commotion from the land of
            the north!
It will make the towns of Judah desolate,
      a haunt of jackals.
²³ LORD, I know that people's lives are not
            their own;
      it is not for them to direct their steps.
²⁴ Discipline me, LORD, but only in due
            measure –
      not in your anger,
      or you will reduce me to nothing.
²⁵ Pour out your wrath on the nations
      that do not acknowledge you,
      on the peoples who do not call on your
            name.
For they have devoured Jacob;
      they have devoured him completely
      and destroyed his homeland.

11 This is the word that came to Jeremiah from the Lord: ² 'Listen to the terms of this covenant and tell them to the people of Judah and to those who live in Jerusalem. ³ Tell them that this is what the Lord, the God of Israel, says: "Cursed is the one who does not obey the terms of this covenant – ⁴ the terms I commanded your ancestors when I brought them out of Egypt, out of the iron-smelting furnace." I said, "Obey me and do everything I command you, and you will be my people, and I will be your God. ⁵ Then I will fulfil the oath I swore

to your ancestors, to give them a land flowing with milk and honey" – the land you possess today.'

I answered, 'Amen, LORD.'

⁶ The LORD said to me, 'Proclaim all these words in the towns of Judah and in the streets of Jerusalem: "Listen to the terms of this covenant and follow them. ⁷ From the time I brought your ancestors up from Egypt until today, I warned them again and again, saying, 'Obey me.' ⁸ But they did not listen or pay attention; instead, they followed the stubbornness of their evil hearts. So I brought on them all the curses of the covenant I had commanded them to follow but that they did not keep."'

⁹ Then the LORD said to me, 'There is a conspiracy among the people of Judah and those who live in Jerusalem. ¹⁰ They have returned to the sins of their ancestors, who refused to listen to my words. They have followed other gods to serve them. Both Israel and Judah have broken the covenant I made with their ancestors. ¹¹ Therefore this is what the LORD says: "I will bring on them a disaster they cannot escape. Although they cry out to me, I will not listen to them. ¹² The towns of Judah and the people of Jerusalem will go and cry out to the gods to whom they burn incense, but they will not help them at all when disaster strikes. ¹³ You, Judah, have as many gods as you have towns; and the altars you have set up to burn incense to that shameful god Baal are as many as the streets of Jerusalem."

¹⁴ 'Do not pray for this people or offer any plea or petition for them, because I will not listen when they call to me in the time of their distress.

¹⁵ 'What is my beloved doing in my temple
      as she, with many others, works out
            her evil schemes?
Can consecrated meat avert your
            punishment?
When you engage in your wickedness,
      then you rejoice.'

¹⁶ The LORD called you a thriving olive tree
     with fruit beautiful in form.
  But with the roar of a mighty storm
     he will set it on fire,
     and its branches will be broken.

¹⁷ The LORD Almighty, who planted you, has decreed disaster for you, because the people of both Israel and Judah have done evil and aroused my anger by burning incense to Baal.

¹⁸ Because the LORD revealed their plot to me, I knew it, for at that time he showed me what they were doing. ¹⁹ I had been like a gentle lamb led to the slaughter; I did not realise that they had plotted against me, saying,

  'Let us destroy the tree and its fruit;
     let us cut him off from the land of the
        living,
     that his name be remembered no
        more.'

²⁰ But you, LORD Almighty, who judge
     righteously
     and test the heart and mind,
  let me see your vengeance on them,
     for to you I have committed my cause.

²¹ Therefore this is what the LORD says about the people of Anathoth who are threatening to kill you, saying, "Do not prophesy in the name of the LORD or you will die by our hands" – ²² therefore this is what the LORD Almighty says: "I will punish them. Their young men will die by the sword, their sons and daughters by famine. ²³ Not even a remnant will be left to them, because I will bring disaster on the people of Anathoth in the year of their punishment.'"

12 You are always righteous, LORD,
     when I bring a case before you.
  Yet I would speak with you about your
     justice:
  Why does the way of the wicked
     prosper?

  Why do all the faithless live at ease?
² You have planted them, and they have
     taken root;
     they grow and bear fruit.
  You are always on their lips
     but far from their hearts.
³ Yet you know me, LORD;
     you see me and test my thoughts about
        you.
  Drag them off like sheep to be butchered!
     Set them apart for the day of
        slaughter!
⁴ How long will the land lie parched
     and the grass in every field be
        withered?
  Because those who live in it are wicked,
     the animals and birds have perished.
  Moreover, the people are saying,
     'He will not see what happens to us.'
⁵ 'If you have raced with men on foot
     and they have worn you out,
     how can you compete with horses?
  If you stumble in safe country,
     how will you manage in the thickets
        by the Jordan?
⁶ Your relatives, members of your own
     family –
     even they have betrayed you;
     they have raised a loud cry against
        you.
  Do not trust them,
     though they speak well of you.

⁷ 'I will forsake my house,
     abandon my inheritance;
  I will give the one I love
     into the hands of her enemies.
⁸ My inheritance has become to me
     like a lion in the forest.
  She roars at me;
     therefore I hate her.
⁹ Has not my inheritance become to me
     like a speckled bird of prey
     that other birds of prey surround and
        attack?
  Go and gather all the wild beasts;

bring them to devour.
¹⁰ Many shepherds will ruin my vineyard
and trample down my field;
they will turn my pleasant field
into a desolate wasteland.
¹¹ It will be made a wasteland,
parched and desolate before me;
the whole land will be laid waste
because there is no one who cares.
¹² Over all the barren heights in the desert
destroyers will swarm,
for the sword of the LORD will devour
from one end of the land to the other;
no one will be safe.
¹³ They will sow wheat but reap thorns;
they will wear themselves out but gain
nothing.
They will bear the shame of their harvest
because of the LORD's fierce anger.'

¹⁴ This is what the LORD says: 'As for all my wicked neighbours who seize the inheritance I gave to my people Israel, I will uproot them from their lands and I will uproot the people of Judah from among them. ¹⁵ But after I uproot them, I will again have compassion and will bring each of them back to their own inheritance and their own country. ¹⁶ And if they learn well the ways of my people and swear by my name, saying, "As surely as the LORD lives" – even as they once taught my people to swear by Baal – then they will be established among my people. ¹⁷ But if any nation does not listen, I will completely uproot and destroy it,' declares the LORD.

▬ PSALM 119:33-36

³³ Teach me, LORD, the way of your decrees,
that I may follow it to the end.
³⁴ Give me understanding, so that I may
keep your law
and obey it with all my heart.
³⁵ Direct me in the path of your commands,

for there I find delight.
³⁶ Turn my heart towards your statutes
and not towards selfish gain.

▬ PROVERBS 25:4-7

⁴ Remove the dross from the silver,
and a silversmith can produce a vessel;
⁵ remove wicked officials from the king's
presence,
and his throne will be established
through righteousness.

⁶ Do not exalt yourself in the king's
presence,
and do not claim a place among his
great men;
⁷ it is better for him to say to you, 'Come
up here,'
than for him to humiliate you before
his nobles.

▬ 1 THESSALONIANS 2:13-3:13

¹³ And we also thank God continually because, when you received the word of God, which you heard from us, you accepted it not as a human word, but as it actually is, the word of God, which is indeed at work in you who believe. ¹⁴ For you, brothers and sisters, became imitators of God's churches in Judea, which are in Christ Jesus: you suffered from your own people the same things those churches suffered from the Jews ¹⁵ who killed the Lord Jesus and the prophets and also drove us out. They displease God and are hostile to everyone ¹⁶ in their effort to keep us from speaking to the Gentiles so that they may be saved. In this way they always heap up their sins to the limit. The wrath of God has come upon them at last.
¹⁷ But, brothers and sisters, when we were orphaned by being separated from you for a

short time (in person, not in thought), out of our intense longing we made every effort to see you. [18] For we wanted to come to you – certainly I, Paul, did, again and again – but Satan blocked our way. [19] For what is our hope, our joy, or the crown in which we will glory in the presence of our Lord Jesus when he comes? Is it not you? [20] Indeed, you are our glory and joy.

3 So when we could stand it no longer, we thought it best to be left by ourselves in Athens. [2] We sent Timothy, who is our brother and co-worker in God's service in spreading the gospel of Christ, to strengthen and encourage you in your faith, [3] so that no one would be unsettled by these trials. For you know quite well that we are destined for them. [4] In fact, when we were with you, we kept telling you that we would be persecuted. And it turned out that way, as you well know. [5] For this reason, when I could stand it no longer, I sent to find out about your faith. I was afraid that in some way the tempter had tempted you and that our labours might have been in vain.

[6] But Timothy has just now come to us from you and has brought good news about your faith and love. He has told us that you always have pleasant memories of us and that you long to see us, just as we also long to see you. [7] Therefore, brothers and sisters, in all our distress and persecution we were encouraged about you because of your faith. [8] For now we really live, since you are standing firm in the Lord. [9] How can we thank God enough for you in return for all the joy we have in the presence of our God because of you? [10] Night and day we pray most earnestly that we may see you again and supply what is lacking in your faith.

[11] Now may our God and Father himself and our Lord Jesus clear the way for us to come to you. [12] May the Lord make your love increase and overflow for each other and for everyone else, just as ours does for you. [13] May he strengthen your hearts so that you will be blameless and holy in the presence of our God and Father when our Lord Jesus comes with all his holy ones.

The Power of Truth

'I have chosen the way of faithfulness; I have set my heart on your laws.' **Psalm 119:30**

We cannot do battle with the Devil until we have girded our waists with truth. Girding the waist was always a symbol of readiness to fight. That is why this comes first. The officers in the Roman army wore short skirts, very much like a Scottish kilt. Over this they had a cloak or tunic which was secured at the waist with a girdle. When they were about to enter battle, they would tuck the tunic up under the girdle so as to leave their legs unencumbered for the fight.

What does Paul's phrase, 'with the belt of truth buckled round your waist' (Eph. 6:14) really mean? What significance does it have for us today? The word 'truth' can be looked at in two ways: one, objective truth, as it is to be found in Jesus Christ, and two, subjective truth as it is to be found in the qualities of honesty and sincerity. The Puritan, William Gurnall, points out that whether the word implies truth of doctrine or truth of heart, one kind of truth will not do without the other.

I believe that in Ephesians 6, Paul is emphasising subjective truth - truth that resides in the inner being. When we are deceitful or hypocritical, or when we resort to intrigue and scheming, we are playing the Devil's game. And we will never be able to beat the Devil at his own game!

What Satan despises is transparent truth. He flees from it as quickly as darkness runs from the dawn. Having our waists girded with truth, then, means being possessed with truth, guided by truth, and controlled by truth. Where truth is absent, we have no power over Satan. It is as simple as that.

PRAYER

O Father, I see that You have set standards by which I rise or fall. When I fulfil them, I rise - when I break them, I fall. Give me the strength I need to fulfil all Your laws, especially the law of truth. In Jesus' name. Amen.

FURTHER STUDY

John 8:34-45; Col. 3:9; Psa. 51:6; Prov. 12:22
- What can protect us from the Devil?
- Where should we desire truth?

October 20

■ JEREMIAH 13:1–15:4

13 This is what the LORD said to me: 'Go and buy a linen belt and put it round your waist, but do not let it touch water.' ²So I bought a belt, as the LORD directed, and put it round my waist.

³Then the word of the LORD came to me a second time: ⁴'Take the belt you bought and are wearing round your waist, and go now to Perath and hide it there in a crevice in the rocks.' ⁵So I went and hid it at Perath, as the LORD told me.

⁶Many days later the LORD said to me, 'Go now to Perath and get the belt I told you to hide there.' ⁷So I went to Perath and dug up the belt and took it from the place where I had hidden it, but now it was ruined and completely useless.

⁸Then the word of the LORD came to me: ⁹'This is what the LORD says: "In the same way I will ruin the pride of Judah and the great pride of Jerusalem. ¹⁰These wicked people, who refuse to listen to my words, who follow the stubbornness of their hearts and go after other gods to serve and worship them, will be like this belt – completely useless! ¹¹For as a belt is bound round the waist, so I bound all the people of Israel and all the people of Judah to me," declares the LORD, "to be my people for my renown and praise and honour. But they have not listened."

¹²'Say to them: "This is what the LORD, the God of Israel, says: every wineskin should be filled with wine." And if they say to you, "Don't we know that every wineskin should be filled with wine?" ¹³then tell them, "This is what the LORD says: I am going to fill with drunkenness all who live in this land, including the kings who sit on David's throne, the priests, the prophets and all those living in Jerusalem. ¹⁴I will smash them one against the other, parents and children alike, declares the LORD. I will allow no pity

or mercy or compassion to keep me from
destroying them."'

¹⁵ Hear and pay attention,
     do not be arrogant,
     for the LORD has spoken.
¹⁶ Give glory to the LORD your God
     before he brings the darkness,
     before your feet stumble
     on the darkening hills.
You hope for light,
     but he will turn it to utter darkness
     and change it to deep gloom.
¹⁷ If you do not listen,
     I will weep in secret
     because of your pride;
my eyes will weep bitterly,
     overflowing with tears,
     because the LORD's flock will be taken
     captive.

¹⁸ Say to the king and to the queen mother,
     'Come down from your thrones,
     for your glorious crowns
     will fall from your heads.'
¹⁹ The cities in the Negev will be shut up,
     and there will be no one to open them.
All Judah will be carried into exile,
     carried completely away.

²⁰ Look up and see
     those who are coming from the north.
Where is the flock that was entrusted to
     you,
     the sheep of which you boasted?
²¹ What will you say when the LORD sets
     over you
     those you cultivated as your special
     allies?
Will not pain grip you
     like that of a woman in labour?
²² And if you ask yourself,
     'Why has this happened to me?' –
     it is because of your many sins
     that your skirts have been torn off
     and your body ill-treated.

²³ Can an Ethiopian change his skin
     or a leopard its spots?
Neither can you do good
     who are accustomed to doing evil.

²⁴ 'I will scatter you like chaff
     driven by the desert wind.
²⁵ This is your lot,
     the portion I have decreed for you,'
         declares the LORD,
     'because you have forgotten me
     and trusted in false gods.
²⁶ I will pull up your skirts over your face
     that your shame may be seen –
²⁷ your adulteries and lustful neighings,
     your shameless prostitution!
I have seen your detestable acts
     on the hills and in the fields.
Woe to you, Jerusalem!
     How long will you be unclean?'

14 This is the word of the Lord that came
to Jeremiah concerning the drought:

² 'Judah mourns,
     her cities languish;
they wail for the land,
     and a cry goes up from Jerusalem.
³ The nobles send their servants for water;
     they go to the cisterns
     but find no water.
They return with their jars unfilled;
     dismayed and despairing,
     they cover their heads.
⁴ The ground is cracked
     because there is no rain in the land;
the farmers are dismayed
     and cover their heads.
⁵ Even the doe in the field
     deserts her newborn fawn
     because there is no grass.
⁶ Wild donkeys stand on the barren
     heights
     and pant like jackals;
their eyes fail
     for lack of food.'

⁷Although our sins testify against us,
  do something, LORD, for the sake of
    your name.
  For we have often rebelled;
    we have sinned against you.
⁸You who are the hope of Israel,
  its Saviour in times of distress,
  why are you like a stranger in the land,
    like a traveller who stays only a night?
⁹Why are you like a man taken by
    surprise,
  like a warrior powerless to save?
  You are among us, LORD,
    and we bear your name;
  do not forsake us!

¹⁰This is what the LORD says about this
people:

'They greatly love to wander;
  they do not restrain their feet.
So the LORD does not accept them;
  he will now remember their
    wickedness
  and punish them for their sins.'

¹¹Then the LORD said to me, 'Do not pray
for the well-being of this people. ¹²Although
they fast, I will not listen to their cry;
though they offer burnt offerings and grain
offerings, I will not accept them. Instead, I
will destroy them with the sword, famine
and plague.'

¹³But I said, 'Alas, Sovereign LORD! The
prophets keep telling them, "You will not
see the sword or suffer famine. Indeed, I
will give you lasting peace in this place."'

¹⁴Then the LORD said to me, 'The prophets are prophesying lies in my name. I have
not sent them or appointed them or spoken
to them. They are prophesying to you false
visions, divinations, idolatries and the delusions of their own minds. ¹⁵Therefore this
is what the LORD says about the prophets
who are prophesying in my name: I did not
send them, yet they are saying, "No sword

or famine will touch this land." Those same
prophets will perish by sword and famine.
¹⁶And the people they are prophesying to
will be thrown out into the streets of Jerusalem because of the famine and sword. There
will be no one to bury them, their wives,
their sons and their daughters. I will pour
out on them the calamity they deserve.

¹⁷'Speak this word to them:

'"Let my eyes overflow with tears
  night and day without ceasing;
for the Virgin Daughter, my people,
  has suffered a grievous wound,
    a crushing blow.
¹⁸If I go into the country,
  I see those slain by the sword;
if I go into the city,
  I see the ravages of famine.
Both prophet and priest
  have gone to a land they know not."'

¹⁹Have you rejected Judah completely?
  Do you despise Zion?
Why have you afflicted us
  so that we cannot be healed?
We hoped for peace
  but no good has come,
for a time of healing
  but there is only terror.
²⁰We acknowledge our wickedness, LORD,
  and the guilt of our ancestors;
  we have indeed sinned against you.
²¹For the sake of your name do not despise
    us;
  do not dishonour your glorious throne.
  Remember your covenant with us
    and do not break it.
²²Do any of the worthless idols of the
    nations bring rain?
  Do the skies themselves send down
    showers?
No, it is you, LORD our God.
  Therefore our hope is in you,
  for you are the one who does all this.

15 Then the LORD said to me: 'Even if Moses and Samuel were to stand before me, my heart would not go out to this people. Send them away from my presence! Let them go! ²And if they ask you, "Where shall we go?" tell them, "This is what the LORD says:

'"Those destined for death, to death;
those for the sword, to the sword;
those for starvation, to starvation;
those for captivity, to captivity."

³'I will send four kinds of destroyers against them,' declares the LORD, 'the sword to kill and the dogs to drag away and the birds and the wild animals to devour and destroy. ⁴I will make them abhorrent to all the kingdoms of the earth because of what Manasseh son of Hezekiah king of Judah did in Jerusalem.

▬ PSALM 119:37–40

³⁷ Turn my eyes away from worthless things;
preserve my life according to your word.
³⁸ Fulfil your promise to your servant,
so that you may be feared.
³⁹ Take away the disgrace I dread,
for your laws are good.
⁴⁰ How I long for your precepts!
In your righteousness preserve my life.

▬ PROVERBS 25:8–10

What you have seen with your eyes
8   do not bring hastily to court,
for what will you do in the end
if your neighbour puts you to shame?

⁹ If you take your neighbour to court,
do not betray another's confidence,

¹⁰ or the one who hears it may shame you
and the charge against you will stand.

▬ 1 THESSALONIANS 4:1–5:7

4 As for other matters, brothers and sisters, we instructed you how to live in order to please God, as in fact you are living. Now we ask you and urge you in the Lord Jesus to do this more and more. ²For you know what instructions we gave you by the authority of the Lord Jesus.

³It is God's will that you should be sanctified: that you should avoid sexual immorality; ⁴that each of you should learn to control your own body in a way that is holy and honourable, ⁵not in passionate lust like the pagans, who do not know God; ⁶and that in this matter no one should wrong or take advantage of a brother or sister. The Lord will punish all those who commit such sins, as we told you and warned you before. ⁷For God did not call us to be impure, but to live a holy life. ⁸Therefore, anyone who rejects this instruction does not reject a human being but God, the very God who gives you his Holy Spirit.

⁹Now about your love for one another we do not need to write to you, for you yourselves have been taught by God to love each other. ¹⁰And in fact, you do love all of God's family throughout Macedonia. Yet we urge you, brothers and sisters, to do so more and more, ¹¹and to make it your ambition to lead a quiet life: you should mind your own business and work with your hands, just as we told you, ¹²so that your daily life may win the respect of outsiders and so that you will not be dependent on anybody.

¹³Brothers and sisters, we do not want you to be uninformed about those who sleep in death, so that you do not grieve like the rest of mankind, who have no hope. ¹⁴For we believe that Jesus died and rose again, and so we believe that God will bring with Jesus

those who have fallen asleep in him. ¹⁵According to the Lord's word, we tell you that we who are still alive, who are left until the coming of the Lord, will certainly not precede those who have fallen asleep. ¹⁶For the Lord himself will come down from heaven, with a loud command, with the voice of the archangel and with the trumpet call of God, and the dead in Christ will rise first. ¹⁷After that, we who are still alive and are left will be caught up together with them in the clouds to meet the Lord in the air. And so we will be with the Lord for ever. ¹⁸Therefore encourage one another with these words.

5 Now, brothers and sisters, about times and dates we do not need to write to you, ²for you know very well that the day of the Lord will come like a thief in the night. ³While people are saying, 'Peace and safety', destruction will come on them suddenly, as labour pains on a pregnant woman, and they will not escape.

⁴But you, brothers and sisters, are not in darkness so that this day should surprise you like a thief. ⁵You are all children of the light and children of the day. We do not belong to the night or to the darkness. ⁶So then, let us not be like others, who are asleep, but let us be awake and sober. ⁷For those who sleep, sleep at night, and those who get drunk, get drunk at night.

Precise Scripture

'This is what the LORD said ...' **Jeremiah 13:1**

Let us focus on what is meant by the phrase – 'the sword of the Spirit, which is the word of God.' The sword is the Word of God – the Bible, the inspired Scriptures.

In Matthew 4:4 and 4:7, we see a perfect illustration of how Jesus used the sword of the Spirit when rebutting the temptations of the Devil when He begins His response, 'It is written ...' and 'It is also written ...' Notice how, prior to the temptation, Jesus was anointed by the Holy Spirit (Matt. 3:13-17). Next we are informed that Jesus was 'led by the Spirit into the wilderness to be tempted by the devil' (4:1).

During the temptation our Lord, filled with the Spirit, resisted every one of the Devil's statements by using the precise words of Scripture. Follow me closely, for this is extremely important: Christ did not merely utter a newly formed statement or something that came to Him on the spur of the moment, but quoted a text which had already been given by God and written down. The weapon used by our Lord was the Word of God, the Scriptures.

Can you see the point I am making? Satan is not rebuffed by clever phrases that are made up on the spur of the moment and sound theologically sophisticated and refined. He is defeated only when we quote to him the precise words of Scripture. If this was the strategy Jesus had to use, then how much more you and I.

Nothing defeats Satan more thoroughly and effectively than the sword of the Spirit, which is the Word of God.

PRAYER

O God, open my eyes that I might see more clearly than ever the power and authority that lies in Your sacred Word, the Bible. Help me to know it better. For Your own dear name's sake. Amen.

FURTHER STUDY

1 Pet. 1:13-25; Psa. 119:89,103; Jer. 15:16
- What did Jeremiah do with God's Word?
- How did the psalmist describe it?

October 21

■ JEREMIAH 15:5–17:18

5 'Who will have pity on you, Jerusalem?
    Who will mourn for you?
    Who will stop to ask how you are?
6 You have rejected me,' declares the LORD.
    'You keep on backsliding.
  So I will reach out and destroy you;
    I am tired of holding back.
7 I will winnow them with a winnowing
      fork
    at the city gates of the land.
  I will bring bereavement and destruction
      on my people,
    for they have not changed their ways.
8 I will make their widows more numerous
      than the sand of the sea.
  At midday I will bring a destroyer
    against the mothers of their young men;
  suddenly I will bring down on them
    anguish and terror.
9 The mother of seven will grow faint
    and breathe her last.
  Her sun will set while it is still day;
    she will be disgraced and humiliated.
  I will put the survivors to the sword
    before their enemies,'
                    declares the LORD.

10 Alas, my mother, that you gave me birth,
    a man with whom the whole land
      strives and contends!

I have neither lent nor borrowed,
    yet everyone curses me.

11 The LORD said,

'Surely I will deliver you for a good
      purpose;
    surely I will make your enemies plead
      with you
    in times of disaster and times of
      distress.

12 'Can a man break iron –
    iron from the north – or bronze?

13 'Your wealth and your treasures
    I will give as plunder, without charge,
  because of all your sins
    throughout your country.
14 I will enslave you to your enemies
    in a land you do not know,
  for my anger will kindle a fire
    that will burn against you.'

15 LORD, you understand;
    remember me and care for me.
  Avenge me on my persecutors.
  You are long-suffering – do not take me
      away;
    think of how I suffer reproach for your
      sake.
16 When your words came, I ate them;

they were my joy and my heart's delight,
for I bear your name,
LORD God Almighty.
¹⁷ I never sat in the company of revellers,
never made merry with them;
I sat alone because your hand was on me
and you had filled me with
indignation.
¹⁸ Why is my pain unending
and my wound grievous and
incurable?
You are to me like a deceptive brook,
like a spring that fails.

¹⁹ Therefore this is what the LORD says:

'If you repent, I will restore you
that you may serve me;
if you utter worthy, not worthless, words,
you will be my spokesman.
Let this people turn to you,
but you must not turn to them.
²⁰ I will make you a wall to this people,
a fortified wall of bronze;
they will fight against you
but will not overcome you,
for I am with you
to rescue and save you,'
declares the LORD.
²¹ 'I will save you from the hands of the
wicked
and deliver you from the grasp of the
cruel.'

16 Then the word of the Lord came to
me: ² 'You must not marry and have
sons or daughters in this place.' ³ For this
is what the Lord says about the sons and
daughters born in this land and about the
women who are their mothers and the men
who are their fathers: ⁴ 'They will die of
deadly diseases. They will not be mourned
or buried but will be like dung lying on the
ground. They will perish by sword and famine, and their dead bodies will become food
for the birds and the wild animals.'

⁵ For this is what the LORD says: 'Do not enter a house where there is a funeral meal; do
not go to mourn or show sympathy, because
I have withdrawn my blessing, my love and
my pity from this people,' declares the LORD.
⁶ 'Both high and low will die in this land.
They will not be buried or mourned, and no
one will cut themselves or shave their head
for the dead. ⁷ No one will offer food to comfort those who mourn for the dead – not even
for a father or a mother – nor will anyone
give them a drink to console them.

⁸ 'And do not enter a house where there is
feasting and sit down to eat and drink. ⁹ For
this is what the LORD Almighty, the God of
Israel, says: Before your eyes and in your
days I will bring an end to the sounds of joy
and gladness and to the voices of bride and
bridegroom in this place.

¹⁰ 'When you tell these people all this and
they ask you, "Why has the LORD decreed
such a great disaster against us? What wrong
have we done? What sin have we committed against the LORD our God?" ¹¹ then say to
them, "It is because your ancestors forsook
me," declares the LORD, "and followed other gods and served and worshipped them.
They forsook me and did not keep my law.
¹² But you have behaved more wickedly than
your ancestors. See how all of you are following the stubbornness of your evil hearts
instead of obeying me. ¹³ So I will throw you
out of this land into a land neither you nor
your ancestors have known, and there you
will serve other gods day and night, for I will
show you no favour."

¹⁴ 'However, the days are coming,' declares
the LORD, 'when it will no longer be said, "As
surely as the LORD lives, who brought the Israelites up out of Egypt," ¹⁵ but it will be said,
"As surely as the LORD lives, who brought
the Israelites up out of the land of the north
and out of all the countries where he had
banished them." For I will restore them to
the land I gave to their ancestors.

¹⁶ 'But now I will send for many fishermen,'

declares the LORD, 'and they will catch them.
After that I will send for many hunters, and
they will hunt them down on every mountain
and hill and from the crevices of the rocks.
¹⁷ My eyes are on all their ways; they are not
hidden from me, nor is their sin concealed
from my eyes. ¹⁸ I will repay them double
for their wickedness and their sin, because
they have defiled my land with the lifeless
forms of their vile images and have filled my
inheritance with their detestable idols.'

¹⁹ LORD, my strength and my fortress,
   my refuge in time of distress,
to you the nations will come
   from the ends of the earth and say,
'Our ancestors possessed nothing but
      false gods,
   worthless idols that did them no good.
²⁰ Do people make their own gods?
   Yes, but they are not gods!'

²¹ 'Therefore I will teach them –
   this time I will teach them
   my power and might.
Then they will know
   that my name is the LORD.

17 'Judah's sin is engraved with an iron
   tool,
   inscribed with a flint point,
on the tablets of their hearts
   and on the horns of their altars.
² Even their children remember
   their altars and Asherah poles
beside the spreading trees
   and on the high hills.
³ My mountain in the land
   and your wealth and all your treasures
I will give away as plunder,
   together with your high places,
   because of sin throughout your
      country.
⁴ Through your own fault you will lose
   the inheritance I gave you.
I will enslave you to your enemies

in a land you do not know,
for you have kindled my anger,
   and it will burn for ever.'

⁵ This is what the LORD says:

'Cursed is the one who trusts in man,
   who draws strength from mere flesh
   and whose heart turns away from the
      LORD.
⁶ That person will be like a bush in the
      wastelands;
   they will not see prosperity when it
      comes.
They will dwell in the parched places of
      the desert,
   in a salt land where no one lives.

⁷ 'But blessed is the one who trusts in the
      LORD,
   whose confidence is in him.
⁸ They will be like a tree planted by the
      water
   that sends out its roots by the stream.
It does not fear when heat comes;
   its leaves are always green.
It has no worries in a year of drought
   and never fails to bear fruit.'

⁹ The heart is deceitful above all things
   and beyond cure.
   Who can understand it?

¹⁰ 'I the LORD search the heart
   and examine the mind,
to reward each person according to their
      conduct,
   according to what their deeds
      deserve.'

¹¹ Like a partridge that hatches eggs it did
      not lay
   are those who gain riches by unjust
      means.
When their lives are half gone, their
   riches will desert them,

and in the end they will prove to be
    fools.
¹² A glorious throne, exalted from the
    beginning,
    is the place of our sanctuary.
¹³ LORD, you are the hope of Israel;
    all who forsake you will be put to
    shame.
Those who turn away from you will be
    written in the dust
    because they have forsaken the LORD,
    the spring of living water.

¹⁴ Heal me, LORD, and I shall be healed;
    save me and I shall be saved,
    for you are the one I praise.
¹⁵ They keep saying to me,
    'Where is the word of the LORD?
    Let it now be fulfilled!'
¹⁶ I have not run away from being your
    shepherd;
    you know I have not desired the day of
    despair.
    What passes my lips is open before
    you.
¹⁷ Do not be a terror to me;
    you are my refuge in the day of
    disaster.
¹⁸ Let my persecutors be put to shame,
    but keep me from shame;
    let them be terrified,
    but keep me from terror.
Bring on them the day of disaster;
    destroy them with double destruction.

■ PSALM 119:41-44

⁴¹ May your unfailing love come to me,
    LORD,
    your salvation, according to your
    promise;
⁴² then I can answer anyone who taunts
    me,
    for I trust in your word.

⁴³ Never take your word of truth from my
    mouth,
    for I have put my hope in your laws.
⁴⁴ I will always obey your law,
    for ever and ever.

■ PROVERBS 25:11-12

¹¹ Like apples of gold in settings of silver
    is a ruling rightly given.
¹² Like an earring of gold or an ornament of
    fine gold
    is the rebuke of a wise judge to a
    listening ear.

■ 1 THESSALONIANS 5:8-28

⁸ But since we belong to the day, let us be
sober, putting on faith and love as a breastplate, and the hope of salvation as a helmet.
⁹ For God did not appoint us to suffer wrath
but to receive salvation through our Lord
Jesus Christ. ¹⁰ He died for us so that, whether we are awake or asleep, we may live together with him. ¹¹ Therefore encourage one
another and build each other up, just as in
fact you are doing.

¹² Now we ask you, brothers and sisters, to
acknowledge those who work hard among
you, who care for you in the Lord and who
admonish you. ¹³ Hold them in the highest
regard in love because of their work. Live in
peace with each other. ¹⁴ And we urge you,
brothers and sisters, warn those who are idle
and disruptive, encourage the disheartened,
help the weak, be patient with everyone.
¹⁵ Make sure that nobody pays back wrong
for wrong, but always strive to do what is
good for each other and for everyone else.

¹⁶ Rejoice always, ¹⁷ pray continually,
¹⁸ give thanks in all circumstances; for this
is God's will for you in Christ Jesus.

¹⁹ Do not quench the Spirit. ²⁰ Do not treat
prophecies with contempt ²¹ but test them

all; hold on to what is good, ²²reject every kind of evil.

²³May God himself, the God of peace, sanctify you through and through. May your whole spirit, soul and body be kept blameless at the coming of our Lord Jesus Christ. ²⁴The one who calls you is faithful, and he will do it.

²⁵Brothers and sisters, pray for us. ²⁶Greet all God's people with a holy kiss. ²⁷I charge you before the Lord to have this letter read to all the brothers and sisters.

²⁸The grace of our Lord Jesus Christ be with you.

Don't Dampen the Spirit

'Do not quench the Spirit.' **1 Thessalonians 5:19**

The sin described in Scripture as 'blasphemy against the Spirit' rarely occurs in the life of a Christian. It is rather a conscious resistance, and anyone worrying about it has not committed it. There is, however, a more frequent sin. It is one that almost all Christians have committed and is known as 'quenching the Spirit'.

How do we 'quench' the Holy Spirit? We can do this in many ways, but the chief way is by refusing to let Him have full control of our lives. *The Amplified Bible* says: 'Do not quench (suppress or subdue) the (Holy) Spirit.' You see, it is possible for you to possess the Holy Spirit without the Holy Spirit possessing you. Dr Handley Moule, who was the Bishop of Durham at the beginning of the 20th century, used to say: 'The difference between someone who is quenching the Spirit and someone who is allowing the Spirit to have free course in their life, is the difference between a well in which there is a spring of water choked, and a well in which the obstruction is removed so that the water springs up and fills the well.' If we are choked by fears, resentments, indecision and self-centredness, then we are suppressing the Holy Spirit who resides in us in order to free us.

We need not be afraid to surrender completely to the Spirit, allowing Him to have full control of our lives.

PRAYER

O God, forgive me, I pray, for not allowing Your Holy Spirit to have full sway in my life and experience. Let Your divine fire burn within me, and help me not to dampen it. For Jesus' sake. Amen.

FURTHER STUDY

Acts 10:34-48; 2 Cor. 3:17; Rom. 8:2; Luke 4:18

• What happened while Peter was preaching?
• What liberty did this bring?

October 22

▬ JEREMIAH 17:19–20:6

¹⁹This is what the LORD said to me: 'Go and stand at the Gate of the People, through which the kings of Judah go in and out; stand also at all the other gates of Jerusalem. ²⁰Say to them, "Hear the word of the LORD, you kings of Judah and all people of Judah and everyone living in Jerusalem who come through these gates. ²¹This is what the LORD says: be careful not to carry a load on the Sabbath day or bring it through the gates of Jerusalem. ²²Do not bring a load out of your houses or do any work on the Sabbath, but keep the Sabbath day holy, as I commanded your ancestors. ²³Yet they did not listen or pay attention; they were stiff-necked and would not listen or respond to discipline. ²⁴But if you are careful to obey me, declares the LORD, and bring no load through the gates of this city on the Sabbath, but keep the Sabbath day holy by not doing any work on it, ²⁵then kings who sit on David's throne will come through the gates of this city with their officials. They and their officials will come riding in chariots and on horses, accompanied by the men of Judah and those living in Jerusalem, and this city will be inhabited for ever. ²⁶People will come from the towns of Judah and the villages around Jerusalem, from the territory of Benjamin and the western foothills, from the hill country and the Negev, bringing burnt offerings and sacrifices, grain offerings and incense, and bringing thank-offerings to the house of the LORD. ²⁷But if you do not obey me to keep the Sabbath day holy by not carrying any load as you come through the gates of Jerusalem on the Sabbath day, then I will kindle an unquenchable fire in the gates of Jerusalem that will consume her fortresses."'

18 This is the word that came to Jeremiah from the LORD: ²'Go down to the potter's house, and there I will give you my message.' ³So I went down to the potter's house, and I saw him working at the wheel. ⁴But the pot he was shaping from the clay was marred in his hands; so the potter formed it into another pot, shaping it as seemed best to him.

⁵Then the word of the LORD came to me. ⁶He said, 'Can I not do with you, Israel, as this potter does?' declares the LORD. 'Like clay in the hand of the potter, so are you in my hand, Israel. ⁷If at any time I announce that a nation or kingdom is to be uprooted, torn down and destroyed, ⁸and if that nation I warned repents of its evil, then I will relent and not inflict on it the disaster I had planned. ⁹And if at another time I announce that a nation or kingdom is to be built up and planted, ¹⁰and if it does evil in my sight and does not obey me, then I will reconsider the good I had intended to do for it.

¹¹'Now therefore say to the people of Judah and those living in Jerusalem, "This is what the LORD says: look! I am preparing a disaster for you and devising a plan against you. So turn from your evil ways, each one of you, and reform your ways and your actions." ¹²But they will reply, "It's no use. We will continue with our own plans; we will all follow the stubbornness of our evil hearts."'

¹³Therefore this is what the LORD says:

'Enquire among the nations:
    who has ever heard anything like this?
A most horrible thing has been done
    by Virgin Israel.

¹⁴ Does the snow of Lebanon
    ever vanish from its rocky slopes?
Do its cool waters from distant sources
    ever stop flowing?
¹⁵ Yet my people have forgotten me;
    they burn incense to worthless idols,
which made them stumble in their ways,
    in the ancient paths.
They made them walk in byways,
    on roads not built up.
¹⁶ Their land will be an object of horror
    and of lasting scorn;
all who pass by will be appalled
    and will shake their heads.
¹⁷ Like a wind from the east,
    I will scatter them before their
        enemies;
    I will show them my back and not my
        face
    in the day of their disaster.'

¹⁸ They said, 'Come, let's make plans against Jeremiah; for the teaching of the law by the priest will not cease, nor will counsel from the wise, nor the word from the prophets. So come, let's attack him with our tongues and pay no attention to anything he says.'

¹⁹ Listen to me, LORD;
    hear what my accusers are saying!
²⁰ Should good be repaid with evil?
    Yet they have dug a pit for me.
Remember that I stood before you
    and spoke on their behalf
    to turn your wrath away from them.
²¹ So give their children over to famine;
    hand them over to the power of the
        sword.
Let their wives be made childless and
        widows;
    let their men be put to death,
    their young men slain by the sword in
        battle.
²² Let a cry be heard from their houses

when you suddenly bring invaders
        against them,
for they have dug a pit to capture me
    and have hidden snares for my feet.
²³ But you, LORD, know
    all their plots to kill me.
Do not forgive their crimes
    or blot out their sins from your sight.
Let them be overthrown before you;
    deal with them in the time of your
        anger.

19 This is what the LORD says: 'Go and buy a clay jar from a potter. Take along some of the elders of the people and of the priests ²and go out to the Valley of Ben Hinnom, near the entrance of the Potsherd Gate. There proclaim the words I tell you, ³and say, "Hear the word of the LORD, you kings of Judah and people of Jerusalem. This is what the LORD Almighty, the God of Israel, says: listen! I am going to bring a disaster on this place that will make the ears of everyone who hears of it tingle. ⁴For they have forsaken me and made this a place of foreign gods; they have burned incense in it to gods that neither they nor their ancestors nor the kings of Judah ever knew, and they have filled this place with the blood of the innocent. ⁵They have built the high places of Baal to burn their children in the fire as offerings to Baal – something I did not command or mention, nor did it enter my mind. ⁶So beware, the days are coming, declares the LORD, when people will no longer call this place Topheth or the Valley of Ben Hinnom, but the Valley of Slaughter.

⁷' "In this place I will ruin the plans of Judah and Jerusalem. I will make them fall by the sword before their enemies, at the hands of those who want to kill them, and I will give their carcasses as food to the birds and the wild animals. ⁸I will devastate this city and make it an object of horror and scorn; all who pass by will be appalled and will scoff because of all its wounds. ⁹I will make

them eat the flesh of their sons and daughters, and they will eat one another's flesh because their enemies will press the siege so hard against them to destroy them."

¹⁰'Then break the jar while those who go with you are watching, ¹¹and say to them, "This is what the LORD Almighty says: I will smash this nation and this city just as this potter's jar is smashed and cannot be repaired. They will bury the dead in Topheth until there is no more room. ¹²This is what I will do to this place and to those who live here, declares the LORD. I will make this city like Topheth. ¹³The houses in Jerusalem and those of the kings of Judah will be defiled like this place, Topheth – all the houses where they burned incense on the roofs to all the starry hosts and poured out drink offerings to other gods."'

¹⁴Jeremiah then returned from Topheth, where the LORD had sent him to prophesy, and stood in the court of the LORD's temple and said to all the people, ¹⁵'This is what the LORD Almighty, the God of Israel, says: "Listen! I am going to bring on this city and all the villages around it every disaster I pronounced against them, because they were stiff-necked and would not listen to my words."'

20 When the priest Pashhur son of Immer, the official in charge of the temple of the LORD, heard Jeremiah prophesying these things, ²he had Jeremiah the prophet beaten and put in the stocks at the Upper Gate of Benjamin at the LORD's temple. ³The next day, when Pashhur released him from the stocks, Jeremiah said to him, 'The LORD's name for you is not Pashhur, but Terror on Every Side. ⁴For this is what the LORD says: "I will make you a terror to yourself and to all your friends; with your own eyes you will see them fall by the sword of their enemies. I will give all Judah into the hands of the king of Babylon, who will carry them away to Babylon or put them to the sword. ⁵I will deliver all the wealth of this city into the hands

of their enemies – all its products, all its valuables and all the treasures of the kings of Judah. They will take it away as plunder and carry it off to Babylon. ⁶And you, Pashhur, and all who live in your house will go into exile to Babylon. There you will die and be buried, you and all your friends to whom you have prophesied lies."'

■ PSALM 119:45-48

⁴⁵I will walk about in freedom,
   for I have sought out your precepts.
⁴⁶I will speak of your statutes before kings
   and will not be put to shame,
⁴⁷for I delight in your commands
   because I love them.
⁴⁸I reach out for your commands, which I love,
   that I may meditate on your decrees.

■ PROVERBS 25:13

¹³Like a snow-cooled drink at harvest time
   is a trustworthy messenger to the one
      who sends him;
   he refreshes the spirit of his master.

■ 2 THESSALONIANS 1:1–2:12

1 Paul, Silas and Timothy,

To the church of the Thessalonians in God our Father and the Lord Jesus Christ:

²Grace and peace to you from God the Father and the Lord Jesus Christ.

³We ought always to thank God for you, brothers and sisters, and rightly so, because your faith is growing more and more, and the love all of you have for one another is increasing. ⁴Therefore, among God's

churches we boast about your perseverance and faith in all the persecutions and trials you are enduring.

⁵ All this is evidence that God's judgment is right, and as a result you will be counted worthy of the kingdom of God, for which you are suffering. ⁶ God is just: he will pay back trouble to those who trouble you ⁷ and give relief to you who are troubled, and to us as well. This will happen when the Lord Jesus is revealed from heaven in blazing fire with his powerful angels. ⁸ He will punish those who do not know God and do not obey the gospel of our Lord Jesus. ⁹ They will be punished with everlasting destruction and shut out from the presence of the Lord and from the glory of his might ¹⁰ on the day he comes to be glorified in his holy people and to be marvelled at among all those who have believed. This includes you, because you believed our testimony to you.

¹¹ With this in mind, we constantly pray for you, that our God may make you worthy of his calling, and that by his power he may bring to fruition your every desire for goodness and your every deed prompted by faith. ¹² We pray this so that the name of our Lord Jesus may be glorified in you, and you in him, according to the grace of our God and the Lord Jesus Christ.

2 Concerning the coming of our Lord Jesus Christ and our being gathered to him, we ask you, brothers and sisters, ² not to become easily unsettled or alarmed by the teaching allegedly from us – whether by a prophecy or by word of mouth or by letter – asserting that the day of the Lord has already come. ³ Don't let anyone deceive you in any way, for that day will not come until the rebellion occurs and the man of lawlessness is revealed, the man doomed to destruction. ⁴ He will oppose and will exalt himself over everything that is called God or is worshipped, so that he sets himself up in God's temple, proclaiming himself to be God.

⁵ Don't you remember that when I was with you I used to tell you these things? ⁶ And now you know what is holding him back, so that he may be revealed at the proper time. ⁷ For the secret power of lawlessness is already at work; but the one who now holds it back will continue to do so till he is taken out of the way. ⁸ And then the lawless one will be revealed, whom the Lord Jesus will overthrow with the breath of his mouth and destroy by the splendour of his coming. ⁹ The coming of the lawless one will be in accordance with how Satan works. He will use all sorts of displays of power through signs and wonders that serve the lie, ¹⁰ and all the ways that wickedness deceives those who are perishing. They perish because they refused to love the truth and so be saved. ¹¹ For this reason God sends them a powerful delusion so that they will believe the lie ¹² and so that all will be condemned who have not believed the truth but have delighted in wickedness.

Their Days Are Numbered

'... the lawless one will be revealed, whom the Lord Jesus will overthrow ... by the splendour of his coming.' **2 Thessalonians 2:8**

Despite all evidence to the contrary, God is in charge of the world's affairs, and the days of rebellious kingdoms on earth are numbered. Our God reigns! The 'power and the glory' spoken of in some versions of the Lord's Prayer are talking about kingdom power and glory. The other type of power and glory, that which is measured by earthly standards alone and rejected by Jesus in His temptation in the wilderness, is doomed to dissolution and decay.

Ezekiel the prophet, speaking centuries ago of the impermanence of anything not founded on kingdom values, said, 'Doom has burst forth, the rod has budded, arrogance has blossomed' (Ezek. 7:10). Note the telltale steps: doom appears, sin blossoms, and pride has budded. And the fruit of all this? Dissolution and decay.

When speaking of a prominent figure who will arise in the last days and challenge the authority of God's kingdom, Moffatt refers to him in his translation as 'the Lawless One, the doomed One' (2 Thess. 2:3). Those who break the laws of God's kingdom, which are written into the very nature of things, are doomed. Perhaps not today, nor tomorrow, but inevitably, anything that is against God's kingdom is destined to destruction. It carries within itself the seeds of its own dissolution and decay.

PRAYER

Gracious Father, I have looked upon the kingdom of the world until my eyes are tired – tired of looking at death. Now lift up my eyes, and let me look at life. Let me look upon You. And I see You, not as a reclining God, but a reigning God. Hallelujah!

FURTHER STUDY

Eph. 6:10-18; John 12:30-31; Heb. 2:14; 1 John 3:8
• What is Paul's exhortation?
• How can we take dominion?

October 23

■ JEREMIAH 20:7–22:30

7 You deceived me, LORD, and I was
      deceived;
   you overpowered me and prevailed.
   I am ridiculed all day long;
      everyone mocks me.
8 Whenever I speak, I cry out
      proclaiming violence and destruction.
   So the word of the LORD has brought me
      insult and reproach all day long.
9 But if I say, 'I will not mention his word
      or speak any more in his name,'
   his word is in my heart like a fire,
      a fire shut up in my bones.
   I am weary of holding it in;

indeed, I cannot.
10 I hear many whispering,
      'Terror on every side!
      Denounce him! Let's denounce him!'
   All my friends
      are waiting for me to slip, saying,
   'Perhaps he will be deceived;
      then we will prevail over him
      and take our revenge on him.'

11 But the LORD is with me like a mighty
      warrior;
   so my persecutors will stumble and
      not prevail.
   They will fail and be thoroughly
      disgraced;

their dishonour will never be
forgotten.
¹² LORD Almighty, you who examine the
righteous
and probe the heart and mind,
let me see your vengeance on them,
for to you I have committed my cause.

¹³ Sing to the LORD!
Give praise to the LORD!
He rescues the life of the needy
from the hands of the wicked.

¹⁴ Cursed be the day I was born!
May the day my mother bore me not
be blessed!
¹⁵ Cursed be the man who brought my
father the news,
who made him very glad, saying,
'A child is born to you – a son!'
¹⁶ May that man be like the towns
the LORD overthrew without pity.
May he hear wailing in the morning,
a battle cry at noon.
¹⁷ For he did not kill me in the womb,
with my mother as my grave,
her womb enlarged for ever.
¹⁸ Why did I ever come out of the womb
to see trouble and sorrow
and to end my days in shame?

21 The word came to Jeremiah from
the Lord when King Zedekiah sent
to him Pashhur son of Malkijah and the
priest Zephaniah son of Maaseiah. They
said: ² 'Enquire now of the Lord for us because Nebuchadnezzar king of Babylon is
attacking us. Perhaps the Lord will perform
wonders for us as in times past so that he
will withdraw from us.'
³ But Jeremiah answered them, 'Tell Zedekiah, ⁴ "This is what the LORD, the God of
Israel, says: I am about to turn against you
the weapons of war that are in your hands,
which you are using to fight the king of Babylon and the Babylonians who are outside

the wall besieging you. And I will gather
them inside this city. ⁵ I myself will fight
against you with an outstretched hand and
a mighty arm in furious anger and in great
wrath. ⁶ I will strike down those who live in
this city – both man and beast – and they
will die of a terrible plague. ⁷ After that, declares the LORD, I will give Zedekiah king of
Judah, his officials and the people in this
city who survive the plague, sword and
famine, into the hands of Nebuchadnezzar
king of Babylon and to their enemies who
want to kill them. He will put them to the
sword; he will show them no mercy or pity
or compassion."

⁸ 'Furthermore, tell the people, "This
is what the LORD says: see, I am setting
before you the way of life and the way of
death. ⁹ Whoever stays in this city will die
by the sword, famine or plague. But whoever goes out and surrenders to the Babylonians who are besieging you will live;
they will escape with their lives. ¹⁰ I have
determined to do this city harm and not
good, declares the LORD. It will be given
into the hands of the king of Babylon, and
he will destroy it with fire."

¹¹ 'Moreover, say to the royal house of Judah, "Hear the word of the LORD. ¹² This is
what the LORD says to you, house of David:

' "Administer justice every morning;
rescue from the hand of the oppressor
the one who has been robbed,
or my wrath will break out and burn like
fire
because of the evil you have done –
burn with no one to quench it.
¹³ I am against you, Jerusalem,
you who live above this valley
on the rocky plateau, declares the
LORD –
you who say, 'Who can come against us?
Who can enter our refuge?'
¹⁴ I will punish you as your deeds deserve,
declares the LORD.

I will kindle a fire in your forests
   that will consume everything around
      you."'

22 This is what the Lord says: 'Go down
to the palace of the king of Judah
and proclaim this message there: ²"Hear
the word of the Lord to you, king of Judah,
you who sit on David's throne – you, your
officials and your people who come through
these gates. ³This is what the Lord says:
do what is just and right. Rescue from the
hand of the oppressor the one who has been
robbed. Do no wrong or violence to the
foreigner, the fatherless or the widow, and
do not shed innocent blood in this place.
⁴For if you are careful to carry out these
commands, then kings who sit on David's
throne will come through the gates of this
palace, riding in chariots and on horses,
accompanied by their officials and their
people. ⁵But if you do not obey these commands, declares the Lord, I swear by myself
that this palace will become a ruin."'

⁶For this is what the LORD says about the
palace of the king of Judah:

'Though you are like Gilead to me,
   like the summit of Lebanon,
I will surely make you like a wasteland,
   like towns not inhabited.
⁷I will send destroyers against you,
   each man with his weapons,
and they will cut up your fine cedar beams
   and throw them into the fire.

⁸'People from many nations will pass by
this city and will ask one another, "Why
has the LORD done such a thing to this great
city?" ⁹And the answer will be: "Because
they have forsaken the covenant of the LORD
their God and have worshipped and served
other gods."'

¹⁰Do not weep for the dead king or mourn
   his loss;

rather, weep bitterly for him who is
      exiled,
   because he will never return
      nor see his native land again.

¹¹For this is what the LORD says about Shallum son of Josiah, who succeeded his father
as king of Judah but has gone from this
place: 'He will never return. ¹²He will die in
the place where they have led him captive;
he will not see this land again.'

¹³'Woe to him who builds his palace by
      unrighteousness,
   his upper rooms by injustice,
making his own people work for nothing,
   not paying them for their labour.
¹⁴He says, "I will build myself a great palace
   with spacious upper rooms."
So he makes large windows in it,
   panels it with cedar
   and decorates it in red.

¹⁵'Does it make you a king
   to have more and more cedar?
Did not your father have food and drink?
   He did what was right and just,
      so all went well with him.
¹⁶He defended the cause of the poor and
         needy,
   and so all went well.
Is that not what it means to know me?'
   declares the LORD.
¹⁷'But your eyes and your heart
   are set only on dishonest gain,
on shedding innocent blood
   and on oppression and extortion.'

¹⁸Therefore this is what the LORD says about
Jehoiakim son of Josiah king of Judah:

'They will not mourn for him:
   "Alas, my brother! Alas, my sister!"
They will not mourn for him:
   "Alas, my master! Alas, his
      splendour!"

19 He will have the burial of a donkey –
dragged away and thrown
outside the gates of Jerusalem.'

20 'Go up to Lebanon and cry out,
let your voice be heard in Bashan,
cry out from Abarim,
for all your allies are crushed.
21 I warned you when you felt secure,
but you said, "I will not listen!"
This has been your way from your youth;
you have not obeyed me.
22 The wind will drive all your shepherds
away,
and your allies will go into exile.
Then you will be ashamed and disgraced
because of all your wickedness.
23 You who live in "Lebanon,"
who are nestled in cedar buildings,
how you will groan when pangs come
upon you,
pain like that of a woman in labour!

24 'As surely as I live,' declares the LORD,
'even if you, Jehoiachin son of Jehoiakim
king of Judah, were a signet ring on my right
hand, I would still pull you off. 25 I will deliver you into the hands of those who want
to kill you, those you fear – Nebuchadnezzar
king of Babylon and the Babylonians. 26 I
will hurl you and the mother who gave you
birth into another country, where neither of
you was born, and there you both will die.
27 You will never come back to the land you
long to return to.'

28 Is this man Jehoiachin a despised,
broken pot,
an object no one wants?
Why will he and his children be hurled
out,
cast into a land they do not know?
29 O land, land, land,
hear the word of the LORD!
30 This is what the LORD says:
'Record this man as if childless,

a man who will not prosper in his
lifetime,
for none of his offspring will prosper,
none will sit on the throne of David
or rule any more in Judah.'

PSALM 119:49–52

49 Remember your word to your servant,
for you have given me hope.
50 My comfort in my suffering is this:
Your promise preserves my life.
51 The arrogant mock me unmercifully,
but I do not turn from your law.
52 I remember, LORD, your ancient laws,
and I find comfort in them.

PROVERBS 25:14–15

14 Like clouds and wind without rain
is one who boasts of gifts never given.

15 Through patience a ruler can be
persuaded,
and a gentle tongue can break a bone.

2 THESSALONIANS 2:13–3:18

13 But we ought always to thank God for
you, brothers and sisters loved by the Lord,
because God chose you as firstfruits to be
saved through the sanctifying work of the
Spirit and through belief in the truth. 14 He
called you to this through our gospel, that
you might share in the glory of our Lord
Jesus Christ.
15 So then, brothers and sisters, stand firm
and hold fast to the teachings we passed on
to you, whether by word of mouth or by letter.
16 May our Lord Jesus Christ himself and
God our Father, who loved us and by his
grace gave us eternal encouragement and

good hope, [17]encourage your hearts and strengthen you in every good deed and word.

3 As for other matters, brothers and sisters, pray for us that the message of the Lord may spread rapidly and be honoured, just as it was with you. [2]And pray that we may be delivered from wicked and evil people, for not everyone has faith. [3]But the Lord is faithful, and he will strengthen you and protect you from the evil one. [4]We have confidence in the Lord that you are doing and will continue to do the things we command. [5]May the Lord direct your hearts into God's love and Christ's perseverance.

[6]In the name of the Lord Jesus Christ, we command you, brothers and sisters, to keep away from every believer who is idle and disruptive and does not live according to the teaching you received from us. [7]For you yourselves know how you ought to follow our example. We were not idle when we were with you, [8]nor did we eat anyone's food without paying for it. On the contrary, we worked night and day, labouring and toiling so that we would not be a burden to any of you. [9]We did this, not because we do not have the right to such help, but in order to offer ourselves as a model for you to imitate. [10]For even when we were with you, we gave you this rule: 'The one who is unwilling to work shall not eat.'

[11]We hear that some among you are idle and disruptive. They are not busy; they are busybodies. [12]Such people we command and urge in the Lord Jesus Christ to settle down and earn the food they eat. [13]And as for you, brothers and sisters, never tire of doing what is good.

[14]Take special note of anyone who does not obey our instruction in this letter. Do not associate with them, in order that they may feel ashamed. [15]Yet do not regard them as an enemy, but warn them as you would a fellow believer.

[16]Now may the Lord of peace himself give you peace at all times and in every way. The Lord be with all of you.

[17]I, Paul, write this greeting in my own hand, which is the distinguishing mark in all my letters. This is how I write.

[18]The grace of our Lord Jesus Christ be with you all.

For New Christians

'... stand firm and hold fast to the teachings we passed on to you ...' **2 Thessalonians 2:15**

Christians need to stand with their feet shod with the preparation of the gospel of peace. The moment we begin to compromise on the Word of God and the great truths of the gospel, we shall not only slide in the understanding of our faith but also in its practice.

Permit me to say a word to those who have been in the Christian life for just a short time. Now that you are a Christian, take your stand unflinchingly on the Lord's side. When you meet your old friends - those you used to hang around with in the days before you came to know the Lord - and they propose that you go on doing the things you used to do that you know are not in harmony with God's Word, then be resolute and refuse. Take a firm stand and watch that you do not slip towards them. Have your feet shod with the preparation of the gospel of peace.

The first thing that strikes everyone who comes into the Christian life is that it is entirely different from one's former life. You must determine to take your stand with Jesus Christ, and when others tempt you, say, 'I cannot betray my Lord. I am bound to Him for all eternity. My feet are shod and I am not moving.' You have to know what you believe and be resolute and determined to stand for it - come what may. If I had not done this in the days following my conversion to Christ, then I would have forfeited an adventure that has taken me deeper and deeper into God.

PRAYER

O God, how can I have faith in You unless I have faith in the words You have spoken to me in the Bible? Help me stand firm in the faith - today and every day. In Jesus' name. Amen.

FURTHER STUDY

Gal. 5:1-13; Phil. 1:27;
1 Pet. 5:7-11
• What did Paul say to the Galatians?
• How should we conduct ourselves?

October 24

■ JEREMIAH 23:1–24:10

23 'Woe to the shepherds who are destroying and scattering the sheep of my pasture!' declares the LORD. ²Therefore this is what the LORD, the God of Israel, says to the shepherds who tend my people: 'Because you have scattered my flock and driven them away and have not bestowed care on them, I will bestow punishment on you for the evil you have done,' declares the LORD. ³'I myself will gather the remnant of my flock out of all the countries where I have driven them and will bring them back to their pasture, where they will be fruitful and increase in number. ⁴I will place shepherds over them who will tend them, and they will no longer be afraid or terrified, nor will any be missing,' declares the LORD.

⁵'The days are coming,' declares the LORD,
'when I will raise up for David a
righteous Branch,
a King who will reign wisely

and do what is just and right in the
land.
⁶In his days Judah will be saved
and Israel will live in safety.
This is the name by which he will be called:
The LORD Our Righteous Saviour.

⁷'So then, the days are coming,' declares the LORD, 'when people will no longer say, "As surely as the LORD lives, who brought the Israelites up out of Egypt," ⁸but they will say, "As surely as the LORD lives, who brought the descendants of Israel up out of the land of the north and out of all the countries where he had banished them." Then they will live in their own land.'

⁹Concerning the prophets:

My heart is broken within me;
all my bones tremble.
I am like a drunken man,
like a strong man overcome by wine,
because of the LORD
and his holy words.

¹⁰ The land is full of adulterers;
   because of the curse the land lies
       parched
   and the pastures in the wilderness are
       withered.
   The prophets follow an evil course
   and use their power unjustly.

¹¹ 'Both prophet and priest are godless;
   even in my temple I find their
       wickedness,'
               declares the LORD.
¹² 'Therefore their path will become slippery;
   they will be banished to darkness
   and there they will fall.
   I will bring disaster on them
   in the year they are punished,'
               declares the LORD.

¹³ 'Among the prophets of Samaria
   I saw this repulsive thing:
   they prophesied by Baal
   and led my people Israel astray.
¹⁴ And among the prophets of Jerusalem
   I have seen something horrible:
   They commit adultery and live a lie.
   They strengthen the hands of evildoers,
       so that not one of them turns from
           their wickedness.
   They are all like Sodom to me;
   the people of Jerusalem are like
       Gomorrah.'

¹⁵ Therefore this is what the LORD
Almighty says concerning the prophets:

   'I will make them eat bitter food
   and drink poisoned water,
   because from the prophets of Jerusalem
   ungodliness has spread throughout
       the land.'

¹⁶ This is what the LORD Almighty says:

   'Do not listen to what the prophets are
       prophesying to you;

they fill you with false hopes.
   They speak visions from their own minds,
       not from the mouth of the LORD.
¹⁷ They keep saying to those who despise me,
   "The LORD says: you will have peace."
   And to all who follow the stubbornness
       of their hearts
   they say, "No harm will come to you."
¹⁸ But which of them has stood in the
       council of the LORD
   to see or to hear his word?
   Who has listened and heard his word?
¹⁹ See, the storm of the LORD
   will burst out in wrath,
   a whirlwind swirling down
   on the heads of the wicked.
²⁰ The anger of the LORD will not turn back
   until he fully accomplishes
   the purposes of his heart.
   In days to come
   you will understand it clearly.
²¹ I did not send these prophets,
   yet they have run with their message;
   I did not speak to them,
   yet they have prophesied.
²² But if they had stood in my council,
   they would have proclaimed my words
       to my people
   and would have turned them from their
       evil ways
   and from their evil deeds.

²³ 'Am I only a God nearby,'
               declares the LORD,
   'and not a God far away?
²⁴ Who can hide in secret places
   so that I cannot see them?'
               declares the LORD.
   'Do not I fill heaven and earth?'
               declares the LORD.

²⁵ 'I have heard what the prophets say
who prophesy lies in my name. They say, "I
had a dream! I had a dream!" ²⁶ How long
will this continue in the hearts of these lying prophets, who prophesy the delusions of

their own minds? [27] They think the dreams they tell one another will make my people forget my name, just as their ancestors forgot my name through Baal worship. [28] Let the prophet who has a dream recount the dream, but let the one who has my word speak it faithfully. For what has straw to do with grain?' declares the LORD. [29] 'Is not my word like fire,' declares the LORD, 'and like a hammer that breaks a rock in pieces?

[30] 'Therefore,' declares the LORD, 'I am against the prophets who steal from one another words supposedly from me. [31] Yes,' declares the LORD, 'I am against the prophets who wag their own tongues and yet declare, "The LORD declares." [32] Indeed, I am against those who prophesy false dreams,' declares the LORD. 'They tell them and lead my people astray with their reckless lies, yet I did not send or appoint them. They do not benefit these people in the least,' declares the LORD.

[33] 'When these people, or a prophet or a priest, ask you, "What is the message from the LORD?" say to them, "What message? I will forsake you, declares the LORD." [34] If a prophet or a priest or anyone else claims, "This is a message from the LORD," I will punish them and their household. [35] This is what each of you keeps saying to your friends and other Israelites: "What is the LORD's answer?" or "What has the LORD spoken?" [36] But you must not mention "a message from the LORD" again, because each one's word becomes their own message. So you distort the words of the living God, the LORD Almighty, our God. [37] This is what you keep saying to a prophet: "What is the LORD's answer to you?" or "What has the LORD spoken?" [38] Although you claim, "This is a message from the LORD," this is what the LORD says: you used the words, "This is a message from the LORD," even though I told you that you must not claim, "This is a message from the LORD." [39] Therefore, I will surely forget you and

cast you out of my presence along with the city I gave to you and your ancestors. [40] I will bring on you everlasting disgrace – everlasting shame that will not be forgotten.'

24 After Jehoiachin son of Jehoiakim king of Judah and the officials, the skilled workers and the craftsmen of Judah were carried into exile from Jerusalem to Babylon by Nebuchadnezzar king of Babylon, the LORD showed me two baskets of figs placed in front of the temple of the LORD. [2] One basket had very good figs, like those that ripen early; the other basket had very bad figs, so bad that they could not be eaten.

[3] Then the LORD asked me, 'What do you see, Jeremiah?'

'Figs,' I answered. 'The good ones are very good, but the bad ones are so bad that they cannot be eaten.'

[4] Then the word of the LORD came to me: [5] 'This is what the LORD, the God of Israel, says: "Like these good figs, I regard as good the exiles from Judah, whom I sent away from this place to the land of the Babylonians. [6] My eyes will watch over them for their good, and I will bring them back to this land. I will build them up and not tear them down; I will plant them and not uproot them. [7] I will give them a heart to know me, that I am the LORD. They will be my people, and I will be their God, for they will return to me with all their heart.

[8] "But like the bad figs, which are so bad that they cannot be eaten," says the LORD, "so will I deal with Zedekiah king of Judah, his officials and the survivors from Jerusalem, whether they remain in this land or live in Egypt. [9] I will make them abhorrent and an offence to all the kingdoms of the earth, a reproach and a byword, a curse and an object of ridicule, wherever I banish them. [10] I will send the sword, famine and plague against them until they are destroyed from the land I gave to them and their ancestors."'

■ PSALM 119:53-56

[53] Indignation grips me because of the
     wicked,
          who have forsaken your law.
[54] Your decrees are the theme of my song
          wherever I lodge.
[55] In the night, LORD, I remember your
     name,
          that I may keep your law.
[56] This has been my practice:
          I obey your precepts.

■ PROVERBS 25:16-17

[16] If you find honey, eat just enough –
          too much of it, and you will vomit.
[17] Seldom set foot in your neighbour's
     house –
          too much of you, and they will hate
          you.

■ 1 TIMOTHY 1:1-20

1 Paul, an apostle of Christ Jesus by the
  command of God our Saviour and of
Christ Jesus our hope,

[2] To Timothy my true son in the faith:

Grace, mercy and peace from God the
Father and Christ Jesus our Lord.
   [3] As I urged you when I went into Macedonia, stay there in Ephesus so that you
may command certain people not to teach
false doctrines any longer [4] or to devote
themselves to myths and endless genealogies. Such things promote controversial
speculations rather than advancing God's
work – which is by faith. [5] The goal of this
command is love, which comes from a
pure heart and a good conscience and a
sincere faith. [6] Some have departed from
these and have turned to meaningless talk.

[7] They want to be teachers of the law, but
they do not know what they are talking
about or what they so confidently affirm.
   [8] We know that the law is good if one
uses it properly. [9] We also know that the
law is made not for the righteous but for
lawbreakers and rebels, the ungodly and
sinful, the unholy and irreligious, for those
who kill their fathers or mothers, for murderers, [10] for the sexually immoral, for those
practising homosexuality, for slave traders
and liars and perjurers – and for whatever
else is contrary to the sound doctrine [11] that
conforms to the gospel concerning the glory of the blessed God, which he entrusted
to me.
   [12] I thank Christ Jesus our Lord, who has
given me strength, that he considered me
trustworthy, appointing me to his service.
[13] Even though I was once a blasphemer and
a persecutor and a violent man, I was shown
mercy because I acted in ignorance and unbelief. [14] The grace of our Lord was poured
out on me abundantly, along with the faith
and love that are in Christ Jesus.
   [15] Here is a trustworthy saying that deserves full acceptance: Christ Jesus came
into the world to save sinners – of whom I
am the worst. [16] But for that very reason I
was shown mercy so that in me, the worst
of sinners, Christ Jesus might display his
immense patience as an example for those
who would believe in him and receive eternal life. [17] Now to the King eternal, immortal, invisible, the only God, be honour and
glory for ever and ever. Amen.
   [18] Timothy, my son, I am giving you this
command in keeping with the prophecies
once made about you, so that by recalling
them you may fight the battle well, [19] holding on to faith and a good conscience,
which some have rejected and so have suffered shipwreck with regard to the faith.
[20] Among them are Hymenaeus and Alexander, whom I have handed over to Satan to
be taught not to blaspheme.

The Burden of Revival

'But you must not mention "a message from the LORD" again, because each one's word becomes their own message.' **Jeremiah 23:36**

God loves His children to be involved with Him in bringing about His purposes, and it is not in God's nature to ignore the great principle of prayer which He himself has established in the universe. Although revival begins in the sovereign purposes of God, it comes into the world through the doorway of believing prayer.

John Wallace, principal of the Bible college I attended prior to entering the ministry, used to say, 'Before somebody can experience a blessing, somebody has to bear a burden.' He used to illustrate the point in this way: 'Before deliverance came to the nation of Israel when they were in Egypt, Moses had to bear a burden. Before the great Temple of God could be built in Jerusalem, Solomon was called to bear a burden. Before the sins of the world could be removed Christ had to bear a burden. Before somebody can experience a blessing, somebody has to bear a burden.'

This is a principle that can be traced throughout the whole of the Bible – from Genesis to Revelation. It can be seen at work, too, in the history of all religious revivals. Before God comes from heaven to work in extraordinary ways He places the burden of revival on the hearts of His people. And whom does He choose to carry this burden? You can be sure that they will be men and women who are drawn to prayer and understand something of its power and potential. Would you, I wonder, be one?

PRAYER

Gracious Father, You know how my heart shrinks from such a great challenge as this. All I can say is – I am willing to be made willing. Help me, dear Father. In Jesus' name. Amen.

FURTHER STUDY

Psa. 21:1-13; 38:9; 73:25; Isa. 26:9; Mark 11:24
• What will God grant to us?
• How can a desire become a burden?

October 25

■ **JEREMIAH 25:1–26:24**

25 The word came to Jeremiah concerning all the people of Judah in the fourth year of Jehoiakim son of Josiah

king of Judah, which was the first year of Nebuchadnezzar king of Babylon. ²So Jeremiah the prophet said to all the people of Judah and to all those living in Jerusalem: ³For twenty-three years – from the thirteenth year of Josiah son of Amon king of Judah until this very day – the word of the LORD has come to me and I have spoken to you again and again, but you have not listened.

⁴ And though the LORD has sent all his servants the prophets to you again and again, you have not listened or paid any attention. ⁵ They said, 'Turn now, each of you, from your evil ways and your evil practices, and you can stay in the land the LORD gave to you and your ancestors for ever and ever. ⁶ Do not follow other gods to serve and worship them; do not arouse my anger with what your hands have made. Then I will not harm you.'

⁷ 'But you did not listen to me,' declares the LORD, 'and you have aroused my anger with what your hands have made, and you have brought harm to yourselves.'

⁸ Therefore the LORD Almighty says this: 'Because you have not listened to my words, ⁹ I will summon all the peoples of the north and my servant Nebuchadnezzar king of Babylon,' declares the LORD, 'and I will bring them against this land and its inhabitants and against all the surrounding nations. I will completely destroy them and make them an object of horror and scorn, and an everlasting ruin. ¹⁰ I will banish from them the sounds of joy and gladness, the voices of bride and bridegroom, the sound of millstones and the light of the lamp. ¹¹ This whole country will become a desolate wasteland, and these nations will serve the king of Babylon for seventy years.

¹² 'But when the seventy years are fulfilled, I will punish the king of Babylon and his nation, the land of the Babylonians, for their guilt,' declares the LORD, 'and will make it desolate for ever. ¹³ I will bring on that land all the things I have spoken against it, all that are written in this book and prophesied by Jeremiah against all the nations. ¹⁴ They themselves will be enslaved by many nations and great kings; I will

repay them according to their deeds and the work of their hands.'

¹⁵ This is what the LORD, the God of Israel, said to me: 'Take from my hand this cup filled with the wine of my wrath and make all the nations to whom I send you drink it. ¹⁶ When they drink it, they will stagger and go mad because of the sword I will send among them.'

¹⁷ So I took the cup from the LORD's hand and made all the nations to whom he sent me drink it: ¹⁸ Jerusalem and the towns of Judah, its kings and officials, to make them a ruin and an object of horror and scorn, a curse – as they are today; ¹⁹ Pharaoh king of Egypt, his attendants, his officials and all his people, ²⁰ and all the foreign people there; all the kings of Uz; all the kings of the Philistines (those of Ashkelon, Gaza, Ekron, and the people left at Ashdod); ²¹ Edom, Moab and Ammon; ²² all the kings of Tyre and Sidon; the kings of the coastlands across the sea; ²³ Dedan, Tema, Buz and all who are in distant places; ²⁴ all the kings of Arabia and all the kings of the foreign people who live in the wilderness; ²⁵ all the kings of Zimri, Elam and Media; ²⁶ and all the kings of the north, near and far, one after the other – all the kingdoms on the face of the earth. And after all of them, the king of Sheshak will drink it too.

²⁷ 'Then tell them, "This is what the LORD Almighty, the God of Israel, says: drink, get drunk and vomit, and fall to rise no more because of the sword I will send among you." ²⁸ But if they refuse to take the cup from your hand and drink, tell them, "This is what the LORD Almighty says: You must drink it! ²⁹ See, I am beginning to bring disaster on the city that bears my Name, and will you indeed go unpunished? You will not go unpunished, for I am calling down a sword on all who live on the earth, declares the LORD Almighty."

³⁰ 'Now prophesy all these words against them and say to them:

' "The LORD will roar from on high;
 he will thunder from his holy dwelling
 and roar mightily against his land.
He will shout like those who tread the
  grapes,
 shout against all who live on the earth.
³¹ The tumult will resound to the ends of
  the earth,
 for the LORD will bring charges against
  the nations;
 he will bring judgment on all mankind
 and put the wicked to the sword," '
        declares the LORD.

³² This is what the LORD Almighty says:

'Look! Disaster is spreading
 from nation to nation;
a mighty storm is rising
 from the ends of the earth.'

³³ At that time those slain by the LORD will
be everywhere – from one end of the earth
to the other. They will not be mourned or
gathered up or buried, but will be like dung
lying on the ground.

³⁴ Weep and wail, you shepherds;
 roll in the dust, you leaders of the
  flock.
For your time to be slaughtered has
  come;
 you will fall like the best of the rams.
³⁵ The shepherds will have nowhere to flee,
 the leaders of the flock no place to
  escape.
³⁶ Hear the cry of the shepherds,
 the wailing of the leaders of the flock,
 for the LORD is destroying their
  pasture.
³⁷ The peaceful meadows will be laid waste
 because of the fierce anger of the LORD.
³⁸ Like a lion he will leave his lair,
 and their land will become desolate
because of the sword of the oppressor
 and because of the LORD's fierce anger.

26 Early in the reign of Jehoiakim son
of Josiah king of Judah, this word
came from the LORD: ² 'This is what the
LORD says: Stand in the courtyard of the
LORD's house and speak to all the people of
the towns of Judah who come to worship in
the house of the LORD. Tell them everything
I command you; do not omit a word. ³ Perhaps they will listen and each will turn from
their evil ways. Then I will relent and not
inflict on them the disaster I was planning
because of the evil they have done. ⁴ Say to
them, "This is what the LORD says: if you do
not listen to me and follow my law, which I
have set before you, ⁵ and if you do not listen
to the words of my servants the prophets,
whom I have sent to you again and again
(though you have not listened), ⁶ then I will
make this house like Shiloh and this city a
curse among all the nations of the earth." '

⁷ The priests, the prophets and all the
people heard Jeremiah speak these words
in the house of the LORD. ⁸ But as soon as
Jeremiah finished telling all the people everything the LORD had commanded him
to say, the priests, the prophets and all the
people seized him and said, 'You must die!
⁹ Why do you prophesy in the LORD's name
that this house will be like Shiloh and this
city will be desolate and deserted?' And all
the people crowded around Jeremiah in the
house of the LORD.

¹⁰ When the officials of Judah heard about
these things, they went up from the royal
palace to the house of the LORD and took their
places at the entrance of the New Gate of
the LORD's house. ¹¹ Then the priests and the
prophets said to the officials and all the people, 'This man should be sentenced to death
because he has prophesied against this city.
You have heard it with your own ears!'

¹² Then Jeremiah said to all the officials
and all the people: 'The LORD sent me to
prophesy against this house and this city
all the things you have heard. ¹³ Now reform your ways and your actions and obey

the LORD your God. Then the LORD will relent and not bring the disaster he has pronounced against you. ¹⁴As for me, I am in your hands; do with me whatever you think is good and right. ¹⁵Be assured, however, that if you put me to death, you will bring the guilt of innocent blood on yourselves and on this city and on those who live in it, for in truth the LORD has sent me to you to speak all these words in your hearing.'

¹⁶Then the officials and all the people said to the priests and the prophets, 'This man should not be sentenced to death! He has spoken to us in the name of the LORD our God.'

¹⁷Some of the elders of the land stepped forward and said to the entire assembly of people, ¹⁸'Micah of Moresheth prophesied in the days of Hezekiah king of Judah. He told all the people of Judah, "This is what the LORD Almighty says:

' "Zion will be ploughed like a field,
    Jerusalem will become a heap of
        rubble,
    the temple hill a mound overgrown
        with thickets."

¹⁹'Did Hezekiah king of Judah or anyone else in Judah put him to death? Did not Hezekiah fear the LORD and seek his favour? And did not the LORD relent, so that he did not bring the disaster he pronounced against them? We are about to bring a terrible disaster on ourselves!'

²⁰(Now Uriah son of Shemaiah from Kiriath Jearim was another man who prophesied in the name of the LORD; he prophesied the same things against this city and this land as Jeremiah did. ²¹When King Jehoiakim and all his officers and officials heard his words, the king was determined to put him to death. But Uriah heard of it and fled in fear to Egypt. ²²King Jehoiakim, however, sent Elnathan son of Akbor to Egypt, along with some other men. ²³They brought Uriah out of

Egypt and took him to King Jehoiakim, who had him struck down with a sword and his body thrown into the burial place of the common people.)

²⁴Furthermore, Ahikam son of Shaphan supported Jeremiah, and so he was not handed over to the people to be put to death.

■ PSALM 119:57-60

⁵⁷You are my portion, LORD;
    I have promised to obey your words.
⁵⁸I have sought your face with all my heart;
    be gracious to me according to your
        promise.
⁵⁹I have considered my ways
    and have turned my steps to your
        statutes.
⁶⁰I will hasten and not delay
    to obey your commands.

■ PROVERBS 25:18-20

¹⁸Like a club or a sword or a sharp arrow
    is one who gives false testimony
        against a neighbour.
¹⁹Like a broken tooth or a lame foot
    is reliance on the unfaithful in a time
        of trouble.
²⁰Like one who takes away a garment on a
        cold day,
    or like vinegar poured on a wound,
    is one who sings songs to a heavy
        heart.

■ 1 TIMOTHY 2:1-3:7

2 I urge, then, first of all, that petitions, prayers, intercession and thanksgiving be made for all people – ²for kings and all those in authority, that we may live peaceful and quiet lives in all godliness and holiness. ³This is good, and pleases

God our Saviour, [4]who wants all people to be saved and to come to a knowledge of the truth. [5]For there is one God and one mediator between God and mankind, the man Christ Jesus, [6]who gave himself as a ransom for all people. This has now been witnessed to at the proper time. [7]And for this purpose I was appointed a herald and an apostle – I am telling the truth, I am not lying – and a true and faithful teacher of the Gentiles.

[8]Therefore I want the men everywhere to pray, lifting up holy hands without anger or disputing. [9]I also want the women to dress modestly, with decency and propriety, adorning themselves, not with elaborate hairstyles or gold or pearls or expensive clothes, [10]but with good deeds, appropriate for women who profess to worship God.

[11]A woman should learn in quietness and full submission. [12]I do not permit a woman to teach or to assume authority over a man; she must be quiet. [13]For Adam was formed first, then Eve. [14]And Adam was not the one deceived; it was the woman who was deceived and became a sinner. [15]But women will be saved through childbearing – if they continue in faith, love and holiness with propriety.

3 Here is a trustworthy saying: whoever aspires to be an overseer desires a noble task. [2]Now the overseer is to be above reproach, faithful to his wife, temperate, self-controlled, respectable, hospitable, able to teach, [3]not given to drunkenness, not violent but gentle, not quarrelsome, not a lover of money. [4]He must manage his own family well and see that his children obey him, and he must do so in a manner worthy of full respect. [5](If anyone does not know how to manage his own family, how can he take care of God's church?) [6]He must not be a recent convert, or he may become conceited and fall under the same judgment as the devil. [7]He must also have a good reputation with outsiders, so that he will not fall into disgrace and into the devil's trap.

The First Thing to Do

'... I want the men everywhere to pray, lifting up holy hands without anger or disputing.' **1 Timothy 2:8**

Although doubt can be turned destructively against error, it is also possible for it to be turned destructively against truth. How do we deal with the darker side of doubt? The first thing we must do is to bring every doubt into the open and examine it. Most Christians fail to do this; they do nothing with their doubts and just hope they will go away.

But the way people react to their doubts is an indication of their attitude to doubt itself. Many feel ashamed when they experience doubt and thus push it below the surface of their minds and refuse to recognise it. Some even regard doubt as the unpardonable sin. Others treat it as an unmentionable subject and never refer to any doubts they have for fear they are letting the team down. I myself sometimes struggle with doubt - even after more than fifty years in the Christian life.

In the months following my conversion, I had doubts about the inspiration and inerrancy of the Bible until I decided to accept it by faith. When I did, all my doubts concerning it were immediately dissolved, and from that day to this I have never had one doubt about the reliability of Scripture. But I have doubted other things – particularly in the area of personal guidance. I have learned, however, not to let doubts threaten or intimidate me, and when they come I simply look them in the face and say, 'I am going to put you in harness and make you work to bring me closer to God.'

Now my doubts get fewer and fewer.

PRAYER

Father, how can I sufficiently thank You for showing me how to take the negative things of life and turn them into positives? Nothing need work against me when I have You within. I am so thankful. Amen.

FURTHER STUDY

1 John 2:1-20; 3:24;
1 Cor. 13:12
• What did Paul admit to?
• What did John affirm?

October 26

■ JEREMIAH 27:1–29:14

27 Early in the reign of Zedekiah son of Josiah king of Judah, this word came to Jeremiah from the LORD: ²this is what the LORD said to me: 'Make a yoke out of straps and crossbars and put it on your neck. ³Then send word to the kings of Edom, Moab, Ammon, Tyre and Sidon through the envoys who have come to Jerusalem to Zedekiah king of Judah. ⁴Give them a message for their masters and say, "This is what the LORD Almighty, the God of Israel, says: 'Tell this to your masters: ⁵with my great power and outstretched arm I made the earth and its people and the animals that are on it, and I give it to anyone I please. ⁶Now I will give all your countries into the hands of my servant Nebuchadnezzar king of Babylon; I will make even the wild animals subject to him. ⁷All nations will serve him and his son and his grandson until the time for his land comes; then many nations and great kings will subjugate him.

⁸'"'If, however, any nation or kingdom will not serve Nebuchadnezzar king of Babylon or bow its neck under his yoke, I will punish that nation with the sword, famine and plague, declares the LORD, until I destroy it by his hand. ⁹So do not listen to your prophets, your diviners, your interpreters of dreams, your mediums or your sorcerers who tell you, "You will not serve the king of Babylon." ¹⁰They prophesy lies to you that will only serve to remove you far from your lands; I will banish you and you will perish. ¹¹But if any nation will bow its neck under the yoke of the king of Babylon and serve him, I will let that nation remain in its own land to till it and to live there, declares the LORD.'"'

¹²I gave the same message to Zedekiah king of Judah. I said, 'Bow your neck under the yoke of the king of Babylon; serve him and his people, and you will live. ¹³Why will you and your people die by the sword, famine and plague with which the LORD has threatened any nation that will not serve the king of Babylon? ¹⁴Do not listen to the words of the prophets who say to you, "You will not serve the king of Babylon," for they are prophesying lies to you. ¹⁵"I have not sent

them," declares the LORD. "They are prophesying lies in my name. Therefore, I will banish you and you will perish, both you and the prophets who prophesy to you."'

[16] Then I said to the priests and all these people, 'This is what the LORD says: do not listen to the prophets who say, "Very soon now the articles from the LORD's house will be brought back from Babylon." They are prophesying lies to you. [17] Do not listen to them. Serve the king of Babylon, and you will live. Why should this city become a ruin? [18] If they are prophets and have the word of the LORD, let them plead with the LORD Almighty that the articles which remain in the house of the LORD and in the palace of the king of Judah and in Jerusalem will not be taken to Babylon. [19] For this is what the LORD Almighty says about the pillars, the bronze Sea, the movable stands and the other articles that are left in this city, [20] which Nebuchadnezzar king of Babylon did not take away when he carried Jehoiachin son of Jehoiakim king of Judah into exile from Jerusalem to Babylon, along with all the nobles of Judah and Jerusalem – [21] yes, this is what the LORD Almighty, the God of Israel, says about the things that are left in the house of the LORD and in the palace of the king of Judah and in Jerusalem: [22] "They will be taken to Babylon and there they will remain until the day I come for them," declares the LORD. "Then I will bring them back and restore them to this place."'

28 In the fifth month of that same year, the fourth year, early in the reign of Zedekiah king of Judah, the prophet Hananiah son of Azzur, who was from Gibeon, said to me in the house of the LORD in the presence of the priests and all the people: [2] 'This is what the LORD Almighty, the God of Israel, says: "I will break the yoke of the king of Babylon. [3] Within two years I will bring back to this place all the articles of the LORD's house that Nebuchadnezzar king of Babylon removed from here and took to

Babylon. [4] I will also bring back to this place Jehoiachin son of Jehoiakim king of Judah and all the other exiles from Judah who went to Babylon", declares the LORD, "for I will break the yoke of the king of Babylon."'

[5] Then the prophet Jeremiah replied to the prophet Hananiah before the priests and all the people who were standing in the house of the LORD. [6] He said, 'Amen! May the LORD do so! May the LORD fulfil the words you have prophesied by bringing the articles of the LORD's house and all the exiles back to this place from Babylon. [7] Nevertheless, listen to what I have to say in your hearing and in the hearing of all the people: [8] from early times the prophets who preceded you and me have prophesied war, disaster and plague against many countries and great kingdoms. [9] But the prophet who prophesies peace will be recognised as one truly sent by the LORD only if his prediction comes true.'

[10] Then the prophet Hananiah took the yoke off the neck of the prophet Jeremiah and broke it, [11] and he said before all the people, 'This is what the LORD says: "In the same way I will break the yoke of Nebuchadnezzar king of Babylon off the neck of all the nations within two years."' At this, the prophet Jeremiah went on his way.

[12] After the prophet Hananiah had broken the yoke off the neck of the prophet Jeremiah, the word of the LORD came to Jeremiah: [13] 'Go and tell Hananiah, "This is what the LORD says: you have broken a wooden yoke, but in its place you will get a yoke of iron. [14] This is what the LORD Almighty, the God of Israel, says: I will put an iron yoke on the necks of all these nations to make them serve Nebuchadnezzar king of Babylon, and they will serve him. I will even give him control over the wild animals."'

[15] Then the prophet Jeremiah said to Hananiah the prophet, 'Listen, Hananiah! The LORD has not sent you, yet you have persuaded this nation to trust in lies. [16] Therefore this is what the LORD says: "I am about to

remove you from the face of the earth. This very year you are going to die, because you have preached rebellion against the LORD."'

[17] In the seventh month of that same year, Hananiah the prophet died.

29 This is the text of the letter that the prophet Jeremiah sent from Jerusalem to the surviving elders among the exiles and to the priests, the prophets and all the other people Nebuchadnezzar had carried into exile from Jerusalem to Babylon. [2] (This was after King Jehoiachin and the queen mother, the court officials and the leaders of Judah and Jerusalem, the skilled workers and the craftsmen had gone into exile from Jerusalem.) [3] He entrusted the letter to Elasah son of Shaphan and to Gemariah son of Hilkiah, whom Zedekiah king of Judah sent to King Nebuchadnezzar in Babylon. It said:

[4] This is what the LORD Almighty, the God of Israel, says to all those I carried into exile from Jerusalem to Babylon: [5] 'Build houses and settle down; plant gardens and eat what they produce. [6] Marry and have sons and daughters; find wives for your sons and give your daughters in marriage, so that they too may have sons and daughters. Increase in number there; do not decrease. [7] Also, seek the peace and prosperity of the city to which I have carried you into exile. Pray to the LORD for it, because if it prospers, you too will prosper.' [8] Yes, this is what the LORD Almighty, the God of Israel, says: 'Do not let the prophets and diviners among you deceive you. Do not listen to the dreams you encourage them to have. [9] They are prophesying lies to you in my name. I have not sent them,' declares the LORD.

[10] This is what the LORD says: 'When seventy years are completed for Babylon, I will come to you and fulfil my good promise to bring you back to this place. [11] For I know the plans I have for you,' declares the LORD, 'plans to prosper you and not to harm you, plans to give you hope and a future. [12] Then you will call on me and come and pray to me, and I will listen to you. [13] You will seek me and find me when you seek me with all your heart. [14] I will be found by you,' declares the LORD, 'and will bring you back from captivity. I will gather you from all the nations and places where I have banished you,' declares the LORD, 'and will bring you back to the place from which I carried you into exile.'

■ PSALM 119:61-64

[61] Though the wicked bind me with ropes,
　　I will not forget your law.
[62] At midnight I rise to give you thanks
　　for your righteous laws.
[63] I am a friend to all who fear you,
　　to all who follow your precepts.
[64] The earth is filled with your love, LORD;
　　teach me your decrees.

■ PROVERBS 25:21-22

[21] If your enemy is hungry, give him food
　　to eat;
　　if he is thirsty, give him water to drink.
[22] In doing this, you will heap burning
　　coals on his head,
　　and the LORD will reward you.

■ 1 TIMOTHY 3:8–4:16

[8] In the same way, deacons are to be worthy of respect, sincere, not indulging in much wine, and not pursuing dishonest gain. [9] They must keep hold of the deep truths of the faith with a clear conscience. [10] They must first be tested; and then if there

is nothing against them, let them serve as deacons.

[11] In the same way, the women are to be worthy of respect, not malicious talkers but temperate and trustworthy in everything.

[12] A deacon must be faithful to his wife and must manage his children and his household well. [13] Those who have served well gain an excellent standing and great assurance in their faith in Christ Jesus.

[14] Although I hope to come to you soon, I am writing to you with these instructions so that, [15] if I am delayed, you will know how people ought to conduct themselves in God's household, which is the church of the living God, the pillar and foundation of the truth. [16] Beyond all question, the mystery from which true godliness springs is great:

He appeared in the flesh,
    was vindicated by the Spirit,
was seen by angels,
    was preached among the nations,
was believed on in the world,
    was taken up in glory.

4 The Spirit clearly says that in later times some will abandon the faith and follow deceiving spirits and things taught by demons. [2] Such teachings come through hypocritical liars, whose consciences have been seared as with a hot iron. [3] They forbid people to marry and order them to abstain from certain foods, which God created to be received with thanksgiving by those who believe and who know the truth.

[4] For everything God created is good, and nothing is to be rejected if it is received with thanksgiving, [5] because it is consecrated by the word of God and prayer.

[6] If you point these things out to the brothers and sisters, you will be a good minister of Christ Jesus, nourished on the truths of the faith and of the good teaching that you have followed. [7] Have nothing to do with godless myths and old wives' tales; rather, train yourself to be godly. [8] For physical training is of some value, but godliness has value for all things, holding promise for both the present life and the life to come. [9] This is a trustworthy saying that deserves full acceptance. [10] That is why we labour and strive, because we have put our hope in the living God, who is the Saviour of all people, and especially of those who believe.

[11] Command and teach these things. [12] Don't let anyone look down on you because you are young, but set an example for the believers in speech, in conduct, in love, in faith and in purity. [13] Until I come, devote yourself to the public reading of Scripture, to preaching and to teaching. [14] Do not neglect your gift, which was given you through prophecy when the body of elders laid their hands on you.

[15] Be diligent in these matters; give yourself wholly to them, so that everyone may see your progress. [16] Watch your life and doctrine closely. Persevere in them, because if you do, you will save both yourself and your hearers.

Missing by Inches

'You will seek me and find me when you seek me with all your heart.' **Jeremiah 29:13**

W e are looking today at what I consider one of the greatest truths we can discover about receiving from God: 'God does not just answer prayer - He answers you.'

The Almighty does not just listen to the words we weave into the air when we pray; He listens also to the attitude of our hearts. If the two are not properly correlated, then we miss out on many of God's blessings. And this missing out is not because God is stingy about the way He dispenses His blessings, but because we short-circuit our own spiritual system and become imperfect receivers. To put it another way: our failure to receive isn't due to the fact that God is not good at giving, but because we are not good at receiving. The fault is always in us, never in Him.

Are you a fully integrated person? When you present your requests to God, are your heart and mind as one? Is what you ask with your lips fully supported by what you are saying in your heart? If not, then when you attempt to climb higher with God, you will not have the precise coordination you need in order to scale the precipitous heights. The awesome fact that has to be faced by all those who want to climb the mountains of God is this – it is possible to miss your step on those steep slopes not by feet, but merely by inches. And it is in those seemingly trivial inches that our spiritual direction is often determined.

PRAYER

O Father, I am seeing more and more the perils that come from being inwardly at cross-purposes. Help me, however, to see that although the challenge is great, the power behind me is greater than the challenge in front of me. In Jesus' name. Amen.

FURTHER STUDY

Joel 2:1-13; Deut. 6:5;
Psa. 119:2
• What was God's message through Joel?
• When are we blessed?

October 27

■ JEREMIAH 29:15–31:14

¹⁵You may say, 'The LORD has raised up prophets for us in Babylon,' ¹⁶but this is what the LORD says about the king who sits on David's throne and all the people who remain in this city, your fellow citizens who did not go with you into exile – ¹⁷yes, this is what the LORD Almighty says: 'I will send the sword, famine and plague against them and I will make them like figs that are so bad they cannot be eaten.

¹⁸I will pursue them with the sword, famine and plague and will make them abhorrent to all the kingdoms of the earth, a curse and an object of horror, of scorn and reproach, among all the nations where I drive them. ¹⁹For they have not listened to my words,' declares the LORD, 'words that I sent to them again and again by my servants the prophets. And you exiles have not listened either,' declares the LORD.

²⁰Therefore, hear the word of the LORD, all you exiles whom I have sent

away from Jerusalem to Babylon. ²¹This is what the LORD Almighty, the God of Israel, says about Ahab son of Kolaiah and Zedekiah son of Maaseiah, who are prophesying lies to you in my name: 'I will deliver them into the hands of Nebuchadnezzar king of Babylon, and he will put them to death before your very eyes. ²²Because of them, all the exiles from Judah who are in Babylon will use this curse: "May the LORD treat you like Zedekiah and Ahab, whom the king of Babylon burned in the fire." ²³For they have done outrageous things in Israel; they have committed adultery with their neighbours' wives, and in my name they have uttered lies – which I did not authorise. I know it and am a witness to it,' declares the LORD.

²⁴Tell Shemaiah the Nehelamite, ²⁵'This is what the Lord Almighty, the God of Israel, says: you sent letters in your own name to all the people in Jerusalem, to the priest Zephaniah son of Maaseiah, and to all the other priests. You said to Zephaniah, ²⁶"The Lord has appointed you priest in place of Jehoiada to be in charge of the house of the Lord; you should put any maniac who acts like a prophet into the stocks and neck-irons. ²⁷So why have you not reprimanded Jeremiah from Anathoth, who poses as a prophet among you? ²⁸He has sent this message to us in Babylon: it will be a long time. Therefore build houses and settle down; plant gardens and eat what they produce."'

²⁹Zephaniah the priest, however, read the letter to Jeremiah the prophet. ³⁰Then the word of the LORD came to Jeremiah: ³¹'Send this message to all the exiles: "This is what the LORD says about Shemaiah the Nehelamite: because Shemaiah has prophesied to you, even though I did not send him, and has persuaded you to trust in lies, ³²this is what the LORD says: I will

surely punish Shemaiah the Nehelamite and his descendants. He will have no one left among this people, nor will he see the good things I will do for my people, declares the LORD, because he has preached rebellion against me."'

30 This is the word that came to Jeremiah from the LORD: ²'This is what the LORD, the God of Israel, says: "Write in a book all the words I have spoken to you. ³The days are coming," declares the LORD, "when I will bring my people Israel and Judah back from captivity and restore them to the land I gave to their ancestors to possess," says the LORD.'

⁴These are the words the LORD spoke concerning Israel and Judah: ⁵'This is what the LORD says:

'"Cries of fear are heard –
    terror, not peace.
⁶Ask and see:
    can a man bear children?
Then why do I see every strong man
    with his hands on his stomach like a
        woman in labour,
    every face turned deathly pale?
⁷How awful that day will be!
    No other will be like it.
It will be a time of trouble for Jacob,
    but he will be saved out of it.

⁸'"In that day," declares the LORD
        Almighty,
    "I will break the yoke off their necks
    and will tear off their bonds;
        no longer will foreigners enslave them.
⁹Instead, they will serve the LORD their
        God
    and David their king,
        whom I will raise up for them.

¹⁰'"So do not be afraid, Jacob my servant;
    do not be dismayed, Israel,"
                declares the LORD.

"I will surely save you out of a distant
    place,
  your descendants from the land of
      their exile.
Jacob will again have peace and security,
  and no one will make him afraid.
[11] I am with you and will save you,"
  declares the LORD.
"Though I completely destroy all the
    nations
  among which I scatter you,
  I will not completely destroy you.
I will discipline you but only in due
    measure;
  I will not let you go entirely
    unpunished."

[12] 'This is what the LORD says:

'"Your wound is incurable,
  your injury beyond healing.
[13] There is no one to plead your cause,
  no remedy for your sore,
  no healing for you.
[14] All your allies have forgotten you;
  they care nothing for you.
I have struck you as an enemy would
  and punished you as would the cruel,
because your guilt is so great
  and your sins so many.
[15] Why do you cry out over your wound,
  your pain that has no cure?
Because of your great guilt and many sins
  I have done these things to you.

[16] ' "But all who devour you will be
    devoured;
  all your enemies will go into exile.
Those who plunder you will be
    plundered;
  all who make spoil of you I will despoil.
[17] But I will restore you to health
  and heal your wounds,"
              declares the LORD,
"because you are called an outcast,
  Zion for whom no one cares."

[18] 'This is what the LORD says:

' "I will restore the fortunes of Jacob's
    tents
  and have compassion on his
    dwellings;
the city will be rebuilt on her ruins,
  and the palace will stand in its proper
    place.
[19] From them will come songs of
    thanksgiving
  and the sound of rejoicing.
I will add to their numbers,
  and they will not be decreased;
I will bring them honour,
  and they will not be disdained.
[20] Their children will be as in days of old,
  and their community will be
    established before me;
  I will punish all who oppress them.
[21] Their leader will be one of their own;
  their ruler will arise from among
    them.
I will bring him near and he will come
    close to me –
  for who is he who will devote himself
    to be close to me?"
              declares the LORD.
[22] ' "So you will be my people,
  and I will be your God."'

[23] See, the storm of the LORD
  will burst out in wrath,
a driving wind swirling down
  on the heads of the wicked.
[24] The fierce anger of the LORD will not turn
    back
  until he fully accomplishes
  the purposes of his heart.
In days to come
  you will understand this.

31 'At that time,' declares the LORD,
    'I will be the God of all the families of
Israel, and they will be my people.'
  [2] This is what the LORD says:

'The people who survive the sword
  will find favour in the wilderness;
  I will come to give rest to Israel.'

³ The LORD appeared to us in the past,
saying:

'I have loved you with an everlasting
  love;
  I have drawn you with unfailing
  kindness.
⁴ I will build you up again,
  and you, Virgin Israel, will be rebuilt.
Again you will take up your tambourines
  and go out to dance with the joyful.
⁵ Again you will plant vineyards
  on the hills of Samaria;
  the farmers will plant them
  and enjoy their fruit.
⁶ There will be a day when watchmen cry
  out
  on the hills of Ephraim,
"Come, let us go up to Zion,
  to the LORD our God."'

⁷ This is what the LORD says:

'Sing with joy for Jacob;
  shout for the foremost of the nations.
Make your praises heard, and say,
  "LORD, save your people,
  the remnant of Israel."
⁸ See, I will bring them from the land of
  the north
  and gather them from the ends of the
  earth.
Among them will be the blind and the
  lame,
  expectant mothers and women in
  labour;
  a great throng will return.
⁹ They will come with weeping;
  they will pray as I bring them back.
I will lead them beside streams of water
  on a level path where they will not
  stumble,

because I am Israel's father,
  and Ephraim is my firstborn son.

¹⁰ 'Hear the word of the LORD, you nations;
  proclaim it in distant coastlands:
"He who scattered Israel will gather
  them
  and will watch over his flock like a
  shepherd."
¹¹ For the LORD will deliver Jacob
  and redeem them from the hand of
  those stronger than they.
¹² They will come and shout for joy on the
  heights of Zion;
  they will rejoice in the bounty of the
  LORD –
the grain, the new wine and the olive oil,
  the young of the flocks and herds.
They will be like a well-watered garden,
  and they will sorrow no more.
¹³ Then young women will dance and be
  glad,
  young men and old as well.
I will turn their mourning into gladness;
  I will give them comfort and joy
  instead of sorrow.
¹⁴ I will satisfy the priests with abundance,
  and my people will be filled with my
  bounty,'

declares the LORD.

━ PSALM 119:65-68

⁶⁵ Do good to your servant
  according to your word, LORD.
⁶⁶ Teach me knowledge and good
  judgment,
  for I trust your commands.
⁶⁷ Before I was afflicted I went astray,
  but now I obey your word.
⁶⁸ You are good, and what you do is good;
  teach me your decrees.

▬ PROVERBS 25:23-24

²³ Like a north wind that brings
  unexpected rain
  is a sly tongue – which provokes a
  horrified look.

²⁴ Better to live on a corner of the roof
  than share a house with a quarrelsome
  wife.

▬ 1 TIMOTHY 5:1-25

5 Do not rebuke an older man harshly,
  but exhort him as if he were your fa-
ther. Treat younger men as brothers, ² older
women as mothers, and younger women as
sisters, with absolute purity.

³ Give proper recognition to those widows
who are really in need. ⁴ But if a widow has
children or grandchildren, these should
learn first of all put their religion into
practice by caring for their own family and
so repaying their parents and grandpar-
ents, for this is pleasing to God. ⁵ The widow
who is really in need and left all alone puts
her hope in God and continues night and
day to pray and to ask God for help. ⁶ But
the widow who lives for pleasure is dead
even while she lives. ⁷ Give the people these
instructions, so that no one may be open
to blame. ⁸ Anyone who does not provide
for their relatives, and especially for their
own household, has denied the faith and is
worse than an unbeliever.

⁹ No widow may be put on the list of wid-
ows unless she is over sixty, has been faithful to her husband, ¹⁰ and is well known for
her good deeds, such as bringing up children, showing hospitality, washing the feet
of the Lord's people, helping those in trouble and devoting herself to all kinds of good
deeds.

¹¹ As for younger widows, do not put
them on such a list. For when their sensual

desires overcome their dedication to Christ,
they want to marry. ¹² Thus they bring judgment on themselves, because they have
broken their first pledge. ¹³ Besides, they get
into the habit of being idle and going about
from house to house. And not only do they
become idlers, but also busybodies who
talk nonsense, saying things they ought not
to. ¹⁴ So I counsel younger widows to marry, to have children, to manage their homes
and to give the enemy no opportunity for
slander. ¹⁵ Some have in fact already turned
away to follow Satan.

¹⁶ If any woman who is a believer has wid-
ows in her care, she should continue to help
them and not let the church be burdened
with them, so that the church can help those
widows who are really in need.

¹⁷ The elders who direct the affairs of the
church well are worthy of double honour,
especially those whose work is preaching
and teaching. ¹⁸ For Scripture says, 'Do not
muzzle an ox while it is treading out the
grain,' and 'The worker deserves his wages.'
¹⁹ Do not entertain an accusation against
an elder unless it is brought by two or three
witnesses. ²⁰ But those elders who are sinning you are to reprove before everyone, so
that the others may take warning. ²¹ I charge
you, in the sight of God and Christ Jesus and
the elect angels, to keep these instructions
without partiality, and to do nothing out of
favouritism.

²² Do not be hasty in the laying on of
hands, and do not share in the sins of
others. Keep yourself pure.

²³ Stop drinking only water, and use a lit-
tle wine because of your stomach and your
frequent illnesses.

²⁴ The sins of some are obvious, reach-
ing the place of judgment ahead of them;
the sins of others trail behind them. ²⁵ In
the same way, good deeds are obvious,
and even those that are not obvious cannot
remain hidden for ever.

What a Tranquilliser!

'"I have loved you with an everlasting love ..."'
Jeremiah 31:3

'How little real love there is for God,' says theologian Arthur W. Pink. He suggests that the level of spirituality in today's church is caused by our hearts being so little occupied with thoughts of the divine love. 'The better we are acquainted with His love – its character, its fullness, its blessedness,' he says, 'the more will our hearts be drawn out in love to Him.'

We focus now on the fact that God's love is eternal.

God being eternal, it follows that His love also is eternal. This means that God loved us before earth and heaven were called into existence, that He has set His heart upon us from all eternity. This is the truth set forth in Ephesians 1:4-5, where we are told that we were chosen in Christ before the foundation of the world. What a tranquilliser this is for our hearts! If God's love for us had no beginning, then it has no ending either. It is from 'everlasting to everlasting' (Psa. 103:17).

Another thing we need to know about the love of God is that it is a holy love. This means that His love is not regulated by whim or caprice or sentiment, but by principle. Just as His grace reigns not at the expense of righteousness but 'through' it (Rom. 5:21), so His love never conflicts with His holiness. This is why John says that God is 'light' before he says God is 'love'. And this is why, too, the Almighty never lets us get away with anything. He loves us too much for that. His love is pure, holy, and unmixed with sentimentality. God will not wink at sin, not even in His own people.

PRAYER

O Father, the more I learn about Your love, the more my heart is set on fire. Increase my understanding, for I see that the more I comprehend how much I am loved, the more secure I am in that love. Amen.

FURTHER STUDY

Rom. 8:18-39; 1 Pet. 1:17-21
• What was Paul convinced of?
• How does Peter portray the eternal perspective?

October 28

■ **JEREMIAH 31:15–32:25**

[15] This is what the LORD says:

'A voice is heard in Ramah,

mourning and great weeping,
Rachel weeping for her children
and refusing to be comforted,
because they are no more.'

¹⁶ This is what the LORD says:

'Restrain your voice from weeping
    and your eyes from tears,
for your work will be rewarded,'
                declares the LORD.
'They will return from the land of the
    enemy.
¹⁷ So there is hope for your descendants,'
                declares the LORD.
'Your children will return to their own
    land.

¹⁸ 'I have surely heard Ephraim's moaning:
    "You disciplined me like an unruly
        calf,
    and I have been disciplined.
Restore me, and I will return,
    because you are the LORD my God.
¹⁹ After I strayed,
    I repented;
after I came to understand,
    I beat my breast.
I was ashamed and humiliated
    because I bore the disgrace of my
        youth."
²⁰ Is not Ephraim my dear son,
    the child in whom I delight?
Though I often speak against him,
    I still remember him.
Therefore my heart yearns for him;
    I have great compassion for him,'
                declares the LORD.

²¹ 'Set up road signs;
    put up guideposts.
Take note of the highway,
    the road that you take.
Return, Virgin Israel,
    return to your towns.
²² How long will you wander,
    unfaithful Daughter Israel?
The LORD will create a new thing on
        earth –
    the woman will return to the man.'

²³ This is what the LORD Almighty, the
God of Israel, says: 'When I bring them back
from captivity, the people in the land of
Judah and in its towns will once again use
these words: "The LORD bless you, you prosperous city, you sacred mountain." ²⁴ People will live together in Judah and all its
towns – farmers and those who move about
with their flocks. ²⁵ I will refresh the weary
and satisfy the faint.'

²⁶ At this I awoke and looked around. My
sleep had been pleasant to me.

²⁷ 'The days are coming,' declares the
LORD, 'when I will plant the kingdoms of
Israel and Judah with the offspring of people and of animals. ²⁸ Just as I watched over
them to uproot and tear down, and to overthrow, destroy and bring disaster, so I will
watch over them to build and to plant,' declares the LORD. ²⁹ 'In those days people will
no longer say,

    "The parents have eaten sour grapes,
        and the children's teeth are set on
            edge."

³⁰ Instead, everyone will die for their own
sin; whoever eats sour grapes – their own
teeth will be set on edge.

³¹ 'The days are coming,' declares the LORD,
    'when I will make a new covenant
        with the people of Israel
            and with the people of Judah.
³² It will not be like the covenant
        I made with their ancestors
    when I took them by the hand
        to lead them out of Egypt,
    because they broke my covenant,
        though I was a husband to them,'
                    declares the LORD.
³³ 'This is the covenant that I will make
        with the people of Israel
    after that time,' declares the LORD.
'I will put my law in their minds
    and write it on their hearts.

I will be their God,
    and they will be my people.
[34] No longer will they teach their neighbour,
    or say to one another, "Know the LORD,"
    because they will all know me,
    from the least of them to the greatest,'
                    declares the LORD.
'For I will forgive their wickedness
    and will remember their sins no more.'

[35] This is what the LORD says,

he who appoints the sun
    to shine by day,
who decrees the moon and stars
    to shine by night,
who stirs up the sea
    so that its waves roar –
    the LORD Almighty is his name:
[36] 'Only if these decrees vanish from my
        sight,'
    declares the LORD,
'will Israel ever cease
    being a nation before me.'

[37] This is what the LORD says:

'Only if the heavens above can be
        measured
    and the foundations of the earth below
        be searched out
will I reject all the descendants of Israel
    because of all they have done,'
                    declares the LORD.

[38] 'The days are coming,' declares the LORD, 'when this city will be rebuilt for me from the Tower of Hananel to the Corner Gate. [39] The measuring line will stretch from there straight to the hill of Gareb and then turn to Goah. [40] The whole valley where dead bodies and ashes are thrown, and all the terraces out to the Kidron Valley on the east as far as the corner of the Horse Gate, will be holy to the LORD. The city will never again be uprooted or demolished.'

32 This is the word that came to Jeremiah from the LORD in the tenth year of Zedekiah king of Judah, which was the eighteenth year of Nebuchadnezzar. [2] The army of the king of Babylon was then besieging Jerusalem, and Jeremiah the prophet was confined in the courtyard of the guard in the royal palace of Judah.

[3] Now Zedekiah king of Judah had imprisoned him there, saying, 'Why do you prophesy as you do? You say, "This is what the LORD says: I am about to give this city into the hands of the king of Babylon, and he will capture it. [4] Zedekiah king of Judah will not escape the Babylonians but will certainly be given into the hands of the king of Babylon, and will speak with him face to face and see him with his own eyes. [5] He will take Zedekiah to Babylon, where he will remain until I deal with him, declares the LORD. If you fight against the Babylonians, you will not succeed."'

[6] Jeremiah said, 'The word of the LORD came to me: [7] Hanamel son of Shallum your uncle is going to come to you and say, "Buy my field at Anathoth, because as nearest relative it is your right and duty to buy it."

[8] 'Then, just as the LORD had said, my cousin Hanamel came to me in the courtyard of the guard and said, "Buy my field at Anathoth in the territory of Benjamin. Since it is your right to redeem it and possess it, buy it for yourself."

'I knew that this was the word of the LORD; [9] so I bought the field at Anathoth from my cousin Hanamel and weighed out for him seventeen shekels of silver. [10] I signed and sealed the deed, had it witnessed, and weighed out the silver on the scales. [11] I took the deed of purchase – the sealed copy containing the terms and conditions, as well as the unsealed copy – [12] and I gave this deed to Baruch son of Neriah, the son of Mahseiah, in the presence of my cousin Hanamel and of the witnesses who had signed the deed and of all the Jews sitting in the courtyard of the guard.

¹³ 'In their presence I gave Baruch these instructions: ¹⁴ "This is what the LORD Almighty, the God of Israel, says: take these documents, both the sealed and unsealed copies of the deed of purchase, and put them in a clay jar so that they will last a long time. ¹⁵ For this is what the LORD Almighty, the God of Israel, says: houses, fields and vineyards will again be bought in this land."

¹⁶ 'After I had given the deed of purchase to Baruch son of Neriah, I prayed to the LORD:

¹⁷ 'Ah, Sovereign LORD, you have made the heavens and the earth by your great power and outstretched arm. Nothing is too hard for you. ¹⁸ You show love to thousands but bring the punishment for the parents' sins into the laps of their children after them. Great and mighty God, whose name is the LORD Almighty, ¹⁹ great are your purposes and mighty are your deeds. Your eyes are open to the ways of all mankind; you reward each person according to their conduct and as their deeds deserve. ²⁰ You performed signs and wonders in Egypt and have continued them to this day, in Israel and among all mankind, and have gained the renown that is still yours. ²¹ You brought your people Israel out of Egypt with signs and wonders, by a mighty hand and an outstretched arm and with great terror. ²² You gave them this land you had sworn to give to their ancestors, a land flowing with milk and honey. ²³ They came in and took possession of it, but they did not obey you or follow your law; they did not do what you commanded them to do. So you brought all this disaster on them.

²⁴ 'See how the siege ramps are built up to take the city. Because of the sword, famine and plague, the city will be given into the hands of the

Babylonians who are attacking it. What you said has happened, as you now see. ²⁵ And though the city will be given into the hands of the Babylonians, you, Sovereign LORD, say to me, "Buy the field with silver and have the transaction witnessed." '

▬ PSALM 119:69-72

⁶⁹ Though the arrogant have smeared me with lies,
    I keep your precepts with all my heart.
⁷⁰ Their hearts are callous and unfeeling,
    but I delight in your law.
⁷¹ It was good for me to be afflicted
    so that I might learn your decrees.
⁷² The law from your mouth is more precious to me
    than thousands of pieces of silver and gold.

▬ PROVERBS 25:25-26

²⁵ Like cold water to a weary soul
    is good news from a distant land.
²⁶ Like a muddied spring or a polluted well
    are the righteous who give way to the wicked.

▬ 1 TIMOTHY 6:1-21

6 All who are under the yoke of slavery should consider their masters worthy of full respect, so that God's name and our teaching may not be slandered. ² Those who have believing masters should not show them disrespect just because they are fellow believers. Instead, they should serve them even better because their masters are dear to them as fellow believers and are devoted to the welfare of their slaves.

These are the things you are to teach and

insist on. [3] If anyone teaches otherwise and does not agree to the sound instruction of our Lord Jesus Christ and to godly teaching, [4] they are conceited and understand nothing. They have an unhealthy interest in controversies and quarrels about words that result in envy, strife, malicious talk, evil suspicions [5] and constant friction between people of corrupt mind, who have been robbed of the truth and who think that godliness is a means to financial gain.

[6] But godliness with contentment is great gain. [7] For we brought nothing into the world, and we can take nothing out of it. [8] But if we have food and clothing, we will be content with that. [9] Those who want to get rich fall into temptation and a trap and into many foolish and harmful desires that plunge people into ruin and destruction. [10] For the love of money is a root of all kinds of evil. Some people, eager for money, have wandered from the faith and pierced themselves with many griefs.

[11] But you, man of God, flee from all this, and pursue righteousness, godliness, faith, love, endurance and gentleness. [12] Fight the good fight of the faith. Take hold of the eternal life to which you were called when you made your good confession in the presence of many witnesses. [13] In the sight of God, who gives life to everything, and of Christ Jesus, who while testifying before Pontius Pilate made the good confession, I charge you [14] to keep this command without spot or blame until the appearing of our Lord Jesus Christ, [15] which God will bring about in his own time – God, the blessed and only Ruler, the King of kings and Lord of lords, [16] who alone is immortal and who lives in unapproachable light, whom no one has seen or can see. To him be honour and might for ever. Amen.

[17] Command those who are rich in this present world not to be arrogant nor to put their hope in wealth, which is so uncertain, but to put their hope in God, who richly provides us with everything for our enjoyment. [18] Command them to do good, to be rich in good deeds, and to be generous and willing to share. [19] In this way they will lay up treasure for themselves as a firm foundation for the coming age, so that they may take hold of the life that is truly life.

[20] Timothy, guard what has been entrusted to your care. Turn away from godless chatter and the opposing ideas of what is falsely called knowledge, [21] which some have professed and in so doing have departed from the faith.

Grace be with you all.

The Shield of Faith

'Fight the good fight of the faith. Take hold of the eternal life to which you were called ...' **1 Timothy 6:12**

The fourth piece of equipment in the Christian soldier's armour is the shield of faith: 'In addition ...' says the apostle, 'take up the shield of faith, with which you can extinguish all the flaming arrows of the evil one' (Eph. 6:16).

Some take Paul's use of the expression 'in addition' to mean 'above everything else in importance', and from this they go on to argue that the last three pieces of armour are more important than the first three. But the phrase only means 'in addition to all this'. It is a transition phrase designed to introduce us to a section of the armour that has a different purpose.

The six pieces of armour fall clearly into two main groups, the first consisting of the belt of truth, the breastplate of righteousness, and the shoes of the preparation of the gospel of peace. The second group comprises the shield of faith, the helmet of salvation, and the sword of the Spirit. The first three pieces of armour were fixed to the body by a special fastening, and hence, to a certain degree, were immovable. But the shield was not fixed to the body; it was something quite separate. The same applies to the helmet; that, too, was something that could be put on or taken off quite easily. And obviously the same was true of the sword of the Spirit.

The lesson, quite clearly, is this - the first three pieces of equipment should be worn at all times, while the other three are to be taken up when and where necessary.

PRAYER

Gracious and loving heavenly Father, I am so thankful for the care and design that have gone into providing for me a sure defence against Satan. I have learned much, yet I see there is still much more to learn. Teach me, my Father. Amen.

FURTHER STUDY

1 Tim. 1:12-20; 6:12;
1 Thess. 5:8; 1 John 5:4
• What had some rejected?
• What was the result?

October 29

■ JEREMIAH 32:26–34:11

²⁶Then the word of the LORD came to Jeremiah: ²⁷'I am the LORD, the God of all mankind. Is anything too hard for me? ²⁸Therefore this is what the LORD says: I am about to give this city into the hands of the Babylonians and to Nebuchadnezzar king of Babylon, who will capture it. ²⁹The Babylonians who are attacking this city will come in and set it on fire; they will burn it down, along with the houses where the people aroused my anger by burning incense on the roofs to Baal and by pouring out drink offerings to other gods.

³⁰'The people of Israel and Judah have done nothing but evil in my sight from their youth; indeed, the people of Israel have done nothing but arouse my anger with what their hands have made, declares the LORD. ³¹From the day it was built until now, this city has so aroused my anger and wrath that I must remove it from my sight. ³²The people of Israel and Judah have provoked me by all the evil they have done – they, their kings and officials, their priests and prophets, the people of Judah and those living in Jerusalem. ³³They turned their backs to me and not their faces; though I taught them again and again, they would not listen or respond to discipline. ³⁴They set up their vile images in the house that bears my Name and defiled it. ³⁵They built high places for Baal in the Valley of Ben Hinnom to sacrifice their sons and daughters to Molek, though I never commanded – nor did it

enter my mind – that they should do such a detestable thing and so make Judah sin. ³⁶'You are saying about this city, "By the sword, famine and plague it will be given into the hands of the king of Babylon"; but this is what the LORD, the God of Israel, says: ³⁷I will surely gather them from all the lands where I banish them in my furious anger and great wrath; I will bring them back to this place and let them live in safety. ³⁸They will be my people, and I will be their God. ³⁹I will give them singleness of heart and action, so that they will always fear me and that all will then go well for them and for their children after them. ⁴⁰I will make an everlasting covenant with them: I will never stop doing good to them, and I will inspire them to fear me, so that they will never turn away from me. ⁴¹I will rejoice in doing them good and will assuredly plant them in this land with all my heart and soul.

⁴²'This is what the LORD says: as I have brought all this great calamity on this people, so I will give them all the prosperity I have promised them. ⁴³Once more fields will be bought in this land of which you say, "It is a desolate waste, without people or animals, for it has been given into the hands of the Babylonians." ⁴⁴Fields will be bought for silver, and deeds will be signed, sealed and witnessed in the territory of Benjamin, in the villages around Jerusalem, in the towns of Judah and in the towns of the hill country, of the western foothills and of the Negev, because I will restore their fortunes, declares the LORD.'

33 While Jeremiah was still confined in the courtyard of the guard, the word of the LORD came to him a second time: ²'This is what the LORD says, he who made the earth, the LORD who formed it and established it – the LORD is his name: ³"Call to me and I will answer you and tell you great and unsearchable things you do not know." ⁴For this is what the LORD, the God of Israel, says about the houses in this city and the royal palaces of Judah that have been torn down to be used against the siege ramps and the sword ⁵in the fight with the Babylonians: "They will be filled with the dead bodies of the people I will slay in my anger and wrath. I will hide my face from this city because of all its wickedness.

⁶'"Nevertheless, I will bring health and healing to it; I will heal my people and will let them enjoy abundant peace and security. ⁷I will bring Judah and Israel back from captivity and will rebuild them as they were before. ⁸I will cleanse them from all the sin they have committed against me and will forgive all their sins of rebellion against me. ⁹Then this city will bring me renown, joy, praise and honour before all nations on earth that hear of all the good things I do for it; and they will be in awe and will tremble at the abundant prosperity and peace I provide for it."

¹⁰'This is what the LORD says: "You say about this place, 'It is a desolate waste, without people or animals.' Yet in the towns of Judah and the streets of Jerusalem that are deserted, inhabited by neither people nor animals, there will be heard once more ¹¹the sounds of joy and gladness, the voices of bride and bridegroom, and the voices of those who bring thank offerings to the house of the LORD, saying,

'Give thanks to the LORD Almighty,
    for the LORD is good;
    his love endures for ever.'

For I will restore the fortunes of the land as they were before," says the LORD. ¹²'This is what the LORD Almighty says: "In this place, desolate and without people or animals – in all its towns there will again be pastures for shepherds to rest their flocks. ¹³In the towns of the hill country, of the western foothills and of the Negev, in the territory of Benjamin, in the villages around Jerusalem and in the towns of

Judah, flocks will again pass under the hand of the one who counts them," says the LORD.

¹⁴"'The days are coming," declares the LORD, "when I will fulfil the good promise I made to the people of Israel and Judah.

¹⁵"'In those days and at that time
    I will make a righteous Branch sprout
      from David's line;
    he will do what is just and right in the
      land.
¹⁶In those days Judah will be saved
    and Jerusalem will live in safety.
This is the name by which it will be
      called:
    The LORD Our Righteous Savior."

¹⁷For this is what the LORD says: "David will never fail to have a man to sit on the throne of Israel, ¹⁸nor will the Levitical priests ever fail to have a man to stand before me continually to offer burnt offerings, to burn grain offerings and to present sacrifices."'

¹⁹The word of the LORD came to Jeremiah: ²⁰'This is what the LORD says: "If you can break my covenant with the day and my covenant with the night, so that day and night no longer come at their appointed time, ²¹then my covenant with David my servant – and my covenant with the Levites who are priests ministering before me – can be broken and David will no longer have a descendant to reign on his throne. ²²I will make the descendants of David my servant and the Levites who minister before me as countless as the stars in the sky and as measureless as the sand on the seashore."'

²³The word of the LORD came to Jeremiah: ²⁴'Have you not noticed that these people are saying, "The LORD has rejected the two kingdoms he chose"? So they despise my people and no longer regard them as a nation. ²⁵This is what the LORD says: "If I have not made my covenant with day and night and established the laws of heaven

and earth, ²⁶then I will reject the descendants of Jacob and David my servant and will not choose one of his sons to rule over the descendants of Abraham, Isaac and Jacob. For I will restore their fortunes and have compassion on them."'

34 While Nebuchadnezzar king of Babylon and all his army and all the kingdoms and peoples in the empire he ruled were fighting against Jerusalem and all its surrounding towns, this word came to Jeremiah from the LORD: ²'This is what the LORD, the God of Israel, says: go to Zedekiah king of Judah and tell him, "This is what the LORD says: I am about to give this city into the hands of the king of Babylon, and he will burn it down. ³You will not escape from his grasp but will surely be captured and given into his hands. You will see the king of Babylon with your own eyes, and he will speak with you face to face. And you will go to Babylon.

⁴"'Yet hear the LORD's promise to you, Zedekiah king of Judah. This is what the LORD says concerning you: you will not die by the sword; ⁵you will die peacefully. As people made a funeral fire in honour of your predecessors, the kings who ruled before you, so they will make a fire in your honour and lament, 'Alas, master!' I myself make this promise, declares the LORD."'

⁶Then Jeremiah the prophet told all this to Zedekiah king of Judah, in Jerusalem, ⁷while the army of the king of Babylon was fighting against Jerusalem and the other cities of Judah that were still holding out – Lachish and Azekah. These were the only fortified cities left in Judah.

⁸The word came to Jeremiah from the LORD after King Zedekiah had made a covenant with all the people in Jerusalem to proclaim freedom for the slaves. ⁹Everyone was to free their Hebrew slaves, both male and female; no one was to hold a fellow Hebrew in bondage. ¹⁰So all the officials and people who entered into this covenant

agreed that they would free their male and female slaves and no longer hold them in bondage. They agreed, and set them free. ¹¹ But afterwards they changed their minds and took back the slaves they had freed and enslaved them again.

▬ PSALM 119:73-77

⁷³ Your hands made me and formed me;
  give me understanding to learn your
    commands.
⁷⁴ May those who fear you rejoice when
    they see me,
  for I have put my hope in your word.
⁷⁵ I know, LORD, that your laws are
    righteous,
  and that in faithfulness you have
    afflicted me.
⁷⁶ May your unfailing love be my comfort,
  according to your promise to your
    servant.
⁷⁷ Let your compassion come to me that I
    may live,
  for your law is my delight.

▬ PROVERBS 25:27-28

²⁷ It is not good to eat too much honey,
  nor is it honourable to search out
    matters that are too deep.

²⁸ Like a city whose walls are broken
    through
  is a person who lacks self-control.

▬ 2 TIMOTHY 1:1-18

1 Paul, an apostle of Christ Jesus by the will of God, in keeping with the promise of life that is in Christ Jesus,

² To Timothy, my dear son:

Grace, mercy and peace from God the Father and Christ Jesus our Lord.

³ I thank God, whom I serve, as my ancestors did, with a clear conscience, as night and day I constantly remember you in my prayers. ⁴ Recalling your tears, I long to see you, so that I may be filled with joy. ⁵ I am reminded of your sincere faith, which first lived in your grandmother Lois and in your mother Eunice and, I am persuaded, now lives in you also.

⁶ For this reason I remind you to fan into flame the gift of God, which is in you through the laying on of my hands. ⁷ For the Spirit God gave us does not make us timid, but gives us power, love and self-discipline. ⁸ So do not be ashamed of the testimony about our Lord or of me his prisoner. Rather, join with me in suffering for the gospel, by the power of God. ⁹ He has saved us and called us to a holy life – not because of anything we have done but because of his own purpose and grace. This grace was given us in Christ Jesus before the beginning of time, ¹⁰ but it has now been revealed through the appearing of our Saviour, Christ Jesus, who has destroyed death and has brought life and immortality to light through the gospel. ¹¹ And of this gospel I was appointed a herald and an apostle and a teacher. ¹² That is why I am suffering as I am. Yet this is no cause for shame, because I know whom I have believed, and am convinced that he is able to guard what I have entrusted to him until that day.

¹³ What you heard from me, keep as the pattern of sound teaching, with faith and love in Christ Jesus. ¹⁴ Guard the good deposit that was entrusted to you – guard it with the help of the Holy Spirit who lives in us.

¹⁵ You know that everyone in the province of Asia has deserted me, including Phygelus and Hermogenes.

¹⁶ May the Lord show mercy to the household of Onesiphorus, because he often

refreshed me and was not ashamed of my chains. [17] On the contrary, when he was in Rome, he searched hard for me until he found me. [18] May the Lord grant that he will find mercy from the Lord on that day! You know very well in how many ways he helped me in Ephesus.

Handling Confusion

'For the Spirit God gave us does not make us timid, but gives us power, love and self-discipline.' **2 Timothy 1:7**

A feeling that Satan delights to arouse in a heart unprotected by a spiritual breastplate is the feeling of confusion. None of us likes confusion, because it erodes our sense of competence. Satan, knowing this, steps in whenever he can to take full advantage of it.

Deep in the centre of our being is a compulsive demand to be in control. And to satisfy that demand, we have to live in a predictable, understandable world. Confusion presents a serious challenge to our desire for control and is the enemy of those who demand to have clear answers for everything.

Whenever Satan sees that we are not wearing our spiritual breastplate, he comes to us and says something like this, 'Look at the great problems that are all around you – earthquakes, famines, violence, cruelty to children. How can you believe in a God of love when these things are going on in the world?' Sometimes he presses home these arguments with such power that you have no clear answers.

There is only one clear answer against such assaults; it is to put on the 'breastplate of righteousness' (Eph. 6:14). You cannot understand particular happenings; you cannot give any explanation. But you do know that the God who clothed you with His righteousness and saved you from a lost eternity must have your highest interests and those of His universe at heart. When you hold on to that, your heart is protected from despair, even if your mind struggles to comprehend what is happening. You can live in peace even though you do not know all the answers.

PRAYER

Father God, I see that I can experience security in my heart even when my mind cannot understand Your ways. Hidden in Christ and His righteousness, I am safe. I am so thankful. Amen.

FURTHER STUDY

2 Tim. 1:1-7; 1 Cor. 14:33; Isa. 26:3; Rom. 8:39
• Where does our peace stem from?
• Where does confusion come from?

October 30

■ JEREMIAH 34:12–36:26

¹²Then the word of the LORD came to Jeremiah: ¹³'This is what the LORD, the God of Israel, says: I made a covenant with your ancestors when I brought them out of Egypt, out of the land of slavery. I said, ¹⁴"Every seventh year each of you must free any fellow Hebrews who have sold themselves to you. After they have served you for six years, you must let them go free." Your ancestors, however, did not listen to me or pay attention to me. ¹⁵Recently you repented and did what is right in my sight: each of you proclaimed freedom to your own people. You even made a covenant before me in the house that bears my Name. ¹⁶But now you have turned round and profaned my name; each of you has taken back the male and female slaves you had set free to go where they wished. You have forced them to become your slaves again.

¹⁷'Therefore this is what the LORD says: you have not obeyed me; you have not proclaimed freedom to your own people. So I now proclaim "freedom" for you, declares the LORD – "freedom" to fall by the sword, plague and famine. I will make you abhorrent to all the kingdoms of the earth. ¹⁸Those who have violated my covenant and have not fulfilled the terms of the covenant they made before me, I will treat like the calf they cut in two and then walked between its pieces. ¹⁹The leaders of Judah and Jerusalem, the court officials, the priests and all the people of the land who walked between the pieces of the calf, ²⁰I will deliver into the hands of their enemies who want to kill them. Their dead bodies will become food for the birds and the wild animals.

²¹'I will deliver Zedekiah king of Judah and his officials into the hands of their enemies who want to kill them, to the army of the king of Babylon, which has withdrawn from you. ²²I am going to give the order, declares the LORD, and I will bring them back to this city. They will fight against it, take it and burn it down. And I will lay waste the towns of Judah so that no one can live there.'

35 This is the word that came to Jeremiah from the LORD during the reign of Jehoiakim son of Josiah king of Judah: ²'Go to the Rekabite family and invite them to come to one of the side rooms of the house of the LORD and give them wine to drink.'

³So I went to get Jaazaniah son of Jeremiah, the son of Habazziniah, and his brothers and all his sons – the whole family of the Rekabites. ⁴I brought them into the house of the LORD, into the room of the sons of Hanan son of Igdaliah the man of God. It was next to the room of the officials, which was over that of Maaseiah son of Shallum the door-keeper. ⁵Then I set bowls full of wine and some cups before the Rekabites and said to them, 'Drink some wine.'

⁶But they replied, 'We do not drink wine, because our forefather Jehonadab son of Rekab gave us this command: "Neither you nor your descendants must ever drink wine. ⁷Also you must never build houses, sow seed or plant vineyards; you must never have any of these things, but must always live in tents. Then you will live a long time in the land where you are nomads." ⁸We have obeyed everything our forefather Jehonadab son of Rekab commanded us. Neither we nor our wives nor our sons and daughters have ever drunk wine ⁹or built houses to live in or had vineyards, fields or crops. ¹⁰We have lived in tents and have

fully obeyed everything our forefather Jehonadab commanded us. [11] But when Nebuchadnezzar king of Babylon invaded this land, we said, "Come, we must go to Jerusalem to escape the Babylonian and Aramean armies." So we have remained in Jerusalem.'

[12] Then the word of the LORD came to Jeremiah, saying: [13] 'This is what the LORD Almighty, the God of Israel, says: go and tell the people of Judah and those living in Jerusalem, "Will you not learn a lesson and obey my words?" declares the LORD. [14] "Jehonadab son of Rekab ordered his descendants not to drink wine and this command has been kept. To this day they do not drink wine, because they obey their forefather's command. But I have spoken to you again and again, yet you have not obeyed me. [15] Again and again I sent all my servants the prophets to you. They said, 'Each of you must turn from your wicked ways and reform your actions; do not follow other gods to serve them. Then you shall live in the land I have given to you and your ancestors.' But you have not paid attention or listened to me. [16] The descendants of Jehonadab son of Rekab have carried out the command their forefather gave them, but these people have not obeyed me."

[17] 'Therefore this is what the LORD God Almighty, the God of Israel, says: "Listen! I am going to bring on Judah and on everyone living in Jerusalem every disaster I pronounced against them. I spoke to them, but they did not listen; I called to them, but they did not answer." '

[18] Then Jeremiah said to the family of the Rekabites, 'This is what the LORD Almighty, the God of Israel, says: "You have obeyed the command of your forefather Jehonadab and have followed all his instructions and have done everything he ordered." [19] Therefore this is what the LORD Almighty, the God of Israel, says: "Jehonadab son of Rekab shall never fail to have a descendant to serve me." '

36 In the fourth year of Jehoiakim son of Josiah king of Judah, this word came to Jeremiah from the LORD: [2] 'Take a scroll and write on it all the words I have spoken to you concerning Israel, Judah and all the other nations from the time I began speaking to you in the reign of Josiah till now. [3] Perhaps when the people of Judah hear about every disaster I plan to inflict on them, they will each turn from their wicked ways; then I will forgive their wickedness and their sin.'

[4] So Jeremiah called Baruch son of Neriah, and while Jeremiah dictated all the words the LORD had spoken to him, Baruch wrote them on the scroll. [5] Then Jeremiah told Baruch, 'I am restricted; I am not allowed to go to the LORD's temple. [6] So you go to the house of the LORD on a day of fasting and read to the people from the scroll the words of the LORD that you wrote as I dictated. Read them to all the people of Judah who come in from their towns. [7] Perhaps they will bring their petition before the LORD and will each turn from their wicked ways, for the anger and wrath pronounced against this people by the LORD are great.'

[8] Baruch son of Neriah did everything Jeremiah the prophet told him to do; at the LORD's temple he read the words of the LORD from the scroll. [9] In the ninth month of the fifth year of Jehoiakim son of Josiah king of Judah, a time of fasting before the LORD was proclaimed for all the people in Jerusalem and those who had come from the towns of Judah. [10] From the room of Gemariah son of Shaphan the secretary, which was in the upper courtyard at the entrance of the New Gate of the temple, Baruch read to all the people at the LORD's temple the words of Jeremiah from the scroll.

[11] When Micaiah son of Gemariah, the son of Shaphan, heard all the words of the LORD from the scroll, [12] he went down to the secretary's room in the royal palace, where all

the officials were sitting: Elishama the secretary, Delaiah son of Shemaiah, Elnathan son of Akbor, Gemariah son of Shaphan, Zedekiah son of Hananiah, and all the other officials. ¹³ After Micaiah told them everything he had heard Baruch read to the people from the scroll, ¹⁴ all the officials sent Jehudi son of Nethaniah, the son of Shelemiah, the son of Cushi, to say to Baruch, 'Bring the scroll from which you have read to the people and come.' So Baruch son of Neriah went to them with the scroll in his hand. ¹⁵ They said to him, 'Sit down, please, and read it to us.'

So Baruch read it to them. ¹⁶ When they heard all these words, they looked at each other in fear and said to Baruch, 'We must report all these words to the king.' ¹⁷ Then they asked Baruch, 'Tell us, how did you come to write all this? Did Jeremiah dictate it?'

¹⁸ 'Yes,' Baruch replied, 'he dictated all these words to me, and I wrote them in ink on the scroll.'

¹⁹ Then the officials said to Baruch, 'You and Jeremiah, go and hide. Don't let anyone know where you are.'

²⁰ After they put the scroll in the room of Elishama the secretary, they went to the king in the courtyard and reported everything to him. ²¹ The king sent Jehudi to get the scroll, and Jehudi brought it from the room of Elishama the secretary and read it to the king and all the officials standing beside him. ²² It was the ninth month and the king was sitting in the winter apartment, with a fire burning in the brazier in front of him. ²³ Whenever Jehudi had read three or four columns of the scroll, the king cut them off with a scribe's knife and threw them into the brazier, until the entire scroll was burned in the fire. ²⁴ The king and all his attendants who heard all these words showed no fear, nor did they tear their clothes. ²⁵ Even though Elnathan, Delaiah and Gemariah urged the king not to burn the scroll, he would not

listen to them. ²⁶ Instead, the king commanded Jerahmeel, a son of the king, Seraiah son of Azriel and Shelemiah son of Abdeel to arrest Baruch the scribe and Jeremiah the prophet. But the LORD had hidden them.

■ PSALM 119:78-81

⁷⁸ May the arrogant be put to shame for
        wronging me without cause;
    but I will meditate on your precepts.
⁷⁹ May those who fear you turn to me,
        those who understand your statutes.
⁸⁰ May I wholeheartedly follow your
        decrees,
    that I may not be put to shame.

⁸¹ My soul faints with longing for your
        salvation,
    but I have put my hope in your word.

■ PROVERBS 26:1-3

26 Like snow in summer or rain in
        harvest,
    honour is not fitting for a fool.
² Like a fluttering sparrow or a darting
        swallow,
    an undeserved curse does not come to
        rest.
³ A whip for the horse, a bridle for the
        donkey,
    and a rod for the backs of fools!

■ 2 TIMOTHY 2:1-21

2 You then, my son, be strong in the grace
    that is in Christ Jesus. ² And the things you have heard me say in the presence of many witnesses entrust to reliable people who will also be qualified to teach others. ³ Join with me in suffering, like a good

soldier of Christ Jesus. [4]No one serving as a soldier gets entangled in civilian affairs, but rather tries to please his commanding officer. [5]Similarly, anyone who competes as an athlete does not receive the victor's crown except by competing according to the rules. [6]The hardworking farmer should be the first to receive a share of the crops. [7]Reflect on what I am saying, for the Lord will give you insight into all this.

[8]Remember Jesus Christ, raised from the dead, descended from David. This is my gospel, [9]for which I am suffering even to the point of being chained like a criminal. But God's word is not chained. [10]Therefore I endure everything for the sake of the elect, that they too may obtain the salvation that is in Christ Jesus, with eternal glory.

[11]Here is a trustworthy saying:

If we died with him,
    we will also live with him;
[12]if we endure,
    we will also reign with him.
If we disown him,
    he will also disown us;
[13]if we are faithless,
    he remains faithful,
    for he cannot disown himself.

[14]Keep reminding God's people of these things. Warn them before God against quarrelling about words; it is of no value, and only ruins those who listen. [15]Do your best to present yourself to God as one approved, a worker who does not need to be ashamed and who correctly handles the word of truth. [16]Avoid godless chatter, because those who indulge in it will become more and more ungodly. [17]Their teaching will spread like gangrene. Among them are Hymenaeus and Philetus, [18]who have departed from the truth. They say that the resurrection has already taken place, and they destroy the faith of some. [19]Nevertheless, God's solid foundation stands firm, sealed with this inscription: 'The Lord knows those who are his,' and, 'Everyone who confesses the name of the Lord must turn away from wickedness.'

[20]In a large house there are articles not only of gold and silver, but also of wood and clay; some are for special purposes and some for common use. [21]Those who cleanse themselves from the latter will be instruments for special purposes, made holy, useful to the Master and prepared to do any good work.

Fear and Cold Feet

'You then, my son, be strong in the grace that is in Christ Jesus.' **2 Timothy 2:1**

When Simon Peter stepped out of the boat and attempted to walk on the water to Jesus, he was afraid: '... and, beginning to sink, cried out, "Lord, save me!"' (Matt. 14:30). Fear makes you sink.

When Jesus healed the paralytic, His first word was, 'Take heart, son,' and His second, 'your sins are forgiven' (Matt. 9:2). When Jesus lifted the guilt, this lifted the fear which, in turn, lifted the paralysis.

When the disciples fell on their faces at the top of the Mount of Transfiguration, terrified because they had heard the voice of God, Jesus said, 'Get up ... Don't be afraid' (Matt. 17:7). Fear puts you down; faith lifts you up.

The man who brought back the unused talent said, 'I was afraid and went out and hid your gold in the ground' (Matt. 25:25). His life investment was in a hole in the ground! Fear did it.

Again, it was said of the disciples that they were gathered 'with the doors locked for fear of the Jewish leaders' (John 20:19). Fear always puts you behind closed doors; it causes you to become an ingrown person.

Joseph of Arimathea was 'a disciple of Jesus, but secretly because he feared the Jewish leaders' (John 19:38). Fear always drives a person underground.

A man I know says that fear gave him cold feet. Prior to the Lord delivering him from fear, his circulation was so bad that he had to wear socks in bed. 'Now,' he says, 'my circulation is normal. God took away my fear and gave me warm feet.'

PRAYER

God, I see that fear is indeed costly. It is so costly that I dare not keep it. But I cannot easily get rid of it, for it has put its roots deep within me. Help me tear it up, root and branch. In Jesus' name I pray. Amen.

FURTHER STUDY

Mark 4:35-41; 5:25-34
• What had Jesus said to His disciples?
• What had this caused Him to do?

October 31

■ JEREMIAH 36:27–38:28

²⁷ After the king burned the scroll containing the words that Baruch had written at Jeremiah's dictation, the word of the LORD came to Jeremiah: ²⁸ 'Take another scroll and write on it all the words that were on the first scroll, which Jehoiakim king of Judah burned up. ²⁹ Also tell Jehoiakim king of Judah, "This is what the LORD says: you burned that scroll and said, 'Why did you write on it that the king of Babylon would certainly come and destroy this land and wipe from it both man and beast?' ³⁰ Therefore this is what the LORD says about Jehoiakim king of Judah: he will have no one to sit on the throne of David; his body will be thrown out and exposed to the heat by day and the frost by night. ³¹ I will punish him and his children and his attendants for their wickedness; I will bring on them and those living in Jerusalem and the people of Judah every disaster I pronounced against them, because they have not listened."'

³² So Jeremiah took another scroll and gave it to the scribe Baruch son of Neriah, and as Jeremiah dictated, Baruch wrote on it all the words of the scroll that Jehoiakim king of Judah had burned in the fire. And many similar words were added to them.

37 Zedekiah son of Josiah was made king of Judah by Nebuchadnezzar king of Babylon; he reigned in place of Jehoiachin son of Jehoiakim. ² Neither he nor his attendants nor the people of the land paid any attention to the words the LORD had spoken through Jeremiah the prophet.

³King Zedekiah, however, sent Jehukal son of Shelemiah with the priest Zephaniah son of Maaseiah to Jeremiah the prophet with this message: 'Please pray to the LORD our God for us.'

⁴Now Jeremiah was free to come and go among the people, for he had not yet been put in prison. ⁵Pharaoh's army had marched out of Egypt, and when the Babylonians who were besieging Jerusalem heard the report about them, they withdrew from Jerusalem.

⁶Then the word of the LORD came to Jeremiah the prophet: ⁷'This is what the LORD, the God of Israel, says: tell the king of Judah, who sent you to enquire of me, "Pharaoh's army, which has marched out to support you, will go back to its own land, to Egypt. ⁸Then the Babylonians will return and attack this city; they will capture it and burn it down."

⁹'This is what the LORD says: do not deceive yourselves, thinking, "The Babylonians will surely leave us." They will not! ¹⁰Even if you were to defeat the entire Babylonian army that is attacking you and only wounded men were left in their tents, they would come out and burn this city down.'

¹¹After the Babylonian army had withdrawn from Jerusalem because of Pharaoh's army, ¹²Jeremiah started to leave the city to go to the territory of Benjamin to get his share of the property among the people there. ¹³But when he reached the Benjamin Gate, the captain of the guard, whose name was Irijah son of Shelemiah, the son of Hananiah, arrested him and said, 'You are deserting to the Babylonians!'

¹⁴'That's not true!' Jeremiah said. 'I am not deserting to the Babylonians.' But Irijah would not listen to him; instead, he arrested Jeremiah and brought him to the officials. ¹⁵They were angry with Jeremiah and had him beaten and imprisoned in the house of Jonathan the secretary, which they had made into a prison.

¹⁶Jeremiah was put into a vaulted cell in a dungeon, where he remained a long time. ¹⁷Then King Zedekiah sent for him and had him brought to the palace, where he asked him privately, 'Is there any word from the LORD?'

'Yes,' Jeremiah replied, 'you will be delivered into the hands of the king of Babylon.'

¹⁸Then Jeremiah said to King Zedekiah, 'What crime have I committed against you or your attendants or this people, that you have put me in prison? ¹⁹Where are your prophets who prophesied to you, "The king of Babylon will not attack you or this land"? ²⁰But now, my lord the king, please listen. Let me bring my petition before you: do not send me back to the house of Jonathan the secretary, or I shall die there.'

²¹King Zedekiah then gave orders for Jeremiah to be placed in the courtyard of the guard and given a loaf of bread from the street of the bakers each day until all the bread in the city was gone. So Jeremiah remained in the courtyard of the guard.

38 Shephatiah son of Mattan, Gedaliah son of Pashhur, Jehukal son of Shelemiah, and Pashhur son of Malkijah heard what Jeremiah was telling all the people when he said, ²'This is what the LORD says: "Whoever stays in this city will die by the sword, famine or plague, but whoever goes over to the Babylonians will live. They will escape with their lives; they will live." ³And this is what the LORD says: "This city will certainly be given into the hands of the army of the king of Babylon, who will capture it."'

⁴Then the officials said to the king, 'This man should be put to death. He is discouraging the soldiers who are left in this city, as well as all the people, by the things he is saying to them. This man is not seeking the good of these people but their ruin.'

⁵'He is in your hands,' King Zedekiah answered. 'The king can do nothing to oppose you.'

⁶So they took Jeremiah and put him into the cistern of Malkijah, the king's son, which was in the courtyard of the guard. They lowered Jeremiah by ropes into the cistern; it had no water in it, only mud, and Jeremiah sank down into the mud.

⁷But Ebed-Melek, a Cushite, an official in the royal palace, heard that they had put Jeremiah into the cistern. While the king was sitting in the Benjamin Gate, ⁸Ebed-Melek went out of the palace and said to him, ⁹'My lord the king, these men have acted wickedly in all they have done to Jeremiah the prophet. They have thrown him into a cistern, where he will starve to death when there is no longer any bread in the city.'

¹⁰Then the king commanded Ebed-Melek the Cushite, 'Take thirty men from here with you and lift Jeremiah the prophet out of the cistern before he dies.'

¹¹So Ebed-Melek took the men with him and went to a room under the treasury in the palace. He took some old rags and worn-out clothes from there and let them down with ropes to Jeremiah in the cistern. ¹²Ebed-Melek the Cushite said to Jeremiah, 'Put these old rags and worn-out clothes under your arms to pad the ropes.' Jeremiah did so, ¹³and they pulled him up with the ropes and lifted him out of the cistern. And Jeremiah remained in the courtyard of the guard.

¹⁴Then King Zedekiah sent for Jeremiah the prophet and had him brought to the third entrance to the temple of the LORD. 'I am going to ask you something,' the king said to Jeremiah. 'Do not hide anything from me.'

¹⁵Jeremiah said to Zedekiah, 'If I give you an answer, will you not kill me? Even if I did give you counsel, you would not listen to me.'

¹⁶But King Zedekiah swore this oath secretly to Jeremiah: 'As surely as the LORD lives, who has given us breath, I will neither kill you nor hand you over to those who want to kill you.'

¹⁷Then Jeremiah said to Zedekiah, 'This is what the LORD God Almighty, the God of Israel, says: "If you surrender to the officers of the king of Babylon, your life will be spared and this city will not be burned down; you and your family will live. ¹⁸But if you will not surrender to the officers of the king of Babylon, this city will be given into the hands of the Babylonians and they will burn it down; you yourself will not escape from them." '

¹⁹King Zedekiah said to Jeremiah, 'I am afraid of the Jews who have gone over to the Babylonians, for the Babylonians may hand me over to them and they will ill-treat me.'

²⁰'They will not hand you over,' Jeremiah replied. 'Obey the LORD by doing what I tell you. Then it will go well with you, and your life will be spared. ²¹But if you refuse to surrender, this is what the LORD has revealed to me: ²²all the women left in the palace of the king of Judah will be brought out to the officials of the king of Babylon. Those women will say to you:

' "They misled you and overcame you –
   those trusted friends of yours.
Your feet are sunk in the mud;
   your friends have deserted you."

²³'All your wives and children will be brought out to the Babylonians. You yourself will not escape from their hands but will be captured by the king of Babylon; and this city will be burned down.'

²⁴Then Zedekiah said to Jeremiah, 'Do not let anyone know about this conversation, or you may die. ²⁵If the officials hear that I talked with you, and they come to you and say, "Tell us what you said to the king and what the king said to you; do not hide it from us or we will kill you," ²⁶then tell them, "I was pleading with the king not to send me back to Jonathan's house to die there." '

²⁷ All the officials did come to Jeremiah and question him, and he told them everything the king had ordered him to say. So they said no more to him, for no one had heard his conversation with the king.

²⁸ And Jeremiah remained in the courtyard of the guard until the day Jerusalem was captured.

▬ PSALM 119:82-88

⁸² My eyes fail, looking for your promise;
I say, 'When will you comfort me?'
⁸³ Though I am like a wineskin in the smoke,
I do not forget your decrees.
⁸⁴ How long must your servant wait?
When will you punish my
persecutors?
⁸⁵ The arrogant dig pits to trap me,
contrary to your law.
⁸⁶ All your commands are trustworthy;
help me, for I am being persecuted
without cause.
⁸⁷ They almost wiped me from the earth,
but I have not forsaken your precepts.
⁸⁸ In your unfailing love preserve my life,
that I may obey the statutes of your
mouth.

▬ PROVERBS 26:4-6

⁴ Do not answer a fool according to his
folly,
or you yourself will be just like him.
⁵ Answer a fool according to his folly,
or he will be wise in his own eyes.
⁶ Sending a message by the hands of a fool
is like cutting off one's feet or
drinking poison.

▬ 2 TIMOTHY 2:22–3:17

²² Flee the evil desires of youth and pursue

righteousness, faith, love and peace, along with those who call on the Lord out of a pure heart. ²³ Don't have anything to do with foolish and stupid arguments, because you know they produce quarrels. ²⁴ And the Lord's servant must not be quarrelsome but must be kind to everyone, able to teach, not resentful. ²⁵ Opponents must be gently instructed, in the hope that God will grant them repentance leading them to a knowledge of the truth, ²⁶ and that they will come to their senses and escape from the trap of the devil, who has taken them captive to do his will.

3 But mark this: there will be terrible times in the last days. ² People will be lovers of themselves, lovers of money, boastful, proud, abusive, disobedient to their parents, ungrateful, unholy, ³ without love, unforgiving, slanderous, without self-control, brutal, not lovers of the good, ⁴ treacherous, rash, conceited, lovers of pleasure rather than lovers of God – ⁵ having a form of godliness but denying its power. Have nothing to do with such people.

⁶ They are the kind who worm their way into homes and gain control over gullible women, who are loaded down with sins and are swayed by all kinds of evil desires, ⁷ always learning but never able to come to a knowledge of the truth. ⁸ Just as Jannes and Jambres opposed Moses, so also these teachers oppose the truth. They are men of depraved minds, who, as far as the faith is concerned, are rejected. ⁹ But they will not get very far because, as in the case of those men, their folly will be clear to everyone.

¹⁰ You, however, know all about my teaching, my way of life, my purpose, faith, patience, love, endurance, ¹¹ persecutions, sufferings – what kinds of things happened to me in Antioch, Iconium and Lystra, the persecutions I endured. Yet the Lord rescued me from all of them. ¹² In fact, everyone who wants to live a godly life in Christ Jesus will be persecuted, ¹³ while evildoers and impostors will go from bad to worse, deceiving

and being deceived. [14] But as for you, continue in what you have learned and have become convinced of, because you know those from whom you learned it, [15] and how from infancy you have known the Holy Scriptures, which are able to make you wise for salvation through faith in Christ Jesus. [16] All Scripture is God-breathed and is useful for teaching, rebuking, correcting and training in righteousness, [17] so that the servant of God may be thoroughly equipped for every good work.

Getting What We Give

'Do not answer a fool according to his folly, or you yourself will be just like him.' **Proverbs 26:4**

Psychologist, Karl Menninger says, 'I know from clinical experience that in some women, the degree of discomfort both in pregnancy and parturition (childbirth) has been directly proportional to the intensity of their resentment at having to live through this phase of the female role.'

Sometimes resentments and grudges can be unconscious. As one doctor put it, 'It is very difficult to get people to see that illness is the price they pay for their unconscious resentments toward the very things they protest they love.' A woman of sixty-five gave her heart to Christ and said, 'I've lived with a stone in my heart ever since my mother said she hated me for stopping her from going to another man. Now this stone has gone. I'm free – for the first time in almost half a century.'

A man gave a golf ball the name of someone he disliked and struck it, but the ball went into the rough. Isn't that instructive? If you bear a grudge against anyone, you can neither see straight nor drive straight. The fact is this – you cannot hurt another person without hurting yourself. As the Chinese put it: 'He who spits against the wind spits in his own face.' We become the product of the qualities we give out. If we give out evil in return for good, then we become evil; we become the thing we give out. But if we give out good for evil, we become good. So mark this and mark it well – you cannot maintain spiritual freshness while you are bearing a grudge.

PRAYER

Heavenly Father, I see that I cannot be an echo of the treatment people give to me. I must echo You and treat people as You treat them. But I cannot do this except by Your grace. I receive that grace now. In Jesus' name I pray. Amen.

FURTHER STUDY

Rom. 12:1-17; Lev. 19:18; Prov. 20:22
• What are we not to do?
• What are we not to say?

November 1

▬ JEREMIAH 39:1–41:18

39 This is how Jerusalem was taken: ¹in the ninth year of Zedekiah king of Judah, in the tenth month, Nebuchadnezzar king of Babylon marched against Jerusalem with his whole army and laid siege to it. ²And on the ninth day of the fourth month of Zedekiah's eleventh year, the city wall was broken through. ³Then all the officials of the king of Babylon came and took seats in the Middle Gate: Nergal-Sharezer of Samgar, Nebo-Sarsekim a chief officer, Nergal-Sharezer a high official and all the other officials of the king of Babylon. ⁴When Zedekiah king of Judah and all the soldiers saw them, they fled; they left the city at night by way of the king's garden, through the gate between the two walls, and headed towards the Arabah.

⁵But the Babylonian army pursued them and overtook Zedekiah in the plains of Jericho. They captured him and took him to Nebuchadnezzar king of Babylon at Riblah in the land of Hamath, where he pronounced sentence on him. ⁶There at Riblah the king of Babylon slaughtered the sons of Zedekiah before his eyes and also killed all the nobles of Judah. ⁷Then he put out Zedekiah's eyes and bound him with bronze shackles to take him to Babylon.

⁸The Babylonians set fire to the royal palace and the houses of the people and broke down the walls of Jerusalem. ⁹Nebuzaradan commander of the imperial guard carried into exile to Babylon the people who remained in the city, along with those who had gone over to him, and the rest of the people. ¹⁰But Nebuzaradan the commander of the guard left behind in the land of Judah some of the poor people, who owned nothing; and at that time he gave them vineyards and fields.

¹¹Now Nebuchadnezzar king of Babylon had given these orders about Jeremiah through Nebuzaradan commander of the imperial guard: ¹²'Take him and look after him; don't harm him but do for him whatever he asks.' ¹³So Nebuzaradan the commander of the guard, Nebushazban a chief officer, Nergal-Sharezer a high official and all the other officers of the king of Babylon ¹⁴sent and had Jeremiah taken out of the courtyard of the guard. They handed him over to Gedaliah son of Ahikam, the son of Shaphan, to take him back to his home. So he remained among his own people.

¹⁵While Jeremiah had been confined in the courtyard of the guard, the word of the LORD came to him: ¹⁶'Go and tell Ebed-Melek the Cushite, "This is what the LORD Almighty, the God of Israel, says: I am about to fulfil my words against this city – words concerning disaster, not prosperity. At that time they will be fulfilled before your eyes. ¹⁷But I will rescue you on that day, declares the LORD; you will not be given into the hands of those you fear. ¹⁸I will save you; you will not fall by the sword but will escape with your life, because you trust in me, declares the LORD."'

40 The word came to Jeremiah from the LORD after Nebuzaradan commander of the imperial guard had released him at Ramah. He had found Jeremiah bound in chains among all the captives from Jerusalem and Judah who were being carried into exile to Babylon. ²When the commander of the guard found Jeremiah, he said to him, 'The LORD your God decreed this disaster for this place. ³And now the LORD has brought it about; he has done just as he said he would. All this happened because you people sinned against the LORD and did not obey him. ⁴But today I am freeing you from the chains on your wrists. Come with me to Babylon, if you like, and I will look after you; but if you do not want to, then don't come. Look, the whole country lies before you; go wherever you please.' [5]However, before Jeremiah turned to go, Nebuzaradan added, 'Go back to Gedaliah son of Ahikam, the son of Shaphan, whom the king of Babylon has appointed over the towns of Judah, and live with him among the people, or go anywhere else you please.'

Then the commander gave him provisions and a present and let him go. [6]So Jeremiah went to Gedaliah son of Ahikam at Mizpah and stayed with him among the people who were left behind in the land.

[7]When all the army officers and their men who were still in the open country heard that the king of Babylon had appointed Gedaliah son of Ahikam as governor over the land and had put him in charge of the men, women and children who were the poorest in the land and who had not been carried into exile to Babylon, [8]they came to Gedaliah at Mizpah – Ishmael son of Nethaniah, Johanan and Jonathan the sons of Kareah, Seraiah son of Tanhumeth, the sons of Ephai the Netophathite, and Jaazaniah the son of the Maakathite, and their men. [9]Gedaliah son of Ahikam, the son of Shaphan, took an oath to reassure them and their men. 'Do not be afraid to serve the Babylonians,' he said. 'Settle down in the land and serve the king of Babylon, and it will go well with you. [10]I myself will stay in Mizpah to represent you before the Babylonians who come to us, but you are to harvest the wine, summer fruit and olive oil, and put them in your storage jars, and live in the towns you have taken over.'

[11]When all the Jews in Moab, Ammon, Edom and all the other countries heard that the king of Babylon had left a remnant in Judah and had appointed Gedaliah son of Ahikam, the son of Shaphan, as governor over them, [12]they all came back to the land of Judah, to Gedaliah at Mizpah, from all the countries where they had been scattered. And they harvested an abundance of wine and summer fruit.

[13]Johanan son of Kareah and all the army officers still in the open country came to Gedaliah at Mizpah [14]and said to him, 'Don't you know that Baalis king of the Ammonites has sent Ishmael son of Nethaniah to take your life?' But Gedaliah son of Ahikam did not believe them.

[15]Then Johanan son of Kareah said privately to Gedaliah in Mizpah, 'Let me go and kill Ishmael son of Nethaniah, and no one will know it. Why should he take your life and cause all the Jews who are gathered around you to be scattered and the remnant of Judah to perish?'

[16]But Gedaliah son of Ahikam said to Johanan son of Kareah, 'Don't do such a thing! What you are saying about Ishmael is not true.'

41 In the seventh month Ishmael son of Nethaniah, the son of Elishama, who was of royal blood and had been one of the king's officers, came with ten men to Gedaliah son of Ahikam at Mizpah. While they were eating together there, [2]Ishmael son of Nethaniah and the ten men who were with him got up and struck down Gedaliah son of Ahikam, the son of Shaphan, with the sword, killing the one whom the king of Babylon had appointed as governor over the land. [3]Ishmael also killed all the men of Judah who were with Gedaliah at Mizpah, as well as the Babylonian soldiers who were there.

[4]The day after Gedaliah's assassination, before anyone knew about it, [5]eighty men who had shaved off their beards, torn their clothes and cut themselves came from Shechem, Shiloh and Samaria, bringing grain offerings and incense with them to the house of the LORD. [6]Ishmael son of Nethaniah went out from Mizpah to meet them, weeping as he went. When he met them, he said, 'Come to Gedaliah son of Ahikam.' [7]When they went into the city, Ishmael son

of Nethaniah and the men who were with him slaughtered them and threw them into a cistern. ⁸ But ten of them said to Ishmael, 'Don't kill us! We have wheat and barley, olive oil and honey, hidden in a field.' So he let them alone and did not kill them with the others. ⁹ Now the cistern where he threw all the bodies of the men he had killed along with Gedaliah was the one King Asa had made as part of his defence against Baasha king of Israel. Ishmael son of Nethaniah filled it with the dead.

¹⁰ Ishmael made captives of all the rest of the people who were in Mizpah – the king's daughters along with all the others who were left there, over whom Nebuzaradan commander of the imperial guard had appointed Gedaliah son of Ahikam. Ishmael son of Nethaniah took them captive and set out to cross over to the Ammonites.

¹¹ When Johanan son of Kareah and all the army officers who were with him heard about all the crimes Ishmael son of Nethaniah had committed, ¹² they took all their men and went to fight Ishmael son of Nethaniah. They caught up with him near the great pool in Gibeon. ¹³ When all the people Ishmael had with him saw Johanan son of Kareah and the army officers who were with him, they were glad. ¹⁴ All the people Ishmael had taken captive at Mizpah turned and went over to Johanan son of Kareah. ¹⁵ But Ishmael son of Nethaniah and eight of his men escaped from Johanan and fled to the Ammonites.

¹⁶ Then Johanan son of Kareah and all the army officers who were with him led away all the people of Mizpah who had survived, whom Johanan had recovered from Ishmael son of Nethaniah after Ishmael had assassinated Gedaliah son of Ahikam – the soldiers, women, children and court officials he had recovered from Gibeon. ¹⁷ And they went on, stopping at Geruth Kimham near Bethlehem on their way to Egypt ¹⁸ to escape the Babylonians. They were afraid of them because Ishmael son of Nethaniah

had killed Gedaliah son of Ahikam, whom the king of Babylon had appointed as governor over the land.

▬ PSALM 119:89–95

⁸⁹ Your word, Lord, is eternal;
    it stands firm in the heavens.
⁹⁰ Your faithfulness continues through all
      generations;
    you established the earth, and it
      endures.
⁹¹ Your laws endure to this day,
    for all things serve you.
⁹² If your law had not been my delight,
    I would have perished in my affliction.
⁹³ I will never forget your precepts,
    for by them you have preserved my life.
⁹⁴ Save me, for I am yours;
    I have sought out your precepts.
⁹⁵ The wicked are waiting to destroy me,
    but I will ponder your statutes.

▬ PROVERBS 26:7–9

⁷ Like the useless legs of one who is lame
    is a proverb in the mouth of a fool.
⁸ Like tying a stone in a sling
    is the giving of honour to a fool.
⁹ Like a thorn-bush in a drunkard's hand
    is a proverb in the mouth of a fool.

▬ 2 TIMOTHY 4:1–22

4 In the presence of God and of Christ Jesus, who will judge the living and the dead, and in view of his appearing and his kingdom, I give you this charge: ² preach the word; be prepared in season and out of season; correct, rebuke and encourage – with great patience and careful instruction. ³ For the time will come when people will not put up with sound doctrine. Instead, to suit

their own desires, they will gather round them a great number of teachers to say what their itching ears want to hear. ⁴They will turn their ears away from the truth and turn aside to myths. ⁵But you, keep your head in all situations, endure hardship, do the work of an evangelist, discharge all the duties of your ministry.

⁶For I am already being poured out like a drink offering, and the time for my departure is near. ⁷I have fought the good fight, I have finished the race, I have kept the faith. ⁸Now there is in store for me the crown of righteousness, which the Lord, the righteous Judge, will award to me on that day – and not only to me, but also to all who have longed for his appearing.

⁹Do your best to come to me quickly, ¹⁰for Demas, because he loved this world, has deserted me and has gone to Thessalonica. Crescens has gone to Galatia, and Titus to Dalmatia. ¹¹Only Luke is with me. Get Mark and bring him with you, because he is helpful to me in my ministry. ¹²I sent Tychicus to Ephesus. ¹³When you come, bring the cloak that I left with Carpus at Troas, and my scrolls, especially the parchments.

¹⁴Alexander the metalworker did me a great deal of harm. The Lord will repay him for what he has done. ¹⁵You too should be on your guard against him, because he strongly opposed our message.

¹⁶At my first defence, no one came to my support, but everyone deserted me. May it not be held against them. ¹⁷But the Lord stood at my side and gave me strength, so that through me the message might be fully proclaimed and all the Gentiles might hear it. And I was delivered from the lion's mouth. ¹⁸The Lord will rescue me from every evil attack and will bring me safely to his heavenly kingdom. To him be glory for ever and ever. Amen.

¹⁹Greet Priscilla and Aquila and the household of Onesiphorus. ²⁰Erastus stayed in Corinth, and I left Trophimus ill in Miletus. ²¹Do your best to get here before winter. Eubulus greets you, and so do Pudens, Linus, Claudia and all the brothers and sisters.

²²The Lord be with your spirit. Grace be with you all.

'Flaming Arrows'

'But the Lord stood at my side and gave me strength
... And I was delivered from the lion's mouth.'
2 Timothy 4:17

The main purpose of the Roman shield was to protect soldiers from the fiery darts thrown at them by the enemy. These darts, made either of wood or metal, were covered with inflammable material and set alight immediately before being thrown. Enemies would throw these at each other in great numbers and from all directions so as to produce confusion. When thus attacked, a soldier would hold up the shield in front of him, allowing the fiery darts to land on the fireproof metal surface, from which they would drop away harmlessly.

The apostle says that we Christians need a 'shield of faith' – in order to 'extinguish all the flaming arrows of the evil one'. An understanding of what these 'flaming arrows' are is essential if we are to stand firm against the adversary. Have you ever gone to bed at night feeling perfectly happy, only to wake in a sad mood? If there was no obvious physical or psychological reason for this, it is possible that you have experienced one of Satan's 'flaming arrows'.

Sometimes they come as negative thoughts that intrude suddenly into our thinking, often at the most incongruous times. We may be reading the Bible, we may be praying, when all of a sudden some inappropriate thought flashes into our mind. It could be a 'flaming arrow'. These do not come from inside us but from outside us. They strike us. Some thoughts do arise from within our carnal nature, but these of which I am speaking come from without – from Satan. And we are foolish if we do not recognise this and deal with them in this light.

PRAYER

O Father, help me to be alert and able to recognise the 'flaming arrows' of Satan when they are hurled at me. For I see that it is only when I recognise them that I can deal effectively with them. Give me insight and understanding. In Jesus' name. Amen.

FURTHER STUDY

James 1:1-22; 1 Cor. 10:13; 2 Cor. 11:3
• What is the progression in temptation?
• What was Paul's concern?

November 2

■ JEREMIAH 42:1–44:14

42 Then all the army officers, including Johanan son of Kareah and Jezaniah son of Hoshaiah, and all the people from the least to the greatest approached ²Jeremiah the prophet and said to him, 'Please hear our petition and pray to the LORD your God for this entire remnant. For as you now see, though we were once many, now only a few are left. ³Pray that the LORD your God will tell us where we should go and what we should do.'

⁴'I have heard you,' replied Jeremiah the prophet. 'I will certainly pray to the LORD your God as you have requested; I will tell you everything the LORD says and will keep nothing back from you.'

⁵Then they said to Jeremiah, 'May the LORD be a true and faithful witness against us if we do not act in accordance with everything the LORD your God sends you to tell us. ⁶Whether it is favourable or unfavourable, we will obey the LORD our God, to whom we are sending you, so that it will go well with us, for we will obey the LORD our God.'

⁷Ten days later the word of the LORD came to Jeremiah. ⁸So he called together Johanan son of Kareah and all the army officers who were with him and all the people from the least to the greatest. ⁹He said to them, 'This is what the LORD, the God of Israel, to whom you sent me to present your petition, says: ¹⁰"If you stay in this land, I will build you up and not tear you down; I will plant you and not uproot you, for I have relented concerning the disaster I have inflicted on you. ¹¹Do not be afraid of the king of Babylon, whom you now fear. Do not be afraid of him, declares the LORD, for I am with you and will

save you and deliver you from his hands.
[12] I will show you compassion so that he will
have compassion on you and restore you to
your land."

[13] 'However, if you say, "We will not stay
in this land," and so disobey the LORD your
God, [14] and if you say, "No, we will go and live
in Egypt, where we will not see war or hear
the trumpet or be hungry for bread," [15] then
hear the word of the LORD, you remnant of
Judah. This is what the LORD Almighty, the
God of Israel, says: "If you are determined
to go to Egypt and you do go to settle there,
[16] then the sword you fear will overtake you
there, and the famine you dread will follow
you into Egypt, and there you will die. [17] Indeed, all who are determined to go to Egypt
to settle there will die by the sword, famine
and plague; not one of them will survive or
escape the disaster I will bring on them."
[18] This is what the LORD Almighty, the God
of Israel, says: "As my anger and wrath have
been poured out on those who lived in Jerusalem, so will my wrath be poured out
on you when you go to Egypt. You will be a
curse and an object of horror, a curse and
an object of reproach; you will never see
this place again."

[19] 'Remnant of Judah, the LORD has told
you, "Do not go to Egypt." Be sure of this: I
warn you today [20] that you made a fatal mistake when you sent me to the LORD your God
and said, "Pray to the LORD our God for us;
tell us everything he says and we will do it."
[21] I have told you today, but you still have not
obeyed the LORD your God in all he sent me
to tell you. [22] So now, be sure of this: you will
die by the sword, famine and plague in the
place where you want to go to settle.'

43 When Jeremiah had finished telling
the people all the words of the LORD
their God – everything the LORD had sent
him to tell them – [2] Azariah son of Hoshaiah
and Johanan son of Kareah and all the arrogant men said to Jeremiah, 'You are lying!
The LORD our God has not sent you to say,

"You must not go to Egypt to settle there."
[3] But Baruch son of Neriah is inciting you
against us to hand us over to the Babylonians, so that they may kill us or carry us into
exile to Babylon.'

[4] So Johanan son of Kareah and all the
army officers and all the people disobeyed
the LORD's command to stay in the land of
Judah. [5] Instead, Johanan son of Kareah
and all the army officers led away all the
remnant of Judah who had come back to
live in the land of Judah from all the nations where they had been scattered. [6] They
also led away all those whom Nebuzaradan
commander of the imperial guard had left
with Gedaliah son of Ahikam, the son of
Shaphan – the men, the women, the children and the king's daughters. And they
took Jeremiah the prophet and Baruch son
of Neriah along with them. [7] So they entered
Egypt in disobedience to the LORD and went
as far as Tahpanhes.

[8] In Tahpanhes the word of the LORD came
to Jeremiah: [9] 'While the Jews are watching,
take some large stones with you and bury
them in clay in the brick pavement at the
entrance to Pharaoh's palace in Tahpanhes.
[10] Then say to them, "This is what the LORD
Almighty, the God of Israel, says: I will send
for my servant Nebuchadnezzar king of
Babylon, and I will set his throne over these
stones I have buried here; he will spread his
royal canopy above them. [11] He will come and
attack Egypt, bringing death to those destined for death, captivity to those destined
for captivity, and the sword to those destined for the sword. [12] He will set fire to the
temples of the gods of Egypt; he will burn
their temples and take their gods captive. As
a shepherd picks his garment clean of lice, so
he will pick Egypt clean and depart. [13] There
in the temple of the sun in Egypt he will demolish the sacred pillars and will burn down
the temples of the gods of Egypt."'

44 This word came to Jeremiah concerning all the Jews living in Lower

Egypt – in Migdol, Tahpanhes and Memphis – and in Upper Egypt: ²'This is what the LORD Almighty, the God of Israel, says: you saw the great disaster I brought on Jerusalem and on all the towns of Judah. Today they lie deserted and in ruins ³because of the evil they have done. They aroused my anger by burning incense to and worshipping other gods that neither they nor you nor your ancestors ever knew. ⁴Again and again I sent my servants the prophets, who said, "Do not do this detestable thing that I hate!" ⁵But they did not listen or pay attention; they did not turn from their wickedness or stop burning incense to other gods. ⁶Therefore, my fierce anger was poured out; it raged against the towns of Judah and the streets of Jerusalem and made them the desolate ruins they are today.

⁷'Now this is what the LORD God Almighty, the God of Israel, says: why bring such great disaster on yourselves by cutting off from Judah the men and women, the children and infants, and so leave yourselves without a remnant? ⁸Why arouse my anger with what your hands have made, burning incense to other gods in Egypt, where you have come to live? You will destroy yourselves and make yourselves a curse and an object of reproach among all the nations on earth. ⁹Have you forgotten the wickedness committed by your ancestors and by the kings and queens of Judah and the wickedness committed by you and your wives in the land of Judah and the streets of Jerusalem? ¹⁰To this day they have not humbled themselves or shown reverence, nor have they followed my law and the decrees I set before you and your ancestors.

¹¹'Therefore this is what the LORD Almighty, the God of Israel, says: I am determined to bring disaster on you and to destroy all Judah. ¹²I will take away the remnant of Judah who were determined to go to Egypt to settle there. They will all perish in Egypt; they will fall by the sword or die

from famine. From the least to the greatest, they will die by sword or famine. They will become a curse and an object of horror, a curse and an object of reproach. ¹³I will punish those who live in Egypt with the sword, famine and plague, as I punished Jerusalem. ¹⁴None of the remnant of Judah who have gone to live in Egypt will escape or survive to return to the land of Judah, to which they long to return and live; none will return except a few fugitives.'

■ PSALM 119:96–100

⁹⁶To all perfection I see a limit,
    but your commands are boundless.
⁹⁷Oh, how I love your law!
    I meditate on it all day long.
⁹⁸Your commands are always with me
    and make me wiser than my enemies.
⁹⁹I have more insight than all my teachers,
    for I meditate on your statutes.
¹⁰⁰I have more understanding than the
        elders,
    for I obey your precepts.

■ PROVERBS 26:10–12

¹⁰Like an archer who wounds at random
    is one who hires a fool or any
        passer-by.
¹¹As a dog returns to its vomit,
    so fools repeat their folly.
¹²Do you see a person wise in their own
        eyes?
    There is more hope for a fool than for
        them.

■ TITUS 1:1–2:8

1 Paul, a servant of God and an apostle of Jesus Christ to further the faith of God's elect and their knowledge of the truth

that leads to godliness – [2]in the hope of eternal life, which God, who does not lie, promised before the beginning of time, [3]and which now at his appointed season he has brought to light through the preaching entrusted to me by the command of God our Saviour,

[4]To Titus, my true son in our common faith:

Grace and peace from God the Father and Christ Jesus our Saviour.

[5]The reason I left you in Crete was that you might put in order what was left unfinished and appoint elders in every town, as I directed you. [6]An elder must be blameless, faithful to his wife, a man whose children believe and are not open to the charge of being wild and disobedient. [7]Since an overseer manages God's household, he must be blameless – not overbearing, not quick-tempered, not given to drunkenness, not violent, not pursuing dishonest gain. [8]Rather, he must be hospitable, one who loves what is good, who is self-controlled, upright, holy and disciplined. [9]He must hold firmly to the trustworthy message as it has been taught, so that he can encourage others by sound doctrine and refute those who oppose it.

[10]For there are many rebellious people, full of meaningless talk and deception, especially those of the circumcision group. [11]They must be silenced, because they are disrupting whole households by teaching things they ought not to teach – and that for the sake of dishonest gain. [12]One of Crete's own prophets has said it: 'Cretans are always liars, evil brutes, lazy gluttons.' [13]This saying is true. Therefore rebuke them sharply, so that they will be sound in the faith [14]and will pay no attention to Jewish myths or to the merely human commands of those who reject the truth. [15]To the pure, all things are pure, but to those who are corrupted and do not believe, nothing is pure. In fact, both their minds and consciences are corrupted. [16]They claim to know God, but by their actions they deny him. They are detestable, disobedient and unfit for doing anything good.

2 You, however, must teach what is appropriate to sound doctrine. [2]Teach the older men to be temperate, worthy of respect, self-controlled, and sound in faith, in love and in endurance.

[3]Likewise, teach the older women to be reverent in the way they live, not to be slanderers or addicted to much wine, but to teach what is good. [4]Then they can urge the younger women to love their husbands and children, [5]to be self-controlled and pure, to be busy at home, to be kind, and to be subject to their husbands, so that no one will malign the word of God.

[6]Similarly, encourage the young men to be self-controlled. [7]In everything set them an example by doing what is good. In your teaching show integrity, seriousness [8]and soundness of speech that cannot be condemned, so that those who oppose you may be ashamed because they have nothing bad to say about us.

Spiritual Digestion

'Oh, how I love your law! I meditate on it all day long ... I have more insight than all my teachers, for I meditate on your statutes.' **Psalm 119:97,99**

One of the highest priorities in order to stay spiritually fresh is to cultivate the art of Scripture meditation.

For some reason, Bible meditation has become a lost art. A survey conducted among Christians in the United States showed that only one in ten thousand knew how to meditate on the Scriptures.

What, then, is the art of Scripture meditation? Is it reading parts of the Bible as slowly as possible so that every word sinks in? No. Is it studying a passage with the aid of a commentary so that one understands exactly what the Scripture is saying? No. Is it memorising certain texts and recalling them to mind whenever one has a spare moment? No. You can do all of these things and still not know how to meditate.

Andrew Murray describes it as 'holding the word of God in your heart and mind until it has affected every area of your life'. My own definition is this: meditation is the process by which we place the Word of God into the digestive system of the soul, where it is transformed into faith and spiritual energy.

Psalm 1:1-3 paints a picture of amazing freshness and vitality: 'Blessed is the one ... whose delight is in the law of the LORD, and who meditates on his law day and night. That person is like a tree planted by streams of water, which yields its fruit in season and whose leaf does not wither ...' What is the secret of this amazing freshness? It is simple - meditation. To draw from Scripture the inspiration and power we need to stay spiritually fresh, we must do more than read it, study it, or even memorise it - we must meditate on it.

PRAYER

O Father, I want so much to learn the art of meditation. Quicken my desire to hide Your Word in my heart so that it becomes the hidden springs of action and determines my character and my conduct. In Jesus' name. Amen.

FURTHER STUDY

Josh. 1:1-9; 24:31
• What was God's promise to Joshua?
• What was the condition - and the result?

November 3

■ JEREMIAH 44:15– 47:7

15 Then all the men who knew that their wives were burning incense to other gods, along with all the women who were present – a large assembly – and all the people living in Lower and Upper Egypt, said to Jeremiah, 16 'We will not listen to the message you have spoken to us in the name of the LORD! 17 We will certainly do everything we said we would: we will burn incense to the Queen of Heaven and will pour out drink offerings to her just as we and our ancestors, our kings and our officials did

in the towns of Judah and in the streets of Jerusalem. At that time we had plenty of food and were well off and suffered no harm. ¹⁸ But ever since we stopped burning incense to the Queen of Heaven and pouring out drink offerings to her, we have had nothing and have been perishing by sword and famine.'

¹⁹ The women added, 'When we burned incense to the Queen of Heaven and poured out drink offerings to her, did not our husbands know that we were making cakes impressed with her image and pouring out drink offerings to her?'

²⁰ Then Jeremiah said to all the people, both men and women, who were answering him, ²¹ 'Did not the LORD remember and call to mind the incense burned in the towns of Judah and the streets of Jerusalem by you and your ancestors, your kings and your officials and the people of the land? ²² When the LORD could no longer endure your wicked actions and the detestable things you did, your land became a curse and a desolate waste without inhabitants, as it is today. ²³ Because you have burned incense and have sinned against the LORD and have not obeyed him or followed his law or his decrees or his stipulations, this disaster has come upon you, as you now see.'

²⁴ Then Jeremiah said to all the people, including the women, 'Hear the word of the LORD, all you people of Judah in Egypt. ²⁵ This is what the LORD Almighty, the God of Israel, says: you and your wives have done what you said you would do when you promised, "We will certainly carry out the vows we made to burn incense and pour out drink offerings to the Queen of Heaven."

'Go ahead then, do what you promised! Keep your vows! ²⁶ But hear the word of the LORD, all you Jews living in Egypt: "I swear by my great name," says the LORD, "that no one from Judah living anywhere in Egypt shall ever again invoke my name or swear, 'As surely as the Sovereign LORD lives.'

²⁷ For I am watching over them for harm, not for good; the Jews in Egypt will perish by sword and famine until they are all destroyed. ²⁸ Those who escape the sword and return to the land of Judah from Egypt will be very few. Then the whole remnant of Judah who came to live in Egypt will know whose word will stand – mine or theirs.

²⁹ ' "This will be the sign to you that I will punish you in this place," declares the LORD, "so that you will know that my threats of harm against you will surely stand." ³⁰ This is what the LORD says: "I am going to deliver Pharaoh Hophra king of Egypt into the hands of his enemies who want to kill him, just as I gave Zedekiah king of Judah into the hands of Nebuchadnezzar king of Babylon, the enemy who wanted to kill him." '

45 When Baruch son of Neriah wrote on a scroll the words Jeremiah the prophet dictated in the fourth year of Jehoiakim son of Josiah king of Judah, Jeremiah said this to Baruch: ² 'This is what the LORD, the God of Israel, says to you, Baruch: ³ You said, "Woe to me! The LORD has added sorrow to my pain; I am worn out with groaning and find no rest." ⁴ But the LORD has told me to say to you, "This is what the LORD says: I will overthrow what I have built and uproot what I have planted, throughout the earth. ⁵ Should you then seek great things for yourself? Do not seek them. For I will bring disaster on all people, declares the LORD, but wherever you go I will let you escape with your life." '

46 This is the word of the LORD that came to Jeremiah the prophet concerning the nations:

² Concerning Egypt:

This is the message against the army of Pharaoh Necho king of Egypt, which was defeated at Carchemish on the River Euphrates by Nebuchadnezzar king of Babylon in the fourth year of Jehoiakim son of Josiah king of Judah:

³ 'Prepare your shields, both large and
      small,
   and march out for battle!
⁴ Harness the horses,
   mount the steeds!
Take your positions
   with helmets on!
Polish your spears,
   put on your armour!
⁵ What do I see?
   They are terrified,
they are retreating,
   their warriors are defeated.
They flee in haste
   without looking back,
   and there is terror on every side,'
                        declares the LORD.
⁶ 'The swift cannot flee
   nor the strong escape.
In the north by the River Euphrates
   they stumble and fall.

⁷ 'Who is this that rises like the Nile,
   like rivers of surging waters?
⁸ Egypt rises like the Nile,
   like rivers of surging waters.
She says, "I will rise and cover the earth;
   I will destroy cities and their people."
⁹ Charge, you horses!
   Drive furiously, you charioteers!
March on, you warriors – men of Cush
   and Put who carry shields,
   men of Lydia who draw the bow.
¹⁰ But that day belongs to the Lord, the
      LORD Almighty –
   a day of vengeance, for vengeance on
      his foes.
The sword will devour till it is satisfied,
   till it has quenched its thirst with blood.
For the Lord, the LORD Almighty, will
      offer sacrifice
   in the land of the north by the River
      Euphrates.

¹¹ 'Go up to Gilead and get balm,
   Virgin Daughter Egypt.

But you try many medicines in vain;
   there is no healing for you.
¹² The nations will hear of your shame;
   your cries will fill the earth.
One warrior will stumble over another;
   both will fall down together.'

¹³ This is the message the LORD spoke to Jeremiah the prophet about the coming of Nebuchadnezzar king of Babylon to attack Egypt:

¹⁴ 'Announce this in Egypt, and proclaim it
      in Migdol;
   proclaim it also in Memphis and
      Tahpanhes:
"Take your positions and get ready,
   for the sword devours those around
      you."
¹⁵ Why will your warriors be laid low?
   They cannot stand, for the LORD will
      push them down.
¹⁶ They will stumble repeatedly;
   they will fall over each other.
They will say, "Get up, let us go back
   to our own people and our native
      lands,
   away from the sword of the
      oppressor."
¹⁷ There they will exclaim,
   "Pharaoh king of Egypt is only a loud
      noise;
   he has missed his opportunity."

¹⁸ 'As surely as I live,' declares the King,
   whose name is the LORD Almighty,
'one will come who is like Tabor among
      the mountains,
   like Carmel by the sea.
¹⁹ Pack your belongings for exile,
   you who live in Egypt,
for Memphis will be laid waste
   and lie in ruins without inhabitant.

²⁰ 'Egypt is a beautiful heifer,
   but a gadfly is coming
   against her from the north.

²¹ The mercenaries in her ranks
  are like fattened calves.
They too will turn and flee together,
  they will not stand their ground,
for the day of disaster is coming upon
    them,
  the time for them to be punished.
²² Egypt will hiss like a fleeing serpent
  as the enemy advances in force;
they will come against her with axes,
  like men who cut down trees.
²³ They will chop down her forest,'
            declares the LORD,
  'dense though it be.
They are more numerous than locusts,
  they cannot be counted.
²⁴ Daughter Egypt will be put to shame,
  given into the hands of the people of
    the north.'

²⁵ The LORD Almighty, the God of Israel,
says: 'I am about to bring punishment on
Amon god of Thebes, on Pharaoh, on Egypt
and her gods and her kings, and on those
who rely on Pharaoh. ²⁶ I will give them into
the hands of those who want to kill them –
Nebuchadnezzar king of Babylon and his
officers. Later, however, Egypt will be inhabited as in times past,' declares the LORD.

²⁷ 'Do not be afraid, Jacob my servant;
  do not be dismayed, Israel.
I will surely save you out of a distant
    place,
  your descendants from the land of
    their exile.
Jacob will again have peace and security,
  and no one will make him afraid.
²⁸ Do not be afraid, Jacob my servant,
  for I am with you,' declares the LORD.
'Though I completely destroy all the
    nations
  among which I scatter you,
I will not completely destroy you.
I will discipline you but only in due
    measure;

I will not let you go entirely
    unpunished.'

47 This is the word of the LORD that
came to Jeremiah the prophet concerning the Philistines before Pharaoh
attacked Gaza:

² This is what the LORD says:

'See how the waters are rising in the north;
  they will become an overflowing
    torrent.
They will overflow the land and
    everything in it,
  the towns and those who live in them.
The people will cry out;
  all who dwell in the land will wail
³ at the sound of the hooves of galloping
    steeds,
  at the noise of enemy chariots
  and the rumble of their wheels.
Parents will not turn to help their
    children;
  their hands will hang limp.
⁴ For the day has come
  to destroy all the Philistines
and to remove all survivors
  who could help Tyre and Sidon.
The LORD is about to destroy the
    Philistines,
  the remnant from the coasts of
    Caphtor.
⁵ Gaza will shave her head in mourning;
  Ashkelon will be silenced.
You remnant on the plain,
  how long will you cut yourselves?
⁶ ' "Alas, sword of the LORD,
  how long till you rest?
Return to your sheath;
  cease and be still."
⁷ But how can it rest
  when the LORD has commanded it,
when he has ordered it
  to attack Ashkelon and the coast?'

▪ PSALM 119:101–104

101 I have kept my feet from every evil path
    so that I might obey your word.
102 I have not departed from your laws,
    for you yourself have taught me.
103 How sweet are your words to my taste,
    sweeter than honey to my mouth!
104 I gain understanding from your precepts;
    therefore I hate every wrong path.

▪ PROVERBS 26:13–16

13 A sluggard says, 'There's a lion in the road,
    a fierce lion roaming the streets!'
14 As a door turns on its hinges,
    so a sluggard turns on his bed.
15 A sluggard buries his hand in the dish;
    he is too lazy to bring it back to his
    mouth.
16 A sluggard is wiser in his own eyes
    than seven people who answer
    discreetly.

▪ TITUS 2:9–3:15

9 Teach slaves to be subject to their masters in everything, to try to please them, not to talk back to them, 10 and not to steal from them, but to show that they can be fully trusted, so that in every way they will make the teaching about God our Saviour attractive.

11 For the grace of God has appeared that offers salvation to all people. 12 It teaches us to say 'No' to ungodliness and worldly passions, and to live self-controlled, upright and godly lives in this present age, 13 while we wait for the blessed hope – the appearing of the glory of our great God and Saviour, Jesus Christ, 14 who gave himself for us to redeem us from all wickedness and to purify for himself a people that are his very own, eager to do what is good.

15 These, then, are the things you should teach. Encourage and rebuke with all authority. Do not let anyone despise you.

3 Remind the people to be subject to rulers and authorities, to be obedient, to be ready to do whatever is good, 2 to slander no one, to be peaceable and considerate, and always to be gentle towards everyone.

3 At one time we too were foolish, disobedient, deceived and enslaved by all kinds of passions and pleasures. We lived in malice and envy, being hated and hating one another. 4 But when the kindness and love of God our Saviour appeared, 5 he saved us, not because of righteous things we had done, but because of his mercy. He saved us through the washing of rebirth and renewal by the Holy Spirit, 6 whom he poured out on us generously through Jesus Christ our Saviour, 7 so that, having been justified by his grace, we might become heirs having the hope of eternal life. 8 This is a trustworthy saying. And I want you to stress these things, so that those who have trusted in God may be careful to devote themselves to doing what is good. These things are excellent and profitable for everyone.

9 But avoid foolish controversies and genealogies and arguments and quarrels about the law, because these are unprofitable and useless. 10 Warn a divisive person once, and then warn them a second time. After that, have nothing to do with them. 11 You may be sure that such people are warped and sinful; they are self-condemned.

12 As soon as I send Artemas or Tychicus to you, do your best to come to me at Nicopolis, because I have decided to winter there. 13 Do everything you can to help Zenas the lawyer and Apollos on their way and see that they have everything they need. 14 Our people must learn to devote themselves to doing what is good, in order to provide for urgent needs and not live unproductive lives.

15 Everyone with me sends you greetings. Greet those who love us in the faith.
Grace be with you all.

What If?

'These ... are the things you should teach. Encourage and rebuke with all authority ...' **Titus 2:15**

A little boy, when asked what the Holy Spirit meant, replied, 'I suppose it is what puts the "oomph" into Christianity'. He was on the right track but failed to use the correct pronoun – not 'it' but 'He'. The Holy Spirit is not an influence but a Person. This is why Scripture, when referring to Him, uses personal pronouns such as 'He', 'who', and 'whom'.

Suppose there had been no Holy Spirit? Then we would have been faced with a religion in which there was little 'oomph'. We would have the four Gospels without the upper room – distinctive, but not dynamic.

Take Mark's Gospel, for example. If there had been no day of Pentecost, if the promised Holy Spirit had not been poured out upon God's people, the message of Christ would have ended with these words: 'Trembling and bewildered, the women went out and fled from the tomb. They said nothing to anyone, because they were afraid' (Mark 16:8).

What a sad plight we would all be in if the message of Christ had ended there. The Resurrection had taken place, the whole of the redemptive process was complete, the gladdest news that had ever burst upon human ears was in the possession of the disciples – but 'they said nothing to anyone, because they were afraid'. If Christianity had ended there, it would not have been a gospel that conquered the world. No amount of good information could have transformed those early disciples. Something else was needed – the Holy Spirit.

PRAYER

O God, help me not to live in the twilight zone between Resurrection and Pentecost. I want to know all the fullness of the upper room in my life. Turn me from a flickering torch into a flaming torch. In Jesus' name. Amen.

FURTHER STUDY

John 16:1-16; 14:26; 15:26-27; Acts 1:8
• What did Jesus say of the Holy Spirit?
• What is another title of the Holy Spirit?

November 4

■ JEREMIAH 48:1–49:6

48 Concerning Moab:

This is what the LORD Almighty, the God

of Israel, says:

'Woe to Nebo, for it will be ruined.
Kiriathaim will be disgraced and
captured;

the stronghold will be disgraced and
    shattered.
² Moab will be praised no more;
    in Heshbon people will plot her
        downfall:
    "Come, let us put an end to that nation."
You, the people of Madmen, will also be
    silenced;
    the sword will pursue you.
³ Cries of anguish arise from Horonaim,
    cries of great havoc and destruction.
⁴ Moab will be broken;
    her little ones will cry out.
⁵ They go up the hill to Luhith,
    weeping bitterly as they go;
on the road down to Horonaim
    anguished cries over the destruction
    are heard.
⁶ Flee! Run for your lives;
    become like a bush in the desert.
⁷ Since you trust in your deeds and riches,
    you too will be taken captive,
and Chemosh will go into exile,
    together with his priests and officials.
⁸ The destroyer will come against every
    town,
    and not a town will escape.
The valley will be ruined
    and the plateau destroyed,
    because the Lord has spoken.
⁹ Put salt on Moab,
    for she will be laid waste;
her towns will become desolate,
    with no one to live in them.

¹⁰ 'A curse on anyone who is lax in doing
    the Lord's work!
    A curse on anyone who keeps their
        sword from bloodshed!
¹¹ 'Moab has been at rest from youth,
    like wine left on its dregs,
not poured from one jar to another –
    she has not gone into exile.
So she tastes as she did,
    and her aroma is unchanged.

¹² But days are coming,'
    declares the Lord,
'when I will send men who pour from
    pitchers,
    and they will pour her out;
they will empty her pitchers
    and smash her jars.
¹³ Then Moab will be ashamed of Chemosh,
    as Israel was ashamed
    when they trusted in Bethel.

¹⁴ 'How can you say, "We are warriors,
    men valiant in battle"?
¹⁵ Moab will be destroyed and her towns
    invaded;
    her finest young men will go down in
        the slaughter,'
    declares the King, whose name is the
        Lord Almighty.
¹⁶ 'The fall of Moab is at hand;
    her calamity will come quickly.
¹⁷ Mourn for her, all who live around her,
    all who know her fame;
say, "How broken is the mighty sceptre,
    how broken the glorious staff!"

¹⁸ 'Come down from your glory
    and sit on the parched ground,
    you inhabitants of Daughter Dibon,
for the one who destroys Moab
    will come up against you
    and ruin your fortified cities.
¹⁹ Stand by the road and watch,
    you who live in Aroer.
Ask the man fleeing and the woman
    escaping,
    ask them, "What has happened?"
²⁰ Moab is disgraced, for she is shattered.
    Wail and cry out!
Announce by the Arnon
    that Moab is destroyed.
²¹ Judgment has come to the plateau –
    to Holon, Jahzah and Mephaath,
²²   to Dibon, Nebo and Beth Diblathaim,
²³   to Kiriathaim, Beth Gamul and Beth
    Meon,

²⁴ to Kerioth and Bozrah –
to all the towns of Moab, far and near.
²⁵ Moab's horn is cut off;
her arm is broken,'
declares the LORD.

²⁶ 'Make her drunk,
for she has defied the LORD.
Let Moab wallow in her vomit;
let her be an object of ridicule.
²⁷ Was not Israel the object of your
ridicule?
Was she caught among thieves,
that you shake your head in scorn
whenever you speak of her?
²⁸ Abandon your towns and dwell among
the rocks,
you who live in Moab.
Be like a dove that makes its nest
at the mouth of a cave.

²⁹ 'We have heard of Moab's pride –
how great is her arrogance! –
of her insolence, her pride, her conceit
and the haughtiness of her heart.
³⁰ I know her insolence but it is futile,'
declares the LORD,
'and her boasts accomplish nothing.
³¹ Therefore I wail over Moab,
for all Moab I cry out,
I moan for the people of Kir Hareseth.
³² I weep for you, as Jazer weeps,
you vines of Sibmah.
Your branches spread as far as the sea;
they reached as far as Jazer.
The destroyer has fallen
on your ripened fruit and grapes.
³³ Joy and gladness are gone
from the orchards and fields of Moab.
I have stopped the flow of wine from the
presses;
no one treads them with shouts of joy.
Although there are shouts,
they are not shouts of joy.

³⁴ 'The sound of their cry rises

from Heshbon to Elealeh and Jahaz,
from Zoar as far as Horonaim and Eglath
Shelishiyah,
for even the waters of Nimrim are
dried up.
³⁵ In Moab I will put an end
to those who make offerings on the
high places
and burn incense to their gods,'
declares the LORD.
³⁶ 'So my heart laments for Moab like the
music of a pipe;
it laments like a pipe for the people of
Kir Hareseth.
The wealth they acquired is gone.
³⁷ Every head is shaved
and every beard cut off;
every hand is slashed
and every waist is covered with
sackcloth.
³⁸ On all the roofs in Moab
and in the public squares
there is nothing but mourning,
for I have broken Moab
like a jar that no one wants,'
declares the LORD.
³⁹ 'How shattered she is! How they wail!
How Moab turns her back in shame!
Moab has become an object of ridicule,
an object of horror to all those around
her.'

⁴⁰ This is what the LORD says:

'Look! An eagle is swooping down,
spreading its wings over Moab.
⁴¹ Kerioth will be captured
and the strongholds taken.
In that day the hearts of Moab's warriors
will be like the heart of a woman in
labour.
⁴² Moab will be destroyed as a nation
because she defied the LORD.
⁴³ Terror and pit and snare await you,
you people of Moab,'
declares the LORD.

⁴⁴ 'Whoever flees from the terror
    will fall into a pit,
  whoever climbs out of the pit
    will be caught in a snare;
  for I will bring on Moab
    the year of her punishment,'
                declares the LORD.

⁴⁵ 'In the shadow of Heshbon
    the fugitives stand helpless,
  for a fire has gone out from Heshbon,
    a blaze from the midst of Sihon;
  it burns the foreheads of Moab,
    the skulls of the noisy boasters.
⁴⁶ Woe to you, Moab!
    The people of Chemosh are destroyed;
  your sons are taken into exile
    and your daughters into captivity.

⁴⁷ 'Yet I will restore the fortunes of Moab
    in days to come,'
                declares the LORD.

Here ends the judgment on Moab.

49 Concerning the Ammonites:

This is what the LORD says:

'Has Israel no sons?
  Has Israel no heir?
Why then has Molek taken possession of
    Gad?
  Why do his people live in its towns?
² But the days are coming,'
    declares the LORD,
  'when I will sound the battle cry
    against Rabbah of the Ammonites;
  it will become a mound of ruins,
    and its surrounding villages will be
      set on fire.
  Then Israel will drive out
    those who drove her out,'
                says the LORD.

³ 'Wail, Heshbon, for Ai is destroyed!
  Cry out, you inhabitants of Rabbah!

Put on sackcloth and mourn;
    rush here and there inside the walls,
  for Molek will go into exile,
    together with his priests and officials.
⁴ Why do you boast of your valleys,
    boast of your valleys so fruitful?
  Unfaithful Daughter Ammon,
    you trust in your riches and say,
    "Who will attack me?"
⁵ I will bring terror on you
    from all those around you,'
                declares the Lord,
                the LORD Almighty.
  'Every one of you will be driven away,
    and no one will gather the fugitives.

⁶ 'Yet afterwards, I will restore the
    fortunes of the Ammonites,'
                declares the LORD.

■ PSALM 119:105–108

¹⁰⁵ Your word is a lamp for my feet,
    a light on my path.
¹⁰⁶ I have taken an oath and confirmed it,
    that I will follow your righteous laws.
¹⁰⁷ I have suffered much;
    preserve my life, LORD, according to
      your word.
¹⁰⁸ Accept, LORD, the willing praise of my
      mouth,
    and teach me your laws.

■ PROVERBS 26:17–19

¹⁷ Like one who grabs a stray dog by the ears
    is someone who rushes into a quarrel
      not their own.

¹⁸ Like a maniac shooting
    flaming arrows of death
¹⁹ is one who deceives their neighbour
    and says, 'I was only joking!'

▬ PHILEMON 1-25

[1] Paul, a prisoner of Christ Jesus, and Timothy our brother,

To Philemon our dear friend and fellow worker – [2] also to Apphia our sister and Archippus our fellow soldier – and to the church that meets in your home:

[3] Grace and peace to you from God our Father and the Lord Jesus Christ.

[4] I always thank my God as I remember you in my prayers, [5] because I hear about your love for all his holy people and your faith in the Lord Jesus. [6] I pray that your partnership with us in the faith may be effective in deepening your understanding of every good thing we share for the sake of Christ. [7] Your love has given me great joy and encouragement, because you, brother, have refreshed the hearts of the Lord's people.

[8] Therefore, although in Christ I could be bold and order you to do what you ought to do, [9] yet I prefer to appeal to you on the basis of love. It is as none other than Paul – an old man and now also a prisoner of Christ Jesus – [10] that I appeal to you for my son Onesimus, who became my son while I was in chains. [11] Formerly he was useless to you, but now he has become useful both to you and to me.

[12] I am sending him – who is my very heart – back to you. [13] I would have liked to keep him with me so that he could take your place in helping me while I am in chains for the gospel. [14] But I did not want to do anything without your consent, so that any favour you do would not seem forced but would be voluntary. [15] Perhaps the reason he was separated from you for a little while was that you might have him back for ever – [16] no longer as a slave, but better than a slave, as a dear brother. He is very dear to me but even dearer to you, both as a fellow man and as a brother in the Lord.

[17] So if you consider me a partner, welcome him as you would welcome me. [18] If he has done you any wrong or owes you anything, charge it to me. [19] I, Paul, am writing this with my own hand. I will pay it back – not to mention that you owe me your very self. [20] I do wish, brother, that I may have some benefit from you in the Lord; refresh my heart in Christ. [21] Confident of your obedience, I write to you, knowing that you will do even more than I ask.

[22] And one thing more: prepare a guest room for me, because I hope to be restored to you in answer to your prayers.

[23] Epaphras, my fellow prisoner in Christ Jesus, sends you greetings. [24] And so do Mark, Aristarchus, Demas and Luke, my fellow workers.

[25] The grace of the Lord Jesus Christ be with your spirit.

Don't Miss the Point

'Your word is a lamp for my feet, a light on my path.'
Psalm 119:105

There are some who claim that having our 'feet fitted with the readiness that comes from the gospel of peace' means that we should always be ready to carry the gospel to others. That interpretation certainly fits in with Romans 10:15: 'How beautiful are the feet of those who bring good news!', but this is not, in my opinion, what Paul had in mind when he wrote the words of Ephesians 6:15.

In Ephesians 6 the apostle is dealing with one thing only – the Christian's engagement with the Devil. He said: '... our struggle is not against flesh and blood, but against ... the powers of this dark world ...' (v. 12). His purpose is to show us how to stand against the 'tactics' of the Devil. Although Paul was an evangelist with a strong evangelistic spirit, he was not thinking here of evangelising, vital though it is. He was rather picturing a Christian who is under attack by Satan, warning us that unless our feet are firmly shod, we can easily be knocked down and disabled.

Those who claim that the phrase the 'readiness that comes from the gospel of peace' relates to evangelism miss the point of his exposition. No one would deny the importance of always being ready to share Christ with others, but the readiness to which Paul is referring here is the readiness to stand firm on the truths of the gospel. In other words, he is saying: don't get into a fight with the Devil in your bare feet. Make sure you are well shod, for if you are not, he will most certainly get the better of you.

PRAYER

O Father, I am so grateful that You breathed into Your servant Paul to write these illuminating words. They are inspired, for they inspire me. Continue to teach me, dear Lord. I am hungry for more and more of Your truth. Amen.

FURTHER STUDY

Psa. 119:97-105; Isa. 40:8; 1 Pet. 1:23-25; 2 Tim. 2:15
- How did the psalmist view God's Word?
- Why is God's Word a sure foundation?

November 5

■ JEREMIAH 49:7–50:23

⁷ Concerning Edom:

This is what the LORD Almighty says:

'Is there no longer wisdom in Teman?
    Has counsel perished from the prudent?
    Has their wisdom decayed?
⁸ Turn and flee, hide in deep caves,
    you who live in Dedan,
for I will bring disaster on Esau
    at the time when I punish him.
⁹ If grape-pickers came to you,
    would they not leave a few grapes?
If thieves came during the night,

would they not steal only as much as
    they wanted?
¹⁰ But I will strip Esau bare;
    I will uncover his hiding-places,
    so that he cannot conceal himself.
His armed men are destroyed,
    also his allies and neighbours,
    so there is no one to say,
¹¹ "Leave your fatherless children; I will
    keep them alive.
    Your widows too can depend on me."'

¹² This is what the LORD says: 'If those who do not deserve to drink the cup must drink it, why should you go unpunished? You will not go unpunished, but must drink it.

¹³ I swear by myself,' declares the LORD, 'that Bozrah will become a ruin and a curse, an object of horror and reproach; and all its towns will be in ruins for ever.'

¹⁴ I have heard a message from the LORD;
  an envoy was sent to the nations to say,
'Assemble yourselves to attack it!
  Rise up for battle!'

¹⁵ 'Now I will make you small among the
    nations,
  despised by mankind.
¹⁶ The terror you inspire
  and the pride of your heart have
    deceived you,
you who live in the clefts of the rocks,
  who occupy the heights of the hill.
Though you build your nest as high as
    the eagle's,
  from there I will bring you down,'
                      declares the LORD.
¹⁷ 'Edom will become an object of horror;
  all who pass by will be appalled and
    will scoff
  because of all its wounds.
¹⁸ As Sodom and Gomorrah were
    overthrown,
  along with their neighbouring towns,'
                      says the LORD,
'so no one will live there;
  no people will dwell in it.

¹⁹ 'Like a lion coming up from Jordan's
    thickets
  to a rich pasture-land,
I will chase Edom from its land in an
    instant.
  Who is the chosen one I will appoint
    for this?
  Who is like me and who can challenge me?
  And what shepherd can stand against
    me?'

²⁰ Therefore, hear what the LORD has
  planned against Edom,
what he has purposed against those
  who live in Teman:
The young of the flock will be dragged
    away;
  their pasture will be appalled at their
    fate.
²¹ At the sound of their fall the earth will
    tremble;
  their cry will resound to the Red Sea.
²² Look! An eagle will soar and swoop down,
  spreading its wings over Bozrah.
In that day the hearts of Edom's warriors
  will be like the heart of a woman in
    labour.

²³ Concerning Damascus:

'Hamath and Arpad are dismayed,
  for they have heard bad news.
They are disheartened,
  troubled like the restless sea.
²⁴ Damascus has become feeble,
  she has turned to flee
  and panic has gripped her;
anguish and pain have seized her,
  pain like that of a woman in labour.
²⁵ Why has the city of renown not been
    abandoned,
  the town in which I delight?
²⁶ Surely, her young men will fall in the
    streets;
  all her soldiers will be silenced in that
    day,'
                      declares the LORD Almighty.
²⁷ 'I will set fire to the walls of Damascus;
  it will consume the fortresses of
    Ben-Hadad.'

²⁸ Concerning Kedar and the kingdoms of Hazor, which Nebuchadnezzar king of Babylon attacked:

This is what the LORD says:

'Arise, and attack Kedar
  and destroy the people of the East.

²⁹ Their tents and their flocks will be taken;
   their shelters will be carried off
   with all their goods and camels.
People will shout to them,
   "Terror on every side!"

³⁰ 'Flee quickly away!
   Stay in deep caves, you who live in
      Hazor,'
                declares the LORD.
'Nebuchadnezzar king of Babylon has
      plotted against you;
   he has devised a plan against you.

³¹ 'Arise and attack a nation at ease,
   which lives in confidence,'
                declares the LORD,
'a nation that has neither gates nor bars;
   its people live far from danger.
³² Their camels will become plunder,
   and their large herds will be spoils of
      war.
I will scatter to the winds those who are
      in distant places
   and will bring disaster on them from
      every side,'
                declares the LORD.
³³ 'Hazor will become a haunt of jackals,
   a desolate place for ever.
No one will live there;
   no people will dwell in it.'

³⁴ This is the word of the Lord that came
to Jeremiah the prophet concerning Elam,
early in the reign of Zedekiah king of Judah:

³⁵ This is what the LORD Almighty says:

'See, I will break the bow of Elam,
   the mainstay of their might.
³⁶ I will bring against Elam the four winds
   from the four quarters of heaven;
I will scatter them to the four winds,
   and there will not be a nation
where Elam's exiles do not go.
³⁷ I will shatter Elam before their foes,

before those who want to kill them;
I will bring disaster on them,
   even my fierce anger,'
                declares the LORD.
'I will pursue them with the sword
   until I have made an end of them.
³⁸ I will set my throne in Elam
   and destroy her king and officials,'
                declares the LORD.

³⁹ 'Yet I will restore the fortunes of Elam
   in days to come,'
                declares the LORD.

50 This is the word the Lord spoke
   through Jeremiah the prophet
concerning Babylon and the land of the
Babylonians:

² 'Announce and proclaim among the
      nations,
   lift up a banner and proclaim it;
   keep nothing back, but say,
"Babylon will be captured;
   Bel will be put to shame,
   Marduk filled with terror.
Her images will be put to shame
   and her idols filled with terror."
³ A nation from the north will attack her
   and lay waste her land.
No one will live in it;
   both people and animals will flee away.

⁴ 'In those days, at that time,'
   declares the LORD,
'the people of Israel and the people of
      Judah together
   will go in tears to seek the LORD their
      God.
⁵ They will ask the way to Zion
   and turn their faces towards it.
They will come and bind themselves to
      the LORD
   in an everlasting covenant
   that will not be forgotten.

⁶'My people have been lost sheep;
  their shepherds have led them astray
  and caused them to roam on the
    mountains.
They wandered over mountain and hill
  and forgot their own resting place.
⁷Whoever found them devoured them;
  their enemies said, "We are not guilty,
for they sinned against the LORD, their
    verdant pasture,
  the LORD, the hope of their ancestors."

⁸'Flee out of Babylon;
  leave the land of the Babylonians,
  and be like the goats that lead the flock.
⁹For I will stir up and bring against Babylon
  an alliance of great nations from the
    land of the north.
They will take up their positions against
    her,
  and from the north she will be captured.
Their arrows will be like skilled warriors
  who do not return empty-handed.
¹⁰So Babylonia will be plundered;
  all who plunder her will have their fill,'
            declares the LORD.

¹¹'Because you rejoice and are glad,
  you who pillage my inheritance,
because you frolic like a heifer threshing
    corn
  and neigh like stallions,
¹²your mother will be greatly ashamed;
  she who gave you birth will be
    disgraced.
She will be the least of the nations –
  a wilderness, a dry land, a desert.
¹³Because of the LORD's anger she will not
    be inhabited
  but will be completely desolate.
All who pass Babylon will be appalled;
  they will scoff because of all her
    wounds.

¹⁴'Take up your positions round Babylon,
  all you who draw the bow.

Shoot at her! Spare no arrows,
  for she has sinned against the LORD.
¹⁵Shout against her on every side!
  She surrenders, her towers fall,
  her walls are torn down.
Since this is the vengeance of the LORD,
  take vengeance on her;
  do to her as she has done to others.
¹⁶Cut off from Babylon the sower,
  and the reaper with his sickle at
    harvest.
Because of the sword of the oppressor
  let everyone return to their own people,
  let everyone flee to their own land.

¹⁷'Israel is a scattered flock
  that lions have chased away.
The first to devour them
  was the king of Assyria;
the last to crush their bones
  was Nebuchadnezzar king of Babylon.'

¹⁸Therefore this is what the LORD
Almighty, the God of Israel, says:

'I will punish the king of Babylon and his
    land
  as I punished the king of Assyria.
¹⁹But I will bring Israel back to their own
    pasture,
  and they will graze on Carmel and
    Bashan;
their appetite will be satisfied
  on the hills of Ephraim and Gilead.
²⁰In those days, at that time,'
    declares the LORD,
'search will be made for Israel's guilt,
  but there will be none,
and for the sins of Judah,
  but none will be found,
  for I will forgive the remnant I spare.

²¹'Attack the land of Merathaim
  and those who live in Pekod.
Pursue, kill and completely destroy them,'
            declares the LORD.

'Do everything I have commanded you.
²² The noise of battle is in the land,
    the noise of great destruction!
²³ How broken and shattered
    is the hammer of the whole earth!
    How desolate is Babylon
    among the nations!

■ PSALM 119:109-112

¹⁰⁹Though I constantly take my life in my
    hands,
    I will not forget your law.
¹¹⁰ The wicked have set a snare for me,
    but I have not strayed from your
    precepts.
¹¹¹ Your statutes are my heritage for ever;
    they are the joy of my heart.
¹¹² My heart is set on keeping your decrees
    to the very end.

■ PROVERBS 26:20-23

²⁰ Without wood a fire goes out;
    without a gossip a quarrel dies down.
²¹ As charcoal to embers and as wood to
    fire,
    so is a quarrelsome person for
    kindling strife.
²² The words of a gossip are like choice
    morsels;
    they go down to the inmost parts.

²³ Like a coating of silver dross on
    earthenware
    are fervent lips with an evil heart.

■ HEBREWS 1:1–2:9

1 In the past God spoke to our ancestors
through the prophets at many times and
in various ways, ²but in these last days he has
spoken to us by his Son, whom he appointed

heir of all things, and through whom also he
made the universe. ³The Son is the radiance
of God's glory and the exact representation of
his being, sustaining all things by his powerful word. After he had provided purification
for sins, he sat down at the right hand of the
Majesty in heaven. ⁴So he became as much
superior to the angels as the name he has
inherited is superior to theirs.

⁵For to which of the angels did God ever
say,

    'You are my Son;
      today I have become your Father'?

Or again,

    'I will be his Father,
      and he will be my Son'?

⁶And again, when God brings his firstborn
into the world, he says,

    'Let all God's angels worship him.'

⁷In speaking of the angels he says,

    'He makes his angels spirits,
      and his servants flames of fire.'

⁸But about the Son he says,

    'Your throne, O God, will last for ever
      and ever;
    a sceptre of justice will be the sceptre
      of your kingdom.
⁹You have loved righteousness and hated
      wickedness;
    therefore God, your God, has set you
      above your companions
    by anointing you with the oil of joy.'

¹⁰He also says,

    'In the beginning, Lord, you laid the
      foundations of the earth,

and the heavens are the work of your
hands.
[11] They will perish, but you remain;
they will all wear out like a garment.
[12] You will roll them up like a robe;
like a garment they will be changed.
But you remain the same,
and your years will never end.'

[13] To which of the angels did God ever say,

'Sit at my right hand
until I make your enemies
a footstool for your feet'?

[14] Are not all angels ministering spirits sent
to serve those who will inherit salvation?

2 We must pay the most careful attention, therefore, to what we have heard,
so that we do not drift away. [2] For since the
message spoken through angels was binding, and every violation and disobedience
received its just punishment, [3] how shall
we escape if we ignore so great a salvation?
This salvation, which was first announced
by the Lord, was confirmed to us by those
who heard him. [4] God also testified to it
by signs, wonders and various miracles,
and by gifts of the Holy Spirit distributed
according to his will.

[5] It is not to angels that he has subjected
the world to come, about which we are
speaking. [6] But there is a place where someone has testified:

'What is mankind that you are mindful
of them,
a son of man that you care for him?
[7] You made them a little lower than the
angels;
you crowned them with glory and
honour
[8]   and put everything under their feet.'

In putting everything under them, God left
nothing that is not subject to them. Yet at
present we do not see everything subject to
them. [9] But we do see Jesus, who was made
lower than the angels for a little while, now
crowned with glory and honour because he
suffered death, so that by the grace of God
he might taste death for everyone.

We See Jesus

'... we do not see everything subject to them. But we
do see Jesus ...' **Hebrews 2:8-9**

Are you troubled as you look out at the situation in the world? Well,
according to the Bible, things are going to get worse. As Jesus
said, 'People will faint from terror, apprehensive of what is coming on
the world ...' (Luke 21:26). How are Christians going to stand when the
darkness deepens and things get very much worse? What will we do
when international tension increases?

Christians have a glorious hope - the hope of salvation. It is this, and
this alone, that enables believers to live out their lives free from mental
distress. I am sure you have already discovered that after reading the
morning newspaper, you move into the day feeling somewhat depressed.
Why is this? It is because almost daily, our newspapers are filled with
murder, rape, violence, economic distress, child abuse. And our
conscience, which through conversion has been sensitised to the moral

laws of God, begins to reverberate as it comes up against the reports of things we know are contrary to the divine principles.

Satan, seeing our concern, attempts to exploit it to his own ends. 'Things are getting worse, aren't they?' he says. 'Why don't you just admit that God has lost control of His world?' If we did not have the helmet of salvation to put on at such a moment, we would finish up with the same attitude as H. G. Wells, who, after the Second World War, wrote: 'The spectacle of evil in the world has come near to breaking my spirit.' There is no protection in the world for the mind.

PRAYER

My Father and my God, where would I be if I could not cling to a text such as that in my reading for today? My spirit, too, would be near to breaking. I am so thankful that in You there is hope – hope with a capital H. Amen.

FURTHER STUDY

John 17; Rom. 8:35-37; 1 John 5:4
• What did Jesus pray for His disciples?
• What was Paul's conviction?

November 6

JEREMIAH 50:24–51:32

24 I set a trap for you, Babylon,
    and you were caught before you knew it;
you were found and captured
    because you opposed the LORD.
25 The LORD has opened his arsenal
    and brought out the weapons of his
        wrath,
for the Sovereign LORD Almighty has
        work to do
    in the land of the Babylonians.
26 Come against her from afar.
    Break open her granaries;
    pile her up like heaps of grain.
Completely destroy her
    and leave her no remnant.
27 Kill all her young bulls;
    let them go down to the slaughter!
Woe to them! For their day has come,
    the time for them to be punished.
28 Listen to the fugitives and refugees from
        Babylon

declaring in Zion
how the LORD our God has taken
        vengeance,
    vengeance for his temple.
29 'Summon archers against Babylon,
    all those who draw the bow.
Encamp all round her;
    let no one escape.
Repay her for her deeds;
    do to her as she has done.
For she defied the LORD,
    the Holy One of Israel.
30 Therefore, her young men will fall in the
        streets;
    all her soldiers will be silenced in that
        day,'
            declares the LORD.
31 'See, I am against you, you arrogant one,'
    declares the Lord, the LORD Almighty,
'for your day has come,
    the time for you to be punished.
32 The arrogant one will stumble and fall

and no one will help her up;
I will kindle a fire in her towns
    that will consume all who are around
        her.'

33 This is what the LORD Almighty says:

'The people of Israel are oppressed,
    and the people of Judah as well.
All their captors hold them fast,
    refusing to let them go.
34 Yet their Redeemer is strong;
    the LORD Almighty is his name.
He will vigorously defend their cause
    so that he may bring rest to their land,
    but unrest to those who live in
        Babylon.

35 'A sword against the Babylonians!'
    declares the LORD –
'against those who live in Babylon
    and against her officials and wise men!
36 A sword against her false prophets!
    They will become fools.
A sword against her warriors!
    They will be filled with terror.
37 A sword against her horses and chariots
    and all the foreigners in her ranks!
    They will become weaklings.
A sword against her treasures!
    They will be plundered.
38 A drought on her waters!
    They will dry up.
For it is a land of idols,
    idols that will go mad with terror.

39 'So desert creatures and hyenas will live
        there,
    and there the owl will dwell.
It will never again be inhabited
    or lived in from generation to generation.
40 As I overthrew Sodom and Gomorrah
    along with their neighbouring towns,'
                        declares the LORD,
'so no one will live there;
    no people will dwell in it.

41 'Look! An army is coming from the north;
    a great nation and many kings
    are being stirred up from the ends of
        the earth.
42 They are armed with bows and spears;
    they are cruel and without mercy.
They sound like the roaring sea
    as they ride on their horses;
they come like men in battle formation
    to attack you, Daughter Babylon.
43 The king of Babylon has heard reports
        about them,
    and his hands hang limp.
Anguish has gripped him,
    pain like that of a woman in labour.
44 Like a lion coming up from Jordan's
        thickets
    to a rich pasture-land,
I will chase Babylon from its land in an
        instant.
    Who is the chosen one I will appoint
        for this?
Who is like me and who can challenge me?
    And what shepherd can stand against
        me?'

45 Therefore, hear what the LORD has
        planned against Babylon,
    what he has purposed against the land
        of the Babylonians:
the young of the flock will be dragged
        away;
    their pasture will be appalled at their
        fate.
46 At the sound of Babylon's capture the
        earth will tremble;
    its cry will resound among the nations.

51 This is what the LORD says:

'See, I will stir up the spirit of a destroyer
    against Babylon and the people of Leb
        Kamai.
2 I will send foreigners to Babylon
    to winnow her and to devastate her land;
    they will oppose her on every side

in the day of her disaster.
³ Let not the archer string his bow,
    nor let him put on his armour.
Do not spare her young men;
    completely destroy her army.
⁴ They will fall down slain in Babylon,
    fatally wounded in her streets.
⁵ For Israel and Judah have not been
        forsaken
    by their God, the Lord Almighty,
though their land is full of guilt
    before the Holy One of Israel.

⁶ 'Flee from Babylon!
    Run for your lives!
    Do not be destroyed because of her sins.
It is time for the Lord's vengeance;
    he will repay her what she deserves.
⁷ Babylon was a gold cup in the Lord's
        hand;
    she made the whole earth drunk.
The nations drank her wine;
    therefore they have now gone mad.
⁸ Babylon will suddenly fall and be broken.
    Wail over her!
Get balm for her pain;
    perhaps she can be healed.

⁹ ' "We would have healed Babylon,
    but she cannot be healed;
let us leave her and each go to our own
        land,
    for her judgment reaches to the skies,
    it rises as high as the heavens." '

¹⁰ ' "The Lord has vindicated us;
    come, let us tell in Zion
what the Lord our God has done." '

¹¹ 'Sharpen the arrows,
    take up the shields!
The Lord has stirred up the kings of the
        Medes,
    because his purpose is to destroy
        Babylon.
The Lord will take vengeance,

vengeance for his temple.
¹² Lift up a banner against the walls of
        Babylon!
    Reinforce the guard,
station the watchmen,
    prepare an ambush!
The Lord will carry out his purpose,
    his decree against the people of
        Babylon.
¹³ You who live by many waters
    and are rich in treasures,
your end has come,
    the time for you to be destroyed.
¹⁴ The Lord Almighty has sworn by
        himself:
    I will surely fill you with troops, as
        with a swarm of locusts,
    and they will shout in triumph over
        you.

¹⁵ 'He made the earth by his power;
    he founded the world by his wisdom
    and stretched out the heavens by his
        understanding.
¹⁶ When he thunders, the waters in the
        heavens roar;
    he makes clouds rise from the ends of
        the earth.
He sends lightning with the rain
    and brings out the wind from his
        storehouses.

¹⁷ 'Everyone is senseless and without
        knowledge;
    every goldsmith is shamed by his idols.
The images he makes are a fraud;
    they have no breath in them.
¹⁸ They are worthless, the objects of
        mockery;
    when their judgment comes, they will
        perish.
¹⁹ He who is the Portion of Jacob is not like
        these,
    for he is the Maker of all things,
including the people of his inheritance –
    the Lord Almighty is his name.

20 'You are my war club,
  my weapon for battle –
with you I shatter nations,
  with you I destroy kingdoms,
21 with you I shatter horse and rider,
  with you I shatter chariot and driver,
22 with you I shatter man and woman,
  with you I shatter old man and youth,
  with you I shatter young man and
    young woman,
23 with you I shatter shepherd and flock,
  with you I shatter farmer and oxen,
  with you I shatter governors and
    officials.

24 'Before your eyes I will repay Babylon and all who live in Babylonia for all the wrong they have done in Zion,' declares the LORD.

25 'I am against you, you destroying
    mountain,
  you who destroy the whole earth,'
        declares the LORD.
'I will stretch out my hand against you,
  roll you off the cliffs,
  and make you a burnt-out mountain.
26 No rock will be taken from you for a
    cornerstone,
  nor any stone for a foundation,
  for you will be desolate for ever,'
        declares the LORD.

27 'Lift up a banner in the land!
  Blow the trumpet among the nations!
Prepare the nations for battle against
    her;
  summon against her these kingdoms:
    Ararat, Minni and Ashkenaz.
  Appoint a commander against her;
    send up horses like a swarm of locusts.
28 Prepare the nations for battle against
    her –
  the kings of the Medes,
  their governors and all their officials,
  and all the countries they rule.

29 The land trembles and writhes,
  for the LORD's purposes against
    Babylon stand –
to lay waste the land of Babylon
  so that no one will live there.
30 Babylon's warriors have stopped
    fighting;
  they remain in their strongholds.
Their strength is exhausted;
  they have become weaklings.
Her dwellings are set on fire;
  the bars of her gates are broken.
31 One courier follows another
  and messenger follows messenger
to announce to the king of Babylon
  that his entire city is captured,
32 the river crossings seized,
  the marshes set on fire,
  and the soldiers terrified.'

....

▬ PSALM 119:113-120

113 I hate double-minded people,
  but I love your law.
114 You are my refuge and my shield;
  I have put my hope in your word.
115 Away from me, you evildoers,
  that I may keep the commands of my
    God!
116 Sustain me, my God, according to your
    promise, and I shall live;
  do not let my hopes be dashed.
117 Uphold me, and I shall be delivered;
  I shall always have regard for your
    decrees.
118 You reject all who stray from your
    decrees,
  for their delusions come to nothing.
119 All the wicked of the earth you discard
    like dross;
  therefore I love your statutes.
120 My flesh trembles in fear of you;
  I stand in awe of your laws.

■ PROVERBS 26:24-26

24 Enemies disguise themselves with their lips,
    but in their hearts they harbour deceit.
25 Though their speech is charming, do not believe them,
    for seven abominations fill their hearts.
26 Their malice may be concealed by deception,
    but their wickedness will be exposed in the assembly.

■ HEBREWS 2:10-3:11

10 In bringing many sons and daughters to glory, it was fitting that God, for whom and through whom everything exists, should make the pioneer of their salvation perfect through what he suffered. 11 Both the one who makes people holy and those who are made holy are of the same family. So Jesus is not ashamed to call them brothers and sisters. 12 He says,

'I will declare your name to my brothers and sisters;
    in the assembly I will sing your praises.'

13 And again,

'I will put my trust in him.'

And again he says,

'Here am I, and the children God has given me.'

14 Since the children have flesh and blood, he too shared in their humanity so that by his death he might break the power of him who holds the power of death – that is, the devil – 15 and free those who all their lives were held in slavery by their fear of death. 16 For surely it is not angels he helps, but Abraham's descendants. 17 For this reason he had to be made like them, fully human in every way, in order that he might become a merciful and faithful high priest in service to God, and that he might make atonement for the sins of the people. 18 Because he himself suffered when he was tempted, he is able to help those who are being tempted.

3 Therefore, holy brothers and sisters, who share in the heavenly calling, fix your thoughts on Jesus, whom we acknowledge as our apostle and high priest. 2 He was faithful to the one who appointed him, just as Moses was faithful in all God's house. 3 Jesus has been found worthy of greater honour than Moses, just as the builder of a house has greater honour than the house itself. 4 For every house is built by someone, but God is the builder of everything. 5 'Moses was faithful as a servant in all God's house,' bearing witness to what would be spoken by God in the future. 6 But Christ is faithful as the Son over God's house. And we are his house, if indeed we hold firmly to our confidence and the hope in which we glory.

7 So, as the Holy Spirit says:

'Today, if you hear his voice,
8   do not harden your hearts
as you did in the rebellion,
    during the time of testing in the wilderness,
9 where your ancestors tested and tried me,
    though for forty years they saw what I did.
10 That is why I was angry with that generation;
I said, "Their hearts are always going astray,
    and they have not known my ways."
11 So I declared on oath in my anger,
    "They shall never enter my rest." '

Two Basic Fears

'... and free those who all their lives were held in slavery by their fear of death.' **Hebrews 2:15**

Psychologists are at pains to point out that fear is different from anxiety. Fear has a specific object, whereas anxiety is a vague and unspecified apprehension.

What, I wonder, is your biggest fear? Benjamin Rank, a social scientist, says that there are basically two forms of fear: the fear of life and the fear of death. The fear of life is the fear of having to live as an isolated individual. The fear of death is the fear of losing individuality. He says: 'Between these two fear possibilities, these poles of fear, the individual is thrown back and forth all his life.'

The first fear - the fear of life - is vividly illustrated by a small boy's comment, 'I suppose the reason for twins is because little children don't like to come into the world alone'. The fear of life makes some retreat into illness. It is a refuge from responsibility. Freud found the cause of neurosis in the past - in childhood; Jung, a disciple of Freud, found it in the present. He said, 'I ask, what is the necessary task which the patient will not accomplish?' Backing out of life's responsibilities through fear of life is a major cause of problems.

But with many, it is the fear of death that paralyses them. Our verse today reads, in speaking of Jesus, that He is able to 'free those who all their lives were held in slavery by their fear of death' (Heb. 2:15). Is it necessary to live under such servitude? Of course not. When Christ has all of you, then fear can have no part of you. It is as simple as that!

PRAYER

Father, I am so thankful that You have made it possible for me not to be enslaved by fear. I can be free, gloriously free - and free now. Touch me in the deepest parts of my being this day and set me free from all and every fear. In Jesus' name. Amen.

FURTHER STUDY

1 Cor. 15; 2 Cor. 5:1; John 11:25-26
• What is the hope of every believer?
• Is this your hope?

November 7

■ JEREMIAH 51:33–52:16

³³ This is what the LORD Almighty, the God of Israel, says:

'Daughter Babylon is like a threshing-floor
     at the time it is trampled;
the time to harvest her will soon come.'

³⁴ 'Nebuchadnezzar king of Babylon has devoured us,
     he has thrown us into confusion,
     he has made us an empty jar.
Like a serpent he has swallowed us
     and filled his stomach with our delicacies,
     and then has spewed us out.
³⁵ May the violence done to our flesh be on Babylon,'
     say the inhabitants of Zion.
'May our blood be on those who live in Babylonia,'
     says Jerusalem.

³⁶ Therefore this is what the LORD says:

'See, I will defend your cause
     and avenge you;
I will dry up her sea
     and make her springs dry.
³⁷ Babylon will be a heap of ruins,
     a haunt of jackals,
an object of horror and scorn,
     a place where no one lives.
³⁸ Her people all roar like young lions,
     they growl like lion cubs.
³⁹ But while they are aroused,
     I will set out a feast for them
     and make them drunk,
so that they shout with laughter –
     then sleep for ever and not awake,'
           declares the LORD.
⁴⁰ 'I will bring them down
     like lambs to the slaughter,
     like rams and goats.

⁴¹ 'How Sheshak will be captured,
     the boast of the whole earth seized!
How desolate Babylon will be
     among the nations!
⁴² The sea will rise over Babylon;
     its roaring waves will cover her.
⁴³ Her towns will be desolate,
     a dry and desert land,
a land where no one lives,
     through which no one travels.
⁴⁴ I will punish Bel in Babylon
     and make him spew out what he has swallowed.
The nations will no longer stream to him.
     And the wall of Babylon will fall.

⁴⁵ 'Come out of her, my people!
     Run for your lives!
     Run from the fierce anger of the LORD.
⁴⁶ Do not lose heart or be afraid
     when rumours are heard in the land;
one rumour comes this year, another the next,
     rumours of violence in the land
     and of ruler against ruler.
⁴⁷ For the time will surely come
     when I will punish the idols of Babylon;
her whole land will be disgraced
     and her slain will all lie fallen within her.
⁴⁸ Then heaven and earth and all that is in them
     will shout for joy over Babylon,
     for out of the north

destroyers will attack her,'
            declares the LORD.

⁴⁹ 'Babylon must fall because of Israel's
        slain,
    just as the slain in all the earth
    have fallen because of Babylon.
⁵⁰ You who have escaped the sword,
        leave and do not linger!
    Remember the LORD in a distant land,
    and call to mind Jerusalem.'

⁵¹ 'We are disgraced,
        for we have been insulted
    and shame covers our faces,
    because foreigners have entered
        the holy places of the LORD's house.'

⁵² 'But days are coming,' declares the LORD,
    'when I will punish her idols,
    and throughout her land
        the wounded will groan.
⁵³ Even if Babylon ascends to the heavens
        and fortifies her lofty stronghold,
    I will send destroyers against her,'
            declares the LORD.

⁵⁴ 'The sound of a cry comes from Babylon,
        the sound of great destruction
    from the land of the Babylonians.
⁵⁵ The LORD will destroy Babylon;
        he will silence her noisy din.
    Waves of enemies will rage like great
            waters;
        the roar of their voices will resound.
⁵⁶ A destroyer will come against Babylon;
        her warriors will be captured,
        and their bows will be broken.
    For the LORD is a God of retribution;
        he will repay in full.
⁵⁷ I will make her officials and wise men
            drunk,
        her governors, officers and warriors
            as well;
        they will sleep for ever and not awake,'

declares the King, whose name is the
    LORD Almighty.

⁵⁸ This is what the LORD Almighty says:

'Babylon's thick wall will be levelled
        and her high gates set on fire;
    the peoples exhaust themselves for
            nothing,
        the nations' labour is only fuel for the
            flames.'

⁵⁹ This is the message Jeremiah the
prophet gave to the staff officer Seraiah
son of Neriah, the son of Mahseiah, when
he went to Babylon with Zedekiah king of
Judah in the fourth year of his reign. ⁶⁰ Jeremiah had written on a scroll about all the
disasters that would come upon Babylon –
all that had been recorded concerning Babylon. ⁶¹ He said to Seraiah, 'When you get to
Babylon, see that you read all these words
aloud. ⁶² Then say, "LORD, you have said you
will destroy this place, so that neither people nor animals will live in it; it will be desolate for ever." ⁶³ When you finish reading
this scroll, tie a stone to it and throw it into
the Euphrates. ⁶⁴ Then say, "So will Babylon
sink to rise no more because of the disaster I
will bring on her. And her people will fall." '

The words of Jeremiah end here.

52 Zedekiah was twenty-one years
old when he became king, and he
reigned in Jerusalem for eleven years. His
mother's name was Hamutal daughter of
Jeremiah; she was from Libnah. ²He did
evil in the eyes of the LORD, just as Jehoiakim had done. ³It was because of the LORD's
anger that all this happened to Jerusalem
and Judah, and in the end he thrust them
from his presence.

Now Zedekiah rebelled against the king
of Babylon.

⁴So in the ninth year of Zedekiah's reign,

on the tenth day of the tenth month, Nebuchadnezzar king of Babylon marched against Jerusalem with his whole army. They encamped outside the city and built siege works all around it. ⁵The city was kept under siege until the eleventh year of King Zedekiah.

⁶By the ninth day of the fourth month the famine in the city had become so severe that there was no food for the people to eat. ⁷Then the city wall was broken through, and the whole army fled. They left the city at night through the gate between the two walls near the king's garden, though the Babylonians were surrounding the city. They fled towards the Arabah, ⁸but the Babylonian army pursued King Zedekiah and overtook him in the plains of Jericho. All his soldiers were separated from him and scattered, ⁹and he was captured.

He was taken to the king of Babylon at Riblah in the land of Hamath, where he pronounced sentence on him. ¹⁰There at Riblah the king of Babylon killed the sons of Zedekiah before his eyes; he also killed all the officials of Judah. ¹¹Then he put out Zedekiah's eyes, bound him with bronze shackles and took him to Babylon, where he put him in prison till the day of his death.

¹²On the tenth day of the fifth month, in the nineteenth year of Nebuchadnezzar king of Babylon, Nebuzaradan commander of the imperial guard, who served the king of Babylon, came to Jerusalem. ¹³He set fire to the temple of the LORD, the royal palace and all the houses of Jerusalem. Every important building he burned down. ¹⁴The whole Babylonian army, under the commander of the imperial guard, broke down all the walls around Jerusalem. ¹⁵Nebuzaradan the commander of the guard carried into exile some of the poorest people and those who remained in the city, along with the rest of the craftsmen and those who had deserted to the king of Babylon. ¹⁶But Nebuzaradan left behind the rest of the poorest people of the land to work the vineyards and fields.

▬ PSALM 119:121–128

¹²¹I have done what is righteous and just;
  do not leave me to my oppressors.
¹²²Ensure your servant's well-being;
  do not let the arrogant oppress me.
¹²³My eyes fail, looking for your salvation,
  looking for your righteous promise.
¹²⁴Deal with your servant according to your love
  and teach me your decrees.
¹²⁵I am your servant; give me discernment
  that I may understand your statutes.
¹²⁶It is time for you to act, LORD;
  your law is being broken.
¹²⁷Because I love your commands
  more than gold, more than pure gold,
¹²⁸and because I consider all your precepts right,
  I hate every wrong path.

▬ PROVERBS 26:27–28

²⁷Whoever digs a pit will fall into it;
  if someone rolls a stone, it will roll back on them.
²⁸A lying tongue hates those it hurts,
  and a flattering mouth works ruin.

▬ HEBREWS 3:12–4:13

¹²See to it, brothers and sisters, that none of you has a sinful, unbelieving heart that turns away from the living God. ¹³But encourage one another daily, as long as it is called 'Today', so that none of you may be hardened by sin's deceitfulness. ¹⁴We have come to share in Christ, if indeed we hold our original conviction firmly to the very end. ¹⁵As has just been said:

'Today, if you hear his voice,
  do not harden your hearts
  as you did in the rebellion.'

¹⁶Who were they who heard and re-belled? Were they not all those Moses led out of Egypt? ¹⁷And with whom was he angry for forty years? Was it not with those who sinned, whose bodies perished in the wilderness? ¹⁸And to whom did God swear that they would never enter his rest if not to those who disobeyed? ¹⁹So we see that they were not able to enter, because of their unbelief.

4 Therefore, since the promise of entering his rest still stands, let us be careful that none of you be found to have fallen short of it. ²For we also have had the good news proclaimed to us, just as they did; but the message they heard was of no value to them, because they did not share the faith of those who obeyed. ³Now we who have believed enter that rest, just as God has said,

'So I declared on oath in my anger,
  "They shall never enter my rest."'

And yet his works have been finished since the creation of the world. ⁴For somewhere he has spoken about the seventh day in these words: 'On the seventh day God rested from all his works.' ⁵And again in the passage above he says, 'They shall never enter my rest.'

⁶Therefore since it still remains for some to enter that rest, and since those who formerly had the good news proclaimed to them did not go in because of their disobedience, ⁷God again set a certain day, calling it 'Today'. This he did when a long time later he spoke through David, as in the passage already quoted:

'Today, if you hear his voice,
  do not harden your hearts.'

⁸For if Joshua had given them rest, God would not have spoken later about another day. ⁹There remains, then, a Sabbath-rest for the people of God; ¹⁰for anyone who enters God's rest also rests from their works, just as God did from his. ¹¹Let us, therefore, make every effort to enter that rest, so that no one will perish by following their example of disobedience.

¹²For the word of God is alive and active. Sharper than any double-edged sword, it penetrates even to dividing soul and spirit, joints and marrow; it judges the thoughts and attitudes of the heart. ¹³Nothing in all creation is hidden from God's sight. Everything is uncovered and laid bare before the eyes of him to whom we must give account.

Talk to Yourself

'For the word of God is alive and active ... it judges the thoughts and attitudes of the heart.' **Hebrews 4:12**

Whatever we do, we must not let any lurking doubts go unchallenged. Pascal said: 'Doubt is an unhappy state, but there is an indispensable duty to seek when we are in doubt, and thus anyone who doubts and does not seek is at once unhappy and in the wrong.'

How do we go about resolving doubts? One way is to bring them to the Lord in prayer and ask Him to help us overcome them. If prayer does not dissolve them, apply the tactic which Nehemiah adopted: 'But we prayed to our God and posted a guard' (Neh. 4:9). Take a verse of Scripture that is the opposite of your doubt and hold it in the centre of your mind, repeating it to yourself many times throughout the day. Dr Martyn Lloyd-Jones once said, 'Have you realised that most of your unhappiness in life is due to the fact that you are listening to yourself instead of talking to yourself? We must talk to ourselves instead of allowing ourselves to talk to us!'

In listening to our doubts instead of talking to them, we fall prey to the same temptation that caught Adam and Eve off guard in the garden of Eden. The order of creation was stood on its head when the first human pair allowed themselves to be dictated to by the animal world (in the form of the serpent), when, in fact, they had been put in a position to dictate to it.

Don't let your doubts dictate to you. Turn the tables and dictate to them. Talk to them with words from the Word of God.

PRAYER

Father, help me never to be nonplussed, for in You there are ways to overcome every problem. Drive the truth I have learned today deeply into my spirit so that I may apply it whenever I am faced with doubt. In Jesus' name. Amen.

FURTHER STUDY

Gen. 3; Psa. 53:5; James 1:6
• What was Satan's strategy?
• What did Adam confess?

November 8

■ JEREMIAH 52:17-34

[17] The Babylonians broke up the bronze pillars, the movable stands and the bronze Sea that were at the temple of the LORD and they carried all the bronze to Babylon. [18] They also took away the pots, shovels, wick trimmers, sprinkling bowls, dishes and all the bronze articles used in the temple service. [19] The commander of the imperial guard took away the basins, censers, sprinkling bowls, pots, lampstands, dishes and bowls used for drink offerings – all that were made of pure gold or silver.

[20] The bronze from the two pillars, the Sea and the twelve bronze bulls under it, and the movable stands, which King Solomon had made for the temple of the LORD, was more than could be weighed.

[21] Each pillar was eighteen cubits high and twelve cubits in circumference; each was four fingers thick, and hollow. [22] The bronze capital on the top of one pillar was five cubits high and was decorated with a network and pomegranates of bronze all around. The other pillar, with its pomegranates, was similar. [23] There were ninety-six pomegranates on the sides; the total number of pomegranates above the surrounding network was a hundred.

[24] The commander of the guard took as prisoners Seraiah the chief priest, Zephaniah the priest next in rank and the three doorkeepers. [25] Of those still in the city, he took the officer in charge of the fighting men, and seven royal advisers. He also took the secretary who was chief officer in charge of conscripting the people of the

land, sixty of whom were found in the city. ²⁶Nebuzaradan the commander took them all and brought them to the king of Babylon at Riblah. ²⁷There at Riblah, in the land of Hamath, the king had them executed.

So Judah went into captivity, away from her land. ²⁸This is the number of the people Nebuchadnezzar carried into exile:

in the seventh year, 3,023 Jews;
²⁹in Nebuchadnezzar's eighteenth year,
832 people from Jerusalem;
³⁰in his twenty-third year,
745 Jews taken into exile by Nebuzaradan the commander of the
imperial guard.
There were 4,600 people in all.

³¹In the thirty-seventh year of the exile of Jehoiachin king of Judah, in the year Awel-Marduk became king of Babylon, on the twenty-fifth day of the twelfth month, he released Jehoiachin king of Judah and freed him from prison. ³²He spoke kindly to him and gave him a seat of honour higher than those of the other kings who were with him in Babylon. ³³So Jehoiachin put aside his prison clothes and for the rest of his life ate regularly at the king's table. ³⁴Day by day the king of Babylon gave Jehoiachin a regular allowance as long as he lived, till the day of his death.

■ PSALM 119:129-136

¹²⁹Your statutes are wonderful;
therefore I obey them.
¹³⁰The unfolding of your words gives light;
it gives understanding to the simple.
¹³¹I open my mouth and pant,
longing for your commands.
¹³²Turn to me and have mercy on me,
as you always do to those who love
your name.

¹³³Direct my footsteps according to your word;
let no sin rule over me.
¹³⁴Redeem me from human oppression,
that I may obey your precepts.
¹³⁵Make your face shine on your servant
and teach me your decrees.
¹³⁶Streams of tears flow from my eyes,
for your law is not obeyed.

■ PROVERBS 27:1-2

27 Do not boast about tomorrow,
for you do not know what a day
may bring.

²Let someone else praise you, and not
your own mouth;
an outsider, and not your own lips.

■ HEBREWS 4:14-6:8

¹⁴Therefore, since we have a great high priest who has ascended into heaven, Jesus the Son of God, let us hold firmly to the faith we profess. ¹⁵For we do not have a high priest who is unable to feel sympathy for our weaknesses, but we have one who has been tempted in every way, just as we are – yet he did not sin. ¹⁶Let us then approach God's throne of grace with confidence, so that we may receive mercy and find grace to help us in our time of need.

5 Every high priest is selected from among the people and is appointed to represent the people in matters related to God, to offer gifts and sacrifices for sins. ²He is able to deal gently with those who are ignorant and are going astray, since he himself is subject to weakness. ³This is why he has to offer sacrifices for his own sins, as well as for the sins of the people. ⁴And no one takes this honour on himself, but he receives it when called by God,

just as Aaron was.

⁵ In the same way, Christ did not take on himself the glory of becoming a high priest. But God said to him,

'You are my Son;
today I have become your Father.'

⁶ And he says in another place,

'You are a priest for ever,
in the order of Melchizedek.'

⁷ During the days of Jesus' life on earth, he offered up prayers and petitions with fervent cries and tears to the one who could save him from death, and he was heard because of his reverent submission. ⁸ Son though he was, he learned obedience from what he suffered ⁹ and, once made perfect, he became the source of eternal salvation for all who obey him ¹⁰ and was designated by God to be high priest in the order of Melchizedek.

¹¹ We have much to say about this, but it is hard to make it clear to you because you no longer try to understand. ¹² In fact, though by this time you ought to be teachers, you need someone to teach you the elementary truths of God's word all over again. You need milk, not solid food! ¹³ Anyone who lives on milk, being still an infant, is not acquainted with the teaching about righteousness. ¹⁴ But solid food is for the mature, who by constant use have trained themselves to distinguish good from evil.

6 Therefore let us move beyond the elementary teachings about Christ and be taken forward to maturity, not laying again the foundation of repentance from acts that lead to death, and of faith in God, ² instruction about cleansing rites, the laying on of hands, the resurrection of the dead, and eternal judgment. ³ And God permitting, we will do so.

⁴ It is impossible for those who have once been enlightened, who have tasted the heavenly gift, who have shared in the Holy Spirit, ⁵ who have tasted the goodness of the word of God and the powers of the coming age ⁶ and who have fallen away, to be brought back to repentance. To their loss they are crucifying the Son of God all over again and subjecting him to public disgrace. ⁷ Land that drinks in the rain often falling on it and that produces a crop useful to those for whom it is farmed receives the blessing of God. ⁸ But land that produces thorns and thistles is worthless and is in danger of being cursed. In the end it will be burned.

Love with a 'Stoop'

'Let us then approach God's throne of grace with confidence ...' **Hebrews 4:16**

G race is more than a synonym for love; it is a characteristic of the Deity which is quite close to love (and mercy) but yet deserves to be seen as different and distinctive. I heard an old Welsh preacher say, 'Grace is a word with a "stoop" in it; love reaches out on the same level, but grace always has to stoop to pick one up.' It was probably this same thought that an anonymous writer had in mind when he said: 'Grace is love at its loveliest, falling on the unlovable and making it lovely.'

But it is to the great Puritan preacher Thomas Goodwin we must turn for the best clarification of the difference between love and grace: 'Grace is more than mercy and love. It superadds to them. It denotes not simply love but love of a sovereign, transcendentally superior One that may do what He will, that may freely choose whether He will love or no. There may be love between equals, and an inferior may love a superior, but love in a Superior – and so superior that He may do what He will – in such a One love is called grace. Grace is attributed to princes; they are said to be "gracious" to their subjects, whereas subjects cannot be gracious to princes.'

Grace then is God's kindness bestowed upon the undeserving; benevolence handed down to those who have no merit; a hand reaching down to those who have fallen into a pit. The Bible bids us believe that on the throne of the universe there is a God like that.

PRAYER

Loving and gracious God, help me understand more deeply than ever what it means to be a recipient of Your grace. I have some idea, but I long to realise it even more. Help me, my Father. In Jesus' name. Amen.

FURTHER STUDY

Dan. 9:1-19; Deut. 9:5; 1 Pet. 5:5

• Is grace the result of righteousness?
• To whom does God give grace?

November 9

■ LAMENTATIONS 1:1–3:12

1 How deserted lies the city,
   once so full of people!
How like a widow is she,
   who once was great among the
      nations!
She who was queen among the provinces
   has now become a slave.

2 Bitterly she weeps at night,
   tears are on her cheeks.
Among all her lovers
   there is no one to comfort her.
All her friends have betrayed her;
   they have become her enemies.

3 After affliction and harsh labour,
   Judah has gone into exile.
She dwells among the nations;
   she finds no resting place.
All who pursue her have overtaken her
   in the midst of her distress.

4 The roads to Zion mourn,
   for no one comes to her appointed
      festivals.
All her gateways are desolate,
   her priests groan,
her young women grieve,
   and she is in bitter anguish.

5 Her foes have become her masters;
   her enemies are at ease.

The LORD has brought her grief
  because of her many sins.
Her children have gone into exile,
  captive before the foe.

⁶ All the splendour has departed
  from Daughter Zion.
Her princes are like deer
  that find no pasture;
in weakness they have fled
  before the pursuer.

⁷ In the days of her affliction and
    wandering
  Jerusalem remembers all the
    treasures
  that were hers in days of old.
When her people fell into enemy hands,
  there was no one to help her.
Her enemies looked at her
  and laughed at her destruction.

⁸ Jerusalem has sinned greatly
  and so has become unclean.
All who honoured her despise her,
  for they have all seen her naked;
she herself groans
  and turns away.

⁹ Her filthiness clung to her skirts;
  she did not consider her future.
Her fall was astounding;
  there was none to comfort her.
'Look, LORD, on my affliction,
  for the enemy has triumphed.'

¹⁰ The enemy laid hands
  on all her treasures;
she saw pagan nations
  enter her sanctuary –
those you had forbidden
  to enter your assembly.

¹¹ All her people groan
  as they search for bread;
they barter their treasures for food

to keep themselves alive.
'Look, LORD, and consider,
  for I am despised.'

¹² 'Is it nothing to you, all you who pass by?
  Look around and see.
Is any suffering like my suffering
  that was inflicted on me,
that the LORD brought on me
  in the day of his fierce anger?

¹³ 'From on high he sent fire,
  sent it down into my bones.
He spread a net for my feet
  and turned me back.
He made me desolate,
  faint all the day long.

¹⁴ 'My sins have been bound into a yoke;
  by his hands they were woven
    together.
They have been hung on my neck,
  and the Lord has sapped my strength.
He has given me into the hands
  of those I cannot withstand.

¹⁵ 'The Lord has rejected
  all the warriors in my midst;
he has summoned an army against me
  to crush my young men.
In his winepress the Lord has trampled
  Virgin Daughter Judah.

¹⁶ 'This is why I weep
  and my eyes overflow with tears.
No one is near to comfort me,
  no one to restore my spirit.
My children are destitute
  because the enemy has prevailed.'

¹⁷ Zion stretches out her hands,
  but there is no one to comfort her.
The LORD has decreed for Jacob
  that his neighbours become his foes;
Jerusalem has become
  an unclean thing among them.

18 'The LORD is righteous,
       yet I rebelled against his command.
   Listen, all you peoples;
       look on my suffering.
   My young men and young women
       have gone into exile.

19 'I called to my allies
       but they betrayed me.
   My priests and my elders
       perished in the city
   while they searched for food
       to keep themselves alive.

20 'See, LORD, how distressed I am!
       I am in torment within,
   and in my heart I am disturbed,
       for I have been most rebellious.
   Outside, the sword bereaves;
       inside, there is only death.

21 'People have heard my groaning,
       but there is no one to comfort me.
   All my enemies have heard of my
           distress;
       they rejoice at what you have done.
   May you bring the day you have
           announced
       so that they may become like me.

22 'Let all their wickedness come before
           you;
       deal with them
   as you have dealt with me
       because of all my sins.
   My groans are many
       and my heart is faint.'

2   How the Lord has covered Daughter
           Zion
       with the cloud of his anger!
   He has hurled down the splendour of
           Israel
       from heaven to earth;
   he has not remembered his footstool
       in the day of his anger.

2 Without pity the Lord has swallowed up
       all the dwellings of Jacob;
   in his wrath he has torn down
       the strongholds of Daughter Judah.
   He has brought her kingdom and its
           princes
       down to the ground in dishonour.

3 In fierce anger he has cut off
       every horn of Israel.
   He has withdrawn his right hand
       at the approach of the enemy.
   He has burned in Jacob like a flaming
           fire
       that consumes everything around it.

4 Like an enemy he has strung his bow;
       his right hand is ready.
   Like a foe he has slain
       all who were pleasing to the eye;
   he has poured out his wrath like fire
       on the tent of Daughter Zion.

5 The Lord is like an enemy;
       he has swallowed up Israel.
   He has swallowed up all her palaces
       and destroyed her strongholds.
   He has multiplied mourning and
           lamentation
       for Daughter Judah.

6 He has laid waste his dwelling like a
           garden;
       he has destroyed his place of meeting.
   The LORD has made Zion forget
       her appointed festivals and her
           Sabbaths;
   in his fierce anger he has spurned
       both king and priest.

7 The Lord has rejected his altar
       and abandoned his sanctuary.
   He has given the walls of her palaces
       into the hands of the enemy;
   they have raised a shout in the house of
       the LORD

as on the day of an appointed festival.

8 The LORD determined to tear down
    the wall around Daughter Zion.
He stretched out a measuring line
    and did not withhold his hand from
        destroying.
He made ramparts and walls lament;
    together they wasted away.

9 Her gates have sunk into the ground;
    their bars he has broken and
        destroyed.
Her king and her princes are exiled
    among the nations,
    the law is no more,
and her prophets no longer find
    visions from the LORD.

10 The elders of Daughter Zion
    sit on the ground in silence;
they have sprinkled dust on their heads
    and put on sackcloth.
The young women of Jerusalem
    have bowed their heads to the ground.

11 My eyes fail from weeping,
    I am in torment within;
my heart is poured out on the ground
    because my people are destroyed,
because children and infants faint
    in the streets of the city.

12 They say to their mothers,
    'Where is bread and wine?'
as they faint like the wounded
    in the streets of the city,
as their lives ebb away
    in their mothers' arms.

13 What can I say for you?
    With what can I compare you,
    Daughter Jerusalem?
To what can I liken you,
    that I may comfort you,
    Virgin Daughter Zion?

Your wound is as deep as the sea.
    Who can heal you?

14 The visions of your prophets
    were false and worthless;
they did not expose your sin
    to ward off your captivity.
The prophecies they gave you
    were false and misleading.

15 All who pass your way
    clap their hands at you;
they scoff and shake their heads
    at Daughter Jerusalem:
'Is this the city that was called
    the perfection of beauty,
    the joy of the whole earth?'

16 All your enemies open their mouths
    wide against you;
they scoff and gnash their teeth
    and say, 'We have swallowed her up.
This is the day we have waited for;
    we have lived to see it.'

17 The LORD has done what he planned;
    he has fulfilled his word,
    which he decreed long ago.
He has overthrown you without pity,
    he has let the enemy gloat over you,
    he has exalted the horn of your foes.

18 The hearts of the people
    cry out to the Lord.
You walls of Daughter Zion,
    let your tears flow like a river
    day and night;
give yourself no relief,
    your eyes no rest.

19 Arise, cry out in the night,
    as the watches of the night begin;
pour out your heart like water
    in the presence of the Lord.
Lift up your hands to him
    for the lives of your children,

who faint from hunger
at every street corner.

20 'Look, LORD, and consider:
whom have you ever treated like this?
Should women eat their offspring,
the children they have cared for?
Should priest and prophet be killed
in the sanctuary of the Lord?

21 'Young and old lie together
in the dust of the streets;
my young men and young women
have fallen by the sword.
You have slain them in the day of your
anger;
you have slaughtered them without
pity.

22 'As you summon to a feast day,
so you summoned against me terrors
on every side.
In the day of the LORD's anger
no one escaped or survived;
those I cared for and reared
my enemy has destroyed.'

3 I am the man who has seen affliction
by the rod of the LORD's wrath.
2 He has driven me away and made me
walk
in darkness rather than light;
3 indeed, he has turned his hand against
me
again and again, all day long.

4 He has made my skin and my flesh grow
old
and has broken my bones.
5 He has besieged me and surrounded me
with bitterness and hardship.
6 He has made me dwell in darkness
like those long dead.

7 He has walled me in so that I cannot
escape;

he has weighed me down with chains.
8 Even when I call out or cry for help,
he shuts out my prayer.
9 He has barred my way with blocks of
stone;
he has made my paths crooked.

10 Like a bear lying in wait,
like a lion in hiding,
11 he dragged me from the path and
mangled me
and left me without help.
12 He drew his bow
and made me the target for his arrows.

◼ PSALM 119:137-140

137 You are righteous, LORD,
and your laws are right.
138 The statutes you have laid down are
righteous;
they are fully trustworthy.
139 My zeal wears me out,
for my enemies ignore your words.
140 Your promises have been thoroughly
tested,
and your servant loves them.

◼ PROVERBS 27:3-4

3 Stone is heavy and sand a burden,
but a fool's provocation is heavier than
both.

4 Anger is cruel and fury overwhelming,
but who can stand before jealousy?

◼ HEBREWS 6:9–7:10

9 Even though we speak like this, dear
friends, we are convinced of better things
in your case – the things that have to do
with salvation. 10 God is not unjust; he will

not forget your work and the love you have shown him as you have helped his people and continue to help them. [11] We want each of you to show this same diligence to the very end, so that what you hope for may be fully realized. [12] We do not want you to become lazy, but to imitate those who through faith and patience inherit what has been promised.

[13] When God made his promise to Abraham, since there was no one greater for him to swear by, he swore by himself, [14] saying, 'I will surely bless you and give you many descendants.' [15] And so after waiting patiently, Abraham received what was promised.

[16] People swear by someone greater than themselves, and the oath confirms what is said and puts an end to all argument. [17] Because God wanted to make the unchanging nature of his purpose very clear to the heirs of what was promised, he confirmed it with an oath. [18] God did this so that, by two unchangeable things in which it is impossible for God to lie, we who have fled to take hold of the hope set before us may be greatly encouraged. [19] We have this hope as an anchor for the soul, firm and secure. It enters the inner sanctuary behind the curtain, [20] where our forerunner, Jesus, has entered on our behalf. He has become a high priest for ever, in the order of Melchizedek.

7 This Melchizedek was king of Salem and priest of God Most High. He met Abraham returning from the defeat of the kings and blessed him, [2] and Abraham gave him a tenth of everything. First, the name Melchizedek means 'king of righteousness'; then also, 'king of Salem' means 'king of peace'. [3] Without father or mother, without genealogy, without beginning of days or end of life, resembling the Son of God, he remains a priest for ever.

[4] Just think how great he was: even the patriarch Abraham gave him a tenth of the plunder! [5] Now the law requires the descendants of Levi who become priests to collect a tenth from the people – that is, from their fellow Israelites – even though they also are descended from Abraham. [6] This man, however, did not trace his descent from Levi, yet he collected a tenth from Abraham and blessed him who had the promises. [7] And without doubt the lesser is blessed by the greater. [8] In the one case, the tenth is collected by people who die; but in the other case, by him who is declared to be living. [9] One might even say that Levi, who collects the tenth, paid the tenth through Abraham, [10] because when Melchizedek met Abraham, Levi was still in the body of his ancestor.

Christ – Our Precursor

'... our forerunner, Jesus, has entered on our behalf.'
Hebrews 6:20

O ut of all the aspects of truth that surround the fact of our Lord's ascension, one of the greatest is surely this – Christ is our Precursor. A precursor is really a forerunner – an advance runner – and that is precisely the term which our text for today applies to the climactic ministry of our ascended Lord.

The 1984 NIV translates the word *prodromos* (forerunner) thus: 'who went before us'. That translation, in my opinion, is not nearly as appealing as that found in the 2011 version of the NIV used above, where the word 'forerunner' is actually used. 'Forerunner' brings to mind a picture of our Lord as a celestial outrider 'bringing many sons and daughters to glory' (Heb. 2:10) and reminds us of a petition in the great high priestly prayer: 'Father, I want those you have given me to be with me where I am, and to see my glory ...' (John 17:24).

Henry Longfellow, in his *Golden Legend*, put it like this:

When Christ ascended
Triumphantly, from start to star,
He left the gates of heaven ajar!

Much as I like Longfellow, I have to disagree. Our Lord left the gates of heaven not just 'ajar' but wide open. One of the creeds expresses it more effectively: 'When Thou hadst overcome the sharpness of death, Thou didst open the kingdom of heaven to all believers.' Whatever the future holds for us, we who are Christ's can be sure of this: our Lord has ascended into heaven. And so, too, shall we.

PRAYER

O Father, I see that not only was there an ascension in the life of Your Son, but there is to be one in mine too. According to Your Word, I am to be 'caught up ... in the clouds' and to be with You forever. Lord Jesus, come quickly. Amen.

FURTHER STUDY

John 17:1–26; 1:12; Gal. 4:7;
1 Cor. 15:39–44
• What does being sons and daughters make us?
• What do we enter into through death?

November 10

▬ LAMENTATIONS 3:13–66

¹³ He pierced my heart
   with arrows from his quiver.
¹⁴ I became the laughing-stock of all my
      people;
   they mock me in song all day long.
¹⁵ He has filled me with bitter herbs
   and given me gall to drink.

¹⁶ He has broken my teeth with gravel;
   he has trampled me in the dust.
¹⁷ I have been deprived of peace;
   I have forgotten what prosperity is.

¹⁸ So I say, 'My splendour is gone
      and all that I had hoped from the
   LORD.'

¹⁹ I remember my affliction and my
      wandering,
   the bitterness and the gall.
²⁰ I well remember them,
   and my soul is downcast within me.
²¹ Yet this I call to mind
   and therefore I have hope:

²² Because of the LORD's great love we are
      not consumed,

for his compassions never fail.
²³ They are new every morning;
    great is your faithfulness.
²⁴ I say to myself, 'The LORD is my portion;
    therefore I will wait for him.'

²⁵ The LORD is good to those whose hope is
        in him,
    to the one who seeks him;
²⁶ it is good to wait quietly
    for the salvation of the LORD.
²⁷ It is good for a man to bear the yoke
    while he is young.

²⁸ Let him sit alone in silence,
    for the LORD has laid it on him.
²⁹ Let him bury his face in the dust –
    there may yet be hope.
³⁰ Let him offer his cheek to one who would
        strike him,
    and let him be filled with disgrace.

³¹ For no one is cast off
    by the Lord for ever.
³² Though he brings grief, he will show
        compassion,
    so great is his unfailing love.
³³ For he does not willingly bring affliction
    or grief to anyone.

³⁴ To crush underfoot
    all prisoners in the land,
³⁵ to deny people their rights
    before the Most High,
³⁶ to deprive them of justice –
    would not the Lord see such things?

³⁷ Who can speak and have it happen
    if the Lord has not decreed it?
³⁸ Is it not from the mouth of the Most High
    that both calamities and good things
        come?
³⁹ Why should the living complain
    when punished for their sins?
⁴⁰ Let us examine our ways and test them,

and let us return to the LORD.
⁴¹ Let us lift up our hearts and our hands
    to God in heaven, and say:
⁴² 'We have sinned and rebelled
    and you have not forgiven.

⁴³ 'You have covered yourself with anger
        and pursued us;
    you have slain without pity.
⁴⁴ You have covered yourself with a cloud
    so that no prayer can get through.
⁴⁵ You have made us scum and refuse
    among the nations.

⁴⁶ 'All our enemies have opened their
        mouths
    wide against us.
⁴⁷ We have suffered terror and pitfalls,
    ruin and destruction.'
⁴⁸ Streams of tears flow from my eyes
    because my people are destroyed.

⁴⁹ My eyes will flow unceasingly,
    without relief,
⁵⁰ until the LORD looks down
    from heaven and sees.
⁵¹ What I see brings grief to my soul
    because of all the women of my city.

⁵² Those who were my enemies without
        cause
    hunted me like a bird.
⁵³ They tried to end my life in a pit
    and threw stones at me;
⁵⁴ the waters closed over my head,
    and I thought I was about to perish.

⁵⁵ I called on your name, LORD,
    from the depths of the pit.
⁵⁶ You heard my plea: 'Do not close your ears
    to my cry for relief.'
⁵⁷ You came near when I called you,
    and you said, 'Do not fear.'

⁵⁸ You, Lord, took up my case;
    you redeemed my life.

⁵⁹ LORD, you have seen the wrong done to
me.
Uphold my cause!
⁶⁰ You have seen the depth of their
vengeance,
all their plots against me.

⁶¹ LORD, you have heard their insults,
all their plots against me –
⁶² what my enemies whisper and mutter
against me all day long.
⁶³ Look at them! Sitting or standing,
they mock me in their songs.

⁶⁴ Pay them back what they deserve, LORD,
for what their hands have done.
⁶⁵ Put a veil over their hearts,
and may your curse be on them!
⁶⁶ Pursue them in anger and destroy them
from under the heavens of the LORD.

■ PSALM 119:141-144

¹⁴¹ Though I am lowly and despised,
I do not forget your precepts.
¹⁴² Your righteousness is everlasting
and your law is true.
¹⁴³ Trouble and distress have come
upon me,
but your commands give me delight.
¹⁴⁴ Your statutes are always righteous;
give me understanding that I may live.

■ PROVERBS 27:5-6

⁵ Better is open rebuke
than hidden love.

⁶ Wounds from a friend can be trusted,
but an enemy multiplies kisses.

■ HEBREWS 7:11–8:6

¹¹ If perfection could have been attained
through the Levitical priesthood – and indeed the law given to the people established
that priesthood – why was there still need
for another priest to come, one in the order
of Melchizedek, not in the order of Aaron?
¹² For when the priesthood is changed, the law
must be changed also. ¹³ He of whom these
things are said belonged to a different tribe,
and no one from that tribe has ever served
at the altar. ¹⁴ For it is clear that our Lord descended from Judah, and in regard to that
tribe Moses said nothing about priests. ¹⁵ And
what we have said is even more clear if another priest like Melchizedek appears, ¹⁶ one
who has become a priest not on the basis of a
regulation as to his ancestry but on the basis
of the power of an indestructible life. ¹⁷ For it
is declared:

'You are a priest for ever,
in the order of Melchizedek.'

¹⁸ The former regulation is set aside because it was weak and useless ¹⁹ (for the law
made nothing perfect), and a better hope is
introduced, by which we draw near to God.
²⁰ And it was not without an oath! Others
became priests without any oath, ²¹ but he
became a priest with an oath when God said
to him:

'The Lord has sworn
and will not change his mind:
"You are a priest for ever."'

²² Because of this oath, Jesus has become
the guarantor of a better covenant.
²³ Now there have been many of those
priests, since death prevented them from
continuing in office; ²⁴ but because Jesus
lives for ever, he has a permanent priesthood. ²⁵ Therefore he is able to save completely those who come to God through

him, because he always lives to intercede for them.

²⁶ Such a high priest truly meets our need – one who is holy, blameless, pure, set apart from sinners, exalted above the heavens. ²⁷ Unlike the other high priests, he does not need to offer sacrifices day after day, first for his own sins, and then for the sins of the people. He sacrificed for their sins once for all when he offered himself. ²⁸ For the law appoints as high priests men in all their weakness; but the oath, which came after the law, appointed the Son, who has been made perfect for ever.

8 Now the main point of what we are saying is this: we do have such a high priest, who sat down at the right hand of the throne of the Majesty in heaven, ² and who serves in the sanctuary, the true tabernacle set up by the Lord, not by a mere human being.

³ Every high priest is appointed to offer both gifts and sacrifices, and so it was necessary for this one also to have something to offer. ⁴ If he were on earth, he would not be a priest, for there are already priests who offer the gifts prescribed by the law. ⁵ They serve at a sanctuary that is a copy and shadow of what is in heaven. This is why Moses was warned when he was about to build the tabernacle: 'See to it that you make everything according to the pattern shown you on the mountain.' ⁶ But in fact the ministry Jesus has received is as superior to theirs as the covenant of which he is mediator is superior to the old one, since the new covenant is established on better promises.

'I Know I'm Saved'

'... [Jesus] is able to save completely those who come to God through him ...' **Hebrews 7:25**

Is it possible to know without any shadow of doubt that one is saved and ready to meet God? This question, says one writer, goes right to the roots of religious experience. Christianity says 'yes'. Other religions are not sure. Without exception they will tell you that it savours of presumption to say one is certain that one is saved.

I know some Christians have difficulty here also. They contend that we can hope to be saved, or claim we are being saved, but that no one can state with any degree of assurance that they *are* saved. It is gross self-centredness, they maintain, and a sign of self-absorption to claim here and now on this earth, 'I am saved'. Yet John Wesley declared it. On May 24, 1738, he walked into a room in Aldersgate Street, London, where he heard someone read the Preface to Luther's commentary on Romans, and as he listened there was given him 'an assurance' that God had taken away his sins and saved him from the law of sin and death.

Millions all over the world can say as Wesley did that they have an assurance they are saved and know that when they die they will go to heaven. It is not presumption to say you are saved providing, of course, you have entered into a personal relationship with Jesus Christ. Indeed, it is offensive for anyone who has given himself or herself to Christ not to say they are saved. As we see from our text today, Christ promises to save and save *completely*. I know I'm saved. How about you?

November 11

▬ LAMENTATIONS 4:1–5:22

4 How the gold has lost its lustre,
 the fine gold become dull!
The sacred gems are scattered
 at every street corner.

² How the precious children of Zion,
 once worth their weight in gold,
are now considered as pots of clay,
 the work of a potter's hands!

³ Even jackals offer their breasts
 to nurse their young,
but my people have become heartless
 like ostriches in the desert.

⁴ Because of thirst the infant's tongue
 sticks to the roof of its mouth;
the children beg for bread,
 but no one gives it to them.

⁵ Those who once ate delicacies
 are destitute in the streets.
Those brought up in royal purple
 now lie on ash heaps.

⁶ The punishment of my people
 is greater than that of Sodom,
which was overthrown in a moment
 without a hand turned to help her.

⁷ Their princes were brighter than snow
 and whiter than milk,
their bodies more ruddy than rubies,
 their appearance like lapis lazuli.

⁸ But now they are blacker than soot;
 they are not recognised in the streets.
Their skin has shrivelled on their bones;
 it has become as dry as a stick.

⁹ Those killed by the sword are better off
 than those who die of famine;
racked with hunger, they waste away
 for lack of food from the field.

¹⁰ With their own hands compassionate
 women
 have cooked their own children,
who became their food
 when my people were destroyed.

¹¹ The LORD has given full vent to his wrath;
 he has poured out his fierce anger.
He kindled a fire in Zion
 that consumed her foundations.

¹² The kings of the earth did not believe,
 nor did any of the peoples of the world,
that enemies and foes could enter
 the gates of Jerusalem.

[13] But it happened because of the sins of her
    prophets
    and the iniquities of her priests,
who shed within her
    the blood of the righteous.

[14] Now they grope through the streets
    as if they were blind.
They are so defiled with blood
    that no one dares to touch their
        garments.

[15] 'Go away! You are unclean!' people cry
    to them.
'Away! Away! Don't touch us!'
When they flee and wander about,
    people among the nations say,
    'They can stay here no longer.'

[16] The LORD himself has scattered them;
    he no longer watches over them.
The priests are shown no honour,
    the elders no favour.

[17] Moreover, our eyes failed,
    looking in vain for help;
from our towers we watched
    for a nation that could not save us.

[18] People stalked us at every step,
    so we could not walk in our streets.
Our end was near, our days were
        numbered,
    for our end had come.

[19] Our pursuers were swifter
    than eagles in the sky;
they chased us over the mountains
    and lay in wait for us in the desert.

[20] The LORD's anointed, our very life breath,
    was caught in their traps.
We thought that under his shadow
    we would live among the nations.

[21] Rejoice and be glad, Daughter Edom,

you who live in the land of Uz.
But to you also the cup will be passed;
    you will be drunk and stripped naked.

[22] Your punishment will end, Daughter
    Zion;
    he will not prolong your exile.
But he will punish your sin, Daughter
    Edom,
    and expose your wickedness.

5 Remember, LORD, what has happened
    to us;
    look, and see our disgrace.
[2] Our inheritance has been turned over to
        strangers,
    our homes to foreigners.
[3] We have become fatherless,
    our mothers are widows.
[4] We must buy the water we drink;
    our wood can be had only at a price.
[5] Those who pursue us are at our heels;
    we are weary and find no rest.
[6] We submitted to Egypt and Assyria
    to get enough bread.
[7] Our ancestors sinned and are no more,
    and we bear their punishment.
[8] Slaves rule over us,
    and there is no one to free us from
        their hands.
[9] We get our bread at the risk of our lives
    because of the sword in the desert.
[10] Our skin is hot as an oven,
    feverish from hunger.
[11] Women have been violated in Zion,
    and virgins in the towns of Judah.
[12] Princes have been hung up by their
        hands;
    elders are shown no respect.
[13] Young men toil at the millstones;
    boys stagger under loads of wood.
[14] The elders are gone from the city gate;
    the young men have stopped their
        music.
[15] Joy is gone from our hearts;
    our dancing has turned to mourning.

¹⁶ The crown has fallen from our head.
   Woe to us, for we have sinned!
¹⁷ Because of this our hearts are faint;
   because of these things our eyes grow
      dim
¹⁸ for Mount Zion, which lies desolate,
   with jackals prowling over it.

¹⁹ You, LORD, reign for ever;
   your throne endures from generation
      to generation.
²⁰ Why do you always forget us?
   Why do you forsake us so long?
²¹ Restore us to yourself, LORD, that we may
      return;
   renew our days as of old
²² unless you have utterly rejected us
   and are angry with us beyond
      measure.

PSALM 119:145–152

¹⁴⁵ I call with all my heart; answer me,
      LORD,
   and I will obey your decrees.
¹⁴⁶ I call out to you; save me
   and I will keep your statutes.
¹⁴⁷ I rise before dawn and cry for help;
   I have put my hope in your word.
¹⁴⁸ My eyes stay open through the watches
      of the night,
   that I may meditate on your promises.
¹⁴⁹ Hear my voice in accordance with your
      love;
   preserve my life, LORD, according to
      your laws.
¹⁵⁰ Those who devise wicked schemes are
      near,
   but they are far from your law.
¹⁵¹ Yet you are near, LORD,
   and all your commands are true.
¹⁵² Long ago I learned from your statutes
   that you established them to last for
      ever.

PROVERBS 27:7–8

⁷ One who is full loathes honey from the
      comb,
   but to the hungry even what is bitter
      tastes sweet.

⁸ Like a bird that flees its nest
   is anyone who flees from home.

HEBREWS 8:7–9:14

⁷ For if there had been nothing wrong
with that first covenant, no place would
have been sought for another. ⁸ But God
found fault with the people and said:

'The days are coming, declares the Lord,
   when I will make a new covenant
with the people of Israel
   and with the people of Judah.
⁹ It will not be like the covenant
   I made with their ancestors
when I took them by the hand
   to lead them out of Egypt,
because they did not remain faithful to
      my covenant,
   and I turned away from them,
      declares the Lord.
¹⁰ This is the covenant I will establish with
      the people of Israel
   after that time, declares the Lord.
I will put my laws in their minds
   and write them on their hearts.
I will be their God,
   and they will be my people.
¹¹ No longer will they teach their
      neighbours,
   or say to one another, "Know the
      Lord,"
because they will all know me,
   from the least of them to the greatest.
¹² For I will forgive their wickedness
   and will remember their sins no
      more.'

[13] By calling this covenant 'new', he has made the first one obsolete; and what is obsolete and outdated will soon disappear.

9 Now the first covenant had regulations for worship and also an earthly sanctuary. [2] A tabernacle was set up. In its first room were the lampstand and the table with its consecrated bread; this was called the Holy Place. [3] Behind the second curtain was a room called the Most Holy Place, [4] which had the golden altar of incense and the gold-covered ark of the covenant. This ark contained the gold jar of manna, Aaron's staff that had budded, and the stone tablets of the covenant. [5] Above the ark were the cherubim of the Glory, overshadowing the atonement cover. But we cannot discuss these things in detail now.

[6] When everything had been arranged like this, the priests entered regularly into the outer room to carry on their ministry. [7] But only the high priest entered the inner room, and that only once a year, and never without blood, which he offered for himself and for the sins the people had committed in ignorance. [8] The Holy Spirit was showing by this that the way into the Most Holy Place had not yet been disclosed as long as the first tabernacle was still functioning. [9] This is an illustration for the present time, indicating that the gifts and sacrifices being offered were not able to clear the conscience of the worshipper. [10] They are only a matter of food and drink and various ceremonial washings – external regulations applying until the time of the new order.

[11] But when Christ came as high priest of the good things that are now already here, he went through the greater and more perfect tabernacle that is not made with human hands, that is to say, is not a part of this creation. [12] He did not enter by means of the blood of goats and calves; but he entered the Most Holy Place once for all by his own blood, so obtaining eternal redemption. [13] The blood of goats and bulls and the ashes of a heifer sprinkled on those who are ceremonially unclean sanctify them so that they are outwardly clean. [14] How much more, then, will the blood of Christ, who through the eternal Spirit offered himself unblemished to God, cleanse our consciences from acts that lead to death, so that we may serve the living God!

The Belt of Truth

'Yet you are near, LORD, and all your commands are true.' **Psalm 119:151**

Paul, in listing the six main pieces of a soldier's equipment, illustrated the six main ways by which we can defend ourselves against the power of Satan – truth, righteousness, steadfastness, faith, salvation, and the Word of God.

Most commentators believe that the reason why Paul chose these six pieces of armour to describe the Christian's protective system against satanic attack was because he was chained to a soldier as he wrote the letter (Eph. 6:20). Although it is probably unlikely that the soldier standing guard in prison would have worn the full armour of an infantryman on the battlefield, the sight of him would have kindled Paul's imagination.

The list begins with the belt of truth. Why, we ask ourselves, does the apostle start with such a seemingly insignificant item? Why did he not begin with one of the bigger and more important pieces of equipment, such as the breastplate, the shield, or the sword of the Spirit? The order in which these pieces are given to us is an inspired order, and if we change the order we make our position extremely perilous. For example, the reason why many Christians fail to wield the sword of the Spirit effectively is because they have not first girded their waist with truth. If we reverse the order, we succeed only in weakening our spiritual defence.

It is very important that we grasp this. Girding our waist with truth is always the place to start whenever we are under satanic attack. If we don't start right, then we will not finish right. We cannot do battle with the Devil until we first gird our waists with truth.

PRAYER

Gracious and loving Father, help me to absorb this thought into my inner being this day so that it will stay with me for the rest of my life: I cannot do battle with the Devil until I first gird my waist with truth. Amen.

FURTHER STUDY

2 Pet. 1:1-12; Prov. 23:23; 3 John 1-4

• In what are we to be established?
• In what did John rejoice?

November 12

■ EZEKIEL 1:1–3:15

1 In my thirtieth year, in the fourth month on the fifth day, while I was among the exiles by the River Kebar, the heavens were opened and I saw visions of God.

2 On the fifth of the month – it was the fifth year of the exile of King Jehoiachin – 3 the word of the LORD came to Ezekiel the priest, the son of Buzi, by the River Kebar in the land of the Babylonians. There the hand of the LORD was on him.

4 I looked, and I saw a violent storm coming out of the north – an immense cloud with flashing lightning and surrounded by brilliant light. The centre of the fire looked like glowing metal, 5 and in the fire was what looked like four living creatures. In appearance their form was human, 6 but each of them had four faces and four wings. 7 Their legs were straight; their feet were like those of a calf and gleamed like burnished bronze. 8 Under their wings on their four sides they had human hands. All four of them had faces and wings, 9 and the wings of one touched the wings of another. Each one went straight ahead; they did not turn as they moved.

10 Their faces looked like this: each of the four had the face of a human being, and on the right side each had the face of a lion, and on the left the face of an ox; each also had the face of an eagle. 11 Such were their faces. They each had two wings spreading

out upwards, each wing touching that of the creature on either side; and each had two other wings covering its body. [12]Each one went straight ahead. Wherever the spirit would go, they would go, without turning as they went. [13]The appearance of the living creatures was like burning coals of fire or like torches. Fire moved back and forth among the creatures; it was bright, and lightning flashed out of it. [14]The creatures sped back and forth like flashes of lightning.

[15]As I looked at the living creatures, I saw a wheel on the ground beside each creature with its four faces. [16]This was the appearance and structure of the wheels: they sparkled like topaz, and all four looked alike. Each appeared to be made like a wheel intersecting a wheel. [17]As they moved, they would go in any one of the four directions the creatures faced; the wheels did not change direction as the creatures went. [18]Their rims were high and awesome, and all four rims were full of eyes all around.

[19]When the living creatures moved, the wheels beside them moved; and when the living creatures rose from the ground, the wheels also rose. [20]Wherever the spirit would go, they would go, and the wheels would rise along with them, because the spirit of the living creatures was in the wheels. [21]When the creatures moved, they also moved; when the creatures stood still, they also stood still; and when the creatures rose from the ground, the wheels rose along with them, because the spirit of the living creatures was in the wheels.

[22]Spread out above the heads of the living creatures was what looked something like a vault, sparkling like crystal, and awesome. [23]Under the vault their wings were stretched out one towards the other, and each had two wings covering its body. [24]When the creatures moved, I heard the sound of their wings, like the roar of rushing waters, like the voice of the Almighty, like the tumult of an army. When they stood still, they lowered their wings.

[25]Then there came a voice from above the vault over their heads as they stood with lowered wings. [26]Above the vault over their heads was what looked like a throne of lapis lazuli, and high above on the throne was a figure like that of a man. [27]I saw that from what appeared to be his waist up he looked like glowing metal, as if full of fire, and that from there down he looked like fire; and brilliant light surrounded him. [28]Like the appearance of a rainbow in the clouds on a rainy day, so was the radiance around him.

This was the appearance of the likeness of the glory of the LORD. When I saw it, I fell face down, and I heard the voice of one speaking.

2 He said to me, 'Son of man, stand up on your feet and I will speak to you.' [2]As he spoke, the Spirit came into me and raised me to my feet, and I heard him speaking to me.

[3]He said: 'Son of man, I am sending you to the Israelites, to a rebellious nation that has rebelled against me; they and their ancestors have been in revolt against me to this very day. [4]The people to whom I am sending you are obstinate and stubborn. Say to them, "This is what the Sovereign LORD says." [5]And whether they listen or fail to listen – for they are a rebellious people – they will know that a prophet has been among them. [6]And you, son of man, do not be afraid of them or their words. Do not be afraid, though briers and thorns are all around you and you live among scorpions. Do not be afraid of what they say or be terrified by them, though they are a rebellious people. [7]You must speak my words to them, whether they listen or fail to listen, for they are rebellious. [8]But you, son of man, listen to what I say to you. Do not rebel like that rebellious people; open your mouth and eat what I give you.'

[9]Then I looked, and I saw a hand stretched out to me. In it was a scroll,

¹⁰which he unrolled before me. On both sides of it were written words of lament and mourning and woe.

3 And he said to me, 'Son of man, eat what is before you, eat this scroll; then go and speak to the people of Israel.' ²So I opened my mouth, and he gave me the scroll to eat.

³Then he said to me, 'Son of man, eat this scroll I am giving you and fill your stomach with it.' So I ate it, and it tasted as sweet as honey in my mouth.

⁴He then said to me: 'Son of man, go now to the people of Israel and speak my words to them. ⁵You are not being sent to a people of obscure speech and strange language, but to the people of Israel – ⁶not to many peoples of obscure speech and strange language, whose words you cannot understand. Surely if I had sent you to them, they would have listened to you. ⁷But the people of Israel are not willing to listen to you because they are not willing to listen to me, for all the Israelites are hardened and obstinate. ⁸But I will make you as unyielding and hardened as they are. ⁹I will make your forehead like the hardest stone, harder than flint. Do not be afraid of them or terrified by them, though they are a rebellious people.'

¹⁰And he said to me, 'Son of man, listen carefully and take to heart all the words I speak to you. ¹¹Go now to your people in exile and speak to them. Say to them, "This is what the Sovereign LORD says," whether they listen or fail to listen.'

¹²Then the Spirit lifted me up, and I heard behind me a loud rumbling sound as the glory of the LORD rose from the place where it was standing. ¹³It was the sound of the wings of the living creatures brushing against each other and the sound of the wheels beside them, a loud rumbling sound. ¹⁴The Spirit then lifted me up and took me away, and I went in bitterness and in the anger of my spirit, with the strong hand of the LORD on me. ¹⁵I came to the exiles who lived at Tel Aviv near the River Kebar. And there, where they were living, I sat among them for seven days – deeply distressed.

PSALM 119:153–160

¹⁵³Look on my suffering and deliver me,
　　for I have not forgotten your law.
¹⁵⁴Defend my cause and redeem me;
　　preserve my life according to your
　　　promise.
¹⁵⁵Salvation is far from the wicked,
　　for they do not seek out your decrees.
¹⁵⁶Your compassion, LORD, is great;
　　preserve my life according to your
　　　laws.
¹⁵⁷Many are the foes who persecute me,
　　but I have not turned from your
　　　statutes.
¹⁵⁸I look on the faithless with loathing,
　　for they do not obey your word.
¹⁵⁹See how I love your precepts;
　　preserve my life, LORD, in accordance
　　　with your love.
¹⁶⁰All your words are true;
　　all your righteous laws are eternal.

PROVERBS 27:9–10

⁹Perfume and incense bring joy to the
　　heart,
　　and the pleasantness of a friend
　　　springs from their heartfelt advice.

¹⁰Do not forsake your friend or a friend of
　　your family,
　　and do not go to your relative's house
　　　when disaster strikes you –
　　better a neighbour nearby than a
　　　relative far away.

▬ HEBREWS 9:15–10:10

¹⁵ For this reason Christ is the mediator of a new covenant, that those who are called may receive the promised eternal inheritance – now that he has died as a ransom to set them free from the sins committed under the first covenant.

¹⁶ In the case of a will, it is necessary to prove the death of the one who made it, ¹⁷ because a will is in force only when somebody has died; it never takes effect while the one who made it is living. ¹⁸ This is why even the first covenant was not put into effect without blood. ¹⁹ When Moses had proclaimed every command of the law to all the people, he took the blood of calves, together with water, scarlet wool and branches of hyssop, and sprinkled the scroll and all the people. ²⁰ He said, 'This is the blood of the covenant, which God has commanded you to keep.' ²¹ In the same way, he sprinkled with the blood both the tabernacle and everything used in its ceremonies. ²² In fact, the law requires that nearly everything be cleansed with blood, and without the shedding of blood there is no forgiveness.

²³ It was necessary, then, for the copies of the heavenly things to be purified with these sacrifices, but the heavenly things themselves with better sacrifices than these. ²⁴ For Christ did not enter a sanctuary made with human hands that was only a copy of the true one; he entered heaven itself, now to appear for us in God's presence. ²⁵ Nor did he enter heaven to offer himself again and again, the way the high priest enters the Most Holy Place every year with blood that is not his own. ²⁶ Otherwise Christ would have had to suffer many times since the creation of the world. But he has appeared once for all at the culmination of the ages to do away with sin by the sacrifice of himself. ²⁷ Just as people are destined to die once, and after that to face judgment, ²⁸ so Christ was sacrificed once to take away the sins of many; and he will appear a second time, not to bear sin, but to bring salvation to those who are waiting for him.

10 The law is only a shadow of the good things that are coming – not the realities themselves. For this reason it can never, by the same sacrifices repeated endlessly year after year, make perfect those who draw near to worship. ²Otherwise, would they not have stopped being offered? For the worshippers would have been cleansed once for all, and would no longer have felt guilty for their sins. ³ But those sacrifices are an annual reminder of sins. ⁴ It is impossible for the blood of bulls and goats to take away sins.

⁵ Therefore, when Christ came into the world, he said:

'Sacrifice and offering you did not desire,
    but a body you prepared for me;
⁶ with burnt offerings and sin offerings
    you were not pleased.
⁷ Then I said, "Here I am – it is written
    about me in the scroll –
I have come to do your will, my God."'

⁸ First he said, 'Sacrifices and offerings, burnt offerings and sin offerings you did not desire, nor were you pleased with them' – though they were offered in accordance with the law. ⁹ Then he said, 'Here I am, I have come to do your will.' He sets aside the first to establish the second. ¹⁰ And by that will, we have been made holy through the sacrifice of the body of Jesus Christ once for all.

A Temple, Not a Trap

'... a body you prepared for me ...' **Hebrews 10:5**

We continue to meditate on things we must do if we are to stay spiritually fresh. My next suggestion may come as a surprise: keep your body in good physical shape.

One of the most disastrous divorces that ever took place in Christendom was that between the physical and the spiritual. In the early days of Christianity, the two were one. When the disciples wanted men to look after the physical nourishment of those who were in need in the early church, the first of those they selected was Stephen, 'a man full of faith and the Holy Spirit' (Acts 6:5). This combination of faith and of the Holy Spirit was to be carried into the satisfying of physical needs, for the early church regarded the physical as being important as well as the spiritual. Not supremely important, of course, but important nevertheless.

In more recent centuries, the physical has been looked upon with greater suspicion in the church. In my youth I heard thundering sermons on the text, 'our vile body' (Phil. 3:21, AV), in which preachers propounded the idea that the body was the enemy of the soul. The suggestion was that the body must be ignored until the day when it is finally discarded and we are given a new resurrection body. These preachers failed to understand that the phrase 'vile body' in the Authorised Version really means 'lowly body' and not something to be treated with contempt. Let's be done with this idea concerning the body that still lingers in parts of the Christian church. Our bodies are not to be seen as traps, but as temples of the Holy Spirit.

PRAYER

Blessed Lord Jesus, help me see my body in the way You saw Yours – not as something to be avoided but as something to be used. Show me the steps I need to take to be healthy in soul and in body. For Your own dear name's sake. Amen.

FURTHER STUDY

Rom. 12:1-8; 6:13; 2 Cor. 6:16
• What are we to offer God?
• What are we to honour God with?

November 13

■ EZEKIEL 3:16–6:14

¹⁶At the end of seven days the word of the LORD came to me: ¹⁷'Son of man, I have made you a watchman for the people of Israel; so hear the word I speak and give them warning from me. ¹⁸When I say to a wicked person, "You will surely die,"

and you do not warn them or speak out to dissuade them from their evil ways in order to save their life, that wicked person will die for their sin, and I will hold you accountable for their blood. ¹⁹But if you do warn the wicked person and they do not turn from their wickedness or from their evil ways, they will die for their sin; but you will have saved yourself.

²⁰'Again, when a righteous person turns from their righteousness and does evil, and I put a stumbling-block before them, they will die. Since you did not warn them, they will die for their sin. The righteous things that person did will not be remembered, and I will hold you accountable for their blood. ²¹But if you do warn the righteous person not to sin and they do not sin, they will surely live because they took warning, and you will have saved yourself.'

²²The hand of the LORD was on me there, and he said to me, 'Get up and go out to the plain, and there I will speak to you.' ²³So I got up and went out to the plain. And the glory of the LORD was standing there, like the glory I had seen by the River Kebar, and I fell face down.

²⁴Then the Spirit came into me and raised me to my feet. He spoke to me and said: 'Go, shut yourself inside your house. ²⁵And you, son of man, they will tie with ropes; you will be bound so that you cannot go out among the people. ²⁶I will make your tongue stick to the roof of your mouth so that you will be silent and unable to rebuke them, for they are a rebellious people. ²⁷But when I speak to you, I will open your mouth and you shall say to them, "This is what the Sovereign LORD says." Whoever will listen let them listen, and whoever will refuse let them refuse; for they are a rebellious people.

4 'Now, son of man, take a block of clay, put it in front of you and draw the city of Jerusalem on it. ²Then lay siege to it: erect siege works against it, build a ramp up to it,

set up camps against it and put battering-rams around it. ³Then take an iron pan, place it as an iron wall between you and the city and turn your face towards it. It will be under siege, and you shall besiege it. This will be a sign to the people of Israel.

⁴'Then lie on your left side and put the sin of the people of Israel upon yourself. You are to bear their sin for the number of days you lie on your side. ⁵I have assigned you the same number of days as the years of their sin. So for 390 days you will bear the sin of the people of Israel.

⁶'After you have finished this, lie down again, this time on your right side, and bear the sin of the people of Judah. I have assigned you 40 days, a day for each year. ⁷Turn your face towards the siege of Jerusalem and with bared arm prophesy against her. ⁸I will tie you up with ropes so that you cannot turn from one side to the other until you have finished the days of your siege.

⁹'Take wheat and barley, beans and lentils, millet and spelt; put them in a storage jar and use them to make bread for yourself. You are to eat it during the 390 days you lie on your side. ¹⁰Weigh out twenty shekels of food to eat each day and eat it at set times. ¹¹Also measure out a sixth of a hin of water and drink it at set times. ¹²Eat the food as you would a loaf of barley bread; bake it in the sight of the people, using human excrement for fuel.' ¹³The LORD said, 'In this way the people of Israel will eat defiled food among the nations where I will drive them.'

¹⁴Then I said, 'Not so, Sovereign LORD! I have never defiled myself. From my youth until now I have never eaten anything found dead or torn by wild animals. No impure meat has ever entered my mouth.'

¹⁵'Very well,' he said, 'I will let you bake your bread over cow dung instead of human excrement.'

¹⁶He then said to me: 'Son of man, I am about to cut off the food supply in Jerusalem. The people will eat rationed food in

anxiety and drink rationed water in despair, [17] for food and water will be scarce. They will be appalled at the sight of each other and will waste away because of their sin.

5 'Now, son of man, take a sharp sword and use it as a barber's razor to shave your head and your beard. Then take a set of scales and divide up the hair. [2] When the days of your siege come to an end, burn a third of the hair inside the city. Take a third and strike it with the sword all around the city. And scatter a third to the wind. For I will pursue them with drawn sword. [3] But take a few hairs and tuck them away in the folds of your garment. [4] Again, take a few of these and throw them into the fire and burn them up. A fire will spread from there to all Israel.

[5] 'This is what the Sovereign LORD says: this is Jerusalem, which I have set in the centre of the nations, with countries all around her. [6] Yet in her wickedness she has rebelled against my laws and decrees more than the nations and countries around her. She has rejected my laws and has not followed my decrees.

[7] 'Therefore this is what the Sovereign LORD says: you have been more unruly than the nations around you and have not followed my decrees or kept my laws. You have not even conformed to the standards of the nations around you.

[8] 'Therefore this is what the Sovereign LORD says: I myself am against you, Jerusalem, and I will inflict punishment on you in the sight of the nations. [9] Because of all your detestable idols, I will do to you what I have never done before and will never do again. [10] Therefore in your midst parents will eat their children, and children will eat their parents. I will inflict punishment on you and will scatter all your survivors to the winds. [11] Therefore as surely as I live, declares the Sovereign LORD, because you have defiled my sanctuary with all your vile images and detestable practices, I myself will shave you; I will not look on you with pity or spare you.

[12] A third of your people will die of the plague or perish by famine inside you; a third will fall by the sword outside your walls; and a third I will scatter to the winds and pursue with drawn sword.

[13] 'Then my anger will cease and my wrath against them will subside, and I will be avenged. And when I have spent my wrath on them, they will know that I the LORD have spoken in my zeal.

[14] 'I will make you a ruin and a reproach among the nations around you, in the sight of all who pass by. [15] You will be a reproach and a taunt, a warning and an object of horror to the nations around you when I inflict punishment on you in anger and in wrath and with stinging rebuke. I the LORD have spoken. [16] When I shoot at you with my deadly and destructive arrows of famine, I will shoot to destroy you. I will bring more and more famine upon you and cut off your supply of food. [17] I will send famine and wild beasts against you, and they will leave you childless. Plague and bloodshed will sweep through you, and I will bring the sword against you. I the LORD have spoken.'

6 The word of the LORD came to me: [2] 'Son of man, set your face against the mountains of Israel; prophesy against them [3] and say: "You mountains of Israel, hear the word of the Sovereign LORD. This is what the Sovereign LORD says to the mountains and hills, to the ravines and valleys: I am about to bring a sword against you, and I will destroy your high places. [4] Your altars will be demolished and your incense altars will be smashed; and I will slay your people in front of your idols. [5] I will lay the dead bodies of the Israelites in front of their idols, and I will scatter your bones around your altars. [6] Wherever you live, the towns will be laid waste and the high places demolished, so that your altars will be laid waste and devastated, your idols smashed and ruined, your incense altars broken down, and what

you have made wiped out. ⁷ Your people will fall slain among you, and you will know that I am the LORD.

⁸ "But I will spare some, for some of you will escape the sword when you are scattered among the lands and nations. ⁹ Then in the nations where they have been carried captive, those who escape will remember me – how I have been grieved by their adulterous hearts, which have turned away from me, and by their eyes, which have lusted after their idols. They will loathe themselves for the evil they have done and for all their detestable practices. ¹⁰ And they will know that I am the LORD; I did not threaten in vain to bring this calamity on them.

¹¹ ' "This is what the Sovereign LORD says: strike your hands together and stamp your feet and cry out 'Alas!' because of all the wicked and detestable practices of the people of Israel, for they will fall by the sword, famine and plague. ¹² One who is far away will die of the plague, and one who is near will fall by the sword, and any one who survives and is spared will die of famine. So will I pour out my wrath on them. ¹³ And they will know that I am the LORD, when their people lie slain among their idols around their altars, on every high hill and on all the mountaintops, under every spreading tree and every leafy oak – places where they offered fragrant incense to all their idols. ¹⁴ And I will stretch out my hand against them and make the land a desolate waste from the desert to Diblah – wherever they live. Then they will know that I am the LORD.' "

■ PSALM 119:161-168

¹⁶¹ Rulers persecute me without cause,
    but my heart trembles at your word.
¹⁶² I rejoice in your promise
    like one who finds great spoil.
¹⁶³ I hate and detest falsehood

    but I love your law.
¹⁶⁴ Seven times a day I praise you
    for your righteous laws.
¹⁶⁵ Great peace have those who love your
    law,
    and nothing can make them stumble.
¹⁶⁶ I wait for your salvation, LORD,
    and I follow your commands.
¹⁶⁷ I obey your statutes,
    for I love them greatly.
¹⁶⁸ I obey your precepts and your statutes,
    for all my ways are known to you.

■ PROVERBS 27:11-13

¹¹ Be wise, my son, and bring joy to my
    heart;
    then I can answer anyone who treats
    me with contempt.

¹² The prudent see danger and take refuge,
    but the simple keep going and pay the
    penalty.

¹³ Take the garment of one who puts up
    security for a stranger;
    hold it in pledge if it is done for an
    outsider.

■ HEBREWS 10:11-31

¹¹ Day after day every priest stands and performs his religious duties; again and again he offers the same sacrifices, which can never take away sins. ¹² But when this priest had offered for all time one sacrifice for sins, he sat down at the right hand of God, ¹³ and since that time he waits for his enemies to be made his footstool. ¹⁴ For by one sacrifice he has made perfect for ever those who are being made holy.

¹⁵ The Holy Spirit also testifies to us about this. First he says:

16 'This is the covenant I will make with
          them
     after that time, says the Lord.
  I will put my laws in their hearts,
     and I will write them on their minds.'

17 Then he adds:

  'Their sins and lawless acts
     I will remember no more.'

18 And where these have been forgiven,
sacrifice for sin is no longer necessary.

19 Therefore, brothers and sisters, since
we have confidence to enter the Most Holy
Place by the blood of Jesus, 20 by a new and
living way opened for us through the curtain, that is, his body, 21 and since we have a
great priest over the house of God, 22 let us
draw near to God with a sincere heart and
with the full assurance that faith brings,
having our hearts sprinkled to cleanse us
from a guilty conscience and having our
bodies washed with pure water. 23 Let us
hold unswervingly to the hope we profess,
for he who promised is faithful. 24 And let
us consider how we may spur one another
on towards love and good deeds, 25 not giving up meeting together, as some are in the
habit of doing, but encouraging one another – and all the more as you see the Day
approaching.

26 If we deliberately keep on sinning after we have received the knowledge of the
truth, no sacrifice for sins is left, 27 but only
a fearful expectation of judgment and of
raging fire that will consume the enemies
of God. 28 Anyone who rejected the law of
Moses died without mercy on the testimony of two or three witnesses. 29 How much
more severely do you think someone deserves to be punished who has trampled the
Son of God underfoot, who has treated as
an unholy thing the blood of the covenant
that sanctified them, and who has insulted
the Spirit of grace? 30 For we know him who
said, 'It is mine to avenge; I will repay,' and
again, 'The Lord will judge his people.' 31 It
is a dreadful thing to fall into the hands of
the living God.

The Spirit - Outraged

'How much more severely do you think someone
deserves to be punished who has ... insulted the Spirit
of grace?' **Hebrews 10:29**

One of the devices Satan uses to keep some Christians from
experiencing all the fullness of the Spirit is to persuade them that
the obsessive or unclean thoughts they might have in connection with
the Holy Spirit are direct 'blasphemy' against the Spirit. Such thoughts
are usually due to emotional and psychological problems and not
deliberate disobedience against the Holy Spirit. They can be forgiven.

Another verse that seems to cause problems for some Christians is the
one before us today. In the days of the early church, there were some
Jews who, after embracing Christianity, decided to abandon it and return
to their old religion: Judaism. Before being readmitted to the faith of their
fathers, they were required to renounce the Christian gospel by figuratively
trampling on the blood of Christ, at the same time saying words to this
effect, 'I renounce the blood of Jesus as unworthy and ineffectual'.

In the religion of the Jews, trampling on the blood was a sign of contempt. What greater insolence, then, to the Christian faith than to tread under foot the blood of the Son of God, and openly state that it was ineffectual and unworthy. Such an act, said the writer to the Hebrews, not only insulted the Holy Spirit, but outraged Him (Heb. 10: 29). Such an action is seldom committed in modern times. Take it from me, most upsets in connection with the Holy Spirit are caused by the Spirit of grace calling us to repentance and forgiveness.

PRAYER

O Father, release me, I pray, from all Satan's attempts to influence my thinking, and enable me to enjoy, from this day forward, the freedom of 'life in the Spirit'. For Jesus' sake. Amen.

FURTHER STUDY

Heb. 9; Matt. 26:28; Rom. 5:9; 1 Pet. 1:18-19
- Why is Christ's shed blood so precious?
- How does it apply to accusing thoughts?

November 14

■ EZEKIEL 7:1–9:11

7 The word of the LORD came to me: ² 'Son of man, this is what the Sovereign LORD says to the land of Israel:

'"The end! The end has come
upon the four corners of the land!
³ The end is now upon you,
and I will unleash my anger against
you.
I will judge you according to your conduct
and repay you for all your detestable
practices.
⁴ I will not look on you with pity;
I will not spare you.
I will surely repay you for your conduct
and for the detestable practices among
you.
'"Then you will know that I am the LORD."

⁵ 'This is what the Sovereign LORD says:

'"Disaster! Unheard-of disaster!
See, it comes!
⁶ The end has come!
The end has come!
It has roused itself against you.
See, it comes!
⁷ Doom has come upon you,
upon you who dwell in the land.
The time has come! The day is near!
There is panic, not joy, on the
mountains.
⁸ I am about to pour out my wrath on you
and spend my anger against you.
I will judge you according to your conduct
and repay you for all your detestable
practices.
⁹ I will not look on you with pity;
I will not spare you.
I will repay you for your conduct
and for the detestable practices among
you.

'"Then you will know that it is I the LORD
who strikes you.

[10] ' "See, the day!
　　See, it comes!
Doom has burst forth,
　　the rod has budded,
　　arrogance has blossomed!
[11] Violence has arisen,
　　a rod to punish the wicked.
None of the people will be left,
　　none of that crowd –
none of their wealth,
　　nothing of value.
[12] The time has come!
　　The day has arrived!
Let not the buyer rejoice
　　nor the seller grieve,
　　for my wrath is on the whole crowd.
[13] The seller will not recover
　　the property that was sold –
　　as long as both buyer and seller live.
For the vision concerning the whole
　　crowd
　　will not be reversed.
Because of their sins, not one of them
　　will preserve their life.

[14] ' "They have blown the trumpet,
　　they have made all things ready,
but no one will go into battle,
　　for my wrath is on the whole crowd.
[15] Outside is the sword;
　　inside are plague and famine.
Those in the country
　　will die by the sword;
those in the city
　　will be devoured by famine and plague.
[16] The fugitives who escape
　　will flee to the mountains.
Like doves of the valleys,
　　they will all moan,
　　each for their own sins.
[17] Every hand will go limp;
　　every leg will be wet with urine.
[18] They will put on sackcloth
　　and be clothed with terror.
Every face will be covered with shame,
　　and every head will be shaved.

[19] ' "They will throw their silver into the
　　streets,
　　and their gold will be treated as a
　　thing unclean.
Their silver and gold
　　will not be able to deliver them
　　in the day of the LORD's wrath.
It will not satisfy their hunger
　　or fill their stomachs,
　　for it has caused them to stumble into
　　sin.
[20] They took pride in their beautiful
　　jewellery
　　and used it to make their detestable
　　idols.
They made it into vile images;
　　therefore I will make it a thing
　　unclean for them.
[21] I will give their wealth as plunder to
　　foreigners
　　and as loot to the wicked of the earth,
　　who will defile it.
[22] I will turn my face away from the people,
　　and robbers will desecrate the place I
　　treasure.
They will enter it
　　and will defile it.

[23] ' "Prepare chains!
　　For the land is full of bloodshed,
　　and the city is full of violence.
[24] I will bring the most wicked of nations
　　to take possession of their houses.
I will put an end to the pride of the
　　mighty,
　　and their sanctuaries will be
　　desecrated.
[25] When terror comes,
　　they will seek peace in vain.
[26] Calamity upon calamity will come,
　　and rumour upon rumour.
They will go searching for a vision from
　　the prophet,
　　priestly instruction in the law will
　　cease,

the counsel of the elders will come to
an end.
²⁷ The king will mourn,
the prince will be clothed with despair,
and the hands of the people of the land
will tremble.
I will deal with them according to their
conduct,
and by their own standards I will
judge them.

' "Then they will know that I am the LORD." '

8 In the sixth year, in the sixth month on the fifth day, while I was sitting in my house and the elders of Judah were sitting before me, the hand of the Sovereign LORD came on me there. ²I looked, and I saw a figure like that of a man. From what appeared to be his waist down he was like fire, and from there up his appearance was as bright as glowing metal. ³He stretched out what looked like a hand and took me by the hair of my head. The Spirit lifted me up between earth and heaven and in visions of God he took me to Jerusalem, to the entrance of the north gate of the inner court, where the idol that provokes to jealousy stood. ⁴And there before me was the glory of the God of Israel, as in the vision I had seen in the plain.

⁵Then he said to me, 'Son of man, look towards the north.' So I looked, and in the entrance north of the gate of the altar I saw this idol of jealousy.

⁶And he said to me, 'Son of man, do you see what they are doing – the utterly detestable things the Israelites are doing here, things that will drive me far from my sanctuary? But you will see things that are even more detestable.'

⁷Then he brought me to the entrance to the court. I looked, and I saw a hole in the wall. ⁸He said to me, 'Son of man, now dig into the wall.' So I dug into the wall and saw a doorway there.

⁹And he said to me, 'Go in and see the wicked and detestable things they are doing here.' ¹⁰So I went in and looked, and I saw portrayed all over the walls all kinds of crawling things and unclean animals and all the idols of Israel. ¹¹In front of them stood seventy elders of Israel, and Jaazaniah son of Shaphan was standing among them. Each had a censer in his hand, and a fragrant cloud of incense was rising.

¹²He said to me, 'Son of man, have you seen what the elders of Israel are doing in the darkness, each at the shrine of his own idol? They say, "The LORD does not see us; the LORD has forsaken the land." ' ¹³Again, he said, 'You will see them doing things that are even more detestable.'

¹⁴Then he brought me to the entrance of the north gate of the house of the LORD, and I saw women sitting there, mourning the god Tammuz. ¹⁵He said to me, 'Do you see this, son of man? You will see things that are even more detestable than this.'

¹⁶He then brought me into the inner court of the house of the LORD, and there at the entrance to the temple, between the portico and the altar, were about twenty-five men. With their backs towards the temple of the LORD and their faces towards the east, they were bowing down to the sun in the east.

¹⁷He said to me, 'Have you seen this, son of man? Is it a trivial matter for the people of Judah to do the detestable things they are doing here? Must they also fill the land with violence and continually arouse my anger? Look at them putting the branch to their nose! ¹⁸Therefore I will deal with them in anger; I will not look on them with pity or spare them. Although they shout in my ears, I will not listen to them.'

9 Then I heard him call out in a loud voice, 'Bring near those who are appointed to execute judgment on the city, each with a weapon in his hand.' ²And I saw six men coming from the direction of the upper gate, which faces north, each with a deadly weapon in his hand. With them was a man clothed in linen who had a writing kit

at his side. They came in and stood beside the bronze altar.

³Now the glory of the God of Israel went up from above the cherubim, where it had been, and moved to the threshold of the temple. Then the LORD called to the man clothed in linen who had the writing kit at his side ⁴and said to him, 'Go throughout the city of Jerusalem and put a mark on the foreheads of those who grieve and lament over all the detestable things that are done in it.'

⁵As I listened, he said to the others, 'Follow him through the city and kill, without showing pity or compassion. ⁶Slaughter the old men, the young men and women, the mothers and children, but do not touch anyone who has the mark. Begin at my sanctuary.' So they began with the old men who were in front of the temple.

⁷Then he said to them, 'Defile the temple and fill the courts with the slain. Go!' So they went out and began killing throughout the city. ⁸While they were killing and I was left alone, I fell face down, crying out, 'Alas, Sovereign LORD! Are you going to destroy the entire remnant of Israel in this outpouring of your wrath on Jerusalem?'

⁹He answered me, 'The sin of the people of Israel and Judah is exceedingly great; the land is full of bloodshed and the city is full of injustice. They say, "The LORD has forsaken the land; the LORD does not see." ¹⁰So I will not look on them with pity or spare them, but I will bring down on their own heads what they have done.'

¹¹Then the man in linen with the writing kit at his side brought back word, saying, 'I have done as you commanded.'

■ PSALM 119:169-176

¹⁶⁹May my cry come before you, LORD;
    give me understanding according to
        your word.
¹⁷⁰May my supplication come before you;

deliver me according to your promise.
¹⁷¹May my lips overflow with praise,
    for you teach me your decrees.
¹⁷²May my tongue sing of your word,
    for all your commands are righteous.
¹⁷³May your hand be ready to help me,
    for I have chosen your precepts.
¹⁷⁴I long for your salvation, LORD,
    and your law gives me delight.
¹⁷⁵Let me live that I may praise you,
    and may your laws sustain me.
¹⁷⁶I have strayed like a lost sheep.
    Seek your servant,
    for I have not forgotten your
        commands.

■ PROVERBS 27:14-16

¹⁴If anyone loudly blesses their neighbour
        early in the morning,
    it will be taken as a curse.

¹⁵A quarrelsome wife is like the dripping
        of a leaky roof in a rainstorm;
¹⁶restraining her is like restraining the
        wind
    or grasping oil with the hand.

■ HEBREWS 10:32–11:12

³²Remember those earlier days after you had received the light, when you endured in a great conflict full of suffering. ³³Sometimes you were publicly exposed to insult and persecution; at other times you stood side by side with those who were so treated. ³⁴You suffered along with those in prison and joyfully accepted the confiscation of your property, because you knew that you yourselves had better and lasting possessions. ³⁵So do not throw away your confidence; it will be richly rewarded. ³⁶You need to persevere so that when you

have done the will of God, you will receive what he has promised. ³⁷For,

'In just a little while,
  he who is coming will come
  and will not delay.'

³⁸And,

'But my righteous one will live by faith.
  And I take no pleasure
  in the one who shrinks back.'

³⁹But we do not belong to those who shrink back and are destroyed, but to those who have faith and are saved.

11 Now faith is confidence in what we hope for and assurance about what we do not see. ²This is what the ancients were commended for.

³By faith we understand that the universe was formed at God's command, so that what is seen was not made out of what was visible.

⁴By faith Abel brought God a better offering than Cain did. By faith he was commended as righteous, when God spoke well of his offerings. And by faith Abel still speaks, even though he is dead.

⁵By faith Enoch was taken from this life, so that he did not experience death: 'He could not be found, because God had taken him away.' For before he was taken, he was commended as one who pleased God. ⁶And without faith it is impossible to please God, because anyone who comes to him must believe that he exists and that he rewards those who earnestly seek him.

⁷By faith Noah, when warned about things not yet seen, in holy fear built an ark to save his family. By his faith he condemned the world and became heir of the righteousness that is in keeping with faith.

⁸By faith Abraham, when called to go to a place he would later receive as his inheritance, obeyed and went, even though he did not know where he was going. ⁹By faith he made his home in the promised land like a stranger in a foreign country; he lived in tents, as did Isaac and Jacob, who were heirs with him of the same promise. ¹⁰For he was looking forward to the city with foundations, whose architect and builder is God. ¹¹And by faith even Sarah, who was past childbearing age, was enabled to bear children because she considered him faithful who had made the promise. ¹²And so from this one man, and he as good as dead, came descendants as numerous as the stars in the sky and as countless as the sand on the seashore.

Faith, Not Demandingness

'Now faith is confidence in what we hope for and assurance about what we do not see.' **Hebrews 11:1**

I am frequently asked, 'Doesn't what you say about demandingness destroy the faith we ought to have when we approach God in prayer? Isn't powerful praying the ability to insist on God giving us the things we know we ought to be receiving?'

There is a world of difference between 'praying in faith' and demandingness. When we 'pray in faith', we have the assurance in our hearts that God wants to bring about a certain purpose for His own glory, whereupon faith reaches into heaven and pulls down the answer through fervent, believing prayer. Demandingness is another thing entirely – it insists on getting the answers that are in accord with its own desires rather than God's purposes. It is an attempt to bring God in line with our will rather than bringing our wills in line with His will.

Dr Francis Schaeffer, when advised that he was suffering from a terminal illness, became assured that his work on earth was finished and that soon he would leave this world and go to his heavenly home. Thousands of people prayed for his healing and when he himself was asked why he did not claim the Bible's promises concerning health and wholeness, he replied, 'When I am in the presence of God, it seems uniquely unbecoming to demand anything'.

Some have interpreted these words as a lack of faith, but I think I understand what he meant. It is one thing to plead and pray with passion for something very personal; it is another to demand that the will of the Almighty be one with our own.

PRAYER

Father, I see that the line between demandingness and faith is so fine that I can easily cross from one to the other without knowing it. Tune my spirit so that I will always be able to discern the difference between these two things. In Jesus' name. Amen.

FURTHER STUDY

Psa. 143:1-10; Matt. 12:50; James 4:1-15
• What was the desire of the psalmist?
• How does James put it?

November 15

■ EZEKIEL 10:1–12:7

10 I looked, and I saw the likeness of a throne of lapis lazuli above the vault that was over the heads of the cherubim. ²The LORD said to the man clothed in linen, 'Go in among the wheels beneath the cherubim. Fill your hands with burning coals from among the cherubim and scatter them over the city.' And as I watched, he went in.

³Now the cherubim were standing on the south side of the temple when the man went in, and a cloud filled the inner court. ⁴Then the glory of the LORD rose from above the cherubim and moved to the threshold of the

temple. The cloud filled the temple, and the court was full of the radiance of the glory of the LORD. ⁵The sound of the wings of the cherubim could be heard as far away as the outer court, like the voice of God Almighty when he speaks.

⁶When the LORD commanded the man in linen, 'Take fire from among the wheels, from among the cherubim,' the man went in and stood beside a wheel. ⁷Then one of the cherubim reached out his hand to the fire that was among them. He took up some of it and put it into the hands of the man in linen, who took it and went out. ⁸(Under the wings of the cherubim could be seen what

looked like human hands.)

⁹I looked, and I saw beside the cherubim four wheels, one beside each of the cherubim; the wheels sparkled like topaz. ¹⁰As for their appearance, the four of them looked alike; each was like a wheel intersecting a wheel. ¹¹As they moved, they would go in any one of the four directions the cherubim faced; the wheels did not turn about as the cherubim went. The cherubim went in whatever direction the head faced, without turning as they went. ¹²Their entire bodies, including their backs, their hands and their wings, were completely full of eyes, as were their four wheels. ¹³I heard the wheels being called 'the whirling wheels'. ¹⁴Each of the cherubim had four faces: one face was that of a cherub, the second the face of a human being, the third the face of a lion, and the fourth the face of an eagle.

¹⁵Then the cherubim rose upward. These were the living creatures I had seen by the River Kebar. ¹⁶When the cherubim moved, the wheels beside them moved; and when the cherubim spread their wings to rise from the ground, the wheels did not leave their side. ¹⁷When the cherubim stood still, they also stood still; and when the cherubim rose, they rose with them, because the spirit of the living creatures was in them.

¹⁸Then the glory of the Lord departed from over the threshold of the temple and stopped above the cherubim. ¹⁹While I watched, the cherubim spread their wings and rose from the ground, and as they went, the wheels went with them. They stopped at the entrance of the east gate of the Lord's house, and the glory of the God of Israel was above them.

²⁰These were the living creatures I had seen beneath the God of Israel by the River Kebar, and I realised that they were cherubim. ²¹Each had four faces and four wings, and under their wings was what looked like human hands. ²²Their faces had the same appearance as those I had seen by the River Kebar. Each one went straight ahead.

11 Then the Spirit lifted me up and brought me to the gate of the house of the Lord that faces east. There at the entrance of the gate were twenty-five men, and I saw among them Jaazaniah son of Azzur and Pelatiah son of Benaiah, leaders of the people. ²The Lord said to me, 'Son of man, these are the men who are plotting evil and giving wicked advice in this city. ³They say, "Haven't our houses been recently rebuilt? This city is a pot, and we are the meat in it." ⁴Therefore prophesy against them; prophesy, son of man.'

⁵Then the Spirit of the Lord came on me, and he told me to say: 'This is what the Lord says: that is what you are saying, you leaders in Israel, but I know what is going through your mind. ⁶You have killed many people in this city and filled its streets with the dead.

⁷'Therefore this is what the Sovereign Lord says: the bodies you have thrown there are the meat and this city is the pot, but I will drive you out of it. ⁸You fear the sword, and the sword is what I will bring against you, declares the Sovereign Lord. ⁹I will drive you out of the city and deliver you into the hands of foreigners and inflict punishment on you. ¹⁰You will fall by the sword, and I will execute judgment on you at the borders of Israel. Then you will know that I am the Lord. ¹¹This city will not be a pot for you, nor will you be the meat in it; I will execute judgment on you at the borders of Israel. ¹²And you will know that I am the Lord, for you have not followed my decrees or kept my laws but have conformed to the standards of the nations around you.'

¹³Now as I was prophesying, Pelatiah son of Benaiah died. Then I fell face down and cried out in a loud voice, 'Alas, Sovereign Lord! Will you completely destroy the remnant of Israel?'

¹⁴The word of the Lord came to me: ¹⁵'Son of man, the people of Jerusalem have said of your fellow exiles and all the other Israelites,

"They are far away from the LORD; this land was given to us as our possession."

¹⁶'Therefore say: "This is what the Sovereign LORD says: although I sent them far away among the nations and scattered them among the countries, yet for a little while I have been a sanctuary for them in the countries where they have gone."

¹⁷'Therefore say: "This is what the Sovereign LORD says: I will gather you from the nations and bring you back from the countries where you have been scattered, and I will give you back the land of Israel again."

¹⁸'They will return to it and remove all its vile images and detestable idols. ¹⁹I will give them an undivided heart and put a new spirit in them; I will remove from them their heart of stone and give them a heart of flesh. ²⁰Then they will follow my decrees and be careful to keep my laws. They will be my people, and I will be their God. ²¹But as for those whose hearts are devoted to their vile images and detestable idols, I will bring down on their own heads what they have done, declares the Sovereign LORD.'

²²Then the cherubim, with the wheels beside them, spread their wings, and the glory of the God of Israel was above them. ²³The glory of the LORD went up from within the city and stopped above the mountain east of it. ²⁴The Spirit lifted me up and brought me to the exiles in Babylonia in the vision given by the Spirit of God.

Then the vision I had seen went up from me, ²⁵and I told the exiles everything the LORD had shown me.

12 The word of the LORD came to me: ²'Son of man, you are living among a rebellious people. They have eyes to see but do not see and ears to hear but do not hear, for they are a rebellious people.

³'Therefore, son of man, pack your belongings for exile and in the daytime, as they watch, set out and go from where you are to another place. Perhaps they will understand, though they are a rebellious

people. ⁴During the daytime, while they watch, bring out your belongings packed for exile. Then in the evening, while they are watching, go out like those who go into exile. ⁵While they watch, dig through the wall and take your belongings out through it. ⁶Put them on your shoulder as they are watching and carry them out at dusk. Cover your face so that you cannot see the land, for I have made you a sign to the Israelites.'

⁷So I did as I was commanded. During the day I brought out my things packed for exile. Then in the evening I dug through the wall with my hands. I took my belongings out at dusk, carrying them on my shoulders while they watched.

PSALM 120:1–7

¹I call on the LORD in my distress,
    and he answers me.
²Save me, LORD,
    from lying lips
    and from deceitful tongues.

³What will he do to you,
    and what more besides,
    you deceitful tongue?
⁴He will punish you with a warrior's
        sharp arrows,
    with burning coals of the broom bush.

⁵Woe to me that I dwell in Meshek,
    that I live among the tents of Kedar!
⁶Too long have I lived
    among those who hate peace.
⁷I am for peace;
    but when I speak, they are for war.

PROVERBS 27:17–18

¹⁷As iron sharpens iron,
    so one person sharpens another.

¹⁸ The one who guards a fig-tree will eat its
fruit,
    and whoever protects their master will
be honoured.

■ HEBREWS 11:13-31

¹³ All these people were still living by faith
when they died. They did not receive the
things promised; they only saw them and
welcomed them from a distance, admitting
that they were foreigners and strangers on
earth. ¹⁴ People who say such things show
that they are looking for a country of their
own. ¹⁵ If they had been thinking of the country they had left, they would have had opportunity to return. ¹⁶ Instead, they were longing
for a better country – a heavenly one. Therefore God is not ashamed to be called their
God, for he has prepared a city for them.

¹⁷ By faith Abraham, when God tested
him, offered Isaac as a sacrifice. He who had
embraced the promises was about to sacrifice his one and only son, ¹⁸ even though God
had said to him, 'It is through Isaac that
your offspring will be reckoned.' ¹⁹ Abraham reasoned that God could even raise the
dead, and so in a manner of speaking he did
receive Isaac back from death.

²⁰ By faith Isaac blessed Jacob and Esau in
regard to their future.

²¹ By faith Jacob, when he was dying,
blessed each of Joseph's sons, and worshipped as he leaned on the top of his staff.

²² By faith Joseph, when his end was
near, spoke about the exodus of the Israelites from Egypt and gave instructions
concerning the burial of his bones.

²³ By faith Moses' parents hid him for
three months after he was born, because
they saw he was no ordinary child, and they
were not afraid of the king's edict.

²⁴ By faith Moses, when he had grown up,
refused to be known as the son of Pharaoh's
daughter. ²⁵ He chose to be ill-treated along
with the people of God rather than to enjoy
the fleeting pleasures of sin. ²⁶ He regarded
disgrace for the sake of Christ as of greater
value than the treasures of Egypt, because
he was looking ahead to his reward. ²⁷ By
faith he left Egypt, not fearing the king's anger; he persevered because he saw him who
is invisible. ²⁸ By faith he kept the Passover
and the application of blood, so that the destroyer of the firstborn would not touch the
firstborn of Israel.

²⁹ By faith the people passed through the
Red Sea as on dry land; but when the Egyptians tried to do so, they were drowned.

³⁰ By faith the walls of Jericho fell, after the army had marched round them for
seven days.

³¹ By faith the prostitute Rahab, because
she welcomed the spies, was not killed with
those who were disobedient.

Seeing the Invisible

'... he persevered because he saw him who is invisible.'
Hebrews 11:27

What is it that prompts some people to take more interest in the
principles of godliness than in God Himself? I think one reason
could be that we are more comfortable dealing in the realm of the
visible than the invisible. We prefer to work with things we can touch,
handle and apply so that we feel an immediate impact rather than to
launch out into the unseen and to simply trust.

I often saw people come up against this problem in the days when much of my time was spent in personal counselling. I would bring people to a place where they could accept that the roots of their problem lay in a deficient relationship with God. However, when a movement of simple basic trust toward Him was called for, terror would appear for a moment in their eyes, and they would say, 'Give me some steps I can take to deal with my problem, some principles I can follow that will act as a ladder on which I can climb out of this pit'.

We all find it easier to do than to be; we prefer a plan to follow rather than a Person to trust. What our carnal nature hates to be faced with is the challenge of throwing ourselves in utter dependency on a God who is invisible and intangible. Yet this is what a relationship with God entails. The thing that marks Moses out as outstanding in the chapter before us today is not his works but his faith. He persevered because he saw Him who is invisible. It is possible to see the invisible, but it is possible only to the eye of faith.

PRAYER

My Father and my God, help me recognise this terrible tendency in myself to be more comfortable with working than trusting. Let Your Word reach deep into my heart today. Teach me how to be. In Jesus' name I pray. Amen.

FURTHER STUDY

Rom. 1:16-23; Heb. 11:1-2; 1 Tim. 1:17
• Why are people without excuse?
• What is the essence of faith?

November 16

■ EZEKIEL 12:8–14:11

⁸In the morning the word of the LORD came to me: ⁹'Son of man, did not the Israelites, that rebellious people, ask you, "What are you doing?"

¹⁰'Say to them, "This is what the Sovereign LORD says: this prophecy concerns the prince in Jerusalem and all the Israelites who are there." ¹¹Say to them, "I am a sign to you."

'As I have done, so it will be done to them. They will go into exile as captives.

¹²'The prince among them will put his things on his shoulder at dusk and leave, and a hole will be dug in the wall for him to go through. He will cover his face so that he cannot see the land. ¹³I will spread my net for him, and he will be caught in my snare; I will bring him to Babylonia, the land of the Chaldeans, but he will not see it, and there he will die. ¹⁴I will scatter to the winds all those around him – his staff and all his troops – and I will pursue them with drawn sword.

¹⁵'They will know that I am the LORD, when I disperse them among the nations and scatter them through the countries. ¹⁶But I will spare a few of them from the sword, famine and plague, so that in the nations where they go they may acknowledge

all their detestable practices. Then they will know that I am the Lord.'

¹⁷The word of the Lord came to me: ¹⁸'Son of man, tremble as you eat your food, and shudder in fear as you drink your water. ¹⁹Say to the people of the land: "This is what the Sovereign Lord says about those living in Jerusalem and in the land of Israel: they will eat their food in anxiety and drink their water in despair, for their land will be stripped of everything in it because of the violence of all who live there. ²⁰The inhabited towns will be laid waste and the land will be desolate. Then you will know that I am the Lord."'

²¹The word of the Lord came to me: ²²'Son of man, what is this proverb you have in the land of Israel: "The days go by and every vision comes to nothing"? ²³Say to them, "This is what the Sovereign Lord says: I am going to put an end to this proverb, and they will no longer quote it in Israel." Say to them, "The days are near when every vision will be fulfilled. ²⁴For there will be no more false visions or flattering divinations among the people of Israel. ²⁵But I the Lord will speak what I will, and it shall be fulfilled without delay. For in your days, you rebellious people, I will fulfil whatever I say, declares the Sovereign Lord."'

²⁶The word of the Lord came to me: ²⁷'Son of man, the Israelites are saying, "The vision he sees is for many years from now, and he prophesies about the distant future."

²⁸'Therefore say to them, "This is what the Sovereign Lord says: none of my words will be delayed any longer; whatever I say will be fulfilled, declares the Sovereign Lord."'

13 The word of the Lord came to me: ²'Son of man, prophesy against the prophets of Israel who are now prophesying. Say to those who prophesy out of their own imagination: "Hear the word of the Lord! ³This is what the Sovereign Lord says: woe to the foolish prophets who follow their own spirit and have seen nothing! ⁴Your prophets, Israel, are like jackals among ruins. ⁵You have not gone up to the breaches in the wall to repair it for the people of Israel so that it will stand firm in the battle on the day of the Lord. ⁶Their visions are false and their divinations a lie. Even though the Lord has not sent them, they say, 'The Lord declares', and expect him to fulfil their words. ⁷Have you not seen false visions and uttered lying divinations when you say, 'The Lord declares', though I have not spoken?

⁸'"Therefore this is what the Sovereign Lord says: because of your false words and lying visions, I am against you, declares the Sovereign Lord. ⁹My hand will be against the prophets who see false visions and utter lying divinations. They will not belong to the council of my people or be listed in the records of Israel, nor will they enter the land of Israel. Then you will know that I am the Sovereign Lord.

¹⁰'"Because they lead my people astray, saying, 'Peace', when there is no peace, and because, when a flimsy wall is built, they cover it with whitewash, ¹¹therefore tell those who cover it with whitewash that it is going to fall. Rain will come in torrents, and I will send hailstones hurtling down, and violent winds will burst forth. ¹²When the wall collapses, will people not ask you, 'Where is the whitewash you covered it with?'

¹³'"Therefore this is what the Sovereign Lord says: in my wrath I will unleash a violent wind, and in my anger hailstones and torrents of rain will fall with destructive fury. ¹⁴I will tear down the wall you have covered with whitewash and will level it to the ground so that its foundation will be laid bare. When it falls, you will be destroyed in it; and you will know that I am the Lord. ¹⁵So I will pour out my wrath against the wall and against those who covered it with whitewash. I will say to you, 'The wall is

gone and so are those who whitewashed it, [16] those prophets of Israel who prophesied to Jerusalem and saw visions of peace for her when there was no peace, declares the Sovereign LORD.'"

[17] 'Now, son of man, set your face against the daughters of your people who prophesy out of their own imagination. Prophesy against them [18] and say, "This is what the Sovereign LORD says: woe to the women who sew magic charms on all their wrists and make veils of various lengths for their heads in order to ensnare people. Will you ensnare the lives of my people but preserve your own? [19] You have profaned me among my people for a few handfuls of barley and scraps of bread. By lying to my people, who listen to lies, you have killed those who should not have died and have spared those who should not live.

[20] '"Therefore this is what the Sovereign LORD says: I am against your magic charms with which you ensnare people like birds and I will tear them from your arms; I will set free the people that you ensnare like birds. [21] I will tear off your veils and save my people from your hands, and they will no longer fall prey to your power. Then you will know that I am the LORD. [22] Because you disheartened the righteous with your lies, when I had brought them no grief, and because you encouraged the wicked not to turn from their evil ways and so save their lives, [23] therefore you will no longer see false visions or practise divination. I will save my people from your hands. And then you will know that I am the LORD."'

14 Some of the elders of Israel came to me and sat down in front of me. [2] Then the word of the LORD came to me: [3] 'Son of man, these men have set up idols in their hearts and put wicked stumbling-blocks before their faces. Should I let them enquire of me at all? [4] Therefore speak to them and tell them, "This is what the Sovereign LORD says: when any of the Israelites

set up idols in their hearts and put a wicked stumbling-block before their faces and then go to a prophet, I the LORD will answer them myself in keeping with their great idolatry. [5] I will do this to recapture the hearts of the people of Israel, who have all deserted me for their idols."

[6] 'Therefore say to the people of Israel, "This is what the Sovereign LORD says: repent! Turn from your idols and renounce all your detestable practices!

[7] '"When any of the Israelites or any foreigner residing in Israel separate themselves from me and set up idols in their hearts and put a wicked stumbling-block before their faces and then go to a prophet to enquire of me, I the LORD will answer them myself. [8] I will set my face against them and make them an example and a byword. I will remove them from my people. Then you will know that I am the LORD.

[9] '"And if the prophet is enticed to utter a prophecy, I the LORD have enticed that prophet, and I will stretch out my hand against him and destroy him from among my people Israel. [10] They will bear their guilt – the prophet will be as guilty as the one who consults him. [11] Then the people of Israel will no longer stray from me, nor will they defile themselves any more with all their sins. They will be my people, and I will be their God, declares the Sovereign LORD."'

■ PSALM 121:1-8

[1] I lift up my eyes to the mountains –
    where does my help come from?
[2] My help comes from the LORD,
    the Maker of heaven and earth.

[3] He will not let your foot slip –
    he who watches over you will not
        slumber;
[4] indeed, he who watches over Israel
    will neither slumber nor sleep.

⁵ The LORD watches over you –
    the LORD is your shade at your right
       hand;
⁶ the sun will not harm you by day,
    nor the moon by night.

⁷ The LORD will keep you from all harm –
    he will watch over your life;
⁸ the LORD will watch over your coming
       and going
    both now and for evermore.

■ PROVERBS 27:19-20

¹⁹ As water reflects the face,
    so one's life reflects the heart.

²⁰ Death and Destruction are never
       satisfied,
    and neither are human eyes.

■ HEBREWS 11:32–12:11

³² And what more shall I say? I do not have time to tell about Gideon, Barak, Samson and Jephthah, about David and Samuel and the prophets, ³³ who through faith conquered kingdoms, administered justice, and gained what was promised; who shut the mouths of lions, ³⁴ quenched the fury of the flames, and escaped the edge of the sword; whose weakness was turned to strength; and who became powerful in battle and routed foreign armies. ³⁵ Women received back their dead, raised to life again. There were others who were tortured, refusing to be released so that they might gain an even better resurrection. ³⁶ Some faced jeers and flogging, and even chains and imprisonment. ³⁷ They were put to death by stoning; they were sawn in two; they were killed by the sword. They went about in sheepskins and goatskins, destitute, persecuted and ill-treated – ³⁸ the world was not

worthy of them. They wandered in deserts and mountains, living in caves and in holes in the ground.

³⁹ These were all commended for their faith, yet none of them received what had been promised, ⁴⁰ since God had planned something better for us so that only together with us would they be made perfect.

12 Therefore, since we are surrounded by such a great cloud of witnesses, let us throw off everything that hinders and the sin that so easily entangles. And let us run with perseverance the race marked out for us, ² fixing our eyes on Jesus, the pioneer and perfecter of faith. For the joy that was set before him he endured the cross, scorning its shame, and sat down at the right hand of the throne of God. ³ Consider him who endured such opposition from sinners, so that you will not grow weary and lose heart.

⁴ In your struggle against sin, you have not yet resisted to the point of shedding your blood. ⁵ And have you completely forgotten this word of encouragement that addresses you as a father addresses his son? It says,

'My son, do not make light of the Lord's
    discipline,
    and do not lose heart when he rebukes
       you,
⁶ because the Lord disciplines the one he
       loves,
    and he chastens everyone he accepts
       as his son.'

⁷ Endure hardship as discipline; God is treating you as his children. For what children are not disciplined by their father? ⁸ If you are not disciplined – and everyone undergoes discipline – then you are not legitimate, not true sons and daughters at all. ⁹ Moreover, we have all had human fathers who disciplined us and we respected them for it. How much more should we submit to

the Father of spirits and live! [10] They disciplined us for a little while as they thought best; but God disciplines us for our good, in order that we may share in his holiness. [11] No discipline seems pleasant at the time, but painful. Later on, however, it produces a harvest of righteousness and peace for those who have been trained by it.

Gaze on His Face

'... let us run with perseverance the race marked out for us, fixing our eyes on Jesus, the pioneer and perfecter of faith.' **Hebrews 12:1-2**

In order to stay spiritually fresh you must keep your eyes fully focused on Jesus.

Our Lord was the most alert and alive person the world has ever seen. Never once do we read that He experienced spiritual staleness or had to confess to being out of touch with heaven. He was always confident, always assured, always in the right place, always doing the right thing at the right time. Even after a period of prolonged fasting in the wilderness when He faced the fiercest of temptations, He turned - not exhausted and limp as a wet rag - but 'in the power of the Spirit' (Luke 4:14). Here was spiritual freshness to the nth degree.

Our text today tells us that one of the ways by which we can become more and more like Christ is to stand with unveiled faces and continually gaze upon Him. It is a breathtaking concept - and so simple. Yet how profound. Look beyond yourself to Another, and thus free yourself from self-preoccupation. Have you noticed how many of the religious cults get their followers to concentrate on the divinity within them? Then what happens? They finish up preoccupied with their own states of mind and emotion. As someone put it, 'If I worship the divinity within me, I will probably end up worshipping myself'.

2 Corinthians 3:18 gets our gaze in the right place - on the face of Christ: 'And we all, who with unveiled faces contemplate the Lord's glory, are being transformed into his image with ever-increasing glory ...'. The attention we give to this is important, for whatever gets our attention gets us. Therefore, when Christ gets our attention, He also gets us. Our gaze must be person-centred, not problem-centred. And that Person must be Jesus Christ.

PRAYER

Blessed Lord Jesus, when I look at myself I feel unworthy and inadequate. But when I look at You, I feel anything is possible. Help me not just to glance at You, but gaze at You - continuously. Amen.

FURTHER STUDY

Rom. 8:29-39; John 1:36; Col. 2:2-3

• What is God's plan for us?
• What was John's declaration?

November 17

■ EZEKIEL 14:12–16:34

¹² The word of the LORD came to me: ¹³ 'Son of man, if a country sins against me by being unfaithful and I stretch out my hand against it to cut off its food supply and send famine upon it and kill its people and their animals, ¹⁴ even if these three men – Noah, Daniel and Job – were in it, they could save only themselves by their righteousness, declares the Sovereign LORD.

¹⁵ 'Or if I send wild beasts through that country and they leave it childless and it becomes desolate so that no one can pass through it because of the beasts, ¹⁶ as surely as I live, declares the Sovereign LORD, even if these three men were in it, they could not save their own sons or daughters. They alone would be saved, but the land would be desolate.

¹⁷ 'Or if I bring a sword against that country and say, "Let the sword pass throughout the land," and I kill its people and their animals, ¹⁸ as surely as I live, declares the Sovereign LORD, even if these three men were in it, they could not save their own sons or daughters. They alone would be saved.

¹⁹ 'Or if I send a plague into that land and pour out my wrath on it through bloodshed, killing its people and their animals, ²⁰ as surely as I live, declares the Sovereign LORD, even if Noah, Daniel and Job were in it, they could save neither son nor daughter. They would save only themselves by their righteousness.

²¹ 'For this is what the Sovereign LORD says: how much worse will it be when I send against Jerusalem my four dreadful judgments – sword and famine and wild beasts and plague – to kill its men and their animals! ²² Yet there will be some survivors – sons and daughters who will be brought out of it. They will come to you, and when you see their conduct and their actions, you will be consoled regarding the disaster I have brought on Jerusalem – every disaster I have brought on it. ²³ You will be consoled when you see their conduct and their actions, for you will know that I have done nothing in it without cause, declares the Sovereign LORD.'

15 The word of the LORD came to me: ² 'Son of man, how is the wood of a vine different from that of a branch from any of the trees in the forest? ³ Is wood ever taken from it to make anything useful? Do they make pegs from it to hang things on? ⁴ And after it is thrown on the fire as fuel and the fire burns both ends and chars the middle, is it then useful for anything? ⁵ If it was not useful for anything when it was whole, how much less can it be made into something useful when the fire has burned it and it is charred?

⁶ 'Therefore this is what the Sovereign LORD says: as I have given the wood of the vine among the trees of the forest as fuel for the fire, so will I treat the people living in Jerusalem. ⁷ I will set my face against them. Although they have come out of the fire, the fire will yet consume them. And when I set my face against them, you will know that I am the LORD. ⁸ I will make the land desolate because they have been unfaithful, declares the Sovereign LORD.'

16 The word of the LORD came to me: ² 'Son of man, confront Jerusalem with her detestable practices ³ and say, "This is what the Sovereign LORD says to Jerusalem: your ancestry and birth were in the land of the Canaanites; your father was an Amorite and your mother a Hittite.

4 On the day you were born your cord was not cut, nor were you washed with water to make you clean, nor were you rubbed with salt or wrapped in cloths. 5 No one looked on you with pity or had compassion enough to do any of these things for you. Rather, you were thrown out into the open field, for on the day you were born you were despised.

6 '"Then I passed by and saw you kicking about in your blood, and as you lay there in your blood I said to you, 'Live!' 7 I made you grow like a plant of the field. You grew and developed and entered puberty. Your breasts had formed and your hair had grown, yet you were stark naked.

8 '"Later I passed by, and when I looked at you and saw that you were old enough for love, I spread the corner of my garment over you and covered your naked body. I gave you my solemn oath and entered into a covenant with you, declares the Sovereign LORD, and you became mine.

9 '"I bathed you with water and washed the blood from you and put ointments on you. 10 I clothed you with an embroidered dress and put sandals of fine leather on you. I dressed you in fine linen and covered you with costly garments. 11 I adorned you with jewellery: I put bracelets on your arms and a necklace round your neck, 12 and I put a ring on your nose, earrings on your ears and a beautiful crown on your head. 13 So you were adorned with gold and silver; your clothes were of fine linen and costly fabric and embroidered cloth. Your food was honey, olive oil and the finest flour. You became very beautiful and rose to be a queen. 14 And your fame spread among the nations on account of your beauty, because the splendour I had given you made your beauty perfect, declares the Sovereign LORD.

15 '"But you trusted in your beauty and used your fame to become a prostitute. You lavished your favours on anyone who passed by and your beauty became his. 16 You took some of your garments to make gaudy high places, where you carried on your prostitution. You went to him, and he possessed your beauty. 17 You also took the fine jewellery I gave you, the jewellery made of my gold and silver, and you made for yourself male idols and engaged in prostitution with them. 18 And you took your embroidered clothes to put on them, and you offered my oil and incense before them. 19 Also the food I provided for you – the flour, olive oil and honey I gave you to eat – you offered as fragrant incense before them. That is what happened, declares the Sovereign LORD.

20 '"And you took your sons and daughters whom you bore to me and sacrificed them as food to the idols. Was your prostitution not enough? 21 You slaughtered my children and sacrificed them to the idols. 22 In all your detestable practices and your prostitution you did not remember the days of your youth, when you were naked and bare, kicking about in your blood.

23 '"Woe! Woe to you, declares the Sovereign LORD. In addition to all your other wickedness, 24 you built a mound for yourself and made a lofty shrine in every public square. 25 At every street corner you built your lofty shrines and degraded your beauty, spreading your legs with increasing promiscuity to anyone who passed by. 26 You engaged in prostitution with the Egyptians, your neighbours with large genitals, and aroused my anger with your increasing promiscuity. 27 So I stretched out my hand against you and reduced your territory; I gave you over to the greed of your enemies, the daughters of the Philistines, who were shocked by your lewd conduct. 28 You engaged in prostitution with the Assyrians too, because you were insatiable; and even after that, you still were not satisfied. 29 Then you increased your promiscuity to include Babylonia, a land of merchants, but even with this you were not satisfied.

30 '"I am filled with fury against you, declares the Sovereign LORD, when you do all

these things, acting like a brazen prostitute! ³¹ When you built your mounds at every street corner and made your lofty shrines in every public square, you were unlike a prostitute, because you scorned payment.

³² ' "You adulterous wife! You prefer strangers to your own husband! ³³ All prostitutes receive gifts, but you give gifts to all your lovers, bribing them to come to you from everywhere for your illicit favours. ³⁴ So in your prostitution you are the opposite of others; no one runs after you for your favours. You are the very opposite, for you give payment and none is given to you.

PSALM 122:1–123:4

¹ I rejoiced with those who said to me,
    'Let us go to the house of the LORD.'
² Our feet are standing
    in your gates, Jerusalem.

³ Jerusalem is built like a city
    that is closely compacted together.
⁴ That is where the tribes go up –
    the tribes of the LORD –
to praise the name of the LORD
    according to the statute given to Israel.
⁵ There stand the thrones for judgment,
    the thrones of the house of David.

⁶ Pray for the peace of Jerusalem:
    'May those who love you be secure.
⁷ May there be peace within your walls
    and security within your citadels.'
⁸ For the sake of my family and friends,
    I will say, 'Peace be within you.'
⁹ For the sake of the house of the LORD our God,
    I will seek your prosperity.

¹ I lift up my eyes to you,
    to you who sit enthroned in heaven.
² As the eyes of slaves look to the hand of their master,

as the eyes of a female slave look to the hand of her mistress,
so our eyes look to the LORD our God,
    till he shows us his mercy.

³ Have mercy on us, LORD, have mercy on us,
    for we have endured no end of contempt.
⁴ We have endured no end
    of ridicule from the arrogant,
    of contempt from the proud.

PROVERBS 27:21-22

²¹ The crucible for silver and the furnace for gold,
    but people are tested by their praise.

²² Though you grind a fool in a mortar,
    grinding them like grain with a pestle,
    you will not remove their folly from them.

HEBREWS 12:12-29

¹² Therefore, strengthen your feeble arms and weak knees. ¹³ 'Make level paths for your feet,' so that the lame may not be disabled, but rather healed.

¹⁴ Make every effort to live in peace with everyone and to be holy; without holiness no one will see the Lord. ¹⁵ See to it that no one falls short of the grace of God and that no bitter root grows up to cause trouble and defile many. ¹⁶ See that no one is sexually immoral, or is godless like Esau, who for a single meal sold his inheritance rights as the oldest son. ¹⁷ Afterwards, as you know, when he wanted to inherit this blessing, he was rejected. Even though he sought the blessing with tears, he could not change what he had done.

¹⁸ You have not come to a mountain that can be touched and that is burning with

fire; to darkness, gloom and storm; [19] to a trumpet blast or to such a voice speaking words that those who heard it begged that no further word be spoken to them, [20] because they could not bear what was commanded: 'If even an animal touches the mountain, it must be stoned to death.' [21] The sight was so terrifying that Moses said, 'I am trembling with fear.'

[22] But you have come to Mount Zion, to the city of the living God, the heavenly Jerusalem. You have come to thousands upon thousands of angels in joyful assembly, [23] to the church of the firstborn, whose names are written in heaven. You have come to God, the Judge of all, to the spirits of the righteous made perfect, [24] to Jesus the mediator of a new covenant, and to the sprinkled blood that speaks a better word than the blood of Abel.

[25] See to it that you do not refuse him who speaks. If they did not escape when they refused him who warned them on earth, how much less will we, if we turn away from him who warns us from heaven? [26] At that time his voice shook the earth, but now he has promised, 'Once more I will shake not only the earth but also the heavens.' [27] The words 'once more' indicate the removing of what can be shaken – that is, created things – so that what cannot be shaken may remain.

[28] Therefore, since we are receiving a kingdom that cannot be shaken, let us be thankful, and so worship God acceptably with reverence and awe, [29] for our 'God is a consuming fire.'

The Consuming Fire

'... our God is a consuming fire.' **Hebrews 12:29**

George MacDonald writes: 'Nothing is inexorable but love, for love loves unto purity. Love has ever in view the absolute loveliness of that which it beholds. Where loveliness is incomplete, and love cannot love its fill of loving, it spends itself to make more lovely, that it may love more; it strives for perfection even that itself may be perfected – not in itself but in the object. Therefore all that is not beautiful in the beloved, all that comes between and is not of love's kind, must be destroyed. Our God is a consuming fire.'

Powerful words.

The nature of God is so terribly pure that it destroys everything that is not as pure as fire. God desires us to worship Him in '... the splendour of his holiness' (Psa. 29:2). This means that He wants the purity in us to match the purity in Him. We cannot arrive at this purity by self-effort, of course, but the more we draw near to Him, the more the fire of His purity will burn out the dross within us.

'It is not the fire that will burn us up if we do not worship,' said George MacDonald, 'but the fire will burn us up until we worship.' And the fire will go on burning within us after everything that is foreign to it has been consumed, no longer with pain and a sense of something unwanted being consumed, but as the highest consciousness of life.

God is a consuming fire. He always was, and always will be – world without end.

PRAYER

O God, I long with all my heart that my worship might be all You want it to be. May Your consuming fire burn out all the dross within me until everything that is foreign to Your nature is part of me no more. In Jesus' name I ask it. Amen.

FURTHER STUDY

Psa. 97:1-5; Isa. 66:15;
1 Cor. 3:12-14
• What does the psalmist say about fire?
• What will the fire do?

November 18

■ EZEKIEL 16:35–17:24

35 "'Therefore, you prostitute, hear the word of the Lord! 36 This is what the Sovereign Lord says: because you poured out your lust and exposed your naked body in your promiscuity with your lovers, and because of all your detestable idols, and because you gave them your children's blood, 37 therefore I am going to gather all your lovers, with whom you found pleasure, those you loved as well as those you hated. I will gather them against you from all around and will strip you in front of them, and they will see you stark naked. 38 I will sentence you to the punishment of women who commit adultery and who shed blood; I will bring on you the blood vengeance of my wrath and jealous anger. 39 Then I will deliver you into the hands of your lovers, and they will tear down your mounds and destroy your lofty shrines. They will strip you of your clothes and take your fine jewellery and leave you stark naked. 40 They will bring a mob against you, who will stone you and hack you to pieces with their swords. 41 They will burn down your houses and inflict punishment on you in the sight of many women. I will put a stop to your prostitution, and you will no longer pay your lovers. 42 Then my wrath against you will subside

and my jealous anger will turn away from you; I will be calm and no longer angry.

43 "'Because you did not remember the days of your youth but enraged me with all these things, I will surely bring down on your head what you have done, declares the Sovereign Lord. Did you not add lewdness to all your other detestable practices?

44 "'Everyone who quotes proverbs will quote this proverb about you: "Like mother, like daughter." 45 You are a true daughter of your mother, who despised her husband and her children; and you are a true sister of your sisters, who despised their husbands and their children. Your mother was a Hittite and your father an Amorite. 46 Your elder sister was Samaria, who lived to the north of you with her daughters; and your younger sister, who lived to the south of you with her daughters, was Sodom. 47 You not only followed their ways and copied their detestable practices, but in all your ways you soon became more depraved than they. 48 As surely as I live, declares the Sovereign Lord, your sister Sodom and her daughters never did what you and your daughters have done.

49 "'Now this was the sin of your sister Sodom: she and her daughters were arrogant, overfed and unconcerned; they did not help the poor and needy. 50 They were haughty and did detestable things before

me. Therefore I did away with them as you have seen. [51] Samaria did not commit half the sins you did. You have done more detestable things than they, and have made your sisters seem righteous by all these things you have done. [52] Bear your disgrace, for you have furnished some justification for your sisters. Because your sins were more vile than theirs, they appear more righteous than you. So then, be ashamed and bear your disgrace, for you have made your sisters appear righteous.

[53] ' "However, I will restore the fortunes of Sodom and her daughters and of Samaria and her daughters, and your fortunes along with them, [54] so that you may bear your disgrace and be ashamed of all you have done in giving them comfort. [55] And your sisters, Sodom with her daughters and Samaria with her daughters, will return to what they were before; and you and your daughters will return to what you were before. [56] You would not even mention your sister Sodom in the day of your pride, [57] before your wickedness was uncovered. Even so, you are now scorned by the daughters of Edom and all her neighbours and the daughters of the Philistines – all those around you who despise you. [58] You will bear the consequences of your lewdness and your detestable practices, declares the LORD.

[59] ' "This is what the Sovereign LORD says: I will deal with you as you deserve, because you have despised my oath by breaking the covenant. [60] Yet I will remember the covenant I made with you in the days of your youth, and I will establish an everlasting covenant with you. [61] Then you will remember your ways and be ashamed when you receive your sisters, both those who are older than you and those who are younger. I will give them to you as daughters, but not on the basis of my covenant with you. [62] So I will establish my covenant with you, and you will know that I am the LORD. [63] Then, when I make atonement for you for all

you have done, you will remember and be ashamed and never again open your mouth because of your humiliation, declares the Sovereign LORD." '

17 The word of the LORD came to me: [2] 'Son of man, set forth an allegory and tell it to the Israelites as a parable. [3] Say to them, "This is what the Sovereign LORD says: a great eagle with powerful wings, long feathers and full plumage of varied colours came to Lebanon. Taking hold of the top of a cedar, [4] he broke off its topmost shoot and carried it away to a land of merchants, where he planted it in a city of traders.

[5] ' "He took one of the seedlings of the land and put it in fertile soil. He planted it like a willow by abundant water, [6] and it sprouted and became a low, spreading vine. Its branches turned towards him, but its roots remained under it. So it became a vine and produced branches and put out leafy boughs.

[7] ' "But there was another great eagle with powerful wings and full plumage. The vine now sent out its roots towards him from the plot where it was planted and stretched out its branches to him for water. [8] It had been planted in good soil by abundant water so that it would produce branches, bear fruit and become a splendid vine."

[9] 'Say to them, "This is what the Sovereign LORD says: will it thrive? Will it not be uprooted and stripped of its fruit so that it withers? All its new growth will wither. It will not take a strong arm or many people to pull it up by the roots. [10] It has been planted, but will it thrive? Will it not wither completely when the east wind strikes it – wither away in the plot where it grew?" '

[11] Then the word of the LORD came to me: [12] 'Say to this rebellious people, "Do you not know what these things mean?" Say to them: "The king of Babylon went to Jerusalem and carried off her king and her nobles, bringing them back with him to Babylon. [13] Then he took a member of the royal family

and made a treaty with him, putting him under oath. He also carried away the leading men of the land, ¹⁴ so that the kingdom would be brought low, unable to rise again, surviving only by keeping his treaty. ¹⁵ But the king rebelled against him by sending his envoys to Egypt to get horses and a large army. Will he succeed? Will he who does such things escape? Will he break the treaty and yet escape?

¹⁶ " "As surely as I live, declares the Sovereign LORD, he shall die in Babylon, in the land of the king who put him on the throne, whose oath he despised and whose treaty he broke. ¹⁷ Pharaoh with his mighty army and great horde will be of no help to him in war, when ramps are built and siege works erected to destroy many lives. ¹⁸ He despised the oath by breaking the covenant. Because he had given his hand in pledge and yet did all these things, he shall not escape.

¹⁹ " "Therefore this is what the Sovereign LORD says: as surely as I live, I will repay him for despising my oath and breaking my covenant. ²⁰ I will spread my net for him, and he will be caught in my snare. I will bring him to Babylon and execute judgment on him there because he was unfaithful to me. ²¹ All his choice troops will fall by the sword, and the survivors will be scattered to the winds. Then you will know that I the LORD have spoken.

²² " "This is what the Sovereign LORD says: I myself will take a shoot from the very top of a cedar and plant it; I will break off a tender sprig from its topmost shoots and plant it on a high and lofty mountain. ²³ On the mountain heights of Israel I will plant it; it will produce branches and bear fruit and become a splendid cedar. Birds of every kind will nest in it; they will find shelter in the shade of its branches. ²⁴ All the trees of the forest will know that I the LORD bring down the tall tree and make the low tree grow tall. I dry up the green tree and make the dry tree flourish.

' "I the LORD have spoken, and I will do it." '

■ PSALM 124:1–8

¹ If the LORD had not been on our side –
  let Israel say –
² if the LORD had not been on our side
    when people attacked us,
³ they would have swallowed us alive
    when their anger flared against us;
⁴ the flood would have engulfed us,
    the torrent would have swept over us,
⁵ the raging waters
    would have swept us away.

⁶ Praise be to the LORD,
    who has not let us be torn by their
      teeth.
⁷ We have escaped like a bird
    from the fowler's snare;
  the snare has been broken,
    and we have escaped.
⁸ Our help is in the name of the LORD,
    the Maker of heaven and earth.

■ PROVERBS 27:23–24

²³ Be sure you know the condition of your
      flocks,
    give careful attention to your herds;
²⁴ for riches do not endure for ever,
    and a crown is not secure for all
      generations.

■ HEBREWS 13:1–25

13 Keep on loving one another as brothers and sisters. ² Do not forget to show hospitality to strangers, for by so doing some people have shown hospitality to angels without knowing it. ³ Continue to remember those in prison as if you were

together with them in prison, and those who are ill-treated as if you yourselves were suffering.

⁴Marriage should be honoured by all, and the marriage bed kept pure, for God will judge the adulterer and all the sexually immoral. ⁵Keep your lives free from the love of money and be content with what you have, because God has said,

'Never will I leave you;
   never will I forsake you.'

⁶So we say with confidence,

'The Lord is my helper; I will not be
      afraid.
   What can mere mortals do to me?'

⁷Remember your leaders, who spoke the word of God to you. Consider the outcome of their way of life and imitate their faith. ⁸Jesus Christ is the same yesterday and today and for ever.

⁹Do not be carried away by all kinds of strange teachings. It is good for our hearts to be strengthened by grace, not by eating ceremonial foods, which is of no benefit to those who do so. ¹⁰We have an altar from which those who minister at the tabernacle have no right to eat.

¹¹The high priest carries the blood of animals into the Most Holy Place as a sin offering, but the bodies are burned outside the camp. ¹²And so Jesus also suffered outside the city gate to make the people holy through his own blood. ¹³Let us, then, go to him outside the camp, bearing the disgrace he bore. ¹⁴For here we do not have an enduring city, but we are looking for the city that is to come.

¹⁵Through Jesus, therefore, let us continually offer to God a sacrifice of praise – the fruit of lips that openly profess his name. ¹⁶And do not forget to do good and to share with others, for with such sacrifices God is pleased.

¹⁷Have confidence in your leaders and submit to their authority, because they keep watch over you as those who must give an account. Do this so that their work will be a joy, not a burden, for that would be of no benefit to you.

¹⁸Pray for us. We are sure that we have a clear conscience and desire to live honourably in every way. ¹⁹I particularly urge you to pray so that I may be restored to you soon.

²⁰Now may the God of peace, who through the blood of the eternal covenant brought back from the dead our Lord Jesus, that great Shepherd of the sheep, ²¹equip you with everything good for doing his will, and may he work in us what is pleasing to him, through Jesus Christ, to whom be glory for ever and ever. Amen.

²²Brothers and sisters, I urge you to bear with my word of exhortation, for in fact I have written to you quite briefly.

²³I want you to know that our brother Timothy has been released. If he arrives soon, I will come with him to see you.

²⁴Greet all your leaders and all the Lord's people. Those from Italy send you their greetings.

²⁵Grace be with you all.

Pray for Me That ...

'Pray for us. We are sure that we have a clear conscience and desire to live honourably in every way. I particularly urge you to pray so that I may be restored to you soon.' **Hebrews 13:18-19**

The apostle ends his discussion of spiritual warfare (Eph. 6:10-20) on the following personal note: 'Pray also for me, that whenever I speak, words may be given me so that I will fearlessly make known the mystery of the gospel ... Pray that I may declare it fearlessly, as I should' (vv. 19-20).

Paul was wise enough to know his own need of supernatural strength in being able to stand against the enemy, and he was humble enough to ask his brothers and sisters to pray for him in this matter.

Imagine this great apostle, probably the most powerful and effective disciple of Christ the world has ever seen, asking his friends to pray for him. Truly, the greater a Christian is, the more he realises his dependence on the prayers of others. Paul knew full well the power that was against him, and he did not hesitate to ask for the prayers of the church in Ephesus.

Notice also that his request for prayer was clear and specific. When you ask someone to pray for you, be equally specific. Don't just say, 'Pray for me', but 'Pray for me that ...' Paul's request was not that he might be delivered from prison, but that through his testimony in prison the gospel of Christ might be advanced. He knew that the most important thing was not to triumph over prison but to triumph in it. He knew he was where God wanted him for that time, and he would allow no self-interest to interfere with the divine schedule.

PRAYER

O Father, teach me, as You taught Your servant Paul, to know Your will and purpose so clearly that I might know just how and what to pray for. I ask this in and through the strong and mighty name of Jesus. Amen.

FURTHER STUDY

2 Thess. 3; 1 Thess. 5:25; Rom. 12:2
• What was Paul's request?
• For whom are you praying regularly?

November 19

EZEKIEL 18:1–19:14

18 The word of the LORD came to me: ²'What do you people mean by quoting this proverb about the land of Israel:

³ '"The parents eat sour grapes,
    and the children's teeth are set on
        edge"?

³'As surely as I live, declares the Sovereign

LORD, you will no longer quote this proverb in Israel. ⁴For everyone belongs to me, the parent as well as the child – both alike belong to me. The one who sins is the one who will die.

⁵'Suppose there is a righteous man
    who does what is just and right.
⁶He does not eat at the mountain shrines
    or look to the idols of Israel.
He does not defile his neighbour's wife

or have sexual relations with a woman
during her period.
⁷ He does not oppress anyone,
but returns what he took in pledge for
a loan.
He does not commit robbery,
but gives his food to the hungry
and provides clothing for the naked.
⁸ He does not lend to them at interest
or take a profit from them.
He withholds his hand from doing
wrong
and judges fairly between two parties.
⁹ He follows my decrees
and faithfully keeps my laws.
That man is righteous;
he will surely live,
declares the Sovereign LORD.

¹⁰ 'Suppose he has a violent son, who
sheds blood or does any of these other
things ¹¹(though the father has done none
of them):

'He eats at the mountain shrines.
He defiles his neighbour's wife.
¹² He oppresses the poor and needy.
He commits robbery.
He does not return what he took in
pledge.
He looks to the idols.
He does detestable things.
¹³ He lends at interest and takes a profit.

Will such a man live? He will not! Because
he has done all these detestable things, he
is to be put to death; his blood will be on his
own head.

¹⁴ 'But suppose this son has a son who sees
all the sins his father commits, and though
he sees them, he does not do such things:

¹⁵ 'He does not eat at the mountain shrines
or look to the idols of Israel.
He does not defile his neighbour's wife.
¹⁶ He does not oppress anyone

or require a pledge for a loan.
He does not commit robbery,
but gives his food to the hungry
and provides clothing for the naked.
¹⁷ He withholds his hand from ill-treating
the poor
and takes no interest or profit from
them.
He keeps my laws and follows my
decrees.

He will not die for his father's sin; he will
surely live. ¹⁸ But his father will die for his
own sin, because he practised extortion,
robbed his brother and did what was wrong
among his people.

¹⁹ 'Yet you ask, "Why does the son not
share the guilt of his father?" Since the son
has done what is just and right and has been
careful to keep all my decrees, he will surely live. ²⁰ The one who sins is the one who
will die. The child will not share the guilt
of the parent, nor will the parent share
the guilt of the child. The righteousness of
the righteous will be credited to them,
and the wickedness of the wicked will be
charged against them.

²¹ 'But if a wicked person turns away from
all the sins they have committed and keeps
all my decrees and does what is just and
right, that person will surely live; they will
not die. ²² None of the offences they have
committed will be remembered against
them. Because of the righteous things they
have done, they will live. ²³ Do I take any
pleasure in the death of the wicked? declares
the Sovereign LORD. Rather, am I not pleased
when they turn from their ways and live?

²⁴ 'But if a righteous person turns from
their righteousness and commits sin and
does the same detestable things the wicked
person does, will they live? None of the righteous things that person has done will be
remembered. Because of the unfaithfulness
they are guilty of and because of the sins they
have committed, they will die.

25 'Yet you say, "The way of the Lord is not just." Hear, you Israelites: is my way unjust? Is it not your ways that are unjust? 26 If a righteous person turns from their righteousness and commits sin, they will die for it; because of the sin they have committed they will die. 27 But if a wicked person turns away from the wickedness they have committed and does what is just and right, they will save their life. 28 Because they consider all the offences they have committed and turn away from them, that person will surely live; they will not die. 29 Yet the Israelites say, "The way of the Lord is not just." Are my ways unjust, people of Israel? Is it not your ways that are unjust?

30 'Therefore, you Israelites, I will judge each of you according to your own ways, declares the Sovereign LORD. Repent! Turn away from all your offences; then sin will not be your downfall. 31 Rid yourselves of all the offences you have committed, and get a new heart and a new spirit. Why will you die, people of Israel? 32 For I take no pleasure in the death of anyone, declares the Sovereign LORD. Repent and live!

19 'Take up a lament concerning the princes of Israel 2 and say:

'"What a lioness was your mother
    among the lions!
She lay down among them
    and reared her cubs.
3 She brought up one of her cubs,
    and he became a strong lion.
He learned to tear the prey
    and he became a man-eater.
4 The nations heard about him,
    and he was trapped in their pit.
They led him with hooks
    to the land of Egypt.

5 '"When she saw her hope unfulfilled,
    her expectation gone,
she took another of her cubs
    and made him a strong lion.

6 He prowled among the lions,
    for he was now a strong lion.
He learned to tear the prey
    and he became a man-eater.
7 He broke down their strongholds
    and devastated their towns.
The land and all who were in it
    were terrified by his roaring.
8 Then the nations came against him,
    those from regions round about.
They spread their net for him,
    and he was trapped in their pit.
9 With hooks they pulled him into a cage
    and brought him to the king of
        Babylon.
They put him in prison,
    so his roar was heard no longer
    on the mountains of Israel.

10 ' "Your mother was like a vine in your
        vineyard
    planted by the water;
it was fruitful and full of branches
    because of abundant water.
11 Its branches were strong,
    fit for a ruler's sceptre.
It towered high
    above the thick foliage,
conspicuous for its height
    and for its many branches.
12 But it was uprooted in fury
    and thrown to the ground.
The east wind made it shrivel,
    it was stripped of its fruit;
its strong branches withered
    and fire consumed them.
13 Now it is planted in the desert,
    in a dry and thirsty land.
14 Fire spread from one of its main
        branches
    and consumed its fruit.
No strong branch is left on it
    fit for a ruler's sceptre."

'This is a lament and is to be used as a lament.'

■ PSALM 125:1–5

¹ Those who trust in the LORD are like
  Mount Zion,
  which cannot be shaken but endures
  for ever.
² As the mountains surround Jerusalem,
  so the LORD surrounds his people
  both now and for evermore.

³ The sceptre of the wicked will not
  remain
  over the land allotted to the righteous,
  for then the righteous might use
  their hands to do evil.

⁴ LORD, do good to those who are good,
  to those who are upright in heart.
⁵ But those who turn to crooked ways
  the LORD will banish with the
  evildoers.

Peace be on Israel.

■ PROVERBS 27:25–27

²⁵ When the hay is removed and new
  growth appears
  and the grass from the hills is
  gathered in,
²⁶ the lambs will provide you with clothing,
  and the goats with the price of a field.
²⁷ You will have plenty of goats' milk to
  feed your family
  and to nourish your female servants.

■ JAMES 1:1–21

1 James, a servant of God and of the Lord
  Jesus Christ,

To the twelve tribes scattered among the
nations:

Greetings.

² Consider it pure joy, my brothers and sisters, whenever you face trials of many kinds, ³ because you know that the testing of your faith produces perseverance. ⁴ Let perseverance finish its work so that you may be mature and complete, not lacking anything. ⁵ If any of you lacks wisdom, you should ask God, who gives generously to all without finding fault, and it will be given to you. ⁶ But when you ask, you must believe and not doubt, because the one who doubts is like a wave of the sea, blown and tossed by the wind. ⁷ That person should not expect to receive anything from the Lord. ⁸ Such a person is double-minded and unstable in all they do.

⁹ Believers in humble circumstances ought to take pride in their high position. ¹⁰ But the rich should take pride in their humiliation – since they will pass away like a wild flower. ¹¹ For the sun rises with scorching heat and withers the plant; its blossom falls and its beauty is destroyed. In the same way, the rich will fade away even while they go about their business.

¹² Blessed is the one who perseveres under trial because, having stood the test, that person will receive the crown of life that the Lord has promised to those who love him.

¹³ When tempted, no one should say, 'God is tempting me.' For God cannot be tempted by evil, nor does he tempt anyone; ¹⁴ but each person is tempted when they are dragged away by their own evil desire and enticed. ¹⁵ Then, after desire has conceived, it gives birth to sin; and sin, when it is full-grown, gives birth to death.

¹⁶ Don't be deceived, my dear brothers and sisters. ¹⁷ Every good and perfect gift is from above, coming down from the Father of the heavenly lights, who does not change like shifting shadows. ¹⁸ He chose to give us birth through the word of truth, that we might be a kind of firstfruits of all he created.

¹⁹My dear brothers and sisters, take note of this: everyone should be quick to listen, slow to speak and slow to become angry, ²⁰because human anger does not produce the righteousness that God desires. ²¹Therefore, get rid of all moral filth and the evil that is so prevalent, and humbly accept the word planted in you, which can save you.

'Some Extra Practice'

'Consider it pure joy, my brothers and sisters, whenever you face trials of many kinds ...' **James 1:2**

The Bible is replete with instances of God's wisdom moving men and women through the most difficult times to the most wonderful ends. Take Abraham, for example. Although he is known in Scripture as the 'the friend of God', he was capable of some shabby behaviour. On one occasion he actually compromised his wife's chastity (Gen. 12:10-20), and later, submitting to her pressure, fathered a child by Hagar, their maid (Gen. 16:1-16). Then, seeking to avoid Sarah's hysterical recriminations, he allowed her to drive Hagar away from their household (Gen. 21:8-21). Clearly, Abraham was not a man of strong principle, and there were great flaws in his character. But God in wisdom dealt with this man and brought him through some great trials until he was changed from a man of the world to a true man of God.

The same wisdom that ordered the path Abraham trod orders our lives. We should never be taken aback when unexpected and upsetting things happen to us. We should recognise that no matter how hard the trial, God's power will be there to get us through, and God's wisdom will ensure that the trial will be worth more than it costs.

I like the way Jim Packer describes what may be God's design when He permits us to go through trials: 'Perhaps he means to strengthen us in patience, good humour, compassion, humility, or meekness by giving us some extra practice in exercising these graces under specially difficult situations.' 'Some extra practice.' Some of us, myself included, sorely need it.

PRAYER

Father, help me grasp this truth once and for all, that Your wisdom ensures the trials I go through are worth far more than they cost. You are more committed to making me like Jesus than I am myself. It hurts sometimes, but deep down I am grateful. Amen.

FURTHER STUDY

Isa. 48:1-10; Psa. 66:10; Mal. 3:3; 1 Pet. 1:7
• What process is God's testing likened to?
• What is the end result?

November 20

▬ EZEKIEL 20:1–21:7

20 In the seventh year, in the fifth month on the tenth day, some of the elders of Israel came to enquire of the LORD, and they sat down in front of me.

² Then the word of the LORD came to me: ³ 'Son of man, speak to the elders of Israel and say to them, "This is what the Sovereign LORD says: have you come to enquire of me? As surely as I live, I will not let you enquire of me, declares the Sovereign LORD."

⁴ 'Will you judge them? Will you judge them, son of man? Then confront them with the detestable practices of their ancestors ⁵ and say to them: "This is what the Sovereign LORD says: on the day I chose Israel, I swore with uplifted hand to the descendants of Jacob and revealed myself to them in Egypt. With uplifted hand I said to them, 'I am the LORD your God.' ⁶ On that day I swore to them that I would bring them out of Egypt into a land I had searched out for them, a land flowing with milk and honey, the most beautiful of all lands. ⁷ And I said to them, 'Each of you, get rid of the vile images you have set your eyes on, and do not defile yourselves with the idols of Egypt. I am the LORD your God.'

⁸ "But they rebelled against me and would not listen to me; they did not get rid of the vile images they had set their eyes on, nor did they forsake the idols of Egypt. So I said I would pour out my wrath on them and spend my anger against them in Egypt. ⁹ But for the sake of my name, I brought them out of Egypt. I did it to keep my name from being profaned in the eyes of the nations among whom they lived and in whose sight I had revealed myself to the Israelites. ¹⁰ Therefore I led them out of Egypt and brought them into the wilderness. ¹¹ I gave them my decrees and made known to them my laws, by which the person who obeys them will live. ¹² Also I gave them my Sabbaths as a sign between us, so they would know that I the LORD made them holy.

¹³ "Yet the people of Israel rebelled against me in the wilderness. They did not follow my decrees but rejected my laws – by which the person who obeys them will live – and they utterly desecrated my Sabbaths. So I said I would pour out my wrath on them and destroy them in the wilderness. ¹⁴ But for the sake of my name I did what would keep it from being profaned in the eyes of the nations in whose sight I had brought them out. ¹⁵ Also with uplifted hand I swore to them in the wilderness that I would not bring them into the land I had given them – a land flowing with milk and honey, the most beautiful of all lands – ¹⁶ because they rejected my laws and did not follow my decrees and desecrated my Sabbaths. For their hearts were devoted to their idols. ¹⁷ Yet I looked on them with pity and did not destroy them or put an end to them in the wilderness. ¹⁸ I said to their children in the wilderness, 'Do not follow the statutes of your parents or keep their laws or defile yourselves with their idols. ¹⁹ I am the LORD your God; follow my decrees and be careful to keep my laws. ²⁰ Keep my Sabbaths holy, that they may be a sign between us. Then you will know that I am the LORD your God.'

²¹ "But the children rebelled against me: they did not follow my decrees, they were not careful to keep my laws, of which I said, 'The person who obeys them will live by them,' and they desecrated my Sabbaths. So I said I would pour out

my wrath on them and spend my anger against them in the wilderness. ²²But I withheld my hand, and for the sake of my name I did what would keep it from being profaned in the eyes of the nations in whose sight I had brought them out. ²³Also with uplifted hand I swore to them in the wilderness that I would disperse them among the nations and scatter them through the countries, ²⁴because they had not obeyed my laws but had rejected my decrees and desecrated my Sabbaths, and their eyes lusted after their parents' idols. ²⁵So I gave them other statutes that were not good and laws through which they could not live; ²⁶I defiled them through their gifts – the sacrifice of every firstborn – that I might fill them with horror so that they would know that I am the LORD."

²⁷'Therefore, son of man, speak to the people of Israel and say to them, "This is what the Sovereign LORD says: in this also your ancestors blasphemed me by being unfaithful to me: ²⁸when I brought them into the land I had sworn to give them and they saw any high hill or any leafy tree, there they offered their sacrifices, made offerings that aroused my anger, presented their fragrant incense and poured out their drink offerings. ²⁹Then I said to them: what is this high place you go to?"' (It is called Bamah to this day.)

³⁰'Therefore say to the Israelites: "This is what the Sovereign LORD says: will you defile yourselves the way your ancestors did and lust after their vile images? ³¹When you offer your gifts – the sacrifice of your children in the fire – you continue to defile yourselves with all your idols to this day. Am I to let you enquire of me, you Israelites? As surely as I live, declares the Sovereign LORD, I will not let you enquire of me.

³²'"You say, 'We want to be like the nations, like the peoples of the world, who serve wood and stone.' But what you have in mind will never happen. ³³As surely as I live, declares the Sovereign LORD, I will reign over you with a mighty hand and an outstretched arm and with outpoured wrath. ³⁴I will bring you from the nations and gather you from the countries where you have been scattered – with a mighty hand and an outstretched arm and with outpoured wrath. ³⁵I will bring you into the wilderness of the nations and there, face to face, I will execute judgment upon you. ³⁶As I judged your ancestors in the wilderness of the land of Egypt, so I will judge you, declares the Sovereign LORD. ³⁷I will take note of you as you pass under my rod, and I will bring you into the bond of the covenant. ³⁸I will purge you of those who revolt and rebel against me. Although I will bring them out of the land where they are living, yet they will not enter the land of Israel. Then you will know that I am the LORD.

³⁹'"As for you, people of Israel, this is what the Sovereign LORD says: go and serve your idols, every one of you! But afterwards you will surely listen to me and no longer profane my holy name with your gifts and idols. ⁴⁰For on my holy mountain, the high mountain of Israel, declares the Sovereign LORD, there in the land all the people of Israel will serve me, and there I will accept them. There I will require your offerings and your choice gifts, along with all your holy sacrifices. ⁴¹I will accept you as fragrant incense when I bring you out from the nations and gather you from the countries where you have been scattered, and I will be proved holy through you in the sight of the nations. ⁴²Then you will know that I am the LORD, when I bring you into the land of Israel, the land I had sworn with uplifted hand to give to your ancestors. ⁴³There you will remember your conduct and all the actions by which you have defiled yourselves, and you will loathe yourselves for all the evil you have done. ⁴⁴You will know that I am the LORD, when I deal with you for my name's sake and not according to your evil

ways and your corrupt practices, you people of Israel, declares the Sovereign LORD."'

⁴⁵The word of the LORD came to me: ⁴⁶'Son of man, set your face towards the south; preach against the south and prophesy against the forest of the southland. ⁴⁷Say to the southern forest: "Hear the word of the LORD. This is what the Sovereign LORD says: I am about to set fire to you, and it will consume all your trees, both green and dry. The blazing flame will not be quenched, and every face from south to north will be scorched by it. ⁴⁸Everyone will see that I the LORD have kindled it; it will not be quenched."'

⁴⁹Then I said, 'Sovereign LORD, they are saying of me, "Isn't he just telling parables?"'

21 The word of the Lord came to me: ²'Son of man, set your face against Jerusalem and preach against the sanctuary. Prophesy against the land of Israel ³and say to her: "This is what the LORD says: I am against you. I will draw my sword from its sheath and cut off from you both the righteous and the wicked. ⁴Because I am going to cut off the righteous and the wicked, my sword will be unsheathed against everyone from south to north. ⁵Then all people will know that I the LORD have drawn my sword from its sheath; it will not return again."

⁶'Therefore groan, son of man! Groan before them with broken heart and bitter grief. ⁷And when they ask you, "Why are you groaning?" you shall say, "Because of the news that is coming. Every heart will melt with fear and every hand go limp; every spirit will become faint and every leg will be wet with urine." It is coming! It will surely take place, declares the Sovereign LORD.'

▬ PSALM 126:1–6

¹When the LORD restored the fortunes of Zion,
   we were like those who dreamed.
²Our mouths were filled with laughter,

our tongues with songs of joy.
Then it was said among the nations,
   'The LORD has done great things for them.'
³The LORD has done great things for us,
   and we are filled with joy.

⁴Restore our fortunes, LORD,
   like streams in the Negev.
⁵Those who sow with tears
   will reap with songs of joy.
⁶Those who go out weeping,
   carrying seed to sow,
will return with songs of joy,
   carrying sheaves with them.

▬ PROVERBS 28:1–3

28 The wicked flee though no one pursues,
   but the righteous are as bold as a lion.

²When a country is rebellious, it has
      many rulers,
   but a ruler with discernment and
      knowledge maintains order.

³A ruler who oppresses the poor
   is like driving rain that leaves no
      crops.

▬ JAMES 1:22–2:17

²²Do not merely listen to the word, and so deceive yourselves. Do what it says. ²³Anyone who listens to the word but does not do what it says is like someone who looks at his face in a mirror ²⁴and, after looking at himself, goes away and immediately forgets what he looks like. ²⁵But whoever looks intently into the perfect law that gives freedom and continues in it – not forgetting what they have heard but doing it – they will be blessed in what they do.

²⁶Those who consider themselves religious and yet do not keep a tight rein on their tongues deceive themselves, and their religion is worthless. ²⁷Religion that God our Father accepts as pure and faultless is this: to look after orphans and widows in their distress and to keep oneself from being polluted by the world.

2 My brothers and sisters, believers in our glorious Lord Jesus Christ must not show favouritism. ²Suppose a man comes into your meeting wearing a gold ring and fine clothes, and a poor man in filthy old clothes also comes in. ³If you show special attention to the man wearing fine clothes and say, 'Here's a good seat for you,' but say to the poor man, 'You stand there' or 'Sit on the floor by my feet,' ⁴have you not discriminated among yourselves and become judges with evil thoughts?

⁵Listen, my dear brothers and sisters: has not God chosen those who are poor in the eyes of the world to be rich in faith and to inherit the kingdom he promised those who love him? ⁶But you have dishonoured the poor. Is it not the rich who are exploiting you? Are they not the ones who are dragging you into court? ⁷Are they not the ones who

are blaspheming the noble name of him to whom you belong?

⁸If you really keep the royal law found in Scripture, 'Love your neighbour as yourself,' you are doing right. ⁹But if you show favouritism, you sin and are convicted by the law as law-breakers. ¹⁰For whoever keeps the whole law and yet stumbles at just one point is guilty of breaking all of it. ¹¹For he who said, 'You shall not commit adultery,' also said, 'You shall not murder.' If you do not commit adultery but do commit murder, you have become a law-breaker.

¹²Speak and act as those who are going to be judged by the law that gives freedom, ¹³because judgment without mercy will be shown to anyone who has not been merciful. Mercy triumphs over judgment.

¹⁴What good is it, my brothers and sisters, if someone claims to have faith but has no deeds? Can such faith save them? ¹⁵Suppose a brother or a sister is without clothes and daily food. ¹⁶If one of you says to them, 'Go in peace; keep warm and well fed,' but does nothing about their physical needs, what good is it? ¹⁷In the same way, faith by itself, if it is not accompanied by action, is dead.

The Glory

'... believers in our glorious Lord Jesus Christ ...'
James 2:1

Can you think of anything that could occupy our attention more profitably than considering how to become more like Jesus? The central condition of this is the 'unveiled face'. As the Scripture says, 'And we all, who with unveiled faces contemplate the Lord's glory, are being transformed into his image with ever-increasing glory ...' (2 Cor. 3:18).

Notice, however, that we must lift the veils if we are to be transformed. When Jesus was crucified, the veil of the temple was rent in two, symbolising the fact that the heart of the universe was laid bare as redemptive love. Since God has unveiled Himself in Jesus, so we in response ought to unveil our faces, drop our masks, gaze in wonder – and in the gazing, be made like Him. It may be that there will be many veils that you will have to lift - veils of dishonesty, hypocrisy, legalism, pride - but I assure you that when they go, He comes.

Just think - we who are born of the dust of the earth are being gradually transformed into the most beautiful image this planet has ever seen: the image of Christ. What a destiny! The wonder of that transformation can only be explained by one word - 'glory'. The drabness, staleness, and dullness of life is replaced by living that has freshness in it. Can we live continuously like that? Yes - in His strength. 'Grace' and 'glory' are often connected in the New Testament. Take the grace, and you get the glory. What a way to live. Glory! Glory! Glory!

PRAYER

Father, help me to lift every veil in my life so that the light of Your countenance may shine through. You are Light and You want to make me light. Let Your radiance steal into every darkened corner of my being now and forever. Amen.

FURTHER STUDY

John 1:10-14; Col. 1:6;
2 Pet. 3:18
• What were the characteristics of Christ's glory?
• Make them the characteristics of your own life.

November 21

■ EZEKIEL 21:8–22:31

⁸The word of the LORD came to me: ⁹'Son of man, prophesy and say, "This is what the Lord says:

'"A sword, a sword,
    sharpened and polished –
¹⁰sharpened for the slaughter,
    polished to flash like lightning!

'"Shall we rejoice in the sceptre of my royal son? The sword despises every such stick.

¹¹'"The sword is appointed to be polished,
    to be grasped with the hand;
it is sharpened and polished,
    made ready for the hand of the slayer.
¹²Cry out and wail, son of man,

for it is against my people;
    it is against all the princes of Israel.
They are thrown to the sword
    along with my people.
Therefore beat your breast.

¹³'"Testing will surely come. And what if even the sceptre, which the sword despises, does not continue? declares the Sovereign LORD."

¹⁴'So then, son of man, prophesy
    and strike your hands together.
Let the sword strike twice,
    even three times.
It is a sword for slaughter –
    a sword for great slaughter,
    closing in on them from every side.
¹⁵So that hearts may melt with fear
    and the fallen be many,

I have stationed the sword for slaughter
   at all their gates.
Look! It is forged to strike like lightning,
   it is grasped for slaughter.
[16] Slash to the right, you sword,
   then to the left,
   wherever your blade is turned.
[17] I too will strike my hands together,
   and my wrath will subside.
I the LORD have spoken.'

[18] The word of the LORD came to me: [19] 'Son of man, mark out two roads for the sword of the king of Babylon to take, both starting from the same country. Make a signpost where the road branches off to the city. [20] Mark out one road for the sword to come against Rabbah of the Ammonites and another against Judah and fortified Jerusalem. [21] For the king of Babylon will stop at the fork in the road, at the junction of the two roads, to seek an omen: he will cast lots with arrows, he will consult his idols, he will examine the liver. [22] Into his right hand will come the lot for Jerusalem, where he is to set up battering-rams, to give the command to slaughter, to sound the battle cry, to set battering-rams against the gates, to build a ramp and to erect siege works. [23] It will seem like a false omen to those who have sworn allegiance to him, but he will remind them of their guilt and take them captive.

[24] 'Therefore this is what the Sovereign LORD says: "Because you people have brought to mind your guilt by your open rebellion, revealing your sins in all that you do – because you have done this, you will be taken captive.

[25] ' "You profane and wicked prince of Israel, whose day has come, whose time of punishment has reached its climax, [26] this is what the Sovereign LORD says: take off the turban, remove the crown. It will not be as it was: The lowly will be exalted and the exalted will be brought low. [27] A ruin! A ruin!

I will make it a ruin! The crown will not be restored until he to whom it rightfully belongs shall come; to him I will give it."

[28] 'And you, son of man, prophesy and say, "This is what the Sovereign LORD says about the Ammonites and their insults:

' "A sword, a sword,
   drawn for the slaughter,
   polished to consume
   and to flash like lightning!
[29] Despite false visions concerning you
   and lying divinations about you,
it will be laid on the necks
   of the wicked who are to be slain,
whose day has come,
   whose time of punishment has
      reached its climax.

[30] ' "Let the sword return to its sheath.
   In the place where you were created,
in the land of your ancestry,
   I will judge you.
[31] I will pour out my wrath on you
   and breathe out my fiery anger against
      you;
I will deliver you into the hands of brutal
      men,
   men skilled in destruction.
[32] You will be fuel for the fire,
   your blood will be shed in your land,
you will be remembered no more;
   for I the LORD have spoken."'

22 The word of the Lord came to me: [2] 'Son of man, will you judge her? Will you judge this city of bloodshed? Then confront her with all her detestable practices [3] and say: "This is what the Sovereign Lord says: you city that brings on herself doom by shedding blood in her midst and defiles herself by making idols, [4] you have become guilty because of the blood you have shed and have become defiled by the idols you have made. You have brought your days to a close, and the end of your years has come. Therefore I will make you an object of scorn to the nations and a laughing-stock to all the countries. [5] Those who are near and those who are far away will mock you, you infamous city, full of turmoil.

[6] ' "See how each of the princes of Israel who are in you uses his power to shed blood. [7] In you they have treated father and mother with contempt; in you they have oppressed the foreigner and ill-treated the fatherless and the widow. [8] You have despised my holy things and desecrated my Sabbaths. [9] In you are slanderers who are bent on shedding blood; in you are those who eat at the mountain shrines and commit lewd acts. [10] In you are those who dishonour their father's bed; in you are those who violate women during their period, when they are ceremonially unclean. [11] In you one man commits a detestable offence with his neighbour's wife, another shamefully defiles his daughter-in-law, and another violates his sister, his own father's daughter. [12] In you are people who accept bribes to shed blood; you take interest and make a profit from the poor. You extort unjust gain from your neighbours. And you have forgotten me, declares the Sovereign LORD.

[13] ' "I will surely strike my hands together at the unjust gain you have made and at the blood you have shed in your midst. [14] Will your courage endure or your hands be strong in the day I deal with you? I the LORD have spoken, and I will do it. [15] I will disperse you among the nations and scatter you through the countries; and I will put an end to your uncleanness. [16] When you have been defiled in the eyes of the nations, you will know that I am the LORD." '

[17] Then the word of the LORD came to me: [18] 'Son of man, the people of Israel have become dross to me; all of them are the copper, tin, iron and lead left inside a furnace. They are but the dross of silver. [19] Therefore this is what the Sovereign LORD says: "Because you

have all become dross, I will gather you into Jerusalem. [20] As silver, copper, iron, lead and tin are gathered into a furnace to be melted with a fiery blast, so will I gather you in my anger and my wrath and put you inside the city and melt you. [21] I will gather you and I will blow on you with my fiery wrath, and you will be melted inside her. [22] As silver is melted in a furnace, so you will be melted inside her, and you will know that I the LORD have poured out my wrath on you." '

[23] Again the word of the LORD came to me: [24] 'Son of man, say to the land, "You are a land that has not been cleansed or rained on in the day of wrath." [25] There is a conspiracy of her princes within her like a roaring lion tearing its prey; they devour people, take treasures and precious things and make many widows within her. [26] Her priests do violence to my law and profane my holy things; they do not distinguish between the holy and the common; they teach that there is no difference between the unclean and the clean; and they shut their eyes to the keeping of my Sabbaths, so that I am profaned among them. [27] Her officials within her are like wolves tearing their prey; they shed blood and kill people to make unjust gain. [28] Her prophets whitewash these deeds for them by false visions and lying divinations. They say, "This is what the Sovereign LORD says" – when the LORD has not spoken. [29] The people of the land practise extortion and commit robbery; they oppress the poor and needy and ill-treat the foreigner, denying them justice.

[30] 'I looked for someone among them who would build up the wall and stand before me in the gap on behalf of the land so that I would not have to destroy it, but I found no one. [31] So I will pour out my wrath on them and consume them with my fiery anger, bringing down on their own heads all they have done, declares the Sovereign LORD.'

PSALM 127:1-5

¹ Unless the LORD builds the house,
    the builders labour in vain.
Unless the LORD watches over the city,
    the guards stand watch in vain.
² In vain you rise early
    and stay up late,
toiling for food to eat –
    for he grants sleep to those he loves.

³ Children are a heritage from the LORD,
    offspring a reward from him.
⁴ Like arrows in the hands of a warrior
    are children born in one's youth.
⁵ Blessed is the man
    whose quiver is full of them.
They will not be put to shame
    when they contend with their
        opponents in court.

PROVERBS 28:4-5

⁴ Those who forsake instruction praise
    the wicked,
but those who heed it resist them.

⁵ Evildoers do not understand what is
    right,
but those who seek the LORD
    understand it fully.

JAMES 2:18–3:12

¹⁸ But someone will say, 'You have faith; I have deeds.'

Show me your faith without deeds, and I will show you my faith by my deeds. ¹⁹ You believe that there is one God. Good! Even the demons believe that – and shudder.

²⁰ You foolish person, do you want evidence that faith without deeds is useless? ²¹ Was not our father Abraham considered righteous for what he did when he offered his son Isaac on the altar? ²² You see that his faith and his actions were working together, and his faith was made complete by what he did. ²³ And the scripture was fulfilled that says, 'Abraham believed God, and it was credited to him as righteousness,' and he was called God's friend. ²⁴ You see that a person is considered righteous by what they do and not by faith alone.

²⁵ In the same way, was not even Rahab the prostitute considered righteous for what she did when she gave lodging to the spies and sent them off in a different direction? ²⁶ As the body without the spirit is dead, so faith without deeds is dead.

3 Not many of you should become teachers, my fellow believers, because you know that we who teach will be judged more strictly. ² We all stumble in many ways. Anyone who is never at fault in what they say is perfect, able to keep their whole body in check.

³ When we put bits into the mouths of horses to make them obey us, we can turn the whole animal. ⁴ Or take ships as an example. Although they are so large and are driven by strong winds, they are steered by a very small rudder wherever the pilot wants to go. ⁵ Likewise, the tongue is a small part of the body, but it makes great boasts. Consider what a great forest is set on fire by a small spark. ⁶ The tongue also is a fire, a world of evil among the parts of the body. It corrupts the whole body, sets the whole course of one's life on fire, and is itself set on fire by hell.

⁷ All kinds of animals, birds, reptiles and sea creatures are being tamed and have been tamed by mankind, ⁸ but no human being can tame the tongue. It is a restless evil, full of deadly poison.

⁹ With the tongue we praise our Lord and Father, and with it we curse human beings, who have been made in God's likeness. ¹⁰ Out of the same mouth come praise

and cursing. My brothers and sisters, this should not be. ¹¹Can both fresh water and salt water flow from the same spring? ¹²My brothers and sisters, can a fig-tree bear olives, or a grapevine bear figs? Neither can a salt spring produce fresh water.

This God Is Your God

'Will your courage endure or your hands be strong in the day I deal with you?' **Ezekiel 22:14**

God is powerful in judgment. When He smites, none can resist Him. The flood of Noah's day is one such example, when the entire race - with the exception of eight people - was swept away (Gen. 6:1-9:18). When a shower of fire and brimstone fell from heaven on Sodom and Gomorrah, all the cities of the plain were destroyed (Gen. 19:1-29). Pharaoh and his hosts found themselves impotent when God blew upon them at the Red Sea (Exod. 14:1-31).

What does the contemplation of God's power do for us?

First, it causes us to tremble before Him. The trouble with many modern men and women is that they do not tremble before God. To treat with impudence the One who can crush us more easily than we can a tiny ant is, as someone put it, 'a suicidal policy'. 'Kiss his son,' said the psalmist, 'or he will be angry and your way will lead to your destruction, for his wrath can flare up in a moment' (Psa. 2:12).

Second, contemplating God's great power causes us to adore Him. Who can consider the might of this awesome God without wanting to worship Him? The rebellious heart will resist this, but the heart cleansed by the blood of Christ will bow in homage and say: 'Who is like you – majestic in holiness, awesome in glory, working wonders?' (Exod. 15:11). No prayer is too hard for Him to answer, no need too great for Him to supply, no predicament too great for Him to solve. Lay hold on this great and gripping truth: this God is your God.

PRAYER

O Father, I see that contemplation of You tilts my soul in Your direction. I realise that without You I am nothing. May I tremble before You until my trembling turns to adoration and ever-increasing trust. Amen.

FURTHER STUDY

Psa. 114:1-8;
1 Chron. 16:30-31; Isa. 66:1-3
• What can the presence of the Lord do?
• Who does the Lord esteem?

November 22

23 The word of the LORD came to me: ²'Son of man, there were two women, daughters of the same mother. ³They became prostitutes in Egypt, engaging in prostitution from their youth. In that land their breasts were fondled and their virgin bosoms caressed. ⁴The elder one was named Oholah, and her sister was Oholibah. They were mine and gave birth to sons and daughters. Oholah is Samaria, and Oholibah is Jerusalem.

⁵'Oholah engaged in prostitution while she was still mine; and she lusted after her lovers, the Assyrians – warriors ⁶clothed in blue, governors and commanders, all of them handsome young men, and mounted horsemen. ⁷She gave herself as a prostitute to all the elite of the Assyrians and defiled herself with all the idols of everyone she lusted after. ⁸She did not give up the prostitution she began in Egypt, when during her youth men slept with her, caressed her virgin bosom and poured out their lust on her.

⁹'Therefore I delivered her into the hands of her lovers, the Assyrians, for whom she lusted. ¹⁰They stripped her naked, took away her sons and daughters and killed her with the sword. She became a byword among women, and punishment was inflicted on her.

¹¹'Her sister Oholibah saw this, yet in her lust and prostitution she was more depraved than her sister. ¹²She too lusted after the Assyrians – governors and commanders, warriors in full dress, mounted horsemen, all handsome young men. ¹³I saw that she too defiled herself; both of them went the same way.

¹⁴'But she carried her prostitution still further. She saw men portrayed on a wall, figures of Chaldeans portrayed in red, ¹⁵with belts round their waists and flowing turbans on their heads; all of them looked like Babylonian chariot officers, natives of Chaldea. ¹⁶As soon as she saw them, she lusted after them and sent messengers to them in Chaldea. ¹⁷Then the Babylonians came to her, to the bed of love, and in their lust they defiled her. After she had been defiled by them, she turned away from them in disgust. ¹⁸When she carried on her prostitution openly and exposed her naked body, I turned away from her in disgust, just as I had turned away from her sister. ¹⁹Yet she became more and more promiscuous as she recalled the days of her youth, when she was a prostitute in Egypt. ²⁰There she lusted after her lovers, whose genitals were like those of donkeys and whose emission was like that of horses. ²¹So you longed for the lewdness of your youth, when in Egypt your bosom was caressed and your young breasts fondled.

²²'Therefore, Oholibah, this is what the Sovereign LORD says: I will stir up your lovers against you, those you turned away from in disgust, and I will bring them against you from every side – ²³the Babylonians and all the Chaldeans, the men of Pekod and Shoa and Koa, and all the Assyrians with them, handsome young men, all of them governors and commanders, chariot officers and men of high rank, all mounted on horses. ²⁴They will come against you with weapons, chariots and wagons and with a throng of people; they will take up positions against you on every side with large and small shields and with helmets.

I will turn you over to them for punishment, and they will punish you according to their standards. ²⁵ I will direct my jealous anger against you, and they will deal with you in fury. They will cut off your noses and your ears, and those of you who are left will fall by the sword. They will take away your sons and daughters, and those of you who are left will be consumed by fire. ²⁶ They will also strip you of your clothes and take your fine jewellery. ²⁷ So I will put a stop to the lewdness and prostitution you began in Egypt. You will not look on these things with longing or remember Egypt any more.

²⁸ 'For this is what the Sovereign LORD says: I am about to deliver you into the hands of those you hate, to those you turned away from in disgust. ²⁹ They will deal with you in hatred and take away everything you have worked for. They will leave you stark naked, and the shame of your prostitution will be exposed. Your lewdness and promiscuity ³⁰ have brought this on you, because you lusted after the nations and defiled yourself with their idols. ³¹ You have gone the way of your sister; so I will put her cup into your hand.

³² 'This is what the Sovereign LORD says:

'You will drink your sister's cup,
    a cup large and deep;
it will bring scorn and derision,
    for it holds so much.
³³ You will be filled with drunkenness and
    sorrow,
    the cup of ruin and desolation,
    the cup of your sister Samaria.
³⁴ You will drink it and drain it dry
    and chew on its pieces –
    and you will tear your breasts.

I have spoken, declares the Sovereign LORD.

³⁵ 'Therefore this is what the Sovereign LORD says: since you have forgotten me and turned your back on me, you must bear the consequences of your lewdness and prostitution.'

³⁶ The LORD said to me: 'Son of man, will you judge Oholah and Oholibah? Then confront them with their detestable practices, ³⁷ for they have committed adultery and blood is on their hands. They committed adultery with their idols; they even sacrificed their children, whom they bore to me, as food for them. ³⁸ They have also done this to me: at that same time they defiled my sanctuary and desecrated my Sabbaths. ³⁹ On the very day they sacrificed their children to their idols, they entered my sanctuary and desecrated it. That is what they did in my house.

⁴⁰ 'They even sent messengers for men who came from far away, and when they arrived you bathed yourself for them, applied eye makeup and put on your jewellery. ⁴¹ You sat on an elegant couch, with a table spread before it on which you had placed the incense and olive oil that belonged to me.

⁴² 'The noise of a carefree crowd was around her; drunkards were brought from the desert along with men from the rabble, and they put bracelets on the wrists of the woman and her sister and beautiful crowns on their heads. ⁴³ Then I said about the one worn out by adultery, "Now let them use her as a prostitute, for that is all she is." ⁴⁴ And they slept with her. As men sleep with a prostitute, so they slept with those lewd women, Oholah and Oholibah. ⁴⁵ But righteous judges will sentence them to the punishment of women who commit adultery and shed blood, because they are adulterous and blood is on their hands.

⁴⁶ 'This is what the Sovereign LORD says: bring a mob against them and give them over to terror and plunder. ⁴⁷ The mob will stone them and cut them down with their swords; they will kill their sons and daughters and burn down their houses.

⁴⁸ 'So I will put an end to lewdness in the land, that all women may take warning and

not imitate you. [49] You will suffer the penalty for your lewdness and bear the consequences of your sins of idolatry. Then you will know that I am the Sovereign LORD.'

24 In the ninth year, in the tenth month on the tenth day, the word of the Lord came to me: [2] 'Son of man, record this date, this very date, because the king of Babylon has laid siege to Jerusalem this very day. [3] Tell this rebellious people a parable and say to them: "This is what the Sovereign Lord says:

' "Put on the cooking pot; put it on
     and pour water into it.
[4] Put into it the pieces of meat,
     all the choice pieces – the leg and the
        shoulder.
Fill it with the best of these bones;
[5]   take the pick of the flock.
Pile wood beneath it for the bones;
     bring it to the boil
     and cook the bones in it.

PSALM 128:1-6

[1] Blessed are all who fear the LORD,
     who walk in obedience to him.
[2] You will eat the fruit of your labour;
     blessings and prosperity will be yours.
[3] Your wife will be like a fruitful vine
     within your house;
your children will be like olive shoots
     round your table.
[4] Yes, this will be the blessing
     for the man who fears the LORD.

[5] May the LORD bless you from Zion;
     may you see the prosperity of
        Jerusalem
all the days of your life.
[6] May you live to see your children's
        children –
     peace be on Israel.

PROVERBS 28:6-8

[6] Better the poor whose way of life is
        blameless
     than the rich whose ways are perverse.

[7] A discerning son heeds instruction,
     but a companion of gluttons disgraces
        his father.

[8] Whoever increases wealth by taking
        interest or profit from the poor
     amasses it for another, who will be
        kind to the poor.

JAMES 3:13–4:17

[13] Who is wise and understanding among you? Let them show it by their good life, by deeds done in the humility that comes from wisdom. [14] But if you harbour bitter envy and selfish ambition in your hearts, do not boast about it or deny the truth. [15] Such 'wisdom' does not come down from heaven but is earthly, unspiritual, demonic. [16] For where you have envy and selfish ambition, there you find disorder and every evil practice.

[17] But the wisdom that comes from heaven is first of all pure; then peace-loving, considerate, submissive, full of mercy and good fruit, impartial and sincere. [18] Peacemakers who sow in peace reap a harvest of righteousness.

4 What causes fights and quarrels among you? Don't they come from your desires that battle within you? [2] You desire but do not have, so you kill. You covet but you cannot get what you want, so you quarrel and fight. You do not have because you do not ask God. [3] When you ask, you do not receive, because you ask with wrong motives, that you may spend what you get on your pleasures.

[4] You adulterous people, don't you know that friendship with the world means

enmity against God? Therefore, anyone who chooses to be a friend of the world becomes an enemy of God. ⁵Or do you think Scripture says without reason that he jealously longs for the spirit he has caused to dwell in us? ⁶But he gives us more grace. That is why Scripture says:

'God opposes the proud
but shows favour to the humble.'

⁷Submit yourselves, then, to God. Resist the devil, and he will flee from you. ⁸Come near to God and he will come near to you. Wash your hands, you sinners, and purify your hearts, you double-minded. ⁹Grieve, mourn and wail. Change your laughter to mourning and your joy to gloom. ¹⁰Humble yourselves before the Lord, and he will lift you up.

¹¹Brothers and sisters, do not slander one another. Anyone who speaks against a brother or sister or judges them speaks against the law and judges it. When you judge the law, you are not keeping it, but sitting in judgment on it. ¹²There is only one Lawgiver and Judge, the one who is able to save and destroy. But you – who are you to judge your neighbour?

¹³Now listen, you who say, 'Today or tomorrow we will go to this or that city, spend a year there, carry on business and make money.' ¹⁴Why, you do not even know what will happen tomorrow. What is your life? You are a mist that appears for a little while and then vanishes. ¹⁵Instead, you ought to say, 'If it is the Lord's will, we will live and do this or that.' ¹⁶As it is, you boast in your arrogant schemes. All such boasting is evil. ¹⁷If anyone, then, knows the good they ought to do and doesn't do it, it is sin for them.

'Nearer My God to Thee'

'Come near to God and he will come near to you.'
James 4:8

The final two verses of Psalm 73 form a conclusion and a resolution. Listen to them here: 'Those who are far from you will perish; you destroy all who are unfaithful to you. But as for me, it is good to be near God. I have made the Sovereign LORD my refuge; I will tell of all your deeds' (vv. 27-28). The psalmist has finished his review of the past and is now hammering out a philosophy with which to face the future. He is resolved that no matter what anyone else may do, he is going to live in close companionship with God. He helps us to see the importance of this resolution by putting it in the form of a contrast: 'Those who are far from you will perish ... But as for me, it is good to be near God.'

Really, when it comes down to it, there are only two positions in life – close to God or far away from Him. I wonder, as the psalmist penned these words, was something like this going through his mind, 'What caused me so much trouble in recent days and accounted for all my difficulties was the fact that I did not keep close to God. I erroneously believed that the cause of my problems was the prosperity of the ungodly, but having entered into the sanctuary of God I see that this was not the cause of my problems at all. My problems came because I had chosen not to remain close to Him. For me there is now only one thing that matters – staying close to God.'

How are things with you at this moment? Do you feel close to God? If you don't, then let me put what I want to say in the words of a wayside pulpit that arrested my attention some years ago: 'If you feel that God is far away, guess who moved?'

PRAYER

Father, I am grateful for the promise of Your Word to me today that when I draw near to You, You will draw near to me. Help me put those words to the test by moving closer to You than I have ever done before. In Jesus' name. Amen.

FURTHER STUDY

Psa. 46:1-11; 2 Sam. 22:3; Psa. 9:9; Psa. 62:1-12
• What does the psalmist affirm?
• What does the psalmist exhort the people?

November 23

■ EZEKIEL 24:6–26:6

6 "For this is what the Sovereign LORD says:

'"Woe to the city of bloodshed,
to the pot now encrusted,
whose deposit will not go away!
Take the meat out piece by piece
in whatever order it comes.

7 "'For the blood she shed is in her midst:
She poured it on the bare rock;
she did not pour it on the ground,
where the dust would cover it.
8 To stir up wrath and take revenge
I put her blood on the bare rock,
so that it would not be covered.

9 "'Therefore this is what the Sovereign LORD says:

'"Woe to the city of bloodshed!
I, too, will pile the wood high.
10 So heap on the wood
and kindle the fire.

Cook the meat well,
mixing in the spices;
and let the bones be charred.
11 Then set the empty pot on the coals
till it becomes hot and its copper
glows,
so that its impurities may be melted
and its deposit burned away.
12 It has frustrated all efforts;
its heavy deposit has not been
removed,
not even by fire.

13 "'Now your impurity is lewdness. Because I tried to cleanse you but you would not be cleansed from your impurity, you will not be clean again until my wrath against you has subsided.

14 "'I the LORD have spoken. The time has come for me to act. I will not hold back; I will not have pity, nor will I relent. You will be judged according to your conduct and your actions, declares the Sovereign LORD.'"

¹⁵ The word of the Lord came to me: ¹⁶ 'Son of man, with one blow I am about to take away from you the delight of your eyes. Yet do not lament or weep or shed any tears. ¹⁷ Groan quietly; do not mourn for the dead. Keep your turban fastened and your sandals on your feet; do not cover your moustache and beard or eat the customary food of mourners.'

¹⁸ So I spoke to the people in the morning, and in the evening my wife died. The next morning I did as I had been commanded.

¹⁹ Then the people asked me, 'Won't you tell us what these things have to do with us? Why are you acting like this?'

²⁰ So I said to them, 'The word of the LORD came to me: ²¹ say to the people of Israel, "This is what the Sovereign LORD says: I am about to desecrate my sanctuary – the stronghold in which you take pride, the delight of your eyes, the object of your affection. The sons and daughters you left behind will fall by the sword. ²² And you will do as I have done. You will not cover your moustache and beard or eat the customary food of mourners. ²³ You will keep your turbans on your heads and your sandals on your feet. You will not mourn or weep but will waste away because of your sins and groan among yourselves. ²⁴ Ezekiel will be a sign to you; you will do just as he has done. When this happens, you will know that I am the Sovereign LORD."

²⁵ 'And you, son of man, on the day I take away their stronghold, their joy and glory, the delight of their eyes, their heart's desire, and their sons and daughters as well – ²⁶ on that day a fugitive will come to tell you the news. ²⁷ At that time your mouth will be opened; you will speak with him and will no longer be silent. So you will be a sign to them, and they will know that I am the LORD.'

25 The word of the Lord came to me: ² 'Son of man, set your face against the Ammonites and prophesy against them. ³ Say to them, "Hear the word of the Sovereign LORD. This is what the Sovereign Lord says: because you said 'Aha!' over my sanctuary when it was desecrated and over the land of Israel when it was laid waste and over the people of Judah when they went into exile, ⁴ therefore I am going to give you to the people of the East as a possession. They will set up their camps and pitch their tents among you; they will eat your fruit and drink your milk. ⁵ I will turn Rabbah into a pasture for camels and Ammon into a resting place for sheep. Then you will know that I am the Lord. ⁶ For this is what the Sovereign Lord says: because you have clapped your hands and stamped your feet, rejoicing with all the malice of your heart against the land of Israel, ⁷ therefore I will stretch out my hand against you and give you as plunder to the nations. I will wipe you out from among the nations and exterminate you from the countries. I will destroy you, and you will know that I am the Lord."'

⁸ 'This is what the Sovereign Lord says: "Because Moab and Seir said, 'Look, Judah has become like all the other nations,' ⁹ therefore I will expose the flank of Moab, beginning at its frontier towns – Beth Jeshimoth, Baal Meon and Kiriathaim – the glory of that land. ¹⁰ I will give Moab along with the Ammonites to the people of the East as a possession, so that the Ammonites will not be remembered among the nations; ¹¹ and I will inflict punishment on Moab. Then they will know that I am the Lord."'

¹² 'This is what the Sovereign Lord says: "Because Edom took revenge on Judah and became very guilty by doing so, ¹³ therefore this is what the Sovereign Lord says: I will stretch out my hand against Edom and kill both man and beast. I will lay it waste, and from Teman to Dedan they will fall by the sword. ¹⁴ I will take vengeance on Edom by

the hand of my people Israel, and they will deal with Edom in accordance with my anger and my wrath; they will know my vengeance, declares the Sovereign Lord."'

¹⁵'This is what the Sovereign LORD says: "Because the Philistines acted in vengeance and took revenge with malice in their hearts, and with ancient hostility sought to destroy Judah, ¹⁶therefore this is what the Sovereign LORD says: I am about to stretch out my hand against the Philistines, and I will wipe out the Kerethites and destroy those remaining along the coast. ¹⁷I will carry out great vengeance on them and punish them in my wrath. Then they will know that I am the LORD, when I take vengeance on them."'

26 In the eleventh month of the twelfth year, on the first day of the month, the word of the Lord came to me: ²'Son of man, because Tyre has said of Jerusalem, "Aha! The gate to the nations is broken, and its doors have swung open to me; now that she lies in ruins I will prosper," ³therefore this is what the Sovereign Lord says: I am against you, Tyre, and I will bring many nations against you, like the sea casting up its waves. ⁴They will destroy the walls of Tyre and pull down her towers; I will scrape away her rubble and make her a bare rock. ⁵Out in the sea she will become a place to spread fishing nets, for I have spoken, declares the Sovereign Lord. She will become plunder for the nations, ⁶and her settlements on the mainland will be ravaged by the sword. Then they will know that I am the Lord.

▬ PSALM 129:1-8

¹'They have greatly oppressed me from
  my youth,'
  let Israel say;
²'they have greatly oppressed me from
  youth,

but they have not gained the victory
  over me.
³Ploughmen have ploughed my back
  and made their furrows long.
⁴But the LORD is righteous;
  he has cut me free from the cords of
  the wicked.'

⁵May all who hate Zion
  be turned back in shame.
⁶May they be like grass on the roof,
  which withers before it can grow;
⁷a reaper cannot fill his hands with it,
  nor one who gathers fill his arms.
⁸May those who pass by not say to them,
  'The blessing of the LORD be on you;
  we bless you in the name of the LORD.'

▬ PROVERBS 28:9-11

⁹If anyone turns a deaf ear to my
  instruction,
  even their prayers are detestable.

¹⁰Whoever leads the upright along an evil
  path
  will fall into their own trap,
  but the blameless will receive a good
  inheritance.

¹¹The rich are wise in their own eyes;
  one who is poor and discerning sees
  how deluded they are.

▬ JAMES 5:1-20

5 Now listen, you rich people, weep and wail because of the misery that is coming on you. ²Your wealth has rotted, and moths have eaten your clothes. ³Your gold and silver are corroded. Their corrosion will testify against you and eat your flesh like fire. You have hoarded wealth in the last days. ⁴Look! The wages you failed to pay the

workers who mowed your fields are crying out against you. The cries of the harvesters have reached the ears of the Lord Almighty. [5] You have lived on earth in luxury and self-indulgence. You have fattened yourselves in the day of slaughter. [6] You have condemned and murdered the innocent one, who was not opposing you.

[7] Be patient, then, brothers and sisters, until the Lord's coming. See how the farmer waits for the land to yield its valuable crop, patiently waiting for the autumn and spring rains. [8] You too, be patient and stand firm, because the Lord's coming is near. [9] Don't grumble against one another, brothers and sisters, or you will be judged. The Judge is standing at the door!

[10] Brothers and sisters, as an example of patience in the face of suffering, take the prophets who spoke in the name of the Lord. [11] As you know, we count as blessed those who have persevered. You have heard of Job's perseverance and have seen what the Lord finally brought about. The Lord is full of compassion and mercy.

[12] Above all, my brothers and sisters, do not swear – not by heaven or by earth or by anything else. All you need to say is a simple 'Yes' or 'No'. Otherwise you will be condemned.

[13] Is anyone among you in trouble? Let them pray. Is anyone happy? Let them sing songs of praise. [14] Is anyone among you ill? Let them call the elders of the church to pray over them and anoint them with oil in the name of the Lord. [15] And the prayer offered in faith will make the sick person well; the Lord will raise them up. If they have sinned, they will be forgiven. [16] Therefore confess your sins to each other and pray for each other so that you may be healed. The prayer of a righteous person is powerful and effective.

[17] Elijah was a human being, even as we are. He prayed earnestly that it would not rain, and it did not rain on the land for three and a half years. [18] Again he prayed, and the heavens gave rain, and the earth produced its crops.

[19] My brothers and sisters, if one of you should wander from the truth and someone should bring that person back, [20] remember this: whoever turns a sinner from the error of their way will save them from death and cover over a multitude of sins.

Down, but Not Out

'... they have greatly oppressed me from my youth, but they have not gained the victory over me.' **Psalm 129:2**

The opening verses of this psalm spell out the simple but powerful message that though the world has always harassed the people of God, the world will never win. '... they have greatly oppressed me from my youth' says the psalmist, 'but they have not gained the victory over me.' The man or woman who clings closely to God outlasts all oppressors. He or she is provided with an inner fortitude that is enduring. Perseverance, patience, stickability – this then is the message of Psalm 129.

There is no better way of seeing the persistency of faith than by setting it in the context of history. God's people have been ostracised, ridiculed, humiliated, scorned, persecuted and beaten, but in the midst of the most horrific trials they have continued to serve God. If the persistence that flows from faith was merely a fad, then we would not be talking about it now.

Faith – persistent faith, that is – is not a fad; it is a fact. It runs like a thread throughout all history and is shared by the men and women of every generation. Those who think of the Christian faith as a plant that flourishes only in good weather ought to take a look at history.

Faith is a hardy perennial that survives all weather conditions – drought, storm, even floods. J. B. Phillips, in his brilliant paraphrase of the New Testament, sums it up admirably: 'We may be knocked down but we are never knocked out!' (2 Cor. 4:9). A preacher friend of mine puts it equally well when he says, 'We may be floored but we are not flattened'.

PRAYER

Gracious Father, help me see that my perseverance is not so much a matter of my persevering but Your persevering in me. I supply the willingness; You supply the power. Together we will make it, You and I. All glory be to Your wonderful name. Amen.

FURTHER STUDY

James 1:1-27; 5:1-11; Gal. 6:9; Heb. 12:1
• What is Paul's exhortation?
• What will enable us to persevere?

November 24

■ EZEKIEL 26:7–27:36

[7] 'For this is what the Sovereign LORD says: from the north I am going to bring against Tyre Nebuchadnezzar king of Babylon, king of kings, with horses and chariots, with horsemen and a great army. [8] He will ravage your settlements on the mainland with the sword; he will set up siege works against you, build a ramp up to your walls and raise his shields against you. [9] He will direct the blows of his battering-rams against your walls and demolish your towers with his weapons. [10] His horses will be so many that they will cover you with dust. Your walls will tremble at the noise of the war horses, wagons and chariots when he enters your gates as men enter a city whose walls have been broken through. [11] The hooves of his horses will trample all your streets; he will kill your people with the sword, and your strong pillars will fall to the ground. [12] They will plunder your wealth and loot your merchandise; they will break down your walls and demolish your fine houses and throw your stones, timber and rubble into the sea. [13] I will put an end to your noisy songs, and the music of your harps will be heard no more. [14] I will make you a bare rock, and you will become a place to spread fishing nets. You will never be rebuilt, for I the LORD have spoken, declares the Sovereign LORD.

[15] 'This is what the Sovereign LORD says to Tyre: will not the coastlands tremble at the sound of your fall, when the wounded groan and the slaughter takes place in you? [16] Then all the princes of the coast will step down from their thrones and lay aside their robes and take off their embroidered garments. Clothed with terror, they will sit on the ground, trembling every moment, appalled at you. [17] Then they will take up a lament concerning you and say to you:

'"How you are destroyed, city of renown,
  peopled by men of the sea!
You were a power on the seas,
  you and your citizens;
you put your terror
  on all who lived there.
18 Now the coastlands tremble
  on the day of your fall;
the islands in the sea
  are terrified at your collapse."

19 'This is what the Sovereign LORD says:
when I make you a desolate city, like cities
no longer inhabited, and when I bring the
ocean depths over you and its vast waters
cover you, 20 then I will bring you down with
those who go down to the pit, to the people
of long ago. I will make you dwell in the
earth below, as in ancient ruins, with those
who go down to the pit, and you will not return or take your place in the land of the living. 21 I will bring you to a horrible end and
you will be no more. You will be sought, but
you will never again be found, declares the
Sovereign LORD.'

27 The word of the Lord came to me:
    2 'Son of man, take up a lament con-
cerning Tyre. 3 Say to Tyre, situated at the
gateway to the sea, merchant of peoples on
many coasts, "This is what the Sovereign
Lord says:

'"You say, Tyre,
  'I am perfect in beauty.'
4 Your domain was on the high seas;
  your builders brought your beauty to
    perfection.
5 They made all your timbers
  of juniper from Senir;
they took a cedar from Lebanon
  to make a mast for you.
6 Of oaks from Bashan
  they made your oars;
of cypress wood from the coasts of
  Cyprus

they made your deck, adorned with
  ivory.
7 Fine embroidered linen from Egypt was
  your sail
and served as your banner;
your awnings were of blue and purple
  from the coasts of Elishah.
8 Men of Sidon and Arvad were your
  oarsmen;
your skilled men, Tyre, were aboard as
  your sailors.
9 Veteran craftsmen of Byblos were on
  board
  as shipwrights to caulk your seams.
All the ships of the sea and their sailors
  came alongside to trade for your wares.

10 '"Men of Persia, Lydia and Put
  served as soldiers in your army.
They hung their shields and helmets on
  your walls,
  bringing you splendour.
11 Men of Arvad and Helek
  guarded your walls on every side;
men of Gammad
  were in your towers.
They hung their shields around your
  walls;
  they brought your beauty to perfection.

12 '"Tarshish did business with you because of your great wealth of goods; they
exchanged silver, iron, tin and lead for your
merchandise.
13 '"Greece, Tubal and Meshek did business with you; they traded human beings
and articles of bronze for your wares.
14 '"Men of Beth Togarmah exchanged
chariot horses, cavalry horses and mules
for your merchandise.
15 '"The men of Rhodes traded with you,
and many coastlands were your customers;
they paid you with ivory tusks and ebony.
16 '"Aram did business with you because
of your many products; they exchanged
turquoise, purple fabric, embroidered

work, fine linen, coral and rubies for your merchandise.

¹⁷ "Judah and Israel traded with you; they exchanged wheat from Minnith and confections, honey, olive oil and balm for your wares.

¹⁸ "Damascus did business with you because of your many products and great wealth of goods. They offered wine from Helbon, wool from Zahar ¹⁹and casks of wine from Izal in exchange for your wares: wrought iron, cassia and calamus.

²⁰ "Dedan traded in saddle blankets with you.

²¹ "Arabia and all the princes of Kedar were your customers; they did business with you in lambs, rams and goats.

²² "The merchants of Sheba and Raamah traded with you; for your merchandise they exchanged the finest of all kinds of spices and precious stones, and gold.

²³ "Harran, Kanneh and Eden and merchants of Sheba, Ashur and Kilmad traded with you. ²⁴In your market-place they traded with you beautiful garments, blue fabric, embroidered work and multicoloured rugs with cords twisted and tightly knotted.

²⁵ "The ships of Tarshish serve
as carriers for your wares.
You are filled with heavy cargo
as you sail the sea.
²⁶ Your oarsmen take you
out to the high seas.
But the east wind will break you to pieces
far out at sea.
²⁷ Your wealth, merchandise and wares,
your mariners, sailors and
shipwrights,
your merchants and all your soldiers,
and everyone else on board
will sink into the heart of the sea
on the day of your shipwreck.
²⁸ The shorelands will quake
when your sailors cry out.
²⁹ All who handle the oars

will abandon their ships;
the mariners and all the sailors
will stand on the shore.
³⁰ They will raise their voice
and cry bitterly over you;
they will sprinkle dust on their heads
and roll in ashes.
³¹ They will shave their heads because of
you
and will put on sackcloth.
They will weep over you with anguish of
soul
and with bitter mourning.
³² As they wail and mourn over you,
they will take up a lament concerning
you:
'Who was ever silenced like Tyre,
surrounded by the sea?'
³³ When your merchandise went out on the
seas,
you satisfied many nations;
with your great wealth and your wares
you enriched the kings of the earth.
³⁴ Now you are shattered by the sea
in the depths of the waters;
your wares and all your company
have gone down with you.
³⁵ All who live in the coastlands
are appalled at you;
their kings shudder with horror
and their faces are distorted with fear.
³⁶ The merchants among the nations scoff
at you;
you have come to a horrible end
and will be no more."'

··

▬ PSALM 130:1-8

¹ Out of the depths I cry to you, LORD;
² Lord, hear my voice.
Let your ears be attentive
to my cry for mercy.

³ If you, LORD, kept a record of sins,
Lord, who could stand?

[4] But with you there is forgiveness,
  so that we can, with reverence, serve
  you.

[5] I wait for the LORD, my whole being waits,
  and in his word I put my hope.
[6] I wait for the Lord
  more than watchmen wait for the
  morning,
  more than watchmen wait for the
  morning.

[7] Israel, put your hope in the LORD,
  for with the LORD is unfailing love
  and with him is full redemption.
[8] He himself will redeem Israel
  from all their sins.

■ PROVERBS 28:12–14

[12] When the righteous triumph, there is
  great elation;
  but when the wicked rise to power,
  people go into hiding.

[13] Whoever conceals their sins does not
  prosper,
  but the one who confesses and
  renounces them finds mercy.

[14] Blessed is the one who always trembles
  before God,
  but whoever hardens their heart falls
  into trouble.

■ 1 PETER 1:1–21

1 Peter, an apostle of Jesus Christ,

To God's elect, exiles, scattered throughout the provinces of Pontus, Galatia, Cappadocia, Asia and Bithynia, [2] who have been chosen according to the foreknowledge of God the Father, through the sanctifying work of the Spirit, to be obedient to Jesus Christ and sprinkled with his blood:

Grace and peace be yours in abundance.

[3] Praise be to the God and Father of our Lord Jesus Christ! In his great mercy he has given us new birth into a living hope through the resurrection of Jesus Christ from the dead, [4] and into an inheritance that can never perish, spoil or fade. This inheritance is kept in heaven for you, [5] who through faith are shielded by God's power until the coming of the salvation that is ready to be revealed in the last time. [6] In all this you greatly rejoice, though now for a little while you may have had to suffer grief in all kinds of trials. [7] These have come so that the proven genuineness of your faith – of greater worth than gold, which perishes even though refined by fire – may result in praise, glory and honour when Jesus Christ is revealed. [8] Though you have not seen him, you love him; and even though you do not see him now, you believe in him and are filled with an inexpressible and glorious joy, [9] for you are receiving the end result of your faith, the salvation of your souls.

[10] Concerning this salvation, the prophets, who spoke of the grace that was to come to you, searched intently and with the greatest care, [11] trying to find out the time and circumstances to which the Spirit of Christ in them was pointing when he predicted the sufferings of the Messiah and the glories that would follow. [12] It was revealed to them that they were not serving themselves but you, when they spoke of the things that have now been told you by those who have preached the gospel to you by the Holy Spirit sent from heaven. Even angels long to look into these things.

[13] Therefore, with minds that are alert and fully sober, set your hope on the grace to be brought to you when Jesus Christ is revealed at his coming. [14] As obedient children, do not conform to the evil desires you had when you lived in ignorance. [15] But just as he who called you is holy, so be holy in all

you do; [16] for it is written: 'Be holy, because I am holy.'

[17] Since you call on a Father who judges each person's work impartially, live out your time as foreigners here in reverent fear. [18] For you know that it was not with perishable things such as silver or gold that you were redeemed from the empty way of life handed down to you from your ancestors, [19] but with the precious blood of Christ, a lamb without blemish or defect. [20] He was chosen before the creation of the world, but was revealed in these last times for your sake. [21] Through him you believe in God, who raised him from the dead and glorified him, and so your faith and hope are in God.

Organising a Quiet Time

'I wait ... and in his word I put my hope. I wait for the Lord more than watchmen wait for morning ...'
Psalm 130:5-6

Someone has described a quiet time as 'turning the dial until we tune in to God's wavelength - then we get the message'. But how do we gain the best results from our quiet time?

First, decide on the amount of time you want to invest in waiting before God. Next, take your Bible and read a portion slowly. Let it soak in. If some words or verses strike you, focus on them in meditation. They will yield up new meanings to you. Write these down.

After the reading, let go, relax, and say to Him, 'Father, have You anything to say to me?' Learn to listen. All those who hear God's voice on a regular basis say that it is something they have had to develop over time and by experience. They pause, they wait, and they learn after a while to disentangle their own thoughts from what God is saying.

Then speak to God in prayer. And finally, thank Him for the answer. He always answers - whether it is 'yes', 'no', or 'wait'. His 'no' is just as much an answer as His 'yes' - sometimes even a better answer.

Not far from my home is the River Thames. Sometimes I walk along the river bank and watch small boats entering the locks from the adjoining rivers. To get into the Thames, these boats must enter the lock and wait there to be lifted up to a higher level. Our quiet time does that. It shuts us in with God. But then infinite resources begin to bubble up from below, and we are lifted silently and without strain onto a higher level. The lifting is the result of being shut in with God.

PRAYER

O Father, help me resolve to spend a quiet time with You every day. May my quiet time at this moment be the open door through which I glide out onto a higher level of life. In Jesus' name. Amen.

FURTHER STUDY

Psa. 130:1-8; 27:14; 37:7; 62:5; Isa. 30:18

- What do we often find the hardest thing to do?
- Take time out today to do this.

November 25

■ EZEKIEL 28:1–30:8

28 The word of the LORD came to me: ²'Son of man, say to the ruler of Tyre, "This is what the Sovereign LORD says:

'"In the pride of your heart
  you say, 'I am a god;
I sit on the throne of a god
  in the heart of the seas.'
But you are a mere mortal and not a god,
  though you think you are as wise as a
    god.
³ Are you wiser than Daniel?
  Is no secret hidden from you?
⁴ By your wisdom and understanding
  you have gained wealth for yourself
and amassed gold and silver
  in your treasuries.
⁵ By your great skill in trading
  you have increased your wealth,
and because of your wealth
  your heart has grown proud.

⁶ '"Therefore this is what the Sovereign LORD says:

'"Because you think you are wise,
  as wise as a god,
⁷ I am going to bring foreigners against you,
  the most ruthless of nations;
they will draw their swords against your
    beauty and wisdom
  and pierce your shining splendour.
⁸ They will bring you down to the pit,
  and you will die a violent death
  in the heart of the seas.
⁹ Will you then say, 'I am a god,'
  in the presence of those who kill you?
You will be but a mortal, not a god,
  in the hands of those who slay you.

¹⁰ You will die the death of the
    uncircumcised
  at the hands of foreigners.

I have spoken, declares the Sovereign LORD."'

¹¹ The word of the LORD came to me: ¹²'Son of man, take up a lament concerning the king of Tyre and say to him: "This is what the Sovereign LORD says:

'"You were the seal of perfection,
  full of wisdom and perfect in beauty.
¹³ You were in Eden,
  the garden of God;
every precious stone adorned you:
  carnelian, chrysolite and emerald,
  topaz, onyx and jasper,
  lapis lazuli, turquoise and beryl.
Your settings and mountings were made
  of gold;
on the day you were created they were
    prepared.
¹⁴ You were anointed as a guardian cherub,
  for so I ordained you.
You were on the holy mount of God;
  you walked among the fiery stones.
¹⁵ You were blameless in your ways
  from the day you were created
  till wickedness was found in you.
¹⁶ Through your widespread trade
  you were filled with violence,
  and you sinned.
So I drove you in disgrace from the
    mount of God,
  and I expelled you, guardian cherub,
  from among the fiery stones.
¹⁷ Your heart became proud
  on account of your beauty,
  and you corrupted your wisdom

because of your splendour.
So I threw you to the earth;
 I made a spectacle of you before kings.
¹⁸ By your many sins and dishonest trade
 you have desecrated your sanctuaries.
So I made a fire come out from you,
 and it consumed you,
and I reduced you to ashes on the ground
 in the sight of all who were watching.
¹⁹ All the nations who knew you
 are appalled at you;
you have come to a horrible end
 and will be no more.'"

²⁰ The word of the Lord came to me:
²¹ 'Son of man, set your face against Sidon;
prophesy against her ²²and say: "This is
what the Sovereign Lord says:

'"I am against you, Sidon,
 and among you I will display my glory.
You will know that I am the LORD,
 when I inflict punishment on you
 and within you am proved to be holy.
²³ I will send a plague upon you
 and make blood flow in your streets.
The slain will fall within you,
 with the sword against you on every side.
Then you will know that I am the LORD.

²⁴ '"No longer will the people of Israel
have malicious neighbours who are painful briers and sharp thorns. Then they will
know that I am the Sovereign LORD.
²⁵ ' "This is what the Sovereign LORD says:
when I gather the people of Israel from the
nations where they have been scattered,
I will be proved holy through them in the
sight of the nations. Then they will live in
their own land, which I gave to my servant
Jacob. ²⁶ They will live there in safety and
will build houses and plant vineyards; they
will live in safety when I inflict punishment on all their neighbours who maligned
them. Then they will know that I am the
LORD their God."'

29 In the tenth year, in the tenth
month on the twelfth day, the word
of the Lord came to me: ² 'Son of man, set
your face against Pharaoh king of Egypt
and prophesy against him and against all
Egypt. ³ Speak to him and say: "This is what
the Sovereign Lord says:

'"I am against you, Pharaoh king of
 Egypt,
you great monster lying among your
 streams.
You say, 'The Nile belongs to me;
 I made it for myself.'
⁴ But I will put hooks in your jaws
 and make the fish of your streams
 stick to your scales.
I will pull you out from among your
 streams,
 with all the fish sticking to your scales.
⁵ I will leave you in the desert,
 you and all the fish of your streams.
You will fall on the open field
 and not be gathered or picked up.
I will give you as food
 to the beasts of the earth and the birds
 of the sky.

⁶ Then all who live in Egypt will know that I
am the LORD.

'"You have been a staff of reed for the people of Israel. ⁷ When they grasped you with
their hands, you splintered and you tore open
their shoulders; when they leaned on you,
you broke and their backs were wrenched.

⁸ '"Therefore this is what the Sovereign
LORD says: I will bring a sword against you
and kill both man and beast. ⁹ Egypt will
become a desolate wasteland. Then they
will know that I am the LORD.

'"Because you said, 'The Nile is mine; I
made it,' ¹⁰ therefore I am against you and
against your streams, and I will make the
land of Egypt a ruin and a desolate waste
from Migdol to Aswan, as far as the border

of Cush. ¹¹The foot of neither man nor beast will pass through it; no one will live there for forty years. ¹²I will make the land of Egypt desolate among devastated lands, and her cities will lie desolate for forty years among ruined cities. And I will disperse the Egyptians among the nations and scatter them through the countries.

¹³ "'Yet this is what the Sovereign LORD says: at the end of forty years I will gather the Egyptians from the nations where they were scattered. ¹⁴I will bring them back from captivity and return them to Upper Egypt, the land of their ancestry. There they will be a lowly kingdom. ¹⁵It will be the lowliest of kingdoms and will never again exalt itself above the other nations. I will make it so weak that it will never again rule over the nations. ¹⁶Egypt will no longer be a source of confidence for the people of Israel but will be a reminder of their sin in turning to her for help. Then they will know that I am the Sovereign LORD.'"

¹⁷In the twenty-seventh year, in the first month on the first day, the word of the LORD came to me: ¹⁸'Son of man, Nebuchadnezzar king of Babylon drove his army in a hard campaign against Tyre; every head was rubbed bare and every shoulder made raw. Yet he and his army got no reward from the campaign he led against Tyre. ¹⁹Therefore this is what the Sovereign LORD says: I am going to give Egypt to Nebuchadnezzar king of Babylon, and he will carry off its wealth. He will loot and plunder the land as pay for his army. ²⁰I have given him Egypt as a reward for his efforts because he and his army did it for me, declares the Sovereign LORD. ²¹'On that day I will make a horn grow for the Israelites, and I will open your mouth among them. Then they will know that I am the LORD.'

30 The word of the LORD came to me: ²'Son of man, prophesy and say:

"This is what the Sovereign LORD says:

"'Wail and say,
    'Alas for that day!'
³ For the day is near,
    the day of the LORD is near –
a day of clouds,
    a time of doom for the nations.
⁴ A sword will come against Egypt,
    and anguish will come upon Cush.
When the slain fall in Egypt,
    her wealth will be carried away
    and her foundations torn down.

⁵ Cush and Libya, Lydia and all Arabia, Kub and the people of the covenant land will fall by the sword along with Egypt.

⁶ "'This is what the LORD says:

"'The allies of Egypt will fall
    and her proud strength will fail.
From Migdol to Aswan
    they will fall by the sword within her,
        declares the Sovereign LORD.
⁷ "'They will be desolate
    among desolate lands,
and their cities will lie
    among ruined cities.
⁸ Then they will know that I am the LORD,
    when I set fire to Egypt
    and all her helpers are crushed.

─ **PSALM 131:1–132:5**

¹ My heart is not proud, LORD,
    my eyes are not haughty;
I do not concern myself with great matters
    or things too wonderful for me.
² But I have calmed and quietened myself,
    I am like a weaned child with its
        mother;
    like a weaned child I am content.

³ Israel, put your hope in the LORD
    both now and for evermore.

[1] LORD, remember David
  and all his self-denial.

[2] He swore an oath to the LORD,
  he made a vow to the Mighty One of
    Jacob:
[3] 'I will not enter my house
  or go to my bed,
[4] I will allow no sleep to my eyes
  or slumber to my eyelids,
[5] till I find a place for the LORD,
  a dwelling for the Mighty One of Jacob.'

▬ PROVERBS 28:15-18

[15] Like a roaring lion or a charging bear
  is a wicked ruler over a helpless
    people.

[16] A tyrannical ruler practises extortion,
  but one who hates ill-gotten gain will
    enjoy a long reign.

[17] Anyone tormented by the guilt of murder
  will seek refuge in the grave;
  let no one hold them back.

[18] The one whose way of life is blameless is
    kept safe,
  but the one whose ways are perverse
    will fall into the pit.

▬ 1 PETER 1:22–2:17

[22] Now that you have purified yourselves by obeying the truth so that you have sincere love for each other, love one another deeply, from the heart. [23] For you have been born again, not of perishable seed, but of imperishable, through the living and enduring word of God. [24] For,

  'All people are like grass,
    and all their glory is like the flowers of
      the field;
    the grass withers and the flowers fall,
[25]   but the word of the Lord endures for
        ever.'

And this is the word that was preached to you.

2 Therefore, rid yourselves of all malice and all deceit, hypocrisy, envy, and slander of every kind. [2] Like newborn babies, crave pure spiritual milk, so that by it you may grow up in your salvation, [3] now that you have tasted that the Lord is good.

[4] As you come to him, the living Stone – rejected by humans but chosen by God and precious to him – [5] you also, like living stones, are being built into a spiritual house to be a holy priesthood, offering spiritual sacrifices acceptable to God through Jesus Christ. [6] For in Scripture it says:

  'See, I lay a stone in Zion,
    a chosen and precious cornerstone,
  and the one who trusts in him
    will never be put to shame.'

[7] Now to you who believe, this stone is precious. But to those who do not believe,

  'The stone the builders rejected
    has become the cornerstone,'

[8] and,

  'A stone that causes people to stumble
    and a rock that makes them fall.'

They stumble because they disobey the message – which is also what they were destined for.

[9] But you are a chosen people, a royal priesthood, a holy nation, God's special possession, that you may declare the praises of him who called you out of darkness into his wonderful light. [10] Once you were

not a people, but now you are the people of God; once you had not received mercy, but now you have received mercy.

¹¹ Dear friends, I urge you, as foreigners and exiles, to abstain from sinful desires, which wage war against your soul. ¹² Live such good lives among the pagans that, though they accuse you of doing wrong, they may see your good deeds and glorify God on the day he visits us.

¹³ Submit yourselves for the Lord's sake to every human authority: whether to the emperor, as the supreme authority, ¹⁴ or to governors, who are sent by him to punish those who do wrong and to commend those who do right. ¹⁵ For it is God's will that by doing good you should silence the ignorant talk of foolish people. ¹⁶ Live as free people, but do not use your freedom as a cover-up for evil; live as God's slaves. ¹⁷ Show proper respect to everyone, love the family of believers, fear God, honour the emperor.

The Devil's Cleft Foot

'You were the seal of perfection, full of wisdom and perfect in beauty ... You were blameless in your ways from the day you were created ...' **Ezekiel 28:12,15**

New Christians often ask: just who is the devil, and where did he come from? The seventeenth-century poet John Donne wrote that there were two things he could not fathom: 'Where all the past years are, and who cleft the devil's foot.' The origin, existence, and activities of the devil have always been among man's most puzzling problems. The books of Isaiah and Ezekiel give us a very clear picture, however, of what someone has called 'The Rise and Fall of the Satanic Empire'.

Jesus said one day to His disciples, 'I saw Satan fall like lightning from heaven' (Luke 10:18). Before he was known as the devil, Satan was called Lucifer and was created as a perfect angelic being. The passages before us today show him to have been a beautiful and morally perfect being. 'You were the seal of perfection, full of wisdom and perfect in beauty ... You were blameless in your ways from the day you were created ...' (Ezek. 28:12,15).

Upright, beautiful, brilliant, and with an enormous capacity for achievement, the angel Lucifer was entrusted by God with the highest of all the offices in the interstellar universe: 'You were anointed as a guardian cherub ... You were on the holy mount of God' (Ezek. 28:14). In his heart, however, arose a rebellious thought: 'I will make myself like the Most High' (Isa. 14:14). Five times that phrase 'I will' is used in this passage. Those two little words – 'I will' – reveal what lies behind the awful blight of sin – a created will coming into conflict with the will of the Creator.

November 26

■ EZEKIEL 30:9–32:16

⁹ "On that day messengers will go out
from me in ships to frighten Cush out of
her complacency. Anguish will take hold
of them on the day of Egypt's doom, for it is
sure to come.

¹⁰ "This is what the Sovereign LORD says:

"'I will put an end to the hordes of Egypt
  by the hand of Nebuchadnezzar king
  of Babylon.
¹¹ He and his army – the most ruthless of
    nations –
  will be brought in to destroy the land.
They will draw their swords against
    Egypt
  and fill the land with the slain.
¹² I will dry up the waters of the Nile
  and sell the land to an evil nation;
by the hand of foreigners
  I will lay waste the land and
    everything in it.

I the LORD have spoken.

¹³ "This is what the Sovereign LORD says:

"'I will destroy the idols
  and put an end to the images in
    Memphis.

No longer will there be a prince in Egypt,
  and I will spread fear throughout the
    land.
¹⁴ I will lay waste Upper Egypt,
  set fire to Zoan
  and inflict punishment on Thebes.
¹⁵ I will pour out my wrath on Pelusium,
  the stronghold of Egypt,
  and wipe out the hordes of Thebes.
¹⁶ I will set fire to Egypt;
  Pelusium will writhe in agony.
Thebes will be taken by storm;
  Memphis will be in constant distress.
¹⁷ The young men of Heliopolis and Bubastis
  will fall by the sword,
  and the cities themselves will go into
    captivity.
¹⁸ Dark will be the day at Tahpanhes
  when I break the yoke of Egypt;
  there her proud strength will come to
    an end.
She will be covered with clouds,
  and her villages will go into captivity.
¹⁹ So I will inflict punishment on Egypt,
  and they will know that I am the
    LORD.'"

²⁰ In the eleventh year, in the first month
on the seventh day, the word of the Lord
came to me: ²¹ "Son of man, I have broken
the arm of Pharaoh king of Egypt. It has
not been bound up to be healed or put in a

splint so that it may become strong enough to hold a sword. ²²Therefore this is what the Sovereign Lord says: I am against Pharaoh king of Egypt. I will break both his arms, the good arm as well as the broken one, and make the sword fall from his hand. ²³I will disperse the Egyptians among the nations and scatter them through the countries. ²⁴I will strengthen the arms of the king of Babylon and put my sword in his hand, but I will break the arms of Pharaoh, and he will groan before him like a mortally wounded man. ²⁵I will strengthen the arms of the king of Babylon, but the arms of Pharaoh will fall limp. Then they will know that I am the Lord, when I put my sword into the hand of the king of Babylon and he brandishes it against Egypt. ²⁶I will disperse the Egyptians among the nations and scatter them through the countries. Then they will know that I am the Lord.'

31 In the eleventh year, in the third month on the first day, the word of the Lord came to me: ²'Son of man, say to Pharaoh king of Egypt and to his hordes:

' "Who can be compared with you in
     majesty?
³Consider Assyria, once a cedar in Lebanon,
     with beautiful branches
          overshadowing the forest;
it towered on high,
     its top above the thick foliage.
⁴The waters nourished it,
     deep springs made it grow tall;
their streams flowed
     all around its base
and sent their channels
     to all the trees of the field.
⁵So it towered higher
     than all the trees of the field;
its boughs increased
     and its branches grew long,
          spreading because of abundant waters.
⁶All the birds of the sky

nested in its boughs,
all the wild animals
     gave birth under its branches;
all the great nations
     lived in its shade.
⁷It was majestic in beauty,
     with its spreading boughs,
for its roots went down
     to abundant waters.
⁸The cedars in the garden of God
     could not rival it,
nor could the junipers
     equal its boughs,
nor could the plane trees
     compare with its branches –
no tree in the garden of God
     could match its beauty.
⁹I made it beautiful
     with abundant branches,
the envy of all the trees of Eden
     in the garden of God.

¹⁰' "Therefore this is what the Sovereign Lord says: because the great cedar towered over the thick foliage, and because it was proud of its height, ¹¹I gave it into the hands of the ruler of the nations, for him to deal with according to its wickedness. I cast it aside, ¹²and the most ruthless of foreign nations cut it down and left it. Its boughs fell on the mountains and in all the valleys; its branches lay broken in all the ravines of the land. All the nations of the earth came out from under its shade and left it. ¹³All the birds settled on the fallen tree, and all the wild animals lived among its branches. ¹⁴Therefore no other trees by the waters are ever to tower proudly on high, lifting their tops above the thick foliage. No other trees so well-watered are ever to reach such a height; they are all destined for death, for the earth below, among mortals who go down to the realm of the dead.

¹⁵' "This is what the Sovereign Lord says: on the day it was brought down to the realm of the dead I covered the deep springs with

mourning for it; I held back its streams, and its abundant waters were restrained. Because of it I clothed Lebanon with gloom, and all the trees of the field withered away. [16] I made the nations tremble at the sound of its fall when I brought it down to the realm of the dead to be with those who go down to the pit. Then all the trees of Eden, the choicest and best of Lebanon, the well-watered trees, were consoled in the earth below. [17] They too, like the great cedar, had gone down to the realm of the dead, to those killed by the sword, along with the armed men who lived in its shade among the nations.

[18] '"Which of the trees of Eden can be compared with you in splendour and majesty? Yet you, too, will be brought down with the trees of Eden to the earth below; you will lie among the uncircumcised, with those killed by the sword.

'"This is Pharaoh and all his hordes, declares the Sovereign Lord."'

32 In the twelfth year, in the twelfth month on the first day, the word of the Lord came to me: [2] 'Son of man, take up a lament concerning Pharaoh king of Egypt and say to him:

'"You are like a lion among the nations;
    you are like a monster in the seas
thrashing about in your streams,
    churning the water with your feet
    and muddying the streams.

[3] '"This is what the Sovereign Lord says:

'"With a great throng of people
    I will cast my net over you,
    and they will haul you up in my net.
[4] I will throw you on the land
    and hurl you on the open field.
I will let all the birds of the sky settle
      on you
    and all the wild animals gorge
      themselves on you.

[5] I will spread your flesh on the mountains
    and fill the valleys with your remains.
[6] I will drench the land with your flowing
      blood
    all the way to the mountains,
    and the ravines will be filled with your
      flesh.
[7] When I snuff you out, I will cover the
      heavens
    and darken their stars;
I will cover the sun with a cloud,
    and the moon will not give its light.
[8] All the shining lights in the heavens
    I will darken over you;
I will bring darkness over your land,
      declares the Sovereign Lord.
[9] I will trouble the hearts of many peoples
    when I bring about your destruction
      among the nations,
    among lands you have not known.
[10] I will cause many peoples to be appalled
      at you,
    and their kings will shudder with
      horror because of you
    when I brandish my sword before them.
On the day of your downfall
    each of them will tremble
    every moment for his life.

[11] '"For this is what the Sovereign Lord says:

'"The sword of the king of Babylon
    will come against you.
[12] I will cause your hordes to fall
    by the swords of mighty men –
    the most ruthless of all nations.
They will shatter the pride of Egypt,
    and all her hordes will be overthrown.
[13] I will destroy all her cattle
    from beside abundant waters
no longer to be stirred by the foot of man
    or muddied by the hooves of cattle.
[14] Then I will let her waters settle
    and make her streams flow like oil,
      declares the Sovereign Lord.

¹⁵ When I make Egypt desolate
and strip the land of everything in it,
when I strike down all who live there,
then they will know that I am the
LORD.'

¹⁶ 'This is the lament they will chant for
her. The daughters of the nations will chant
it; for Egypt and all her hordes they will
chant it, declares the Sovereign LORD.'

....

■ PSALM 132:6-12

⁶ We heard it in Ephrathah,
we came upon it in the fields of Jaar:
⁷ 'Let us go to his dwelling-place,
let us worship at his footstool, saying,
⁸ "Arise, LORD, and come to your resting
place,
you and the ark of your might.
⁹ May your priests be clothed with your
righteousness;
may your faithful people sing for joy."'

¹⁰ For the sake of your servant David,
do not reject your anointed one.

¹¹ The LORD swore an oath to David,
a sure oath he will not revoke:
'One of your own descendants
I will place on your throne.
¹² If your sons keep my covenant
and the statutes I teach them,
then their sons shall sit
on your throne for ever and ever.'

....

■ PROVERBS 28:19-22

¹⁹ Those who work their land will have
abundant food,
but those who chase fantasies will
have their fill of poverty.

²⁰ A faithful person will be richly blessed,

but one eager to get rich will not go
unpunished.

²¹ To show partiality is not good –
yet a person will do wrong for a piece
of bread.

²² The stingy are eager to get rich
and are unaware that poverty awaits
them.

....

■ 1 PETER 2:18–3:12

¹⁸ Slaves, in reverent fear of God submit
yourselves to your masters, not only to those
who are good and considerate, but also to
those who are harsh. ¹⁹ For it is commendable if someone bears up under the pain of
unjust suffering because they are conscious
of God. ²⁰ But how is it to your credit if you
receive a beating for doing wrong and endure it? But if you suffer for doing good and
you endure it, this is commendable before
God. ²¹ To this you were called, because
Christ suffered for you, leaving you an
example, that you should follow in his steps.

²² 'He committed no sin,
and no deceit was found in his mouth.'

²³ When they hurled their insults at him, he
did not retaliate; when he suffered, he made
no threats. Instead, he entrusted himself to
him who judges justly. ²⁴ 'He himself bore
our sins' in his body on the cross, so that
we might die to sins and live for righteousness; 'by his wounds you have been healed.'
²⁵ For 'you were like sheep going astray,' but
now you have returned to the Shepherd and
Overseer of your souls.

3 Wives, in the same way submit yourselves to your own husbands so that,
if any of them do not believe the word, they
may be won over without words by the behaviour of their wives, ² when they see the

purity and reverence of your lives. [3] Your beauty should not come from outward adornment, such as elaborate hairstyles and the wearing of gold jewellery or fine clothes. [4] Rather, it should be that of your inner self, the unfading beauty of a gentle and quiet spirit, which is of great worth in God's sight. [5] For this is the way the holy women of the past who put their hope in God used to adorn themselves. They submitted themselves to their own husbands, [6] like Sarah, who obeyed Abraham and called him her lord. You are her daughters if you do what is right and do not give way to fear.

[7] Husbands, in the same way be considerate as you live with your wives, and treat them with respect as the weaker partner and as heirs with you of the gracious gift of life, so that nothing will hinder your prayers.

[8] Finally, all of you, be like-minded, be sympathetic, love one another, be compassionate and humble. [9] Do not repay evil with evil or insult with insult. On the contrary, repay evil with blessing, because to this you were called so that you may inherit a blessing. [10] For,

'Whoever would love life
    and see good days
must keep their tongue from evil
    and their lips from deceitful speech.
[11] They must turn from evil and do good;
    they must seek peace and pursue it.
[12] For the eyes of the Lord are on the
        righteous
    and his ears are attentive to their
        prayer,
but the face of the Lord is against those
        who do evil.'

The Breastplate

'May your priests be clothed with your righteousness; may your faithful people sing for joy.' **Psalm 132:9**

The second piece of armour with which we are to defend ourselves against the tactics of the Devil is the breastplate of righteousness.

A soldier's breastplate generally extended from the base of the neck to the upper part of the thighs so it would cover many important parts of the body, in particular the heart. Some commentators think that the word breastplate suggests that this piece of equipment covered only the front of the chest and thus gave no protection for the back. They deduce from this that a Christian should face the Devil and never turn his back on him, or else he will expose a part that is unguarded. It is an interesting idea, but it must not be given too much credence, for the soldier's breastplate often covered his back as well as his front.

What spiritual lesson can we draw from the 'breastplate of righteousness'? Most commentators believe that because the soldier's breastplate primarily covered his heart, the spiritual application of this is that in Christ we have all the protection we need against negative or desolating feelings – the heart being seen as the focal point of the emotions.

What an exciting thought: by putting on the breastplate of righteousness, we have the spiritual resources to deal with all those debilitating feelings that tend to bring us down into despair – unworthiness, inadequacy, fear, and so on. When I mentioned this to a friend who asked me what I thought the breastplate of righteousness was for, he said, 'It sounds too good to be true'. I replied, 'It's too good not to be true'.

PRAYER

Gracious Lord and Master, how can I sufficiently thank You for providing a defence against this most difficult of problems – emotional distress. Show me how to apply Your truth to this part of my personality. In Jesus' name. Amen.

FURTHER STUDY

Matt. 15:10-20; Mark 7:21; Prov. 4:23; 28:9
• What comes out of the heart?
• How are we to guard our hearts?

November 27

■ EZEKIEL 32:17–33:33

[17] In the twelfth year, on the fifteenth day of the month, the word of the LORD came to me: [18] 'Son of man, wail for the hordes of Egypt and consign to the earth below both her and the daughters of mighty nations, along with those who go down to the pit. [19] Say to them, "Are you more favoured than others? Go down and be laid among the uncircumcised." [20] They will fall among those killed by the sword. The sword is drawn; let her be dragged off with all her hordes. [21] From within the realm of the dead the mighty leaders will say of Egypt and her allies, "They have come down and they lie with the uncircumcised, with those killed by the sword."

[22] 'Assyria is there with her whole army; she is surrounded by the graves of all her slain, all who have fallen by the sword. [23] Their graves are in the depths of the pit and her army lies around her grave. All who had spread terror in the land of the living

are slain, fallen by the sword.

[24] 'Elam is there, with all her hordes around her grave. All of them are slain, fallen by the sword. All who had spread terror in the land of the living went down uncircumcised to the earth below. They bear their shame with those who go down to the pit. [25] A bed is made for her among the slain, with all her hordes around her grave. All of them are uncircumcised, killed by the sword. Because their terror had spread in the land of the living, they bear their shame with those who go down to the pit; they are laid among the slain.

[26] 'Meshek and Tubal are there, with all their hordes around their graves. All of them are uncircumcised, killed by the sword because they spread their terror in the land of the living. [27] But they do not lie with the fallen warriors of old, who went down to the realm of the dead with their weapons of war – their swords placed under their heads and their shields resting on their bones – though these warriors also

had terrorised the land of the living.

28 'You too, Pharaoh, will be broken and will lie among the uncircumcised, with those killed by the sword.

29 'Edom is there, her kings and all her princes; despite their power, they are laid with those killed by the sword. They lie with the uncircumcised, with those who go down to the pit.

30 'All the princes of the north and all the Sidonians are there; they went down with the slain in disgrace despite the terror caused by their power. They lie uncircumcised with those killed by the sword and bear their shame with those who go down to the pit.

31 'Pharaoh – he and all his army – will see them and he will be consoled for all his hordes that were killed by the sword, declares the Sovereign LORD. 32 Although I allowed him to spread terror in the land of the living, Pharaoh and all his hordes will be laid among the uncircumcised, with those killed by the sword, declares the Sovereign LORD.'

33 The word of the LORD came to me: 2 'Son of man, speak to your people and say to them: "When I bring the sword against a land, and the people of the land choose one of their men and make him their watchman, 3 and he sees the sword coming against the land and blows the trumpet to warn the people, 4 then if anyone hears the trumpet but does not heed the warning and the sword comes and takes their life, their blood will be on their own head. 5 Since they heard the sound of the trumpet but did not heed the warning, their blood will be on their own head. If they had heeded the warning, they would have saved themselves. 6 But if the watchman sees the sword coming and does not blow the trumpet to warn the people and the sword comes and takes someone's life, that person's life will be taken because of their sin, but I will hold the watchman accountable for their blood."

7 'Son of man, I have made you a watchman for the people of Israel; so hear the word I speak and give them warning from me. 8 When I say to the wicked, "You wicked person, you will surely die," and you do not speak out to dissuade them from their ways, that wicked person will die for their sin, and I will hold you accountable for their blood. 9 But if you do warn the wicked person to turn from their ways and they do not do so, they will die for their sin, though you yourself will be saved.

10 'Son of man, say to the Israelites, "This is what you are saying: 'Our offences and sins weigh us down, and we are wasting away because of them. How then can we live?'" 11 Say to them, "As surely as I live, declares the Sovereign LORD, I take no pleasure in the death of the wicked, but rather that they turn from their ways and live. Turn! Turn from your evil ways! Why will you die, people of Israel?"

12 'Therefore, son of man, say to your people, "If someone who is righteous disobeys, that person's former righteousness will count for nothing. And if someone who is wicked repents, that person's former wickedness will not bring condemnation. The righteous person who sins will not be allowed to live even though they were formerly righteous." 13 If I tell a righteous person that they will surely live, but then they trust in their righteousness and do evil, none of the righteous things that person has done will be remembered; they will die for the evil they have done. 14 And if I say to a wicked person, "You will surely die," but they then turn away from their sin and do what is just and right – 15 if they give back what they took in pledge for a loan, return what they have stolen, follow the decrees that give life, and do no evil – that person will surely live; they will not die. 16 None of the sins that person has committed will be remembered against them. They have done what is just and right; they will surely live.

17 'Yet your people say, "The way of the Lord is not just." But it is their way that is not just. 18 If a righteous person turns from their righteousness and does evil, they will die for it. 19 And if a wicked person turns away from their wickedness and does what is just and right, they will live by doing so. 20 Yet you Israelites say, "The way of the Lord is not just." But I will judge each of you according to your own ways.'

21 In the twelfth year of our exile, in the tenth month on the fifth day, a man who had escaped from Jerusalem came to me and said, 'The city has fallen!' 22 Now the evening before the man arrived, the hand of the LORD was on me, and he opened my mouth before the man came to me in the morning. So my mouth was opened and I was no longer silent.

23 Then the word of the LORD came to me: 24 'Son of man, the people living in those ruins in the land of Israel are saying, "Abraham was only one man, yet he possessed the land. But we are many; surely the land has been given to us as our possession." 25 Therefore say to them, "This is what the Sovereign LORD says: since you eat meat with the blood still in it and look to your idols and shed blood, should you then possess the land? 26 You rely on your sword, you do detestable things, and each of you defiles his neighbour's wife. Should you then possess the land?"

27 'Say this to them: "This is what the Sovereign LORD says: as surely as I live, those who are left in the ruins will fall by the sword, those out in the country I will give to the wild animals to be devoured, and those in strongholds and caves will die of a plague. 28 I will make the land a desolate waste, and her proud strength will come to an end, and the mountains of Israel will become desolate so that no one will cross them. 29 Then they will know that I am the LORD, when I have made the land a desolate

waste because of all the detestable things they have done."

30 'As for you, son of man, your people are talking together about you by the walls and at the doors of the houses, saying to each other, "Come and hear the message that has come from the LORD." 31 My people come to you, as they usually do, and sit before you to hear your words, but they do not put them into practice. Their mouths speak of love, but their hearts are greedy for unjust gain. 32 Indeed, to them you are nothing more than one who sings love songs with a beautiful voice and plays an instrument well, for they hear your words but do not put them into practice.

33 'When all this comes true – and it surely will – then they will know that a prophet has been among them.'

■ PSALM 132:13-18

13 For the LORD has chosen Zion,
    he has desired it for his dwelling,
        saying,
14 'This is my resting place for ever and
        ever;
    here I will sit enthroned, for I have
        desired it.
15 I will bless her with abundant
        provisions;
    her poor I will satisfy with food.
16 I will clothe her priests with salvation,
    and her faithful people shall ever sing
        for joy.

17 'Here I will make a horn grow for David
    and set up a lamp for my anointed one.
18 I will clothe his enemies with shame,
    but his head shall be adorned with a
        radiant crown.'

■ PROVERBS 28:23-25

²³ Whoever rebukes a person will in the
    end gain favour
    rather than one who has a flattering
    tongue.

²⁴ Whoever robs their father or mother
    and says, 'It's not wrong,'
    is partner to one who destroys.

²⁵ The greedy stir up conflict,
    but those who trust in the LORD will
    prosper.

■ 1 PETER 3:13–4:11

¹³ Who is going to harm you if you are
eager to do good? ¹⁴ But even if you should
suffer for what is right, you are blessed.
'Do not fear their threats; do not be frightened.' ¹⁵ But in your hearts revere Christ as
Lord. Always be prepared to give an answer
to everyone who asks you to give the reason for the hope that you have. But do this
with gentleness and respect, ¹⁶ keeping a
clear conscience, so that those who speak
maliciously against your good behaviour
in Christ may be ashamed of their slander. ¹⁷ For it is better, if it is God's will, to
suffer for doing good than for doing evil.
¹⁸ For Christ also suffered once for sins, the
righteous for the unrighteous, to bring you
to God. He was put to death in the body
but made alive in the Spirit. ¹⁹ After being
made alive, he went and made proclamation to the imprisoned spirits – ²⁰ to those
who were disobedient long ago when God
waited patiently in the days of Noah while
the ark was being built. In it only a few
people, eight in all, were saved through
water, ²¹ and this water symbolises baptism

that now saves you also – not the removal
of dirt from the body but the pledge of a
clear conscience towards God. It saves you
by the resurrection of Jesus Christ, ²² who
has gone into heaven and is at God's right
hand – with angels, authorities and powers
in submission to him.

4 Therefore, since Christ suffered in his
body, arm yourselves also with the
same attitude, because whoever suffers in
the body has finished with sin. ² As a result, they do not live the rest of their earthly
lives for evil human desires, but rather for
the will of God. ³ For you have spent enough
time in the past doing what pagans choose
to do – living in debauchery, lust, drunkenness, orgies, carousing and detestable
idolatry. ⁴ They are surprised that you do
not join them in their reckless, wild living,
and they heap abuse on you. ⁵ But they will
have to give account to him who is ready to
judge the living and the dead. ⁶ For this is
the reason the gospel was preached even to
those who are now dead, so that they might
be judged according to human standards in
regard to the body, but live according to God
in regard to the spirit.

⁷ The end of all things is near. Therefore be alert and of sober mind so that
you may pray. ⁸ Above all, love each other
deeply, because love covers over a multitude of sins. ⁹ Offer hospitality to one
another without grumbling. ¹⁰ Each of
you should use whatever gift you have
received to serve others, as faithful stewards of God's grace in its various forms.
¹¹ If anyone speaks, they should do so as
one who speaks the very words of God. If
anyone serves, they should do so with the
strength God provides, so that in all things
God may be praised through Jesus Christ.
To him be the glory and the power for ever
and ever. Amen.

The Dividing Line

'He was put to death in the body but made alive in the Spirit.' **1 Peter 3:18**

It was the Holy Spirit who transformed the early disciples from timid and disconsolate men into ones who were ablaze and invincible.

If you draw a line through the pages of the New Testament, you will find on one side a good deal of spiritual staleness while on the other an abundance of spiritual freshness. That line runs straight through an upper room where a group of people waited in simple confidence for the promise their Master had made to them to be fulfilled. We read in Acts 2:4: 'All of them were filled with the Holy Spirit ...' That filling was the dividing line in the moral and spiritual development of humanity. It marked a new era - the era of the Holy Spirit.

On the other side of that dividing line, prior to Pentecost, the disciples were spasmodic in their allegiance and achievements. Sometimes they could rejoice that evil spirits were subject to them, and sometimes they had to ask, 'Why could we not cast it out?' Sometimes they appeared ready to go to death with Jesus, and sometimes they quarrelled over who should have first place in His kingdom. Simon Peter could whip out a sword and cut off the ear of the high priest's servant and then quail before the gaze of a serving maid.

Then came Pentecost. A divine reinforcement took place. They were new men doing new work - no longer spasmodic, but stable. On which side of that dividing line are you? Are you a pre-Pentecost Christian, spasmodic and intermittent, or a post-Pentecost Christian - dynamic and different?

PRAYER

O God, forgive me that so often I am crouching behind closed doors instead of being out on the open road. Make me a post-Pentecost Christian. In Jesus' name. Amen.

FURTHER STUDY

2 Cor. 3:1-6; John 6:63; Rom. 8:11
• What does the letter of the law do?
• What changes this?

November 28

■ **EZEKIEL 34:1–36:12**

34 The word of the LORD came to me: ²'Son of man, prophesy against the shepherds of Israel; prophesy and say to them: "This is what the Sovereign LORD says: woe to you shepherds of Israel who only take care of yourselves! Should not shepherds take care of the flock? ³You eat the curds, clothe yourselves with the wool and slaughter the choice animals, but you do not take care of the flock. ⁴You have not strengthened the weak or healed those who are ill or bound up the injured. You have not brought back the strays or searched for the lost. You have ruled them harshly and brutally. ⁵So they were scattered because there was no shepherd, and when they were scattered they became food for all the wild animals. ⁶My sheep wandered over all the mountains and on every high hill. They were scattered over the whole earth, and no one searched or looked for them.

⁷'Therefore, you shepherds, hear the word of the LORD: ⁸as surely as I live, declares the Sovereign LORD, because my flock lacks a shepherd and so has been plundered and has become food for all the wild animals, and because my shepherds did not search for my flock but cared for themselves rather than for my flock, ⁹therefore, you shepherds, hear the word of the LORD: ¹⁰this is what the Sovereign LORD says: I am against the shepherds and will hold them accountable for my flock. I will remove them from tending the flock so that the shepherds can no longer feed themselves. I will rescue my flock from their mouths, and it will no longer be food for them.

¹¹'For this is what the Sovereign LORD says: I myself will search for my sheep and look after them. ¹²As a shepherd looks after his scattered flock when he is with them, so will I look after my sheep. I will rescue them from all the places where they were scattered on a day of clouds and darkness. ¹³I will bring them out from the nations and gather them from the countries, and I will bring them into their own land. I will pasture them on the mountains of Israel, in the ravines and in all the settlements in the land. ¹⁴I will tend them in a good pasture, and the mountain heights of Israel will be their grazing land. There they will lie down in good grazing land, and there they will feed in a rich pasture on the mountains of

Israel. ¹⁵I myself will tend my sheep and make them lie down, declares the Sovereign LORD. ¹⁶I will search for the lost and bring back the strays. I will bind up the injured and strengthen the weak, but the sleek and the strong I will destroy. I will shepherd the flock with justice.

¹⁷'As for you, my flock, this is what the Sovereign LORD says: I will judge between one sheep and another, and between rams and goats. ¹⁸Is it not enough for you to feed on the good pasture? Must you also trample the rest of your pasture with your feet? Is it not enough for you to drink clear water? Must you also muddy the rest with your feet? ¹⁹Must my flock feed on what you have trampled and drink what you have muddied with your feet?

²⁰'Therefore this is what the Sovereign LORD says to them: see, I myself will judge between the fat sheep and the lean sheep. ²¹Because you shove with flank and shoulder, butting all the weak sheep with your horns until you have driven them away, ²²I will save my flock, and they will no longer be plundered. I will judge between one sheep and another. ²³I will place over them one shepherd, my servant David, and he will tend them; he will tend them and be their shepherd. ²⁴I the LORD will be their God, and my servant David will be prince among them. I the LORD have spoken.

²⁵'I will make a covenant of peace with them and rid the land of savage beasts so that they may live in the wilderness and sleep in the forests in safety. ²⁶I will make them and the places surrounding my hill a blessing. I will send down showers in season; there will be showers of blessing. ²⁷The trees will yield their fruit and the ground will yield its crops; the people will be secure in their land. They will know that I am the LORD, when I break the bars of their yoke and rescue them from the hands of those who enslaved them. ²⁸They will no longer be plundered by the nations, nor will wild

animals devour them. They will live in safety, and no one will make them afraid. ²⁹I will provide for them a land renowned for its crops, and they will no longer be victims of famine in the land or bear the scorn of the nations. ³⁰Then they will know that I, the LORD their God, am with them and that they, the Israelites, are my people, declares the Sovereign LORD. ³¹You are my sheep, the sheep of my pasture, and I am your God, declares the Sovereign LORD."'

35 The word of the Lord came to me: ²'Son of man, set your face against Mount Seir; prophesy against it ³and say: "This is what the Sovereign Lord says: I am against you, Mount Seir, and I will stretch out my hand against you and make you a desolate waste. ⁴I will turn your towns into ruins and you will be desolate. Then you will know that I am the Lord.

⁵ "Because you harboured an ancient hostility and delivered the Israelites over to the sword at the time of their calamity, the time their punishment reached its climax, ⁶therefore as surely as I live, declares the Sovereign LORD, I will give you over to bloodshed and it will pursue you. Since you did not hate bloodshed, bloodshed will pursue you. ⁷I will make Mount Seir a desolate waste and cut off from it all who come and go. ⁸I will fill your mountains with the slain; those killed by the sword will fall on your hills and in your valleys and in all your ravines. ⁹I will make you desolate for ever; your towns will not be inhabited. Then you will know that I am the LORD.

¹⁰ "Because you have said, 'These two nations and countries will be ours and we will take possession of them,' even though I the LORD was there, ¹¹therefore as surely as I live, declares the Sovereign LORD, I will treat you in accordance with the anger and jealousy you showed in your hatred of them and I will make myself known among them when I judge you. ¹²Then you will know that

I the LORD have heard all the contemptible things you have said against the mountains of Israel. You said, 'They have been laid waste and have been given over to us to devour.' ¹³You boasted against me and spoke against me without restraint, and I heard it. ¹⁴This is what the Sovereign LORD says: while the whole earth rejoices, I will make you desolate. ¹⁵Because you rejoiced when the inheritance of Israel became desolate, that is how I will treat you. You will be desolate, Mount Seir, you and all of Edom. Then they will know that I am the LORD."'

36 'Son of man, prophesy to the mountains of Israel and say, "Mountains of Israel, hear the word of the Lord. ²This is what the Sovereign Lord says: the enemy said of you, 'Aha! The ancient heights have become our possession.'" ³Therefore prophesy and say, "This is what the Sovereign Lord says: because they ravaged and crushed you from every side so that you became the possession of the rest of the nations and the object of people's malicious talk and slander, ⁴therefore, mountains of Israel, hear the word of the Sovereign Lord: this is what the Sovereign Lord says to the mountains and hills, to the ravines and valleys, to the desolate ruins and the deserted towns that have been plundered and ridiculed by the rest of the nations around you – ⁵this is what the Sovereign Lord says: in my burning zeal I have spoken against the rest of the nations, and against Edom, for with glee and with malice in their hearts they made my land their own possession so that they might plunder its pasture-land." ⁶Therefore prophesy concerning the land of Israel and say to the mountains and hills, to the ravines and valleys: "This is what the Sovereign Lord says: I speak in my jealous wrath because you have suffered the scorn of the nations. ⁷Therefore this is what the Sovereign Lord says: I swear with uplifted hand that the nations around you will also suffer scorn.

8 ' "But you, mountains of Israel, will produce branches and fruit for my people Israel, for they will soon come home. 9 I am concerned for you and will look on you with favour; you will be ploughed and sown, 10 and I will cause many people to live on you – yes, all of Israel. The towns will be inhabited and the ruins rebuilt. 11 I will increase the number of people and animals living on you, and they will be fruitful and become numerous. I will settle people on you as in the past and will make you prosper more than before. Then you will know that I am the Lord. 12 I will cause people, my people Israel, to live on you. They will possess you, and you will be their inheritance; you will never again deprive them of their children.

■ PSALM 133:1–134:3

1 How good and pleasant it is
    when God's people live together in
    unity!

2 It is like precious oil poured on the head,
    running down on the beard,
    running down on Aaron's beard,
    down on the collar of his robe.
3 It is as if the dew of Hermon
    were falling on Mount Zion.
For there the Lord bestows his blessing,
    even life for evermore.

1 Praise the Lord, all you servants of the
    Lord
    who minister by night in the house of
    the Lord.
2 Lift up your hands in the sanctuary
    and praise the Lord.

3 May the Lord bless you from Zion,
    he who is the Maker of heaven and
    earth.

■ PROVERBS 28:26–28

26 Those who trust in themselves are fools,
    but those who walk in wisdom are
    kept safe.

27 Those who give to the poor will lack
    nothing,
    but those who close their eyes to them
    receive many curses.

28 When the wicked rise to power, people
    go into hiding;
    but when the wicked perish, the
    righteous thrive.

■ 1 PETER 4:12–5:14

12 Dear friends, do not be surprised at the fiery ordeal that has come on you to test you, as though something strange were happening to you. 13 But rejoice inasmuch as you participate in the sufferings of Christ, so that you may be overjoyed when his glory is revealed. 14 If you are insulted because of the name of Christ, you are blessed, for the Spirit of glory and of God rests on you. 15 If you suffer, it should not be as a murderer or thief or any other kind of criminal, or even as a meddler. 16 However, if you suffer as a Christian, do not be ashamed, but praise God that you bear that name. 17 For it is time for judgment to begin with God's household; and if it begins with us, what will the outcome be for those who do not obey the gospel of God? 18 And,

'If it is hard for the righteous to be saved,
    what will become of the ungodly and
    the sinner?'

19 So then, those who suffer according to God's will should commit themselves to their faithful Creator and continue to do good.

5 To the elders among you, I appeal as a fellow elder and a witness of Christ's sufferings who also will share in the glory to be revealed: ²be shepherds of God's flock that is under your care, watching over them – not because you must, but because you are willing, as God wants you to be; not pursuing dishonest gain, but eager to serve; ³not lording it over those entrusted to you, but being examples to the flock. ⁴And when the Chief Shepherd appears, you will receive the crown of glory that will never fade away.

⁵In the same way, you who are younger, submit yourselves to your elders. All of you, clothe yourselves with humility towards one another, because,

'God opposes the proud
but shows favour to the humble.'

⁶Humble yourselves, therefore, under God's mighty hand, that he may lift you up in due time. ⁷Cast all your anxiety on him because he cares for you.

⁸Be alert and of sober mind. Your enemy the devil prowls around like a roaring lion looking for someone to devour. ⁹Resist him, standing firm in the faith, because you know that the family of believers throughout the world is undergoing the same kind of sufferings.

¹⁰And the God of all grace, who called you to his eternal glory in Christ, after you have suffered a little while, will himself restore you and make you strong, firm and steadfast. ¹¹To him be the power for ever and ever. Amen.

¹²With the help of Silas, whom I regard as a faithful brother, I have written to you briefly, encouraging you and testifying that this is the true grace of God. Stand fast in it.

¹³She who is in Babylon, chosen together with you, sends you her greetings, and so does my son Mark. ¹⁴Greet one another with a kiss of love.

Peace to all of you who are in Christ.

Danger – the Devil at Work

'Your enemy the devil prowls around like a roaring lion looking for someone to devour.' **1 Peter 5:8**

A woman said to me once, 'I think you are giving too much credit to the devil. He is such an insignificant person compared to God that we ought not even mention his name.' In one way I can sympathise with this view, for when you listen to some Christians talk, you get the impression that they have a small God and a big devil.

It would be unrealistic to think, however, that we can go through life without coming into direct contact with Satan and his forces. What is even more unrealistic is to think that many (though certainly not all) of the problems which confront us day by day have no devilish strategy behind them.

Satan is responsible for more of our individual woes and international wars, our crime and violence, our human sorrow, sickness and death than we may believe. The late Dr Martyn Lloyd-Jones said: 'I am certain that one of the main causes of the ill state of the church today is the fact that the devil is being forgotten ... We are ignorant of this great objective fact – the being, the existence of the devil, the adversary, the accuser, and his fiery darts.'

Does the thought of doing battle with the devil frighten you? Then heed the words of Corrie ten Boom, who said: 'The fear of the devil is most likely from the devil himself.' God has given us all the protection we need to defend ourselves against the attacks of Satan, and when we know how to avail ourselves of this protection, we will no longer be afraid of the devil. Rather, he will be afraid of us.

PRAYER

O God, as I go deeper into this subject, I am becoming increasingly aware of the intensity of the spiritual battle in which I am engaged. Dispel every fear that may arise in me, and show me the way to power and victory. In Jesus' name. Amen.

FURTHER STUDY

2 Cor. 2:1-11; 11:3; 2 Thess. 2:9
• What did Paul say about his knowledge of the devil?
• What was his reason?

November 29

■ EZEKIEL 36:13–37:28

¹³ "'This is what the Sovereign LORD says: because some say to you, 'You devour people and deprive your nation of its children,' ¹⁴ therefore you will no longer devour people or make your nation childless, declares the Sovereign LORD. ¹⁵ No longer will I make you hear the taunts of the nations, and no longer will you suffer the scorn of the peoples or cause your nation to fall, declares the Sovereign LORD.'"

¹⁶ Again the word of the Lord came to me: ¹⁷ 'Son of man, when the people of Israel were living in their own land, they defiled it by their conduct and their actions. Their conduct was like a woman's monthly uncleanness in my sight. ¹⁸ So I poured out my wrath on them because they had shed blood in the land and because they had defiled it with their idols. ¹⁹ I dispersed them among the nations, and they were scattered through the countries; I judged them according to their conduct and their actions.

²⁰ And wherever they went among the nations they profaned my holy name, for it was said of them, "These are the Lord's people, and yet they had to leave his land." ²¹ I had concern for my holy name, which the people of Israel profaned among the nations where they had gone.

²² 'Therefore say to the Israelites, "This is what the Sovereign LORD says: it is not for your sake, people of Israel, that I am going to do these things, but for the sake of my holy name, which you have profaned among the nations where you have gone. ²³ I will show the holiness of my great name, which has been profaned among the nations, the name you have profaned among them. Then the nations will know that I am the LORD, declares the Sovereign LORD, when I am proved holy through you before their eyes.

²⁴ "'For I will take you out of the nations; I will gather you from all the countries and bring you back into your own land. ²⁵ I will sprinkle clean water on you, and you will be clean; I will cleanse you from all your impurities and from all your idols. ²⁶ I will give

you a new heart and put a new spirit in you; I will remove from you your heart of stone and give you a heart of flesh. ²⁷ And I will put my Spirit in you and move you to follow my decrees and be careful to keep my laws. ²⁸ Then you will live in the land I gave your ancestors; you will be my people, and I will be your God. ²⁹ I will save you from all your uncleanness. I will call for the corn and make it plentiful and will not bring famine upon you. ³⁰ I will increase the fruit of the trees and the crops of the field, so that you will no longer suffer disgrace among the nations because of famine. ³¹ Then you will remember your evil ways and wicked deeds, and you will loathe yourselves for your sins and detestable practices. ³² I want you to know that I am not doing this for your sake, declares the Sovereign LORD. Be ashamed and disgraced for your conduct, people of Israel!

³³ ' "This is what the Sovereign LORD says: on the day I cleanse you from all your sins, I will resettle your towns, and the ruins will be rebuilt. ³⁴ The desolate land will be cultivated instead of lying desolate in the sight of all who pass through it. ³⁵ They will say, 'This land that was laid waste has become like the garden of Eden; the cities that were lying in ruins, desolate and destroyed, are now fortified and inhabited.' ³⁶ Then the nations around you that remain will know that I the LORD have rebuilt what was destroyed and have replanted what was desolate. I the LORD have spoken, and I will do it."

³⁷ 'This is what the Sovereign LORD says: once again I will yield to Israel's plea and do this for them: I will make their people as numerous as sheep, ³⁸ as numerous as the flocks for offerings at Jerusalem during her appointed festivals. So will the ruined cities be filled with flocks of people. Then they will know that I am the LORD.'

37 The hand of the Lord was on me, and he brought me out by the Spirit of the Lord and set me in the middle of a valley; it was full of bones. ² He led me to and fro among them, and I saw a great many bones on the floor of the valley, bones that were very dry. ³ He asked me, 'Son of man, can these bones live?'

I said, 'Sovereign LORD, you alone know.'

⁴ Then he said to me, 'Prophesy to these bones and say to them, "Dry bones, hear the word of the LORD! ⁵ This is what the Sovereign LORD says to these bones: I will make breath enter you, and you will come to life. ⁶ I will attach tendons to you and make flesh come upon you and cover you with skin; I will put breath in you, and you will come to life. Then you will know that I am the LORD."'

⁷ So I prophesied as I was commanded. And as I was prophesying, there was a noise, a rattling sound, and the bones came together, bone to bone. ⁸ I looked, and tendons and flesh appeared on them and skin covered them, but there was no breath in them.

⁹ Then he said to me, 'Prophesy to the breath; prophesy, son of man, and say to it, "This is what the Sovereign LORD says: come, breath, from the four winds and breathe into these slain, that they may live."' ¹⁰ So I prophesied as he commanded me, and breath entered them; they came to life and stood up on their feet – a vast army.

¹¹ Then he said to me: 'Son of man, these bones are the people of Israel. They say, "Our bones are dried up and our hope is gone; we are cut off." ¹² Therefore prophesy and say to them: "This is what the Sovereign LORD says: my people, I am going to open your graves and bring you up from them; I will bring you back to the land of Israel. ¹³ Then you, my people, will know that I am the LORD, when I open your graves and bring you up from them. ¹⁴ I will put my Spirit in you and you will live, and I will settle you in your own land. Then you will know that I the LORD have spoken, and I have done it, declares the LORD."'

¹⁵ The word of the LORD came to me: ¹⁶ 'Son of man, take a stick of wood and write on it, "Belonging to Judah and the Israelites associated with him." Then take another stick of wood, and write on it, "Belonging to Joseph (that is, to Ephraim) and all the Israelites associated with him." ¹⁷ Join them together into one stick so that they will become one in your hand.

¹⁸ 'When your people ask you, "Won't you tell us what you mean by this?" ¹⁹ say to them, "This is what the Sovereign LORD says: I am going to take the stick of Joseph – which is in Ephraim's hand – and of the Israelite tribes associated with him, and join it to Judah's stick. I will make them into a single stick of wood, and they will become one in my hand." ²⁰ Hold before their eyes the sticks you have written on ²¹ and say to them, "This is what the Sovereign LORD says: I will take the Israelites out of the nations where they have gone. I will gather them from all around and bring them back into their own land. ²² I will make them one nation in the land, on the mountains of Israel. There will be one king over all of them and they will never again be two nations or be divided into two kingdoms. ²³ They will no longer defile themselves with their idols and vile images or with any of their offences, for I will save them from all their sinful backsliding, and I will cleanse them. They will be my people, and I will be their God.

²⁴ ' "My servant David will be king over them, and they will all have one shepherd. They will follow my laws and be careful to keep my decrees. ²⁵ They will live in the land I gave to my servant Jacob, the land where your ancestors lived. They and their children and their children's children will live there for ever, and David my servant will be their prince for ever. ²⁶ I will make a covenant of peace with them; it will be an everlasting covenant. I will establish them and increase their numbers, and I will put my sanctuary among them for ever.

²⁷ My dwelling-place will be with them; I will be their God, and they will be my people. ²⁸ Then the nations will know that I the LORD make Israel holy, when my sanctuary is among them for ever." '

▬ PSALM 135:1-7

¹ Praise the LORD.

Praise the name of the LORD;
    praise him, you servants of the LORD,
² you who minister in the house of the
        LORD,
    in the courts of the house of our God.

³ Praise the LORD, for the LORD is good;
    sing praise to his name, for that is
        pleasant.
⁴ For the LORD has chosen Jacob to be his
        own,
    Israel to be his treasured possession.

⁵ I know that the LORD is great,
    that our Lord is greater than all gods.
⁶ The LORD does whatever pleases him,
    in the heavens and on the earth,
    in the seas and all their depths.
⁷ He makes clouds rise from the ends of
        the earth;
    he sends lightning with the rain
    and brings out the wind from his
        storehouses.

▬ PROVERBS 29:1-3

29 Whoever remains stiff-necked
    after many rebukes
    will suddenly be destroyed – without
        remedy.

² When the righteous thrive, the people
        rejoice;

when the wicked rule, the people
groan.

³ A man who loves wisdom brings joy to
his father,
but a companion of prostitutes
squanders his wealth.

▬ 2 PETER 1:1-21

1 Simon Peter, a servant and apostle of
Jesus Christ,

To those who through the righteousness
of our God and Saviour Jesus Christ have
received a faith as precious as ours:

² Grace and peace be yours in abundance
through the knowledge of God and of Jesus
our Lord.

³ His divine power has given us everything we need for a godly life through our
knowledge of him who called us by his
own glory and goodness. ⁴ Through these
he has given us his very great and precious
promises, so that through them you may
participate in the divine nature, having escaped the corruption in the world caused
by evil desires.

⁵ For this very reason, make every effort to
add to your faith goodness; and to goodness,
knowledge; ⁶ and to knowledge, self-control;
and to self-control, perseverance; and to
perseverance, godliness; ⁷ and to godliness,
mutual affection; and to mutual affection,
love. ⁸ For if you possess these qualities in
increasing measure, they will keep you from
being ineffective and unproductive in your
knowledge of our Lord Jesus Christ. ⁹ But
whoever does not have them is short-sighted

and blind, forgetting that they have been
cleansed from their past sins.

¹⁰ Therefore, my brothers and sisters,
make every effort to confirm your calling
and election. For if you do these things, you
will never stumble, ¹¹ and you will receive a
rich welcome into the eternal kingdom of
our Lord and Saviour Jesus Christ.

¹² So I will always remind you of these
things, even though you know them and
are firmly established in the truth you now
have. ¹³ I think it is right to refresh your
memory as long as I live in the tent of this
body, ¹⁴ because I know that I will soon put
it aside, as our Lord Jesus Christ has made
clear to me. ¹⁵ And I will make every effort to
see that after my departure you will always
be able to remember these things.

¹⁶ For we did not follow cleverly devised
stories when we told you about the coming of our Lord Jesus Christ in power, but
we were eye-witnesses of his majesty. ¹⁷ He
received honour and glory from God the
Father when the voice came to him from
the Majestic Glory, saying, 'This is my Son,
whom I love; with him I am well pleased.'
¹⁸ We ourselves heard this voice that came
from heaven when we were with him on the
sacred mountain.

¹⁹ We also have the prophetic message as
something completely reliable, and you will
do well to pay attention to it, as to a light
shining in a dark place, until the day dawns
and the morning star rises in your hearts.
²⁰ Above all, you must understand that no
prophecy of Scripture came about by the
prophet's own interpretation of things.
²¹ For prophecy never had its origin in the
human will, but prophets, though human,
spoke from God as they were carried along
by the Holy Spirit.

Standing on Promises

'... he has given us his very great and precious promises ...' **2 Peter 1:4**

I t is one thing to accept the faithfulness of God as a clear biblical truth; it is quite another to act upon it. God has given us many great and precious promises, as our text for today puts it, but do we actually count on them being fulfilled?

We have to be careful that we do not hold God to promises He has not given. I have seen a good deal of heartache suffered by Christians because someone encouraged them to take a statement from the Word of God, turn it into a 'promise', and believe for it to come to pass. Then when nothing happened, they became deeply discouraged.

One woman told me that many years ago she had taken the words found in Acts 16:31, 'Believe in the Lord Jesus, and you will be saved – you and your household', and claimed them as a promise. When her husband and son died unrepentant, she was devastated. I pointed out to her that even God cannot save those who don't want to be saved, and that the promise given by Paul and Silas was for the Philippian jailer, not anyone else.

There are hundreds of promises that God has given in His Word that we can claim without equivocation. Someone who has counted all God's promises in the Bible numbers them as being over 3,000. That ought to be enough to keep you going if you lived to be a hundred. Be careful, however, that it is a general promise you are banking on, not a specific one.

PRAYER

Father, I have Your promise that You will guide me into all truth, so my trust is in You that You will give me the wisdom to discern between a promise which is general and one that is specific. In Jesus' name. Amen.

FURTHER STUDY

Heb. 1:1-12; 13:8; 2 Cor. 4:18
• Why is Jesus so dependable?
• Where do we fix our eyes?

November 30

▬ EZEKIEL 38:1–39:29

38 The word of the LORD came to me: ²'Son of man, set your face against Gog, of the land of Magog, the chief prince of Meshek and Tubal; prophesy against him ³and say: "This is what the Sovereign LORD says: I am against you, Gog, chief prince of Meshek and Tubal. ⁴I will turn you around, put hooks in your jaws and bring you out with your whole army – your horses, your horsemen fully armed, and a great horde with large and small shields, all of them brandishing their swords. ⁵Persia, Cush and Put will be with them, all with shields and helmets, ⁶also Gomer with all its troops, and Beth Togarmah from the far north with all its troops – the many nations with you.

⁷ "Get ready; be prepared, you and all the hordes gathered about you, and take command of them. ⁸After many days you will be called to arms. In future years you will invade a land that has recovered from war, whose people were gathered from many nations to the mountains of Israel, which had long been desolate. They had been brought out from the nations, and now all of them live in safety. ⁹You and all your troops and the many nations with you will go up, advancing like a storm; you will be like a cloud covering the land.

¹⁰ "This is what the Sovereign LORD says: on that day thoughts will come into your mind and you will devise an evil scheme. ¹¹You will say, 'I will invade a land of unwalled villages; I will attack a peaceful and unsuspecting people – all of them living without walls and without gates and bars. ¹²I will plunder and loot and turn my hand against the resettled ruins and the people gathered from the nations, rich in livestock and goods, living at the centre of the land.' ¹³Sheba and Dedan and the merchants of Tarshish and all her villages will say to you, 'Have you come to plunder? Have you gathered your hordes to loot, to carry off silver and gold, to take away livestock and goods and to seize much plunder?'"

¹⁴'Therefore, son of man, prophesy and say to Gog: "This is what the Sovereign LORD says: in that day, when my people Israel are living in safety, will you not take notice of it? ¹⁵You will come from your place in the far north, you and many nations with you, all of them riding on horses, a great horde, a mighty army. ¹⁶You will advance against my people Israel like a cloud that covers the land. In days to come, Gog, I will bring you against my land, so that the nations may know me when I am proved holy through you before their eyes.

¹⁷ "This is what the Sovereign LORD says: you are the one I spoke of in former days by my servants the prophets of Israel. At that time they prophesied for years that I would bring you against them. ¹⁸This is what will happen in that day: when Gog attacks the land of Israel, my hot anger will be aroused, declares the Sovereign LORD. ¹⁹In my zeal and fiery wrath I declare that at that time there shall be a great earthquake in the land of Israel. ²⁰The fish in the sea, the birds in the sky, the beasts of the field, every creature that moves along the ground, and all the people on the face of the earth will tremble at my presence. The mountains will be overturned, the cliffs will crumble and every wall will fall to the ground. ²¹I will summon a sword against Gog on all my mountains, declares the Sovereign LORD. Every man's sword will be against his brother. ²²I will execute judgment on him with plague and bloodshed; I will pour down torrents of rain, hailstones and burning sulphur on him and on his troops and on the many nations with him. ²³And so I will show my greatness and my holiness, and I will make myself known in the sight of many nations. Then they will know that I am the LORD."

39 'Son of man, prophesy against Gog and say: "This is what the Sovereign LORD says: I am against you, Gog, chief prince of Meshek and Tubal. ²I will turn you around and drag you along. I will bring you from the far north and send you against the mountains of Israel. ³Then I will strike your bow from your left hand and make your arrows drop from your right hand. ⁴On the mountains of Israel you will fall, you and all your troops and the nations with you. I will give you as food to all kinds of carrion birds and to the wild animals. ⁵You will fall in the open field, for I have spoken, declares the Sovereign LORD. ⁶ I will send fire on Magog and on those who live in safety in the coastlands, and they will know that I am the LORD.

⁷ "I will make known my holy name among my people Israel. I will no longer let my holy name be profaned, and the nations will know that I the LORD am the Holy One in Israel. ⁸ It is coming! It will surely take place, declares the Sovereign LORD. This is the day I have spoken of.

⁹ "Then those who live in the towns of Israel will go out and use the weapons for fuel and burn them up – the small and large shields, the bows and arrows, the war clubs and spears. For seven years they will use them for fuel. ¹⁰ They will not need to gather wood from the fields or cut it from the forests, because they will use the weapons for fuel. And they will plunder those who plundered them and loot those who looted them, declares the Sovereign LORD.

¹¹ "On that day I will give Gog a burial place in Israel, in the valley of those who travel east of the Sea. It will block the way of travellers, because Gog and all his hordes will be buried there. So it will be called the Valley of Hamon Gog.

¹² "For seven months the Israelites will be burying them in order to cleanse the land. ¹³ All the people of the land will bury them, and the day I display my glory will be a memorable day for them, declares the Sovereign LORD. ¹⁴ People will be continually employed in cleansing the land. They will spread out across the land and, along with others, they will bury any bodies that are lying on the ground.

'"After the seven months they will carry out a more detailed search. ¹⁵ As they go through the land, anyone who sees a human bone will leave a marker beside it until the gravediggers bury it in the Valley of Hamon Gog, ¹⁶ near a town called Hamonah. And so they will cleanse the land."

¹⁷ "Son of man, this is what the Sovereign LORD says: call out to every kind of bird and all the wild animals: "Assemble and come together from all around to the sacrifice I am preparing for you, the great sacrifice on the mountains of Israel. There you will eat flesh and drink blood. ¹⁸ You will eat the flesh of mighty men and drink the blood of the princes of the earth as if they were rams and lambs, goats and bulls – all of them fattened animals from Bashan. ¹⁹ At the sacrifice I am preparing for you, you will eat fat till you are glutted and drink blood till you are drunk. ²⁰ At my table you will eat your fill of horses and riders, mighty men and soldiers of every kind," declares the Sovereign LORD.

²¹ "I will display my glory among the nations, and all the nations will see the punishment I inflict and the hand I lay on them. ²² From that day forward the people of Israel will know that I am the LORD their God. ²³ And the nations will know that the people of Israel went into exile for their sin, because they were unfaithful to me. So I hid my face from them and handed them over to their enemies, and they all fell by the sword. ²⁴ I dealt with them according to their uncleanness and their offences, and I hid my face from them.

²⁵ "Therefore this is what the Sovereign LORD says: I will now restore the fortunes of Jacob and will have compassion on all the people of Israel, and I will be zealous for my holy name. ²⁶ They will forget their shame and all the unfaithfulness they showed towards me when they lived in safety in their land with no one to make them afraid. ²⁷ When I have brought them back from the nations and have gathered them from the countries of their enemies, I will be proved holy through them in the sight of many nations. ²⁸ Then they will know that I am the LORD their God, for though I sent them into exile among the nations, I will gather them to their own land, not leaving any behind. ²⁹ I will no longer hide my face from them,

for I will pour out my Spirit on the people of Israel, declares the Sovereign LORD.'

■ PSALM 135:8-12

8 He struck down the firstborn of Egypt,
    the firstborn of people and animals.
9 He sent his signs and wonders into your
        midst, Egypt,
    against Pharaoh and all his servants.
10 He struck down many nations
    and killed mighty kings –
11 Sihon king of the Amorites,
    Og king of Bashan,
    and all the kings of Canaan –
12 and he gave their land as an inheritance,
    an inheritance to his people Israel.

■ PROVERBS 29:4-6

4 By justice a king gives a country stability,
    but those who are greedy for bribes
        tear it down.

5 Those who flatter their neighbours
    are spreading nets for their feet.

6 Evildoers are snared by their own sin,
    but the righteous shout for joy and
        are glad.

■ 2 PETER 2:1-22

2 But there were also false prophets among the people, just as there will be false teachers among you. They will secretly introduce destructive heresies, even denying the sovereign Lord who bought them – bringing swift destruction on themselves. 2 Many will follow their depraved conduct and will bring the way of truth into disrepute. 3 In their greed these teachers will exploit you with fabricated stories. Their condemnation has long been hanging over them, and their destruction has not been sleeping.

4 For if God did not spare angels when they sinned, but sent them to hell, putting them in chains of darkness to be held for judgment; 5 if he did not spare the ancient world when he brought the flood on its ungodly people, but protected Noah, a preacher of righteousness, and seven others; 6 if he condemned the cities of Sodom and Gomorrah by burning them to ashes, and made them an example of what is going to happen to the ungodly; 7 and if he rescued Lot, a righteous man, who was distressed by the depraved conduct of the lawless 8 (for that righteous man, living among them day after day, was tormented in his righteous soul by the lawless deeds he saw and heard) – 9 if this is so, then the Lord knows how to rescue the godly from trials and to hold the unrighteous for punishment on the day of judgment. 10 This is especially true of those who follow the corrupt desire of the flesh and despise authority.

Bold and arrogant, they are not afraid to heap abuse on celestial beings; 11 yet even angels, although they are stronger and more powerful, do not heap abuse on such beings when bringing judgment on them from the Lord. 12 But these people blaspheme in matters they do not understand. They are like unreasoning animals, creatures of instinct, born only to be caught and destroyed, and like animals they too will perish.

13 They will be paid back with harm for the harm they have done. Their idea of pleasure is to carouse in broad daylight. They are blots and blemishes, revelling in their pleasures while they feast with you. 14 With eyes full of adultery, they never stop sinning; they seduce the unstable; they are experts in greed – an accursed brood! 15 They have left the straight way and wandered off to follow the way of Balaam son of Bezer, who loved the wages of wickedness. 16 But he was rebuked for his wrongdoing

by a donkey – an animal without speech – who spoke with a human voice and restrained the prophet's madness.

[17] These people are springs without water and mists driven by a storm. Blackest darkness is reserved for them. [18] For they mouth empty, boastful words and, by appealing to the lustful desires of the flesh, they entice people who are just escaping from those who live in error. [19] They promise them freedom, while they themselves are slaves of depravity – for 'people are slaves to whatever has mastered them.' [20] If they have escaped the corruption of the world by knowing our Lord and Saviour Jesus Christ and are again entangled in it and are overcome, they are worse off at the end than they were at the beginning. [21] It would have been better for them not to have known the way of righteousness, than to have known it and then to turn their backs on the sacred command that was passed on to them. [22] Of them the proverbs are true: 'A dog returns to its vomit,' and, 'A sow that is washed returns to her wallowing in the mud.'

The Upper Room

'... I will pour out my Spirit on the people of Israel ...'
Ezekiel 39:29

The upper room has been described as 'the birthplace of the church'. Certainly it was there that power was loosed which changed the world. Some commentators believe that the upper room was part of someone's home – someone sympathetic to Jesus and His ministry. Why did the Holy Spirit come upon the disciples in a home and not in a sacred place such as the temple? If the Holy Spirit had come upon them in the temple, then His coming would have been associated with a sacred place, sacred services, or sacred occasions. The Holy Spirit came in the most common of all places – a home – as if He was saying, 'I am here not just for "sacred" occasions, but for all occasions, for all of life.'

One writer said in commenting on the ordinariness of the upper room, 'The Holy Spirit is not a spiritual luxury to be imported into the unusual, but a spiritual necessity for the usual.' He is to be the pulse-beat of all we do – the usual as well as the unusual, the ordinary as well as the extraordinary. In the coming of the Holy Spirit, the ordinary and seemingly insignificant things of life are touched with divine significance: every bush is aflame with the glory of God, every moment is packed with eternity, and every contact we make is part of His perfect purposes.

PRAYER

O God, I am so thankful that I don't have to wander from sacred place to sacred place in search of Your power and Your glory. You come to me just where I am until my heart glows with Your shekinah glory. Amen.

FURTHER STUDY

Joel 2:18-32; Isa. 32:15; 59:21
• What did God say would follow the coming of the Spirit?
• What is the Lord exhorting the Israelites to do?

December 1

■ EZEKIEL 40:1–41:7

40 In the twenty-fifth year of our exile, at the beginning of the year, on the tenth of the month, in the fourteenth year after the fall of the city – on that very day the hand of the LORD was on me and he took me there. ²In visions of God he took me to the land of Israel and set me on a very high mountain, on whose south side were some buildings that looked like a city. ³He took me there, and I saw a man whose appearance was like bronze; he was standing in the gateway with a linen cord and a measuring rod in his hand. ⁴The man said to me, 'Son of man, look carefully and listen closely and pay attention to everything I am going to show you, for that is why you have been brought here. Tell the people of Israel everything you see.'

⁵I saw a wall completely surrounding the temple area. The length of the measuring rod in the man's hand was six long cubits, each of which was a cubit and a handbreadth. He measured the wall; it was one measuring rod thick and one rod high.

⁶Then he went to the east gate. He climbed its steps and measured the threshold of the gate; it was one rod deep. ⁷The alcoves for the guards were one rod long and one rod wide, and the projecting walls between the alcoves were five cubits thick. And the threshold of the gate next to the portico facing the temple was one rod deep.

⁸Then he measured the portico of the gateway; ⁹it was eight cubits deep and its jambs were two cubits thick. The portico of the gateway faced the temple.

¹⁰Inside the east gate were three alcoves on each side; the three had the same measurements, and the faces of the projecting walls on each side had the same measurements. ¹¹Then he measured the width of the entrance of the gateway; it was ten cubits and its length was thirteen cubits. ¹²In front of each alcove was a wall one cubit high, and the alcoves were six cubits square. ¹³Then he measured the gateway from the top of the rear wall of one alcove to the top of the opposite one; the distance was twenty-five cubits from one parapet opening to the opposite one. ¹⁴He measured along the faces of the projecting walls all around the inside of the gateway – sixty cubits. The measurement was up to the portico facing the courtyard. ¹⁵The distance from the entrance of the gateway to the far end of its portico was fifty cubits. ¹⁶The alcoves and the projecting walls inside the gateway were surmounted by narrow parapet openings all round, as was the portico; the openings all round faced inward. The faces of the projecting walls were decorated with palm trees.

¹⁷Then he brought me into the outer court. There I saw some rooms and a pavement that had been constructed all round the court; there were thirty rooms along the pavement. ¹⁸It abutted the sides of the gateways and was as wide as they were long; this was the lower pavement. ¹⁹Then he measured the distance from the inside of the lower gateway to the outside of the inner court; it was a hundred cubits on the east side as well as on the north.

²⁰Then he measured the length and width of the north gate, leading into the outer court. ²¹Its alcoves – three on each side – its projecting walls and its portico had the same measurements as those of the first gateway. It was fifty cubits long and twenty-five cubits wide. ²²Its openings, its portico and its palm tree decorations had

the same measurements as those of the gate facing east. Seven steps led up to it, with its portico opposite them. ²³ There was a gate to the inner court facing the north gate, just as there was on the east. He measured from one gate to the opposite one; it was a hundred cubits.

²⁴ Then he led me to the south side and I saw the south gate. He measured its jambs and its portico, and they had the same measurements as the others. ²⁵ The gateway and its portico had narrow openings all round, like the openings of the others. It was fifty cubits long and twenty-five cubits wide. ²⁶ Seven steps led up to it, with its portico opposite them; it had palm tree decorations on the faces of the projecting walls on each side. ²⁷ The inner court also had a gate facing south, and he measured from this gate to the outer gate on the south side; it was a hundred cubits.

²⁸ Then he brought me into the inner court through the south gate, and he measured the south gate; it had the same measurements as the others. ²⁹ Its alcoves, its projecting walls and its portico had the same measurements as the others. The gateway and its portico had openings all round. It was fifty cubits long and twenty-five cubits wide. ³⁰ (The porticoes of the gateways around the inner court were twenty-five cubits wide and five cubits deep.) ³¹ Its portico faced the outer court; palm trees decorated its jambs, and eight steps led up to it.

³² Then he brought me to the inner court on the east side, and he measured the gateway; it had the same measurements as the others. ³³ Its alcoves, its projecting walls and its portico had the same measurements as the others. The gateway and its portico had openings all round. It was fifty cubits long and twenty-five cubits wide. ³⁴ Its portico faced the outer court; palm trees decorated the jambs on either side, and eight steps led up to it.

³⁵ Then he brought me to the north gate and measured it. It had the same measurements as the others, ³⁶ as did its alcoves, its projecting walls and its portico, and it had openings all round. It was fifty cubits long and twenty-five cubits wide. ³⁷ Its portico faced the outer court; palm trees decorated the jambs on either side, and eight steps led up to it.

³⁸ A room with a doorway was by the portico in each of the inner gateways, where the burnt offerings were washed. ³⁹ In the portico of the gateway were two tables on each side, on which the burnt offerings, sin offerings and guilt offerings were slaughtered. ⁴⁰ By the outside wall of the portico of the gateway, near the steps at the entrance of the north gateway were two tables, and on the other side of the steps were two tables. ⁴¹ So there were four tables on one side of the gateway and four on the other – eight tables in all – on which the sacrifices were slaughtered. ⁴² There were also four tables of dressed stone for the burnt offerings, each a cubit and a half long, a cubit and a half wide and a cubit high. On them were placed the utensils for slaughtering the burnt offerings and the other sacrifices. ⁴³ And double-pronged hooks, each a handbreadth long, were attached to the wall all round. The tables were for the flesh of the offerings.

⁴⁴ Outside the inner gate, within the inner court, were two rooms, one at the side of the north gate and facing south, and another at the side of the south gate and facing north. ⁴⁵ He said to me, 'The room facing south is for the priests who guard the temple, ⁴⁶ and the room facing north is for the priests who guard the altar. These are the sons of Zadok, who are the only Levites who may draw near to the LORD to minister before him.'

⁴⁷ Then he measured the court: it was square – a hundred cubits long and a hundred cubits wide. And the altar was in front of the temple.

48 He brought me to the portico of the temple and measured the jambs of the portico; they were five cubits wide on either side. The width of the entrance was fourteen cubits and its projecting walls were three cubits wide on either side. 49 The portico was twenty cubits wide, and twelve cubits from front to back. It was reached by a flight of stairs, and there were pillars on each side of the jambs.

41 Then the man brought me to the main hall and measured the jambs; the width of the jambs was six cubits on each side. 2 The entrance was ten cubits wide, and the projecting walls on each side of it were five cubits wide. He also measured the main hall; it was forty cubits long and twenty cubits wide.

3 Then he went into the inner sanctuary and measured the jambs of the entrance; each was two cubits wide. The entrance was six cubits wide, and the projecting walls on each side of it were seven cubits wide. 4 And he measured the length of the inner sanctuary; it was twenty cubits, and its width was twenty cubits across the end of the main hall. He said to me, 'This is the Most Holy Place.'

5 Then he measured the wall of the temple; it was six cubits thick, and each side room round the temple was four cubits wide. 6 The side rooms were on three levels, one above another, thirty on each level. There were ledges all round the wall of the temple to serve as supports for the side rooms, so that the supports were not inserted into the wall of the temple. 7 The side rooms all round the temple were wider at each successive level. The structure surrounding the temple was built in ascending stages, so that the rooms widened as one went upwards. A stairway went up from the lowest floor to the top floor through the middle floor.

■ PSALM 135:13-21

13 Your name, LORD, endures for ever,
  your renown, LORD, through all
    generations.
14 For the LORD will vindicate his people
  and have compassion on his servants.

15 The idols of the nations are silver and
    gold,
  made by human hands.
16 They have mouths, but cannot speak,
  eyes, but cannot see.
17 They have ears, but cannot hear,
  nor is there breath in their mouths.
18 Those who make them will be like them,
  and so will all who trust in them.

19 All you Israelites, praise the LORD;
  house of Aaron, praise the LORD;
20 house of Levi, praise the LORD;
  you who fear him, praise the LORD.
21 Praise be to the LORD from Zion,
  to him who dwells in Jerusalem.

Praise the LORD.

■ PROVERBS 29:7-9

7 The righteous care about justice for the
    poor,
  but the wicked have no such concern.

8 Mockers stir up a city,
  but the wise turn away anger.

9 If a wise person goes to court with a fool,
  the fool rages and scoffs, and there is
    no peace.

■ 2 PETER 3:1-18

3 Dear friends, this is now my second letter to you. I have written both of

them as reminders to stimulate you to wholesome thinking. [2] I want you to recall the words spoken in the past by the holy prophets and the command given by our Lord and Saviour through your apostles.

[3] Above all, you must understand that in the last days scoffers will come, scoffing and following their own evil desires. [4] They will say, 'Where is this "coming" he promised? Ever since our ancestors died, everything goes on as it has since the beginning of creation.' [5] But they deliberately forget that long ago by God's word the heavens came into being and the earth was formed out of water and by water. [6] By these waters also the world of that time was deluged and destroyed. [7] By the same word the present heavens and earth are reserved for fire, being kept for the day of judgment and destruction of the ungodly.

[8] But do not forget this one thing, dear friends: with the Lord a day is like a thousand years, and a thousand years are like a day. [9] The Lord is not slow in keeping his promise, as some understand slowness. Instead he is patient with you, not wanting anyone to perish, but everyone to come to repentance.

[10] But the day of the Lord will come like a thief. The heavens will disappear with a roar; the elements will be destroyed by fire, and the earth and everything done in it will be laid bare.

[11] Since everything will be destroyed in this way, what kind of people ought you to be? You ought to live holy and godly lives [12] as you look forward to the day of God and speed its coming. That day will bring about the destruction of the heavens by fire, and the elements will melt in the heat. [13] But in keeping with his promise we are looking forward to a new heaven and a new earth, where righteousness dwells.

[14] So then, dear friends, since you are looking forward to this, make every effort to be found spotless, blameless and at peace with him. [15] Bear in mind that our Lord's patience means salvation, just as our dear brother Paul also wrote to you with the wisdom that God gave him. [16] He writes the same way in all his letters, speaking in them of these matters. His letters contain some things that are hard to understand, which ignorant and unstable people distort, as they do the other Scriptures, to their own destruction.

[17] Therefore, dear friends, since you have been forewarned, be on your guard so that you may not be carried away by the error of the lawless and fall from your secure position. [18] But grow in the grace and knowledge of our Lord and Saviour Jesus Christ. To him be glory both now and for ever! Amen.

Slow Growth - Good Growth

'But grow in the grace and knowledge of our Lord and Saviour Jesus Christ.' **2 Peter 3:18**

Resentment poisons the one who holds it. Think how free of resentment our Lord was. His 'first word' from the cross shows how He dealt with any possible temptation to be resentful. I believe that He was as free to walk away from Calvary as he was to walk away from the cliff-edge above Nazareth. He accepted death. Sin and love were in decisive battle. Had He drawn back, sin would have won. And He who lives in us can love in us - if we let Him.

We must allow time for change. Change is more often than not a process. I want to emphasise this because many, when once they see the way out of their dilemma, want change to take place too quickly. Some changes in our lives take place quickly. The night I surrendered my life to Jesus Christ, a lot of my sinful habits left me. But some didn't, and the process of change was long and tedious. Deep healing and supernatural change can take place in a moment, but often it takes months of struggle, trial and error, learning and unlearning.

All of us have different timetables when it comes to growing, and no one should judge another's timetable. There is an assumption that when God is involved, then all change will be instantaneous. It can happen that way, but be prepared also for it to take place over a period of time. A gardener friend of mine says, 'Slow growth is good growth'. It is the same in the garden of the soul.

PRAYER

Father, help me to be content with Your timetable for my spiritual growth. Sometimes I want to grow more quickly than is good for me. Help me be patient with Your patience. In Jesus' name. Amen.

FURTHER STUDY

2 Pet. 1:2-8; Psa. 1:1-3; Jer. 17:7-8; Ezek. 31:3-9
• What do we grow in?
• Compare spiritual growth to the growth of a tree.

December 2

■ EZEKIEL 41:8–43:12

⁸ I saw that the temple had a raised base all round it, forming the foundation of the side rooms. It was the length of the rod, six long cubits. ⁹ The outer wall of the side rooms was five cubits thick. The open area between the side rooms of the temple ¹⁰ and the priests' rooms was twenty cubits wide all round the temple. ¹¹ There were entrances to the side rooms from the open area, one on the north and another on the south; and the base adjoining the open area was five cubits wide all round.

¹² The building facing the temple courtyard on the west side was seventy cubits wide. The wall of the building was five cubits thick all round, and its length was ninety cubits.

¹³ Then he measured the temple; it was a hundred cubits long, and the temple courtyard and the building with its walls were also a hundred cubits long. ¹⁴ The width of the temple courtyard on the east, including the front of the temple, was a hundred cubits.

¹⁵ Then he measured the length of the building facing the courtyard at the rear of the temple, including its galleries on each side; it was a hundred cubits.

The main hall, the inner sanctuary and the portico facing the court, ¹⁶ as well as the thresholds and the narrow windows and galleries round the three of them – everything beyond and including the threshold was covered with wood. The floor, the wall up to the windows, and the windows were covered. ¹⁷ In the space above the outside of the entrance to the inner sanctuary and on the walls at regular intervals all round the inner and outer sanctuary ¹⁸ were carved cherubim and palm trees. Palm trees alternated with cherubim. Each cherub had two faces: ¹⁹ the face of a human being towards the palm tree on one side and the face of a lion towards the palm tree on the other. They were carved all round the whole temple. ²⁰ From the floor to the area above the entrance, cherubim and palm trees were carved on the wall of the main hall.

²¹ The main hall had a rectangular doorframe, and the one at the front of the Most Holy Place was similar. ²² There was a wooden altar three cubits high and two cubits square; its corners, its base and its sides were of wood. The man said to me, 'This is the table that is before the LORD.' ²³ Both the main hall and the Most Holy Place had double doors. ²⁴ Each door had two leaves – two hinged leaves for each door. ²⁵ And on the doors of the main hall were carved cherubim and palm trees like those carved on the walls, and there was a wooden overhang on the front of the portico. ²⁶ On the side walls of the portico were narrow windows with palm trees carved on each side. The side rooms of the temple also had overhangs.

42 Then the man led me northward into the outer court and brought me to the rooms opposite the temple courtyard and opposite the outer wall on the north side. ² The building whose door faced north was a hundred cubits long and fifty cubits wide. ³ Both in the section twenty cubits from the inner court and in the section opposite the pavement of the outer court, gallery faced gallery at the three levels. ⁴ In front of the rooms was an inner passageway ten cubits wide and a hundred cubits long. Their doors were on the north. ⁵ Now the upper rooms were narrower, for the galleries took more space from them than from the rooms on the lower and middle floors of the building. ⁶ The rooms on the top floor had no pillars, as the courts had; so they were smaller in floor space than those on the lower and middle floors. ⁷ There was an outer wall parallel to the rooms and the outer court; it extended in front of the rooms for fifty cubits. ⁸ While the row of rooms on the side next to the outer court was fifty cubits long, the row on the side nearest the sanctuary was a hundred cubits long. ⁹ The lower rooms had an entrance on the east side as one enters them from the outer court.

¹⁰ On the south side along the length of the wall of the outer court, adjoining the temple courtyard and opposite the outer wall, were rooms ¹¹ with a passageway in front of them. These were like the rooms on the north; they had the same length and width, with similar exits and dimensions. Similar to the doorways on the north ¹² were the doorways of the rooms on the south. There was a doorway at the beginning of the passageway that was parallel to the corresponding wall extending eastward, by which one enters the rooms.

¹³ Then he said to me, 'The north and south rooms facing the temple courtyard are the priests' rooms, where the priests who approach the LORD will eat the most holy offerings. There they will put the most holy offerings – the grain offerings, the sin offerings and the guilt offerings – for the place is holy. ¹⁴ Once the priests enter the holy precincts, they are not to go into the outer court until they leave behind the garments in which they minister, for these are holy. They are to put on other clothes before they go near the places that are for the people.'

¹⁵ When he had finished measuring what was inside the temple area, he led me out by the east gate and measured the area all around: ¹⁶ he measured the east side with the measuring rod; it was five hundred cubits. ¹⁷ He measured the north side; it was five hundred cubits by the measuring rod. ¹⁸ He measured the south side;

it was five hundred cubits by the measuring rod. [19]Then he turned to the west side and measured; it was five hundred cubits by the measuring rod. [20]So he measured the area on all four sides. It had a wall round it, five hundred cubits long and five hundred cubits wide, to separate the holy from the common.

43 Then the man brought me to the gate facing east, [2]and I saw the glory of the God of Israel coming from the east. His voice was like the roar of rushing waters, and the land was radiant with his glory. [3]The vision I saw was like the vision I had seen when he came to destroy the city and like the visions I had seen by the River Kebar, and I fell face down. [4]The glory of the LORD entered the temple through the gate facing east. [5]Then the Spirit lifted me up and brought me into the inner court, and the glory of the LORD filled the temple.

[6]While the man was standing beside me, I heard someone speaking to me from inside the temple. [7]He said: 'Son of man, this is the place of my throne and the place for the soles of my feet. This is where I will live among the Israelites for ever. The people of Israel will never again defile my holy name – neither they nor their kings – by their prostitution and the funeral offerings for their kings at their death. [8]When they placed their threshold next to my threshold and their doorposts beside my doorposts, with only a wall between me and them, they defiled my holy name by their detestable practices. So I destroyed them in my anger. [9]Now let them put away from me their prostitution and the funeral offerings for their kings, and I will live among them for ever.

[10]'Son of man, describe the temple to the people of Israel, that they may be ashamed of their sins. Let them consider its perfection, [11]and if they are ashamed of all they have done, make known to them the design of the temple – its arrangement, its exits and entrances – its whole design and all its regulations and laws. Write these down before them so that they may be faithful to its design and follow all its regulations.

[12]'This is the law of the temple: all the surrounding area on top of the mountain will be most holy. Such is the law of the temple.

PSALM 136:1-9

[1]Give thanks to the LORD, for he is good.
    His love endures for ever.
[2]Give thanks to the God of gods.
    His love endures for ever.
[3]Give thanks to the Lord of lords:
    His love endures for ever.

[4]to him who alone does great wonders,
    His love endures for ever.
[5]who by his understanding made the
        heavens,
    His love endures for ever.
[6]who spread out the earth upon the
        waters,
    His love endures for ever.
[7]who made the great lights –
    His love endures for ever.
[8]the sun to govern the day,
    His love endures for ever.
[9]the moon and stars to govern the night;
    His love endures for ever.

PROVERBS 29:10-12

[10]The bloodthirsty hate a person of
        integrity
    and seek to kill the upright.

[11]Fools give full vent to their rage,
    but the wise bring calm in the end.

[12]If a ruler listens to lies,
    all his officials become wicked.

▬ 1 JOHN 1:1–2:11

1 That which was from the beginning, which we have heard, which we have seen with our eyes, which we have looked at and our hands have touched – this we proclaim concerning the Word of life. [2] The life appeared; we have seen it and testify to it, and we proclaim to you the eternal life, which was with the Father and has appeared to us. [3] We proclaim to you what we have seen and heard, so that you also may have fellowship with us. And our fellowship is with the Father and with his Son, Jesus Christ. [4] We write this to make our joy complete.

[5] This is the message we have heard from him and declare to you: God is light; in him there is no darkness at all. [6] If we claim to have fellowship with him and yet walk in the darkness, we lie and do not live out the truth. [7] But if we walk in the light, as he is in the light, we have fellowship with one another, and the blood of Jesus, his Son, purifies us from all sin.

[8] If we claim to be without sin, we deceive ourselves and the truth is not in us. [9] If we confess our sins, he is faithful and just and will forgive us our sins and purify us from all unrighteousness. [10] If we claim we have not sinned, we make him out to be a liar and his word is not in us.

2 My dear children, I write this to you so that you will not sin. But if anybody does sin, we have an advocate with the Father – Jesus Christ, the Righteous One. [2] He is the atoning sacrifice for our sins, and not only for ours but also for the sins of the whole world.

[3] We know that we have come to know him if we keep his commands. [4] Whoever says, 'I know him,' but does not do what he commands is a liar, and the truth is not in that person. [5] But if anyone obeys his word, love for God is truly made complete in them. This is how we know we are in him: [6] whoever claims to live in him must live as Jesus did.

[7] Dear friends, I am not writing you a new command but an old one, which you have had since the beginning. This old command is the message you have heard. [8] Yet I am writing you a new command; its truth is seen in him and in you, because the darkness is passing and the true light is already shining.

[9] Anyone who claims to be in the light but hates a brother or sister is still in the darkness. [10] Anyone who loves their brother and sister lives in the light, and there is nothing in them to make them stumble. [11] But anyone who hates a brother or sister is in the darkness and walks around in the darkness. They do not know where they are going, because the darkness has blinded them.

Logically Necessary

'Give thanks to the God of gods. *His love endures for ever.*' **Psalm 136:2**

The Trinity is implicit in the whole Bible from the beginning, though it might not be evident to someone unfamiliar with the Book who started reading at Genesis until they had reached the books of the New Testament.

Ian Macpherson, in his book *The Faith Once Delivered*, says that when the island now known as Trinidad was discovered by Columbus, he thought at first it was three islands, as all he could see were three hills silhouetted against the sky. When he got closer, however, he found that what he had seen was not three islands at all but just one island. From a distance it looked like three, but close up it was only one. Hence he named the island 'Trinidad' – Spanish for 'Trinity'.

That is the kind of experience you get when reading the Bible. At first it seems to be talking about three Gods, but as you go deeper into the Scriptures you discover there are not three Gods but one – one God in three Persons.

It must be noted, though, that it is not only in isolated texts that one encounters the doctrine of the Trinity. The very concept of God's love presupposes plurality in the Godhead. Love, to be love, must have an object. Self-love is love's opposite. Since God is eternal love, He must have had objects of eternal affection. The objects of His affection were the Son and the Spirit. The doctrine of the Trinity, therefore, is not only theologically but logically necessary to an understanding of the nature of the Deity.

PRAYER

Father, help me understand that a being fully comprehended could not be God. In Your unfathomable depths all my thoughts are drowned. Symbolically I remove my shoes, for I sense I stand on holy ground. Amen.

FURTHER STUDY

Eph. 4:1-6; Deut. 4:35; Psa. 83:18; 1 Cor. 8:4
• What did Paul confirm to the Ephesians and Corinthians?
• What was the psalmist's conviction?

December 3

■ EZEKIEL 43:13–44:31

13 'These are the measurements of the altar in long cubits, that cubit being a cubit and a handbreadth: its gutter is a cubit deep and a cubit wide, with a kerb of one span around the edge. And this is the height of the altar: 14 from the gutter on the ground up to the lower ledge that goes round the altar it is two cubits high, and the ledge is a cubit wide. From this lower ledge to the upper ledge that goes round the altar it is four cubits high, and that ledge is also a cubit wide. 15 Above that, the altar hearth is four cubits high, and four horns project upwards from the hearth. 16 The altar hearth is

square, twelve cubits long and twelve cubits wide. 17 The upper ledge also is square, fourteen cubits long and fourteen cubits wide. All round the altar is a gutter of one cubit with a kerb of half a cubit. The steps of the altar face east.'

18 Then he said to me, 'Son of man, this is what the Sovereign LORD says: these will be the regulations for sacrificing burnt offerings and splashing blood against the altar when it is built: 19 you are to give a young bull as a sin offering to the Levitical priests of the family of Zadok, who come near to minister before me, declares the Sovereign LORD. 20 You are to take some of its blood and put it on the four horns of the altar

and on the four corners of the upper ledge and all round the rim, and so purify the altar and make atonement for it. ²¹You are to take the bull for the sin offering and burn it in the designated part of the temple area outside the sanctuary.

²²'On the second day you are to offer a male goat without defect for a sin offering, and the altar is to be purified as it was purified with the bull. ²³When you have finished purifying it, you are to offer a young bull and a ram from the flock, both without defect. ²⁴You are to offer them before the LORD, and the priests are to sprinkle salt on them and sacrifice them as a burnt offering to the LORD.

²⁵'For seven days you are to provide a male goat daily for a sin offering; you are also to provide a young bull and a ram from the flock, both without defect. ²⁶For seven days they are to make atonement for the altar and cleanse it; thus they will dedicate it. ²⁷At the end of these days, from the eighth day on, the priests are to present your burnt offerings and fellowship offerings on the altar. Then I will accept you, declares the Sovereign LORD.'

44 Then the man brought me back to the outer gate of the sanctuary, the one facing east, and it was shut. ²The LORD said to me, 'This gate is to remain shut. It must not be opened; no one may enter through it. It is to remain shut because the LORD, the God of Israel, has entered through it. ³The prince himself is the only one who may sit inside the gateway to eat in the presence of the LORD. He is to enter by way of the portico of the gateway and go out the same way.'

⁴Then the man brought me by way of the north gate to the front of the temple. I looked and saw the glory of the LORD filling the temple of the LORD, and I fell face down.

⁵The LORD said to me, 'Son of man, look carefully, listen closely and give attention to everything I tell you concerning all the regulations and instructions regarding the temple of the LORD. Give attention to the entrance to the temple and all the exits of the sanctuary. ⁶Say to rebellious Israel, "This is what the Sovereign LORD says: enough of your detestable practices, people of Israel! ⁷In addition to all your other detestable practices, you brought foreigners uncircumcised in heart and flesh into my sanctuary, desecrating my temple while you offered me food, fat and blood, and you broke my covenant. ⁸Instead of carrying out your duty in regard to my holy things, you put others in charge of my sanctuary. ⁹This is what the Sovereign LORD says: no foreigner uncircumcised in heart and flesh is to enter my sanctuary, not even the foreigners who live among the Israelites.

¹⁰' "The Levites who went far from me when Israel went astray and who wandered from me after their idols must bear the consequences of their sin. ¹¹They may serve in my sanctuary, having charge of the gates of the temple and serving in it; they may slaughter the burnt offerings and sacrifices for the people and stand before the people and serve them. ¹²But because they served them in the presence of their idols and made the people of Israel fall into sin, therefore I have sworn with uplifted hand that they must bear the consequences of their sin, declares the Sovereign LORD. ¹³They are not to come near to serve me as priests or come near any of my holy things or my most holy offerings; they must bear the shame of their detestable practices. ¹⁴And I will appoint them to guard the temple for all the work that is to be done in it.

¹⁵' "But the Levitical priests, who are descendants of Zadok and who guarded my sanctuary when the Israelites went astray from me, are to come near to minister before me; they are to stand before me to offer sacrifices of fat and blood, declares the Sovereign LORD. ¹⁶They alone are to enter my sanctuary; they alone are to come near my table to minister before me and serve me as guards.

17 ' "When they enter the gates of the inner court, they are to wear linen clothes; they must not wear any woollen garment while ministering at the gates of the inner court or inside the temple. 18 They are to wear linen turbans on their heads and linen undergarments round their waists. They must not wear anything that makes them perspire. 19 When they go out into the outer court where the people are, they are to take off the clothes they have been ministering in and leave them in the sacred rooms, and put on other clothes, so that the people are not consecrated through contact with their garments.

20 ' "They must not shave their heads or let their hair grow long, but they are to keep the hair of their heads trimmed. 21 No priest is to drink wine when he enters the inner court. 22 They must not marry widows or divorced women; they may marry only virgins of Israelite descent or widows of priests. 23 They are to teach my people the difference between the holy and the common and show them how to distinguish between the unclean and the clean.

24 ' "In any dispute, the priests are to serve as judges and decide it according to my ordinances. They are to keep my laws and my decrees for all my appointed festivals, and they are to keep my Sabbaths holy.

25 ' "A priest must not defile himself by going near a dead person; however, if the dead person was his father or mother, son or daughter, brother or unmarried sister, then he may defile himself. 26 After he is cleansed, he must wait seven days. 27 On the day he goes into the inner court of the sanctuary to minister in the sanctuary, he is to offer a sin offering for himself, declares the Sovereign LORD.

28 ' "I am to be the only inheritance the priests have. You are to give them no possession in Israel; I will be their possession. 29 They will eat the grain offerings, the sin offerings and the guilt offerings; and

everything in Israel devoted to the LORD will belong to them. 30 The best of all the firstfruits and of all your special gifts will belong to the priests. You are to give them the first portion of your ground meal so that a blessing may rest on your household. 31 The priests must not eat anything, whether bird or animal, found dead or torn by wild animals.

■ PSALM 136:10-16

10 to him who struck down the firstborn of
      Egypt
            His love endures for ever.
11 and brought Israel out from among them
            His love endures for ever.
12 with a mighty hand and outstretched
      arm;
            His love endures for ever.

13 to him who divided the Red Sea asunder
            His love endures for ever.
14 and brought Israel through the midst
      of it,
            His love endures for ever.
15 but swept Pharaoh and his army into the
      Red Sea;
            His love endures for ever.

16 to him who led his people through the
      wilderness;
            His love endures for ever.

■ PROVERBS 29:13-14

13 The poor and the oppressor have this in
      common:
      the LORD gives sight to the eyes of
      both.

14 If a king judges the poor with fairness,
      his throne will be established for ever.

▬ 1 John 2:12-29

¹²I am writing to you, dear children,
    because your sins have been forgiven
        on account of his name.
¹³I am writing to you, fathers,
    because you know him who is from
        the beginning.
I am writing to you, young men,
    because you have overcome the evil one.

¹⁴I write to you, dear children,
    because you know the Father.
I write to you, fathers,
    because you know him who is from
        the beginning.
I write to you, young men,
    because you are strong,
    and the word of God lives in you,
    and you have overcome the evil one.

¹⁵Do not love the world or anything in the world. If anyone loves the world, love for the Father is not in them. ¹⁶For everything in the world – the lust of the flesh, the lust of the eyes, and the pride of life – comes not from the Father but from the world. ¹⁷The world and its desires pass away, but whoever does the will of God lives for ever.

¹⁸Dear children, this is the last hour; and as you have heard that the antichrist is coming, even now many antichrists have come. This is how we know it is the last hour. ¹⁹They went out from us, but they did not really belong to us. For if they had belonged to us, they would have remained with us; but their going showed that none of them belonged to us. ²⁰But you have an anointing from the Holy One, and all of you know the truth. ²¹I do not write to you because you do not know the truth, but because you do know it and because no lie comes from the truth. ²²Who is the liar? It is whoever denies that Jesus is the Christ. Such a person is the antichrist – denying the Father and the Son. ²³No one who denies the Son has the Father; whoever acknowledges the Son has the Father also.

²⁴As for you, see that what you have heard from the beginning remains in you. If it does, you also will remain in the Son and in the Father. ²⁵And this is what he promised us – eternal life.

²⁶I am writing these things to you about those who are trying to lead you astray. ²⁷As for you, the anointing you received from him remains in you, and you do not need anyone to teach you. But as his anointing teaches you about all things and as that anointing is real, not counterfeit – just as it has taught you, remain in him.

²⁸And now, dear children, continue in him, so that when he appears we may be confident and unashamed before him at his coming.

²⁹If you know that he is righteous, you know that everyone who does what is right has been born of him.

God Is a Father

'I am writing to you, fathers, because you know him who is from the beginning.' **1 John 2:13**

God is a Father in the creative sense and the familial sense. So, for whom was the Lord's Prayer designed – for everyone or only for God's redeemed children? There is no doubt in my mind that it was intended for Christ's true disciples. Obviously many people outside the Christian church find the words of the Lord's Prayer greatly appealing, but much of the appeal is sentimental rather than spiritual.

To understand the Lord's Prayer and apply its principles in the way our Lord intended, one needs to have experienced a genuine conversion. Then, and only then, does its meaning become apparent. Jesus shows us in the first sentence of His prayer pattern that true prayer must begin with a concept of God as Father. Someone has pointed out that the term 'Father' answers all the philosophical questions about the nature of God. A father is a person; therefore God is not an impersonal being, aloof from all our troubles and trials. And, above all, a father is predisposed, by reason of his familial relationship, to give careful attention to what his child says.

When we pray, then, to the Father, we must hold in our minds the picture of our eternal Creator as a being who has a father's heart, a father's love, and a father's strength. This, then, must be the second note we strike when praying – God is a Father, and we must come to Him with all the trust and frankness of a child. Otherwise it is not a prayer.

PRAYER

O God, I am so grateful that in the word 'Father' I discover the greatest truth about You. My heart pillows itself on that glorious and wonderful fact. Thank You – Father. Amen.

FURTHER STUDY

John 5:17-47; 1:12;
2 Cor. 6:17-18; Gal. 4:5-6
• How did Jesus speak of His Father?
• What is God's promise to those who believe?

December 4

▪ EZEKIEL 45:1–47:5

45 ¹ "When you allot the land as an inheritance, you are to present to the LORD a portion of the land as a sacred district, 25,000 cubits long and 20,000 cubits wide; the entire area will be holy. ²Of this, a section 500 cubits square is to be for the sanctuary, with 50 cubits around it for open land. ³In the sacred district, measure off a section 25,000 cubits long and 10,000 cubits wide. In it will be the sanctuary, the Most Holy Place. ⁴It will be the sacred portion of the land for the priests, who minister in the sanctuary and who draw near to minister before the LORD. It will be a place for their houses as well as a holy place for the

sanctuary. ⁵An area 25,000 cubits long and 10,000 cubits wide will belong to the Levites, who serve in the temple, as their possession for towns to live in.

⁶ "You are to give the city as its property an area 5,000 cubits wide and 25,000 cubits long, adjoining the sacred portion; it will belong to all Israel.

⁷ "The prince will have the land bordering each side of the area formed by the sacred district and the property of the city. It will extend westward from the west side and eastward from the east side, running lengthwise from the western to the eastern border parallel to one of the tribal portions. ⁸This land will be his possession in Israel. And my princes will no longer oppress my

people but will allow the people of Israel to possess the land according to their tribes.

9 ' "This is what the Sovereign LORD says: you have gone far enough, princes of Israel! Give up your violence and oppression and do what is just and right. Stop dispossessing my people, declares the Sovereign LORD. 10 You are to use accurate scales, an accurate ephah and an accurate bath. 11 The ephah and the bath are to be the same size, the bath containing a tenth of a homer and the ephah a tenth of a homer; the homer is to be the standard measure for both. 12 The shekel is to consist of twenty gerahs. Twenty shekels plus twenty-five shekels plus fifteen shekels equal one mina.

13 ' "This is the special gift you are to offer: a sixth of an ephah from each homer of wheat and a sixth of an ephah from each homer of barley. 14 The prescribed portion of olive oil, measured by the bath, is a tenth of a bath from each cor (which consists of ten baths or one homer, for ten baths are equivalent to a homer). 15 Also one sheep is to be taken from every flock of two hundred from the well-watered pastures of Israel. These will be used for the grain offerings, burnt offerings and fellowship offerings to make atonement for the people, declares the Sovereign LORD. 16 All the people of the land will be required to give this special offering to the prince in Israel. 17 It will be the duty of the prince to provide the burnt offerings, grain offerings and drink offerings at the festivals, the New Moons and the Sabbaths – at all the appointed festivals of Israel. He will provide the sin offerings, grain offerings, burnt offerings and fellowship offerings to make atonement for the Israelites.

18 ' "This is what the Sovereign LORD says: in the first month on the first day you are to take a young bull without defect and purify the sanctuary. 19 The priest is to take some of the blood of the sin offering and put it on the doorposts of the temple, on the four corners of the upper ledge of the altar and on the gateposts of the inner court. 20 You are to do the same on the seventh day of the month for anyone who sins unintentionally or through ignorance; so you are to make atonement for the temple.

21 ' "In the first month on the fourteenth day you are to observe the Passover, a festival lasting seven days, during which you shall eat bread made without yeast. 22 On that day the prince is to provide a bull as a sin offering for himself and for all the people of the land. 23 Every day during the seven days of the Festival he is to provide seven bulls and seven rams without defect as a burnt offering to the LORD, and a male goat for a sin offering. 24 He is to provide as a grain offering an ephah for each bull and an ephah for each ram, along with a hin of olive oil for each ephah.

25 ' "During the seven days of the Festival, which begins in the seventh month on the fifteenth day, he is to make the same provision for sin offerings, burnt offerings, grain offerings and oil.

46 ' "This is what the Sovereign LORD says: the gate of the inner court facing east is to be shut on the six working days, but on the Sabbath day and on the day of the New Moon it is to be opened. 2 The prince is to enter from the outside through the portico of the gateway and stand by the gatepost. The priests are to sacrifice his burnt offering and his fellowship offerings. He is to bow down in worship at the threshold of the gateway and then go out, but the gate will not be shut until evening. 3 On the Sabbaths and New Moons the people of the land are to worship in the presence of the LORD at the entrance of that gateway. 4 The burnt offering the prince brings to the LORD on the Sabbath day is to be six male lambs and a ram, all without defect. 5 The grain offering given with the ram is to be an ephah, and the grain offering with the lambs is to be as much as he pleases, along with a hin of olive oil for each ephah. 6 On the day of the New

Moon he is to offer a young bull, six lambs and a ram, all without defect. [7] He is to provide as a grain offering one ephah with the bull, one ephah with the ram, and with the lambs as much as he wants to give, along with a hin of oil for each ephah. [8] When the prince enters, he is to go in through the portico of the gateway, and he is to come out the same way.

[9] " 'When the people of the land come before the LORD at the appointed festivals, whoever enters by the north gate to worship is to go out by the south gate; and whoever enters by the south gate is to go out by the north gate. No one is to return through the gate by which they entered, but each is to go out by the opposite gate. [10] The prince is to be among them, going in when they go in and going out when they go out. [11] At the feasts and the appointed festivals, the grain offering is to be an ephah with a bull, an ephah with a ram, and with the lambs as much as he pleases, along with a hin of oil for each ephah.

[12] " 'When the prince provides a freewill offering to the LORD – whether a burnt offering or fellowship offerings – the gate facing east is to be opened for him. He shall offer his burnt offering or his fellowship offerings as he does on the Sabbath day. Then he shall go out, and after he has gone out, the gate will be shut.

[13] " 'Every day you are to provide a year-old lamb without defect for a burnt offering to the LORD; morning by morning you shall provide it. [14] You are also to provide with it morning by morning a grain offering, consisting of a sixth of an ephah with a third of a hin of oil to moisten the flour. The presenting of this grain offering to the LORD is a lasting ordinance. [15] So the lamb and the grain offering and the oil shall be provided morning by morning for a regular burnt offering.

[16] " 'This is what the Sovereign LORD says: if the prince makes a gift from his inheritance to one of his sons, it will also belong to his descendants; it is to be their property by inheritance. [17] If, however, he makes a gift from his inheritance to one of his servants, the servant may keep it until the year of freedom; then it will revert to the prince. His inheritance belongs to his sons only; it is theirs. [18] The prince must not take any of the inheritance of the people, driving them off their property. He is to give his sons their inheritance out of his own property, so that not one of my people will be separated from their property.' "

[19] Then the man brought me through the entrance at the side of the gate to the sacred rooms facing north, which belonged to the priests, and showed me a place at the western end. [20] He said to me, 'This is the place where the priests are to cook the guilt offering and the sin offering and bake the grain offering, to avoid bringing them into the outer court and consecrating the people.'

[21] He then brought me to the outer court and led me round to its four corners, and I saw in each corner another court. [22] In the four corners of the outer court were enclosed courts, forty cubits long and thirty cubits wide; each of the courts in the four corners was the same size. [23] Around the inside of each of the four courts was a ledge of stone, with places for fire built all round under the ledge. [24] He said to me, 'These are the kitchens where those who minister at the temple are to cook the sacrifices of the people.'

47 The man brought me back to the entrance to the temple, and I saw water coming out from under the threshold of the temple towards the east (for the temple faced east). The water was coming down from under the south side of the temple, south of the altar. [2] He then brought me out through the north gate and led me round the outside to the outer gate facing east, and the water was trickling from the south side.

[3] As the man went eastward with a measuring line in his hand, he measured off a thousand cubits and then led me through

water that was ankle-deep. ⁴He measured off another thousand cubits and led me through water that was knee-deep. He measured off another thousand and led me through water that was up to the waist. ⁵He measured off another thousand, but now it was a river that I could not cross, because the water had risen and was deep enough to swim in – a river that no one could cross.

PSALM 136:17-26

¹⁷ to him who struck down great kings,
His love endures for ever.
¹⁸ and killed mighty kings –
His love endures for ever.
¹⁹ Sihon king of the Amorites
His love endures for ever.
²⁰ and Og king of Bashan –
His love endures for ever.
²¹ and gave their land as an inheritance,
His love endures for ever.
²² an inheritance to his servant Israel.
His love endures for ever.

²³ He remembered us in our low estate
His love endures for ever.
²⁴ and freed us from our enemies.
His love endures for ever.
²⁵ He gives food to every creature.
His love endures for ever.

²⁶ Give thanks to the God of heaven.
His love endures for ever.

PROVERBS 29:15-17

¹⁵ A rod and a reprimand impart wisdom,
but a child left undisciplined
disgraces its mother.

¹⁶ When the wicked thrive, so does sin,
but the righteous will see their
downfall.

¹⁷ Discipline your children, and they will
give you peace;
they will bring you the delights you
desire.

1 JOHN 3:1-24

3 See what great love the Father has lavished on us, that we should be called children of God! And that is what we are! The reason the world does not know us is that it did not know him. ²Dear friends, now we are children of God, and what we will be has not yet been made known. But we know that when Christ appears, we shall be like him, for we shall see him as he is. ³All who have this hope in him purify themselves, just as he is pure.

⁴Everyone who sins breaks the law; in fact, sin is lawlessness. ⁵But you know that he appeared so that he might take away our sins. And in him is no sin. ⁶No one who lives in him keeps on sinning. No one who continues to sin has either seen him or known him.

⁷Dear children, do not let anyone lead you astray. The one who does what is right is righteous, just as he is righteous. ⁸The one who does what is sinful is of the devil, because the devil has been sinning from the beginning. The reason the Son of God appeared was to destroy the devil's work. ⁹No one who is born of God will continue to sin, because God's seed remains in them; they cannot go on sinning, because they have been born of God. ¹⁰This is how we know who the children of God are and who the children of the devil are: anyone who does not do what is right is not God's child, nor is anyone who does not love their brother and sister.

¹¹For this is the message you heard from the beginning: we should love one another. ¹²Do not be like Cain, who belonged to the evil one and murdered his brother. And why did he murder him? Because his

own actions were evil and his brother's were righteous. [13] Do not be surprised, my brothers and sisters, if the world hates you. [14] We know that we have passed from death to life, because we love each other. Anyone who does not love remains in death. [15] Anyone who hates a brother or sister is a murderer, and you know that no murderer has eternal life residing in him.

[16] This is how we know what love is: Jesus Christ laid down his life for us. And we ought to lay down our lives for our brothers and sisters. [17] If anyone has material possessions and sees a brother or sister in need but has no pity on them, how can the love of God be in that person? [18] Dear children, let us not love with words or speech but with actions and in truth.

[19] This is how we know that we belong to the truth and how we set our hearts at rest in his presence: [20] if our hearts condemn us, we know that God is greater than our hearts, and he knows everything. [21] Dear friends, if our hearts do not condemn us, we have confidence before God [22] and receive from him anything we ask, because we keep his commands and do what pleases him. [23] And this is his command: to believe in the name of his Son, Jesus Christ, and to love one another as he commanded us. [24] The one who keeps God's commands lives in him, and he in them. And this is how we know that he lives in us: we know it by the Spirit he gave us.

Self-Protection

'And this is his command: to believe in the name of his Son, Jesus Christ, and to love one another ...'
1 John 3:23

An advantage of being willing to feel disappointment is that it enables us to come in touch with another hidden sin of the heart – self-protection.

Whenever we are disappointed, we naturally feel hurt and experience inner pain. Some people are so affected by this that a pool of pain builds up inside them, and they say to themselves, 'People are a source of hurt. Stay away from them, and don't get too closely involved.' They see non-involvement as the best way to avoid the pain of possible disappointment.

But this attitude is a violation of the law of love. Larry Crabb, a Christian psychologist, says: 'Deficient love is always central to our problems.' Behind most of our problems is a failure to love others as we love ourselves. If we refuse to move towards someone in the spirit of love for fear they may disappoint us, then we are more interested in protecting ourselves from pain than we are in loving – and that is sin.

Did you ever think of self-protection as a sin? Well, it is, and in my estimation it is one of the most subtle of all. Many of our relationships are ruined by this – particularly marriage relationships. A man who shouts angrily at his wife early in his marriage is setting up a self-protective system that says, 'Disappoint me, and you will have to suffer the consequences.' What is he doing? He is protecting himself more than he is loving his wife. And that, no matter how one might attempt to rationalise it, is sin.

PRAYER

Father, Your challenges are sometimes more than I can bear, yet I see the sense and wisdom that lies behind them. Reveal to me my own self-protective devices, and help me be willing to give them up in favour of loving as I have been loved. Amen.

FURTHER STUDY

Luke 10:25-37; Rom. 13:10; James 1:27
• What did the priest and Levite display?
• What did the Samaritan display?

December 5

■ EZEKIEL 47:6–48:35

⁶He asked me, 'Son of man, do you see this?'

Then he led me back to the bank of the river. ⁷When I arrived there, I saw a great number of trees on each side of the river. ⁸He said to me, 'This water flows towards the eastern region and goes down into the Arabah, where it enters the Dead Sea. When it empties into the sea, the salty water there becomes fresh. ⁹Swarms of living creatures will live wherever the river flows. There will be large numbers of fish, because this water flows there and makes the salt water fresh; so where the river flows everything will live. ¹⁰Fishermen will stand along the shore; from En Gedi to En Eglaim there will be places for spreading nets. The fish will be of many kinds – like the fish of the Mediterranean Sea. ¹¹But the swamps and marshes will not become fresh; they will be left for salt. ¹²Fruit trees of all kinds will grow on both banks of the river. Their leaves will not wither, nor will their fruit fail. Every month they will bear fruit, because the water from the sanctuary flows to them. Their fruit will serve for food and their leaves for healing.'

¹³This is what the Sovereign LORD says: 'These are the boundaries of the land that you will divide among the twelve tribes of Israel as their inheritance, with two portions for Joseph. ¹⁴You are to divide it equally among them. Because I swore with uplifted hand to give it to your ancestors, this land will become your inheritance.

¹⁵'This is to be the boundary of the land:

'On the north side it will run from the Mediterranean Sea by the Hethlon road past Lebo Hamath to Zedad, ¹⁶Berothah and Sibraim (which lies on the border between Damascus and Hamath), as far as Hazer Hattikon, which is on the border of Hauran. ¹⁷The boundary will extend from the sea to Hazar Enan, along the northern border of Damascus, with the border of Hamath to the north. This will be the northern boundary.
¹⁸'On the east side the boundary will run between Hauran and Damascus, along the Jordan between Gilead and the land of Israel, to the Dead Sea and as far as Tamar. This will be the eastern boundary.
¹⁹'On the south side it will run from Tamar as far as the waters of Meribah Kadesh, then along the Wadi of Egypt to the Mediterranean Sea. This will be the southern boundary.

²⁰'On the west side, the Mediterranean Sea will be the boundary to a point opposite Lebo Hamath. This will be the western boundary.

²¹'You are to distribute this land among yourselves according to the tribes of Israel. ²²You are to allot it as an inheritance for yourselves and for the foreigners residing among you and who have children. You are to consider them as native-born Israelites; along with you they are to be allotted an inheritance among the tribes of Israel. ²³In whatever tribe a foreigner resides, there you are to give them their inheritance,' declares the Sovereign LORD.

48 'These are the tribes, listed by name: at the northern frontier, Dan will have one portion; it will follow the Hethlon road to Lebo Hamath; Hazar Enan and the northern border of Damascus next to Hamath will be part of its border from the east side to the west side.

²'Asher will have one portion; it will border the territory of Dan from east to west.

³'Naphtali will have one portion; it will border the territory of Asher from east to west.

⁴'Manasseh will have one portion; it will border the territory of Naphtali from east to west.

⁵'Ephraim will have one portion; it will border the territory of Manasseh from east to west.

⁶'Reuben will have one portion; it will border the territory of Ephraim from east to west.

⁷'Judah will have one portion; it will border the territory of Reuben from east to west.

⁸'Bordering the territory of Judah from east to west will be the portion you are to present as a special gift. It will be 25,000 cubits wide, and its length from east to west will equal one of the tribal portions; the sanctuary will be in the centre of it.

⁹'The special portion you are to offer to the LORD will be 25,000 cubits long and 10,000 cubits wide. ¹⁰This will be the sacred portion for the priests. It will be 25,000 cubits long on the north side, 10,000 cubits wide on the west side, 10,000 cubits wide on the east side and 25,000 cubits long on the south side. In the centre of it will be the sanctuary of the LORD. ¹¹This will be for the consecrated priests, the Zadokites, who were faithful in serving me and did not go astray as the Levites did when the Israelites went astray. ¹²It will be a special gift to them from the sacred portion of the land, a most holy portion, bordering the territory of the Levites.

¹³'Alongside the territory of the priests, the Levites will be allotted a portion of land 25,000 cubits long and 10,000 cubits wide. Its total length will be 25,000 cubits and its width 10,000 cubits. ¹⁴They must not sell or exchange any of it. This is the best of the land and must not pass into other hands, because it is holy to the LORD.

¹⁵'The remaining area, 5,000 cubits wide and 25,000 cubits long, will be for the common use of the city, for houses and for pasture-land. The city will be in the centre of it ¹⁶and will have these measurements: the north side 4,500 cubits, the south side 4,500 cubits, the east side 4,500 cubits, and the west side 4,500 cubits. ¹⁷The pasture-land for the city will be 250 cubits on the north, 250 cubits on the south, 250 cubits on the east, and 250 cubits on the west. ¹⁸What remains of the area, bordering on the sacred portion and running the length of it, will be 10,000 cubits on the east side and 10,000 cubits on the west side. Its produce will supply food for the workers of the city. ¹⁹The workers from the city who farm it will come from all the tribes of Israel. ²⁰The entire portion will be a square, 25,000 cubits on each side. As a special gift you will set aside the sacred portion, along with the property of the city.

²¹'What remains on both sides of the area

formed by the sacred portion and the property of the city will belong to the prince. It will extend eastward from the 25,000 cubits of the sacred portion to the eastern border, and westward from the 25,000 cubits to the western border. Both these areas running the length of the tribal portions will belong to the prince, and the sacred portion with the temple sanctuary will be in the centre of them. ²² So the property of the Levites and the property of the city will lie in the centre of the area that belongs to the prince. The area belonging to the prince will lie between the border of Judah and the border of Benjamin.

²³ 'As for the rest of the tribes: Benjamin will have one portion; it will extend from the east side to the west side.

²⁴ 'Simeon will have one portion; it will border the territory of Benjamin from east to west.

²⁵ 'Issachar will have one portion; it will border the territory of Simeon from east to west.

²⁶ 'Zebulun will have one portion; it will border the territory of Issachar from east to west.

²⁷ 'Gad will have one portion; it will border the territory of Zebulun from east to west.

²⁸ 'The southern boundary of Gad will run south from Tamar to the waters of Meribah Kadesh, then along the Wadi of Egypt to the Mediterranean Sea.

²⁹ 'This is the land you are to allot as an inheritance to the tribes of Israel, and these will be their portions,' declares the Sovereign LORD.

³⁰ 'These will be the exits of the city: beginning on the north side, which is 4,500 cubits long, ³¹ the gates of the city will be named after the tribes of Israel. The three gates on the north side will be the gate of Reuben, the gate of Judah and the gate of Levi.

³² 'On the east side, which is 4,500 cubits long, will be three gates: the gate of Joseph, the gate of Benjamin and the gate of Dan.

³³ 'On the south side, which measures 4,500 cubits, will be three gates: the gate of Simeon, the gate of Issachar and the gate of Zebulun.

³⁴ 'On the west side, which is 4,500 cubits long, will be three gates: the gate of Gad, the gate of Asher and the gate of Naphtali.

³⁵ 'The distance all around will be 18,000 cubits.

'And the name of the city from that time on will be:

THE LORD IS THERE.'

PSALM 137:1–6

¹ By the rivers of Babylon we sat and wept
    when we remembered Zion.
² There on the poplars
    we hung our harps,
³ for there our captors asked us for songs,
    our tormentors demanded songs of
        joy;
    they said, 'Sing us one of the songs of
        Zion!'

⁴ How can we sing the songs of the LORD
    while in a foreign land?
⁵ If I forget you, Jerusalem,
    may my right hand forget its skill.
⁶ May my tongue cling to the roof of my
        mouth
    if I do not remember you,
    if I do not consider Jerusalem
    my highest joy.

PROVERBS 29:18–21

¹⁸ Where there is no revelation, people cast
        off restraint;
    but blessed is the one who heeds
        wisdom's instruction.

[19] Servants cannot be corrected by mere
     words;
     though they understand, they will not
     respond.

[20] Do you see someone who speaks in
     haste?
     There is more hope for a fool than for
     them.

[21] A servant pampered from youth
     will turn out to be insolent.

■ 1 JOHN 4:1-21

4 Dear friends, do not believe every
  spirit, but test the spirits to see whether
they are from God, because many false
prophets have gone out into the world.
[2] This is how you can recognise the Spirit of God: every spirit that acknowledges
that Jesus Christ has come in the flesh is
from God, [3] but every spirit that does not
acknowledge Jesus is not from God. This is
the spirit of the antichrist, which you have
heard is coming and even now is already in
the world.

[4] You, dear children, are from God and
have overcome them, because the one who
is in you is greater than the one who is in the
world. [5] They are from the world and therefore speak from the viewpoint of the world,
and the world listens to them. [6] We are from
God, and whoever knows God listens to us;
but whoever is not from God does not listen
to us. This is how we recognise the Spirit of
truth and the spirit of falsehood.

[7] Dear friends, let us love one another,
for love comes from God. Everyone who
loves has been born of God and knows God.
[8] Whoever does not love does not know
God, because God is love. [9] This is how God
showed his love among us: he sent his one
and only Son into the world that we might
live through him. [10] This is love: not that
we loved God, but that he loved us and sent
his Son as an atoning sacrifice for our sins.
[11] Dear friends, since God so loved us, we
also ought to love one another. [12] No one
has ever seen God; but if we love one another, God lives in us and his love is made
complete in us.

[13] This is how we know that we live in him
and he in us: he has given us of his Spirit.
[14] And we have seen and testify that the Father has sent his Son to be the Saviour of the
world. [15] If anyone acknowledges that Jesus
is the Son of God, God lives in them and
they in God. [16] And so we know and rely on
the love God has for us.

God is love. Whoever lives in love lives in
God, and God in them. [17] This is how love is
made complete among us so that we will
have confidence on the day of judgment:
in this world we are like Jesus. [18] There
is no fear in love. But perfect love drives
out fear, because fear has to do with punishment. The one who fears is not made
perfect in love.

[19] We love because he first loved us.
[20] Whoever claims to love God yet hates a
brother or sister is a liar. For whoever does
not love their brother and sister, whom they
have seen, cannot love God, whom they
have not seen. [21] And he has given us this
command: anyone who loves God must also
love their brother and sister.

God – the Aggressive Lover

'This is love: not that we loved God, but that he
loved us ...' 1 John 4:10

When we perceive how much God loves us, an amazing effect is produced in our personalities – we begin to love like Him. We cannot help it. Love – *agape* love – is not the fruit of labour; it is a response. When we stand at the foot of Calvary, the place where the love of God is fully focused and caught up, the scales drop from our eyes, and our own love flames in response. We love Him because He first loved us.

Teresa of Avila tells how one day, going into her private room, she noticed a picture of our Lord being scourged before His crucifixion. She must have seen it hundreds of times, but in that moment of revelation she saw it as she had never seen it before. She saw God suffering – suffering for love and suffering for her. The revelation sent her to her knees sobbing in pain and wonder, and when she arose, she was a changed woman. The revelation of Calvary's love was the great divide in her life. She said that she arose with a sense of 'unpayable debt' and went out to share God's realised love with others.

Don't try to manufacture love. Linger in the shadow of the Cross. The love of God finds its most burning expression there. Meditate on it. Contemplate it. Remember that heaven knows no higher strategy for begetting love in mortal hearts than by granting us a vision of how much we are loved, a vision strong enough to evoke a response in our hearts – and by that answering love begotten in us by the Holy Spirit, we are freed and purged and saved.

PRAYER

Gracious Father, I see that before I can love, I must comprehend how much I am loved. Help me be aware that in my heart I have the most aggressive Lover in the universe. I am eternally grateful. Amen.

FURTHER STUDY

Rom. 5:1-8; Jer. 31:3;
Eph. 2:4-5; 1 John 3:1
• How has God demonstrated His love for us?
• What kind of love is God's love?

December 6

■ DANIEL 1:1–2:35

1 In the third year of the reign of Jehoiakim king of Judah, Nebuchadnezzar king of Babylon came to Jerusalem and besieged it. ² And the Lord delivered Jehoiakim king of Judah into his hand, along with some of the articles from the temple of God. These he carried off to the temple of his god in Babylonia and put in the treasure-house of his god.

³ Then the king ordered Ashpenaz, chief of his court officials, to bring into the king's service some of the Israelites from the royal family and the nobility – ⁴young men without any physical defect, handsome, showing aptitude for every kind of learning, well informed, quick to understand, and qualified to serve in the king's palace. He was to teach them the language

and literature of the Babylonians. ⁵The king assigned them a daily amount of food and wine from the king's table. They were to be trained for three years, and after that they were to enter the king's service.

⁶Among those who were chosen were some from Judah: Daniel, Hananiah, Mishael and Azariah. ⁷The chief official gave them new names: to Daniel, the name Belteshazzar; to Hananiah, Shadrach; to Mishael, Meshach; and to Azariah, Abednego.

⁸But Daniel resolved not to defile himself with the royal food and wine, and he asked the chief official for permission not to defile himself in this way. ⁹Now God had caused the official to show favour and compassion to Daniel, ¹⁰but the official told Daniel, 'I am afraid of my lord the king, who has assigned your food and drink. Why should he see you looking worse than the other young men of your age? The king would then have my head because of you.'

¹¹Daniel then said to the guard whom the chief official had appointed over Daniel, Hananiah, Mishael and Azariah, ¹²'Please test your servants for ten days: Give us nothing but vegetables to eat and water to drink. ¹³Then compare our appearance with that of the young men who eat the royal food, and treat your servants in accordance with what you see.' ¹⁴So he agreed to this and tested them for ten days.

¹⁵At the end of the ten days they looked healthier and better nourished than any of the young men who ate the royal food. ¹⁶So the guard took away their choice food and the wine they were to drink and gave them vegetables instead.

¹⁷To these four young men God gave knowledge and understanding of all kinds of literature and learning. And Daniel could understand visions and dreams of all kinds.

¹⁸At the end of the time set by the king to bring them into his service, the chief official presented them to Nebuchadnezzar. ¹⁹The king talked with them, and he found none

equal to Daniel, Hananiah, Mishael and Azariah; so they entered the king's service. ²⁰In every matter of wisdom and understanding about which the king questioned them, he found them ten times better than all the magicians and enchanters in his whole kingdom.

²¹And Daniel remained there until the first year of King Cyrus.

2 In the second year of his reign, Nebuchadnezzar had dreams; his mind was troubled and he could not sleep. ²So the king summoned the magicians, enchanters, sorcerers and astrologers to tell him what he had dreamed. When they came in and stood before the king, ³he said to them, 'I have had a dream that troubles me and I want to know what it means.'

⁴Then the astrologers answered the king, 'May the king live for ever! Tell your servants the dream, and we will interpret it.'

⁵The king replied to the astrologers, 'This is what I have firmly decided: if you do not tell me what my dream was and interpret it, I will have you cut into pieces and your houses turned into piles of rubble. ⁶But if you tell me the dream and explain it, you will receive from me gifts and rewards and great honour. So tell me the dream and interpret it for me.'

⁷Once more they replied, 'Let the king tell his servants the dream, and we will interpret it.'

⁸Then the king answered, 'I am certain that you are trying to gain time, because you realise that this is what I have firmly decided: ⁹if you do not tell me the dream, there is only one penalty for you. You have conspired to tell me misleading and wicked things, hoping the situation will change. So then, tell me the dream, and I will know that you can interpret it for me.'

¹⁰The astrologers answered the king, 'There is no one on earth who can do what the king asks! No king, however great and mighty, has ever asked such a thing of any

magician or enchanter or astrologer. ¹¹ What the king asks is too difficult. No one can reveal it to the king except the gods, and they do not live among humans.'

¹² This made the king so angry and furious that he ordered the execution of all the wise men of Babylon. ¹³ So the decree was issued to put the wise men to death, and men were sent to look for Daniel and his friends to put them to death.

¹⁴ When Arioch, the commander of the king's guard, had gone out to put to death the wise men of Babylon, Daniel spoke to him with wisdom and tact. ¹⁵ He asked the king's officer, 'Why did the king issue such a harsh decree?' Arioch then explained the matter to Daniel. ¹⁶ At this, Daniel went in to the king and asked for time, so that he might interpret the dream for him.

¹⁷ Then Daniel returned to his house and explained the matter to his friends Hananiah, Mishael and Azariah. ¹⁸ He urged them to plead for mercy from the God of heaven concerning this mystery, so that he and his friends might not be executed with the rest of the wise men of Babylon. ¹⁹ During the night the mystery was revealed to Daniel in a vision. Then Daniel praised the God of heaven ²⁰ and said:

'Praise be to the name of God for ever
    and ever;
    wisdom and power are his.
²¹ He changes times and seasons;
    he deposes kings and raises up others.
He gives wisdom to the wise
    and knowledge to the discerning.
²² He reveals deep and hidden things;
    he knows what lies in darkness,
    and light dwells with him.
²³ I thank and praise you, God of my
    ancestors:
You have given me wisdom and power,
you have made known to me what we
    asked of you,

you have made known to us the dream
    of the king.'

²⁴ Then Daniel went to Arioch, whom the king had appointed to execute the wise men of Babylon, and said to him, 'Do not execute the wise men of Babylon. Take me to the king, and I will interpret his dream for him.'

²⁵ Arioch took Daniel to the king at once and said, 'I have found a man among the exiles from Judah who can tell the king what his dream means.'

²⁶ The king asked Daniel (also called Belteshazzar), 'Are you able to tell me what I saw in my dream and interpret it?'

²⁷ Daniel replied, 'No wise man, enchanter, magician or diviner can explain to the king the mystery he has asked about, ²⁸ but there is a God in heaven who reveals mysteries. He has shown King Nebuchadnezzar what will happen in days to come. Your dream and the visions that passed through your mind as you were lying in bed are these:

²⁹ 'As Your Majesty was lying there, your mind turned to things to come, and the revealer of mysteries showed you what is going to happen. ³⁰ As for me, this mystery has been revealed to me, not because I have greater wisdom than anyone else alive, but so that Your Majesty may know the interpretation and that you may understand what went through your mind.

³¹ 'Your Majesty looked, and there before you stood a large statue – an enormous, dazzling statue, awesome in appearance. ³² The head of the statue was made of pure gold, its chest and arms of silver, its belly and thighs of bronze, ³³ its legs of iron, its feet partly of iron and partly of baked clay. ³⁴ While you were watching, a rock was cut out, but not by human hands. It struck the statue on its feet of iron and clay and smashed them. ³⁵ Then the iron, the clay, the bronze, the silver and the gold were all

broken to pieces and became like chaff on a threshing-floor in the summer. The wind swept them away without leaving a trace. But the rock that struck the statue became a huge mountain and filled the whole earth.

▬ PSALM 137:7–138:3

7 Remember, LORD, what the Edomites did
   on the day Jerusalem fell.
'Tear it down,' they cried,
   'tear it down to its foundations!'
8 Daughter Babylon, doomed to
      destruction,
   happy is the one who repays you
   according to what you have done
      to us.
9 Happy is the one who seizes your infants
   and dashes them against the rocks.

1 I will praise you, LORD, with all my heart;
   before the 'gods' I will sing your
      praise.
2 I will bow down towards your holy
      temple
   and will praise your name
   for your unfailing love and your
      faithfulness,
   for you have so exalted your solemn
      decree
   that it surpasses your fame.
3 When I called, you answered me;
   you greatly emboldened me.

▬ PROVERBS 29:22–23

22 An angry person stirs up conflict,
   and a hot-tempered person commits
      many sins.

23 Pride brings a person low,
   but the lowly in spirit gain honour.

▬ 1 JOHN 5:1–21

5 Everyone who believes that Jesus is the Christ is born of God, and everyone who loves the father loves his child as well. 2 This is how we know that we love the children of God: by loving God and carrying out his commands. 3 In fact, this is love for God: to keep his commands. And his commands are not burdensome, 4 for everyone born of God overcomes the world. This is the victory that has overcome the world, even our faith. 5 Who is it that overcomes the world? Only the one who believes that Jesus is the Son of God.

6 This is the one who came by water and blood – Jesus Christ. He did not come by water only, but by water and blood. And it is the Spirit who testifies, because the Spirit is the truth. 7 For there are three that testify: 8 the Spirit, the water and the blood; and the three are in agreement. 9 We accept human testimony, but God's testimony is greater because it is the testimony of God, which he has given about his Son. 10 Whoever believes in the Son of God accepts this testimony. Whoever does not believe God has made him out to be a liar, because they have not believed the testimony God has given about his Son. 11 And this is the testimony: God has given us eternal life, and this life is in his Son. 12 Whoever has the Son has life; whoever does not have the Son of God does not have life.

13 I write these things to you who believe in the name of the Son of God so that you may know that you have eternal life. 14 This is the confidence we have in approaching God: that if we ask anything according to his will, he hears us. 15 And if we know that he hears us – whatever we ask – we know that we have what we asked of him.

16 If you see any brother or sister commit a sin that does not lead to death, you should pray and God will give them life. I refer to those whose sin does not lead to death. There is a sin that leads to death. I am not

saying that you should pray about that. ¹⁷ All wrongdoing is sin, and there is sin that does not lead to death.

¹⁸ We know that anyone born of God does not continue to sin; the One who was born of God keeps them safe, and the evil one cannot harm them. ¹⁹ We know that we are children of God, and that the whole world is under the control of the evil one. ²⁰ We know also that the Son of God has come and has given us understanding, so that we may know him who is true. And we are in him who is true by being in his Son Jesus Christ. He is the true God and eternal life.

²¹ Dear children, keep yourselves from idols.

Truth in a Nutshell

'When I called, you answered me; you greatly emboldened me.' **Psalm 138:3**

What are the benefits of keeping our gaze continually focused on God? I can think of at least three.

First, the more we study Him, the more we will want to become like Him. The most natural thing in the world, when there is a good relationship between parents and their children, is for that child to want to become like them. That is the way it is also with God our Father. The more we discover of His love, His holiness, His purity, His trustworthiness, His strength, His patience, the more we want to emulate Him.

Second, the more we study God, the better we will know ourselves. When Isaiah stepped into the Temple and had a vision of God, he also saw the truth about himself. Things that were hidden deep within him came to light in the presence of the Eternal.

Third, the more we study Him, the clearer will be our perspective on the world. When you see that God is in charge, then you won't panic every time you open the newspaper. You can only know God, of course, through Christ, and because You have Him, instead of saying, 'Look what the world has come to,' you will be able to say, 'Look what has come to the world.'

The people who know their God will firmly resist the Adversary, says Daniel. He writes, 'the people who know their God will firmly resist him' (Dan. 11:32). I can do no more than to say – there you have it in a nutshell. The more you know God, the stronger you will be.

PRAYER

My Father and my God, now I set my course for the wide seas. With Your truth as my compass and Your Word as my chart, I set sail on this great adventure to know You better. I can count on You, but can I count on me? With Christ's help I can. Amen.

FURTHER STUDY

2 Tim. 1:1-12; John 17:3; Job 19:25
- What did Jesus pray?
- What was the key to Job's facing his difficult circumstances?

December 7

■ DANIEL 2:36–3:30

36 'This was the dream, and now we will interpret it to the king. 37 Your Majesty, you are the king of kings. The God of heaven has given you dominion and power and might and glory; 38 in your hands he has placed all mankind and the beasts of the field and the birds in the sky. Wherever they live, he has made you ruler over them all. You are that head of gold.

39 'After you, another kingdom will arise, inferior to yours. Next, a third kingdom, one of bronze, will rule over the whole earth. 40 Finally, there will be a fourth kingdom, strong as iron – for iron breaks and smashes everything – and as iron breaks things to pieces, so it will crush and break all the others. 41 Just as you saw that the feet and toes were partly of baked clay and partly of iron, so this will be a divided kingdom; yet it will have some of the strength of iron in it, even as you saw iron mixed with clay. 42 As the toes were partly iron and partly clay, so this kingdom will be partly strong and partly brittle. 43 And just as you saw the iron mixed with baked clay, so the people will be a mixture and will not remain united, any more than iron mixes with clay.

44 'In the time of those kings, the God of heaven will set up a kingdom that will never be destroyed, nor will it be left to another people. It will crush all those kingdoms and bring them to an end, but it will itself endure for ever. 45 This is the meaning of the vision of the rock cut out of a mountain, but not by human hands – a rock that broke the iron, the bronze, the clay, the silver and the gold to pieces.

'The great God has shown the king what will take place in the future. The dream is true and its interpretation is trustworthy.'

46 Then King Nebuchadnezzar fell prostrate before Daniel and paid him honour and ordered that an offering and incense be presented to him. 47 The king said to Daniel, 'Surely your God is the God of gods and the Lord of kings and a revealer of mysteries, for you were able to reveal this mystery.'

48 Then the king placed Daniel in a high position and lavished many gifts on him. He made him ruler over the entire province of Babylon and placed him in charge of all its wise men. 49 Moreover, at Daniel's request the king appointed Shadrach, Meshach and Abednego chief ministers over the province of Babylon, while Daniel himself remained at the royal court.

3 King Nebuchadnezzar made an image of gold, sixty cubits high and six cubits wide, and set it up on the plain of Dura in the province of Babylon. 2 He then summoned the satraps, prefects, governors, advisors, treasurers, judges, magistrates and all the other provincial officials to come to the dedication of the image he had set up. 3 So the satraps, prefects, governors, advisors, treasurers, judges, magistrates and all the other provincial officials assembled for the dedication of the image that King Nebuchadnezzar had set up, and they stood before it.

4 Then the herald loudly proclaimed, 'Nations and peoples of every language, this is what you are commanded to do: 5 as soon as you hear the sound of the horn, flute, zither, lyre, harp, pipe and all kinds of music, you must fall down and worship the image of gold that King Nebuchadnezzar has set up. 6 Whoever does not fall down and worship will immediately be thrown into a blazing furnace.'

⁷Therefore, as soon as they heard the sound of the horn, flute, zither, lyre, harp and all kinds of music, all the nations and peoples of every language fell down and worshipped the image of gold that King Nebuchadnezzar had set up.

⁸At this time some astrologers came forward and denounced the Jews. ⁹They said to King Nebuchadnezzar, 'May the king live for ever! ¹⁰Your Majesty has issued a decree that everyone who hears the sound of the horn, flute, zither, lyre, harp, pipe and all kinds of music must fall down and worship the image of gold, ¹¹and that whoever does not fall down and worship will be thrown into a blazing furnace. ¹²But there are some Jews whom you have set over the affairs of the province of Babylon – Shadrach, Meshach and Abednego – who pay no attention to you, Your Majesty. They neither serve your gods nor worship the image of gold you have set up.'

¹³Furious with rage, Nebuchadnezzar summoned Shadrach, Meshach and Abednego. So these men were brought before the king, ¹⁴and Nebuchadnezzar said to them, 'Is it true, Shadrach, Meshach and Abednego, that you do not serve my gods or worship the image of gold I have set up? ¹⁵Now when you hear the sound of the horn, flute, zither, lyre, harp, pipe and all kinds of music, if you are ready to fall down and worship the image I made, very good. But if you do not worship it, you will be thrown immediately into a blazing furnace. Then what god will be able to rescue you from my hand?'

¹⁶Shadrach, Meshach and Abednego replied to him, 'King Nebuchadnezzar, we do not need to defend ourselves before you in this matter. ¹⁷If we are thrown into the blazing furnace, the God we serve is able to deliver us from it, and he will deliver us from Your Majesty's hand. ¹⁸But even if he does not, we want you to know, Your Majesty, that we will not serve your gods or worship the image of gold you have set up.'

¹⁹Then Nebuchadnezzar was furious with Shadrach, Meshach and Abednego, and his attitude towards them changed. He ordered the furnace to be heated seven times hotter than usual ²⁰and commanded some of the strongest soldiers in his army to tie up Shadrach, Meshach and Abednego and throw them into the blazing furnace. ²¹So these men, wearing their robes, trousers, turbans and other clothes, were bound and thrown into the blazing furnace. ²²The king's command was so urgent and the furnace so hot that the flames of the fire killed the soldiers who took up Shadrach, Meshach and Abednego, ²³and these three men, firmly tied, fell into the blazing furnace.

²⁴Then King Nebuchadnezzar leaped to his feet in amazement and asked his advisors, 'Weren't there three men that we tied up and threw into the fire?'

They replied, 'Certainly, Your Majesty.'

²⁵He said, 'Look! I see four men walking around in the fire, unbound and unharmed, and the fourth looks like a son of the gods.'

²⁶Nebuchadnezzar then approached the opening of the blazing furnace and shouted, 'Shadrach, Meshach and Abednego, servants of the Most High God, come out! Come here!'

So Shadrach, Meshach and Abednego came out of the fire, ²⁷and the satraps, prefects, governors and royal advisors crowded around them. They saw that the fire had not harmed their bodies, nor was a hair of their heads singed; their robes were not scorched, and there was no smell of fire on them.

²⁸Then Nebuchadnezzar said, 'Praise be to the God of Shadrach, Meshach and Abednego, who has sent his angel and rescued his servants! They trusted in him and defied the king's command and were willing to give up their lives rather than serve or worship any god except their own God. ²⁹Therefore I decree that the people of any nation or language who say anything against the God of Shadrach, Meshach

and Abednego be cut into pieces and their houses be turned into piles of rubble, for no other god can save in this way.'

³⁰ Then the king promoted Shadrach, Meshach and Abednego in the province of Babylon.

■ PSALM 138:4-8

⁴ May all the kings of the earth praise you, LORD,
   when they hear what you have decreed.
⁵ May they sing of the ways of the LORD,
   for the glory of the LORD is great.

⁶ Though the LORD is exalted, he looks
      kindly on the lowly;
   though lofty, he sees them from afar.
⁷ Though I walk in the midst of trouble,
   you preserve my life.
You stretch out your hand against the
      anger of my foes;
   with your right hand you save me.
⁸ The LORD will vindicate me;
   your love, LORD, endures for ever –
   do not abandon the works of your
      hands.

■ PROVERBS 29:24-25

²⁴ The accomplices of thieves are their own
      enemies;
   they are put under oath and dare not
      testify.

²⁵ Fear of man will prove to be a snare,
   but whoever trusts in the LORD is
      kept safe.

■ 2 JOHN 1-13

¹ The elder,

To the lady chosen by God and to her children, whom I love in the truth – and not I only, but also all who know the truth – ² because of the truth, which lives in us and will be with us for ever:

³ Grace, mercy and peace from God the Father and from Jesus Christ, the Father's Son, will be with us in truth and love.

⁴ It has given me great joy to find some of your children walking in the truth, just as the Father commanded us. ⁵ And now, dear lady, I am not writing you a new command but one we have had from the beginning. I ask that we love one another. ⁶ And this is love: that we walk in obedience to his commands. As you have heard from the beginning, his command is that you walk in love.

⁷ I say this because many deceivers, who do not acknowledge Jesus Christ as coming in the flesh, have gone out into the world. Any such person is the deceiver and the antichrist. ⁸ Watch out that you do not lose what we have worked for, but that you may be rewarded fully. ⁹ Anyone who runs ahead and does not continue in the teaching of Christ does not have God; whoever continues in the teaching has both the Father and the Son. ¹⁰ If anyone comes to you and does not bring this teaching, do not take them into your house or welcome them. ¹¹ Anyone who welcomes them shares in their wicked work.

¹² I have much to write to you, but I do not want to use paper and ink. Instead, I hope to visit you and talk with you face to face, so that our joy may be complete.

¹³ The children of your sister, who is chosen by God, send their greetings.

Demandingness in Action

'… we want you to know, Your Majesty, that we will not serve your gods or worship the image of gold you have set up.' **Daniel 3:18**

How does demandingness manifest itself? One way is by an insistence that God answer our prayers in the way we think He should. I talked with a woman whose husband had abandoned her and their three small children. As she talked, I grew uncomfortable, for she told me, 'I know God is going to bring him back. If He doesn't, then He is not as faithful as He says He is. That can't be, so my husband will come back.'

Can you hear the spirit of demandingness in these words? I sympathised with her hurt to such a degree that it was painful for me to have to explain this: that faith is one thing but demandingness is another. Her 'faith' in God was based not on unconditional confidence in His character and sovereign purposes, but rather in the hope that He would relieve her suffering in the way she thought best.

Deep hurt is an environment in which we can wrongfully nourish a demanding spirit. Nothing convinces us more that God must answer our prayers in the way we think He should than when we are experiencing continued heartache. And the line between legitimate desiring and illegitimate demanding is a thin one which is easily crossed.

How can we be sure our desiring does not turn into demanding? When we are willing to say, 'If God does not grant what I desire, then I can still go on because I know that He will never abandon me, and in His love I have all the strength I need to handle whatever comes.'

PRAYER

O God, save me from an insistent and demanding spirit. You who are always reaching out to me in love and awakening me, help me to recognise the difference between a desire and a demand. In Jesus' name. Amen.

FURTHER STUDY

Matt. 26:36-46; Psa. 40:8; Eph. 6:6; Phil. 1:1
- How did Jesus express desire without demandingness?
- How did Paul express it?

December 8

■ **DANIEL 4:1–5:31**

4 King Nebuchadnezzar,

To the nations and peoples of every language, who live in all the earth:

May you prosper greatly!

² It is my pleasure to tell you about the miraculous signs and wonders that the Most High God has performed for me.

³ How great are his signs,
    how mighty his wonders!
His kingdom is an eternal
    kingdom;
his dominion endures from
    generation to generation.

⁴ I, Nebuchadnezzar, was at home in my palace, contented and prosperous. ⁵ I had a dream that made me afraid. As I was lying in bed, the images and visions that passed through my mind terrified me. ⁶ So I commanded that all the wise men of Babylon be brought before me to interpret the dream for me. ⁷ When the magicians, enchanters, astrologers and diviners came, I told them the dream, but they could not interpret it for me. ⁸ Finally, Daniel came into my presence and I told him the dream. (He is called Belteshazzar, after the name of my god, and the spirit of the holy gods is in him.) ⁹ I said, 'Belteshazzar, chief of the magicians, I know that the spirit of the holy gods is in you, and no mystery is too difficult for you. Here is my dream;

interpret it for me. ¹⁰ These are the visions I saw while lying in bed: I looked, and there before me stood a tree in the middle of the land. Its height was enormous. ¹¹ The tree grew large and strong and its top touched the sky; it was visible to the ends of the earth. ¹² Its leaves were beautiful, its fruit abundant, and on it was food for all. Under it the wild animals found shelter, and the birds lived in its branches; from it every creature was fed.

¹³ 'In the visions I saw while lying in bed, I looked, and there before me was a holy one, a messenger, coming down from heaven. ¹⁴ He called in a loud voice: "Cut down the tree and trim off its branches; strip off its leaves and scatter its fruit. Let the animals flee from under it and the birds from its branches. ¹⁵ But let the stump and its roots, bound with iron and bronze, remain in the ground, in the grass of the field.

' "Let him be drenched with the dew of heaven, and let him live with the animals among the plants of the earth. ¹⁶ Let his mind be changed from that of a man and let him be given the mind of an animal, till seven times pass by for him.

¹⁷ ' "The decision is announced by messengers, the holy ones declare the verdict, so that the living may know that the Most High is sovereign over all kingdoms on earth and gives them to anyone he wishes and sets over them the lowliest of people."

¹⁸ 'This is the dream that I, King Nebuchadnezzar, had. Now, Belteshazzar, tell me what it means, for none of the

wise men in my kingdom can interpret it for me. But you can, because the spirit of the holy gods is in you.'

[19] Then Daniel (also called Belteshazzar) was greatly perplexed for a time, and his thoughts terrified him. So the king said, 'Belteshazzar, do not let the dream or its meaning alarm you.'

Belteshazzar answered, 'My lord, if only the dream applied to your enemies and its meaning to your adversaries! [20] The tree you saw, which grew large and strong, with its top touching the sky, visible to the whole earth, [21] with beautiful leaves and abundant fruit, providing food for all, giving shelter to the wild animals, and having nesting places in its branches for the birds – [22] Your Majesty, you are that tree! You have become great and strong; your greatness has grown until it reaches the sky, and your dominion extends to distant parts of the earth.

[23] 'Your Majesty saw a holy one, a messenger, coming down from heaven and saying, "Cut down the tree and destroy it, but leave the stump, bound with iron and bronze, in the grass of the field, while its roots remain in the ground. Let him be drenched with the dew of heaven; let him live with the wild animals, until seven times pass by for him."

[24] 'This is the interpretation, Your Majesty, and this is the decree the Most High has issued against my lord the king: [25] you will be driven away from people and will live with the wild animals; you will eat grass like the ox and be drenched with the dew of heaven. Seven times will pass by for you until you acknowledge that the Most High is sovereign over all kingdoms on earth and gives them to anyone he wishes. [26] The command to leave the stump of the tree with its roots means that

your kingdom will be restored to you when you acknowledge that Heaven rules. [27] Therefore, Your Majesty, be pleased to accept my advice: renounce your sins by doing what is right, and your wickedness by being kind to the oppressed. It may be that then your prosperity will continue.'

[28] All this happened to King Nebuchadnezzar. [29] Twelve months later, as the king was walking on the roof of the royal palace of Babylon, [30] he said, 'Is not this the great Babylon I have built as the royal residence, by my mighty power and for the glory of my majesty?'

[31] Even as the words were on his lips, a voice came from heaven, 'This is what is decreed for you, King Nebuchadnezzar: your royal authority has been taken from you. [32] You will be driven away from people and will live with the wild animals; you will eat grass like the ox. Seven times will pass by for you until you acknowledge that the Most High is sovereign over all kingdoms on earth and gives them to anyone he wishes.'

[33] Immediately what had been said about Nebuchadnezzar was fulfilled. He was driven away from people and ate grass like the ox. His body was drenched with the dew of heaven until his hair grew like the feathers of an eagle and his nails like the claws of a bird.

[34] At the end of that time, I, Nebuchadnezzar, raised my eyes towards heaven, and my sanity was restored. Then I praised the Most High; I honoured and glorified him who lives for ever.

His dominion is an eternal dominion;
    his kingdom endures from generation
      to generation.
[35] All the peoples of the earth
    are regarded as nothing.
He does as he pleases

with the powers of heaven
and the peoples of the earth.
No one can hold back his hand
or say to him: 'What have you done?'

³⁶ At the same time that my sanity was restored, my honour and splendour were returned to me for the glory of my kingdom. My advisors and nobles sought me out, and I was restored to my throne and became even greater than before. ³⁷ Now I, Nebuchadnezzar, praise and exalt and glorify the King of heaven, because everything he does is right and all his ways are just. And those who walk in pride he is able to humble.

5 King Belshazzar gave a great banquet for a thousand of his nobles and drank wine with them. ² While Belshazzar was drinking his wine, he gave orders to bring in the gold and silver goblets that Nebuchadnezzar his father had taken from the temple in Jerusalem, so that the king and his nobles, his wives and his concubines might drink from them. ³ So they brought in the gold goblets that had been taken from the temple of God in Jerusalem, and the king and his nobles, his wives and his concubines drank from them. ⁴ As they drank the wine, they praised the gods of gold and silver, of bronze, iron, wood and stone.

⁵ Suddenly the fingers of a human hand appeared and wrote on the plaster of the wall, near the lampstand in the royal palace. The king watched the hand as it wrote. ⁶ His face turned pale and he was so frightened that his legs became weak and his knees were knocking.

⁷ The king summoned the enchanters, astrologers and diviners. Then he said to these wise men of Babylon, 'Whoever reads this writing and tells me what it means will be clothed in purple and have a gold chain placed round his neck, and he will be made the third highest ruler in the kingdom.'

⁸ Then all the king's wise men came in, but they could not read the writing or tell the king what it meant. ⁹ So King Belshazzar became even more terrified and his face grew more pale. His nobles were baffled.

¹⁰ The queen, hearing the voices of the king and his nobles, came into the banquet hall. 'May the king live for ever!' she said. 'Don't be alarmed! Don't look so pale! ¹¹ There is a man in your kingdom who has the spirit of the holy gods in him. In the time of your father he was found to have insight and intelligence and wisdom like that of the gods. Your father, King Nebuchadnezzar, appointed him chief of the magicians, enchanters, astrologers and diviners. ¹² He did this because Daniel, whom the king called Belteshazzar, was found to have a keen mind and knowledge and understanding, and also the ability to interpret dreams, explain riddles and solve difficult problems. Call for Daniel, and he will tell you what the writing means.'

¹³ So Daniel was brought before the king, and the king said to him, 'Are you Daniel, one of the exiles my father the king brought from Judah? ¹⁴ I have heard that the spirit of the gods is in you and that you have insight, intelligence and outstanding wisdom. ¹⁵ The wise men and enchanters were brought before me to read this writing and tell me what it means, but they could not explain it. ¹⁶ Now I have heard that you are able to give interpretations and to solve difficult problems. If you can read this writing and tell me what it means, you will be clothed in purple and have a gold chain placed round your neck, and you will be made the third highest ruler in the kingdom.'

¹⁷ Then Daniel answered the king, 'You may keep your gifts for yourself and give your rewards to someone else. Nevertheless, I will read the writing for the king and tell him what it means.

¹⁸ 'Your Majesty, the Most High God gave your father Nebuchadnezzar sovereignty and greatness and glory and splendour.

¹⁹ Because of the high position he gave him, all the nations and peoples of every language dreaded and feared him. Those the king wanted to put to death, he put to death; those he wanted to spare, he spared; those he wanted to promote, he promoted; and those he wanted to humble, he humbled. ²⁰ But when his heart became arrogant and hardened with pride, he was deposed from his royal throne and stripped of his glory. ²¹ He was driven away from people and given the mind of an animal; he lived with the wild donkeys and ate grass like the ox; and his body was drenched with the dew of heaven, until he acknowledged that the Most High God is sovereign over all kingdoms on earth and sets over them anyone he wishes.

²² 'But you, Belshazzar, his son, have not humbled yourself, though you knew all this. ²³ Instead, you have set yourself up against the Lord of heaven. You had the goblets from his temple brought to you, and you and your nobles, your wives and your concubines drank wine from them. You praised the gods of silver and gold, of bronze, iron, wood and stone, which cannot see or hear or understand. But you did not honour the God who holds in his hand your life and all your ways. ²⁴ Therefore he sent the hand that wrote the inscription.

²⁵ 'This is the inscription that was written:

MENE, MENE, TEKEL, PARSIN

²⁶ 'Here is what these words mean:

Mene: God has numbered the days of your reign and brought it to an end.

²⁷ *Tekel*: You have been weighed on the scales and found wanting.

²⁸ *Peres*: Your kingdom is divided and given to the Medes and Persians.'

²⁹ Then at Belshazzar's command, Daniel was clothed in purple, a gold chain was placed round his neck, and he was proclaimed the third highest ruler in the kingdom.

³⁰ That very night Belshazzar, king of the Babylonians, was slain, ³¹ and Darius the Mede took over the kingdom, at the age of sixty-two.

■ PSALM 139:1-6

¹ You have searched me, LORD,
  and you know me.
² You know when I sit and when I rise;
  you perceive my thoughts from afar.
³ You discern my going out and my lying down;
  you are familiar with all my ways.
⁴ Before a word is on my tongue
  you, LORD, know it completely.
⁵ You hem me in behind and before,
  and you lay your hand upon me.
⁶ Such knowledge is too wonderful for me,
  too lofty for me to attain.

■ PROVERBS 29:26-27

²⁶ Many seek an audience with a ruler,
  but it is from the LORD that one gets justice.

²⁷ The righteous detest the dishonest;
  the wicked detest the upright.

■ 3 JOHN 1-14

¹ The elder,

To my dear friend Gaius, whom I love in the truth.

² Dear friend, I pray that you may enjoy

good health and that all may go well with you, just as you are progressing spiritually. ³It gave me great joy when some believers came and testified about your faithfulness to the truth, telling how you continue to walk in it. ⁴I have no greater joy than to hear that my children are walking in the truth.

⁵Dear friend, you are faithful in what you are doing for the brothers and sisters, even though they are strangers to you. ⁶They have told the church about your love. Please send them on their way in a manner that honours God. ⁷It was for the sake of the Name that they went out, receiving no help from the pagans. ⁸We ought therefore to show hospitality to such people so that we may work together for the truth.

⁹I wrote to the church, but Diotrephes, who loves to be first, will not welcome us.

¹⁰So when I come, I will call attention to what he is doing, spreading malicious nonsense about us. Not satisfied with that, he even refuses to welcome other believers. He also stops those who want to do so and puts them out of the church.

¹¹Dear friend, do not imitate what is evil but what is good. Anyone who does what is good is from God. Anyone who does what is evil has not seen God. ¹²Demetrius is well spoken of by everyone – and even by the truth itself. We also speak well of him, and you know that our testimony is true.

¹³I have much to write to you, but I do not want to do so with pen and ink. ¹⁴I hope to see you soon, and we will talk face to face.

Peace to you. The friends here send their greetings. Greet the friends there by name.

'Do It Yourself'

'... you did not honour the God who holds in his hand your life and all your ways.' **Daniel 5:23**

Most Christians do not pant after God in the way the psalmist described in Psalm 42:1. Now I must attempt to make clear what I mean.

First, let me pull into focus the major problem with which we all struggle as soon as we are born. When God created us in the beginning, He designed us to have a relationship with Him. This means that deep within our being is a thirst for God which will not go away. It can be ignored, disguised, misunderstood, wrongly labelled, or submerged underneath a wealth of activity, but it will not disappear. And for good reason. We were designed to enjoy something better than this world can give us, particularly in the sphere of relationships. No human relationship can satisfy in the way that a relationship with God does.

This deep thirst for God that resides within us makes us dependent on God for satisfaction, and that is something our sinful human nature deeply resents. You see, due to Adam and Eve's sin in the garden of Eden, we have all been left a legacy called 'Do It Yourself'. There is something within every single one of us that wants to take charge and have a hand in bringing about our own salvation. So here is the problem: facing the fact realistically that we inwardly thirst after God puts us in touch with a level of helplessness from which our sinful human nature shrinks. It reinforces the conviction that we are dependent on someone outside of ourselves for satisfaction. And that is something we don't care to acknowledge.

PRAYER

O Father, I recognise this elemental drive in my nature which causes me to resist standing in utter helplessness before You. But I sense that there can be no breakthrough in my life until I face this issue and deal with it. Help me, Father. In Jesus' name. Amen.

FURTHER STUDY

Psa. 143:1-6; 42:2; 63:1
• What did the psalmist recognise?
• What does it mean to 'thirst'?

December 9

■ DANIEL 6:1–7:28

6 It pleased Darius to appoint 120 satraps to rule throughout the kingdom, ²with three chief ministers over them, one of whom was Daniel. The satraps were made accountable to them so that the king might not suffer loss. ³Now Daniel so distinguished himself among the chief ministers and the satraps by his exceptional qualities that the king planned to set him over the whole kingdom. ⁴At this, the chief ministers and the satraps tried to find grounds for charges against Daniel in his conduct of government affairs, but they were unable to do so. They could find no corruption in him, because he was trustworthy and neither corrupt nor negligent. ⁵Finally these men said, 'We will never find any basis for charges against this man Daniel unless it has something to do with the law of his God.'

⁶So these chief ministers and satraps went as a group to the king and said: 'May King Darius live for ever! ⁷The royal ministers, prefects, satraps, advisors and governors have all agreed that the king should issue an edict and enforce the decree that anyone who prays to any god or human being during the next thirty days, except to you, Your Majesty, shall be thrown into the lions' den. ⁸Now, Your Majesty, issue the decree and put it in writing so that it cannot be altered – in accordance with the law of the Medes and Persians, which cannot be repealed.' ⁹So King Darius put the decree in writing.

¹⁰Now when Daniel learned that the decree had been published, he went home to his upstairs room where the windows opened towards Jerusalem. Three times a day he got down on his knees and prayed, giving thanks to his God, just as he had done before. ¹¹Then these men went as a group and found Daniel praying and asking God for help. ¹²So they went to the king and spoke to him about his royal decree: 'Did you not publish a decree that during the next thirty days anyone who prays to any god or human being except to you, Your Majesty, would be thrown into the lions' den?'

The king answered, 'The decree stands – in accordance with the law of the Medes and Persians, which cannot be repealed.'

¹³ Then they said to the king, 'Daniel, who is one of the exiles from Judah, pays no attention to you, Your Majesty, or to the decree you put in writing. He still prays three times a day.' ¹⁴ When the king heard this, he was greatly distressed; he was determined to rescue Daniel and made every effort until sunset to save him.

¹⁵ Then the men went as a group to King Darius and said to him, 'Remember, Your Majesty, that according to the law of the Medes and Persians no decree or edict that the king issues can be changed.'

¹⁶ So the king gave the order, and they brought Daniel and threw him into the lions' den. The king said to Daniel, 'May your God, whom you serve continually, rescue you!'

¹⁷ A stone was brought and placed over the mouth of the den, and the king sealed it with his own signet ring and with the rings of his nobles, so that Daniel's situation might not be changed. ¹⁸ Then the king returned to his palace and spent the night without eating and without any entertainment being brought to him. And he could not sleep.

¹⁹ At the first light of dawn, the king got up and hurried to the lions' den. ²⁰ When he came near the den, he called to Daniel in an anguished voice, 'Daniel, servant of the living God, has your God, whom you serve continually, been able to rescue you from the lions?'

²¹ Daniel answered, 'May the king live for ever! ²² My God sent his angel, and he shut the mouths of the lions. They have not hurt me, because I was found innocent in his sight. Nor have I ever done any wrong before you, Your Majesty.'

²³ The king was overjoyed and gave orders to lift Daniel out of the den. And when Daniel was lifted from the den, no wound was found on him, because he had trusted in his God.

²⁴ At the king's command, the men who had falsely accused Daniel were brought in and thrown into the lions' den, along with their wives and children. And before they reached the floor of the den, the lions overpowered them and crushed all their bones.

²⁵ Then King Darius wrote to all the nations and peoples of every language in all the earth:

'May you prosper greatly!

²⁶ 'I issue a decree that in every part of my kingdom people must fear and reverence the God of Daniel.

'For he is the living God
    and he endures for ever;
his kingdom will not be destroyed,
    his dominion will never end.
²⁷ He rescues and he saves;
    he performs signs and wonders
    in the heavens and on the earth.
He has rescued Daniel
    from the power of the lions.'

²⁸ So Daniel prospered during the reign of Darius and the reign of Cyrus the Persian.

7 In the first year of Belshazzar king of Babylon, Daniel had a dream, and visions passed through his mind as he was lying in bed. He wrote down the substance of his dream.

² Daniel said: 'In my vision at night I looked, and there before me were the four winds of heaven churning up the great sea. ³ Four great beasts, each different from the others, came up out of the sea.

⁴ 'The first was like a lion, and it had the wings of an eagle. I watched until its wings were torn off and it was lifted from the ground so that it stood on two feet like a human being, and the mind of a human was given to it.

⁵ 'And there before me was a second beast, which looked like a bear. It was raised up on one of its sides, and it had three ribs in its mouth between its teeth. It was told,

"Get up and eat your fill of flesh!"

6'After that, I looked, and there before me was another beast, one that looked like a leopard. And on its back it had four wings like those of a bird. This beast had four heads, and it was given authority to rule.

7'After that, in my vision at night I looked, and there before me was a fourth beast – terrifying and frightening and very powerful. It had large iron teeth; it crushed and devoured its victims and trampled underfoot whatever was left. It was different from all the former beasts, and it had ten horns.

8'While I was thinking about the horns, there before me was another horn, a little one, which came up among them; and three of the first horns were uprooted before it. This horn had eyes like the eyes of a human being and a mouth that spoke boastfully.

9'As I looked,

'thrones were set in place,
    and the Ancient of Days took his seat.
His clothing was as white as snow;
    the hair of his head was white like wool.
His throne was flaming with fire,
    and its wheels were all ablaze.
10A river of fire was flowing,
    coming out from before him.
Thousands upon thousands attended him;
    ten thousand times ten thousand
        stood before him.
The court was seated,
    and the books were opened.

11'Then I continued to watch because of the boastful words the horn was speaking. I kept looking until the beast was slain and its body destroyed and thrown into the blazing fire. 12(The other beasts had been stripped of their authority, but were allowed to live for a period of time.)

13'In my vision at night I looked, and there before me was one like a son of man, coming with the clouds of heaven. He approached the Ancient of Days and was led

into his presence. 14He was given authority, glory and sovereign power; all nations and peoples of every language worshipped him. His dominion is an everlasting dominion that will not pass away, and his kingdom is one that will never be destroyed.

15'I, Daniel, was troubled in spirit, and the visions that passed through my mind disturbed me. 16I approached one of those standing there and asked him the meaning of all this.

'So he told me and gave me the interpretation of these things: 17"The four great beasts are four kings that will rise from the earth. 18But the holy people of the Most High will receive the kingdom and will possess it for ever – yes, for ever and ever."

19'Then I wanted to know the meaning of the fourth beast, which was different from all the others and most terrifying, with its iron teeth and bronze claws – the beast that crushed and devoured its victims and trampled underfoot whatever was left. 20I also wanted to know about the ten horns on its head and about the other horn that came up, before which three of them fell – the horn that looked more imposing than the others and that had eyes and a mouth that spoke boastfully. 21As I watched, this horn was waging war against the holy people and defeating them, 22until the Ancient of Days came and pronounced judgment in favour of the holy people of the Most High, and the time came when they possessed the kingdom.

23'He gave me this explanation: "The fourth beast is a fourth kingdom that will appear on earth. It will be different from all the other kingdoms and will devour the whole earth, trampling it down and crushing it. 24The ten horns are ten kings who will come from this kingdom. After them another king will arise, different from the earlier ones; he will subdue three kings. 25He will speak against the Most High and oppress his holy people and try to change the set times and the laws. The holy people will be delivered into his hands for a time, times and half a time.

²⁶ ' "But the court will sit, and his power will be taken away and completely destroyed for ever. ²⁷ Then the sovereignty, power and greatness of all the kingdoms under heaven will be handed over to the holy people of the Most High. His kingdom will be an everlasting kingdom, and all rulers will worship and obey him."

²⁸ 'This is the end of the matter. I, Daniel, was deeply troubled by my thoughts, and my face turned pale, but I kept the matter to myself.'

■ PSALM 139:7-12

⁷ Where can I go from your Spirit?
   Where can I flee from your presence?
⁸ If I go up to the heavens, you are there;
   if I make my bed in the depths, you
      are there.
⁹ If I rise on the wings of the dawn,
   if I settle on the far side of the sea,
¹⁰ even there your hand will guide me,
   your right hand will hold me fast.
¹¹ If I say, 'Surely the darkness will hide me
   and the light become night around me,'
¹² even the darkness will not be dark to
      you;
   the night will shine like the day,
   for darkness is as light to you.

■ PROVERBS 30:1-2

30 The sayings of Agur son of Jakeh –
   an inspired utterance.

This man's utterance to Ithiel:

'I am weary, God,
   but I can prevail.
² Surely I am only a brute, not a man;

I do not have human understanding.

■ JUDE 1-13

¹ Jude, a servant of Jesus Christ and a brother of James,

To those who have been called, who are loved in God the Father and kept for Jesus Christ:

² Mercy, peace and love be yours in abundance.

³ Dear friends, although I was very eager to write to you about the salvation we share, I felt compelled to write and urge you to contend for the faith that was once for all entrusted to God's holy people. ⁴ For certain individuals whose condemnation was written about long ago have secretly slipped in among you. They are ungodly people, who pervert the grace of our God into a licence for immorality and deny Jesus Christ our only Sovereign and Lord.

⁵ Though you already know all this, I want to remind you that the Lord at one time delivered his people out of Egypt, but later destroyed those who did not believe. ⁶ And the angels who did not keep their positions of authority but abandoned their proper dwelling – these he has kept in darkness, bound with everlasting chains for judgment on the great Day. ⁷ In a similar way, Sodom and Gomorrah and the surrounding towns gave themselves up to sexual immorality and perversion. They serve as an example of those who suffer the punishment of eternal fire.

⁸ In the very same way, on the strength of their dreams these ungodly people pollute their own bodies, reject authority and heap abuse on celestial beings. ⁹ But even the archangel Michael, when he was disputing with the devil about the body of Moses, did not himself dare to condemn him for

slander but said, 'The Lord rebuke you!'
[10] Yet these people slander whatever they do not understand, and the very things they do understand by instinct – as irrational animals do – will destroy them.

[11] Woe to them! They have taken the way of Cain; they have rushed for profit into Balaam's error; they have been destroyed in Korah's rebellion.

[12] These people are blemishes at your love feasts, eating with you without the slightest qualm – shepherds who feed only themselves. They are clouds without rain, blown along by the wind; autumn trees, without fruit and uprooted – twice dead. [13] They are wild waves of the sea, foaming up their shame; wandering stars, for whom blackest darkness has been reserved for ever.

Satanic Forces

'And the angels who did not keep their positions of authority but abandoned their proper dwelling – these he has kept in darkness, bound with everlasting chains for judgment on the great Day.' **Jude 6**

The devil was created as a wise and morally perfect being (then known as Lucifer) who aspired to take over the throne of God and thus usurp the position of his Creator. Once that happened, Lucifer was expelled from heaven, together with the other angels who had sensed and shared his rebellious attitude. This is the fall from heaven that Jesus told His disciples He had witnessed.

Since his fall from heaven, Satan, apparently losing little of his administrative skill, has marshalled these fallen angels (now known as demons) into a hostile force to work against God and His creation. We do not know just how many angels fell with Satan, but doubtless it must have been a colossal number. When Jesus once asked a demoniac, 'What is your name?' (Luke 8:30), the demons answered, 'Legion'. If they were telling the truth, the man was controlled by thousands of demons. A Roman legion contained six thousand men!

It is little wonder, then, that the Apostle Paul warned the Ephesians that they were involved in a tremendous spiritual conflict: 'For our struggle is not against flesh and blood, but against the rulers, against the authorities, against the powers of this dark world and against the spiritual forces of evil in the heavenly realms' (Eph. 6:12).

One of America's founding fathers said, 'If men will not be governed by God, then they will be ruled by tyrants'. How sad that people actually choose to be governed by Satan rather than by God.

December 10

■ DANIEL 8:1–9:27

8 In the third year of King Belshazzar's reign, I, Daniel, had a vision, after the one that had already appeared to me. ²In my vision I saw myself in the citadel of Susa in the province of Elam; in the vision I was beside the Ulai Canal. ³I looked up, and there before me was a ram with two horns, standing beside the canal, and the horns were long. One of the horns was longer than the other but grew up later. ⁴I watched the ram as it charged towards the west and the north and the south. No animal could stand against it, and none could rescue from its power. It did as it pleased and became great.

⁵As I was thinking about this, suddenly a goat with a prominent horn between its eyes came from the west, crossing the whole earth without touching the ground. ⁶It came towards the two-horned ram I had seen standing beside the canal and charged at it in great rage. ⁷I saw it attack the ram furiously, striking the ram and shattering its two horns. The ram was powerless to stand against it; the goat knocked it to the ground and trampled on it, and none could rescue the ram from its power. ⁸The goat became very great, but at the height of its power the large horn was broken off, and in its place four prominent horns grew up towards the four winds of heaven.

⁹Out of one of them came another horn, which started small but grew in power to the south and to the east and towards the Beautiful Land. ¹⁰It grew until it reached the host of the heavens, and it threw some of the starry host down to the earth and trampled on them. ¹¹It set itself up to be as great as the commander of the army of the LORD; it took away the daily sacrifice from the LORD, and his sanctuary was thrown down. ¹²Because of rebellion, the LORD's people and the daily sacrifice were given over to it. It prospered in everything it did, and truth was thrown to the ground.

¹³Then I heard a holy one speaking, and another holy one said to him, 'How long will it take for the vision to be fulfilled – the vision concerning the daily sacrifice, the rebellion that causes desolation, the surrender of the sanctuary and the trampling underfoot of the LORD's people?'

¹⁴He said to me, 'It will take 2,300 evenings and mornings; then the sanctuary will be reconsecrated.'

¹⁵While I, Daniel, was watching the vision and trying to understand it, there before me stood one who looked like a man. ¹⁶And I heard a man's voice from the Ulai calling, 'Gabriel, tell this man the meaning of the vision.'

¹⁷As he came near the place where I was standing, I was terrified and fell prostrate. 'Son of man,' he said to me, 'understand that the vision concerns the time of the end.'

¹⁸While he was speaking to me, I was in a deep sleep, with my face to the ground. Then he touched me and raised me to my feet.

¹⁹He said: 'I am going to tell you what will happen later in the time of wrath, because the vision concerns the appointed time of the end. ²⁰The two-horned ram that you saw represents the kings of Media and Persia. ²¹The shaggy goat is the king of Greece, and the large horn between its eyes is the first king. ²²The four horns that replaced the one that was broken off represent four kingdoms that will emerge from his nation but will not have the same power.

²³'In the latter part of their reign, when rebels have become completely wicked, a fierce-looking king, a master of intrigue, will arise. ²⁴He will become very strong, but not by his own power. He will cause astounding devastation and will succeed in whatever he does. He will destroy those who are mighty, the holy people. ²⁵He will cause deceit to prosper, and he will consider himself superior. When they feel secure, he will destroy many and take his stand against the Prince of princes. Yet he will be destroyed, but not by human power.

²⁶'The vision of the evenings and mornings that has been given you is true, but seal up the vision, for it concerns the distant future.'

²⁷I, Daniel, was worn out. I lay exhausted for several days. Then I got up and went about the king's business. I was appalled by the vision; it was beyond understanding.

9 In the first year of Darius son of Xerxes (a Mede by descent), who was made ruler over the Babylonian kingdom – ²in the first year of his reign, I, Daniel, understood from the Scriptures, according to the word of the LORD given to Jeremiah the prophet, that the desolation of Jerusalem would last seventy years. ³So I turned to the Lord God and pleaded with him in prayer and petition, in fasting, and in sackcloth and ashes.

⁴I prayed to the LORD my God and confessed:

'Lord, the great and awesome God, who keeps his covenant of love with those who love him and keep his commandments, ⁵we have sinned and done wrong. We have been wicked and have rebelled; we have turned away from your commands and laws. ⁶We have not listened to your servants the prophets, who spoke in your name to our kings, our princes and our ancestors, and to all the people of the land.

⁷'Lord, you are righteous, but this day we are covered with shame – the people of Judah and the inhabitants of Jerusalem and all Israel, both near and far, in all the countries where you have scattered us because of our unfaithfulness to you. ⁸We and our kings, our princes and our ancestors are covered with shame, LORD, because we have sinned against you. ⁹The Lord our God is merciful and forgiving, even though we have rebelled against him; ¹⁰we have not obeyed the LORD our God or kept the laws he gave us through his servants the prophets. ¹¹All Israel has transgressed your law and turned away, refusing to obey you.

'Therefore the curses and sworn judgments written in the Law of Moses, the servant of God, have been poured out on us, because we have sinned against you. ¹²You have fulfilled the words spoken against us and against our rulers by bringing on us great disaster. Under the whole heaven nothing has ever been done like what has been done to Jerusalem. ¹³Just as it is written in the Law of Moses, all this disaster has come on us, yet we have not sought the favour of the LORD our God by turning from our sins and giving attention to your truth. ¹⁴ The LORD did not hesitate to bring the disaster on us, for the LORD our God is righteous in everything he does; yet we have not obeyed him.

¹⁵ 'Now, Lord our God, who brought your people out of Egypt with a mighty hand and who made for yourself a name that endures to this day, we have sinned, we have done wrong. ¹⁶ Lord, in keeping with all your righteous acts, turn away your anger and your wrath from Jerusalem, your city, your holy hill. Our sins and the iniquities of our ancestors have made Jerusalem and your people an object of scorn to all those around us.

¹⁷ 'Now, our God, hear the prayers and petitions of your servant. For your sake, Lord, look with favour on your desolate sanctuary. ¹⁸ Give ear, our God, and hear; open your eyes and see the desolation of the city that bears your Name. We do not make requests of you because we are righteous, but because of your great mercy. ¹⁹ Lord, listen! Lord, forgive! Lord, hear and act! For your sake, my God, do not delay, because your city and your people bear your Name.'

²⁰ While I was speaking and praying, confessing my sin and the sin of my people Israel and making my request to the LORD my God for his holy hill – ²¹ while I was still in prayer, Gabriel, the man I had seen in the earlier vision, came to me in swift flight about the time of the evening sacrifice. ²² He instructed me and said to me, 'Daniel, I have now come to give you insight and understanding. ²³ As soon as you began to pray, a word went out, which I have come to tell you, for you are highly

esteemed. Therefore, consider the word and understand the vision:

²⁴ 'Seventy "sevens" are decreed for your people and your holy city to finish transgression, to put an end to sin, to atone for wickedness, to bring in everlasting righteousness, to seal up vision and prophecy and to anoint the Most Holy Place.

²⁵ 'Know and understand this: From the time the word goes out to restore and rebuild Jerusalem until the Anointed One, the ruler, comes, there will be seven "sevens", and sixty-two "sevens". It will be rebuilt with streets and a trench, but in times of trouble. ²⁶ After the sixty-two "sevens", the Anointed One will be put to death and will have nothing. The people of the ruler who will come will destroy the city and the sanctuary. The end will come like a flood: war will continue until the end, and desolations have been decreed. ²⁷ He will confirm a covenant with many for one "seven". In the middle of the "seven" he will put an end to sacrifice and offering. And at the temple he will set up an abomination that causes desolation, until the end that is decreed is poured out on him.'

■ PSALM 139:13-18

¹³ For you created my inmost being;
    you knit me together in my mother's
        womb.
¹⁴ I praise you because I am fearfully and
        wonderfully made;
    your works are wonderful,
    I know that full well.
¹⁵ My frame was not hidden from you
    when I was made in the secret place,
    when I was woven together in the
        depths of the earth.
¹⁶ Your eyes saw my unformed body;
    all the days ordained for me were
        written in your book
    before one of them came to be.

[17] How precious to me are your thoughts,
　　God!
　　How vast is the sum of them!
[18] Were I to count them,
　　they would outnumber the grains
　　　of sand –
　　when I awake, I am still with you.

- ## PROVERBS 30:3-4

[3] I have not learned wisdom,
　　nor have I attained to the knowledge
　　　of the Holy One.
[4] Who has gone up to heaven and come
　　　down?
　　Whose hands have gathered up the
　　　wind?
　　Who has wrapped up the waters in a
　　　cloak?
　　Who has established all the ends of
　　　the earth?
　　What is his name, and what is the name
　　　of his son?
　　Surely you know!

- ## JUDE 14-25

[14] Enoch, the seventh from Adam,
prophesied about them: 'See, the Lord is
coming with thousands upon thousands
of his holy ones [15] to judge everyone, and to
convict all of them of all the ungodly acts
they have committed in their ungodliness,
and of all the defiant words ungodly sinners have spoken against him.' [16] These
people are grumblers and fault-finders;
they follow their own evil desires; they
boast about themselves and flatter others
for their own advantage.
[17] But, dear friends, remember what the
apostles of our Lord Jesus Christ foretold.
[18] They said to you, 'In the last times there
will be scoffers who will follow their own
ungodly desires.' [19] These are the people
who divide you, who follow mere natural
instincts and do not have the Spirit.
[20] But you, dear friends, by building yourselves up in your most holy faith and praying
in the Holy Spirit, [21] keep yourselves in God's
love as you wait for the mercy of our Lord
Jesus Christ to bring you to eternal life.
[22] Be merciful to those who doubt; [23] save
others by snatching them from the fire;
to others show mercy, mixed with fear –
hating even the clothing stained by
corrupted flesh.
[24] To him who is able to keep you from
stumbling and to present you before his glorious presence without fault and with great
joy – [25] to the only God our Saviour be glory, majesty, power and authority, through
Jesus Christ our Lord, before all ages, now
and for evermore! Amen.

'Plenty of Time for You'

'How precious to me are your thoughts, God! How vast
is the sum of them!' **Psalm 139:17**

The constituent parts of personality are predicted of God on almost
every page of the Bible. 'I will raise up for myself a faithful priest,
who will do according to what is in my heart and mind,' said the Lord to
Eli in 1 Samuel 2:35. This shows (if it needs showing) that God has a
mind with which He thinks.

God has emotions also - another aspect of personality. Some modern-day theologians claim that God is unable to feel, but clearly this is not supported by Scripture. God can be angry (Psa. 2:12), jealous (Zech. 1:14-15), merciful (Psa. 78:38), and joyful (Deut. 30:9). These are just a few of the emotions which Scripture talks about, but there are many more. Again, God chooses and decides. 'The LORD regretted that he had made human beings on the earth ... So the LORD said, "I will wipe from the face of the earth the human race ... and with them the animals, the birds and the creatures that move along the ground"' (Gen. 6:6-7).

While the majority of people believe in some kind of God, many view Him as being so great that He cannot possibly take a personal interest in such insignificant creatures as ourselves. Dr Henry Norris Russell, one of the great astronomers of the twentieth century and a Christian, once gave a talk on the vastness of the universe. Afterwards, someone asked him this question, 'How is it possible for such a great and infinite God to have time for me?' This was his reply, 'An infinite God can dispatch the affairs of this universe in the twinkling of an eye, thus giving Him plenty of time for you.'

PRAYER

O Father, help me in the midst of every trial and difficulty to rest securely in this reassuring and encouraging revelation: no matter what my problem, You always have plenty of time to give to me. I am so deeply, deeply thankful. Amen.

FURTHER STUDY

Heb. 4:12-16; Psa. 2:12; Zech. 1:14-15; Psa. 78:38; Deut. 30:9

• Can you think of other Scriptures showing God's emotions?
• What is God able to do through Christ?

December 11

■ DANIEL 10:1–11:45

10 In the third year of Cyrus king of Persia, a revelation was given to Daniel (who was called Belteshazzar). Its message was true and it concerned a great war. The understanding of the message came to him in a vision.

² At that time I, Daniel, mourned for three weeks. ³ I ate no choice food; no meat or wine touched my lips; and I used no lotions at all until the three weeks were over.

⁴ On the twenty-fourth day of the first month, as I was standing on the bank of the great river, the Tigris, ⁵ I looked up and there before me was a man dressed in linen, with a belt of fine gold from Uphaz round his waist. ⁶ His body was like topaz, his face like lightning, his eyes like flaming torches, his arms and legs like the gleam of burnished bronze, and his voice like the sound of a multitude.

⁷ I, Daniel, was the only one who saw the vision; those who were with me did not see it, but such terror overwhelmed them that they fled and hid themselves. ⁸ So I was

left alone, gazing at this great vision; I had no strength left, my face turned deathly pale and I was helpless. ⁹Then I heard him speaking, and as I listened to him, I fell into a deep sleep, my face to the ground.

¹⁰A hand touched me and set me trembling on my hands and knees. ¹¹He said, 'Daniel, you who are highly esteemed, consider carefully the words I am about to speak to you, and stand up, for I have now been sent to you.' And when he said this to me, I stood up trembling.

¹²Then he continued, 'Do not be afraid, Daniel. Since the first day that you set your mind to gain understanding and to humble yourself before your God, your words were heard, and I have come in response to them. ¹³But the prince of the Persian kingdom resisted me twenty-one days. Then Michael, one of the chief princes, came to help me, because I was detained there with the king of Persia. ¹⁴Now I have come to explain to you what will happen to your people in the future, for the vision concerns a time yet to come.'

¹⁵While he was saying this to me, I bowed with my face towards the ground and was speechless. ¹⁶Then one who looked like a man touched my lips, and I opened my mouth and began to speak. I said to the one standing before me, 'I am overcome with anguish because of the vision, my lord, and I feel very weak. ¹⁷How can I, your servant, talk with you, my lord? My strength is gone and I can hardly breathe.'

¹⁸Again the one who looked like a man touched me and gave me strength. ¹⁹'Do not be afraid, you who are highly esteemed,' he said. 'Peace! Be strong now; be strong.'

When he spoke to me, I was strengthened and said, 'Speak, my lord, since you have given me strength.'

²⁰So he said, 'Do you know why I have come to you? Soon I will return to fight against the prince of Persia, and when I go, the prince of Greece will come; ²¹but

first I will tell you what is written in the Book of Truth. (No one supports me against them except Michael, your prince. ¹And in the first year of Darius the Mede, I took my stand to support and protect him.)

11

²'Now then, I tell you the truth: three more kings will arise in Persia, and then a fourth, who will be far richer than all the others. When he has gained power by his wealth, he will stir up everyone against the kingdom of Greece. ³Then a mighty king will arise, who will rule with great power and do as he pleases. ⁴After he has arisen, his empire will be broken up and parcelled out towards the four winds of heaven. It will not go to his descendants, nor will it have the power he exercised, because his empire will be uprooted and given to others.

⁵'The king of the South will become strong, but one of his commanders will become even stronger than he and will rule his own kingdom with great power. ⁶After some years, they will become allies. The daughter of the king of the South will go to the king of the North to make an alliance, but she will not retain her power, and he and his power will not last. In those days she will be betrayed, together with her royal escort and her father and the one who supported her.

⁷'Someone from within her family will arise to take her place. He will attack the forces of the king of the North and enter his fortress; he will fight against them and be victorious. ⁸He will also seize their gods, their metal images and their valuable articles of silver and gold and carry them off to Egypt. For some years he will leave the king of the North alone. ⁹Then the king of the North will invade the realm of the king of the South but will retreat to his own country. ¹⁰His sons will prepare for war and assemble a great army, which will sweep on like an irresistible flood and carry the battle as far as his fortress.

¹¹'Then the king of the South will march out in a rage and fight against the king of the North, who will raise a large army, but it will be defeated. ¹²When the army is carried off, the king of the South will be filled with pride and will slaughter many thousands, yet he will not remain triumphant. ¹³For the king of the North will muster another army, larger than the first; and after several years, he will advance with a huge army fully equipped.

¹⁴'In those times many will rise against the king of the South. Those who are violent among your own people will rebel in fulfilment of the vision, but without success. ¹⁵Then the king of the North will come and build up siege ramps and will capture a fortified city. The forces of the South will be powerless to resist; even their best troops will not have the strength to stand. ¹⁶The invader will do as he pleases; no one will be able to stand against him. He will establish himself in the Beautiful Land and will have the power to destroy it. ¹⁷He will determine to come with the might of his entire kingdom and will make an alliance with the king of the South. And he will give him a daughter in marriage in order to overthrow the kingdom, but his plans will not succeed or help him. ¹⁸Then he will turn his attention to the coastlands and will take many of them, but a commander will put an end to his insolence and will turn his insolence back on him. ¹⁹After this, he will turn back towards the fortresses of his own country but will stumble and fall, to be seen no more.

²⁰'His successor will send out a tax collector to maintain the royal splendour. In a few years, however, he will be destroyed, yet not in anger or in battle.

²¹'He will be succeeded by a contemptible person who has not been given the honour of royalty. He will invade the kingdom when its people feel secure, and he will seize it through intrigue. ²²Then an overwhelming army will be swept away before him; both it and a prince of the covenant will be destroyed. ²³After coming to an agreement with him, he will act deceitfully, and with only a few people he will rise to power. ²⁴When the richest provinces feel secure, he will invade them and will achieve what neither his fathers nor his forefathers did. He will distribute plunder, loot and wealth among his followers. He will plot the overthrow of fortresses – but only for a time.

²⁵'With a large army he will stir up his strength and courage against the king of the South. The king of the South will wage war with a large and very powerful army, but he will not be able to stand because of the plots devised against him. ²⁶Those who eat from the king's provisions will try to destroy him; his army will be swept away, and many will fall in battle. ²⁷The two kings, with their hearts bent on evil, will sit at the same table and lie to each other, but to no avail, because an end will still come at the appointed time. ²⁸The king of the North will return to his own country with great wealth, but his heart will be set against the holy covenant. He will take action against it and then return to his own country.

²⁹'At the appointed time he will invade the South again, but this time the outcome will be different from what it was before. ³⁰Ships of the western coastlands will oppose him, and he will lose heart. Then he will turn back and vent his fury against the holy covenant. He will return and show favour to those who forsake the holy covenant.

³¹'His armed forces will rise up to desecrate the temple fortress and will abolish the daily sacrifice. Then they will set up the abomination that causes desolation. ³²With flattery he will corrupt those who have violated the covenant, but the people who know their God will firmly resist him.

³³'Those who are wise will instruct many, though for a time they will fall by the sword

or be burned or captured or plundered. [34] When they fall, they will receive a little help, and many who are not sincere will join them. [35] Some of the wise will stumble, so that they may be refined, purified and made spotless until the time of the end, for it will still come at the appointed time.

[36] 'The king will do as he pleases. He will exalt and magnify himself above every god and will say unheard-of things against the God of gods. He will be successful until the time of wrath is completed, for what has been determined must take place. [37] He will show no regard for the gods of his ancestors or for the one desired by women, nor will he regard any god, but will exalt himself above them all. [38] Instead of them, he will honour a god of fortresses; a god unknown to his ancestors he will honour with gold and silver, with precious stones and costly gifts. [39] He will attack the mightiest fortresses with the help of a foreign god and will greatly honour those who acknowledge him. He will make them rulers over many people and will distribute the land at a price.

[40] 'At the time of the end the king of the South will engage him in battle, and the king of the North will storm out against him with chariots and cavalry and a great fleet of ships. He will invade many countries and sweep through them like a flood. [41] He will also invade the Beautiful Land. Many countries will fall, but Edom, Moab and the leaders of Ammon will be delivered from his hand. [42] He will extend his power over many countries; Egypt will not escape. [43] He will gain control of the treasures of gold and silver and all the riches of Egypt, with the Libyans and Cushites in submission. [44] But reports from the east and the north will alarm him, and he will set out in a great rage to destroy and annihilate many. [45] He will pitch his royal tents between the seas at the beautiful holy mountain. Yet he will come to his end, and no one will help him.

■ PSALM 139:19-24

[19] If only you, God, would slay the wicked!
    Away from me, you who are
        bloodthirsty!
[20] They speak of you with evil intent;
    your adversaries misuse your name.
[21] Do I not hate those who hate you, LORD,
    and abhor those who are in rebellion
        against you?
[22] I have nothing but hatred for them;
    I count them my enemies.
[23] Search me, God, and know my heart;
    test me and know my anxious
        thoughts.
[24] See if there is any offensive way in me,
    and lead me in the way everlasting.

■ PROVERBS 30:5-6

[5] 'Every word of God is flawless;
    he is a shield to those who take refuge
        in him.
[6] Do not add to his words,
    or he will rebuke you and prove you
        a liar.

■ REVELATION 1:1-20

1 The revelation from Jesus Christ, which God gave him to show his servants what must soon take place. He made it known by sending his angel to his servant John, [2] who testifies to everything he saw – that is, the word of God and the testimony of Jesus Christ. [3] Blessed is the one who reads aloud the words of this prophecy, and blessed are those who hear it and take to heart what is written in it, because the time is near.

[4] John,

To the seven churches in the province of Asia:

Grace and peace to you from him who is, and who was, and who is to come, and from the seven spirits before his throne, ⁵and from Jesus Christ, who is the faithful witness, the firstborn from the dead, and the ruler of the kings of the earth.

To him who loves us and has freed us from our sins by his blood, ⁶and has made us to be a kingdom and priests to serve his God and Father – to him be glory and power for ever and ever! Amen.

⁷'Look, he is coming with the clouds,'
   and 'every eye will see him,
even those who pierced him';
   and all peoples on earth 'will mourn
      because of him.'
                     So shall it be! Amen.

⁸'I am the Alpha and the Omega,' says the Lord God, 'who is, and who was, and who is to come, the Almighty.'

⁹I, John, your brother and companion in the suffering and kingdom and patient endurance that are ours in Jesus, was on the island of Patmos because of the word of God and the testimony of Jesus. ¹⁰On the Lord's Day I was in the Spirit, and I heard behind me a loud voice like a trumpet, ¹¹which said: 'Write on a scroll what you see and send it to the seven churches: to Ephesus, Smyrna,

Pergamum, Thyatira, Sardis, Philadelphia and Laodicea.'

¹²I turned round to see the voice that was speaking to me. And when I turned I saw seven golden lampstands, ¹³and among the lampstands was someone like a son of man, dressed in a robe reaching down to his feet and with a golden sash round his chest. ¹⁴The hair on his head was white like wool, as white as snow, and his eyes were like blazing fire. ¹⁵His feet were like bronze glowing in a furnace, and his voice was like the sound of rushing waters. ¹⁶In his right hand he held seven stars, and coming out of his mouth was a sharp, double-edged sword. His face was like the sun shining in all its brilliance.

¹⁷When I saw him, I fell at his feet as though dead. Then he placed his right hand on me and said: 'Do not be afraid. I am the First and the Last. ¹⁸I am the Living One; I was dead, and now look, I am alive for ever and ever! And I hold the keys of death and Hades.

¹⁹'Write, therefore, what you have seen, what is now and what will take place later. ²⁰The mystery of the seven stars that you saw in my right hand and of the seven golden lampstands is this: the seven stars are the angels of the seven churches, and the seven lampstands are the seven churches.

The Searchlight of Truth

'Search me, God, and know my heart; test me and know my anxious thoughts.' **Psalm 139:23**

To have 'the belt of truth buckled round [our] waist' means to be possessed by truth. If we are to defend ourselves effectively against the attacks of Satan, then truth and honesty are vital necessities.

The mental health experts tell us that being willing to face the truth about ourselves is an important part of our growth towards maturity. The same is true in the realm of the spiritual. How easy it is to hide from the truth and imagine ourselves to be truthful when really we are not.

Whatever his personal idiosyncrasies and his rebellious attitude towards Christianity, Sigmund Freud made an interesting contribution to our understanding of human personality when he documented with true genius the incredibly subtle ways in which we lie to ourselves. Psychologists call them 'defence mechanisms', but a more biblical view of them would be 'lying mechanisms'. We would all much prefer to be called defensive than dishonest. But whenever we allow ourselves to be self-deceived, we not only impede our spiritual growth – we also lower our defences against Satan. He thrives on deception, and if he can push us towards self-deception, he maintains a definite advantage over us.

Many of us might react with horror to the suggestion that we are being dishonest, for we would not dream of doing or saying anything that was not according to the truth. Yet it is possible to be open and honest on the outside and yet hide from truth on the inside. All of us, even mature and experienced Christians, are capable of hiding from truth.

PRAYER

O Father, I see that if I am to overcome Satan, then I must know truth inwardly as well as outwardly. Search my heart today, dear Lord, and bring to the surface the things within me that are untrue. In Jesus' name I ask it. Amen.

FURTHER STUDY

2 Chron. 7:1-14; Isa. 44:20; James 1:22
• What are God's people to turn from?
• What does James warn against?

December 12

■ DANIEL 12:1 – HOSEA 3:5

12 'At that time Michael, the great prince who protects your people, will arise. There will be a time of distress such as has not happened from the beginning of nations until then. But at that time your people – everyone whose name is found written in the book – will be delivered. ²Multitudes who sleep in the dust of the earth will awake: some to everlasting life, others to shame and everlasting contempt. ³Those who are wise will shine like the brightness of the heavens, and those who lead many to righteousness, like the stars for ever and ever. ⁴But you, Daniel, roll up and seal the words of the scroll until the time of the end. Many will go here and there to increase knowledge.'

⁵Then I, Daniel, looked, and there before me stood two others, one on this bank of the river and one on the opposite bank. ⁶One of them said to the man clothed in linen, who was above the waters of the river, 'How long will it be before these astonishing things are fulfilled?'

⁷The man clothed in linen, who was above the waters of the river, lifted his right hand and his left hand towards heaven, and I heard him swear by him who lives for ever, saying, 'It will be for a time, times and half

a time. When the power of the holy people has been finally broken, all these things will be completed.'

⁸ I heard, but I did not understand. So I asked, 'My lord, what will the outcome of all this be?'

⁹ He replied, 'Go your way, Daniel, because the words are rolled up and sealed until the time of the end. ¹⁰ Many will be purified, made spotless and refined, but the wicked will continue to be wicked. None of the wicked will understand, but those who are wise will understand.

¹¹ 'From the time that the daily sacrifice is abolished and the abomination that causes desolation is set up, there will be 1,290 days. ¹² Blessed is the one who waits for and reaches the end of the 1,335 days.

¹³ 'As for you, go your way till the end. You will rest, and then at the end of the days you will rise to receive your allotted inheritance.'

1 The word of the Lord that came to Hosea son of Beeri during the reigns of Uzziah, Jotham, Ahaz and Hezekiah, kings of Judah, and during the reign of Jeroboam son of Joash king of Israel:

² When the LORD began to speak through Hosea, the LORD said to him, 'Go, marry a promiscuous woman and have children with her, for like an adulterous wife this land is guilty of unfaithfulness to the LORD.' ³ So he married Gomer daughter of Diblaim, and she conceived and bore him a son.

⁴ Then the LORD said to Hosea, 'Call him Jezreel, because I will soon punish the house of Jehu for the massacre at Jezreel, and I will put an end to the kingdom of Israel. ⁵ In that day I will break Israel's bow in the Valley of Jezreel.'

⁶ Gomer conceived again and gave birth to a daughter. Then the LORD said to Hosea, 'Call her Lo-Ruhamah (which means "not loved"), for I will no longer show love to Israel, that I should at all forgive them.

⁷ Yet I will show love to Judah; and I will save them – not by bow, sword or battle, or by horses and horsemen, but I, the LORD their God, will save them.'

⁸ After she had weaned Lo-Ruhamah, Gomer had another son. ⁹ Then the LORD said, 'Call him Lo-Ammi (which means "not my people"), for you are not my people, and I am not your God.

¹⁰ 'Yet the Israelites will be like the sand on the seashore, which cannot be measured or counted. In the place where it was said to them, "You are not my people", they will be called "children of the living God". ¹¹ The people of Judah and the people of Israel will come together; they will appoint one leader and will come up out of the land, for great will be the day of Jezreel.

2 'Say of your brothers, "My people", and of your sisters, "My loved one".

² 'Rebuke your mother, rebuke her,
    for she is not my wife,
    and I am not her husband.
Let her remove the adulterous look from
        her face
    and the unfaithfulness from between
        her breasts.
³ Otherwise I will strip her naked
    and make her as bare as on the day she
        was born;
I will make her like a desert,
    turn her into a parched land,
    and slay her with thirst.
⁴ I will not show my love to her children,
    because they are the children of
        adultery.
⁵ Their mother has been unfaithful
    and has conceived them in disgrace.
She said, "I will go after my lovers,
    who give me my food and my water,
    my wool and my linen, my olive oil
        and my drink."
⁶ Therefore I will block her path with
        thornbushes;
    I will wall her in so that she cannot
        find her way.

⁷ She will chase after her lovers but not
    catch them;
  she will look for them but not find
    them.
  Then she will say,
  "I will go back to my husband as at
    first,
  for then I was better off than now."
⁸ She has not acknowledged that I was the
    one
  who gave her the grain, the new wine
    and oil,
  who lavished on her the silver and gold –
  which they used for Baal.

⁹ 'Therefore I will take away my corn when
    it ripens,
  and my new wine when it is ready.
  I will take back my wool and my linen,
  intended to cover her naked body.
¹⁰ So now I will expose her lewdness
  before the eyes of her lovers;
  no one will take her out of my hands.
¹¹ I will stop all her celebrations:
  her yearly festivals, her New Moons,
  her Sabbath days – all her appointed
    festivals.
¹² I will ruin her vines and her fig-trees,
  which she said were her pay from her
    lovers;
  I will make them a thicket,
  and wild animals will devour them.
¹³ I will punish her for the days
  she burned incense to the Baals;
  she decked herself with rings and
    jewellery,
  and went after her lovers,
  but me she forgot,'
                        declares the LORD.

¹⁴ 'Therefore I am now going to allure her;
  I will lead her into the wilderness
  and speak tenderly to her.
¹⁵ There I will give her back her vineyards,
  and will make the Valley of Achor a
    door of hope.

There she will respond as in the days of
    her youth,
  as in the day she came up out of Egypt.

¹⁶ 'In that day,' declares the LORD,
  'you will call me "my husband";
  you will no longer call me "my master".
¹⁷ I will remove the names of the Baals
    from her lips;
  no longer will their names be invoked.
¹⁸ In that day I will make a covenant for
    them
  with the beasts of the field, the birds in
    the sky
  and the creatures that move along the
    ground.
  Bow and sword and battle
  I will abolish from the land,
  so that all may lie down in safety.
¹⁹ I will betroth you to me for ever;
  I will betroth you in righteousness
    and justice,
  in love and compassion.
²⁰ I will betroth you in faithfulness,
  and you will acknowledge the LORD.

²¹ 'In that day I will respond,'
    declares the LORD –
  'I will respond to the skies,
  and they will respond to the earth;
²² and the earth will respond to the grain,
  the new wine and the olive oil,
  and they will respond to Jezreel.
²³ I will plant her for myself in the land;
  I will show my love to the one I called
    "Not my loved one".
  I will say to those called "Not my
    people", "You are my people";
  and they will say, "You are my God." '

3 The LORD said to me, 'Go, show your love
to your wife again, though she is loved
by another man and is an adulteress. Love
her as the LORD loves the Israelites, though
they turn to other gods and love the sacred
raisin cakes.'

²So I bought her for fifteen shekels of silver and about a homer and a lethek of barley. ³Then I told her, 'You are to live with me for many days; you must not be a prostitute or be intimate with any man, and I will behave the same way toward you.'

⁴For the Israelites will live for many days without king or prince, without sacrifice or sacred stones, without ephod or household gods. ⁵Afterwards the Israelites will return and seek the LORD their God and David their king. They will come trembling to the LORD and to his blessings in the last days.

■ PSALM 140:1-5

¹Rescue me, LORD, from evildoers;
  protect me from the violent,
²who devise evil plans in their hearts
  and stir up war every day.
³They make their tongues as sharp as a
    serpent's;
  the poison of vipers is on their lips.

⁴Keep me safe, LORD, from the hands of
    the wicked;
  protect me from the violent,
  who devise ways to trip my feet.
⁵The arrogant have hidden a snare for me;
  they have spread out the cords of their
    net
  and have set traps for me along my
    path.

■ PROVERBS 30:7-9

⁷'Two things I ask of you, LORD;
  do not refuse me before I die:
⁸keep falsehood and lies far from me;
  give me neither poverty nor riches,
  but give me only my daily bread.
⁹Otherwise, I may have too much and
    disown you
  and say, "Who is the LORD?"

Or I may become poor and steal,
  and so dishonour the name of my God.

■ REVELATION 2:1-17

2 'To the angel of the church in Ephesus write:

These are the words of him who holds the seven stars in his right hand and walks among the seven golden lampstands. ²I know your deeds, your hard work and your perseverance. I know that you cannot tolerate wicked people, that you have tested those who claim to be apostles but are not, and have found them false. ³You have persevered and have endured hardships for my name, and have not grown weary.

⁴Yet I hold this against you: you have forsaken the love you had at first. ⁵Consider how far you have fallen! Repent and do the things you did at first. If you do not repent, I will come to you and remove your lampstand from its place. ⁶But you have this in your favour: you hate the practices of the Nicolaitans, which I also hate.

⁷Whoever has ears, let them hear what the Spirit says to the churches. To the one who is victorious, I will give the right to eat from the tree of life, which is in the paradise of God.

⁸'To the angel of the church in Smyrna write:

These are the words of him who is the First and the Last, who died and came to life again. ⁹I know your afflictions and your poverty – yet you are rich! I know about the slander of those who say they are Jews and are not, but are a synagogue of Satan. ¹⁰Do not be afraid of what you are about to suffer. I tell you, the devil will put some of you in prison to test you, and you will suffer persecution for ten days. Be faithful, even to the point of death, and I will give you life as your victor's crown.

¹¹Whoever has ears, let them hear what the Spirit says to the churches. The one who is victorious will not be hurt at all by the second death.

¹²'To the angel of the church in Pergamum write:

These are the words of him who has the sharp, double-edged sword. ¹³I know where you live – where Satan has his throne. Yet you remain true to my name. You did not renounce your faith in me, not even in the days of Antipas,

my faithful witness, who was put to death in your city – where Satan lives.

¹⁴Nevertheless, I have a few things against you: there are some among you who hold to the teaching of Balaam, who taught Balak to entice the Israelites to sin so that they ate food sacrificed to idols and committed sexual immorality. ¹⁵Likewise, you also have those who hold to the teaching of the Nicolaitans. ¹⁶Repent therefore! Otherwise, I will soon come to you and will fight against them with the sword of my mouth.

¹⁷Whoever has ears, let them hear what the Spirit says to the churches. To the one who is victorious, I will give some of the hidden manna. I will also give that person a white stone with a new name written on it, known only to the one who receives it.

God Is Not Father of All

'... where it was said to them, "You are not my people", they will be called "children of the living God".'
Hosea 1:10

Jim Packer said: 'You sum up the whole of New Testament teaching in a single phrase if you speak of it as a revelation of the Fatherhood of the Holy Creator. In the same way you sum up the whole of the New Testament religion if you describe it as the knowledge of God as one's Holy Father. Father is the Christian name for God.'

There are those who claim that the teaching given in the Old Testament is quite different. There, they say, God is viewed as being the Father of all. But is He? Consider this: 'Israel is my firstborn son ... "Let my son go ..."' (Exod. 4:22-23). There are many such passages. The Old Testament as well and the New shows God as the Father, not of all men and women but of His own people, Abraham's descendants. Galatians 3:26 tells us that God is not the Father of all, but only of those who know themselves to be sinners and have accepted His Son into their hearts. When we have done this, Paul says, we belong to Christ and are ourselves Abraham's offspring.

Divine sonship is not ours because we have been born into this world; it is ours because we have been born again into another realm –

the kingdom of God. Sonship is a gift, a gift of grace. It is not a natural sonship but an adoptive sonship. God takes those who receive His Son and makes them His adopted children, to see and share His glory into which His one and only Son has already come.

PRAYER

O Father, once again I want to record my deepest thanks that because of Your Son I am an heir of God and a joint heir with Christ. How wonderful. How truly wonderful. All honour and glory be to Your precious name. Amen.

FURTHER STUDY

Rom. 9:4-12; Jer. 31:9; Hos. 11:1; 2 Cor. 6:18
• What makes people children of God?
• What does 'Abraham's children' mean?

December 13

■ HOSEA 4:1–7:16

4 Hear the word of the LORD, you
    Israelites,
  because the LORD has a charge to bring
    against you who live in the land:
  'There is no faithfulness, no love,
    no acknowledgment of God in the
      land.
² There is only cursing, lying and murder,
    stealing and adultery;
  they break all bounds,
    and bloodshed follows bloodshed.
³ Because of this the land dries up,
    and all who live in it waste away;
  the beasts of the field, the birds in the sky
    and the fish in the sea are swept away.

⁴ 'But let no one bring a charge,
    let no one accuse another,
  for your people are like those
    who bring charges against a priest.
⁵ You stumble day and night,
    and the prophets stumble with you.
  So I will destroy your mother –
⁶   my people are destroyed from lack
      of knowledge.

'Because you have rejected knowledge,
    I also reject you as my priests;
  because you have ignored the law of your
    God,
  I also will ignore your children.
⁷ The more priests there were,
    the more they sinned against me;
  they exchanged their glorious God for
    something disgraceful.
⁸ They feed on the sins of my people
    and relish their wickedness.
⁹ And it will be: like people, like priests.
  I will punish both of them for their
    ways
  and repay them for their deeds.

¹⁰ 'They will eat but not have enough;
    they will engage in prostitution but
      not flourish,
  because they have deserted the LORD
    to give themselves ¹¹ to prostitution;
  old wine and new wine
    take away their understanding.
¹² My people consult a wooden idol,
    and a diviner's rod speaks to them.
  A spirit of prostitution leads them
    astray;

they are unfaithful to their God.
¹³ They sacrifice on the mountaintops
    and burn offerings on the hills,
under oak, poplar and terebinth,
    where the shade is pleasant.
Therefore your daughters turn to
        prostitution
    and your daughters-in-law to adultery.

¹⁴ 'I will not punish your daughters
    when they turn to prostitution,
nor your daughters-in-law
    when they commit adultery,
because the men themselves consort
        with harlots
    and sacrifice with shrine-prostitutes –
    a people without understanding will
        come to ruin!

¹⁵ 'Though you, Israel, commit adultery,
    do not let Judah become guilty.

'Do not go to Gilgal;
    do not go up to Beth Aven.
    And do not swear, "As surely as the
        LORD lives!"
¹⁶ The Israelites are stubborn,
    like a stubborn heifer.
How then can the LORD pasture them
    like lambs in a meadow?
¹⁷ Ephraim is joined to idols;
    leave him alone!
¹⁸ Even when their drinks are gone,
    they continue their prostitution;
    their rulers dearly love shameful ways.
¹⁹ A whirlwind will sweep them away,
    and their sacrifices will bring them
        shame.

5 'Hear this, you priests!
    Pay attention, you Israelites!
Listen, royal house!
    This judgment is against you:
you have been a snare at Mizpah,
    a net spread out on Tabor.
² The rebels are knee-deep in slaughter.

I will discipline all of them.
³ I know all about Ephraim;
    Israel is not hidden from me.
Ephraim, you have now turned to
        prostitution;
    Israel is corrupt.

⁴ 'Their deeds do not permit them
    to return to their God.
A spirit of prostitution is in their heart;
    they do not acknowledge the LORD.
⁵ Israel's arrogance testifies against them;
    the Israelites, even Ephraim, stumble
        in their sin;
Judah also stumbles with them.
⁶ When they go with their flocks and herds
    to seek the LORD,
they will not find him;
    he has withdrawn himself from them.
⁷ They are unfaithful to the LORD;
    they give birth to illegitimate children.
When they celebrate their New Moon
        feasts,
    he will devour their fields.

⁸ 'Sound the trumpet in Gibeah,
    the horn in Ramah.
Raise the battle cry in Beth Aven;
    lead on, Benjamin.
⁹ Ephraim will be laid waste
    on the day of reckoning.
Among the tribes of Israel
    I proclaim what is certain.
¹⁰ Judah's leaders are like those
    who move boundary stones.
I will pour out my wrath on them
    like a flood of water.
¹¹ Ephraim is oppressed,
    trampled in judgment,
    intent on pursuing idols.
¹² I am like a moth to Ephraim,
    like rot to the people of Judah.

¹³ 'When Ephraim saw his sickness,
    and Judah his sores,
    then Ephraim turned to Assyria,

and sent to the great king for help.
But he is not able to cure you,
    not able to heal your sores.
¹⁴ For I will be like a lion to Ephraim,
    like a great lion to Judah.
I will tear them to pieces and go away;
    I will carry them off, with no one to
        rescue them.
¹⁵ Then I will return to my lair
    until they have borne their guilt
    and seek my face –
in their misery
    they will earnestly seek me.'

6 'Come, let us return to the Lord.
He has torn us to pieces
    but he will heal us;
he has injured us
    but he will bind up our wounds.
² After two days he will revive us;
    on the third day he will restore us,
    that we may live in his presence.
³ Let us acknowledge the LORD;
    let us press on to acknowledge him.
As surely as the sun rises,
    he will appear;
he will come to us like the winter rains,
    like the spring rains that water the
        earth.'

⁴ 'What can I do with you, Ephraim?
    What can I do with you, Judah?
Your love is like the morning mist,
    like the early dew that disappears.
⁵ Therefore I cut you in pieces with my
        prophets,
    I killed you with the words of my
        mouth –
    then my judgments go forth like the
        sun.
⁶ For I desire mercy, not sacrifice,
    and acknowledgment of God rather
        than burnt offerings.
⁷ As at Adam, they have broken the
        covenant;
    they were unfaithful to me there.

⁸ Gilead is a city of evildoers,
    stained with footprints of blood.
⁹ As marauders lie in ambush for a victim,
    so do bands of priests;
they murder on the road to Shechem,
    carrying out their wicked schemes.
¹⁰ I have seen a horrible thing in Israel:
    there Ephraim is given to prostitution,
    Israel is defiled.

¹¹ 'Also for you, Judah,
    a harvest is appointed.

'Whenever I would restore the fortunes
        of my people,

7 ¹ whenever I would heal Israel,
    the sins of Ephraim are exposed
    and the crimes of Samaria revealed.
They practise deceit,
    thieves break into houses,
    bandits rob in the streets;
² but they do not realise
    that I remember all their evil deeds.
Their sins engulf them;
    they are always before me.

³ 'They delight the king with their
        wickedness,
    the princes with their lies.
⁴ They are all adulterers,
    burning like an oven
whose fire the baker need not stir
    from the kneading of the dough till it
        rises.
⁵ On the day of the festival of our king
    the princes become inflamed with
        wine,
    and he joins hands with the mockers.
⁶ Their hearts are like an oven;
    they approach him with intrigue.
Their passion smoulders all night;
    in the morning it blazes like a flaming
        fire.
⁷ All of them are hot as an oven;
    they devour their rulers.
All their kings fall,

and none of them calls on me.

8 'Ephraim mixes with the nations;
  Ephraim is a flat loaf not turned over.
9 Foreigners sap his strength,
  but he does not realise it.
His hair is sprinkled with grey,
  but he does not notice.
10 Israel's arrogance testifies against him,
  but despite all this
he does not return to the LORD his God
  or search for him.

11 'Ephraim is like a dove,
  easily deceived and senseless –
now calling to Egypt,
  now turning to Assyria.
12 When they go, I will throw my net over
  them;
  I will pull them down like the birds in
  the sky.
When I hear them flocking together,
  I will catch them.
13 Woe to them,
  because they have strayed from me!
Destruction to them,
  because they have rebelled against
  me!
I long to redeem them
  but they speak about me falsely.
14 They do not cry out to me from their
  hearts
  but wail on their beds.
They slash themselves, appealing to
  their gods
  for grain and new wine,
  but they turn away from me.
15 I trained them and strengthened their
  arms,
  but they plot evil against me.
16 They do not turn to the Most High;
  they are like a faulty bow.
Their leaders will fall by the sword
  because of their insolent words.
For this they will be ridiculed
  in the land of Egypt.

PSALM 140:6-13

6 I say to the LORD, 'You are my God.'
  Hear, LORD, my cry for mercy.
7 Sovereign LORD, my strong deliverer,
  you shield my head in the day of battle.
8 Do not grant the wicked their desires,
  LORD;
  do not let their plans succeed.

9 Those who surround me proudly rear
  their heads;
  may the mischief of their lips engulf
  them.
10 May burning coals fall on them;
  may they be thrown into the fire,
  into miry pits, never to rise.
11 May slanderers not be established in the
  land;
  may disaster hunt down the violent.

12 I know that the LORD secures justice for
  the poor
  and upholds the cause of the needy.
13 Surely the righteous will praise your
  name,
  and the upright will live in your
  presence.

PROVERBS 30:10-12

10 'Do not slander a servant to their master,
  or they will curse you, and you will
  pay for it.

11 'There are those who curse their fathers
  and do not bless their mothers;
12 those who are pure in their own eyes
  and yet are not cleansed of their filth;

REVELATION 2:18–3:6

18 'To the angel of the church in Thyatira
write:

These are the words of the Son of God, whose eyes are like blazing fire and whose feet are like burnished bronze. [19] I know your deeds, your love and faith, your service and perseverance, and that you are now doing more than you did at first.

[20] Nevertheless, I have this against you: you tolerate that woman Jezebel, who calls herself a prophet. By her teaching she misleads my servants into sexual immorality and the eating of food sacrificed to idols. [21] I have given time to repent of her immorality, but she is unwilling. [22] So I will cast her on a bed of suffering, and I will make those who commit adultery with her suffer intensely, unless they repent of her ways. [23] I will strike her children dead. Then all the churches will know that I am he who searches hearts and minds, and I will repay each of you according to your deeds.

[24] Now I say to the rest of you in Thyatira, to you who do not hold to her teaching and have not learned Satan's so-called deep secrets, "I will not impose any other burden on you, [25] except to hold on to what you have until I come."

[26] To the one who is victorious and does my will to the end, I will give authority over the nations – [27] that one "will rule them with an iron sceptre and will dash them to pieces like pottery" – just as I have received authority from my Father. [28] I will also give that one the morning star. [29] Whoever has ears, let them hear what the Spirit says to the churches.

3 'To the angel of the church in Sardis write:

These are the words of him who holds the seven spirits of God and the seven stars. I know your deeds; you have a reputation of being alive, but you are dead. [2] Wake up! Strengthen what remains and is about to die, for I have found your deeds unfinished in the sight of my God. [3] Remember, therefore, what you have received and heard; hold it fast, and repent. But if you do not wake up, I will come like a thief, and you will not know at what time I will come to you.

[4] Yet you have a few people in Sardis who have not soiled their clothes. They will walk with me, dressed in white, for they are worthy. [5] The one who is victorious will, like them, be dressed in white. I will never blot out the name of that person from the book of life, but will acknowledge that name before my Father and his angels. [6] Whoever has ears, let them hear what the Spirit says to the churches.

'Nutty' Is the Word

'Your love is like the morning mist, like the early dew that disappears.' **Hosea 6:4**

A danger with which we must acquaint ourselves as we discuss the need to contemplate God more deeply is that of becoming more interested in godliness than in God Himself. Theologian Jim Packer puts the point effectively when he writes in *Meeting God* that, 'moving in evangelical circles as I do, I am often troubled by what I find. While my fellow believers are constantly seeking to advance in godliness, they show little direct interest in God Himself. When they study Scripture, only the principles of personal godliness get their attention; their heavenly Father does not. It is as if they should concentrate on the ethics of marriage and fail to spend time with their spouse!' He goes on to say, 'There is something narcissistic, and, to tell the truth, nutty in being more concerned with godliness than about God.'

I think 'nutty' is the right word.

I knew a man who went to every seminar he could find on the subject of marriage, and whenever he came upon a new idea or a deep insight, he would reflect for hours on its wonder and profundity. The only trouble was he never got past the reflecting stage, and while he indulged himself in new and profound ideas, his wife was left languishing at home.

How sad that a man can take more interest in the principles that undergird his marriage than in the partner whom he has pledged to love, honour, and cherish. Let's be watchful that we don't care more for the principles of godliness than for the God we are called to praise and please every day of our lives.

PRAYER

Gracious and loving heavenly Father, forgive me, I pray, if I have been caught up more in the mechanics of my faith than in the dynamics of it. May nothing ever become more important to me than my relationship with You. Amen.

FURTHER STUDY

2 Tim. 3:1-5; 2 Chron. 25:1-2; Isa. 29:13
• What is one of the signs of the last days?
• What is said of Amaziah?

December 14

■ HOSEA 8:1–10:15

8 'Put the trumpet to your lips!
An eagle is over the house of the LORD
because the people have broken my
    covenant
and rebelled against my law.
² Israel cries out to me,
    "Our God, we acknowledge you!"
³ But Israel has rejected what is good;
    an enemy will pursue him.
⁴ They set up kings without my consent;

they choose princes without my
    approval.
With their silver and gold
    they make idols for themselves
    to their own destruction.
⁵ Throw out your calf-idol, Samaria!
    My anger burns against them.
How long will they be incapable of purity?
⁶   They are from Israel!
This calf – a metalworker has made it;
    it is not God.
It will be broken in pieces,
    that calf of Samaria.

⁷'They sow the wind
  and reap the whirlwind.
The stalk has no head;
  it will produce no flour.
Were it to yield grain,
  foreigners would swallow it up.
⁸Israel is swallowed up;
  now she is among the nations
  like something no one wants.
⁹For they have gone up to Assyria
  like a wild donkey wandering alone.
  Ephraim has sold herself to lovers.
¹⁰Although they have sold themselves
    among the nations,
  I will now gather them together.
They will begin to waste away
  under the oppression of the mighty
    king.

¹¹'Though Ephraim built many altars for
    sin offerings,
  these have become altars for sinning.
¹²I wrote for them the many things of my
    law,
  but they regarded them as something
    foreign.
¹³Though they offer sacrifices as gifts to
    me,
  and though they eat the meat,
  the LORD is not pleased with them.
Now he will remember their wickedness
  and punish their sins:
  They will return to Egypt.
¹⁴Israel has forgotten his Maker
  and built palaces;
  Judah has fortified many towns.
But I will send fire on their cities
  that will consume their fortresses.'

9 Do not rejoice, Israel;
  do not be jubilant like the other nations.
For you have been unfaithful to your
    God;
  you love the wages of a prostitute
  at every threshing-floor.

²Threshing-floors and winepresses will
  not feed the people;
  the new wine will fail them.
³They will not remain in the LORD's land;
  Ephraim will return to Egypt
  and eat unclean food in Assyria.
⁴They will not pour out wine offerings to
    the LORD,
  nor will their sacrifices please him.
Such sacrifices will be to them like the
    bread of mourners;
  all who eat them will be unclean.
This food will be for themselves;
  it will not come into the temple of the
    LORD.

⁵What will you do on the day of your
    appointed festivals,
  on the feast days of the LORD?
⁶Even if they escape from destruction,
  Egypt will gather them,
  and Memphis will bury them.
Their treasures of silver will be taken
    over by briers,
  and thorns will overrun their tents.
⁷The days of punishment are coming,
  the days of reckoning are at hand.
  Let Israel know this.
Because your sins are so many
  and your hostility so great,
  the prophet is considered a fool,
  the inspired person a maniac.
⁸The prophet, along with my God,
  is the watchman over Ephraim,
  yet snares await him on all his paths,
  and hostility in the house of his God.
⁹They have sunk deep into corruption,
  as in the days of Gibeah.
God will remember their wickedness
  and punish them for their sins.

¹⁰'When I found Israel,
  it was like finding grapes in the desert;
when I saw your ancestors,
  it was like seeing the early fruit on the
    fig-tree.

But when they came to Baal Peor,
  they consecrated themselves to that
      shameful idol
  and became as vile as the thing they
      loved.
¹¹ Ephraim's glory will fly away like a
      bird –
  no birth, no pregnancy, no
      conception.
¹² Even if they bring up children,
  I will bereave them of every one.
  Woe to them
    when I turn away from them!
¹³ I have seen Ephraim, like Tyre,
    planted in a pleasant place.
  But Ephraim will bring out
    their children to the slayer.'

¹⁴ Give them, LORD –
    what will you give them?
  Give them wombs that miscarry
    and breasts that are dry.

¹⁵ 'Because of all their wickedness in
      Gilgal,
    I hated them there.
  Because of their sinful deeds,
    I will drive them out of my house.
  I will no longer love them;
    all their leaders are rebellious.
¹⁶ Ephraim is blighted,
    their root is withered,
    they yield no fruit.
  Even if they bear children,
    I will slay their cherished offspring.'

¹⁷ My God will reject them
    because they have not obeyed him;
    they will be wanderers among the
      nations.

10

Israel was a spreading vine;
  he brought forth fruit for himself.
As his fruit increased,
  he built more altars;
as his land prospered,

he adorned his sacred stones.
² Their heart is deceitful,
  and now they must bear their guilt.
The LORD will demolish their altars
  and destroy their sacred stones.

³ Then they will say, 'We have no king
    because we did not revere the LORD.
  But even if we had a king,
    what could he do for us?'
⁴ They make many promises,
    take false oaths
    and make agreements;
  therefore lawsuits spring up
    like poisonous weeds in a ploughed
      field.
⁵ The people who live in Samaria fear
    for the calf-idol of Beth Aven.
  Its people will mourn over it,
    and so will its idolatrous priests,
  those who had rejoiced over its
      splendour,
    because it is taken from them into
      exile.
⁶ It will be carried to Assyria
    as tribute for the great king.
  Ephraim will be disgraced;
    Israel will be ashamed of its foreign
      alliances.
⁷ Samaria's king will be destroyed,
    swept away like a twig on the surface
      of the waters.
⁸ The high places of wickedness will be
      destroyed –
    it is the sin of Israel.
  Thorns and thistles will grow up
    and cover their altars.
  Then they will say to the mountains,
    'Cover us!'
    and to the hills, 'Fall on us!'

⁹ 'Since the days of Gibeah, you have
      sinned, Israel,
    and there you have remained.
  Will not war again overtake
    the evildoers in Gibeah?

¹⁰ When I please, I will punish them;
    nations will be gathered against them
    to put them in bonds for their double
        sin.
¹¹ Ephraim is a trained heifer
    that loves to thresh;
  so I will put a yoke
    on her fair neck.
  I will drive Ephraim,
    Judah must plough,
    and Jacob must break up the ground.
¹² Sow righteousness for yourselves,
    reap the fruit of unfailing love,
  and break up your unploughed ground;
    for it is time to seek the LORD,
  until he comes
    and showers his righteousness on you.
¹³ But you have planted wickedness,
    you have reaped evil,
    you have eaten the fruit of deception.
  Because you have depended on your own
        strength
    and on your many warriors,
¹⁴ the roar of battle will rise against your
        people,
    so that all your fortresses will be
        devastated –
  as Shalman devastated Beth Arbel on the
        day of battle,
    when mothers were dashed to the
        ground with their children.
¹⁵ So will it happen to you, Bethel,
    because your wickedness is great.
  When that day dawns,
    the king of Israel will be completely
        destroyed.

■ PSALM 141:1-6

¹ I call to you, LORD, come quickly to me;
    hear me when I call to you.
² May my prayer be set before you like
        incense;
    may the lifting up of my hands be like
        the evening sacrifice.

³ Set a guard over my mouth, LORD;
    keep watch over the door of my lips.
⁴ Do not let my heart be drawn to what is
        evil
  so that I take part in wicked deeds
  along with those who are evildoers;
    do not let me eat their delicacies.

⁵ Let a righteous man strike me – that is a
        kindness;
    let him rebuke me – that is oil on my
        head.
  My head will not refuse it,
    for my prayer will still be against the
        deeds of evildoers.

⁶ Their rulers will be thrown down from
        the cliffs,
    and the wicked will learn that my
        words were well spoken.

■ PROVERBS 30:13-14

¹³ those whose eyes are ever so haughty,
    whose glances are so disdainful;
¹⁴ those whose teeth are swords
    and whose jaws are set with knives
  to devour the poor from the earth
    and the needy from among the human
        race.

■ REVELATION 3:7-22

⁷ 'To the angel of the church in Philadelphia
write:

    These are the words of him who is
holy and true, who holds the key of
David. What he opens no one can shut,
and what he shuts no one can open. ⁸ I
know your deeds. See, I have placed
before you an open door that no one
can shut. I know that you have little
strength, yet you have kept my word

and have not denied my name. ⁹I will make those who are of the synagogue of Satan, who claim to be Jews though they are not, but are liars – I will make them come and fall down at your feet and acknowledge that I have loved you. ¹⁰Since you have kept my command to endure patiently, I will also keep you from the hour of trial that is going to come on the whole world to test the inhabitants of the earth.

¹¹I am coming soon. Hold on to what you have, so that no one will take your crown. ¹²The one who is victorious I will make a pillar in the temple of my God. Never again will they leave it. I will write on them the name of my God and the name of the city of my God, the new Jerusalem, which is coming down out of heaven from my God; and I will also write on them my new name. ¹³Whoever has ears, let them hear what the Spirit says to the churches.

¹⁴'To the angel of the church in Laodicea write:

These are the words of the Amen, the faithful and true witness, the ruler of God's creation. ¹⁵I know your deeds, that you are neither cold nor hot. I wish you were either one or the other! ¹⁶So, because you are lukewarm – neither hot nor cold – I am about to spit you out of my mouth. ¹⁷You say, "I am rich; I have acquired wealth and do not need a thing." But you do not realise that you are wretched, pitiful, poor, blind and naked. ¹⁸I counsel you to buy from me gold refined in the fire, so that you can become rich; and white clothes to wear, so that you can cover your shameful nakedness; and salve to put on your eyes, so that you can see.

¹⁹Those whom I love I rebuke and discipline. So be earnest and repent. ²⁰Here I am! I stand at the door and knock. If anyone hears my voice and opens the door, I will come in and eat with that person, and they with me.

²¹To the one who is victorious, I will give the right to sit with me on my throne, just as I was victorious and sat down with my Father on his throne. ²²Whoever has ears, let them hear what the Spirit says to the churches.'

A Disciplined Tongue

'Set a guard over my mouth, LORD; keep watch over the door of my lips.' **Psalm 141:3**

Proverbs 10:19 states, 'the prudent hold their tongues'. I'm glad God included in the Psalms and Proverbs the words that are before us today about controlling our speech. It's important to talk, but talking too much is as bad as not talking at all. Proverbs extols rationing our words.

Once, when Thomas Edison the inventor was at a reception, the toastmaster stood up and complimented him on his many inventions, especially the talking machine. After the toastmaster sat down, the aged inventor rose to his feet and said, 'Thank you for those remarks, but I must correct one thing. It was God who invented the talking machine. I only invented the first one that can be shut off.'

A doctor told me that once, while writing out a prescription, he asked a woman to put out her tongue. When he had finished, she said to him, 'But doctor, you never even looked at my tongue.' The doctor replied, 'It wasn't necessary, I just wanted you to keep quiet while I wrote the prescription.' Amidst the humour of today's notes, don't miss the point - words are important, but don't overdo them. I like the advice of an anonymous poet who wrote:

If your lips would keep from slips
Five things observe with care:
Of whom you speak, to whom you speak,
And how and when and where.

A wise person has a disciplined tongue. Many need to learn this, for, like the tongue in old shoes, our tongue is often the last thing to be worn out. If a disciplined tongue is your need, ask God to help you, for an undisciplined tongue is an unloving tongue.

PRAYER

Father, I realise that often my tongue is the most difficult thing to bring under control. Yet I have the promise of Your help even in this. I give you my tongue to be bridled – take over the reins. In Jesus' name I pray. Amen.

FURTHER STUDY

Matt. 12:30-37; Titus 1:1-10; Job 11:3
• What did Jesus say we will have to account for?
• What did Paul mean by 'meaningless talk' (Titus 1:10)?

December 15

■ HOSEA 11:1–14:9

11 ¹ 'When Israel was a child, I loved him, and out of Egypt I called my son.
² But the more they were called, the more they went away from me.
They sacrificed to the Baals and they burned incense to images.
³ It was I who taught Ephraim to walk, taking them by the arms;
but they did not realise it was I who healed them.
⁴ I led them with cords of human kindness, with ties of love.

To them I was like one who lifts a little child to the cheek, and I bent down to feed them.
⁵ 'Will they not return to Egypt and will not Assyria rule over them because they refuse to repent?
⁶ A sword will flash in their cities; it will devour their false prophets and put an end to their plans.
⁷ My people are determined to turn from me.
Even though they call me God Most High,

I will by no means exalt them.

8 'How can I give you up, Ephraim?
　How can I hand you over, Israel?
How can I treat you like Admah?
　How can I make you like Zeboyim?
My heart is changed within me;
　all my compassion is aroused.
9 I will not carry out my fierce anger,
　nor will I devastate Ephraim again.
For I am God, and not a man –
　the Holy One among you.
I will not come against their cities.
10 They will follow the LORD;
　he will roar like a lion.
When he roars,
　his children will come trembling from
　　the west.
11 They will come from Egypt,
　trembling like sparrows,
　from Assyria, fluttering like doves.
I will settle them in their homes,'
　declares the LORD.
12 Ephraim has surrounded me with lies,
　Israel with deceit.
And Judah is unruly against God,
　even against the faithful Holy One.

12 ¹Ephraim feeds on the wind;
　he pursues the east wind all day
and multiplies lies and violence.
He makes a treaty with Assyria
　and sends olive oil to Egypt.
2 The LORD has a charge to bring against
　　Judah;
　he will punish Jacob according to his
　　ways
　and repay him according to his deeds.
3 In the womb he grasped his brother's
　　heel;
　as a man he struggled with God.
4 He struggled with the angel and
　　overcame him;
　he wept and begged for his favour.
He found him at Bethel
　and talked with him there –
5 the LORD God Almighty,

the LORD is his name!
6 But you must return to your God;
　maintain love and justice,
　and wait for your God always.

7 The merchant uses dishonest scales
　and loves to defraud.
8 Ephraim boasts,
　'I am very rich; I have become wealthy.
With all my wealth they will not find in me
　any iniquity or sin.'

9 'I have been the LORD your God
　ever since you came out of Egypt;
I will make you live in tents again,
　as in the days of your appointed
　　festivals.
10 I spoke to the prophets,
　gave them many visions
　and told parables through them.'

11 Is Gilead wicked?
　Its people are worthless!
Do they sacrifice bulls in Gilgal?
　Their altars will be like piles of stones
　on a ploughed field.
12 Jacob fled to the country of Aram;
　Israel served to get a wife,
　and to pay for her he tended sheep.
13 The LORD used a prophet to bring Israel
　　up from Egypt,
　by a prophet he cared for him.
14 But Ephraim has aroused his bitter
　　anger;
　his Lord will leave on him the guilt of
　　his bloodshed
　and will repay him for his contempt.

13 When Ephraim spoke, people
　　trembled;
　he was exalted in Israel.
But he became guilty of Baal worship
　and died.
2 Now they sin more and more;
　they make idols for themselves from
　　their silver,

cleverly fashioned images,
    all of them the work of craftsmen.
It is said of these people,
    'They offer human sacrifices!
    They kiss calf-idols!'
3 Therefore they will be like the morning
    mist,
    like the early dew that disappears,
    like chaff swirling from a
        threshing-floor,
    like smoke escaping through a
        window.

4 'But I have been the LORD your God
    ever since you came out of Egypt.
You shall acknowledge no God but me,
    no Saviour except me.
5 I cared for you in the wilderness,
    in the land of burning heat.
6 When I fed them, they were satisfied;
    when they were satisfied, they became
        proud;
    then they forgot me.
7 So I will be like a lion to them,
    like a leopard I will lurk by the path.
8 Like a bear robbed of her cubs,
    I will attack them and rip them open;
like a lion I will devour them –
    a wild animal will tear them apart.

9 'You are destroyed, Israel,
    because you are against me, against
        your helper.
10 Where is your king, that he may save
        you?
    Where are your rulers in all your
        towns,
of whom you said,
    "Give me a king and princes"?
11 So in my anger I gave you a king,
    and in my wrath I took him away.
12 The guilt of Ephraim is stored up,
    his sins are kept on record.
13 Pains as of a woman in childbirth come
        to him,
    but he is a child without wisdom;

when the time arrives,
    he doesn't have the sense to come out
        of the womb.

14 'I will deliver this people from the power
    of the grave;
    I will redeem them from death.
Where, O death, are your plagues?
    Where, O grave, is your destruction?

'I will have no compassion,
15   even though he thrives among his
        brothers.
An east wind from the LORD will come,
    blowing in from the desert;
his spring will fail
    and his well dry up.
His storehouse will be plundered
    of all its treasures.
16 The people of Samaria must bear their
    guilt,
    because they have rebelled against
        their God.
They will fall by the sword;
    their little ones will be dashed to the
        ground,
    their pregnant women ripped open.'

14 Return, Israel, to the LORD your God.
    Your sins have been your
        downfall!
2 Take words with you
    and return to the LORD.
Say to him:
    'Forgive all our sins
and receive us graciously,
    that we may offer the fruit of our lips.
3 Assyria cannot save us;
    we will not mount war-horses.
We will never again say "Our gods"
    to what our own hands have made,
for in you the fatherless find
        compassion.'

4 'I will heal their waywardness
    and love them freely,

for my anger has turned away from
   them.
⁵ I will be like the dew to Israel;
   he will blossom like a lily.
Like a cedar of Lebanon
   he will send down his roots;
⁶   his young shoots will grow.
His splendour will be like an olive tree,
   his fragrance like a cedar of Lebanon.
⁷ People will dwell again in his shade;
   they will flourish like the corn,
they will blossom like the vine –
   Israel's fame will be like the wine of
      Lebanon.
⁸ Ephraim, what more have I to do with
      idols?
   I will answer him and care for him.
I am like a flourishing juniper;
   your fruitfulness comes from me.'

⁹ Who is wise? Let them realise these
      things.
   Who is discerning? Let them
      understand.
The ways of the LORD are right;
   the righteous walk in them,
   but the rebellious stumble in them.

PSALM 141:7–10

⁷ They will say, 'As one ploughs and
      breaks up the earth,
   so our bones have been scattered at
      the mouth of the grave.'

⁸ But my eyes are fixed on you, Sovereign
      LORD;
   in you I take refuge – do not give me
      over to death.
⁹ Keep me safe from the traps set by
      evildoers,
   from the snares they have laid for me.
¹⁰ Let the wicked fall into their own nets,
   while I pass by in safety.

PROVERBS 30:15–17

¹⁵ 'The leech has two daughters.
   "Give! Give!" they cry.

'There are three things that are never
      satisfied,
   four that never say, "Enough!":
¹⁶ the grave, the barren womb,
   land, which is never satisfied with
      water,
   and fire, which never says, "Enough!"

¹⁷ 'The eye that mocks a father,
   that scorns an aged mother,
will be pecked out by the ravens of the
      valley,
   will be eaten by the vultures.

REVELATION 4:1–5:14

4 After this I looked, and there before me
   was a door standing open in heaven.
And the voice I had first heard speaking
to me like a trumpet said, 'Come up here,
and I will show you what must take place
after this.' ² At once I was in the Spirit, and
there before me was a throne in heaven with
someone sitting on it. ³ And the one who sat
there had the appearance of jasper and ruby.
A rainbow that shone like an emerald encircled the throne. ⁴ Surrounding the throne
were twenty-four other thrones, and seated
on them were twenty-four elders. They were
dressed in white and had crowns of gold on
their heads. ⁵ From the throne came flashes
of lightning, rumblings and peals of thunder. In front of the throne, seven lamps were
blazing. These are the seven spirits of God.
⁶ Also in front of the throne there was what
looked like a sea of glass, clear as crystal.
   In the centre, round the throne, were four
living creatures, and they were covered with
eyes, in front and behind. ⁷ The first living
creature was like a lion, the second was

like an ox, the third had a face like a man, the fourth was like a flying eagle. [8] Each of the four living creatures had six wings and was covered with eyes all round, even under its wings. Day and night they never stop saying:

> ' "Holy, holy, holy
> is the Lord God Almighty,"
> who was, and is, and is to come.'

[9] Whenever the living creatures give glory, honour and thanks to him who sits on the throne and who lives for ever and ever, [10] the twenty-four elders fall down before him who sits on the throne and worship him who lives for ever and ever. They lay their crowns before the throne and say:

> [11] 'You are worthy, our Lord and God,
> to receive glory and honour and power,
> for you created all things,
> and by your will they were created
> and have their being.'

5 Then I saw in the right hand of him who sat on the throne a scroll with writing on both sides and sealed with seven seals. [2] And I saw a mighty angel proclaiming in a loud voice, 'Who is worthy to break the seals and open the scroll?' [3] But no one in heaven or on earth or under the earth could open the scroll or even look inside it. [4] I wept and wept because no one was found who was worthy to open the scroll or look inside. [5] Then one of the elders said to me, 'Do not weep! See, the Lion of the tribe of Judah, the Root of David, has triumphed. He is able to open the scroll and its seven seals.'

[6] Then I saw a Lamb, looking as if it had been slain, standing at the centre of the throne, encircled by the four living creatures and the elders. The Lamb had seven horns and seven eyes, which are the seven spirits of God sent out into all the earth.

[7] He went and took the scroll from the right hand of him who sat on the throne. [8] And when he had taken it, the four living creatures and the twenty-four elders fell down before the Lamb. Each one had a harp and they were holding golden bowls full of incense, which are the prayers of God's people. [9] And they sang a new song, saying:

> 'You are worthy to take the scroll
> and to open its seals,
> because you were slain,
> and with your blood you purchased for God
> persons from every tribe and language
> and people and nation.
> [10] You have made them to be a kingdom
> and priests to serve our God,
> and they will reign on the earth.'

[11] Then I looked and heard the voice of many angels, numbering thousands upon thousands, and ten thousand times ten thousand. They encircled the throne and the living creatures and the elders. [12] In a loud voice they were saying:

> 'Worthy is the Lamb, who was slain,
> to receive power and wealth and wisdom and strength
> and honour and glory and praise!'

[13] Then I heard every creature in heaven and on earth and under the earth and on the sea, and all that is in them, saying:

> 'To him who sits on the throne and to the Lamb
> be praise and honour and glory and power,
> for ever and ever!'

[14] The four living creatures said, 'Amen', and the elders fell down and worshipped.

The Only Cure

'Take words with you and return to the LORD.'
Hosea 14:2

How do we deal with demandingness? We must repent of it. Our passage today tells us how.

First: 'Return to the LORD.' The key to ridding ourselves of anything that is spiritually injurious is to return to God. The pursuit of God involves a shift away from dependence on one's own resources to dependence on God. Doing good and correcting wrong behaviour does not automatically make us good people. Obedience is extremely important, but it must be accompanied by deep, heart repentance.

Second, the passage says: 'Take words of repentance with you' (HCSB). This phrase means that we must put into words a clear description of what we are repenting of. If we are not clear about what is going on inside us, how can we repent of it?

Next: 'Forgive all our sins.' Repentance puts us in touch with God's forgiveness. We can work to bring about change also, but the greatest catalyst for change is humbly positioning ourselves before God and asking for His forgiveness.

Then: 'Receive us graciously, that we may offer the fruit of our lips.' The thought here is: 'Receive us that we may worship You more effectively.' The purpose of all restoration is to worship God. We will be drawn into true worship when we give up insisting on our own way and learn to trust God for our own happiness. When repentance moves us from a spirit of demandingness to absolute trust in God, then we are in the place where God is able to make our feet like 'hinds' feet' and equip us with the ability to ascend into the heights with Him.

PRAYER

Invade my heart Lord as I yield to You, and ask for healing and wholeness. Drain every drop of demandingness from my being. For I want not only to be better but to be whole. In Jesus' name. Amen.

FURTHER STUDY

Joel 2:12-18; Isa. 55:7; Psa. 34:18; 51:17
• What does God not despise?
• What does it mean to 'rend your heart'?

December 16

■ JOEL 1:1–2:32

1 The word of the LORD that came to Joel son of Pethuel.

² Hear this, you elders;
   listen, all who live in the land.
Has anything like this ever happened in
      your days
   or in the days of your ancestors?
³ Tell it to your children,
   and let your children tell it to their
      children,
   and their children to the next
      generation.
⁴ What the locust swarm has left
   the great locusts have eaten;
what the great locusts have left
   the young locusts have eaten;
what the young locusts have left
   other locusts have eaten.

⁵ Wake up, you drunkards, and weep!
   Wail, all you drinkers of wine;
wail because of the new wine,
   for it has been snatched from your
      lips.
⁶ A nation has invaded my land,
   a mighty army without number;
it has the teeth of a lion,
   the fangs of a lioness.
⁷ It has laid waste my vines
   and ruined my fig-trees.
It has stripped off their bark
   and thrown it away,
   leaving their branches white.

⁸ Mourn like a virgin in sackcloth
   grieving for the betrothed of her
      youth.
⁹ Grain offerings and drink offerings
   are cut off from the house of the LORD.

The priests are in mourning,
   those who minister before the LORD.
¹⁰ The fields are ruined,
   the ground is dried up;
the grain is destroyed,
   the new wine is dried up,
   the olive oil fails.

¹¹ Despair, you farmers,
   wail, you vine growers;
grieve for the wheat and the barley,
   because the harvest of the field is
      destroyed.
¹² The vine is dried up
   and the fig-tree is withered;
the pomegranate, the palm and the apple
      tree –
   all the trees of the field – are dried up.
Surely the people's joy
   is withered away.

¹³ Put on sackcloth, you priests, and mourn;
   wail, you who minister before the
      altar.
Come, spend the night in sackcloth,
   you who minister before my God;
for the grain offerings and drink
      offerings
   are withheld from the house of your
      God.
¹⁴ Declare a holy fast;
   call a sacred assembly.
Summon the elders
   and all who live in the land
to the house of the LORD your God,
   and cry out to the LORD.

¹⁵ Alas for that day!
   For the day of the LORD is near;
   it will come like destruction from the
      Almighty.

[16] Has not the food been cut off
　　before our very eyes –
joy and gladness
　　from the house of our God?
[17] The seeds are shrivelled
　　beneath the clods.
The storehouses are in ruins,
　　the granaries have been broken down,
　　for the grain has dried up.
[18] How the cattle moan!
　　The herds mill about
because they have no pasture;
　　even the flocks of sheep are suffering.

[19] To you, Lord, I call,
　　for fire has devoured the pastures in
　　　　the wilderness
　　and flames have burned up all the
　　　　trees of the field.
[20] Even the wild animals pant for you;
　　the streams of water have dried up
　　and fire has devoured the pastures in
　　　　the wilderness.

2 Blow the trumpet in Zion;
　　sound the alarm on my holy hill.

Let all who live in the land tremble,
　　for the day of the Lord is coming.
It is close at hand –
[2]　a day of darkness and gloom,
　　a day of clouds and blackness.
Like dawn spreading across the mountains
　　a large and mighty army comes,
such as never was in ancient times
　　nor ever will be in ages to come.

[3] Before them fire devours,
　　behind them a flame blazes.
Before them the land is like the garden
　　　　of Eden,
　　behind them, a desert waste –
　　nothing escapes them.
[4] They have the appearance of horses;
　　they gallop along like cavalry.
[5] With a noise like that of chariots

they leap over the mountaintops,
　　like a crackling fire consuming stubble,
　　like a mighty army drawn up for battle.

[6] At the sight of them, nations are in
　　　　anguish;
　　every face turns pale.
[7] They charge like warriors;
　　they scale walls like soldiers.
They all march in line,
　　not swerving from their course.
[8] They do not jostle each other;
　　each marches straight ahead.
They plunge through defences
　　without breaking ranks.
[9] They rush upon the city;
　　they run along the wall.
They climb into the houses;
　　like thieves they enter through the
　　　　windows.

[10] Before them the earth shakes,
　　the heavens tremble,
the sun and moon are darkened,
　　and the stars no longer shine.
[11] The Lord thunders
　　at the head of his army;
his forces are beyond number,
　　and mighty is the army that obeys his
　　　　command.
The day of the Lord is great;
　　it is dreadful.
　　Who can endure it?

[12] 'Even now,' declares the Lord,
　　'return to me with all your heart,
　　with fasting and weeping and
　　　　mourning.'

[13] Rend your heart
　　and not your garments.
Return to the Lord your God,
　　for he is gracious and compassionate,
slow to anger and abounding in love,
　　and he relents from sending calamity.
[14] Who knows? He may turn and relent

and leave behind a blessing –
grain offerings and drink offerings
for the LORD your God.

¹⁵ Blow the trumpet in Zion,
declare a holy fast,
call a sacred assembly.
¹⁶ Gather the people,
consecrate the assembly;
bring together the elders,
gather the children,
those nursing at the breast.
Let the bridegroom leave his room
and the bride her chamber.
¹⁷ Let the priests, who minister before the
LORD,
weep between the portico and the
altar.
Let them say, 'Spare your people, LORD.
Do not make your inheritance an
object of scorn,
a byword among the nations.
Why should they say among the peoples,
"Where is their God?"'

¹⁸ Then the Lord was jealous for his land
and took pity on his people.

¹⁹ The LORD replied to them:

'I am sending you grain, new wine and
olive oil,
enough to satisfy you fully;
never again will I make you
an object of scorn to the nations.

²⁰ 'I will drive the northern horde far from
you,
pushing it into a parched and barren
land;
its eastern ranks will drown in the Dead
Sea
and its western ranks in the
Mediterranean Sea.
And its stench will go up;
its smell will rise.'

Surely he has done great things!
²¹ Do not be afraid, land of Judah;
be glad and rejoice.
Surely the LORD has done great things!
²² Do not be afraid, you wild animals,
for the pastures in the wilderness are
becoming green.
The trees are bearing their fruit;
the fig-tree and the vine yield their
riches.
²³ Be glad, people of Zion,
rejoice in the LORD your God,
for he has given you the autumn rains
because he is faithful.
He sends you abundant showers,
both autumn and spring rains, as before.
²⁴ The threshing-floors will be filled with
grain;
the vats will overflow with new wine
and oil.

²⁵ 'I will repay you for the years the locusts
have eaten –
the great locust and the young locust,
the other locusts and the locust
swarm –
my great army that I sent among you.
²⁶ You will have plenty to eat, until you are
full,
and you will praise the name of the
LORD your God,
who has worked wonders for you;
never again will my people be shamed.
²⁷ Then you will know that I am in Israel,
that I am the LORD your God,
and that there is no other;
never again will my people be shamed.

²⁸ 'And afterwards,
I will pour out my Spirit on all people.
Your sons and daughters will prophesy,
your old men will dream dreams,
your young men will see visions.
²⁹ Even on my servants, both men and
women,
I will pour out my Spirit in those days.

³⁰ I will show wonders in the heavens
    and on the earth,
    blood and fire and billows of smoke.
³¹ The sun will be turned to darkness
    and the moon to blood
    before the coming of the great and
        dreadful day of the Lord.
³² And everyone who calls
    on the name of the Lord will be saved;
for on Mount Zion and in Jerusalem
    there will be deliverance,
    as the Lord has said,
even among the survivors
    whom the Lord calls.

■ PSALM 142:1–7

¹ I cry aloud to the Lord;
    I lift up my voice to the Lord for
        mercy.
² I pour out before him my complaint;
    before him I tell my trouble.

³ When my spirit grows faint within me,
    it is you who watch over my way.
In the path where I walk
    people have hidden a snare for me.
⁴ Look and see, there is no one at my right
        hand;
    no one is concerned for me.
I have no refuge;
    no one cares for my life.

⁵ I cry to you, Lord;
    I say, 'You are my refuge,
    my portion in the land of the living.'

⁶ Listen to my cry,
    for I am in desperate need;
rescue me from those who pursue me,
    for they are too strong for me.
⁷ Set me free from my prison,
    that I may praise your name.
Then the righteous will gather about me
    because of your goodness to me.

■ PROVERBS 30:18–20

¹⁸ 'There are three things that are too
        amazing for me,
    four that I do not understand:
¹⁹ the way of an eagle in the sky,
    the way of a snake on a rock,
    the way of a ship on the high seas,
    and the way of a man with a young
        woman.

²⁰ 'This is the way of an adulterous woman:
    she eats and wipes her mouth
    and says, "I've done nothing wrong."

■ REVELATION 6:1–17

6 I watched as the Lamb opened the first of the seven seals. Then I heard one of the four living creatures say in a voice like thunder, 'Come!' ² I looked, and there before me was a white horse! Its rider held a bow, and he was given a crown, and he rode out as a conqueror bent on conquest.

³ When the Lamb opened the second seal, I heard the second living creature say, 'Come!' ⁴ Then another horse came out, a fiery red one. Its rider was given power to take peace from the earth and to make people kill each other. To him was given a large sword.

⁵ When the Lamb opened the third seal, I heard the third living creature say, 'Come!' I looked, and there before me was a black horse! Its rider was holding a pair of scales in his hand. ⁶ Then I heard what sounded like a voice among the four living creatures, saying, 'A kilogram of wheat for a day's wages, and three kilograms of barley for a day's wages, and do not damage the oil and the wine!'

⁷ When the Lamb opened the fourth seal, I heard the voice of the fourth living creature say, 'Come!' ⁸ I looked, and there before me was a pale horse! Its rider was

named Death, and Hades was following close behind him. They were given power over a quarter of the earth to kill by sword, famine and plague, and by the wild beasts of the earth.

⁹When he opened the fifth seal, I saw under the altar the souls of those who had been slain because of the word of God and the testimony they had maintained. ¹⁰They called out in a loud voice, 'How long, Sovereign Lord, holy and true, until you judge the inhabitants of the earth and avenge our blood?' ¹¹Then each of them was given a white robe, and they were told to wait a little longer, until the full number of their fellow servants, their brothers and sisters, were killed just as they had been.

¹²I watched as he opened the sixth seal.

There was a great earthquake. The sun turned black like sackcloth made of goat hair, the whole moon turned blood red, ¹³and the stars in the sky fell to earth, as figs drop from a fig-tree when shaken by a strong wind. ¹⁴The heavens receded like a scroll being rolled up, and every mountain and island was removed from its place.

¹⁵Then the kings of the earth, the princes, the generals, the rich, the mighty, and everyone else, both slave and free, hid in caves and among the rocks of the mountains. ¹⁶They called to the mountains and the rocks, 'Fall on us and hide us from the face of him who sits on the throne and from the wrath of the Lamb! ¹⁷For the great day of their wrath has come, and who can withstand it?'

Under the Surface

'... I will pour out my Spirit on all people.' **Joel 2:28**

What are some evidences of the Spirit-filled life? How do we know when we are fully indwelt by the divine Paraclete?

I am not going to begin where you might expect, in the area of spiritual gifts, but in a realm I believe to be equally important yet seldom mentioned. I refer to the area of the subconscious.

The longer I live, the more I feel the church has missed its way here. We have talked much about the works of the Spirit on the conscious level but little of His work at a subconscious level. We have failed to see, generally speaking, that part of the work of the Holy Spirit in the life of a Christian is to project His power and presence into the depths of the personality – even the subconscious.

We are told that about one-tenth of the mind is conscious and the other nine-tenths subconscious. Like the iceberg, which is nine-tenths submerged, life is largely lived in the submerged part of our being. Now, if this is so, then it becomes evident at once that if the submerged nine-tenths is not working with the conscious purposes of the one-tenth, then there is going to be a serious division, and a division this serious becomes divisive. Whatever controls the nine-tenths greatly influences the one-tenth. The Holy Spirit wants to project Himself into that submerged part of our being in order to harness those untamed forces and make them work for us and not against us. Then the subconscious is no longer an enemy but a friend.

PRAYER

O God, my Father, I am grateful that You have provided for my deepest need – the need of unifying and controlling the depths within me. My heart tingles at the thought that I can be unified – on the inside. Thank You, Father. Amen.

FURTHER STUDY

Joel 2:18-32; Rom. 12:2; 1 Cor. 14:3; 2 Tim. 1:7; Matt. 12:25
• What did Joel prophesy?
• What is the difference between dreams and visions?

December 17

■ JOEL 3:1–AMOS 2:16

3 ¹'In those days and at that time,
when I restore the fortunes of Judah
and Jerusalem,
² I will gather all nations
and bring them down to the Valley of
Jehoshaphat.
There I will put them on trial
for what they did to my inheritance,
my people Israel,
because they scattered my people among
the nations
and divided up my land.
³ They cast lots for my people
and traded boys for prostitutes;
they sold girls for wine to drink.

⁴ 'Now what have you against me, Tyre and Sidon and all you regions of Philistia? Are you repaying me for something I have done? If you are paying me back, I will swiftly and speedily return on your own heads what you have done. ⁵ For you took my silver and my gold and carried off my finest treasures to your temples. ⁶ You sold the people of Judah and Jerusalem to the Greeks, that you might send them far from their homeland.

⁷ 'See, I am going to rouse them out of the places to which you sold them, and I will

return on your own heads what you have done. ⁸ I will sell your sons and daughters to the people of Judah, and they will sell them to the Sabeans, a nation far away.' The LORD has spoken.

⁹ Proclaim this among the nations:
Prepare for war!
Rouse the warriors!
Let all the fighting men draw near and
attack.
¹⁰ Beat your ploughshares into swords
and your pruning hooks into spears.
Let the weakling say,
'I am strong!'
¹¹ Come quickly, all you nations from every
side,
and assemble there.

Bring down your warriors, LORD!

¹² 'Let the nations be roused;
let them advance into the Valley of
Jehoshaphat,
for there I will sit
to judge all the nations on every side.
¹³ Swing the sickle,
for the harvest is ripe.
Come, trample the grapes,
for the winepress is full
and the vats overflow –

so great is their wickedness!'

¹⁴ Multitudes, multitudes
    in the valley of decision!
For the day of the LORD is near
    in the valley of decision.
¹⁵ The sun and moon will be darkened,
    and the stars no longer shine.
¹⁶ The LORD will roar from Zion
    and thunder from Jerusalem;
    the earth and the heavens will
        tremble.
But the LORD will be a refuge for his
        people,
    a stronghold for the people of Israel.

¹⁷ 'Then you will know that I, the Lord
        your God,
    dwell in Zion, my holy hill.
Jerusalem will be holy;
    never again will foreigners invade her.

¹⁸ 'In that day the mountains will drip new
        wine,
    and the hills will flow with milk;
    all the ravines of Judah will run with
        water.
A fountain will flow out of the LORD's
        house
    and will water the valley of acacias.
¹⁹ But Egypt will be desolate,
    Edom a desert waste,
    because of violence done to the people of
        Judah,
    in whose land they shed innocent
        blood.
²⁰ Judah will be inhabited for ever
    and Jerusalem through all
        generations.
²¹ Shall I leave their innocent blood
        unavenged?
    No, I will not.'

    The LORD dwells in Zion!

1 The words of Amos, one of the shep-
    herds of Tekoa – the vision he saw con-
cerning Israel two years before the earthquake, when Uzziah was king of Judah and
Jeroboam son of Jehoash was king of Israel.
² He said:

    'The LORD roars from Zion
        and thunders from Jerusalem;
    the pastures of the shepherds dry up,
        and the top of Carmel withers.'

³ This is what the Lord says:

    'For three sins of Damascus,
        even for four, I will not relent.
    Because she threshed Gilead
        with sledges having iron teeth,
⁴ I will send fire on the house of Hazael
        that will consume the fortresses of
            Ben-Hadad.
⁵ I will break down the gate of Damascus;
    I will destroy the king who is in the
            Valley of Aven
    and the one who holds the sceptre in
            Beth Eden.
    The people of Aram will go into exile
            to Kir,'
                    says the LORD.

⁶ This is what the LORD says:

    'For three sins of Gaza,
        even for four, I will not relent.
    Because she took captive whole
            communities
        and sold them to Edom,
⁷ I will send fire on the walls of Gaza
        that will consume her fortresses.
⁸ I will destroy the king of Ashdod
    and the one who holds the sceptre in
            Ashkelon.
    I will turn my hand against Ekron,
        till the last of the Philistines are dead,'
                    says the Sovereign LORD.

⁹ This is what the LORD says:

'For three sins of Tyre,
    even for four, I will not relent.
Because she sold whole communities of
    captives to Edom,
    disregarding a treaty of brotherhood,
¹⁰ I will send fire on the walls of Tyre
    that will consume her fortresses.'

¹¹ This is what the LORD says:

'For three sins of Edom,
    even for four, I will not relent.
Because he pursued his brother with a
    sword
    and slaughtered the women of the
    land,
because his anger raged continually
    and his fury flamed unchecked,
¹² I will send fire on Teman
    that will consume the fortresses of
    Bozrah.'

¹³ This is what the LORD says:

'For three sins of Ammon,
    even for four, I will not relent.
Because he ripped open the pregnant
    women of Gilead
    in order to extend his borders,
¹⁴ I will set fire to the walls of Rabbah
    that will consume her fortresses
amid war cries on the day of battle,
    amid violent winds on a stormy day.
¹⁵ Her king will go into exile,
    he and his officials together,'
                            says the LORD.

2 This is what the LORD says:

'For three sins of Moab,
    even for four, I will not relent.
Because he burned to ashes
    the bones of Edom's king,
² I will send fire on Moab

that will consume the fortresses of
    Kerioth.
Moab will go down in great tumult
    amid war cries and the blast of the
    trumpet.
³ I will destroy her ruler
    and kill all her officials with him,'
                            says the LORD.

⁴ This is what the LORD says:

'For three sins of Judah,
    even for four, I will not relent.
Because they have rejected the law of the
    LORD
    and have not kept his decrees,
because they have been led astray by
    false gods,
    the gods their ancestors followed,
⁵ I will send fire on Judah
    that will consume the fortresses of
    Jerusalem.'

⁶ This is what the Lord says:

'For three sins of Israel,
    even for four, I will not relent.
They sell the innocent for silver,
    and the needy for a pair of sandals.
⁷ They trample on the heads of the poor
    as on the dust of the ground
    and deny justice to the oppressed.
Father and son use the same girl
    and so profane my holy name.
⁸ They lie down beside every altar
    on garments taken in pledge.
In the house of their god
    they drink wine taken as fines.

⁹ 'Yet I destroyed the Amorites before them,
    though they were tall as the cedars
    and strong as the oaks.
I destroyed their fruit above
    and their roots below.
¹⁰ I brought you up out of Egypt

and led you for forty years in the
wilderness
to give you the land of the Amorites.

[11] 'I also raised up prophets from among
your children
and Nazirites from among your youths.
Is this not true, people of Israel?'
declares the LORD.
[12] 'But you made the Nazirites drink wine
and commanded the prophets not to
prophesy.

[13] 'Now then, I will crush you
as a cart crushes when loaded with
grain.
[14] The swift will not escape,
the strong will not muster their strength,
and the warrior will not save his life.
[15] The archer will not stand his ground,
the fleet-footed soldier will not get
away,
and the horseman will not save his life.
[16] Even the bravest warriors
will flee naked on that day,'
declares the LORD.

■ PSALM 143:1-6

[1] LORD, hear my prayer,
listen to my cry for mercy;
in your faithfulness and righteousness
come to my relief.
[2] Do not bring your servant into judgment,
for no one living is righteous before you.
[3] The enemy pursues me,
he crushes me to the ground;
he makes me dwell in the darkness
like those long dead.
[4] So my spirit grows faint within me;
my heart within me is dismayed.
[5] I remember the days of long ago;
I meditate on all your works
and consider what your hands have
done.

[6] I spread out my hands to you;
I thirst for you like a parched land.

■ PROVERBS 30:21-23

[21] 'Under three things the earth trembles,
under four it cannot bear up:
[22] a servant who becomes king,
a godless fool who gets plenty to eat,
[23] a contemptible woman who gets married,
and a servant who displaces her
mistress.

■ REVELATION 7:1-17

7 After this I saw four angels standing at
the four corners of the earth, holding
back the four winds of the earth to prevent
any wind from blowing on the land or on the
sea or on any tree. [2] Then I saw another angel
coming up from the east, having the seal of
the living God. He called out in a loud voice to
the four angels who had been given power to
harm the land and the sea: [3] 'Do not harm the
land or the sea or the trees until we put a seal
on the foreheads of the servants of our God.'
[4] Then I heard the number of those who were
sealed: 144,000 from all the tribes of Israel.

[5] From the tribe of Judah 12,000 were
sealed,
from the tribe of Reuben 12,000,
from the tribe of Gad 12,000,
[6] from the tribe of Asher 12,000,
from the tribe of Naphtali 12,000,
from the tribe of Manasseh 12,000,
[7] from the tribe of Simeon 12,000,
from the tribe of Levi 12,000,
from the tribe of Issachar 12,000,
[8] from the tribe of Zebulun 12,000,
from the tribe of Joseph 12,000,
from the tribe of Benjamin 12,000.

[9] After this I looked, and there before me

was a great multitude that no one could count, from every nation, tribe, people and language, standing before the throne and before the Lamb. They were wearing white robes and were holding palm branches in their hands. [10] And they cried out in a loud voice:

'Salvation belongs to our God,
who sits on the throne,
and to the Lamb.'

[11] All the angels were standing round the throne and round the elders and the four living creatures. They fell down on their faces before the throne and worshipped God, [12] saying:

'Amen!
Praise and glory
and wisdom and thanks and honour
and power and strength
be to our God for ever and ever.
Amen!'

[13] Then one of the elders asked me, 'These in white robes – who are they, and where did they come from?'

[14] I answered, 'Sir, you know.'

And he said, 'These are they who have come out of the great tribulation; they have washed their robes and made them white in the blood of the Lamb. [15] Therefore,

'they are before the throne of God
and serve him day and night in his
temple;
and he who sits on the throne
will shelter them with his presence.
[16] "Never again will they hunger;
never again will they thirst.
The sun will not beat down on them,"
nor any scorching heat.
[17] For the Lamb at the centre of the throne
will be their shepherd;
"he will lead them to springs of living
water."
"And God will wipe away every tear
from their eyes."'

Fresh Water

'... the Lamb ... "will lead them to springs of living water. And God will wipe away every tear from their eyes."' **Revelation 7:17**

I once received a letter from a reader of my notes which said: 'Over the past year or so, my Christian life has become stale - insufferably so. I have lost the freshness and spontaneity I once knew. Can you say something that will help bring back the sparkle into my Christian experience? What is the remedy?'

But can we expect always to live in a state of spiritual alertness and freshness? Isn't that being unrealistically optimistic? Well, what does Scripture say? It shows us that the people of God are meant to be beautiful gardens in the midst of a dry desert. The prophet Isaiah puts it like this: 'You will be like a well-watered garden, like a spring whose waters never fail' (Isa. 58:11).

In Ezekiel 47:8, Ezekiel says that the river flows into the Dead Sea and 'the salty water there becomes fresh'. How thrilling! The river of God flowing into our dead seas turns them fresh. Whatever reasons there are for our lives becoming spiritually stale, it is quite clear from Scripture that they need not be so. God offers to exchange His strength daily for our weakness, His freshness for our staleness.

PRAYER

My Father and my God, I come to You to ask that You will make my life like a well watered garden. Let the fresh rivers of Your grace run into my dead seas so that my whole being is revived – day after day after day. Amen.

FURTHER STUDY

John 4:1-29; 7:37-38;
Rev. 7:17
• What is the quality of the water that Christ gives?
• How did Jesus describe it to the woman?

December 18

▬ AMOS 3:1–5:27

3 Hear this word, people of Israel, the word the LORD has spoken against you – against the whole family I brought up out of Egypt:

2 'You only have I chosen
of all the families of the earth;
therefore I will punish you
for all your sins.'

3 Do two walk together
unless they have agreed to do so?
4 Does a lion roar in the thicket
when it has no prey?
Does it growl in its den
when it has caught nothing?
5 Does a bird swoop down to a trap on the ground
when no bait is there?
Does a trap spring up from the ground
if it has not caught anything?
6 When a trumpet sounds in a city,
do not the people tremble?
When disaster comes to a city,
has not the LORD caused it?

7 Surely the Sovereign LORD does nothing
without revealing his plan
to his servants the prophets.

8 The lion has roared –
who will not fear?
The Sovereign LORD has spoken –
who can but prophesy?

9 Proclaim to the fortresses of Ashdod
and to the fortresses of Egypt:
'Assemble yourselves on the mountains
of Samaria;
see the great unrest within her
and the oppression among her people.'

10 'They do not know how to do right,'
declares the LORD,
'who store up in their fortresses
what they have plundered and looted.'

11 Therefore this is what the Sovereign LORD says:

'An enemy will overrun your land,
pull down your strongholds
and plunder your fortresses.'

¹²This is what the Lord says:

'As a shepherd rescues from the lion's
    mouth
      only two leg bones or a piece of an ear,
so will the Israelites living in Samaria be
    rescued,
    with only the head of a bed
    and a piece of fabric from a couch.'

¹³'Hear this and testify against the
descendants of Jacob,' declares the Lord,
the Lord God Almighty.

¹⁴'On the day I punish Israel for her sins,
    I will destroy the altars of Bethel;
the horns of the altar will be cut off
    and fall to the ground.
¹⁵I will tear down the winter house
    along with the summer house;
the houses adorned with ivory will be
    destroyed
      and the mansions will be demolished,'
                  declares the Lord.

4 Hear this word, you cows of Bashan on
  Mount Samaria,
    you women who oppress the poor and
      crush the needy
    and say to your husbands, 'Bring us
      some drinks!'
²The Sovereign Lord has sworn by his
    holiness:
'The time will surely come
when you will be taken away with hooks,
    the last of you with fishhooks.
³You will each go straight out
    through breaches in the wall,
    and you will be cast out towards
      Harmon,'
                  declares the Lord.
⁴'Go to Bethel and sin;
    go to Gilgal and sin yet more.
Bring your sacrifices every morning,
    your tithes every three years.
⁵Burn leavened bread as a thank-offering

and brag about your freewill
    offerings –
boast about them, you Israelites,
    for this is what you love to do,'
             declares the Sovereign Lord.

⁶'I gave you empty stomachs in every city
    and lack of bread in every town,
    yet you have not returned to me,'
               declares the Lord.

⁷'I also withheld rain from you
    when the harvest was still three
      months away.
I sent rain on one town,
    but withheld it from another.
One field had rain;
    another had none and dried up.
⁸People staggered from town to town for
    water
    but did not get enough to drink,
    yet you have not returned to me,'
               declares the Lord.

⁹'Many times I struck your gardens and
    vineyards,
    destroying them with blight and
      mildew.
Locusts devoured your fig and olive
    trees,
    yet you have not returned to me,'
               declares the Lord.

¹⁰'I sent plagues among you
    as I did to Egypt.
I killed your young men with the sword,
    along with your captured horses.
I filled your nostrils with the stench of
    your camps,
    yet you have not returned to me,'
               declares the Lord.

¹¹'I overthrew some of you
    as I overthrew Sodom and Gomorrah.
You were like a burning stick snatched
    from the fire,

yet you have not returned to me,'
   declares the LORD.

12 'Therefore this is what I will do to you,
  Israel,
 and because I will do this to you, Israel,
  prepare to meet your God.'

13 He who forms the mountains,
 who creates the wind,
 and who reveals his thoughts to
   mankind,
who turns dawn to darkness,
 and treads on the heights of the
   earth –
 the LORD God Almighty is his name.

5 Hear this word, Israel, this lament I take
up concerning you:

2 'Fallen is Virgin Israel,
 never to rise again,
deserted in her own land,
 with no one to lift her up.'

3 This is what the Sovereign LORD says to
Israel:

'Your city that marches out a thousand
  strong
 will have only a hundred left;
your town that marches out a hundred
  strong
 will have only ten left.'

4 This is what the LORD says to Israel:

'Seek me and live;
5 do not seek Bethel,
do not go to Gilgal,
 do not journey to Beersheba.
For Gilgal will surely go into exile,
 and Bethel will be reduced to nothing.'
6 Seek the LORD and live,
 or he will sweep through the tribes of
  Joseph like a fire;

it will devour them,
 and Bethel will have no one to
  quench it.

7 There are those who turn justice into
  bitterness
 and cast righteousness to the ground.

8 He who made the Pleiades and Orion,
 who turns midnight into dawn
 and darkens day into night,
who calls for the waters of the sea
 and pours them out over the face of
  the land –
 the LORD is his name.
9 With a blinding flash he destroys the
  stronghold
 and brings the fortified city to ruin.

10 There are those who hate the one who
  upholds justice in court
 and detest the one who tells the truth.

11 You levy a straw tax on the poor
 and impose a tax on their grain.
Therefore, though you have built stone
  mansions,
 you will not live in them;
though you have planted lush vineyards,
 you will not drink their wine.
12 For I know how many are your offences
 and how great your sins.

There are those who oppress the
  innocent and take bribes
 and deprive the poor of justice in the
  courts.
13 Therefore the prudent keep quiet in such
  times,
 for the times are evil.

14 Seek good, not evil,
 that you may live.
Then the LORD God Almighty will be
  with you,
 just as you say he is.

¹⁵ Hate evil, love good;
  maintain justice in the courts.
Perhaps the LORD God Almighty will
    have mercy
  on the remnant of Joseph.

¹⁶ Therefore this is what the Lord, the
LORD God Almighty, says:

'There will be wailing in all the streets
  and cries of anguish in every public
    square.
The farmers will be summoned to weep
  and the mourners to wail.
¹⁷ There will be wailing in all the
    vineyards,
  for I will pass through your midst,'
              says the LORD.

¹⁸ Woe to you who long
  for the day of the LORD!
Why do you long for the day of the LORD?
  That day will be darkness, not light.
¹⁹ It will be as though a man fled from a
    lion
  only to meet a bear,
as though he entered his house
  and rested his hand on the wall
  only to have a snake bite him.
²⁰ Will not the day of the LORD be darkness,
    not light –
  pitch-dark, without a ray of
    brightness?

²¹ 'I hate, I despise your religious festivals;
  your assemblies are a stench to me.
²² Even though you bring me burnt
    offerings and grain offerings,
  I will not accept them.
Though you bring choice fellowship
    offerings,
  I will have no regard for them.
²³ Away with the noise of your songs!
  I will not listen to the music of your
    harps.
²⁴ But let justice roll on like a river,

righteousness like a never-failing
    stream!

²⁵ 'Did you bring me sacrifices and
    offerings
  for forty years in the wilderness,
    people of Israel?
²⁶ You have lifted up the shrine of your
    king,
  the pedestal of your idols,
  the star of your god –
  which you made for yourselves.
²⁷ Therefore I will send you into exile
    beyond Damascus,'
  says the LORD, whose name is God
    Almighty.

■ PSALM 143:7–12

⁷ Answer me quickly, LORD;
  my spirit fails.
Do not hide your face from me
  or I will be like those who go down to
    the pit.
⁸ Let the morning bring me word of your
    unfailing love,
  for I have put my trust in you.
Show me the way I should go,
  for to you I entrust my life.
⁹ Rescue me from my enemies, LORD,
  for I hide myself in you.
¹⁰ Teach me to do your will,
  for you are my God;
may your good Spirit
  lead me on level ground.

¹¹ For your name's sake, LORD, preserve my
    life;
  in your righteousness, bring me out of
    trouble.
¹² In your unfailing love, silence my
    enemies;
  destroy all my foes,
  for I am your servant.

■ PROVERBS 30:24-28

24 'Four things on earth are small,
     yet they are extremely wise:
25 ants are creatures of little strength,
     yet they store up their food in the
         summer;
26 hyraxes are creatures of little power,
     yet they make their home in the crags;
27 locusts have no king,
     yet they advance together in ranks;
28 a lizard can be caught with the hand,
     yet it is found in kings' palaces.

■ REVELATION 8:1–9:12

8 When he opened the seventh seal, there was silence in heaven for about half an hour.

2 And I saw the seven angels who stand before God, and seven trumpets were given to them.

3 Another angel, who had a golden censer, came and stood at the altar. He was given much incense to offer, with the prayers of all God's people, on the golden altar in front of the throne. 4 The smoke of the incense, together with the prayers of God's people, went up before God from the angel's hand. 5 Then the angel took the censer, filled it with fire from the altar, and hurled it on the earth; and there came peals of thunder, rumblings, flashes of lightning and an earthquake.

6 Then the seven angels who had the seven trumpets prepared to sound them.

7 The first angel sounded his trumpet, and there came hail and fire mixed with blood, and it was hurled down on the earth. A third of the earth was burned up, a third of the trees were burned up, and all the green grass was burned up.

8 The second angel sounded his trumpet, and something like a huge mountain, all ablaze, was thrown into the sea. A third of the sea turned into blood, 9 a third of the living creatures in the sea died, and a third of the ships were destroyed.

10 The third angel sounded his trumpet, and a great star, blazing like a torch, fell from the sky on a third of the rivers and on the springs of water – 11 the name of the star is Wormwood. A third of the waters turned bitter, and many people died from the waters that had become bitter.

12 The fourth angel sounded his trumpet, and a third of the sun was struck, a third of the moon, and a third of the stars, so that a third of them turned dark. A third of the day was without light, and also a third of the night.

13 As I watched, I heard an eagle that was flying in mid-air call out in a loud voice: 'Woe! Woe! Woe to the inhabitants of the earth, because of the trumpet blasts about to be sounded by the other three angels!'

9 The fifth angel sounded his trumpet, and I saw a star that had fallen from the sky to the earth. The star was given the key to the shaft of the Abyss. 2 When he opened the Abyss, smoke rose from it like the smoke from a gigantic furnace. The sun and sky were darkened by the smoke from the Abyss. 3 And out of the smoke locusts came down on the earth and were given power like that of scorpions of the earth. 4 They were told not to harm the grass of the earth or any plant or tree, but only those people who did not have the seal of God on their foreheads. 5 They were not allowed to kill them but only to torture them for five months. And the agony they suffered was like that of the sting of a scorpion when it strikes. 6 During those days people will seek death but will not find it; they will long to die, but death will elude them.

7 The locusts looked like horses prepared for battle. On their heads they wore something like crowns of gold, and their faces resembled human faces. 8 Their hair was like women's hair, and their teeth were like

lions' teeth. ⁹They had breastplates like breastplates of iron, and the sound of their wings was like the thundering of many horses and chariots rushing into battle. ¹⁰They had tails with stings, like scorpions, and in their tails they had power to torment people for five months. ¹¹They had as king over them the angel of the Abyss, whose name in Hebrew is Abaddon and in Greek is Apollyon (that is, Destroyer).

¹²The first woe is past; two other woes are yet to come.

The Standard Note

'Let the morning bring me word of your unfailing love, for I have put my trust in you.' **Psalm 143:8**

Jesus felt the need for three simple habits in His earthly life: (1) He stood up to read; (2) He went up a mountain to pray; (3) He taught people the Scriptures – all 'as was his custom' (Luke 4:16).

These three habits – reading the Scriptures, exposing oneself to God in prayer, and passing on to others what one has found – are basic to the spiritual life. If Jesus Himself couldn't get along without them, how can we?

I am often asked by interviewers how I maintain my spiritual life. I usually reply that it centres on a daily quiet time with God. There are some days when a morning quiet time is not possible, but most of my mornings begin with a time closeted with God in prayer.

Someone sent me a brochure once, telling me of a home that had opened, which they described as 'a place in the country where those who have lost their spiritual freshness may come to tone up and be invigorated'. My quiet time is such a 'place'.

A sheep rancher in Australia found that his violin was out of tune, and being unable to find another musical instrument to provide him with a standard note, he wrote to a radio station asking them to strike that note. They did just that – stopped a programme and struck the note. The sheep rancher caught it, and the violin was in tune again. Your daily quiet time will help you hear God's 'standard notes'. Then you can tune your flattened notes to His.

PRAYER

O God, I know there is nothing better than what I have found in You – except more of what I have found in You. Help me today to catch Your 'standard note' and tune every part of my life to it. In Christ's name I ask it. Amen.

FURTHER STUDY

Acts 10:1-8; Luke 6:12; 2 Chron. 29:2
- What is recorded of Cornelius?
- What is said about Hezekiah?

December 19

■ AMOS 6:1–8:14

6 Woe to you who are complacent in Zion,
and to you who feel secure on
Mount Samaria,
you notable men of the foremost nation,
to whom the people of Israel come!
² Go to Kalneh and look at it;
go from there to great Hamath,
and then go down to Gath in Philistia.
Are they better off than your two
kingdoms?
Is their land larger than yours?
³ You put off the day of disaster
and bring near a reign of terror.
⁴ You lie on beds adorned with ivory
and lounge on your couches.
You dine on choice lambs
and fattened calves.
⁵ You strum away on your harps like
David
and improvise on musical
instruments.
⁶ You drink wine by the bowlful
and use the finest lotions,
but you do not grieve over the ruin of
Joseph.
⁷ Therefore you will be among the first to
go into exile;
your feasting and lounging will end.

⁸ The Sovereign Lord has sworn by himself – the Lord God Almighty declares:

'I abhor the pride of Jacob
and detest his fortresses;
I will deliver up the city
and everything in it.'

⁹ If ten people are left in one house, they
too will die. ¹⁰ And if the relative who comes
to carry the bodies out of the house to burn
them asks anyone who might be hiding
there, 'Is anyone else with you?' and he
says, 'No,' then he will go on to say, 'Hush!
We must not mention the name of the LORD.'

¹¹ For the LORD has given the command,
and he will smash the great house into
pieces
and the small house into bits.

¹² Do horses run on the rocky crags?
Does one plough the sea with oxen?
But you have turned justice into poison
and the fruit of righteousness into
bitterness –
¹³ you who rejoice in the conquest of Lo
Debar
and say, 'Did we not take Karnaim by
our own strength?'
¹⁴ For the LORD God Almighty declares,
'I will stir up a nation against you,
Israel,
that will oppress you all the way
from Lebo Hamath to the valley of the
Arabah.'

7 This is what the Sovereign Lord showed
me: he was preparing swarms of locusts
after the king's share had been harvested
and just as the late crops were coming up.
² When they had stripped the land clean, I
cried out, 'Sovereign Lord, forgive! How can
Jacob survive? He is so small!'
³ So the LORD relented.
'This will not happen,' the LORD said.
⁴ This is what the Sovereign LORD showed
me: the Sovereign LORD was calling for
judgment by fire; it dried up the great deep
and devoured the land. ⁵ Then I cried out,

'Sovereign LORD, I beg you, stop! How can Jacob survive? He is so small!'

⁶ So the LORD relented.

'This will not happen either,' the Sovereign LORD said.

⁷ This is what he showed me: the Lord was standing by a wall that had been built true to plumb, with a plumb-line in his hand. ⁸ And the LORD asked me, 'What do you see, Amos?'

'A plumb-line,' I replied.

Then the Lord said, 'Look, I am setting a plumb-line among my people Israel; I will spare them no longer.

⁹ 'The high places of Isaac will be
     destroyed
    and the sanctuaries of Israel will be
     ruined;
    with my sword I will rise against the
     house of Jeroboam.'

¹⁰ Then Amaziah the priest of Bethel sent a message to Jeroboam king of Israel: 'Amos is raising a conspiracy against you in the very heart of Israel. The land cannot bear all his words. ¹¹ For this is what Amos is saying:

' "Jeroboam will die by the sword,
    and Israel will surely go into exile,
     away from their native land." '

¹² Then Amaziah said to Amos, 'Get out, you seer! Go back to the land of Judah. Earn your bread there and do your prophesying there. ¹³ Don't prophesy any more at Bethel, because this is the king's sanctuary and the temple of the kingdom.'

¹⁴ Amos answered Amaziah, 'I was neither a prophet nor the son of a prophet, but I was a shepherd, and I also took care of sycamore-fig trees. ¹⁵ But the LORD took me from tending the flock and said to me, "Go, prophesy to my people Israel." ¹⁶ Now then, hear the word of the LORD. You say,

' "Do not prophesy against Israel,
    and stop preaching against the
     descendants of Isaac."

¹⁷ 'Therefore this is what the LORD says:

' "Your wife will become a prostitute in
     the city,
    and your sons and daughters will fall
     by the sword.
Your land will be measured and divided
     up,
    and you yourself will die in a pagan
     country.
And Israel will surely go into exile,
    away from their native land." '

8 This is what the Sovereign LORD showed me: a basket of ripe fruit. ² 'What do you see, Amos?' he asked.

'A basket of ripe fruit,' I answered.

Then the LORD said to me, 'The time is ripe for my people Israel; I will spare them no longer.

³ 'In that day,' declares the Sovereign LORD, 'the songs in the temple will turn to wailing. Many, many bodies – flung everywhere! Silence!'

⁴ Hear this, you who trample the needy
    and do away with the poor of the land,

⁵ saying,

'When will the New Moon be over
    that we may sell grain,
and the Sabbath be ended
    that we may market wheat?' –
skimping on the measure,
    boosting the price
    and cheating with dishonest scales,
⁶ buying the poor with silver
    and the needy for a pair of sandals,
    selling even the sweepings with the
     wheat.

⁷The LORD has sworn by himself, the Pride of Jacob: 'I will never forget anything they have done.

⁸'Will not the land tremble for this,
and all who live in it mourn?
The whole land will rise like the Nile;
it will be stirred up and then sink
like the river of Egypt.

⁹'In that day,' declares the Sovereign LORD,

'I will make the sun go down at noon
and darken the earth in broad
daylight.
¹⁰ I will turn your religious festivals into
mourning
and all your singing into weeping.
I will make all of you wear sackcloth
and shave your heads.
I will make that time like mourning for
an only son
and the end of it like a bitter day.

¹¹ 'The days are coming,' declares the
Sovereign LORD,
'when I will send a famine through the
land –
not a famine of food or a thirst for water,
but a famine of hearing the words of
the LORD.
¹² People will stagger from sea to sea
and wander from north to east,
searching for the word of the LORD,
but they will not find it.

¹³ 'In that day

'the lovely young women and strong
young men
will faint because of thirst.
¹⁴ Those who swear by the sin of Samaria –
who say, "As surely as your god lives,
Dan",

or, "As surely as the god of Beersheba
lives" –
they will fall, never to rise again.'

■ PSALM 144:1-8

¹ Praise be to the LORD my Rock,
who trains my hands for war,
my fingers for battle.
² He is my loving God and my fortress,
my stronghold and my deliverer,
my shield, in whom I take refuge,
who subdues peoples under me.

³ LORD, what are human beings that you
care for them,
mere mortals that you think of them?
⁴ They are like a breath;
their days are like a fleeting shadow.

⁵ Part your heavens, LORD, and come
down;
touch the mountains, so that they
smoke.
⁶ Send forth lightning and scatter the
enemy;
shoot your arrows and rout them.
⁷ Reach down your hand from on high;
deliver me and rescue me
from the mighty waters,
from the hands of foreigners
⁸ whose mouths are full of lies,
whose right hands are deceitful.

■ PROVERBS 30:29-33

²⁹ 'There are three things that are stately in
their stride,
four that move with stately bearing:
³⁰ a lion, mighty among beasts,
who retreats before nothing;
³¹ a strutting cock, a he-goat,
and a king secure against revolt.

32 'If you play the fool and exalt yourself,
    or if you plan evil,
  clap your hand over your mouth!
33 For as churning cream produces butter,
    and as twisting the nose produces
      blood,
  so stirring up anger produces strife.'

··

■ REVELATION 9:13–10:11

13 The sixth angel sounded his trumpet, and I heard a voice coming from the four horns of the golden altar that is before God. 14 It said to the sixth angel who had the trumpet, 'Release the four angels who are bound at the great river Euphrates.' 15 And the four angels who had been kept ready for this very hour and day and month and year were released to kill a third of mankind. 16 The number of the mounted troops was twice ten thousand times ten thousand. I heard their number.

17 The horses and riders I saw in my vision looked like this: their breastplates were fiery red, dark blue, and yellow as sulphur. The heads of the horses resembled the heads of lions, and out of their mouths came fire, smoke and sulphur. 18 A third of mankind was killed by the three plagues of fire, smoke and sulphur that came out of their mouths. 19 The power of the horses was in their mouths and in their tails; for their tails were like snakes, having heads with which they inflict injury.

20 The rest of mankind who were not killed by these plagues still did not repent of the work of their hands; they did not stop worshipping demons, and idols of gold, silver, bronze, stone and wood – idols that cannot see or hear or walk. 21 Nor did they repent of their murders, their magic arts, their sexual immorality or their thefts.

10 Then I saw another mighty angel coming down from heaven. He was robed in a cloud, with a rainbow above his head; his face was like the sun, and his legs were like fiery pillars. 2 He was holding a little scroll, which lay open in his hand. He planted his right foot on the sea and his left foot on the land, 3 and he gave a loud shout like the roar of a lion. When he shouted, the voices of the seven thunders spoke. 4 And when the seven thunders spoke, I was about to write; but I heard a voice from heaven say, 'Seal up what the seven thunders have said and do not write it down.'

5 Then the angel I had seen standing on the sea and on the land raised his right hand to heaven. 6 And he swore by him who lives for ever and ever, who created the heavens and all that is in them, the earth and all that is in it, and the sea and all that is in it, and said, 'There will be no more delay! 7 But in the days when the seventh angel is about to sound his trumpet, the mystery of God will be accomplished, just as he announced to his servants the prophets.'

8 Then the voice that I had heard from heaven spoke to me once more: 'Go, take the scroll that lies open in the hand of the angel who is standing on the sea and on the land.'

9 So I went to the angel and asked him to give me the little scroll. He said to me, 'Take it and eat it. It will turn your stomach sour, but "in your mouth it will be as sweet as honey."' 10 I took the little scroll from the angel's hand and ate it. It tasted as sweet as honey in my mouth, but when I had eaten it, my stomach turned sour. 11 Then I was told, 'You must prophesy again about many peoples, nations, languages and kings.'

How to Forgive

'... as twisting the nose produces blood, so stirring up anger produces strife.' **Proverbs 30:33**

If difficulties concerning basic trust on a natural level can hinder our ability to trust at a spiritual level, how do we as Christians overcome this? The first thing we must do is demonstrate a willingness to forgive those who hurt us. 'That's hard', you might say. My reply is, 'Yes, in the case of those who have been badly let down, it is hard – but not impossible.'

Here's how you do it. Focus first on how much you have been forgiven. The key to forgiving others is to enter into a realised awareness of how much God has forgiven you. When people say to me during a counselling session, 'My problem is that I can't forgive', I usually respond by saying, 'No, that's not your problem. Your problem is that you don't know how much you have been forgiven'. It may be difficult for some to see this, especially those who have gone through deep hurt, but nothing others have done to you is as awful as what you have done to God.

If you have difficulty with the last statement, it is because you do not understand the nature of sin. Sin is taking the Creator of the universe and relegating Him to irrelevance; it is saying to the One who made us, 'I can run my life on my own terms.' Sin is insanity – and you and I have been guilty of that. Yet in Christ God has forgiven us, pardoned us, and bestowed upon us His royal favour. Having been given such forgiveness, can we, dare we, withhold it from anyone who has betrayed our trust, no matter how horrifying that hurt has been?

PRAYER

Father, Your Word is frank and open – help me to respond to it in the same way. Take from me any anger, every fear and apprehension, every refusal to accept responsibility. In Jesus' name I pray. Amen.

FURTHER STUDY

Col. 3:1-14; Mark 11:25; Luke 17:4; Eph. 4:32
• How are we to forgive?
• Do you need to forgive someone today?

December 20

■ AMOS 9:1–OBADIAH 1–21

9 I saw the Lord standing by the altar, and he said:

'Strike the tops of the pillars
    so that the thresholds shake.
Bring them down on the heads of all the
    people;

those who are left I will kill with the
        sword.
Not one will get away,
        none will escape.
² Though they dig down to the depths
        below,
    from there my hand will take them.
Though they climb up to the heavens
        above,
    from there I will bring them down.
³ Though they hide themselves on the top
        of Carmel,
    there I will hunt them down and seize
        them.
Though they hide from my eyes at the
        bottom of the sea,
    there I will command the serpent to
        bite them.
⁴ Though they are driven into exile by
        their enemies,
    there I will command the sword to
        slay them.

'I will keep my eye on them
    for harm and not for good.'

⁵ The Lord, the LORD Almighty –
he touches the earth and it melts,
    and all who live in it mourn;
the whole land rises like the Nile,
    then sinks like the river of Egypt;
⁶ he builds his lofty palace in the heavens
    and sets its foundation on the earth;
he calls for the waters of the sea
    and pours them out over the face of
        the land –
    the LORD is his name.

⁷ 'Are not you Israelites
    the same to me as the Cushites?'
                        declares the LORD.
'Did I not bring Israel up from Egypt,
    the Philistines from Caphtor
    and the Arameans from Kir?

⁸ 'Surely the eyes of the Sovereign LORD

are on the sinful kingdom.
I will destroy it
    from the face of the earth.
Yet I will not totally destroy
    the descendants of Jacob,'
                        declares the LORD.
⁹ 'For I will give the command,
    and I will shake the people of Israel
    among all the nations
as grain is shaken in a sieve,
    and not a pebble will reach the ground.
¹⁰ All the sinners among my people
    will die by the sword,
all those who say,
    "Disaster will not overtake or meet us."

¹¹ 'In that day

'I will restore David's fallen shelter –
    I will repair its broken walls
    and restore its ruins –
    and will rebuild it as it used to be,
¹² so that they may possess the remnant of
        Edom
    and all the nations that bear my name,'
                        declares the LORD,
            who will do these things.

¹³ 'The days are coming,' declares the
LORD,

'when the reaper will be overtaken by the
        ploughman
    and the planter by the one treading
        grapes.
New wine will drip from the mountains
    and flow from all the hills,
¹⁴   and I will bring my people Israel back
        from exile.

'They will rebuild the ruined cities and
        live in them.
They will plant vineyards and drink
        their wine;
they will make gardens and eat their
        fruit.

¹⁵ I will plant Israel in their own land,
  never again to be uprooted
  from the land I have given them,'

                    says the LORD your God.

1

The vision of Obadiah.

  This is what the Sovereign LORD says
about Edom –

  We have heard a message from the LORD:
    an envoy was sent to the nations to
      say,
  'Rise, let us go against her for battle' –

² 'See, I will make you small among the
      nations;
  you will be utterly despised.
³ The pride of your heart has deceived you,
  you who live in the clefts of the rocks
    and make your home on the heights,
  you who say to yourself,
    "Who can bring me down to the
      ground?"
⁴ Though you soar like the eagle
    and make your nest among the stars,
    from there I will bring you down,'
                  declares the LORD.
⁵ 'If thieves came to you,
    if robbers in the night –
  oh, what a disaster awaits you –
    would they not steal only as much as
      they wanted?
  If grape pickers came to you,
    would they not leave a few grapes?
⁶ But how Esau will be ransacked,
    his hidden treasures pillaged!
⁷ All your allies will force you to the
      border;
    your friends will deceive and
      overpower you;
  those who eat your bread will set a trap
      for you,
    but you will not detect it.

⁸ 'In that day,' declares the LORD,
  'will I not destroy the wise men of
      Edom,
    those of understanding in the
      mountains of Esau?
⁹ Your warriors, Teman, will be terrified,
    and everyone in Esau's mountains
    will be cut down in the slaughter.
¹⁰ Because of the violence against your
      brother Jacob,
  you will be covered with shame;
    you will be destroyed for ever.
¹¹ On the day you stood aloof
    while strangers carried off his wealth
  and foreigners entered his gates
    and cast lots for Jerusalem,
    you were like one of them.
¹² You should not gloat over your brother
    in the day of his misfortune,
  nor rejoice over the people of Judah
    in the day of their destruction,
  nor boast so much
    in the day of their trouble.
¹³ You should not march through the gates
      of my people
    in the day of their disaster,
  nor gloat over them in their calamity
    in the day of their disaster,
  nor seize their wealth
    in the day of their disaster.
¹⁴ You should not wait at the crossroads
    to cut down their fugitives,
  nor hand over their survivors
    in the day of their trouble.
¹⁵ 'The day of the LORD is near
    for all nations.
  As you have done, it will be done to you;
    your deeds will return upon your own
      head.
¹⁶ Just as you drank on my holy hill,
    so all the nations will drink
      continually;
  they will drink and drink
    and be as if they had never been.
¹⁷ But on Mount Zion will be deliverance;

it will be holy,
and Jacob will possess his inheritance.
¹⁸ Jacob will be a fire
and Joseph a flame;
Esau will be stubble,
and they will set him on fire and
destroy him.
There will be no survivors
from Esau.'
                        The LORD has spoken.

¹⁹ People from the Negev will occupy
the mountains of Esau,
and people from the foothills will
possess
the land of the Philistines.
They will occupy the fields of Ephraim
and Samaria,
and Benjamin will possess Gilead.
²⁰ This company of Israelite exiles who are
in Canaan
will possess the land as far as
Zarephath;
the exiles from Jerusalem who are in
Sepharad
will possess the towns of the Negev.
²¹ Deliverers will go up on Mount Zion
to govern the mountains of Esau.
And the kingdom will be the LORD's.

■ PSALM 144:9-15

⁹ I will sing a new song to you, my God;
on the ten-stringed lyre I will make
music to you,
¹⁰ to the One who gives victory to kings,
who delivers his servant David.

From the deadly sword ¹¹ deliver me;
rescue me from the hands of
foreigners
whose mouths are full of lies,
whose right hands are deceitful.

¹² Then our sons in their youth

will be like well-nurtured plants,
and our daughters will be like pillars
carved to adorn a palace.
¹³ Our barns will be filled
with every kind of provision.
Our sheep will increase by thousands,
by tens of thousands in our fields;
¹⁴ our oxen will draw heavy loads.
There will be no breaching of walls,
no going into captivity,
no cry of distress in our streets.
¹⁵ Blessed is the people of whom this is
true;
blessed is the people whose God is the
LORD.

■ PROVERBS 31:1-3

31 The sayings of King Lemuel – an
inspired utterance his mother taught
him.

² Listen, my son! Listen, son of my womb!
Listen, my son, the answer to my
prayers!
³ Do not spend your strength on women,
your vigour on those who ruin kings.

■ REVELATION 11:1-19

11 I was given a reed like a measuring
rod and was told, 'Go and measure
the temple of God and the altar, with its
worshippers. ² But exclude the outer court;
do not measure it, because it has been giv-
en to the Gentiles. They will trample on the
holy city for 42 months. ³ And I will appoint
my two witnesses, and they will prophesy
for 1,260 days, clothed in sackcloth.' ⁴ They
are 'the two olive trees' and the two lampstands, and 'they stand before the Lord of
the earth.' ⁵ If anyone tries to harm them,
fire comes from their mouths and devours
their enemies. This is how anyone who

wants to harm them must die. ⁶They have power to shut up the heavens so that it will not rain during the time they are prophesying; and they have power to turn the waters into blood and to strike the earth with every kind of plague as often as they want.

⁷Now when they have finished their testimony, the beast that comes up from the Abyss will attack them, and overpower and kill them. ⁸Their bodies will lie in the public square of the great city – which is figuratively called Sodom and Egypt – where also their Lord was crucified. ⁹For three and a half days some from every people, tribe, language and nation will gaze on their bodies and refuse them burial. ¹⁰The inhabitants of the earth will gloat over them and will celebrate by sending each other gifts, because these two prophets had tormented those who live on the earth.

¹¹But after the three and a half days the breath of life from God entered them, and they stood on their feet, and terror struck those who saw them. ¹²Then they heard a loud voice from heaven saying to them, 'Come up here.' And they went up to heaven in a cloud, while their enemies looked on.

¹³At that very hour there was a severe earthquake and a tenth of the city collapsed. Seven thousand people were killed in the earthquake, and the survivors were terrified and gave glory to the God of heaven.

¹⁴The second woe has passed; the third woe is coming soon.

¹⁵The seventh angel sounded his trumpet, and there were loud voices in heaven, which said:

'The kingdom of the world has become
the kingdom of our Lord and of his
Messiah,
and he will reign for ever and ever.'

¹⁶And the twenty-four elders, who were seated on their thrones before God, fell on their faces and worshipped God, ¹⁷saying:

'We give thanks to you, Lord God
Almighty,
the One who is and who was,
because you have taken your great power
and have begun to reign.
¹⁸The nations were angry,
and your wrath has come.
The time has come for judging the dead,
and for rewarding your servants the
prophets
and your people who revere your name,
both great and small –
and for destroying those who destroy the
earth.'

¹⁹Then God's temple in heaven was opened, and within his temple was seen the ark of his covenant. And there came flashes of lightning, rumblings, peals of thunder, an earthquake and a severe hailstorm.

The Doxology

'The kingdom of the world has become the kingdom of
our Lord and of his Messiah ...' **Revelation 11:15**

The end of the Lord's Prayer – 'For Yours is the kingdom and the power and the glory forever. Amen' – is a doxology so beautiful that it somehow seems almost irreverent to try to dissect it. Some believe that Jesus did not actually say these words. They claim that they were added by someone else at a later date, which is why they are not included in some versions of the Bible. Some manuscripts have it, and some do not. I have looked long at the evidence for and against their inclusion in the sacred Scriptures, and I am perfectly satisfied myself that they were part of Jesus' original pattern of prayer.

The prayer ends as it begins, with an assertion of God's majesty and glory: 'Yours is the kingdom.' I believe that the emphasis here should be placed on the word 'is', to read, 'Yours *is* the kingdom' – now.

Despite all appearances to the contrary, God has never abdicated His position as ruler of the universe. What a heartening thought this can be in these days, a thought to fill the soul with song and flood the heart with hope and gladness. It is true that there are many things in the world that militate against His authority – war, poverty, unemployment, drink, gambling, social impurity, and so on. All these seem a flat and final refutation of the phrase 'Yours is the kingdom', but their days are numbered. The hour will come when the kingdoms of this world will signal their final surrender and pledge allegiance to their rightful Lord.

PRAYER

O Father, help me to see, despite all the situations and circumstances which might deny Your eternal Kingship, that You are reigning over the world now. Yours is the final control. I am so thankful. Amen.

FURTHER STUDY

Matt. 4:1-11; Obad. 21; Heb. 12:28; 2 Pet. 1:11
• Why was Satan's temptation foolish?
• How did Jesus respond?

December 21

■ JONAH 1:1–4:11

1 The word of the LORD came to Jonah son of Amittai: ²'Go to the great city of Nineveh and preach against it, because its wickedness has come up before me.'

³But Jonah ran away from the LORD and headed for Tarshish. He went down to Joppa, where he found a ship bound for that port. After paying the fare, he went aboard and sailed for Tarshish to flee from the LORD.

⁴Then the LORD sent a great wind on the sea, and such a violent storm arose that the ship threatened to break up. ⁵All the sailors were afraid and each cried out to his own

god. And they threw the cargo into the sea to lighten the ship.

But Jonah had gone below deck, where he lay down and fell into a deep sleep. ⁶The captain went to him and said, 'How can you sleep? Get up and call on your god! Maybe he will take notice of us so that we will not perish.'

⁷Then the sailors said to each other, 'Come, let us cast lots to find out who is responsible for this calamity.' They cast lots and the lot fell on Jonah. ⁸So they asked him, 'Tell us, who is responsible for making all this trouble for us? What kind of work do you do? Where do you come from? What is your country? From what people are you?'

⁹He answered, 'I am a Hebrew and I worship the LORD, the God of heaven, who made the sea and the dry land.'

¹⁰This terrified them and they asked, 'What have you done?' (They knew he was running away from the LORD, because he had already told them so.)

¹¹The sea was getting rougher and rougher. So they asked him, 'What should we do to you to make the sea calm down for us?'

¹²'Pick me up and throw me into the sea,' he replied, 'and it will become calm. I know that it is my fault that this great storm has come upon you.'

¹³Instead, the men did their best to row back to land. But they could not, for the sea grew even wilder than before. ¹⁴Then they cried out to the LORD, 'Please, LORD, do not let us die for taking this man's life. Do not hold us accountable for killing an innocent man, for you, LORD, have done as you pleased.' ¹⁵Then they took Jonah and threw him overboard, and the raging sea grew calm. ¹⁶At this the men greatly feared the LORD, and they offered a sacrifice to the LORD and made vows to him.

¹⁷Now the LORD provided a huge fish to swallow Jonah, and Jonah was in the belly of the fish three days and three nights.

2 ¹From inside the fish Jonah prayed to the LORD his God. ²He said:

'In my distress I called to the LORD,
    and he answered me.
From deep in the realm of the dead I
        called for help,
    and you listened to my cry.
³You hurled me into the depths,
    into the very heart of the seas,
    and the currents swirled about me;
all your waves and breakers
    swept over me.
⁴I said, "I have been banished
    from your sight;
yet I will look again
    towards your holy temple."

⁵The engulfing waters threatened me,
    the deep surrounded me;
seaweed was wrapped around my
    head.
⁶To the roots of the mountains I sank
    down;
    the earth beneath barred me in for
        ever.
But you, LORD my God,
    brought my life up from the pit.

⁷'When my life was ebbing away,
    I remembered you, LORD,
and my prayer rose to you,
    to your holy temple.

⁸'Those who cling to worthless idols
    turn away from God's love for them.
⁹But I, with shouts of grateful praise,
    will sacrifice to you.
What I have vowed I will make good.
    I will say, "Salvation comes from the
        LORD."'

¹⁰And the LORD commanded the fish, and it vomited Jonah onto dry land.

3 Then the word of the LORD came to Jonah a second time: ²'Go to the great city of Nineveh and proclaim to it the message I give you.'

³Jonah obeyed the word of the LORD and went to Nineveh. Now Nineveh was a very large city; it took three days to go through it. ⁴Jonah began by going a day's journey into the city, proclaiming, 'Forty more days and Nineveh will be overthrown.' ⁵The Ninevites believed God. A fast was proclaimed, and all of them, from the greatest to the least, put on sackcloth.

⁶When Jonah's warning reached the king of Nineveh, he rose from his throne, took off his royal robes, covered himself with sackcloth and sat down in the dust. ⁷This is the proclamation he issued in Nineveh:

'By the decree of the king and his nobles:

Do not let people or animals, herds or flocks, taste anything; do not let them eat or drink. ⁸But let people and animals be covered with sackcloth. Let everyone call urgently on God. Let them give up their evil ways and their violence. ⁹Who knows? God may yet relent and with compassion turn from his fierce anger so that we will not perish.'

¹⁰When God saw what they did and how they turned from their evil ways, he relented and did not bring on them the destruction he had threatened.

4 But to Jonah this seemed very wrong, and he became angry. ²He prayed to the LORD, 'Isn't this what I said, LORD, when I was still at home? That is what I tried to forestall by fleeing to Tarshish. I knew that you are a gracious and compassionate God, slow to anger and abounding in love, a God who relents from sending calamity. ³Now, LORD, take away my life, for it is better for me to die than to live.'

⁴But the LORD replied, 'Is it right for you to be angry?'

⁵Jonah had gone out and sat down at a place east of the city. There he made himself a shelter, sat in its shade and waited to see what would happen to the city. ⁶Then the LORD God provided a leafy plant and made it grow up over Jonah to give shade for his head to ease his discomfort, and Jonah was very happy about the plant. ⁷But at dawn the next day God provided a worm, which chewed the plant so that it withered. ⁸When the sun rose, God provided a scorching east wind, and the sun blazed on Jonah's head so that he grew faint. He wanted to die, and said, 'It would be better for me to die than to live.'

⁹But God said to Jonah, 'Is it right for you to be angry about the plant?'

'It is,' he said. 'And I'm so angry I wish I were dead.'

¹⁰But the LORD said, 'You have been concerned about this plant, though you did not tend it or make it grow. It sprang up overnight and died overnight. ¹¹And should I not have concern for the great city of Nineveh, in which there are more than a hundred and twenty thousand people who cannot tell their right hand from their left – and also many animals?'

························

▬ PSALM 145:1–7

¹I will exalt you, my God the King;
   I will praise your name for ever and
      ever.
²Every day I will praise you
   and extol your name for ever and ever.

³Great is the LORD and most worthy of
      praise;
   his greatness no one can fathom.
⁴One generation commends your works
      to another;
   they tell of your mighty acts.
⁵They speak of the glorious splendour of
      your majesty –
   and I will meditate on your wonderful
      works.
⁶They tell of the power of your awesome
      works –
   and I will proclaim your great deeds.
⁷They celebrate your abundant goodness
   and joyfully sing of your
      righteousness.

························

▬ PROVERBS 31:4–7

⁴It is not for kings, Lemuel –
   it is not for kings to drink wine,
   not for rulers to crave beer,
⁵lest they drink and forget what has been
      decreed,
   and deprive all the oppressed of their
      rights.

⁶ Let beer be for those who are perishing,
  wine for those who are in anguish!
⁷ Let them drink and forget their poverty
  and remember their misery no more.

▬ REVELATION 12:1-17

12 A great sign appeared in heaven: a woman clothed with the sun, with the moon under her feet and a crown of twelve stars on her head. ²She was pregnant and cried out in pain as she was about to give birth. ³Then another sign appeared in heaven: an enormous red dragon with seven heads and ten horns and seven crowns on its heads. ⁴Its tail swept a third of the stars out of the sky and flung them to the earth. The dragon stood in front of the woman who was about to give birth, so that it might devour her child the moment he was born. ⁵She gave birth to a son, a male child, who 'will rule all the nations with an iron sceptre.' And her child was snatched up to God and to his throne. ⁶The woman fled into the wilderness to a place prepared for her by God, where she might be taken care of for 1,260 days.

⁷Then war broke out in heaven. Michael and his angels fought against the dragon, and the dragon and his angels fought back. ⁸But he was not strong enough, and they lost their place in heaven. ⁹The great dragon was hurled down – that ancient snake called the devil, or Satan, who leads the whole world astray. He was hurled to the earth, and his angels with him.

¹⁰Then I heard a loud voice in heaven say:

'Now have come the salvation and the
  power

and the kingdom of our God,
  and the authority of his Messiah.
For the accuser of our brothers and
  sisters,
  who accuses them before our God day
  and night,
  has been hurled down.
¹¹ They triumphed over him
  by the blood of the Lamb
  and by the word of their testimony;
they did not love their lives so much
  as to shrink from death.
¹² Therefore rejoice, you heavens
  and you who dwell in them!
But woe to the earth and the sea,
  because the devil has gone down to
  you!
He is filled with fury,
  because he knows that his time is
  short.'

¹³When the dragon saw that he had been hurled to the earth, he pursued the woman who had given birth to the male child. ¹⁴The woman was given the two wings of a great eagle, so that she might fly to the place prepared for her in the wilderness, where she would be taken care of for a time, times and half a time, out of the snake's reach. ¹⁵Then from his mouth the snake spewed water like a river, to overtake the woman and sweep her away with the torrent. ¹⁶But the earth helped the woman by opening its mouth and swallowing the river that the dragon had spewed out of his mouth. ¹⁷Then the dragon was enraged at the woman and went off to wage war against the rest of her offspring – those who keep God's commands and hold fast their testimony about Jesus.

Reflect on Perfection

'They speak of the glorious splendour of your majesty and I will meditate on your wonderful works.' **Psalm 145:5**

The fact that God knows everything ought to strengthen our faith and cause us to bow down in adoration before Him. Yet how little do we reflect on this divine perfection! Those who are inclined to rebel against God hate this aspect of His being and would do away with it if they could. They wish there might be no Witness to their sin, no Searcher of their hearts, no Judge of their deeds. How very solemn are the words of the psalmist recorded in Psalm 90:8: 'You have set our iniquities before you, our secret sins in the light of your presence.'

To the believer, however, the truth of God's omniscience (His all-knowledge) ought to be one of tremendous comfort and security. In times of perplexity we ought to say like Job: 'But he knows the way I take; when he has tested me, I shall come forth as gold' (Job 23:10). Whatever might be going on in our lives that is profoundly mysterious to us and quite incomprehensible to those who are around us, we must never lose sight of the fact that 'He knows the way [we] take'. The psalmist, when seeking to stir his soul to confidence and hope, reminded himself in the midst of his weakness and weariness: 'he knows how we are formed, he remembers that we are dust' (Psa. 103:14). And Simon Peter, when his failure brought him almost to the point of despair and the searching question came, 'Do you love me?' said, 'Lord, you know all things, you know that I love you' (John 21:17). Such knowledge should ever cause us to worship.

PRAYER

Father, help me reflect on this fact that You know everything, for I see that the more I understand it, the more secure I will feel in my soul. Teach me still more, dear Lord. In Jesus' name. Amen.

FURTHER STUDY

Isa. 55:1-9; Heb. 4:12-13; 1 John 3:20
- What statement did God make?
- What did the writer to the Hebrews confirm?

December 22

■ MICAH 1:1–4:13

1 The word of the LORD that came to Micah of Moresheth during the reigns of Jotham, Ahaz and Hezekiah, kings of Judah – the vision he saw concerning Samaria and Jerusalem.

² Hear, you peoples, all of you,
listen, earth and all who live in it,

that the Sovereign Lord may bear
    witness against you,
    the Lord from his holy temple.
³ Look! The Lord is coming from his
    dwelling-place;
    he comes down and treads on the
    heights of the earth.
⁴ The mountains melt beneath him
    and the valleys split apart,
    like wax before the fire,
    like water rushing down a slope.
⁵ All this is because of Jacob's
    transgression,
    because of the sins of the people of
    Israel.
What is Jacob's transgression?
    Is it not Samaria?
What is Judah's high place?
    Is it not Jerusalem?

⁶ 'Therefore I will make Samaria a heap
    of rubble,
    a place for planting vineyards.
I will pour her stones into the valley
    and lay bare her foundations.
⁷ All her idols will be broken to pieces;
    all her temple gifts will be burned
    with fire;
    I will destroy all her images.
Since she gathered her gifts from the
    wages of prostitutes,
    as the wages of prostitutes they will
    again be used.'

⁸ Because of this I will weep and wail;
    I will go about barefoot and naked.
I will howl like a jackal
    and moan like an owl.
⁹ For Samaria's plague is incurable;
    it has spread to Judah.
It has reached the very gate of my people,
    even to Jerusalem itself.
¹⁰ Tell it not in Gath;
    weep not at all.
In Beth Ophrah
    roll in the dust.

¹¹ Pass by naked and in shame,
    you who live in Shaphir.
Those who live in Zaanan
    will not come out.
Beth Ezel is in mourning;
    it no longer protects you.
¹² Those who live in Maroth writhe in pain,
    waiting for relief,
because disaster has come from the Lord,
    even to the gate of Jerusalem.
¹³ You who live in Lachish,
    harness fast horses to the chariot.
You are where the sin of Daughter Zion
    began,
    for the transgressions of Israel were
    found in you.
¹⁴ Therefore you will give parting gifts
    to Moresheth Gath.
The town of Akzib will prove deceptive
    to the kings of Israel.
¹⁵ I will bring a conqueror against you
    who live in Mareshah.
The nobles of Israel
    will flee to Adullam.
¹⁶ Shave your head in mourning
    for the children in whom you delight;
make yourself as bald as the vulture,
    for they will go from you into exile.

2 Woe to those who plan iniquity,
    to those who plot evil on their beds!
At morning's light they carry it out
    because it is in their power to do it.
² They covet fields and seize them,
    and houses, and take them.
They defraud people of their homes,
    they rob them of their inheritance.

³ Therefore, the Lord says:

'I am planning disaster against this
    people,
    from which you cannot save
    yourselves.
You will no longer walk proudly,
    for it will be a time of calamity.

⁴In that day people will ridicule you;
    they will taunt you with this mournful
        song:
"We are utterly ruined;
    my people's possession is divided up.
He takes it from me!
    He assigns our fields to traitors."'

⁵Therefore you will have no one in the
        assembly of the LORD
    to divide the land by lot.

⁶'Do not prophesy,' their prophets say.
    'Do not prophesy about these things;
    disgrace will not overtake us.'
⁷You descendants of Jacob, should it be
        said,
    'Does the LORD become impatient?
    Does he do such things?'

'Do not my words do good
    to the one whose ways are upright?
⁸Lately my people have risen up
    like an enemy.
You strip off the rich robe
    from those who pass by without a care,
    like men returning from battle.
⁹You drive the women of my people
    from their pleasant homes.
You take away my blessing
    from their children for ever.
¹⁰Get up, go away!
    For this is not your resting place,
because it is defiled,
    it is ruined, beyond all remedy.
¹¹If a liar and deceiver comes and says,
    "I will prophesy for you plenty of wine
        and beer,"
    that would be just the prophet for this
        people!

¹²'I will surely gather all of you, Jacob;
    I will surely bring together the
        remnant of Israel.
I will bring them together like sheep in a
        sheepfold,

like a flock in its pasture;
    the place will throng with people.
¹³The One who breaks open the way will go
        up before them;
    they will break through the gate and
        go out.
Their King will pass through before them,
    the LORD at their head.'

3 Then I said,
    'Listen, you leaders of Jacob,
    you rulers of Israel.
Should you not embrace justice,
²   you who hate good and love evil;
who tear the skin from my people
    and the flesh from their bones;
³who eat my people's flesh,
    strip off their skin
    and break their bones in pieces;
who chop them up like meat for the pan,
    like flesh for the pot.'

⁴Then they will cry out to the LORD,
    but he will not answer them.
At that time he will hide his face from
        them
    because of the evil they have done.

⁵This is what the LORD says:

'As for the prophets
    who lead my people astray,
they proclaim "peace"
    if they have something to eat,
but prepare to wage war against anyone
    who refuses to feed them.
⁶Therefore night will come over you,
        without visions,
    and darkness, without divination.
The sun will set for the prophets,
    and the day will go dark for them.
⁷The seers will be ashamed
    and the diviners disgraced.
They will all cover their faces
    because there is no answer from God.'
⁸But as for me, I am filled with power,

with the Spirit of the LORD,
and with justice and might,
to declare to Jacob his transgression,
to Israel his sin.

⁹ Hear this, you leaders of Jacob,
you rulers of Israel,
who despise justice
and distort all that is right;
¹⁰ who build Zion with bloodshed,
and Jerusalem with wickedness.
¹¹ Her leaders judge for a bribe,
her priests teach for a price,
and her prophets tell fortunes for money.
Yet they look for the LORD's support and
say,
'Is not the LORD among us?
No disaster will come upon us.'
¹² Therefore because of you,
Zion will be ploughed like a field,
Jerusalem will become a heap of rubble,
the temple hill a mound overgrown
with thickets.

4 In the last days

the mountain of the LORD's temple will
be established
as the highest of the mountains;
it will be exalted above the hills,
and peoples will stream to it.

² Many nations will come and say,

'Come, let us go up to the mountain of
the LORD,
to the temple of the God of Jacob.
He will teach us his ways,
so that we may walk in his paths.'
The law will go out from Zion,
the word of the LORD from Jerusalem.
³ He will judge between many peoples
and will settle disputes for strong
nations far and wide.
They will beat their swords into
ploughshares

and their spears into pruning hooks.
Nation will not take up sword against
nation,
nor will they train for war any more.
⁴ Everyone will sit under their own vine
and under their own fig-tree,
and no one will make them afraid,
for the LORD Almighty has spoken.
⁵ All the nations may walk
in the name of their gods,
but we will walk in the name of the LORD
our God for ever and ever.

⁶ 'In that day,' declares the Lord,
'I will gather the lame;
I will assemble the exiles
and those I have brought to grief.
⁷ I will make the lame my remnant,
those driven away a strong nation.
The LORD will rule over them in Mount
Zion
from that day and for ever.
⁸ As for you, watchtower of the flock,
stronghold of Daughter Zion,
the former dominion will be restored to
you;
kingship will come to Daughter
Jerusalem.'

⁹ Why do you now cry aloud –
have you no king?
Has your ruler perished,
that pain seizes you like that of a
woman in labour?
¹⁰ Writhe in agony, Daughter Zion,
like a woman in labour,
for now you must leave the city
to camp in the open field.
You will go to Babylon;
there you will be rescued.
There the LORD will redeem you
out of the hand of your enemies.

¹¹ But now many nations
are gathered against you.
They say, 'Let her be defiled,

let our eyes gloat over Zion!'
¹² But they do not know
    the thoughts of the LORD;
  they do not understand his plan,
    that he has gathered them like sheaves
      to the threshing-floor.
¹³ 'Rise and thresh, Daughter Zion,
  for I will give you horns of iron;
I will give you hooves of bronze,
  and you will break to pieces many
    nations.'
You will devote their ill-gotten gains to
    the LORD,
  their wealth to the Lord of all the earth.

■ PSALM 145:8-13

⁸ The LORD is gracious and compassionate,
  slow to anger and rich in love.

⁹ The LORD is good to all;
  he has compassion on all he has made.
¹⁰ All your works praise you, LORD;
  your faithful people extol you.
¹¹ They tell of the glory of your kingdom
  and speak of your might,
¹² so that all people may know of your
      mighty acts
  and the glorious splendour of your
    kingdom.
¹³ Your kingdom is an everlasting kingdom,
  and your dominion endures through
    all generations.

The LORD is trustworthy in all he promises
  and faithful in all he does.

■ PROVERBS 31:8-9

⁸ Speak up for those who cannot speak for
    themselves,
  for the rights of all who are destitute.
⁹ Speak up and judge fairly;
  defend the rights of the poor and needy.

■ REVELATION 13:1-18

13 The dragon stood on the shore of the sea. And I saw a beast coming out of the sea. It had ten horns and seven heads, with ten crowns on its horns, and on each head a blasphemous name. ² The beast I saw resembled a leopard, but had feet like those of a bear and a mouth like that of a lion. The dragon gave the beast his power and his throne and great authority. ³ One of the heads of the beast seemed to have had a fatal wound, but the fatal wound had been healed. The whole world was filled with wonder and followed the beast. ⁴ People worshipped the dragon because he had given authority to the beast, and they also worshipped the beast and asked, 'Who is like the beast? Who can wage war against it?'

⁵ The beast was given a mouth to utter proud words and blasphemies and to exercise its authority for forty-two months. ⁶ It opened its mouth to blaspheme God, and to slander his name and his dwelling-place and those who live in heaven. ⁷ It was given power to wage war against God's holy people and to conquer them. And it was given authority over every tribe, people, language and nation. ⁸ All inhabitants of the earth will worship the beast – all whose names have not been written in the Lamb's book of life, the Lamb who was slain from the creation of the world.

⁹ Whoever has ears, let them hear.

¹⁰ 'If anyone is to go into captivity,
  into captivity they will go.
If anyone is to be killed with the sword,
  with the sword they will be killed.'

This calls for patient endurance and faithfulness on the part of God's people.

¹¹ Then I saw a second beast, coming out of the earth. It had two horns like a lamb, but it spoke like a dragon. ¹² It exercised all the authority of the first beast on its behalf,

and made the earth and its inhabitants worship the first beast, whose fatal wound had been healed. ¹³And it performed great signs, even causing fire to come down from heaven to the earth in full view of the people. ¹⁴Because of the signs it was given power to perform on behalf of the first beast, it deceived the inhabitants of the earth. It ordered them to set up an image in honour of the beast who was wounded by the sword and yet lived. ¹⁵The second beast was given power to give breath to the image of the first beast, so that the image could speak and cause all who refused to worship the image to be killed. ¹⁶It also forced all people, great and small, rich and poor, free and slave, to receive a mark on their right hands or on their foreheads, ¹⁷so that they could not buy or sell unless they had the mark, which is the name of the beast or the number of its name.

¹⁸This calls for wisdom. Let the person who has insight calculate the number of the beast, for it is the number of a man. That number is 666.

The 'marshmallow test'

'But as for me, I watch in hope for the LORD, I wait for God my Saviour ...' **Micah 7:7**

The willingness to wait for God to give us an answer in His own time and in the way He thinks best is without doubt one of the greatest marks of spiritual maturity. I know many Christians who can pass almost all the other tests of spiritual maturity but fail this one.

Have you heard of the 'marshmallow test'? It was devised a few decades ago by psychologists at Stanford University in the USA. One by one, a group of four-year-olds was placed in a room, a marshmallow was put on a table and then a psychologist said, 'I have to go out for a while and if, when I come back, you have not eaten the marshmallow, I will give you two. If you eat the marshmallow, it's the only one you are going to get.' The children developed all kinds of strategies to kill the waiting time until the psychologist returned. They would sing, sit on their hands, and one little boy actually licked the table near the marshmallow thinking that perhaps the flavour had transferred to the wood. Some children, of course, couldn't wait and ate the marshmallow.

Following this test, the researchers tracked all those children into adolescence and found that the 'marshmallow grabbers' grew up to be more hesitant and indecisive, more easily upset by frustration and more resentful about not getting enough. Those who were able to wait grew up to be more socially competent, better able to handle stress and less likely to give up under pressure than those who could not wait.

The waiting times, said a philosopher, 'are the times that try men's souls'. They most certainly are. Ask yourself now: How good am I at waiting for God's answers to my prayers? The ability to wait says more about your spirituality than almost any other thing.

PRAYER

O Father, Your Word goes like an
arrow to the core of my problem. I
find it so difficult to wait. Teach me
the art of putting everything in Your
hands and waiting for the outcome
which You decide in Your own good
time. In Jesus' name I ask it. Amen.

FURTHER STUDY

Num. 3:10; 16:40;
1 Sam. 10:8; 13:3–14
• Why did Saul act
  foolishly?
• What was the result?

December 23

■ MICAH 5:1–7:20

5 Marshal your troops now, city of troops,
for a siege is laid against us.
They will strike Israel's ruler
on the cheek with a rod.

2 'But you, Bethlehem Ephrathah,
though you are small among the clans
of Judah,
out of you will come for me
one who will be ruler over Israel,
whose origins are from of old,
from ancient times.'

3 Therefore Israel will be abandoned
until the time when she who is in
labour bears a son,
and the rest of his brothers return
to join the Israelites.

4 He will stand and shepherd his flock
in the strength of the LORD,
in the majesty of the name of the LORD
his God.
And they will live securely, for then his
greatness
will reach to the ends of the earth.

5 And he will be our peace
when the Assyrians invade our land

and march through our fortresses.
We will raise against them seven
shepherds,
even eight commanders,
6 who will rule the land of Assyria with
the sword,
the land of Nimrod with drawn sword.
He will deliver us from the Assyrians
when they invade our land
and march across our borders.

7 The remnant of Jacob will be
in the midst of many peoples
like dew from the LORD,
like showers on the grass,
which do not wait for anyone
or depend on man.
8 The remnant of Jacob will be among the
nations,
in the midst of many peoples,
like a lion among the beasts of the forest,
like a young lion among flocks of
sheep,
which mauls and mangles as it goes,
and no one can rescue.
9 Your hand will be lifted up in triumph
over your enemies,
and all your foes will be destroyed.

10 'In that day,' declares the LORD,

'I will destroy your horses from among
     you
  and demolish your chariots.
¹¹ I will destroy the cities of your land
  and tear down all your strongholds.
¹² I will destroy your witchcraft
  and you will no longer cast spells.
¹³ I will destroy your idols
  and your sacred stones from among
     you;
  you will no longer bow down
  to the work of your hands.
¹⁴ I will uproot from among you your
     Asherah poles
  when I demolish your cities.
¹⁵ I will take vengeance in anger and wrath
  on the nations that have not obeyed
     me.'

6 Listen to what the Lord says:

'Stand up, plead my case before the
     mountains;
  let the hills hear what you have to say.
² 'Hear, you mountains, the LORD's
     accusation;
  listen, you everlasting foundations of
     the earth.
  For the LORD has a case against his
     people;
  he is lodging a charge against Israel.

³ 'My people, what have I done to you?
  How have I burdened you? Answer me.
⁴ I brought you up out of Egypt
  and redeemed you from the land of
     slavery.
  I sent Moses to lead you,
  also Aaron and Miriam.
⁵ My people, remember
  what Balak king of Moab plotted
  and what Balaam son of Beor
     answered.
  Remember your journey from Shittim to
     Gilgal,

that you may know the righteous acts
     of the LORD.'

⁶ With what shall I come before the LORD
  and bow down before the exalted God?
  Shall I come before him with burnt
     offerings,
  with calves a year old?
⁷ Will the LORD be pleased with thousands
     of rams,
  with ten thousand rivers of oil?
  Shall I offer my firstborn for my
     transgression,
  the fruit of my body for the sin of my
     soul?
⁸ He has shown you, O mortal, what is
     good.
  And what does the LORD require of
     you?
  To act justly and to love mercy
  and to walk humbly with your God.

⁹ Listen! The Lord is calling to the city –
  and to fear your name is wisdom –
  'Heed the rod and the One who
     appointed it.
¹⁰ Am I still to forget your ill-gotten
     treasures, you wicked house,
  and the short ephah, which is
     accursed?
¹¹ Shall I acquit someone with dishonest
     scales,
  with a bag of false weights?
¹² Your rich people are violent;
  your inhabitants are liars
  and their tongues speak deceitfully.
¹³ Therefore, I have begun to destroy you,
  to ruin you because of your sins.
¹⁴ You will eat but not be satisfied;
  your stomach will still be empty.
  You will store up but save nothing,
  because what you save I will give to
     the sword.
¹⁵ You will plant but not harvest;
  you will press olives but not use the
     oil,

you will crush grapes but not drink
the wine.
¹⁶ You have observed the statutes of Omri
and all the practices of Ahab's house;
you have followed their traditions.
Therefore I will give you over to ruin
and your people to derision;
you will bear the scorn of the nations.'

7 What misery is mine!
I am like one who gathers summer fruit
at the gleaning of the vineyard;
there is no cluster of grapes to eat,
none of the early figs that I crave.
² The faithful have been swept from the
land;
not one upright person remains.
Everyone lies in wait to shed blood;
they hunt each other with nets.
³ Both hands are skilled in doing evil;
the ruler demands gifts,
the judge accepts bribes,
the powerful dictate what they
desire –
they all conspire together.
⁴ The best of them is like a brier,
the most upright worse than a thorn
hedge.
The day God visits you has come,
the day your watchmen sound the
alarm.
Now is the time of your confusion.
⁵ Do not trust a neighbour;
put no confidence in a friend.
Even with the woman who lies in your
embrace
guard the words of your lips.
⁶ For a son dishonours his father,
a daughter rises up against her
mother,
a daughter-in-law against her
mother-in-law –
a man's enemies are the members of
his own household.

⁷ But as for me, I watch in hope for the
LORD,
I wait for God my Saviour;
my God will hear me.

⁸ Do not gloat over me, my enemy!
Though I have fallen, I will rise.
Though I sit in darkness,
the LORD will be my light.
⁹ Because I have sinned against him,
I will bear the LORD's wrath,
until he pleads my case
and upholds my cause.
He will bring me out into the light;
I will see his righteousness.
¹⁰ Then my enemy will see it
and will be covered with shame,
she who said to me,
'Where is the LORD your God?'
My eyes will see her downfall;
even now she will be trampled
underfoot
like mire in the streets.

¹¹ The day for building your walls will come,
the day for extending your
boundaries.
¹² In that day people will come to you
from Assyria and the cities of Egypt,
even from Egypt to the Euphrates
and from sea to sea
and from mountain to mountain.
¹³ The earth will become desolate because
of its inhabitants,
as the result of their deeds.

¹⁴ Shepherd your people with your staff,
the flock of your inheritance,
which lives by itself in a forest,
in fertile pasture-lands.
Let them feed in Bashan and Gilead
as in days long ago.

¹⁵ 'As in the days when you came out of
Egypt,
I will show them my wonders.'

¹⁶ Nations will see and be ashamed,
    deprived of all their power.
They will put their hands over their
        mouths
    and their ears will become deaf.
¹⁷ They will lick dust like a snake,
    like creatures that crawl on the
        ground.
They will come trembling out of their
        dens;
    they will turn in fear to the LORD our
        God
    and will be afraid of you.
¹⁸ Who is a God like you,
    who pardons sin and forgives the
        transgression
    of the remnant of his inheritance?
You do not stay angry for ever
    but delight to show mercy.
¹⁹ You will again have compassion on us;
    you will tread our sins underfoot
    and hurl all our iniquities into the
        depths of the sea.
²⁰ You will be faithful to Jacob,
    and show love to Abraham,
    as you pledged on oath to our ancestors
        in days long ago.

PSALM 145:14-21

¹⁴ The LORD upholds all who fall
    and lifts up all who are bowed down.
¹⁵ The eyes of all look to you,
    and you give them their food at the
        proper time.
¹⁶ You open your hand
    and satisfy the desires of every living
        thing.

¹⁷ The LORD is righteous in all his ways
    and faithful in all he does.
¹⁸ The LORD is near to all who call on him,
    to all who call on him in truth.
¹⁹ He fulfils the desires of those who fear
        him;

he hears their cry and saves them.
²⁰ The LORD watches over all who love him,
    but all the wicked he will destroy.

²¹ My mouth will speak in praise of the
        LORD.
    Let every creature praise his holy
        name
    for ever and ever.

PROVERBS 31:10-12

¹⁰ A wife of noble character who can find?
    She is worth far more than rubies.
¹¹ Her husband has full confidence in her
    and lacks nothing of value.
¹² She brings him good, not harm,
    all the days of her life.

REVELATION 14:1-20

14 Then I looked, and there before me
was the Lamb, standing on Mount
Zion, and with him 144,000 who had his
name and his Father's name written on
their foreheads. ² And I heard a sound from
heaven like the roar of rushing waters and
like a loud peal of thunder. The sound I
heard was like that of harpists playing their
harps. ³ And they sang a new song before the
throne and before the four living creatures
and the elders. No one could learn the song
except the 144,000 who had been redeemed
from the earth. ⁴ These are those who did
not defile themselves with women, for they
remained virgins. They follow the Lamb
wherever he goes. They were purchased
from among mankind and offered as firstfruits to God and the Lamb. ⁵ No lie was
found in their mouths; they are blameless.

⁶ Then I saw another angel flying in mid-
air, and he had the eternal gospel to proclaim to those who live on the earth – to
every nation, tribe, language and people.

[7] He said in a loud voice, 'Fear God and give him glory, because the hour of his judgment has come. Worship him who made the heavens, the earth, the sea and the springs of water.'

[8] A second angel followed and said, '"Fallen! Fallen is Babylon the Great," which made all the nations drink the maddening wine of her adulteries.'

[9] A third angel followed them and said in a loud voice: 'If anyone worships the beast and its image and receives its mark on their forehead or on their hand, [10] they, too, will drink the wine of God's fury, which has been poured full strength into the cup of his wrath. They will be tormented with burning sulphur in the presence of the holy angels and of the Lamb. [11] And the smoke of their torment will rise for ever and ever. There will be no rest day or night for those who worship the beast and its image, or for anyone who receives the mark of its name.' [12] This calls for patient endurance on the part of the people of God who keep his commands and remain faithful to Jesus.

[13] Then I heard a voice from heaven say, 'Write this: blessed are the dead who die in the Lord from now on.'

'Yes,' says the Spirit, 'they will rest from their labour, for their deeds will follow them.'

[14] I looked, and there before me was a white cloud, and seated on the cloud was one like a son of man with a crown of gold on his head and a sharp sickle in his hand. [15] Then another angel came out of the temple and called in a loud voice to him who was sitting on the cloud, 'Take your sickle and reap, because the time to reap has come, for the harvest of the earth is ripe.' [16] So he who was seated on the cloud swung his sickle over the earth, and the earth was harvested.

[17] Another angel came out of the temple in heaven, and he too had a sharp sickle. [18] Still another angel, who had charge of the fire, came from the altar and called in a loud voice to him who had the sharp sickle, 'Take your sharp sickle and gather the clusters of grapes from the earth's vine, because its grapes are ripe.' [19] The angel swung his sickle on the earth, gathered its grapes and threw them into the great winepress of God's wrath. [20] They were trampled in the winepress outside the city, and blood flowed out of the press, rising as high as the horses' bridles for a distance of 1,600 stadia.

Familiar with Failure

'The LORD is near to all who call on him, to all who call on him in truth.' **Psalm 145:18**

Many years ago, a young man came to see me and said, 'I am not making a success of my life spiritually. I want with all my heart to become a successful Christian, but I seem to be failing in everything I do.' At that time I was not as aware of the subtleties of the human heart as I am today, and I encouraged him to keep trying. I said, 'Responsible effort and dogged obedience will bring you what you need; keep going no matter what.' The advice I gave him was good, but it was not complete.

About a year later, after God had allowed me to see the subtleties and deceptions of my own heart, and after putting some personal things right before Him myself, I sat down once again with the young man and asked him how things were going. 'A little better', he said, 'but even though I keep asking God to help me become a successful Christian, I am still failing.'

I took a deep breath and tentatively suggested that perhaps, deep down in his heart, he preferred failure to success. He looked at me in amazement and after a few seconds said, 'Say some more about that. I feel you are touching something very vulnerable inside me.'

We talked for hours, and he told me how all his life he had lived with failure, and it soon became obvious that he preferred the familiar feelings of failure to the unfamiliar feelings of success – even spiritual success. This one insight was all he needed to open up the whole of his being to God and call upon Him in truth.

PRAYER

Father, if I too need something to trigger off a deeper openness and self-awareness in my heart, then give it to me today. I want nothing more than to be an honest person, not only on the surface but also at the depths. Help me – in Jesus' name. Amen.

FURTHER STUDY

Exod. 16:1-3;
Num. 11:1-6; 13:17-33
• What was the problem of the children of Israel?
• Why were they not prepared to move forward?

December 24

■ NAHUM 1:1–3:19

1 A prophecy concerning Nineveh. The book of the vision of Nahum the Elkoshite.

[2] The Lord is a jealous and avenging God;
    the LORD takes vengeance and is filled with wrath.
The LORD takes vengeance on his foes
    and vents his wrath against his enemies.
[3] The LORD is slow to anger but great in power;
    the LORD will not leave the guilty unpunished.
His way is in the whirlwind and the storm,
    and clouds are the dust of his feet.
[4] He rebukes the sea and dries it up;

he makes all the rivers run dry.
Bashan and Carmel wither
    and the blossoms of Lebanon fade.
[5] The mountains quake before him
    and the hills melt away.
The earth trembles at his presence,
    the world and all who live in it.
[6] Who can withstand his indignation?
    Who can endure his fierce anger?
His wrath is poured out like fire;
    the rocks are shattered before him.
[7] The LORD is good,
    a refuge in times of trouble.
He cares for those who trust in him,
[8]   but with an overwhelming flood
he will make an end of Nineveh;
    he will pursue his foes into the realm of darkness.

⁹ Whatever they plot against the LORD
    he will bring to an end;
    trouble will not come a second time.
¹⁰ They will be entangled among thorns
    and drunk from their wine;
    they will be consumed like dry stubble.
¹¹ From you, Nineveh, has one come forth
    who plots evil against the LORD
    and devises wicked plans.

¹² This is what the LORD says:

'Although they have allies and are
        numerous,
    they will be destroyed and pass away.
Although I have afflicted you, Judah,
    I will afflict you no more.
¹³ Now I will break their yoke from your neck
    and tear your shackles away.'

¹⁴ The LORD has given a command
        concerning you, Nineveh:
    'You will have no descendants to bear
        your name.
I will destroy the images and idols
    that are in the temple of your gods.
I will prepare your grave,
    for you are vile.'

¹⁵ Look, there on the mountains,
    the feet of one who brings good news,
    who proclaims peace!
Celebrate your festivals, Judah,
    and fulfil your vows.
No more will the wicked invade you;
    they will be completely destroyed.

2 An attacker advances against you,
    Nineveh.
    Guard the fortress,
    watch the road,
    brace yourselves,
    marshal all your strength!

² The LORD will restore the splendour
        of Jacob

like the splendour of Israel,
    though destroyers have laid them waste
    and have ruined their vines.

³ The shields of the soldiers are red;
    the warriors are clad in scarlet.
The metal on the chariots flashes
    on the day they are made ready;
    the spears of juniper are brandished.
⁴ The chariots storm through the streets,
    rushing back and forth through the
        squares.
They look like flaming torches;
    they dart about like lightning.

⁵ Nineveh summons her picked troops,
    yet they stumble on their way.
They dash to the city wall;
    the protective shield is put in place.
⁶ The river gates are thrown open
    and the palace collapses.
⁷ It is decreed that Nineveh
    be exiled and carried away.
Her female slaves moan like doves
    and beat on their breasts.
⁸ Nineveh is like a pool
    whose water is draining away.
'Stop! Stop!' they cry,
    but no one turns back.
⁹ Plunder the silver!
    Plunder the gold!
The supply is endless,
    the wealth from all its treasures!
¹⁰ She is pillaged, plundered, stripped!
    Hearts melt, knees give way,
    bodies tremble, every face grows pale.

¹¹ Where now is the lions' den,
    the place where they fed their young,
where the lion and lioness went,
    and the cubs, with nothing to fear?
¹² The lion killed enough for his cubs
    and strangled the prey for his mate,
filling his lairs with the kill
    and his dens with the prey.

¹³ 'I am against you,'
   declares the LORD Almighty.
'I will burn up your chariots in smoke,
   and the sword will devour your young
      lions.
I will leave you no prey on the earth.
The voices of your messengers
   will no longer be heard.'

3 Woe to the city of blood,
   full of lies,
full of plunder,
   never without victims!
² The crack of whips,
   the clatter of wheels,
galloping horses
   and jolting chariots!
³ Charging cavalry,
   flashing swords
   and glittering spears!
Many casualties,
   piles of dead,
bodies without number,
   people stumbling over the corpses –
⁴ all because of the wanton lust of a
      prostitute,
   alluring, the mistress of sorceries,
who enslaved nations by her prostitution
   and peoples by her witchcraft.

⁵ 'I am against you,' declares the LORD
      Almighty.
'I will lift your skirts over your face.
I will show the nations your nakedness
   and the kingdoms your shame.
⁶ I will pelt you with filth,
   I will treat you with contempt
   and make you a spectacle.
⁷ All who see you will flee from you and say,
   "Nineveh is in ruins – who will mourn
      for her?"
   Where can I find anyone to comfort
      you?'

⁸ Are you better than Thebes,
   situated on the Nile,

with water around her?
The river was her defence,
   the waters her wall.
⁹ Cush and Egypt were her boundless
      strength;
   Put and Libya were among her allies.
¹⁰ Yet she was taken captive
   and went into exile.
Her infants were dashed to pieces
   at every street corner.
Lots were cast for her nobles,
   and all her great men were put in chains.
¹¹ You too will become drunk;
   you will go into hiding
   and seek refuge from the enemy.

¹² All your fortresses are like fig-trees
   with their first ripe fruit;
when they are shaken,
   the figs fall into the mouth of the eater.
¹³ Look at your troops –
   they are all weaklings.
The gates of your land
   are wide open to your enemies;
   fire has consumed the bars of your
      gates.

¹⁴ Draw water for the siege,
   strengthen your defences!
Work the clay,
   tread the mortar,
   repair the brickwork!
¹⁵ There the fire will consume you;
   the sword will cut you down –
   and it will devour you like a swarm of
      locusts.
Multiply like grasshoppers,
   multiply like locusts!
¹⁶ You have increased the number of your
      merchants
   till they are more numerous than the
      stars in the sky,
but like locusts they strip the land
   and then fly away.
¹⁷ Your guards are like locusts,
   your officials like swarms of locusts

that settle in the walls on a cold day –
but when the sun appears they fly away,
    and no one knows where.

¹⁸ King of Assyria, your shepherds
    slumber;
your nobles lie down to rest.
Your people are scattered on the
    mountains
    with no one to gather them.
¹⁹ Nothing can heal you;
    your wound is fatal.
All who hear the news about you
    clap their hands at your fall,
for who has not felt
    your endless cruelty?

PSALM 146:1–10

¹ Praise the LORD.

Praise the LORD, my soul.

² I will praise the LORD all my life;
    I will sing praise to my God as long as
    I live.
³ Do not put your trust in princes,
    in human beings, who cannot save.
⁴ When their spirit departs, they return to
    the ground;
    on that very day their plans come to
    nothing.
⁵ Blessed are those whose help is the God
    of Jacob,
    whose hope is in the LORD their God.

⁶ He is the Maker of heaven and earth,
    the sea, and everything in them –
    he remains faithful for ever.
⁷ He upholds the cause of the oppressed
    and gives food to the hungry.
The LORD sets prisoners free,
⁸   the LORD gives sight to the blind,
the LORD lifts up those who are bowed
    down,

the LORD loves the righteous.
⁹ The LORD watches over the foreigner
    and sustains the fatherless and the
    widow,
    but he frustrates the ways of the
    wicked.

¹⁰ The LORD reigns for ever,
    your God, O Zion, for all generations.

Praise the LORD.

PROVERBS 31:13–14

¹³ She selects wool and flax
    and works with eager hands.
¹⁴ She is like the merchant ships,
    bringing her food from afar.

REVELATION 15:1–16:11

15 I saw in heaven another great and
marvellous sign: seven angels with
the seven last plagues – last, because with
them God's wrath is completed. ² And I saw
what looked like a sea of glass glowing with
fire and, standing beside the sea, those who
had been victorious over the beast and its
image and over the number of its name.
They held harps given them by God ³ and
sang the song of God's servant Moses and
of the Lamb:

'Great and marvellous are your deeds,
    Lord God Almighty.
Just and true are your ways,
    King of the nations.
⁴ Who will not fear you, Lord,
    and bring glory to your name?
For you alone are holy.
All nations will come
    and worship before you,
for your righteous acts have been
    revealed.'

⁵After this I looked, and I saw in heaven the temple – that is, the tabernacle of the covenant law – and it was opened. ⁶Out of the temple came the seven angels with the seven plagues. They were dressed in clean, shining linen and wore golden sashes round their chests. ⁷Then one of the four living creatures gave to the seven angels seven golden bowls filled with the wrath of God, who lives for ever and ever. ⁸And the temple was filled with smoke from the glory of God and from his power, and no one could enter the temple until the seven plagues of the seven angels were completed.

16 Then I heard a loud voice from the temple saying to the seven angels, 'Go, pour out the seven bowls of God's wrath on the earth.'

²The first angel went and poured out his bowl on the land, and ugly, festering sores broke out on the people who had the mark of the beast and worshipped its image.

³The second angel poured out his bowl on the sea, and it turned into blood like that of a dead person, and every living thing in the sea died.

⁴The third angel poured out his bowl on the rivers and springs of water, and they became blood. ⁵Then I heard the angel in charge of the waters say:

'You are just in these judgments, O Holy One,
    you who are and who were;
⁶for they have shed the blood of your holy people and your prophets,
    and you have given them blood to drink as they deserve.'

⁷And I heard the altar respond:

'Yes, Lord God Almighty,
    true and just are your judgments.'

⁸The fourth angel poured out his bowl on the sun, and the sun was allowed to scorch people with fire. ⁹They were seared by the intense heat and they cursed the name of God, who had control over these plagues, but they refused to repent and glorify him.

¹⁰The fifth angel poured out his bowl on the throne of the beast, and its kingdom was plunged into darkness. People gnawed their tongues in agony ¹¹and cursed the God of heaven because of their pains and their sores, but they refused to repent of what they had done.

Climbing Higher

'Look, there on the mountains, the feet of one who brings good news, who proclaims peace!' **Nahum 1:15**

There are numerous references in Scripture where the pursuit of God is likened to a deer climbing steadily, sure-footedly towards the high mountain peaks, and the more we consider the simile, the more rich and rewarding are the truths that flow out of it.

Why does God liken the pursuit of Himself to a deer making its way upward to the high places? And why does He focus so much attention upon the deer's feet? Well, the deer has an amazing ability, when climbing a steep mountain slope, of ensuring that its back feet alight on the exact spot where its front feet were positioned. This perfect correlation between its front and back feet enables the deer to avoid the dangers that would befall a less coordinated animal.

The Bible writers, in drawing attention to the sure-footedness of the deer, are attempting to show (so I believe) that what the deer experiences in the natural realm, we can experience in the spiritual realm. Do you really want to climb higher with God than you have ever gone before? Is there a deep longing in your heart to ascend, like the prophets and seers of old, into the mountain of the Lord? Then take heart - you can. This can be the greatest time of spiritual advance you have ever known. If you supply the willingness, then I promise you - God will supply the power.

PRAYER

O Father, my prayer is - make this the greatest time of my life. I long more than anything to ascend into the mountain peaks with You. I am willing - now send the power. In Jesus' name. Amen.

FURTHER STUDY

Isa. 55; Psa. 42:2; 63:1; 143:6
• What did the psalmist express continually?
• What does God promise?

December 25

■ HABAKKUK 1:1–3:19

1 The prophecy that Habakkuk the prophet received.

² How long, Lord, must I call for help,
  but you do not listen?
 Or cry out to you, 'Violence!'
  but you do not save?
³ Why do you make me look at injustice?
  Why do you tolerate wrongdoing?
 Destruction and violence are before me;
  there is strife, and conflict abounds.
⁴ Therefore the law is paralysed,
  and justice never prevails.
 The wicked hem in the righteous,
  so that justice is perverted.

⁵ 'Look at the nations and watch –
  and be utterly amazed.
 For I am going to do something in your days
  that you would not believe,

even if you were told.
⁶ I am raising up the Babylonians,
  that ruthless and impetuous people,
 who sweep across the whole earth
  to seize dwellings not their own.
⁷ They are a feared and dreaded people;
  they are a law to themselves
  and promote their own honour.
⁸ Their horses are swifter than leopards,
  fiercer than wolves at dusk.
 Their cavalry gallops headlong;
  their horsemen come from afar.
 They fly like an eagle swooping to devour;
⁹   they all come intent on violence.
 Their hordes advance like a desert wind
  and gather prisoners like sand.
¹⁰ They mock kings
  and scoff at rulers.
 They laugh at all fortified cities;
  by building earthen ramps they
   capture them.
¹¹ Then they sweep past like the wind and
  go on –

guilty people, whose own strength is
their god.'

¹² Lord, are you not from everlasting?
My God, my Holy One, you will never
die.
You, LORD, have appointed them to
execute judgment;
you, my Rock, have ordained them to
punish.
¹³ Your eyes are too pure to look on evil;
you cannot tolerate wrongdoing.
Why then do you tolerate the
treacherous?
Why are you silent while the wicked
swallow up those more righteous than
themselves?
¹⁴ You have made people like the fish in the
sea,
like the sea creatures that have no
ruler.
¹⁵ The wicked foe pulls all of them up with
hooks,
he catches them in his net,
he gathers them up in his drag-net;
and so he rejoices and is glad.
¹⁶ Therefore he sacrifices to his net
and burns incense to his drag-net,
for by his net he lives in luxury
and enjoys the choicest food.
¹⁷ Is he to keep on emptying his net,
destroying nations without mercy?

2 I will stand at my watch
and station myself on the ramparts;
I will look to see what he will say to me,
and what answer I am to give to this
complaint.

² Then the Lord replied:

'Write down the revelation
and make it plain on tablets
so that a herald may run with it.
³ For the revelation awaits an appointed
time;

it speaks of the end
and will not prove false.
Though it linger, wait for it;
it will certainly come
and will not delay.

⁴ 'See, the enemy is puffed up;
his desires are not upright –
but the righteous person will live by
his faithfulness –
⁵ indeed, wine betrays him;
he is arrogant and never at rest.
Because he is as greedy as the grave
and like death is never satisfied,
he gathers to himself all the nations
and takes captive all the peoples.

⁶ 'Will not all of them taunt him with
ridicule and scorn, saying,

' "Woe to him who piles up stolen goods
and makes himself wealthy by
extortion!
How long must this go on?"
⁷ Will not your creditors suddenly arise?
Will they not wake up and make you
tremble?
Then you will become their prey.
⁸ Because you have plundered many
nations,
the peoples who are left will plunder
you.
For you have shed human blood;
you have destroyed lands and cities
and everyone in them.

⁹ 'Woe to him who builds his house by
unjust gain,
setting his nest on high
to escape the clutches of ruin!
¹⁰ You have plotted the ruin of many peoples,
shaming your own house and
forfeiting your life.
¹¹ The stones of the wall will cry out,
and the beams of the woodwork will
echo it.

¹² 'Woe to him who builds a city with
    bloodshed
and establishes a town by injustice!
¹³ Has not the LORD Almighty determined
    that the people's labour is only fuel for
    the fire,
    that the nations exhaust themselves
    for nothing?
¹⁴ For the earth will be filled with the
    knowledge of the glory of the LORD
as the waters cover the sea.

¹⁵ 'Woe to him who gives drink to his
    neighbours,
    pouring it from the wineskin till they
    are drunk,
    so that he can gaze on their naked
    bodies!
¹⁶ You will be filled with shame instead of
    glory.
    Now it is your turn! Drink and let your
    nakedness be exposed!
The cup from the LORD's right hand is
    coming round to you,
and disgrace will cover your glory.
¹⁷ The violence you have done to Lebanon
    will overwhelm you,
    and your destruction of animals will
    terrify you.
For you have shed human blood;
    you have destroyed lands and cities
    and everyone in them.

¹⁸ 'Of what value is an idol carved by a
    craftsman?
    Or an image that teaches lies?
For the one who makes it trusts in his
    own creation;
    he makes idols that cannot speak.
¹⁹ Woe to him who says to wood, "Come to
    life!"
    Or to lifeless stone, "Wake up!"
Can it give guidance?
    It is covered with gold and silver;
    there is no breath in it.'

²⁰ The LORD is in his holy temple;
    let all the earth be silent before him.

3 A prayer of Habakkuk the prophet.
On *shigionoth*.

² LORD, I have heard of your fame;
    I stand in awe of your deeds, LORD.
Repeat them in our day,
    in our time make them known;
    in wrath remember mercy.

³ God came from Teman,
    the Holy One from Mount Paran.
His glory covered the heavens
    and his praise filled the earth.
⁴ His splendour was like the sunrise;
    rays flashed from his hand,
    where his power was hidden.
⁵ Plague went before him;
    pestilence followed his steps.
⁶ He stood, and shook the earth;
    he looked, and made the nations
    tremble.
The ancient mountains crumbled
    and the age-old hills collapsed –
    but he marches on for ever.
⁷ I saw the tents of Cushan in distress,
    the dwellings of Midian in anguish.

⁸ Were you angry with the rivers, LORD?
    Was your wrath against the streams?
Did you rage against the sea
    when you rode your horses
    and your chariots to victory?
⁹ You uncovered your bow,
    you called for many arrows.
You split the earth with rivers;
¹⁰   the mountains saw you and writhed.
Torrents of water swept by;
    the deep roared
    and lifted its waves on high.

¹¹ Sun and moon stood still in the heavens
    at the glint of your flying arrows,
    at the lightning of your flashing spear.

[12] In wrath you strode through the earth
  and in anger you threshed the nations.
[13] You came out to deliver your people,
  to save your anointed one.
You crushed the leader of the land of
  wickedness,
  you stripped him from head to foot.
[14] With his own spear you pierced his head
  when his warriors stormed out to
    scatter us,
gloating as though about to devour
  the wretched who were in hiding.
[15] You trampled the sea with your horses,
  churning the great waters.

[16] I heard and my heart pounded,
  my lips quivered at the sound;
decay crept into my bones,
  and my legs trembled.
Yet I will wait patiently for the day of
    calamity
  to come on the nation invading us.
[17] Though the fig-tree does not bud
  and there are no grapes on the vines,
though the olive crop fails
  and the fields produce no food,
though there are no sheep in the
    sheepfold
  and no cattle in the stalls,
[18] yet I will rejoice in the LORD,
  I will be joyful in God my Saviour.

[19] The Sovereign LORD is my strength;
  he makes my feet like the feet of a deer,
  he enables me to tread on the heights.

For the director of music. On my
    stringed instruments.

■ PSALM 147:1–6

[1] Praise the LORD.

How good it is to sing praises to our God,

how pleasant and fitting to praise
    him!
[2] The LORD builds up Jerusalem;
  he gathers the exiles of Israel.
[3] He heals the broken-hearted
  and binds up their wounds.
[4] He determines the number of the stars
  and calls them each by name.
[5] Great is our Lord and mighty in power;
  his understanding has no limit.
[6] The LORD sustains the humble
  but casts the wicked to the ground.

■ PROVERBS 31:15–17

[15] She gets up while it is still night;
  she provides food for her family
  and portions for her female servants.
[16] She considers a field and buys it;
  out of her earnings she plants a
    vineyard.
[17] She sets about her work vigorously;
  her arms are strong for her tasks.

■ REVELATION 16:12–17:8

[12] The sixth angel poured out his bowl on
the great river Euphrates, and its water was
dried up to prepare the way for the kings
from the East. [13] Then I saw three impure
spirits that looked like frogs; they came
out of the mouth of the dragon, out of the
mouth of the beast and out of the mouth of
the false prophet. [14] They are demonic spirits that perform signs, and they go out to the
kings of the whole world, to gather them for
the battle on the great day of God Almighty.

[15] 'Look, I come like a thief! Blessed is
the one who stays awake and remains
clothed, so as not to go naked and be
shamefully exposed.'

¹⁶Then they gathered the kings together to the place that in Hebrew is called Armageddon.

¹⁷The seventh angel poured out his bowl into the air, and out of the temple came a loud voice from the throne, saying, 'It is done!' ¹⁸Then there came flashes of lightning, rumblings, peals of thunder and a severe earthquake. No earthquake like it has ever occurred since mankind has been on earth, so tremendous was the quake. ¹⁹The great city split into three parts, and the cities of the nations collapsed. God remembered Babylon the Great and gave her the cup filled with the wine of the fury of his wrath. ²⁰Every island fled away and the mountains could not be found. ²¹From the sky huge hailstones, each weighing about forty kilograms fell on people. And they cursed God on account of the plague of hail, because the plague was so terrible.

17 One of the seven angels who had the seven bowls came and said to me, 'Come, I will show you the punishment of the great prostitute, who sits by many waters. ²With her the kings of the earth committed adultery, and the inhabitants of the earth were intoxicated with the wine of her adulteries.'

³Then the angel carried me away in the Spirit into a desert. There I saw a woman sitting on a scarlet beast that was covered with blasphemous names and had seven heads and ten horns. ⁴The woman was dressed in purple and scarlet, and was glittering with gold, precious stones and pearls. She held a golden cup in her hand, filled with abominable things and the filth of her adulteries. ⁵The name written on her forehead was a mystery:

BABYLON THE GREAT
THE MOTHER OF PROSTITUTES
AND OF THE ABOMINATIONS OF THE EARTH.

⁶I saw that the woman was drunk with the blood of God's holy people, the blood of those who bore testimony to Jesus.

When I saw her, I was greatly astonished. ⁷Then the angel said to me: 'Why are you astonished? I will explain to you the mystery of the woman and of the beast she rides, which has the seven heads and ten horns. ⁸The beast, which you saw, once was, now is not, and yet will come up out of the Abyss and go to its destruction. The inhabitants of the earth whose names have not been written in the book of life from the creation of the world will be astonished when they see the beast, because it once was, now is not, and yet will come.

God Knows All

'Great is our Lord and mighty in power; his understanding has no limit.' **Psalm 147:5**

Two aspects of God's nature which cannot be examined separately are His knowledge and His wisdom. I link these two characteristics together because really it is almost impossible to consider one without considering the other.

The difference between knowledge and wisdom has been described like this, 'Knowledge is what we know; wisdom is the right application of what we know'. God, of course, knows everything: everything possible, everything actual. He is perfectly acquainted with every detail in the life of every being in heaven, in earth, and in hell. Daniel said of Him: 'He knows what lies in the darkness, and light dwells with him' (Dan. 2:22). Nothing escapes His notice, nothing can be hidden from Him, and nothing can be forgotten by Him.

Many Christians, when referring to their conversion, say that God has forgotten their sins, but strictly speaking that is not so. God never forgets anything. What He promises to do with our sins is 'remember ... no more' (Jer. 31:34). There is a great difference between forgetting something and deciding not to remember it. Realising, then, as we do, that God knows everything ought to strengthen our faith and cause us to bow in adoration before Him. The hymnist put it effectively when he wrote these words:

> *The knowledge of this life is small,*
> *The eye of faith is dim,*
> *But 'tis enough that God knows all*
> *And I shall be with Him.*

PRAYER

O Father, how consoling it is to know that You know everything. Nothing ever escapes Your attention. This means I can relax, for what I don't know You know. And because You know it, then what I don't know can't hurt me. Amen.

FURTHER STUDY

Job 31:1-4; 34:21-25;
Psa. 147:5; Ezek. 11:5
• What was Job's question?
• What was Elihu's response?

December 26

▪ ZEPHANIAH 1:1–3:20

1 The word of the LORD that came to Zephaniah son of Cushi, the son of Gedaliah, the son of Amariah, the son of Hezekiah, during the reign of Josiah son of Amon king of Judah:

² 'I will sweep away everything
    from the face of the earth,'
                declares the LORD.
³ 'I will sweep away both man and beast;
    I will sweep away the birds in the sky
    and the fish in the sea –

and the idols that cause the wicked to
    stumble.'

'When I destroy all mankind
    on the face of the earth,'
                declares the LORD,
⁴ 'I will stretch out my hand against Judah
    and against all who live in Jerusalem.
I will destroy every remnant of Baal
    worship in this place,
    the very names of the idolatrous
        priests –
⁵ those who bow down on the roofs
    to worship the starry host,

those who bow down and swear by the
LORD
and who also swear by Molek,
⁶ those who turn back from following the
LORD
and neither seek the LORD nor enquire
of him.'

⁷ Be silent before the Sovereign LORD,
for the day of the LORD is near.
The LORD has prepared a sacrifice;
he has consecrated those he has
invited.

⁸ 'On the day of the LORD's sacrifice
I will punish the officials
and the king's sons
and all those clad
in foreign clothes.
⁹ On that day I will punish
all who avoid stepping on the
threshold,
who fill the temple of their gods
with violence and deceit.

¹⁰ 'On that day,'
declares the LORD,
'a cry will go up from the Fish Gate,
wailing from the New Quarter,
and a loud crash from the hills.
¹¹ Wail, you who live in the market district;
all your merchants will be wiped out,
all who trade with silver will be
destroyed.
¹² At that time I will search Jerusalem with
lamps
and punish those who are complacent,
who are like wine left on its dregs,
who think, "The LORD will do nothing,
either good or bad."
¹³ Their wealth will be plundered,
their houses demolished.
Though they build houses,
they will not live in them;
though they plant vineyards,
they will not drink the wine.'

¹⁴ The great day of the LORD is near –
near and coming quickly.
The cry on the day of the LORD is bitter;
the Mighty Warrior shouts his battle
cry.
¹⁵ That day will be a day of wrath –
a day of distress and anguish,
a day of trouble and ruin,
a day of darkness and gloom,
a day of clouds and blackness –
¹⁶ a day of trumpet and battle cry
against the fortified cities
and against the corner towers.

¹⁷ 'I will bring such distress on all people
that they will grope about like those
who are blind,
because they have sinned against the
LORD.
Their blood will be poured out like dust
and their entrails like dung.
¹⁸ Neither their silver nor their gold
will be able to save them
on the day of the LORD's wrath.'

In the fire of his jealousy
the whole earth will be consumed,
for he will make a sudden end
of all who live on the earth.

2 Gather together, gather yourselves
together,
you shameful nation,
² before the decree takes effect
and that day passes like windblown
chaff,
before the LORD's fierce anger
comes upon you,
before the day of the LORD's wrath
comes upon you.
³ Seek the LORD, all you humble of the land,
you who do what he commands.
Seek righteousness, seek humility;
perhaps you will be sheltered
on the day of the LORD's anger.

⁴Gaza will be abandoned
    and Ashkelon left in ruins.
At midday Ashdod will be emptied
    and Ekron uprooted.
⁵Woe to you who live by the sea,
    you Kerethite people;
the word of the LORD is against you,
    Canaan, land of the Philistines.
He says, 'I will destroy you,
    and none will be left.'
⁶The land by the sea will become pastures
    having wells for shepherds
    and sheepfolds for flocks.
⁷That land will belong
    to the remnant of the people of Judah;
    there they will find pasture.
In the evening they will lie down
    in the houses of Ashkelon.
The LORD their God will care for them;
    he will restore their fortunes.

⁸'I have heard the insults of Moab
    and the taunts of the Ammonites,
who insulted my people
    and made threats against their land.
⁹Therefore, as surely as I live,'
    declares the LORD Almighty,
    the God of Israel,
'surely Moab will become like Sodom,
    the Ammonites like Gomorrah –
a place of weeds and salt pits,
    a wasteland for ever.
The remnant of my people will plunder
    them;
    the survivors of my nation will inherit
    their land.'

¹⁰This is what they will get in return for
    their pride,
    for insulting and mocking
    the people of the LORD Almighty.
¹¹The LORD will be awesome to them
    when he destroys all the gods of the
    earth.
Distant nations will bow down to him,
    all of them in their own lands.

¹²'You Cushites, too,
    will be slain by my sword.'
¹³He will stretch out his hand against the
    north
    and destroy Assyria,
leaving Nineveh utterly desolate
    and dry as the desert.
¹⁴Flocks and herds will lie down there,
    creatures of every kind.
The desert owl and the screech owl
    will roost on her columns.
Their hooting will echo through the
    windows,
    rubble will fill the doorways,
    the beams of cedar will be exposed.
¹⁵This is the city of revelry
    that lived in safety.
She said to herself,
    'I am the one! And there is none
        besides me.'
What a ruin she has become,
    a lair for wild beasts!
All who pass by her scoff
    and shake their fists.

3 Woe to the city of oppressors,
    rebellious and defiled!
²She obeys no one,
    she accepts no correction.
She does not trust in the LORD,
    she does not draw near to her God.
³Her officials within her
    are roaring lions;
her rulers are evening wolves,
    who leave nothing for the morning.
⁴Her prophets are unprincipled;
    they are treacherous people.
Her priests profane the sanctuary
    and do violence to the law.
⁵The LORD within her is righteous;
    he does no wrong.
Morning by morning he dispenses his
    justice,
    and every new day he does not fail,
    yet the unrighteous know no shame.

6 'I have destroyed nations;
    their strongholds are demolished.
I have left their streets deserted,
    with no one passing through.
Their cities are laid waste;
    they are deserted and empty.
7 Of Jerusalem I thought,
    "Surely you will fear me
    and accept correction!"
Then her place of refuge would not be
    destroyed,
    nor all my punishments come upon her.
But they were still eager
    to act corruptly in all they did.
8 Therefore wait for me,'
    declares the LORD,
    'for the day I will stand up to testify.
I have decided to assemble the nations,
    to gather the kingdoms
and to pour out my wrath on them –
    all my fierce anger.
The whole world will be consumed
    by the fire of my jealous anger.

9 'Then I will purify the lips of the peoples,
    that all of them may call on the name
      of the LORD
    and serve him shoulder to shoulder.
10 From beyond the rivers of Cush
    my worshippers, my scattered people,
    will bring me offerings.
11 On that day you, Jerusalem, will not be
      put to shame
    for all the wrongs you have done to me,
because I will remove from you
    your arrogant boasters.
Never again will you be haughty
    on my holy hill.
12 But I will leave within you
    the meek and humble.
The remnant of Israel
    will trust in the name of the LORD.
13 They will do no wrong;
    they will tell no lies.
A deceitful tongue
    will not be found in their mouths.

They will eat and lie down
    and no one will make them afraid.'

14 Sing, Daughter Zion;
    shout aloud, Israel!
Be glad and rejoice with all your heart,
    Daughter Jerusalem!
15 The LORD has taken away your
      punishment,
    he has turned back your enemy.
The LORD, the King of Israel, is with you;
    never again will you fear any harm.
16 On that day
    they will say to Jerusalem,
'Do not fear, Zion;
    do not let your hands hang limp.
17 The LORD your God is with you,
    the Mighty Warrior who saves.
He will take great delight in you;
    in his love he will no longer rebuke you,
    but will rejoice over you with singing.'

18 'I will remove from you
    all who mourn over the loss of your
      appointed festivals,
    which is a burden and reproach for you.
19 At that time I will deal
    with all who oppressed you.
I will rescue the lame;
    I will gather the exiles.
I will give them praise and honour
    in every land where they have suffered
      shame.
20 At that time I will gather you;
    at that time I will bring you home.
I will give you honour and praise
    among all the peoples of the earth
when I restore your fortunes
    before your very eyes,'
                  says the LORD

■ PSALM 147:7–14

7 Sing to the LORD with grateful praise;
    make music to our God on the harp.

⁸ He covers the sky with clouds;
    he supplies the earth with rain
    and makes grass grow on the hills.
⁹ He provides food for the cattle
    and for the young ravens when they call.

¹⁰ His pleasure is not in the strength of the
        horse,
    nor his delight in the legs of the
        warrior;
¹¹ the LORD delights in those who fear him,
    who put their hope in his unfailing
        love.

¹² Extol the LORD, Jerusalem;
    praise your God, Zion.

¹³ He strengthens the bars of your gates
    and blesses your people within you.
¹⁴ He grants peace to your borders
    and satisfies you with the finest of wheat.

■ PROVERBS 31:18–19

¹⁸ She sees that her trading is profitable,
    and her lamp does not go out at night.
¹⁹ In her hand she holds the distaff
    and grasps the spindle with her fingers.

■ REVELATION 17:9–18:8

⁹ 'This calls for a mind with wisdom. The
seven heads are seven hills on which the
woman sits. ¹⁰ They are also seven kings. Five
have fallen, one is, the other has not yet come;
but when he does come, he must remain for
only a little while. ¹¹ The beast who once was,
and now is not, is an eighth king. He belongs
to the seven and is going to his destruction.
¹² 'The ten horns you saw are ten kings who
have not yet received a kingdom, but who
for one hour will receive authority as kings
along with the beast. ¹³ They have one purpose and will give their power and authority

to the beast. ¹⁴ They will wage war against
the Lamb, but the Lamb will triumph over
them because he is Lord of lords and King
of kings – and with him will be his called,
chosen and faithful followers.'

¹⁵ Then the angel said to me, 'The waters
you saw, where the prostitute sits, are peoples, multitudes, nations and languages.
¹⁶ The beast and the ten horns you saw will
hate the prostitute. They will bring her to
ruin and leave her naked; they will eat her
flesh and burn her with fire. ¹⁷ For God has
put it into their hearts to accomplish his purpose by agreeing to hand over to the beast
their royal authority, until God's words are
fulfilled. ¹⁸ The woman you saw is the great
city that rules over the kings of the earth.'

18 After this I saw another angel coming down from heaven. He had great
authority, and the earth was illuminated
by his splendour. ² With a mighty voice he
shouted:

' "Fallen! Fallen is Babylon the Great!"
    She has become a dwelling for demons
and a haunt for every impure spirit,
    a haunt for every unclean bird,
    a haunt for every unclean and
        detestable animal.
³ For all the nations have drunk
    the maddening wine of her adulteries.
The kings of the earth committed
        adultery with her,
    and the merchants of the earth grew
        rich from her excessive luxuries.'

⁴ Then I heard another voice from heaven
say:

' "Come out of her, my people,"
    so that you will not share in her sins,
    so that you will not receive any of her
        plagues;
⁵ for her sins are piled up to heaven,
    and God has remembered her crimes.
⁶ Give back to her as she has given;

pay her back double for what she has
done.
Pour her a double portion from her
own cup.
⁷ Give her as much torment and grief
as the glory and luxury she gave herself.
In her heart she boasts,
"I sit enthroned as queen.

I am not a widow;
I will never mourn."
⁸ Therefore in one day her plagues will
overtake her:
death, mourning and famine.
She will be consumed by fire,
for mighty is the Lord God who judges
her.

Staying Close to the Shepherd

'The LORD, the King of Israel, is with you; never again will you fear any harm.' **Zephaniah 3:15**

A classic example of the way in which the divine Shepherd ministers to His children is seen in Luke 22:24-32. Jesus tells Simon Peter that Satan has sought to tempt him and sift him like wheat but that He has prayed that Peter's faith might not fail in that moment of overwhelming testing. Where would I have been, where would you have been, but for that blessed ministry of the divine Shepherd - going before us, anticipating our circumstances, and supportively working and praying for us, so that we might not be overtaken by the enemy of our souls? If He did not minister to us in this way ... where should we be?

This does not mean, of course, that the responsibility for our safety and security rests entirely on our divine Shepherd. We, too, have a responsibility - a responsibility to make sure that we keep as close to Him as we possibly can. This is the one sure place of safety. 'It is always the distant sheep, the roamers, the wanderers', says one shepherd, 'which are picked off by predators in an unsuspecting moment. Sometimes the sheep is so overtaken by fear that it is too frightened to even cry out. It might give a plaintive bleat before its blood is spilled.' The divine Shepherd wants to forestall every calamity that would come our way and strives to keep our lives free from serious dangers and hazards. And, of course, our lives will be danger-free if we stay close to Him, where He can provide for us and protect us.

PRAYER

My Father and my God, thank You for reminding me that although You make Yourself responsible for my safety and security, I also have a responsibility - to stay as close as I possibly can to You. Help me to do just that - today and every day. For Jesus' sake. Amen.

FURTHER STUDY

Heb. 2; 7:25; 1 Cor. 10:13;
James 4:7; Rom. 16:20
• What does Christ do in
our times of temptation?
• What should we do?

December 27

■ HAGGAI 1:1 –ZECHARIAH 1:21

1 In the second year of King Darius, on the first day of the sixth month, the word of the LORD came through the prophet Haggai to Zerubbabel son of Shealtiel, governor of Judah, and to Joshua son of Jozadak, the high priest:

² This is what the LORD Almighty says: 'These people say, "The time has not yet come to rebuild the LORD's house."'

³ Then the word of the LORD came through the prophet Haggai: ⁴ 'Is it a time for you yourselves to be living in your panelled houses, while this house remains a ruin?'

⁵ Now this is what the LORD Almighty says: 'Give careful thought to your ways. ⁶ You have planted much, but harvested little. You eat, but never have enough. You drink, but never have your fill. You put on clothes, but are not warm. You earn wages, only to put them in a purse with holes in it.'

⁷ This is what the LORD Almighty says: 'Give careful thought to your ways. ⁸ Go up into the mountains and bring down timber and build my house, so that I may take pleasure in it and be honoured,' says the LORD. ⁹ 'You expected much, but see, it turned out to be little. What you brought home, I blew away. Why?' declares the LORD Almighty. 'Because of my house, which remains a ruin, while each of you is busy with your own house. ¹⁰ Therefore, because of you the heavens have withheld their dew and the earth its crops. ¹¹ I called for a drought on the fields and the mountains, on the grain, the new wine, the olive oil and everything else the ground produces, on people and livestock, and on all the labour of your hands.'

¹² Then Zerubbabel son of Shealtiel, Joshua son of Jozadak, the high priest, and the whole remnant of the people obeyed the voice of the LORD their God and the message of the prophet Haggai, because the LORD their God had sent him. And the people feared the LORD.

¹³ Then Haggai, the LORD's messenger, gave this message of the LORD to the people: 'I am with you,' declares the LORD. ¹⁴ So the LORD stirred up the spirit of Zerubbabel son of Shealtiel, governor of Judah, and the spirit of Joshua son of Jozadak, the high priest, and the spirit of the whole remnant of the people. They came and began to work on the house of the LORD Almighty, their God, ¹⁵ on the twenty-fourth day of the sixth month.

2 In the second year of King Darius, ¹ on the twenty-first day of the seventh month, the word of the LORD came through the prophet Haggai: ² 'Speak to Zerubbabel son of Shealtiel, governor of Judah, to Joshua son of Jozadak, the high priest, and to the remnant of the people. Ask them, ³ "Who of you is left who saw this house in its former glory? How does it look to you now? Does it not seem to you like nothing? ⁴ But now be strong, Zerubbabel," declares the LORD. "Be strong, Joshua son of Jozadak, the high priest. Be strong, all you people of the land," declares the LORD, "and work. For I am with you," declares the LORD Almighty. ⁵ "This is what I covenanted with you when you came out of Egypt. And my Spirit remains among you. Do not fear."

⁶ 'This is what the LORD Almighty says: "In a little while I will once more shake the heavens and the earth, the sea and the dry land. ⁷ I will shake all nations, and what is desired by all nations will come, and I will fill this house with glory," says the LORD

Almighty. [8] "The silver is mine and the gold is mine," declares the LORD Almighty. [9] "The glory of this present house will be greater than the glory of the former house," says the LORD Almighty. "And in this place I will grant peace," declares the LORD Almighty.'

[10] On the twenty-fourth day of the ninth month, in the second year of Darius, the word of the LORD came to the prophet Haggai: [11] 'This is what the LORD Almighty says: "Ask the priests what the law says: [12] if someone carries consecrated meat in the fold of their garment, and that fold touches some bread or stew, some wine, olive oil or other food, does it become consecrated?"'

The priests answered, 'No.'

[13] Then Haggai said, 'If a person defiled by contact with a dead body touches one of these things, does it become defiled?'

'Yes,' the priests replied, 'it becomes defiled.'

[14] Then Haggai said, '"So it is with this people and this nation in my sight," declares the LORD. "Whatever they do and whatever they offer there is defiled.

[15] "'Now give careful thought to this from this day on – consider how things were before one stone was laid on another in the LORD's temple. [16] When anyone came to a heap of twenty measures, there were only ten. When anyone went to a wine vat to draw fifty measures, there were only twenty. [17] I struck all the work of your hands with blight, mildew and hail, yet you did not return to me," declares the LORD. [18] "From this day on, from this twenty-fourth day of the ninth month, give careful thought to the day when the foundation of the LORD's temple was laid. Give careful thought: [19] is there yet any seed left in the barn? Until now, the vine and the fig-tree, the pomegranate and the olive tree have not borne fruit.

'"From this day on I will bless you."'

[20] The word of the LORD came to Haggai a second time on the twenty-fourth day of the month: [21] 'Tell Zerubbabel governor of Judah that I am going to shake the heavens and the earth. [22] I will overturn royal thrones and shatter the power of the foreign kingdoms. I will overthrow chariots and their drivers; horses and their riders will fall, each by the sword of his brother.

[23] "On that day," declares the LORD Almighty, "I will take you, my servant Zerubbabel son of Shealtiel," declares the LORD, "and I will make you like my signet ring, for I have chosen you," declares the LORD Almighty.'

1 In the eighth month of the second year of Darius, the word of the LORD came to the prophet Zechariah son of Berekiah, the son of Iddo:

[2] 'The LORD was very angry with your ancestors. [3] Therefore tell the people: this is what the LORD Almighty says: "Return to me," declares the LORD Almighty, "and I will return to you," says the LORD Almighty. [4] Do not be like your ancestors, to whom the earlier prophets proclaimed: this is what the LORD Almighty says: "Turn from your evil ways and your evil practices." But they would not listen or pay attention to me, declares the LORD. [5] Where are your ancestors now? And the prophets, do they live for ever? [6] But did not my words and my decrees, which I commanded my servants the prophets, overtake your ancestors?

'Then they repented and said, "The LORD Almighty has done to us what our ways and practices deserve, just as he determined to do."'

[7] On the twenty-fourth day of the eleventh month, the month of Shebat, in the second year of Darius, the word of the LORD came to the prophet Zechariah son of Berekiah, the son of Iddo.

[8] During the night I had a vision, and there before me was a man mounted on a red horse. He was standing among the myrtle trees in a ravine. Behind him were red, brown and white horses.

⁹ I asked, 'What are these, my lord?'

The angel who was talking with me answered, 'I will show you what they are.'

¹⁰ Then the man standing among the myrtle trees explained, 'They are the ones the LORD has sent to go throughout the earth.'

¹¹ And they reported to the angel of the LORD who was standing among the myrtle trees, 'We have gone throughout the earth and found the whole world at rest and in peace.'

¹² Then the angel of the LORD said, 'LORD Almighty, how long will you withhold mercy from Jerusalem and from the towns of Judah, which you have been angry with these seventy years?' ¹³ So the LORD spoke kind and comforting words to the angel who talked with me.

¹⁴ Then the angel who was speaking to me said, 'Proclaim this word: this is what the LORD Almighty says: "I am very jealous for Jerusalem and Zion, ¹⁵ and I am very angry with the nations that feel secure. I was only a little angry, but they went too far with the punishment."

¹⁶ 'Therefore this is what the LORD says: "I will return to Jerusalem with mercy, and there my house will be rebuilt. And the measuring line will be stretched out over Jerusalem," declares the LORD Almighty.

¹⁷ 'Proclaim further: this is what the LORD Almighty says: "My towns will again overflow with prosperity, and the LORD will again comfort Zion and choose Jerusalem."'

¹⁸ Then I looked up, and there before me were four horns. ¹⁹ I asked the angel who was speaking to me, 'What are these?'

He answered me, 'These are the horns that scattered Judah, Israel and Jerusalem.'

²⁰ Then the LORD showed me four craftsmen. ²¹ I asked, 'What are these coming to do?'

He answered, 'These are the horns that scattered Judah so that no one could raise their head, but the craftsmen have come to terrify them and throw down these horns of the nations who lifted up their horns against the land of Judah to scatter its people.'

▬ PSALM 147:15-20

¹⁵ He sends his command to the earth;
　　his word runs swiftly.
¹⁶ He spreads the snow like wool
　　and scatters the frost like ashes.
¹⁷ He hurls down hail like pebbles.
　　Who can withstand his icy blast?
¹⁸ He sends his word and melts them;
　　he stirs up his breezes, and the waters
　　　flow.

¹⁹ He has revealed his word to Jacob,
　　his laws and decrees to Israel.
²⁰ He has done this for no other nation;
　　they do not know his laws.

Praise the LORD.

▬ PROVERBS 31:20-22

²⁰ She opens her arms to the poor
　　and extends her hands to the needy.
²¹ When it snows, she has no fear for her
　　household;
　　for all of them are clothed in scarlet.
²² She makes coverings for her bed;
　　she is clothed in fine linen and purple.

▬ REVELATION 18:9-24

⁹ 'When the kings of the earth who committed adultery with her and shared her luxury see the smoke of her burning, they will weep and mourn over her. ¹⁰ Terrified at her torment, they will stand far off and cry:

'"Woe! Woe to you, great city,
　　you mighty city of Babylon!
In one hour your doom has come!"

¹¹ 'The merchants of the earth will weep and mourn over her because no one buys their cargoes any more – ¹² cargoes of gold,

silver, precious stones and pearls; fine linen, purple, silk and scarlet cloth; every sort of citron wood, and articles of every kind made of ivory, costly wood, bronze, iron and marble; [13] cargoes of cinnamon and spice, of incense, myrrh and frankincense, of wine and olive oil, of fine flour and wheat; cattle and sheep; horses and carriages; and human beings sold as slaves.

[14] 'They will say, "The fruit you longed for is gone from you. All your luxury and splendour have vanished, never to be recovered." [15] The merchants who sold these things and gained their wealth from her will stand far off, terrified at her torment. They will weep and mourn [16] and cry out:

'"Woe! Woe to you, great city,
    dressed in fine linen, purple and scarlet,
    and glittering with gold, precious
        stones and pearls!
[17] In one hour such great wealth has been
        brought to ruin!"

'Every sea captain, and all who travel by ship, the sailors, and all who earn their living from the sea, will stand far off. [18] When they see the smoke of her burning, they will exclaim, "Was there ever a city like this great city?" [19] They will throw dust on their heads, and with weeping and mourning cry out:

'"Woe! Woe to you, great city,
    where all who had ships on the sea
    became rich through her wealth!

In one hour she has been brought to ruin!"

[20] 'Rejoice over her, you heavens!
    Rejoice, you people of God!
    Rejoice, apostles and prophets!
For God has judged her
    with the judgment she imposed on you.'

[21] Then a mighty angel picked up a boulder the size of a large millstone and threw it into the sea, and said:

'With such violence
    the great city of Babylon will be
        thrown down,
    never to be found again.
[22] The music of harpists and musicians,
        pipers and trumpeters,
    will never be heard in you again.
No worker of any trade
    will ever be found in you again.
The sound of a millstone
    will never be heard in you again.
[23] The light of a lamp
    will never shine in you again.
The voice of bridegroom and bride
    will never be heard in you again.
Your merchants were the world's
        important people.
By your magic spell all the nations
        were led astray.
[24] In her was found the blood of prophets
        and of God's holy people,
    of all who have been slaughtered on
        the earth.'

The Divine Design

'... his word runs swiftly.' **Psalm 147:15**

When we come to God's Word, laying aside all preconceived ideas and depending entirely on the Holy Spirit to reveal its truth to us, we put ourselves in a position where the Holy Spirit can impress the truth of the Scriptures into our innermost being. There it takes root within us, and whenever we stand in need of a word with which to rebut the Devil, the Holy Spirit brings it to our remembrance.

And here's the most wonderful thing – the Word of God on our lips will have the same effect upon the Devil as if he were hearing it from the lips of Jesus Himself! Every time we open the Bible, we must be careful to pray for the illumination of the Spirit so that we don't finish up making the Bible say what we want it to say. When we receive that help, we are following the divine design – letting the Spirit bring home to our hearts the truth and meaning of His own Word.

This attitude of humility and receptivity gives the Holy Spirit the opportunity He needs to build the truth of the Word of God into our spirits. Approaching the Bible in this way, said the late J. B. Phillips, 'is like rewiring a house where the electricity has not been turned off'. As we read the Scriptures, we are touching something that has a current of power flowing through its pages – a power not put there by any man. The Holy Spirit has gone into it, so is it any wonder that the Holy Spirit comes out of it?

PRAYER

My Father and my God, I know the Spirit dwells in Your Word. I come to ask that He might dwell also in me, to open up my whole being to the truth and power that lies in its inspired pages. In Jesus' name I ask it. Amen.

FURTHER STUDY

John 14:26; 15:18-27; Luke 12:11-12; Rom. 8:14
- What did Jesus declare about the Holy Spirit's ministry?
- What promise did Jesus give to His disciples?

December 28

▬ ZECHARIAH 2:1–6:15

2 Then I looked up, and there before me was a man with a measuring line in his hand. ²I asked, 'Where are you going?'

He answered me, 'To measure Jerusalem, to find out how wide and how long it is.'

³While the angel who was speaking to me was leaving, another angel came to meet him ⁴and said to him: 'Run, tell that young man, "Jerusalem will be a city without walls because of the great number of people and animals in it. ⁵And I myself will be a wall of fire around it," declares the LORD, "and I will be its glory within."

⁶'Come! Come! Flee from the land of the north,' declares the LORD, 'for I have scattered you to the four winds of heaven,' declares the LORD.

⁷'Come, Zion! Escape, you who live in Daughter Babylon!' ⁸For this is what the LORD Almighty says: 'After the Glorious One has sent me against the nations that have plundered you – for whoever touches you touches the apple of his eye – ⁹I will surely raise my hand against them so that their slaves will plunder them. Then you will know that the LORD Almighty has sent me.

¹⁰'Shout and be glad, Daughter Zion. For I am coming, and I will live among you,' declares the LORD. ¹¹'Many nations will be joined with the LORD in that day and will

become my people. I will live among you and you will know that the LORD Almighty has sent me to you. ¹²The LORD will inherit Judah as his portion in the holy land and will again choose Jerusalem. ¹³Be still before the LORD, all mankind, because he has roused himself from his holy dwelling.'

3 Then he showed me Joshua the high priest standing before the angel of the Lord, and Satan standing at his right side to accuse him. ²The Lord said to Satan, 'The Lord rebuke you, Satan! The Lord, who has chosen Jerusalem, rebuke you! Is not this man a burning stick snatched from the fire?'

³Now Joshua was dressed in filthy clothes as he stood before the angel. ⁴The angel said to those who were standing before him, 'Take off his filthy clothes.'

Then he said to Joshua, 'See, I have taken away your sin, and I will put fine garments on you.'

⁵Then I said, 'Put a clean turban on his head.' So they put a clean turban on his head and clothed him, while the angel of the LORD stood by.

⁶The angel of the LORD gave this charge to Joshua: ⁷'This is what the LORD Almighty says: "If you will walk in obedience to me and keep my requirements, then you will govern my house and have charge of my courts, and I will give you a place among these standing here.

⁸ "Listen, High Priest Joshua, you and your associates seated before you, who are men symbolic of things to come: I am going to bring my servant, the Branch. ⁹See, the stone I have set in front of Joshua! There are seven eyes on that one stone, and I will engrave an inscription on it," says the LORD Almighty, "and I will remove the sin of this land in a single day.

¹⁰ "In that day each of you will invite your neighbour to sit under your vine and fig-tree," declares the LORD Almighty.'

4 Then the angel who talked with me returned and woke me up, like someone awakened from sleep. ²He asked me, 'What do you see?'

I answered, 'I see a solid gold lampstand with a bowl at the top and seven lamps on it, with seven channels to the lamps. ³Also there are two olive trees by it, one on the right of the bowl and the other on its left.'

⁴I asked the angel who talked with me, 'What are these, my lord?'

⁵He answered, 'Do you not know what these are?'

'No, my lord,' I replied.

⁶So he said to me, 'This is the word of the LORD to Zerubbabel: "Not by might nor by power, but by my Spirit," says the LORD Almighty.

⁷'What are you, mighty mountain? Before Zerubbabel you will become level ground. Then he will bring out the capstone to shouts of "God bless it! God bless it!"'

⁸Then the word of the LORD came to me: ⁹'The hands of Zerubbabel have laid the foundation of this temple; his hands will also complete it. Then you will know that the LORD Almighty has sent me to you.

¹⁰'Who dares despise the day of small things, since the seven eyes of the LORD that range throughout the earth will rejoice when they see the chosen capstone in the hand of Zerubbabel?'

¹¹Then I asked the angel, 'What are these two olive trees on the right and the left of the lampstand?'

¹²Again I asked him, 'What are these two olive branches beside the two gold pipes that pour out golden oil?'

¹³He replied, 'Do you not know what these are?'

'No, my lord,' I said.

¹⁴So he said, 'These are the two who are anointed to serve the Lord of all the earth.'

5 I looked again, and there before me was a flying scroll.

²He asked me, 'What do you see?'

I answered, 'I see a flying scroll, twenty cubits long and ten cubits wide.'

³And he said to me, 'This is the curse that is going out over the whole land; for according to what it says on one side, every thief will be banished, and according to what it says on the other, everyone who swears falsely will be banished. ⁴The LORD Almighty declares, "I will send it out, and it will enter the house of the thief and the house of anyone who swears falsely by my name. It will remain in that house and destroy it completely, both its timbers and its stones."'

⁵Then the angel who was speaking to me came forward and said to me, 'Look up and see what is appearing.'

⁶I asked, 'What is it?'

He replied, 'It is a basket.' And he added, 'This is the iniquity of the people throughout the land.'

⁷Then the cover of lead was raised, and there in the basket sat a woman! ⁸He said, 'This is wickedness,' and he pushed her back into the basket and pushed its lead cover down on it.

⁹Then I looked up – and there before me were two women, with the wind in their wings! They had wings like those of a stork, and they lifted up the basket between heaven and earth.

¹⁰'Where are they taking the basket?' I asked the angel who was speaking to me.

¹¹He replied, 'To the country of Babylonia to build a house for it. When the house is ready, the basket will be set there in its place.'

6 I looked up again, and there before me were four chariots coming out from between two mountains – mountains of bronze. ²The first chariot had red horses, the second black, ³the third white, and the fourth dappled – all of them powerful. ⁴I asked the angel who was speaking to me, 'What are these, my lord?'

⁵The angel answered me, 'These are the four spirits of heaven, going out from standing in the presence of the Lord of the whole world. ⁶The one with the black horses is going towards the north country, the one with the white horses towards the west, and the one with the dappled horses towards the south.'

⁷When the powerful horses went out, they were straining to go throughout the earth. And he said, 'Go throughout the earth!' So they went throughout the earth.

⁸Then he called to me, 'Look, those going towards the north country have given my Spirit rest in the land of the north.'

⁹The word of the LORD came to me: ¹⁰'Take silver and gold from the exiles Heldai, Tobijah and Jedaiah, who have arrived from Babylon. Go the same day to the house of Josiah son of Zephaniah. ¹¹Take the silver and gold and make a crown, and set it on the head of the high priest, Joshua son of Jozadak. ¹²Tell him this is what the LORD Almighty says: "Here is the man whose name is the Branch, and he will branch out from his place and build the temple of the LORD. ¹³It is he who will build the temple of the LORD, and he will be clothed with majesty and will sit and rule on his throne. And he will be a priest on his throne. And there will be harmony between the two." ¹⁴The crown will be given to Heldai, Tobijah, Jedaiah and Hen son of Zephaniah as a memorial in the temple of the LORD. ¹⁵Those who are far away will come and help to build the temple of the LORD, and you will know that the LORD Almighty has sent me to you. This will happen if you diligently obey the LORD your God.'

■ PSALM 148:1-6

¹Praise the LORD.

Praise the LORD from the heavens;
    praise him in the heights above.
²Praise him, all his angels;

praise him, all his heavenly hosts.
³ Praise him, sun and moon;
    praise him, all you shining stars.
⁴ Praise him, you highest heavens
    and you waters above the skies.

⁵ Let them praise the name of the LORD,
    for at his command they were created,
⁶ and he established them for ever and
    ever –
    he issued a decree that will never pass
    away.

PROVERBS 31:23-25

²³ Her husband is respected at the city gate,
    where he takes his seat among the
        elders of the land.
²⁴ She makes linen garments and sells
        them,
    and supplies the merchants with
        sashes.
²⁵ She is clothed with strength and dignity;
    she can laugh at the days to come.

REVELATION 19:1-21

19 After this I heard what sounded
   like the roar of a great multitude in
heaven shouting:

'Hallelujah!
Salvation and glory and power belong to
    our God,
²   for true and just are his judgments.
He has condemned the great prostitute
    who corrupted the earth by her
        adulteries.
He has avenged on her the blood of his
        servants.'

³ And again they shouted:

'Hallelujah!

The smoke from her goes up for ever and
        ever.'

⁴ The twenty-four elders and the four
living creatures fell down and worshipped
God, who was seated on the throne. And
they cried:

'Amen, Hallelujah!'

⁵ Then a voice came from the throne,
saying:

'Praise our God,
    all you his servants,
you who fear him,
    both great and small!'

⁶ Then I heard what sounded like a great
multitude, like the roar of rushing waters
and like loud peals of thunder, shouting:

'Hallelujah!
    For our Lord God Almighty reigns.
⁷ Let us rejoice and be glad
    and give him glory!
For the wedding of the Lamb has come,
    and his bride has made herself ready.
⁸ Fine linen, bright and clean,
    was given her to wear.'
(Fine linen stands for the righteous acts
of God's holy people.)

⁹ Then the angel said to me, 'Write this:
Blessed are those who are invited to the
wedding supper of the Lamb!' And he
added, 'These are the true words of God.'

¹⁰ At this I fell at his feet to worship him.
But he said to me, 'Don't do that! I am a fellow
servant with you and with your brothers and
sisters who hold to the testimony of Jesus.
Worship God! For it is the Spirit of prophecy
who bears testimony to Jesus.'

¹¹ I saw heaven standing open and there
before me was a white horse, whose rider
is called Faithful and True. With justice

he judges and wages war. [12] His eyes are like blazing fire, and on his head are many crowns. He has a name written on him that no one knows but he himself. [13] He is dressed in a robe dipped in blood, and his name is the Word of God. [14] The armies of heaven were following him, riding on white horses and dressed in fine linen, white and clean. [15] Coming out of his mouth is a sharp sword with which to strike down the nations. 'He will rule them with an iron sceptre.' He treads the winepress of the fury of the wrath of God Almighty. [16] On his robe and on his thigh he has this name written:

KING OF KINGS AND LORD OF LORDS.

[17] And I saw an angel standing in the sun, who cried in a loud voice to all the birds flying in mid-air, 'Come, gather together for the great supper of God, [18] so that you may eat the flesh of kings, generals, and the mighty, of horses and their riders, and the flesh of all people, free and slave, great and small.'

[19] Then I saw the beast and the kings of the earth and their armies gathered together to wage war against the rider on the horse and his army. [20] But the beast was captured, and with it the false prophet who had performed the signs on its behalf. With these signs he had deluded those who had received the mark of the beast and worshipped its image. The two of them were thrown alive into the fiery lake of burning sulphur. [21] The rest were killed with the sword coming out of the mouth of the rider on the horse, and all the birds gorged themselves on their flesh.

We win!

'I saw heaven standing open and there before me was a white horse, whose rider is called Faithful and True.'
Revelation 19:11

The theme of judgment comes to an end with chapter 19 verse 8 and another theme emerges in verse 9 - the end of all things. This section begins with the angel prompting John to write of the blessedness of those who are invited to the marriage supper of the Lamb. When John hears the voice of the angel he falls at his feet to worship him, but he is told not to. Though we may admire angels, we do not worship them. The statement which forms part of the angel's reply - 'For it is the Spirit of prophecy who bears testimony to Jesus' (v.10) - is to be understood, I believe, as meaning that at the heart of all true prophecy is Jesus. All prophecy in some way has to do with Him.

Very quickly and dramatically we move from a wedding to a war, and we see once again Jesus riding on a white horse, victoriously robed, leading the armies of heaven into battle against the beast and the false prophet. When we compare Revelation 19:20 with 13:14 we can see that the false prophet is almost certainly the beast from the earth. The battle ends with these two enemies, who have caused so much havoc in the world, being thrown alive into the lake of burning sulphur, and those who followed them being destroyed by the victor's sword.

It is predicted from the early pages of the Bible that evil will ultimately be eliminated, and here we see its death throes. I am reminded of the story of a new Christian who became discouraged as he read in Genesis of the entrance of evil into the world. Quickly he turned to Revelation to see how it all ends. Coming to the passage before us today he breathed a sigh of relief and exclaimed, 'Thank God we win!' Keep hope; we do.

PRAYER

Father, I am grateful that I am on the winning side. Your victory is my victory. May I walk through life conscious that though at times it appears some battles are being lost, the outcome is certain and secure. We win. Amen.

FURTHER STUDY

1 Cor. 9:24-25; 2 Tim. 4:6-8
- What do we win?
- Who will receive the prize?

December 29

■ ZECHARIAH 7:1–10:12

7 In the fourth year of King Darius, the word of the LORD came to Zechariah on the fourth day of the ninth month, the month of Kislev. ²The people of Bethel had sent Sharezer and Regem-Melek, together with their men, to entreat the LORD ³by asking the priests of the house of the LORD Almighty and the prophets, 'Should I mourn and fast in the fifth month, as I have done for so many years?'

⁴Then the word of the LORD Almighty came to me: ⁵'Ask all the people of the land and the priests, "When you fasted and mourned in the fifth and seventh months for the past seventy years, was it really for me that you fasted? ⁶And when you were eating and drinking, were you not just feasting for yourselves? ⁷Are these not the words the LORD proclaimed through the earlier prophets when Jerusalem and its surrounding towns were at rest and prosperous, and the Negev and the western foothills were settled?"'

⁸And the word of the LORD came again to Zechariah: ⁹'This is what the LORD Almighty said: "Administer true justice; show mercy and compassion to one another. ¹⁰Do not oppress the widow or the fatherless, the foreigner or the poor. Do not plot evil against each other."

¹¹'But they refused to pay attention; stubbornly they turned their backs and covered their ears. ¹²They made their hearts as hard as flint and would not listen to the law or to the words that the LORD Almighty had sent by his Spirit through the earlier prophets. So the LORD Almighty was very angry.

¹³'"When I called, they did not listen; so when they called, I would not listen," says the LORD Almighty. ¹⁴"I scattered them with a whirlwind among all the nations, where they were strangers. The land they left behind them was so desolate that no one travelled through it. This is how they made the pleasant land desolate."'

8 The word of the Lord Almighty came to me.
²This is what the LORD Almighty says: 'I am very jealous for Zion; I am burning with jealousy for her.'

³ This is what the LORD says: 'I will return to Zion and dwell in Jerusalem. Then Jerusalem will be called the Faithful City, and the mountain of the LORD Almighty will be called the Holy Mountain.'

⁴ This is what the LORD Almighty says: 'Once again men and women of ripe old age will sit in the streets of Jerusalem, each of them with cane in hand because of their age. ⁵ The city streets will be filled with boys and girls playing there.'

⁶ This is what the LORD Almighty says: 'It may seem marvellous to the remnant of this people at that time, but will it seem marvellous to me?' declares the LORD Almighty.

⁷ This is what the LORD Almighty says: 'I will save my people from the countries of the east and the west. ⁸ I will bring them back to live in Jerusalem; they will be my people, and I will be faithful and righteous to them as their God.'

⁹ This is what the LORD Almighty says: 'Now hear these words, "Let your hands be strong so that the temple may be built." This is also what the prophets said who were present when the foundation was laid for the house of the LORD Almighty. ¹⁰ Before that time there were no wages for people or hire for animals. No one could go about their business safely because of their enemies, since I had turned everyone against their neighbour. ¹¹ But now I will not deal with the remnant of this people as I did in the past,' declares the LORD Almighty.

¹² 'The seed will grow well, the vine will yield its fruit, the ground will produce its crops, and the heavens will drop their dew. I will give all these things as an inheritance to the remnant of this people. ¹³ Just as you, Judah and Israel, have been a curse among the nations, so I will save you, and you will be a blessing. Do not be afraid, but let your hands be strong.'

¹⁴ This is what the LORD Almighty says: 'Just as I had determined to bring disaster on you and showed no pity when your ancestors angered me,' says the LORD Almighty, ¹⁵ 'so now I have determined to do good again to Jerusalem and Judah. Do not be afraid. ¹⁶ These are the things you are to do: Speak the truth to each other, and render true and sound judgment in your courts; ¹⁷ do not plot evil against each other, and do not love to swear falsely. I hate all this,' declares the LORD.

¹⁸ The word of the LORD Almighty came to me. ¹⁹ This is what the LORD Almighty says: 'The fasts of the fourth, fifth, seventh and tenth months will become joyful and glad occasions and happy festivals for Judah. Therefore love truth and peace.'

²⁰ This is what the LORD Almighty says: 'Many peoples and the inhabitants of many cities will yet come, ²¹ and the inhabitants of one city will go to another and say, "Let us go at once to entreat the LORD and seek the LORD Almighty. I myself am going." ²² And many peoples and powerful nations will come to Jerusalem to seek the LORD Almighty and to entreat him.'

²³ This is what the LORD Almighty says: 'In those days ten people from all languages and nations will take firm hold of one Jew by the hem of his robe and say, "Let us go with you, because we have heard that God is with you."'

9 A prophecy:

The word of the LORD is against the land
    of Hadrak
        and will come to rest on Damascus –
for the eyes of all people and all the
            tribes of Israel
        are on the LORD –
² and on Hamath too, which borders on it,
        and on Tyre and Sidon, though they
            are very skilful.
³ Tyre has built herself a stronghold;
        she has heaped up silver like dust,
            and gold like the dirt of the streets.

⁴ But the Lord will take away her
    possessions
  and destroy her power on the sea,
  and she will be consumed by fire.
⁵ Ashkelon will see it and fear;
  Gaza will writhe in agony,
  and Ekron too, for her hope will
    wither.
 Gaza will lose her king
  and Ashkelon will be deserted.
⁶ A mongrel people will occupy Ashdod,
  and I will put an end to the pride of the
    Philistines.
⁷ I will take the blood from their mouths,
  the forbidden food from between their
    teeth.
 Those who are left will belong to our God
  and become a clan in Judah,
  and Ekron will be like the Jebusites.
⁸ But I will encamp at my temple
  to guard it against marauding forces.
 Never again will an oppressor overrun
    my people,
  for now I am keeping watch.

⁹ Rejoice greatly, Daughter Zion!
  Shout, Daughter Jerusalem!
 See, your king comes to you,
  righteous and victorious,
 lowly and riding on a donkey,
  on a colt, the foal of a donkey.
¹⁰ I will take away the chariots from Ephraim
  and the war-horses from Jerusalem,
  and the battle-bow will be broken.
 He will proclaim peace to the nations.
  His rule will extend from sea to sea
  and from the River to the ends of the
    earth.
¹¹ As for you, because of the blood of my
    covenant with you,
  I will free your prisoners from the
    waterless pit.
¹² Return to your fortress, you prisoners of
    hope;
  even now I announce that I will
    restore twice as much to you.

¹³ I will bend Judah as I bend my bow
  and fill it with Ephraim.
 I will rouse your sons, Zion,
  against your sons, Greece,
  and make you like a warrior's sword.
¹⁴ Then the LORD will appear over them;
  his arrow will flash like lightning.
 The Sovereign LORD will sound the
    trumpet;
  he will march in the storms of the
    south,
¹⁵   and the LORD Almighty will shield
    them.
 They will destroy
  and overcome with slingstones.
 They will drink and roar as with wine;
  they will be full like a bowl
  used for sprinkling the corners of the
    altar.
¹⁶ The LORD their God will save his people
    on that day
  as a shepherd saves his flock.
 They will sparkle in his land
  like jewels in a crown.
¹⁷ How attractive and beautiful they will
    be!
  Grain will make the young men thrive,
  and new wine the young women.

10 Ask the Lord for rain in the
    springtime;
  it is the LORD who sends the
    thunderstorms.
 He gives showers of rain to all people,
  and plants of the field to everyone.
² The idols speak deceitfully,
  diviners see visions that lie;
 they tell dreams that are false,
  they give comfort in vain.
 Therefore the people wander like sheep
  oppressed for lack of a shepherd.

³ 'My anger burns against the shepherds,
  and I will punish the leaders;
 for the LORD Almighty will care
  for his flock, the people of Judah,

and make them like a proud horse in
    battle.
⁴ From Judah will come the cornerstone,
    from him the tent peg,
    from him the battle-bow,
    from him every ruler.
⁵ Together they will be like warriors in
    battle
    trampling their enemy into the mud of
    the streets.
They will fight because the LORD is with
    them,
    and they will put the enemy horsemen
    to shame.

⁶ 'I will strengthen Judah
    and save the tribes of Joseph.
I will restore them
    because I have compassion on them.
They will be as though
    I had not rejected them,
for I am the LORD their God
    and I will answer them.
⁷ The Ephraimites will become like
    warriors,
    and their hearts will be glad as with
    wine.
Their children will see it and be joyful;
    their hearts will rejoice in the LORD.
⁸ I will signal for them
    and gather them in.
Surely I will redeem them;
    they will be as numerous as before.
⁹ Though I scatter them among the
    peoples,
    yet in distant lands they will
    remember me.
They and their children will survive,
    and they will return.
¹⁰ I will bring them back from Egypt
    and gather them from Assyria.
I will bring them to Gilead and Lebanon,
    and there will not be room enough for
    them.
¹¹ They will pass through the sea of trouble;
    the surging sea will be subdued

and all the depths of the Nile will dry
    up.
Assyria's pride will be brought down
    and Egypt's sceptre will pass away.
¹² I will strengthen them in the LORD
    and in his name they will live securely,'
        declares the LORD.

- -

▬ PSALM 148:7-14

⁷ Praise the LORD from the earth,
    you great sea creatures and all ocean
    depths,
⁸ lightning and hail, snow and clouds,
    stormy winds that do his bidding,
⁹ you mountains and all hills,
    fruit trees and all cedars,
¹⁰ wild animals and all cattle,
    small creatures and flying birds,
¹¹ kings of the earth and all nations,
    you princes and all rulers on earth,
¹² young men and women,
    old men and children.

¹³ Let them praise the name of the LORD,
    for his name alone is exalted;
    his splendour is above the earth and
    the heavens.
¹⁴ And he has raised up for his people a
    horn,
    the praise of all his faithful servants,
    of Israel, the people close to his heart.

Praise the LORD.

- -

▬ PROVERBS 31:26-27

²⁶ She speaks with wisdom,
    and faithful instruction is on her
    tongue.
²⁷ She watches over the affairs of her
    household
    and does not eat the bread of idleness.

■ REVELATION 20:1–21:4

20 And I saw an angel coming down out of heaven, having the key to the Abyss and holding in his hand a great chain. ²He seized the dragon, that ancient snake, who is the devil, or Satan, and bound him for a thousand years. ³He threw him into the Abyss, and locked and sealed it over him, to keep him from deceiving the nations any more until the thousand years were ended. After that, he must be set free for a short time.

⁴I saw thrones on which were seated those who had been given authority to judge. And I saw the souls of those who had been beheaded because of their testimony about Jesus and because of the word of God. They had not worshipped the beast or its image and had not received its mark on their foreheads or their hands. They came to life and reigned with Christ for a thousand years. ⁵(The rest of the dead did not come to life until the thousand years were ended.) This is the first resurrection. ⁶Blessed and holy are those who share in the first resurrection. The second death has no power over them, but they will be priests of God and of Christ and will reign with him for a thousand years.

⁷When the thousand years are over, Satan will be released from his prison ⁸and will go out to deceive the nations in the four corners of the earth – Gog and Magog – and to gather them for battle. In number they are like the sand on the seashore. ⁹They marched across the breadth of the earth and surrounded the camp of God's people, the city he loves. But fire came down from heaven and devoured them. ¹⁰And the devil, who deceived them, was thrown into the lake of burning sulphur, where the beast and the false prophet had been thrown. They will be tormented day and night for ever and ever.

¹¹Then I saw a great white throne and him who was seated on it. The earth and the heavens fled from his presence, and there was no place for them. ¹²And I saw the dead, great and small, standing before the throne, and books were opened. Another book was opened, which is the book of life. The dead were judged according to what they had done as recorded in the books. ¹³The sea gave up the dead that were in it, and death and Hades gave up the dead that were in them, and each person was judged according to what they had done. ¹⁴Then death and Hades were thrown into the lake of fire. The lake of fire is the second death. ¹⁵Anyone whose name was not found written in the book of life was thrown into the lake of fire.

21 Then I saw 'a new heaven and a new earth,' for the first heaven and the first earth had passed away, and there was no longer any sea. ²I saw the Holy City, the new Jerusalem, coming down out of heaven from God, prepared as a bride beautifully dressed for her husband. ³And I heard a loud voice from the throne saying, 'Look! God's dwelling-place is now among the people, and he will dwell with them. They will be his people, and God himself will be with them and be their God. ⁴"He will wipe every tear from their eyes. There will be no more death" or mourning or crying or pain, for the old order of things has passed away.'

Kindness and Generosity

'She speaks with wisdom, and faithful instruction is on her tongue.' **Proverbs 31:26**

The fifth fruit of the Spirit is kindness. In the unforgettable description of a model wife in Proverbs 31, there is this statement:

'She speaks with wisdom, and faithful instruction is on her tongue' (v. 26). Note the use of the word 'faithful'. A model wife passes an inner law in the legislature of her personality that everything she says and does will be loving. Kindness is not something set in her emotions – it is set in her will and thus becomes a life attitude. May we, on bended knee, this day pass the same law in the legislature of our own hearts and so come under its sway forever.

The sixth fruit of the Spirit is goodness. The Greek word *agathosune* means, according to the experts, 'kindness at work'. This is why the word is best understood as it is sometimes translated: 'generosity'. This leads us to an interesting statement which Jesus once made: 'If your Eye is generous, the whole of your body will be illumined' (Matt. 6:22, Moffatt). If your 'Eye' (your outlook on life, your whole way of looking at things) is generous, then your whole personality will be illuminated or lit up.

Jesus was generous towards everyone – the poor, the meek, the sinful and the unlovely – and His whole personality was full of light. By the ministry of the Holy Spirit, this characteristic of Jesus is generated in us – if we let it. And when we do, then we begin to see everyone with 'the generous Eye'.

PRAYER

Lord Jesus, your generous Eye saw in me something that wasn't there – and then it was there! Help me to thus create what I see in others. For Your own dear name's sake. Amen.

FURTHER STUDY

2 Pet. 1; Rom. 12:10; 1 Cor. 13:4; Eph. 4:32; Col. 3:12
• From what does kindness flow out?
• How can you show kindness today?

December 30

■ ZECHARIAH 11:1–14:21

11 Open your doors, Lebanon,
so that fire may devour your cedars!
² Wail, you juniper, for the cedar has fallen;
the stately trees are ruined!
Wail, oaks of Bashan;
the dense forest has been cut down!
³ Listen to the wail of the shepherds:
their rich pastures are destroyed!
Listen to the roar of the lions;
the lush thicket of the Jordan is ruined!

⁴ This is what the LORD my God says: 'Shepherd the flock marked for slaughter. ⁵ Their buyers slaughter them and go unpunished. Those who sell them say, "Praise the LORD, I am rich!" Their own shepherds do not spare them. ⁶ For I will no longer have pity on the people of the land,' declares the LORD. 'I will give everyone into the hands of their neighbours and their king. They will devastate the land, and I will not rescue anyone from their hands.'

⁷ So I shepherded the flock marked for

slaughter, particularly the oppressed of the flock. Then I took two staffs and called one Favour and the other Union, and I shepherded the flock. [8] In one month I got rid of the three shepherds.

The flock detested me, and I grew weary of them [9] and said, 'I will not be your shepherd. Let the dying die, and the perishing perish. Let those who are left eat one another's flesh.'

[10] Then I took my staff called Favour and broke it, revoking the covenant I had made with all the nations. [11] It was revoked on that day, and so the oppressed of the flock who were watching me knew it was the word of the LORD.

[12] I told them, 'If you think it best, give me my pay; but if not, keep it.' So they paid me thirty pieces of silver.

[13] And the LORD said to me, 'Throw it to the potter' – the handsome price at which they valued me! So I took the thirty pieces of silver and threw them to the potter at the house of the LORD.

[14] Then I broke my second staff called Union, breaking the family bond between Judah and Israel.

[15] Then the LORD said to me, 'Take again the equipment of a foolish shepherd. [16] For I am going to raise up a shepherd over the land who will not care for the lost, or seek the young, or heal the injured, or feed the healthy, but will eat the meat of the choice sheep, tearing off their hooves.

[17] 'Woe to the worthless shepherd,
    who deserts the flock!
May the sword strike his arm and his
    right eye!
May his arm be completely withered,
    his right eye totally blinded!'

12 A prophecy: the word of the LORD concerning Israel.

The LORD, who stretches out the heavens, who lays the foundation of the earth,

and who forms the human spirit within a person, declares: [2] 'I am going to make Jerusalem a cup that sends all the surrounding peoples reeling. Judah will be besieged as well as Jerusalem. [3] On that day, when all the nations of the earth are gathered against her, I will make Jerusalem an immovable rock for all the nations. All who try to move it will injure themselves. [4] On that day I will strike every horse with panic and its rider with madness,' declares the LORD. 'I will keep a watchful eye over Judah, but I will blind all the horses of the nations. [5] Then the clans of Judah will say in their hearts, "The people of Jerusalem are strong, because the LORD Almighty is their God."

[6] 'On that day I will make the clans of Judah like a brazier in a woodpile, like a flaming torch among sheaves. They will consume all the surrounding peoples right and left, but Jerusalem will remain intact in her place.

[7] 'The LORD will save the dwellings of Judah first, so that the honour of the house of David and of Jerusalem's inhabitants may not be greater than that of Judah. [8] On that day the LORD will shield those who live in Jerusalem, so that the feeblest among them will be like David, and the house of David will be like God, like the angel of the LORD going before them. [9] On that day I will set out to destroy all the nations that attack Jerusalem.

[10] 'And I will pour out on the house of David and the inhabitants of Jerusalem a spirit of grace and supplication. They will look on me, the one they have pierced, and they will mourn for him as one mourns for an only child, and grieve bitterly for him as one grieves for a firstborn son. [11] On that day the weeping in Jerusalem will be as great as the weeping of Hadad Rimmon in the plain of Megiddo. [12] The land will mourn, each clan by itself, with their wives by themselves: the clan of the house of David and their wives, the clan of the house of Nathan and their

wives, [13]the clan of the house of Levi and their wives, the clan of Shimei and their wives, [14]and all the rest of the clans and their wives.

13 [1]'On that day a fountain will be opened to the house of David and the inhabitants of Jerusalem, to cleanse them from sin and impurity.

[2]'On that day, I will banish the names of the idols from the land, and they will be remembered no more,' declares the LORD Almighty. 'I will remove both the prophets and the spirit of impurity from the land. [3]And if anyone still prophesies, their father and mother, to whom they were born, will say to them, "You must die, because you have told lies in the LORD's name." Then their own parents will stab the one who prophesies.

[4]'On that day every prophet will be ashamed of their prophetic vision. They will not put on a prophet's garment of hair in order to deceive. [5]Each will say, "I am not a prophet. I am a farmer; the land has been my livelihood since my youth." [6]If someone asks, "What are these wounds on your body?" they will answer, "The wounds I was given at the house of my friends."

[7]'Awake, sword, against my shepherd,
     against the man who is close to me!'
        declares the LORD Almighty.
   'Strike the shepherd,
        and the sheep will be scattered,
        and I will turn my hand against the
           little ones.
[8]In the whole land,' declares the LORD,
     'two-thirds will be struck down and
           perish;
        yet one-third will be left in it.
[9]This third I will put into the fire;
        I will refine them like silver
        and test them like gold.
     They will call on my name
        and I will answer them;
   I will say, "They are my people,"

and they will say, "The LORD is our
        God."'

14 A day of the LORD is coming, Jerusalem, when your possessions will be plundered and divided up within your very walls.

[2]I will gather all the nations to Jerusalem to fight against it; the city will be captured, the houses ransacked, and the women raped. Half of the city will go into exile, but the rest of the people will not be taken from the city. [3]Then the LORD will go out and fight against those nations, as he fights on a day of battle. [4]On that day his feet will stand on the Mount of Olives, east of Jerusalem, and the Mount of Olives will be split in two from east to west, forming a great valley, with half of the mountain moving north and half moving south. [5]You will flee by my mountain valley, for it will extend to Azel. You will flee as you fled from the earthquake in the days of Uzziah king of Judah. Then the LORD my God will come, and all the holy ones with him.

[6]On that day there will be neither sunlight nor cold, frosty darkness. [7]It will be a unique day – a day known only to the LORD – with no distinction between day and night. When evening comes, there will be light.

[8]On that day living water will flow out from Jerusalem, half of it east to the Dead Sea and half of it west to the Mediterranean Sea, in summer and in winter.

[9]The LORD will be king over the whole earth. On that day there will be one LORD, and his name the only name.

[10]The whole land, from Geba to Rimmon, south of Jerusalem, will become like the Arabah. But Jerusalem will be raised up high from the Benjamin Gate to the site of the First Gate, to the Corner Gate, and from the Tower of Hananel to the royal winepresses, and will remain in its place. [11]It will be inhabited; never again will it be destroyed. Jerusalem will be secure.

¹²This is the plague with which the LORD will strike all the nations that fought against Jerusalem: their flesh will rot while they are still standing on their feet, their eyes will rot in their sockets, and their tongues will rot in their mouths. ¹³On that day people will be stricken by the LORD with great panic. They will seize each other by the hand and attack one another. ¹⁴Judah too will fight at Jerusalem. The wealth of all the surrounding nations will be collected – great quantities of gold and silver and clothing. ¹⁵A similar plague will strike the horses and mules, the camels and donkeys, and all the animals in those camps.

¹⁶Then the survivors from all the nations that have attacked Jerusalem will go up year after year to worship the King, the LORD Almighty, and to celebrate the Festival of Tabernacles. ¹⁷If any of the peoples of the earth do not go up to Jerusalem to worship the King, the LORD Almighty, they will have no rain. ¹⁸If the Egyptian people do not go up and take part, they will have no rain. The LORD will bring on them the plague he inflicts on the nations that do not go up to celebrate the Festival of Tabernacles. ¹⁹This will be the punishment of Egypt and the punishment of all the nations that do not go up to celebrate the Festival of Tabernacles.

²⁰On that day HOLY TO THE LORD will be inscribed on the bells of the horses, and the cooking pots in the LORD's house will be like the sacred bowls in front of the altar. ²¹Every pot in Jerusalem and Judah will be holy to the LORD Almighty, and all who come to sacrifice will take some of the pots and cook in them. And on that day there will no longer be a Canaanite in the house of the LORD Almighty.

▬ PSALM 149:1-9

¹Praise the LORD.

Sing to the LORD a new song,
    his praise in the assembly of his
        faithful people.

²Let Israel rejoice in their Maker;
    let the people of Zion be glad in their
        King.
³Let them praise his name with dancing
    and make music to him with
        tambourine and harp.
⁴For the LORD takes delight in his people;
    he crowns the humble with victory.
⁵Let his faithful people rejoice in this
        honour
    and sing for joy on their beds.

⁶May the praise of God be in their mouths
    and a double-edged sword in their
        hands,
⁷to inflict vengeance on the nations
    and punishment on the peoples,
⁸to bind their kings with fetters,
    their nobles with shackles of iron,
⁹to carry out the sentence written against
        them –
    this is the glory of all his faithful
        people.

Praise the LORD.

▬ PROVERBS 31:28-29

²⁸Her children arise and call her blessed;
    her husband also, and he praises her:
²⁹'Many women do noble things,
    but you surpass them all.'

▬ REVELATION 21:5-27

⁵ He who was seated on the throne said, 'I am making everything new!' Then he said, 'Write this down, for these words are trustworthy and true.'

⁶ He said to me: 'It is done. I am the Alpha and the Omega, the Beginning and the End. To the thirsty I will give water without cost from the spring of the water of life. ⁷ Those who are victorious will inherit all this, and I will be their God and they will be my children. ⁸ But the cowardly, the unbelieving, the vile, the murderers, the sexually immoral, those who practise magic arts, the idolaters and all liars – they will be consigned to the fiery lake of burning sulphur. This is the second death.'

⁹ One of the seven angels who had the seven bowls full of the seven last plagues came and said to me, 'Come, I will show you the bride, the wife of the Lamb.' ¹⁰ And he carried me away in the Spirit to a mountain great and high, and showed me the Holy City, Jerusalem, coming down out of heaven from God. ¹¹ It shone with the glory of God, and its brilliance was like that of a very precious jewel, like a jasper, clear as crystal. ¹² It had a great, high wall with twelve gates, and with twelve angels at the gates. On the gates were written the names of the twelve tribes of Israel. ¹³ There were three gates on the east, three on the north, three on the south and three on the west. ¹⁴ The wall of the city had twelve foundations, and on them were the names of the twelve apostles of the Lamb.

¹⁵ The angel who talked with me had a measuring rod of gold to measure the city, its gates and its walls. ¹⁶ The city was laid out like a square, as long as it was wide. He measured the city with the rod and found it to be 12,000 stadia in length, and as wide and high as it is long. ¹⁷ The angel measured the wall using human measurement, and it was 144 cubits thick. ¹⁸ The wall was made of jasper, and the city of pure gold, as pure as glass. ¹⁹ The foundations of the city walls were decorated with every kind of precious stone. The first foundation was jasper, the second sapphire, the third agate, the fourth emerald, ²⁰ the fifth onyx, the sixth ruby, the seventh chrysolite, the eighth beryl, the ninth topaz, the tenth turquoise, the eleventh jacinth, and the twelfth amethyst. ²¹ The twelve gates were twelve pearls, each gate made of a single pearl. The great street of the city was of gold, as pure as transparent glass.

²² I did not see a temple in the city, because the Lord God Almighty and the Lamb are its temple. ²³ The city does not need the sun or the moon to shine on it, for the glory of God gives it light, and the Lamb is its lamp. ²⁴ The nations will walk by its light, and the kings of the earth will bring their splendour into it. ²⁵ On no day will its gates ever be shut, for there will be no night there. ²⁶ The glory and honour of the nations will be brought into it. ²⁷ Nothing impure will ever enter it, nor will anyone who does what is shameful or deceitful, but only those whose names are written in the Lamb's book of life.

Subdued Puppies?

'For the Lord takes delight in his people; he crowns the humble with victory.' **Psalm 149:4**

Part of Christ's prescription for happiness is 'Blessed are the meek, for they shall inherit the earth' (Matt. 5:5, AV). How we have shied away from that word 'meek'. We have thought of meekness as a weakness and thus have a totally wrong concept of what Jesus meant. *The Amplified Bible* translates it thus: 'Blessed are the meek (the mild, patient, long-suffering), for they shall inherit the earth.' The dictionary defines 'meek' as 'humble, compliant, and submissive'. Does this mean that Jesus expects the children of the kingdom to be like subdued puppies who crawl into their master's presence and cower at his feet? Or to become the type of people who lack inner fortitude and gumption, who can be easily pushed around and manipulated?

The truly meek person - in the biblical sense of the word - is not timid, shy, hesitant and unassuming, but trusting, confident and secure. The root meaning of the word 'meekness' is that of yieldedness or surrender - a characteristic without which no real progress can be made in the Christian life. What happens, for example, to the scientist who approaches the mysteries of the universe in a spirit of meekness? He finds its richest secrets unfolding themselves to him, and he is able to harness the mighty forces around him to advantage. The Christian who approaches life in the same spirit - the spirit of meekness and submission - discovers the true meaning of his existence and the purpose of God in all his affairs.

PRAYER

Gracious Father, help me to understand clearly the difference between meekness and weakness. And show me how to apply this principle in all I say and in all I do. This I ask in Christ's powerful and precious name. Amen.

FURTHER STUDY

James 1:12-21; Zeph. 2:3; Gal. 5:22-23; 1 Pet. 3:4
• What are we to receive with humility?
• Does the biblical definition of meekness fit you?

December 31

■ MALACHI 1:1–4:6

1 A prophecy: the word of the LORD to Israel through Malachi.

²'I have loved you,' says the LORD.

'But you ask, "How have you loved us?"

'Was not Esau Jacob's brother?' declares the LORD. 'Yet I have loved Jacob, ³but Esau I have hated, and I have turned his hill country into a wasteland and left his inheritance to the desert jackals.'

⁴Edom may say, 'Though we have been crushed, we will rebuild the ruins.'

But this is what the LORD Almighty says: 'They may build, but I will demolish. They will be called the Wicked Land, a people always under the wrath of the LORD. ⁵You will see it with your own eyes and say, "Great is the LORD – even beyond the borders of Israel!"

⁶'A son honours his father, and a slave his master. If I am a father, where is the honour due to me? If I am a master, where is the respect due to me?' says the LORD Almighty.

'It is you priests who show contempt for my name.

'But you ask, "How have we shown contempt for your name?"

⁷'By offering defiled food on my altar.

'But you ask, "How have we defiled you?"

'By saying that the LORD's table is contemptible. ⁸When you offer blind animals for sacrifice, is that not wrong? When you sacrifice lame or diseased animals, is that not wrong? Try offering them to your governor! Would he be pleased with you? Would he accept you?' says the LORD Almighty.

⁹'Now plead with God to be gracious to us. With such offerings from your hands, will he accept you?' – says the LORD Almighty.

¹⁰'Oh, that one of you would shut the temple doors, so that you would not light useless fires on my altar! I am not pleased with you,' says the LORD Almighty, 'and I will accept no offering from your hands. ¹¹My name will be great among the nations, from where the sun rises to where it sets. In every place incense and pure offerings will be brought to me, because my name will be great among the nations,' says the LORD Almighty.

¹²'But you profane it by saying, "The Lord's table is defiled," and, "Its food is contemptible." ¹³And you say, "What a burden!" and you sniff at it contemptuously,' says the LORD Almighty.

'When you bring injured, lame or diseased animals and offer them as sacrifices, should I accept them from your hands?' says the LORD. ¹⁴'Cursed is the cheat who has an acceptable male in his flock and vows to give it, but then sacrifices a blemished animal to the Lord. For I am a great king,' says the LORD Almighty, 'and my name is to be feared among the nations.

2 'And now, you priests, this warning is for you. ²If you do not listen, and if you do not resolve to honour my name,' says the LORD Almighty, 'I will send a curse on you, and I will curse your blessings. Yes, I have already cursed them, because you have not resolved to honour me.

³'Because of you I will rebuke your descendants; I will smear on your faces the dung from your festival sacrifices, and you will be carried off with it. ⁴And you will know that I have sent you this warning so that my covenant with Levi may continue,' says the LORD Almighty. ⁵'My covenant was with him, a covenant of life and peace, and I gave them to him; this called for reverence and he revered me and stood in awe of my name. ⁶True instruction was in his mouth and nothing false was found on his lips. He walked with me in peace and uprightness, and turned many from sin.

⁷'For the lips of a priest ought to preserve knowledge, because he is the messenger of the LORD Almighty and people seek instruction from his mouth. ⁸But you have turned from the way and by your teaching have caused many to stumble; you have violated the covenant with Levi,' says the LORD Almighty. ⁹'So I have caused you to be despised and humiliated before all the people, because you have not followed my ways but have shown partiality in matters of the law.'

¹⁰Do we not all have one Father? Did not one God create us? Why do we profane the covenant of our ancestors by being unfaithful to one another?

¹¹Judah has been unfaithful. A detestable thing has been committed in Israel and in Jerusalem: Judah has desecrated the sanctuary the LORD loves by marrying women who worship a foreign god. ¹²As for the man

who does this, whoever he may be, may the LORD remove him from the tents of Jacob – even though he brings an offering to the LORD Almighty.

¹³ Another thing you do: you flood the LORD's altar with tears. You weep and wail because he no longer looks with favour on your offerings or accepts them with pleasure from your hands. ¹⁴ You ask, 'Why?' It is because the LORD is the witness between you and the wife of your youth. You have been unfaithful to her, though she is your partner, the wife of your marriage covenant.

¹⁵ Has not the one God made you? You belong to him in body and spirit. And what does the one God seek? Godly offspring. So be on your guard, and do not be unfaithful to the wife of your youth.

¹⁶ 'The man who hates and divorces his wife,' says the LORD, the God of Israel, 'does violence to the one he should protect,' says the LORD Almighty.

So be on your guard, and do not be unfaithful.

¹⁷ You have wearied the LORD with your words.

'How have we wearied him?' you ask.

By saying, 'All who do evil are good in the eyes of the LORD, and he is pleased with them' or 'Where is the God of justice?'

3 'I will send my messenger, who will prepare the way before me. Then suddenly the Lord you are seeking will come to his temple; the messenger of the covenant, whom you desire, will come,' says the LORD Almighty.

² But who can endure the day of his coming? Who can stand when he appears? For he will be like a refiner's fire or a launderer's soap. ³ He will sit as a refiner and purifier of silver; he will purify the Levites and refine them like gold and silver. Then the LORD will have men who will bring offerings in righteousness, ⁴ and the offerings of Judah and Jerusalem will be

acceptable to the LORD, as in days gone by, as in former years.

⁵ 'So I will come to put you on trial. I will be quick to testify against sorcerers, adulterers and perjurers, against those who defraud labourers of their wages, who oppress the widows and the fatherless, and deprive the foreigners among you of justice, but do not fear me,' says the LORD Almighty.

⁶ 'I the LORD do not change. So you, the descendants of Jacob, are not destroyed. ⁷ Ever since the time of your ancestors you have turned away from my decrees and have not kept them. Return to me, and I will return to you,' says the LORD Almighty.

'But you ask, "How are we to return?"

⁸ 'Will a mere mortal rob God? Yet you rob me.

'But you ask, "How are we robbing you?"

'In tithes and offerings. ⁹ You are under a curse – your whole nation – because you are robbing me. ¹⁰ Bring the whole tithe into the storehouse, that there may be food in my house. Test me in this,' says the LORD Almighty, 'and see if I will not throw open the floodgates of heaven and pour out so much blessing that there will not be room enough to store it. ¹¹ I will prevent pests from devouring your crops, and the vines in your fields will not drop their fruit before it is ripe,' says the LORD Almighty. ¹² 'Then all the nations will call you blessed, for yours will be a delightful land,' says the LORD Almighty.

¹³ 'You have spoken arrogantly against me,' says the LORD.

'Yet you ask, "What have we said against you?"

¹⁴ 'You have said, "It is futile to serve God. What do we gain by carrying out his requirements and going about like mourners before the LORD Almighty? ¹⁵ But now we call the arrogant blessed. Certainly evildoers prosper, and even when they put God to the test, they get away with it."'

¹⁶ Then those who feared the LORD talked

with each other, and the LORD listened and heard. A scroll of remembrance was written in his presence concerning those who feared the LORD and honoured his name.

17'On the day when I act,' says the LORD Almighty, 'they will be my treasured possession. I will spare them, just as a father has compassion and spares his son who serves him. 18 And you will again see the distinction between the righteous and the wicked, between those who serve God and those who do not.

4 'Surely the day is coming; it will burn like a furnace. All the arrogant and every evildoer will be stubble, and that day that is coming will set them on fire,' says the LORD Almighty. 'Not a root or a branch will be left to them. 2 But for you who revere my name, the sun of righteousness will rise with healing in its rays. And you will go out and frolic like well-fed calves. 3 Then you will trample on the wicked; they will be ashes under the soles of your feet on the day when I act,' says the LORD Almighty.

4'Remember the law of my servant Moses, the decrees and laws I gave him at Horeb for all Israel.

5'See, I will send the prophet Elijah to you before that great and dreadful day of the LORD comes. 6 He will turn the hearts of the parents to their children, and the hearts of the children to their parents; or else I will come and strike the land with total destruction.'

▬ PSALM 150:1-6

1 Praise the LORD.

Praise God in his sanctuary;
    praise him in his mighty heavens.
2 Praise him for his acts of power;
    praise him for his surpassing
        greatness.

3 Praise him with the sounding of the
        trumpet,
    praise him with the harp and lyre,
4 praise him with tambourine and dancing,
    praise him with the strings and pipe,
5 praise him with the clash of cymbals,
    praise him with resounding cymbals.

6 Let everything that has breath praise the
    LORD.

Praise the LORD.

▬ PROVERBS 31:30-31

30 Charm is deceptive, and beauty is fleeting;
    but a woman who fears the LORD is to
        be praised.
31 Honour her for all that her hands have
        done,
    and let her works bring her praise at
        the city gate.

▬ REVELATION 22:1-21

22 Then the angel showed me the river of the water of life, as clear as crystal, flowing from the throne of God and of the Lamb 2 down the middle of the great street of the city. On each side of the river stood the tree of life, bearing twelve crops of fruit, yielding its fruit every month. And the leaves of the tree are for the healing of the nations. 3 No longer will there be any curse. The throne of God and of the Lamb will be in the city, and his servants will serve him. 4 They will see his face, and his name will be on their foreheads. 5 There will be no more night. They will not need the light of a lamp or the light of the sun, for the Lord God will give them light. And they will reign for ever and ever.

6 The angel said to me, 'These words are trustworthy and true. The Lord, the God

who inspires the prophets, sent his angel to show his servants the things that must soon take place.'

⁷'Look, I am coming soon! Blessed is the one who keeps the words of the prophecy written in this scroll.'

⁸I, John, am the one who heard and saw these things. And when I had heard and seen them, I fell down to worship at the feet of the angel who had been showing them to me. ⁹But he said to me, 'Don't do that! I am a fellow servant with you and with your fellow prophets and with all who keep the words of this scroll. Worship God!'

¹⁰Then he told me, 'Do not seal up the words of the prophecy of this scroll, because the time is near. ¹¹Let the one who does wrong continue to do wrong; let the vile person continue to be vile; let the one who does right continue to do right; and let the holy person continue to be holy.'

¹²'Look, I am coming soon! My reward is with me, and I will give to each person according to what they have done. ¹³I am the Alpha and the Omega, the First and the Last, the Beginning and the End.

¹⁴'Blessed are those who wash their robes, that they may have the right to the tree of life and may go through the gates into the city. ¹⁵Outside are the dogs, those who practise magic arts, the sexually immoral, the murderers, the idolaters and everyone who loves and practises falsehood.

¹⁶'I, Jesus, have sent my angel to give you this testimony for the churches. I am the Root and the Offspring of David, and the bright Morning Star.'

¹⁷The Spirit and the bride say, 'Come!' And let the one who hears say, 'Come!' Let the one who is thirsty come; and let the one who wishes take the free gift of the water of life.

¹⁸I warn everyone who hears the words of the prophecy of this scroll: if anyone adds anything to them, God will add to that person the plagues described in this scroll. ¹⁹And if anyone takes words away from this scroll of prophecy, God will take away from that person any share in the tree of life and in the Holy City, which are described in this scroll.

²⁰He who testifies to these things says, 'Yes, I am coming soon.'

Amen. Come, Lord Jesus.

²¹The grace of the Lord Jesus be with God's people. Amen.

Commending Our Saviour

'Then those who feared the LORD talked with each other ...' **Malachi 3:16**

It is vital to share Christ with others: experience and expression are the alternate beats of the Christian heart. And if these two things are not in operation, the Christian heart ceases to beat. Then what happens? We settle down to dead forms, dead attitudes and dead prayers.

This matter of sharing, however, must not be limited only to evangelism. It applies also to sharing with other Christians the things God has shared with us.

If God has shown you something today from His Word, then it is imperative that you share it with another Christian. As we have been saying, nothing is really ours until we share it – the expression will deepen the impression. So in seeking to stay spiritually fresh, discipline yourself to share appropriate issues with your Christian and non-Christian friends. Many do not do this. They are disciplined in their quiet time or their study of the Scriptures, but they have never disciplined themselves to share. Someone has defined a Christian as one who says by word or deed: 'Let me commend my Saviour to you.' There is no better definition.

I saw a cartoon in a newspaper which showed a woman putting a garment around the shivering body of a little girl. Behind the woman stood Christ throwing a cloak around her shoulders. The title of the cartoon was this: 'A proven assembly line.' It is indeed. Give out to others, and it will be given to you – pressed down and running over. Especially running over.

PRAYER

Father, I reach up to You with one hand and reach out to those in need with the other. Give me some word or message to pass on to a non-Christian or one of my Christian brothers or sisters this day. In Jesus' name. Amen.

FURTHER STUDY

Jer. 20:1-9; Acts 4:20;
2 Cor. 4:13

• What was Jeremiah's confession?
• What does believing produce?

NATIONAL DISTRIBUTORS

UK: (and countries not listed below)
CWR, Waverley Abbey House, Waverley Lane, Farnham, Surrey GU9 8EP.
Tel: (01252) 784700 Outside UK (44) 1252 784700. Email: mail@cwr.org.uk

AUSTRALIA: KI Entertainment, Unit 21 317-321 Woodpark Road, Smithfield, New South Wales 2164.
Tel: 1 800 850 777 Fax: 02 9604 3077. Email: sales@keientertainment.com.au

CANADA: David C Cook Distribution Canada, PO Box 98, 55 Woodslee Avenue, Paris, Ontario N3L 3E5.
Tel: 1800 263 2664. Email: sandi.swanson@davidccook.ca

GHANA: Challenge Enterprises of Ghana, PO Box 5723, Accra.
Tel: (021) 222437/223249 Fax: (021) 226227. Email: ceg-africaonline.com.gh

HONG KONG: Cross Communications Ltd, 1/F, 562A Nathan Road, Kowloon.
Tel: 2780 1188 Fax: 2770 6229. Email: cross@crossltd.com

INDIA: Crystal Communications, 10-3-18/4/1, East Marredpally, Secunderabad - 500026, Andhra Pradesh.
Tel/Fax: (040) 27737145. Email: crystal_edwj@rediffmail.com

KENYA: Keswick Books and Gifts Ltd, PO Box 10242, 00400 Nairobi.
Tel: (020) 4402167/2226047/312029. Email: sales.keswick@gilgalministries.co.ke

MALAYSIA: Canaanland, No 25, Jalan PJU 1A/41B, NZX Commercial Centre, Ara Jaya, 47301 Petaling Jaya,
Selangor. Tel: (03) 7885 0540/2 Fax: (03) 7885 0545. Email: info@canaanland.com.my

Salvation Publishing & Distribution Sdn Bhd, 23, Jalan SS 2/64, 47300 Petaling Jaya, Selangor.
Tel: (03) 78766411/78766422 Fax: (03) 78766433. Email: info@salvationbookcentre.com

NEW ZEALAND: KI Entertainment, Unit 21 317-321 Woodpark Road, Smithfield, New South Wales 2164,
Australia. Tel: 0 800 850 777 Fax: +612 9604 3073. Email: sales@keientertainment.com.au

NIGERIA: FBFM, Helen Baugh House, 96 St Finbarr's College Road, Akoka, Lagos.
Tel: (01) 7747429/4720218/7749726 8128, 234 8033 88 1479. Email: fbfm_1@yahoo.com

PHILIPPINES: OMF Literature Inc, 776 Boni Avenue, Mandaluyong City.
Tel: (02) 531 2183 Fax: (02) 531 1960. Email: gloadela@omflit.com

SINGAPORE: Alby Commercial Enterprises Pte Ltd, 95 Kallang Avenue #04-00, AIS Industrial Building
339420. Tel: (65) 629 2738 Fax: (65) 629 4708. Email: marketing@alby.com.sg

SRI LANKA: Assembly Publications (PVT) Ltd, Barrizo House, 65 Brownrigg Place, Colombo 2.
Tel: (94) 24210/2447668. Email: christombu@dynabook.lbhsomail.com

USA: David C Cook Distribution Canada, PO Box 98, 55 Woodslee Avenue, Paris, Ontario N3L 3E5, Canada.
Tel: 1800 263 2664. Email: sandi.swanson@davidccook.ca

NATIONAL DISTRIBUTORS

UK: (and countries not listed below)
CWR, Waverley Abbey House, Waverley Lane, Farnham, Surrey GU9 8EP.
Tel: (01252) 784700 Outside UK (44) 1252 784700 Email: mail@cwr.org.uk

AUSTRALIA: KI Entertainment, Unit 21 317-321 Woodpark Road, Smithfield, New South Wales 2164.
Tel: 1 800 850 777 Fax: 02 9604 3699 Email: sales@kientertainment.com.au

CANADA: David C Cook Distribution Canada, PO Box 98, 55 Woodslee Avenue, Paris, Ontario N3L 3E5.
Tel: 1800 263 2664 Email: sandi.swanson@davidccook.ca

GHANA: Challenge Enterprises of Ghana, PO Box 5723, Accra.
Tel: (021) 222437/223249 Fax: (021) 226227 Email: ceg@africaonline.com.gh

HONG KONG: Cross Communications Ltd, 1/F, 562A Nathan Road, Kowloon.
Tel: 2780 1188 Fax: 2770 6229 Email: cross@crosshk.com

INDIA: Crystal Communications, 10-3-18/4/1, East Marredpalli, Secunderabad – 500026, Andhra Pradesh.
Tel/Fax: (040) 27737145 Email: crystal_edwj@rediffmail.com

KENYA: Keswick Books and Gifts Ltd, PO Box 10242-00400, Nairobi.
Tel: (020) 2226047/312639 Email: sales.keswick@africaonline.co.ke

MALAYSIA: Canaanland, No. 25 Jalan PJU 1A/41B, NZX Commercial Centre, Ara Jaya, 47301 Petaling Jaya,
Selangor. Tel: (03) 7885 0540/1/2 Fax: (03) 7885 0545 Email: info@canaanland.com.my

Salvation Publishing & Distribution Sdn Bhd, 23 Jalan SS 2/64, 47300 Petaling Jaya, Selangor.
Tel: (03) 78766411/78766797 Fax: (03) 78757066/78756360 Email: info@salvationbookcentre.com

NEW ZEALAND: KI Entertainment, Unit 21 317-321 Woodpark Road, Smithfield, New South Wales 2164,
Australia. Tel: 0 800 850 777 Fax: +612 9604 3699 Email: sales@kientertainment.com.au

NIGERIA: FBFM, Helen Baugh House, 96 St Finbarr's College Road, Akoka, Lagos.
Tel: (01) 7747429/4700218/825775/827264 Email: fbfm_1@yahoo.com

PHILIPPINES: OMF Literature Inc, 776 Boni Avenue, Mandaluyong City.
Tel: (02) 531 2183 Fax: (02) 531 1960 Email: gloadlaon@omflit.com

SINGAPORE: Alby Commercial Enterprises Pte Ltd, 95 Kallang Avenue #04-00, AIS Industrial Building,
339420. Tel: (65) 629 27238 Fax: (65) 629 27235 Email: marketing@alby.com.sg

SRI LANKA: Christombu Publications (Pvt) Ltd, Bartleet House, 65 Braybrooke Place, Colombo 2.
Tel: (9411) 2421073/2447665 Email: christombupublications@gmail.com

USA: David C Cook Distribution Canada, PO Box 98, 55 Woodslee Avenue, Paris, Ontario N3L 3E5, Canada.
Tel: 1800 263 2664 Email: sandi.swanson@davidccook.ca

EVERY DAY WITH JESUS DAILY DEVOTIONAL

With around half a million readers, this bi-monthly devotional is one of the world's most popular daily Bible-reading resources.

- Get practical help with life's challenges
- Gain insight into the deeper truths of Scripture
- Be challenged, comforted and encouraged
- Study six topics in depth each year
- Explore each theme further using additional free resources for individual or group study, including video and discussion starters, at www.cwr.org.uk/extra

For current prices of our annual subscriptions or individual issues please visit www.cwr.org.uk/store

Also available in Large Print format, by daily email, eBook and Kindle. For more information on *Every Day with Jesus* and all other CWR publications please visit **www.cwr.org.uk**

Every Day with Jesus

HONOUR
GLORIFY EXTOL
BEAUTIFY
LOVE
ADULATION
AWE

The Heart of W

'Glorify the LORD with me
let us exalt his name tog
Psalm 34:3

Transforming lives

Courses and seminars

Publishing and media

Conference facilities

CWR's vision is to enable people to experience personal transformation through applying God's Word to their lives and relationships.

Our Bible-based training and resources help people around the world to:
• Grow in their walk with God
• Understand and apply Scripture to their lives
• Resource themselves and their church
• Develop pastoral care and counselling skills
• Train for leadership
• Strengthen relationships, marriage and family life
and much more.

Our insightful writers provide daily Bible-reading notes and other resources for all ages, and our experienced course designers and presenters have gained an international reputation for excellence and effectiveness.

CWR's Training and Conference Centres in Surrey and East Sussex, England, provide excellent facilities in idyllic settings – ideal for both learning and spiritual refreshment.

 CWR Applying God's Word
to everyday life and relationships

CWR, Waverley Abbey House,
Waverley Lane, Farnham,
Surrey GU9 8EP, UK

Telephone: +44 (0)1252 784700
Email: info@cwr.org.uk
Website: www.cwr.org.uk

Registered Charity No 294387
Company Registration No 1990308